# Chambers
# Thesaurus

# Chambers
# Thesaurus

*Managing Editor*

Catherine Schwarz

*Editors*

Anne Seaton, George Davidson
John Simpson

# Chambers

This edition published 1991 by W & R Chambers Ltd
43-45 Annandale Street, Edinburgh EH7 4AZ

First published as *Chambers 20th Century Thesaurus* 1986
Published as *Chambers Thesaurus* 1988

ISBN 0 550 10572 7 Standard
ISBN 0 550 10574 3 Thumb Index

A catalogue record for this book is available from the British Library

Typeset by Hewer Text Composition Services, Edinburgh
Printed in England by Clays Ltd, St Ives plc

# Contents

# Preface

In the five years since the first edition of *Chambers Thesaurus* was published, the English language has benefited from the vocabulary of recent medical, scientific and technical advances, of national and international politics, of widening cultural horizons, and even of war.

These and many other areas have contributed to the Chambers English language database, on which this new edition of the *Thesaurus* is based. It is up-to-date and authoritative, and even more comprehensive and accessible than its highly regarded predecessor.

As with the previous edition, the scope and versatility of the *Thesaurus* will be enhanced by using it in conjunction with a dictionary — the standard *Chambers Concise Dictionary* (1991) or the fuller *Chambers English Dictionary* (1988).

# Preface to first edition

## What is a thesaurus?

Clearly it is a kind of dictionary; but whereas an ordinary dictionary gives the meanings of a word, a thesaurus supplies alternatives for it. It is the essential companion for anyone who wants to create something satisfying out of words — a quick, convenient source of synonymous and related terms that will help the user to express himself in as precise, succinct, and yet varied a manner as possible.

It is 130 years since Peter Mark Roget published his *Thesaurus*. His purpose was to provide the reader not only with synonyms for a word, but, more generally, with a wide choice of expressions relevant to a particular concept. His method was to classify these within a framework of ideas on seventeenth-century philosophical and scientific principles. This meant that a very full alphabetical index was needed to open up the classified lists to the user. It was probably the complications of this system that ensured the continued popularity of the more 'user-friendly' type of word-finding book already in production in Roget's time — the simple alphabetical list of words, each followed by its own group of synonyms. More recently there has emerged the type of thesaurus that, while preserving the alphabetical arrangement, acknowledges the value of Roget's approach by supplying with each entry related vocabulary on a rather broader, more comprehensive basis than that of mere synonymity.

*Chambers 20th Century Thesaurus* belongs to this last type — it contains 18 000 of the commonest, most synonym-rich words in the language, alphabetically listed, each with a plentiful supply of alternative and connected expressions; selected antonyms have also been added wherever appropriate. It has all the recognised usefulness of any thesaurus — but its special advantage is that it draws on the resources of *Chambers 20th Century Dictionary*, known to dictionary connoisseurs and word-game enthusiasts alike as a mine of useful, interesting and diverting items of vocabulary.

## What are the advantages of a thesaurus?

To a regular thesaurus-user they become ever more apparent. A thesaurus jogs the memory — it offers help to the person struggling to encapsulate his meaning in a forgotten *mot juste* that might remain tantalisingly on the tip of his tongue. It is indispensable to the journalist, writer and reporter. A thesaurus is fun to use, and with the fun comes the opportunity to enhance one's personal command of words and increase one's general knowledge; words that may not be well known to the reader will trigger off investigations in his dictionary and lead him to explore the remoter corners of the language. Finally, a thesaurus is a tool that the word-gamester — compiler, player or solver — cannot do without.

The thing one notices about a thesaurus is that it rarely yields completely interchangeable alternatives for a word — but this is one of its beauties. What it gives is a list of possibles that have more or less of a particular ingredient, are more or less formal, are more or less euphonious, that, in short, have more or less of the precise flavour sought by the user. English has its international origins largely to thank for its richness and subtle variety, and a thesaurus of English words, with their diversity of shape, size, sound and association, will surely yield that ideal, unmistakably usable expression to fit a particular context.

The bias towards abstract terms in the main text has been balanced by the addition of a section that is a newcomer to this type of thesaurus: an appendix of concrete and technical terms drawn from the *20th Century Dictionary* and collected alphabetically into categories such as architecture, furniture, vehicles, garments, rhetorical terms, legal terms, anatomical terms. There are also useful lists of collective nouns, names for collectors and enthusiasts, ranks in the armed forces, and wine-bottle sizes. Such words do not fit readily into synonym lists but may be no less sought-after for that. A list of the categories included appears on the Contents page [in the New Edition lists appear on pages 705 and 706].

A second appendix contains words listed by suffix. The *20th Century Dictionary* has been combed to produce exhaustive lists of -ologies, -ocracies, -ographies, -philias, -phobias, -manias, -therapies, -hoods, -doms and some seventy other such groups. This is another innovative and intriguing addition to the standard thesaurus. These two appendices will be invaluable extras not only for the crossword-solver, but for all types of thesaurus-user.

## How to use this thesaurus

Little explanation is needed, as the arrangement is deliberately simple. To take the word **ailment** as an example: the part of speech, *n*, is given, and then a list of related and synonymous words in straightforward alphabetical order — affliction, complaint, disability, disease, disorder, illness, indisposition, infection, infirmity, malady, sickness, weakness. If none of the synonyms will do, many (in this case all) have entries of their own, providing further alternatives. It is the same with the antonyms: at **abiding** the word 'transient' is supplied as an antonym; the entry **transient** will give further opposites to 'abiding'.

Separate parts of speech have separate lists of synonyms: thus at **act**, two distinct lists are provided for the word as noun and as verb; the list for each new part of speech begins on a new line.

There is coverage of phrases too: again at **act**, there are the sub-entries **act up** and **act upon**, each with its list of synonymous expressions. Some phrases occur as independent entries rather than as sub-entries, and are ordered according to their first word. This means that all the phrases beginning with the word **in**, for example, will be found in an alphabetically arranged group *before* the word **inability**, and the phrase **de trop** must be looked for *before* the word **dead**.

Among the listed synonyms the user will find the occasional abstruse or colourfully unusual word, reflecting the broad coverage of *Chambers 20th Century Dictionary*. At **aftermath**, for instance, the words 'lattermath' and 'rowen', which correspond to the original meaning of aftermath (a second crop of grass), are included in the synonym list. As a general policy, however, the editors have excluded dialect and obsolete terms, unless such terms make an appearance in, say, a well-known song, poem or play.

The simple alphabetical arrangement of synonyms means that there is no classification of meanings within an entry, but many words that have strongly distinct senses are given two or more entries. For example, **bear** (carry . . . transport . . . sustain . . . endure . . . weather, etc) and **bear** (breed . . . engender . . . give birth to . . . produce . . . propagate, etc) have been entered as **bear**[1] and **bear**[2].

It is recommended that the thesaurus should be used in conjunction with a dictionary. *Chambers Concise 20th Century Dictionary* will be a useful standard companion; the obscurer terms will be found in the fuller *Chambers 20th Century Dictionary*.

The editors hope that the readers will get as much enjoyment out of using this thesaurus as they have had in compiling it, and that it will be found to live up to the definition of **thesaurus** in the *20th Century Dictionary* — 'a treasury, a storehouse of knowledge'.

#### Acknowledgement

W & R Chambers would like to thank Peter Schwarz for the invaluable contribution in time and technical expertise that he has made to this project.

# A

**abandon** *v* abdicate, back-pedal, cede, chuck, desert, desist, discontinue, ditch, drop, evacuate, forgo, forsake, give up, jilt, leave, leave behind, leave in the lurch, quit, relinquish, renounce, repudiate, resign, scrap, sink, surrender, vacate, waive, withdraw from, yield.

*antonyms* continue, persist, support.

*n* dash, recklessness, unrestraint, wantonness, wildness.

*antonym* restraint.

**abandoned** *adj* cast aside, cast away, cast out, corrupt, debauched, depraved, derelict, deserted, desolate, discarded, dissipated, dissolute, dropped, forlorn, forsaken, jilted, left, neglected, outcast, profligate, rejected, relinquished, reprobate, scorned, sinful, unoccupied, vacant, wanton, wicked.

*antonyms* cherished, restrained.

**abandonment** *n* apostasy, cession, decampment, dereliction, desertion, desistance, discontinuance, discontinuation, dropping, evacuation, forsaking, giving up, jilting, leaving, neglect, relinquishment, renegation, renunciation, resignation, sacrifice, scrapping, surrender, waiver.

**abase** *v* belittle, cast down, debase, degrade, demean, discredit, disgrace, dishonour, downgrade, humble, humiliate, lower, malign, mortify, reduce, vitiate.

*antonyms* elevate, honour.

**abasement** *n* belittlement, debasement, degradation, demotion, depravation, deterioration, disgrace, dishonour, downgrading, humbling, humiliation, lowering, mortification, reduction, shame, vitiation.

*antonyms* elevation, promotion.

**abashed** *adj* affronted, ashamed, astounded, bewildered, chagrined, confounded, confused, cowed, discomfited, discomposed, disconcerted, discountenanced, discouraged, dismayed, dum(b)founded, embarrassed, floored, humbled, humiliated, mortified, nonplussed, perturbed, shamefaced, taken aback.

*antonyms* at ease, audacious, composed.

**abate** *v* alleviate, appease, attenuate, bate, decline, decrease, deduct, diminish, discount, dull, dwindle, ease, ebb, fade, faik, fall off, lessen, let up, mitigate, moderate, mollify, pacify, quell, rebate, reduce, relieve, remit, sink, slacken, slake, slow, subside, subtract, taper off, wane, weaken.

*antonyms* increase, strengthen.

**abatement** *n* alleviation, allowance, assuagement, attenuation, cessation, decline, decrease, deduction, diminution, discount, dulling, dwindling, easing, ebb, extenuation, fading, fall-off, lessening, let-up, mitigation, moderation, mollification, palliation, quelling, rebatement, reduction, relief, remission, slackening, slowing, softening, subsidence, subtraction, tapering off, tempering, waning, weakening.

*antonyms* crescendo, increase.

**abbey** *n* abbacy, cloister, convent, friary, monastery, nunnery, priory, seminary.

**abbot** *n* abbe, archimandrite, general, head, prior, superior.

**abbreviate** *v* abridge, abstract, clip, compress, condense, contract, curtail, cut, digest, epitomise, lessen, precis, reduce, shorten, shrink, summarise, trim, truncate.

*antonyms* amplify, extend.

**abbreviation** *n* abridgement, abstract, abstraction, clipping, compendium, compression, condensation, conspectus, contraction, curtailment, digest, epitome, precis, reduction, resume, shortening, summarisation, summary, summation, synopsis, trimming, truncation.

*antonyms* expansion, extension.

**abdicate** *v* abandon, abjure, abnegate, cede, demit, forgo, give up, quit, relinquish, renounce, repudiate, resign, retire, surrender, vacate, yield.

**abdication** *n* abandonment, abjuration, abnegation, cession, giving up, quitting, relinquishment, renunciation, resignation, retiral, retirement, surrender.

**abdomen** *n* belly, bread-basket, corporation, guts, hind-body, midriff, paunch, pot, stomach, tum, tummy, venter.

**abdominal** *adj* coeliac, gastric, intestinal, stomachic(al), ventral, ventricular, visceral.

**abduct** *v* abduce, appropriate, carry off, kidnap, lay hold of, make off with, rape, run away with, run off with, seduce, seize, snatch, spirit away.

**abducted** *adj* appropriated, enleve, kidnapped, seduced, seized, snatched, stolen.

**abduction** *n* appropriation, enlevement, kidnap, rape, seduction, seizure, theft.

**aberrant** *adj* abnormal, anomalous, atypical, corrupt, corrupted, defective, degenerate, depraved, deviant, different, divergent, eccentric, egregious, erroneous, incongruous, irregular, odd, peculiar, perverse, perverted, queer, quirky, rambling, roving, straying, untypical, wandering, wrong.

*antonyms* normal, straight.

**aberration** *n* aberrancy, abnormality, anomaly, defect, delusion, deviation, divergence, eccentricity, freak, hallucination, illusion, irregularity, lapse, nonconformity, oddity, peculiarity, quirk, rambling, rogue, straying, vagary, wandering.

*antonym* conformity.

**abet** *v* aid, assist, back, condone, connive, egg on, encourage, goad, help, incite, promote, prompt, sanction, second, spur, succour, support, sustain, uphold, urge.

*antonym* discourage.

**abettor** *n* accessory, accomplice, assistant, associate, backer, confederate, conniver, co-operator, encourager, fautor, fomenter, goad, helper, henchman, inciter, instigator, particeps criminis, prompter, second, supporter.

**abeyance** *n* adjournment, deferral, discontinuation, inactivity, intermission, lull, postponement, recess, remission, reservation, suspension, waiting.

*antonyms* activity, continuation.

**abhor** *v* abominate, despise, detest, execrate, hate, loathe, recoil from, shrink from, shudder at, spurn.

*antonyms* adore, love.

**abhorrence** *n* abomination, animosity, aversion, despite, detestation, disgust, distaste, enmity, execration, hate, hatred, horror, loathing, malice, odium, repugnance, revulsion.

*antonyms* adoration, love.

**abhorrent** *adj* abominable, absonant, despiteful, detestable, disgusting, distasteful, execrable, hated, hateful, heinous, horrible, horrid, loathsome, nauseating, obnoxious, odious, offensive, repellent, repugnant, repulsive, revolting.

*antonym* attractive.

**abide** *v* accept, bear, brook, continue, endure, last, outlive, persist, put up with, remain, stand, stay, stomach, submit to, suffer, survive, tarry, tolerate.

*antonyms* dispute, quit.

**abide by** acknowledge, acquiesce in, adhere to, agree to, carry out, comply with, conform to, discharge, follow, fulfil, go along with, hold to, keep to, obey, observe, stand by, submit to.

**abiding** *adj* constant, continual, continuing, continuous, durable, enduring, eternal, everlasting, fast, firm, immortal, immutable, indissoluble, lasting, permanent, persistent, persisting, stable, steadfast, surviving, tenacious, unchangeable, unchanging, unending.

*antonyms* ephemeral, transient.

**ability** *n* adeptness, adroitness, aptitude, capability, capacity, competence, competency,

deftness, dexterity, endowment, energy, expertise, expertness, facility, faculty, flair, forte, genius, gift, knack, know-how, long suit, nous, potentiality, power, proficiency, qualification, savoir-faire, savvy, skill, strength, talent, touch.

*antonyms* inability, incompetence.

**abject** *adj* base, contemptible, cringing, debased, degenerate, degraded, deplorable, despicable, dishonourable, execrable, fawning, forlorn, grovelling, hopeless, humiliating, ignoble, ignominious, low, mean, miserable, outcast, pathetic, pitiable, servile, slavish, sordid, submissive, vile, worthless, wretched.

*antonym* exalted.

**abjuration** *n* abnegation, abstention, denial, disavowal, disclaiming, disclamation, eschewal, forswearing, recantation, refusal, rejection, relinquishment, renunciation, retraction, self-denial.

*antonyms* agreement, assent, support.

**abjure** *v* abandon, abnegate, abstain from, deny, disavow, discard, disclaim, disown, eschew, forsake, forswear, give up, recant, refrain from, reject, relinquish, renegue on, renounce, retract.

*antonyms* agree, assent, support.

**ablaze** *adj* afire, aflame, aglow, alight, angry, aroused, blazing, brilliant, burning, enthusiastic, excited, exhilarated, fervent, fiery, flaming, flashing, frenzied, fuming, furious, glaring, gleaming, glowing, ignited, illuminated, impassioned, incandescent, incensed, lighted, luminous, on fire, passionate, radiant, raging, sparkling, stimulated.

**able** *adj* accomplished, adept, adequate, adroit, capable, clever, competent, deft, dexterous, effective, efficient, experienced, expert, fere, fit, fitted, gifted, ingenious, masterful, masterly, powerful, practised, proficient, qualified, skilful, skilled, strong, talented.

*antonyms* incapable, incompetent.

**able-bodied** *adj* firm, fit, hale, hardy, healthy, hearty, lusty, powerful, robust, sound, stalwart, staunch, stout, strapping, strong, sturdy, tough, vigorous.

*antonyms* delicate, infirm.

**ablution** *n* bath, bathing, cleansing, lavation, purgation, purging, purification, shower, wash, washing.

**abnegate** *v* abandon, abdicate, abjure, abstain from, acquiesce, concede, decline, deny, disallow, eschew, forbear, forgo, forsake, give up, refrain from, reject, relinquish, renounce, sacrifice, submit, surrender, yield.

**abnegation** *n* abandonment, abjuration, abstinence, acquiescence, continence, disallowance, eschewal, forbearance, giving up, refusal, rejection, relinquishment, renunciation, sacrifice, self-denial, submission, surrender, temperance.

*antonyms* acceptance, support.

**abnormal** *adj* aberrant, anomalous, atypical, curious, deviant, different, divergent, eccentric, erratic, exceptional, extraordinary, irregular, monstrous, odd, paranormal, peculiar, queer, singular, strange, uncanny, uncommon, unexpected, unnatural, untypical, unusual, wayward, weird.

*antonyms* normal, straight.

**abnormality** *n* aberration, anomaly, atypicalness, bizarreness, deformity, deviation, difference, divergence, dysfunction, eccentricity, exception, flaw, irregularity, monstrosity, oddity, peculiarity, queerness, singularity, strangeness, uncommonness, unexpectedness, unnaturalness, untypicalness, unusualness, weirdness.

*antonym* normality.

**abode** *n* domicile, dwelling, dwelling-place, habitat, habitation, home, house, lodging, pad, place, quarters, residence.

**abolish** *v* abrogate, annihilate, annul, blot out, cancel, destroy, do away with, eliminate, end, eradicate, expunge, exterminate, extinguish, extirpate, get rid of, invalidate, kibosh, nullify, obliterate, overthrow, overturn, put an end to, put the kibosh on, quash, repeal, repudiate, rescind, revoke, sink, stamp out, subvert, suppress, terminate, vitiate, void, wipe out.

*antonyms* continue, retain.

**abolition** *n* abolishment, abrogation, annihilation, annulment, cancellation, destruction, dissolution, elimination, end, ending, eradication, expunction, extermination, extinction, extirpation, invalidation, nullification, obliteration, overthrow, overturning, quashing, repeal, repudiation, rescission, revocation, subversion, suppression, termination, vitiation, voiding, withdrawal.

*antonyms* continuance, retention.

**abominable** *adj* abhorrent, accursed, appalling, atrocious, base, beastly, contemptible, despicable, detestable, disgusting, execrable, foul, hateful, heinous, hellish, horrible, horrid, loathsome, nauseating, nauseous, nefandous, nefast, obnoxious, odious, repellent, reprehensible, repugnant, repulsive, revolting, terrible, vile, villainous, wretched.

*antonyms* delightful, desirable.

**abominate** *v* abhor, condemn, despise, detest, execrate, hate, loathe.

*antonyms* adore, esteem, love.

**abomination** *n* abhorrence, anathema, animosity, animus, antipathy, aversion, bête noire, bugbear, curse, detestation, disgrace, disgust, distaste, evil, execration, hate, hatred, horror, hostility, loathing, odium, offence, plague, repugnance, revulsion, torment.

*antonyms* adoration, delight.

**aboriginal** *adj* ancient, autochthonic, autochthonous, domestic, earliest, enchorial, endemic, first, indigenous, native, original, primal, primary, primeval, primitive, primordial, pristine.

**aborigine** *n* aboriginal, autochthon, indigene, native, warragal.

*antonyms* immigrant, incomer.

**abort** *v* arrest, call off, check, end, fail, frustrate, halt, miscarry, nullify, stop, terminate, thwart.

*antonym* continue.

**abortion** *n* aborticide, disappointment, failure, fiasco, foeticide, freak, frustration, misadventure, misbirth, miscarriage, monster, monstrosity, termination, thwarting.

*antonyms* continuation, success.

**abortive** *adj* barren, bootless, failed, failing, fruitless, futile, idle, ineffective, ineffectual, misborn, miscarried, sterile, unavailing, unproductive, unsuccessful, useless, vain.

*antonym* successful.

**abound** *v* be plentiful, brim over, crowd, exuberate, flourish, increase, infest, luxuriate, overflow, proliferate, run riot, superabound, swarm, swell, teem, thrive.

*antonym* be in short supply.

**abounding** *adj* abundant, bountiful, copious, filled, flourishing, flowing, flush, full, lavish, luxuriant, overflowing, plenteous, plentiful, prodigal, profuse, prolific, rank, replete, rich, superabundant, teeming, unstinting.

*antonym* lacking.

**about** *prep* adjacent to, all over, anent, around, as regards, beside, busy with, circa, close to, concerned with, concerning, connected with, encircling, encompassing, engaged on, in respect to, in the matter of, near, nearby, of, on, over, re, referring to, regarding, relating to, relative to, respecting, round, surrounding, through, throughout, touching, with reference to, with regard to, with respect to.

*adv* active, almost, approaching, approximately, around, astir, close to, from place to place, here and there, hither and thither, in motion, in the region of, more or less, nearing, nearly, present, roughly, stirring, to and fro.

**about to** all but, intending to, on the point of, on the verge of, preparing to, ready to.

**about-turn** *n* about-face, apostasy, backtrack, enantiodromia, reversal, right-about (face), turnabout, turn(a)round, uey, U-turn, volte-face.

**above** *prep* atop, before, beyond, exceeding, higher than, in excess of, on top of, over, prior to, superior to, surpassing, upon.

*antonyms* below, under.

*adv* aloft, atop, earlier, heavenwards, in heaven, on high, overhead, supra.

*antonym* below.

*adj* above-mentioned, above-stated, aforementioned, aforesaid, earlier, foregoing, preceding, previous, prior.

**above suspicion** above reproach, blameless, guiltless, honourable, innocent, irreproachable, pure, sinless, unimpeachable, virtuous.

**above-board** *adj* candid, fair, fair and square, forthright, frank, guileless, honest, honourable, legitimate, on the level, open, overt, reputable, square, straight, straightforward, true, trustworthy, truthful, upright, veracious.

*antonyms* shady, underhand.

**abrade** v chafe, erase, erode, file, grind, levigate, rub off, scour, scrape, triturate, wear away, wear down, wear off.

**abrasion** n abrading, chafe, chafing, erosion, friction, grating, graze, grinding, levigation, rubbing, scouring, scrape, scraping, scratch, scratching, scuff, scuffing, trituration, wearing away, wearing down.

**abrasive** adj abradant, annoying, attritional, biting, caustic, chafing, erodent, erosive, frictional, galling, grating, hurtful, irritating, nasty, rough, scraping, scratching, scratchy, scuffing, sharp, unpleasant.

*antonyms* pleasant, smooth.

**abreast** adj acquainted, au courant, au fait, conversant, familiar, in the picture, in touch, informed, knowledgeable, on the ball, up to date.

*antonyms* out of touch, unaware.

**abridge** v abbreviate, abstract, circumscribe, clip, compress, concentrate, condense, contract, curtail, cut, cut down, decrease, digest, diminish, dock, epitomise, lessen, lop, precis, prune, reduce, shorten, summarise, synopsise, trim, truncate.

*antonyms* amplify, pad.

**abridgement** n abbreviation, abrege, abstract, compendium, compression, concentration, condensation, conspectus, contraction, curtailment, cutting, decrease, digest, diminishing, diminution, epitome, lessening, limitation, outline, precis, pruning, reduction, restriction, resume, shortening, summary, synopsis, truncation.

*antonyms* expansion, padding.

**abroad** adv about, at large, away, circulating, current, elsewhere, extensively, far, far and wide, forth, in circulation, in foreign parts, out, out of the country, out-of-doors, outside, overseas, publicly, widely.

**abrogate** v abolish, annul, cancel, countermand, disannul, discontinue, disenact, dissolve, end, invalidate, nullify, override, overrule, quash, recall, repeal, repudiate, rescind, retract, reverse, revoke, scrap, set aside, terminate, void, withdraw.

*antonyms* establish, institute.

**abrogation** n abolition, annulling, annulment, cancellation, countermanding, defeasance, disannulment, discontinuation, ending, invalidation, nullification, overriding, overruling, quashing, repeal, repudiation, rescission, retraction, reversal, revocation, scrapping, setting aside, termination, voiding, withdrawal.

*antonyms* continuation, retention.

**abrupt** adj blunt, brief, brisk, broken, brusque, curt, direct, disconnected, discontinuous, discourteous, gruff, hasty, headlong, hurried, impolite, irregular, jerky, precipitate, precipitous, prerupt, quick, rapid, rough, rude, sharp, sheer, short, snappy, steep, sudden, surprising, swift, terse, unannounced, unceremonious, uncivil, uneven, unexpected, unforeseen, ungracious.

*antonyms* ceremonious, expansive, leisurely.

**abscond** v absquatulate, beat it, bolt, clear out, decamp, disappear, do a bunk, escape, flee, flit, fly, hightail it, levant, make off, quit, run off, scram, skedaddle, skive, take French leave, vamoose.

**absconder** n absentee, bolter, escapee, levanter, quitter, truant.

**absence** n absenteeism, absent-mindedness, abstraction, dearth, default, defect, deficiency, distraction, inattention, lack, need, non-appearance, non-attendance, non-existence, omission, paucity, preoccupation, privation, reverie, scarcity, truancy, unavailability, vacancy, vacuity, want.

*antonyms* existence, presence.

**absent** adj absent-minded, absorbed, abstracted, away, bemused, blank, day-dreaming, distracted, distrait(e), dreamy, elsewhere, empty, faraway, gone, heedless, inattentive, lacking, missing, musing, non-existent, not present, oblivious, out, preoccupied, truant, unavailable, unaware, unconscious, unheeding, unthinking, vacant, vague, wanting, withdrawn, wool-gathering.

*antonyms* aware, present.

**absent-minded** adj absent, absorbed, abstracted, bemused, distracted, distrait(e), dreaming, dreamy, engrossed, faraway, forgetful, heedless, impractical, inattentive, musing, oblivious, otherwordly, pensive, preoccupied, scatterbrained, unaware, unconscious, unheeding, unthinking, withdrawn, wool-gathering.

*antonyms* matter-of-fact, attentive, practical.

**absent-mindedness** n absence, absorption, abstraction, distraction, dreaminess, forgetfulness, heedlessness, inattention, muse, preoccupation, unawareness, vacancy, vagueness.

*antonym* alertness.

**absolute** adj absolutist, actual, almighty, arbitrary, autarchical, autocratic, autonomous, categorical, certain, complete, conclusive, consummate, decided, decisive, definite, definitive, despotic, dictatorial, downright, entire, exact, exhaustive, final, flawless, free, full, genuine, independent, indubitable, infallible, omnipotent, out-and-out, outright, peremptory, perfect, positive, precise, pure, sheer, sovereign, supreme, sure, terminative, thorough, total, totalitarian, tyrannical, unadulterated, unalloyed, unambiguous, unbounded, unconditional, uncontrolled, undivided, unequivocal, unlimited, unmitigated, unmixed, unqualified, unquestionable, unrestrained, unrestricted, utter.

*antonyms* conditional, partial.

**absolutely** adv actually, arbitrarily, autocratically, autonomously, bang, categorically, certainly, completely, conclusively, consummately, dead, decidedly, decisively, definitely, despotically, diametrically, dictatorially, entirely, exactly, exhaustively, finally, fully, genuinely, indubitably, infallibly, peremptorily, perfectly, positively, precisely, purely, sovereignly, supremely, surely, thoroughly, totally, truly, tyrannically, unambiguously, unconditionally, unequivocally, unmitigatedly, unquestionably, unrestrainedly, utterly, wholly.

**absolution** *n* acquittal, acquittance, amnesty, compurgation, deliverance, discharge, dispensation, emancipation, exculpation, exemption, exoneration, forgiveness, forgiving, freeing, indulgence, liberation, mercy, pardon, purgation, redemption, release, remission, shriving, vindication.

*antonym* condemnation.

**absolve** *v* acquit, clear, deliver, discharge, emancipate, exculpate, excuse, exempt, exonerate, forgive, free, justify, let off, liberate, loose, pardon, ransom, redeem, release, remit, set free, shrive, vindicate.

*antonym* charge.

**absorb** *v* adsorb, apprehend, assimilate, captivate, consume, co-opt, devour, digest, drink in, engage, engross, engulf, enthral(l), enwrap, exhaust, fascinate, fill (up), fix, grip, hold, imbibe, immerse, incorporate, ingest, involve, monopolise, occupy, osmose, preoccupy, receive, retain, rivet, soak up, sorb, submerge, suck up, take in, understand, utilise.

*antonyms* dissipate, exude.

**absorbed** *adj* captivated, concentrating, engaged, engrossed, enthralled, fascinated, fixed, gripped, held, immersed, intent, involved, lost, obsessed, occupied, preoccupied, rapt, riveted, wrapped up.

*antonyms* bored, distracted.

**absorbent** *adj* absorptive, assimilative, blotting, penetrable, permeable, pervious, porous, receptive, resorbent, retentive, sorbefacient, sorbent, spongy.

*antonym* impermeable.

**absorbing** *adj* amusing, arresting, captivating, compulsive, diverting, engrossing, entertaining, enthralling, fascinating, gripping, interesting, intriguing, preoccupying, riveting, spellbinding, unputdownable.

*antonyms* boring, off-putting.

**absorption** *n* adsorption, assimilation, attentiveness, captivation, concentration, consumption, digestion, engagement, exhaustion, fascination, holding, imbibition, immersion, incorporation, ingestion, intentness, involvement, occupation, osmosis, preoccupation, raptness, soaking up, sucking up.

**abstain** *v* avoid, cease, decline, deny, desist, eschew, forbear, forgo, give up, keep from, refrain, refuse, reject, renounce, resist, shun, stop, swear off, withhold.

*antonym* indulge.

**abstemious** *adj* abstinent, ascetic, austere, continent, disciplined, frugal, moderate, restrained, self-denying, self-disciplined, sober, sparing, temperate.

*antonyms* gluttonous, intemperate, luxurious.

**abstention** *n* abstaining, abstinence, avoidance, continence, desistance, eschewal, forbearance, frugality, nephalism, non-indulgence, refraining, refusal, restraint, self-control, self-denial, self-discipline, self-restraint, sobriety.

**abstinence** *n* abstemiousness, abstinency, asceticism, avoidance, continence, forbearance, frugality, moderation, nephalism, non-indulgence, refraining, self-denial, self-discipline, self-restraint, soberness, sobriety, teetotalism, temperance.

*antonym* self-indulgence.

**abstinent** *adj* abstaining, abstemious, continent, disciplined, forbearing, frugal, moderate, self-controlled, self-denying, self-disciplined, self-restrained, sober, temperate.

*antonyms* self-indulgent, voluptuous, wanton.

**abstract** *adj* abstruse, academic, arcane, complex, conceptual, deep, discrete, general, generalised, hypothetical, indefinite, intellectual, metaphysical, non-concrete, occult, philosophical, profound, recondite, separate, subtle, theoretic, theoretical, unpractical, unrealistic.

*antonym* concrete.

*n* abbreviation, abridgement, abstractive, compendium, compression, condensation, conspectus, digest, epitome, essence, outline, precis, recapitulation, resume, summary, synopsis.

*v* abbreviate, abridge, compress, condense, detach, digest, dissociate, epitomise, extract, isolate, outline, precis, purloin, remove, separate, shorten, steal, summarise, withdraw.

*antonyms* expand, insert.

**abstracted** *adj* absent, absent-minded, bemused, distrait(e), dreamy, faraway, inattentive, pensive, preoccupied, remote, withdrawn, wool-gathering.

*antonyms* alert, on the ball.

**abstraction** *n* absence, absent-mindedness, absorption, bemusedness, concept, conception, dissociation, distraction, dream, dreaminess, formula, generalisation, generality, hypothesis, idea, inattention, notion, pensiveness, preoccupation, remoteness, separation, theorem, theory, thought, withdrawal, wool-gathering.

**abstruse** *adj* abstract, arcane, complex, cryptic, dark, deep, devious, difficult, enigmatic, esoteric, hermetic, hidden, incomprehensible, mysterious, mystical, obscure, occult, perplexing, profound, puzzling, recondite, subtle, tortuous, unfathomable, unobvious, vague.

*antonyms* concrete, obvious.

**absurd** *adj* anomalous, comical, crazy, daft, derisory, fantastic, farcical, foolish, funny, humorous, idiotic, illogical, implausible, incongruous, irrational, laughable, ludicrous, meaningless, nonsensical, paradoxical, preposterous, ridiculous, risible, senseless, silly, stupid, unreasonable, untenable.

*antonyms* logical, rational, sensible.

**absurdity** *n* comicality, craziness, daftness, farce, farcicality, farcicalness, fatuity, fatuousness, folly, foolery, foolishness, idiocy, illogicality, illogicalness, incongruity, irrationality, joke, ludicrousness, meaninglessness, nonsense, nonsensicality, preposterousness, ridiculousness, senselessness, silliness, stupidity, unreasonableness.

**abundance** *n* affluence, ampleness, amplitude, bonanza, bounty, copiousness, exuberance, fortune, fullness, glut, heap, lavishness, luxuriance, luxuriancy, milk and honey, munificence, oodles, opulence, plenitude, plenteousness, plenty, pleroma, plethora, prodigality, profusion, riches, richness, routh, uberty, wealth.

*antonyms* dearth, scarcity.

**abundant** *adj* ample, bounteous, bountiful, copious, exuberant, filled, full, generous, in plenty, lavish, luxuriant, overflowing, plenteous, plentiful, prodigal, profuse, rank, rich, superabundant, teeming, uberous, unstinted, well-provided, well-supplied.

*antonyms* scarce, sparse.

**abuse** *v* batter, calumniate, castigate, curse, damage, deceive, defame, denigrate, disparage, exploit, harm, hurt, ill-treat, impose on, injure, insult, inveigh against, libel, malign, maltreat, manhandle, mar, misapply, miscall, misemploy, misuse, molest, objurgate, oppress, oppugn, revile, scold, slander, slate, smear, spoil, swear at, take advantage of, traduce, upbraid, vilify, violate, vituperate, wrong.

*antonyms* cherish, compliment, praise.

*n* affront, blame, calumniation, calumny, castigation, censure, contumely, curses, cursing, damage, defamation, denigration, derision, diatribe, disparagement, execration, exploitation, flyting, harm, hurt, ill-treatment, imposition, injury, insults, invective, libel, malediction, maltreatment, manhandling, misapplication, misconduct, misdeed, misuse, obloquy, offence, oppression, opprobrium, reproach, revilement, scolding, sin, slander, spoiling, swearing, tirade, traducement, upbraiding, vilification, violation, vitriol, vituperation, wrong, wrong-doing.

*antonyms* attention, care.

**abusive** *adj* brutal, calumniating, calumnious, castigating, censorious, contumelious, cruel, defamatory, denigrating, derisive, derogatory, destructive, disparaging, harmful, hurtful, injurious, insulting, invective, libellous, maligning, objurgatory, offensive, opprobrious, pejorative, reproachful, reviling, rough, rude, scathing, scolding, slanderous, traducing, upbraiding, vilifying, vituperative.

*antonym* complimentary.

**abut** *v* adjoin, border, conjoin, connect, impinge, join, meet, touch, verge.

**abysmal** *adj* abyssal, bottomless, boundless, complete, deep, endless, extreme, immeasurable, incalculable, infinite, profound, thorough, unending, unfathomable, vast, yawning.

**abyss** *n* abysm, Avernus, barathrum, canyon, chasm, crater, crevasse, depth, fissure, gorge, gulf, pit, profound, swallow, void.

**academic** *adj* abstract, bookish, collegiate, conjectural, donnish, educational, erudite, highbrow, hypothetical, impractical, instructional, learned, lettered, literary, notional, pedagogical, scholarly, scholastic, speculative, studious, theoretical, well-read.

*n* academe, academician, don, fellow, lecturer, man of letters, master, pedant, professor, pundit, savant, scholar, scholastic, schoolman, student, tutor.

**accede** *v* accept, acquiesce, admit, agree, assent, assume, attain, capitulate, comply, concede, concur, consent, defer, endorse, grant, inherit, submit, succeed (to), yield.

*antonyms* demur, object.

**accelerate** *v* advance, antedate, dispatch, expedite, facilitate, festinate, forward, further, hasten, hurry, pick up speed, precipitate, promote, quicken, speed, speed up, spur, step on the gas, step on the juice, step up, stimulate.

*antonyms* delay, slow down.

**accent** *n* accentuation, arsis, articulation, beat, cadence, emphasis, enunciation, force, ictus, inflection, intensity, intonation, modulation, pitch, pronunciation, pulsation, pulse, rhythm, stress, thesis, timbre, tonality, tone.

*v* accentuate, emphasise, stress, underline, underscore.

**accentuate** *v* accent, deepen, emphasise, highlight, intensify, italicise, spotlight, strengthen, stress, underline, underscore.

*antonyms* play down, weaken.

**accept** *v* abide by, accede, acknowledge, acquiesce, acquire, admit, adopt, affirm, agree to, approve, assume, avow, bear, believe, bow to, brook, concur with, consent to, co-operate with, defer to, gain, get, have, jump at, obtain, put up with, receive, recognise, secure, stand, stomach, submit to, suffer, swallow, take, take on, tolerate, undertake, wear, yield to.

*antonyms* demur, reject.

**acceptable** *adj* adequate, admissible, agreeable, all right, conventional, correct, delightful, desirable, done, grateful, gratifying, moderate, passable, pleasant, pleasing, satisfactory, standard, suitable, tolerable, U, unexceptionable, unobjectionable, welcome.

*antonyms* unsatisfactory, unwelcome.

**acceptance** *n* accedence, accepting, accession, acknowledgement, acquiescence, acquiring, admission, adoption, affirmation, agreement, approbation, approval, assent, belief, compliance, concession, concurrence, consent, credence, gaining, getting, having, obtaining, OK, permission, ratification, receipt, recognition, seal of approval, securing, stamp of approval, taking, tolerance, toleration, undertaking.

*antonyms* dissent, refusal.

**accepted** *adj* acceptable, acknowledged, admitted, agreed, agreed upon, approved, authorised, common, confirmed, consuetudinary, conventional, correct, customary, established, normal, ratified, received, recognised, regular, sanctioned, standard, time-honoured, traditional, universal, unwritten, usual.

*antonym* unorthodox.

**access** n adit, admission, admittance, approach, avenue, course, door, entering, entrance, entree, entry, gateway, increase, ingress, key, onset, passage, passageway, path, road, upsurge, upsurgence.

*antonyms* egress, outlet.

**accessible** adj achievable, affable, approachable, at hand, attainable, available, come-at-able, conversable, cordial, exposed, friendly, get-at-able, handy, informal, liable, near, nearby, obtainable, on hand, open, possible, procurable, reachable, ready, sociable, subject, susceptible, user-friendly, vulnerable, wide-open.

*antonym* inaccessible.

**accession** n accedence, acceptance, acquiescence, acquisition, addition, agreement, assumption, attaining, attainment, augmentation, concurrence, consent, enlargement, entering upon, extension, increase, installation, purchase, submission, succession, taking over, yielding.

**accessory** n abettor, accompaniment, accomplice, addition, adjunct, adjuvant, adornment, aid, appendage, assistant, associate, attachment, colleague, component, confederate, conniver, convenience, decoration, embellishment, extension, extra, frill, help, helper, particeps criminis, partner, supplement, trim, trimming.

adj abetting, additional, adjuvant, adventitious, aiding, ancillary, assisting, auxiliary, contributory, extra, incidental, secondary, subordinate, subsidiary, supplemental, supplementary.

**accident** n blow, calamity, casualty, chance, collision, contingency, contretemps, crash, disaster, fate, fluke, fortuity, fortune, happenstance, hazard, luck, misadventure, miscarriage, mischance, misfortune, mishap, pile-up, prang, serendipity, shunt.

**accidental** adj adventitious, adventive, casual, chance, contingent, fluky, fortuitous, haphazard, inadvertent, incidental, random, serendipitous, unanticipated, uncalculated, uncertain, unexpected, unforeseen, unintended, unintentional, unlooked-for, unplanned, unpremeditated, unwitting.

*antonyms* intentional, premeditated.

**accidentally** adv adventitiously, bechance, by accident, by chance, by mistake, casually, fortuitously, haphazardly, inadvertently, incidentally, involuntarily, randomly, serendipitously, unconsciously, undesignedly, unexpectedly, unintentionally, unwittingly.

*antonym* intentionally.

**acclaim** v announce, applaud, approve, celebrate, cheer, clap, commend, crown, declare, eulogise, exalt, extol, fanfare, hail, honour, laud, praise, salute, welcome.

*antonym* demean.

n acclamation, applause, approbation, approval, celebration, cheering, clapping, commendation, eulogising, eulogy, exaltation, fanfare, honour, laudation, ovation, plaudits, praise, welcome.

*antonyms* brickbats, criticism, vituperation.

**acclamation** n acclaim, adulation, applause, approbation, bravos, cheer, cheering, cheers, commendation, declaration, eclat, endorsement, enthusiasm, extolment, homage, laudation, ovation, paean, panegyric, plaudit, praise, salutation, shouting, tribute.

*antonym* disapproval.

**acclimatise** v accommodate, acculturate, accustom, adapt, adjust, attune, conform, familiarise, find one's legs, get used to, habituate, inure, naturalise.

**acclivity** n ascent, gradient, hill, rise, rising ground, slope.

**accolade** n award, honour, kudos, laurels, praise.

**accommodate** v acclimatise, accustom, adapt, adjust, afford, aid, assist, attune, billet, board, cater for, comply, compose, conform, domicile, entertain, fit, furnish, harbour, harmonise, help, house, lodge, modify, oblige, provide, put up, quarter, reconcile, serve, settle, shelter, supply.

**accommodating** adj complaisant, considerate, co-operative, friendly, helpful, hospitable, indulgent, kind, obliging, polite, sympathetic, unselfish, willing.

*antonym* disobliging.

**accommodation**[1] n adaptation, adjustment, assistance, compliance, composition, compromise, conformity, fitting, harmonisation, harmony, help, modification, reconciliation, settlement.

**accommodation**[2] n bed and breakfast, billet, board, digs, domicile, dwelling, harbouring, house, housing, lodgings, quartering, quarters, residence, shelter, sheltering.

**accompaniment** n accessory, attendance, background, back-up, complement, concomitant, obligato, support, vamp.

**accompany** v attend, belong to, chaperon, co-exist, coincide, complement, conduct, consort, convoy, escort, follow, go with, occur with, squire, supplement, usher.

**accompanying** adj accessory, added, additional, appended, associate, associated, attached, attendant, background, complementary, concomitant, concurrent, connected, fellow, joint, related, subsidiary, supplemental, supplementary.

**accomplice** n abettor, accessory, ally, assistant, associate, coadjutor, collaborator, colleague, confederate, conspirator, helper, helpmate, henchman, mate, particeps criminis, participator, partner, practisant, shill.

**accomplish** v achieve, attain, bring about, bring off, carry out, compass, complete, conclude, consummate, discharge, do, effect, effectuate, engineer, execute, finish, fulfil, manage, obtain, perform, produce, realise.

**accomplished** adj adept, adroit, consummate, cultivated, expert, facile, gifted, masterly, polished, practised, professional, proficient, skilful, skilled, talented.

*antonym* inexpert.

**accomplishment** n ability, achievement, act, aptitude, art, attainment, capability, carrying out, completion, conclusion, consummation, coup, deed, discharge, doing, effecting, execution, exploit, faculty, feat, finishing, forte, fruition, fulfilment, futurition, gift, management, perfection, performance, production, proficiency, realisation, skill, stroke, talent, triumph.

**accord** *v* agree, allow, assent, bestow, concede, concur, confer, conform, correspond, endow, fit, give, grant, harmonise, jibe, match, present, render, suit, tally, tender, vouchsafe.

*antonym* disagree.

*n* accordance, agreement, assent, concert, concurrence, conformity, congruence, congruity, consort, correspondence, harmony, rapport, symmetry, sympathy, unanimity, unity.

*antonym* discord.

**accordance** *n* accord, agreement, assent, concert, concurrence, conformity, congruence, consistency, consonance, correspondence, harmony, rapport, sympathy, unanimity.

**accordingly** *adv* appropriately, as a result, as requested, consequently, correspondingly, ergo, fitly, hence, in accord with, in accordance, in consequence, properly, so, suitably, therefore, thus.

**according to** after, after the manner of, agreeably to, commensurate with, consistent with, in accordance with, in compliance with, in conformity with, in keeping with, in line with, in obedience to, in proportion, in relation, in the light of, in the manner of, obedient to.

**accost** *v* address, approach, button-hole, confront, detain, greet, hail, halt, importune, salute, solicit, stop, waylay.

**account¹** *n* advantage, basis, battels, benefit, cause, chronicle, communique, concern, consequence, consideration, description, detail, distinction, esteem, estimation, explanation, ground, grounds, history, honour, import, importance, interest, memoir, merit, motive, narration, narrative, note, performance, portrayal, presentation, profit, rank, reason, recital, record, regard, relation, report, reputation, repute, sake, score, significance, sketch, standing, statement, story, tale, use, value, version, worth, write-up.

*v* adjudge, appraise, assess, believe, consider, count, deem, esteem, estimate, explain, gauge, hold, judge, rate, reckon, regard, think, value, weigh.

**account for** answer for, clarify, clear up, destroy, elucidate, explain, illuminate, incapacitate, justify, kill, put paid to, rationalise, vindicate.

**account²** *n* balance, battels, bill, book, books, charge, check, computation, inventory, invoice, ledger, reckoning, register, score, statement, tab, tally, tick.

**accountability** *n* amenability, answerability, blamableness, blameworthiness, chargeability, liability, responsibility.

**accountable** *adj* amenable, answerable, blamable, bound, charged with, liable, obligated, obliged, responsible.

**accoutrements** *n* adornments, apparel, appurtenances, array, attire, caparison, clothes, clothing, decorations, dress, equipage, equipment, fittings, fixtures, furnishings, garb, gear, habiliments, kit, ornamentation, outfit, paraphernalia, tackle, trappings, traps, trimmings.

**accredit** *v* appoint, approve, ascribe, assign, attribute, authorise, certificate, certify, commission, credit, depute, empower, enable, endorse, entrust, guarantee, license, okay, qualify, recognise, sanction, vouch for.

**accredited** *adj* appointed, approved, attested, authorised, certificated, certified, commissioned, deputed, deputised, empowered, endorsed, guaranteed, licensed, official, qualified, recognised, sanctioned, vouched for.

*antonym* unauthorised.

**accretion** *n* accession, accrual, accumulation, addition, amplification, augmentation, coherence, cohesion, enlargement, fusion, growth, increase, increment, supplement.

*antonyms* decrease, deduction.

**accrue** *v* accumulate, amass, arise, be added, build up, collect, emanate, enlarge, ensue, fall due, flow, follow, gather, grow, increase, issue, proceed, redound, result, spring up.

**accumulate** *v* accrue, agglomerate, aggregate, amass, assemble, build up, collect, cumulate, gather, grow, hoard, increase, multiply, pile up, stash, stockpile, store.

*antonyms* diffuse, disseminate.

**accumulation** *n* accretion, aggregation, assemblage, augmentation, backlog, build-up, collection, conglomeration, gathering, growth, heap, hoard, increase, mass, pile, reserve, stack, stock, stockpile, store.

**accuracy** *n* accurateness, actuality, authenticity, carefulness, closeness, correctness, exactitude, exactness, faithfulness, faultlessness, fidelity, meticulousness, minuteness, niceness, nicety, precision, rigorousness, scrupulosity, scrupulousness, strictness, truth, truthfulness, veracity, veridicality, verity.

*antonym* inaccuracy.

**accurate** *adj* authentic, careful, close, correct, exact, factual, faithful, faultless, just, letter-perfect, mathematical, meticulous, minute, nice, perfect, precise, proper, regular, right, rigorous, scrupulous, sound, spot-on, strict, true, truthful, unerring, veracious, veridical, well-aimed, well-directed, well-judged, word-perfect.

*antonyms* inaccurate, wrong.

**accursed** *adj* abominable, anathematised, bedevilled, bewitched, blighted, condemned, cursed, damned, despicable, detestable, doomed, execrable, foredoomed, hateful, hellish, hopeless, horrible, ill-fated, ill-omened, jinxed, luckless, maledict, ruined, star-crossed, undone, unfortunate, unholy, unlucky, wretched.

*antonym* blessed.

**accusation** *n* accusal, allegation, arraignment, attribution, charge, citation, complaint, crimination, delation, denunciation, gravamen, impeachment, imputation, incrimination, indictment, plaint, recrimination, threap.

**accuse** *v* allege, arraign, attaint, attribute, blame, censure, charge, cite, criminate, delate, denounce, impeach, impugn, impute, incriminate, indict, inform against, recriminate, tax.

**accustom** *v* acclimatise, acculturate, acquaint, adapt, adjust, discipline, exercise, familiarise, habituate, harden, inure, season, train.

**accustomed** *adj* acclimatised, acquainted, adapted, common, confirmed, consuetudinary, conventional, customary, disciplined, established, everyday, exercised, expected, familiar, familiarised, fixed, general, given to, habitual, habituated, in the habit of, inured, normal, ordinary, prevailing, regular, routine, seasoned, set, traditional, trained, used, usual, wonted.

*antonym* unaccustomed.

**ace** *n* adept, champion, dab hand, dabster, expert, genius, maestro, master, nonpareil, star, talent, virtuoso, winner, wizard.

*antonyms* colt, novice.

*adj* brilliant, champion, excellent, expert, fine, first-class, great, hell of a, masterly, matchless, nonpareil, outstanding, superb, superlative, tiptop, virtuoso.

**acerbic** *adj* abrasive, acid, acidulous, acrid, acrimonious, astringent, bitter, brusque, caustic, churlish, corrosive, harsh, incisive, mordant, nasty, rancorous, rude, sarcastic, severe, sharp, sour, stern, tart, trenchant, unfriendly, unkind.

*antonym* mild.

**acerbity** *n* acidity, acidulousness, acridity, acridness, acrimoniousness, acrimony, asperity, astringency, bitterness, brusqueness, causticity, churlishness, harshness, mordacity, mordancy, nastiness, rancour, rudeness, severity, sharpness, sourness, sternness, tartness, trenchancy, unfriendliness, unkindness.

*antonym* mildness.

**ache** *v* agonise, covet, crave, desire, grieve, hanker, hunger, hurt, itch, long, mourn, need, pain, pine, pound, rack, smart, sorrow, suffer, throb, twinge, yearn.

*n* anguish, craving, desire, grief, hankering, hunger, hurt, itch, longing, misery, mourning, need, pain, pang, pining, pounding, smart, smarting, soreness, sorrow, suffering, throb, throbbing, yearning.

**achieve** *v* accomplish, acquire, attain, bring about, carry out, compass, complete, consummate, do, earn, effect, effectuate, execute, finish, fulfil, gain, get, manage, obtain, perform, procure, produce, reach, realise, score, strike, succeed, win.

*antonyms* fail, miss.

**achievement** *n* accomplishment, acquirement, act, attainment, completion, deed, effort, execution, exploit, feat, fruition, fulfilment, magnum opus, performance, production, qualification, realisation, stroke, success.

**achiever** *n* doer, goer, go-getter, performer, succeeder.

**acid** *adj* acerbic, acidulous, acrid, astringent, biting, bitter, caustic, corrosive, cutting, harsh, hurtful, ill-natured, incisive, mordant, morose, pungent, sharp, sour, stinging, tart, trenchant, vinegarish, vinegary, vitriolic.

**acid test** experimentum crucis, proof of the pudding.

**acidity** *n* acerbity, acidulousness, acridity, acridness, asperity, astringency, bitterness, causticity, causticness, corrosiveness, harshness, hurtfulness, incisiveness, mordancy, pungency, sharpness, sourness, tartness, trenchancy, vinegariness, vinegarishness.

**acidulous** *adj* acerbic, acid, astringent, biting, bitter, caustic, cutting, harsh, incisive, pungent, sharp, sour, tart, vinegarish, vinegary.

*antonyms* saccharine, sugary, sweet.

**acknowledge** *v* accede, accept, acquiesce, address, admit, affirm, agnise, allow, answer, attest, avouch, concede, confess, confirm, declare, endorse, grant, greet, hail, notice, own, profess, react to, recognise, reply to, respond to, return, salute, vouch for, witness, yield.

**acknowledged** *adj* accepted, accredited, admitted, affirmed, answered, approved, attested, avowed, conceded, confessed, declared, endorsed, professed, recognised, returned.

**acknowledgement** *n* acceptance, accession, acquiescence, addressing, admission, affirmation, allowing, answer, appreciation, confession, credit, declaration, endorsement, gratitude, greeting, hail, hailing, honour, notice, profession, reaction, realisation, recognition, recompense, reply, response, return, salutation, salute, thanks, tribute, yielding.

**acme** *n* apex, apogee, climax, crest, crown, culmination, height, high point, maximum, optimum, peak, pinnacle, sublimation, sublimity, summit, top, vertex, zenith.

*antonym* nadir.

**acolyte** *n* acolyth, adherent, admirer, altar boy, assistant, attendant, follower, helper, lackey, slave.

**acoustic** *adj* audile, auditory, aural.

**acquaint** *v* accustom, advise, announce, apprise, brief, disclose, divulge, enlighten, familiarise, inform, notify, reveal, tell.

**acquaintance** *n* associate, association, awareness, chum, cognisance, colleague, companionship, confrère, consociate, contact, conversance, conversancy, experience, familiarity, fellowship, intimacy, knowledge, relationship, understanding.

**acquainted** *adj* abreast, conversant, familiar, in the know, informed.

**acquiesce** *v* accede, accept, agree, allow, approve, assent, comply, concur, conform, consent, defer, give in, submit, yield.

*antonyms* disagree, object.

**acquiescence** *n* acceptance, accession, agreement, approval, assent, compliance, concurrence, conformity, consent, deference, giving in, obedience, sanction, submission, yielding.

*antonyms* disagreement, rebelliousness.

**acquiescent** *adj* acceding, accepting, agreeable, amenable, approving, assenting, biddable, complaisant, compliant, concurrent, conforming, consenting, docile, obedient, submissive, yielding.

**acquire** *v* achieve, amass, appropriate, attain, buy, collect, cop, earn, gain, gather, get, net, obtain, pick up, procure, realise, receive, secure, win.

*antonyms* forfeit, forgo, relinquish.

**acquirements** *n* accomplishments, achievements, acquisitions, attainments, attributes, culture, erudition, knowledge, learning, mastery, qualifications, skills.

**acquisition** *n* accession, achievement, acquest, acquirement, appropriation, attainment, buy, gain, gaining, learning, obtainment, possession, prize, procurement, property, purchase, pursuit, securing, take-over.

**acquisitive** *adj* avaricious, avid, covetous, grabbing, grasping, greedy, insatiable, mercenary, possessive, predatory, rapacious, voracious.

*antonym* generous.

**acquisitiveness** *n* avarice, avidity, avidness, covetousness, graspingness, greed, predatoriness, rapaciousness, rapacity, voracity.

**acquit** *v* absolve, bear, behave, clear, comport, conduct, deliver, discharge, dismiss, exculpate, excuse, exonerate, free, fulfil, liberate, pay, pay off, perform, release, relieve, repay, reprieve, satisfy, settle, vindicate.

*antonym* convict.

**acquittal** *n* absolution, clearance, compurgation, deliverance, discharge, dismissal, dispensation, exculpation, excusing, exoneration, freeing, liberation, release, relief, reprieve, vindication.

*antonym* conviction.

**acquittance** *n* discharge, dispensation, payment, quittance, release, satisfaction, settlement.

**acrid** *adj* acerbic, acid, acrimonious, astringent, biting, bitter, burning, caustic, cutting, empyreumatic, harsh, incisive, irritating, malicious, mordant, nasty, pungent, sarcastic, sardonic, sharp, stinging, trenchant, venomous, virulent, vitriolic.

**acridity** *n* acidity, acrimoniousness, acrimony, astringency, bitterness, causticity, empyreuma, harshness, mordancy, sharpness, trenchancy.

**acrimonious** *adj* abusive, acerbic, astringent, atrabilious, biting, bitter, caustic, censorious, churlish, crabbed, cutting, ill-tempered, irascible, mordant, peevish, petulant, pungent, rancorous, sarcastic, severe, sharp, spiteful, splenetic, tart, testy, trenchant, virulent, waspish.

*antonyms* irenic, kindly, peaceable.

**acrimony** *n* acerbity, asperity, astringency, bitterness, churlishness, gall, harshness, ill-temper, ill-will, irascibility, mordancy, peevishness, petulance, rancour, resentment, sarcasm, spleen, tartness, trenchancy, virulence, waspishness.

**acrobat** *n* aerialist, balancer, contortionist, equilibrist, funambulist, gymnast, somersaulter, stunt-girl, stuntman, tumbler, voltigeur.

**act** *n* accomplishment, achievement, action, affectation, attitude, bill, blow, counterfeit, decree, deed, dissimulation, doing, edict, enactment, enterprise, execution, exertion, exploit, fake, feat, feigning, front, gest, gig, law, make-believe, manoeuvre, measure, move, operation, ordinance, performance, pose, posture, pretence, proceeding, resolution, routine, sham, show, sketch, spiel, stance, statute, step, stroke, transaction, turn, undertaking.

*v* acquit, act out, affect, assume, bear, behave, carry, carry out, characterise, comport, conduct, counterfeit, dissimulate, do, enact, execute, exert, feign, function, go about, imitate, impersonate, make, mime, mimic, move, operate, perform, personate, personify, play, portray, pose, posture, pretend, put on, react, represent, seem, serve, sham, simulate, strike, take effect, undertake, work.

**act up** carry on, cause trouble, give bother, give trouble, horse around, make waves, malfunction, mess about, misbehave, muck about, play up, rock the boat.

**act (up)on** affect, alter, carry out, change, comply with, conform to, execute, follow, fulfil, heed, influence, modify, obey, sway, transform, yield to.

**acting** *adj* interim, pro tem, provisional, reserve, stand-by, stop-gap, substitute, supply, surrogate, temporary.

*n* affectation, assuming, bluff, characterisation, counterfeiting, dissimulation, dramatics, enacting, feigning, histrionicism, histrionics, histrionism, imitating, imitation, impersonation, imposture, melodrama, performance, performing, play-acting, playing, portrayal, portraying, posing, posturing, pretence, pretending, putting on, seeming, shamming, stagecraft, theatre, theatricals.

**action** *n* accomplishment, achievement, act, activity, affray, agency, battle, case, cause, clash, combat, conflict, contest, deed, effect, effort, encounter, endeavour, energy, engagement, enterprise, exercise, exertion, exploit, feat, fight, fighting, force, fray, functioning, influence, lawsuit, litigation, liveliness, mechanism, motion, move, movement, operation, performance, power, proceeding, process, prosecution, skirmish, sortie, spirit, stop, stroke, suit, undertaking, vigour, vim, vitality, warfare, work, working, works.

**actions** *n* address, air, bearing, behaviour, comportment, conduct, demeanour, deportment, manners, mein, port, ways.

**activate** *v* actuate, animate, arouse, bestir, energise, excite, fire, galvanise, impel, initiate, mobilise, motivate, move, prompt, propel, rouse, set in motion, set off, start, stimulate, stir, switch on, trigger.

*antonyms* arrest, deactivate, stop.

**active** *adj* acting, activist, aggressive, agile, alert, ambitious, animated, assertive, assiduous, astir, bustling, busy, committed, deedy, devoted, diligent, doing, effectual, energetic, engaged, enterprising, enthusiastic, forceful, forward, full, functioning, hard-working, in force, in operation, industrious, involved, light-footed, live, lively, militant, moving, nimble, occupied, on the go, on the move, operate, quick, running, sedulous, spirited, sprightly, spry, stirabout, stirring, strenuous, through-going, vibrant, vigorous, vital, vivacious, working, zealous.

*antonyms* dormant, inactive, inert, passive.

**activity** *n* act, action, activeness, animation, avocation, bustle, commotion, deed, endeavour, enterprise, exercise, exertion, hobby, hurly-burly, hustle, industry, interest, job, kerfuffle, labour, life, liveliness, motion, movement, occupation, pastime, project, pursuit, scheme, stir, task, undertaking, venture, work.

**actor** *n* actress, agent, artist, comedian, doer, executor, factor, functionary, guiser, ham, hamfatter, histrio, histrion, impersonator, masquerader, mime, mummer, operative, operator, participant, participator, performer, perpetrator, personator, play-actor, player, practitioner, Roscius, Thespian, tragedian, trouper, worker.

**actual** *adj* absolute, authentic, bona fide, categorical, certain, concrete, confirmed, corporeal, current, de facto, definite, existent, extant, factual, genuine, indisputable, indubitable, legitimate, live, living, material, physical, positive, present, present-day, prevailing, real, realistic, substantial, tangible, thingy, true, truthful, unquestionable, verified, veritable.

*antonyms* apparent, imaginary, theoretical.

**actuality** *n* corporeality, fact, factuality, historicity, materiality, reality, realness, substance, substantiality, truth, verity.

**actually** *adv* absolutely, as a matter of fact, de facto, essentially, in fact, in reality, in truth, indeed, literally, really, truly, verily, veritably.

**actuate** *v* activate, animate, arouse, cause, circulate, dispose, drive, excite, impel, incite, induce, influence, inspire, instigate, lead, mobilise, motivate, move, prod, prompt, propel, quicken, rouse, spur, stimulate, stir, urge.

**acumen** *n* acuteness, astuteness, cleverness, discernment, discrimination, gumption, ingenuity, insight, intelligence, intuition, judgement, judiciousness, keenness, penetration, perception, perceptiveness, percipience, perspicacity, perspicuity, quickness, sagacity, sapience, sharpness, shrewdness, smartness, wisdom, wit.

*antonym* obtuseness.

**acute**[1] *adj* astute, canny, clever, critical, crucial, cutting, dangerous, decisive, discerning, discriminating, distressing, essential, excruciating, exquisite, extreme, fierce, grave, important, incisive, ingenious, insightful, intense, intuitive, judicious, keen, lancinating, observant, overpowering, overwhelming, penetrating, perceptive, percipient, perspicacious, piercing, poignant, pointed, powerful, racking, sagacious, sapient, sensitive, serious, severe, sharp, shooting, shrewd, shrill, smart, stabbing, subtle, sudden, urgent, violent, vital.

*antonyms* chronic, mild, obtuse.

**acute**[2] *adj* acicular, apiculate, cuspate, cuspidate, needle-shaped, peaked, pointed, sharp, sharpened.

*antonym* obtuse.

**acuteness** *n* acuity, astuteness, canniness, cleverness, criticality, danger, dangerousness, discernment, discrimination, fierceness, gravity, importance, ingenuity, insight, intensity, intuition, intuitiveness, keenness, perception, perceptiveness, percipience, perspicacity, poignancy, powerfulness, sagacity, sapience, sensitivity, seriousness, severity, sharpness, shrewdness, shrillness, smartness, subtlety, suddenness, urgency, violence, wit.

**adage** *n* aphorism, apophthegm, axiom, byword, dictum, gnome, maxim, motto, paroemia, precept, proverb, saw, saying, sentence.

**adamant** *adj* adamantine, determined, firm, fixed, flinty, hard, immovable, impenetrable, indestructible, inexorable, inflexible, infrangible, insistent, intransigent, obdurate, resolute, rigid, rock-like, rocky, set, steely, stiff, stony, stubborn, tough, unbending, unbreakable, uncompromising, unrelenting, unshakable, unyielding.

*antonyms* flexible, pliant, yielding.

**adapt** *v* acclimatise, accommodate, adjust, alter, apply, attemper, change, comply, conform, contemper, convert, customise, familiarise, fashion, fit, habituate, harmonise, match, metamorphose, modify, prepare, proportion, qualify, refashion, remodel, shape, suit, tailor.

**adaptable** *adj* adjustable, alterable, amenable, changeable, compliant, conformable, convertible, easy-going, flexible, malleable, modifiable, plastic, pliant, resilient, tractable, variable, versatile.

*antonyms* inflexible, refractory.

**adaptation** *n* acclimatisation, accommodation, accustomedness, adaption, adjustment, alteration, change, conversion, familiarisation, habituation, modification, naturalisation, refashioning, refitting, remodelling, reshaping, reworking, shift, transformation, variation, version.

**add** *v* adjoin, affix, amplify, annex, append, attach, augment, combine, compute, count, include, join, reckon, subjoin, sum up, superimpose, supplement, tack on, tot up, total.

*antonym* subtract.

**add up** add, amount, be consistent, be plausible, be reasonable, come to, compute, count, count up, hang together, hold water, imply, indicate, make sense, mean, reckon, reveal, ring true, signify, stand to reason, sum up, tally, tot up, total.

**added** *adj* additional, adjective, adjunct, extra, fresh, further, increased, new, supplementary.

**addendum** *n* addition, adjunct, affix, allonge, appendage, appendix, attachment, augmentation, codicil, endorsement, epilogue, extension, extra, postscript, supplement.

**addict** *n* acid-head, adherent, buff, devotee, dope-fiend, enthusiast, fan, fiend, follower, freak, head, hop-head, junkie, mainliner, nut, pillhead, pillpopper, pot-head, tripper, user.

**addicted** *adj* absorbed, accustomed, dedicated, dependent, devoted, disposed, enslaved, fond, habituated, hooked, inclined, obsessed, prone, spaced out.

**addiction** *n* a monkey on one's back, craving, dependence, enslavement, habit, monkey, obsession.

**addition** *n* accession, accessory, accretion, addend, addendum, adding, additament, additive, adjoining, adjunct, adjunction, affix, affixing, amplification, annexation, annexure, appendage, appendix, appurtenance, attachment, augmentation, computation, counting, enlargement, extension, extra, gain, inclusion, increase, increasing, increment, inpouring, reckoning, summation, summing-up, supplement, totalling, totting-up.

**additional** *adj* added, additive, adscititious, adventitious, adventive, affixed, appended, excrescent, extra, fresh, further, increased, more, new, other, spare, supplementary.

**addled** *adj* bad, bamboozled, befuddled, bewildered, confused, flustered, foolish, gone bad, mixed-up, muddled, off, perplexed, putrid, rancid, rotten, silly, turned, unbalanced.

*antonyms* clear, fresh.

**address**[1] *n* abode, department, direction, domicile, dwelling, home, house, inscription, location, lodging, place, residence, situation, superscription, whereabouts.

**address**[2] *n* adroitness, air, allocution, application, art, bearing, declamation, deftness, dexterity, discourse, discretion, dispatch, disquisition, dissertation, expedition, expertise, expertness, facility, harangue, ingenuity, lecture, manner, oration, sermon, skilfulness, skill, speech, tact, talk.

*v* accost, address (oneself) to, apostrophise, apply (oneself) to, approach, attend to, bespeak, button-hole, concentrate on, devote (oneself) to, discourse, engage in, focus on, greet, hail, harangue, invoke, lecture, orate, salute, sermonise, speak, speak to, take care of, talk, talk to, turn to, undertake.

**addresses** *n* advances, approaches, attentions, courting, courtship, lovemaking, proposals, wooing.

**adept** *adj* able, accomplished, ace, adroit, deft, dexterous, experienced, expert, masterful, masterly, nimble, polished, practised, proficient, skilful, skilled, versed.

*antonyms* bungling, incompetent, inept.

*n* ace, dab hand, dabster, deacon, don, expert, genius, maestro, mahatma, master, old hand, pastmaster, wizard.

*antonyms* bungler, incompetent.

**adequacy** *n* adequateness, capability, commensurateness, competence, competency, efficacy, fairness, fitness, passability, requisiteness, satisfactoriness, serviceability, sufficiency, suitability, tolerability.

*antonyms* inadequacy, insufficiency.

**adequate** *adj* able, acceptable, capable, commensurate, competent, condign, efficacious, enough, fair, fit, passable, presentable, requisite, respectable, satisfactory, serviceable, sufficient, suitable, tolerable.

*antonyms* inadequate, insufficient.

**adhere** *v* abide by, accrete, agree, attach, cement, cleave, cleave to, cling, coalesce, cohere, combine, comply with, fasten, fix, follow, fulfil, glue, heed, hold, hold fast, join, keep, link, maintain, mind, obey, observe, paste, respect, stand by, stick, stick fast, support, unite.

**adherent** *n* admirer, advocate, aficionado, devotee, disciple, enthusiast, fan, follower, freak, hanger-on, henchman, nut, partisan, satellite, sectary, supporter, upholder, votary.

**adhering** *adj* adherent, clinging, coalescent, cohering, cohesive, holding, osculant, tenacious.

**adhesion** *n* adherence, adhesiveness, allegiance, attachment, bond, coherence, cohesion, constancy, devotion, faithfulness, fidelity, fulfilment, grip, heed, holding fast, loyalty, obedience, observation, respect, sticking, support, union.

**adhesive** *adj* adherent, adhering, attaching, clinging, cohesive, emplastic, gluey, glutinous, gummy, holding, mucilaginous, sticking, sticky, tacky, tenacious.

*n* cement, glue, gum, mountant, mucilage, paste, tape.

**adieu** *n* bon voyage, cheerio, conge, departure, farewell, goodbye, leave-taking, parting, valediction, valedictory.

**adjacent** *adj* abutting, adjoining, alongside, beside, bordering, close, conterminant, conterminate, conterminous, contiguous, juxtaposed, near, neighbouring, next, proximate, touching, vicinal.

**adjoin** *v* abut, add, affix, annex, append, approximate, attach, border, combine, communicate with, connect, couple, impinge, interconnect, join, juxtapose, link, meet, neighbour, touch, unite, verge.

**adjoining** *adj* abutting, adjacent, bordering, connecting, contiguous, impinging, interconnecting, joined, juxtaposed, near, neighbouring, next, next door, proximate, touching, verging, vicinal.

**adjourn** *v* continue, defer, delay, discontinue, interrupt, postpone, prorogue, put off, recess, stay, suspend.

*antonym* convene.

**adjournment** *n* break, deferment, deferral, delay, discontinuation, dissolution, interruption, pause, postponement, prorogation, putting off, recess, stay, suspension.

**adjudicate** *v* adjudge, arbitrate, decide, determine, judge, pronounce, ref, referee, settle, umpire.

**adjudication** *n* adjudgement, arbitration, conclusion, decision, determination, finding, judgement, pronouncement, reffing, ruling, settlement, verdict.

**adjunct** *n* accessory, addendum, addition, appanage, appendage, appendix, appurtenance, auxiliary, complement, extension, supplement.

**adjure** *v* appeal to, beg, beseech, charge, command, conjure, direct, enjoin, entreat, implore, importune, invoke, order, plead with, pray, request, supplicate.

**adjust** *v* acclimatise, accommodate, accustom, adapt, alter, arrange, balance, change, coapt, compose, concert, conform, convert, dispose, fine-tune, fit, fix, harmonise, jiggle, measure, modify, order, proportion, reconcile, rectify, redress, refashion, regulate, remodel, reshape, set, settle, shape, square, suit, temper, tune.

*antonyms* derange, disarrange, upset.

**adjustable** *adj* adaptable, alterable, flexible, malleable, modifiable, mouldable, movable, tractable.

*antonyms* fixed, inflexible.

**adjustment** *n* acclimatisation, accommodation, adaptation, alteration, arrangement, arranging, conforming, conversion, fitting, fixing, harmonisation, modification, naturalisation, ordering, orientation, reconciliation, rectification, redress, refashioning, regulation, remodelling, setting, settlement, settling in, shaping, tuning.

**ad-lib** *v* extemporise, improvise, invent, make up.

*adj* extemporaneous, extempore, extemporised, impromptu, improvised, made up, off-the-cuff, spontaneous, unpremeditated, unprepared, unrehearsed.

*antonym* prepared.

*adv* extemporaneously, extempore, impromptu, impulsively, off the cuff, off the top of one's head, spontaneously.

**administer** *v* adhibit, apply, assign, conduct, contribute, control, direct, disburse, dispense, dispose, distribute, dole out, execute, give, govern, head, impose, lead, manage, measure out, mete out, officiate, organise, oversee, perform, preside over, provide, regulate, rule, run, superintend, supervise, supply.

**administration** *n* adhibition, administering, application, conduct, control, direction, directorship, disbursement, dispensation, disposal, distribution, execution, executive, governing, governing body, government, leadership, management, ministry, organisation, overseeing, performance, provision, regime, regulation, rule, ruling, running, settlement, superintendence, supervision, supply, term of office.

**administrative** *adj* authoritative, directorial, executive, governmental, gubernatorial, legislative, management, managerial, organisational, regulatory, supervisory.

**administrator** *n* boss, controller, curator, custodian, director, factor, governor, guardian, leader, manager, organiser, overseer, ruler, superintendent, supervisor, trustee.

**admirable** *adj* choice, commendable, creditable, deserving, estimable, excellent, exquisite, fine, laudable, meritorious, praiseworthy, rare, respected, superior, valuable, wonderful, worthy.

*antonym* despicable.

**admiration** *n* adoration, affection, amazement, appreciation, approbation, approval, astonishment, awe, delight, esteem, fureur, idolism, pleasure, praise, regard, respect, reverence, surprise, veneration, wonder, wonderment, worship.

*antonym* contempt.

**admire** *v* adore, applaud, appreciate, approve, esteem, iconise, idolise, laud, praise, prize, respect, revere, value, venerate, worship.

*antonym* despise.

**admirer** *n* adherent, aficionado, beau, boyfriend, devotee, disciple, enthusiast, fan, follower, gallant, idolator, idoliser, lover, partisan, suitor, supporter, sweetheart, votary, wooer, worshipper.

*antonyms* critic, opponent.

**admissible** *adj* acceptable, allowable, allowed, equitable, justifiable, lawful, legitimate, licit, passable, permissible, permitted, tolerable, tolerated.

*antonyms* illegitimate, inadmissible.

**admission** *n* acceptance, access, acknowledgement, adhibition, admittance, admitting, affirmation, allowance, avowal, concession, confession, declaration, disclosure, divulgence, entrance, entree, entry, expose, granting, inclusion, ingress, initiation, introduction, owning, profession, revelation.

*antonyms* denial, exclusion.

**admit** *v* accept, acknowledge, adhibit, affirm, agree, allow, allow to enter, avow, concede, confess, declare, disclose, divulge, give access, grant, initiate, introduce, intromit, let, let in, permit, profess, receive, recognise, reveal, take in.

*antonyms* exclude, gainsay.

**admittance** *n* acceptance, access, admitting, allowing, entrance, entree, entry, ingress, letting in, passage, reception.

**admixture** *n* addition, amalgamation, blend, combination, commixture, fusion, intermixture, mingling, tincture, trace.

**admonish** *v* advise, berate, caution, censure, check, chide, counsel, enjoin, exhort, forewarn, rebuke, reprehend, reprimand, reproach, reprove, scold, upbraid, warn.

**admonition** *n* advice, berating, caution, censure, counsel, pi-jaw, rebuke, reprehension, reprimand, reproach, reproof, scolding, warning.

**admonitory** *adj* admonishing, advisory, cautionary, censorious, rebuking, reprimanding, reproachful, reproving, scolding, warning.

**ado** *n* agitation, bother, business, bustle, ceremony, commotion, confusion, delay, disturbance, excitement, ferment, flurry, fuss, hassle, hurly-burly, kerfuffle, labour, pother, romage, stir, to-do, trouble, tumult, turmoil.

*antonyms* calm, tranquillity.

**adolescence** *n* boyhood, boyishness, childishness, development, girlhood, girlishness, immaturity, juvenescence, juvenility, minority, puberty, puerility, teens, transition, youth, youthfulness.

*antonym* senescence.

**adolescent** *adj* boyish, girlish, growing, immature, juvenescent, juvenile, maturing, puerile, teenage, young, youthful.

*n* bobbysoxer, Halbstarker, halfling, juvenile, minor, teenager, youngster, youth.

**Adonis** *n* charmer, dish, Ganymede, god, golden boy, good-looker, he-man, idol, knockout, matinee idol.

**adopt** *v* accept, affect, appropriate, approve, assume, back, choose, embrace, endorse, espouse, follow, foster, maintain, ratify, sanction, select, support, take in, take on, take up.

*antonyms* disown, repudiate.

**adoption** *n* acceptance, affectation, approbation, appropriation, approval, assumption, cherishment, choice, embracement, embracing, endorsement, espousal, following, fosterage, fostering, maintenance, ratification, sanction, select, selection, support.

**adorable** *adj* appealing, attractive, bewitching, captivating, charming, darling, dear, delightful, enchanting, fetching, lovable, pleasing, precious, winning, winsome.

*antonym* hateful.

**adoration** *n* admiration, esteem, estimation, exaltation, glorification, honour, idolatry, idolisation, love, magnification, reverence, veneration, worship.

*antonyms* abhorrence, detestation.

**adore** *v* admire, cherish, dote on, esteem, exalt, glorify, honour, idolatrise, idolise, love, magnify, revere, reverence, venerate, worship.

*antonyms* abhor, hate.

**adorn** *v* adonise, apparel, array, beautify, bedeck, bedight, bedizen, begem, bejewel, bestick, crown, deck, decorate, dight, doll up, embellish, emblazon, enhance, enrich, furbish, garnish, gild, grace, impearl, miniate, ornament, tart up, trick out, trim.

**adornment** *n* accessory, beautification, bedizenment, decorating, decoration, embellishment, falbala, fallal, fallalery, fandangle, figgery, flounce, frill, frippery, furbelow, garnish, garnishry, garniture, gilding, ornament, ornamentation, ornateness, trappings, trimming.

**adrift** *adj* aimless, amiss, anchorless, astray, at sea, directionless, goalless, insecure, off course, purposeless, rootless, rudderless, unsettled, wrong.

*antonyms* anchored, stable.

**adroit** *adj* able, adept, apt, artful, clever, cunning, deft, dexterous, expert, habile, ingenious, masterful, neat, nimble, proficient, quick, resourceful, skilful, skilled, slick.

*antonyms* clumsy, inept, maladroit.

**adroitness** *n* ability, ableness, address, adeptness, aptness, artfulness, cleverness, cunning, deftness, dexterity, expertise, facility, finesse, ingeniousness, ingenuity, legerdemain, masterfulness, mastery, neatness, nimbleness, proficiency, quickness, resourcefulness, skilfulness, skill.

*antonyms* clumsiness, ineptitude.

**adulation** *n* blandishment, bootlicking, fawning, flattery, idolatory, idolisation, personality cult, sycophancy, worship.

*antonym* abuse.

**adulatory** *adj* blandishing, bootlicking, fawning, flattering, fulsome, grovelling, idolatrous, obsequious, praising, servile, slavish, sycophantic, unctuous, worshipping.

*antonym* unflattering.

**adult** *adj* developed, full-grown, fully grown, grown-up, mature, of age, ripe, ripened.

*antonym* immature.

**adulterate** *v* attenuate, bastardise, contaminate, corrupt, dash, debase, defile, depreciate, deteriorate, devalue, dilute, doctor, infect, load, pollute, taint, thin, vitiate, water down, weaken.

*antonym* refine.

**adumbrate** *v* augur, bedim, chart, conceal, darken, delineate, draft, eclipse, forecast, foreshadow, foretell, hint at, indicate, obfuscate, obscure, outline, overshadow, portend, predict, prefigure, presage, prognosticate, prophesy, silhouette, sketch, suggest, trace, veil.

**advance** *v* accelerate, adduce, allege, ameliorate, assist, benefit, bring forward, cite, elevate, expedite, facilitate, foster, furnish, further, go ahead, go forward, grow, hasten, improve, increase, lend, move on, multiply, offer, pay beforehand, present, press on, proceed, proffer, profit, progress, promote, prosper, provide, raise, send forward, speed, submit, suggest, supply, thrive, upgrade.

*antonyms* impede, retard, retreat.

*n* advancement, amelioration, betterment, breakthrough, credit, deposit, development, down payment, furtherance, gain, growth, headway, improvement, increase, loan, preferment, prepayment, profit, progress, promotion, retainer, rise, step.

*antonym* recession.

*adj* beforehand, early, foremost, forward, in front, leading, preliminary, prior.

**advanced** *adj* ahead, avant-garde, extreme, foremost, forward, forward-looking, higher, imaginative, late, leading, original, precocious, progressive.

*antonyms* backward, retarded.

**advancement** *n* advance, amelioration, betterment, development, forward movement, gain, growth, headway, improvement, maturation, onward movement, preferment, progress, promotion, rise.

*antonyms* demotion, retardation.

**advances** *n* addresses, approach, approaches, attentions, moves, overtures, proposals, proposition.

**advantage** *n* account, aid, ascendancy, asset, assistances, avail, benefit, blessing, boon, boot, convenience, dominance, edge, expediency, fruit, gain, good, help, hold, interest, lead, leverage, precedence, pre-eminence, profit, purchase, service, start, superiority, sway, upper hand, use, usefulness, utility, welfare.

*antonyms* disadvantage, hindrance.

**advantageous** *adj* beneficial, convenient, favourable, furthersome, gainful, helpful, opportune, profitable, propitious, remunerative, rewarding, superior, useful, valuable, worthwhile.

*antonym* disadvantageous.

**advent** *n* accession, appearance, approach, arrival, coming, dawn, entrance, inception, introduction, occurrence, onset, visitation.

**adventitious** *adj* accidental, casual, chance, contingent, extraneous, extrinsic, foreign, fortuitous, incidental, non-essential, serendipitous, supervenient, unexpected.

*antonyms* inherent, intrinsic.

**adventure** *n* chance, contingency, enterprise, experience, exploit, gest, hazard, incident, occurrence, risk, speculation, undertaking, venture.

**adventurer** *n* cowboy, daredevil, derring-doer, filibuster, fortune-hunter, freebooter, freelancer, gambler, hero, heroine, knight-errant, madcap, mercenary, opportunist, rogue, soldier of fortune, speculator, swashbuckler, traveller, venturer, voyager, wanderer.

**adventuress** *n* bloodsucker, gold-digger, harpy, man-eater, seductress, siren, temptress, vamp.

**adventurous** *adj* adventuresome, audacious, bold, dangerous, daredevil, daring, dauntless, doughty, enterprising, foolhardy, game, hazardous, headstrong, impetuous, intrepid, perilous, plucky, rash, reckless, risky, spunky, swashbuckling, temerarious, venturesome.

*antonyms* cautious, chary, prudent.

**adversary** *n* antagonist, assailant, attacker, competitor, contestant, enemy, foe, foeman, opponent, opposer, rival.

*antonyms* ally, supporter.

**adverse** *adj* antagonistic, conflicting, contrary, counter, counter-productive, detrimental, disadvantageous, hostile, hurtful, inauspicious, inexpedient, inimical, injurious, inopportune, negative, noxious, opposing, opposite, reluctant, repugnant, uncongenial, unfavourable, unfortunate, unfriendly, unlucky, unpropitious, untoward, unwilling.

*antonyms* advantageous, propitious.

**adversity** *n* affliction, ambs-ace, bad luck, calamity, catastrophe, contretemps, disaster, distress, hard times, hardship, ill-fortune, ill-luck, mischance, misery, misfortune, mishap, reverse, sorrow, suffering, trial, tribulation, trouble, woe, wretchedness.

*antonym* prosperity.

**advertise** *v* advise, announce, apprise, blazon, broadcast, bruit, declare, display, flaunt, herald, inform, make known, notify, plug, praise, proclaim, promote, promulgate, publicise, publish, puff, push, tout, trumpet.

**advertisement** *n* ad, advert, announcement, bill, blurb, circular, commercial, display, handbill, handout, hype, leaflet, notice, placard, plug, poster, promotion, propaganda, propagation, publicity, puff, puffery, trumpet-blowing.

**advice** *n* admonition, caution, communication, conseil, counsel, direction, do's and don'ts, guidance, help, information, injunction, instruction, intelligence, memorandum, notice, notification, opinion, recommendation, rede, suggestion, view, warning, wisdom, word.

**advisable** *adj* advantageous, appropriate, apt, beneficial, correct, desirable, expedient, fit, fitting, judicious, meet, politic, profitable, proper, prudent, recommended, seemly, sensible, sound, suggested, suitable, wise.

*antonyms* inadvisable, injudicious.

**advise** *v* acquaint, apprise, bethink, caution, commend, counsel, enjoin, forewarn, guide, inform, instruct, make known, notify, recommend, report, suggest, teach, tell, tutor, urge, warn.

**adviser** *n* admonitor, aide, authority, coach, confidant, consultant, counsel, counsellor, eminence grise, guide, helper, instructor, lawyer, mentor, monitor, preceptor, righthand man, solicitor, teacher, therapist, tutor.

**advisory** *adj* advising, consultative, consultatory, consulting, counselling, helping, hortatory, recommending.

**advocacy** *n* adoption, advancement, backing, campaigning, championing, championship, defence, encouragement, espousal, justification, patronage, pleading, promotion, promulgation, propagation, proposal, recommendation, spokesmanship, support, upholding, urging.

**advocate** *v* adopt, advise, argue for, campaign for, champion, countenance, defend, encourage, endorse, espouse, favour, justify, patronise, plead for, press for, promote, propose, recommend, subscribe to, support, uphold, urge.

*antonyms* deprecate, disparage, impugn.

*n* apologist, apostle, attorney, backer, barrister, campaigner, champion, counsel, counsellor, defender, interceder, intercessor, lawyer, mediator, paraclete, patron, pleader, promoter, proponent, proposer, solicitor, speaker, spokesman, supporter, upholder, vindicator.

*antonyms* critic, opponent.

**aegis** *n* advocacy, auspices, backing, championship, favour, guardianship, patronage, protection, shelter, sponsorship, support, wing.

**aerial** *adj* aeolian, aery, atmospheric, elevated, ethereal, incorporeal, insubstantial, lofty, unreal.

**affability** n accessibility, amiability, amicability, approachability, benevolence, benignity, civility, congeniality, conversableness, cordiality, courtesy, easiness, friendliness, geniality, good humour, good nature, graciousness, kindliness, mildness, obligingness, openness, pleasantness, sociability, suavity, urbanity, warmth.

*antonyms* coolness, reserve, reticence.

**affable** adj agreeable, amiable, amicable, approachable, benevolent, benign, civil, congenial, cordial, courteous, expansive, free, friendly, genial, good-humoured, good-natured, gracious, kindly, mild, obliging, open, pleasant, sociable, suave, urbane, warm.

*antonyms* cool, reserved, reticent, unfriendly.

**affair** n activity, adventure, amour, amourette, business, circumstance, concern, connection, episode, event, happening, incident, interest, intrigue, liaison, matter, occurrence, operation, organisation, party, proceeding, project, question, reception, relationship, responsibility, romance, subject, topic, transaction, undertaking.

**affect¹** v act on, agitate, alter, apply to, attack, bear upon, change, concern, disturb, grieve, grip, impinge upon, impress, influence, interest, involve, melt, modify, move, overcome, penetrate, pertain to, perturb, prevail over, regard, relate to, seize, soften, stir, strike, sway, touch, transform, trouble, upset.

**affect²** v adopt, aspire to, assume, contrive, counterfeit, fake, feign, imitate, pretend, profess, put on, sham, simulate.

**affectation** n act, affectedness, appearance, artificiality, euphuism, façade, fakery, false display, imitation, insincerity, ladyism, mannerism, minanderie, pose, pretence, pretension, pretentiousness, sham, show, simulation, staginess, theatricality, theatricism, unnaturalness.

*antonyms* artlessness, ingenuousness.

**affected¹** adj afflicted, agitated, altered, changed, concerned, damaged, distressed, gripped, hurt, impaired, impressed, influenced, injured, melted, moved, perturbed, smitten, stimulated, stirred, swayed, touched, troubled, upset.

**affected²** adj alembicated, artificial, assumed, bogus, chichi, conceited, contrived, counterfeit, debby, euphuistic, fake, feigned, fussy, greenery-yallery, hyperaesthesic, hyperaesthetic, insincere, lah-di-dah, literose, mannered, mincing, minikin, namby-pamby, niminy-piminy, phoney, pompous, precious, pretended, pretentious, put-on, sham, simulated, spurious, stiff, studied, unnatural.

*antonyms* genuine, natural.

**affecting** adj impressive, moving, pathetic, piteous, pitiable, pitiful, poignant, sad, saddening, stirring, touching, troubling.

**affection** n amity, attachment, care, desire, devotion, favour, feeling, fondness, friendliness, good will, inclination, kindness, liking, love, partiality, passion, penchant, predilection, predisposition, proclivity, propensity, regard, tenderness, warmth.

*antonyms* antipathy, dislike.

**affectionate** adj amiable, amorous, attached, caring, cordial, devoted, doting, fond, friendly, kind, loving, passionate, responsive, solicitous, tender, warm, warm-hearted.

*antonyms* cold, undemonstrative.

**affiliate** v ally, amalgamate, annex, associate, band together, combine, confederate, conjoin, connect, federate, incorporate, join, merge, syndicate, unite.

**affiliation** n alliance, amalgamation, association, coalition, combination, confederation, connection, federation, incorporation, joining, league, merger, merging, relationship, syndication, union.

**affinity** n alliance, analogy, attraction, closeness, compatibility, connection, correspondence, fondness, homogeneity, inclination, kinship, leaning, likeness, liking, partiality, predisposition, proclivity, propensity, rapport, relation, relationship, resemblance, similarity, similitude, sympathy.

*antonym* dissimilarity.

**affirm** v assert, asseverate, attest, aver, avouch, avow, certify, confirm, corroborate, declare, depose, endorse, maintain, pronounce, ratify, state, swear, testify, witness.

**affirmation** n affirmance, assertion, asseveration, attestation, averment, avouchment, avowal, certification, confirmation, corroboration, declaration, deposition, endorsement, oath, pronouncement, ratification, statement, testimony, witness.

**affirmative** adj affirmatory, agreeing, approving, assenting, assertory, asseverative, concurring, confirming, consenting, corroborative, emphatic, positive.

*antonyms* dissenting, negative.

**affix** v add, adjoin, annex, append, assign, attach, attribute, bind, connect, fasten, glue, join, paste, pin on, stick, subjoin, tack, tag.

*antonym* detach.

**afflict** v beset, burden, distress, grieve, harass, harm, harrow, hurt, oppress, pain, plague, rack, smite, strike, torment, torture, trouble, try, visit, wound, wring.

*antonyms* comfort, solace.

**affliction** n adversity, calamity, cross, curse, depression, disaster, disease, distress, grief, hardship, illness, misery, misfortune, ordeal, pain, plague, scourge, sickness, sorrow, suffering, torment, trial, tribulation, trouble, visitation, woe, wretchedness.

*antonyms* comfort, consolation, solace.

**affluence** n abundance, exuberance, fortune, opulence, plenty, profusion, property, prosperity, riches, substance, wealth, wealthiness.

*antonym* poverty.

**affluent** adj comfortable, flourishing, flush, loaded, moneyed, opulent, pecunious, prosperous, rich, wealthy, well-heeled, well-off, well-to-do.

*antonyms* impecunious, impoverished, poor.

**afford** v bear, bestow, cope with, engender, furnish, generate, give, grant, impart, manage, offer, produce, provide, render, spare, stand, supply, sustain, yield.

**affray** *n* brawl, brush, contest, disturbance, dogfight, Donnybrook, encounter, feud, fight, fisticuffs, fracas, fray, free-for-all, mêlee, quarrel, riot, row, scrap, scrimmage, scuffle, set-to, skirmish, squabble, tussle, wrangle.

**affront** *v* abuse, anger, annoy, displease, gall, incense, insult, irritate, nettle, offend, outrage, pique, provoke, slight, snub, vex.

*antonyms* appease, compliment.

*n* abuse, discourtesy, disrespect, facer, indignity, injury, insult, offence, outrage, provocation, rudeness, slap in the face, slight, slur, snub, vexation, wrong.

*antonym* compliment.

**afoot** *adv* about, abroad, afloat, agate, astir, brewing, circulating, current, going about, in preparation, in progress, in the air, in the wind, up.

**afraid** *adj* aghast, alarmed, anxious, apprehensive, cowardly, diffident, distrustful, faint-hearted, fearful, frightened, intimidated, nervous, regretful, reluctant, scared, sorry, suspicious, timid, timorous, tremulous, unhappy.

*antonyms* confident, unafraid.

**afresh** *adv* again, anew, da capo, de integro, de novo, newly, once again, once more, over again.

**after** *adv, prep* afterwards, as a result of, behind, below, following, in consequence of, later, post, subsequent to, subsequently, succeeding, thereafter.

*antonym* before.

**aftermath** *n* afterclap, after-effects, backwash, consequences, effects, end, fall-out, lattermath, outcome, repercussion, results, rowen, upshot, wake.

**afternoon** *n* mid-life, pip-emma, pm, post meridiem, siesta.

**again** *adv* afresh, also, anew, another time, au contraire, besides, bis, conversely, da capo, de integro, de novo, ditto, encore, furthermore, in addition, moreover, on the contrary, on the other hand, once more.

**against** *prep* abutting, across, adjacent to, athwart, close up to, confronting, contra, counter to, facing, fronting, hostile to, in contact with, in contrast to, in defiance of, in exchange for, in opposition to, in the face of, on, opposed to, opposing, opposite to, resisting, touching, versus.

*antonyms* for, pro.

**age** *n* (a)eon, agedness, anility, caducity, date, day, days, decline, decrepitude, dotage, duration, eld, elderliness, epoch, era, generation, lifetime, majority, maturity, old age, period, senescence, senility, seniority, span, the sere and yellow, time, years.

*antonyms* salad days, youth.

*v* decline, degenerate, deteriorate, grow old, mature, mellow, obsolesce, ripen, season.

**aged** *adj* advanced, age-old, ancient, antiquated, antique, decrepit, elderly, geriatric, grey, hoary, old, patriarchal, senescent, sere, superannuated, time-worn, venerable, worn-out.

*antonyms* young, youthful.

**agency** *n* action, activity, bureau, business, department, effect, effectuation, efficiency, finger, force, handling, influence, instrumentality, intercession, intervention, means, mechanism, mediation, medium, office, offices, operation, organisation, power, work, workings.

**agenda** *n* calendar, diary, list, menu, plan, programme, schedule, timetable.

**agent** *n* actor, agency, author, cause, channel, delegate, deputy, doer, emissary, envoy, executor, factor, force, functionary, go-between, instrument, intermediary, legate, means, middleman, mover, negotiator, operative, operator, organ, performer, power, practisant, rep, representative, substitute, surrogate, vehicle, vicar, worker.

**ages** *n* (a)eons, centuries, decades, donkey's years, years, yonks.

**aggrandise** *v* advance, amplify, augment, dignify, elevate, enhance, enlarge, ennoble, enrich, exaggerate, exalt, glamorise, glorify, increase, inflate, magnify, promote, upgrade, widen.

*antonyms* belittle, debase.

**aggravate** *v* annoy, exacerbate, exaggerate, exasperate, harass, hassle, heighten, incense, increase, inflame, intensify, irk, irritate, magnify, needle, nettle, peeve, pester, provoke, tease, vex, worsen.

*antonyms* alleviate, appease, mollify.

**aggravation** *n* annoyance, bore, drag, exacerbation, exacerbescence, exaggeration, exasperation, hassle, heightening, increase, inflammation, intensification, irksomeness, irritant, irritation, magnification, provocation, teasing, thorn in the flesh, vexation, worsening.

**aggregate** *n* accumulation, agglomeration, aggregation, amount, assemblage, body, bulk, collection, combination, entirety, generality, heap, herd, lump, mass, mixture, pile, sum, throng, total, totality, whole.

*adj* accumulated, added, assembled, collected, collective, combined, complete, composite, corporate, cumulative, mixed, total, united.

*antonyms* individual, particular.

*v* accumulate, add up, agglomerate, amass, amount to, assemble, cluster, collect, combine, conglomerate, heap, mix, pile, total.

**aggregation** *n* accumulation, agglomeration, amassment, asemblage, cluster, collection, combination, congeries, conglomeration, heap, mass, pile, stack.

**aggression** *n* aggressiveness, antagonism, assault, attack, bellicosity, belligerence, combativeness, destructiveness, encroachment, hostility, impingement, incursion, injury, intrusion, invasion, jingoism, militancy, offence, offensive, onslaught, provocation, pugnacity, raid.

**aggressive** *adj* argumentative, assertive, bare-knuckle, bellicose, belligerent, bold, butch, combative, contentious, destructive, disputatious, dynamic, energetic, enterprising, forceful, go-ahead, hostile, intrusive, invasive, jingoistic, militant, offensive, provocative, pugnacious, pushful, pushing, pushy, quarrelsome, scrappy, vigorous, zealous.

*antonyms* peaceable, submissive.

**aggressor** *n* assailant, assaulter, attacker, intruder, invader, offender, provoker.

*antonym* victim.

**aggrieved** *adj* afflicted, affronted, distressed, disturbed, harmed, hurt, ill-used, injured, insulted, maltreated, offended, pained, peeved, saddened, unhappy, woeful, wronged.

*antonym* pleased.

**aghast** *adj* afraid, amazed, appalled, astonished, astounded, awestruck, confounded, dismayed, frightened, horrified, horror-struck, shocked, startled, stunned, stupefied, terrified, thunder-struck.

**agile** *adj* active, acute, adroit, alert, brisk, clever, fleet, flexible, limber, lissome, lithe, lively, mobile, nimble, prompt, quick, quick-witted, sharp, sprightly, spry, supple, swift, withy.

*antonyms* clumsy, stiff, torpid.

**agility** *n* activity, acuteness, adroitness, alertness, briskness, cleverness, flexibility, lissomeness, litheness, liveliness, mobility, nimbleness, promptitude, promptness, quickness, quick-wittedness, sharpness, sprightliness, spryness, suppleness, swiftness.

*antonyms* sluggishness, stiffness, torpidity.

**aging** *adj* elderly, gerontic, obsolescent, senescent.

**agitate** *v* alarm, arouse, beat, churn, confuse, convulse, discompose, disconcert, disquiet, distract, disturb, excite, ferment, flurry, fluster, incite, inflame, perturb, rattle, rock, rouse, ruffle, shake, stimulate, stir, toss, trouble, unnerve, unsettle, upset, work up, worry.

*antonyms* calm, tranquillise.

**agitated** *adj* anxious, discomposed, distracted, dithery, feverish, flappable, flurried, flustered, in a lather, insecure, jumpy, nervous, perturbed, restive, restless, ruffled, tumultuous, twitchy, uneasy, unnerved, unsettled, upset, wrought-up.

*antonyms* calm, composed.

**agitation** *n* agitprop, alarm, anxiety, arousal, churning, clamour, commotion, confusion, controversy, convulsion, discomposure, disquiet, distraction, disturbance, doodah, ebullition, excitement, ferment, flurry, fluster, fomentation, hassle, incitement, inflammation, outcry, rocking, shake, shaking, solicitude, stimulation, stir, stirring, tail-spin, taking, tizz(y), tossing, trepidation, trouble, tumult, turbulence, turmoil, uneasiness, unrest, upset, welter, worry.

*antonyms* calm, tranquillity.

**agitator** *n* agent provocateur, bell-wether, demagogue, firebrand, fomenter, inciter, instigator, mob orator, rabble-rouser, revolutionary, soap-box orator, stirrer, troublemaker, tub-thumper.

**agog** *adj* avid, breathless, curious, desirous, eager, enthralled, enthusiastic, excited, expectant, impatient, in suspense, keen, on tenterhooks.

*antonyms* incurious, laid-back.

**agonise** *v* afflict, anguish, bleed, distress, excruciate, harrow, labour, pain, rack, strain, strive, struggle, suffer, toil, torment, torture, trouble, worry, wrestle, writhe.

**agony** *n* affliction, anguish, distress, misery, pain, pangs, paroxysm, spasm, suffering, throes, torment, torture, tribulation, woe, wretchedness.

**agrarian** *adj* agricultural, agronomic, farming, geoponic, georgic, praedial.

**agree** *v* accede, accord, acquiesce, admit, allow, answer, assent, chime, coincide, comply, concede, concord, concur, conform, consent, consort, contract, correspond, cotton, covenant, engage, fadge, fit, fix, get on, grant, harmonise, homologate, jibe, match, permit, promise, see eye to eye, settle, side with, square, suit, tally, yield.

*antonyms* conflict, disagree.

**agreeable** *adj* acceptable, acquiescent, amenable, amicable, appropriate, approving, attractive, befitting, compatible, complying, concurring, conformable, congenial, consenting, consistent, d'accord, delectable, delightful, enjoyable, fitting, gemütlich, gratifying, in accord, likeable, palatable, pleasant, pleasing, pleasurable, proper, responsive, satisfying, suitable, sympathetic, well-disposed, willing.

*antonyms* disagreeable, distasteful, incompatible, nasty.

**agreement**[1] *n* acceptance, accord, accordance, adherence, affinity, analogy, closing, compact, compatibility, complaisance, compliance, concert, concord, concordat, concurrence, conformity, congruence, congruity, consentience, consistency, consonance, consort, convention, correspondence, harmony, modus vivendi, preconcert, resemblance, respondence, similarity, suitableness, sympathy, unanimity, union, unison.

*antonym* disagreement.

**agreement**[2] *n* arrangement, bargain, compact, concordat, contract, covenant, deal, pact, settlement, treaty, understanding.

**agricultural** *adj* agrarian, agronomic, farming, geoponic, georgic, praedial.

**agriculture** *n* agribusiness, agronomics, agronomy, cultivation, culture, farming, geoponics, husbandry, tillage.

**aground** *adj, adv* ashore, beached, foundered, grounded, high and dry, marooned, on the rocks, stranded, stuck, wrecked.

*antonym* afloat.

**ague** *n* fever, fit, malaria, quaking, shivering, trembling, tremor.

**ahead** *adj, adv* advanced, along, at an advantage, at the head, before, earlier on, forwards, in advance, in front, in the forefront, in the lead, in the vanguard, leading, onwards, superior, to the fore, winning.

**aid** *v* abet, accommodate, adminiculate, assist, befriend, boost, ease, encourage, expedite, facilitate, favour, help, oblige, promote, prop, rally round, relieve, second, serve, subsidise, succour, support, sustain.

*antonyms* impede, obstruct.

*n* a leg up, adminicle, aidance, assistance, assistant, benefit, contribution, donation, encouragement, favour, help, helper, patronage, prop, relief, service, sponsorship, subsidy, subvention, succour, support, supporter.

*antonyms* impediment, obstruction.

**aide** *n* adjutant, adviser, advocate, aide de camp, assistant, attache, confidant, disciple, follower, galloper, henchman, right-hand man, supporter.

**ail** *v* afflict, annoy, be indisposed, bother, decline, distress, droop, fail, irritate, languish, pain, pine, sicken, trouble, upset, weaken, worry.

*antonyms* comfort, flourish.

**ailing** *adj* debilitated, diseased, feeble, frail, ill, indisposed, infirm, invalid, languishing, off-colour, out of sorts, peaky, poorly, sick, sickly, suffering, under the weather, unsound, unwell, weak, weakly.

*antonyms* flourishing, healthy.

**ailment** *n* affliction, complaint, disability, disease, disorder, illness, indisposition, infection, infirmity, malady, sickness, weakness.

**aim** *v* address, aspire, attempt, beam, design, direct, draw a bead, endeavour, essay, ettle, intend, level, mean, plan, point, propose, purpose, resolve, seek, set one's sights on, sight, strive, take aim, target, train, try, want, wish, zero in on.

*n* ambition, aspiration, course, desideratum, design, desire, direction, dream, end, goal, hope, intent, intention, mark, motive, object, objective, plan, purpose, scheme, target, telos, wish.

**aimless** *adj* chance, desultory, directionless, erratic, feckless, frivolous, goalless, haphazard, irresolute, pointless, purposeless, rambling, random, stray, undirected, unguided, unmotivated, unpredictable, vagrant, wayward.

*antonyms* determined, positive, purposeful.

**air** *n* ambience, ambient, appearance, aria, atmosphere, aura, bearing, blast, breath, breeze, character, demeanour, draught, effect, ether, feeling, flavour, heavens, impression, lay, look, manner, melody, mood, motif, oxygen, puff, quality, sky, song, strain, style, theme, tone, tune, waft, welkin, whiff, wind, zephyr.

*v* aerate, broadcast, circulate, communicate, declare, disclose, display, disseminate, divulge, exhibit, expose, express, freshen, give vent to, make known, make public, parade, proclaim, publicise, publish, reveal, tell, utter, vaunt, ventilate, voice.

**airily** *adv* animatedly, blithely, breezily, brightly, buoyantly, cheerfully, daintily, delicately, ethereally, flippantly, gaily, gracefully, happily, high-spiritedly, insouciantly, jauntily, light-heartedly, lightly, nonchalantly, unconcernedly.

*antonyms* concernedly, thoughtfully.

**airless** *adj* breathless, close, frowsty, frowsy, fusty, heavy, muggy, musty, oppressive, stale, stifling, stuffy, suffocating, sultry, unventilated.

*antonyms* airy, fresh.

**airman** *n* ace, aviator, erk, flyer, pilot.

**airs** *n* affectation, affectedness, arrogance, artificiality, haughtiness, hauteur, pomposity, posing, pretensions, pretentiousness, staginess, superciliousness, swank.

**air-tight** *adj* closed, impenetrable, impermeable, sealed, tight-fitting, wind-tight.

**airy** *adj* aerial, blithe, blowy, bodiless, breezy, buoyant, cheerful, cheery, debonair, delicate, disembodied, draughty, ethereal, fanciful, flimsy, fresh, frolicsome, gay, graceful, gusty, happy, high-spirited, illusory, imaginary, immaterial, incorporeal, insouciant, insubstantial, jaunty, light, light-hearted, lively, lofty, merry, nimble, nonchalant, offhand, open, roomy, spacious, spectral, sportive, sprightly, trifling, uncluttered, unreal, unsubstantial, vaporous, visionary, weightless, well-ventilated, windy.

*antonyms* close, heavy, oppressive, stuffy.

**aisle** *n* alleyway, ambulatory, corridor, deambulatory, division, gangway, lane, passage, passageway, path, walkway.

**akin** *adj* affiliated, agnate, alike, allied, analogous, cognate, comparable, congenial, connected, consanguineous, consonant, corresponding, kin, kindred, like, parallel, related, similar.

*antonym* alien.

**alacrity** *n* alertness, avidity, briskness, celerity, cheerfulness, dispatch, eagerness, enthusiasm, gaiety, liveliness, promptitude, promptness, quickness, readiness, speed, sprightliness, swiftness, willingness, zeal.

*antonyms* dilatoriness, slowness.

**alarm** *v* affright, agitate, daunt, dismay, distress, frighten, give (someone) a turn, panic, put the wind up (someone), scare, startle, terrify, terrorise, unnerve.

*antonyms* calm, reassure, soothe.

*n* alarm-bell, alert, anxiety, apprehension, bell, bleeper, consternation, danger signal, dismay, distress, distress signal, fear, fright, horror, larum, larum-bell, nervousness, panic, scare, siren, terror, tocsin, trepidation, unease, uneasiness, warning.

*antonym* composure.

**alarming** *adj* daunting, direful, dismaying, distressing, disturbing, dreadful, frightening, ominous, scaring, shocking, startling, terrifying, threatening, unnerving.

*antonym* reassuring.

**alarmist** *n* doomsman, doomwatcher, jitterbug, pessimist, scaremonger.

*antonym* optimist.

**alas** *interj* alack, alack-a-day, ewhow, good lack, waesucks, welladay, wel(l)away, woe.

**albeit** *conj* although, even if, even though, howbeit, notwithstanding that, though.

**albumen** *n* glair.

**alchemy** *n* hermetics, magic, sorcery, thaumaturgy, witchcraft, wizardry.

**alcohol** *n* bev(v)y, booze, firewater, hard stuff, hooch, John Barleycorn, (jungle) juice, liquor, medicine, moonshine, mountain dew, rotgut, spirits.

**alcoholic** *adj* ardent, brewed, distilled, fermented, hard, inebriant, inebriating, intoxicating, spirituous, strong, vinous.

*n* bibber, boozer, dipso, dipsomaniac, drunk, drunkard, hard drinker, inebriate, lush, piss artist, soak, sot, sponge, tippler, toper, tosspot, wino.

**alcoholism** *n* alcohol-addiction, crapulence, dipsomania, drunkenness, methomania, vinosity.

**alcove** *n* bay, booth, bower, carrel, compartment, corner, cubby-hole, cubicle, niche, nook, recess.

**ale** *n* beer, bitter, mild, morocco, nappy, swipes, wallop.

**alert** *adj* active, agile, attentive, brisk, careful, circumspect, gleg, heedful, lively, nimble, observant, on the ball, on the lookout, on the qui vive, perceptive, prepared, quick, ready, sharp-eyed, sharp-witted, spirited, sprightly, streetwise, vigilant, wary, watchful, wide-awake.
*antonyms* listless, slow.

*n* alarm, signal, siren, tocsin, warning.

*v* alarm, forewarn, inform, notify, signal, tip off, warn.

**alertness** *n* activeness, agility, attention, attentiveness, briskness, carefulness, circumspection, heedfulness, liveliness, nimbleness, perceptiveness, preparedness, promptitude, quickness, readiness, spiritedness, sprightliness, vigilance, wakefulness, wariness, watchfulness.
*antonyms* listlessness, slowness.

**alias** *n* allonym, anonym, assumed name, false name, nickname, nom de guerre, nom de plume, pen name, pseudonym, soubriquet, stage name.
*adv* alias dictus, also, also called, also known as, formerly, otherwise, otherwise called.

**alibi** *n* cover-up, defence, excuse, explanation, justification, plea, pretext, reason, story.

**alien** *adj* adverse, antagonistic, conflicting, contrary, estranged, exotic, extraneous, foreign, inappropriate, incompatible, incongruous, inimical, opposed, outlandish, remote, repugnant, separated, strange, unfamiliar.
*antonym* akin.

*n* emigrant, foreigner, immigrant, metic, newcomer, outlander, outsider, stranger.
*antonym* native.

**alienate** *v* antagonise, disaffect, divert, divorce, estrange, separate, set against, turn away, turn off, withdraw.
*antonyms* disarm, unite.

**alienation** *n* antagonisation, disaffection, disjunction, disunion, diversion, divorce, estrangement, indifference, remoteness, rupture, separation, severance, turning away, withdrawal.
*antonym* endearment.

**alight**[1] *v* come down, come to rest, debark, descend, detrain, disembark, disentrain, dismount, get down, get off, land, light, perch, settle, touch down.
*antonyms* ascend, board, rise.

**alight**[2] *adj* ablaze, afire, aflame, aglow, blazing, bright, brilliant, burning, fiery, flaming, flaring, ignited, illuminated, illumined, lighted, lit, lit up, on fire, radiant, shining.
*antonym* dark.

**align** *v* affiliate, agree, ally, arrange in line, associate, co-operate, co-ordinate, even, even up, join, line up, make parallel, order, range, regularise, regulate, side, straighten, sympathise.

**alignment** *n* adjustment, affiliation, agreement, alliance, arrangement, association, conformity, co-operation, co-ordination, evening, evening up, line, lining up, order, ranging, regularisation, regulating, regulation, sequence, straightening, sympathy, union.

**alike** *adj* akin, analogous, cognate, comparable, corresponding, duplicate, equal, equivalent, even, homologous, identical, parallel, resembling, similar, the same, uniform.
*antonyms* different, unlike.

*adv* analogously, correspondingly, equally, evenly, identically, in common, similarly, uniformly.

**alive** *adj* active, alert, animate, animated, awake, breathing, brisk, cheerful, eager, energetic, existent, existing, extant, functioning, having life, in existence, in force, life-like, live, lively, living, operative, quick, real, spirited, sprightly, spry, subsisting, vibrant, vigorous, vital, vivacious, zestful.
*antonyms* dead, lifeless.

**alive with** abounding in, bristling with, bustling with, buzzing with, crawling with, crowded with, infested with, lousy with, overflowing with, overrun by, stiff with, swarming with, teeming with, thronged with.

**all** *adj* complete, each, each and every, entire, every, every bit of, every one of, every single, full, greatest, gross, outright, perfect, the complete, the entire, the sum of, the total of, the totality of, the whole of, total, utter.
*antonym* none.

*n* aggregate, comprehensiveness, entirety, everything, sum, sum total, total, total amount, totality, universality, utmost, whole, whole amount.

*adv* altogether, completely, entirely, fully, holus-bolus, totally, utterly, wholesale, wholly.

**all being well** Deo volente, DV, God willing, if I'm spared, volente Deo.

**all right** *adj* acceptable, adequate, allowable, average, fair, hale, healthy, OK, passable, permissible, right as rain, safe, satisfactory, secure, sound, standard, unharmed, unhurt, unimpaired, uninjured, unobjectionable, well, whole.

*antonyms* unacceptable, uninjured.

*adv* acceptably, adequately, appropriately, OK, passably, reasonably, satisfactorily, suitably, unobjectionably, well enough.

*antonyms* unacceptably, unsatisfactorily.

**all the time** always, constantly, continually, continuously, ever, everlastingly, perpetually, unceasingly.

**all thumbs** butter-fingered, cack-handed, clumsy, ham-fisted, ham-handed, inept, maladroit, unhandy.

**allay** *v* allege, alleviate, appease, assuage, blunt, calm, check, compose, diminish, dull, ease, lessen, lull, mitigate, moderate, mollify, pacify, quell, quiet, reduce, relieve, slake, smooth, soften, soothe, subdue, tranquillise.

*antonyms* exacerbate, intensify.

**allegation** *n* accusation, affirmation, assertion, asseveration, attestation, averment, avowal, charge, claim, declaration, deposition, plea, profession, statement, testimony.

**allege** *v* adduce, advance, affirm, assert, asseverate, attest, aver, avow, charge, claim, contend, declare, depose, hold, insist, maintain, plead, profess, put forward, state.

**alleged** *adj* affirmed, asserted, averred, claimed, declared, described, designated, doubtful, dubious, inferred, ostensible, professed, purported, reputed, so-called, stated, supposed, suspect, suspicious.

**allegiance** *n* adherence, constancy, devotion, duty, faithfulness, fealty, fidelity, friendship, homage, loyalty, obedience, obligation, support.

*antonyms* disloyalty, enmity.

**allegorical** *adj* emblematic, figurative, parabolic, representative, significative, symbolic, symbolising, typical.

**allegory** *n* analogy, apologue, comparison, emblem, fable, metaphor, myth, parable, story, symbol, symbolism, tale.

**allergic** *adj* affected, antipathetic, averse, disinclined, dyspathetic, hostile, hypersensitive, loath, opposed, sensitised, sensitive, susceptible.

*antonym* tolerant.

**allergy** *n* antipathy, aversion, disinclination, dislike, dyspathy, hostility, hypersensitivity, loathing, opposition, sensitivity, susceptibility, vulnerability, weakness.

*an.onyms* affinity, tolerance.

**alleviate** *v* abate, allay, assuage, blunt, check, cushion, deaden, diminish, dull, ease, lessen, lighten, mitigate, moderate, modify, mollify, palliate, quell, quench, quiet, reduce, relieve, slacken, slake, smooth, soften, soothe, subdue, temper.

*antonym* aggravate.

**alleviation** *n* abatement, allegeance, assuagement, diminution, dulling, easing,

lessening, lightening, mitigation, moderation, mollification, palliation, quelling, quenching, reduction, relief, slackening, slaking.

*antonym* aggravation.

**alley** *n* alleyway, back street, close, entry, gate, ginnel, lane, mall, passage, passageway, pathway, walk.

**alliance** *n* affiliation, affinity, agreement, association, bloc, bond, cartel, coalition, combination, compact, concordat, confederacy, confederation, conglomerate, connection, consociation, consortium, faction, federation, guild, league, marriage, pact, partnership, syndicate, treaty, union.

*antonyms* divorce, enmity, estrangement, hostility.

**allied** *adj* affiliated, agnate, amalgamated, associate, associated, bound, combined, confederate, congeric, connected, correlate(d), hand in glove, in cahoots, in league, joined, joint, kindred, leagued, linked, married, related, unified, united, wed.

*antonym* estranged.

**allocate** *v* allot, apportion, appropriate, assign, budget, designate, disperse, distribute, earmark, mete, ration, set aside, share out.

**allocation** *n* allotment, allowance, apportionment, appropriation, budget, grant, lot, measure, portion, quota, ration, share, stint.

**allot** *v* allocate, apportion, appropriate, assign, budget, designate, dispense, distribute, earmark, grant, mete, render, set aside, share out.

**allotment** *n* allocation, allowance, apportionment, appropriation, division, grant, lot, measure, partition, percentage, portion, quota, ration, share, stint.

**all-out** *adj* complete, determined, energetic, exhaustive, full, full-scale, intensive, maximum, no-holds-barred, optimum, powerful, resolute, supreme, thorough, thoroughgoing, total, undivided, unlimited, unremitting, unrestrained, unstinted, utmost, vigorous, wholesale.

*antonyms* half-hearted, perfunctory.

**allow** *v* accord, acknowledge, acquiesce, admeasure, admit, allocate, allot, apportion, approve, assign, authorise, bear, brook, concede, confess, deduct, endure, give, give leave, grant, let, own, permit, provide, put up with, remit, sanction, spare, stand, suffer, tolerate.

*antonyms* deny, forbid.

**allow for** arrange for, bear in mind, consider, foresee, include, keep in mind, keep in view, make allowances for, make concessions for, make provision for, plan for, provide for, take into account.

*antonym* discount.

**allowable** *adj* acceptable, admissible, all right, appropriate, approved, apt, legal(ised), legitimate, licit, permissible, sanctionable, sufferable, suitable, supportable, tolerable.

*antonym* unacceptable.

**allowance** *n* admission, allocation, allotment, amount, annuity, apportionment, batta, concession, deduction, discount, grant, lot, measure, pension, portion, quota, ration, rebate, reduction, remittance, sanction, share, stint, stipend, subsidy, sufferance, tolerance, weighting, X-factor.

**alloy** n admixture, amalgam, blend, coalescence, combination, composite, compound, fusion, hybrid, mix, mixture.

v admix, amalgamate, blend, combine, compound, debase, fuse, impair, mix, qualify, temper.

**all-rounder** n generalist, pancratist, Renaissance man.

*antonym* specialist.

**allude** v adumbrate, advert, cite, glance, hint, imply, infer, insinuate, intimate, mention, refer, remark, speak of, suggest, touch upon.

**allure** v attract, beguile, cajole, captivate, charm, coax, decoy, disarm, enchant, enrapture, entice, entrance, fascinate, interest, inveigle, lead on, lure, persuade, seduce, tempt, win over.

*antonym* repel.

n appeal, attraction, captivation, charm, enchantment, enticement, fascination, glamour, lure, magnetism, persuasion, seductiveness, temptation.

**alluring** adj agaçant(e), arousing, attractive, beguiling, bewitching, captivating, come-hither, enchanting, engaging, enticing, fascinating, fetching, intriguing, seductive, sensuous, sexy, tempting, voluptuous, winning.

*antonyms* repellant, unattractive.

**allusion** n citation, glance, hint, implication, innuendo, insinuation, intimation, mention, observation, quotation, reference, remark, suggestion.

**ally** n abettor, accessory, accomplice, associate, coadjutor, collaborator, colleague, confederate, confrere, consort, co-worker, friend, helper, helpmate, leaguer, partner, side-kick.

*antonyms* antagonist, enemy.

v affiliate, amalgamate, associate, band together, collaborate, combine, confederate, conjoin, connect, fraternise, join, join forces, league, marry, team up, unify, unite.

*antonym* estrange.

**almanac** n annual, calendar, ephemeris, register, year-book.

**almighty** adj absolute, all-powerful, awful, desperate, enormous, excessive, great, intense, invincible, loud, omnipotent, overpowering, overwhelming, plenipotent, severe, supreme, terrible, unlimited.

*antonyms* impotent, insignificant, weak.

**almost** adv about, all but, approaching, approximately, as good as, close to, just about, nearing, nearly, not far from, not quite, practically, towards, virtually, well-nigh.

**alms** n benefaction, beneficence, bounty, charity, donation, gift, largess(e), offerings, relief.

**alone** adj, adv abandoned, apart, by itself, by oneself, deserted, desolate, detached, discrete, forlorn, forsaken, incomparable, isolated, just, lonely, lonesome, matchless, mere, nonpareil, on one's own, on one's tod, only, peerless, separate, simply, single, single-handed, singular, sole, solitary, unaccompanied, unaided, unassisted, unattended, uncombined, unconnected, unequalled, unescorted, unique, unparalleled, unsurpassed.

**aloof** adj chilly, cold, cool, detached, distant, forbidding, formal, haughty, inaccessible, indifferent, offish, remote, reserved, reticent, stand-offish, supercilious, unapproachable, uncompanionable, unforthcoming, unfriendly, uninterested, unresponsive, unsociable, unsympathetic.

*antonyms* concerned, sociable.

**aloofness** n coolness, distance, indifference, offishness, remoteness, reservation, reserve, uncompanionability.

*antonyms* concern, sociability.

**aloud** adv audibly, clamorously, clangorously, clearly, distinctly, intelligibly, loudly, noisily, out loud, plainly, resoundingly, sonorously, vociferously.

*antonym* silently.

**already** adv at present, before now, beforehand, by now, by that time, by then, by this time, even now, heretofore, hitherto, just now, previously.

**also** adv additionally, along with, and, as well, as well as, besides, ditto, eke, further, furthermore, in addition, including, moreover, plus, therewithal, to boot, too.

**alter** v adapt, adjust, amend, bushel, castrate, change, convert, diversify, emend, metamorphose, modify, qualify, recast, reform, remodel, reshape, revise, shift, take liberties with, transform, transmute, transpose, turn, vary.

*antonym* fix.

**alteration** n adaptation, adjustment, amendment, castration, change, conversion, difference, diversification, emendation, interchanging, metamorphosis, modification, reciprocation, reformation, remodelling, reshaping, revision, rotation, shift, transfiguration, transformation, transmutation, transposition, variance, variation, vicissitude.

*antonym* fixity.

**altercation** n argument, bickering, clash, contention, controversy, debate, disagreement, discord, dispute, dissension, fracas, logomachy, quarrel, row, sparring, squabble, wrangle.

**alternate** v alter, change, fluctuate, follow one another, interchange, intersperse, oscillate, reciprocate, rotate, substitute, take turns, transpose, vary.

adj alternating, alternative, another, different, every other, every second, interchanging, reciprocal, reciprocating, reciprocative, rotating, second, substitute.

**alternative** n back-up, choice, option, other, preference, recourse, selection, substitute.

*adj* alternate, another, different, fall-back, fringe, other, second, substitute, unconventional, unorthodox.

**although** *conj* admitting that, albeit, conceding that, even if, even supposing, even though, granted that, howbeit, notwithstanding, though, while.

**altitude** *n* elevation, height, loftiness, stature, tallness.

*antonym* depth.

**altogether** *adv* absolutely, all in all, all told, as a whole, collectively, completely, entirely, fully, generally, holus-bolus, in all, in general, in sum, in toto, on the whole, perfectly, quite, thoroughly, totally, utterly, wholesale, wholly.

**altruism** *n* considerateness, disinterestedness, generosity, humanity, philanthropy, public spirit, self-abnegation, self-sacrifice, social conscience, unself, unselfishness.

*antonym* selfishness.

**altruistic** *adj* benevolent, charitable, considerate, disinterested, generous, humane, humanitarian, philanthropic, public-spirited, self-abnegating, self-sacrificing, unselfish.

**always** *adv* aye, consistently, constantly, continually, endlessly, eternally, ever, everlastingly, evermore, every time, forever, in perpetuum, invariably, perpetually, regularly, repeatedly, sempiternally, unceasingly, unfailingly, without exception.

*antonym* never.

**amalgam** *n* admixture, aggregate, alloy, amalgamation, blend, coalescence, combination, commixture, composite, compound, fusion, mixture, union.

**amalgamate** *v* alloy, ally, blend, coalesce, coalise, combine, commingle, compound, fuse, homogenise, incorporate, integrate, intermix, merge, mingle, synthesise, unify, unite.

*antonym* separate.

**amalgamation** *n* admixture, alliance, alloy, amalgam, amalgamating, blend, coalescence, coalition, combination, commingling, composite, compound, fusion, homogenisation, incorporation, integration, joining, merger, mingling, mixing, mixture, synthesis, unification, union.

**amass** *v* accumulate, agglomerate, agglutinate, aggregate, assemble, collect, compile, foregather, garner, gather, heap up, hoard, pile up, rake up, scrape together.

**amateur** *n* aficionado, buff, dabbler, dilettante, do-it-yourselfer, fancier, ham, layman, non-professional.

*antonym* professional.

**amateurish** *adj* amateur, clumsy, crude, dilettantish, hammy, incompetent, inept, inexpert, unaccomplished, unprofessional, unskilful, untrained.

*antonyms* professional, skilled.

**amatory** *adj* amatorial, amatorious, amorous, aphrodisiac, erogenous, erotic, erotogenous,

lascivious, libidinous, love, passionate, romantic, sensual, sexual, sexy.

**amaze** *v* alarm, astonish, astound, bewilder, confound, daze, disconcert, dismay, dumbfound, electrify, flabbergast, floor, shock, stagger, startle, stun, stupefy, surprise, wow.

**amazement** *n* admiration, astonishment, bewilderment, confusion, dismay, incomprehension, marvel, perplexity, shock, stupefaction, surprise, wonder, wonderment.

**ambassador** *n* agent, apostle, consul, deputy, diplomat, elchi, embassador, emissary, envoy, legate, minister, nuncio, plenipotentiary, representative.

**ambassadorial** *adj* diplomatic, fetial, legatine, plenipotentiary, representative.

**ambience** *n* air, atmosphere, aura, character, climate, environment, feel, feeling, flavour, impression, milieu, mood, quality, setting, spirit, surroundings, tenor, tone, vibes, vibrations.

**ambiguity** *n* ambivalence, confusion, doubt, doubtfulness, dubiety, dubiousness, enigma, equivocacy, equivocality, equivocation, inconclusiveness, indefiniteness, indeterminateness, obscurity, puzzle, tergiversation, uncertainty, unclearness, vagueness, weasel word(s), woolliness.

*antonym* clarity.

**ambiguous** *adj* ambivalent, amphibolic, amphibological, amphibolous, confused, confusing, cryptic, Delphic, double-barrelled, double-meaning, doubtful, dubious, enigmatic, enigmatical, equivocal, inconclusive, indefinite, indeterminate, louche, multivocal, obscure, oracular, puzzling, uncertain, unclear, vague, woolly.

*antonym* clear.

**ambit** *n* circuit, compass, confines, environs, precincts, scope.

**ambition** *n* aim, aspiration, avidity, craving, design, desire, dream, drive, eagerness, end, enterprise, goal, hankering, hope, hunger, ideal, intent, longing, object, objective, purpose, push, striving, target, wish, yearning, zeal.

*antonyms* apathy, diffidence.

**ambitious** *adj* arduous, aspiring, assertive, avid, bold, challenging, demanding, desirous, difficult, driving, eager, elaborate, energetic, enterprising, enthusiastic, exacting, fervid, formidable, go-ahead, grandiose, hard, hopeful, impressive, industrious, intent, keen, pretentious, purposeful, pushy, severe, strenuous, striving, zealous.

*antonym* unassuming.

**ambivalence** *n* ambiguity, clash, conflict, confusion, contradiction, doubt, equivocation, fluctuation, hesitancy, inconsistency, indecision, instability, irresolution, opposition, uncertainty, vacillation, wavering.

*antonym* certainty.

**ambivalent** *adj* ambiguous, clashing, conflicting, confused, contradictory, debatable, doubtful, equivocal, fluctuating, hesitant, inconclusive, inconsistent, irresolute, mixed, opposed, uncertain, undecided, unresolved, unsettled, unsure, vacillating, warring, wavering.

*antonym* unequivocal.

**amble** *v* dawdle, drift, meander, mosey, perambulate, promenade, ramble, saunter, stroll, toddle, walk, wander.

*antonyms* march, stride.

**ambush** *n* ambuscade, concealment, cover, emboscata, hiding, hiding-place, retreat, shelter, snare, trap, waylaying.

*v* ambuscade, bushwhack, ensnare, entrap, surprise, trap, waylay.

**ameliorate** *v* advance, alleviate, amend, assuage, benefit, better, ease, elevate, emend, enhance, improve, meliorate, mend, mitigate, promote, raise, redress, reform, relieve, revise.

*antonyms* exacerbate, worsen.

**amenable** *adj* accountable, acquiescent, agreeable, answerable, biddable, chargeable, complaisant, conformable, docile, flexible, liable, open, persuadable, responsible, responsive, submissive, susceptible, tractable.

*antonym* intractable.

**amend** *v* adjust, alter, ameliorate, better, change, correct, emend, emendate, enhance, fix, improve, mend, modify, qualify, rectify, redress, reform, remedy, repair, revise.

*antonyms* impair, worsen.

**amendment** *n* addendum, addition, adjunct, adjustment, alteration, amelioration, betterment, change, clarification, correction, corrigendum, emendation, enhancement, improvement, mending, modification, qualification, rectification, redress, reform, remedy, repair, revision.

*antonyms* deterioration, impairment.

**amends** *n* atonement, compensation, expiation, indemnification, indemnity, mitigation, quittance, recompense, redress, reparation, requital, restitution, restoration, satisfaction.

**amenity** *n* advantage, attraction, beauty, charm, comfort, convenience, facility, pleasantness, refinement, service.

*antonyms* eyesore, inconvenience.

**amiable** *adj* accessible, affable, agreeable, approachable, attractive, benign, biddable, charming, cheerful, companionable, complaisant, congenial, conversable, couthie, delightful, engaging, friendly, gemütlich, genial, good-humoured, good-natured, good-tempered, kind, kindly, likable, lovable, obliging, pleasant, pleasing, sociable, sweet, winning, winsome.

*antonyms* hostile, unfriendly.

**amicable** *adj* amiable, brotherly, civil, civilised, cordial, courteous, easy, frank, fraternal, friendly, good-natured, harmonious, kind, kindly, neighbourly, open, peaceable, peaceful, polite, sociable, unreserved.

*antonym* hostile.

**amid** *conj* amidst, among, amongst, in the middle of, in the midst of, in the thick of, surrounded by.

**amiss** *adj* awry, defective, erroneous, fallacious, false, faulty, improper, inaccurate, inappropriate, incorrect, out of order, unsuitable, untoward, wonky, wrong.

*adv* ill, imperfect, imprecise, out of kilter.

*antonyms* right, well.

**amity** *n* accord, amicability, brotherhood, brotherliness, comity, comradeship, concord, cordiality, fellowship, fraternity, friendliness, friendship, goodwill, harmony, kindliness, kindness, peace, peacefulness, sympathy, tranquillity, understanding.

*antonyms* discord, hostility.

**amnesty** *n* absolution, condonation, dispensation, forgiveness, immunity, indulgence, lenience, mercy, oblivion, pardon, remission, reprieve.

**amok** *adv* amuck, berserk, crazy, in a frenzy, in a fury, insane, like a madman, mad, wild.

**among** *prep* amid, amidst, amongst, between, in the middle of, in the midst of, in the thick of, midst, mongst, surrounded by, together with, with.

**amoral** *adj* abandoned, free-living, intemperate, lax, loose, non-moral, uninhibited, unmoral, unrestrained.

*antonym* moral.

**amorous** *adj* affectionate, amatory, ardent, attached, doting, enamoured, erotic, fond, impassioned, in love, lovesick, loving, lustful, passionate, randy, tender, uxorious.

*antonyms* cold, indifferent.

**amorphous** *adj* chaotic, characterless, featureless, formless, inchoate, indeterminate, indistinct, irregular, nebulous, nondescript, shapeless, undefined, unformed, unshaped, unshapen, unstructured, vague.

*antonyms* definite, distinctive, shapely.

**amount** *n* addition, aggregate, bulk, entirety, expanse, extent, lot, magnitude, mass, measure, number, quantity, quantum, quota, sum, sum total, supply, total, volume, whole.

**amount to** add up to, aggregate, approximate to, be equivalent to, be tantamount to, become, come to, equal, grow, mean, purport, run to, total.

**amour** *n* affair, affaire de coeur, entanglement, intimacy, intrigue, liaison, love affair, relationship, romance.

**ample** *adj* abundant, big, bountiful, broad, capacious, commodious, considerable, copious, expansive, extensive, full, generous, goodly, great, handsome, large, lavish, liberal, munificent, plenteous, plentiful, plenty, profuse, rich, roomy, spacious, substantial, sufficient, unrestricted, voluminous, wide.

*antonyms* insufficient, meagre.

**amplify** *v* add to, augment, boost, broaden, bulk out, deepen, develop, dilate, elaborate, enhance, enlarge, expand, expatiate, extend, fill out, heighten, increase, intensify, lengthen, magnify, raise, strengthen, supplement, widen.

*antonym* reduce.

**amplitude** *n* abundance, ampleness, bigness, breadth, bulk, capaciousness, capacity, compass, completeness, copiousness, dimension, expanse, extent, fullness, greatness, hugeness, largeness, magnitude, mass, plenitude, plentifulness, plethora, profusion, range, reach, richness, scope, size, spaciousness, sweep, vastness, volume, width.

**amply** *adv* abundantly, bountifully, completely, copiously, extensively, fully, generously, greatly, handsomely, lavishly, liberally, munificently, plenteously, plentifully, profusely, richly, substantially, sufficiently, thoroughly, unstintingly, well.

*antonym* inadequately.

**amputate** *v* curtail, cut off, dissever, dock, excise, lop, remove, separate, sever, truncate.

**amulet** *n* abraxas, charm, fetish, juju, lucky charm, pentacle, periapt, phylactory, talisman, telesm.

**amuse** *v* absorb, beguile, charm, cheer, cheer up, delight, disport, divert, engross, enliven, entertain, enthral, gladden, interest, occupy, please, popjoy, recreate, regale, relax, slay, tickle.

*antonym* bore.

**amusement** *n* beguilement, delight, disportment, distraction, diversion, enjoyment, entertainment, fun, game, gladdening, hilarity, hobby, interest, joke, lark, laughter, merriment, mirth, pastime, pleasure, prank, recreation, regalement, sport.

*antonyms* bore, boredom.

**amusing** *adj* amusive, charming, cheerful, cheering, comical, delightful, diverting, droll, enjoyable, entertaining, facetious, funny, gladdening, hilarious, humorous, interesting, jocular, jolly, killing, laughable, lively, ludicrous, merry, pleasant, pleasing, rib-tickling, risible, sportive, witty.

*antonym* boring.

**an eye for an eye** justice, reciprocation, repayment, reprisal, requital, retaliation, retribution, revenge, tit for tat, vengeance.

**anachronism** *n* antique, archaism, back number, dinosaur, fogey, fossil, metachronism, parachronism, prochronism.

**anaemic** *adj* ashen, bloodless, chalky, characterless, colourless, dull, enervated, exsanguine, exsanguin(e)ous, feeble, frail, ineffectual, infirm, insipid, pale, pallid, pasty, peelie-wally, sallow, sickly, spiritless, wan, weak, whey-faced.

*antonyms* full-blooded, ruddy, sanguine.

**anaesthetic** *n* analgesic, anodyne, narcotic, opiate, pain-killer, palliative, sedative, soporific, stupefacient, stupefactive.

**anaesthetise** *v* benumb, deaden, desensitise, dope, dull, etherise, lull, mull, numb, stupefy.

**analogous** *adj* agreeing, akin, alike, comparable, correlative, corresponding, equivalent, homologous, like, matching, parallel, reciprocal, related, resembling, similar.

*antonym* disparate.

**analogy** *n* agreement, comparison, correlation, correspondence, equivalence, homologue, homology, likeness, parallel, parallelism, relation, resemblance, semblance, similarity, similitude.

**analyse** *v* anatomise, assay, break down, consider, dissect, dissolve, divide, estimate, evaluate, examine, interpret, investigate, judge, reduce, resolve, review, scrutinise, separate, sift, study, test.

**analysis** *n* anatomisation, anatomy, assay, breakdown, dissection, dissolution, division, enquiry, estimation, evaluation, examination, exegesis, explanation, explication, exposition, interpretation, investigation, judgement, opinion, reasoning, reduction, resolution, review, scrutiny, separation, sifting, study, test.

**analytic** *adj* analytical, anatomical, critical, detailed, diagnostic, discrete, dissecting, enquiring, explanatory, expository, inquisitive, interpretative, interpretive, investigative, investigatory, logical, methodical, questioning, rational, searching, studious, systematic.

**anarchic** *adj* anarchical, anarchistic, chaotic, confused, disordered, disorganised, iconoclastic, lawless, libertarian, nihilist, rebellious, revolutionary, riotous, ungoverned.

*antonyms* orderly, submissive.

**anarchist** *n* anarch, apostate, iconoclast, insurgent, libertarian, nihilist, rebel, revolutionary, terrorist.

**anarchy** *n* anarchism, apostasy, bedlam, chaos, confusion, disorder, disorganisation, iconoclasm, insurrection, lawlessness, libertarianism, misgovernment, misrule, mutiny, nihilism, pandemonium, rebellion, revolution, riot, unrule.

*antonyms* control, order, rule.

**anathema** *n* abhorrence, abomination, aversion, ban, bane, bête noire, bugbear, condemnation, curse, damnation, denunciation, excommunication, execration, imprecation, malediction, object of loathing, pariah, proscription, taboo.

**anatomise** *v* analyse, break down, dissect, dissolve, divide, examine, pull apart, resolve, scrutinise, separate, study, vivisect.

**anatomy** *n* analysis, build, composition, constitution, construction, dissection, frame, framework, make-up, structure, vivisection, zootomy.

**ancestor** *n* antecedent, antecessor, forebear, forefather, forerunner, precursor, predecessor, primogenitor, progenitor, progenitress, progenitrix.

*antonym* descendant.

**ancestral** *adj* atavistic, avital, familial, genealogical, genetic, hereditary, lineal, parental.

**ancestry** *n* ancestors, antecedents, antecessors, blood, derivation, descent, extraction, family, forebears, forefathers, genealogy, heredity, heritage, house, line, lineage, origin, parentage, pedigree, progenitors, race, roots, stirps, stock.

**anchor** *n* grapnel, kedge, killick, mainstay, mud-hook, pillar of strength, prop, security, staff, support.

*v* affix, attach, fasten, fix, make fast, moor.

**anchorage** n bield, harbour, harbourage, haven, mooring, port, protection, refuge, sanctuary, shelter.

**anchorite** n anchoress, anchoret, ancress, ascetic, eremite, hermit, holy man, marabout, recluse, solitaire, solitarian, solitary, stylite.

**ancient** adj aged, age-old, antediluvian, antiquated, antique, archaic, bygone, demode, early, fossilised, hoary, immemorial, obsolete, old, olden, old-fashioned, original, outmoded, out-of-date, preadamic, prehistoric, primeval, primordial, pristine, superannuated, time-worn, venerable, world-old.

*antonym* modern.

**ancillary** adj accessory, additional, adjuvant, adminicular, auxiliary, contributory, extra, secondary, subordinate, subsidiary, supplementary.

**androgynous** adj bisexual, epicene, gynandrous, hermaphrodite, hermaphroditic.

**anecdote** n exemplum, fable, reminiscence, sketch, story, tale, yarn.

**angel** n archangel, backer, benefactor, cherub, darling, divine messenger, fairy godmother, guardian spirit, ideal, paragon, principality, saint, seraph, supporter, treasure.

*antonyms* devil, fiend.

**angelic** adj adorable, beatific, beautiful, celestial, cherubic, divine, entrancing, ethereal, exemplary, heavenly, holy, innocent, lovely, pious, pure, saintly, seraphic, unworldly, virtuous.

*antonyms* devilish, fiendish.

**anger** n annoyance, antagonism, bad blood, bile, bitterness, choler, dander, displeasure, dudgeon, exasperation, fury, gall, indignation, ire, irritability, irritation, monkey, outrage, passion, pique, rage, rancour, resentment, spleen, temper, vexation, wrath.

*antonym* forbearance.

v affront, aggravate, annoy, antagonise, bother, bug, displease, enrage, exasperate, fret, frustrate, gall, incense, infuriate, irk, irritate, madden, miff, needle, nettle, offend, outrage, pique, provoke, rile, ruffle, vex.

*antonyms* appease, calm, please.

**angle** n approach, aspect, bend, corner, crook, crotch, cusp, direction, edge, elbow, facet, flexure, hook, nook, outlook, perspective, point, point of view, position, side, slant, standpoint, turn, viewpoint.

**angle for** aim for, be after, be out for, contrive, fish for, have one's beady eye on, hunt, invite, scheme, seek, solicit.

**angler** n fisherman, piscator, piscatrix, rodman, rodsman, rodster.

**angling** n ars piscatoria, fishing, gentle craft.

**angry** adj aggravated, annoyed, antagonised, bitter, burned up, choked, choleric, chuffed, disgruntled, displeased, enraged, exasperated, furious, heated, hot, incensed, indignant, infuriated, irascible, irate, ireful, irked, irritable, irritated, mad, miffed, needled, nettled, outraged, passionate, piqued, provoked, raging, rancorous, ratty, red-headed, resentful, riled, shirty, splenetic, stomachful, tumultuous, uptight, waxy, wrathful, wroth.

*antonyms* calm, content.

**angst** n agony, angoisse, anguish, anxiety, apprehension, depression, dread, foreboding, future shock, mal du siècle, malaise, mid-life crisis, Weltschmerz, worry.

**anguish** n agony, angst, anxiety, desolation, distress, dole, dolour, grief, heartache, heartbreak, misery, pain, pang, rack, sorrow, suffering, torment, torture, tribulation, woe, wretchedness.

*antonyms* happiness, solace.

**anguished** adj afflicted, agonised, angst-ridden, distressed, dolorous, harrowed, miserable, racked, stricken, suffering, tormented, tortured, wretched.

**angular** adj bony, gauche, gaunt, gawky, lank, lanky, lean, rangy, rawboned, scrawny, skinny, spare, ungainly.

**animal** n barbarian, beast, brute, creature, critter, cur, hound, mammal, monster, pig, savage, swine.

adj animalic, bestial, bodily, brutish, carnal, faunal, feral, ferine, fleshly, gross, inhuman, instinctive, physical, piggish, savage, sensual, wild, zoic.

**animate** v activate, arouse, embolden, encourage, energise, enliven, excite, fire, galvanise, goad, impel, incite, inspire, inspirit, instigate, invest, invigorate, irradiate, kindle, move, quicken, reactivate, revive, revivify, rouse, spark, spur, stimulate, stir, suffuse, urge, vitalise, vivify.

*antonyms* dull, inhibit.

adj alive, breathing, conscious, live, living, sentient.

*antonyms* dull, spiritless.

**animated** adj active, airy, alive, ardent, brisk, buoyant, eager, ebullient, energetic, enthusiastic, excited, fervent, gay, glowing, impassioned, lively, passionate, quick, radiant, spirited, sprightly, vehement, vibrant, vigorous, vital, vivacious, vivid, zestful.

*antonyms* inert, sluggish.

**animation** n action, activity, ardour, briskness, buoyancy, ebullience, elation, energy, enthusiasm, excitement, exhilaration, fervour, gaiety, high spirits, life, liveliness, passion, pep, radiance, sparkle, spirit, sprightliness, verve, vibrancy, vigour, vitality, vivacity, zeal, zest, zing.

*antonyms* dullness, inertia.

**animosity** n acrimony, animus, antagonism, antipathy, bad blood, bitterness, enmity, feud, feuding, hate, hatred, hostility, ill-will, loathing, malevolence, malice, malignity, odium, rancour, resentment, spite.

*antonym* goodwill.

**animus** *n* acrimony, animosity, antagonism, antipathy, bad blood, bitterness, enmity, hate, hatred, hostility, ill-feeling, ill-will, impetus, intention, loathing, malevolence, malice, malignance, malignity, motive, odium, purpose, rancour, resentment, will.

*antonym* sympathy.

**annals** *n* accounts, archives, chronicles, history, journals, memoirs, memorials, records, registers, reports.

**annex** *v* acquire, add, adjoin, affix, append, appropriate, arrogate, attach, connect, conquer, expropriate, fasten, incorporate, join, occupy, purloin, seize, subjoin, tack, take over, unite, usurp.

*n* addendum, additament, addition, adjunct, appendix, attachment, supplement.

**annexation** *n* amalgamation, annexing, appropriation, arrogation, augmentation, combination, conquest, expropriation, occupation, seizure, takeover, usurpation.

**annexe** *n* addition, ell, expansion, extension, wing.

**annihilate** *v* abolish, assassinate, destroy, eliminate, eradicate, erase, exterminate, extinguish, extirpate, liquidate, murder, nullify, obliterate, raze, rub out, thrash, trounce, wipe out.

**annihilation** *n* abolition, assassination, defeat, destruction, elimination, eradication, erasure, extermination, extinction, extirpation, liquidation, nullification, obliteration.

**annotate** *v* comment, commentate, elucidate, explain, gloss, gloze, interpret, marginalise, note.

**annotation** *n* apparatus criticus, comment, commentary, elucidation, exegesis, explanation, explication, footnote, gloss, interpretation, marginalia, note, scholia, scholion, scholium.

**announce** *v* advertise, blazon, broadcast, declare, disclose, divulge, intimate, leak, make known, notify, preconise, proclaim, promulgate, propound, publicise, publish, report, reveal, state.

*antonym* suppress.

**announcement** *n* advertisement, broadcast, bulletin, communique, declaration, disclosure, dispatch, divulgation, divulgence, intimation, notification, proclamation, promulgation, publication, report, revelation, statement.

**announcer** *n* anchor man, broadcaster, commentator, commère, compère, crier, harbinger, herald, messenger, newscaster, news-reader, reporter.

**annoy** *v* aggravate, anger, badger, bore, bother, bug, chagrin, contrary, displease, disturb, exasperate, fash, gall, get, give the pigs, harass, harm, harry, hip, hump, incommode, irk, irritate, madden, miff, molest, needle, nettle, peeve, pester, pique, plague, provoke, rile, ruffle, tease, trouble, vex.

*antonyms* gratify, please.

**annoyance** *n* aggravation, anger, bind, bore, bother, desagrement, displeasure, disturbance, exasperation, fash, gêne, harassment, headache, irritant, irritation, nuisance, pain, pest, pique, plague, provocation, tease, trouble, vexation.

*antonym* pleasure.

**annoyed** *adj* bored, bugged, chagrined, displeased, exasperated, galled, harassed, hipped, irked, irritated, miffed, narked, peeved, piqued, provoked, shirty, vexed.

*antonym* pleased.

**annoying** *adj* aggravating, boring, bothersome, displeasing, disturbing, exasperating, fashious, galling, harassing, irksome, irritating, maddening, offensive, peeving, pesky, pesterous, pestful, pestiferous, pestilent, pestilential, plaguesome, plaguey, provoking, teasing, troublesome, vexatious.

*antonyms* pleasing, welcome.

**annual** *n* almanac, annal, ephemeris, year-book.

**annul** *v* abolish, abrogate, cancel, cashier, countermand, disannul, invalidate, negate, nullify, quash, recall, repeal, rescind, retract, reverse, revoke, suspend, void.

*antonyms* enact, restore.

**annulment** *n* abolition, abrogation, cancellation, cassation, countermanding, disannulment, invalidation, negation, nullification, quashing, recall, repeal, rescindment, rescission, retraction, reversal, revocation, suspension, voiding.

*antonyms* enactment, restoration.

**anodyne** *adj* analgesic, bland, blunting, calmative, deadening, desensitising, dulling, febrifugal, inoffensive, narcotic, numbing, pain-killing, pain-relieving, palliative, sedative.

*antonym* irritant.

*n* alleviative, analgesic, febrifuge, narcotic, pain-killer, pain-reliever, palliative, sedative.

*antonym* irritant.

**anoint** *v* anele, bless, consecrate, daub, dedicate, embrocate, grease, hallow, lard, lubricate, oil, rub, sanctify, smear.

**anointing** *n* aneling, blessing, consecration, dedication, embrocation, hallowing, sanctification, unction.

**anomalous** *adj* aberrant, abnormal, atypical, bizarre, deviant, eccentric, exceptional, freakish, incongruous, inconsistent, irregular, odd, peculiar, quirky, rare, singular, untypical, unusual.

*antonyms* normal, regular.

**anomaly** *n* aberration, abnormality, departure, deviant, deviation, divergence, eccentricity, exception, freak, incongruity, inconsistency, irregularity, misfit, oddity, peculiarity, rarity.

**anonymous** *adj* characterless, faceless, impersonal, incognito, innominate, nameless, nondescript, unacknowledged, unattested, unauthenticated, uncredited, unexceptional, unidentified, unknown, unnamed, unsigned, unspecified.

*antonyms* distinctive, identifiable, named.

**anorak** *n* blouson, golf-jacket, jerkin, lumber-jacket, parka, waterproof, windcheater, windjammer.

**answer** *n* acknowledgement, apology, comeback, counterbuff, countercharge, defence, explanation, outcome, plea, reaction, rebuttal, reciprocation, refutation, rejoinder, reply, report, resolution, response, retaliation, retort, return, riposte, solution, vindication.

*v* acknowledge, agree, balance, conform, correlate, correspond, do, echo, explain, fill, fit, fulfil, match up to, meet, pass, qualify, react, reciprocate, refute, rejoin, reply, resolve, respond, retaliate, retort, return, satisfy, serve, solve, succeed, suffice, suit, work.

**answer back** argue, cheek, contradict, disagree, dispute, rebut, retaliate, retort, riposte, talk back.

*antonym* acquiesce.

**answerable¹** *adj* accountable, amenable, blameable, blameworthy, chargeable, liable, responsible, to blame.

**answerable²** *adj* defensible, deniable, disprovable, explicable, rebuttable, refutable, repudiable.

**answering** *adj* respondent, responsory.

**ant** *n* emmet, hymenopteran, pismire, termite.

**antagonise** *v* alienate, anger, annoy, disaffect, embitter, estrange, incense, insult, irritate, offend, provoke, repel.

*antonym* disarm.

**antagonism** *n* animosity, animus, antipathy, competition, conflict, contention, discord, dissension, friction, hostility, ill-feeling, ill-will, opposition, rivalry.

*antonyms* rapport, sympathy.

**antagonist** *n* adversary, competitor, contender, contestant, disputant, enemy, foe, opponent, opposer, rival.

*antonyms* ally, supporter.

**antagonistic** *adj* adverse, antipathetic, at variance, averse, bellicose, belligerent, conflicting, contentious, hostile, ill-disposed, incompatible, inimical, opposed, pugnacious, unfriendly.

*antonyms* friendly, sympathetic.

**antecedents** *n* ancestors, ancestry, antecessors, background, blood, descent, dossier, extraction, family, forebears, forefathers, genealogy, history, line, lineage, past, pedigree, prodromi, progenitors, record, stock.

**antedate** *v* antecede, anticipate, forego, forerun, go before, precede, predate.

*antonym* follow.

**antediluvian** *adj* anachronistic, ancient, antiquated, antique, archaic, bygone, demode, fossilised, obsolete, old-fashioned, out of the ark, out-of-date, passe, prehistoric, primal, primeval, primitive, primordial, superannuated.

*antonyms* up-to-date, with it.

**anterior** *adj* antecedent, earlier, foregoing, former, introductory, preceding, previous, prior, prodromal, prodromic.

*antonym* subsequent.

**anthem** *n* canticle, chant, chorale, hymn, introit, paean, psalm, song.

**anthology** *n* analects, choice, collection, compendium, compilation, digest, divan, florilegium, garland, miscellany, selection, spicilegium, treasury.

**anticipate** *v* antedate, apprehend, await, bank on, beat to it, count upon, earlierise, expect, forecast, foredate, foresee, forestall, foretaste, foretell, forethink, hope for, intercept, look for, look forward to, predict, pre-empt, prevent.

**anticipation** *n* apprehension, awaiting, expectancy, expectation, foresight, foretaste, forethought, forewarning, hope, preconception, premonition, prescience, presentiment, prodrome, prolepsis.

**anticipatory** *adj* anticipative, expectant, hopeful, intuitive, preparatory, proleptic, proleptical.

**anticlimax** *n* bathos, comedown, damp squib, disappointment, disenchantment, fiasco, let-down.

**anticlockwise** *adj* dextrorse, l(a)evorotatory.

**antics** *n* buffoonery, capers, clownery, clowning, didoes, doings, escapades, foolery, foolishness, frolics, larks, mischief, monkey tricks, playfulness, pranks, silliness, skylarking, stunts, tomfoolery, tricks, zanyism.

**antidote** *n* antitoxin, antivenin, corrective, counter-agent, countermeasure, cure, detoxicant, mithridate, neutraliser, preventive, remedy, specific, theriac, treacle.

**antipathetic** *adj* abhorrent, allergic, anathematical, antagonistic, antipathetical, averse, disgusting, distasteful, hateful, horrible, hostile, incompatible, inimical, invidious, loathsome, obnoxious, odious, offensive, repellent, repugnant, repulsive, revolting.

*antonyms* agreeable, harmonious, sympathetic.

**antipathy** *n* abhorrence, allergy, animosity, animus, antagonism, aversion, bad blood, contrariety, disgust, dislike, distaste, enmity, hate, hatred, hostility, ill-will, incompatibility, loathing, odium, opposition, rancour, repugnance, repulsion, resentment.

*antonyms* rapport, sympathy.

**antipodes** *n* underworld.

**antiquary** *n* antiquarian, archaeologist, archaist, bibliophile, collector, Dryasdust, palaeologist, virtuoso.

**antiquated** *adj* anachronistic, ancient, antediluvian, antique, archaic, dated, demode, elderly, fogeyish, fogram, fossilised, obsolete, old, old hat, old-fashioned, old-fogeyish, outdated, outmoded, out-of-date, outworn, passe, quaint, superannuated, unfashionable.

*antonyms* forward-looking, modern.

**antique** *adj* aged, ancient, antiquarian, archaic, elderly, obsolete, old, old-fashioned, outdated, quaint, superannuated, vintage.

*n* antiquity, bibelot, bygone, curio, curiosity, heirloom, knick-knack, museum-piece, object of virtu, period piece, rarity, relic.

**antiquity** n age, agedness, ancient times, ancientness, antique, distant past, e(i)ld, elderliness, fogramity, hoariness, old age, olden days, oldness, time immemorial, venerableness.

*antonyms* modernity, novelty.

**antiseptic** adj aseptic, bactericidal, clean, disinfectant, germ-free, germicidal, hygienic, medicated, pure, sanitary, sanitised, sterile, uncontaminated, unpolluted.

n bactericide, cleanser, decontaminant, disinfectant, germicide, purifier.

**antisocial** adj alienated, anarchic, antagonistic, asocial, belligerent, disorderly, disruptive, hostile, menacing, misanthropic, rebellious, reserved, retiring, unacceptable, unapproachable, uncommunicative, unfriendly, unsociable, withdrawn.

*antonyms* acceptable, sociable.

**antithesis** n antipode, contradiction, contradistinction, contraposition, contrariety, contrary, contrast, converse, inverse, inversion, opposite, opposite extreme, opposition, polarity, reversal, reverse.

**antithetical** adj antipodal, antipodean, antithetic, contradictory, contrary, contrasted, contrasting, converse, counter, inverse, opposed, opposite, polarised, poles apart, reverse.

**anxiety** n angst, anxiousness, apprehension, care, concern, craving, desire, disquiet, disquietude, distress, dread, dysthymia, eagerness, foreboding, fretfulness, impatience, keenness, misgiving, nervousness, presentiment, restlessness, solicitude, suspense, tension, torment, torture, unease, uneasiness, watchfulness, willingness, worriment, worry.

*antonym* composure.

**anxious** adj afraid, angst-ridden, apprehensive, avid, careful, concerned, desirous, disquieted, distressed, disturbed, eager, expectant, fearful, fretful, impatient, in suspense, intent, itching, keen, nervous, on tenterhooks, overwrought, restless, solicitous, taut, tense, tormented, tortured, troubled, uneasy, unquiet, watchful, worried, yearning.

*antonym* composed.

**apace** adv at full speed, at top speed, double-quick, expeditiously, fast, hastily, posthaste, quickly, rapidly, speedily, swiftly, without delay.

**apart** adv afar, alone, aloof, aside, asunder, away, by oneself, cut off, distant, distinct, divorced, excluded, in bits, in pieces, independent, independently, individually, into parts, isolated, on one's own, piecemeal, privately, separate, separated, separately, singly, to bits, to one side, to pieces.

**apartment** n accommodation, chambers, compartment, condominium, flat, living quarters, lodgings, maisonette, pad, penthouse, quarters, room, rooms, suite, tenement.

**apathetic** adj cold, cool, dispassionate, emotionless, impassive, indifferent, insensible, insentient, listless, numb, passive, phlegmatic, sluggish, stoic, torpid, unambitious, unconcerned, unemotional, unfeeling, uninterested, uninvolved, unmotivated, unmoved, unresponsive.

*antonyms* concerned, responsive.

**apathy** n accidie, acedia, coldness, coolness, emotionlessness, impassibility, impassivity, incuriousness, indifference, inertia, insensibility, lethargy, listlessness, passiveness, passivity, phlegm, sluggishness, torpor, unconcern, unfeelingness, uninterestedness, unresponsiveness.

*antonyms* concern, warmth.

**ape** v affect, caricature, copy, counterfeit, echo, imitate, mimic, mirror, mock, parody, parrot, take off.

n baboon, boor, brute, chimpanzee, gibbon, gorilla, jocko, monkey, oaf, orang-utan, pongid, pongo, savage.

**aperture** n breach, chink, cleft, crack, eye, eyelet, fissure, foramen, gap, hole, interstice, opening, orifice, passage, perforation, rent, rift, slit, slot, space, vent.

**apex** n acme, apogee, climax, consummation, crest, crown, crowning point, culmination, fastigium, height, high point, peak, pinnacle, point, summit, tip, top, vertex, zenith.

*antonym* nadir.

**aphorism** n adage, apothegm, axiom, dictum, epigram, gnome, maxim, mot, precept, proverb, saw, saying, sentence.

**aphrodisiac** adj amative, amatory, erogenous, erotic, erotogenous, venerous.

**aplomb** n assurance, audacity, balance, calmness, composure, confidence, coolness, equanimity, poise, sang-froid, savoir faire, self-assurance, self-confidence, self-possession.

*antonym* discomposure.

**apocalyptic** adj fatidic, ominous, oracular, portentous, prophetic, revelational, revelatory, signal, threatening, vatic.

**apocryphal** adj concocted, doubtful, dubious, equivocal, fabricated, fictitious, imaginary, legendary, mythical, phony, questionable, spurious, unauthenticated, uncanonical, unsubstantiated, unsupported, unverified.

*antonym* true.

**apogee** n acme, apex, climax, consummation, crest, crown, culmination, height, high point, meridian, peak, pinnacle, summit, tip, top, vertex, zenith.

*antonyms* nadir, perigee.

**apologetic** adj compunctious, conscience-stricken, contrite, excusatory, penitent, regretful, remorseful, repentant, rueful, sorry.

*antonym* defiant.

**apologist** n advocate, champion, defender, endorser, justifier, pleader, seconder, spokesman, supporter, upholder, vindicator.

*antonym* critic.

**apology** n acknowledgement, apologia, confession, defence, excuse, explanation, extenuation, justification, palliation, plea, semblance, substitute, travesty, vindication.

*antonym* defiance.

**apophthegm** *n* adage, aphorism, axiom, dictum, epigram, gnome, maxim, precept, proverb, saw, saying, sentence.

**apostasy** *n* defection, desertion, disloyalty, faithlessness, falseness, heresy, perfidy, rattery, ratting, recidivism, recreance, recreancy, renegation, renunciation, treachery, unfaithfulness.

*antonyms* loyalty, orthodoxy.

**apostate** *n* defector, deserter, heretic, recidivist, recreant, renegade, renegado, runagate, tergiversator, traitor, turncoat.

*antonyms* adherent, convert, loyalist.

*adj* disloyal, faithless, false, heretical, perfidious, recreant, renegate, traitorous, treacherous, unfaithful, unorthodox, untrue.

*antonym* faithful.

**apostatise** *v* backslide, defect, lapse, recant, renegue, renig, tergiversate, withdraw.

**apostle** *n* advocate, champion, crusader, evangelist, exponent, herald, messenger, missionary, pioneer, preacher, promoter, propagandist, propagator, proponent, proselytiser.

**apotheosis** *n* deification, elevation, exaltation, glorification, godding, idealisation, idolisation, immortalisation.

**apotheosise** *v* deify, elevate, exalt, glorify, god, idealise, idolise, immortalise.

**appal** *v* alarm, astound, daunt, disconcert, disgust, dishearten, dismay, frighten, harrow, horrify, intimidate, outrage, petrify, scare, shock, terrify, unnerve.

*antonyms* encourage, reassure.

**appalling** *adj* alarming, astounding, awful, daunting, dire, disheartening, dismaying, dreadful, fearful, frightening, frightful, ghastly, grim, harrowing, hideous, horrible, horrid, horrific, horrifying, intimidating, loathsome, petrifying, scaring, shocking, startling, terrible, terrifying, unnerving, wretched.

*antonym* reassuring.

**apparatus** *n* appliance, bureaucracy, contraption, device, equipment, framework, gadget, gear, gismo, hierarchy, implements, machine, machinery, materials, means, mechanism, network, organisation, outfit, set-up, structure, system, tackle, tools, utensils.

**apparel** *n* accoutrements, array, attire, clothes, clothing, costume, dress, equipment, garb, garments, garniture, gear, guise, habiliments, habit, outfit, raiment, rig-out, robes, suit, trappings, vestiture, vestments, wardrobe, weeds.

**apparent** *adj* clear, conspicuous, declared, discernible, distinct, evident, indubitable, manifest, marked, noticeable, obvious, on paper, open, ostensible, outward, overt, patent,

perceptible, plain, seeming, specious, superficial, unmistakable, visible.

*antonyms* obscure, real.

**apparently** *adv* clearly, manifestly, obviously, ostensibly, outwardly, patently, plainly, seemingly, speciously, superficially.

**apparition** *n* chimera, eidolon, ghost, manifestation, materialisation, phantasm, phantom, presence, revenant, shade, spectre, spirit, spook, umbra, vision, visitant, visitation, wraith.

**appeal**¹ *n* adjuration, application, entreaty, imploration, invocation, orison, petition, plea, prayer, request, solicitation, suit, supplication.

*v* address, adjure, apply, ask, beg, beseech, call, call upon, entreat, implore, invoke, petition, plead, pray, refer, request, resort to, solicit, sue, supplicate.

**appeal**² *n* allure, attraction, attractiveness, beauty, charisma, charm, enchantment, fascination, interest, magnetism, winsomeness.

*v* allure, attract, charm, draw, engage, entice, fascinate, interest, invite, lure, please, tempt.

**appear** *v* act, arise, arrive, attend, be published, bob up, come into sight, come into view, come out, come to light, crop up, develop, emerge, enter, issue, leak out, look, loom, materialise, occur, perform, play, rise, seem, show, show up, surface, take part, transpire, turn out, turn up.

*antonym* disappear.

**appearance** *n* advent, air, appearing, arrival, aspect, bearing, brow, cast, character, coming, debut, demeanour, emergence, expression, façade, face, facies, favour, figure, form, front, guise, illusion, image, impression, introduction, look, looks, manner, mien, physiognomy, presence, pretence, seeming, semblance, show, the cut of one's jib.

*antonyms* disappearance, reality.

**appease** *v* allay, assuage, blunt, calm, compose, conciliate, diminish, ease, give a sop to, humour, lessen, lull, mitigate, mollify, pacify, placate, propitiate, quell, quench, quiet, reconcile, satisfy, soften, soothe, subdue, tranquillise.

*antonym* aggravate.

**appeasement** *n* acceding, accommodation, assuagement, compromise, concession, conciliation, humouring, lessening, mitigation, mollification, Munich, Munichism, pacification, placation, propitiation, quelling, quieting, satisfaction, softening, sop.

*antonyms* aggravation, resistance.

**appellation** *n* address, denomination, description, designation, epithet, label, monicker, name, nickname, sobriquet, style, term, title.

**append** *v* add, adjoin, affix, annex, attach, conjoin, fasten, join, subjoin, tack on.

**appendage** *n* accessory, addendum, addition, adjunct, affix, ancillary, annexe, appendix, appurtenance, attachment, auxiliary, excrescence, extremity, limb, member, projection, prosthesis, protuberance, supplement, tab, tag.

**appendix** *n* addendum, additament, addition, adjunct, appendage, codicil, epilogue, excursus, postscript, rider, supplement.

**appertaining** *adj* applicable, applying, belonging, characteristic, connected, germane, pertinent, related, relevant.

**appetiser** *n* antipasto, aperitif, bonne bouche, canape, cocktail, foretaste, hors d'oeuvre, preview, sample, taste, taster, titbit, whet.

**appetising** *adj* appealing, delicious, inviting, lip-smacking, moreish, mouthwatering, palatable, piquant, savoury, scrumptious, succulent, tasty, tempting, toothsome, yummy.

*antonym* disgusting.

**appetite** *n* appetence, appetency, craving, demand, desire, eagerness, hankering, hunger, inclination, keenness, liking, limosis, longing, orexis, passion, predilection, proclivity, propensity, relish, stomach, taste, willingness, yearning, zeal, zest.

*antonym* distaste.

**applaud** *v* acclaim, approve, cheer, clap, commend, compliment, congratulate, encourage, eulogise, extol, laud, ovate, praise.

*antonyms* censure, disparage.

**applauding** *adj* acclamatory, adulatory, approving, commendatory, complimentary, congratulatory, laudatory, plauditory, plausive.

*antonym* abusive.

**applause** *n* acclaim, acclamation, accolade, approbation, approval, cheering, cheers, commendation, congratulation, encomium, eulogies, eulogising, hand, laudation, ovation, plaudits, praise.

*antonyms* censure, disparagement.

**appliance** *n* apparatus, contraption, contrivance, device, gadget, gismo, implement, instrument, machine, mechanism, tool.

**applicable** *adj* apposite, appropriate, apropos, apt, befitting, fit, fitting, germane, legitimate, pertinent, proper, related, relevant, suitable, suited, useful, valid.

*antonym* inapplicable.

**applicant** *n* aspirant, candidate, claimant, competitor, contestant, inquirer, interviewee, petitioner, postulant, suitor.

**application**[1] *n* adhibition, appeal, appositeness, apposition, assiduity, attention, attentiveness, claim, commitment, dedication, diligence, effort, exercise, extension, function, germaneness, industry, inquiry, keenness, lesson, moral, perseverance, pertinence, petition, practice, purpose, reference, relevance, request, requisition, sedulity, sedulousness, solicitation, suit, use, value.

**application**[2] *n* balm, cream, dressing, emollient, lotion, medication, ointment, poultice, preparation, salve, unguent.

**apply**[1] *v* adhibit, administer, appose, assign, bring into play, bring to bear, direct, employ, engage, execute, exercise, implement, ply, practise, resort to, set, use, utilise, wield.

**apply**[2] *v* appertain, be relevant, fit, have force, pertain, refer, relate, suit.

**apply**[3] *v* anoint, cover with, lay on, paint, place, put on, rub, smear, spread on, use.

**apply**[4] *v* appeal, ask for, claim, indent for, inquire, petition, put in, request, requisition, solicit, sue.

**apply**[5] *v* address, bend, buckle down, commit, concentrate, dedicate, devote, direct, give, persevere, settle down, study, throw.

**appoint** *v* allot, arrange, assign, charge, choose, command, commission, constitute, co-opt, decide, decree, delegate, designate, destine, detail, determine, devote, direct, elect, engage, enjoin, equip, establish, fit out, fix, furnish, install, name, nominate, ordain, outfit, plenish, provide, select, set, settle, supply.

*antonyms* dismiss, reject.

**appointed** *adj* allotted, arranged, assigned, chosen, commanded, commissioned, co-opted, dative, decided, decreed, delegated, designated, determined, directed, elected, enjoined, equipped, established, fitted out, fixed, furnished, installed, invested, named, nominated, ordained, plenished, preordained, provided, selected, set, settled, supplied.

**appointment** *n* allotment, arrangement, assignation, assignment, choice, choosing, commissioning, consultation, date, delegation, election, engagement, installation, interview, job, meeting, naming, nomination, office, place, position, post, rendezvous, selection, session, situation, station, tryst.

**appointments** *n* accoutrements, appurtenances, equipage, fittings, fixtures, furnishings, furniture, gear, outfit, paraphernalia, plenishings, trappings.

**apportion** *v* accord, admeasure, allocate, allot, assign, award, deal, dispense, distribute, divide, dole out, grant, measure out, mete, morsel, portion out, ration, share.

**apportionment** *n* allocation, allotment, assignment, dealing, dispensation, dispensing, distribution, division, divvying up, doling, measuring, meting, partitioning, sharing.

**apposite** *adj* applicable, appropriate, apropos, apt, befitting, condign, felicitous, germane, in point, pertinent, proper, relevant, suitable, suited, to the point, to the purpose.

*antonym* inapposite.

**appraisal** *n* appreciation, assay, assaying, assessment, estimate, estimation, evaluation, examination, inspection, judgement, once-over, opinion, pricing, rating, reckoning, review, sizing-up, survey, valuation.

**appraise** *v* assay, assess, estimate, evaluate, examine, gauge, inspect, judge, price, rate, review, size up, survey, valuate, value.

**appreciable** *adj* apparent, ascertainable, clear-cut, considerable, definite, detectable, discernible, distinguishable, evident, marked, material, measurable, noticeable, obvious, perceivable, perceptible, pronounced, recognisable, significant, substantial, undeniable, visible.

*antonyms* imperceptible, negligible.

**appreciate¹** *v* acknowledge, admire, be sensible of, be sensitive to, cherish, comprehend, dig, do justice to, enjoy, esteem, estimate, know, like, perceive, prize, realise, recognise, regard, relish, respect, savour, sympathise with, take kindly to, treasure, understand, value.

*antonyms* despise, overlook.

**appreciate²** *v* enhance, gain, grow, improve, increase, inflate, mount, rise, strengthen.

*antonym* depreciate.

**appreciation¹** *n* acclamation, acknowledgement, admiration, appraisal, assessment, awareness, cognisance, comprehension, criticism, critique, enjoyment, esteem, estimation, gratefulness, gratitude, indebtedness, judgement, knowledge, liking, notice, obligation, perception, praise, realisation, recognition, regard, relish, respect, responsiveness, review, sensitivity, sympathy, thankfulness, thanks, tribute, understanding, valuation.

*antonyms* ingratitude, neglect.

**appreciation²** *n* climb, enhancement, gain, growth, improvement, increase, inflation, rise, the up-and-up.

*antonym* depreciation.

**appreciative** *adj* admiring, aware, beholden, cognisant, conscious, encouraging, enthusiastic, grateful, indebted, knowledgeable, mindful, obliged, perceptive, pleased, regardful, respectful, responsive, sensible, sensitive, supportive, sympathetic, thankful, understanding.

*antonym* ungrateful.

**apprehend¹** *v* arrest, bust, capture, catch, collar, detain, get, grab, nab, nick, pinch, run in, seize, take.

**apprehend²** *v* appreciate, believe, comprehend, conceive, consider, discern, grasp, imagine, know, perceive, realise, recognise, see, twig, understand.

**apprehension¹** *n* arrest, capture, catching, seizure, taking.

**apprehension²** *n* alarm, anxiety, apprehensiveness, awareness, belief, comprehension, concept, conception, concern, conjecture, discernment, disquiet, doubt, dread, fear, foreboding, grasp, idea, impression, intellect, intellection, intelligence, ken, knowledge, misgiving, mistrust, nervousness, notion, opinion, perception, premonition, presentiment, qualm, sentiment, suspicion, thought, understanding, unease, uneasiness, uptake, view, worry.

**apprehensive** *adj* afraid, alarmed, anxious, concerned, disquieted, distrustful, disturbed, doubtful, fearful, mistrustful, nervous, solicitous, suspicious, uneasy, worried.

*antonym* confident.

**apprentice** *n* beginner, cub, learner, neophyte, newcomer, novice, probationer, pupil, recruit, starter, student, trainee, tyro.

*antonym* expert.

**apprise** *v* acquaint, advise, brief, communicate, enlighten, inform, intimate, notify, tell, tip off, warn.

**approach** *v* advance, anear, appeal to, apply to, approximate, be like, begin, broach, catch up, come close, come near to, commence, compare with, draw near, embark on, gain on, introduce, make advances, make overtures, meet, mention, near, reach, resemble, set about, sound out, undertake.

*n* access, advance, advent, appeal, application, approximation, arrival, attitude, avenue, course, doorway, entrance, gesture, invitation, landfall, likeness, manner, means, method, mode, modus operandi, motion, nearing, offer, overture, passage, procedure, proposal, proposition, resemblance, road, semblance, style, system, technique, threshold, way.

**approachable** *adj* accessible, affable, agreeable, attainable, congenial, conversable, cordial, easy, friendly, informal, open, reachable, sociable.

*antonym* unapproachable.

**approbation** *n* acceptance, acclaim, acclamation, applause, approval, assent, commendation, congratulation, encouragement, endorsement, esteem, favour, kudos, laudation, praise, ratification, recognition, regard, sanction, support.

*antonym* disapprobation.

**appropriate** *adj* applicable, apposite, appurtenant, apropos, apt, becoming, befitting, belonging, condign, congruous, correct, felicitous, fit, fitting, germane, meet, merited, opportune, pertinent, proper, relevant, right, seasonable, seemly, spot-on, suitable, timely, to the point, well-chosen, well-suited, well-timed.

*antonym* inappropriate.

*v* allocate, allot, annex, apportion, arrogate, assign, assume, commandeer, confiscate, devote, earmark, embezzle, expropriate, filch, impound, impropriate, misappropriate, pilfer, pocket, possess oneself of, pre-empt, purloin, seize, set apart, steal, take, usurp.

**appropriateness** *n* applicability, appositeness, aptness, becomingness, condignness, congruousness, correctness, felicitousness, felicity, fitness, germaneness, justness, opportuneness, pertinence, properness, propriety, relevance, rightness, seemliness, suitability, timeliness.

**appropriation** *n* allocation, allotment, annexation, apportionment, arrogation, assignment, assumption, commandeering, confiscation, dispensation, earmarking, expropriation, impoundment, misappropriation, pre-emption, seizure, setting apart, usurpation.

**approval** *n* acclaim, acclamation, acquiescence, admiration, adoption, agreement, applause, appreciation, approbation, approof, assent, authorisation, blessing, certification, commendation, compliance, concurrence, confirmation, consent, countenance, endorsement, esteem, favour, go-ahead, good opinion, green light, honour, imprimatur, leave, licence, liking, mandate, OK, permission, plaudits, praise, ratification, recommendation, regard, respect, sanction, support, thumbs-up, validation.

*antonym* disapproval.

**approve** *v* accede to, accept, acclaim, admire, adopt, advocate, agree to, allow, applaud, appreciate, assent to, authorise, back, bless, commend, comply with, concur in, confirm, consent to, countenance, dig, endorse, esteem, favour, homologate, like, mandate, OK, pass, permit, praise, ratify, recommend, regard, respect, rubber-stamp, sanction, second, support, take kindly to, uphold, validate.

*antonym* disapprove.

**approved** *adj* acceptable, accepted, authorised, comme il faut, correct, favoured, official, permissible, permitted, preferred, proper, recognised, recommended, sanctioned.

*antonym* unorthodox.

**approximate** *adj* ballpark, close, comparable, conjectural, estimated, extrapolated, guessed, inexact, like, loose, near, relative, rough, similar, verging on.

*antonym* exact.

*v* approach, be tantamount to, border on, resemble, verge on.

**approximately** *adv* about, almost, around, circa, close to, coming up to, in round numbers, in the region of, in the vicinity of, just about, loosely, more or less, nearly, not far off, pushing, relatively, roughly, round about, well-nigh.

*antonym* exactly.

**approximation** *n* approach, conjecture, correspondence, estimate, estimation, extrapolation, guess, guesstimate, guesswork, likeness, proximity, resemblance, rough calculation, rough idea, semblance.

*antonyms* exactitude, precision.

**appurtenance** *n* accessory, accompaniment, addition, adjunct, annexe, appanage, appendage, appurtenant, attachment, auxiliary, concomitant, incidental, subordinate, subsidiary, supplement.

**appurtenances** *n* accessories, accompaniments, accoutrements, appendages, equipment, gear, impedimenta, kit, paraphernalia, trappings, traps.

**apropos** *adj* applicable, apposite, appropriate, apt, befitting, belonging, condign, correct, fit, fitting, germane, meet, opportune, pertinent, proper, related, relevant, right, seemly, suitable, timely, to the point.

*antonym* inappropriate.

*adv* appositely, appropriately, aptly, by the bye, by the way, en passant, in passing, incidentally, opportunely, pat, pertinently, properly, relevantly, suitably, to the point.

*antonym* inappropriately.

**apropos of** in connection with, in relation to, in respect of, on the subject of, re, regarding, respecting, with reference to, with regard to, with respect to.

**apt** *adj* accurate, adept, applicable, apposite, appropriate, apropos, astute, befitting, bright, clever, condign, correct, disposed, expert, fair, fit, fitting, germane, gifted, given, gleg, inclined, ingenious, intelligent, liable, likely, meet, pertinent, prompt, prone, proper, quick, ready, relevant, seasonable, seemly, sharp, skilful, smart, spot-on, suitable, talented, teachable, tending, timely.

*antonym* inapt.

**aptitude** *n* ability, aptness, bent, capability, capacity, cleverness, disposition, facility, faculty, flair, gift, inclination, intelligence, knack, leaning, penchant, predilection, proclivity, proficiency, proneness, propensity, quickness, talent, tendency.

*antonym* inaptitude.

**aptness** *n* ability, accuracy, applicability, appositeness, appropriateness, aptitude, becomingness, bent, capability, capacity, cleverness, condignness, congruousness, correctness, disposition, facility, faculty, felicitousness, felicity, fitness, fittingness, flair, germaneness, gift, inclination, intelligence, knack, leaning, liability, likelihood, likeliness, opportuneness, pertinence, predilection, proclivity, proficiency, proneness, propensity, properness, quickness, readiness, relevance, rightness, seemliness, suitability, talent, tendency, timeliness.

**arbiter** *n* adjudicator, arbiter elegantiarum, arbitrator, authority, controller, dictator, expert, intermediary, judge, master, mediator, negotiator, pundit, referee, ruler, umpire.

**arbitrariness** *n* absoluteness, capriciousness, despotism, dogmatism, fancifulness, high-handedness, imperiousness, inconsistency, irrationality, irresponsibility, peremptoriness, randomness, subjectivity, summariness, tyranny, unreasonableness, waywardness, whimsicality, wilfulness.

**arbitrary** *adj* absolute, autocratic, capricious, chance, despotic, dictatorial, discretionary, dogmatic, domineering, erratic, fanciful, high-handed, imperious, inconsistent, instinctive, magisterial, optional, overbearing, peremptory, personal, random, subjective, summary, tyrannical, tyrannous, unreasonable, unreasoned, unsupported, whimsical, wilful.

*antonyms* circumspect, rational, reasoned.

**arbitrate** *v* adjudge, adjudicate, decide, determine, judge, pass judgement, referee, settle, umpire.

**arbitration** *n* adjudication, arbitrament, decision, determination, intervention, judgement, mediation, negotiation, settlement.

**arbitrator** *n* adjudicator, arbiter, intermediary, judge, mediator, moderator, negotiator, referee, umpire.

**arcade** *n* cloister, colonnade, covered way, gallery, loggia, mall, peristyle, portico, precinct, stoa.

**arcane** *adj* abstruse, cabbalistic, cryptic, enigmatic, esoteric, hidden, mysterious, mystical, obscure, occult, profound, recondite, secret.

*antonym* commonplace.

**arch**[1] n arc, archway, bend, bow, concave, cupola, curvature, curve, dome, flexure, semicircle, span, vault.

v arc, bend, bow, camber, curve, embow, extend, vault.

**arch**[2] adj accomplished, chief, consummate, coy, egregious, espiègle, expert, finished, first, first-class, foremost, frolicsome, greatest, highest, knowing, leading, main, major, master, mischievous, pert, playful, pre-eminent, primary, principal, provocative, roguish, saucy, sly, top, waggish, wily.

**archaic** adj ancient, antediluvian, antiquated, antique, bygone, demode, fogram, obsolete, old, old hat, old-fashioned, outdated, outmoded, out-of-date, passe, primitive, quaint, superannuated, Wardour Street.

*antonym* modern.

**archetype** n classic, conception, exemplar, form, idea, ideal, model, original, paradigm, pattern, precursor, prototype, standard, type.

**architect** n artist, author, constructor, contriver, creator, designer, deviser, engineer, fabricator, fashioner, founder, instigator, inventor, maker, master builder, originator, planner, prime mover, shaper.

**architecture** n architectonics, arrangement, building, composition, construction, design, framework, make-up, planning, structure, style.

**archive** n library, muniment room, museum, record office, registry, repository.

**archives** n annals, chronicles, deeds, documents, ledgers, memorabilia, memorials, muniments, papers, records, registers, roll.

**ardent** adj amorous, avid, devoted, eager, enthusiastic, fervent, fervid, fierce, fiery, hot, hot-blooded, impassioned, intense, keen, lusty, passionate, perfervid, spirited, vehement, warm, zealous.

*antonym* dispassionate.

**ardour** n animation, avidity, devotion, eagerness, earnestness, empressement, enthusiasm, feeling, fervour, fire, heat, intensity, keenness, lust, passion, spirit, vehemence, warmth, zeal, zest.

*antonyms* coolness, indifference.

**arduous** adj backbreaking, burdensome, daunting, difficult, exhausting, fatiguing, formidable, gruelling, hard, harsh, herculean, laborious, onerous, punishing, rigorous, severe, strenuous, taxing, tiring, toilsome, tough, troublesome, trying, uphill, wearisome.

*antonym* easy.

**area** n arena, bailiwick, ball-park, breadth, canvas, compass, department, district, domain, environs, expanse, extent, field, locality, neighbourhood, part, patch, pidgin, portion, province, range, realm, region, scope, section, sector, size, sphere, stretch, terrain, territory, tract, width, zone.

**arena** n amphitheatre, area, battlefield, battleground, bowl, coliseum, field, ground, lists, park, ring, scene, stadium, stage.

**argot** n cant, dialect, idiom, jargon, lingo, parlance, patois, slang, terminology, usage, vernacular, vocabulary.

**argue** v altercate, argufy, assert, bicker, chop logic, claim, contend, convince, debate, demonstrate, denote, disagree, discuss, display, dispute, evidence, evince, exhibit, expostulate, fall out, fence, feud, fight, haggle, hold, imply, indicate, join issue, logicise, maintain, manifest, moot, persuade, plead, prevail upon, prove, quarrel, question, reason, remonstrate, show, squabble, suggest, talk into, wrangle.

**argument** n abstract, altercation, argumentation, assertion, barney, beef, bickering, case, claim, clash, contention, controversy, debate, defence, demonstration, dialectic, difference, disagreement, discussion, dispute, exposition, expostulation, feud, fight, gist, ground, lemma, logic, logomachy, outline, plea, pleading, plot, polemic, quarrel, questioning, quodlibet, reason, reasoning, remonstrance, remonstration, row, set-to, shouting-match, squabble, story, story line, subject, summary, synopsis, theme, thesis, wrangle.

**argumentative** adj belligerent, captious, combative, contentious, contrary, disputatious, disputative, dissentious, litigious, opinionated, perverse, polemical, quarrelsome, wranglesome.

*antonym* complaisant.

**arid** adj baked, barren, boring, colourless, desert, desiccated, dreary, droughty, dry, dull, empty, flat, infertile, jejune, lifeless, moistureless, monotonous, parched, spiritless, sterile, tedious, torrid, torrefied, uninspired, uninteresting, unproductive, vapid, waste, waterless.

*antonyms* fertile, lively.

**aridity** n aridness, barrenness, boredom, colourlessness, dreariness, dryness, dullness, emptiness, flatness, infertility, jejuneness, jejunity, lifelessness, monotony, sterility, tedium, vapidity, vapidness.

*antonyms* fertility, liveliness, productivity, variety.

**aright** adv accurately, aptly, correctly, de règle, deasil, duly, en règle, exactly, fitly, justly, properly, rightly, suitably, truly.

**arise** v appear, ascend, begin, climb, come to light, commence, crop up, derive, emanate, emerge, ensue, flow, follow, get up, go up, grow, happen, issue, lift, mount, occur, originate, proceed, result, rise, set in, soar, spring, stand up, start, stem, tower, wake up.

**aristocracy** n elite, gentility, gentry, haut monde, nobility, noblemen, noblesse, optimates, patricians, patriciate, peerage, quality, ruling class, top drawer, upper class, upper crust.

*antonyms* canaille, the plebs.

**aristocrat** n eupatrid, grand seigneur, grande dame, grandee, lady, lord, lordling, nob, noble, nobleman, noblewoman, optimate, patrician, peer, peeress, swell, toff.

*antonym* commoner.

**aristocratic** adj blue-blooded, courtly, dignified, elegant, elite, fine, gentle, gentlemanly, haughty, highborn, lordly, noble, patricianly, polished, refined, supercilious, thoroughbred, titled, upper-class, upper-crust, well-born, well-bred.

*antonyms* plebeian, vulgar.

**arithmetic** *n* algorism, algorithm, calculation, ciphering, computation, count, counting, mathematics, numeration, reckoning.

**arm**[1] *n* appendage, authority, bough, brachium, branch, channel, department, detachment, division, estuary, extension, firth, inlet, limb, offshoot, projection, section, sector, sound, strait, sway, tributary, upper limb.

**arm**[2] *v* accoutre, ammunition, array, brace, empanoply, equip, forearm, fortify, furnish, gird, issue with, munition, nuclearise, outfit, prepare, prime, protect, provide, reinforce, rig, steel, strengthen, supply.

**armaments** *n* ammunition, arms, artillery, cannon, guns, materiel, munitions, ordnance, weaponry, weapons.

**armed** *adj* accoutred, armoured, arrayed, braced, briefed, equipped, fitted out, forearmed, fortified, furnished, girded, guarded, prepared, primed, protected, provided, steeled, strengthened, thorny.

*antonyms* unarmed, unprepared.

**armour** *n* armature, carapace, chain-mail, garniture, iron-cladding, mail, shell, steel-plating.

**armoured** *adj* armour-plated, bomb-proof, bullet-proof, iron-clad, mail-clad, mailed, protected, steel-plated.

**armoury** *n* ammunition dump, arsenal, depot, garderobe, magazine, ordnance depot, repertoire, repository, stock, stock-in-trade, stockpile.

**arms**[1] *n* armaments, firearms, guns, instruments of war, ordnance, weaponry, weapons.

**arms**[2] *n* armorial bearings, blazonry, crest, escutcheon, hatchment, heraldry, insignia, scutcheon, shield.

**army** *n* armed force, array, arrière-ban, cohorts, fyrd, gang, horde, host, land forces, legions, military, militia, mob, multitude, pack, soldiers, soldiery, swarm, the junior service, throng, troops.

**aroma** *n* bouquet, fragrance, fumet(te), odour, perfume, redolence, savour, scent, smell.

**aromatic** *adj* balmy, fragrant, odoriferous, perfumed, pungent, redolent, savoury, spicy, sweet-smelling.

*antonym* acrid.

**around** *prep* about, approximately, circa, circling, circumambient, circumjacent, encircling, enclosing, encompassing, environing, more or less, on all sides of, on every side of, roughly, surrounding.

*adv* about, abroad, all over, at hand, close, close by, everywhere, here and there, in all directions, in the air, near, nearby, nigh, on all sides, to and fro.

**arouse** *v* agitate, animate, awaken, bestir, call forth, disentrance, enliven, evoke, excite,

foment, foster, galvanise, goad, incite, inflame, instigate, kindle, move, prompt, provoke, quicken, rouse, sharpen, spark, spur, startle, stimulate, stir up, summon up, wake up, waken, warm, whet, whip up.

*antonyms* calm, lull, quieten.

**arraign** *v* accuse, attack, call to account, charge, denounce, impeach, impugn, incriminate, indict, prosecute.

**arrange**[1] *v* adjust, align, array, categorise, class, classify, collocate, concert, construct, contrive, co-ordinate, design, determine, devise, dispose, distribute, fettle, file, fix, form, format, group, lay out, marshal, methodise, order, organise, plan, position, prepare, project, range, rank, regulate, schedule, set out, settle, sift, sort, sort out, stage-manage, style, swing, systematise, tidy, trim.

**arrange**[2] *v* adapt, harmonise, instrument, orchestrate, score, set.

**arrangement**[1] *n* adjustment, agreement, alignment, array, Ausgleich, battery, classification, compact, compromise, construction, deal, design, display, disposition, form, grouping, layout, line-up, marshalling, method, modus vivendi, order, ordering, organisation, plan, planning, preconcert, preparation, provision, ranging, rank, schedule, scheme, settlement, set-up, spacing, structure, system, tabulation, taxis, terms.

**arrangement**[2] *n* adaptation, harmonisation, instrumentation, interpretation, orchestration, score, setting, version.

**arrant** *adj* absolute, atrocious, barefaced, blatant, brazen, complete, downright, egregious, extreme, flagrant, gross, incorrigible, infamous, monstrous, notorious, out-and-out, outright, rank, thorough, thoroughgoing, undisguised, unmitigated, unregenerate, utter, vile.

**array** *n* apparel, arrangement, assemblage, attire, battery, clothes, collection, display, disposition, dress, equipage, exhibition, exposition, finery, formation, garb, garments, line-up, marshalling, muster, order, parade, raiment, regalia, robes, show, supply.

*v* accoutre, adorn, align, apparel, arrange, assemble, attire, bedeck, bedizen, caparison, clothe, deck, decorate, display, dispose, draw up, dress, equip, exhibit, form up, garb, group, habilitate, line up, marshal, muster, order, outfit, parade, range, rig out, robe, show, supply, trick out, wrap.

**arrest** *v* absorb, apprehend, block, bust, capture, catch, check, collar, delay, detain, divert, end, engage, engross, fascinate, grip, halt, hinder, hold, impede, inhibit, interrupt, intrigue, lay, nab, nick, nip, obstruct, occupy, pinch, prevent, restrain, retard, run in, seize, slow, stall, stanch, stay, stem, stop, suppress.

*n* apprehension, blockage, bust, caption, capture, cessation, check, cop, delay, detention, end, halt, hindrance, inhibition, interruption, obstruction, prevention, restraint, seizure, stalling, stay, stoppage, suppression, suspension.

**arresting** *adj* amazing, conspicuous, engaging, extraordinary, impressive, notable, noteworthy, noticeable, outstanding, remarkable, striking, stunning, surprising.

*antonyms* inconspicuous, unremarkable.

**arrival** *n* accession, advent, appearance, approach, caller, comer, coming, debutant(e), entrance, entrant, happening, incomer, landfall, newcomer, occurrence, visitant, visitor.

*antonym* departure.

**arrive** *v* alight, appear, attain, befall, come, enter, fetch, get to the top, happen, land, make it, materialise, occur, reach, show, show up, succeed, turn up.

*antonym* depart.

**arrogance** *n* airs, conceit, conceitedness, condescension, contempt, contemptuousness, contumely, disdain, disdainfulness, haughtiness, hauteur, high-handedness, hubris, imperiousness, insolence, loftiness, lordliness, morgue, presumption, presumptuousness, pretension, pretentiousness, pride, scorn, scornfulness, superciliousness, superiority, uppishness.

*antonym* humility.

**arrogant** *adj* assuming, conceited, condescending, contemptuous, contumelious, disdainful, fastuous, haughty, high and mighty, high-handed, hubristic, imperious, insolent, lordly, on the high ropes, overbearing, overweening, presumptuous, proud, scornful, supercilious, superior, uppish.

*antonym* humble.

**arrogate** *v* appropriate, assume, commandeer, confiscate, demand, expropriate, misappropriate, possess oneself of, presume, seize, usurp.

**arrow** *n* bolt, dart, flight, indicator, pointer, shaft.

**arsenal** *n* ammunition dump, armoury, depot, magazine, ordnance depot, repository, stock, stockpile, store, storehouse, supply, warehouse.

**arson** *n* fire-raising, incendiarism, pyromania.

**arsonist** *n* fire-bug, fire-raiser, incendiary, pyromaniac.

**art** *n* address, adroitness, aptitude, artfulness, artifice, artistry, artwork, astuteness, contrivance, craft, craftiness, craftsmanship, cunning, deceit, dexterity, draughtsmanship, drawing, expertise, facility, finesse, guile, ingenuity, knack, knowledge, mastery, method, metier, painting, profession, sculpture, skill, slyness, subtlety, trade, trick, trickery, virtu, virtuosity, visuals, wiliness.

**artful** *adj* adept, adroit, canny, clever, crafty, cunning, deceitful, designing, devious, dexterous, fly, foxy, ingenious, masterly, politic, resourceful, ruse, scheming, sharp, shrewd, skilful, sly, smart, subtle, tricksy, tricky, vulpine, wily.

*antonyms* artless, ingenuous, naïve.

**article** *n* account, bit, clause, commodity, composition, constituent, count, detail, discourse, division, element, essay, feature, head, heading, item, matter, object, paper, paragraph, part, particular, piece, point, portion, report, review, section, story, thing, unit.

**articulate**[1] *adj* clear, coherent, comprehensible, distinct, eloquent, expressive, facile, fluent, intelligible, lucid, meaningful, understandable, vocal, well-spoken.

*v* breathe, elocute, enounce, enunciate, express, pronounce, say, speak, state, talk, utter, verbalise, vocalise, voice.

**articulate**[2] *v* attach, connect, couple, fasten, fit together, hinge, interlock, join, joint, link.

**articulation**[1] *n* delivery, diction, enunciation, expression, pronunciation, saying, speaking, talking, utterance, verbalisation, vocalisation, voicing.

**articulation**[2] *n* arthrosis, conjunction, connection, coupling, hinge, interlinking, interlock, joint, jointing, juncture, link.

**artifice** *n* adroitness, artfulness, chicanery, cleverness, contrivance, cozenage, craft, craftiness, cunning, deception, deftness, device, dodge, duplicity, expedient, facility, finesse, fraud, guile, hoax, invention, machination, manipulation, manoeuvre, ruse, scheme, shift, skill, slyness, stratagem, strategy, subterfuge, subtlety, tactic, trick, trickery, wile.

**artificer** *n* architect, artisan, builder, constructer, contriver, craftsman, creator, designer, deviser, fabricator, fashioner, framer, inventor, maker, mechanic, opificer, originator.

**artificial** *adj* affected, assumed, bogus, contrived, counterfeit, ersatz, factitious, fake, false, feigned, forced, hyped up, imitation, insincere, made-up, man-made, mannered, manufactured, meretricious, mock, non-natural, phoney, plastic, pretended, pseudo, sham, simulated, specious, spurious, stagey, synthetic, unnatural.

*antonyms* genuine, natural.

**artillery** *n* battery, cannon, cannonry, enginery, field-guns, field-pieces, gunnage, gunnery, guns, heavy metal, ordnance.

**artisan** *n* artificer, craftsman, expert, handicraftsman, journeyman, mechanic, operative, technician, workman.

**artist** *n* colourist, craftsman, draughtsman, expert, maestro, master, muralist, painter, portraitist, portrait-painter, sculptor, water-colourist.

**artiste** *n* actor, comedian, comedienne, comic, entertainer, moke, performer, player, trouper, variety artist, vaudevillian.

**artistic** *adj* aesthetic, beautiful, bohemian, creative, cultivated, cultured, decorative, elegant, exquisite, graceful, harmonious, imaginative, ornamental, refined, sensitive, skilled, stylish, talented, tasteful.

*antonym* inelegant.

**artistry** *n* accomplishment, art, brilliance, craft, craftsmanship, creativity, deftness, expertise, finesse, flair, genius, mastery, proficiency, sensibility, sensitivity, skill, style, talent, taste, touch, virtuosity, workmanship.

*antonym* ineptitude.

**artless** *adj* candid, childlike, direct, frank, genuine, guileless, honest, humble, ingenuous, innocent, naïf, naïve, naked, natural, open, plain, primitive, pure, simple, sincere, straightforward, true, trustful, trusting, unadorned, unaffected, uncontrived, undesigning, unpretentious, unsophisticated, unwary, unworldly.

*antonym* artful.

**artlessness** n candour, directness, frankness, genuineness, honesty, humbleness, humility, ingenuousness, innocence, naïvete, naïvety, naturalness, openness, purity, simplicity, sincerity, straightforwardness, trustfulness, unpretentiousness, unwariness, unworldliness.

*antonym* cunning.

**as** *conj, prep* because, being, considering that, for example, for instance, in that, in the character of, in the manner of, in the part of, in the role of, inasmuch as, like, seeing that, since, such as, that, to wit, what, when, which, while.

**as a rule** characteristically, customarily, generally, habitually, mainly, normally, ordinarily, regularly, typically, usually.

**as for** as regards, in connection with, in reference to, on the subject of, with reference to, with regard to, with relation to, with respect to.

**as it were** as it might be, in a manner of speaking, in a way, in some way, so to say, so to speak.

**as long as** assuming, on condition that, provided, supposing, with the provision that.

**ascend** v climb, float up, fly up, go up, lift off, mount, move up, rise, scale, slope upwards, soar, take off, tower.

*antonym* descend.

**ascendancy** n authority, command, control, dominance, domination, dominion, edge, hegemony, influence, leadership, lordship, mastery, power, predominance, pre-eminence, prestige, prevalence, reign, rule, sovereignty, superiority, supremacy, sway, upper hand.

*antonyms* decline, subordination.

**ascendant** adj ascending, authoritative, climbing, commanding, controlling, dominant, influential, levitating, lifting, mounting, powerful, predominant, pre-eminent, prevailing, rising, ruling, superior, supreme, upgoing, uphill, uppermost.

*antonyms* descending, subordinate.

**ascension** n arising, ascent, climb, levitation, lifting, mounting, raising, rise, rising.

*antonym* descent.

**ascent** n acclivity, advancement, anabasis, ascending, ascension, brae, clamber, clambering, climb, climbing, elevation, escalation, gradient, hill, incline, mounting, ramp, rise, rising, scaling, slope.

*antonym* descent.

**ascertain** v confirm, detect, determine, discover, establish, find out, fix, identify, learn, locate, make certain, settle, verify.

**ascetic** n abstainer, anchorite, celibate, flagellant, hermit, monk, nun, puritan, recluse, solitary, Spartan, stylite.

*antonym* voluptuary.

adj abstemious, abstinent, austere, celibate, continent, frugal, harsh, plain, puritanical, rigorous, self-controlled, self-denying, self-disciplined, severe, Spartan, stern, strict, temperate.

*antonym* voluptuous.

**asceticism** n abstemiousness, abstinence, ascesis, austerity, celibacy, continence, frugality, harshness, moderation, monasticism, plainness, puritanism, rigorousness, rigour, self-abnegation, self-control, self-denial, self-discipline, temperance.

*antonym* voluptuousness.

**ascribe** v accredit, arrogate, assign, attribute, chalk up to, charge, credit, impute, put down.

**ashamed** adj abashed, apologetic, bashful, blushing, chagrined, confused, conscience-stricken, crestfallen, discomfited, discomposed, distressed, embarrassed, guilty, hesitant, humbled, humiliated, modest, mortified, prudish, red in the face, redfaced, reluctant, remorseful, self-conscious, shamefaced, sheepish, shy, sorry, unwilling, verecund.

*antonyms* defiant, shameless.

**ashen** adj anaemic, ashy, blanched, bleached, colourless, ghastly, grey, leaden, livid, pale, pallid, pasty, wan, white.

*antonym* ruddy.

**aside** adv alone, apart, away, in isolation, in reserve, on one side, out of the way, privately, secretly, separately.

n departure, digression, excursion, excursus, interpolation, interposition, parenthesis, soliloquy, whisper.

**asinine** adj absurd, brainless, cretinous, daft, doltish, dunderheaded, fatuous, foolish, goofy, gormless, half-witted, idiotic, imbecile, imbecilic, inane, moronic, obstinate, potty, senseless, silly, stupid, witless.

*antonyms* intelligent, sensible.

**ask** v appeal, apply, beg, beseech, bid, catechise, claim, clamour, crave, demand, enquire, entreat, implore, importune, indent, interrogate, invite, order, petition, plead, pray, press, query, question, quiz, request, require, seek, solicit, sue, summon, supplicate.

**askance** adv contemptuously, disapprovingly, disdainfully, distrustfully, doubtfully, dubiously, indirectly, mistrustfully, obliquely, sceptically, scornfully, sideways, suspiciously.

**askew** adv, adj aglee, agley, aslant, asymmetric, awry, cock-eyed, crooked, crookedly, lopsided, oblique, off-centre, out of line, skew, skew-whiff, squint.

**asleep** adj benumbed, comatose, dead to the world, dormant, dormient, dozing, fast asleep, inactive, inert, napping, numb, reposing, sleeping, slumbering, snoozing, sound asleep, unconscious.

**aspect** n air, angle, appearance, attitude, bearing, condition, countenance, demeanour, direction, elevation, exposure, expression, face, facet, feature, look, manner, mien, outlook, physiognomy, point of view, position, prospect, scene, side, situation, standpoint, view, visage.

**asperity** *n* acerbity, acidity, acrimony, astringency, bitterness, causticity, churlishness, crabbedness, crossness, harshness, irascibility, irritability, peevishness, roughness, severity, sharpness, sourness.

*antonym* mildness.

**aspersion** *n* abuse, animadversion, calumny, censure, criticism, defamation, denigration, derogation, detraction, disparagement, mud-slinging, obloquy, reproach, slander, slur, smear, traducement, vilification, vituperation.

*antonyms* commendation, compliment.

**asphyxiate** *v* burke, choke, garrotte, smother, stifle, strangle, strangulate, suffocate, throttle.

**aspirant** *n* applicant, aspirer, candidate, competitor, contestant, hopeful, postulant, seeker, striver, suitor.

**aspiration** *n* aim, ambition, craving, desire, dream, eagerness, endeavour, goal, hankering, hope, ideal, intent, longing, object, objective, purpose, wish, yearning.

**aspire** *v* aim, crave, desire, dream, ettle, hanker, hope, intend, long, purpose, pursue, seek, wish, yearn.

**aspiring** *adj* ambitious, aspirant, eager, endeavouring, enterprising, hopeful, keen, longing, optimistic, striving, wishful, would-be.

**ass**[1] *n* blockhead, bonehead, cretin, dolt, dope, dunce, fool, half-wit, idiot, moron, nincompoop, ninny, nitwit, numskull, schmuck, simpleton, twerp, twit.

**ass**[2] *n* burro, cardophagus, cuddy, donkey, hinny, jackass, jenny, Jerusalem pony, moke, mule.

**assail** *v* abuse, assault, attack, belabour, berate, beset, bombard, charge, criticise, encounter, fall upon, impugn, invade, lay into, malign, maltreat, pelt, revile, set about, set upon, strike, vilify.

**assailant** *n* abuser, adversary, aggressor, assailer, assaulter, attacker, invader, opponent, reviler.

**assassin** *n* bravo, cut-throat, eliminator, executioner, hatchet man, hit-man, homicide, killer, liquidator, murderer, ninja, slayer, thug.

**assassinate** *v* dispatch, eliminate, hit, kill, liquidate, murder, rub out, slay.

**assault** *n* aggression, attack, blitz, charge, incursion, invasion, offensive, onset, onslaught, raid, storm, storming, strike.

*v* assail, attack, beset, charge, fall on, hit, invade, lay violent hands on, set upon, storm, strike.

**assay** *v* analyse, appraise, assess, estimate, evaluate, examine, inspect, investigate, prove, test, try, weigh.

*n* analysis, assaying, attempt, docimasy, endeavour, essay, examination, inspection, investigation, test, trial, try, valuation, venture.

**assemblage** *n* accumulation, aggregation, array, assembly, body, collection, company, congeries, conglomeration, crowd, flock, galaxy, gathering, group, mass, multitude, rally, throng.

**assemble** *v* accumulate, amass, build, collect, compose, congregate, construct, convene, convocate, convoke, erect, fabricate, flock, forgather, gather, group, join up, levy, make, manufacture, marshal, meet, mobilise, muster, muster (up), piece, rally, round up, set up, summon, together.

*antonym* disperse.

**assembly** *n* agora, assemblage, ball, body, building, collection, company, conclave, conference, congregation, congress, consistory, construction, convocation, council, crowd, diet, divan, ecclesia, erection, fabrication, fitting, flock, folkmoot, gathering, gemot, gorsedd, group, indaba, joining, kgotla, levy, manufacture, mass, meeting, moot, multitude, panegyry, rally, reception, setting up, soiree, synod, throng.

**assent** *v* accede, accept, acquiesce, agree, allow, approve, comply, concede, concur, consent, grant, permit, sanction, submit, subscribe, yield.

*antonym* disagree.

*n* acceptance, accession, accord, acquiescence, agreement, approval, capitulation, compliance, concession, concurrence, consent, permission, sanction, submission.

**assert** *v* advance, affirm, allege, asseverate, attest, aver, avouch, avow, claim, constate, contend, declare, defend, dogmatise, insist, lay down, maintain, predicate, press, profess, promote, pronounce, protest, state, stress, swear, testify to, thrust forward, uphold, vindicate.

*antonym* deny.

**assertion** *n* affirmance, affirmation, allegation, asseveration, attestation, averment, avowal, claim, constatation, contention, declaration, dictum, gratis dictum, ipse dixit, predication, profession, pronouncement, statement, vindication, vouch, word.

*antonym* denial.

**assertive** *adj* aggressive, assuming, bold, bumptious, confident, decided, dogmatic, domineering, emphatic, firm, forceful, forward, insistent, opinionated, overbearing, presumptuous, pushy, self-assured, strong-willed.

*antonym* diffident.

**assertiveness** *n* aggressiveness, boldness, bumptiousness, decisiveness, dogmatism, forcefulness, forwardness, insistence, overbearingness, positiveness, presumption, presumptuousness, pushiness, self-assurance, self-confidence.

**assess** *v* affeer, appraise, compute, consider, demand, determine, estimate, evaluate, fix, gauge, impose, investigate, judge, levy, rate, review, size up, tax, value, weigh.

**assessment** *n* affeerment, appraisal, calculation, consideration, determination, estimate, estimation, evaluation, gauging, judgement, opinion, rating, review, taxation, valuation.

**asset** *n* advantage, aid, benefit, blessing, help, plus, resource, service, strength, virtue.

*antonym* liability.

**assets** *n* capital, estate, funds, goods, holdings, means, money, possessions, property, reserves, resources, securities, wealth, wherewithal.

**asseverate** *v* affirm, assert, attest, aver, avouch, avow, certify, declare, maintain, profess, pronounce, protest, state, swear, testify.

**asseveration** *n* affirmation, assertion, assurance, attestation, averment, avowal, declaration, deposition, predication, profession, pronouncement, protestation, statement, vow.

**assiduity** *n* application, assiduousness, attentiveness, conscientiousness, constancy, dedication, devotion, diligence, indefatigability, industriousness, industry, labour, perseverance, persistence, sedulity, sedulousness, steadiness, tirelessness.

*antonym* negligence.

**assiduous** *adj* attentive, conscientious, constant, dedicated, devoted, diligent, hard-working, indefatigable, industrious, persevering, persistent, sedulous, steady, studious, unflagging, untiring.

*antonym* negligent.

**assign** *v* accredit, adjudge, allocate, allot, apart, appoint, apportion, arrogate, ascribe, attribute, choose, consign, delegate, designate, determine, dispense, distribute, fix, give, grant, name, nominate, put down, select, set, specify, stipulate.

**assignation** *n* allocation, allotment, appointment, arrangement, date, engagement, meeting, rendezvous, tryst.

**assignment** *n* allocation, allotment, appointment, apportionment, ascription, attribution, charge, commission, consignment, delegation, designation, determination, dispensation, distribution, duty, errand, giving, grant, imposition, job, mission, nomination, position, post, responsibility, selection, specification, task.

**assimilate** *v* absorb, accept, acclimatise, accommodate, acculturate, accustom, adapt, adjust, blend, conform, digest, fit, homogenise, imbibe, incorporate, ingest, intermix, learn, merge, mingle, take in, tolerate.

*antonym* reject.

**assimilation** *n* absorption, acceptance, acclimatisation, accommodation, acculturation, adaptation, adjustment, conformity, homogenisation, incorporation, ingestion, learning, toleration.

*antonym* rejection.

**assist** *v* abet, accommodate, aid, back, benefit, bestead, boost, collaborate, co-operate, enable, expedite, facilitate, further, help, rally round, reinforce, relieve, second, serve, succour, support, sustain.

*antonym* thwart.

**assistance** *n* a leg up, abetment, accommodation, adjutancy, aid, backing, benefit, boost, collaboration, comfort, co-operation, furtherance, help, reinforcement, relief, succour, support, sustainment.

*antonym* hindrance.

**assistant** *n* abettor, accessory, accomplice, adjutant, aide, ally, ancillary, associate, auxiliary, backer, coadjutor, collaborator, colleague, confederate, co-operator, Girl Friday, helper, helpmate, henchman, Man Friday, partner, Person Friday, right-hand man, second, subordinate, subsidiary, supporter.

**associate** *v* accompany, affiliate, ally, amalgamate, combine, company, confederate, conjoin, connect, consort, correlate, couple, fraternise, hang around, hobnob, identify, join, league, link, mingle, mix, pair, relate, socialise, unite, yoke.

*n* affiliate, ally, assistant, bedfellow, coadjutor, collaborator, colleague, companion, compeer, comrade, confederate, confrère, co-worker, fellow, follower, friend, leaguer, mate, partner, peer, side-kick.

**association** *n* affiliation, alliance, analogy, band, blend, bloc, bond, cartel, clique, club, coalition, combination, combine, companionship, company, compound, comradeship, concomitance, confederacy, confederation, connection, consociation, consortium, conspiracy, co-operative, corporation, correlation, familiarity, federation, fellowship, fraternisation, fraternity, friendship, Gesellschaft, group, intimacy, joining, juxtaposition, league, linkage, mixture, organisation, pairing, partnership, relation, relations, relationship, resemblance, society, syndicate, syndication, tie, trust, union, Verein.

**assorted** *adj* different, differing, divergent, divers, diverse, diversified, heterogeneous, manifold, miscellaneous, mixed, motley, multifarious, multiform, several, sundry, varied, variegated, various.

**assortment** *n* arrangement, array, assemblage, categorisation, choice, classification, collection, disposition, distribution, diversity, farrago, grading, grouping, hotchpotch, jumble, medley, melange, miscellany, mishmash, mixture, olio, olla-podrida, pot-pourri, ranging, salad, salmagundi, selection, sift, sifting, sorting, variety.

**assuage** *v* allay, alleviate, appease, calm, dull, ease, lessen, lighten, lower, lull, mitigate, moderate, mollify, pacify, palliate, quench, quieten, reduce, relieve, satisfy, slake, soften, soothe, still, temper, tranquillise.

*antonym* exacerbate.

**assume** *v* accept, acquire, adopt, affect, appropriate, arrogate, believe, commandeer, counterfeit, deduce, don, embrace, expect, expropriate, fancy, feign, guess, imagine, infer, opine, postulate, pre-empt, premise, presume, presuppose, pretend to, put on, seize, sham, shoulder, simulate, strike, suppose, surmise, suspect, take, take for granted, take on, take over, take up, think, understand, undertake, usurp.

**assumed** *adj* accepted, adopted, affected, bogus, conjectural, counterfeit, expected, fake, false, feigned, fictitious, fiducial, hypothetical, made-up, phoney, presumed, presupposed, pretended, pseudonymous, seized, sham, simulated, specious, spurious, supposed, suppositional, surmised, usurped.

**assuming** *adj* arrogant, assertive, audacious, bold, brazen, bumptious, conceited, forward, impertinent, impudent, overconfident, presumptuous, pretentious, pushy, self-assertive, self-important, uppish.

*antonym* unassuming.

**assumption** *n* acceptance, acquisition, adoption, appropriation, arrogance, arrogation, audacity, belief, bumptiousness, conceit, conjecture, expectation, expropriation, fancy, guess, guesswork, hypothesis, impudence, inference, postulate, postulation, pre-emption, premise, premiss, presumption, presumptuousness, presupposition, pride, seizure, self-importance, supposition, surmise, suspicion, theory, understanding, undertaking, usurpation.

**assurance** *n* affirmation, aplomb, assertion, asseveration, assuredness, audacity, boldness, certainty, certitude, chutzpah, confidence, conviction, coolness, courage, declaration, firmness, gall, guarantee, nerve, oath, pledge, plerophory, poise, positiveness, profession, promise, protestation, security, self-confidence, self-reliance, sureness, vow, word.

*antonym* uncertainty.

**assure** *v* affirm, attest, boost, certify, clinch, comfort, confirm, convince, embolden, encourage, ensure, guarantee, hearten, persuade, pledge, promise, reassure, seal, secure, soothe, strengthen, swear, tell, vow, warrant.

**assured** *adj* assertive, audacious, belt-and-braces, bold, certain, clinched, cocksure, confident, confirmed, definite, ensured, fixed, guaranteed, indisputable, indubitable, irrefutable, overconfident, pert, poised, positive, secure, self-assured, self-confident, self-possessed, settled, sure, unquestionable.

*antonym* uncertain.

**assuredly** *adv* certainly, definitely, indisputably, indubitably, surely, truly, unquestionably.

**astir** *adj, adv* about, active, afoot, awake, circulating, in motion, in the air, roused, up.

**astonish** *v* amaze, astound, baffle, bewilder, confound, daze, dumbfound, electrify, flabbergast, floor, nonplus, shock, stagger, startle, stun, stupefy, surprise, wow.

**astonished** *adj* amazed, astounded, baffled, bewildered, bug-eyed, confounded, dazed, dumbfounded, electrified, flabbergasted, incredulous, staggered, startled, stunned, surprised, thunder-struck.

**astonishing** *adj* amazing, astounding, baffling, bewildering, breathtaking, dazzling, impressive, incredible, prodigious, staggering, startling, striking, stunning, stupefying, surprising.

**astonishment** *n* amazement, awe, bafflement, bewilderment, confusion, consternation, dismay, shock, stupefaction, surprise, wonder, wonderment.

**astound** *v* abash, amaze, astonish, baffle, bewilder, confound, daze, dumbfound, electrify, flabbergast, overwhelm, shake, shock, stagger, stun, stupefy, surprise, wow.

**astounded** *adj* abashed, amazed, baffled, bewildered, confounded, dazed, dumbfounded, electrified, flabbergasted, incredulous, overwhelmed, shaken, shocked, staggered, stunned, stupefied, wowed.

**astounding** *adj* amazing, astonishing, baffling, bewildering, breathtaking, electrifying, impressive, incredible, overwhelming, shocking, staggering, striking, stunning, stupefying, surprising.

**astray** *adv* adrift, amiss, awry, lost, off course, off the mark, off the rails, to the bad, wrong.

**astringent** *adj* acerb, acerbic, acid, astrictive, austere, biting, caustic, contractile, contractive, exacting, grim, hard, harsh, puckery, restringent, rigorous, scathing, severe, stern, strict, stringent, styptic, trenchant.

*antonym* bland.

**astrology** *n* astromancy, horoscopy, star-gazing.

**astronomical** *adj* astrophysical, celestial, cosmological, enormous, high, huge, Uranian.

**astronomy** *n* astrodynamics, astrography, astrophysics, cosmography, cosmology, star-gazing, uranography, uranology.

**astute** *adj* acute, adroit, artful, astucious, calculating, canny, clever, crafty, cunning, discerning, fly, foxy, intelligent, keen, knowing, penetrating, perceptive, percipient, perspicacious, politic, prudent, sagacious, sharp, shrewd, sly, subtle, wily, wise.

*antonym* stupid.

**astuteness** *n* acumen, acuteness, adroitness, artfulness, astucity, canniness, cleverness, craftiness, cunning, discernment, insight, intelligence, penetration, perceptiveness, percipience, perspicacity, sagacity, sharpness, shrewdness, slyness, subtlety, wiliness.

*antonym* stupidity.

**asunder** *adv* apart, in half, in pieces, in twain, in two, into pieces, to bits, to pieces.

**asylum** *n* bedlam, bughouse, cover, funny farm, harbour, haven, hospital, institution, loony-bin, madhouse, mental hospital, nuthouse, preserve, refuge, reserve, retreat, safety, sanctuary, shelter.

**asymmetrical** *adj* asymmetric, awry, crooked, disproportionate, disymmetric, gibbous, irregular, unbalanced, unequal, uneven, unsymmetrical.

*antonym* symmetrical.

**asymmetry** *n* disproportion, disymmetry, imbalance, inequality, irregularity, misproportion, unevenness, unsymmetry.

*antonym* symmetry.

**at a loss** baffled, bewildered, confounded, confused, helpless, nonplussed, perplexed, puzzled, resourceless, stuck, stumped.

**at bay** caught, cornered, trapped, up against it, with one's back to the wall.

**at fault** accountable, answerable, blamable, blameworthy, culpable, guilty, responsible.

**at first sight** on first acquaintance, on the surface, prima facie, superficially, to the outsider.

**at hand** approaching, at one's elbow, available, close, handy, immediate, imminent, impending, near, nearby, on tap, ready.

**at home** at ease, comfortable, contented, conversant, experienced, familiar, knowledgeable, proficient, relaxed, skilled, well-versed.

**at large** at liberty, footloose, free, independent, liberated, on the loose, on the run, roaming, unconfined, unconstrained.

**at last** at length, at long last, eventually, finally, in conclusion, in due course, in the end, in time, ultimately.

**at leisure** at ease, at liberty, disengaged, free, idle, off the hook, unbusy, unengaged.

**at length** at last, at long last, completely, eventually, exhaustively, finally, for ages, for hours, fully, in depth, in detail, in the end, in time, interminably, thoroughly, to the full, ultimately.

**at liberty** at large, at leisure, disengaged, footloose, free, idle, not confined, on the loose, unconstrained, unrestricted.

**at odds** at daggers drawn, at enmity, at loggerheads, at one another's throats, at outs, at variance, feuding, in conflict, in dispute, opposed, quarrelling.

**at once** at one go, at the same time, directly, ek dum, forthwith, immediately, in concert, in unison, incontinent, instantly, now, promptly, right away, simultaneously, straight away, straightway, this minute, together, unhesitatingly, without delay.

**at one's wits' end** at a loss, at the end of one's tether, baffled, bewildered, desperate, in despair, in dire straits, lost, resourceless, stuck, stumped.

**at random** accidentally, adventitiously, aimlessly, arbitrarily, casually, desultorily, fortuitously, haphazardly, indiscriminately, irregularly, purposelessly, randomly, unsystematically.

**at rest** asleep, at a standstill, calm, dead, idle, inactive, motionless, peaceful, resting, sleeping, still, stopped, tranquil, unmoving.

**at sea** adrift, astray, baffled, bewildered, confused, disoriented, insecure, lost, mystified, perplexed, puzzled, upset.

**at the double** at full speed, at once, briskly, immediately, in double-quick time, lickety-split, like lightning, posthaste, quickly, quick-sticks, without delay.

**at work** on the job.

**atheism** n disbelief, free-thinking, godlessness, heathenism, impiety, infidelity, irreligion, non-belief, paganism, rationalism, scepticism, unbelief, ungodliness.

**atheist** n disbeliever, free-thinker, heathen, infidel, irreligionist, non-believer, nullifidian, pagan, sceptic, unbeliever.

**atheistic** adj atheistical, disbelieving, free-thinking, heathen, impious, irreligious, irreverent, rationalistic, sceptical, unbelieving, ungodly, unreligious.

*antonym* religious.

**athlete** n agonist, competitor, contender, contestant, gymnast, jock, runner, sportsman, sportswoman.

**athletic** adj active, brawny, energetic, fit, husky, muscular, powerful, robust, sinewy, strapping, strong, sturdy, thewy, vigorous, well-knit, well-proportioned, wiry.

*antonym* puny.

**athletics** n agonistics, callisthenics, contests, events, exercises, games, gymnastics, races, sports, track events.

**atmosphere** n aerospace, aerosphere, air, ambience, aura, character, climate, environment, feel, feeling, flavour, heavens, milieu, mood, quality, sky, spirit, surroundings, tenor, tone, vibrations.

**atmospheric** adj aerial, climatic, epedaphic, meteorological.

**atom** n atomy, bit, crumb, grain, hint, iota, jot, mite, molecule, morsel, particle, scintilla, scrap, shred, smidgen, speck, spot, tittle, trace, whit.

**atone** v aby(e), compensate, expiate, make amends, make up for, offset, pay for, propitiate, recompense, reconcile, redeem, redress, remedy.

**atonement** n amends, compensation, expiation, indemnity, payment, penance, propitiation, recompense, redress, reparation, repayment, restitution, restoration, satisfaction.

**atrocious** adj abominable, barbaric, brutal, cruel, diabolical, execrable, fell, fiendish, flagitious, ghastly, grievous, heinous, hideous, horrible, horrifying, infamous, infernal, inhuman, monstrous, piacular, ruthless, savage, shocking, terrible, vicious, vile, villainous, wicked.

**atrocity** n abomination, atrociousness, barbarity, barbarousness, brutality, crime, cruelty, enormity, evil, flagitiousness, ghastliness, heinousness, hideousness, horror, infamy, inhumanity, monstrosity, monstrousness, outrage, ruthlessness, savagery, viciousness, vileness, villainy, wickedness.

**atrophy** n decay, decline, degeneration, deterioration, diminution, emaciation, marasmus, shrivelling, tabefaction, tabes, wasting, withering.

v decay, decline, degenerate, deteriorate, diminish, dwindle, emaciate, fade, shrink, shrivel, tabefy, waste, wither.

**attach** v add, adhere, adhibit, affix, annex, append, articulate, ascribe, assign, associate, attract, attribute, belong, bind, captivate, combine, connect, couple, fasten, fix, impute, join, link, place, put, relate to, secure, stick, tie, unite, weld.

*antonyms* detach, unfasten.

**attached** *adj* affectionate, affiliated, associated, connected, fond, loving.

**attachment** *n* accessory, accoutrement, adapter, addition, adhesion, adhibition, adjunct, affection, affinity, appendage, appurtenance, attraction, bond, codicil, cohesion, confiscation, connection, connector, coupling, devotion, esteem, extension, extra, fastener, fastening, fidelity, fitting, fixture, fondness, friendship, joint, junction, liking, link, love, loyalty, partiality, predilection, regard, seizure, supplement, tenderness, tie.

**attack** *n* abuse, access, aggression, assailment, assault, battery, blitz, bombardment, bout, broadside, censure, charge, convulsion, criticism, fit, foray, impugnment, incursion, inroad, invasion, invective, kamikaze, offensive, onset, onslaught, paroxysm, raid, rush, seizure, spasm, spell, strike, stroke.

*v* abuse, assail, assault, belabour, berate, blame, censure, charge, chastise, criticise, denounce, do over, fake, fall on, flay, have one's knife in, impugn, invade, inveigh against, lash, lay into, light into, make at, malign, mob, put the boot in, raid, rate, revile, rush, set about, set on, snipe, storm, strafe, strike, vilify, visit, wade into.

**attacker** *n* abuser, aggressor, assailant, assaulter, critic, invader, mugger, persecutor, raider, reviler, traducer.

*antonyms* defender, supporter.

**attain** *v* accomplish, achieve, acquire, arrive at, bag, compass, complete, earn, effect, fulfil, gain, get, grasp, net, obtain, procure, reach, realise, reap, secure, touch, win.

**attainability** *n* accessibility, availability, feasibility, obtainability, practicalness, procurability, realisability.

**attainable** *adj* accessible, achievable, available, feasible, manageable, obtainable, possible, potential, practicable, probable, procurable, reachable, realistic, within reach.

*antonym* unattainable.

**attainment** *n* ability, accomplishment, achievement, acquirement, acquisition, aptitude, art, capability, competence, completion, consummation, facility, feat, fulfilment, gift, mastery, procurement, proficiency, reaching, realisation, skill, success, talent.

**attempt** *n* assault, assay, attack, bash, bid, coup d'essai, crack, effort, endeavour, essay, experiment, go, move, push, shot, shy, stab, struggle, trial, try, undertaking, venture.

*v* aspire, endeavour, essay, experiment, have a bash, have a crack, have a go, have a shot, seek, strive, tackle, try, try one's hand at, try one's luck at, undertake, venture.

**attend** *v* accompany, appear, arise from, assist, be all ears, be present, care for, chaperon, companion, convoy, escort, follow, frequent, give ear, guard, hear, hearken, heed, help, lend an ear, listen, look after, mark, mind, minister to, note, notice, nurse, observe, pay attention, pay heed, pin back one's ears, regard, result from, serve, squire, succour, take care of, tend, usher, visit, wait upon, watch.

**attend to** concentrate on, control, cope with, deal with, direct, look after, manage, oversee, see to, supervise, take care of.

**attendance** *n* appearance, assistance, attending, audience, crowd, escortage, gate, house, ministration, presence, turn-out.

**attendant** *n* acolyte, aide, assistant, auxiliary, batman, bed captain, chaperon, companion, custodian, equerry, escort, famulus, flunkey, follower, ghillie, guard, guide, helper, jäger, Jeames, kavass, lackey, lady-help, lady-in-waiting, lady's-maid, livery-servant, marshal, menial, page, poursuivant, retainer, servant, steward, underling, usher, waiter.

*adj* accessory, accompanying, associated, attached, concomitant, consequent, incidental, related, resultant, subsequent.

**attention** *n* advertence, advertency, alertness, attentiveness, awareness, care, civility, concentration, concern, consciousness, consideration, contemplation, courtesy, deference, ear, gallantry, heed, heedfulness, intentness, mindfulness, ministration, notice, observation, politeness, recognition, regard, respect, service, thought, thoughtfulness, treatment, vigilance.

*antonyms* disregard, inattention.

**attentive** *adj* accommodating, advertent, alert, awake, careful, civil, concentrating, conscientious, considerate, courteous, deferential, devoted, gallant, gracious, heedful, intent, kind, mindful, obliging, observant, polite, regardant, studious, thoughtful, vigilant, watchful.

*antonyms* heedless, inattentive, inconsiderate.

**attenuate** *v* adulterate, debase, decrease, devaluate, dilute, diminish, draw out, elongate, enervate, enfeeble, extend, lengthen, rarefy, reduce, refine, sap, stretch out, taper, thin, thin out, water down, weaken.

*antonyms* expand, intensify, thicken.

**attenuated** *adj* adulterated, attenuate, debased, decreased, devalued, dilute, diluted, diminished, drawn out, elongated, enervated, enfeebled, extended, lengthened, rarefied, reduced, refined, sapped, slender, spun out, stretched out, tapering, thinned, watered down, weakened.

**attest** *v* adjure, affirm, assert, authenticate, aver, certify, confirm, corroborate, declare, demonstrate, depose, display, endorse, evidence, evince, exhibit, manifest, prove, ratify, seal, show, substantiate, swear, testify, verify, vouch, warrant, witness.

**attestation** *n* affirmation, asseveration, assurance, averment, avowal, certification, confirmation, corroboration, declaration, deposition, endorsement, evidence, evincement, testification, testimony, vouch, witness.

**attire** *n* accoutrements, apparel, array, clothes, clothing, costume, dress, finery, garb, garments, gear, get-up, habiliments, habit, outfit, raiment, rig-out, robes, togs, uniform, vestment, wear, weeds.

*v* accoutre, adorn, apparel, array, caparison, clothe, costume, deck out, dress, equip, garb, habilitate, outfit, prepare, rig out, robe, turn out.

**attitude** n affectation, air, Anschauung, approach, aspect, bearing, carriage, condition, demeanour, disposition, feeling, manner, mien, mood, opinion, outlook, perspective, point of view, pose, position, posture, stance, view, Weltanschauung.

**attract** v allure, appeal to, bewitch, captivate, charm, decoy, draw, enchant, engage, entice, fascinate, incline, induce, interest, inveigle, invite, lure, pull, seduce, tempt.

*antonym* repel.

**attraction** n allure, amenity, appeal, attractiveness, bait, captivation, charm, crowd-puller, draw, enchantment, entertainment, enticement, event, fascination, inducement, interest, invitation, lure, magnetism, pull, seduction, show, temptation.

*antonym* repulsion.

**attractive** adj agreeable, alluring, appealing, appetible, beautiful, beddable, captivating, catching, catchy, charming, comely, enchanting, engaging, enticing, epigamous, fair, fascinating, fetching, glamorous, good-looking, gorgeous, handsome, hunky, interesting, inviting, jolie laide, lovely, magnetic, nubile, personable, pleasant, pleasing, prepossessing, pretty, seductive, snazzy, stunning, taky, tempting, toothsome, voluptuous, winning, winsome.

*antonyms* repellent, unattractive.

**attribute** v accredit, apply, arrogate, ascribe, assign, blame, charge, credit, impute, put down, refer.

n affection, aspect, character, characteristic, facet, feature, idiosyncrasy, mark, note, peculiarity, point, property, quality, quirk, sign, symbol, trait, virtue.

**attribution** n accreditation, application, ascription, assignment, charge, crediting, imputation.

**attrition** n abrasion, attenuation, chafing, debilitation, detrition, erosion, fretting, friction, grinding, harassment, harrying, rubbing, scraping, weakening, wear, wearing away, wearing down.

**attune** v acclimatise, accustom, adapt, adjust, assimilate, co-ordinate, familiarise, harmonise, homologise, modulate, reconcile, regulate, set, tune.

**atypical** adj aberrant, abnormal, anomalous, deviant, divergent, eccentric, exceptional, extraordinary, freakish, untypical, unusual.

*antonym* typical.

**au fait** abreast of, acquainted, au courant, clued-up, conversant, hep, in the know, in the stream, in the swim, in touch, knowledgeable, on the ball, posted, up-to-date, well up, well-informed.

**auburn** adj chestnut, copper, henna, nutbrown, red, russet, rust, tawny, titian.

**auction** n cant, roup, sale, vendue.

**audacious** adj adventurous, assuming, assured, bold, brave, brazen, cheeky, courageous, dare-devil, daring, dauntless, death-defying, der-doing, disrespectful, enterprising, fearless, forward, impertinent, impudent, insolent, intrepid, pert, plucky, presumptuous, rash, reckless, risky, rude, shameless, unabashed, valiant, venturesome.

*antonyms* cautious, reserved, timid.

**audacity** n adventurousness, assurance, audaciousness, boldness, brass neck, bravery, brazenness, cheek, chutzpah, courage, daring, dauntlessness, defiance, derring-do, disrespectfulness, effrontery, enterprise, fearlessness, foolhardiness, forwardness, gall, guts, impertinence, impudence, insolence, intrepidity, nerve, pertness, presumption, rashness, recklessness, rudeness, shamelessness, valour, venturesomeness.

*antonyms* caution, reserve, timidity.

**audible** adj appreciable, clear, detectable, discernible, distinct, hearable, perceptible, recognisable.

*antonym* inaudible.

**audience** n assemblage, assembly, auditorium, congregation, crowd, devotees, fans, following, gallery, gathering, hearing, house, interview, listeners, market, meeting, onlookers, public, ratings, reception, regulars, spectators, turn-out, viewers.

**audit** n analysis, balancing, check, checking, examination, inspection, investigation, review, scrutiny, statement, verification.

v analyse, balance, check, examine, inspect, investigate, review, scrutinise, verify.

**auditor** n accountant, actuary, analyst, examiner, inspector, scrutator, scrutiniser.

**augment** v add to, amplify, boost, dilate, eke out, enhance, enlarge, expand, extend, grow, heighten, increase, inflate, intensify, magnify, multiply, raise, reinforce, strengthen, supplement, swell.

*antonym* decrease.

**augur** n auspex, divinator, diviner, haruspex, oracle, prognosticator, prophet, seer, soothsayer.

v auspicate, bespeak, betoken, bode, forebode, foreshadow, foretoken, harbinger, haruspicate, herald, import, portend, predict, prefigure, presage, promise, prophesy, signify.

**augury** n auspice, divination, foreboding, forerunner, forewarning, harbinger, haruspication, herald, omen, portent, precursor, prediction, presage, prodrome, prognostication, promise, prophecy, sign, soothsaying, token, warning.

**august** adj awful, dignified, exalted, glorious, grand, imposing, impressive, lofty, magnificent, majestic, monumental, noble, portentous, regal, revered, solemn, splendid, stately, venerable.

**aura** n air, ambience, aroma, atmosphere, effluvium, emanation, feel, feeling, hint, mood, nimbus, odour, quality, scent, suggestion, vibes, vibrations.

**auspices** n aegis, authority, backing, care, championship, charge, control, guidance, influence, patronage, protection, responsibility, sponsorship, superintendence, supervision, support, tutelage.

**auspicious** adj bright, cheerful, encouraging, favourable, felicitous, fortunate, happy, hopeful, lucky, opportune, optimistic, promising, propitious, prosperous, rosy, white.

*antonyms* inauspicious, ominous.

**austere** *adj* abstemious, abstinent, ascetic, astringent, bitter, bleak, chaste, cold, conservative, continent, Dantean, Dantesque, economical, exacting, forbidding, formal, grave, grim, hard, harsh, plain, puritanical, restrained, rigid, rigorous, self-denying, self-disciplined, serious, severe, simple, sober, solemn, sour, spare, Spartan, stark, stern, strict, stringent, unadorned, unembellished, unornamented, unrelenting.

*antonyms* elaborate, extravagant, genial.

**austerity** *n* abstemiousness, abstinence, asceticism, chasteness, chastity, coldness, continence, economy, formality, gravity, grimness, hardness, harshness, inflexibility, plainness, puritanism, reserve, restraint, rigidity, rigour, self-control, self-denial, self-discipline, seriousness, severity, simplicity, sobriety, solemnity, spareness, Spartanism, starkness, sternness, strictness.

*antonyms* elaborateness, extravagant, geniality.

**authentic** *adj* accurate, actual, authoritative, bona fide, certain, dependable, dinkum, factual, faithful, genuine, honest, kosher, legitimate, original, pure, real, reliable, simon-pure, true, true-to-life, trustworthy, valid, veracious, veritable.

*antonyms* counterfeit, inauthentic, spurious.

**authenticate** *v* accredit, attest, authorise, avouch, certify, confirm, corroborate, endorse, guarantee, validate, verify, vouch for, warrant.

**authentication** *n* accreditation, attestation, authorisation, certification, confirmation, corroboration, endorsement, guarantee, validation, verification, voucher, warrant.

**authenticity** *n* accuracy, actuality, authoritativeness, certainty, correctness, dependability, factualness, faithfulness, fidelity, genuineness, honesty, legitimacy, purity, reality, realness, reliability, trustworthiness, truth, truthfulness, validity, veracity, veritableness, verity.

*antonyms* invalidity, spuriousness.

**author** *n* architect, begetter, composer, creator, designer, fabricator, fashioner, father, forger, founder, framer, initiator, inventor, maker, mover, originator, paper-stainer, parent, pen, penman, penwoman, planner, prime mover, producer, volumist, writer.

**authorisation** *n* accreditation, approval, certification, credentials, go-ahead, green light, leave, licence, permission, permit, sanction, warrant.

**authorise** *v* accredit, allow, approve, commission, confirm, consent to, countenance, empower, enable, entitle, legalise, license, permit, ratify, sanction, validate, warrant.

**authoritarian** *adj* absolute, autocratic, despotic, dictatorial, disciplinarian, doctrinaire, dogmatic, domineering, harsh, heavy, imperious, inflexible, oppressive, repressive, rigid, severe, strict, tyrannical, unyielding.

*antonym* liberal.

*n* absolutist, autocrat, despot, dictator, disciplinarian, fascist, Hitler, tyrant.

**authoritarianism** *n* absolutism, autocracy, despotism, dictatorship, fascism, fascismo, Hildebrandism, Hitlerism, totalitarianism, tyranny.

*antonyms* laissez faire, liberalism.

**authoritative** *adj* accepted, accurate, approved, assured, authentic, authorised, cathedratic, commanding, confident, convincing, decisive, definitive, dependable, factual, faithful, learned, legitimate, magisterial, magistral, masterly, official, reliable, sanctioned, scholarly, sound, sovereign, true, trustworthy, truthful, valid, veritable.

*antonym* unreliable.

**authoritatively** *adv* confidently, decisively, ex cathedra, legitimately, reliably, soundly.

**authority**[1] *n* administration, ascendancy, attestation, authorisation, avowal, charge, command, control, declaration, domination, dominion, evidence, force, government, imperium, influence, jurisdiction, justification, licence, management, might, officialdom, permission, permit, power, prerogative, profession, right, rule, sanction, sovereignty, statement, strength, supremacy, sway, testimony, textbook, warrant, weight, word.

**authority**[2] *n* arbiter, bible, connoisseur, expert, judge, master, professional, pundit, sage, scholar, specialist.

**autocracy** *n* absolutism, authoritarianism, despotism, dictatorship, fascism, Hitlerism, totalitarianism, tyranny.

*antonym* democracy.

**autocrat** *n* absolutist, authoritarian, Caesar, cham, despot, dictator, fascist, Hitler, panjandrum, totalitarian, tyrant.

**autocratic** *adj* absolute, all-powerful, authoritarian, despotic, dictatorial, dictatory, domineering, imperious, overbearing, totalitarian, tyrannical, tyrannous.

*antonyms* democratic, liberal.

**automatic** *adj* automated, certain, habitual, inescapable, inevitable, instinctive, involuntary, mechanical, mechanised, natural, necessary, perfunctory, push-button, reflex, robot, robot-like, routine, self-acting, self-activating, self-moving, self-propelling, self-regulating, spontaneous, unavoidable, unbidden, unconscious, unthinking, unwilled, vegetative.

**automaton** *n* Dalek, machine, mechanical man, robot.

**autonomous** *adj* autarkic, free, independent, self-determining, self-governing, sovereign, voluntary.

*antonym* subject.

**autonomy** *n* autarky, free will, freedom, home rule, independence, self-determination, self-government, self-rule, sovereignty.

*antonyms* compulsion, subjection.

**auxiliary** *adj* accessory, adjuvant, adminicular, aiding, ancillary, assistant, assisting, back-up, emergency, helping, reserve, secondary, subsidiary, substitute, supplementary, supporting, supportive.

*n* accessory, accomplice, adminicle, ally, ancillary, assistant, associate, companion, confederate, foederatus, helper, partner, reserve, subordinate, supporter.

**avail** v advance, advantage, aid, assist, benefit, boot, dow, exploit, help, make the most of, profit, serve, work.

n advantage, aid, assistance, benefit, boot, good, help, profit, purpose, service, use, value.

**avail oneself of** capitalise on, make use of, profit by, profit from, take advantage of, turn to account, use, utilise.

**available** adj accessible, at hand, attainable, convenient, disengaged, free, handy, obtainable, on hand, on tap, procurable, ready, to hand, vacant, within reach.

antonym unavailable.

**avalanche** n barrage, cascade, cataclysm, deluge, flood, inundation, landslide, landslip, laurine, torrent.

**avant-garde** adj advanced, enterprising, experimental, far-out, forward-looking, goey, innovative, innovatory, inventive, pioneering, progressive, unconventional, way-out.

antonyms conservative, dyed-in-the-wool.

**avarice** n acquisitiveness, cheese-paring, covetousness, cupidity, greed, greediness, meanness, miserliness, niggardliness, parsimoniousness, parsimony, penny-pinching, penuriousness, pleonexia, predatoriness, rapacity, stinginess, tight-fistedness.

antonym generosity.

**avaricious** adj acquisitive, cheese-paring, covetous, gare, grasping, greedy, gripple, mean, miserable, miserly, money-grubbing, niggardly, parsimonious, penny-pinching, penurious, pleonectic, predatory, rapacious, stingy, tight-fisted.

antonym generous.

**avenge** v punish, repay, requite, take revenge for, take vengeance for, vindicate.

**avengement** n punishment, repayment, reprisal, requital, retaliation, retribution, revenge, ultion, vengeance.

**avenger** n retributor, vindicator.

**avenging** adj retaliatory, retributive, vengeful, vindictive, wreakful.

**avenue** n access, alley, approach, boulevard, channel, course, drive, driveway, entrance, entree, entry, means, pass, passage, path, pathway, road, route, street, thoroughfare, vista, walk, way.

**aver** v affirm, allege, assert, asseverate, attest, avouch, avow, declare, insist, maintain, proclaim, profess, pronounce, protest, say, state, swear, testify, witness.

**average** n mean, mediocrity, medium, midpoint, norm, par, rule, run, standard.

antonyms exception, extreme.

adj common, commonplace, everyday, fair, general, indifferent, intermediate, mean, medial, median, mediocre, medium, middle, middling, moderate, normal, ordinary, passable, regular, run-of-the-mill, satisfactory, so-so, standard, tolerable, typical, undistinguished, unexceptional, unremarkable, usual.

antonyms exceptional, extreme.

**averse** adj antagonistic, antipathetic, disapproving, disinclined, hostile, ill-disposed, inimical, loath, opposed, reluctant, unfavourable, unwilling.

antonyms sympathetic, willing.

**aversion** n abhorrence, abomination, anathema, animosity, antagonism, antipathy, detestation, disapproval, disgust, disinclination, dislike, distaste, hate, hatred, horror, hostility, loathing, odium, opposition, phobia, phobism, reluctance, repugnance, repulsion, revulsion, unwillingness.

antonyms liking, sympathy.

**avert** v avoid, deflect, evade, fend off, forestall, frustrate, obviate, parry, preclude, prevent, stave off, turn, turn aside, turn away, ward off.

**aviary** n birdcage, birdhouse, volary.

**aviation** n aeronautics, flight, flying.

**aviator** n ace, aeronaut, airman, erk, flier, pilot.

**avid** adj acquisitive, ardent, avaricious, covetous, dedicated, devoted, eager, earnest, enthusiastic, fanatical, fervent, grasping, greedy, hungry, insatiable, intense, keen, passionate, rapacious, ravenous, thirsty, voracious, zealous.

antonym indifferent.

**avidity** n acquisitiveness, ardour, avarice, covetousness, craving, cupidity, desire, devotion, eagerness, enthusiasm, fervour, greed, greediness, hankering, hunger, insatiability, keenness, longing, rapacity, ravenousness, thirst, voracity, zeal.

antonym indifference.

**avocation** n business, calling, distraction, diversion, employment, hobby, interest, job, occupation, pastime, profession, pursuit, recreation, relaxation, sideline, trade, vocation, work.

**avoid** v abstain from, avert, balk, bypass, circumvent, dodge, duck, elude, escape, eschew, evade, evite, funk, get out of, obviate, prevent, refrain from, shirk, shun, side-step, steer clear of.

**avoidable** adj avertible, eludible, escapable, evadable, evitable, preventable, voidable.

antonym inevitable.

**avoidance** n abstention, abstinence, circumvention, dodge, dodging, eluding, elusion, escape, eschewal, evasion, evitation, prevention, refraining, shirking, shunning.

**avow** v acknowledge, admit, affirm, allege, assert, asseverate, attest, aver, confess, declare, maintain, own, proclaim, profess, recognise, state, swear, testify.

**avowal** n acknowledgment, admission, affirmation, allegation, assertion, asseveration, attestation, averment, confession, declaration, oath, owning, proclamation, profession, recognition, statement, swearing, testimony.

**avowed** adj acknowledged, admitted, confessed, declared, open, overt, professed, self-confessed, self-proclaimed, sworn.

**avowedly** adv admittedly, candidly, confessedly, ex professo, frankly, openly, overtly, professedly.

antonym secretly.

**await** v anticipate, attend, be in store for, expect, hope for, lie in wait, look for, look forward to, wait for.

**awake** v arouse, awaken, rouse, wake, wake up.

adj alert, alive, aroused, astir, attentive, awakened, aware, conscious, heedful, observant, sensitive, vigilant, wakeful, waking, watchful, wide-awake.

**awaken** v activate, alert, animate, arouse, awake, call forth, enliven, evoke, excite, fan, kindle, prompt, provoke, revive, rouse, stimulate, stir up, vivify, wake, waken.

*antonyms* lull, quell, quench.

**awakening** n activation, animating, arousal, awaking, birth, enlivening, evocation, kindling, prompting, provocation, revival, rousing, stimulation, vivification, wakening, waking.

**award** v accord, adjudge, allot, allow, apportion, assign, bestow, confer, determine, dispense, distribute, endow, gift, give, grant, present.

n adjudication, allotment, allowance, bestowal, conferment, conferral, decision, decoration, dispensation, endowment, gift, grant, judgement, order, presentation, prize, trophy.

**aware** adj acquainted, alive to, appreciative, apprised, attentive, au courant, cognisant, conscient, conscious, conversant, enlightened, familiar, heedful, hep, hip, informed, knowing, knowledgeable, mindful, observant, on the ball, on the qui vive, sensible, sensitive, sentient, sharp, shrewd.

*antonyms* insensitive, unaware.

**awareness** n acquaintance, appreciation, attention, cognisance, consciousness, enlightenment, familiarity, knowledge, observation, perception, realisation, recognition, sensibility, sensitivity, sentience, understanding.

*antonyms* insensitivity, unawareness.

**awe** n admiration, amazement, apprehension, astonishment, dread, fear, respect, reverence, terror, veneration, wonder, wonderment.

*antonym* contempt.

v amaze, astonish, cow, daunt, frighten, horrify, impress, intimidate, overwhelm, stun, terrify.

**awe-inspiring** adj amazing, astonishing, awesome, awful, breathtaking, daunting, fearsome, formidable, impressive, intimidating, magnificent, overwhelming, wonderful, wondrous.

*antonyms* contemptible, tame.

**awesome** adj alarming, amazing, astonishing, august, awe-inspiring, awful, breathtaking, daunting, dread, dreadful, fearful, fearsome, formidable, frightening, imposing, impressive, intimidating, magnificent, majestic, moving, overwhelming, redoubtable, solemn, stunning, stupefying, stupendous, terrible, terrifying, wonderful, wondrous.

**awe-struck** adj afraid, amazed, astonished, awed, awe-inspired, awe-stricken, cowed, daunted, dumbfounded, fearful, frightened, impressed, intimidated, speechless, struck dumb, stunned, terrified, wonder-struck.

**awful** adj abysmal, alarming, amazing, atrocious, august, awe-inspiring, awesome, blood-curdling, dire, dread, dreadful, eldritch, fearful, fearsome, frightful, ghastly, gruesome, harrowing, hideous, horrendous, horrible, horrific, horrifying, majestic, nasty, portentous, shocking, solemn, spine-chilling, terrible, tremendous, ugly, unpleasant.

**awfully** adv abysmally, badly, disgracefully, disputably, dreadfully, exceedingly, exceptionally, excessively, extremely, greatly, immensely, inadequately, quite, reprehensibly, shockingly, shoddily, terribly, unforgivably, unpleasantly, very, wickedly, woefully, wretchedly.

**awkward** adj annoying, bloody-minded, blundering, bungling, chancy, chuckle-headed, clownish, clumsy, coarse, compromising, cubbish, cumbersome, delicate, difficult, disobliging, embarrassed, embarrassing, exasperating, farouche, fiddly, gauche, gawky, graceless, ham-fisted, ham-handed, hazardous, ill at ease, inconvenient, inelegant, inept, inexpedient, inexpert, inopportune, intractable, intransigent, irritable, left-handed, maladroit, obstinate, painful, perplexing, perverse, prickly, risky, rude, spastic, sticky, stubborn, thorny, ticklish, touchy, troublesome, trying, uncomfortable, unco-operative, unco-ordinated, uncouth, ungainly, ungraceful, unhandy, unhelpful, unmanageable, unpleasant, unrefined, unskilful, untimely, untoward, unwieldy, vexatious, vexing.

*antonyms* amenable, convenient, elegant, graceful, straightforward.

**awkwardness** n bloody-mindedness, clumsiness, coarseness, cumbersomeness, delicacy, difficulty, discomfort, embarrassment, gaucheness, gaucherie, gawkihood, gracelessness, inconvenience, inelegance, ineptness, inexperience, intractability, intransigence, irritability, left-handedness, left-handiness, maladresse, maladroitness, obstinacy, painfulness, perilousness, perversity, prickliness, risk, riskiness, rudeness, stiffness, stubbornness, touchiness, troublesomeness, unco-operativeness, ungainliness, unhandiness, unhelpfulness, unmanageability, unpleasantness, untimeliness, unwieldiness.

*antonyms* amenability, convenience, elegance, grace, straightforwardness.

**awning** n baldachin, canopy, covering, sunshade, tarpaulin, velarium, wind-break.

**awry** adv, adj aglee, amiss, askew, asymmetrical, cock-eyed, crooked, misaligned, oblique, off-centre, out of kilter, skew-whiff, twisted, uneven, unevenly, wonky, wrong.

*antonyms* straight, symmetrical.

**axe** v cancel, chop, cleave, cut, cut down, discharge, discontinue, dismiss, eliminate, fell, fire, get rid of, hew, remove, sack, split, terminate, throw out, withdraw.

**axiom** n adage, aphorism, apophthegm, byword, dictum, fundamental, gnome, maxim, postulate, precept, principle, truism, truth.

**axiomatic** adj absolute, accepted, aphoristic, apodictic, apophthegmatic, assumed, certain, fundamental, given, gnomic, granted, indubitable, manifest, presupposed, proverbial, self-evident, understood, unquestioned.

**axis** n alliance, arbor, axle, bloc, centre-line, coalition, compact, entente, league, longitude, pact, pivot, plumb-line, shaft, spindle, vertical.

**axle** n arbor, axis, hinge, mandrel, pin, pivot, shaft, spindle.

# B

**babble** v blab, burble, cackle, chatter, gabble, gibber, gurgle, jabber, mumble, murmur, mutter, prate, prattle, purl, twattle.

n burble, clamour, drivel, gabble, gibberish, lallation, lalling, murmur, purl, purling, twattle.

**babbling** adj burbling, cackling, chattering, drivelling, drooling, gabbling, gibbering, gurgling, incoherent, jabbering, long-tongued, murmuring, prattling, rambling, unco-ordinated, unintelligible.

**babe** n bab, baby, bairn, child, infant, nursling, papoose, suckling, wean, weanling, youngling.

**babel** n bedlam, chaos, clamour, commotion, confusion, din, disorder, hubbub, hullabaloo, pandemonium, tumult, turmoil, uproar.

*antonyms* calm, order.

**baby** n babe, bairn, child, infant, nursling, papoose, suckling, tiny, toddler, wean, weanling, youngling.

adj diminutive, dwarf, Lilliputian, little, midget, mini, miniature, minute, pygmy, small, small-scale, tiny, toy, wee.

v cocker, coddle, cosset, humour, indulge, mollycoddle, overindulge, pamper, pander to, pet, spoil, spoon-feed.

**babyish** adj baby, childish, foolish, immature, infantile, jejune, juvenile, naïve, namby-pamby, puerile, silly, sissy, soft, spoilt.

*antonyms* mature, precocious.

**bacchanalian** adj bacchaic, debauched, Dionysian, dissolute, drunken, frenzied, intemperate, licentious, maenadic, orgiastic, riotous, saturnalian, wanton.

**back¹** v advocate, assist, boost, buttress, champion, countenance, countersign, encourage, endorse, favour, finance, sanction, second, side with, sponsor, subsidise, support, sustain, underwrite.

*antonym* discourage.

**back up** aid, assist, bolster, champion, confirm, corroborate, endorse, reinforce, second, substantiate, support.

*antonym* let down.

**back²** n backside, end, hind part, hindquarters, posterior, rear, reverse, stern, tail, tail end, tergum, verso.

adj end, hind, hindmost, posterior, rear, reverse, tail.

**back³** v backtrack, recede, recoil, regress, retire, retreat, reverse, withdraw.

**back down** accede, back-pedal, concede, give in, retreat, submit, surrender, withdraw, yield.

**back out** abandon, apostatise, bunk off, cancel, chicken out, give up, go back on, recant, renegue, resign, withdraw.

**back⁴** adj delayed, earlier, elapsed, former, outdated, overdue, past, previous, prior, superseded.

**backbite** v abuse, attack, calumniate, criticise, defame, denigrate, disparage, libel, malign, revile, slag, slander, traduce, vilify, vituperate.

*antonym* praise.

**backbiting** n abuse, aspersion, bitchiness, calumniation, calumny, cattiness, criticism, defamation, denigration, detraction, disparagement, gossip, malice, revilement, scandalmongering, slagging, slander, spite, spitefulness, vilification, vituperation.

*antonym* praise.

**backbone** n basis, bottle, character, core, courage, determination, firmness, foundation, grit, hardihood, mainstay, mettle, nerve, pluck, power, resolution, resolve, spine, stamina, staunchness, steadfastness, strength, support, tenacity, toughness, vertebral column, will.

*antonyms* spinelessness, weakness.

**backbreaking** adj arduous, crushing, exhausting, gruelling, hard, heavy, killing, laborious, punishing, strenuous, tiring, toilsome, wearing, wearisome.

*antonym* easy.

**backer** n advocate, benefactor, bottle-holder, champion, funder, patron, promoter, second, seconder, sponsor, subscriber, supporter, underwriter, well-wisher.

**backfire** v boomerang, come home to roost, fail, flop, miscarry, rebound, recoil, ricochet.

**background** n breeding, circumstances, credentials, culture, dossier, education, environment, experience, fond, grounding, history, milieu, preparation, record, surroundings, tradition, upbringing.

**back-handed** adj ambiguous, double-edged, doubtful, dubious, equivocal, ironic, oblique, sarcastic, sardonic, two-edged.

*antonyms* sincere, wholehearted.

**backing** n accompaniment, advocacy, aid, assistance, championing, championship, encouragement, endorsement, favour, funds, grant, helpers, moral support, patronage, sanction, seconding, sponsorship, subsidy, support.

**backlash** n backfire, boomerang, counterblast, kickback, reaction, recoil, repercussion, reprisal, resentment, response, retaliation.

**backlog** n accumulation, excess, hoard, leeway, mountain, reserve, reserves, resources, stock, supply.

**backslide** v apostatise, default, defect, fall from grace, lapse, regress, relapse, renegue, retrogress, revert, sin, slip, stray, weaken.

*antonym* persevere.

**backslider** n apostate, defaulter, defector, deserter, recidivist, recreant, renegade, reneguer, turncoat.

**backsliding** n apostasy, defaulting, defection, desertion, lapse, recidivism, recreancy, relapse, renegation.

**backward** adj bashful, behind, behindhand, diffident, dull, hesitant, hesitating, immature, late, reluctant, retarded, shy, slow, sluggish, stupid, subnormal, tardy, underdeveloped, unwilling, wavering.

*antonyms* forward, precocious.

**backwoods** n back of beyond, boondocks, bush, outback, sticks.

**bacteria** n bacilli, bugs, germs, listerias, microbes, micro-organisms, pathogens, schizomycetes, viruses.

**bad** adj adverse, ailing, base, blameworthy, conscience-stricken, contrite, corrupt, criminal, damaging, dangerous, decayed, defective, deficient, deleterious, delinquent, despondent, detrimental, disastrous, discouraged, discouraging, diseased, disobedient, distressed, distressing, evil, fallacious, faulty, gloomy, grave, grim, grotty, guilty, harmful, harsh, ill, illaudable, immoral, imperfect, inadequate, incorrect, inferior, injurious, mean, melancholy, mischievous, mouldy, naughty, no-good, noxious, off, offensive, onkus, painful, piacular, poor, putrid, rancid, regretful, remorseful, ropy, rotten, rueful, ruinous, sad, serious, severe, shoddy, sick, sinful, sombre, sorry, sour, spoilt, stormy, substandard, terrible, troubled, unfortunate, unwell, upset, vile, wicked, wrong.

**bad blood** acrimony, anger, animosity, antagonism, bad feeling, dislike, distrust, enmity, feud, hatred, hostility, malevolence, malice, nastiness, odium, rancour, resentment, upset, vendetta.

**bad form** bad style, barbarism, gaucherie, impropriety, indecorum, inelegance, infelicity, mauvais ton, solecism.

**bad luck** adversity, blow, deuce-ace, hard cheese, hard lines, hard luck, hoodoo, ill luck, mischance, misfortune, misluck, reverse, setback.

*antonym* luck.

**bad manners** boorishness, coarseness, discourtesy, disrespect, gaucherie, impoliteness, incivility, inconsideration, indelicacy, mismanners, unmannerliness.

*antonym* politeness.

**bad taste** coarseness, crudeness, grossness, indecency, indelicacy, mauvais goût, obscenity, offensiveness, poor taste, smuttiness, tactlessness, tastelessness, vulgarity.

*antonyms* delicacy, tastefulness.

**bad time** agony, going-over, grilling, mauvais moment, mauvais quart d'heure, nasty moment, suspense, third degree, torture.

**badge** n brand, cognisance, device, emblem, episemon, identification, insignia, logo, mark, sign, stamp, token, trademark.

**badger** v bait, bully, bullyrag, chivvy, goad, harass, harry, hassle, hound, importune, nag, pester, plague, torment.

**badinage** n banter, chaff, dicacity, drollery, give and take, humour, jocularity, mockery, persiflage, raillery, repartee, ribbing, teasing, waggery, word-play.

**badly**[1] adv carelessly, criminally, defectively, faultily, immorally, imperfectly, improperly, inadequately, incompetently, incorrectly, ineptly, negligently, poorly, shamefully, shoddily, unethically, unfairly, unfavourably, unfortunately, unsatisfactorily, unsuccessfully, wickedly, wrong, wrongly.

*antonym* mildly.

**badly**[2] adv acutely, bitterly, critically, crucially, deeply, desperately, exceedingly, extremely, gravely, greatly, intensely, painfully, seriously, severely.

*antonym* mildly.

**bad-tempered** adj cantankerous, captious, choleric, crabbed, cross, crotchety, dyspeptic, fractious, franzy, girnie, impatient, irascible, irritable, peevish, petulant, querulous, snappy, splenetic, stroppy, testy, vixenish, vixenly.

*antonyms* equable, genial.

**baffle** v amaze, astound, balk, bamboozle, bemuse, bewilder, check, confound, confuse, daze, defeat, disconcert, dumbfound, flabbergast, floor, flummox, foil, frustrate, hinder, mystify, nonplus, perplex, puzzle, stump, stun, stymie, thwart, upset.

*antonyms* enlighten, help.

**baffling** adj amazing, astounding, bemusing, confusing, extraordinary, frustrating, mysterious, perplexing, stupefying, surprising, thwarting, unfathomable.

*antonyms* enlightening, explanatory.

**bag** v acquire, appropriate, capture, catch, commandeer, corner, gain, get, grab, kill, land, obtain, reserve, shoot, take, trap.

n carrier, container, dorlach, Dorothy bag, dressing-case, Gladstone bag, grab-bag, grip, gripsack, handbag, haversack, hold-all, holder, pack, poke, reticule, rucksack, sack, satchel, satchet, scrip, shoulder-bag, tote-bag, valise.

**baggage** n accoutrements, bags, belongings, equipment, gear, impedimenta, luggage, paraphernalia, suit-cases, things, traps, viaticals.

**baggy** *adj* billowing, bulging, droopy, flaccid, floppy, ill-fitting, loose, oversize, pouchy, roomy, sagging, slack.

*antonyms* firm, tight.

**bail** *n* bond, guarantee, guaranty, pledge, security, surety, warranty.

**bail out**[1] aid, assist, finance, help, relieve, rescue.

**bail out**[2], bale out back out, back out, cop out, escape, quit, retreat, withdraw.

**bailiff** *n* agent, beagle, constable, deputy, factor, huissier, magistrate, office, Philistine, sheriff.

**bait** *n* allurement, attraction, bribe, carrot, decoy, enticement, inducement, lure, temptation.

*antonym* disincentive.

*v* annoy, gall, goad, harass, hound, irk, irritate, needle, persecute, provoke, tease, torment.

**balance** *v* adjust, assess, calculate, compare, compute, consider, counteract, counterbalance, counterpoise, deliberate, equalise, equate, equilibrate, equipoise, equiponderate, estimate, evaluate, level, librate, match, neutralise, offset, parallel, poise, settle, square, stabilise, steady, tally, total, weigh.

*antonyms* overbalance, unbalance.

*n* composure, correspondence, difference, equality, equanimity, equilibrium, equipoise, equity, equivalence, evenness, parity, poise, remainder, residue, rest, self-possession, stability, stasis, steadiness, surplus, symmetry.

*antonyms* imbalance, instability.

**balanced** *adj* calm, equitable, even-handed, fair, impartial, just, self-possessed, sensible, unbiased, unprejudiced, well-rounded.

*antonyms* prejudiced, unbalanced.

**balcony** *n* gallery, gods, moucharaby, terrace, upper circle, veranda.

**bald** *adj* bald-headed, baldpated, bare, barren, bleak, depilated, direct, downright, exposed, forthright, glabrate, glabrous, hairless, naked, outright, peeled, plain, severe, simple, stark, straight, straightforward, treeless, unadorned, uncompromising, uncovered, undisguised, unvarnished.

*antonyms* adorned, hirsute.

**balderdash** *n* balls, bollocks, bullshit, bunk, bunkum, claptrap, drivel, gibberish, nonsense, poppycock, rot, rubbish, tommyrot, trash, tripe, twaddle.

**baldness** *n* alopecia, bald-headedness, bareness, calvities, calvousness, directness, glabrousness, hairlessness, psilosis, starkness.

*antonym* hirsuteness.

**bale** *n* bundle, fardel, pack, package, parcel, truss.

**bale out** *see* **bail out**.

**baleful** *adj* deadly, destructive, evil, fell, harmful, hurtful, injurious, malevolent, malignant, menacing, mournful, noxious, ominous, pernicious, ruinous, sad, sinister, venomous, woeful.

*antonyms* auspicious, favourable.

**balk, baulk** *v* baffle, bar, boggle, check, counteract, defeat, demur, disconcert, dodge, evade, flinch, foil, forestall, frustrate, hesitate, hinder, jib, make difficulties, obstruct, prevent, recoil, refuse, resist, shirk, shrink, stall, thwart.

**ball**[1] *n* bauble, bobble, bullet, clew, conglomeration, drop, globe, globule, orb, pellet, pill, shot, slug, sphere, spheroid.

**ball**[2] *n* assembly, carnival, dance, dinner-dance, fandango, hop, masquerade, party, ridotto, rout, soirée.

**ballad** *n* carol, composition, ditty, folk-song, forebitter, lay, poem, shanty, song.

**ballet** *n* ballet-dancing, dancing, leg-business.

**balloon** *v* bag, belly, billow, blow up, bulge, dilate, distend, enlarge, expand, inflate, puff out, swell.

**ballot** *n* election, plebiscite, poll, polling, referendum, vote, voting.

**ballyhoo** *n* advertising, agitation, build-up, clamour, commotion, disturbance, excitement, fuss, hubbub, hue and cry, hullabaloo, hype, noise, promotion, propaganda, publicity, racket, tumult.

**balm** *n* anodyne, balsam, bromide, calmative, comfort, consolation, cream, curative, embrocation, emollient, lenitive, lotion, ointment, palliative, restorative, salve, sedative, solace, unguent.

*antonyms* irritant, vexation.

**balmy**[1] *adj* clement, gentle, mild, pleasant, soft, summery, temperate.

*antonym* inclement.

**balmy**[2] *adj* barmy, crazy, daft, dippy, dotty, foolish, idiotic, insane, loony, mad, nuts, nutty, odd, round the bend, silly, stupid.

*antonyms* rational, sane, sensible.

**bamboozle** *v* baffle, befool, befuddle, bemuse, cheat, con, confound, confuse, cozen, deceive, defraud, delude, dupe, fool, hoax, hoodwink, mystify, perplex, puzzle, stump, swindle, trick.

**ban** *v* anathematise, banish, bar, debar, disallow, exclude, forbid, interdict, ostracise, outlaw, prohibit, proscribe, restrict, suppress.

*antonym* permit.

*n* anathematisation, boycott, censorship, condemnation, curse, denunciation, embargo, interdiction, outlawry, prohibition, proscription, restriction, stoppage, suppression, taboo.

*antonyms* dispensation, permission.

**banal** *adj* boring, clichéd, cliché-ridden, commonplace, corny, empty, everyday, hackneyed, humdrum, jejune, old hat, ordinary, pedestrian, platitudinous, stale, stereotyped, stock, threadbare, tired, trite, unimaginative, unoriginal, vapid.

*antonym* original.

**banality** *n* bromide, cliché, commonplace, dullness, platitude, prosaicism, triteness, triviality, truism, vapidity.

*antonym* originality.

**band**[1] *n* bandage, bandeau, belt, binding, bond, chain, cord, fascia, fasciole, fetter, fillet, ligature, manacle, ribbon, shackle, strap, strip, swath, tape, tie, vitta.

**band**[2] *n* association, body, clique, club, combo, company, coterie, crew, ensemble, flock, gang, group, herd, horde, orchestra, party, range, society, troop, waits.

*v* affiliate, ally, amalgamate, collaborate, consolidate, federate, gather, group, join, merge, unite.

*antonyms* disband, disperse.

**bandage** *n* compress, dressing, gauze, ligature, plaster, swaddle, swathe, tourniquet.

*v* bind, cover, dress, swaddle, swathe.

**bandit** *n* brigand, buccaneer, cowboy, dacoit, desperado, footpad, freebooter, gangster, gunman, highwayman, hijacker, marauder, outlaw, pirate, racketeer, robber, ruffian, thief.

**banditry** *n* brigandage, dacoitage, dacoity, freebooting, heist, hijacking, hold-up, latrociny, robbery, stickup, theft.

**bandy**[1] *v* barter, exchange, interchange, pass, reciprocate, swap, throw, toss, trade.

**bandy**[2] *adj* bandy-legged, bent, bowed, bow-legged, crooked, curved, valgous.

**bane** *n* adversity, affliction, annoyance, bête noire, blight, burden, calamity, curse, despair, destruction, disaster, distress, downfall, evil, irritation, misery, misfortune, nuisance, ordeal, pest, pestilence, plague, ruin, scourge, sorrow, torment, trial, trouble, vexation, woe.

*antonym* blessing.

**baneful** *adj* deadly, deleterious, destructive, disastrous, fell, harmful, hurtful, injurious, malevolent, noxious, pernicious, pestilential, ruinous, sinister, venomous.

*antonym* beneficent.

**bang** *n* blow, boom, box, bump, clang, clap, clash, collision, crash, cuff, detonation, explosion, hit, knock, noise, peal, pop, punch, report, shot, slam, smack, stroke, thud, thump, wallop, whack.

*v* bash, boom, bump, burst, clang, clatter, crash, detonate, drum, echo, explode, hammer, knock, peal, pound, pummel, rap, resound, slam, stamp, strike, thump, thunder.

*adv* directly, hard, headlong, noisily, plumb, precisely, right, slap, smack, straight, suddenly.

**banish** *v* ban, bar, blacklist, debar, deport, discard, dislodge, dismiss, dispel, eject, eliminate, eradicate, evict, exclude, excommunicate, exile, expatriate, expel, get rid of, ostracise, oust, outlaw, remove, shut out, transport.

*antonyms* recall, welcome.

**banishment** *n* deportation, eviction, exile, exilement, expatriation, expulsion, ostracisation, outlawry, proscription, transportation.

*antonyms* recall, return, welcome.

**bank**[1] *n* accumulation, cache, depository, fund, hoard, pool, repository, reserve, reservoir, savings, stock, stockpile, store, storehouse, treasury.

*v* accumulate, deposit, keep, save, stockpile, store.

*antonym* spend.

**bank**[2] *n* acclivity, banking, brink, bund, earthwork, edge, embankment, fail-dike, heap, margin, mass, mound, pile, rampart, ridge, rivage, shallow, shoal, shore, side, slope, tilt.

*v* accumulate, aggrade, amass, camber, cant, drift, heap, incline, mass, mound, pile, pitch, slant, slope, stack, tilt, tip.

**bank**[3] *n* array, bench, echelon, file, group, line, rank, row, sequence, series, succession, tier, train.

**bank-note** *n* bill, flimsy, greenback, note, paper money, treasury note.

**bankrupt** *adj* beggared, broke, depleted, destitute, exhausted, failed, impecunious, impoverished, insolvent, lacking, penurious, ruined, spent.

*antonyms* solvent, wealthy.

*n* debtor, duck, dyvour, insolvent, pauper.

**bankruptcy** *n* beggary, disaster, dyvoury, exhaustion, failure, indebtedness, insolvency, lack, liquidation, penury, ruin, ruination.

*antonyms* solvency, wealth.

**banner** *n* banderol(e), bannerol, burgee, colours, ensign, fanion, flag, gonfalon, labarum, oriflamme, pennant, pennon, standard, streamer, vexillum.

**banquet** *n* binge, dinner, feast, meal, repast, revel, treat, wayzgoose.

**banter** *n* badinage, chaff, chaffing, cross-talk, derision, dicacity, jesting, joking, kidding, mockery, persiflage, pleasantry, quiz, raillery, repartee, ribbing, ridicule, word play.

**baptise** *v* admit, call, christen, cleanse, dub, enrol, immerse, initiate, introduce, name, purify, recruit, sprinkle, style, term, title.

**baptism** *n* beginning, chrism, christening, début, dedication, immersion, initiation, introduction, launch, launching, purification, sprinkling.

**bar**[1] *n* barricade, barrier, batten, check, cross-piece, deterrent, deterrment, hindrance, impediment, obstacle, obstruction, overslaugh, paling, pole, preventive, rail, railing, rod, shaft, stake, stanchion, stick, stop.

*v* ban, barricade, blackball, bolt, debar, exclude, fasten, forbid, hinder, latch, lock, obstruct, preclude, prevent, prohibit, restrain, secure.

**bar**[2] *n* bierkeller, boozer, canteen, counter, dive, doggery, dram-shop, estaminet, exchange, gin-palace, ginshop, groggery, grogshop, honky-tonk, howff, inn, joint, lounge, nineteenth hole, pub, public house, saloon, tavern, vaults, watering-hole.

**bar**[3] *n* advocates, attorneys, barristers, bench, counsel, court, courtroom, dock, law court, tribunal.

**bar⁴** *n* block, chunk, ingot, lump, nugget, slab, wedge.

**barb** *n* affront, arrow, barbule, bristle, cut, dig, fluke, gibe, home-thrust, home-truth, insult, point, prickle, prong, quill, rebuff, sarcasm, sneer, spicule, spike, spur, stab, thorn, thrust.

**barbarian** *n* ape, boor, brute, clod, hooligan, hottentot, hun, ignoramus, illiterate, lout, lowbrow, oaf, philistine, ruffian, savage, tramontane, vandal, vulgarian, yahoo.
*adj* boorish, brutish, coarse, crude, lowbrow, philistine, rough, tramontane, uncivilised, uncouth, uncultivated, uncultured, unsophisticated, vulgar.

**barbaric** *adj* barbarous, boorish, brutal, brutish, coarse, crude, cruel, ferocious, fierce, inhuman, primitive, rude, savage, uncivilised, uncouth, vulgar, wild.
*antonyms* civilised, humane.

**barbarism** *n* abuse, atrocity, barbarity, brutishness, coarseness, corruption, crudity, cruelty, enormity, misuse, outrage, savagery, solecism, vulgarism.

**barbarity** *n* barbarousness, boorishness, brutality, brutishness, cruelty, ferocity, inhumanity, rudeness, ruthlessness, savagery, viciousness, wildness.
*antonyms* civilisation, civility, humanity.

**barbarous** *adj* barbarian, barbaric, brutal, brutish, coarse, crude, cruel, ferocious, heartless, heathenish, ignorant, inhuman, monstrous, philistine, primitive, rough, rude, ruthless, savage, uncivilised, uncouth, uncultured, unlettered, unrefined, vicious, vulgar, wild.
*antonyms* civilised, cultured, educated.

**barbed** *adj* acerbic, acid, catty, caustic, critical, cutting, hooked, hostile, hurtful, jagged, nasty, pointed, prickly, pronged, snide, spiked, spiny, thorny, toothed, unkind.

**bare** *adj* austere, bald, barren, basic, blank, defoliate, defoliated, denudated, denuded, disfurnished, empty, essential, explicit, exposed, hard, lacking, literal, mean, naked, napless, nude, open, peeled, plain, poor, scanty, scarce, severe, sheer, shorn, simple, spare, stark, stripped, unadorned, unarmed, unclad, unclothed, uncovered, undisguised, undressed, unembellished, unforested, unfurnished, unprovided, unsheathed, untimbered, unvarnished, unwooded, vacant, void, wanting, woodless.

**barefaced** *adj* arrant, audacious, bald, blatant, bold, brash, brazen, flagrant, glaring, impudent, insolent, manifest, naked, obvious, open, palpable, patent, shameless, transparent, unabashed, unconcealed.

**barefooted** *adj* barefoot, discalced, shoeless, unshod.
*antonym* shod.

**barely¹** *adv* almost, hardly, just, scarcely, sparingly, sparsely.

**barely²** *adv* explicitly, nakedly, openly, plainly.

**bargain** *n* agreement, arrangement, compact, contract, discount, giveaway, negotiation, pact, pledge, promise, reduction, snip, steal, stipulation, transaction, treaty, understanding.
*v* agree, barter, broke, buy, chaffer, contract, covenant, deal, dicker, haggle, higgle, negotiate, promise, sell, stipulate, trade, traffic, transact.

**bargain for** anticipate, consider, contemplate, expect, foresee, imagine, include, look for, plan for, reckon on.

**bargaining** *n* barter, bartering, dealing, dicker, haggling, higgling, horse-dealing, horse-trading, negotiation, trading, trafficking, wheeler-dealing.

**barge¹** *v* bump, butt in, cannon, collide, elbow, encroach, gatecrash, hit, impinge, interfere, interrupt, intrude, muscle in, push, push in, shove.

**barge²** *n* birlinn, Bucentaur, canal boat, flatboat, house-boat, lighter, narrow-boat, transport.

**bark** *n* bawl, bay, growl, shout, snap, snarl, woof, yap, yell, yelp.
*v* advertise, bawl, bay, bluster, cough, growl, shout, snap, snarl, yap, yell, yelp.

**barking** *n* latration.
*adj* latrant.

**barmy** *adj* balmy, crazy, daft, dippy, dotty, foolish, idiotic, insane, loony, mad, nuts, nutty, odd, silly, stupid.
*antonyms* rational, sane, sensible.

**baroque** *adj* bizarre, bold, convoluted, elaborate, extravagant, exuberant, fanciful, fantastic, flamboyant, florid, grotesque, ornate, overdecorated, overwrought, rococo, vigorous, whimsical.
*antonym* plain.

**barracks** *n* accommodation, billet, camp, cantonment, caserne, encampment, garrison, guard-house, lodging, quarters.

**barrage** *n* assault, attack, battery, bombardment, broadside, burst, cannonade, deluge, fusillade, gunfire, hail, mass, onset, onslaught, plethora, profusion, rain, salvo, shelling, shower, storm, stream, torrent, volley.

**barred** *adj* banned, blackballed, disallowed, excluded, forbidden, outlawed, prohibited, proscribed, taboo.
*antonym* permissible.

**barrel** *n* butt, cade, cask, hogshead, keg, kilderkin, puncheon, rundlet, tierce, tun, water-butt, wood.

**barren** *adj* arid, boring, childless, desert, desolate, dry, dull, empty, flat, fruitless, infecund, infertile, jejune, lacklustre, pointless, profitless, stale, sterile, unbearing, unfruitful, uninformative, uninspiring, uninstructive, uninteresting, unproductive, unprolific, unrewarding, useless, vapid, waste.
*antonyms* fertile, productive, useful.

**barricade** *n* barrier, blockade, bulwark, fence, obstruction, palisade, protection, rampart, screen, stockade.

*v* bar, block, blockade, defend, fortify, obstruct, palisade, protect, screen.

**barrier** *n* bail, bar, barricade, blockade, boom, boundary, bulkhead, check, difficulty, ditch, drawback, fence, fortification, handicap, hindrance, hurdle, impediment, limitation, obstacle, obstruction, railing, rampart, restriction, stop, stumbling-block, transverse, wall.

**barrow** *n* hand-barrow, handcart, hurly, push-cart, wheelbarrow.

**bartender** *n* bar-keeper, barmaid, barman, publican, tapster.

**barter** *v* bargain, chaffer, deal, dicker, exchange, haggle, higgle, negotiate, niffer, sell, swap, trade, traffic, truck.

**base**[1] *n* basis, bed, bottom, camp, centre, core, essence, essential, foot, foundation, fundamental, groundwork, headquarters, heart, home, key, keystone, origin, pedestal, plinth, post, principal, rest, root, settlement, socle, source, stand, standard, starting-point, station, substrate, substructure, support, underpinning, understructure.

*v* build, construct, depend, derive, establish, found, ground, hinge, locate, station.

**base**[2] *adj* abject, contemptible, corrupt, counterfeit, depraved, disgraceful, disreputable, dog, evil, grovelling, humble, ignoble, ignominious, immoral, infamous, low, lowly, low-minded, low-thoughted, mean, menial, miserable, paltry, pitiful, poor, scandalous, servile, shameful, slavish, sordid, sorry, valueless, vile, villainous, vulgar, wicked, worthless, wretched.

**base**[3] *adj* adulterated, alloyed, artificial, bastard, counterfeit, debased, fake, forged, fraudulent, impure, inferior, pinchbeck, spurious.

**base-born** *adj* bastard, common, humble, illegitimate, low-born, low-bred, lowly, misborn, plebeian, proletarian, vulgar.

*antonym* highborn.

**baseless** *adj* gratuitous, groundless, unattested, unauthenticated, uncalled-for, unconfirmed, uncorroborated, unfounded, ungrounded, unjustifiable, unjustified, unsubstantiated, unsupported.

*antonym* justifiable.

**baseness** *n* contemptibility, degradation, depravation, depravity, despicability, ignominy, infamy, knavery, lowliness, meanness, misery, poverty, servility, slavishness, sordidness, sorriness, subservience, turpitude, vileness, villainy, worthlessness, wretchedness.

**bash** *v* belt, biff, break, crash, crush, ding, dunt, hit, punch, slosh, slug, smack, smash, sock, strike, swipe, wallop.

*n* attempt, crack, go, shot, stab, try, turn, whirl.

**bashful** *adj* abashed, backward, blushing, confused, coy, diffident, embarrassed, hesitant, inhibited, modest, nervous, reserved, reticent, retiring, self-conscious, self-effacing, shamefaced, sheepish, shrinking, shy, timid, timorous, unforthcoming, verecund.

*antonym* confident.

**bashfulness** *n* coyness, diffidence, embarrassment, hesitancy, inhibition, mauvaise honte, modesty, reserve, self-consciousness, shamefacedness, sheepishness, shyness, timidity, timorousness.

*antonym* confidence.

**basic** *adj* central, elementary, essential, fundamental, important, indispensable, inherent, intrinsic, key, necessary, primary, radical, root, underlying, vital.

*antonyms* inessential, peripheral.

**basically** *adv* à fond, at bottom, at heart, au fond, essentially, fundamentally, inherently, intrinsically, primarily, principally, radically.

**basics** *n* bedrock, brass tacks, core, essentials, facts, fundamentals, grass roots, necessaries, nitty-gritty, nuts and bolts, practicalities, principles, rock bottom, rudiments.

**basin** *n* aquamanile, bowl, cavity, crater, depression, dip, dish, hollow, porringer, sink.

**basis** *n* approach, base, bottom, core, essential, fond, footing, foundation, fundamental, ground, groundwork, heart, keynote, premise, principle, support, thrust.

**bask** *v* apricate, delight in, enjoy, laze, lie, lounge, luxuriate, relax, relish, revel, savour, sunbathe, wallow.

**basket** *n* bassinet, corf, creel, dosser, frail, hamper, junket, pannier, pottle, punnet, skep, trug.

**bass** *adj* deep, deep-toned, grave, low, low-pitched, low-toned, resonant, sepulchral, sonorous.

**bastard** *n* by-blow, filius nullius, git, illegitimate, love child, love-child, lucky-piece, misfortune, mother-fucker, natural child, whoreson.

*adj* abnormal, adulterated, anomalous, artificial, base, baseborn, counterfeit, false, illegitimate, imperfect, impure, inferior, irregular, misbegotten, sham, spurious, synthetic.

*antonyms* genuine, legitimate.

**bastardise** *v* adulterate, cheapen, corrupt, debase, defile, degrade, demean, depreciate, devalue, distort, pervert, vitiate.

**bastion** *n* bulwark, citadel, defence, fastness, fortress, mainstay, pillar, prop, redoubt, rock, stronghold, support, tower of strength.

**batch** *n* amount, assemblage, assortment, bunch, collection, consignment, contingent, group, lot, pack, parcel, quantity, set.

**bath** *n* ablution, balneary, cleansing, douche, douse, hamman, Jacuzzi"trade", scrubbing, shower, soak, tub, wash.

*v* bathe, clean, douse, lave, shower, soak, tub, wash.

**bathe** *v* cleanse, cover, dook, dunk, encompass, flood, immerse, moisten, rinse, soak, steep, stew, suffuse, swim, wash, wet.

*n* dip, dook, rinse, soak, swim, wash.

**bathetic** *adj* anticlimactic, sublime to ridiculous.

**bathos** *n* anticlimax, comedown, let-down.

**battalion** *n* army, brigade, company, contingent, division, force, herd, horde, host, legion, mass, multitude, phalanx, platoon, regiment, squadron, throng.

**batten** *v* barricade, board up, clamp down, fasten, fix, nail down, secure, tighten.

**batter** *v* abuse, assault, bash, beat, belabour, bruise, buffet, crush, dash, deface, demolish, destroy, disfigure, distress, hurt, injure, lash, maltreat, mangle, manhandle, mar, maul, pelt, pound, pummel, ruin, shatter, smash, thrash, wallop.

**battered** *adj* abused, beaten, bruised, crumbling, crushed, damaged, dilapidated, ill-treated, injured, ramshackle, tumbledown, weather-beaten.

**battery** *n* artillery, assault, attack, barrage, beating, cannon, cannonry, emplacements, guns, mayhem, onslaught, progression, sequence, series, set, thrashing, violence.

**battle** *n* action, attack, campaign, clash, combat, conflict, contest, controversy, crusade, debate, disagreement, dispute, encounter, engagement, fight, fray, hostilities, row, skirmish, stour, strife, struggle, war, warfare.
*v* agitate, argue, campaign, clamour, combat, contend, contest, crusade, dispute, feud, fight, strive, struggle, war.

**battle-axe** *n* disciplinarian, harridan, martinet, Tartar, termagant, virago.

**battle-cry** *n* catchword, motto, slogan, war cry, war whoop, warsong, watchword.

**batty** *adj* barmy, bats, bonkers, cracked, crackers, crazy, daffy, daft, demented, dippy, dotty, eccentric, idiotic, insane, loony, lunatic, mad, nuts, nutty, odd, off one's rocker, peculiar, potty, queer, screwy, touched.
*antonym* sane.

**bauble** *n* bagatelle, flamfew, gewgaw, gimcrack, kickshaw, knick-knack, plaything, tinsel, toy, trifle, trinket.

**baulk, balk** *v* baffle, bar, boggle, check, counteract, defeat, demur, disconcert, dodge, evade, flinch, foil, forestall, frustrate, hesitate, hinder, jib, make difficulties, obstruct, prevent, recoil, refuse, resist, shirk, shrink, stall, thwart.

**bawd** *n* brothel-keeper, madam, panderess, pimp, procuress.

**bawdy** *adj* blue, coarse, dirty, erotic, gross, improper, indecent, indecorous, indelicate, lascivious, lecherous, lewd, libidinous, licentious, lustful, obscene, pornographic, prurient, ribald, risqué, rude, salacious, smutty, suggestive, vulgar.
*antonyms* chaste, clean.

**bawl** *v* bellow, blubber, call, caterwaul, clamour, cry, halloo, howl, roar, shout, sob, squall, vociferate, wail, waul, weep, yell.

**bay¹** *n* arm, bight, cove, embayment, gulf, inlet, voe.

**bay²** *n* alcove, booth, carrel, compartment, cubicle, embrasure, niche, nook, opening, recess, stall.

**bay³** *v* bark, bawl, bell, bellow, cry, holler, howl, roar.

**bayonet** *v* impale, knife, pierce, spear, stab, stick.

**bazaar** *n* agora, alcaicería, alcázar, bring-and-buy, exchange, fair, fête, market, market-place, mart, sale.

**be** *v* abide, arise, befall, breathe, come about, come to pass, continue, develop, dwell, endure, exist, happen, inhabit, inhere, last, live, obtain, occur, persist, prevail, remain, reside, stand, stay, survive, take place.

**beach** *n* coast, foreshore, lido, littoral, machair, margin, plage, sand, sands, seaboard, seashore, seaside, shingle, shore, strand, water's edge.

**beachcomber** *n* Autolycus, forager, loafer, loiterer, scavenger, scrounger, wayfarer.

**beacon** *n* beam, bonfire, fanal, flare, lighthouse, pharos, rocket, sign, signal, watch-fire.

**bead** *n* blob, bubble, dot, drop, droplet, glob, globule, pearl, pellet, pill, spherule.

**beak** *n* bill, bow, mandibles, neb, nib, nose, nozzle, proboscis, projection, prow, ram, rostrum, snout, stem.

**beaked** *adj* curved, hooked, pointed, rostrate, rostrated, sharp.

**beam** *n* arbor, bar, boom, girder, gleam, glimmer, glint, glow, joist, plank, radiation, rafter, ray, shaft, spar, stanchion, stream, support, timber, transom.
*v* broadcast, effulge, emit, fulgurate, glare, glimmer, glitter, glow, grin, laugh, radiate, shine, smile, transmit.

**beaming** *adj* beautiful, bright, brilliant, cheerful, effulgent, flashing, gleaming, glistening, glittering, glowing, grinning, happy, joyful, lambent, radiant, refulgent, scintillating, shining, smiling, sparkling, sunny.
*antonyms* lowering, sullen.

**bear¹** *v* abide, admit, allow, beget, bring, brook, carry, cherish, convey, endure, entertain, exhibit, hack, harbour, have, hold, maintain, move, permit, possess, put up with, shoulder, stomach, suffer, support, sustain, take, tolerate, tote, transport, undergo, uphold, weather, weigh upon.

**bear down** advance on, approach, attack, burden, close in, compress, converge on, encumber, near, oppress, press down, push, strain, weigh down.

**bear in mind** be cognisant of, be mindful of, beware, consider, heed, include, mind out for, note, remember.

**bear on** affect, appertain to, concern, connect with, involve, pertain to, refer to, relate to, touch on.

**bear oneself** acquit oneself, act, behave, comport oneself, demean oneself, deport oneself, perform.

**bear out** confirm, corroborate, demonstrate, endorse, justify, prove, substantiate, support, testify, uphold, vindicate.

**bear up** carry on, endure, keep one's pecker up, persevere, soldier on, suffer, withstand.

**bear with** be patient with, endure, forbear, make allowances for, put up with, suffer, tolerate.

**bear witness** attest, confirm, corroborate, demonstrate, depone, depose, evidence, evince, prove, show, testify, testify to, vouch for.

**bear$^2$** v breed, bring forth, develop, drop, engender, generate, give birth to, give up, produce, propagate, yield.

**bearable** adj acceptable, endurable, livable(-with), manageable, sufferable, supportable, sustainable, tolerable.

**beard** v brave, challenge, confront, dare, defy, face, oppose.

n beaver, excrement, face fungus, goatee, imperial, moustache, mutton chops, sideburns, tuft, vandyke, whiskers.

**bearded** adj awned, bewhiskered, bristly, bushy, hairy, hirsute, shaggy, tufted, unshaven, whiskered.

antonyms beardless, clean-shaven, smooth.

**bearer** n beneficiary, carrier, consignee, conveyor, courier, holder, messenger, payee, porter, possessor, post, runner, servant.

**bearing** n air, application, aspect, attitude, behaviour, carriage, comportment, connection, course, demeanour, deportment, direction, import, manner, mien, pertinence, poise, posture, presence, reference, relation, relevance, significance.

**bearings** n aim, course, direction, inclination, location, orientation, position, situation, tack, track, way, whereabouts.

**beast** n animal, ape, barbarian, brute, creature, devil, fiend, monster, pig, sadist, savage, swine.

**beastly** adj barbarous, bestial, brutal, brutish, coarse, cruel, depraved, disagreeable, foul, inhuman, mean, monstrous, nasty, repulsive, rotten, sadistic, savage, sensual, swinish, terrible, unpleasant, vile.

**beat$^1$** v bang, bash, baste, bastinade, bastinado, batter, belabour, bethump, bethwack, bless, bludgeon, bruise, buffet, cane, contuse, cudgel, curry, ding, drub, dunt, fashion, flog, forge, form, fustigate, hammer, hit, impinge, knobble, knock, knout, knubble, lam, lash, lay into, malleate, maul, mill, model, nubble, pelt, pound, punch, shape, slat, strap, strike, swipe, tan, thrash, thwack, trounce, vapulate, verberate, warm, welt, whale, wham, whip, work.

n blow, hit, lash, punch, shake, slap, strike, swing, thump.

adj exhausted, fatigued, jiggered, tired, wearied, worn out, zonked.

**beat it** go away, hop it, leave, scarper, scram, shoo, skedaddle, vamoose.

**beat up** assault, attack, batter, do over, duff over, duff up, fill in, hammer, knock about, knock around, thrash.

**beat$^2$** v best, conquer, defeat, excel, hammer, outdo, outrun, outstrip, overcome, overwhelm, slaughter, subdue, surpass, trounce, vanquish.

**beat$^3$** v flutter, palpitate, patter, pound, pulsate, pulse, quake, quiver, race, shake, throb, thump, tremble, vibrate.

n accent, cadence, flutter, measure, metre, palpitation, pulsation, pulse, rhyme, rhythm, stress, throb, time.

**beat$^4$** n circuit, course, journey, path, round, rounds, route, territory, way.

**beaten$^1$** adj baffled, cowed, defeated, disappointed, disheartened, frustrated, overcome, ruined, surpassed, thwarted, vanquished, worsted.

**beaten$^2$** adj fashioned, forged, formed, hammered, malleated, shaped, stamped, worked.

**beaten$^3$** adj blended, foamy, frothy, mixed, pounded, stirred, tenderised, whipped, whisked.

**beatific** adj angelic, blessed, blissful, divine, ecstatic, exalted, glorious, heavenly, joyful, rapturous, seraphic, serene, sublime.

**beatify** v bless, exalt, glorify, macarise, sanctify.

**beating** n belting, caning, chastisement, conquest, corporal punishment, defeat, downfall, dressing, drubbing, flogging, laldie, lamming, overthrow, rout, ruin, slapping, smacking, thrashing, vapulation, verberation, warming, whaling, whipping.

adj pounding, pulsatile, pulsating, pulsative, pulsatory, pulsing, racing, throbbing, thumping.

**beatitude** n beatification, blessedness, bliss, ecstasy, exaltation, felicity, happiness, holiness, joy, macarism, saintliness, sanctity.

**beau** n admirer, Adonis, boyfriend, cavalier, coxcomb, dandy, escort, fancy man, fiancé, fop, gallant, Jack-a-dandy, ladies' man, lover, popinjay, suitor, swain, sweetheart, swell.

**beautician** n beauty specialist, cosmetician, friseur, hairdresser, visagiste.

**beautiful** adj alluring, appealing, attractive, beau, beauteous, belle, charming, comely, delightful, exquisite, fair, fine, good-looking, gorgeous, graceful, handsome, lovely, pleasing, pulchritudinous, radiant, ravishing, stunning.

antonyms plain, ugly.

**beautify** v adorn, array, bedeck, bedizen, deck, decorate, embellish, enhance, garnish, gild, glamorise, grace, improve, ornament, tart up, titivate.

antonyms disfigure, spoil.

**beauty$^1$** n allure, attractiveness, bloom, charm, comeliness, elegance, excellence, exquisitness, fairness, glamour, grace, handsomeness, loveliness, pleasure, pulchritude, seemliness, symmetry.

antonym ugliness.

**beauty$^2$** n belle, charmer, corker, cracker, femme fatale, goddess, good-looker, knockout, lovely, siren, stunner, Venus.

antonym frump.

**becalmed** adj at a standstill, idle, motionless, still, stranded, stuck.

**because** conj as, by reason of, for, forasmuch, forwhy, in that, inasmuch as, on account of, owing to, since, thanks to.

**beckon** v allure, attract, bid, call, coax, decoy, draw, entice, gesticulate, gesture, invite, lure, motion, nod, pull, signal, summon, tempt, waft.

**become** v befit, behove, embellish, enhance, fit, flatter, grace, harmonise, ornament, set off, suit.

**becoming** adj appropriate, attractive, befitting, charming, comely, comme il faut, compatible, congruous, decent, decorous, enhancing, fit, fitting, flattering, graceful, maidenly, meet, neat, pretty, proper, seemly, suitable, tasteful, worthy.
antonym unbecoming.

**bed¹** n bedstead, berth, bunk, cot, cote, couch, divan, kip, mattress, pallet, palliasse, sack, the downy.

**bed²** n base, border, bottom, channel, foundation, garden, groundwork, layer, matrix, patch, plot, row, stratus, strip, substratum, wadi, watercourse.
v base, embed, establish, fix, found, ground, implant, insert, plant, settle.

**bedaub** v begrime, besmear, blotch, daub, smear, smirch, soil, spatter, splash, stain.

**bedclothes** n bedding, bed-linen, blankets, counterpanes, coverlets, covers, downies, eiderdowns, pillows, quilts, sheets.

**bedeck** v adorn, array, beautify, bedight, bedizen, decorate, embellish, festoon, garnish, ornament, trick out, trim.
antonym strip.

**bedevil** v afflict, annoy, besiege, confound, distress, fret, frustrate, harass, irk, irritate, pester, plague, tease, torment, torture, trouble, vex, worry.

**bedew** v dampen, drench, imbue, moisten, shower, soak, spray, sprinkle, water, wet.

**bedim** v becloud, bedarken, befog, cloak, cloud, darken, dim, fog, obscure, overcast, shade, shadow, veil.

**bedlam** n anarchy, babel, chaos, clamour, commotion, confusion, furore, hubbub, hullabaloo, madhouse, noise, pandemonium, tumult, turmoil, uproar.
antonym calm.

**bedraggled** adj dirty, dishevelled, disordered, messy, muddied, muddy, scruffy, slovenly, sodden, soiled, stained, sullied, unkempt, untidy.
antonym tidy.

**beef¹** n beefiness, brawn, bulk, flesh, fleshiness, heftiness, muscle, robustness, sinew, strength.

**beef²** n complaint, criticism, dispute, dissatisfaction, grievance, gripe, grouse, grumble, objection, protest.
v complain, criticise, gripe, grumble, moan, object.
antonym approve.

**beefy** adj brawny, bulky, burly, corpulent, fat, fleshy, heavy, hefty, hulking, muscular, plump, podgy, pudgy, rotund, stalwart, stocky, strapping, sturdy.
antonym slight.

**beetle** v dash, hurry, nip, run, rush, scamper, scoot, scurry, tear, zip.

**beetling** adj beetle, jutting, overhanging, pendent, poking, projecting, prominent, protruding.

**befall** v arrive, betide, chance, ensue, fall, follow, happen, materialise, occur, supervene, take place.

**befitting** adj appropriate, becoming, correct, decent, fit, fitting, meet, proper, right, seemly, suitable.
antonym unbecoming.

**before** adv ahead, earlier, formerly, in advance, in front, previously, sooner.
antonyms after, later.
prep ahead of, earlier than, in advance of, in anticipation of, in front of, in preparation for, previous to, prior to, sooner than.
conj in case, rather than.

**beforehand** adv already, before, earlier, in advance, preliminarily, previously, sooner.

**befoul** v bedung, begrime, besmirch, bespatter, defile, dirty, foul, muddy, pollute, soil, stain, sully, tarnish.

**befriend** v aid, assist, back, benefit, comfort, encourage, favour, help, patronise, stand by, succour, support, sustain, take a liking to, take under one's wing, uphold, welcome.
antonym neglect.

**befuddle** v baffle, bamboozle, befog, bewilder, confuse, daze, disorient, hocus, muddle, puzzle, stupefy.

**befuddled** adj baffled, bewildered, confused, dazed, fuddled, groggy, hazy, inebriated, intoxicated, muddled, woozy.
antonym lucid.

**beg** v beseech, cadge, crave, desire, entreat, fleech, implore, importune, petition, plead, pray, prog, request, require, schnorr, scrounge, shool, skelder, solicit, sponge on, supplicate, touch.
**beg the question** avoid, dodge, duck, equivocate, evade, hedge, shirk, shun, side-step, take for granted.

**beget** v breed, bring, cause, create, effect, engender, father, gender, generate, get, give rise to, occasion, procreate, produce, propagate, result in, sire, spawn.

**beggar¹** n Abraham-man, bankrupt, beadsman, besognio, bluegown, cadger, canter, craver, down-and-out, gaberlunzie, lazzarone, mendicant, palliard, pauper, schnorrer, scrounger, sponger, starveling, supplicant, toe-rag, toe-ragger, tramp, vagrant.

**beggar²** v baffle, challenge, defy, exceed, surpass, transcend.

**beggarly** adj abject, contemptible, despicable, destitute, impoverished, inadequate, indigent, low, meagre, mean, miserly, needy, niggardly, paltry, pathetic, penurious, pitiful, poor, poverty-stricken, stingy, vile, wretched.
antonyms affluent, generous.

**beggary** n bankruptcy, destitution, indigence, mendicancy, need, neediness, pauperism, penury, poverty, vagrancy, want, wretchedness.
*antonyms* affluence, plenty.

**begging** adj beseeching, entreating, imploratory, imploring, longing, pleading, precative, precatory, wistful.

n cadging, entreaty, mendicancy, mendicity, petitioning, prayers, scrounging, soliciting, sponging, supplication.

**begin** v activate, actuate, appear, arise, commence, crop up, dawn, emerge, happen, inaugurate, initiate, instigate, institute, introduce, originate, prepare, set about, set in, spring, start.
*antonyms* end, finish.

**beginner** n abecedarian, alphabetarian, amateur, apprentice, cheechako, cub, fledgling, freshman, greenhorn, initiate, Johnny-raw, learner, neophyte, novice, recruit, rookie, rooky, starter, student, tenderfoot, tiro, trainee.
*antonyms* expert, old hand, veteran.

**beginning** n birth, commencement, embryo, establishment, fons et origo, fountainhead, germ, inauguration, inception, inchoation, initiation, introduction, onset, opening, origin, outset, preface, prelude, prime, rise, root, rudiments, seed, source, start, starting point.
*antonyms* end, finish.

adj early, elementary, inaugural, inauguratory, inceptive, inchoative, incipient, initial, introductory, nascent, primal, primary, primeval.

**begrudge** v covet, envy, grudge, mind, resent, stint.
*antonym* allow.

**beguile** v amuse, charm, cheat, cheer, cozen, deceive, delight, delude, distract, divert, dupe, engross, entertain, fool, hoodwink, mislead, occupy, pass, solace, trick, wile.

**beguiling** adj alluring, appealing, attractive, bewitching, captivating, charming, diverting, enchanting, entertaining, enticing, interesting, intriguing.
*antonyms* offensive, repulsive.

**behalf** n account, advantage, authority, benefit, defence, good, interest, name, part, profit, sake, side, support.

**behave** v acquit, act, bear, comport, conduct, demean, deport, function, operate, perform, react, respond, run, work.

**behaviour** n action, actions, bearing, carriage, comportment, conduct, dealings, demeanour, deportment, doings, functioning, habits, manner, manners, operation, performance, reaction, response, ways.

**behead** v decapitate, decollate, execute, guillotine, unhead.

**behest** n authority, bidding, charge, command, commandment, decree, dictate, direction, fiat, injunction, instruction, mandate, order, ordinance, precept, wish.

**behind** prep after, backing, causing, following, for, initiating, instigating, later than, responsible for, supporting.

adv after, afterwards, behindhand, en arrière, following, in arrears, in debt, in the wake of, next, overdue, subsequently.

n backside, bottom, butt, buttocks, derrière, posterior, prat, rear, rump, seat, sit-upon, tail.

**behind one's back** covertly, deceitfully, secretly, sneakily, sub rosa, surreptitiously, treacherously.

**behind the times** antiquated, dated, démodé, fogram, obsolete, old hat, old-fashioned, out of date, outdated, outmoded, passé, square.

**behind-hand** adj backward, dilatory, ill-provided, lag, late, remiss, slow, tardy.
*antonym* provident.

**behold** v consider, contemplate, descry, discern, espy, eye, look at, note, observe, perceive, regard, scan, survey, view, watch, witness.

interj ecce, lo, look, mark, observe, see, voici, voilà, watch.

**beholden** adj bound, grateful, indebted, obligated, obliged, owing, thankful.

**behove** v advance, be to one's advantage, befit, benefit, beseem, profit.

**beige** adj biscuit, buff, café au lait, camel, cinnamon, coffee, cream, ecru, fawn, greige, khaki, mushroom, neutral, oatmeal, sand, tan.

**being**[1] n actuality, animation, entity, essence, existence, haecceity, life, living, nature, quiddity, reality, soul, spirit, substance.

**being**[2] n animal, beast, body, creature, human being, individual, mortal, sentient, thing.

**belabour** v attack, bash, batter, beat, belt, berate, castigate, censure, chastise, criticise, flay, flog, lambast, lay into, thrash, whip.

**belated** adj behind-hand, delayed, late, overdue, retarded, tardy, unpunctual.
*antonyms* punctual, timely.

**belch** v burp, discharge, disgorge, emit, eruct, eructate, erupt, gush, hiccup, spew, vent.

n burp, eructation, eruption, hiccup.

**beleaguered** adj badgered, beset, besieged, bothered, harassed, hedged about, hedged in, persecuted, plagued, surrounded, vexed, worried.

**belie** v conceal, confute, contradict, deceive, deny, disguise, disprove, falsify, gainsay, mislead, misrepresent, negate, refute, repudiate, run counter to, understate.
*antonym* attest.

**belief** n assurance, confidence, conviction, credence, credit, credo, creed, doctrine, dogma, expectation, faith, feeling, ideology, impression, intuition, ism, judgement, notion, opinion, persuasion, presumption, principle, principles, reliance, sureness, surety, tenet, theory, trust, view.
*antonym* disbelief.

**believable** adj acceptable, authentic, authoritative, conceivable, credible, creditable, imaginable, likely, plausible, possible, probable, reliable, thinkable, trustworthy.
*antonym* unconvincing.

**believe** v accept, assume, be under the impression, conjecture, consider, count on, credit, deem, depend on, gather, guess, hold, imagine, judge, maintain, postulate, presume, reckon, rely on, speculate, suppose, swallow, swear by, think, trust, wear.

*antonym* disbelieve.

**believer** n adherent, catechumen, convert, devotee, disciple, follower, proselyte, supporter, upholder, votary, zealot.

*antonyms* apostate, sceptic, unbeliever.

**belittle** v decry, deprecate, depreciate, deride, derogate, detract, diminish, dismiss, disparage, downgrade, lessen, minimise, ridicule, run down, scorn, underestimate, underrate, undervalue, vilipend.

*antonym* exaggerate.

**bellicose** adj aggressive, antagonistic, argumentative, bare-knuckle, belligerent, combative, contentious, defiant, hawkish, hostile, jingoistic, militant, militaristic, provocative, pugnacious, quarrelsome, sabre-rattling, warlike, war-loving, warmongering.

*antonym* peacable.

**belligerence** n aggression, aggressiveness, animosity, antagonism, bellicosity, combativeness, contentiousness, pugnacity, quarrelsomeness, unfriendliness, violence.

*antonym* complaisance.

**belligerent** adj aggressive, antagonistic, argumentative, bellicose, bullying, combative, contentious, forceful, militant, pugnacious, quarrelsome, violent, warlike, warring.

*antonym* peaceable.

**bellow** v bell, call, clamour, cry, howl, roar, scream, shout, shriek, troat, yell.

**belly** n abdomen, bowels, bread-basket, corporation, gut, guts, insides, paunch, pot, sound-board, stomach, tummy, uterus, venter, vitals, womb.

v bag, balloon, billow, blow up, bulge, dilate, distend, expand, fill out, inflate, swell.

*antonyms* deflate, shrink.

**belong** v attach to, be connected with, be part of, be relevant to, be tied to, fit, go with, inhere, link up with, pertain to, relate to, tie up with.

**belonging** n acceptance, affinity, association, attachment, closeness, compatibility, fellow-feeling, fellowship, inclusion, kinship, link, linkage, loyalty, rapport, relationship.

*antonym* antipathy.

**belonging to** affiliated to, associated with, essential to, held by, included in, inherent in, intrinsic in, native to, owned by.

*antonym* alien to.

**belongings** n accoutrements, chattels, effects, gear, goods, impedimenta, paraphernalia, possessions, stuff, things, traps.

**beloved** adj admired, adored, cherished, darling, dear, dearest, favourite, loved, pet, precious, prized, revered, sweet, treasured.

n adored, darling, dear, dearest, favourite, inamorata, inamorato, lover, pet, precious, sweet, sweetheart.

**below** adv beneath, down, infra, lower, lower down, under, underneath.

*prep* inferior to, lesser than, 'neath, subject to, subordinate to, under, underneath, unworthy of.

**below par** below average, imperfect, inferior, lacking, not oneself, off, off-colour, off-form, poor, poorly, second-rate, substandard, under the weather, unfit, unhealthy, wanting.

**below the belt** cowardly, dirty, dishonest, foul, unfair, unjust, unscrupulous, unsporting, unsportsmanlike.

**belt[1]** n area, band, ceinture, cincture, cingulum, cummerbund, district, girdle, girth, layer, region, sash, strait, stretch, strip, swathe, tract, waistband, zone, zonule, zonulet.

v circle, encircle, girdle, ring, surround.

**belt up** be quiet, cut it out, leave it out, put a sock in, shut one's mouth, shut up, stow it.

**belt[2]** v bolt, career, charge, dash, hurry, race, rush, speed.

**bemoan** v bewail, deplore, grieve for, lament, mourn, regret, rue, sigh for, sorrow over, weep for.

*antonym* gloat.

**bemuse** v amaze, bewilder, confuse, daze, distract, muddle, overwhelm, perplex, pixillate, puzzle, stun.

*antonyms* enlighten, illuminate.

**bemused** adj absent-minded, befuddled, bewildered, confused, dazed, distracted, engrossed, fuddled, half-drunk, muddled, mused, perplexed, pixillated, stunned, stupefied, tipsy.

*antonyms* clear, clear-headed, lucid.

**bench[1]** n bleachers, board, counter, form, ledge, pew, seat, settle, stall, table, terrace, tier, work-bench, work-table.

**bench[2]** n court, courtroom, judge, judges, judicature, judiciary, magistrate, magistrates, tribunal.

**benchmark** n criterion, example, level, model, norm, reference, reference-point, standard, touchstone, yardstick.

**bend** v aim, bow, brace, buckle, compel, constrain, contort, couch, crankle, crimp, crouch, curve, deflect, direct, dispose, diverge, dog-leg, embow, fasten, flex, incline, incurvate, incurve, influence, lean, mould, nerve, persuade, shape, stoop, string, subdue, submit, sway, swerve, turn, twist, veer, warp, yield.

n angle, arc, bight, bought, bow, corner, crank, crook, curvature, curve, dog-leg, elbow, flexure, genu, hook, incurvation, incurvature, incurve, inflexure, loop, turn, twist, zigzag.

**beneath** adv below, lower, lower down, under, underneath.

*prep* below, inferior to, infra dig(nitatem), lower than, 'neath, subject to, subordinate to, unbefitting, under, underneath, unworthy of.

**benediction** *n* beatitude, Benedictus, benison, blessing, consecration, favour, grace, invocation, orison, prayer, thanksgiving.

*antonyms* anathema, curse, execration.

**benefaction** *n* aid, alms-giving, backing, beneficence, benevolence, bequest, boon, bounty, charity, contribution, donation, endowment, generosity, gift, grant, gratuity, help, legacy, liberality, munificence, offering, philanthropy, present, sponsorship, subsidy.

**benefactor** *n* angel, backer, contributor, donor, endower, friend, helper, patron, philanthropist, promoter, provider, sponsor, subscriber, subsidiser, supporter, well-wisher.

*antonyms* opponent, persecutor.

**beneficence** *n* aid, altruism, benefaction, benevolence, bestowal, bounty, charity, compassion, donation, generosity, gift, goodness, helpfulness, kindness, largess, largition, liberality, love, munificence, present, relief, succour, unselfishness, virtue.

*antonym* meanness.

**beneficent** *adj* altruistic, benevolent, benign, bounteous, bountiful, charitable, compassionate, generous, helpful, kind, liberal, munificent, unselfish.

*antonym* mean.

**beneficial** *adj* advantageous, benign, benignant, edifying, favourable, gainful, healthful, helpful, improving, nourishing, nutritious, profitable, restorative, rewarding, salubrious, salutary, serviceable, useful, valuable, wholesome.

*antonym* harmful.

**beneficiary** *n* assignee, devisee, donee, fructuary, heir, heiress, heritor, inheritor, legatee, payee, receiver, recipient, successor.

**benefit** *n* advantage, aid, asset, assistance, avail, betterment, blessing, boon, favour, gain, good, help, interest, plus, profit, service, use, weal, welfare.

*antonym* harm.

*v* advance, advantage, aid, ameliorate, amend, assist, avail, better, enhance, further, improve, profit, promote, serve.

*antonyms* harm, hinder, undermine.

**benefits** *n* advantages, bonuses, extras, freebies, loaves and fishes, perks, perquisites, pluses.

*antonym* disadvantages.

**benevolence** *n* altruism, benignity, bounty, charity, compassion, fellow-feeling, generosity, goodness, goodwill, humanity, kind-heartedness, kindliness, kindness, munificence, sympathy.

*antonym* meanness.

**benevolent** *adj* altruistic, beneficent, benign, bounteous, bountiful, caring, charitable, compassionate, considerate, generous, good-will, Grandisonian, humane, humanitarian, kind, kind-hearted, kindly, liberal, loving, philanthropic, solicitous, well-disposed.

*antonym* mean.

**benign** *adj* advantageous, amiable, auspicious, balmy, benefic, beneficent, beneficial,

benevolent, complaisant, curable, curative, encouraging, favourable, friendly, generous, genial, gentle, good, gracious, harmless, healthful, kind, kindly, liberal, lucky, mild, obliging, propitious, refreshing, restorative, salubrious, salutary, sympathetic, temperate, warm, wholesome.

*antonyms* harmful, hostile, malign, malignant.

**bent** *adj* angled, arched, bowed, coudé, criminal, crooked, curved, dishonest, doubled, falcate, folded, homosexual, hunched, inbent, inflexed, retorted, retroverted, stolen, stooped, twisted, untrustworthy.

*antonym* straight.

*n* ability, aptitude, capacity, facility, faculty, flair, forte, gift, inclination, knack, leaning, penchant, preference, proclivity, propensity, talent, tendency.

**bent on** determined, disposed, fixed, heading for, inclined, insistent, resolved, set on.

**benumbed** *adj* anaesthetised, dazed, deadened, desensitised, dull, frozen, immobilised, insensible, insensitive, numb, numbed, paralysed, stunned, stupefied, unfeeling, unresponsive.

**bequeath** *v* assign, bestow, commit, demise, devise, endow, entrust, gift, give, grant, hand down, impart, pass on, settle, transmit, will.

**bequest** *n* bequeathal, bequeathment, bestowal, devisal, devise, donation, dower, endowment, estate, gift, heritage, inheritance, legacy, patrimony, settlement, trust.

**berate** *v* castigate, censure, chastise, chide, criticise, flyte, jump down the throat of, rail at, rate, rebuke, reprimand, reproach, reprove, revile, scold, tell off, upbraid, vituperate.

*antonym* praise.

**bereave** *v* afflict, deprive, despoil, dispossess, divest, orphan, rob, strip, widow.

**bereavement** *n* death, defiliation, deprivation, despoliation, dispossession, loss.

*antonyms* addition, increase.

**bereft** *adj* denuded, deprived, despoiled, destitute, devoid, lacking, minus, robbed, shorn, stripped, wanting.

**berserk** *adj* amok, crazy, demented, deranged, enraged, frantic, frenetic, frenzied, furious, insane, mad, maniacal, manic, rabid, raging, raving, uncontrollable, violent, wild.

*antonyms* calm, sane.

**berth** *n* anchorage, bed, billet, bunk, cot, dock, employment, hammock, harbour, harbourage, haven, job, landfall, pier, port, position, post, quay, shelter, sinecure, situation, slip, wharf.

*v* anchor, dock, drop anchor, land, moor, tie up.

*antonym* weigh anchor.

**beseech** *v* adjure, ask, beg, call on, conjure, crave, desire, entreat, implore, importune, obsecrate, petition, plead, pray, solicit, sue, supplicate.

**beset** *v* assail, attack, badger, bamboozle, bedevil, besiege, embarrass, encircle, enclose, encompass, entangle, environ, faze, harass, hassle, hem in, perplex, pester, plague, surround.

**besetting** adj compulsive, constant, dominant, habitual, harassing, inveterate, irresistible, obsessive, persistent, prevalent, recurring, troublesome, uncontrollable.

**beside** prep abreast of, abutting on, adjacent, bordering on, close to, near, neighbouring, next door to, next to, overlooking, upsides with.

**beside oneself** berserk, crazed, delirious, demented, deranged, distracted, distraught, frantic, frenetic, frenzied, furious, insane, mad, unbalanced, unhinged.

**beside the point** extraneous, immaterial, inapplicable, incidental, inconsequential, irrelevant, pointless, unimportant, unrelated.

*antonym* relevant.

**besides** adv additionally, also, as well, extra, further, furthermore, in addition, into the bargain, moreover, otherwise, to boot, too, withal.

prep apart from, in addition to, other than, over and above.

**besiege** v assail, badger, belay, beleaguer, beset, blockade, bother, confine, dun, encircle, encompass, environ, harass, harry, hound, importune, nag, pester, plague, surround, trouble.

**besmirch** v begrime, bespatter, daub, defame, defile, dirty, dishonour, muddy, slander, smear, soil, spatter, stain, sully, tarnish.

*antonym* enhance.

**besotted** adj befuddled, bewitched, confused, doting, drunk, foolish, hypnotised, inebriated, infatuated, intoxicated, muddled, obsessed, smitten, stupefied, witless.

*antonyms* disenchanted, indifferent, sober.

**bespeak** v attest, betoken, demonstrate, denote, display, evidence, evince, exhibit, forebode, foretell, imply, indicate, predict, proclaim, reveal, show, signify, suggest, testify to.

**best** adj advantageous, apt, correct, excellent, finest, first, first-class, first-rate, foremost, greatest, highest, incomparable, largest, leading, makeless, matchless, nonpareil, optimal, optimum, outstanding, perfect, pre-eminent, preferable, principal, right, superlative, supreme, transcendent, unequalled, unsurpassed.

*antonym* worst.

adv excellently, exceptionally, extremely, greatly, superlatively, surpassingly.

*antonym* worst.

n choice, cream, crème de la crème, élite, favourite, finest, first, flower, hardest, nonpareil, pick, prime, the tops, top, utmost.

*antonym* worst.

v beat, conquer, defeat, get the better of, have the laugh of, lick, outclass, outdo, outwit, surpass, thrash, trounce, vanquish, worst.

**bestial** adj animal, barbaric, barbarous, beastly, brutal, brutish, carnal, degraded, depraved, feral, gross, inhuman, savage, sensual, sordid, subhuman, swinish, vile.

*antonyms* civilised, humane.

**bestir** v activate, actuate, animate, arouse, awaken, energise, exert, galvanise, incite, motivate, rouse, stimulate.

*antonyms* calm, lull, quell.

**bestow** v accord, allot, apportion, award, bequeath, commit, confer, donate, dower, endow, entrust, give, grant, impart, lavish, lend, present, transmit, wreak.

*antonym* deprive.

**bestowal** n benefaction, bequeathal, bequeathment, conferring, distribution, donation, gift, giving, imparting, largition, presentation, transmission.

**bestride** v bestraddle, command, dominate, horse, overshadow, sit astride, stand astride, straddle.

**bet** n accumulator, ante, bid, flutter, gamble, hazard, pledge, risk, speculation, stake, venture, wager.

v ante, bid, chance, gamble, hazard, lay, pledge, punt, risk, speculate, stake, venture, wager.

**bête noire** abomination, anathema, aversion, bane, bogey, bugbear, curse, pet hate.

*antonym* favourite.

**betide** v bechance, befall, chance, develop, ensue, hap, happen, occur, overtake, supervene.

**betimes** adv early, expeditiously, punctually, seasonably, soon, speedily, timeously.

*antonym* late.

**betoken** v augur, bespeak, bode, declare, denote, evidence, forebode, foreshow, import, indicate, manifest, mark, portend, presage, prognosticate, promise, represent, signify, suggest.

**betray** v abandon, beguile, corrupt, deceive, delude, desert, disclose, discover, divulge, dob in, double-cross, dupe, ensnare, entrap, evince, expose, forsake, give away, grass, inform on, jilt, manifest, mislead, reveal, seduce, sell, sell down the river, sell out, shop, show, tell, turn Queen's (King's) evidence, undo.

*antonyms* defend, fulfil, protect.

**betrayal** n deception, disclosure, discovery, disloyalty, divulgence, double-dealing, duplicity, exposure, falseness, Judas-kiss, perfidy, rattery, ratting, revelation, sell-out, treachery, treason, trickery, unfaithfulness.

*antonyms* loyalty, protection.

**betrayer** n apostate, conspirator, , deceiver, double-crosser, grass, informer, renegade, supergrass, traitor.

*antonyms* protector, supporter.

**betroth** v affiance, contract, espouse, plight, plight one's troth, promise.

**betrothal** n engagement, espousal, fiançailles, handfast, plight, promise, troth, vow.

**better** adj bigger, cured, finer, fitter, greater, healthier, improving, larger, longer, on the mend, preferable, progressing, recovered, recovering, restored, stronger, superior, surpassing, worthier.

*antonym* worse.

*v* advance, ameliorate, amend, beat, cap, correct, enhance, exceed, excel, forward, further, go one further than, improve, improve on, increase, meliorate, mend, outdo, outstrip, overtake, overtop, promote, raise, rectify, redress, reform, strengthen, surpass, top, transcend.

*antonyms* deteriorate, worsen.

**betterment** *n* advancement, amelioration, edification, enhancement, furtherance, improvement, melioration.

*antonyms* deterioration, impairment.

**betterness** *n* advantage, ascendancy, meliority, preferability, superiority, transcendancy.

**between** *prep* amidst, among, amongst, betwixt, inter-, mid.

**between ourselves** entre nous, in confidence, in secret, privately, within these four walls.

**bevel** *n* angle, basil, bezel, bias, cant, chamfer, diagonal, mitre, oblique, slant, slope.

*v* bias, cant, chamfer, mitre, slant.

**beverage** *n* bevvy, draught, drink, libation, liquid, liquor, poison, potable, potation.

**bevy** *n* band, bunch, collection, company, crowd, flock, gaggle, gathering, group, pack, phalanx, throng, troupe.

**bewail** *v* bemoan, cry over, deplore, greet, grieve for, keen, lament, moan, mourn, regret, repent, rue, sigh over, sorrow over.

*antonyms* gloat, glory, vaunt.

**beware** *v* avoid, give a wide berth to, guard against, heed, look out, mind, shun, steer clear of, take heed, watch out.

*antonym* court.

*interj* fore, nix.

**bewilder** *v* baffle, bamboozle, befuddle, bemuse, buffalo, confound, confuse, daze, disconcert, disorient, fuddle, maze, muddle, mystify, perplex, puzzle, stupefy, tie in knots.

**bewildered** *adj* awed, baffled, bamboozled, bemused, confused, désorienté, disconcerted, disoriented, dizzy, giddy, muddled, mystified, nonplussed, perplexed, pixillated, pixy-led, puzzled, stunned, surprised, uncertain.

*antonyms* collected, unperturbed.

**bewilderment** *n* awe, confusion, daze, disconcertion, disorientation, mizmaze, mystification, perplexity, puzzledom, puzzlement, stupefaction, surprise, uncertainty.

*antonyms* composure, confidence.

**bewitch** *v* allure, attract, beguile, captivate, charm, elf-shoot, enchant, enrapture, ensorcell, entrance, fascinate, forspeak, hex, hoodoo, hypnotise, jinx, obsess, possess, spellbind, voodoo, witch.

**bewitched** *adj* charmed, elf-shot, enchanted, enthralled, entranced, fascinated, hexed, jinxed, mesmerised, obsessed, possessed, spellbound, transfixed, transformed.

*antonym* disenchanted.

**bewitching** *adj* beguiling, charming, enchanting, entrancing, fascinating, glamorous, hypnotic, intriguing, seductive, tantalising, witching.

*antonym* repellent.

**beyond** *prep* above, across, apart from, away from, before, further than, out of range, out of reach of, over, past, remote from, superior to, yonder.

**beyond price** inestimable, invaluable, irreplaceable, precious, priceless.

**bias** *n* angle, bent, bigotry, distortion, editorialisation, favouritism, inclination, intolerance, leaning, one-sidedness, parti pris, partiality, penchant, predilection, predisposition, prejudice, proclivity, proneness, propensity, slant, tendency, tendentiousness, turn, unfairness, viewiness.

*antonyms* fairness, impartiality.

*v* angle, distort, earwig, editorialise, influence, jaundice, load, load the dice, predispose, prejudice, slant, sway, twist, warp, weight.

**biased** *adj* angled, bigoted, blinkered, distorted, embittered, jaundiced, loaded, one-sided, partial, predisposed, prejudiced, slanted, swayed, tendentious, twisted, unfair, verkrampte, viewy, warped, weighted.

*antonyms* fair, impartial.

**bibulous** *adj* alcoholic, crapulous, dipsomaniac, drunken, inebriate, intemperate, sottish, thirsty, tipsy.

*antonyms* sober, temperate.

**bicker** *v* altercate, argue, clash, disagree, dispute, feud, fight, quarrel, row, scrap, spar, squabble, wrangle.

*antonym* agree.

**bicycle** *n* bike, boneshaker, cycle, dandy-horse, draisine, ordinary, penny-farthing, push-bike, racer, safety bicycle, tandem, two-wheeler, velocipede.

**bid** *v* ask, call, charge, command, desire, direct, enjoin, greet, instruct, invite, offer, proclaim, propose, request, require, say, solicit, summon, tell, wish.

*n* advance, amount, ante, attempt, crack, effort, endeavour, go, offer, price, proposal, proposition, submission, sum, tender, try, venture.

**biddable** *adj* acquiescent, agreeable, amenable, complaisant, co-operative, docile, obedient, responsive, teachable, tractable.

*antonym* recalcitrant.

**bidding** *n* behest, call, charge, command, demand, dictate, direction, injunction, instruction, invitation, order, request, requirement, summons.

**big** *adj* adult, altruistic, beefy, benevolent, boastful, bombastic, bulky, burly, buxom, colossal, considerable, corpulent, elder, elephantine, eminent, enormous, extensive, gargantuan, generous, gigantic, gracious, great, grown, grown-up, heroic, huge, hulking, immense, important, influential, large, leading, lofty, magnanimous, main, mammoth, man-sized, massive, mature, momentous, noble, paramount, plonking, ponderous, powerful, prime, principal, prodigious, prominent, serious, significant, sizable, skelping, spacious, stout, substantial, titanic, tolerant, unselfish, valuable, vast, voluminous, weighty.

*antonyms* little, small.

**big shot** big noise, bigwig, celebrity, dignitary, heavyweight, mogul, mugwump, nob, notability, notable, panjandrum, personage, somebody, VIP.

*antonym* nonentity.

**bigamy** *n* diandry.

**bigot** *n* chauvinist, dogmatist, fanatic, racist, religionist, sectarian, sexist, verkrampte, zealot.

*antonyms* humanitarian, liberal.

**bigoted** *adj* biased, blinkered, chauvinist, closed, dogmatic, illiberal, intolerant, narrow, narrow-minded, obstinate, opinionated, prejudiced, sectarian, twisted, verkrampte, warped.

*antonyms* broad-minded, enlightened, liberal.

**bigotry** *n* bias, chauvinism, discrimination, dogmatism, fanaticism, ignorance, illiberality, injustice, intolerance, jingoism, mindlessness, narrow-mindedness, prejudice, racialism, racism, religionism, sectarianism, sexism, unfairness.

**bigwig** *n* big gun, big noise, big shot, celebrity, dignitary, heavyweight, huzoor, mogul, mugwump, nabob, nob, notability, notable, panjandrum, personage, somebody, VIP.

*antonym* nobody.

**bile** *n* anger, bitterness, choler, gall, ill-humour, irascibility, irritability, peevishness, rancour, spleen, testiness.

**bilingual** *adj* diglot.

**bilious** *adj* choleric, crabby, cross, crotchety, grouchy, grumpy, irritable, liverish, nauseated, out of sorts, peevish, queasy, sick, sickly, testy.

**bilk** *v* balk, bamboozle, cheat, con, cozen, deceive, defraud, do, do out of, fleece, foil, rook, sting, swindle, thwart, trick.

**bill**[1] *n* account, advertisement, battels, broadsheet, broadside, bulletin, card, catalogue, charges, chit, circular, greenback, handbill, hand-out, inventory, invoice, leaflet, legislation, list, listing, measure, note, notice, placard, playbill, poster, programme, proposal, reckoning, roster, schedule, score, sheet, statement, syllabus, tab, tally.

*v* advertise, announce, charge, debit, invoice, list, post, reckon, record.

**bill**[2] *n* beak, mandible, neb, nib, rostrum.

**billet** *n* accommodation, barracks, berth, employment, housing, lodgement, lodging, occupation, post, quarterage, quarters.

*v* accommodate, berth, lodge, quarter, station.

**billow** *v* balloon, belly, expand, fill out, heave, puff out, roll, seethe, spread, surge, swell, undulate.

**billowy** *adj* billowing, heaving, rippling, rolling, surging, swelling, swirling, tossing, undulating, waving.

**bind** *v* astrict, astringe, attach, bandage, border, cinch, clamp, colligate, compel, complain, confine, constipate, constrain, cover, detain, dress, edge, encase, engage, fasten, finish, force, glue, hamper, harden, hinder, hitch, indenture, lash, necessitate, obligate, oblige, prescribe, require, restrain, restrict, rope, seal, secure, stick, strap, swathe, thirl, tie, trim, truss, wrap.

*n* bore, difficulty, dilemma, embarrassment, hole, impasse, nuisance, predicament, quandary.

**binding** *adj* compulsory, conclusive, imperative, indissoluble, irrevocable, mandatory, necessary, obligatory, permanent, requisite, strict, unalterable, unbreakable.

*n* bandage, border, covering, deligation, edging, stricture, syndesis, tape, trimming, wrapping.

**binge** *n* banquet, beano, bender, blind, bout, do, feast, fling, guzzle, jag, orgy, spree.

*antonym* fast.

**biographical** *adj* prosopographical.

**biography** *n* account, adventures, autobiography, biopic, curriculum vitae, exposé, fortunes, history, life, life story, memoir, memoirs, prosopography, recollections, record.

**bird-like** *adj* aquiline, avian, aviform, avine, hawk-like, ornithoid, volucrine.

**birdwatcher** *n* birder, twitcher.

**birth** *n* ancestry, background, beginning, birthright, blood, breeding, childbirth, delivery, derivation, descent, emergence, extraction, family, fell, genealogy, genesis, geniture, line, lineage, nativity, nobility, origin, parentage, parturition, pedigree, race, rise, source, stirps, stock, strain.

**birthday** *n* anniversary, day of birth, (dies) natalis, natalitium.

*adj* anniversary, genethliac, genethliacal, natal, natalitial.

**birthmark** *n* angioma, mole, mother's mark, motherspot, naevus, port wine stain.

**birthplace** *n* fount, incunabula, native country, native town, place of origin, provenance, roots, source.

**biscuit** *n* cake, cookie, cracker, hardtack, rusk, wafer.

**bisect** *v* bifurcate, cross, divide, fork, furcate, halve, intersect, separate, split.

**bisexual** *adj* androgynous, epicene, gynandromorphic, gynandromorphous, gynandrous, hermaphrodite, hermaphroditic, monoclinous.

*antonyms* heterosexual, homosexual.

**bishop** *n* abba, archbishop, diocesan, exarch, metropolitan, patriarch, prelate, primate, suffragan.

**bit** *n* atom, chip, crumb, fragment, grain, instant, iota, jiffy, jot, mammock, minute, mite, moment, morsel, part, period, piece, scrap, second, segment, sippet, slice, snippet, speck, spell, tick, time, tittle, while, whit.

**bit by bit** gradatim, gradually, insidiously, little by little, piecemeal, seriatim, step by step.

*antonym* wholesale.

**bitch** *n* back-biter, cat, doggess, fury, harridan, shrew, termagant, virago, vixen.

**bitchy** *adj* back-biting, catty, cruel, malicious, mean, nasty, poisonous, snide, spiteful, venomous, vicious, vindictive, vixenish, vixenly, waspish.

*antonym* kind.

**bite** *v* burn, champ, chew, clamp, corrode, crunch, crush, cut, gnaw, knap, masticate, nibble, nip, pierce, pinch, rend, seize, smart, snap, sting, tear, tingle, wound.

*n* edge, food, grip, kick, morsel, morsure, mouthful, nip, piece, pinch, piquancy, prick, punch, pungency, refreshment, smarting, snack, spice, sting, taste, wound.

**bite the dust** crumple, die, drop, drop dead, expire, fall, perish.

**biting** *adj* astringent, bitter, blighting, caustic, cold, cutting, cynical, freezing, harsh, hurtful, incisive, mordant, nipping, penetrating, piercing, raw, sarcastic, scathing, severe, sharp, stinging, tart, trenchant, withering.

*antonyms* bland, mild.

**bitter** *adj* acerb, acerbic, acid, acrid, acrimonious, astringent, begrudging, biting, calamitous, crabbed, cruel, cynical, dire, distressing, embittered, fierce, freezing, galling, grievous, harsh, hateful, heartbreaking, hostile, intense, ironic, jaundiced, merciless, morose, odious, painful, poignant, rancorous, raw, resentful, ruthless, sarcastic, savage, severe, sharp, sore, sour, stinging, sullen, tart, unsweetened, vexatious, vinegary, waspish.

*antonyms* contented, genial, sweet.

**bitterness** *n* acerbity, acidity, acrimoniousness, animosity, asperity, astringency, causticity, grudge, hostility, irony, mordancy, pique, rancour, resentment, sarcasm, sharpness, sourness, tartness, venom, virulence, wormwood.

*antonyms* contentment, geniality, sweetness.

**bizarre** *adj* abnormal, comical, curious, deviant, eccentric, extraordinary, extravagant, fantastic, freakish, grotesque, ludicrous, odd, off-beat, outlandish, outré, peculiar, Pythonesque, quaint, queer, ridiculous, strange, unusual, way-out, weird.

*antonym* normal.

**bizarreness** *n* bizarrerie, curiousness, eccentricity, freakishness, grotesqueness, grotesquerie, oddity, oddness, outlandishness, queerness, singularity, strangeness, weirdness.

*antonym* normality.

**blab** *v* blurt, disclose, divulge, gossip, leak, reveal, squeal, tattle, tell.

*antonyms* hide, hush up.

**blabber** *v* blather, blether, chatter, chinwag, earbash, gab, gabble, jabber, natter, prattle, whitter.

**black** *adj* angry, atrocious, bad, begrimed, coal-black, collied, dark, darksome, depressing, dingy, dirty, dismal, doleful, dusky, ebony, evil, filthy, funereal, furious, gloomy, grim, grimy, grubby, hopeless, horrible, hostile, inky, jet, jet-black, jetty, lugubrious, menacing, moonless, morel, mournful, murky, nefarious, ominous, overcast, pitchy, raven, resentful, sable, sad, sloe, soiled, sombre, sooty, stained, starless, Stygian, sullen, swarthy, threatening, thunderous, villainous, wicked.

*v* ban, bar, blacklist, boycott, taboo.

**black eye** keeker, mouse, shiner.

**black magic** black art, demonolatry, devil-worship, diabolism, hoodoo, necromancy, sorcery, voodoo, witchcraft, wizardry.

**black out** censor, collapse, conceal, cover up, darken, eclipse, extinguish, faint, flake out, gag, keel over, obfuscate, obliterate, pass out, shade, suppress, swoon, withhold.

**black sheep** disgrace, drop-out, ne'er-do-well, outcast, pariah, prodigal, reject, renegade, reprobate, wastrel.

*antonym* pride.

**blackball** *v* ban, bar, blacklist, debar, exclude, expel, ostracise, oust, pip, reject, repudiate, snub, veto.

**blacken** *v* befoul, begrime, besmirch, calumniate, cloud, colly, darken, decry, defame, defile, denigrate, detract, dishonour, malign, nigrify, revile, slander, smear, smirch, smudge, soil, stain, sully, taint, tarnish, traduce, vilify.

*antonyms* enhance, praise.

**blackguard** *n* bleeder, blighter, bounder, cur, devil, knave, miscreant, rascal, reprobate, rogue, rotter, scoundrel, stinker, swine, villain, wretch.

**blackhead** *n* comedo.

**blackleg** *n* fink, strike-breaker.

**blacklist** *v* ban, bar, blackball, boycott, debar, disallow, exclude, expel, ostracise, preclude, proscribe, reject, repudiate, snub, taboo, veto.

*antonyms* accept, allow.

**blackmail** *n* blood-sucking, chantage, exaction, extortion, hush money, intimidation, milking, pay-off, protection, ransom.

*v* bleed, bribe, coerce, compel, demand, force, hold to ransom, lean on, milk, put the black on, squeeze, threaten.

**blackmailer** *n* bloodsucker, extortioner, extortionist, highbinder, vampire.

**blackness** *n* darkness, duskiness, filthiness, gloom, griminess, inkiness, melanism, murkiness, nigrescence, nigritude, swarthiness, wickedness.

**blackout** *n* censorship, coma, concealment, cover-up, faint, oblivion, power cut, secrecy, suppression, swoon, syncope, unconsciousness.

**bladder** *n* aveole, bag, bursa, caecum, capsule, cell, cyst, pocket, pouch, receptacle, sac, saccule, theca, utricle, vesica, vesicle, vesicula.

**blade** *n* dagger, edge, knife, rapier, scalpel, sword, vane.

**blamable** *adj* accountable, answerable, at fault, blameworthy, culpable, guilty, liable, reprehensible, reproachable, reprovable, responsible, wrong.

**blame** *n* accountability, accusation, animadversion, castigation, censure, charge, complaint, condemnation, criticism, culpability, discommendation, fault, guilt, incrimination, liability, obloquy, onus, rap, recrimination, reprimand, reproach, reproof, responsibility, stick, stricture.

*v* accuse, admonish, censure, charge, chide, condemn, criticise, disapprove, discommend, dispraise, find fault with, rebuke, reprehend, reprimand, reproach, reprove, tax, upbraid.

*antonym* exonerate.

**blameless** *adj* above reproach, clean, clear, faultless, guiltless, immaculate, impeccable, inculpable, innocent, irreprehensible, irreproachable, irreprovable, perfect, sinless, stainless, unblamable, unblemished, unimpeachable, unspotted, unsullied, untarnished, upright, virtuous.

*antonym* guilty.

**blameworthy** *adj* censurable, culpable, discreditable, disreputable, flagitious, guilty, indefensible, inexcusable, reprehensible, reproachable, shameful, unworthy.

*antonym* blameless.

**blanch** *v* bleach, blench, drain, etiolate, fade, pale, wan, whiten.

*antonyms* blush, colour, redden.

**bland** *adv* affable, amiable, balmy, boring, calm, characterless, congenial, courteous, demulcent, dull, fair-spoken, flat, friendly, gentle, gracious, humdrum, hypo-allergenic, impassive, inscrutable, insipid, mild, mollifying, monotonous, nondescript, non-irritant, smooth, soft, soothing, suave, tasteless, tedious, temperate, unexciting, uninspiring, uninteresting, urbane, vapid, weak.

*antonyms* piquant, sharp.

**blandishments** *n* blarney, cajolery, coaxing, compliments, enticements, fawning, flattery, inducements, ingratiation, inveiglement, lip-salve, persuasiveness, soft soap, sweet talk, sycophancy, wheedling.

**blank** *adj* apathetic, bare, bewildered, clean, clear, confounded, confused, deadpan, disconcerted, dull, dumbfounded, empty, expressionless, featureless, glazed, hollow, immobile, impassive, inane, inscrutable, lifeless, muddled, nonplussed, plain, poker-faced, sheer, spotless, staring, uncomprehending, unfilled, unmarked, unrhymed, vacant, vacuous, vague, void, white.

*n* break, emptiness, gap, nothingness, space, tabula rasa, vacancy, vacuity, vacuum, void.

**blanket** *n* carpet, cloak, coat, coating, cover, covering, coverlet, envelope, film, housing, layer, mackinaw, manta, mantle, rug, sheet, wrapper, wrapping.

*adj* across-the-board, all-embracing, all-inclusive, comprehensive, inclusive, overall, sweeping, wide-ranging.

*v* cloak, cloud, coat, conceal, cover, deaden, eclipse, hide, mask, muffle, obscure, surround.

**blankness** *n* abstraction, bareness, emptiness, immobility, impassivity, inanity, incomprehension, indifference, inscrutability, obliviousness, vacancy, vacuity, void.

**blare** *v* blast, boom, clamour, clang, honk, hoot, peal, resound, ring, roar, scream, shriek, toot, trumpet.

**blarney** *n* blandishment, cajolery, coaxing, eloquence, flattery, persuasiveness, plausibility, soft soap, spiel, sweet talk, wheedling.

**blasé** *adj* apathetic, bored, dulled, glutted, indifferent, jaded, nonchalant, offhand, sated, satiated, surfeited, unconcerned, unexcited, unimpressed, unimpressible, uninspired, uninterested, unmoved, weary, world-weary.

*antonyms* enthusiastic, excited.

**blaspheme** *v* abuse, curse, damn, defile, desecrate, execrate, imprecate, profane, revile, swear.

**blasphemous** *adj* execrative, godless, hubristic, impious, imprecatory, irreligious, irreverent, profane, sacrilegious, ungodly.

**blasphemy** *n* curse, cursing, defilement, desecration, execration, expletive, hubris, impiety, impiousness, imprecation, irreverence, outrage, profanation, profaneness, profanity, sacrilege, swearing, violation.

**blast**[1] *n, v* blare, blow, boom, honk, hoot, peal, roar, scream, shriek, sound, wail.

**blast**[2] *n* bang, bluster, burst, clap, crack, crash, detonation, discharge, draught, eruption, explosion, flatus, gale, gust, hail, outburst, salvo, squall, storm, tempest, volley.

*v* assail, attack, blight, blow up, burst, castigate, demolish, destroy, explode, flay, kill, lash, ruin, shatter, shrivel, storm at, wither.

**blasted** *adj* blighted, desolated, destroyed, devastated, ravaged, ruined, scorched, shattered, wasted, withered.

**blatant** *adj* arrant, bald, barefaced, brazen, clamorous, conspicuous, egregious, flagrant, flaunting, glaring, harsh, loud, naked, noisy, obtrusive, obvious, ostentatious, outright, overt, prominent, pronounced, sheer, unmitigated.

**blaze** *n* blast, bonfire, brilliance, burst, conflagration, eruption, explosion, fire, flame, flames, flare, flare-up, flash, fury, glare, gleam, glitter, glow, light, outbreak, outburst, radiance, rush, storm.

*v* beam, burn, burst, erupt, explode, fire, flame, flare, flare up, flash, fume, glare, gleam, glow, seethe, shine.

**blazon** *v* announce, broadcast, bruit, celebrate, flaunt, flourish, proclaim, publicise, trumpet, vaunt.

*antonyms* deprecate, hush up.

**bleach** *v* blanch, decolorise, etiolate, fade, lighten, pale, peroxide, whiten.

**bleak** *adj* bare, barren, blae, blasted, cheerless, chilly, cold, colourless, comfortless, delightless, depressing, desolate, discouraging, disheartening, dismal, dreary, empty, exposed, gaunt, gloomy, grim, hopeless, joyless, leaden, loveless, open, raw, sombre, unsheltered, weather-beaten, windswept, windy.

*antonyms* cheerful, congenial.

**bleary** *adj* blurred, blurry, cloudy, dim, fogged, foggy, fuzzy, hazy, indistinct, misty, muddy, murky, obscured, rheumy, watery.

**bleat** *v* baa, bitch, blat, complain, growl, grumble, moan, whine, whinge.

**bleed** *v* blackmail, deplete, drain, exhaust, exploit, exsanguinate, extort, extract, extravasate, exude, fleece, flow, gush, haemorrhage, leech, milk, ooze, reduce, run, sap, seep, spurt, squeeze, suck dry, trickle, weep.

**blemish** *n* birthmark, blot, blotch, blur, botch, defect, deformity, disfigurement, disgrace, dishonour, fault, flaw, imperfection, mackle, macula, maculation, mark, naevus, smudge, speck, spot, stain, taint.

*v* besmirch, blot, blotch, blur, damage, deface, disfigure, flaw, impair, injure, maculate, mar, mark, smirch, smudge, spoil, spot, stain, sully, taint, tarnish.

**blench** *v* balk, boggle, cower, falter, flinch, hesitate, jib, quail, quake, quiver, recoil, shrink, shudder, shy, start, wince.

**blend** *v* amalgamate, coalesce, combine, complement, compound, contemper, fit, fuse, harmonise, intermix, meld, merge, mingle, mix, synthesise, unite.

*antonym* separate.

*n* alloy, amalgam, amalgamation, combination, composite, compound, concoction, fusion, interunion, meld, mix, mixture, synthesis, union.

**bless** *v* anoint, approve, bestow, consecrate, countenance, dedicate, endow, exalt, extol, favour, glorify, grace, hallow, magnify, ordain, praise, provide, sanctify, thank.

*antonyms* condemn, curse.

**blessed** *adj* adored, beatified, blissful, contented, divine, endowed, favoured, fortunate, glad, hallowed, happy, holy, joyful, joyous, lucky, prosperous, revered, sacred, sanctified, seely.

*antonym* cursed.

**blessedness** *n* beatitude, bliss, blissfulness, content, felicity, happiness, joy, sanctity, seel.

**blessing** *n* advantage, approbation, approval, authority, backing, benedicite, benediction, benefit, benison, boon, bounty, commendation, concurrence, consecration, consent, countenance, darshan, dedication, favour, gain, gift, godsend, grace, help, invocation, kiddush, kindness, leave, permission, profit, sanction, service, support, thanksgiving, windfall.

*antonyms* blight, condemnation, curse.

**blether** *n* blather, chatter, chatterbox, chatterer, chit-chat, claptrap, drivel, gibberish, gibble-gabble, gobbledegook, haverel, jabbering, loquacity, moonshine, nonsense, prattle, prattler, twaddle.

*v* blabber, chatter, gab, gabble, haver, jabber, prattle.

**blight** *n* affliction, bane, cancer, canker, check, contamination, corruption, curse, decay, depression, disease, evil, fungus, infestation, mildew, pest, pestilence, plague, pollution, rot, scourge, set-back, woe.

*antonyms* blessing, boon.

*v* annihilate, blast, crush, dash, destroy, disappoint, frustrate, injure, mar, ruin, shatter, shrivel, spoil, undermine, wither, wreck.

*antonym* bless.

**blind** *adj* amaurotic, beetle-eyed, blinkered, careless, closed, concealed, dark, dim, eyeless, hasty, heedless, hidden, ignorant, impetuous, inattentive, inconsiderate, indifferent, indiscriminate, injudicious, insensate, insensitive, irrational, mindless, neglectful, oblivious, obscured, obstructed, prejudiced, purblind, rash, reckless, sand-blind, senseless, sightless, stone-blind, thoughtless, unaware, uncontrollable, uncritical, undiscerning, unobservant, unobserving, unreasoning, unseeing, unsighted, unthinking, violent, visionless, wild.

*antonyms* aware, clear, sighted.

*n* camouflage, cloak, cover, cover-up, distraction, façade, feint, front, mask, masquerade, screen, smoke-screen.

**blindfold** *v* bamboozle, beguile, blind, deceive, delude, fool, hoodwink, mislead.

*antonym* enlighten.

**blindly** *adv* aimlessly, carelessly, confusedly, frantically, headlong, heedlessly, impetuously, impulsively, incautiously, inconsiderately, indiscriminately, madly, passionately, precipitately, purposelessly, recklessly, regardlessly, senselessly, thoughtlessly, wildly, wilfully.

*antonym* cautiously.

**blindness** *n* cecity, ignorance, indifference, insensitivity, narrow-mindedness, neglect, prejudice, prestriction, sightlessness, unawareness.

*antonyms* awareness, sight, sightedness.

**blink** *v* bat, condone, connive at, disregard, flash, flicker, flutter, gleam, glimmer, glimpse, ignore, nictate, nictitate, overlook, peer, pink, scintillate, shine, sparkle, squint, twinkle, wink.

**bliss** *n* beatitude, blessedness, blissfulness, ecstasy, euphoria, felicity, gladness, happiness, heaven, joy, nirvana, paradise, rapture, seel.

*antonyms* damnation, misery.

**blissful** *adj* beatific, delighted, ecstatic, elated, enchanted, enraptured, euphoric, happy, heavenly, joyful, joyous, rapturous.

*antonym* wretched.

**blister** *n* abscess, blain, bleb, boil, bubble, bulla, canker, carbuncle, cyst, furuncle, papilla, papula, papule, pimple, pompholyx, pustule, sore, swelling, ulcer, vesicle, vesicula, welt, wen.

**blistering** *adj* cruel, excoriating, hot, intense, sarcastic, savage, scathing, scorching, strenuous, vesicant, vesicatory, vicious, virulent, withering.

*antonym* mild.

**blithe** *adj* animated, buoyant, carefree, careless, casual, cheerful, cheery, debonair, gay, gladsome, happy, heedless, jaunty, light-hearted, lightsome, lively, merry, mirthful, nonchalant, sprightly, sunny, thoughtless, unconcerned, untroubled, vivacious.

*antonym* morose.

**blizzard** *n* snow-squall, snowstorm, squall, storm, tempest.

**bloated** *adj* blown up, bombastic, dilated, distended, dropsical, enlarged, expanded, inflated, oedematous, sated, swollen, tumescent, tumid, turgid.

*antonyms* shrivelled, shrunken, thin.

**blob** *n* ball, bead, bobble, bubble, dab, dew-drop, drop, droplet, glob, globule, gob, lump, mass, pearl, pellet, pill, spot.

**bloc** *n* alliance, axis, cabal, cartel, clique, coalition, combine, entente, faction, group, league, ring.

**block** *n* bar, barrier, blockage, brick, cake, chunk, cube, delay, hang-up, hindrance, hunk, impediment, ingot, jam, let, lump, mass, obstacle, obstruction, piece, resistance, square, stoppage, tranche.

*v* arrest, bar, check, choke, clog, close, dam up, deter, halt, hinder, impede, obstruct, obturate, oppilate, plug, scotch, stonewall, stop, stop up, thwart, trig.

**blockade** *n* barricade, barrier, beleaguerment, closure, encirclement, obstruction, restriction, siege, stoppage.

**blockage** *n* block, blocking, clot, embolism, hindrance, impediment, jam, log-jam, obstruction, occlusion, stoppage.

**blockhead** *n* bonehead, boodle, chump, dolt, dullard, dunce, fool, idiot, ignoramus, jobernowl, leather-head, loggerhead, log-head, noodle, numskull, pigsconce, pinhead, pot-head, thickhead, thickskin, thick-skull.

*antonyms* brain, genius.

**bloke** *n* bastard, bod, body, bugger, chap, character, cove, customer, fellow, individual, Johnny, oik, personage, punter.

**blond, blonde** *adj* bleached, fair, fair-haired, fair-skinned, flaxen, golden-haired, light-coloured, tow-headed.

**blood** *n* ancestry, anger, birth, bloodshed, consanguinity, descendants, descent, extraction, family, kindred, kinship, lineage, murder, relations, relationship, temper, temperament.

**bloodcurdling** *adj* appalling, chilling, dreadful, eldritch, fearful, frightening, hair-raising, horrendous, horrible, horrid, horrifying, scaring, spine-chilling, terrifying, weird.

**bloodless** *adj* anaemic, ashen, chalky, cold, colourless, drained, feeble, insipid, languid,

lifeless, listless, pale, pallid, passionless, pasty, sallow, sickly, spiritless, torpid, unemotional, unfeeling, wan.

*antonyms* bloody, ruddy, vigorous.

**bloodshed** *n* bloodletting, butchery, carnage, gore, killing, massacre, murder, slaughter, slaying.

**blood-sucker** *n* blackmailer, extortioner, extortionist, leech, parasite, sponger.

**bloodthirsty** *adj* barbaric, barbarous, brutal, cruel, ferocious, inhuman, murderous, ruthless, sanguinary, savage, slaughterous, vicious, warlike.

**bloody** *adj* bleeding, bloodstained, blooming, brutal, cruel, ferocious, fierce, gaping, murderous, raw, sanguinary, sanguine, sanguineous, sanguinolent, savage.

**bloom** *n* beauty, blossom, blossoming, blow, blush, bud, efflorescence, florescence, flourishing, flower, flush, freshness, glaucescence, glow, health, heyday, lustre, perfection, prime, radiance, rosiness, vigour.

*v* blossom, blow, bud, burgeon, develop, flourish, grow, open, prosper, sprout, succeed, thrive, wax.

*antonym* wither.

**blooming** *adj* blossoming, bonny, florescent, flowering, healthful, healthy, rosy, ruddy.

*antonym* ailing.

**blossom** *n* bloom, bud, floret, flower, flowers.

*v* bloom, blow, burgeon, develop, effloresce, flourish, flower, grow, mature, progress, prosper, thrive.

*antonym* wither.

**blot** *n* blemish, blotch, defect, disgrace, fault, flaw, mackle, macula, mark, patch, smear, smudge, speck, splodge, spot, stain, taint.

*v* bespatter, blur, disfigure, disgrace, maculate, mar, mark, smudge, spoil, spot, stain, sully, taint, tarnish.

**blot out** cancel, darken, delete, destroy, eclipse, efface, erase, expunge, obliterate, obscure, shadow.

**blotch** *n* blemish, blot, mark, patch, pustule, smudge, splash, splodge, spot, stain.

**blotchy** *adj* blemished, macular, maculose, patchy, reddened, smeary, spotted, spotty, uneven.

**blow**[1] *v* bear, blare, blast, breathe, buffet, drive, exhale, fan, fling, flow, flutter, mouth, pant, pipe, play, puff, rush, sound, stream, sweep, toot, trumpet, vibrate, waft, whirl, whisk, wind.

*n* blast, draught, flurry, gale, gust, puff, squall, tempest, wind.

**blow in(to)** insufflate.

**blow over** cease, die down, disappear, dissipate, end, finish, fizzle out, pass, peter out, subside, vanish.

**blow up** balloon, belly out, bloat, dilate, distend, enlarge, exaggerate, expand, fill, fill out, heighten, inflate, magnify, overstate, puff up, pump up, swell.

**blow²** *n* affliction, bang, bash, bat, belt, biff, bombshell, bop, box, buff, buffet, calamity, catastrophe, clap, clip, clout, clump, comedown, concussion, counterbluff, devvel, disappointment, disaster, douse, fourpenny one, haymaker, jolt, knock, knuckle sandwich, misfortune, oner, paik, punch, rap, reverse, setback, shock, siserary, slap, slat, slosh, smack, sock, sockdologer, souse, stroke, swash, swat, swipe, thump, upset, wallop, wap, welt, whack, whang, winder.

**blow up** blast, blow one's top, bomb, burst, castigate, detonate, dynamite, erupt, explode, go off, go off the deep end, hit the roof, lose one's cool, lose one's rag, lose one's temper, rage, reprimand, rupture, scold, shatter.

**blown** *adj* breathless, effete, jaded, stale, tired, worthless.

**blow-out** *n* beanfeast, binge, blast, burst, carousal, detonation, eruption, escape, explosion, feast, fuse, leak, party, puncture, rupture, spree, tear.

**blowy** *adj* blustery, breezy, draughty, fresh, gusty, squally, stormy, windy.

**blowzy** *adj* bedraggled, dishevelled, draggle-tailed, flushed, frowzy, messy, ruddy, slatternly, slipshod, sloppy, slovenly, sluttish, tousled, ungroomed, unkempt, untidy.

*antonyms* neat, smart.

**bludgeon** *n* baton, club, cosh, cudgel, knobkerrie, life-preserver, night-stick, sap, shillelagh, truncheon.

*v* badger, batter, beat, browbeat, bulldoze, bully, club, coerce, cosh, cudgel, force, harass, hector, intimidate, sap, steam-roller, strike, terrorise, torment.

**blue¹** *adj* aquamarine, azure, cerulean, cobalt, cyan, indigo, navy, sapphire, turquoise, ultramarine, watchet.

**blue²** *adj* black, bleak, dejected, depressed, despondent, dismal, dispirited, doleful, down in the dumps, downcast, down-hearted, fed up, gloomy, glum, low, melancholy, miserable, morose, sad, unhappy.

*antonym* cheerful.

**blue³** *adv* bawdy, coarse, dirty, improper, indecent, lewd, naughty, near the bone, near the knuckle, obscene, offensive, pornographic, risqué, smutty, vulgar.

*antonym* decent.

**blue-pencil** *v* bowdlerise, censor, clean up, correct, edit, expurgate, purge.

**blueprint** *n* archetype, design, draft, guide, model, outline, pattern, pilot, plan, project, prototype, sketch.

**blues** *n* blue devils, dejection, depression, despondency, doldrums, dumps, gloom, gloominess, glumness, melancholy, miseries, moodiness.

*antonym* euphoria.

**blue-stocking** *n* bas-bleu, femme savante, learned lady.

**bluff¹** *n* bank, brow, cliff, crag, escarp, escarpment, foreland, headland, height, knoll, peak, precipice, promontory, ridge, scarp, slope.

*adj* affable, blunt, candid, direct, downright, frank, genial, good-natured, hearty, open, outspoken, plain-spoken, straightforward.

*antonyms* diplomatic, refined.

**bluff²** *v* bamboozle, blind, deceive, defraud, delude, fake, feign, grift, hoodwink, humbug, lie, mislead, pretend, sham.

*n* bluster, boast, braggadocio, bravado, deceit, deception, fake, fanfaronade, feint, fraud, grift, humbug, idle boast, lie, pretence, sham, show, subterfuge, trick.

**blunder** *n* bêtise, bevue, bish, bloomer, boner, boob, boo-boo, clanger, clinker, error, fault, faux pas, floater, fluff, gaffe, gaucherie, goof, howler, impropriety, inaccuracy, indiscretion, mistake, oversight, pratfall, slip, slip-up, solecism.

*v* blow it, botch, bumble, bungle, err, flounder, flub, fluff, fumble, goof, miscalculate, misjudge, mismanage, muff it, slip up, stumble.

**blunderer** *n* botcher, bungler, duffer, fool, goof, incompetent, josser.

**blunt** *adj* abrupt, bluff, brusque, candid, curt, direct, discourteous, downright, dull, dulled, edgeless, explicit, forthright, frank, honest, impolite, insensitive, obtuse, outspoken, plain-spoken, pointless, retuse, rounded, rude, straightforward, stubbed, stumpy, tactless, thick, trenchant, unceremonious, uncivil, unpolished, unsharpened.

*antonyms* sharp, tactful.

*v* abate, allay, alleviate, anaesthetise, bate, dampen, deaden, disedge, dull, hebetate, numb, obtund, palliate, rebate, retund, soften, stupefy, unedge, weaken.

*antonyms* intensify, sharpen.

**bluntness** *n* abruptness, brusqueness, candidness, dullness, forthrightness, frankness, hebetude, hebetudinarity, insensitivity, lack of ceremony, obtuseness, obtusity, tactlessness.

*antonyms* sharpness, tact.

**blur** *v* becloud, befog, blear, blemish, blot, blotch, cloud, darken, dim, fog, mask, obfuscate, obscure, scumble, smear, smutch, soften, spot, stain.

*n* blear, blot, blotch, cloudiness, confusion, dimness, fog, fuzziness, haze, indistinctness, muddle, obscurity, smear, smudge, spot, stain.

**blurb** *n* advertisement, commendation, copy, hype, puff, spiel.

**blurred** *adj* beclouded, bleary, blurry, clouded, confused, dim, faint, foggy, fuzzy, hazy, ill-defined, indistinct, misty, nebulous, unclear, vague.

*antonym* distinct.

**blurt** *v* babble, blab, cry, disclose, divulge, ejaculate, exclaim, gush, leak, let slip, let the cat out of the bag, reveal, spill, spill the beans, spout, utter.

*antonym* hush up.

**blush** *v* colour, crimson, flush, glow, mantle, redden.

*antonym* blanch.

*n* colour, erubescence, flush, glow, reddening, rosiness, ruddiness, suffusion.

**blushing** *adj* confused, discomfited, embarrassed, erubescent, flushed, glowing, red, rosy, rubescent, suffused.

*antonyms* composed, pale.

**bluster** *v* boast, brag, bully, domineer, fanfaronade, hector, rant, roar, rodomontade, roist, roister, storm, strut, swagger, swell, talk big, vapour, vaunt.

*n* bluff, boasting, bombast, braggadocio, bragging, bravado, crowing, fanfaronade, parade, racket, rodomontade, swagger, swaggering, vapour, vauntery.

**blusterer** *n* big mouth, big talker, boaster, braggart, fanfaron, rodomontader, roister, roisterer, show-off, swaggerer, swank, swashbuckler, swasher, vapourer, windbag.

**blustery** *adj* boisterous, gusty, noisy, squally, stormy, tempestuous, tumultuous, violent, wild, windy.

*antonym* calm.

**board¹** *n* beam, clapboard, deal, lath, panel, plank, sheet, slab, slat, timber, two-by-four.

**board²** commons, food, grub, meals, provisions, rations, repasts, table, victuals.

*v* accommodate, bed, billet, feed, house, lodge, put up, quarter, room, table.

**board³** *n* advisers, chamber, commission, committee, conclave, council, directorate, directors, jury, panel, trustees.

**board⁴** *v* catch, embark, embus, emplane, enter, entrain, mount.

**boarding-house** *n* pension.

**boast** *v* be all mouth, blazon, blow, bluster, bounce, brag, claim, crow, exaggerate, exhibit, gasconade, possess, puff, rodomontade, show off, strut, swagger, talk big, trumpet, vaunt.

*antonym* deprecate.

*n* avowal, brag, claim, fanfaronade, gasconade, gem, joy, pride, rodomontade, swank, treasure, vaunt.

**boaster** *n* bangster, big mouth, big talker, blowhard, Bobadil, braggart, fanfaron, galah, gascon, gasconader, rodomontader, show-off, swaggerer, swank, vapourer, vaunter.

**boastful** *adj* blowhard, braggart, bragging, cocky, conceited, crowing, egotistical, proud, puffed-up, self-glorious, swaggering, swanky, swollen-headed, thrasonic, thrasonical, vain, vainglorious, vaunting, windy.

*antonym* modest.

**boasting** *n* bluster, bragging, conceit, fanfaronade, gasconade, gasconism, jactation,

jactitation, ostentation, rodomontade, swagger, swank, vaingloriousness, vainglory, vauntery, vaunting, windiness.

*antonym* modesty.

**boat** *n* bateau, canoe, dahabiyah, dinghy, funny, gondola, ketch, punt, rowing-boat, speed-boat, water-craft.

**boatman** *n* ferryman, gondolier, oarsman, rower, sailor, voyageur, waterman, water-rat, wet bob, yachtsman.

**bob** *v* bounce, duck, hop, jerk, jolt, jounce, jump, leap, nod, oscillate, popple, quiver, shake, skip, spring, twitch, waggle, weave, wobble.

**bob up** appear, arise, arrive, crop up, emerge, materialise, pop up, rise, show up, spring up, surface.

**bode** *v* adumbrate, augur, betoken, forebode, foreshadow, foreshow, foretell, forewarn, import, indicate, intimate, omen, portend, predict, presage, prophesy, signify, threaten, warn.

**bodily** *adj* actual, carnal, concrete, corporal, corporeal, earthly, fleshly, incarnate, material, physical, real, somatic, substantial, tangible.

*antonym* spiritual.

*adv* altogether, as a whole, bag and baggage, collectively, completely, en masse, entirely, fully, in toto, totally, wholly.

*antonym* piecemeal.

**body¹** *n* being, bod, build, bulk, cadaver, carcass, consistency, corpse, corpus, creature, density, essence, figure, firmness, form, frame, human, individual, mass, material, matter, mortal, opacity, person, physique, relics, remains, richness, shape, solidity, stiff, substance, substantiality, tabernacle, torso, trunk.

**body²** *n* association, band, bevy, bloc, cartel, collection, company, confederation, congress, corporation, crowd, group, horde, majority, mass, mob, multitude, society, syndicate, throng.

**bodyguard** *n* minder, praetorian, protector.

**body-snatcher** *n* desecrator, resurrectionist, resurrection-man.

**boffin** *n* backroom-boy, brain, designer, egghead, engineer, genius, headpiece, intellect, intellectual, inventor, mastermind, planner, scientist, thinker, wizard.

**bog** *n* fen, marsh, marshland, mire, morass, moss, muskeg, quag, quagmire, quicksands, slough, swamp, swampland, wetlands.

**bog down** delay, deluge, halt, hinder, impede, overwhelm, retard, sink, slow down, slow up, stall, stick.

**boggle** *v* blench, demur, dither, doubt, equivocate, falter, fight shy, flinch, funk, hang back, hesitate, hover, jib, jump, pause, recoil, shillyshally, shrink, shy, stagger, start, startle, vacillate, waver.

**boggy** *adj* fennish, fenny, marshy, miry, morassy, muddy, oozy, paludal, quaggy, soft, spongy, swampy, waterlogged.

*antonym* arid.

**bogus** *adj* artificial, counterfeit, dummy, ersatz, fake, false, forged, fraudulent, imitation, phoney, pinchbeck, pseudo, sham, spoof, spurious, unauthentic.

*antonym* genuine.

**bogy, bogey** *n* bête noire, bogeyman, boggart, bogle, bugaboo, bugbear, goblin, hobgoblin, imp, incubus, nightmare, spectre, spook.

**bohemian** *adj* alternative, artistic, arty, bizarre, eccentric, exotic, irregular, left-bank, nonconformist, offbeat, outré, unconventional, unorthodox, way-out.

*antonyms* bourgeois, conventional.

*n* beatnik, drop-out, hippie, iconoclast, nonconformist.

*antonyms* bourgeois, conformist.

**boil**[1] *v* agitate, brew, bubble, churn, decoct, effervesce, erupt, explode, fizz, foam, froth, fulminate, fume, gurgle, mantle, parboil, rage, rave, seethe, simmer, sizzle, spume, steam, stew, storm, wallop.

**boil down** abridge, abstract, concentrate, condense, decrease, digest, distil, epitomise, reduce, summarise, synopsise.

**boil**[2] *n* abscess, anthrax, blain, bleb, blister, carbuncle, furuncle, gathering, gumboil, inflammation, papule, parulis, pimple, pock, pustule, tumour, ulcer, whelk.

**boiling** *adj* angry, baking, blistering, bubbling, enraged, flaming, fuming, furious, gurgling, hot, incensed, indignant, infuriated, roasting, scorching, seething, torrid, turbulent.

**boisterous** *adj* blusterous, blustery, bouncy, clamorous, disorderly, exuberant, gusty, impetuous, loud, noisy, obstreperous, rackety, raging, rambunctious, riotous, roisting, rollicking, rough, rowdy, rumbustious, squally, tempestuous, termagant, tumultous, turbulent, unrestrained, unruly, uproarious, vociferous, wild.

*antonyms* calm, quiet, restrained.

**bold** *adj* adventurous, audacious, brash, brave, brazen, bright, cheeky, colourful, confident, conspicuous, courageous, daring, dauntless, enterprising, extrovert, eye-catching, fearless, flamboyant, flashy, forceful, forward, fresh, gallant, heroic, impudent, insolent, intrepid, jazzy, lively, loud, malapert, outgoing, pert, plucky, prominent, pronounced, saucy, shameless, showy, spirited, striking, strong, unabashed, unashamed, unbashful, valiant, valorous, venturesome, vivid.

*antonyms* diffident, restrained.

**bolster** *v* aid, assist, augment, boost, brace, buoy up, buttress, firm up, help, maintain, prop, reinforce, shore up, stay, stiffen, strengthen, supplement, support.

*antonym* undermine.

**bolt** *n* arrow, bar, bound, catch, dart, dash, elopement, escape, fastener, flight, flit, latch, lock, missile, peg, pin, projectile, rivet, rod, rush, shaft, sneck, sprint, thunderbolt.

*v* abscond, bar, bound, cram, dart, dash, devour, discharge, elope, escape, expel, fasten, fetter, flee, fly, gobble, gorge, gulp, guzzle, hurtle, jump, latch, leap, lock, run, rush, secure, spring, sprint, stuff, wolf.

**bomb** *n* A-bomb, bombshell, charge, egg, explosive, grenade, mine, missile, mortar-bomb, petrol bomb, projectile, rocket, shell, torpedo.

*v* attack, blow up, bombard, collapse, come a cropper, come to grief, destroy, fail, flop, misfire, shell, strafe, torpedo.

**bombard** *v* assail, assault, attack, barrage, batter, beset, besiege, blast, blitz, bomb, cannonade, dun, harass, hound, importune, pelt, pester, pound, shell, strafe.

**bombardment** *n* air-raid, assault, attack, barrage, blitz, bombing, cannonade, fire, flak, fusillade, salvo, shelling, strafe.

**bombast** *n* ampollosity, bluster, brag, braggadocio, euphuism, fustian, gasconade, Gongorism, grandiloquence, grandiosity, heroics, magniloquence, pomposity, portentiousness, pretentiousness, rant, rodomontade, verbosity, wordiness.

*antonyms* reserve, restraint.

**bombastic** *adj* bloated, declamatory, euphuistic, fustian, Gongoristic, grandiloquent, grandiose, high-flown, histrionic, inflated, magniloquent, pompous, turgid, verbose, windy, wordy.

**bon viveur** bon vivant, epicure, epicurean, gastronome, gourmet, hedonist, luxurist, pleasure-seeker, voluptuary.

*antonym* ascetic.

**bona fide** actual, authentic, genuine, honest, kosher, lawful, legal, legitimate, real, true, valid.

*antonym* bogus.

**bond** *n* affiliation, affinity, agreement, attachment, band, binding, chain, compact, connection, contract, copula, cord, covenant, fastening, fetter, ligament, ligature, link, manacle, nexus, obligation, pledge, promise, relation, shackle, tie, union, vinculum, word.

*v* bind, connect, fasten, fuse, glue, gum, paste, seal, unite.

**bondage** *n* captivity, confinement, durance, duress, enslavement, enthralment, imprisonment, incarceration, restraint, serfdom, servitude, slavery, subjection, subjugation, subservience, thraldom, vassalage, yoke.

*antonyms* freedom, independence.

**bonfire** *n* beacon, conflagration, feu de joie, pyre.

**bonny** *adj* attractive, beautiful, blithe, blooming, bouncing, buxom, cheerful, cheery, chubby, comely, fair, fine, gay, goodly, handsome, joyful, lovely, merry, pretty, shapely, sunny, sweet, wholesome, winsome.

*antonym* ill-favoured.

**bonus** *n* advantage, benefit, bounty, bribe, commission, dividend, douceur, extra, freebie, gift, gratuity, hand-out, honorarium, lagniappe, perk, perquisite, plus, premium, prize, profit, reward, tip.

*antonyms* disadvantage, disincentive, liability.

**bony** *adj* angular, drawn, emaciated, gangling, gaunt, gawky, knobbly, lanky, lean, osseous, rawboned, sclerous, scrawny, skinny, thin.
*antonym* plump.

**boob** *n* balls-up, bêtise, blunder, botch, clanger, error, fault, faux pas, gaffe, gaucherie, howler, inaccuracy, indiscretion, mistake, oversight, pratfall, slip, slip-up, solecism.

**booby** *n* blockhead, clod, clodpate, clodpoll, clot, dimwit, duffer, dunce, dunderhead, fool, goof, halfwit, idiot, muggins, nickumpoop, ni(n)compoop, ninny, palooka, prat, schmuck, simpleton.
*antonym* genius.

**booby prize** consolation prize, wooden spoon.

**book** *n* album, booklet, codex, companion, diary, hornbook, incunable, incunabulum, jotter, lectionary, manual, manuscript, notebook, pad, paperback, publication, roll, scroll, textbook, tome, tract, volume, work.
*v* arrange, arrest, bag, charter, engage, enter, insert, list, log, note, organise, post, procure, programme, record, register, reserve, schedule.
*antonym* cancel.

**bookish** *adj* academic, cultured, donnish, erudite, highbrow, intellectual, learned, lettered, literary, pedantic, scholarly, scholastic, studious, well-read.
*antonyms* lowbrow, unlettered.

**boom¹** *v* bang, blare, blast, crash, explode, resound, reverberate, roar, roll, rumble, sound, thunder.
*n* bang, blast, burst, clang, clap, crash, explosion, reverberation, roar, rumble, thunder.

**boom²** *v* develop, escalate, expand, explode, flourish, gain, go from strength to strength, grow, increase, intensify, prosper, spurt, strengthen, succeed, swell, thrive.
*antonyms* collapse, fail.
*n* advance, boost, development, escalation, expansion, explosion, gain, growth, improvement, increase, jump, spurt, upsurge, upturn.
*antonyms* collapse, failure.

**boon** *n* advantage, benefaction, benefit, blessing, donation, favour, gift, godsend, grant, gratification, gratuity, kindness, petition, present, windfall.
*antonyms* blight, disadvantage.

**boor** *n* barbarian, brute, bumpkin, chuff, churl, clodhopper, goop, Goth, Grobian, hedgehog, hog, keelie, kerne, lout, oaf, peasant, philistine, rustic, vulgarian.
*antonyms* aesthete, charmer.

**boorish** *adj* awkward, barbaric, bearish, churlish, clodhopping, clownish, coarse, crude, goustrous, gross, gruff, ill-bred, jungli, kernish, loutish, lubberly, lumpen, oafish, rude, rustic, swailish, uncivilised, uncouth, uneducated, unrefined, vulgar.
*antonyms* cultured, polite, refined.

**boorishness** *n* awkwardness, barbarity, bluntness, coarseness, crudeness, gaucherie,

Gothicism, grossièreté, grossness, hoggery, ignorance, impoliteness, loutishness, lubberliness, philistinism, roughness, rudeness, rudery, rusticity, uncouthness, vulgarity.
*antonyms* politeness, refinement.

**boost** *n* addition, advancement, ego-trip, encouragement, enhancement, expansion, fillip, heave, help, hoist, hype, improvement, increase, increment, jump, lift, praise, promotion, push, rise, supplement, thrust.
*antonyms* blow, setback.
*v* advance, advertise, aid, amplify, assist, augment, bolster, develop, elevate, encourage, enhance, enlarge, expand, foster, further, heave, heighten, hoist, improve, increase, inspire, jack up, lift, plug, praise, promote, push, raise, supplement, support, sustain, thrust.
*antonyms* hinder, undermine.

**boot¹** *n* bootee, galosh, gumboot, jemima, Kletterschuh, larrigan, moon-boot, muckluck, overshoe, riding-boot, rubber, top-boot, wader, wellie, wellington.
*v* bounce, dismiss, eject, expel, fire, give the bum's rush, give the heave, kick, kick out, knock, oust, punt, sack, shove.

**boot²** *v* advantage, aid, avail, benefit, help, profit, serve.

**booth** *n* bay, carrel, cart, compartment, guichet, hut, kiosk, stall, stand, ticket-office.

**bootless** *adj* barren, fruitless, futile, ineffective, on a hiding to nothing, pointless, profitless, sterile, unavailing, unproductive, unsuccessful, useless, vain, worthless.
*antonyms* profitable, useful.

**bootlicking** *n* arse-licking, back-scratching, crawling, cringing, deference, faggery, fagging, fawning, flattery, grovelling, heepishness, ingratiation, lackeying, obsequiousness, servility, sycophancy, toadying.

**booty** *n* boodle, bunce, gains, haul, loot, pickings, pillage, plunder, spoil, spoils, swag, takings, winnings.

**border** *n* borderline, bound, boundary, bounds, brim, brink, circumference, confine, confines, demarcation, edge, fringe, frontier, hem, limit, limits, lip, list, march, margin, perimeter, periphery, rand, rim, screed, selvage, skirt, surround, trimming, valance, verge.
*adj* boundary, circumscriptive, dividing, frontier, limitary, limitrophe, marginal, perimeter, separating, side.
**border on** abut, adjoin, appear like, approach, approximate, communicate with, connect, contact, impinge, join, march, neighbour, resemble, touch, verge on.

**bordered** *adj* bounded, circumscribed, edged, fringed, hemmed, limbate, marginate, margined, rimmed, skirted, surrounded, trimmed.

**borderline** *adj* ambivalent, doubtful, iffy, indecisive, indefinite, indeterminate, marginal, problematic, uncertain.
*antonyms* certain, definite.

**bore¹** *v* burrow, countermine, drill, gouge, mine, penetrate, perforate, pierce, sap, sink, thirl, thrill, tunnel, undermine.

*antonyms* accomplish, succeed.

**bore²** *v* annoy, bother, bug, fatigue, irk, irritate, jade, pester, tire, trouble, vex, weary, worry.

*antonyms* charm, interest.

*n* annoyance, bind, bother, drag, dullard, headache, nuisance, pain, pain in the neck, pest, schmo, terebrant, trial, turn-off, vexation, vieux jeu, yawn.

*antonym* pleasure.

**bored** *adj* brassed off, browned off, ennuied, ennuyé.

*antonym* interested.

**boredom** *n* acedia, apathy, doldrums, dullness, ennui, flatness, irksomeness, listlessness, monotony, sameness, tediousness, tedium, vapours, weariness, wearisomeness, world-weariness.

*antonym* interest.

**boring** *adj* commonplace, dead, draggy, dreary, dry, dull, ennuying, flat, ho-hum, humdrum, insipid, irksome, monotonous, repetitious, routine, stale, stupid, tedious, tiresome, tiring, trite, unamusing, undiverting, unedifying, uneventful, unexciting, unfunny, unimaginative, uninspired, uninteresting, unvaried, unwitty, vapid, wearisome.

*antonyms* interesting, original.

**borrow** *v* adopt, ape, appropriate, cadge, copy, crib, derive, draw, echo, filch, imitate, list, mimic, obtain, pilfer, pirate, plagiarise, scrounge, sponge, steal, take, use, usurp.

**borrowing** *n* adoption, appropriation, cadging, calque, copy, copying, crib, imitation, loan, loan-translation, loan-word, plagiarisation, scrounging, sponging.

**bosom** *n* breast, bust, centre, chest, circle, core, heart, midst, protection, sanctuary, shelter.

*adj* boon, cherished, close, confidential, dear, favourite, inseparable, intimate.

**boss¹** *n* administrator, baron, captain, chief, director, employer, executive, foreman, gaffer, governor, head, leader, manager, master, overseer, owner, superintendent, supervisor, supremo.

*v* administrate, command, control, direct, employ, manage, oversee, run, superintend, supervise.

**boss around** browbeat, bulldoze, bully, dominate, domineer, dragoon, hector, oppress, order about, overbear, push around, tyrannise.

**boss²** *n* knob, knub, knubble, nub, nubble, omphalos, point, protuberance, stud, tip, umbo.

**bossy** *adj* arrogant, authoritarian, autocratic, demanding, despotic, dictatorial, domineering, exacting, hectoring, high-handed, imperious, insistent, lordly, oppressive, overbearing, tyrannical.

*antonym* unassertive.

**botch** *v* balls up, blunder, bungle, butcher, cobble, cock up, corpse, flub, fuck up, fudge, fumble, goof, louse up, mar, mend, mess, mismanage, muff, patch, ruin, screw up, spoil.

*antonyms* accomplish, succeed.

*n* balls-up, blunder, bungle, cock-up, failure, farce, hash, mess, miscarriage, muddle, shambles.

*antonym* success.

**bother** *v* alarm, annoy, bore, chivvy, concern, dismay, distress, disturb, dog, harass, harry, hassle, inconvenience, irk, irritate, molest, nag, pester, plague, pother, pudder, trouble, upset, vex, worry.

*n* aggravation, annoyance, bustle, consternation, difficulty, flurry, fuss, hassle, inconvenience, irritation, kerfuffle, molestation, nuisance, palaver, perplexity, pest, pother, problem, pudder, shtook, strain, trouble, vexation, worry.

**bothersome** *adj* aggravating, annoying, boring, distressing, exasperating, inconvenient, infuriating, irksome, irritating, laborious, tedious, tiresome, troublesome, vexatious, vexing, wearisome.

**bottle** *n* carafe, carboy, dead-man, decanter, demijohn, flacket, flacon, flagon, flask, jack, jar, phial, vial.

**bottle up** check, conceal, contain, curb, enclose, hide, hold in, inhibit, quell, restrain, restrict, suppress.

*antonyms* unbosom, unburden.

**bottleneck** *n* block, blockage, clogging, congestion, hindrance, hold-up, jam, obstacle, obstruction, snarl-up, traffic-jam.

**bottom** *n* arse, backside, base, basis, bed, behind, bum, butt, buttocks, core, depths, derrière, essence, floor, foot, foundation, fundament, fundus, ground, groundwork, heart, jacksie, nadir, origin, pedestal, plinth, posterior, principle, rear, rear end, root, rump, seat, sit-upon, socle, sole, source, substance, substratum, substructure, support, tail, underneath, underside, understratum.

**bottom drawer** hope chest.

**bottomless** *adj* abysmal, abyssal, boundless, deep, fathomless, immeasurable, inexhaustible, infinite, limitless, measureless, profound, unfathomable, unfathomed, unlimited, unplumbed.

*antonym* shallow.

**bottomless pit** Abaddon, abode of the damned, abysm, abyss, chasm, crevasse, fire and brimstone, Gehenna, gulf, Hades, Hell, hellfire, infernal regions, inferno, maw.

**boulevard** *n* avenue, mall, parade, promenade, prospect, row, street, terrace, thoroughfare.

**bounce** *v* bob, bound, bump, dap, dismiss, eject, jounce, jump, kick out, leap, oust, rebound, recoil, resile, ricochet, spring, stot, throw out.

*n* animation, bound, dap, dynamism, ebullience, elasticity, energy, exuberance, give, go, life, liveliness, pep, rebound, recoil, resilience, spring, springiness, vigour, vitality, vivacity, zip.

**bouncing** *adj* blooming, bonny, healthy, lively, robust, strong, thriving, vigorous.

**bound¹** *adj* bandaged, beholden, cased, certain, chained, committed, compelled, constrained, destined, doomed, duty-bound, fastened, fated, fixed, forced, held, liable, manacled, obligated, obliged, pinioned, pledged, required, restricted, secured, sure, tied, tied up.

**bound²** *v* bob, bounce, caper, frisk, gallumph, gambol, hurdle, jump, leap, lope, loup, lunge, pounce, prance, skip, spring, vault.

*n* bob, bounce, caper, dance, frisk, gambado, gambol, jump, leap, lope, loup, lunge, pounce, prance, scamper, skip, spring, vault.

**boundary** *n* abuttal, barrier, border, borderline, bounds, bourne, brink, confines, demarcation, edge, extremity, fringe, frontier, junction, limes, limits, line, march, margin, mete, perimeter, termination, verge.

*adj* border, demarcation, frontier, limitary, limitrophe, perimeter.

**bounded** *adj* bordered, circumscribed, confined, controlled, defined, delimited, demarcated, edged, encircled, enclosed, encompassed, hemmed in, limit ed, restrained, restricted, surrounded, terminated.

**bounder** *n* blackguard, blighter, cad, cheat, cur, dastard, dirty dog, heel, knave, miscreant, oik, pig, rat, rip, rogue, rotter, swine.

**boundless** *adj* countless, endless, illimitable, immeasurable, immense, incalculable, indefatigable, inexhaustible, infinite, interminable, interminate, limitless, measureless, prodigious, unbounded, unconfined, unending, unflagging, unlimited, untold, vast.

*antonym* limited.

**bounds** *n* borders, boundaries, circumference, confines, edges, extremities, fringes, frontiers, limits, marches, margins, periphery, rim, verges.

**bountiful** *adj* abundant, ample, boundless, bounteous, copious, exuberant, generous, lavish, liberal, luxuriant, magnanimous, munificent, open-handed, overflowing, plenteous, plentiful, princely, profuse, prolific, ungrudging, unstinting.

*antonyms* meagre, mean, sparse.

**bounty** *n* allowance, almsgiving, annuity, assistance, beneficence, benevolence, bonus, charity, donation, generosity, gift, grace, grant, gratuity, kindness, largesse, liberality, philanthropy, premium, present, recompense, reward.

**bouquet** *n* anthology, aroma, boutonnière, bunch, buttonhole, corsage, florilegium, fragrance, garland, nosegay, odour, perfume, posy, redolence, savour, scent, smell, spray, wreath.

**bourgeois** *adj* Biedermeier, circumscribed, commonplace, conformist, conservative, conventional, dull, hide-bound, humdrum, kitsch, materialistic, middle-class, pedestrian, tawdry, traditional, trite, trivial, unadventurous, unimaginative, uninspired, unoriginal, vulgar.

*antonyms* bohemian, original, unconventional.

*n* conformist, petit bourgeois, philistine, plebeian, Pooter, stick-in-the-mud.

*antonyms* bohemian, nonconformist.

**bout** *n* battle, competition, contest, course, encounter, engagement, fight, fit, go, heat, match, period, round, run, session, set-to, spell, spree, stint, stretch, struggle, term, time, turn, venue.

**bovine** *adj* beefy, dense, dull, dumb, heavy, hulking, obtuse, slow, slow-witted, sluggish, stolid, stupid, thick.

*antonym* quick.

**bow¹** *v* accept, acquiesce, bend, bob, capitulate, comply, concede, conquer, consent, crush, curtsey, defer, depress, droop, genuflect, give in, incline, kowtow, nod, overpower, stoop, subdue, subjugate, submit, surrender, vanquish, yield.

*n* acknowledgement, bending, bob, curtsey, genuflexion, inclination, kowtow, nod, obeisance, salaam, salutation.

**bow out** abandon, back out, bunk off, chicken out, defect, desert, give up, opt out, pull out, quit, resign, retire, stand down, step down, withdraw.

**bow²** *n* beak, head, prow, rostrum, stem.

**bowdlerise** *v* blue-pencil, censor, clean up, cut, edit, excise, expunge, expurgate, launder, modify, mutilate, purge, purify.

**bowels** *n* belly, centre, core, depths, entrails, guts, heart, hold, innards, inside, insides, interior, intestines, middle, viscera, vitals.

**bower** *n* alcove, arbour, bay, belvedere, boudoir, dwelling, gazebo, grot, grotto, hideaway, pleasance, recess, retreat, sanctuary, shelter, summer-house.

**bowl¹** *n* basin, bicker, cruse, dish, pan, piggin, porringer, quaich, receptacle, sink, tureen, vessel.

**bowl²** *n* jack, wood.

*v* fling, hurl, pitch, revolve, roll, rotate, spin, throw, trundle, whirl.

**bowl over** amaze, astonish, astound, dumbfound, fell, flabbergast, floor, stagger, startle, stun, surprise, topple, unbalance.

**bow-legs** *n* bandiness, bandy legs, valgus.

**bowler** *n* billycock, bowler hat, hard hat, pot-hat.

**box¹** *n* bijou, carton, case, casket, chest, coffer, coffin, coffret, consignment, container, coop, fund, pack, package, portmanteau, present, pyx, pyxis, receptacle, trunk.

*v* case, embox, encase, pack, package, wrap.

**box in** cage, circumscribe, confine, contain, coop up, cordon off, corner, enclose, hem in, imprison, restrict, surround, trap.

**box²** *v* buffet, butt, clout, cuff, fight, hit, punch, slap, sock, spar, strike, thwack, wallop, whack, wham, whang.

*n* blow, buffet, clout, cuff, punch, slap, stroke, thump, wallop, wham, whang.

**boxing** *n* fisticuffs, prize-fighting, pugilism, sparring, the noble art.

*adj* fistic, fistical, pugilistic.

**boxing-match** *n* bout, mill.

**boy** *n* callant, cub, dandiprat, fellow, gamin, gossoon, halfling, imp, junior, kid, lad, loon, loonie, man-child, nipper, puppy, schoolboy, spalpeen, stripling, urchin, whippersnapper, youngster, youth.

**boycott** v ban, bar, black, blackball, blacklist, cold-shoulder, disallow, embargo, exclude, ignore, ostracise, outlaw, prohibit, proscribe, refuse, reject, spurn.

*antonyms* encourage, support.

**boyfriend** n admirer, beau, date, fancy man, follower, lover, man, steady, suitor, swain, sweetheart, young man.

**boyish** adj adolescent, childish, gamine, immature, innocent, juvenile, puerile, tomboy, unfeminine, unmaidenly, young, youthful.

**brace¹** n binder, bracer, bracket, buttress, cleat, corset, nogging, prop, reinforcement, shoring, stanchion, stay, strap, strut, support, truss.

v bandage, bind, bolster, buttress, fasten, fortify, prop, reinforce, shore (up), steady, strap, strengthen, support, tie, tighten.

**brace²** n couple, doubleton, duo, pair, twosome.

**braces** n gallowses, galluses, suspenders.

**bracing** adj brisk, crisp, energetic, energising, enlivening, exhilarating, fortifying, fresh, invigorating, refreshing, restorative, reviving, rousing, stimulating, strengthening, tonic, vigorous.

*antonym* debilitating.

**brackish** adj bitter, briny, saline, salt, saltish, salty.

*antonym* fresh.

**brag** v bluster, boast, crow, fanfaronade, rodomontade, swagger, talk big, trumpet, vapour, vaunt.

*antonym* deprecate.

**braggart** n bangster, big mouth, bluffer, blusterer, boaster, braggadocio, Brobadil, fanfaron, gascon, gasconader, rodomontader, show-off, swaggerer, swashbuckler, vapourer, whiffler.

**bragging** n bluster, boastfulness, boasting, bravado, exaggeration, fanfaronade, gasconade, jactation, jactitation, rodomontade, showing off, strutting, swagger, swank, talk, vauntery.

*antonyms* modesty, unobtrusiveness.

**braid** v entwine, interlace, intertwine, interweave, lace, plait, ravel, twine, twist, weave, wind.

*antonyms* undo, untwist.

**brain¹** n boffin, egghead, expert, genius, highbrow, intellect, intellectual, mastermind, prodigy, pundit, sage, savant, scholar, wizard.

*antonym* simpleton.

**brain²** n cerebrum, grey matter, intellect, mind, sensorium, sensory.

**brainless** adj crazy, daft, foolish, half-witted, hen-witted, idiotic, incompetent, inept, mindless, senseless, stupid, thoughtless, unintelligent, witless.

*antonyms* sensible, shrewd, wise.

**brains** n capacity, common sense, grey matter, head, intellect, intelligence, mind, nous, reason, sagacity, savvy, sense, shrewdness, understanding, wit.

**brain-teaser** n conundrum, mind-bender, poser, problem, puzzle, riddle.

**brainwash** v alter, bludgeon, condition, grill, indoctrinate, persuade, pressure, pressurise, re-educate, verbal.

**brainwashing** n conditioning, double-think, grilling, indoctrination, menticide, mind-bending, persuasion, pressure, pressurisation, re-education, unlearning, verballing.

**brainy** adj bright, brilliant, clever, intellectual, intelligent, sapient, smart.

*antonym* dull.

**brake** n check, constraint, control, curb, drag, rein, restraint, restriction, retardment.

v check, decelerate, drag, halt, moderate, pull up, retard, slacken, slow, stop.

*antonym* accelerate.

**branch** n arm, bough, chapter, department, division, grain, limb, lodge, office, offshoot, part, prong, ramification, ramus, section, shoot, sprig, subdivision, subsection, whip, wing, witty.

**branch out** bifurcate, broaden out, develop, divaricate, diversify, enlarge, expand, extend, increase, move on, multiply, proliferate, ramify, vary.

**brand** n brand-name, class, emblem, grade, hallmark, kind, label, line, logo, make, mark, marker, marque, quality, sign, sort, species, stamp, symbol, trademark, type, variety.

v burn, censure, denounce, discredit, disgrace, label, mark, scar, stain, stamp, stigmatise, taint, type.

**brandish** v display, exhibit, flash, flaunt, flourish, parade, raise, shake, swing, wave, wield.

**brand-new** adj fire-new, fresh.

**brash** adj assuming, assured, audacious, bold, brazen, bumptious, cocky, foolhardy, forward, hasty, heedless, impertinent, impetuous, impudent, impulsive, incautious, indiscreet, insolent, precipitate, rash, reckless, rude, temerarious.

*antonyms* cautious, reserved, unobtrusive.

**brass** n assurance, audacity, brass neck, brazenness, cheek, effrontery, gall, impertinence, impudence, insolence, nerve, presumption, rudeness, self-assurance, temerity.

*antonyms* circumspection, timidity.

**brassy** adj blaring, blatant, bold, brash, brazen, cheap, dissonant, flamboyant, flashy, forward, garish, gaudy, grating, hard, harsh, jangling, jarring, jazzy, loud, loud-mouthed, meretricious, noisy, obtrusive, pert, piercing, raucous, saucy, showy, shrill, strident, tawdry, vulgar.

**brat** n cub, gamin, get, guttersnipe, jackanapes, kid, nipper, puppy, rascal, ruffian, toe-rag, urchin, varmint, whippersnapper, youngster.

**bravado** *n* bluster, boast, boastfulness, boasting, bombast, brag, braggadocio, bragging, fanfaronade, parade, pretence, rodomontade, show, showing off, swagger, swaggering, swank, swashbuckling, talk, vauntery, vaunting.

*antonyms* modesty, restraint.

**brave** *adj* audacious, bold, courageous, daring, dauntless, doughty, fearless, fine, gallant, game, glorious, hardy, heroic, indomitable, intrepid, plucky, resolute, resplendent, splendid, stalwart, stoic, stoical, stout-hearted, unafraid, undaunted, unflinching, valiant, valorous.

*antonyms* cowardly, timid.

*v* accost, bear, beard, challenge, confront, dare, defy, encounter, endure, face, face up to, stand up to, suffer, withstand.

*antonyms* capitulate, crumple.

**bravely** *adv* courageously, dauntlessly, fearlessly, gallantly, gamely, heroically, intrepidly, manfully, pluckily, resolutely, splendidly, stoically, unflinchingly, valiantly, womanfully.

*antonym* cravenly.

**bravery** *n* audacity, boldness, courage, daring, dauntlessness, doughtiness, fearlessness, fortitude, gallantry, grit, guts, hardihood, hardiness, heroism, indomitability, intrepidity, mettle, pluck, pluckiness, resoluteness, resolution, spirit, spunk, stalwartness, stoicism, stout-heartedness, valiance, valour.

*antonyms* cowardice, timidity.

**bravura** *n* animation, audacity, boldness, brilliance, brio, daring, dash, display, élan, energy, exhibitionism, extravagance, flamboyance, liveliness, ostentation, panache, pizzazz, punch, spirit, verve, vigour, virtuosity.

*antonym* restraint.

**brawl** *n* affray, altercation, argument, bagarre, battle, broil, bust-up, clash, disorder, dispute, dog-fight, Donnybrook, dust-up, fight, fracas, fray, free-for-all, mêlée, punch-up, quarrel, row, ruckus, rumpus, scrap, scuffle, squabble, tumult, uproar, wrangle.

*v* altercate, argue, argy-bargy, battle, dispute, fight, flyte, quarrel, row, scrap, scuffle, squabble, tussle, wrangle, wrestle.

**brawn** *n* beef, beefiness, brawniness, bulk, bulkiness, flesh, meat, might, muscle, muscles, muscularity, power, robustness, sinews, strength, thews.

**brawny** *adj* athletic, beefy, bovine, bulky, burly, fleshy, hardy, hefty, herculean, hulking, husky, lusty, massive, muscular, powerful, robust, sinewy, solid, stalwart, strapping, strong, sturdy, thewy, vigorous, well-built, well-knit.

*antonyms* frail, slight.

**bray** *v* blare, hoot, roar, screech, trumpet.

*n* bawl, bellow, blare, blast, cry, hoot, roar, screech, shout, shriek.

**brazen** *adj* assured, audacious, barefaced, blatant, bold, brash, brassy, defiant, flagrant, forward, immodest, impudent, insolent, malapert, pert, saucy, shameless, unabashed, unashamed.

*antonym* shamefaced.

**breach** *n* alienation, aperture, break, break-up, chasm, cleft, contravention, crack, crevice, difference, disaffection, disagreement, discontinuity, disobedience, disruption, dissension, dissociation, division, estrangement, fissure, gap, hole, infraction, infringement, lapse, offence, opening, parting, quarrel, rent, rift, rupture, schism, scission, scissure, secession, separation, severance, split, transgression, trespass, variance, violation.

**bread** *n* aliment, cash, diet, dough, fare, finance, food, funds, money, moolah, necessities, nourishment, nutriment, provisions, rooty, spondulicks, subsistence, sustenance, viands, victuals, wherewithal.

**breadth** *n* amplitude, area, beam, broadness, bulk, compass, comprehensiveness, dimension, expanse, extensiveness, extent, latitude, magnitude, measure, range, reach, scale, scope, size, space, span, spread, sweep, thickness, vastness, volume, wideness, width.

**break** *v* abandon, absorb, announce, appear, bankrupt, batter, beat, better, breach, burst, bust, contravene, cow, crack, crash, cripple, cushion, cut, dash, defeat, degrade, demolish, demoralise, destroy, diminish, discharge, disclose, discontinue, disintegrate, disobey, dispirit, disregard, divide, divulge, emerge, enervate, enfeeble, erupt, escape, exceed, excel, explode, flee, flout, fly, fract, fracture, fragment, go phut, happen, humiliate, impair, impart, incapacitate, inform, infract, infringe, interrupt, jigger, knacker, knap, lessen, moderate, modify, occur, outdo, outstrip, part, pause, proclaim, reduce, rend, rest, retard, reveal, ruin, separate, sever, shatter, shiver, smash, snap, soften, splinter, split, stave, stop, subdue, surpass, suspend, tame, tear, tell, transgress, undermine, undo, violate, weaken, worst.

*n* abruption, advantage, alienation, breach, breather, chance, cleft, crack, crevice, disaffection, discontinuity, dispute, disruption, divergence, division, estrangement, fissure, fortune, fracture, gap, gash, halt, hiatus, hole, interlude, intermission, interruption, interval, lapse, let-up, lull, opening, opportunity, pause, quarrel, recess, rent, respite, rest, rift, rupture, schism, separation, split, suspension, tear, time-out.

**break away** apostasise, depart, detach, escape, flee, fly, leave, part company, quit, renegue, revolt, run away, secede, separate, split.

**break down** analyse, anatomise, collapse, conk out, crack up, crush, demolish, dissect, fail, give way, go phut, seize up, stop.

**break in** burgle, encroach, impinge, interfere, interject, interpose, interrupt, intervene, intrude, invade, irrupt.

**break off** cease, desist, detach, disconnect, discontinue, dissever, divide, end, finish, halt, interrupt, part, pause, separate, sever, snap off, splinter, stop, suspend, terminate.

**break out** abscond, arise, begin, bolt, burst, commence, emerge, erupt, escape, flare up, flee, happen, occur, start.

**break the ice** begin, lead the way, oil the works, relax, set at ease, start the ball rolling, unbend.

**break through** achieve, emerge, gain ground, leap forward, make headway, pass, penetrate, progress, succeed.

**break up** adjourn, analyse, anatomise, demolish, destroy, disband, dismantle, disperse, disrupt, dissolve, divide, divorce, part, scatter, separate, sever, split, stop, suspend, terminate.

**break with** ditch, drop, finish with, jilt, part with, reject, renounce, repudiate, separate.

**breakable** *adj* brittle, crumbly, delicate, flimsy, fragile, frail, frangible, friable, insubstantial, murly.

*antonyms* durable, sturdy.

**breakaway** *adj* apostate, dissenting, heretical, rebel, renegade, schismatic, seceding, secessionist.

**breakdown** *n* analysis, cataclasm, categorisation, classification, collapse, disintegration, disruption, dissection, failure, interruption, itemisation, mishap, stoppage.

**breakfast** *n* dejeune, déjeuner, disjune, petit déjeuner.

**break-in** *n* burglary, housebreaking, intrusion, larceny, robbery, theft.

**breakthrough** *n* advance, development, discovery, find, finding, gain, headway, improvement, invention, leap, progress, step.

**break-up** *n* breakdown, crack-up, crumbling, disintegration, dispersal, dissolution, divorce, finish, parting, rift, separation, split, splitting, termination.

**breakwater** *n* dock, groyne, jetty, mole, pier, quay, wharf.

**breast** *n* bosom, bust, chest, front, heart, thorax.

**breasts** *n* boobs, bristols, bust, cans, dugs, knockers, paps, teats, tits.

**breath** *n* air, animation, aroma, breathing, breeze, energy, exhalation, existence, flatus, flutter, gasp, gulp, gust, hint, inhalation, life, murmur, odour, pant, pneuma, puff, respiration, sigh, smell, spirit, suggestion, suspicion, undertone, vapour, vitality, waft, wheeze, whiff, whisper.

**breathe** *v* articulate, exercise, exhale, expire, express, imbue, impart, infuse, inhale, inject, inspire, instil, live, murmur, pant, puff, respire, say, sigh, suspire, tire, transfuse, utter, voice, whisper.

**breather** *n* break, breathing-space, constitutional, halt, pause, recess, relaxation, respite, rest, walk.

**breathless** *adj* agog, anxious, avid, choking, eager, excited, exhausted, expectant, gasping, gulping, hushed, impatient, panting, peching, puffing, short-winded, spent, wheezing, wheezy, winded.

**breathlessness** *n* air-hunger, dyspnoea, gasping, panting, short-windedness, wheeziness.

**breathtaking** *adj* affecting, amazing, astonishing, awe-inspiring, awesome, exciting, impressive, magnificent, moving, overwhelming, stirring, stunning, thrilling.

**breeches** *n* galligaskins, knee-breeches, knee-cords, knickerbockers, knickers, moleskins, pantaloons, pants, plus-fours, trews, trousers.

**breed** *v* arouse, bear, beget, bring forth, bring up, cause, create, cultivate, develop, discipline, educate, engender, foster, generate, hatch, induce, instruct, make, multiply, nourish, nurture, occasion, originate, procreate, produce, propagate, raise, rear, reproduce, train.

*n* family, ilk, kind, line, lineage, pedigree, progeny, race, sort, species, stamp, stock, strain, type, variety.

**breeding** *n* ancestry, background, civility, courtesy, cultivation, culture, development, education, gentility, lineage, manners, nurture, polish, politeness, raising, rearing, refinement, reproduction, stock, strain, training, upbringing, urbanity.

*antonym* vulgarity.

**breeding-ground** *n* hotbed, nest, nursery, school, training ground.

**breeze** *n* air, breath, cat's-paw, draught, flurry, gale, gust, waft, whiff, wind, zephyr.

*v* flit, glide, hurry, sail, sally, sweep, trip, wander.

**breezy** *adj* airy, animated, blithe, blowing, blowy, blustery, bright, buoyant, carefree, careless, casual, cheerful, debonair, easy-going, exhilarating, fresh, gusty, informal, insouciant, jaunty, light, light-hearted, lively, nonchalant, sprightly, squally, sunny, untroubled, vivacious, windy.

*antonyms* calm, staid.

**brevity** *n* abruptness, briefness, brusqueness, conciseness, concision, crispness, curtness, economy, ephemerality, evanescence, fugacity, impermanence, incisiveness, laconicism, laconism, pithiness, shortness, succinctness, summariness, terseness, transience, transitoriness.

*antonyms* longevity, permanence, verbosity.

**brew** *v* boil, build up, concoct, contrive, cook, decoct, develop, devise, excite, ferment, foment, gather, hatch, infuse, mix, plan, plot, prepare, project, scheme, seethe, soak, steep, stew.

*n* beverage, blend, bouillon, brewage, broth, concoction, distillation, drink, fermentation, gruel, infusion, liquor, mixture, potion, preparation, stew.

**bribable** *adj* bent, buyable, corrupt, corruptible, purchasable, venal.

*antonym* incorruptible.

**bribe** *n* allurement, back-hander, baksheesh, boodle, dash, enticement, graft, grease, hush money, incentive, inducement, kickback, pay-off, payola, protection money, refresher, slush fund, sweetener.

*v* buy off, buy over, corrupt, reward, square, suborn.

**bribery** *n* corruption, graft, greasing, inducement, lubrication, palm-greasing, payola, protection, subornation.

**bric-à-brac** *n* antiques, baubles, bibelots, curios, curiosities, gewgaws, kickshaws, knick-knacks, ornaments, rattle-trap, trinkets, virtu.

**brick** *n* adobe, block, breeze block, brickbat, clanger, closer, faux pas, firebrick, fletton, gaffe, gaucherie, header, klinker, nogging, quoin, stretcher.

**bridal** *adj* conjugal, connubial, hymeneal, hymenean, marital, marriage, matrimonial, nuptial, sponsal, spousal, wedding.

**bridge** *n* arch, band, bond, causeway, connection, flyover, link, overpass, pontoon bridge, span, tie, viaduct, yoke.

*v* attach, bind, connect, couple, cross, fill, join, link, span, traverse, unite, yoke.

**bridle** *v* check, contain, control, curb, govern, master, moderate, rein in, repress, restrain, subdue.

**brief** *adj* abrupt, aphoristic, blunt, brusque, capsular, compendious, compressed, concise, crisp, cursory, curt, ephemeral, fast, fleeting, fugacious, fugitive, hasty, laconic, limited, momentary, passing, pithy, quick, sharp, short, short-lived, succinct, surly, swift, temporary, terse, thumbnail, transient, transitory.

*antonyms* long, long-lived, verbose.

*n* advice, argument, briefing, case, contention, data, defence, demonstration, directions, directive, dossier, instructions, mandate, orders, outline, précis, remit, summary.

*v* advise, direct, explain, fill in, gen up, guide, inform, instruct, prepare, prime.

**briefing** *n* advice, conference, directions, filling-in, gen, guidance, information, instruction, instructions, intimation, low-down, meeting, notification, orders, preamble, preparation, priming.

**briefly** *adv* abruptly, brusquely, concisely, cursorily, curtly, fleetingly, hastily, hurriedly, laconically, momentarily, precisely, quickly, shortly, summarily, temporarily, tersely.

*antonyms* fully, permanently.

**brigade** *n* band, body, company, contingent, corps, crew, force, group, guard, outfit, party, squad, team, troop, unit.

**brigand** *n* bandit, cateran, dacoit, desperado, footpad, freebooter, gangster, haiduk, heister, highwayman, klepht, marauder, outlaw, plunderer, robber, ruffian.

**brigandage** *n* banditry, brigandry, dacoitage, dacoity, freebootery, freebooting, gangsterism, heist, hold-up, robbery.

**bright** *adj* ablaze, acute, astute, auspicious, beaming, blazing, brainy, breezy, brilliant, burnished, cheerful, clear, clear-headed, clever, cloudless, dazzling, effulgent, encouraging, excellent, favourable, flashing, fulgent, gay, genial, glad, glaring, gleaming, glistening, glittering, glorious, glowing, golden, happy, hopeful, illuminated, illustrious, ingenious, intelligent, intense, inventive, jolly, joyful, joyous, keen, lambent, lamping, light-hearted, limpid, lively, lucent, lucid, luculent, luminous, lustrous, magnificent, merry, observant, optimistic, pellucid, perceptive, percipient, perspicacious, polished, prefulgent, promising, propitious, prosperous, quick, quick-witted, radiant, resplendent, rosy, scintillating, sharp, sheeny,

shimmering, shining, smart, sparkling, splendid, sunny, translucent, transparent, twinkling, unclouded, undulled, untarnished, vivacious, vivid, wide-awake.

*antonyms* depressing, dull, stupid.

**brighten** *v* burnish, cheer up, clear up, encourage, enliven, flash, gladden, gleam, glow, hearten, illuminate, light up, lighten, perk up, polish, rub up, shine.

*antonyms* darken, dull, tarnish.

**brightness** *n* blaze, braininess, brains, breeziness, brilliance, brilliancy, cheer, cheerfulness, cleverness, effulgence, fulgency, fulgor, gladness, glare, glitter, glory, hopefulness, illumination, joy, liveliness, lucency, luminance, luminosity, lustre, magnificence, optimism, promise, propitiousness, radiance, refulgence, resplendence, sheen, sparkle, splendour, vivacity, vividness.

*antonyms* cheerlessness, darkness, dullness.

**brilliance** *n* animation, aptitude, blaze, braininess, bravura, brightness, brilliancy, cleverness, coruscation, dazzle, distinction, éclat, effulgence, excellence, fulgency, gaiety, genius, giftedness, glamour, glare, gleam, glitter, glory, gloss, gorgeousness, grandeur, greatness, illustriousness, intensity, inventiveness, lambency, lucency, luminosity, lustre, magnificence, pizzazz, radiance, refulgence, resplendence, scintillation, sheen, sparkle, splendour, talent, vivacity, vividness, wit.

**brilliant** *adj* ablaze, accomplished, adroit, animated, astute, blazing, brainy, bright, celebrated, clever, coruscating, dazzling, effulgent, eminent, exceptional, expert, famous, gemmy, gifted, glaring, glittering, glorious, glossy, illustrious, ingenious, intellectual, intelligent, intense, inventive, lambent, luminous, magnificent, masterly, outstanding, quick, refulgent, scintillating, shining, showy, skilful, sparkling, splendid, star, star-like, superb, talented, vivacious, vivid, witty.

*antonyms* dull, restrained, stupid, undistinguished.

**brim** *n* border, brink, circumference, edge, lip, marge, margin, perimeter, periphery, rim, skirt, verge.

**bring** *v* accompany, accustom, add, attract, bear, carry, cause, command, conduct, convey, convince, create, deliver, dispose, draw, earn, effect, engender, escort, fetch, force, gather, generate, get beget, gross, guide, induce, inflict, influence, introduce, lead, make, move, net, occasion, persuade, produce, prompt, return, sway, take, transfer, transport, usher, wreak, yield.

**bring about** accomplish, achieve, cause, compass, create, effect, effectuate, engender, engineer, fulfil, generate, manage, manipulate, manoeuvre, occasion, produce, realise.

**bring down** abase, break, debase, degrade, fell, floor, humble, lay low, level, lower, overthrow, overturn, reduce, ruin, shoot, topple, undermine.

**bring forth** afford, bear, beget, engender, furnish, generate, produce, provide, supply, yield.

**bring home to** convince, drive home, emphasise, impress upon, persuade, prove.

**bring in** accrue, earn, fetch, gross, introduce, net, produce, profit, realise, return, yield.

**bring off** accomplish, achieve, bring about, compass, discharge, execute, fulfil, perform, rescue.

**bring on** accelerate, advance, cause, expedite, generate, give rise to, induce, inspire, lead to, occasion, precipitate, prompt, provoke.

*antonym* inhibit.

**bring out** draw out, emphasise, enhance, highlight, introduce, issue, print, publish, utter.

**bring to light** dig up, disclose, discover, disinter, exhume, expose, reveal, show, uncover, unearth, unveil.

**bring to nothing** destroy, knock the bottom out of, mar, nullify, ruin, scupper, spoil, undermine, vitiate.

**bring up** advance, broach, disgorge, educate, form, foster, introduce, mention, nurture, propose, puke, raise, rear, regurgitate, submit, succeed, succour, support, teach, throw up, train, vomit.

**brink** *n* bank, border, boundary, brim, edge, extremity, fringe, limit, lip, marge, margin, point, rim, skirt, threshold, verge, waterside.

**briny** *adj* muriatic, salty.

**brisk** *adj* active, agile, alert, allegro, bracing, bright, brushy, bustling, busy, crank, crisp, effervescing, energetic, exhilarating, expeditious, fresh, galliard, invigorating, keen, lively, nimble, nippy, no-nonsense, prompt, quick, refreshing, sharp, snappy, speedy, spirited, sprightly, spry, stimulating, vigorous.

*antonym* sluggish.

**briskly** *adv* abruptly, actively, allegro, brightly, decisively, efficiently, energetically, expeditiously, incisively, nimbly, promptly, quickly, rapidly, readily, smartly, vigorously.

*antonym* sluggishly.

**bristle** *n* barb, hair, prickle, spine, stubble, thorn, vibrissa, whisker.

*v* bridle, draw oneself up, horripilate, prickle, react, rise, seethe, spit.

**bristling** *adj* abounding, crawling, horrent, horrid, horripilant, humming, incensed, indignant, seething, spitting, swarming, teeming.

**bristly** *adj* bearded, bewhiskered, bristling, hairy, hirsute, hispid, horrent, horripilant, prickly, rough, stubbly, thorny, unshaven, whiskered.

*antonyms* clean-shaven, smooth.

**brittle** *adj* anxious, breakable, crackly, crisp, crumbling, crumbly, curt, delicate, edgy, fragile, frail, frangible, friable, frush, irritable, nervous, nervy, shattery, shivery, short, spalted, tense.

*antonyms* durable, resilient, sturdy.

**broach** *v* crack open, introduce, launch into, mention, pierce, propose, puncture, raise, start, suggest, tap, uncork, utter.

**broad** *adj* all-embracing, ample, beamy, blue, capacious, catholic, coarse, comprehensive, eclectic, encyclopaedic, enlightened, expansive, extensive, far-reaching, general, generous, gross, improper, inclusive, indecent, indelicate, large, latitudinous, roomy, spacious, square, sweeping, tolerant, universal, unlimited, unrefined, vast, voluminous, vulgar, wide, wide-ranging, widespread.

*antonym* narrow.

**broadcast** *v* advertise, air, announce, beam, cable, circulate, disseminate, proclaim, promulgate, publicise, publish, radio, relay, report, show, spread, televise, transmit.

*n* programme, relay, show, telecast, transmission.

**broaden** *v* augment, branch out, develop, diversify, enlarge, enlighten, expand, extend, increase, open up, spread, stretch, supplement, swell, thicken, widen.

**broad-minded** *adj* catholic, cosmopolitan, dispassionate, enlightened, flexible, free-thinking, indulgent, liberal, open-minded, permissive, receptive, tolerant, unbiased, unprejudiced, verligte.

**broadside** *n* assault, attack, battering, blast, bombardment, brickbat, broadsheet, cannonade, counterblast, denunciation, diatribe, fulmination, harangue, invective, pamphlet, philippic.

**brochure** *n* advertisement, booklet, broadsheet, broadside, circular, folder, handbill, hand-out, leaflet, pamphlet.

**broil** *n* affray, altercation, argument, brawl, brouhaha, dispute, disturbance, fracas, fray, imbraglio, quarrel, scrimmage, scrum, stramash, strife, tumult, wrangle.

**broke** *adj* bankrupt, bust, destitute, impecunious, impoverished, insolvent, penniless, penurious, ruined, skint, stony-broke, strapped.

*antonyms* affluent, solvent.

**broken** *adj* bankrupt, beaten, betrayed, browbeaten, burst, crippled, crushed, defeated, defective, demolished, demoralised, destroyed, disconnected, discontinuous, dishonoured, disjointed, dismantled, dispersed, disregarded, disturbed, down, dud, duff, erratic, exhausted, faulty, feeble, forgotten, fracted, fractured, fragmentary, fragmented, halting, hesitating, humbled, ignored, imperfect, incoherent, incomplete, infirm, infringed, intermittent, interrupted, isolated, jiggered, kaput, knackered, oppressed, out of order, overpowered, prerupt, rent, retracted, routed, ruined, run-down, ruptured, separated, severed, shattered, shivered, spasmodic, spent, stammering, subdued, tamed, traduced, transgressed, uncertain, vanquished, variegated, weak.

**broken-down** *adj* collapsed, decayed, dilapidated, disintegrated, inoperative, kaput, out of order, ruined.

**broken-hearted** *adj* crestfallen, dejected, desolate, despairing, despondent, devastated, disappointed, disconsolate, grief-stricken, hard-hit, heartbroken, heart-sick, heartsore, inconsolable, miserable, mournful, prostrated, sorrowful, unhappy, wretched.

**broker** *n* agent, dealer, factor, handler, intermediary, middleman, negotiator, stockbroker.

**bromide** *n* anodyne, banality, cliché, commonplace, platitude, stereotype, truism.

**bronze** *adj* auburn, brazen, chestnut, copper, copper-coloured, reddish-brown, rust, tan, titian.

**brooch** *n* badge, breastpin, clasp, clip, pin, prop.

**brood** *v* agonise, cover, dwell on, fret, go over, hatch, incubate, meditate, mope, mull over, muse, ponder, rehearse, repine, ruminate.

*n* birth, chicks, children, clutch, family, get, hatch, issue, litter, nide, offspring, progeny, young.

**brook**[1] *n* beck, burn, channel, freshet, gill, inlet, mill, rill, rivulet, runnel, stream, streamlet, watercourse.

**brook**[2] *v* abide, accept, allow, bear, countenance, endure, permit, stand, stomach, submit to, suffer, support, swallow, thole, tolerate, withstand.

**broom** *n* besom, brush, sweeper, wisp.

**brothel** *n* bagnio, bawdy-house, bordello, cathouse, flash-house, house of ill fame, house of ill repute, kip, kip-shop, knocking-shop, red light, stews, vaulting-house, whorehouse.

**brother** *n* associate, blood-brother, brer, chum, colleague, companion, compeer, comrade, confrère, cousin, fellow, fellow-creature, friar, friend, kin, kinsman, mate, monk, pal, partner, relation, relative, religieux, religious, sibling.

**brotherhood** *n* affiliation, alliance, association, clan, clique, community, confederacy, confederation, confraternity, confrèrie, coterie, fraternity, guild, league, society, union.

**brotherly** *adj* affectionate, amicable, benevolent, caring, concerned, cordial, fraternal, friendly, kind, loving, neighbourly, philanthropic, supervisory, sympathetic.

*antonyms* callous, unbrotherly.

**brow** *n* appearance, aspect, bearing, brink, cliff, countenance, crown, edge, eyebrow, face, forehead, front, mien, peak, ridge, rim, summit, temples, tip, top, verge, visage.

**browbeat** *v* awe, batter, bludgeon, bulldoze, bully, coerce, cow, domineer, dragoon, hector, hound, intimidate, oppress, overbear, threaten, tyrannise.

*antonym* coax.

**brown** *adj* auburn, bay, brick, bronze, bronzed, browned, brunette, chestnut, chocolate, coffee, dark, donkey, dun, dusky, fuscous, ginger, hazel, mahogany, russet, rust, rusty, sunburnt, tan, tanned, tawny, titian, toasted, umber, vandyke brown.

**brown study** absence, absent-mindedness, absorption, abstraction, contemplation, meditation, musing, pensiveness, preoccupation, reflection, reverie, rumination.

**browned off** bored, bored stiff, brassed off, cheesed off, discontented, discouraged, disgruntled, disheartened, fed up, pissed off, weary.

*antonyms* fascinated, interested.

**brownie** *n* elf, fairy, goblin, hob, kobold, leprechaun, lob-lie-by-the-fire, lubber fiend, nix, nixie, pixie, Puck, Robin Goodfellow, sprite.

**browse** *v* crop, dip into, eat, feed, flick through, graze, leaf through, nibble, pasture, peruse, scan, skim, survey.

**bruise** *v* blacken, blemish, contund, contuse, crush, discolour, grieve, hurt, injure, insult, mar, mark, offend, pound, pulverise, stain, wound.

*n* blemish, contusion, discoloration, injury, mark, rainbow, shiner, swelling.

**brunt** *n* burden, force, impact, impetus, pressure, shock, strain, stress, thrust, violence, weight.

**brush**[1] *n* besom, broom, sweeper.

*v* buff, burnish, caress, clean, contact, flick, glance, graze, kiss, paint, polish, rub, scrape, shine, stroke, sweep, touch, wash.

**brush aside** belittle, dismiss, disregard, flout, ignore, override, pooh-pooh.

**brush off** cold-shoulder, discourage, disdain, dismiss, disown, disregard, ignore, rebuff, refuse, reject, repudiate, repulse, scorn, slight, snub, spurn.

*antonyms* cultivate, encourage.

**brush up** cram, freshen up, improve, read up, refresh, relearn, revise, study, swot.

**brush**[2] *n* brushwood, bushes, frith, ground cover, scrub, shrubs, thicket, undergrowth, underwood.

**brush**[3] *n* clash, conflict, confrontation, dust-up, encounter, fight, fracas, incident, run-in, scrap, set-to, skirmish, tussle.

**brush-off** *n* cold shoulder, discouragement, dismissal, go-by, rebuff, refusal, rejection, repudiation, repulse, slight, snub.

*antonym* encouragement.

**brusque** *adj* abrupt, blunt, curt, discourteous, gruff, hasty, impolite, sharp, short, surly, tactless, tart, terse, uncivil, undiplomatic.

*antonyms* courteous, tactful.

**brutal** *adj* animal, barbarous, bearish, beastly, bestial, bloodthirsty, boarish, brute, brutish, callous, carnal, coarse, crude, cruel, doggish, ferocious, gruff, harsh, heartless, impolite, inhuman, inhumane, insensitive, merciless, pitiless, remorseless, rough, rude, ruthless, savage, sensual, severe, uncivil, uncivilised, unfeeling, unmannerly, unsympathetic, vicious.

*antonyms* humane, kindly.

**brutalise** *v* decivilise, dehumanise, desensitise, harden, inure.

*antonym* civilise.

**brutality** *n* atrocity, barbarism, barbarity, bloodthirstiness, brutishness, callosity, callousness, coarseness, cruelty, ferocity, inhumanity, roughness, ruthlessness, savageness, savagery, viciousness.

*antonyms* gentleness, kindness.

**brutally** *adv* barbarically, barbarously, brutishly, callously, coarsely, cruelly, ferociously, fiercely, hard-heartedly, harshly, heartlessly, inhumanly, meanly, mercilessly, murderously, pitilessly, remorselessly, roughly, ruthlessly, savagely, unkindly, viciously.

*antonyms* gently, kindly.

**brute** *n* animal, barbarian, beast, bête, boor, creature, devil, fiend, lout, monster, ogre, sadist, savage, swine.

*antonym* gentleman.

*adj* bestial, bodily, carnal, coarse, depraved, fleshly, gross, instinctive, mindless, physical, senseless, sensual, unthinking.

*antonym* refined.

**brutish** *adj* barbarian, barbaric, barbarous, boorish, coarse, crass, crude, cruel, feral, ferine, gross, loutish, savage, stupid, subhuman, swinish, uncouth, vulgar.

*antonym* refined.

**bubble¹** *n* ball, bead, bladder, blister, blob, drop, droplet, globule, vesicle.

*v* babble, boil, burble, effervesce, fizz, foam, froth, gurgle, murmur, percolate, purl, ripple, seethe, sparkle, trickle, trill, wallop.

**bubble²** *n* bagatelle, delusion, fantasy, fraud, illusion, sting, toy, trifle, vanity.

**bubbles** *n* effervescence, fizz, foam, froth, head, lather, spume, suds.

**bubbly** *adj* animated, bouncy, carbonated, curly, effervescent, elated, excited, fizzy, happy, lively, merry, sudsy.

*antonym* flat.

**buccaneer** *n* corsair, filibuster, freebooter, pirate, privateer, sea-robber, sea-rover, sea-wolf.

**buck¹** *n* beau, blade, blood, coxcomb, dandy, fop, gallant, playboy, popinjay, spark, swell.

**buck²** *v* bound, cheer, dislodge, encourage, gladden, gratify, hearten, inspirit, jerk, jump, leap, please, prance, spring, start, throw, unseat, vault.

**buck up** brighten, cheer, cheer up, encourage, hearten, improve, inspirit, perk up, rally, stimulate, take heart.

*antonym* dishearten.

**bucket** *n* bail, barrel, basin, can, cask, kibble, pail, pan, pitcher, vessel.

**buckle** *n* bend, bulge, catch, clasp, clip, contortion, distortion, fastener, hasp, kink, twist, warp.

*v* bend, bulge, catch, cave in, clasp, close, collapse, connect, contort, crumple, distort, fasten, fold, hitch, hook, secure, twist, warp, wrinkle.

**bucolic** *adj* agrarian, agricultural, countrified, country, pastoral, rural, rustic.

*antonyms* industrial, urban.

**bud** *n* embryo, germ, knosp, shoot, sprig, sprout.

*v* burgeon, develop, grow, pullulate, shoot, sprout.

*antonyms* waste away, wither.

**budding** *adj* burgeoning, developing, embryonic, fledgling, flowering, germinal, growing, hopeful, incipient, intending, nascent, potential, promising.

*antonym* experienced.

**budge** *v* bend, change, convince, dislodge, give (way), inch, influence, move, persuade, propel, push, remove, roll, shift, slide, stir, sway, yield.

**budget** *n* allocation, allotment, allowance, cost, estimate, finances, fonds, funds, means, resources.

*v* allocate, apportion, cost, estimate, plan, ration.

**buff¹** *adj* fawn, fulvid, fulvous, khaki, sandy, straw, tan, yellowish, yellowish-brown.

*v* brush, burnish, polish, polish up, rub, shine, smooth.

**buff²** *n* addict, admirer, aficionado, bug, cognoscente, connoisseur, devotee, enthusiast, expert, fan, fiend, freak.

**buffer** *n* bulwark, bumper, cushion, fender, intermediary, pad, pillow, safeguard, screen, shield, shock-absorber.

**buffet¹** *n* café, cafeteria, counter, snack-bar, snack-counter.

**buffet²** *v* bang, batter, beat, box, bump, clobber, clout, cuff, flail, hit, jar, knock, pound, pummel, push, rap, shove, slap, strike, thump, wallop.

*n* bang, blow, box, bump, clout, cuff, jar, jolt, knock, push, rap, shove, slap, smack, thump, wallop.

**buffoon** *n* clown, comedian, comic, droll, fool, goliard, harlequin, jester, joker, merry-andrew, mountebank, scaramouch, Scoggin, tomfool, vice, wag, zany.

**buffoonery** *n* clowning, drollery, farce, harlequinade, jesting, nonsense, pantomime, silliness, tomfoolery, waggishness, zanyism.

**bug** *n* addict, admirer, bacterium, blemish, buff, catch, craze, defect, disease, enthusiast, error, fad, failing, fan, fault, fiend, flaw, freak, germ, gremlin, imperfection, infection, mania, micro-organism, obsession, rage, snarl-up, virus.

*v* annoy, badger, bother, disturb, get, harass, irk, irritate, needle, nettle, pester, plague, vex.

**bugbear** *n* anathema, bane, bête noire, bloody-bones, bogey, bugaboo, devil, dread, fiend, horror, Mumbo-jumbo, nightmare, pet hate, poker, rawhead.

**build** *v* assemble, augment, base, begin, big, constitute, construct, develop, edify, enlarge, erect, escalate, establish, extend, fabricate, form, formulate, found, improve, inaugurate, increase, initiate, institute, intensify, knock together, make, originate, raise, strengthen.

*antonyms* destroy, knock down, lessen, weaken.

*n* body, figure, form, frame, physique, shape, size, structure.

**build up** advertise, amplify, assemble, boost, develop, enhance, expand, extend, fortify, heighten, hype, improve, increase, intensify, plug, promote, publicise, reinforce, strengthen.

*antonyms* lessen, weaken.

**building** *n* architecture, construction, domicile, dwelling, edifice, erection, fabric, fabrication, house, megastructure, pile, structure.

*antonym* destruction.

**build-up** *n* accretion, accumulation, ballyhoo, development, enlargement, escalation, expansion, gain, growth, heap, hype, increase, load, mass, plug, promotion, publicity, puff, stack, stockpile, store.

*antonyms* decrease, reduction.

**built-in** *adj* essential, fundamental, implicit, in-built, included, incorporated, inherent, inseparable, integral, intrinsic, necessary.

**bulbous** *adj* bellied, bellying, bloated, bulging, convex, distended, pulvinate(d), rounded, swelling, swollen.

**bulge** *n* belly, boost, bump, distension, hump, increase, intensification, lump, projection, protrusion, protuberance, rise, surge, swelling, upsurge.

*v* bag, belly, bulb, dilate, distend, enlarge, expand, hump, project, protrude, sag, strout, swell.

**bulging** *adj* bellied, bulbous, bunchy, convex, pulvinate, pulvinated, rounded, swelling, swollen.

**bulk** *n* amplitude, bigness, body, dimensions, extensity, extent, generality, immensity, largeness, magnitude, majority, mass, most, plurality, preponderance, size, substance, volume, weight.

**bulky** *adj* big, colossal, cumbersome, enormous, heavy, hefty, huge, hulking, immense, large, lumping, mammoth, massive, massy, ponderous, substantial, unmanageable, unwieldy, volumed, voluminous, weighty.

*antonyms* handy, insubstantial, small.

**bulldoze** *v* browbeat, buffalo, bully, clear, coerce, cow, demolish, drive, flatten, force, hector, intimidate, knock down, level, propel, push, push through, raze, shove, thrust.

**bullet** *n* ball, missile, pellet, plumb, projectile, shot, sinker, slug, weight.

**bulletin** *n* announcement, communication, communiqué, dispatch, dope, message, newsflash, notification, report, sitrep, statement.

**bull's-eye** *n* bull, centre, gold.

*antonym* miss.

**bully** *n* bouncer, browbeater, bucko, bully-boy, bully-rook, coercionist, Drawcansir, intimidator, killcrow, oppressor, persecutor, ruffian, termagant, tormentor, tough, tyrant.

*v* bluster, browbeat, bulldoze, bullyrag, coerce, cow, domineer, haze, hector, intimidate, oppress, overbear, persecute, push around, swagger, terrorise, tyrannise.

*antonyms* coax, persuade.

**bulwark** *n* bastion, buffer, buttress, defence, embankment, fortification, guard, mainstay, outwork, partition, rampart, redoubt, safeguard, security, support.

**bumbling** *adj* awkward, blundering, botching, bungling, clumsy, footling, foozling, incompetent, inefficient, inept, lumbering, maladroit, muddled, stumbling.

*antonyms* competent, efficient.

**bump** *v* bang, bounce, budge, collide (with), crash, dislodge, displace, hit, jar, jerk, jolt, jostle,

jounce, knock, move, rattle, remove, shake, shift, slam, strike.

*n* bang, blow, bulge, collision, contusion, crash, hit, hump, impact, jar, jolt, knob, knock, knot, lump, node, nodule, protuberance, rap, shock, smash, swelling, thud, thump.

**bump off** assassinate, dispatch, do in, eliminate, kill, liquidate, murder, remove, rub out, top.

**bumper** *adj* abundant, bountiful, enormous, excellent, exceptional, great, huge, jumbo, large, massive, prodigal, spanking, teeming, unusual, whacking, whopping.

*antonyms* miserly, small.

**bumpkin** *n* boor, chaw-bacon, clodhopper, clown, corn-ball, hick, hillbilly, jake, looby, lout, lubbard, lubber, lummox, oaf, peasant, provincial, rustic, yokel.

*antonym* man of the world.

**bumptious** *adj* arrogant, boastful, brash, cocky, conceited, egotistic, forward, full of oneself, impudent, overbearing, over-confident, pompous, presumptuous, pushy, self-assertive, self-important, showy, swaggering, vainglorious, vaunting.

*antonyms* humble, modest.

**bumpy** *adj* bouncy, choppy, irregular, jarring, jerky, jolting, jolty, knobbly, knobby, lumpy, rough, rutted, uneven.

*antonym* smooth.

**bunch** *n* assortment, band, batch, bouquet, bundle, clump, cluster, collection, crew, crowd, fascicle, fascicule, flock, gang, gathering, group-knot, heap, lot, mass, mob, multitude, number, parcel, party, pile, quantity, sheaf, spray, stack, swarm, team, troop, tuft.

*v* assemble, bundle, cluster, collect, congregate, crowd, flock, group, herd, huddle, mass, pack.

*antonyms* scatter, spread out.

**bunched** *adj* clustered, concentrated, fascicled, fascicular, fasciculate(d), gathered, grouped.

*antonyms* scattered, spread out.

**bundle** *n* accumulation, assortment, bag, bale, batch, box, bunch, carton, collection, consignment, crate, dorlach, drum, fascicle, fascicule, group, heap, mass, Matilda, pack, package, packet, pallet, parcel, pile, quantity, roll, shock, shook, stack, stook, swag.

*v* bale, bind, fasten, pack, palletise, tie, truss, wrap.

**bundled** *adj* clustered, fascicled, fascicular, fasciculate(d), gathered, grouped, parcelled, tied.

*antonyms* loose, scattered.

**bung** *n* cork, dook, stopper.

**bungle** *v* blunder, bodge, boob, botch, bumble, cock up, duff, flub, footle, foozle, foul up, fuck up, fudge, goof, louse up, mar, mess up, miscalculate, mismanage, muff, mull, ruin, screw up, spoil.

*n* blunder, boob, boo-boo, botch-up, cock-up, foul-up, mull.

**bungler** *n* blunderer, botcher, butterfingers, duffer, footler, foozler, fumbler, incompetent, lubber, muddler, muff.

**bungling** *adj* awkward, blundering, botching, cack-handed, clumsy, footling, foozling, ham-fisted, ham-handed, incompetent, inept, maladroit, unskilful.

**bunkum** *n* balderdash, baloney, bilge, bosh, bunk, garbage, havers, hooey, horsefeathers, nonsense, piffle, poppycock, rot, rubbish, stuff and nonsense, tar(r)adiddle, tomfoolery, tommyrot, tosh, trash, tripe, twaddle.

*antonym* sense.

**buoy** *n* beacon, dolphin, float, marker, signal.

**buoy up** boost, cheer, encourage, hearten, lift, raise, support, sustain.

*antonym* depress.

**buoyant** *adj* afloat, animated, blithe, bouncy, breezy, bright, bullish, carefree, cheerful, debonair, floatable, floating, happy, jaunty, joyful, light, light-hearted, lively, peppy, rising, sprightly, sunny, weightless.

*antonym* depressed.

**burble** *n* babble, gurgle, lapping, murmur, purl, purling.

*v* babble, gurgle, lap, murmur, purl.

**burden** *n* affliction, anxiety, bear, care, cargo, clog, dead weight, encumbrance, grievance, load, millstone, obligation, obstruction, onus, responsibility, sorrow, strain, stress, trial, trouble, weight, worry.

*v* bother, encumber, handicap, lade, lie hard on, lie heavy on, load, oppress, overload, overwhelm, strain, tax, worry.

*antonyms* disburden, lighten, relieve.

**burdensome** *adj* crushing, difficult, distressing, exacting, heavy, irksome, onerous, oppressive, taxing, troublesome, trying, wearisome, weighty.

*antonyms* easy, light.

**bureau** *n* agency, branch, counter, department, desk, division, office, service.

**bureaucracy** *n* administration, city hall, civil service, directorate, government, ministry, officialdom, officialese, officials, red tape, regulations, the authorities, the system.

**bureaucrat** *n* administrator, apparatchik, bureaucratist, chinovnik, civil servant, functionary, mandarin, minister, office-holder, officer, official.

**burglar** *n* cat-burglar, cracksman, house-breaker, picklock, pilferer, robber, thief, yegg.

**burglary** *n* break-in, cat-burglary, house-breaking, larceny, pilferage, robbery, stealing, theft, thieving.

**burial** *n* burying, entombment, exequies, funeral, inhumation, interment, obsequies, sepulchre, sepulture.

**burlesque** *n* caricature, mickey-taking, mock, mockery, parody, ridicule, satire, send-up, spoof, take-off, travesty.

*adj* caricatural, comic, derisive, droll, farcical, hudibrastic, mocking, parodying, satirical.

*antonym* serious.

*v* ape, caricature, exaggerate, imitate, lampoon, mock, parody, ridicule, satirise, send up, spoof, take off, travesty.

**burly** *adj* athletic, beefy, big, brawny, bulky, heavy, hefty, hulking, husky, muscular, powerful, stocky, stout, strapping, strong, sturdy, thickset, well-built.

*antonyms* puny, slim, small, thin.

**burn** *v* bite, blaze, brand, calcine, cauterise, char, combust, conflagrate, consume, corrode, deflagrate, desire, expend, flame, flare, flash, flicker, fume, glow, hurt, ignite, incinerate, kindle, light, oxidise, pain, parch, scorch, seethe, shrivel, simmer, singe, smart, smoke, smoulder, sting, tingle, toast, use, wither, yearn.

**burning** *adj* acrid, acute, alight, ardent, biting, blazing, caustic, compelling, consuming, corrosive, critical, crucial, eager, earnest, essential, excessive, fervent, fiery, flaming, flashing, frantic, frenzied, gleaming, glowing, hot, illuminated, impassioned, important, intense, irritating, painful, passionate, piercing, pressing, prickling, pungent, reeking, scorching, significant, smarting, smouldering, stinging, tingling, urent, urgent, vehement, vital, zealous.

*antonyms* apathetic, cold, mild, unimportant.

**burnish** *v* brighten, buff, furbish, glaze, polish, polish up, rub, shine.

*antonym* tarnish.

*n* gloss, lustre, patina, polish, sheen, shine.

**burrow** *n* den, earth, hole, lair, retreat, set(t), shelter, tunnel, warren.

*v* delve, dig, earth, excavate, mine, tunnel, undermine.

**burst** *v* barge, blow up, break, crack, dehisce, disintegrate, erupt, explode, fragment, gush, puncture, run, rupture, rush, shatter, shiver, split, spout, tear.

*n* bang, blast, blasting, blow-out, blow-up, breach, break, crack, discharge, eruption, explosion, fit, gallop, gush, gust, outbreak, outburst, outpouring, rupture, rush, spate, split, spurt, surge, torrent.

*adj* broken, flat, kaput, punctured, rent, ruptured, split, torn.

**burst-up** *n* break, collapse, commotion, disruption, failure, separation.

**bury** *v* absorb, conceal, cover, embed, enclose, engage, engross, engulf, enshroud, entomb, hide, immerse, implant, inearth, inhume, inter, interest, lay to rest, occupy, secrete, sepulchre, shroud, sink, submerge.

*antonyms* disinter, uncover.

**bus** *n* charabanc, coach, jitney, mammy-wagon, omnibus.

**bush** *n* backwoods, brush, hedge, plant, scrub, scrubland, shrub, shrubbery, thicket, wilds, woodland.

**bushy** *adj* bosky, bristling, bristly, dasyphyllous, dumose, dumous, fluffy, fuzzy, luxuriant, rough, shaggy, spreading, stiff, thick, unruly, wiry.

*antonyms* neat, tidy, trim, well-kept.

**busily** *adv* actively, assiduously, briskly, diligently, earnestly, energetically, hard, industriously, intently, purposefully, speedily, strenuously.

**business** *n* affair, assignment, bargaining, calling, career, commerce, company, concern, corporation, craft, dealings, duty, employment, enterprise, establishment, firm, function, industry, issue, job, line, line of country, manufacturing, matter, merchandising, métier, occupation, organisation, palaver, point, problem, profession, pursuit, question, responsibility, selling, subject, task, topic, trade, trading, transaction(s), venture, vocation, work.

**business-like** *adj* correct, efficient, formal, impersonal, matter-of-fact, methodical, orderly, organised, practical, precise, professional, regular, routine, systematic, thorough, well-ordered.

*antonyms* disorganised, inefficient.

**businessman** *n* capitalist, employer, entrepreneur, executive, financier, homme d'affaires, industrialist, merchant, trader, tradesman, tycoon.

**buskers** *n* German-band, mariachi, street-entertainers, street-musicians.

**bust** *n* bosom, breast, carving, chest, head, statue, statuette, torso.

**bustle** *v* dash, flutter, fuss, hasten, hurry, rush, scamper, scramble, scurry, scuttle, stir, tear.
*n* activity, ado, agitation, commotion, excitement, flurry, fuss, haste, hurly-burly, hurry, palaver, pother, stir, to-do, toing and froing, tumult.

**bustling** *adj* active, astir, busy, buzzing, crowded, energetic, eventful, full, humming, lively, restless, rushing, stirring, swarming, teeming, thronged.

*antonym* quiet.

**bust-up** *n* brawl, disruption, disturbance, quarrel, separation.

**busy** *adj* active, assiduous, brisk, diligent, eident, employed, energetic, engaged, engrossed, exacting, full, fussy, hectic, industrious, inquisitive, interfering, lively, meddlesome, meddling, nosy, occupied, officious, persevering, prying, restless, slaving, stirabout, stirring, strenuous, tireless, tiring, troublesome, unleisured, versant, working.

*antonyms* idle, quiet.

*v* absorb, bother, concern, employ, engage, engross, immerse, interest, occupy.

**busybody** *n* eavesdropper, gossip, intriguer, intruder, meddler, nosey parker, pantopragmatic, prodnose, pry, scandalmonger, snoop, snooper, troublemaker.

**butcher** *n* destroyer, killcow, killer, murderer, slaughterer, slayer.
*v* assassinate, botch, carve, clean, cut, destroy, dress, exterminate, joint, kill, liquidate, massacre, mutilate, prepare, ruin, slaughter, slay, spoil, wreck.

**butchery** *n* blood-letting, bloodshed, carnage, killing, mass destruction, massacre, murder, slaughter.

**butler** *n* sommelier, wine-waiter.

**butt**[1] *n* base, end, foot, haft, handle, hilt, shaft, shank, stock, stub, tail, tip.

**butt**[2] *n* dupe, laughing-stock, mark, object, point, subject, target, victim.

**butt**[3] *v, n* buck, buffet, bump, bunt, hit, jab, knock, poke, prod, punch, push, ram, shove, thrust.

**butt in** cut in, interfere, interpose, interrupt, intrude, meddle.

**butter up** blarney, cajole, coax, flatter, soft-soap, wheedle.

**buttocks** *n* arse, backside, beam end, behind, bottom, breach, bum, derrière, doup, fanny, fud, haunches, hinder-end, hinderlin(g)s, hindquarters, hurdies, natch, nates, posterior, prat, rear, rump, seat.

**button** *n* bud, catch, clasp, fastening, frog, knob, pimple.

**buttonhole** *v* accost, bore, catch, detain, grab, importune, nab, pin, waylay.

**buttress** *n* abutment, brace, mainstay, pier, prop, reinforcement, shore, stanchion, stay, strut, support.
*v* bolster up, brace, hold up, prop up, reinforce, shore up, strengthen, support, sustain, uphold.

*antonym* weaken.

**buxom** *adj* ample, bosomy, busty, chesty, comely, debonair, hearty, jocund, jolly, lively, lusty, merry, plump, robust, voluptuous, well-rounded, winsome.

*antonyms* petite, slim, small.

**buy** *v* acquire, bribe, corrupt, fix, get, obtain, procure, purchase, square, suborn.

*antonym* sell.

*n* acquisition, bargain, deal, purchase.

**buyer** *n* emptor, purchaser, vendee.

*antonyms* seller, vendor.

**buying** *n* acquisition, emption, purchase.

**buzz** *n* bombilation, bombination, buzzing, drone, gossip, hearsay, hiss, hum, murmur, news, purr, report, ring, ringing, rumour, scandal, susurration, susurrus, whir(r), whisper, whizz.
*v* bombilate, bombinate, drone, hum, murmur, reverberate, ring, susurrate, whir(r), whisper, whizz.

**by** *prep* along, beside, near, next to, over, past, through, via.

*adv* aside, at hand, away, beyond, close, handy, near, past.

**by all means** absolutely, certainly, doubtlessly, of course, positively, surely.

**by any means** anyhow.

**by chance** perchance.

**by degrees** bit by bit, gently, gradually, imperceptibly, inch by inch, little by little, slowly, step by step.

*antonyms* all at one go, quickly, suddenly.

**by far** by a long chalk, by a long shot, easily, far and away, immeasurably, incomparably, much.

**by fits and starts** erratically, fitfully, intermittently, irregularly, now and again, on and off, spasmodically, sporadically, unsystematically.

*antonyms* constantly, continuously.

**by force** vi et armis.

**by halves** imperfectly, incompletely, scrappily, skimpily.

*antonyms* completely, totally.

**by heart** by rote, memoriter, off pat, parrot-fashion, pat, word for word.

**by mistake** in error, misapprehensively, mistakenly.

**by no means** in no way, not at all, not in the least, not the least bit, on no account.

**by repute** reputatively, reputedly, supposedly.

**by the way** en passant, in passing.

**bygone** *adj* ancient, antiquated, departed, erstwhile, forepast, forgotten, former, lost, olden, past, previous.

*antonyms* modern, recent.

*n* antique, grievance, oldie.

**bypass** *v* avoid, circumvent, ignore, neglect, outflank.

*n* detour, ring road.

**by-product** *n* after-effect, consequence, epiphenomenon, fall-out, repercussion, result, side-effect.

**bystander** *n* eye-witness, looker-on, observer, onlooker, passer-by, spectator, watcher, witness.

**byword** *n* adage, aphorism, apophthegm, catchword, dictum, epithet, gnome, maxim, motto, precept, proverb, saw, saying, slogan.

# C

**cab** *n* hackney carriage, minicab, taxi, taxicab, vettura.

**cabal** *n* caucus, clique, coalition, conclave, confederacy, conspiracy, coterie, faction, intrigue, junta, junto, league, machination, party, plot, plotters, scheme, set.

**cabin** *n* berth, bothy, chalet, compartment, cot, cot-house, cottage, crib, deck-house, hovel, hut, lodge, quarters, room, shack, shanty, shed.

**cabin boy** grummet.

**cabinet** *n* almirah, case, chiffonier, closet, commode, cupboard, dresser, escritoire, locker.

**cabinetmaker** *n* ebeniste.

**cable** *n* chain, cord, hawser, line, mooring, rope.

**cabman** *n* cabby, taxi-driver, vetturino.

**cache** *n* accumulation, fund, garner, hoard, repository, reserve, stockpile, store, storehouse, supply, treasure-store.
*v* bury, conceal, hide, secrete, stash, store, stow.

**cackle** *v,n* babble, chatter, chuckle, crow, gabble, gibber, giggle, jabber, laugh, prattle, snicker, snigger, titter.

**cacophonous** *adj* discordant, dissonant, grating, harsh, horrisonant, inharmonious, jarring, raucous, strident.

*antonyms* harmonious, pleasant.

**cacophony** *n* caterwauling, discord, disharmony, dissonance, horrisonance, stridency.

*antonym* harmony.

**cad** *n* blackguard, bounder, caitiff, churl, cur, dastard, heel, knave, oik, poltroon, rat, rotter, skunk, swine, worm.

*antonym* gentleman.

**cadence** *n* accent, beat, inflection, intonation, lilt, measure, metre, modulation, pattern, pulse, rate, rhythm, stress, swing, tempo, throb.

**cadge** *v* beg, bum, freeload, hitch, scrounge, sponge.

**cadre** *n* basis, core, framework, hierarchy, infrastructure, nucleus, official.

**cafe** *n* cafeteria, coffee bar, coffee shop, estaminet, greasy spoon, restaurant, snack bar, tea-room.

**cage** *v* confine, coop up, encage, fence in, immure, impound, imprison, incarcerate, lock up, mew, restrain, shut up.

*antonyms* free, let out.

*n* aviary, coop, corral, enclosure, pen, pound.

**cag(e)y** *adj* careful, chary, circumspect, discreet, guarded, non-committal, secretive, shrewd, wary, wily.

*antonyms* frank, indiscreet, open.

**cajole** *v* beguile, blandish, blarney, coax, decoy, dupe, entice, entrap, flatter, fleech, inveigle, lure, manoeuvre, mislead, seduce, soothe, sweet-talk, tempt, wheedle, whillywha(w), wile.

*antonyms* bully, force.

**cajolery** *n* beguilement, blandishments, blarney, coaxing, enticement, flattery, inducement(s), inveigling, persuasion, soft soap, sweet talk, wheedling.

*antonyms* bullying, force.

**cake** *v* bake, cement, coagulate, coat, condense, congeal, consolidate, cover, dry, encrust, harden, inspissate, ossify, solidify, thicken.

*n* block, jumbal, loaf, lump, madeleine, mass, slab.

**calamitous** *adj* cataclysmic, catastrophic, deadly, devastating, dire, disastrous, dreadful, fatal, ghastly, grievous, pernicious, ruinous, tragic, woeful.

*antonyms* fortunate, happy.

**calamity** *n* adversity, affliction, cataclysm, catastrophe, desolation, disaster, distress, downfall, misadventure, mischance, misfortune, mishap, reverse, ruin, scourge, tragedy, trial, tribulation, woe, wretchedness.

*antonyms* blessing, godsend.

**calculate** *v* aim, cipher, compute, consider, count, determine, enumerate, estimate, figure, gauge, intend, judge, plan, rate, reckon, value, weigh, work out.

**calculated** *adj* considered, deliberate, intended, intentional, planned, premeditated, purposed, purposeful, purposive, wilful.

*antonyms* unintended, unplanned.

**calculating** *adj* canny, cautious, contriving, crafty, cunning, designing, devious, Machiavellian, manipulative, politic, scheming, sharp, shrewd, sly.

*antonyms* artless, naïve, open.

**calculation** *n* answer, caution, ciphering, circumspection, computation, deliberation, estimate, estimation, figurework, figuring, forecast, foresight, forethought, judgement, planning, precaution, reckoning, result.

**calibre** *n* ability, bore, capacity, character, diameter, distinction, endowment, faculty, force, gauge, gifts, league, measure, merit, parts, quality, scope, size, stature, strength, talent, worth.

**call** *v* announce, appoint, arouse, assemble, awaken, bid, christen, collect, consider, contact, convene, convoke, cry, declare, decree, denominate, designate, dub, elect, entitle, estimate, gather, hail, halloo, invite, judge, label, muster, name, ordain, order, phone, proclaim, rally, regard, rouse, shout, style, summon, telephone, term, think, waken, yell.

*n* announcement, appeal, cause, claim, command, cry, demand, excuse, grounds, hail, invitation, justification, need, notice, occasion, order, plea, reason, request, right, ring, scream, shout, signal, summons, supplication, urge, visit, whoop, yell.

**call for[1]** demand, entail, involve, necessitate, need, occasion, require, suggest.

**call for[2]** collect, fetch, pick up, uplift.

**call it a day** finish, knock off, leave off, pack it in, pack up, shut up shop, stop, throw in the towel.

**call off** abandon, break off, cancel, desist, discontinue, drop, withdraw.

**call on** appeal, appeal to, ask, bid, call round, entreat, gam, go and see, invite, invoke, request, summon, supplicate, visit.

**call the tune** call the shots, command, dictate, give the orders, govern, lead, rule, rule the roost.

**calling** *n* business, career, employment, field, job, line, line of country, metier, mission, occupation, profession, province, pursuit, trade, vocation, work.

**callous** *adj* case-hardened, cold, hard-bitten, hard-boiled, hardened, hard-hearted, heartless, indifferent, indurated, insensate, insensible, insensitive, inured, obdurate, soulless, thick-skinned, uncaring, unfeeling, unresponsive, unsouled, unsusceptible, unsympathetic.

*antonyms* kind, sensitive, sympathetic.

**callow** *adj* fledgling, green, guileless, immature, inexperienced, jejune, juvenile, naïve, puerile, raw, unfledged, uninitiated, unsophisticated, untried.

*antonym* experienced.

**calm** *adj* balmy, collected, composed, cool, dispassionate, equable, halcyon, impassive, imperturbable, laid back, mild, pacific, passionless, peaceful, placid, quiet, relaxed, restful, sedate, self-collected, self-possessed, serene, smooth, still, stilly, tranquil, unapprehensive, unclouded, undisturbed, unemotional, uneventful, unexcitable, unexcited, unflappable, unflustered, unmoved, unperturbed, unruffled, untroubled, windless.

*antonyms* excitable, rough, stormy, wild, worried.

*v* compose, hush, mollify, pacify, placate, quieten, relax, soothe.

*antonyms* excite, irritate, worry.

*n* calmness, dispassion, hush, peace, peacefulness, quiet, repose, serenity, stillness.

*antonyms* restlessness, storminess.

**calmness** *n* ataraxia, ataraxy, calm, composure, cool, coolness, dispassion, equability, equanimity, hush, impassiveness, impassivity, imperturbability, motionless, peace, peacefulness, placidity, poise, quiet, repose, restfulness, sang-froid, self-possession, serenity, smoothness, stillness, tranquillity, unexcitableness, unflappableness.

*antonyms* excitability, restlessness, storminess.

**calumniate** *v* asperse, backbite, blacken, defame, denigrate, detract, disparage, lampoon, libel, malign, misrepresent, revile, slag, slander, stigmatise, traduce, vilify, vilipend.

**calumny** *n* abuse, aspersion, backbiting, calumniation, defamation, denigration, derogation, detraction, disparagement, insult, libel, lying, misrepresentation, obloquy, revilement, slagging, slander, smear, stigma, vilification, vituperation.

**camaraderie** *n* brotherhood, brotherliness, companionship, comradeship, esprit de corps, fellowship, fraternisation, good-fellowship, intimacy, togetherness.

**camouflage** *n* blind, cloak, concealment, cover, covering, deception, disguise, front, guise, mask, masquerade, screen, subterfuge.

*v* cloak, conceal, cover, disguise, hide, mask, obfuscate, obscure, screen, veil.

*antonyms* reveal, uncover.

**camp[1]** *adj* affected, artificial, campy, effeminate, exaggerated, homosexual, mannered, ostentatious, over the top, poncy, posturing, theatrical.

**camp[2]** *n* caucus, clique, crowd, faction, group, party, section, set, side.

**campaign** *n* attack, crusade, drive, excursion, expedition, jihad, movement, offensive, operation, promotion, push.

*v* advocate, attack, crusade, fight, promote, push.

**camp-follower** *n* hanger-on, henchman, lackey, lascar, leaguer-lady, leaguer-lass, toady.

**can** *n* canister, cannikin, container, jar, jerrycan, pail, receptacle, tin.

**canal** *n* waterway, zanja.

**cancel** *v* abolish, abort, abrogate, adeem, annul, compensate, counterbalance, countermand, delete, efface, eliminate, erase, expunge, neutralise, nullify, obliterate, offset, quash, redeem, repeal, repudiate, rescind, revoke, scrub, strike.

**cancellation** *n* abandoning, abandonment, abolition, ademption, annulment, deletion, elimination, neutralisation, nullifying, quashing, repeal, revocation.

**cancer** *n* blight, canker, carcinoma, corruption, evil, growth, malignancy, melanoma, pestilence, rot, sickness, tumour.

**candelabrum** *n* candlestick, menorah.

**candid** *adj* blunt, clear, fair, forthright, frank, free, guileless, ingenuous, just, open, outspoken, plain, shining, sincere, straightforward, truthful, unbiased, uncontrived, unequivocal, unposed, unprejudiced, upfront.

*antonyms* cagey, devious, evasive.

**candidate** *n* applicant, aspirant, claimant, competitor, contender, contestant, doctorand, entrant, nominee, possibility, pretendant, pretender, runner, solicitant, suitor.

**candle** *n* cerge, taper, wax-light.

**candour** *n* artlessness, directness, fairness, forthrightness, franchise, frankness, guilelessness, honesty, ingenuousness, naïvety, openness, outspokenness, plain-dealing, simplicity, sincerity, straightforwardness, truthfulness, unequivocalness.

*antonyms* cageyness, deviousness, evasiveness.

**cane** *n* ferula, ferule, Malacca-cane, Penang-lawyer, stick, walking-stick.

**canker** *n* bane, blight, boil, cancer, corrosion, corruption, infection, lesion, rot, scourge, sore, ulcer.

**cannabis** *n* benj, bhang, grass, hash, hashish, marijuana, pot.

**cannibal** *n* anthropophagite, man-eater.

**cannibalism** *n* anthropophagy, endophagy, exophagy.

**canny** *adj* acute, artful, astute, careful, cautious, circumspect, clever, comfortable, gentle, harmless, innocent, judicious, knowing, lucky, perspicacious, prudent, sagacious, sharp, shrewd, skilful, sly, subtle, wise, worldly-wise.

*antonyms* foolish, imprudent.

**canon** *n* catalogue, criterion, dictate, formula, list, precept, principle, regulation, roll, rule, standard, statute, yardstick.

**canonical** *adj* accepted, approved, authorised, authoritative, orthodox, recognised, regular, sanctioned.

*antonym* uncanonical.

**canopy** *n* awning, baldachin, covering, dais, shade, sunshade, tabernacle, tester, umbrella.

**cant**[1] *n* argot, humbug, hypocrisy, insincerity, jargon, lingo, pretentiousness, sanctimoniousness, slang, thieves' Latin, vernacular.

**cant**[2] *n* angle, bevel, incline, jerk, rise, slant, slope, tilt, toss.

**cantankerous** *adj* bad-tempered, captious, carnaptious, choleric, contrary, crabbed, crabby, cranky, crotchety, crusty, disagreeable, feisty, grouchy, grumpy, ill-humoured, ill-natured, irascible, irritable, peevish, perverse, piggish, quarrelsome, testy.

*antonyms* good-natured, pleasant.

**canter** *n* amble, dogtrot, jog, jog-trot, lope.

*v* amble, jog, lollop, lope, run.

**canvass** *v* agitate, analyse, ask for, campaign, debate, discuss, dispute, electioneer, examine, inspect, investigate, poll, scan, scrutinise, seek, sift, solicit, study.

*n* examination, investigation, poll, scrutiny, survey, tally.

**canyon** *n* box-canyon, cañon, coulée, gorge, gulch, gully, ravine.

**cap** *v* beat, better, complete, cover, crown, eclipse, exceed, excel, finish, outdo, outstrip, surpass, top, transcend.

*n* beret, biretta, bonnet, chapka, cowl, fez, hat, shako, skullcap, Tam o' Shanter, yarmulka.

**capability** *n* ability, capacity, competence, facility, faculty, means, potential, potentiality, power, proficiency, qualification, skill, talent.

**capable** *adj* able, accomplished, adept, adequate, apt, clever, competent, disposed, efficient, experienced, fitted, gifted, intelligent, liable, masterly, predisposed, proficient, qualified, skilful, suited, susceptible, talented.

*antonyms* incapable, incompetent, useless.

**capacious** *adj* ample, big, broad, comfortable, commodious, comprehensive, expansive, extensive, generous, huge, large, liberal, roomy, sizable, spacious, substantial, vast, voluminous, wide.

*antonyms* cramped, small.

**capacity** *n* ability, amplitude, appointment, aptitude, aptness, brains, calibre, capability, cleverness, compass, competence, competency, dimensions, efficiency, extent, facility, faculty, forte, function, genius, gift, intelligence, magnitude, office, position, post, power, province, range, readiness, role, room, scope, service, size, space, sphere, strength, volume.

**cape**[1] *n* chersonese, head, headland, ness, peninsula, point, promontory, tongue.

**cape**[2] *n* cloak, coat, cope, mantle, pelerine, pelisse, poncho, robe, shawl, wrap.

**caper** *v* bounce, bound, capriole, cavort, dance, frisk, frolic, gambol, hop, jump, leap, romp, skip, spring.

*n* affair, antic, business, capriole, dido, escapade, gambado, gambol, high jinks, hop, jape, jest, jump, lark, leap, mischief, prank, revel, sport, stunt.

**capital**[1] *adj* cardinal, central, chief, controlling, essential, excellent, fine, first, first-rate, foremost, great, important, leading, main, major, overruling, paramount, pre-eminent, primary, prime, principal, splendid, superb, upper-case.

*antonyms* minor, sad, unfortunate.

**capital**[2] *n* assets, cash, finance, finances, financing, fonds, funds, investment(s), means, money, principal, property, resources, stock, wealth, wherewithal.

**capitulate** *v* give in, relent, submit, succumb, surrender, throw in the towel/sponge, yield.

*antonym* fight on.

**capitulation** *n* accedence, relentment, submission, surrender, yielding.

**caprice** *n* boutade, changeableness, concetto, fad, fancy, fantasia, fantasy, fickleness, fitfulness, freak, humoresque, humour, impulse, inconstancy, notion, quirk, vagary, vapour, whim, whimsy.

**capricious** *adj* changeable, crotchety, erratic, fanciful, fickle, fitful, freakish, humorous, impulsive, inconstant, mercurial, odd, queer, quirky, uncertain, unpredictable, variable, wayward, whimsical.

*antonyms* sensible, steady.

**capsize** *v* invert, keel over, overturn, turn over, turn turtle, upset.

**capsule** *n* bolus, case, lozenge, module, pericarp, pill, pod, receptacle, sheath, shell, space-ship, tablet, troche, vessel.

**captain** *n* boss, chief, chieftain, commander, head, leader, master, officer, patron, pilot, skip, skipper.

**captious** *adj* acrimonious, cantankerous, carping, cavilling, censorious, crabbed, critical, cross, disparaging, exceptious, fault-finding, hypercritical, irritable, nagging, narky, nit-picking, peevish, testy, touchy.

*antonyms* amiable, good-natured, pleasant.

**captivate** *v* allure, attract, beguile, besot, bewitch, charm, dazzle, enamour, enchain, enchant, enrapture, enslave, ensnare, enthrall, entrance, fascinate, hypnotise, infatuate, lure, mesmerise, seduce, win.

*antonyms* appal, repel.

**captivated** *adj* beguiled, besotted, bewitched, crazy, enchanted, epris, infatuated.

**captivating** *adj* attractive, beautiful, beguiling, bewitching, catching, dazzling, enchanting.

*antonyms* ugly, unattractive.

**captive** *n* convict, detainee, hostage, internee, prisoner, slave.

*adj* caged, confined, enchained, enslaved, ensnared, imprisoned, incarcerated, restricted, secure, subjugated.

*antonym* free.

**captivity** *n* bondage, confinement, custody, detention, durance, duress, enchainment, enthralment, imprisonment, incarceration, internment, restraint, servitude, slavery, thraldom, vassalage.

*antonym* freedom.

**capture** *v* apprehend, arrest, bag, catch, collar, cop, feel someone's collar, lift, nab, secure, seize, snaffle, take.

*n* apprehension, arrest, catch, imprisonment, seizure, taking, trapping.

**car** *n* auto, autocar, automobile, banger, buggy, crate, drag, dragster, flivver, horseless carriage, hot rod, jalop(p)y, jalopy, machine, motor, motor-car, vehicle, vettura.

**carafe** *n* bottle, decanter, flagon, flask, jug, pitcher.

**caravan** *n* camel train, kafila.

**carbuncle** *n* anthrax, boil, inflammation, pimple, sore.

**carcass** *n* body, cadaver, corpse, framework, hulk, relics, remains, shell, skeleton, stiff.

**card**[1] *n* dial, domino, map, playing-card, programme.

**card**[2] *n* eccentric, person, wag.

**cardinal** *adj* capital, central, chief, essential, first, foremost, fundamental, greatest, highest, important, key, leading, main, paramount, pre-eminent, primary, prime, principal.

**cardinal** *n* red-hat.

**cards** *n* devil's (picture-)books.

**care** *n* affliction, anxiety, attention, burden, carefulness, caution, charge, circumspection, concern, consideration, control, custody, direction, disquiet, forethought, guardianship, hardship, heed, interest, keeping, leading-strings, management, meticulousness, ministration, pains, perplexity, pressure, protection, prudence, regard, responsibility, solicitude, stress, supervision, tribulation, trouble, vexation, vigilance, ward, watchfulness, woe, worry.

*antonyms* carelessness, inattention, thoughtlessness.

**care for** attend, delight in, desire, enjoy, foster, like, love, mind, nurse, prize, protect, take pleasure in, tend, want, watch over.

**career** *n* calling, course, employment, job, life-work, livelihood, occupation, passage, path, procedure, progress, pursuit, race, vocation, walk.

*v* bolt, dash, gallop, hurtle, race, run, rush, shoot, speed, tear.

**carefree** *adj* airy, blithe, breezy, buoyant, careless, cheerful, cheery, easy-going, happy, happy-go-lucky, insouciant, jaunty, laid-back, light-hearted, lightsome, radiant, sunny, untroubled, unworried.

*antonyms* anxious, worried.

**careful** *adj* accurate, alert, attentive, cautious, chary, circumspect, concerned, conscientious, discreet, fastidious, heedful, judicious, meticulous, mindful, painstaking, particular, precise, protective, prudent, punctilious, scrupulous, softly-softly, solicitous, thoughtful, thrifty, vigilant, wary, watchful.

*antonyms* careless, inattentive, thoughtless.

**carefully** *adv* cautiously, painstakingly, point-device, punctiliously, warily.

*antonym* carelessly.

**careless** *adj* absent-minded, casual, cursory, derelict, forgetful, heedless, hit-or-miss, inaccurate, incautious, inconsiderate, indiscreet, irresponsible, lackadaisical, messy, neglectful, negligent, nonchalant, offhand, perfunctory, regardless, remiss, slap-dash, slipshod, sloppy, thoughtless, uncaring, unconcerned, unguarded, unmindful, unstudied, untenty, unthinking.

*antonyms* accurate, careful, meticulous, thoughtful.

**carelessness** *n* absent-mindedness, heedlessness, inaccuracy, inattention, inconsiderateness, indiscretion, irresponsibility, messiness, neglect, negligence, omission, remissness, slackness, slipshodness, sloppiness, thoughtlessness.

*antonyms* accuracy, care, thoughtfulness.

**caress** *v* canoodle, cuddle, embrace, fondle, hug, kiss, lallygag (lollygag), nuzzle, paw, pet, rub, stroke, touch.

*n* cuddle, embrace, fondle, hug, kiss, pat, stroke.

**caretaker** *n* concierge, curator, custodian, dvornik, janitor, keeper, porter, superintendent, warden, watchman.

**careworn** *adj* exhausted, fatigued, gaunt, haggard, tired, weary, worn, worn-out.

*antonyms* lively, sprightly.

**cargo** *n* baggage, consignment, contents, freight, goods, haul, lading, load, merchandise, pay-load, shipment, tonnage, ware.

**caricature** *n* burlesque, cartoon, distortion, farce, lampoon, mimicry, parody, Pasquil, Pasquin, pasquinade, representation, satire, send-up, take-off, travesty.

*v* burlesque, distort, lampoon, mimic, mock, parody, pasquinade, ridicule, satirise, send up, take off.

**carnage** *n* blood-bath, bloodshed, butchery, havoc, holocaust, massacre, murder, shambles, slaughter.

**carnal** *adj* animal, bodily, corporeal, earthly, erotic, fleshly, human, impure, lascivious, lecherous, lewd, libidinous, licentious, lustful, mundane, natural, physical, profane, prurient, salacious, secular, sensual, sensuous, sexual, sublunary, temporal, unchaste, unregenerate, unspiritual, voluptuous, wanton, worldly.

*antonyms* chaste, pure, spiritual.

**carnality** *n* bestiality, brutishness, corporeality, fleshliness, lasciviousness, lechery, lust, lustfulness, prurience, salaciousness, sensuality, voluptuousness, worldliness.

*antonyms* chastity, purity, spirituality.

**carnival** *n* celebration, fair, Fasching, festival, fête, fiesta, gala, holiday, jamboree, jubilee, Mardi Gras, merrymaking, revelry, wassail, wassail-bout, wassailry.

**carnivorous** *adj* creophagous, meat-eating, zoophagous.

**carol** *n* canticle, canzonet, chorus, ditty, hymn, lay, noel, song, strain, wassail.

**carouse** *v* booze, drink, imbibe, quaff, revel, roister, wassail.

*n* beer-up, drinking-bout, party, wassail.

**carousing** *n* celebrating, drinking, mallemaroking, party, partying.

**carp** *v* cavil, censure, complain, criticise, hypercriticise, knock, nag, quibble, reproach, ultracrepidate.

*antonym* praise.

**carpet** *n* Axminster, kali, kilim, mat, rug, Wilton.

**carping** *adj* biting, bitter, captious, cavilling, critical, fault-finding, grouchy, hypercritical, nagging, nit-picking, picky, reproachful, Zoilean.

*n* censure, complaints, criticism, disparagement, knocking, reproofs, Zoilism.

*antonyms* compliments, praise.

**carriage** *n* air, bearing, behaviour, cab, carrying, coach, comportment, conduct, conveyance, conveying, delivery, demeanour, deportment, freight, gait, manner, mien, posture, presence, transport, transportation, vehicle, vettura, voiture, wagon, wagonette.

**carrier** *n* bearer, conveyor, delivery-man, messenger, porter, runner, transmitter, transporter, vector.

**carry** *v* accomplish, bear, bring, broadcast, capture, chair, communicate, conduct, convey, display, disseminate, drive, effect, fetch, gain, give, haul, hip, impel, influence, lift, lug, maintain, motivate, move, offer, publish, relay, release, secure, shoulder, spur, stand, stock, suffer, support, sustain, take, tote, transfer, transmit, transport, underpin, uphold, urge, win.

**carry on** administer, continue, endure, flirt, last, maintain, manage, misbehave, operate, perpetuate, persevere, persist, proceed, run.

**carry out** accomplish, achieve, bring off, discharge, do, effect, execute, fulfil, implement, perform, realise.

**cart** *n* barrow, buggy, chaise, curricle, float, gig, gurney, shay, trap, tray, truck, tumbrel, wagon, wain, wheel-barrow.

*v* bear, carry, convey, haul, hump, humph, jag, lug, move, tote, transport.

**carton** *n* box, case, container, pack, package, packet, parcel.

**cartoon** *n* animation, caricature, comic strip, drawing, fumetto, lampoon, parody, representation, sketch, take-off.

**cartridge** *n* canister, capsule, case, cassette, charge, container, cylinder, magazine, round, shell.

**carve** *v* chip, chisel, cut, divide, engrave, etch, fashion, form, grave, hack, hew, incise, indent, make, mould, sculp(t), sculpture, slash, slice, tool, whittle.

**carving** *n* bust, dendroglyph, incision, lithoglyph, petroglyph, sculpture, statue, statuette.

**cascade** *n* avalanche, cataract, deluge, falls, flood, force, fountain, outpouring, rush, shower, torrent, waterfall, water-works.

*antonym* trickle.

*v* descend, flood, gush, overflow, pitch, plunge, pour, rush, shower, spill, surge, tumble.

**case**[1] *n* box, cabinet, canister, capsule, carton, cartridge, casing, casket, chest, compact, container, cover, covering, crate, envelope, etui, folder, holder, integument, jacket, receptacle, sheath, shell, showcase, suit-case, tray, trunk, wrapper, wrapping.

*v* encase, enclose, skin.

**case²** *n* argument, circumstances, condition, context, contingency, dilemma, event, example, illustration, instance, occasion, occurrence, plight, point, position, predicament, situation, specimen, state, thesis.

*v* investigate, reconnoitre.

**case³** *n* action, argument, cause, dispute, lawsuit, proceedings, process, suit, trial.

**cash** *n* bank-notes, bread, bullion, change, coin, coinage, currency, dough, funds, hard currency, hard money, money, notes, payment, readies, ready, ready money, resources, specie, wherewithal.

*v* encash, liquidate, realise.

**cashier¹** *n* accountant, assistant, banker, bursar, check-out girl, clerk, purser, teller, treasurer.

**cashier²** *v* break, discard, discharge, dismiss, drum out, expel, sack, unfrock.

**cask** *n* barrel, barrico, butt, cade, firkin, hogshead, puncheon, tub, tun, vat, wood.

**casket** *n* box, case, chest, coffer, jewel-box, kist, pyxis.

**casserole** *n* pot-au-feu, stew-pan.

**cast¹** *v* abandon, add, allot, appoint, assign, bestow, calculate, categorise, choose, chuck, compute, deposit, diffuse, distribute, drive, drop, emit, figure, fling, forecast, form, found, give, hurl, impel, launch, lob, model, mould, name, pick, pitch, project, radiate, reckon, reject, scatter, select, set, shape, shed, shy, sling, spread, throw, thrust, toss, total.

*n* air, appearance, complexion, demeanour, fling, form, lob, look, manner, mien, quality, semblance, shade, stamp, style, throw, thrust, tinge, tone, toss, turn.

**cast down** crush, deject, depress, desolate, discourage, dishearten, dispirit, sadden.

*antonyms* encourage, lift up.

**cast²** *n* actors, artistes, characters, company, dramatis personae, entertainers, performers, players, troupe.

**caste** *n* class, degree, estate, grade, lineage, order, position, race, rank, species, station, status, stratum.

**castigate** *v* beat, berate, cane, censure, chasten, chastise, chide, correct, discipline, flail, flay, flog, flyte, lash, rebuke, reprimand, scold, scourge, whip.

**castle** *n* casbah (kasba, kasbah), château, citadel, donjon, fastness, fortress, keep, mansion, motte and bailey, palace, peel, schloss, stronghold, tower.

**castrate** *v* emasculate, evirate, geld, neuter, unman, unsex.

**casual** *adj* accidental, apathetic, blasé, chance, contingent, cursory, fortuitous, incidental, indifferent, informal, insouciant, irregular, lackadaisical, negligent, nonchalant, occasional, offhand, perfunctory, random, relaxed, serendipitous, stray, unceremonious, uncertain, unconcerned, unexpected, unforeseen, unintentional, unpremeditated.

*antonyms* deliberate, painstaking, planned.

**casualty** *n* death, injured, injury, loss, sufferer, victim, wounded.

**casuistry** *n* chicanery, equivocation, Jesuitism, Jesuitry, sophism, sophistry, speciousness.

**cat** *n* feline, gib, grimalkin, malkin, mawkin, mog, moggy, mouser, puss, pussy, tabby.

**cataclysm** *n* blow, calamity, catastrophe, collapse, convulsion, debacle (débâcle), devastation, disaster, upheaval.

**catacomb** *n* burial-vault, crypt, ossuary, tomb, vault.

**catalogue** *n* directory, gazetteer, index, inventory, list, litany, record, register, roll, roster, schedule, table.

*v* accession, alphabetise, classify, codify, file, index, inventory, list, record, register.

**catapult** *v* heave, hurl, hurtle, launch, pitch, plunge, propel, shoot, throw, toss.

**cataract** *n* cascade, deluge, downpour, falls, force, rapids, torrent, waterfall.

**catastrophe** *n* adversity, affliction, blow, calamity, cataclysm, conclusion, culmination, curtain, debacle (débâcle), denouement, devastation, disaster, end, failure, fiasco, finale, ill, mischance, misfortune, mishap, reverse, ruin, termination, tragedy, trial, trouble, upheaval, upshot, winding-up.

**catcall** *n* barracking, boo, gibe, hiss, jeer, raspberry, whistle.

*v* barrack, boo, deride, gibe, give (someone) the bird, hiss, jeer, whistle.

**catch** *v* apprehend, arrest, benet, bewitch, captivate, capture, charm, clutch, contract, cop, delight, detect, develop, discern, discover, enchant, enrapture, ensnare, entangle, entrap, expose, fascinate, feel, follow, grab, grasp, grip, hear, incur, nab, nail, perceive, recognise, seize, sense, snare, snatch, surprise, take, twig, unmask.

*antonyms* drop, free, miss.

*n* bolt, clasp, clip, detent, disadvantage, drawback, fastener, hasp, hitch, hook, latch, obstacle, parti, snag, sneck, snib, trap, trick.

**catch sight of** espy, glimpse, notice, recognise, spot, view.

**catch up** draw level with, gain on, make up leeway, overtake.

**catching** *adj* attractive, captivating, charming, communicable, contagious, enchanting, fascinating, fetching, infectious, infective, taking, transferable, transmissible, transmittable, winning, winsome.

*antonyms* boring, ugly, unattractive.

**catchword** *n* byword, catch-phrase, motto, parrot-cry, password, refrain, slogan, watchword.

**catchy** *adj* attractive, captivating, confusing, deceptive, haunting, memorable, popular.

*antonyms* boring, dull.

**catechise** *v* cross-examine, drill, examine, grill, instruct, interrogate, question, test.

**catechumen** *v* convert, disciple, initiate, learner, neophyte, novice, probationer, proselyte, pupil, tyro.

**categorical** *adj* absolute, clear, direct, downright, emphatic, explicit, express, positive, total, unambiguous, unconditional, unequivocal, unqualified, unquestionable, unreserved.

*antonyms* qualified, tentative, vague.

**categorise** *v* class, classify, grade, group, list, order, pigeonhole, rank, sort.

**category** *n* chapter, class, classification, department, division, grade, grouping, head, heading, list, order, rank, section, sort, type.

**cater** *v* furnish, humour, indulge, outfit, pander, provide, provision, purvey, supply, victual.

**caterwaul** *v* bawl, cry, howl, miaow, miaul, scream, screech, shriek, squall, wail, yowl.

**catharsis** *n* abreaction, abstersion, cleansing, epuration, lustration, purgation, purging, purification, purifying, release.

**cathedral** *n* dome, duomo, minster.

**catholic** *adj* all-embracing, all-inclusive, broad, broad-minded, charitable, comprehensive, eclectic, ecumenical, general, global, inclusive, liberal, tolerant, universal, whole, wide, wide-ranging, world-wide.

*antonyms* narrow, narrow-minded.

**cattle** *n* beasts, cows, kine, livestock, neat, nowt, stock.

**catty** *adj* back-biting, bitchy, ill-natured, malevolent, malicious, mean, rancorous, spiteful, venomous, vicious.

*antonyms* kind, pleasant.

**caucus** *n* assembly, clique, conclave, convention, gathering, get-together, meeting, parley, session, set.

**causative** *adj* factitive, factive, root.

**cause** *n* account, agency, agent, aim, attempt, basis, beginning, belief, causation, consideration, conviction, creator, end, enterprise, genesis, grounds, ideal, impulse, incentive, inducement, mainspring, maker, motivation, motive, movement, object, origin, originator, producer, purpose, reason, root, source, spring, stimulus, undertaking.

*antonyms* effect, result.

*v* begin, compel, create, effect, engender, gar, generate, give rise to, incite, induce, motivate, occasion, precipitate, produce, provoke, result in.

**caustic** *adj* acidulous, acrid, acrimonious, astringent, biting, bitter, burning, corroding, corrosive, cutting, escharotic, keen, mordant, pungent, sarcastic, scathing, severe, stinging, trenchant, virulent, waspish.

*antonyms* mild, soothing.

**caution** *n* admonition, advice, alertness, care, carefulness, circumspection, counsel, deliberation, discretion, forethought, heed, heedfulness, injunction, prudence, via trita, via tuta, vigilance, wariness, warning, watchfulness.

*v* admonish, advise, urge, warn.

**cautious** *adj* alert, cagey, careful, chary, circumspect, discreet, Fabian, guarded, heedful, judicious, prudent, scrupulous, softly-softly, tentative, unadventurous, vigilant, wary, watchful.

*antonyms* heedless, imprudent, incautious.

**cautiousness** *n* caginess, care, carefulness, caution, chariness, via trita, via tuta, wariness.

*antonym* heedlessness.

**cavalcade** *n* array, march-past, parade, procession, retinue, spectacle, train, troop.

**cavalier** *n* attendant, beau, blade, chevalier, equestrian, escort, gallant, gentleman, horseman, knight, partner, royalist.

*adj* arrogant, cavalierish, condescending, curt, disdainful, free-and-easy, gay, haughty, insolent, lofty, lordly, misproud, off-hand, scornful, supercilious, swaggering.

**cave** *n* antre, cavern, cavity, den, grotto, hollow, mattamore, pothole.

**cave in** collapse, fall, give way, slip, subside, yield.

**caveat** *n* admonition, alarm, caution, warning.

**cavern** *n* cave, cavity, den, grotto, hollow, pothole, vault.

**cavernous** *adj* concave, deep, deep-set, echoing, gaping, hollow, resonant, reverberant, sepulchral, sunken, yawning.

**cavil** *v* carp, censure, complain, hypercriticise, nit-pick, object, quibble.

*n* complaint, criticism, objection, quibble, quiddit, quiddity.

**cavilling** *adj* captious, carping, censorious, critical, fault-finding, hypercritical, nit-picking, quibbling, quidditative.

**cavity** *n* antrum, belly, caries, crater, dent, gap, hole, hollow, pit, pot-hole, sinus, vacuole, ventricle, well, womb.

**cavort** *v* caper, caracole, dance, frisk, frolic, gambol, hop, prance, romp, skip, sport.

**cease** *v* call a halt, call it a day, conclude, culminate, desist, die, discontinue, end, fail, finish, halt, pack in, poop out, refrain, stay, stop, terminate.

*antonyms* begin, start.

**ceaseless** *adj* constant, continual, continuous, endless, eternal, everlasting, incessant, indefatigable, interminable, never-ending, non-stop, perennial, perpetual, persistent, unending, unremitting, untiring.

*antonyms* irregular, occasional.

**cede** *v* abandon, abdicate, allow, concede, convey, give up, grant, relinquish, renounce, resign, surrender, transfer, yield.

**celebrate** *v* bless, commemorate, commend, emblazon, eulogise, exalt, extol, glorify, honour, keep, laud, live it up, observe, perform, praise, proclaim, publicise, rejoice, reverance, solemnise, toast, wassail, whoop it up.

**celebrated** *adj* acclaimed, big, distingue, distinguished, eminent, exalted, famed, famous, glorious, illustrious, lionised, notable, outstanding, popular, pre-eminent, prominent, renowned, revered, well-known.

*antonyms* obscure, unknown.

**celebration** *n* anniversary, carousal, commemoration, festival, festivity, gala, honouring, jollification, jubilee, junketing, merry-make, merrymaking, observance, orgy, party, performance, rave-up, rejoicings, remembrance, revelry, shindig, solemnisation.

**celebrity** *n* big name, big shot, bigwig, celeb, dignitary, distinction, eclat, eminence, fame, glory, honour, lion, luminary, name, notability, personage, personality, popularity, pre-eminence, prestige, prominence, renown, reputation, repute, star, stardom, superstar, VIP.

*antonyms* nobody, obscurity.

**celerity** *n* dispatch, expedition, fastness, fleetness, haste, promptness, quickness, rapidity, speed, swiftness, velocity.

*antonyms* sloth, slowness.

**celestial** *adj* angelic, astral, divine, elysian, empyrean, eternal, ethereal, godlike, heavenly, immortal, paradisaic(al), seraphic, spiritual, starry, sublime, supernatural, transcendental.

*antonyms* earthly, mundane.

**celibacy** *n* bachelorhood, chastity, continence, singleness, spinsterhood, virginity.

**cell** *n* caucus, cavity, chamber, compartment, coterie, cubicle, dungeon, group, little-ease, nucleus, peter, stall, unit.

**cellar** *n* basement, crypt, store-room, vault, wine-store.

**cement** *v* attach, bind, bond, cohere, combine, fix together, glue, gum, join, plaster, seal, solder, stick, unite, weld.

*n* adhesive, concrete, glue, gum, mortar, paste, plaster, sealant.

**cemetery** *n* boneyard, burial-ground, churchyard, God's acre, graveyard, necropolis.

**censor** *v* amend, blue-pencil, bowdlerise, cut, edit, expurgate.

**censorious** *adj* captious, carping, cavilling, condemnatory, critical, disapproving, disparaging, fault-finding, hypercritical, severe.

*antonyms* approving, complimentary, laudatory.

**censure** *n* admonishment, admonition, blame, castigation, condemnation, criticism, disapproval, obloquy, rebuke, remonstrance, reprehension, reprimand, reproach, reprobation, reproof, stricture, telling-off, vituperation.

*antonyms* approval, compliments, praise.

*v* abuse, admonish, animadvert, berate, blame, castigate, chide, condemn, criticise, decry, denounce, inveigh against, jump on, rebuke,

reprehend, reprimand, reproach, reprobate, reprove, scold, slam, tell off, upbraid.

*antonyms* approve, compliment, praise.

**central** *adj* chief, essential, focal, fundamental, important, inner, interior, key, main, mean, median, mid, middle, pivotal, primary, principal, vital.

*antonyms* minor, peripheral.

**centralise** *v* amalgamate, compact, concentrate, condense, converge, gather together, incorporate, rationalise, streamline, unify.

*antonym* decentralise.

**centre** *n* bull's-eye, core, crux, focus, heart, hub, Mecca, mid, middle, mid-point, nave, nucleus, omphalos, pivot.

*antonyms* edge, outskirts, periphery.

*v* cluster, concentrate, converge, focus, gravitate, hinge, pivot, revolve.

**centre-piece** *n* cynosure, epergne, focus, highlight, ornament.

**centrifugal** *adj* diffusive, divergent, diverging, efferent, radial, radiating, scattering, spreading.

*antonym* centripetal.

**centripetal** *adj* afferent, clustering, concentrating, convergent, converging.

*antonym* centrifugal.

**ceremonial** *adj* dress, formal, liturgical, ritual, ritualistic, solemn, stately.

*antonym* informal.

*n* ceremony, formality, protocol, rite, ritual, solemnity.

**ceremonious** *adj* civil, courteous, courtly, deferential, dignified, exact, formal, grand, polite, pompous, precise, punctilious, ritual, solemn, starchy, stately, stiff.

*antonyms* informal, relaxed, unceremonious.

**ceremony** *n* celebration, ceremonial, commemoration, decorum, etiquette, event, form, formality, function, niceties, observance, parade, pomp, propriety, protocol, rite, ritual, service, show, solemnities.

**certain** *adj* ascertained, assured, banker, bound, conclusive, confident, constant, convinced, convincing, decided, definite, dependable, destined, determinate, established, express, fated, fixed, incontrovertible, individual, indubitable, ineluctable, inescapable, inevitable, inexorable, irrefutable, known, one, particular, plain, positive, precise, regular, reliable, resolved, satisfied, settled, some, special, specific, stable, steady, sure, true, trustworthy, undeniable, undoubted, unequivocal, unfailing, unmistakable, unquestionable, valid.

*antonyms* doubtful, hesitant, uncertain, unsure.

**certainly** *adv* doubtlessly, naturally, of course, without question.

**certainty** *n* assurance, authoritativeness, certitude, confidence, conviction, fact, faith, indubitableness, inevitability, nap, plerophoria, plerophory, positiveness, reality, sure thing, sureness, surety, trust, truth, validity.

*antonyms* doubt, hesitation, uncertainty.

**certificate** *n* attestation, authorisation, award, coupon, credentials, diploma, document, endorsement, guarantee, licence, pass, qualification, testimonial, validation, voucher, warrant.

**certify** *v* ascertain, assure, attest, authenticate, authorise, aver, avow, confirm, corroborate, declare, endorse, evidence, guarantee, notify, show, testify, validate, verify, vouch, witness.

**certitude** *n* assurance, certainty, confidence, conviction, plerophoria, plerophory.

*antonym* doubt.

**cessation** *n* abeyance, arrest, arresting, break, ceasing, desistance, discontinuance, discontinuation, discontinuing, end, ending, halt, halting, hiatus, intermission, interruption, interval, let-up, pause, recess, remission, respite, rest, standstill, stay, stoppage, stopping, suspension, termination.

*antonym* commencement.

**cession** *n* abandoning, abandonment, abnegation, capitulation, ceding, conceding, concession, conveyance, grant, relinquishing, relinquishment, renouncing, renunciation, surrender, yielding.

**chafe** *v* abrade, anger, annoy, enrage, exasperate, fret, fume, gall, get, grate, heat, incense, inflame, irritate, offend, provoke, rage, rasp, rub, scrape, scratch, vex, wear, worry.

**chaff** *n* badinage, banter, jesting, jokes, joking, persiflage, raillery, teasing.

*v* banter, chip, deride, jeer, laugh at, mock, pull (someone's) leg, rib, ridicule, scoff, taunt, tease.

**chagrin** *n* annoyance, discomfiture, discomposure, displeasure, disquiet, dissatisfaction, embarrassment, exasperation, fretfulness, humiliation, indignation, irritation, mortification, peevishness, spleen, vexation.

*antonyms* delight, pleasure.

*v* annoy, displease, disquiet, dissatisfy, embarrass, exasperate, humiliate, irk, irritate, mortify, peeve, vex.

**chain** *n* bond, catena, concatenation, coupling, fetter, fob, link, manacle, progression, restraint, sequence, series, set, shackle, string, succession, train, union, vinculum.

*v* bind, confine, enslave, fasten, fetter, gyve, handcuff, manacle, restrain, secure, shackle, tether, trammel.

*antonyms* free, release.

**chairman** *n* chair, chairperson, chairwoman, convenor, director, master of ceremonies, MC, president, presider, speaker, spokesman, toastmaster.

**chalk up** accumulate, achieve, ascribe, attain, attribute, charge, credit, enter, gain, log, mark, record, register, score, tally, win.

**chalky** *adj* ashen, calcareous, cretaceous, pale, pallid, powdery, wan, white.

**challenge** *v* accost, beard, brave, confront, dare, defy, demand, dispute, impugn, provoke, query, question, stimulate, summon, tax, test, throw down the gauntlet, try.

*n* confrontation, dare, defiance, gauntlet, hurdle, interrogation, obstacle, poser, provocation, question, test, trial, ultimatum.

**chamber** *n* apartment, assembly, bed-chamber, bedroom, boudoir, camera, cavity, closet, compartment, council, cubicle, enclosure, hall, legislature, parliament, room, vault.

**chamberpot** *n* jerry, po, pot, potty.

**champion** *n* backer, challenger, conqueror, defender, guardian, hero, kemper, kempery-man, nonpareil, paladin, Palmerin, patron, peer, promachos, protector, Roland, upholder, victor, vindicator, warrior, winner.

*v* advocate, back, defend, espouse, maintain, promote, stand up for, support, uphold.

**chance** *n* accident, act of God, coincidence, contingency, destiny, fate, fortuity, fortune, gamble, happenstance, hazard, jeopardy, liability, likelihood, luck, misfortune, occasion, odds, opening, opportunity, peril, possibility, probability, prospect, providence, risk, scope, speculation, time, uncertainty.

*antonyms* certainty, law, necessity.

*v* befall, gamble, happen, hazard, occur, risk, stake, transpire, try, venture, wager.

*adj* accidental, casual, contingent, fortuitous, inadvertent, incidental, random, serendipitous, unforeseeable, unforeseen, unintended, unintentional, unlooked-for.

*antonyms* certain, deliberate, intentional.

**chancy** *adj* dangerous, dicey, dodgy, fraught, hazardous, problematical, risky, speculative, tricky, uncertain.

*antonyms* safe, secure.

**chandelier** *n* corona, girandole, lustre.

**change** *v* alter, alternate, barter, convert, denature, displace, diversify, exchange, fluctuate, interchange, metamorphose, moderate, modify, mutate, reform, remodel, remove, reorganise, replace, restyle, shift, substitute, swap, take liberties with, trade, transfigure, transform, transmit, transmute, transpose, vacillate, vary, veer.

*n* alteration, break, chop, conversion, difference, diversion, exchange, innovation, interchange, metamorphosis, metanoia, modification, mutation, novelty, permutation, revolution, satisfaction, sea-change, shift, substitution, trade, transformation, transition, transmutation, transposition, upheaval, variation, variety, vicissitude.

**change of heart** metanoia.

**changeable** *adj* capricious, chameleon(ic), changeful, erratic, fickle, fitful, fluid, inconstant, irregular, kaleidoscopic, labile, mercurial, mobile, mutable, protean, shifting, uncertain, unpredictable, unreliable, unsettled, unstable, unsteady, vacillating, variable, vicissitudinous, volatile, wavering, windy.

*antonyms* constant, reliable, unchangeable.

**changeling** *n* elf-child, killcrop.

**changing** *adj* different, diverse, fluctuating, fluid, inconstant, kaleidoscopic, mobile, unstable, various, varying.

**channel** *n* approach, artery, avenue, canal, chamber, chamfer, communication, conduit, course, duct, euripus, fairway, fleet, flume, fluting, furrow, gat, groove, gullet, gut, gutter, level, main, means, medium, overflow, passage, path, route, sound, start, strait, trough, watercourse, waterway, way.

*v* conduct, convey, direct, force, furrow, guide, send, transmit.

**chant** *n* carol, chorus, mantra(m), melody, psalm, slogan, song, war-cry.

*v* cantillate, carol, chorus, croon, decantate, descant, intone, recite, sing.

**chaos** *n* anarchy, bedlam, confusion, disorder, disorganisation, entropy, lawlessness, mayhem, pandemonium, snafu, tohu bohu, tumult, unreason.

*antonym* order.

**chaotic** *adj* anarchic, confused, deranged, disordered, disorganised, lawless, purposeless, rampageous, riotous, shambolic, snafu, topsy-turvy, tumultous, tumultuary, uncontrolled.

*antonyms* organised, purposive.

**chap** *n* bloke, buffer, character, codger, cove, customer, fellow, guy, individual, Johnny, josser, oik, person, punter, shaver, sort, type.

**chapel** *n* bethel, Bethesda, Beulah, church, ebenezer, meeting-house, sacellum.

**chaperon** *n* companion, duenna, escort, gooseberry, gouvernante, governess.

*v* accompany, attend, escort, guard, matronise, protect, safeguard, shepherd, watch over.

**chapter** *n* assembly, branch, chapel, clause, division, episode, part, period, phase, section, stage, topic.

**char** *v* brown, burn, carbonise, cauterise, scorch, sear, singe.

**character**[1] *n* attributes, bent, calibre, cast, complexion, constitution, disposition, feature, honour, individuality, integrity, kidney, make-up, nature, peculiarity, personality, physiognomy, position, quality, rank, rectitude, reputation, stamp, status, strength, temper, temperament, type, uprightness.

**character**[2] *n* card, cove, customer, eccentric, fellow, guy, individual, oddball, oddity, original, part, person, persona, portrayal, role, sort, type.

**character**[3] *n* cipher, device, emblem, figure, hieroglyph, ideogram, ideograph, letter, logo, mark, rune, sign, symbol, type.

**characterise** *v* brand, distinguish, identify, indicate, inform, mark, represent, stamp, symptomise, typify.

**characteristic** *adj* discriminative, distinctive, distinguishing, idiosyncratic, individual, peculiar, representative, singular, special, specific, symbolic, symptomatic, typical, vintage.

*antonyms* uncharacteristic, untypical.

*n* attribute, faculty, feature, hallmark, idiosyncrasy, jizz, lineament, mannerism, mark, peculiarity, property, quality, symptom, thing, trait.

**charade** *n* fake, farce, mockery, pantomime, parody, pasquinade, pretence, travesty.

**charge** *v* accuse, adjuration, afflict, arraign, ask, assail, assault, attack, behest, bid, blame, burden, command, commit, count, demand, enjoin, entrust, exact, exhort, fill, impeach, incriminate, inculpate, indict, instil, instruct, involve, lade, load, onset, order, require, rush, storm, suffuse, tax, terms.

*n* accusation, allegation, amount, assault, attack, burden, care, command, concern, cost, custody, damage, demand, dictate, direction, duty, exhortation, expenditure, expense, imputation, indictment, injunction, instruction, mandate, office, onset, onslaught, order, outlay, payment, precept, price, rate, responsibility, rush, safekeeping, sortie, trust, ward.

**charitable** *adj* accommodating, beneficent, benevolent, benign, benignant, bountiful, broad-minded, clement, compassionate, considerate, eleemosynary, favourable, forgiving, generous, gracious, humane, indulgent, kind, kindly, lavish, lenient, liberal, magnanimous, mild, philanthropic, sympathetic, tolerant, understanding.

*antonyms* uncharitable, unforgiving.

**charity** *n* affection, agape, alms-giving, altruism, assistance, benefaction, beneficence, benevolence, benignity, benignness, bountifulness, bounty, clemency, compassion, endowment, fund, generosity, gift, goodness, hand-out, humanity, indulgence, love, philanthropy, relief, tender-heartedness.

**charlatan** *n* cheat, con man, fake, fraud, impostor, mountebank, phoney, pretender, quack, quacksalver, sham, swindler, trickster.

**charm** *v* allure, attract, becharm, beguile, bewitch, cajole, captivate, delight, enamour, enchant, enrapture, entrance, fascinate, mesmerise, please, win.

*n* abraxas, allure, allurement, amulet, appeal, attraction, attractiveness, desirability, enchantment, fascination, fetish, grisgris, idol, ju-ju, magic, magnetism, mascot, medicine, obeah, obi, phylactery, porte-bonheur, sorcery, spell, talisman, trinket, weird.

**charming** *adj* appealing, attractive, bewitching, captivating, delectable, delightful, engaging, eye-catching, fetching, honeyed, irresistible, lovely, pleasant, pleasing, seductive, sweet, winning, winsome.

*antonyms* ugly, unattractive.

**chart** *n* abac, alignment chart, blueprint, diagram, graph, map, nomograph, plan, table, tabulation.

*v* delineate, draft, draw, graph, map out, mark, outline, place, plot, shape, sketch.

**charter** *n* accreditation, authorisation, bond, concession, contract, deed, document, franchise, indenture, licence, permit, prerogative, privilege, right.

*v* authorise, commission, employ, engage, hire, lease, rent, sanction.

**chary** *adj* careful, cautious, circumspect, guarded, heedful, leery, prudent, reluctant, slow, suspicious, uneasy, unwilling, wary.

*antonyms* heedless, unwary.

**chase** *v* course, drive, expel, follow, hunt, hurry, pursue, rush, track.

*n* coursing, hunt, hunting, pursuit, race, run, rush, venery.

**chasm** *n* abysm, abyss, breach, canyon, cavity, cleft, crater, crevasse, fissure, gap, gorge, gulf, hiatus, hollow, opening, ravine, rent, rift, split, void.

**chassis** *n* anatomy, bodywork, bones, frame, framework, fuselage, skeleton, structure, substructure, undercarriage.

**chaste** *adj* austere, decent, decorous, elegant, immaculate, incorrupt, innocent, maidenly, modest, moral, neat, pure, refined, restrained, simple, unaffected, undefiled, unsullied, unvulgar, vestal, virginal, virginly, virtuous, wholesome.

*antonyms* indecorous, lewd.

**chasten** *v* admonish, afflict, castigate, chastise, correct, cow, curb, discipline, humble, humiliate, repress, reprove, soften, subdue, tame.

**chastise** *v* beat, berate, castigate, censure, correct, discipline, flog, flyte, lash, punish, reprove, scold, scourge, smack, spank, upbraid, whip.

**chastity** *n* abstinence, celibacy, continence, innocence, maidenhood, modesty, purity, restraint, self-restraint, temperateness, virginity, virtue.

*antonym* lechery.

**chat** *n* chatter, chinwag, confab, coze, crack, gossip, heart-to-heart, natter, rap, talk, tête-à-tête, visit.

*v* chatter, chew the fat, crack, gossip, jaw, natter, rabbit (on), talk, visit, yackety-yak.

**chatter** *n* babble, blather, blether, chat, chinwag, gab, gabnash, gossip, jabber, nashgab, natter, prate, prattle, prattlement, tattle, tongue-work, twaddle.

*v* babble, blather, blether, chat, clack, clatter, gab, gossip, jabber, natter, prate, prattle, prittle-prattle, talk like a pen-gun, tattle, twaddle, yackety-yak.

**chatterer** *n* big mouth, blabber, blatherskite, bletherskate, chatterbox, gabber, gabnash, gossip, loudmouth, nashgab, pie, prattlebox, windbag.

**chattering** *adj* blathering, blethering, clacking, long-tongued, prattling, tattling.

**chatty** *adj* colloquial, conversative, familiar, friendly, gossipy, informal, long-tongued, newsy, prattling, talkative.

*antonym* quiet.

**chauvinist** *adj* flag-flapping, jingoish, jingoistic, nationalistic, parochial.

**cheap** *adj* à bon marche, bargain, base, budget, common, contemptible, cut-price, despicable, dirt-cheap, dog-cheap, economical, economy, inexpensive, inferior, jitney, keen, knock-down, low, low-cost, low-priced, mean, paltry, poor, reasonable, reduced, sale, scurvy, second-rate, shoddy, sordid, tatty, tawdry, uncostly, vulgar, worthless.

*antonyms* costly, excellent, noble, superior.

**cheapen** *v* belittle, debase, degrade, demean, denigrate, depreciate, derogate, devalue, discredit, disparage, downgrade, lower, prostitute.

*antonym* enhance.

**cheat** *v* baffle, bam, bamboozle, beguile, bilk, check, chisel, chouse, cog, con, cozen, deceive, defeat, defraud, deprive, diddle, do, double-cross, dupe, finagle, fleece, fob, foil, fool, frustrate, fudge, grift, gudgeon, gull, gyp, hand (someone) a lemon, hoax, hocus, hoodwink, mislead, prevent, queer, rip off, screw, short-change, skin, smouch, swindle, thwart, touch, trick, trim, victimise.

*n* artifice, bilker, charlatan, cheater, chouse, cogger, con man, cozener, deceit, deceiver, deception, dodger, double-crosser, extortioner, fraud, grifter, impostor, imposture, knave, picaroon, rip-off, rogue, shark, sharp, sharper, short-changer, snap, swindle, swindler, trickery, trickster, welsher.

**check¹** *v* compare, confirm, examine, give the once-over, inspect, investigate, monitor, note, probe, research, scrutinise, study, test, verify.

*n* audit, examination, inspection, investigation, research, scrutiny, tab, test.

**check out** examine, investigate, test.

**check²** *v* arrest, bar, blame, bridle, chide, control, curb, damp, delay, halt, hinder, impede, inhibit, limit, obstruct, pause, rebuke, repress, reprimand, reprove, restrain, retard, scold, stop, thwart.

*n* blow, constraint, control, curb, damp, damper, disappointment, frustration, hindrance, impediment, inhibition, limitation, obstruction, rejection, restraint, reverse, setback, stoppage.

**check³** *n* bill, counterfoil, token.

**cheek¹** *n* audacity, brass, brass neck, brazenness, brazenry, disrespect, effrontery, gall, impertinence, impudence, insolence, lip, nerve, sauce, temerity.

**cheek²** *n* chap, face, gena, jowl.

**cheeky** *adj* audacious, disrespectful, forward, impertinent, impudent, insolent, insulting, lippy, malapert, pert, saucy.

*antonyms* polite, respectful.

**cheer** *v* acclaim, animate, applaud, brighten, clap, comfort, console, elate, elevate, encheer, encourage, enhearten, enliven, exhilarate, gladden, hail, hearten, hurrah, incite, inspirit, solace, uplift, warm.

*antonyms* boo, dishearten, jeer.

*n* acclamation, animation, applause, bravo, buoyancy, cheerfulness, comfort, gaiety, gladness, glee, hoorah, hopefulness, hurrah, joy, liveliness, merriment, merry-making, mirth, optimism, ovation, plaudits, solace.

**cheerful** *adj* animated, blithe, bobbish, bright, bucked, buoyant, canty, cheery, chipper, chirpy, chirrupy, contented, enlivening, enthusiastic, eupeptic, gay, gaysome, genial, glad, gladsome, happy, hearty, jaunty, jolly, jovial, joyful, joyous, light-hearted, lightsome, light-spirited, merry, optimistic, perky, pleasant, sparkling, sprightly, sunny, upbeat, winsome.

*antonym* sad.

**cheerfulness** *n* blitheness, buoyancy, cheeriness, exuberance, gaiety, geniality, gladness, happiness, jauntiness, joyfulness, joyousness, light-heartedness, sprightliness.

*antonym* sadness.

**cheering** *adj* auspicious, bright, comforting, encouraging, heartening, inspiring, promising, propitious, reassuring, stirring.

*antonyms* depressing, disheartening.

**cheerless** *adj* austere, barren, bleak, cold, comfortless, dank, dark, dejected, depressed, desolate, despondent, dingy, disconsolate, dismal, dolorous, drab, dreary, dull, forlorn, gloomy, grim, joyless, lonely, melancholy, miserable, mournful, sad, sombre, sorrowful, sullen, sunless, unhappy, uninviting, winterly, woebegone, woeful.

*antonyms* bright, cheerful.

**cheers** *interj* bottoms up, drink-hail, prosit, skoal, skol, slàinte.

**cheery** *adj* blithe, breezy, bright, carefree, cheerful, chipper, gay, good-humoured, happy, jovial, lightsome, light-spirited, lively, merry, pleasant, sparkling, sunny.

*antonyms* downcast, sad.

**chemical** *n* compound, element, substance, synthetic.

**cherish** *v* comfort, cosset, encourage, entertain, foster, harbour, make much of, nourish, nurse, nurture, prize, shelter, support, sustain, tender, treasure, value.

**cherubic** *adj* adorable, angelic, appealing, cute, heavenly, innocent, lovable, lovely, seraphic, sweet.

**chest** *n* ark, box, case, casket, coffer, crate, kist, strongbox, trunk.

**chestnut** *n* cliche, vieux jeu, war-horse.

**chew** *v* champ, crunch, gnaw, grind, manducate, masticate, munch.

**chic** *adj* à la mode, chichi, elegant, fashionable, modish, smart, stylish, trendy.

*antonyms* out-moded, unfashionable.

**chicanery** *n* artifice, cheating, chicane, deception, deviousness, dodge, double-dealing, duplicity, intrigue, jiggery-pokery, sharp practice, skulduggery, sophistry, stratagems, subterfuge, trickery, underhandedness, wiles, wire-pulling.

**chick** *n* baby, broad, chicken, girl, girlfriend, peeper.

**chicken** *n* chick, chook(ie), chuck(ie), fowl, hen, pullet.

**chicken-feed** *n* coppers, peanuts, pennies, pin money, pittance.

**chide** *v* admonish, berate, blame, censure, check, criticise, lecture, objurgate, rate, rebuke, reprehend, reprimand, reproach, reprove, scold, tell off, upbraid.

*antonym* praise.

**chief** *adj* capital, cardinal, central, especial, essential, foremost, grand, highest, key, leading, main, outstanding, paramount, predominant, pre-eminent, premier, prevailing, primal, primary, prime, principal, superior, supreme, uppermost, vital.

*antonyms* junior, minor, unimportant.

*n* boss, captain, chieftain, cock of the loft, commander, coryphaeus, director, duke, gaffer, governor, head, kaid, leader, lord, manager, master, paramount, paramount chief, principal, ringleader, ruler, superintendent, superior, supremo, suzerain.

**chiefly** *adv* especially, essentially, for the most part, generally, mainly, mostly, predominantly, primarily, principally, usually.

**child** *n* babe, baby, bairn, bambino, bantling, brat, chit, dandiprat, descendant, elf, get, git, gyte, infant, issue, juvenile, kid, kiddiewinkie, kiddywink, kinchin, littling, minor, nipper, nursling, offspring, papoose, pickaninny, progeny, shaver, sprog, suckling, toddler, tot, wean, youngling, youngster.

**child prodigy** wunderkind.

**childbirth** *n* accouchement, child-bearing, childbed, confinement, delivery, labour, lying-in, parturition, travail.

**childhood** *n* adolescence, babyhood, boyhood, girlhood, immaturity, infancy, minority, schooldays, youth.

**childish** *adj* boyish, foolish, frivolous, girlish, hypocoristic, hypocoristical, immature, infantile, juvenile, puerile, silly, simple, trifling, weak, young.

*antonyms* adult, sensible.

**childlike** *adj* artless, credulous, guileless, ingenuous, innocent, naïve, natural, simple, trustful, trusting.

**children** *n* line, offspring, progeny.

**chill** *adj* aloof, biting, bleak, chilly, cold, cool, depressing, distant, freezing, frigid, hostile, parky, raw, sharp, stony, unfriendly, unresponsive, unwelcoming, wintry.

*antonyms* friendly, warm.

*v* congeal, cool, dampen, depress, discourage, dishearten, dismay, freeze, frighten, refrigerate, terrify.

*n* bite, cold, coldness, coolness, coolth, crispness, frigidity, nip, rawness, sharpness.

**chilly** *adj* aloof, blowy, breezy, brisk, cold, cool, crisp, draughty, fresh, frigid, hostile, nippy, parky, penetrating, sharp, stony, unfriendly, unresponsive, unsympathetic, unwelcoming.

*antonyms* friendly, warm.

**chime** *v* clang, dong, jingle, mark, peal, ping, ring, sound, strike, tell, ting, tinkle, tintinnabulate, toll.

**chimera** *n* bogy, delusion, dream, fancy, fantasy, figment, hallucination, idle fancy, ignis fatuus, illusion, monster, monstrosity, snare, spectre, will-o'-the-wisp.

**chimeric** *adj* chimerical, delusive, fabulous, fanciful, fantastic, hallucinatory, illusive, illusory, imaginary, quixotic, unfounded, unreal, vain, visionary, whimsical, wild.

*antonym* real.

**chimney** *n* cleft, crevice, femerall, funnel, lum, shaft, vent.

**chimpanzee** *n* ape, jocko, pongo.

**china** *adj* ceramic, earthenware, porcelain, pottery, terracotta, wally.

**chink**[1] *n* aperture, cleft, crack, crevice, cut, fissure, flaw, gap, opening, rift, slot, space.

**chink**[2] *n* clink, ding, jangle, jingle, ping, ring, ting, tinkle.

**chip** *n* dent, flake, flaw, fragment, nick, notch, paring, scrap, scratch, shard, shaving, sliver, spall, wafer.

*v* chisel, damage, gash, nick, notch, spall, whittle.

**chip in** contribute, donate, interpose, interrupt, participate, pay, subscribe.

**chiropodist** *n* pedicurist.

**chiropody** *n* pedicure.

**chirp** *v, n* cheep, chirrup, peep, pipe, tweet, twitter, warble, whistle.

**chirpy** *adj* blithe, bright, cheerful, cheery, chipper, gay, happy, jaunty, merry, perky, sunny.

*antonyms* downcast, sad.

**chivalrous** *adj* bold, brave, chivalric, courageous, courteous, courtly, gallant, gentlemanly, Grandisonian, heroic, honourable, knightly, polite, true, valiant.

*antonyms* cowardly, ungallant.

**chivalry** *n* boldness, bravery, courage, courtesy, courtliness, gallantry, gentlemanliness, knight-errantry, knighthood, politeness.

**chivvy** *v* badger, harass, hassle, hound, importune, nag, pester, plague, pressure, prod, torment.

**choice** *n* alternative, choosing, decision, dilemma, discrimination, election, espousal, opting, option, pick, preference, say, selection, variety.

*adj* best, dainty, elect, elite, excellent, exclusive, exquisite, hand-picked, nice, plum, precious, prime, prize, rare, select, special, superior, uncommon, unusual, valuable.

*antonym* inferior.

**choke** *v* asphyxiate, bar, block, clog, close, congest, constrict, dam, gag, obstruct, occlude, overpower, reach, retch, smother, stifle, stop, strangle, suffocate, suppress, throttle.

**choleric** *adj* angry, bad-tempered, crabbed, crabby, crotchety, fiery, hasty, hot, hot-tempered, ill-tempered, irascible, irritable, petulant, quick-tempered, testy, touchy.

*antonyms* calm, placid.

**choose** *v* adopt, cull, designate, desire, elect, espouse, fix on, opt for, pick, plump for, predestine, prefer, see fit, select, settle on, single out, take, vote for, wish.

**choosing** *n* proairesis.

**choosy** *adj* discriminating, exacting, faddy, fastidious, fikish, fiky, finicky, fussy, particular, picky, selective.

*antonym* undemanding.

**chop** *v* cleave, cut, divide, fell, hack, hew, lop, sever, shear, slash, slice, truncate.

**chop up** cube, cut up, dice, divide, fragment, mince, slice (up).

**choppy** *adj* blustery, broken, rough, ruffled, squally, stormy, tempestuous, wavy, white.

*antonym* calm.

**chore** *n* burden, duty, errand, fag, job, stint, task, trouble.

**chortle** *v* cackle, chuckle, crow, guffaw, laugh, snigger.

**chorus** *n* burden, call, choir, choristers, ensemble, refrain, response, shout, singers, strain, vocalists.

**chosen** *adj* elect, elite, peculiar, predilect, predilected, selected.

**christen** *v* baptise, besprinkle, call, designate, dub, inaugurate, name, sprinkle, style, term, title, use.

**Christmas** *n* Noel (Nowell), Xmas, Yule, Yuletide.

**chronic** *adj* appalling, atrocious, awful, confirmed, deep-rooted, deep-seated, dreadful, habitual, incessant, incurable, ineradicable, ingrained, inveterate, persistent, terrible.

*antonym* temporary.

**chronicle** *n* account, annals, chanson de geste, diary, epic, gest(e), history, journal, narrative, record, register, saga, story.

*v* enter, list, narrate, record, recount, register, relate, report, tell, write down.

**chronicler** *n* annalist, chronographer, chronologer, diarist, historian, historiographer, narrator, recorder, reporter, scribe.

**chronological** *adj* consecutive, historical, ordered, progressive, sequential.

**chubby** *adj* buxom, flabby, fleshy, paunchy, plump, podgy, portly, rotund, round, stout, tubby.

*antonyms* skinny, slim.

**chuck** *v* cast, discard, fling, heave, hurl, jettison, pitch, reject, shy, sling, throw, toss.

**chuckle** *v* chortle, crow, exult, giggle, laugh, snigger, snort, titter.

**chum** *n* china, cobber, companion, comrade, crony, friend, mate, pal.

*antonym* enemy.

**chummy** *adj* affectionate, close, friendly, intimate, matey, pally, sociable, thick.

**chunk** *n* block, chuck, dod, dollop, hunk, lump, mass, piece, portion, slab, wad, wodge.

**chunky** *adj* beefy, blocky, brawny, dumpy, fat, square, stocky, stubby, thick, thickset.

*antonym* slim.

**church** *n* basilica, bethel, Bethesda, Beulah, cathedral, house of God, house of prayer, kirk, minster, preaching-house, steeple-house.

*adj* ecclesiastic, ecclesiastical, ecclesiological.

**churl** *n* boor, bumpkin, clodhopper, clown, curmudgeon, hill-billy, labourer, lout, oaf, peasant, rustic, yokel.

**churlish** *adj* boorish, brusque, crabbed, doggish, harsh, ill-tempered, impolite, loutish, morose, oafish, rude, sullen, surly, uncivil, unmannerly, unneighbourly, unsociable, vulgar.

*antonyms* polite, urbane.

**churn** *v* agitate, beat, boil, convulse, foam, froth, knot, seethe, swirl, toss, writhe.

**chute** *n* channel, funnel, gutter, incline, ramp, runway, shaft, slide, slope, trough.

**cigarette** *n* cancer-stick, cig, ciggy, coffin-nail, fag, gasper, joint, smoke, snout, whiff.

**cinch** *n* doddle, piece of cake, snip, stroll, walk-over.

**cinema** *n* big screen, filmhouse, flicks, movies, picture-house, picture-palace.

**cipher** *n* character, code, cryptograph, device, digit, figure, logo, mark, monogram, nil, nobody, nonentity, nothing, nought, number, numeral, symbol, yes-man, zero.

**circle** *n* area, assembly, band, bounds, circuit, circumference, class, clique, club, coil, company, compass, cordon, coterie, crowd, cycle, disc, domain, enclosure, fellowship, field, fraternity, globe, group, gyre, lap, loop, orb, orbit, perimeter, periphery, province, range, realm, region, revolution, ring, round, roundance, roundel, roundlet, rundle, scene, school, set, society, sphere, turn.

*v* belt, circumambulate, circumnavigate, circumscribe, coil, compass, curl, curve, encircle, enclose, encompass, envelop, gird, girdle, hem in, loop, pivot, revolve, ring, rotate, surround, tour, whirl.

**circling** *adj* eddying, vortical, wheeling, whirling.

**circuit** *n* ambit, area, boundary, bounds, circumference, compass, course, district, eyre, journey, lap, limit, orbit, perambulation, range, region, revolution, round, route, tour, track, tract.

**circuitous** *adj* ambagious, anfractuous, cagey, devious, indirect, labyrinthine, meandering, oblique, periphrastic, rambling, roundabout, tortuous, winding.

*antonyms* direct, straight.

**circular** *adj* annular, discoid(al), disc-shaped, hoop-shaped, ring-shaped, round.

*n* advert, announcement, handbill, leaflet, letter, notice, pamphlet.

**circulate** *v* broadcast, diffuse, disseminate, distribute, flow, go around, go the rounds, gyrate, issue, promulgate, propagate, publicise, publish, radiate, revolve, rotate, spread, spread abroad, swirl, whirl.

**circulation** *n* blood-flow, circling, currency, dissemination, distribution, flow, motion, rotation, spread, spreading, transmission.

**circumference** *n* border, boundary, bounds, circuit, edge, extremity, fringe, limits, margin, outline, perimeter, periphery, rim, verge.

**circumlocution** *n* diffuseness, discursiveness, euphemism, indirectness, periphrasis, prolixity, redundancy, roundaboutness, wordiness.

**circumscribe** *v* bound, confine, curtail, define, delimit, delineate, demarcate, encircle, enclose, encompass, environ, hem in, limit, pen in, restrain, restrict, surround, trim.

**circumspect** *adj* attentive, canny, careful, cautious, chary, deliberate, discreet, discriminating, guarded, heedful, judicious, leery, observant, politic, sagacious, sage, vigilant, wary, watchful.

*antonyms* unguarded, unwary.

**circumspection** *n* canniness, care, caution, chariness, deliberation, discretion, guardedness, prudence, wariness.

**circumstance** *n* accident, condition, contingency, detail, element, event, fact, factor, happening, happenstance, incident, item, occurrence, particular, position, respect, situation.

**circumstances** *n* conditions, galère, lifestyle, means, position, resources, situation, state, state of affairs, station, status, times.

**circumstantial** *adj* conjectural, contingent, detailed, evidential, exact, hearsay, incidental, indirect, inferential, minute, particular, presumptive, provisional, specific.

*antonyms* hard, inexact, vague.

**circumvent** *v* beguile, bypass, deceive, dupe, elude, ensnare, entrap, evade, get out of, get past, hoodwink, mislead, outflank, outgeneral, outwit, overreach, sidestep, steer clear of, thwart, trick.

**circumvention** *n* bypassing, chicanery, deceit, deception, dodge, duplicity, evasion, fraud, guile, imposition, imposture, thwarting, trickery, wiles.

**cistern** *n* basin, pool, reservoir, sink, tank, vat.

**citadel** *n* acropolis, bastion, castle, fortification, fortress, keep, stronghold, tower.

**citation** *n* award, commendation, cutting, excerpt, illustration, mention, passage, quotation, quote, reference, source.

**cite** *v* accite, adduce, advance, call, enumerate, evidence, extract, mention, name, quote, specify, subpoena, summon.

**citizen** *n* burgess, burgher, city-dweller, denizen, dweller, freeman, inhabitant, oppidan, ratepayer, resident, subject, townsman, urbanite.

**city** n conurbation, megalopolis, metropolis, municipality, town.

**civic** adj borough, city, communal, community, local, municipal, oppidan, public, urban.

**civil** adj accommodating, affable, civic, civilised, complaisant, courteous, courtly, domestic, home, interior, internal, internecine, lay, municipal, obliging, polished, polite, political, refined, secular, temporal, urbane, well-bred, well-mannered.

*antonym* uncivil.

**civil servant** bureaucrat, fonctionnaire.

**civilisation** n advancement, cultivation, culture, development, education, enlightenment, kultur, progress, refinement, sophistication, urbanity.

*antonyms* barbarity, primitiveness.

**civilise** v ameliorate, cultivate, educate, enlighten, humanise, improve, meliorate, perfect, polish, refine, sophisticate, tame.

**civilised** adj advanced, cultured, educated, enlightened, humane, polite, refined, sophisticated, tolerant, urbane.

*antonyms* barbarous, primitive.

**civility** n affability, amenity, amiability, attention, breeding, comity, complaisance, cordiality, courteousness, courtesy, graciousness, politeness, politesse, tact, urbanity.

*antonyms* rudeness, uncouthness.

**claim** v affirm, allege, arrogate, ask, assert, challenge, collect, demand, exact, hold, insist, maintain, need, profess, request, require, state, take, uphold.

n affirmation, allegation, application, assertion, call, demand, insistence, petition, pretension, privilege, protestation, request, requirement, right, title.

**claimant** n applicant, petitioner, pretendant, pretender, suppliant, supplicant.

**clairvoyant** adj extra-sensory, fey, oracular, prescient, prophetic, psychic, second-sighted, sibylline, telepathic, vatic, visionary.

n augur, diviner, fortune-teller, haruspex, oracle, prophet, prophetess, seer, sibyl, soothsayer, spaeman, spaer, spaewife, telepath, telepathist, visionary.

**clamber** v ascend, claw, climb, crawl, descend, scale, scrabble, scramble, shin.

**clammy** adj close, damp, dank, heavy, moist, muggy, pasty, slimy, sticky, sweating, sweaty, viscid.

**clamorous** adj blaring, deafening, insistent, lusty, noisy, riotous, tumultuous, uproarious, vehement, vociferant, vociferous.

*antonym* silent.

**clamour** n agitation, babel, blare, brouhaha, commotion, complaint, din, exclamation, hubbub, hue, hullabaloo, katzenjammer, noise, outcry, racket, shout, shouting, uproar, vociferation.

*antonym* silence.

**clamp** n brace, bracket, fastener, grip, press, vice.

v brace, clinch, fasten, fix, impose, secure.

**clan** n band, brotherhood, clique, confraternity, coterie, faction, family, fraternity, gens, group, house, phratry, race, sect, sept, set, society, sodality, tribe.

**clandestine** adj backroom, behind-door, cloak-and-dagger, closet, concealed, covert, fraudulent, furtive, hidden, private, secret, sly, sneaky, stealthy, subreptitious, surreptitious, underground, underhand, under-the-counter.

*antonym* open.

**clandestinely** adv covertly, furtively, on the q.t., on the quiet, quietly, secretly, surreptitiously.

**clang** v bong, chime, clank, clash, jangle, peal, resound, reverberate, ring, toll.

n bong, clank, clash, clatter, jangle, peal.

**clannish** adj cliqu(e)y, cliquish, close, exclusive, insular, narrow, parochial, sectarian, select, unfriendly.

*antonyms* friendly, open.

**clap** v acclaim, applaud, bang, cheer, pat, slap, smack, thrust, thwack, wallop, whack.

**claptrap** n affectation, balderdash, blarney, bombast, bunk, bunkum, codswallop, drivel, flannel, guff, hokum, hot air, humbug, nonsense, rodomontade, rubbish, tripe.

**clarification** n definition, elucidation, explanation, exposition, gloss, illumination, interpretation, simplification.

*antonym* obfuscation.

**clarify** v cleanse, define, elucidate, explain, gloss, illuminate, purify, refine, resolve, shed/throw light on, simplify.

*antonym* obscure.

**clarity** n clearness, comprehensibility, definition, explicitness, intelligibility, limpidity, lucidity, lucidness, obviousness, precision, simplicity, transparency, unambiguousness.

*antonyms* obscurity, vagueness.

**clash** v bang, clang, clank, clatter, conflict, crash, disagree, feud, fight, grapple, jangle, jar, quarrel, rattle, war, wrangle.

n brush, clank, clatter, collision, conflict, confrontation, disagreement, fight, jangle, jar, noise, show-down.

**clasp** n agraffe, brooch, buckle, catch, clip, embrace, fastener, fastening, grasp, grip, hasp, hold, hook, hug, pin, snap, tach(e).

v attach, clutch, concatenate, connect, embrace, enclasp, enfold, fasten, grapple, grasp, grip, hold, hug, press, seize, squeeze.

**class**[1] n calibre, caste, category, classification, collection, denomination, department, description, division, genre, genus, grade, group, grouping, ilk, kidney, kind, kingdom, league, order, phylum, quality, rank, section, set, sort, species, sphere, status, style, taxon, type, value.

v assort, brand, categorise, classify, codify, designate, grade, group, rank, rate.

**class**[2] n course, lecture, seminar, teach-in, tutorial.

**classic** *adj* abiding, ageless, archetypal, Augustan, best, characteristic, chaste, consummate, deathless, definitive, enduring, established, excellent, exemplary, finest, first-rate, ideal, immortal, lasting, master, masterly, model, paradigmatic, quintessential, refined, regular, restrained, standard, time-honoured, traditional, typical, undying, usual.

*antonym* second-rate.

*n* chef d'oeuvre, exemplar, masterpiece, masterwork, model, paradigm, pièce de resistance, prototype, standard.

**classical** *adj* attic, Attic, Augustan, chaste, elegant, established, excellent, grecian, Greek, harmonious, Hellenic, Latin, pure, refined, restrained, Roman, standard, symmetrical, traditional, well-proportioned.

**classification** *n* analysis, arrangement, cataloguing, categorisation, codification, digestion, grading, pigeon-holing, sorting, taxis, taxonomy.

**classify** *v* arrange, assort, catalogue, categorise, codify, digest, dispose, distribute, file, grade, pigeon-hole, rank, sort, systematise, tabulate.

**classy** *adj* elegant, exclusive, exquisite, fine, gorgeous, grand, high-class, posh, select, stylish, superior, swanky, up-market.

*antonyms* dowdy, plain, unstylish.

**clause** *n* article, chapter, condition, demand, heading, item, paragraph, part, passage, point, provision, proviso, section, specification, stipulation, subsection.

**claw** *n* griff(e), gripper, nail, nipper, pincer, pounce, talon, tentacle, unguis.

*v* dig, graze, lacerate, mangle, maul, rip, scrabble, scrape, scratch, tear.

**clean** *adj* antiseptic, chaste, clarified, complete, conclusive, decent, decisive, decontaminated, delicate, elegant, entire, exemplary, faultless, final, flawless, fresh, good, graceful, guiltless, honest, honourable, hygienic, immaculate, innocent, laundered, moral, natural, neat, perfect, pure, purified, respectable, sanitary, simple, spotless, sterile, sterilised, thorough, tidy, total, trim, unblemished, unadulterated, uncluttered, uncontaminated, undefiled, unimpaired, unpolluted, unsoiled, unspotted, unstained, unsullied, upright, virtuous, washed, whole.

*antonyms* dirty, indecent, polluted, unsterile.

*v* bath, cleanse, deodorise, deterge, disinfect, dust, launder, lave, mop, purge, purify, rinse, sanitise, scour, scrub, sponge, swab, sweep, vacuum, wash, wipe.

*antonyms* defile, dirty.

**clean up** sanitise, tidy, wash.

**cleaner** *n* char, charlady, charwoman, daily.

**cleanse** *v* absolve, absterge, catharise, clean, clear, deterge, detoxicate, detoxify, lustrate, porge, purge, purify, rinse, scavenge, scour, scrub, wash.

*antonyms* defile, dirty.

**cleanser** *n* abstergent, detergent, detersive, disinfectant, purifier, scourer, scouring-powder, soap, solvent.

**cleansing** *n* abstersion, detergence, detergency, detersion.

*adj* abstergent, abstersive, cathartic(al), detergent, detersive, purgative, purgatory.

**clear** *adj* apparent, audible, bright, certain, clean, cloudless, coherent, comprehensible, conspicuous, convinced, crystalline, decided, definite, diaphanous, disengaged, distinct, eidetic, empty, evident, explicit, express, fair, fine, free, glassy, guiltless, halcyon, hyaline, immaculate, incontrovertible, innocent, intelligible, light, limpid, lucid, luculent, luminous, manifest, obvious, open, palpable, patent, pellucid, perceptible, perspicuous, plain, positive, pronounced, pure, recognisable, resolved, satisfied, see-through, serene, sharp, shining, smooth, stainless, sunny, sure, translucent, transparent, unambiguous, unblemished, unclouded, undefiled, undimmed, undulled, unequivocal, unhampered, unhindered, unimpeded, unlimited, unmistakable, unobstructed, unquestionable, untarnished, untroubled, well-defined.

*antonyms* cloudy, fuzzy, guilty, vague.

*v* absolve, acquire, acquit, brighten, clarify, clean, cleanse, decode, decongest, deoppilate, disengage, disentangle, earn, emancipate, erase, excuse, exonerate, extricate, fix, free, gain, jump, justify, leap, liberate, lighten, loosen, make, miss, open, pass over, purify, reap, refine, rid, secure, strip, tidy, unblock, unclog, uncloud, unload, unpack, unscramble, vault, vindicate, wipe.

*antonyms* block, condemn, defile, dirty.

**clear out** beat it, clear off, decamp, depart, empty, exhaust, leave, retire, sort, throw out, withdraw.

**clear up** answer, clarify, elucidate, explain, fix, order, rearrange, remove, resolve, solve, sort, tidy, unravel.

**clearance** *n* allowance, authorisation, consent, endorsement, gap, go-ahead, headroom, leave, margin, OK, permission, riddance, sanction, space, the green light.

**clear-cut** *adj* clear, definite, distinct, explicit, plain, precise, specific, straightforward, unambiguous, unequivocal, well-defined.

*antonyms* ambiguous, vague.

**clearing** *n* dell, glade, hollow, opening, space.

*adj* deobstruent.

**clearly** *adv* distinctly, evidently, incontestably, incontrovertibly, manifestly, markedly, obviously, openly, plainly, undeniably, undoubtedly.

*antonyms* indistinctly, vaguely.

**clearness** *n* audibility, brightness, clarity, coherence, distinctness, explicitness, glassiness, intelligibility, limpidity, lucidity, lucidness, luminosity, transparency, transparentness, unambiguousness.

**cleave**[1] *v* adhere, attach, cling, cohere, hold, remain, stick, unite.

**cleave**[2] *v* chop, crack, dissever, disunite, divide, halve, hew, open, part, pierce, rend, rive, separate, sever, slice, split, sunder.

*antonyms* join, unite.

**cleft** *n* breach, break, chasm, chink, crack, cranny, crevice, fissure, fracture, gap, opening, rent, split.
*adj* cloven, divided, parted, rent, riven, ruptured, separated, split, sundered, torn.
*antonym* solid.

**clemency** *n* compassion, forebearance, forgiveness, generosity, humanity, indulgence, kindness, lenience, leniency, lenity, magnanimity, mercifulness, mercy, mildness, moderation, soft-heartedness, tenderness.
*antonyms* harshness, ruthlessness.

**clement** *adj* balmy, calm, compassionate, fair, fine, forbearing, forgiving, generous, gentle, humane, indulgent, kind, kind-hearted, lenient, magnanimous, merciful, mild, soft-hearted, temperate, tender.
*antonyms* harsh, ruthless.

**clench** *v* clasp, close, clutch, double, grasp, grip, grit, hold.

**clergy** *n* churchmen, clergymen, clerics, ecclesiastics, ministry, presbyterate, priesthood, the church, the cloth.

**clergyman** *n* chaplain, churchman, cleric, curate, deacon, dean, divine, father, levite, man of God, minister, padre, parson, pastor, presbyter, priest, rabbi, rector, reverend, sky-pilot, vicar.

**clerical** *adj* ecclesiastical, pastoral, priestly, sacerdotal.

**clerk** *n* account-keeper, assistant, copyist, official, pen-driver, pen-pusher, protocolist, quill-driver, quillman, receptionist, shop-assistant, writer.

**clever** *adj* able, adroit, apt, astute, brainy, bright, canny, capable, cunning, deep, dexterous, discerning, elegant, expert, gifted, gleg, good-natured, habile, ingenious, intelligent, inventive, keen, knowing, knowledgeable, quick, quick-witted, rational, resourceful, sagacious, sensible, shrewd, skilful, smart, talented, witty.
*antonyms* foolish, naïve, senseless.

**clever dick** smart Alec, smart-ass, smartypants, wiseling, witling, wit-monger.

**cleverness** *n* ability, adroitness, astuteness, brains, brightness, canniness, cunning, dexterity, flair, gift, gumption, ingenuity, intelligence, nous, quickness, resourcefulness, sagacity, sense, sharpness, shrewdness, smartness, smeddum, talent, wit.
*antonyms* foolishness, naïvety, senselessness.

**cliche** *n* banality, bromide, chestnut, penny-a-lineism, platitude, stereotype, tag, truism.

**click** *n, v* beat, clack, snap, snick, snip, tick.

**client** *n* applicant, buyer, consumer, customer, dependant, habitue, patient, patron, protege, shopper.

**clientèle** *n* business, clients, customers, following, market, patronage, patrons, regulars, trade.

**cliff** *n* bluff, crag, escarpment, face, overhang, precipice, rock-face, scar, scarp.

**climactic** *adj* climactical, critical, crucial, decisive, exciting, orgasmic, orgastic, paramount.
*antonyms* bathetic, trivial.

**climate** *n* ambience, atmosphere, clime, country, disposition, feeling, milieu, mood, region, setting, temper, temperature, tendency, trend, weather.

**climax** *n* acme, apogee, culmination, head, height, high point, highlight, orgasm, peak, summit, top, zenith.
*antonyms* bathos, low point, nadir.

**climb** *v* ascend, clamber, mount, rise, scale, shin up, soar, swarm (up), top.

**climb down** back down, clamber down, descend, dismount, eat crow, eat one's words, retract, retreat.

**clinch** *v* assure, bolt, cap, clamp, conclude, confirm, cuddle, decide, determine, embrace, fasten, fix, grasp, hug, nail, neck, rivet, seal, secure, settle, squeeze, verify.

**cling** *v* adhere, clasp, cleave, clutch, embrace, fasten, grasp, grip, hug, stick.

**clinical** *adj* analytic, business-like, cold, detached, disinterested, dispassionate, emotionless, impersonal, objective, scientific, unemotional.
*antonyms* biased, subjective.

**clip¹** *v* crop, curtail, cut, dock, pare, poll, pollard, prune, shear, shorten, snip, trim.

**clip²** *v* box, clobber, clout, cuff, hit, knock, punch, skelp, slap, smack, sock, thump, wallop, whack.
*n* blow, box, clout, cuff, hit, knock, punch, skelp, slap, smack, sock, thump, wallop, whack.

**clip³** *n* gallop, lick, rate, speed.

**clip⁴** *v* attach, fasten, fix, hold, pin, staple.

**clipping** *n* citation, cutting, excerpt, extract, piece.

**clique** *n* bunch, circle, clan, coterie, crew, crowd, faction, gang, group, grouplet, mates, mob, pack, set.

**cloak** *n* blind, cape, coat, cover, front, mantle, mask, pretext, shield, wrap.
*v* camouflage, conceal, cover, disguise, hide, mask, obscure, screen, veil.

**clodhopper** *n* booby, boor, bumpkin, galoot, lout, lummox, lumpkin, oaf, ox, yokel.

**clog** *v* ball, block, burden, congest, dam up, gaum, hamper, hinder, impede, jam, obstruct, occlude, shackle, stop up, stuff.
*antonym* unblock.
*n* burden, dead-weight, drag, encumbrance, hindrance, impediment, obstruction.

**cloistered** *adj* cloistral, confined, enclosed, hermitic, insulated, protected, reclusive, restricted, secluded, sequestered, sheltered, shielded, withdrawn.
*antonyms* open, urbane.

**close¹** *v* bar, block, cease, choke, clog, cloture, complete, conclude, confine, connect, cork, couple, culminate, discontinue, end, fill, finish, fuse, grapple, join, lock, mothball, obstruct, plug, seal, secure, shut, stop, terminate, unite, wind up.

*n* cadence, cessation, completion, conclusion, culmination, denouement, end, ending, finale, finish, junction, pause, stop, termination, wind-up.

**close²** *adj* accurate, adjacent, adjoining, airless, alert, approaching, approximative, assiduous, at hand, attached, attentive, careful, compact, concentrated, confidential, confined, congested, conscientious, cramped, cropped, crowded, dear, dense, detailed, devoted, dogged, earnest, exact, faithful, familiar, fixed, frowsty, fuggy, handy, hard by, heavy, hidden, humid, illiberal, imminent, impending, impenetrable, inseparable, intense, intent, intimate, jam-packed, keen, literal, loving, mean, mingy, minute, miserly, muggy, narrow, near, near-by, neighbouring, niggardly, nigh, oppressive, packed, painstaking, parsimonious, penurious, precise, private, reserved, reticent, retired, rigorous, searching, secluded, secret, secretive, short, solid, stale, stifling, stingy, strict, stuffy, suffocating, sweltering, taciturn, thick, thorough, tight, tight-fisted, uncommunicative, unforthcoming, ungenerous, unventilated.

*antonyms* careless, cool, far, unfriendly.

**closed** *adj* concluded, decided, ended, exclusive, fastened, finished, locked, over, resolved, restricted, sealed, settled, shut, terminated, wound-up.

*antonyms* open, unfastened, unsettled.

**closure** *n* cap, cessation, closing, cloture, conclusion, end, finish, guillotine, lid, plug, seal, stoppage, stopper, stricture, winding-up.

*antonym* opening.

**clot¹** *n* clotting, coagulation, curdling, embolism, embolus, gob, grume, lump, mass, occlusion, thrombus.

*v* coagulate, coalesce, congeal, curdle, jell, thicken.

**clot²** *n* ass, buffoon, dolt, dope, dunderhead, fathead, fool, idiot, nincompoop, nit, nitwit, numbskull, twerp.

**cloth** *n* dish-cloth, duster, fabric, face-cloth, material, rag, stuff, textiles, tissue, towel.

**clothe** *v* accoutre, apparel, array, attire, bedizen, caparison, cover, deck, drape, dress, enclothe, endow, enwrap, equip, garb, habilitate, habit, invest, outfit, rig, robe, swathe, vest.

*antonyms* unclothe, undress.

**clothes** *n* apparel, attire, clobber, clothing, costume, dress, duds, ensemble, garb, garments, garmenture, gear, get-up, habiliments, habit(s), outfit, raiment, rig-out, threads, toggery, togs, vestiture, vestments, vesture, wardrobe, wear, weeds.

**cloud** *n* billow, crowd, darkness, flock, fog, gloom, haze, horde, host, mist, multitude, murk, nebula, nebulosity, obscurity, shower, swarm, throng, vapour, water-dog, weft, woolpack.

*v* becloud, confuse, darken, defame, dim, disorient, distort, dull, eclipse, impair, muddle, obfuscate, obscure, overcast, overshadow, shade, shadow, stain, veil.

*antonym* clear.

**cloudiness** *n* blurredness, dimness, haziness, murkiness, nebula, opacity.

*antonym* clearness.

**cloudy** *adj* blurred, blurry, confused, dark, dim, dismal, dull, emulsified, hazy, indistinct, leaden, lightless, lowering, muddy, murky, nebulous, nubilous, obscure, opaque, overcast, sombre, sullen, sunless.

*antonyms* clear, sunny.

**clout** *v* box, clobber, cuff, hit, skelp, slap, smack, sock, strike, thump, wallop, whack, wham.

*n* authority, cuff, influence, power, prestige, pull, skelp, slap, smack, sock, standing, thump, wallop, weight, whack.

**cloven** *adj* bisected, cleft, divided, split.

*antonym* solid.

**clown** *n* august(e), boor, buffoon, chuff, clodhopper, clout-shoe, comedian, dolt, fool, gracioso, harlequin, hob, jester, Joey, joker, joskin, merry-andrew, mountebank, peasant, pierrot, Pierrot, prankster, punchinello, swain, yahoo, yokel, zany.

**clowning** *n* buffoonery, jesting, joking, messing about, pantaloonery, pranks, skylarking.

**clownish** *adj* awkward, clumsy, comic, foolish, galumphing, hobbish, ill-bred, rough, rude, rustic, slapstick, uncivil, ungainly, vulgar, zany.

*antonyms* graceful, sophisticated.

**cloy** *v* choke, disgust, glut, gorge, nauseate, sate, satiate, sicken, surfeit, tire, weary.

*antonyms* please, whet.

**cloying** *adj* excessive, nauseating, oversweet, sickening, sickly.

**club¹** *n* bat, bludgeon, cosh, cudgel, mace, mere, stick, truncheon, waddy.

*v* bash, baste, batter, beat, bludgeon, clobber, clout, cosh, hammer, hit, pummel, strike.

**club²** *n* association, bunch, circle, clique, combination, company, fraternity, group, guild, lodge, order, set, society, sodality, union.

**clue** *n* clavis, evidence, hint, idea, indication, inkling, intimation, lead, notion, pointer, sign, suggestion, suspicion, tip, tip-off, trace.

**clump** *n* bunch, bundle, cluster, mass, shock, thicket, tuffet, tuft.

*v* clomp, lumber, plod, stamp, stomp, stump, thud, thump, tramp, tread.

**clumsiness** *n* awkwardness, bungling, cack-handedness, gaucheness, indexterity, maladdress, maladroitness, unhandiness.

**clumsy** *adj* awkward, blundering, bumbling, bungling, cack-handed, chuckle, chuckle-headed, clumping, crude, gauche, gawky, ham-fisted, ham-handed, hammy, heavy, hulking, ill-made, inept, inexpert, looby, lubber, lubberly, lumbering, maladroit, ponderous, rough, shapeless, spastic, squab, unco-ordinated, uncouth, ungainly, ungraceful, unhandy, unskilful, unwieldy.

*antonym* graceful.

**cluster** *n* assemblage, batch, bunch, clump, collection, gathering, glomeration, group, knot, mass.

*v* assemble, bunch, collect, flock, gather, group.

**clustered** *adj* assembled, bunched, gathered, glomerate, grouped, massed.

**clutch** *v* catch, clasp, embrace, fasten, grab, grapple, grasp, grip, hang on to, seize, snatch.

**clutches** *n* claws, control, custody, dominion, embrace, grasp, grip, hands, keeping, mercy, possession, power, sway.

**clutter** *n* confusion, disarray, disorder, hotchpotch, jumble, litter, mess, muddle, untidiness.

*v* cover, encumber, fill, litter, scatter, strew.

**coach**[1] *n* grinder, instructor, repetiteur, teacher, trainer, tutor.

*v* cram, drill, instruct, prepare, teach, train, tutor.

**coach**[2] *n* bus, carriage, charabanc, landau, motor-bus, motor-coach, omnibus.

**coagulate** *v* clot, congeal, curdle, jell, solidify, thicken.

*antonym* melt.

**coal** *n* black diamonds.

**coalesce** *v* amalgamate, blend, cohere, combine, commingle, commix, consolidate, fuse, incorporate, integrate, merge, mix, unite.

**coalition** *n* affiliation, alliance, amalgam, amalgamation, association, bloc, coadunation, combination, compact, confederacy, confederation, conjunction, federation, fusion, integration, league, merger, union.

**coal-scuttle** *n* purdonium.

**coarse** *adj* barrack-room, bawdy, blowzy, boorish, brutish, coarse-grained, crude, earthly, foul-mouthed, homespun, immodest, impolite, improper, impure, indelicate, inelegant, loutish, mean, offensive, porterly, Rabelaisian, ribald, rough, rude, smutty, Sotadic, uncivil, unfinished, unpolished, unprocessed, unpurified, unrefined, vulgar.

*antonyms* fine, polite, refined, sophisticated.

**coarsen** *v* anaesthetise, blunt, deaden, desensitise, dull, harden, indurate, roughen.

*antonyms* civilise, sensitise.

**coarseness** *n* bawdiness, boorishness, crassitude, crudity, earthiness, grossièrete, indelicacy, offensiveness, ribaldry, roughness, smut, smuttiness, uncouthness, unevenness.

*antonyms* delicacy, politeness, sophistication.

**coast** *n* coastline, littoral, seaboard, seaside, shore.

*v* cruise, drift, free-wheel, glide, sail.

**coat** *n* Burberry, cloak, coating, covering, fleece, fur, hair, hide, layer, mac, mackinaw, mackintosh, mantle, overlay, pelt, raincoat, skin, wash, wool.

*v* apply, cover, plaster, smear, spread.

**coated** *adj* covered, furred, painted, proofed.

**coating** *n* blanket, coat, covering, dusting, film, finish, fur, glaze, lamination, layer, membrane, patina, pellicle, sheet, skin, varnish, veneer, wash.

**coax** *v* allure, beguile, cajole, decoy, entice, flatter, inveigle, persuade, soft-soap, sweet-talk, wheedle, whilly, whillywha(w), wile.

*antonym* force.

**cobble** *v* botch, bungle, knock up, mend, patch, put together, tinker.

**cock** *n* capon, chanticleer, rooster.

**cock-eyed** *adj* absurd, askew, asymmetrical, awry, crazy, crooked, daft, lop-sided, ludicrous, nonsensical, preposterous, skew-whiff, squint, tiddly, tipsy.

*antonyms* sensible, sober.

**cocksure** *adj* arrogant, brash, bumptious, cocky, hubristic, overconfident, presumptuous, self-confident.

*antonym* modest.

**cocky** *adj* arrogant, bouncy, brash, cocksure, conceited, egotistical, fresh, pert, swaggering, swollen-headed, vain.

**cocoon** *v* cover, cushion, envelop, insulate, pad, preserve, protect, sheathe, swaddle, swathe, wrap.

**coddle** *v* baby, cocker, cosset, humour, indulge, mollycoddle, nurse, pamper, pet, spoil.

**code** *n* canon, cipher, convention, cryptograph, custom, ethics, etiquette, manners, maxim, regulations, rules, system.

*v* encipher, encode.

**coded** *adj* cryptic, encrypted, hidden, secret.

**codify** *v* catalogue, classify, code, digest, organise, summarise, systematise, tabulate, write down.

**coding** *n* encryption.

**coerce** *v* bludgeon, browbeat, bulldoze, bully, compel, constrain, dragoon, drive, drum, force, intimidate, press-gang, pressurise.

*antonyms* coax, persuade.

**coercion** *n* browbeating, bullying, compulsion, constraint, direct action, duress, force, intimidation, pressure, threats.

*antonym* persuasion.

**co-existent** *adj* coetaneous, coeval, co-existing, concomitant, contemporaneous, contemporary, synchronous.

**coffer** *n* ark, case, casket, chest, kist, repository, strongbox, treasure, treasury.

**cogency** *n* conviction, force, persuasion, potency, power, strength.

*antonym* weakness.

**cogent** *adj* compelling, conclusive, convincing, effective, forceful, forcible, influential, irresistible, persuasive, potent, powerful, strong, unanswerable, urgent, weighty.

*antonyms* ineffective, unsound.

**cogitate** v cerebrate, consider, contemplate, deliberate, meditate, muse, ponder, reflect, ruminate, think.

**cogitation** n cerebration, consideration, contemplation, deliberation, meditation, reflection, rumination, thought.

**cognate** adj affiliated, agnate, akin, alike, allied, analogous, associated, connected, kindred, related, similar.

antonym unconnected.

**cognisance** n acknowledgement, apprehension, cognition, knowledge, notice, perception, percipience, recognition, regard.

antonym unawareness.

**cognisant** adj acquainted, aware, conscious, conversant, familiar, informed, knowledgeable, versed, witting.

antonym unaware.

**cognition** n apprehension, awareness, comprehension, discernment, insight, intelligence, perception, reasoning, understanding.

**cohere** v adhere, agree, bind, cling, coalesce, combine, consolidate, correspond, fuse, glue, hang together, harmonise, hold, square, stick, unite.

antonym separate.

**coherence** n agreement, comprehensibility, concordance, congruity, connection, consistency, consonance, correspondence, intelligibility, rationality, sense, union, unity.

antonym incoherence.

**coherent** adj articulate, comprehensible, consistent, intelligible, logical, lucid, meaningful, orderly, organised, rational, reasoned, sensible, systematic.

**cohort** n accomplice, assistant, associate, band, companion, company, comrade, contingent, crony, division, follower, henchman, legion, mate, myrmidon, partner, regiment, sidekick, squadron, supporter, toady, troop.

**coil** v convolute, curl, entwine, loop, snake, spiral, twine, twist, wind, wreathe, writhe.

n bight, convolution, curl, fank, loop, spiral, twist.

**coin** v conceive, create, devise, fabricate, forge, form, formulate, frame, introduce, invent, make up, mint, mould, originate, produce, think up.

n bit, cash, change, copper, jitney, loose change, lucky-piece, money, piece, silver, small change, specie.

**coincide** v accord, agree, co-exist, concur, correspond, harmonise, match, square, tally.

**coincidence** n accident, chance, concomitance, concurrence, conjunction, correlation, correspondence, eventuality, fluke, fortuity, luck, synchronism.

**coincidental** adj accident, casual, chance, coincident, concomitant, concurrent, fluky, fortuitous, lucky, simultaneous, synchronous, unintentional, unplanned.

antonyms deliberate, planned.

**coitus** n coition, congress, copulation, coupling, love-making, marriage-bed, mating, sexual intercourse, union.

**cold** adj agued, algid, aloof, apathetic, arctic, benumbed, biting, bitter, bleak, brumal, chill, chilled, chilly, cold-blooded, cool, dead, distant, freezing, frigid, frosty, frozen, gelid, glacial, icy, inclement, indifferent, inhospitable, lukewarm, numbed, parky, passionless, phlegmatic, raw, reserved, shivery, spiritless, stand-offish, stony, undemonstrative, unfeeling, unfriendly, unheated, unmoved, unresponsive, unsympathetic, wintry.

antonyms friendly, warm.

n catarrh, chill, chilliness, coldness, frigidity, frostiness, hypothermia, iciness, inclemency.

antonyms friendliness, warmth.

**cold fish** iceberg.

**cold-blooded** adj barbaric, barbarous, brutal, callous, cruel, dispassionate, fell, flinty, heartless, inhuman, merciless, obdurate, pitiless, ruthless, savage, steely, stony-hearted, uncompassionate, unemotional, unfeeling, unmoved.

antonyms compassionate, merciful.

**cold-hearted** adj callous, cold, detached, flinty, frigid, frozen, heartless, indifferent, inhuman, insensitive, stony-hearted, uncaring, uncompassionate, unfeeling, unkind, unsympathetic.

antonym warm-hearted.

**collaborate** v coact, collude, conspire, co-operate, co-produce, fraternise, participate, team up.

**collaboration** n alliance, association, coactivity, concert, co-operation, partnership, teamwork.

**collaborator** n assistant, associate, caballer, collaborationist, colleague, confederate, co-worker, fellow-traveller, partner, quisling, team-mate, traitor, turncoat.

**collapse** v crumple, fail, faint, fall, fold, founder, peg out, sink, subside.

n breakdown, cave-in, debacle (débâcle), detumescence, disintegration, downfall, efoulement, exhaustion, failure, faint, flop, subsidence.

**collar** v apprehend, appropriate, arrest, capture, catch, grab, nab, nick, seize.

n dog-collar, gorget, neckband, ring, ruff.

**collate** v adduce, analogise, arrange, collect, compare, compose, gather, sort.

**collateral** n assurance, deposit, funds, guarantee, pledge, security, surety.

adj concurrent, confirmatory, corroborative, indirect, parallel, related, supporting.

**colleague** n aide, aider, ally, assistant, associate, auxiliary, bedfellow, coadjutor, collaborator, companion, comrade, confederate, confrère, helper, partner, team-mate, workmate.

**collect** v accumulate, acquire, aggregate, amass, assemble, cluster, congregate, convene, converge, forgather, gather, gather together, heap, hoard, muster, obtain, raise, rally, save, secure, stockpile, uplift.

**collected** *adj* assembled, calm, composed, confident, cool, efficient, gathered, imperturbable, placid, poised, self-possessed, serene, together, unperturbed, unruffled.

*antonyms* disorganised, dithery, worried.

**collection** *n* accumulation, anthology, assemblage, assembly, assortment, caboodle, cluster, company, compilation, congeries, conglomerate, conglomeration, congregation, convocation, crowd, festschrift, gathering, group, harvesting, heap, hoard, ingathering, inning, jingbang, job-lot, mass, pile, set, spicilege, stockpile, store, whip-round.

**collective** *adj* aggregate, combined, common, composite, concerted, congregated, co-operative, corporate, cumulative, joint, shared, unified, united.

*n* aggregate, assemblage, corporation, gathering, group.

**collision** *n* accident, bump, clash, clashing, conflict, confrontation, crash, encounter, impact, opposition, pile-up, prang, rencontre, rencounter, skirmish, smash.

**colloquial** *adj* conversational, demotic, everyday, familiar, idiomatic, informal, non-technical, vernacular.

*antonym* formal.

**collude** *v* abet, cabal, coact, collaborate, complot, connive, conspire, contrive, intrigue, machinate, plot, scheme.

**collusion** *n* artifice, cahoots, coactivity, complicity, connivance, conspiracy, craft, deceit, fraudulent, intrigue.

**colonise** *v* people, pioneer, populate, settle.

**colonist** *n* colonial, coloniser, emigrant, frontiersman, homesteader, immigrant, oecist, oikist, pioneer, planter, settler.

**colonnade** *n* arcade, cloisters, columniation, peristyle, portico.

**colony** *n* dependency, dominion, outpost, possession, province, settlement, territory.

**colossal** *adj* Brobdingnagian, elephantine, enormous, gargantuan, gigantic, herculean, heroic, huge, immense, leviathan, mammoth, massive, monstrous, monumental, mountainous, prodigious, titanic, vast.

*antonym* tiny.

**colour**[1] *n* animation, appearance, bloom, blush, brilliance, chroma, colorant, coloration, complexion, disguise, dye, façade, flush, glow, guise, hue, liveliness, paint, pigment, pigmentation, plausibility, pretence, pretext, race, reason, rosiness, ruddiness, semblance, shade, timbre, tincture, tinge, tint, variety, vividness, wash, water-colour.

*v* blush, burn, colourwash, disguise, distort, dye, embroider, encolour, exaggerate, falsify, flush, misrepresent, paint, pervert, prejudice, redden, slant, stain, strain, taint, tinge, tint.

**colour**[2] *n* colours, ensign, flag, standard.

**colour-blind** *adj* dichromatic.

**coloured** *n* Asian, black, Hottentot, Negro.

*adj* Asian, black, brown-skinned, dark-skinned, Negro.

**colourful** *adj* bright, brilliant, distinctive, graphic, intense, interesting, jazzy, kaleidoscopic, lively, motley, multicoloured, parti-coloured, picturesque, psychedelic, rich, stimulating, unusual, variegated, vibrant, vivid.

*antonyms* colourless, drab, plain.

**colourless** *adj* achromatic, achromic, anaemic, ashen, bleached, characterless, drab, dreary, fade, faded, insipid, lacklustre, livid, neutral, pale, sickly, tame, transparent, uninteresting, unmemorable, vacuous, vapid, wan, washed out.

*antonym* colourful.

**colours** *n* banner, colour, emblem, ensign, flag, standard.

**column** *n* anta, cavalcade, file, line, list, obelisk, pilaster, pillar, post, procession, queue, rank, row, shaft, string, support, train, upright.

**columnist** *n* correspondent, critic, editor, journalist, reporter, reviewer, writer.

**coma** *n* catalepsy, drowsiness, hypnosis, insensibility, lethargy, oblivion, somnolence, sopor, stupor, torpor, trance, unconsciousness.

**comatose** *adj* cataleptic, drowsy, insensible, lethargic, sleepy, sluggish, somnolent, soporose, stupefied, torpid, unconscious.

*antonym* conscious.

**comb** *v* hackle, hunt, rake, ransack, rummage, scour, screen, search, sift, sweep.

*n* crest, hackle.

**combat** *n* action, battle, bout, clash, conflict, contest, duel, encounter, engagement, fight, hostilities, j(i)u-jitsu, judo, karate, kendo, kung fu, skirmish, struggle, war, warfare.

*v* battle, contend, contest, defy, engage, fight, oppose, resist, strive, struggle, withstand.

**combatant** *n* adversary, antagonist, belligerent, contender, enemy, fighter, opponent, serviceman, soldier, warrior.

*adj* active, battling, belligerent, combating, contending, fighting, opposing, warring.

**combative** *adj* aggressive, antagonistic, argumentative, bellicose, belligerent, contentious, militant, pugnacious, quarrelsome, truculent, warlike.

*antonyms* pacific, peaceful.

**combination** *n* alliance, amalgam, amalgamation, association, blend, cabal, cartel, coalescence, coalition, combine, composite, composition, compound, confederacy, confederation, conjunction, connection, consortium, conspiracy, federation, meld, merger, mix, mixture, syndicate, unification, union.

**combine** *v* amalgamate, associate, bind, blend, bond, coadunate, compound, conjoin, connect, cooperate, fuse, incorporate, integrate, join, link, marry, meld, merge, mix, peace, pool, synthesise, unify, unite.

*antonym* separate.

**combustible** *adj* excitable, explosive, flammable, incendiary, inflammable.

*antonyms* incombustible, non-flammable.

**come** *v* advance, appear, approach, arrive, attain, become, draw near, ejaculate, enter, happen, materialise, move, near, occur, originate, reach.

*antonyms* depart, go, leave.

**come about** arise, befall, come to pass, happen, occur, result, transpire.

**come across** bump into, chance upon, discover, encounter, find, happen on, meet, notice, unearth.

**come along** arise, arrive, develop, happen, improve, mend, progress, rally, recover, recuperate.

**come apart** break, crumble, disintegrate, fall to bits, separate, split, tear.

**come between** alienate, disunite, divide, estrange, interfere, meddle, part, separate, split up.

**come by** acquire, get, obtain, procure, secure.

*antonyms* give, lose.

**come clean** acknowledge, admit, confess, own, own up, reveal, spill the beans.

**come down** decline, degenerate, descend, deteriorate, fall, reduce, worsen.

**come in** appear, arrive, enter, finish, show up.

**come on** advance, appear, begin, develop, improve, proceed, progress, take place, thrive.

**come out** conclude, emerge, end, result, terminate.

**come out with** affirm, declare, disclose, divulge, own, say, state.

**come round** accede, acquiesce, allow, awake, awaken, concede, grant, mellow, recover, relent, revive, wake, waken, yield.

**come through** accomplish, achieve, endure, prevail, succeed, survive, triumph, withstand.

**come to grief** bomb, come unstuck, fail, miscarry.

*antonyms* succeed, triumph.

**come to life** revive, rouse.

*antonym* collapse.

**come to light** appear, come out, transpire, turn up.

**come up with** advance, create, discover, find, furnish, offer, present, produce, propose, provide, submit, suggest, think of, think out.

**come-back** *n* quip, rally, rebound, recovery, rejoinder, repartee, reply, response, resurgence, retaliation, retort, return, revival, riposte, triumph.

**comedian** *n* card, clown, comic, droll, funny man, gagster, humorist, jester, joker, jokesmith, laugh, wag, wit.

**come-down** *n* anticlimax, blow, decline, deflation, degradation, demotion, descent, disappointment, humiliation, let-down, reverse.

**comedy** *n* chaffing, clowning, drollery, facetiousness, farce, fun, hilarity, humour, jesting, joking, sitcom, slapstick, wisecracking, witticisms.

**comely** *adj* attractive, beautiful, becoming, blooming, bonny, buxom, callipygian, callipygous, decent, decorous, fair, fit, fitting, gainly, good-looking, graceful, handsome, lovely, pleasing, pretty, proper, pulchritudinous, seemly, suitable, wholesome, winsome.

**come-uppance** *n* chastening, deserts, dues, merit, punishment, rebuke, recompense, requital, retribution.

**comfort** *v* alleviate, assuage, cheer, console, ease, encheer, encourage, enliven, gladden, hearten, inspirit, invigorate, reassure, refresh, relieve, solace, soothe, strengthen.

*n* aid, alleviation, cheer, compensation, consolation, cosiness, ease, easy street, encouragement, enjoyment, help, luxury, opulence, relief, satisfaction, snugness, succour, support, well-being.

*antonyms* distress, torment.

**comfortable** *adj* adequate, affluent, agreeable, ample, canny, commodious, contented, convenient, cosy, delightful, easy, enjoyable, gemütlich, gratified, happy, homely, loose, loose-fitting, pleasant, prosperous, relaxed, relaxing, restful, roomy, serene, snug, well-off, well-to-do.

*antonyms* poor, uncomfortable.

**comforting** *adj* analeptic, cheering, consolatory, consoling, encouraging, heart-warming, inspiriting, reassuring, soothing.

*antonym* worrying.

**comic** *adj* amusing, comical, droll, facetious, farcical, funny, humorous, jocular, joking, light, rich, waggish, witty.

*antonyms* serious, tragic, unfunny.

*n* buffoon, clown, comedian, droll, funny, gagster, humorist, jester, joker, jokesmith, man, wag, wit.

**comical** *adj* absurd, amusing, comic, diverting, droll, entertaining, farcical, funny, hilarious, humorous, laughable, ludicrous, priceless, ridiculous, risible, side-splitting, silly, whimsical.

*antonyms* sad, unamusing.

**coming** *adj* approaching, aspiring, due, forthcoming, future, imminent, impending, near, next, nigh, promising, rising, up-and-coming.

*n* accession, advent, approach, arrival.

**command** *v* bid, charge, compel, control, demand, direct, dominate, enjoin, govern, head, lead, manage, order, reign over, require, rule, supervise, sway.

*n* authority, behest, bidding, charge, commandment, control, decree, dictation, diktat, direction, directive, domination, dominion, edict, fiat, government, grasp, injunction, instruction, management, mandate, mastery, order, power, precept, requirement, rule, supervision, sway, ukase, ultimatum.

**commandeer** *v* appropriate, confiscate, expropriate, hijack, requisition, seize, sequester, sequestrate, usurp.

**commander** *n* admiral, boss, captain, chief, commander-in-chief, commanding officer, director, general, head, imperator, leader, marshal, officer, ruler.

**commanding** *adj* advantageous, assertive, authoritative, autocratic, compelling, controlling, decisive, dominant, dominating, forceful, imposing, impressive, peremptory, superior.

**commando** *n* fedayee, Green Beret, soldier.

**commemorate** *v* celebrate, honour, immortalise, keep, memorialise, observe, remember, salute, solemnise.

**commemoration** *n* ceremony, honouring, observance, recordation, remembrance, tribute.

**commemorative** *adj* celebratory, dedicatory, in memoriam, memorial.

**commence** *v* begin, embark on, inaugurate, initiate, open, originate, start.

*antonyms* cease, finish.

**commend** *v* acclaim, applaud, approve, commit, compliment, confide, consign, deliver, entrust, eulogise, extol, praise, recommend, yield.

*antonym* criticise.

**commendable** *adj* admirable, creditable, deserving, estimable, excellent, exemplary, laudable, meritorious, noble, praiseworthy, worthy.

*antonyms* blameworthy, poor.

**commendation** *n* acclaim, acclamation, accolade, applause, approbation, approval, credit, encomium, encouragement, panegyric, praise, recommendation.

*antonyms* blame, criticism.

**commensurate** *adj* acceptable, adequate, appropriate, co-extensive, comparable, compatible, consistent, corresponding, due, equivalent, fitting, just, meet, proportionate, sufficient.

*antonym* inappropriate.

**comment** *v* animadvert, annotate, criticise, descant, elucidate, explain, gloss, interpose, interpret, mention, note, observe, opine, remark, say.

*n* animadversion, annotation, commentary, criticism, elucidation, explanation, exposition, footnote, illustration, marginal note, marginalia, note, observation, remark, statement.

**commentary** *n* analysis, critique, description, elucidation, exegesis, explanation, narration, notes, postil, review, treatise, voice-over.

**commentator** *n* annotator, commenter, critic, expositor, glossator, glosser, glossographer, interpreter, reporter, scholiast, sportscaster.

**commerce** *n* business, communication, dealing(s), exchange, intercourse, merchandising, relations, trade, traffic.

**commercial** *adj* business, exploited, marketable, materialistic, mercantile, mercenary, monetary, pecuniary, popular, profitable, profit-making, saleable, sales, sellable, trade, trading, venal.

**commiseration** *n* compassion, condolence, consolation, pity, sympathy.

**commission** *n* allowance, appointment, authority, board, brokerage, brok(er)age, charge, committee, compensation, cut, delegation, deputation, duty, employment, errand, fee, function, mandate, mission, percentage, rake-off, representative, task, trust, warrant.

*v* appoint, ask for, authorise, contract, delegate, depute, empower, engage, nominate, order, request, select, send.

**commit** *v* align, bind, commend, compromise, confide, confine, consign, deliver, deposit, do, enact, endanger, engage, entrust, execute, give, imprison, involve, obligate, perform, perpetrate, pledge.

**commit oneself** bind oneself, decide, promise, take the plunge, undertake.

**commitment** *n* adherence, assurance, dedication, devotion, duty, engagement, guarantee, involvement, liability, loyalty, obligation, pledge, promise, responsibility, tie, undertaking, vow, word.

**committed** *adj* active, card-carrying, engage, fervent, red-hot.

*antonyms* apathetic, uncommitted.

**committee** *n* advisory group, board, cabinet, commission, council, jury, panel, table, task force, think-tank, working party.

**commodious** *adj* ample, capacious, comfortable, expansive, extensive, large, loose, roomy, spacious.

*antonym* cramped.

**commodities** *n* goods, merchandise, output, produce, products, stock, things, wares.

**common** *adj* accepted, average, coarse, collective, commonplace, communal, conventional, customary, daily, everyday, familiar, flat, frequent, general, habitual, hackneyed, humdrum, inferior, low, mutual, obscure, ordinary, pedestrian, plain, plebby, plebeian, popular, prevailing, prevalent, public, regular, routine, run-of-the-mill, simple, social, stale, standard, stock, trite, tritical, undistinguished, unexceptional, universal, usual, vulgar, widespread, workaday.

*antonyms* noteworthy, uncommon.

**common sense** gumption, judgement, level-headedness, mother-wit, nous, practicality, prudence, soundness, wit.

**commonly** *adv* for the most part, generally, normally, usually, vulgo.

*antonym* rarely.

**commonplace** *adj* common, customary, everyday, humdrum, obvious, ordinary, pedestrian, quotidian, stale, threadbare, trite, uninteresting, widespread, worn out.

*antonyms* exceptional, rare.

*n* banality, cliche, platitude, truism.

**common-sense** *adj* astute, common-sensical, down-to-earth, hard-headed, judicious, level-headed, matter-of-fact, practical, pragmatical, realistic, reasonable, sane, savvy, sensible, shrewd, sound.

*antonym* foolish.

**commotion** *n* ado, agitation, ballyhoo, bobbery, brouhaha, burst-up, bustle, bust-up, carfuffle, disorder, disturbance, excitement, ferment, fracas, fraise, furore, fuss, hoo-ha, hubbub, hullabaloo, hurly-burly, perturbation, pother, pudder, racket, riot, rumpus, to-do, toss, tumult, turmoil, uproar.

**communal** *adj* collective, common, communistic, community, general, joint, public, shared.

*antonyms* personal, private.

**commune** *n* collective, colony, community, co-operative, encampment, fellowship, kibbutz, settlement.

*v* communicate, confer, converse, discourse, hold converse with, make contact with.

**communicable** *adj* catching, contagious, conveyable, impartible, infectious, infective, spreadable, transferable, transmittable.

**communicate** *v* acquaint, announce, bestow, connect, contact, convey, correspond, declare, diffuse, disclose, disseminate, divulge, fax, impart, inform, intimate, notify, proclaim, promulgate, publish, report, reveal, signify, spread, telex, transmit, unfold.

**communication** *n* announcement, bulletin, communique, connection, contact, conversation, converse, correspondence, disclosure, dispatch, dissemination, fax, information, intelligence, intercourse, intimation, message, news, promulgation, report, statement, telex, transmission, word.

**communicative** *adj* candid, chatty, conversable, conversational, expansive, extrovert, forthcoming, frank, free, friendly, informative, loquacious, open, outgoing, sociable, talkative, unreserved, voluble.

*antonym* reticent.

**communion** *n* accord, affinity, agreement, closeness, communing, concord, converse, empathy, Eucharist, fellow-feeling, fellowship, harmony, Holy Communion, housel, intercourse, Lord's Supper, Mass, participation, rapport, Sacrament, sympathy, togetherness, unity.

**communique** *n* announcement, bulletin, communication, dispatch, message, report, statement.

**communism** *n* Bolshevism, collectivism, Leninism, Marxism, socialism, sovietism, Stalinism, totalitarianism, Trotskyism.

**communist** *n* Bolshevik, collectivist, Leninist, Marxist, Red, socialist, soviet, Stalinist, totalitarian, Trot, Trotskyist, Trotskyite.

**community** *n* affinity, agreement, association, body politic, brotherhood, coincidence, colony, commonness, commonwealth, company, concurrence, confraternity, confrèrie, correspondence, district, fellowship, fraternity, identity, kibbutz, kindredness, likeness, locality, nest, people, populace, population, public, residents, sameness, similarity, society, state.

**commute**[1] *v* adjust, alter, curtail, decrease, lighten, mitigate, modify, reduce, remit, shorten, soften.

**commute**[2] *v* alternate, journey, strap-hang, travel.

**commuter** *n* exurbanite, strap-hanger, suburbanite, traveller.

*antonym* urbanite.

**compact**[1] *adj* brief, close, compendious, compressed, concise, condensed, dense, firm, impenetrable, solid, stocky, succinct, thick, well-knit.

*antonyms* diffuse, rambling, rangy.

*v* compress, condense, consolidate, cram, flatten, ram, squeeze, tamp.

**compact**[2] *n* agreement, alliance, arrangement, bargain, bond, concordat, contract, covenant, deal, entente, pact, settlement, treaty, understanding.

**companion** *n* accomplice, aide, ally, assistant, associate, attendant, attender, buddy, chaperon, cohort, colleague, compeer, complement, comrade, confederate, confidant, confidante, consort, counterpart, crony, duenna, escort, fellow, fere, follower, friend, intimate, mate, partner, satellite, shadow, squire, twin.

**companionable** *adj* affable, amiable, approachable, congenial, conversable, convivial, extrovert, familiar, friendly, genial, gregarious, informal, neighbourly, outgoing, sociable, sympathetic.

*antonym* unfriendly.

**companionship** *n* camaraderie, companionhood, company, comradeship, confraternity, consociation, conviviality, esprit de corps, fellowship, fraternity, friendship, rapport, support, sympathy, togetherness.

**company**[1] *n* assemblage, assembly, association, band, body, business, cartel, circle, collection, community, concern, concourse, consociation, consortium, convention, corporation, coterie, crew, crowd, ensemble, establishment, firm, fraternity, gathering, group, house, league, line, partnership, party, set, set-out, syndicate, throng, troop, troupe.

**company**[2] *n* attendance, callers, companionhood, companionship, fellowship, guests, party, presence, society, support, visitors.

**comparable** *adj* akin, alike, analogous, cognate, commensurate, correspondent, corresponding, equal, equivalent, kindred, parallel, proportionate, related, similar, tantamount.

*antonym* unlike.

**compare** *v* balance, collate, confront, contrast, correlate, emulate, equal, equate, juxtapose, liken, match, parallel, resemble, similise, vie, weigh.

**comparison** *n* analogy, collation, comparability, contrast, correlation, distinction, juxtaposition, likeness, parallel, parallelism, resemblance, similarity, similitude.

**compartment** *n* alcove, area, bay, berth, booth, box, carrel, carriage, category, cell, chamber, cubby-hole, cubicle, department, division, locker, niche, pigeon-hole, section, stall, subdivision.

**compass** *n* area, boundary, bounds, circle, circuit, circumference, diapason, enclosure, extent, field, gamut, girth, limit, range, reach, realm, round, scale, scope, space, sphere, stretch, zone.

*v* accomplish, achieve, beset, besiege, blockade, circumscribe, contrive, devise, effect, encircle, enclose, encompass, environ, manage, realise, surround.

**compassion** *n* charity, clemency, commiseration, concern, condolence, fellow-feeling, heart, humanity, kindness, loving-kindness, mercy, pity, ruth, sorrow, sympathy, tenderness, understanding, weltschmerz, yearning.

*antonym* indifference.

**compassionate** *adj* benevolent, caring, charitable, clement, humane, humanitarian, indulgent, kind-hearted, kindly, lenient, merciful, piteous, pitying, supportive, sympathetic, tender, tender-hearted, understanding, warm-hearted.

*antonym* indifferent.

**compatibility** *n* accord, affinity, agreement, amity, concord, congeniality, consistency, consonance, correspondence, empathy, fellowship, harmony, like-mindedness, rapport, reconcilability, sympathy, understanding, unity.

*antonyms* antagonism, antipathy, incompatibility.

**compatible** *adj* accordant, adaptable, agreeable, conformable, congenial, congruent, congruous, consistent, consonant, harmonious, kindred, like-minded, reconcilable, suitable, sympathetic.

*antonyms* antagonistic, antipathetic, incompatible.

**compel** *v* browbeat, bulldoze, bully, coact, coerce, constrain, dragoon, drive, enforce, exact, force, gar, hustle, impel, make, necessitate, obligate, oblige, press-gang, pressurise, strongarm, urge.

**compelling** *adj* binding, coercive, cogent, compulsive, conclusive, convincing, enchanting, enthralling, forceful, gripping, hypnotic, imperative, incontrovertible, irrefragable, irrefutable, irresistible, mesmeric, overriding, peremptory, persuasive, powerful, pressing, spellbinding, telling, unanswerable, unavoidable, unputdownable, urgent, weighty.

**compendious** *adj* abbreviated, abridged, brief, compact, comprehensive, concise, condensed, contracted, epitomised, short, shortened, succinct, summarised, summary, synoptic.

*antonym* enlarged.

**compendium** *n* abbreviation, abridgement, abstract, brief, companion, condensation, conspectus, digest, encapsulation, epitome, handbook, manual, precis, recapitulation, summary, synopsis, vade-mecum.

**compensate** *v* atone, balance, cancel, counteract, counterbalance, countervail, expiate, guerdon, indemnify, offset, recompense, recover, recuperate, redeem, redress, refund, reimburse, remunerate, repay, requite, restore, reward, satisfy.

**compensation** *n* amends, atonement, comfort, consolation, damages, guerdon, indemnification, indemnity, payment, quittance, recompense, redress, refund, reimbursement, remuneration, reparation, repayment, requital, restitution, restoration, return, reward, satisfaction, solatium.

**compère** *n* anchor-man, announcer, commère, emcee, host, link man, master of ceremonies, MC, presenter, ringmaster.

**compete** *v* battle, challenge, contend, contest, duel, emulate, fight, oppose, rival, strive, struggle, tussle, vie.

**competence** *n* ability, adequacy, appropriateness, aptitude, capability, capacity, competency, experience, expertise, facility, fitness, proficiency, skill, suitability, technique.

*antonym* incompetence.

**competent** *adj* able, adapted, adequate, appropriate, belonging, capable, clever, efficient, endowed, equal, fit, legitimate, masterly, pertinent, proficient, qualified, satisfactory, strong, sufficient, suitable, trained, well-qualified.

*antonym* incompetent.

**competition** *n* challenge, challengers, championship, combativeness, competitiveness, competitors, contention, contest, corrivalry, cup, emulation, event, field, match, opposition, quiz, race, rivalry, rivals, series, strife, struggle, tournament, tourney, trial.

**competitive** *adj* aggressive, ambitious, antagonistic, combative, contentious, cut-throat, emulative, emulous, keen, pushy, vying.

*antonyms* sluggish, unambitious.

**competitiveness** *n* aggression, aggressiveness, ambition, ambitiousness, antagonism, assertiveness, challenge, combativeness, contention, contentiousness, emulation, keenness, pugnacity, pushiness, rivalry, self-assertion.

*antonyms* backwardness, sluggishness.

**competitor** *n* adversary, agonist, antagonist, challenger, competition, contender, contestant, corrival, emulator, entrant, opponent, opposition, rival.

**compilation** *n* accumulation, amassment, anthology, arrangement, assemblage, assortment, collection, composition, florilegium, opus, selection, thesaurus, treasury, work.

**compile** *v* accumulate, amass, anthologise, arrange, assemble, collect, compose, cull, garner, gather, marshal, organise.

**complacency** *n* content, contentment, gloating, gratification, pleasure, pride, satisfaction, self-content, self-satisfaction, serenity, smugness, triumph.

*antonyms* diffidence, discontent.

**complacent** *adj* contented, gloating, gratified, pleased, proud, satisfied, self-assured, self-congratulatory, self-contented, self-righteous, self-satisfied, serene, smug, triumphant, unconcerned.

*antonyms* diffident, discontented.

**complain** *v* beef, belly-ache, bemoan, bewail, bind, bitch, bleat, carp, deplore, fuss, girn, grieve, gripe, groan, grouse, growl, grumble, kvetch, lament, moan, protest, squeal, whine, whinge.

**complainer** *n* belly-acher, bleater, fuss-pot, girner, grouser, grumbler, kvetch(er), moaner, nit-picker, protester, whiner, whinger, winger.

**complaining** *adj* bleating, cantankerous, captious, critical, fault-finding, fussy, hypercritical, moaning, nagging, nit-picking, peevish, protesting, querimonious, querulous, whingeing.

*antonym* contented.

**complaint**[1] *n* accusation, annoyance, beef, bellyache, bitch, bleat, censure, charge, criticism, dissatisfaction, fault-finding, girn, gravamen, grievance, gripe, grouse, grumble, lament, moan, nit-picking, plaint, protest, querimony, remonstrance, squawk, stricture, wail, whinge, winge.

**complaint**[2] *n* affliction, ailment, disease, disorder, illness, indisposition, malady, malaise, sickness, trouble, upset.

**complaisance** *n* acquiescence, agreeableness, amenability, biddableness, compliance, conformability, deference, docility, obligingness.

*antonyms* obstinacy, perversity.

**complaisant** *adj* accommodating, agreeable, amenable, amiable, biddable, compliant, conciliatory, conformable, deferential, docile, douce, obedient, obliging, solicitous, tractable.

*antonyms* obstinate, perverse.

**complement** *n* aggregate, capacity, companion, completion, consummation, counterpart, entirety, fellow, quota, sum, supplement, total, totality, wholeness.

**complementary** *adj* companion, correlative, corresponding, dove-tailed, fellow, interdependent, interrelated, interrelating, interwoven, matched, reciprocal, reciprocative, reciprocatory.

**complete** *adj* absolute, accomplished, achieved, all, concluded, consummate, ended, entire, equipped, faultless, finished, full, intact, integral, integrate, out-and-out, perfect, plenary, root-and-branch, self-contained, thorough, thoroughgoing, thorough-paced, total, unabbreviated, unabridged, unbroken, uncut, undivided, unedited, unexpurgated, unimpaired, utter, whole, whole-hog.

*antonyms* imperfect, incomplete.

*v* accomplish, achieve, cap, clinch, close, conclude, consummate, crown, discharge, do, effect, end, execute, finalise, finish, fulfil, perfect, perform, realise, settle, terminate, wind up.

**completely** *adv* absolutely, altogether, diametrically, en bloc, en masse, entirely, every inch, from first to last, fully, heart and soul, in full, in toto, lock stock and barrel, perfectly, quite, root and branch, solidly, thoroughly, totally, utterly, wholly.

**completion** *n* accomplishment, achievement, attainment, close, conclusion, consummation, crowning, culmination, discharge, end, expiration, finalisation, finish, fruition, fulfilment, perfection, plenitude, realisation, settlement, telos, termination.

**complex** *adj* ambagious, Byzantine, circuitous, complicated, composite, compound, compounded, convoluted, Daedalian, devious, diverse, elaborate, heterogeneous, intricate, involved, knotty, labyrinthine, manifold, mingled, mixed, multifarious, multipartite, multiple, plexiform, polymerous, ramified, tangled, tortuous.

*antonym* simple.

*n* aggregate, composite, establishment, fixation, hang-up, idee fixe, institute, network, obsession, organisation, phobia, preoccupation, scheme, structure, syndrome, synthesis, system.

**complexion** *n* appearance, aspect, cast, character, colour, colouring, composition, countenance, disposition, guise, hue, kind, light, look, make-up, nature, pigmentation, rud, skin, stamp, temperament, type.

**complexity** *n* complication, convolution, deviousness, diversity, elaboration, entanglement, intricacy, involution, involvement, multifariousness, multiplicity, ramification, repercussion, tortuousness, variation, variety.

*antonym* simplicity.

**compliance** *n* acquiescence, agreement, assent, complaisance, concession, concurrence, conformability, conformity, consent, co-operation, deference, obedience, observance, passivity, submission, submissiveness, yielding.

*antonyms* defiance, disobedience.

**compliant** *adj* accommodating, acquiescent, agreeable, amenable, biddable, complaisant, conformable, deferential, docile, obedient, obliging, passive, submissive, tractable, yielding.

*antonyms* disobedient, intractable.

**complicate** *v* complexify, compound, confuse, elaborate, embroil, entangle, foul up, involve, mix up, muddle, tangle.

*antonym* simplify.

**complicated** *adj* ambivalent, baroque, Byzantine, complex, convoluted, devious, difficult, elaborate, entangled, Heath-Robinson, intricate, involved, labyrinthine, perplexing, problematic, puzzling, rigmarole, tangled, tortuous, troublesome.

*antonyms* easy, simple.

**complication** *n* aggravation, ambage, complexification, complexity, complicatedness, confusion, difficulty, drawback, elaboration, embarrassment, entanglement, factor, intricacy, mixture, obstacle, problem, ramification, repercussion, snag, web.

**complicity** *n* abetment, agreement, approval, collaboration, collusion, concurrence, connivance, involvement, knowledge.

*antonyms* ignorance, innocence.

**compliment** *n* accolade, admiration, bouquet, commendation, congratulations, courtesy, douceur, encomium, eulogy, favour, felicitation, flattery, honour, plaudit, praise, tribute.

*antonyms* criticism, insult.

*v* admire, applaud, commend, congratulate, eulogise, extol, felicitate, flatter, laud, praise, salute.

*antonyms* condemn, insult.

**complimentary** *adj* admiring, appreciative, approving, commendatory, congratulatory, courtesy, encomiastic, eulogistic, favourable, flattering, free, gratis, honorary, laudatory, panegyrical.

*antonyms* critical, insulting, unflattering.

**compliments** *n* best wishes, congratulations, devoirs, greetings, regards, remembrances, respects, salutation.

**comply** *v* accede, accommodate, accord, acquiesce, agree, assent, conform, consent, defer, discharge, fall in, follow, fulfil, obey, oblige, observe, perform, respect, satisfy, submit, yield.

*antonyms* disobey, resist.

**component** *n* bit, constituent, element, factor, ingredient, item, part, piece, spare part, unit.

**comport** *v* acquit, act, bear, behave, carry, conduct, demean, deport, perform.

**compose** *v* adjust, arrange, build, calm, collect, compound, comprise, constitute, construct, contrive, control, create, devise, fashion, form, frame, govern, imagine, indite, invent, make, meditate the muse, pacify, produce, quell, quiet, recollect, reconcile, regulate, resolve, settle, soothe, still, structure, tranquillise, write.

**composed** *adj* calm, collected, complacent, confident, cool, imperturbable, level-headed, placid, poised, relaxed, self-possessed, serene, together, tranquil, unflappable, unruffled, unworried.

*antonym* agitated.

**composer** *n* arranger, author, bard, creator, makar, maker, originator, poet, songsmith, songwriter, tunesmith, writer.

**composite** *adj* agglutinate, blended, combined, complex, compound, conglomerate, fused, mixed, patchwork, synthesised.

*antonyms* homogeneous, uniform.

*n* agglutination, alloy, amalgam, blend, combination, compound, conglomerate, fusion, mixture, pastiche, patchwork, synthesis.

**composition** *n* arrangement, balance, combination, compilation, compromise, concord, confection, configuration, congruity, consonance, constitution, creation, design, essay, exaration, exercise, form, formation, formulation, harmony, invention, lay-out, lucubration, make-up, making, mixture, opus, organisation, piece, placing, production, proportion, structure, study, symmetry, work, writing.

**composure** *n* aplomb, assurance, calm, calmness, confidence, cool, coolness, dignity, dispassion, ease, equanimity, impassivity, imperturbability, placidity, poise, sang-froid, savoir-faire, sedateness, self-assurance, self-possession, serenity, tranquillity.

*antonym* discomposure.

**compound** *v* aggravate, alloy, amalgamate, augment, blend, coalesce, combine, complicate, compose, concoct, exacerbate, fuse, heighten, increase, intensify, intermingle, magnify, mingle, mix, synthesise, unite, worsen.

*n* alloy, amalgam, amalgamation, blend, combination, composite, composition, confection,

conglomerate, conglomeration, fusion, medley, mixture, synthesis.

*adj* complex, complicated, composite, conglomerate, intricate, mixed, multiple.

**comprehend** *v* appreciate, apprehend, assimilate, compass, comprise, conceive, cover, discern, embrace, encompass, fathom, grasp, include, know, penetrate, perceive, see, see daylight, tumble to, twig, understand.

*antonym* misunderstand.

**comprehensible** *adj* clear, coherent, conceivable, explicit, graspable, intelligible, knowable, lucid, plain, rational, simple, straightforward, understandable.

*antonym* incomprehensible.

**comprehension** *n* appreciation, apprehension, capacity, conception, discernment, grasp, intellection, intelligence, intension, judgement, knowledge, perception, realisation, sense, understanding.

*antonym* incomprehension.

**comprehensive** *adj* across-the-board, all-embracing, all-inclusive, blanket, broad, catholic, compendious, complete, encyclopedic, exhaustive, extensive, full, general, inclusive, omnibus, sweeping, thorough, wide.

*antonyms* incomplete, selective.

**compress** *v* abbreviate, astrict, astringe, compact, concentrate, condense, constrict, contract, cram, crowd, crush, flatten, impact, jam, precis, press, shorten, squash, squeeze, stuff, summarise, synopsise, telescope, wedge.

*antonyms* diffuse, expand, separate.

**compressed** *adj* abridged, coarctate, compact, compacted, compendious, concentrated, concise, condensed, consolidated, constricted, flattened, impacted, pressed, reduced, shortened, squashed, squeezed, synopsised.

**compression** *n* abbreviation, abridgement, astriction, concentration, condensation, consolidation, constriction, crushing, digest, impaction, pressure, reduction, squeezing, thlipsis.

*antonyms* enlargement, expansion.

**comprise** *v* comprehend, consist of, contain, cover, embody, embrace, encompass, include, incorporate, involve, subsume.

**compromise**[1] *v* adapt, adjust, agree, arbitrate, bargain, concede, make concessions, negotiate, retire, retreat, settle.

*antonyms* differ, quarrel.

*n* accommodation, accord, adjustment, agreement, bargain, concession, co-operation, settlement, trade-off, via media.

*antonyms* disagreement, intransigence.

**compromise**[2] *v* discredit, dishonour, embarrass, embroil, expose, hazard, imperil, implicate, involve, jeopardise, prejudice, undermine, weaken.

**compulsion** *n* coercion, constraint, demand, distress, drive, duress, exigency, force, impulse, necessity, need, obligation, obsession, preoccupation, pressure, pressurisation, urge, urgency.

*antonyms* freedom, liberty.

**compulsive** *adj* besetting, compelling, driving, hardened, hopeless, incorrigible, incurable, irredeemable, irresistible, obsessive, overmastering, overpowering, overwhelming, uncontrollable, unputdownable, urgent.

**compulsory** *adj* binding, de rigueur, forced, imperative, mandatory, obligatory, required, requisite, stipulated, stipulatory.

*antonyms* optional, voluntary.

**compunction** *n* contrition, hesitance, hesitation, misgiving, penitence, qualm, regret, reluctance, remorse, repentance, sorrow, unease, uneasiness.

*antonyms* callousness, defiance.

**compute** *v* assess, calculate, count, enumerate, estimate, evaluate, figure, measure, rate, reckon, sum, tally, total.

**computer** *n* adding machine, analogue computer, calculator, data processor, digital computer, mainframe, processor, word processor.

**comrade** *n* Achates, ally, associate, brother, buddy, bully-rook, butty, china, cobber, colleague, companion, compatriot, compeer, confederate, co-worker, crony, fellow, frater, friend, mate, pal, partner, sidekick.

**con** *v* bamboozle, beguile, bilk, bluff, bunko, cheat, cozen, deceive, defraud, double-cross, dupe, fiddle, grift, gull, hoax, hoodwink, humbug, inveigle, mislead, racket, rip off, rook, swindle, trick.

*n* bluff, deception, fraud, grift, kidology, scam, swindle, trick.

**concatenation** *n* chain, connection, course, interlinking, interlocking, linking, nexus, procession, progress, progression, sequence, series, string, succession, thread, trail, train.

**concave** *adj* cupped, depressed, emaciated, excavated, hollow, hollowed, incurved, indented, scooped, sunken.

*antonym* convex.

**concavity** *n* basin, bowl, cavity, depression, dimple, dint, dip, dish, fossa, fossula, fovea, foveola, foveole, hole, hollow, hollowness, indentation, invagination, pit, recess, sag, sink, umbilicus, vacuity.

*antonyms* convexity, mound, protuberance.

**conceal** *v* bury, camouflage, cloak, cover, disguise, dissemble, hide, keep dark, mask, obscure, screen, secrete, shelter, sink, smother, submerge, suppress, veil.

*antonym* reveal.

**concealed** *adj* clandestine, covered, covert, disguised, hidden, inconspicuous, masked, perdu(e), screened, secret, secreted, ulterior, unseen, veiled.

*antonyms* clear, plain.

**concealment** *n* ambush, camouflage, cloak, cover, disguise, hide-away, hideout, hiding, protection, screen, secrecy, shelter.

*antonyms* openness, revelation.

**concede** *v* accept, acknowledge, admit, allow, cede, confess, forfeit, grant, own, recognise, relinquish, sacrifice, surrender, yield.

*antonyms* deny, dispute.

**conceit**[1] *n* arrogance, assumption, cockiness, complacency, conceitedness, egotism, narcissism, pride, self-assumption, self-conceit, self-importance, self-love, self-pride, self-satisfaction, swagger, vainglory, vainness, vanity.

*antonyms* diffidence, modesty.

**conceit**[2] *n* belief, caprice, concetto, fancy, fantasy, freak, humour, idea, image, imagination, impulse, jeu d'esprit, judgement, notion, opinion, quip, quirk, thought, vagary, whim, whimsy, wit.

**conceited** *adj* arrogant, assuming, bigheaded, cocky, complacent, egotistical, highty-tighty, hoity-toity, immodest, narcissistic, overweening, self-important, self-satisfied, stuck-up, swell-headed, swollen-headed, toffee-nose(d), uppish, uppity, vain, vainglorious, windy.

*antonyms* diffident, modest.

**conceivable** *adj* believable, credible, imaginable, likely, possible, probable, supposable, tenable, thinkable.

*antonym* inconceivable.

**conceive** *v* appreciate, apprehend, believe, comprehend, contrive, create, design, develop, devise, envisage, fancy, form, formulate, germinate, grasp, ideate, imagine, invent, originate, produce, project, purpose, realise, suppose, think, understand, visualise.

**concentrate** *v* absorb, accumulate, attend, attract, centre, cluster, collect, condense, congregate, converge, crowd, draw, engross, focus, foregather, gather, huddle, intensify.

*antonyms* disperse, distract, separate.

*n* apozem, decoction, decocture, distillate, distillation, elixir, essence, extract, juice, quintessence.

**concentrated** *adj* all-out, compact, condensed, deep, dense, evaporated, hard, intense, intensive, reduced, rich, thickened, undiluted.

*antonyms* desultory, diffuse, diluted.

**concentration** *n* absorption, accumulation, agglomeration, aggregation, application, centralisation, centring, cluster, collection, combination, compression, conglomeration, consolidation, convergence, crowd, denseness, focusing, grouping, heed, horde, intensification, intensity, mass, single-mindedness.

*antonyms* dilution, dispersal, distraction.

**concept** *n* abstraction, conception, conceptualisation, construct, hyphothesis, idea, image, impression, invention, notion, pattern, picture, plan, theory, type, view, visualisation.

**conception** *n* appreciation, apprehension, beginning, birth, clue, comprehension, concept, design, envisagement, fertilisation, formation, germination, idea, image, impregnation, impression, inauguration, inception, initiation, inkling, insemination, invention, knowledge, launching, notion, origin, outset, perception, picture, plan, understanding, visualisation.

**concern** v affect, bother, disquiet, distress, disturb, interest, involve, pertain to, perturb, refer to, regard, relate to, touch, trouble, upset, worry.

n affair, anxiety, apprehension, attention, bearing, burden, business, care, charge, company, consideration, corporation, disquiet, disquietude, distress, enterprise, establishment, field, firm, heed, house, importance, interest, involvement, job, matter, mission, occupation, organisation, perturbation, reference, relation, relevance, responsibility, solicitude, stake, task, transaction, unease, uneasiness, worry.

*antonym* unconcern.

**concerned** adj active, anxious, apprehensive, attentive, bothered, caring, connected, disquieted, distressed, disturbed, exercised, implicated, interested, involved, perturbed, solicitous, troubled, uneasy, unhappy, upset, worried.

*antonym* unconcerned.

**concerning** prep about, anent, apropos of, as regards, germane to, in regard to, in the matter of, re, regarding, relating to, relevant to, respecting, touching, with reference to, with regard to.

**concert¹** n accord, agreement, concord, concordance, consonance, diapason, harmony, unanimity, union, unison.

*antonym* disunity.

**concert²** n appearance, engagement, gig, performance, presentation, production, recital, rendering, rendition, show.

**concerted** adj collaborative, collective, combined, co-ordinated, joint, organised, planned, prearranged, shared, united.

*antonyms* disorganised, separate, unco-ordinated.

**concert-hall** n assembly room, auditorium, chamber, music hall, odeon, town hall.

**concession** n acknowledgement, adjustment, admission, allowance, assent, boon, compromise, exception, favour, grant, indulgence, permit, privilege, relaxation, sacrifice, surrender, yielding.

**conciliate** v appease, disarm, disembitter, mollify, pacify, placate, propitiate, satisfy, soften, soothe.

*antonym* antagonise.

**conciliation** n appeasement, indulgence, mollification, pacification, peace-making, placation, propitiation, reconciliation, satisfaction.

*antonyms* alienation, antagonisation.

**conciliator** n dove, intercessor, intermediary, mediator, negotiator, peace-maker, reconciler.

*antonym* trouble-maker.

**conciliatory** adj disarming, irenic, mollifying, pacific, pacificatory, peaceable, placatory, propitiative, propitiatory, reconciliatory.

*antonym* antagonistic.

**concise** adj abbreviated, abridged, aphoristic, brief, compact, compendious, compressed, condensed, epigrammatic, gnomic, laconic, pithy, short, succinct, summary, synoptic, terse, thumbnail.

*antonyms* diffuse, expansive.

**conclave** n assembly, cabal, cabinet, confabulation, conference, conspiracy, conventicle, council, meeting, parley, powwow, session.

**conclude** v accomplish, assume, cease, clinch, close, complete, consummate, culminate, decide, deduce, determine, effect, end, establish, finish, fix, gather, infer, judge, opine, reckon, resolve, settle, suppose, surmise, terminate.

**concluding** adj closing, epilogic, epilogistic, final, last, perorating, terminal, ultimate.

*antonym* introductory.

**conclusion** n answer, assumption, clincher, close, come-off, completion, consequence, consummation, conviction, culmination, decision, deduction, end, explicit, finale, fine, finis, finish, illation, inference, issue, judgement, opinion, outcome, resolution, result, settlement, solution, termination, upshot, verdict.

**conclusive** adj clear, clinching, convincing, decisive, definite, definitive, final, incontrovertible, irrefragable, irrefutable, manifest, ultimate, unanswerable, unappealable, unarguable, undeniable.

*antonym* inconclusive.

**concoct** v brew, contrive, decoct, design, develop, devise, digest, fabricate, form, formulate, hatch, invent, mature, plan, plot, prepare, project, refine.

**concoction** n blend, brew, combination, compound, contrivance, creation, decoction, fable, mixture, myth, potion, preparation, story.

**concomitant** adj accompanying, associative, attendant, co-existent, coincidental, collateral, complementary, concurrent, contemporaneous, conterminous, contributing, incidental, simultaneous, synchronous, syndromic.

*antonyms* accidental, unrelated.

n accompaniment, by-product, epiphenomenon, incidental, secondary, symptom.

**concord** n accord, agreement, amicability, amity, brotherliness, compact, concert, concordat, consensus, consonance, convention, diapason, entente, friendship, harmony, peace, protocol, rapport, treaty, unanimity, unison.

*antonym* discord.

**concourse** n assemblage, assembly, collection, confluence, convergence, crowd, crush, entrance, foyer, frequence, gathering, hall, lobby, lounge, meeting, multitude, piazza, plaza, press, swarm, throng.

**concrete** adj actual, calcified, compact, compressed, conglomerated, consolidated, definite, explicit, factual, firm, material, perceptible, petrified, physical, real, seeable, sensible, solid, solidified, specific, substantial, tactile, tangible, touchable, visible.

*antonym* abstract.

**concubine** *n* apple-squire, courtesan, hetaira, leman, lorette, lover, mistress, odalisque, paramour.

**concupiscence** *n* appetite, desire, horniness, lasciviousness, lechery, lewdness, libidinousness, libido, lickerishness, lubricity, lust, lustfulness, randiness, ruttishness.

**concupiscent** *adj* horny, lascivious, lecherous, lewd, libidinous, lickerish, lubricious, lustful, randy, ruttish.

**concur** *v* accede, accord, acquiesce, agree, approve, assent, coincide, combine, comply, consent, co-operate, harmonise, join, meet, unite.
*antonym* disagree.

**concurrence** *n* acquiescence, agreement, assent, association, co-existence, coincidence, common ground, community, concomitance, conjunction, consilience, contemporaneity, convergence, juxtaposition, simultaneity, synchrony, syndrome.
*antonyms* difference, disagreement.

**concurrent** *adj* co-existing, coincident, coinciding, concerted, concomitant, confluent, consilient, contemporaneous, convergent, converging, simultaneous, synchronous, syndromic, uniting.

**condemn** *v* ban, blame, castigate, censure, convict, damn, decry, denounce, disapprove, disparage, doom, pan, proscribe, reprehend, reproach, reprobate, reprove, revile, sentence, slam, slate, upbraid.
*antonyms* approve, praise.

**condemnation** *n* ban, blame, castigation, censure, conviction, damnation, denouncement, denunciation, disapproval, disparagement, judgement, proscription, reproach, reprobation, reproof, sentence, slating, stricture, thumbs-down.
*antonyms* approval, praise.

**condemnatory** *adj* accusatory, accusing, censorious, critical, damnatory, denunciatory, deprecatory, disapproving, discouraging, incriminating, proscriptive, reprobative, reprobatory, unfavourable.
*antonyms* approving, complimentary, indulgent, laudatory.

**condensation** *n* abridgement, compression, concentrate, concentration, condensate, consolidation, contraction, crystallisation, curtailment, decoction, deliquescence, digest, distillate, distillation, encapsulation, liquefaction, precipitate, precipitation, precis, reduction, synopsis.

**condense** *v* abbreviate, abridge, capsulise, coagulate, compact, compress, concentrate, contract, crystallise, curtail, decoct, distil, encapsulate, epitomise, evaporate, inspissate, precipitate, precis, reduce, shorten, solidify, summarise, synopsise, thicken.
*antonyms* dilute, expand.

**condensed** *adj* abbreviated, abridged, abstracted, capsular, clotted, coagulated, compact, compressed, concentrated, concise, contracted, crystallised, curtailed, distilled, epitomised, evaporated, precipitated, reduced, shortened, shrunken, summarised, thickened.
*antonyms* diluted, expanded.

**condescend** *v* bend, deign, patronise, see fit, stoop, submit, unbend, vouchsafe.

**condescending** *adj* de haut en bas, disdainful, gracious, haughty, imperious, lofty, lordly, patronising, snooty, stooping, supercilious, superior, unbending.
*antonyms* approachable, humble.

**condescension** *n* affability, airs, civility, courtesy, deference, disdain, favour, generosity, graciousness, haughtiness, loftiness, lordliness, superciliousness, superiority.
*antonym* humility.

**condign** *adj* adequate, apposite, appropriate, deserved, earned, fitting, just, meet, merited, suitable, well-earned, well-merited.
*antonym* unjust.

**condition** *n* ailment, arrangement, article, case, caste, circumstances, class, complaint, defect, demand, diathesis, disease, disorder, estate, fettle, fitness, grade, health, infirmity, kilter, level, liability, limitation, malady, modification, nick, obligation, order, plight, position, predicament, prerequisite, problem, provision, proviso, qualification, rank, requirement, requisite, restriction, rule, shape, situation, state, status, stipulation, stratum, terms, trim, understanding, weakness.

*v* accustom, adapt, adjust, attune, determine, educate, equip, groom, habituate, hone, indoctrinate, inure, limit, prepare, prime, ready, restrict, season, temper, train, tune.

**conditional** *adj* contingent, dependent, limited, provisional, qualified, relative, restricted, tied.
*antonym* unconditional.

**conditioned** *adj* acclimatised, accustomed, adapted, adjusted, attuned, familiarised, groomed, habituated, honed, indoctrinated, inured, prepared, primed, seasoned, tempered, trained, tuned, used.

**conditioning** *n* acculturation, adjustment, education, familiarisation, grooming, hardening, honing, indoctrination, inurement, preparation, priming, reorientation, seasoning, tempering, training, tuning.

**conditions** *n* atmosphere, background, circumstances, context, environment, habitat, medium, milieu, setting, situation, state, surroundings.

**condolence** *n* commiseration, compassion, condolences, consolation, pity, support, sympathy.
*antonym* congratulation.

**condom** *n* French letter, johnnie, johnny, protective, rubber, safe, scumbag, sheath.

**condone** *v* allow, brook, disregard, excuse, forgive, ignore, indulge, overlook, pardon, tolerate.
*antonyms* censure, disallow.

**conducive** *adj* advantageous, beneficial, contributive, contributory, encouraging, favourable, helpful, leading, productive, promotive, stimulative, tending.

*antonyms* adverse, unfavourable.

**conduct** *n* actions, administration, attitude, bearing, behaviour, carriage, comportment, control, co-ordination, demeanour, deportment, direction, discharge, escort, guidance, guide, leadership, management, manners, mien, orchestration, organisation, running, supervision, ways.

*v* accompany, acquit, act, administer, attend, bear, behave, carry, chair, comport, control, convey, demean, deport, direct, escort, govern, guide, handle, lead, manage, orchestrate, organise, pilot, regulate, run, solicit, steer, supervise, transact, usher.

**conduit** *n* canal, channel, chute, culvert, ditch, drain, duct, flume, gutter, lade, main, passage, pipe, rhine, tube, water-course, waterway.

**confab** *n* blether, chat, chinwag, conclave, confabulation, conference, conversation, discussion, gossip, jaw, natter, powwow, session, talk.

**confabulate** *v* blether, chat, clash, claver, confer, converse, discuss, gossip, natter, talk.

**confederacy** *n* alliance, Bund, cabal, coalition, compact, confederation, conspiracy, covenant, federation, junta, league, partnership, union.

**confederate** *adj* allied, associated, combined, federal, federated.

*n* abettor, accessory, accomplice, ally, assistant, associate, collaborator, colleague, conspirator, friend, leaguer, partner, practisant, supporter.

*v* ally, amalgamate, associate, bind, combine, federate, join, merge, unite, weld.

**confer** *v* accord, award, bestow, consult, converse, deliberate, discourse, discuss, give, grant, impart, lay heads together, lend, parley, powwow, present, talk, vouchsafe.

**conference** *n* colloquium, confab, confabulation, congress, consultation, convention, convocation, debate, diet, discussion, forum, indaba, meeting, moot, powwow, seminar, symposium, synod, teach-in.

**confess** *v* acknowledge, admit, affirm, agnise, allow, assert, attest, aver, betray, concede, confide, confirm, declare, disclose, divulge, evince, expose, grant, manifest, own, own up, profess, prove, recognise, reveal, show.

*antonyms* conceal, deny.

**confession** *n* acknowledgement, admission, affirmation, assertion, attestation, averment, avowal, confidences, confiteor, declaration, disclosure, divulgence, expose, exposure, profession, revelation, unbosoming, unburdening, verbal.

*antonyms* concealment, denial.

**confidant** *n* companion, confidante, crony, duenna, familiar, friend, inseparable, intimate, repository.

**confide** *v* admit, breathe, confess, disclose, divulge, impart, reveal, unburden, whisper.

*antonyms* hide, suppress.

**confidence** *n* aplomb, assurance, belief, boldness, calmness, communication, composure, confession, coolness, courage, credence, dependence, disclosure, divulgence, faith, firmness, morale, nerve, reliance, savoir-faire, secret, self-assurance, self-confidence, self-possession, self-reliance, trust.

*antonyms* diffidence, distrust.

**confident** *adj* assured, bold, certain, composed, convinced, cool, dauntless, fearless, persuaded, positive, sanguine, satisfied, secure, self-assured, self-confident, self-possessed, self-reliant, sure, unabashed, unbashful, unselfconscious.

*antonyms* diffident, sceptical.

**confidential** *adj* classified, close, closed, faithful, familiar, hush-hush, in camera, intimate, private, privy, secret, tête-à-tête, trusted, trustworthy, trusty.

*antonyms* common, public.

**confidentially** *adv* behind closed doors, between you me and the bed-post (lamp-post, gate-post), in camera, in confidence, in privacy, in private, in secret, on the quiet, personally, privately, under the rose, within these four walls.

*antonym* openly.

**configuration** *n* arrangement, cast, composition, conformation, contour, deployment, disposition, figure, form, Gestalt, outline, shape.

**confine** *v* bind, bound, cage, chamber, circumscribe, constrain, cramp, crib, emmew, enclose, immew, immure, imprison, incarcerate, inhibit, intern, keep, keep prisoner, limit, mew, repress, restrain, restrict, shackle, shut up, thirl, trammel.

*antonym* free.

**confined** *adj* circumscribed, enclosed, housebound, limited, pokey, poking, restricted.

*antonyms* free, unrestricted.

**confinement** *n* accouchement, birth, childbed, childbirth, constraint, custody, delivery, detention, down-lying, gander-month, gander-moon, house-arrest, imprisonment, incarceration, internment, labour, lying-in, parturition, time, travail.

*antonym* freedom.

**confines** *n* border, boundaries, bounds, circumference, edge, frontier, limits, perimeter, periphery, precincts.

**confirm** *v* approve, assure, attest, authenticate, back, buttress, clinch, corroborate, endorse, establish, evidence, fix, fortify, homologate, prove, ratify, reinforce, sanction, settle, strengthen, substantiate, support, validate, verify, witness to.

*antonym* deny.

**confirmation** *n* acceptance, agreement, approval, assent, attestation, authentication, backing, clincher, corroboration, endorsement, evidence, proof, ratification, sanction, substantiation, support, testimony, validation, verification, witness.

*antonym* denial.

**confirmed** *adj* authenticated, chronic, committed, corroborated, deep-dyed, dyed-in-the-wool, entrenched, established, habitual, hardened, incorrigible, incurable, ingrained, inured, inveterate, irredeemable, long-established, long-standing, proved, proven, rooted, seasoned, substantiated, unredeemed.

*antonyms* uncommitted, unconfirmed.

**confiscate** *v* appropriate, commandeer, distrain, escheat, expropriate, impound, remove, seize, sequester, sequestrate.

*antonym* restore.

**confiscation** *n* appropriation, distrainment, distraint, escheat, expropriation, forfeiture, impounding, seizure, sequestration, takeover.

*antonym* restoration.

**conflagration** *n* blaze, deflagration, fire, hellfire, holocaust, inferno, wildfire.

**conflict** *n* agony, ambivalence, antagonism, antipathy, Armageddon, battle, brawl, clash, collision, combat, confrontation, contention, contest, difference, disagreement, discord, dissension, encounter, engagement, feud, fight, fracas, friction, hostility, interference, opposition, quarrel, set-to, skirmish, strife, turmoil, unrest, variance, war, warfare.

*antonyms* agreement, concord.

*v* battle, clash, collide, combat, contend, contest, contradict, differ, disagree, fight, interfere, oppose, strive, struggle, war, wrangle.

*antonym* agree.

**conflicting** *adj* ambivalent, antagonistic, clashing, contradictory, contrary, discordant, inconsistent, opposed, opposing, opposite, paradoxical, turbulent, warring.

*antonym* compatible.

**confluence** *n* assemblage, assembly, concourse, concurrence, conflux, conjunction, convergence, crowd, disemboguement, host, junction, meeting, multitude, union, watersmeet.

**conform** *v* accommodate, accord, adapt, adjust, agree, assimilate, comply, correspond, follow, harmonise, match, obey, quadrate, square, suit, tally, yield.

*antonym* differ.

**conformation** *n* anatomy, arrangement, build, composition, configuration, form, framework, Gestalt, outline, shape, structure.

**conformist** *n* Babbit, bourgeois, conventionalist, rubber-stamp, stick-in-the-mud, traditionalist, yes-man.

*antonyms* bohemian, nonconformist.

**conformity** *n* affinity, agreement, allegiance, Babbitry, compliance, congruity, consonance, conventionalism, conventionality, correspondence, Gleichschaltung, harmony, likeness, observance, orthodoxy, resemblance, similarity, traditionalism.

*antonyms* difference, nonconformity.

**confound** *v* abash, amaze, astonish, astound, baffle, bamboozle, bewilder, confuse, contradict, demolish, destroy, discombobulate, dismay, dumbfound, flabbergast, mystify, nonplus, overthrow, overwhelm, perplex, ruin, spif(f)licate, startle, stupefy, surprise, thwart, unshape, upset.

**confounded** *adj* arrant, astounded, baffled, bewildered, confused, consummate, cursed, discomfited, dismayed, dumbfounded, egregious, embarrassed, flabbergasted, frustrated, insufferable, mystified, nonplussed, notorious, outrageous, perplexed, rank, thwarted.

**confront** *v* accost, address, appose, beard, brave, challenge, defy, encounter, eyeball, face, front, oppose.

*antonym* evade.

**confrontation** *n* battle, collision, conflict, contest, crisis, disagreement, encounter, engagement, face-off, fight, quarrel, set-to, showdown.

**confuse** *v* abash, addle, baffle, befuddle, bemuse, bewilder, buffalo, burble, confound, darken, demoralise, disarrange, discomfit, discompose, disconcert, discountenance, disorder, disorient, disorientate, embarrass, embrangle, flummox, fluster, intermingle, involve, jumble, maze, mingle, mistake, mix up, mortify, muddle, mystify, nonplus, obscure, perplex, puzzle, rattle, shame, tangle, tie in knots, upset.

*antonyms* clarify, enlighten, reassure.

**confused** *adj* addle-brained, addle(d), addle-headed, addle-pated, baffled, bewildered, bushed, chaotic, dazed, desoriente, disarranged, discombobulated, disordered, disorderly, disorganised, disorientated, distracted, embarrassed, flummoxed, fuddled, higgledy-piggledy, jumbled, maffled, mistaken, misunderstood, muddled, muddle-headed, muzzy, nonplussed, perplexed, puzzled, puzzle-headed, streaked, topsy-turvy, tosticated, untidy, upset.

*antonym* clear.

**confusing** *adj* ambiguous, baffling, bewildering, complicated, contradictory, cryptic, difficult, inconclusive, inconsistent, involved, misleading, muddling, perplexing, puzzling, tortuous, unclear.

*antonyms* clear, definite.

**confusion** *n* abashment, Babel, balls-up, befuddlement, bemusement, bewilderment, bustle, chagrin, chaos, clutter, cock-up, combustion, commotion, demoralisation, disarrangement, discomfiture, disorder, disorganisation, disorientation, distraction, dudder, egarement, embarrassment, embroglio, embroilment, fluster, hotchpotch, hubble-bubble, hugger-mugger, imbroglio, jumble, mess, mix-up, muddle, mystification, overthrow, palaver, perdition, perplexity, perturbation, pie, puzzlement, shambles, shame, tangle, tizz(y), topsyturviness, topsyturvy, topsyturvydom, toss, turmoil, untidiness, upheaval, welter.

*antonyms* clarity, composure, order.

**confute** *v* annihilate, confound, controvert, disprove, give the lie to, impune, invalidate, nullify, oppugn, overthrow, overturn, rebut, refute, vitiate.

*antonyms* confirm, prove.

**congeal** v clot, coagulate, coalesce, concrete, condense, curdle, freeze, fuse, geal, gelatinate, gelatinise, harden, jell, jelly, pectise, set, solidify, stiffen, thicken.

*antonyms* dissolve, melt, separate.

**congealment** n clotting, coalescence, concretion, condensing, congelation, curdling, freezing, fusion, gelatination, gelatinisation, hardening, jelling, setting, solidification, stiffening, thickening.

*antonyms* liquefaction, melting, separation.

**congenial** adj agreeable, companionable, compatible, complaisant, cosy, delightful, favourable, friendly, gemütlich, genial, homely, kindly, kindred, like-minded, pleasant, pleasing, relaxing, suitable, sympathetic, well-suited.

*antonym* disagreeable.

**congenital** adj complete, connate, constitutional, hereditary, inborn, inbred, ingenerate, inherent, inherited, innate, inveterate, natural, thorough, utter.

**congested** adj blocked, clogged, crammed, engorged, full, jammed, overcharged, overcrowded, overfilled, overflowing, overfull, packed, saturated, stuffed, swollen, teeming.

*antonym* clear.

**congestion** n bottle-neck, clogging, engorgement, fullness, gridlock, jam, log-jam, mass, overcrowding, overfullness, snarl-up, surfeit, traffic-jam.

**conglomerate** adj agglutinated, amassed, clustered, coherent, composite, conglutinated, heterogeneous, massed.

v accumulate, agglomerate, agglutinate, aggregate, amass, assemble, clump, cohere, collect, congregate, foregather, gather, mass.

*antonym* separate.

n agglomerate, aggregate, composite, congeries, mass, multinational.

**conglomeration** n accumulation, agglomeration, agglutination, aggregation, assemblage, combination, composite, congeries, hotchpotch, mass, medley.

**congratulate** v compliment, felicitate, gratulate.

*antonym* commiserate.

**congratulations** n compliments, felicitations, good wishes, greetings.

*antonyms* commiserations, condolences.

**congregate** v accumulate, assemble, bunch, clump, cluster, collect, concentrate, conglomerate, convene, converge, convoke, crowd, flock, foregather, gather, mass, meet, muster, rally, rendezvous, throng.

*antonyms* dismiss, disperse.

**congregation** n assemblage, assembly, brethren, concourse, crowd, fellowship, flock, host, laity, multitude, parish, parishioners, throng.

**congress** n assembly, conclave, conference, convention, convocation, council, diet, forum, legislature, meeting, parliament, synod.

**congruity** n agreement, coincidence, compatibility, concinnity, concurrence, conformity, congruence, congruousness, consistency, correspondence, harmony, identity, match, parallelism.

*antonym* incongruity.

**conical** adj cone-shaped, conic, conoid, fastigiate(d), funnel-shaped, infundibular, infundibulate, infundibuliform, pointed, pyramidal, tapered, tapering.

**conjectural** adj academic, assumed, hypothetical, posited, postulated, speculative, supposed, suppositional, surmised, tentative, theoretical.

*antonyms* factual, real.

**conjecture** v assume, estimate, extrapolate, fancy, guess, hypothesise, imagine, infer, opine, reckon, speculate, suppose, surmise, suspect, theorise.

n assumption, conclusion, estimate, extrapolation, fancy, guess, guesstimate, guesswork, hypothesis, inference, notion, opinion, presumption, projection, speculation, supposition, surmise, theorising, theory.

**conjugal** adv bridal, connubial, epithalamic, hymeneal, marital, married, matrimonial, nuptial, spousal, wedded.

**conjunction** n amalgamation, association, coincidence, combination, concurrence, juxtaposition, syzygy, unification, union, unition.

**conjuncture** n combination, concomitance, concurrence, connection, crisis, crossroads, emergency, exigency, juncture, pass, predicament, simultaneity, stage.

**conjure** v adjure, beseech, bewitch, charm, compel, crave, enchant, entreat, fascinate, implore, importune, invoke, juggle, pray, raise, rouse, summon, supplicate.

**conjure up** awaken, contrive, create, evoke, excite, produce, recall, recollect.

**conjuror, conjurer** n illusionist, magician, miracle-worker, prestidigitator, prestigiator, sorcerer, thaumaturge, wizard.

**conk out** break down, collapse, fail, fall asleep.

**connect** v affix, ally, associate, cohere, combine, compaginate, concatenate, couple, enlink, fasten, join, link, relate, unite.

*antonym* disconnect.

**connected** adj affiliated, akin, allied, associate, associated, bracketed, combined, confederate, coupled, joined, linked, related, united.

*antonyms* disconnected, unconnected.

**connection** n acquaintance, affinity, alliance, ally, arthrosis, associate, association, attachment, bond, catenation, coherence, commerce, communication, compagination, conjunction, contact, context, correlation, correspondence, coupling, fastening, friend, hook-up, intercourse, interrelation, intimacy, junction, kin, kindred, kinsman, kith, link, marriage, reference, relation, relationship, relative, relevance, sponsor, tie, tie-in, union.

*antonym* disconnection.

**connivance** *n* abetment, abetting, collusion, complicity, condoning, consent, jobbery.

**connive** *v* cabal, coact, collude, complot, conspire, intrigue, plot, scheme.

**connive at** abet, aid, blink at, condone, disregard, let go, overlook, turn a blind eye to, wink at.

**connoisseur** *n* aficionado, appreciator, arbiter, authority, buff, cognoscente, devotee, expert, iconophilist, judge, savant, specialist, virtuoso.

**connoisseurship** *n* virtuosity.

**connotation** *n* association, colouring, hint, implication, nuance, overtone, significance, suggestion, undertone.

**connote** *v* betoken, hint at, imply, import, indicate, intimate, involve, purport, signify, suggest.

**connubial** *adj* conjugal, epithalamic, hymeneal, marital, married, matrimonial, nuptial, wedded.

**conquer** *v* acquire, annex, beat, best, checkmate, crush, defeat, discomfit, get the better of, humble, master, obtain, occupy, overcome, overpower, overrun, overthrow, prevail, quell, rout, seize, subdue, subjugate, succeed, surmount, triumph, vanquish, win, worst.

*antonyms* surrender, yield.

**conqueror** *n* champ, champion, conquistador, defeater, hero, lord, master, number one, subjugator, vanquisher, victor, winner.

**conquest** *n* acquisition, annexation, appropriation, captivation, coup, defeat, discomfiture, enchantment, enthralment, enticement, invasion, inveiglement, mastery, occupation, overthrow, rout, seduction, subjection, subjugation, takeover, triumph, vanquishment, victory.

**conscience** *n* ethics, morals, principles, scruples, standards.

**conscience-stricken** *adj* ashamed, compunctious, contrite, disturbed, guilt-ridden, guilty, penitent, regretful, remorseful, repentant, sorry, troubled.

*antonyms* unashamed, unrepentant.

**conscientious** *adj* careful, diligent, exact, faithful, hard-working, high-minded, high-principled, honest, honourable, incorruptible, just, meticulous, moral, painstaking, particular, punctilious, responsible, scrupulous, solicitous, straightforward, strict, thorough, upright.

*antonyms* careless, irresponsible.

**conscious** *adj* alert, alive, awake, aware, calculated, cognisant, deliberate, heedful, intentional, knowing, mindful, percipient, premeditated, rational, reasoning, reflective, regardful, responsible, responsive, self-conscious, sensible, sentient, studied, wilful, witting.

*antonym* unconscious.

**consciousness** *n* apprehension, awareness, intuition, knowledge, realisation, recognition, sensibility, sentience.

*antonym* unconciousness.

**consecrate** *v* beatify, dedicate, devote, exalt, hallow, ordain, revere, sanctify, venerate.

**consecutive** *adj* chronological, continuous, following, running, sequential, seriatim, succeeding, successive, unbroken, uninterrupted.

*antonym* discontinuous.

**consensus** *n* agreement, concord, concurrence, consent, consentience, harmony, unanimity, unity.

*antonym* disagreement.

**consent** *v* accede, acquiesce, admit, agree, allow, approve, assent, comply, concede, concur, grant, homologate, permit, yield.

*antonyms* oppose, refuse.

*n* accordance, acquiescence, agreement, approval, assent, compliance, concession, concurrence, consentience, go-ahead, green light, permission, sanction.

*antonyms* opposition, refusal.

**consequence** *n* account, concern, distinction, effect, eminence, end, event, fall-out, import, importance, interest, issue, moment, notability, note, outcome, portent, rank, repercussion, repute, result, side effect, significance, standing, status, upshot, value, weight.

*antonym* cause.

**consequent** *adj* ensuing, following, resultant, resulting, sequent, sequential, subsequent, successive.

**consequential** *adj* arrogant, bumptious, conceited, consequent, eventful, far-reaching, grave, important, impressive, indirect, inflated, momentous, noteworthy, pompous, pretentious, resultant, self-important, serious, significant, supercilious, vainglorious, weighty.

*antonyms* inconsequential, unimportant.

**consequently** *adv* accordingly, consequentially, ergo, hence, inferentially, necessarily, subsequently, therefore, thus.

**conservation** *n* custody, ecology, economy, guardianship, husbandry, keeping, maintenance, preservation, protection, safeguarding, safe-keeping, saving, upkeep.

*antonyms* destruction, neglect, waste.

**conservatism** *n* conservativeness, conventionalism, orthodoxy, traditionalism, via trita, via truta.

*antonym* radicalism.

**conservative** *adj* cautious, conventional, die-hard, establishmentarian, guarded, hidebound, middle-of-the-road, moderate, quiet, reactionary, right-wing, sober, Tory, traditional, unexaggerated, unprogressive, verkrampte.

*antonyms* left-wing, radical.

*n* diehard, moderate, moss-back, reactionary, right-winger, stick-in-the-mud, Tory, traditionalist.

*antonyms* left-winger, radical.

**conservatory** *n* academy, conservatoire, glasshouse, greenhouse, hothouse, institute.

**conserve** *v* guard, hoard, husband, keep, maintain, nurse, preserve, protect, save.

*antonyms* squander, use, waste.

**consider** v believe, bethink, cogitate, consult, contemplate, count, deem, deliberate, discuss, examine, judge, meditate, mull over, muse, perpend, ponder, rate, reflect, regard, remember, respect, revolve, ruminate, study, think, weigh.

*antonym* ignore.

**considerable** adj abundant, ample, appreciable, big, comfortable, distinguished, goodly, great, important, influential, large, lavish, marked, much, noteworthy, noticeable, plentiful, reasonable, renowned, significant, siz(e)able, substantial, tidy, tolerable, venerable.

*antonyms* insignificant, slight.

**considerably** adv abundantly, appreciably, greatly, markedly, much, noticeably, remarkably, significantly, substantially.

*antonym* slightly.

**considerate** adj attentive, charitable, circumspect, concerned, discreet, forbearing, gracious, kind, kindly, mindful, obliging, patient, solicitous, tactful, thoughtful, unselfish.

*antonyms* selfish, thoughtless.

**consideration** n analysis, attention, cogitation, concern, considerateness, contemplation, deliberation, discussion, examination, factor, fee, friendliness, issue, kindliness, kindness, meditation, payment, perquisite, point, recompense, reflection, regard, remuneration, respect, review, reward, rumination, scrutiny, solicitude, study, tact, thought, thoughtfulness, tip.

*antonyms* disdain, disregard.

**consign** v commit, convey, deliver, devote, entrust, hand over, relegate, seal, ship, sign, transfer, transmit.

**consignment** n assignment, batch, cargo, committal, delivery, dispatch, distribution, goods, load, relegation, sending, shipment, transmittal.

**consist of** amount to, comprise, contain, embody, embrace, include, incorporate, involve.

**consist in** inhere, lie, reside.

**consistency** n accordance, agreement, coherence, compactness, compatibility, concordance, congruity, constancy, correspondence, density, evenness, firmness, harmony, identity, regularity, sameness, steadfastness, steadiness, thickness, uniformity, viscosity.

*antonym* inconsistency.

**consistent** adj accordant, agreeing, coherent, compatible, congruous, consonant, constant, dependable, harmonious, logical, of a piece, persistent, regular, steady, unchanging, undeviating, unfailing, uniform.

*antonyms* erratic, inconsistent.

**consolation** n aid, alleviation, assuagement, cheer, comfort, ease, easement, encouragement, help, relief, solace, succour, support.

*antonym* discouragement.

**console** v assuage, calm, cheer, comfort, encourage, hearten, solace, soothe.

*antonyms* agitate, upset.

**consolidate** v affiliate, amalgamate, cement, combine, compact, condense, confederate, conjoin, federate, fortify, fuse, harden, join, reinforce, secure, solidify, stabilise, strengthen, thicken, unify, unite.

**consolidation** n affiliation, alliance, amalgamation, association, compression, condensation, confederation, federation, fortification, fusion, reinforcement, strengthening.

**consonance** n accord, agreement, compatibility, concord, conformity, congruence, congruity, consistency, correspondence, harmony, suitableness.

*antonym* dissonance.

**consonant** adj accordant, according, compatible, concordant, congruous, consistent, correspondent, harmonious, suitable.

*antonym* dissonant.

**consort** n associate, companion, fellow, helpmate, helpmeet, husband, partner, spouse, wife.

v accord, agree, associate, correspond, fraternise, harmonise, jibe, mingle, mix, square, tally.

**conspectus** n abstract, compendium, digest, epitome, outline, precis, report, resume, review, statement, summary, survey, syllabus, synopsis.

**conspicuous** adj apparent, blatant, clear, discernible, evident, flagrant, flashy, garish, glaring, kenspeck(le), manifest, noticeable, obvious, patent, perceptible, remarked, showy, visible.

*antonym* inconspicuous.

**conspiracy** n cabal, collusion, complot, confederacy, fix, frame-up, intrigue, league, machination, omerta, plot, scheme, treason.

**conspirator** n caballer, conspirer, highbinder, intriguer, plotter, practisant, schemer, traitor.

**conspire** v cabal, collude, combine, complot, concur, conduce, confederate, contribute, contrive, co-operate, devise, hatch, intrigue, machinate, manoeuvre, plot, scheme, tend, treason.

**constancy** n determination, devotion, faithfulness, fidelity, firmness, fixedness, loyalty, permanence, perseverance, regularity, resolution, stability, steadfastness, steadiness, tenacity, uniformity.

*antonyms* inconstancy, irregularity.

**constant** adj attached, ceaseless, changeless, continual, continuous, dependable, determined, devoted, dogged, endless, eternal, even, everlasting, faithful, firm, fixed, habitual, immutable, incessant, interminable, invariable, loyal, never-ending, non-stop, permanent, perpetual, persevering, persistent, regular, relentless, resolute, stable, staunch, steadfast, steady, sustained, tried-and-true, true, trustworthy, trusty, unalterable, unbroken, unchangeable, unfailing, unflagging, uniform, uninterrupted, unrelenting, unremitting, unshaken, unvarying, unwavering.

*antonyms* fickle, fitful, irregular, occasional, variable.

**constantly** *adv* always, continually, continuously, endlessly, everlastingly, incessantly, interminably, invariably, non-stop, perpetually, relentlessly, steadfastly, uniformly.

*antonym* occasionally.

**consternation** *n* alarm, amazement, anxiety, awe, bewilderment, confusion, dismay, disquietude, distress, dread, fear, fright, horror, panic, perturbation, shock, terror, trepidation.

*antonym* composure.

**constituent** *adj* basic, component, elemental, essential, inherent, integral, intrinsic.

*n* bit, component, element, essential, factor, ingredient, part, portion, principle, section, unit.

*antonym* whole.

**constitute** *v* appoint, authorise, commission, compose, comprise, create, delegate, depute, empower, enact, establish, fix, form, found, inaugurate, make, name, nominate, ordain.

**constitution** *n* build, character, composition, configuration, construction, disposition, establishment, form, formation, habit, health, make-up, nature, organisation, physique, structure, temper, temperament.

**constitutional** *adj* chartered, congenital, immanent, inborn, inherent, innate, intrinsic, organic, statutory, vested.

*n* airing, promenade, stroll, turn, walk.

**constrain** *v* bind, bulldoze, chain, check, coerce, compel, confine, constrict, curb, drive, force, impel, necessitate, oblige, pressure, pressurise, railroad, restrain, urge.

**constrained** *adj* embarrassed, forced, guarded, inhibited, reserved, reticent, stiff, subdued, uneasy, unnatural.

*antonyms* free, relaxed.

**constraint** *n* check, coaction, coercion, compulsion, curb, damper, deterrent, duress, force, hindrance, limitation, necessity, pressure, restraint, restriction.

**constrict** *v* choke, compact, compress, constringe, contract, cramp, inhibit, limit, narrow, pinch, restrict, shrink, squeeze, strangle, strangulate, tighten.

*antonym* expand.

**constriction** *n* blockage, compression, constraint, constringency, cramp, impediment, limitation, narrowing, pressure, reduction, restriction, squeezing, stenosis, stricture, tightening, tightness.

*antonym* expansion.

**construct** *v* assemble, build, compose, create, design, elevate, engineer, erect, establish, fabricate, fashion, form, formulate, found, frame, knock together, make, manufacture, model, organise, raise, shape.

*antonyms* demolish, destroy.

**construction** *n* assembly, building, composition, constitution, creation, edifice, erection, fabric, fabrication, figure, form, formation, model, organisation, shape, structure.

*antonym* destruction.

**constructive** *adj* advantageous, beneficial, helpful, positive, practical, productive, useful, valuable.

*antonyms* destructive, negative, unhelpful.

**construe** *v* analyse, decipher, deduce, explain, expound, infer, interpret, parse, read, render, take, translate.

**consult** *v* ask, commune, confer, consider, debate, deliberate, interrogate, parley, powwow, question, regard, respect.

**consultant** *n* adviser, authority, expert, specialist.

**consultation** *n* appointment, colloquy, conference, council, deliberation, dialogue, discussion, examination, hearing, interview, meeting, parley, session.

**consumables** *n* comestibles, eatables, fungibles.

**consume** *v* absorb, annihilate, decay, demolish, deplete, destroy, devastate, devour, discuss, dissipate, drain, eat, employ, engulf, envelop, exhaust, expend, gobble, guzzle, lessen, ravage, spend, squander, swallow, use (up), utilise, vanish, waste, wear out.

**consumed** *adj* absorbed, devoured, dominated, engrossed, monopolised, obsessed, preoccupied.

**consumer** *n* buyer, customer, end-user, purchaser, shopper, user.

**consuming** *adj* absorbing, compelling, devouring, dominating, engrossing, excruciating, gripping, immoderate, monopolising, overwhelming, tormenting.

**consummate** *v* accomplish, achieve, cap, compass, complete, conclude, crown, effectuate, end, finish, fulfil, perfect, perform, terminate.

*adj* absolute, accomplished, complete, conspicuous, distinguished, finished, matchless, perfect, polished, practised, skilled, superb, superior, supreme, total, transcendent, ultimate, unqualified, utter.

*antonym* imperfect.

**consummation** *n* achievement, actualisation, completion, culmination, end, fulfilment, perfection, realisation, termination.

**consumption** *n* consuming, decay, decline, decrease, depletion, destruction, diminution, dissipation, emaciation, exhaustion, expenditure, loss, phthisis, tabefaction, tabes, TB, tuberculosis, use, utilisation, waste.

**contact** *n* acquaintance, approximation, association, communication, connection, contiguity, contingence, impact, junction, juxtaposition, meeting, tangency, touch, union.

*v* approach, call, get hold of, notify, phone, reach, ring.

**contagious** *adj* catching, communicable, epidemic, epizootic, infectious, pestiferous, pestilential, spreading, transmissible, zymotic.

**contain** *v* accommodate, check, comprehend, comprise, control, curb, embody, embrace, enclose, entomb, hold, include, incorporate, involve, limit, repress, restrain, seat, stifle.

*antonym* exclude.

**container** *n* holder, hopper, receptacle, repository, vessel.

**contaminate** *v* adulterate, befoul, besmirch, corrupt, debase, defile, deprave, infect, pollute, soil, stain, sully, taint, tarnish, vitiate.

*antonym* purify.

**contamination** *n* adulteration, contagion, corruption, decay, defilement, desecration, filth, foulness, impurity, infection, poisoning, pollution, rottenness, taint, vitiation.

*antonym* purification.

**contemplate** *v* behold, cerebrate, consider, deliberate, design, envisage, examine, expect, eye, foresee, inspect, intend, mean, meditate, mull over, observe, plan, ponder, propose, reflect on, regard, ruminate, scrutinise, study, survey, view.

**contemplation** *n* cerebration, cogitation, consideration, deliberation, examination, inspection, meditation, musing, observation, pondering, reflection, reverie, rumination, scrutiny, survey, thought, viewing.

**contemplative** *adj* cerebral, intent, introspective, meditative, musing, pensive, rapt, reflective, ruminative, thoughtful.

*antonyms* impulsive, thoughtless.

**contemporary** *adj* à la mode, coetaneous, coeval, co-existent, co-existing, concurrent, contemporaneous, conterminous, coterminous, current, latest, modern, newfangled, present, present-day, recent, synchronous, ultra-modern, up-to-date, up-to-the-minute, with it.

*antonyms* preceding, succeeding.

**contempt** *n* condescension, contumely, derision, despite, detestation, disdain, disgrace, dishonour, disregard, disrespect, floccinaucinihilipilification, humiliation, loathing, mockery, neglect, scorn, shame, slight.

*antonyms* admiration, regard.

**contemptible** *adj* abject, base, cheap, degenerate, despicable, detestable, ignominious, loathsome, low, low-down, mean, paltry, pitiful, scurvy, shabby, shameful, vile, worthless, wretched.

*antonyms* admirable, honourable.

**contemptuous** *adj* arrogant, cavalier, condescending, contumacious, contumelious, cynical, derisive, disdainful, haughty, high and mighty, insolent, insulting, scornful, sneering, supercilious, tossy, withering.

*antonyms* humble, polite, respectful.

**contemptuously** *adv* arrogantly, de haut en bas, derisively, disdainfully, haughtily, insolently, pompously, scornfully, superciliously.

*antonyms* humbly, politely, respectfully.

**contend** *v* affirm, allege, argue, assert, aver, avow, clash, compete, contest, cope, debate, declare, dispute, emulate, grapple, hold, jostle, litigate, maintain, skirmish, strive, struggle, vie, wrestle.

**content**[1] *v* appease, delight, gladden, gratify, humour, indulge, mollify, pacify, placate, please, reconcile, satisfy, suffice.

*antonym* displease.

*n* comfort, contentment, delight, ease, gratification, happiness, peace, pleasure, satisfaction.

*antonym* discontent.

*adj* agreeable, comfortable, contented, fulfilled, pleased, satisfied, untroubled.

*antonym* dissatisfied.

**content**[2] *n* burden, capacity, essence, gist, ideas, load, matter, meaning, measure, significance, size, subject matter, substance, text, thoughts, volume.

**contented** *adj* cheerful, comfortable, complacent, content, glad, gratified, happy, placid, pleased, relaxed, satisfied, serene, thankful.

*antonym* discontented.

**contention** *n* affirmation, allegation, argument, assertion, asseveration, belief, claim, competition, contest, controversy, debate, declaration, discord, dispute, dissension, enmity, feuding, ground, hostility, idea, opinion, position, profession, rivalry, stand, strife, struggle, thesis, view, wrangling.

**contentious** *adj* antagonistic, argumentative, bickering, captious, cavilling, combative, controversial, cross, debat(e)able, disputatious, factious, hostile, litigious, peevish, perverse, pugnacious, quarrelsome, querulous, wrangling.

*antonyms* co-operative, peaceable, uncontroversial.

**contentment** *n* comfort, complacency, content, contentedness, ease, equanimity, fulfilment, gladness, gratification, happiness, peace, peacefulness, placidity, pleasure, repletion, satisfaction, serenity.

*antonym* dissatisfaction.

**contents** *n* chapters, constituents, divisions, elements, ingredients, items, load, parts, subjects, themes, topics.

**contest** *n* affray, altercation, battle, combat, competition, concours, conflict, controversy, debate, discord, dispute, encounter, fight, game, match, olympiad, set-to, shock, struggle, tournament, trial.

*v* argue against, challenge, compete, contend, debate, deny, dispute, doubt, fight, litigate, oppose, question, refute, strive, vie.

**contestant** *n* agonist, aspirant, candidate, competitor, contender, entrant, participant, player.

**context** *n* ambience, associations, background, circumstances, conditions, connection, frame of reference, framework, relation, situation.

**contiguous** *adj* abutting, adjacent, adjoining, beside, bordering, conjoining, conterminous, juxtaposed, juxtapositional, near, neighbouring, next, tangential, touching.

*antonyms* distort, separate.

**continence** *n* abstemiousness, abstinence, asceticism, celibacy, chastity, moderation, self-control, self-restraint, sobriety, temperance.

*antonym* incontinence.

**continent** *adj* abstemious, abstinent, ascetic, austere, celibate, chaste, pure, restrained, self-restrained, sober, virginal.

*antonym* incontinent.

**contingency** *n* accident, arbitrariness, chance, emergency, event, eventuality, fortuity, happening, incident, juncture, possibility, randomness, uncertainty.

**contingent** *n* batch, body, bunch, company, complement, deputation, detachment, group, mission, quota, section, set.

**continual** *adj* ceaseless, constant, continuous, endless, eternal, everlasting, frequent, incessant, interminable, oft-repeated, perpetual, recurrent, regular, repeated, repetitive, unbroken, unceasing, uninterrupted, unremitting.

*antonyms* intermittent, occasional, temporary.

**continually** *adv* always, ceaselessly, constantly, endlessly, eternally, everlastingly, forever, incessantly, interminably, non-stop, perpetually, persistently, repeatedly.

*antonym* occasionally.

**continuance** *n* continuation, duration, endurance, period, permanence, protraction, term.

**continuation** *n* addition, appendix, epilogue, extension, furtherance, maintenance, perpetuation, postscript, prolongation, resumption, sequel, supplement.

*antonyms* cessation, termination.

**continue** *v* abide, aby(e), adjourn, carry on, endure, extend, go on, last, lengthen, maintain, persevere, persist, proceed, project, prolong, pursue, reach, recommence, remain, rest, resume, stay, stick at, survive, sustain.

*antonyms* discontinue, stop.

**continuing** *adj* abiding, enduring, lasting, on-going, progressing, sustained.

**continuity** *n* cohesion, connection, extension, flow, interrelationship, linkage, progression, sequence, succession.

*antonym* discontinuity.

**continuous** *adj* connected, consecutive, constant, continued, extended, non-stop, prolonged, unbroken, unceasing, undivided, uninterrupted.

*antonyms* discontinuous, intermittent, sporadic.

**contort** *v* convolute, deform, disfigure, distort, gnarl, knot, misshape, squirm, twist, warp, wrench, wriggle, writhe.

**contortionist** *n* acrobat, gymnast, posture-maker, posture-master, tumbler.

**contour** *n* aspect, character, contorno, curve, figure, form, lines, outline, profile, relief, shape, silhouette.

**contraband** *adj* banned, black-market, bootleg, forbidden, hot, illegal, illicit, interdicted, prohibited, proscribed, smuggled, unlawful, verboten.

**contract** *v* abbreviate, abridge, acquire, agree, arrange, bargain, catch, clinch, close, compress, condense, confine, constrict, constringe, covenant, curtail, develop, dwindle, engage, epitomise, incur, lessen, narrow, negotiate, pledge, purse, reduce, shrink, shrivel, stipulate, tighten, wither, wrinkle.

*antonyms* enlarge, expand, lengthen.

*n* agreement, arrangement, bargain, bond, commission, commitment, compact, concordat, convention, covenant, deal, engagement, handfast, instrument, pact, settlement, stipulation, transaction, treaty, understanding.

**contraction** *n* abbreviation, astringency, compression, constriction, cramp, diminution, elision, narrowing, reduction, retrenchment, shortening, shrinkage, shrivelling, tensing, tightening.

*antonyms* expansion, growth.

**contradict** *v* belie, challenge, contravene, controvert, counter, counteract, deny, disaffirm, dispute, gainsay, impugn, negate, oppose.

*antonyms* agree, confirm, corroborate.

**contradiction** *n* conflict, confutation, contravention, denial, disaffirmance, disaffirmation, gainsay, Hibernicism, incongruity, inconsistency, negation, opposite.

*antonyms* agreement, confirmation, corroboration.

**contradictory** *adj* antagonistic, antithetical, conflicting, contrary, discrepant, dissident, double-mouthed, incompatible, inconsistent, irreconcilable, opposed, opposite, paradoxical, repugnant, unreconciled.

*antonym* consistent.

**contraption** *n* apparatus, contrivance, device, gadget, gizmo, mechanism, rig, thingumajig, widget.

**contrary** *adj* adverse, antagonistic, arsy-versy, awkward, balky, cantankerous, clashing, contradictory, counter, cross-grained, cussed, difficult, discordant, disobliging, froward, hostile, inconsistent, inimical, intractable, intractible, obstinate, opposed, opposite, paradoxical, perverse, stroppy, thrawn, unaccommodating, wayward, wilful.

*antonyms* like, obliging, similar.

*n* antithesis, converse, opposite, reverse.

**contrast** *n* comparison, contraposition, contrariety, counter-view, difference, differentiation, disparity, dissimilarity, distinction, divergence, foil, opposition, set-off.

*antonym* similarity.

*v* compare, differ, differentiate, discriminate, distinguish, oppose, set off.

**contravene** *v* break, contradict, counteract, cross, disobey, hinder, infract, infringe, interfere, oppose, refute, thwart, transgress, trespass, violate.

*antonym* uphold.

**contretemps** n accident, calamity, difficulty, hitch, misadventure, misfortune, mishap, mistake, predicament.

**contribute** v add, afford, bestow, conduce, dob in, donate, furnish, give, help, kick in, lead, provide, subscribe, supply, tend.

*antonyms* subtract, withhold.

**contribution** n addition, bestowal, donation, gift, grant, gratuity, handout, input, offering, subscription.

**contributor** n backer, benefactor, bestower, conferrer, correspondent, donor, freelance, freelancer, giver, journalist, patron, reporter, subscriber, supporter.

**contrite** adj chastened, conscience-stricken, guilt-ridden, humble, penitent, penitential, penitentiary, regretful, remorseful, repentant, sorrowful, sorry.

**contrition** n compunction, humiliation, penitence, remorse, repentance, sackcloth and ashes, self-reproach, sorrow.

**contrivance** n apparatus, appliance, artifice, contraption, design, device, dodge, equipment, excogitation, expedient, fabrication, formation, gadget, gear, implement, intrigue, invention, inventiveness, knack, machination, machine, measure, mechanism, plan, plot, project, ruse, scheme, stratagem, trick.

**contrive** v arrange, compass, concoct, construct, create, design, devise, effect, engineer, excogitate, fabricate, frame, improvise, invent, manage, manoeuvre, plan, plot, scheme, wangle.

**contrived** adj artificial, elaborate, false, forced, laboured, mannered, overdone, planned, recherche, strained, unnatural.

*antonym* natural.

**control** v boss, bridle, check, command, conduct, confine, constrain, contain, curb, determine, direct, dominate, govern, lead, limit, manage, manipulate, master, monitor, oversee, pilot, regiment, regulate, repress, restrain, rule, run, stage-manage, steer, subdue, superintend, supervise, suppress, verify.

n authority, brake, charge, check, clutches, command, curb, direction, dirigism(e), discipline, governance, government, guidance, jurisdiction, leading-strings, leash, limitation, management, mastery, oversight, regulation, rule, superintendence, supervision, supremacy.

**controller** n administrator, captain, compère, director, executive, executor, gerent, governor, gubernator, manager, marshal, navigator, pilot, ringmaster, ruler, steward.

**controversial** adj attacking, contentious, controvertible, debatable, disputable, disputed, doubtful, polemic, polemical, questionable.

**controversy** n altercation, argument, contention, debate, disagreement, discussion, dispute, dissension, polemic, quarrel, squabble, strife, war of words, wrangle, wrangling.

*antonyms* accord, agreement.

**controvert** v argue, challenge, contest, contradict, counter, debate, deny, disaffirm, discuss, dispute, gainsay, oppose, refute, wrangle.

**contumacious** adj haughty, headstrong, insubordinate, intractable, intransigent, mulish, obdurate, obstinate, perverse, pig-headed, rebellious, recalcitrant, refractory, stiff-necked, stubborn, wilful.

*antonym* obedient.

**contumely** n abuse, affront, arrogance, contempt, derision, disdain, humiliation, incivility, indignity, insolence, insult, invective, obloquy, opprobrium, rudeness, scorn, superciliousness.

**contusion** n bruise, bump, discolouration, injury, knock, lump, swelling.

**conundrum** n anagram, brain-teaser, enigma, poser, problem, puzzle, riddle.

**convalescence** n improvement, recovery, recuperation, rehabilitation, restoration.

**convene** v assemble, call, collect, congregate, convoke, gather, meet, muster, rally, summon.

**convenience** n accessibility, accommodation, advantage, amenity, appliance, appropriateness, availability, benefit, chance, comfort, ease, enjoyment, facility, fitness, handiness, help, leisure, opportuneness, opportunity, satisfaction, service, serviceability, suitability, timeliness, use, usefulness, utility.

**convenient** adj accessible, adapted, advantageable, appropriate, at hand, available, beneficial, commodious, fit, fitted, handy, helpful, labour-saving, nearby, opportune, seasonable, serviceable, suitable, suited, timely, useful, utile, well-timed.

*antonyms* awkward, inconvenient.

**convention** n agreement, assembly, bargain, code, compact, conclave, concordat, conference, congress, contract, convocation, council, custom, delegates, etiquette, formality, matter of form, meeting, pact, practice, propriety, protocol, representatives, stipulation, synod, tradition, treaty, understanding, usage.

**conventional** adj accepted, arbitrary, bourgeois, common, commonplace, copybook, correct, customary, decorous, expected, formal, formalist, habitual, hackneyed, hidebound, iconic, nomic, normal, ordinary, orthodox, pedestrian, prevailing, prevalent, proper, prosaic, regular, ritual, routine, run-of-the-mill, standard, stereotyped, straight, stylised, traditional, unoriginal, uptight, usual, wonted.

*antonyms* exotic, unconventional, unusual.

**converge** v approach, coincide, combine, concentrate, concur, focus, gather, join, meet, merge, mingle.

*antonyms* disperse, diverge.

**convergence** n approach, blending, coincidence, concentration, concurrence, confluence, conflux, conjunction, intersection, junction, meeting, merging, mingling, union.

*antonym* divergence.

**conversant with** acquainted with, apprised of, au fait with, experienced in, familiar with, informed about, knowledgeable about, practised in, proficient in, skilled in, versant with, versed in.

*antonym* ignorant of.

**conversation** *n* chat, chinwag, chitchat, colloquy, communication, communion, confab, confabulation, conference, converse, dialogue, discourse, discussion, exchange, gossip, intercourse, interlocution, powwow, talk, tête-à-tête.

**conversational** *adj* chatty, colloquial, communicative, confabulatory, informal, relaxed.

**conversationalist** *n* deipnosophist, table-philosopher.

**converse**[1] *v* chat, colloquise, commune, confabulate, confer, discourse, talk.

**converse**[2] *n* antithesis, contrary, counterpart, obverse, opposite, reverse.

*adj* antipodal, antipodean, contrary, counter, opposite, reverse, reversed, transposed.

**conversion** *n* adaptation, alteration, change, metamorphosis, metanoia, modification, permutation, proselytisation, rebirth, reconstruction, reformation, regeneration, remodelling, reorganisation, transfiguration, transformation, transmogrification, transmutation.

**convert** *v* adapt, alter, apply, appropriate, baptise, change, convince, interchange, metamorphose, modify, permute, proselytise, reform, regenerate, remodel, reorganise, restyle, revise, save, transform, transmogrify, transmute, transpose, turn.

*n* catechumen, disciple, neophyte, proselyte, vert.

**convertible** *adj* adaptable, adjustable, exchangeable, interchangeable, permutable.

**convex** *adj* bulging, gibbous, protuberant, rounded, tumid.

*antonym* concave.

**convey** *v* bear, bequeath, bring, carry, cede, communicate, conduct, deliver, demise, devolve, disclose, fetch, forward, grant, guide, impart, lease, move, relate, reveal, send, steal, support, tell, transfer, transmit, transport, waft, will.

**conveyance** *n* carriage, movement, shipment, transfer, transference, transmission, transport, transportation, tran(s)shipment, vehicle, wagonage.

**convict** *v* attaint, condemn, imprison, sentence.

*n* con, criminal, culprit, felon, forçat, jail-bird, lag, malefactor, prisoner.

**conviction** *n* assurance, belief, certainty, certitude, confidence, convincement, creed, earnestness, faith, fervour, firmness, opinion, persuasion, plerophory, principle, reliance, tenet, view.

**convince** *v* assure, confirm, persuade, reassure, satisfy, sway, win over.

**convincing** *adj* cogent, conclusive, credible, impressive, incontrovertible, likely, luculent,

persuasive, plausible, powerful, probable, telling, verisimiliar.

*antonyms* dubious, improbable.

**convivial** *adj* back-slapping, cheerful, festive, friendly, fun-loving, gay, genial, hearty, hilarious, jolly, jovial, lively, merry, mirthful, sociable.

*antonym* taciturn.

**conviviality** *n* bonhomie, cheer, cordiality, festivity, gaiety, geniality, jollification, jollity, joviality, liveliness, merrymaking, mirth, sociability.

**convocation** *n* assemblage, assembly, conclave, concourse, congregation, congress, convention, council, diet, for(e)gathering, meeting, muster, synod.

**convoke** *v* assemble, collect, convene, gather, muster, rally, round up, summon.

**convoluted** *adj* complex, complicated, gyrose, involved, meandering, tangled, twisting, winding.

*antonym* straightforward.

**convolution** *n* coil, coiling, complexity, contortion, curlicue, gyrus, helix, intricacy, involution, loop, sinousness, sinuosity, spiral, tortuousness, twist, undulation, volution, whorl, winding.

**convoy** *n* attendance, attendant, escort, fleet, guard, protection, train.

**convulsion** *n* agitation, commotion, contortion, contraction, cramp, disturbance, eruption, fit, furore, outburst, paroxysm, seizure, shaking, spasm, throe, tremor, tumult, turbulence, upheaval.

**convulsive** *adj* churning, fitful, jerky, paroxysmal, spasmodic, spastic, sporadic, twitchy, violent.

**cook** *n* chef, chef de cuisine, confectioner, cuisinier, pastrycook.

*v* bake, boil, braise, broil, fry, grill, heat, prepare, roast, saute, simmer, steam, stew, toast.

**cook up** brew, concoct, contrive, devise, fabricate, improvise, invent, plan, plot, prepare, scheme.

**cool** *adj* aloof, apathetic, audacious, bold, brazen, calm, cheeky, chilled, chilling, chilly, coldish, collected, composed, cosmopolitan, degage, deliberate, dispassionate, distant, down-beat, elegant, frigid, impertinent, imperturbable, impudent, incurious, indifferent, laid-back, level-headed, lukewarm, nippy, offhand, placid, pleasant, presumptuous, quiet, refreshing, relaxed, reserved, satisfying, self-controlled, self-possessed, serene, shameless, sophisticated, stand-offish, together, uncommunicative, unconcerned, unemotional, unenthusiastic, unexcited, unfriendly, unheated, uninterested, unresponsive, unruffled, unwelcoming, urbane.

*antonyms* excited, friendly, hot, warm.

*v* abate, allay, assuage, calm, chill, dampen, defuse, fan, freeze, lessen, moderate, quiet, refrigerate, temper.

*antonyms* excite, heat, warm.

*n* calmness, collectedness, composure, control, poise, sangfroid, self-control, self-discipline, self-possession, temper.

**cooling** *n* air-conditioning, chilling, defervescence, defervescency, refrigeration, ventilation.

*antonyms* heating, warming.

*adj* freezing, refrigerant, refrigerative, refrigeratory.

*antonym* warming.

**coop** *n* box, cage, enclosure, hutch, mew, pen, pound.

*v* cage, confine, immure, impound, imprison, intern, pen.

**co-operate** *v* abet, aid, assist, collaborate, combine, concur, conduce, conspire, contribute, co-ordinate, help, play along, play ball.

**co-operation** *n* assistance, coaction, collaboration, concert, concurrence, give-and-take, helpfulness, participation, responsiveness, synergy, teamwork, unity.

**co-operative** *adj* accommodating, coactive, collective, combined, concerted, co-ordinated, helpful, joint, obliging, responsive, shared, supportive, synergetic, synergic, unified, united.

*antonym* unco-operative.

**co-ordinate** *v* codify, correlate, grade, graduate, harmonise, integrate, match, mesh, organise, relate, synchronise, systematise, tabulate.

*adj* coequal, correlative, correspondent, equal, equipotent, equivalent, parallel, reciprocal.

**cop out** abandon, desert, dodge, evade, quit, renege, renounce, revoke, shirk, skip, skive, withdraw.

**cope** *v* carry on, get by, make (a) shift, make do, manage, survive.

**cope with** contend with, deal with, dispatch, encounter, grapple with, handle, manage, struggle with, tangle with, tussle with, weather, wrestle with.

**copious** *adj* abundant, ample, bounteous, bountiful, extensive, exuberant, full, generous, great, huge, inexhaustible, lavish, liberal, luxuriant, overflowing, plenteous, plentiful, profuse, rich, superabundant.

*antonyms* meagre, scarce.

**copiousness** *n* abundance, amplitude, bountifulness, bounty, cornucopia, exuberance, fullness, lavishness, luxuriance, plenitude, plentifulness, plenty, prodigality, profusion, richness, superabundance.

*antonym* scarcity.

**cop-out** *n* alibi, dodge, evasion, fraud, pretence, pretext.

**copulate** *v* bonk, cover, enjoy, fuck, gender, horse, know, line, make love, mate, serve, tread.

**copulation** *n* carnal knowledge, coition, coitus, congress, coupling, covering, joining, love, lovemaking, mating, serving, sex, sexual intercourse, treading.

**copy** *n* apograph, archetype, autotype, borrowing, calque, carbon copy, counterfeit, crib, duplicate, ectype, engrossment, exemplar, facsimile, fax, flimsy, forgery, image, imitation, likeness, loan translation, loan-word, model, Ozalid®, pattern, photocopy, Photostat®, plagiarisation, print, replica, replication, representation, reproduction, tenor, tracing, transcript, transcription, Xerox®.

*antonym* original.

*v* ape, borrow, counterfeit, crib, duplicate, echo, emulate, engross, exemplify, extract, facsimile, follow, imitate, mimic, mirror, parrot, personate, photocopy, Photostat®, plagiarise, repeat, replicate, reproduce, simulate, transcribe, Xerox®.

**coquettish** *adj* amorous, arch, come-hither, coy, dallying, flighty, flirtatious, flirty, inviting, teasing, vampish.

**cord** *n* bond, connection, funicle, gimp, line, link, rope, strand, string, tie, twine.

**cordial** *adj* affable, affectionate, agreeable, cheerful, earnest, friendly, genial, heartfelt, hearty, invigorating, pleasant, restorative, sociable, stimulating, warm, warm-hearted, welcoming, whole-hearted.

*antonyms* aloof, cool, hostile.

**cordiality** *n* affability, affection, amiability, friendliness, geniality, goodwill, heartiness, sincerity, warmth, whole-heartedness.

*antonyms* coolness, hostility.

**cordon** *n* barrier, chain, fence, line, ring.

**cordon off** encircle, enclose, fence off, isolate, separate, surround.

**core** *n* centre, crux, essence, germ, gist, heart, kernel, nitty-gritty, nub, nucleus, pith.

*antonyms* exterior, perimeter, surface.

**corner** *n* angle, bend, cantle, cavity, cranny, crook, hide-away, hideout, hidey-hole, hole, joint, neuk, niche, nook, pickle, predicament, recess, retreat, spot.

**corny** *adj* banal, cliched, commonplace, dull, feeble, hackneyed, maudlin, mawkish, old-fashioned, platitudinous, sentimental, stale, stereotyped, trite.

*antonyms* new, original.

**corollary** *n* conclusion, consequence, deduction, fall-out, illation, induction, inference, result, upshot.

**corporal** *adj* anatomical, bodily, carnal, concrete, corporeal, fleshly, material, physical, somatic, tangible.

*antonym* spiritual.

**corporate** *adj* allied, amalgamated, collaborative, collective, combined, communal, concerted, joint, merged, pooled, shared, united.

**corporation¹** *n* association, authorities, body, combine, conglomerate, council, society.

**corporation²** *n* beer belly, paunch, pod, pot, pot-belly, spare tyre.

**corporeal** *adj* actual, bodily, fleshly, human, hylic, material, mortal, physical, substantial, tangible.

*antonym* spiritual.

**corps** n band, body, brigade, company, contingent, crew, detachment, division, phalanx, regiment, squad, squadron, team, troop, unit.

**corpse** n body, cadaver, carcass, deader, remains, skeleton, stiff.

**corpulence** n adiposity, blubber, burliness, embonpoint, fatness, fleshiness, obesity, plumpness, portliness, rotundity, stoutness, tubbiness.

*antonym* thinness.

**corpulent** adj adipose, beefy, bulky, burly, fat, fattish, fleshy, large, lusty, obese, overweight, plump, poddy, podgy, portly, pot-bellied, pudgy, roly-poly, rotund, stout, tubby, well-padded.

*antonym* thin.

**corpus** n aggregation, body, collection, compilation, entirety, oeuvre, whole.

**corral** n coop, enclosure, fold, kraal, pound, stall, sty.

**correct** v adjust, admonish, amend, blue-pencil, chasten, chastise, chide, counterbalance, cure, debug, discipline, emend, emendate, improve, punish, rectify, redress, reform, regulate, remedy, reprimand, reprove, right.

adj acceptable, accurate, appropriate, comme il faut, diplomatic, equitable, exact, faultless, fitting, flawless, jake, just, OK, precise, proper, regular, right, seemly, standard, strict, true, well-formed, word-perfect.

*antonyms* inaccurate, incorrect, wrong.

**correction** n adjustment, admonition, alteration, amendment, castigation, chastisement, discipline, emendation, improvement, modification, punishment, rectification, reformation, reproof, righting.

**corrective** adj curative, disciplinary, emendatory, medicinal, palliative, penal, punitive, reformatory, rehabilitative, remedial, restorative, therapeutic.

**correctly** adv accurately, aright, faithfully, faultlessly, perfectly, precisely, properly, right, rightly.

*antonyms* incorrectly, wrongly.

**correctness** n accuracy, breeding, civility, decorum, exactitude, exactness, faithfulness, faultlessness, fidelity, perfection, preciseness, precision, propriety, regularity, seemliness, truth.

**correlate** v associate, compare, connect, co-ordinate, correspond, equate, interact, link, parallel, relate, tie in.

**correlation** n alternation, correspondence, equivalence, interaction, interchange, interdependence, interrelationship, link, reciprocity, relationship.

**correspond** v accord, agree, answer, coincide, communicate, complement, concur, conform, correlate, dovetail, fit, harmonise, match, square, tally, write.

**correspondence** n agreement, analogy, assonance, coincidence, communication, comparability, comparison, concurrence, conformity, congruity, correlation, equivalence, fitness, harmony, homology, homotypy, letters, mail, match, post, relation, resemblance, respondence, responding, similarity, writing.

*antonyms* divergence, incongruity.

**correspondent** n contributor, journalist, penpal, reporter, writer.

adj analogous, comparable, equivalent, like, matching, parallel, reciprocal, similar.

**corresponding** adj accordant, analogous, answering, collateral, complementary, correlative, correspondent, equivalent, homologous, homotypal, homotypic, identical, interrelated, matching, reciprocal, similar, synonymous.

**corridor** n aisle, ambulatory, foyer, hallway, lobby, passage, passageway, vestibule.

**corroborate** v authenticate, bear out, confirm, document, endorse, establish, prove, ratify, substantiate, support, sustain, underpin, validate.

*antonym* contradict.

**corroborative** adj confirmative, confirmatory, evidential, evidentiary, supportive, verificatory.

**corrode** v canker, consume, corrupt, crumble, deteriorate, disintegrate, eat away, erode, fret, impair, oxidise, rust, waste, wear away.

**corrosive** adj abrasive, acid, acrid, biting, caustic, consuming, corroding, cutting, incisive, mordant, sarcastic, trenchant, venomous, virulent, wasting, wearing.

**corrugated** adj channelled, creased, crinkled, fluted, furrowed, grooved, puckered, ribbed, ridged, rumpled, striate(d), wrinkled.

**corrupt** adj abandoned, adulterate(d), altered, bent, bribed, contaminated, crooked, debased, decayed, defiled, degenerate, demoralised, depraved, dishonest, dishonoured, dissolute, distorted, doctored, falsified, fraudulent, infected, polluted, profligate, putrescent, putrid, rotten, shady, tainted, unethical, unprincipled, unscrupulous, venal, vicious.

*antonyms* honest, trustworthy, upright.

v adulterate, barbarise, bribe, canker, contaminate, debase, debauch, defile, demoralise, deprave, doctor, empoison, entice, fix, infect, lure, pervert, putrefy, seduce, spoil, square, suborn, subvert, taint, vitiate.

*antonym* purify.

**corruption** n adulteration, baseness, bribery, bribing, crookedness, debasement, decadence, decay, defilement, degeneration, degradation, demoralisation, depravity, dishonesty. distortion, doctoring, evil, extortion, falsification, fiddling, foulness, fraud, fraudulence, fraudulency, graft, immorality, impurity, infection, iniquity, jobbery, leprosy, malversation, perversion, pollution, profiteering, profligacy, putrefaction, putrescence, rot, rottenness, shadiness, sinfulness, turpitude, ulcer, unscrupulousness, venality, vice, viciousness, virus, wickedness.

*antonyms* honesty, purification.

**corset** n belt, bodice, check, corselet, curb, curtailment, foundation garment, girdle, limit, limitation, panty girdle, restriction, stays.

**cortège** n cavalcade, column, entourage, parade, procession, retinue, suite, train.

**cosmetic** adj non-essential, superficial, surface.
antonym essential.

**cosmetics** n grease paint, make-up, maquillage, pancake.

**cosmic** adj boundless, grandiose, huge, illimitable, immense, infinite, limitless, measureless, universal, vast.

**cosmopolitan** adj catholic, international, sophisticated, universal, unprejudiced, urbane, well-travelled, worldly, worldy-wise.
antonyms insular, parochial, rustic.

**cosmos** n creation, galaxy, system, universe, world.

**cosset** v baby, cherish, coddle, cuddle, mollycoddle, pamper, pet.

**cost** n amount, charge, damage, deprivation, detriment, disbursement, expenditure, expense, figure, harm, hurt, injury, loss, outlay, payment, penalty, price, rate, sacrifice, worth.

**costly** adj catastrophic, damaging, dear, deleterious, disastrous, excessive, exorbitant, expensive, extortionate, gorgeous, harmful, highly-priced, lavish, loss-making, luxurious, opulent, precious, priceless, pricy, rich, ruinous, sacrificial, splendid, steep, sumptuous, valuable.
antonyms cheap, inexpensive.

**costs** n budget, expenses, oncosts, outgoings, overheads.

**costume** n apparel, attire, clothing, dress, ensemble, garb, get-up, livery, outfit, raiment, robes, uniform, vestment.

**cosy** adj comfortable, comfy, homelike, homely, intimate, secure, sheltered, snug, warm.
antonyms cold, uncomfortable.

**coterie** n camp, caucus, cenacle, circle, clique, galère, gang, group, outfit, set.

**cottage** n bothy, bungalow, but-and-ben, cabin, chalet, cot, hut, lodge, shack.

**couch** v bear, cradle, express, frame, phrase, support, utter, word.
n bed, chaise-longue, chesterfield, day-bed, divan, lounge, ottoman, settee, sofa.

**cough** n bark, hack, tussis.
v bark, hack, harrumph, hawk, hem, hoast.
**cough up** deliver, fork out, give, hand over, pay, pay out, shell out, surrender.

**council** n assembly, board, cabinet, chamber, committee, conclave, conference, congress, consistory, consult, convention, convocation, diet, divan, ministry, panchayat, panel, parliament, soviet, syndicate, synod, volost.

**counsel** n admonition, advice, advocate, attorney, barrister, caution, consideration, consultation, deliberation, direction, forethought, guidance, information, lawyer, plan, purpose, recommendation, solicitor, suggestion, warning.
v admonish, advise, advocate, caution, direct, exhort, guide, instruct, recommend, suggest, urge, warn.

**counsellor** n adviser, attorney, councillor, lawyer, representative, vizier, wazir.

**count** v add, ascribe, calculate, check, compute, consider, deem, enumerate, esteem, estimate, hold, impute, include, judge, list, matter, number, rate, reckon, regard, score, signify, tally, tell, think, tot up, total, weigh.
n addition, calculation, computation, enumeration, numbering, poll, reckoning, sum, tally, total.
**count for nothing** cut no ice, make no difference.
**count on** bank on, believe, depend on, expect, reckon on, rely on, trust.
**count out** exclude, include out.
antonym include.

**countenance** n acquiescence, aid, air, appearance, approval, aspect, assistance, backing, demeanour, endorsement, expression, face, favour, features, help, look, mien, physiognomy, sanction, support, visage.
v abet, acquiesce, agree to, aid, approve, back, brook, champion, condone, encourage, endorse, endure, help, sanction, support, tolerate.

**counter**[1] adv against, contrarily, contrariwise, conversely, in opposition.
adj adverse, against, antithetical, conflicting, contradictory, contrary, contrasting, obverse, opposed, opposing, opposite.
antonyms concurring, corroborating.
v answer, meet, offset, parry, resist, respond, retaliate, retort, return.

**counter**[2] n coin, disc, jet(t)on, marker, tiddlywink, token.

**counteract** v act against, annul, check, contravene, counterbalance, countervail, cross, defeat, foil, frustrate, hinder, invalidate, negate, neutralise, offset, oppose, resist, thwart, undo.
antonyms assist, support.

**counterbalance** v balance, compensate for, counterpoise, countervail, equalise, neutralise, offset.

**counterfeit** v copy, fabricate, fake, feign, forge, imitate, impersonate, phoney, pretend, sham, simulate.
adj bogus, Brummagem, copied, ersatz, faked, false, feigned, forged, fraudulent, imitation, phoney, postiche, pretend(ed), pseud, pseudo, sham, simular, simulated, simulate(d), spurious, supposititious.
antonym genuine.
n copy, fake, forgery, fraud, imitant, imitation, phantasm(a), phoney, reproduction, sham.

**countermand** v abrogate, annul, cancel, override, repeal, rescind, reverse, revoke.

**counterpart** n complement, copy, correlative, duplicate, equal, fellow, homologue, homotype, match, mate, opposite number, supplement, tally, twin, vis-à-vis.

**countless** *adj* endless, immeasurable, incalculable, infinite, innumerable, legion, limitless, measureless, multitudinous, myriad, numberless, uncounted, unnumbered, unsummed, untold.

*antonym* limited.

**countrified** *adj* agrestic, arcadian, bucolic, hick, homespun, idyllic, pastoral, provincial, rural, rustic.

*antonyms* oppidan, urban.

**country** *n* backwoods, boondocks, citizenry, citizens, clime, commonwealth, community, countryside, electors, farmland, fatherland, green belt, homeland, inhabitants, kingdom, land, motherland, nation, nationality, outback, outdoors, part, people, populace, provinces, public, realm, region, society, sovereign state, state, sticks, terrain, territory, voters.

*adj* agrarian, agrestic, arcadian, bucolic, georgic, landed, pastoral, provincial, rude, rural, rustic.

*antonyms* oppidan, urban.

**countryman** *n* bumpkin, compatriot, farmer, fellow countryman, hayseed, hind, husbandman, peasant, provincial, rustic, swain, yokel.

**countryside** *n* country, farmland, green belt, landscape, outback, outdoors, panorama, sticks.

**county** *n* airt, comitatus, district, province, region, shire.

**coup** *n* accomplishment, action, blow, coup d'etat, deed, exploit, feat, manoeuvre, masterstroke, putsch, revolution, stratagem, stroke, stunt, tour de force.

**coup de grâce** clincher, come-uppance, death-blow, kibosh, kill, quietus.

**coup d'etat** coup, overthrow, palace revolution, putsch, rebellion, revolt, revolution, takeover, uprising.

**couple** *n* brace, Darby and Joan, duo, dyad, pair, span, team, twain, twosome, yoke.

*v* accompany, buckle, clasp, conjoin, connect, copulate, fornicate, hitch, join, link, marry, pair, unite, wed, yoke.

**coupon** *n* billet, card, certificate, check, slip, ticket, token, voucher.

**courage** *n* boldness, bottle, bravery, daring, dauntlessness, fearlessness, firmness, fortitude, gallantry, grit, guts, hardihood, heroism, mettle, moxie, nerve, pluck, resolution, spirit, spunk, stomach, valour.

*antonym* cowardice.

**courageous** *adj* audacious, bold, brave, daring, dauntless, dreadless, fearless, gallant, gutsy, hardy, heroic, high-hearted, indomitable, intrepid, lion-hearted, plucky, resolute, stout-hearted, valiant, valorous.

*antonym* cowardly.

**courier** *n* bearer, carrier, emissary, envoy, estafette, guide, herald, legate, messenger, nuncio, pursuivant, representative, runner.

**course** *n* advance, advancement, channel, circuit, circus, classes, continuity, current, curriculum, development, diadrom, direction, duration, flight-path, flow, furtherance, hippodrome, lap, lapse, lectures, line, march, method, mode, movement, orbit, order, passage, passing, path, piste, plan, policy, procedure, programme, progress, progression, race, race-course, race-track, raik, regimen, road, round, route, schedule, sequence, series, studies, succession, sweep, syllabus, tack, term, time, track, trail, trajectory, unfolding, vector, voyage, way, wheel.

*v* chase, dash, flow, follow, gush, hunt, move, pour, pursue, race, run, scud, scurry, speed, stream, surge, tumble.

**court** *n* attendants, bailey, bar, bench, cloister, cortège, courtyard, durbar, entourage, hall, Hof, law-court, manor, palace, piazza, plaza, quad, quadrangle, retinue, square, suite, train, tribunal, yard.

*v* attract, chase, cultivate, date, flatter, incite, invite, lionise, pander to, prompt, provoke, pursue, seek, serenade, solicit, woo.

**courteous** *adj* affable, attentive, ceremonious, civil, considerate, courtly, debonair, elegant, gallant, gracious, mannerly, obliging, polished, polite, refined, respectful, urbane, well-bred, well-mannered.

*antonyms* discourteous, rude.

**courtesan** *n* call girl, Delilah, demi-mondaine, fille de joie, harlot, hetaira, kept woman, lorette, mistress, paramour, prostitute, scarlet woman, whore, woman of easy virtue, woman of the night, woman of the town.

**courtesy** *n* affability, attention, benevolence, breeding, civility, comity, consent, consideration, courteousness, courtliness, elegance, favour, gallantness, gallantry, generosity, gentilesse, graciousness, indulgence, kindness, manners, polish, politeness, urbanity.

*antonyms* discourtesy, rudeness.

**courtier** *n* attendant, chamberlain, follower, henchman, lady, lord, major-domo, noble, nobleman, page, pursuivant, squire, steward, sycophant, toady, train-bearer.

**courtly** *adj* affable, aristocratic, aulic, ceremonious, chivalric, chivalrous, civil, decorous, dignified, elegant, flattering, formal, gallant, high-bred, lordly, obliging, polished, polite, refined, stately.

*antonyms* inelegant, provincial, rough.

**courtyard** *n* area, cortile, enclosure, patio, peristyle, playground, quad, quadrangle, yard.

**cove** *n* anchorage, bay, bight, creek, estuary, fiord, firth, frith, harbour, inlet, sound.

**covenant** *n* arrangement, bargain, bond, commitment, compact, concordat, contract, convention, deed, engagement, pact, pledge, promise, stipulation, treaty, trust, undertaking.

*v* agree, bargain, contract, engage, pledge, promise, stipulate, undertake.

**cover** *v* balance, camouflage, canopy, clad, cloak, clothe, coat, compensate, comprehend, comprise, conceal, consider, contain, counterbalance, curtain, daub, defend, describe, detail, disguise, dress, eclipse, embody, embrace, encase, encompass, enshroud, envelop, examine, guard, hide, hood, house, include, incorporate, insure, invest, investigate, involve, layer, mantle, mask, narrate, obscure, offset, overlay, overspread, protect, recount, reinforce, relate, report, screen, secrete, shade, sheathe, shelter, shield, shroud, suffuse, survey, veil.

*n* bedspread, binding, camouflage, canopy, cap, case, cloak, clothing, coating, compensation, concealment, confederate, covering, cover-up, defence, disguise, dress, envelope, façade, front, guard, indemnity, insurance, jacket, lid, mask, payment, pretence, pretext, protection, refuge, reimbursement, sanctuary, screen, sheath, shelter, shield, smoke, spread, top, undergrowth, veil, woods, wrapper.

**cover up** coat, conceal, cover, dissemble, dissimulate, encrust, envelop, hide, hush up, plaster, repress, stonewall, suppress, swathe, whitewash.

*antonym* uncover.

**coverage** *n* analysis, assurance, description, insurance, protection, reportage, reporting, treatment.

**covering** *n* blanket, capping, casing, cloak, clothing, coating, cocoon, cope, cover, exoskeleton, housing, integument, layer, mask, masking, overlay, protection, sheath, shelter, tegmen, tegument, top, umbrella, wash, wrap, wrappage, wrapper, wrapping.

*adj* accompanying, descriptive, explanatory, introductory, masking, obscuring, protective.

**covert** *adj* clandestine, concealed, disguised, dissembled, hidden, private, secret, sneaky, stealthy, subreptitious, surreptitious, ulterior, under the table, underhand, unsuspected, veiled.

*antonym* open.

**cover-up** *n* complicity, concealment, conspiracy, dissemblance, dissimulation, front, pretence, smoke-screen, whitewash.

**covet** *v* after, begrudge, crave, desire, envy, fancy, hanker, long for, lust after, thirst for, want, yearn for, yen for.

*antonym* abjure.

**covetous** *adj* acquisitive, avaricious, close-fisted, envious, grasping, greedy, insatiable, jealous, mercenary, rapacious, thirsting, yearning.

*antonyms* generous, temperate.

**covey** *n* bevy, cluster, flight, flock, group, nide, nye, skein.

**cow** *v* awe, break, browbeat, bulldoze, bully, daunt, dishearten, dismay, domineer, frighten, intimidate, overawe, scare, subdue, terrorise, unnerve.

*antonym* encourage.

**coward** *n* caitiff, chicken, craven, dastard, faint-heart, funk, hilding, nithing, poltroon, recreant, renegade, scaredy-cat, skulker, sneak, viliaco, viliago, yellow-belly, yellow-dog.

*antonym* hero.

**cowardice** *n* faint-heartedness, fear, funk, gutlessness, pusillanimity, spinelessness.

*antonyms* courage, valour.

**cowardly** *adj* base, caitiff, chicken, chicken-hearted, chicken-livered, craven, dastard(ly), faint-hearted, fearful, gutless, hilding, lily-livered, nesh, nithing, pusillanimous, recreant, scared, shrinking, soft, spineless, timorous, unheroic, weak, weak-kneed, white-livered, yellow, yellow-bellied.

*antonym* courageous.

**cowboy** *n* bronco-buster, buckaroo, cattleman, cowhand, cowpoke, cowpuncher, drover, gaucho, herder, herdsman, rancher, ranchero, stockman, vaquero, waddy, wrangler.

**cower** *v* cringe, crouch, flinch, grovel, quail, ruck, shake, shiver, shrink, skulk, tremble.

**coxcomb** *n* beau, Beau Brummell, dandy, dude, exquisite, fop, Jack-a-dandy, jackanapes, macaroni, peacock, popinjay, princox, swell.

**coy** *adj* arch, backward, bashful, coquettish, demure, diffident, evasive, flirtatious, kittenish, maidenly, modest, prudish, reserved, retiring, self-effacing, shrinking, shy, skittish, timid, virginal.

*antonyms* forward, impudent, sober.

**coyness** *n* affectation, archness, bashfulness, coquettishness, demureness, diffidence, evasiveness, modesty, primness, prudery, prudishness, reserve, shyness, skittishness, timidity.

*antonyms* forwardness, impudence.

**cozen** *v* bamboozle, bilk, cheat, circumvent, con, deceive, diddle, double-cross, dupe, finagle, gull, hoodwink, inveigle, swindle, trick.

**crabbed** *adj* acid, acrid, acrimonious, awkward, bad-tempered, captious, churlish, crabby, cross, cross-grained, crotchety, cynical, difficult, fretful, grouchy, harsh, ill-humoured, ill-tempered, iracund, iracundulous, irascible, irritable, misanthropic, morose, perverse, petulant, prickly, snappish, snappy, sour, splenetic, surly, tart, testy, tough, trying.

*antonyms* calm, placid.

**crack** *v* break, buffet, burst, chap, chip, chop, cleave, clip, clout, collapse, crackle, crash, craze, cuff, decipher, detonate, explode, fathom, fracture, pop, ring, rive, slap, snap, solve, splinter, split, succumb, thump, wallop, whack, yield.

*n* attempt, blow, breach, break, buffet, burst, chap, chink, chip, clap, cleft, clip, clout, cranny, crash, craze, crevasse, crevice, cuff, dig, expert, explosion, fent, fissure, flaw, fracture, gag, gap, go, insult, interstice, jibe, joke, moment, opportunity, pop, quip, report, rift, slap, smack, snap, stab, thump, try, wallop, whack, wisecrack, witticism.

*adj* ace, choice, elite, excellent, first-class, first-rate, hand-picked, superior, top-notch.

**crack down on** act against, check, clamp down on, end, put a stop to, stop.

**crack up** break down, collapse, go crackers, go crazy, go to pieces.

**crackdown** *n* clampdown, crushing, end, repression, stop, suppression.

**cracked** *adj* bats, batty, broken, chipped, crackbrained, crackpot, crazed, crazy, daft, damaged, defective, deranged, eccentric, faulty, fissured, flawed, imperfect, insane, loony, nuts, nutty, rent, split, torn.

*antonyms* flawless, perfect, sane.

**crackers** *adj* cracked, crazy, daft, foolish, idiotic, loony, mad, nuts.

*antonym* sane.

**crackle** *v* crepitate, decrepitate, rustle.

*n* crepitation, crepitus, decrepitation, rustle.

**crackpot** *n* crackbrain, idiot, loony, nut, nutter.

**cradle** *n* bassinet, bed, beginning, berceau, birthplace, cot, crib, fount, fountain-head, holder, incunabula, origin, rest, source, spring, stand, well-spring.

*v* bear, couch, hold, lull, nestle, nurse, rock, support, tend.

**craft** *n* ability, aircraft, aptitude, art, artfulness, artifice, artistry, barque, boat, business, calling, cleverness, contrivance, craftiness, cunning, deceit, dexterity, duplicity, employment, expertise, expertness, guile, handicraft, handiwork, ingenuity, knack, know-how, line, occupation, plane, pursuit, ruse, scheme, ship, shrewdness, skill, spacecraft, spaceship, stratagem, subterfuge, subtlety, technique, trade, trickery, vessel, vocation, wiles, work, workmanship.

*antonyms* naïvety, openness.

**craftiness** *n* artfulness, astuteness, canniness, cunning, deceit, deviousness, double-dealing, duplicity, foxiness, guile, shrewdness, slyness, subtlety, trickiness, underhandedness, vulpinism, wiliness.

*antonyms* naïvety, openness.

**craftsman** *n* artificer, artisan, maker, master, opificer, smith, technician, wright.

**craftsmanship** *n* artistry, expertise, facture, mastery, technique, workmanship.

**crafty** *adj* artful, astute, calculating, canny, cunning, deceitful, designing, devious, duplicitous, foxy, fraudulent, guileful, insidious, knowing, machiavellian, scheming, sharp, shrewd, sly, subtle, tricksy, tricky, versute, vulpine, wily.

*antonyms* naïve, open.

**crag** *n* aiguille, bluff, cliff, peak, pinnacle, rock, tor(r).

**craggy** *adj* broken, brusque, cragged, jagged, jaggy, precipitous, rocky, rough, rugged, stony, surly, uneven.

*antonyms* pleasant, smooth.

**cram** *v* bag, compact, compress, con, crowd, crush, force, glut, gorge, gormandise, grind, guzzle, jam, mug up, overcrowd, overeat, overfeed, overfill, pack, press, ram, satiate, shove, squeeze, stodge, study, stuff, swot.

**cramming** *n* gavage, gluttony, gormandise, gourmandise, greed, packing, pressing, stuffing.

**cramp**[1] *v* check, circumscribe, clog, confine, constrain, encumber, frustrate, hamper, hamstring, handicap, hinder, impede, inhibit, obstruct, restrict, shackle, stymie, thwart, tie.

**cramp**[2] *n* ache, contraction, convulsion, crick, pain, pang, pins and needles, spasm, stiffness, stitch, twinge.

**cramped** *adj* awkward, circumscribed, confined, congested, crowded, incapacious, jam-packed, narrow, overcrowded, packed, restricted, riggling, squashed, squeezed, squeezy, tight, uncomfortable.

*antonym* spacious.

**crane** *n* block and tackle, davit, derrick, hoist, tackle, winch.

**crank** *n* eccentric, loony, madman, nutter.

**cranky** *adj* bizarre, capricious, crabbed, cross, crotchety, dotty, eccentric, erratic, Fifish, freakish, freaky, funny, idiosyncratic, irritable, odd, peculiar, prickly, queer, quirky, strange, surly, viewy, wacky.

*antonyms* normal, placid, sensible.

**cranny** *n* chink, cleavage, cleft, crack, crevice, fissure, gap, hole, interstice, nook, opening.

**crash** *n* accident, bang, bankruptcy, boom, bump, clang, clash, clatter, clattering, collapse, collision, debacle (debâcle), depression, din, downfall, failure, fragor, jar, jolt, pile-up, prang, racket, ruin, smash, smashing, smash-up, thud, thump, thunder, wreck.

*v* bang, break, bump, collapse, collide, dash, disintegrate, fail, fall, fold (up), fracture, fragment, go bust, go under, hurtle, lurch, overbalance, pitch, plunge, prang, shatter, shiver, smash, splinter, sprawl, topple.

*adj* concentrated, emergency, immediate, intensive, round-the-clock, telescoped, urgent.

**crass** *adj* asinine, blundering, boorish, bovine, coarse, dense, doltish, gross, indelicate, insensitive, lumpish, oafish, obtuse, stupid, tactless, unrefined, unsubtle, witless.

*antonyms* refined, sensitive.

**crate** *n* box, case, container, packing case, packing-box, tea-chest.

**crave** *v* ask, beg, beseech, desire, entreat, fancy, hanker after, hunger after, implore, long for, need, petition, pine for, require, seek, solicit, supplicate, thirst for, want, yearn for, yen for.

*antonyms* dislike, spurn.

**craven** *adj* caitiff, chicken-hearted, cowardly, dastardly, fearful, lily-livered, mean-spirited, nithing, pusillanimous, scared, spiritless, timorous, unheroic, weak, whey-faced, yellow.

*antonym* courageous.

*n* caitiff, coward, dastard, nithing, poltroon, recreant.

*antonyms* hero, renegade, yellow-belly.

**craving** *n* appetence, appetency, appetite, cacoethes, desire, hankering, hunger, longing, lust, thirst, urge, yearning, yen.

*antonyms* dislike, distaste.

**craw** n crop, gizzard, gullet, maw, oesophagous, throat.

**crawl** v creep, cringe, drag, eat crow, eat dirt, eat humble pie, fawn, grovel, inch, slither, swarm, teem, toady, truckle, wriggle, writhe.

**craze** n dernier cri, enthusiasm, fad, fashion, frenzy, infatuation, mania, mode, novelty, obsession, passion, preoccupation, rage, thing, trend, vogue.

v bewilder, confuse, dement, derange, distemper, distract, enrage, infatuate, inflame, madden, unbalance, unhinge.

**crazed** adj demented, maddened, maenadic, possessed.

antonym sane.

**crazy** adj absurd, ardent, bananas, barmy, bats, batty, berserk, bird-brained, bizarre, bonkers, cockeyed, cracked, crazed, cuckoo, daffy, daft, delirious, demented, deranged, derisory, devoted, dippy, eager, eccentric, enamoured, enthusiastic, fanatical, fantastic, fatuous, foolhardy, foolish, fruity, half-baked, hysterical, idiotic, ill-conceived, impracticable, imprudent, inane, inappropriate, infatuated, insane, irresponsible, ludicrous, lunatic, mad, maniacal, mental, nonsensical, nuts, nutty, odd, off one's rocker, outrageous, passionate, peculiar, pixil(l)ated, potty, preposterous, puerile, quixotic, ridiculous, scatty, senseless, short-sighted, silly, smitten, strange, touched, unbalanced, unhinged, unrealistic, unwise, unworkable, up the pole, wacky, weird, wild, zany, zealous.

antonyms sane, sensible.

**creak** v grate, grind, groan, rasp, scrape, scratch, screak, screech, squeak, squeal.

**creaky** adj creaking, grating, rasping, rusty, screaky, squeaking, squeaky, unoiled.

**cream** n best, cosmetic, crème de la crème, elite, emulsion, essence, flower, liniment, lotion, oil, ointment, paste, pick, prime, salve, the four hundred, unguent.

**creamy** adj buttery, cream-coloured, creamed, lush, milky, off-white, oily, rich, smooth, soft, velvety.

**crease** v corrugate, crimp, crinkle, crumple, fold, pucker, ridge, ruckle, rumple, wrinkle.

n bulge, corrugation, crumple, fold, groove, line, overlap, pucker, ridge, ruck, ruckle, rumple, tuck, wrinkle.

**create** v appoint, beget, cause, coin, compose, concoct, constitute, design, develop, devise, engender, establish, form, formulate, found, generate, hatch, initiate, install, institute, invent, invest, make, occasion, originate, produce, set up, sire, spawn.

antonym destroy.

**creation** n achievement, brainchild, chef d'oeuvre, concept, conception, concoction, constitution, cosmos, development, establishment, fathering, formation, foundation, generation, genesis, handiwork, inception, institution, invention, life, magnum opus, making, nature, origination, pièce de resistance, procreation, production, siring, universe, world.

antonym destruction.

**creative** adj adept, artistic, clever, fertile, gifted, imaginative, ingenious, inspired, inventive, original, productive, resourceful, stimulating, talented, visionary.

antonym unimaginative.

**creativity** n artistry, cleverness, fecundity, fertility, imagination, imaginativeness, ingenuity, inspiration, inventiveness, originality, resourcefulness, talent, vision.

antonym unimaginativeness.

**creator** n architect, auteur, author, begetter, demiurge, demiurgus, designer, father, framer, God, initiator, inventor, maker, originator.

**creature** n animal, beast, being, body, brute, character, critter, dependant, fellow, hanger-on, henchman, hireling, individual, instrument, lackey, man, minion, mortal, person, puppet, retainer, soul, toady, tool, wight, woman, wretch.

**credence** n belief, confidence, credit, dependence, faith, reliance, support, trust.

antonym distrust.

**credentials** n accreditation, attestation, authorisation, card, certificate, deed, diploma, docket, endorsement, letters of credence, licence, missive, passport, permit, recommendation, reference, testament, testimonial, title, voucher, warrant.

**credibility** n believableness, integrity, likeliness, plausibility, probability, reliability, tenability, trustworthiness.

antonym implausibility.

**credible** adj believable, conceivable, convincing, dependable, honest, imaginable, likely, persuasive, plausible, possible, probable, reasonable, reliable, sincere, supposable, tenable, thinkable, trustworthy, trusty.

antonyms implausible, unreliable.

**credit** n acclaim, acknowledgement, approval, belief, character, clout, commendation, confidence, credence, distinction, esteem, estimation, faith, fame, glory, honour, influence, kudos, merit, position, praise, prestige, recognition, regard, reliance, reputation, repute, standing, status, thanks, tribute, trust.

antonym discredit.

v accept, believe, buy, subscribe to, swallow, trust.

antonym disbelieve.

**creditable** adj admirable, commendable, deserving, estimable, excellent, exemplary, good, honourable, laudable, meritorious, praiseworthy, reputable, respectable, sterling, worthy.

antonyms blameworthy, shameful.

**creditor** n debtee, dun, lender.

**credulity** n credulousness, dupability, gullibility, naïvety, silliness, simplicity, stupidity.

antonym scepticism.

**credulous** *adj* dupable, green, gullible, naïve, trusting, uncritical, unsuspecting, unsuspicious, wide-eyed.

*antonym* sceptical.

**creed** *n* articles, belief, canon, catechism, confession, credo, doctrine, dogma, faith, persuasion, principles, tenets.

**creek** *n* bay, bight, brook, cove, fiord, firth, frith, inlet, rivulet, stream, streamlet, tributary, voe, watercourse.

**creep** *v* bootlick, cower, crawl, cringe, dawdle, drag, edge, fawn, grovel, inch, insinuate, kowtow, scrape, skulk, slink, slither, snail, sneak, squirm, steal, tiptoe, toady, truckle, worm, wriggle, writhe.

*n* bootlicker, Jack Nasty, jerk, sneak, sycophant, toady.

**creeper** *n* climber, liana, plant, rambler, runner, trailing vine.

**creepy** *adj* awful, direful, disturbing, eerie, frightening, ghoulish, gruesome, hair-raising, horrible, macabre, menacing, nightmarish, ominous, scary, sinister, spookish, spooky, terrifying, threatening, unearthly, unpleasant, weird.

*antonyms* normal, pleasant.

**crescent-shaped** *adj* bow-shaped, falcate(d), falciform, lunate(d), lunular, sickle-shaped.

**crest** *n* aigrette, apex, badge, caruncle, cockscomb, coma, comb, crown, device, emblem, head, height, insignia, mane, panache, peak, pinnacle, plume, ridge, summit, symbol, tassel, top, topknot, tuft.

**crestfallen** *adj* chopfallen, dejected, depressed, despondent, disappointed, disconsolate, discouraged, disheartened, dispirited, downcast, downhearted, woebegone.

*antonym* elated.

**crevasse** *n* abyss, bergschrund, chasm, cleavage, cleft, crack, fissure, gap.

**crevice** *n* chink, cleavage, cleft, crack, cranny, fissure, fracture, gap, hole, interstice, opening, rent, rift, slit, split.

**crew** *n* assemblage, band, bunch, company, complement, corps, crowd, galère, gang, hands, henchmen, herd, horde, lot, lower deck, mob, pack, party, posse, set, squad, swarm, team, troop.

**crib** *n* bassinet, bed, bin, borrowing, box, bunker, cot, cradle, key, manger, plagiarism, rack, stall, translation.

*v* borrow, cheat, copy, pinch, pirate, plagiarise, purloin, steal.

**crick** *n* convulsion, cramp, pain, spasm, stiffness, twinge.

*v* jar, rax, rick, sprain, twist, wrench.

**crime** *n* atrocity, corruption, delinquency, fault, felony, flagitiousness, guilt, illegality, iniquity, law-breaking, malefaction, malfeasance, misconduct, misdeed, misdemeanour, offence, outrage, sin, transgression, trespass, unrighteousness, vice, villainy, violation, wickedness, wrong, wrong-doing.

**criminal** *n* con, convict, crook, culprit, delinquent, evil-doer, felon, fraudsman, infractor, jail-bird, law-breaker, malefactor, offender, sinner, transgressor.

*adj* bent, corrupt, crooked, culpable, deplorable, felonious, flagitious, foolish, illegal, immoral, indictable, iniquitous, lawless, malfeasant, nefarious, peccant, preposterous, ridiculous, scandalous, senseless, unlawful, unrighteous, vicious, villainous, wicked, wrong.

*antonyms* honest, upright.

**cringe** *v* bend, blench, bootlick, bow, cower, crawl, creep, crouch, dodge, duck, fawn, flinch, grovel, kneel, kowtow, quail, quiver, recoil, shrink, shy, sneak, start, stoop, submit, toady, tremble, truckle, wince.

**crinkle** *n* curl, fold, pucker, ruffle, rumple, rustle, scallop, twist, wave, wrinkle.

*v* crimp, crimple, crumple, curl, fold, pucker, ruffle, rumple, rustle, scallop, twist, wrinkle.

**crinkly** *adj* curly, fluted, frizzy, furrowed, gathered, kinky, puckered, ruffled, scalloped, wrinkled, wrinkly.

*antonyms* smooth, straight.

**cripple** *v* cramp, damage, debilitate, destroy, disable, enfeeble, halt, hamstring, impair, incapacitate, lame, maim, mutilate, paralyse, ruin, sabotage, spoil, vitiate, weaken.

**crippled** *adj* deformed, disabled, enfeebled, handicapped, incapacitated, invalid, lame, paralysed.

**crisis** *n* calamity, catastrophe, climacteric, climax, confrontation, conjuncture, crunch, crux, culmination, difficulty, dilemma, disaster, emergency, exigency, extremity, height, impasse, mess, pinch, plight, predicament, quandary, strait, trouble.

**crisp** *adj* bracing, brief, brisk, brittle, brusque, clear, crispy, crumbly, crunchy, decisive, firm, forthright, fresh, incisive, invigorating, neat, orderly, pithy, refreshing, short, smart, snappy, spruce, succinct, tart, terse, tidy, vigorous.

*antonyms* flabby, limp, vague.

**criterion** *n* bench-mark, canon, gauge, measure, norm, precedent, principle, proof, rule, shibboleth, standard, test, touchstone, yardstick.

**critic** *n* analyst, animadverter, arbiter, Aristarch, attacker, authority, carper, caviller, censor, censurer, commentator, connoisseur, detractor, expert, expositor, fault-finder, feuilletonist, judge, knocker, Momus, pundit, reviewer, reviler, ultracrepidarian, vilifier, Zoilist.

**critical** *adj* accurate, all-important, analytical, captious, carping, cavilling, censorious, climacteric, crucial, dangerous, deciding, decisive, derogatory, diagnostic, disapproving, discerning, discriminating, disparaging, fastidious, fault-finding, grave, hairy, high-priority, judgemental, judicious, momentous, nagging, niggling, nit-picking, penetrating, perceptive, perilous, pivotal, precarious, precise, pressing, psychological, risky, serious, sharp-tongued, ultracrepidarian, uncomplimentary, urgent, vital, Zoilean.

*antonyms* uncritical, unimportant.

**criticise** *v* analyse, animadvert, appraise, assess, badmouth, blame, carp, censure, condemn, crab, decry, disparage, evaluate, excoriate, judge, knock, pan, review, roast, scarify, slag, slam, slash, slate, snipe, ultracrepidate.

*antonym* praise.

**criticism** *n* analysis, animadversion, appraisal, appreciation, assessment, blame, brickbat, censure, comment, commentary, critique, disapproval, disparagement, elucidation, evaluation, fault-finding, flak, judgement, knocking, knocking-copy, notice, panning, review, slating, stick, stricture, ultracrepidation, vivisection, Zoilism.

*antonym* praise.

**critique** *n* analysis, appraisal, assessment, commentary, essay, evaluation, examination, review.

**croak** *v* caw, die, expire, gasp, grunt, kick the bucket, pass away, perish, snuff it, squawk, wheeze.

**crockery** *n* ceramics, china, dishes, earthenware, holloware, pottery, stoneware, whiteware.

**croft** *n* farm, pightle, plot, smallholding.

**crone** *n* bag, bat, beldam, gammer, grandam, grannam, hag, witch.

**crony** *n* accomplice, ally, associate, buddy, china, chum, colleague, companion, comrade, follower, friend, henchman, mate, pal, sidekick.

**crook** *n* cheat, criminal, knave, racketeer, robber, rogue, shark, shyster, swindler, thief, villain.

**crooked¹** *adj* bent, corrupt, crafty, criminal, deceitful, discreditable, dishonest, dishonourable, dubious, fraudulent, illegal, knavish, nefarious, questionable, shady, shifty, treacherous, underhand, unethical, unlawful, unprincipled, unscrupulous.

*antonym* honest.

**crooked²** *adj* anfractuous, angled, askew, asymmetric, awry, bent, bowed, crank, cranky, crippled, crump, curved, deformed, deviating, disfigured, distorted, hooked, irregular, lopsided, meandering, misshapen, off-centre, skew-whiff, slanted, slanting, squint, tilted, tortuous, twisted, twisting, uneven, warped, winding, zigzag.

*antonym* straight.

**crookedness** *n* distortion, squintness, twistedness, warp.

*antonym* straightness.

**crop¹** *n* fruits, gathering, growth, harvest, ingathering, produce, vintage, yield.

*v* browse, clip, collect, curtail, cut, garner, gather, graze, harvest, lop, mow, nibble, pare, pick, prune, reap, reduce, shear, shingle, shorten, snip, top, trim, yield.

**crop up** appear, arise, arrive, emerge, happen, occur.

**crop²** *n* craw, gizzard, gullet, maw, oesophagus, throat.

**cross** *adj* adverse, angry, annoyed, cantankerous, captious, churlish, contrary, cranky, crosswise, crotchety, crusty, disagreeable, displeased, fractious, fretful, grouchy, grumpy, hybrid, ill-humoured, ill-tempered, impatient, interchanged, intersecting, irascible, irritable, oblique, opposed, opposing, opposite, peeved, peevish, pettish, petulant, querulous, reciprocal, shirty, short, snappish, snappy, splenetic, sullen, surly, testy, transverse, unfavourable, vexed, waspish.

*antonyms* calm, placid, pleasant.

*v* annoy, bestride, blend, block, bridge, cancel, criss-cross, crossbreed, cross-fertilise, cross-pollinate, decussate, deny, foil, ford, frustrate, hinder, hybridise, impede, interbreed, intercross, interfere, intersect, intertwine, lace, meet, mix, mongrelise, obstruct, oppose, resist, span, thwart, traverse, zigzag.

*n* affliction, amalgam, blend, burden, combination, crossbreed, crossing, crossroads, crucifix, cur, grief, holy-rood, hybrid, hybridisation, intersection, load, misery, misfortune, mixture, mongrel, rood, trial, tribulation, trouble, woe, worry.

**cross swords** argue, dispute, fight, spar, take issue, wrangle.

**cross-examine** *v* catechise, give (someone) the third degree, grill, interrogate, pump, question, quiz.

**crosspatch** *n* bear, crank, crotcheteer, curmudgeon, grump, kill-joy, scold, shrew, sorehead, sourpuss.

**cross-question** *v* cross-examine, debrief, examine, grill.

**crosswise** *adv* across, aslant, athwart, awry, crisscross, crossways, diagonally, over, sideways, transversely.

**crotchety** *adj* awkward, bad-tempered, cantankerous, contrary, crabbed, crabby, cross, crusty, curmudgeonly, difficult, disagreeable, fractious, grumpy, iracund, iracundulous, irascible, irritable, obstreperous, peevish, prickly, surly, testy.

*antonyms* clam, placid, pleasant.

**crouch** *v* bend, bow, cower, cringe, duck, hunch, kneel, ruck, squat, stoop.

**crow** *v* bluster, boast, brag, exult, flourish, gloat, prate, rejoice, triumph, vaunt.

**crowbar** *n* gavelock, jemmy, jimmy.

**crowd** *n* army, assembly, attendance, audience, boodle, bunch, caboodle, circle, clique, company, concourse, flock, gate, group, herd, hoi polloi, horde, host, house, lot, many-headed beast/monster, mass, masses, mob, multitude, pack, people, populace, press, proletariat, public, rabble, riff-raff, set, spectators, squash, swarm, the many, throng, troupe.

*v* bundle, cluster, compress, congest, congregate, cram, elbow, flock, for(e)gather,

gather, huddle, jostle, mass, muster, pack, pile, press, push, shove, squeeze, stream, surge, swarm, throng.

**crowded** *adj* busy, congested, cramped, crushed, filled, full, huddled, jammed, jam-packed, mobbed, overflowing, packed, populous, swarming, teeming, thronged.

*antonym* empty.

**crown** *n* acme, apex, bays, chaplet, circlet, coronal, coronet, crest, diadem, distinction, forehead, garland, head, honour, kudos, laurel wreath, laurels, monarch, monarchy, pate, perfection, pinnacle, prize, royalty, ruler, skull, sovereign, sovereignty, summit, tiara, tip, top, trophy, ultimate, zenith.

*v* adorn, biff, box, cap, clout, complete, consummate, cuff, dignify, festoon, finish, fulfil, honour, instal, perfect, punch, reward, surmount, terminate, top.

**crowned** *adj* capped, incoronate(d), royal, ruling, sovereign, surmounted, topped, wreathed.

**crowning** *adj* climactic, consummate, culminating, final, paramount, perfect, sovereign, supreme, top, ultimate, unmatched, unsurpassed.

*n* coronation, incoronation, installation.

**crucial** *adj* central, critical, decisive, essential, important, key, momentous, pivotal, pressing, psychological, searching, testing, trying, urgent, vital.

*antonym* unimportant.

**crucifix** *n* cross, holy-rood, rood.

**crucify** *v* criticise, execute, harrow, lampoon, mock, pan, persecute, rack, ridicule, slam, torment, torture.

**crude** *adj* amateurish, blue, boorish, clumsy, coarse, crass, dirty, earthy, gross, half-baked, immature, inartistic, indecent, lewd, makeshift, natural, obscene, outline, primitive, raw, rough, rough-hewn, rude, rudimentary, sketchy, smutty, tactless, tasteless, uncouth, undeveloped, undigested, unfinished, unformed, unpolished, unprepared, unprocessed, unrefined, unsubtle, vulgar.

*antonyms* finished, polite, refined, tasteful.

**crudity** *n* bawdiness, brutalism, clumsiness, coarseness, crudeness, impropriety, indecency, indelicacy, lewdness, loudness, obscenity, offensiveness, primitiveness, roughness, rudeness, smuttiness, vulgarity.

*antonyms* polish, politeness, tastefulness.

**cruel** *adj* atrocious, barbarous, bitter, bloodthirsty, brutal, brutish, butcherly, callous, cold-blooded, cutting, depraved, excruciating, fell, ferocious, fierce, flinty, grim, hard, hard-hearted, harsh, heartless, heathenish, hellish, immane, implacable, inclement, inexorable, inhuman, inhumane, malevolent, marble-breasted, merciless, murderous, painful, pitiless, poignant, ravening, raw, relentless, remorseless, ruthless, sadistic, sanguinary, savage, severe, spiteful, stony-hearted, unfeeling, ungentle, unkind, unmerciful, unnatural, unrelenting, vengeful, vicious.

*antonyms* compassionate, kind, merciful.

**cruelty** *n* barbarity, bestiality, bloodthirstiness, brutality, brutishness, callousness, depravity, ferocity, fiendishness, hard-heartedness, harshness, heartlessness, immanity, inhumanity, mercilessness, murderousness, ruthlessness, sadism, savagery, severity, spite, spitefulness, tyranny, ungentleness, venom, viciousness.

*antonyms* compassion, kindness, mercy.

**crumb** *n* atom, bit, grain, iota, jot, mite, morsel, nirl, particle, scrap, shred, sliver, snippet, soupçon, speck.

**crumble** *v* break up, collapse, comminute, crumb, crush, decay, decompose, degenerate, deteriorate, disintegrate, fragment, granulate, grind, levigate, moulder, murl, perish, pound, powder, pulverise, triturate.

**crumbly** *adj* brittle, friable, murly, powdery, pulverulent, short.

**crummy** *adj* cheap, contemptible, grotty, half-baked, inferior, miserable, pathetic, poor, rotten, rubbishy, second-rate, shoddy, third-rate, trashy, useless, weak, worthless.

*antonym* excellent.

**crumple** *v* collapse, crease, crunkle, crush, fall, pucker, raffle, rumple, wrinkle.

**crunch** *v* champ, chomp, grind, masticate, munch, scranch.

*n* crisis, crux, emergency, pinch, test.

**crusade** *n* campaign, cause, drive, expedition, holy war, jihad, movement, push, undertaking.

**crusader** *n* advocate, campaigner, champion, enthusiast, fighter, missionary, reformer, zealot.

**crush** *v* abash, break, browbeat, bruise, chagrin, champ, comminute, compress, conquer, contuse, crease, crumble, crumple, crunch, embrace, enfold, extinguish, hug, humiliate, mash, mortify, overcome, overpower, overwhelm, pound, press, pulverise, quash, quell, rumple, shame, smash, squabash, squeeze, squelch, steam-roller, subdue, vanquish, wrinkle.

*n* check, crowd, huddle, jam.

**crust** *n* caking, coat, coating, concretion, covering, exterior, film, heel, impertinence, incrustation, layer, outside, rind, scab, shell, skin, surface.

**crusty** *adj* brittle, brusque, cantankerous, captious, choleric, crabbed, crabby, crisp, crispy, cross, curt, friable, grouchy, gruff, hard, ill-humoured, irritable, peevish, prickly, short, short-tempered, snappish, snappy, snarling, splenetic, surly, testy, touchy.

*antonyms* calm, pleasant, soft, soggy.

**crux** *n* core, essence, heart, nub, vexata quaestio, vexed question.

**cry** *v* advertise, announce, bark, bawl, beg, bellow, beseech, bewail, blubber, boo-hoo, broadcast, bruit, call, caterwaul, clamour, ejaculate, entreat, exclaim, greet, hail, halloo, hawk, holler, howl, implore, keen, lament, mewl, miaow, miaul, noise, plead, pray, proclaim, promulgate, pule, roar, scream, screech, shout, shriek, snivel, sob, squall, squeal, trumpet, vociferate, wail, weep, whimper, whine, whinge, whoop, yell, yowl.

*n* announcement, appeal, battle-cry, bawl(ing), bellow, blubber(ing), call, caterwaul, caterwaul(ing), ejaculation, entreaty, exclamation, greet, holler, hoot, howl, keening, lament, lamentation, miaow, miaul, outcry, petition, plaint, plea, prayer, proclamation, report, roar, rumour, scream, screech, shriek, slogan, snivel(ling), sob(bing), sorrowing, squall, squawk, squeal, supplication, utterance, wail(ing), watch-word, weep(ing), whoop, yell, yelp, yoo-hoo.

**cry-baby** *n* cissy, mardy, softy.

**crypt** *n* catacomb, mausoleum, tomb, undercroft, vault.

**cryptic** *adj* abstruse, ambiguous, apocryphal, arcane, bizarre, cabbalistic, dark, Delphic, enigmatic, equivocal, esoteric, hidden, mysterious, obscure, occult, oracular, perplexing, puzzling, recondite, secret, strange, vague, veiled.

*antonyms* clear, obvious, straightforward.

**crystallise** *v* appear, coalesce, emerge, form, harden, materialise, solidify.

**cub** *n* babe, beginner, fledgling, greenhorn, lad, learner, offspring, pup, puppy, recruit, tenderfoot, trainee, whelp, whippersnapper, young, youngster, youth.

*antonym* adult.

**cubby-hole** *n* compartment, den, hide-away, hole, niche, pigeonhole, priest hole, recess, slot, snug.

**cube** *n* cuboid, dice, die, hexahedron, solid.

**cuddle** *v* canoodle, clasp, cosset, dandle, doodle, embrace, fondle, hug, nestle, pet, smuggle, snuggle.

**cuddly** *adj* buxom, cosy, cuddlesome, curvaceous, huggable, lovable, plump, soft, warm.

**cudgel** *n* alpeen, bastinado, baton, bludgeon, club, cosh, plant, shillelagh, stick, truncheon.

*v* bang, baste, bastinado, batter, beat, bludgeon, cane, clobber, cosh, drub, maul, pound, pummel, thrash, thump, thwack.

**cue** *n* catchword, hint, feed-line, incentive, key, nod, prompt(ing), reminder, sign, signal, stimulus, suggestion.

**cuff** *v* bat, beat, belt, biff, box, buffet, clap, clobber, clout, knock, pummel, punch, slap, smack, smite, strike, thump, whack.

*n* belt, biff, blow, box, buffet, clout, knock, punch, rap, slap, smack, swat, thump, whack.

**cull** *v* amass, choose, collect, decimate, destroy, gather, glean, kill, pick, pick out, pluck, select, sift, thin, winnow.

**culminate** *v* climax, close, conclude, consummate, end (up), finish, peak, terminate.

*antonyms* begin, start.

**culmination** *n* acme, apex, apogee, climax, completion, conclusion, consummation, crown,

finale, height, meridian, ne plus ultra, peak, perfection, pinnacle, summit, top, zenith.

*antonyms* beginning, start.

**culpable** *adj* answerable, blam(e)able, blameworthy, censurable, guilty, liable, offending, peccant, reprehensible, sinful, to blame, wrong.

*antonyms* blameless, innocent.

**culprit** *n* criminal, delinquent, evil-doer, felon, guilty party, law-breaker, malefactor, miscreant, offender, rascal, sinner, transgressor, wrong-doer.

**cult** *n* admiration, believers, body, clique, craze, denomination, devotion, faith, following, idolisation, party, religion, reverence, school, sect, veneration, worship.

**cultivate** *v* aid, ameliorate, better, cherish, civilise, court, develop, discipline, elevate, encourage, enrich, farm, fertilise, forward, foster, further, harvest, help, improve, patronise, plant, plough, polish, prepare, promote, pursue, refine, school, support, tend, till, train, work.

*antonym* neglect.

**cultivation** *n* advancement, advocacy, agronomy, breeding, civilisation, civility, culture, development, discernment, discrimination, education, encouragement, enhancement, enlightenment, farming, fostering, furtherance, gardening, gentility, help, husbandry, learning, letters, manners, nurture, patronage, planting, ploughing, polish, promotion, pursuit, refinement, schooling, study, support, taste, tillage, tilling, tilth, working.

**cultural** *adj* aesthetic, artistic, arty, broadening, civilising, developmental, edifying, educational, educative, elevating, enlightening, enriching, humane, humanising, liberal.

**culture** *n* accomplishment, aestheticism, agriculture, agronomy, art, breeding, civilisation, cultivation, customs, education, elevation, enlightenment, erudition, farming, gentility, husbandry, improvement, Kultur, lifestyle, mores, polish, politeness, refinement, society, taste, the arts, urbanity.

**cultured** *adj* accomplished, advanced, aesthetic, arty, civilised, educated, enlightened, erudite, genteel, highbrow, knowledgeable, polished, refined, scholarly, urbane, versed, well-bred, well-informed, well-read.

*antonyms* ignorant, uncultured.

**culvert** *n* channel, conduit, drain, duct, gutter, sewer, watercourse.

**cumbersome** *adj* awkward, bulky, burdensome, clumsy, cumbrous, embarrassing, heavy, hefty, incommodious, inconvenient, onerous, oppressive, ponderous, unmanageable, unwieldy, weighty.

*antonyms* convenient, manageable.

**cumulative** *adj* accumulative, additive, aggregate, collective, increasing.

**cunning** *adj* adroit, arch, artful, astute, canny, crafty, deep, deft, devious, dexterous, foxy, guileful, imaginative, ingenious, knowing, leery,

Machiavellian, ruse, sharp, shifty, shrewd, skilful, sneeky, subtle, tricky, vulpine, wily.

*antonyms* gullible, naïve.

*n* ability, adroitness, art, artfulness, artifice, astuteness, cleverness, craftiness, deceitfulness, deftness, deviousness, dexterity, finesse, foxiness, guile, ingenuity, policy, shrewdness, skill, slyness, subtlety, trickery, vulpinism, wiliness.

*antonyms* openness, simplicity.

**cup** *n* beaker, bidon, cannikin, cantharus, chalice, cupful, cylix, demitasse, dish, draught, drink, fingan, goblet, mazer, pokal, potion, tankard, tass, tazza, teacup, tig, trophy.

**cupboard** *n* almirah, ambry, armoire, cabinet, closet, locker, press.

**cupidity** *n* acquisitiveness, avarice, avidity, covetousness, eagerness, graspingness, greed, greediness, hankering, hunger, itching, longing, rapaciousness, rapacity, voracity, yearning.

**cur** *n* blackguard, canine, coward, dastard, good-for-nothing, heel, hound, mongrel, mutt, rat, rotter, scoundrel, stray, swine, villain, wretch.

**curative** *adj* alleviative, corrective, febrifugal, healing, healthful, health-giving, medicinal, remedial, restorative, salutary, therapeutic, tonic, vulnerary.

**curb** *v* bit, bridle, check, constrain, contain, control, hamper, hinder, hobble, impede, inhibit, moderate, muzzle, repress, restrain, restrict, retard, subdue, suppress.

*antonyms* encourage, foster, goad.

*n* brake, bridle, check, control, deterrent, hamper, hobble, limitation, rein, restraint.

**curdle** *v* clot, coagulate, condense, congeal, earn, ferment, sour, thicken, turn.

**cure**[1] *v* alleviate, correct, ease, heal, help, mend, rehabilitate, relieve, remedy, restore.

*n* alleviation, antidote, corrective, detoxicant, febrifuge, healing, medicine, panacea, panpharmacon, recovery, remedy, restorative, specific, treatment, vulnerary.

**cure**[2] *v* brine, dry, kipper, pickle, preserve, salt, smoke.

**curio** *n* antique, bibelot, bygone, curiosity, knick-knack, object of virtu, objet de vertu, trinket.

**curiosity** *n* bibelot, bygone, celebrity, curio, freak, inquisitiveness, interest, knick-knack, marvel, nosiness, novelty, object of virtu, objet d'art, objet de vertu, oddity, phenomenon, prying, rarity, sight, snooping, spectacle, trinket, wonder.

**curiosities** *n* exotica, novelties, virtu.

**curious** *adj* bizarre, enquiring, exotic, extraordinary, ferly, funny, inquisitive, interested, marvellous, meddling, mysterious, nosy, novel, odd, peculiar, peeping, peering, prying, puzzled, puzzling, quaint, queer, questioning, rare, searching, singular, snoopy, strange, unconventional, unexpected, unique, unorthodox, unusual, wonderful.

*antonyms* incurious, indifferent, normal, ordinary, uninterested.

**curl** *v* bend, coil, convolute, corkscrew, crimp, crimple, crinkle, crisp, curve, entwine, frizz, loop, meander, ripple, scroll, spiral, turn, twine, twirl, wind, wreathe, writhe.

*antonym* uncurl.

*n* coil, curlicue, kink, ringlet, spiral, swirl, tress, twist, whorl.

**curly** *adj* corkscrew, crimped, crimpy, crinkly, curled, curling, frizzy, fuzzy, kinky, spiralled, waved, wavy, whorled, winding.

*antonym* straight.

**currency** *n* acceptance, bills, circulation, coinage, coins, exposure, legal tender, money, notes, popularity, prevalence, publicity, reign, transmission, vogue.

**current** *adj* accepted, circulating, common, contemporary, customary, extant, fashionable, general, on-going, popular, present, present-day, prevailing, prevalent, reigning, rife, trendy, up-to-date, up-to-the-minute, widespread.

*antonyms* antiquated, old-fashioned.

*n* atmosphere, course, draught, drift, feeling, flow, inclination, jet, juice, mood, progression, river, stream, tendency, thermal, tide, trend, undercurrent.

**curse** *n* affliction, anathema, ban, bane, blasphemy, burden, calamity, cross, damn, denunciation, disaster, evil, excommunication, execration, expletive, imprecation, jinx, malediction, malison, misfortune, oath, obscenity, ordeal, plague, scourge, swearing, swear-word, torment, tribulation, trouble, vexation, woe.

*antonyms* advantage, blessing.

*v* accurse, afflict, anathematise, blaspheme, blight, blind, blow, burden, cuss, damn, destroy, doom, excommunicate, execrate, fulminate, imprecate, plague, scourge, swear, torment, trouble, vex.

*antonym* bless.

**cursed** *adj* abominable, accursed, bedevilled, bewitched, blessed, blighted, confounded, damnable, damned, destestable, devilish, doomed, excommunicate, execrable, fell, fey, fiendish, foredoomed, hateful, hexed, ill-fated, infamous, infernal, loathsome, odious, pernicious, pestilential, star-crossed, unholy, unsanctified, vile, villainous.

**cursory** *adj* brief, careless, casual, desultory, fleeting, hasty, hurried, offhand, passing, perfunctory, quick, rapid, slap-dash, slight, summary, superficial.

*antonyms* painstaking, thorough.

**curt** *adj* abrupt, blunt, brief, brusque, concise, gruff, laconic, offhand, pithy, rude, sharp, short, short-spoken, snappish, succinct, summary, tart, terse, unceremonious, uncivil, ungracious.

*antonym* voluble.

**curtail** *v* abbreviate, abridge, circumscribe, contract, cut, decrease, dock, lessen, lop, pare, prune, reduce, restrict, retrench, shorten, trim, truncate.

*antonyms* extend, lengthen, prolong.

**curtailment** *n* abbreviation, abridgement, contraction, cutback, cutting, docking, guillotine, pruning, restriction, retrenchment, truncation.

*antonyms* extension, lengthening, prolongation.

**curtain** *v* conceal, drape, hide, screen, shield, shroud, shutter, veil.

*n* arras, backdrop, drapery, hanging, portière, tab, tapestry, vitrage.

**curtsy** *n* bob, bow, genuflection, kowtow, salaam.

**curvaceous** *adj* bosomy, buxom, comely, curvy, Junoesque, shapely, voluptuous, well-proportioned, well-rounded, well-stacked.

**curve** *v* arc, arch, bend, bow, coil, decurve, hook, incurvate, incurve, inflect, spiral, swerve, turn, twist, wind.

*n* arc, bend, camber, curvature, half-moon, incurvation, incurvature, inflexure, loop, trajectory, turn.

**curved** *adj* arched, arc(k)ed, arcuate, bent, bowed, crooked, falcate, humped, inbent, incurvate, incurved, inflexed, rounded, serpentine, sinuous, sweeping, turned, twisted.

*antonym* straight.

**cushion** *n* bean-bag, bolster, buffer, hassock, headrest, pad, pillion, pillow, shock absorber, squab.

*v* allay, bolster, buttress, cradle, dampen, deaden, lessen, mitigate, muffle, pillow, protect, soften, stifle, support, suppress.

**cushy** *adj* comfortable, easy, jammy, plum, soft, undemanding.

*antonyms* demanding, tough.

**custodian** *n* caretaker, castellan, chatelaine, claviger, conservator, curator, guardian, keeper, overseer, protector, superintendent, warden, warder, watch-dog, watchman.

**custody** *n* aegis, arrest, auspices, care, charge, confinement, custodianship, detention, durance, duress, guardianship, holding, imprisonment, incarceration, keeping, observation, possession, preservation, protection, retention, safe-keeping, supervision, trusteeship, tutelage, ward, wardship, watch.

**custom** *n* consuetude, convention, customers, etiquette, fashion, form, formality, habit, habitualness, habitude, manner, mode, observance, observation, patronage, policy, practice, praxis, procedure, ritual, routine, rule, style, thew, trade, tradition, usage, use, way, wont.

**customarily** *adv* commonly, generally, habitually, normally, ordinarily, popularly, regularly, routinely, traditionally, usually.

*antonyms* occasionally, rarely.

**customary** *adj* accepted, accustomed, acknowledged, common, confirmed, conventional, established, everyday, familiar, fashionable, favourite, general, habitual, nomic, normal, ordinary, popular, prevailing, regular, routine, traditional, usual, wonted.

*antonyms* occasional, rare, unusual.

**customer** *n* buyer, client, consumer, habitue, patron, prospect, punter, purchaser, regular, shopper, vendee.

**cut** *v* abbreviate, abridge, avoid, bisect, carve, castrate, chip, chisel, chop, cleave, clip, cold-shoulder, condense, contract, crop, cross, curtail, decrease, delete, dissect, divide, dock, dod, edit, engrave, excise, fashion, fell, form, gash, gather, gride, grieve, hack, harvest, hew, hurt, ignore, incise, insult, interrupt, intersect, jump-cut, lacerate, lop, lower, mow, nick, notch, pain, pare, part, penetrate, pierce, precis, prune, rationalise, reap, reduce, saw, scissor, score, sculpt, sculpture, segment, sever, shape, share, shave, shorten, slash, slice, slight, slim, slit, sned, snub, split, spurn, sting, sunder, trim, truncate, whittle, wound.

*n* abscission, blow, chop, configuration, cutback, decrease, decrement, diminution, division, economy, fall, fashion, form, gash, graze, groove, incision, incisure, insection, kerf, kickback, laceration, look, lowering, mode, nick, percentage, piece, portion, race, rake-off, reduction, rent, rip, saving, section, shape, share, slash, slice, slit, snick, stroke, style, wound.

**cut and dried** automatic, fixed, organised, prearranged, predetermined, settled, sewn up.

**cut back** check, crop, curb, decrease, economise, lessen, lop, lower, prune, reduce, retrench, slash, trim.

**cut down** decrease, diminish, dispatch, fell, hew, kill, lessen, level, lop, lower, massacre, raze, reduce, slaughter, slay.

**cut in** interjaculate, interject, interpose, interrupt, intervene, intrude.

**cut off** abscind, block, disconnect, discontinue, disinherit, disown, end, excide, excise, exscind, halt, intercept, interclude, interrupt, intersect, isolate, obstruct, prescind, renounce, separate, sever, stop, suspend.

**cut out** cease, contrive, debar, delete, displace, eliminate, excise, exclude, exsect, extract, oust, remove, sever, shape, stop, supersede, supplant.

**cut out for** adapted, adequate, competent, designed, equipped, fitted, made, qualified, right, suitable, suited.

**cut short** abbreviate, abort, arrest, check, crop, curtail, dock, halt, interrupt, postpone, prune, reduce, stop, terminate.

*antonym* prolong.

**cut up** carve, chop, criticise, crucify, dice, divide, injure, knife, lacerate, mince, pan, ridicule, slash, slate, slice, vilify, wound.

**cutback** *n* cut, decrease, decrement, economy, lessening, reduction, retrenchment.

**cut-price** *adj* bargain, cheap, cut-rate, low-priced, reduced, sale.

**cut-throat** *n* assassin, bravo, butcher, executioner, hatchet man, hit-man, homicide, killer, liquidator, murderer, slayer, thug.

*adj* barbarous, bloodthirsty, bloody, brutal, competitive, cruel, dog-eat-dog, ferine, ferocious, fierce, homicidal, murderous, relentless, ruthless, savage, thuggish, unprincipled, vicious, violent.

**cutting** *adj* acid, acrimonious, barbed, biting, bitter, caustic, chill, hurtful, incisive, keen, malicious, mordant, numbing, penetrating, piercing, pointed, raw, sarcastic, sardonic, scathing, severe, sharp, stinging, trenchant, wounding.

*n* bit, cleavage, clipping, piece, scion, scission, slice.

**cycle** *n* aeon, age, circle, epoch, era, period, phase, revolution, rotation, round, sequence.

**cyclist** *n* velocipedean, velocipeder, velocipedestrian, velocipedian, velocipedist, wheeler.

**cyclone** *n* hurricane, monsoon, tempest, tornado, twister, typhoon, whirlwind.

**cylinder** *n* barrel, bobbin, column, drum, reel, spindle, spool, trunk.

**cynic** *n* doubter, killjoy, knocker, misanthrope, misanthropist, pessimist, sceptic, scoffer, spoilsport.

**cynical** *adj* contemptuous, derisive, distrustful, ironic, mephistophelian, mephistophilic, misanthropic(al), mocking, mordant, pessimistic, sarcastic, sardonic, sceptical, scoffing, scornful, sharp-tongued, sneering, streetwise.

**cynicism** *n* disbelief, distrust, doubt, misanthropy, pessimism, sarcasm, scepticism.

**cyst** *n* atheroma, bladder, bleb, blister, growth, sac, vesicle, wen.

# D

**dab**[1] *v* blot, daub, pat, stipple, swab, tap, touch, wipe.

*n* bit, dollop, drop, fingerprint, fleck, flick, pat, peck, smear, smidgen, smudge, speck, spot, stroke, tap, touch, trace.

**dab**[2] ace, adept, dab hand, dabster, expert, pastmaster, wizard.

**dabble** *v* dally, dip, fiddle, guddle, moisten, paddle, potter, spatter, splash, sprinkle, tinker, toy, trifle, wet.

**dabbler** *n* amateur, dilettante, potterer, sciolist, tinkerer, trifler.

*antonyms* connoisseur, expert, professional.

**daft** *adj* absurd, asinine, berserk, besotted, crackers, crazy, daffy, delirious, demented, deranged, dop(e)y, doting, dotty, foolish, giddy, hysterical, idiotic, inane, infatuated, insane, lunatic, mad, mental, nuts, nutty, potty, scatty, screwy, silly, simple, stupid, touched, unhinged, witless.

*antonyms* bright, sane.

**dagger** *n* bayonet, dah, dirk, jambiya(h), kris, kukri, misericord(e), poniard, skean, skean-dhu, stiletto, whinger, whiniard, yatag(h)an.

**daily** *adj* circadian, common, commonplace, customary, day-to-day, diurnal, everyday, normal, ordinary, quotidian, regular, routine.

**dainty** *adj* charming, choice, choos(e)y, delectable, delicate, delicious, dinky, elegant, exquisite, fastidious, fine, finical, finicking, finicky, friand(e), fussy, genty, graceful, lickerish, liquorish, meticulous, mignon(ne), mincing, minikin, neat, nice, palatable, particular, petite, pretty, refined, savoury, scrupulous, tasty, tender, toothsome.

*antonyms* clumsy, gross.

*n* bonbon, bonne-bouche, delicacy, fancy, sweetmeat, titbit.

**dale** *n* bottom, clough, coomb, dell, dingle, ghyll, gill, glen, strath, vale, valley.

**dally** *v* canoodle, dawdle, delay, dilly-dally, fiddle-faddle, flirt, frivol, linger, loiter, play, procrastinate, sport, tamper, tarry, toy, trifle.

*antonyms* hasten, hurry.

**dam** *n* an(n)icut, barrage, barrier, blockage, embankment, hindrance, obstruction, wall.

*v* barricade, block, check, choke, confine, obstruct, restrict, stanch, staunch, stem.

**damage** *n* destruction, detriment, devastation, disprofit, harm, hurt, impairment, injury, loss, mischief, mutilation, scathe, suffering.

*antonym* repair.

*v* deface, harm, hurt, impair, incapacitate, injure, mar, mutilate, play havoc with, play hell with, ruin, spoil, tamper with, weaken, wreck.

*antonyms* fix, repair.

**damages** *n* amercement, compensation, fine, indemnity, reimbursement, reparation, satisfaction.

**damaging** *adj* deleterious, detrimental, disadvantageous, harmful, hurtful, injurious, pernicious, prejudicial, ruinous, unfavourable.

*antonyms* favourable, helpful.

**dame** *n* baroness, broad, dowager, female, lady, matron, noblewoman, peeress, woman.

**damn** *v* abuse, anathematise, blaspheme, blast, castigate, censure, condemn, criticise, curse, dang, darn, dash, denounce, denunciate, doom, excoriate, execrate, imprecate, pan, revile, sentence, slam, slate, swear.

*antonym* bless.

*n* brass farthing, darn, dash, hoot, iota, jot, monkey's, tinker's cuss, two hoots, whit.

**damnable** *adj* abominable, accursed, atrocious, culpable, cursed, despicable, detestable, execrable, hateful, horrible, iniquitous, offensive, sinful, wicked.

*antonyms* admirable, praiseworthy.

**damnation** *n* anathema, ban, condemnation, denunciation, doom, excommunication, malison, objurgation, perdition, proscription.

**damned** *adj* accursed, anathematised, condemned, confounded, danged, darned, dashed, despicable, detestable, deuced, doggone(d), doomed, dratted, effing, flipping, fucking, goddam(n), goddamned, hateful, infamous, infernal, loathsome, lost, reprobate, revolting, unhappy.

*antonym* blessed.

**damning** *adj* accusatorial, condemnatory, damnatory, dooming, implicative, incriminating, inculpatory.

**damp** *n* clamminess, dampness, dankness, dew, drizzle, fog, humidity, mist, moisture, mugginess, muzziness, vapour, wet.

*antonym* dryness.

**dampen** *adj* clammy, dank, dewy, dripping, drizzly, humid, misty, moist, muggish, muggy, sodden, soggy, sopping, vaporous, vapourish, vapoury, wet.

*antonyms* arid, dry.

*v* allay, bedew, check, chill, cool, curb, dampen, dash, deaden, deject, depress, diminish, discourage, dispirit, dull, inhibit, moderate, moisten, restrain, stifle, wet.

*antonym* dry.

**dampen** *v* bedew, besprinkle, check, dash, deaden, decrease, depress, deter, diminish, dishearten, dismay, dull, lessen, moderate, moisten, muffle, reduce, restrain, smother, spray, stifle, wet.

*antonyms* dry, encourage.

**dance** *v* caper, frolic, gambol, hoof it, hop, jig, jive, juke, kantikoy, prance, rock, skip, spin, stomp, sway, swing, tread a measure, whirl.

*n* bal masque, bal pare, ball, hop, kantikoy, kick-up, knees-up, prom, shindig, social.

**dancer** *n* ballerina, ballet dancer, belly-dancer, coryphee, danseur, danseuse, hoofer, prima ballerina, tap-dancer.

**dandy** *n* Adonis, beau, blade, blood, buck, Corinthian, coxcomb, dapperling, dude, exquisite, fop, Jack-a-dandy, jay, macaroni, man-about-town, masher, muscadin, musk-cat, peacock, popinjay, swell, toff.

*adj* capital, dinky, excellent, fine, first-rate, great, splendid.

**danger** *n* endangerment, hazard, insecurity, jeopardy, liability, menace, peril, precariousness, risk, threat, trouble, venture, vulnerability.

*antonyms* safety, security.

**dangerous** *adj* alarming, breakneck, chancy, critical, daring, exposed, grave, hairy, harmful, hazardous, insecure, menacing, nasty, parlous, perilous, precarious, reckless, risky, serious, severe, threatening, tickly, treacherous, ugly, unsafe, vulnerable.

*antonyms* harmless, safe, secure.

**dangle** *v* droop, flap, flaunt, flourish, hang, lure, sway, swing, tantalise, tempt, trail, wave.

**dangling** *adj* disconnected, drooping, hanging, loose, pendulous, swaying, swinging, trailing.

**dank** *adj* chilly, clammy, damp, dewy, dripping, moist, rheumy, slimy, soggy.

*antonym* dry.

**dapper** *adj* active, brisk, chic, dainty, natty, neat, nimble, smart, spiffy, spruce, spry, stylish, trig, trim, well-dressed, well-groomed.

*antonyms* dishevelled, dowdy, scruffy, shabby, sloppy.

**dappled** *adj* bespeckled, brindled, checkered, dotted, flecked, freckled, mottled, piebald, pied, speckled, spotted, stippled, variegated.

**dare** *v* adventure, brave, challenge, defy, endanger, gamble, goad, have the gall, hazard, presume, provoke, risk, stake, taunt, venture.

*n* challenge, gauntlet, provocation, taunt.

**daredevil** *n* adventurer, desperado, exhibitionist, Hotspur, madcap, stuntman.

*antonym* coward.

*adj* adventurous, audacious, bold, daring, death-defying, fearless, madcap, rash, reckless.

*antonyms* cautious, prudent, timid.

**daring** *adj* adventurous, audacious, bold, brave, brazen, dauntless, fearless, game, impulsive, intrepid, plucky, rash, reckless, valiant, venturesome.

*antonyms* afraid, timid.

*n* audacity, boldness, bottle, bravery, bravura, courage, defiance, derring-do, fearlessness, gall, grit, guts, intrepidity, nerve, pluck, prowess, rashness, spirit, spunk, temerity.

*antonyms* cowardice, timidity.

**dark** *adj* abstruse, angry, aphotic, arcane, atrocious, benighted, black, bleak, brunette, caliginous, cheerless, cloudy, concealed, cryptic, damnable, darkling, dark-skinned, darksome, deep, dim, dingy, dismal, doleful, dour, drab, dusky, ebony, enigmatic, evil, forbidding, foul, frowning, gloomy, glowering, glum, grim, hellish, hidden, horrible, ignorant, indistinct, infamous, infernal, joyless, lightless, melanic, melanous, midnight, mirk, mirky, morbid, morose, mournful, murk, murky, mysterious, mystic, nefarious, obscure, occult, ominous, overcast, pitch-black, pitchy, puzzling, recondite, sable, satanic, scowling, secret, shadowy, shady, sinful, sinister, sombre, sulky, sullen, sunless, swarthy, tenebr(i)ous, threatening, uncultivated, unenlightened, unillumed, unilluminated, unlettered, unlit, vile, wicked.

*antonyms* bright, happy, light, lucid.

*n* concealment, darkness, dimness, dusk, evening, gloom, ignorance, mirk, mirkiness, murk, murkiness, night, nightfall, night-time, obscurity, secrecy, twilight, yin.

*antonyms* brightness, light.

**darken** *v* becloud, blacken, cloud, cloud over, darkle, deepen, deject, depress, dim, disilluminate, dispirit, dusken, eclipse, embrown, obscure, overshade, overshadow, sadden, shade, shadow.

*antonyms* brighten, lighten.

**darkness** *n* blackness, blindness, concealment, dark, dimness, dusk, duskiness, gloom, ignorance, mirk, mirkiness, murk, murkiness, mystery, nightfall, obscurity, privacy, secrecy, shade, shadiness, shadows, tenebr(os)ity.

*antonyms* brightness, daylight, lightness.

**darling** *n* acushla, apple of one's eye, asthore, beloved, blue-eyed boy, dear, dearest, fair-haired boy, favourite, jo(e), lady-love, love, lovey, machree, mavourneen, minikin, pet, poppet, sweetheart, true-love.

*adj* adored, beloved, cherished, dear, precious, treasured, white-headed.

**dart** *v* bound, cast, dartle, dash, flash, fling, flit, fly, hurl, launch, propel, race, run, rush, scoot, send, shoot, sling, spring, sprint, start, tear, throw, whistle, whiz.

*n* arrow, barb, bolt, flechette, flight, shaft.

**dash**[1] *v* abash, blight, break, cast, chagrin, confound, crash, dampen, destroy, ding, disappoint, discomfort, discourage, fling, foil, frustrate, hurl, ruin, shatter, shiver, slam, sling, smash, splinter, spoil, throw, thwart.

*n* bit, bravura, brio, da(u)d, drop, elan, flair, flavour, flourish, hint, little, panache, pinch, smack, soupçon, spirit, sprinkling, style, suggestion, tinge, touch, verve, vigour, vivacity.

**dash**[2] *v* be off like a shot, bolt, bound, dart, dartle, fly, haste(n), hurry, race, run, rush, speed, spring, sprint, tear.

*n* bolt, dart, race, run, rush, sprint, spurt.

**dashing** *adj* bold, dapper, daring, dazzling, debonair, doggy, elegant, exuberant, flamboyant, gallant, impressive, jaunty, lively, plucky, showy, smart, spirited, sporty, stylish, swashbuckling, swish.

*antonym* drab.

**dastard** *n* caitiff, coward, craven, cur, milksop, poltroon, worm.

**dastardly** *adj* base, caitiff, contemptible, cowardly, craven, despicable, faint-hearted, lily-livered, low, mean, niddering, pusillanimous, recreant, sneaking, sneaky, spiritless, timorous, underhand, vile.

*antonyms* heroic, noble.

**data** *n* details, documents, dope, facts, figures, info, information, input, materials, statistics.

**date**[1] *n* age, epoch, era, period, point, point in time, stage, time.

**date**[2] *n* appointment, assignation, engagement, escort, friend, meeting, partner, rendezvous, steady, tryst.

**dated** *adj* antiquated, archaic, demode, obsolescent, obsolete, old hat, old-fashioned, out, outdated, outmoded, out-of-date, passe, superseded, unfashionable.

*antonyms* fashionable, up-to-the-minute.

**daub** *v* begrime, besmear, blur, coat, cover, dedaub, deface, dirty, gaum, grime, paint, plaster, smear, smirch, smudge, spatter, splatter, stain, sully.

*n* blot, blotch, smear, splash, splodge, splotch, spot, stain.

**daunt** *v* alarm, appal, cow, deter, discourage, dishearten, dismay, dispirit, frighten, intimidate, overawe, put off, scare, shake, subdue, terrify, unnerve.

*antonyms* encourage, hearten.

**daunted** *adj* alarmed, cowed, demoralised, deterred, discouraged, disheartened, disillusioned, dismayed, dismayful, dispirited, downcast, frightened, hesitant, intimidated, overcome, put off, unnerved.

*antonyms* encouraged, heartened.

**dauntless** *adj* bold, brave, courageous, daring, doughty, fearless, gallant, game, heroic, indomitable, intrepid, lion-hearted, plucky, resolute, stout-hearted, undaunted, unflinching, valiant, valorous.

*antonyms* discouraged, disheartened.

**dawdle** *v* daidle, dally, delay, dilly-dally, fiddle, fritter, hang about, idle, lag, loaf, loiter, potter, shilly-shally, trail.

*antonym* hurry.

**dawdler** *n* laggard, lingerer, loafer, loiterer, shilly-shallier, slowcoach, snail, tortoise.

**dawn** *n* advent, aurora, beginning, birth, cock-crow(ing), dawning, daybreak, daylight, day-peep, dayspring, emergence, genesis, inception, morning, onset, origin, outset, peep of day, rise, start, sunrise, sun-up.

*antonyms* dusk, sundown, sunset.

*v* appear, begin, break, brighten, develop, emerge, gleam, glimmer, hit, initiate, lighten, occur, open, originate, register, rise, strike, unfold.

**day** *n* age, ascendancy, childhood, cycle, date, daylight, daytime, epoch, era, generation, height, heyday, period, prime, time, young days, youth, zenith.

*antonym* night.

**day after day** continually, endlessly, forever, monotonously, perpetually, persistently, regularly, relentlessly.

**day by day** daily, gradually, progressively, slowly but surely, steadily.

**daybreak** *n* break of day, cock-crow(ing), crack of dawn, dawn, day-peep, dayspring, first light, morning, peep of day, sunrise, sun-up.

*antonyms* sundown, sunset.

**daydream** *n* castles in Spain, castles in the air, dream, dwa(l)m, fantasy, figment, fond hope, imagining, musing, phantasm, pipe dream, reverie, star-gazing, vision, wish, wool-gathering.

*v* dream, fancy, fantasise, hallucinate, imagine, muse, stargaze.

**daydreamer** *n* fantasiser, rêveur, rêveuse, stargazer.

**daze** *v* amaze, astonish, astound, befog, benumb, bewilder, blind, confuse, dazzle, dumbfound, flabbergast, numb, paralyse, perplex, shock, stagger, startle, stun, stupefy, surprise.

*n* bewilderment, confusion, distraction, dwa(l)m, shock, stupor, trance.

**dazed** *adj* baffled, bemused, bewildered, confused, disorien(ta)ted, dizzy, dop(e)y, dumbstruck, flabbergasted, fuddled, groggy, light-headed, muddled, nonplussed, numbed, perplexed, punch-drunk, shocked, staggered, stunned, stupefied, totty, woozy.

**dazzle** *v* amaze, astonish, awe, bedazzle, blind, blur, confuse, daze, fascinate, hypnotise, impress, overawe, overpower, overwhelm, scintillate, sparkle, stupefy.

*n* brilliance, glitter, magnificence, razzle-dazzle, razzmatazz, scintillation, sparkle, splendour.

**dazzling** *adj* brilliant, foudroyant, glaring, glary, glittering, glorious, radiant, ravishing, scintillating, sensational, shining, sparkling, splendid, stunning, sublime, superb, virtuoso.

**de facto** *adv* actually, in effect, really.

*adj* actual, existing, real.

**de jure** legally, rightfully.

**de luxe** choice, costly, elegant, exclusive, expensive, grand, luxurious, opulent, palatial, plush, rich, select, special, splendid, sumptuous, superior.

**de rigueur** comme il faut, conventional, correct, decent, decorous, done, fitting, necessary, proper, required, right, the done thing.

**de trop** needless, redundant, supererogatory, superfluous, supernumerary, surplus, unnecessary, unneeded, unwanted, unwelcome.

**dead**[1] *adj* ad patres, apathetic, barren, boring, breathless, callous, cold, dead-and-alive, dead-beat, deceased, defunct, departed, dull, exhausted, extinct, flat, frigid, glassy, glazed, gone, inactive, inanimate, indifferent, inert, inoperative, insipid, late, lifeless, lukewarm, napoo, numb, obsolete, paralysed, perished, spent, spiritless, stagnant, stale, sterile, stiff, still, tasteless, tired, torpid, unemployed, uninteresting, unprofitable, unresponsive, useless, vapid, wooden, worn out.

*antonyms* active, alive, animated.

**dead**[2] *adj* absolute, complete, downright, entire, outright, perfect, thorough, total, unqualified, utter.

*adv* absolutely, completely, entirely, exactly, perfectly, quite, totally.

**deaden** *v* abate, allay, alleviate, anaesthetise, benumb, blunt, check, cushion, damp, dampen, desensitise, diminish, dull, hush, impair, lessen, muffle, mute, numb, obtund, paralyse, quieten, reduce, smother, stifle, suppress, weaken.

*antonym* enliven.

**deadlock** *n* halt, impasse, stalemate, standstill.

**deadly** *adj* accurate, ashen, baleful, baneful, boring, cruel, dangerous, death-dealing, deathful, deathlike, deathly, destructive, devastating, dull, effective, exact, fatal, feral, funest, ghastly, ghostly, grim, implacable, lethal, malignant, monotonous, mortal, noxious, pallid, pernicious, pestilent, poisonous, precise, ruthless, savage, sure, tedious, thanatoid, true, unerring, unfailing, uninteresting, unrelenting, venomous, wearisome, white.

*antonyms* harmless, healthy.

**deadpan** *adj* blank, dispassionate, empty, expressionless, impassive, inexpressive, inscrutable, poker-faced, straight-faced, unexpressive.

**deaf** *adj* hard of hearing, heedless, indifferent, oblivious, stone-deaf, unconcerned, unmindful, unmoved.

*antonyms* aware, conscious.

**deafening** *adj* booming, dinning, ear-piercing, ear-splitting, fortissimo, piercing, resounding, ringing, roaring, thunderous.

*antonyms* pianissimo, quiet.

**deal** *v* allot, apportion, assign, bargain, bestow, dispense, distribute, divide, dole out, give, mete out, negotiate, reward, sell, share, stock, trade, traffic, treat.

*n* agreement, amount, arrangement, bargain, buy, contract, degree, distribution, extent, hand, pact, portion, quantity, round, share, transaction, understanding.

**deal with** attend to, concern, consider, cope with, handle, manage, oversee, see to, treat.

**dealer** *n* chandler, chapman, marketer, merchandiser, merchant, monger, trader, tradesman, wholesaler.

**dealings** *n* business, commerce, intercourse, intertraffic, trade, traffic, transactions, truck.

**dear** *adj* beloved, cherished, close, costly, darling, esteemed, expensive, familiar, favourite, high-priced, intimate, loved, overpriced, precious, pric(e)y, prized, respected, treasured, valued.

*antonyms* cheap, hateful.

*n* angel, beloved, darling, dearie, deary, loved one, precious, treasure.

**dearly** *adv* affectionately, devotedly, extremely, fondly, greatly, lovingly, profoundly, tenderly.

**dearth** *n* absence, barrenness, deficiency, exiguousness, famine, inadequacy, insufficiency, lack, need, paucity, poverty, scantiness, scarcity, shortage, sparseness, sparsity, want.

*antonyms* abundance, excess.

**death** *n* annihilation, bane, bereavement, cessation, curtains, decease, demise, departure, destruction, dissolution, dormition, downfall, dying, end, eradication, exit, expiration, extermination, extinction, fatality, finish, grave, loss, obliteration, passing, quietus, release, ruin, ruination, undoing.

*antonyms* birth, life.

**deathless** *adj* eternal, everlasting, immortal, imperishable, incorruptible, never-ending, timeless, undying, unforgettable.

**deathly** *adj* ashen, cadaverous, deadly, deathlike, fatal, gaunt, ghastly, grim, haggard, intense, mortal, pale, pallid, terrible, wan.

**debacle** *n* cataclysm, catastrophe, collapse, defeat, devastation, disaster, downfall, farce, fiasco, havoc, overthrow, reversal, rout, ruin, ruination, stampede.

**debar** *v* bar, blackball, deny, eject, exclude, expel, hamper, hinder, obstruct, preclude, prevent, prohibit, restrain, segregate, shut out, stop.

*antonym* admit.

**debase** *v* abase, adulterate, allay, bastardise, cheapen, contaminate, corrupt, defile, degrade, demean, depreciate, devalue, diminish, disgrace, dishonour, embase, humble, humiliate, impair, lower, pollute, reduce, shame, taint, vitiate.

*antonyms* elevate, upgrade.

**debased** *adj* abandoned, adulterated, base, corrupt, debauched, degenerate, degraded, depraved, depreciated, devalued, diminished, fallen, impure, low, lowered, mixed, perverted, polluted, reduced, sordid, vile.

*antonyms* elevated, pure.

**debasement** *n* abasement, adulteration, baseness, contamination, corruption, degeneration, degradation, depravation, depreciation, devaluation, dishonour, perversion, pollution, reduction.

*antonyms* elevation, purification.

**deceit**

**debatable** *adj* arguable, borderline, contentious, contestable, controversial, controvertible, disputable, doubtful, dubious, moot, open to question, problematical, questionable, uncertain, undecided, unsettled.

*antonyms* certain, questionable.

**debate** *v* argue, cogitate, consider, contend, contest, controvert, deliberate, discuss, dispute, logicise, meditate on, mull over, ponder, question, reflect, revolve, ruminate, weigh, wrangle.

*antonym* agree.

*n* altercation, argument, cogitation, consideration, contention, controversy, deliberation, discussion, disputation, dispute, meditation, polemic, quodlibet, reflection.

*antonym* agreement.

**debauch** *v* corrupt, deflower, demoralise, deprave, over-indulge, pervert, pollute, ravish, ruin, seduce, subvert, violate, vitiate.

*antonyms* cleanse, purge, purify.

*n* bacchanalia, bender, bevvy, binge, booze-up, bout, fling, orgy, pub-crawl, saturnalia, spree, wet.

**debauched** *adj* abandoned, corrupt, corrupted, debased, degenerate, degraded, depraved, dissipated, dissolute, immoral, intemperate, lewd, licentious, perverted, profligate, raddled, rakehell, rakehelly, wanton.

*antonyms* decent, pure, virtuous.

**debauchee** *n* hell-bender, libertine, Lothario, playboy, profligate, rake, rake-hell, roue, sensualist, wanton.

**debauchery** *n* carousal, debauchedness, debauchment, depravity, dissipation, dissoluteness, excess, gluttony, immorality, incontinence, indulgence, intemperance, lewdness, licentiousness, lust, orgy, overindulgence, rakery, revel, riot, wantonness.

**debilitate** *v* devitalise, enervate, enfeeble, exhaust, impair, incapacitate, prostrate, relax, sap, undermine, unman, weaken, wear out.

*antonyms* energise, invigorate, strengthen.

**debilitating** *adj* enervating, enervative, enfeebling, exhausting, fatiguing, tiring, weakening.

*antonyms* invigorating, strengthening.

**debility** *n* asthenia, atonicity, atony, decrepitude, enervation, enfeeblement, exhaustion, faintness, feebleness, frailty, incapacity, infirmity, languor, malaise, sickliness, weakness.

*antonyms* strength, vigour.

**debonair** *adj* affable, breezy, buoyant, charming, cheerful, courteous, dashing, elegant, gay, jaunty, light-hearted, refined, smooth, sprightly, suave, urbane, well-bred.

**debris** *n* bits, brash, detritus, drift, dross, duff, eluvium, exuviae, fragments, litter, moraine, pieces, remains, rubbish, rubble, ruins, sweepings, trash, waste, wreck, wreckage.

**debt** *n* arrears, bill, claim, commitment, debit, due, duty, indebtedness, liability, obligation, score, sin.

*antonyms* asset, credit.

**debtor** *n* bankrupt, borrower, defaulter, insolvent, mortgagee, mortgagor.

*antonym* creditor.

**debunk** *v* deflate, disparage, explode, expose, lampoon, mock, puncture, ridicule, show up.

**debut** *n* appearance, beginning, bow, entrance, inauguration, initiation, introduction, launching, première, presentation.

**decadence** *n* corruption, debasement, decadency, decay, decline, degenerateness, degeneration, deterioration, dissipation, dissolution, fall, perversion, retrogression, symbolism.

*antonyms* flourishing, rise.

**decadent** *adj* corrupt, debased, debauched, decaying, declining, degenerate, degraded, depraved, dissolute, effete, fin-de-siècle, immoral, self-indulgent, symbolist.

*antonym* moral.

**decamp** *v* abscond, absquatulate, bolt, desert, do a bunk, escape, flee, flit, fly, guy, hightail it, levant, make off, mizzle, run away, scarper, skedaddle.

**decapitate** *v* behead, execute, guillotine, unhead.

**decay** *v* atrophy, canker, cavitate, corrode, crumble, decline, decompose, decompound, degenerate, deteriorate, disintegrate, dissolve, dote, dwindle, mortify, moulder, perish, putrefy, rot, shrivel, sink, spoil, wane, waste away, wear away, wither.

*antonyms* flourish, grow, ripen.

*n* atrophy, caries, collapse, consenescence, decadence, decline, decomposition, decrepitness, decrepitude, degeneracy, degeneration, deterioration, disintegration, dying, fading, failing, gangrene, labefactation, labefaction, mortification, perishing, putrefaction, putrescence, putridity, putridness, rot, rotting, wasting, withering.

**decayed** *adj* addled, bad, carious, carrion, corroded, decomposed, off, perished, putrefied, putrid, rank, rotten, spoiled, wasted, withered.

**decaying** *adj* crumbling, decrepit, deteriorating, disintegrating, doty, dricksie, druxy, gangrenous, perishing, putrescent, rotting.

**decease** *n* death, demise, departure, dissolution, dying, passing, release.

*v* cease, croak, die, expire, give up the ghost, kick the bucket, pass away, pass on, pass over, perish.

**deceased** *adj* dead, defunct, departed, expired, extinct, finished, former, gone, late, lifeless, lost.

*n* dead, decedent, departed.

**deceit** *n* abuse, artifice, blind, cheat, cheating, chicanery, con, cozenage, craftiness, cunning, deceitfulness, deception, dissimulation, double-dealing, duplicity, fake, feint, fraud, fraudulence, guile, hypocrisy, imposition, imposture, misrepresentation, phenakism, pretence, ruse, sham, shift, slyness, stratagem, subterfuge, swindle, treachery, trick, trickery, underhandedness, wile.

*antonyms* honesty, openness.

**deceitful** *adj* collusive, counterfeit, crafty, deceiving, deceptive, designing, dishonest, disingenuous, double-dealing, duplicitous, elusory, fallacious, false, fraudulent, guileful, hypocritical, illusory, insincere, knavish, prestigious, Punic, ruse, sneaky, treacherous, tricky, two-faced, underhand, untrustworthy.

*antonyms* honest, open, trustworthy.

**deceive** *v* abuse, bamboozle, befool, beguile, betray, camouflage, cheat, cog, con, cozen, delude, diddle, disappoint, dissemble, dissimulate, double-cross, dupe, ensnare, entrap, flam, fool, gag, gammon, gloze, gull, have on, hoax, hoodwink, impose upon, lead on, mislead, outwit, seel, swindle, take for a ride, take in, trick, two-time.

*antonym* enlighten.

**deceiver** *n* abuser, betrayer, charlatan, cheat, con man, cozener, crook, deluder, diddler, dissembler, dissimulator, double-dealer, fake, fraud, hypocrite, impostor, inveigler, mountebank, pretender, sharper, swindler, trickster.

**decency** *n* appropriateness, civility, correctness, courtesy, decorum, etiquette, fitness, good form, good manners, helpfulness, modesty, propriety, respectability, seemliness, thoughtfulness.

*antonyms* discourtesy, indecency.

**decent** *adj* acceptable, accommodating, adequate, ample, appropriate, average, becoming, befitting, chaste, comely, comme il faut, competent, courteous, decorous, delicate, fair, fit, fitting, friendly, generous, gracious, gradely, helpful, kind, modest, nice, obliging, passable, polite, presentable, proper, pure, reasonable, respectable, satisfactory, seemly, sufficient, suitable, thoughtful, tolerable.

*antonyms* disobliging, indecent, poor.

**decentralisation** *n* delegation, development, devolution.

*antonym* centralisation.

**deception** *n* artifice, bluff, cheat, conning, craftiness, cunning, deceifulness, deceit, deceptiveness, decoy, defraudation, defraudment, dissembling, dissimulation, duplicity, false-pretences, feint, flim-flam, fraud, fraudulence, guile, gullery, hoax, hype, hypocrisy, illusion, imposition, imposture, insincerity, legerdemain, leg-pull, lie, ruse, sell, sham, snare, stratagem, subterfuge, take-in, treachery, trick, trickery, wile.

*antonyms* artlessness, openness.

**deceptive** *adj* ambiguous, catchy, delusive, delusory, dishonest, elusory, fake, fallacious, false, fraudulent, illusive, illusory, misleading, mock, specious, spurious, unreliable.

*antonyms* artless, genuine, open.

**decide** *v* adjudge, adjudicate, choose, conclude, decree, determine, dijudicate, elect, end, fix, judge, opt, purpose, reach a decision, resolve, settle.

**decided** *adj* absolute, assertive, categorical, certain, clear-cut, decisive, definite, deliberate, determined, distinct, emphatic, express, firm, forthright, indisputable, marked, noticeable, positive, pronounced, resolute, strong-willed, unambiguous, undeniable, undisputed, unequivocal, unfaltering, unhesitating, unmistakable, unquestionable.

*antonyms* indecisive, undecided.

**decidedly** *adv* absolutely, certainly, clearly, decisively, definitely, distinctly, downright, positively, quite, unequivocally, unmistakably, very.

**decider** *n* clincher, coup de grâce, determiner, floorer.

**deciding** *adj* chief, conclusive, critical, crucial, crunch, decisive, determining, final, influential, prime, principal, significant, supreme.

*antonym* insignificant.

**decipher** *v* construe, crack, decode, decrypt, deduce, explain, figure out, interpret, make out, read, solve, transliterate, uncipher, understand, unfold, unravel, unscramble.

*antonym* encode.

**decipherment** *n* decryption, interpretation, translation, transliteration, unscrambling.

*antonym* encoding.

**decision** *n* arbitrament, arbitration, arrêt, conclusion, decisiveness, determination, fetwa, finding, firmness, judgement, outcome, parti, purpose, purposefulness, resoluteness, resolution, resolve, result, ruling, settlement, verdict.

**decisive** *adj* absolute, conclusive, critical, crucial, crunch, decided, definite, definitive, determinate, determined, fateful, final, firm, forceful, forthright, incisive, influential, momentous, positive, resolute, significant, strong-minded, supreme, trenchant.

*antonyms* indecisive, insignificant.

**deck** *v* adorn, apparel, array, attire, beautify, bedeck, bedight, bedizen, betrim, clothe, decorate, doll up, dress, embellish, festoon, garland, grace, ornament, prettify, pretty up, primp, prink, rig out, smarten, titivate, tog out, tog up, trick out, trim.

**declaim** *v* bespout, harangue, hold forth, lecture, mouth, orate, perorate, preach, proclaim, rant, recite, rhetorise, speak, speechify, spiel, spout, tub-thump.

**declamation** *n* address, harangue, lecture, oration, rant, recitation, rhetoric, speech, speechifying, tirade.

**declamatory** *adj* bombastic, discursive, fustian, grandiloquent, grandiose, high-flown, inflated, magniloquent, oratorical, oro(ro)tund, overblown, pompous, rhetorical, stagy, stilted, theatrical, turgid.

**declaration** *n* acknowledgement, affirmation, announcement, assertion, asseveration, attestation, averment, avouchment, avowal, deposition, disclosure, edict, manifesto, notification, proclamation, profession, promulgation, pronouncement, pronunciamento, protestation, revelation, statement, testimony.

**declare** *v* affirm, announce, assert, attest, aver, avouch, avow, certify, claim, confess, confirm, convey, disclose, maintain, manifest, nuncupate, proclaim, profess, pronounce, reveal, show, state, swear, testify, validate, witness.

**decline¹** *v* avoid, balk, decay, decrease, degenerate, deny, deteriorate, deviate, diminish, droop, dwindle, ebb, fade, fail, fall, fall off, flag, forgo, languish, lessen, pine, refuse, reject, shrink, sink, turn down, wane, weaken, worsen.

*n* abatement, consumption, decay, declension, decrepitude, degeneration, deterioration, deviation, diminution, downturn, dwindling, enfeeblement, failing, falling-off, lessening, paracme, phthisis, recession, senility, slump, tuberculosis, weakening, worsening.

**decline²** *v* descend, dip, sink, slant, slope.

*n* brae, declination, declivity, descent, deviation, dip, divergence, hill, incline, obliqueness, obliquity, slope.

**declivity** *n* brae, declination, decline, descent, incline, slant, slope.

*antonym* acclivity.

**decode** *v* decipher, decrypt, interpret, translate, transliterate, uncipher, unscramble.

*antonym* encode.

**decomposable** *adj* biodegradable, decompoundable, degradable, destructible.

**decompose** *v* analyse, atomise, break down, break up, crumble, decay, decompound, degrade, disintegrate, dissolve, distil, fall apart, fester, fractionate, putrefy, rot, separate, spoil.

*antonyms* combine, unite.

**decomposition** *n* atomisation, breakdown, corruption, decay, degradation, disintegration, dissolution, distillation, division, electrolysis, fractionation, hydrolysis, putrefaction, putrescence, putridity, rot.

*antonyms* combination, unification.

**decor** *n* colour-scheme, decoration, embellishments, furnishings, ornamentation, scenery.

**decorate¹** *v* adorn, beautify, bedeck, colour, daiker, deck, do up, embellish, enrich, furbish, grace, impearl, miniate, ornament, paint, paper, prettify, renovate, tart up, trick out, trim, wallpaper.

**decorate²** *v* bemedal, cite, crown, garland, honour.

**decorated** *adj* baroque, elaborate, embellished, figured, garnished, ornate, rococo.

*antonym* plain.

**decoration¹** *n* adornment, arabesque, bauble, beautification, curlicue, elaboration, embellishment, enrichment, falderal, flounce, flourish, frill, frou-frou, furbelow, garnish, ornament, ornamentation, pass(e)ment, passementerie, scroll, spangle, trimming, trinket.

**decoration²** *n* award, badge, colours, crown, emblem, garland, garter, laurel, laurel-wreath, medal, order, ribbon, star.

**decorative** *adj* adorning, arty-crafty, baroque, beautifying, embellishing, enhancing, fancy, non-functional, ornamental, ornate, pretty, rococo, superfluous.

*antonyms* plain, ugly.

**decorous** *adj* appropriate, becoming, befitting, comely, comme il faut, correct, courtly, decent, dignified, fit, maidenly, mannerly, modest, polite, proper, refined, sedate, seemly, staid, suitable, well-behaved.

*antonym* indecorous.

**decorum** *n* behaviour, breeding, courtliness, decency, deportment, dignity, etiquette, gentility, good manners, grace, gravity, modesty, politeness, politesse, propriety, protocol, punctilio, respectability, restraint, seemliness.

*antonyms* bad manners, indecorum.

**decoy** *n* attraction, bait, ensnarement, enticement, inducement, lure, pretence, roper(-in), shill, trap.

*v* allure, attract, bait, beguile, deceive, draw, ensnare, entice, entrap, inveigle, lead, lure, seduce, tempt.

**decrease** *v* abate, ablate, contract, curtail, cut down, decline, decrement, diminish, drop, dwindle, ease, fall off, lessen, lower, peter out, reduce, shrink, slacken, slim, subside, taper, wane.

*antonym* increase.

*n* abatement, ablation, contraction, cutback, decline, decrement, degression, diminution, downturn, dwindling, ebb, falling-off, lessening, loss, reduction, shrinkage, step-down, subsidence.

*antonym* increase.

**decree** *n* act, command, decretal, dictum, edict, enactment, firman, hatti-sherif, indiction, interlocution, interlocutor, law, mandate, order, ordinance, precept, proclamation, regulation, ruling, statute, ukase.

*v* command, decide, determine, dictate, enact, lay down, ordain, order, prescribe, proclaim, pronounce, rescript, rule.

**decreed** *adj* enacted, ordained, proclaimed, stated, writ, written.

**decrepit** *adj* aged, antiquated, battered, broken-backed, broken-down, crippled, debilitated, deteriorated, dilapidated, doddering, doddery, feeble, frail, incapacitated, infirm, ramshackle, rickety, run-down, superannuated, tumble-down, warby, wasted, weak, worn-out.

*antonyms* fit, well-cared-for, youthful.

**decrepitude** *n* debility, decay, degeneration, deterioration, dilapidation, disability, dotage, feebleness, incapacity, infirmity, invalidity, old age, senescence, senility, wasting, weakness.

*antonyms* good repair, youth.

**decry** *v* abuse, belittle, blame, censure, condemn, criticise, cry down, declaim against, denounce, depreciate, derogate, detract, devalue, discredit, disparage, inveigh against, rail against, run down, traduce, underestimate, underrate, undervalue.

*antonyms* praise, value.

**dedicate** v address, assign, bless, commit, consecrate, devote, give over to, hallow, inscribe, offer, pledge, present, sacrifice, sanctify, set apart, surrender.

**dedicated** adj committed, devoted, enthusiastic, given over to, purposeful, single-hearted, single-minded, sworn, whole-hearted, zealous.

antonyms apathetic, uncommitted.

**dedication**[1] n adherence, allegiance, attachment, commitment, devotedness, devotion, faithfulness, loyalty, self-sacrifice, single-mindedness, whole-heartedness.

antonym apathy.

**dedication**[2] n address, consecration, donation, hallowing, inscription, presentation, sanctification.

**deduce** v conclude, derive, draw, gather, glean, infer, reason, surmise, understand.

**deducible** adj a fortiori, a posteriori, derivable, inferable, traceable.

**deduct** v decrease by, knock off, reduce by, remove, subduct, subtract, take away, withdraw.

antonym add.

**deduction**[1] n assumption, conclusion, consectary, corollary, finding, inference, reasoning, result.

**deduction**[2] n abatement, allowance, decrease, diminution, discount, reduction, subduction, subtraction, withdrawal.

antonyms addition, increase.

**deed**[1] n achievement, act, action, exploit, fact, factum, feat, gest(e), performance, reality, truth.

**deed**[2] n contract, document, indenture, instrument, record, title, transaction.

**deem** v account, adjudge, believe, conceive, consider, esteem, estimate, hold, imagine, judge, reckon, regard, suppose, think.

**deep** adj absorbed, abstract, abstruse, abyssal, acute, arcane, artful, astute, bass, booming, bottomless, broad, canny, cryptic, cunning, dark, designing, devious, discerning, engrossed, esoteric, extreme, far, fathomless, full-toned, grave, great, hidden, immersed, inmost, inner, innermost, insidious, intense, knowing, learned, lost, low, low-pitched, mysterious, obscure, penetrating, preoccupied, profound, rapt, recondite, resonant, rich, sagacious, scheming, secret, shrewd, sonorous, strong, unfathomable, unfathomed, unplumbed, unsoundable, unsounded, vivid, wide, wise, yawning.

antonyms open, shallow.

n briny, drink, high seas, main, ocean, sea.

**deepen** v dredge, excavate, grow, hollow, increase, intensify, magnify, reinforce, scoop out, strengthen.

antonym fill in.

**deeply** adv acutely, affectingly, completely, distressingly, feelingly, gravely, intensely, mournfully, movingly, passionately, profoundly, sadly, seriously, severely, thoroughly, to the quick, very much.

antonym slightly.

**deep-seated** adj confirmed, deep, deep-rooted, entrenched, fixed, ineradicable, ingrained, inveterate, rooted, settled, subconscious, unconscious.

antonyms eradicable, temporary.

**deer** n buck, doe, hart, reindeer, roe, stag.

**deface** v blemish, damage, deform, destroy, disfeature, disfigure, impair, injure, mar, mutilate, obliterate, spoil, sully, tarnish, vandalise.

antonym repair.

**defamation** n aspersion, calumny, denigration, derogation, disparagement, innuendo, libel, mud-slinging, obloquy, opprobrium, scandal, slander, slur, smear, traducement, vilification.

antonym praise.

**defamatory** adj abusive, calumnious, contumelious, denigrating, derogatory, disparaging, injurious, insulting, libellous, pejorative, slanderous, vilifying, vituperative.

antonym complimentary.

**defame** v asperse, belie, besmirch, blacken, calumniate, cast aspersions on, cloud, denigrate, detract, discredit, disgrace, dishonour, disparage, infame, libel, malign, slander, smear, speak evil of, stigmatise, traduce, vilify, vituperate.

antonyms compliment, praise.

**default** n absence, defalcation, defect, deficiency, dereliction, failure, fault, lack, lapse, neglect, non-payment, omission, want.

v backslide, bilk, defraud, dodge, evade, fail, levant, neglect, rat, renegue, swindle, waddle, welsh.

**defaulter** n defalcator, defector, delinquent, duck, embezzler, levanter, non-payer, offender, peculator, welsher.

**defeat** v baffle, balk, beat, best, checkmate, clobber, confound, conquer, counteract, crush, disappoint, discomfit, down, foil, frustrate, get the better of, outbargain, overpower, overthrow, overwhelm, psych out, quell, repulse, rout, ruin, stump, subdue, subjugate, tank, thump, thwart, trounce, vanquish, vote down, whop.

n beating, conquest, debâcle, disappointment, discomfiture, failure, frustration, overthrow, rebuff, repulse, reverse, rout, setback, thwarting, trouncing, vanquishment, Waterloo.

**defeated** adj balked, beaten, bested, checkmated, confounded, conquered, crushed, licked, nonplussed, overcome, overpowered, overwhelmed, routed, thrashed, thwarted, trounced, vanquished, worsted.

antonyms conquering, triumphant.

**defeatist** n futilitarian, pessimist, prophet of doom, quitter.

antonym optimist.

adj cynical, despairing, despondent, fatalistic, gloomy, helpless, hopeless, pessimistic, resigned, resourceless.

antonym optimistic.

**defecate** v ease oneself, egest, empty, evacuate, excrete, pass a motion, poo, relieve oneself, shit, void (excrement).

**defecation** *n* dejection, egestion, elimination, evacuation, excrement, excretion, motion, movement, poo, shit, voiding.

**defect** *n* absence, blemish, bug, default, deficiency, error, failing, fault, flaw, frailty, hamartia, imperfection, inadequacy, lack, mistake, shortcoming, spot, taint, want, weakness.

*v* apostatise, break faith, desert, rebel, renegue, revolt, tergiversate.

**defection** *n* abandonment, apostasy, backsliding, defalcation, dereliction, desertion, rebellion, renegation, revolt.

**defective** *adj* abnormal, broken, deficient, faulty, flawed, imperfect, inadequate, incomplete, insufficient, kaput, out of order, retarded, scant, short, subnormal.

*antonyms* normal, operative.

**defector** *n* apostate, deserter, Grenzgänger, Judas, quisling, rat, recreant, renegade, runagate, tergiversator, turncoat.

**defence**[1] *n* aegis, armament, barricade, bastion, buckler, bulwark, buttress, cover, deterrence, fastness, fortification, guard, immunity, muniment, munition, protection, rampart, resistance, safeguard, security, shelter, shield.

*antonym* attack.

**defence**[2] *n* alibi, apologia, apology, argument, case, declaration, denial, excuse, exoneration, explanation, extenuation, justification, palliation, plea, pleading, rebuttal, testimony, vindication.

**defenceless** *adj* endangered, exposed, helpless, imperilled, naked, powerless, unarmed, undefended, unguarded, unprotected, unshielded, vulnerable, wide open.

*antonym* protected.

**defend** *v* assert, bulwark, champion, contest, cover, endorse, espouse, fortify, guard, justify, maintain, plead, preserve, protect, safeguard, screen, secure, shelter, shield, speak up for, stand by, stand up for, support, sustain, uphold, vindicate, watch over.

*antonym* attack.

**defendant** *n* accused, appellant, defender, litigant, offender, prisoner, respondent.

**defender** *n* advocate, bodyguard, champion, counsel, escort, guard, patron, promachos, protector, sponsor, supporter, vindicator.

*antonym* attacker.

**defensible** *adj* arguable, holdable, impregnable, justifiable, pardonable, permissible, plausible, safe, secure, tenable, unassailable, valid, vindicable.

*antonyms* indefensible, insecure.

**defensive** *adj* apologetic, aposematic, averting, cautious, defending, opposing, protective, safeguarding, self-justifying, wary, watchful, withstanding.

*antonym* bold.

**defer**[1] *v* adjourn, delay, hold over, postpone, procrastinate, prorogue, protract, put off, put on ice, shelve, suspend, waive.

**defer**[2] *v* accede, bow, capitulate, comply, give way, kowtow, respect, submit, yield.

**deference** *n* acquiescence, attention, capitulation, civility, complaisance, compliance, consideration, courtesy, esteem, homage, honour, morigeration, obedience, obeisance, obsequiousness, politeness, regard, respect, reverence, submission, submissiveness, thoughtfulness, veneration, yielding.

**deferential** *adj* civil, complaisant, considerate, courteous, dutiful, ingratiating, morigerous, obedient, obeisant, obsequious, polite, regardful, respectful, reverential, submissive.

*antonyms* arrogant, immodest.

**deferment** *n* adjournment, deferral, delay, moratorium, postponement, procrastination, putting off, stay, suspension.

**defiance** *n* challenge, confrontation, contempt, contumacy, disobedience, disregard, insolence, insubordination, obstinacy, opposition, provocation, rebelliousness, recalcitrance, spite.

*antonyms* acquiescence, submissiveness.

**defiant** *adj* aggressive, audacious, bold, challenging, contumacious, daring, disobedient, insolent, insubordinate, intransigent, mutinous, obstinate, provocative, rebellious, recalcitrant, refractory, truculent, unco-operative.

*antonyms* acquiescent, submissive.

**deficiency** *n* absence, dearth, defalcation, defect, deficit, demerit, failing, fault, flaw, frailty, imperfection, inadequacy, insufficiency, lack, paucity, scantiness, scarcity, shortage, shortcoming, want, wantage, weakness.

*antonym* superfluity.

**deficient** *adj* defectible, defective, exiguous, faulty, flawed, impaired, imperfect, inadequate, incomplete, inferior, insufficient, lacking, meagre, scanty, scarce, short, skimpy, unsatisfactory, wanting, weak.

*antonyms* excessive, superfluous.

**deficit** *n* arrears, defalcation, default, deficiency, lack, loss, shortage, shortfall.

*antonym* excess.

**defile**[1] *v* abuse, befoul, besmirch, contaminate, corrupt, debase, deflower, defoul, degrade, desecrate, dirty, disgrace, dishonour, inquinate, make foul, molest, pollute, profane, rape, ravish, seduce, smear, soil, stain, sully, taint, tarnish, violate, vitiate.

*antonym* cleanse.

**defile**[2] *n* gorge, gulch, gully, pass, passage, ravine.

**defiled** *adj* besmirched, desecrated, dishonoured, impure, maculate, polluted, profaned, ravished, spoilt, sullied, tainted, unclean.

*antonyms* clean, cleansed, pure.

**definable** *adj* ascertainable, definite, describable, determinable, explicable, perceptible, specific.

*antonym* indefinable.

**define** *v* bound, characterise, circumscribe, delimit, delimitate, delineate, demarcate, describe, designate, detail, determine, explain, expound, interpret, limit, mark out, outline, specify, spell out.

**definite** *adj* assured, certain, clear, clear-cut, decided, determined, exact, explicit, express, fixed, guaranteed, marked, obvious, particular, positive, precise, settled, specific, substantive, sure.

*antonyms* indefinite, vague.

**definitely** *adv* absolutely, beyond doubt, categorically, certainly, clearly, decidedly, doubtless, doubtlessly, easily, finally, indeed, indubitably, obviously, plainly, positively, surely, undeniably, unequivocally, unmistakably, unquestionably, without doubt, without fail.

**definition**[1] *n* clarification, delimitation, delineation, demarcation, description, determination, elucidation, explanation, exposition, interpretation, outlining, settling.

**definition**[2] *n* clarity, clearness, contrast, distinctness, focus, precision, sharpness.

**definitive** *adj* absolute, authoritative, complete, conclusive, correct, decisive, exact, exhaustive, final, perfect, reliable, standard, ultimate.

*antonym* interim.

**deflate**[1] *v* chasten, collapse, contract, dash, debunk, disconcert, dispirit, empty, exhaust, flatten, humble, humiliate, mortify, press, puncture, put down, shrink, squash, squeeze, void.

*antonym* inflate.

**deflate**[2] *v* decrease, depreciate, depress, devalue, diminish, lessen, lower, reduce.

*antonym* increase.

**deflect** *v* avert, bend, deviate, diverge, glance off, ricochet, shy, sidetrack, slew, swerve, turn, turn aside, twist, veer, wind.

**deflection** *n* aberration, bend, bending, declination, deviation, divergence, drift, refraction, swerve, turning, veer.

**deflower** *v* assault, defile, deflorate, desecrate, despoil, force, harm, mar, molest, rape, ravish, ruin, seduce, spoil, violate.

**deflowering** *n* defloration, green gown, rape, ravishment, violation.

**deform** *v* corrupt, disfigure, distort, mangle, mar, pervert, ruin, spoil, twist, warp.

**deformation** *n* bend, curve, diastrophism, distortion, malformation, twist, warp.

**deformed** *adj* bent, blemished, buckled, contorted, corrupted, crippled, crooked, defaced, depraved, disfigured, distorted, gnarled, maimed, malformed, mangled, marred, misbegotten, misborn, miscreate(d), misshapen, mutilated, perverted, ruined, spoilt, twisted, warped.

**deformity** *n* abnormality, corruption, defect, depravity, disfigurement, distortion, dysmelia, irregularity, malformation, misfeature, misproportion, misshape, misshapenness, ugliness.

**defraud** *v* beguile, bilk, cheat, con, cozen, deceive, delude, diddle, do, dupe, embezzle, fleece, gull, gyp, outwit, rip off, rob, rock, sting, swindle, trick.

**defray** *v* clear, cover, discharge, foot, meet, pay, refund, repay, settle.

*antonym* incur.

**defrayal** *n* clearance, defrayment, discharge, payment, refund, settlement.

*antonym* incurrence.

**deft** *adj* able, adept, adroit, agile, clever, dexterous, expert, feat, habile, handy, neat, nifty, nimble, proficient, skilful.

*antonym* clumsy.

**defunct** *adj* dead, deceased, departed, expired, extinct, gone, inoperative, invalid, kaput, non-existent, obsolete, passe.

*antonyms* alive, live, operative.

**defy** *v* baffle, beard, beat, brave, challenge, confront, contemn, dare, defeat, despise, disregard, elude, face, flout, foil, frustrate, outdare, provoke, repel, repulse, resist, scorn, slight, spurn, thwart, withstand.

*antonyms* flinch, quail, yield.

**degeneracy** *n* corruption, debasement, decadence, decay, decline, decrease, degradation, depravation, depravity, deterioration, dissoluteness, effeteness, falling-off, immorality, inferiority, lapsing, meanness, poorness, turpitude.

*antonyms* morality, uprightness.

**degenerate** *adj* base, corrupt, debased, debauched, decadent, degenerated, degraded, depraved, deteriorated, dissolute, effete, fallen, immoral, low, mean, perverted.

*antonyms* upright, virtuous.

*v* age, decay, decline, decrease, deteriorate, fall off, lapse, regress, retrogress, rot, sink, slip, worsen.

*antonym* improve.

**degeneration** *n* debasement, decline, degeneracy, descent, deterioration, dissipation, dissolution, falling-off, lapse, lapsing, regression, retrogress, retrogression.

*antonyms* improvement, uprightness, virtue.

**degradation** *n* abasement, debasedness, debasement, decadence, decline, degeneracy, degeneration, demission, demotion, derogation, destitution, deterioration, discredit, disgrace, dishonour, downgrading, humiliation, ignominy, mortification, perversion, shame.

*antonyms* enhancement, virtue.

**degrade** *v* abase, adulterate, break, brutalise, cashier, cheapen, corrupt, debase, declass, demean, demote, depose, deprive, deteriorate, discredit, disennoble, disgrace, disgrade, dishonour, disrank, disrate, downgrade, embase, humble, humiliate, impair, injure, lower, pervert, shame, unfrock, ungown, vitiate, weaken.

*antonyms* enhance, improve.

**degraded** *adj* abandoned, abased, base, corrupt, debased, debauched, decadent, declasse, depraved, despicable, disgraced, disreputable, dissolute, low, mean, profligate, sordid, vicious, vile.

*antonyms* moral, upright.

**degrading** *adj* base, cheapening, contemptible, debasing, demeaning, disgraceful, dishonourable, humiliating, ignoble, infra dig, lowering, shameful, undignified, unworthy.

*antonym* enhancing.

**degree** *n* calibre, class, division, doctorate, extent, gradation, grade, intensity, interval, level, limit, mark, masterate, measure, notch, order, point, position, proportion, quality, quantity, range, rank, rate, ratio, run, scale, scope, severity, stage, standard, standing, station, status, step, unit.

**dehydrate** *v* desiccate, drain, dry out, dry up, effloresce, evaporate, exsiccate, parch.

**deification** *n* apotheosis, divinification, divinisation, elevation, ennoblement, exaltation, glorification, idolisation.

**deify** *v* apotheosise, divinify, divinise, elevate, ennoble, enthrone, exalt, extol, glorify, idealise, idolise, immortalise, venerate, worship.

**deign** *v* condescend, consent, demean oneself, lower oneself, stoop, vouchsafe.

**deity** *n* Allah, demigod, demigoddess, deva, divinity, god, goddess, godhead, godhood, idol, immortal, Jehovah, kami, power.

**deject** *v* cast down, crush, dampen, daunt, demoralise, depress, discourage, dishearten, dismay, dispirit, sadden.

**dejected** *adj* abattu, alamort, blue, cast down, crestfallen, depressed, despondent, disconsolate, disheartened, dismal, doleful, down, downcast, downhearted, gloomy, glum, jaw-fallen, low, low-spirited, melancholy, miserable, morose, sad, spiritless, woebegone, wretched.

*antonyms* bright, happy, high-spirited.

**dejection** *n* blues, depression, despair, despondency, disconsolateness, disconsolation, doldrums, downheartedness, dumps, gloom, gloominess, low spirits, melancholy, sadness, sorrow, unhappiness.

*antonyms* happiness, high spirits.

**delay** *v* arrest, bog down, check, dawdle, defer, detain, dilly-dally, drag, halt, hinder, hold back, hold over, hold up, impede, lag, linger, loiter, obstruct, play for time, postpone, procrastinate, prolong, protract, put off, retard, set back, shelve, stall, stave off, stop, suspend, table, tarry, temporise.

*antonyms* accelerate, expedite, hurry.

*n* ambage, check, cunctation, dawdling, deferment, detention, dilly-dallying, hindrance, hold-up, impediment, interruption, interval, lingering, loitering, obstruction, postponement, procrastination, setback, stay, stoppage, suspension, tarrying, wait.

*antonyms* hastening, hurry.

**delaying** *adj* cunctatious, cunctative, cunctatory, filibusterous, retardative, retardatory.

*antonyms* advancing, expediting.

**delectable** *adj* adorable, agreeable, ambrosial, ambrosian, appetising, charming, dainty, delicious, delightful, enjoyable, enticing, flavoursome, gratifying, inviting, luscious, lush, palatable, pleasant, pleasurable, satisfying, scrumptious, tasty, toothsome, yummy.

*antonyms* horrid, unpleasant.

**delectation** *n* amusement, comfort, contentment, delight, diversion, enjoyment, entertainment, gratification, happiness, pleasure, refreshment, relish, satisfaction.

*antonym* distaste.

**delegate** *n* agent, ambassador, commissioner, deputy, envoy, legate, messenger, nuncio, representative.

*v* accredit, appoint, assign, authorise, charge, commission, consign, depute, designate, devolve, empower, entrust, give, hand over, mandate, name, nominate, pass on, relegate, transfer.

**delegated** *adj* assigned, devolved, relegated, vicarate, vicarial, vicariate.

**delegation** *n* commission, contingent, deputation, embassy, legation, mission.

**delete** *v* blot out, blue-pencil, cancel, cross out, dele, edit, edit out, efface, erase, expunge, obliterate, remove, rub out, strike, strike out.

*antonym* add in.

**deleterious** *adj* bad, damaging, destructive, detrimental, harmful, hurtful, injurious, noxious, pernicious, prejudicial, ruinous.

*antonyms* enhancing, helpful.

**deliberate** *v* cogitate, consider, consult, debate, discuss, meditate, mull over, ponder, reflect, ruminate, think, weigh.

*adj* advised, calculated, careful, cautious, circumspect, conscious, considered, designed, heedful, intentional, measured, methodical, planned, ponderous, prearranged, premeditated, prudent, purposeful, slow, studied, thoughtful, unhurried, volitive, voulu, wary, wilful, willed, witting.

*antonyms* chance, unintentional.

**deliberately** *adv* by design, calculatingly, consciously, determinedly, emphatically, in cold blood, intentionally, knowingly, on purpose, pointedly, resolutely, wilfully, with malice aforethought, wittingly.

*antonym* unintentionally.

**deliberation** *n* calculation, canniness, care, carefulness, caution, circumspection, cogitation, conference, consideration, consultation, coolness, debate, discussion, forethought, meditation, prudence, purpose, reflection, rumination, speculation, study, thought, wariness.

**delicacy** *n* accuracy, bonne bouche, daintiness, dainty, discrimination, elegance, exquisiteness, fastidiousness, fineness, finesse, lightness, luxury, niceness, nicety, precision, purity, refinement, relish, savoury, sensibility, sensitiveness, sensitivity, subtlety, sweetmeat, tact, taste, titbit, treat.

*antonyms* indelicacy, tactlessness.

**delicate** *adj* accurate, ailing, careful, choice, considerate, critical, dainty, debilitated, deft, delicious, detailed, diaphanous, difficult, diplomatic, discreet, discriminating, eggshell, elegant, elfin, exquisite, faint, fastidious, fine, flimsy, fragile, frail, friand(e), gauzy, graceful, hazardous, kid-glove, minikin, minute, muted, nesh, pastel, precarious, precise, prudish, pure, refined, risky, savoury, scrupulous, sensible, sensitive, sickly, skilled, slender, slight, soft, softly-softly, squeamish, sticky, subdued, subtle, tactful, tender, ticklish, touchy, weak.

*antonyms* harsh, imprecise, strong.

**delicious** *adj* agreeable, ambrosial, ambrosian, appetising, charming, choice, dainty, delectable, delightful, enjoyable, entertaining, exquisite, flavoursome, goluptious, lip-smacking, luscious, mouthwatering, nectareous, palatable, pleasant, pleasing, savoury, scrummy, scrumptious, tasty, toothsome, yummy.

*antonym* unpleasant.

**delight** *n* bliss, ecstasy, enjoyment, felicity, gladness, gratification, happiness, heaven, joy, jubilation, pleasure, rapture, transport.

*antonyms* dismay, displeasure.

*v* amuse, charm, cheer, divert, enchant, gladden, gratify, please, ravish, rejoice, satisfy, thrill, tickle.

*antonyms* dismay, displease.

**delight in** appreciate, enjoy, gloat over, glory in, indulge in, like, love, relish, revel in, savour, take pride in.

**delighted** *adj* captivated, charmed, cock-a-hoop, ecstatic, elated, enchanted, gladdened, happy, joyous, jubilant, overjoyed, pleased, pleased as Punch, thrilled.

*antonyms* dismayed, displeased.

**delightful** *adj* agreeable, amusing, captivating, charming, congenial, delectable, delightsome, enchanting, engaging, enjoyable, entertaining, fascinating, fetching, gratifying, heavenly, pleasant, pleasing, pleasurable, rapturous, ravishing, scrummy, scrumptious, sweet, thrilling, wizard.

*antonym* horrible.

**delimit** *v* bound, define, demarcate, determine, establish, fix, mark.

**delineate** *v* characterise, chart, depict, describe, design, draw, figure, limn, outline, paint, picture, portray, render, represent, sketch, trace.

**delineation** *n* account, characterisation, chart, depiction, description, design, diagram, drawing, outline, picture, portrait, portrayal, representation, sketch, tracing.

**delinquency** *n* crime, criminality, fault, law-breaking, misbehaviour, misconduct, misdeed, misdemeanour, offence, wrong-doing.

**delinquent** *n* criminal, culprit, defaulter, hooligan, law-breaker, malefactor, miscreant, offender, rough, tough, wrong-doer, young offender.

*adj* careless, culpable, guilty, neglectful, negligent, remiss.

*antonyms* blameless, careful.

**delirious** *adj* bacchic, beside oneself, corybantic, crazy, demented, deranged, ecstatic, excited, frantic, frenzied, hysterical, incoherent, insane, light-headed, mad, maenadic, raving, unhinged, wild.

*antonym* sane.

**delirium** *n* derangement, ecstasy, fever, frenzy, fury, hallucination, hysteria, insanity, jimjams, lunacy, madness, passion, rage, raving.

**deliver** *v* acquit, administer, aim, announce, bear, bring, carry, cart, cede, commit, convey, deal, declare, direct, discharge, dispense, distribute, emancipate, feed, free, give, give forth, give up, grant, hand over, inflict, launch, liberate, loose, make over, pass, present, proclaim, pronounce, publish, ransom, read, redeem, release, relinquish, rescue, resign, save, strike, supply, surrender, throw, transfer, transport, turn over, utter, yield.

**deliverance** *n* emancipation, escape, extrication, liberation, ransom, redemption, release, rescue, salvation.

**delivery¹** *n* consignment, conveyance, dispatch, distribution, shipment, surrender, transfer, transmission, transmittal, transport.

**delivery²** *n* articulation, elocution, enunciation, intonation, presentation, speech, utterance.

**delivery³** *n* accouchement, childbirth, confinement, labour, parturition, travail.

**dell** *n* dargle, dean, dimble, dingle, hollow, vale, valley.

**delude** *v* bamboozle, beguile, cheat, con, cozen, deceive, dupe, fool, gull, hoax, hoodwink, impose on, misguide, misinform, mislead, snow, take in, trick.

**deluge** *n* avalanche, barrage, cataclysm, downpour, flood, hail, inundation, rush, spate, torrent.

*v* bury, douse, drench, drown, engulf, flood, inundate, overload, overrun, overwhelm, soak, submerge, swamp.

**delusion** *n* deception, error, fallacy, fancy, fata Morgana, hallucination, illusion, mirage, misapprehension, misbelief, misconception, mistake, phantasm.

**delve** *v* burrow, dig into, examine, explore, investigate, poke, probe, ransack, research, root, rummage, search.

**demagogue** *n* agitator, Boanerges, firebrand, haranguer, mob-orator, orator, rabble-rouser, tub-thumper.

**demand** *v* ask, call for, challenge, claim, exact, expect, inquire, insist on, interrogate, involve, necessitate, need, order, question, request, require, take, want.

*antonyms* cede, supply.

*n* bidding, call, charge, claim, desire, inquiry, interrogation, necessity, need, order, question, request, requirement, requisition, want.

*antonym* supply.

**demanding** *adj* back-breaking, challenging, clamorous, difficult, exacting, exhausting, exigent, fatiguing, hard, imperious, importunate, insistent, nagging, pressing, taxing, tough, trying, urgent, wearing.

*antonyms* easy, easy-going, undemanding.

**demarcate**  *v*  define, delimit, determine, differentiate, distinguish, establish, fix, mark, mark out, separate.

**demarcation** *n* bound, boundary, bourn, confine, delimitation, differentiation, distinction, division, enclosure, limit, line, margin, pale, separation.

**demean** *v* abase, condescend, debase, degrade, deign, descend, humble, lower, stoop.

*antonym* enhance.

**demeanour** *n* air, bearing, behaviour, carriage, comportment, conduct, deportment, manner, mien, port.

**demented** *adj* crazed, crazy, deranged, distracted, distraught, dotty, foolish, frenzied, idiotic, insane, lunatic, mad, maenadic, maniacal, manic, non compos mentis, nutty, unbalanced, unhinged.

*antonym* sane.

**demigod** *n* demigoddess, kami, power, spirit.

**demise¹** *n* collapse, death, decease, departure, dissolution, downfall, end, expiration, failure, fall, passing, ruin, termination.

**demise²** *n* alienation, conveyance, inheritance, transfer, transmission.

*v* bequeath, convey, grant, leave, transfer, will.

**democracy** *n* autonomy, commonwealth, populism, republic, self-government.

**democratic** *adj* autonomous, egalitarian, popular, populist, representative, republican, self-governing.

**demolish** *v* annihilate, bulldoze, consume, defeat, delapidate, destroy, devour, dismantle, down, eat, flatten, gobble, gulp, guzzle, knock down, level, overthrow, overturn, pull down, pulverize, raze, ruin, tear down, unbuild, undo, wreck.

*antonym* build up.

**demolition** *n* bulldozing, destruction, dismantling, levelling, razing, wrecking.

**demon¹** *n* afrit, daemon, daimon, devil, evil spirit, fallen angel, fiend, genius, goblin, guardian spirit, incubus, monster, numen, rakshas, rakshasa, succubus, villain, warlock.

**demon²** *n* ace, addict, dab hand, fanatic, fiend, master, pastmaster, wizard.

**demoniac** *adj* crazed, d(a)emonic, demoniacal, devilish, diabolic, diabolical, fiendish, frantic, frenetic, frenzied, furious, hectic, hellish, infernal, mad, maniacal, manic, possessed, satanic.

**demonstrable** *adj* arguable, attestable, axiomatic, certain, clear, evident, evincible, incontrovertible, indubitable, irrefutable, obvious, palpable, positive, provable, self-evident, substantiable, undeniable, unmistakable, verifiable.

*antonyms* untestable, unverifiable.

**demonstrate¹** *v* describe, display, establish, evidence, evince, exhibit, explain, expound, illustrate, indicate, manifest, prove, show, substantiate, teach, testify to.

**demonstrate²** *v* march, parade, picket, protest, rally, sit in.

**demonstration¹** *n* affirmation, confirmation, deixis, description, display, evidence, exhibition, explanation, exposition, expression, illustration, manifestation, presentation, proof, substantiation, test, testimony, trial, validation.

**demonstration²** *v* demo, march, parade, picket, protest, rally, sit-in, work-in.

**demonstrative** *adj* affectionate, deictic, effusive, emotional, endeictic, evincive, expansive, explanatory, expository, expressive, illustrative, indicative, loving, open, symptomatic, unreserved, unrestrained.

*antonyms* cold, undemonstrative.

**demoralisation** *n* agitation, corruption, crushing, debasement, dejection, depravation, depression, despondency, devitalisation, discomfiture, enervation, lowering, panic, perturbation, perversion, trepidation, unmanning, vitiation, weakening.

*antonym* encouragement.

**demoralise** *v* corrupt, cripple, crush, daunt, debase, debauch, deject, deprave, depress, disconcert, discourage, dishearten, dispirit, enfeeble, lower, panic, pervert, rattle, sap, shake, undermine, unnerve, vitiate, weaken.

*antonym* encourage.

**demoralised** *adj* bad, base, broken, corrupt, crushed, degenerate, dejected, depraved, depressed, despondent, discouraged, disheartened, dispirited, dissolute, downcast, immoral, low, reprobate, sinful, subdued, unmanned, unnerved, weakened, wicked.

*antonyms* encouraged, heartened.

**demote** *v* declass, degrade, disrate, downgrade, reduce, relegate.

*antonyms* promote, upgrade.

**demotic** *adj* enchorial, enchoric, popular, vernacular, vulgar.

**demur** *v* balk, cavil, disagree, dispute, dissent, doubt, hesitate, object, pause, protest, refuse, take exception, waver.

*n* arrière pensee, compunction, demurral, demurrer, dissent, hesitation, misgiving, objection, protest, qualm, reservation, scruple.

**demure** *adj* coy, decorous, diffident, grave, maidenly, modest, priggish, prim, prissy, prudish, reserved, reticent, retiring, sedate, shy, sober, staid, strait-laced.

*antonym* forward.

**den** *n* cave, cavern, cloister, cubby-hole, earth, haunt, hide-away, hide-out, hole, lair, retreat, sanctuary, sanctum, set(t), shelter, study.

**denial** *n* abjuration, abnegation, contradiction, denegation, disaffirmance, disaffirmation, disavowal, disclaimer, dismissal, dissent, gainsay, negation, prohibition, rebuff, refusal, rejection, renunciation, repudiation, repulse, retraction, veto.

**denigrate** v abuse, assail, belittle, besmirch, blacken, calumniate, criticise, decry, defame, disparage, impugn, malign, revile, run down, slander, vilify, vilipend.

*antonym* praise.

**denigration** n aspersion, backbiting, decrial, defamation, derogation, detraction, disparagement, mud-slinging, obloquy, scandal, scurrility, slander, vilification.

*antonym* praise.

**denizen** n citizen, dweller, habitant, habitue, inhabitant, occupant, resident.

**denominate** v baptise, call, christen, designate, dub, entitle, name, phrase, style, term, title.

**denomination** n appellation, belief, body, category, class, classification, communion, creed, designation, grade, group, label, name, persuasion, religion, school, sect, size, style, taxon, term, title, unit, value.

**denote** v betoken, designate, express, imply, import, indicate, mark, mean, show, signify, stand for, symbolise, typify.

**denouement** n climax, close, conclusion, culmination, finale, finish, outcome, pay-off, resolution, solution, termination, upshot.

**denounce** v accuse, anathematise, arraign, assail, attack, brand, castigate, censure, condemn, declaim against, decry, denunciate, fulminate, hereticate, impugn, inveigh against, proscribe, revile, stigmatise, vilify, vilipend.

*antonym* praise.

**dense** adj blockish, close, close-knit, compact, compressed, condensed, crass, crowded, dull, heavy, impenetrable, jam-packed, obtuse, opaque, packed, slow, slow-witted, solid, stolid, stupid, substantial, thick, thickset, thick-witted.

*antonyms* clever, sparse.

**denseness** n crassness, density, dullness, obtuseness, slowness, stolidity, stupidity, thickness.

*antonym* acuteness.

**density** n body, bulk, closeness, compactness, consistency, crassitude, denseness, impenetrability, mass, solidity, solidness, spissitude, thickness, tightness.

*antonym* sparseness.

**dent** n bang, chip, concavity, crater, depression, dimple, dint, dip, dunt, hollow, impression, indentation, pit.

v depress, dint, gouge, indent, push in.

**dentures** n false teeth, wallies.

**denude** v bare, defoliate, deforest, divest, expose, strip, uncover.

*antonym* cover.

**denunciation** n accusation, assailment, castigation, censure, condemnation, criticism, decrial, decrying, denouncement, fulmination, incrimination, invective, obloquy, stigmatisation.

*antonyms* compliment, praise.

**denunciatory** adj accusatory, censorious, comminatory, condemnatory, decrying, execrative, fulminatory, incriminatory, recriminatory, reproachful.

*antonym* complimentary.

**deny** v abjure, begrudge, contradict, decline, disaffirm, disagree with, disallow, disavow, discard, disclaim, disown, disprove, forbid, gainsay, negative, oppose, rebuff, recant, refuse, refute, reject, renounce, repudiate, revoke, traverse, turn down, veto, withhold.

*antonyms* admit, allow.

**deodorant** n air-freshener, antiperspirant, deodoriser, disinfectant, fumigant, fumigator.

**deodorise** v aerate, disinfect, freshen, fumigate, purify, refresh, sweeten, ventilate.

**depart** v absent oneself, decamp, deviate, differ, digress, disappear, diverge, escape, exit, go, leave, levant, make off, migrate, mizzle, quit, remove, retire, retreat, set forth, stray, swerve, take one's leave, toddle, vanish, vary, veer, withdraw.

*antonyms* arrive, keep to.

**departed** adj dead, deceased, defunct, expired, late.

**department** n area, branch, bureau, district, division, domain, field, function, line, line of country, office, province, realm, region, responsibility, section, sector, speciality, sphere, station, subdivision, unit.

**departure** n abandonment, branching, branching out, change, decession, deviation, difference, digression, divergence, exit, exodus, going, innovation, leave-taking, leaving, lucky, novelty, removal, retirement, shift, variation, veering, withdrawal.

*antonym* arrival.

**depend on** anticipate, bank on, build upon, calculate on, count on, expect, hang on, hinge on, lean on, reckon on, rely upon, rest on, revolve around, trust in, turn to.

**dependable** adj certain, conscientious, faithful, gilt-edged, honest, reliable, responsible, steady, sure, trustworthy, trusty, unfailing.

*antonyms* undependable, unreliable.

**dependant** n child, client, galloglass, hanger-on, henchman, minion, minor, protege, relative, retainer, subordinate, vassal.

**dependence** n addiction, assurance, attachment, belief, confidence, craving, dependency, expectation, faith, helplessness, hope, need, reliance, subordination, subservience, trust, vassalage, vulnerability, weakness.

*antonym* independence.

**dependent** adj adjective, conditional, contingent, defenceless, depending, determined by, feudal, helpless, immature, liable to, relative, reliant, relying on, subject, subject to, subordinate, tributary, vulnerable, weak.

*antonym* independent.

**depict** *v* caricature, characterise, delineate, describe, detail, draw, illustrate, limn, narrate, outline, paint, picture, portray, render, reproduce, sculpt, sketch, trace.

**depiction** *n* caricature, delineation, description, drawing, illustration, image, likeness, outline, picture, portrayal, representation, sketch.

**depilation** *n* electrolysis, epilation, hair-removing.

**deplete** *v* attenuate, bankrupt, consume, decrease, drain, empty, evacuate, exhaust, expend, impoverish, lessen, reduce, use up.

**depleted** *adj* attenuated, consumed, decreased, depreciated, drained, emptied, exhausted, lessened, reduced, spent, wasted, weakened, worn out.

*antonyms* augmented, increased.

**depletion** *n* attenuation, consumption, decimation, decrease, deficiency, diminution, dwindling, exhaustion, expenditure, lessening, lowering, reduction, shrinkage.

*antonyms* increase, supply.

**deplorable** *adj* blameworthy, calamitous, dire, disastrous, disgraceful, dishonourable, disreputable, distressing, execrable, grievous, heartbreaking, lamentable, melancholy, miserable, opprobrious, pitiable, regrettable, reprehensible, sad, scandalous, shameful, unfortunate, wretched.

*antonyms* excellent, praiseworthy.

**deplore** *v* abhor, bemoan, bewail, censure, condemn, denounce, deprecate, grieve for, lament, mourn, regret, repent of, rue.

*antonym* praise.

**deploy** *v* arrange, darraign, dispose, distribute, embattle, extend, position, station, use, utilise.

**depopulate** *v* dispeople, empty, unpeople.

**deport**[1] *v* banish, exile, expatriate, expel, extradite, ostracise, oust.

**deport**[2] *v* acquit, act, bear, behave, carry, comport, conduct, hold, manage.

**deportation** *n* banishment, eviction, exile, expatriation, expulsion, extradition, ostracism, transportation.

**deportment** *n* air, appearance, aspect, bearing, behaviour, carriage, cast, comportment, conduct, demeanour, etiquette, manner, mien, pose, posture, stance.

**depose** *v* break, cashier, decrown, degrade, demote, dethrone, discrown, disestablish, dismiss, displace, downgrade, oust, topple, unking.

**deposit**[1] *v* drop, dump, lay, locate, park, place, precipitate, put, settle, sit.

*n* accumulation, alluvium, deposition, dregs, hypostasis, lees, precipitate, sediment, silt.

**deposit**[2] *v* amass, bank, consign, depone, entrust, file, hoard, lodge, reposit, save, store.

*n* bailment, down payment, instalment, money, part payment, pledge, retainer, security, stake, warranty.

**deposition**[1] *n* dethronement, dismissal, displacement, ousting, removal, toppling.

**deposition**[2] *n* affidavit, declaration, denunciation, evidence, information, statement, testimony.

**depository** *n* bond, depot, dump, godown, repository, store, storehouse, warehouse.

**depot** *n* arsenal, bond, depository, dump, garage, receiving-house, repository, station, storehouse, terminus, warehouse.

**deprave** *v* brutalise, contaminate, corrupt, debase, debauch, degrade, demoralise, infect, pervert, seduce, subvert, vitiate.

*antonym* improve.

**depraved** *adj* abandoned, base, corrupt, debased, debauched, degenerate, degraded, dissolute, evil, immoral, lewd, libertine, licentious, perverted, profligate, reprobate, shameless, sinful, vicious, vile, wicked.

*antonym* upright.

**depravity** *n* baseness, contamination, corruption, criminality, debasement, debauchery, degeneracy, degradation, depravation, depravedness, depravement, dissoluteness, evil, immorality, iniquity, lewdness, libertinage, licence, perversion, profligacy, reprobacy, sinfulness, turpitude, vice, viciousness, vileness, wickedness.

*antonym* uprightness.

**deprecate** *v* condemn, deplore, disapprove of, disparage, object to, protest at, reject.

*antonyms* approve, commend.

**deprecation** *n* condemnation, deploration, disapproval, dismissal, disparagement, protestation, rejection.

*antonyms* commendation, encouragement.

**deprecatory** *adj* apologetic, censorious, condemnatory, disapproving, dismissive, protesting, regretful, reproachful.

*antonyms* commendatory, encouraging.

**depreciate** *v* belittle, decrease, decry, deflate, denigrate, deride, derogate, detract, devaluate, devalue, disparage, downgrade, drop, fall, lessen, lower, minimise, misprise, reduce, ridicule, scorn, slump, traduce, underestimate, underrate, undervalue.

*antonyms* appreciate, overrate, praise.

**depreciation** *n* belittlement, deflation, depression, derogation, detraction, devaluation, disparagement, downgrading, drop, fall, misprising, misprision, pejoration, slump.

*antonyms* appreciation, exaggeration, praise.

**depredation** *n* denudation, desolation, despoiling, despoliation, destruction, devastation, harrying, laying waste, looting, marauding, pillage, plunder, raiding, ransacking, rapine, ravaging, ravin, robbery, spoliation, stripping, theft.

**depress** *v* burden, cheapen, chill, damp, daunt, debilitate, deject, depreciate, devaluate, devalue, devitalise, diminish, discourage, dishearten, dispirit, downgrade, drain, enervate, engloom, exhaust, flatten, hip, impair, lessen, level, lower, oppress, overburden, press, reduce, sadden, sap, squash, tire, undermine, upset, weaken, weary.

*antonym* cheer.

**depressant** *n* calmant, calmative, downer, relaxant, sedative, tranquilliser.

*antonym* stimulant.

**depressed¹** *adj* a peg too low, accable, blue, cast down, crestfallen, debilitated, dejected, deprived, despondent, desponding, destitute, disadvantaged, discouraged, disheartened, dispirited, distressed, down, down-beat, downcast, downhearted, exanimate, fed up, glum, jaw-fallen, low, low-spirited, melancholy, miserable, Mondayish, moody, morose, needy, pessimistic, poor, sad, unhappy.

*antonym* cheerful.

**depressed²** *adj* concave, dented, dinted, dished, hollow, indented, invaginated, recessed, sunken.

*antonyms* convex, prominent, protuberant.

**depressing** *adj* black, bleak, cheerless, daunting, dejecting, discouraging, disheartening, dismal, dispiriting, distressing, dreary, gloomy, grey, heartbreaking, hopeless, lugubrious, melancholy, Mondayish, sad, saddening, sombre.

*antonym* encouraging.

**depression¹** *n* blues, cafard, decline, dejection, demission, despair, despondency, doldrums, dolefulness, downheartedness, dullness, dumps, examination, gloominess, glumness, hard times, heart-heaviness, hopelessness, inactivity, low spirits, lowness, mal du siècle, megrims, melancholia, melancholy, panophobia, recession, sadness, slump, stagnation, vapours.

*antonyms* cheerfulness, prosperity.

**depression²** *n* basin, bowl, cavity, concavity, dent, dimple, dint, dip, dish, excavation, fossa, fossula, fovea, foveola, hollow, hollowness, impression, indentation, pit, sag, sink, umbilicus, valley.

*antonyms* convexity, prominence, protuberance.

**deprivation** *n* degradation, denial, denudation, deprival, despoliation, destitution, disadvantage, dispossession, distress, divestment, expropriation, hardship, need, privation, removal, want, withdrawal, withholding.

*antonym* bestowal.

**deprive** *v* amerce, bereave, denude, deny, despoil, dispossess, divest, expropriate, mulct, rob, starve, strip.

*antonym* bestow.

**deprived** *adj* benighted, bereft, denuded, depressed, destitute, disadvantaged, forlorn, impoverished, lacking, necessitous, needy, poor.

*antonyms* fortunate, prosperous.

**depth** *n* abstruseness, abysm, abyss, complexity, deepness, discernment, drop, exhaustiveness, extent, gulf, insight, intensity, measure, obscurity, penetration, pit, profoundness, profundity, reconditeness, richness, sagacity, shrewdness, strength, thoroughness, wisdom.

**deputation** *n* appointment, assignment, commission, delegates, delegation, deputies, deputing, designation, embassy, legation, mission, nomination, representatives.

**depute** *v* accredit, appoint, authorise, charge, commission, delegate, empower, entrust, mandate, nominate.

**deputise** *n* commission, delegate, depute, double, replace, represent, stand in for, substitute, understudy.

**deputy** *n* agent, alternate, ambassador, commis, commissary, commissioner, delegate, henchman, legate, lieutenant, nuncio, proxy, representative, second-in-command, substitute, suffragan, surrogate, vicar, vicegerent.

*adj* assistant, coadjutor, depute, subordinate, suffragan.

**derange** *v* confound, confuse, craze, dement, disarrange, disarray, discompose, disconcert, disorder, displace, disturb, drive crazy, madden, ruffle, unbalance, unhinge, unsettle, upset.

**deranged** *adj* aberrant, batty, berserk, brainsick, confused, crazed, crazy, delirious, demented, disarranged, disordered, distracted, distraught, disturbed, frantic, frenzied, insane, irrational, loony, lunatic, mad, maddened, nutty, unbalanced, unhinged.

*antonyms* calm, sane.

**derangement** *n* aberration, agitation, alienation, confusion, delirium, dementia, disarrangement, disarray, disorder, distraction, disturbance, frenzy, hallucination, insanity, irregularity, jumble, lunacy, madness, mania, muddle.

*antonyms* order, sanity.

**derelict** *adj* abandoned, deserted, desolate, dilapidated, discarded, forlorn, forsaken, neglected, ruined.

*n* dosser, down-and-out, drifter, hobo, outcast, toe-rag, tramp, vagrant, wastrel.

**dereliction** *n* abandonment, abdication, apostasy, betrayal, delinquency, desertion, evasion, failure, faithlessness, fault, forsaking, neglect, negligence, relinquishment, remissness, renegation, renunciation.

*antonyms* devotion, faithfulness, fulfilment.

**deride** *v* belittle, chiack, condemn, detract, disdain, disparage, flout, gibe, insult, jeer, knock, mock, pillory, pooh-pooh, rail at, ridicule, satirise, scoff, scorn, sneer, taunt, vilipend.

*antonym* praise.

**derision** *n* chiack, contempt, contumely, dicacity, disdain, disparagement, disrespect, insult, irrision, laughter, mockery, raillery, ridicule, satire, scoffing, scorn, sneering.

*antonym* praise.

**derisive** *adj* contemptuous, disdainful, disrespectful, irreverent, irrisory, jeering, mocking, scornful, taunting.

*antonyms* appreciative, flattering.

**derisory** *adj* absurd, contemptible, insulting, laughable, ludicrous, mockable, outrageous, paltry, preposterous, ridiculous, risible.

**derivation** n acquisition, ancestry, basis, beginning, deduction, descent, etymology, extraction, foundation, genealogy, inference, origin, root, source.

**derivative** adj acquired, borrowed, copied, cribbed, daughter, derived, hackneyed, imitative, inferred, obtained, plagiarised, plagiaristic, procured, regurgitated, rehashed, secondary, second-hand, transmitted, trite, unadventurous, uninventive, unoriginal.

n branch, by-product, derivation, descendant, development, formative, offshoot, outgrowth, product, refinement, spin-off.

**derive** v acquire, arise, borrow, collect, crib, deduce, descend, develop, draw, elicit, emanate, extract, flow, follow, gain, gather, get, glean, grow, infer, issue, lift, obtain, originate, proceed, procure, receive, spring, stem, trace.

**derogate** v belittle, decry, defame, denigrate, depreciate, detract, devalue, diminish, disparage, insult, lessen, misprise, slight, take away from.

*antonyms* add to, appreciate, praise.

**derogatory** adj aspersory, belittling, critical, damaging, defamatory, depreciative, destructive, detractive, detractory, disparaging, injurious, insulting, offensive, pejorative, slighting, snide, uncomplimentary, unfavourable, unflattering.

*antonyms* appreciative, favourable, flattering.

**descend** v alight, arrive, assail, assault, attack, condescend, degenerate, degringoler, deign, derive, deteriorate, develop, dip, dismount, drop, fall, gravitate, incline, invade, issue, leap, originate, plummet, plunge, pounce, proceed, raid, sink, slant, slope, spring, stem, stoop, subside, swoop, tumble.

**descendants** n children, epigones, epigoni, epigons, family, issue, line, lineage, offspring, posterity, progeny, race, scions, seed, sons and daughters, successors.

**descent** n ancestry, assault, attack, comedown, debasement, decadence, declination, decline, declivity, degradation, degringolade, deterioration, dip, drop, extraction, fall, family tree, foray, genealogy, heredity, incline, incursion, invasion, lineage, origin, parentage, plunge, pounce, raid, slant, slope, stoop, swoop.

*antonyms* ascent, improvement.

**describe** v characterise, define, delineate, depict, detail, draw, enlarge on, explain, express, illustrate, mark out, narrate, outline, portray, present, recount, relate, report, sketch, specify, tell, trace.

**description** n account, brand, breed, category, characterisation, class, delineation, depiction, detail, explanation, exposition, genre, genus, hypotyposis, ilk, kidney, kind, narration, narrative, order, outline, portrayal, presentation, report, representation, sketch, sort, species, specification, type, variety, word-painting, word-picture.

**descriptive** adj blow-by-blow, circumstantial, colourful, depictive, detailed, explanatory, expressive, graphic, illustrative, immediate, pictorial, picturesque, specific, vivid.

*antonyms* cursory, laconic.

**descry** v detect, discern, discover, distinguish, espy, glimpse, mark, notice, observe, perceive, recognise, see, sight, spot, spy.

**desecrate** v abuse, blaspheme, contaminate, debase, defile, despoil, dishallow, dishonour, insult, invade, pervert, pollute, profane, vandalise, violate.

**desecration** n blasphemy, debasement, defilement, dishonouring, impiety, insult, invasion, pollution, profanation, sacrilege, violation.

**desert**[1] n solitude, vacuum, vast, void, waste, wasteland, wilderness, wilds.

adj arid, bare, barren, desolate, droughty, dry, eremic, infertile, lonely, solitary, sterile, uncultivated, uninhabited, unproductive, untilled, waste, waterless, wild.

**desert**[2] v abandon, abscond, apostatise, backslide, betray, decamp, deceive, defect, forsake, give up, jilt, leave, leave in the lurch, maroon, quit, rat on, relinquish, renegue, renounce, resign, strand, tergiversate, vacate.

**desert**[3] n come-uppance, demerit, deserts, due, guerdon, meed, merit, payment, recompense, remuneration, requital, retribution, return, reward, right, virtue, worth.

**deserted** adj abandoned, benighted, bereft, betrayed, derelict, desolate, empty, forlorn, forsaken, friendless, godforsaken, isolated, left in the lurch, lonely, neglected, solitary, stranded, underpopulated, unfriended, unoccupied, unpopulous, vacant, vacated.

*antonym* populous.

**deserter** n absconder, apostate, backslider, betrayer, defector, delinquent, escapee, fugitive, rat, renegade, runaway, traitor, truant.

**desertion** n abandonment, absconding, apostasy, betrayal, defection, delinquency, departure, dereliction, escape, evasion, flight, forsaking, relinquishment, renegation, tergiversation, truancy.

**deserve** v ask for, earn, gain, incur, justify, merit, procure, rate, warrant, win.

**deserved** adj apposite, appropriate, apt, condign, due, earned, fair, fitting, just, justifiable, justified, legitimate, meet, merited, proper, right, rightful, suitable, warranted, well-earned.

*antonyms* gratuitous, undeserved.

**deserving** adj admirable, commendable, creditable, estimable, exemplary, laudable, meritorious, praiseworthy, righteous, worthy.

*antonyms* undeserving, unworthy.

**desiccated** adj arid, dead, dehydrated, drained, dried, dry, dry-as-dust, exsiccated, lifeless, parched, passionless, powdered, spiritless, sterile.

**desiccation** n aridity, dehydration, dryness, exsiccation, parching, sterility, xeransis.

**desideratum** n aim, aspiration, besoin, dream, essential, gap, goal, heart's desire, hope, ideal, lack, lacuna, need, object, objective, sine qua non, want, wish.

**design** *n* aim, arrangement, blueprint, composition, configuration, conformation, conspiracy, construction, contrivance, delineation, draft, drawing, end, enterprise, exemplar, figure, form, goal, guide, intent, intention, intrigue, logo, machination, manoeuvre, meaning, model, motif, object, objective, organisation, outline, pattern, plan, plot, project, prototype, purpose, schema, scheme, shape, sketch, structure, style, target, undertaking.

*v* aim, conceive, construct, contrive, create, delineate, describe, destine, develop, devise, draft, draw, draw up, fabricate, fashion, form, intend, invent, make, mean, model, originate, outline, plan, project, propose, purpose, scheme, shape, sketch, structure, tailor, trace.

**designate** *v* allot, appoint, assign, bill, call, characterise, choose, christen, code-name, deem, define, delegate, denominate, denote, depute, describe, docket, dub, earmark, entitle, indicate, label, name, nickname, nominate, select, show, specify, stipulate, style, term, ticket, title.

**designation** *n* appointment, category, characterisation, classification, code-name, definition, delegation, denomination, description, docket, epithet, indication, label, mark, name, nickname, nomination, selection, specification, title.

**designedly** *adv* calculatedly, consciously, deliberately, intentionally, knowingly, on purpose, premeditatedly, purposely, studiously, wilfully, willingly, with malice aforethought, wittingly.

*antonyms* innocently, unwittingly.

**designer** *n* architect, artificer, author, contriver, couturier, creator, deccie, deviser, fashioner, framer, inventor, maker, originator, stylist.

**designing** *adj* artful, conniving, conspiring, contriving, crafty, cunning, deceitful, devious, disingenuous, guileful, insidious, intriguing, Machiavellian, plotting, scheming, sharp, shrewd, sly, treacherous, tricky, underhand, unscrupulous, wily.

*antonym* artless.

**desirability** *n* advantage, advisability, attraction, attractiveness, beauty, benefit, merit, profit, seductiveness, usefulness, value, worth.

*antonyms* disadvantage, inadvisability, undesirability.

**desirable** *adj* adorable, advantageous, advisable, agreeable, alluring, appetible, appropriate, attractive, beneficial, captivating, covetable, eligible, enviable, expedient, fascinating, fetching, good, nubile, pleasing, plummy, preferable, profitable, seductive, sensible, sexy, tempting, worthwhile.

*antonym* undesirable.

**desire** *v* ask, aspire to, beg, covet, crave, desiderate, entreat, fancy, hanker after, hunger for, importune, lack, long for, need, petition, request, solicit, want, wish for, yearn for.

*n* appeal, appetence, appetency, appetite, ardour, aspiration, besoin, concupiscence, covetousness, craving, cupidity, desideration, entreaty, greed, hankering, hot pants, importunity, kama, kamadeva, lasciviousness, lechery, libido, longing, lust, lustfulness, month's mind, need, passion, petition, request, solicitation, supplication, velleity, want, wish, yearning, yen.

**desired** *adj* accurate, appropriate, correct, exact, expected, express, fitting, longed-for, looked-for, necessary, particular, proper, required, right, sought-after, wanted, wished-for.

*antonyms* undesired, unintentional.

**desirous** *adj* ambitious, anxious, appetent, aspiring, avid, burning, craving, cupidinous, eager, enthusiastic, hopeful, hoping, itching, keen, longing, ready, willing, wishing, yearning.

*antonyms* reluctant, unenthusiastic.

**desist** *v* abstain, break off, cease, come to a halt, discontinue, end, forbear, give over, give up, halt, leave off, pause, peter out, refrain, remit, stop, suspend.

*antonyms* continue, resume.

**desk** *n* bureau, davenport, ecritoire, lectern, prie-dieu, secretaire, writing-table.

**desolate** *adj* abandoned, arid, bare, barren, benighted, bereft, bleak, cheerless, comfortless, companionless, dejected, depopulated, depressed, depressing, desert, desolated, despondent, disconsolate, disheartened, dismal, dismayed, distressed, downcast, dreary, forlorn, forsaken, gloomy, god-forsaken, grieved, inconsolable, lonely, melancholy, miserable, ravaged, ruined, solitary, unfrequented, uninhabited, unpopulous, unsolaced, waste, wild, wretched.

*antonym* cheerful.

*v* denude, depopulate, despoil, destroy, devastate, lay waste, pillage, plunder, ravage, ruin, spoil, waste, wreck.

**desolation** *n* anguish, barrenness, bleakness, dejection, depopulation, desolateness, despair, desperation, despondency, destruction, devastation, disconsolateness, distress, emptiness, forlornness, gloom, gloominess, grief, havoc, isolation, loneliness, melancholy, misery, ravages, ruin, ruination, sadness, solitariness, solitude, sorrow, unhappiness, wildness, woe, wretchedness.

**despair** *v* capitulate, collapse, crumple, despond, give in, give up, lose heart, lose hope, quit, surrender.

*antonym* hope.

*n* anguish, dejection, depression, desperation, despond, despondency, emptiness, gloom, hopelessness, inconsolableness, melancholy, misery, ordeal, pain, resourcelessness, sorrow, trial, tribulation, wretchedness.

*antonyms* cheerfulness, resilience.

**despairing** *adj* anxious, broken-hearted, dejected, depressed, desolate, desperate, despondent, disconsolate, disheartened, distracted, distraught, downcast, frantic, grief-stricken, hopeless, inconsolable, melancholy, miserable, sorrowful, suicidal, wretched.

*antonyms* cheerful, resilient.

**despatch** *see* **dispatch**.

**desperado** *n* bandit, brigand, cateran, criminal, cut-throat, dacoit, gangster, gunman, heavy, hood, hoodlum, law-breaker, mugger, outlaw, ruffian, thug.

**desperate** *adj* grave, abandoned, acute, audacious, critical, dangerous, daring, despairing, despondent, determined, dire, do-or-die, drastic, extreme, foolhardy, forlorn, frantic, frenzied, furious, great, hasty, hazardous, headlong, headstrong, hopeless, impetuous, inconsolable, irremediable, irretrievable, madcap, precipitate, rash, reckless, risky, serious, severe, temerarious, urgent, violent, wild, wretched.

**desperately** *adv* appallingly, badly, critically, dangerously, distractedly, fearfully, frantically, frenziedly, frightfully, gravely, hopelessly, perilously, seriously, severely, shockingly.

**desperation** *n* agony, anguish, anxiety, defiance, despair, despondency, disconsolateness, distraction, distress, foolhardiness, franticness, frenzy, hastiness, heedlessness, hopelessness, madness, misery, pain, rashness, recklessness, sorrow, trouble, unhappiness, worry.

**despicable** *adj* abhorrent, abject, base, cheap, contemptible, degrading, detestable, disgraceful, disgusting, disreputable, hateful, ignoble, ignominious, infamous, low, mean, reprehensible, reprobate, scurvy, shameful, sordid, unprincipled, vile, worthless, wretched.

*antonyms* laudable, noble.

**despise** *v* abhor, condemn, deplore, deride, detest, disdain, dislike, disregard, ignore, loathe, misprise, revile, scorn, slight, spurn, undervalue, vilipend.

*antonyms* appreciate, prize.

**despite** *prep* against, defying, heedless of, in spite of, in the face of, in the teeth of, notwithstanding, regardless of, undeterred by.

**despoil** *v* bereave, denude, depredate, deprive, destroy, devastate, disgarnish, dispossess, divest, loot, maraud, pillage, plunder, ransack, ravage, rifle, rob, spoliate, strip, vandalise, wreck.

*antonyms* adorn, enrich.

**despoliation** *n* depredation, despoilment, destruction, devastation, havoc, looting, marauding, pillage, plunder, rapine, ravaging, ravin, ruin, spoliation, vandalism, wreckage.

*antonyms* adornment, enrichment.

**despond** *v* capitulate, despair, lose courage, lose heart, lose hope, mourn, quit, sorrow, surrender.

*antonym* hope.

**despondency** *n* broken-heartedness, dejection, depression, despair, desperation, disconsolateness, discouragement, dispiritedness, downheartedness, gloom, glumness, hopelessness, inconsolability, melancholia, melancholy, misery, sadness, sorrow, wretchedness.

*antonyms* cheerfulness, hopefulness.

**despondent** *adj* blue, broken-hearted, dejected, depressed, despairing, disconsolate, discouraged, disheartened, dispirited, doleful, down, downcast, downhearted, gloomy, glum, hopeless, inconsolable, low, low-spirited, melancholy, miserable, morose, mournful, overwhelmed, sad, sorrowful, woebegone, wretched.

*antonyms* cheerful, hopeful.

**despot** *n* absolutist, autocrat, boss, dictator, Hitler, monocrat, oppressor, tyrant.

*antonyms* democrat, egalitarian, liberal.

**despotic** *adj* absolute, absolutist, arbitrary, arrogant, authoritarian, autocratic, bossy, dictatorial, domineering, imperious, monocratic, oppressive, overbearing, peremptory, tyrannical.

*antonyms* democratic, egalitarian, liberal, tolerant.

**despotism** *n* absolutism, autarchy, autocracy, dictatorship, monarchism, monocracy, oppression, repression, totalitarianism, tyranny.

*antonyms* democracy, egalitarianism, liberalism, tolerance.

**dessert** *n* afters, doucet, pudding, sweet, sweet course.

**destination** *n* aim, ambition, aspiration, design, end, end in view, goal, harbour, haven, intention, journey's end, object, objective, port of call, purpose, station, stop, target, terminus.

**destine** *v* allot, appoint, assign, consecrate, decree, design, designate, devote, doom, earmark, fate, foredoom, head, intend, mark out, mean, ordain, predetermine, preordain, purpose, reserve.

**destined** *adj* assigned, booked, bound, certain, designed, directed, doomed, en route, fated, foreordained, headed, heading, ineluctable, inescapable, inevitable, intended, meant, ordained, predestined, predetermined, preordained, routed, scheduled, unavoidable.

**destiny** *n* cup, doom, fate, fortune, joss, karma, kismet, lot, Moira, portion, predestiny, weird.

**destitute** *adj* bankrupt, beggared, bereft, deficient, depleted, deprived, devoid of, distressed, down and out, impecunious, impoverished, indigent, innocent of, insolvent, lacking, necessitous, needy, penniless, penurious, poor, poverty-stricken, skint, strapped, wanting.

*antonyms* prosperous, wealthy.

**destitution** *n* bankruptcy, beggary, distress, impecuniousness, indigence, neediness, pauperdom, pauperism, pennilessness, penury, poverty, privation, starvation, straits, want.

*antonyms* prosperity, wealth.

**destroy** *v* annihilate, banjax, break, canker, crush, demolish, destruct, devastate, dismantle, dispatch, eliminate, eradicate, extinguish, extirpate, gut, kill, level, nullify, overthrow, ravage, raze, ruin, sabotage, scuttle, shatter, slay, slight, smash, stonker, thwart, torpedo, undermine, undo, unshape, vaporise, waste, wreck, zap.

*antonym* create.

**destroyer** *n* annihilator, demolisher, desolater, despoiler, iconoclast, Juggernaut, kiss of death, locust, Luddite, maelstrom, ransacker, ravager, vandal, wrecker.

*antonym* creator.

**destruction** *n* annihilation, bane, confutation, crushing, defeat, demolition, depopulation, desolation, devastation, downfall, elimination, end, eradication, estrepement, extermination, extinction, extirpation, havoc, liquidation, massacre, nullification, overthrow, ravagement, ruin, ruination, shattering, slaughter, undoing, wastage, wrack, wreckage.

*antonym* creation.

**destructive** *adj* adverse, antagonistic, baleful, baneful, calamitous, cataclysmic, catastrophic, contrary, damaging, deadly, deathful, deleterious, derogatory, detrimental, devastating, disastrous, discouraging, disparaging, disruptive, fatal, harmful, hostile, hurtful, injurious, invalidating, lethal, malignant, mischievous, negative, noxious, nullifying, pernicious, pestful, pestiferous, pestilent, pestilential, ruinous, slaughterous, subversive, undermining, vexatious, vicious.

*antonyms* creative, positive, productive.

**desultory** *adj* aimless, capricious, cursory, disconnected, discursive, disorderly, disorganised, erratic, fitful, haphazard, inconsistent, inconstant, inexact, irregular, loose, maundering, random, spasmodic, unco-ordinated, undirected, unmethodical, unsystematic.

*antonyms* concerted, methodical, systematic.

**detach** *v* abstract, alienate, cut off, deglutinate, disconnect, disengage, disentangle, disjoin, dissociate, disunite, divide, estrange, free, isolate, loosen, remove, segregate, separate, sever, uncouple, undo, unfasten, unfix, unhitch.

*antonym* attach.

**detached** *adj* aloof, disconnected, discrete, disinterested, disjoined, dispassionate, dissociated, divided, free, free-standing, impartial, impassive, impersonal, independent, loosened, neutral, objective, reserved, separate, severed, unattached, unbiased, uncommitted, unconcerned, unconnected, unimpassioned, uninvolved, unprejudiced.

*antonyms* concerned, connected, involved.

**detachment**[1] *n* aloofness, coolness, disconnection, disengagement, disinterestedness, disjoining, fairness, impartiality, impassivity, indifference, laissez-faire, neutrality, non-partisanship, objectivity, remoteness, separation, severance, severing, unconcern.

*antonym* concern.

**detachment**[2] *n* body, brigade, corps, detail, force, party, patrol, squad, task force, unit.

**detail** *n* aspect, attribute, complexity, complication, component, count, elaborateness, elaboration, element, fact, factor, feature, ingredient, intricacy, item, meticulousness, nicety, particular, particularity, point, refinement, respect, specific, specificity, technicality, thoroughness, triviality.

*v* allocate, appoint, assign, catalogue, charge, commission, delegate, delineate, depict, depute, describe, detach, enarrate, enumerate, individualise, itemise, list, narrate, overname, particularise, portray, recount, rehearse, relate, send, specify.

**detailed** *adj* blow-by-blow, circumstantial, complex, complicated, comprehensive, descriptive, elaborate, exact, exhaustive, fine, full, intricate, itemised, meticulous, minute, particular, particularised, refined, specific, thorough, unsparing.

*antonyms* brief, cursory, summary.

**details** *n* complexities, complications, ins and outs, intricacies, minutiae, niceties, particularities, particulars, specifics, trivia, trivialities.

**detain** *v* arrest, buttonhole, check, confine, delay, hinder, hold, hold up, impede, intern, keep, prevent, restrain, retard, slow, stay, stop.

*antonym* release.

**detect** *v* ascertain, catch, descry, discern, disclose, discover, distinguish, espy, expose, find, identify, note, notice, observe, perceive, recognise, reveal, scent, sight, spot, spy, track down, uncover, unmask.

**detection** *n* discernment, discovery, expose, exposure, identification, revelation, smelling out, sniffing out, tracking down, uncovering, unearthing, unmasking.

**detective** *n* busy, constable, cop, copper, dick, gumshoe, investigator, jack, private dick, private eye, private investigator, shamus, sleuth, sleuth-hound, tec, thief-catcher, thief-taker.

**detention** *n* confinement, constraint, custody, delay, detainment, duress, hindrance, holding back, imprisonment, incarceration, quarantine, restraint, withholding.

*antonym* release.

**deter** *v* caution, check, damp, daunt, debar, discourage, disincline, dissuade, frighten, hinder, inhibit, intimidate, prevent, prohibit, put off, repel, restrain, stop, turn off, warn.

*antonym* encourage.

**detergent** *n* abstergent, cleaner, cleanser, soap.

*adj* abstergent, abstersive, cleaning, cleansing, detersive.

**deteriorate** *v* backslide, crumble, decay, decline, decompose, degenerate, depreciate, disintegrate, ebb, fade, fail, fall off, go downhill, lapse, relapse, slide, slip, weaken, worsen.

*antonym* improve.

**deterioration** *n* atrophy, corrosion, debasement, decline, degeneration, degradation, degringolade, depreciation, descent, dilapidation, disintegration, downturn, drop, failing, fall, falling-off, lapse, pejoration, retrogression, slump, tabes, tabescence, vitiation, wastage, worsening.

*antonym* improvement.

**determinate** *adj* absolute, certain, clear-cut, conclusive, decided, decisive, defined, definite, definitive, delimited, determined, distinct, established, explicit, express, fixed, limited, positive, precise, quantified, settled, specific, specified.

*antonym* indeterminate.

**determination** *n* backbone, conclusion, constancy, conviction, decision, dedication, doggedness, drive, firmness, fortitude, indomitability, insistence, intention, judgement, obstinacy, perseverance, persistence, pertinacity, purpose, resoluteness, resolution, resolve, result, settlement, single-mindedness, solution, steadfastness, stubbornness, tenacity, verdict, will, will-power.

*antonym* irresolution.

**determine** *v* affect, arbitrate, ascertain, certify, check, choose, conclude, control, decide, detect, dictate, direct, discover, elect, end, establish, finish, fix, govern, guide, identify, impel, impose, incline, induce, influence, intend, lead, learn, modify, ordain, point, purpose, regulate, resolve, rule, settle, shape, terminate, undertake, verify.

**determined** *adj* backboned, bent, constant, convinced, decided, dogged, firm, fixed, indivertible, insistent, intent, obstinate, persevering, persistent, pertinacious, purposeful, resolute, set, single-minded, steadfast, strong-minded, strong-willed, stubborn, tenacious, tough-minded, undissuadable, unflinching, unhesitating, unwavering.

*antonym* irresolute.

**deterrent** *n* bar, barrier, check, curb, determent, difficulty, discouragement, disincentive, hindrance, impediment, obstacle, obstruction, repellent, restraint, turn-off.

*antonym* incentive.

**detest** *v* abhor, abominate, deplore, despise, dislike, execrate, hate, loathe, recoil from.

*antonym* adore.

**detestable** *adj* abhorred, abhorrent, abominable, accursed, despicable, disgusting, execrable, foul, hated, hateful, heinous, loathsome, nauseating, noisome, obnoxious, odious, offensive, pestiferous, pestilent, pestilential, repellent, repugnant, repulsive, revolting, rotten, shocking, sordid, swinish, vile, villainous.

*antonyms* admirable, adorable, pleasant.

**detestation** *n* abhorrence, abomination, anathema, animosity, animus, antipathy, aversion, despite, disgust, dislike, enmity, execration, hate, hatred, hostility, loathing, odium, repugnance, revulsion.

*antonyms* adoration, approval, love.

**dethrone** *v* depose, oust, topple, uncrown, unking, unseat, unthrone.

*antonyms* crown, enthrone.

**detonate** *v* blast, blow up, discharge, displode, explode, fulminate, ignite, kindle, set off, spark off.

**detonation** *n* bang, blast, blow-up, boom, burst, discharge, displosion, explosion, fulmination, igniting, ignition, report.

**detour** *n* bypass, bypath, byroad, byway, circumbendibus, deviation, digression, diversion, excursus.

**detract** *v* belittle, depreciate, derogate, devaluate, diminish, lessen, lower, negate, nullify, reduce, vilipend, vitiate.

*antonyms* add to, praise.

**detraction** *n* abuse, aspersion, belittlement, calumniation, calumny, defamation, denigration, depreciation, derogation, disparagement, innuendo, insinuation, misprision, misrepresentation, muck-raking, revilement, scandalmongering, scurrility, slander, traducement, vituperation.

*antonyms* appreciation, praise.

**detractor** *n* backbiter, belittler, defamer, denigrator, disparager, enemy, muck-raker, reviler, scandalmonger, slanderer, traducer, vilifier.

*antonyms* flatterer, supporter.

**detriment** *n* damage, disadvantage, disservice, evil, harm, hurt, ill, impairment, injury, loss, mischief, prejudice.

*antonym* advantage.

**detrimental** *adj* adverse, baleful, damaging, deleterious, destructive, disadvantageous, harmful, hurtful, inimical, injurious, mischievous, noxious, pernicious, prejudicial, unfavourable, untoward.

*antonym* advantageous.

**detritus** *n* debris, fragments, garbage, junk, litter, remains, rubbish, scum, waste, wreckage.

**devaluation** *n* decrease, deflation, devalorisation, lowering, reduction.

**devalue** *v* decrease, deflate, devalorise, devaluate, lower, reduce.

**devastate** *v* confound, demolish, depredate, desolate, despoil, destroy, discomfit, discompose, disconcert, floor, lay waste, level, maraud, nonplus, overwhelm, pillage, plunder, ransack, ravage, raze, ruin, sack, spoil, spoliate, waste, wreck.

**devastation** *n* annihilation, demolition, denudation, depredation, desolation, despoliation, destruction, havoc, pillage, plunder, ravages, ruin, ruination, spoliation, wrack, wreckage.

**devastator** *n* demolisher, desolater, despoiler, destroyer, devourer, locust, plunderer, ravager, spoliator, vandal, wrecker.

**develop** *v* acquire, advance, amplify, augment, begin, bloom, blossom, branch out, breed, broaden, commence, contract, cultivate, dilate, diversify, elaborate, engender, enlarge, ensue, establish, evolve, expand, flourish, follow, form, foster, generate, grow, happen, invent, make headway, mature, move on, originate, pick up, progress, promote, prosper, result, ripen, sprout, start, unfold.

**development** *n* advance, advancement, blooming, blossoming, change, circumstance, detail, elaboration, event, evolution, expansion, extension, furtherance, growth, happening, improvement, incident, increase, issue, maturation, maturity, occurrence, outcome, phenomenon, phylogenesis, phylogeny, progress, progression, promotion, refinement, result, ripening, situation, spread, unfolding, unravelling, upbuilding, upshot.

**deviant** *adj* aberrant, abnormal, anomalous, bent, bizarre, deviate, devious, divergent, freakish, freaky, heretical, heteromorphic, heteromorphous, heterotypic, irregular, kinky, perverse, perverted, queer, twisted, wayward.

*antonym* normal.

*n* deviate, freak, kook, misfit, oddball, pervert, queer, vert.

*antonym* straight.

**deviate** *v* aberrate, depart, differ, digress, divagate, diverge, drift, err, go astray, go off the rails, part, stray, swerve, turn, turn aside, vary, veer, wander, yaw.

**deviation** *n* aberrance, aberrancy, aberration, abnormality, alteration, ambage, anomaly, change, deflection, departure, detour, digression, discrepancy, disparity, divagation, divergence, driftage, eccentricity, fluctuation, freak, heteromorphism, heteromorphy, inconsistency, irregularity, kinkiness, quirk, shift, variance, variation, wandering.

*antonym* conformity.

**device** *n* apparatus, appliance, artifice, badge, blazon, colophon, contraption, contrivance, crest, design, dodge, emblem, episemon, expedient, figure, gadget, gambit, gimmick, gismo, implement, improvisation, insignia, instrument, invention, logo, machination, manoeuvre, motif, motto, plan, plot, ploy, project, ruse, scheme, shield, shift, stratagem, strategy, stunt, symbol, tactic, token, tool, trick, utensil, wile.

**devil** *n* Abaddon, Adversary, Apollyon, arch-fiend, bastard, beast, Beelzebub, Belial, bog(e)y-man, brute, bugger, cad, Clootie, creature, deil, demon, enthusiast, Evil One, fiend, goodman, Hornie, imp, incubus, jumpy, Lucifer, Mahoun(d), man of sin, Mephisto, Mephistopheles, monkey, monster, ogre, Old Harry, Old Nick, Old Scratch, Prince of Darkness, ragman, rascal, rogue, rotter, Satan, savage, scamp, scoundrel, shaitan, Slanderer, succubus, swine, terror, unfortunate, villain, wirricow, worricow, wretch.

**devilish** *adj* accursed, black-hearted, damnable, demoniac, demoniacal, diabolic, diabolical, execrable, fiendish, hellish, impious, infernal, iniquitous, mischievous, monstrous, nefarious, satanic, wicked.

**devil-may-care** *adj* careless, casual, cavalier, easy-going, flippant, frivolous, happy-go-lucky, heedless, insouciant, jaunty, lackadaisical, nonchalant, pococurante, reckless, swaggering, swashbuckling, unconcerned, unworried.

**devilment** *n* devilry, knavery, mischief, mischievousness, naughtiness, rascality, roguery, roguishness, sport, teasing.

**devilry** *n* black magic, chicanery, cruelty, devilment, deviltry, diablerie, diabolism, evil, jiggery-pokery, knavery, malevolence, malice, mischief, mischievousness, monkey-business, rascality, roguery, sorcery, trickiness, vice, viciousness, villainy, wickedness.

**devious** *adj* calculating, circuitous, confusing, crooked, cunning, deceitful, deviating, dishonest, disingenuous, double-dealing, erratic, evasive, excursive, indirect, insidious, insincere, misleading, rambling, roundabout, scheming,

slippery, sly, subtle, surreptitious, tortuous, treacherous, tricky, underhand, wandering, wily, winding.

*antonyms* artless, candid, straightforward.

**deviousness** *n* cunning, deceit, dishonesty, disingenuity, evasion, evasiveness, indirectness, insincerity, slipperiness, slyness, subtlety, trickiness.

*antonyms* artlessness, openness.

**devise** *v* arrange, compass, compose, conceive, concoct, construct, contrive, design, excogitate, forge, form, formulate, frame, imagine, invent, plan, plot, prepare, project, scheme, shape.

**devoid** *adj* barren, bereft, deficient, denuded, destitute, empty, free, innocent, lacking, sans, vacant, void, wanting, without.

*antonyms* blessed, endowed.

**devolution** *n* decentralisation, delegation, dispersal, distribution, transference.

*antonym* centralisation.

**devolve** *v* alienate, be handed down, commission, consign, convey, delegate, deliver, depute, entrust, fall to, hand down, rest with, transfer.

**devote** *v* allocate, allot, apply, appropriate, assign, commit, consecrate, dedicate, enshrine, give, oneself, pledge, reserve, sacrifice, set apart, set aside, surrender.

**devoted** *adj* ardent, attentive, caring, committed, concerned, constant, dedicated, devout, faithful, fond, loving, loyal, staunch, steadfast, tireless, true, unremitting, unswerving.

*antonyms* inconstant, indifferent, negligent.

**devotee** *n* addict, adherent, admirer, aficionado, buff, devil, devot, disciple, enthusiast, fan, fanatic, fiend, follower, hound, merchant, supporter, votary, voteen, zealot.

*antonyms* adversary, sceptic.

**devotion** *n* adherence, adoration, affection, allegiance, ardour, assiduity, attachment, commitment, consecration, constancy, dedication, devoutness, earnestness, faith, faithfulness, fervour, fidelity, fondness, godliness, holiness, indefatigability, love, loyalty, partiality, passion, piety, prayer, regard, religiousness, reverence, sanctity, sedulousness, spirituality, steadfastness, support, worship, zeal.

*antonyms* inconstancy, negligence.

**devotional** *adj* devout, dutiful, holy, pietistic, pious, religious, reverential, sacred, solemn, spiritual.

**devour** *v* absorb, annihilate, bolt, consume, cram, destroy, dispatch, down, eat, engulf, feast on, feast one's eyes on, gluttonise, gobble, gorge, gormandise, gulp, guzzle, polish off, ravage, ravin, relish, revel in, spend, stuff, swallow, waste, wolf.

**devourer** *n* consumer, glutton, gobbler, gormandiser, gourmand, guzzler, locust, waster.

**devout** *adj* ardent, constant, deep, devoted, earnest, faithful, fervent, genuine, godly, heartfelt, holy, intense, orthodox, passionate, pious, prayerful, profound, pure, religious, reverent, saintly, serious, sincere, staunch, steadfast, unswerving, whole-hearted, zealous.

*antonyms* insincere, uncommitted.

**devoutly** *adv* deeply, faithfully, fervently, profoundly, sincerely, staunchly, steadfastly, whole-heartedly.

**dewy** *adj* blooming, innocent, roral, roric, rorid, roscid, starry-eyed, youthful.

**dexterity** *n* ability, address, adroitness, agility, aptitude, art, artistry, cleverness, cunning, deftness, effortlessness, expertise, expertness, facility, finesse, handiness, ingenuity, knack, legerdemain, mastery, neatness, nimbleness, proficiency, readiness, skilfulness, skill, smoothness, tact, touch.

*antonyms* clumsiness, ineptitude.

**dexterous** *adj* able, active, acute, adept, adroit, agile, apt, clever, cunning, deft, expert, facile, feat, habile, handy, ingenious, light-handed, masterly, neat, neat-handed, nifty, nimble, nimble-fingered, nippy, proficient, prompt, quick, skilful.

*antonyms* clumsy, inept.

**diabolical** *adj* damnable, devilish, diabolic, difficult, disastrous, dreadful, excruciating, fiendish, hellish, infernal, knavish, nasty, outrageous, shocking, tricky, unpleasant, vile, villainous, wicked.

**diadem** *n* circlet, coronet, crown, mitre, round, tiara.

**diagnose** *v* analyse, determine, distinguish, explain, identify, interpret, investigate, isolate, pinpoint, pronounce, recognise.

**diagnosis** *n* analysis, answer, conclusion, examination, explanation, identification, interpretation, investigation, isolation, opinion, pronouncement, scrutiny, verdict.

**diagnostic** *adj* analytical, demonstrative, distinctive, distinguishing, idiosyncratic, indicative, interpretative, interpretive, particular, peculiar, recognisable, symptomatic.

**diagonal** *adj* angled, cater-cornered, cornerways, crooked, cross, crossways, crosswise, oblique, slanting, slantwise, sloping.

**diagonally** *adv* aslant, at an angle, cornerwise, crosswise, obliquely, on the bias, on the cross, on the slant, slantwise.

**diagram** *n* abac, chart, drawing, figure, graph, illustration, lay-out, nomogram, outline, picture, plan, representation, schema, sketch, table.

**diagrammatic** *adj* diagrammatical, graphic, illustrative, representational, schematic, tabular.

*antonyms* imaginative, impressionistic.

**dialect** *n* accent, diction, Doric, idiom, jargon, language, lingo, localism, patois, pronunciation, provincialism, regionalism, speech, tongue, vernacular.

**dialectic** *adj* analytic, argumentative, deductive, dialectical, disceptatorial, inductive, logical, logistic, polemical, ratiocinative, ratiocinatory, rational, rationalistic.

*n* analysis, argumentation, casuistry, contention, debate, deduction, dialectics, disceptation, discussion, disputation, induction, logic, polemics, ratiocination, rationale, reasoning, sophistry.

**dialogue** *n* causerie, colloquy, communication, confabulation, conference, conversation, converse, debate, discourse, discussion, duologue, exchange, interchange, interlocution, lines, script, stichomythia, table talk, talk.

**diametric** *adj* antipodal, antithetical, contrary, contrasting, counter, diametral, diametrical, opposed, opposite.

**diaphanous** *adj* cobwebby, delicate, filmy, fine, gauzy, gossamer, gossamery, light, pellucid, see-through, sheer, thin, translucent, transparent, veily.

*antonyms* heavy, opaque, thick.

**diarrhoea** *n* dysentery, gippy tummy, holiday tummy, looseness, Montezuma's revenge, Spanish tummy, the runs, the trots.

*antonym* constipation.

**diary** *n* appointment book, chronicle, commonplace book, day-book, diurnal, engagement book, journal, journal intime, logbook, year-book.

**diatribe** *n* abuse, attack, castigation, criticism, denunciation, flyting, harangue, insult, invective, onslaught, philippic, reviling, stricture, tirade, upbraiding, vituperation.

*antonyms* bouquet, encomium, praise.

**dice** *n* astragals, bones, cubes, devil's bones, die, hazard.

**dicey** *adj* chancy, dangerous, difficult, dubious, hairy, iffy, problematic, risky, ticklish, tricky.

*antonyms* certain, easy.

**dicky** *adj* ailing, frail, infirm, queer, shaky, unreliable, unsound, unsteady, weak.

*antonyms* healthy, robust.

**dictate** *v* announce, command, decree, direct, enjoin, impose, instruct, ordain, order, prescribe, pronounce, rule, say, speak, transmit, utter.

*n* behest, bidding, code, command, decree, dictation, dictum, direction, edict, fiat, injunction, law, mandate, order, ordinance, precept, principle, requirement, rule, ruling, statute, ultimatum, word.

**dictator** *n* autarch, autocrat, Big Brother, boss, despot, Hitler, supremo, tyrant.

**dictatorial** *adj* absolute, almighty, arbitrary, autarchic, authoritarian, autocratic, bossy, despotic, dogmatic, domineering, imperious, magisterial, oppressive, overbearing, peremptory, repressive, totalitarian, tyrannical.

*antonyms* democratic, egalitarian, liberal, tolerant.

**dictatorship** *n* absolute rule, absolutism, autarchy, authoritarianism, autocracy, despotism, dictature, fascism, Hitlerism, totalitarianism, tyranny.

*antonyms* democracy, egalitarianism.

**diction** *n* articulation, delivery, elocution, enunciation, expression, fluency, idiom, inflection, intonation, language, phraseology, phrasing, pronunciation, speech, style, terminology, usage, vocabulary, wording.

**dictionary** *n* concordance, encyclopaedia, glossary, idioticon, lexicon, onomasticon, thesaurus, vocabulary, wordbook.

**dictum** *n* adage, axiom, command, decree, dictate, edict, fiat, gnome, maxim, order, precept, pronouncement, proverb, ruling, saw, saying, utterance.

**didactic** *adj* didascalic, educational, educative, homiletic, instructive, moral, moralising, pedagogic, pedantic, preceptive, prescriptive.

**die** *v* breathe one's last, croak, decay, decease, decline, depart, desire, disappear, dwindle, ebb, end, expire, fade, finish, fizzle out, gangrene, go over to the majority, go to one's (long) account, hunger, kick in, kick it, kick the bucket, languish, lapse, long for, pass, pass away, pass over, peg out, perish, peter out, pine for, pop off, run down, sink, slip the cable, snuff it, starve, stop, subside, succumb, suffer, vanish, wane, wilt, wither, yearn.

**die-hard** *n* blimp, Colonel Blimp, fanatic, fogey, hardliner, intransigent, reactionary, rightist, stick-in-the-mud, ultra-conservative, zealot.

*adj* blimpish, confirmed, dyed-in-the-wool, entrenched, hardcore, hardline, immovable, incorrigible, incurable, inflexible, intransigent, irreconcilable, obstinate, reactionary, rigid, stubborn, ultra-conservative, uncompromising, unyielding.

*antonyms* enlightened, flexible, progressive.

**diet¹** *n* abstinence, aliment, board, comestibles, commons, dietary, edibles, fare, fast, food, foodstuffs, nourishment, nutriment, nutrition, provisions, rations, regime, regimen, subsistence, sustenance, viands, victuals.

*v* abstain, bant, fast, lose weight, reduce, slim, weight-watch.

**diet²** *n* assembly, chamber, congress, convention, convocation, council, divan, legislature, meeting, parliament, session, sitting, synod.

**differ** *v* argue, be at odds with, clash, conflict, contend, contradict, contrast, debate, demur, depart from, deviate, disagree, dispute, dissent, diverge, fall out, oppose, part company with, quarrel, take issue, vary.

*antonyms* agree, conform.

**difference** *n* alteration, argument, balance, change, clash, conflict, contention, contrariety, contrast, contretemps, controversy, debate, deviation, differentia, differentiation, difformity, disagreement, discordance, discrepancy, discreteness, disparateness, disparity, dispute, dissimilarity, distinction, distinctness, divergence, diversity, exception, idiosyncrasy, jizz, nuance, particularity, peculiarity, quarrel, remainder, rest, set-to, singularity, strife, tiff, unlikeness, variation, variety, wrangle.

*antonyms* agreement, conformity, uniformity.

**different** *adj* altered, anomalous, assorted, at odds, at variance, atypical, bizarre, changed, clashing, contrasting, deviating,

discrepant, discrete, disparate, dissimilar, distinct, distinctive, divergent, divers, diverse, eccentric, extraordinary, inconsistent, individual, manifold, many, miscellaneous, multifarious, numerous, opposed, original, other, peculiar, rare, separate, several, singular, special, strange, sundry, unalike, uncommon, unconventional, unique, unlike, unusual, varied, various.

*antonyms* conventional, normal, same, similar, uniform.

**differentiate** *v* adapt, alter, change, contrast, convert, demarcate, discern, discriminate, distinguish, individualise, mark off, modify, nuance, particularise, separate, tell apart, transform.

*antonyms* assimilate, associate, confuse, link.

**differentiation** *n* contrast, demarcation, differentia, discrimination, distinction, distinguishing, individualisation, jizz, modification, particularisation, separation.

*antonyms* assimilation, association, confusion, connection.

**difficult** *adj* abstract, abstruse, arduous, Augean, awkward, baffling, burdensome, captious, complex, complicated, dark, delicate, demanding, difficile, disruptive, enigmatical, fastidious, formidable, fractious, fussy, Gordian, grim, hard, herculean, iffy, intractable, intricate, involved, knotty, laborious, obscure, obstinate, obstreperous, onerous, painful, perplexing, perverse, problematic, problematical, recalcitrant, refractory, rigid, steep, sticky, stiff, straitened, strenuous, stubborn, thorny, ticklish, tiresome, toilsome, tough, troublesome, trying, unamenable, unco-operative, unmanageable, uphill, wearisome.

*antonyms* easy, straightforward.

**difficulty** *n* a bad patch, arduousness, awkwardness, block, complication, dilemma, distress, embarrassment, fix, hang-up, hardship, hiccup, hindrance, hole, hurdle, impediment, jam, laboriousness, labour, mess, nineholes, objection, obstacle, opposition, pain, painfulness, perplexity, pickle, pinch, pitfall, plight, predicament, problem, protest, quandary, scruple, spot, strain, strait, straits, strenuousness, stumbling-block, trial, tribulation, trouble, vexata quaestio, vexed question.

*antonyms* advantage, ease.

**diffidence** *n* abashment, backwardness, bashfulness, constraint, doubt, fear, hesitancy, hesitation, humility, inhibition, insecurity, meekness, modesty, reluctance, reserve, self-consciousness, self-distrust, self-doubt, self-effacement, shamefacedness, shamefast, sheepishness, shyness, tentativeness, timidity, timidness, timorousness, unassertiveness.

*antonym* confidence.

**diffident** *adj* abashed, backward, bashful, constrained, distrustful, doubtful, hesitant, inhibited, insecure, meek, modest, reluctant, reserved, self-conscious, self-effacing, shamefaced, shamefast, sheepish, shrinking, shy, suspicious, tentative, timid, timorous, unadventurous, unassertive, unassuming, unobtrusive, unsure, withdrawn.

*antonym* confident.

**diffuse** adj ambagious, circuitous, circumlocutory, copious, diffused, digressive, disconnected, discursive, dispersed, long-winded, loose, maundering, meandering, prolix, rambling, scattered, unconcentrated, unco-ordinated, vague, verbose, waffling, wordy.

antonyms concentrated, succinct.

v circulate, dispense, disperse, disseminate, dissipate, distribute, propagate, scatter, spread, winnow.

antonyms concentrate, suppress.

**dig¹** v burrow, delve, drive, excavate, go into, gouge, graft, grub, hoe, howk, investigate, jab, mine, penetrate, pierce, poke, probe, prod, punch, quarry, research, scoop, search, spit, thrust, till, tunnel.

n aspersion, barb, crack, cut, gibe, insinuation, insult, jab, jeer, poke, prod, punch, quip, sneer, taunt, thrust, wisecrack.

antonym compliment.

**dig up** discover, disinter, dredge, exhumate, exhume, expose, extricate, find, retrieve, track down, uncover, unearth.

antonyms bury, obscure.

**dig²** v adore, appreciate, be into, enjoy, fancy, follow, get a kick out of, get off on, go a bundle on, go for, go overboard about, groove, have the hots for, like, love, understand, warm to.

antonym hate.

**digest** v abridge, absorb, arrange, assimilate, classify, codify, compress, condense, consider, contemplate, dispose, dissolve, grasp, incorporate, ingest, macerate, master, meditate, methodise, ponder, process, reduce, shorten, stomach, study, summarise, systematise, tabulate, take in, understand.

n abbreviation, abridgement, abstract, compendium, compression, condensation, epitome, precis, reduction, resume, summary, synopsis.

**digestion** n absorption, assimilation, dyspepsia, eupepsia, ingestion, transformation.

**dignified** adj august, decorous, distinguished, exalted, formal, grave, honourable, imposing, impressive, lofty, lordly, majestic, noble, oro(ro)tund, reserved, solemn, stately, upright.

antonym undignified.

**dignify** v adorn, advance, aggrandise, apotheosise, distinguish, elevate, ennoble, exalt, glorify, honour, promote, raise.

antonyms degrade, demean.

**dignitary** n bigwig, celeb, celebrity, dignity, high-up, notability, notable, personage, pillar of society, VIP, worthy.

**dignity** n amour-propre, courtliness, decorum, elevation, eminence, excellence, glory, grandeur, gravitas, gravity, greatness, hauteur, honour, importance, loftiness, majesty, nobility, nobleness, pride, propriety, rank, respectability, self-esteem, self-importance, self-possession, self-regard, self-respect, solemnity, standing, stateliness, station, status.

**digress** v depart, deviate, divagate, diverge, drift, excurse, expatiate, go off at a tangent, ramble, stray, wander.

**digression** n apostrophe, aside, departure, detour, deviation, divagation, divergence, diversion, evagation, excursion, footnote, obiter dictum, parenthesis, straying, vagary, wandering.

**dilapidated** adj battered, broken-down, crumbling, decayed, decaying, decrepit, mouldering, neglected, ramshackle, rickety, ruined, ruinous, run-down, shabby, shaky, tumble-down, uncared-for, worn-out.

**dilapidation** n collapse, decay, demolition, destruction, deterioration, disintegration, disrepair, dissolution, downfall, ruin, ruination, waste.

**dilate** v amplify, broaden, descant, detail, develop, distend, dwell on, elaborate, enlarge, expand, expatiate, expound, extend, increase, puff out, spin out, stretch, swell, widen.

antonyms abbreviate, constrict, curtail.

**dilated** adj bloated, distended, enlarged, expanded, extended, inflated, outspread, swollen, tumescent, varicose.

antonyms contracted, shortened.

**dilation** n broadening, dilatation, distension, enlargement, expansion, extension, increase, spread, swelling, widening.

antonyms constriction, contraction.

**dilatory** adj backward, behind-hand, dallying, delaying, indolent, lackadaisical, laggard, lingering, loitering, procrastinating, slack, slothful, slow, sluggish, tardy, tarrying.

antonym diligent.

**dilemma** n bind, corner, difficulty, embarrassment, fix, jam, mess, perplexity, pickle, pinch, plight, predicament, problem, puzzle, quandary, spot, strait.

**dilettante** n aesthete, amateur, dabbler, sciolist, trifler.

**diligence** n activity, application, assiduity, assiduousness, attention, attentiveness, care, constancy, earnestness, heedfulness, industry, intentness, laboriousness, perseverance, pertinacity, sedulousness.

antonym laziness.

**diligent** adj active, assiduous, attentive, busy, careful, conscientious, constant, dogged, earnest, hard-working, indefatigable, industrious, laborious, painstaking, persevering, persistent, pertinacious, sedulous, studious, tireless.

antonyms dilatory, lazy.

**dilly-dally** v dally, dawdle, delay, dither, falter, hesitate, hover, linger, loiter, potter, procrastinate, shilly-shally, swither, tarry, trifle, vacillate, waver.

**dilute** v adulterate, allay, attenuate, cut, dash, decrease, diffuse, diminish, lessen, mitigate, reduce, temper, thin (out), water down, weaken.

antonym concentrate.

adj adulterated, attenuate(d), cut, diluted, thin, watered (down), waterish, weak.

antonym concentrated.

**dim** adj bleary, blurred, caliginous, cloudy, confused, dark, darkish, dense, depressing, dingy, discouraging, dull, dumb, dusky, faint, feeble, foggy, fuzzy, gloomy, grey, hazy, ill-defined, imperfect, indistinct, intangible, lack-lustre, misty, muted, obscure, obscured, obtuse, opaque, overcast, pale, remote, shadowy, slow, sombre, stupid, sullied, tarnished, tenebrious, thick, unclear, unfavourable, unilluminated, unpromising, vague, weak.

*antonyms* bright, distinct.

*v* becloud, bedim, blear, blur, cloud, darken, dull, fade, lower, obscure, tarnish.

*antonyms* brighten, illuminate.

**dimension(s)** *n* amplitude, bulk, capacity, extent, greatness, importance, largeness, magnitude, measure, range, scale, scope, size.

**diminish** *v* abate, bate, belittle, cheapen, contract, curtail, cut, deactivate, decline, decrease, de-emphasise, demean, depreciate, devalue, dwindle, ebb, fade, lessen, lower, minify, peter out, recede, reduce, retrench, shrink, shrivel, sink, slacken, subside, taper off, wane, weaken.

*antonyms* enhance, enlarge, increase.

**diminishing** *adj* abating, contracting, declining, decreasing, decrescent, dwindling, ebbing, fading, lessening, lowering, receding, reducing, shrinking, shrivelling, subsiding, waning.

*antonyms* growing, increasing.

**diminution** *n* abatement, contraction, curtailment, cut, cutback, deactivation, decay, decline, decrease, deduction, ebb, lessening, reduction, retrenchment, shortening, shrinkage, subsidence, weakening.

*antonyms* enlargement, increase.

**diminutive** *adj* bantam, dinky, Lilliputian, little, midget, mini, miniature, minute, petite, pint-size(d), pocket(-sized), pygmy, small, tiny, undersized, wee.

*antonyms* big, great, huge, large.

*n* hypocorisma, pet-name.

**dimple** *n* concavity, depression, dint, fovea, hollow, umbilicus.

**dimwit** *n* blockhead, bonehead, booby, dullard, dunce, dunderhead, ignoramus, nitwit, numskull, thick, thick-skull, twit.

**din** *n* babble, chirm, clamour, clangour, clash, clatter, commotion, crash, hubbub, hullaballoo, noise, outcry, pandemonium, racket, randan, row, shout, uproar.

*antonyms* calm, quiet.

**dine** *v* banquet, break bread, eat, feast, feed, lunch, sup.

**dine on** banquet, consume, dine off, eat, feast, feed, regale oneself.

**dingy** *adj* bedimmed, colourless, dark, dim, dirty, discoloured, drab, dreary, dull, dusky, faded, fuscous, gloomy, grimy, murky, obscure, run-down, seedy, shabby, soiled, sombre, tacky, worn.

*antonyms* bright, clean.

**dining-room** *n* dinette, frater, mess, refectory, triclinium.

**dinky** *adj* dainty, fine, mini, miniature, natty, neat, petite, small, trig, trim.

**dinner** *n* banquet, beanfeast, blow-out, collation, feast, meal, refection, repast, spread, supper, tea.

**dint** *n* blow, concavity, dent, depression, hollow, impression, indentation, stroke.

**dip** *v* bathe, decline, descend, disappear, dook, dop, douse, droop, drop, duck, dunk, fade, fall, immerse, ladle, lower, plunge, rinse, sag, scoop, set, sink, slope, slump, souse, spoon, subside, tilt.

*n* basin, bathe, concavity, concoction, decline, depression, dilution, dive, dook, douche, drenching, ducking, fall, hole, hollow, immersion, incline, infusion, lowering, mixture, plunge, preparation, sag, slip, slope, slump, soaking, solution, suspension, swim.

**dip into** browse, dabble, peruse, sample, skim, try.

**diplomacy** *n* artfulness, craft, delicacy, discretion, finesse, manoeuvring, savoir-faire, skill, statecraft, statesmanship, subtlety, tact, tactfulness.

**diplomat** *n* conciliator, go-between, mediator, moderator, negotiator, peacemaker, politician, tactician.

**diplomatic** *adj* discreet, judicious, polite, politic, prudent, sagacious, sensitive, subtle, tactful.

*antonyms* rude, tactless, thoughtless.

**dire** *adj* alarming, appalling, awful, calamitous, cataclysmic, catastrophic, critical, crucial, cruel, crying, desperate, disastrous, dismal, distressing, drastic, dreadful, exigent, extreme, fearful, gloomy, grave, grim, horrible, horrid, ominous, portentous, pressing, ruinous, terrible, urgent, woeful.

**direct¹** *v* address, administer, advise, aim, bid, case, charge, command, conduct, control, dictate, dispose, enjoin, fix, focus, govern, guide, handle, indicate, instruct, intend, label, lead, level, mail, manage, mastermind, mean, order, oversee, point, regulate, route, rule, run, send, show, stage-manage, superintend, superscribe, supervise, train, turn.

**direct²** *adj* absolute, blunt, candid, categorical, downright, explicit, express, face-to-face, first-hand, frank, head-on, honest, immediate, man-to-man, matter-of-fact, non-stop, open, outright, outspoken, personal, plain, plain-spoken, point-blank, shortest, sincere, straight, straightforward, through, unambiguous, unbroken, undeviating, unequivocal, uninterrupted.

*antonyms* crooked, devious, indirect.

**direction** *n* address, administration, aim, approach, bearing, bent, bias, charge, command, control, course, current, drift, end, government, guidance, label, leadership, line, management, mark, order, orientation, oversight, path, proclivity, purpose, road, route, superintendence, superscription, supervision, tack, tendency, tenor, track, trend, way.

**directions** *n* briefing, guidance, guidelines, indication, instructions, orders, plan, recipe, recommendations, regulations.

**directive** *n* charge, command, decree, dictate, diktat, edict, fiat, imperative, injunction, instruction, mandate, notice, order, ordinance, regulation, ruling.

**directly** *adv* bluntly, candidly, dead, due, exactly, face-to-face, forthwith, frankly, honestly, immediately, instantaneously, instantly, openly, personally, plainly, point-blank, precisely, presently, promptly, pronto, quickly, right away, soon, speedily, straight, straightaway, straightforwardly, truthfully, unequivocally, unerringly, unswervingly.

*antonym* indirectly.

**directness** *n* bluffness, bluntness, candour, forthrightness, frankness, honesty, outspoken-ness, plain-speaking, sincerity, straightforwardness.

**director** *n* administrator, auteur, boss, chairman, chief, conductor, controller, corrector, executive, governor, head, leader, manager, monitor, organiser, principal, producer, supervisor.

**dirge** *n* coronach, dead-march, elegy, lament, monody, requiem, threnody.

**dirt** *n* clay, crud, dust, earth, excrement, filth, grime, impurity, indecency, loam, mire, muck, mud, obscenity, ordure, pornography, slime, smudge, smut, smutch, soil, sordor, stain, tarnish, vomit, yuck.

*antonyms* cleanliness, cleanness.

**dirty** *adj* angry, base, beggarly, begrimed, bitter, blue, clouded, contemptible, corrupt, cowardly, crooked, cruddy, dark, despicable, dishonest, dull, filthy, foul, fraudulent, grimy, grubby, grungy, ignominious, illegal, indecent, low, low-down, maculate, manky, mean, messy, miry, mucky, muddy, nasty, obscene, off-colour, piggish, polluted, pornographic, risque, salacious, scruffy, scurvy, shabby, sluttish, smutty, soiled, sordid, squalid, sullied, treacherous, unclean, unfair, unscrupulous, unsporting, unsterile, unswept, vile, vulgar, yucky.

*antonyms* clean, spotless.

*v* bedaub, begrime, besmear, besmirch, besmut, bespatter, blacken, defile, foul, mess up, muddy, pollute, smear, smirch, smudge, soil, soss, spoil, stain, sully.

*antonyms* clean, cleanse.

**disability** *n* affliction, ailment, complaint, crippledom, defect, disablement, disorder, disqualification, handicap, impairment, impotency, inability, incapacitation, incapacity, incompetency, infirmity, malady, unfitness, weakness.

**disable** *v* cripple, damage, debilitate, disenable, disqualify, enfeeble, hamstring, handicap, immobilise, impair, incapacitate, invalidate, lame, paralyse, prostrate, unfit, unman, weaken.

**disabled** *adj* bedridden, crippled, handicapped, hors de combat, immobilised, incapacitated, infirm, lame, maimed, mangled, mutilated, paralysed, weak, weakened, wrecked.

*antonyms* able, able-bodied.

**disadvantage** *n* burden, damage, debit, detriment, disamenity, disbenefit, disservice, drawback, flaw, fly in the ointment, handicap, hardship, harm, hindrance, hurt, impediment, inconvenience, injury, liability, loss, minus, nuisance, prejudice, privation, snag, trouble, unfavourableness, weakness.

*antonyms* advantage, benefit.

*v* hamper, handicap, hinder, inconvenience, wrong-foot.

*antonyms* aid, help.

**disadvantaged** *adj* deprived, handicapped, hindered, impeded, impoverished, struggling, underprivileged.

*antonym* privileged.

**disadvantageous** *adj* adverse, burdensome, damaging, deleterious, detrimental, harmful, hurtful, ill-timed, inauspicious, inconvenient, inexpedient, injurious, inopportune, prejudicial, unfavourable.

*antonym* advantageous.

**disaffected** *adj* alienated, antagonistic, antipathetic(al), discontented, disgruntled, disloyal, dissatisfied, estranged, hostile, mutinous, rebellious, seditious.

*antonym* contented.

**disaffection** *n* alienation, animosity, antagonism, antipathy, aversion, breach, coolness, disagreement, discontentment, discord, disharmony, dislike, disloyalty, dissatisfaction, estrangement, hostility, ill-will, repugnance, resentment, unfriendliness.

*antonym* contentment.

**disagree** *v* altercate, argue, bicker, bother, clash, conflict, contend, contest, contradict, counter, depart, deviate, differ, disaccord, discomfort, dissent, distress, diverge, fall out, hurt, nauseate, object, oppose, quarrel, run counter to, sicken, spat, squabble, take issue with, tiff, trouble, upset, vary, wrangle.

*antonym* agree.

**disagreeable** *adj* bad-tempered, brusque, churlish, contrary, cross, difficult, disgusting, dislik(e)able, disobliging, displeasing, distasteful, ill-natured, irritable, nasty, objectionable, obnoxious, offensive, peevish, repellent, repugnant, repulsive, rude, surly, unamiable, unappetising, unfriendly, ungracious, uninviting, unpalatable, unpleasant, unsavoury.

*antonyms* agreeable, friendly, pleasant.

**disagreement** *n* altercation, argument, clash, conflict, debate, difference, disaccord, discord, discrepancy, disparity, dispute, dissent, dissimilarity, dissimilitude, divergence, diversity, division, falling-out, incompatibility, incongruity, misunderstanding, quarrel, squabble, strife, tiff, unlikeness, variance, wrangle.

*antonym* agreement.

**disallow** *v* abjure, ban, cancel, chalk off, debar, disaffirm, disavow, disclaim, dismiss, disown, embargo, forbid, prohibit, proscribe, rebuff, refuse, reject, repudiate, veto.

*antonyms* allow, permit.

**disallowed** *adj* debarred, excepted, excluded, forbidden, impermissible, interdicted, prohibited, proscribed, rejected.

*antonyms* allowed, permissible.

**disappear** v cease, dematerialise, depart, dissolve, ebb, end, escape, evanesce, evaporate, expire, fade, flee, fly, go, pass, perish, recede, retire, scarper, vamoose, vanish, wane, withdraw.

*antonym* appear.

**disappearance** n dematerialisation, departure, desertion, disappearing, dispersal, dispersion, dissipation, eclipse, evanescence, evaporation, fading, flight, going, loss, melting, passing, vanishing.

*antonym* appearance.

**disappoint** v baffle, balk, chagrin, dash, deceive, defeat, delude, disconcert, disenchant, disgruntle, dishearten, disillusion, dismay, dissatisfy, fail, foil, frustrate, hamper, hinder, let down, miff, sadden, thwart, vex.

*antonyms* delight, please, satisfy.

**disappointed** adj balked, depressed, despondent, discontented, discouraged, disenchanted, disgruntled, disillusioned, dissatisfied, distressed, down-hearted, foiled, frustrated, let down, miffed, saddened, thwarted, upset.

*antonyms* delighted, pleased, satisfied.

**disappointing** adj anti-climactic, depressing, disagreeable, disconcerting, discouraging, inadequate, inferior, insufficient, pathetic, sad, sorry, unhappy, unsatisfactory, unworthy.

*antonyms* encouraging, pleasant, satisfactory.

**disappointment**[1] n bafflement, chagrin, discontent, discouragement, disenchantment, disillusionment, displeasure, dissatisfaction, distress, failure, frustration, mortification, regret.

*antonyms* delight, pleasure, satisfaction.

**disappointment**[2] n blow, calamity, comedown, disaster, drop, failure, fiasco, frost, lemon, let-down, misfortune, setback, swiz, swizzle.

*antonyms* boost, success.

**disapprobation** n blame, censure, condemnation, denunciation, disapproval, disfavour, dislike, displeasure, dissatisfaction, objection, reproach, reproof.

*antonyms* approbation, approval.

**disapproval** n censure, condemnation, criticism, denunciation, deprecation, disapprobation, disfavour, dislike, disparagement, displeasure, dissatisfaction, objection, reproach, thumbs-down.

*antonyms* approbation, approval, thumbs-up.

**disapprove of** blame, censure, condemn, denounce, deplore, deprecate, disallow, discountenance, dislike, disparage, object to, reject, spurn, take exception to.

*antonym* approve of.

**disapproving** adj censorious, condemnatory, critical, deprecatory, disapprobative, disapprobatory, disparaging, improbative, improbatory, reproachful.

**disarm**[1] v deactivate, demilitarise, demobilise, disable, disband, unarm, unweapon.

*antonym* arm.

**disarm**[2] appease, conciliate, modify, persuade, win over.

**disarming** adj charming, conciliatory, irresistible, likeable, mollifying, persuasive, winning.

**disarrange** v confuse, derange, disarray, discompose, dislocate, disorder, disorganise, disrank, disturb, jumble, muss(e), shuffle, unsettle, untidy.

*antonym* arrange.

**disarray** n chaos, clutter, confusion, discomposure, disharmony, dishevelment, dislocation, dismay, disorder, disorderliness, disorganisation, displacement, disunity, guddle, indiscipline, jumble, mess, muddle, shambles, tangle, unruliness, untidiness, upset.

*antonyms* array, order.

**disaster** n accident, act of God, blow, calamity, cataclysm, catastrophe, curtains, debacle, melt, misadventure, mischance, misfortune, mishap, reverse, ruin, ruination, stroke, tragedy, trouble.

*antonyms* success, triumph.

**disastrous** adj adverse, calamitous, cataclysmal, cataclysmic, catastrophic, destructive, detrimental, devastating, dire, dreadful, fatal, grievous, hapless, harmful, ill-fated, ill-starred, miserable, ruinous, terrible, tragic, unfortunate, unlucky.

*antonyms* successful, triumphant.

**disband** v break up, demobilise, dismiss, disperse, dissolve, part company, retire, scatter, separate.

*antonyms* assemble, band, combine.

**disbelief** n distrust, doubt, dubiety, incredulity, mistrust, rejection, scepticism, suspicion, unbelief.

*antonym* belief.

**disbelieve** v discount, discredit, miscredit, mistrust, reject, repudiate, suspect, unbelieve.

*antonyms* believe, trust.

**disbeliever** n agnostic, atheist, doubter, doubting Thomas, nullifidian, questioner, sceptic, scoffer, unbeliever.

*antonym* believer.

**disbursement** n disbursal, disposal, expenditure, outlay, payment, spending.

**disc** n circle, disk, diskette, face, plate, record, ring, roundel, roundlet, rundle.

**discard** v abandon, cashier, cast aside, dispense with, dispose of, ditch, drop, dump, jettison, leave off, reject, relinquish, remove, repudiate, scrap, shed.

*antonyms* adopt, embrace, espouse.

**discern** v ascertain, behold, descry, detect, determine, differentiate, discover, discriminate, distinguish, espy, judge, make out, notice, observe, perceive, recognise, see, wot.

**discernible** adj apparent, appreciable, clear, detectable, discoverable, distinct, distinguishable, manifest, noticeable, observable, obvious, patent, perceptible, plain, recognisable, sensible, visible.

*antonym* invisible.

**discerning** *adj* acute, astute, clear-sighted, critical, discriminating, eagle-eyed, eagle-sighted, ingenious, intelligent, judicious, knowing, penetrating, perceptive, percipient, perspicacious, piercing, sagacious, sensitive, sharp, shrewd, subtle, wise.

*antonym* obtuse.

**discernment** *n* acumen, acuteness, ascertainment, astuteness, awareness, clear-sightedness, cleverness, discrimination, ingenuity, insight, intelligence, judgement, keenness, penetration, perception, perceptiveness, percipience, perspicacity, sagacity, sharpness, understanding, wisdom.

**discharge** *v* absolve, accomplish, acquit, carry out, cashier, clear, detonate, disburden, discard, disembogue, dismiss, dispense, drum out, effectuate, egest, eject, emit, empty, excrete, execute, exonerate, expel, explode, exude, fire, free, fulfil, give off, gush, honour, leak, let off, liberate, meet, offload, ooze, oust, pardon, pay, perform, release, relieve, remove, sack, satisfy, set off, settle, shoot, unburden, unload, vent, void, volley.

*antonyms* employ, engage, hire.

*n* accomplishment, achievement, acquittal, acquittance, blast, burst, clearance, conge, defluxion, demobilisation, detonation, disburdening, discharging, dismissal, effluent, ejecta, ejectamenta, ejection, emission, emptying, excretion, execution, exoneration, explosion, firing, flight, flow, flux, fluxion, fulfilment, fusillade, gleet, glit, liberation, mittimus, observance, ooze, pardon, payment, performance, pus, quietus, quittance, release, remittance, report, salvo, satisfaction, secretion, seepage, settlement, shot, suppuration, the boot, the sack, unburdening, unloading, vent, voidance, voiding, volley, whiff.

**disciple** *n* acolyte, adherent, apostle, believer, catechumen, chela, convert, devotee, follower, learner, partisan, proselyte, pupil, student, supporter, votary.

**disciplinarian** *n* authoritarian, autocrat, despot, martinet, stickler, taskmaster, tyrant.

**discipline** *n* castigation, chastisement, conduct, control, correction, course, curriculum, drill, exercise, martinetism, method, orderliness, practice, punishment, regimen, regulation, restraint, self-control, speciality, strictness, subject, training.

*antonyms* carelessness, negligence.

*v* break in, castigate, chasten, chastise, check, control, correct, drill, educate, exercise, form, govern, habituate, instruct, inure, penalise, prepare, punish, regulate, reprimand, reprove, restrain, toughen, train.

**disclaim** *v* abandon, abjure, abnegate, decline, deny, disacknowledge, disaffirm, disallow, disavow, disown, forswear, reject, renounce, repudiate.

*antonyms* accept, acknowledge, claim.

**disclaimer** *n* abjuration, abnegation, contradiction, denial, disavowal, disownment, rejection, renunciation, repudiation, retraction.

**disclose** *v* broadcast, communicate, confess, discover, divulge, exhibit, expose, impart, lay, lay bare, leak, let slip, propale, publish, relate, reveal, show, tell, unbare, unbosom, unburden, uncover, unfold, unveil, utter.

*antonyms* conceal, hide.

**disclosure** *n* acknowledgement, admission, announcement, Apocalypse, broadcast, confession, declaration, discovery, divulgence, expose, exposure, leak, publication, revelation, uncovering.

**discoloration** *n* blemish, blot, blotch, dyschroa, ecchymosis, mark, patch, splotch, spot, stain.

**discolour** *v* disfigure, fade, mar, mark, rust, soil, stain, streak, tarnish, tinge, weather.

**discomfit** *v* abash, baffle, balk, beat, checkmate, confound, confuse, defeat, demoralise, discompose, disconcert, embarrass, faze, flurry, fluster, foil, frustrate, humble, humiliate, outwit, overcome, perplex, perturb, rattle, ruffle, thwart, trump, unsettle, vanquish, worry, worst.

**discomfiture** *n* abashment, beating, chagrin, confusion, defeat, demoralisation, disappointment, discomposure, embarrassment, failure, frustration, humiliation, overthrow, repulse, rout, ruin, shame, undoing, unease, vanquishment.

**discomfort** *n* ache, annoyance, disquiet, distress, hardship, hurt, inquietude, irritant, irritation, malaise, trouble, uneasiness, unpleasantness, unpleasantry, vexation.

*antonyms* comfort, ease.

**discompose** *v* agitate, annoy, bewilder, confuse, discomfit, disconcert, dishevel, displease, disturb, embarrass, faze, flurry, fluster, fret, irritate, perturb, rattle, ruffle, rumple, tousle, unsettle, upset, vex, worry.

*antonym* compose.

**discomposure** *n* agitation, anxiety, confusion, discomfiture, dislocation, disorder, disquiet, disquietude, distraction, disturbance, embarrassment, fluster, inquietude, malaise, nervousness, perturbation, uneasiness.

*antonym* composure.

**disconcert** *v* abash, agitate, baffle, balk, bewilder, confuse, discombobulate, discomfit, discompose, disturb, flurry, fluster, frustrate, hinder, nonplus, perplex, perturb, put someone's nose out of joint, rattle, ruffle, thwart, trouble, unbalance, undo, unsettle, upset, worry.

**disconcerted** *adj* annoyed, bewildered, confused, discombobulated, discomfited, distracted, disturbed, embarrassed, fazed, flurried, flustered, mixed-up, nonplussed, perturbed, rattled, ruffled, taken aback, thrown, troubled, unsettled, upset.

**disconcerting** *adj* alarming, awkward, baffling, bewildering, bothersome, confusing, discombobulating, dismaying, distracting, disturbing, embarrassing, off-putting, perplexing, upsetting.

**disconnect** *v* cut off, detach, disengage, divide, part, separate, sever, uncouple, ungear, unhitch, unhook, unlink, unplug, unyoke.

*antonyms* attach, connect, engage.

**disconnected** *adj* confused, disjointed, free, garbled, illogical, incoherent, irrational, jumbled, loose, rambling, unco-ordinated, unintelligible, wandering.

*antonyms* attached, coherent, connected.

**disconsolate** *adj* crushed, dejected, desolate, despairing, dispirited, forlorn, gloomy, grief-stricken, heartbroken, heavy-hearted, hopeless, inconsolable, melancholy, miserable, sad, unhappy, unsolaced, woeful, wretched.

*antonyms* cheerful, cheery.

**discontent** *n* discontentment, displeasure, disquiet, dissatisfaction, envy, fretfulness, impatience, regret, restlessness, uneasiness, unhappiness, unrest, vexation.

*antonym* content.

**discontented** *adj* brassed off, browned off, cheesed off, complaining, disaffected, disgruntled, displeased, dissatisfied, exasperated, fed up, fretful, impatient, miserable, scunnered, unhappy, vexed.

*antonyms* contented, happy, satisfied.

**discontinue** *v* abandon, break off, cancel, cease, drop, end, finish, halt, interrupt, pause, quit, stop, suspend, terminate.

*antonym* continue.

**discontinuity** *n* breach, disconnectedness, disconnection, disjointedness, disruption, disunion, incoherence, interruption, rupture.

*antonym* continuity.

**discontinuous** *adj* broken, disconnected, fitful, intermittent, interrupted, irregular, periodic, punctuated, spasmodic.

*antonym* continuous.

**discord** *n* cacophony, clashing, conflict, contention, difference, din, disagreement, discordance, disharmony, dispute, dissension, dissonance, disunity, division, friction, harshness, incompatibility, jangle, jarring, opposition, racket, rupture, split, strife, tumult, variance, wrangling.

*antonyms* agreement, concord, harmony.

**discordant** *adj* absonant, at odds, cacophonous, clashing, conflicting, contradictory, contrary, different, disagreeing, disharmonic, disharmonious, dissonant, grating, harsh, incompatible, incongruous, inconsistent, inharmonious, jangling, jarring, opposite, shrill, strident, unmelodious, untuneful.

*antonyms* concordant, harmonious.

**discount**[1] *v* disbelieve, disregard, gloss over, ignore, overlook.

**discount**[2] *n* abatement, allowance, concession, cut, deduction, mark-down, rebate, rebatement, reduction.

**discountenance** *v* abash, chagrin, confuse, discompose, disconcert, discourage, embarrass, humble, humiliate, shame.

*antonyms* countenance, support.

**discourage** *v* abash, awe, check, chill, cow, curb, damp, dampen, dash, daunt, deject, demoralise, deprecate, depress, deter, discountenance,

disfavour, dishearten, dismay, dispirit, dissuade, frighten, hinder, inhibit, intimidate, overawe, prevent, put off, restrain, scare, unman, unnerve.

*antonyms* encourage, favour, hearten, inspire.

**discouraged** *adj* chopfallen, crestfallen, dashed, daunted, depressed, deterred, disheartened, dismayed, dispirited, downcast, glum, pessimistic.

*antonyms* encouraged, heartened.

**discouragement** *n* constraint, curb, damp, damper, dejection, depression, despair, despondency, deterrent, disappointment, discomfiture, disincentive, dismay, dismayedness, downheartedness, hindrance, hopelessness, impediment, obstacle, opposition, pessimism, rebuff, restraint, setback.

*antonyms* encouragement, incentive.

**discouraging** *adj* dampening, daunting, dehortatory, depressing, disappointing, disheartening, dispiriting, dissuasive, dissuasory, inauspicious, off-putting, unfavourable, unpropitious.

*antonyms* encouraging, heartening.

**discourse** *n* address, chat, communication, conversation, converse, descant, dialogue, discussion, disquisition, dissertation, essay, exercitation, homily, lecture, oration, sermon, speech, talk, treatise.

*v* confer, converse, debate, declaim, descant, dialogise, discuss, dissent, dissertate, expatiate, jaw, lecture, lucubrate, talk.

**discourteous** *adj* abrupt, bad-mannered, boorish, brusque, curt, disrespectful, ill-bred, ill-mannered, impolite, insolent, offhand, rude, slighting, unceremonious, uncivil, uncourteous, ungracious, unmannerly.

*antonyms* courteous, polite, respectful.

**discourtesy** *n* affront, bad manners, disrespectfulness, ill-breeding, impertinence, impoliteness, incivility, indecorousness, indecorum, insolence, insult, rebuff, rudeness, slight, snub, ungraciousness, unmannerliness.

*antonyms* courtesy, politeness.

**discover** *v* ascertain, conceive, contrive, descry, design, detect, determine, devise, dig up, discern, disclose, espy, find, invent, learn, light on, locate, notice, originate, perceive, pioneer, realise, recognise, reveal, see, spot, suss out, uncover, unearth.

*antonyms* conceal, hide.

**discoverer** *n* author, explorer, finder, founder, initiator, inventor, originator, pioneer.

**discovery** *n* ascertainment, breakthrough, coup, detection, disclosure, espial, eureka, exploration, find, finding, innovation, introduction, invention, locating, location, origination, revelation, uncovering.

*antonym* concealment.

**discredit** *v* blame, censure, challenge, defame, degrade, deny, disbelieve, discount, disgrace, dishonour, disparage, dispute, distrust, doubt, explode, mistrust, question, reproach, slander, slur, smear, vilify.

*antonyms* believe, credit.

*n* aspersion, blame, censure, disgrace, dishonour, disrepute, distrust, doubt, ignominy, ill-repute, imputation, mistrust, odium, opprobium, question, reproach, scandal, scepticism, shame, slur, smear, stigma, suspicion.

*antonym* credit.

**discreditable** *adj* blameworthy, degrading, disgraceful, dishonourable, humiliating, ignoble, ignominious, improper, infamous, reprehensible, scandalous, shameful, unbecoming, unprincipled, unworthy.

*antonyms* creditable, worthy.

**discredited** *adj* debunked, discarded, disgraced, dishonoured, exploded, exposed, outworn, refuted, rejected.

**discreet** *adj* careful, cautious, circumspect, considerate, delicate, diplomatic, discerning, guarded, judicious, politic, prudent, reserved, sagacious, sensible, softly-softly, tactful, wary.

*antonyms* careless, indiscreet, tactless.

**discrepancy** *n* conflict, contrariety, difference, disagreement, discordance, disparity, dissimilarity, dissonance, divergence, imparity, incongruity, inconsistency, inequality, variance, variation.

**discrete** *adj* detached, disconnected, discontinuous, disjoined, disjunct, distinct, individual, separate, unattached.

**discretion** *n* acumen, care, carefulness, caution, choice, circumspection, consideration, diplomacy, discernment, disposition, heedfulness, inclination, judgement, judiciousness, liking, maturity, mind, option, pleasure, predilection, preference, prudence, responsibility, sagacity, tact, volition, wariness, will, wisdom, wish.

*antonym* indiscretion.

**discriminate[1]** *v* assess, differentiate, discern, distinguish, evaluate, make a distinction, segregate, separate, sift, tell apart.

*antonyms* confound, confuse.

**discriminate[2]** (against) *v* be biased, be prejudiced, disfavour, victimise.

**discriminating** *adj* acute, astute, critical, cultivated, discerning, discriminant, fastidious, nasute, particular, perceptive, selective, sensitive, tasteful.

**discrimination[1]** *n* bias, bigotry, favouritism, inequity, intolerance, Jim Crow, prejudice, unfairness.

**discrimination[2]** *n* acumen, acuteness, discernment, insight, judgement, keenness, penetration, perception, percipience, refinement, sagacity, subtlety, taste.

**discriminatory[1]** *adj* biased, discriminative, favouring, inequitable, loaded, one-sided, partial, partisan, preferential, prejudiced, prejudicial, unfair, unjust, weighted.

*antonyms* fair, impartial, unbiased.

**discriminatory[2]** *adj* analytical, astute, differentiating, discerning, discriminating, perceptive, percipient, perspicacious.

**discursive** *adj* circuitous, desultory, diffuse, digressive, discursory, erratic, long-winded, loose, meandering, prolix, rambling, wide-ranging.

*antonyms* brief, short.

**discuss** *v* argue, confer, consider, consult, converse, debate, deliberate, examine, lay heads together, rap.

**discussion** *n* analysis, argument, colloquium, colloquy, confabulation, conference, conferencing, consideration, consultation, conversation, debate, deliberation, dialogue, discourse, examination, exchange, gabfest, moot, quodlibet, rap, review, scrutiny, seminar, symposium, talkfest, talk-in, teleconferencing.

**disdain** *v* belittle, contemn, deride, despise, disavow, disregard, misprise, pooh-pooh, rebuff, reject, scorn, slight, sneer at, spurn, undervalue.

*antonyms* admire, respect.

*n* arrogance, contempt, contumely, deprecation, derision, dislike, haughtiness, hauteur, imperiousness, indifference, scorn, sneering, snobbishness, superciliousness.

*antonyms* admiration, respect.

**disdainful** *adj* aloof, arrogant, contemptuous, derisive, haughty, hoity-toity, imperious, insolent, proud, scornful, sneering, supercilious, superior, uppish.

*antonyms* admiring, respectful.

**disease** *n* affection, affliction, ailment, blight, cancer, canker, complaint, condition, contagion, contamination, disorder, distemper, epidemic, epizootic, idiopathy, ill-health, illness, indisposition, infection, infirmity, lurgy, malady, malaise, murrain, pest, plague, sickness, upset.

*antonym* health.

**diseased** *adj* ailing, contaminated, distemperate, infected, poisoned, rotten, sick, sickly, tainted, unhealthy, unsound, unwell, unwholesome.

*antonym* healthy.

**disembark** *v* alight, arrive, debark, debus, deplane, detrain, disbark, land.

*antonym* embark.

**disembodied** *adj* bodiless, disbodied, discorporate, disfleshed, ghostly, immaterial, incorporeal, intangible, phantom, spectral, spiritual, unbodied.

**disembowel** *v* disbowel, draw, embowel, eviscerate, exenterate, gralloch, gut, paunch.

**disenchanted** *adj* blase, cynical, disappointed, disillusioned, fed up, indifferent, jaundiced, scunnered, soured, undeceived.

**disenchantment** *n* cynicism, disappointment, disillusion, disillusionment, revulsion, scunner.

**disengage** *v* detach, disconnect, disentangle, disentwine, disinvolve, disjoin, disunite, divide, ease, extricate, free, liberate, loosen, release, separate, undo, unloose, untie, untwine, withdraw.

*antonyms* attach, connect, engage.

**disengaged** *adj* disentangled, free(d), heart-free, heart-whole, inactive, liberated, loose, released, separate(d), unattached, unconnected, unhitched, unoccupied.

*antonyms* connected, joined, united.

**disentangle** *v* clarify, debarrass, detach, disconnect, disembarrass, disengage, disentwine, disinvolve, extricate, free, loose, ravel out, resolve, separate, sever, simplify, unfold, unravel, unsnarl, untangle, untwine, untwist.

*antonym* entangle.

**disfavour** *n* disapprobation, disapproval, discredit, disesteem, disgrace, disgust, dislike, displeasure, unpopularity.

*antonym* favour.

**disfigure** *v* blemish, damage, deface, deform, disfeature, distort, injure, maim, mar, mutilate, scar, spoil, uglify.

*antonym* adorn.

**disfigured** *adj* damaged, defaced, deformed, flawed, ruined, scarred, spoilt, ugly.

*antonym* adorned.

**disfigurement** *n* blemish, defacement, defect, deformity, disgrace, distortion, impairment, injury, mutilation, scar, spot, stain, uglification.

*antonym* adornment.

**disgorge** *v* belch, discharge, effuse, eject, empty, expel, regorge, regurgitate, relinquish, renounce, spew, spout, surrender, throw up, vomit.

**disgrace** *n* aspersion, attaint, baseness, blemish, blot, contempt, defamation, degradation, discredit, disesteem, disfavour, dishonour, disrepute, dog-house, ignominy, infamy, obloquy, odium, opprobium, reproach, scandal, shame, slur, stain, stigma.

*antonyms* esteem, honour, respect.

*v* abase, attaint, defame, degrade, discredit, disfavour, dishonour, disparage, humiliate, reproach, scandalise, shame, slur, stain, stigmatise, sully, taint.

*antonyms* honour, respect.

**disgraced** *adj* branded, degraded, discredited, dishonoured, humiliated, in the doghouse, stigmatised.

*antonyms* honoured, respected.

**disgraceful** *adj* appalling, blameworthy, contemptible, degrading, detestable, discreditable, dishonourable, disreputable, dreadful, ignominious, infamous, low, mean, opprobrious, scandalous, shameful, shocking, unworthy.

*antonyms* honourable, respectable.

**disgruntled** *adj* annoyed, brassed off, browned off, cheesed off, discontented, displeased, dissatisfied, grumpy, irritated, malcontent, peeved, peevish, petulant, put out, scunnered, sulky, sullen, testy, vexed.

*antonyms* pleased, satisfied.

**disguise** *v* camouflage, cloak, conceal, cover, deceive, dissemble, dissimulate, dress up, explain away, fake, falsify, fudge, hide, mask, misrepresent, screen, secrete, shroud, veil.

*antonyms* expose, reveal, uncover.

*n* camouflage, cloak, concealment, costume, cover, coverture, deception, dissimulation, façade, front, get-up, mask, masquerade, pretence, screen, semblance, travesty, trickery, veil, veneer, visor.

**disguised** *adj* camouflaged, cloaked, covert, fake, false, feigned, incognito, made up, masked, undercover, unrecognisable, visored.

**disgust** *v* displease, nauseate, offend, outrage, put off, repel, revolt, scandalise, scunner, sicken.

*antonyms* delight, gratify, tempt.

*n* abhorrence, abomination, antipathy, aversion, detestation, dislike, disrelish, distaste, hatefulness, hatred, loathing, nausea, odium, repugnance, repulsion, revulsion.

*antonyms* admiration, liking.

**disgusted** *adj* appalled, nauseated, offended, outraged, repelled, repulsed, scandalised, scunnered, sick (and tired), sickened.

*antonyms* attracted, delighted.

**disgusting** *adj* abominable, detestable, distasteful, foul, gross, hateful, loathsome, nasty, nauseating, nauseous, objectionable, obnoxious, obscene, odious, offensive, repellent, repugnant, revolting, shameless, sickening, sick-making, stinking, ugsome, unappetising, vile, vulgar.

*antonyms* attractive, delightful, pleasant.

**dish¹** *n* bowl, fare, food, plate, platter, porringer, ramekin, recipe, salver, trencher.

**dish out** allocate, distribute, dole out, give out, hand out, hand round, inflict, mete out.

**dish up** dispense, ladle, prepare, present, produce, scoop, serve, spoon.

**dish²** *v* finish, ruin, spoil, torpedo, wreck.

**disharmony** *n* clash, conflict, disaccord, discord, discordance, dissonance, friction, incompatibility.

*antonym* harmony.

**dishearten** *v* cast down, crush, damp, dampen, dash, daunt, deject, depress, deter, discourage, dismay, dispirit, frighten, weary.

*antonyms* encourage, hearten.

**disheartened** *adj* crestfallen, crushed, daunted, dejected, depressed, disappointed, discouraged, dismayed, dispirited, downcast, downhearted, frightened, weary.

*antonyms* encouraged, heartened.

**dishevelled** *adj* bedraggled, blowsy, disarranged, disordered, frowsy, messy, mussy, ruffled, rumpled, slovenly, tousled, uncombed, unkempt, untidy.

*antonyms* neat, spruce, tidy.

**dishonest** *adj* bent, cheating, corrupt, crafty, crooked, deceitful, deceiving, deceptive, designing, disreputable, double-dealing, false, fraudulent, guileful, immoral, knavish, lying, mendacious, perfidious, shady, snide, swindling, treacherous, unethical, unfair, unprincipled, unscrupulous, untrustworthy, untruthful, wrongful.

*antonyms* fair, honest, scrupulous, trustworthy.

**dishonesty** *n* cheating, chicanery, corruption, craft, criminality, crookedness, deceit, duplicity, falsehood, falsity, fraud, fraudulence, graft, immorality, improbity, insincerity, mendacity, perfidy, stealing, treachery, trickery, unscrupulousness, wiliness.

*antonyms* honesty, truthfulness.

**dishonour** *v* abase, blacken, corrupt, debase, debauch, defame, defile, deflower, degrade, demean, discredit, disgrace, disparage, pollute, rape, ravish, seduce, shame, sully.

*antonym* honour.

*n* abasement, abuse, affront, aspersion, degradation, discourtesy, discredit, disfavour, disgrace, disrepute, ignominy, imputation, indignity, infamy, insult, obloquy, odium, offence, opprobrium, outrage, reproach, scandal, shame, slight, slur.

*antonym* honour.

**dishonourable** *adj* base, blackguardly, contemptible, corrupt, despicable, discreditable, disgraceful, disreputable, ignoble, ignominous, infamous, scandalous, shameful, shameless, treacherous, unethical, unprincipled, unscrupulous, untrustworthy, unworthy.

*antonym* honourable.

**disillusioned** *adj* disabused, disappointed, disenchanted, enlightened, indifferent, undeceived, unenthusiastic.

**disincentive** *n* barrier, constraint, damper, determent, deterrent, discouragement, dissuasion, hindrance, impediment, obstacle, repellent, restriction, turn-off.

*antonyms* encouragement, incentive.

**disinclination** *n* alienation, antipathy, averseness, aversion, demur, dislike, loathness, objection, opposition, reluctance, repugnance, resistance, unwillingness.

*antonym* inclination.

**disinclined** *adj* antipathetic, averse, hesitant, indisposed, loath, opposed, reluctant, resistant, undisposed, unenthusiastic, unwilling.

*antonyms* inclined, willing.

**disinfect** *v* clean, cleanse, decontaminate, deodorise, depurate, fumigate, purge, purify, sanitise, sterilise.

*antonyms* contaminate, infect.

**disinfectant** *n* antiseptic, decontaminative, depurant, germicide, sanitiser, steriliser.

**disinfection** *n* cleansing, decontamination, depuration, fumigation, purification, sanitisation, sterilisation.

**disingenuous** *adj* artful, cunning, deceitful, designing, devious, dishonest, duplicitous, guileful, insidious, insincere, shifty, two-faced, uncandid, wily.

*antonyms* artless, frank, ingenuous, naive.

**disintegrate** *v* break up, crumble, decompose, disunite, fall apart, moulder, rot, separate, shatter, splinter.

*antonyms* combine, merge, unite.

**disinterest** *n* candidness, detachment, disinterestedness, dispassionateness, equitableness, equity, fairness, impartiality, justice, neutrality, unbiasedness.

*antonym* interest.

**disinterested** *adj* candid, detached, dispassionate, equitable, even-handed, impartial, impersonal, neutral, open-minded, unbiased, uninvolved, unprejudiced, unselfish.

*antonyms* biased, concerned, interested, prejudiced.

**disjoin** *v* detach, disannex, disconnect, disengage, dismember, dissociate, disunite, divide, divorce, isolate, partition, segregate, separate, sever, split, uncouple.

*antonyms* connect, join.

**disjoint** *v* anatomise, disarrange, disarticulate, discompose, dislocate, dismember, disorder, displace, dissect, unjoint.

**disjointed** *adj* aimless, broken, confused, dearticulated, disarticulated, disconnected, dislocated, disordered, displaced, disunited, divided, fitful, incoherent, loose, rambling, separated, spasmodic, split, unconnected, unjointed.

*antonym* coherent.

**dislike** *n* animosity, animus, antagonism, antipathy, aversion, detestation, disapprobation, disapproval, disgust, disinclination, displeasure, disrelish, distaste, dyspathy, enmity, hatred, hostility, loathing, repugnance.

*antonyms* attachment, liking, predilection.

*v* abhor, abominate, despise, detest, disapprove, disfavour, disrelish, hate, keck, loathe, scorn, shun.

*antonyms* favour, like, prefer.

**dislocate** *v* derange, disarray, disarticulate, disconnect, disengage, disjoint, disorder, displace, disrupt, disturb, disunite, luxate, misplace, shift, unhinge.

**dislocation** *n* derangement, disarray, disarticulation, disconnection, disengagement, disorder, disorganisation, disruption, disturbance, luxation, misarrangement, misarray, misplacement, unhingement, unhinging.

*antonym* order.

**dislodge** *v* displace, disturb, eject, extricate, move, oust, remove, shift, uproot.

**disloyal** *adj* apostate, disaffected, faithless, false, perfidious, seditious, subversive, traitorous, treacherous, treasonable, two-faced, unfaithful, unleal, unpatriotic, untrustworthy, unwifely.

*antonym* loyal.

**disloyalty** *n* apostasy, betrayal, double-dealing, falseness, falsity, inconstancy, infidelity, lese-majesty, perfidiousness, perfidy, sedition, treachery, treason, unfaithfulness.

*antonym* loyalty.

**dismal** *adj* black, bleak, burdan, cheerless, dark, depressing, despondent, discouraging, doleful, dolorous, dowie, dreary, dreich, forlorn, funereal, ghostful, gloomy, gruesome, hopeless, incompetent, inept, lac(h)rymose, lonesome, long-faced, long-visaged, lowering, low-spirited, lugubrious, melancholy, poor, sad, sepulchral, sombre, sorrowful, stupid, thick, useless.

*antonyms* bright, cheerful.

**dismantle** *v* demolish, demount, disassemble, dismount, raze, strike, strip, unrig.

*antonym* assemble.

**dismay** *v* affright, alarm, appal, consternate, daunt, depress, disappoint, disconcert, discourage, dishearten, disillusion, dispirit, distress, frighten, horrify, paralyse, put off, scare, terrify, unnerve, unsettle.

*antonym* encourage.

*n* agitation, alarm, anxiety, apprehension, consternation, disappointment, distress, dread, fear, fright, funk, horror, panic, terror, trepidation, upset.

*antonyms* boldness, encouragement.

**dismember** *v* amputate, anatomise, disject, disjoint, dislimb, dislocate, dissect, divellicate, divide, mutilate, piecemeal, rend, sever.

*antonyms* assemble, join.

**dismemberment** *n* amputation, anatomisation, disjection, dislocation, dissection, division, mutilation.

*antonyms* assembly, joining, unifying.

**dismiss** *v* axe, banish, bounce, bowler-hat, cashier, chasse, chuck, disband, discharge, discount, dispel, disperse, disregard, dissolve, drop, fire, free, give (someone) the push, lay off, let go, oust, pooh-pooh, reject, release, relegate, remove, repudiate, sack, send packing, set aside, shelve, spurn.

*antonyms* accept, appoint.

**dismissal** *n* adjournment, cards, conge, dear John letter, discharge, dismission, end, expulsion, marching orders, mittimus, notice, release, removal, the boot, the bum's rush, the elbow, the mitten, the push, the sack, walking-orders, walking-papers, walking-ticket.

*antonym* appointment.

**dismissive** *adj* contemptuous, disdainful, dismissory, off-hand, scornful, sneering.

*antonyms* concerned, interested.

**dismount** *v* alight, descend, get down, light, unmount.

*antonym* mount.

**disobedience** *n* contrariness, contumacity, contumacy, indiscipline, infraction, insubordination, mutiny, non-observance, recalcitrance, revolt, unruliness, waywardness.

*antonym* obedience.

**disobedient** *adj* contrary, contumacious, defiant, disorderly, froward, insubordinate, intractable, mischievous, naughty, obstreperous, refractory, unruly, wayward, wilful.

*antonym* obedient.

**disobey** *v* contravene, defy, disregard, flout, ignore, infringe, overstep, rebel, resist, transgress, violate.

*antonym* obey.

**disoblige** *v* deny, disserve, refuse.

*antonym* oblige.

**disobliging** *adj* awkward, bloody-minded, cussed, disagreeable, discourteous, inaccommodating, rude, unaccommodating, uncivil, unco-operative, unhelpful.

*antonym* obliging.

**disorder** *n* affliction, ailment, brawl, chaos, clamour, clutter, commotion, complaint, confusion, derangement, disarray, disease, disorderliness, disorganisation, disturbance, fight, fracas, hubbub, hullabaloo, illness, indisposition, irregularity, jumble, malady, mess, misarrangement, misarray, misorder, misrule, muddle, muss(e), mussiness, quarrel, riot, rumpus, shambles, sickness, tumult, untidiness, uproar.

*antonym* order.

*v* clutter, confound, confuse, derange, disarrange, discompose, disorganise, disrank, disturb, jumble, mess up, misorder, mix up, muddle, scatter, unsettle, upset.

*antonyms* arrange, organise.

**disordered** *adj* confused, deranged, disarranged, dislocated, disorganised, displaced, higgledy-piggledy, indigest, jumbled, misplaced, muddle, mussy, onkus, out of kilter, turbid, untidy.

*antonyms* ordered, tidy.

**disorderly** *adj* chaotic, confused, disordinate, disorganised, disruptive, higgledy-piggledy, indiscriminate, irregular, jumbled, lawless, messy, obstreperous, rebellious, refractory, riotous, rowdy, shambolic, stormy, tumultuous, turbulent, undisciplined, ungovernable, unlawful, unmanageable, unruly, unsystematic, untidy.

*antonyms* tidy, well-behaved.

**disorganisation** *n* chaos, confusion, derangement, disarray, disjointedness, dislocation, disorder, disruption, incoherence, unconnectedness.

*antonyms* order, tidiness.

**disorganise** *v* break up, confuse, derange, destroy, disarrange, discompose, disorder, disrank, disrupt, disturb, jumble, muddle, play havoc with, play hell with, unsettle, upset.

*antonym* organise.

**disorganised** *adj* chaotic, confused, disordered, haphazard, jumbled, muddled, shambolic, shuffled, topsy-turvy, unmethodical, unorganised, unregulated, unsifted, unsorted, unstructured, unsystematic, unsystematised.

*antonyms* organised, tidy.

**disorientate** *v* confuse, dislocate, disorient, faze, feeze, mislead, muddle, perplex, puzzle, upset.

**disorientated** *adj* adrift, astray, at sea, bewildered, confused, disoriented, lost, mixed up, muddled, perplexed, puzzled, unbalanced, unsettled, upset.

**disown** *v* abandon, abnegate, cast off, deny, disacknowledge, disallow, disavow, disclaim, reject, renounce, repudiate, unget.

*antonym* accept.

**disparage** *v* belittle, criticise, decry, defame, degrade, denigrate, deprecate, depreciate, deride, derogate, detract from, discredit, disdain, dishonour, dismiss, disvalue, malign, minimise, ridicule, run down, scorn, slander, traduce, underestimate, underrate, undervalue, vilify, vilipend.

*antonym* praise.

**disparagement** *n* aspersion, belittlement, condemnation, contempt, contumely, criticism, debasement, decrial, decrying, degradation, denunciation, deprecation, depreciation, derision, derogation, detraction, discredit, disdain, ridicule, scorn, slander, underestimation, vilification.

*antonym* praise.

**disparate** *adj* contrary, contrasting, different, discordant, discrepant, dissimilar, distinct, diverse, unequal, unlike.

*antonyms* equal, similar.

**disparity** *n* contrast, difference, discrepancy, disproportion, dissimilarity, dissimilitude, distinction, gap, imbalance, imparity, incongruity, inequality, unevenness, unlikeness.

*antonyms* equality, similarity.

**dispassionate** *adj* calm, candid, collected, composed, cool, detached, disinterested, fair, impartial, impersonal, imperturbable, indifferent, moderate, neutral, objective, quiet, serene, sober, temperate, unbiased, unemotional, unexcitable, unexcited, uninvolved, unmoved, unprejudiced, unruffled.

*antonyms* biased, emotional.

**dispatch**[1], despatch *v* accelerate, conclude, discharge, dismiss, dispose of, expedite, finish, hasten, hurry, perform, quicken, settle.

*antonym* impede.

*n* alacrity, celerity, depêche, expedition, haste, precipitateness, promptitude, promptness, quickness, rapidity, speed, swiftness.

*antonym* slowness.

**dispatch**[2], despatch *v* consign, express, forward, remit, send, transmit.

*n* account, bulletin, communication, communique, document, instruction, item, letter, message, missive, news, piece, report, story.

**dispatch**[3], despatch *v* assassinate, bump off, execute, kill, murder, rub out, slaughter, slay, waste.

**dispel** *v* allay, banish, discuss, dismiss, disperse, dissipate, drive off, eliminate, expel, melt away, resolve, rout, scatter.

*antonym* give rise to.

**dispensable** *adj* disposable, expendable, inessential, needless, non-essential, replaceable, superfluous, unnecessary, useless.

*antonym* indispensable.

**dispensation** *n* administration, allotment, appointment, apportionment, award, bestowal, conferment, consignment, derogation, direction, disbursement, distribution, dole, economy, endowment, exception, exemption, immunity, indulgence, licence, management, part, permission, plan, portion, privilege, quota, regulation, relaxation, relief, remission, reprieve, scheme, share, stewardship, supplying, system.

**dispensatory** *adj* derogative, disobligatory, dispensative.

**dispense** *v* administer, allocate, allot, apply, apportion, assign, deal out, direct, disburse, discharge, distribute, dole out, enforce, except, excuse, execute, exempt, exonerate, implement, let off, measure, mete out, mix, operate, prepare, release, relieve, reprieve, share, supply, undertake.

**dispense with** abolish, cancel, dispose of, disregard, forgo, ignore, omit, pass over, relinquish, waive.

*antonyms* accept, use.

**disperse** *v* broadcast, circulate, diffuse, disappear, disband, dismiss, dispel, disseminate, dissipate, dissolve, distribute, drive off, evanesce, melt away, rout, scatter, separate, spread, strew, vanish.

*antonym* gather.

**dispersion** *n* broadcast, circulation, diaspora, diffusion, discussion, dispersal, dissemination, dissipation, distribution, galut(h), scattering, spread.

**dispirit** *v* damp, dampen, dash, deject, depress, deter, discourage, dishearten, put a damper on, sadden.

*antonym* encourage.

**dispirited** *adj* brassed off, browned off, cast down, crestfallen, dejected, depressed, despondent, discouraged, disheartened, down, downcast, fed up, gloomy, glum, low, morose, sad.

*antonym* encouraged.

**displace** *v* cashier, crowd out, depose, derange, disarrange, discard, discharge, dislocate, dislodge, dismiss, dispossess, disturb, eject, evict, fire, luxate, misplace, move, oust, remove, replace, sack, shift, succeed, supersede, supplant, transpose, unsettle.

**displaced** *adj* disarranged, ectopic, misplaced.

**displacement** *n* disarrangement, disturbance, ectopia, ectopy, heterotaxis, heterotopia, misplacement.

*antonym* order.

**display** *v* betray, blazon, boast, demonstrate, disclose, evidence, evince, exhibit, expand, expose, extend, flash, flaunt, flourish, manifest, model, parade, present, reveal, show, show off, showcase, splash, sport, unfold, unfurl, unveil, vaunt, wear.

*antonym* hide.

*n* array, demonstration, etalage, exhibition, exposition, exposure, flourish, manifestation, ostentation, pageant, parade, pomp, presentation, revelation, show, spectacle, splurge.

**displease** *v* aggravate, anger, annoy, disgust, dissatisfy, exasperate, gall, get, incense, infuriate, irk, irritate, nettle, offend, peeve, pique, provoke, put out, rile, upset, vex.

*antonyms* calm, please.

**displeased** *n* aggravated, angry, annoyed, chuffed, exasperated, furious, irritated, peeved, piqued, put out, upset.

*antonym* pleased.

**displeasure** *n* anger, annoyance, disapprobation, disapproval, discontent, disfavour, disgruntlement, dudgeon, huff, indignation, irritation, offence, pique, resentment, vexation, wrath.

*antonyms* gratification, pleasure.

**disport** *v* amuse, beguile, bound, caper, cavort, cheer, delight, divert, entertain, frisk, frolic, gambol, play, revel, romp, sport.

**disposal** *n* arrangement, array, assignment, authority, bequest, bestowal, clearance, conduct, consignment, control, conveyance, determination, direction, discarding, discretion, dispensation, disposition, distribution, dumping, ejection, gift, government, jettisoning, management, ordering, position, regulation, relinquishment, removal, responsibility, riddance, scrapping, settlement, transfer.

*antonym* provision.

**dispose** *v* actuate, adapt, adjust, align, arrange, array, bias, condition, determine, dispone, distribute, fix, group, incline, induce, influence, lay, lead, marshal, motivate, move, order, place, position, predispose, prompt, put, range, rank, regulate, set, settle, situate, stand, tempt.

**dispose of** bestow, deal with, decide, destroy, determine, discard, dump, end, get rid of, give, jettison, kibosh, make over, put the kibosh on, scrap, sell, settle, transfer, unload.

*antonym* provide.

**disposed** *adj* apt, given, inclined, liable, likely, minded, moved, predisposed, prone, ready, subject, willing.

*antonym* disinclined.

**disposition** *n* adjustment, arrangement, bent, bias, character, classification, constitution, control, direction, disposal, distribution, grain, grouping, habit, inclination, kidney, leaning, make-up, management, nature, ordering, organisation, placement, predisposition, proclivity, proneness, propensity, readiness, regulation, spirit, temper, temperament, tendency, velleity.

**dispossess** *v* deprive, dislodge, disseise, divest, eject, evict, expel, expropriate, oust, rob, strip, unhouse.

*antonyms* give, provide.

**dispossession** *n* dethronement, dethroning, disseisin, ejection, ejectment, eviction, expulsion, ousting.

*antonym* possession.

**disproportion** *n* asymmetry, discrepancy, disparity, imbalance, imparity, inadequacy, inequality, insufficiency, lopsidedness, unevenness.

*antonyms* balance, equality.

**disproportionate** *adj* excessive, inappropriate, incommensurate, inordinate, unbalanced, unequal, uneven, unreasonable.

*antonyms* appropriate, balanced.

**disprove** *v* answer, confute, contradict, controvert, discredit, explode, expose, invalidate, negate, rebut, refute.

*antonym* prove.

**disputable** *adj* arguable, controversial, debatable, doubtful, dubious, litigious, moot, questionable, uncertain.

*antonym* indisputable.

**disputation** *n* argumentation, controversy, debate, dispute, dissension, polemics, quodlibet.

**disputatious** *adj* argumentative, cantankerous, captious, cavilling, contentious, litigious, polemical, pugnacious, quarrelsome, wranglesome.

**dispute** *v* altercate, argue, brawl, challenge, clash, contend, contest, contradict, controvert, debate, deny, discuss, doubt, gainsay, impugn, litigate, moot, oppugn, quarrel, question, spar, squabble, traverse, wrangle.

*antonym* agree.

*n* altercation, argument, brawl, conflict, contention, controversy, debate, disagreement, discord, discussion, dissension, disturbance, feud, friction, quarrel, spar, squabble, strife, wrangle.

*antonym* agreement.

**disputer** *n* adversary, antagonist, arguer, contender, contestant, debater, discursist, discutant, opponent.

**disqualified** *adj* debarred, eliminated, ineligible.

*antonyms* accepted, eligible, qualified.

**disqualify** *v* debar, disable, disauthorise, disentitle, dishabilitate, disprivilege, incapacitate, invalidate, preclude, prohibit, rule out, unfit.

*antonyms* accept, allow.

**disquiet** *n* alarm, angst, anxiety, concern, disquietude, distress, disturbance, fear, foreboding, fretfulness, nervousness, restlessness, trouble, uneasiness, unrest, worry.

*antonym* calmness.

*v* agitate, annoy, bother, concern, discompose, distress, disturb, fret, harass, hassle, incommode, perturb, pester, plague, shake, trouble, unsettle, upset, vex, worry.

*antonym* calm.

**disquieting** *adj* annoying, bothersome, disconcerting, disquietful, disquietive, distressing, disturbing, irritating, perturbing, troubling, unnerving, unsettling, upsetting, vexing, worrying.

*antonym* calming.

**disquisition** *n* descant, discourse, dissertation, essay, exposition, monograph, paper, sermon, thesis, treatise.

**disregard** *v* brush aside, cold-shoulder, contemn, despise, discount, disdain, disobey, disparage, ignore, laugh off, make light of, neglect, overlook, pass over, pooh-pooh, slight, snub, turn a blind eye to.

*antonyms* note, pay attention to.

*n* brush-off, contempt, disdain, disesteem, disrespect, heedlessness, ignoring, inattention, indifference, neglect, negligence, oversight, slight.

*antonym* attention.

**disrepair** *n* collapse, decay, deterioration, dilapidation, ruin, ruination, shabbiness, unrepair.

*antonyms* good repair, restoration.

**disreputable** *adj* base, contemptible, derogatory, discreditable, disgraceful, dishonourable, disorderly, disrespectable, ignominious, infamous, louche, low, mean, notorious, opprobrious, scandalous, seedy, shady, shameful, shocking, unprincipled.

*antonyms* decent, honourable.

**disrepute** *n* discredit, disesteem, disfavour, disgrace, dishonour, disreputation, ignominy, infamy, obloquy, shame.

*antonyms* esteem, honour.

**disrespect** *n* cheek, contempt, discourtesy, dishonour, disregard, impertinence, impoliteness, impudence, incivility, insolence, irreverence, misesteem, rudeness, unmannerliness.

*antonym* respect.

**disrespectful** *adj* bad-tempered, cheeky, contemptuous, discourteous, impertinent, impolite, impudent, insolent, insulting, irreverent, rude, uncivil, unmannerly.

*antonym* respectful.

**disrobe** *v* bare, denude, disapparel, divest, remove, shed, strip, take off, unclothe, uncover, undress.

*antonyms* cover, dress.

**disrupt** *v* agitate, break into, break up, confuse, derange, dislocate, disorder, disorganise, disturb, interrupt, intrude, obstruct, spoil, unsettle, upset.

**disruption** *n* burst-up, bust-up, cataclasm, confusion, disarray, disorder, disorderliness, dissembly, dissolution, disturbance, interference, interruption, stoppage, upheaval.

**disruptive** *adj* boisterous, disorderly, distracting, disturbing, obstreperous, troublesome, turbulent, undisciplined, unruly, unsettling, upsetting.

*antonym* well-behaved.

**dissatisfaction** *n* annoyance, chagrin, disappointment, discomfort, discontent, dislike, dismay, displeasure, distress, exasperation, frustration, irritation, non-fulfilment, regret, resentment, unfulfilment, unhappiness.

*antonyms* fulfilment, satisfaction.

**dissatisfied** *adj* chuffed, disappointed, discontented, disgruntled, displeased, fed up, frustrated, unfulfilled, unhappy, unsatisfied.

*antonyms* fulfilled, satisfied.

**dissatisfy** *v* annoy, disappoint, discontent, disgruntle, displease, exasperate, frustrate, irritate, put out, vex.

**dissect** *v* analyse, anatomise, break down, dismember, examine, explore, inspect, investigate, pore over, scrutinise, study.

**dissection** *n* analysis, anatomisation, anatomy, autopsy, breakdown, dismemberment,

examination, inspection, investigation, necropsy, scrutiny, study.

**dissemble** *v* affect, camouflage, cloak, conceal, counterfeit, cover up, disguise, dissimulate, fake, falsify, feign, hide, mask, play possum, pretend, sham, simulate.

*antonym* admit.

**dissembler** *n* charlatan, con man, deceiver, dissimulator, fake, feigner, fraud, humbug, hypocrite, impostor, pretender, trickster, whited sepulchre.

**disseminate** *v* broadcast, circulate, diffuse, disperse, dissipate, distribute, evangelise, proclaim, promulgate, propagate, publicise, publish, scatter, sow, spread.

**dissemination** *n* broadcasting, circulation, diffusion, dispersion, distribution, evangelisation, evangelism, promulgation, propagation, publication, publishing, spread.

**dissension** *n* conflict, contention, difference, disagreement, discord, discordance, dispeace, dispute, dissent, friction, quarrel, strife, variance.

*antonyms* agreement, peace.

**dissent** *v* decline, differ, disagree, disconsent, object, protest, quibble, refuse.

*antonyms* agree, consent.

*n* difference, disagreement, discord, dissension, dissidence, nonconformity, objection, opposition, quibble, refusal, resistance.

*antonym* agreement.

**dissenter** *n* disputant, dissident, nonconformist, objector, protestant, protestor, recusant, schismatic, sectary.

**dissentient** *adj* conflicting, differing, disagreeing, dissenting, dissident, opposing, protesting, recusant.

*antonym* arguing.

**dissertation** *n* critique, discourse, disquisition, essay, exposition, monograph, paper, prolegomena, propaedeutic, thesis, treatise.

**disservice** *n* bad turn, disfavour, harm, injury, injustice, unkindness, wrong.

*antonym* favour.

**dissever** *v* cleave, disunite, divorce, part, rend, rift, rive, separate, sever, split, sunder.

**dissidence** *n* disagreement, discordance, dispute, dissent, feud, recusancy, rupture, schism, variance.

*antonyms* agreement, peace.

**dissident** *adj* differing, disagreeing, discordant, dissentient, dissenting, heterodox, nonconformist, recusant, schismatic.

*antonyms* acquiescent, agreeing.

*n* agitator, dissenter, protestor, rebel, recusant, refus(e)nik, schismatic.

*antonym* assenter.

**dissimilar** *adj* different, disparate, divergent, diverse, heterogeneous, incompatible, mismatched, unlike, unrelated, various.

*antonyms* compatible, similar.

**dissimilarity** *n* difference, discrepancy, disparity, dissimilitude, distinction, divergence, diversity, heterogeneity, incomparability, incompatibility, unlikeness, unrelatedness.

*antonyms* compatibility, similarity.

**dissimulate** *v* camouflage, cloak, conceal, disguise, dissemble, fake, feign, hide, mask, pretend.

**dissimulation** *n* act, affectation, concealment, deceit, deception, dissembling, double-dealing, duplicity, feigning, hypocrisy, play-acting, pretence, sham, wile.

*antonym* openness.

**dissipate** *v* burn up, consume, deplete, disappear, dispel, disperse, dissolve, evaporate, expend, fritter away, lavish, rig, scatter, spend, squander, vanish, wanton, waste.

*antonym* accumulate.

**dissipated** *adj* abandoned, consumed, debauched, destroyed, dissolute, exhausted, intemperate, profligate, rakehell, rakehelly, rakish, scattered, squandered, wasted.

*antonyms* conserved, virtuous.

**dissipation** *n* abandonment, debauchery, disappearance, disintegration, dispersion, dissemination, dissoluteness, dissolution, excess, extravagance, intemperance, prodigality, profligacy, rakery, rakishness, scattering, squandering, vanishing, wantonness, waste.

*antonyms* conservation, virtue.

**dissociate** *v* break off, detach, disband, disconnect, disrupt, distance, divorce, isolate, leave, quit, segregate, separate.

*antonyms* attach, share.

**dissociation** *n* break, detachment, disconnection, disengagement, dissevering, distancing, disunion, division, divorce, isolation, segregation, separation, severance, severing, split.

*antonyms* association, union.

**dissolute** *adj* abandoned, corrupt, debauched, degenerate, depraved, dissipated, immoral, lax, lewd, libertine, licentious, loose, profligate, rakehell, rakehelly, rakish, unrestrained, vicious, wanton, wide, wild.

*antonym* virtuous.

**dissoluteness** *n* abandon, corruption, debauchery, degeneracy, depravity, dissipation, immorality, lewdness, licence, licentiousness, profligacy, rakery, vice, wantonness.

*antonym* virtue.

**dissolution** *n* adjournment, break-up, conclusion, death, decay, decomposition, demise, destruction, disappearance, disbandment, discontinuation, disintegration, dismissal, dispersal, disruption, dissembly, division, divorce, end, ending, evaporation, extinction, finish, liquefaction, melting, overthrow, parting, resolution, ruin, separation, solution, suspension, termination.

*antonym* unification.

**dissolve** *v* break up, crumble, decompose, deliquesce, destroy, diffuse, disappear, discontinue, disintegrate, dismiss, disorganise, disperse, dissipate, disunite, divorce, dwindle, end, evanesce, evaporate, fade, flux, fuse, liquefy, loose, melt, overthrow, perish, ruin, separate, sever, soften, suspend, terminate, thaw, vanish, wind up.

**dissonance** *n* cacophony, difference, disagreement, discord, discordance, discrepancy, disharmony, disparity, dissension, harshness, incongruity, inconsistency, jangle, jarring, variance.

*antonym* harmony.

**dissonant** *adj* anomalous, cacophonous, different, differing, disagreeing, discordant, discrepant, disharmonious, dissentient, grating, harsh, incompatible, incongruous, inconsistent, inharmonious, irreconcilable, irregular, jangling, jarring, raucous, strident, tuneless, unmelodious.

*antonyms* compatible, harmonious.

**dissuade** *v* dehort, deter, discourage, disincline, divert, expostulate, put off, remonstrate, warn.

*antonym* persuade.

**dissuasion** *n* caution, dehortation, determent, deterrence, deterring, discouragement, expostulation, remonstrance, remonstration, setback.

*antonym* persuasion.

**distance** *n* absence, aloofness, coldness, coolness, extent, farness, frigidity, gap, interval, isolation, lapse, length, range, reach, remoteness, remove, reserve, restraint, separation, space, span, stand-offishness, stiffness, stretch, width.

**distant** *adj* abroad, afar, aloof, apart, ceremonious, cold, cool, disparate, dispersed, distinct, faint, far, faraway, far-flung, far-off, formal, haughty, indirect, indistinct, isolated, obscure, outlying, out-of-the-way, remote, removed, reserved, restrained, reticent, scattered, separate, slight, stand-offish, stiff, unapproachable, uncertain, unfriendly, withdrawn.

*antonyms* close, friendly.

**distaste** *n* abhorrence, antipathy, aversion, detestation, discontent, discontentment, disfavour, disgust, disinclination, dislike, displeasure, disrelish, dissatisfaction, horror, loathing, repugnance, revulsion.

*antonym* inclination.

**distasteful** *adj* abhorrent, aversive, disagreeable, displeasing, dissatisfying, loathsome, nasty, nauseous, objectionable, obnoxious, offensive, repugnant, repulsive, undesirable, uninviting, unpalatable, unpleasant, unsavoury.

*antonym* pleasing.

**distend** *v* balloon, bloat, bulge, dilate, enlarge, expand, fill out, increase, inflate, intumesce, puff, stretch, swell, widen.

*antonym* deflate.

**distended** *adj* astrut, bloated, dilated, emphysematous, enlarged, expanded, inflated, puffed-out, puffy, stretched, swollen, tumescent, varicose.

*antonym* deflated.

**distension** *n* dilatation, dilation, emphysema, enlargement, expansion, extension, inflation, intumescence, spread, swelling, tumescence.

**distil** *v* condense, drip, evaporate, extract, flow, purify, rectify, refine, sublimate, trickle, vaporise.

**distinct** *adj* apparent, clear, clear-cut, decided, definite, detached, different, discrete, dissimilar, evident, individual, lucid, manifest, marked, noticeable, obvious, palpable, patent, plain, recognisable, separate, several, sharp, unambiguous, unconnected, unmistakable, well-defined.

*antonyms* fuzzy, hazy, indistinct.

**distinction**[1] *n* characteristic, contradistinction, contrast, difference, differential, differentiation, diorism, discernment, discrimination, dissimilarity, distinctiveness, division, feature, individuality, mark, nuance, particularity, peculiarity, penetration, perception, quality, separation.

**distinction**[2] *n* account, celebrity, consequence, credit, eminence, excellence, fame, glory, greatness, honour, importance, merit, name, note, prestige, prominence, quality, rank, renown, reputation, repute, significance, superiority, worth.

*antonym* insignificance.

**distinctive** *adj* characteristic, different, discriminative, discriminatory, distinguishing, extraordinary, idiosyncratic, individual, inimitable, original, peculiar, singular, special, typical, uncommon, unique.

*antonym* common.

**distinctness** *n* clarity, clearness, difference, discreteness, disparateness, dissimilarity, dissociation, distinctiveness, individuality, lucidity, obviousness, plainness, sharpness, vividness.

*antonyms* fuzziness, haziness, indistinctness.

**distinguish** *v* ascertain, categorise, celebrate, characterise, classify, decide, determine, differentiate, dignify, discern, discriminate, honour, immortalise, individualise, judge, know, make out, mark, perceive, pick out, recognise, see, separate, signalise, tell, tell apart.

**distinguishable** *adj* appreciable, clear, conspicuous, discernible, evident, manifest, noticeable, observable, obvious, perceptible, plain, recognisable.

*antonym* indistinguishable.

**distinguished** *adj* acclaimed, celebrated, conspicuous, distingue, eminent, eximious, extraordinary, famed, famous, illustrious, marked, nameworthy, notable, noted, outstanding, renowned, signal, striking, well-known.

*antonyms* insignificant, ordinary.

**distinguishing** *adj* characteristic, different, differentiating, discriminative, discriminatory, distinctive, individual, individualistic, marked, peculiar, typical, unique.

**distort** *v* bend, bias, buckle, colour, contort, deform, disfigure, falsify, garble, miscolour, misrepresent, misshape, pervert, skew, slant, torture, twist, warp, wrench, wrest, wring.

**distorted** *adj* awry, biased, deformed, false, misshapen, skew, skewed, twisted, warped, wry.

*antonym* straight.

**distortion** *n* bend, bias, buckle, colouring, contortion, crookedness, deformity, falsification, malformation, misrepresentation, obliquity, perversion, skew, slant, twist, warp.

**distract** *v* agitate, amuse, beguile, bewilder, confound, confuse, derange, discompose, disconcert, disturb, divert, engross, entertain, faze, feeze, harass, madden, occupy, perplex, puzzle, sidetrack, torment, trouble.

**distracted** *adj* agitated, bemused, bewildered, confounded, confused, crazy, deranged, distraught, eperdu(e), flustered, frantic, frenzied, grief-stricken, harassed, hassled, insane, mad, maddened, overwrought, perplexed, puzzled, raving, troubled, wild, worked up, wrought up.

*antonyms* calm, untroubled.

**distracting** *adj* annoying, bewildering, confusing, disconcerting, disturbing, irritating, off-putting, perturbing.

**distraction** *n* aberration, abstraction, agitation, alienation, amusement, beguilement, bewilderment, commotion, confusion, delirium, derangement, desperation, discord, disorder, disturbance, diversion, divertissement, entertainment, frenzy, hallucination, harassment, incoherence, insanity, interference, interruption, mania, pastime, recreation.

**distraught** *adj* agitated, anxious, beside oneself, crazed, crazy, distracted, distressed, frantic, hysterical, mad, overwrought, raving, wild, worked up, wrought up.

*antonyms* calm, untroubled.

**distress** *n* adversity, affliction, agony, anguish, anxiety, calamity, depravation, desolation, destitution, difficulties, discomfort, grief, hardship, heartache, indigence, katzenjammer, misery, misfortune, need, pain, pauperism, poverty, privation, sadness, sorrow, strait(s), suffering, torment, torture, trial, trouble, woe, worry, wretchedness.

*antonyms* comfort, ease, security.

*v* afflict, agonise, bother, constrain, cut up, disturb, grieve, harass, harrow, pain, perplex, sadden, straiten, torment, trouble, upset, worry, wound.

*antonyms* assist, comfort.

**distressed** *adj* afflicted, agitated, anxious, cut up, destitute, distracted, distraught, indigent, needy, poor, poverty-stricken, saddened, straitened, tormented, troubled, upset, worried, wretched.

*antonyms* calm, untroubled.

**distressing** *adj* affecting, afflicting, afflictive, disquieting, distressful, disturbing, grievous, heart-breaking, hurtful, lamentable, nerve-racking, painful, perturbing, sad, trying, unnerving, upsetting, worrying.

*antonyms* assuaging, pleasant.

**distribute** *v* administer, allocate, allot, apportion, arrange, assign, assort, bestow, carve up, categorise, circulate, class, classify, convey, deal, deliver, diffuse, dish out, dispense, disperse, dispose, disseminate, divide, dole, file, give, group, hand out, mete, scatter, share, spread, strew.

*antonyms* collect, gather in.

**distribution** *n* allocation, allotment, apportionment, arrangement, assortment, bestowal, bestowing, circulation, classification, dealing, delivery, diffusion, dispensation, dispersal, dispersion, disposition, dissemination, division, dole, handling, largition, location, mailing, marketing, partition, placement, propagation, scattering, sharing, spreading, trading, transport, transportation.

*antonyms* collection, gathering.

**district** *n* area, canton, cantred, cantret, community, gau, hundred, locale, locality, neighbourhood, parish, precinct, quarter, region, sector, vicinity, ward.

**distrust** *v* disbelieve, discredit, doubt, misbelieve, miscredit, misdeem, mistrust, question, suspect.

*antonym* trust.

*n* disbelief, doubt, misfaith, misgiving, mistrust, qualm, question, scepticism, suspicion, untrust, wariness.

*antonym* trust.

**distrustful** *adj* chary, cynical, disbelieving, distrusting, doubtful, doubting, dubious, mistrustful, sceptical, suspicious, uneasy, untrustful, untrusting, wary.

*antonyms* trustful, unsuspecting.

**disturb** *v* affray, agitate, alarm, annoy, bother, concuss, confound, confuse, derange, disarrange, discompose, disorder, disorganise, disrupt, distract, distress, excite, fluster, harass, interrupt, muddle, perturb, pester, rouse, ruffle, shake, startle, trouble, unsettle, upset, worry.

*antonyms* calm, quiet, reassure.

**disturbance** *n* agitation, annoyance, bother, brawl, breeze, broil, burst-up, bust-up, commotion, confusion, derangement, disorder, distraction, fracas, fray, hindrance, hubbub, interruption, intrusion, katzenjammer, kick-up, misarrangement, molestation, muss(e), perturbation, riot, ruckus, ruction, shake-up, stour, stramash, tumult, turmoil, unrest, upheaval, uproar, upset, upturn.

*antonyms* peace, quiet.

**disturbed** *adj* agitated, anxious, apprehensive, bothered, concerned, confused, discomposed, disordered, disquieted, flustered, maladjusted, neurotic, troubled, unbalanced, uneasy, unrestful, upset, worried.

*antonyms* calm, sane.

**disturbing** *adj* agitating, alarming, disconcerting, discouraging, dismaying, disquieting, distressful, distressing, disturbant, disturbative, frightening, perturbing, startling, threatening, troubling, unsettling, upsetting, worrying.

*antonym* reassuring.

**disunion** *n* alienation, breach, detachment, disagreement, disconcert, disconnection, discord,

disjunction, dissension, dissevering, dissidence, division, estrangement, feud, partition, rift, rupture, schism, separation, severance, split.

*antonym* unification.

**disunite** *v* alienate, detach, disband, disconnect, disengage, disjoin, disrupt, divide, estrange, part, segregate, separate, sever, split, sunder.

*antonym* unify.

**disunity** *n* alienation, breach, conflict, disagreement, discord, discordance, dissension, dissent, estrangement, rupture, schism, split, strife, variance.

*antonym* unity.

**disuse** *n* abandonment, decay, desuetude, discontinuance, disusage, idleness, neglect.

*antonym* use.

**ditch** *n* channel, drain, dyke, furrow, gully, ha-ha, level, moat, rhine, stank, trench, watercourse.

*v* abandon, discard, dispose of, drop, dump, jettison, scrap.

**dither** *v* faff about, falter, footer, haver, hesitate, oscillate, shilly-shally, swither, teeter, vacillate, waver.

*antonym* decide.

*n* bother, flap, fluster, flutter, indecision, panic, pother, stew, tizzy, twitter.

*antonym* decision.

**diuretic** *adj* emictory.

**divan** *n* chaise-longue, couch, lounger, ottoman, settee, sofa.

**dive**[1] *v* descend, dip, drop, duck, fall, jump, leap, nose-dive, pitch, plummet, plunge, rush, sound, submerge, swoop.

*n* dash, header, jump, leap, lunge, nose-dive, plunge, rush, spring, swoop.

**dive**[2] *n* den, honky-tonk, joint, lush-house.

**diverge** *v* bifurcate, branch, conflict, depart, deviate, differ, digress, disagree, dissent, divaricate, divide, fork, part, radiate, separate, split, spread, stray, vary, wander.

*antonyms* agree, come together, join.

**divergence** *n* branching-out, deflection, departure, deviation, difference, digression, disparity, divagation, parting, radiating, ramification, separation, variation.

*antonym* convergence.

**divergent** *adj* conflicting, deviating, different, differing, disagreeing, dissimilar, diverging, diverse, forking, parting, radial, radiating, separate, spreading, variant, varying.

*antonym* convergent.

**divers** *adj* different, manifold, many, miscellaneous, multifarious, numerous, several, some, sundry, varied, various.

**diverse** *adj* assorted, different, differing, discrete, disparate, dissimilar, distinct, divergent, diversified, heterogeneous, manifold, many, miscellaneous, multifarious, multiform, numerous, separate, several, some, sundry, unlike, varied, various, varying.

*antonym* identical.

**diversify** *v* alter, assort, branch out, change, expand, mix, spread out, variegate, vary.

**diversion** *n* alteration, amusement, beguilement, change, deflection, delight, departure, detour, deviation, digression, disportment, distraction, divertissement, enjoyment, entertainment, game, gratification, pastime, play, pleasure, recreation, relaxation, sport, variation.

**diversionary** *adj* distracting, divertive.

**diversity** *n* assortment, difference, dissimilarity, distinctiveness, divergence, diverseness, diversification, heterogeneity, medley, multifariousness, multiplicity, range, unlikeness, variance, variegation, variety.

*antonyms* sameness, similarity.

**divert** *v* amuse, avert, beguile, deflect, delight, detract, distract, entertain, gratify, hive off, recreate, redirect, regale, side-track, switch, tickle.

*antonyms* direct, irritate.

**diverting** *adj* amusing, beguiling, enjoyable, entertaining, fun, funny, humorous, pleasant, witty.

*antonym* irritating.

**divest** *v* denude, deprive, despoil, disinvest, dispossess, disrobe, disseise, doff, remove, strip, unclothe, undress.

*antonym* clothe.

**divide** *v* alienate, allocate, allot, apportion, arrange, bisect, break up, categorise, classify, cleave, cut, deal out, departmentalise, detach, disconnect, dispense, distribute, disunite, divvy, estrange, grade, group, part, partition, portion, segment, segregate, separate, sever, share, shear, sort, split, subdivide, sunder.

*antonyms* collect, gather, join.

**divide out** allocate, allot, apportion, dole out, measure out, morsel, parcel out, share, share out.

**dividend** *n* bonus, cut, divvy, extra, gain, gratuity, interest, lagniappe, plus, portion, share, surplus, whack.

**divination** *n* augury, clairvoyance, divining, dukkeripen, foretelling, fortune-telling, hariolation, -mancy, prediction, presage, prognostication, prophecy, second sight, soothsaying, taghairm.

**divine** *adj* angelic, beatific, beautiful, blissful, celestial, consecrated, exalted, excellent, glorious, godlike, heavenly, holy, marvellous, mystical, perfect, rapturous, religious, sacred, sanctified, spiritual, splendid, superhuman, superlative, supernatural, supreme, transcendent, transcendental, transmundane, wonderful.

*n* churchman, clergyman, cleric, ecclesiastic, minister, parson, pastor, prelate, priest, reverend.

*v* apprehend, conjecture, deduce, foretell, guess, hariolate, haruspicate, infer, intuit, perceive, prognosticate, suppose, surmise, suspect, understand.

**diviner** *n* astrologer, augur, divinator, dowser, haruspex, oracle, prophet, seer, sibyl, soothsayer, water-finder.

**divinity** *n* daemon, deity, deva, genius, god, goddess, godhead, godhood, godliness, godship, holiness, kami, sanctity, spirit.

**divisible** *adj* dividable, dividual, fractional, partible, separable, splittable.

**division** *n* allotment, apportionment, bisection, border, boundary, branch, breach, category, class, compartment, cutting, demarcation, department, detaching, dichotomy, disagreement, discord, distribution, disunion, divide, divider, dividing, estrangement, feud, group, head, part, partition, portion, rupture, schism, scission, section, sector, segment, separation, sept, sharing, side, split, splitting, stream, variance, wapentake, ward, watershed, wing.

*antonyms* agreement, multiplication, unification.

**divisive** *adj* alienating, discordant, disruptive, inharmonious.

*antonyms* harmonious, unifying.

**divorce** *n* annulment, breach, break, break-up, decree nisi, diffarreation, dissolution, disunion, rupture, separation, severance, split-up, talaq.

*v* annul, cancel, disconnect, dissever, dissociate, dissolve, disunite, divide, part, separate, sever, split up, sunder.

*antonyms* marry, unify.

**divulge** *v* betray, broadcast, communicate, confess, declare, disclose, evulgate, exhibit, expose, impart, leak, let slip, proclaim, promulgate, publish, reveal, spill, tell, uncover.

**divvy** *n* bit, cut, dividend, lagniappe, percentage, portion, quota, share, whack.

*v* apportion, cut, distribute, divide, parcel out, share, share out, split.

**dizzy** *adj* befuddled, bemused, bewildered, capricious, confused, dazed, dazzled, faint, fickle, flighty, foolish, frivolous, giddy, light-headed, lofty, muddled, reeling, scatter-brained, shaky, staggering, steep, swimming, vertiginous, wobbly, woozy.

**do** *v* accomplish, achieve, act, adapt, answer, arrange, behave, carry out, cause, cheat, complete, con, conclude, cover, cozen, deceive, decipher, decode, defraud, discharge, dupe, effect, end, execute, explore, fare, fix, fleece, give, hoax, implement, make, manage, organise, pass muster, perform, prepare, present, proceed, produce, put on, render, resolve, satisfy, serve, solve, suffice, suit, swindle, tour, transact, translate, transpose, travel, trick, undertake, visit, work, work out.

*n* affair, event, function, gathering, occasion, party.

**do away with** abolish, bump off, destroy, discard, discontinue, do in, eliminate, exterminate, get rid of, kill, liquidate, murder, remove, slay.

**do for** defeat, destroy, finish (off), kill, ruin, shatter, slay.

**do in** butcher, dispatch, eliminate, execute, exhaust, fag, fatigue, kill, knacker, liquidate, murder, rub out, shatter, slaughter, slay, tire, waste, wear out, weary.

**do out of** balk, bilk, cheat, con, deprive, diddle, fleece, rook, swindle, trick.

**do's and don'ts** code, customs, etiquette, instructions, niceties, p's and q's, punctilios, regulations, rules, standards.

**do without** abstain from, dispense with, forgo, give up, relinquish, waive.

**docile** *adj* amenable, biddable, complaisant, compliant, ductile, manageable, obedient, obliging, pliable, pliant, submissive, teachable, tractable, unmurmuring, unprotesting, unquestioning.

*antonyms* truculent, unco-operative.

**docility** *n* amenability, biddableness, complaisance, compliance, ductility, manageability, meekness, obedience, pliability, pliancy, submissiveness, tractability.

*antonyms* truculence, unco-operativeness.

**dock**[1] *n* boat-yard, harbour, marina, pier, quay, waterfront, wharf.

*v* anchor, berth, drop anchor, join up, land, link up, moor, put in, rendezvous, tie up, unite.

**dock**[2] *v* clip, crop, curtail, cut, decaudate, decrease, deduct, diminish, lessen, reduce, shorten, subtract, truncate, withhold.

**docket** *n* bill, certificate, chit, chitty, counterfoil, label, receipt, tab, tag, tally, ticket.

*v* catalogue, file, index, label, mark, register, tab, tag, ticket.

**doctor** *n* clinician, doctoress, doctress, general practitioner, GP, hakim, internist, leech, medic, medical officer, medical practitioner, medicaster, medico, physician, pill(s).

*v* adulterate, alter, botch, change, cobble, cook, cut, dilute, disguise, falsify, fix, fudge, hocus, load, medicate, mend, misrepresent, patch, pervert, repair, spike, tamper with, treat.

**doctrinaire** *adj* biased, doctrinarian, dogmatic, fanatical, hypothetical, ideological, impractical, inflexible, insistent, opinionated, pedantic, rigid, speculative, theoretical, unrealistic.

*antonym* flexible.

**doctrine** *n* belief, canon, concept, conviction, creed, dogma, ism, opinion, precept, principle, teaching, tenet.

**document** *n* certificate, chirograph, deed, form, instrument, paper, parchment, record, report.

*v* authenticate, back, certify, cite, corroborate, detail, enumerate, instance, list, particularise, prove, substantiate, support, validate, verify.

**documentary** *n* faction, feature, programme.

**doddery** *adj* aged, decrepit, doddering, doited, faltering, feeble, infirm, rambling, senile, shaky, shambling, tottery, trembly, unsteady, weak.

*antonyms* hale, youthful.

**dodge** *v* avoid, dart, deceive, duck, elude, equivocate, evade, fend off, fudge, hedge, parry, shift, shirk, shuffle, side-step, skive, swerve, swing the lead, trick.

*n* chicane, contrivance, device, fakery, feint, machination, manoeuvre, ploy, ruse, scheme, stratagem, subterfuge, trick, wheeze, wile.

**dodger** *n* evader, lead-swinger, shirker, skiver, slacker, slyboots, trickster.

**dodgy** *adj* chancy, dangerous, delicate, dicey, dicky, difficult, problematical, risky, ticklish, tricky, uncertain, unreliable, unsafe.

*antonyms* easy, safe.

**doer** *n* accomplisher, achiever, activist, bustler, dynamo, executer, go-getter, live wire, organiser, power-house, wheeler-dealer.

**doff** *v* discard, lift, raise, remove, shed, take off, throw off, tip, touch, undress.

*antonym* don.

**dog** *n* beast, bitch, blackguard, bowwow, canid, canine, cur, heel, hound, knave, mongrel, moppet, mutt, pooch, pup, puppy, scoundrel, tyke, villain, yapper, yapster.

*v* harry, haunt, hound, plague, pursue, shadow, tail, track, trail, trouble, worry.

**dogged** *adj* determined, firm, indefatigable, indomitable, obstinate, persevering, persistent, pertinacious, relentless, resolute, single-minded, staunch, steadfast, steady, stubborn, tenacious, unflagging, unshakable, unyielding.

*antonym* irresolute.

**doggedness** *n* determination, endurance, indomitablity, obstinacy, perseverance, persistence, pertinacity, relentlessness, resolution, single-mindedness, steadfastness, steadiness, stubbornness, tenaciousness, tenacity.

**dogma** *n* article, article of faith, belief, conviction, credendum, credo, creed, doctrine, opinion, precept, principle, teaching, tenet.

**dogmatic** *adj* affirmative, arbitrary, assertive, authoritative, canonical, categorical, dictatorial, didactic, doctrinaire, doctrinal, downright, emphatic, ex cathedra, high-dried, imperious, magisterial, obdurate, opinionated, oracular, overbearing, peremptory, pontific(al), positive.

**dogmatism** *n* arbitrariness, assertiveness, bigotry, dictatorialness, imperiousness, opinionatedness, peremptoriness, positiveness, presumption.

**dogsbody** *n* doormat, drudge, factotum, galley-slave, lackey, maid-of-all-work, man-of-all-work, menial, skivvy, slave.

**doings** *n* actions, activities, acts, adventures, affairs, concerns, dealings, deeds, events, exploits, goings-on, handiwork, happenings, proceedings, transactions.

**doldrums** *n* accidie, acedia, apathy, blues, boredom, depression, dullness, dumps, ennui, gloom, inertia, lassitude, listlessness, low-spiritedness, malaise, stagnation, tedium, torpor.

**dole** *n* allocation, allotment, allowance, alms, apportionment, benefit, dispensation, dispersal, distribution, division, donation, gift, grant, gratuity, issuance, modicum, parcel, pittance, portion, quota, share.

**dole out** administer, allocate, allot, apportion, assign, deal, dispense, distribute, divide, give, hand out, issue, mete, ration, share.

**doleful** *adj* blue, cheerless, depressing, dismal, distressing, dolorous, dreary, forlorn, funereal, gloomy, lugubrious, melancholy, mournful, painful, pathetic, pitiful, rueful, sad, sombre, sorrowful, woebegone, woeful, wretched.

*antonym* cheerful.

**doll** *n* dolly, figurine, kewpie doll, marionette, moppet, plaything, puppet, toy.

**doll up** deck out, dress up, preen, primp, prink, tart up, titivate, trick out.

**dollar** *n* buck, greenback, smacker, wheel.

**dollop** *n* ball, blob, bunch, clump, glob, gob, gobbet, lump.

**dolorous** *adj* anguished, distressing, doleful, grievous, harrowing, heart-rending, lugubrious, melancholy, miserable, mournful, painful, rueful, sad, sombre, sorrowful, woebegone, woeful, wretched.

*antonym* happy.

**dolour** *n* anguish, distress, grief, heartache, heartbreak, lamentation, misery, mourning, ruth, sadness, sorrow, suffering.

*antonym* beatitude.

**dolt** *n* ass, beetlebrain, beetlehead, besom-head, blockhead, bonehead, booby, boodle, bufflehead, bull-calf, calf, chump, clod, clodhopper, clodpate, clodpoll, clot, clunk, dimwit, dope, dullard, dunce, fool, galoot, half-wit, idiot, ignoramus, leather-head, loggerhead, log-head, lurdan(e), lurden, mutt, mutton-head, nitwit, nutcase, palooka, sheep's-head, simpleton, turnip.

**doltish** *adj* boneheaded, brainless, clottish, daffy, dense, dimwitted, dopey, dumb, foolish, half-witted, idiotic, mindless, obtuse, silly, stupid, thick.

*antonyms* brainy, clever.

**domain** *n* area, authority, bailiwick, business, concern, demesne, department, discipline, dominion, empire, estate, field, jurisdiction, kingdom, lands, orbit, pidgin, policies, power, province, realm, region, scope, speciality, sphere, sway, territory.

**domestic** *adj* autochthonic, domal, domesticated, domiciliary, family, home, home-bred, home-loving, homely, house, household, house-trained, housewifely, indigenous, internal, native, pet, private, stay-at-home, tame, trained.

*n* au pair, char, charwoman, daily, daily help, help, maid, scullery maid, servant, slavey, woman.

**domesticate** *v* acclimatise, accustom, break, domesticise, familiarise, habituate, house-train, naturalise, tame, train.

**domesticated** *adj* broken (in), domestic, home-loving, homely, house-proud, housewifely, naturalised, tame, tamed.

*antonyms* feral, wild.

**domesticity** *n* domestic science, domestication, familism, home economics, homecraft, homemaking, housecraft, housekeeping, housewifery, housewifeship.

**domicile** *n* abode, dwelling, habitation, home, house, lodging(s), mansion, quarters, residence, residency, settlement.

**dominance** *n* ascendancy, authority, command, control, domination, government, hegemony, leadership, mastery, paramountcy, power, rule, supremacy, sway.

**dominant** *adj* ascendant, assertive, authoritative, besetting, chief, commanding, controlling, governing, influential, leading, main, outstanding, paramount, predominant, pre-eminent, presiding, prevailing, prevalent, primary, prime, principal, prominent, ruling, superior, supreme.

*antonym* subordinate.

**dominate** *v* bestride, control, direct, domineer, dwarf, eclipse, govern, have the whip hand, keep under one's thumb, lead, master, monopolise, outshine, overbear, overgang, overlook, overrule, overshadow, predominate, prevail, rule, tyrannise.

**domination** *n* ascendancy, authority, command, control, despotism, dictatorship, hegemony, influence, leadership, mastery, oppression, power, repression, rule, subjection, subordination, superiority, suppression, supremacy, sway, tyranny.

**domineer** *v* bluster, boss, browbeat, bully, command, hector, intimidate, jackboot, lord it over, menace, overbear, ride roughshod, rule, swagger, threaten, tyrannise.

**domineering** *adj* arrogant, authoritarian, autocratic, bossy, coercive, despotic, dictatorial, harsh, high-handed, imperious, iron-handed, magisterial, masterful, oppressive, overbearing, severe, tyrannical.

*antonyms* meek, obsequious, servile.

**dominion** *n* ascendancy, authority, colony, command, control, country, domain, domination, empire, government, hegemony, jurisdiction, kingdom, lordship, mastery, power, province, realm, region, rule, sovereignty, supremacy, sway, territory.

**don** *v* affect, assume, clothe oneself in, dress in, get into, put on.

*antonym* doff.

**Don Juan** *n* amoretto, amoroso, amourette, Casanova, gigolo, ladies' man, lady-killer, lover, muff, philander(er), romeo.

**donate** *v* bequeath, bestow, chip in, confer, contribute, cough up, fork out, gift, give, impart, present, proffer, subscribe.

**donation** *n* alms, benefaction, boon, conferment, contribution, gift, grant, gratuity, largess(e), offering, present, presentation, subscription.

**done** *adj* acceptable, accomplished, advised, agreed, completed, concluded, consummated, conventional, cooked, cooked to a turn, de rigueur, depleted, drained, ended, executed, exhausted, fatigued, finished, OK, over, perfected, proper, ready, realised, settled, spent, terminated, through, U, used up.

**done for** beaten, broken, dashed, defeated, destroyed, doomed, finished, foiled, for the high jump, lost, ruined, undone, vanquished, wrecked.

**done in** all in, bushed, dead, dead beat, dog-tired, exhausted, fagged, jiggered, knackered, pooped, worn to a frazzle, zonked.

**donkey** *n* ass, burro, cardophagus, cuddy, hinny, jackass, jennet, jenny, moke, mule.

**donnish** *adj* academic, bookish, erudite, formalistic, learned, pedagogic, pedantic, precise, scholarly, scholastic.

**donor** *n* benefactor, contributor, donator, fairy godmother, giver, granter, philanthropist, provider.

*antonym* beneficiary.

**doom** *n* Armageddon, catastrophe, condemnation, death, death-knell, decision, decree, destiny, destruction, Doomsday, downfall, fate, fortune, judgement, Judgement Day, karma, kismet, lot, portion, ruin, sentence, the Last Judgement, the last trump, verdict.

*v* condemn, consign, damn, decree, destine, foredoom, foreordain, judge, predestine, preordain, sentence, threaten.

**doomed** *adj* accursed, bedevilled, bewitched, condemned, cursed, fated, fey, hopeless, ill-fated, ill-omened, ill-starred, luckless, star-crossed.

**door** *n* doorstead, doorway, egress, entrance, entry, exit, ingress, opening, portal, vomitorium, vomitory.

**doorkeeper** *n* commissionaire, gate-keeper, huissier, janitor, jobsworth, ostiary, porter.

**dope**[1] *n* details, drugs, facts, gen, hallucinogen, info, information, low-down, narcotic, news, opiate, tip.

*v* anaesthetise, doctor, drug, inject, load, medicate, narcotise, sedate, stupefy.

**dope**[2] *n* blockhead, bonehead, clot, dimwit, dolt, dullard, dunce, fool, half-wit, idiot, simpleton.

**dop(e)y** *adj* dazed, dense, doltish, dozy, drowsy, drugged, dumb, foolish, groggy, hazy, idiotic, muzzy, senseless, silly, simple, slow, stupefied, stupid, thick, woozy.

*antonyms* alert, bright.

**dormant** *adj* asleep, comatose, fallow, hibernating, inactive, inert, inoperative, latent, latescent, quiescent, sleeping, sluggish, slumbering, suspended, torpid, undeveloped, unrealised.

*antonym* active.

**dose** *n* dosage, draught, drench, hit, measure, portion, potion, prescription, quantity, shot, slug.

*v* administer, dispense, drench, medicate, treat.

**dot** *n* atom, circle, dab, decimal point, dit, fleck, full stop, iota, jot, mark, mite, mote, pin-point, point, speck, spot.

*v* bespeckle, dab, dabble, fleck, punctuate, spot, sprinkle, stipple, stud.

**dotage** *n* anility, decrepitude, feebleness, imbecility, old age, second childhood, senility, weakness.

*antonym* youth.

**dote on** admire, adore, idolise, indulge, pamper, prize, spoil, treasure.

**doting** *adj* adoring, devoted, fond, foolish, indulgent, lovesick, soft.

**dotty** *adj* batty, crazy, eccentric, feeble-minded, loopy, peculiar, potty, touched, weird.

*antonym* sensible.

**double** *adj* bifarious, bifold, binate, coupled, diploid, doubled, dual, duple, duplex, duplicate, paired, twice, twin, twofold.

*v* duplicate, enlarge, fold, geminate, grow, increase, magnify, multiply, repeat.

*n* clone, copy, counterpart, dead ringer, dead spit, doppelgänger, duplicate, fellow, image, impersonator, lookalike, mate, replica, ringer, spitting image, twin.

**double back** backtrack, circle, dodge, evade, loop, retrace one's steps, return, reverse.

**double entendre** ambiguity, double meaning, innuendo, play on words, pun, suggestiveness, word-play.

**double-cross** *v* betray, cheat, con, cozen, defraud, hoodwink, mislead, swindle, trick, two-time.

**double-dealer** *n* betrayer, cheat, con man, cozener, deceiver, dissembler, double-crosser, fraud, hypocrite, Machiavellian, rogue, swindler, traitor, two-timer.

**double-dealing** *n* bad faith, betrayal, cheating, deceit, deception, dishonesty, duplicity, foul play, hypocrisy, Machiavellianism, mendacity, perfidy, treachery, trickery, two-timing.

*adj* cheating, crooked, deceitful, dishonest, duplicitous, fraudulent, hypocritical, lying, Machiavellian, perfidious, scheming, shifty, sneaky, swindling, treacherous, tricky, two-faced, two-timing, underhanded, unscrupulous, untrustworthy, wily.

**doubly** *adv* again, bis, twice, twofold.

**doubt** *v* be dubious, be uncertain, demur, discredit, distrust, dubitate, fear, fluctuate, hesitate, misgive, mistrust, query, question, scruple, suspect, vacillate, waver.

*antonyms* believe, trust.

*n* ambiguity, apprehension, arrière pensee, confusion, difficulty, dilemma, disquiet, distrust, dubiety, fear, hesitancy, hesitation, incredulity, indecision, irresolution, misgiving, mistrust, perplexity, problem, qualm, quandary, reservation, scepticism, suspense, suspicion, uncertainty, vacillation.

*antonyms* belief, certainty, confidence, trust.

**doubter** *n* agnostic, cynic, disbeliever, doubting Thomas, questioner, questionist, sceptic, scoffer, unbeliever.

*antonym* believer.

**doubtful** *adj* ambiguous, debatable, disreputable, distrustful, dubious, dubitable, equivocal, hazardous, hesitant, hesitating, iffy, inconclusive, indefinite, indeterminate, irresolute, litigious, obscure, perplexed, precarious, problematic, problematical, questionable, sceptical, shady, suspect, suspicious, tentative, uncertain, unclear, unconfirmed, unconvinced, undecided, unresolved, unsettled, unsure, vacillating, vague, wavering.

*antonyms* certain, definite.

**doubtless** adv apparently, assuredly, certainly, clearly, indisputably, most likely, of course, ostensibly, out of question, precisely, presumably, probably, questionless, seemingly, supposedly, surely, truly, undoubtedly, unquestionably, without doubt.

**doughty** adj able, bold, brave, courageous, daring, dauntless, fearless, gallant, game, hardy, heroic, intrepid, redoubtable, resolute, stout-hearted, strong, valiant, valorous.

*antonyms* cowardly, weak.

**dour** adj austere, dismal, dreary, forbidding, gloomy, grim, hard, humourless, inflexible, morose, obstinate, rigid, rigorous, severe, sour, Spartan, strict, sullen, uncompromising, unfriendly, unyielding.

*antonyms* bright, cheery, easy-going.

**douse, dowse** v blow out, dip, drench, duck, dunk, extinguish, immerge, immerse, plunge, put out, saturate, smother, snuff, soak, souse, steep, submerge.

**dovetail** v accord, agree, coincide, conform, correspond, fit, harmonise, interlock, join, link, match, mortise, splice, tailor, tally, tenon, unite.

**dowdy** adj dingy, drab, frowzy, frumpish, frumpy, ill-dressed, old-fashioned, scrubby, shabby, slovenly, tacky, tatty, unfashionable, unmodish, unsmart.

*antonyms* dressy, smart, spruce.

**down**[1] n bloom, floccus, floss, flue, fluff, fuzz, nap, pile, shag, thistledown, wool.

**down**[2] v drink, fell, floor, gulp, knock back, swallow, throw, topple, toss off.

**down and out** derelict, destitute, impoverished, on one's uppers, penniless, ruined.

**down at heel** dowdy, impoverished, out at elbows, run-down, seedy, shabby, slipshod, slovenly, slummy, worn.

**down in the mouth** blue, chopfallen, crestfallen, dejected, depressed, disheartened, dispirited, down, down in the dumps, downcast, in low spirits, in the doldrums, melancholy, sad, unhappy.

**down the drain** lost, out of the window, ruined, up the spout, wasted.

**down with** away with, exterminate, get rid of.

**down-and-out** n beggar, bum, derelict, dosser, loser, outcast, pauper, tramp, vagabond, vagrant.

**downcast** adj cheerless, chopfallen, crestfallen, daunted, dejected, depressed, despondent, disappointed, disconsolate, discouraged, disheartened, dismayed, dispirited, down, miserable, sad, unhappy.

*antonyms* cheerful, elated, happy.

**downfall** n breakdown, cloudburst, collapse, comedown, come-uppance, debacle, deluge, descent, destruction, disgrace, downpour, failure, fall, humiliation, overthrow, rainstorm, ruin, undoing, Waterloo.

**downgrade** v belittle, decry, degrade, demote, denigrate, detract from, disparage, humble, lower, reduce in rank, run down.

*antonyms* improve, upgrade.

**downhearted** adj blue, chopfallen, crestfallen, dejected, depressed, despondent, discouraged, disheartened, dismayed, dispirited, downcast, gloomy, glum, jaw-fallen, low-spirited, sad, sorrowful, unhappy.

*antonyms* cheerful, enthusiastic, happy.

**downpour** n cloudburst, deluge, downcome, flood, inundation, rainstorm, torrent, water-spout.

**downright** adj absolute, blatant, blunt, candid, categorical, clear, complete, explicit, forthright, frank, honest, open, out-and-out, outright, outspoken, plain, positive, simple, sincere, straightforward, thoroughgoing, total, undisguised, unequivocal, unqualified, utter, wholesale.

**down-to-earth** adj commonsense, commonsensical, hard-headed, matter-of-fact, mundane, no-nonsense, plain-spoken, practical, realistic, sane, sensible, unsentimental.

*antonyms* fantastic, impractical.

**down-trodden** adj abused, afflicted, distressed, exploited, helpless, oppressed, subjugated, subservient, trampled on, trampled underfoot, tyrannised, victimised.

**downward** adj declining, descending, downhill, sliding, slippery, slipping.

*antonym* upward.

**downy** adj eriophorous, feathery, fleecy, floccose, fluffy, lanuginose, lanuginous, nappy, plumate, plumulate, silky, soft, velvety, woolly.

**dowry** n dot, dower, endowment, faculty, gift, inheritance, legacy, portion, provision, share, talent, wedding-dower.

**dowse** see **douse**.

**doze** v catnap, dove, dover, drop off, drowse, kip, nap, nod, nod off, sleep, slumber, snooze, zizz.

n catnap, dogsleep, forty winks, kip, nap, shut-eye, siesta, snooze, zizz.

**drab** adj cheerless, colourless, dingy, dismal, dreary, dull, dun-coloured, flat, gloomy, grey, lack-lustre, mous(e)y, shabby, sombre, uninspired, vapid.

*antonym* bright.

**draft**[1] v compose, delineate, design, draw, draw up, formulate, outline, plan, sketch.

n abstract, delineation, ebauche, outline, plan, protocol, rough, sketch, version.

**draft**[2] n bill, cheque, order, postal order.

**drag** v crawl, creep, dawdle, draggle, draw, hale, harl, haul, inch, lag, linger, loiter, lug, pull, schlep, shamble, shuffle, straggle, sweep, tow, trail, tug, yank.

n annoyance, bore, bother, brake, drogue, nuisance, pain, pest, pill.

**drag on, drag out** draw out, extend, hang on, lengthen, persist, prolong, protract, spin out.

**drag one's feet** delay, obstruct, procrastinate, stall.

**dragoon** v browbeat, bully, coact, coerce, compel, constrain, drive, force, impel, intimidate, strong-arm.

**drain** v bleed, consume, deplete, discharge, dissipate, down, draw off, drink up, dry, effuse, empty, emulge, evacuate, exhaust, exude, finish, flow out, lade, leak, milk, ooze, quaff, remove, sap, seep, strain, swallow, tap, tax, trickle, use up, weary, withdraw.

*antonym* fill.

n channel, conduit, culvert, depletion, ditch, drag, duct, exhaustion, expenditure, grip, outlet, pipe, reduction, sap, sewer, sink, sough, stank, strain, trench, watercourse, withdrawal.

**drainage** n bilge, leaching, seepage, sewage, sewerage, waste.

**dram** n caulker, drop, glass, measure, nobbler, shot, slug, snifter, snort, tot.

**drama** n acting, crisis, dramatics, dramatisation, dramaturgy, excitement, histrionics, kabuki, kathakali, melodrama, play, scene, show, spectacle, stage-craft, theatre, theatricals, Thespian art, turmoil.

**dramatic** adj affecting, breathtaking, climactic, dramaturgic, dramaturgical, effective, electrifying, emotional, exciting, expressive, graphic, impressive, meaningful, melodramatic, moving, powerful, sensational, startling, striking, sudden, suspenseful, tense, theatrical, Thespian, thrilling, vivid.

*antonyms* normal, ordinary.

**dramatise** v act, exaggerate, overdo, overstate, play-act, put on, stage.

**dramatist** n comedian, dramaturge, dramaturgist, playwright, play-writer, screen-writer, scriptwriter, tragedian.

**drape** v adorn, array, cloak, cover, dangle, droop, drop, enrap, fold, hang, suspend, swathe, vest, wrap.

**drapery** n arras, backdrop, blind(s), covering(s), curtain(s), hanging(s), portière, tapestry, valance.

**drastic** adj desperate, dire, draconian, extreme, far-reaching, forceful, harsh, heroic, radical, severe, strong.

*antonym* mild.

**draught** n cup, current, dose, dragging, drawing, drench, drink, flow, haulage, influx, movement, portion, potation, puff, pulling, quantity, traction.

**draw¹** v allure, attenuate, attract, borrow, breathe in, bring forth, choose, deduce, delineate, depict, derive, design, drag, drain, elicit, elongate, engage, entice, entrain, evoke, extend, extort, extract, get, haul, induce, infer, influence, inhale, inspire, invite, lengthen, make, map out, mark out, outline, paint, pencil, persuade, pick, portray, puff, pull, respire, select, sketch, stretch, suck, take, tow, trace, tug, unsheathe.

*antonyms* propel, push.

n appeal, attraction, bait, enticement, interest, lure, pull.

**draw back** recoil, resile, retract, retreat, shrink, start back, withdraw.

**draw lots** choose, decide, draw straws, pick, select, spin a coin, toss up.

**draw on** employ, exploit, extract, make use of, quarry, rely on, take from, use.

**draw out** drag out, elongate, extend, lengthen, prolong, prolongate, protract, spin out, stretch, string out.

*antonym* curtail.

**draw the line** lay down the law, object, put one's foot down, restrict, say no, set a limit.

**draw up** compose, draft, embattle, formulate, frame, halt, prepare, pull up, run in, stop, stop short, write out.

**draw²** v be equal, be even, be neck and neck, dead-heat, tie.

n dead-heat, deadlock, impasse, stalemate, tie.

**drawback** n block, defect, deficiency, desagrement, detriment, difficulty, disability, disadvantage, fault, flaw, fly in the ointment, handicap, hindrance, hitch, impediment, imperfection, nuisance, obstacle, pull-back, snag, stumbling, trouble.

*antonym* advantage.

**drawing** n cartoon, delineation, depiction, graphic, illustration, outline, picture, portrait, portrayal, representation, sketch, study.

**drawl** v dra(u)nt, drone, haw-haw, protract, twang.

**drawn** adj fatigued, fraught, haggard, harassed, harrowed, hassled, pinched, sapped, strained, stressed, taut, tense, tired, worn.

**dread** v cringe at, fear, flinch, quail, shrink from, shudder, shy, tremble.

n alarm, apprehension, aversion, awe, dismay, disquiet, fear, fright, funk, heebie-jeebies, horror, misgiving, terror, trepidation, worry.

*antonyms* confidence, security.

adj alarming, awe-inspiring, awful, dire, dreaded, dreadful, frightening, frightful, ghastly, grisly, gruesome, horrible, terrible, terrifying.

**dreadful** adj alarming, appalling, awful, dire, distressing, fearful, formidable, frightful, ghastly, grievous, grisly, gruesome, harrowing, hideous, horrendous, horrible, monstrous, shocking, terrible, tragic, tremendous.

*antonym* comforting.

**dream** n aisling, ambition, aspiration, beauty, castle in Spain, castle in the air, daydream, delight, delusion, design, desire, fantasy, goal, hallucination, hope, illusion, imagination, joy, marvel, notion, phantasm, pipe-dream, pleasure, reverie, speculation, trance, treasure, vagary, vision, wish.

v conjure, daydream, envisage, fancy, fantasise, hallucinate, imagine, muse, star-gaze, think, visualise.

**dream up** conceive, concoct, contrive, cook up, create, devise, hatch, imagine, invent, spin, think up.

**dreamer** n daydreamer, Don Quixote, fantasiser, fantasist, fantast, idealist, John o'dreams, Johnny-head-in-the-air, romancer, star-gazer, theoriser, utopian, visionary, Walter Mitty, wool-gatherer.

*antonyms* pragmatist, realist.

**dreaminess** n absent-mindedness, abstraction, dimness, dwam, ethereality, fancifulness, insubstantiality, kef, preoccupation, vagueness, whimsicality.

**dreamlike** *adj* chimerical, hallucinatory, illusory, insubstantial, phantasmagoric, phantasmagorical, phantom, surreal, trance-like, unreal, unsubstantial, visionary.

**dreamy** absent, abstracted, chimerical, daydreaming, dreamlike, fanciful, fantastic, faraway, gentle, imaginary, impractical, intangible, lulling, misty, musing, pensive, phantasmagoric, phantasmagorical, phantasmal, preoccupied, quixotic, romantic, shadowy, speculative, unreal, vague, visionary.

*antonyms* down-to-earth, realistic.

**dreary** *adj* bleak, boring, cheerless, colourless, comfortless, commonplace, depressing, dismal, doleful, downcast, drab, drear, dreich, dull, forlorn, gloomy, glum, gousty, humdrum, joyless, lifeless, lonely, lonesome, melancholy, monotonous, mournful, routine, sad, solitary, sombre, sorrowful, tedious, trite, uneventful, uninteresting, wearisome, wretched.

*antonyms* bright, interesting.

**dredge** *v* dig up, discover, drag up, draw up, expose, fish up, raise, rake up, scoop up, uncover, unearth.

**dregs** *n* canaille, deposit, draff, dross, excrement, faeces, fag-end, fecula, grounds, lags, lees, left-overs, mother, outcasts, rabble, residue, residuum, riff-raff, scourings, scum, sediment, tailings, trash, waste.

**drench** *v* douse, drouk, drown, duck, flood, imbrue, imbue, immerse, inundate, saturate, soak, souse, steep, wet.

**dress** *n* apparel, attire, caparison, clothes, clothing, costume, ensemble, frock, garb, garment, garments, gear, get-up, gown, guise, habiliments, habit, outfit, raiment, rig-out, robe, suit, togs, vestment.

*v* accoutre, adjust, adorn, align, apparel, arrange, array, attire, bandage, bedeck, bedizen, betrim, bind up, boun, busk, caparison, change, clothe, deck, decorate, dispose, don, drape, embellish, fit, furbish, garb, garnish, groom, habilitate, habit, ornament, plaster, prepare, put on, rig, robe, set, straighten, tend, treat, trim.

*antonyms* disrobe, strip, undress.

**dress down** berate, castigate, chide, flyte, haul over the coals, rebuke, reprimand, reprove, scold, tear off a strip, tell off, upbraid.

**dress up** adorn, beautify, dandify, deck, disguise, doll up, embellish, fig out, gild, improve, play-act, tart up, titivate, trick out.

**dressing** *n* bandage, compress, emplastron, emplastrum, ligature, pad, plaster, pledget, poultice, spica, tourniquet.

**dressing-gown** *n* housecoat, negligee, peignoir.

**dressmaker** *n* couturier, midinette, modiste, seamstress, sewing woman, tailor, tailoress.

**dressy** *adj* classy, elaborate, elegant, formal, natty, ornate, ritzy, smart, stylish, swanky, swish.

*antonyms* dowdy, scruffy.

**dribble** *v* drip, drivel, drool, drop, leak, ooze, run, saliva, seep, slaver, slobber, sprinkle, trickle.

*n* drip, droplet, gobbet, leak, seepage, sprinkling, trickle.

**dried** *adj* arid, dehydrated, desiccated, drained, exsiccated, mummified, parched, shrivelled, wilted, withered, wizened.

**drift** *v* accumulate, amass, coast, drive, float, freewheel, gather, meander, pile up, stray, waft, wander.

*n* accumulation, aim, bank, course, current, design, direction, dune, flow, gist, heap, implication, import, impulse, intention, mass, meaning, mound, movement, object, pile, purport, ridge, rush, scope, significance, sweep, tendency, tenor, thrust, trend.

**drifter** *n* beachcomber, hobo, intinerant, rolling stone, rover, swagman, tramp, vagabond, vagrant, wanderer.

**drill¹** *v* coach, discipline, exercise, instruct, practise, rehearse, teach, train, tutor.

*n* coaching, discipline, exercise, instruction, practice, preparation, repetition, training, tuition.

**drill²** *v* bore, penetrate, perforate, pierce, puncture, transpierce.

*n* awl, bit, borer, gimlet.

**drink** *v* absorb, bib, booze, carouse, down, drain, dram, gulp, guzzle, hit the bottle, imbibe, indulge, knock back, liquefy, liquor up, partake of, quaff, revel, sip, suck, sup, swallow, swig, swill, tank up, tipple, tope, toss off, wassail, water.

*n* alcohol, ambrosia, beverage, bev(v)y, booze, deoch-an-doris, dose, dram, draught, glass, gulp, hooch, liquid, liquor, noggin, plonk, potion, refreshment, sensation, sip, slug, snifter, snort, spirits, stiffener, suck, swallow, swig, swizzle, taste, the bottle, tickler, tiff, tipple, toss, tot.

**drink in** absorb, assimilate, attend to, be absorbed by, ingest, soak up.

**drink to** pledge (the health of), salute, toast.

**drinker** *n* alcoholic, bibber, boozer, carouser, dipso, dipsomaniac, drunk, drunkard, guzzler, inebriate, lush, soak, sot, souse, sponge, tippler, toper, wino.

*antonyms* abstainer, teetotaller.

**drip** *v* dribble, drizzle, drop, exude, filter, plop, splash, sprinkle, trickle, weep.

*n* dribble, dripping, drop, leak, milk-sop, ninny, softy, stillicide, trickle, weakling, weed, wet.

**drive** *v* actuate, bear, coerce, compel, constrain, dash, dig, direct, force, goad, guide, hammer, handle, harass, herd, hurl, impel, manage, motivate, motor, oblige, operate, overburden, overwork, plunge, press, prod, propel, push, ram, ride, rush, send, sink, spur, stab, steer, task, tax, thrust, travel, urge.

*n* action, advance, ambition, appeal, campaign, crusade, determination, effort, energy, enterprise, excursion, get-up-and-go, hurl, initiative, jaunt, journey, motivation, outing, pressure, push, ride, run, spin, surge, trip, turn, vigour, vim, zip.

**drive at** aim, allude to, get at, imply, indicate, insinuate, intend, intimate, mean, refer to, signify, suggest.

**drive up the wall** annoy, dement, derange, drive round the bend, exasperate, infuriate, irritate, madden.

**drivel** n blathering, bunkum, eyewash, fosh, gibberish, gobbledegook, guff, gush, jive, mumbo-jumbo, nonsense, slush, stultiloquy, twaddle, waffle.

**driver** n cabbie, cabman, charioteer, chauffeur, coachman, Jehu, motorist, trucker, vetturino, voiturier, wag(g)oner.

**driving** adj compelling, dynamic, energetic, forceful, forthright, galvanic, heavy, sweeping, vigorous, violent.

**drizzle** n drow, mizzle, Scotch mist, serein.

v dribble, mizzle, rain, shower, spit, spot, spray, sprinkle.

**droll** adj amusing, clownish, comic, comical, diverting, eccentric, entertaining, farcical, funny, humorous, jocular, laughable, ludicrous, pawky, quaint, ridiculous, risible, waggish, whimsical, witty.

**drollery** n absurdity, archness, banter, buffoonery, comicality, farce, fun, humour, jocularity, pleasantry, waggery, waggishness, whimsicality, wit.

**drone** v bombilate, bombinate, buzz, chant, drawl, hum, intone, purr, thrum, vibrate, whirr.

n buzz, chant, hum, murmuring, purr, thrum, vibration, whirr, whirring.

**drool** v dote, dribble, drivel, enthuse, fondle, gloat, gush, rave, salivate, slaver, slobber, water at the mouth.

**droop** v bend, dangle, decline, despond, diminish, drop, fade, faint, fall down, falter, flag, hang (down) sag, languish, lose heart, sink, slouch, slump, stoop, wilt, wither.

antonyms rise, straighten.

**drooping** adj blue, dejected, disheartened, dispirited, doleful, downcast, droopy, flabby, flaccid, floppy, languid, languorous, lassitudinous, limp, pendulous, sagging, stooped, wilting.

antonyms stiff, straight.

**drop** n abyss, bead, bubble, chasm, cut, dab, dash, decline, declivity, decrease, descent, deterioration, downturn, drib, driblet, drip, droplet, fall, falling-off, glob, globule, globulet, goutte, gutta, lowering, mouthful, nip, pearl, pinch, plunge, precipice, reduction, shot, sip, slope, slump, spot, taste, tear, tot, trace, trickle.

v abandon, cease, chuck, decline, depress, descend, desert, diminish, discontinue, disown, dive, dribble, drip, droop, fall, forsake, give up, jilt, kick, leave, lower, plummet, plunge, quit, reject, relinquish, remit, renounce, repudiate, sink, stop, terminate, throw over, trickle, tumble.

antonyms mount, rise.

**drop off** catnap, decline, decrease, deliver, depreciate, diminish, doze, drowse, dwindle, fall off, have forty winks, leave, lessen, nod, nod off, set down, slacken, snooze.

antonym increase.

**drop out** abandon, back out, cry off, forsake, leave, quit, renegue, stop, withdraw.

**drop-out** n Bohemian, deviant, dissenter, dissentient, hippie, loner, malcontent, non-conformist, rebel, renegade.

**droppings** n dung, egesta, excrement, excreta, faeces, fumet, guano, manure, ordure, spraint, stools.

**dross** n crust, debris, dregs, impurity, lees, recrement, refuse, remains, rubbish, scoria, scum, trash, waste.

**drought** n aridity, dearth, deficiency, dehydration, desiccation, drouth, dryness, insufficiency, lack, need, parchedness, scarcity, shortage, want.

**drove** n collection, company, crowd, drift, flock, gathering, herd, horde, mob, multitude, press, swarm, throng.

**drown** v deaden, deluge, drench, engulf, extinguish, flood, go under, immerse, inundate, muffle, obliterate, overcome, overpower, overwhelm, silence, sink, stifle, submerge, swallow up, swamp, wipe out.

**drowsiness** n dopeyness, doziness, grogginess, lethargy, narcosis, oscitancy, sleepiness, sluggishness, somnolence, torpor.

**drowsy** adj comatose, dazed, dopey, dozy, dreamy, drugged, heavy, lethargic, lulling, nodding, restful, sleepy, somniculous, somnolent, soothing, soporific, tired, torpid.

antonyms alert, awake.

**drubbing** n beating, clobbering, defeat, flogging, hammering, licking, pounding, pummelling, thrashing, trouncing, walloping, whipping, whitewash.

**drudge** n afterguard, devil, dogsbody, factotum, galley-slave, hack, jackal, lackey, maid-of-all-work, man-of-all-work, menial, scullion, servant, skivvy, slave, toiler, worker.

v beaver, droil, grind, labour, moil, plod, plug away, slave, toil, work.

antonyms idle, laze.

**drudgery** n chore, collar-work, donkey-work, drudgism, fag, faggery, grind, hack-work, labor improbus, labour, skivvying, slavery, slog, sweat, sweated labour, toil.

**drug** n depressant, dope, kef, medicament, medication, medicine, Mickey, Mickey Finn, narcotic, opiate, physic, poison, potion, remedy, stimulant.

v anaesthetise, deaden, dope, dose, drench, knock out, load, medicate, numb, poison, stupefy, treat.

**drug-addict** n acid head, acidfreak, dope-fiend, head, hop-head, hype, junkie, tripper.

**drugged** adj comatose, doped, dopey, high, looped, spaced out, stoned, stupefied, tripping, turned on, zonked.

**drum** v beat, pulsate, rap, reverberate, tap, tattoo, throb, thrum.

**drum into** din into, drive home, hammer, harp on, instil, reiterate.

**drum up** attract, canvass, collect, gather, obtain, petition, round up, solicit.

**drunk** *adj* a peg too low, a sheet (three sheets) in the wind, bevvied, blind, blotto, bonkers, bottled, canned, cockeyed, corked, corny, drunken, fou, fuddled, half-seas-over, in liquor, inebriate, inebriated, intoxicated, legless, liquored, lit up, loaded, lushy, maggoty, maudlin, merry, moony, moppy, mops and brooms, mortal, muddled, nappy, obfuscated, paralytic, pickled, pie-eyed, pissed, pixil(l)ated, plastered, shickered, sloshed, smashed, soaked, sottish, soused, sow-drunk, sozzled, stewed, stoned, stotious, tanked up, temulent, tiddly, tight, tipsy, up the pole, well-oiled, wet.

*antonym* sober.

*n* boozer, drunkard, inebriate, lush, soak, sot, toper, wino.

**drunkard** *n* alcoholic, bacchant, carouser, dipsomaniac, drinker, drunk, lush, soak, sot, souse, sponge, tippler, toper, tosspot, wino.

**drunken** *adj* bacchanalian, bacchic, bibulous, boozing, boozy, crapulent, crapulous, debauched, Dionysiac, dissipated, drunk, inebriate, intoxicated, orgiastic, riotous, saturnalian, sodden, sottish, spongy, tippling, toping, under the influence.

*antonym* sober.

**drunkenness** *n* alcoholism, bibulousness, dipsomania, inebriety, insobriety, intemperance, intoxication, ivresse, methysis, sottishness, tipsiness.

*antonym* sobriety.

**dry** *adj* arid, barren, boring, cutting, cynical, deadpan, dehydrated, desiccated, dreary, dried up, droll, droughty, drouthy, dull, juiceless, keen, low-key, moistureless, monotonous, parched, pawky, plain, sapless, sarcastic, sec, secco, sharp, sly, tedious, thirsty, tiresome, torrid, uninteresting, waterless, withered, xeric.

*antonyms* interesting, sweet, wet.

*v* dehumidify, dehydrate, desiccate, drain, exsiccate, harden, mummify, parch, sear, shrivel, welt, wilt, wither, wizen.

*antonyms* soak, wet.

**drying** *n* dehumidification, dehydration, desiccation, exsiccation.

**dryness** *n* aridity, aridness, cynicality, dehydration, drought, drouth, pawkiness, sarcasm, thirst, thirstiness, xerosis.

*antonym* wetness.

**dual** *adj* binary, combined, coupled, double, duplex, duplicate, geminate, matched, paired, twin, twofold.

**dub** *v* bestow, call, christen, confer, denominate, designate, entitle, knight, label, name, nickname, style, tag, term.

**dubiety** *n* doubt, doubtfulness, dubiosity, dubiousness, equivocality, incertitude, indecision, misgiving, mistrust, qualm, scepticism, suspicion, uncertainty.

*antonym* certainty.

**dubious** *adj* ambiguous, debatable, doubtful, equivocal, fishy, hesitant, iffy, indefinite, indeterminate, obscure, problematical, questionable, sceptical, shady, speculative, suspect, suspicious, uncertain, unclear, unconvinced, undecided, undependable, unreliable, unsettled, unsure, untrustworthy, wavering.

*antonyms* certain, reliable, trustworthy.

**duck**[1] *v* avoid, bend, bob, bow, crouch, dodge, drop, escape, evade, lower, shirk, shun, sidestep, squat, stoop.

**duck**[2] *v* dip, dive, dook, douse, dunk, immerse, plunge, souse, submerge, wet.

**duct** *n* blood, canal, channel, conduit, fistula, funnel, passage, pipe, tube, vas, vessel.

**ductile** *adj* amenable, biddable, complaint, docile, extensible, flexible, malleable, manageable, manipul(at)able, plastic, pliable, pliant, tractable, yielding.

*antonyms* intractable, refractory.

**dud** *n* bum steer, failure, flop, lemon, stumer, wash-out.

*adj* broken, bust, duff, failed, inoperative, kaput, nugatory, valueless, worthless.

**due** *adj* adequate, ample, appropriate, becoming, bounden, deserved, enough, expected, fit, fitting, in arrears, just, justified, mature, merited, obligatory, outstanding, owed, owing, payable, plenty of, proper, requisite, returnable, right, rightful, scheduled, sufficient, suitable, unpaid, well-earned.

*n* birthright, come-uppance, deserts, merits, prerogative, privilege, right(s).

*adv* dead, direct, directly, exactly, precisely, straight.

**duel** *n* affair of honour, clash, competition, contest, duello, encounter, engagement, fight, monomachia, monomachy, rivalry, single combat, struggle.

*v* battle, clash, compete, contend, contest, fight, rival, struggle, vie.

**dues** *n* charge(s), contribution, fee, levy, subscription.

**duffer** *n* blunderer, bonehead, booby, bungler, clod, clot, dolt, galoot, lubber, lummox, muff, oaf.

**dull** *adj* apathetic, blank, blockish, blunt, blunted, Boeotian, boring, bovine, callous, cloudy, commonplace, corny, dead, dead-and-alive, dense, depressed, dim, dimwitted, dismal, doltish, dowie, drab, dreary, dry, dulled, edgeless, empty, faded, featureless, feeble, flat, gloomy, heavy, humdrum, inactive, indifferent, indistinct, insensible, insensitive, insipid, lack-lustre, leaden, lifeless, listless, monotonous, mopish, muffled, mumpish, murky, muted, opaque, opiate, opioid, overcast, passionless, pedestrian, plain, prosaic, run-of-the-mill, slack, sleepy, slow, sluggish, sombre, stodgy, stolid, stultifying, stupid, subdued, subfusc, sullen, sunless, tame, tedious, thick, tiresome, toneless, torpid, turbid, uneventful, unexciting, unfunny, ungifted, unidea'd, unimaginative, unintelligent, uninteresting, unlively, unresponsive, unsharpened, unsunny, unsympathetic, untalented, vacuous, vapid.

*antonyms* alert, bright, clear, exciting, sharp.

**dullard** v allay, alleviate, assuage, blunt, cloud, dampen, darken, deject, depress, dim, discourage, disedge, dishearten, dispirit, fade, hebetate, lessen, mitigate, moderate, muffle, obscure, obtund, opiate, palliate, paralyse, rebate, relieve, sadden, soften, stain, stupefy, subdue, sully, tarnish.

*antonyms* brighten, sharpen, stimulate.

**dullard** n blockhead, bonehead, chump, clod, clot, dimwit, dolt, dope, dummy, dunce, dunderhead, flat tyre, idiot, ignoramus, imbecile, moron, nitwit, noodle, numskull, oaf, simpleton, vegetable.

*antonym* brain.

**dullness** n dreariness, dryness, emptiness, fadeur, flatness, hebetude, hebetudinosity, monotony, plainness, slowness, sluggishness, stolidity, stupidity, tedium, torpor, vacuity, vapidity.

*antonyms* brightness, clarity, excitement, interest, sharpness.

**duly** adv accordingly, appropriately, befittingly, condignly, correctly, decorously, deservedly, fitly, fittingly, properly, punctually, rightfully, suitably, sure enough.

**dumb** adj aphonic, aphonous, dense, dimwitted, dull, foolish, inarticulate, mum, mute, silent, soundless, speechless, stupid, thick, tongue-tied, unintelligent, voiceless, wordless.

*antonym* intelligent.

**dum(b)founded** adj amazed, astonished, astounded, bewildered, bowled over, breathless, confounded, confused, dumb, flabbergasted, floored, knocked sideways, nonplussed, overcome, overwhelmed, paralysed, speechless, staggered, startled, stunned, taken aback, thrown, thunderstruck.

**dummy** n blockhead, copy, counterfeit, dimwit, dolt, dullard, dunce, duplicate, figure, fool, form, imitation, lay-figure, manikin, mannequin, model, numskull, pacifier, sham, simpleton, substitute, teat.

adj artificial, bogus, dry, fake, false, imitation, mock, phoney, practice, sham, simulated, trial.

**dump** v deposit, discharge, dispose of, ditch, drop, empty out, get rid of, jettison, let fall, offload, park, scrap, throw away, throw down, tip, unload.

n coup, hole, hovel, joint, junk-yard, landhill, mess, midden, pigsty, rubbish-heap, rubbish-tip, shack, shanty, slum, tip.

**dumpy** adj chubby, chunky, fatling, homely, plump, podgy, pudgy, roly-poly, short, squab, squat, stout, stubby, tubby.

*antonyms* rangy, tall.

**dun** v beset, harass, harry, importune, pester, plague, press, urge.

**dunce** n ass, blockhead, bonehead, dimwit, dolt, donkey, duffer, dullard, dunderhead, goose, half-wit, ignoramus, loggerhead, log-head, loon, moron, nincompoop, numskull, simpleton.

*antonyms* brain, intellectual.

**dung** n excrement, faeces, fumet, guano, manure, ordure, spraint.

**dungeon** n cage, cell, donjon, lock-up, oubliette, pit, prison, vault.

**dunghill** n midden, middenstead, mixen, muck-heap, muck-midden.

**dupe** n cat's-paw, fall guy, flat, geck, gull, instrument, mug, pawn, pigeon, puppet, pushover, sap, simpleton, sitter, soft mark, stooge, sucker, tool, victim.

v bamboozle, beguile, cheat, con, cozen, deceive, defraud, delude, gammon, grift, gudgeon, gull, hoax, hoodwink, humbug, outwit, overreach, pigeon, rip off, swindle, trick.

**duplicate** adj corresponding, geminate, identical, matched, matching, twin, twofold.

n carbon copy, copy, facsimile, match, photocopy, Photostat®, replica, reproduction, Xerox®.

v clone, copy, ditto, double, echo, geminate, photocopy, Photostat®, repeat, replicate, reproduce, Xerox®.

**duplication** n clone, cloning, copy(ing), dittography, gemination, photocopy(ing), repetition, replication, reproduction.

**duplicity** n artifice, chicanery, deceit, deception, dishonesty, dissimulation, double-dealing, falsehood, fraud, guile, hypocrisy, mendacity, perfidy, treachery.

**durability** n constancy, durableness, endurance, imperishability, lastingness, longevity, permanence, persistence, stability, strength.

*antonyms* fragility, impermanence, weakness.

**durable** adj abiding, constant, dependable, enduring, fast, firm, fixed, hard-wearing, lasting, long-lasting, perdurable, permanent, persistent, reliable, resistant, sound, stable, strong, sturdy, substantial, tough, unfading.

*antonyms* fragile, impermanent, perishable, weak.

**duration** n continuance, continuation, extent, fullness, length, period, perpetuation, prolongation, span, spell, stretch, term-time.

*antonym* shortening.

**duress** n bullying, captivity, coaction, coercion, compulsion, confinement, constraint, force, hardship, imprisonment, incarceration, pressure, restraint, threat.

**dusk** n crepuscle, crepuscule, dark, darkness, evening, eventide, gloaming, gloom, murk, nightfall, obscurity, shade, shadowiness, sundown, sunset, twilight.

*antonyms* brightness, dawn.

**duskiness** n caliginosity, darkness, fuliginosity, murkiness, swarthiness.

*antonyms* brightness, lightness, whiteness.

**dusky** adj caliginous, cloudy, crepuscular, dark, dark-hued, darkish, dim, fuliginous, gloomy, murky, obscure, overcast, sable, shadowy, shady, sooty, subfusc, swarthy, tenebr(i)ous, twilight, twilit, umbrose, veiled.

*antonyms* bright, light, white.

**dust** n coom, dirt, earth, grime, grit, ground, particles, powder, soil.

*v* burnish, clean, cover, dredge, polish, powder, scatter, sift, spray, spread, sprinkle, wipe.

**dustman** *n* garbo, garbologist.

**dust-storm** *n* dust-devil, sand-storm.

**dust-up** *n* argument, argy-bargy, brawl, brush, commotion, conflict, disagreement, disturbance, encounter, fight, fracas, punch-up, quarrel, scrap, scuffle, set-to, shindig, skirmish, tussle.

**dusty** *adj* chalky, crumbly, dirty, filthy, friable, granular, grubby, powdery, pulverous, sandy, sooty, unswept.

*antonyms* clean, hard, polished, solid.

**dutiful** *adj* acquiescent, complaisant, compliant, conscientious, deferential, devoted, docile, duteous, filial, obedient, punctilious, regardful, respectful, reverential, submissive.

**duty** *n* allegiance, assignment, business, calling, charge, chore, customs, debt, deference, devoir, due, engagement, excise, function, impost, job, levy, loyalty, mission, obedience, obligation, office, onus, province, respect, responsibility, reverence, role, service, tariff, task, tax, toll, work.

**dwarf** *n* droich, durgan, elf, gnome, goblin, homuncle, homuncule, homunculus, hop-o'-my-thumb, Lilliputian, man(n)ikin, midget, pygmy, Tom Thumb.

*adj* baby, bonsai, diminutive, dwarfed, dwarfish, Lilliputian, mini, miniature, petite, pint-size(d), pocket, small, tiny, undersized.

*antonym* large.

*v* check, dim, diminish, dominate, lower, minimise, overshadow, retard, stunt.

**dwarfish** *adj* diminutive, durgy, pocket, pygmean, pygmy, small, stunted, undersized.

*antonym* large.

**dwell** *v* abide, bide, hang out, inhabit, live, lodge, people, populate, quarter, remain, reside, rest, settle, sojourn, stay, stop, tenant.

**dwell on** elaborate, emphasise, expatiate, harp on, harp on about, linger over, mull over.

*antonym* pass over.

**dweller** *n* denizen, inhabitant, occupant, occupier, resident.

**dwelling** *n* abode, domicile, dwelling-house, establishment, habitation, home, house, lodge, lodging, quarters, residence, tent, tepee, woning.

**dwindle** *v* abate, contract, decay, decline, decrease, die, die out, diminish, disappear, ebb, fade, fall, lessen, peter out, pine, shrink, shrivel, sink, subside, tail off, taper off, vanish, wane, waste away, weaken, wither.

*antonym* increase.

**dye** *n* colorant, colour, colouring, grain, pigment, stain, tinge, tint.

*v* colour, grain, imbue, pigment, stain, tincture, tinge, tint.

**dyed-in-the-wool** *adj* card-carrying, complete, confirmed, deep-rooted, die-hard, entrenched, established, fixed, hard-core, hardened, inflexible, inveterate, long-standing, settled, unchangeable, uncompromising, unshakable.

*antonym* superficial.

**dying** *adj* at death's door, declining, disappearing, ebbing, expiring, fading, failing, final, going, in articulo mortis, in extremis, moribund, mortal, not long for this world, obsolescent, passing, perishing, sinking, vanishing.

*antonyms* coming, reviving.

**dynamic** *adj* active, driving, electric, energetic, forceful, go-ahead, go-getting, high-powered, lively, powerful, self-starting, spirited, vigorous, vital, zippy.

*antonyms* apathetic, inactive, slow.

**dynamism** *n* drive, energy, enterprise, forcefulness, get-up-and-go, go, initiative, liveliness, pep, pizzazz, push, vigour, vim, zap, zip.

*antonyms* apathy, inactivity, slowness.

**dynasty** *n* ascendancy, authority, dominion, empire, government, house, regime, rule, sovereignty, succession, sway.

**dyspeptic** *adj* bad-tempered, crabbed, crabby, crotchety, gloomy, grouchy, indigested, peevish, short-tempered, snappish, testy, touchy.

# E

**each** *adv* apiece, individually, per capita, per head, per person, respectively, separately, singly.

**eager** *adj* agog, anxious, ardent, athirst, avid, desirous, earnest, empressé, enthusiastic, fervent, fervid, fervorous, freck, greedy, gung-ho, hot, hungry, impatient, intent, keen, longing, perfervid, raring, unshrinking, vehement, yearning, zealous.

*antonyms* apathetic, unenthusiastic.

**eagerly** *adv* ardently, avidly, earnestly, enthusiastically, fain, fervently, greedily, intently, keenly, zealously.

*antonyms* apathetically, listlessly.

**eagerness** *n* ardour, avidity, earnestness, enthusiasm, fainness, fervency, fervidity, fervour, greediness, heartiness, hunger, impatience, impetuosity, intentness, keenness, longing, thirst, vehemence, yearning, zeal.

*antonyms* apathy, disinterest.

**ear** *n* ability, appreciation, attention, consideration, discrimination, hearing, heed, notice, perception, regard, sensitivity, skill, taste.

**early** *adj* advanced, forward, matutinal, matutine, prehistoric, premature, primeval, primitive, primordial, undeveloped, untimely, young.

*adv* ahead of time, beforehand, betimes, in advance, in good time, prematurely, too soon.

*antonym* late.

**earmark** *v* allocate, designate, keep back, label, put aside, reserve, set aside, tag.

**earn** *v* acquire, attain, bring in, collect, deserve, draw, gain, get, gross, make, merit, net, obtain, procure, rate, realise, reap, receive, warrant, win.

*antonyms* lose, spend.

**earnest** *adj* ardent, close, constant, determined, devoted, eager, enthusiastic, fervent, fervid, firm, fixed, grave, heartfelt, impassioned, intent, keen, passionate, purposeful, resolute, resolved, serious, sincere, solemn, stable, staid, steady, thoughtful, urgent, vehement, warm, zealous.

*antonyms* apathetic, flippant, unenthusiastic.

*n* assurance, deposit, determination, down payment, guarantee, pledge, promise, resolution, security, seriousness, sincerity, token, truth.

**earnestly** *adv* eagerly, ex animo, fervently, firmly, intently, keenly, resolutely, seriously, sincerely, warmly, zealously.

*antonyms* flippantly, listlessly.

**earnestness** *n* ardour, determination, devotion, eagerness, enthusiasm, fervency, fervour, gravity, intentness, keenness, passion, purposefulness, resolution, seriousness, sincerity, urgency, vehemence, warmth, zeal.

*antonyms* apathy, flippancy.

**earnings** *n* emoluments, gain, income, pay, proceeds, profits, receipts, remuneration, return, revenue, reward, salary, stipend, takings, wages.

*antonyms* expenses, outgoings.

**earring** *n* earbob, ear-drop.

**earth**[1] *n* Gaia, geosphere, globe, middle-earth, middle-world, Midgard, orb, planet, sphere, world.

**earth**[2] *n* clay, clod, dirt, ground, humus, land, loam, mould, sod, soil, topsoil.

**earthenware** *n* ceramics, crockery, crocks, pots, pottery.

*adj* ceramic, clay, fictile, figuline, terra-cotta, wally.

**earthly** *adj* base, carnal, conceivable, earthern, feasible, fleshly, gross, human, imaginable, likely, low, material, materialistic, mortal, mundane, physical, possible, practical, profane, secular, sensual, slight, slightest, sordid, sublunar, sublunary, tellurian, telluric, temporal, terrene, terrestrial, vile, worldly.

*antonyms* heavenly, spiritual.

**earthquake** *n* earth-tremor, quake, seism, shake, upheaval.

**earthy** *adj* bawdy, blue, coarse, crude, down-to-earth, homely, indecorous, lusty, natural, raunchy, ribald, robust, rough, simple, uninhibited, unrefined, unsophisticated, vulgar.

*antonyms* cultured, refined.

**ease** *n* affluence, aplomb, calmness, comfort, composure, content, contentment, dexterity, easiness, effortlessness, enjoyment, facileness, facility, flexibility, freedom, happiness, informality, insouciance, leisure, liberty, naturalness, nonchalance, peace, peace of mind, poise, quiet, quietude, readiness, relaxation, repose, rest, restfulness, serenity, simplicity, solace, tranquillity, unaffectedness, unconstraint, unreservedness.

*antonyms* difficulty, discomfort.

*v* abate, aid, allay, alleviate, appease, assist, assuage, calm, comfort, disburden, edge, expedite, facilitate, forward, further, guide, inch, lessen, lighten, manoeuvre, mitigate, moderate, mollify, pacify, palliate, quiet, relax, relent, relieve, simplify, slacken, slide, slip, smooth, solace, soothe, speed up, squeeze, steer, still, tranquillise.

*antonyms* hinder, retard, torment.

**ease off** abate, decrease, die away, die down, moderate, relent, slacken, subside, wane.

*antonym* increase.

**easily**[1] *adv* comfortably, effortlessly, facilely, readily, simply, smoothly, standing on one's head, with one arm tied behind one's back.

*antonym* laboriously.

**easily**[2] *adv* absolutely, by far, certainly, clearly, definitely, doubtlessly, far and away, indisputably, indubitably, plainly, probably, simply, surely, undeniably, undoubtedly, unequivocally, unquestionably, well.

**easy** *adj* a doddle, a piece of cake, a pushover, accommodating, affable, amenable, biddable, calm, carefree, casual, child's play, clear, comfortable, compliant, contented, cushy, docile, easeful, easy-going, effortless, facile, flexible, friendly, gentle, graceful, gracious, gullible, idiot-proof, indulgent, informal, leisurely, lenient, liberal, light, manageable, mild, moderate, natural, no bother, open, painless, peaceful, permissive, pleasant, pliant, quiet, relaxed, satisfied, serene, simple, smooth, soft, straightforward, submissive, suggestible, susceptible, temperate, tolerant, tractable, tranquil, trusting, unaffected, unburdensome, unceremonious, uncomplicated, unconstrained, undemanding, undisturbed, unexacting, unforced, unhurried, unlaboured, unoppressive, unpretentious, untroubled, unworried, user-friendly, well-to-do, yielding.

*antonyms* demanding, difficult, fast, impossible, intolerant.

**easy-going** *adj* amenable, calm, carefree, casual, complacent, downbeat, easy, easy-osy, even-tempered, flexible, happy-go-lucky, indulgent, insouciant, laid-back, lenient, liberal, mild, moderate, nonchalant, permissive, placid, relaxed, serene, tolerant, unconcerned, uncritical, undemanding, unhurried, unworried.

*antonyms* fussy, intolerant.

**eat** *v* banquet, break bread, chew, chop, consume, corrode, crumble, decay, devour, dine, dissolve, erode, feed, grub, ingest, knock back, manducate, munch, pig, rot, scoff, swallow, wear away.

**eat one's words** abjure, recant, rescind, retract, take back, unsay.

**eatable** *adj* comestible, digestible, edible, esculent, good, harmless, palatable, wholesome.

*antonym* unpalatable.

**eatables** *n* comestibles, food, grub, nosh, scoff.

**eavesdrop** *v* bug, earwig, listen in, monitor, overhear, snoop, spy, tap.

**eavesdropper** *n* listener, monitor, snoop, snooper, spy.

**ebb** *v* abate, decay, decline, decrease, degenerate, deteriorate, diminish, drop, dwindle,

fade away, fall away, fall back, flag, flow back, go out, lessen, peter out, recede, reflow, retire, retreat, retrocede, shrink, sink, slacken, subside, wane, weaken, withdraw.

*antonyms* increase, rise.

*n* decay, decline, decrease, degeneration, deterioration, diminution, drop, dwindling, ebb tide, flagging, lessening, low tide, low water, reflow, refluence, reflux, regression, retreat, retrocession, shrinkage, sinking, slackening, subsidence, wane, waning, weakening, withdrawal.

*antonyms* flow, increase, rising.

**ebony** *adj* black, dark, jet, jet-black, jetty, sable, sooty.

**ebullience** *n* boiling, breeziness, brightness, bubbling, buoyancy, chirpiness, ebullition, effervescence, effusiveness, elation, enthusiasm, excitement, exhilaration, exuberance, ferment, fermentation, foaming, frothing, high spirits, seething, vivacity, zest.

*antonyms* apathy, dullness, lifelessness.

**ebullient** *adj* boiling, breezy, bright, bubbling, buoyant, chirpy, effervescent, effusive, elated, enthusiastic, excited, exhilarated, exuberant, foaming, frothing, frothy, gushing, irrepressible, seething, vivacious, zestful.

*antonyms* apathetic, dull, lifeless.

**eccentric** *adj* aberrant, abnormal, anomalous, bizarre, capricious, dotty, erratic, fey, freakish, fruity, idiosyncratic, irregular, nuts, nutty, odd, offbeat, outlandish, peculiar, queer, quirky, screwball, screwy, singular, spac(e)y, strange, uncommon, unconventional, way-out, weird, whimsical.

*antonyms* normal, sane.

*n* case, character, crank, freak, fruit-cake, nonconformist, nut, nutter, oddball, oddity, queer fish, screwball, weirdie, weirdo.

**eccentricity** *n* aberration, abnormality, anomaly, bizarreness, bizarrerie, caprice, capriciousness, foible, freakishness, idiosyncrasy, irregularity, nonconformity, oddity, outlandishness, peculiarity, queerness, quirk, singularity, strangeness, unconventionality, waywardness, weirdness, whimsicality.

*antonyms* normalcy, normality, ordinariness.

**ecclesiastic** *n* abbé, churchman, clergyman, cleric, divine, man of the cloth, minister, parson, priest.

**ecclesiastic(al)** *adj* church, churchly, churchy, clerical, divine, holy, pastoral, priestly, religious, spiritual, templar.

**echelon** *n* degree, grade, level, place, position, rank, status, step, tier.

**echo** *v* ape, copy, echoise, imitate, mimic, mirror, parallel, parrot, recall, reflect, reiterate, repeat, reproduce, resemble, resound, reverberate, ring, second.

*n* allusion, answer, copy, evocation, hint, image, imitation, intimation, memory, mirror image, parallel, reflection, reiteration, reminder, repetition, reproduction, reverberation, suggestion, sympathy, trace.

**echoic** *adj* imitative, onomatopoeic, onomatopoetic.

**éclat** *n* acclaim, acclamation, applause, approval, brilliance, celebrity, display, distinction, effect, fame, glory, lustre, ostentation, plaudits, pomp, renown, show, showmanship, splendour, success.

*antonyms* disapproval, dullness.

**eclectic** *adj* all-embracing, broad, catholic, comprehensive, dilettantish, diverse, diversified, general, heterogeneous, liberal, many-sided, multifarious, selective, varied, wide-ranging.

*antonyms* narrow, one-sided.

**eclipse** *v* blot out, cloud, darken, dim, dwarf, exceed, excel, extinguish, obscure, outdo, outshine, overshadow, shroud, surpass, transcend, veil.

*n* darkening, decline, deliquium, diminution, dimming, extinction, failure, fall, loss, obscuration, occultation, overshadowing, shading.

**economic** *adj* budgetary, business, cheap, commercial, cost-effective, economical, economy-size, fair, financial, fiscal, industrial, inexpensive, low, low-priced, mercantile, modest, monetary, money-making, pecuniary, productive, profitable, profit-making, reasonable, remunerative, solvent, trade, viable.

*antonyms* expensive, uneconomic.

**economical** *adj* careful, cheap, cost-effective, economic, economising, efficient, fair, frugal, inexpensive, labour-saving, low, low-priced, modest, prudent, reasonable, saving, scrimping, sparing, thrifty, time-saving.

*antonyms* expensive, uneconomical.

**economics** *n* plutology, plutonomy, political economy.

**economise** *v* cut back, cut corners, husband, retrench, save, scrimp, tighten one's belt.

*antonym* squander.

**economy** *n* frugality, frugalness, husbandry, parsimony, providence, prudence, restraint, retrenchment, saving, scrimping, sparingness, thrift, thriftiness.

*antonym* improvidence.

**ecstasy** *n* bliss, delight, ecstasis, elation, enthusiasm, euphoria, exaltation, fervour, frenzy, joy, rapture, ravishment, rhapsody, seventh heaven, sublimation, trance, transport.

*antonym* torment.

**ecstatic** *adj* blissful, delirious, elated, enraptured, enthusiastic, entranced, euphoric, exultant, fervent, frenzied, joyful, joyous, on cloud nine, over the moon, overjoyed, rapturous, rhapsodic, transported.

*antonym* downcast.

**eddy** *n* counter-current, counterflow, pirl, purl, swirl, vortex, well, whirlpool.

*v* swirl, whirl.

**edge** *n* acuteness, advantage, animation, arris, ascendancy, bezel, bite, border, bound, boundary, brim, brink, cantle, contour, dominance, effectiveness, force, fringe, incisiveness, interest, keenness, lead, limit, line, lip, margin, outline, perimeter, periphery, point, pungency, rim, sharpness, side, sting, superiority, threshold, upper hand, urgency, verge, zest.

*v* bind, border, creep, drib, ease, fringe, gravitate, hem, hone, inch, rim, shape, sharpen, sidle, steal, strop, trim, verge, whet, work, worm.

**edgy** *adj* anxious, ill at ease, irascible, irritable, keyed-up, nervous, on edge, prickly, restive, tense, testy, touchy.

*antonym* calm.

**edible** *adj* comestible, digestible, eatable, esculent, good, harmless, palatable, safe, wholesome.

*antonym* inedible.

**edict** *n* act, command, decree, dictate, dictum, enactment, fiat, injunction, law, mandate, manifesto, order, ordinance, proclamation, pronouncement, pronunciamento, regulation, rescript, ruling, statute, ukase.

**edification** *n* enlightenment, guidance, improvement, instruction, upbuilding.

**edifice** *n* building, construction, erection, structure.

**edify** *v* educate, elevate, enlighten, guide, improve, inform, instruct, nurture, school, teach, train, tutor.

**edit** *v* adapt, annotate, assemble, blue-pencil, bowdlerise, censor, check, compose, condense, correct, emend, polish, rearrange, redact, reorder, rephrase, revise, rewrite, select.

**edition** *n* copy, exemplar, impression, issue, number, printing, programme, version, volume.

**educable** *adj* instructible, teachable, trainable.

*antonym* ineducable.

**educate** *v* catechise, civilise, coach, cultivate, develop, discipline, drill, edify, exercise, improve, indoctrinate, inform, instruct, learn, mature, rear, school, teach, train, tutor.

**educated** *adj* civilised, coached, cultivated, cultured, enlightened, experienced, informed, instructed, knowledgeable, learned, lettered, literary, nurtured, polished, refined, schooled, sophisticated, taught, trained, tutored, well-bred.

*antonyms* uncultured, uneducated.

**education** *n* breeding, civilisation, coaching, cultivation, culture, development, discipline, drilling, edification, enlightenment, erudition, guidance, improvement, indoctrination, instruction, knowledge, nurture, scholarship, schooling, teaching, training, tuition, tutelage, tutoring.

**educational** *adj* cultural, didactic, edifying, educative, enlightening, improving, informative, instructive, scholastic.

*antonym* uninformative.

**educative** *adj* catechetic, catechismal, catechistic(al), didactic, edifying, educational, enlightening, improving, informative, instructive.

*antonym* uninformative.

**educator** *n* coach, dominie, edifier, educationalist, educationist, instructor, lecturer, pedagogue, schoolmaster, schoolmistress, schoolteacher, teacher, trainer, tutor.

**eerie** *adj* awesome, chilling, creepy, eldritch, fearful, frightening, ghastly, ghostly, mysterious, scary, spectral, spine-chilling, spooky, strange, uncanny, unearthly, unnatural, weird.

*antonyms* natural, ordinary.

**efface** *v* annihilate, blank out, blot out, blue-pencil, cancel, cross out, delete, destroy, dim, eliminate, eradicate, erase, excise, expunge, extirpate, humble, lower, obliterate, raze, remove, rub out, wipe out, withdraw.

**effect** *n* action, aftermath, clout, conclusion, consequence, drift, éclat, effectiveness, efficacy, efficiency, enforcement, essence, event, execution, fact, force, fruit, impact, implementation, import, impression, influence, issue, meaning, operation, outcome, power, purport, purpose, reality, result, sense, significance, strength, tenor, upshot, use, validity, vigour, weight, work.

*v* accomplish, achieve, actuate, cause, complete, consummate, create, effectuate, execute, fulfil, initiate, make, perform, produce, wreak.

**effective** *adj* able, active, adequate, capable, cogent, compelling, competent, convincing, current, effectual, efficacious, efficient, emphatic, energetic, forceful, forcible, implemental, impressive, moving, operative, perficient, persuasive, potent, powerful, productive, real, serviceable, striking, telling, useful.

*antonyms* ineffective, useless.

**effectiveness** *n* ability, capability, clout, cogency, effect, efficacy, efficiency, force, influence, potency, power, strength, success, use, validity, vigour, weight.

*antonyms* ineffectiveness, uselessness.

**effects** *n* belongings, chattels, gear, goods, movables, paraphernalia, possessions, property, things, trappings, traps.

**effectual** *adj* authoritative, binding, capable, effective, efficacious, efficient, forcible, influential, lawful, legal, licit, operative, perficient, potent, powerful, productive, serviceable, sound, successful, telling, useful, valid.

*antonyms* ineffective, useless.

**effeminate** *adj* delicate, epicene, feminine, pansy, poofy, sissy, soft, tender, unmanly, weak, womanish, womanlike, womanly.

*antonym* manly.

**effervesce** *v* boil, bubble, ferment, fizz, foam, froth, sparkle.

**effervescence** *n* animation, bubbles, bubbling, buoyancy, ebullience, ebulliency, enthusiasm, excitedness, excitement, exhilaration, exuberance, ferment, fermentation, fizz, foam, foaming, froth, frothing, gaiety, high spirits, liveliness, sparkle, vim, vitality, vivacity, zing, zip.

**effervescent** *adj* animated, bubbling, bubbly, buoyant, carbonated, ebullient, enthusiastic, excited, exhilarated, exuberant, fermenting, fizzing, fizzy, foaming, frothing, frothy, gay, irrepressible, lively, merry, sparkling, vital, vivacious, zingy.

*antonyms* apathetic, dull, flat.

**effete** *adj* barren, corrupt, debased, debilitated, decadent, decayed, decrepit, degenerate, dissipated, drained, enervated, enfeebled, exhausted, feeble, fruitless, incapable, ineffectual, infecund, infertile, overrefined, played out, spent, spoiled, sterile, tired out, unfruitful, unproductive, unprolific, used up, wasted, weak, worn out.

*antonym* vigorous.

**efficacious** *adj* active, adequate, capable, competent, effective, effectual, efficient, energetic, operative, potent, powerful, productive, serviceable, strong, successful, sufficient, useful.

*antonyms* ineffective, useless.

**efficacy** *n* ability, capability, competence, effect, effectiveness, efficaciousness, efficiency, energy, force, influence, potency, power, strength, success, use, virtue.

*antonyms* ineffectiveness, uselessness.

**efficiency** *n* ability, adeptness, capability, competence, competency, economy, effectiveness, efficacy, mastery, power, productivity, proficiency, readiness, skilfulness, skill.

*antonym* inefficiency.

**efficient** *adj* able, adept, businesslike, capable, competent, economic, effective, effectual, powerful, productive, proficient, ready, skilful, streamlined, well-conducted, well-ordered, well-organised, well-regulated, workmanlike.

*antonym* inefficient.

**effigy** *n* carving, dummy, figure, guy, icon, idol, image, likeness, mumbo-jumbo, picture, portrait, representation, statue.

**effluent** *n* discharge, effluence, effluvium, efflux, emanation, emission, exhalation, outflow, pollutant, pollution, sewage, waste.

**effort** *n* accomplishment, achievement, application, attempt, conatus, creation, deed, endeavour, energy, essay, exertion, feat, force, go, job, labour, molimen, nisus, pains, power, product, production, shot, stab, strain, stress, stretch, striving, struggle, toil, travail, trouble, try, work.

**effortless** *adj* easy, facile, painless, simple, smooth, uncomplicated, undemanding, unlaboured.

*antonym* difficult.

**effrontery** *n* arrogance, assurance, audacity, boldness, brashness, brass (neck), brazenness, cheek, cheekiness, disrespect, face, front, gall, impertinence, impudence, incivility, insolence, neck, nerve, presumption, rudeness, shamelessness, temerity.

**effusion** *n* address, discharge, effluence, efflux, emission, gush, outflow, outpouring, shedding, speech, stream, talk, utterance, voidance, word salad, writing.

**effusive** *adj* demonstrative, ebullient, enthusiastic, expansive, extravagant, exuberant, fulsome, gushing, gushy, lavish, overflowing, profuse, talkative, unreserved, unrestrained, voluble, wordy.

*antonyms* quiet, restrained.

**egg on** coax, encourage, exhort, goad, incite, prick, prod, prompt, push, spur, stimulate, urge, wheedle.

*antonym* discourage.

**egghead** *n* brain, Einstein, genius, headpiece, intellect, intellectual, scholar.

**egoism** *n* amour-propre, egocentricity, egomania, egotism, narcissism, self-absorption, self-centredness, self-importance, self-interest, selfishness, self-love, self-regard, self-seeking.

*antonym* altruism.

**egoist** *n* egomaniac, egotist, narcissist, self-seeker.

**egoistic** *adj* egocentric, egoistical, egomaniacal, egotistic, egotistical, narcissistic, self-absorbed, self-centred, self-important, self-involved, self-pleasing, self-seeking.

*antonym* altruistic.

**egotism** *n* bigheadedness, conceitedness, egocentricity, egoism, egomania, narcissism, self-admiration, self-centredness, self-conceit, self-esteem, self-importance, self-love, self-praise, self-pride, superiority, vainglory, vanity.

*antonym* humility.

**egotist** *n* bighead, boaster, braggadocio, braggart, egoist, egomaniac, swaggerer.

**egotistic** *adj* bigheaded, boasting, bragging, conceited, egocentric, egoistic, egoistical, egomaniacal, egotistical, narcissistic, opinionated, self-centred, self-important, superior, swollen-headed, vain, vainglorious.

*antonym* humble.

**egregious** *adj* arrant, flagrant, frabjous, glaring, grievous, gross, heinous, infamous, insufferable, intolerable, monstrous, notorious, outrageous, rank, scandalous, shocking.

*antonym* slight.

**egress** *n* emergence, escape, exit, exodus, issue, outlet, vent.

**ejaculate**[1] *v* discharge, eject, emit, spurt.

**ejaculate**[2] *v* blurt, call, cry, exclaim, scream, shout, utter, yell.

**ejaculation**[1] *n* discharge, ejection, emission, spurt.

**ejaculation**[2] *n* call, cry, exclamation, scream, shout, utterance, yell.

**eject** *v* banish, belch, boot out, bounce, deport, discharge, disgorge, dislodge, dismiss, dispossess, drive out, emit, evacuate, evict, exile, expel, fire, kick out, oust, remove, sack, spew, spout, throw out, turn out, unhouse, vomit.

**ejection** *n* banishment, defenestration, deportation, discharge, disgorgement, dislodgement, dismissal, dispossession, evacuation, eviction, exile, expulsion, firing, ouster, ousting, removal, sacking, spouting, the boot, the sack.

**eke out** add to, economise on, husband, increase, make (something) stretch, stretch, supplement.

**elaborate** *adj* careful, complex, complicated, daedal(ic), decorated, dedal(ian), detailed, exact, extravagant, fancy, fussy, Heath-Robinson, intricate, involved, laboured, minute, ornamental, ornate, ostentatious, painstaking, perfected, precise, showy, skilful, studied, thorough.

*antonyms* plain, simple.

*v* amplify, complicate, decorate, detail, develop, devise, embellish, enhance, enlarge, expand, expatiate, explain, flesh out, garnish, improve, ornament, polish, refine.

*antonyms* précis, simplify.

**élan** *n* animation, brio, dash, esprit, flair, flourish, impetuosity, liveliness, oomph, panache, pizzazz, spirit, style, verve, vigour, vivacity, zest.

*antonyms* apathy, lifelessness.

**elapse** *v* go by, lapse, pass, slip away.

**elastic** *adj* accommodating, adaptable, adjustable, bouncy, buoyant, complaisant, compliant, distensible, ductile, flexible, irrepressible, plastic, pliable, pliant, resilient, rubbery, springy, stretchable, stretchy, supple, tolerant, variable, yielding.

*antonym* rigid.

**elasticity** *n* adaptability, adjustability, bounce, buoyancy, complaisance, compliance, compliancy, compliantness, ductileness, ductility, flexibility, give, irrepressibility, plasticity, pliability, pliancy, resilience, rubberiness, springiness, stretch, stretchiness, suppleness, tolerance, variability.

*antonym* rigidity.

**elated** *adj* animated, blissful, cheered, delighted, ecstatic, euphoric, excited, exhilarated, exultant, gleeful, joyful, joyous, jubilant, on the high ropes, over the moon, overjoyed, pleased, proud, roused.

*antonym* downcast.

**elation** *n* bliss, delight, ecstasy, euphoria, exaltation, exhilaration, exultation, glee, high spirits, joy, joyfulness, joyousness, jubilation, rapture, transports of delight.

*antonym* depression.

**elbow** *v* bulldoze, bump, crowd, hustle, jostle, knock, nudge, plough, push, shoulder, shove.

**elbow-room** *n* freedom, latitude, Lebensraum, leeway, play, room, scope, space.

**elder** *adj* aîné(e), ancient, eigne, first-born, older, senior.

*antonym* younger.

*n* deacon, doyen, presbyter, senior.

**elderly** *adj* aged, aging, badgerly, hoary, old, senile.

*antonyms* young, youthful.

**eldest** *adj* first, first-begotten, first-born, oldest.

*antonym* youngest.

**elect** v adopt, appoint, choose, designate, determine, opt for, pick, prefer, select, vote.

adj choice, chosen, designate, designated, elite, hand-picked, picked, preferred, presumptive, prospective, select, selected, to be.

**election** n appointment, ballot-box, choice, choosing, decision, determination, judgement, preference, selection, vote, voting.

**elector** n constituent, selector, voter.

**electric** adj charged, dynamic, electrifying, exciting, rousing, stimulating, stirring, tense, thrilling.

antonyms tedious, unexciting.

**electrify** v amaze, animate, astonish, astound, excite, fire, galvanise, invigorate, jolt, rouse, shock, stagger, startle, stimulate, stir, stun, thrill.

antonym bore.

**elegance** n beauty, chic, concinnity, courtliness, dignity, discernment, distinction, exquisiteness, gentility, grace, gracefulness, grandeur, luxury, polish, politeness, propriety, refinement, style, sumptuousness, taste.

antonym inelegance.

**elegant** adj à la mode, appropriate, apt, artistic, beautiful, chic, choice, clever, comely, concinnous, courtly, cultivated, debonair, delicate, effective, exquisite, fashionable, fine, genteel, graceful, handsome, ingenious, luxurious, modish, neat, nice, polished, refined, simple, smart, smooth, stylish, sumptuous, tasteful.

antonym inelegant.

**elegiac** adj doleful, funereal, keening, lamenting, melancholy, mournful, nostalgic, plaintive, sad, threnetic, threnetical, threnodial, threnodic, valedictory.

antonym happy.

**elegy** n coronach, dirge, keen, lament, plaint, requiem, threnode, threnody.

**element** n basis, component, constituent, domain, environment, factor, feature, field, fragment, habitat, hint, ingredient, medium, member, milieu, part, piece, section, sphere, subdivision, trace, unit.

**elementary** adj basic, clear, easy, elemental, facile, fundamental, initial, introductory, original, plain, primary, principial, rudimentary, simple, straightforward, uncomplicated.

antonyms advanced, complex.

**elements** n basics, essentials, foundations, fundamentals, introduction, principia, principles, rudiments, weather.

**elevate** v advance, aggrandise, animate, augment, boost, brighten, buoy up, cheer, elate, exalt, excite, exhilarate, hearten, heighten, hoist, increase, intensify, lift, magnify, prefer, promote, raise, rouse, sublimate, swell, upgrade, uplift, upraise.

antonyms lessen, lower.

**elevated** adj animated, cheerful, cheery, dignified, elated, exalted, excited, exhilarated, grand, high, high-flown, high-minded, inflated, lofty, noble, overjoyed, raised, sublime, tipsy.

antonyms base, informal, lowly.

**elevation** n acclivity, advancement, aggrandisement, altitude, eminence, exaltation, exaltedness, grandeur, height, hill, hillock, loftiness, mountain, nobility, nobleness, preferment, promotion, rise, sublimation, sublimity, upgrading, uplift.

antonyms baseness, informality.

**elfin** adj arch, charming, delicate, elfish, elflike, elvish, frolicsome, impish, mischievous, petite, playful, puckish, small, sprightly.

**elicit** v cause, derive, draw out, educe, evoke, evolve, exact, extort, extract, fish, mole out, obtain, wrest, wring.

**eligible** adj acceptable, appropriate, available, desirable, fit, proper, qualified, suitable, suited, worthy.

antonym ineligible.

**eliminate** v annihilate, bump off, cut out, delete, dispense with, dispose of, disregard, do away with, drop, eject, eradicate, exclude, expel, expunge, exterminate, extinguish, get rid of, ignore, kill, knock out, liquidate, murder, omit, reject, remove, rub out, slay, stamp out, take out, terminate, waste.

antonym accept.

**elite** n aristocracy, best, cream, crème de la crème, elect, establishment, flower, gentry, high society, meritocracy, nobility, pick.

adj aristocratic, best, choice, crack, exclusive, first-class, noble, pick, selected, top, top-class, upper-class.

antonyms ordinary, run-of-the-mill.

**elixir** n concentrate, cure-all, daffy, essence, extract, mixture, nostrum, panacea, pith, potion, principle, quintessence, remedy, solution, syrup, tincture, treacle.

**elliptical**[1] adj egg-shaped, oval, oviform, ovoid(al).

**elliptical**[2] adj abstruse, ambiguous, concentrated, concise, condensed, cryptic, incomprehensible, laconic, obscure, recondite, terse, unfathomable.

antonym clear.

**elocution** n articulation, declamation, delivery, diction, enunciation, oratory, pronunciation, rhetoric, speech, speechmaking, utterance.

**elongated** adj extended, lengthened, long, prolonged, protracted, stretched.

**elope** v abscond, bolt, decamp, disappear, do a bunk, escape, leave, run away, run off, slip away, steal away.

**eloquence** n dick, expression, expressiveness, facundity, fluency, forcefulness, oratory, persuasiveness, rhetoric.

antonym inarticulateness.

**eloquent** adj articulate, Demosthenic, expressive, fluent, forceful, graceful, honeyed, meaningful, moving, persuasive, plausible, pregnant, revealing, silver-tongued, stirring, suggestive, telling, vivid, vocal, voluble, well-expressed.

antonyms inarticulate, tongue-tied.

**elucidate** v annotate, clarify, explain, explicate, expound, gloss, illuminate, illustrate, interpret, spell out, unfold.

antonyms confuse, obscure.

**elucidation** n annotation, clarification, comment, commentary, explanation, explication, exposition, foot-note, gloss, illumination, illustration, interpretation, marginalia.

**elude** v avoid, baffle, beat, circumvent, confound, dodge, duck, escape, evade, flee, foil, frustrate, outrun, puzzle, shirk, shun, stump, thwart.

**elusive** adj ambiguous, baffling, deceitful, deceptive, elusory, equivocal, evasive, fallacious, fleeting, fraudulent, fugitive, illusory, indefinable, intangible, misleading, puzzling, shifty, slippery, subtle, transient, transitory, tricky, unanalysable.

**emaciated** adj atrophied, attenuate, attenuated, cadaverous, gaunt, haggard, lank, lean, meagre, pinched, scrawny, skeletal, tabefied, tabescent, thin, wasted.

antonyms plump, well-fed.

**emaciation** n atrophy, attenuation, gauntness, haggardness, leanness, meagreness, scrawniness, tabefaction, tabes, tabescence, thinness.

antonym plumpness.

**emanate** v arise, come, derive, discharge, emerge, emit, exhale, flow, give off, give out, issue, originate, proceed, radiate, send out, spring, stem.

**emanation** n arising, derivation, discharge, ectoplasm, effluence, effluent, effluvium, efflux, effluxion, effusion, emergence, emission, exhalation, exoplasm, flow, generation, mephitis, origination, proceeding, procession, radiation.

**emancipate** v deliver, discharge, disencumber, disenthral, enfranchise, free, liberate, manumit, release, set free, unbind, unchain, unfetter, unshackle.

antonym enslave.

**emancipation** n deliverance, discharge, enfranchisement, freedom, liberation, liberty, manumission, release, unbinding, unchaining.

antonym enslavement.

**emasculate** v castrate, cripple, debilitate, enervate, geld, impoverish, neuter, soften, spay, weaken.

antonyms boost, vitalise.

**embalm** v cherish, consecrate, conserve, enshrine, immortalise, mummify, preserve, store, treasure.

**embankment** n bund, causeway, causey, defences, earthwork, levee, rampart.

**embargo** n ban, bar, barrier, blockage, check, hindrance, impediment, interdict, interdiction, prohibition, proscription, restraint, restriction, seizure, stoppage.

v ban, bar, block, check, embar, impede, interdict, prohibit, proscribe, restrict, seize, stop.

antonym allow.

**embark** v board ship, emplane, entrain, take ship.

antonym disembark.

**embark on** begin, broach, commence, engage, enter, initiate, launch, start, undertake.

antonym finish.

**embarkation** n boarding, entrainment.

antonym disembarkation.

**embarrass** v abash, chagrin, confuse, discomfit, discomfort, discompose, disconcert, discountenance, distress, fluster, mortify, shame, show up.

**embarrassed** adj abashed, constrained, discomfited, disconcerted, mortified, shamed, shown up, uncomfortable.

antonym unembarrassed.

**embarrassing** adj awkward, compromising, discomfiting, discomfortable, disconcerting, distressing, humiliating, mortifying, sensitive, shameful, shaming, touchy, tricky, uncomfortable.

**embarrassment** n awkwardness, bashfulness, bind, chagrin, confusion, constraint, difficulty, discomfiture, discomfort, discomposure, distress, excess, gêne, humiliation, mess, mortification, overabundance, pickle, predicament, scrape, self-consciousness, shame, superabundance, superfluity, surfeit, surplus.

**embassy** n consulate, delegation, deputation, embassade, embassage, legation, mission.

**embed** v fix, imbed, implant, insert, plant, root, set, sink.

**embellish** v adorn, beautify, bedeck, deck, decorate, dress up, elaborate, embroider, enhance, enrich, exaggerate, festoon, garnish, gild, grace, ornament, trim, varnish.

antonyms denude, simplify.

**embellishment** n adornment, decoration, elaboration, embroidery, enhancement, enrichment, exaggeration, fioritura, garnish, gilding, melisma, ornament, ornamentation, trimming, vignette.

**embers** n ashes, cinders.

**embezzle** v abstract, appropriate, defalcate, filch, misapply, misappropriate, misuse, peculate, pilfer, pinch, purloin, steal, sting.

**embezzlement** n abstraction, appropriation, defalcation, filching, fraud, larceny, misapplication, misappropriation, misuse, peculation, pilferage, pilfering, purloining, stealing, sting, theft, thieving.

**embezzler** n cheat, defalcator, fraud, peculator, thief.

**embitter** v acerbate, aggravate, alienate, anger, disaffect, disillusion, empoison, envenom, exacerbate, exasperate, poison, sour, worsen.

antonym pacify.

**embittered** adj bitter, disaffected, disillusioned, empoisoned, sour, soured.

antonym pacified.

**emblazon** v adorn, blazon, colour, decorate, depict, embellish, extol, glorify, illuminate, laud, ornament, paint, praise, proclaim, publicise, publish, trumpet.

**emblem** n badge, crest, device, figure, ichthys, image, insignia, mark, representation, sigil, sign, symbol, token, type.

**emblematic** adj emblematical, figurative, representative, representing, symbolic, symbolical.

**embodiment** n codification, collection, combination, comprehension, concentration, consolidation, example, exemplar, exemplification, expression, incarnation, inclusion, incorporation, integration, manifestation, organisation, personification, realisation, reification, representation, symbol, systematisation, type.

**embody** v codify, collect, combine, comprehend, comprise, concentrate, concretise, consolidate, contain, encarnalise, exemplify, express, incarnate, include, incorporate, integrate, manifest, organise, personify, realise, reify, represent, stand for, symbolise, systematise, typify.

**embolden** v animate, cheer, encourage, enhearten, fire, hearten, inflame, inspire, inspirit, invigorate, nerve, reassure, rouse, stimulate, stir, strengthen, vitalise.

*antonym* dishearten.

**embrace** v accept, canoodle, clasp, complect, comprehend, comprise, contain, cover, cuddle, dally, embody, embosom, encircle, enclose, encompass, enfold, enlace, espouse, grab, grasp, halse, hold, hug, inarm, include, incorporate, involve, neck, receive, seize, snog, squeeze, subsume, take up, welcome.

n abrazo, accolade, clasp, clinch, cuddle, hug, squeeze.

**embrocation** n cream, epithem, lotion, ointment, salve.

**embroglio** see **imbroglio**.

**embroidery** n fancywork, needle-point, needlework, sewing, tapestry, tatting.

**embroil** v confound, confuse, distract, disturb, encumber, enmesh, ensnare, entangle, implicate, incriminate, involve, mire, mix up, muddle, perplex, trouble.

**embryo** n beginning, embryon, germ, nucleus, root, rudiment.

**embryonic** adj beginning, early, germinal, immature, inchoate, incipient, primary, rudimentary, seminal, underdeveloped.

*antonyms* advanced, developed.

**emend** v alter, amend, correct, edit, improve, rectify, redact, revise, rewrite.

**emendation** n alteration, amendment, correction, corrigendum, editing, improvement, rectification, redaction, revision.

**emerge** v appear, arise, crop up, debouch, develop, eclose, emanate, issue, materialise, proceed, rise, surface, transpire, turn up.

*antonyms* disappear, fade.

**emergence** n advent, apparition, appearance, arrival, coming, dawn, development, disclosure, eclosion, emanation, emersion, issue, materialisation, rise.

*antonyms* decline, disappearance.

**emergency** n crisis, crunch, danger, difficulty, exigency, extremity, necessity, pass, pinch, plight, predicament, quandary, scrape, strait.

adj alternative, back-up, extra, fall-back, reserve, spare, substitute.

**emergent** adj budding, coming, developing, emerging, independent, rising.

*antonyms* declining, disappearing.

**emetic** adj emetical, vomitive, vomitory.

n vomit, vomitary, vomitive.

**emigration** n departure, exodus, journey, migration, removal.

**eminence** n celebrity, dignity, distinction, elevation, esteem, fame, greatness, height, hill, hillock, illustriousness, importance, knob, knoll, notability, note, peak, pre-eminence, prestige, prominence, rank, renown, reputation, repute, ridge, rise, summit, superiority.

**eminent** adj august, celebrated, conspicuous, distinguished, elevated, esteemed, exalted, famous, grand, great, high, high-ranking, illustrious, important, notable, noted, noteworthy, outstanding, paramount, pre-eminent, prestigious, prominent, renowned, reputable, respected, revered, signal, superior, well-known.

*antonyms* unimportant, unknown.

**eminently** adv conspicuously, exceedingly, exceptionally, extremely, greatly, highly, notably, outstandingly, par excellence, prominently, remarkably, signally, strikingly, surpassingly.

**emissary** n agent, ambassador, courier, delegate, deputy, envoy, herald, legate, messenger, nuncio, plenipotentiary, representative, scout, spy.

**emission** n diffusion, discharge, ejaculation, ejection, emanation, exhalation, exudation, issuance, issue, mephitis, radiation, release, shedding, transmission, utterance, vent, venting.

**emit** v diffuse, discharge, eject, emanate, exhale, exude, give off, give out, issue, radiate, shed, vent.

*antonym* absorb.

**emollient** adj assuaging, assuasive, balsamic, demulcent, lenitive, mitigative, mollifying, softening, soothing.

n balm, cream, lenitive, liniment, lotion, moisturiser, oil, ointment, poultice, salve, unguent.

**emolument** n allowance, benefit, compensation, earnings, fee, gain, hire, honorarium, pay, payment, profits, recompense, remuneration, return, reward, salary, stipend, wages.

**emotion** n affect, agitation, ardour, excitement, feeling, fervour, passion, perturbation, reaction, sensation, sentiment, vehemence, warmth.

**emotional** adj affecting, ardent, demonstrative, emotive, enthusiastic, excitable, exciting, feeling, fervent, fervid, fiery, heart-warming, heated, hot-blooded, impassioned, moved, moving, overcharged, passionate, pathetic, poignant, responsive, roused, sensitive, sentimental, stirred, stirring, susceptible, tear-jerking, temperamental, tempestuous, tender, thrilling, touching, volcanic, warm, zealous.

*antonyms* calm, cold, detached, emotionless, unemotional.

**emotionless** *adj* blank, cold, cold-blooded, cool, detached, distant, frigid, glacial, impassive, imperturbable, indifferent, phlegmatic, remote, toneless, undemonstrative, unemotional, unfeeling.

*antonym* emotional.

**emotive** *adj* affecting, ardent, controversial, delicate, emotional, enthusiastic, exciting, fervent, fervid, fiery, heart-warming, heated, impassioned, inflammatory, moving, passionate, pathetic, poignant, roused, sensitive, sentimental, stirred, stirring, tear-jerking, thrilling, touching, touchy, zealous.

**emperor** *n* imperator, kaiser, mikado, ruler, shogun, sovereign, tsar.

**emphasis** *n* accent, accentuation, attention, force, import, importance, impressiveness, insistence, intensity, mark, moment, positiveness, power, pre-eminence, priority, prominence, significance, strength, stress, underscoring, urgency, weight.

**emphasise** *v* accent, accentuate, dwell on, feature, highlight, insist on, intensify, play up, point up, press home, punctuate, spotlight, strengthen, stress, underline, underscore, weight.

*antonyms* depreciate, play down, understate.

**emphatic** *adj* absolute, categorical, certain, decided, definite, direct, distinct, earnest, energetic, forceful, forcible, graphic, important, impressive, insistent, marked, momentous, positive, powerful, pronounced, punctuated, resounding, significant, striking, strong, telling, trenchant, unequivocal, unmistakable, vigorous, vivid.

*antonyms* quiet, understated, unemphatic.

**empire** *n* authority, bailiwick, command, commonwealth, control, domain, dominion, government, imperium, jurisdiction, kingdom, power, realm, rule, sovereignty, supremacy, sway, territory.

**empirical** *adj* empiric, experiential, experimental, observed, practical, pragmatic.

*antonyms* conjectural, speculative, theoretical.

**employ** *v* apply, apprentice, bring to bear, commission, engage, enlist, exercise, exert, fill, hire, indent(ure), occupy, ply, retain, spend, take on, take up, use, utilise.

*n* employment, hire, pay, service.

**employed** *adj* active, busy, earning, engaged, hired, occupied, working.

*antonym* unemployed.

**employee** *n* hand, job-holder, member of staff, staffer, wage-earner, worker, workman.

**employer** *n* boss, business, company, establishment, firm, gaffer, organisation, outfit,

owner, padrone, patron, proprietor, taskmaster, workmaster, workmistress.

**employment** *n* application, avocation, business, calling, craft, employ, engagement, enlistment, errand, exercise, exercitation, exertion, hire, job, line, métier, occupation, profession, pursuit, service, trade, use, utilisation, vocation, work.

*antonym* unemployment.

**emporium** *n* bazaar, establishment, market, mart, shop, store.

**empower** *v* accredit, allow, authorise, commission, delegate, enable, enfranchise, entitle, license, permit, qualify, sanction, warrant.

**emptiness** *n* absentness, aimlessness, banality, bareness, barrenness, blankness, cheapness, desertedness, desire, desolation, destitution, expressionlessness, frivolity, futility, hollowness, hunger, idleness, inanity, ineffectiveness, insincerity, insubstantiality, meaninglessness, purposelessness, ravening, senselessness, silliness, triviality, trivialness, unreality, unsatisfactoriness, vacancy, vacantness, vacuity, vacuousness, vacuum, vainness, valuelessness, vanity, void, waste, worthlessness.

*antonym* fullness.

**empty** *adj* absent, aimless, banal, bare, blank, bootless, cheap, clear, deserted, desolate, destitute, expressionless, famished, frivolous, fruitless, futile, hollow, hungry, idle, inane, ineffective, insincere, insubstantial, meaningless, purposeless, ravenous, senseless, silly, starving, superficial, trivial, unfed, unfilled, unfrequented, unfurnished, uninhabited, unintelligent, unoccupied, unreal, unsatisfactory, unsubstantial, untenanted, vacant, vacuous, vain, valueless, viduous, void, waste, worthless.

*antonyms* filled, full, replete.

*v* clear, consume, deplete, discharge, drain, dump, evacuate, exhaust, gut, lade, pour out, unburden, unload, vacate, void.

*antonym* fill.

**empty-headed** *adj* batty, brainless, dizzy, dotty, flighty, frivolous, giddy, hare-brained, inane, scatter-brained, scatty, silly, skittish, vacuous.

**emulate** *v* challenge, compete with, contend with, copy, echo, follow, imitate, match, mimic, rival, vie with.

**emulation** *n* challenge, competition, contention, contest, copying, echoing, envy, following, imitation, jealousy, matching, mimicry, rivalry, strife.

**en masse** all at once, all together, as a group, as a whole, as one, en bloc, ensemble, in a body, together, wholesale.

**enable** *v* accredit, allow, authorise, capacitate, commission, empower, endue, equip, facilitate, fit, license, permit, prepare, qualify, sanction, warrant.

*antonyms* inhibit, prevent.

**enact** *v* act (out), authorise, command, decree, depict, establish, impersonate, legislate, ordain, order, pass, perform, personate, play, portray, proclaim, ratify, represent, sanction.

*antonym* repeal.

**enactment** n acting, authorisation, command, commandment, decree, depiction, dictate, edict, impersonation, law, legislation, order, ordinance, performance, personation, play-acting, playing, portrayal, proclamation, ratification, regulation, representation, statute.

*antonym* repeal.

**enamoured** adj besotted, bewitched, captivated, charmed, enchanted, enraptured, entranced, fascinated, fond, infatuated, smitten, taken.

**encampment** n base, bivouac, camp, camping-ground, campsite, cantonment, duar, hutment, quarters, tents.

**encapsulate** v abridge, capture, compress, condense, digest, epitomise, exemplify, incapsulate, précis, represent, sum up, summarise, typify.

**enchant** v becharm, beguile, bewitch, captivate, charm, delight, enamour, enrapture, enravish, ensorcell, enthral, fascinate, hypnotise, mesmerise, spellbind.

*antonyms* bore, disenchant.

**enchanter** n conjurer, magician, magus, mesmerist, necromancer, reim-kennar, sorcerer, spellbinder, warlock, witch, wizard.

**enchanting** adj alluring, appealing, attractive, bewitching, captivating, charming, delightful, endearing, entrancing, fascinating, lovely, mesmerising, pleasant, ravishing, winsome, wonderful.

*antonyms* boring, repellent.

**enchantment** n allure, allurement, beguilement, bliss, charm, conjuration, delight, fascination, glamour, gramary(e), hypnotism, incantation, magic, mesmerism, necromancy, rapture, ravishment, sorcery, spell, transport, witchcraft, wizardry.

*antonym* disenchantment.

**enchantress** n charmer, Circe, conjurer, femme fatale, lamia, magician, necromancer, reim-kennar, seductress, siren, sorceress, spellbinder, vamp, witch.

**encircle** v begird, circle, circumscribe, compass, enclose, encompass, enfold, engird, engirdle, enlace, enring, envelop, environ, enwreathe, gird, girdle, hem in, ring, surround.

**enclose** v bound, circumscribe, compass, comprehend, confine, contain, cover, embale, embosom, embrace, encase, encircle, encompass, enlock, environ, fence, hedge, hem in, hold, inclose, include, incorporate, insert, pen, shut in, wall in, wrap.

**enclosed** adj bound, caged, cocooned, confined, contained, corralled, encased, encircled, encompassed, ensheathed, immured, imprisoned, included, sacculated, surrounded.

*antonyms* open, unenclosed.

**enclosure** n arena, bawn, boma, cloister, compound, corral, court, encasement, enceinte, fold, haining, hope, kraal, paddock, pen, pightle, pinfold, pound, ring, sept, seraglio, stockade, sty.

**encompass** v admit, begird, bring about, cause, circle, circumscribe, comprehend, comprise, contain, contrive, cover, devise, effect, embody, embrace, encircle, enclose, envelop, environ, girdle, hem in, hold, include, incorporate, involve, manage, ring, subsume, surround.

**encounter** v chance upon, clash with, combat, come upon, confront, contend, cross swords with, engage, experience, face, fight, grapple with, happen on, meet, rencontre, rencounter, run across, run into, strive, struggle.

n action, battle, brush, clash, collision, combat, conflict, confrontation, contest, dispute, engagement, fight, meeting, rencontre, rencounter, run-in, set-to, skirmish.

**encourage** v abet, advance, advocate, aid, animate, boost, buoy up, cheer, comfort, console, egg on, embolden, embrave, favour, forward, foster, further, hearten, help, incite, inspire, inspirit, promote, rally, reassure, rouse, second, spirit, spur, stimulate, strengthen, succour, support, urge.

*antonyms* depress, discourage, dissuade.

**encouragement** n advocacy, aid, boost, cheer, come-on, consolation, favour, help, hortation, incentive, incitement, inspiration, promotion, reassurance, stimulation, stimulus, succour, support, urging.

*antonyms* disapproval, discouragement.

**encouraging** adj auspicious, bright, cheerful, cheering, cohortative, comforting, heartening, hopeful, hortatory, incentive, proceleusmatic, promising, protreptic, reassuring, rosy, satisfactory, stimulating, uplifting.

*antonym* discouraging.

**encroach** v appropriate, arrogate, impinge, infringe, intrude, invade, make inroads, muscle in, obtrude, overstep, trench, trespass, usurp.

**encroachment** n appropriation, arrogation, impingement, incursion, infringement, inroad, intrusion, invasion, obtrusion, trespass, usurpation, violation.

**encumber** v burden, clog, cramp, cumber, embarrass, hamper, handicap, hinder, impede, incommode, inconvenience, lumber, obstruct, oppress, overload, retard, saddle, slow down, trammel, weigh down.

**encumbrance** n burden, clog, cumbrance, difficulty, drag, embarrassment, handicap, hindrance, impediment, inconvenience, liability, load, lumber, millstone, obstacle, obstruction, onus.

*antonym* aid.

**encyclopaedic** adj all-embracing, all-encompassing, all-inclusive, broad, compendious, complete, comprehensive, exhaustive, thorough, universal, vast, wide-ranging.

*antonyms* incomplete, narrow.

**end** n aim, annihilation, aspiration, attainment, bit, bound, boundary, butt, cessation, close, closure, completion, conclusion, consequence, consummation, culmination, curtain, death, demise, dénouement, design, destruction, dissolution, doom, downfall, drift, edge, ending, expiration, expiry, extent, extermination, extinction, extreme, extremity, finale, fine, finis, finish, fragment, goal, intent, intention, issue, left-over, limit, object, objective, outcome, part, pay-off, piece, point, portion, purpose, reason, remainder, remnant, resolution, responsibility, result, ruin, ruination, scrap, share, side, stop, stub, telos, termination, terminus, tip, upshot, wind-up.

*antonyms* beginning, opening, start.

*v* abate, abolish, annihilate, cease, close, complete, conclude, culminate, destroy, dissolve, expire, exterminate, extinguish, fetch up, finish, resolve, ruin, sopite, stop, terminate, wind up.

*antonyms* begin, start.

**endanger** *v* compromise, expose, hazard, imperil, jeopardise, risk, threaten.

*antonyms* protect, shelter, shield.

**endearing** *adj* adorable, attractive, captivating, charming, delightful, enchanting, engaging, lovable, sweet, winning, winsome.

**endearment** *n* affection, attachment, diminutive, fondness, hypocorisma, love, pet-name, sweet nothing.

**endeavour** *n* aim, attempt, conatus, crack, effort, enterprise, essay, go, nisus, shot, stab, trial, try, undertaking, venture.

*v* aim, aspire, attempt, essay, labour, strive, struggle, take pains, try, undertake, venture.

**ending** *n* catastrophe, cessation, climax, close, completion, conclusion, consummation, culmination, dénouement, desinence, end, epilogue, finale, finish, resolution, termination, wind-up.

*antonyms* beginning, start.

**endless** *adj* boundless, ceaseless, constant, continual, continuous, eternal, everlasting, immortal, incessant, infinite, interminable, interminate, limitless, measureless, monotonous, overlong, perpetual, Sisyphean, termless, unbounded, unbroken, undivided, undying, unending, uninterrupted, unlimited, whole.

**endorse** *v* adopt, advocate, affirm, approve, authorise, back, champion, confirm, countenance, countersign, favour, indorse, ratify, recommend, sanction, sign, subscribe to, superscribe, support, sustain, undersign, vouch for, warrant.

*antonyms* denounce, disapprove.

**endorsement** *n* advocacy, affirmation, approbation, approval, authorisation, backing, championship, commendation, comment, confirmation, corroboration, countersignature, favour, fiat, indorsement, OK, qualification, ratification, recommendation, sanction, seal of approval, signature, superscription, support, testimonial, warrant.

*antonyms* denouncement, disapproval.

**endow** *v* award, bequeath, bestow, confer, donate, dower, endue, enrich, favour, finance, fund, furnish, give, grant, invest, leave, make over, present, provide, settle on, supply, will.

*antonym* divest.

**endowment** *n* ability, aptitude, attribute, award, benefaction, bequest, bestowal, boon, capability,

capacity, donation, dotation, dowry, faculty, flair, fund, genius, gift, grant, income, largesse, legacy, power, presentation, property, provision, qualification, quality, revenue, talent.

**endurable** *adj* bearable, sufferable, supportable, sustainable, tolerable.

*antonyms* intolerable, unbearable.

**endurance** *n* bearing, continuation, continuity, durability, fortitude, immutability, lastingness, longevity, patience, permanence, perseverance, persistence, pertinacity, resignation, resolution, stability, stamina, staying power, strength, submission, sufferance, sustainment, sustenance, tenacity, toleration.

**endure** *v* abear, abide, aby(e), allow, bear, brave, brook, continue, cope with, countenance, digest, dree, experience, go through, hold, last, live, perdure, permit, persist, prevail, put up with, remain, stand, stay, stick, stomach, submit to, suffer, support, survive, sustain, swallow, thole, tolerate, undergo, weather, withstand.

*antonyms* cease, end.

**enduring** *adj* abiding, continuing, durable, eternal, firm, immortal, imperishable, lasting, living, long(a)evous, long-lasting, perennial, permanent, persistent, persisting, prevailing, remaining, steadfast, steady, surviving, unfaltering, unwavering.

*antonyms* changeable, fleeting.

**enemy** *n* adversary, antagonist, competitor, foe, foeman, opponent, opposer, Philistine, rival, the opposition.

*antonyms* ally, friend.

**energetic** *adj* active, animated, brisk, dynamic, forceful, forcible, high-powered, indefatigable, lively, pithy, potent, powerful, spirited, strenuous, strong, throughgoing, tireless, vigorous, zippy.

*antonyms* idle, inactive, lazy, sluggish.

**energise** *v* activate, animate, electrify, enliven, galvanise, inspirit, invigorate, liven, motivate, pep up, quicken, stimulate, vitalise, vivify.

*antonym* daunt.

**energy** *n* activity, animation, ardour, brio, drive, efficiency, élan, exertion, fire, force, forcefulness, get-up-and-go, intensity, inworking, jism, juice, life, liveliness, pluck, power, spirit, stamina, steam, strength, strenuousness, verve, vigour, vim, vitality, vivacity, vroom, zeal, zest, zip.

*antonyms* inertia, lethargy, weakness.

**enervate** *v* debilitate, deplete, devitalise, enfeeble, exhaust, fatigue, incapacitate, paralyse, prostrate, sap, tire, unman, unnerve, weaken, wear out.

*antonyms* activate, energise.

**enervated** *adj* debilitated, depleted, devitalised, done in, effete, enervate, enfeebled, exhausted, fatigued, feeble, incapacitated, limp, paralysed, prostrate, prostrated, run-down, sapped, spent, tired, undermined, unmanned, unnerved, washed out, weak, weakened, worn out.

*antonyms* active, energetic.

**enervation** *n* debilitation, debility, depletion, effeteness, enfeeblement, exhaustedness, exhaustion, fatigue, feebleness, impotence, incapacity, infirmity, lassitude, paralysis, powerlessness, prostration, tiredness, unmanning, weakening, weakness.

**enfeeble** v debilitate, deplete, devitalise, diminish, enervate, exhaust, fatigue, geld, reduce, sap, undermine, unhinge, unnerve, weaken, wear out.
*antonym* strengthen.

**enfold** v clasp, embrace, encircle, enclose, encompass, envelop, enwrap, fold, hold, hug, shroud, swathe, wimple, wrap (up).

**enforce** v administer, apply, carry out, coact, coerce, compel, constrain, discharge, exact, execute, implement, impose, insist on, oblige, prosecute, reinforce, require, urge.

**enforced** adj binding, compelled, compulsory, constrained, dictated, imposed, involuntary, necessary, ordained, prescribed, required, unavoidable.

**enforcement** n administration, application, coaction, coercion, compulsion, constraint, execution, implementation, imposition, insistence, obligation, pressure, prosecution, requirement.

**enfranchise** v affranchise, emancipate, free, liberate, manumit, release.
*antonym* disenfranchise.

**enfranchisement** n affranchisement, emancipation, freedom, freeing, liberating, liberation, manumission, release, suffrage.
*antonym* disenfranchisement.

**engage** v absorb, activate, affiance, agree, allure, apply, appoint, arrest, assail, attach, attack, attract, bespeak, betroth, bind, book, busy, captivate, catch, charm, charter, combat, commission, commit, contract, covenant, draw, embark, employ, enamour, enchant, encounter, energise, engross, enlist, enrol, enter, fascinate, fit, fix, gain, grip, guarantee, hire, interact, interconnect, interlock, involve, join, lease, meet, mesh, obligate, oblige, occupy, operate, partake, participate, pledge, practise, prearrange, preoccupy, promise, rent, reserve, retain, secure, take on, tie up, undertake, vouch, vow, win.
*antonyms* discharge, disengage, dismiss.

**engaged** adj absorbed, affianced, betrothed, busy, committed, employed, engrossed, immersed, involved, occupied, pledged, preoccupied, promised, spoken for, tied up, unavailable.

**engagement** n action, affiance, appointment, arrangement, assurance, battle, betrothal, bond, combat, commission, commitment, compact, conflict, confrontation, contest, contract, date, employment, encounter, fight, gig, job, meeting, oath, obligation, pact, pledge, post, promise, situation, stint, subarr(h)ation, troth, undertaking, vow, word, work.
*antonym* disengagement.

**engaging** adj agreeable, appealing, attractive, beguiling, captivating, charming, enchanting, fascinating, fetching, lik(e)able, lovable, pleasant, pleasing, prepossessing, winning, winsome.
*antonyms* boring, loathsome.

**engender** v beget, breed, bring about, cause, create, encourage, excite, father, foment, generate, give rise to, hatch, incite, induce, instigate, lead to, make, nurture, occasion, precipitate, procreate, produce, propagate, provoke, sire, spawn.

**engine** n agency, agent, apparatus, appliance, contraption, contrivance, device, dynamo, implement, instrument, machine, means, mechanism, motor, tool, turbine, weapon.

**engineer** n architect, contriver, designer, deviser, driver, inventor, operator, originator, planner.
v cause, concoct, contrive, control, create, devise, effect, encompass, finagle, machinate, manage, manipulate, manoeuvre, mastermind, originate, plan, plot, scheme, wangle.

**engrave** v blaze, carve, chase, chisel, cut, embed, enchase, etch, fix, grave, impress, imprint, infix, ingrain, inscribe, lodge, mark, print.

**engraved** adj carved, chased, chiselled, cut, enchased, etched, graven, imprinted, incised, intagliated, marked, printed.

**engraving** n blaze, block, carving, chasing, chiselling, cutting, dendroglyph, dry-point, enchasing, etching, impression, inscribing, inscription, lithoglyph, mark, plate, print, woodcut.

**engross** v absorb, arrest, corner, engage, engulf, fixate, hold, immerse, involve, monopolise, occupy, preoccupy, rivet.

**engrossed** adj absorbed, captivated, caught up, enthralled, fascinated, fixated, gripped, immersed, intent, intrigued, lost, preoccupied, rapt, riveted, taken.
*antonyms* bored, disinterested.

**engrossing** adj absorbing, captivating, compelling, enthralling, fascinating, gripping, interesting, intriguing, riveting, suspenseful, taking, unputdownable.
*antonym* boring.

**engulf** v absorb, bury, consume, deluge, drown, encompass, engross, envelop, flood, immerse, ingulf, inundate, overrun, overwhelm, plunge, submerge, swallow up, swamp.

**enhance** v amplify, augment, boost, complement, deodorise, elevate, embellish, escalate, exalt, heighten, improve, increase, intensify, lift, magnify, raise, reinforce, strengthen, swell.
*antonyms* decrease, minimise.

**enigma** n brain-teaser, conundrum, mystery, poser, problem, puzzle, riddle.

**enigmatic** adj ambiguous, cryptic, Delphic, doubtful, enigmatical, equivocal, impenetrable, incomprehensible, indecipherable, inexplicable, inscrutable, mysterious, obscure, perplexing, puzzling, recondite, riddling, strange, uncertain, unfathomable, unintelligible.
*antonyms* simple, straightforward.

**enjoin** v advise, ban, bar, bid, call upon, charge, command, comply, counsel, demand, direct, disallow, forbid, instruct, interdict, obey, order, preclude, prescribe, prohibit, proscribe, require, restrain, urge, warn.

**enjoy** *v* appreciate, delight in, dig, experience, have, like, make a meal of, own, possess, rejoice in, relish, revel in, savour, take pleasure in, use.

*antonyms* abhor, detest.

**enjoy oneself** have a ball, have a good time, have fun, make merry, party.

**enjoyable** *adj* agreeable, amusing, delectable, delicious, delightful, entertaining, fun, good, gratifying, pleasant, pleasing, pleasurable, satisfying.

*antonyms* disagreeable, unpleasant.

**enjoyment** *n* advantage, amusement, benefit, comfort, delectation, delight, diversion, ease, entertainment, exercise, fun, gaiety, gladness, gratification, gusto, happiness, indulgence, jollity, joy, ownership, pleasure, possession, recreation, relish, satisfaction, use, zest.

*antonyms* displeasure, dissatisfaction.

**enlarge** *v* add to, amplify, augment, blow up, broaden, descant, develop, diffuse, dilate, distend, elaborate, elongate, expand, expatiate, extend, greaten, grow, heighten, increase, inflate, intumesce, jumboise, lengthen, magnify, multiply, stretch, swell, wax, widen.

*antonyms* decrease, diminish, shrink.

**enlargement** *n* ampliation, amplification, aneurysm, augmentation, blow-up, dilation, distension, emphysema, expansion, extension, growth, increase, increment, intumescence, magnification, oedema, protuberation, supplementation, swelling.

*antonyms* contraction, decrease.

**enlighten** *v* advise, apprise, civilise, counsel, edify, educate, illuminate, indoctrinate, inform, instruct, teach, undeceive.

*antonyms* confuse, puzzle.

**enlightened** *adj* aware, broad-minded, civilised, conversant, cultivated, educated, informed, knowledgeable, liberal, literate, open-minded, reasonable, refined, sophisticated, verligte, wise.

*antonyms* confused, ignorant.

**enlightenment** *n* awareness, broad-mindedness, civilisation, comprehension, cultivation, edification, education, erudition, information, insight, instruction, knowledge, learning, literacy, open-mindedness, refinement, sapience, sophistication, teaching, understanding, wisdom.

*antonyms* confusion, ignorance.

**enlist** *v* conscript, employ, engage, enrol, enter, gather, join (up), muster, obtain, procure, recruit, register, secure, sign up, volunteer.

**enliven** *v* animate, brighten, buoy up, cheer (up), excite, exhilarate, fire, gladden, hearten, inspire, inspirit, invigorate, juice up, kindle, liven (up), pep up, perk up, quicken, rouse, spark, stimulate, vitalise, vivify, wake up.

*antonym* subdue.

**enmity** *n* acrimony, animosity, animus, antagonism, antipathy, aversion, bad blood, bitterness, feud, hate, hatred, hostility, ill-will, invidiousness, malevolence, malice, malignity, rancour, spite, venom.

*antonyms* amity, friendship.

**ennoble** *v* aggrandise, dignify, elevate, enhance, exalt, gentle, glorify, honour, magnify, nobilitate, raise.

**ennoblement** *n* aggrandisement, dignification, elevation, exaltation, glorification, lionisation, magnification, nobilitation.

**ennui** *n* accidie, acedia, boredom, dissatisfaction, lassitude, listlessness, tedium, the doldrums.

**enormity** *n* abomination, atrociousness, atrocity, crime, depravity, disgrace, evil, evilness, flagitiousness, heinousness, horror, iniquity, monstrosity, monstrousness, nefariousness, outrage, outrageousness, turpitude, viciousness, vileness, villainy, wickedness.

*antonyms* triviality, unimportance.

**enormous** *adj* abominable, astronomic(al), atrocious, Brobdingnagian, colossal, cyclopean, depraved, disgraceful, evil, excessive, gargantuan, gigantic, gross, heinous, herculean, huge, hulking, immense, jumbo, leviathan, mammoth, massive, monstrous, mountainous, nefarious, odious, outrageous, prodigious, titanic, tremendous, vast, vasty, vicious, vile, villainous, wicked.

*antonyms* small, tiny.

**enough** *adj* abundant, adequate, ample, enow, plenty, sufficient.

*n* abundance, adequacy, plenitude, plenty, repletion, sufficiency.

*adv* abundantly, adequately, amply, aplenty, enow, fairly, moderately, passably, reasonably, satisfactorily, sufficiently, tolerably.

**enquire, inquire** *v* ask, examine, explore, inspect, investigate, probe, query, question, quiz, scrutinise, search, speir.

**enquiry, inquiry** *n* examination, exploration, inquest, inspection, investigation, probe, query, quest, question, research, scrutiny, search, study, survey.

**enrage** *v* acerbate, aggravate, anger, exasperate, incense, incite, inflame, infuriate, irritate, madden, make someone's hackles rise, provoke.

*antonyms* calm, placate, soothe.

**enraged** *adj* aggravated, angered, angry, exasperated, fizzing, fuming, furious, incensed, inflamed, infuriated, irate, irritated, livid, mad, raging, storming, wild.

*antonym* calm.

**enrapture** *v* beguile, bewitch, captivate, charm, delight, enchant, enravish, enthrall, entrance, fascinate, ravish, spellbind, thrill, transport.

**enrich** *v* adorn, aggrandise, ameliorate, augment, cultivate, decorate, develop, embellish, endow, enhance, fortify, grace, improve, ornament, prosper, refine, supplement.

*antonym* impoverish.

**enrol** *v* accept, admit, chronicle, empanel, engage, enlist, enregister, inscribe, join up, list, matriculate, note, record, recruit, register, sign on, sign up, take on.

*antonyms* leave, reject.

**enrolment** *n* acceptance, admission, empanelment, engagement, enlistment, matriculation, recruitment, register, registration.

**enthusiastic**

**ensconce** v entrench, establish, install, locate, lodge, nestle, place, protect, put, screen, settle, shelter, shield.

**ensemble** n aggregate, assemblage, band, case, chorus, collection, company, corps de ballet, costume, entirety, get-up, group, outfit, rig-out, set, suit, sum, total, totality, troupe, whole.

**enshrine** v apotheosise, cherish, consecrate, dedicate, embalm, exalt, hallow, idolise, preserve, revere, sanctify, treasure.

**enshroud** v cloak, cloud, conceal, cover, enclose, enfold, envelop, enwrap, enwreathe, hide, obscure, pall, shroud, veil, wrap.

**ensign** n badge, banner, colours, flag, gonfalon, jack, oriflamme, pennant, pennon, standard, streamer.

**enslave** v bind, conquer, dominate, enchain, enthrall, overcome, subject, subjugate, yoke.

*antonyms* emancipate, free.

**enslavement** n bondage, captivity, dulosis, duress, enthralment, oppression, repression, serfdom, servitude, slavery, subjection, subjugation, thraldom, vassalage.

*antonym* emancipation.

**ensnare** v catch, embroil, enmesh, entangle, entrap, gin, illaqueate, net, snare, snarl, trap, trepan.

**ensue** v arise, attend, befall, derive, eventuate, flow, follow, happen, issue, proceed, result, stem, succeed, supervene, turn out, turn up.

*antonym* precede.

**ensure** v certify, clinch, confirm, effect, guarantee, guard, insure, protect, safeguard, secure, warrant.

**entail** v cause, demand, encompass, give rise to, impose, involve, lead to, necessitate, occasion, predetermine, require, result in.

**entangle** v ball, bewilder, catch, complicate, compromise, confuse, embroil, enlace, enmesh, ensnare, entoil, entrap, foul, implicate, involve, jumble, knot, mat, mix up, muddle, perplex, puzzle, ravel, snag, snare, snarl, tangle, trammel, trap, twist.

*antonym* disentangle.

**entanglement** n complication, confusion, difficulty, embarrassment, ensnarement, entoilment, entrapment, imbroglio, involvement, jumble, knot, liaison, mesh, mess, mix-up, muddle, predicament, snare, snarl-up, tangle, tie, toils, trap.

*antonym* disentanglement.

**entente** n agreement, arrangement, compact, deal, entente cordiale, friendship, pact, treaty, understanding.

**enter** v arrive, begin, board, commence, embark upon, enlist, enrol, inscribe, insert, introduce, join, list, log, note, offer, participate, participate in, penetrate, pierce, present, proffer, record, register, set about, set down, sign up, start, submit, take down, take up, tender.

*antonyms* delete, issue, leave.

**enterprise** n activity, adventure, adventurousness, alertness, audacity, boldness, business, company, concern, daring, dash, drive, eagerness, effort, emprise, endeavour, energy, enthusiasm, essay, establishment, firm, get-up-and-go, gumption, imagination, initiative, operation, plan, programme, project, push, readiness, resource, resourcefulness, spirit, undertaking, venture, vigour, zeal.

*antonyms* apathy, inertia.

**enterprising** adj active, adventurous, alert, ambitious, aspiring, audacious, bold, daring, dashing, eager, energetic, enthusiastic, go-ahead, goey, imaginative, intrepid, keen, pushful, ready, resourceful, self-reliant, spirited, stirring, up-and-coming, venturesome, vigorous, zealous.

*antonyms* lethargic, unadventurous.

**entertain** v accommodate, accourt, amuse, charm, cheer, cherish, conceive, consider, contemplate, countenance, delight, divert, fête, foster, harbour, hold, imagine, lodge, maintain, occupy, please, ponder, put up, recreate, regale, support, treat.

*antonyms* bore, reject.

**entertainer** n artiste, diseur, diseuse, performer, troubadour, trouper.

**entertaining** adj amusing, charming, cheering, delightful, diverting, droll, fun, funny, humorous, interesting, pleasant, pleasing, pleasurable, recreative, witty.

*antonym* boring.

**entertainment** n amusement, cheer, distraction, diversion, enjoyment, extravaganza, fun, pastime, play, pleasure, recreation, satisfaction, show, spectacle, sport, table, treat.

**enthral(l)** v beguile, captivate, charm, enchant, enrapture, enravish, entrance, fascinate, grip, hypnotise, intrigue, mesmerise, rivet, spellbind, thrill.

*antonyms* bore, weary.

**enthralling** adj beguiling, captivating, charming, compelling, compulsive, enchanting, entrancing, fascinating, gripping, hypnotising, intriguing, mesmeric, mesmerising, riveting, spellbinding, thrilling.

*antonym* boring.

**enthuse** v absorb, drool, ecstasise, effervesce, emote, excite, gush, impassion, inflame, involve, possess, wax lyrical.

**enthusiasm** n ardour, avidity, craze, devotion, eagerness, earnestness, empressement, entraînement, estro, excitement, fad, fervour, frenzy, hobby, hobby-horse, interest, keenness, mania, oomph, passion, rage, relish, spirit, vehemence, warmth, zeal, zest.

*antonym* apathy.

**enthusiast** n addict, admirer, aficionado, buff, bug, devotee, eager beaver, fan, fanatic, fiend, follower, freak, lover, supporter, whole-hogger, zealot.

*antonym* detractor.

**enthusiastic** adj ardent, avid, devoted, eager, earnest, ebullient, empressé, excited, exuberant, fervent, fervid, forceful, gung-ho, hearty, keen, keen as mustard, lively, passionate, spirited, unstinting, vehement, vigorous, warm, whole-hearted, zealous.

*antonyms* apathetic, reluctant, unenthusiastic.

**entice** *v* allure, attract, beguile, blandish, cajole, coax, decoy, draw, induce, inveigle, lead on, lure, persuade, prevail on, seduce, sweet-talk, tempt, wheedle.

**enticement** *n* allurement, attraction, bait, beguilement, blandishments, cajolery, coaxing, come-on, decoy, inducement, inveiglement, lure, persuasion, seduction, sweet-talk, temptation.

**entire** *adj* absolute, all-in, complete, continuous, full, intact, integrated, outright, perfect, sound, thorough, total, unabridged, unbroken, uncut, undamaged, undiminished, undivided, unified, unmarked, unmarred, unmitigated, unreserved, unrestricted, whole.

*antonyms* impaired, incomplete, partial.

**entirely** *adv* absolutely, altogether, completely, every inch, exclusively, fully, hook line and sinker, in toto, lock stock and barrel, only, perfectly, solely, thoroughly, totally, unreservedly, utterly, wholly, without exception, without reservation.

*antonym* partially.

**entirety** *n* absoluteness, aggregate, completeness, fullness, sum, total, totality, unity, universality, whole, wholeness.

*antonyms* element, incompleteness, part.

**entitle** *v* accredit, allow, authorise, call, christen, denominate, designate, dub, empower, enable, enfranchise, label, license, name, permit, style, term, title, warrant.

**entity** *n* being, body, creature, essence, existence, haecceity, individual, individuum, object, organism, presence, quantity, quiddity, quintessence, substance, thing.

**entombment** *n* burial, inhumation, interment, inurnment, sepulture.

**entourage** *n* associates, attendants, claque, companions, company, cortège, coterie, court, escort, followers, following, retainers, retinue, staff, suite, train.

**entrails** *n* bowels, entera, gralloch, guts, harigal(d)s, ha(r)slet, innards, insides, intestines, offal, umbles, viscera.

**entrance**[1] *n* access, admission, admittance, appearance, arrival, atrium, avenue, beginning, commencement, debut, door, doorway, entrée, entry, gate, ingress, initiation, inlet, introduction, opening, outset, passage, portal, start.

*antonyms* departure, exit.

**entrance**[2] *v* bewitch, captivate, charm, delight, enchant, enrapture, enravish, enthrall, fascinate, gladden, hypnotise, magnetise, mesmerise, ravish, spellbind, transport.

*antonyms* bore, repel.

**entrant** *n* beginner, candidate, competitor, contender, contestant, convert, entry, initiate, neophyte, newcomer, novice, participant, player, probationer, tyro.

**entrap** *v* allure, beguile, capture, catch, decoy, embroil, enmesh, ensnare, entangle, entice, gin, implicate, inveigle, involve, lure, net, seduce, snare, trap, trepan, trick.

**entreat** *v* appeal to, ask, beg, beseech, conjure, crave, enjoin, exhort, flagitate, implore, importune, invoke, petition, plead with, pray, request, sue, supplicate.

**entreaty** *n* appeal, entreatment, exhortation, importunity, invocation, petition, plea, prayer, request, solicitation, suing, suit, supplication.

**entrench** *v* anchor, dig in, embed, encroach, ensconce, establish, fix, fortify, impinge, infix, infringe, ingrain, install, interlope, intrench, intrude, lodge, plant, root, seat, set, settle, trespass.

*antonym* dislodge.

**entrenched** *adj* deep-rooted, deep-seated, firm, fixed, implanted, inbred, indelible, ineradicable, ingrained, rooted, set, unshakable, well-established.

**entrepreneur** *n* businessman, businesswoman, contractor, financier, impresario, industrialist, magnate, tycoon, undertaker.

**entrust** *v* assign, authorise, charge, commend, commit, confide, consign, delegate, deliver, depute, invest, trust, turn over.

**entry**[1] *n* access, admission, admittance, appearance, avenue, door, doorway, entering, entrance, entrée, gate, ingress, initiation, inlet, introduction, opening, passage, passageway, portal, threshold.

*antonym* exit.

**entry**[2] *n* account, attempt, bulletin, candidate, competitor, contestant, effort, entrant, item, jotting, listing, memo, memorandum, minute, note, participant, player, record, registration, statement, submission.

**entwine** *v* braid, embrace, encircle, enlace, entwist, interlace, interlink, intertwine, interweave, intwine, knit, plait, splice, surround, thatch, twine, twist, weave, wind.

*antonym* unravel.

**enumerate** *v* calculate, cite, count, detail, itemise, list, mention, name, number, quote, recapitulate, recite, reckon, recount, rehearse, relate, specify, spell out, tell.

**enunciate** *v* articulate, broadcast, declare, enounce, proclaim, promulgate, pronounce, propound, publish, say, sound, speak, state, utter, vocalise, voice.

**envelop** *v* blanket, cloak, conceal, cover, embrace, encase, encircle, enclose, encompass, enfold, engulf, enshroud, enwrap, enwreathe, hide, obscure, sheathe, shroud, surround, swaddle, swathe, veil, wrap.

**envelope** *n* case, casing, coating, cover, covering, integument, jacket, sheath, shell, skin, theca, wrapper, wrapping.

**enviable** *adj* advantageous, blessed, covetable, desirable, excellent, favoured, fine, fortunate, good, lucky, privileged.

*antonym* unenviable.

**envious** *adj* begrudging, covetous, dissatisfied, green, green with envy, green-eyed, grudging, jaundiced, jealous, malcontent, malicious, resentful, spiteful.

**environment** *n* ambience, atmosphere, background, conditions, context, domain, element, entourage, habitat, locale, medium, milieu, scene, setting, situation, surroundings, territory.

**environmentalist** *n* conservationist, doomwatcher, ecofreak, econut, green.

**environs** *n* circumjacencies, district, locality, neighbourhood, outskirts, precincts, purlieus, suburbs, surround(ing)s, vicinage, vicinity.

**envisage** *v* anticipate, conceive of, conceptualise, contemplate, envision, fancy, foresee, ideate, image, imagine, picture, preconceive, predict, see, visualise.

**envoy** *n* agent, ambassador, courier, delegate, deputy, diplomat, elchi, emissary, intermediary, legate, messenger, minister, nuncio, plenipotentiary, representative.

**envy** *n* covetousness, cupidity, dissatisfaction, enviousness, grudge, hatred, ill-will, jealousy, malice, malignity, resentfulness, resentment, spite.

*v* begrudge, covet, crave, grudge, resent.

**enwrap** *v* encase, enclose, enfold, enshroud, envelop, enwind, enwreathe, parcel, sheathe, sheet, shroud, swaddle, swathe, wimple, wind.

**ephemeral** *adj* brief, evanescent, fleeting, flitting, fugacious, fugitive, fungous, impermanent, momentary, passing, short, short-lived, temporary, transient, transitory.

*antonyms* enduring, lasting, perpetual.

**epic** *adj* colossal, elevated, exalted, grand, grandiloquent, great, heroic, Homeric, huge, imposing, impressive, lofty, majestic, sublime, vast.

*antonym* ordinary.

**epicure** *n* arbiter elegantiae, bon vivant, bon viveur, connoisseur, epicurean, gastronome, glutton, gourmand, gourmet, hedonist, sensualist, sybarite, voluptuary.

**epicurean** *adj* gluttonous, gourmandising, hedonistic, libertine, luscious, lush, luxurious, self-indulgent, sensual, sybaritic, unrestrained, voluptuous.

*n* bon vivant, bon viveur, epicure, gastronome, gourmet, hedonist, sensualist, voluptuary.

**epidemic** *adj* epizootic, general, pandemic, prevailing, prevalent, rampant, rife, sweeping, wide-ranging, widespread.

*n* growth, outbreak, pandemic, plague, rash, spread, upsurge, wave.

**epigram** *n* aphorism, apophthegm, bon mot, gnome, quip, witticism.

**epigrammatic** *adj* aphoristic, apophthegmatic, concise, gnomic, laconic, piquant, pithy, pointed, pungent, sharp, short, succinct, terse, witty.

**epilogue** *n* afterword, coda, conclusion, exode, postscript.

*antonyms* foreword, preface, prologue.

**episode** *n* adventure, affaire, business, chapter, circumstance, event, experience, happening, incident, instalment, matter, occasion, occurrence, part, passage, scene, section.

**episodic** *adj* anecdotal, digressive, disconnected, disjointed, episod(i)al, intermittent, irregular, occasional, picaresque, spasmodic, sporadic.

**epistle** *n* communication, encyclical, letter, line, message, missive, note.

**epithet** *n* appellation, denomination, description, designation, epitheton, name, nickname, so(u)briquet, tag, title.

**epitome** *n* abbreviation, abridgement, abstract, archetype, compendium, compression, condensation, conspectus, contraction, digest, embodiment, essence, exemplar, personification, préis, quintessence, reduction, representation, résumé, summary, syllabus, synopsis, type.

**epitomise** *v* abbreviate, abridge, abstract, compress, condense, contract, curtail, cut, embody, encapsulate, exemplify, illustrate, incarnate, personify, précis, reduce, represent, shorten, summarise, symbolise, typify.

*antonyms* elaborate, expand.

**epoch** *n* age, date, epocha, era, period, time.

**equable** *adj* agreeable, calm, composed, consistent, constant, easy-going, even, even-tempered, imperturbable, level-headed, phlegmatic, placid, regular, serene, smooth, stable, steady, temperate, tranquil, unchanging, unexcitable, unflappable, uniform, unruffled, unvarying, unworrying.

*antonyms* excitable, variable.

**equal** *adj* able, adequate, alike, balanced, capable, commensurate, competent, corresponding, egalitarian, equable, equivalent, even, even-handed, evenly-balanced, evenly-matched, evenly-proportioned, fair, fifty-fifty, fit, identical, impartial, just, level-pegging, like, matched, proportionate, ready, regular, sufficient, suitable, symmetrical, tantamount, the same, unbiased, uniform, unvarying, up to.

*antonyms* different, inequitable, unequal.

*n* brother, coequal, compeer, counterpart, equivalent, fellow, match, mate, parallel, peer, rival, twin.

*v* balance, commeasure, correspond to, equalise, equate, even, level, match, parallel, rival, square with, tally with.

**equalise** *v* balance, compensate, draw level, equal, equate, even up, level, match, regularise, smooth, square, standardise.

**equality** *n* balance, coequality, correspondence, egalitarianism, equitability, equivalence, evenness, fairness, identity, likeness, par, parity, proportion, sameness, similarity, uniformity.

*antonym* inequality.

**equanimity** *n* aplomb, calm, calmness, composure, coolness, equability, equableness, imperturbability, level-headedness, peace, phlegm, placidity, poise, presence of mind, sang-froid, self-possession, serenity, steadiness, tranquillity.

*antonyms* alarm, anxiety, discomposure.

**equate** v agree, balance, compare, correspond to, correspond with, equalise, juxtapose, liken, match, offset, pair, parallel, square, tally.

**equation** n agreement, balancing, bracketing, comparison, correspondence, equalisation, equality, equating, equivalence, juxtaposition, likeness, match, pairing, parallel.

**equestrian** n cavalier, horseman, knight, postilion, rider.

**equilibrium** n balance, calm, calmness, collectedness, composure, cool, coolness, counterpoise, equanimity, equipoise, equiponderance, evenness, poise, rest, self-possession, serenity, stability, steadiness, symmetry.

antonym imbalance.

**equip** v accoutre, arm, array, attire, bedight, deck out, dight, dress, endow, fit out, fit up, furnish, habilitate, kit out, outfit, prepare, provide, rig, stock, supply.

**equipage** n accoutrements, apparatus, baggage, carriage, coach, equipment, gear, impedimenta, material, munitions, outfit, retinue, stores, suite, train, traps, turn-out.

**equipment** n accessories, accoutrements, apparatus, appurtenances, baggage, equipage, furnishings, furniture, gear, graith, impedimenta, implements, material, matériel, muniments, outfit, paraphernalia, rig-out, stuff, supplies, tackle, things, tools, traps.

**equipoise** n balance, ballast, counterbalance, counterpoise, counter-weight, equibalance, equilibrium, equiponderance, evenness, offset, poise, stability, steadiness, symmetry.

antonym imbalance.

**equitable** adj disinterested, dispassionate, due, ethical, even-handed, fair, fair-and-square, honest, impartial, just, legitimate, objective, proper, proportionate, right, rightful, square, unbiased, unprejudiced.

antonyms inequitable, unfair.

**equitably** adv disinterestedly, dispassionately, even-handedly, ex aequo, fairly, fairly and squarely, honestly, impartially, justly, objectively, properly, reasonably, rightly.

antonym inequitably.

**equity** n disinterestedness, equality, equitableness, even-handedness, fair play, fair-mindedness, fairness, honesty, impartiality, integrity, justice, justness, objectivity, reasonableness, rectitude, righteousness, uprightness.

antonym inequity.

**equivalence** n agreement, alikeness, conformity, correspondence, equality, evenness, homology, identity, interchangeability, interchangeableness, likeness, match, parallel, parity, sameness, similarity, substitutability, synonymy.

antonyms dissimilarity, inequality, unlikeness.

**equivalent** adj alike, commensurate, comparable, convertible, correlative, correspondent, corresponding, equal, equipollent, equipotent, even, homologous, homotypal, homotypic, interchangeable, same, similar, substitutable, synonymous, tantamount, twin.

antonyms dissimilar, unlike.

n correlative, correspondent, counterpart, equal, homologue, homotype, match, opposite number, parallel, peer, twin.

**equivocal** adj ambiguous, ambivalent, casuistical, confusing, Delphic, doubtful, dubious, evasive, indefinite, indeterminate, misleading, oblique, obscure, oracular, questionable, suspicious, uncertain, vague.

antonyms clear, unequivocal.

**equivocate** v dodge, evade, fence, fudge, hedge, mislead, palter, parry, prevaricate, pussyfoot, quibble, shift, shuffle, sidestep, tergiversate, weasel.

**equivocation** n ambiguity, casuistry, confusion, double talk, doubtfulness, equivocacy, equivocality, equivocalness, equivoke, evasion, hedging, prevarication, quibbling, shifting, shuffling, sophistry, tergiversation, waffle, weasel-words.

antonym directness.

**era** n aeon, age, century, cycle, date, day, days, epoch, generation, period, stage, time.

**eradicable** adj destroyable, destructible, effaceable, eliminable, erasable, exterminable, extinguishable, extirpable, removable, washable.

antonyms ineradicable, permanent.

**eradicate** v abolish, annihilate, deracinate, destroy, efface, eliminate, erase, expunge, exterminate, extinguish, extirpate, get rid of, obliterate, rase, remove, root out, stamp out, suppress, unroot, uproot, weed out.

**eradication** n abolition, annihilation, deracination, destruction, effacement, elimination, erasure, expunction, extermination, extinction, extirpation, obliteration, removal, riddance, suppression.

**erasable** adj effaceable, eradicable, removable, washable.

antonyms ineradicable, permanent.

**erase** v blot out, cancel, cleanse, delete, efface, eliminate, eradicate, expunge, get rid of, obliterate, remove, rub out.

**erasure** n cancellation, cleansing, deletion, effacement, elimination, eradication, erasement, expunction, obliteration, rasure, razure, removal.

**erect** adj elevated, engorged, firm, hard, perpendicular, pricked, raised, rigid, standing, stiff, straight, taut, tense, tumescent, upright, upstanding, vertical.

antonyms limp, relaxed.

v assemble, build, constitute, construct, create, elevate, establish, fabricate, form, found, initiate, institute, lift, mount, organise, pitch, put up, raise, rear, set up.

**erection** n assembly, building, construction, creation, edifice, elevation, establishment, fabrication, manufacture, pile, raising, rigidity, stiffness, structure, tumescence.

**ergo** adv accordingly, consequently, for this reason, hence, in consequence, so, then, therefore, this being the case, thus.

**erode** *v* abrade, consume, corrade, corrode, denude, destroy, deteriorate, disintegrate, eat away, grind down, spoil, wear away, wear down.

**eroded** *adj* abraded, attrite, corraded, denuded, destroyed, disintegrated, eaten away, fragmented, ground down, undermined, worn away.

**erosion** *n* abrasion, attrition, consumption, corrasion, corrosion, denudation, destruction, deterioration, diminishment, disintegration, fragmentation, undermining.

**erosive** *adj* caustic, corrosive, denuding, destructive, disruptive, erodent, gnawing, nibbling, undermining.

**erotic** *adj* amatorial, amatorious, amatory, amorous, aphrodisiac, carnal, concupiscent, erogenic, erogenous, erotogenic, erotogenous, libidinous, lustful, page-three, rousing, seductive, sensual, sexy, stimulating, suggestive, titillating, venereal, voluptuous.

**err** *v* blunder, deviate, fail, go astray, lapse, misapprehend, misbehave, miscalculate, misjudge, mistake, misunderstand, offend, sin, slip up, stray, stumble, transgress, trespass, trip up, wander.

**errand** *n* assignment, charge, commission, duty, job, message, mission, task.

**errant** *adj* aberrant, deviant, erring, itinerant, journeying, loose, nomadic, offending, peccant, peripatetic, rambling, roaming, roving, sinful, sinning, stray, straying, vagrant, wandering, wayward, wrong.

**erratic** *adj* aberrant, abnormal, capricious, changeable, desultory, directionless, eccentric, fitful, fluctuating, inconsistent, inconstant, irregular, meandering, planetary, shifting, unpredictable, unreliable, unstable, variable, wandering, wayward.

*antonyms* consistent, reliable, stable, straight.

**erring** *adj* aberrant, backsliding, delinquent, disobedient, errant, faithless, guilty, peccant, sinful, sinning, straying, wandering, wayward.

**erroneous** *adj* amiss, fallacious, false, faulty, flawed, illogical, inaccurate, incorrect, inexact, invalid, mistaken, specious, spurious, unfounded, unsound, untrue, wrong.

*antonym* correct.

**error** *n* barbarism, bêtise, bish, bloomer, blunder, boner, boob, corrigendum, delinquency, delusion, deviation, erratum, fallacy, fault, faux pas, flaw, gaucherie, howler, ignorance, ignoratio elenchi, illusion, inaccuracy, inexactitude, lapse, lapsus calami, lapsus linguae, lapsus memoriae, literal, malapropism, misapprehension, miscalculation, misconception, miscopy, miscorrection, misdeed, misprint, mistake, misunderstanding, mumpsimus, offence, omission, oversight, overslip, sin, slip, slip-up, solecism, transgression, trespass, wrong, wrongdoing.

**erstwhile** *adj* bygone, ex, former, late, old, once, one-time, past, previous, quondam, sometime, umwhile, whilom.

**erudite** *adj* academic, cultivated, cultured, educated, highbrow, knowledgeable, learned, lettered, literate, profound, recondite, scholarly, scholastic, well-educated, well-read, wise.

*antonym* unlettered.

**erudition** *n* culture, data, education, facts, knowledge, knowledgeableness, learnedness, learning, letters, lore, profoundness, profundity, reconditeness, scholarliness, scholarship, wisdom.

**erupt** *v* belch, break, break out, burst, discharge, eruct, eructate, explode, flare, gush, rift, spew, spout, vent, vomit.

**eruption** *n* discharge, ejection, emphysis, empyesis, eructation, explosion, inflammation, outbreak, outburst, rash, sally, venting.

**escalate** *v* accelerate, amplify, ascend, climb, enlarge, expand, extend, grow, heighten, increase, intensify, magnify, mount, raise, rise, spiral, step up.

*antonym* diminish.

**escalator** *n* elevator, lift, moving staircase.

**escapable** *adj* avertible, avoidable, eludible, evadable, evitable.

*antonym* inevitable.

**escapade** *n* adventure, antic, caper, doing, escapado, exploit, fling, fredaine, gest, lark, prank, romp, scrape, spree, stunt, trick.

**escape** *v* abscond, avoid, baffle, bolt, break free, break loose, break off, break out, circumvent, decamp, discharge, do a bunk, dodge, drain, duck, elude, emanate, evade, flee, flit, flow, fly, foil, get away, gush, issue, leak, ooze, pass, pour forth, scape, scarper, seep, shake off, shun, skedaddle, skip, slip, slip away, spurt, take it on the run, take to one's heels, trickle, vamoose.

*n* abscondence, avoidance, bolt, break, break-out, circumvention, decampment, discharge, distraction, diversion, drain, effluence, effluent, efflux, effluxion, elusion, emanation, emission, escapism, evasion, flight, flit, getaway, gush, jailbreak, leak, leakage, meuse, out, outflow, outlet, outpour, pastime, recreation, relaxation, relief, safety-valve, seepage, spurt, vent.

**escape route** bolthole, egress, escape road, exit, loophole, meuse, out, outlet, secret passage, slip road, vent.

**escapee** *n* absconder, defector, deserter, fugitive, jail-breaker, runaway.

**escapist** *n* daydreamer, dreamer, fantasiser, non-realist, ostrich, Walter Mitty, wishful thinker.

*antonym* realist.

**eschew** *v* abandon, abjure, abstain from, avoid, disdain, forgo, forswear, give up, keep clear of, refrain from, renounce, repudiate, shun, spurn, swear off.

*antonym* embrace.

**escort** *n* aide, attendant, beau, bodyguard, chaperon, cicisbeo, companion, company, convoy, cortège, entourage, gigolo, guard, guardian, guide, partner, pilot, procession, protection, protector, retinue, safeguard, squire, suite, train.

*v* accompany, chaperon, chum, company, conduct, convoy, guard, guide, lead, partner, protect, shepherd, squire, usher.

**esoteric** *adj* abstruse, acroamatic, acroamatical, arcane, cabbalistic, confidential, cryptic, hermetic, hidden, inner, inscrutable, inside, mysterious, mystic, mystical, obscure, occult, private, recondite, secret.

*antonyms* familiar, popular.

**especial** *adj* chief, conspicuous, distinguished, eminent, exceptional, exclusive, express, extraordinary, individual, marked, notable, noteworthy, outstanding, particular, peculiar, personal, pre-eminent, principal, private, proper, remarkable, signal, singular, special, specific, striking, uncommon, unique, unusual.

**especially** *adv* chiefly, conspicuously, eminently, exceedingly, exceptionally, exclusively, expressly, extraordinarily, mainly, markedly, notably, noticeably, outstandingly, particularly, passing, peculiarly, pre-eminently, principally, remarkably, signally, singularly, specially, specifically, strikingly, supremely, uncommonly, uniquely, unusually, very.

**espionage** *n* counter-intelligence, infiltration, intelligence, investigation, probing, reconnaissance, spying, surveillance, undercover operations.

**espousal** *n* adoption, advocacy, affiance, alliance, backing, betrothal, betrothing, bridal, championing, championship, defence, embracing, engagement, espousing, maintenance, marriage, matrimony, nuptials, plighting, spousal, support, wedding.

**espouse** *v* adopt, advocate, affiance, back, befriend, betroth, champion, choose, defend, embrace, maintain, marry, opt for, patronise, support, take to wife, take up, wed.

**espy** *v* behold, descry, detect, discern, discover, distinguish, glimpse, make out, notice, observe, perceive, see, sight, spot, spy.

**essay**[1] *n* article, assignment, commentary, composition, critique, discourse, disquisition, dissertation, essayette, leader, paper, piece, review, thesis, tract, treatise.

**essay**[2] *n* attempt, bash, bid, crack, effort, endeavour, exertion, experiment, go, shot, stab, struggle, test, trial, try, undertaking, venture, whack, whirl.

*v* attempt, endeavour, go for, have a bash, have a crack, have a go, have a stab, strain, strive, struggle, tackle, take on, test, try, undertake.

**essence** *n* alma, attar, attributes, being, centre, character, characteristics, concentrate, core, crux, decoction, decocture, distillate, elixir, ens, entity, esse, extract, fragrance, haecceity, heart, hypostasis, inscape, kernel, life, lifeblood, marrow, meaning, nature, perfume, pith, principle, properties, qualities, quality, quiddit, quiddity, quintessence, scent, significance, soul, spirit, spirits, substance, tincture, virtuality, whatness.

**essential**[1] *adj* absolute, basic, cardinal, characteristic, complete, constituent, constitutional, constitutive, crucial, definitive, elemental, elementary, formal, fundamental, ideal, important, indispensable, inherent, innate, intrinsic, key, main, must, necessary, needed, perfect, principal, quintessential, required, requisite, typical, vital.

*antonym* inessential.

*n* basic, fundamental, must, necessary, necessity, prerequisite, principle, qualification, quality, requirement, requisite, rudiment, sine qua non.

*antonym* inessential.

**essential**[2] *adj* concentrated, decocted, distilled, ethereal, extracted, pure, purified, rectified, refined, volatile.

**establish** *v* affirm, attest to, authenticate, authorise, base, certify, confirm, constitute, corroborate, create, decree, demonstrate, enact, ensconce, entrench, fix, form, found, ground, implant, inaugurate, install, institute, introduce, invent, lodge, ordain, organise, plant, prove, radicate, ratify, root, sanction, seat, secure, set up, settle, show, start, station, substantiate, validate, verify.

**established** *adj* accepted, attested, confirmed, conventional, ensconced, entrenched, experienced, fixed, proved, proven, radicate, radicated, respected, routed, secure, settled, stated, steadfast, traditional.

*antonyms* impermanent, unreliable.

**establishment** *n* abode, building, business, company, concern, construction, corporation, creation, domicile, dwelling, edifice, enactment, enterprise, erection, factory, firm, formation, foundation, founding, hacienda, home, house, household, implantation, inauguration, inception, installation, institute, institution, introduction, invention, office, ordination, organisation, outfit, plant, quarters, radication, residence, ruling class, set-up, structure, system, the powers that be, the system.

**estate** *n* area, assets, barony, belongings, caste, class, condition, demesne, domain, effects, estancia, fortune, goods, grade, hacienda, holdings, lands, latifundium, lot, manor, order, period, place, position, possessions, property, quality, ranch, rank, situation, standing, state, station, status, wealth.

**esteem** *v* account, adjudge, admire, believe, calculate, cherish, consider, count, deem, estimate, hold, honour, include, judge, like, love, prize, rate, reckon, regard, regard highly, respect, revere, reverence, think, treasure, value, venerate, view.

*n* account, admiration, consideration, count, credit, estimation, good opinion, honour, judgement, love, reckoning, regard, respect, reverence, veneration.

**esteemed** *adj* admirable, admired, distinguished, excellent, highly-regarded, honourable, honoured, prized, reputable, respectable, respected, revered, treasured, valued, venerated, well-respected, well-thought-of, worthy.

**estimable** *adj* admirable, commendable, considerable, distinguished, egregious, esteemed, excellent, good, honourable, laudable, meritorious, notable, noteworthy, praiseworthy, reputable, respectable, respected, valuable, valued, worthy.

*antonyms* despicable, insignificant.

**estimate** *v* appraise, approximate, assess, believe, calculate, compute, conjecture, consider, count, evaluate, gauge, guess, judge, number, opine, rank, rate, reckon, surmise, think, value.

*n* appraisal, appraisement, approximation, assessment, belief, computation, conceit, conception, conjecture, estimation, evaluation, guess, guesstimate, judgement, opinion, reckoning, surmise, valuation.

**estimation** *n* account, admiration, appraisal, appreciation, assessment, belief, calculation, computation, conception, consideration, credit, esteem, estimate, evaluation, good opinion, honour, judgement, opinion, rating, reckoning, regard, respect, reverence, veneration, view.

**estrange** *v* alienate, antagonise, disaffect, disunite, divide, drive a wedge between, drive apart, part, put a barrier between, separate, set at variance, sever, sunder, withdraw, withhold.

*antonyms* ally, attract, bind, unite.

**estrangement** *n* alienation, antagonisation, antipathy, breach, break-up, disaffection, dissociation, disunity, division, hostility, parting, separation, severance, split, sunderance, sundering, unfriendliness, withdrawal, withholding.

**estuary** *n* arm, creek, firth, fjord, inlet, mouth, sea-loch, wash, wick.

**et cetera** and so forth, and so on, and the like, and the rest, &c, et ainsi de suite, et al, et alia, et alii, et hoc genus omne, et sequentia, et sic de ceteris, et sic de similibus, etc, kai ta leipomena, kai ta loipa, ktl, und so weiter, usw.

**etch** *v* bite, burn, carve, corrode, cut, dig, engrave, furrow, grave, groove, hatch, impress, imprint, incise, ingrain, inscribe, stamp.

**etching** *n* carving, cut, engraving, impression, imprint, print, sketch.

**eternal** *adj* abiding, aeonian, ceaseless, changeless, constant, deathless, durable, endless, enduring, eterne, everlasting, eviternal, illimitable, immortal, immutable, imperishable, incessant, indestructible, infinite, interminable, lasting, limitless, never-ending, perennial, permanent, perpetual, sempiternal, timeless, unbegotten, unceasing, unchanging, undying, unending, unextinguishable, unremitting.

*antonyms* changeable, ephemeral, temporary.

**eternally** *adv* ceaselessly, constantly, endlessly, everlastingly, immutably, incessantly, indestructibly, interminably, lastingly, never-endingly, perennially, permanently, perpetually, unendingly.

*antonyms* briefly, temporarily.

**eternity** *n* aeon, afterlife, age, ages, changelessness, endlessness, everlasting, everlastingness, eviternity, Ewigkeit, heaven, hereafter, illimitability, immortality, immutability, imperishability, incorruptibility, incorruption, infinitude, infinity, next world, paradise, perpetuity, sempiternity, timelessness, world to come.

**ethereal** *adj* aerial, airy, celestial, dainty, delicate, diaphanous, elemental, empyreal, empyrean,

essential, etheric, etherical, exquisite, fairy, fine, gossamer, heavenly, impalpable, insubstantial, intangible, light, rarefied, rectified, refined, spiritual, subtle, tenuous, unearthly, unworldly.

*antonyms* earthly, solid.

**ethical** *adj* commendable, conscientious, correct, decent, fair, fitting, good, honest, honourable, just, meet, moral, noble, principled, proper, right, righteous, seemly, upright, virtuous.

*antonym* unethical.

**ethics** *n* code, conscience, deontics, deontology, equity, mind philosophy, moral ethology, moral philosophy, moral values, morality, principles, probity, propriety, rule, rules, seemliness, standards.

**ethnic** *adj* aboriginal, ancestral, autochthonous, cultural, folk, gentilic, historic, indigenous, national, native, racial, traditional, traditive, tribal.

**ethos** *n* attitude, beliefs, character, code, disposition, ethic, geist, manners, moeurs, morality, principles, rationale, spirit, standards, tenor.

**etiquette** *n* ceremony, civility, code, convention, conventionalities, correctness, courtesy, customs, decency, decorum, formalities, manners, politeness, politesse, propriety, protocol, rules, seemliness, usage, use.

**etymology** *n* derivation, descent, lexicology, linguistics, origin, pedigree, philology, semantics, source, word history, word-lore.

**eulogise** *v* acclaim, adulate, applaud, approve, belaud, celebrate, commend, compliment, congratulate, cry up, exalt, extol, flatter, glorify, honour, laud, magnify, panegyrise, praise.

*antonym* condemn.

**eulogistic** *adj* adulatory, approbatory, commendatory, complimentary, encomiastic, epaenetic, favourable, flattering, laudatory, panegyrical.

*antonym* unfavourable.

**eulogy** *n* acclaim, acclamation, accolade, applause, commendation, compliment, encomium, exaltation, glorification, laud, laudation, laudatory, paean, panegyric, plaudit, praise, tribute.

*antonym* condemnation.

**euphemism** *n* evasion, fig-leaf, genteelism, hypocorism, hypocorisma, polite term, politeness, substitution, understatement.

**euphonious** *adj* canorous, clear, consonant, dulcet, dulcifluous, dulciloquent, euphonic, harmonious, honeyed, mellifluent, mellifluous, mellow, melodic, melodious, musical, silvery, soft, sugared, sweet, sweet-sounding, sweet-toned, symphonious, tunable, tuneful.

*antonym* cacophonous.

**euphony** *n* consonance, dulciloquy, euphoniousness, harmoniousness, harmony, mellifluousness, mellowness, melodiousness, melody, music, musicality, tunefulness.

*antonym* cacophony.

**euphoria** *n* bliss, buoyancy, cheerfulness, cloud nine, ecstasy, elation, enthusiasm, euphory, exaltation, exhilaration, exultation, glee, high, high spirits, intoxication, joy, joyousness, jubilation, rapture, transport.

*antonym* depression.

**euphoric** *adj* blissful, buoyant, cheerful, ecstatic, elated, enraptured, enthusiastic, exhilarated, exultant, exulted, gleeful, happy, high, intoxicated, joyful, joyous, jubilant, rapturous.

*antonym* depressed.

**euthanasia** *n* euthanasy, mercy killing, quietus.

**evacuate**[1] *v* abandon, clear, clear out, decamp, depart, desert, forsake, leave, quit, relinquish, remove, retire from, vacate, withdraw.

**evacuate**[2] *v* defecate, discharge, eject, eliminate, empty, excrete, expel, purge, void.

**evacuation**[1] *n* abandonment, clearance, departure, desertion, exodus, quitting, relinquishment, removal, retiral, retreat, vacation, withdrawal.

**evacuation**[2] *n* catharsis, defecation, discharge, ejection, elimination, emptying, excretion, expulsion, purgation, purging, urination, voidance.

**evade** *v* avert, avoid, balk, blink, chicken out of, circumvent, cop out, decline, dodge, duck, elude, equivocate, escape, fence, fend off, fudge, give the runaround, hedge, parry, prevaricate, quibble, scrimshank, shirk, shun, sidestep, skive, steer clear of, temporise.

*antonym* face.

**evaluate** *v* appraise, assay, assess, calculate, compute, estimate, gauge, judge, rank, rate, reckon, size up, value, weigh.

**evaluation** *n* appraisal, assessment, calculation, computation, estimate, estimation, judgement, opinion, rating, reckoning, valuation.

**evanescence** *n* brevity, briefness, ephemerality, ephemeralness, fleetingness, fugaciousness, fugacity, fugitiveness, impermanence, inconstancy, instability, momentariness, temporariness, transience, transitoriness.

*antonym* permanence.

**evanescent** *adj* brief, changing, disappearing, ephemeral, fading, fleeting, fugacious, fugitive, impermanent, insubstantial, momentary, passing, perishable, short-lived, temporary, transient, transitory, unstable, vanishing.

*antonym* permanent.

**evangelical** *adj* campaigning, crusading, evangelistic, missionary, propagandising, propagandist, proselytising, zealous.

**evangelise** *v* baptise, campaign, convert, crusade, gospelise, missionarise, missionise, preach, propagandise, proselytise.

**evaporate** *v* condense, dehydrate, dematerialise, desiccate, disappear, dispel, disperse, dissipate, dissolve, distil, dry, evanesce, exhale, fade, melt (away), vanish, vaporise, vapour.

**evaporation** *n* condensation, dehydration, dematerialisation, desiccation, disappearance, dispelling, dispersal, dissipation, dissolution,

distillation, drying, evanescence, fading, melting, vanishing, vaporisation, water-smoke.

**evasion** *n* artifice, avoidance, casuistry, circumvention, cop-out, cunning, dodge, elusion, equivocation, escape, euphemism, evasiveness, excuse, fudging, obfuscation, obliqueness, pretext, prevarication, put-off, ruse, shift, shirking, shuffling, sophism, sophistry, subterfuge, trickery, weasel-words.

*antonyms* directness, frankness.

**evasive** *adj* ambiguous, cag(e)y, casuistic, casuistical, cunning, deceitful, deceptive, devious, disingenuous, dissembling, elusive, elusory, equivocating, indirect, misleading, oblique, prevaricating, secretive, shifty, shuffling, slippery, sophistical, tricky, unforthcoming, vacillating.

*antonyms* direct, frank.

**eve** *n* brink, edge, evening, moment, point, threshold, verge, vigil.

**even** *adj* abreast, alongside, balanced, calm, coequal, commensurate, comparable, complanate, composed, constant, cool, disinterested, dispassionate, drawn, equable, equal, equalised, equanimous, equitable, even-tempered, fair, fair and square, fifty-fifty, flat, fluent, flush, horizontal, identical, impartial, impassive, imperturbable, just, level, level-pegging, like, matching, metrical, monotonous, neck and neck, on a par, parallel, peaceful, placid, plane, plumb, proportionate, quits, regular, rhythmical, serene, side by side, similar, smooth, square, stable, steady, straight, symmetrical, tied, tranquil, true, unbiased, unbroken, undisturbed, unexcitable, unexcited, uniform, uninterrupted, unprejudiced, unruffled, unvarying, unwavering, well-balanced.

*antonyms* unequal, uneven.

*adv* all the more, also, although, as well, at all, directly, exactly, hardly, including, just, much, scarcely, so much as, still, yet.

*v* align, balance, equal, equalise, flatten, flush, level, match, regularise, regulate, smooth, square, stabilise, steady, straighten.

**even so** all the same, despite that, however, however that may be, in spite of that, natheless, nevertheless, nonetheless, notwithstanding that, still, yet.

**even-handed** *adj* balanced, disinterested, dispassionate, equitable, fair, fair and square, impartial, just, neutral, non-discriminatory, reasonable, square, unbiased, unprejudiced, without fear or favour.

*antonym* inequitable.

**evening** *n* crepuscule, dusk, eve, even, eventide, forenight, gloaming, Hesper, Hesperus, nightfall, sundown, sunset, twilight, vesper.

*adj* crepuscular, twilight, vesperal, vespertinal, vespertine.

**evenness** *n* alikeness, balance, calmness, commensurateness, comparability, composure, constancy, coolness, equability, equableness, equality, equanimity, flatness, fluency, identicalness, impassivity, imperturbability, levelness, monotony, peacableness, placidity, proportion, regularity, rhythmicality, serenity, similarity, smoothness, stability, steadiness, straightness, symmetry, tranquillity, trueness, uniformity.

*antonyms* inequality, unevenness.

**event** *n* adventure, affair, bout, business, case, circumstance, competition, conclusion, consequence, contest, effect, end, engagement, episode, eventuality, experience, fact, game, happening, incident, issue, match, matter, milestone, occasion, occurrence, outcome, possibility, result, termination, tournament, upshot.

**even-tempered** *adj* calm, composed, cool, cool-headed, equable, equanimous, impassive, imperturbable, level-headed, peaceable, peaceful, placid, serene, stable, steady, tranquil, unexcitable, unfussed, unruffled.

*antonym* excitable.

**eventful** *adj* active, busy, consequential, critical, crucial, decisive, epochal, exciting, fateful, full, historic, important, interesting, lively, memorable, momentous, notable, noteworthy, portentous, remarkable, significant, unforgettable.

*antonyms* dull, ordinary, uneventful.

**eventual** *adj* concluding, consequent, ensuing, final, future, impending, last, later, overall, planned, projected, prospective, resulting, subsequent, ultimate.

**eventuality** *n* case, chance, circumstance, contingency, crisis, emergency, event, happening, happenstance, likelihood, mishap, outcome, possibility, probability.

**eventually** *adv* after all, at last, at length, finally, in one's own good time, sooner or later, subsequently, ultimately.

**ever** *adv* always, at all, at all times, at any time, ceaselessly, constantly, continually, endlessly, eternally, everlastingly, evermore, for ever, in any case, in any circumstances, incessantly, on any account, perpetually, unceasingly, unendingly.

**everlasting** *adj* abiding, boring, ceaseless, changeless, constant, continual, continuous, deathless, durable, endless, enduring, eternal, immarcescible, immortal, imperishable, incessant, indestructible, infinite, interminable, lasting, monotonous, never-ending, perdurable, permanent, perpetual, relentless, tedious, timeless, unceasing, unchanging, undying, unfading, uninterrupted, unremitting.

*antonyms* temporary, transient.

**evermore** *adv* always, eternally, ever, ever after, for aye, for ever, for ever and a day, for ever and ever, henceforth, hereafter, in perpetuum, in saecula saeculorum, till doomsday, to the end of time, unceasingly.

**evert** *v* evaginate, turn inside out, turn out.

**everted** *adj* evaginated, extrorse, turned inside out.

**everybody** *n* all and sundry, each one, everyone, one and all, the whole world, tout le monde.

**everyday** *adj* accustomed, banal, boring, circadian, common, common-or-garden, commonplace, conventional, customary, daily, diurnal, dull, familiar, frequent, habitual, informal, monotonous, mundane, normal, ordinary, plain, prosaic, quotidian, regular, routine, run-of-the-mill, simple, stock, unexceptional, unimaginative, usual, wonted, workaday.

*antonyms* exceptional, special.

**everyone** *n* all and sundry, each one, every man-jack, every mother's son, everybody, one and all, the whole jingbang, the whole world, tout le monde.

**everything** *n* all, lock stock and barrel, the aggregate, the entirety, the lot, the sum, the total, the whole caboodle, the whole lot, the whole shoot, the whole shooting-match.

**everywhere** *adv* all along the line, all around, all over, far and near, far and wide, high and low, left right and centre, omnipresent, passim, ubique, ubiquitous.

**evict** *v* boot out, cast out, chuck out, defenestrate, dislodge, dispossess, disseise, eject, expel, expropriate, give the bum's rush, kick out, oust, put out, remove, show the door, turf out.

**eviction** *n* clearance, defenestration, dislodgement, dispossession, disseisin, ejection, expropriation, expulsion, ouster, removal, the bum's rush.

**evidence** *n* affirmation, attestation, betrayal, confirmation, corroboration, data, declaration, demonstration, deposition, documentation, grounds, hint, indication, manifestation, mark, pledge, proof, sign, substantiation, suggestion, testimony, token, voucher, witness.

*v* affirm, attest, betray, confirm, demonstrate, denote, display, establish, evince, exhibit, indicate, manifest, prove, reveal, show, signify, testify to, witness.

**evident** *adj* apparent, clear, clear-cut, confessed, conspicuous, detectable, discernible, distinct, incontestable, incontrovertible, indisputable, manifest, noticeable, obvious, ostensible, palpable, patent, perceptible, plain, tangible, undeniable, unmistakable, visible.

*antonym* uncertain.

**evidently** *adv* apparently, clearly, distinctly, doubtless, doubtlessly, incontestably, incontrovertibly, indisputably, indubitably, irrefragably, manifestly, obviously, ostensibly, outwardly, patently, plainly, seemingly, undoubtedly, unmistakably, unquestionably.

**evil** *adj* adverse, bad, baleful, baneful, base, blackguardly, black-hearted, calamitous, catastrophic, corrupt, cruel, deadly, deleterious, depraved, destructive, detrimental, devilish, dire, disastrous, facinorous, flagitious, foul, ghastly, grim, harmful, heinous, hurtful, immoral, inauspicious, inimical, iniquitous, injurious, knavish, malefactory, malefic, maleficent, malevolent, malicious, malignant, mephitic, mischievous, miscreant, nefarious, nefast, nocuous, noisome, noxious, offensive, painful, perfidious, pernicious, pestiferous, pestilential, poisonous, putrid, reprobate, ruinous, sinful, sorrowful, ugly, unfortunate, unlucky, unpleasant, unspeakable, vicious, vile, villainous, wicked, woeful, wrong.

*n* adversity, affliction, amiss, badness, bane, baseness, blow, calamity, catastrophe, corruption, curse, demonry, depravity, disaster, distress, facinorousness, flagitiousness, foulness, harm, heinousness, hurt, hydra, ill, immorality, impiety, improbity, iniquity, injury, knavery, maleficence, malignity, mischief, misery, misfortune, pain, perfidy, ruin, sin, sinfulness, sorrow, suffering, turpitude, ulcer, vice, viciousness, villainy, wickedness, woe, wrong, wrong-doing.

**evil eye** blight, cantrip, charm, curse, hoodoo, jettatura, jinx, malocchio, spell, voodoo.

**evil spirit** bogey, bogle, cacodaemon, demon, devil, fiend, ghost, goblin, gremlin, hobgoblin, imp, incubus, jumby, kelpie, kobold, nicker, nightmare, nix, nixie, succubus, troll.

**evil-doer** *n* blackguard, caitiff, criminal, delinquent, knave, malefactor, malfeasant, miscreant, offender, reprobate, rogue, scamp, scapegrace, scoundrel, sinner, villain, wrong-doer.

**evince** *v* attest, bespeak, betoken, betray, confess, declare, demonstrate, display, establish, evidence, exhibit, express, indicate, manifest, reveal, show, signify.

*antonyms* conceal, suppress.

**eviscerate** *v* disembowel, draw, exenterate, gralloch, gut.

**evisceration** *n* disembowelment, drawing, exenteration, gralloching, gutting.

**evocation** *n* activation, actuation, arousal, echo, eduction, elicitation, excitation, kindling, recall, stimulation, stirring, suggestion, summoning-up.

**evoke** *v* activate, actuate, arouse, awaken, call, call forth, call up, conjure up, educe, elicit, excite, induce, invoke, produce, provoke, raise, recall, rekindle, stimulate, stir, summon, summon up.

*antonyms* quell, suppress.

**evolution** *n* convolution, Darwinism, derivation, descent, development, evolvement, expansion, growth, gyration, increase, maturation, progress, progression, ripening, unfolding, unrolling.

**evolve** *v* derive, descend, develop, disclose, elaborate, emerge, enlarge, expand, grow, increase, mature, progress, result, unravel.

**exacerbate** *v* aggravate, deepen, embitter, enrage, envenom, exaggerate, exasperate, excite, heighten, increase, inflame, infuriate, intensify, irritate, provoke, sharpen, vex, worsen.

*antonym* soothe.

**exact** *adj* accurate, blow-by-blow, careful, close, correct, definite, detailed, explicit, express, factual, faithful, faultless, finical, finicky, flawless, identical, letter-perfect, literal, methodical, meticulous, nice, orderly, painstaking, particular, perfectionist, perjink, precise, punctilious, right, rigorous, scrupulous, severe, specific, square, strict, true, unambiguous, unequivocal, unerring, veracious, very, word-perfect.

*antonym* inexact.

*v* bleed, claim, command, compel, demand, extort, extract, force, impose, insist on, milk, require, requisition, squeeze, wrest, wring.

**exactable** *adj* demandable, exigible, imposable, requirable.

**exacting** *adj* arduous, demanding, difficult, exig(e)ant, exigent, hard, harsh, imperious, laborious, oppressive, painstaking, rigid, rigorous, severe, stern, strict, stringent, taxing, toilsome, tough, trying, tyrannical, unsparing, uphill.

*antonyms* easy, tolerant.

**exaction** *n* blackmail, bleeding, compulsion, contribution, demand, extortion, imposition, milking, rapacity, requirement, requisition, tribute.

**exactitude** *n* accuracy, authenticity, care, carefulness, clarity, conscientiousness, correctness, detail, exactness, faithfulness, faultlessness, fidelity, meticulousness, nicety, orderliness, painstakingness, perfectionism, preciseness, precision, promptitude, promptness, punctilio, punctuality, regularity, rigorousness, rigour, scrupulosity, scrupulousness, strictness, thoroughness, truth, veracity.

*antonyms* carelessness, inaccuracy.

**exactly** *adv* absolutely, accurately, bang, carefully, correctly, dead, definitely, explicitly, expressly, faithfully, faultlessly, just, literally, literatim, methodically, particularly, plumb, precisely, punctiliously, quite, rigorously, scrupulously, severely, specifically, strictly, to the letter, truly, truthfully, unambiguously, unequivocally, unerringly, veraciously, verbatim.

*interj* absolutely, agreed, certainly, indeed, just so, of course, precisely, quite, right, true.

**exactness** *n* accuracy, authenticity, carefulness, correctness, detail, exactitude, faithfulness, faultlessness, fidelity, meticulousness, nicety, orderliness, painstakingness, perfectionism, preciseness, precision, promptitude, punctilio, regularity, rigorousness, rigour, scrupulousness, strictness, truth, veracity, verity.

*antonyms* carelessness, inaccuracy.

**exaggerate** *v* amplify, bounce, caricature, distend, embellish, embroider, emphasise, enlarge, exalt, hyperbolise, inflate, magnify, overdo, overdraw, overemphasise, overestimate, oversell, overstate, pile it on.

*antonyms* belittle, understate.

**exaggerated** *adj* amplified, bloated, bombastic, burlesqued, caricatured, embellished, euphuistic, exalted, excessive, extravagant, hyperbolic, hyperbolical, inflated, overblown, overcharged, overdone, overestimated, overstated, pretentious, tall, turgid.

*antonym* understated.

**exaggeration** *n* amplification, burlesque, caricature, embellishment, emphasis, enlargement, exaltation, excess, extravagance, hyperbole, inflation, magnification, overemphasis, overestimation, overstatement, parody, pretension, pretentiousness, stretcher.

*antonyms* meiosis, understatement.

**exalt** *v* acclaim, advance, aggrandise, animate, apotheosise, applaud, arouse, bless, crown, deify, delight, dignify, elate, electrify, elevate, enliven, ennoble, enthrone, excite, exhilarate, extol, fire, glorify, heighten, honour, idolise, inspire, inspirit, laud, magnify, praise, promote, raise, revere, reverence, stimulate, sublimise, thrill, upgrade, uplift, venerate, worship.

*antonym* debase.

**exaltation** *n* acclaim, acclamation, adoration, adulation, advancement, aggrandisement, animation, apotheosis, applause, blessing, bliss, canonisation, deification, delight, dignification, dignity, ecstasy, elation, elevation, eminence, ennoblement, enthusiasm, excitement, exhilaration, extolment, exultation, glorification, glory, grandeur, homage, honour, idealisation, idolisation, inspiration, joy, joyfulness, joyousness, jubilation, laudation, lionisation, loftiness, magnification, panegyric, plaudits, praise, prestige, promotion, rapture, reverence, rise, stimulation, transport, tribute, upgrading, uplift, veneration, worship.

*antonym* debasement.

**exalted** *adj* animated, august, blissful, dignified, ecstatic, elate, elated, elevated, eminent, enhanced, enlivened, enthusiastic, exaggerated, excessive, excited, exhilarated, exultant, glorified, glorious, grand, happy, high, high-minded, high-ranking, honoured, ideal, idealised, in high spirits, in seventh heaven, inflated, inspired, inspirited, intellectual, joyful, joyous, jubilant, lofty, lordly, noble, overblown, prestigious, pretentious, princely, rapturous, stately, stimulated, sublime, superior, transcendent, transported, uplifted, uplifting.

*antonym* debased.

**examination** *n* analysis, appraisal, assay, audit, catechism, check, check-up, critique, cross-examination, cross-questioning, docimasy, exam, exploration, inquiry, inquisition, inspection, interrogation, investigation, observation, once-over, perusal, probe, questioning, quiz, research, review, scan, scrutinisation, scrutiny, search, sift, study, survey, test, trial, visitation, viva.

**examine** *v* analyse, appraise, assay, audit, case, catechise, check (out), consider, cross-examine, cross-question, explore, eyeball, grill, inquire, inspect, interrogate, investigate, jerque, peruse, ponder, pore over, probe, question, quiz, review, scan, scrutinise, sift, study, survey, sus out, test, vet, visit, weigh.

**examinee** *n* applicant, candidate, competitor, contestant, entrant, examinant, examinate, interviewee.

**examiner** *n* adjudicator, analyst, arbiter, assayer, assessor, auditor, censor, critic, examinant, examinator, inspector, interlocutor, interviewer, judge, marker, questioner, reader, reviewer, scrutator, scrutineer, scrutiniser, tester.

**example** *n* admonition, archetype, case, case in point, caution, citation, ensample, exemplar, exemplification, exemplum, ideal, illustration, instance, lesson, mirror, model, occurrence, paradigm, paragon, parallel, pattern, praxis, precedent, prototype, sample, specimen, standard, type, warning.

**exasperate** *v* aggravate, anger, annoy, bug, enrage, exacerbate, excite, exulcerate, gall, get, get in someone's hair, get on someone's nerves, get on someone's wick, get to, goad, incense,

inflame, infuriate, irk, irritate, madden, needle, nettle, peeve, pique, plague, provoke, rankle, rile, rouse, vex.

*antonyms* calm, soothe.

**exasperated** *adj* aggravated, angered, angry, annoyed, at the end of one's tether, bored, bugged, fed up, galled, goaded, incensed, indignant, infuriated, irked, irritated, maddened, needled, nettled, peeved, piqued, provoked, riled, vexed.

**exasperating** *adj* aggravating, annoying, boring, bothersome, disagreeable, galling, infuriating, irksome, irritating, maddening, pernicious, pesky, pestiferous, pestilential, provoking, troublesome, vexatious, vexing.

**exasperation** *n* aggravation, anger, annoyance, arousal, discontent, disgust, displeasure, dissatisfaction, enragement, exacerbation, exulceration, fury, gall, indignation, inflammation, ire, irritation, passion, pique, provocation, rage, resentment, vexation, wrath.

*antonym* calmness.

**excavate** *v* burrow, cut, delve, dig, dig out, dig up, disinter, drive, exhume, gouge, hollow, mine, quarry, sap, scoop, stope, trench, tunnel, uncover, undermine, unearth.

**excavation** *n* burrow, cavity, cut, cutting, delf, dig, diggings, ditch, dugout, hole, hollow, mine, pit, quarry, sap, sapping, shaft, souterrain, stope, trench, trough, undermining.

**exceed** *v* beat, better, cap, contravene, eclipse, excel, outdistance, outdo, outreach, outrival, outrun, outshine, outstrip, overdo, overstep, overtake, pass, surmount, surpass, take liberties with, top, transcend, transgress.

**exceeding** *adj* amazing, astonishing, enormous, exceptional, excessive, extraordinary, great, huge, outstanding, pre-eminent, superior, superlative, surpassing, transcendent, unequalled, unprecedented, unusual, vast.

**exceedingly** *adv* amazingly, astonishingly, enormously, especially, exceeding, exceptionally, excessively, extraordinarily, extremely, greatly, highly, hugely, inordinately, passing, superlatively, surpassingly, unprecedentedly, unusually, vastly, very.

**excel** *v* beat, better, cap, eclipse, exceed, outclass, outdo, outperform, outrank, outrival, outshine, outstrip, overshadow, pass, predominate, shine, stand out, surmount, surpass, top, transcend, trump.

**excellence** *n* distinction, eminence, fineness, goodness, greatness, merit, perfection, pre-eminence, purity, quality, superiority, supremacy, transcendence, virtue, water, worth.

*antonym* inferiority.

**excellent** *adj* A1, admirable, beaut, bonzer, boshta, bosker, boss, brave, bully, capital, champion, choice, commendable, copacetic, corking, crack, cracking, dilly, distinguished, estimable, exemplary, eximious, exquisite, fine, first-class, first-rate, good, great, hot stuff, laudable, meritorious, nonpareil, notable, noted, noteworthy, outstanding, peerless, prime, remarkable, ripping, select, splendid, sterling, stunning, superb, supereminent, superior, superlative, surpassing, tipping, tiptop, top-flight, top-notch, topping, unequalled, unexceptionable, up to dick, way-out, wonderful, worthy.

*antonym* inferior.

**except** *prep* apart from, bar, barring, besides, but, except for, excepting, excluding, exclusive of, leaving out, less, minus, not counting, omitting, other than, save, saving.

*v* ban, bar, debar, disallow, eliminate, exclude, leave out, omit, pass over, reject, rule out.

**exception** *n* abnormality, anomaly, curiosity, debarment, departure, deviation, disallowment, eccentricity, excepting, exclusion, exemption, freak, inconsistency, irregularity, oddity, omission, peculiarity, prodigy, quirk, rarity, rejection, special case.

**exceptional** *adj* aberrant, abnormal, anomalous, atypical, curious, deviant, eccentric, excellent, extraordinary, freakish, inconsistent, irregular, marvellous, notable, noteworthy, odd, outstanding, peculiar, phenomenal, prodigious, quirky, rare, remarkable, singular, special, strange, superior, superlative, uncommon, unconventional, unequalled, unexpected, unusual.

*antonyms* mediocre, unexceptional.

**exceptionally** *adv* amazingly, especially, excellently, extraordinarily, marvellously, notably, outstandingly, peculiarly, phenomenally, prodigiously, remarkably, singularly, specially, splendidly, superlatively, uncommonly, unusually, wonderfully.

**excerpt** *n* citation, extract, fragment, gobbet, part, passage, pericope, portion, quotation, quote, scrap, section, selection.

*v* borrow, cite, crib, cull, extract, lift, mine, quarry, quote, select.

**excess** *n* debauchery, diarrhoea, dissipation, dissoluteness, excesses, exorbitance, extravagance, glut, gluttony, immoderateness, immoderation, intemperance, left-over, libertinism, licentiousness, nimiety, overabundance, overdose, overflow, overflush, overindulgence, overkill, overload, plethora, prodigality, remainder, superabundance, superfluity, surfeit, surplus, unrestraint.

*antonym* dearth.

*adj* additional, extra, left-over, redundant, remaining, residual, spare, superfluous, supernumerary, surplus.

**excessive** *adj* disproportionate, exaggerated, exorbitant, extravagant, extreme, fanatical, immoderate, inordinate, intemperate, needless, nimious, overdone, overmuch, prodigal, profligate, steep, stiff, supererogatory, superfluous, unasked-for, uncalled-for, unconscionable, undue, unnecessary, unneeded, unreasonable.

*antonym* insufficient.

**excessively** *adv* disproportionately, exaggeratedly, exorbitantly, extravagantly, extremely, fanatically, immoderately, inordinately,

intemperately, needlessly, overly, overmuch, prodigally, superfluously, unconscionably, unduly, unnecessarily, unreasonably.

*antonym* insufficiently.

**exchange** *v* bandy, bargain, barter, change, commute, convert, interchange, reciprocate, replace, substitute, swap, switch, toss about, trade, truck.

*n* bargain, barter, bourse, brush, chat, commerce, conversation, converse, conversion, dealing, interchange, intercourse, market, quid pro quo, reciprocity, replacement, substitution, swap, switch, tit for tat, trade, traffic, truck.

**excise**[1] *n* customs, duty, impost, levy, surcharge, tariff, tax, toll, VAT.

**excise**[2] *v* bowdlerise, cut, cut out, delete, destroy, eradicate, erase, expunge, expurgate, exterminate, extirpate, extract, remove, rescind.

**excision** *n* bowdlerisation, deletion, destruction, eradication, expunction, expurgation, extermination, extirpation, removal.

**excitable** *adj* edgy, emotional, explosive, feisty, fiery, hasty, highly-strung, high-strung, hot-headed, hot-tempered, inflammable, irascible, mercurial, nervous, nervy, passionate, quick-tempered, restive, restless, sensitive, susceptible, temperamental, unstable, violent, volatile.

*antonyms* calm, impassive.

**excite** *v* activate, actuate, aerate, affect, agitate, animate, arouse, awaken, discompose, disturb, elate, electrify, elicit, engender, evoke, fire, foment, galvanise, generate, ignite, impress, incite, induce, inflame, initiate, inspire, instigate, kindle, motivate, move, provoke, quicken, rouse, stimulate, stir up, suscitate, sway, thrill, titillate, touch, turn on, upset, waken, warm, whet.

*antonyms* bore, quell.

**excited** *adj* aflame, agitated, animated, aroused, awakened, breathless, corybantic, discomposed, disturbed, eager, elated, enthused, enthusiastic, feverish, flurried, flustered, fluttered, frantic, frenzied, high, impassioned, moved, nervous, overwrought, restive, restless, roused, ruffled, stimulated, stirred, thrilled, titillated, upset, wild, worked up, wrought-up.

*antonyms* apathetic, bored.

**excitement** *n* action, activity, ado, adventure, agitation, animation, brouhaha, clamour, commotion, deliriousness, delirium, discomposure, eagerness, elation, enthusiasm, excitation, ferment, fever, flurry, furore, fuss, heat, hubbub, hue and cry, hurly-burly, kerfuffle, kicks, passion, perturbation, restlessness, stimulation, stimulus, tew, thrill, titillation, tumult, unrest, urge.

*antonyms* apathy, calm.

**exciting** *adj* cliff-hanging, electrifying, encouraging, enthralling, exhilarating, impressive, inspiring, intoxicating, moving, nail-biting, promising, provocative, rousing, sensational, stimulating, stirring, striking, suspenseful, swashbuckling, thrilling, titillating.

*antonyms* boring, unexciting.

**exclaim** *v* blurt, call, cry, declare, ejaculate, interject, proclaim, shout, utter, vociferate.

**exclamation** *n* call, cry, ecphonesis, ejaculation, expletive, interjection, outcry, shout, utterance, vociferation.

**exclamatory** *adj* dramatic, ejaculatory, exclamative, interjaculatory, interjectional, interjectionary, interjectural, melodramatic, sensationalist.

**exclude** *v* anathematise, ban, bar, blackball, blacklist, bounce, boycott, debar, disallow, eject, eliminate, embargo, evict, except, excommunicate, expel, forbid, ignore, include out, interclude, interdict, keep out, leave out, omit, ostracise, oust, preclude, prohibit, proscribe, refuse, reject, remove, repudiate, rule out, shut out, veto.

*antonyms* admit, allow, include.

**exclusion** *n* ban, bar, boycott, debarment, disfellowship, ejection, elimination, embargo, eviction, exception, expulsion, forbiddal, forbiddance, interdict, non-admission, omission, ostracisation, preclusion, prohibition, proscription, refusal, rejection, removal, repudiation, veto.

*antonyms* admittance, allowance, inclusion.

**exclusive** *adj* absolute, arrogant, chic, choice, clannish, classy, cliquey, cliquish, closed, complete, confined, discriminative, elegant, entire, esoteric, exclusory, fashionable, full, limited, luxurious, monopolistic, narrow, only, peculiar, posh, private, restricted, restrictive, select, selective, selfish, single, snobbish, sole, total, undivided, unique, unshared, whole.

**exclusive of** barring, debarring, except, except for, excepting, excluding, omitting, ruling out.

*antonym* inclusive of.

**excommunicate** *v* anathematise, ban, banish, bar, blacklist, debar, denounce, disfellowship, eject, exclude, execrate, expel, outlaw, proscribe, remove, repudiate, unchurch.

**excrescence** *n* appendage, bump, excrement, growth, intumescence, knob, lump, misgrowth, outgrowth, process, projection, prominence, protrusion, protuberance, swelling, tumour, wart.

**excrete** *v* crap, defecate, discharge, egest, eject, eliminate, evacuate, expel, exude, secrete, shit, urinate, void.

**excretion** *n* crap, defecation, discharge, droppings, dung, eccrisis, egesta, ejection, elimination, evacuation, excrement, excreta, expulsion, exudation, ordure, perspiration, rejectamenta, shit(e), skat, stool, sudation, urination, voidance.

**excretory** *adj* defecatory, egestive, emunctory, excremental, excrementitial, excrementitious, exudative, faecal, perspiratory, sudatory, urinary, urinative.

**excruciating** *adj* acute, agonising, atrocious, bitter, burning, exquisite, extreme, harrowing, insufferable, intense, intolerable, painful, piercing, racking, savage, searing, severe, sharp, tormenting, torturing, torturous, unbearable, unendurable.

**exculpate** *v* absolve, acquit, clear, deliver, discharge, disculpate, excuse, exonerate, forgive, free, justify, let off, pardon, release, vindicate.

*antonyms* blame, condemn.

**exculpation** *n* absolution, acquittal, clearance, discharge, excuse, exoneration, expurgation, freedom, justification, pardon, release, vindication.

*antonym* condemnation.

**excursion** *n* airing, breather, day trip, detour, deviation, digression, divagation, ecbole, episode, excursus, expedition, jaunt, journey, outing, ramble, ride, sashay, tour, trip, walk, wandering, wayzgoose.

**excusable** *adj* allowable, defensible, explainable, explicable, forgivable, ignorable, justifiable, minor, pardonable, permissible, slight, understandable, venial, vindicable, warrantable.

*antonym* blameworthy.

**excuse** *v* absolve, acquit, apologise for, condone, defend, discharge, exculpate, exempt, exonerate, explain, extenuate, forgive, free, ignore, indulge, justify, let off, liberate, mitigate, overlook, palliate, pardon, release, relieve, sanction, spare, tolerate, vindicate, warrant, wink at.

*n* alibi, apology, cop-out, defence, disguise, evasion, exculpation, exoneration, expedient, explanation, extenuation, grounds, justification, makeshift, mitigation, mockery, palliation, parody, plea, pretence, pretext, put-off, reason, semblance, shift, substitute, subterfuge, travesty, vindication.

**ex-directory** *adj* unlisted.

**execrable** *adj* abhorrent, abominable, accursed, appalling, atrocious, damnable, deplorable, despicable, detestable, disgusting, foul, hateful, heinous, horrible, loathsome, nauseous, obnoxious, odious, offensive, repulsive, revolting, shocking, sickening, vile.

*antonyms* admirable, esteemable.

**execrate** *v* abhor, abominate, anathematise, blast, condemn, curse, damn, denounce, denunciate, deplore, despise, detest, excoriate, fulminate, hate, imprecate, inveigh against, loathe, revile, vilify.

*antonyms* commend, praise.

**execration** *n* abhorrence, abomination, anathema, condemnation, contempt, curse, damnation, detestation, excoriation, fulmination, hate, hatred, imprecation, invective, loathing, malediction, odium, revilement, vilification, vituperation.

*antonyms* commendation, praise.

**execute**[1] *v* behead, burn, crucify, decapitate, decollate, electrocute, guillotine, hang, kill, liquidate, put to death, shoot.

**execute**[2] *v* accomplish, achieve, administer, complete, consummate, deliver, discharge, dispatch, do, effect, effectuate, enact, enforce, expedite, finish, fulfil, implement, perform, prosecute, realise, render, seal, serve, sign, validate.

**execution**[1] *n* auto-da-fé, beheading, burning, capital punishment, crucifixion, death, death penalty, decapitation, decollation, electrocution, firing squad, fusillation, guillotining, hanging, killing, shooting.

**execution**[2] *n* accomplishment, achievement, administration, completion, consummation, delivery, discharge, dispatch, effect, effectuation, enactment, enforcement, exercitation, implementation, manner, mode, operation, performance, prosecution, realisation, rendering, rendition, style, technique, warrant, writ.

**executioner** *n* assassin, exterminator, hangman, headsman, hit man, killer, liquidator, murderer, slayer.

**executive** *n* administration, administrator, controller, director, directorate, directors, government, hierarchy, leadership, management, manager, official, organiser.

*adj* administrative, controlling, decision-making, directing, directorial, governing, gubernatorial, guiding, leading, managerial, organisational, organising, regulating, supervisory.

**exemplar** *n* archetype, copy, criterion, embodiment, epitome, example, exemplification, ideal, illustration, instance, model, paradigm, paragon, pattern, prototype, specimen, standard, type, yardstick.

**exemplary** *adj* admirable, admonitory, cautionary, commendable, correct, estimable, excellent, faultless, flawless, good, honourable, ideal, laudable, meritorious, model, monitory, perfect, praiseworthy, punctilious, sterling, unerring, unexceptionable, warning, worthy.

*antonyms* imperfect, unworthy.

**exemplify** *v* demonstrate, depict, display, embody, ensample, epitomise, evidence, example, exhibit, illustrate, instance, manifest, represent, show, typify.

**exempt** *v* absolve, discharge, dismiss, except, excuse, exonerate, free, let off, liberate, make an exception of, release, relieve, spare.

*adj* absolved, clear, discharged, excepted, excluded, excused, favoured, free, immune, liberated, released, spared.

*antonym* liable.

**exemption** *n* absolution, discharge, dispensation, exception, exclusion, exoneration, freedom, immunity, indulgence, overslaugh, privilege, release.

*antonym* liability.

**exercise** *v* afflict, agitate, annoy, apply, burden, discharge, discipline, distress, disturb, drill, employ, enjoy, exert, habituate, inure, occupy, operate, pain, perturb, practise, preoccupy, train, trouble, try, upset, use, utilise, vex, wield, work out, worry.

*n* accomplishment, action, activity, aerobics, application, assignment, daily dozen, discharge, discipline, drill, drilling, effort, employment, enjoyment, exercitation, exertion, fulfilment, implementation, krieg(s)spiel, labour, lesson, operation, physical jerks, practice, problem, schooling, school-work, task, toil, training, use, utilisation, war-game, work, work-out.

**exert** *v* apply, bring to bear, employ, exercise, expend, use, utilise, wield.

**exert oneself** apply oneself, concentrate, endeavour, labour, strain, strive, struggle, sweat, take pains, toil, work.

**exertion** *n* action, application, assiduity, attempt, diligence, effort, employment, endeavour, exercise, industry, labour, operation, pains, perseverance, sedulousness, strain, stretch, struggle, toil, travail, trial, use, utilisation, work.

*antonyms* idleness, rest.

**exhalation** *n* air, aura, breath, discharge, ectoplasm, effluvium, efflux, emanation, emission, evaporation, exhaust, expiration, flow, fog, fume, fumes, mist, respiration, smoke, steam, vapour, vapours.

*antonym* inhalation.

**exhale** *v* breathe (out), discharge, eject, emanate, emit, evaporate, expel, expire, give off, issue, respire, steam.

*antonym* inhale.

**exhaust** *v* bankrupt, beggar, bugger, consume, cripple, debilitate, deplete, disable, dissipate, drain, dry, empty, enervate, enfeeble, expend, fatigue, finish, impoverish, overtax, overtire, overwork, prostrate, run through, sap, spend, squander, strain, tax, tire (out), use up, void, waste, weaken, wear out, weary.

*antonym* refresh.

*n* discharge, eduction, effluvium, emanation, emission, exhalation, fumes.

**exhausted** *adj* all in, bare, beat, buggered, burned out, clapped-out, consumed, crippled, dead, dead tired, dead-beat, debilitated, depleted, disabled, dissipated, dog-tired, done, done in, drained, dry, effete, empty, enervated, enfeebled, expended, fatigued, finished, fogged out, forjeskit, forswunk, gone, jaded, jiggered, knackered, out for the count, outspent, pooped, prostrated, sapped, spent, squandered, tired out, used up, void, washed-out, washed-up, wasted, weak, weary, whacked, worn out, zonked.

*antonyms* conserved, fresh, vigorous.

**exhausting** *adj* arduous, backbreaking, crippling, debilitating, difficult, draining, enervating, fatiguing, formidable, gruelling, hard, knackering, laborious, punishing, sapping, severe, strenuous, taxing, testing, tiring, vigorous.

*antonym* refreshing.

**exhaustion** *n* consumption, debilitation, depletion, effeteness, emptying, enervation, fatigue, feebleness, inanition, jet-lag, lassitude, prostration, tiredness, weariness.

*antonym* freshness.

**exhaustive** *adj* all-embracing, all-inclusive, all-out, complete, comprehensive, definitive, detailed, encyclopaedic, expansive, extensive, far-reaching, full, full-scale, in-depth, intensive, sweeping, thorough, thoroughgoing, total.

*antonym* incomplete.

**exhibit** *v* air, demonstrate, disclose, display, evidence, evince, expose, express, flaunt, indicate, manifest, offer, parade, present, reveal, show, showcase, sport.

*antonym* hide.

*n* display, exhibition, illustration, model, show.

**exhibition** *n* airing, array, demonstration, display, exhibit, expo, exposition, fair, manifestation, panopticon, performance, presentation, representation, show, showcase, showing, spectacle.

**exhibitionist** *n* extrovert, flasher, pervert, self-advertiser, show-off.

**exhilarate** *v* animate, cheer, delight, elate, energise, enhearten, enliven, exalt, excite, gladden, hearten, inspirit, invigorate, lift, stimulate, thrill, vitalise.

*antonyms* bore, discourage.

**exhilarating** *adj* breathtaking, cheering, enlivening, euphoriant, exalting, exciting, exhilarant, exhilarative, exhilaratory, gladdening, heartsome, invigorating, mind-blowing, stimulating, thrilling, vitalising.

*antonyms* boring, discouraging.

**exhilaration** *n* animation, ardour, cheerfulness, dash, delight, élan, elation, exaltation, excitement, gaiety, gladness, glee, gleefulness, gusto, high spirits, hilarity, joy, joyfulness, liveliness, mirth, sprightliness, vivacity, zeal.

*antonyms* boredom, discouragement.

**exhort** *v* admonish, advise, beseech, bid, call upon, caution, counsel, encourage, enjoin, entreat, goad, implore, incite, inflame, inspire, instigate, persuade, press, spur, urge, warn.

**exhortation** *n* admonition, advice, allocution, beseeching, bidding, caution, counsel, encouragement, enjoinder, entreaty, goading, incitement, lecture, paraenesis, persuasion, protreptic, sermon, urging, warning.

**exhortative** *adj* begging, beseeching, imploring, paraenetic(al), persuasive, protreptic, protreptical.

**exhume** *v* dig up, disentomb, disinhume, disinter, excavate, unbury, unearth.

*antonym* bury.

**exigency** *n* acuteness, bind, constraint, crisis, criticalness, crunch, demand, difficulty, distress, emergency, exigence, extremity, fix, hardship, imperativeness, jam, juncture, necessity, need, needfulness, pass, pickle, pinch, plight, predicament, pressure, quandary, requirement, scrape, stew, strait, stress, urgency.

**exigent** *adj* acute, arduous, constraining, critical, crucial, demanding, difficult, exacting, exhausting, hard, harsh, imperative, importunate, insistent, necessary, needful, pressing, rigorous, severe, stiff, strict, stringent, taxing, tough, urgent.

*antonym* mild.

**exile** *n* banishment, deportation, deportee, émigré, exilement, expatriate, expatriation, expulsion, galut(h), ostracism, outcast, proscription, refugee, separation.

*v* banish, deport, drive out, expatriate, expel, ostracise, oust, proscribe.

**exist** *v* abide, be, be available, be extant, breathe, continue, endure, happen, have one's being, last, live, obtain, occur, prevail, remain, stand, subsist, survive.

**existence** *n* actuality, animation, being, breath, continuance, continuation, creation, creature, duration, endurance, entity, esse, haecceity, inbeing, life, reality, subsistence, survival, the world, thing.

*antonym* non-existence.

**existent** *adj* abiding, actual, around, current, enduring, existing, extant, living, obtaining, present, prevailing, real, remaining, standing, surviving.

*antonym* non-existent.

**exit** *n* adieu, aperture, congé, departure, door, doorway, egress, evacuation, exodus, farewell, gate, going, leave-taking, outlet, retirement, retreat, vent, way out, withdrawal.

*antonym* entrance.

*v* arrive, depart, enter, issue, leave, retire, retreat, take one's leave, withdraw.

**exodus** *n* departure, evacuation, exit, flight, hegira, leaving, long march, migration, retirement, retreat, withdrawal.

**exonerate** *v* absolve, acquit, clear, discharge, disculpate, dismiss, except, exculpate, excuse, exempt, free, justify, let off, liberate, pardon, release, relieve, vindicate.

*antonym* incriminate.

**exoneration** *n* absolution, acquittal, amnesty, deliverance, discharge, dismissal, exception, exculpation, exemption, freeing, immunity, indemnity, justification, liberation, pardon, release, relief, vindication.

*antonym* incrimination.

**exorbitance** *n* excess, excessiveness, extravagance, immoderateness, immoderation, inordinateness, monstrousness, nimiety, preposterousness, unreasonableness.

*antonyms* fairness, reasonableness.

**exorbitant** *adj* enormous, excessive, extortionate, extravagant, extreme, immoderate, inordinate, monstrous, outrageous, preposterous, unconscionable, undue, unreasonable, unwarranted.

*antonyms* fair, reasonable.

**exorcise** *v* adjure, cast out, drive out, expel, exsufflate, purify.

**exorcism** *n* adjuration, deliverance, expulsion, exsufflation, purification.

**exotic** *adj* alien, bizarre, colourful, curious, different, external, extraneous, extraordinary, extrinsic, fascinating, foreign, foreign-looking, glamorous, imported, introduced, mysterious, naturalised, outlandish, outré, peculiar, recherché, strange, striking, unfamiliar, unusual.

*antonym* ordinary.

**expand** *v* amplify, augment, bloat, blow up, branch out, broaden, develop, diffuse, dilate, dispread, distend, diversify, elaborate, embellish, enlarge, expatiate, expound, extend, fatten, fill out, flesh out, grow, heighten, increase, inflate, lengthen, magnify, multiply, open, outspread, prolong, protract, snowball, spread, stretch, swell, thicken, unfold, unfurl, unravel, unroll, wax, widen.

*antonyms* contract, précis.

**expanded** *adj* bloated, blown out, blown up, dilated, distended, enlarged, increased, inflated, puffed out, swollen.

**expanse** *n* area, breadth, extent, field, plain, range, space, stretch, sweep, tract, vast, vastness.

**expansible** *adj* distensible, distensile, expansile, inflatable.

**expansion** *n* amplification, augmentation, development, diffusion, dilatation, dilation, distension, diversification, enlargement, expanse, extension, growth, increase, inflation, magnification, multiplication, spread, swelling, unfolding, unfurling.

*antonym* contraction.

**expansive** *adj* affable, all-embracing, broad, communicative, comprehensive, dilating, distending, easy, effusive, elastic, expanding, expatiative, expatiatory, extendable, extensive, far-reaching, free, friendly, garrulous, genial, inclusive, loquacious, open, outgoing, sociable, stretching, stretchy, swelling, talkative, thorough, unreserved, voluminous, warm, wide, wide-ranging, widespread.

*antonyms* cold, reserved.

**expatiate** *v* amplify, descant, develop, dilate, dwell on, elaborate, embellish, enlarge, expound.

**expatriate** *n* displaced person, emigrant, émigré, exile, ex-pat, refugee.

*v* banish, deport, exile, expel, ostracise, oust, proscribe.

*adj* banished, emigrant, émigré, exiled.

**expect** *v* anticipate, assume, await, bank on, bargain for, believe, calculate, conjecture, contemplate, count on, demand, envisage, forecast, foresee, hope for, imagine, insist on, look for, look forward to, predict, presume, project, reckon, rely on, require, suppose, surmise, think, trust, want, wish.

**expectancy** *n* anticipation, assumption, belief, conjecture, curiosity, eagerness, expectation, hope, likelihood, outlook, prediction, presumption, probability, prospect, supposition, surmise, suspense, waiting.

**expectant** *adj* agog, anticipating, anxious, apprehensive, awaiting, curious, eager, enceinte, expecting, gravid, hopeful, in suspense, pregnant, ready, watchful.

**expectantly** *adv* eagerly, expectingly, hopefully, in anticipation, optimistically.

**expectation** *n* anticipation, apprehension, assumption, assurance, belief, calculation, chance, confidence, conjecture, demand, eagerness, expectancy, fear, forecast, hope, insistence, likelihood, optimism, outlook, possibility, prediction, presumption, probability, projection, promise, prospect, reliance, requirement, supposition, surmise, suspense, trust, want, wish.

**expected** *adj* anticipated, awaited, en l'aire, hoped-for, longed-for, predicted, promised.

*antonym* unexpected.

**expecting** *adj* enceinte, expectant, gravid, in the club, in the family way, pregnant, with child.

**expedience** *n* advantage, advantageousness, advisability, appropriateness, aptness, benefit, convenience, desirability, effectiveness, expediency, fitness, gainfulness, helpfulness, judiciousness, meetness, practicality, pragmatism, profitability, profitableness, properness, propriety, prudence, suitability, usefulness, utilitarianism, utility.

**expedient** *adj* advantageous, advisable, appropriate, beneficial, convenient, desirable, effective, fit, helpful, judicious, meet, opportune, politic, practical, pragmatic, profitable, proper, prudent, serviceable, suitable, useful, utilitarian, worthwhile.

*antonym* inexpedient.

*n* contrivance, device, dodge, makeshift, manoeuvre, means, measure, method, resort, resource, ruse, scheme, shift, stop-gap, stratagem, substitute.

**expedite** *v* accelerate, advance, aid, assist, dispatch, facilitate, forward, further, hasten, hurry, precipitate, press, promote, quicken, rush, speed.

*antonym* delay.

**expedition**[1] *n* company, crusade, enterprise, excursion, exploration, explorers, hike, journey, mission, pilgrimage, quest, raid, ramble, safari, sail, team, tour, travellers, trek, trip, undertaking, voyage, voyagers.

**expedition**[2] *n* alacrity, briskness, celerity, dispatch, expeditiousness, haste, hurry, immediacy, promptness, quickness, rapidity, readiness, speed, swiftness.

*antonym* delay.

**expeditious** *adj* active, alert, brisk, diligent, efficient, fast, hasty, immediate, instant, meteoric, prompt, quick, rapid, ready, speedy, swift.

*antonym* slow.

**expel** *v* ban, banish, bar, belch, blackball, cast out, disbar, discharge, dislodge, dismiss, drive out, drum out, egest, eject, evict, exclude, exile, expatriate, hoof out, oust, proscribe, remove, send packing, spew, throw out, turf out.

*antonym* admit.

**expend** *v* consume, disburse, dissipate, employ, exhaust, fork out, pay, shell out, spend, use, use up.

*antonym* save.

**expendable** *adj* dispensable, disposable, inessential, non-essential, replaceable, unimportant, unnecessary.

*antonyms* indispensable, necessary.

**expenditure** *n* application, charge, consumption, cost, disbursement, expense, outgo, outgoings, outlay, output, payment, spending.

*antonyms* profit, savings.

**expense** *n* charge, consumption, cost, damage, disbursement, expenditure, loss, outlay, output, payment, sacrifice, spending, toll, use.

**expenses** *n* costs, incidentals, outgoings, outlay, overheads.

**expensive** *adj* costly, dear, excessive, exorbitant, extortionate, extravagant, high-priced, inordinate, lavish, overpriced, rich, steep, stiff.

*antonyms* cheap, inexpensive.

**experience** *n* adventure, affair, assay, contact, doing, encounter, episode, event, evidence, exposure, familiarity, happening, incident, involvement, know-how, knowledge, observation, occurrence, ordeal, participation, practice, proof, taste, test, training, trial, understanding.

*antonym* inexperience.

*v* apprehend, behold, empathise, encounter, endure, face, feel, have, know, meet, observe, perceive, sample, sense, suffer, sustain, taste, try, undergo.

**experienced** *adj* accomplished, adept, capable, competent, expert, familiar, knowing, knowledgeable, master, mature, practised, professional, qualified, schooled, seasoned, skilful, sophisticated, streetwise, tested, trained, travailed, travelled, tried, veteran, well-versed, wise, worldly, worldly-wise.

*antonym* inexperienced.

**experiment** *n* assay, attempt, ballon d'essai, examination, experimentation, heurism, investigation, procedure, proof, research, test, trial, trial and error, trial run, venture.

*v* assay, examine, investigate, research, sample, test, try, verify.

**experimental** *adj* empiric(al), exploratory, heuristic, peirastic, pilot, preliminary, probationary, provisional, speculative, tentative, test, trial, trial-and-error.

**expert** *n* ace, adept, authority, boffin, connoisseur, dab hand, dabster, deacon, dean, maestro, master, pastmaster, pro, professional, specialist, virtuoso, wizard.

*adj* able, adept, adroit, apt, clever, crack, deft, dexterous, experienced, facile, handy, knowledgeable, master, masterly, practised, professional, proficient, qualified, skilful, skilled, trained, virtuoso.

*antonym* novice.

**expertise** *n* ableness, adroitness, aptness, cleverness, command, deftness, dexterity, expertness, facility, judgement, knack, know-how, knowledge, masterliness, mastery, proficiency, skilfulness, skill, virtuosity.

*antonym* inexpertness.

**expertness** *n* ableness, adroitness, aptness, command, deftness, dexterity, expertise, facility, finesse, judgement, know-how, knowledge, masterliness, mastery, proficiency, savoir-faire, skilfulness, skill.

*antonym* inexpertness.

**expiation** *n* amends, atonement, penance, ransom, redemption, redress, shrift.

**expiatory** *adj* atoning, piacular, purgative, purgatory, redemptive.

**expire** *v* cease, close, conclude, decease, depart, die, discontinue, emit, end, exhale, finish, lapse, perish, run out, stop, terminate.

*antonyms* begin, continue.

**expiry** *n* cease, cessation, close, conclusion, death, decease, demise, departure, end, expiration, finis, finish, termination.

*antonyms* beginning, continuation.

**explain** *v* account for, clarify, clear up, construe, decipher, decode, define, demonstrate, describe,

disclose, elucidate, enucleate, excuse, explicate, expound, gloss, gloze, illustrate, interpret, justify, resolve, simplify, solve, spell out, teach, translate, unfold, unravel, untangle.

*antonyms* obfuscate, obscure.

**explanation** *n* account, answer, cause, clarification, definition, demonstration, description, éclaircissement, elucidation, enucleation, excuse, exegesis, explication, exposition, gloss, illustration, interpretation, justification, legend, meaning, mitigation, motive, reason, resolution, sense, significance, solution, vindication, voice-over.

**explanatory** *adj* demonstrative, descriptive, elucidative, elucidatory, exegetic, exegetical, explicative, expositive, expository, illuminative, illustrational, illustrative, illustratory, interpretive, justifying.

**explicable** *adj* accountable, definable, determinable, explainable, exponible, intelligible, interpretable, justifiable, resolvable, solvable, understandable.

**explicate** *v* clarify, construct, develop, devise, elucidate, evolve, explain, expound, formulate, interpret, set forth, unfold, unravel, untangle, work out.

*antonyms* confuse, obscure.

**explicit** *adj* absolute, accurate, categorical, certain, clear, declared, definite, detailed, direct, distinct, exact, express, frank, open, outspoken, patent, plain, positive, precise, specific, stated, straightforward, unambiguous, unequivocal, unqualified, unreserved.

*antonyms* inexplicit, vague.

**explode** *v* belie, blow up, burst, debunk, detonate, discharge, discredit, disprove, erupt, give the lie to, go off, invalidate, rebut, refute, repudiate, set off, shatter, shiver.

*antonym* prove.

**exploit** *n* accomplishment, achievement, adventure, attainment, deed, feat, gest(e), stunt.

*v* abuse, bleed, capitalise on, cash in on, fleece, impose on, make capital out of, manipulate, milk, misuse, profit by, rip off, skin, soak, take advantage of, turn to account, use, utilise.

**exploitation** *n* abuse, imposition, manipulation, misuse, rip-off, sexploitation, speciesism.

**exploration** *n* analysis, examination, expedition, inquiry, inquisition, inspection, investigation, probe, reconnaissance, research, safari, scrutiny, search, study, survey, tour, travel, trip, voyage.

**exploratory** *adj* analytic(al), experimental, fact-finding, investigative, pilot, probing, searching, tentative, trial, wildcat.

**explore** *v* analyse, case, examine, inspect, investigate, probe, prospect, reconnoitre, research, scout, scrutinise, search, survey, tour, travel, traverse.

**explosion** *n* bang, blast, burst, clap, crack, debunking, detonation, discharge, discrediting, eruption, fit, outbreak, outburst, paroxysm, refutation, report.

**explosive** *adj* charged, dangerous, fiery, hazardous, overwrought, perilous, stormy, tense, touchy, ugly, unstable, vehement, violent, volatile, volcanic.

*antonym* calm.

*n* cordite, dynamite, gelignite, gun-powder, jelly, lyddite, melinite, nitroglycerine, TNT.

**exponent** *n* advocate, backer, champion, commentator, defender, demonstrator, elucidator, example, executant, exegetist, exemplar, expositor, expounder, illustration, illustrator, indication, interpreter, model, performer, player, presenter, promoter, propagandist, proponent, representative, sample, specimen, spokesman, spokeswoman, supporter, type, upholder.

**expose** *v* air, betray, bring to light, denounce, detect, disclose, display, divulge, endanger, exhibit, hazard, imperil, jeopardise, manifest, present, reveal, risk, show, uncover, unearth, unmask, unveil, wash one's dirty linen in public.

*antonym* cover.

**expose to** acquaint with, bring into contact with, familiarise with, introduce to, lay open to, subject to.

*antonym* protect.

**exposé** *n* account, article, disclosure, divulgence, expose, exposure, revelation, uncovering.

**exposed** *adj* bare, exhibited, laid bare, liable, on display, on show, on view, open, prey to, revealed, shown, susceptible, unconcealed, uncovered, unprotected, unsheltered, unveiled, vulnerable.

*antonyms* covered, sheltered.

**exposition** *n* account, commentary, critique, demonstration, description, discourse, display, elucidation, exegesis, exhibition, explanation, explication, expo, fair, illustration, interpretation, monograph, paper, presentation, show, study, thesis.

**expository** *adj* declaratory, descriptive, elucidative, exegetic, explanatory, explicative, explicatory, hermeneutic, illustrative, interpretative, interpretive.

**expostulate** *v* argue, dissuade, plead, protest, reason, remonstrate.

**exposure** *n* acquaintance, airing, aspect, betrayal, cold, contact, conversance, conversancy, danger, denunciation, detection, disclosure, discovery, display, divulgence, divulging, exhibition, experience, exposé, familiarity, frontage, hazard, introduction, jeopardy, knowledge, lack of shelter, location, manifestation, outlook, position, presentation, publicity, revelation, risk, setting, showing, uncovering, unmasking, unveiling, view, vulnerability.

**expound** *v* describe, elucidate, explain, explicate, illustrate, interpet, preach, sermonise, set forth, spell out, unfold.

**express** *v* articulate, assert, asseverate, bespeak, communicate, conceive, convey, couch, declare, denote, depict, designate, disclose, divulge, embody, enunciate, evince, exhibit, extract, force out, formulate, formulise, indicate, intimate, manifest, phrase, pronounce, put, put across, represent, reveal, say, show, signify, speak, stand for, state, symbolise, tell, testify, utter, verbalise, voice, word.

*adj* accurate, categorical, certain, clear, clear-cut, definite, direct, distinct, especial, exact, explicit, fast, high-speed, manifest, non-stop, outright, particular, plain, pointed, precise, quick, rapid, singular, special, speedy, stated, swift, unambiguous, unqualified.

*antonym* vague.

**expression** *n* air, announcement, appearance, aspect, assertion, asseveration, communication, countenance, declaration, delivery, demonstration, diction, embodiment, emphasis, enunciation, execution, exhibition, face, idiom, indication, intonation, language, locution, look, manifestation, mention, mien, phrase, phraseology, phrasing, pronouncement, reflex, remark, representation, set phrase, show, sign, speaking, speech, statement, style, symbol, term, token, turn of phrase, utterance, verbalisation, verbalism, voicing, word, wording.

**expressionless** *adj* blank, dead-pan, dull, empty, glassy, impassive, inscrutable, poker-faced, straight-faced, vacuous, wooden.

*antonym* expressive.

**expressive** *adj* allusive, demonstrative, eloquent, emphatic, energetic, forcible, indicative, informative, lively, meaningful, mobile, moving, poignant, pointed, pregnant, representative, revealing, significant, striking, strong, suggestive, sympathetic, telling, thoughtful, vivid.

*antonyms* expressionless, poker-faced.

**expressly** *adv* absolutely, categorically, clearly, decidedly, definitely, distinctly, especially, exactly, explicitly, intentionally, manifestly, on purpose, outright, particularly, plainly, pointedly, positively, precisely, purposely, specially, specifically, unambiguously, unequivocally.

**expropriate** *v* annex, appropriate, arrogate, assume, commandeer, confiscate, dispossess, disseise, impound, requisition, seize, sequester, take, unhouse.

**expulsion** *n* banishment, debarment, disbarment, discharge, dislodgement, dislodging, dismissal, ejection, ejectment, eviction, exclusion, exile, expatriation, extrusion, proscription, removal.

**expunge** *v* abolish, annihilate, annul, blot out, cancel, delete, destroy, efface, eradicate, erase, exterminate, extinguish, extirpate, obliterate, raze, remove, uncreate, unmake, wipe out.

**expurgate** *v* blue-pencil, bowdlerise, censor, clean up, cut, emend, purge, purify, sanitise.

**exquisite** *adj* acute, admirable, alembicated, appreciative, attractive, beautiful, charming, choice, comely, consummate, cultivated, dainty, delicate, delicious, discerning, discriminating, elegant, excellent, excruciating, fastidious, fine, flawless, impeccable, incomparable, intense, keen, lovely, matchless, meticulous, outstanding, peerless, perfect, piercing, pleasing, poignant, polished, precious, rare, refined, select, selective, sensitive, sharp, splendid, striking, superb, superlative, too-too.

*antonyms* flawed, imperfect, poor, ugly.

**extant** *adj* alive, existent, existing, in existence, living, remaining, subsistent, subsisting, surviving.

*antonyms* dead, extinct, non-existent.

**extemporary** *adj* ad-lib, expedient, extemporaneous, extempore, free, impromptu, improvisatory, improvised, jazz, made-up, makeshift, offhand, off-the-cuff, on-the-spot, spontaneous, temporary, unplanned, unpremeditated, unprepared, unrehearsed.

*antonym* planned.

**extemporise** *v* ad-lib, autoschediaze, improvise, make up, play by ear.

**extend** *v* advance, amplify, attain, augment, bestow, broaden, confer, continue, develop, dilate, drag out, draw out, elongate, enhance, enlarge, expand, give, grant, hold out, impart, increase, last, lengthen, offer, present, proffer, prolong, protract, pull out, reach, spin out, spread, stretch, supplement, take, uncoil, unfold, unfurl, unroll, widen, yield.

*antonym* shorten.

**extension** *n* accretion, addendum, addition, adjunct, amplification, annexe, appendage, appendix, augmentation, branch, broadening, continuation, delay, development, dilatation, distension, el, elongation, enhancement, enlargement, expansion, extent, increase, lengthening, postponement, prolongation, protraction, spread, stretching, supplement, widening, wing.

**extensive** *adj* all-inclusive, broad, capacious, commodious, comprehensive, expanded, expansive, extended, far-flung, far-reaching, general, great, huge, large, large-scale, lengthy, long, pervasive, prevalent, protracted, roomy, spacious, sweeping, thorough, thoroughgoing, universal, unrestricted, vast, voluminous, wholesale, wide, widespread.

*antonyms* narrow, restricted.

**extent** *n* amount, amplitude, area, bounds, breadth, bulk, compass, degree, dimension(s), duration, expanse, expansion, length, magnitude, measure, play, proportions, quantity, range, reach, scope, size, sphere, spread, stretch, sweep, term, time, volume, width.

**extenuate** *v* decrease, diminish, excuse, lessen, minimise, mitigate, moderate, modify, palliate, qualify, reduce, soften, temper, weaken.

**extenuating** *adj* exculpatory, extenuative, extenuatory, justifying, mitigating, moderating, palliative, qualifying.

**exterior** *n* appearance, aspect, coating, covering, externals, façade, face, finish, outside, shell, skin, superficies, surface.

*antonym* interior.

*adj* alien, exotic, external, extraneous, extrinsic, foreign, outer, outermost, outside, outward, peripheral, superficial, surface, surrounding.

*antonym* interior.

**exterminate** *v* abolish, annihilate, deracinate, destroy, eliminate, eradicate, extirpate, massacre, wipe out.

**extermination** *n* annihilation, deracination, destruction, elimination, eradication, extirpation, genocide, massacre.

**external** *adj* alien, apparent, exoteric, exotic, exterior, extern, externe, extramural, extraneous, extrinsic, foreign, independent, outer, outermost, outside, outward, superficial, surface, visible.

*antonym* internal.

**extinct** *adj* abolished, dead, defunct, doused, ended, exterminated, extinguished, gone, inactive, lost, obsolete, out, quenched, terminated, vanished, void.

*antonyms* extant, living.

**extinction** *n* abolition, annihilation, death, destruction, eradication, excision, extermination, extinguishment, extirpation, obliteration, oblivion, quietus.

**extinguish** *v* abolish, annihilate, destroy, douse, dout, eliminate, end, eradicate, erase, expunge, exterminate, extirpate, kill, obscure, put out, quench, remove, slake, smother, snuff out, stifle, suppress.

**extirpate** *v* abolish, annihilate, cut out, deracinate, destroy, eliminate, eradicate, erase, expunge, exterminate, extinguish, remove, root out, uproot, wipe out.

**extol** *v* acclaim, applaud, celebrate, commend, cry up, eulogise, exalt, glorify, laud, magnify, panegyrise, praise, puff.

*antonyms* blame, denigrate.

**extort** *v* blackmail, bleed, bully, coerce, exact, extract, force, milk, squeeze, wrest, wring.

**extortion** *n* blackmail, coercion, compulsion, demand, exaction, exorbitance, expensiveness, force, milking, oppression, overcharging, rapacity.

**extortionate** *adj* blood-sucking, exacting, excessive, exorbitant, extorsive, extortive, extravagant, grasping, hard, harsh, immoderate, inflated, inordinate, oppressive, outrageous, preposterous, rapacious, rigorous, severe, sky-high, unreasonable, usurious.

*antonym* reasonable.

**extra** *adj* accessory, added, additional, ancillary, auxiliary, excess, extraneous, for good measure, fresh, further, gash, inessential, leftover, more, needless, new, other, redundant, reserve, spare, supererogatory, superfluous, supernumerary, supplemental, supplementary, surplus, unnecessary, unneeded, unused.

*antonym* integral.

*n* accessory, addendum, addition, adjunct, affix, appendage, appurtenance, attachment, bonus, complement, extension, lagniappe, plus(s)age, supernumerary, supplement.

*adv* especially, exceptionally, extraordinarily, extremely, particularly, remarkably, uncommonly, unusually.

**extract** *v* abstract, choose, cite, cull, decoct, deduce, derive, develop, distil, draw, draw out, educe, elicit, enucleate, evoke, evolve, evulse, exact, express, extirpate, gather, get, glean, obtain, quote, reap, remove, select, uproot, withdraw, wrest, wring.

*antonym* insert.

*n* abstract, apozem, citation, clip, clipping, concentrate, cutting, decoction, decocture, distillate, distillation, essence, excerpt, juice, passage, quotation, selection.

**extraction** *n* ancestry, birth, blood, derivation, descent, distillation, drawing, educt, enucleation, extirpation, family, lineage, origin, parentage, pedigree, pulling, race, removal, separation, stock, withdrawal.

*antonym* insertion.

**extraneous** *adj* accidental, additional, adventitious, alien, exotic, exterior, external, extra, extrinsic, foreign, immaterial, impertinent, inadmissible, inapplicable, inapposite, inappropriate, inapt, incidental, inessential, irrelevant, needless, non-essential, peripheral, redundant, strange, superfluous, supplementary, tangential, unconnected, unessential, unnecessary, unneeded, unrelated.

*antonym* integral.

**extraordinary** *adj* amazing, bizarre, curious, exceptional, fantastic, marvellous, notable, noteworthy, odd, outstanding, particular, peculiar, phenomenal, rare, remarkable, significant, singular, special, strange, striking, surprising, uncommon, uncontemplated, unfamiliar, unheard-of, unimaginable, unique, unprecedented, unusual, unwonted, weird, wonderful.

*antonyms* commonplace, ordinary.

**extravagance** *n* absurdity, dissipation, exaggeration, excess, exorbitance, folly, hyperbole, immoderation, improvidence, lavishness, outrageousness, overspending, preposterousness, prodigality, profligacy, profusion, recklessness, squandering, unreasonableness, unrestraint, unthrift, unthriftiness, waste, wastefulness, wildness.

*antonyms* moderation, thrift.

**extravagant** *adj* absurd, costly, exaggerated, excessive, exorbitant, expensive, extortionate, fanciful, fancy, fantastic, flamboyant, flashy, foolish, garish, gaudy, grandiose, hyperbolic, hyperbolical, immoderate, improvident, imprudent, inordinate, lavish, ornate, ostentatious, outrageous, outré, overpriced, preposterous, pretentious, prodigal, profligate, reckless, showy, spendthrift, steep, thriftless, unreasonable, unrestrained, unthrifty, wasteful, wild.

*antonyms* moderate, thrifty.

**extravaganza** *n* display, féerie, pageant, show, spectacle, spectacular.

**extravert** *see* **extrovert**.

**extreme** *adj* acute, deep-dyed, dire, double-dyed, downright, Draconian, drastic, egregious, exaggerated, exceptional, excessive, exquisite, extraordinary, extravagant, fanatical, faraway, far-off, farthest, final, great, greatest, harsh, high, highest, immoderate, inordinate, intemperate, intense, last, maximum, out-and-out, outermost, outrageous, radical, red-hot, remarkable, remotest, rigid, severe, sheer, stern, strict, supreme, terminal, ultimate, ultra, unbending, uncommon, uncompromising, unconventional,

unreasonable, unusual, utmost, utter, uttermost, worst, zealous.

*antonyms* mild, moderate.

*n* acme, apex, apogee, boundary, climax, consummation, depth, edge, end, excess, extremity, height, limit, maximum, minimum, nadir, peak, pinnacle, pole, termination, top, ultimate, utmost, zenith.

**extremely** *adv* acutely, awfully, exceedingly, exceptionally, excessively, extraordinarily, greatly, highly, inordinately, intensely, markedly, mortal, passing, quite, severely, terribly, too, too-too, ultra, uncommonly, unusually, utterly, very.

**extremism** *n* fanaticism, radicalism, terrorism, ultraism, zeal, zealotism, zealotry.

*antonym* moderation.

**extremist** *n* die-hard, fanatic, militant, radical, terrorist, ultra, ultraconservative, zealot.

*antonym* moderate.

**extremity** *n* acme, acuteness, adversity, apex, apogee, border, bound, boundary, brim, brink, climax, consummation, crisis, crunch, depth, disaster, edge, emergency, end, excess, exigency, extreme, foot, frontier, hand, hardship, height, limit, margin, maximum, minimum, nadir, peak, pinnacle, plight, pole, rim, setback, terminal, termination, terminus, tip, top, trouble, ultimate, utmost, verge, zenith.

**extricate** *v* clear, deliver, disembarrass, disembrangle, disembroil, disengage, disentangle, disintricate, free, liberate, release, relieve, remove, rescue, withdraw.

*antonym* involve.

**extrinsic** *adj* accidental, alien, exotic, exterior, external, extraneous, foreign, imported, inessential, non-essential, outside, superficial.

*antonym* essential.

**extroversion** *n* amiability, amicability, extraversion, exuberance, friendliness, heartiness, sociability, viscerotonia.

**extrovert** *adj* amiable, amicable, extravert, exuberant, friendly, hail-fellow-well-met, hearty, outgoing, social, viscerotonic.

*antonym* introvert.

*n* joiner, life and soul of the party, mixer, socialiser.

*antonyms* introvert, loner.

**exuberance** *n* abundance, animation, buoyancy, cheerfulness, copiousness, eagerness, ebullience, effervescence, effusiveness, energy, enthusiasm, exaggeration, excessiveness, excitement, exhilaration, fulsomeness, high spirits, lavishness, life, liveliness, lushness, luxuriance, pizzazz, plenitude, prodigality, profusion, rankness, richness, spirit, sprightliness, superabundance, superfluity, vigour, vitality, vivacity, zest.

*antonyms* apathy, lifelessness, scantiness.

**exuberant** *adj* abundant, animated, baroque, buoyant, cheerful, copious, eager, ebullient, effervescent, effusive, elated, energetic, enthusiastic, exaggerated, excessive, excited, exhilarated, fulsome, high-spirited, lavish, lively, lush, luxuriant, overdone, overflowing, plenteous, plentiful, prodigal, profuse, rambunctious, rank, rich, sparkling, spirited, sprightly, superabundant, superfluous, teeming, vigorous, vivacious, zestful.

*antonyms* apathetic, lifeless, scant.

**exude** *v* bleed, discharge, display, emanate, emit, excrete, exhibit, flow out, issue, leak, manifest, ooze, perspire, radiate, secrete, seep, show, sweat, trickle, weep, well.

**exult** *v* boast, brag, celebrate, crow, delight, gloat, glory, jubilate, rejoice, relish, revel, taunt, triumph.

**exultant** *adj* cock-a-hoop, delighted, elated, exulting, gleeful, joyful, joyous, jubilant, over the moon, overjoyed, rejoicing, revelling, transporting, triumphant.

*antonym* depressed.

**exultation** *n* boasting, bragging, celebration, crowing, delight, elation, glee, gloating, glory, glorying, joy, joyfulness, joyousness, jubilation, merriness, paean, rejoicing, revelling, transport, triumph.

*antonym* depression.

**eye** *n* appreciation, belief, discernment, discrimination, eyeball, glim, judgement, keeker, mind, opinion, optic, orb, peeper, perception, recognition, taste, viewpoint.

*v* contemplate, examine, eye up, gaze at, glance at, inspect, leer at, look at, make eyes at, observe, ogle, peruse, regard, scan, scrutinise, stare at, study, survey, view, watch.

**eye-catching** *adj* arresting, attractive, beautiful, captivating, gorgeous, imposing, impressive, showy, spectacular, striking, stunning.

*antonyms* plain, unattractive.

**eyeful** *n* beauty, dazzler, knockout, show, sight, sight for sore eyes, spectacle, stunner, view, vision.

**eyeglasses** *n* glasses, lorgnette, lorgnon, monocle, pince-nez, specs, spectacles.

**eyesight** *n* observation, perception, sight, view, vision.

**eyesore** *n* atrocity, blemish, blight, blot, disfigurement, disgrace, dissight, horror, mess, monstrosity, sight, ugliness.

**eye-witness** *n* beholder, bystander, looker-on, observer, onlooker, passer-by, spectator, viewer, watcher, witness.

# F

**fable** *n* allegory, apologue, fabliau, fabrication, fairy story, falsehood, fantasy, fib, fiction, figment, invention, legend, lie, Märchen, myth, narrative, old wives' tale, parable, romance, saga, story, tale, tall story, untruth, yarn.

**fabled** *adj* fabulous, famed, famous, feigned, fictional, legendary, mythical, renowned, storied.
*antonym* unknown.

**fabric** *n* cloth, constitution, construction, foundations, framework, infrastructure, make-up, material, organisation, structure, stuff, textile, texture, web.

**fabricate** *v* assemble, build, coin, concoct, construct, create, devise, erect, fake, falsify, fashion, feign, forge, form, frame, invent, make, manufacture, shape, trump up.

**fabrication** *n* assemblage, assembly, building, cock-and-bull story, concoction, construction, erection, fable, fairy story, fake, falsehood, fiction, figment, forgery, frame-up, invention, lie, manufacture, myth, production, story, untruth.
*antonym* truth.

**fabulous** *adj* amazing, apocryphal, astounding, breathtaking, fabled, false, fantastic, feigned, fictitious, imaginary, immense, inconceivable, incredible, invented, legendary, marvellous, mythical, phenomenal, renowned, spectacular, superb, unbelievable, unreal, wonderful.
*antonyms* moderate, real, small.

**façade** *n* appearance, cloak, cover, disguise, exterior, face, front, frontage, guise, mask, pretence, semblance, show, veil, veneer.

**face** *n* air, appearance, aspect, assurance, audacity, authority, boatrace, boldness, brass neck, cheek, confidence, countenance, cover, dial, dignity, disguise, display, effrontery, expression, exterior, façade, facet, favour, features, front, frown, gall, grimace, honour, image, impudence, kisser, lineaments, look, mask, metope, moue, mug, nerve, outside, phiz, phizog, physiognomy, pout, prestige, presumption, pretence, reputation, sauce, scowl, self-respect, semblance, show, side, smirk, snoot, standing, status, surface, visage.
*v* clad, coat, confront, cope with, cover, deal with, defy, dress, encounter, experience, finish, front, give on to, level, line, meet, oppose, overlay, overlook, sheathe, surface, tackle, veneer.

**face to face** à deux, confronting, eye to eye, eyeball to eyeball, in confrontation, opposite, tête-à-tête, vis-à-vis.

**face up to** accept, acknowledge, come to terms with, confront, cope with, deal with, meet head-on, recognise, square up to, stand up to.

**face-lift** *n* cosmetic surgery, plastic surgery, redecoration, renovation, restoration, rhytidectomy.

**facet** *n* angle, aspect, characteristic, face, feature, part, phase, plane, point, side, slant, surface.

**facetious** *adj* amusing, comical, droll, facete, flippant, frivolous, funny, humorous, jesting, jocose, jocular, merry, playful, pleasant, tongue-in-cheek, unserious, waggish, witty.
*antonym* serious.

**facile** *adj* adept, adroit, complaisant, cursory, dexterous, easy, effortless, fluent, glib, hasty, light, plausible, proficient, quick, ready, shallow, simple, skilful, slick, smooth, superficial, uncomplicated, yielding.
*antonyms* clumsy, implausible, profound.

**facilitate** *v* assist, ease, expedite, forward, further, grease, help, promote, speed up.

**facilities** *n* amenity, appliance, convenience, equipment, means, mod cons, opportunity, prerequisites, resource.

**facility** *n* ability, adeptness, adroitness, bent, dexterity, ease, efficiency, effortlessness, expertness, fluency, gift, knack, proficiency, quickness, readiness, skilfulness, skill, smoothness, talent, turn.

**facing** *n* cladding, coating, façade, false front, overlay, reinforcement, revetment, skin, surface, trimming, veneer.

**facsimile** *n* carbon, carbon copy, copy, duplicate, image, mimeograph, photocopy, Photostat®, print, replica, repro, reproduction, transcript, Xerox®.

**fact** *n* act, actuality, certainty, circumstance, datum, deed, detail, event, fait accompli, feature, gospel, happening, incident, item, occurrence, particular, point, reality, specific, truth.

**faction**[1] *n* band, bloc, cabal, cadre, camp, caucus, clique, coalition, combination, confederacy, contingent, coterie, crowd, division, gang, ginger group, group, grouplet, junta, lobby, minority, party, pressure group, ring, section, sector, set, splinter group, splinter party, troop.

**faction**[2] *n* conflict, disagreement, discord, disharmony, dissension, disunity, division, divisiveness, fighting, friction, infighting, quarrelling, rebellion, sedition, strife, tumult, turbulence.

*antonyms* agreement, peace.

**factious** *adj* conflicting, contentious, disputatious, dissident, divisive, insurrectionary, litigious, malcontent, mutinous, partisan, quarrelling, quarrelsome, rebellious, refractory, rival, sectarian, seditious, troublemaking, tumultuous, turbulent, warring.

*antonyms* calm, co-operative.

**factitious** *adj* affected, artificial, assumed, contrived, counterfeit, engineered, fabricated, fake, false, imitation, insincere, made-up, manufactured, mock, phoney, pinchbeck, put-on, sham, simulated, spurious, supposititious, synthetic, unnatural, unreal.

*antonym* genuine.

**factor** *n* agent, aspect, cause, circumstance, component, consideration, deputy, determinant, element, estate manager, influence, item, joker, middleman, parameter, part, point, reeve, steward, thing, unknown quantity.

**factors** *n* considerations, details, pros and cons.

**factory** *n* hacienda, manufactory, mill, plant, shop, shop-floor, works.

**factotum** *n* do-all, famulus, handyman, jack-of-all-trades, Johnnie a'thing, maid-of-all-work, Man (or Girl) Friday, odd-jobman, orra man.

**facts** *n* data, details, gen, info, information, story, the low-down, the score.

**factual** *adj* accurate, authentic, circumstantial, close, correct, credible, detailed, exact, faithful, genuine, literal, objective, precise, real, straight, sure, true, unadorned, unbiased, veritable.

*antonym* false.

**faculties** *n* capabilities, functions, intelligence, powers, reason, senses, wits.

**faculty¹** *n* academics, department, discipline, lecturers, profession, school, staff.

**faculty²** *n* ability, adroitness, aptitude, bent, brain-power, capability, capacity, cleverness, dexterity, facility, gift, knack, power, propensity, readiness, skill, talent, turn.

**faculty³** *n* authorisation, authority, licence, prerogative, privilege, right.

**fad** *n* affectation, craze, crotchet, cult, fancy, fashion, mania, mode, rage, trend, vogue, whim.

**fade** *v* blanch, bleach, blench, decline, die, dim, diminish, disappear, discolour, disperse, dissolve, droop, dull, dwindle, ebb, etiolate, evanesce, fail, fall, flag, languish, pale, perish, shrivel, vanish, wane, wilt, wither, yellow.

**faded** *adj* bleached, dim, discoloured, dull, etiolated, indistinct, lustreless, pale, passé, past one's best, washed-out.

*antonym* bright.

**faeces** *n* dregs, droppings, dung, excrement, excreta, ordure, scat, sediment, stools.

**fag** *n* bind, bore, bother, chore, drag, inconvenience, irritation, nuisance, pest.

**fagged** *adj* all in, beat, exhausted, fatigued, jaded, jiggered, knackered, on one's last legs, wasted, weary, worn out, zonked.

*antonym* refreshed.

**fail** *v* abandon, cease, come to grief, conk out, crack up, crash, cut out, decline, desert, die, disappoint, droop, dwindle, fade, fall, flop, flub, flunk, fold, forget, forsake, founder, fudge, give out, give up, go bankrupt, go bust, go to the wall, go under, gutter, languish, lay an egg, let down, miscarry, misfire, miss, miss one's trip, neglect, omit, peter out, plough, sink, smash, underachieve, underperform, wane, weaken.

*antonyms* gain, improve, prosper, succeed.

**failing** *n* blemish, blind spot, decay, decline, defect, deficiency, deterioration, drawback, error, failure, fault, flaw, foible, frailty, hamartia, imperfection, lapse, miscarriage, misfortune, peccadillo, shortcoming, weakness.

*antonyms* advantage, strength.

*adj* collapsing, decaying, declining, deteriorating, drooping, dwindling, dying, flagging, languishing, moribund, waning, weak, weakening.

*antonyms* thriving, vigorous.

*prep* in default of, in the absence of, lacking, wanting, without.

**failure** *n* abortion, also-ran, bankruptcy, breakdown, bummer, collapse, crash, cropper, damp squib, dead duck, decay, decline, default, defeat, deficiency, dereliction, deterioration, disappointment, downfall, dud, failing, fiasco, flivver, flop, folding, frost, frustration, goner, incompetent, insolvency, loser, loss, melt, miscarriage, neglect, negligence, no-hoper, non-performance, omission, remissness, ruin, shortcoming, slip-up, stoppage, turkey, unsuccess, wash-out, wreck.

*antonym* success.

**faint** *adj* bleached, delicate, dim, distant, dizzy, drooping, dull, enervated, exhausted, faded, faltering, fatigued, feeble, feint, giddy, hazy, hushed, ill-defined, indistinct, languid, lethargic, light, light-headed, low, muffled, muted, muzzy, remote, slight, soft, subdued, thin, unenthusiastic, vague, vertiginous, weak, whispered, woozy.

*antonyms* clear, strong.

*v* black out, collapse, droop, drop, flag, flake out, keel over, pass out, swoon.

*n* blackout, collapse, deliquium, swoon, syncope, unconsciousness.

**faint-hearted** *adj* diffident, faint-heart, half-hearted, hen-hearted, irresolute, lily-livered, spiritless, timid, timorous, weak.

*antonym* courageous.

**fair¹** *adj* adequate, all right, average, beauteous, beautiful, bonny, bright, clean, clear, clement, cloudless, comely, decent, disinterested, dispassionate, dry, equal, equitable, even-handed, favourable, fine, handsome, honest, honourable, impartial, just, lawful, legitimate, lovely, mediocre, middling, moderate, not bad, objective, OK, on the level, passable, pretty, proper, reasonable, respectable, satisfactory, so-so, square, sunny, sunshiny, tolerable, trustworthy, unbiased, unclouded, unprejudiced, upright, well-favoured.

*antonyms* cloudy, inclement, poor, unfair.

**fair²** *adj* blond(e), fair-haired, fair-headed, flaxen, light, tow-headed.

*antonym* dark.

**fair³** *n* bang, bazaar, carnival, expo, exposition, festival, fête, gaff, gala, kermis, market, show.

**fairly** *adv* absolutely, adequately, deservedly, equitably, ex aequo, fully, honestly, impartially, justly, moderately, objectively, plainly, positively, pretty, properly, quite, rather, really, reasonably, somewhat, tolerably, unbiasedly, veritably.

*antonym* unfairly.

**fairness** *n* decency, disinterestedness, equitableness, equity, impartiality, justice, legitimacy, legitimateness, rightfulness, rightness, unbiasedness, uprightness.

*antonym* unfairness.

**fairy** *n* brownie, buggane, elf, fay, fée, hob, hobgoblin, leprechaun, Mab, peri, pisky, pixie, Robin Goodfellow, rusalka, sprite.

**fairy tale** cock-and-bull story, fabrication, fairy story, fantasy, fiction, folk-tale, invention, lie, Märchen, Munch(h)ausen, myth, romance, tall story, untruth.

**fairyland** *n* féerie, never-never-land, toyland.

**faith** *n* allegiance, assurance, belief, church, communion, confidence, constancy, conviction, credence, credit, creed, denomination, dependence, dogma, faithfulness, fealty, fidelity, honesty, honour, loyalty, persuasion, pledge, promise, reliance, religion, sincerity, trust, truth, truthfulness, uberrima fides, vow, word, word of honour.

*antonyms* mistrust, treachery, unfaithfulness.

**faithful** *adj* accurate, attached, card-carrying, close, constant, convinced, dependable, devoted, exact, just, leal, loyal, precise, reliable, soothfast, soothful, staunch, steadfast, strict, true, true-blue, true-hearted, trusty, truthful, unswerving, unwavering.

*antonyms* disloyal, inaccurate, treacherous.

*n* adherents, believers, brethren, communicants, congregation, followers, supporters.

**faithfulness** *n* accuracy, adherence, closeness, constancy, dependability, devotion, exactness, fealty, fidelity, justice, loyalty, scrupulousness, staunchness, strictness, trustworthiness, truth.

*antonyms* disloyalty, inaccuracy, treachery.

**faithless** *adj* adulterous, delusive, disloyal, doubting, false, false-hearted, fickle, inconstant, perfidious, punic, recreant, traitorous, treacherous, unbelieving, unfaithful, unreliable, untrue, untrustworthy, untruthful.

*antonyms* believing, faithful.

**faithlessness** *n* adultery, apostasy, betrayal, disloyalty, fickleness, inconstancy, infidelity, perfidy, treachery, unfaithfulness.

*antonyms* belief, faithfulness.

**fake** *v* affect, assume, copy, counterfeit, fabricate, feign, forge, phon(e)y, pretend, put on, sham, simulate.

*n* charlatan, copy, forgery, fraud, hoax, imitant, imitation, impostor, mountebank, phon(e)y, reproduction, sham, simulation.

*adj* affected, artificial, assumed, bastard, bogus, counterfeit, ersatz, false, forged, hyped up, imitation, mock, phon(e)y, pinchbeck, pretended, pseudo, reproduction, sham, simulated, spurious.

*antonym* genuine.

**fall** *v* abate, backslide, become, befall, capitulate, cascade, chance, collapse, come about, come to pass, crash, decline, decrease, depreciate, descend, die, diminish, dive, drop, drop down, dwindle, ebb, err, fall away, fall off, fall out, flag, give in, give up, give way, go a purler, go astray, go down, happen, incline, keel over, lapse, lessen, measure one's length, meet one's end, nose-dive, occur, offend, perish, pitch, plummet, plunge, push, resign, settle, sin, sink, slope, slump, souse, stumble, subside, succumb, surrender, take place, topple, transgress, trespass, trip, trip over, tumble, yield, yield to temptation.

*antonym* rise.

*n* capitulation, collapse, cropper, cut, death, decline, declivity, decrease, defeat, degradation, descent, destruction, diminution, dip, dive, downfall, downgrade, drop, dwindling, failure, incline, lapse, lessening, lowering, nose-dive, overthrow, plummet, plunge, pusher, reduction, resignation, ruin, sin, slant, slip, slope, slump, souse, spill, surrender, transgression, tumble, voluntary.

*antonym* rise.

**fall apart** break, crumble, decay, decompose, disband, disintegrate, disperse, dissolve, rot, shatter.

**fall asleep** doze off, drop off, nod off.

**fall back on** have recourse to, look to, resort to, turn to, use.

**fall for** accept, be taken in by, swallow.

**fall guy** dupe, patsy, scapegoat, victim.

**fall in** cave in, collapse, come down, crumble, give way, sink.

**fall in with** accept, acquiesce, agree with, assent, come across, comply, concur with, co-operate with, go along with, meet, support.

**fall off** decelerate, decline, decrease, deteriorate, drop, slacken, slow, slump, wane, worsen.

**fall on** assail, assault, attack, descend on, lay into, pounce on, snatch.

**fall out¹** altercate, argue, bicker, clash, differ, disagree, fight, quarrel, squabble.

*antonym* agree.

**fall out²** befall, chance, happen, occur, result, take place.

**fall through** collapse, come to nothing, fail, fizzle out, founder, miscarry.

*antonym* succeed.

**fall to** apply oneself, begin, commence, get stuck in, set about, start.

**fallacious** *adj* casuistical, deceptive, delusive, delusory, erroneous, false, fictitious, illogical, illusory, incorrect, misleading, mistaken, sophistic, sophistical, spurious, untrue, wrong.

*antonyms* correct, true.

**fallacy** *n* casuistry, deceit, deception, deceptiveness, delusion, error, falsehood, faultiness, flaw, illusion, inconsistency, misapprehension, misconception, mistake, sophism, sophistry, untruth.

*antonym* truth.

**fallible** *adj* errant, erring, frail, human, ignorant, imperfect, mortal, uncertain, weak.

*antonym* infallible.

**fallow** *adj* dormant, idle, inactive, inert, resting, uncultivated, undeveloped, unplanted, unsown, untilled, unused.

**false** *adj* artificial, bastard, bogus, concocted, counterfeit, deceitful, deceiving, deceptive, delusive, dishonest, dishonourable, disloyal, double-dealing, double-faced, duplicitous, erroneous, ersatz, faithless, fake, fallacious, false-hearted, faulty, feigned, fictitious, forged, fraudulent, hypocritical, illusive, imitation, improper, inaccurate, incorrect, inexact, invalid, lying, mendacious, misleading, mistaken, mock, perfidious, postiche, pretended, pseud, pseudo, sham, simulated, spurious, synthetic, treacherous, treasonable, trumped-up, truthless, two-faced, unfaithful, unfounded, unreal, unreliable, unsound, untrue, untrustworthy, untruthful, wrong.

*antonyms* honest, reliable, true.

**falsehood** *n* deceit, deception, dishonesty, dissimulation, fable, fabrication, fib, fiction, inexactitude, inveracity, lie, mendacity, misstatement, perjury, prevarication, pseudery, story, unfact, untruth, untruthfulness.

*antonyms* truth, truthfulness.

**falsification** *n* adulteration, alteration, change, deceit, dissimulation, distortion, forgery, misrepresentation, perversion, tampering.

**falsify** *v* adulterate, alter, belie, cook, counterfeit, distort, doctor, fake, forge, garble, misrepresent, misstate, pervert, sophisticate, take liberties with, tamper with.

**falter** *v* break, fail, flag, flinch, halt, hem and haw, hesitate, shake, stammer, stumble, stutter, totter, tremble, vacillate, waver.

**faltering** *adj* broken, failing, flagging, hesitant, irresolute, stammering, stumbling, tentative, timid, uncertain, unsteady, weak.

*antonyms* firm, strong.

**fame** *n* celebrity, credit, eminence, esteem, glory, honour, illustriousness, kudos, name, prominence, renown, reputation, repute, stardom.

**famed** *adj* acclaimed, celebrated, famous, noted, recognised, renowned, well-known, widely-known.

*antonym* unknown.

**familiar** *adj* abreast, accustomed, acquainted, amicable, au courant, au fait, aware, bold, chummy, close, common, common-or-garden, confidential, conscious, conventional, conversant, cordial, customary, disrespectful, domestic, easy, everyday, forward, free, free-and-easy, frequent, friendly, household, impudent, informal, intimate, intrusive, knowledgeable, mundane, near, open, ordinary, overfree, presuming, presumptuous, private, recognisable, relaxed, repeated, routine, stock, unceremonious, unconstrained, unreserved, versed, well-known.

*antonyms* formal, reserved, unfamiliar, unversed.

**familiarise** *v* acclimatise, accustom, brief, coach, habituate, instruct, inure, prime, school, season, train.

**familiarity** *n* acquaintance, acquaintanceship, awareness, boldness, cheek, closeness, conversance, disrespect, ease, experience, fellowship, forwardness, freedom, friendliness, grasp, impertinence, impudence, informality, intimacy, liberties, liberty, licence, naturalness, openness, presumption, sociability, unceremoniousness, understanding.

*antonyms* formality, reservation, unfamiliarity.

**family** *n* ancestors, ancestry, birth, blood, brood, children, clan, class, classification, descendants, descent, dynasty, extraction, folk, forebears, forefathers, genealogy, genre, group, house, household, issue, kin, kind, kindred, kinsmen, kith and kin, line, lineage, ménage, network, offspring, parentage, pedigree, people, progeny, quiverful, race, relations, relatives, sept, stemma, stirps, strain, subdivision, system, tribe.

**family tree** ancestry, extraction, genealogy, line, lineage, pedigree, stemma, stirps.

**famine** *n* dearth, destitution, hunger, scarcity, starvation, want.

*antonym* plenty.

**famished** *adj* famishing, hungry, ravening, ravenous, starved, starving, voracious.

*antonym* sated.

**famous** *adj* acclaimed, celebrated, conspicuous, distinguished, eminent, excellent, famed, far-famed, glorious, great, honoured, illustrious, legendary, lionised, notable, noted, prominent, remarkable, renowned, signal, well-known.

*antonym* unknown.

**fan**[1] *v* aggravate, agitate, air-condition, air-cool, arouse, blow, cool, enkindle, excite, impassion, increase, provoke, refresh, rouse, stimulate, stir up, ventilate, whip up, winnow, work up.

*n* air-conditioner, blower, extractor fan, flabellum, propeller, punkah, vane, ventilator.

**fan**[2] *n* adherent, admirer, aficionado, buff, devotee, enthusiast, fiend, follower, freak, groupie, lover, rooter, supporter, zealot.

**fanatic** *n* activist, addict, bigot, demoniac, devotee, energumen, enthusiast, extremist, fiend, freak, militant, visionary, zealot.

**fanatical** *adj* bigoted, burning, demoniac, demoniacal, enthusiastic, extreme, fervent, fervid, frenzied, immoderate, mad, obsessive, overenthusiastic, passionate, rabid, visionary, wild, zealous.

*antonyms* moderate, unenthusiastic.

**fanaticism** *n* bigotry, dedication, devotion, enthusiasm, extremism, fervidness, fervour, immoderacy, immoderateness, immoderation, infatuation, madness, monomania, obsessiveness, overenthusiasm, single-mindedness, zeal, zealotism, zealotry.

*antonym* moderation.

**fanciful** *adj* airy-fairy, capricious, chimeric(al), curious, extravagant, fabulous, fairy-tale, fantastic, ideal, imaginary, imaginative, metaphysical, mythical, poetic, romantic, unreal, vaporous, visionary, whimsical, wild.

*antonym* ordinary.

**fancy** *v* be attracted to, believe, conceive, conjecture, crave, desire, dream of, favour, go for, guess, hanker after, have an eye for, imagine, infer, like, long for, lust after, picture, prefer, reckon, relish, suppose, surmise, take a liking to, take to, think, think likely, whim, wish for, yearn for, yen for.

*antonym* dislike.

*n* caprice, chim(a)era, conception, daydream, delusion, desire, dream, fantasy, fondness, hankering, humour, idea, image, imagination, impression, impulse, inclination, liking, nightmare, notion, partiality, penchant, phantasm, predilection, preference, relish, thought, urge, vapour, velleity, vision, whim.

*antonyms* dislike, fact, reality.

*adj* baroque, capricious, chimerical, decorated, decorative, delusive, elaborate, elegant, embellished, extravagant, fanciful, fantastic, far-fetched, illusory, ornamented, ornate, rococo, whimsical.

*antonym* plain.

**fanfare** *n* fanfarade, fanfaronade, flourish, trump, trumpet call, tucket.

**fang** *n* prong, tang, tooth, tusk, venom-tooth.

**fantasise** *v* build castles in the air, daydream, dream, hallucinate, imagine, invent, live in a dream, romance.

**fantastic** *adj* absurd, ambitious, capricious, chimerical, comical, eccentric, enormous, excellent, exotic, extravagant, extreme, fanciful, fantasque, far-fetched, first-rate, freakish, grandiose, great, grotesque, illusory, imaginative, implausible, incredible, irrational, ludicrous, mad, marvellous, odd, out of this world, outlandish, outré, overwhelming, peculiar, phantasmagorical, preposterous, Pythonesque, quaint, queer, ridiculous, rococo, sensational, severe, strange, superb, tremendous, unlikely, unreal, unrealistic, visionary, weird, whimsical, wild, wonderful.

*antonyms* ordinary, plain, poor.

**fantasy** *n* apparition, caprice, creativity, daydream, delusion, dream, dreamery, fancy, fantasia, fantasque, flight of fancy, hallucination, illusion, imagination, invention, mirage, nightmare, originality, phantasy, pipe-dream, reverie, vision, whims(e)y.

*antonym* reality.

**far** *adv* a good way, a long way, afar, considerably, decidedly, deep, extremely, greatly, incomparably, miles, much.

*antonym* near.

*adj* distal, distant, faraway, far-flung, far-off, far-removed, further, god-forsaken, long, opposite, other, outlying, out-of-the-way, remote, removed.

*antonyms* close, nearby.

**far and wide** all about, broadly, everywhere, extensively, far and near, widely, worldwide.

**faraway** *adj* absent, absent-minded, abstracted, distant, dreamy, far, far-flung, far-off, lost, outlying, remote.

*antonyms* alert, nearby.

**farce** *n* absurdity, buffoonery, burlesque, comedy, commedia dell'arte, exode, joke, lazzo, low comedy, mockery, nonsense, parody, ridiculousness, satire, sham, slapstick, travesty.

**farcical** *adj* absurd, amusing, comic, derisory, diverting, droll, facetious, funny, laughable, ludicrous, nonsensical, preposterous, ridiculous, risible, silly, slapstick, stupid.

*antonym* sensible.

**fare**[1] *n* charge, cost, fee, passage, passenger, pick-up, price, traveller.

**fare**[2] *n* board, commons, diet, eatables, food, meals, menu, provisions, rations, sustenance, table, victuals.

**fare**[3] *v* be, do, get along, get on, go, go on, happen, make out, manage, proceed, prosper, turn out.

**farewell** *n* adieu, departure, good-bye, leave-taking, parting, send-off, valediction.

*antonym* hello.

*adj* final, parting, valedictory.

*interj* aloha, bye-bye, cheers, ciao, good-bye.

**far-fetched** *adj* crazy, doubtful, dubious, fantastic, forced, implausible, improbable, incredible, preposterous, strained, unbelievable, unconvincing, unlikely, unnatural, unrealistic.

*antonym* plausible.

**farm** *n* acreage, acres, bowery, croft, farmstead, grange, holding, homestead, kolkhoz, land, mains, plantation, ranch, smallholding, station.

*v* cultivate, operate, plant, till, work the land.

**farmer** *n* agriculturist, agronomist, countryman, crofter, gebur, husbandman, smallholder, yeoman.

**farming** *n* agriculture, agronomy, crofting, husbandry.

**farrago** *n* dog's breakfast, gallimaufry, hash, hotchpotch, jumble, medley, mélange, miscellany, mishmash, mixture, pot-pourri, salmagundi.

**far-reaching** *adj* broad, consequential, extensive, important, momentous, pervasive, significant, sweeping, widespread.

*antonym* insignificant.

**far-sighted** *adj* acute, canny, cautious, circumspect, discerning, far-seeing, judicious, politic, prescient, provident, prudent, sage, shrewd, wise.

*antonyms* imprudent, unwise.

**fascinate** *v* absorb, allure, beguile, bewitch, captivate, charm, delight, enchant, engross, enrapture, enravish, enthrall, entrance, hypnotise, infatuate, intrigue, mesmerise, rivet, spellbind, transfix.

*antonym* bore.

**fascinated** *adj* absorbed, beguiled, bewitched, captivated, charmed, engrossed, enthralled, entranced, hooked, hypnotised, infatuated, mesmerised, smitten, spellbound.

*antonyms* bored, uninterested.

**fascinating** *adj* alluring, bewitching, captivating, charming, compelling, delightful, enchanting, engaging, engrossing, enticing, gripping, interesting, intriguing, irresistible, mesmerising, ravishing, riveting, seductive, witching.

*antonyms* boring, uninteresting.

**fascination** *n* allure, attraction, charm, enchantment, glamour, interest, lure, magic, magnetism, pull, sorcery, spell, witchery.

*antonym* boredom.

**fascism** *n* absolutism, authoritarianism, autocracy, dictatorship, Hitlerism, totalitarianism.

**fascist** *n* absolutist, authoritarian, autocrat, Blackshirt, Hitlerist, Hitlerite, totalitarian.

*adj* absolutist, authoritarian, autocratic, fascistic, Hitlerist, Hitlerite, totalitarian.

**fashion** *n* appearance, attitude, beau monde, configuration, convention, craze, cult, custom, cut, demeanour, dernier cri, description, fad, figure, form, guise, haut ton, haute couture, high society, jet set, kind, latest, line, look, make, manner, method, mode, model, mould, pattern, rage, shape, sort, style, trend, type, usage, vogue, way.

*v* accommodate, adapt, adjust, alter, construct, contrive, create, design, fit, forge, form, make, manufacture, mould, shape, suit, tailor, work.

**fashionable** *adj* à la mode, alamode, all the rage, chic, chichi, contemporary, cult, current, customary, funky, genteel, in, in vogue, latest, modern, modish, mondain, popular, prevailing, smart, snazzy, stylish, swagger, tippy, ton(e)y, ton(n)ish, trendsetting, trendy, up-to-date, up-to-the-minute, usual, with it.

*antonym* unfashionable.

**fast¹** *adj* accelerated, brisk, fleet, flying, hasty, hurried, mercurial, nippy, quick, rapid, spanking, speedy, swift, winged.

*antonym* slow.

*adv* apace, hastily, hell for leather, hurriedly, like a flash, like a shot, posthaste, presto, quickly, rapidly, speedily, swiftly, ventre à terre.

*antonym* slowly.

**fast²** *adj* close, constant, fastened, firm, fixed, fortified, immovable, impregnable, lasting, loyal, permanent, secure, sound, staunch, steadfast, tight, unflinching, unwavering.

*antonyms* impermanent, loose.

*adv* close, deeply, firmly, fixedly, near, rigidly, securely, soundly, sound(ly), tightly, unflinchingly.

*antonym* loosely.

**fast³** *adj* dissipated, dissolute, extravagant, immoral, intemperate, licentious, loose, profligate, promiscuous, rakehell, rakehelly, rakish, reckless, self-indulgent, wanton, whorish, wild.

*antonyms* chaste, moral.

**fast⁴** *v* abstain, bant, diet, go hungry, starve.

*n* abstinence, diet, fasting, starvation, xerophagy.

*antonyms* gluttony, self-indulgence.

**fasten** *v* affix, aim, anchor, attach, belay, bend, bind, bolt, chain, clamp, concentrate, connect, direct, fix, focus, grip, infibulate, join, lace, link, lock, nail, rivet, seal, secure, spar, tie, unite.

*antonym* unfasten.

**fasten together** interdigitate, interlink, interlock, join, link, unite.

*antonyms* unfasten, untie.

**fastened** *adj* anchored, attached, bolted, chained, clamped, closed, fixed, joined, knotted, linked, locked, lockfast, nailed, sealed, secured, shut, tied.

**fastening** *n* bond, catch, clasp, clip, copula, fastness, hasp, holder, hook, latch, latchet, link, lock, nexus, tach(e), tie, vinculum.

**fastidious** *adj* choosy, critical, dainty, difficult, discriminating, finical, finicky, fussy, hypercritical, meticulous, overnice, particular, pernickety, picky, precise, punctilious, squeamish.

*antonym* undemanding.

**fasting** *n* abstinence, banting, dieting, reducing, self-denial, slimming, starvation, xerophagy.

*antonyms* gluttony, self-indulgence.

**fat** *adj* abdominous, adipose, affluent, beefy, blowzy, corpulent, cushy, elephantine, fatling, fatty, fertile, fleshed, fleshy, flourishing, fozy, fruitful, greasy, gross, heavy, jammy, lucrative, lush, obese, oily, oleaginous, overweight, paunchy, pinguid, plump, poddy, podgy, portly, pot-bellied, productive, profitable, prosperous, pudgy, remunerative, rich, roly-poly, rotund, round, solid, squab, stout, suety, thriving, tubbish, tubby, well-upholstered.

*antonyms* thin, unproductive.

*n* adipose tissue, blubber, brown fat, cellulite, corpulence, degras, embonpoint, fatness, flab, obesity, overweight, paunch, pot (belly), speck.

**fatal** *adj* baleful, baneful, calamitous, catastrophic, deadly, destructive, disastrous, final, incurable, killing, lethal, malignant, mortal, mortiferous, mortific, pernicious, ruinous, terminal, vital.

*antonym* harmless.

**fatality** *n* casualty, deadliness, death, disaster, lethalness, loss, mortality, unavoidability.

**fate** *n* chance, cup, death, destiny, destruction, divine will, doom, downfall, end, fortune, future, horoscope, issue, joss, karma, kismet, lot, Moira, nemesis, outcome, portion, predestination, predestiny, providence, ruin, stars, upshot, weird.

**fated** *adj* destined, doomed, foreordained, ineluctable, inescapable, inevitable, predestined, pre-elected, preordained, sure, unavoidable, written.

*antonym* avoidable.

**fateful** *adj* critical, crucial, deadly, decisive, destructive, disastrous, fatal, important, lethal, momentous, ominous, portentous, ruinous, significant.

*antonym* unimportant.

**Fates** n Fatal Sisters, Moirai, Norns, Parcae, Providence, Three Sisters, Weird Sisters.

**fathead** n ass, booby, dimwit, dolt, dope, dumb-cluck, dumbo, dunderhead, fool, goose, idiot, imbecile, jackass, nincompoop, nitwit, numskull, twerp, twit.

**father** n abbé, ancestor, architect, author, begetter, confessor, creator, curé, dad, daddy, elder, forebear, forefather, founder, generant, genitor, governor, inventor, leader, maker, old boy, old man, originator, pa, padre, papa, pappy, parent, pastor, pater, paterfamilias, patriarch, patron, pop, poppa, pops, predecessor, priest, prime mover, procreator, progenitor, senator, sire.

v beget, conceive, create, dream up, engender, establish, found, get, institute, invent, originate, procreate, produce, sire.

**fatherland** n home, homeland, mother-country, motherland, native land, old country.

**fatherly** adj affectionate, avuncular, benevolent, benign, forbearing, indulgent, kind, kindly, paternal, patriarchal, protective, supportive, tender.

antonyms cold, harsh, unkind.

**fathom** v comprehend, deduce, divine, estimate, gauge, get to the bottom of, grasp, interpret, measure, penetrate, plumb, plummet, probe, see, sound, understand, work out.

**fatigue** v do in, drain, exhaust, fag, jade, knacker, overtire, shatter, tire, weaken, wear out, weary, whack.

antonym refresh.

n debility, decay, degeneration, ennui, failure, heaviness, languor, lethargy, listlessness, overtiredness, tiredness.

antonyms energy, freshness.

**fatigued** adj all in, beat, bushed, dead-beat, exhausted, fagged, jaded, jiggered, knackered, overtired, tired, tired out, wasted, weary, whacked, zonked.

antonym refreshed.

**fatness** n bulk, bulkiness, corpulence, embonpoint, flab, flesh, fleshiness, girth, grossness, heaviness, obesity, overweight, podginess, portliness, rotundity, size, stoutness, tubbiness, weight.

**fatten** v bloat, broaden, build up, coarsen, cram, distend, expand, feed, feed up, fertilise, nourish, overfeed, pinguefy, spread, stuff, swell, thicken, thrive.

**fatty** adj adipose, fat, greasy, oily, oleaginous, suet(t)y.

n fatso, fustilugs, gor-belly, heavyweight, horse-godmother, podge, pudding, pudge, roly-poly.

**fatuity** n absurdity, asininity, brainlessness, daftness, denseness, fatuousness, folly, foolishness, idiocy, imbecility, inanity, insanity, ludicrousness, lunacy, mindlessness, stupidity.

antonym sense.

**fatuous** adj absurd, asinine, brainless, daft, dense, dull, fatuitous, foolish, idiotic, imbecile,

inane, ludicrous, lunatic, mindless, moony, moronic, puerile, silly, stupid, vacuous, weak-minded, witless.

antonym sensible.

**fault** n accountability, blemish, blunder, boner, boob, booboo, culpability, defect, deficiency, delict, delinquency, demerit, disdemeanour, dislocation, drawback, error, failing, flaw, frailty, goof, hamartia, imperfection, inaccuracy, indiscretion, infirmity, lack, lapse, liability, misconduct, misdeed, mistake, negligence, offence, omission, oversight, peccadillo, responsibility, shortcoming, sin, slip, slip-up, snag, solecism, transgression, trespass, weakness, wrong.

antonyms advantage, strength.

v blame, call to account, censure, criticise, find fault with, impugn, pick a hole in someone's coat, pick at, pick holes in.

antonym praise.

**fault-finder** n carper, caviller, grumbler, hair-splitter, hypercritic, kvetch(er), nagger, niggler, nit-picker, pettifogger, ultracrepidarian.

**fault-finding** n carping, cavilling, finger-pointing, grumbling, hair-splitting, hypercriticism, kvetching, nagging, niggling, nit-picking, ultracrepidation.

antonym praise.

adj captious, carping, cavilling, censorious, critical, grumbling, hypercritical, nagging, pettifogging, querulous, ultracrepidarian.

antonym complimentary.

**faultless** adj accurate, blameless, classic, correct, exemplary, faithful, flawless, foolproof, guiltless, immaculate, impeccable, innocent, irreproachable, model, perfect, pure, sinless, spotless, stainless, unblemished, unspotted, unsullied, untainted, word-perfect.

antonym imperfect.

**faulty** adj bad, blemished, broken, casuistic, damaged, defective, erroneous, fallacious, flawed, illogical, impaired, imperfect, imprecise, inaccurate, incorrect, invalid, malfunctioning, out of order, specious, unsound, weak, wrong.

**faux pas** blunder, boner, boob, booboo, clanger, gaffe, gaucherie, goof, impropriety, indiscretion, solecism.

**favour** n acceptance, approbation, approval, backing, badge, benefit, bias, boon, championship, courtesy, decoration, esteem, favouritism, friendliness, gift, good turn, goodwill, grace, indulgence, keepsake, kindness, knot, love-token, memento, obligement, partiality, patronage, present, regard, rosette, service, smile, souvenir, support, token.

antonym disfavour.

v abet, accommodate, advance, advocate, aid, approve, assist, back, befriend, champion, choose, commend, countenance, ease, encourage, esteem, extenuate, facilitate, fancy, have in one's good books, help, indulge, like, oblige, opt for, pamper, patronise, prefer, promote, resemble, spare, spoil, succour, support, take after, take kindly to, value.

antonyms disfavour, hinder, thwart.

**favourable** *adj* advantageous, affirmative, agreeable, amicable, appropriate, approving, auspicious, beneficial, benign, convenient, encouraging, enthusiastic, fair, Favonian, fit, friendly, good, helpful, hopeful, kind, opportune, positive, promising, propitious, reassuring, roseate, suitable, sympathetic, timely, understanding, welcoming, well-disposed, well-minded, white.

*antonym* unfavourable.

**favourably** *adv* advantageously, agreeably, approvingly, auspiciously, benignly, conveniently, enthusiastically, fortunately, genially, graciously, helpfully, opportunely, profitably, propitiously, sympathetically, well.

*antonym* unfavourably.

**favoured** *adj* advantaged, blessed, chosen, elite, favourite, lucky, pet, predilect, predilected, preferred, privileged, recommended, selected.

**favourite** *adj* best-loved, choice, dearest, esteemed, favoured, pet, preferred.

*antonyms* hated, unfavourite.

*n* beloved, blue-eyed boy, choice, darling, dear, form horse, idol, pet, pick, preference, teacher's pet, the apple of one's eye, whitehead, whiteheaded boy.

*antonym* pet hate.

**favouritism** *n* bias, biasedness, injustice, jobs for the boys, nepotism, old school tie, one-sidedness, partiality, partisanship, preference, preferential treatment.

*antonym* impartiality.

**fawn**[1] *v* bootlick, bow and scrape, court, crawl, creep, cringe, curry favour, dance attendance, flatter, grovel, ingratiate oneself, kneel, kowtow, pay court, smarm, toady, truckle.

**fawn**[2] *adj* beige, buff, khaki, sand-coloured, sandy.

**fawning** *adj* abject, bootlicking, crawling, cringing, deferential, flattering, grovelling, knee-crooking, obsequious, servile, slavish, sycophantic, toad-eating, toadying, toadyish, unctuous.

*antonyms* cold, proud.

**fear** *n* agitation, alarm, anxiety, apprehension, apprehensiveness, awe, bogey, bugbear, concern, consternation, cravenness, danger, dismay, disquietude, distress, doubt, dread, foreboding(s), fright, funk, heart-quake, horror, likelihood, misgiving(s), nightmare, panic, phobia, phobism, qualms, reverence, risk, solicitude, spectre, suspicion, terror, timidity, tremors, trepidation, unease, uneasiness, veneration, wonder, worry.

*antonyms* courage, fortitude.

*v* anticipate, apprehend, dread, expect, foresee, respect, reverence, shudder at, suspect, take fright, tremble, venerate, worry.

**fear for** tremble for, worry about.

**fearful**[1] *adj* afraid, alarmed, anxious, apprehensive, diffident, faint-hearted, feared, frightened, hesitant, intimidated, jittery, jumpy, nervous, nervy, panicky, pusillanimous, scared, shrinking, tense, timid, timorous, uneasy.

*antonym* courageous.

**fearful**[2] *adj* appalling, atrocious, awful, dire, distressing, dreadful, fearsome, ferly, frightful, ghastly, grievous, grim, gruesome, hair-raising, hideous, horrendous, horrible, horrific, monstrous, shocking, terrible, unspeakable.

*antonym* delightful.

**fearless** *adj* aweless, bold, brave, confident, courageous, daring, dauntless, doughty, gallant, game, gutsy, heroic, impavid, indomitable, intrepid, lion-hearted, plucky, unabashed, unafraid, unapprehensive, unblenching, unblinking, undaunted, unflinching, valiant, valorous.

*antonyms* afraid, timid.

**fearlessness** *n* boldness, bravery, confidence, courage, dauntlessness, guts, indomitability, intrepidity, intrepidness, lion-heartedness, nerve, pluck, pluckiness, prowess, valour.

*antonyms* fear, timidness.

**fearsome** *adj* alarming, appalling, awe-inspiring, awesome, awful, daunting, dismaying, formidable, frightening, frightful, hair-raising, horrendous, horrible, horrific, horrifying, menacing, terrible, unco, unnerving.

*antonym* delightful.

**feasible** *adj* achievable, attainable, likely, possible, practicable, practical, realisable, reasonable, viable, workable.

*antonym* impossible.

**feast** *n* banquet, barbecue, beanfeast, beano, binge, blow-out, carousal, carouse, celebration, delight, dinner, enjoyment, entertainment, epulation, festival, fête, gala day, gaudy, gratification, holiday, holy day, jollification, junket, pig, pleasure, potlatch, repast, revels, saint's day, spread, treat.

*v* delight, eat one's fill, entertain, gladden, gorge, gormandise, gratify, indulge, overindulge, regale, rejoice, stuff, stuff one's face, thrill, treat, wine and dine.

**feat** *n* accomplishment, achievement, act, attainment, deed, exploit, gest(e), performance.

**feather** *n* aigrette, egret, penna, pinion, plume, plumula, plumule, quill.

**feathery** *adj* downy, feathered, featherlike, fluffy, pennaceous, penniform, plumate, plumed, plumose, plumy, wispy.

**feature** *n* article, aspect, attraction, attribute, character, characteristic, column, comment, draw, facet, factor, hallmark, highlight, innovation, item, lineament, mark, peculiarity, piece, point, property, quality, report, special, speciality, specialty, story, trait.

*v* accentuate, emphasise, headline, highlight, play up, present, promote, push, recommend, show, spotlight, star.

**features** *n* countenance, face, lineaments, looks, mug, phiz, phizog, physiognomy.

**febrile** *adj* burning, delirious, febrific, fevered, feverish, fiery, flushed, hot, inflamed, pyretic.

**feckless** *adj* aimless, étourdi(e), feeble, futile, gormless, hopeless, incompetent, ineffectual, irresponsible, shiftless, useless, weak, worthless.

*antonyms* efficient, sensible.

**fecund** *adj* feracious, fertile, fructiferous, fructuous, fruitful, productive, prolific, teeming.

*antonym* infertile.

**fecundity** *n* feracity, fertility, fructiferousness, fruitfulness, productiveness.

*antonym* infertility.

**fed up** annoyed, blue, bored, brassed off, browned off, cheesed off, depressed, discontented, dismal, dissatisfied, down, gloomy, glum, scunnered, sick and tired, tired, weary.

*antonym* contented.

**federate** *v* amalgamate, associate, combine, confederate, integrate, join together, league, syndicate, unify, unite.

*antonyms* disunite, separate.

**federation** *n* alliance, amalgamation, association, Bund, coalition, combination, confederacy, confederation, copartnership, copartnery, entente, federacy, league, syndicate, union.

**fee** *n* account, bill, charge, compensation, emolument, hire, honorarium, pay, payment, recompense, remuneration, retainer, reward, terms, toll.

**feeble** *adj* debilitated, delicate, doddering, effete, enervated, enfeebled, exhausted, failing, faint, flat, flimsy, forceless, frail, fushionless, inadequate, incompetent, indecisive, ineffective, ineffectual, inefficient, inform, insignificant, insufficient, lame, languid, paltry, poor, powerless, puny, shilpit, sickly, silly, slight, tame, thin, unconvincing, vacillating, weak, weakened, weakly.

*antonyms* strong, worthy.

**feeble-minded** *adj* addle-pated, cretinised, cretinoid, cretinous, deficient, dim-witted, dull, dumb, half-witted, idiotic, imbecilic, irresolute, lacking, moronic, retarded, simple, slow on the uptake, slow-witted, soft in the head, stupid, two bricks short of a load, vacant, weak-minded.

*antonyms* bright, intelligent.

**feebleness** *n* debility, delicacy, effeteness, enervation, etiolation, exhaustion, faintness, flimsiness, forcelessness, foziness, frailness, frailty, inadequacy, incapacity, incompetence, indecisiveness, ineffectualness, infirmity, insignificance, insufficiency, lameness, languor, lassitude, sickliness, weakness.

*antonyms* strength, weariness.

**feed** *v* augment, bolster, cater for, dine, eat, encourage, fare, foster, fuel, graze, grub, nourish, nurture, pasture, provide for, provision, strengthen, subsist, supply, sustain, victual.

*n* banquet, feast, fodder, food, forage, meal, nosh, pasturage, pasture, provender, repast, silage, spread, tuck-in, victuals.

**feed in** inject, input, key in, supply.

**feed on** consume, devour, eat, exist on, live on, partake of.

**feel** *v* appear, believe, caress, consider, deem, empathise, endure, enjoy, experience, explore, finger, fondle, fumble, go through, grope, handle, have, have a hunch, hold, intuit, judge, know,

manipulate, maul, notice, observe, paw, perceive, reckon, resemble, seem, sense, sound, stroke, suffer, take to heart, test, think, touch, try, undergo.

*n* bent, feeling, finish, gift, impression, knack, quality, sense, surface, texture, touch, vibes.

**feel for** be sorry for, bleed for, commiserate (with), compassionate, condole, empathise with, pity, sympathise with.

**feel like** desire, fancy, want.

**feeler** *n* advance, antenna, approach, ballon d'essai, horn, overture, probe, tentacle, trawl, trial balloon.

**feeling** *n* (a)esthesia, (a)esthesis, affection, air, ambience, appreciation, apprehension, ardour, atmosphere, aura, compassion, concern, consciousness, emotion, empathy, Empfindung, feel, fervour, fondness, heat, hunch, idea, impression, inclination, inkling, instinct, intensity, mood, notion, opinion, passion, perception, pity, point of view, presentiment, quality, sensation, sense, sensibility, sensitivity, sentiment, sentimentality, suspicion, sympathy, touch, understanding, vibes, vibrations, view, warmth.

**feelings** *n* affections, ego, emotions, passions, self-esteem, sensitivities, susceptibilities.

**feign** *v* act, affect, assume, counterfeit, devise, dissemble, dissimulate, fabricate, fake, forge, imitate, invent, make a show of, pretend, put on, sham, simulate.

**feigned** *adj* affected, artificial, assumed, counterfeit, fabricated, fake, false, imitation, insincere, personated, pretend, pretended, pseudo, sham, simulated, spurious.

*antonyms* genuine, sincere.

**feint** *n* artifice, blind, bluff, deception, distraction, dodge, dummy, expedient, gambit, manoeuvre, mock-assault, play, pretence, ruse, stratagem, subterfuge, wile.

**felicitous** *adj* apposite, appropriate, apropos, apt, delightful, fitting, happy, inspired, neat, opportune, pat, propitious, prosperous, suitable, timely, well-chosen, well-timed, well-turned.

*antonyms* inappropriate, inept.

**felicity** *n* applicability, appropriateness, aptness, becomingness, blessedness, blessing, bliss, blissfulness, delectation, delight, ecstasy, effectiveness, eloquence, grace, happiness, joy, propriety, suitability, suitableness.

*antonyms* inappropriateness, ineptitude, sadness.

**feline** *adj* catlike, graceful, leonine, seductive, sensual, sinuous, sleek, slinky, smooth, stealthy.

**fell[1]** *v* cut down, demolish, flatten, floor, hew down, lay level, level, prostrate, raze, strike down.

**fell[2]** *adj* baneful, barbarous, bloody, cruel, deadly, destructive, fatal, ferocious, fierce, grim, implacable, inhuman, maleficent, malevolent, malicious, malign, malignant, merciless, mortal, nefarious, noxious, pernicious, pestilential, pitiless, relentless, ruinous, ruthless, sanguinary, savage, vicious.

*antonyms* benign, gentle, kind.

**fellow[1]** *n* bloke, boy, buffer, bugger, cat, chal, chap, character, codger, cove, cuss, customer, dandiprat, dog, fucker, gadgie, gink, guy, hangdog, individual, Johnny, joker, josser, kipper, man, person, punter.

**fellow²** *n* associate, brother, colleague, companion, compeer, comrade, counterpart, co-worker, double, equal, fellow-member, friend, like, match, mate, member, partner, peer, twin. *adj* associate, associated, co-, like, related, similar.

**fellow-feeling** *n* commiseration, compassion, empathy, sympathy, understanding.

**fellowship** *n* amity, association, brotherhood, camaraderie, club, communion, companionability, companionableness, companionship, endowment, familiarity, fraternisation, fraternity, guild, intercourse, intimacy, kindliness, league, order, sisterhood, sociability, society, sodality.

**female** *adj* distaff, feminal, feminine, petticoat, womanish, womanly, yin. *antonym* male.

**femaleness** *n* feminality, femineity, feminility, feminineness, femininity, feminity. *antonym* maleness.

**feminine** *adj* delicate, effeminate, effete, gentle, girlish, graceful, ladylike, modest, petticoat, sissy, soft, tender, unmanly, unmasculine, weak, womanish, womanly. *antonym* masculine.

**femininity** *n* delicacy, effeminacy, effeteness, feminineness, gentleness, girlishness, muliebrity, sissiness, softness, unmanliness, womanhood, womanishness, womanliness, Yin. *antonym* masculinity.

**feminism** *n* female emancipation, women's emancipation, women's liberation, women's movement, women's rights.

**femme fatale** charmer, enchantress, seductress, siren, temptress, vamp.

**fen** *n* bog, marsh, morass, moss, quag, quagmire, slough, swamp.

**fence¹** *n* barricade, barrier, defence, guard, hedge, paling, palisade, railings, rampart, sepiment, sept, shield, stockade, wall, windbreak. *v* bound, circumscribe, confine, coop, defend, encircle, enclose, fortify, guard, hedge, pen, protect, restrict, secure, separate, surround.

**fence²** *v* beat about the bush, cavil, digladiate, dodge, equivocate, evade, hedge, parry, prevaricate, pussyfoot, quibble, shift, stonewall, tergiversate.

**fencing¹** *n* iaido, kendo, swordplay, swordsmanship.

**fencing²** *n* beating about the bush, double talk, equivocation, evasiveness, hedging, parrying, prevarication, pussyfooting, quibbling, stonewalling, tergiversation, weasel-words.

**fend for** look after, maintain, provide for, shift for, support, sustain.

**fend off** avert, beat off, defend, deflect, hold at bay, keep off, parry, repel, repulse, resist, shut out, stave off, ward off.

**feral** *adj* bestial, brutal, brutish, fell, ferae naturae, ferine, ferocious, fierce, savage, unbroken, uncultivated, undomesticated, untamed, vicious, wild. *antonym* tame.

**ferment** *v* agitate, boil, brew, bubble, concoct, effervesce, excite, fester, foam, foment, froth, heat, incite, inflame, leaven, provoke, rise, rouse, seethe, smoulder, stir up, work, work up. *n* agitation, brouhaha, commotion, disruption, excitement, fever, frenzy, furore, glow, heat, hubbub, imbroglio, stew, stir, tumult, turbulence, turmoil, unrest, uproar, yeast, zymosis. *antonym* calm.

**ferocious** *adj* barbaric, barbarous, bloodthirsty, bloody, brutal, brutish, catamountain, cruel, fearsome, feral, fiendish, fierce, homicidal, inhuman, merciless, murderous, pitiless, predatory, rapacious, ravening, relentless, ruthless, sadistic, sanguinary, savage, truculent, vicious, violent, wild. *antonyms* gentle, mild.

**ferocity** *n* barbarity, bloodthirstiness, brutality, cruelty, ferity, ferociousness, fiendishness, fierceness, inhumanity, murderousness, rapacity, ruthlessness, sadism, savageness, savagery, truculence, viciousness, wildness. *antonyms* gentleness, mildness.

**ferret out** dig up, disclose, discover, disinter, drive out, elicit, extract, find, hunt down, nose out, root out, run to earth, smell out, sniff out, sus out, trace, track down, unearth, worm out.

**ferry** *v* carry, chauffeur, convey, drive, move, remove, run, shift, ship, shuttle, taxi, transport.

**fertile** *adj* abundant, fat, fecund, feracious, flowering, fructiferous, fructuous, frugiferous, fruit-bearing, fruitful, generative, lush, luxuriant, plenteous, plentiful, potent, productive, prolific, rich, teeming, uberous, virile, yielding. *antonyms* arid, barren.

**fertilisation** *n* dressing, dunging, enrichment, fecundation, implantation, impregnation, insemination, manuring, mulching, pollination, procreation, propagation, top-dressing.

**fertilise** *v* compost, dress, dung, enrich, fecundate, feed, fructify, impregnate, inseminate, manure, mulch, pollinate, top-dress.

**fertiliser** *n* compost, dressing, dung, guano, manure, marl, plant-food.

**fertility** *n* abundance, fatness, fecundity, feracity, fruitfulness, lushness, luxuriance, plenteousness, potency, productiveness, prolificity, prolificness, richness, uberty, virility. *antonyms* aridity, barrenness.

**fervent** *adj* animated, ardent, devout, eager, earnest, emotional, empressé, energetic, enthusiastic, excited, fervid, fiery, full-blooded, heartfelt, impassioned, intense, passionate, perfervid, spirited, vehement, vigorous, warm, whole-hearted, zealous.

**fervour** *n* animation, ardour, eagerness, earnestness, empressment, energy, enthusiasm, excitement, fervency, fervidity, fervidness, hwyl, intensity, passion, spirit, unction, unctuousness, vehemence, verve, vigour, warmth, zeal.

*antonym* apathy.

**fester** *v* chafe, decay, discharge, gall, gather, irk, maturate, putrefy, rankle, smoulder, suppurate, ulcerate.

*antonyms* dissipate, heal.

**festering** *n* discharging, galling, gathering, infected, inflamed, mattering, mattery, maturating, poisonous, purulent, pussy, putrescent, rankling, septic, smouldering, suppurating, ulcerated, venomous, virulent.

**festival** *n* anniversary, carnival, celebration, commemoration, eisteddfod, entertainment, feast, festa, festivities, fête, field day, fiesta, gala, holiday, holy day, jubilee, junketing, merry-make, merrymaking, merry-night, mod, potlatch, puja, saint's day, treat.

**festive** *adj* carnival, celebratory, cheery, Christmassy, convivial, cordial, en fête, festal, festivous, gala, gay, gleeful, happy, hearty, holiday, jolly, jovial, joyful, joyous, jubilant, merry, mirthful, rollicking, sportive, uproarious.

*antonyms* gloomy, sober, sombre.

**festivities** *n* bacchanalia, banqueting, carousal, celebration, entertainment, feasting, festival, fun and games, glorification, jollification, jollities, junketings, party, rejoicings, revelries, revels.

**festivity** *n* amusement, conviviality, enjoyment, feasting, festal, fun, gaiety, jollification, jollity, joviality, joyfulness, junketing, merriment, merrymaking, mirth, pleasure, revelry, sport, wassail.

**festoon** *n* chaplet, decoration, garbe, garland, lei, swag, swathe, wreathe.

*v* adorn, array, bedeck, bedizen, beribbon, deck, decorate, drape, garland, garnish, hang, swathe, wreath.

**fetch** *v* be good for, bring, bring in, carry, conduct, convey, deliver, draw, earn, elicit, escort, evoke, get, go for, lead, make, obtain, produce, realise, retrieve, sell for, transport, uplift, utter, yield.

**fetch up** arrive, come, come to a halt, end up, finish, finish up, halt, land, reach, stop, turn up.

**fetching** *adj* alluring, attractive, beguiling, captivating, charming, cute, disarming, enchanting, enticing, fascinating, pretty, sweet, taking, winning, winsome.

*antonym* repellent.

**fête** *n* bazaar, carnival, fair, festival, gala, garden party, sale of work.

*v* banquet, bring out the red carpet for, entertain, honour, lionise, make much of, regale, treat, welcome, wine and dine.

**fetid** *adj* corrupt, disgusting, filthy, foul, malodorous, mephitic, nauseating, noisome, noxious, odorous, offensive, rancid, rank, reeking, sickly, smelly, stinking.

*antonym* fragrant.

**fetish** *n* amulet, charm, cult object, fixation, idée fixe, idol, image, ju-ju, mania, obsession, periapt, phylactery, talisman, thing, totem.

**fetter** *v* bind, chain, confine, curb, encumber, entrammel, gyve, hamper, hamshackle, hamstring, hobble, manacle, pinion, restrain, restrict, shackle, tie (up), trammel, truss.

*antonym* free.

**fetters** *n* bilboes, bondage, bonds, bracelets, captivity, chains, check, constraint, curb, gyve, gyves, hampers, hamshackle, handcuffs, hindrance, hobble, hopple, inhibition, irons, manacles, obstruction, restraint, shackles, trammel.

**feud** *n* animosity, antagonism, argument, bad blood, bickering, bitterness, conflict, contention, disagreement, discord, dispute, dissension, enmity, estrangement, faction, feuding, grudge, hostility, ill will, quarrel, rivalry, row, strife, variance, vendetta.

*antonyms* agreement, peace.

*v* altercate, argue, be at odds, bicker, brawl, clash, contend, dispute, duel, fight, quarrel, row, squabble, war, wrangle.

*antonym* agree.

**fever** *n* agitation, calenture, delirium, ecstasy, excitement, febricity, febricula, febricule, ferment, fervour, feverishness, flush, frenzy, heat, intensity, passion, pyrexia, restlessness, temperature, turmoil, unrest.

**fevered** *adj* burning, febrile, feverish, feverous, fever-ridden, fiery, flushed, hectic, hot, pyretic, pyrexial, pyrexic.

*antonym* cool.

**feverish** *adj* agitated, anxious, burning, distracted, eager, excited, fanatical, febrile, fevered, feverous, flurried, flushed, flustered, frantic, frenetic, frenzied, hasty, hectic, hot, hurried, impatient, inflamed, nervous, obsessive, overwrought, pyretic, restless.

*antonyms* calm, cool.

**feverishness** *n* agitation, bustle, commotion, distraction, excitement, febricity, febrility, ferment, fever, flurry, flush, franticness, frenzy, fuss, haste, hurry, kerfuffle, pother, pyrexia, restlessness, stir, turmoil.

*antonyms* calmness, coolness.

**few** *adj* few and far between, hard to come by, in short supply, inadequate, inconsiderable, infrequent, insufficient, meagre, negligible, rare, scant, scanty, scarce, scattered, sparse, sporadic, thin, uncommon.

*pron* a couple, handful, not many, oddments, one or two, scarcely any, scattering, small number, small quantity, some, sprinkling.

**fewness** *n* dearth, inadequacy, infrequency, insufficiency, lack, negligibility, paucity, rareness, rarity, scantiness, scarceness, scarcity, sparseness, thinness, uncommonness, want.

*antonyms* abundance, glut.

**fiancé(e)** *n* betrothed, bridegroom-to-be, bride-to-be, husband-to-be, intended, wife-to-be.

**fiasco** *n* bummer, calamity, catastrophe, collapse, cropper, damp squib, debacle, disaster, failure, flivver, flop, mess, non-success, rout, ruin, turkey, unsuccess, wash-out.

*antonym* success.

**fiat** *n* authorisation, command, decree, dictate, dictum, diktat, directive, edict, injunction, mandate, OK, order, ordinance, permission, precept, prescript, proclamation, sanction, ukase, warrant.

**fib** *n* concoction, evasion, falsehood, fantasy, fiction, invention, lie, misrepresentation, prevarication, story, tale, untruth, white lie, whopper, yarn.

*v* dissemble, evade, fabricate, falsify, fantasise, invent, lie, prevaricate, sidestep.

**fibre** *n* backbone, bast, calibre, character, courage, determination, essence, fibril, filament, filasse, funicle, grit, guts, nature, nerve, pile, pluck, quality, resolution, sinew, spirit, stamina, staple, strand, strength, substance, temperament, tenacity, tendril, texture, thread, toughness.

**fibrous** *adj* fibred, fibriform, fibrillar, fibrillary, fibrillate, fibrillose, fibrillous, fibroid, filamentous, filiform, filose, funicular, funiculate, penicillate, sinewy, stringy, tendinous, thread-like, wiry.

**fickle** *adj* capricious, chameleon(ic), changeable, disloyal, dizzy, erratic, faithless, fitful, flighty, fluctuating, inconstant, irresolute, mercurial, mutable, quicksilver, treacherous, unfaithful, unpredictable, unreliable, unstable, unsteady, vacillating, variable, volage, volageous, volatile, wind-changing.

*antonym* constant.

**fickleness** *n* capriciousness, changeability, changeableness, disloyalty, faithlessness, fitfulness, flightiness, inconstancy, mutability, treachery, unfaithfulness, unpredictability, unreliability, unsteadiness, volatility.

*antonym* constancy.

**fiction** *n* canard, cock-and-bull story, concoction, fable, fabrication, falsehood, fancy, fantasy, feuilleton, fib, figment, imagination, improvisation, invention, legend, lie, myth, novel, parable, romance, story, story-telling, tale, tall story, untruth, whopper, yarn.

*antonym* truth.

**fictional** *adj* fabulous, imaginary, invented, legendary, made-up, mythical, non-existent, unreal.

*antonyms* real, true.

**fictitious** *adj* aprocryphal, artificial, assumed, bogus, counterfeit, fabricated, false, fanciful, feigned, fictive, fraudulent, imaginary, imagined, improvised, invented, made-up, make-believe, mythical, non-existent, spurious, supposed, suppositional, supposititious, unreal, untrue.

*antonyms* genuine, real.

**fiddle**[1] *v* cheat, cook, cook the books, diddle, fidget, finagle, finger, fix, gerrymander, graft, interfere, juggle, manoeuvre, mess around, play, racketeer, swindle, tamper, tinker, toy, trifle, wangle.

*n* chicanery, con, fix, fraud, graft, monkey-business, racket, rip-off, sharp practice, swindle, trickery, wangle.

**fiddle**[2] *n* viol, viola, viola da braccio, viola da spalla, viola d'amore, violin.

**fiddling** *adj* footling, futile, insignificant, negligible, paltry, pettifogging, petty, trifling, trivial.

*antonyms* important, significant.

**fidelity** *n* accuracy, adherence, allegiance, authenticity, closeness, constancy, correspondence, dedication, dependability, devotedness, devotion, dutifulness, exactitude, exactness, faith, faithfulness, fealty, incorruptibility, integrity, loyalty, loyalty, preciseness, precision, reliability, scrupulousness, staunchness, steadfastness, true-heartedness, trustworthiness.

*antonyms* inaccuracy, inconstancy, treachery.

**fidget** *v* bustle, chafe, fiddle, fidge, fike, fret, jerk, jiggle, jitter, jump, mess about, play around, squirm, toy, twitch, worry.

*n* agitation, anxiety, creeps, discomposure, edginess, fidgetiness, fidgets, heebie-jeebies, jimjams, jitteriness, jitters, jumpiness, nerves, nerviness, nervousness, restlessness, shakes, twitchiness, unease, uneasiness, willies.

**fidgety** *adj* agitated, frisky, impatient, jerky, jittery, jumpy, nervous, nervy, on edge, restive, restless, skittish, twitchy, uneasy.

*antonym* still.

**field**[1] *n* arena, battlefield, battleground, glebe, grassland, green, greensward, lawn, lay, lea, mead, meadow, padang, paddock, pasture, pitch, playing-field, theatre.

**field**[2] *n* applicants, candidates, competition, competitors, contenders, contestants, entrants, opponents, opposition, possibilities, runners.

**field**[3] *n* area, bailiwick, ball park, bounds, confines, department, discipline, domain, environment, forte, limits, line, métier, period, pidgin, province, purview, range, scope, speciality, specialty, territory.

**field**[4] *v* answer, catch, cope with, deal with, deflect, handle, parry, pick up, receive, retrieve, return, stop.

**fiend** *n* addict, aficionado, barbarian, beast, brute, degenerate, demon, devil, devotee, enthusiast, evil spirit, fanatic, freak, ghoul, goblin, hellhound, hobgoblin, incubus, lamia, maniac, monster, nut, ogre, Satan, savage, succubus.

**fiendish** *adj* accursed, atrocious, baleful, black-hearted, cruel, damnable, demoniac, devilish, diabolic, diabolical, hellish, impious, implacable, infernal, inhuman, malefic, maleficent, malevolent, malicious, malign, malignant, Mephistophelean, Mephistophelic, mischievous, monstrous, nefarious, satanic, savage, ungodly, unspeakable, vicious, vile, wicked.

**fierce** *adj* baleful, barbarous, blustery, boisterous, brutal, cruel, cut-throat, dangerous, fearsome, fell, feral, ferocious, fiery, frightening, furious, grim, howling, intense, keen, menacing, merciless, murderous, passionate, powerful, raging, relentless, savage, stern, stormy, strong, tempestuous, threatening, truculent, tumultuous, uncontrollable, unrelenting, untamed, vicious, violent, wild.

*antonyms* calm, gentle, kind.

**fiercely** *adv* ardently, bitterly, fanatically, ferociously, furiously, implacably, intensely, keenly, menacingly, mercilessly, murderously, passionately, relentlessly, savagely, sternly, tempestuously, tigerishly, tooth and nail, viciously, violently, wildly, zealously.

*antonyms* gently, kindly.

**fierceness** *n* ardour, avidity, bitterness, bluster, destructiveness, fanaticism, fearsomeness, ferocity, fervidness, fervour, fieriness, intensity, keenness, mercilessness, passion, relentlessness, roughness, ruthlessness, savageness, savagery, sternness, storminess, strength, tempestuousness, turbulence, viciousness, violence, wildness, zeal.

*antonyms* gentleness, kindness.

**fiery** *adj* ablaze, afire, aflame, aglow, ardent, blazing, burning, choleric, excitable, febrile, fervent, fervid, fevered, feverish, fierce, flaming, flushed, glowing, heated, hot, hot-headed, impatient, impetuous, impulsive, inflamed, irascible, irritable, passionate, peppery, perfervid, precipitate, red-hot, sultry, torrid, truculent, violent, volcanic.

*antonyms* cold, impassive.

**fight** *v* altercate, argue, assault, battle, bear arms against, bicker, box, brawl, clash, close, combat, conduct, conflict, contend, contest, cross swords, defy, dispute, do battle, engage, exchange blows, fence, feud, grapple, joust, lock horns, measure strength, measure swords, mell, mix it, oppose, prosecute, quarrel, resist, scrap, scuffle, skirmish, spar, squabble, stand up to, strive, struggle, take the field, tilt, tussle, wage, wage war, war, withstand, wrangle, wrestle.

*n* action, affray, altercation, argument, barney, battle, belligerence, bicker, bout, brawl, brush, clash, combat, conflict, contest, courage, dispute, dissension, dogfight, duel, encounter, engagement, fisticuffs, fracas, fray, free-for-all, gameness, hostilities, joust, luctation, mêlée, mettle, militancy, monomachy, passage of arms, pluck, pugnacity, quarrel, rammy, resilience, resistance, riot, row, ruck, rumble, scrap, scuffle, set-to, skirmish, spirit, strength, struggle, tenacity, tussle, war.

**fight back**[1] defend oneself, give as good as one gets, put up a fight, reply, resist, retaliate, retort.

**fight back**[2] bottle up, contain, control, curb, hold back, hold in check, repress, resist, restrain, suppress.

**fight off** beat off, hold off, keep at bay, put to flight, rebuff, repel, repress, repulse, resist, rout, stave off, ward off.

**fight shy of** avoid, disdain, eschew, give a wide berth, keep at arm's length, shun, spurn, steer clear of.

**fighter** *n* adventurer, antagonist, battler, belligerent, boxer, brave, bruiser, champion, combatant, contender, contestant, disputant, fighting man, filibuster, free lance, gladiator, man-at-arms, mercenary, militant, prize-fighter, pugilist, soldier, soldier of fortune, swordsman, trouper, warrior, wrestler.

**fighting** *adj* aggressive, argumentative, bellicose, belligerent, combative, contentious, disputatious, fierce, hawkish, martial, militant, militaristic, pugnacious, quarrelsome, sabre-rattling, truculent, warfaring, warlike.

*n* battle, bloodshed, boxing, brawling, clash, combat, conflict, encounter, engagement, fisticuffs, fray, handicuffs, hostilities, mêlée, quarrelling, scuffle, scuffling, struggle, war, warfare, wrangling, wrestling.

**figment** *n* concoction, creation, deception, delusion, fable, fabrication, falsehood, fancy, fiction, illusion, improvisation, invention, mare's nest, production, work.

**figurative** *adj* allegorical, analogous, descriptive, embellished, emblematic, emblematical, fanciful, florid, flowery, metaphorical, ornate, parabolic, pictorial, picturesque, poetical, representative, symbolic, symbolical, tropical, typical.

*antonym* literal.

**figure** *n* amount, body, build, celebrity, character, chassis, cipher, configuration, conformation, cost, depiction, design, device, diagram, digit, dignitary, drawing, embellishment, emblem, form, frame, illustration, image, leader, motif, notability, notable, number, numeral, outline, pattern, personage, personality, physique, presence, price, proportions, representation, shadow, shape, sign, silhouette, sketch, somebody, sum, symbol, torso, total, trope, value.

*v* act, add, appear, believe, calculate, compute, count, estimate, feature, guess, judge, opine, reckon, sum, surmise, tally, think, tot up, work out.

**figure of speech** conceit, concetto, figure, image, imagery, rhetorical device, trope, turn of phrase.

**figure out** calculate, comprehend, compute, decipher, excogitate, explain, fathom, make out, puzzle out, reason out, reckon, resolve, see, understand, work out.

**figured** *adj* adorned, decorated, embellished, marked, ornamented, patterned, printed, sprigged, variegated.

*antonym* plain.

**figurehead** *n* bust, carving, cipher, dummy, front man, image, leader, man of straw, mouthpiece, name, nominal head, nonentity, puppet, straw man, titular head, token.

**filament** *n* cilium, fibre, fibril, file, funicle, hair, pile, staple, strand, string, thread, whisker, wire.

**filch** *v* abstract, borrow, crib, drib, embezzle, fake, finger, half-inch, lift, misappropriate, nick, palm, peculate, pilfer, pinch, plagiarise, prig, purloin, rip off, snaffle, snitch, steal, swipe, take, thieve.

**file**[1] *v* abrade, burnish, furbish, grate, hone, pare, plane, polish, rasp, refine, rub (down), sand, scour, scrape, shape, shave, smooth, trim, whet.

**file**[2] *n* binder, cabinet, case, date, documents, dossier, folder, information, portfolio, record.

*v* capture, document, enter, memorise, pigeonhole, process, record, register, slot in, store.

**file**[3] *n* column, cortège, line, list, procession, queue, row, stream, string, trail, train.

*v* defile, march, parade, stream, trail, troop.

**filial** *adj* affectionate, daughterly, devoted, dutiful, fond, loving, loyal, respectful, sonlike, sonly.

*antonyms* disloyal, unfilial.

**filibuster**[1] *n* delay, hindrance, impediment, obstruction, peroration, postponement, procrastination, speechifying.

*v* delay, hinder, impede, obstruct, perorate, prevent, procrastinate, put off, speechify.

*antonym* expedite.

**filibuster**[2] *n* adventurer, buccaneer, corsair, free lance, freebooter, pirate, rover, sea rat, sea-robber, sea-rover, soldier of fortune.

**filigree** *n* fret-work, interlace, lace, lacework, lattice, lattice-work, scrollwork, tracery, wirework.

**fill** *v* assign, block, bung, charge, clog, close, congest, cork, cram, crowd, discharge, drench, engage, englut, engorge, execute, fulfil, furnish, glut, gorge, hold, imbue, impregnate, inflate, load, occupy, officiate, overspread, pack, perform, permeate, pervade, plug, replenish, sate, satiate, satisfy, saturate, seal, soak, stock, stop, stuff, suffuse, supply, surfeit, swell, take up.

*antonyms* clear, empty.

*n* abundance, ample, enough, plenty, sufficiency, sufficient.

**fill in** acquaint, act for, advise, answer, apprise, brief, bring up to date, complete, deputise, fill out, inform, put wise, replace, represent, stand in, sub, substitute, understudy.

**filling** *n* contents, filler, grouting, infill, infilling, innards, inside, insides, nogging, padding, rubble, stuffing, wadding.

*adj* ample, big, bulky, generous, heavy, large, nutritious, satisfying, solid, square, substantial, sustaining, tidy.

*antonym* insubstantial.

**fillip** *n* boost, flick, goad, impetus, incentive, prod, push, shove, spice, spur, stimulus, zest.

*antonym* damper.

**film**[1] *n* bloom, blur, cloud, coat, coating, covering, dusting, gauze, glaze, haze, haziness, integument, layer, membrane, mist, opacity, pellicle, screen, scum, sheet, skin, tissue, veil, web, weft.

*v* blear, blur, cloud, dull, glaze, haze, mist, screen, veil.

**film**[2] *n* documentary, epic, feature film, flick, horse-opera, motion picture, movie, oldie, picture, short, spaghetti western, video, western.

*v* photograph, shoot, take, video, videotape.

**filmy** *adj* cobwebby, delicate, diaphanous, fine, flimsy, floaty, fragile, gauzy, gossamer, gossamery, insubstantial, light, see-through, sheer, shimmering, thin, translucent, transparent.

*antonym* opaque.

**filter** *v* clarify, dribble, escape, exude, filtrate, leach, leak, ooze, penetrate, percolate, purify, refine, screen, seep, sieve, sift, strain, transpire, transude, trickle, well.

*n* colander, gauze, membrane, mesh, riddle, sieve, sifter, strainer.

**filth** *n* bilge, carrion, coarseness, colluvies, contamination, coprolalia, coprophilia, corruption, crud, defilement, dirt, dirty-mindedness, dung, excrement, excreta, faeces,, faex, filthiness, foulness, garbage, grime, grossness, gunge, impurity, indecency, muck, nastiness, obscenity, ordure, pollution, pornography, putrefaction, putrescence, refuse, scatology, sewage, slime, sludge, smt, smuttiness, soil, sordes, sordidness, squalor, sullage, uncleanness, vileness, vulgarity.

*antonyms* cleanliness, decency, purity.

**filthy** *adj* Augean, base, bawdy, begrimed, black, blackened, blue, coarse, contemptible, coprolaliac, coprophilous, corrupt, depraved, despicable, dirty, dirty-minded, faecal, feculent, foul, foul-mouthed, grimy, gross, grubby, impure, indecent, lavatorial, lewd, licentious, low, mean, miry, mucky, muddy, nasty, nasty-minded, obscene, offensive, polluted, pornographic, putrid, scatological, scurrilous, slimy, smoky, smutty, sooty, sordid, squalid, suggestive, swinish, unclean, unwashed, vicious, vile, vulgar.

*antonyms* clean, decent, inoffensive, pure.

**final** *adj* absolute, clinching, closing, concluding, conclusive, conclusory, decided, decisive, definite, definitive, desinent, desinential, determinate, dying, eleventh-hour, end, eventual, finished, incontrovertible, irrefragable, irrefutable, irrevocable, last, last-minute, latest, settled, terminal, terminating, ultimate, undeniable.

**finale** *n* climax, close, conclusion, crescendo, crowning glory, culmination, curtain, dénouement, epilogue, final curtain, finis, last act, supreme moment.

**finalise** *v* agree, clinch, complete, conclude, decide, dispose of, finish, get signed and sealed, get taped, resolve, round off, seal, settle, sew up, tie up, work out, wrap up.

**finality** *n* certitude, conclusiveness, conviction, decidedness, decisiveness, definiteness, firmness, inevitability, inevitableness, irreversibility, irrevocability, resolution, ultimacy, unavoidability.

**finally** *adv* absolutely, at last, at length, completely, conclusively, convincingly, decisively, definitely, eventually, for ever, for good, for good and all, in conclusion, in the end, inescapably, inexorably, irreversibly, irrevocably, lastly, once and for all, permanently, ultimately.

**finance** *n* accounting, accounts, banking, business, commerce, economics, investment, money, money management, stock market, trade.

*v* back, bail out, bankroll, capitalise, float, fund, guarantee, habilitate, pay for, set up, subsidise, support, underwrite.

**finances** *n* affairs, assets, bank account, bread, budget, capital, cash, coffers, dibs, fisc, funds, income, liquidity, money, moolah, purse, resources, revenue, spondulicks, wealth, wherewithal.

**financial** *adj* budgetary, chrematistic, commercial, economic, fiscal, monetary, money, pecuniary.

**financier** *n* banker, broker, cambist, financialist, gnome, investor, money-maker, speculator, stockbroker.

**find** *v* achieve, acquire, ascertain, attain, bring, catch, chance on, come across, consider, contribute, cough up, descry, detect, discover, earn, encounter, espy, experience, expose, ferret out, furnish, gain, get, hit on, judge, learn, light on, locate, meet, note, notice, observe, obtain, perceive, procure, provide, reach, realise, recognise, recover, rediscover, regain, remark, repossess, retrieve, spot, stumble on, supply, think, track down, turn up, uncover, unearth, win.

*n* acquisition, asset, bargain, catch, coup, discovery, good buy, unconsidered trifle.

**find fault** bitch, carp, cavil, censure, complain, criticise, depreciate, disparage, gripe, hypercriticise, kvetch, nag, niggle, nitpick, pick holes, pull to pieces, quarrel with, quibble, reprove, take to task, ultracrepidate.

*antonym* praise.

**find out** ascertain, catch, detect, dig up, disclose, discover, establish, expiscate, expose, learn, note, observe, perceive, realise, reveal, rumble, show up, speir, sus out, tumble to, uncover, unmask.

**finding** *n* award, breakthrough, conclusion, decision, decree, discovery, evidence, find, judgement, pronouncement, recommendation, verdict.

**fine¹** *adj* abstruse, acceptable, acute, admirable, agreeable, all right, attractive, balmy, beau, beaut, beautiful, bonny, brave, braw, bright, brilliant, choice, clear, clement, cloudless, convenient, critical, cutting, dainty, dandy, delicate, diaphanous, discriminating, dry, elegant, elusive, excellent, exceptional, expensive, exquisite, fair, fastidious, fine-drawn, first-class, first-rate, flimsy, four-square, fragile, gauzy, good, good-looking, goodly, gorgeous, gossamer, great, hair-splitting, handsome, honed, hunky, hunky-dory, impressive, intelligent, jake, keen, light, lovely, magnificent, masterly, minute, nice, OK, ornate, outstanding, pleasant, polished, powdery, precise, pure, quick, rare, refined, robust, satisfactory, select, sensitive, sharp, sheer, showy, skilful, skilled, slender, small, smart, solid, splendid, sterling, strong, sturdy, stylish, sublime, subtle, suitable, sunny, superior, supreme, tasteful, tenuous, thin, tickety-boo, unalloyed, virtuoso, well-favoured, wiredrawn.

**fine²** *v* amerce, mulct, penalise, punish, sting.

*n* amercement, amerciament, damages, forfeit, forfeiture, mulct, penalty, punishment.

**finery** *n* bedizenment, decorations, frills and furbelows, frippery, gaud, gaudery, gauds, gear, gewgaws, glad rags, jewellery, ornaments, showiness, splendour, Sunday best, trappings.

**finesse** *n* address, adeptness, adroitness, artfulness, artifice, cleverness, craft, deftness, delicacy, diplomacy, discretion, elegance, expertise, gracefulness, know-how, neatness, polish, quickness, refinement, savoir-faire, skill, sophistication, subtlety, tact.

*v* bluff, evade, manipulate, manoeuvre, trick.

**finger** *v* caress, feel, fiddle with, fondle, handle, manipulate, maul, meddle with, palpate, paw, play about with, stroke, touch, toy with.

*n* claw, digit, digital, index, phalanges, talon.

**finical** *adj* choosy, dainty, dandified, dandyish, fastidious, finicky, foppish, fussy, natty, neat, nice, nipperty-tipperty, particular, pernickety, precise.

**finicky** *adj* choosy, critical, dainty, delicate, difficult, fastidious, finical, finicking, fussy, hypercritical, meticulous, nice, nit-picking, overnice, particular, pernickety, scrupulous, squeamish, tricky.

*antonyms* easy, easy-going.

**finish** *v* accomplish, achieve, annihilate, best, buff, burnish, cease, close, coat, complete, conclude, consume, consummate, culminate, deal with, defeat, destroy, devour, discharge, dispatch, dispose of, do, drain, drink, eat, elaborate, empty, encompass, end, execute, exhaust, expend, exterminate, face, finalise, fulfil, get rid of, gild, hone, kill, lacquer, overcome, overpower, overthrow, perfect, polish, put an end to, put the last hand to, refine, round off, rout, ruin, settle, smooth, smooth off, sophisticate, spend, stain, stop, terminate, texture, use (up), veneer, wax, wind up, worst, zap.

*n* annihilation, appearance, bankruptcy, burnish, cessation, close, closing, completion, conclusion, coup de grâce, culmination, cultivation, culture, curtain, curtains, death, defeat, dénouement, elaboration, end, end of the road, ending, finale, gloss, grain, liquidation, lustre, patina, perfection, polish, refinement, ruin, shine, smoothness, sophistication, surface, termination, texture, wind-up.

**finished** *adj* accomplished, bankrupt, clapped-out, classic, consummate, cultivated, defeated, done, done for, doomed, drained, elegant, empty, exhausted, expert, faultless, flawless, impeccable, jiggered, lost, masterly, napoo, overpast, perfected, played out, polished, professional, proficient, refined, ruined, skilled, smooth, sophisticated, spent, through, undone, urbane, virtuoso, washed up, wrecked, zonked.

*antonyms* coarse, crude, unfinished.

**finite** *adj* bounded, calculable, circumscribed, compassable, definable, delimited, demarcated, fixed, limited, measurable, restricted, terminable.

*antonym* infinite.

**fire** *n* animation, ardour, bale-fire, barrage, blaze, bombardment, bonfire, brio, broadside, burning, cannonade, combustion, conflagration, dash, eagerness, earnestness, élan, enthusiasm, excitement, feeling, fervency, fervidity, fervidness, fervour, feu de joie, fierceness, flak, flames, force, fusillade, hail, heat, impetuosity, inferno, intensity, life, light, lustre, passion, radiance, salvo, scintillation, shelling, sniping, sparkle, spirit, splendour, verve, vigour, virtuosity, vivacity, volley, warmth, zeal.

*v* activate, animate, arouse, boot out, cashier, depose, detonate, discharge, dismiss, eject, electrify, enkindle, enliven, excite, explode, galvanise, give marching orders, give the bum's rush, hurl, ignite, impassion, incite, inflame, inspire, inspirit, kindle, launch, let off, light, loose, put a match to, quicken, rouse, sack, send off, set alight, set fire to, set off, set on fire, shell, shoot, show the door, stimulate, stir, touch off, trigger off, whet.

**firearm** *n* automatic, gun, handgun, musket, musketoon, muzzle-loader, muzzler, pistol, revolver, rifle, shooter, shooting-iron, shotgun, weapon.

**fireworks** n devils, explosions, feux d'artifice, firecrackers, gerbes, hysterics, illuminations, maroon, pyrotechnics, rage, rockets, rows, sparks, storm, temper, trouble, uproar.

**firm¹** adj abiding, adamant, anchored, balanced, braced, cast-iron, cemented, changeless, committed, compact, compressed, concentrated, congealed, constant, convinced, crisp, definite, dense, dependable, determined, dogged, durable, embedded, enduring, established, fast, fastened, fixed, grounded, hard, hardened, immovable, impregnable, indurate, inelastic, inflexible, iron-hearted, jelled, jellified, motionless, obdurate, reliable, resolute, resolved, rigid, robust, secure, secured, set, settled, solid, solidified, stable, stationary, staunch, steadfast, steady, stiff, strict, strong, sturdy, substantial, sure, taut, tight, true, unalterable, unassailable, unbending, unchanging, undeviating, unfaltering, unflinching, unmoved, unmoving, unshakable, unshakeable, unshaken, unshifting, unswerving, unwavering, unyielding, well-knit.

*antonyms* infirm, soft, unsound.

**firm²** n association, business, company, concern, conglomerate, corporation, enterprise, establishment, house, institution, organisation, outfit, partnership, set-up, syndicate.

**firmly** adv compactly, decisively, definitely, determinedly, doggedly, enduringly, four-square, immovably, inflexibly, motionlessly, resolutely, robustly, securely, solidly, squarely, stably, staunchly, steadfastly, steadily, strictly, strongly, sturdily, surely, tightly, unalterably, unchangeably, unflinchingly, unshakeably, unwaveringly.

*antonyms* hesitantly, uncertainly, unsoundly.

**firmness** n changelessness, compactness, constancy, conviction, density, dependability, determination, doggedness, durability, fixedness, fixity, hardness, immovability, impregnability, indomitability, inelasticity, inflexibility, obduracy, reliability, resistance, resolution, resolve, rigidity, solidity, soundness, stability, staunchness, steadfastness, steadiness, stiffness, strength, strength of will, strictness, sureness, tautness, tension, tightness, will, will-power.

*antonyms* infirmity, uncertainty, unsoundness.

**first** adj basic, cardinal, chief, earliest, eldest, elementary, embryonic, foremost, fundamental, head, highest, initial, introductory, key, leading, maiden, main, oldest, opening, original, paramount, predominant, pre-eminent, premier, primal, primary, prime, primeval, primitive, primordial, principal, prior, pristine, rudimentary, ruling, senior, sovereign, uppermost.

adv at the outset, before all else, beforehand, early on, firstly, in preference, in the beginning, initially, originally, primarily, rather, sooner, to begin with, to start with.

**first name** baptismal name, Christian name, font name, forename, given name.

**first-born** adj aîné(e), eigne, elder, eldest, older, primogenit, senior.

**first-fruits** n annates, primitiae, tribute.

**firsthand** adj direct, immediate, personal, straight from the horse's mouth.

*antonyms* hearsay, indirect.

**first-rate** adj A1, admirable, crack, élite, excellent, exceptional, exclusive, fine, first-class, jake, leading, matchless, nonpareil, outstanding, peerless, prime, second-to-none, splendid, superb, superior, superlative, tiptop, top, top-flight, top-notch, tops.

*antonym* inferior.

**fiscal** adj budgetary, bursal, economic, financial, monetary, money, pecuniary, treasury.

**fish** v angle, cast, delve, elicit, hint, hunt, invite, seek, solicit, trawl, troll.

n aquatic, chap, drip, fellow.

**fish out** come up with, dredge up, extract, extricate, find, haul up, produce.

**fish out of water** freak, horse marine, maverick, misfit, nonconformist, rogue, square peg in a round hole.

*antonym* conformist.

**fisherman** n angler, fisher, peter-man, piscator, piscatorian, rod-fisher, rodman, rodsman, rodster.

**fishing** n angling, fishery, halieutics, piscary, trawling, trolling.

adj halieutic, piscatorial, piscatory.

**fishy** adj doubtful, dubious, fish-like, funny, glassy, implausible, improbable, irregular, odd, piscatorial, piscatory, pisciform, piscine, queer, questionable, rummy, shady, suspect, suspicious, unlikely, vacant.

*antonyms* honest, legitimate.

**fissile** adj cleavable, divisible, easily split, fissionable, fissive, flaky, scissile, separable, severable.

**fission** n breaking, cleavage, division, parting, rending, rupture, schism, scission, severance, splitting.

**fissure** n breach, break, chasm, chink, cleavage, cleft, crack, cranny, crevasse, crevice, fault, foramen, fracture, gap, gash, grike, hole, interstice, opening, rent, rift, rupture, scissure, slit, split, sulcus, vein.

**fist** n duke, mitt, nieve, paw, pud, puddy.

**fit¹** adj able, able-bodied, adapted, adequate, apposite, appropriate, apt, becoming, blooming, capable, commensurate, competent, condign, convenient, correct, deserving, due, eligible, equipped, expedient, fit as a fiddle, fitted, fitting, hale, hale and hearty, healthy, in fine fettle, in good form, in good nick, in good shape, in good trim, in the pink, meet, prepared, proper, qualified, ready, right, robust, satisfactory, seemly, sound, strapping, strong, sturdy, suitable, suited, trained, trim, well, well-suited, worthy.

*antonym* unfit.

v accommodate, accord, adapt, adjust, agree, alter, arrange, assimilate, belong, change, concur, conform, correspond, dispose, dovetail, fashion, fay, figure, follow, gee, go, harmonise, interlock, join, match, meet, modify, place, position, reconcile, shape, suit, tally.

**fit out** accommodate, accoutre, arm, caparison, equip, kit out, outfit, prepare, provide, rig out, supply.

**fit²** *n* access, attack, bout, burst, caprice, convulsion, eruption, exies, explosion, fancy, humour, mood, outbreak, outburst, paroxysm, seizure, spasm, spell, storm, surge, whim.

**fitful** *adj* broken, desultory, disturbed, erratic, fluctuating, haphazard, intermittent, irregular, occasional, spasmodic, sporadic, uneven, unstable, unsteady, variable.

*antonyms* regular, steady.

**fitfully** *adv* desultorily, erratically, haphazardly, in fits and starts, in snatches, intermittently, interruptedly, irregularly, off and on, spasmodically, sporadically, unevenly, unsteadily.

*antonyms* regularly, steadily.

**fitness** *n* adaptation, adequacy, applicability, appropriateness, aptness, competence, condition, eligibility, haleness, health, healthiness, pertinence, preparedness, propriety, qualifications, readiness, robustness, seemliness, strength, suitability, vigour.

*antonym* unfitness.

**fitted** *adj* accoutred, adapted, appointed, armed, booted and spurred, built-in, caparisoned, equipped, fit, furnished, kitted, outfitted, permanent, prepared, provided, qualified, rigged out, right, suitable, supplied, tailor-made.

*antonym* unfitted.

**fitting** *adj* apposite, appropriate, apt, becoming, comme il faut, condign, correct, decent, decorous, deserved, desirable, harmonious, meet, merited, proper, right, seasonable, seemly, suitable.

*antonym* unsuitable.

*n* accessory, attachment, component, connection, fitment, fixture, part, piece, unit.

**fittings** *n* accessories, accoutrements, appointments, appurtenances, conveniences, equipment, extras, fitments, fixtures, furnishings, furniture, plenishing, trimmings.

**fivefold** *adj* pentaploid, quintuple, quintuplicate.

**fix¹** *v* adjust, agree on, anchor, appoint, arrange, arrive at, attach, bind, cement, conclude, confirm, congeal, connect, consolidate, correct, couple, decide, define, determine, direct, embed, establish, fasten, fiddle, finalise, firm, focus, freeze, glue, harden, implant, inculcate, influence, install, irradicate, limit, link, locate, make, manipulate, manoeuvre, mend, nail, name, ordain, pin, place, plant, point, position, prearrange, preordain, produce, regulate, repair, resolve, restore, rigidify, rigidise, rivet, root, seal, seat, secure, see to, set, settle, solidify, sort, sort out, specify, stabilise, stick, stiffen, straighten, swing, thicken, tidy, tie.

*n* corner, difficulty, dilemma, embarrassment, hole, jam, mess, muddle, nineholes, pickle, plight, predicament, quagmire, quandary, scrape, spot.

**fix up** accommodate, agree on, arrange (for), bring about, equip, fix, furnish, lay on, organise, plan, produce, provide, settle, sort out, supply.

**fix²** *n* dose, hit, injection, jag, score, shot, slug.

**fixation** *n* complex, compulsion, fetish, hang up, idée fixe, infatuation, mania, monomania, obsession, preoccupation, thing.

**fixed** *adj* agreed, anchored, arranged, attached, decided, definite, determinate, entrenched, established, fast, fiddled, fiducial, firm, framed, immovable, inflexible, ingrained, intent, invariable, lasting, level, manipulated, packed, permanent, planned, put-up, radicate, resolute, resolved, rigged, rigid, rooted, secure, set, settled, standing, steadfast, steady, sure, unalterable, unbending, unblinking, unchanging, undeviating, unflinching, unvarying, unwavering, unyielding.

*antonyms* alterable, variable.

**fixity** *n* determination, doggedness, fixedness, intentness, perseverance, persistence, resoluteness, resolve, stability, steadiness, strength, tenacity.

**fizz** *v* bubble, effervesce, fizzle, froth, fume, hiss, sizzle, sparkle, spit, sputter.

**fizzle out** abort, collapse, come to nothing, die away, die down, disappear, dissipate, evaporate, fail, fall through, fold, peter out, stop, subside, taper off.

**fizzy** *adj* aerated, bubbling, bubbly, carbonated, effervescent, frothy, gassy, sparkling.

**flabbergasted** *adj* amazed, astonished, astounded, bowled over, confounded, dazed, disconcerted, dumbfounded, nonplussed, overcome, overwhelmed, speechless, staggered, stunned, stupefied.

**flabbiness** *n* bloat, bloatedness, embonpoint, fat, flab, flaccidity, flesh, fleshiness, heaviness, laxness, limpness, looseness, overweight, pendulousness, plumpness, slackness.

*antonyms* firmness, leanness, strength.

**flabby** *adj* baggy, drooping, effete, enervated, feckless, feeble, flaccid, fleshy, floppy, fushionless, hanging, impotent, ineffective, ineffectual, inert, lax, limp, loose, nerveless, pendulous, plump, sagging, slack, sloppy, spineless, toneless, unfit, weak, yielding.

*antonyms* firm, lean, strong.

**flaccid** *adj* clammy, drooping, flabby, floppy, hypotonic, inert, lax, limp, loose, nerveless, relaxed, sagging, slack, soft, toneless, weak.

*antonym* firm.

**flaccidity** *n* clamminess, droopiness, flabbiness, floppiness, limpness, looseness, nervelessness, slackness, softness, tonelessness.

*antonym* firmness.

**flag¹** *v* abate, decline, degenerate, deteriorate, die, diminish, droop, dwindle, ebb, fade, fail, faint, fall (off), falter, flop, languish, lessen, peter out, sag, sink, slow, slump, subside, succumb, taper off, tire, wane, weaken, weary, wilt.

*antonym* revive.

**flag²** *n* banderole, banner, burgee, colours, ensign, fanion, gonfalon, jack, Jolly Roger, labarum, oriflamme, pennant, pennon, pen(n)oncel(le), standard, streamer, vane.

*v* docket, hail, indicate, label, mark, motion, note, salute, signal, tab, tag, warn, wave.

**flagellation** *n* beating, castigation, chastisement, flaying, flogging, lashing, scourging, thrashing, vapulation, verberation, whaling, whipping.

**flagging** *adj* declining, decreasing, deteriorating, diminishing, drooping, dwindling, ebbing, fading, failing, faltering, lessening, sagging, sinking, slowing, subsiding, tiring, waning, weakening, wilting.

*antonyms* returning, reviving.

**flagrant** *adj* arrant, atrocious, audacious, barefaced, blatant, bold, brazen, conspicuous, crying, egregious, enormous, flagitious, flaunting, glaring, heinous, immodest, infamous, notorious, open, ostentatious, outrageous, overt, rank, scandalous, shameless, unashamed, undisguised.

*antonyms* covert, secret.

**flail** *v* beat, scutch, swinge, thrash, thresh, whip.

**flair** *n* ability, accomplishment, acumen, aptitude, chic, dash, discernment, elegance, facility, faculty, feel, genius, gift, knack, mastery, nose, panache, skill, style, stylishness, talent, taste.

*antonym* ineptitude.

**flak** *n* abuse, animadversions, aspersions, bad press, brickbats, censure, complaints, condemnation, criticism, disapprobation, disapproval, disparagement, fault-finding, hostility, invective, opposition, stick, strictures.

**flake** *n* chip, disc, flaught, floccule, flocculus, lamina, layer, paring, peeling, scale, shaving, sliver, squama, wafer.
*v* blister, chip, delaminate, desquamate, exfoliate, peel, scale.

**flaky** *adj* desquamative, desquamatory, dry, exfoliative, furfuraceous, laminar, layered, scabrous, scaly, scurfy.

**flamboyance** *n* brilliance, colour, dash, élan, extravagance, glamour, ostentation, panache, pizzazz, showiness, style, theatricality.

*antonyms* diffidence, restraint.

**flamboyant** *adj* baroque, brilliant, colourful, dashing, dazzling, elaborate, exciting, extravagant, flashy, florid, gaudy, glamorous, jaunty, ornate, ostentatious, rich, showy, striking, stylish, swashbuckling, theatrical.

*antonyms* modest, restrained.

**flame** *v* beam, blaze, burn, flare, flash, glare, glow, radiate, shine.
*n* affection, ardour, beau, blaze, brightness, enthusiasm, fervency, fervour, fire, flake, flammule, heart-throb, intensity, keenness, light, lover, passion, radiance, sweetheart, warmth, zeal.

**flaming** *adj* ablaze, afire, alight, angry, ardent, aroused, blazing, brilliant, burning, fervid, fiery, frenzied, glowing, hot, impassioned, intense, raging, red, red-hot, scintillating, smouldering, vehement, vivid.

**flammable** *adj* combustible, combustive, deflagrable, ignitable, inflammable.

*antonyms* fire-resistant, flameproof, incombustible, non-flammable, non-inflammable.

**flange** *n* flanch, flare, lip, rim, skirt, splay.

**flank** *n* edge, flitch, ham, haunch, hip, loin, quarter, side, thigh, wing.
*v* accompany, border, bound, confine, edge, fringe, line, screen, skirt, wall.

**flap¹** *v* agitate, beat, dither, flacker, flaff, flaffer, flail, flutter, fuss, panic, shake, swing, swish, thrash, thresh, vibrate, wag, wave.
*n* agitation, commotion, dither, fluster, flutter, fuss, kerfuffle, pother, state, stew, sweat, tizzy, twitter.

**flap²** *n* aileron, apron, cover, fly, fold, lapel, lappet, lug, overlap, skirt, slat, tab, tag, tail.

**flare** *v* blaze, burn (up), burst, dazzle, erupt, explode, flame, flash, flicker, flutter, fulgurate, glare, waver.
*n* bell-bottom, blaze, broadening, burst, dazzle, flame, flanch, flange, flash, flicker, glare, gore, splay, widening.
**flare out** broaden, flanch, flaunch, splay, spread out, widen.
**flare up** blaze, blow one's top, erupt, explode, fly off the handle, lose one's cool.

**flash** *v* blaze, bolt, brandish, coruscate, dart, dash, display, exhibit, expose, flare, flaunt, flicker, flourish, fly, fulgurate, fulminate, glare, gleam, glint, glisten, glitter, light, race, scintillate, shimmer, shoot, show, sparkle, speed, sprint, streak, sweep, twinkle, whistle.
*n* blaze, bluette, burst, coruscation, dazzle, demonstration, display, flare, flaught, flicker, fulguration, gleam, hint, instant, jiff, jiffy, manifestation, moment, outburst, ray, scintillation, second, shaft, shake, shimmer, show, sign, spark, sparkle, split second, streak, touch, trice, twinkle, twinkling.

**flashing** *adj* coruscant, coruscating, dancing, flaring, flickering, fulgid, fulgurant, fulgurous, glittering, lambent, scintillating, sparkling, twinkling.

*antonym* steady.

**flashy** *adj* bold, brassy, cheap, flamboyant, flash, garish, gaudy, glamorous, glittery, glitzy, jazzy, loud, meretricious, obtrusive, ostentatious, raffish, rakish, ritzy, showy, snazzy, tacky, tasteless, tawdry, tig(e)rish, tinselly, vulgar.

*antonyms* plain, simple, tasteful.

**flask** *n* carafe, flacket, lekythos, matrass, pocket-pistol.

**flat¹** *adj* even, horizontal, lamellar, lamelliform, level, levelled, low, outstretched, planar, plane, prone, prostrate, reclining, recumbent, smooth, spread-eagled, supine, unbroken, uniform.
*n* lowland, marsh, morass, moss, mud flat, plain, shallow, shoal, strand, swamp.
**flat out** all out, at full speed, at full tilt, at top speed, double-quick, for all one is worth, hell for leather, posthaste.

**flat²** *adj* bored, boring, burst, collapsed, dead, deflated, depressed, dull, empty, flavourless, insipid, jejune, lacklustre, lifeless, monotonous, pointless, prosaic, punctured, spiritless, stale, tedious, uninteresting, unpalatable, vapid, watery, weak.

**flat³** *adj* absolute, categorical, direct, downright, explicit, final, fixed, out-and-out, peremptory, plain, point-blank, positive, straight, total, uncompromising, unconditional, unequivocal, unqualified.

*antonym* equivocal.

*adv* absolutely, categorically, completely, entirely, exactly, point-blank, precisely, totally, utterly.

**flat⁴** *n* apartment, bed-sit, bed-sitter, maison(n)ette, pad, penthouse, pied-à-terre, rooms, tenement.

**flatly** *adv* absolutely, categorically, completely, peremptorily, point-blank, positively, uncompromisingly, unconditionally, unhesitatingly.

**flatness** *n* boredom, dullness, emptiness, evenness, horizontality, insipidity, languor, levelness, monotony, smoothness, staleness, tastelessness, tedium, uniformity, vapidity.

**flatten** *v* compress, crush, demolish, even out, fell, floor, iron out, knock down, level, overwhelm, planish, plaster, prostrate, raze, roll, slight, smooth, squash, subdue, trample.

**flatter** *v* adulate, become, beslobber, blandish, blarney, butter up, cajole, claw, collogue, compliment, court, enhance, eulogise, fawn, flannel, fleech, gloze, humour, inveigle, laud, play up to, praise, sawder, set off, show to advantage, soap, soft-soap, soothe, suit, sweet-talk, sycophantise, wheedle.

*antonym* criticise.

**flatterer** *n* adulator, back-scratcher, bootlicker, earwig, encomiast, eulogiser, fawner, flunkey, groveller, incenser, lackey, sycophant, toady.

*antonyms* critic, opponent.

**flattering** *adj* adulatory, becoming, complimentary, effective, effusive, enhancing, favourable, fawning, fulsome, gnathonic, gratifying, honeyed, honey-tongued, ingratiating, kind, laudatory, obsequious, servile, smooth-spoken, smooth-tongued, sugared, sugary, sycophantic, unctuous.

*antonyms* candid, uncompromising, unflattering.

**flattery** *n* adulation, backscratching, blandishment, blarney, bootlicking, butter, cajolement, cajolery, eulogy, fawning, flannel, flapdoodle, fleechment, fulsomeness, ingratiation, obsequiousness, servility, soap, soft sawder, soft soap, sugar, sweet talk, sycophancy, sycophantism, taffy, toadyism, unctuousness.

*antonym* criticism.

**flatulence** *n* borborygmus, eructation, flatulency, flatus, gas, gassiness, pomposity, prolixity, turgidity, ventosity, wind, windiness.

**flatulent** *v* gassy, pompous, prolix, swollen, turgid, ventose, windy.

**flaunt** *v* air, boast, brandish, dangle, display, disport, exhibit, flash, flourish, parade, show off, sport, vaunt, wield.

**flavour** *n* aroma, aspect, character, essence, extract, feel, feeling, flavouring, hint, odour, piquancy, property, quality, relish, sapidity, savour, savouriness, seasoning, smack, soupçon, stamp, style, suggestion, tang, taste, tastiness, tinge, tone, touch, zest, zing.

*v* contaminate, ginger up, imbue, infuse, lace, leaven, season, spice, taint.

**flavourful** *adj* delicious, flavorous, flavoursome, high-tasted, palatable, sapid, savoury, tasty, toothsome.

*antonyms* insipid, tasteless.

**flavouring** *n* essence, extract, seasoning, spirit, tincture, zest.

**flaw** *n* blemish, breach, break, cleft, crack, craze, crevice, defect, disfigurement, failing, fallacy, fault, fissure, fracture, hamartia, imperfection, lapse, macula, mark, mistake, rent, rift, shortcoming, slip, speck, split, spot, tear, weakness, wreath.

**flawed** *adj* blemished, broken, chipped, cracked, damaged, defective, disfigured, erroneous, faulty, imperfect, marked, marred, spoilt, unsound, vicious, vitiated.

*antonyms* flawless, perfect.

**flawless** *adj* faultless, immaculate, impeccable, intact, irreproachable, perfect, sound, spotless, stainless, unblemished, unbroken, undamaged, unsullied, whole.

*antonyms* flawed, imperfect.

**flay** *v* castigate, excoriate, execrate, flench, flog, lambast, pull to pieces, revile, scourge, skin, skin alive, tear a strip off, upbraid.

**flea-ridden** *adj* crawling, decrepit, dingy, flea-bitten, fly-blown, frowsty, grotty, grubby, infested, insalubrious, lousy, mangy, mean, moth-eaten, mucky, pediculous, run-down, scabby, scruffy, scurfy, sleazy, slummy, sordid, squalid, tatty, unhealthy, unhygienic.

*antonym* salubrious.

**fleck** *v* bespeckle, besprinkle, dapple, dot, dust, freak, mark, mottle, speckle, spinkle, spot, stipple, streak, variegate.

*n* dot, freak, macula, mark, point, speck, speckle, spot, streak.

**fledgling** *n* apprentice, beginner, chick, greenhorn, learner, neophyte, nestling, newcomer, novice, novitiate, recruit, rookie, tenderfoot, trainee, tyro.

**flee** *v* abscond, avoid, beat a hasty retreat, bolt, bunk (off), cut and run, decamp, depart, escape, fly, get away, leave, make off, make oneself scarce, scarper, scram, shun, skedaddle, split, take flight, take it on the lam, take off, take to one's heels, vamoose, vanish, withdraw.

*antonyms* stand, stay.

**fleece** *v* bilk, bleed, cheat, clip, con, defraud, diddle, mulct, overcharge, plunder, rifle, rip off, rob, rook, shear, skin, soak, squeeze, steal, sting, swindle.

**fleecy** *adj* downy, eriophorous, floccose, flocculate, fluffy, hairy, lanuginose, nappy, pilose, shaggy, soft, velvety, woolly.

*antonyms* bald, smooth.

**fleet**[1] *n* argosy, armada, escadrille, flota, flotilla, navy, squadron, task force.

**fleet**[2] *adj* expeditious, fast, flying, light-footed, mercurial, meteoric, nimble, quick, rapid, speedy, swift, velocipede, winged.

*antonym* slow.

**fleeting** *adj* brief, disappearing, ephemeral, evanescent, flitting, flying, fugacious, fugitive, impermanent, momentary, passing, short, short-lived, temporary, transient, transitory, vanishing.

*antonym* lasting.

**fleetness** *n* celerity, dispatch, expedition, expeditiousness, light-footedness, nimbleness, quickness, rapidity, speed, speediness, swiftness, velocity.

*antonym* sluggishness.

**flesh** *n* animality, beef, blood, body, brawn, carnality, corporeality, dead-meat, family, fat, fatness, flesh and blood, food, human nature, kin, kindred, kinsfolk, kith and kin, matter, meat, physicality, pulp, relations, relatives, sensuality, substance, tissue.

**fleshiness** *n* adiposity, chubbiness, corpulence, embonpoint, flabbiness, heaviness, obesity, plumpness, portliness, stoutness, tubbiness.

**fleshly** *adj* animal, bestial, bodily, brutish, carnal, corporal, corporeal, earthly, earthy, erotic, human, lustful, material, mundane, physical, secular, sensual, terrestrial, wordly.

*antonym* spiritual.

**fleshy** *adj* ample, beefy, brawny, carneous, carnose, chubby, chunky, corpulent, fat, flabby, hefty, meaty, obese, overweight, paunchy, plump, podgy, portly, rotund, stout, tubby, well-padded.

*antonym* thin.

**flex** *v* angle, bend, bow, contract, crook, curve, double up, ply, tighten.

*antonyms* extend, straighten.

**flexibility** *n* adaptability, adjustability, agreeability, amenability, bendability, complaisance, elasticity, flexion, give, pliability, pliancy, resilience, spring, springiness, suppleness, tensility.

*antonym* inflexibility.

**flexible** *adj* accommodating, adaptable, adjustable, agreeable, amenable, bendable, biddable, complaisant, compliant, discretionary, docile, double-jointed, ductile, elastic, flexile, gentle, limber, lissome, lithe, loose-limbed, manageable, mobile, mouldable, open, plastic, pliable, pliant, responsive, springy, stretchy, supple, tensile, tractable, variable, whippy, willowy, withy, yielding.

*antonym* inflexible.

**flibbertigibbet** *n* backfisch, bird-brain, butterfly, featherbrain, fizgig, flapper, giddy goat, madcap, rattle-brain, rattle-head, rattle-pate, scatterbrain, tearaway.

**flick** *v* bat, click, dab, fillip, flap, flicker, flip, flirt, hit, jab, peck, rap, strike, tap, touch, whip.

*n* click, fillip, flap, flip, flutter, jab, peck, rap, tap, touch.

**flick through** flip, glance, riffle, scan, skim, skip, thumb.

**flicker** *v* coruscate, flare, flash, flutter, glimmer, gutter, quiver, scintillate, shimmer, sparkle, twinkle, vibrate, waver.

*n* atom, breath, coruscation, drop, flare, flash, gleam, glimmer, glint, indication, inkling, iota, scintillation, spark, trace, vestige.

**flickering** *n* coruscant, coruscating, guttering, lambent, sparkling, twinkling, unsteady.

**flight**[1] *n* aeronautics, air transport, air travel, aviation, cloud, echelon, escadrille, flip, flock, flying, formation, journey, mounting, soaring, squadron, swarm, trip, unit, volitation, voyage, wing, winging.

**flight**[2] *n* breakaway, departure, escape, exit, exodus, fleeing, getaway, guy, hegira, retreat, running away.

**flightiness** *n* capriciousness, changeability, dizziness, fickleness, flippancy, frivolity, giddiness, inconstancy, irresponsibility, levity, lightness, mercurialness, volatility, wildness.

*antonym* steadiness.

**flighty** *adj* bird-brained, bird-witted, bubble-headed, capricious, changeable, dizzy, fickle, frivolous, giddy, hare-brained, impetuous, impulsive, inconstant, irresponsible, light-headed, mercurial, rattle-brained, rattle-headed, rattle-pated, scatterbrained, silly, skittish, thoughtless, unbalanced, unstable, unsteady, volage, volageous, volatile, whisky-frisky, wild.

*antonym* steady.

**flimsy** *adj* cardboard, chiffon, cobwebby, delicate, diaphanous, ethereal, feeble, fragile, frail, frivolous, gauzy, gimcrack, gossamer, implausible, inadequate, insubstantial, light, makeshift, meagre, poor, rickety, shaky, shallow, sheer, slight, superficial, thin, transparent, trivial, unconvincing, unsatisfactory, unsubstantial, vaporous, weak.

*antonym* sturdy.

**flinch** *v* baulk, blench, cower, cringe, draw back, duck, flee, quail, quake, recoil, retreat, shake, shirk, shiver, shrink, shudder, shy away, start, swerve, tremble, wince, withdraw.

**fling** *v* bung, cant, cast, catapult, chuck, heave, hurl, jerk, let fly, lob, pitch, precipitate, propel, send, shoot, shy, sling, slug, souse, throw, toss.

*n* attempt, bash, binge, cast, crack, gamble, go, heave, indulgence, lob, pitch, shot, spree, stab, throw, toss, trial, try, turn, venture, whirl.

**flip** *v* cast, fillip, flap, flick, jerk, pitch, snap, spin, throw, toss, turn, twirl, twist.

*n* bob, fillip, flap, flick, jerk, toss, turn, twirl, twist.

**flippancy** *n* cheek, cheekiness, disrespect, disrespectfulness, frivolity, glibness, impertinence, irreverence, levity, persiflage, pertness, sauciness, superficiality.

*antonym* earnestness.

**flippant** *adj* brash, cheeky, cocky, disrespectful, flip, frivolous, glib, impertinent, impudent, irreverent, malapert, nonchalant, offhand, pert, pococurante, rude, saucy, superficial, unserious.

*antonym* earnest.

**flirt** *v* chat up, coquet, dally, ogle, philander, tease.

*n* chippy, coquet(te), gillet, gillflirt, heart-breaker, hussy, philanderer, tease, trifler, wanton.

**flirt with** consider, dabble in, entertain, make up to, play with, toy with, trifle with, try.

**flirtation** *n* affair, amorousness, amour, chatting up, coquetry, dalliance, dallying, intrigue, philandering, sport, teasing, toying, trifling.

**flirtatious** *adj* amorous, arch, come-hither, come-on, coquettish, coy, flirty, loose, promiscuous, provocative, sportive, teasing, wanton.

**flit** *v* beat, bob, dance, dart, elapse, flash, fleet, flutter, fly, pass, skim, slip, speed, volitate, whisk, wing.

**flitting** *adj* bobbing, dancing, darting, ephemeral, fleet, fleeting, flittering, fluttering, skimming, volitant.

**float** *v* bob, drift, glide, hang, hover, initiate, launch, poise, promote, ride, sail, set up, slide, swim, waft.

*antonym* sink.

**floating** *adj* afloat, bobbing, buoyant, buoyed up, fluctuating, free, migratory, movable, ocean-going, sailing, swimming, unattached, uncommitted, unfixed, unsinkable, unsubmerged, variable, wandering, water-borne.

**flock** *v* bunch, cluster, collect, congregate, converge, crowd, gather, gravitate, group, herd, huddle, mass, swarm, throng, troop.

*n* assembly, bevy, collection, colony, company, congregation, convoy, crowd, drove, flight, gaggle, gathering, group, herd, horde, host, mass, multitude, pack, shoal, skein, swarm, throng.

**flog** *v* beat, birch, breech, chastise, drive, drub, flagellate, flay, hide, knout, k(o)urbash, larrup, lash, overexert, overtax, overwork, punish, push, scourge, strain, swish, tat, tax, thrash, trounce, vapulate, verberate, welt, whack, whale, whang, whip, whop.

**flogging** *n* beating, caning, drubbing, flagellation, flaying, hiding, horsewhipping, lashing, scourging, thrashing, trouncing, vapulation, verberation, whaling, whipping, whopping.

**flood** *v* bog down, brim, choke, deluge, drench, drown, engulf, fill, flow, glut, gush, immerse, inundate, overflow, oversupply, overwhelm, pour, rush, saturate, soak, submerge, surge, swamp, swarm, sweep.

*n* abundance, alluvion, bore, cataclysm, debacle, deluge, diluvion, diluvium, downpour, eagre, flash flood, flow, freshet, glut, inundation, multitude, outpouring, overflow, plethora, profusion, rush, spate, stream, superfluity, tide, torrent.

*antonyms* dearth, drought, trickle.

**floor** *n* base, basis, deck, étage, landing, level, stage, storey, tier.

*v* baffle, beat, bewilder, confound, conquer, defeat, discomfit, disconcert, down, dumbfound, frustrate, nonplus, overthrow, overwhelm, perplex, prostrate, puzzle, stump, stun, throw, trounce, worst.

**flop** *v* bomb, close, collapse, dangle, droop, drop, fail, fall, fall flat, flap, flump, fold, founder, hang, misfire, plump, sag, slump, topple, tumble.

*n* balls-up, cock-up, debacle, disaster, failure, fiasco, loser, no go, non-starter, turkey, wash-out.

**floppy** *adj* baggy, dangling, droopy, flabby, flaccid, flapping, flappy, flopping, hanging, limp, loose, pendulous, sagging, soft.

*antonym* firm.

**flora** *n* botany, herbage, plantage, plant-life, plants, vegetable kingdom, vegetation.

**florid** *adj* baroque, blowzy, bombastic, busy, coloratura, elaborate, embellished, euphuistic, figurative, flamboyant, flourishy, flowery, flushed, fussy, grandiloquent, high-coloured, high-falutin(g), high-flown, melismatic, ornate, overelaborate, purple, raddled, red, rococo, rubicund, ruddy.

*antonyms* pale, plain.

**flotsam** *n* debris, detritus, jetsam, junk, oddments, scum, sweepings, waveson, wreckage.

**flounce** *v* bob, bounce, fling, jerk, spring, stamp, storm, throw, toss, twist.

*n* falbala, frill, fringe, furbelow, ruffle, trimming, valance.

**flounder** *v* blunder, bungle, falter, flail, fumble, grope, muddle, plunge, stagger, struggle, stumble, thrash, toss, tumble, wallop, wallow, welter.

**flourish¹** *v* advance, bloom, blossom, boom, burgeon, develop, do well, flower, get on, grow, increase, mushroom, progress, prosper, succeed, thrive, wax.

*antonyms* fail, languish.

**flourish²** *v* brandish, display, flaunt, flutter, parade, shake, sweep, swing, swish, twirl, vaunt, wag, wave, wield.

*n* arabesque, brandishing, ceremony, curlicue, dash, decoration, display, élan, embellishment, fanfare, ornament, ornamentation, panache, parade, paraph, pizzazz, plume, shaking, show, sweep, twirling, wave.

**flourishing** *adj* blooming, booming, burgeoning, developing, going strong, in the pink, lush, luxuriant, mushrooming, progressing, prospering, rampant, rank, riotous, successful, thriving.

*antonyms* failing, languishing.

**flout** *v* affront, contemn, defy, deride, disregard, insult, jeer at, mock, outrage, reject, ridicule, scoff at, scorn, scout, spurn, taunt.

*antonym* respect.

**flow** *v* arise, bubble, cascade, circulate, course, deluge, derive, distil, drift, emanate, emerge, flood, glide, gush, inundate, issue, move, originate, overflow, pour, proceed, purl, result, ripple, roll, run, rush, slide, slip, spew, spill, spring, spurt, squirt, stream, surge, sweep, swirl, teem, well, whirl.

*n* abundance, cascade, course, current, deluge, drift, effluence, efflux, effusion, emanation, flood, flowage, flux, fluxion, gush, outflow, outpouring, plenty, plethora, spate, spurt, stream, succession, tide, train, wash.

**flower** *n* best, bloom, blossom, choice, cream, crème de la crème, efflorescence, élite, fleuret, fleuron, floret, floscule, floweret, freshness, height, pick, prime, vigour.

*v* blossom, blow, burgeon, dehisce, effloresce, flourish, mature, open, unfold.

**flowering** *adj* blooming, bloomy, blossoming, efflorescent, florescent.

*n* anthesis, blooming, blossoming, burgeoning, development, florescence, flourishing, flowerage, maturing.

**flowery** *adj* affected, baroque, elaborate, embellished, euphuistic, fancy, figurative, floral, floriated, florid, fulsome, high-flown, ornate, overelaborate, overwrought, rhetorical, Wardour Street.

*antonym* plain.

**flowing** *adj* abounding, brimming, cantabile, cascading, continuous, cursive, easy, facile, falling, flooded, fluent, full, gushing, overrun, prolific, rich, rolling, rushing, smooth, streaming, surging, sweeping, teeming, unbroken, uninterrupted, voluble.

*antonyms* hesitant, interrupted.

**fluctuate** *v* alter, alternate, change, ebb and flow, float, hesitate, oscillate, pendulate, rise and fall, seesaw, shift, shuffle, sway, swing, undulate, vacillate, vary, veer, waver.

**fluctuating** *adj* capricious, changeable, fickle, fluctuant, irresolute, mutable, oscillating, oscillatory, rising and falling, swaying, swinging, unstable, unsteady, vacillant, vacillating, vacillatory, variable, wavering.

*antonym* stable.

**fluctuation** *n* alternation, ambivalence, capriciousness, change, ficklessness, inconstancy, instability, irresolution, oscillation, shift, swing, unsteadiness, vacillation, variability, variableness, variation, wavering.

**fluency** *n* articulateness, assurance, command, control, ease, eloquence, facility, facundity, glibness, readiness, slickness, smoothness, volubility.

*antonym* incoherence.

**fluent** *adj* articulate, easy, effortless, eloquent, facile, flowing, fluid, glib, mellifluous, natural, ready, smooth, smooth-talking, voluble, well-versed.

*antonym* tongue-tied.

**fluff** *n* down, dust, dustball, floccus, flosh, floss, flue, fug, fuzz, lint, nap, oose, pile.

*v* balls up, botch, bungle, cock up, fumble, mess up, muddle, muff, screw up, spoil.

*antonym* bring off.

**fluffy** *adj* downy, eriophorous, feathery, fleecy, floccose, flocculate, flossy, fuzzy, gossamer, hairy, lanuginose, lanuginous, nappy, oozy, shaggy, silky, soft, velvety, woolly.

*antonym* smooth.

**fluid** *adj* adaptable, adjustable, aqueous, changeable, diffluent, easy, elegant, feline, flexible, floating, flowing, fluctuating, fluent, fluidal, fluidic, graceful, inconstant, indefinite, liquefied, liquid, melted, mercurial, mobile, molten, mutable, protean, running, runny, shifting, sinuous, smooth, unstable, watery.

*antonyms* solid, stable.

*n* humour, juice, liquid, liquor, sanies, sap, solution.

**fluke** *n* accident, blessing, break, chance, coincidence, fortuity, freak, lucky break, quirk, serendipity, stroke, windfall.

**fluky** *adj* accidental, chance, chancy, coincidental, fortuitous, fortunate, freakish, incalculable, lucky, serendipitous, uncertain.

**flummox** *v* baffle, bamboozle, befuddle, bewilder, confound, confuse, defeat, fox, mystify, nonplus, perplex, puzzle, stump, stymie.

**flummoxed** *adj* at a loss, at sea, baffled, befuddled, bewildered, confounded, confused, foxed, mystified, nonplussed, perplexed, puzzled, stumped, stymied.

**flunkey** *n* assistant, boot-licker, creature, cringer, drudge, footman, hanger-on, healer, lackey, manservant, menial, minion, slave, toady, tool, underling, valet, yes-man.

**flurry** *n* ado, agitation, burst, bustle, commotion, disturbance, excitement, ferment, flap, flaw, fluster, flutter, furore, fuss, gust, hubbub, hurry, kerfuffle, outbreak, pother, spell, spurt, squall, stir, to-do, tumult, upset, whirl.

*v* abash, agitate, bewilder, bother, bustle, confuse, disconcert, discountenance, disturb, fluster, flutter, fuss, hassle, hurry, hustle, perturb, rattle, ruffle, unsettle, upset.

**flush¹** *v* blush, burn, colour, crimson, flame, glow, go red, mantle, redden, rouge, suffuse.

*antonym* pale.

*n* bloom, blush, colour, freshness, glow, redness, rosiness, rud, vigour.

**flush²** *v* cleanse, douche, drench, eject, empty, evacuate, expel, hose, rinse, swab, syringe, wash.

*adj* abundant, affluent, full, generous, in funds, lavish, liberal, moneyed, overflowing, prodigal, prosperous, rich, rolling, wealthy, well-heeled, well-off, well-supplied, well-to-do.

**flush³** *adj* even, flat, level, plane, smooth, square, true.

**flush⁴** *v* discover, disturb, drive out, force out, rouse, run to earth, start, uncover.

**flushed** *adj* ablaze, aflame, aglow, animated, aroused, blowzy, blushing, burning, crimson, elated, embarrassed, enthused, excited, exhilarated, exultant, febrile, feverish, glowing, hectic, high, hot, inspired, intoxicated, red, rosy, rubicund, ruddy, sanguine, scarlet, thrilled.

*antonym* pale.

**fluster** *v* abash, agitate, bother, bustle, confound, confuse, discombobulate, disconcert, discountenance, disturb, embarrass, excite, faze, flurry, hassle, heat, hurry, perturb, pother, pudder, rattle, ruffle, unnerve, unsettle, upset.

*antonym* calm.

*n* agitation, bustle, commotion, discomposure, distraction, disturbance, dither, embarrassment, faze, flap, flurry, flutter, furore, kerfuffle, perturbation, ruffle, state, tizzy, turmoil.

*antonym* calm.

**fluted** *adj* chamfered, channelled, corrugated, furrowed, gouged, grooved, ribbed, ridged, rutted, valleculate.

**flutter** *v* agitate, bat, beat, dance, discompose, flap, flichter, flicker, flit, flitter, fluctuate, hover, palpitate, quiver, ripple, ruffle, shiver, toss, tremble, vibrate, volitate, wave, waver.

*n* agitation, commotion, confusion, discomposure, dither, excitement, flurry, fluster, nervousness, palpitation, perturbation, quiver, quivering, shiver, shudder, state, tremble, tremor, tumult, twitching, upset, vibration, volitation.

**fluttering** *adj* beating, dancing, flapping, flickering, flitting, hovering, palpitating, quivering, tossing, trembling, volitant, waving.

**flux** *n* alteration, change, chaos, development, flow, fluctuation, fluidity, instability, modification, motion, movement, mutability, mutation, stir, transition, unrest.

*antonym* stability.

**fly**[1] *v* abscond, aviate, avoid, bolt, career, clear out, dart, dash, decamp, disappear, display, elapse, escape, flap, flee, flit, float, flutter, get away, glide, hare, hasten, hasten away, hedgehop, hightail it, hoist, hover, hurry, light out, mount, operate, pass, pilot, race, raise, retreat, roll by, run, run for it, rush, sail, scamper, scarper, scoot, shoot, show, shun, skim, soar, speed, sprint, take flight, take off, take to one's heels, take wing, tear, vamoose, volitate, wave, whisk, whiz, wing, zoom.

**fly at** assail, assault, attack, fall upon, go for, have at, light into, pitch into, rush at.

**fly in the face of** affront, defy, disobey, flout, insult, oppose.

**fly**[2] *adj* alert, artful, astute, canny, careful, cunning, knowing, nobody's fool, on the ball, prudent, sagacious, sharp, shrewd, smart, wide-awake.

**fly-by-night** *adj* brief, cowboy, discreditable, disreputable, dubious, ephemeral, here today - gone tomorrow, impermanent, irresponsible, questionable, shady, short-lived, undependable, unreliable, untrustworthy.

*antonym* reliable.

**flying** *adj* airborne, brief, express, fast, flapping, fleet, fleeting, floating, fluttering, fugacious, fugitive, gliding, hasty, hovering, hurried, mercurial, mobile, rapid, rushed, short-lived, soaring, speedy, streaming, transitory, vanishing, volant, volatic, volitant, volitational, volitorial, waving, wind-borne, winged, winging.

**foam** *n* barm, bubbles, effervescence, foaminess, froth, frothiness, head, lather, scum, spume, spumescence, suds, surf.

*v* boil, bubble, effervesce, fizz, froth, lather, spume.

**foamy** *adj* barmy, bubbly, foaming, frothy, lathery, spumescent, spumous, spumy, sudsy.

**fob off** appease, deceive, dump, foist, get rid of, give a sop to, impose, inflict, palm off, pass off, placate, put off, stall, unload.

**focus** *n* axis, centre, centre of attraction, core, crux, cynosure, focal point, headquarters, heart, hinge, hub, kernel, linchpin, nucleus, pivot, target.

*v* aim, centre, concentrate, concentre, converge, direct, fix, focalise, home in, join, meet, rivet, spotlight, zero in, zoom in.

**fodder** *n* browsing, feed, food, foodstuff, forage, fuel, nourishment, pabulum, provand, provend, provender, proviant, rations, silage.

**foe** *n* adversary, antagonist, enemy, foeman, ill-wisher, opponent, rival.

*antonym* friend.

**fog** *n* bewilderment, blanket, blindness, brume, confusion, daze, gloom, haze, London particular, miasma, mist, muddle, murk, murkiness, obscurity, pea-souper, perplexity, puzzlement, smog, stupor, trance, vagueness.

*v* becloud, bedim, befuddle, bewilder, blanket, blind, cloud, confuse, darken, daze, dim, dull, mist, muddle, obfuscate, obscure, perplex, shroud, steam up, stupefy.

**fog(e)y** *n* anachronism, antique, archaism, dodo, eccentric, fossil, fuddy-duddy, moss-back, mumpsimus, oddity, period piece, relic, square, stick-in-the-mud.

**foggy** *adj* beclouded, befuddled, bewildered, blurred, blurry, brumous, clouded, cloudy, confused, dark, dazed, dim, grey, hazy, indistinct, misty, muddled, muggish, muggy, murky, muzzy, nebulous, obscure, shadowy, smoggy, stupefied, stupid, unclear, vague, vaporous.

*antonym* clear.

**foible** *n* crotchet, defect, eccentricity, failing, fault, habit, idiosyncrasy, imperfection, infirmity, oddity, oddness, peculiarity, quirk, shortcoming, strangeness, weakness.

**foil**[1] *v* baffle, balk, check, checkmate, circumvent, counter, defeat, disappoint, elude, frustrate, nullify, obstruct, outsmart, outwit, spike (someone's) guns, stop, stump, thwart.

*antonym* abet.

**foil**[2] *n* antithesis, background, balance, complement, contrast, relief, setting.

**foist** *v* fob off, force, get rid of, impose, insert, insinuate, interpolate, introduce, palm off, pass off, thrust, unload, wish on.

**fold** *v* bend, clasp, close, collapse, crash, crease, crimp, crumple, dog-ear, double, embrace, enclose, enfold, entwine, envelop, fail, fake, gather, go bust, hug, intertwine, overlap, pleat, ply, shut down, tuck, wrap, wrap up.

*n* bend, corrugation, crease, crimp, duplicature, furrow, knife-edge, layer, overlap, pleat, ply, turn, wimple, wrinkle.

**folder** *n* binder, envelope, file, folio, holder, portfolio.

**foliage** *n* foliation, foliature, frondescence, greenery, leafage, verdure, vernation.

**folk** *n* clan, family, kin, kindred, kinfolk, kinsmen, nation, people, race, society, tribe.

*adj* ancestral, ethnic, indigenous, national, native, traditional, tribal.

**folklore** *n* fables, folk-tales, legends, lore, mythology, myths, superstitions, tales, tradition.

**follow** *v* accompany, accord, act according to, appreciate, arise, attend, catch, catch on, chase, come after, come next, comply, comprehend, conform, cultivate, dangle, develop, dog, emanate, ensue, escort, fathom, get, get the picture, grasp, haunt, heed, hound, hunt, imitate, keep abreast of, live up to, mind, note, obey, observe, pursue, realise, regard, result, second, see, shadow, stag, stalk, succeed, supersede, supervene, supplant, support, tag along, tail, track, trail, twig, understand, watch.

*antonyms* desert, precede.

**follow through** complete, conclude, consummate, continue, finish, fulfil, implement, pursue, see through.

**follow up** check out, consolidate, continue, investigate, pursue, reinforce, substantiate.

**follower** *n* acolyte, adherent, admirer, aficionado, Anthony, apostle, attendant, backer, believer, buff, cohort, companion, convert, devotee, disciple, emulator, fan, fancier, freak, galloglass, habitué, hanger-on, heeler, helper, henchman, imitator, lackey, minion, partisan, poodle-dog, poursuivant, pupil, representative, retainer, running dog, servitor, sidekick, supporter, tantony, votary, worshipper.

*antonyms* leader, opponent.

**following** *adj* coming, consecutive, consequent, consequential, ensuing, later, next, resulting, sequent, subsequent, succeeding, successive.

*n* audience, backing, circle, claque, clientèle, coterie, entourage, fans, followers, patronage, public, retinue, suite, support, supporters, train.

**folly**[1] *n* absurdity, craziness, daftness, fatuity, foolishness, idiocy, illogicality, imbecility, imprudence, indiscretion, insanity, irrationality, irresponsibility, lunacy, madness, moonraking, moria, nonsense, preposterousness, rashness, recklessness, senselessness, silliness, stupidity, unreason, unwisdom.

*antonym* prudence.

**folly**[2] *n* belvedere, gazebo, monument, tower, whim.

**foment** *v* activate, agitate, arouse, brew, encourage, excite, foster, goad, incite, instigate, kindle, promote, prompt, provoke, quicken, raise, rouse, spur, stimulate, stir up, whip up, work up.

*antonym* quell.

**fomenter** *n* abettor, agitator, demagogue, firebrand, incendiary, inciter, instigator, mob-orator, rabble-rouser, troublemaker, tub-thumper.

**fond** *adj* absurd, adoring, affectionate, amorous, caring, credulous, deluded, devoted, doting, empty, foolish, indiscreet, indulgent, loving, naive, over-optimistic, sanguine, tender, uxorious, vain, warm.

*antonyms* hostile, realistic.

**fond of** addicted to, attached to, enamoured of, hooked on, keen on, partial to, predisposed towards, stuck on, sweet on.

**fondle** *v* caress, cocker, coddle, cuddle, dandle, lallygag, pat, pet, smuggle, stroke.

**fondly** *adv* absurdly, adoringly, affectionately, credulously, dearly, foolishly, indulgently, lovingly, naïvely, over-optimistically, sanguinely, stupidly, tenderly, vainly.

**fondness** *n* affection, attachment, devotion, engouement, enthusiasm, fancy, inclination, kindness, leaning, liking, love, partiality, penchant, predilection, preference, soft spot, susceptibility, taste, tenderness, weakness.

*antonym* aversion.

**food** *n* aliment, ambrosia, board, bread, cheer, chow, comestibles, commons, cooking, cuisine, diet, eatables, eats, edibles, fare, feed, fodder, foodstuffs, forage, grub, larder, meat, menu, nosh, nourishment, nouriture, nutriment, nutrition, pabulum, pap, prog, provand, provend, provender, proviant, provisions, rations, refreshment, scoff, scran, stores, subsistence, sustenance, table, tack, tommy, tuck, tucker, viands, victuals, vittles, vivers.

**fool** *n* ass, bécasse, berk, besom-head, bête, bird-brain, blockhead, bonehead, boodle, buffethead, buffoon, burk, butt, capocchia, Charlie, chump, clodpate, clot, clown, cluck, comic, coxcomb, cuckoo, daftie, daw, dawcock, dimwit, dizzard, Dogberry, dolt, dope, dottle, droll, drongo, dumb-bell, dumb-cluck, dumbo, dunce, dunderhead, dunderpate, dupe, easy mark, fall guy, fathead, fon, galah, gaupus, git, goon, goop, goose, greenhorn, gudgeon, gull, halfwit, harlequin, idiot, ignoramus, illiterate, imbecile, jackass, Jack-fool, jerk, jester, jobernowl, josh, joskin, leather-head, loggerhead, log-head, loon, madhaun, merry-andrew, mooncalf, moron, motley, mug, nerd, nig-nog, nincompoop, ninny, nit, nitwit, nong, noodle, numskull, nurd, pierrot, pillock, pot-head, prat, prick, punchinello, sap, saphead, sawney, schlep, schmo, schmuck, silly, silly-billy, simpleton, soft, soft-head, softie, softy, stooge, stupe, stupid, sucker, thicko, tomfool, Tom-noddy, turnip, twerp, twit, wally, want-wit, wimp, witling, wooden-head, yap, zany, zombie.

*v* act dido, act the fool, act up, bamboozle, be silly, beguile, bluff, cavort, cheat, clown, con, cozen, cut capers, daff, deceive, delude, diddle, dupe, feign, fiddle, fon, frolic, gull, have on, hoax, hoodwink, horse around, jest, joke, kid, lark, meddle, mess, mess about, mislead, monkey, play, play the fool, play the goat, play up, pretend, put one over on, string, string along, swindle, take in, tamper, tease, toy, trick, trifle.

**fool about** dawdle, idle, kill time, lark, lark about, mess about, play about, trifle.

**foolery** *n* antics, buffoonery, capers, carry-on, childishness, clowning, desipience, dido, drollery, espièglerie, farce, folly, fooling, high jinks, horseplay, larks, mischief, monkey tricks, nonsense, practical jokes, pranks, shenanigans, silliness, tomfoolery, waggery, zanyism.

**foolhardy** *adj* adventurous, bold, dare-devil, hot-headed, ill-advised, ill-considered, impetuous, imprudent, incautious, irresponsible, madcap, precipitate, rash, reckless, temerarious, unheeding, unwary, venturesome, venturous.

*antonym* cautious.

**fooling** *n* bluffing, buffoonery, clownishness, desipience, drollery, farce, jesting, joking, kidding, kidology, mockery, nonsense, pretence, shamming, skylarking, teasing, tricks, trifling, waggery, zanyism.

**foolish** *adj* absurd, brainless, cockle-brained, crazy, daft, desipient, dilly, doited, doltish, dotish, dottled, dunderheaded, étourdi(e), fatuous, glaikit, gudgeon, half-baked, half-witted, hare-brained, idiotic, idle-headed, ill-advised, illaudable, ill-considered, ill-judged, imbecile, imbecilic, imprudent, incautious, indiscreet, inept, injudicious, insipient, lean-witted, ludicrous, mad, moronic, nonsensical, potty, ridiculous, senseless, short-sighted, silly, simple, simple-minded, sottish, stupid, tomfool, unintelligent, unreasonable, unwise, weak, wet, witless.
*antonym* wise.

**foolishly** *adv* absurdly, fatuously, fondly, idiotically, ill-advisedly, imprudently, incautiously, indiscreetly, ineptly, injudiciously, mistakenly, ridiculously, senselessly, short-sightedly, stupidly, unwisely.
*antonym* wisely.

**foolishness** *n* absurdity, bunk, bunkum, claptrap, étourderie, folly, foolery, imprudence, inanity, incaution, incautiousness, indiscretion, ineptitude, insipience, irresponsibility, malarkey, niaiserie, nonsense, rubbish, silliness, stupidity, unreason, unwisdom, weakness.
*antonyms* prudence, wisdom.

**foolproof** *adj* certain, fail-safe, guaranteed, idiot-proof, infallible, never-failing, safe, sure-fire, unassailable, unbreakable.
*antonym* unreliable.

**footing** *n* base, basis, condition, conditions, establishment, foot-hold, foundation, grade, ground, groundwork, installation, position, purchase, rank, relations, relationship, settlement, standing, state, status, terms.

**footnotes** *n* annotations, apparatus criticus, commentary, marginalia, notes, scholia.

**footprint** *n* footmark, spoor, trace, track, trail, vestige.

**footstep** *n* footfall, plod, step, tramp, tread, trudge.

**fop** *n* beau, coxcomb, dandy, dude, exquisite, Jack-a-dandy, Jessie, macaroni, muscadin, musk-cat, pansy, peacock, petit maître, popinjay, spark, swell.

**foppish** *adj* affected, coxcombical, dainty, dandiacal, dandified, dandyish, dapper, dressy, finical, la-di-da, natty, overdressed, preening, prinking, spruce, vain.
*antonym* unkempt.

**for dear life** desperately, energetically, for all one is worth, intensely, strenuously, urgently, vigorously, with might and main.

**for example** eg, exempli gratia, par exemple, zum Beispiel.

**for fun** facetiously, for kicks, for thrills, in jest, jokingly, light-heartedly, mischievously, playfully, roguishly, sportively, teasingly, tongue in cheek.

**for good** finally, for ever, irreparably, irreversibly, irrevocably, once and for all, permanently, sine die.

**for good measure** as a bonus, as an extra, besides, gratis, in addition, into the bargain, to boot.

**for love** for nothing, for pleasure, free of charge, freely, gratis, voluntarily.

**for love or money** by any means, ever, for anything, on any condition, under any circumstances.

**for the most part** chiefly, commonly, generally, in the main, largely, mainly, mostly, on the whole, principally, usually.

**for the present** for a while, for now, for the moment, for the nonce, for the time being, in the interim, in the meantime, pro tem, pro tempore, provisionally, temporarily.

**for the time being** for now, for the moment, for the nonce, for the present, in the meantime, meantime, meanwhile, pro tem, pro tempore, temporarily.

**forage** *n* étape, feed, fodder, food, foodstuffs, pabulum, pasturage, provender.
*v* cast about, explore, hunt, plunder, prog, raid, ransack, rummage, scavenge, scour, scrounge, search, seek.

**foray** *n* depredation, descent, excursion, incursion, inroad, invasion, irruption, offensive, raid, razzia, reconnaissance, sally, sortie, spreagh, swoop.

**forbear** *v* abstain, avoid, cease, decline, desist, eschew, hesitate, hold, hold back, keep from, omit, pause, refrain, restrain oneself, stay, stop, withhold.

**forbearance** *n* abstinence, avoidance, clemency, endurance, indulgence, leniency, lenity, longanimity, long-suffering, mildness, moderation, patience, refraining, resignation, restraint, self-control, sufferance, temperance, tolerance, toleration.
*antonym* intolerance.

**forbearing** *adj* clement, easy, forbearant, forgiving, indulgent, lenient, longanimous, long-suffering, merciful, mild, moderate, patient, restrained, self-controlled, tolerant.
*antonyms* intolerant, merciless.

**forbid** *v* ban, block, contraindicate, debar, deny, disallow, exclude, hinder, inhibit, interdict, outlaw, preclude, prevent, prohibit, proscribe, refuse, rule out, veto.
*antonym* allow.

**forbidden** *adj* banned, barred, debarred, disallowed, interdit, out of bounds, outlawed, prohibited, proscribed, taboo, verboten, vetoed.

**forbidding** *adj* abhorrent, awesome, daunting, formidable, frightening, gaunt, grim, hostile, inhospitable, menacing, off-putting, ominous, repellent, repulsive, sinister, stern, threatening, unapproachable, unfriendly.
*antonyms* approachable, congenial.

**force**[1] *n* aggression, arm-twisting, beef, big stick, bite, coercion, cogency, compulsion, constraint, drive, duress, dynamism, effect, effectiveness, efficacy, emphasis, energy, enforcement, fierceness, foison, forcefulness, fushion, impact, impetus, impulse, incentive, influence, intensity, jism, life, mailed fist, might, momentum, motivation, muscle, persistence, persuasiveness, potency, power, pressure, punch, shock, steam, stimulus, strength, stress, validity, vehemence, vigour, violence, vis, vitality, weight.

*v* bulldoze, coerce, compel, constrain, drag, drive, exact, extort, impel, impose, lean on, make, necessitate, obligate, oblige, press, pressgang, pressure, pressurise, prise, propel, push, strong-arm, thrust, urge, wrench, wrest, wring.

**force²** *n* army, battalion, body, corps, detachment, detail, division, effective, enomoty, host, legion, patrol, phalanx, regiment, squad, squadron, troop, unit, Wehrmacht.

**forced** *adj* affected, artificial, compulsory, contrived, enforced, false, feigned, insincere, involuntary, laboured, mandatory, obligatory, stiff, stilted, strained, synthetic, unnatural, unspontaneous, wooden.

*antonyms* spontaneous, voluntary.

**forceful** *adj* cogent, compelling, convincing, domineering, drastic, dynamic, effective, emphatic, energetic, persuasive, pithy, potent, powerful, strong, telling, urgent, vigorous, weighty.

*antonym* feeble.

**forcible** *adj* active, aggressive, coercive, cogent, compelling, compulsory, drastic, effective, efficient, energetic, forceful, impressive, mighty, pithy, potent, powerful, strong, telling, urgent, vehement, violent, weighty.

*antonym* feeble.

**forcibly** *adv* against one's will, by main force, compulsorily, emphatically, obligatorily, under compulsion, under duress, vehemently, vigorously, violently, willy-nilly.

**ford** *n* causeway, crossing, drift.

**forebear** *n* ancestor, antecedent, antecessor, father, forefather, forerunner, predecessor, primogenitor, progenitor.

*antonym* descendant.

**forebode** *v* augur, betoken, foreshadow, foreshow, foretell, foretoken, forewarn, import, indicate, omen, portend, predict, presage, prognosticate, promise, signify, warn.

**foreboding** *n* anticipation, anxiety, apprehension, apprehensiveness, augury, boding, chill, dread, fear, foreshadowing, foretoken, hoodoo, intuition, misgiving, omen, portent, prediction, prefigurement, premonition, presage, presentiment, prodrome, prodromus, prognostication, sign, token, warning, worry.

**forecast** *v* augur, bode, calculate, conjecture, divine, estimate, expect, foresee, foretell, plan, predict, prognosticate, prophesy.

*n* augury, conjecture, foresight, forethought, guess, guesstimate, outlook, planning, prediction, prognosis, prognostication, projection, prophecy.

**forefather** *n* ancestor, antecedent, antecessor, father, forebear, forerunner, predecessor,

primogenitor, primogenitrix, procreator, progenitor, progenitress, progenitrix.

*antonym* descendant.

**forefront** *n* avant-garde, centre, firing line, fore, foreground, front, front line, lead, prominence, spearhead, van, vanguard.

*antonym* rear.

**forego** *see* **forgo**.

**foregoing** *adj* above, aforementioned, antecedent, anterior, earlier, former, preceding, previous, prior, prodromal, prodromic.

**foregone** *adj* anticipated, cut-and-dried, foreseen, inevitable, open and shut, predetermined, predictable.

*antonym* unpredictable.

**foreground** *n* centre, fore, forefront, front, limelight, prominence.

*antonym* background.

**forehead** *n* brow, front, metope, temples.

**foreign** *adj* adventitious, adventive, alien, borrowed, distant, exotic, external, extraneous, extrinsic, fremd, imported, incongruous, irrelevant, outlandish, outside, overseas, remote, strange, tramontane, unassimilable, uncharacteristic, unfamiliar, unknown, unnative, unrelated.

*antonym* native.

**foreigner** *n* alien, Ausländer, barbarian, dago, étranger, étrangère, immigrant, incomer, metic, newcomer, outlander, stranger, uitlander, wog, wop.

*antonym* native.

**foreknowledge** *n* clairvoyance, foresight, forewarning, precognition, premonition, prescience, prevision, prognostication, second sight.

**foreman** *n* charge-hand, charge-man, gaffer, ganger, gangsman, overman, overseer, oversman, steward, straw boss, supervisor.

**foremost** *adj* cardinal, central, chief, first, front, headmost, highest, inaugural, initial, leading, main, paramount, pre-eminent, primary, prime, principal, salient, supreme, uppermost.

**foreordain** *v* appoint, destine, doom, fate, foredoom, ordain, prearrange, predestine, predetermine, preordain.

**foreordained** *adj* appointed, foredoomed, prearranged, predestined, predetermined, predevote, preordained.

**forerunner** *n* ancestor, announcer, antecedent, antecessor, envoy, forebear, foregoer, foretoken, harbinger, herald, indication, omen, portent, precursor, predecessor, premonition, prodrome, prodromus, progenitor, prognostic, prototype, sign, token, vaunt-courier.

*antonyms* aftermath, result.

**foresee** *v* anticipate, augur, divine, envisage, expect, forebode, forecast, foreknow, foretell, predict, previse, prognosticate, prophesy, vaticinate.

**foreshadow** *v* adumbrate, anticipate, augur, betoken, bode, forebode, forepoint, foreshow,

**foresight** foresignify, foretoken, imply, import, indicate, omen, portend, predict, prefigure, presage, promise, prophesy, signal.

**foresight** *n* anticipation, care, caution, circumspection, far-sightedness, forethought, perspicacity, precaution, preparedness, prescience, prevision, providence, provision, prudence, readiness, vision.

*antonym* improvidence.

**forest** *n* greenwood, monte, plantation, urman, wood, woodland.

**forestall** *v* anticipate, avert, balk, circumvent, frustrate, head off, hinder, intercept, obstruct, obviate, parry, preclude, pre-empt, prevent, thwart, ward off.

*antonyms* encourage, facilitate.

**forester** *n* gamekeeper, woodman, woodsman, woodward.

**forestry** *n* afforestation, arboriculture, dendrology, forestation, silviculture, woodcraft, woodmanship.

**foretaste** *n* example, foretoken, forewarning, indication, pregustation, prelibation, prelude, preview, sample, specimen, trailer, warning, whiff.

**foretell** *v* adumbrate, augur, bode, forebode, forecast, foresay, foreshadow, foreshow, forespeak, forewarn, portend, predict, presage, presignify, prognosticate, prophesy, signify, soothsay, vaticinate.

**forethought** *n* anticipation, circumspection, far-sightedness, foresight, precaution, preparation, providence, provision, prudence.

*antonym* improvidence.

**foretold** *adj* forecast, foreshown, forespoken, predicted, prophesied, written.

*antonym* unforeseen.

**forever** *adv* always, ceaselessly, constantly, continually, endlessly, eternally, everlastingly, evermore, for all time, for good and all, for keeps, in perpetuity, in saecula saeculorum, incessantly, interminably, permanently, perpetually, persistently, till the cows come home, till the end of time, unremittingly, world without end.

**forewarn** *v* admonish, advise, alert, apprise, caution, dissuade, previse, tip off.

**foreword** *n* exordium, introduction, preamble, preface, preliminary, proem, prolegomenon, prologue.

*antonyms* epilogue, postscript.

**forfeit** *n* amercement, damages, escheat, fine, forfeiture, loss, mulct, penalisation, penalty, surrender.

*v* abandon, forgo, give up, lose, relinquish, renounce, sacrifice, surrender.

**forfeiture** *n* attainder, confiscation, déchéance, escheat, forgoing, giving up, loss, relinquishment, sacrifice, sequestration, surrender.

**forge¹** *v* beat out, cast, coin, construct, contrive, copy, counterfeit, create, devise, fabricate, fake, falsify, fashion, feign, form, frame, hammer out, imitate, invent, make, mould, shape, simulate, work.

**forge²** *v* advance, gain ground, improve, make great strides, make headway, press on, proceed, progress, push on.

**forger** *n* coiner, contriver, counterfeiter, creator, deviser, fabricator, faker, falsifier, framer, truqueur.

**forgery** *n* coining, counterfeit, counterfeiting, dud, fake, falsification, fraud, fraudulence, imitation, phoney, sham, stumer.

*antonym* original.

**forget** *v* consign to oblivion, discount, dismiss, disregard, fail, ignore, lose sight of, misremember, neglect, omit, overlook, think no more of, unlearn.

*antonym* remember.

**forgetful** *adj* absent-minded, amnesiac, amnesic, careless, dreamy, heedless, inattentive, lax, neglectful, negligent, oblivious, unmindful, unretentive.

*antonyms* attentive, heedful.

**forgetfulness** *n* absent-mindedness, abstraction, amnesia, carelessness, dreaminess, heedlessness, inattention, lapse, laxness, Lethe, oblivion, obliviousness, obliviscence, wool-gathering.

*antonyms* attentiveness, heedfulness.

**forgivable** *adj* excusable, innocent, minor, pardonable, petty, slight, trifling, venial.

*antonym* unforgivable.

**forgive** *v* absolve, acquit, condone, exculpate, excuse, exonerate, let off, overlook, pardon, remit, shrive.

*antonym* censure.

**forgiveness** *n* absolution, acquittal, amnesty, condonation, exculpation, exoneration, mercy, pardon, remission, shrift, shriving.

*antonyms* blame, censure.

**forgiving** *adj* clement, compassionate, forbearing, humane, indulgent, lenient, magnanimous, merciful, mild, remissive, soft-hearted, sparing, tolerant.

*antonym* censorious.

**forgo, forego** *v* abandon, abjure, abstain from, cede, do without, eschew, forfeit, give up, pass up, refrain from, relinquish, renounce, resign, sacrifice, surrender, waive, yield.

*antonyms* claim, indulge in, insist on.

**forgotten** *adj* blotted out, buried, bygone, disregarded, ignored, irrecoverable, irretrievable, lost, neglected, obliterated, omitted, out of mind, overlooked, past, past recall, past recollection, unrecalled, unremembered, unretrieved.

*antonym* remembered.

**fork** *v* bifurcate, branch, branch off, divaricate, diverge, divide, part, ramify, separate, split.

*n* bifurcation, branching, divarication, divergence, division, furcation, intersection, junction, ramification, separation, split.

**forked** *adj* bifurcate, branched, branching, cloven, divaricated, divided, forficate, furcal, furcate, furcular, pronged, ramified, split, tined, zigzag.

**forlorn** *adj* abandoned, abject, bereft, cheerless, comfortless, deserted, desolate, desperate, destitute, disconsolate, forgotten, forsaken, friendless, helpless, homeless, hopeless, lonely, lost, miserable, pathetic, piteous, pitiable, pitiful, unhappy, woebegone, woeful, wretched.

*antonym* hopeful.

**form** *v* accumulate, acquire, appear, arrange, assemble, bring up, build, combine, compose, comprise, concoct, constitute, construct, contract, contrive, create, crystallise, cultivate, design, develop, devise, discipline, dispose, draw up, educate, establish, evolve, fabricate, fashion, forge, formulate, found, frame, group, grow, hatch, instruct, invent, make, make up, manufacture, materialise, model, mould, organise, pattern, plan, produce, put together, rear, rise, school, serve as, settle, shape, take shape, teach, train.

*n* anatomy, appearance, application, arrangement, behaviour, being, body, build, cast, ceremony, character, class, condition, conduct, configuration, construction, convention, custom, cut, description, design, document, etiquette, fashion, fettle, figure, fitness, formality, format, formation, frame, framework, genre, Gestalt, grade, guise, harmony, health, kind, manifestation, manner, manners, matrix, method, mode, model, mould, nature, nick, order, orderliness, organisation, outline, paper, pattern, person, physique, plan, practice, procedure, proportion, protocol, questionnaire, rank, ritual, rule, schedule, semblance, shape, sheet, silhouette, sort, species, spirits, stamp, structure, style, symmetry, system, trim, type, variety, way.

**formal** *adj* academic, aloof, approved, ceremonial, ceremonious, conventional, correct, exact, explicit, express, fixed, full-dress, impersonal, lawful, legal, methodical, nominal, official, perfunctory, precise, prescribed, prim, punctilious, recognised, regular, reserved, rigid, ritualistic, set, solemn, starch, starched, starchy, stiff, stiff-necked, stilted, strict, unbending.

*antonym* informal.

**formality** *n* ceremoniousness, ceremony, convenance, convention, conventionality, correctness, custom, decorum, etiquette, form, formalism, gesture, matter of form, politeness, politesse, procedure, propriety, protocol, punctilio, red tape, rite, ritual.

*antonym* informality.

**format** *n* appearance, arrangement, configuration, construction, dimensions, form, lay-out, look, make-up, pattern, plan, shape, structure, style, type.

**formation** *n* accumulation, appearance, arrangement, compilation, composition, configuration, constitution, construction, creation, crystallisation, design, development, disposition, emergence, establishment, evolution, fabrication, figure, format, forming, generation, genesis, grouping, manufacture, organisation, pattern, production, rank, shaping, structure.

**formative** *adj* controlling, determinative, determining, developmental, dominant, guiding, impressionable, influential, malleable, mouldable, moulding, pliant, sensitive, shaping, susceptible.

*antonym* destructive.

**former** *adj* above, aforementioned, aforesaid, ancient, antecedent, anterior, bygone, departed, earlier, erstwhile, ex-, first mentioned, foregoing, late, long ago, of yore, old, old-time, one-time, past, preceding, pre-existent, previous, prior, pristine, quondam, sometime, umwhile, whilom.

*antonyms* current, future, later, present, prospective, subsequent.

**formerly** *adv* already, at one time, before, earlier, erstwhile, heretofore, hitherto, lately, once, previously, umwhile, while-ere, whilom.

*antonyms* currently, later, now, presently, subsequently.

**formidable** *adj* alarming, appalling, arduous, awesome, challenging, colossal, dangerous, daunting, difficult, dismaying, dreadful, enormous, fearful, frightening, frightful, great, horrible, huge, impressive, indomitable, intimidating, leviathan, mammoth, menacing, mighty, onerous, overwhelming, powerful, puissant, redoubtable, shocking, staggering, terrific, terrifying, threatening, toilsome, tremendous.

*antonyms* easy, genial.

**formless** *adj* amorphous, chaotic, confused, disorganised, inchoate, incoherent, indefinite, indeterminate, indigest, nebulous, shapeless, unformed, unshaped, vague.

*antonyms* definite, orderly.

**formula** *n* blueprint, code, form, formulary, method, modus operandi, password, precept, prescription, principle, procedure, recipe, rite, ritual, rubric, rule, rule of thumb, way, wording.

**formulate** *v* block out, codify, create, define, detail, develop, devise, evolve, express, form, frame, invent, originate, particularise, plan, specify, systematise, work out.

**forsake** *v* abandon, abdicate, cast off, desert, discard, disown, forgo, forswear, give up, jettison, jilt, leave, leave in the lurch, quit, reject, relinquish, renounce, repudiate, surrender, throw over, turn one's back on, vacate, yield.

*antonyms* resume, revert to.

**forsaken** *adj* abandoned, cast off, deserted, desolate, destitute, discarded, disowned, forlorn, friendless, ignored, isolated, jilted, left in the lurch, lonely, lorn, lovelorn, marooned, outcast, rejected, shunned, solitary.

**forswear** *v* abandon, abjure, burn one's faggot, deny, disavow, disclaim, disown, drop, forgo, forsake, give up, lie, perjure oneself, recant, reject, renegue, renounce, repudiate, retract, swear off.

*antonym* revert to.

**fort** *n* acropolis, blockhouse, camp, castle, citadel, fastness, fortification, fortress, garrison, hill-fort, rath, redoubt, station, stronghold, tower.

**forte** *n* aptitude, bent, gift, long suit, métier, skill, speciality, strength, strong point, talent.

*antonyms* inadequacy, weak point.

**forthcoming**[1] *adj* accessible, approaching, at hand, available, coming, expected, future, imminent, impending, obtainable, projected, prospective, ready.

**forthcoming**[2] *adj* chatty, communicative, conversational, expansive, frank, free, informative, loquacious, open, sociable, talkative, unreserved.

*antonyms* bygone, distant, lacking, reserved.

**forthright** *adj* above-board, blunt, bold, candid, direct, four-square, frank, open, outspoken, plain-speaking, plain-spoken, straightforward, straight-from-the-shoulder, trenchant, unequivocal.

*antonyms* devious, tactful.

**forthwith** *adv* at once, directly, eftsoons, immediately, incontinent, instanter, instantly, posthaste, pronto, quickly, right away, straightaway, tout de suite, without delay.

**fortification** *n* abatis, bastion, bulwark, buttressing, castle, citadel, defence, earthwork, embattlement, entrenchment, fastness, fort, fortress, keep, munition, outwork, protection, rampart, redoubt, reinforcement, stockade, strengthening, stronghold.

**fortify** *v* boost, brace, bulwark, buttress, cheer, confirm, embattle, embolden, encourage, entrench, garrison, hearten, invigorate, lace, load, mix, munify, protect, reassure, reinforce, secure, shore up, spike, steel, stiffen, strengthen, support, sustain.

*antonyms* dilute, weaken.

**fortitude** *n* backbone, bottle, braveness, bravery, courage, dauntlessness, determination, endurance, fearlessness, firmness, grit, guts, hardihood, indomitability, intrepidity, long-suffering, patience, perseverance, pluck, resoluteness, resolution, staying power, stout-heartedness, strength, strength of mind, valour.

*antonyms* cowardice, weakness.

**fortress** *n* alcázar, burg, castle, citadel, fastness, fortification, kasbah, stronghold.

**fortuitous** *adj* accidental, adventitious, arbitrary, casual, chance, coincidental, contingent, felicitous, fluky, fortunate, happy, incidental, lucky, providential, random, serendipitous, unexpected, unforeseen, unintentional, unplanned.

*antonym* intentional.

**fortunate** *adj* advantageous, auspicious, blessed, bright, convenient, encouraging, favourable, favoured, felicitous, fortuitous, golden, happy, helpful, lucky, opportune, profitable, promising, propitious, prosperous, providential, rosy, serendipitous, successful, timely, well-off, well-timed.

*antonym* unfortunate.

**fortunately** *adv* happily, luckily, providentially.

*antonym* unfortunately.

**fortune**[1] *n* affluence, assets, bomb, bundle, estate, income, king's ransom, means, mint, opulence, packet, pile, possessions, property, prosperity, riches, treasure, wealth.

**fortune**[2] *n* accident, adventures, chance, circumstances, contingency, cup, destiny, doom, expectation, experience, fate, fortuity, hap, happenstance, hazard, history, kismet, life, lot, luck, portion, providence, star, success, weird.

**fortune-telling** *n* augury, chiromancy, crystal-gazing, divination, dukkeripen, palmistry, prediction, prognostication, prophecy, second sight.

**forward**[1] *adj* advance, advanced, early, enterprising, first, fore, foremost, forward-looking, front, go-ahead, head, leading, onward, precocious, premature, progressive, well-advanced, well-developed.

*antonym* retrograde.

*adv* ahead, en avant, forth, forwards, into view, on, onward, out, outward, to light, to the fore, to the surface.

*antonym* backward.

*v* accelerate, advance, aid, assist, back, dispatch, encourage, expedite, facilitate, favour, foster, freight, further, hasten, help, hurry, post, promote, route, send, send on, ship, speed, support, transmit.

*antonyms* impede, obstruct.

**forward**[2] *adj* assertive, assuming, audacious, bare-faced, bold, brash, brass-necked, brazen, brazen-faced, cheeky, confident, familiar, fresh, impertinent, impudent, malapert, officious, overweening, pert, presuming, presumptuous, pushy.

*antonym* diffident.

**forward-looking** *adj* avant-garde, dynamic, enlightened, enterprising, far-sighted, go-ahead, goey, go-getting, innovative, liberal, modern, progressive, reforming.

*antonyms* conservative, retrograde.

**forwardness** *n* assurance, audacity, boldness, brashness, brazenness, cheek, cheekiness, impertinence, impudence, malapertness, overconfidence, pertness, presumption, presumptuousness.

*antonyms* reserve, retiring.

**fossilised** *adj* anachronistic, antediluvian, antiquated, archaic, archaistic, dead, démodé, extinct, exuvial, inflexible, obsolete, old-fashioned, old-fog(e)yish, ossified, out of date, outmoded, passé, petrified, prehistoric, stony, superannuated.

*antonym* up-to-date.

**foster** *v* accommodate, bring up, care for, cherish, cultivate, encourage, entertain, feed, foment, harbour, make much of, nourish, nurse, nurture, promote, raise, rear, stimulate, support, sustain, take care of.

*antonyms* discourage, neglect.

**foul** *adj* abhorrent, abominable, abusive, bad, base, blasphemous, blue, blustery, choked, coarse, contaminated, crooked, despicable, detestable, dirty, disagreeable, disfigured, disgraceful, disgusting, dishonest, dishonourable, entangled, fetid, filthy, foggy, foul-mouthed, fraudulent, gross, hateful, heinous, impure, indecent, inequitable, infamous, iniquitous, lewd, loathsome, low, malodorous, mephitic, murky, nasty, nauseating, nefarious, noisome, notorious, obscene, offensive, polluted, profane, putrid, rainy, rank, repulsive, revolting, rotten, rough, scandalous, scatological, scurrilous, shady, shameful, smutty, squalid, stinking, stormy, sullied, tainted, unclean, underhand, unfair, unfavourable, unjust, unsportsmanlike, untidy, vicious, vile, virose, vulgar, wet, wicked, wild.

*antonyms* clean, fair, pure, worthy.

*v* befoul, begrime, besmear, besmirch, block, catch, choke, clog, contaminate, defile, dirty, ensnare, entangle, foul up, jam, pollute, smear, snarl, soil, stain, sully, taint, twist.

*antonyms* clean, clear, disentangle.

**foul play** chicanery, corruption, crime, deception, dirty work, double-dealing, duplicity, fraud, funny business, jiggery-pokery, perfidy, roguery, sharp practice, skulduggery, treachery, villainy.

*antonyms* fair play, justice.

**foul-mouthed** *adj* abusive, blasphemous, coarse, foul-spoken, obscene, offensive, profane.

**found** *v* base, bottom, build, constitute, construct, create, endow, erect, establish, fix, ground, inaugurate, initiate, institute, organise, originate, plant, raise, rest, root, set up, settle, start, sustain.

**foundation** *n* base, basis, bedrock, bottom, endowment, establishment, fond, footing, ground, groundwork, inauguration, institution, organisation, setting up, settlement, substance, substratum, substructure, underpinning.

**founder**[1] *n* architect, author, beginner, benefactor, builder, constructor, designer, endower, establisher, father, framer, generator, initiator, institutor, inventor, maker, organiser, originator, patriarch.

**founder**[2] *v* abort, break down, collapse, come to grief, come to nothing, fail, fall, fall through, go lame, lurch, miscarry, misfire, sink, sprawl, stagger, stick, stumble, submerge, subside, trip.

**foundling** *n* enfant trouvé, orphan, outcast, stray, urchin, waif.

**fountain** *n* fons et origo, font, fount, fountain-head, gerbe, inspiration, jet, origin, reservoir, source, spout, spray, spring, waterworks, well, well-head, well-spring.

**fourfold** *adj* quadruple, quadruplex, quadruplicate, tetraploid.

**four-square** *adv* firmly, frankly, honestly, resolutely, squarely.

*adj* firm, forthright, frank, honest, immovable, resolute, solid, steady, strong, unyielding.

*antonyms* uncertain, wavering.

**fox** *n* cunning devil, Lowrie, Lowrie-tod, reynard, sly one, slyboots, tod, Tod-Lowrie.

**foxy** *adj* artful, astute, canny, crafty, cunning, devious, fly, guileful, knowing, sharp, shrewd, sly, tricky, vulpine, wily.

*antonyms* naïve, open.

**foyer** *n* antechamber, anteroom, entrance hall, hall, lobby, reception, vestibule.

**fracas** *n* affray, aggro, bagarre, barney, brawl, disturbance, Donnybrook, fight, free-for-all, mêlée, quarrel, riot, row, ruckus, ruction, rumpus, scrimmage, scuffle, shindy, trouble, uproar.

**fractious** *adj* awkward, captious, choleric, crabbed, crabby, cross, crotchety, fretful, froward, grouchy, irritable, peevish, pettish, petulant, quarrelsome, querulous, recalcitrant, refractory, testy, touchy, unruly.

*antonyms* complaisant, placid.

**fracture** *n* breach, break, cleft, crack, fissure, gap, opening, rent, rift, rupture, schism, scission, split.

*v* break, crack, rupture, splinter, split.

*antonym* join.

**fragile** *adj* breakable, brittle, dainty, delicate, feeble, fine, flimsy, frail, frangible, infirm, insubstantial, shattery, slight, weak.

*antonyms* durable, robust, tough.

**fragility** *n* breakableness, brittleness, delicacy, feebleness, frailty, frangibility, infirmity, weakness.

*antonyms* durability, robustness, strength.

**fragment** *n* bit, cantlet, chip, flinder, fraction, frazzle, fritter, morceau, morsel, ort, part, particle, piece, portion, remnant, scrap, shard, shatter, sheave, shiver, shred, sliver.

*v* break, break up, come apart, come to pieces, crumble, disintegrate, disunite, divide, fractionalise, fritter, shatter, shiver, splinter, split, split up.

*antonyms* hold together, join.

**fragmentary** *adj* bitty, broken, disconnected, discrete, disjointed, fractionary, incoherent, incomplete, partial, piecemeal, scattered, scrappy, separate, sketchy, unsystematic.

*antonym* complete.

**fragrance** *n* aroma, balm, balminess, bouquet, fragrancy, odour, perfume, redolence, scent, smell.

**fragrant** *adj* aromatic, balmy, balsamy, odoriferous, odorous, perfumed, redolent, suaveolent, sweet, sweet-scented, sweet-smelling.

*antonyms* smelly, unscented.

**frail** *adj* breakable, brittle, decrepit, delicate, feeble, flimsy, fragile, frangible, infirm, insubstantial, puny, slight, tender, unchaste, unsound, vulnerable, weak.

*antonyms* firm, robust, strong, tough.

**frailty** *n* blemish, defect, deficiency, failing, fallibility, fault, feebleness, flaw, foible, frailness, imperfection, infirmity, peccability, peccadillo, peccancy, puniness, shortcoming, susceptibility, unchasteness, unchastity, vice, weakness.

*antonyms* firmness, robustness, strength, toughness.

**frame** *v* assemble, block out, build, case, compose, conceive, concoct, constitute, construct, contrive, cook up, devise, draft, draw up, enclose, enframe, fabricate, fashion, forge, form, formulate, hatch, institute, invent, make, manufacture, map out, model, mould, mount, plan, put together, redact, set up, shape, sketch, surround, trap, victimise.

*n* anatomy, body, bodyshell, bodywork, build, carcass, casing, chassis, construction, fabric, flake, form, framework, monture, morphology, mount, mounting, physique, scaffolding, scheme, setting, shell, skeleton, structure, system.

**frame of mind** attitude, disposition, fettle, humour, mood, morale, outlook, spirit, state, temper, vein.

**frame-up** n fabrication, fit-up, fix, put-up job, trap, trumped-up charge.

**framework** n bare bones, core, fabric, foundation, frame, gantry, groundwork, plan, schema, shell, skeleton, structure.

**franchise** n authorisation, charter, concession, exemption, freedom, immunity, liberty, prerogative, privilege, right, suffrage, vote.

**frank** adj artless, blunt, candid, direct, downright, forthright, four-square, free, honest, ingenuous, open, outright, outspoken, plain, plain-spoken, simple-hearted, sincere, straight, straightforward, transparent, truthful, unconcealed, undisguised, unreserved, unrestricted.
*antonyms* evasive, insincere.

**frankly** adv bluntly, candidly, directly, freely, honestly, in truth, openly, plainly, straight, to be frank, to be honest, unreservedly, without reserve.
*antonyms* evasively, insincerely.

**frankness** n bluntness, candour, forthrightness, franchise, glasnost, ingenuousness, openness, outspokenness, plain speaking, truthfulness, unreserve.

**frantic** adj berserk, beside oneself, desperate, distracted, distraught, fraught, frenetic, frenzied, furious, hairless, hectic, mad, overwrought, raging, raving, wild.
*antonym* calm.

**fraternise** v affiliate, associate, concur, consort, cooperate, forgather, hobnob, mingle, mix, socialise, sympathise, unite.
*antonyms* ignore, shun.

**fraternity** n association, brotherhood, camaraderie, circle, clan, club, companionship, company, comradeship, confraternity, confrèrie, fellowship, fratry, guild, kinship, league, set, society, sodality, union.

**fraud¹** n artifice, cheat, chicane, chicanery, craft, deceit, deception, double-dealing, duplicity, fake, forgery, guile, hoax, humbug, imposture, sham, sharp practice, spuriousness, swindling, swiz, swizzle, take-in, treachery, trickery.

**fraud²** n bluffer, charlatan, cheat, counterfeit, double-dealer, hoaxer, impostor, malingerer, mountebank, phoney, pretender, pseud, quack, swindler.

**fraudulent** adj bogus, counterfeit, crafty, criminal, crooked, deceitful, deceptive, dishonest, double-dealing, duplicitous, false, knavish, phoney, sham, specious, spurious, swindling, treacherous.
*antonyms* genuine, honest.

**fraught** adj abounding, accompanied, agitated, anxious, attended, bristling, charged, difficult, distracted, distressed, distressing, emotive, filled, full, heavy, hotching, laden, replete, stuffed, tense, tricky, troublesome, trying, uptight, worrisome.
*antonyms* calm, untroublesome.

**fray** n affray, bagarre, barney, battle, brawl, broil, clash, combat, conflict, disturbance, Donnybrook, dust-up, fight, free-for-all, mêlée, quarrel, rammy, riot, row, ruckus, ruction, rumble, rumpus, scuffle, set-to, shindy.

**frayed** adj edgy, frazzled, on edge, ragged, shreddy, tattered, threadbare, worn.
*antonyms* calm, tidy.

**freak¹** n aberration, abnormality, abortion, anomaly, caprice, crotchet, fad, fancy, folly, grotesque, humour, irregularity, lusus naturae, malformation, misgrowth, monster, monstrosity, mutant, oddity, queer fish, quirk, rara avis, sport, teratism, turn, twist, vagary, weirdie, weirdo, whim, whimsy.
adj aberrant, abnormal, atypical, bizarre, capricious, erratic, exceptional, fluky, fortuitous, odd, queer, surprise, unaccountable, unexpected, unforeseen, unparalleled, unpredictable, unpredicted, unusual.
*antonyms* common, expected.

**freak²** n addict, aficionado, buff, devotee, enthusiast, fan, fanatic, fiend, monomaniac, nut, votary.

**freakish** adj aberrant, abnormal, arbitrary, bizarre, capricious, changeable, erratic, fanciful, fantastic, fitful, freakful, freaky, grotesque, malformed, monstrous, odd, outlandish, outré, preternatural, strange, teratoid, unconventional, unpredictable, unusual, vagarious, vagarish, wayward, weird, whimsical.
*antonym* ordinary.

**freckle** n ephelis, fernitickle, heatspot, lentigo.

**free** adj able, allowed, at large, at leisure, at liberty, autarchic, autonomous, available, bounteous, bountiful, buckshee, casual, charitable, clear, complimentary, cost-free, dégagé, democratic, désoevré, disengaged, eager, easy, emancipated, empty, extra, familiar, footloose, forward, frank, free and easy, free of charge, generous, gratis, hospitable, idle, independent, informal, laid-back, lavish, lax, leisured, liberal, liberated, loose, munificent, natural, off the hook, on the house, on the loose, open, open-handed, permitted, prodigal, relaxed, self-governing, self-ruling, solute, sovereign, spare, spontaneous, unattached, unbidden, unbowed, unceremonious, uncommitted, unconstrained, unemployed, unencumbered, unengaged, unfettered, unforced, unhampered, unhindered, unimpeded, uninhabited, uninhibited, unobstructed, unoccupied, unpaid, unpent, unpreoccupied, unregimented, unregulated, unrestrained, unrestricted, unsparing, unstinting, untrammelled, unused, vacant, willing, without charge.
*antonyms* attached, confined, costly, formal, mean, niggardly, restricted, tied.

adv abundantly, copiously, for free, for love, for nothing, freely, gratis, idly, loosely, without charge.
*antonym* meanly.

v absolve, affranchise, clear, debarrass, declassify, decolonise, decontrol, deliver, disburden, discage, discharge, disembarrass, disembrangle, disenchain, disengage, disenslave, disentangle, disenthral, disimprison, disprison, emancipate, exempt, extricate, let go, liberate, loose, manumit, ransom, release, relieve, rescue, rid, set free, turn loose, unbind, unburden, uncage, unchain, undo, unfetter, unhand, unleash, unlock, unloose, unmanacle, unmew, unpen, unshackle, unstick, untether, untie, unyoke.

*antonyms* confine, enslave, imprison.

**free hand** authority, carte-blanche, discretion, freedom, latitude, liberty, permission, power, scope.

**free of** devoid of, exempt from, immune to, innocent of, lacking, not liable to, safe from, sans, unaffected by, unencumbered by, untouched by, without.

**freebooter** *n* bandit, brigand, buccaneer, cateran, filibuster, highwayman, looter, marauder, mosstrooper, pillager, pirate, plunderer, raider, reiver, robber, rover.

**freedom** *n* abandon, ability, affranchisement, autonomy, boldness, brazenness, candour, carte-blanche, deliverance, directness, discretion, disrespect, ease, elbow-room, emancipation, exemption, facility, familiarity, flexibility, forwardness, frankness, free rein, home rule, immunity, impertinence, impunity, independence, informality, ingenuousness, lack of restraint or reserve, latitude, laxity, leeway, liberty, Liberty Hall, licence, manumission, openness, opportunity, overfamiliarity, play, power, presumption, privilege, range, release, scope, self-government, uhuru, unconstraint.

*antonyms* confinement, reserve, restriction.

**freely** *adv* abundantly, amply, bountifully, candidly, cleanly, copiously, easily, extravagantly, frankly, generously, lavishly, liberally, loosely, of one's own accord, open-handedly, openly, plainly, readily, smoothly, spontaneously, sponte sua, unchallenged, unreservedly, unstintingly, voluntarily, willingly.

*antonyms* evasively, meanly, roughly, under duress.

**free-thinker** *n* agnostic, deist, doubter, esprit fort, infidel, rationalist, sceptic, unbeliever.

**free-will** *n* autarky, autonomy, election, freedom, independence, liberty, self-determination, self-sufficiency, spontaneity, volition.

**freeze** *v* benumb, chill, congeal, enfreeze, fix, glaciate, harden, hold, ice, ice over, inhibit, peg, rigidify, shelve, solidify, stiffen, stop, suspend.

*n* abeyance, discontinuation, embargo, freeze-up, frost, halt, interruption, moratorium, postponement, shut-down, standstill, stay, stoppage, suspension.

**freezing** *adj* arctic, biting, bitter, brumous, chill, chilled, chilly, cutting, frigorific, frosty, gelid, glacial, icy, numbing, penetrating, polar, raw, Siberian, wintry.

*antonyms* hot, warm.

**freight** *n* bulk, burden, cargo, carriage, charge, consignment, contents, conveyance, fee, goods, haul, lading, load, merchandise, pay-load, shipment, tonnage, transportation.

**frenetic** *adj* demented, distraught, excited, fanatical, frantic, frenzical, frenzied, hyperactive, insane, mad, maniacal, obsessive, overwrought, phrenetic, unbalanced, wild.

*antonyms* calm, placid.

**frenzied** *adj* agitated, convulsive, distracted, distraught, excited, feverish, frantic, frenetic, frenzical, furious, hysterical, mad, maniacal, must, musty, rabid, uncontrolled, wild.

*antonyms* calm, placid.

**frenzy** *n* aberration, agitation, bout, burst, convulsion, delirium, derangement, distraction, fit, fury, hysteria, insanity, lunacy, madness, mania, must, oestrus, outburst, paroxysm, passion, rage, seizure, spasm, transport, turmoil.

*antonyms* calm, placidness.

**frequency** *n* constancy, frequence, frequentness, oftenness, periodicity, prevalence, recurrence, repetition.

*antonym* infrequency.

**frequent**[1] *adj* common, commonplace, constant, continual, customary, everyday, familiar, habitual, incessant, numerous, persistent, recurrent, recurring, regular, reiterated, repeated, usual.

*antonym* infrequent.

**frequent**[2] *v* associate with, attend, crowd, hang about, hang out at, haunt, haunt about, patronise, resort, visit.

**frequenter** *n* client, customer, denizen, habitué, haunter, patron, regular.

**frequently** *adv* commonly, continually, customarily, habitually, many a time, many times, much, oft, often, oftentimes, over and over, persistently, repeatedly.

*antonyms* infrequently, seldom.

**fresh** *adj* added, additional, alert, artless, auxiliary, blooming, bold, bouncing, bracing, brazen, bright, brisk, callow, cheeky, chipper, clean, clear, cool, crisp, crude, dewy, different, disrespectful, energetic, extra, fair, familiar, flip, florid, forward, further, glowing, green, hardy, healthy, impudent, inexperienced, innovative, insolent, inventive, invigorated, invigorating, keen, latest, lively, malapert, modern, modernistic, more, natural, new, new-fangled, novel, original, other, pert, presumptuous, pure, raw, recent, refreshed, refreshing, renewed, rested, restored, revived, rosy, ruddy, saucy, span, spanking, sparkling, spick, sprightly, spry, stiff, supplementary, sweet, unblown, unconventional, uncultivated, undimmed, unhackneyed, unjaded, unjaundiced, unpolluted, unsoured, unspoilt, untrained, untried, unusual, unwarped, unwearied, up-to-date, verdant, vernal, vigorous, virescent, vital, vivid, warm, wholesome, young, youthful.

*antonyms* experienced, faded, old hat, polite, stale, tired.

**freshen** *v* air, enliven, liven, purify, refresh, reinvigorate, restore, resuscitate, revitalise, spruce up, tart up, titivate, ventilate, vernalise.

*antonym* tire.

**freshman** *n* bajan, bejant, first-year, fresher, pennal, sophomore, underclassman.

**freshness** *n* bloom, brightness, cleanness, clearness, dewiness, fraîcheur, glow, newness, novelty, originality, shine, sparkle, vigour, virescence, wholesomeness.

*antonyms* staleness, tiredness.

**fret** *v* abrade, agitate, agonise, annoy, bother, brood, chafe, chagrin, corrode, distress, disturb, eat into, erode, fray, gall, goad, grieve, harass, irk, irritate, nag, nettle, peeve, pique, provoke, rankle, repine, rile, ripple, rub, ruffle, torment, trouble, vex, wear, wear away, worry.

*antonym* calm.

**fretful** *adj* cantankerous, captious, complaining, cross, crotchety, edgy, fractious, irritable, peevish, petulant, querulous, short-tempered, snappish, snappy, splenetic, testy, thrawn, touchy, uneasy.

*antonym* calm.

**friable** *adj* brittle, crisp, crumbly, murly, powdery, pulverisable.

*antonyms* clayey, solid.

**friar** *n* mendicant, monk, religieux, religionary, religioner, religious.

**friction** *n* abrasion, animosity, antagonism, attrition, bad blood, bad feeling, bickering, chafing, conflict, contention, disagreement, discontent, discord, disharmony, dispute, dissension, erosion, fretting, grating, hostility, ill-feeling, incompatibility, irritation, limation, opposition, quarrelling, rasping, resentment, resistance, rivalry, rubbing, scraping, wearing away, wrangling, xerotripsis.

**friend** *n* Achates, adherent, advocate, ally, alter ego, associate, backer, benefactor, boon companion, bosom friend, buddy, china, chum, cobber, companion, comrade, confidant, crony, familiar, gossip, intimate, mate, paisano, pal, partisan, partner, patron, playmate, side-kick, soul mate, supporter, well-wisher.

*antonym* enemy.

**friendless** *adj* abandoned, alienated, alone, deserted, estranged, forlorn, forsaken, isolated, lonely, lonely-heart, lonesome, ostracised, shunned, solitary, unattached, unbefriended, unbeloved, unfriended, unloved.

**friendliness** *n* affability, amiability, approachability, companionability, congeniality, conviviality, Gemütlichkeit, geniality, kindliness, matyness, neighbourliness, sociability, warmth.

*antonyms* coldness, unsociableness.

**friendly** *adj* affable, affectionate, amiable, amicable, approachable, attached, attentive, auspicious, beneficial, benevolent, benign, chummy, close, clubby, companionable, comradely, conciliatory, confiding, convivial, cordial, familiar, Favonian, favourable, fond, fraternal, gemütlich, genial, good, helpful, intimate, kind, kindly, maty, neighbourly, outgoing, palsy-walsy, peaceable, propitious, receptive, sociable, sympathetic, thick, welcoming, well-disposed.

*antonyms* cold, unsociable.

**friendship** *n* affection, affinity, alliance, amity, attachment, benevolence, closeness, concord, familiarity, fellowship, fondness, friendliness, goodwill, harmony, intimacy, love, neighbourliness, rapport, regard.

*antonym* enmity.

**fright** *n* alarm, apprehension, consternation, dismay, dread, eyesore, fear, fleg, funk, horror, mess, monstrosity, panic, quaking, scare, scarecrow, shock, sight, spectacle, sweat, terror, the shivers, trepidation.

**frighten** *v* affray, affright, affrighten, alarm, appal, cow, daunt, dismay, fleg, intimidate, petrify, scare, scare stiff, shock, spook, startle, terrify, terrorise, unman, unnerve.

*antonyms* calm, reassure.

**frightened** *adj* affrighted, affrightened, afraid, alarmed, cowed, dismayed, frightsome, frozen, panicky, petrified, scared, scared stiff, startled, terrified, terrorised, terror-stricken, unnerved, windy.

*antonyms* calm, courageous.

**frightening** *adj* alarming, appalling, bloodcurdling, daunting, dismaying, dreadful, fearful, fearsome, hair-raising, horrifying, intimidating, menacing, scary, shocking, spine-chilling, spooky, terrifying, traumatic, unnerving.

*antonym* reassuring.

**frightful** *adj* alarming, appalling, awful, dire, disagreeable, dread, dreadful, fearful, fearsome, frightsome, ghastly, great, grim, grisly, gruesome, harrowing, hideous, horrendous, horrible, horrid, insufferable, macabre, petrifying, shocking, terrible, terrific, terrifying, traumatic, unnerving, unpleasant, unspeakable.

*antonyms* agreeable, pleasant.

**frigid** *adj* aloof, arctic, austere, brumous, chill, chilly, cold, cold-hearted, cool, forbidding, formal, frore, frost-bound, frosty, frozen, gelid, glacial, icy, lifeless, passionless, passive, repellent, rigid, stand-offish, stiff, unanimated, unapproachable, unbending, unfeeling, unloving, unresponsive, wintry.

*antonyms* responsive, warm.

**frigidity** *n* aloofness, austerity, chill, chilliness, cold-heartedness, coldness, frostiness, iciness, impassivity, lifelessness, passivity, stiffness, unapproachability, unresponsiveness, wintriness.

*antonyms* responsiveness, warmth.

**frill** *n* flounce, furbelow, gathering, orphrey, purfle, ruche, ruching, ruff, ruffle, trimming, tuck, valance.

**frills** *n* accessories, additions, affectation, decoration, embellishment, extras, fanciness, fandangles, finery, frilliness, frippery, froth, frothery, frou-frous, gewgaws, mannerisms, nonsense, ornamentation, ostentation, superfluities, tomfoolery, trimmings.

**frilly** *adj* fancy, flouncy, frothy, lacy, ornate, overornate, ruched, ruffled.

*antonyms* plain, unadorned.

**fringe** *n* borderline, edge, fimbriation, frisette, limits, march, marches, margin, outskirts, perimeter, periphery.

*adj* alternative, unconventional, unofficial, unorthodox.

*v* border, edge, enclose, fimbriate, skirt, surround, trim.

**fringed** *adj* bordered, edged, fimbriated, fringy, tasselled, tasselly, trimmed.

**frippery** *n* adornments, baubles, decorations, fanciness, fandangles, finery, flashiness, foppery, frilliness, frills, froth, frothery, fussiness, gaudiness, gewgaws, glad rags, knick-knacks, meretriciousness, nonsense, ornaments, ostentation, pretentiousness, showiness, tawdriness, trifles, trinkets, trivia, triviality.

*antonym* plainness.

**frisk**[1] *v* bounce, caper, cavort, curvet, dance, frolic, gambol, hop, jump, leap, pirouette, play, prance, rollick, romp, skip, sport, trip.

**frisk**[2] *v* check, inspect, search, shake down.

**frisky** *adj* bouncy, buckish, coltish, frolicsome, gamesome, high-spirited, kittenish, lively, playful, rollicking, romping, skittish, spirited, sportive.

*antonym* quiet.

**fritter** *v* blow, dissipate, idle, misspend, run through, squander, waste.

**frivolity** *n* childishness, flightiness, flippancy, flummery, folly, frivolousness, froth, fun, gaiety, giddiness, jest, levity, light-heartedness, lightness, nonsense, puerility, shallowness, silliness, skittishness, superficiality, trifling, triviality.

*antonym* seriousness.

**frivolous** *adj* bubble-headed, childish, dizzy, empty-headed, extravagant, facetious, flighty, flip, flippant, foolish, giddy, idle, ill-considered, impractical, jocular, juvenile, light, light-minded, petty, pointless, puerile, shallow, silly, skittish, superficial, trifling, trivial, unimportant, unserious, vacuous, vain.

*antonym* serious.

**frizzy** *adj* corrugated, crimped, crisp, curled, curly, frizzed, wiry.

*antonym* straight.

**frolic** *v* caper, cavort, cut capers, frisk, gambol, gammock, lark, make merry, play, rollick, romp, skylark, sport, wanton.

*n* amusement, antic, drollery, escapade, fun, gaiety, gambado, gambol, game, gammock, gilravage, high jinks, lark, merriment, prank, razzle-dazzle, revel, rig, romp, skylarking, sport, spree.

**frolicsome** *adj* coltish, espiègle, frisky, gamesome, gay, kittenish, kitteny, lively, merry, playful, rollicking, sportive, sprightly, wanton.

*antonym* quiet.

**from hand to mouth** dangerously, from day to day, improvidently, in poverty, insecurely, necessitously, on the breadline, precariously, uncertainly.

**from time to time** at times, every now and then, every so often, intermittently, now and then, occasionally, on occasion, once in a while, sometimes, spasmodically, sporadically.

*antonym* constantly.

**front** *n* air, anterior, appearance, aspect, bearing, beginning, blind, countenance, cover, cover-up, demeanour, disguise, expression, exterior, façade, face, facing, fore, forefront, foreground, forepart, front line, frontage, head, lead, manner, mask, metope, mien, obverse, pretence, pretext, show, top, van, vanguard.

*antonym* back.

*adj* anterior, anticous, first, fore, foremost, head, lead, leading.

*antonyms* back, last, least, posterior.

*v* confront, face, look over, meet, oppose, overlook.

**frontier** *n* borderland, borderline, bound, boundary, bourn(e), confines, edge, limit, march, marches, perimeter, verge.

*adj* backwoods, limitrophe, outlying, pioneering.

**frost** *n* coldness, disappointment, failure, freeze, freeze-up, hoar-frost, rime.

**frosty** *adj* chilly, cold, discouraging, frigid, frozen, hoar, ice-capped, icicled, icy, off-putting, rimy, stand-offish, stiff, unfriendly, unwelcoming, wintry.

*antonym* warm.

**froth** *n* bubbles, effervescence, foam, frivolity, frothery, head, lather, scum, spume, suds, triviality.

*v* bubble, effervesce, ferment, fizz, foam, lather.

**frothy** *adj* barmy, bubbling, bubbly, empty, foaming, foamy, frilly, frivolous, insubstantial, light, slight, spumescent, spumous, spumy, sudsy, trifling, trivial, trumpery, vain.

*antonym* flat.

**frown** *v* glare, glower, grimace, lower, scowl.

*n* dirty look, glare, glower, grimace, moue, scowl.

**frown on** deprecate, disapprove of, discountenance, discourage, dislike, look askance at, object to, take a dim view of.

*antonym* approve of.

**frowzy** *adj* blowzed, blowzy, dirty, dishevelled, draggle-tailed, frumpish, frumpy, messy, slatternly, sloppy, slovenly, sluttish, ungroomed, unkempt, untidy, unwashed.

*antonym* well-groomed.

**frozen** *adj* arctic, chilled, fixed, frigid, frore, frosted, icebound, ice-cold, ice-covered, icy, in abeyance, numb, pegged, petrified, rigid, rooted, shelved, solidified, stiff, stock-still, stopped, suspended, turned to stone.

*antonym* warm.

**frugal** *adj* abstemious, careful, cheese-paring, economical, meagre, niggardly, parsimonious, penny-wise, provident, prudent, saving, sparing, Spartan, thrifty, ungenerous.

*antonym* wasteful.

**frugality** *n* carefulness, conservation, economising, economy, frugalness, good management, husbandry, providence, prudence, thrift, thriftiness.

*antonym* wastefulness.

**fruit** *n* advantage, benefit, consequence, crop, effect, fruitage, fruitery, harvest, outcome, produce, product, profit, result, return, reward, yield.

**fruitful** *adj* abundant, advantageous, beneficial, copious, effective, fecund, feracious, fertile, flush, fructiferous, fructuous, gainful, plenteous, plentiful, productive, profitable, profuse, prolific, rewarding, rich, spawning, successful, teeming, uberous, useful, well-spent, worthwhile.

*antonyms* barren, fruitless.

**fruitfulness** *n* fecundity, feracity, fertility, productiveness, profitability, uberty, usefulness.

*antonym* fruitlessness.

**fruition** *n* accomplishment, actualisation, attainment, completion, consummation, enjoyment, fulfilment, materialisation, maturation, maturity, perfection, realisation, ripeness, success.

*antonym* failure.

**fruitless** *adj* abortive, barren, bootless, futile, hopeless, idle, ineffectual, pointless, profitless, unavailing, unfruitful, unproductive, unprofitable, unsuccessful, useless, vain.

*antonyms* fruitful, successful.

**fruity** *adj* bawdy, blue, full, indecent, indelicate, juicy, mellow, racy, resonant, rich, ripe, risqué, salacious, saucy, sexy, smutty, spicy, suggestive, titillating, vulgar.

*antonyms* decent, light.

**frump** *n* dowd, dowdy, draggle-tail, fright, Judy, mopsy, scarecrow, slattern, sloven, slut.

**frumpish** badly-dressed, blowzed, blowzy, dated, dingy, dowdy, drab, dreary, frumpy, ill-dressed, out of date.

*antonyms* chic, well-groomed.

**frustrate** *v* baffle, balk, block, bugger, check, circumvent, confront, counter, countermine, crab, defeat, depress, disappoint, discourage, dishearten, foil, forestall, inhibit, neutralise, nullify, scotch, spike, stymie, thwart.

*antonyms* fulfil, further, promote.

**frustrated** *adj* disappointed, discontented, discouraged, disheartened, embittered, foiled, irked, resentful, scunnered, thwarted.

*antonym* fulfilled.

**frustration** *n* annoyance, balking, circumvention, contravention, curbing, disappointment, dissatisfaction, failure, foiling, irritation, non-fulfilment, non-success, obstruction, resentment, thwarting, vexation.

*antonyms* fulfilment, furthering, promoting.

**fuddled** *adj* bemused, confused, drunk, groggy, hazy, inebriated, intoxicated, muddled, mused, muzzy, sozzled, stupefied, tipsy, woozy.

*antonyms* clear, sober.

**fuddy-duddy** *n* back number, carper, conservative, dodo, fogey, fossil, museum piece, old fog(e)y, square, stick-in-the-mud, stuffed shirt.

*adj* carping, censorious, old-fashioned, old-fog(e)yish, prim, stick-in-the-mud, stuffy.

*antonym* up-to-date.

**fudge** *v* avoid, cook, dodge, equivocate, evade, fake, falsify, fiddle, fix, hedge, misrepresent, shuffle, stall.

**fuel** *n* ammunition, eilding, encouragement, fodder, food, incitement, material, means, nourishment, provocation.

*v* charge, encourage, fan, feed, fire, incite, inflame, nourish, stoke up, sustain.

*antonyms* damp down, discourage.

**fug** *n* fetidity, fetidness, fetor, frowst, frowstiness, fustiness, reek, staleness, stink, stuffiness.

*antonym* airiness.

**fuggy** *adj* airless, close, fetid, foul, frowsty, fusty, noisome, noxious, stale, stuffy, suffocating, unventilated.

*antonym* airy.

**fugitive** *n* deserter, escapee, refugee, runagate, runaway.

*adj* brief, elusive, ephemeral, evanescent, fleeing, fleeting, flitting, flying, fugacious, intangible, momentary, passing, short, short-lived, temporary, transient, transitory, unstable.

*antonym* permanent.

**fulfil** *v* accomplish, achieve, answer, carry out, complete, comply with, conclude, conform to, consummate, discharge, effect, effectuate, execute, fill, finish, implement, keep, meet, obey, observe, perfect, perform, realise, satisfy.

*antonyms* break, defect, fail, frustrate.

**fulfilment** *n* accomplishment, achievement, attainment, bringing about, carrying out, completion, consummation, crowning, discharge, discharging, effecting, effectuation, end, implementation, observance, perfection, performance, realisation, success.

*antonyms* failure, frustration.

**full** *adj* abundant, adequate, all-inclusive, ample, baggy, brimful, brimming, broad, buxom, capacious, chock-a-block, chock-full, clear, complete, comprehensive, copious, crammed, crowded, curvaceous, deep, detailed, distinct, entire, exhaustive, extensive, filled, generous, gorged, intact, jammed, large, loaded, loud, maximum, occupied, orotund, packed, plenary, plenteous, plentiful, plump, replete, resonant, rich, rounded, sated, satiated, satisfied, saturated, stocked, sufficient, taken, thorough, unabbreviated, unabridged, uncut, unedited, unexpurgated, voluminous, voluptuous.

*antonyms* empty, incomplete.

**full-blooded** *adj* gutsy, hearty, lusty, mettlesome, red-blooded, thoroughbred, vigorous, virile, whole-hearted.

**full-grown** *adj* adult, developed, full-aged, full-blown, full-scale, grown-up, marriageable, mature, nubile, of age, ripe.

*antonyms* undeveloped, young.

**fullness** *n* abundance, adequateness, ampleness, broadness, clearness, completeness, comprehensiveness, copiousness, curvaceousness, dilation, distension, enlargement, entirety, extensiveness, fill, glut, loudness, orotundity, plenitude, plenty, pleroma, profusion, repletion, resonance, richness, roundness, satiety, saturation, strength, sufficiency, swelling, totality, tumescence, vastness, voluptuousness, wealth, wholeness. *antonyms* emptiness, incompleteness.

**full-scale** *adj* all-encompassing, all-out, comprehensive, exhaustive, extensive, full-dress, in-depth, intensive, major, proper, sweeping, thorough, thoroughgoing, wide-ranging. *antonym* partial.

**fully** *adv* absolutely, abundantly, adequately, altogether, amply, completely, comprehensively, enough, entirely, every inch, from first to last, heart and soul, in all respects, intimately, perfectly, plentifully, positively, quite, satisfactorily, sufficiently, thoroughly, totally, utterly, wholly, without reserve. *antonym* partly.

**fully-fledged** *adj* experienced, full-blown, full-fledged, graduate, mature, professional, proficient, qualified, senior, trained. *antonym* inexperienced.

**fulminate** *v* animadvert, criticise, curse, denounce, detonate, fume, inveigh, protest, rage, rail, thunder, vilipend, vituperate. *antonym* praise.

**fulmination** *n* condemnation, denunciation, detonation, diatribe, invective, obloquy, philippic, reprobation, thundering, tirade. *antonym* praise.

**fulsome** *adj* adulatory, cloying, effusive, excessive, extravagant, fawning, gross, immoderate, ingratiating, inordinate, insincere, nauseating, nauseous, offensive, overdone, rank, saccharine, sickening, smarmy, sycophantic, unctuous. *antonym* sincere.

**fumble** *v* botch, bumble, bungle, faff, flail, flounder, fluff, footer, grope, misfield, mishandle, mismanage, muff, mumble, paw, scrabble, spoil.

**fume** *v* boil, chafe, fizz, get steamed up, give off, rage, rant, rave, reek, seethe, smoke, smoulder, storm.

**fumes** *n* effluvium, exhalation, exhaust, gas, haze, mephitis, miasma, pollution, reek, smog, smoke, stench, vapour.

**fumigate** *v* cleanse, deodorise, disinfect, purify, sanitise, sterilise.

**fuming** *adj* angry, boiling, enraged, fizzing, incensed, raging, roused, seething, spitting, steamed up. *antonym* calm.

**fun** *n* amusement, buffoonery, cheer, clowning, distraction, diversion, enjoyment, entertainment, foolery, frolic, gaiety, game, gammock, high jinks, horseplay, jesting, jocularity, joking, jollification, jollity, joy, junketing, merriment, merrymaking, mirth, nonsense, play, playfulness, pleasure, recreation, romp, skylarking, sport, teasing, tomfoolery, treat, waggery, whoopee.

**function**[1] *n* activity, business, capacity, charge, concern, duty, employment, exercise, faculty, job, mission, occupation, office, operation, part, post, province, purpose, raison d'être, responsibility, role, situation, task.

*v* act, be in running order, behave, do duty, functionate, go, officiate, operate, perform, run, serve, work.

**function**[2] *n* affair, dinner, do, gathering, junket, luncheon, party, reception, shindig.

**functional** *adj* hard-wearing, operational, operative, plain, practical, serviceable, useful, utilitarian, utility, working. *antonyms* effective, inoperative, ornate, useless.

**functionary** *n* bureaucrat, dignitary, employee, office-bearer, office-holder, officer, official.

**functionless** *adj* aimless, decorative, futile, hollow, idle, inactive, inert, irrelevant, needless, otiose, pointless, redundant, superfluous, useless. *antonym* useful.

**fund** *n* cache, capital, endowment, foundation, hoard, kitty, mine, pool, repository, reserve, reservoir, source, stack, stock, store, storehouse, supply, treasury, vein, well.

*v* back, capitalise, endow, finance, float, promote, stake, subsidise, support, underwrite.

**fundamental** *adj* axiomatic, basal, basic, basilar, cardinal, central, constitutional, crucial, elementary, essential, first, important, indispensable, integral, intrinsic, key, keynote, necessary, organic, primal, primary, prime, principal, rudimentary, underlying, vital. *antonym* advanced.

*n* axiom, basic, cornerstone, essential, first principle, keystone, law, principle, rudiment, rule, sine qua non.

**fundamentally** *adv* à fond, at bottom, at heart, au fond, basically, essentially, intrinsically, primarily, radically.

**fundamentals** *n* basics, brass tacks, business, nitty-gritty, practicalities.

**funds** *n* backing, bread, capital, cash, dough, finance, hard cash, money, moola(h), pelf, ready money, resources, savings, spondulicks, the ready, the wherewithal.

**funeral** *n* burial, inhumation, interment, obit, obsequies.

**funereal** *adj* dark, deathlike, depressing, dirgelike, dismal, dreary, exequial, feral, funebral, funebrial, gloomy, grave, lamenting, lugubrious, mournful, sad, sepulchral, solemn, sombre, woeful. *antonyms* happy, lively.

**funk** *v* balk at, blench, chicken out of, cop out, dodge, duck out of, flinch from, recoil from, shirk from.

**funnel** *v* channel, conduct, convey, direct, filter, move, pass, pour, siphon, transfer.

**funny** *adj* a card, a caution, a scream, absurd, amusing, comic, comical, curious, diverting, droll, dubious, entertaining, facetious, farcical, funny ha-ha, funny peculiar, hilarious, humorous, jocose, jocular, jolly, killing, laughable, ludicrous, mirth-provoking, mysterious, odd, peculiar, perplexing, puzzling, queer, remarkable, rib-tickling, rich, ridiculous, riotous, risible, side-splitting, silly, slapstick, strange, suspicious, unusual, waggish, weird, witty.

*antonyms* sad, solemn, unamusing, unfunny.

**fur** *n* coat, down, fell, fleece, flix, flue, hide, pelage, pelt, skin, wool.

**Furies** *n* Dirae, Erinyes, Eumenides, Furiae, Semnai.

**furious** *adj* acharné, agitated, angry, boiling, boisterous, enraged, fierce, fizzing, frantic, frenzied, fuming, furibund, impetuous, incensed, infuriated, intense, livid, mad, maddened, maenadic, raging, savage, stormy, tempestuous, tumultuous, turbulent, up in arms, vehement, violent, waxy, wild, wrathful, wroth.

*antonyms* calm, pleased.

**furnish** *v* afford, appoint, bedight, bestow, decorate, endow, equip, fit out, fit up, give, grant, offer, outfit, present, provide, provision, reveal, rig, stake, stock, store, suit, supply.

*antonym* divest.

**furniture** *n* appliances, appointments, appurtenances, chattels, effects, equipment, fittings, furnishing, goods, household goods, movables, plenishing, possessions, things.

**furore** *n* commotion, craze, disturbance, enthusiasm, excitement, flap, frenzy, fury, fuss, hullabaloo, mania, outburst, outcry, rage, stir, to-do, tumult, uproar.

*antonym* calm.

**furrow** *n* chamfer, channel, corrugation, crease, crow's-foot, flute, fluting, groove, hollow, line, rut, seam, trench, vallecula, wrinkle.

*v* corrugate, crease, draw together, flute, knit, seam, wrinkle.

**furrowed** *adj* channelled, corrugated, exarate, fluted, gouged, grooved, ribbed, ridged, rutted, seamed, vallecular, valleculate, wrinkled.

**further** *adj* additional, distant, extra, far, fresh, more, new, opposite, other, supplementary.

*v* accelerate, advance, aid, assist, champion, contribute to, ease, encourage, expedite, facilitate, forward, foster, hasten, help, patronise, plug, promote, push, speed, succour.

*antonyms* frustrate, stop.

**furtherance** *n* advancement, advancing, advocacy, backing, boosting, carrying-out, championship, promoting, promotion, prosecution, pursuit.

**furthermore** *adv* additionally, also, as well, besides, further, in addition, into the bargain, likewise, moreover, not to mention, to boot, too, what's more.

**furthest** *adj* extreme, farthest, furthermost, most distant, outermost, outmost, remotest, ultimate, uttermost.

*antonym* nearest.

**furtive** *adj* back-door, backstairs, clandestine, cloaked, conspiratorial, covert, hidden, secret, secretive, skulking, slinking, sly, sneaking, sneaky, stealthy, surreptitious, underhand.

*antonym* open.

**fury¹** *n* anger, desperation, ferocity, fierceness, force, frenzy, impetuosity, intensity, ire, madness, passion, power, rage, savagery, severity, tempestuousness, turbulence, vehemence, violence, wax, wrath.

*antonym* calm.

**fury²** *n* bacchante, hag, harridan, hell-cat, shrew, spitfire, termagant, virago, vixen.

**fuse** *v* agglutinate, amalgamate, ankylose, blend, coalesce, combine, commingle, federate, integrate, intermingle, intermix, join, meld, melt, merge, smelt, solder, unite, weld.

**fusillade** *n* barrage, broadside, burst, discharge, fire, haii, mitraille, outburst, salvo, volley.

**fusion** *n* alloy, amalgam, amalgamation, blend, blending, coalescence, commingling, commixture, federation, integration, liquefaction, liquefying, melting, merger, merging, mixture, smelting, synthesis, union, uniting, welding.

**fuss** *n* ado, agitation, bother, brouhaha, bustle, coil, commotion, confusion, difficulty, display, doodah, excitement, fantigue, fash, fidget, fikery, flap, flurry, fluster, flutter, furore, hassle, hoo-ha, hurry, kerfuffle, objection, palaver, pother, pudder, row, squabble, stew, stir, to-do, trouble, unrest, upset, worry.

*antonym* calm.

*v* bustle, chafe, complain, emote, fash, fidget, flap, fret, fume, niggle, pother, pudder, take pains, worry.

**fussiness** *n* busy-ness, choosiness, daintiness, elaborateness, faddiness, faddishness, fastidiousness, finicality, finicalness, meticulousness, niceness, niggling, particularity, perfectionism, pernicketiness.

*antonym* unfastidiousness.

**fuss-pot** *n* fantod, fidget, fuss-budget, hypercritic, nit-picker, old woman, perfectionist, worrier.

**fussy** *adj* busy, chichi, choosy, cluttered, dainty, difficult, discriminating, exacting, faddish, faddy, fastidious, finical, finicking, finicky, finikin, hard to please, niggling, nipperty-tipperty, nit-picking, old womanish, old-maidish, overdecorated, overelaborate, overparticular, particular, pernickety, picky, squeamish.

*antonyms* plain, uncritical, undemanding.

**fustiness** *n* airlessness, closeness, dampness, frowst, frowstiness, fug, fust, mouldiness, mustiness, staleness, stuffiness.

*antonym* airiness.

**fusty** *adj* airless, antediluvian, antiquated, archaic, close, damp, dank, frowsty, fuggy, ill-smelling, malodorous, mildewed, mildewy, mouldering, mouldy, musty, old-fashioned, old-fog(e)yish, outdated, out-of-date, passé, rank, stale, stuffy, unventilated.

*antonyms* airy, chic, up-to-date.

**futile** *adj* abortive, barren, bootless, empty, forlorn, fruitless, hollow, idle, ineffectual, nugatory, otiose, pointless, profitless, Sisyphean, sterile, trifling, trivial, unavailing, unimportant, unproductive, unprofitable, unsuccessful, useless, vain, valueless, worthless.

*antonyms* fruitful, profitable.

**futility** *n* aimlessness, bootlessness, emptiness, fruitlessness, hollowness, idleness, ineffectiveness, otioseness, pointlessness, triviality, unimportance, uselessness, vanity.

*antonyms* fruitfulness, profitability.

**future** *n* expectation, futurition, futurity, hereafter, outlook, prospects.

*antonym* past.

*adj* approaching, coming, designate, destined, eventual, expected, fated, forthcoming, impending, in the offing, later, prospective, rising, subsequent, to be, to come, ultimate, unborn.

*antonym* past.

**fuzz** *n* down, fibre, flock, floss, flue, fluff, fug, hair, lint, nap, ooze, pile.

**fuzzy** *adj* bleary, blurred, blurry, distanceless, distorted, downy, faint, fluffy, frizzy, hazy, ill-defined, indistinct, linty, muffled, napped, shadowy, unclear, unfocused, vague, woolly.

*antonyms* base, distinct.

# G

**gab** v babble, blabber, blather, blether, buzz, chatter, drivel, gossip, jabber, jaw, prattle, talk, tattle, yabber, yak, yatter.

n blab, blarney, blethering, blethers, chat, chatter, chitchat, conversation, drivel, gossip, loquacity, palaver, prattle, prattling, small talk, tête-à-tête, tittle-tattle, tongue-wagging, yabber, yackety-yak, yak, yatter.

**gabble** v babble, blab, blabber, blether, cackle, chatter, gaggle, gibber, gush, jabber, prattle, rattle, splutter, spout, sputter, yabber, yatter.

n babble, blabber, blethering, cackling, chatter, drivel, gibberish, jargon, nonsense, prattle, twaddle, waffle, yabber, yatter.

**gad about** dot about, gallivant, ramble, range, roam, rove, run around, stray, traipse, wander.

**gadabout** n gallivanter, pleasure-seeker, rambler, rover, runabout, stravaiger, wanderer.

**gadget** n appliance, contraption, contrivance, device, doodad, gimmick, gismo, gizmo, invention, jiggumbob, jigjam, jigmaree, novelty, thing, thingumajig, tool, widget.

**gaffe** n bloomer, blunder, boner, boob, boo-boo, brick, clanger, faux pas, gaucherie, goof, howler, indiscretion, mistake, slip, solecism.

**gaffer** n boss, foreman, ganger, manager, overman, overseer, superintendent, supervisor.

**gag¹** v choke, choke up, curb, disgorge, gasp, heave, muffle, muzzle, puke, quiet, retch, silence, spew, stifle, still, stop up, suppress, throttle, throw up, vomit.

**gag²** n funny, hoax, jest, joke, one-liner, pun, quip, wisecrack, witticism.

**gaiety** n animation, blitheness, blithesomeness, brightness, brilliance, celebration, cheerfulness, colour, colourfulness, conviviality, effervescence, elation, exhilaration, festivity, fun, galliardise, gaudiness, glee, glitter, good humour, high spirits, hilarity, joie de vivre, jollification, jollity, joviality, joyousness, light-heartedness, liveliness, merriment, merrymaking, mirth, revelry, revels, show, showiness, sparkle, sprightliness, vivacity.

*antonyms* drabness, dreariness, sadness.

**gaily** adv blithely, brightly, brilliantly, cheerfully, colourfully, fancily, flamboyantly, flashily, gaudily, gleefully, happily, joyfully, joyously, light-heartedly, merrily, showily.

*antonyms* dully, sadly.

**gain** v achieve, acquire, advance, arrive at, attain, avail, bag, bring in, capture, clear, collect, come to, earn, enlist, gather, get, get to, glean, harvest, impetrate, improve, increase, make, net, obtain, pick up, procure, produce, profit, progress, reach, realise, reap, secure, win, win over, yield.

*antonym* lose.

n accretion, achievement, acquisition, advance, advancement, advantage, attainment, benefit, bunce, dividend, earnings, emolument, growth, headway, improvement, income, increase, increment, lucre, proceeds, produce, profit, progress, pudding, return, rise, winnings, yield.

*antonyms* loss, losses.

**gain on** approach, catch up, catch up with, close with, come up with, encroach on, leave behind, level with, narrow the gap, outdistance, overtake, widen the gap.

**gain time** delay, drag one's feet, procrastinate, stall, temporise.

**gainful** adj advantageous, beneficial, feracious, fructuous, fruitful, lucrative, moneymaking, paying, productive, profitable, remunerative, rewarding, useful, worthwhile.

*antonym* useless.

**gains** n booty, bunce, earnings, fruits, gainings, loaves and fishes, pickings, prize, proceeds, profits, revenue, takings, velvet, winnings.

*antonym* losses.

**gainsay** v contradict, contravene, controvert, deny, disaffirm, disagree with, dispute, nay-say.

*antonym* agree.

**gait** n bearing, carriage, manner, pace, step, stride, tread, walk.

**gala** n carnival, celebration, festival, festivity, fête, glorification, jamboree, jubilee, Mardi Gras, pageant, party, procession.

**gale** n blast, burst, cyclone, eruption, explosion, fit, howl, hurricane, outbreak, outburst, peal, ripsnorter, shout, shriek, squall, storm, tempest, tornado, typhoon.

**gall¹** n acrimony, animosity, animus, antipathy, assurance, bad blood, bile, bitterness, brass, brass neck, brazenness, cheek, effrontery, enmity, hostility, impertinence, impudence, insolence, malevolence, malice, malignity, neck, nerve, presumption, presumptuousness, rancour, sauciness, sourness, spite, spleen, venom, virulence.

*antonyms* friendliness, modesty, reserve.

**gall²** v abrade, aggravate, annoy, bark, bother, chafe, exasperate, excoriate, fret, get, get to, graze, harass, hurt, irk, irritate, nag, nettle, peeve, pester, plague, provoke, rankle, rile, rub raw, ruffle, scrape, skin, vex.

**gallant** adj attentive, august, bold, brave, chivalrous, courageous, courteous, courtly, daring, dashing, dauntless, dignified, doughty, elegant, fearless, game, gentlemanly, glorious, gracious, grand, heroic, high-spirited, honourable, imposing, indomitable, intrepid, lion-hearted, lofty, magnanimous, magnificent, manful, manly, mettlesome, noble, plucky, polite, splendid, stately, valiant, valorous.

*antonyms* cowardly, craven, ungentlemanly.

n admirer, adventurer, beau, blade, boyfriend, buck, cavalier, champion, cicisbeo, dandy, daredevil, escort, fop, hero, knight, ladies' man, lady-killer, lover, paramour, suitor, wooer.

**gallantry** n attention, attentiveness, audacity, boldness, bravery, chivalry, courage, courageousness, courteousness, courtesy, courtliness, daring, dauntlessness, derring-do, elegance, fearlessness, gentlemanliness, graciousness, heroism, intrepidity, manliness, mettle, nerve, nobility, pluck, politeness, politesse, prowess, spirit, valiance, valour.

*antonyms* cowardice, ungentlemanliness.

**gallery** n arcade, art-gallery, balcony, circle, gods, grandstand, loggia, museum, passage, pawn, spectators, walk.

**galley** n bireme, long-ship, lymphad, quadrireme, quinquereme, trireme.

**galling** adj aggravating, annoying, bitter, bothersome, exasperating, harassing, humiliating, infuriating, irksome, irritating, nettling, plaguing, provoking, rankling, vexatious, vexing.

*antonym* pleasing.

**gallivant** v dot about, gad about, ramble, range, roam, rove, run around, stravaig, stray, traipse, travel, wander.

**gallop** v bolt, career, dart, dash, fly, gal(l)umph, hasten, hie, hurry, lope, race, run, rush, scud, shoot, speed, sprint, tear, zoom.

**gallows** n dule-tree, hempen caudle, nubbing-cleat, scaffold, the rope.

**galore** adv aplenty, everywhere, heaps of, in abundance, in numbers, in profusion, lots of, millions of, stacks of, to spare, tons of.

*antonym* scarce.

**galvanise** v animate, arouse, awaken, electrify, excite, fire, inspire, invigorate, jolt, move, prod, provoke, quicken, shock, spur, startle, stimulate, stir, thrill, vitalise, wake.

*antonym* retard.

**gambit** n artifice, device, manoeuvre, move, ploy, stratagem, trick, wile.

**gamble** v back, bet, chance, gaff, game, have a flutter, hazard, play, punt, risk, speculate, stake, stick one's neck out, take a chance, try one's luck, venture, wager.

n bet, chance, flutter, leap in the dark, lottery, punt, risk, speculation, uncertainty, venture, wager.

**gambler** n better, gaffer, gamester, punter, throwster, wagerer.

**gambol** v bounce, bound, caper, cavort, curvet, cut a caper, frisk, frolic, hop, jump, prance, rollick, skip.

n antic, bound, caper, frisk, frolic, gambado, hop, jump, prance, skip, spring.

**game¹** n adventure, amusement, business, competition, contest, design, device, distraction, diversion, enterprise, entertainment, event, frolic, fun, jest, joke, lark, line, main, match, meeting, merriment, merry-making, occupation, pastime, plan, play, plot, ploy, proceeding, recreation, romp, round, scheme, sport, stratagem, strategy, tactic, tournament, trick, undertaking.

**game²** n animals, bag, flesh, game-birds, meat, prey, quarry, spoils.

**game³** adj bold, brave, courageous, dauntless, desirous, disposed, dogged, eager, fearless, gallant, gamy, heroic, inclined, interested, intrepid, persevering, persistent, plucky, prepared, ready, resolute, spirited, spunky, unflinching, valiant, valorous, willing.

*antonyms* cowardly, unwilling.

**game⁴** adj bad, crippled, deformed, disabled, gammy, gouty, hobbling, incapacitated, injured, lame, maimed.

**gamekeeper** n keeper, venerer, verderer, warden.

**gamut** n area, catalogue, compass, field, gamme, range, scale, scope, series, spectrum, sweep.

**gang** n band, circle, clique, club, coffle, company, core, coterie, crew, crowd, group, herd, horde, lot, mob, pack, party, ring, set, shift, squad, team, troupe.

**gangling** adj angular, awkward, bony, gangly, gauche, gawky, lanky, loose-jointed, rangy, raw-boned, skinny, spindly, tall, ungainly.

**gangster** n bandit, brigand, crook, desperado, heavy, hood, hoodlum, mobster, racketeer, robber, rough, ruffian, thug, tough.

**gaol** see **jail**.

**gap** n blank, breach, break, chink, cleft, crack, cranny, crevice, diastema, difference, disagreement, discontinuity, disparateness, disparity, divergence, divide, hiatus, hole, inconsistency, interlude, intermission, interruption, interspace, interstice, interval, lacuna, lull, opening, pause, recess, rent, rift, space, vacuity, void.

**gape** v crack, dehisce, gawk, gawp, goggle, open, split, stare, wonder, yawn.

**gaping** adj broad, cavernous, dehiscent, fatiscent, great, hiant, open, ringent, vast, wide, yawning.

*antonym* tiny.

**garage** n lock-up, petrol station, service station.

**garb** *n* accoutrements, apparel, appearance, array, aspect, attire, clothes, clothing, costume, covering, cut, dress, fashion, garment, gear, guise, habiliment, habit, look, mode, outfit, raiment, robes, style, uniform, vestments, wear.

*v* apparel, array, attire, clothe, cover, dress, habilitate, rig out, robe.

**garbage** *n* bits and pieces, debris, detritus, dross, filth, gash, junk, litter, muck, odds and ends, offal, refuse, rubbish, scourings, scraps, slops, sweepings, swill, trash, waste.

**garble** *v* confuse, corrupt, distort, doctor, edit, falsify, jumble, misinterpret, misquote, misreport, misrepresent, misstate, mistranslate, mix up, muddle, mutilate, pervert, slant, tamper with, twist.

*antonym* decipher.

**garden** *n* backyard, garth, orchard, park, plot, yard.

**gargantuan** *adj* big, Brobdingnag(ian), colossal, elephantine, enormous, giant, gigantic, huge, immense, large, leviathan, mammoth, massive, monstrous, monumental, mountainous, prodigious, titanic, towering, tremendous, vast.

*antonym* small.

**gargoyle** *n* grotesque, spout.

**garish** *adj* brassy, brummagem, cheap, criant, flash, flashy, flaunting, flaunty, gaudy, glaring, glittering, glitzy, loud, meretricious, raffish, showy, tasteless, tawdry, vulgar.

*antonyms* modest, plain, quiet.

**garland** *n* bays, chaplet, coronal, crown, festoon, honours, laurels, lei, stemma, swag, wreath.

*v* adorn, crown, deck, engarland, festoon, wreathe.

**garments** *n* apparel, array, attire, clothes, clothing, costume, dress, duds, garb, gear, get-up, habiliment, habit, outfit, raiment, robes, togs, uniform, vestments, wear.

**garner** *v* accumulate, amass, assemble, collect, cull, deposit, gather, hoard, husband, lay up, put by, reserve, save, stockpile, store, stow away, treasure.

*antonym* dissipate.

**garnish** *v* adorn, beautify, bedeck, deck, decorate, embellish, enhance, furnish, grace, ornament, set off, trim.

*antonym* divest.

*n* adornment, decoration, embellishment, enhancement, garnishment, garnishry, garniture, ornament, ornamentation, relish, trim, trimming.

**garrison** *n* armed force, barracks, base, camp, casern(e), command, detachment, encampment, fort, fortification, fortress, post, station, stronghold, troops, unit, zareba.

*v* assign, defend, furnish, guard, man, mount, occupy, place, position, post, protect, station.

**garrulity** *n* babble, babbling, chatter, chattering, chattiness, diffuseness, effusiveness, gabbiness, garrulousness, gassing, gift of the gab, glibness, long-windedness, loquaciousness, loquacity, prating, prattle, prolixity, prosiness, talkativeness, verbosity, volubility, windiness, wordiness.

*antonyms* taciturnity, terseness.

**garrulous** *adj* babbling, chattering, chatty, diffuse, effusive, gabby, gassy, glib, gossiping, gushing, long-winded, loquacious, mouthy, prating, prattling, prolix, prosy, talkative, verbose, voluble, windy, wordy, yabbering.

*antonyms* taciturn, terse.

**gash** *v* cleave, cut, gouge, incise, lacerate, nick, notch, rend, score, slash, slit, split, tear, wound.

*n* cleft, cut, gouge, incision, laceration, nick, notch, rent, score, slash, slit, split, tear, wound.

**gasp** *v* blow, breathe, choke, ejaculate, gulp, pant, puff, utter.

*n* blow, breath, ejaculation, exclamation, gulp, pant, puff.

**gate** *n* barrier, door, doorway, entrance, exit, gateway, opening, passage, port, portal, portcullis, wicket.

**gather** *v* accumulate, amass, assemble, assume, build, clasp, collect, conclude, congregate, convene, crop, cull, deduce, deepen, draw, embrace, enfold, enlarge, expand, flock, fold, foregather, garner, glean, group, grow, harvest, heap, hear, heighten, hoard, hold, hug, increase, infer, intensify, learn, make, marshal, mass, muster, pick, pile up, pleat, pluck, pucker, rake up, reap, rise, round up, ruche, ruffle, select, shirr, stockpile, surmise, swell, thicken, tuck, understand, wax.

*antonyms* dissipate, scatter.

**gathering** *n* accumulation, acquisition, aggregate, assemblage, assembly, collection, company, concentration, conclave, concourse, congregation, congress, convention, convocation, crowd, fest, flock, gain, galère, get-together, group, heap, hoard, jamboree, kgotla, knot, mass, meeting, moot, muster, omnium-gatherum, party, pile, procurement, rally, round-up, rout, stock, stockpile, throng, turn-out.

*antonym* scattering.

**gauche** *adj* awkward, clumsy, farouche, gawky, graceless, ignorant, ill-bred, ill-mannered, inelegant, inept, insensitive, maladroit, tactless, uncultured, ungainly, ungraceful, unpolished, unsophisticated.

*antonym* graceful.

**gaucherie** *n* awkwardness, bad taste, bloomer, blunder, boner, boob, brick, clanger, clumsiness, faux pas, gaffe, gaucheness, goof, gracelessness, ignorance, ill-breeding, indiscretion, inelegance, ineptness, insensitivity, maladroitness, mistake, slip, solecism, tactlessness.

*antonym* elegance.

**gaudy** *adj* bright, brilliant, brummagem, chintzy, flash, flashy, florid, garish, gay, glaring, glitzy, loud, meretricious, ostentatious, raffish, showy, tasteless, tawdry, tinsel(ly), vulgar.

*antonyms* drab, plain, quiet.

**gauge**[1] *v* adjudge, adjust, appraise, ascertain, assess, calculate, check, compute, count, determine, estimate, evaluate, figure, guess, judge, measure, rate, reckon, value, weigh.

*n* basis, criterion, example, exemplar, guide, guideline, indicator, measure, meter, micrometer, model, pattern, rule, sample, standard, test, touchstone, yardstick.

**gauge**[2] *n* bore, calibre, capacity, degree, depth, extent, height, magnitude, measure, scope, size, span, thickness, width.

**gaunt** *adj* angular, attenuated, bare, bleak, bony, cadaverous, desolate, dismal, dreary, emaciated, forbidding, forlorn, grim, haggard, hagged, harsh, hollow-eyed, lank, lean, meagre, pinched, rawboned, scraggy, scrawny, skeletal, skinny, spare, thin, wasted.

*antonyms* hale, plump.

**gauzy** *adj* delicate, diaphanous, filmy, flimsy, gossamer, insubstantial, light, see-through, sheer, thin, transparent, unsubstantial.

*antonyms* heavy, thick.

**gawk** *v* gape, gaup, gaze, goggle, look, ogle, stare.

**gawky** *adj* awkward, clownish, clumsy, gangling, gauche, loutish, lumbering, lumpish, maladroit, oafish, uncouth, ungainly, ungraceful.

*antonym* graceful.

**gay**[1] *adj* animated, blithe, boon, bright, brilliant, carefree, cavalier, cheerful, colourful, convivial, debonair, festive, flamboyant, flashy, fresh, frivolous, frolicsome, fun-loving, gamesome, garish, gaudy, glad, gleeful, happy, hilarious, insouciant, jolly, jovial, joyful, joyous, lifesome, light-hearted, lightsome, lively, merry, playful, pleasure-seeking, rakish, riant, rich, rollicking, rorty, showy, sparkish, sparkling, sportive, sunny, tit(t)upy, vivacious, vivid, waggish.

*antonyms* gloomy, sad.

**gay**[2] *adj* bent, dikey, homosexual, lesbian, queer.

*antonyms* heterosexual, straight.

*n* dike, homo, homosexual, lesbian, poof, queer, sapphist.

*antonym* heterosexual.

**gaze** *v* contemplate, gape, gaup, gawp, look, ogle, regard, stare, view, watch.

*n* gaup, gawp, look, stare.

**gazebo** *n* belvedere, hut, pavilion, shelter, summer-house.

**gazette** *n* despatch, journal, magazine, newspaper, news-sheet, notice, organ, paper, periodical.

**gear** *n* accessories, accoutrements, affair, apparatus, apparel, armour, array, attire, baggage, belongings, business, clothes, clothing, cog, costume, doings, dress, effects, equipment, garb, garments, gearing, get-up, habit, harness, instruments, kit, luggage, machinery, matter, mechanism, outfit, paraphernalia, possessions, rigging, rig-out, stuff, supplies, tackle, things, togs, tools, trappings, traps, wear, works.

*v* adapt, adjust, equip, fit, harness, rig, suit, tailor.

**gears** *n* cams, cam-wheels, cogs, cogwheels, engrenage, gear-wheels, mechanism, workings, works.

**gelatinous** *adj* congealed, gluey, glutinous, gooey, gummy, jellied, jellified, jelly, jellyform, jelly-like, mucilaginous, rubbery, sticky, viscid, viscous.

**gem** *n* angel, bijou, brick, flower, honey, jewel, masterpiece, pearl, pick, pièce de résistance, precious stone, prize, stone, treasure.

**gen** *n* background, data, details, facts, info, information, low-down.

**genealogy** *n* ancestry, background, blood-line, derivation, descent, extraction, family, family tree, line, lineage, pedigree, progeniture, stemma, stirps, stock, strain.

**general** *adj* accepted, accustomed, across-the-board, all-inclusive, approximate, blanket, broad, catholic, collective, common, comprehensive, conventional, customary, ecumenic, ecumenical, encyclop(a)edic, everyday, extensive, generic, habitual, ill-defined, imprecise, inaccurate, indefinite, indiscriminate, inexact, loose, miscellaneous, normal, ordinary, panoramic, popular, prevailing, prevalent, public, regular, sweeping, total, typical, universal, unspecific, usual, vague, widespread.

*antonyms* limited, novel, particular.

*n* chief, c-in-c, commander, commander in chief, generalissimo, hetman, leader, marshal, officer.

**generality** *n* approximateness, breadth, catholicity, commonness, comprehensiveness, ecumenicity, extensiveness, generalisation, impreciseness, indefiniteness, inexactness, looseness, miscellaneity, popularity, prevalence, sweeping statement, universality, vagueness.

*antonyms* detail, exactness, particular, uncommonness.

**generally** *adv* approximately, as a rule, broadly, by and large, characteristically, chiefly, commonly, conventionally, customarily, extensively, for the most part, habitually, in the main, largely, mainly, mostly, normally, on average, on the whole, ordinarily, popularly, predominantly, principally, publicly, regularly, typically, universally, usually, widely.

*antonym* rarely.

**generate** *v* beget, breed, bring about, cause, create, engender, father, form, gender, give rise to, initiate, make, originate, procreate, produce, propagate, spawn, whip up.

*antonym* prevent.

**generation** *n* age, age group, begetting, breed, breeding, creation, crop, day, days, engendering, engenderment, engend(r)ure, epoch, era, formation, generating, genesis, geniture, origination, period, procreation, production, progeniture, propagation, reproduction, time, times.

**generic** *adj* all-inclusive, blanket, collective, common, comprehensive, general, inclusive, sweeping, universal, wide.

*antonym* particular.

**generosity** *n* beneficence, benevolence, big-heartedness, bounteousness, bounty, charity, goodness, high-mindedness, kindness, large-heartedness, liberality, magnanimity, munificence, nobleness, open-handedness, soft-heartedness, unselfishness, unsparingness.

*antonyms* meanness, selfishness.

**generous** *adj* abundant, ample, beneficent, benevolent, big-hearted, bounteous, bountiful, charitable, copious, disinterested, free, full, good, high-minded, hospitable, kind, large-hearted, large-minded, lavish, liberal, lofty, magnanimous, munificent, noble, open-handed, overflowing, plentiful, princely, rich, soft-boiled, soft-hearted, ungrudging, unreproachful, unresentful, unselfish, unsparing, unstinted, unstinting.

*antonyms* mean, selfish.

**genesis** *n* beginning, birth, commencement, creation, dawn, engendering, formation, foundation, founding, generation, inception, initiation, origin, outset, propagation, root, source, start.

*antonym* end.

**genial** *adj* affable, agreeable, amiable, cheerful, cheery, congenial, convivial, cordial, easy-going, expansive, friendly, glad, good-natured, happy, hearty, jolly, jovial, joyous, kind, kindly, merry, pleasant, sunny, sunshiny, warm, warm-hearted.

*antonym* cold.

**geniality** *n* affability, agreeableness, amiability, cheerfulness, cheeriness, congenialness, conviviality, cordiality, friendliness, gladness, good nature, happiness, heartiness, jollity, joviality, kindliness, kindness, mirth, openness, pleasantness, sunniness, warm-heartedness, warmth.

*antonym* coldness.

**genie** *n* demon, (d)jinni, fairy, jann, jinnee, spirit.

**genitals** *n* fanny, genitalia, private parts, privates, pudenda, pudendum, pussy, quim, yoni.

**genius**[1] *n* adept, brain, expert, intellect, maestro, master, master-hand, mastermind, pastmaster, virtuoso.

**genius**[2] *n* ability, aptitude, bent, brightness, brilliance, capacity, endowment, faculty, flair, gift, inclination, intellect, knack, propensity, talent, turn.

**genius**[3] *n* daemon, double, genie, ka, spirit.

**genocide** *n* ethnocide, extermination, massacre, slaughter.

**genre** *n* brand, category, character, class, fashion, genus, group, kind, race, school, sort, species, strain, style, type, variety.

**genteel** *adj* aristocratic, civil, courteous, courtly, cultivated, cultured, elegant, fashionable, formal, gentlemanly, graceful, ladylike, mannerly, polished, polite, refined, respectable, stylish, urbane, well-bred, well-mannered.

*antonyms* crude, rough, unpolished.

**Gentile** *n* goy.

**gentility** *n* aristocracy, blue blood, breeding, civility, courtesy, courtliness, cultivation, culture, decorum, elegance, elite, etiquette, formality, gentilesse, gentle birth, gentlefolk, gentrice, gentry, good family, high birth, mannerliness, manners, nobility, nobles, polish, politeness, propriety, rank, refinement, respectability, upper class, urbanity.

*antonyms* crudeness, discourteousness, roughness.

**gentle** *adj* amiable, aristocratic, balmy, benign, biddable, bland, broken, calm, canny, clement, compassionate, courteous, cultured, docile, easy, elegant, genteel, gentlemanlike, gentlemanly, gradual, high-born, humane, imperceptible, kind, kindly, ladylike, lamb-like, lenient, light, low, maidenly, manageable, meek, merciful, mild, moderate, muted, noble, pacific, peaceful, placid, polished, polite, quiet, refined, serene, slight, slow, smooth, soft, soothing, sweet, sweet-tempered, tame, temperate, tender, tractable, tranquil, untroubled, upper-class, well-born, well-bred.

*antonyms* crude, rough, unkind, unpolished.

**gentleman** *n* duniewassal, gemman, gent, gentilhomme, hidalgo, sahib, Sen^•or, Signor(e), sir.

**gentlemanly** *adj* civil, civilised, courteous, cultivated, gallant, genteel, gentlemanlike, gentlewomanly, honourable, mannerly, noble, obliging, polished, polite, refined, reputable, suave, urbane, well-bred, well-mannered.

*antonyms* impolite, rough.

**gentry** *n* aristocracy, elite, gens de condition, gentility, gentlefolk, nobility, nobles, quality, squirearchy, upper class.

**genuine** *adj* actual, artless, authentic, bona fide, candid, earnest, frank, heartfelt, honest, kosher, legitimate, natural, original, pukka, pure, real, simon-pure, sincere, sound, sterling, sure-enough, true, unadulterate(d), unaffected, unalloyed, unfeigned, unsophisticated, veritable.

*antonyms* artificial, insincere.

**genus** *n* breed, category, class, division, genre, group, kind, order, race, set, sort, species, taxon, type.

**geography** *n* chorography, layout, lie.

**geology** *n* geognosy, geogony, geotectonics.

**germ** *n* bacterium, beginning, bud, bug, cause, egg, embryo, microbe, micro-organism, nucleus, origin, ovule, ovum, root, rudiment, seed, source, spark, spore, sprout, virus, zyme.

**germane** *adj* akin, allied, applicable, apposite, appropriate, apropos, apt, cognate, connected, fitting, kin, kindred, material, pertinent, proper, related, relevant, suitable.

*antonym* irrelevant.

**germinal** *adj* developing, embryonic, preliminary, rudimentary, seminal, undeveloped.

**germinate** *v* bud, develop, generate, grow, originate, pullulate, root, shoot, sprout, swell, vegetate.

**gestation** *n* conception, development, drafting, evolution, incubation, maturation, planning, pregnancy, ripening.

**gesticulate** *v* gesture, indicate, motion, point, sign, signal, wave.

**gesticulation** *n* ch(e)ironomy, motion, sign, signal, wave.

**gesture** *n* act, action, gesticulation, indication, motion, sign, signal, wave.
*v* gesticulate, indicate, motion, point, sign, signal, wave.

**get** *v* achieve, acquire, affect, annoy, arouse, arrange, arrest, arrive, attain, baffle, bag, become, bother, bring, bug, capture, catch, coax, collar, come, come by, come down with, communicate with, comprehend, confound, contact, contract, contrive, convince, earn, excite, fathom, fetch, fix, follow, gain, glean, grab, grow, hear, impetrate, impress, induce, influence, inherit, irk, irritate, make, make it, manage, move, mystify, net, nonplus, notice, obtain, perceive, perplex, persuade, pick up, pique, prevail upon, procure, puzzle, reach, realise, reap, receive, secure, see, seize, stimulate, stir, stump, succeed, sway, take, touch, trap, turn, twig, understand, upset, vex, wangle, wax, wheedle, win.
*antonyms* lose, misunderstand, pacify.

**get a move on** get cracking, get going, go to it, hurry (up), jump to it, make haste, shake a leg, speed up, step on it.
*antonym* slow down.

**get across** bring home to, communicate, convey, cross, ford, impart, negotiate, put over, transmit, traverse.

**get ahead** advance, flourish, get there, go places, make good, make it, progress, prosper, succeed, thrive.
*antonyms* fail, fall behind.

**get along** cope, develop, fare, get by, get on, harmonise, hit it off, make (a) shift, make out, manage, progress, shift, survive.
*antonym* argue.

**get at** acquire, annoy, attack, attain, blame, bribe, buy off, carp, corrupt, criticise, find fault with, hint, imply, influence, intend, irritate, make fun of, mean, mock, nag, pervert, pick on, poke fun at, suborn, suggest, tamper with, taunt.
*antonym* praise.

**get away** break out, decamp, depart, disappear, escape, flee, get out, leave, run away.

**get back** get even, get one's own back (on), recoup, recover, regain, repossess, retaliate, retrieve, return, revenge oneself (on), revert, revisit.

**get by** contrive, cope, exist, fare, get along, make both ends meet, manage, negotiate, pass muster, shift, subsist, survive.

**get down** alight, depress, descend, disembark, dishearten, dismount, dispirit, lower, sadden.
*antonyms* board, encourage.

**get even** even the score, get one's own back, pay back, reciprocate, repay, requite, revenge oneself, settle the score.

**get in** alight, appear, arrive, collect, come, embark, enter, gather in, include, infiltrate, insert, interpose, land, mount, penetrate, take.
*antonym* get out.

**get off** alight, depart, descend, detach, disembark, dismount, doff, escape, exit, learn, leave, remove, shed, swot up.
*antonyms* arrive, board, put on.

**get on** advance, agree, ascend, board, climb, concur, cope, embark, fare, get along, harmonise, hit it off, make out, manage, mount, proceed, progress, prosper, succeed.
*antonyms* alight, argue.

**get out** alight, break out, clear out, decamp, deliver, escape, evacuate, extricate oneself, flee, flit, free oneself, leave, produce, publish, quit, scarper, vacate, withdraw.
*antonym* board.

**get out of** avoid, dodge, escape, evade, shirk, skive.

**get over** communicate, convey, cross, defeat, explain, ford, get the better of, impart, master, overcome, pass, put across, recover from, shake off, surmount, survive, traverse.

**get ready** arrange, fix up, get psyched up, gird one's loins, inspan, prepare, psych oneself up, ready, rehearse, set out.

**get rid of** dispense with, dispose of, do away with, dump, eject, eliminate, expel, jettison, remove, rid oneself of, shake off, unload.
*antonyms* accumulate, acquire.

**get round** bypass, cajole, circumvent, coax, convert, edge, evade, outmanoeuvre, persuade, prevail upon, skirt, talk over, talk round, wheedle.

**get the better of** beat, best, defeat, outdo, outfox, outsmart, outwit, surpass, worst.

**get the hang of** absorb, comprehend, grasp, understand.

**get the message** catch on, comprehend, get it, get the point, see, take the hint, twig, understand.
*antonym* misunderstand.

**get there** advance, arrive, go places, make good, make it, prosper, succeed.

**get together** accumulate, assemble, collaborate, collect, congregate, convene, converge, gather, join, meet, muster, rally, unite.

**get under one's skin** annoy, get, get to, infuriate, irk, irritate, needle, nettle.
*antonym* pacify.

**get up** arise, arrange, ascend, climb, fix up, increase, learn, memorise, mount, organise, rise, scale, stand.

**getaway** *n* break, break-out, decampment, escape, flight, start.

**get-together** *n* do, function, gabfest, gathering, party, reception, social, soirée.

**gewgaw** *n* bagatelle, bauble, bijou, gaud, gimcrack, kickshaw(s), knick-knack, novelty, plaything, toy, trifle, trinket.

**ghastly** *adj* ashen, cadaverous, deathlike, deathly, dreadful, frightful, ghostly, grim, grisly, gruesome, hideous, horrendous, horrible, horrid, livid, loathsome, lurid, pale, pallid, repellent, shocking, spectral, terrible, terrifying, wan.

*antonym* delightful.

**ghost** *n* apparition, astral body, duppy, eidolon, fetch, glimmer, gytrash, hint, jumby, larva, lemur, manes, phantasm, phantom, possibility, revenant, semblance, shade, shadow, simulacrum, soul, spectre, spirit, spook, suggestion, trace, umbra, visitant, white-lady.

**ghostly** *adj* chthonian, eerie, eldritch, faint, ghostlike, illusory, insubstantial, phantasmal, phantom, spectral, spooky, supernatural, uncanny, unearthly, weird, wraith-like.

**ghoulish** *adj* grisly, gruesome, macabre, morbid, revolting, sick, unhealthy, unwholesome.

**giant** *n* behemoth, colossus, Goliath, Hercules, jotun, leviathan, monster, Patagonian, titan.

*adj* Atlantean, Babylonian, Brobdingnag(ian), colossal, cyclopean, elephantine, enormous, gargantuan, gigantean, gigantesque, gigantic, huge, immense, jumble, king-size, large, leviathan, mammoth, monstrous, Patagonian, prodigious, rounceval, titanic, vast.

**gibber** *v* babble, blab, blabber, blather, cackle, cant, chatter, claptrap, gabble, jabber, prattle.

**gibberish** *n* abracadabra, babble, balderdash, blather, drivel, gabble, gobbledegook, jabber, jabberwock(y), jargon, mumbo-jumbo, nonsense, prattle, slipslop, twaddle, yammer.

*antonym* sense.

**gibe** *see* **jibe**.

**giddiness** *n* dizziness, faintness, light-headedness, nausea, vertigo, wobbliness, wooziness.

**giddy** *adj* capricious, careless, changeable, changeful, dizzy, dizzying, erratic, faint, fickle, flighty, frivolous, heedless, impulsive, inconstant, irresolute, irresponsible, light-headed, reckless, reeling, scatterbrained, scatty, silly, thoughtless, unbalanced, unstable, unsteady, vacillating, vertiginous, volage, volageous, volatile, wild.

*antonyms* sensible, sober.

**gift** *n* ability, aptitude, attribute, benefaction, benificence, bent, bequest, bonus, boon, bounty, cadeau, capability, capacity, contribution, cumshaw, deodate, dolly, donary, donation, donative, douceur, earnest, endowment, faculty, flair, foy, freebie, genius, grant, gratuity, knack, largess(e), legacy, manna, offering, potlatch, power, present, sop, talent, turn, xenium.

**gifted** *adj* able, accomplished, ace, adroit, bright, brilliant, capable, clever, expert, ingenious, intelligent, masterly, skilful, skilled, talented.

*antonym* dull.

**gigantic** *adj* Atlantean, Babylonian, Brobdingnag(ian), colossal, cyclopean, elephantine, enormous, gargantuan, giant, herculean, huge, immense, leviathan, mammoth, monstrous, Patagonian, prodigious, rounceval, stupendous, titanic, tremendous, vast.

*antonym* small.

**giggle** *v* chortle, chuckle, laugh, snigger, tee-hee, titter.

*n* chortle, chuckle, fou rire, laugh, snigger, tee-hee, titter.

**gild** *v* adorn, array, beautify, bedeck, brighten, coat, deck, dress up, embellish, embroider, enhance, enrich, festoon, garnish, grace, ornament, paint, trim.

**gilded** *adj* gilt, gold, golden, inaurate.

**gimcrack** *adj* cheap, rubbishy, shoddy, tawdry, trashy, trumpery.

*antonyms* solid, well-made.

**gimmick** *n* angle, attraction, contrivance, device, dodge, gadget, gambit, gizmo, manoeuvre, ploy, scheme, stratagem, stunt, trick.

**gin** *n* mother's ruin (mothers' ruin).

**gingerly** *adv* carefully, cautiously, charily, circumspectly, daintily, delicately, fastidiously, gently, hesitantly, reluctantly, squeamishly, suspiciously, timidly, warily.

*antonyms* carelessly, roughly.

**gipsy** *see* **gypsy**.

**gird** *v* belt, bind, blockade, brace, encircle, enclose, encompass, enfold, engird, environ, enzone, fortify, girdle, hem in, pen, prepare, ready, ring, steel, surround.

**girdle** *n* band, belt, ceinture, cestus, cincture, cingulum, corset, cummerbund, fillet, sash, waistband, zona, zone, zonule.

*v* bind, bound, encirle, enclose, encompass, engird, environ, enzone, gird, gird round, go round, hem, ring, surround.

**girl** *n* backfisch, bird, chick, chicken, chit, colleen, damsel, daughter, demoiselle, filly, fizgig, flapper, flibbertigibbet, floosie, fluff, fräulein, gal, giglet, girl-friend, gouge, grisette, judy, lass, lassie, maid, maiden, miss, moppet, peach, piece, popsy(-wopsy), quean, quine, sheila, sweetheart, wench.

**girth** *n* band, belly-band, bulk, circumference, measure, saddle-band, size, strap.

**gist** *n* core, direction, drift, essence, force, idea, import, marrow, matter, meaning, nub, pith, point, quintessence, sense, significance, substance.

**give** *v* accord, administer, admit, allow, announce, award, bend, bestow, break, cause, cede, collapse, commit, communicate, concede, confer, consign, contribute, deliver, demonstrate, devote, display, do, donate, emit, engender, entrust, evidence, fall, furnish, grant, hand, hand over, impart, indicate, issue, lead, lend, make, make over, manifest, notify, occasion, offer, pay, perform, permit, present, produce, proffer, pronounce, provide, publish, recede, relinquish, render, retire, set forth, show, sink, state, supply, surrender, transmit, utter, vouchsafe, yield.

*antonyms* hold out, take, withstand.

**give away** betray, disclose, divulge, expose, grass, inform on, leak, let out, let slip, rat, reveal, uncover.

**give in** capitulate, collapse, comply, concede, crack, give way, quit, submit, surrender, yield.

*antonym* hold out.

**give off** discharge, emit, exhale, exude, outpour, pour out, produce, release, send out, throw out, vent.

**give on to** lead to, open on to, overlook.

**give out** announce, broadcast, communicate, discharge, disseminate, emit, exhale, exude, give off, impart, notify, outpour, pour out, produce, publish, release, send out, transmit, utter, vent.

*antonym* take in.

**give rise to** breed, bring about, bring on, cause, effect, engender, generate, produce, provoke, result in.

**give up** abandon, capitulate, cease, cede, cut out, desist, despair, forswear, hand over, leave off, quit, relinquish, renounce, resign, stop, surrender, throw in the towel, throw up the sponge, waive.

*antonym* hold out.

**give way** accede, acquiesce, back down, bend, break (down), cave in, cede, collapse, concede, crack, crumple, fall, give ground, give place, sink, submit, subside, withdraw, yield.

*antonyms* hold out, withstand.

**give-and-take** *n* adaptability, compliance, flexibility, giff-gaff, good-will, willingness.

**given** *adj* addicted, admitted, agreed, apt, bestowed, disposed, granted, inclined, liable, likely, prone, specified.

**glacial** *adj* antagonistic, arctic, biting, bitter, brumous, chill, chilly, cold, freezing, frigid, frore, frosty, frozen, gelid, hostile, icy, inimical, piercing, polar, raw, Siberian, stiff, unfriendly, wintry.

*antonym* warm.

**glad** *adj* animated, blithe, blithesome, bright, cheerful, cheering, cheery, chuffed, contented, delighted, delightful, felicitous, gay, gleeful, gratified, gratifying, happy, jocund, jovial, joyful, joyous, merry, over the moon, overjoyed, pleasant, pleased, pleasing, willing.

*antonym* sad.

**gladden** *v* brighten, cheer, delight, elate, enliven, exhilarate, gratify, hearten, please, rejoice.

*antonym* sadden.

**gladly** *adv* blithely, blithesomely, cheerfully, fain, freely, gaily, gleefully, happily, jovially, joyfully, joyously, merrily, readily, willingly, with good grace, with pleasure.

*antonyms* sadly, unwillingly.

**gladness** *n* animation, blitheness, blithesomeness, brightness, cheerfulness, delight, felicity, gaiety, glee, happiness, high spirits, hilarity, jollity, joy, joyousness, mirth, pleasure.

*antonym* sadness.

**glamorous** *adj* alluring, attractive, beautiful, bewitching, captivating, charming, classy, dazzling, elegant, enchanting, entrancing, exciting, exotic, fascinating, glittering, glossy, gorgeous, lovely, prestigious, smart.

*antonyms* boring, drab, plain.

**glamour** *n* lure, appeal, attraction, beauty, bewitchment, charm, enchantment, fascination, magic, magnetism, prestige, ravishment, witchery.

**glance¹** *v* browse, dip, flip, gaze, glimpse, leaf, look, peek, peep, riffle, scan, skim, thumb, touch on, view.

*n* allusion, coup d'oeil, dekko, gander, glimpse, look, mention, once over, peek, peep, reference, squint, view.

**glance²** *v* bounce, brush, cannon, carom, coruscate, flash, gleam, glimmer, glint, glisten, glister, glitter, graze, rebound, reflect, ricochet, shimmer, shine, skim, twinkle.

**glare** *v* blaze, coruscate, dazzle, flame, flare, frown, glower, look daggers, lower, scowl, shine.

*n* black look, blaze, brilliance, dazzle, dirty look, flame, flare, flashiness, floridness, frown, gaudiness, glow, glower, light, look, loudness, lower, scowl, showiness, stare, tawdriness.

**glaring** *adj* audacious, blatant, blazing, bright, conspicuous, dazzling, dreadful, egregious, flagrant, flashy, florid, garish, glowing, gross, horrendous, loud, manifest, obvious, open, outrageous, outstanding, overt, patent, rank, terrible, unconcealed, visible.

*antonyms* dull, hidden, minor.

**glass** *n* beaker, crystal, goblet, lens, looking-glass, magnifying glass, pane, pocket-lens, roemer, rummer, schooner, tumbler, vitrics, window.

**glass case** display cabinet, vitrine, vivarium, Wardian case.

**glassiness** *n* vitreosity, vitreousness.

**glassware** *n* crystal, glass, vitrics.

**glassy** *adj* blank, clear, cold, dazed, dull, empty, expressionless, fixed, glasslike, glazed, glazy, glossy, hyaline, icy, lifeless, shiny, slick, slippery, smooth, transparent, vacant, vitreous, vitriform.

**glaze** *v* burnish, coat, crystallise, enamel, furbish, gloss, lacquer, polish, varnish.

*n* coat, enamel, finish, gloss, lacquer, lustre, patina, polish, shine, varnish.

**gleam** *n* beam, brightness, brilliance, coruscation, flash, flicker, glimmer, glint, gloss, glow, hint, inkling, lustre, ray, sheen, shimmer, sparkle, splendour, suggestion, trace.

*v* coruscate, flare, flash, glance, glimmer, glint, glisten, glister, glitter, glow, scintillate, shimmer, shine, sparkle.

**gleaming** *adj* ablaze, bright, brilliant, burnished, glistening, glowing, lustrous, polished, shining.

*antonym* dull.

**glean** *v* accumulate, amass, collect, cull, find out, garner, gather, harvest, learn, pick (up), reap, select.

**glee** *n* cheerfulness, delight, elation, exhilaration, exuberance, exultation, fun, gaiety, gladness, gratification, hilarity, jocularity, jollity, joviality, joy, joyfulness, joyousness, liveliness, merriment, mirth, pleasure, sprightliness, triumph, verve.

**gleeful** *adj* beside oneself, cheerful, cock-a-hoop, delighted, elated, exuberant, exultant, gay, gleesome, gratified, happy, jovial, joyful, joyous, jubilant, merry, mirthful, over the moon, overjoyed, pleased, triumphant.

*antonym* sad.

**glib** *adj* artful, easy, facile, fast-talking, fluent, garrulous, insincere, logodaedalic, plausible, quick, ready, slick, slippery, smooth, smooth-spoken, smooth-tongued, suave, talkative, voluble.

*antonyms* implausible, tongue-tied.

**glibness** *n* logodaedaly, patter, plausibility, slickness, smoothness, suaveness, suavity.

**glide** *v* coast, drift, float, flow, fly, glissade, roll, run, sail, skate, skim, slide, slip, soar, volplane.

**glimmer** *v* blink, flicker, gleam, glint, glisten, glitter, glow, shimmer, shine, sparkle, twinkle.

*n* blink, flicker, gleam, glimmering, glint, glow, grain, hint, inkling, ray, shimmer, sparkle, suggestion, trace, twinkle.

**glimpse** *n* glance, gliff, glim, glisk, look, peek, peep, sight, sighting, squint.

*v* descry, espy, sight, spot, spy, view.

**glint** *v* flash, gleam, glimmer, glitter, reflect, shine, sparkle, twinkle.

*n* flash, gleam, glimmer, glimmering, glitter, shine, sparkle, twinkle, twinkling.

**glisten** *v* coruscate, flash, glance, glare, gleam, glimmer, glint, glister, glitter, scintillate, shimmer, shine, sparkle, twinkle.

**glitter** *v* coruscate, flare, flash, glare, gleam, glimmer, glint, glisten, scintillate, shimmer, shine, spangle, sparkle, twinkle.

*n* beam, brightness, brilliance, clinquant, display, flash, gaudiness, glamour, glare, gleam, lustre, pageantry, radiance, scintillation, sheen, shimmer, shine, show, showiness, sparkle, splendour, tinsel.

**gloat** *v* crow, exult, eye, glory, ogle, rejoice, relish, revel in, rub it in, triumph, vaunt.

**global** *adj* all-encompassing, all-inclusive, all-out, comprehensive, encylopaedic, exhaustive, general, globular, international, pandemic, planetary, spherical, thorough, total, unbounded, universal, unlimited, world, world-wide.

*antonyms* limited, parochial.

**globe** *n* ball, earth, orb, planet, round, roundure, sphere, world.

**globular** *adj* globate, globated, globoid, globous, globulous, orbicular, round, spherical, spheroid.

**globule** *n* bead, bubble, drop, droplet, globulet, particle, pearl, pellet, vesicle, vesicula.

**gloom** *n* blackness, blues, cloud, cloudiness, damp, dark, darkness, dejection, depression, desolation, despair, despondency, dimness, downheartedness, dullness, dusk, duskiness, gloominess, glumness, low spirits, melancholy, misery, murk, murkiness, obscurity, sadness, shade, shadow, sorrow, twilight, unhappiness, woe.

*antonym* brightness.

**gloominess** *n* cheerlessness, darkness, dejection, depression, despondency, dreariness, dullness, gloom, glumness, melancholy, mirkiness, misery, moroseness, mumps, murkiness, pessimism.

*antonym* brightness.

**gloomy** *adj* bad, black, blue, chapfallen, cheerless, comfortless, crepuscular, crestfallen, dark, darksome, dejected, delightless, depressing, despondent, dim, disheartening, dismal, dispirited, dispiriting, down, down in the dumps, down in the mouth, downbeat, downcast, downhearted, dreary, dreich, dull, dusky, gloomful, glum, joyless, long-faced, long-visaged, low-spirited, melancholy, mirk(y), miserable, moody, morose, murk(y), obscure, overcast, pessimistic, sad, saddening, saturnine, sepulchral, shadowy, sombre, Stygian, sullen, tenebrous.

*antonym* bright.

**glorification** *n* doxology, exaltation, glorifying, idolising, magnification, panegyric, praise, praising, romanticising.

*antonyms* blame, vilification.

**glorify** *v* adore, adorn, aggrandise, apotheosise, augment, beatify, bless, canonise, celebrate, deify, dignify, elevate, enhance, ennoble, enshrine, eulogise, exalt, extol, honour, hymn, idolise, illuminate, immortalise, laud, lift up, magnify, panegyrise, praise, raise, revere, sanctify, venerate, worship.

*antonyms* denounce, vilify.

**glorious** *adj* beautiful, bright, brilliant, celebrated, dazzling, delightful, distinguished, divine, drunk, effulgent, elated, elevated, eminent, enjoyable, excellent, famed, famous, fine, gorgeous, grand, great, heavenly, honoured, illustrious, intoxicated, magnificent, majestic, marvellous, noble, noted, pleasurable, radiant, renowned, resplendent, shining, splendid, sublime, superb, tipsy, triumphant, wonderful.

*antonyms* dreadful, inglorious, plain, unknown.

**glory** *n* adoration, beauty, benediction, blessing, brightness, brilliance, celebrity, dignity, distinction, effulgence, eminence, exaltation, fame, gloire, gloria, gorgeousness, grandeur, gratitude, greatness, heaven, homage, honour, illustriousness, immortality, kudos, laudation, lustre, magnificence, majesty, nobility, pageantry, pomp, praise, prestige, radiance, renown, resplendence, richness, splendour, sublimity, thanksgiving, triumph, veneration, worship.

*antonyms* blame, restraint.

*v* boast, crow, delight, exult, gloat, pride oneself, rejoice, relish, revel, triumph.

**gloss**[1] *n* appearance, brightness, brilliance, burnish, façade, front, gleam, lustre, mask, polish, semblance, sheen, shine, show, surface, varnish, veneer, window-dressing.

**gloss over** camouflage, conceal, disguise, double-glaze, explain away, gild, glaze over, hide, mask, smooth over, veil, whitewash.

**gloss²** *n* annotation, comment, commentary, elucidation, explanation, footnote, interpretation, note, postillation, scholion, scholium, translation.

*v* annotate, comment, construe, elucidate, explain, interpret, postil, postillate, translate.

**glossary** *n* dictionary, idioticon, lexicon, phrase-book, vocabulary, word-book, word-list.

**glossy** *adj* bright, brilliant, burnished, enamelled, glacé, glassy, glazed, lustrous, polished, sheeny, shining, shiny, silken, silky, sleek, smooth.

*antonym* mat(t).

**glow** *n* ardour, bloom, blush, brightness, brilliance, burning, earnestness, effulgence, enthusiasm, excitement, fervour, flush, gleam, glimmer, gusto, impetuosity, incandescence, intensity, lambency, light, luminosity, passion, phosphorescence, radiance, reddening, redness, rosiness, splendour, vehemence, vividness, warmth.

*v* blush, brighten, burn, colour, fill, flush, gleam, glimmer, glowing, radiate, redden, shine, smoulder, thrill, tingle.

**glower** *v* frown, glare, look daggers, lower, scowl.

*n* black look, dirty look, frown, glare, look, lower, scowl, stare.

**glowing** *adj* adulatory, aglow, beaming, bright, complimentary, ecstatic, enthusiastic, eulogistic, flaming, florid, flushed, gleamy, lambent, laudatory, luminous, panegyrical, rave, red, rhapsodic, rich, ruddy, suffused, vibrant, vivid, warm.

*antonyms* dull, restrained.

**glue** *n* adhesive, cement, fish-glue, gum, isinglass, mucilage, paste, size.

*v* affix, agglutinate, cement, fix, gum, paste, seal, stick.

**gluey** *adj* adhesive, glutinous, gummy, sticky, viscid, viscous.

**glum** *adj* chapfallen, churlish, crabbed, crestfallen, dejected, doleful, down, gloomy, glumpish, glumpy, gruff, grumpy, ill-humoured, low, moody, morose, pessimistic, saturnine, sour, sulky, sullen, surly.

*antonyms* ecstatic, happy.

**glut** *n* excess, overabundance, oversupply, pleroma, plethora, saturation, superabundance, superfluity, surfeit, surplus.

*antonyms* lack, scarcity.

*v* choke, clog, cram, deluge, englut, fill, flesh, flood, gorge, inundate, overfeed, overload, oversupply, sate, satiate, saturate, stuff.

**glutinous** *adj* adhesive, cohesive, emplastic, gluey, gummy, mucilaginous, ropy, sticky, viscid, viscous.

**glutton** *n* cormorant, free-liver, gannet, gobbler, gorger, gormandiser, gourmand, guzzler, hog, omnivore, pig, trencherman, vulture, whale.

*antonym* ascetic.

**gluttonous** *adj* edacious, esurient, gluttonish, gormandising, greedy, gutsy, hoggish, insatiable, omnivorous, piggish, rapacious, ravenous, ventripotent, voracious.

*antonyms* abstemious, ascetic.

**gluttony** *n* edacity, esurience, gormandising, go(u)rmandise, go(u)rmandism, greed, greediness, gulosity, insatiability, omnivorousness, piggishness, rapaciousness, rapacity, voraciousness, voracity.

*antonyms* abstinence, asceticism.

**gnarled** *adj* contorted, distorted, gnarly, gnarred, knarred, knotted, knotty, knurled, leathery, rough, rugged, twisted, weather-beaten, wrinkled.

**gnaw** *v* bite, chew, consume, devour, distress, eat, erode, fret, harry, haunt, munch, nag, nibble, niggle, plague, prey, trouble, wear, worry.

**go** *v* accord, advance, agree, avail, beat it, blend, chime, complement, concur, conduce, connect, contribute, correspond, decamp, decease, depart, develop, die, disappear, elapse, eventuate, expire, extend, fare, fit, flow, function, gee, happen, harmonise, incline, jib, journey, lapse, lead, lead to, leave, levant, make for, match, mosey, move, naff off, nip, operate, pass, pass away, perform, perish, proceed, progress, rate, reach, repair, result, retreat, roll, run, sally, scram, serve, shift, shove off, slip, sod off, span, spread, stretch, suit, take one's leave, tend, travel, trot, vanish, wag, walk, wend, withdraw, work.

*n* animation, attempt, bid, crack, drive, dynamism, effort, energy, essay, force, get-up-and-go, life, oomph, pep, shot, spirit, stab, try, turn, verve, vigour, vim, vitality, vivacity, whack, whirl, zest.

**go about** address, approach, begin, circulate, get abroad, journey, set about, tackle, travel, undertake, wander.

**go ahead** advance, begin, continue, march on, move, proceed, progress.

**go at** argue, attack, blame, criticise, impugn, set about, turn on.

**go away** bugger off, decamp, depart, disappear, eff off, exit, fuck off, get lost, hop it, imshi, leave, piss off, recede, retreat, scat, scram, vanish, withdraw.

**go back** backslide, desert, forsake, renege, repudiate, retract, retreat, return, revert.

**go by** adopt, elapse, flow, follow, heed, observe, pass, proceed, trust.

**go down** collapse, decline, decrease, degenerate, deteriorate, drop, fail, fall, founder, go under, lose, set, sink, submerge, submit, succumb.

**go far** advance, blaze a trail, do well, progress, succeed.

**go for** admire, assail, assault, attack, be into, choose, clutch at, dig, enjoy, fall on, favour, fetch, hold with, like, lunge at, obtain, prefer, reach, seek, set about.

**go ill with** destroy, endanger, harm, imperil, injure, jeopardise, put at hazard, put at risk, ruin.

**go in for** adopt, embrace, engage in, enter, enter for, espouse, follow, participate in, practise, pursue, take part in, take up, undertake.

**go into** analyse, begin, check out, consider, delve into, develop, discuss, dissect, enquire into, enter, examine, investigate, make a study of, participate in, probe, pursue, review, scrutinise, study, sus out, undertake.

**go mad** go bonkers, go crazy, go nuts, take leave of one's senses.

**go missing** be nowhere to be found, disappear, get lost, scarper, vamoose, vanish.

**go off** abscond, blow up, decamp, depart, deteriorate, detonate, dislike, explode, fire, happen, leave, occur, part, proceed, quit, rot, turn, vamoose, vanish.

**go on** behave, blether, chatter, continue, endure, happen, last, last out, occur, persist, prattle, proceed, ramble on, stay, waffle, witter.

**go out** depart, die out, exit, expire, fade out, leave, obsolesce.

**go over** detail, examine, inspect, list, overname, peruse, read, recall, recapitulate, rehearse, reiterate, review, revise, scan, skim, study.

**go through** bear, brave, check, consume, endure, examine, exhaust, experience, explore, face, hunt, investigate, look, rehearse, search, squander, suffer, tolerate, undergo, use, withstand.

**go to bed** bed down, go to sleep, hit the hay, hit the sack, kip, kip down, retire, turn in.

**go together** accord, agree, chime, fit, gee, harmonise, jibe, match.

**go to pieces** break down, capitulate, collapse, crack up, crumble, crumple, disintegrate, fall apart, lose control, lose one's head.

**go to seed** decay, decline, degenerate, deteriorate, go downhill, go to pot, go to waste, underachieve.

**go to the dogs** be ruined, degenerate, deteriorate, fail, go down the drain, go to pot, go to rack and ruin.

**go under** close down, collapse, default, die, drown, fail, fold, founder, go down, sink, submerge, succumb.

**go with** accompany, agree, blend, chime, complement, concur, correspond, court, date, fit, gee, go steady, harmonise, jibe, match, suit.

**go wrong** boob, break, break down, come to grief, come to nothing, come ungummed, come unstuck, conk out, cut out, err, fail, fall through, flop, go astray, go off the rails, go on the blink, go phut, lapse, malfunction, miscarry, misfire, sin, slip up.

**goad** n fillip, impetus, incentive, incitement, irritation, jab, motivation, poke, pressure, prod, push, spur, stimulation, stimulus, thrust, urge.

v annoy, arouse, badger, bullyrag, chivvy, drive, egg on, exasperate, exhort, harass, hassle, hector, hound, impel, incite, infuriate, instigate, irritate, lash, madden, nag, needle, persecute, prick, prod, prompt, propel, push, spur, stimulate, sting, urge, vex, worry.

**go-ahead** n agreement, assent, authorisation, clearance, consent, fiat, green light, leave, OK, permission, sanction.

*antonyms* ban, embargo, moratorium, veto.

*adj* ambitious, avant-garde, enterprising, goey, go-getting, pioneering, progressive, up-and-coming.

*antonyms* sluggish, unenterprising.

**goal** n aim, ambition, aspiration, bourn(e), design, destination, destiny, end, grail, intention, limit, mark, object, objective, purpose, target.

**goat-like** adj capriform, caprine, concupiscent, foolish, giddy, goatish, hircine, horny, lascivious, libidinous, lustful, randy, silly.

**gobble** v bolt, consume, cram, devour, gorge, gulp, guttle, guzzle, hog, put away, shovel, slabber, stuff, swallow, wire into, wolf.

**go-between** n agent, broker, contact, dealer, factor, informer, intermediary, internuncio, liaison, mediator, medium, messenger, middleman, ombudsman, pander, pimp, procuress.

**goblet** n balloon glass, brandy-glass, chalice, drinking-cup, hanap, Paris goblet, quaich, rummer, tass, wine-glass.

**goblin** n barghest, bogey, bogle, brownie, bugbear, demon, esprit follet, fiend, gremlin, hobgoblin, imp, kelpie, kobold, lubber fiend, nis, nix, nixie, pooka, red-cap, red-cowl, spirit, sprite.

**God, god** n Allah, avatar, Brahma, deity, divinity, genius, Godhead, Holy One, idol, Jah, Jehovah, joss, Jove, kami, jar, Lord, Lord God, monad, Mumbo-jumbo, numen, penates, power, Providence, spirit, the Almighty, the Creator, tutelar, tutelary, Yahweh, Zeus.

**god-forsaken** adj abandoned, backward, benighted, bleak, deserted, desolate, dismal, dreary, forlorn, gloomy, isolated, lonely, miserable, neglected, remote, unfrequented, wretched.

*antonym* congenial.

**godless** adj atheistic, depraved, evil, heathen, impious, irreligious, irreverent, nullifidian, pagan, profane, sacrilegious, ungodly, unholy, unprincipled, unrighteous, wicked.

*antonyms* godly, pious.

**godlike** adj celestial, deiform, divine, exalted, heavenly, saintly, sublime, superhuman, theomorphic, transcendent.

**godly** adj blameless, devout, god-fearing, good, holy, innocent, pious, pure, religious, righteous, saintly, virtuous.

*antonyms* godless, impious.

**godsend** n blessing, boon, fluke, lucky break, manna, miracle, stroke of luck, windfall.

*antonyms* blow, bolt from the blue, bombshell, setback.

**going-over** n analysis, beating, buffeting, castigation, chastisement, check, check-up, chiding, doing, dressing-down, drubbing, examination, inspection, investigation, lecture, probe, rebuke, reprimand, review, row, scolding, scrutiny, study, survey, thrashing, thumping, treatment, trouncing, whipping.

**golden** adj advantageous, aureate, auric, auspicious, best, blissful, blond(e), bright, brilliant, delightful, excellent, fair, favourable, favoured, flaxen, flourishing, glorious, happy, inaurate, invaluable, joyful, lustrous, opportune, precious, priceless, promising, propitious, prosperous, resplendent, rich, rosy, shining, successful, timely, valuable, xanthous, yellow.

**goldmine** n dripping roast, Golconda, gold-dust, golden goose, widow's cruse.

**gone** adj absent, astray, away, broken, bygone, closed, concluded, consumed, dead, deceased, defunct, departed, disappeared, done, elapsed, ended, extinct, finished, kaput, lacking, lost, missed, missing, over, over and done with, past, pregnant, spent, used, vanished, wanting.

**goo** n crud, glaur, grease, grime, gunge, gunk, matter, mire, muck, mud, ooze, scum, slime, sludge, slush, stickiness.

**good** adj able, acceptable, accomplished, adept, adequate, admirable, adroit, advantageous, agreeable, altruistic, amiable, ample, appropriate, approved, approving, auspicious, authentic, balmy, beneficent, beneficial, benevolent, benign, bona fide, bonzer, boshta, bosker, bright, brotherly, budgeree, buoyant, calm, capable, capital, charitable, cheerful, choice, clear, clever, cloudless, commendable, competent, complete, congenial, considerate, convenient, convivial, correct, decorous, dependable, deserving, dexterous, dutiful, eatable, efficient, enjoyable, entire, estimable, ethical, excellent, exemplary, expert, extensive, fair, favourable, fine, first-class, first-rate, fit, fitting, friendly, full, genuine, gracious, gratifying, great, happy, healthy, helpful, honest, honourable, humane, kind, kindly, large, legitimate, long, loyal, mannerly, merciful, meritorious, mild, moral, nice, noble, nourishing, nutritious, obedient, obliging, opportune, orderly, pious, pleasant, pleasing, pleasurable, polite, positive, praiseworthy, precious, presentable, professional, proficient, profitable, proper, propitious, rattling, real, reliable, right, righteous, safe, salubrious, salutary, satisfactory, satisfying, seemly, serviceable, sizeable, skilful, skilled, solid, sound, special, splendid, substantial, sufficient, suitable, sunny, super, superior, sustaining, talented, tested, thorough, tranquil, true, trustworthy, uncorrupted, untainted, upright, useful, valid, valuable, virtuous, well-behaved, well-disposed, well-mannered, whole, wholesome, worthwhile, worthy.

n advantage, avail, behalf, behoof, benefit, boon, convenience, excellence, gain, goodness, interest, merit, morality, probity, profit, rectitude, right, righteousness, service, uprightness, use, usefulness, virtue, weal, welfare, well-being, worth, worthiness.

**good health** interj à votre santé, cheers, Gesundheit, kia-ora, prosit, salud, salute, your health.

n haleness, hardiness, health, healthiness, heartiness, lustiness, robustness, soundness, strength, vigour, vitality.

antonyms ill health, invalidism.

**good-bye** n, interj adieu, adiós, arrivederci, au revoir, auf Wiedersehen, chin-chin, ciao, farewell, leave-taking, parting, valediction, valedictory.

**good-for-nothing** n black sheep, bum, drone, idler, layabout, lazy-bones, loafer, lorel, losel, mauvais sujet, ne'er-do-well, profligate, rapscallion, reprobate, scapegrace, vaurien, waster, wastrel.

antonyms achiever, success, winner.

adj do-nothing, feckless, idle, indolent, irresponsible, lorel, losel, no-good, profligate, reprobate, slothful, useless, worthless.

antonyms conscientious, successful.

**good-humoured** adj affable, amiable, approachable, blithe, cheerful, congenial, expansive, genial, good-tempered, happy, jocund, jovial, pleasant.

antonym ill-humoured.

**good-looking** adj attractive, beautiful, bonny, comely, easy on the eye, fair, handsome, personable, presentable, pretty, well-favoured, well-looking, well-proportioned, well-set-up.

antonyms ill-favoured, plain, ugly.

**good-luck charm** amulet, periapt, phylactery, porte-bonheur, talisman.

antonym evil eye.

**goodly** adj ample, considerable, good, large, significant, sizeable, substantial, sufficient, tidy.

antonym inadequate.

**good-natured** adj agreeable, amenable, approachable, benevolent, broad-minded, friendly, gentle, good-hearted, helpful, kind, kind-hearted, kindly, neighbourly, open-minded, sympathetic, tolerant, warm-hearted.

antonym ill-natured.

**goodness** n advantage, altruism, beneficence, benefit, benevolence, condescension, excellence, fairness, friendliness, generosity, goodwill, graciousness, honesty, honour, humaneness, humanity, integrity, justness, kindliness, kindness, mercy, merit, morality, nourishment, nutrition, piety, probity, quality, rectitude, righteousness, salubriousness, superiority, unselfishness, uprightness, value, virtue, wholesomeness, worth.

antonyms badness, inferiority, wickedness.

**goods** n appurtenances, bags and baggage, belongings, chattels, commodities, effects, furnishings, furniture, gear, merchandise, movables, paraphernalia, plenishing, possessions, property, stock, stuff, traps, vendibles, wares.

**goodwill** n altruism, amity, benevolence, compassion, earnestness, favour, friendliness, friendship, generosity, heartiness, kindliness, loving-kindness, sincerity, sympathy, zeal.

antonym ill-will.

**goody-goody** adj pious, priggish, sanctimonious, self-righteous, ultra-virtuous, unctuous.

**gooey** adj clarty, gluey, glutinous, gummy, gungy, maudlin, mawkish, mucilaginous, sentimental, slushy, soft, sticky, syrupy, tacky, thick, viscid, viscous.

**gooseberry** n goosegob, goosegog, groser, groset, third person.

**gooseflesh** *n* creeps, duck bumps, formication, goose bumps, goose-pimples, grue, heebie-jeebies, horripilation, horrors, shivers, shudders.

**gore**[1] *n* blood, bloodiness, bloodshed, butchery, carnage, cruor, grume, slaughter.

**gore**[2] *v* impale, penetrate, pierce, rend, spear, spit, stab, stick, transfix, wound.

*n* flare, gair, godet, gusset.

**gorge**[1] *n* abyss, barranca, canyon, chasm, cleft, clough, defile, fissure, gap, gulch, gully, pass, ravine.

**gorge**[2] *v* bolt, cram, devour, feed, fill, fill one's face, glut, gluttonise, gobble, gormandise, gulp, guzzle, hog, make a pig of oneself, overeat, ravin, sate, satiate, stuff, surfeit, swallow, wolf.

*antonym* abstain.

**gorgeous** *adj* attractive, beautiful, bright, brilliant, dazzling, delightful, elegant, enjoyable, exquisite, fine, flamboyant, glamorous, glittering, glorious, good, good-looking, grand, lovely, luxuriant, luxurious, magnificent, opulent, pleasing, ravishing, resplendent, rich, showy, splendid, splendiferous, stunning, sumptuous, superb.

*antonyms* dull, plain, seedy.

**gory** *adj* blood-soaked, bloodstained, bloodthirsty, bloody, brutal, ensanguined, murderous, sanguinary, sanguineous, sanguinolent, savage.

**gospel** *n* certainty, credo, creed, doctrine, evangel, fact, kerygma, message, news, revelation, teaching, testament, tidings, truth, verity.

**gossamer** *adj* airy, cobwebby, delicate, diaphanous, fine, flimsy, gauzy, insubstantial, light, sheer, shimmering, silky, thin, translucent, transparent.

*antonyms* heavy, opaque, thick.

**gossip**[1] *n* blether, bush telegraph, causerie, chinwag, chitchat, clash, clash-ma-clavers, clish-clash, clishmaclaver, gup, hearsay, idle talk, jaw, newsmongering, prattle, report, rumour, scandal, schmooze, small talk, tittle-tattle, yackety-yak.

**gossip**[2] *n* babbler, blatherskite, blether, bletherskate, busybody, chatterbox, chatterer, gossip-monger, newsmonger, nosy parker, prattler, quidnunc, rumourer, scandalmonger, tabby, talebearer, tattler, telltale, whisperer.

*v* blather, blether, bruit, chat, clash, gabble, jaw, prattle, rumour, tattle, tell tales, whisper.

**gouge** *v* chisel, claw, cut, dig, extract, force, gash, grave, groove, hack, hollow, incise, scoop, score, scratch, slash.

*n* cut, furrow, gash, groove, hack, hollow, incision, notch, scoop, score, scratch, slash, trench.

**gourmand** *n* cormorant, free-liver, gannet, glutton, gorger, gormandiser, guzzler, hog, omnivore, pig, trencherman, whale.

*antonym* ascetic.

**gourmet** *n* arbiter elegantiae, arbiter elegantiarum, bon vivant, bon viveur, connoisseur, dainty eater, epicure, epicurean, gastronome, gastronomer, gastrosoph, gastrosopher.

*antonym* omnivore.

**govern** *v* administer, allay, bridle, check, command, conduct, contain, control, curb, decide, determine, direct, discipline, guide, influence, inhibit, lead, manage, master, order, oversee, pilot, preside, quell, regulate, reign, restrain, rule, steer, subdue, superintend, supervise, sway, tame, underlie.

**governess** *n* companion, duenna, gouvernante, guide, instructress, mentor, teacher, tutoress, tutress.

**governing** *adj* commanding, dominant, dominative, guiding, leading, overriding, predominant, prevailing, reigning, ruling, supreme, transcendent, uppermost.

**government** *n* administration, authority, charge, command, conduct, control, direction, domination, dominion, Establishment, executive, governance, guidance, kingcraft, law, management, ministry, polity, powers-that-be, raj, régime, regimen, regulation, restraint, rule, sovereignty, state, statecraft, superintendence, supervision, surveillance, sway.

**governor** *n* adelantado, administrator, alcalde, alderman, boss, chief, commander, commissioner, comptroller, controller, corrector, director, executive, gubernator, hakim, head, leader, manager, naik, overseer, ruler, superintendent, supervisor, vali.

**gown** *n* costume, creation, dress, dressing-gown, frock, garb, garment, habit, kirtle, négligé, robe.

**grab** *v* affect, annex, appropriate, bag, capture, catch, catch hold of, clutch, collar, commandeer, grasp, grip, impress, latch on to, nab, pluck, ramp, rap, seize, snap up, snatch, strike, usurp.

**grace**[1] *n* attractiveness, beauty, benefaction, beneficence, benevolence, benignity, benison, breeding, charity, charm, clemency, comeliness, compassion, compassionateness, consideration, courtesy, cultivation, decency, decorum, deftness, ease, elegance, eloquence, etiquette, favour, finesse, fluency, forgiveness, generosity, goodness, goodwill, gracefulness, graciousness, indulgence, kindliness, kindness, leniency, lenity, love, loveliness, mannerliness, manners, mercifulness, mercy, merit, pardon, pleasantness, poise, polish, propriety, quarter, refinement, reprieve, shapeliness, tact, tastefulness, unction, virtue.

*v* adorn, beautify, bedeck, deck, decorate, dignify, distinguish, dress, elevate, embellish, enhance, enrich, favour, garnish, glorify, honour, ornament, prettify, set off, trim.

*antonyms* deface, detract from, spoil.

**grace**[2] *n* benediction, benedictus, blessing, consecration, prayer, thanks, thanksgiving.

**graceful** *adj* agile, balletic, beautiful, becoming, charming, comely, deft, easy, elegant, facile, feat, feline, fine, flowing, fluid, gainly, genty, gracile, lightsome, natural, pleasing, pliant, slender, smooth, suave, supple, tasteful, willowish, willowy.

*antonym* graceless.

**graceless** *adj* awkward, barbarous, boorish, brazen, clumsy, coarse, crude, forced, gauche, gawky, ill-mannered, improper, incorrigible, indecorous, inelegant, inept, loutish, reprobate, rough, rude, shameless, uncouth, ungainly, ungraceful, unmannerly, unsophisticated, untutored, vulgar.

*antonym* graceful.

**gracious** *adj* accommodating, affable, affluent, amenable, amiable, beneficent, benevolent, benign, benignant, charitable, chivalrous, civil, compassionate, complaisant, condescending, considerate, cordial, courteous, courtly, elegant, friendly, grand, hospitable, indulgent, kind, kindly, lenient, loving, luxurious, merciful, mild, obliging, pleasant, pleasing, polite, refined, sweet, well-mannered.

*antonym* ungracious.

**gradation** *n* ablaut, arrangement, array, classification, degree, depth, grade, grading, grouping, level, mark, measurement, notch, ordering, place, point, position, progress, progression, rank, sequence, series, shading, sorting, stage, step, succession.

**grade** *n* acclivity, bank, brand, category, class, condition, dan, declivity, degree, downgrade, echelon, gradation, gradient, group, hill, incline, level, mark, notch, order, place, position, quality, rank, rise, rung, size, slope, stage, station, step, upgrade.

*v* arrange, blend, brand, categorise, class, classify, docket, evaluate, group, label, mark, order, pigeonhole, range, rank, rate, shade, size, sort, type, value.

**gradient** *n* acclivity, bank, decline, declivity, downgrade, grade, hill, incline, rise, slope, upgrade.

**gradual** *adj* cautious, continuous, deliberate, even, gentle, graduated, leisurely, measured, moderate, piecemeal, progressive, regular, slow, steady, step-by-step, successive, unhurried.

*antonyms* precipitate, sudden.

**gradually** *adv* bit by bit, by degrees, cautiously, drop by drop, evenly, gently, gingerly, imperceptibly, in penny numbers, inch by inch, inchmeal, little by little, moderately, piece by piece, piecemeal, progressively, slowly, steadily, step by step, unhurriedly.

**graduate**[1] *v* arrange, calibrate, classify, grade, group, make the grade, mark off, measure out, order, pass, proportion, qualify, range, rank, regulate, sort.

**graduate**[2] *n* alumna, alumnus, bachelor, diplomate, diplômé, diplômée, doctor, fellow, graduand, licentiate, literate, master, member.

**graft** *n* bud, engraft, engraftation, engraftment, heteroplasty, imp, implant, implantation, insert, scion, shoot, splice, sprout, transplant.

*v* engraft, implant, insert, join, splice, transplant.

**grain** *n* atom, bit, cereals, corn, crumb, doit, fibre, fragment, granule, grist, grits, iota, jot, kernel, marking, mite, modicum, molecule, morsel, mote, nap, ounce, panic, particle, pattern, piece, scintilla, scrap, scruple, seed, smidgeon, spark, speck, surface, suspicion, texture, trace, weave, whit.

**grammarian** *n* grammaticaster, grammatist, linguist, linguistician, philologist, Priscianist.

**grand** *adj* A1, admirable, affluent, ambitious, august, chief, condescending, dignified, elevated, eminent, exalted, excellent, fine, first-class, first-rate, glorious, gracious, grandiose, great, haughty, head, highest, illustrious, imperious, imposing, impressive, large, leading, lofty, lordly, luxurious, magnificent, main, majestic, marvellous, monumental, noble, opulent, ostentatious, outstanding, palatial, patronising, pompous, pre-eminent, pretentious, princely, principal, regal, senior, smashing, splendid, stately, striking, sublime, sumptuous, super, superb, supreme, wonderful.

**grandeur** *n* augustness, dignity, graciousness, gravitas, greatness, hauteur, imperiousness, importance, loftiness, magnificence, majesty, morgue, nobility, pomp, splendour, state, stateliness, sublimity.

*antonyms* humbleness, lowliness, simplicity.

**grandfather** *n* gaffer, goodsire, grandad, grand(d)addy, grandpa, grandsire, granfer, gutcher.

**grandiloquence** *n* affectation, bombast, euphuism, fustian, Gongorism, magniloquence, orotundity, pomposity, pretentiousness, rhetoric, turgidity.

*antonyms* plainness, restraint, simplicity.

**grandiloquent** *adj* bombastic, euphuistic, flowery, fustian, Gongoristic, grandiloquous, high-flown, high-sounding, inflated, magniloquent, orotund, pompous, pretentious, rhetorical, swollen, turgid.

*antonyms* plain, restrained, simple.

**grandiose** *adj* affected, ambitious, bombastic, euphuistic, extravagant, flamboyant, grand, high-flown, imposing, impressive, lofty, magnificent, majestic, monumental, ostentatious, pompous, ponderous, pretentious, showy, stately, Wagnerian, weighty.

*antonym* unpretentious.

**grandmother** *n* gammer, gran, grandma, grandmama, granny.

**grant** *v* accede to, accord, acknowledge, admit, agree to, allocate, allot, allow, apportion, assign, award, bestow, cede, concede, confer, consent to, convey, deign, dispense, donate, give, impart, permit, present, provide, transfer, transmit, vouchsafe, yield.

*antonyms* deny, refuse.

*n* accord, admission, allocation, allotment, allowance, annuity, award, benefaction, bequest, boon, bounty, bursary, concession, donation, endowment, gift, honorarium, present, scholarship, subsidy, subvention.

**granular** *adj* crumbly, grainy, granulase, granulated, granulous, gravelly, gritty, murly, rough, sabulose, sabulous, sandy.

**granule** *n* atom, bead, crumb, fragment, grain, iota, jot, molecule, particle, pellet, scrap, seed, speck.

**graph** *n* chart, diagram, grid, histogram, table.

**graphic** *adj* blow-by-blow, clear, cogent, delineated, delineative, descriptive, detailed, diagrammatic, drawn, explicit, expressive, forcible, illustrative, lively, lucid, pictorial, picturesque, representational, seen, specific, striking, telling, visible, visual, vivid.

*antonyms* impressionistic, vague.

**grapple** *v* attack, battle, catch, clash, clasp, clinch, close, clutch, combat, come to grips, confront, contend, cope, deal with, encounter, engage, face, fasten, fight, grab, grasp, grip, gripe, hold, hug, lay hold, make fast, seize, snatch, struggle, tackle, tussle, wrestle.

*antonyms* avoid, evade.

**grasp** *v* catch, catch on, clasp, clinch, clutch, comprehend, follow, get, grab, grapple, grip, gripe, hold, lay hold of, realise, savvy, see, seize, snatch, twig, understand.

*n* acquaintance, apprehension, awareness, capacity, clasp, clutches, compass, competence, comprehension, control, conversance, conversancy, embrace, expertness, extent, familiarity, grip, hold, holt, intimacy, ken, knowledge, mastery, perception, possession, power, range, reach, realisation, scope, sway, sweep, tenure, understanding.

**grasping** *adj* acquisitive, avaricious, close-fisted, covetous, greedy, mean, mercenary, miserly, niggardly, parsimonious, penny-pinching, rapacious, selfish, stingy, tight-fisted, usurious.

*antonym* generous.

**grass** *n* fog, foggage, grama, grassland, green, greensward, hay, herbage, lawn, pasturage, pasture, sward, turf, verdure.

**grasshopper** *n* cicada, cigale, cricket, grig, katydid, locust.

**grassland** *n* downs, lay, lea, ley, llano, meadow, meadowland, pampas, pasture, prairie, savanna, steppe, sward, veldt.

**grate** *v* aggravate, annoy, chafe, comminute, creak, exasperate, fret, gall, get on one's nerves, granulate, gride, grind, irk, irritate, jar, mince, nettle, peeve, pulverise, rankle, rasp, rub, scrape, scratch, set one's teeth on edge, shred, triturate, vex.

**grateful** *adj* appreciative, aware, beholden, indebted, mindful, obligated, obliged, sensible, thankful.

*antonym* ungrateful.

**gratification** *n* contentment, delight, elation, enjoyment, fruition, fulfilment, glee, indulgence, joy, jubilation, kicks, pleasure, recompense, relish, reward, satisfaction, thrill, triumph.

*antonym* frustration.

**gratify** *v* appease, cater to, content, delight, favour, fulfil, gladden, humour, indulge, pander to, please, pleasure, recompense, requite, satisfy, thrill.

*antonyms* frustrate, thwart.

**grating**[1] *adj* annoying, cacophonous, disagreeable, discordant, displeasing, grinding, harsh, horrisonant, irksome, irritating, jarring, rasping, raucous, scraping, squeaky, strident, unharmonious, unmelodious, unpleasant, vexatious.

*antonyms* harmonious, pleasing.

**grating**[2] *n* grid, grill, grille, hack, heck, lattice, lattice-work, treillage, treille, trellis, trelliswork.

**gratitude** *n* acknowledgement, appreciation, awareness, gratefulness, indebtedness, mindfulness, obligation, recognition, thankfulness, thanks.

*antonym* ingratitude.

**gratuitous** *adj* assumed, baseless, buckshee, causeless, complimentary, free, gratis, groundless, irrelevant, needless, spontaneous, superfluous, unasked-for, uncalled-for, undeserved, unearned, unfounded, unjustified, unmerited, unnecessary, unpaid, unprovoked, unrewarded, unsolicited, unwarranted, voluntary, wanton.

*antonyms* justified, reasonable.

**gratuity** *n* baksheesh, beer-money, benefaction, bonus, boon, bounty, dash, donation, donative, douceur, drink-money, gift, lagniappe, largess, perquisite, pourboire, present, recompense, reward, tip, Trinkgeld.

**grave**[1] *n* barrow, burial-place, burying-place, cairn, cist, crypt, long home, mausoleum, pit, sepulchre, tomb, vault.

**grave**[2] *adj* acute, Catonian, critical, crucial, dangerous, depressing, dignified, disquieting, dour, dull, earnest, exigent, gloomy, grim, grim-faced, hazardous, heavy, important, leaden, long-faced, momentous, muted, perilous, ponderous, preoccupied, pressing, quiet, reserved, restrained, sad, sage, saturnine, sedate, serious, severe, significant, sober, solemn, sombre, staid, subdued, thoughtful, threatening, unsmiling, urgent, vital, weighty.

*antonyms* cheerful, light, slight, trivial.

**gravel** *n* chesil, grail, hogging, shingle.

**gravelly** *adj* ginny, glareous, grainy, granular, grating, gritty, gruff, guttural, harsh, hoarse, pebbly, sabulose, sabulous, shingly, throaty.

*antonyms* clear, fine, powdery.

**graveyard** *n* boneyard, burial-ground, burial-place, burying-place, cemetery, churchyard, God's acre, Golgotha, necropolis.

**gravitate** *v* descend, drop, fall, head for, incline, lean, move, precipitate, settle, sink, tend.

**gravity** *n* acuteness, consequence, demureness, dignity, earnestness, exigency, gloom, gravitas, grimness, hazardousness, importance, magnitude, moment, momentousness, perilousness, ponderousness, reserve, restraint, sedateness, seriousness, severity, significance, sobriety, solemnity, sombreness, thoughtfulness, urgency, weightiness.

*antonyms* gaiety, levity, triviality.

**graze**[1] *v* batten, browse, crop, feed, fodder, pasture.

**graze**[2] *v* abrade, bark, brush, chafe, gride, rub, scart, score, scotch, scrape, scratch, shave, skim, skin, touch.

*n* abrasion, score, scrape, scratch.

**grease** *n* dope, dripping, fat, gunge, lard, oil, ointment, sebum, tallow, unction, unguent, wax.

**greasy** *adj* fatty, fawning, glib, grovelling, ingratiating, lardy, oily, oleaginous, sebaceous, slick, slimy, slippery, smarmy, smeary, smooth, sycophantic, tallowy, toadying, unctuous, waxy.

**great** *adj* able, ace, active, adept, admirable, adroit, august, big, bulky, capital, celebrated, chief, colossal, consequential, considerable, crack, critical, crucial, decided, devoted, dignified, distinguished, eminent, enormous, enthusiastic, exalted, excellent, excessive, expert, extended, extensive, extravagant, extreme, fab, fabulous, famed, famous, fantastic, fine, finished, first-rate, generous, gigantic, glorious, good, grand, grave, great-hearted, grievous, heavy, heroic, high, high-minded, huge, idealistic, illustrious, immense, important, impressive, inordinate, invaluable, jake, keen, large, leading, lengthy, lofty, long, magnanimous, main, major, mammoth, manifold, marked, marvellous, massive, masterly, momentous, multitudinous, munificent, noble, nonpareil, notable, noteworthy, noticeable, outstanding, paramount, ponderous, precious, pre-eminent, priceless, primary, princely, principal, prodigious, proficient, prolific, prolonged, prominent, pronounced, protracted, remarkable, renowned, senior, serious, significant, skilful, skilled, strong, stupendous, sublime, superb, superior, superlative, swingeing, talented, terrific, tremendous, valuable, vast, virtuoso, voluminous, weighty, wonderful, zealous.

*antonyms* insignificant, pusillanimous, small, unimportant.

**greatly** *adv* abundantly, considerably, enormously, exceedingly, extremely, highly, hugely, immensely, impressively, markedly, mightily, much, notably, noticeably, powerfully, remarkably, significantly, substantially, tremendously, vastly.

**greatness** *n* amplitude, bulk, celebrity, dignity, distinction, eminence, excellence, fame, force, generosity, genius, glory, grandeur, gravity, great-heartedness, heaviness, heroism, high-mindedness, hugeness, idealism, illustriousness, immensity, import, importance, intensity, largeness, length, loftiness, lustre, magnanimity, magnitude, majesty, mass, moment, momentousness, nobility, nobleness, note, potency, power, prodigiousness, renown, seriousness, significance, size, stateliness, strength, sublimity, superbness, urgency, vastness, weight.

*antonyms* insignificance, pettiness, pusillanimity, smallness.

**greed** *n* acquisitiveness, anxiety, avidity, covetousness, craving, cupidity, desire, eagerness, edacity, esurience, esuriency, gluttony, gormandising, gormandism, gourmandise, greediness, gulosity, hunger, insatiability, insatiableness, itchy palm, land-hunger, longing, pleonexia, plutolatry, rapacity, ravenousness, selfishness, voraciousness, voracity.

*antonym* abstemiousness.

**greedy** *adj* acquisitive, anxious, avaricious, avid, covetous, craving, curious, desirous, eager, edacious, esurient, gare, gluttonish, gluttonous, gormandising, grasping, gripple, gutsy, hoggery, hoggish, hungry, impatient, insatiable, itchy-palmed, land-grabbing, money-grubbing, piggish, pleonectic, rapacious, ravenous, selfish, ventripotent, voracious.

*antonym* abstemious.

**green** *adj* blooming, budding, callow, covetous, credulous, emerald, envious, flourishing, fresh, glaucous, grassy, grudging, gullible, ignorant, ill, immature, inexperienced, inexpert, ingenuous, innocent, jealous, leafy, naive, nauseous, new, pale, pliable, raw, recent, resentful, sick, starry-eyed, supple, tender, unhealthy, unpractised, unripe, unseasoned, unsophisticated, untrained, untried, unversed, verdant, verdurous, vert, virescent, virid, viridescent, vitreous, wan, wet behind the ears, young.

*n* common, grass, greensward, lawn, sward, turf.

**greenery** *n* foliage, greenness, greenth, vegetation, verdancy, verdure, virescence, viridescence, viridity.

**greenhorn** *n* apprentice, beginner, catechumen, fledgling, ignoramus, ingénué, initiate, Johnnie raw, learner, naïf, neophyte, newcomer, novice, novitiate, recruit, rookie, simpleton, tenderfoot, tyro.

*antonyms* old hand, veteran.

**greenhouse** *n* conservatory, glasshouse, hothouse, nursery, pavilion, vinery.

**greet** *v* accost, acknowledge, address, compliment, hail, hallo, halloo, meet, receive, salute, wave to, welcome.

*antonym* ignore.

**greeting** *n* abrazo, accost, acknowledgement, address, aloha, hail, kiss of peace, reception, salaam, salutation, salute, salve, the time of day, welcome.

**greetings** *n* best wishes, civilities, compliments, devoirs, formalities, good wishes, love, regards, respects, salutations.

**gregarious** *adj* affable, chummy, companionable, convivial, cordial, extrovert, friendly, outgoing, pally, sociable, social, warm.

*antonym* unsociable.

**grey** *adj* aged, ancient, anonymous, ashen, bloodless, characterless, cheerless, cloudy, colourless, dark, depressing, dim, dismal, drab, dreary, dull, elderly, experienced, glaucous, gloomy, grège, greige, griseous, grizzle, grizzled, hoar, hoary, indistinct, leaden, liard, livid, mature, murksome, murky, neutral, old, overcast, pale, pallid, sunless, uncertain, unclear, unidentifiable, venerable, wan.

**grid** *n* graticule, grating, gridison, grill, grille, lattice.

**grief** *n* ache, affliction, agony, anguish, bereavement, blow, burden, dejection, desiderium, desolation, distress, dole, grievance, heartache, heartbreak, lamentation, misery, mournfulness, mourning, pain, regret, remorse, sadness, sorrow, suffering, tragedy, trial, tribulation, trouble, woe.

*antonym* happiness.

**grief-stricken** *adj* afflicted, agonised, broken, broken-hearted, crushed, desolate, despairing, devastated, disconsolate, distracted, grieving, heartbroken, inconsolable, mourning, overcome, overwhelmed, sad, sorrowful, sorrowing, stricken, unhappy, woebegone, wretched.

*antonym* overjoyed.

**grievance** *n* affliction, beef, bitch, charge, complaint, damage, distress, gravamen, grief, gripe, grouse, hardship, injury, injustice, moan, peeve, resentment, sorrow, trial, tribulation, trouble, unhappiness, wrong.

**grieve** *v* ache, afflict, agonise, bemoan, bewail, complain, crush, cut to the quick, deplore, distress, disturb, eat one's heart out, harrow, hurt, injure, lament, mourn, pain, regret, rue, sadden, sorrow, suffer, upset, wail, weep, wound.

**grieved** *adj* abashed, affronted, ashamed, desolated, displeased, distressed, horrified, hurt, injured, offended, pained, sad, saddened, shocked, sorry, upset, wounded.

**grievous** *adj* appalling, atrocious, burdensome, calamitous, damaging, deplorable, devastating, distressing, dreadful, flagrant, glaring, grave, harmful, heart-rending, heavy, heinous, hurtful, injurious, intolerable, lamentable, monstrous, mournful, offensive, oppressive, outrageous, overwhelming, painful, pitiful, plightful, severe, shameful, shocking, sorrowful, tragic, unbearable, wounding.

**grievously** *adv* appallingly, badly, deplorably, dernly, desperately, distressingly, dreadfully, gravely, heinously, lamentably, monstrously, outrageously, painfully, seriously, severely, shamefully, shockingly, unforgivably.

**grim** *adj* adamant, cruel, doom-laden, dour, fearsome, ferocious, fierce, forbidding, formidable, frightening, frightful, ghastly, grisly, gruesome, harsh, hideous, horrible, horrid, implacable, merciless, morose, relentless, repellent, resolute, ruthless, severe, shocking, sinister, stern, sullen, surly, terrible, unpleasant, unrelenting, unwelcome, unyielding.

*antonyms* benign, congenial, pleasant.

**grimace** *n* face, fit of the face, frown, moue, mouth, pout, scowl, smirk, sneer, wry face.

*v* fleer, frown, girn, make a face, mop, mop and mow, mouth, mow, mug, pout, scowl, smirk, sneer.

**grime** *n* dirt, filth, muck, smut, soot, squalor.

**grimy** *adj* begrimed, besmeared, besmirched, contaminated, dirty, filthy, foul, grubby, murky, reechy, smudgy, smutty, soiled, sooty, squalid.

*antonyms* clean, pure.

**grind** *v* abrade, beaver, bray, comminute, crush, drudge, file, gnash, granulate, grate, grit, kibble, labour, levigate, lucubrate, mill, polish, pound, powder, pulverise, sand, scrape, sharpen, slave, smooth, sweat, swot, toil, triturate, whet.

*n* chore, drudgery, exertion, grindstone, labour, round, routine, slavery, sweat, task, toil.

**grind down** afflict, crush, harass, harry, hound, oppress, persecute, plague, trouble, tyrannise.

**grip** *n* acquaintance, clasp, clutches, comprehension, control, domination, embrace, grasp, handclasp, hold, influence, keeping, mastery, perception, possession, power, purchase, sway, tenure, understanding.

*v* absorb, catch, clasp, clutch, compel, divert, engross, enthrall, entrance, fascinate, grasp, hold, involve, latch on to, mesmerise, rivet, seize, spellbind, thrill, vice.

**gripe** *v* beef, bellyache, bitch, carp, complain, groan, grouch, grouse, grumble, moan, nag, whine, whinge.

*n* ache, aching, affliction, beef, bitch, colic, collywobbles, complaint, cramps, distress, grievance, griping, groan, grouch, grouse, grumble, moan, objection, pain, pang, pinching, spasm, stomach-ache, twinge.

**gripping** *adj* absorbing, compelling, compulsive, diverting, engrossing, enthralling, entrancing, exciting, fascinating, riveting, spellbinding, suspenseful, thrilling, unputdownable.

**grisly** *adj* abominable, appalling, awful, dreadful, eldritch, frightful, ghastly, grim, gruesome, hair-raising, hideous, horrible, horrid, macabre, shocking, sickening, terrible, terrifying, weird.

*antonym* delightful.

**grit**[1] *n* chesil, dust, grail, gravel, hogging, pebbles, sand, shingle, swarf.

*v* clench, gnash, grate, grind, lock.

**grit**[2] backbone, bottle, bravery, courage, determination, doggedness, foison, fortitude, fushion, gameness, guts, hardihood, mettle, nerve, perseverance, pluck, resolution, spine, spirit, spunk, stamina, staying power, tenacity, toughness.

**gritty** *adj* abrasive, brave, courageous, determined, dogged, dusty, game, grainy, granular, gravelly, hardy, mettlesome, pebbly, plucky, resolute, rough, sabulose, sabulous, sandy, shingly, spirited, spunky, steadfast, tenacious, tough.

*antonyms* fine, smooth, spineless.

**grizzle** *v* cry, fret, girn, mewl, pule, sniffle, snivel, snuffle, whimper, whine, whinge.

**grizzled** *adj* canescent, grey, grey-haired, grey-headed, greying, griseous, grizzly, hoar, hoary, pepper-and-salt.

**groan** *n* complaint, cry, moan, objection, outcry, protest, sigh, wail.

*antonym* cheer.

*v* complain, cry, lament, moan, object, protest, sigh, wail.

*antonym* cheer.

**grocer** *n* dealer, épicier, greengrocer, Italian warehouseman, purveyor, spicer, storekeeper, supplier, victualler.

**groggy** *adj* befuddled, confused, dazed, dizzy, dopey, faint, fuddled, knocked-up, muzzy, punch-drunk, reeling, shaky, stunned, stupefied, unsteady, weak, wobbly, woozy.

*antonym* lucid.

**groom** *v* brush, clean, coach, curry, dress, drill, educate, neaten, nurture, preen, prepare, prime, primp, prink, ready, school, smarten, spruce up, tart up, tend, tidy, titivate, train, turn out, tutor.

**groove** *n* canal, cannelure, chamfer, channel, chase, cut, cutting, flute, furrow, gutter, hollow, indentation, kerf, rabbet, rebate, rigol, rut, score, scrobe, sulcus, trench, vallecula.

*antonym* ridge.

**grooved** *adj* chamfered, channelled, exarate, fluted, furrowed, rabbeted, rutted, scored, scrobiculate, sulcal, sulcate.

*antonym* ridged.

**grope** *v* cast about, feel, feel about, feel up, finger, fish, flounder, fumble, goose, grabble, probe, scrabble, search.

**gross¹** *adj* apparent, arrant, bawdy, bestial, big, blatant, blue, boorish, broad, brutish, bulky, callous, coarse, colossal, corpulent, crass, crude, cumbersome, dense, downright, dull, earthy, egregious, fat, flagrant, foul, glaring, great, grievous, heavy, heinous, huge, hulking, ignorant, immense, imperceptive, improper, impure, indecent, indelicate, insensitive, large, lewd, low, lumpish, manifest, massive, obese, obscene, obtuse, obvious, offensive, outrageous, outright, overweight, plain, rank, ribald, rude, sensual, serious, shameful, shameless, sheer, shocking, slow, sluggish, smutty, tasteless, thick, uncivil, uncouth, uncultured, undiscriminating, undisguised, unfeeling, unmitigated, unseemly, unsophisticated, unwieldy, utter, vulgar.

*antonyms* delicate, fine, seemly, slight.

**gross²** *n* aggregate, bulk, entirety, sum, total, totality, whole.

*adj* aggregate, all-inclusive, complete, entire, inclusive, total, whole.

*v* accumulate, aggregate, bring, earn, make, rake in, take, total.

**grossness** *n* bawdiness, bestiality, bigness, blatancy, brutishness, bulkiness, coarseness, corpulence, crassness, crudity, earthiness, egregiousness, fatness, flagrancy, foulness, greatness, grievousness, grossièreté, heaviness, hugeness, ignorance, immensity, impurity, incivility, indecency, indelicacy, insensitivity, licentiousness, lumpishness, obesity, obscenity, obtuseness, obviousness, offensiveness, rankness, ribaldry, rudeness, sensuality, seriousness, shamefulness, shamelessness, sluggishness, smut, smuttiness, tastelessness, thickness, uncouthness, unseemliness, unwieldiness, vulgarity.

*antonyms* delicacy, fineness, seemliness, slightness.

**grotesque** *adj* absurd, antic, bizarre, deformed, distorted, extravagant, fanciful, fantastic, freakish, gruesome, hideous, incongruous, laughable, ludicrous, macabre, malformed, misshapen, monstrous, odd, outlandish, preposterous, ridiculous, rococo, strange, ugly, unnatural, unsightly, weird.

*n* bizarrerie, extravaganza, fantastic figure, gargoyle, gobbo, grotesquerie, manikin.

**grotto** *n* catacomb, cave, cavern, chamber, dene-hole, grot, souterrain, subterranean (chamber), subterrene, underground chamber.

**grouch** *v* beef, bellyache, bitch, carp, complain, find fault, gripe, grouse, grumble, moan, whine, whinge.

*antonym* acquiesce.

*n* belly-acher, churl, complainer, complaint, crab, crosspatch, crotcheteer, curmudgeon, fault-finder, grievance, gripe, grouse, grouser, grumble, grumbler, malcontent, moan, moaner, murmer, murmurer, mutterer, objection, whiner, whinge, whinger.

**grouchy** *adj* bad-tempered, cantankerous, captious, churlish, complaining, cross, crotchety, discontented, dissatisfied, grumbling, grumpy, ill-tempered, irascible, irritable, mutinous, peevish, petulant, querulous, sulky, surly, testy, truculent.

*antonym* contented.

**ground** *n* arena, background, ball-park, bottom, clay, clod, deck, dirt, dry land, dust, earth, field, foundation, land, loam, mould, park, pitch, sod, soil, solum, stadium, surface, terra firma, terrain, turf.

*v* acquaint with, base, build up, coach, drill, establish, familiarise with, fix, found, inform, initiate, instruct, introduce, prepare, set, settle, teach, train, tutor.

**groundless** *adj* absurd, baseless, chimerical, empty, false, gratuitous, idle, illusory, imaginary, irrational, unauthorised, uncalled-for, unfounded, unjustified, unproven, unprovoked, unreasonable, unsubstantiated, unsupported, unwarranted.

*antonyms* justified, reasonable.

**grounds¹** *n* acres, area, country, district, domain, estate, fields, gardens, habitat, holding, land, park, property, realm, surroundings, terrain, territory, tract.

**grounds²** *n* account, argument, base, basis, call, cause, excuse, factor, foundation, inducement, justification, motive, occasion, premise, pretext, principle, rationale, reason, score, vindication.

**grounds³** *n* deposit, dregs, grouts, lees, precipitate, precipitation, sediment, settlings.

**groundwork** *n* base, basis, cornerstone, essentials, footing, foundation, fundamentals, homework, preliminaries, preparation, research, spadework, underpinnings.

**group** *n* accumulation, aggregation, assemblage, association, band, batch, bracket, bunch, category, caucus, circle, class, classification, classis, clique, clump, cluster, clutch, cohort, collection, collective, combination, company, conclave, conglomeration, congregation, constellation, core, coterie, covey, crowd, detachment, faction, formation, front, galère, gang, gathering, Gemeinschaft, genus, grouping, knot, lot, nexus, organisation, pack, parti, party, pop-group, set, shower, species, squad, squadron, team, troop.

*v* arrange, assemble, associate, assort, band, bracket, categorise, class, classify, cluster, collect, congregate, consort, deploy, dispose, fraternise, gather, get together, link, marshal, mass, order, organise, range, sort.

**grouse** *v* beef, belly-ache, bitch, carp, complain, find fault, fret, fuss, gripe, grouch, grumble, moan, mutter, whine, whinge.

*antonym* acquiesce.

*n* belly-ache, complaint, grievance, gripe, grouch, grumble, moan, murmur, mutter, objection, peeve, whine, whinge.

**grove** *n* arbour, avenue, bosk, bosket, brake, coppice, copse, covert, hurst, plantation, spinney, thicket, wood, woodland.

**grovel** *v* abase oneself, backscratch, bootlick, cower, crawl, creep, cringe, crouch, defer, demean oneself, fawn, flatter, kowtow, sneak, sycophantise, toady.

**grovelling** *adj* backscratching, bootlicking, fawning, flattering, ingratiating, obsequious, sycophantic, wormy.

*antonyms* outspoken, straightforward.

**grow** *v* advance, arise, augment, become, branch out, breed, broaden, burgeon, cultivate, develop, diversify, enlarge, evolve, expand, extend, farm, flourish, flower, germinate, get, heighten, improve, increase, issue, mature, multiply, nurture, originate, produce, progress, proliferate, propagate, prosper, raise, ripen, rise, shoot, spread, spring, sprout, stem, stretch, succeed, swell, thicken, thrive, turn, vegetate, wax, widen.

*antonyms* decrease, fail, halt.

**growing** *adj* accrescent, blossoming, broadening, burgeoning, crescent, crescive, deepening, developing, elongating, enlarging, escalating, expanding, extending, flourishing, heightening, increasing, increscent, intumescent, lengthening, maturing, mounting, multiplying, proliferating, rising, spreading, swelling, thickening, thriving, tumescent, waxing, widening.

*antonyms* decreasing, failing, stagnant, static, waning.

**growl** *v* gnar, gnarl, gnarr, knar, snap, snarl, yap.

**grown-up** *adj* adult, full-grown, fully-fledged, fully-grown, mature, of age.

*antonyms* childish, immature.

*n* adult, gentleman, lady, man, woman.

*antonym* child.

**growth** *n* accrescence, accretion, advance, advancement, aggrandisement, augmentation, auxesis, broadening, change, crop, cultivation, development, diversification, enlargement, evolution, excrement, excrescence, expansion, extension, flowering, gall, germination,

growing, heightening, improvement, increase, intumescence, lump, maturation, multiplication, outgrowth, produce, production, progress, proliferation, prosperity, protuberance, ripening, rise, shooting, sprouting, stretching, success, swelling, thickening, transformation, tumour, vegetation, waxing, widening.

*antonyms* decrease, failure, stagnation, stoppage.

**grub**[1] *v* burrow, delve, dig, explore, ferret, forage, grout, hunt, investigate, nose, probe, pull up, root, rootle, rummage, scour, uproot.

*n* caterpillar, chrysalis, larva, maggot, nymph, pupa, worm.

**grub**[2] *n* chow, commons, eats, edibles, fodder, food, nosh, provisions, rations, scoff, sustenance, victuals.

**grubby** *adj* crummy, dirty, filthy, fly-blown, frowzy, grimy, manky, mean, messy, mucky, scruffy, seedy, shabby, slovenly, smutty, soiled, sordid, squalid, unkempt, untidy, unwashed.

*antonyms* clean, smart.

**grudge** *n* animosity, animus, antagonism, antipathy, aversion, bitterness, dislike, enmity, envy, grievance, hard feelings, hate, ill-will, jealousy, malevolence, malice, pique, rancour, resentment, spite.

*antonyms* favour, regard.

*v* begrudge, covet, dislike, envy, mind, niggard, object to, regret, repine, resent, stint, take exception to.

*antonyms* applaud, approve.

**grudging** *adj* cautious, guarded, half-hearted, hesitant, reluctant, secret, unenthusiastic, unwilling.

**gruelling** *adj* arduous, backbreaking, brutal, crushing, demanding, difficult, exhausting, fatiguing, fierce, grinding, hard, hard-going, harsh, laborious, punishing, severe, stern, stiff, strenuous, taxing, tiring, tough, trying, uphill, wearing, wearying.

*antonym* easy.

**gruesome** *adj* abominable, awful, chilling, eldritch, fearful, fearsome, ghastly, grim, grisly, grooly, hideous, horrible, horrid, horrific, horrifying, loathsome, macabre, monstrous, repellent, repugnant, repulsive, shocking, sick, spine-chilling, terrible, weird.

*antonyms* charming, congenial.

**gruff** *adj* abrupt, bad-tempered, bearish, blunt, brusque, churlish, crabbed, croaking, crusty, curt, discourteous, gravelly, grouchy, grumpy, guttural, harsh, hoarse, husky, ill-humoured, ill-natured, impolite, low, rasping, rough, rude, sour, sullen, surly, throaty, uncivil, ungracious, unmannerly.

*antonyms* clear, courteous, sweet.

**grumble** *v* beef, bellyache, bitch, bleat, carp, chunter, complain, croak, find fault, gripe, grouch, grouse, growl, gurgle, moan, murmur, mutter, nark, repine, roar, rumble, whine.

*antonym* acquiesce.

*n* beef, bitch, bleat, complaint, grievance, gripe, grouch, grouse, growl, gurgle, moan, murmur, muttering, objection, roar, rumble, whinge.

**grumpy** *adj* bad-tempered, cantankerous, churlish, crabbed, cross, crotchety, discontented, grouchy, grumbling, ill-tempered, irritable, mutinous, peevish, petulant, querulous, sulky, sullen, surly, testy, truculent.

*antonyms* civil, contented.

**guarantee** *n* assurance, attestation, bond, certainty, collateral, covenant, earnest, endorsement, guaranty, insurance, oath, pledge, promise, security, surety, testimonial, undertaking, voucher, warranty, word, word of honour.

*v* answer for, assure, avouch, certify, ensure, insure, maintain, make certain, make sure of, pledge, promise, protect, secure, swear, underwrite, vouch for, warrant.

**guarantor** *n* angel, backer, bailsman, bondsman, covenanter, guarantee, referee, sponsor, supporter, surety, underwriter, voucher, warrantor.

**guard** *v* be on the qui vive, be on the watch, beware, conserve, cover, defend, escort, keep, look out, mind, oversee, patrol, police, preserve, protect, safeguard, save, screen, secure, sentinel, shelter, shield, supervise, tend, ward, watch.

*n* attention, backstop, barrier, buffer, bulwark, bumper, care, caution, convoy, custodian, defence, defender, escort, guarantee, heed, lookout, minder, pad, patrol, picket, precaution, protection, protector, rampart, safeguard, screen, security, sentinel, sentry, shield, vigilance, wall, warder, wariness, watch, watchfulness, watchman.

**guarded** *adj* cagey, careful, cautious, circumspect, discreet, disingenuous, non-committal, prudent, reserved, restrained, reticent, secretive, suspicious, uncommunicative, unforthcoming, wary, watchful.

*antonyms* frank, whole-hearted.

**guardian** *n* attendant, carer, champion, conservator, curator, custodian, defender, depositary, depository, escort, fiduciary, guard, keeper, minder, preserver, protector, trustee, warden, warder.

**guardianship** *n* aegis, attendance, care, companionship, curatorship, custodianship, custody, defence, escort, guard, guidance, hands, keeping, patronage, protection, safekeeping, trust, trusteeship, wardenry, wardenship, wardship.

**guerrilla** *n* bushwhacker, franc-tireur, freedom-fighter, guerrillero, haiduck, irregular, maquisard, partisan, resistance fighter, sniper.

**guess** *v* assume, believe, conjecture, dare say, deem, divine, estimate, fancy, fathom, feel, guesstimate, hazard, hypothesise, imagine, intuit, judge, opine, penetrate, predict, reckon, solve, speculate, suppose, surmise, suspect, think, work out.

*n* assumption, belief, conjecture, fancy, feeling, guesstimate, hypothesis, intuition, judgement, notion, opinion, prediction, reckoning, shot (in the dark), speculation, supposition, surmise, suspicion, theory.

**guesswork** *n* assumption, conjecture, estimation, intuition, presumption, presupposition, reckoning, speculation, supposition, surmise, suspicion, theory.

**guest** *n* boarder, caller, company, freeloader, habitué, lodger, parasite, regular, roomer, visitant, visitor.

**guest-house** *n* boarding-house, hospice, hospitium, hostel, hostelry, hotel, inn, pension, rooming-house, xenodochium.

**guidance** *n* advice, aegis, auspices, clues, conduct, control, counsel, counselling, direction, government, guidelines, help, illumination, indications, instruction, leadership, management, pointers, recommendation, regulation, steering, teaching.

**guide** *v* accompany, advise, attend, command, conduct, control, convoy, counsel, direct, educate, escort, govern, handle, head, influence, instruct, lead, manage, manoeuvre, oversee, pilot, point, regulate, rule, shape, shepherd, steer, superintend, supervise, sway, teach, train, usher, vector.

*n* ABC, adviser, attendant, beacon, catalogue, chaperon, cicerone, clue, companion, conductor, controller, counsellor, courier, criterion, director, directory, dragoman, escort, example, exemplar, guide-book, guideline, handbook, ideal, index, indication, informant, inspiration, instructions, key, landmark, leader, lodestar, manual, mark, marker, master, mentor, model, monitor, paradigm, pilot, pointer, praxis, sign, signal, signpost, standard, steersman, teacher, template, usher, vade-mecum.

**guiding** *adj* advisory, consultant, consultative, consultatory, consulting, controlling, counselling, directorial, directory, formative, governing, influential, instructional, instructive, managing, monitoring, piloting, shepherding, steering, supervisory, tutorial.

**guild** *n* association, brotherhood, chapel, club, company, corporation, fellowship, fraternity, incorporation, league, lodge, order, organisation, society, union.

**guile** *n* art, artfulness, artifice, cleverness, craft, craftiness, cunning, deceit, deception, deviousness, disingenuity, duplicity, gamesmanship, knavery, ruse, slyness, treachery, trickery, trickiness, wiliness.

*antonyms* artlessness, guilelessness.

**guileful** *adj* artful, clever, crafty, cunning, deceitful, devious, disingenuous, duplicitous, foxy, sly, sneaky, treacherous, tricky, underhand, wily.

*antonyms* artless, guileless.

**guileless** *adj* artless, candid, direct, frank, genuine, honest, ingenuous, innocent, naïve, natural, open, simple, sincere, straightforward, transparent, trusting, truthful, unreserved, unsophisticated, unworldly.

*antonyms* artful, guileful.

**guilt** *n* blamability, blame, blameworthiness, compunction, conscience, contrition, criminality, culpability, delinquency, disgrace, dishonour, guiltiness, guilty conscience, infamy, iniquity, mens rea, regret, remorse, responsibility, self-condemnation, self-reproach, self-reproof, shame, sinfulness, stigma, wickedness, wrong.

*antonyms* innocence, shamelessness.

**guiltless** *adj* blameless, clean, clear, immaculate, impeccable, inculpable, innocent, irreproachable, pure, sinless, spotless, unimpeachable, unspotted, unsullied, untainted, untarnished.

*antonyms* guilty, tainted.

**guilty** *adj* ashamed, blamable, blameworthy, compunctious, conscience-stricken, contrite, convicted, criminal, culpable, delinquent, errant, erring, evil, felonious, guilt-ridden, hangdog, illicit, iniquitous, nefarious, nocent, offending, penitent, regretful, remorseful, repentant, reprehensible, responsible, rueful, shamefaced, sheepish, sinful, sorry, wicked, wrong.

*antonyms* guiltless, innocent.

**guise** *n* air, appearance, aspect, behaviour, custom, demeanour, disguise, dress, façade, face, fashion, features, form, front, likeness, manner, mask, mode, pretence, semblance, shape, show.

**gulf** *n* abyss, basin, bay, bight, breach, chasm, cleft, gap, gorge, opening, rent, rift, separation, split, void, whirlpool.

**gull** *n* maw, mew, seagull, sea-mew.

**gullet** *n* craw, crop, maw, oesophagus, the Red Lane, throat, weasand.

**gullibility** *n* credulity, glaikitness, innocence, naïvety, simplicity, trustfulness, verdancy.

*antonym* astuteness.

**gullible** *adj* born yesterday, credulous, foolish, glaikit, green, innocent, naïve, trusting, unsuspecting, verdant.

*antonym* astute.

**gully** *n* channel, ditch, donga, geo, gio, gulch, gutter, ravine, watercourse.

**gulp** *v* bolt, choke, devour, gasp, gobble, gollop, gormandise, guzzle, knock back, quaff, stifle, stuff, swallow, swig, swill, toss off, wolf.

*antonyms* nibble, sip.

*n* draught, mouthful, slug, swallow, swig.

**gum** *n* adhesive, cement, glue, goo, mucilage, paste, resin, sap.

*v* affix, block, cement, clog, fix, glue, paste, seal, stick.

**gumboil** *n* abscess, parulis, swelling.

**gummy** *adj* adhesive, gluey, gooey, sticky, tacky, viscid, viscous.

**gumption** *n* ability, acumen, acuteness, astuteness, cleverness, common sense, discernment, enterprise, horse sense, initiative, mother wit, nous, resourcefulness, sagacity, savvy, shrewdness, smeddum, spirit, wit(s).

*antonym* foolishness.

**gun** *n* equaliser, gat, heater, peacemaker, persuader, piece, pistol, shooter, shooting-iron, tool.

**gunman** *n* assassin, bandit, bravo, desperado, gangster, gunsel, gunslinger, hatchet man, hit man, killer, mobster, murderer, shootist, sniper, terrorist, thug.

**gurgle** *v* babble, bubble, burble, crow, guggle, lap, murmur, plash, purl, ripple, splash.

*n* babble, guggle, murmur, purl, ripple.

**guru** *n* authority, instructor, leader, luminary, maharishi, master, mentor, pundit, sage, Svengali, swami, teacher, tutor.

**gush** *v* babble, blather, burst, cascade, chatter, drivel, effuse, enthuse, flood, flow, fountain, jabber, jet, pour, run, rush, spout, spurt, stream, yatter.

*n* babble, burst, cascade, chatter, ebullition, effusion, eruption, exuberance, flood, flow, jet, outburst, outflow, rush, spout, spurt, stream, tide, torrent.

**gushing** *adj* cloying, effusive, emotional, excessive, fulsome, gushy, mawkish, over-enthusiastic, saccharine, sentimental, sickly.

*antonyms* restrained, sincere.

**gust** *n* blast, blow, breeze, burst, flaught, flaw, flurry, gale, puff, rush, squall, williwaw.

*v* blast, blow, bluster, breeze, puff, squall.

**gusto** *n* appetite, appreciation, brio, delight, élan, enjoyment, enthusiasm, exhilaration, exuberance, fervour, liking, pleasure, relish, savour, verve, zeal, zest.

*antonyms* apathy, distaste.

**gusty** *adj* blowy, blustering, blustery, breezy, gustful, squally, stormy, tempestuous, windy.

*antonym* calm.

**gut** *v* clean, clean out, despoil, disembowel, draw, dress, empty, eviscerate, exenterate, gill, pillage, plunder, ransack, ravage, rifle, sack, strip.

*adj* basic, deep-seated, emotional, heartfelt, innate, instinctive, intuitive, involuntary, natural, spontaneous, strong, unthinking, visceral.

**gutless** *adj* abject, chicken, chicken-hearted, chicken-livered, cowardly, craven, faint-hearted, feeble, irresolute, lily-livered, spineless, submissive, timid, weak.

*antonym* courageous.

**guts** *n* audacity, backbone, belly, boldness, bottle, bowels, courage, daring, endurance, entrails, forcefulness, grit, hardihood, innards, insides, intestines, inwards, mettle, nerve, paunch, pluck, spirit, spunk, stamina, staying power, stomach, tenacity, toughness, viscera.

*antonym* spinelessness.

**gutsy** *adj* bold, brave, courageous, determined, gallant, game, indomitable, lusty, mettlesome, passionate, plucky, resolute, spirited, staunch.

*antonyms* quiet, timid.

**gutter** *n* channel, conduit, ditch, drain, duct, grip, kennel, pipe, rigol(l), sluice, trench, trough, tube.

**guttersnipe** *n* gamin, mudlark, ragamuffin, street Arab, tatterdemalion, urchin, waif.

**guttural** *adj* deep, grating, gravelly, gruff, harsh, hoarse, husky, low, rasping, rough, thick, throaty. *antonym* dulcet.

**guy** *n* bloke, buffer, cat, chap, codger, cove, customer, fellow, individual, josser, lad, man, oik, person, punter, youth.

**guzzle** *v* bolt, carouse, cram, devour, gobble, gormandise, stuff, wolf.

**gypsy** *n* Bohemian, diddicoy, faw, gipsy, gitana, gitano, nomad, rambler, roamer, Romany, rover, tink, tinker, traveller, tsigane, tzigany, vagabond, vagrant, wanderer, Zigeuner, Zincalo, Zingaro.

**gyrate** *v* circle, gyre, pirouette, revolve, rotate, spin, spiral, twirl, whirl.

**gyrating** *adj* gyral, gyrant, revolving, rotating, spinning, twirling, whirling.

**gyration** *n* convolution, pirouette, revolution, rotation, spin, spinning, spiral, twirl, vertigo, whirl, whirling.

# H

**habit¹** *n* accustomedness, addiction, assuetude, bent, constitution, convention, custom, dependence, diathesis, disposition, fixation, frame of mind, habitude, inclination, make-up, manner, mannerism, mode, mores, nature, obsession, practice, proclivity, propensity, quirk, routine, rule, second nature, tendency, usage, vice, way, weakness, wont.

**habit²** *n* apparel, attire, clothes, clothing, dress, garb, garment, habiliment.

**habitat** *n* abode, domain, element, environment, home, locality, surroundings, terrain, territory.

**habitation** *n* abode, cottage, domicile, dwelling, dwelling-place, home, house, hut, inhabitance, inhabitancy, inhabitation, living quarters, lodging, mansion, occupancy, occupation, quarters, residence, tenancy.

**habitual** *adj* accustomed, chronic, common, confirmed, constant, customary, established, familiar, fixed, frequent, hardened, ingrained, inveterate, natural, normal, ordinary, persistent, recurrent, regular, routine, standard, traditional, usual, wonted.

*antonym* occasional.

**habituate** *v* acclimatise, accustom, break in, condition, discipline, familiarise, harden, inure, school, season, tame, train.

**habitué** *n* denizen, frequenter, patron, regular, regular customer.

**hack¹** *v* bark, chop, cough, cut, gash, haggle, hew, kick, lacerate, mangle, mutilate, notch, rasp, slash.

*n* bark, chop, cough, cut, gash, notch, rasp, slash.

**hack²** *adj* banal, hackneyed, mediocre, pedestrian, poor, stereotyped, tired, undistinguished, uninspired, unoriginal.

*n* crock, drudge, horse, jade, journalist, nag, paper-stainer, penny-a-liner, scribbler, slave.

**hackneyed** *adj* banal, clichéd, common, commonplace, corny, hack, hand-me-down, overworked, pedestrian, percoct, played-out, run-of-the-mill, second-hand, stale, stereotyped, stock, threadbare, time-worn, tired, trite, unoriginal, worn-out.

*antonyms* arresting, new.

**hack-work** *n* drudgery, pot-boiler.

**haemorrhoids** *n* emerods, piles.

**hag** *n* battle-axe, beldame, crone, fury, harpy, harridan, ogress, shrew, termagant, virago, vixen, witch.

**haggard** *adj* cadaverous, careworn, drawn, emaciated, gaunt, ghastly, hagged, hollow-eyed, pinched, shrunken, thin, wan, wasted, wrinkled.

*antonym* hale.

**haggle** *v* bargain, barter, bicker, cavil, chaffer, dicker, dispute, higgle, palter, quarrel, squabble, wrangle.

**hail¹** *n* barrage, bombardment, rain, shower, storm, torrent, volley.

*v* assail, barrage, batter, bombard, pelt, rain, shower, storm, volley.

**hail²** *v* acclaim, accost, acknowledge, address, applaud, call, cheer, exalt, flag down, glorify, greet, halloo, honour, salute, shout, signal to, wave, welcome.

*n* call, cry, halloo, holla, shout.

**hair** *n* locks, mane, mop, shock, tresses, vibrissa, villus.

**hair removal** depilation, electrolysis, epilation.

**hair-do** *n* coiffure, cut, haircut, hairstyle, perm, set, style.

**hairdresser** *n* barber, coiffeur, coiffeuse, friseur, hair-stylist, stylist.

**hairless** *adj* bald, bald-headed, beardless, clean-shaven, depilated, desperate, frantic, glabrate, glabrous, shorn, tonsured.

*antonym* hairy.

**hairpiece** *n* postiche, wig.

**hair-raising** *adj* alarming, bloodcurdling, breathtaking, creepy, eerie, exciting, frightening, ghastly, ghostly, horrifying, petrifying, scary, shocking, spine-chilling, startling, terrifying, thrilling.

*antonym* calming.

**hair's-breadth** *n* fraction, hair, inch, jot, whisker.

*antonym* mile.

**hair-splitting** *adj* captious, carping, cavilling, fault-finding, fine, finicky, nice, niggling, nit-picking, overnice, over-refined, pettifogging, quibbling, subtle, word-splitting.

*antonym* unfussy.

**hairy** *adj* bearded, bewhiskered, bushy, crinigerous, crinite, crinose, dangerous, dicey, difficult, fleecy, furry, hazardous, hirsute, hispid, lanuginose, lanuginous, perilous, pilose, pilous, risky, scaring, shaggy, stubbly, tricky, villose, villous, woolly.

*antonyms* bald, clean-shaven.

**halcyon** *adj* balmy, calm, carefree, flourishing, gentle, golden, happy, mild, pacific, peaceful, placid, prosperous, quiet, serene, still, tranquil, undisturbed.
*antonym* stormy.

**hale** *adj* able-bodied, athletic, blooming, fit, flourishing, healthy, hearty, in fine fettle, in the pink, robust, sound, strong, vigorous, well, youthful.
*antonym* ill.

**half** *n* bisection, division, fifty per cent, fraction, half-back, half-share, hemisphere, portion, section, segment, term.
*adj* divided, fractional, halved, incomplete, limited, moderate, part, partial, semi-.
*antonym* whole.
*adv* barely, imperfectly, in part, inadequately, incompletely, partially, partly, slightly.
*antonym* completely.

**half-baked** *adj* brainless, crazy, foolish, harebrained, ill-conceived, ill-judged, impractical, senseless, short-sighted, silly, stupid, unplanned.
*antonym* sensible.

**half-breed, half-caste** *n* griff(e), mestee, mestiza, mestizo, metif, métis, métisse, miscegen, miscegene, miscegine, mongrel, mulatta, mulatto, mulattress, mustee, quadroon, quarter-blood, quarteroon, quintroon, zambo.

**half-hearted** *adj* apathetic, cool, indifferent, lackadaisical, lacklustre, listless, lukewarm, neutral, passive, perfunctory, uninterested.
*antonym* enthusiastic.

**halfway** *adv* barely, imperfectly, in the middle, incompletely, midway, moderately, nearly, partially, partly, rather, slightly.
*antonym* completely.
*adj* central, equidistant, incomplete, intermediate, mid, middle, midway, partial, part-way.
*antonym* complete.

**half-wit** *n* cretin, dimwit, dolt, dullard, dunce, dunderhead, fool, gaupus, idiot, imbecile, moron, nitwit, nut, simpleton, underwit, witling.
*antonym* brain.

**half-witted** *adj* addle-brained, barmy, batty, crazy, cretinous, dull, dull-witted, feeble-minded, foolish, idiotic, moronic, nuts, nutty, silly, simple, simple-minded, stupid, two bricks short of a load.
*antonym* clever.

**hall** *n* assembly-room, auditorium, aula, basilica, chamber, concert-hall, concourse, corridor, entrance-hall, entry, foyer, hallway, lobby, salon, saloon, vestibule.

**hallmark** *n* authentication, badge, brand-name, device, emblem, endorsement, indication, mark, seal, sign, stamp, symbol, trademark.

**hallo!** *see* hello.

**hallowed** *adj* age-old, beatified, blessed, consecrated, dedicated, established, holy, honoured, inviolable, revered, sacred, sacrosanct, sanctified.

**hallucinate** *v* aberrate, daydream, envision, fantasise, freak out, imagine, trip.

**hallucination** *n* aberration, apparition, delusion, dream, fantasy, figment, illusion, mirage, phantasmagoria, pink elephants, vision.

**halo** *n* aura, aureola, aureole, corona, gloria, gloriole, glory, halation, nimbus, radiance.

**halt** *v* arrest, block, break off, call it a day, cease, check, curb, desist, draw up, end, impede, obstruct, pack it in, quit, rest, stem, stop, terminate, wait.
*antonyms* assist, continue, start.
*n* arrest, break, close, end, étape, impasse, interruption, pause, stand, standstill, stop, stoppage, termination, way point.
*antonyms* continuation, start.

**halting** *adj* awkward, broken, faltering, hesitant, imperfect, laboured, stammering, stumbling, stuttering, uncertain.
*antonym* fluent.

**halve** *v* bisect, cut down, divide, go Dutch, lessen, reduce, share, split.

**halved** *adj* bisected, dimidiate, divided, split.

**hammer** *v* bang, beat, clobber, defeat, din, dolly, drive, drive home, drub, drum, form, grind, hit, impress upon, instruct, knock, make, malleate, pan, repeat, shape, slate, thrash, trounce, worst.
*n* beetle, gavel, madge, mall, mallet, maul, monkey.

**hammer out** accomplish, bring about, complete, contrive, excogitate, fashion, finish, negotiate, produce, settle, sort out, thrash out.

**hamper** *v* bind, cramp, cumber, curb, curtail, distort, embarrass, encumber, entangle, fetter, frustrate, hamshackle, hamstring, handicap, hinder, hobble, hold up, impede, interfere with, obstruct, pinch, prevent, restrain, restrict, shackle, slow down, tangle, thwart, trammel.
*antonyms* aid, expedite.

**hamstrung** *adj* balked, crippled, disabled, foiled, frustrated, handicapped, helpless, hors de combat, incapacitated, paralysed, stymied.

**hand[1]** *n* ability, agency, aid, applause, art, artistry, assistance, calligraphy, cheirography, clap, daddle, direction, fist, flipper, handwriting, help, influence, mitt, ovation, palm, part, participation, paw, penmanship, pud, puddy, script, share, skill, support.
*v* aid, assist, conduct, convey, deliver, give, guide, help, lead, offer, pass, present, provide, transmit, yield.

**hand down** bequeath, give, grant, pass on, transfer, will.

**hand in glove** allied, in cahoots, in collusion, in league, intimate.

**hand out** deal out, disburse, dish out, dispense, disseminate, distribute, give out, mete, share out.

**hand over** deliver, donate, fork out, present, release, relinquish, surrender, turn over, yield.
*antonym* retain.

**hand[2]** *n* artificer, artisan, craftsman, employee, farm-hand, hired man, hireling, labourer, operative, orra man, redneck, worker, workman.

**handbook** *n* Baedeker, book of words, companion, guide, guidebook, instruction book, manual, vade-mecum.

**handcuff** *v* fasten, fetter, manacle, secure, shackle, tie.

**handcuffs** *n* bracelets, cuffs, darbies, fetters, manacles, mittens, shackles, wristlets.

**handful** *n* few, scattering, smattering, sprinkling, wheen.

*antonym* lot.

**handicap** *n* barrier, block, defect, disability, disadvantage, drawback, encumbrance, hindrance, impairment, impediment, impost, limitation, millstone, obstacle, odds, penalty, restriction, shortcoming, stumbling-block.

*antonyms* assistance, benefit.

*v* burden, disadvantage, encumber, hamper, hamstring, hinder, impede, limit, restrict, retard.

*antonyms* assist, further.

**handicraft** *n* art, artisanship, craft, craftsmanship, handiwork, skill, workmanship.

**handiness** *n* accessibility, adroitness, aptitude, availability, cleverness, closeness, convenience, deftness, dexterity, efficiency, expertise, knack, practicality, proficiency, proximity, skill, usefulness, workability.

*antonym* clumsiness.

**handiwork** *n* achievement, artefact, craft, creation, design, doing, handicraft, handwork, invention, product, production, result, work.

**handkerchief** *n* fogle, handkercher, hanky, monteith, mouchoir, nose-rag, romal, rumal, sudary, wipe.

**handle** *n* ear, grip, haft, handfast, handgrip, heft, helve, hilt, knob, lug, stock, wythe.

*v* administer, carry, conduct, control, cope with, deal in, deal with, direct, discourse, discuss, feel, finger, fondle, grasp, guide, hold, manage, manipulate, manoeuvre, market, maul, operate, paw, pick up, poke, sell, steer, stock, supervise, touch, trade, traffic in, treat, use, wield.

**handling** *n* administration, approach, conduct, direction, discussion, management, manipulation, operation, running, transaction, treatment.

**hand-out**[1] *n* alms, charity, dole, freebie, issue, largess(e), share, share-out.

**hand-out**[2] *n* bulletin, circular, free sample, leaflet, literature, press release, statement.

**hand-picked** *adj* choice, chosen, elect, elite, picked, recherché, screened, select, selected.

**hands** *n* authority, care, charge, command, control, custody, disposal, guardianship, guidance, jurisdiction, keeping, possession, power, supervision, tutelage.

**hands down** easily, effortlessly, in a canter, with ease.

*antonym* with difficulty.

**handsome** *adj* abundant, admirable, ample, attractive, beau, becoming, bountiful, braw, comely, considerable, elegant, feat(e)ous, featuous, featurely, fine, generous, good-looking, graceful, gracious, large, liberal, magnanimous, majestic, personable, plentiful, seemly, sizeable, stately, well-favoured, well-looking, well-proportioned, well-set-up.

*antonyms* mean, stingy, ugly.

**handsomely** *adv* abundantly, amply, bountifully, generously, lavishly, liberally, magnanimously, munificently, plentifully, richly, unsparingly, unstintingly.

*antonym* stingily.

**handwriting** *n* cacography, calligraphy, cheirography, fist, hand, longhand, penmanship, scrawl, script.

**handy** *adj* accessible, adept, adroit, at hand, available, clever, close, convenient, deft, dexterous, expert, helpful, manageable, near, nearby, neat, nimble, practical, proficient, ready, serviceable, skilful, skilled, useful.

*antonyms* clumsy, inconvenient, unwieldy.

**handyman** *n* DIYer, factotum, famulus, hobjobber, Jack-of-all-trades, man-of-the-world, odd-jobman, orra man.

**hang** *v* adhere, attach, bow, cling, cover, dangle, deck, decorate, depend, drape, drift, droop, drop, execute, fasten, fix, float, furnish, gibbet, hold, hover, incline, lean, loll, lower, remain, rest, sag, stick, string up, suspend, suspercollate, swing, trail, weep.

**hang about/around** associate with, dally, frequent, haunt, linger, loiter, resort, roam, tarry, waste time.

**hang back** demur, hesitate, hold back, recoil, shy away.

**hang fire** delay, hang back, hold back, hold on, procrastinate, stall, stick, stop, vacillate, wait.

*antonym* press on.

**hang on** carry on, cling, clutch, continue, depend on, endure, grasp, grip, hang fire, hang in there, hinge, hold fast, hold on, hold out, hold the line, persevere, persist, remain, rest, stop, turn on, wait.

*antonym* give up.

**hang over** impend, loom, menace, threaten.

**hangdog** *adj* abject, browbeaten, cowed, cringing, defeated, downcast, furtive, guilty, miserable, shamefaced, sneaking, wretched.

*antonym* bold.

**hanger-on** *n* camp follower, dependant, follower, freeloader, lackey, leech, minion, parasite, sponger, sycophant, toad-eater, toady.

**hanging**[1] *adj* dangling, drooping, flapping, flopping, floppy, loose, pendent, pendulous, pensile, suspended, swinging, unattached, undecided, unresolved, unsettled, unsupported.

**hanging**[2] *n* dossal, dossel, drape, drapery, drop, drop-scene, frontal.

**hangman** *n* Jack Ketch.

**hang-out** *n* den, dive, haunt, home, howf(f), joint, local, resort, watering-hole.

**hangover** *n* after-effects, crapulence, katzenjammer.

**hang-up** *n* block, difficulty, idée fixe, inhibition, mental block, obsession, preoccupation, problem, thing.

**hank** *n* coil, fank, length, loop, piece, roll, skein.

**hanker for/after** covet, crave, desire, hunger for, itch for, long for, lust after, pine for, thirst for, want, wish, yearn for, yen for.

*antonym* dislike.

**hankering** *n* craving, desire, hunger, itch, longing, pining, thirst, urge, wish, yearning, yen.

*antonym* dislike.

**hanky-panky** *n* cheating, chicanery, deception, devilry, dishonesty, funny business, jiggery-pokery, knavery, machinations, mischief, monkey business, nonsense, shenanigans, subterfuge, trickery, tricks.

*antonym* openness.

**haphazard** *adj* accidental, aimless, arbitrary, careless, casual, chance, disorderly, disorganised, flukey, hit-or-miss, indiscriminate, promiscuous, random, slapdash, slipshod, unmethodical, unsystematic.

*antonyms* deliberate, planned.

**hapless** *adj* cursed, ill-fated, ill-starred, jinxed, luckless, miserable, star-crossed, unfortunate, unhappy, unlucky, wretched.

*antonym* lucky.

**happen** *v* appear, arise, befall, chance, come about, crop up, develop, ensue, eventuate, fall out, follow, materialise, occur, result, supervene, take place, transpire, turn out.

**happen on** chance on, come on, discover, find, hit on, light on, stumble on.

**happening** *n* accident, adventure, affair, case, chance, circumstance, episode, event, experience, incident, occasion, occurrence, phenomenon, proceeding, scene.

**happily** *adv* agreeably, appropriately, aptly, auspiciously, blithely, by chance, cheerfully, contentedly, delightedly, enthusiastically, favourably, felicitously, fittingly, fortunately, freely, gaily, gladly, gleefully, gracefully, heartily, joyfully, joyously, luckily, merrily, opportunely, perhaps, propitiously, providentially, seasonably, successfully, willingly.

*antonym* unhappily.

**happiness** *n* beatitude, blessedness, bliss, cheer, cheerfulness, cheeriness, chirpiness, contentment, delight, ecstasy, elation, enjoyment, exuberance, felicity, gaiety, gladness, high spirits, joy, joyfulness, jubilation, light-heartedness, merriment, pleasure, satisfaction, well-being.

*antonym* unhappiness.

**happy** *adj* advantageous, appropriate, apt, auspicious, befitting, blessed, blest, blissful, blithe, chance, cheerful, content, contented, convenient, delighted, ecstatic, elated, enviable, favourable, felicitous, fit, fitting, fortunate, glad, gratified, gruntled, idyllic, jolly, joyful, joyous, jubilant, lucky, merry, opportune, over the moon, overjoyed, pleased, promising, propitious, satisfactory, Saturnian, seasonable, starry-eyed, successful, sunny, thrilled, timely, well-timed.

*antonym* unhappy.

**happy medium** aurea mediocritas, golden mean, juste milieu.

*antonym* excess.

**happy-go-lucky** *adj* blithe, carefree, casual, cheerful, devil-may-care, easy-going, heedless, improvident, insouciant, irresponsible, light-hearted, nonchalant, reckless, unconcerned, untroubled, unworried.

*antonyms* anxious, wary.

**harangue** *n* address, declamation, diatribe, discourse, exhortation, homily, lecture, oration, paternoster, peroration, philippic, sermon, speech, spiel, tirade.

*v* address, declaim, descant, exhort, hold forth, lecture, monolog(u)ise, orate, perorate, preach, rant, rhetorise, sermonise, spout.

**harass** *v* annoy, badger, bait, beleaguer, bother, chivvy, distress, disturb, exasperate, exhaust, fatigue, harry, hassle, hound, perplex, persecute, pester, plague, tease, tire, torment, trash, trouble, vex, wear out, weary, worry.

*antonym* assist.

**harassed** *adj* careworn, distraught, distressed, harried, hassled, hounded, pestered, plagued, pressured, pressurised, strained, stressed, tormented, troubled, vexed, worried.

*antonym* carefree.

**harassment** *n* aggravation, annoyance, badgering, bedevilment, bother, distress, hassle, irritation, molest, molestation, nuisance, persecution, pestering, pressuring, torment, trouble, vexation.

*antonym* assistance.

**harbinger** *n* avant-courier, forerunner, foretoken, herald, indication, messenger, omen, portent, precursor, presage, sign, warning.

**harbour** *n* anchorage, asylum, covert, destination, haven, marina, port, refuge, roadstead, sanctuary, sanctum, security, shelter.

*v* believe, cherish, cling to, conceal, entertain, foster, hide, hold, imagine, lodge, maintain, nurse, nurture, protect, retain, secrete, shelter, shield.

**hard** *adj* acrimonious, actual, adamantine, alcoholic, angry, antagonistic, arduous, backbreaking, baffling, bare, bitter, burdensome, calamitous, callous, cast-iron, cold, compact, complex, complicated, cruel, crusty, dark, definite, dense, difficult, disagreeable, disastrous, distressing, driving, exacting, exhausting, fatiguing, fierce, firm, flinty, forceful, formidable, grievous, grim, habit-forming, hard-hearted, harsh, heavy, Herculean, hostile, impenetrable, implacable, indisputable, inflexible, intolerable, intricate, involved, irony, knotty, laborious, marbly, obdurate, painful, perplexing, pitiless, plain, powerful, puzzling, rancorous, resentful, rigid, rigorous, ruthless, sclerous, severe, shrewd, solid, stern, stiff, stony, strenuous, strict, strong, stubborn, tangled, thorny, toilsome, tough, undeniable, unfathomable, unfeeling, ungentle, unjust, unkind, unpleasant, unrelenting, unsparing, unsympathetic, unvarnished, unyielding, uphill, verified, violent, wearying.

**antonyms** harmless, kind, mild, non-alcoholic, pleasant, pleasing, soft, yielding.

*adv* agonisingly, assiduously, badly, bitterly, close, completely, determinedly, diligently, distressingly, doggedly, earnestly, energetically, fiercely, forcefully, forcibly, fully, hardly, harshly, heavily, industriously, intensely, intently, keenly, laboriously, near, painfully, persistently, powerfully, rancorously, reluctantly, resentfully, roughly, severely, sharply, slowly, sorely, steadily, strenuously, strongly, uneasily, untiringly, vigorously, violently, with difficulty.

**antonyms** gently, mildly, moderately, unenthusiastically.

**hard and fast** binding, fixed, immutable, incontrovertible, inflexible, invariable, rigid, set, strict, stringent, unalterable, unchangeable, unchanging.

**antonym** flexible.

**hard up** bankrupt, broke, bust, cleaned out, destitute, impecunious, impoverished, in the red, penniless, penurious, poor, short, skint, strapped for cash.

**antonym** rich.

**hard-bitten** *adj* callous, case-hardened, cynical, down-to-earth, hard-boiled, hard-headed, hard-nosed, matter-of-fact, practical, realistic, ruthless, shrewd, tough, unsentimental.

**antonym** callow.

**hard-core** *adj* blatant, dedicated, die-hard, dyed-in-the-wool, explicit, extreme, intransigent, obstinate, rigid, staunch, steadfast.

**antonym** moderate.

**harden** *v* accustom, anneal, bake, brace, brutalise, buttress, cake, case-harden, concrete, fortify, freeze, gird, habituate, indurate, inure, nerve, reinforce, sclerose, season, set, solidify, steel, stiffen, strengthen, toughen, train.

**antonym** soften.

**hardened** *adj* accustomed, chronic, fixed, habitual, habituated, incorrigible, inured, inveterate, irredeemable, obdurate, reprobate, seasoned, set, shameless, toughened, unfeeling.

**antonyms** callow, soft.

**hardening** *n* annealing, clotting, coagulation, congealing, sclerosis, setting, solidifying, vulcanisation.

**hard-headed** *adj* astute, clear-thinking, cool, hard-boiled, level-headed, practical, pragmatic, realistic, sensible, shrewd, tough, unsentimental.

**antonym** unrealistic.

**hard-hearted** *adj* callous, cold, cruel, hard, heartless, indifferent, inhuman, insensitive, intolerant, iron-hearted, marble-breasted, marble-hearted, merciless, pitiless, stony, uncaring, uncompassionate, unfeeling, unkind, unsympathetic.

**antonyms** kind, merciful.

**hard-hitting** *adj* condemnatory, critical, forceful, no-holds-barred, strongly-worded, tough, unsparing, vigorous.

**antonym** mild.

**hardihood** *n* assurance, audacity, backbone, boldness, bottle, bravery, courage, daring, determination, effrontery, firmness, foolhardiness, grit, guts, hardiness, impertinence, impetuousness, intrepidity, mettle, nerve, pluck, prowess, rashness, recklessness, resolution, spirit, spunk, strength, temerity.

**antonyms** sense, timidity.

**hardiness** *n* boldness, courage, fortitude, hardihood, intrepidity, resilience, resolution, robustness, ruggedness, sturdiness, toughness, valour.

**antonym** timidity.

**hardline** *adj* definite, extreme, immoderate, inflexible, intransigent, militant, tough, uncompromising, undeviating, unyielding.

**antonym** moderate.

**hardly** *adv* barely, by no means, faintly, harshly, infrequently, just, no way, not at all, not quite, only, only just, roughly, scarcely, severely, with difficulty.

**antonyms** easily, very.

**hardness** *n* coldness, difficulty, firmness, harshness, inhumanity, insensitivity, laboriousness, pitilessness, rigidity, severity, solidity, steel, sternness, toughness.

**antonyms** ease, mildness, softness.

**hard-pressed** *adj* hard-pushed, harassed, harried, pushed, under pressure, up against it, with one's back to the wall.

**antonym** untroubled.

**hardship** *n* adversity, affliction, austerity, burden, calamity, destitution, difficulty, fatigue, grievance, labour, misery, misfortune, need, oppression, persecution, privation, strait, suffering, toil, torment, trial, tribulation, trouble, want.

**antonym** ease.

**hard-wearing** *adj* durable, resilient, rugged, stout, strong, sturdy, tough.

**antonym** delicate.

**hard-working** *adj* assiduous, busy, conscientious, diligent, energetic, indefatigable, industrious, sedulous, workaholic, zealous.

**antonym** lazy.

**hardy** *adj* audacious, bold, brave, brazen, courageous, daring, firm, fit, foolhardy, hale, headstrong, healthy, hearty, heroic, impudent, intrepid, lusty, manly, plucky, rash, reckless, resolute, robust, rugged, sound, spartan, stalwart, stout, stout-hearted, strong, sturdy, tough, valiant, valorous, vigorous.

**antonyms** unhealthy, weak.

**hare-brained** *adj* asinine, careless, daft, empty-headed, flighty, foolish, giddy, half-baked, harum-scarum, headlong, heedless, inane, mindless, rash, reckless, scatter-brained, scatty, unstable, unsteady, wild.

**antonym** sensible.

**harem** *n* gynaeceum, seraglio, serai(l), women's quarters, zenana.

**hark** *v* attend, give ear, hear, hearken, listen, mark, note, notice, pay attention, pay heed.

**hark back** go back, recall, recollect, regress, remember, revert.

**harlot** *n* call-girl, fallen woman, hussy, loon, loose fish, loose woman, lorette, Paphian, pro, prostitute, scrubber, street-walker, strumpet, tart, tramp, whore.

**harm** *n* abuse, damage, detriment, disservice, evil, hurt, ill, immorality, impairment, iniquity, injury, loss, mischief, misfortune, scathe, sin, sinfulness, vice, wickedness, wrong.

*antonyms* benefit, service.

*v* abuse, blemish, damage, hurt, ill-treat, ill-use, impair, injure, maltreat, mar, molest, ruin, scathe, spoil, wound.

*antonyms* benefit, improve.

**harmful** *adj* baleful, baneful, damaging, deleterious, destructive, detrimental, disadvantageous, evil, hurtful, injurious, noxious, pernicious, pestful, pestiferous, pestilent, scatheful.

*antonym* harmless.

**harmless** *adj* gentle, innocent, innocuous, innoxious, inoffensive, non-toxic, safe, scatheless, unharmed, uninjured, unobjectionable, unscathed.

*antonym* harmful.

**harmonious** *adj* according, agreeable, amicable, compatible, concinnous, concordant, congenial, congruous, consonant, consonous, co-ordinated, cordial, correspondent, dulcet, euharmonic, euphonic, euphonious, eurhythmic, friendly, harmonic, harmonising, matching, mellifluous, melodious, musical, sweet-sounding, sympathetic, symphonious, tuneful.

*antonym* inharmonious.

**harmonise** *v* accommodate, accord, adapt, agree, arrange, attune, blend, chime, cohere, compose, co-ordinate, correspond, jibe, match, reconcile, suit, tally, tone.

*antonym* clash.

**harmony** *n* accord, agreement, amicability, amity, balance, chime, compatibility, concinnity, concord, conformity, congruity, consensus, consistency, consonance, co-operation, co-ordination, correspondence, correspondency, diapason, euphony, eurhythmy, fitness, friendship, goodwill, like-mindedness, melodiousness, melody, parallelism, peace, rapport, suitability, symmetry, sympathy, tune, tunefulness, unanimity, understanding, unity.

*antonym* discord.

**harness** *n* equipment, gear, reins, straps, tack, tackle, trappings.

*v* apply, channel, control, couple, employ, exploit, make use of, mobilise, saddle, turn to account, use, utilise, yoke.

**harp on (about)** dwell on, labour, press, reiterate, renew, repeat.

**harpoon** *n* arrow, barb, dart, grains, spear, trident.

**harpy** *n* gold-digger, harriden, man-eater, vamp, vampire.

**harridan** *n* battle-axe, dragon, fury, gorgon, harpy, hell-cat, nag, scold, shrew, tartar, termagant, virago, vixen, witch, Xanthippe.

**harried** *adj* agitated, anxious, beset, bothered, distressed, hag-ridden, harassed, hard-pressed, hassled, plagued, pressured, pressurised, ravaged, tormented, troubled, worried.

*antonym* untroubled.

**harrow** *v* agonise, daunt, dismay, distress, harass, lacerate, perturb, rack, rend, tear, torment, torture, vex, wound, wring.

*antonyms* assuage, hearten.

**harrowing** *adj* agonising, alarming, chilling, distressing, disturbing, excruciating, frightening, heart-rending, lacerant, nerve-racking, racking, soaring, terrifying, tormenting, traumatic.

*antonyms* calming, heartening.

**harry** *v* annoy, badger, bedevil, chivvy, depredate, despoil, devastate, disturb, fret, harass, hassle, maraud, molest, persecute, pester, pillage, plague, plunder, raid, ravage, rob, sack, tease, torment, trouble, vex, worry.

*antonyms* aid, calm.

**harsh** *adj* abrasive, abusive, austere, bitter, bleak, brutal, coarse, comfortless, croaking, crude, cruel, discordant, dissonant, dour, Draconian, glaring, grating, grim, guttural, hard, jarring, pitiless, punitive, rasping, raucous, relentless, rough, ruthless, scabrous, severe, sharp, Spartan, stark, stern, strident, stringent, unfeeling, ungentle, unkind, unmelodious, unpleasant, unrelenting.

*antonyms* mild, smooth, soft.

**harshness** *n* abrasiveness, acerbity, acrimony, asperity, austerity, bitterness, brutality, churlishness, coarseness, crudity, hardness, ill-temper, rigour, roughness, severity, sourness, starkness, sternness, strictness.

*antonyms* mildness, softness.

**harum-scarum** *adj* careless, erratic, flighty, giddy, haphazard, hare-brained, hasty, ill-considered, impetuous, imprudent, irresponsible, precipitate, rash, reckless, scatter-brained, scatty, wild.

*antonym* sensible.

**harvest** *n* collection, consequence, crop, effect, fruition, harvesting, harvest-time, hockey, ingathering, inning, produce, product, reaping, result, return, vendage, yield.

*v* accumulate, acquire, amass, collect, garner, gather, mow, pick, pluck, reap.

**hash**[1] *n* botch, confusion, cow's arse, fuck-up, hotchpotch, jumble, mess, mishmash, mix-up, muddle, shambles.

**hash**[2] *n* goulash, hotpot, lob's course, lobscouse, stew.

**hash**[3] *see* hashish.

**hashish** *n* bhang, cannabis, charas, churrus, dope, ganja, grass, hash, hemp, marijuana, pot.

**hassle** *n* altercation, argument, bickering, bother, difficulty, disagreement, dispute, fight, inconvenience, nuisance, problem, quarrel, squabble, struggle, trial, trouble, tussle, upset, wrangle.

*antonyms* agreement, peace.

*v* annoy, badger, bother, bug, chivvy, harass, harry, hound, pester.

*antonyms* assist, calm.

**haste** *n* alacrity, briskness, bustle, celerity, dispatch, expedition, fleetness, hastiness, hurry, hustle, impetuosity, nimbleness, precipitance, precipitancy, precipitateness, precipitation, promptitude, quickness, rapidity, rapidness, rashness, recklessness, rush, speed, swiftness, urgency, velocity.

*antonyms* care, deliberation, slowness.

**hasten** *v* accelerate, advance, bolt, dash, dispatch, expedite, fly, gallop, goad, haste, have it on one's toes, hightail it, hurry, make haste, precipitate, press, quicken, race, run, rush, scurry, scuttle, speed, speed up, sprint, step on it, step up, tear, trot, urge.

*antonym* dawdle.

**hastily** *adv* apace, chop-chop, double-quick, fast, heedlessly, hurriedly, impetuously, impulsively, posthaste, precipitately, promptly, quickly, rapidly, rashly, recklessly, speedily, straightaway.

*antonyms* carefully, deliberately, slowly.

**hasty** *adj* brief, brisk, brusque, cursory, eager, excited, expeditious, fast, fiery, fleet, fleeting, foolhardy, headlong, heedless, hot-headed, hot-tempered, hurried, impatient, impetuous, impulsive, indiscreet, irascible, irritable, passing, passionate, perfunctory, precipitant, precipitate, prompt, quick-tempered, rapid, rash, reckless, rushed, short, snappy, speedy, subitaneous, superficial, swift, thoughtless, urgent.

*antonyms* careful, deliberate, placid, slow.

**hat** *n* beret, biretta, boater, bonnet, bowler, cap, lid, night-cap, poke-bonnet, skull-cap, sombrero, sou'wester, titfer, top-hat, trilby, yarmulka.

**hatch** *v* breed, brood, conceive, concoct, contrive, cook up, design, develop, devise, dream up, incubate, originate, plan, plot, project, scheme, think up.

**hate** *v* abhor, abominate, despise, detest, dislike, execrate, loathe, spite.

*antonym* like.

*n* abhorrence, abomination, animosity, animus, antagonism, antipathy, averseness, aversion, detestation, dislike, enmity, execration, hatred, hostility, loathing, odium, odium theologicum.

*antonym* like.

**hateful** *adj* abhorrent, abominable, damnable, despicable, detestable, disgusting, execrable, forbidding, foul, hateworthy, heinous, horrible, loathsome, obnoxious, odious, offensive, repellent, repugnant, repulsive, revolting, vile.

*antonym* pleasing.

**hatred** *n* abomination, animosity, animus, antagonism, antipathy, aversion, despite, detestation, dislike, enmity, execration, hate, ill-will, misandry, misanthropy, odium, repugnance, revulsion.

*antonym* like.

**haughtiness** *n* airs, aloofness, arrogance, conceit, contempt, contemptuousness, disdain, hauteur, insolence, loftiness, pomposity, pride, snobbishness, snootiness, superciliousness.

*antonyms* friendliness, humility.

**haughty** *adj* arrogant, assuming, cavalier, conceited, contemptuous, disdainful, fastuous, high, high and mighty, highty-tighty, hoity-toity, imperious, lofty, overweening, proud, scornful, snobbish, snooty, stiff-necked, stomachful, stuck-up, supercilious, superior, uppish.

*antonyms* friendly, humble.

**haul** *v* bouse, carry, cart, convey, drag, draw, hale, heave, hump, lug, move, pull, tow, trail, transport, trice, tug.

*n* booty, bunce, catch, drag, find, gain, harvest, heave, loot, pull, spoils, swag, takings, tug, yield.

**haunches** *n* buttocks, huckles, hucks, hunkers, nates, thighs.

**haunt** *v* beset, frequent, obsess, plague, possess, prey on, recur, repair, resort, torment, trouble, visit, walk.

*n* den, gathering-place, hangout, howf(f), meeting place, rendezvous, resort, stamping ground.

**haunted** *adj* cursed, eerie, ghostly, hag-ridden, jinxed, obsessed, plagued, possessed, preoccupied, spooky, tormented, troubled, worried.

**haunting** *adj* disturbing, eerie, evocative, indelible, memorable, nostalgic, persistent, poignant, recurrent, recurring, unforgettable.

*antonym* unmemorable.

**have** *v* accept, acquire, allow, bear, beget, cheat, comprehend, comprise, consider, contain, deceive, deliver, dupe, embody, endure, enjoy, entertain, experience, feel, fool, gain, get, give birth to, hold, include, keep, obtain, occupy, outwit, own, permit, possess, procure, produce, put up with, receive, retain, secure, suffer, sustain, swindle, take, tolerate, trick, undergo.

**have done with** be through with, cease, desist, finish with, give up, stop, throw over, wash one's hands of.

**have to** be compelled, be forced, be obliged, be required, have got to, must, ought, should.

**haven** *n* anchorage, asylum, harbour, hithe, port, refuge, retreat, roads, roadstead, sanctuary, sanctum, shelter.

**havoc** *n* carnage, chaos, confusion, damage, depopulation, desolation, despoliation, destruction, devastation, disorder, disruption, mayhem, rack and ruin, ravages, ruin, shambles, slaughter, waste, wreck.

**hawk**[1] *v* bark, cry, market, offer, peddle, sell, tout, vend.

**hawk**[2] *n* buzzard, falcon, goshawk, haggard, t(i)ercel, warmonger.

**hawker** *n* barrow-boy, cheap-jack, colporteur, coster, costermonger, crier, huckster, pedlar, vendor.

**haywire** *adj* amiss, chaotic, confused, crazy, disarranged, disordered, disorganised, erratic, kaput, mad, shambolic, tangled, topsy-turvy, wild.

*antonyms* correct, in order.

**hazard** *n* accident, chance, coincidence, danger, death-trap, endangerment, fluke, imperilment, jeopardy, luck, mischance, misfortune, mishap, peril, risk, threat.

*antonym* safety.

*v* advance, attempt, chance, conjecture, dare, endanger, expose, gamble, imperil, jeopardise, offer, presume, proffer, risk, speculate, stake, submit, suggest, suppose, threaten, venture, volunteer.

**hazardous** *adj* chancy, dangerous, dicey, difficult, fraught, hairy, haphazard, insecure, perilous, precarious, risky, thorny, ticklish, uncertain, unpredictable, unsafe.

*antonyms* safe, secure.

**haze** *n* cloud, dimness, film, fog, mist, nebulosity, obscurity, smog, smokiness, steam, unclearness, vapour.

**hazy** *adj* blurry, clouded, cloudy, dim, distanceless, dull, faint, foggy, fuzzy, ill-defined, indefinite, indistinct, loose, milky, misty, muddled, muzzy, nebulous, obscure, overcast, smoky, uncertain, unclear, vague, veiled.

*antonyms* clear, definite.

**head** *n* ability, apex, aptitude, bean, beginning, bonce, boss, brain, brains, branch, capacity, cape, captain, caput, category, chief, chieftain, chump, class, climax, commander, commencement, conclusion, conk, cop, cranium, crest, crisis, crown, culmination, department, director, division, end, faculty, flair, fore, forefront, foreland, front, godfather, head teacher, heading, headland, headmaster, headmistress, height, intellect, intelligence, knowledge box, leader, loaf, manager, master, mastermind, mentality, mind, nab, napper, nob, noddle, nut, origin, pate, peak, pitch, point, principal, promontory, rise, sconce, section, skull, source, start, subject, summit, superintendent, supervisor, talent, tête, thought, tip, top, topic, topknot, turning-point, understanding, upperworks, van, vanguard, vertex.

*antonyms* foot, subordinate, tail.

*adj* arch, chief, dominant, first, foremost, front, highest, leading, main, pre-eminent, premier, prime, principal, supreme, top, topmost.

*v* aim, cap, command, control, crown, direct, govern, guide, lead, make a beeline, make for, manage, oversee, point, precede, rule, run, steer, superintend, supervise, top, turn.

**head for** aim for, direct towards, gravitate towards, make for, point to, steer for, turn for, zero in on.

**head off** avert, deflect, distract, divert, fend off, forestall, intercept, interpose, intervene, parry, prevent, stop, ward off.

**head over heels** completely, intensely, recklessly, thoroughly, uncontrollably, utterly, whole-heartedly, wildly.

**headache** *n* bane, bother, cephalalgia, hassle, hemicrania, inconvenience, migraine, neuralgia, nuisance, problem, trouble, vexation, worry.

**heading** *n* caption, category, class, descriptor, division, headline, lemma, name, rubric, section, superscription, title.

**headland** *n* bill, bluff, cape, cliff, foreland, head, morro, mull, naze, point, promontory.

**headlong** *adj* breakneck, dangerous, hasty, head-first, head-foremost, head-on, hell-for-leather, impetuous, impulsive, inconsiderate, precipitate, reckless, thoughtless.

*adv* hastily, head first, head foremost, head-on, heedlessly, hell for leather, helter-skelter, hurriedly, lickety-split, pell-mell, precipitately, rashly, thoughtlessly, wildly.

**head-man** *n* captain, chief, leader, muqaddam, ruler, sachem.

**headquarters** *n* base camp, head office, high command, HQ, nerve centre, praetorium.

**headstrong** *adj* bull-headed, contrary, foolhardy, fractious, froward, heedless, imprudent, impulsive, intractable, mulish, obstinate, perverse, pig-headed, rash, reckless, self-willed, stubborn, ungovernable, unruly, wilful.

*antonyms* biddable, docile, obedient.

**headway** *n* advance, improvement, inroad(s), progress, progression, way.

**heady** *adj* exciting, exhilarating, hasty, impetuous, impulsive, inconsiderate, inebriant, intoxicating, overpowering, potent, precipitate, rash, reckless, spirituous, stimulating, strong, thoughtless, thrilling.

**heal** *v* alleviate, ameliorate, balsam, compose, conciliate, cure, harmonise, mend, patch up, physic, reconcile, regenerate, remedy, restore, salve, settle, soothe, treat.

**healing** *adj* analeptic, assuaging, comforting, curative, emollient, epulotic, gentle, lenitive, medicinal, mild, mitigative, palliative, remedial, restorative, restoring, sanative, sanatory, soothing, styptic, therapeutic, vulnerary.

**health** *n* condition, constitution, fettle, fitness, form, good condition, haleness, heal, healthiness, robustness, salubrity, shape, soundness, state, strength, tone, vigour, weal, welfare, well-being.

*antonyms* disease, infirmity.

**healthy** *adj* active, beneficial, blooming, bracing, fine, fit, flourishing, good, hale (and hearty), hardy, healthful, health-giving, hearty, hygienic, in fine feather, in fine fettle, in fine form, in good condition, in good shape, in the pink, invigorating, nourishing, nutritious, physically fit, robust, salubrious, salutary, salutiferous, sound, strong, sturdy, vigorous, well, wholesome.

*antonyms* diseased, ill, infirm, sick, unhealthy.

**heap** *n* accumulation, acervation, aggregation, bing, clamp, cock, collection, cumulus, hoard, lot, mass, mound, mountain, pile, ruck, stack, stockpile, store.

*v* accumulate, amass, assign, augment, bank, bestow, build, burden, collect, confer, gather, hoard, increase, lavish, load, mound, pile, shower, stack, stockpile, store.

**heaps** *n* a lot, abundance, great deal, lashings, load(s), lots, mass, millions, mint, ocean(s), oodles, plenty, pot(s), quantities, scores, stack(s), tons.

**hear** *v* acknowledge, ascertain, attend, catch, discover, eavesdrop, examine, find, gather, hark, hearken, heed, investigate, judge, learn, listen, overhear, pick up, try, understand.

**hearing** *n* audience, audition, auditory, auditory range, ear, ear-shot, inquest, inquiry, inquisition, interview, investigation, perception, range, reach, review, sound, trial.

**hearsay** *n* bruit, buzz, gossip, grapevine, on-dit, report, rumour, talk, talk of the town, tittle-tattle, word of mouth.

**heart** *n* affection, benevolence, boldness, bravery, centre, character, compassion, concern, core, courage, crux, disposition, emotion, essence, feeling, fortitude, guts, hub, humanity, inclination, kernel, love, marrow, mettle, middle, mind, nature, nerve, nerve centre, nub, nucleus, pith, pity, pluck, purpose, quintessence, resolution, root, sentiment, soul, spirit, spunk, sympathy, temperament, tenderness, ticker, understanding, will.

**heart and soul** absolutely, completely, devotedly, eagerly, entirely, gladly, heartily, unreservedly, whole-heartedly.

**heartache** *n* affliction, agony, anguish, bitterness, dejection, despair, despondency, distress, grief, heartbreak, heart-sickness, pain, remorse, sorrow, suffering, torment, torture.

**heartbreak** *n* agony, anguish, dejection, desolation, despair, grief, misery, pain, sorrow, suffering.

*antonyms* elation, joy, relief.

**heartbreaking** *adj* agonising, bitter, desolating, disappointing, distressing, grievous, harrowing, heart-rending, pitiful, poignant, sad, tragic.

*antonyms* heartening, heartwarming, joyful.

**heartbroken** *adj* broken-hearted, crestfallen, crushed, dejected, desolate, despondent, disappointed, disconsolate, disheartened, dispirited, down, downcast, grieved, heart-sick, miserable, woebegone.

*antonyms* delighted, elated.

**hearten** *v* animate, assure, buck up, buoy up, cheer, comfort, console, embolden, encourage, gladden, incite, inspire, inspirit, pep up, reassure, revivify, rouse, stimulate.

*antonym* dishearten.

**heart-felt** *adj* ardent, cordial, deep, devoted, devout, earnest, fervent, genuine, hearty, honest, impassioned, infelt, profound, sincere, unfeigned, warm, whole-hearted.

*antonyms* false, insincere.

**heartily** *adv* absolutely, completely, cordially, deeply, eagerly, earnestly, enthusiastically, feelingly, genuinely, gladly, profoundly, resolutely, sincerely, thoroughly, totally, unfeignedly, very, vigorously, warmly, zealously.

**heartless** *adj* brutal, callous, cold, cold-blooded, cold-hearted, cruel, hard, hard-hearted, harsh, inhuman, merciless, pitiless, stern, uncaring, unfeeling, unkind.

*antonyms* considerate, kind, merciful, sympathetic.

**heart-rending** *adj* affecting, distressing, harrowing, heartbreaking, moving, pathetic, piteous, pitiful, poignant, sad, tear-jerking, tragic.

**heart-throb** *n* dreamboat, matinée idol, pin-up, star.

**heartwarming** *adj* affecting, cheering, encouraging, gladsome, gratifying, heartening, moving, pleasing, rewarding, satisfying, touching, warming.

*antonym* heart-breaking.

**hearty** *adj* active, affable, ample, ardent, cordial, doughty, eager, earnest, ebullient, effusive, energetic, enthusiastic, exuberant, filling, friendly, generous, genial, genuine, hale, hardy, healthy, heartfelt, honest, jovial, nourishing, real, robust, sincere, sizeable, solid, sound, square, stalwart, strong, substantial, true, unfeigned, unreserved, vigorous, warm, well, whole-hearted.

*antonyms* cold, emotionless.

**heat** *n* agitation, ardour, calefaction, earnestness, excitement, fervour, fever, fieriness, fury, hotness, impetuosity, incandescence, intensity, passion, sizzle, sultriness, swelter, torridity, vehemence, violence, warmness, warmth, zeal.

*antonyms* cold(ness), coolness.

*v* animate, calefy, chafe, excite, flush, glow, impassion, inflame, inspirit, reheat, rouse, stimulate, stir, toast, warm up.

*antonyms* chill, cool.

**heated** *adj* acrimonious, angry, bitter, excited, fierce, fiery, frenzied, furious, impassioned, intense, passionate, perfervid, raging, stormy, tempestuous, vehement, violent.

*antonym* dispassionate.

**heathen** *n* barbarian, gentile, idolator, idolatress, infidel, nations, nullifidian, pagan, philistine, savage, unbeliever.

*antonym* believer.

*adj* barbaric, gentile, godless, heathenish, idolatrous, infidel, irreligious, nullifidian, pagan, philistine, savage, uncivilised, unenlightened.

*antonyms* Christian, godly.

**heave** *v* billow, breathe, cast, chuck, dilate, drag, elevate, exhale, expand, fling, gag, groan, haul, heft, hitch, hoist, hurl, let fly, lever, lift, palpitate, pant, pitch, puff, pull, raise, retch, rise, send, sigh, sling, sob, spew, surge, suspire, swell, throb, throw, throw up, toss, tug, vomit, yomp.

**heaven** *n* bliss, ecstasy, Elysian fields, Elysium, empyrean, enchantment, ether, felicity, fiddler's green, firmament, happiness, happy hunting-ground(s), hereafter, Land of the Leal, next world, nirvana, paradise, rapture, sky, Swarga, transport, utopia, Valhalla, welkin, Zion.

*antonym* hell.

**heavenly** *adj* alluring, ambrosial, angelic, beatific, beautiful, blessed, blest, blissful, celestial, delightful, divine, empyrean, entrancing, exquisite, extra-terrestrial, glorious, godlike, holy, immortal, lovely, paradisaic(al), paradisal, paradisean, paradisial, paradisian, paradisic, rapturous, ravishing, seraphic, sublime, superhuman, supernal, supernatural, Uranian, wonderful.

*antonym* hellish.

**heavens** *n* ether, firmament, sky, the blue, the wild blue yonder, welkin.

**heavily** *adv* awkwardly, closely, clumsily, compactly, completely, considerably, copiously, decisively, deep, deeply, dejectedly, densely, dully, excessively, fast, frequently, gloomily, hard, heftily, laboriously, painfully, ponderously, profoundly, roundly, sluggishly, solidly, sound, soundly, thick, thickly, thoroughly, to excess, utterly, weightily, woodenly.

*antonym* lightly.

**heaviness** *n* arduousness, burdensomeness, deadness, dejection, depression, despondency, drowsiness, dullness, gloom, gloominess, glumness, gravity, grievousness, heftiness, languor, lassitude, melancholy, numbness, onerousness, oppression, oppressiveness, ponderousness, sadness, seriousness, severity, sleepiness, sluggishness, somnolence, torpor, weight, weightiness.

*antonyms* lightness, liveliness.

**heavy** *adj* abundant, apathetic, boisterous, bulky, burdened, burdensome, clumpy, complex, considerable, copious, crestfallen, deep, dejected, depressed, despondent, difficult, disconsolate, downcast, drowsy, dull, encumbered, excessive, gloomy, grave, grieving, grievous, hard, harsh, hefty, inactive, indolent, inert, intolerable, laborious, laden, large, leaden, listless, loaded, lumping, lumpish, massive, melancholy, onerous, oppressed, oppressive, ponderous, portly, profound, profuse, rough, sad, serious, severe, slow, sluggish, solemn, sorrowful, squabbish, stodgy, stormy, stupid, tedious, tempestuous, torpid, turbulent, vexatious, violent, wearisome, weighted, weighty, wild, wooden.

*antonyms* airy, insignificant, light.

**heavy-handed** *adj* autocratic, awkward, bungling, clumsy, domineering, graceless, ham-fisted, ham-handed, harsh, inconsiderate, inept, inexpert, insensitive, maladroit, oppressive, overbearing, tactless, thoughtless, unsubtle.

**heavy-hearted** *adj* crushed, depressed, despondent, discouraged, disheartened, downcast, downhearted, forlorn, glum, heart-sick, heart-sore, melancholy, miserable, morose, mournful, sad, sorrowful.

*antonym* light-hearted.

**heckle** *v* bait, barrack, catcall, disrupt, gibe, interrupt, jeer, pester, shout down, taunt.

**hectic** *adj* animated, boisterous, chaotic, excited, fast, fevered, feverish, flurrying, flustering, frantic, frenetic, frenzied, furious, heated, rapid, riotous, rumbustious, tumultuous, turbulent, wild.

*antonym* leisurely.

**hector** *v* badger, bluster, boast, browbeat, bully, bullyrag, chivvy, harass, huff, intimidate, menace, nag, provoke, roister, threaten, worry.

**hedge** *n* barrier, boundary, compensation, counterbalance, dike, dyke, guard, hedgerow, insurance, protection, quickset, screen, wind-break.

*v* block, circumscribe, confine, cover, dodge, duck, equivocate, fortify, guard, hem in, hinder, insure, obstruct, protect, quibble, restrict, safeguard, shield, sidestep, stall, temporise, waffle.

**hedonism** *n* dolce vita, epicureanism, epicurism, gratification, luxuriousness, pleasure-seeking, self-indulgence, sensualism, sensuality, sybaritism, voluptuousness.

*antonym* asceticism.

**hedonist** *n* bon vivant, epicure, epicurean, pleasure-seeker, sensualist, swinger, sybarite, voluptuary.

*antonym* ascetic.

**hedonistic** *adj* epicurean, luxurious, pleasure-seeking, self-indulgent, swinging, sybaritic, voluptuous.

*antonyms* ascetic, austere.

**heed** *n* animadversion, attention, care, caution, consideration, ear, heedfulness, mind, note, notice, reck, regard, respect, thought, watchfulness.

*antonyms* inattention, indifference, unconcern.

*v* animadvert, attend, consider, follow, listen, mark, mind, note, obey, observe, regard, take notice of.

*antonyms* disregrad, ignore.

**heedful** *adj* attentive, careful, cautious, chary, circumspect, mindful, observant, prudent, regardful, vigilant, wary, watchful.

*antonym* heedless.

**heedless** *adj* careless, étourdi(e), foolhardy, imprudent, inattentive, incautious, incurious, inobservant, neglectful, negligent, oblivious, precipitate, rash, reckless, thoughtless, uncaring, unconcerned, unheedful, unheedy, unmindful, unobservant, unthinking.

*antonym* heedful.

**heel** *n* blackguard, bounder, cad, crust, end, hallux, hock, remainder, rotter, rump, scoundrel, spur, stub, stump, swine.

**hefty** *adj* ample, awkward, beefy, big, brawny, bulky, burly, colossal, cumbersome, forceful, heavy, hulking, husky, large, massive, muscular, ponderous, powerful, robust, solid, strapping, strong, substantial, thumping, tremendous, unwieldy, vigorous, weighty.

*antonyms* slight, small.

**height** *n* acme, altitude, apex, apogee, ceiling, celsitude, climax, crest, crown, culmination, degree, dignity, elevation, eminence, exaltation, extremity, grandeur, highness, hill, limit, loftiness, maximum, mountain, ne plus ultra, peak, pinnacle, prominence, stature, summit, tallness, top, ultimate, utmost, uttermost, vertex, zenith.

*antonym* depth.

**heighten** *v* add to, aggrandise, aggravate, amplify, augment, elevate, enhance, ennoble, exalt, greaten, improve, increase, intensify, magnify, raise, sharpen, strengthen, uplift.

*antonyms* decrease, diminish.

**heinous** *adj* abhorrent, abominable, atrocious, awful, evil, execrable, facinorous, flagrant, grave, hateful, hideous, immitigable, infamous, iniquitous, monstrous, nefarious, odious, outrageous, revolting, shocking, unspeakable, vicious, villainous.

**heir** *n* beneficiary, co-heir, heiress, heritor, inheritor, inheritress, inheritrix, parcener, scion, successor.

**hell** *n* Abaddon, abyss, Acheron, affliction, agony, anguish, Erebus, Gehenna, Hades, hellfire, infernal regions, inferno, lower regions, Malebolge, martyrdom, misery, nether world, nightmare, ordeal, suffering, Tartarus, Tophet, torment, trial, underworld, wretchedness.

*antonym* heaven.

**hell-bent** *adj* bent, determined, dogged, fixed, inflexible, intent, intransigent, obdurate, resolved, set, settled, tenacious, unhesitating, unwavering.

**hellish** *adj* abominable, accursed, atrocious, barbarous, cruel, damnable, damned, demoniacal, detestable, devilish, diabolical, execrable, fiendish, infernal, inhuman, monstrous, nefarious, Stygian, sulphurous, vicious, wicked.

*antonym* heavenly.

**helm** *n* command, control, direction, driving seat, leadership, reins, rudder, rule, saddle, tiller, wheel.

**hello** *interj* chin-chin, ciao, hail, hi, hiya, how-do-you-do, howdy, salve, what cheer, wotcher.

*antonym* good-bye.

**help**[1] *v* abet, abstain, aid, alleviate, ameliorate, assist, avoid, back, befriend, bestead, control, co-operate, cure, ease, eschew, facilitate, forbear, heal, hinder, improve, keep from, lend a hand, mitigate, prevent, promote, rally round, refrain from, relieve, remedy, resist, restore, save, second, serve, shun, stand by, succour, support, withstand.

*antonym* hinder.

*n* adjuvant, advice, aid, aidance, assistance, avail, benefit, co-operation, guidance, leg up, service, support, use, utility.

*antonym* hindrance.

**help**[2] *n* assistant, daily, employee, hand, helper, worker.

**helper** *n* abettor, adjutant, aide, aider, ally, assistant, attendant, auxiliary, coadjutor, collaborator, colleague, deputy, girl Friday, helpmate, man Friday, mate, PA, partner, person Friday, right-hand man, Samaritan, second, subsidiary, supporter.

**helpful** *adj* accommodating, adjuvant, advantageous, beneficent, beneficial, benevolent, caring, considerate, constructive, co-operative, favourable, fortunate, friendly, furthersome, kind, neighbourly, practical, productive, profitable, serviceable, supportive, sympathetic, timely, useful.

*antonyms* futile, useless, worthless.

**helping** *n* amount, dollop, piece, plateful, portion, ration, serving, share.

**helpless** *adj* abandoned, adynamic, aidless, debilitated, defenceless, dependent, destitute, disabled, exposed, feeble, forlorn, friendless, impotent, incapable, incompetent, infirm, paralysed, powerless, unfit, unprotected, vulnerable, weak.

*antonyms* competent, enterprising, independent resourceful, strong.

**helpmate** *n* assistant, associate, better half companion, consort, helper, helpmeet, husband other half, partner, spouse, support, wife.

**helter-skelter** *adv* carelessly, confusedly, hastily headlong, hurriedly, impulsively, pell-mell, rashly recklessly, wildly.

*adj* anyhow, confused, disordered, disorganised, haphazard, higgledy-piggledy, hit-or-miss, jumbled, muddled, random, topsy-turvy, unsystematic.

**hem** *n* border, edge, fringe, margin, skirt, trimming.

*v* beset, border, circumscribe, confine, edge, enclose, engird, environ, fimbriate, gird, hedge, restrict, skirt, surround.

**hence** *adv* accordingly, ergo, therefore, thus.

**henceforth** *adv* hence, henceforward, hereafter, hereinafter.

**henchman** *n* aide, associate, attendant, bodyguard, cohort, crony, follower, gallo(w)glass, heavy, heeler, house-carl, jackal, led captain, minder, minion, myrmidon, right-hand man, running dog, satellite, sidekick, subordinate, supporter.

**henpeck** *v* badger, browbeat, bully, carp, cavil, chide, chivvy, criticise, domineer, find fault, harass, hector, intimidate, nag, niggle, pester, scold, torment.

**henpecked** *adj* browbeaten, bullied, cringing, dominated, intimidated, meek, subject, subjugated, timid.

*antonym* dominant.

**herald** *n* courier, crier, forerunner, harbinger, indication, messenger, omen, precursor, sign, signal, token, vaunt-courier.

*v* advertise, announce, broadcast, forebode, foretoken, harbinger, indicate, pave the way, portend, precede, presage, proclaim, prognosticate, promise, publicise, publish, show, trumpet, usher in.

**heraldry** *n* arms, badge, blazonry, crest, emblazonry, emblem, ensign, (e)scutcheon, hatchment, insignia, pageantry, regalia.

**herculean** *adj* arduous, athletic, brawny, colossal, daunting, demanding, difficult, enormous, exacting, exhausting, formidable, gigantic, great, gruelling, hard, heavy, huge, husky, laborious, large, mammoth, massive, mighty, muscular, onerous, powerful, prodigious, rugged, sinewy, stalwart, strapping, strenuous, strong, sturdy, titanic, toilsome, tough, tremendous.

**herd** *n* assemblage, canaille, collection, cowherd, crowd, crush, drove, flock, herdboy, herdsman, horde, mass, mob, multitude, populace, press, rabble, riff-raff, shepherd, swarm, the hoi polloi, the masses, the plebs, throng, vulgus.

*v* assemble, associate, collect, congregate, drive, flock, force, gather, goad, guard, guide, huddle, lead, muster, protect, rally, shepherd, spur, watch.

**herdsman** *n* cowherd, cowman, drover, grazier, stockman, vaquero, wrangler.

**here and there** from pillar to post, hither and thither, passim, sporadically, to and fro.

**hereafter** adv eventually, hence, henceforth, henceforward, in future, later.
n after-life, Elysian fields, happy hunting-ground, heaven, life after death, next world.

**hereditary** adj ancestral, bequeathed, congenital, family, genetic, handed down, inborn, inbred, inheritable, inherited, patrimonial, traditional, transmissible, transmittable, transmitted, willed.

**heresy** n apostasy, dissidence, error, free-thinking, heterodoxy, iconoclasm, impiety, revisionism, schism, unorthodoxy.
antonym orthodoxy.

**heretic** n apostate, dissenter, dissident, free-thinker, nonconformist, renegade, revisionist, schismatic, sectarian, separatist.
antonym conformist.

**heretical** adj free-thinking, heterodox, iconoclastic, idolatrous, impious, infidel, irreverent, rationalistic, revisionist, schismatic.
antonyms conformist, conventional, orthodox.

**heritage** n bequest, birthright, deserts, due, endowment, estate, history, inheritance, legacy, lot, past, patrimony, portion, record, share, tradition.

**hermetic** adj airtight, hermetical, sealed, shut, watertight.

**hermit** n anchoret, anchorite, ascetic, eremite, monk, recluse, solitaire, solitarian, solitary, stylite.

**hero** n celebrity, champion, conqueror, exemplar, goody, heart-throb, idol, male lead, paragon, protagonist, star, superstar, victor.

**heroic** adj bold, brave, classic, classical, courageous, daring, dauntless, doughty, elevated, epic, exaggerated, extravagant, fearless, gallant, game, grand, grandiose, gritty, high-flown, Homeric, inflated, intrepid, legendary, lion-hearted, mythological, spunky, stout-hearted, undaunted, valiant, valorous.
antonyms cowardly, pusillanimous, timid.

**heroin** n horse, shit, smack.

**heroine** n celebrity, female lead, goddess, ideal, idol, protagonist, star, superstar.

**heroism** n boldness, bravery, courage, courageousness, daring, derring-do, fearlessness, fortitude, gallantry, gameness, grit, intrepidity, prowess, spirit, valour.
antonyms cowardice, pusillanimity, timidity.

**hero-worship** n admiration, adoration, adulation, deification, idealisation, idolisation, veneration.

**hesitancy** n demur, disinclination, doubt, doubtfulness, dubiousness, dubitance, dubitation, indecision, irresolution, misgiving, qualm, reluctance, reservation, swithering, uncertainty, unwillingness, wavering.
antonyms certainty, willingness.

**hesitant** adj diffident, dilatory, doubtful, half-hearted, halting, hesitating, hesitative, hesitatory, irresolute, reluctant, sceptical, shy, swithering, timid, uncertain, unsure, vacillating, wavering.
antonyms resolute, staunch.

**hesitate** v balk, be reluctant, be uncertain, be unwilling, boggle, delay, demur, dither, doubt, dubitate, falter, fumble, halt, haver, pause, scruple, shillyshally, shrink from, stammer, stumble, stutter, swither, think twice, vacillate, wait, waver.

**hesitation** n delay, demurral, doubt, dubiety, faltering, fumbling, hesitancy, indecision, irresolution, misdoubt, misgiving(s), qualm(s), reluctance, scruple(s), second thought(s), stammering, stumbling, stuttering, swithering, uncertainty, unwillingness, vacillation.
antonyms alacrity, assurance, eagerness.

**heterodox** adj dissident, free-thinking, heretical, iconoclastic, revisionist, schismatic, unorthodox, unsound.
antonym orthodox.

**heterogeneous** adj assorted, catholic, contrary, contrasted, different, discrepant, disparate, dissimilar, divergent, diverse, diversified, incongruous, miscellaneous, mixed, motley, multiform, opposed, polymorphic, unlike, unrelated, varied.
antonym homogeneous.

**hew** v axe, carve, chop, cut, fashion, fell, form, hack, lop, make, model, sculpt, sculpture, sever, shape, smooth, split.

**heyday** n bloom, boom time, florescence, floruit, flower, flowering, golden age, pink, prime, salad days, vigour.

**hiatus** n aperture, blank, breach, break, chasm, discontinuance, discontinuity, gap, interruption, interval, lacuna, lapse, opening, rift, space, void.

**hidden** adj abstruse, cabbalistic(al), clandestine, close, concealed, covered, covert, cryptic, dark, de(a)rn, delitescent, doggo, hermetic, hermetical, latent, mysterious, mystic, mystical, obscure, occult, recondite, secret, shrouded, ulterior, unapparent, unseen, veiled.
antonyms open, showing.

**hide¹** v abscond, bury, cache, camouflage, cloak, conceal, cover, disguise, earth, eclipse, ensconce, feal, go to ground, go underground, hole up, keep dark, lie low, mask, obscure, occult, screen, secrete, shadow, shelter, shroud, stash, suppress, take cover, tappice, veil, withhold.
antonyms display, reveal, show.

**hide²** n deacon, fell, flaught, nebris, pelt, skin.

**hide-away** n cloister, haven, hideout, hiding-place, nest, refuge, retreat, sanctuary.

**hidebound** adj conventional, entrenched, narrow, narrow-minded, rigid, set, set in one's ways, strait-laced, ultra-conservative, unprogressive.
antonyms liberal, unconventional.

**hideous** adj abominable, appalling, awful, detestable, disgusting, dreadful, frightful, gash, gashful, gashly, ghastly, grim, grisly, grotesque, gruesome, horrendous, horrible, horrid, loathsome, macabre, monstrous, odious, repulsive, revolting, shocking, sickening, terrible, terrifying, ugly, ugsome, unsightly.
antonym beautiful.

**hideout** n den, hide-away, hiding-place, hole, lair, retreat, shelter.

**hiding**[1] n beating, caning, drubbing, flogging, hammering, larruping, lathering, leathering, licking, spanking, tanning, thrashing, walloping, whaling, whipping.

**hiding**[2] n camouflage, concealment, de(a)rn, disguise, screening, secretion, veiling.

**hiding-place** n den, haven, hide-away, hideout, hole, lair, lurking-place, mew, priest hole, refuge, retreat, sanctuary, starting-hole, stash.

**hierarchy** n echelons, grading, peck(ing) order, ranking, scale, strata.

**higgledy-piggledy** adv any old how, anyhow, confusedly, haphazardly, helter-skelter, indiscriminately, pell-mell, topsy-turvy.

adj confused, disorderly, disorganised, haphazard, indiscriminate, jumbled, muddled, topsy-turvy.

**high** adj acute, altissimo, alto, arch, arrogant, boastful, boisterous, bouncy, bragging, capital, cheerful, chief, consequential, costly, dear, delirious, despotic, distinguished, domineering, elated, elevated, eminent, euphoric, exalted, excessive, excited, exhilarated, exorbitant, expensive, extraordinary, extravagant, extreme, exuberant, freaked out, gamy, grand, grave, great, haughty, high-pitched, important, inebriated, influential, intensified, intoxicated, joyful, lavish, leading, light-hearted, lofty, lordly, luxurious, merry, mountain(s)-high, niffy, orthian, ostentatious, overbearing, penetrating, piercing, piping, pongy, powerful, prominent, proud, rich, ruling, serious, sharp, shrill, significant, soaring, soprano, spaced out, steep, stiff, stoned, strident, strong, superior, tainted, tall, towering, treble, tripping, tumultuous, turbulent, tyrannical, vainglorious, whiffy.

antonyms deep, low, lowly, short.

n apex, apogee, delirium, ecstasy, euphoria, height, intoxication, level, peak, record, summit, top, trip, zenith.

antonyms low, nadir.

**high and dry** abandoned, bereft, destitute, helpless, marooned, stranded.

**high and mighty** arrogant, cavalier, conceited, disdainful, haughty, imperious, overbearing, overweening, self-important, snobbish, stuck-up, superior.

**high society** aristocracy, beautiful people, crème de la crème, éite, gentry, grand monde, haut monde, jet set, nobility, upper crust.

antonym hoi polloi.

**high spirits** boisterousness, bounce, buoyancy, exhilaration, exuberance, good cheer, hilarity, joie de vivre, liveliness, sparkle, vivacity.

**high-born** adj aristocratic, blue-blooded, gentle, noble, patrician, pedigreed, thoroughbred, well-born, well-connected.

**highbrow** n aesthete, boffin, Brahmin, brain, egghead, intellectual, long-hair, mandarin, mastermind, savant, scholar.

adj bookish, brainy, cultivated, cultured, deep, intellectual, long-haired, serious, sophisticated.

antonym lowbrow.

**high-class** adj A1, choice, classy, de luxe, elite, exclusive, first-rate, high-quality, posh, quality, select, superior, tiptop, top-flight, tops, U, upper class.

antonyms mediocre, ordinary.

**highest** adj apical, apogaeic, peak, record, top, topmost, upmost, uppermost, zenithal.

antonyms bottom(most), lowest.

**high-falutin(g)** adj affected, big, bombastic, florid, grandiose, high-flown, high-sounding, la(h)-di-da(h), lofty, magniloquent, pompous, pretentious, supercilious, swanky.

**high-flown** adj elaborate, elevated, exaggerated, extravagant, florid, grandiose, high-falutin(g), inflated, la(h)-di-da(h), lofty, magniloquent, overblown, pretentious, turgid.

**high-handed** adj arbitrary, autocratic, bossy, despotic, dictatorial, discourteous, disdainful, domineering, imperious, inconsiderate, oppressive, overbearing, peremptory, self-willed, tyrannical, wilful.

**highlight** n best, climax, cream, feature, focal point, focus, high point, high spot, peak, zenith.

v accent, accentuate, emphasise, feature, focus on, illuminate, play up, point up, set off, show up, spotlight, stress, underline.

**highly** adv appreciatively, approvingly, considerably, decidedly, eminently, enthusiastically, exceptionally, extraordinarily, extremely, favourably, greatly, immensely, supremely, tremendously, vastly, very, warmly, well.

**highly-strung** adj edgy, excitable, irascible, irritable, jittery, nervous, nervy, neurotic, restless, sensitive, skittish, stressed, taut, temperamental, tense.

antonyms calm, relaxed.

**high-minded** adj elevated, ethical, fair, good, honourable, idealistic, lofty, magnanimous, moral, noble, principled, pure, righteous, scrupulous, upright, virtuous, worthy.

antonyms immoral, unscrupulous.

**high-powered** adj aggressive, driving, dynamic, effective, energetic, enterprising, forceful, go-ahead, go-getting, industrious, vigorous.

**high-priced** adj costly, dear, excessive, exorbitant, expensive, extortionate, high, pricy, steep, stiff, unreasonable.

antonym cheap.

**high-quality** adj blue-chip, choice, classy, de luxe, gilt-edged, quality, select, superior, tiptop, top-class.

**high-sounding** adj affected, artificial, bombastic, extravagant, flamboyant, florid, grandiloquent, grandiose, high-flown, magniloquent, orotund, ostentatious, overblown, pompous, ponderous, pretentious, stilted, strained.

**high-spirited** adj animated, boisterous, bold, bouncy, daring, dashing, ebullient, effervescent, energetic, exuberant, frolicsome, lively, mettlesome, peppy, sparkling, spirited, spunky, vibrant, vital, vivacious.

antonyms downcast, glum.

**highwayman** n bandit, bandolero, footpad, knight of the road, land-pirate, rank-rider, robber.

**hijack** v commandeer, expropriate, kidnap, seize, skyjack, snatch, steal.

**hike** v back-pack, footslog, hoof it, leg it, plod, ramble, tramp, treck, trudge, walk.

n march, plod, ramble, tramp, trek, trudge, walk.

**hilarious** adj amusing, comical, convivial, entertaining, funny, gay, happy, humorous, hysterical, jolly, jovial, joyful, joyous, killing, merry, mirthful, noisy, rollicking, side-splitting, uproarious.

antonyms grave, serious.

**hilarity** n amusement, boisterousness, cheerfulness, conviviality, entertainment, exhilaration, exuberance, frivolity, gaiety, glee, high spirits, jollification, jollity, joviality, joyousness, laughter, levity, merriment, mirth, uproariousness.

antonyms gravity, seriousness.

**hill** n acclivity, berg, brae, butte, climb, dod, down, drift, elevation, eminence, fell, gradient, heap, height, hillock, hilltop, how, hummock, incline, knoll, knowe, kop, koppie, law, mamelon, mesa, mound, mount, pike, pile, prominence, rise, slope, stack, tor.

**hillock** n barrow, dune, hummock, knap, knoll, knowe, monticulus, mote, motte, mound, tump.

**hilt** n grip, haft, handgrip, handle, heft, helve.

**hind** adj after, back, caudal, hinder, posterior, rear, tail.

antonym fore.

**hinder** v arrest, check, counteract, debar, delay, deter, embar, encumber, forelay, frustrate, hamper, hamstring, handicap, hold back, hold up, impede, interrupt, obstruct, oppose, prevent, retard, slow down, stop, stymie, thwart, trammel.

antonyms aid, assist, help.

**hindmost** adj concluding, endmost, final, furthest, lag, last, rearmost, remotest, tail, terminal, trailing, ultimate.

antonym foremost.

**hindrance** n bar, barrier, check, demurrage, deterrent, difficulty, drag, drawback, encumbrance, handicap, hitch, impediment, interruption, limitation, obstacle, obstruction, pull-back, remora, restraint, restriction, snag, stoppage, stumbling-block, trammel.

antonyms aid, assistance, help.

**hinge** v be contingent, centre, depend, hang, pivot, rest, revolve around, turn.

n articulation, condition, foundation, garnet, joint, premise, principle.

**hint** n advice, allusion, breath, clue, dash, help, implication, indication, inkling, innuendo, insinuation, intimation, mention, pointer, reminder, scintilla, sign, signal, soupçon, speck, subindication, suggestion, suspicion, taste, tinge, tip, tip-off, touch, trace, undertone, whiff, whisper, wrinkle.

v allude, imply, indicate, inkle, innuendo, insinuate, intimate, mention, prompt, subindicate, suggest, tip off.

**hinterland** n back-blocks, back-country, backveld, hinderland, interior.

**hip** n buttocks, croup, haunch, hindquarters, huck, huckle, loin, pelvis, posterior, rump.

**hippy** n beatnik, bohemian, drop-out, flower child, hippie.

**hire** v appoint, book, charter, commission, employ, engage, lease, let, rent, reserve, retain, sign up, take on.

antonyms dismiss, fire.

n charge, cost, fare, fee, price, rent, rental, toll.

**hire-purchase** n easy terms, never-never.

**hirsute** adj bearded, bewhiskered, bristly, crinigerous, crinite, crinose, hairy, hispid, shaggy, unshaven.

antonyms bald, hairless.

**hiss** n boo, buzz, catcall, contempt, derision, hissing, hoot, jeer, mockery, raspberry, sibilance, sibilation, whistle.

v boo, catcall, condemn, damn, decry, deride, hoot, jeer, mock, rasp, revile, ridicule, shrill, sibilate, siffle, wheeze, whirr, whiss, whistle, whiz.

**historic** adj celebrated, consequential, epoch-making, extraordinary, famed, famous, momentous, notable, outstanding, red-letter, remarkable, renowned, significant.

**historical** adj actual, archival, attested, authentic, documented, factual, real, traditional, verifiable.

**history** n account, annals, antecedents, antiquity, autobiography, biography, chronicle, chronology, days of old, days of yore, genealogy, memoirs, narration, narrative, olden days, recapitulation, recital, record, relation, saga, story, tale, the past.

**histrionic** adj affected, artificial, bogus, dramatic, forced, ham, insincere, melodramatic, ranting, sensational, theatrical, unnatural.

**histrionics** n dramatics, overacting, performance, ranting and raving, scene, staginess, tantrums, temperament, theatricality.

**hit** v accomplish, achieve, affect, arrive at, attain, bang, bash, batter, bean, beat, belt, bump, clip, clobber, clock, clonk, clout, collide with, crown, cuff, damage, devastate, flog, frap, fustigate, gain, impinge on, influence, knock, lob, move, overwhelm, prop, punch, reach, secure, slap, slog, slosh, slug, smack, smash, smite, sock, strike, swat, thump, touch, volley, wallop, whack, wham, whap, w(h)op, wipe.

n blow, bump, clash, clout, collision, cuff, impact, knock, rap, sell-out, sensation, shot, slap, slog, slosh, smack, smash, sock, stroke, success, swipe, triumph, venue, wallop, winner.

**hit back** recalcitrate, reciprocate, retaliate.

**hit on** arrive at, chance on, contrive, discover, guess, invent, light on, realise, stumble on.

**hit out** assail, attack, castigate, condemn, criticise, denounce, inveigh, lash, lay about one, rail.

**hitch** v attach, connect, couple, fasten, harness, heave, hike (up), hitch-hike, hoi(c)k, hoist, jerk, join, pull, tether, thumb a lift, tie, tug, unite, yank, yoke.

antonyms unfasten, unhitch.

*n* catch, check, delay, difficulty, drawback, hiccup, hindrance, hold-up, impediment, mishap, problem, snag, stick, stoppage, trouble.

**hitherto** *adv* beforehand, heretofore, previously, so far, thus far, till now, until now, up to now.

**hit-or-miss** *adj* aimless, apathetic, casual, cursory, disorganised, haphazard, indiscriminate, lackadaisical, perfunctory, random, undirected, uneven.

**hoard** *n* accumulation, cache, fund, heap, mass, pile, profusion, reserve, reservoir, stockpile, store, supply, treasure-trove.

*v* accumulate, amass, cache, coffer, collect, deposit, garner, gather, hive, husband, lay up, put by, reposit, save, stash away, stockpile, store, treasure.

*antonyms* spend, squander, use.

**hoarder** *n* collector, gatherer, magpie, miser, niggard, squirrel.

**hoarse** *adj* croaky, discordant, grating, gravelly, growling, gruff, guttural, harsh, husky, rasping, raspy, raucous, rough, throaty.

*antonyms* clear, smooth.

**hoary** *adj* aged, ancient, antiquated, antique, canescent, frosty, grey, grey-haired, grizzled, hoar, old, senescent, silvery, venerable, white, white-haired.

**hoax** *n* bam, cheat, cod, con, deception, fast one, fraud, grift, hum, huntiegowk, hunt-the-gowk, imposture, joke, josh, leg-pull, practical joke, prank, put-on, quiz, ruse, spoof, string, swindle, trick.

*v* bam, bamboozle, befool, bluff, cod, con, deceive, delude, dupe, fool, gammon, gull, have on, hoodwink, hornswoggle, hum, lead on, pull someone's leg, spoof, string, stuff, swindle, take for a ride, trick.

**hoaxer** *n* bamboozler, grifter, hoodwinker, humbug, joker, mystifier, practical joker, prankster, quiz, quizzer, spoofer, trickster.

**hobble** *v* clog, dodder, falter, fasten, fetter, halt, hamshackle, hamstring, hirple, limp, restrict, shackle, shamble, shuffle, stagger, stumble, tie, totter.

**hobby** *n* avocation, diversion, pastime, pursuit, recreation, relaxation, sideline.

**hobgoblin** *n* apparition, bog(e)y, bugaboo, bugbear, buggan(e), buggin, goblin, hob, imp, spectre, spirit, sprite.

**hobnob** *v* associate, consort, fraternise, hang about, keep company, mingle, mix, pal around, socialise.

**hocus-pocus** *n* abracadabra, artifice, cant, cheat, chicanery, conjuring, deceit, deception, delusion, finesse, gibberish, gobbledegook, hoax, humbug, imposture, jargon, jugglery, legerdemain, mumbo-jumbo, nonsense, prestidigitation, rigmarole, sleight of hand, swindle, trickery, trompe-l'oeil.

**hogwash** *n* balderdash, bilge, bunk, bunkum, claptrap, drivel, eyewash, hooey, nonsense, piffle, rot, rubbish, tar(r)adiddle, tosh, trash, tripe, twaddle.

**hoi polloi** *n* admass, canaille, citizenry, commonalty, riff-raff, the common people, the great unwashed, the herd, the masses, the plebs, the populace, the proles, the proletariat, the rabble, the third estate.

*antonyms* aristocracy, élite, nobility.

**hoist** *v* elevate, erect, heave, jack up, lift, raise, rear, uplift, upraise.

*n* crane, davit, elevator, jack, lift, tackle, winch.

**hoity-toity** *adj* arrogant, conceited, disdainful, haughty, high and mighty, lofty, overweening, pompous, proud, scornful, snobbish, snooty, stuck-up, supercilious, toffee-nosed, uppish, uppity.

**hold** *v* accommodate, account, adhere, apply, arrest, assemble, assume, be in force, be the case, bear, believe, bond, brace, call, carry, carry on, celebrate, check, clasp, cleave, clinch, cling, clip, clutch, comprise, conduct, confine, consider, contain, continue, convene, cradle, curb, deem, delay, detain, embrace, endure, enfold, entertain, esteem, exist, grasp, grip, have, hold good, imprison, judge, keep, last, maintain, occupy, operate, own, persevere, persist, possess, preside over, presume, prop, reckon, regard, remain, remain true, remain valid, resist, restrain, retain, run, seat, shoulder, solemnise, stand up, stay, stick, stop, summon, support, suspend, sustain, take, think, view, wear.

*n* anchorage, asendancy, authority, clasp, clout, clutch, control, dominance, dominion, foothold, footing, grasp, grip, holt, influence, leverage, mastery, prop, pull, purchase, stay, support, sway, vantage.

**hold back** check, control, curb, desist, forbear, inhibit, refuse, repress, restrain, retain, stifle, suppress, withhold.

*antonym* release.

**hold forth** declaim, descant, discourse, go on, harangue, lecture, orate, preach, sermonise, speak, speechify, spiel, spout.

**hold off** avoid, defer, delay, fend off, keep off, postpone, put off, rebuff, refrain, repel, repulse, stave off, wait.

**hold out** continue, endure, extend, give, hang on, last, offer, persevere, persist, porrect, present, proffer, stand fast.

**hold over** adjourn, defer, delay, postpone, put off, shelve, suspend.

**hold up** brace, delay, detain, display, endure, exhibit, hinder, impede, last, lift, present, raise, retard, show, slow, stop, survive, sustain, waylay, wear.

**hold water** bear scrutiny, convince, make sense, pass the test, ring true, wash, work.

**hold with** accept, agree to, approve of, countenance, go along with, subscribe to, support.

**holder** *n* bearer, case, container, cover, cradle, custodian, housing, incumbent, keeper, occupant, owner, possessor, proprietor, purchaser, receptacle, rest, sheath, stand.

**holdings** *n* assets, bonds, estate, investments, land, possessions, property, real estate, resources, securities, shares, stocks.

**hold-up**[1] *n* bottle-neck, delay, difficulty, gridlock, hitch, obstruction, setback, snag, stoppage, (traffic) jam, trouble, wait.

**hold-up**[2] *n* heist, robbery, stick-up.

**hole** *n* aperture, breach, break, burrow, cave, cavern, cavity, chamber, covert, crack, defect, den, depression, dilemma, dimple, discrepancy, dive, dump, earth, error, excavation, eyelet, fallacy, fault, fissure, fix, flaw, foramen, fovea, gap, hollow, hovel, imbroglio, inconsistency, jam, joint, lair, loophole, mess, nest, opening, orifice, outlet, perforation, pit, pocket, pore, predicament, puncture, quandary, rent, retreat, scoop, scrape, shaft, shelter, slum, split, spot, tangle, tear, tight spot, vent, ventage.

**hole-and-corner** *adj* back-door, backstairs, back-stairs, clandestine, covert, furtive, hugger-mugger, hush-hush, secret, secretive, sneaky, stealthy, surreptitious, underhand, under-the-counter.

*antonyms* open, public.

**holiday** *n* anniversary, break, celebration, exeat, feast, festival, festivity, fête, furlough, gala, hols, leave, recess, respite, rest, sabbatical, saint's day, time off, vacation.

**holier-than-thou** *adj* complacent, goody-goody, pietistic(al), pious, priggish, religiose, sanctimonious, self-approving, self-righteous, self-satisfied, smug, unctuous.

*antonyms* humble, meek.

**holiness** *n* blessedness, devoutness, divinity, evangelicism, godliness, halidom, pietism, piety, priggishness, purity, religiosity, religiousness, righteousness, sacredness, saintliness, sanctimoniousness, sanctity, self-righteousness, spirituality, unctuosity, unctuousness, virtuousness.

*antonyms* impiety, wickedness.

**holler** *n, v* bawl, bellow, call, cheer, clamour, cry, hail, halloo, hollo, howl, hurrah, huzzah, roar, shout, shriek, whoop, yell, yelp, yowl.

**hollow** *adj* artificial, cavernous, concave, coreless, cynical, deaf, deceitful, deceptive, deep, deep-set, depressed, dished, dull, empty, expressionless, faithless, false, famished, flat, fleeting, flimsy, fruitless, futile, gaunt, glenoid(al), hungry, hypocritical, indented, insincere, lantern-jawed, low, meaningless, muffled, muted, pointless, Pyrrhic, ravenous, reverberant, rumbling, sepulchral, specious, starved, sunken, toneless, treacherous, unavailing, unfilled, unreal, unreliable, unsound, useless, vacant, vain, void, weak, worthless.

*n* basin, bottom, bowl, cave, cavern, cavity, channel, concave, concavity, coomb, crater, cup, dale, dell, den, dent, depression, dimple, dingle, dint, dish, druse, excavation, fossa, fossula, fovea, foveola, foveole, geode, gilgie, glen, gnamma hole, groove, hole, hope, how(e), indentation, invagination, pit, trough, umbilicus, vacuity, valley, vlei, well, womb.

*v* burrow, channel, dent, dig, dint, dish, excavate, furrow, gouge, groove, indent, pit, scoop.

**holocaust** *n* annihilation, carnage, conflagration, destruction, devastation, extermination, extinction, flames, genocide, hecatomb, immolation, inferno, mass murder, massacre, pogrom, sacrifice, slaughter.

**holy** *adj* blessed, consecrated, dedicated, devout, divine, evangelical, evangelistic, faithful, god-fearing, godly, good, hallowed, perfect, pietistic, pious, pure, religiose, religious, righteous, sacred, sacrosanct, saintly, sanctified, sanctimonious, spiritual, sublime, unctuous, venerable, venerated, virtuous.

*antonyms* impious, unsanctified, wicked.

**homage** *n* acknowledgement, admiration, adoration, adulation, allegiance, awe, deference, devotion, duty, esteem, faithfulness, fealty, fidelity, honour, loyalty, obeisance, praise, recognition, regard, respect, reverence, service, tribute, veneration, worship.

**home** *n* abode, almshouse, asylum, birthplace, blighty, clinic, domicile, dwelling, dwelling-place, element, environment, family, fireside, habitat, habitation, haunt, hearth, home ground, home town, homestead, hospice, hospital, house, household, institution, native heath, nest, nursing-home, old people's home, pad, pied-à-terre, range, residence, roof, sanatorium, stamping-ground, territory.

*adj* candid, central, direct, domestic, domiciliary, familiar, family, household, incisive, inland, internal, intimate, local, national, native, penetrating, plain, pointed, unanswerable, uncomfortable, wounding.

**homeland** *n* fatherland, mother country, motherland, native country, native heath, native land, native soil.

**homeless** *adj* abandoned, destitute, disinherited, displaced, dispossessed, down-and-out, exiled, forlorn, forsaken, houseless, itinerant, outcast, unsettled, vagabond, wandering.

*n* derelicts, dossers, down-and-outs, nomads, squatters, tramps, travellers, vagrants.

**homely** *adj* comfortable, comfy, congenial, cosy, domestic, easy, everyday, familiar, folksy, friendly, gemütlich, homelike, homespun, hom(e)y, informal, intimate, modest, natural, ordinary, plain, relaxed, simple, snug, unaffected, unassuming, unpretentious, unsophisticated, welcoming.

*antonyms* formal, unfamiliar.

**Homeric** *adj* epic, grand, heroic, imposing, impressive, Virgilian.

**homesickness** *n* Heimweh, mal du pays, nostalgia, nostomania.

*antonym* wanderlust.

**homespun** *adj* amateurish, artless, coarse, crude, folksy, homely, home-made, inelegant, plain, rough, rude, rustic, unpolished, unrefined, unsophisticated.

*antonym* sophisticated.

**homicidal** *adj* blood-thirsty, deadly, death-dealing, lethal, maniacal, mortal, murderous, sanguinary, violent.

**homicide** *n* assassin, assassination, bloodshed, cut-throat, killer, killing, liquidator, manslaughter, murder, murderer, slayer, slaying.

**homily** *n* address, discourse, harangue, heart-to-heart, lecture, postil, preachment, sermon, spiel, talk.

**homogeneity** *n* agreement, akinness, analogousness, comparability, consistency, consonancy, correspondence, identicalness, likeness, oneness, resemblance, sameness, similarity, similitude, uniformity.

*antonyms* difference, disagreement.

**homogeneous** *adj* akin, alike, analogous, cognate, comparable, consistent, consonant, harmonious, identical, indiscrete, kindred, of a piece, similar, uniform, unvarying.

*antonym* different.

**homologous** *adj* analogous, comparable, correspondent, corresponding, equivalent, like, matching, parallel, related, similar.

*antonyms* different, dissimilar.

**homosexual** *n* catamite, dike, dyke, fag, fairy, fruit, Ganymede, gunsel, homophile, invert, les, lesbian, lez, Nancy, paederast, poof, pooftah, poove, puff, punk, queen, queer, rent-boy, sapphist, tribade, urning.

*antonyms* heterosexual, straight.

*adj* bent, camp, dikey, dykey, fruity, gay, homoerotic, lesbian, paederastic, poofy, poovy, queer, sapphic.

*antonyms* heterosexual, straight.

**homosexuality** *n* gayness, homoeroticism, homoerotism, homosexualism, paederasty, poovery, queerdom, sapphism, tribadism, tribady.

*antonym* heterosexuality.

**hone** *v* edge, file, grind, point, polish, rasp, sharpen, strop, whet.

**honest** *adj* above-board, authentic, bona fide, candid, chaste, conscientious, decent, direct, equitable, ethical, fair, fair and square, forthright, four-square, frank, genuine, high-minded, honourable, humble, impartial, ingenuous, jake, just, law-abiding, legitimate, modest, objective, on the level, open, outright, outspoken, plain, plain-hearted, proper, real, reliable, reputable, respectable, scrupulous, seemly, simple, sincere, soothfast, square, straight, straightforward, true, trustworthy, trusty, truthful, undisguised, unequivocal, unfeigned, unreserved, upright, veracious, virtuous, well-gotten, well-won, white.

*antonyms* covert, devious, dishonest, dishonourable.

**honestly** *adv* by fair means, candidly, cleanly, conscientiously, directly, dispassionately, equitably, ethically, fairly, frankly, honourably, in all sincerity, in good faith, justly, lawfully, legally, legitimately, objectively, on the level, openly, outright, plainly, really, scrupulously, sincerely, straight, straight out, truly, truthfully, undisguisedly, unreservedly, uprightly, verily.

*antonyms* dishonestly, dishonourably.

**honesty** *n* artlessness, bluntness, candour, equity, even-handedness, explicitness, fairness, faithfulness, fidelity, frankness, genuineness, honour, incorruptibility, integrity, justness, morality, objectivity, openness, outspokenness, plain-heartedness, plainness, plain-speaking, probity, rectitude, reputability, scrupulousness, sincerity, sooth, squareness, straightforwardness, straightness, trustworthiness, truthfulness, unreserve, uprightness, veracity, verity, virtue.

*antonyms* deviousness, dishonesty.

**honorary** *adj* complimentary, ex officio, formal, honorific, honoris causa, in name only, nominal, titular, unofficial, unpaid, virtute officii.

*antonyms* gainful, paid, salaried, waged.

**honour** *n* acclaim, accolade, acknowledgement, admiration, adoration, chastity, commendation, compliment, credit, decency, deference, dignity, distinction, duty, elevation, esteem, fairness, favour, good name, goodness, homage, honesty, honorificabilitudinity, honourableness, innocence, integrity, kudos, laudation, laurels, loyalty, modesty, morality, pleasure, praise, principles, privilege, probity, purity, rank, recognition, rectitude, regard, renown, reputation, repute, respect, reverence, righteousness, self-respect, tribute, trust, trustworthiness, uprightness, veneration, virginity, virtue, worship.

*antonyms* disgrace, dishonour, obloquy.

*v* accept, acclaim, acknowledge, admire, adore, applaud, appreciate, carry out, cash, celebrate, clear, commemorate, commend, compliment, credit, crown, decorate, dignify, discharge, esteem, exalt, execute, fulfil, glorify, hallow, homage, keep, laud, laureate, lionise, observe, pass, pay, pay homage, perform, praise, prize, remember, respect, revere, reverence, take, value, venerate, worship.

*antonyms* betray, debase, disgrace, dishonour.

**honourable** *adj* creditable, distinguished, eminent, equitable, estimable, ethical, fair, great, high-minded, honest, illustrious, irreproachable, just, meritorious, moral, noble, prestigious, principled, proper, renowned, reputable, respectable, respected, right, righteous, sincere, straight, true, trustworthy, trusty, unexceptionable, upright, upstanding, venerable, virtuous, worthful, worthy.

*antonyms* dishonest, dishonourable, unworthy.

**honours** *n* awards, crowns, decorations, dignities, distinctions, laurels, prizes, rewards, titles, trophies.

*antonyms* aspersions, indignities.

**hood** *n* capeline, capuche, cowl, domino.

**hoodwink** *v* bamboozle, befool, blear, cheat, con, cozen, deceive, delude, dupe, fool, gammon, gull, gyp, have on, hoax, impose, mislead, rook, seel, swindle, take in, trick.

**hoof** *n* cloot, cloven hoof, foot, trotter, ungula.

**hoofed** *adj* cloven-footed, cloven-hoofed, ungulate, unguligrade.

**hook** *n* agraffe, barb, catch, clasp, fastener, fluke, hamulus, hasp, holder, link, lock, peg, sickle, snag, snare, springe, trap, uncus.

*v* bag, catch, clasp, collar, enmesh, ensnare, entangle, entrap, fasten, fix, grab, hasp, hitch, nab, secure, snare, trap.

**hooked** *adj* addicted, adunc, aquiline, barbed, beaked, beaky, bent, curled, curved, devoted, enamoured, falcate, hamate, hamose, hamous, hamular, hamulate, obsessed, sickle-shaped, uncate, unciform, uncinate.

**hooligan** *n* apache, bovver boy, delinquent, droog, hood, hoodlum, lout, mobster, ned, rough, roughneck, rowdy, ruffian, thug, tityre-tu, tough, toughie, vandal, yob, yobbo.

**hoop** *n* annulus, bail, band, circlet, gird, girdle, loop, ring, round, wheel.

**hoot** *n* beep, boo, call, card, catcall, caution, cry, hiss, howl, jeer, laugh, raspberry, scream, shout, shriek, toot, whistle, whoop, yell.

*v* beep, boo, catcall, condemn, cry, decry, deride, explode, hiss, howl down, jeer, ridicule, scream, shout, shriek, toot, ululate, whistle, whoop, yell, yell at.

**hop** *v* bound, caper, dance, fly, frisk, hitch, hobble, jump, leap, limp, nip, prance, skip, spring, vault.

*n* ball, barn-dance, bounce, bound, crossing, dance, flight, jump, leap, skip, social, spring, step, trip, vault.

**hope** *n* ambition, anticipation, aspiration, assumption, assurance, belief, confidence, conviction, desire, dream, expectancy, expectation, faith, hopefulness, longing, optimism, promise, prospect, wish.

*antonyms* apathy, despair, pessimism.

*v* anticipate, aspire, assume, await, believe, contemplate, desire, expect, foresee, long, reckon on, rely, trust, wish.

*antonym* despair.

**hopeful** *adj* assured, auspicious, bright, bullish, buoyant, cheerful, confident, encouraging, expectant, favourable, heartening, optimistic, promising, propitious, reassuring, rosy, sanguine.

*antonyms* despairing, discouraging, pessimistic.

*n* great white hope, white hope, wunderkind.

**hopefully** *adv* all being well, bullishly, conceivably, confidently, deo volente, eagerly, expectantly, expectedly, feasibly, optimistically, probably, sanguinely, with a bit of luck.

**hopeless** *adj* defeatist, dejected, demoralised, despairing, desperate, despondent, disconsolate, downhearted, foolish, forlorn, futile, helpless, impossible, impracticable, inadequate, incompetent, incorrigible, incurable, ineffectual, irredeemable, irremediable, irreparable, irreversible, lost, madcap, no-win, past cure, pessimistic, pointless, poor, reckless, unachievable, unattainable, useless, vain, woebegone, worthless, wretched.

*antonyms* curable, hopeful, optimistic.

**horde** *n* band, bevy, concourse, crew, crowd, drove, flock, gang, herd, host, mob, multitude, pack, press, swarm, throng, troop.

**horizon** *n* compass, ken, perspective, prospect, purview, range, realm, scope, skyline, sphere, stretch, verge, vista.

**hornless** *adj* muley, polled.

**horny**[1] *adj* callous, ceratoid, corneous, corny.

**horny**[2] *adj* ardent, concupiscent, lascivious, lecherous, libidinous, lickerish, lubricious, lustful, priapic, randy, ruttish.

*antonyms* cold, frigid.

**horrible** *adj* abhorrent, abominable, appalling, atrocious, awful, beastly, bloodcurdling, cruel, disagreeable, dreadful, fearful, fearsome, frightful, ghastly, grim, grisly, gruesome, heinous, hideous, horrid, horrific, loathsome, macabre, nasty, repulsive, revolting, shameful, shocking, terrible, terrifying, unkind, unpleasant, weird.

*antonyms* agreeable, pleasant.

**horrid** *adj* abominable, alarming, appalling, awful, beastly, bloodcurdling, cruel, despicable, disagreeable, disgusting, dreadful, formidable, frightening, hair-raising, harrowing, hateful, hideous, horrible, horrific, mean, nasty, odious, offensive, repulsive, revolting, shocking, terrible, terrifying, unkind, unpleasant.

*antonyms* agreeable, lovely, pleasant.

**horrific** *adj* appalling, awful, dreadful, frightening, frightful, ghastly, grim, grisly, hair-raising, harrowing, horrendous, horrifying, scaring, shocking, spine-chilling, terrifying.

**horrify** *v* abash, affright, alarm, appal, disgust, dismay, frighten, harrow, intimidate, outrage, petrify, scandalise, scare, shock, sicken, startle, terrify, unnerve.

*antonyms* delight, gratify, please.

**horror** *n* abhorrence, abomination, alarm, antipathy, apprehension, aversion, awe, awfulness, consternation, detestation, disgust, dismay, dread, fear, fright, frightfulness, ghastliness, gooseflesh, goose-pimples, grimness, hatred, hideousness, horripilation, loathing, outrage, panic, repugnance, revulsion, shock, terror.

**horror-struck** *adj* aghast, appalled, frightened, horrified, horror-stricken, petrified, shocked, stunned.

*antonyms* delighted, pleased.

**horse** *n* bayard, bronc(h)o, brumby, caple, cayuse, charger, cob, crock, cuddy, destrier, dobbin, garran, gee-gee, hack, hackney, hobbler, hobby, horseflesh, hoss, jade, jennet, mare, mount, mustang, nag, pad, palfrey, pony, stallion, steed, tit, waler, war-horse, warragal.

**horse sense** brains, common sense, gumption, head, judgement, mother wit, native intelligence, nous, practicality, sense.

*antonym* stupidity.

**horse-cloth** *n* caparison, horse-blanket, housing, manta, trap, trappings.

**horseman** *n* broncobuster, buckaroo, cavalier, cavalryman, cowboy, dragoon, equestrian, gaucho, horse-soldier, hussar, jockey, rider.

**horsemanship** *n* equestrianism, equitation, haute école, manège.

**horseplay** *n* buffoonery, capers, clowning, desipience, fooling, fooling around, fun and games, high jinks, pranks, romping, rough-and-tumble, rough-housing, rough-stuff, rumpus, skylarking.

**horse-trainer** *n* breaker, broncobuster, cowboy, handler, hippodamist, horse-breaker, horse-tamer, trainer.

**hortatory** *adj* didactic, edifying, encouraging, exhortative, exhortatory, heartening, homiletic,

**hortative**, incitative, inspiriting, instructive, pep, practical, preceptive, stimulating.

**horticulture** *n* arboriculture, cultivation, floriculture, gardening.

**hospitable** *adj* accessible, amenable, amicable, approachable, bountiful, congenial, convivial, cordial, couthie, friendly, gemütlich, generous, genial, gracious, kind, liberal, liv(e)able, open-minded, receptive, responsive, sociable, tolerant, welcoming.
*antonyms* hostile, inhospitable.

**hospital** *n* clinic, lazaret, lazaretto, leprosarium, leproserie, leprosery, sanatorium.

**hospitality** *n* cheer, congeniality, conviviality, cordiality, friendliness, generosity, graciousness, open-handedness, philoxenia, sociability, warmth, welcome.
*antonyms* hostility, inhospitality.

**host**[1] *n* anchor-man, announcer, compère, emcee, entertainer, innkeeper, landlord, link man, master of ceremonies, MC, presenter, proprietor, visitee.
*v* compère, introduce, present.

**host**[2] *n* army, array, band, company, drove, horde, legion, multitude, myriad, pack, swarm, throng.

**hostel** *n* boarding-house, dormitory, doss-house, flophouse, Gasthaus, Gasthof, guest-house, hospice, hospital, hospitium, hostelry, hotel, inn, residence, xenodochium, youth hostel.

**hostile** *adj* adverse, alien, antagonistic, anti, antipathetic, bellicose, belligerent, contrary, ill-disposed, inhospitable, inimical, malevolent, opposed, opposite, oppugnant, rancorous, unfriendly, ungenial, unkind, unpropitious, unsympathetic, unwelcoming, warlike.
*antonyms* friendly, sympathetic.

**hostilities** *n* battle, bloodshed, conflict, encounter, fighting, state of war, strife, war, warfare.

**hostility** *n* abhorrence, animosity, animus, antagonism, antipathy, aversion, breach, detestation, disaffection, dislike, enmity, estrangement, hate, hatred, ill-will, malevolence, malice, opposition, resentment, unfriendliness.
*antonyms* friendliness, sympathy.

**hot** *adj* acrid, animated, approved, ardent, biting, blistering, boiling, burning, candent, clever, close, dangerous, eager, excellent, excited, exciting, favoured, febrile, fervent, fervid, fevered, feverish, fierce, fiery, flaming, fresh, heated, hotheaded, impetuous, impulsive, in demand, in vogue, incandescent, inflamed, intense, irascible, latest, lustful, near, new, passionate, peppery, perfervid, piping, piquant, popular, pungent, quick, raging, recent, risky, roasting, scalding, scorching, searing, sensual, sharp, sizzling, skilful, sought-after, spicy, steaming, stormy, strong, sultry, sweltering, torrid, touchy, tropical, vehement, violent, voluptuous, warm, zealous.
*antonyms* calm, cold, mild, moderate.

**hot air** balderdash, blather, blether, bluster, bombast, bosh, bullshit, bunk, bunkum, cant, claptrap, emptiness, flatulence, foam, froth, gas, guff, jejuneness, nonsense, rant, vapour, verbiage, wind, words.
*antonym* wisdom.

**hotbed** *n* breeding-ground, cradle, den, forcing-house, hive, nest, nidus, nursery, school, seedbed.

**hot-blooded** *adj* ardent, bold, eager, excitable, fervent, fiery, heated, high-spirited, homothermous, impetuous, impulsive, lustful, lusty, passionate, perfervid, precipitate, rash, sensual, spirited, temperamental, warm-blooded, wild.
*antonyms* cool, dispassionate.

**hotchpotch** *n* collection, commixture, confusion, congeries, conglomeration, farrago, gallimaufry, hash, jumble, medley, mélange, mess, miscellany, mishmash, mix, mixture, olio, olla-podrida, omnium gatherum, pot-pourri.

**hotel** *n* auberge, boarding-house, doss-house, flophouse, Gasthaus, Gasthof, guest-house, hostelry, hydro, hydropathic, inn, motel, pension, pub, public house, tavern.

**hotfoot** *adv* at top speed, hastily, helter-skelter, hurriedly, in haste, pell-mell, posthaste, quickly, rapidly, speedily, without delay.
*antonyms* dilatorily, slowly.

**hothead** *n* daredevil, desperado, hotspur, madcap, madman, tearaway, terror.

**hotheaded** *adj* daredevil, fiery, foolhardy, hasty, headstrong, hot-tempered, impetuous, impulsive, intemperate, madcap, over-eager, precipitate, quick-tempered, rash, reckless, unruly, volatile.
*antonyms* calm, cool.

**hothouse** *n* conservatory, glasshouse, greenhouse, nursery, plant-house, vinery.

**hot-tempered** *adj* choleric, explosive, fiery, hasty, irascible, irritable, petulant, quick-tempered, short-tempered, testy, violent, volcanic, wrathy.
*antonyms* calm, cool, imperturbable.

**hound** *v* badger, chase, chivvy, drive, dun, goad, harass, harry, hunt (down), impel, importune, persecute, pester, prod, provoke, pursue.

**house** *n* abode, ancestry, biggin, blood, building, business, clan, company, concern, domicile, dwelling, dynasty, edifice, establishment, family, family tree, firm, gens, habitation, home, homestead, hostelry, hotel, household, inn, kindred, line, lineage, lodgings, maison, maison(n)ette, ménage, organisation, outfit, parliament, partnership, pied-à-terre, public house, race, residence, roof, stem, tavern, tribe.
*v* accommodate, bed, billet, board, contain, cover, domicile, domiciliate, harbour, hold, keep, lodge, place, protect, put up, quarter, sheathe, shelter, store, take in.

**household** *n* establishment, family, family circle, home, house, ménage, set-up.
*adj* common, domestic, domiciliary, established, everyday, familiar, family, home, ordinary, plain, well-known.

**householder** *n* franklin, freeholder, goodman, head of the household, home-owner, housefather, landlord, occupant, occupier, owner, property owner, proprietor, resident, tenant.

**housekeeper**    *n*    châtelaine, concièrge, gouvernante, home economist, housewife, lady-help.

**houseman**   *n*   house-physician, house-surgeon, intern(e), resident.

**house-trained** *adj* domesticated, house-broken, tame, tamed, well-mannered.

*antonym* unsocial.

**housewife** *n* consort, hausfrau, home economist, homemaker, housekeeper, hussif, mate.

**housing** *n* accommodation, case, casing, container, cover, covering, dwellings, enclosure, habitation, holder, homes, houses, living quarters, matrix, protection, roof, sheath, shelter.

**hovel** *n* bothy, but-and-ben, cabin, cot, croft, cruve, den, doghole, dump, hole, hut, hutch, shack, shanty, shed.

**hover** *v* alternate, dally, dither, drift, falter, flap, float, fluctuate, flutter, fly, hang, hang about, hesitate, impend, linger, loom, menace, oscillate, pause, poise, seesaw, threaten, vacillate, waver.

**however** *conj* anyhow, but, even so, howbeit, in spite of that, natheless, nevertheless, nonetheless, notwithstanding, still, though, yet.

**howl** *n* bay, bellow, clamour, cry, groan, holler, hoot, outcry, roar, scream, shriek, ululation, wail, yell, yelp, yowl.

*v* bellow, cry, holler, hoot, lament, quest, roar, scream, shout, shriek, ululate, wail, waul, weep, yawl, yell, yelp.

**howler** *n* bêtise, bloomer, blunder, boner, bull, clanger, error, gaffe, malapropism, mistake, solecism.

**hub** *n* axis, centre, core, focal point, focus, heart, linchpin, middle, nave, nerve centre, pivot.

**hubbub** *n* ado, agitation, babel, bedlam, brouhaha, chaos, clamour, coil, confusion, din, disorder, disturbance, hue and cry, hullabaloo, hurly-burly, kerfuffle, noise, palaver, pandemonium, racket, riot, rowdedow, rowdydow, ruckus, ruction, rumpus, tumult, turbulence, uproar, upset.

*antonym* calm.

**huckster** *n* barker, chapman, dealer, haggler, hawker, packman, pedlar, pitcher, salesman, tinker, vendor.

**huddle** *n* clump, clutch, conclave, confab, conference, confusion, crowd, discussion, disorder, heap, jumble, knot, mass, meeting, mess, muddle.

*v* cluster, conglomerate, congregate, converge, crouch, crowd, cuddle, curl up, flock, gather, gravitate, hunch, nestle, press, ruck, snuggle, throng.

*antonym* disperse.

**hue** *n* aspect, cast, character, colour, complexion, dye, light, nuance, shade, tincture, tinge, tint, tone.

**hue and cry** ado, brouhaha, chase, clamour, furore, howls, hullabaloo, humdudgeon, outcry, pursuit, ruction, rumpus, uproar.

**huff** *n* anger, bad mood, mood, passion, pet, pique, sulks, tiff.

**huffy** *adj* angry, crabbed, cross, crotchety, crusty, disgruntled, grumpy, hoity-toity, huffish, irritable, miffed, miffy, moody, moping, morose, offended, peevish, pettish, petulant, querulous, resentful, shirty, short, snappy, sulky, surly, testy, touchy, waspish.

*antonyms* cheery, happy.

**hug** *v* cherish, clasp, cling to, cuddle, embrace, enclose, enfold, follow, grip, hold, lock, nurse, retain, skirt, squeeze.

*n* clasp, clinch, cuddle, embrace, squeeze.

**huge** *adj* Babylonian, Brobdingnagian, bulky, colossal, Cyclopean, enormous, extensive, gargantuan, giant, gigantean, gigantesque, gigantic, great, gross, immense, jumbo, large, leviathan, mammoth, massive, monumental, mountainous, Patagonian, prodigious, rounceval, stupendous, swingeing, thundering, titanic, tremendous, unwieldy, vast, walloping, whacking.

*antonyms* dainty, tiny.

**hugeness** *n* bulkiness, enormousness, extensiveness, gigantism, greatness, grossness, immensity, largeness, massiveness, overdevelopment, overgrowth, prodigiousness, size, stupendousness, tremendousness, unwieldiness, vastness.

*antonyms* daintiness, smallness.

**hulk** *n* clod, derelict, frame, hull, lout, lubber, lump, oaf, ox, shell, shipwreck, wreck.

**hulking** *adj* awkward, bulky, cloddish, clodhopping, clumsy, cumbersome, galumphing, gross, hulky, loutish, lubberly, lumbering, lumpish, massive, oafish, overgrown, ponderous, ungainly, unwieldy.

*antonyms* delicate, small.

**hull**[1] *n* body, casing, covering, frame, framework, hulk, skeleton, structure.

**hull**[2] *n* capsule, epicarp, husk, legume, peel, pod, rind, shell, shuck, skin, theca.

*v* husk, pare, peel, shell, shuck, skin, strip, trim.

**hullabaloo** *n* agitation, babel, bedlam, brouhaha, chaos, clamour, commotion, confusion, din, disturbance, furore, fuss, hubbub, hue and cry, hurly-burly, kerfuffle, noise, outcry, pandemonium, panic, racket, ruckus, ruction, rumpus, to-do, tumult, turmoil, uproar.

**hum** *v* bombilate, bombinate, bum, bustle, buzz, croon, drone, lilt, move, mumble, murmur, pulsate, pulse, purr, sing, stir, susurrate, throb, thrum, vibrate, whirr, zoom.

*n* bombilation, bombination, bustle, busyness, buzz, drone, mumble, murmur, noise, pulsation, pulse, purr, purring, singing, stir, susurration, susurrus, throb, thrum, vibration, whirr.

**human** *adj* anthropoid, approachable, compassionate, considerate, fallible, fleshly, forgivable, hominoid, humane, kind, kindly, man-like, mortal, natural, reasonable, susceptible, understandable, understanding, vulnerable.

*antonym* inhuman.

*n* body, child, creature, hominid, homo sapiens, human being, individual, living soul, man, mortal, person, soul, wight, woman.

**humane** *adj* beneficent, benevolent, benign, charitable, civilising, clement, compassionate, forbearing, forgiving, gentle, good, good-natured, human, humanising, kind, kind-hearted, kindly, lenient, loving, magnanimous, merciful, mild, sympathetic, tender, understanding.

*antonym* inhumane.

**humanise** *v* break, civilise, cultivate, domesticate, edify, educate, enlighten, improve, mellow, polish, reclaim, refine, soften, tame, temper.

*antonym* brutalise.

**humanitarian** *adj* altruistic, beneficent, benevolent, charitable, compassionate, humane, philanthropic, philanthropical, public-spirited.

*n* altruist, benefactor, do-gooder, Good Samaritan, philanthrope, philanthropist.

*antonyms* egoist, self-seeker.

**humanitarianism** *n* beneficence, benevolence, charitableness, charity, compassionateness, do-goodery, generosity, goodwill, humanism, loving-kindness, philanthropy.

*antonyms* egoism, self-seeking.

**humanity** *n* altruism, benevolence, benignity, brotherly love, charity, compassion, everyman, fellow-feeling, flesh, generosity, gentleness, goodwill, Homo sapiens, human nature, human race, humankind, humaneness, kind-heartedness, kindness, loving-kindness, man, mandom, mankind, men, mercy, mortality, people, philanthropy, sympathy, tenderness, tolerance, understanding.

*antonym* inhumanity.

**humble** *adj* common, commonplace, courteous, deferential, demiss, docile, homespun, humdrum, insignificant, low, low-born, lowly, mean, meek, modest, obedient, obliging, obscure, obsequious, ordinary, plebeian, polite, poor, respectful, self-effacing, servile, simple, submissive, subservient, supplicatory, unassertive, unassuming, undistinguished, unimportant, unostentatious, unpretending, unpretentious.

*antonyms* assertive, important, pretentious, proud.

*v* abase, abash, break, bring down, bring low, chagrin, chasten, confound, crush, debase, deflate, degrade, demean, discomfit, discredit, disgrace, humiliate, lower, mortify, reduce, shame, sink, subdue, take down a peg.

*antonyms* exalt, raise.

**humbleness** *n* abjectness, courtesy, deference, fawning, grovelling, heepishness, insignificance, lowliness, meanness, meekness, modestness, modesty, obscurity, obsequiousness, ordinariness, politeness, respectfulness, servility, simplicity, slavishness, smarminess, submissiveness, subservience, unimportance, unpretentiousness.

*antonyms* assertiveness, pride.

**humbly** *adv* deferentially, diffidently, docilely, heepishly, meekly, modestly, obsequiously, respectfully, servilely, simply, submissively, subserviently, unassumingly, unpretentiously.

*antonyms* confidently, defiantly.

**humbug** *n* baloney, berley, blague, bluff, bounce, bullshit, bunk, bunkum, burley, cant, charlatan, charlatanry, cheat, claptrap, con, con man, deceit, deception, dodge, eyewash, faker, feint, fraud, fudge, gaff, gammon, hoax, hollowness, hype, hypocrisy, imposition, impostor, imposture, mountebank, nonsense, phoney, pretence, pseud, quack, quackery, rubbish, ruse, sham, shenanigans, swindle, swindler, trick, trickery, trickster, wile.

*v* bamboozle, befool, beguile, cajole, cheat, cozen, deceive, delude, dupe, fool, gammon, gull, hoax, hoodwink, impose, mislead, swindle, trick.

**humdrum** *adj* boring, commonplace, dreary, droning, dull, everyday, humble, monotonous, mundane, ordinary, prosy, repetitious, routine, tedious, tiresome, uneventful, uninteresting, unvaried, wearisome.

*antonyms* exceptional, unusual.

**humid** *adj* clammy, damp, dank, moist, muggy, soggy, steamy, sticky, sultry, vaporous, watery, wet.

*antonym* dry.

**humidity** *n* clamminess, damp, dampness, dankness, dew, humidness, moistness, moisture, mugginess, sogginess, steaminess, vaporosity, vaporousness, wetness.

*antonym* dryness.

**humiliate** *v* abase, abash, bring low, chagrin, chasten, confound, crush, debase, deflate, degrade, discomfit, discredit, disgrace, embarrass, humble, mortify, shame, subdue, undignify.

*antonyms* boost, dignify, exalt, vindicate.

**humiliating** *adj* chastening, crushing, deflating, degrading, discomfiting, disgraceful, disgracing, embarrassing, humbling, humiliant, humiliative, humiliatory, ignominious, inglorious, mortifying, shaming, snubbing.

*antonyms* gratifying, triumphant.

**humiliation** *n* abasement, affront, chagrin, condescension, deflation, degradation, discomfiture, discrediting, disgrace, dishonour, embarrassment, humbling, ignominy, indignity, mortification, put-down, rebuff, resignation, shame, snub.

*antonyms* gratification, triumph.

**humility** *n* deference, diffidence, humbleness, lowliness, meekness, modesty, obedience, resignation, self-abasement, servility, submissiveness, unassertiveness, unpretentiousness.

*antonym* pride.

**hummock** *n* barrow, elevation, hillock, hump, knoll, mound, prominence.

**humorist** *n* buffoon, clown, comedian, comédienne, comic, droll, eccentric, entertainer, funny man, jester, joker, parodist, satirist, wag, wisecracker, wit, zany.

**humorous** *adj* absurd, amusing, comic, comical, entertaining, facetious, farcical, funny, hilarious, humoristic, jocose, jocular, laughable, ludicrous, merry, playful, pleasant, Rabelaisian, satirical, side-splitting, waggish, whimsical, wisecracking, witty, zany.

*antonym* humourless.

**humour** *n* amusement, badinage, banter, bent, bias, caprice, choler, comedy, conceit, disposition, drollery, facetiousness, fancy, farce, frame of mind, fun, funniness, gags, jesting, jests, jocoseness, jocosity, jocularity, jokes, joking, ludicrousness, melancholy, mood, phlegm, pleasantries, propensity, quirk, raillery, repartee, spirits, temper, temperament, vagary, vein, whim, wisecracks, wit, witticisms, wittiness.

*v* accommodate, appease, coax, comply with, cosset, favour, flatter, go along with, gratify, indulge, mollify, pamper, spoil.

*antonym* thwart.

**humourless** *adj* austere, boring, crass, dour, dry, dull, glum, heavy-going, inflated, mirthless, morose, obtuse, po, po-faced, self-important, tedious, thick, thick-skinned, unamused, unamusing, unfunny, unwitty.

*antonyms* humorous, witty.

**hump** *n* bulge, bump, excrescence, hunch, knob, lump, mound, projection, prominence, protrusion, protuberance, swelling.

*v* arch, carry, curve, heave, hoist, hunch, lift, lug, shoulder, yomp.

**humpback** *n* crookback, gibbosity, gibbus, gobbo, hunchback, kyphosis, Quasimodo, torticollis, wry-neck.

**hump-backed** *adj* crookbacked, crooked, deformed, gibbous, humped, hunchbacked, hunched, kyphotic, misshapen, stooped.

*antonyms* straight, upright.

**humped** *adj* arched, bent, crooked, curved, gibbous, hunched.

*antonyms* flat, straight.

**hunch** *n* feeling, guess, guesswork, idea, impression, inkling, intuition, premonition, presentiment, suspicion.

*v* arch, bend, crouch, curl up, curve, draw in, huddle, hump, shrug, squat, stoop, tense.

**hunger** *n* appetence, appetency, appetite, craving, desire, emptiness, esurience, esuriency, famine, greediness, hungriness, itch, lust, rapacity, ravenousness, starvation, voracity, yearning, yen, yird-hunger.

*antonyms* appeasement, satisfaction.

*v* ache, crave, desire, hanker, itch, long, lust, pine, starve, thirst, want, wish, yearn.

**hungry** *adj* aching, appetitive, athirst, avid, bulimic, covetous, craving, desirous, eager, empty, esurient, famished, famishing, greedy, hollow, hungerful, keen, lean, longing, peckish, ravenous, sharp-set, starved, starving, underfed, undernourished, voracious, yearning.

*antonyms* replete, satisfied.

**hunk** *n* block, chunk, clod, dod, dollop, gobbet, lump, mass, piece, slab, wedge, wodge.

**hunt** *v* chase, chevy, course, dog, ferret, forage, gun for, hound, investigate, look for, pursue, rummage, scour, search, seek, stalk, track, trail.

*n* battue, chase, chevy, hue and cry, hunting, investigation, pursuit, quest, search, venation.

**hunted** *adj* angst-ridden, careworn, desperate, distraught, gaunt, haggard, hag-ridden, harassed, harried, henpecked, persecuted, stricken, terror-stricken, tormented, worn, worried.

*antonym* serene.

**hunting** *adj* cynegetic, venatic, venatical, venatorial.

**huntsman** *n* chaser, chasseur, hunter, jaeger, jäger, montero, venator, venerer, woodman, woodsman.

**hurdle** *n* barricade, barrier, complication, difficulty, fence, handicap, hedge, hindrance, impediment, jump, obstacle, obstruction, problem, snag, stumbling-block, wall.

**hurl** *v* cast, catapult, chuck, dash, fire, fling, heave, launch, let fly, pitch, project, propel, send, shy, sling, throw, toss.

**hurly-burly** *n* agitation, bedlam, brouhaha, bustle, chaos, commotion, confusion, disorder, distraction, frenzy, furore, hassle, hubbub, hustle, storm and stress, Sturm und Drang, tumult, turbulence, turmoil, upheaval.

**hurricane** *n* baguio, cordonazo, cyclone, gale, squall, storm, tempest, tornado, twister, typhoon, whirlwind, willy-willy.

**hurried** *adj* breakneck, brief, careless, cursory, hasty, headlong, hectic, passing, perfunctory, precipitate, quick, rushed, shallow, short, slapdash, speedy, superficial, swift, unthorough.

*antonym* leisurely.

**hurry** *v* accelerate, belt, bustle, dash, dispatch, expedite, festinate, fly, get a move on, goad, hasten, hightail it, hump, hustle, jump to it, look lively, move, pike, quicken, rush, scoot, scurry, scutter, scuttle, shake a leg, shift, speed up, step on it, step on the gas, urge.

*antonyms* dally, delay.

*n* bustle, celerity, commotion, dispatch, expedition, flurry, haste, precipitance, precipitancy, precipitation, promptitude, quickness, rush, scurry, speed, sweat, urgency.

*antonyms* calm, leisureliness.

**hurt** *v* abuse, ache, afflict, aggrieve, annoy, bruise, burn, damage, disable, distress, grieve, harm, impair, injure, maim, maltreat, mar, pain, sadden, smart, spoil, sting, throb, tingle, torture, upset, wound.

*n* abuse, bruise, damage, detriment, disadvantage, discomfort, distress, harm, injury, lesion, loss, mischief, pain, pang, scathe, sore, soreness, suffering, wound, wrong.

*adj* aggrieved, annoyed, bruised, crushed, cut, damaged, displeased, grazed, harmed, huffed, injured, maimed, miffed, offended, pained, piqued, rueful, sad, saddened, scarred, scraped, scratched, wounded.

**hurtful** *adj* catty, cruel, cutting, damaging, derogatory, destructive, detrimental, disadvantageous, distressing, harmful, humiliating, injurious, malefactory, malefic, maleficent, malicious, malificious, malignant, mean, mischievous, nasty, nocuous, pernicious, pestful, pestiferous, pestilent(ial), pointed, prejudicial, scathing, spiteful, unkind, upsetting, vicious, wounding.

*antonyms* helpful, kind.

**hurtle** *v* bowl, charge, chase, crash, dash, fly, plunge, race, rattle, rush, scoot, scramble, shoot, speed, spin, spurt, tear.

**husband¹** *v* budget, conserve, economise, eke out, hoard, ration, save, save up, store, use sparingly.

*antonyms* squander, waste.

**husband²** *n* Benedick, consort, goodman, hubby, man, married man, mate, old man, spouse.

**husbandry** *n* agriculture, agronomics, agronomy, conservation, cultivation, economy, farming, frugality, good housekeeping, land management, management, thrift, thriftiness, tillage.

*antonym* wastefulness.

**hush** *v* calm, compose, mollify, mute, muzzle, quieten, settle, shush, silence, soothe, still.

*antonyms* disturb, rouse.

*n* calm, calmness, peace, peacefulness, quiet, quietness, repose, serenity, silence, still, stillness, tranquillity.

*antonyms* clamour, uproar.

*interj* belt up, euphemeite, favete linguis, hold your tongue, leave it out, not another word, pipe down, quiet, say no more, shush, shut up, ssh, stow it, unberufen, wheesht, whisht.

**hush up** conceal, cover up, gag, keep dark, muzzle, smother, soft-pedal, squash, stifle, suppress.

*antonym* publicise.

**hush-hush** *adj* classified, confidential, hushy, restricted, secret, top-secret, under wraps, unpublished.

*antonyms* open, public.

**husk** *n* bark, bract, bran, case, chaff, covering, glume, hull, pod, rind, shell, shuck, tegmen.

**huskiness** *n* croakiness, dryness, gruffness, gutturalness, harshness, hoarseness, roughness, throatiness.

*antonym* clarity.

**husky¹** *adj* croaking, croaky, gruff, guttural, harsh, hoarse, low, rasping, raucous, rough, roupy, throaty.

**husky²** *adj* beefy, brawny, burly, hefty, muscular, powerful, rugged, stocky, strapping, strong, sturdy, thickset, tough.

**hussy** *n* baggage, broad, floozy, jade, minx, piece, scrubber, slut, strumpet, tart, temptress, tramp, trollop, vamp, wanton, wench.

**hustle** *v* bustle, crowd, elbow, force, frog-march, haste, hasten, hurry, impel, jog, jostle, pressgang, pressure, push, rush, shove, thrust.

**hut** *n* booth, bothan, bothy, cabin, caboose, crib, den, hogan, hovel, kraal, lean-to, shack, shanty, shebang, shed, shelter, shiel, shieling, tilt.

**hybrid** *n* amalgam, combination, composite, compound, conglomerate, cross, crossbreed, half-blood, half-breed, heterogeny, mixture, mongrel, mule, pastiche.

*adj* bastard, combined, composite, compound, cross, heterogeneous, hybridous, hyphenated, mixed, mongrel, mule, patchwork.

*antonyms* pure, pure-bred.

**hybridity** *n* bastardisation, compositeness, cross-breeding, crossing, heterogeneity, hybridism, interbreeding, pastiche.

*antonym* purity.

**hygiene** *n* asepsis, cleanliness, disinfection, hygienics, purity, salubriousness, salubrity, salutariness, sanitariness, sanitation, sterility, wholesomeness.

*antonyms* filth, insanitariness.

**hygienic** *adj* aseptic, clean, cleanly, disinfected, germ-free, healthy, pure, salubrious, salutary, sanitary, sterile, wholesome.

*antonym* unhygenic.

**hymn** *n* anthem, bhajan, cantata, canticle, canticum, carol, chant, choral(e), dithyramb, doxology, introit, mantra(m), motet, offertory, om, paean, paraphrase, psalm, song of praise.

**hype** *n* advertisement, advertising, ballyhoo, build-up, deception, fuss, kidology, plugging, publicity, puffery, puffing, racket, razzmatazz, trumpet-blowing.

**hyperbole** *n* enlargement, exaggeration, excess, extravagance, magnification, overkill, overplay, overstatement.

*antonyms* meiosis, understatement.

**hypercritical** *adj* captious, carping, cavilling, censorious, exceptious, fault-finding, finicky, fussy, hair-splitting, niggling, nit-picking, over-particular, pedantic, pernickety, quibbling, strict, ultracrepidarian, Zoilean.

*antonyms* tolerant, uncritical.

**hypnotic** *adj* compelling, dazzling, fascinating, irresistible, magnetic, mesmeric, mesmerising, narcotic, opiate, sleep-inducing, somniferous, soothing, soporific, spellbinding.

**hypnotise** *v* bewitch, captivate, dazzle, entrance, fascinate, magnetise, mesmerise, spellbind, stupefy.

**hypnotism** *n* animal magnetism, hypnosis, hypnotherapy, mesmerism, suggestion.

**hypochondria** *n* hypochondrianism, hypochondriasis, neurosis, valetudinarianism.

**hypochondriac** *n* hypochondriast, valetudinarian.

*adj* hypochondriacal, neurotic, valetudinarian.

**hypocrisy** *n* cant, deceit, deceitfulness, deception, dissembling, double-talk, duplicity, falsity, imposture, insincerity, lip-service, pharisaicalness, pharisaism, phariseeism, phoneyness, pietism, pretence, quackery, sanctimoniousness, self-righteousness, speciousness, Tartuffism, two-facedness.

*antonyms* humility, sincerity.

**hypocrite** *n* canter, charlatan, deceiver, dissembler, fraud, Holy Willie, impostor, mountebank, Pharisee, phon(e)y, pretender, pseud, pseudo, Tartuffe, whited sepulchre.

**hypocritical** *adj* canting, deceitful, deceptive, dissembling, double-faced, duplicitous, false, fraudulent, hollow, insincere, Pecksniffian, pharisaic(al), phoney, pietistic, sanctimonious, self-pious, self-righteous, specious, spurious, Tartuffian, Tartuffish, two-faced.

*antonyms* genuine, humble, sincere.

**hypothesis** *n* assumption, conjecture, guess, postulate, postulatum, premise, premiss, presumption, proposition, starting-point, supposition, theory, thesis.

**hypothetical** *adj* academic, assumed, conjectural, imaginary, postulated, proposed, putative, speculative, supposed, suppositional, theoretical.

*antonyms* actual, real.

**hysteria** *n* agitation, frenzy, hysterics, hysteromania, instability, madness, neurosis, panic, psychoneurosis, unreason.

*antonyms* calm, composure, reason.

**hysterical** *adj* berserk, comical, crazed, distracted, distraught, falling about, farcical, frantic, frenzied, hairless, hilarious, mad, neurotic, overwrought, priceless, psychoneurotic, psychosomatic, raving, side-splitting, uncontrollable, uproarious.

*antonyms* calm, composed.

**hysterics** *n* drama, dramatics, emotionalism, emotionality, histrionics, melodrama, (screaming) habdabs.

**I**

**ice** *n* chill, chilliness, coldness, distance, formality, frazil, frigidity, frost, frostiness, ice-cream, iciness, icing, reserve, rime, stiffness, verglas.

*v* freeze, frost, glaciate, glaze.

**ice-cold** *adj* algid, arctic, biting, bitter, chilled to the bone, freezing, frigid, frozen, frozen to the marrow, gelid, glacial, icy, icy cold, raw, refrigerated.

**iced** *adj* frappé(e), frosted, glazed.

**icon** *n* figure, idol, ikon, image, portrait, portrayal, representation, symbol.

**iconoclasm** *n* criticism, demythologisation, denunciation, disabusing, dissent, dissidence, heresy, irreverence, opposition, questioning, radicalism, scepticism, subversion, unbelief, undeceiving.

*antonyms* credulity, trustfulness.

**iconoclast** *n* critic, denouncer, denunciator, dissenter, dissident, heretic, idoloclast, image-breaker, opponent, questioner, radical, rebel, sceptic, unbeliever.

*antonyms* believer, devotee.

**iconoclastic** *adj* critical, denunciatory, dissentient, dissident, heretical, impious, innovative, irreverent, questioning, radical, rebellious, sceptical, subversive.

*antonyms* trustful, uncritical, unquestioning.

**icy** *adj* algid, aloof, arctic, biting, bitter, chill, chilling, chilly, cold, distant, forbidding, formal, freezing, frigid, frore, frost-bound, frosty, frozen over, gelid, glacial, glassy, hoar, hostile, ice-cold, indifferent, raw, reserved, rimy, slippery, slippy, steely, stiff, stony, unfriendly.

**idea** *n* abstraction, aim, approximation, archetype, belief, clue, conceit, concept, conception, conceptualisation, conclusion, conjecture, construct, conviction, design, doctrine, end, essence, estimate, fancy, form, guess, guesstimate, hint, hypothesis, idée fixe, image, import, impression, inkling, intention, interpretation, intimation, judgement, meaning, monomania, notion, object, opinion, pattern, perception, plan, purpose, reason, recept, recommendation, scheme, sense, significance, solution, suggestion, surmise, suspicion, teaching, theory, thought, type, understanding, view, viewpoint, vision.

**ideal** *n* archetype, criterion, dreamboat, epitome, example, exemplar, image, last word, model, ne

plus ultra, nonpareil, paradigm, paragon, pattern, perfection, pink of perfection, principle, prototype, standard, type.

*adj* abstract, archetypal, best, classic, complete, conceptual, consummate, fanciful, highest, hypothetical, imaginary, impractical, model, optimal, optimum, perfect, quintessential, supreme, theoretical, transcendent, transcendental, unattainable, unreal, Utopian, visionary.

**idealisation** *n* apotheosis, ennoblement, exaltation, glorification, romanticisation, romanticising, worship.

**idealise** *v* apotheosise, deify, ennoble, exalt, glorify, romanticise, utopianise, worship.

*antonyms* caricature, travesty.

**idealism** *n* impracticality, perfectionism, romanticism, utopianism, utopism.

*antonyms* pragmatism, realism.

**idealist** *n* dreamer, perfectionist, romantic, romanticist, utopian, utopianiser, utopiast, utopist, visionary.

*antonyms* pragmatist, realist.

**idealistic** *adj* impracticable, impractical, optimistic, perfectionist, quixotic, romantic, starry-eyed, unrealistic, utopian, visionary.

*antonyms* pragmatic, realistic.

**idée fixe** complex, fixation, fixed idea, hang-up, leitmotiv, monomania, obsession.

**identical** *adj* alike, clonal, coincident, corresponding, duplicate, equal, equivalent, identic, indistinguishable, interchangeable, like, matching, monozygotic, same, self-same, synonymous, twin.

*antonym* different.

**identifiable** *adj* ascertainable, detectable, discernible, distinguishable, known, noticeable, perceptible, recognisable, unmistakable.

*antonyms* indefinable, unfamiliar, unidentifiable, unknown.

**identification** *n* association, cataloguing, classifying, connection, credentials, detection, diagnosis, documents, empathy, fellow-feeling, ID, involvement, labelling, naming, papers, pinpointing, rapport, recognition, relating, relationship, sympathy.

**identify** *v* catalogue, classify, detect, diagnose, distinguish, finger, know, label, make out, name, pick out, pinpoint, place, recognise, single out, specify, spot, tag.

**identify with** ally with, associate with, connect with, empathise with, equate with, feel for, relate to, respond to.

**identity** *n* accord, coincidence, correspondence, empathy, existence, haecceity, individuality, oneness, particularity, personality, quiddity, rapport, sameness, self, selfhood, singularity, unanimity, uniqueness, unity.

**ideologist** *n* ideologue, theorist, thinker, visionary.

**ideology** *n* belief(s), convictions, creed, doctrine(s), dogma, ethic, faith, ideas, metaphysics, philosophy, principles, speculation, tenets, Weltanschauung, world view.

**idiocy** *n* amentia, asininity, cretinism, dementia, fatuity, fatuousness, folly, foolishness, imbecility, inanity, insanity, irrationality, lunacy, mental deficiency, senselessness, silliness, stupidity, tomfoolery.

*antonyms* sanity, wisdom.

**idiom** *n* colloquialism, expression, idiolect, idiotism, jargon, language, locution, parlance, phrase, regionalism, set phrase, style, talk, turn of phrase, usage, vernacular.

**idiomatic** *adj* colloquial, correct, dialectal, dialectical, grammatical, idiolectal, idiolectic, native, vernacular.

*antonym* unidiomatic.

**idiosyncrasy** *n* characteristic, eccentricity, feature, freak, habit, kink, mannerism, oddity, oddness, peculiarity, quirk, singularity, trait.

**idiosyncratic** *adj* characteristic, distinctive, eccentric, individual, individualistic, inimitable, odd, peculiar, quirky, typical.

*antonyms* common, general.

**idiot** *n* ament, ass, bampot, blockhead, booby, crazy, cretin, cuckoo, dimwit, dolt, dumbbell, dummy, dunderhead, fat-head, featherbrain, fool, golem, half-wit, imbecile, klutz, knuckle-head, mental defective, mooncalf, moron, natural, nidget, nig-nog, nincompoop, nitwit, nong, noodle, omadhaun, pillock, saphead, schlep, schmo, schmuck, simpleton, thick, thickhead, thicko.

**idiotic** *adj* asinine, crazy, cretinous, daft, dumb, fat-headed, fatuous, foolhardy, foolish, hair-brained, half-witted, harebrained, idiotical, imbecile, imbecilic, inane, insane, knuckle-headed, loony, lunatic, moronic, nutty, screwy, senseless, simple, stupid, tomfool, unintelligent.

*antonyms* sane, sensible.

**idle** *adj* abortive, bootless, dead, dormant, dronish, empty, foolish, frivolous, fruitless, futile, good-for-nothing, groundless, inactive, indolent, ineffective, ineffectual, inoperative, jobless, lackadaisical, lazy, mothballed, nugatory, of no avail, otiose, pointless, purposeless, redundant, shiftless, slothful, sluggish, stationary, superficial, torpid, trivial, unavailing, unbusy, unemployed, unproductive, unsuccessful, unused, useless, vain, work-shy, worthless.

*antonyms* active, effective, purposeful.

*v* coast, dally, dawdle, drift, fool, fritter, kill time, lallygag, laze, lie up, loiter, lounge, potter, rest on one's laurels, shirk, skive, slack, take it easy, tick over, vegetate, waste, while.

*antonyms* act, work.

**idleness** *n* dolce far niente, ease, flânerie, idlesse, inaction, inactivity, indolence, inertia, inoccupation, laziness, lazing, leisure, loafing, pottering, shiftlessness, skiving, sloth, slothfulness, sluggishness, torpor, unemployment, vegetating.

*antonyms* activity, employment.

**idler** *n* clock-watcher, dawdler, dodger, do-naught, donnat, donnot, do-nothing, do-nought, drone, fainéant, flâneur, good-for-nothing, laggard, layabout, lazybones, loafer, lotus-eater, lounger, malingerer, shirker, skiver, slacker, sloth, slouch, sluggard, waster, wastrel.

**idling** *adj* dawdling, drifting, ligging, loafing, pottering, resting, resting on one's oars, shirking, skiving, taking it easy, ticking over.

**idol** *n* beloved, darling, deity, favourite, fetish, god, graven image, hero, icon, image, joss, ju-ju, mammet, Mumbo-jumbo, pet, pin-up, superstar.

**idolater** *n* admirer, adorer, devotee, iconolater, idolatress, idolist, idol-worshipper, votary, worshipper.

**idolatrous** *adj* adoring, adulatory, idolising, idol-worshipping, reverential, uncritical, worshipful.

**idolatry** *n* adoration, adulation, deification, exaltation, glorification, hero-worship, iconolatry, idolising, idolism, mammetry, whoredom.

*antonym* vilification.

**idolise** *v* admire, adore, apotheosise, deify, dote on, exalt, glorify, hero-worship, iconise, lionise, love, revere, reverence, venerate, worship.

*antonym* vilify.

**idyllic** *adj* arcadian, charming, delightful, halcyon, happy, heavenly, idealised, innocent, pastoral, peaceful, picturesque, rustic, unspoiled.

*antonym* disagreeable.

**ignite** *v* burn, catch fire, combust, conflagrate, fire, flare up, inflame, kindle, light, set alight, set fire to, spark off, touch off.

*antonym* quench.

**ignoble** *adj* abject, base, base-born, caddish, common, contemptible, cowardly, craven, dastardly, degenerate, degraded, despicable, disgraceful, dishonourable, heinous, humble, infamous, low, low-born, lowly, mean, petty, plebeian, shabby, shameless, unworthy, vile, vulgar, worthless, wretched.

*antonyms* honourable, noble.

**ignominious** *adj* abject, crushing, degrading, despicable, discreditable, disgraceful, dishonourable, disreputable, humiliating, indecorous, inglorious, mortifying, scandalous, shameful, sorry, undignified.

*antonyms* honourable, triumphant.

**ignominy** *n* contempt, degradation, discredit, disgrace, dishonour, disrepute, humiliation, indignity, infamy, mortification, obloquy, odium, opprobrium, reproach, scandal, shame, stigma.

*antonyms* credit, honour.

**ignoramus** *n* ass, blockhead, bonehead, booby, dolt, donkey, duffer, dullard, dunce, fool, ignaro, illiterate, know-nothing, lowbrow, num(b)skull, simpleton.

*antonyms* high-brow, intellectual, scholar.

**ignorance** *n* benightedness, blindness, crassness, denseness, greenness, illiteracy, illiterateness, inexperience, innocence, naïvety, nescience, oblivion, unawareness, unconsciousness, unfamiliarity.

*antonyms* knowledge, wisdom.

**ignorant** *adj* as thick as two short planks, benighted, blind, bookless, clueless, crass, dense, green, gross, half-baked, idealess, ill-informed, illiterate, ill-versed, inexperienced, innocent, innumerate, insensitive, know-nothing, naïve, nescient, oblivious, pig-ignorant, stupid, thick, unacquainted, unaware, unconscious, uncultivated, uneducated, unenlightened, unidea'd, uninformed, uninitiated, uninstructed, unknowing, unlearned, unlettered, unread, unscholarly, unschooled, untaught, untrained, untutored, unwitting.

*antonyms* knowlegeable, wise.

**ignore** *v* blink, cold-shoulder, cut, disregard, neglect, omit, overlook, pass over, pay no attention to, pidgeon-hole, reject, send to Coventry, set aside, shut one's eyes to, slight, take no notice of, turn a blind eye to, turn a deaf ear to, turn one's back on.

*antonym* note.

**ilk** *n* brand, breed, cast cut, character, class, description, kidney, kind, make, sort, stamp, style, type, variety.

**ill¹** *adj* ailing, dicky, diseased, frail, funny, indisposed, infirm, laid up, not up to snuff, off-colour, on the sick list, out of sorts, peelie-wally, poorly, queasy, queer, seedy, sick, under the weather, unhealthy, unwell, valetudinarian.

*antonym* well.

*n* affliction, ailment, complaint, disease, disorder, illness, indisposition, infection, infirmity, malady, malaise, sickness.

**ill²** *adj* acrimonious, adverse, antagonistic, bad, cantankerous, cross, damaging, deleterious, detrimental, difficult, disturbing, evil, foul, harmful, harsh, hateful, hostile, hurtful, inauspicious, incorrect, inimical, iniquitous, injurious, malevolent, malicious, ominous, reprehensible, ruinous, sinister, sullen, surly, threatening, unfavourable, unfortunate, unfriendly, unhealthy, unkind, unlucky, unpromising, unpropitious, unwholesome, vile, wicked, wrong.

*antonyms* beneficial, fortunate, good, kind.

*n* abuse, affliction, badness, cruelty, damage, depravity, destruction, evil, harm, hurt, ill-usage, injury, malice, mischief, misery, misfortune, pain, sorrow, suffering, trial, tribulation, trouble, unpleasantness, wickedness, woe.

*antonym* benefit.

*adv* amiss, badly, by no means, hard, hardly, inauspiciously, insufficiently, poorly, scantily, scarcely, unfavourably, unluckily, wrongfully.

*antonym* well.

**ill at ease** anxious, awkward, disquieted, disturbed, edgy, embarrassed, fidgety, hesitant, like a cat on hot bricks, nervous, on edge, on tenterhooks, restless, self-conscious, strange, tense, uncomfortable, uneasy, unrelaxed, unsettled, unsure, worried.

*antonym* at ease.

**ill-advised** *adj* daft, foolhardy, foolish, hasty, hazardous, ill-considered, ill-judged, impolitic, imprudent, inappropriate, incautious, indiscreet, injudicious, misguided, overhasty, rash, reckless, short-sighted, thoughtless, unseemly, unwise, wrong-headed.

*antonym* sensible.

**ill-assorted** *adj* discordant, incompatible, incongruous, inharmonious, misallied, mismatched, uncongenial, unsuited.

*antonym* harmonious.

**ill-bred** *adj* bad-mannered, boorish, churlish, coarse, crass, crude, discourteous, ill-mannered, impolite, indelicate, non-U, rude, uncivil, uncivilised, uncouth, ungallant, ungentlemanly, ungracious, unladylike, unmannerly, unrefined, vulgar.

*antonym* urbane.

**ill-considered** *adj* careless, follish, hasty, heedless, ill-advised, ill-judged, improvident, imprudent, injudicious, overhasty, precipitate, rash, unwise.

*antonym* sensible.

**ill-defined** *adj* blurred, blurry, dim, fuzzy, hazy, imprecise, indefinite, indistinct, nebulous, shadowy, unclear, vague, woolly.

*antonym* clear.

**ill-disposed** *adj* against, antagonistic, anti, antipathetic, averse, hostile, inimical, opposed, unco-operative, unfriendly, unsympathetic, unwelcoming.

*antonym* well-disposed.

**illegal** *adj* actionable, backyard, banned, black-market, contraband, criminal, felonious, forbidden, illicit, outlawed, pirate, prohibited, proscribed, unauthorised, unconstitutional, under-the-counter, unlawful, unlicensed, wrongful, wrongous.

*antonym* legal.

**illegality** *n* crime, criminality, felony, illegitimacy, illicitness, lawlessness, unconstitutionality, unlawfulness, wrong, wrongfulness, wrongness.

*antonym* legality.

**illegible** *adj* crabbed, faint, hieroglyphic, indecipherable, indistinct, obscure, scrawled, undecipherable, unreadable.

*antonym* legible.

**illegitimacy** *n* bar-sinister, bastardism, bastardy, baton-sinister, illegality, illicitness, irregularity, unconstitutionality, unlawfulness.

*antonym* legitimacy.

**illegitimate** *adj* bastard, born on the wrong side of the blanket, born out of wedlock, fatherless, illegal, illicit, illogical, improper, incorrect, invalid, misbegotten, natural, spurious, unauthorised, unconstitutional, unfathered, unjustifiable, unjustified, unlawful, unsanctioned, unsound, unwarrantable, unwarranted.

*antonym* legitimate.

**ill-fated** *adj* blighted, doomed, forlorn, hapless, ill-omened, ill-starred, infaust, luckless, star-crossed, unfortunate, unhappy, unlucky.

*antonym* lucky.

**ill-favoured** *adj* hideous, homely, plain, repulsive, ugly, unattractive, unlovely, unprepossessing, unsightly.

*antonym* beautiful.

**ill-feeling** *n* animosity, animus, antagonism, bad blood, bitterness, disgruntlement, dissatisfaction, dudgeon, enmity, frustration, grudge, hard-feelings, hostility, ill-will, odium, offence, rancour, resentment, sourness, spite.

*antonyms* friendship, goodwill.

**ill-humour** *n* acrimony, choler, crabbiness, crassness, disagreeableness, dishumour, distemper, grumpiness, irascibility, moroseness, petulance, spleen, sulkiness, the dods.

*antonym* amiability.

**ill-humoured** *adj* acrimonious, bad-tempered, cantankerous, crabbed, crabby, cross, cross-grained, disagreeable, grumpy, huffy, impatient, irascible, irritable, moody, morose, peevish, petulant, sharp, snappish, snappy, sulky, sullen, tart, testy, waspish.

*antonym* amiable.

**illiberal** *adj* bigoted, close-fisted, hidebound, intolerant, mean, miserly, narrow-minded, niggardly, parsimonious, petty, prejudiced, reactionary, small-minded, sordid, stingy, tight, tightfisted, uncharitable, ungenerous, verkrampte.

*antonym* liberal.

**illiberality** *n* bigotry, intolerance, meanness, miserliness, narrow-mindedness, narrowness, niggardliness, parsimony, pettiness, prejudice, small-mindedness, stinginess.

*antonym* liberality.

**illicit** *adj* black, black-market, bootleg, clandestine, contraband, criminal, felonious, forbidden, furtive, guilty, illegal, illegitimate, ill-gotten, immoral, improper, inadmissible, prohibited, unauthorised, unlawful, unlicensed, unsanctioned, wrong.

*antonyms* legal, licit.

**illiterate** *adj* analphabetic, benighted, ignorant, uncultured, uneducated, unlettered, untaught, untutored.

*antonym* literate.

**ill-judged** *adj* daft, foolhardy, foolish, hasty, ill-advised, ill-considered, impolitic, imprudent, incautious, indiscreet, injudicious, misguided, overhasty, rash, reckless, short-sighted, unwise, wrong-headed.

*antonym* sensible.

**ill-mannered** *adj* badly-behaved, boorish, churlish, coarse, crude, discourteous, ill-behaved, ill-bred, impolite, insensitive, insolent, loutish, rude, uncivil, uncouth, ungallant, unmannerly.

*antonym* polite.

**ill-natured** *adj* bad-tempered, churlish, crabbed, cross, cross-grained, disagreeable, disobliging, malevolent, malicious, malignant, mean, nasty, perverse, petulant, spiteful, sulky, sullen, surly, unfriendly, unkind, unpleasant, vicious, vindictive.

*antonym* good-natured.

**illness** *n* affliction, ailment, attack, complaint, disability, disease, disorder, distemper, dyscrasia, idiopathy, ill-being, ill-health, indisposition, infirmity, lurgy, malady, malaise, sickness.

*antonym* health.

**illogical** *adj* absurd, fallacious, faulty, Fifish, illegitimate, inconclusive, inconsistent, incorrect, invalid, Irish, irrational, meaningless, senseless, sophistical, specious, spurious, unreasonable, unscientific, unsound.

*antonym* logical.

**illogicality** *n* absurdity, fallaciousness, fallacy, inconsistency, invalidity, Irishness, irrationality, senselessness, speciousness, unreason, unsoundness.

*antonym* logicality.

**ill-omened** *adj* doomed, ill-fated, inauspicious, infaust, star-crossed, unfortunate, unhappy, unlucky.

*antonym* fortunate.

**ill-tempered** *adj* bad-tempered, choleric, cross, curt, grumpy, ill-humoured, ill-natured, impatient, irascible, irritable, sharp, spiteful, testy, tetchy, touchy, vicious, vixenish, vixenly.

*antonym* good-tempered.

**ill-timed** *adj* awkward, crass, inappropriate, inconvenient, inept, inopportune, tactless, unseasonable, untimely, unwelcome, wrong-timed.

*antonym* well-timed.

**ill-treat** *v* abuse, damage, harass, harm, harry, ill-use, injure, maltreat, manhandle, mishandle, mistreat, misuse, neglect, oppress, wrong.

*antonym* care for.

**ill-treatment** *n* abuse, damage, harm, ill-use, injury, maltreatment, manhandling, mishandling, mistreatment, misuse, neglect.

*antonym* care.

**illuminate** *v* adorn, beacon, brighten, clarify, clear up, decorate, edify, elucidate, enlighten, explain, illumine, illustrate, instruct, irradiate, light, light up, limn, miniate, ornament.

*antonyms* darken, deface, divest.

**illuminating** *adj* edifying, enlightening, explanatory, helpful, informative, instructive, revealing, revelatory.

*antonym* unhelpful.

**illumination** *n* adornment, awareness, beam, brightening, brightness, clarification, decoration, edification, enlightenment, insight, inspiration, instruction, light, lighting, lights, limning, miniation, ornamentation, perception, radiance, ray, revelation, splendour, understanding.

*antonym* darkness.

**illusion** *n* apparition, chimera, daydream, deception, delusion, error, fallacy, fancy, fantasy, figment, hallucination, ignis fatuus, maya, mirage, misapprehension, misconception, phantasm, semblance, will-o'-the-wisp.

*antonym* reality.

**illusory** *adj* apparent, Barmecidal, beguiling, chimerical, deceitful, deceptive, deluding, delusive, fallacious, false, hallucinatory, illusive, misleading, mistaken, seeming, sham, unreal, unsubstantial, untrue, vain.

*antonym* real.

**illustrate** *v* adorn, clarify, decorate, demonstrate, depict, draw, elucidate, emphasise, exemplify, exhibit, explain, illuminate, instance, interpret, miniate, ornament, picture, show, sketch.

**illustrated** *adj* decorated, embellished, illuminated, miniated, pictorial.

**illustration** *n* adornment, analogy, case, case in point, clarification, decoration, delineation, demonstration, drawing, elucidation, example, exemplification, explanation, figure, graphic, half-tone, instance, interpretation, photograph, picture, plate, representation, sketch, specimen.

**illustrative** *adj* delineative, descriptive, diagrammatic, explanatory, explicatory, expository, graphic, illustrational, illustratory, interpretive, pictorial, representative, sample, specimen, typical.

**illustrious** *adj* brilliant, celebrated, distinguished, eminent, exalted, excellent, famed, famous, glorious, great, magnificent, noble, notable, noted, outstanding, prominent, remarkable, renowned, resplendent, signal, splendid.

*antonyms* inglorious, shameful.

**ill-will** *n* acrimony, animosity, animus, antagonism, antipathy, aversion, bad blood, dislike, enmity, envy, grudge, hard feelings, hatred, hostility, malevolence, malice, odium, rancour, resentment, spite, unfriendliness, venom.

*antonyms* friendship, good-will.

**image** *n* appearance, conceit, concept, conception, counterpart, dead ringer, Doppelgänger, double, effigies, effigy, eidolon, eikon, facsimile, figure, icon, idea, idol, impression, likeness, perception, picture, portrait, reflection, replica, representation, semblance, similitude, simulacrum, spit, spitting image, statue, trope.

**imaginable** *adj* believable, comprehensible, conceivable, credible, likely, plausible, possible, predictable, supposable, thinkable, visualisable.

*antonym* unimaginable.

**imaginary** *adj* assumed, Barmecidal, chimerical, dreamlike, fancied, fanciful, fictional, fictitious, hallucinatory, hypothetical, ideal, illusive,

illusory, imagined, insubstantial, invented, legendary, made-up, mythological, non-existent, phantasmal, shadowy, supposed, unreal, unsubstantial, visionary.

*antonym* real.

**imagination** *n* chimera, conception, creativity, enterprise, fancy, idea, ideality, illusion, image, imaginativeness, ingenuity, innovativeness, innovatoriness, insight, inspiration, invention, inventiveness, notion, originality, resourcefulness, supposition, unreality, vision, wit, wittiness.

*antonyms* reality, unimaginativeness.

**imaginative** *adj* clever, creative, dreamy, enterprising, fanciful, fantastic, fertile, ingenious, innovative, inspired, inventive, original, poetical, resourceful, visionary, vivid.

*antonym* unimaginative.

**imagine** *v* apprehend, assume, believe, conceive, conceptualise, conjecture, conjure up, create, deduce, deem, devise, dream up, envisage, envision, fancy, fantasise, frame, gather, guess, ideate, infer, invent, judge, picture, plan, project, realise, scheme, suppose, surmise, suspect, take it, think, think of, think up, visualise.

**imbalance** *n* bias, disparity, disproportion, imparity, inequality, lopsidedness, partiality, top-heaviness, unequalness, unevenness, unfairness.

*antonym* parity.

**imbecile** *n* ament, blockhead, bungler, clown, cretin, dolt, dotard, fool, half-wit, idiot, moron, thickhead.

*adj* anile, asinine, doltish, fatuous, feeble-minded, foolish, idiotic, imbecilic, inane, ludicrous, moronic, senile, simple, stupid, thick, witless.

*antonyms* intelligent, sensible.

**imbecility** *n* amentia, anility, asininity, childishness, cretinism, fatuity, foolishness, idiocy, inanity, incompetency, senility, stupidity.

*antonyms* intelligence, sense.

**imbibe** *v* absorb, acquire, assimilate, consume, drink, drink in, gain, gather, gulp, ingest, knock back, lap up, quaff, receive, sink, sip, soak in, soak up, swallow, swig, take in.

**imbroglio, embroglio** *n* confusion, difficulty, dilemma, embroilment, entanglement, involvement, mess, muddle, quandary, scrape, tangle.

**imbue** *v* bathe, colour, dye, fill, impregnate, inculcate, infuse, ingrain, instil, moisten, permeate, pervade, saturate, stain, steep, suffuse, tinge, tint.

**imitate** *v* affect, ape, burlesque, caricature, clone, copy, copy-cat, counterfeit, do, duplicate, echo, emulate, follow, follow suit, forge, impersonate, mimic, mirror, mock, monkey, parody, parrot, personate, repeat, reproduce, send up, simulate, spoof, take off, travesty.

**imitation** *n* apery, aping, copy, counterfeit, counterfeiting, duplication, echoing, echopraxia, echopraxis, fake, forgery, impersonation, impression, likeness, me-tooism, mimesis, mimicry, mockery, parody, reflection, replica, reproduction, resemblance, sham, simulation, substitution, take-off, travesty.

*adj* artificial, dummy, ersatz, man-made, mock, phoney, pinchbeck, pseudo, repro, reproduction, sham, simulated, synthetic.

*antonym* genuine.

**imitative** *adj* apish, copied, copycat, copying, derivative, echoic, me-too, mimetic, mimicking, mock, onomatopoeic, parodistic, parrot-like, plagiarised, pseudo, put-on, second-hand, simulated, unoriginal.

**imitator** *n* ape, aper, copier, copy-cat, echo, epigone, follower, impersonator, impressionist, me-tooer, mimic, parodist, parrot.

**immaculate** *adj* blameless, clean, faultless, flawless, guiltless, impeccable, incorrupt, innocent, neat, perfect, pure, scrupulous, sinless, spick-and-span, spotless, spruce, stainless, trim, unblemished, uncontaminated, undefiled, unexceptionable, unpolluted, unsullied, untainted, untarnished, virtuous.

*antonyms* contaminated, spoiled.

**immaterial** *adj* airy, disembodied, ethereal, extraneous, ghostly, impertinent, inapposite, inconsequential, inconsiderable, incorporeal, inessential, insignificant, insubstantial, irrelevant, metaphysical, minor, spiritual, trifling, trivial, unimportant, unnecessary, unsubstantial.

*antonyms* important, material, solid.

**immature** *adj* adolescent, babyish, callow, childish, crude, green, immatured, imperfect, inexperienced, infantile, jejune, juvenile, premature, puerile, raw, under-age, undeveloped, unfinished, unfledged, unformed, unripe, unseasonable, untimely, young.

*antonym* mature.

**immaturity** *n* babyishness, callowness, childishness, crudeness, crudity, greenness, immatureness, imperfection, inexperience, juvenility, prematureness, prematurity, puerility, rawness, unpreparedness, unripeness.

*antonym* maturity.

**immeasurable** *adj* bottomless, boundless, endless, illimitable, immense, immensurable, incalculable, inestimable, inexhaustible, infinite, limitless, measureless, unbounded, unfathomable, unlimited, unmeasureable, vast.

*antonym* limited.

**immediacy** *n* directness, imminence, instancy, instantaneity, promptness, simultaneity, spontaneity, swiftness.

*antonym* remoteness.

**immediate** *adj* actual, adjacent, close, contiguous, current, direct, existing, extant, instant, instantaneous, near, nearest, neighbouring, next, on hand, present, pressing, primary, prompt, proximate, recent, unhesitating, up-to-date, urgent.

*antonym* distant.

**immediately** *adv* at once, closely, directly, ek dum, forthwith, incontinent, instantly, lickety-split, nearly, now, off the top of one's head, on the instant, posthaste, promptly, pronto, right away, soonest, straight away, straight off, straight way, tout de suite, unhesitatingly, without delay.

*antonyms* eventually, never.

**immemorial** *adj* age-old, ancestral, ancient, archaic, fixed, hoary, long-standing, time-honoured, traditional.

*antonym* recent.

**immense** *adj* Brobdingnag(ian), colossal, cyclopean, elephantine, enormous, extensive, giant, gigantic, great, herculean, huge, illimitable, immeasurable, infinite, interminable, jumbo, large, limitless, mammoth, massive, monstrous, monumental, prodigious, rounceval, stupendous, Titanesque, titanic, tremendous, vast.

*antonym* minute.

**immensity** *n* bulk, enormousness, expanse, extent, greatness, hugeness, infinity, magnitude, massiveness, scope, size, sweep, vastness.

*antonym* minuteness.

**immerse** *v* bathe, demerge, demerse, dip, douse, duck, dunk, plunge, sink, submerge, submerse.

**immersed** *adj* absorbed, buried, busy, consumed, deep, engrossed, involved, occupied, preoccupied, rapt, sunk, taken up, wrapped up.

**immersion** *n* absorption, baptism, bathe, concentration, demersion, dip, dipping, dousing, ducking, dunking, involvement, plunging, preoccupation, submersion.

**immigrant** *n* incomer, newcomer, settler, wetback.

*antonym* emigrant.

**immigrate** *v* come in, migrate, move in, remove, resettle, settle.

*antonym* emigrate.

**imminence** *n* approach, immediacy, impendency, instancy, menace, propinquity, threat.

*antonym* remoteness.

**imminent** *adj* afoot, approaching, at hand, brewing, close, coming, forthcoming, gathering, impending, in the air, in the offing, looming, menacing, near, nigh, overhanging, threatening.

*antonym* far-off.

**immobile** *adj* at a standstill, at rest, cataplectic, expressionless, fixed, frozen, immobilised, immotile, immovable, motionless, rigid, riveted, rooted, solid, stable, static, stationary, stiff, still, stock-still, stolid, unexpressive, unmoving.

*antonyms* mobile, moving.

**immobilise** *v* cripple, disable, fix, freeze, halt, paralyse, stop, transfix.

*antonym* mobilise.

**immobility** *n* disability, firmness, fixedness, fixity, immovability, inertness, motionlessness, stability, steadiness, stillness.

*antonym* mobility.

**immoderate** *adj* distemperate, egregious, enormous, exaggerated, excessive, exorbitant, extravagant, extreme, hubristic, inordinate, intemperate, over the top, profligate, steep, uncalled-for, unconscionable, uncontrolled, undue, unjustified, unreasonable, unrestrained, unwarranted, wanton.

*antonym* moderate.

**immoderately** *adv* exaggeratedly, excessively, exorbitantly, extravagantly, extremely, inordinately, unduly, unjustifiably, unreasonably, unrestrainedly, wantonly, without measure.

*antonym* moderately.

**immoderation** *n* excess, exorbitance, extravagance, immoderateness, intemperance, overindulgence, prodigality, unreason, unrestraint.

*antonym* moderation.

**immodest** *adj* bawdy, bold, brass-necked, brazen, coarse, depraved, forward, fresh, gross, immoral, improper, impudent, impure, indecent, indecorous, indelicate, lewd, obscene, pushy, revealing, risqué, shameless, titillating, unblushing, unchaste, unmaidenly.

*antonym* modest.

**immodesty** *n* audacity, bawdiness, boldness, brass, coarseness, forwardness, gall, impudence, impurity, indecorousness, indecorum, indelicacy, lewdness, obscenity, shamelessness, temerity.

*antonym* modesty.

**immoral** *adj* abandoned, bad, corrupt, debauched, degenerate, depraved, dishonest, dissolute, evil, foul, impure, indecent, iniquitous, lecherous, lewd, licentious, nefarious, obscene, pornographic, profligate, reprobate, sinful, unchaste, unethical, unprincipled, unrighteous, unscrupulous, vicious, vile, wanton, wicked, wrong.

*antonym* moral.

**immorality** *n* badness, corruption, debauchery, depravity, dissoluteness, evil, iniquity, libertinage, licence, licentiousness, profligacy, sin, turpitude, vice, wickedness, wrong.

*antonym* morality.

**immortal** *adj* abiding, ambrosial, constant, deathless, endless, enduring, eternal, everlasting, imperishable, incorruptible, indestructable, lasting, perennial, perpetual, sempiternal, timeless, undying, unfading, unforgettable.

*antonym* mortal.

*n* deity, divinity, genius, god, goddess, great, hero, Olympian.

**immortalise** *v* apotheosise, celebrate, commemorate, deify, enshrine, eternalise, eternise, exalt, glorify, hallow, memorialise, perpetuate, solemnise.

**immortality** *n* athanasy, celebrity, deathlessness, deification, endlessness, eternity, everlasting life, fame, glorification, gloriousness, glory, greatness, incorruptibility, indestructibility, perpetuity, renown, timelessness.

*antonym* mortality.

**immovable** *adj* adamant, constant, determined, entrenched, fast, firm, fixed, immutable, impassive, inflexible, jammed, marble-constant, moveless, obdurate, obstinate, resolute, rooted, secure, set, stable, stationary, steadfast, stony, stuck, unbudgeable, unchangeable, unimpressionable, unmovable, unshakable, unshaken, unwavering, unyielding.

*antonym* movable.

**immune** *adj* clear, exempt, free, insusceptible, insusceptive, invulnerable, proof, protected, resistant, safe, unaffected, unsusceptible.

*antonym* susceptible.

**immunisation** *n* injection, inoculation, jab, jag, protection, vaccination.

**immunise** *v* inject, inoculate, protect, safeguard, vaccinate.

**immunity** *n* amnesty, charter, exemption, exoneration, franchise, freedom, immunisation, indemnity, insusceptibility, invulnerability, liberty, licence, mithridatism, prerogative, privilege, protection, release, resistance, right.

*antonym* susceptibility.

**immure** *v* cage, cloister, confine, enclose, enwall, imprison, incarcerate, jail, shut up, wall in.

*antonym* free.

**immutability** *n* changelessness, constancy, durability, fixedness, immutableness, invariability, permanence, stability, unalterableness, unchangeableness.

*antonym* mutability.

**immutable** *adj* abiding, changeless, constant, enduring, fixed, inflexible, invariable, lasting, permanent, perpetual, sacrosanct, solid, stable, steadfast, unalterable, unchangeable.

*antonym* mutable.

**imp** *n* brat, demon, devil, flibbertigibbet, gamin, minx, prankster, rascal, rogue, scamp, sprite, trickster, urchin.

**impact** *n* aftermath, bang, blow, brunt, bump, burden, collision, concussion, consequences, contact, crash, effect, force, impression, influence, jolt, knock, knock-on effect, meaning, power, repercussions, shock, significance, smash, stroke, thrust, thump, weight.

*v* clash, collide, crash, crush, fix, hit, press together, strike, wedge.

**impair** *v* blunt, craze, damage, debilitate, decrease, deteriorate, devalue, diminish, enervate, enfeeble, harm, hinder, injure, lessen, mar, reduce, spoil, undermine, vitiate, weaken, worsen.

*antonym* enhance.

**impaired** *adj* damaged, defective, faulty, flawed, imperfect, poor, unsound, vicious, vitiated.

*antonym* enhanced.

**impairment** *n* damage, deterioration, disablement, dysfunction, fault, flaw, harm, hurt, injury, reduction, ruin, vitiation.

*antonym* enhancement.

**impale** *v* ga(u)nch, lance, perforate, pierce, puncture, run through, skewer, spear, spike, spit, stick, transfix.

**impalpable** *adj* airy, delicate, disembodied, elusive, fine, imperceptible, inapprehensible, incorporeal, indistinct, insubstantial, intangible, shadowy, tenuous, thin, unsubstantial.

*antonym* palpable.

**impalpably** *adv* imperceptibly, insensibly, intangibly, slightly.

*antonym* perceptibly.

**imparity** *n* bias, disparity, disproportion, imbalance, inequality, inequity, partiality, unequalness, unevenness, unfairness.

*antonym* parity.

**impart** *v* accord, afford, bestow, communicate, confer, contribute, convey, disclose, discover, divulge, give, grant, hand over, lend, make known, offer, pass on, relate, reveal, tell, yield.

**impartial** *adj* crossbench, detached, disinterested, dispassionate, equal, equitable, even-handed, fair, just, neutral, non-discriminating, non-partisan, objective, open-minded, umcommitted, unbiased, unprejudiced.

*antonym* biased.

**impartiality** *n* detachment, disinterest, disinterestedness, dispassion, equality, equity, even-handedness, fairness, neutrality, non-partisanship, objectivity, open-mindedness, unbiasedness.

*antonym* bias.

**impassable** *adj* blocked, closed, impenetrable, invious, obstructed, pathless, trackless, unnavigable, unpassable.

*antonym* passable.

**impasse** *n* blind alley, cul-de-sac, dead end, deadlock, halt, nonplus, stalemate, stand-off, standstill.

**impassioned** *adj* animated, ardent, blazing, enthusiastic, excited, fervent, fervid, fiery, furious, glowing, heated, inflamed, inspired, intense, passionate, rousing, spirited, stirring, vehement, vigorous, violent, vivid, warm.

*antonyms* apathetic, mild.

**impassive** *adj* aloof, apathetic, blockish, callous, calm, composed, cool, dispassionate, emotionless, expressionless, immobile, impassible, imperturbable, indifferent, inscrutable, insensible, insusceptible, laid back, phlegmatic, poker-faced, reserved, serene, stoical, stolid, unconcerned, unemotional, unexcitable, unfeeling, unimpressible, unmoved, unruffled.

*antonyms* moved, responsive, warm.

**impassivity** *n* aloofness, calmness, composure, coolness, dispassion, impassibility, impassiveness, imperturbability, indifference, inscrutability, insensibility, phlegm, sang-froid, stoicism, stolidity.

*antonyms* compassion, responsiveness, warmth.

**impatience** *n* agitation, anxiety, avidity, avidness, eagerness, edginess, haste, hastiness, heat, impetuosity, intolerance, irritability, irritableness, nervousness, rashness, restiveness, restlessness, shortness, snappishness, testiness, uneasiness, vehemence.

*antonym* patience.

**impatient** *adj* abrupt, brusque, chafing, champing at the bit, curt, demanding, eager, edgy, fretful, hasty, headlong, hot-tempered, impetuous, intolerant, irritable, precipitate, quick-tempered, restless, snappy, testy, vehement, violent.

*antonym* patient.

**impeach** *v* accuse, arraign, blame, cast doubt on, censure, challenge, charge, denounce, disparage, grass on, impugn, indict, peach on, question, tax.

**impeachment** *n* accusation, arraignment, charge, disparagement, indictment.

**impeccable** *adj* blameless, exact, exquisite, flawless, immaculate, incorrupt, innocent, irreproachable, perfect, precise, pure, scrupulous, sinless, squeaky-clean, stainless, unblemished, unerring, unimpeachable.

*antonym* flawed.

**impecunious** *adj* broke, cleaned out, destitute, impoverished, indigent, insolvent, penniless, penurious, poor, poverty-stricken, skint, stony.

*antonym* rich.

**impede** *v* bar, block, brake, check, clog, curb, delay, disrupt, hamper, hinder, hobble, hold up, let, obstruct, restrain, retard, slow, stop, thwart, trammel.

*antonym* aid.

**impediment** *n* bar, barrier, block, burr, check, clog, curb, defect, difficulty, encumbrance, hindrance, let, log, obstacle, obstruction, snag, stammer, stumbling-block, stutter.

*antonym* aid.

**impel** *v* actuate, chivvy, compel, constrain, drive, excite, force, goad, incite, induce, influence, inspire, instigate, motivate, move, oblige, poke, power, prod, prompt, propel, push, spur, stimulate, urge.

*antonym* dissuade.

**impending** *adj* approaching, brewing, close, collecting, coming, forthcoming, gathering, hovering, imminent, in store, looming, menacing, near, nearing, threatening.

*antonym* remote.

**impenetrable** *adj* arcane, baffling, cabbalistic, cryptic, dark, dense, enigmatic(al), fathomless, hermetic, hidden, impassable, impermeable, impervious, incomprehensible, indiscernible, inexplicable, inscrutable, inviolable, mysterious, obscure, solid, thick, unfathomable, unintelligible, unpiercable.

*antonyms* imtelligible, penetrable.

**impenitence** *n* defiance, hard-heartedness, impenitency, incorrigibility, obduracy, recidivism, stubbornness.

*antonym* penitence.

**impenitent** *adj* defiant, hardened, incorrigible, obdurate, recidivisitic, remorseless, unabashed, unashamed, uncontrite, unreformed, unregenerate, unremorseful, unrepentant.

*antonym* penitent.

**imperative** *adj* authoritative, autocratic, bossy, commanding, compulsory, crucial, dictatorial, domineering, essential, exigent, high-handed, imperious, indispensable, insistent, lordly, magisterial, obligatory, peremptory, pressing, tyrannical, tyrannous, urgent, vital.

*antonyms* humble, optional.

**imperceptible** *adj* faint, fine, gradual, impalpable, inapparent, inappreciable, inaudible, inconsensequential, indiscernible, indistinguishable, infinitesimal, insensible, invisible, microscopic, minute, shadowy, slight, small, subtle, tiny, undetectable, unnoticeable.

*antonym* perceptible.

**imperceptibly** *adv* inappreciably, indiscernibly, insensibly, invisibly, little by little, slowly, subtly, unnoticeably, unobtrusively, unseen.

*antonym* perceptibly.

**imperceptive** *adj* crass, dim, dull, impercipient, insensitive, obtuse, superficial, unappreciative, unaware, undiscerning, unobservant, unseeing.

*antonym* perceptive.

**imperfect** *adj* abortive, broken, damaged, defective, deficient, faulty, flawed, impaired, incomplete, inexact, limited, partial, patchy, rudimentary, unfinished, unideal.

*antonym* perfect.

**imperfection** *n* blemish, blot, blotch, crack, defect, deficiency, dent, failing, fallibility, fault, flaw, foible, frailty, glitch, inadequacy, incompleteness, insufficiency, peccadillo, shortcoming, stain, taint, weakness.

*antonyms* asset, perfection.

**imperial** *adj* august, exalted, grand, great, imperatorial, imperious, kingly, lofty, magnificent, majestic, noble, princely, queenly, regal, royal, sovereign, superior, supreme.

**imperialism** *n* acquisitiveness, adventurism, colonialism, empire-building, expansionism.

**imperil** *v* compromise, endanger, expose, hazard, jeopardise, risk, threaten.

**imperious** *adj* arrogant, authoritarian, autocratic, bossy, commanding, demanding, despotic, dictatorial, domineering, exacting, haughty, high-and-mighty, high-handed, imperative, lordly, magisterial, overbearing, overweening, peremptory, tyrannical, tyrannous.

*antonym* humble.

**imperishable** *adj* abiding, deathless, enduring, eternal, everlasting, immortal, incorruptible, indestructible, inextinguishable, perennial, permanent, perpetual, undying, unfading, unforgettable.

*antonym* perishable.

**impermanent** *adj* brief, elusive, ephemeral, evanescent, fleeting, fly-by-night, flying, fugacious, fugitive, inconstant, momentary, mortal, passing, perishable, short-lived, temporary, transient, transitory, unfixed, unsettled, unstable.

*antonym* permanent.

**impermeable** *adj* damp-proof, hermetic, impassable, impenetrable, impervious, non-porous, proof, resistant, waterproof, water-repellent, water-resistant.

*antonym* permeable.

**impersonal** *adj* aloof, bureaucratic, businesslike, cold, detached, dispassionate, faceless, formal, frosty, glassy, inhuman, neutral, official, remote, unfriendly, unsympathetic.

*antonym* friendly.

**impersonate** *v* act, ape, caricature, do, imitate, masquerade as, mimic, mock, parody, personate, pose as, take off.

**impersonation** *n* apery, aping, burlesque, caricature, imitation, impression, mimicry, parody, take-off.

**impertinence** *n* assurance, audacity, backchat, boldness, brass, brazenness, cheek, discourtesy, disrespect, effrontery, forwardness, impoliteness, impudence, incivility, insolence, malapertness, nerve, pertness, politeness, presumption, rudeness, sauce, sauciness.

**impertinent** *adj* bold, brattish, brazen, bumptious, cheeky, discourteous, disrespectful, forward, fresh, ill-mannered, impolite, impudent, insolent, interfering, malapert, pert, presumptuous, rude, saucy, uncivil, unmannerly.

*antonym* polite.

**imperturbability** *n* calmness, complacency, composure, coolness, equanimity, self-possession, tranquility.

*antonyms* jitteriness, touchiness.

**imperturbable** *adj* calm, collected, complacent, composed, cool, equanimous, impassible, optimistic, sanguine, sedate, self-possessed, stoical, tranquil, unexcitable, unflappable.

*antonyms* jittery, touchy.

**impervious** *adj* closed, damp-proof, hermetic, immune, impassable, impenetrable, impermeable, imperviable, invulnerable, resistant, sealed, unaffected, unmoved, unreceptive, unswayable, untouched.

*antonyms* pervious, responsive.

**impetuosity** *n* dash, élan, haste, hastiness, impetuousness, impulsiveness, precipitancy, precipitateness, rashness, vehemence, violence.

*antonym* circumspection.

**impetuous** *adj* ardent, bull-headed, eager, furious, hasty, headlong, impassioned, impulsive, overhasty, passionate, precipitate, rash, spontaneous, tearaway, unplanned, unpremeditated, unreflecting, unrestrained, unthinking.

*antonym* circumspect.

**impetuously** *adv* impulsively, passionately, precipitately, rashly, recklessly, spontaneously, unthinkingly, vehemently.

*antonym* circumspectly.

**impetus** *n* drive, energy, force, goad, impulse, impulsion, incentive, momentum, motivation, motive, power, push, spur, stimulus.

**impiety** *n* blasphemy, godlessness, hubris, iniquity, irreligion, irreverence, profaneness, profanity, sacrilege, sacrilegiousness, sinfulness, ungodliness, unholiness, unrighteousness, wickedness.

*antonym* piety.

**impinge** *v* affect, clash, collide, dash, encroach, enter, hit, influence, infringe, intrude, invade, obtrude, strike, touch, touch on, trespass, violate.

**impious** *adj* blasphemous, godless, hubristic, iniquitous, irreligious, irreverent, profane, sacrilegious, sinful, ungodly, unholy, unrighteous, wicked.

*antonym* pious.

**impish** *adj* arch, devilish, elfin, frolicsome, gamin, mischievous, naughty, pranksome, puckish, rascally, roguish, sportive, tricksome, tricksy, waggish, wanton, wicked.

**impishness** *n* archness, devilry, deviltry, gaminerie, mischief, naughtiness, puckishness, roguery, roguishness, sportiveness, waggishness, wickedness.

**implacability** *n* implacableness, inexorability, inflexibility, intransigence, intractability, irreconcilability, mercilessness, pitilessness, rancorousness, relentlessness, remorselessness, ruthlessness, unforgivingness, vengefulness.

*antonym* placability.

**implacable** *adj* cruel, immovable, inappeasable, inexorable, inflexible, intractable, intransigent, irreconcilable, merciless, pitiless, rancorous, relentless, remorseless, ruthless, unappeasable, unbending, uncompromising, unforgiving, unrelenting, unyielding.

*antonym* placable.

**implant** *v* embed, fix, graft, inculcate, infix, infuse, ingraft, inoculate, inseminate, insert, inset, instil, place, plant, root, sow.

**implausible** *adj* dubious, far-fetched, flimsy, improbable, incredible, suspect, thin, transparent, unbelievable, unconvincing, unlikely, unplausible, unreasonable, weak.

*antonym* plausible.

**implement** *n* agent, apparatus, appliance, device, gadget, gimmick, gismo, instrument, tool, utensil.
*v* accomplish, bring about, carry out, complete, discharge, do, effect, enforce, execute, fulfil, perfect, perform, realise.

**implementation** *n* accomplishment, carrying out, completion, discharge, effecting, enforcement, execution, fulfilling, fulfilment, performance, performing, realisation.

**implicate** *v* associate, compromise, connect, embroil, entangle, include, incriminate, inculpate, involve, throw suspicion on.

*antonyms* absolve, exonerate.

**implicated** *adj* associated, compromised, embroiled, entangled, incriminated, inculpated, involved, suspected.

*antonym* exonerated.

**implication** *n* association, assumption, conclusion, connection, entanglement, hint, incrimination, inference, innuendo, insinuation, involvement, meaning, overtone, presupposition, ramification, repercusssion, significance, signification, suggestion, undertone.

**implicit** *adj* absolute, constant, contained, entire, firm, fixed, full, implied, inherent, latent, presupposed, steadfast, tacit, total, undeclared, understood, unhesitating, unqualified, unquestioning, unreserved, unshakable, unshaken, unspoken, wholehearted.

*antonym* explicit.

**implicitly** *adv* absolutely, by implication, completely, firmly, unconditionally, unhesitatingly, unquestioningly, unreservedly, utterly.

*antonym* explicitly.

**implied** *adj* assumed, hinted, implicit, indirect, inherent, insinuated, suggested, tacit, undeclared, understood, unexpressed, unspoken, unstated.

*antonym* stated.

**implore** *v* ask, beg, beseech, crave, entreat, importune, plead, pray, solicit, supplicate, wheedle.

**imply** *v* betoken, connote, denote, entail, evidence, hint, import, indicate, insinuate, intimate, involve, mean, point to, presuppose, require, signify, suggest.

*antonym* state.

**impolite** *adj* abrupt, bad-mannered, boorish, churlish, clumsy, coarse, cross, discourteous, disrespectful, gauche, ill-bred, ill-mannered, indecorous, indelicate, inept, insolent, loutish, rough, rude, uncivil, uncourteous, ungallant, ungentlemanly, ungracious, unladylike, unmannerly, unrefined.

*antonym* polite.

**impoliteness** *n* abruptness, bad manners, boorishness, churlishness, clumsiness, coarseness, crassness, discourtesy, disrespect, gaucherie, incivility, indelicacy, ineptitude, insolence, rudeness, unmannerliness.

*antonym* politeness.

**impolitic** *adj* daft, foolish, ill-advised, ill-judged, imprudent, indiscreet, inexpedient, injudicious, maladroit, misguided, rash, undiplomatic, unwise.

*antonym* politic.

**import** *n* bearing, consequence, drift, essence, gist, implication, importance, intention, magnitude, meaning, message, moment, nub, purport, sense, significance, substance, thrust, weight.
*v* betoken, bring in, imply, indicate, introduce, mean, purport, signify.

**importance** *n* concern, concernment, consequence, consideration, distinction, eminence, esteem, gravitas, import, influence, interest, mark, moment, momentousness, pith, pre-eminence, prestige, prominence, significance, signification, standing, status, substance, usefulness, value, weight, worth.

*antonym* unimportance.

**important** *adj* basic, earthshaking, earthshattering, eminent, essential, far-reaching, foremost, grave, heavy, high-level, high-ranking, influential, key, keynote, large, leading, material, meaningful, momentous, notable, noteworthy, on the map, outstanding, powerful, pre-eminent, primary, prominent, relevant, salient, seminal, serious, signal, significant, substantial, urgent, valuable, valued, weighty.

*antonym* unimportant.

**importunate** *adj* impatient, insistent, persistent, pertinacious, pressing, tenacious, urgent, wheedlesome, wheedling, whilly, whillywha(w).

**importune** *v* badger, beset, besiege, cajole, dun, earwig, entreat, flagitate, harass, hound, pester, plague, plead with, press, solicit, urge.

**importunity** *n* cajolery, entreaties, harassment, insistence, persistence, solicitation, urgency, urging.

**impose**[1] *v* appoint, burden, charge (with), decree, dictate, encumber, enforce, enjoin, establish, exact, fix, impone, inflict, institute, introduce, lay, levy, ordain, place, prescribe, promulgate, put, saddle, set.

**impose**[2] *v* butt in, encroach, foist, force oneself, gate crash, horn in, impone, interpose, intrude, obtrude, presume, take liberties, trespass.

**impose on** abuse, deceive, exploit, fool, hoodwink, mislead, play on, take advantage of, trick, use.

**imposing** *adj* august, commanding, dignified, distinguished, effective, grand, grandiose, impressive, majestic, ortund, pompous, stately, striking.

*antonyms* modest, unimposing.

**imposition**[1] *n* application, decree, exaction, infliction, introduction, levying, promulgation.

**imposition**[2] *n* burden, charge, cheek, constraint, deception, duty, encroachment, intrusion, levy, liberty, lines, presumption, punishment, task, tax.

**impossibility** *n* hopelessness, impracticability, inability, inconceivability, unattainableness, unobtainableness, untenability, unviability.

*antonym* possibility.

**impossible** *adj* absurd, hopeless, impracticable, inadmissible, inconceivable, insoluble, intolerable, ludicrous, outrageous, preposterous, unacceptable, unachievable, unattainable, ungovernable, unobtainable, unreasonable, untenable, unthinkable, unviable, unworkable.

*antonym* possible.

**impostor** *n* charlatan, cheat, con man, deceiver, faitor, fake, fraud, grifter, hypocrite, impersonator, mountebank, phoney, pretender, quack, rogue, sham, swindler, trickster.

**imposture** *n* artifice, cheat, con, con trick, counterfeit, deception, fraud, grift, hoax, impersonation, quackery, swindle, trick.

**impotence** *n* disability, enervation, feebleness, frailty, helplessness, impuissance, inability, inadequacy, incapacity, incompetence, ineffectiveness, inefficacy, inefficiency, infirmity, ligature, paralysis, powerlessness, resourcelessness, uselessness, weakness.

*antonym* strength.

**impotent** *adj* disabled, enervated, feeble, frail, helpless, impuissant, inadequate, incapable, incapacitated, incompetent, ineffective, infirm, paralysed, powerless, resourceless, unable, unmanned, weak.

*antonyms* potent, strong.

**impoverish** *v* bankrupt, beggar, break, denude, depauperate, deplete, diminish, drain, exhaust, pauperise, reduce, ruin, weaken.

*antonym* enrich.

**impoverished** *adj* arid, bankrupt, barren, decayed, denuded, depauperate(d), depleted, destitute, distressed, drained, empty, exhausted, impecunious, in reduced circumstances, indigent, jejune, necessitous, needy, on the rocks, penurious, poor, poorly off, reduced, skint, spent, straitened.

*antonym* rich.

**impracticability** *n* futility, hopelessness, impossibility, impracticality, infeasibility, unsuitableness, unviability, unworkability, uselessness.

*antonym* practicability.

**impracticable** *adj* awkward, doctrinaire, impossible, impractical, inapplicable, inconvenient, infeasible, unachievable, unattainable, unfeasible, unpractical, unserviceable, unsuitable, unworkable, useless, visionary.

*antonym* practicable.

**impractical** *adj* academic, idealistic, impossible, impracticable, inoperable, ivory-tower, non-viable, romantic, starry-eyed, unbusinesslike, unrealistic, unserviceable, unworkable, visionary, wild.

*antonym* practical.

**impracticality** *n* hopelessness, idealism, impossibility, infeasibility, romanticism, unworkability, unworkableness.

*antonym* practicality.

**imprecation** *n* abuse, anathema, blasphemy, curse, denunciation, execration, malediction, profanity, vilification, vituperation.

**imprecise** *adj* ambiguous, careless, equivocal, estimated, fluctuating, hazy, ill-defined, inaccurate, indefinite, indeterminate, inexact, inexplicit, loose, rough, sloppy, unprecise, unscholarly, unscientific, vague, woolly.

*antonym* precise.

**impregnable** *adj* fast, fortified, immovable, impenetrable, impugnable, indestructible, invincible, invulnerable, secure, solid, strong, unassailable, unbeatable, unconquerable.

*antonym* vulnerable.

**impregnate** *v* fecundate, fertilise, fill, fructify, imbrue, imbue, infuse, inseminate, knock up, percolate, permeate, pervade, saturate, soak, steep, suffuse.

**impregnation** *n* fecundation, fertilisation, fertilising, fructification, fructifying, imbruement, imbruing, imbuing, insemination, saturation.

**impress** *v* affect, emboss, emphasise, engrave, excite, fix, grab, imprint, inculcate, indent, influence, inspire, instil, make one's mark, mark, move, namedrop, print, slay, stamp, stand out, stir, strike, sway, touch, wow.

**impressed** *adj* affected, épris, excited, grabbed, imprinted, indented, influenced, marked, moved, stamped, stirred, struck, taken, touched, turned on.

*antonym* unimpressed.

**impression**[1] *n* awareness, belief, concept, consciousness, conviction, effect, fancy, feeling, hunch, idea, impact, influence, memory, notion, opinion, reaction, recollection, sense, suspicion, sway.

**impression**[2] *n* dent, edition, engram, engramma, hollow, impress, imprint, imprinting, incuse, indentation, issue, mark, niello, outline, pressure, printing, stamp, stamping.

**impression**[3] *n* apery, aping, burlesque, imitation, impersonation, parody, send-up, take-off.

**impressionability** *n* greenness, impressibility, ingenuousness, naïvety, receptiveness, receptivity, sensitivity, suggestibility, susceptibility, vulnerability.

**impressionable** *adj* gullible, impressible, ingenuous, naïve, open, receptive, responsive, sensitive, suggestible, susceptible, vulnerable.

**impressive** *adj* affecting, effective, exciting, forcible, foudroyant, frappant, imposing, moving, powerful, stirring, striking, touching.

*antonym* unimpressive.

**imprint** *n* badge, brand mark, impression, indentation, logo, mark, print, sign, stamp.

*v* brand, engrave, etch, fix, impress, mark, print, stamp.

**imprison** *v* cage, confine, constrain, detain, encage, enchain, immure, incarcerate, intern, jail, lock up, put away, quod, send down.

*antonym* free.

**imprisoned** *adj* bars, behind, caged, captive, confined, doing bird, doing time, immured, incarcerated, jailed, locked up, put away, sent down.

*antonym* free.

**imprisonment** *n* bird, confinement, custody, detention, durance, duress(e), enchainment, incarceration, internment, porridge, quod.

*antonym* freedom.

**improbability** *n* doubt, doubtfulness, dubiety, dubiousness, far-fetchedness, implausibility, uncertainty, unlikelihood, unlikeliness.

*antonym* probability.

**improbable** *adj* doubtful, dubious, fanciful, far-fetched, implausible, preposterous, questionable,

tall, unbelievable, uncertain, unconvincing, unlikely, weak.

*antonym* probable.

**impromptu** *adj* ad-lib, autoschediastic, extemporaneous, extempore, extemporised, improvised, off the cuff, off-hand, offhand, spontaneous, unpremeditated, unprepared, unrehearsed, unscripted, unstudied.

*antonyms* planned, rehearsed.

*adv* ad lib, extempore, off the cuff, off the top of one's head, on the spur of the moment, spontaneously.

*n* autoschediasm, extemporisation, improvisation, voluntary.

**improper** *adj* abnormal, erroneous, false, illegitimate, ill-timed, impolite, inaccurate, inadmissible, inapplicable, inapposite, inappropriate, inapt, incongruous, incorrect, indecent, indecorous, indelicate, infelicitous, inopportune, irregular, malapropos, off-colour, out of place, risqué, smutty, suggestive, unbecoming, uncalled-for, unfit, unfitting, unmaidenly, unparliamentary, unprintable, unquotable, unrepeatable, unseasonable, unseemly, unsuitable, unsuited, untoward, unwarranted, vulgar, wrong.

*antonym* proper.

**impropriety** *n* bad taste, blunder, faux pas, gaffe, gaucherie, immodesty, incongruity, indecency, indecorousness, indecorum, lapse, mistake, slip, solecism, unseemliness, unsuitability, vulgarity.

*antonym* propriety.

**improve** *v* advance, ameliorate, amend, augment, better, correct, culture, deodorise, develop, embourgeoise, enhance, gentrify, help, increase, look up, meliorate, mend, mend one's ways, perk up, pick up, polish, progress, rally, recover, rectify, recuperate, reform, rise, touch up, turn over a new leaf, turn the corner, up, upgrade.

*antonyms* decline, diminish.

**improvement** *n* advance, advancement, amelioration, amendment, augmentation, bettering, betterment, correction, development, embourgeoisement, enhancement, furtherance, gain, gentrification, increase, melioration, progress, rally, recovery, rectification, reformation, rise, upswing.

*antonyms* decline, retrogression.

**improvidence** *n* carelessness, extravagance, fecklessness, heedlessness, imprudence, Micawberism, negligence, prodigality, profligacy, thriftlessness, wastefulness.

*antonym* thrift.

**improvident** *adj* careless, feckless, heedless, imprudent, Micawberish, negligent, prodigal, profligate, reckless, shiftless, spendthrift, thoughtless, thriftless, underprepared, uneconomical, unprepared, unthrifty, wasteful.

*antonym* thrifty.

**improving** *adj* convalescing, edifying, educational, instructive, meliorative, on the mend, recuperating, uplifting.

*antonyms* harmful, unedifying.

**improvisation** *n* ad hocery, ad-lib, ad-libbing, autoschediasm, expedient, extemporising, impromptu, invention, makeshift, spontaneity, vamp.

**improvise** *v* ad-lib, autoschediaze, coin, concoct, contrive, devise, extemporise, improvisate, invent, make do, noodle, play it by ear, throw together, vamp.

**improvised** *adj* ad-lib, extemporaneous, extempore, extemporised, improvisational, improvisatory, makeshift, off-the-cuff, spontaneous, unprepared, unrehearsed.

*antonym* rehearsed.

**imprudence** *n* carelessness, folly, foolhardiness, foolishness, haste, hastiness, heedlessness, improvidence, inadvisability, incaution, incautiousness, inconsiderateness, indiscretion, irresponsibility, rashness, recklessness, short-sightedness, temerity.

*antonym* prudence.

**imprudent** *adj* careless, foolhardy, foolish, hasty, heedless, ill-advised, ill-considered, ill-judged, impolitic, improvident, incautious, inconsiderate, indiscreet, injudicious, irresponsible, overhasty, rash, reckless, short-sighted, temerarious, unthinking, unwise.

*antonym* prudent.

**impudence** *n* assurance, audacity, backchat, boldness, brass neck, brazenness, cheek, chutzpah, effrontery, face, impertinence, impudicity, insolence, lip, malapertness, neck, nerve, pertness, presumption, presumptuousness, rudeness, sauciness, shamelessness.

*antonym* politeness.

**impudent** *adj* audacious, bold, bold-faced, brazen, brazen-faced, cheeky, cocky, forward, fresh, immodest, impertinent, insolent, malapert, pert, presumptuous, rude, saucy, shameless.

*antonym* polite.

**impugn** *v* assail, attack, call in question, challenge, criticise, dispute, oppose, question, resist, revile, traduce, vilify, vilipend, vituperate.

*antonym* praise.

**impulse** *n* caprice, catalyst, conatus, desire, drive, feeling, force, impetus, incitement, inclination, influence, instinct, momentum, motive, movement, notion, passion, pressure, push, resolve, stimulus, surge, thrust, urge, whim, wish.

**impulsive** *adj* hasty, headlong, impetuous, instinctive, intuitive, passionate, precipitant, precipitate, quick, rash, reckless, spontaneous, unconsidered, unpredictable, unpremeditated.

*antonym* cautious.

**impulsiveness** *n* haste, hastiness, impetuosity, impetuousness, precipitateness, precipitation, rashness, recklessness.

*antonym* caution.

**impunity** *n* amnesty, dispensation, excusal, exemption, freedom, immunity, liberty, licence, permission, security.

*antonym* liability.

**impure** *adj* admixed, adulterated, alloyed, carnal, coarse, contaminated, corrupt, debased, defiled, dirty, feculent, filthy, foul, gross, immodest, immoral, indecent, indelicate, infected, lascivious, lewd, licentious, lustful, mixed, obscene, polluted, prurient, salacious, smutty, sullied, tainted, turbid, unchaste, unclean, unrefined, unwholesome, vicious, vitiated.

*antonyms* chaste, pure.

**impurity** *n* admixture, adulteration, befoulment, carnality, coarseness, contaminant, contamination, corruption, defilement, dirt, dirtiness, dross, feculence, filth, foreign body, foreign matter, foulness, grime, grossness, immodesty, immorality, indecency, infection, lasciviousness, lewdness, licentiousness, mark, mixture, obscenity, pollutant, pollution, prurience, salaciousness, scum, smuttiness, spot, stain, taint, turbidity, turbidness, unchastity, uncleanness, vulgarity.

*antonyms* chasteness, purity.

**imputable** *adj* ascribable, attributable, blameable, chargeable, referable, traceable.

**imputation** *n* accusation, arrogation, ascription, aspersion, attribution, blame, censure, charge, insinuation, reproach, slander, slur, suggestion.

**impute** *v* accredit, ascribe, assign, attribute, charge, credit, put down to, refer.

**in a state** agitated, anxious, distressed, disturbed, flustered, hassled, het up, in a stew, in a tizzy, panic-stricken, ruffled, steamed up, troubled, upset, worked up, worried.

*antonym* calm.

**in a word** briefly, concisely, in a nutshell, in short, succinctly, to be brief, to put it briefly, to sum up.

*antonym* at length.

**in abeyance** dormant, hanging fire, on ice, pending, shelved, suspended.

**in addition** additionally, also, as well, besides, further, furthermore, into the bargain, moreover, over and above, to boot, too, withal.

**in advance** ahead, beforehand, earlier, in front, in the forefront, in the lead, in the van, previously, sooner.

*antonyms* behind, later.

**in ambush** embusqué, lying in wait.

**in camera** behind closed doors, hugger-mugger, in private, in secret, privately, secretly, sub rosa, under the rose.

*antonym* openly.

**in confidence** in private, privately, secretly, sub rosa, under the rose.

**in conflict** at daggers drawn, at loggerheads, at odds, at variance, at war, disagreeing, disunited, in disagreement, opposed.

*antonyms* at peace, in agreement.

**in crowds** gregatim, in droves, in flocks, in force, in herds, in hordes, in large numbers, in strength, in troops.

*antonym* in penny numbers.

**in depth** comprehensively, exhaustively, extensively, in detail, intensively, thoroughly.

*antonyms* broadly, superficially.

**in detail** comprehensively, exhaustively, in depth, in particular, inside out, item by item, particularly, point by point, thoroughly.

*antonyms* broadly, superficially.

**in difficulties** in a hole, in dire straights, in the shit, up shit creek, up the creek, up the pole.

**in effect** actually, effectively, essentially, for practical purposes, in actuality, in fact, in reality, in the end, in truth, really, to all intents and purposes, virtually, when all is said and done.

**in fact** actually, en effet, in point of fact, in reality, in truth, indeed, really, truly.

**in favour of** all for, backing, for, on the side of, pro, supporting, to the advantage of.

*antonym* against.

**in force** binding, current, effective, gregatim, in crowds, in droves, in flocks, in hordes, in large numbers, in operation, in strength, on the statute book, operative, valid, working.

*antonym* inoperative.

**in French** Gallice.

**in front** ahead, before, first, in advance, in the van, leading, preceding, to the fore.

*antonym* behind.

**in full** completely, entirely, in its entirety, in total, in toto, unabridged, uncut, wholly.

*antonyms* partially, partly.

**in German** Germanice.

**in good part** cheerfully, cordially, good-naturedly, laughingly, well.

*antonyms* angrily, touchily.

**in Greek** Graece.

**in gross** en bloc, en masse, in aggregate, in bulk, in toto, wholesale.

*antonym* retail.

**in hiding** concealed, doggo, hidden, latitant.

**in keeping** appropriate, befitting, fit, fitting, harmonious, in harmony, of a piece, suitable.

*antonym* inappropriate.

**in kind** in like manner, similarly, tit for tat.

**in Latin** Latine.

**in league** allied, collaborating, conniving, conspiring, hand in glove, in cahoots, in collusion.

*antonym* at odds.

**in love** besotted, charmed, doting, enamoured, enraptured, hooked, infatuated, smitten.

**in motion** afoot, functioning, going, in progress, moving, on the go, operational, running, sailing, travelling, under way.

*antonym* stationary.

**in my opinion** for my money, me judice.

**in order** acceptable, all right, allowed, appropriate, arranged, called for, correct, done, fitting, in sequence, neat, OK, orderly, permitted, right, shipshape, suitable, tidy.

*antonyms* disallowed, out of order.

**in order to** intending to, so that, to, with a view to, with the intention of, with the purpose of.

**in part** a little, in some measure, part way, partially, partly, slightly, somewhat, to a certain extent, to some degree.

*antonym* wholly.

**in particular** distinctly, especially, exactly, expressly, in detail, particularly, specifically.

**in passing** accidentally, by the by(e), by the way, en passant, incidentally.

**in penny numbers** in dribs and drabs, in ones and twos.

*antonyms* in crowds, in force.

**in person** as large as life, bodily, in propria persona, personally.

**in pieces** broken, burst, damaged, disintegrated, in bits, in smithereens, kaput, piecemeal, ruined, shattered, smashed.

**in place of** as a replacement for, as a substitute for, as an alternative to, in exchange for, in lieu of, instead of.

**in principle** en principe, ideally, in essence, in theory, theoretically.

**in private** behind closed doors, hugger-mugger, in camera, in confidence, in secret, privately, secretly, sub rosa, under the rose.

*antonym* openly.

**in progress** going on, happening, occurring, proceeding, under way.

**in proportion** pro rata.

**in public** coram populo, for all to see, in full view, in open view, in the open, openly, publicly.

*antonyms* in camera, in secret.

**in return** en revanche.

**in secret** hugger-mugger, in confidence, in gremio, in pectore, in petto, inly, inwardly, on the q.t., on the quiet, sub rosa, under the rose.

*antonym* openly.

**in spite of** despite, notwithstanding.

**in the interest(s) of** for the sake of, on behalf of, on the part of, to the advantage of, to the benefit of.

**in the light of** bearing/keeping in mind, because of, considering, in view of, taking into account.

**in the making** budding, coming, developing, emergent, growing, nascent, potential, up and coming.

**in the middle of** among, busy with, during, engaged in, in the midst of, in the process of, occupied with, surrounded by, while.

**in the midst of** among, during, in the middle of, in the thick of, surrounded by.

**in the money** affluent, flush, loaded, opulent, prosperous, rich, rolling in it, wealthy, well-heeled, well-off, well-to-do.

*antonym* poor.

**in the mood** disposed, in the right frame of mind, inclined, interested, keen, minded, of a mind, willing.

**in the offing** at hand, close at hand, coming up, imminent, in sight, on the horizon, on the way.

*antonym* far off.

**in the red** bankrupt, in arrears, in debt, insolvent, on the rocks, overdrawn.

*antonym* in credit.

**in the right** justified, right.

*antonym* in the wrong.

**in the wrong** at fault, blameworthy, guilty, in error, mistaken, to blame.

*antonym* in the right.

**in toto** as a whole, completely, entirely, in its entirety, in total, totally, unabridged, uncut, wholly.

**in two minds** dithering, hesitant, hesitating, shilly-shallying, swithering, uncertain, undecided, unsure, vacillating, wavering.

*antonym* certain.

**in vain** bootlessly, fruitlessly, ineffectually, to no avail, unsuccessfully, uselessly, vainly.

*antonym* successfully.

**inability** *n* disability, disqualification, handicap, impotence, inadequacy, incapability, incapacity, incompetence, ineptitude, ineptness, powerlessness, weakness.

*antonym* ability.

**inaccessible** *adj* impassible, isolated, remote, solitary, unapproachable, unattainable, uncom(e)atable, unfrequented, unget-at-able, unreachable.

*antonym* accessible.

**inaccuracy** *n* blunder, boob, carelessness, corrigendum, defect, erratum, erroneousness, error, fault, faultiness, howler, imprecision, incorrectness, inexactness, looseness, miscalculation, mistake, slip, unreliability.

*antonym* accuracy.

**inaccurate** *adj* careless, defective, discrepant, erroneous, faulty, imprecise, in error, incorrect, inexact, loose, mistaken, out, unfaithful, unreliable, unrepresentative, unsound, wide of the mark, wild, wrong.

*antonym* accurate.

**inaccurately** *adv* carelessly, clumsily, imprecisely, inexactly, loosely, unfaithfully, unreliably, wildly.

*antonym* accurately.

**inaction** *n* dormancy, idleness, immobility, inactivity, inertia, rest, stagnation, stasis, torpidity, torpor.

*antonym* activeness.

**inactivate** *v* cripple, disable, immobilise, knock the bottom out of, mothball, paralyse, scupper, stabilise, stop.

*antonym* activate.

**inactive** *adj* abeyant, dormant, dull, idle, immobile, indolent, inert, inoperative, jobless, kicking one's heels, latent, lazy, lethargic, low-key, mothballed, out of service, out of work, passive, quiet, sedentary, sleepy, slothful, slow, sluggish, somnolent, stagnant, stagnating, torpid, unemployed, unoccupied, unused.

*antonym* active.

**inactivity** *n* abeyance, abeyancy, dilatoriness, dolce far niente, dormancy, dullness, heaviness, hibernation, idleness, immobility, inaction, indolence, inertia, inertness, languor, lassitude, laziness, lethargy, passivity, quiescence, sloth, sluggishness, stagnation, stasis, torpor, unemployment, vegetation.

*antonym* activeness.

**inadequacy** *n* dearth, defect, defectiveness, deficiency, failing, faultiness, imperfection, inability, inadequateness, inaptness, incapacity, incompetence, incompetency, incompleteness, ineffectiveness, ineffectuality, ineffectualness, inefficacy, inefficiency, insufficiency, lack, meagreness, paucity, poverty, scantiness, shortage, shortcoming, skimpiness, unfitness, unsuitableness, want, weakness.

*antonym* adequacy.

**inadequate** *adj* defective, deficient, faulty, imperfect, inapt, incapable, incommensurate, incompetent, incomplete, ineffective, ineffectual, inefficacious, inefficient, insubstantial, insufficient, leaving a little/a lot/much to be desired, meagre, niggardly, scanty, short, sketchy, skimpy, sparse, unequal, unfitted, unqualified, wanting.

*antonym* adequate.

**inadequately** *adv* badly, carelessly, imperfectly, insufficiently, meagrely, poorly, scantily, sketchily, skimpily, sparsely, thinly.

*antonym* adequately.

**inadmissible** *adj* disallowed, immaterial, improper, inappropriate, incompetent, irrelevant, prohibited, unacceptable, unallowable, unqualified.

*antonym* admissible.

**inadvertence** *n* blunder, boob, boo-boo, carelessness, clanger, error, heedlessness, inadvertency, inattention, inconsideration, inobservance, mistake, neglect, negligence, oversight, remissness, thoughtlessness.

*antonym* care.

**inadvertent** *adj* accidental, careless, chance, heedless, inattentive, negligent, thoughtless, unguarded, unheeding, unintended, unintentional, unplanned, unpremeditated, unthinking, unwitting.

*antonym* deliberate.

**inadvertently** *adv* accidentally, by accident, by mistake, carelessly, heedlessly, involuntarily, mistakenly, negligently, remissly, thoughtlessly, unguardedly, unintentionally, unthinkingly, unwittingly.

*antonym* deliberately.

**inadvisable** *adj* daft, foolish, ill-advised, ill-judged, impolitic, imprudent, incautious, indiscreet, inexpedient, injudicious, misguided, unwise.

*antonym* advisable.

**inalienable** *adj* absolute, entailed, imprescriptible, indefeasible, infrangible, inherent, inviolable, non-negotiable, non-transferable, permanent, sacrosanct, unassailable, unremovable, untransferable.

*antonym* impermanent.

**inane** *adj* asinine, daft, drippy, empty, fatuous, foolish, frivolous, futile, idiotic, imbecilic, mindless, nutty, puerile, senseless, silly, stupid, trifling, unintelligent, vacuous, vain, vapid, worthless.

*antonym* sensible.

**inanimate** *adj* abiotic, dead, defunct, dormant, dull, exanimate, extinct, heavy, inactive, inert, inorganic, insensate, insentient, leaden, lifeless, listless, slow, spiritless, stagnant, torpid.

*antonyms* alive, animate, lively, living.

**inanity** *n* asininity, bêtise, daftness, drippiness, emptiness, fatuity, folly, foolishness, frivolity, imbecility, puerility, senselessness, silliness, vacuity, vapidity, waffle.

*antonym* sense.

**inapplicable** *adj* inapposite, inappropriate, inapt, inconsequent, irrelevant, unrelated, unsuitable, unsuited.

*antonym* applicable.

**inappropriate** *adj* disproportionate, ill-fitted, ill-suited, ill-timed, improper, incongruous, infelicitous, malapropos, out of place, tactless, tasteless, unbecoming, unbefitting, unfit, unfitting, unseemly, unsuitable, untimely.

*antonym* appropriate.

**inappropriately** *adv* malapropos, tactlessly, tastelessly.

*antonym* appropriately.

**inapt** *adj* awkward, clumsy, crass, dull, gauche, ill-fitted, ill-suited, ill-timed, inapposite, inappropriate, incompetent, inept, inexpert, infelicitous, inopportune, maladroit, slow, stupid, tactless, unapt, unfortunate, unhappy, unsuitable, unsuited.

*antonym* apt.

**inaptitude** *n* awkwardness, clumsiness, crassness, inaptness, incompetence, inopportuneness, maladroitness, tactlessness, unfitness, unreadiness, unsuitableness.

*antonym* aptitude.

**inarticulacy** *n* inarticulateness, incoherence, mumbling, speechlessness, tongue-tiedness, unintelligibility.

*antonym* articulacy.

**inarticulate** *adj* blurred, dumb, dysarthric, dysphasic, dyspraxic, faltering, halting, hesitant, incoherent, incomprehensible, indistinct, muffled, mumbled, mute, silent, speechless, tongue-tied, unclear, unintelligible, unspoken, unuttered, unvoiced, voiceless, wordless.

*antonym* articulate.

**inattention** *n* absence of mind, absent-mindedness, carelessness, daydreaming, disregard, dwam, forgetfulness, heedlessness, inadvertence, inattentiveness, neglect, preoccupation, wool-gathering.

*antonym* attentiveness.

**inattentive** *adj* absent-minded, careless, deaf, distracted, distrait, dreaming, dreamy, heedless, inadvertent, neglectful, negligent, preoccupied, regardless, remiss, unheeding, unmindful, unobservant, vague.

*antonym* attentive.

**inaudible** *adj* faint, imperceptible, indistinct, low, muffled, mumbled, mumbling, muted, noiseless, out of earshot, silent.

*antonym* audible.

**inaugural** *adj* consecratory, dedicatory, exordial, first, initial, introductory, launching, maiden, opening.

**inaugurate** *v* begin, christen, commence, commission, consecrate, dedicate, enthrone, han(d)sel, induct, initiate, install, instate, institute, introduce, invest, kick off, launch, open, ordain, originate, set up, start, start off, usher in.

**inauguration** *n* consecration, enthronement, han(d)sel, induction, initiation, installation, installing, institution, investiture, launch, launching, opening, setting up.

**inauspicious** *adj* bad, black, discouraging, ill-boding, ill-omened, ominous, threatening, unfavourable, unfortunate, unlucky, unpromising, unpropitious, untoward.

*antonym* auspicious.

**inborn** *adj* congenital, connate, hereditary, inbred, ingenerate, ingrained, inherent, inherited, innate, instinctive, intuitive, native, natural.

*antonym* learned.

**inbred** *adj* connate, constitutional, ingenerate, ingrained, inherent, innate, native, natural.

*antonym* learned.

**inbreeding** *n* endogamy, homogamy.

**incalculable** *adj* boundless, countless, enormous, immense, incomputable, inestimable, infinite, innumerable, limitless, measureless, numberless, uncountable, unforeseeable, unlimited, unmeasureable, unpredictable, untold, vast.

*antonym* limited.

**incantation** *n* abracadabra, chant, charm, conjuration, formula, hex, invocation, mantra(m), om, rune, spell.

**incapable** *adj* disqualified, drunk, feeble, helpless, impotent, inadequate, incompetent, ineffective, ineffectual, inept, insufficient, powerless, tipsy, unable, unfit, unfitted, unqualified, weak.

*antonyms* capable, sober.

**incapacitate** *v* cripple, disable, disqualify, hamstring, immobilise, lay up, paralyse, prostrate, put out of action, scupper, unfit.

*antonyms* facilitate, set up.

**incapacitated** *adj* disqualified, drunk, hamstrung, immobilised, indisposed, laid up, out of action, prostrate, scuppered, tipsy, unfit, unwell.

*antonym* operative.

**incapacity** *n* disability, disqualification, feebleness, impotence, inability, inadequacy, incapability, incompetency, ineffectiveness, powerlessness, unfitness, weakness.

*antonym* capability.

**incapsulate** *see* encapsulate.

**incarcerate** *v* cage, commit, confine, coop up, detain, encage, gaol, immure, impound, imprison, intern, jail, lock up, put away, restrain, restrict, send down, wall in.

*antonym* free.

**incarceration** *n* bondage, captivity, confinement, custody, detention, imprisonment, internment, jail, restraint, restriction.

*antonym* freedom.

**incarnate** *adj* embodied, made flesh, personified, typified.

**incarnation** *n* avatar, embodiment, exemplification, impersonation, manifestation, personification, type.

**incautious** *adj* careless, hasty, heedless, ill-advised, ill-judged, improvident, imprudent, impulsive, inconsiderate, indiscreet, injudicious, negligent, overhasty, precipitate, rash, reckless, thoughtless, unchary, unguarded, unthinking, unwary, wareless.

*antonym* cautious.

**incendiary**[1] *n* arsonist, firebug, fire-raiser, pétroleur, pétroleuse, pyromaniac.

**incendiary**[2] *n* agitator, demagogue, firebrand, insurgent, rabble-rouser, revolutionary.

*adj* dissentious, inciting, inflammatory, proceleusmatic, protreptic, provocative, rabble-rousing, seditious, subversive.

*antonym* calming.

**incense**[1] *n* adulation, aroma, balm, bouquet, fragrance, homage, joss-stick, perfume, scent, worship.

**incense**[2] *v* anger, enrage, exasperate, excite, inflame, infuriate, irritate, madden, make one see red, make one's blood boil, make one's hackles rise, provoke, raise one's hackles, rile.

*antonym* calm.

**incensed** *adj* angry, enraged, exasperated, fuming, furibund, furious, in a paddy, indignant, infuriated, irate, ireful, mad, maddened, on the warpath, steamed up, up in arms, waxy, wrathful.

*antonym* calm.

**incentive** *n* bait, carrot, cause, consideration, encouragement, enticement, impetus, impulse, inducement, lure, motivation, motive, reason, reward, spur, stimulant, stimulus.

*antonym* disincentive.

**inception** *n* beginning, birth, commencement, dawn, inauguration, initiation, installation, kick-off, origin, outset, rise, start.

*antonym* end.

**incessant** *adj* ceaseless, constant, continual, continuous, endless, eternal, everlasting, interminable, never-ending, non-stop, perpetual, persistent, relentless, unbroken, unceasing, unending, unrelenting, unremitting, weariless.

*antonym* intermittent.

**incidence** *n* amount, commonness, degree, extent, frequency, occurrence, prevalence, range, rate.

**incident** *n* adventure, affair(e), brush, circumstance, clash, commotion, confrontation, contretemps, disturbance, episode, event, fight, happening, mishap, occasion, occurrence, scene, skirmish.

**incidental** *adj* accidental, accompanying, ancillary, attendant, casual, chance, concomitant, contingent, contributory, fortuitous, incident, inconsequential, inessential, irrelevant, minor, non-essential, occasional, odd, random, related, secondary, subordinate, subsidiary.

*antonym* essential.

**incidentally** *adv* accidentally, by chance, by the by(e), by the way, casually, digressively, en passant, fortuitously, in passing, parenthetically.

**incidentals** *n* contingencies, epiphenomena, extras, odds and ends.

*antonym* essentials.

**incinerate** *v* burn, char, cremate, reduce to ashes.

**incipient** *adj* beginning, commencing, developing, embryonic, inceptive, inchoate, nascent, originating, rudimentary, starting.

*antonym* developed.

**incise** *v* carve, chisel, cut, cut into, engrave, etch, gash.

**incised** *adj* carved, cut, engraved, intagliated.

**incision** *n* cut, discission, gash, incisure, insection, notch, opening, slash, slit.

**incisive** *adj* acid, acute, astucious, astute, biting, caustic, cutting, keen, mordant, penetrating, perceptive, perspicacious, piercing, sarcastic, sardonic, satirical, severe, sharp, tart, trenchant.

*antonym* woolly.

**incisiveness** *n* acidity, astucity, astuteness, keenness, penetration, perspicacity, pungency, sarcasm, sharpness, tartness, trenchancy.

*antonym* woolliness.

**incite** *v* abet, animate, drive, egg on, encourage, excite, foment, goad, impel, inflame, instigate, prompt, provoke, put up to, rouse, set on, solicit, spur, stimulate, stir up, urge, whip up.

*antonym* restrain.

**incitement** *n* abetment, agitation, encouragement, goad, hortation, impetus, impulse, inducement, instigation, motivation, motive, prompting, provocation, spur, stimulus.

*antonyms* check, discouragement.

**inciting** *adj* exciting, incendiary, inflammatory, proceleusmatic, protreptic, protreptical, provocative, rabble-rousing.

*antonym* calming.

**incivility** *n* bad manners, boorishness, coarseness, discourteousness, discourtesy, disrespect, ill-breeding, impoliteness, inurbanity, roughness, rudeness, unmannerliness, vulgarity.

*antonym* civility.

**inclemency** *n* bitterness, boisterousness, callousness, cruelty, harshness, mercilessness, pitilessness, rawness, rigour, roughness, severity, storminess, tyranny, unfeelingness, ungeniality.

*antonym* clemency.

**inclement** *adj* bitter, boisterous, callous, cruel, draconian, foul, harsh, intemperate, merciless, pitiless, rigorous, rough, severe, stormy, tempestuous, tyrannical, unfeeling, ungenial, unmerciful.

*antonym* clement.

**inclination**[1] *n* affection, aptitude, bent, bias, clinamen, desire, disposition, fancy, fondness, ingenium, leaning, liking, month's mind, partiality, penchant, predilection, predisposition, prejudice, proclivity, proneness, propensity, stomach, taste, tendency, turn, turn of mind, velleity, wish.

*antonym* disinclination.

**inclination**[2] *n* angle, bend, bending, bow, bowing, clinamen, deviation, gradient, incline, leaning, nod, pitch, slant, slope, tilt.

**incline**[1] *v* affect, bias, dispose, influence, nod, persuade, predispose, prejudice, stoop, sway.

**incline**[2] *v* bend, bevel, bow, cant, deviate, diverge, lean, slant, slope, tend, tilt, tip, veer.

*n* acclivity, ascent, brae, declivity, descent, dip, grade, gradient, hill, ramp, rise, slope.

**inclined** *adj* apt, bent, disposed, given, liable, likely, minded, oblique, of a mind, predisposed, prone, sloping, tilted, willing.

*antonym* flat.

**inclose** *see* enclose.

**include** *v* add, allow for, comprehend, comprise, connote, contain, cover, embody, embrace, enclose, encompass, incorporate, involve, number among, rope in, subsume, take in, take into account.

*antonyms* exclude, ignore.

**inclusion** *n* addition, incorporation, insertion, involvement.

*antonym* exclusion.

**inclusive** *adj* across-the-board, all in, all-embracing, blanket, catch-all, compendious, comprehensive, full, general, overall, sweeping, umbrella.

*antonyms* exclusive, narrow.

**incognito** *adj* disguised, in disguise, masked, unknown, unrecognisable, unrecognised, veiled.

*antonyms* openly, undisguised.

**incoherence** *n* confusion, disconnectedness, disjointedness, illogicality, inarticulateness, inconsistency, unintelligibility, wildness.

*antonym* coherence.

**incoherent** *adj* confused, disconnected, disjointed, dislocated, disordered, inarticulate, inconsequent, inconsistent, jumbled, loose, muddled, rambling, stammering, stuttering, unconnected, unco-ordinated, unintelligible, unjointed, wandering, wild.

*antonym* coherent.

**incombustible** *adj* fireproof, fire-resistant, flameproof, flame-resistant, non-flammable, non-inflammable.

*antonym* combustible.

**income** *n* earnings, gains, interest, means, pay, proceeds, profits, receipts, returns, revenue, salary, takings, wages, yield.

*antonym* expenses.

**incoming** *adj* accruing, approaching, arriving, coming, ensuing, entering, homeward, landing, new, next, returning, succeeding.

*antonym* outgoing.

**incommensurate** *adj* disproportionate, excessive, extravagant, extreme, inadequate, inequitable, inordinate, insufficient, unequal.

*antonym* appropriate.

**incommunicable** *adj* indescribable, ineffable, inexpressible, unimpartable, unspeakable, unutterable.

*antonym* expressible.

**incomparable** *adj* brilliant, inimitable, matchless, paramount, peerless, superb, superlative, supreme, transcendent, unequalled, unmatched, unparalleled, unrivalled.

*antonyms* poor, run-of-the-mill.

**incomparably** *adv* brilliantly, by far, eminently, far and away, immeasurably, superbly, superlatively.

*antonyms* poorly, slightly.

**incompatibility** *n* antagonism, clash, conflict, difference, discrepancy, disparateness, disparity, incongruity, inconsistency, irreconcilability, mismatch, uncongeniality.

*antonym* compatibility.

**incompatible** *adj* antagonistic, antipathetic, clashing, conflicting, contradictory, discordant, discrepant, disparate, ill-assorted, incongruous, inconsistent, inconsonant, inharmonious, irreconcilable, mismatched, uncongenial, unsuitable, unsuited.

*antonym* compatible.

**incompetence** n bungling, inability, inadequacy, incapability, incapacity, incompetency, ineffectiveness, ineffectuality, ineffectualness, inefficiency, ineptitude, ineptness, insufficiency, stupidity, unfitness, uselessness.

*antonym* competence.

**incompetent** adj bungling, floundering, incapable, incapacitated, ineffective, ineffectual, inept, inexpert, insufficient, stupid, unable, unfit, unfitted, unskilful, useless.

*antonym* competent.

**incomplete** adj broken, defective, deficient, fragmentary, imperfect, incondite, inexhaustive, insufficient, lacking, part, partial, short, unaccomplished, undeveloped, undone, unexecuted, unfinished, wanting.

*antonym* complete.

**incomprehensible** adj above one's head, all Greek, arcane, baffling, beyond one's comprehension, beyond one's grasp, double-Dutch, enigmatic, impenetrable, inapprehensible, inconceivable, inscrutable, mysterious, obscure, opaque, perplexing, puzzling, unfathomable, unimaginable, unintelligible, unthinkable.

*antonym* comprehensible.

**inconceivable** adj implausible, incogitable, incredible, mind-boggling, out of the question, staggering, unbelievable, unheard-of, unimaginable, unknowable, unthinkable.

*antonym* conceivable.

**inconclusive** adj ambiguous, indecisive, indeterminate, open, uncertain, unconvincing, undecided, unsatisfying, unsettled, vague.

*antonym* conclusive.

**incongruity** n conflict, discrepancy, disparity, dissociability, dissociableness, inappropriateness, inaptness, incompatibility, inconcinnity, inconsistency, inharmoniousness, unsuitability.

*antonyms* consistency, harmoniousness.

**incongruous** adj absurd, conflicting, contradictory, contrary, disconsonant, discordant, dissociable, extraneous, improper, inappropriate, inapt, incoherent, incompatible, inconcinnous, inconsistent, out of keeping, out of place, unbecoming, unsuitable, unsuited.

*antonyms* consistent, harmonious.

**inconsequential** adj illogical, immaterial, inconsequent, inconsiderable, insignificant, minor, negligible, paltry, petty, trifling, trivial, unimportant.

*antonym* important.

**inconsiderable** adj exiguous, inconsequential, insignificant, light, minor, negligible, petty, piddling, piffling, slight, small, small-time, trifling, trivial, unimportant, unnoticeable.

*antonym* considerable.

**inconsiderate** adj careless, imprudent, indelicate, insensitive, intolerant, rash, rude, self-centred, selfish, tactless, thoughtless, unconcerned, ungracious, unkind, unthinking.

*antonym* considerate.

**inconsiderateness** n carelessness, étourderie, indelicacy, insensitivity, rudeness, selfishness, tactlessness, thoughtlessness, unconcern, unkindness.

*antonym* considerateness.

**inconsistency** n changeableness, contrariety, disagreement, discrepancy, disparity, divergence, fickleness, incompatibility, incongruity, inconsonance, inconstancy, instability, paradox, unpredictability, unreliability, unsteadiness, variance.

*antonym* consistency.

**inconsistent** adj at odds, at variance, capricious, changeable, conflicting, contradictory, contrary, discordant, discrepant, erratic, fickle, incoherent, incompatible, incongruous, inconstant, irreconcilable, irregular, unpredictable, unstable, unsteady, variable, varying.

*antonym* constant.

**inconsistently** adv contradictorily, differently, eccentrically, erratically, illogically, inequably, randomly, unequally, unfairly, unpredictably, variably.

*antonym* consistently.

**inconsolable** adj brokenhearted, desolate, desolated, despairing, devastated, disconsolate, heartbroken, wretched.

*antonym* consolable.

**inconspicuous** adj camouflaged, hidden, insignificant, low-key, modest, muted, ordinary, plain, quiet, retiring, unassuming, unnoticeable, unobtrusive, unostentatious.

*antonym* conspicuous.

**inconstant** adj capricious, chameleon(ic), changeable, changeful, erratic, fickle, fluctuating, inconsistent, irresolute, mercurial, moonish, mutable, uncertain, undependable, unreliable, unsettled, unstable, unsteady, vacillating, variable, varying, volatile, wavering, wayward.

*antonym* constant.

**incontestable** adj certain, clear, evident, incontrovertible, indisputable, indubitable, irrefutable, obvious, self-evident, sure, undeniable, unquestionable.

*antonym* uncertain.

**incontinence** n enuresis.

**incontinent** adj debauched, dissipated, dissolute, enuretic, lascivious, lecherous, lewd, licentious, loose, lustful, profligate, promiscuous, unbridled, unchaste, unchecked, uncontrollable, uncontrolled, ungovernable, ungoverned, unrestrained, wanton.

*antonym* continent.

**incontrovertible** adj certain, clear, established, evident, incontestable, indisputable, indubitable, irrefutable, positive, self-evident, sure, undeniable, unquestionable, unshakable.

*antonym* uncertain.

**inconvenience** n annoyance, awkwardness, bother, cumbersomeness, difficulty, disadvantage, disruption, disturbance, disutility, drawback, fuss, hindrance, nuisance, trouble, uneasiness, unhandiness, unsuitableness, untimeliness, unwieldiness, upset, vexation.

*antonym* convenience.

*v* bother, disaccommodate, discommode, disrupt, disturb, irk, put out, put to trouble, trouble, upset.

*antonym* convenience.

**inconvenient** *adj* annoying, awkward, bothersome, cumbersome, difficult, disadvantageous, disturbing, embarrassing, inopportune, tiresome, troublesome, unhandy, unmanageable, unseasonable, unsocial, unsuitable, untimely, untoward, unwieldy, vexatious.

*antonym* convenient.

**incorporate** *v* absorb, amalgamate, assimilate, blend, coalesce, combine, consolidate, embody, fuse, incarnate, include, integrate, merge, mix, subsume, unite.

*antonyms* separate, split off.

**incorporation** *n* absorption, amalgamation, assimilation, association, blend, coalescence, company, federation, fusion, inclusion, integration, merger, society, unification, unifying.

*antonyms* separation, splitting off.

**incorporeal** *adj* bodiless, ethereal, ghostly, illusory, intangible, phantasmal, phantasmic, spectral, spiritual, unfleshy, unreal.

*antonym* real.

**incorrect** *adj* erroneous, false, faulty, flawed, illegitimate, imprecise, improper, inaccurate, inappropriate, inexact, mistaken, out, specious, ungrammatical, unidiomatic, unsuitable, untrue, wrong.

*antonym* correct.

**incorrectness** *n* erroneousness, error, fallacy, falseness, faultiness, illegitimacy, impreciseness, imprecision, impropriety, inaccuracy, inexactness, speciousness, ungrammaticalness, unsoundness, unsuitability, wrongness.

*antonym* correctness.

**incorrigible** *adj* hardened, hopeless, impenitent, incurable, indocile, intractable, inveterate, irreclaimable, irredeemable, irreformable, unreformable, unreformed, unteachable.

*antonym* reformable.

**incorruptibility** *n* honesty, honour, integrity, justness, nobility, probity, uprightness, virtue.

*antonym* corruptibility.

**incorruptible** *adj* everlasting, honest, honourable, imperishable, incorrupt, just, straight, trustworthy, unbribable, undecaying, upright.

*antonym* corruptible.

**increase** *v* add to, advance, aggrandise, amplify, augment, boost, build up, develop, dilate, eke, eke out, enhance, enlarge, escalate, expand, extend, greaten, grow, heighten, inflate, intensify, magnify, mount, multiply, proliferate, prolong,

pullulate, raise, snowball, soar, spread, step up, strengthen, swell, wax.

*antonym* decrease.

*n* accrescence, addition, augment, augmentation, auxesis, boost, development, enlargement, escalation, expansion, extension, gain, growth, increment, intensification, proliferation, rise, step-up, surge, upsurge, upsurgence, upturn.

*antonym* decrease.

**increasing** *adj* accrescent, addititious, advancing, broadening, crescent, crescive, developing, expanding, growing, intensifying, mounting, rising, rocketing, sprouting, waxing, widening.

*antonym* decreasing.

**incredible** *adj* absurd, amazing, astonishing, astounding, extraordinary, fabulous, far-fetched, great, implausible, impossible, improbable, inconceivable, inspired, marvellous, preposterous, prodigious, superb, superhuman, unbelievable, unimaginable, unthinkable, wonderful.

*antonyms* believable, run-of-the-mill.

**incredulity** *n* disbelief, distrust, doubt, doubting, incredulousness, scepticism, unbelief.

*antonym* credulity.

**incredulous** *adj* disbelieving, distrustful, doubtful, doubting, dubious, mistrustful, sceptical, suspicious, unbelieving, uncertain, unconvinced.

*antonym* credulous.

**increment** *n* accretion, accrual, accrument, addendum, addition, advancement, augmentation, enlargement, expansion, extension, gain, growth, increase, step up, supplement.

*antonym* decrease.

**incriminate** *v* accuse, arraign, blame, charge, criminate, impeach, implicate, inculpate, indict, involve, point the finger at, recriminate, stigmatise.

*antonym* exonerate.

**incubator** *n* eccaleobion, hatchery.

**incubus** *n* affliction, angst, burden, cacod(a)emon, cross, demon, devil, dread, ephialtes, evil spirit, fear, fiend, load, nightmare, oppression, pressure, sorrow, spirit, stress, succubus, trial, worry.

**inculcate** *v* drill into, drum into, engrain, hammer into, implant, impress, indoctrinate, infuse, instil, teach.

**inculpate** *v* accuse, blame, censure, charge, connect, criminate, drag into, impeach, implicate, incriminate, involve, recriminate.

*antonym* exonerate.

**incumbent** *adj* binding, compulsory, mandatory, necessary, obligatory, prescribed, up to.

**incur** *v* arouse, bring upon, contract, draw, earn, expose oneself to, gain, induce, meet with, provoke, run up, suffer.

**incurable** *adj* dyed-in-the-wool, fatal, hopeless, immedicable, incorrigible, inoperable, inveterate, irrecoverable, irremediable, recidivistic, remediless, terminal, unmedicinable, untreatable.

*antonym* curable.

**incurious** *adj* apathetic, careless, inattentive, indifferent, unconcerned, uncurious, unenquiring, uninquiring, uninquisitive, uninterested, unreflective.

*antonym* curious.

**incursion** *n* attack, foray, infiltration, inroads, invasion, irruption, penetration, raid.

**indebted** *adj* beholden, grateful, in debt, obligated, obliged, thankful.

**indecency** *n* bawdiness, coarseness, crudity, foulness, grossness, immodesty, impropriety, impurity, indecorum, indelicacy, lewdness, licentiousness, obscenity, outrageousness, pornography, Rabelaisianism, smut, smuttiness, unseemliness, vileness, vulgarity.

*antonyms* decency, modesty.

**indecent** *adj* blue, coarse, crude, dirty, filthy, foul, gross, immodest, improper, impure, indecorous, indelicate, lewd, licentious, near the knuckle, offensive, outrageous, pornographic, Rabelaisian, salacious, scatological, smutty, tasteless, unbecoming, uncomely, unseemly, vile, vulgar.

*antonyms* decent, modest.

**indecipherable** *adj* crabbed, cramped, illegible, indistinct, indistinguishable, tiny, unclear, unintelligible, unreadable.

*antonym* readable.

**indecision** *n* ambivalence, doubt, hesitancy, hesitation, indecisiveness, irresoluteness, irresolution, shilly-shallying, swither, uncertainty, vacillation, wavering.

*antonym* decisiveness.

**indecisive** *adj* doubtful, faltering, hesitating, hung, in two minds, inconclusive, indefinite, indeterminate, irresolute, pussyfooting, swithering, tentative, uncertain, unclear, undecided, undetermined, unsure, vacillating, wavering.

*antonym* decisive.

**indecorous** *adj* boorish, churlish, coarse, crude, ill-bred, immodest, impolite, improper, indecent, rough, rude, tasteless, uncivil, uncouth, undignified, unmannerly, unseemly, untoward, vulgar.

*antonym* decorous.

**indeed** *adv* actually, certainly, doubtlessly, forsooth, positively, really, strictly, to be sure, truly, undeniably, undoubtedly, verily, veritably.

**indefatigable** *adj* assiduous, diligent, dogged, inexhaustible, patient, persevering, pertinacious, relentless, sedulous, tireless, undying, unfailing, unflagging, unremitting, unresting, untireable, untiring, unweariable, unwearied, unwearying.

*antonyms* flagging, slothful.

**indefensible** *adj* faulty, inexcusable, insupportable, unforgivable, unjustifiable, unjustified, unpardonable, untenable, unwarrantable, wrong.

*antonym* defensible.

**indefinable** *adj* dim, hazy, impalpable, indescribable, indistinct, inexpressible, nameless, obscure, subtle, unclear, unrealised, vague.

*antonym* definable.

**indefinite** *adj* ambiguous, confused, doubtful, equivocal, evasive, general, ill-defined, imprecise, indeterminate, indistinct, inexact, loose, obscure, uncertain, unclear, undecided, undefined, undetermined, unfixed, unfocus(s)ed, unformed, unformulated, unknown, unlimited, unresolved, unsettled, vague.

*antonyms* clear, limited.

**indefinitely** *adv* ad infinitum, continually, endlessly, eternally, for ever, for life, sine die, time without end, world without end.

**indelible** *adj* enduring, indestructible, ineffaceable, ineradicable, inerasable, inexpungible, inextirpable, ingrained, lasting, permanent, unerasable.

*antonyms* erasable, impermanent.

**indelicacy** *n* bad taste, coarseness, crudity, grossness, immodesty, impropriety, indecency, obscenity, offensiveness, rudeness, smuttiness, suggestiveness, tastelessness, underniceness, vulgarity.

*antonym* delicacy.

**indelicate** *adj* blue, coarse, crude, embarrassing, gross, immodest, improper, indecent, indecorous, low, obscene, off-colour, offensive, risqué, rude, suggestive, tasteless, unbecoming, unmaidenly, unseemly, untoward, vulgar, warm.

*antonym* delicate.

**indemnify** *v* compensate, endorse, exempt, free, guarantee, insure, pay, protect, reimburse, remunerate, repair, repay, requite, satisfy, secure, underwrite.

**indemnity** *n* amnesty, compensation, excusal, exemption, guarantee, immunity, impunity, insurance, privilege, protection, redress, reimbursement, remuneration, reparation, requital, restitution, satisfaction, security.

**indent**[1] *v* cut, dent, dint, mark, nick, notch, pink, scallop, serrate.

**indent**[2] *v* ask for, demand, order, request, requisition.

**indentation** *n* bash, cut, dent, depression, dimple, dint, dip, hollow, jag, nick, notch, pit.

**indented** *adj* dancetté, dented, impressed, notched, zigzag.

**independence** *n* affranchisement, autarchy, autarky, autonomy, decolonisation, freedom, home rule, individualism, liberty, manumission, self-determination, self-government, self-reliance, self-rule, self-sufficiency, separation, sovereignty, uhuru, unconventionality.

*antonyms* conventionality, dependence.

**independent** *adj* absolute, autarchical, autocephalous, autogenous, autonomous, bold, crossbench, decontrolled, free, individualistic, liberated, non-aligned, one's own man, self-contained, self-determining, self-governing, self-reliant, self-sufficient, self-supporting, separate, separated, sovereign, unaided, unbiased, unconnected, unconstrained, uncontrolled, unconventional, unrelated, upon one's legs.

*antonyms* conventional, dependent, timid.

**independently** *adv* alone, autonomously, by oneself, individually, on one's own, on one's tod, separately, solo, unaided.

*antonym* together.

**indescribable** *adj* incommunicable, indefinable, ineffable, inexpressible, phraseless, unutterable.

*antonym* describable.

**indestructible** *adj* abiding, durable, enduring, eternal, everlasting, immortal, imperishable, incorruptible, indissoluble, infrangible, lasting, permanent, unbreakable, unfading.

*antonyms* breakable, mortal.

**indeterminacy** *n* impreciseness, inconclusiveness, indefiniteness, inexactness, open-endedness, uncertainty, vagueness.

*antonym* definiteness.

**indeterminate** *adj* imprecise, inconclusive, indefinite, inexact, open-ended, uncertain, undecided, undefined, undetermined, unfixed, unspecified, unstated, unstipulated, vague.

*antonyms* exact, limited.

**index** *n* clue, guide, hand, indication, indicator, mark, needle, pointer, sign, symptom, table, token.

**indicate** *v* add up to, bespeak, betoken, denote, designate, display, evince, express, imply, manifest, mark, point out, point to, read, record, register, reveal, show, signify, specify, suggest, telegraph, tip.

**indicated** *adj* advisable, called-for, desirable, necessary, needed, recommended, required, suggested.

**indication** *n* clue, endeixis, evidence, explanation, forewarning, hint, index, inkling, intimation, manifestation, mark, note, omen, portent, prognostic, sign, signal, signpost, suggestion, symptom, warning.

**indicative** *adj* denotative, exhibitive, indicatory, indicial, significant, suggestive, symptomatic.

**indicator** *n* display, gauge, gnomon, guide, index, mark, marker, meter, pointer, sign, signal, signpost, symbol, winker.

**indict** *v* accuse, arraign, charge, criminate, impeach, incriminate, prosecute, recriminate, summon, summons, tax.

*antonym* exonerate.

**indictment** *n* accusation, allegation, charge, crimination, impeachment, incrimination, prosecution, recrimination, summons.

*antonym* exoneration.

**indifference** *n* aloofness, apathy, callousness, coldness, coolness, detachment, disinterestedness, dispassion, disregard, equity, heedlessness, impartiality, inattention, insignificance, irrelevance, latitudinarianism, negligence, neutrality, objectivity, pococurant(e)ism, stoicalness, unconcern, unimportance.

*antonyms* bias, interest.

**indifferent** *adj* aloof, apathetic, average, callous, careless, cold, cool, detached, disinterested, dispassionate, distant, equitable, fair, heedless, immaterial, impartial, impervious, inattentive, incurious, insignificant, jack easy, mediocre, middling, moderate, neutral, non-aligned, objective, ordinary, passable, perfunctory, pococurante, regardless, so-so, unbiased, uncaring, unconcerned, undistinguished, unenquiring, unenthusiastic, unexcited, unimportant, unimpressed, uninspired, uninterested, uninvolved, unmoved, unprejudiced, unresponsive, unsympathetic.

*antonyms* biased, interested.

**indigence** *n* deprivation, destitution, distress, necessity, need, penury, poverty, privation, want.

*antonym* affluence.

**indigenous** *adj* aboriginal, autochthonous, home-grown, indigene, local, native, original.

*antonym* foreign.

**indigent** *adj* destitute, impecunious, impoverished, in forma pauperis, in want, necessitous, needy, penniless, penurious, poor, poverty-stricken, straitened.

*antonym* affluent.

**indigestion** *n* cardialgia, dyspepsia, dyspepsy, heartburn, water-brash.

**indignant** *adj* angry, annoyed, disgruntled, exasperated, fuming, furibund, furious, heated, huffy, in a paddy, in a wax, incensed, irate, livid, mad, marked, miffed, peeved, provoked, resentful, riled, scornful, sore, waxy, wrathful, wroth.

*antonym* pleased.

**indignation** *n* anger, exasperation, fury, ire, pique, rage, resentment, scorn, umbrage, wax, wrath.

*antonym* pleasure.

**indignity** *n* abuse, affront, contempt, contumely, disgrace, dishonour, disrespect, humiliation, incivility, injury, insult, obloquy, opprobrium, outrage, reproach, slight, snub.

*antonym* honour.

**indirect** *adj* ancillary, backhanded, circuitous, circumlocutory, collateral, contingent, crooked, devious, incidental, meandering, mediate, oblique, periphrastic, rambling, roundabout, secondary, slanted, subsidiary, tortuous, unintended, wandering, winding, zigzag.

*antonym* direct.

**indirectly** *adv* circumlocutorily, deviously, hintingly, obliquely, periphrastically, roundaboutedly, roundaboutly, second-hand.

*antonym* directly.

**indiscernible** *adj* hidden, impalpable, imperceptible, indistinct, indistinguishable, invisible, minuscule, minute, tiny, unapparent, undiscernible.

*antonym* clear.

**indiscreet** *adj* careless, foolish, hasty, heedless, ill-advised, ill-considered, ill-judged, impolitic, imprudent, incautious, injudicious, naïve, rash, reckless, tactless, temerarious, temerous, undiplomatic, unthinking, unwise.

*antonym* discreet.

**indiscretion** *n* boob, brick, error, faux pas, folly, foolishness, gaffe, imprudence, mistake, rashness, recklessness, slip, slip of the tongue, tactlessness, temerarity.

*antonym* discretion.

**indiscriminate** *adj* aimless, careless, chaotic, confused, desultory, general, haphazard, higgledy-piggledy, hit or miss, indiscriminating, indiscriminative, jumbled, mingled, miscellaneous, mixed, mongrel, motley, promiscuous, random, sweeping, uncritical, undifferentiated, undiscriminating, undistinguishable, unmethodical, unparticular, unselective, unsystematic, wholesale.

*antonyms* deliberate, selective.

**indiscriminately** *adv* carelessly, haphazardly, in the mass, randomly, unsystematically, wholesale, without fear or favour.

*antonyms* deliberately, selectively.

**indispensable** *adj* basic, crucial, essential, imperative, key, necessary, needed, needful, required, requisite, vital.

*antonym* unnecessary.

**indisposed¹** *adj* ailing, ill, laid up, poorly, sick, sickly, under the weather, unwell.

*antonym* well.

**indisposed²** *adj* averse, disinclined, loath, not of a mind (to), not willing, reluctant, unwilling.

*antonym* inclined.

**indisposition¹** *n* ailment, illness, sickness.

*antonym* health.

**indisposition²** *n* aversion, disinclination, dislike, distaste, hesitancy, reluctance, unwillingness.

*antonym* inclination.

**indisputable** *adj* absolute, certain, evident, incontestable, incontrovertible, indubitable, irrebuttable, irrefragable, irrefutable, positive, sure, unanswerable, unassailable, undeniable, unquestionable.

*antonym* doubtful.

**indissoluble** *adj* abiding, binding, enduring, eternal, fixed, imperishable, incorruptible, indestructible, inseparable, inviolable, lasting, permanent, sempiternal, solid, unbreakable.

*antonym* impermanent.

**indistinct** *adj* ambiguous, bleary, blurred, confused, dim, distant, doubtful, faint, fuzzy, hazy, ill-defined, indefinite, indeterminate, indiscernible, indistinguishable, misty, muffled, mumbled, obscure, shadowy, slurred, unclear, undefined, unintelligible, vague.

*antonym* distinct.

**indistinguishable** *adj* alike, identical, interchangeable, same, tantamount, twin.

*antonyms* distinguishable, unalike.

**individual** *n* being, bloke, body, chap, character, creature, fellow, individuum, mortal, party, person, personage, punter, soul.

*adj* characteristic, discrete, distinct, distinctive, exclusive, identical, idiosyncratic, own, particular, peculiar, personal, personalised, proper, respective, separate, several, single, singular, special, specific, unique.

**individualism** *n* anarchism, egocentricity, egoism, free-thinking, free-thought, independence, libertarianism, originality, self-direction, self-interest, self-reliance.

*antonym* conventionality.

**individualist** *n* anarchist, free-thinker, independent, libertarian, lone wolf, loner, maverick, nonconformist, original.

*antonym* conventionalist.

**individualistic** *adj* anarchistic, characteristic, distinctive, egocentric, egoistic, iconoclastic, idiosyncratic, independent, individual, libertarian, non-conformist, original, particular, self-reliant, special, typical, unconventional, unique.

*antonym* conventionalistic.

**individuality** *n* character, discreteness, distinction, distinctiveness, haecceity, originality, peculiarity, personality, separateness, singularity, unicity, uniqueness.

*antonym* sameness.

**individually** *adv* independently, particularly, separately, seriatim et privatim, severally, singly.

*antonym* together.

**indivisible** *adj* impartible, indiscerptible, inseparable, undividable.

*antonym* divisible.

**indoctrinate** *v* brainwash, catechise, drill, ground, imbue, initiate, instruct, school, teach, train.

**indoctrination** *n* brainwashing, catechesis, catechetics, inculcation, instruction, schooling, training.

**indolence** *n* do-nothingism, fainéance, heaviness, idleness, inactivity, inertia, inertness, languidness, languor, laziness, lethargy, shirking, slacking, sloth, sluggishness, torpidity, torpidness, torpitude, torpor.

*antonyms* activeness, enthusiasm, industriousness.

**indolent** *adj* fainéant, idle, inactive, inert, lackadaisical, languid, lazy, lethargic, listless, lumpish, slack, slothful, slow, sluggard, sluggish, torpid.

*antonyms* active, enthusiastic, industrious.

**indomitable** *adj* bold, intrepid, invincible, resolute, staunch, steadfast, unbeatable, unconquerable, undaunted, unflinching, untameable, unyielding.

*antonyms* compliant, timid.

**indoor** *adj* inside, umbratile, umbratilous.

*antonym* outdoor.

**indubitable** *adj* certain, evident, incontestable, incontrovertible, indisputable, irrebuttable, irrefragable, irrefutable, obvious, sure, unanswerable, unarguable, undeniable, undoubtable, undoubted, unquestionable, veritable.

*antonym* arguable.

**induce** *v* actuate, bring about, cause, convince, draw, effect, encourage, engender, generate, get, give rise to, impel, incite, influence, instigate, lead to, move, occasion, persuade, press, prevail upon, produce, prompt, talk into.

**inducement** *n* attraction, bait, carrot, cause, come-on, consideration, encouragement, impulse, incentive, incitement, influence, lure, motive, reason, reward, spur, stimulus.

*antonym* disincentive.

**induct** *v* consecrate, enthrone, inaugurate, initiate, install, introduce, invest, ordain, swear in.

**induction** *n* conclusion, consecration, deduction, enthronement, generalisation, inauguration, inference, initiation, installation, institution, introduction, investiture, ordination.

**indulge** *v* baby, cocker, coddle, cosset, favour, foster, give in to, go along with, gratify, humour, mollycoddle, pamper, pander to, pet, regale, satiate, satisfy, spoil, treat (oneself), yield to.

**indulge in** give free rein to, give oneself up to, give way to, luxuriate in, revel in, wallow in.

**indulgence** *n* appeasement, courtesy, excess, extravagance, favour, forbearance, good will, gratification, immoderateness, immoderation, intemperance, intemperateness, kindness, leniency, luxury, pampering, partiality, patience, permissiveness, privilege, prodigality, profligacy, profligateness, satiation, satisfaction, self-gratification, self-indulgence, spoiling, tolerance, treat, understanding.

*antonyms* moderation, strictness.

**indulgent** *adj* complaisant, compliant, easy-going, favourable, fond, forbearing, gentle, gratifying, intemperate, kind, kindly, lenient, liberal, mild, permissive, prodigal, self-indulgent, tender, tolerant, understanding.

*antonyms* moderate, strict.

**industrialist** *n* baron, boss, capitalist, captain of industry, financier, magnate, manufacturer, mill-owner, producer, tycoon.

**industrious** *adj* active, assiduous, busy, conscientious, deedy, diligent, energetic, hard-working, laborious, persevering, persistent, productive, purposeful, sedulous, steady, tireless, zealous.

*antonym* indolent.

**industriously** *adv* assiduously, conscientiously, diligently, doggedly, hard, perseveringly, sedulously, steadily, with one's nose to the grindstone.

*antonym* indolently.

**industry** *n* activity, application, assiduity, business, commerce, determination, diligence, effort, labour, manufacturing, perseverance, persistence, production, tirelessness, toil, trade, vigour, zeal.

*antonym* indolence.

**inebriate** *v* addle, animate, arouse, carry away, excite, exhilarate, fire, fuddle, intoxicate, stimulate, stupefy.

*antonyms* dampen, sober up.

**inebriated** *adj* befuddled, blind drunk, blotto, drunk, glorious, half seas over, half-cut, half-drunk, in one's cups, incapable, inebriate, intoxicated, legless, merry, paralytic, pie-eyed, plastered, sloshed, smashed, sozzled, stoned, stotious, three sheets in the wind, tight, tipsy, tired and emotional, under the influence.

*antonym* sober.

**inebriation** *n* drunkenness, inebriety, insobriety, intemperance, intoxication, sottishness, tipsiness.

*antonym* sobriety.

**inedible** *adj* deadly, harmful, inesculent, injurious, noxious, poisonous, uneatable.

*antonym* edible.

**ineducable** *adj* incorrigible, indocile, unteachable.

*antonym* educable.

**ineffable** *adj* incommunicable, indescribable, inexpressible, unimpartible, unspeakable, unutterable.

*antonym* describable.

**ineffective, ineffectual** *adj* abortive, barren, bootless, emasculate, feeble, fruitless, futile, idle, impotent, inadequate, incompetent, ineffective, ineffectual, inefficacious, inefficient, inept, lame, powerless, unavailing, unproductive, useless, vain, void, weak, worthless.

*antonyms* effective, effectual.

**inefficacy** *n* futility, inadequacy, ineffectiveness, ineffectuality, ineffectualness, unproductiveness, uselessness.

*antonym* efficacy.

**inefficiency** *n* carelessness, disorganisation, incompetence, muddle, negligence, slackness, sloppiness, waste, wastefulness.

*antonym* efficiency.

**inefficient** *adj* incompetent, inept, inexpert, money-wasting, negligent, slipshod, sloppy, time-wasting, unworkmanlike, wasteful.

*antonym* efficient.

**inelegant** *adj* awkward, barbarous, clumsy, coarse, crass, crude, gauche, graceless, indelicate, laboured, rough, uncourtly, uncouth, uncultivated, ungainly, ungraceful, unpolished, unrefined, unsophisticated.

*antonym* elegant.

**ineligible** *adj* disqualified, improper, inappropriate, incompetent, objectionable, unacceptable, undesirable, unequipped, unfit, unfitted, unqualified, unsuitable, unworthy.

*antonym* eligible.

**inept** *adj* absurd, awkward, bungling, cack-handed, clumsy, fatuous, futile, gauche, improper, inappropriate, inapt, incompetent, inexpert, infelicitous, irrelevant, maladroit, malapropos, meaningless, ridiculous, unfit, unhandy, unskilful, unworkmanlike.

*antonyms* adroit, apt.

**ineptitude** *n* absurdity, clumsiness, crassness, fatuity, futility, gaucheness, gaucherie, inappropriateness, incapacity, incompetence, ineptness, inexpertness, irrelevance, pointlessness, stupidity, unfitness, unhandiness, uselessness.

*antonyms* aptitude, skill.

**inequality** *n* bias, difference, disparity, disproportion, dissimilarity, diversity, imparity, inadequacy, irregularity, preferentiality, prejudice, unequalness, unevenness.

*antonym* equality.

**inequitable** *adj* biased, discriminatory, one-sided, partial, partisan, preferential, prejudiced, unequal, unfair, unjust, wrongful.

*antonym* equitable.

**inequity** *n* abuse, bias, discrimination, injustice, maltreatment, mistreatment, one-sidedness, partiality, prejudice, unfairness, unjustness.

*antonym* equity.

**inert** *adj* apathetic, dead, dormant, dull, idle, immobile, inactive, inanimate, indolent, insensible, lazy, leaden, lifeless, motionless, nerveless, numb, passive, quiescent, senseless, slack, sleepy, slothful, sluggish, somnolent, static, still, torpid, unmoving, unreacting, unresponsive.

*antonyms* alive, animated.

**inertia** *n* accedia, accidie, apathy, deadness, drowsiness, dullness, idleness, immobility, inactivity, indolence, insensibility, languor, lassitude, laziness, lethargy, listlessness, nervelessness, numbness, passivity, sleepiness, sloth, sluggishness, somnolence, stillness, stupor, torpor, unresponsiveness.

*antonyms* activity, liveliness.

**inescapable** *adj* certain, destined, fated, ineluctable, inevitable, inexorable, irrevocable, sure, unalterable, unavoidable, unpreventable.

*antonym* escapable.

**inessential** *adj* accidental, dispensable, expendable, extraneous, extrinsic, irrelevant, needless, non-essential, optional, redundant, secondary, spare, superfluous, surplus, unasked-for, uncalled-for, unessential, unimportant, unnecessary.

*antonym* essential.

*n* accessory, appendage, expendable, extra, extravagance, luxury, non-essential, superfluity, trimming.

*antonym* essential.

**inestimable** *adj* immeasurable, immense incalculable, incomputable, infinite, invaluable measureless, precious, priceless, prodigious uncountable, unfathomable, unlimited, untold vast.

*antonym* insignificant.

**inevitable** *adj* assured, automatic, certain, compulsory, decreed, destined, fated, fixed, ineluctable, inescapable, inexorable, irrevocable, mandatory, necessary, obligatory, ordained, settled, sure, unalterable, unavertable, unavoidable, unpreventable, unshunnable.

*antonyms* alterable, avoidable, uncertain.

**inevitably** *adv* automatically, certainly, incontestably, ineluctably, inescapably, necessarily, of necessity, perforce, surely, unavoidably.

**inexact** *adj* erroneous, fuzzy, imprecise, inaccurate, incorrect, indefinite, indeterminate, indistinct, lax, loose, muddled, woolly.

*antonym* exact.

**inexactitude** *n* blunder, error, impreciseness, imprecision, inaccuracy, incorrectness, indefiniteness, inexactness, laxness, looseness, miscalculation, mistake, woolliness.

*antonym* exactitude.

**inexcusable** *adj* blameworthy, indefensible, inexpiable, intolerable, outrageous, reprehensible, shameful, unacceptable, unforgivable, unjustifiable, unpardonable, unwarrantable.

*antonyms* excusable, venial.

**inexhaustible** *adj* abundant, bottomless, boundless, copious, endless, exhaustless, illimitable, indefatigable, infinite, lavish, limitless, measureless, never-ending, never-failing, tireless, unbounded, undaunted, unfailing, unflagging, unlimited, untiring, unwearied, unwearying.

*antonym* limited.

**inexorable** *adj* adamant, cruel, hard, harsh, immovable, implacable, ineluctable, inescapable, inflexible, intransigent, irreconcilable, irresistible, irrevocable, merciless, obdurate, pitiless, relentless, remorseless, severe, unalterable, unappeasable, unavertable, unbending, uncompromising, unrelenting, unyielding.

*antonyms* flexible, lenient, yielding.

**inexorably** *adv* implacably, ineluctably, inescapably, irresistibly, irrevocably, mercilessly, pitilessly, relentlessly, remorselessly, resistlessly.

**inexpedient** *adj* detrimental, disadvantageous, foolish, ill-advised, ill-chosen, ill-judged, impolitic, impractical, imprudent, inadvisable, inappropriate, indiscreet, injudicious, misguided, senseless, unadvisable, undesirable, undiplomatic, unfavourable, unsuitable, unwise, wrong.

*antonym* expedient.

**inexpensive** *adj* bargain, bon marché, budget, cheap, economical, low-cost, low-priced, modest, reasonable, uncostly.

*antonym* expensive.

**inexperience** *n* callowness, greenness, ignorance, inexpertness, innocence, naïvety, nescience, newness, rawness, strangeness, unexpertness, unfamiliarity, unsophistication, verdancy.

*antonym* experience.

**inexperienced** *adj* amateur, callow, fresh, green, immature, inexpert, innocent, nescient, new, raw, unaccustomed, unacquainted, unbearded, unfamiliar, unpractical, unpractised, unschooled, unseasoned, unskilled, unsophisticated, untrained, untravelled, untried, unused, unversed, verdant.

*antonym* experienced.

**inexpert** *adj* amateurish, awkward, blundering, bungling, clumsy, hammy, incompetent, inept, maladroit, unhandy, unpractised, unprofessional, unskilful, unskilled, untaught, untrained, untutored, unworkmanlike.

*antonym* expert.

**inexplicable** *adj* baffling, enigmatic, impenetrable, incomprehensible, incredible, inscrutable, insoluble, intractable, miraculous, mysterious, mystifying, puzzling, strange, unaccountable, unexplainable, unfathomable, unintelligible, unsolvable.

*antonym* explicable.

**inexplicably** *adv* bafflingly, incomprehensibly, incredibly, miraculously, mysteriously, mystifyingly, puzzlingly, strangely, unaccountably, unexplainably.

*antonym* explicably.

**inexpressible** *adj* incommunicable, indefinable, indescribable, ineffable, nameless, undescribable, unsayable, unspeakable, untellable, unutterable.

**inexpressive** *adj* bland, blank, dead-pan, emotionless, empty, expressionless, immobile, impassive, inanimate, inscrutable, lifeless, poker-faced, stolid, stony, unexpressive, vacant.

*antonym* expressive.

**inextinguishable** *adj* deathless, enduring, eternal, everlasting, immortal, imperishable, indestructible, irrepressible, lasting, unconquerable, undying, unquellable, unquenchable, unsuppressible.

*antonyms* impermanent, perishable.

**inextricably** *adv* indissolubly, indistinguishably, inseparably, intricately, irresolubly, irretrievably, irreversibly.

**infallibility** *n* accuracy, dependability, faultlessness, impeccability, inerrancy, inevitability, irrefutability, irreproachability, omniscience, perfection, reliability, safety, supremacy, sureness, trustworthiness, unerringness.

*antonym* fallibility.

**infallible** *adj* accurate, certain, dependable, fail-safe, faultless, foolproof, impeccable, inerrable, inerrant, irreproachable, omniscient, perfect, reliable, sound, sure, sure-fire, trustworthy, unbeatable, unerring, unfailing, unfaltering, unfaulty, unimpeachable.

*antonym* fallible.

**infamous** *adj* abhorrent, abominable, atrocious, base, dastardly, despicable, detestable, discreditable, disgraceful, dishonourable, disreputable, egregious, execrable, facinorous, flagitious, hateful, heinous, ignoble, ignominious, ill-famed, iniquitous, knavish, loathsome, monstrous, nefarious, notorious, odious, opprobrious, outrageous, scandalous, scurvy, shameful, shocking, vile, villainous, wicked.

*antonym* glorious.

**infamy** *n* atrocity, baseness, crime, dastardliness, depravity, discredit, disgrace, dishonour, disrepute, enormity, ignominy, improbity, notoriety, obloquy, odium, opprobrium, outrageousness, scandal, shame, stain, stigma, turpitude, villainy, wickedness.

*antonym* glory.

**infancy** *n* babyhood, beginnings, birth, childhood, commencement, cradle, dawn, embryonic stage, emergence, genesis, inception, origins, outset, start, youth.

*antonym* adulthood.

**infant** *n* babe, babe in arms, baby, bairn, bambino, child, neonate, nipper, nurseling, papoose, suckling, tiny, toddler, tot, wean, weanling, youngling.

*antonym* adult.

*adj* baby, childish, dawning, developing, early, emergent, growing, immature, inchoate, incipient, initial, juvenile, nascent, newborn, rudimentary, unfledged, unformed, young, youthful.

*antonym* adult.

**infantile** *adj* adolescent, babyish, childish, immature, juvenile, puerile, tender, undeveloped, young, youthful.

*antonyms* adult, mature.

**infatuated** *adj* befooled, beguiled, besotted, bewitched, captivated, crazy, deluded, enamoured, enraptured, fascinated, fixated, hypnotised, intoxicated, mad, mesmerised, obsessed, possessed, ravished, smitten, spellbound.

*antonyms* disenchanted, indifferent.

**infatuation** *n* besottedness, crush, dotage, engouement, fascination, fixation, folly, fondness, intoxication, madness, mania, obsession, passion, possession.

*antonyms* disenchantment, indifference.

**infect** *v* affect, blight, canker, contaminate, corrupt, defile, enthuse, influence, inject, inspire, pervert, poison, pollute, taint, touch, vitiate.

**infection** *n* contagion, contamination, corruption, defilement, disease, epidemic, illness, inflammation, influence, miasma, pestilence, poison, pollution, sepsis, septicity, taint, virus.

**infectious** *adj* catching, communicable, contagious, contaminating, corrupting, deadly, defiling, epidemic, infective, miasmic, miasmous, pestilential, poisoning, poisonous, polluting, spreading, transmissible, transmittable, venemous, virulent, vitiating.

**infelicitous** *adj* gauche, ill-timed, inappropriate, inopportune, maladroit, tactless, unapt, unfortunate, unhappy, unsuitable, untimely.

*antonym* felicitous.

**infelicity** *n* despair, gaucheness, inappositeness, inappropriateness, inaptness, incongruity, inopportuneness, misery, misfortune, sadness, sorrow, tactlessness, unfortunateness, unhappiness, unsuitability, untimeliness, woe, wretchedness, wrongness.

*antonyms* aptness, felicity, happiness.

**infer** *v* assume, conclude, conjecture, construe, deduce, derive, extract, extrapolate, gather, presume, surmise, understand.

**inference** *n* assumption, conclusion, conjecture, consequence, construction, corollary, deduction, extrapolation, illation, interpretation, presumption, reading, surmise.

**inferior** *adj* bad, crummy, dog, grotty, humble, imperfect, indifferent, junior, lesser, low, lower, low-grade, mean, mediocre, menial, minor, one-horse, paravail, poor, poorer, provant, schlock, secondary, second-class, second-rate, shoddy, slipshod, slovenly, subordinate, subsidiary, substandard, under, underneath, undistinguished, unsatisfactory, unworthy, worse.

*antonym* superior.

*n* junior, menial, minion, subordinate, underling, understrapper, vassal.

*antonym* superior.

**inferiority** *n* badness, baseness, deficiency, humbleness, imperfection, inadequacy, insignificance, lowliness, meanness, mediocrity, shoddiness, slovenliness, subordination, subservience, unimportance, unworthiness, worthlessness.

*antonym* superiority.

**infernal** *adj* accursed, Acherontic, chthonian, chthonic, damnable, damned, demonic, devilish, diabolical, fiendish, Hadean, hellish, malevolent, malicious, Mephistophelian, Plutonian, satanic, Stygian, Tartarean, underworld.

*antonym* heavenly.

**infertile** *adj* acarpous, arid, barren, dried-up, effete, infecund, infructuous, non-productive, parched, sterile, unbearing, unfruitful, unproductive.

*antonym* fertile.

**infertility** *n* aridity, aridness, barrenness, effeteness, infecundity, sterility, unfruitfulness, unproductiveness.

*antonym* fertility.

**infest** *v* beset, flood, infiltrate, invade, overrun, overspread, penetrate, permeate, pervade, ravage, swarm, throng.

**infested** *adj* alive, beset, bristling, crawling, infiltrated, lousy, overrun, overspread, permeated, pervaded, plagued, ravaged, ridden, swarming, teeming, vermined, verminy.

**infidel** *n* atheist, disbeliever, free-thinker, giaour, heathen, heretic, iconoclast, irreligionist, nullifidian, pagan, sceptic, unbeliever.

*antonym* believer.

**infidelity** *n* adultery, apostasy, bad faith, betrayal, cheating, disbelief, disloyalty, duplicity, faithlessness, false-heartedness, falseness, iconoclasm, irreligion, perfidy, recreancy, renegation, scepticism, traitorhood, traitorousness, treachery, unbelief, unfaithfulness.

*antonym* fidelity.

**infiltrate** *v* creep into, filter, infilter, insinuate, interpenetrate, intrude, penetrate, percolate, permeate, pervade, sift.

**infiltration** *n* entr(y)ism, insinuation, interpenetration, intrusion, penetration, percolation, permeation, pervasion.

**infiltrator** *n* entr(y)ist, insinuator, intruder, penetrator, seditionary, spy, subversive, subverter.

**infinite** *adj* absolute, bottomless, boundless, countless, enormous, eternal, everlasting, fathomless, illimitable, immeasurable, immense, incomputable, inestimable, inexhaustible, interminable, limitless, measureless, never-ending, numberless, perpetual, stupendous, total, unbounded, uncountable, uncounted, unfathomable, untold, vast, wide.

*antonym* finite.

**infinitesimal** *adj* atomic, exiguous, imperceptible, inappreciable, inconsiderable, insignificant, microscopic, minuscule, minute, negligible, paltry, teeny, tiny, unnoticeable, wee.

*antonyms* significant, substantial.

**infinity** *n* boundlessness, countlessness, endlessness, eternity, everlasting, everlastingness, for ever, illimitibleness, immeasurableness, immensity, inexhaustibility, infinitude, interminableness, limitlessness, perpetuity, vastness.

*antonyms* finiteness, limitation.

**infirm** *adj* ailing, crippled, debilitated, decrepit, dicky, doddering, doddery, enfeebled, failing, faltering, feeble, fickle, frail, hesitant, indecisive, insecure, irresolute, lame, poorly, sickly, unreliable, wavering, weak, wobbly.

*antonyms* healthy, strong.

**infirmity** *n* ailment, complaint, debility, decrepitude, defect, deficiency, dickiness, disease, disorder, failing, fault, feebleness, foible, frailty, ill health, illness, imperfection, instability, malady, sickliness, sickness, vulnerability, weakness.

*antonyms* health, strength.

**inflame** *v* aggravate, agitate, anger, arouse, dynamise, embitter, enkindle, enrage, exacerbate, exasperate, excite, fan, fire, foment, fuel, galvanise, heat, ignite, impassion, incense, increase, infatuate, infuriate, intensify, intoxicate, kindle, madden, provoke, ravish, rile, rouse, stimulate, worsen.

*antonyms* cool, quench.

**inflamed** *adj* angry, chafing, enraged, erythematous, excited, festering, fevered, heated, hot, impassioned, incensed, infected, poisoned, red, septic, sore, swollen.

**inflammable** *adj* burnable, choleric, combustible, deflagrable, flammable, incendiary, irascible, piceous, pyrophorous, short-tempered, volatile.

*antonyms* flame-proof, incombustible, non-flammable, non-inflammable.

**inflammation** *n* abscess, burning, empyema, erythema, heat, infection, painfulness, rash, redness, sepsis, septicity, sore, soreness, tenderness.

**inflammatory** *adj* anarchic, demagogic, explosive, fiery, incendiary, incitative, inflaming, instigative, insurgent, intemperate, provocative, rabble-rousing, rabid, riotous, seditious.

*antonyms* calming, pacific.

**inflate** *v* aerate, aggrandise, amplify, balloon, bloat, blow out, blow up, bombast, boost, dilate, distend, enlarge, escalate, exaggerate, expand, increase, puff out, puff up, pump up, swell, tumefy.

*antonym* deflate.

**inflated** *adj* ballooned, bloated, blown up, bombastic, dilated, distended, euphuistic, exaggerated, flatulent, grandiloquent, magniloquent, ostentatious, overblown, pompous, puffed out, swollen, tumefied, tumid, turgid.

*antonym* deflated.

**inflation** *n* aggrandisement, ballooning, bloating, dilation, distension, enhancement, enlargement, escalation, expansion, extension, hyperinflation, increase, intensification, rise, spread, swelling, tumefaction.

*antonym* deflation.

**inflexibility** *n* fixity, hardness, immovability, immutability, immutableness, inelasticity, intractability, intransigence, obduracy, obstinacy, rigidity, steeliness, stiffness, stringency, stubbornness, unsuppleness.

*antonym* flexibility.

**inflexible** *adj* adamant, dyed-in-the-wool, entrenched, fast, firm, fixed, hard, hardened, immovable, immutable, implacable, inelastic, inexorable, intractable, intransigent, iron, non-flexible, obdurate, obstinate, relentless, resolute, rigid, rigorous, set, steadfast, steely, stiff, strict, stringent, stubborn, taut, unaccommodating, unadaptable, unbending, unchangeable, uncompromising, unpliable, unpliant, unsupple, unyielding.

*antonym* flexible.

**inflict** *v* administer, afflict, apply, burden, deal, deliver, enforce, exact, force, impose, lay, levy, mete, perpetrate, visit, wreak.

**infliction** *n* administration, affliction, burden, castigation, chastisement, exaction, imposition, nemesis, penalty, perpetration, punishment, retribution, trouble, visitation, worry, wreaking.

**influence** *n* agency, ascendancy, authority, bias, charisma, clout, connections, control, credit, direction, domination, drag, effect, éminence grise, good offices, guidance, hold, importance, leverage, magnetism, mastery, power, pressure, prestige, pull, reach, rule, scope, spell, standing, strength, string-pulling, sway, teaching, training, weight, wire-pulling.

*v* affect, alter, arouse, bias, change, control, direct, dispose, dominate, edge, guide, head, impel, impress, incite, incline, induce, instigate, manipulate, manoeuvre, modify, motivate, move, persuade, point, predispose, prompt, pull, pull wires, rouse, strings, sway, teach, train, weigh with.

**influential** *adj* ascendant, authoritative, charismatic, cogent, compelling, controlling, dominant, dominating, effective, efficacious, forcible, guiding, important, instrumental, leading, momentous, moving, persuasive, potent, powerful, significant, strong, telling, weighty, well-placed.

*antonym* ineffectual.

**influenza** *n* dog's disease, flu, grip, grippe.

**influx** *n* access, accession, arrival, consignment, convergence, flood, flow, incursion, inflow, inrush, instreaming, inundation, invasion, rush.

**inform**[1] *v* acquaint, advise, apprise, brief, clue up, communicate, conscientise, enlighten, fill in, illuminate, impart, instruct, intimate, leak, notify, teach, tell, tip off, wise up.

**inform on** accuse, betray, blab, blow the whistle, clype, denounce, denunciate, dob (in), grass, incriminate, inculpate, nark, peach, rat, sing, snitch, squeal, tell on, whistle.

**inform**[2] *v* animate, characterise, endue, fill, illuminate, imbue, inspire, invest, irradiate, light up, permeate, suffuse, typify.

**informal** *adj* approachable, casual, colloquial, congenial, cosy, easy, familiar, free, homely, irregular, natural, relaxed, relaxing, simple, unbuttoned, unceremonious, unconstrained, unofficial, unorthodox, unpretentious, unsolemn.

*antonym* formal.

**informality** *n* approachability, casualness, congeniality, cosiness, ease, familiarity, freedom, homeliness, irregularity, naturalness, relaxation, simplicity, unceremoniousness, unpretentiousness.

*antonym* formality.

**informally** *adj* casually, colloquially, confidentially, cosily, easily, en famille, familiarly, freely, on the quiet, privately, simply, unceremoniously, unofficially.

*antonym* formally.

**information** *n* advices, blurb, briefing, bulletin, bumf, clues, communiqué, conscientisation, data, databank, database, dope, dossier, enlightenment, facts, gen, illumination, info, input, instruction, intelligence, knowledge, low-down, message, news, notice, report, tidings, word.

**informative** *adj* chatty, communicative, constructive, edifying, educational, enlightening, forthcoming, gossipy, illuminating, informatory, instructive, newsy, revealing, revelatory, useful, valuable.

*antonym* uninformative.

**informed** *adj* abreast, acquainted, apprised, au courant, au fait, authoritative, briefed, clued up, conversant, enlightened, erudite, expert, familiar, filled in, genned up, hep, in the know, knowledgeable, learned, posted, primed, scholarly, trained, up to date, versed, well-informed, well-read, well-researched.

*antonyms* ignorant, unaware.

**informer** *n* betrayer, canary, denouncer, denunciator, fink, fiz(z)gig, grass, Judas, nark, singer, sneak, snitch(er), snout, squeak, squealer, stool pigeon, stoolie, supergrass, whistle-blower.

**infrequent** *adj* exceptional, intermittent, occasional, rare, scanty, sparse, spasmodic, sporadic, uncommon, unusual.

*antonym* frequent.

**infringe** *v* break, contravene, defy, disobey, encroach, flout, ignore, infract, intrude, invade, overstep, transgress, trespass, violate.

**infringement** *n* breach, contravention, defiance, encroachment, evasion, infraction, intrusion, invasion, non-compliance, non-observance, transgression, trespass, violation.

**infuriate** *v* anger, antagonise, bug, enrage, exasperate, incense, irritate, madden, provoke, put someone's back up, rile, rouse, vex.

*antonyms* calm, mollify.

**infuriated** *adj* agitated, angry, beside oneself, enraged, exasperated, flaming, furious, heated, incensed, irate, irritated, maddened, provoked, roused, vexed, violent, wild.

*antonyms* calm, gratified, pleased.

**infuriating** *adj* aggravating, annoying, exasperating, frustrating, galling, intolerable, irritating, maddening, mortifying, pesky, pestiferous, pestilential, provoking, thwarting, unbearable, vexatious.

*antonyms* agreeable, pleasing.

**infuse** *v* breathe into, brew, draw, imbue, impart to, implant, inculcate, inject, inspire, instil, introduce, leach, macerate, saturate, soak, steep.

**infusion** *n* brew, implantation, inculcation, infusing, instillation, leachate, maceration, soaking, steeping.

**ingenious** *adj* adroit, bright, brilliant, clever, crafty, creative, cunning, daedal, Daedalian, daedalic, dedalian, deft, dexterous, fertile, Gordian, Heath-Robinson, imaginative, innovative, intricate, inventive, masterly, original, pretty, ready, resourceful, shrewd, skilful, sly, subtle.

*antonyms* clumsy, unimaginative.

**ingenuity** *n* adroitness, cleverness, cunning, deftness, faculty, flair, genius, gift, ingeniousness, innovativeness, invention, inventiveness, knack, originality, resourcefulness, sharpness, shrewdness, skill, slyness, turn.

*antonyms* clumsiness, dullness.

**ingenuous** *adj* artless, candid, childlike, frank, guileless, honest, innocent, naïf, naïve, open, plain, simple, sincere, trustful, trusting, unreserved, unsophisticated, unstudied.

*antonyms* artful, sly.

**ingenuousness** *n* artlessness, candour, frankness, guilelessness, innocence, naïvety, openness, trustfulness, unreserve, unsophisticatedness.

*antonyms* artfulness, slyness, subterfuge.

**inglorious** *adj* discreditable, disgraceful, dishonourable, disreputable, humiliating, ignoble, ignominious, infamous, mortifying, obscure, shameful, unheroic, unhonoured, unknown, unsuccessful, unsung.

*antonym* glorious.

**ingrain** *v* dye, embed, engrain, entrench, fix, imbue, implant, impress, imprint, infix, instil, root.

**ingrained** *adj* constitutional, deep-rooted, deep-seated, entrenched, fixed, fundamental, hereditary, immovable, inborn, inbred, inbuilt, indelible, ineradicable, infixed, inherent, intrinsic, inveterate, permanent, rooted.

*antonym* superficial.

**ingratiate** *v* blandish, crawl, curry, favour, fawn, flatter, get in with, grovel, insinuate, suck up, toady, worm.

**ingratiating** *adj* bland, bootlicking, crawling, fawning, flattering, obsequious, servile, smooth-tongued, suave, sycophantic, time-serving, toadying, unctuous, whilly, whillywha(w).

**ingratitude** *n* thanklessness, unappreciativeness, ungraciousness, ungratefulness.

*antonym* gratitude.

**ingredient** *n* component, constituent, element, factor, part.

**inhabit** *v* abide, bide, dwell, habit, live, lodge, make one's home, occupy, people, populate, possess, reside, settle, settle in, stay, take up one's abode, tenant.

**inhabitant** *n* aborigine, autochthon, burgher, citizen, denizen, dweller, habitant, indigene, indweller, inmate, lodger, native, occupant, occupier, resident, residentiary, resider, settler, tenant.

**inhabited** *adj* colonised, developed, held, lived-in, occupied, overrun, peopled, populated, possessed, settled, tenanted.

*antonym* uninhabited.

**inhalation** *n* breath, breathing, inhaling, inspiration, respiration, spiration, suction, toke.

**inhale** *v* breathe in, draw, draw in, inbreathe, inspire, respire, suck in, toke, whiff.

**inharmonious** *adj* antipathetic, atonal, cacophonous, clashing, conficting, discordant, dissonant, grating, harsh, horrisonant, incompatible, inconsonant, jangling, jarring, raucous, strident, tuneless, unharmonious, unmelodious, unmusical, untuneful.

*antonym* harmonious.

**inherent** *adj* basic, characteristic, congenital, connate, essential, fundamental, hereditary, immanent, inborn, inbred, inbuilt, ingrained, inherited, innate, instinctive, intrinsic, inwrought, native, natural.

**inherit** *v* accede to, assume, be bequeathed, be left, come in for, come into, fall heir to, receive, succeed to.

**inheritance** *n* accession, bequest, birthright, descent, heredity, heritage, heritament, legacy, patrimony, succession.

**inheritor** *n* beneficiary, co-heir, co-heiress, coheritor, devisee, heir, heiress, heritor, heritrix, inheritress, inheritrix, legatee, recipient, reversionary, successor.

**inhibit** *v* arrest, bar, bridle, check, constrain, cramp, curb, debar, discourage, forbid, frustrate, hinder, hold, impede, interfere with, obstruct, prevent, prohibit, repress, restrain, stanch, stem, stop, suppress, thwart.

**inhibited** *adj* bashful, constrained, diffident, frustrated, guarded, repressed, reserved, reticent, self-conscious, shamefaced, shy, strained, subdued, tense, uptight, withdrawn.

*antonym* uninhibited.

**inhibition** *n* bar, check, constraint, embargo, hang-up, hindrance, impediment, interdict, interference, obstacle, obstruction, prohibition, repression, reserve, restraint, restriction, reticence, self-consciousness, shyness, suppression.

*antonym* freedom.

**inhospitable** *adj* antisocial, bare, barren, bleak, cold, cool, desolate, forbidding, hostile, inimical, intolerant, sterile, unaccommodating, uncivil, uncongenial, unfavourable, unfriendly, ungenerous, uninhabitable, unkind, unneighbourly, unreceptive, unsociable, unwelcoming, xenophobic.

*antonyms* favourable, hospitable.

**inhospitality** *n* coldness, coolness, hostility, incivility, inimicality, intolerance, uncongeniality, unfriendliness, unkindness, unneighbourliness, unreceptiveness, unsociability, xenophobia.

*antonym* hospitality.

**inhuman** *adj* animal, barbaric, barbarous, bestial, brutal, brutish, callous, cold-blooded, cruel, diabolical, fiendish, heartless, inhumane, insensate, merciless, pitiless, remorseless, ruthless, savage, sublime, unfeeling, vicious.

*antonym* human.

**inhumane** *adj* brutal, callous, cold-hearted, cruel, heartless, indurate, inhuman, insensitive, pitiless, uncaring, uncompassionate, unfeeling, unkind, unsympathetic.

*antonym* humane.

**inhumanity** *n* atrocity, barbarism, barbarity, brutality, brutishness, callousness, cold-bloodedness, cold-heartedness, cruelty, hard-heartedness, heartlessness, pitilessness, ruthlessness, sadism, unkindness, viciousness.

*antonym* humanity.

**inimical** *adj* adverse, antagonistic, antipathetic, contrary, destructive, disaffected, harmful, hostile, hurtful, ill-disposed, inhospitable, injurious, intolerant, noxious, opposed, oppugnant, pernicious, repugnant, unfavourable, unfriendly, unwelcoming.

*antonyms* favourable, friendly, sympathetic.

**inimitable** *adj* consummate, distinctive, exceptional, incomparable, matchless, nonpareil, peerless, sublime, superlative, supreme, unequalled, unexampled, unique, unmatched, unparalleled, unrivalled, unsurpassable, unsurpassed.

**iniquitous** *adj* abominable, accursed, atrocious, awful, base, criminal, dreadful, evil, facinorous, flagitious, heinous, immoral, infamous, nefarious, nefast, reprehensible, reprobate, sinful, unjust, unrighteous, vicious, wicked.

*antonym* virtuous.

**iniquity** *n* abomination, baseness, crime, enormity, evil, evil-doing, heinousness, impiety, infamy, injustice, misdeed, offence, sin, sinfulness, ungodliness, unrighteousness, vice, viciousness, wickedness, wrong, wrong-doing.

*antonym* virtue.

**initial** *adj* beginning, commencing, early, embryonic, first, formative, inaugural, inauguratory, inceptive, inchoate, incipient, infant, introductory, opening, original, primary.

*antonym* final.

**initially** *adv* at first, at the beginning, at the outset, at the start, first, first of all, firstly, in the beginning, introductorily, originally, prefatorily, to begin with, to start with.

*antonym* finally.

**initiate** *v* activate, actuate, begin, cause, coach, commence, inaugurate, indoctrinate, induce, induct, instate, institute, instruct, introduce, invest, launch, open, originate, prompt, start, stimulate, teach, train.

*n* authority, beginner, catechumen, cognoscente, connoisseur, convert, entrant, epopt, expert, insider, learner, member, newcomer, novice, novitiate, probationer, proselyte, recruit, sage, savant, tenderfoot, tiro.

**initiation** *n* admission, commencement, début, enrolment, entrance, entry, inauguration, inception, induction, installation, instatement, instruction, introduction, investiture, reception, rite of passage.

**initiative** *n* advantage, ambition, drive, dynamism, energy, enterprise, forcefulness, get-up-and-go, goeyness, innovativeness, inventiveness, lead, move, originality, prompting, push, recommendation, resource, resourcefulness, suggestion.

**inject** *v* add, bring, fix, hit, infuse, inoculate, insert, instil, interject, introduce, jab, mainline, pop, shoot, shoot up, skin-pop, vaccinate.

**injection** *n* dose, fix, hit, infusion, inoculation, insertion, interjection, introduction, jab, mainlining, popping, shot, skin-popping, vaccination, vaccine.

**injudicious** *adj* foolish, hasty, ill-advised, ill-judged, ill-timed, impolitic, imprudent, inadvisable, incautious, inconsiderate, indiscreet, inexpedient, misguided, rash, stupid, unthinking, unwise, wrong-headed.

*antonym* judicious.

**injunction** *n* admonition, behest, command, dictate, direction, directive, enjoinment, exhortation, instruction, interdict, mandate, order, precept, ruling.

**injure** *v* abuse, aggrieve, blemish, blight, break, cripple, damage, deface, disable, disfigure, disserve, harm, hurt, ill-treat, impair, maim, maltreat, mar, ruin, scathe, spoil, tarnish, undermine, vandalise, vitiate, weaken, wound, wrong.

**injured** *adj* abused, aggrieved, blemished, broken, cut to the quick, defamed, disabled, disgruntled, displeased, grieved, hurt, ill-treated, insulted, lamed, long-suffering, maligned, maltreated, misused, offended, pained, put out, stung, tarnished, undermined, unhappy, upset, vilified, weakened, wounded, wronged.

**injurious** *adj* adverse, bad, baneful, calumnious, corrupting, damaging, deleterious, destructive, detrimental, disadvantageous, harmful, hurtful, iniquitous, insulting, libellous, mischievous, noxious, pernicious, prejudicial, ruinous, slanderous, unconducive, unhealthy, unjust, wrongful.

*antonyms* beneficial, favourable.

**injury** *n* abuse, annoyance, damage, damnification, detriment, disservice, evil, grievance, harm, hurt, ill, impairment, injustice, insult, lesion, loss, mischief, noyance, prejudice, ruin, scathe, trauma, vexation, wound, wrong.

**injustice** *n* bias, discrimination, disparity, favouritism, imposition, inequality, inequitableness, inequity, iniquity, one-sidedness, oppression, partiality, partisanship, prejudice, unevenness, unfairness, unjustness, unlawfulness, unreason, wrong.

*antonym* justice.

**inkling** *n* allusion, clue, conception, earthly, faintest, foggiest, glimmering, hint, idea, indication, intimation, notion, pointer, sign, suggestion, suspicion, umbrage, whisper.

**inlaid** *adj* damascened, empaestic, enchased, set, studded, tessellated.

**inland** *adj* central, domestic, inner, interior, internal, up-country.

**inlay** *n* damascene, emblema, tessellation.

**inlet** *n* bay, bight, cove, creek, entrance, fjord, fleet, hope, ingress, opening, passage, wick.

**inmost** *adj* basic, buried, central, closest, dearest, deep, deepest, esoteric, essential, hidden, innermost, intimate, personal, private, secret.

**inn** *n* albergo, alehouse, auberge, caravanserai, hostelry, hotel, howff, khan, local, public, public house, roadhouse, saloon, serai, tavern.

**innards** *n* entera, entrails, gralloch, guts, insides, interior, intestines, inwards, mechanism, organs, umbles, viscera, vitals, works.

**innate** *adj* basic, congenital, connate, constitutional, essential, fundamental, immanent, inborn, inbred, ingenerate, ingrained, inherent, inherited, instinctive, intrinsic, intuitive, native, natural.

**inner** *adj* central, concealed, emotional, esoteric, essential, hidden, inly, inside, interior, internal, intimate, inward, mental, middle, personal, private, psychical, psychological, secret, spiritual.

*antonyms* outer, patent.

**innkeeper** *n* aubergiste, boniface, host, hostess, hotelier, hotel-keeper, innholder, landlady, landlord, mine host, padrone, publican, restaurateur.

**innocence** *n* artlessness, blamelessness, chastity, credulousness, freshness, greenness, guilelessness, guiltlessness, gullibility, harmlessness, honesty, ignorance, incorruptibility, incorruption, inexperience, ingenuousness, innocuity, innocuousness, inoffensiveness, irreproachability, naïvety, naturalness, nescience, probity, purity, righteousness, simplicity, sinlessness, stainlessness, trustfulness, unawareness, unfamiliarity, unimpeachability, unsophistication, unworldliness, virginity, virtue.

*antonyms* experience, guilt, knowledge.

**innocent** *adj* Arcadian, artless, benign, bereft of, blameless, canny, chaste, childlike, clear, credulous, dewy-eyed, faultless, frank, free of, fresh, green, guileless, guiltless, gullible, harmless, honest, immaculate, impeccable, incorrupt, ingenuous, innocuous, inoffensive, intact, irreproachable, naïve, natural, nescient, open, pristine, pure, righteous, simple, sinless, spotless, stainless, trustful, trusting, unblemished, uncontaminated, unimpeachable, unobjectionable, unoffending, unsullied, unsuspicious, untainted, untouched, unworldly, verdant, virginal, well-intentioned, well-meaning, well-meant.

*antonyms* experienced, guilty, knowing.

*n* babe, babe in arms, beginner, child, greenhorn, infant, ingénu, ingénue, neophyte, tenderfoot.

*antonyms* connoisseur, expert.

**innocently** *adv* artlessly, blamelessly, credulously, harmlessly, ingenuously, innocuously, inoffensively, like a lamb to the slaughter, simply, trustfully, trustingly, unoffendingly, unsuspiciously.

**innocuous** *adj* bland, harmless, hypo-allergenic, innocent, innoxious, inoffensive, non-irritant, safe, unimpeachable, unobjectionable.

*antonym* harmful.

**innovation** *n* alteration, change, departure, introduction, modernisation, modernism, neologism, neoterism, newness, novation, novelty, progress, reform, variation.

**innovative** *adj* adventurous, bold, daring, enterprising, fresh, go-ahead, goey, groundbreaking, imaginative, inventive, modernising, new, on the move, original, progressive, reforming, resourceful, revolutionary.

*antonyms* conservative, unimaginative.

**innuendo** *n* aspersion, hint, implication, imputation, insinuation, intimation, overtone, slant, slur, suggestion, whisper.

**innumerable** *adj* countless, incalculable, incomputable, infinite, many, multitudinous, myriad, numberless, numerous, uncountable, uncounted, unnumbered, untold.

**inoculate** *v* immunise, inject, jag, protect, safeguard, vaccinate.

**inoculation** *n* immunisation, injection, jag, protection, shot, vaccination.

**inoffensive** *adj* gentle, harmless, humble, innocent, innocuous, innoxious, mild, mousy, non-provocative, peaceable, quiet, retiring, unassertive, unobjectionable, unobtrusive, unoffending.

*antonyms* malicious, offensive.

**inoperable** *adj* impracticable, impractical, intractable, irremovable, non-viable, unrealistic, unworkable.

*antonyms* operable, practicable.

**inoperative** *adj* broken, broken-down, defective, hors de combat, idle, ineffective, ineffectual, inefficacious, invalid, non-active, non-functioning, nugatory, out of action, out of commission, out of order, out of service, unserviceable, unused, unworkable, useless.

*antonym* operative.

**inopportune** *adj* clumsy, ill-chosen, ill-timed, inappropriate, inauspicious, inconvenient, infelicitous, malapropos, mistimed, tactless, unfortunate, unpropitious, unseasonable, unsuitable, untimely, wrong-timed.

*antonym* opportune.

**inordinate** *adj* disproportionate, excessive, exorbitant, extravagant, hubristic, immoderate, intemperate, overweening, preposterous, prohibitive, unconscionable, undue, unreasonable, unrestrained, unwarranted.

*antonyms* moderate, reasonable.

**input** *v* capture, code, feed in, insert, key in, process, store.

**inquietude** *n* agitation, anxiety, apprehension, discomposure, disquiet, disquietude, jumpiness, nervousness, perturbation, restlessness, solicitude, unease, uneasiness, worry.

*antonym* composure.

**inquire** *v* ask, catechise, delve, enquire, examine, explore, inspect, interrogate, investigate, look into, probe, query, quest, question, reconnoitre, scout, scrutinise, search, speir.

**inquirer** *n* explorer, interrogator, investigator, querist, quester, questioner, researcher, searcher, seeker, student.

**inquiring** *adj* analytical, curious, doubtful, eager, inquisitive, interested, interrogatory, investigative, investigatory, nosy, outward-looking, probing, prying, questing, questioning, sceptical, searching, wondering, zetetic.

*antonym* incurious.

**inquiry** *n* enquiry, examination, exploration, inquest, interrogation, investigation, perquisition, post-mortem, probe, query, question, research, scrutiny, search, study, survey, witch-hunt, zetetic.

**inquisition** *n* catechism, cross-examination, cross-questioning, examination, grilling, inquest, inquiry, interrogation, investigation, questioning, quizzing, third degree, witch-hunt.

**inquisitive** *adj* curious, eager, inquiring, intrusive, investigative, meddlesome, nosy, peeping, peering, probing, prying, questing, questioning, snooping, snoopy.

*antonym* incurious.

**inroad** *n* advance, encroachment, foray, impingement, incursion, intrusion, invasion, irruption, onslaught, raid, sally, sortie, trespass.

**insane** *adj* barmy, batty, bizarre, bonkers, brainsick, cracked, crackers, crazed, cuckoo, daft, delirious, demented, deranged, distracted, disturbed, fatuous, foolish, idiotic, impractical, irrational, irresponsible, loony, loopy, lunatic, mad, manic, mental, mentally ill, non compos mentis, nuts, nutty, preposterous, psychotic, queer, schizoid, schizophrenic, screwy, senseless, stupid, touched, unbalanced, unhinged.

*antonym* sane.

**insanitary** *adj* contaminated, dirty, disease-ridden, feculent, filthy, foul, impure, infected, infested, insalubrious, insalutary, noisome, noxious, polluted, unclean, unhealthful, unhealthy, unhygienic, unsanitary.

*antonym* sanitary.

**insanity** *n* aberration, alienation, amentia, brainsickness, brainstorm, craziness, delirium, dementia, derangement, folly, frenzy, infatuation, irresponsibility, lunacy, madness, mania, mental illness, neurosis, preposterousness, psychoneurosis, psychosis, senselessness, stupidity.

*antonym* sanity.

**insatiable** *adj* esurient, gluttonous, greedy, immoderate, incontrollable, inordinate, insatiate, intemperate, persistent, quenchless, rapacious, ravenous, unappeasable, uncurbable, unquenchable, unsatisfiable, voracious.

*antonym* moderate.

**inscribe**[1] *v* carve, cut, engrave, etch, grave, impress, imprint, incise, stamp.

**inscribe**[2] *v* address, autograph, dedicate, enlist, enrol, enter, record, register, sign, write.

**inscription** *n* autograph, caption, dedication, engraving, epigraph, epitaph, label, legend, lettering, saying, signature, words.

**inscrutable** *adj* baffling, blank, cryptic, dead-pan, deep, enigmatic, esoteric, expressionless, hidden, impassive, impenetrable, incomprehensible, inexplicable, mysterious, poker-faced, sphinx-like, undiscoverable, unexplainable, unfathomable, unintelligible, unknowable, unsearchable.

*antonyms* clear, comprehensible, expressive.

**insecure** *adj* afraid, anxious, apprehensive, dangerous, defenceless, diffident, exposed, expugnable, flimsy, frail, hazardous, insubstantial, jerry-built, loose, nervous, perilous, precarious, pregnable, rickety, rocky, shaky, shoogly, uncertain, unconfident, uneasy, unguarded, unprotected, unsafe, unshielded, unsound, unstable, unsteady, unsure, vulnerable, weak, wobbly, worried.

*antonyms* confident, safe, secure.

**insecurity** *n* anxiety, apprehension, danger, defencelessness, diffidence, dubiety, fear, flimsiness, frailness, hazard, instability, nervousness, peril, precariousness, ricketiness, risk, shakiness, uncertainty, uneasiness, unsafeness, unsafety, unsteadiness, unsureness, vulnerability, weakness, worry.

*antonyms* confidence, safety, security.

**insensibility** *n* apathy, blindness, callousness, coma, crassness, deafness, dullness, indifference, inertness, insensitivity, lethargy, nervelessness, numbness, oblivion, thoughtlessness, torpor, unawareness, unconsciousness.

*antonyms* consciousness, sensibilty.

**insensible¹** *adj* anaesthetised, apathetic, blind, callous, cataleptic, cold, deaf, dull, hard-hearted, impassive, impercipient, impervious, indifferent, inert, insensate, marble, nerveless, numb, numbed, oblivious, senseless, stupid, torpid, unaffected, unaware, unconscious, unfeeling, unmindful, unmoved, unnoticing, unobservant, unresponsive, unsusceptible, untouched.

*antonyms* conscious, sensible.

**insensible²** *adj* imperceivable, imperceptible, inappreciable, minuscule, minute, negligible, tiny, unnoticeable.

*antonym* appreciable.

**insensitive** *adj* blunted, callous, crass, dead, hardened, immune, impenetrable, imperceptive, impercipient, impervious, indifferent, insusceptible, obtuse, pachydermatous, proof, resistant, tactless, thick-skinned, tough, unaffected, uncaring, unconcerned, unfeeling, unimpressionable, unmoved, unreactive, unresponsive, unsensitive, unsusceptible.

*antonym* sensitive.

**insensitivity** *n* bluntness, callousness, crassness, hard-headedness, hypalgesia, hypalgia, impenetrability, imperceptiveness, impercipience, imperviousness, indifference, obtuseness, tactlessness, unconcern, unresponsiveness.

*antonym* sensitivity.

**inseparable** *adj* bosom, close, conjoined, devoted, impartible, inalienable, indiscerptible, indissociable, indissoluble, individuate, indivisible, inextricable, inseverable, intimate, undividable.

*antonym* separable.

**insert** *v* embed, engraft, enter, immit, implant, infix, inset, intercalate, interject, interlaminate, interlard, interleave, interline, interpolate, interpose, introduce, intromit, let in, place, pop in, put, put in, set, stick in.

*n* ad, advertisement, empiecement, enclosure, engraftment, godet, graft, gusset, implant, insertion, inset, notice.

**insertion** *n* addition, entry, implant, inclusion, insert, inset, intercalation, interpolation, introduction, intromission, intrusion, supplement.

**inside** *n* content, contents, interior.

*adv* indoors, inly, internally, inwardly, privately, secretly, within.

*adj* classified, confidential, esoteric, exclusive, hush-hush, inner, innermost, interior, internal, intramural, inward, private, restricted, secret.

**insides** *n* belly, bowels, entera, entrails, gut, guts, innards, organs, stomach, viscera, vitals.

**insidious** *adj* artful, crafty, crooked, cunning, deceitful, deceptive, designing, devious, disingenuous, duplicitous, furtive, guileful, intriguing, Machiavellian, slick, sly, smooth, sneaking, stealthy, subtle, surreptitious, treacherous, tricky, wily.

**insight** *n* acumen, acuteness, apprehension, awareness, comprehension, discernment, grasp, ingenuity, intelligence, intuition, intuitiveness, judgement, knowledge, observation, penetration, perception, percipience, perspicacity, sensitivity, shrewdness, understanding, vision, wisdom.

**insightful** *adj* acute, astute, discerning, intelligent, knowledgeable, observant, penetrating, perceptive, percipient, perspicacious, prudent, sagacious, sage, shrewd, understanding, wise.

*antonym* superficial.

**insignia** *n* badge, brand, crest, decoration, emblem, ensign, hallmarks, mark, regalia, signs, symbol, trademark.

**insignificance** *n* immateriality, inconsequence, inconsequentiality, insubstantiality, irrelevance, meaninglessness, meanness, negligibility, nugatoriness, paltriness, pettiness, tininess, triviality, unimportance, worthlessness.

*antonym* significance.

**insignificant** *adj* dinky, flimsy, humble, immaterial, inappreciable, inconsequential, inconsiderable, insubstantial, irrelevant, meagre, meaningless, Mickey Mouse, minor, negligible, nondescript, nonessential, nugatory, paltry, petty, piddling, scanty, scrub, tiny, trifling, trivial, unimportant, unsubstantial.

*antonym* significant.

**insincere** *adj* artificial, canting, deceitful, deceptive, devious, dishonest, disingenuous, dissembling, dissimulating, double-dealing, duplicitous, evasive, faithless, false, hollow, hypocritical, lip-deep, lying, mendacious, perfidious, phoney, pretended, synthetic, two-faced, unfaithful, ungenuine, untrue, untruthful.

*antonym* sincere.

**insincerity** *n* artificiality, cant, deceitfulness, deviousness, dishonesty, disingenuousness, dissembling, dissimulation, duplicity, evasiveness, faithlessness, falseness, falsity, hollowness, hypocrisy, lip service, mendacity, perfidy, phoniness, pretence, untruthfulness.

*antonym* sincerity.

**insinuate** *v* allude, get at, hint, imply, indicate, innuendo, intimate, suggest.

**insinuate oneself** curry favour, get in with, ingratiate, sidle, work, worm, wriggle.

**insinuation** *n* allusion, aspersion, hint, implication, infiltration, ingratiating, innuendo, intimation, introduction, slant, slur, suggestion.

**insipid** *adj* anaemic, banal, bland, characterless, colourless, dilute, drab, dry, dull, fade, flat, flavourless, insulse, jejune, lash, lifeless, limp, missish, missy, monotonous, pointless, prosaic, prosy, savourless, spiritless, stale, tame, tasteless, trite, unappetising, unimaginative, uninteresting, unsavoury, vapid, watery, weak, wearish, weedy, wishy-washy.

*antonyms* appetising, piquant, punchy, tasty.

**insipidity** *n* anaemicness, banality, blandness, characterlessness, colournessness, diluteness, drabness, dryness, dullness, fadeur, flatness, jejuneness, jejunity, lifelessness, limpness, monotony, prosiness, spiritlessness, staleness, tameness, tastelessness, triteness, vapidity, wateriness, weakness, weediness.

*antonyms* character, liveliness, piquancy, punch, tastiness.

**insist** *v* assert, asseverate, aver, claim, contend, demand, dwell on, emphasise, harp on, hold, maintain, persist, reiterate, repeat, request, require, stand firm, stress, swear, urge, vow.

**insistence** *n* advice, assertion, averment, certainty, contention, demand, determination, emphasis, encouragement, entreaty, exhortation, firmness, importunity, instance, persistence, persuasion, pressing, reiteration, solicitations, stress, urgency, urging.

**insistent** *adj* demanding, dogged, emphatic, exigent, forceful, importunate, incessant, peremptory, persevering, persistent, pressing, relentless, tenacious, unrelenting, unremitting, urgent.

**insobriety** *n* crapulence, drunkenness, inebriation, inebriety, intemperance, intoxication, tipsiness.

*antonym* sobriety.

**insolence** *n* abuse, arrogance, assurance, audacity, backchat, boldness, cheek, cheekiness, chutzpah, contemptuousness, contumely, defiance, disrespect, effrontery, forwardness, gall, gum, hubris, impertinence, impudence, incivility, insubordination, lip, malapertness, offensiveness, pertness, presumption, presumptuousness, rudeness, sauce, sauciness.

*antonyms* politeness, respect.

**insolent** *adj* abusive, arrogant, bold, brazen, cheeky, contemptuous, contumelious, defiant, disrespectful, forward, fresh, hubristic, impertinent, impudent, insubordinate, insulting,

malapert, pert, presumptuous, rude, saucy, uncivil.

*antonyms* polite, respectful.

**insoluble** *adj* baffling, impenetrable, indecipherable, inexplicable, inextricable, intractable, mysterious, mystifying, obscure, perplexing, unaccountable, unexplainable, unfathomable, unsolvable.

*antonym* explicable.

**insolvency** *n* bankruptcy, default, failure, liquidation, ruin.

*antonym* solvency.

**insolvent** *adj* bankrupt, broke, bust, defaulting, destitute, failed, flat broke, in queer street, on the rocks, ruined.

*antonym* solvent.

**insomnia** *n* insomnolence, restlessness, sleeplessness, wakefulness.

*antonym* sleep.

**insouciance** *n* airiness, breeziness, carefreeness, ease, flippancy, heedlessness, indifference, jauntiness, light-heartedness, nonchalance, pococurantism, unconcern.

*antonyms* anxiety, care.

**insouciant** *adj* airy, breezy, buoyant, carefree, casual, easy-going, flippant, gay, happy-go-lucky, heedless, indifferent, jaunty, light-hearted, nonchalant, pococurante, sunny, unconcerned, untroubled, unworried.

*antonyms* anxious, careworn.

**inspect** *v* audit, check, examine, give the once-over, investigate, look over, oversee, peruse, reconnoitre, scan, scrutinise, search, study, superintend, supervise, survey, vet, visit.

**inspection** *n* audit, autopsy, check, check-up, examination, investigation, once-over, post-mortem, reconnaissance, review, scan, scrutiny, search, superintendence, supervision, surveillance, survey, vidimus, visitation.

**inspector** *n* censor, checker, conner, controller, critic, examiner, investigator, overseer, reviewer, scrutineer, scrutiniser, superintendent, supervisor, surveyor, tester, viewer.

**inspiration** *n* afflation, afflatus, Aganippe, arousal, awakening, brainstorm, brain-wave, creativity, elevation, encouragement, enthusiasm, estro, exaltation, genius, Hippocrene, hwyl, illumination, influence, insight, muse, Muse, revelation, spur, stimulation, stimulus, Svengali, taghairm.

**inspire** *v* activate, animate, arouse, encourage, enkindle, enliven, enthuse, excite, fill, galvanise, hearten, imbue, influence, infuse, inhale, inspirit, instil, motivate, produce, quicken, spark off, spur, stimulate, stir, trigger.

**inspired** *adj* afflated, aroused, brilliant, dazzling, elated, enthralling, enthused, enthusiastic, exalted, exciting, exhilarated, fired, galvanised, impressive, invigorated, memorable, outstanding, possessed, reanimated, stimulated, superlative, thrilled, thrilling, uplifted, wonderful.

*antonyms* dull, uninspired.

**inspiring** *adj* affecting, emboldening, encouraging, exciting, exhilarating, heartening, inspiriting, invigorating, moving, rousing, stimulating, stirring, uplifting.

*antonyms* dull, uninspiring.

**inspirit** *v* animate, cheer, embolden, encourage, enliven, exhilarate, fire, galvanise, gladden, hearten, incite, inspire, invigorate, move, nerve, quicken, refresh, reinvigorate, rouse, stimulate.

**instability** *n* capriciousness, changeableness, fickleness, fitfulness, flimsiness, fluctuation, fluidity, frailty, imbalance, impermanence, inconstancy, insecurity, insolidity, irresolution, lability, mutability, oscillation, precariousness, restlessness, shakiness, transience, uncertainty, undependableness, unpredictability, unreliability, unsafeness, unsoundness, unsteadiness, vacillation, variability, volatility, wavering, weakness.

*antonym* stability.

**instal(l)** *v* consecrate, ensconce, establish, fix, inaugurate, induct, instate, institute, introduce, invest, lay, locate, lodge, ordain, place, plant, position, put, set, set up, settle, site, situate, station.

**installation** *n* base, consecration, equipment, establishment, fitting, inauguration, induction, instalment, instatement, investiture, location, machinery, ordination, placing, plant, positioning, post, siting, station, system.

**instalment** *n* chapter, consignment, delivery, division, episode, fascicule, heft, part, portion, repayment, section.

**instance¹** *n* case, case in point, citation, example, illustration, occasion, occurrence, precedent, sample, situation, time.

*v* adduce, cite, mention, name, point to, quote, refer to, specify.

**instance²** *n* advice, application, behest, demand, entreaty, exhortation, importunity, impulse, incitement, initiative, insistence, instigation, pressure, prompting, request, solicitation, urging.

**instant** *n* flash, jiffy, juncture, minute, mo, moment, occasion, point, second, shake, split second, tick, time, trice, twinkling, two shakes.

*adj* convenience, direct, fast, immediate, instantaneous, on-the-spot, precooked, prompt, quick, rapid, ready-mixed, split-second, unhesitating, urgent.

**instantaneous** *adj* direct, immediate, instant, on-the-spot, prompt, rapid, unhesitating.

*antonym* eventual.

**instantaneously** *adv* at once, directly, forthwith, immediately, instantly, on the spot, promptly, rapidly, straight away, there and then, unhesitatingly.

*antonym* eventually.

**instantly** *adv* at once, directly, ek dum, forthwith, immediately, instantaneously, now, on the spot, pronto, quick-sticks, right away, straight away, there and then, tout de suite, without delay.

*antonym* eventually.

**instead** *adv* alternatively, as a substitute, as an alternative, in lieu, in preference, preferably, rather.

**instead of** as proxy for, in default of, in lieu of, in place of, in preference to, on behalf of, rather than.

**instigate** *v* actuate, cause, encourage, excite, foment, generate, impel, incite, influence, initiate, inspire, kindle, move, persuade, prompt, provoke, rouse, set on, spur, start, stimulate, stir up, urge, whip up.

**instigation** *n* behest, bidding, encouragement, incentive, incitement, initiative, insistence, instance, prompting, urging.

**instigator** *n* agent provocateur, agitator, firebrand, fomenter, goad, incendiary, inciter, leader, mischief-maker, motivator, prime mover, provoker, ringleader, spur, troublemaker.

**instil** *v* din into, engender, engraft, imbue, implant, impress, inculcate, infix, infuse, inject, insinuate, introduce.

**instinct** *n* ability, aptitude, faculty, feel, feeling, flair, gift, gut feeling, gut reaction, id, impulse, intuition, knack, nose, predisposition, proclivity, sixth sense, talent, tendency, urge.

**instinctive** *adj* automatic, gut, immediate, impulsive, inborn, inherent, innate, instinctual, intuitional, intuitive, involuntary, mechanical, native, natural, reflex, spontaneous, unlearned, unpremeditated, unthinking, visceral.

*antonyms* conscious, deliberate, voluntary.

**instinctively** *adv* automatically, intuitively, involuntarily, mechanically, naturally, spontaneously, unthinkingly, without thinking.

*antonyms* consciously, deliberately, voluntarily.

**institute¹** *v* appoint, begin, commence, constitute, create, enact, establish, fix, found, inaugurate, induct, initiate, install, introduce, invest, launch, open, ordain, organise, originate, pioneer, set up, settle, start.

*antonyms* abolish, cancel, discontinue.

**institute²** *n* custom, decree, doctrine, dogma, edict, firman, indiction, irade, law, maxim, precedent, precept, principle, regulation, rescript, rule, tenet, ukase.

**institute³** *n* academy, association, college, conservatory, foundation, guild, institution, organisation, poly, polytechnic, school, seminary, society.

**institution¹** *n* constitution, creation, enactment, establishment, formation, foundation, founding, inception, initiation, installation, introduction, investiture, organisation, protectory.

**institution²** *n* convention, custom, fixture, law, practice, ritual, rule, tradition, usage.

**institution³** *n* academy, college, concern, corporation, establishment, foundation, hospital, institute, organisation, school, seminary, society, university.

**institutional** *adj* accepted, bureaucratic, cheerless, clinical, cold, conventional, customary, drab, dreary, dull, established, establishment, forbidding, formal, impersonal, institutionary, monotonous, orthodox, regimented, ritualistic, routine, set, societal, uniform, unwelcoming.

*antonyms* individualistic, unconventional.

**instruct** *v* acquaint, advise, apprise, bid, brief, catechise, charge, coach, command, counsel, direct, discipline, drill, educate, enjoin, enlighten, ground, guide, inform, mandate, notify, order, school, teach, tell, train, tutor.

**instruction** *n* apprenticeship, briefing, catechesis, catechising, coaching, command, direction, directive, discipline, drilling, education, enlightenment, grounding, guidance, information, injunction, lesson(s), mandate, order, preparation, ruling, schooling, teaching, training, tuition, tutelage.

**instructions** *n* advice, book of words, commands, directions, guidance, handbook, information, key, legend, orders, recommendations, rules.

**instructive** *adj* cautionary, didactic, edificatory, edifying, educational, educative, educatory, enlightening, helpful, illuminating, improving, inculcative, informative, instructional, revealing, useful.

*antonym* unenlightening.

**instructor** *n* adviser, catechiser, catechist, coach, demonstrator, edifier, Egeria, exponent, guide, guru, instructress, maharishi, master, mentor, mistress, pedagogue, preceptor, schoolmaster, schoolmistress, teacher, trainer, tutor.

**instrument** *n* agency, agent, apparatus, appliance, cat's-paw, channel, contraption, contrivance, device, doodad, dupe, factor, force, gadget, implement, means, mechanism, medium, organ, pawn, puppet, tool, utensil, vehicle, way, widget.

**instrumental** *adj* active, assisting, auxiliary, conducive, contributive, contributory, helpful, helping, implemental, influential, involved, subsidiary, useful.

*antonyms* obstructive, unhelpful.

**insubordinate** *adj* contumacious, defiant, disobedient, disorderly, fractious, impertinent, impudent, insurgent, mutinous, rebellious, recalcitrant, refractory, riotous, rude, seditious, turbulent, undisciplined, ungovernable, unruly.

*antonyms* docile, obedient.

**insubordination** *n* defiance, disobedience, impertinence, impudence, indiscipline, insurrection, mutinousness, mutiny, rebellion, recalcitrance, revolt, riotousness, rudeness, sedition, ungovernability.

*antonyms* docility, obedience.

**insubstantial** *adj* chimerical, ephemeral, false, fanciful, feeble, flimsy, frail, idle, illusory, imaginary, immaterial, incorporeal, moonshine, poor, slight, tenuous, thin, unreal, vaporous, weak, windy, yeasty.

*antonyms* real, strong.

**insufferable** *adj* detestable, dreadful, hateful, impossible, insupportable, intolerable,

loathsome, outrageous, unbearable, unendurable, unliv(e)able, unspeakable.

*antonyms* pleasant, tolerable.

**insufficiency** *n* dearth, deficiency, inadequacy, inadequateness, lack, need, paucity, poverty, scantiness, scarcity, shortage, sparsity, want.

*antonyms* excess, sufficiency.

**insufficient** *adj* deficient, inadequate, incapable, incommensurate, lacking, scanty, scarce, short, sparse, wanting.

*antonyms* excessive, sufficient.

**insular** *adj* blinkered, circumscribed, closed, contracted, cut off, detached, illiberal, inward-looking, isolated, limited, narrow, narrow-minded, parish-pump, parochial, petty, prejudiced, provincial, xenophobic.

*antonym* cosmopolitan.

**insularity** *n* isolation, narrow-mindedness, parochiality, parochialness, prejudice, xenophobia.

*antonyms* open-mindedness, openness.

**insulate** *v* cocoon, cushion, cut off, isolate, protect, quarantine, separate off, sequester, shield.

**insulation** *n* cushioning, deadening, deafening, padding, protection, stuffing.

**insult** *v* abuse, affront, call names, fling/throw mud at, give offence to, injure, libel, miscall, offend, outrage, revile, slag, slander, slight, snub, vilify, vilipend.

*antonyms* compliment, honour.

*n* abuse, affront, aspersion, contumely, indignity, insolence, libel, offence, outrage, rudeness, slander, slap in the face, slight, snub.

*antonyms* compliment, honour.

**insulting** *adj* abusive, affronting, contemptuous, degrading, disparaging, insolent, libellous, offensive, rude, scurrilous, slanderous, slighting.

*antonyms* complimentary, respectful.

**insuperable** *adj* formidable, impassable, insurmountable, invincible, overwhelming, unconquerable.

*antonym* surmountable.

**insupportable** *adj* detestable, dreadful, hateful, indefensible, insufferable, intenable, intolerable, invalid, loathsome, unbearable, unendurable, unjustifiable, untenable.

*antonym* bearable.

**insuppressible** *adj* energetic, go-getting, incorrigible, irrepressible, lively, obstreperous, uncontrollable, ungovernable, unruly, unstoppable, unsubduable.

*antonym* suppressible.

**insurance** *n* assurance, cover, coverage, guarantee, indemnification, indemnity, policy, premium, protection, provision, safeguard, security, warranty.

**insure** *v* assure, cover, guarantee, indemnify, protect, underwrite, warrant.

**insurer** *n* assurer, underwriter.

**insurgent** n insurrectionist, mutineer, partisan, rebel, resister, revolter, revoluntionist, revolutionary, rioter.

adj disobedient, insubordinate, insurrectionary, mutinous, partisan, rebellious, revolting, revolutionary, riotous, seditious.

**insurmountable** adj hopeless, impassable, impossible, insuperable, invincible, overwhelming, unclimable, unconquerable, unscalable, unsurmountable.

antonym surmountable.

**insurrection** n coup, inqilab, insurgence, insurgency, mutiny, putsch, rebellion, revolt, revolution, riot, rising, sedition, uprising.

**intact** adj all in one piece, complete, entire, inviolate, perfect, scatheless, sound, together, unbroken, undamaged, undefiled, unharmed, unhurt, unimpaired, uninjured, unscathed, untouched, unviolated, virgin, whole.

antonyms broken, damaged, harmed.

**intaglio** n diaglyph.

**intangible** adj airy, bodiless, dim, elusive, ethereal, evanescent, impalpable, imperceptible, incorporeal, indefinite, insubstantial, invisible, shadowy, unreal, unsubstantial, vague.

antonyms real, tangible.

**integral** adj basic, complete, component, constituent, elemental, entire, essential, full, fundamental, indispensable, intact, intrinsic, necessary, requisite, undivided, unitary, whole.

antonyms accessory, partial.

**integrate** v accommodate, amalgamate, assimilate, blend, coalesce, combine, commingle, desegregate, fuse, harmonise, incorporate, intermix, join, knit, merge, mesh, mix, unite.

antonym separate.

**integrated** adj cohesive, concordant, connected, desegregated, harmonious, interrelated, part and parcel, unified, unsegregated, unseparated.

antonym unintegrated.

**integration** n amalgamation, assimilation, blending, combining, commingling, desegregation, fusing, harmony, incorporation, mixing, unification.

antonym separation.

**integrity** n candour, coherence, cohesion, completeness, entireness, goodness, honesty, honour, incorruptibility, principle, probity, purity, rectitude, righteousness, soundness, unity, uprightness, virtue, wholeness.

antonyms dishonesty, incompleteness, unreliability.

**intellect** n brain, brain power, brains, egghead, genius, highbrow, intellectual, intelligence, judgement, mind, nous, reason, sense, thinker, understanding.

antonym dunce.

**intellectual** adj bookish, cerebral, deep-browed, discursive, highbrow, intelligent, mental, noetic, rational, scholarly, studious, thoughtful.

antonym low-brow.

n academic, egghead, headpiece, highbrow, mastermind, thinker.

antonym low-brow.

**intelligence** n acuity, acumen, advice, alertness, aptitude, brain power, brains, brightness, capacity, cleverness, comprehension, data, discernment, disclosure, facts, findings, gen, grey matter, information, intellect, intellectuality, knowledge, low-down, mind, news, notice, notification, nous, penetration, perception, quickness, reason, report, rumour, tidings, tip-off, understanding, word.

antonym foolishness.

**intelligent** adj acute, alert, apt, brainy, bright, clever, deep-browed, discerning, enlightened, instructed, knowing, penetrating, perspicacious, quick, quick-witted, rational, razor-sharp, sharp, smart, thinking, well-informed.

antonyms foolish, unintelligent.

**intelligentsia** n academics, brains, eggheads, eggmass, highbrows, illuminati, intellectuals, literati.

**intelligibility** n clarity, clearness, comprehensibility, comprehensibleness, distinctness, explicitness, lucidity, lucidness, plainness, precision, simplicity.

antonym unintelligibility.

**intelligible** adj clear, comprehensible, decipherable, distinct, fathomable, lucid, open, penetrable, plain, understandable.

antonym unintelligible.

**intemperance** n crapulence, drunkenness, excess, extravagance, immoderation, inebriation, insobriety, intoxication, licence, overindulgence, self-indulgence, unrestraint.

antonym temperance.

**intemperate** adj drunken, excessive, extravagant, extreme, immoderate, incontinent, inordinate, intoxicated, irrestrainable, licentious, over the top, passionate, prodigal, profligate, self-indulgent, severe, tempestuous, unbridled, uncontrollable, ungovernable, unrestrained, violent, wild.

antonym temperate.

**intend** v aim, consign, contemplate, design, destine, determine, earmark, have a mind, mark out, mean, meditate, plan, project, propose, purpose, scheme, set apart.

**intended** adj betrothed, deliberate, designate, designated, destined, future, intentional, planned, proposed, prospective.

antonym accidental.

n betrothed, fiancé, fiancée, husband-to-be, wife-to-be.

**intense** adj acute, agonising, ardent, burning, close, concentrated, consuming, eager, earnest, energetic, fanatical, fervent, fervid, fierce, forceful, forcible, great, harsh, heightened, impassioned, intensive, keen, passionate, powerful, profound, severe, strained, strong, vehement.

antonyms apathetic, mild.

**intensely** *adv* ardently, deeply, extremely, fervently, fiercely, greatly, passionately, profoundly, strongly, very.

*antonym* mildly.

**intensification** *n* acceleration, building-up, build-up, deepening, escalation, exacerbescence, heightening, increase, worsening.

*antonym* lessening.

**intensify** *v* add to, aggravate, boost, concentrate, deepen, emphasise, enhance, escalate, exacerbate, fire, fuel, heighten, hot up, increase, magnify, quicken, redouble, reinforce, sharpen, step up, strengthen, whet, whip up.

*antonyms* damp down, die down.

**intensity** *n* accent, ardour, concentration, depth, earnestness, emotion, energy, excess, extremity, fanaticism, fervency, fervour, fierceness, fire, force, intenseness, keenness, passion, potency, power, severity, strain, strength, tension, vehemence, vigour, voltage.

**intensive** *adj* all-out, comprehensive, concentrated, demanding, detailed, exhaustive, in detail, in-depth, thorough, thoroughgoing.

*antonym* superficial.

**intent** *adj* absorbed, alert, attentive, bent, committed, concentrated, concentrating, determined, eager, earnest, engrossed, fixed, hell-bent, industrious, intense, mindful, occupied, piercing, preoccupied, rapt, resolute, resolved, set, steadfast, steady, watchful, wrapped up.

*antonyms* absent-minded, distracted.

*n* aim, design, end, goal, intention, meaning, object, objective, plan, purpose.

**intention** *n* aim, concept, design, end, end in view, goal, idea, intent, meaning, object, objective, plan, point, purpose, scope, target, view.

**intentional** *adj* calculated, deliberate, designed, intended, meant, planned, prearranged, preconcerted, premeditated, purposed, studied, wilful.

*antonym* accidental.

**intentionally** *adv* by design, deliberately, designedly, meaningly, on purpose, wilfully, with malice aforethought.

*antonym* accidentally.

**intently** *adv* attentively, carefully, closely, fixedly, hard, keenly, searchingly, staringly, steadily, watchfully.

*antonym* absent-mindedly.

**inter** *v* bury, entomb, inhume, inurn, lay to rest, sepulchre.

*antonym* exhume.

**interbreed** *v* cross, cross-breed, hybridise, miscegenate.

**interbreeding** *n* cross-breeding, crossing, hybridisation, miscegenation.

**intercede** *v* advocate, arbitrate, interpose, intervene, mediate, plead, speak.

**intercept** *v* arrest, block, catch, check, cut off, deflect, delay, frustrate, head off, impede, interrupt, obstruct, retard, seize, stop, take, thwart.

**intercession** *n* advocacy, agency, beseeching, entreaty, good offices, intervention, mediation, plea, pleading, prayer, solicitation, supplication.

**interchange** *n* alternation, crossfire, exchange, interplay, intersection, junction, reciprocation, trading.

**interchangeable** *adj* commutable, equal, equivalent, exchangeable, identical, reciprocal, similar, standard, synonymous, the same, transposable.

*antonym* different.

**intercourse**[1] *n* association, commerce, communication, communion, congress, connection, contact, conversation, converse, correspondence, dealings, intercommunication, traffic, truck.

**intercourse**[2] *n* carnal knowledge, coition, coitus, copulation, embraces, greens, intimacy, love-making, sex, sexual relations, venery.

**interdict** *v* ban, bar, debar, disallow, forbid, outlaw, preclude, prevent, prohibit, proscribe, rule out, veto.

*antonym* allow.

*n* ban, disallowance, injunction, interdiction, prohibition, proscription, taboo, veto.

*antonym* permission.

**interest** *n* activity, advantage, affair, affection, attention, attentiveness, attraction, authority, bag, benefit, business, care, claim, commitment, concern, consequence, curiosity, diversion, finger, gain, good, hobby, importance, influence, investment, involvement, line of country, matter, moment, note, notice, participation, pastime, portion, preoccupation, profit, pursuit, regard, relaxation, relevance, right, share, significance, stake, study, suspicion, sympathy, weight.

*antonyms* boredom, irrelevance.

*v* affect, amuse, attract, concern, divert, engage, engross, fascinate, intrigue, involve, move, touch, warm.

*antonym* bore.

**interested** *adj* affected, attentive, attracted, biased, concerned, curious, drawn, engrossed, fascinated, implicated, intent, involved, keen, partisan, predisposed, prejudiced, responsive, simulated.

*antonyms* apathetic, indifferent, unaffected.

**interesting** *adj* absorbing, amusing, amusive, appealing, attractive, compelling, curious, engaging, engrossing, entertaining, gripping, intriguing, provocative, stimulating, thought-provoking, unusual, viewable, visitable.

*antonym* boring.

**interfere** *v* block, butt in, clash, collide, conflict, cramp, frustrate, hamper, handicap, hinder, impede, inhibit, interlope, intermeddle, interpose, intervene, intrude, meddle, obstruct, poke one's nose in, stick one's oar in, tamper, trammel.

*antonyms* assist, forbear.

**interference** n clashing, collision, conflict, do-goodery, do-goodism, impedance, intervention, intrusion, meddlesomeness, meddling, mush, obstruction, opposition, paternalism, prying, shash, statics, white noise.

*antonyms* assistance, forbearance.

**interim** *adj* acting, caretaker, improvised, intervening, makeshift, permanent, pro tem, provisional, stand-in, stop-gap, temporary.

n interregnum, interval, meantime, meanwhile.

**interior** *adj* central, domestic, hidden, home, inland, inly, inner, inside, internal, intimate, inward, mental, pectoral, personal, private, remote, secret, spiritual, up-country.

*antonyms* exterior, external.

n bowels, centre, core, heart, heartland, hinterland, inside, up-country.

**interject** v call, cry, exclaim, interjaculate, interpolate, interpose, interrupt, introduce, shout.

**interjection** n call, cry, ejaculation, exclamation, interpolation, interposition, shout.

**interlace** v braid, cross, enlace, entwine, interlock, intermix, intersperse, intertwine, interweave, interwreathe, knit, plait, reticulate, twine.

**interlink** v clasp together, interconnect, intergrow, interlock, intertwine, interweave, knit, link, link together, lock together, mesh.

*antonym* separate.

**interlock** v interdigitate, intertwine, lock together.

**interloper** n gate-crasher, intruder, trespasser, uninvited guest.

**interlude** n break, breathing-space, breathing-time, breathing-while, delay, episode, halt, hiatus, intermission, interval, pause, respite, rest, spell, stop, stoppage, wait.

**intermarriage** n miscegenation.

**intermediary** n agent, broker, entrepreneur, go-between, in-between, internuncio, mediator, middleman, ombudsman, ombudswoman.

**intermediate** *adj* halfway, in-between, intermediary, interposed, intervening, mean, medial, median, mid, middle, midway, transitional.

*antonym* extreme.

**interment** n burial, burying, funeral, inhumation, obsequies, obsequy, sepulture.

*antonym* exhumation.

**interminable** *adj* boundless, ceaseless, dragging, endless, everlasting, immeasurable, infinite, limitless, long, long-drawn-out, long-winded, never-ending, perpetual, prolix, protracted, unbounded, unlimited, wearisome.

*antonym* limited.

**intermingle** v amalgamate, blend, combine, commingle, commix, fuse, interlace, intermix, interweave, merge, mix, mix together, mix up.

*antonym* separate.

**intermission** n break, breather, breathing-space, breathing-while, cessation, entr'acte, interlude, interruption, interval, let-up, lull, pause, recess, remission, respite, rest, stop, stoppage, suspense, suspension.

**intermittent** *adj* broken, discontinuous, fitful, irregular, occasional, periodic, periodical, punctuated, recurrent, recurring, remittent, spasmodic, sporadic, stop-go.

*antonym* continuous.

**intern** v confine, detain, hold, imprison, jail.

*antonym* free.

**internal** *adj* domestic, in-house, inner, inside, interior, intimate, inward, private, subjective.

*antonym* external.

**international** *adj* cosmopolitan, general, global, intercontinental, interterritorial, universal, worldwide.

*antonym* parochial.

**internecine** *adj* bloody, civil, deadly, destructive, exterminating, exterminatory, family, fatal, internal, internecive, mortal, murderous, ruinous.

**interplay** n exchange, give-and-take, interaction, interchange, meshing, reciprocation, reciprocity.

**interpolate** v add, insert, intercalate, interjaculate, interject, introduce.

**interpolation** n addition, aside, insert, insertion, intercalation, interjaculation, interjection, introduction.

**interpose** v come between, insert, intercede, interfere, interjaculate, interject, interrupt, intervene, introduce, intrude, mediate, offer, place between, step in, thrust in.

*antonym* forbear.

**interpret** v adapt, clarify, construe, decipher, decode, define, elucidate, explain, explicate, expound, paraphrase, read, render, solve, take, throw light on, translate, understand, unfold.

**interpretation** n anagoge, anagogy, analysis, clarification, construction, diagnosis, elucidation, exegesis, explanation, explication, exposition, meaning, performance, portrayal, reading, rendering, rendition, sense, signification, translation, understanding, version.

**interpretative** *adj* clarificatory, exegetic, explanatory, explicatory, expository, hermeneutic, interpretive.

**interpreter** n annotator, commentator, dobhash, dragoman, elucidator, exegete, exegetist, exponent, expositor, hermeneutist, interpretress, linguister, munshi, scholiast, translator, truchman, ulema.

**interrogate** v ask, catechise, cross-examine, cross-question, debrief, enquire, examine, give (someone) the third degree, grill, inquire, investigate, pump, question, quiz.

**interrogation** n catachesis, cross-examination, cross-questioning, enquiry, examination, grilling, inquiry, inquisition, probing, questioning, third degree.

**interrogative** adj catechetical, curious, erotetic, inquiring, inquisitional, inquisitive, inquisitorial, interrogatory, questioning, quizzical.

**interrupt** v barge in, break, break in, break off, butt in, check, cut, cut off, cut short, delay, disconnect, discontinue, disjoin, disturb, disunite, divide, heckle, hinder, hold up, interfere, interjaculate, interject, intrude, obstruct, punctuate, separate, sever, stay, stop, suspend.

*antonym* forbear.

**interrupted** adj broken, cut off, disconnected, discontinuous, disturbed, incomplete, intermittent, uneven, unfinished.

*antonyms* complete, continuous.

**interruption** n break, cessation, Derby dog, disconnection, discontinuance, disruption, dissolution, disturbance, disuniting, division, halt, hiatus, hindrance, hitch, impediment, intrusion, obstacle, obstruction, pause, separation, severance, stop, stoppage, suspension.

**intersect** v bisect, criss-cross, cross, cut, cut across, decussate, divide, divide up, meet.

**intersection** n bisection, crossing, crossroads, decussation, division, interchange, junction.

**intersperse** v diversify, dot, interlard, intermix, pepper, scatter, sprinkle.

**intertwine** v braid, convolute, cross, entwine, interlace, intertangle, intertwist, interweave, interwreathe, inweave, link, reticulate, twist.

**interval** n break, delay, distance, entr'acte, gap, hiatus, in-between, interim, interlude, intermission, interspace, interstice, meantime, meanwhile, opening, pause, period, playtime, rest, season, space, spell, term, time, wait.

**intervene** v arbitrate, befall, ensue, happen, intercede, interfere, interpose oneself, interrupt, intrude, involve, mediate, occur, step in, succeed, supervene, take a hand.

**intervening** adj between, interjacent, interposing, intervenient, mediate.

**intervention** n agency, intercession, interference, interposition, intervening, intrusion, mediation.

**interview** n audience, conference, consultation, dialogue, enquiry, evaluation, inquisition, meeting, oral, oral examination, press conference, talk, viva.

v examine, interrogate, question, viva.

**interviewer** n examiner, inquisitor, inquisitress, interlocutor, interrogant, interrogator, investigator, questioner, reporter.

**interweave** v blend, braid, criss-cross, cross, interlace, intertangle, intertwine, intertwist, interwork, interwreathe, reticulate, splice.

**interweaving** n interramification, intertangling, intertwining, intertwisting.

**interwoven** adj blended, connected, entwined, inmixed, interconnected, interlaced, interlocked, intermingled, intertangled, intertwisted, interworked, interwreathed, interwrought, knit.

**intestinal** adj abdominal, coeliac, duodenal, ileac, internal, stomachic, visceral.

**intestines** n bowels, chitterlings, entrails, guts, innards, insides, offal, umbles, viscera, vitals.

**intimacy** n brotherliness, closeness, coition, coitus, confidence, confidentiality, copulating, copulation, familiarity, fornication, fraternisation, friendship, intercourse, sexual intercourse, sisterliness, understanding.

**intimate**[1] v allude, announce, communicate, declare, hint, impart, imply, indicate, insinuate, state, suggest, tell.

**intimate**[2] adj as thick as thieves, bosom, cherished, close, confidential, cosy, dear, deep, deep-seated, detailed, exhaustive, friendly, gremial, informal, innermost, internal, near, palsy-walsy, penetrating, personal, private, privy, profound, secret, warm.

*antonyms* cold, distant, unfriendly.

n Achates, associate, bosom buddy, buddy, china, chum, comrade, confidant, confidante, crony, familiar, friend, mate, mucker, pal, repository.

*antonym* stranger.

**intimately** adv affectionately, closely, confidentially, confidingly, exhaustively, familiarly, fully, in detail, inside out, personally, tenderly, thoroughly, warmly.

*antonyms* coldly, distantly.

**intimation** n allusion, announcement, communication, declaration, hint, indication, inkling, insinuation, notice, reminder, statement, suggestion, warning.

**intimidate** v alarm, appal, browbeat, bulldoze, bully, coerce, cow, daunt, dishearten, dismay, dispirit, frighten, lean on, overawe, psych out, put the frighteners on, scare, subdue, terrify, terrorise, threaten.

*antonym* persuade.

**intimidation** n arm-twisting, browbeating, bullying, coercion, fear, menaces, pressure, terror, terrorisation, terrorising, threats.

*antonym* persuasion.

**intolerable** adj beyond the pale, excruciating, impossible, insufferable, insupportable, painful, unbearable, unendurable.

*antonym* tolerable.

**intolerance** n bigotry, chauvinism, discrimination, dogmatism, fanaticism, illiberality, impatience, jingoism, narrow-mindedness, narrowness, opinionativeness, prejudice, racialism, racism, xenophobia.

*antonym* tolerance.

**intolerant** adj bigoted, chauvinistic, dictatorial, dogmatic, fanatical, illiberal, impatient, narrow, narrow-minded, opinionated, opinionative, opinioned, persecuting, prejudiced, racialist, racist, small-minded, uncharitable.

*antonym* tolerant.

**intonation** n accentuation, cadence, chant, incantation, inflection, mantra(m), modulation, tone.

**intone** *v* chant, croon, declaim, intonate, monotone, pronounce, recite, sing, utter.

**intoxicate** *n* addle, befuddle, elate, excite, exhilarate, fuddle, inebriate, inflame, stimulate, stupefy.

*antonym* sober.

**intoxicated** *adj* blotto, canned, cut, disguised in liquor, dizzy, drunk, drunken, ebriate, ebriated, ebriose, elated, enraptured, euphoric, excited, exhilarated, fuddled, glorious, half seas over, high, in one's cups, incapable, inebriate, inebriated, infatuated, legless, lit up, looped, pickled, pissed, pixil(l)ated, plastered, sent, sloshed, smashed, sozzled, stewed, stiff, stimulated, stoned, stotious, three sheets in the wind, tight, tipsy, under the influence, up the pole, zonked.

*antonym* sober.

**intoxicating** *adj* alcoholic, dizzy, euphoric, exciting, exhilarating, heady, inebriant, intoxicant, spirituous, stimulating, strong, thrilling.

*antonym* sobering.

**intoxication** *n* delirium, drunkenness, ebriety, ebriosity, elation, euphoria, exaltation, excitement, exhilaration, inebriation, inebriety, infatuation, insobriety, tipsiness.

*antonym* sobriety.

**intractability** *n* awkwardness, cantankerousness, contrariness, incorrigibility, indiscipline, indocility, mulishness, obduracy, obstinacy, perverseness, perversity, pig-headedness, stubbornness, unamenability, unco-operativeness, ungovernability, waywardness.

*antonym* amenability.

**intractable** *adj* awkward, bull-headed, cantankerous, contrary, difficult, fractious, haggard, headstrong, incurable, insoluble, intransigent, obdurate, obstinate, perverse, pig-headed, refractory, self-willed, stubborn, unamenable, unbending, unco-operative, undisciplined, ungovernable, unmanageable, unruly, unyielding, wayward, wild, wilful.

*antonym* amenable.

**intransigent** *adj* hardline, immovable, intractable, irreconcilable, obdurate, obstinate, stubborn, tenacious, tough, unamenable, unbending, unbudgeable, uncompromising, unpersuadable, unyielding, uppity.

*antonym* amenable.

**intrepid** *adj* audacious, bold, brave, courageous, daring, dashing, dauntless, doughty, fearless, gallant, game, gutsy, heroic, lion-hearted, nerveless, plucky, resolute, stalwart, stout-hearted, unafraid, undashed, undaunted, unflinching, valiant, valorous.

*antonyms* cowardly, timid.

**intrepidness** *n* audacity, boldness, bravery, courage, daring, dauntlessness, doughtiness, fearlessness, fortitude, gallantry, guts, heroism, intrepidity, lion-heartedness, nerve, pluck, prowess, spirit, stout-heartedness, undauntedness, valour.

*antonyms* cowardice, timidity.

**intricacy** *n* complexedness, complexity, complexness, complication, convolutions, elaborateness, entanglement, intricateness, involution, involvement, knottiness, obscurity.

*antonym* simplicity.

**intricate** *adj* Byzantine, complex, complicated, convoluted, daedal(e), Daedalian, daedalic, dedal, dedalian, difficult, elaborate, entangled, fancy, Gordian, involved, knotty, labyrinthine, perplexing, rococo, sophisticated, tangled, tortuous.

*antonym* simple.

**intrigue**[1] *v* attract, charm, fascinate, interest, puzzle, rivet, tantalise, tickle one's fancy, titillate.

*antonym* bore.

**intrigue**[2] *n* affair, amour, brigue, cabal, chicanery, collusion, conspiracy, double-dealing, intimacy, knavery, liaison, machination, machination(s), manipulation, manoeuvre, plot, romance, ruse, scheme, sharp practice, stratagem, string-pulling, trickery, wheeler-dealing, wile, wire-pulling.

*v* connive, conspire, machinate, manoeuvre, plot, scheme.

**intriguer** *n* conniver, intrigant(e), Machiavellian, machinator, plotter, schemer, wangler, wheeler-dealer, wire-puller.

**intriguing** *adj* beguiling, compelling, diverting, exciting, fascinating, interesting, puzzling, tantalising, titillating.

*antonyms* boring, uninteresting.

**intrinsic** *adj* basic, basically, built-in, central, congenital, constitutional, constitutionally, elemental, essential, essentially, fundamental, fundamentally, genuine, inborn, inbred, inherent, intrinsically, inward, native, natural, underlying.

*antonym* extrinsic.

**introduce** *v* acquaint, add, advance, air, announce, begin, bring in, bring up, broach, commence, conduct, establish, familiarise, found, inaugurate, initiate, inject, insert, institute, interpolate, interpose, launch, lead in, lead into, moot, offer, open, organise, pioneer, preface, present, propose, put forward, put in, recommend, set forth, start, submit, suggest, throw in, ventilate.

*antonym* take away.

**introduction** *n* addition, baptism, commencement, debut, establishment, exordium, foreword, inauguration, induction, initiation, insertion, institution, interpolation, intro, launch, lead-in, opening, overture, pioneering, preamble, preface, preliminaries, prelude, presentation, prodrome, prodromus, proem, prolegomena, prolegomenon, prologue, prooemion, prooemium.

*antonym* withdrawal.

**introductory** *adj* early, elementary, exordial, first, inaugural, initial, initiatory, opening, precursory, prefatory, preliminary, preparatory, proemial, prolegomenary, prolegomenous, prolusory, starting.

**introspection** *n* brooding, heart-searching, introversion, self-analysis, self-examination, self-observation, soul-searching.

**introspective** *adj* brooding, contemplative, introverted, inward-looking, meditative, pensive, ruminative, subjective, thoughtful.

*antonym* outward-looking.

**introverted** *adj* indrawn, intervertive, introspective, introversive, inward-looking, self-centred, self-contained, withdrawn.

*antonym* extroverted.

**intrude** *v* aggress, butt in, encroach, infringe, interfere, interrupt, meddle, obtrude, trespass, violate.

*antonyms* stand back, withdraw.

**intruder** *n* burglar, Derby dog, gate-crasher, infiltrator, interloper, invader, prowler, raider, snooper, trespasser.

**intrusion** *n* aggression, encroachment, incursion, infringement, ingression, interference, interruption, invasion, trespass, violation.

*antonym* withdrawal.

**intrusive** *adj* disturbing, forward, impertinent, importunate, interfering, invasive, meddlesome, nosy, obtrusive, officious, presumptuous, pushy, uncalled-for, unwanted, unwelcome.

*antonyms* unintrusive, welcome.

**intuition** *n* discernment, feeling, gut feeling, hunch, insight, instinct, perception, presentiment, sixth sense.

*antonym* reasoning.

**intuitive** *adj* innate, instinctive, instinctual, involuntary, spontaneous, unreflecting, untaught.

*antonym* reasoned.

**inundate** *v* bury, deluge, drown, engulf, fill, flood, glut, immerse, overflow, overrun, overwhelm, submerge, swamp.

**inundation** *n* deluge, deluvion, deluvium, flood, glut, overflow, tidal wave, torrent.

*antonym* trickle.

**inure** *v* accustom, desensitise, familiarise, flesh, habituate, harden, strengthen, temper, toughen, train.

**invade** *v* assail, assault, attack, burst in, come upon, descend upon, encroach, enter, fall upon, infest, infringe, irrupt, occupy, overrun, overspread, penetrate, pervade, raid, rush into, seize, swarm over, violate.

*antonym* withdraw.

**invader** *n* aggressor, attacker, intruder, raider, trespasser.

**invalid**[1] *adj* ailing, bedridden, disabled, feeble, frail, ill, infirm, invalidish, poorly, sick, sickly, valetudinarian, valetudinary, weak.

*antonym* healthy.

*n* case, convalescent, patient, sufferer, valetudinarian, valetudinary.

**invalid**[2] *adj* baseless, fallacious, false, ill-founded, illogical, incorrect, inoperative, irrational, nugatory, null, null and void, unfounded, unscientific, unsound, untrue, void, worthless.

*antonym* valid.

**invalidate** *v* abrogate, annul, cancel, nullify, overrule, overthrow, quash, rescind, undermine, undo, vitiate, weaken.

*antonym* validate.

**invalidity** *n* fallaciousness, fallacy, falsity, illogicality, inconsistency, incorrectness, invalidness, irrationality, sophism, speciousness, unsoundness, voidness.

**invaluable** *adj* costly, exquisite, inestimable, precious, priceless, valuable.

*antonym* worthless.

**invariable** *adj* changeless, consistent, constant, fixed, immutable, inflexible, permanent, regular, rigid, set, static, unalterable, unchangeable, unchanging, unfailing, uniform, unvarying, unwavering.

*antonym* variable.

**invariably** *adv* always, consistently, customarily, habitually, inevitably, perpetually, regularly, unfailingly, without exception, without fail.

*antonym* variably.

**invasion** *n* aggression, assault, attack, breach, encroachment, foray, incursion, infiltration, infraction, infringement, inroad, intrusion, irruption, offensive, onslaught, raid, seizure, usurpation, violation.

*antonym* withdrawal.

**invective** *n* abuse, berating, billingsgate, castigation, censure, contumely, denunciation, diatribe, flyting, obloquy, philippic, philippic(s), reproach, revilement, sarcasm, scolding, tirade, tongue-lashing, vilification, vituperation.

*antonym* praise.

**inveigh** *v* berate, blame, castigate, censure, condemn, denounce, expostulate, flite, fulminate, lambast, rail, recriminate, reproach, scold, sound off, tongue-lash, upbraid, vituperate.

*antonym* praise.

**inveigle** *v* allure, bamboozle, beguile, cajole, coax, con, decoy, ensnare, entice, entrap, lead on, lure, manipulate, manoeuvre, persuade, seduce, sweet-talk, wheedle, wile.

*antonym* force.

**invent** *v* coin, conceive, concoct, contrive, cook up, create, design, devise, discover, dream up, fabricate, formulate, frame, imagine, improvise, make up, originate, think up, trump up.

**invention** *n* brainchild, coinage, contraption, contrivance, contrivement, creation, creativeness, creativity, deceit, design, development, device, discovery, excogitation, fabrication, fake, falsehood, fantasy, fib, fiction, figment of (someone's) imagination, forgery, gadget, genius, imagination, ingenuity, inspiration, inventiveness, inveracity, lie, originality, prevarication, resourcefulness, sham, story, tall story, untruth, yarn.

*antonym* truth.

**inventive** *adj* creative, daedal(e), Daedalian, daedalic, dedal, excogitative, fertile, gifted, imaginative, ingenious, innovative, inspired, original, resourceful.

*antonym* uninventive.

**inventor** *n* architect, author, builder, coiner, creator, designer, father, framer, inventress, maker, originator.

**inventory** *n* account, catalogue, equipment, file, list, listing, record, register, roll, roster, schedule, stock.

**inverse** *adj* contrary, converse, inverted, opposite, reverse, reversed, transposed, upside down.

**inversion** *n* antipode, antithesis, contraposition, contrariety, contrary, hysteron-proteron, opposite, reversal, transposal, transposition.

**invert** *v* capsize, introvert, inverse, overturn, reverse, transpose, turn turtle, turn upside down, upset, upturn.

*antonym* right.

**invest** *v* adopt, advance, authorise, charge, consecrate, devote, empower, endow, endue, enthrone, establish, inaugurate, induct, install, lay out, license, ordain, provide, put in, sanction, sink, spend, supply, vest.

*antonym* divest.

**investigate** *v* consider, enquire into, examine, explore, go into, inspect, look into, probe, scrutinise, search, see how the land lies, sift, study, suss out.

**investigation** *n* analysis, enquiry, examination, exploration, fact finding, hearing, inquest, inquiry, inspection, probe, research, review, scrutiny, search, study, survey, witch-hunt, zetetic.

**investigative** *adj* fact-finding, heuristic, inspecting, investigating, research, researching, zetetic.

**investigator** *n* detective, dick, enquirer, examiner, gumshoe, inquisitor, private detective, private eye, researcher, shamus, sleuth, sleuth-hound.

**investiture** *n* admission, coronation, enthronement, inauguration, induction, installation, instatement, investing, investment, ordination.

**investment** *n* ante, asset, besieging, blockade, contribution, investing, investiture, siege, speculation, stake, transaction, venture.

**inveterate** *adj* chronic, confirmed, deep-dyed, deep-rooted, deep-seated, diehard, dyed-in-the-wool, entrenched, established, habitual, hard-core, hardened, incorrigible, incurable, ineradicable, ingrained, irreformable, long-standing, obstinate.

*antonym* impermanent.

**invidious** *adj* discriminating, discriminatory, hateful, objectionable, obnoxious, odious, offensive, repugnant, slighting, undesirable.

*antonym* desirable.

**invigorate** *v* animate, brace, buck up, energise, enliven, exhilarate, fortify, freshen, galvanise, harden, inspirit, liven up, nerve, pep up, perk up, quicken, refresh, rejuvenate, revitalise, stimulate, strengthen, vitalise, vivify.

*antonyms* dishearten, weary.

**invigorating** *adj* bracing, energising, exhilarating, fresh, generous, healthful, inspiriting, refreshing, rejuvenating, rejuvenative, restorative, salubrious, stimulating, tonic, uplifting, vivifying.

*antonyms* disheartening, wearying.

**invincible** *adj* impenetrable, impregnable, indestructible, indomitable, inseparable, insuperable, invulnerable, irreducible, unassailable, unbeatable, unconquerable, unreducible, unsurmountable, unyielding.

*antonym* beatable.

**inviolability** *n* holiness, inalienability, inviolableness, inviolacy, invulnerability, sacredness, sacrosanctness, sanctity.

*antonym* violability.

**inviolable** *adj* hallowed, holy, inalienable, intemerate, sacred, sacrosanct, unalterable.

*antonym* violable.

**inviolate** *adj* entire, intact, pure, sacred, stainless, unbroken, undefiled, undisturbed, unhurt, uninjured, unpolluted, unprofaned, unstained, unsullied, untouched, virgin, whole.

*antonym* sullied.

**invisible** *adj* concealed, disguised, hidden, imperceptible, inappreciable, inconspicuous, indetectable, indiscernible, infinitesimal, microscopic, out of sight, unperceivable, unseeable, unseen.

*antonym* visible.

**invitation** *n* allurement, asking, begging, bidding, call, challenge, come-on, coquetry, enticement, exhortation, glad eye, incitement, inducement, invite, overture, provocation, request, solicitation, summons, supplication, temptation.

**invite** *v* allure, ask, ask for, attract, beckon, beg, bid, bring on, call, court, draw, encourage, entice, lead, provoke, request, seek, solicit, summon, tempt, welcome.

*antonyms* force, order.

**inviting** *adj* alluring, appealing, appetising, attractive, beguiling, captivating, delightful, engaging, enticing, fascinating, intriguing, magnetic, mouthwatering, pleasing, seductive, tantalising, tempting, warm, welcoming, winning.

*antonym* uninviting.

**invocation** *n* appeal, beseeching, conjuration, entreaty, epiclasis, imploration, petition, prayer, supplication.

**invoke** *v* adjure, appeal to, apply, base on, beg, beseech, call upon, conjure, conjure up, entreat, implement, implore, initiate, petition, pray, put into effect, refer to, resort to, solicit, supplicate, use.

**involuntary** *adj* automatic, blind, compulsory, conditioned, forced, instinctive, instinctual, obligatory, reflex, reluctant, spontaneous, unconscious, uncontrolled, unintentional, unthinking, unwilled, unwilling, vegetative.

*antonym* voluntary.

**involve** *v* absorb, affect, associate, bind, commit, comprehend, comprise, compromise, concern, connect, contain, cover, draw in, embrace, engage, engross, entail, grip, hold, implicate, imply, include, incorporate, incriminate, inculpate, mean, mix up, necessitate, number among, preoccupy, presuppose, require, rivet, take in, touch.

**involved** adj anfractuous, caught up/in, complex, complicated, concerned, confusing, convoluted, difficult, elaborate, implicated, in on, intricate, knotty, labyrinthine, mixed up in/with, occupied, participating, sophisticated, tangled, tortuous.

antonyms simple, uninvolved.

**involvement** n association, commitment, complexity, complication, concern, connection, dedication, difficulty, embarrassment, entanglement, imbroglio, implication, interest, intricacy, participation, problem, ramification, responsibility.

**invulnerability** n impenetrability, inviolability, safety, security, strength, unassailability.

antonym vulnerability.

**invulnerable** adj impenetrable, indestructible, insusceptible, invincible, proof against, safe, secure, unassailable, unwoundable.

antonym vulnerable.

**inward** adj confidential, entering, hidden, inbound, incoming, inflowing, ingoing, inly, inmost, inner, innermost, inpouring, inside, interior, internal, penetrating, personal, private, privy, secret.

antonyms external, outward.

**inwardly** adv at heart, deep down, in gremio, in pectore, in petto, inly, inside, privately, secretly, to oneself, within.

antonyms externally, outwardly.

**iota** n atom, bit, drop, grain, hint, jot, mite, particle, scintilla, scrap, smidgeon, soupçon, speck, tittle, trace, whit.

**IOU** n debenture.

**irascibility** n asperity, bad temper, cantankerousness, choler, crabbiness, crossness, edginess, fieriness, ill-temper, impatience, irritability, irritation, petulance, shortness, snappishness, testiness, touchiness.

antonym placidness.

**irascible** adj bad-tempered, cantankerous, choleric, crabbed, crabby, cross, hasty, hot-tempered, ill-natured, ill-tempered, iracund, iracundulous, irritable, narky, peppery, petulant, prickly, quick-tempered, short-tempered, testy, touchy, volcanic.

antonym placid.

**irate** adj angered, angry, annoyed, enraged, exasperated, fuming, furibund, furious, gusty, in a paddy, incensed, indignant, infuriated, ireful, irritated, livid, mad, piqued, provoked, riled, up in arms, waxy, worked up, wrathful, wroth.

antonym calm.

**ire** n anger, annoyance, choler, displeasure, exasperation, fury, indignation, passion, rage, wax, wrath.

antonym calmness.

**iridescence** n glittering, iridisation, opalescence, reflet, shimmering.

**iridescent** adj glittering, iridial, iridian, irisated, irised, nacreous, opalescent, opaline, pearly, polychromatic, prismatic, rainbow, rainbow-coloured, rainbow-like, shimmering, shot.

**iris** n flag, fleur-de-lis, gladdon.

**Irish** adj green, Hibernian, Milesian.

**irk** v aggravate, annoy, bug, disgust, distress, gall, get, get to, irritate, miff, nettle, peeve, provoke, put out, rile, rub up the wrong way, ruffle, vex, weary.

antonym please.

**irksome** adj aggravating, annoying, boring, bothersome, burdensome, disagreeable, exasperating, infuriating, irritating, tedious, tiresome, troublesome, trying, vexatious, vexing, wearisome.

antonym pleasing.

**iron** adj adamant, cruel, fast-binding, fixed, grating, hard, harsh, heavy, immovable, implacable, indomitable, inflexible, insensitive, obdurate, rigid, robust, steel, steely, strong, tough, unbending, unyielding.

antonyms pliable, weak.

v flatten, press, smooth, uncrease.

n flatiron, goose.

**iron out** clear up, deal with, eliminate, eradicate, erase, expedite, fix, get rid of, harmonise, put right, reconcile, resolve, settle, smooth over, solve, sort out, straighten out.

**ironic** adj contemptuous, derisive, incongruous, ironical, irrisory, mocking, paradoxical, sarcastic, sardonic, satirical, scoffing, scornful, sneering, wry.

**irons** n bilboes, bonds, chains, fetters, gyves, manacles, shackles, trammels.

**irony** n asteism, contrariness, incongruity, irrision, mockery, paradox, sarcasm, satire.

**irradiate** v brighten, enlighten, expose, illume, illuminate, illumine, light up, lighten, radiate, shine on.

**irrational** adj aberrant, absurd, alogical, brainless, crazy, demented, foolish, illogical, injudicious, insane, mindless, muddle-headed, nonsensical, preposterous, raving, senseless, silly, unreasonable, unreasoning, unsound, unstable, unthinking, unwise, wild.

antonym rational.

**irrationality** n absurdity, brainlessness, illogicality, insanity, lunacy, madness, preposterousness, senselessness, unreason, unreasonableness, unsoundness.

antonym rationality.

**irreconcilable** adj clashing, conflicting, hardline, implacable, incompatible, incongruous, inconsistent, inexorable, inflexible, intransigent, opposed, unappeasable, uncompromising, unreconcilable.

antonym reconcilable.

**irrecoverable** *adj* irreclaimable, irredeemable, irremediable, irreparable, irretrievable, lost, unrecoverable, unsalvageable, unsavable.

*antonym* recoverable.

**irrefutable** *adj* apod(e)ictic, certain, impregnable, incontestable, incontrovertible, indisputable, indubitable, invincible, irrebuttable, irrefragable, irresistible, sure, unanswerable, unassailable, undeniable, ungainsayable, unquestionable.

*antonym* refutable.

**irregular** *adj* abnormal, anomalistic(al), anomalous, asymmetrical, broken, bumpy, capricious, craggy, crooked, difform, disconnected, disorderly, eccentric, erratic, exceptional, extraordinary, extravagant, fitful, fluctuating, fragmentary, haphazard, holey, immoderate, improper, inappropriate, incondite, inordinate, intermittent, jagged, lop-sided, lumpy, occasional, odd, patchy, peculiar, pitted, queer, quirky, ragged, random, rough, serrated, shifting, snatchy, spasmodic, sporadic, uncertain, unconventional, unequal, uneven, unofficial, unorthodox, unprocedural, unpunctual, unsteady, unsuitable, unsymmetrical, unsystematic, unusual, variable, wavering.

*antonyms* conventional, regular, smooth.

**irregularity** *n* aberration, abnormality, anomaly, asymmetry, breach, bumpiness, confusion, crookedness, desultoriness, deviation, difformity, disorderliness, disorganisation, eccentricity, freak, haphazardness, heterodoxy, jaggedness, lop-sidedness, lumpiness, malfunction, malpractice, oddity, patchiness, peculiarity, raggedness, randomness, roughness, singularity, uncertainty, unconventionality, unevenness, unorthodoxy, unpunctuality, unsteadiness.

*antonyms* conventionality, regularity, smoothness.

**irregularly** *adv* anyhow, by fits and starts, disconnectedly, eccentrically, erratically, fitfully, haphazardly, intermittently, jerkily, now and again, occasionally, off and on, spasmodically, unevenly, unmethodically.

*antonym* regularly.

**irrelevance** *n* inappositeness, inappropriateness, inaptness, inconsequence, irrelevancy, unimportance.

*antonym* relevance.

**irrelevant** *adj* alien, extraneous, foreign, immaterial, impertinent, inapplicable, inapposite, inappropriate, inapt, inconsequent, inessential, peripheral, tangential, unapt, unconnected, unnecessary, unrelated.

*antonym* relevant.

**irreligious** *adj* agnostic, atheistic, blasphemous, free-thinking, godless, heathen, heathenish, iconoclastic, impious, irreverent, nullifidian, pagan, profane, rationalistic, sacrilegious, sceptical, sinful, unbelieving, undevout, ungodly, unholy, unreligious, unrighteous, wicked.

*antonyms* pious, religious.

**irremediable** *adj* deadly, fatal, final, hopeless, incorrigible, incurable, inoperable, irrecoverable, irredeemable, irreparable, irretrievable,

irreversible, mortal, remediless, terminal, unmedicinable.

*antonym* remediable.

**irremovable** *adj* durable, fast, fixed, immovable, indestructible, ineradicable, ingrained, inoperable, obdurate, obstinate, permanent, persistent, rooted, set, stuck.

*antonym* removable.

**irreparable** *adj* incurable, irreclaimable, irrecoverable, irremediable, irretrievable, irreversible, unrepairable.

*antonyms* recoverable, remediable.

**irreplaceable** *adj* essential, indispensable, inimitable, invaluable, matchless, peerless, priceless, sublime, unique, unmatched, vital.

*antonym* replaceable.

**irrepressible** *adj* boisterous, bubbling over, buoyant, ebullient, effervescent, inextinguishable, insuppressible, resilient, uncontainable, uncontrollable, ungovernable, uninhibited, unmanageable, unquenchable, unrestrainable, unstoppable.

*antonyms* depressed, depressive, despondent, resistible.

**irreproachable** *adj* blameless, faultless, guiltless, immaculate, impeccable, inculpable, innocent, irreprehensible, irreprovable, perfect, pure, reproachless, stainless, taintless, unblemished, unimpeachable.

*antonyms* blameworthy, culpable.

**irresistible** *adj* alluring, beckoning, beguiling, charming, compelling, enchanting, fascinating, imperative, ineluctable, inescapable, inevitable, inexorable, overmastering, overpowering, overwhelming, potent, pressing, ravishing, resistless, seductive, tempting, unavoidable, uncontrollable, urgent.

*antonyms* avoidable, resistible.

**irresolute** *adj* dithering, doubtful, faint-hearted, fickle, fluctuating, half-hearted, hesitant, hesitating, indecisive, infirm, shifting, shilly-shallying, swithering, tentative, undecided, undetermined, unsettled, unstable, unsteady, vacillating, variable, wavering, weak.

*antonym* resolute.

**irresolution** *n* dithering, faint-heartedness, fluctuation, half-heartedness, hesitancy, hesitation, inconsistency, inconstancy, indecisiveness, infirmity, infirmness, shifting, shilly-shally, shilly-shallying, tentativeness, uncertainty, unsteadiness, vacillation, wavering.

*antonym* resolution.

**irresponsible** *adj* carefree, careless, feather-brained, feckless, flibbertigibbet, flighty, foot-loose, giddy, harebrained, harum-scarum, heedless, ill-considered, immature, light-hearted, madcap, negligent, rash, reckless, scatter-brained, shiftless, thoughtless, undependable, unreliable, untrustworthy, wild.

*antonym* responsible.

**irretrievable** *adj* damned, hopeless, irrecoverable, irredeemable, irremediable, irreparable, irreversible, irrevocable, lost, unrecallable, unrecoverable, unsalvageable.

*antonyms* recoverable, reversible.

**irreverence** *n* blasphemy, cheek, cheekiness, derision, discourtesy, disrespect, disrespectfulness, flippancy, godlessness, iconoclasm, impertinence, impiety, impudence, levity, mockery, profanity, sauce.

*antonym* reverence.

**irreverent** *adj* blasphemous, cheeky, contemptuous, derisive, discourteous, disrespectful, flip, flippant, godless, iconoclastic, impertinent, impious, impudent, mocking, profane, rude, sacrilegious, saucy, tongue-in-cheek.

*antonym* reverent.

**irreversible** *adj* final, hopeless, immedicable, incurable, inoperable, irremediable, irreparable, irretrievable, irrevocable, lasting, lost, permanent, remediless, unalterable, unmedicinable.

*antonyms* curable, remediable, reversible.

**irrevocable** *adj* changeless, fated, fixed, hopeless, immutable, inexorable, invariable, irremediable, irrepealable, irretrievable, irreversible, predestined, predetermined, settled, unalterable, unchangeable.

*antonyms* alterable, flexible, mutable, reversible.

**irrigate** *v* dampen, flood, humect, humify, inundate, moisten, water, wet.

**irritability** *n* edge, edginess, erethism, fractiousness, fretfulness, hypersensitivity, ill-humour, ill-temper, impatience, irascibility, peevishness, petulance, prickliness, testiness, tetchiness, touchiness.

*antonyms* bonhomie, cheerfulness, complacence, good humour.

**irritable** *adj* bad-tempered, cantankerous, captious, choleric, crabbed, crabby, cross, crotchety, crusty, edgy, feisty, fractious, fretful, hasty, hypersensitive, ill-humoured, ill-tempered, impatient, irascible, narky, nettlesome, peevish, petulant, prickly, querulous, short, short-tempered, snappish, snappy, snarling, sore, tense, testy, te(t)chy, thin-skinned, touchy.

*antonyms* cheerful, complacent.

**irritant** *n* annoyance, bore, bother, goad, menace, nuisance, pain, pest, pin-prick, plague, provocation, rankle, tease, thorn in the flesh, trouble, vexation.

*antonyms* pleasure, sop, sweetness.

**irritate** *v* acerbate, aggravate, anger, annoy, bedevil, bother, bug, chafe, emboil, enrage, exacerbate, exasperate, faze, fret, get on one's nerves, get to, give the pip, gravel, grig, harass, incense, inflame, infuriate, irk, needle, nettle, offend, pain, peeve, pester, pique, provoke, put out, rankle, rile, rouse, rub, ruffle, vex.

*antonyms* gratify, mollify, placate, please.

**irritated** *adj* angry, annoyed, bothered, cross, discomposed, displeased, edgy, exasperated, fazed, flappable, flustered, harassed, impatient, irked, irritable, nettled, peeved, piqued, put out, ratty, riled, roused, ruffled, uptight, vexed.

*antonyms* composed, gratified, pleased.

**irritating** *adj* abrasive, aggravating, annoying, bothersome, displeasing, disturbing, galling, infuriating, irksome, maddening, nagging, pesky, pesterous, pestful, pestiferous, pestilent, pestilential, plaguey, provoking, thorny, troublesome, trying, upsetting, urticant, vexatious, vexing, worrisome.

*antonyms* pleasant, pleasing.

**irritation** *n* aggravation, anger, annoyance, crossness, displeasure, dissatisfaction, exasperation, fury, goad, impatience, indignation, irritability, irritant, itch, nuisance, pain, pain in the neck, pest, pin-prick, provocation, rankle, resentment, shortness, snappiness, tease, testiness, vexation, wrath.

*antonyms* pleasure, satisfaction.

**island** *n* ait, atoll, cay, eyot, holm, inch, isle, islet, key.

**isolate** *v* abstract, cut off, detach, disconnect, divorce, exclude, identify, insulate, keep apart, ostracise, pinpoint, quarantine, remove, seclude, segregate, separate, sequester, set apart.

*antonyms* assimilate, incorporate.

**isolated** *adj* abnormal, anomalous, atypical, backwoods, deserted, detached, dissociated, eremitic, exceptional, freak, godforsaken, hermitical, hidden, incommunicado, insular, lonely, monastic, outlying, out-of-the-way, random, reclusive, remote, retired, secluded, single, solitary, special, sporadic, unfrequented, unique, unrelated, untrodden, untypical, unusual, unvisited.

*antonyms* populous, typical.

**isolation** *n* aloofness, detachment, disconnection, dissociation, exile, insularity, insulation, lazaretto, loneliness, quarantine, reclusion, remoteness, retirement, seclusion, segregation, self-sufficiency, separation, solitariness, solitude, withdrawal.

**issue**[1] *n* affair, argument, concern, controversy, crux, debate, matter, point, problem, question, subject, topic.

**issue**[2] *n* announcement, broadcast, circulation, copy, delivery, dispersal, dissemination, distribution, edition, emanation, flow, granting, handout, impression, instalment, issuance, issuing, number, printing, promulgation, propagation, publication, release, supply, supplying, vent.

*v* announce, broadcast, circulate, deal out, deliver, distribute, emit, give out, mint, produce, promulgate, publicise, publish, put out, release, supply.

**issue**[3] *n* conclusion, consequence, culmination, dénouement, effect, end, finale, outcome, pay-off, product, result, termination, upshot.

*v* arise, burst forth, debouch, emanate, emerge, flow, leak, originate, proceed, rise, spring, stem.

**issue**[4] *n* brood, children, descendants, heirs, offspring, progeny, scions, seed, young.

**itch** *v* crawl, prickle, tickle, tingle, yuke.

*n* cacoethes, craving, desire, eagerness, formication, hankering, hunger, irritation, itchiness, keenness, longing, lust, passion, prickling, scabies, tingling, yearning, yen.

**itching** *adj* aching, avid, burning, dying, eager, greedy, hankering, impatient, inquisitive, itch, longing, raring, spoiling.

**itchy** *adj* avaricious, eager, edgy, fidgety, greedy, impatient, restive, restless, roving, unsettled, yuky.

**item** *n* account, article, aspect, bulletin, component, consideration, detail, element, entry, factor, feature, ingredient, matter, minute, note, notice, object, paragraph, particular, piece, point, report, thing.

**itemise** *v* count, detail, document, enumerate, instance, inventory, list, mention, number, overname, particularise, record, specify, tabulate.

**itinerancy** *n* drifting, nomadism, peregrination, roaming, rootlessness, roving, travelling, vagabondism, vagrancy, wandering, wanderlust, wayfaring.

**itinerant** *adj* ambulatory, drifting, journeying, migratory, nomadic, peregrinatory, peripatetic, rambling, roaming, rootless, roving, travelling, vagabond, vagrant, wandering, wayfaring.

*antonyms* settled, stationary.

*n* diddicoy, dusty-foot, gypsy, hobo, nomad, perigrinator, peripatetic, piepowder, pilgrim, Romany, tinker, toe-rag, tramp, traveller, vagabond, vagrant, wanderer, wayfarer.

**itinerary** *n* circuit, course, journey, line, plan, programme, route, schedule, tour.

# J

**jab** *v* dig, elbow, jag, lunge, nudge, poke, prod, punch, push, shove, stab, tap, thrust.

**jabber** *v* babble, blather, blether, chatter, drivel, gab, gabble, gash, jaw, mumble, prate, rabbit, ramble, tattle, witter, yap.

**jacket** *n* blouson, case, casing, coat, cover, covering, envelope, folder, jerkin, jupon, mackinaw, sheath, shell, skin, wrap, wrapper, wrapping.

**jackpot** *n* award, big time, bonanza, kitty, pool, pot, prize, reward, stakes, winnings.

**jade** *n* baggage, broad, draggle-tail, floosie, harridan, hussy, nag, shrew, slattern, slut, strumpet, tart, trollop, vixen, wench.

**jaded** *adj* blunted, bored, cloyed, disjaskit, dulled, effete, exhausted, fagged, fatigued, played-out, satiated, spent, surfeited, tired, tired out, weary.

*antonyms* fresh, refreshed.

**jag** *n* barb, denticle, dentil, notch, point, projection, protrusion, snag, spur, tooth.

**jagged** *adj* barbed, broken, craggy, denticulate, hackly, indented, irregular, notched, pointed, ragged, ridged, rough, saw-edged, serrate, serrated, snagged, snaggy, spiked, spiky, toothed, uneven.

*antonym* smooth.

**jail, gaol** *n* borstal, bridewell, brig, calaboose, can, cells, choky, clink, cooler, coop, custody, guardhouse, hoos(e)gow, house of correction, inside, jailhouse, jankers, jug, lock-up, nick, pen, penitentiary, pokey, porridge, prison, quod, reformatory, slammer, stir, tollbooth.

*v* confine, detain, immure, impound, imprison, incarcerate, intern, lock up, quod, send down.

**jailer, gaoler** *n* captor, guard, keeper, prison officer, screw, turnkey, warden, warder.

**jam**[1] *v* block, clog, compact, confine, congest, cram, crowd, crush, force, obstruct, pack, press, ram, sandwich, squash, squeeze, stall, stick, stuff, throng, thrust, vice, wedge.

*n* bottle-neck, concourse, crowd, crush, gridlock, herd, horde, mass, mob, multitude, pack, press, swarm, throng, traffic jam.

**jam**[2] *n* bind, contretemps, difficulty, dilemma, fix, hitch, hole, hot water, imbroglio, impasse, pickle, plight, predicament, quandary, scrape, spot, straits, tangle, tight corner, trouble.

**jam**[3] *n* confiture, confyt, conserve, jelly, marmalade, preserve, spread.

**jamboree** *n* carnival, carouse, celebration, convention, festival, festivity, fête, field day, frolic, gathering, get-together, jubilee, junket, merriment, party, potlatch, rally, revelry, shindig, spree.

**jangle** *v* chime, clank, clash, clatter, jar, jingle, rattle, upset, vibrate.

*n* cacophony, clang, clangour, clash, din, dissonance, jar, racket, rattle, reverberation, stridence, stridency, stridor.

*antonyms* euphony, harmony.

**janitor** *n* caretaker, concierge, custodian, doorkeeper, doorman, janitress, janitrix, ostiary, porter.

**jar**[1] *n* amphora, aquamanile, bellarmine, can, carafe, container, crock, cruet, cruse, ewer, flagon, jug, kang, mug, olla, pitcher, pot, receptacle, stamnos, stoup, urn, vase, vessel.

**jar**[2] *v* agitate, annoy, clash, convulse, disagree, discompose, disturb, grate, grind, interfere, irk, irritate, jangle, jolt, nettle, offend, quarrel, rasp, rattle, rock, shake, upset, vibrate.

*n* clash, disagreement, discord, dissonance, grating, irritation, jangle, jolt, quarrel, rasping, wrangling.

**jargon** *n* argot, balderdash, baragouin, bunkum, cant, computerese, criminalese, dialect, diplomatese, double-Dutch, drivel, gabble, gibberish, gobbledegook, gobbledygook, Greek, idiom, jive, lingo, mumbo-jumbo, nonsense, palaver, parlance, patois, rigmarole, slang, tongue, twaddle, vernacular.

**jarring** *adj* cacophonous, discordant, dissonant, disturbing, grating, horrisonant, irritating, jangling, jolting, rasping, strident, upsetting.

**jaundiced** *adj* biased, bitter, cynical, disbelieving, distorted, distrustful, envious, hostile, jaded, jealous, misanthropic, partial, pessimistic, preconceived, prejudiced, resentful, sceptical, suspicious.

*antonyms* fresh, naïve, optimistic.

**jaunty** *adj* airy, breezy, buoyant, carefree, cheeky, chipper, dapper, debonair, gay, high-spirited, insouciant, lively, perky, self-confident, showy, smart, sparkish, sprightly, spruce, trim.

*antonyms* anxious, depressed, dowdy, seedy.

**jaw**[1] *n* chops, dewlap, flews, jaws, mandible, masticator, maw, maxilla, mouth, muzzle, proboscis, trap.

**jaw²** *v* abuse, babble, censure, chat, chatter, criticise, gab, gabble, gossip, lecture, prate, revile, scold, talk.

*n* chat, chinwag, conversation, discussion, gab, gossip, natter, talk.

**jazz** *n* bebop, blues, boogie, boogie-woogie, crap, Dixieland, guff, hard rock, heavy metal, lies, New Wave, ragtime, rhythm, rock, spiel, swing, talk.

**jazzy** *adj* animated, avant-garde, bold, fancy, flashy, gaudy, goey, lively, smart, snazzy, spirited, stylish, swinging, vivacious, wild, zestful.

*antonyms* conservative, prosaic, square.

**jealous** *adj* anxious, apprehensive, attentive, careful, covetous, desirous, emulous, envious, green, green-eyed, grudging, guarded, heedful, invidious, mistrustful, possessive, proprietorial, protective, resentful, rival, solicitous, suspicious, vigilant, wary, watchful, zealous.

**jealousy** *n* covetousness, distrust, emulation, envy, grudge, heart-burning, ill-will, mistrust, possessiveness, resentment, spite, suspicion, vigilance, watchfulness, zelotypia.

**jeer** *v* banter, barrack, chaff, contemn, deride, explode, fleer, flout, flyte, gibe, heckle, hector, knock, mock, rail, razz, ridicule, scoff, sneer, taunt, twit.

*n* abuse, aspersion, catcall, chaff, derision, dig, fleer, flyte, flyting, gibe, hiss, hoot, mockery, raillery, raspberry, ridicule, scoff, sneer, taunt, thrust.

**jejune** *adj* arid, banal, barren, callow, childish, colourless, dry, dull, empty, foolish, immature, impoverished, inane, insipid, juvenile, meagre, naïve, pointless, prosaic, puerile, senseless, silly, simple, spiritless, trite, uninteresting, unoriginal, unsophisticated, vapid, wishy-washy.

*antonyms* mature, meaningful.

**jell, gel** *v* coagulate, congeal, crystallise, finalise, form, gee, gel, gelatinate, gelatinise, harden, jelly, materialise, set, solidify, take form, take shape, thicken.

*antonym* disintegrate.

**jeopardise** *v* chance, endanger, expose, gamble, hazard, imperil, jeopard, menace, risk, stake, threaten, venture.

*antonyms* protect, safeguard.

**jeopardy** *n* danger, endangerment, exposure, hazard, imperilment, insecurity, liability, peril, plight, precariousness, risk, venture, vulnerability.

*antonyms* safety, security.

**jerk¹** *n* bounce, jog, jolt, lurch, pluck, pull, shrug, throw, thrust, tug, tweak, twitch, wrench, yank.

*v* bounce, flirt, jigger, jog, jolt, jounce, lurch, peck, pluck, pull, shrug, throw, thrust, tug, tweak, twitch, wrench, yank.

**jerk²** *n* bum, clod, clot, clown, creep, dimwit, dolt, dope, fool, halfwit, idiot, klutz, ninny, prick, schlep, schmo, schmuck, twit.

**jerky** *adj* bouncy, bumpy, convulsive, disconnected, fitful, incoherent, jolting, jumpy, rough, shaky, spasmodic, tremulous, twitchy, uncontrolled, unco-ordinated.

*antonym* smooth.

**jerry-built** *adj* cheap, cheapjack, defective, faulty, flimsy, insubstantial, ramshackle, rickety, shoddy, slipshod, unsubstantial.

*antonyms* firm, stable, substantial.

**jersey** *n* guernsey, jumper, lammy, pullover, sweater, sweat-shirt, woolly.

**jest** *n* banter, bon mot, clowning, cod, crack, desipience, foolery, fooling, fun, gag, hoax, jape, jeu d'esprit, joke, josh, kidding, leg-pull, pleasantry, prank, quip, sally, sport, trick, trifling, waggery, wisecrack, witticism.

*v* banter, chaff, clown, deride, fool, gibe, jeer, joke, josh, kid, mock, quip, scoff, tease, trifle.

**jester** *n* buffoon, clown, comedian, comic, droll, fool, goliard, harlequin, humorist, joculator, joker, juggler, merry-andrew, merryman, motley, mummer, pantaloon, patch, prankster, quipster, wag, wit, zany.

**jet¹** *n* atomiser, flow, fountain, gush, issue, nose, nozzle, rose, rush, spout, spray, sprayer, spring, sprinkler, spurt, squirt, stream, surge.

**jet²** *adj* atramentous, black, coal-black, ebon, ebony, inky, jetty, pitch-black, pitchy, raven, sable, sloe, sooty.

**jetsam** *n* jetsom, jetson, lagan, waif, wreckage.

**jettison** *v* abandon, chuck, discard, ditch, dump, eject, expel, heave, offload, scrap, unload.

*antonyms* load, take on.

**jetty** *n* breakwater, dock, groyne, jutty, mole, pier, quay, wharf.

**jewel** *n* bijou, brilliant, charm, find, flower, gaud, gem, gemstone, humdinger, locket, masterpiece, ornament, paragon, pearl, precious stone, pride, prize, rarity, rock, sparkler, stone, treasure, wonder.

**jewellery** *n* bijouterie, bijoux, finery, gauds, gemmery, gems, jewels, ornaments, regalia, treasure, trinkets.

**Jezebel** *n* Delilah, femme fatale, harlot, hussy, jade, man-eater, scarlet woman, seductress, temptress, vamp, wanton, whore, witch.

**jib** *v* back off, balk, recoil, refuse, retreat, shrink, stall, stop short.

**jibe, gibe** *v* deride, fleer, flout, jeer, mock, rail, ridicule, scoff, scorn, sneer, taunt, twit.

*n* barb, crack, derision, dig, fleer, fling, jeer, mockery, poke, quip, raillery, ridicule, sarcasm, scoff, slant, sneer, taunt, thrust.

**jiffy** *n* flash, instant, minute, moment, no time, sec, second, split second, tick, trice, twinkling, two shakes, two ticks, whiff.

*antonym* age.

**jig** *v* bob, bobble, bounce, caper, hop, jerk, jiggle, jounce, jump, prance, shake, skip, twitch, wiggle, wobble.

**jigger** *v* balls up, botch up, break, bugger up, destroy, kibosh, louse up, make a pig's ear of, queer, ruin, scupper, spoil, undermine, vitiate, wreck.

**jiggery-pokery** *n* chicanery, deceit, deception, dishonesty, fraud, funny business, hanky-panky, monkey-business, subterfuge, trickery.

**jiggle** *v* agitate, bounce, fidget, jerk, jig, jog, joggle, shake, shift, shimmy, twitch, waggle, wiggle, wobble.

**jilt** *v* abandon, betray, brush off, chuck, deceive, desert, discard, ditch, drop, forsake, reject, repudiate, spurn, throw over.

*antonym* cleave to.

**jingle¹** *v* chime, chink, clatter, clink, jangle, rattle, ring, tink, tinkle, tintinnabulate.

*n* clang, clangour, clink, rattle, reverberation, ringing, tink, tinkle, tintinnabulation.

**jingle²** *n* chant, chime, chorus, couplet, ditty, doggerel, limerick, melody, poem, rhyme, song, tune, verse.

**jingoism** *n* chauvinism, flag-waving, imperialism, insularity, nationalism, parochialism, patriotism, xenophobia.

**jinx** *n* black magic, charm, curse, evil eye, gremlin, hex, hoodoo, jettatura, Jonah, plague, spell, voodoo.

*v* bedevil, bewitch, curse, doom, hex, hoodoo, plague.

**jitters** *n* anxiety, fidgets, habdabs, heebie-jeebies, jimjams, nerves, nervousness, tenseness, the creeps, the shakes, the shivers, the willies.

**jittery** *adj* agitated, anxious, edgy, fidgety, flustered, jumpy, nervous, panicky, perturbed, quaking, quivering, shaky, shivery, trembling, uneasy.

*antonyms* calm, composed, confident.

**job** *n* activity, affair, allotment, assignment, batch, business, calling, capacity, career, charge, chore, commission, concern, consignment, contract, contribution, craft, duty, employment, enterprise, errand, function, livelihood, lot, message, métier, mission, occupation, office, output, part, piece, place, portion, position, post, proceeding, product, profession, project, province, pursuit, responsibility, role, share, situation, stint, task, trade, undertaking, venture, vocation, work.

**jobless** *adj* idle, inactive, laid off, on the dole, out of work, unemployed, unoccupied, unused, workless.

*antonym* employed.

**jockey** *v* cajole, coax, ease, edge, engineer, finagle, induce, inveigle, manage, manipulate, manoeuvre, negotiate, wheedle.

**jocose** *adj* blithe, comical, droll, facetious, funny, humorous, jesting, jocular, jocund, jovial, joyous, lepid, merry, mirthful, mischievous, playful, pleasant, sportive, teasing, waggish, witty.

*antonym* morose.

**jocular** *adj* amusing, arch, blithe, comical, desipient, droll, entertaining, facetious, frolicsome, funny, humorous, jesting, jocose, jocund, joking, jolly, jovial, merry, playful, roguish, sportive, teasing, waggish, whimsical, witty.

*antonym* serious.

**jocularity** *n* absurdity, comicality, desipience, drollery, facetiousness, fooling, gaiety, hilarity, humour, jesting, jocoseness, jocosity, jolliness,

joviality, laughter, merriment, playfulness, pleasantry, roguishness, sport, sportiveness, teasing, waggery, waggishness, whimsicality, whimsy, wit.

**jog¹** *v* activate, arouse, bounce, jar, jerk, joggle, jolt, jostle, jounce, nudge, poke, prod, prompt, push, remind, rock, shake, shove, stimulate, stir.

*n* jerk, jiggle, jolt, nudge, poke, prod, push, reminder, shake, shove.

**jog²** *v, n* bump, canter, dogtrot, jogtrot, lope, lumber, pad, run, trot.

**joie de vivre** blitheness, bounce, buoyancy, cheerfulness, ebullience, enjoyment, enthusiasm, gaiety, get-up-and-go, gusto, joy, joyfulness, merriment, mirth, pleasure, relish, zest.

*antonym* depression.

**join** *v* abut, accompany, accrete, add, adhere, adjoin, affiliate, alligate, amalgamate, annex, append, associate, attach, border, border on, butt, cement, coincide, combine, compaginate, conglutinate, conjoin, conjugate, connect, couple, dock, enlist, enrol, enter, fasten, knit, link, march with, marry, meet, merge, reach, sign up, splice, team, tie, touch, unite, verge on, yoke.

*antonyms* leave, separate.

**join in** chip in, contribute, co-operate, help, lend a hand, muck in, partake, participate, pitch in.

**join up** enlist, enroll, enter, sign up, take the king's shilling.

**joint¹** *n* articulation, commissure, connection, geniculation, gimmel, ginglymus, gomphosis, hinge, intersection, junction, juncture, knot, nexus, node, seam, union.

*adj* adjunct, amalgamated, collective, combined, communal, concerted, consolidated, co-operative, co-ordinated, joined, mutual, shared, united.

*v* articulate, carve, connect, couple, cut up, dismember, dissect, divide, fasten, fit, geniculate, join, segment, sever, sunder, unite.

**joint²** *n* dance-hall, dive, haunt, honky-tonk, jerry-shop, night-club, place, pub.

**joint³** *n* reefer, roach, stick.

**jointed** *adj* articulate, geniculate(d), gimmelled.

**joke** *n* buffoon, butt, clown, conceit, concetto, frolic, fun, funny, gag, guy, hoot, jape, jest, jeu d'esprit, lark, laughing-stock, play, pun, quip, quirk, sally, simpleton, sport, target, whimsy, wisecrack, witticism, yarn, yell.

*v* banter, chaff, clown, deride, fool, frolic, gambol, jest, kid, laugh, mock, quip, ridicule, spoof, taunt, tease, wisecrack.

**joke-book** *n* jest-book, Joe Miller.

**joker** *n* buffoon, card, character, clown, comedian, comic, droll, humorist, jester, joculator, jokesmith, kidder, prankster, sport, trickster, wag, wit.

**jollification** *n* beanfeast, beano, celebration, frolic, jollity, junket, knees-up, merriment, merry-making, party, rave-up, shindig, spree, thrash.

*antonym* lamentation.

**jolly** *adj* blithe, blithesome, buxom, carefree, cheerful, cheery, convivial, exuberant, festive, frisky, frolicsome, funny, gay, gladsome, happy, hearty, hilarious, jaunty, jocund, jovial, joyful, joyous, jubilant, merry, mirthful, playful, sportive, sprightly, sunny.

*antonym* sad.

**jolt** *v* astonish, bounce, bump, discompose, disconcert, dismay, disturb, jar, jerk, jog, jostle, jounce, knock, nonplus, perturb, push, shake, shock, shove, stagger, startle, stun, surprise, upset.

*n* blow, bolt from the blue, bombshell, bump, hit, impact, jar, jerk, jog, jump, lurch, quiver, reversal, setback, shake, shock, start, surprise, thunderbolt.

**jostle** *v* bump, butt, crowd, elbow, force, hustle, jog, joggle, jolt, press, push, rough up, scramble, shake, shoulder, shove, squeeze, throng, thrust.

**jot** *n* ace, atom, bit, detail, fraction, gleam, glimmer, grain, hint, iota, mite, morsel, particle, scintilla, scrap, smidgen, speck, tittle, trace, trifle, whit.

**jot down** enter, list, note, record, register, scribble, take down, write down.

**journal** *n* book, chronicle, commonplace, daily, daybook, diary, ephemeris, gazette, log, magazine, monthly, newspaper, organ, paper, periodical, publication, record, register, review, tabloid, waste-book, weekly.

**journalism** *n* copy-writing, correspondence, feature-writing, Fleet Street, fourth estate, gossip-writing, Grub Street, news, press, reportage, reporting, writing.

**journalist** *n* broadcaster, chronicler, columnist, commentator, contributor, correspondent, diarist, feature-writer, hack, hackette, hatchet man, journo, newshound, newsman, newspaperman, news-writer, periodicalist, pressman, reporter, scribe, stringer, sub, subeditor.

**journey** *n* career, course, excursion, expedition, eyre, hadj, itinerary, jaunt, odyssey, outing, passage, peregrination, pilgrimage, progress, raik, ramble, route, safari, tour, travel, trek, trip, voyage, wanderings.

*v* fare, fly, gallivant, go, jaunt, peregrinate, proceed, ramble, range, roam, rove, safari, tour, tramp, travel, traverse, trek, voyage, wander, wend.

**journeyer** *n* hadji, peregrinator, pilgrim, rambler, tourist, traveller, trekker, tripper, viator, voyager, wanderer, wayfarer.

**joust** *n* contest, encounter, engagement, pas d'armes, skirmish, tilt, tournament, tourney, trial.

**jovial** *adj* affable, airy, animated, blithe, buoyant, cheery, convivial, cordial, ebullient, expansive, Falstaffian, gay, glad, happy, hilarious, jaunty, jocose, jocund, jolly, jubilant, merry, mirthful.

*antonyms* morose, sad, saturnine.

**joviality** *n* affability, buoyancy, cheerfulness, cheeriness, ebullience, fun, gaiety, gladness, glee, happiness, hilarity, jollity, merriment, mirth.

*antonyms* moroseness, sadness.

**joy** *n* blessedness, bliss, charm, delight, ecstasy, elation, exaltation, exultation, felicity, festivity, gaiety, gem, gladness, gladsomeness, glee, gratification, happiness, hilarity, jewel, joyance, joyfulness, joyousness, pleasure, pride, prize, rapture, ravishment, satisfaction, seel, transport, treasure, treat, triumph, wonder.

*antonyms* mourning, sorrow.

**joyful** *adj* blithe, blithesome, delighted, ecstatic, elated, enraptured, glad, gladsome, gratified, happy, jocund, jolly, jovial, jubilant, light-hearted, merry, pleased, rapturous, satisfied, seely, transported, triumphant.

*antonyms* mournful, sorrowful.

**joyless** *adj* bleak, cheerless, dejected, depressed, despondent, discouraged, discouraging, dismal, dispirited, doleful, dour, downcast, dreary, forlorn, gloomy, glum, grim, miserable, sad, sombre, sunless, unhappy.

*antonym* joyful.

**joyous** *adj* cheerful, ecstatic, festal, festive, frabjous, glad, gladsome, gleeful, happy, joyful, jubilant, merry, rapturous.

*antonym* sad.

**jubilant** *adj* celebratory, delighted, elated, enraptured, euphoric, excited, exuberant, exultant, flushed, glad, gratified, joyous, over the moon, overjoyed, rejoicing, thrilled, triumphal, triumphant.

*antonyms* defeated, depressed.

**jubilation** *n* celebration, ecstasy, elation, euphoria, excitement, exultation, festivity, jamboree, jollification, joy, jubilee, triumph.

*antonyms* depression, lamentation.

**jubilee** *n* anniversary, carnival, celebration, commemoration, festival, festivity, fête, gala, holiday.

**Judas** *n* betrayer, deceiver, quisling, renegade, tergiversator, traitor, turncoat.

**judge** *n* adjudicator, alcalde, arbiter, arbiter elegantiae, arbitrator, arbitratrix, assessor, authority, beak, connoisseur, critic, Daniel, deemster, dempster, doomster, elegantiarum, evaluator, expert, hakim, justice, justiciar, justiciary, Law Lord, magistrate, mediator, moderator, pundit, referee, umpire, virtuoso, wig.

*v* adjudge, adjudicate, appraise, appreciate, arbitrate, ascertain, assess, conclude, condemn, consider, criticise, decern, decide, decree, determine, dijudicate, discern, distinguish, doom, esteem, estimate, evaluate, examine, find, gauge, mediate, opine, rate, reckon, referee, review, rule, sentence, sit, try, umpire, value.

**judgement** *n* acumen, appraisal, arbitration, arrêt, assessment, assize, award, belief, common sense, conclusion, conviction, damnation, decision, decree, decreet, deduction, determination, diagnosis, discernment, discretion, discrimination, doom, enlightenment, estimate, expertise, fate, fetwa, finding, intelligence, mediation, misfortune, opinion, order, penetration, perceptiveness, percipience, perspicacity, prudence, punishment, result, retribution, ruling, sagacity, sense, sentence, shrewdness, taste, understanding, valuation, verdict, view, virtuosity, wisdom.

**judicial** *adj* critical, decretory, discriminating, distinguished, forensic, impartial, judiciary, juridical, legal, magisterial, magistral, official.

**judicious** *adj* acute, astute, canny, careful, cautious, circumspect, considered, diplomatic, discerning, discreet, discriminating, enlightened, expedient, informed, percipient, perspicacious, politic, prescient, prudent, rational, reasonable, sagacious, sage, sane, sapient, sensible, shrewd, skilful, sober, sound, thoughtful, wary, well-advised, well-judged, well-judging, wise.

*antonym* injudicious.

**jug** *n* amphora, aquamanile, bellarmine, blackjack, carafe, churn, container, crock, ewer, flagon, jar, pitcher, stoup, urn, vessel.

**juggle** *v* alter, change, cook, disguise, doctor, fake, falsify, fix, hocus-pocus, manipulate, manoeuvre, misrepresent, modify, rig, tamper with.

**juice** *n* essence, extract, fluid, latex, liquid, liquor, nectar, sap, secretion, serum, succus.

**juicy** *adj* colourful, gamy, interesting, lactiferous, lush, moist, naughty, provocative, racy, risqué, salacious, sappy, scatological, sensational, serous, spicy, succose, succous, succulent, suggestive, vivid, watery.

*antonym* dry.

**jumble** *v* confuse, disarrange, disarray, disorder, disorganise, mingle-mangle, mix, mix up, muddle, shuffle, tangle, tumble, wuzzle.

*antonym* order.

*n* agglomeration, chaos, clutter, collection, confusion, congeries, conglomeration, disarrangement, disarray, disorder, farrago, gallimaufry, hotch-potch, medley, mess, mingle-mangle, miscellany, mishmash, mixture, mix-up, muddle, olio, olla-podrida, pastiche, pot-pourri, raffle, salad.

**jumbled** *adj* chaotic, confused, disarrayed, disordered, disorganised, mingle-mangle, miscellaneous, mixed-up, muddled, shuffled, tangled, tumbled, unsorted, untidy.

*antonym* orderly.

**jump**[1] *v* bounce, bound, caper, clear, dance, frisk, frolic, gambol, hop, hurdle, jig, leap, pounce, prance, skip, spring, vault.

*n* bounce, bound, capriole, curvet, dance, frisk, frolic, gambado, hop, jeté, leap, pounce, prance, saltation, skip, spring, vault.

**jump**[2] *v* avoid, bypass, digress, disregard, evade, ignore, leave out, miss, omit, overshoot, pass over, skip, switch.

*n* breach, break, gap, hiatus, interruption, interval, lacuna, lapse, omission, saltation, saltus, switch.

**jump**[3] *v* advance, appreciate, ascend, boost, escalate, gain, hike, increase, mount, rise, spiral, surge.

*n* advance, ascent, augmentation, boost, escalation, increase, increment, mounting, rise, upsurge, upturn.

**jump**[4] *v* flinch, jerk, jump out of one's skin, leap in the air, quail, recoil, resile, shrink, start, wince.

*n* jar, jerk, jolt, lurch, quiver, shiver, shock, spasm, start, swerve, twitch, wrench.

**jump**[5] *n* barricade, barrier, fence, gate, hedge, hurdle, impediment, obstacle, pons asinorum, rail.

**jump at** accept, agree to, fall for, grab, pounce on, seize, snatch, swallow, swoop on.

*antonym* recoil.

**jump on** berate, blame, castigate, censure, chide, criticise, fly at, flyte, rate, rebuke, reprimand, reproach, reprove, revile, scold, tick off, upbraid.

**jumper** *n* guernsey, jersey, lammy, pullover, sweater, sweat-shirt, woolly.

**jumping** *adj* desultory, disconnected, incoherent, jumpy, salient, saltatorial, saltatorious, saltatory, saltigrade, unco-ordinated.

**jumpy** *adj* agitated, anxious, apprehensive, discomposed, edgy, fidgety, jittery, nervous, nervy, restive, restless, shaky, tense, tremulous, uneasy.

*antonyms* calm, composed.

**junction** *n* abutment, combination, confluence, conjunction, connection, coupling, disemboguement, intersection, interstice, join, joining, joint, juncture, linking, meeting-point, nexus, seam, union.

**juncture** *n* bond, conjunction, connection, convergence, crisis, crux, emergency, intersection, join, joining, junction, link, minute, moment, nexus, occasion, period, point, predicament, seam, stage, time, union, weld.

**junior** *adj* inferior, lesser, lower, minor, puisne, secondary, subordinate, subsidiary, younger.

*antonym* senior.

**junk** *n* clutter, debris, detritus, dregs, garbage, litter, oddments, refuse, rejectamenta, rubbish, rummage, scrap, trash, waste, wreckage.

**junta** *n* cabal, camarilla, cartel, clique, combination, conclave, confederacy, convocation, coterie, council, crew, faction, gang, league, oligarchy, party, ring, set.

**jurisdiction** *n* area, authority, bailiwick, bounds, cognisance, command, control, domination, dominion, field, influence, judicature, orbit, power, prerogative, province, range, reach, rule, scope, sovereignty, sphere, sway, verge, zone.

**jury** *n* jurors, jurymen, jurywomen, panel, tales, talesmen, veniremen.

**just** *adj* accurate, apposite, appropriate, apt, blameless, condign, conscientious, correct, decent, deserved, disinterested, due, equitable, even-handed, exact, fair, fair-minded, faithful, fitting, four-square, good, honest, honourable, impartial, impeccable, irreproachable, justified, lawful, legitimate, merited, normal, precise, proper, pure, reasonable, regular, right, righteous, rightful, sound, suitable, true, unbiased, unimpeachable, unprejudiced, upright, virtuous, well-deserved.

*antonym* unjust.

**justice**[1] *n* amends, appositeness, appropriateness, compensation, correction, dharma, equitableness, equity, fairness, honesty, impartiality, integrity, justifiableness, justness, law, legality, legitimacy, nemesis, penalty, propriety, reasonableness, recompense, rectitude, redress, reparation, requital, right, rightfulness, rightness, satisfaction.

*antonym* injustice.

**justice²** *n* beak, JP, judge, Justice of the Peace, justiciar, magistrate.

**justifiable** *adj* acceptable, allowable, defensible, excusable, explainable, explicable, fit, forgivable, justified, lawful, legitimate, licit, maintainable, pardonable, proper, reasonable, right, sound, tenable, understandable, valid, vindicable, warrantable, warranted, well-founded.

*antonyms* culpable, illicit, unjustifiable.

**justification** *n* absolution, apology, approval, authorisation, basis, defence, exculpation, excuse, exoneration, explanation, extenuation, foundation, grounds, mitigation, palliation, plea, rationalisation, reason, substance, vindication, warrant.

**justify** *v* absolve, acquit, condone, confirm, defend, establish, exculpate, excuse, exonerate, explain, forgive, legalise, legitimise, maintain, pardon, substantiate, support, sustain, uphold, validate, vindicate, warrant.

**justly** *adv* accurately, condignly, conscientiously, correctly, duly, equally, equitably, even-handedly, fairly, honestly, impartially, lawfully, legitimately, objectively, properly, rightfully, rightly.

*antonym* unjustly.

**jut** *v* beetle, bulge, extend, impend, overhang, poke, project, protrude, stick out.

*antonym* recede.

**juvenile** *n* adolescent, boy, child, girl, halfling, infant, kid, minor, young person, youngster, youth.

*antonym* adult.

*adj* adolescent, babyish, boyish, callow, childish, girlish, immature, impressionable, inexperienced, infantile, jejune, puerile, tender, undeveloped, unsophisticated, young, youthful.

*antonym* mature.

**juxtaposition** *n* adjacency, closeness, contact, contiguity, immediacy, nearness, propinquity, proximity, vicinity.

*antonyms* dissociation, separation.

# K

**kaleidoscopic** *adj* changeable, ever-changing, fluctuating, fluid, manifold, many-coloured, many-splendoured, mobile, motley, multicoloured, multifarious, poikilitic, polychromatic, polychrome, variegated.

*antonyms* dull, monochrome, monotonous.

**kaput** *adj* broken, conked out, dead, defunct, destroyed, extinct, fini, finished, phut, ruined, smashed, undone, wrecked.

**keel over** black out, capsize, collapse, crumple, drop, faint, fall, founder, go out like a light, overturn, pass out, stagger, swoon, topple over, upset.

**keen** *adj* acid, acute, anxious, ardent, argute, assiduous, astute, avid, biting, brilliant, canny, caustic, clever, cutting, devoted, diligent, discerning, discriminating, eager, earnest, ebullient, edged, enthusiastic, fervid, fierce, fond, forthright, gleg, impassioned, incisive, industrious, intense, intent, mordant, penetrating, perceptive, perfervid, perspicacious, piercing, pointed, pungent, quick, razorlike, sagacious, sapient, sardonic, satirical, scathing, sedulous, sensitive, sharp, shrewd, shrill, tart, trenchant, wise, zealous.

*antonyms* apathetic, blunt, dull.

**keenness** *n* acerbity, anxiety, ardour, assiduity, astuteness, avidity, avidness, canniness, cleverness, diligence, discernment, eagerness, earnestness, ebullience, enthusiasm, fervour, forthrightness, harshness, impatience, incisiveness, industriousness, industry, insight, intensity, intentness, mordancy, passion, penetration, perfervidity, pungency, rigour, sagacity, sapience, sedulity, sensitivity, severity, sharpness, shrewdness, sternness, trenchancy, virulence, wisdom, zeal, zest.

*antonyms* apathy, bluntness, dullness.

**keep¹** *v* accumulate, amass, carry, collect, conserve, control, deal in, deposit, furnish, garner, hang on to, heap, hold, hold on to, maintain, pile, place, possess, preserve, retain, stack, stock, store.

**keep an eye on** guard, keep tabs on, keep under surveillance, look after, look to, monitor, observe, regard, scrutinise, supervise, survey, watch.

**keep at** be steadfast, beaver away at, carry on, complete, continue, drudge, endure, finish, grind, labour, last, maintain, persevere, persist, plug away at, remain, slave, slog at, stay, stick at, toil.

*antonyms* abandon, neglect.

**keep on** carry on, continue, endure, hold on, keep at it, last, maintain, persevere, persist, prolong, remain, retain, soldier on, stay, stay the course.

**keep on at** badger, chivvy, dun, go on at, harass, harry, importune, nag, pester, plague, pursue.

**keep one's distance** avoid, be aloof, give a wide berth, keep at arm's length, keep oneself to oneself, shun, withdraw.

**keep secret** conceal, dissemble, hide, keep back, keep dark, keep under one's hat, keep under wraps, suppress, wash one's dirty linen at home.

*antonym* reveal.

**keep track of** follow, grasp, keep up with, monitor, oversee, plot, record, trace, track, understand, watch.

**keep up** be on a par with, compete, contend, continue, emulate, equal, keep pace, maintain, match, pace, persevere, preserve, rival, support, sustain, vie.

**keep²** *v* be responsible for, board, care for, defend, feed, foster, guard, have charge of, have custody of, look after, maintain, manage, mind, nourish, nurture, operate, protect, provide for, provision, safeguard, shelter, shield, subsidise, support, sustain, tend, victual, watch, watch over.

*n* board, food, livelihood, living, maintenance, means, nourishment, nurture, subsistence, support, upkeep.

**keep³** *v* arrest, block, check, constrain, control, curb, delay, detain, deter, hamper, hamstring, hinder, hold, hold back, hold up, impede, inhibit, interfere with, keep back, limit, obstruct, prevent, restrain, retard, shackle, stall, trammel, withhold.

**keep back** censor, check, conceal, constrain, control, curb, delay, hide, hold back, hush up, impede, limit, prohibit, quell, ration, reserve, restrain, restrict, retain, retard, stifle, stop, suppress, withhold.

**keep in** bottle up, conceal, confine, control, detain, hide, inhibit, keep back, quell, restrain, retain, stifle, stop up, suppress.

*antonyms* declare, release.

**keep⁴** *v* adhere to, celebrate, commemorate, comply with, fulfil, hold, honour, keep faith with, keep up, maintain, obey, observe, perform, perpetuate, recognise, respect, ritualise, solemnise.

**keep⁵** *n* castle, citadel, donjon, dungeon, fastness, fort, fortress, motte, peel-house, peel-tower, stronghold, tower.

**keeper** *n* attendant, caretaker, conservator, conservatrix, curator, custodian, defender, gaoler, governor, guard, guardian, inspector, jailer, mahout, nab, overseer, steward, superintendent, supervisor, surveyor, warden, warder.

**keeping** *n* accord, accordance, aegis, agreement, auspices, balance, care, charge, compliance, conformity, congruity, consistency, correspondence, cure, custody, guardianship, harmony, keep, maintenance, obedience, observance, patronage, possession, proportion, protection, safe-keeping, supervision, surveillance, trust, tutelage, ward.

**keepsake** *n* emblem, favour, memento, pledge, relic, remembrance, reminder, souvenir, token.

**keg** *n* barrel, butt, cask, drum, firkin, hogshead, puncheon, round, rundlet, tierce, tun, vat.

**ken** *n* acquaintance, appreciation, awareness, cognisance, compass, comprehension, field, grasp, knowledge, notice, perception, range, reach, realisation, scope, sight, understanding, view, vision.

**kerchief** *n* babushka, bandana, cravat, fichu, headscarf, headsquare, kaffiyeh, madras, neck-cloth, neckerchief, scarf, shawl, square, sudary, veronica.

**kernel** *n* core, essence, germ, gist, grain, heart, marrow, nitty-gritty, nub, pith, seed, substance.

**key** *n* answer, clavis, clue, code, crib, cue, digital, explanation, glossary, guide, index, indicator, interpretation, lead, means, pointer, secret, sign, solution, table, translation.

*adj* basic, cardinal, central, chief, core, crucial, decisive, essential, fundamental, hinge, important, leading, main, major, pivotal, principal, salient.

**key in** capture, input, load, process, store.

**keynote** *n* accent, centre, core, emphasis, essence, flavour, flavour of the month, gist, heart, kernel, leitmotiv, marrow, motif, pith, stress, substance, theme.

**keystone** *n* base, basis, core, cornerstone, crux, foundation, fundamental, ground, linchpin, mainspring, motive, principle, quoin, root, source, spring.

**kick** *v* abandon, boot, break, desist from, drop, foot, give up, leave off, leave out, punt, quit, spurn, stop, toe.

*n* bite, buzz, dash, élan, enjoyment, excitement, feeling, force, fun, gratification, gusto, intensity, panache, pep, pizzazz, pleasure, power, punch, pungency, relish, snap, sparkle, stimulation, strength, tang, thrill, verve, vitality, zest, zing, zip.

**kick off** begin, break the ice, commence, get under way, inaugurate, initiate, introduce, open, open the proceedings, set the ball rolling, start.

**kick out** chuck out, defenestrate, discharge, dismiss, eject, evict, expel, get rid of, give the bum's rush, oust, reject, remove, sack, throw out, toss out.

**kick-off** *n* beginning, bully-off, commencement, face-off, inception, introduction, opening, outset, start, word go.

**kid¹** *n* babe, baby, bairn, bambino, boy, child, dandiprat, girl, halfling, infant, juvenile, kiddy, lad, nipper, shaver, stripling, teenager, tot, wean, whippersnapper, youngster, youth.

**kid²** *v* bamboozle, befool, beguile, con, cozen, delude, dupe, fool, gull, have on, hoax, hoodwink, humbug, jest, joke, josh, mock, pretend, pull someone's leg, put one over on, rag, ridicule, tease, trick.

**kidnap** *v* abduct, capture, hijack, rape, remove, seize, skyjack, snatch, steal.

**kidnapped** *adj* abducted, enlevé, hijacked, rapt, seized, stolen.

**kidnapping** *n* abduction, child-stealing, enlevement, kidnap, plagium, rape, seizure.

**kill** *v* abolish, annihilate, assassinate, beguile, bump off, butcher, cancel, cease, deaden, defeat, destroy, dispatch, do away with, do in, do to death, eliminate, eradicate, execute, exterminate, extinguish, extirpate, fill, finish off, halt, kibosh, knock off, knock on the head, liquidate, mar, martyr, massacre, murder, napoo, neutralise, nip in the bud, nullify, obliterate, occupy, pass, pip, put to death, quash, quell, rub out, ruin, scotch, slaughter, slay, smite, smother, spoil, stifle, still, stonker, stop, suppress, top, veto, vitiate, while away, zap.

*n* climax, conclusion, coup de grâce, death, death-blow, dénouement, dispatch, end, finish, mop-up, shoot-out.

**killer** *n* assassin, butcher, cut-throat, destroyer, executioner, exterminator, fratricide, gunman, hatchet man, hit-man, homicide, infanticide, liquidator, matricide, murderer, parricide, patricide, regicide, ripper, shootist, slaughterer, slayer, sororicide, triggerman, uxoricide.

**killing¹** *n* assassination, bloodshed, carnage, elimination, ethnocide, execution, extermination, fatality, fratricide, homicide, infanticide, liquidation, mactation, manslaughter, massacre, matricide, murder, parricide, patricide, pogrom, regicide, slaughter, slaying, sororicide, thuggee, uxoricide.

*adj* deadly, death-dealing, deathly, debilitating, enervating, exhausting, fatal, fatiguing, final, lethal, lethiferous, mortal, mortiferous, murderous, prostrating, punishing, tiring, vital.

**killing²** *n* big hit, bomb, bonanza, bunce, clean-up, coup, fortune, gain, hit, lucky break, profit, success, windfall, winner.

**killing³** *adj* absurd, amusing, comical, funny, hilarious, ludicrous, side-splitting, uproarious.

**killjoy** *n* complainer, cynic, dampener, damper, grouch, misery, moaner, pessimist, prophet of doom, sceptic, spoil-sport, trouble-mirth, Weary Willie, wet blanket, whiner.

*antonyms* enthusiast, optimist, sport.

**kin** *n* affines, affinity, blood, clan, connection, connections, consanguinity, cousins, extraction, family, flesh and blood, kindred, kinsfolk, kinship, kinsmen, kith, lineage, people, relations, relationship, relatives, stock, tribe.

*adj* affine, akin, allied, close, cognate, congener, connected, consanguine, consanguineous, interconnected, kindred, linked, near, related, similar, twin.

**kind¹** *n* brand, breed, category, character, class, description, essence, family, genus, habit, ilk, kidney, manner, mould, nature, persuasion, race, set, sort, species, stamp, style, temperament, type, variety.

**kind²** *adj* accommodating, affectionate, altruistic, amiable, amicable, avuncular, beneficent, benevolent, benign, benignant, bonhomous, boon, bounteous, bountiful, brotherly, charitable, clement, compassionate, congenial, considerate, cordial, courteous, diplomatic, fatherly, friendly, generous, gentle, giving, good, gracious, hospitable, humane, indulgent, kind-hearted, kindly, lenient, loving, mild, motherly, neighbourly, obliging, philanthropic, propitious, sisterly, soft-boiled, soft-hearted, sweet, sympathetic, tactful, tender-hearted, thoughtful, understanding.

*antonyms* cruel, inconsiderate, unhelpful.

**kind-hearted** *adj* altruistic, amicable, benign, big-hearted, compassionate, considerate, generous, good-hearted, good-natured, gracious, helpful, humane, humanitarian, kind, kindly, obliging, philanthropic, sympathetic, tender-hearted, warm, warm-hearted.

*antonym* ill-natured.

**kindle** *v* activate, actuate, agitate, animate, arouse, awaken, deflagrate, enkindle, exasperate, excite, fan, fire, foment, ignite, incite, induce, inflame, initiate, inspire, inspirit, light, provoke, rouse, set alight, sharpen, stimulate, stir, thrill.

**kindliness** *n* amiability, beneficence, benevolence, benignity, charity, compassion, friendliness, generosity, kindness, loving-kindness, sympathy, warmth.

*antonyms* cruelty, meanness, unkindness.

**kindly** *adj* benefic, beneficent, beneficial, benevolent, benign, charitable, comforting, compassionate, cordial, favourable, generous, genial, gentle, giving, good-natured, good-willy, hearty, helpful, indulgent, kind, mild, patient, pleasant, polite, sympathetic, tender, warm.

*adv* agreeably, charitably, comfortingly, considerately, cordially, generously, gently, graciously, indulgently, patiently, politely, tenderly, thoughtfully.

*antonyms* cruel, inconsiderate, uncharitable, unpleasant.

**kindness** *n* affection, aid, aloha, altruism, amiability, assistance, benefaction, beneficence, benevolence, benignity, bonhomie, bounty, charity, chivalry, clemency, compassion, cordiality, courtesy, favour, forbearance, friendliness, gallantry, generosity, gentilesse, gentleness, good will, goodness, grace, help, hospitality, humaneness, humanity, indulgence, kindliness, liberality, loving-kindness, magnanimity, mildness, munificence, obligingness, patience, philanthropy, service, tenderness, tolerance, understanding.

*antonyms* cruelty, illiberality, inhumanity.

**kindred** *n* affines, affinity, clan, connections, consanguinity, family, flesh, folk, kin, kinsfolk, kinship, kinsmen, lineage, people, relations, relationship, relatives.

*adj* affiliated, affine, akin, allied, cognate, common, congenial, connected, corresponding, kin, like, matching, related, similar.

**king** *n* boss, chief, chieftain, doyen, emperor, kingpin, leading light, luminary, majesty, monarch, overlord, paramount, patriarch, potentate, prince, royalet, ruler, sovereign, supremo, suzerain.

**kingdom** *n* area, commonwealth, country, division, domain, dominion, dynasty, empire, field, land, monarchy, nation, palatinate, principality, province, realm, reign, royalty, sovereignty, sphere, state, territory, tract.

**kingly** *adj* august, basilical, glorious, grand, grandiose, imperial, imperious, imposing, lordly, majestic, monarchical, noble, regal, royal, sovereign, splendid, stately, sublime, supreme.

**kink¹** *n* bend, coil, complication, corkscrew, crick, crimp, defect, dent, difficulty, entanglement, flaw, hitch, imperfection, indentation, knot, loop, tangle, twist, wrinkle.

*v* bend, coil, crimp, curl, tangle, twist, wrinkle.

**kink²** *n* caprice, crotchet, eccentricity, fetish, foible, freak, idiosyncracy, idiosyncrasy, oddity, quirk, singularity, vagary, whim.

**kinky¹** *adj* coiled, crimped, crumpled, curled, curly, frizzy, tangled, twisted, wrinkled.

**kinky²** *adj* bizarre, capricious, crotchety, degenerate, depraved, deviant, eccentric, freakish, idiosyncratic, licentious, odd, outlandish, peculiar, perverted, queer, quirky, strange, unconventional, unnatural, warped, weird, whimsical.

**kinsfolk** *n* affines, clan, connections, cousins, family, kin, kindred, kinsmen, relations, relatives.

**kinship** *n* affinity, alliance, association, bearing, community, conformity, connection, consanguinity, correspondence, kin, relation, relationship, similarity.

**kinsman** *n* affine, cousin, relation, relative.

**kiosk** *n* bookstall, booth, box, cabin, counter, hut, news-stand, stall, stand.

**kismet** *n* destiny, doom, fate, fortune, joss, karma, lot, portion, predestiny, providence, weird.

**kiss¹** *v* buss, canoodle, neck, osculate, peck, salute, smooch, snog.

*n* buss, osculation, peck, plonker, salute, smack, smacker, snog.

**kiss²** *v* brush, caress, fan, glance, graze, lick, scrape, touch.

**kit** *n* accoutrements, apparatus, appurtenances, baggage, effects, equipage, equipment, gear, impedimenta, implements, instruments, luggage, matériel, muniments, outfit, paraphernalia, provisions, rig, rig-out, set, supplies, tackle, tools, trappings, traps, utensils.

**kit out** accoutre, arm, deck out, dight, dress, equip, fit out, fix up, furnish, habilitate, outfit, prepare, supply.

**kittenish** *adj* arch, coquettish, coy, cute, flirtatious, frisky, frolicsome, playful, sportive.

*antonym* staid.

**knack** *n* ability, adroitness, aptitude, bent, capacity, dexterity, expertise, expertness, facility, faculty, flair, forte, genius, gift, handiness, hang, ingenuity, propensity, quickness, skilfulness, skill, talent, trick, trick of the trade, turn.

**knapsack** *n* backpack, bag, dufflebag, haversack, musette, pack, rucksack, tuckerbag.

**knave** *n* bastard, blackguard, blighter, bounder, cheat, dastard, drôle, fripon, rapscallion, rascal, reprobate, rogue, rotter, scallywag, scamp, scapegrace, scoundrel, stinker, swindler, swine, varlet, villain.

**knavery** *n* chicanery, corruption, deceit, deception, devilry, dishonesty, double-dealing, duplicity, fraud, friponnerie, hanky-panky, imposture, knavishness, mischief, monkey-business, rascality, roguery, ropery, trickery, villainy.

**knavish** *adj* contemptible, corrupt, damnable, dastardly, deceitful, deceptive, devilish, dishonest, dishonourable, fiendish, fraudulent, furciferous, lying, mischievous, rascally, reprobate, roguish, scoundrelly, unprincipled, unscrupulous, villainous, wicked.

*antonyms* honest, honourable, scrupulous.

**knead** *v* form, knuckle, manipulate, massage, mould, ply, press, rub, shape, squeeze, work.

**kneel** *v* fall to one's knees, genuflect.

**knell** *n* chime, knoll, peel, ringing, sound, tintinnabulation, toll.

**knickers** *n* bloomers, breeks, briefs, Directoire knickers, drawers, knickerbockers, panties, pants, smalls, underwear.

**knick-knack** *n* bagatelle, bauble, bibelot, bric-à-brac, gadget, gaud, gewgaw, gimcrack, gismo, jimjam, kickshaw, object of virtu, plaything, pretty, pretty-pretty, quip, rattle-trap, toy, trifle, trinket, whigmaleerie, whim-wham.

**knife** *n* blade, carver, chakra, chiv, cutter, dagger, dah, flick-knife, jack-knife, machete, parang, pen-knife, pocket-knife, skean, skene, skene-dhu, skene-occle, switchblade, whittle.

*v* cut, impale, lacerate, pierce, rip, slash, stab, wound.

**knight** *n* cavalier, champion, chevalier, free-lance, gallant, horseman, kemper, kempery-man, knight-at-arms, knight-errant, man-at-arms, preux chevalier, ritter, soldier, warrior.

**knightly** *adj* bold, chivalrous, courageous, courtly, dauntless, gallant, gracious, heroic, honourable, intrepid, noble, soldierly, valiant, valorous.

*antonyms* cowardly, ignoble, ungallant.

**knit** *v* ally, bind, connect, crease, crotchet, fasten, furrow, heal, interlace, intertwine, join, knot, link, loop, mend, secure, tie, unite, weave, wrinkle.

**knob** *n* boll, boss, bump, caput, door-handle, knot, knub, knurl, lump, nub, projection, protrusion, protuberance, snib, stud, swell, swelling, tuber, tumour, umbo.

**knock**[1] *v* buffet, clap, cuff, ding, hit, knobble, (k)nubble, punch, rap, slap, smack, smite, strike, thump, thwack.

*n* blow, box, chap, clip, clout, con, cuff, hammering, rap, slap, smack, thump.

**knock about**[1] associate, go around, loaf, ramble, range, roam, rove, saunter, traipse, travel, wander.

**knock about**[2] abuse, bash, batter, beat up, biff, bruise, buffet, damage, hit, hurt, maltreat, manhandle, maul, mistreat.

**knock down** batter, clout, demolish, destroy, fell, floor, level, pound, prop, raze, smash, wallop, wreck.

**knock off**[1] cease, clock off, clock out, complete, conclude, finish, pack (it) in, stop, terminate.

**knock off**[2] deduct, filch, nick, pilfer, pinch, purloin, rob, steal, take away, thieve.

**knock off**[3] assassinate, bump off, do away with, do in, kill, liquidate, murder, rub out, slay, waste.

**knock up** achieve, build, construct, erect, make.

*antonym* demolish.

**knock**[2] *v* abuse, belittle, carp, cavil, censure, condemn, criticise, deprecate, disparage, find fault, lambaste, run down, slam, vilify, vilipend.

*n* blame, censure, condemnation, criticism, defeat, failure, rebuff, rejection, reversal, setback, stricture.

*antonyms* boost, praise.

**knockout** *n* bestseller, coup de grâce, hit, kayo, KO, sensation, smash, smash-hit, stunner, success, triumph, winner.

*antonyms* flop, loser.

**knoll** *n* barrow, hill, hillock, hummock, knowe, koppie, mound.

**knot** *v* bind, entangle, entwine, knit, loop, secure, tangle, tether, tie, weave.

*n* aggregation, bond, bow, braid, bunch, burl, clump, cluster, collection, connection, gnar, gnarl, heap, hitch, joint, knag, knar, knarl, ligature, loop, mass, pile, rosette, tie, tuft.

**knotty** *adj* anfractuous, baffling, bumpy, Byzantine, complex, complicated, difficult, gnarled, hard, intricate, knobby, knotted, mystifying, nodose, nodous, nodular, perplexing, problematical, puzzling, rough, rugged, thorny, tricky, troublesome.

**know** *v* apprehend, comprehend, discern, distinguish, experience, fathom, identify, intuit, ken, learn, make out, notice, perceive, realise, recognise, see, tell, undergo, understand, wist.

**know-all** *n* Besserwisser, clever-clogs, smart Alec, smarty-pants.

**know-how** *n* ability, adroitness, aptitude, capability, dexterity, experience, expertise, faculty, flair, gumption, ingenuity, knack, knowledge, proficiency, savoir-faire, savvy, skill, talent.

**knowing** *adj* acute, astute, aware, clever, competent, conscious, cunning, discerning, downy, eloquent, experienced, expert, expressive, gnostic, gnostical, hep, intelligent, meaningful, perceptive, qualified, sagacious, shrewd, significant, skilful, well-informed.

*antonyms* ignorant, obtuse.

**knowingly** *adv* consciously, deliberately, designedly, intentionally, on purpose, purposely, studiedly, wilfully, wittingly.

**knowledge** *n* ability, acquaintance, acquaintanceship, apprehension, book-learning, booklore, cognisance, cognition, comprehension, consciousness, cum-savvy, discernment, education, enlightenment, erudition, familiarity, gnosis, grasp, information, instruction, intelligence, intimacy, judgement, know-how, learning, multiscience, notice, pansophy, recognition, scholarship, schooling, science, tuition, understanding, wisdom.

*antonym* ignorance.

**knowledgeable** *adj* acquainted, au courant, au fait, aware, book-learned, bright, cognisant, conscious, conversant, educated, erudite, experienced, familiar, in the know, intelligent, learned, lettered, scholarly, well-informed.

*antonym* ignorant.

**known** *adj* acknowledged, admitted, avowed, celebrated, commonplace, confessed, familiar, famous, manifest, noted, obvious, patent, plain, published, recognised, well-known.

**knuckle under** accede, acquiesce, capitulate, defer, give in, give way, submit, succumb, surrender, truckle, yield.

**kowtow** *v* bow, court, cringe, defer, fawn, flatter, genuflect, grovel, kneel, pander, suck up, toady, truckle.

**kudos** *n* acclaim, applause, distinction, esteem, fame, glory, honour, laudation, laurels, plaudits, praise, prestige, regard, renown, repute.

# L

**label** *n* badge, brand, categorisation, characterisation, classification, company, description, docket, epithet, mark, marker, sticker, tag, tally, ticket, trademark.

*v* brand, call, categorise, characterise, class, classify, define, describe, designate, docket, dub, identify, mark, name, stamp, tag.

**laborious** *adj* arduous, assiduous, backbreaking, burdensome, difficult, diligent, fatiguing, forced, hard, hard-working, heavy, herculean, indefatigable, industrious, laboured, onerous, operose, painstaking, persevering, ponderous, sedulous, strained, strenuous, tireless, tiresome, toilsome, tough, unflagging, uphill, wearing, wearisome.

*antonyms* easy, effortless, relaxing, simple.

**labour¹** *n* chore, donkey-work, drudgery, effort, employees, exertion, grind, hands, industry, job, labor improbus, labourers, moil, pains, painstaking, slog, sweat, task, toil, undertaking, work, workers, workforce, workmen.

*antonyms* ease, leisure, relaxation, rest.

*v* drudge, endeavour, grind, heave, moil, pitch, plod, roll, slave, strive, struggle, suffer, sweat, toil, toss, travail, work.

*antonyms* idle, laze, loaf, lounge.

**labour²** *n* birth, childbirth, contractions, delivery, labour pains, pains, parturition, throes, travail.

*v* dwell on, elaborate, overdo, overemphasise, overstress, strain.

**laboured** *adj* affected, awkward, complicated, contrived, difficult, forced, heavy, overdone, overwrought, ponderous, stiff, stilted, strained, studied, unnatural.

*antonyms* easy, natural.

**labourer** *n* drudge, farm-hand, hand, hireling, hobbler, hobo, hodman, hunky, husbandman, land-girl, manual worker, navvy, redneck, worker, working man, workman.

**labyrinth** *n* circumvolution, coil, complexity, complication, convolution, entanglement, Gordian knot, intricacy, jungle, maze, perplexity, puzzle, riddle, tangle, windings.

**labyrinthine** *adj* Byzantine, complex, confused, convoluted, Daedalian, dedalian, faveolate, Gordian, intricate, involved, knotty, mazy, mizmaze, perplexing, puzzling, tangled, tortuous, winding.

*antonyms* simple, straightforward.

**lace¹** *n* crochet, dentelle, filigree, mesh-work, netting, open-work, orris, tatting.

**lace²** *n* babiche, bootlace, cord, lanyard, shoe-lace, string, thong, tie.

*v* attach, bind, close, do up, fasten, intertwine, interweave, interwork, string, thread, tie.

**lace³** *v* add to, fortify, intermix, mix in, spike.

**lacerate** *v* afflict, claw, cut, distress, gash, ga(u)nch, harrow, jag, lancinate, maim, mangle, rend, rip, slash, tear, torment, torture, wound.

**laceration** *n* cut, gash, injury, lancination, maim, mutilation, rent, rip, slash, tear, wound.

**lachrymose** *adj* crying, dolorous, lugubrious, mournful, sad, sobbing, tearful, teary, weeping, weepy, woeful.

*antonyms* happy, laughing.

**lack** *n* absence, dearth, deficiency, deprivation, destitution, emptiness, insufficiency, need, privation, scantiness, scarcity, shortage, shortcoming, shortness, vacancy, void, want.

*antonyms* abundance, profusion.

*v* miss, need, require, want.

**lackadaisical** *adj* abstracted, apathetic, dreamy, dronish, dull, enervated, fainéant, half-hearted, idle, indifferent, indolent, inert, languid, languorous, lazy, lethargic, limp, listless, spiritless, supine.

*antonyms* active, dynamic, energetic, vigorous.

**lackey** *n* attendant, creature, fawner, flatterer, flunky, footman, gofer, hanger-on, instrument, manservant, menial, minion, parasite, pawn, servitor, sycophant, toady, tool, valet, yes-man.

**lacking** *adj* defective, deficient, flawed, impaired, inadequate, minus, missing, needing, sans, short of, wanting, without.

**lacklustre** *adj* boring, dim, drab, dry, dull, flat, leaden, lifeless, lustreless, mundane, muted, prosaic, sombre, spiritless, unimaginative, uninspired, vapid.

*antonyms* brilliant, polished.

**laconic** *adj* brief, close-mouthed, compact, concise, crisp, curt, pithy, sententious, short, succinct, taciturn, terse.

*antonyms* garrulous, verbose, wordy.

**lacuna** *n* blank, break, cavity, gap, hiatus, omission, space, void.

**lad** *n* boy, bucko, callant, chap, fellow, guy, halfling, juvenile, kid, laddie, nipper, schoolboy, shaver, stripling, youngster, youth.

**laden** *adj* burdened, charged, chock-a-block, chock-full, encumbered, fraught, full, hampered, jammed, loaded, oppressed, packed, stuffed, taxed, weighed down, weighted.

*antonym* empty.

**la-di-da** *adj* affected, conceited, foppish, high-falutin(g), mannered, mincing, over-refined, posh, precious, pretentious, put-on, snobbish, snooty, stuck-up, toffee-nosed, too-too.

**ladies' man** Casanova, Don Juan, gigolo, lady-killer, libertine, muff, poodle-faker, womaniser.

**ladle** *v* bail, dip, dish, lade, scoop, shovel, spoon.

**ladle out** disburse, dish out, distribute, dole out, hand out.

**lady** *n* begum, dame, damsel, don(n)a, Frau, gentlewoman, hidalga, madam(e), matron, memsahib, milady, noblewoman, Sen^•ora, signora, woman.

**lady-killer** *n* Casanova, Don Juan, heartbreaker, ladies' man, libertine, Lothario, philanderer, rake, roué, stud, wolf, womaniser.

**ladylike** *adj* courtly, cultured, decorous, elegant, genteel, matronly, modest, polite, proper, queenly, refined, respectable, well-bred.

**lag** *v* dawdle, delay, hang back, idle, linger, loiter, mosey, saunter, shuffle, straggle, tarry, trail.

*antonym* lead.

**laggard** *n* dawdler, idler, lingerer, loafer, loiterer, lounger, saunterer, slowcoach, slowpoke, slug-a-bed, sluggard, snail, straggler.

*antonyms* dynamo, go-getter, livewire.

**lagoon** *n* bayou, bog, fen, haff, lake, marsh, pond, pool, shallows, shoal, swamp.

**laid up** bedridden, disabled, hors de combat, housebound, ill, immobilised, incapacitated, injured, on the sick list, out of action, sick.

**laid-back** *adj* at ease, calm, casual, cool, easy-going, free and easy, passionless, relaxed, unflappable, unhurried, untroubled, unworried.

*antonyms* tense, uptight.

**lair** *n* burrow, den, earth, form, hideout, hole, nest, refuge, retreat, roost, sanctuary, stronghold.

**lake** *n* lagoon, loch, lochan, lough, mere, reservoir, tarn.

**lam** *v* batter, beat, clout, hit, knock, lambaste, leather, pelt, pound, pummel, strike, thrash, thump.

**lambast** *v* beat, berate, bludgeon, castigate, censure, cudgel, drub, flay, flog, leather, rebuke, reprimand, roast, scold, strike, thrash, upbraid, whip.

**lambent** *adj* brilliant, dancing, flickering, fluttering, gleaming, glistening, glowing, incandescent, licking, light, luminous, lustrous, radiant, refulgent, shimmering, sparkling, touching, twinkling.

**lame** *adj* crippled, defective, disabled, disappointing, feeble, flimsy, game, half-baked, halt, handicapped, hobbling, inadequate, insufficient, limping, poor, thin, unconvincing, unsatisfactory, weak.

*v* cripple, damage, disable, hamstring, hobble, hurt, incapacitate, injure, maim, wing.

**lament** *v* bemoan, bewail, beweep, complain, deplore, grieve, keen, mourn, regret, sorrow, wail, weep, yammer.

*antonyms* celebrate, rejoice.

*n* complaint, coronach, dirge, dumka, elegy, jeremiad, keening, lamentation, moan, moaning, monody, plaint, requiem, threnody, ululation, wail, wailing.

**lamentable** *adj* deplorable, disappointing, distressing, funest, grievous, inadequate, insufficient, low, meagre, mean, miserable, mournful, pitiful, poor, regrettable, sorrowful, tragic, unfortunate, unsatisfactory, woeful, wretched.

**lamentation** *n* deploration, dirge, grief, grieving, jeremiad, keen, keening, lament, moan, mourning, plaint, sobbing, sorrow, ululation, wailing, weeping.

*antonyms* celebration, rejoicing.

**laminate** *v* coat, cover, exfoliate, face, flake, foliate, layer, plate, separate, split, stratify, veneer.

**lamp** *n* beacon, flare, floodlight, lampad, lantern, light, limelight, searchlight, torch, veilleuse.

**lampoon** *n* burlesque, caricature, mickey-take, parody, Pasquil, Pasquin, pasquinade, satire, send-up, skit, spoof, squib, take-off.

*v* burlesque, caricature, make fun of, mock, parody, Pasquil, Pasquin, pasquinade, ridicule, satirise, send up, spoof, squib, take off, take the mickey out of.

**lampooner** *n* caricaturist, parodist, pasquilant, pasquiler, pasquinader, satirist.

**land¹** *n* country, countryside, dirt, district, earth, estate, farmland, fatherland, ground, grounds, loam, motherland, nation, property, province, real estate, realty, region, soil, terra firma, territory, tract.

*v* alight, arrive, berth, bring, carry, cause, come to rest, debark, deposit, disembark, dock, drop, end up, plant, touch down, turn up, wind up.

**land²** *v* achieve, acquire, capture, gain, get, net, obtain, secure, win.

**landlord** *n* freeholder, host, hotelier, hotel-keeper, innkeeper, lessor, letter, owner, proprietor, publican.

*antonym* tenant.

**landmark** *n* beacon, boundary, cairn, feature, milestone, monument, signpost, turning-point, watershed.

**lands** *n* acreage, acres, demesne, estate(s), grounds, manor, policies, spread.

**landscape** *n* aspect, countryside, outlook, panorama, prospect, scene, scenery, view, vista.

**landslide** *n* avalanche, earthfall, éboulement, landslip, lauwine, rock-fall.

*adj* decisive, emphatic, overwhelming, runaway.

**lane** *n* alley(way), avenue, boreen, byroad, byway, channel, driveway, footpath, footway, gut, loan, passage(way), path(way), towpath, vennel, way, wynd.

**language** *n* argot, cant, conversation, dialect, diction, discourse, expression, idiolect, idiom, interchange, jargon, langue, lingo, lingua franca, parlance, parole, patois, phraseology, phrasing, speech, style, talk, terminology, tongue, utterance, vernacular, vocabulary, wording.

**languid** *adj* debilitated, drooping, dull, enervated, faint, feeble, heavy, inactive, indifferent, inert, lackadaisical, languorous, lazy, lethargic, limp, listless, pining, sickly, slow, sluggish, spiritless, torpid, unenthusiastic, uninterested, weak, weary.

*antonyms* alert, lively, vivacious.

**languish** *v* brood, decline, desire, despond, droop, fade, fail, faint, flag, grieve, hanker, hunger, long, mope, pine, repine, rot, sicken, sigh, sink, sorrow, suffer, sulk, want, waste, waste away, weaken, wilt, wither, yearn.

*antonym* flourish.

**languishing** *adj* brooding, declining, deteriorating, dreamy, drooping, droopy, fading, failing, flagging, longing, lovelorn, lovesick, melancholic, moping, nostalgic, pensive, pining, sickening, sinking, soulful, sulking, tender, wasting away, weak, weakening, wilting, wistful, withering, woebegone, yearning.

*antonyms* flourishing, thriving.

**languor** *n* apathy, asthenia, calm, debility, dreaminess, drowsiness, enervation, ennui, faintness, fatigue, feebleness, frailty, heaviness, hush, indolence, inertia, lassitude, laziness, lethargy, listlessness, lull, oppressiveness, relaxation, silence, sleepiness, sloth, stillness, torpor, weakness, weariness.

*antonyms* alacrity, gusto.

**lank** *adj* attenuated, drooping, dull, emaciated, flabby, flaccid, gaunt, lanky, lean, lifeless, limp, long, lustreless, rawboned, scraggy, scrawny, skinny, slender, slim, spare, straggling, thin.

*antonym* burly.

**lanky** *adj* angular, bony, gangling, gangly, gaunt, loose-jointed, rangy, rawboned, scraggy, scrawny, spare, tall, thin, twiggy, weedy.

*antonyms* short, squat.

**lap**[1] *v* drink, lick, sip, sup, tongue.

**lap**[2] *v* gurgle, plash, purl, ripple, slap, slosh, splash, swish, wash.

**lap**[3] *n* ambit, circle, circuit, course, distance, loop, orbit, round, tour.

*v* cover, encase, enfold, envelop, fold, surround, swaddle, swathe, turn, twist, wrap.

**lapse** *n* aberration, backsliding, break, caducity, decline, descent, deterioration, drop, error, failing, fall, fault, gap, indiscretion, intermission, interruption, interval, lull, mistake, negligence, omission, oversight, passage, pause, relapse, slip.

*v* backslide, decline, degenerate, deteriorate, drop, end, expire, fail, fall, run out, sink, slide, slip, stop, terminate, worsen.

**lapsed** *adj* discontinued, ended, expired, finished, invalid, obsolete, out of date, outdated, outworn, run out, unrenewed.

**larceny** *n* burglary, expropriation, heist, misappropriation, pilfering, piracy, purloining, robbery, stealing, theft.

**large** *adj* abundant, ample, big, broad, bulky, capacious, colossal, comprehensive, considerable, copious, decuman, enormous, extensive, full, generous, giant, gigantic, goodly, grand, grandiose, great, huge, immense, jumbo, king-sized, liberal, mammoth, man-sized, massive, monumental, outsize, Patagonian, plentiful, plonking, roomy, sizeable, spacious, spanking, substantial, sweeping, swingeing, tidy, vast, wide.

*antonyms* diminutive, little, slight, small, tiny.

**largely** *adv* abundantly, by and large, chiefly, considerably, extensively, generally, greatly, highly, mainly, mostly, predominantly, primarily, principally, widely.

**largeness** *n* bigness, breadth, broadness, bulk, bulkiness, dimension, enormity, enormousness, expanse, extent, greatness, heaviness, heftiness, height, immensity, magnitude, mass, massiveness, measure, mightiness, obesity, prodigiousness, size, vastness, wideness, width.

*antonym* smallness.

**large-scale** *adj* broad, country-wide, epic, expansive, extensive, far-reaching, global, nation-wide, sweeping, vast, wholesale, wide, wide-ranging.

*antonym* minor.

**largess(e)** *n* aid, allowance, alms, benefaction, bequest, bounty, charity, donation, endowment, generosity, gift, grant, handout, liberality, munificence, open-handedness, philanthropy, present.

*antonym* meanness.

**lark** *n* antic, caper, escapade, fling, fredaine, frolic, fun, gambol, game, gammock, guy, jape, mischief, prank, revel, rollick, romp, skylark, spree.

*v* caper, cavort, frolic, gambol, gammock, play, rollick, romp, skylark, sport.

**lascivious** *adj* bawdy, blue, coarse, crude, dirty, horny, indecent, lecherous, lewd, libidinous, licentious, lustful, obscene, offensive, Paphian, pornographic, prurient, randy, ribald, salacious, scurrilous, sensual, smutty, suggestive, tentiginous, unchaste, voluptuous, vulgar, wanton.

**lash**[1] *n* blow, cat, cat-o'-nine-tails, hit, quirt, stripe, stroke, swipe, whip.

*v* attack, beat, belabour, berate, birch, buffet, castigate, censure, chastise, criticise, dash, drum, flagellate, flay, flog, hammer, hit, horsewhip, knock, lace, lam, lambast, lampoon, larrup, pound, ridicule, satirise, scold, scourge, smack, strike, tear into, thrash, upbraid, welt, whip.

**lash**[2] *v* affix, bind, fasten, join, make fast, rope, secure, strap, tether, tie.

**lass** *n* bird, chick, colleen, damsel, girl, lassie, maid, maiden, miss, quean, quine, schoolgirl.

**lassitude** *n* apathy, drowsiness, dullness, enervation, ennui, exhaustion, fatigue, heaviness, languor, lethargy, listlessness, oscitancy, prostration, sluggishness, tiredness, torpor, weariness.

*antonyms* energy, vigour.

**last**[1] *adj* aftermost, closing, concluding, conclusive, definitive, extreme, final, furthest, hindmost, latest, rearmost, remotest, terminal, ultimate, utmost.

*antonyms* first, initial.

*adv* after, behind, finally, ultimately.

*antonyms* first, firstly.

*n* close, completion, conclusion, curtain, end, ending, finale, finish, termination.

*antonyms* beginning, start.

**last word**[1] final decision, final say, ultimatum.

**last word**[2] best, cream, crème de la crème, dernier cri, latest, ne plus ultra, perfection, pick, quintessence, rage, ultimate, vogue.

**last**[2] *v* abide, carry on, continue, endure, hold on, hold out, keep (on), perdure, persist, remain, stand up, stay, survive, wear.

**last-ditch** *adj* all-out, desperate, eleventh-hour, final, frantic, heroic, last-gasp, straining, struggling.

**lasting** *adj* abiding, continuing, deep-rooted, durable, enduring, immutable, indelible, indestructible, lifelong, long-standing, long-term, perennial, permanent, perpetual, sempiternal, unceasing, unchanging, undying, unending.

*antonyms* ephemeral, fleeting, short-lived.

**lastly** *adv* finally, in conclusion, in fine, in the end, to sum up, ultimately.

*antonym* firstly.

**latch** *n* bar, bolt, catch, fastening, hasp, hook, lock, sneck.

**latch on to** apprehend, attach oneself to, comprehend, twig, understand.

**late**[1] *adj* behind, behind-hand, belated, delayed, dilatory, last-minute, overdue, slow, tardy, unpunctual.

*antonyms* early, punctual.

*adv* behind-hand, belatedly, dilatorily, formerly, recently, slowly, tardily, unpunctually.

*antonyms* early, punctually.

**late**[2] *adj* dead, deceased, defunct, departed, ex-, former, old, past, preceding, previous.

**lately** *adv* formerly, heretofore, latterly, recently.

**lateness** *n* belatedness, delay, dilatoriness, retardation, tardiness, unpunctuality.

*antonym* earliness.

**latent** *adj* concealed, delitescent, dormant, hidden, inherent, invisible, lurking, potential, quiescent, secret, underlying, undeveloped, unexpressed, unrealised, unseen, veiled.

*antonyms* active, live, patent.

**later** *adv* after, afterwards, next, sequentially, subsequently, successively, thereafter.

*antonym* earlier.

**lateral** *adj* edgeways, flanking, marginal, oblique, side, sideward, sideways.

*antonym* central.

**latest** *adj* current, fashionable, in, modern, newest, now, ultimate, up-to-date, up-to-the-minute, with it.

*antonym* earliest.

**lather**[1] *n* bubbles, foam, froth, shampoo, soap, soap-suds, suds.

*v* foam, froth, shampoo, soap, whip up.

**lather**[2] *n* agitation, dither, fever, flap, fluster, flutter, fuss, pother, state, stew, sweat, tizzy, twitter.

**lather**[3] *v* beat, cane, drub, flog, lambast, lash, leather, strike, thrash, whip.

**latitude** *n* breadth, clearance, compass, elbow-room, extent, field, freedom, indulgence, laxity, leeway, liberty, licence, play, range, reach, room, scope, space, span, spread, sweep, width.

**latrine** *n* bog, head, jakes, outhouse, privy, rear, toilet.

**latter** *adj* closing, concluding, ensuing, last, last-mentioned, later, latest, modern, recent, second, succeeding, successive.

*antonym* former.

**latterly** *adv* hitherto, lately, of late, recently.

*antonym* formerly.

**lattice** *n* espalier, fret-work, grate, grating, grid, grille, lattice-work, mesh, network, open-work, reticulation, tracery, trellis, web.

**laud** *v* acclaim, applaud, approve, celebrate, extol, glorify, hail, honour, magnify, praise.

*antonyms* blame, condemn, curse, damn.

**laudable** *adj* admirable, commendable, creditable, estimable, excellent, exemplary, meritorious, of note, praiseworthy, sterling, worthy.

*antonyms* damnable, execrable.

**laudation** *n* acclaim, acclamation, accolade, adulation, blessing, celebrity, commendation, devotion, encomion, encomium, eulogy, extolment, glorification, glory, homage, kudos, paean, panegyric, praise, reverence, tribute, veneration.

*antonyms* condemnation, criticism.

**laudatory** *adj* acclamatory, adulatory, approbatory, approving, celebratory, commendatory, complimentary, encomiastic(al), epaenetic, eulogistic, glorifying, panegyrical.

*antonym* damning.

**laugh** *v* cachinnate, chortle, chuckle, crease up, fall about, giggle, guffaw, snicker, snigger, split one's sides, te(e)hee, titter, yok.

*antonym* cry.

*n* belly-laugh, card, case, caution, chortle, chuckle, clown, comedian, comic, cure, entertainer, giggle, guffaw, hoot, humorist, joke, lark, scream, snicker, snigger, te(e)hee, titter, wag, wit, yok.

**laugh at** belittle, deride, jeer, lampoon, make fun of, mock, ridicule, scoff at, scorn, take the mickey out of, taunt.

**laugh off** belittle, brush aside, dismiss, disregard, ignore, make little of, minimise, pooh-pooh, shrug off.

**laughable** *adj* absurd, amusing, comical, derisive, derisory, diverting, droll, farcical, funny, gelastic, hilarious, humorous, laughworthy, ludicrous, mirthful, mockable, nonsensical, preposterous, ridiculous, risible.

*antonyms* impressive, serious, solemn.

**laughing** *adj* cackling, cheerful, cheery, chortling, chuckling, giggling, gleeful, guffawing, happy, jocund, jolly, jovial, merry, mirthful, riant, rident, snickering, sniggering, tittering.

**laughing-stock** *n* Aunt Sally, butt, derision, fair game, figure of fun, pointing-stock, target, victim.

**laughter** *n* amusement, asbestos gelos, cachinnation, chortling, chuckling, convulsions, fou rire, giggling, glee, guffawing, hilarity, Homeric laughter, horselaugh, laughing, merriment, mirth, tittering.

**launch** *v* begin, cast, commence, discharge, dispatch, embark on, establish, fire, float, found, inaugurate, initiate, instigate, introduce, open, project, propel, send off, set in motion, start, throw.

**lavatory** *n* bathroom, bog, can, cloakroom, cludge, cludgie, comfort station, convenience, dike, draught-house, dunnakin, dunny, dyke, earth-closet, garderobe, Gents, George, head(s), jakes, john, Ladies, latrine, lav, loo, office, powder-room, privy, public convenience, smallest room, toilet, urinal, washroom, water-closet, WC.

**lavish** *adj* abundant, bountiful, copious, effusive, exaggerated, excessive, extravagant, exuberant, free, generous, gorgeous, immoderate, improvident, intemperate, liberal, lush, luxuriant, munificent, open-handed, opulent, plentiful, princely, prodigal, profuse, prolific, sumptuous, thriftless, unlimited, unreasonable, unrestrained, unstinting, wasteful, wild.

*antonyms* economical, frugal, parsimonious, scanty, sparing, thrifty.

*v* bestow, deluge, dissipate, expend, heap, pour, shower, spend, squander, waste.

**law** *n* act, axiom, brocard, canon, charter, code, command, commandment, constitution, consuetudinary, covenant, criterion, decree, dharma, edict, enactment, formula, institute, jurisprudence, order, ordinance, precept, principle, regulation, rule, standard, statute.

*antonym* chance.

**law-abiding** *adj* compliant, decent, dutiful, good, honest, honourable, lawful, obedient, orderly, peaceable, peaceful, upright.

*antonym* lawless.

**law-breaker** *n* convict, criminal, crook, culprit, delinquent, felon, infractor, miscreant, offender, outlaw, sinner, transgressor, trespasser, wrong-doer.

**lawful** *adj* allowable, authorised, constitutional, hal(l)al, kosher, legal, legalised, legitimate, licit, permissible, proper, rightful, valid, warranted.

*antonyms* illegal, illicit, lawless, unlawful.

**lawless** *adj* anarchic(al), chaotic, disorderly, felonious, insubordinate, insurgent, mutinous, rebellious, reckless, riotous, ruleless, seditious, unbridled, ungoverned, unrestrained, unruly, wild.

*antonym* lawful.

**lawlessness** *n* anarchy, chaos, disorder, insurgency, mobocracy, mob-rule, ochlocracy, piracy, racketeering, rent-a-mob.

*antonym* order.

**lawsuit** *n* action, argument, case, cause, contest, dispute, litigation, proceedings, process, prosecution, suit, trial.

**lawyer** *n* advocate, attorney, barrister, counsel, counsellor, green-bag, jurisconsult, law-agent, lawmonger, legist, solicitor.

**lax** *adj* broad, careless, casual, derelict, easy-going, flabby, flaccid, general, imprecise, inaccurate, indefinite, inexact, lenient, loose, neglectful, negligent, overindulgent, remiss, shapeless, slack, slipshod, soft, vague, wide, wide-open, yielding.

*antonyms* rigid, strict, stringent.

**laxative** *n* aperient, cathartic, eccoprotic, loosener, purgative, purge, salts.

*adj* aperient, cathartic, eccoprotic, lenitive, purgative.

**laxness** *n* carelessness, freedom, heedlessness, imprecision, indifference, indulgence, laissez-faire, latitude, latitudinarianism, laxism, laxity, leniency, looseness, neglect, negligence, nonchalance, permissiveness, slackness, sloppiness, slovenliness, softness, tolerance.

*antonyms* severity, strictness.

**lay**[1] *v* advance, allay, alleviate, allocate, allot, appease, apply, arrange, ascribe, assess, assign, assuage, attribute, bet, burden, calm, charge, concoct, contrive, deposit, design, devise, dispose, encumber, establish, gamble, hatch, hazard, impose, impute, leave, locate, lodge, offer, organise, place, plan, plant, plot, posit, position, prepare, present, put, quiet, relieve, risk, saddle, set, set down, set out, settle, soothe, spread, stake, still, submit, suppress, tax, wager, work out.

**lay aside** abandon, cast aside, discard, dismiss, pigeon-hole, postpone, put aside, put off, reject, shelve, store.

**lay bare** disclose, divulge, exhibit, exhume, explain, expose, reveal, show, uncover, unveil.

**lay down** affirm, assert, assume, couch, discard, drop, establish, formulate, give, give up, ordain, postulate, prescribe, relinquish, state, stipulate, surrender, yield.

**lay down the law** crack down, dictate, dogmatise, emphasise, pontificate, read the riot act, rule the roost.

**lay hands on** acquire, assault, attack, beat up, bless, clasp, clutch, confirm, consecrate, discover, find, get, get hold of, grab, grasp, grip, lay hold of, lay into, ordain, seize, set on, unearth.

**lay in** accumulate, amass, build up, collect, gather, glean, hoard, stock up, stockpile, store (up).

**lay into** assail, attack, belabour, berate, chastise, lambast, let fly at, pitch into, set about, slam, tear into, turn on.

**lay it on** butter up, exaggerate, flatter, overdo it, overpraise, soft-soap, sweet-talk.

**lay off** axe, cease, desist, discharge, dismiss, drop, give it a rest, give over, give up, leave alone, leave off, let go, let up, make redundant, oust, pay off, quit, stop, withhold.

**lay on** contribute, furnish, give, provide, set up, supply.

**lay out** arrange, demolish, design, disburse, display, exhibit, expend, fell, flatten, fork out, give, invest, knock out, pay, plan, set out, shell out, spend, spread out.

**lay up** accumulate, amass, garner, hive, hoard, hospitalise, incapacitate, keep, preserve, put away, salt away, save, squirrel away, store up, treasure.

**lay waste** depredate, desolate, despoil, destroy, devastate, pillage, rape, ravage, raze, ruin, sack, spoil, vandalise.

**lay²** *adj* amateur, inexpert, laic, laical, non-professional, non-specialist, secular.

**lay³** *n* ballad, canzone(t), lyric, madrigal, ode, poem, roundelay, song.

**layabout** *n* beachcomber, good-for-nothing, idler, laggard, loafer, lounger, ne'er-do-well, shirker, skiver, slug-a-bed, waster.

**layer** *n* bed, blanket, coat, coating, cover, covering, film, folium, lame, lamella, lamina, mantle, plate, ply, row, seam, sheet, stratum, table, thickness, tier, touch.

**layman** *n* amateur, layperson, outsider, parishioner.

**lay-off** *n* discharge, dismissal, redundancy, unemployment.

**layout** *n* arrangement, blueprint, design, draft, formation, geography, map, outline, plan, sketch.

**laze** *v* idle, lie around, loaf, loll, lounge, sit around.

**laziness** *n* dilatoriness, faineance, fainéancy, idleness, inactivity, indolence, otiosity, pococurant(e)ism, slackness, sloth, slothfulness, slowness, sluggishness, tardiness.
*antonym* industriousness.

**lazy** *adj* dormant, drowsy, idle, inactive, indolent, inert, languid, languorous, lethargic, otiose, remiss, shiftless, slack, sleepy, slobby, slothful, slow, slow-moving, sluggish, somnolent, torpid, work-shy.
*antonyms* active, diligent, energetic, industrious.

**lazy-bones** *n* hallion, idler, laggard, loafer, lounger, shirker, skiver, sleepy-head, slouch, slug-a-bed, sluggard.

**leach** *v* drain, extract, filter, filtrate, lixiviate, osmose, percolate, seep, strain.

**lead** *v* antecede, cause, command, conduct, direct, dispose, draw, escort, exceed, excel, experience, govern, guide, have, head, incline, induce, influence, live, manage, outdo, outstrip, pass, persuade, pilot, precede, preside over, prevail, prompt, spend, steer, supervise, surpass, transcend, undergo, usher.
*antonym* follow.

*n* advance, advantage, clue, direction, edge, example, first place, guidance, guide, hint, indication, leadership, margin, model, precedence, primacy, principal, priority,

protagonist, starring role, start, suggestion, supremacy, tip, title role, trace, van, vanguard.
*adj* chief, first, foremost, head, leading, main, premier, primary, prime, principal, star.

**lead off** begin, commence, get going, inaugurate, initiate, kick off, open, start, start off, start out, start the ball rolling.

**lead on** beguile, deceive, draw on, entice, hoax, inveigle, lure, persuade, seduce, string along, tempt, trick.

**lead to** bring about, bring on, cause, conduce, contribute to, produce, result in, tend towards.

**lead up to** approach, intimate, introduce, make advances, make overtures, overture, pave the way, prepare (the way) for.

**leaden** *adj* ashen, burdensome, crushing, cumbersome, dingy, dismal, dreary, dull, gloomy, grey, greyish, heavy, humdrum, inert, laboured, lacklustre, languid, lead, lifeless, listless, lowering, lustreless, onerous, oppressive, overcast, plodding, sluggish, sombre, spiritless, stiff, stilted, wooden.

**leader** *n* bell-wether, boss, captain, chief, chieftain, commander, conductor, coryphaeus, counsellor, director, doyen, figurehead, flagship, guide, head, mahatma, principal, ringleader, ruler, skipper, superior, supremo.
*antonym* follower.

**leadership** *n* administration, authority, command, control, direction, directorship, domination, guidance, hegemony, influence, initiative, management, pre-eminence, premiership, running, superintendency, supremacy, sway.

**leading** *adj* chief, dominant, first, foremost, governing, greatest, highest, main, number one, outstanding, paramount, pre-eminent, primary, principal, ruling, superior, supreme.
*antonym* subordinate.

**leaf** *n* blade, bract, calyx, cotyledon, flag, folio, foliole, frond, needle, pad, page, sepal, sheet.
*v* browse, flip, glance, riffle, skim, thumb (through).

**leaflet** *n* advert, bill, booklet, brochure, circular, handbill, handout, pamphlet.

**leafy** *adj* bosky, dasyphyllous, foliose, frondescent, frondose, green, leafed, leaved, shaded, shady, verdant, wooded, woody.

**league** *n* alliance, association, band, Bund, cartel, category, class, coalition, combination, combine, compact, confederacy, confederation, consortium, federation, fellowship, fraternity, group, guild, level, partnership, sorority, syndicate, union.
*v* ally, amalgamate, associate, band, collaborate, combine, confederate, consort, join forces, unite.

**leak** *n* aperture, chink, crack, crevice, disclosure, divulgence, drip, fissure, hole, leakage, leaking, oozing, opening, percolation, perforation, puncture, seepage.
*v* discharge, disclose, divulge, drip, escape, exude, give away, let slip, let the cat out of the bag, make known, make public, make water,

ooze, pass, pass on, percolate, reveal, seep, spill, spill the beans, tell, trickle, weep.

**leaky** *adj* cracked, holey, leaking, perforated, permeable, porous, punctured, split, waterlogged.

**lean¹** *v* bend, confide, count on, depend, favour, incline, list, prefer, prop, recline, rely, repose, rest, slant, slope, tend, tilt, tip, trust.

**lean²** *adj* angular, bare, barren, bony, emaciated, gaunt, inadequate, infertile, lank, meagre, pitiful, poor, rangy, scanty, scragged, scraggy, scrawny, skinny, slender, slim, slink(y), spare, sparse, thin, unfruitful, unproductive, wiry.

*antonyms* fat, fleshy.

**lean on** force, persuade, pressurise, put pressure on.

**leaning** *n* aptitude, bent, bias, disposition, inclination, liking, partiality, penchant, predilection, proclivity, proneness, propensity, susceptibility, taste, tendency, velleity.

**leap** *v* advance, bounce, bound, caper, capriole, cavort, clear, curvet, escalate, frisk, gambol, hasten, hop, hurry, increase, jump, jump (over), reach, rocket, rush, salto, skip, soar, spring, surge, vault.

*antonyms* drop, fall, sink.

*n* bound, caper, capriole, curvet, escalation, frisk, hop, increase, jump, rise, sally, salto, skip, spring, surge, upsurge, upswing, vault, volt(e).

**learn** *v* acquire, ascertain, assimilate, attain, cognise, con, detect, determine, discern, discover, find out, gather, get off pat, grasp, hear, imbibe, learn by heart, master, memorise, pick up, see, understand.

**learned** *adj* academic, adept, blue, cultured, erudite, experienced, expert, highbrow, intellectual, lettered, literate, proficient, sage, scholarly, skilled, versed, well-informed, well-read, wise.

*antonyms* ignorant, illiterate, uneducated.

**learner** *n* abecedarian, alphabetarian, apprentice, beginner, catechumen, cheechako, disciple, neophyte, novice, pupil, scholar, student, tenderfoot, trainee, tyro.

**learning** *n* acquirements, attainments, culture, edification, education, enlightenment, erudition, information, knowledge, letters, literature, lore, research, scholarship, schoolcraft, schooling, study, tuition, wisdom.

**lease** *v* charter, farm out, hire, let, loan, rent, sublet.

**leash** *n* check, control, curb, discipline, hold, lead, lyam, rein, restraint, tether.

**least** *adj* fewest, last, lowest, meanest, merest, minimum, minutest, poorest, slightest, smallest, tiniest.

*antonym* most.

**leathery** *adj* coriaceous, corious, durable, hard, hardened, leathern, rough, rugged, tough, wrinkled.

**leave¹** *v* abandon, allot, assign, bequeath, cause, cease, cede, commit, consign, decamp, depart, deposit, desert, desist, disappear, do a bunk, drop, entrust, exit, flit, forget, forsake, generate, give over, give up, go, go away, hand down, leave behind, levant, move, produce, pull out, quit, refer, refrain, relinquish, renounce, retire, set out, stop, surrender, take off, transmit, will, withdraw.

*antonym* arrive.

**leave off** abstain, break off, cease, desist, discontinue, end, give over, halt, knock off, lay off, quit, refrain, stop, terminate.

**leave out** bar, cast aside, count out, cut (out), disregard, eliminate, except, exclude, ignore, neglect, omit, overlook, pass over, reject.

**leave²** *n* allowance, authorisation, concession, consent, dispensation, exeat, freedom, furlough, holiday, indulgence, liberty, permission, sabbatical, sanction, time off, vacation.

*antonyms* refusal, rejection.

**leaven** *v* elevate, expand, ferment, imbue, inspire, lighten, permeate, pervade, quicken, raise, stimulate, suffuse, work.

**leavings** *n* bits, detritus, dregs, dross, fragments, left-overs, orts, pieces, refuse, remains, remnants, residue, scraps, spoil, sweepings, waste.

**lecher** *n* adulterer, Casanova, debauchee, Don Juan, fornicator, goat, letch, lewdsby, lewdster, libertine, libidinist, profligate, rake, roué, satyr, seducer, sensualist, wanton, whoremonger, wolf, womaniser.

**lecherous** *adj* carnal, concupiscent, goatish, lascivious, lewd, libidinous, licentious, lickerish, liquorish, lubricous, lustful, prurient, randy, raunchy, salacious, unchaste, wanton, womanising.

**lechery** *n* carnality, concupiscence, debauchery, goatishness, lasciviousness, lecherousness, leching, lewdness, libertinism, libidinousness, licentiousness, lubricity, lust, lustfulness, profligacy, prurience, rakishness, randiness, raunchiness, salaciousness, sensuality, wantonness, womanising.

**lecture** *n* address, castigation, censure, chiding, discourse, disquisition, dressing-down, going-over, harangue, instruction, lesson, prelection, rebuke, reprimand, reproof, scolding, speech, talk, talking-to, telling-off, wigging.

*v* address, admonish, berate, carpet, castigate, censure, chide, discourse, expound, harangue, hold forth, jawbone, lucubrate, prelect, rate, reprimand, reprove, scold, speak, talk, teach, tell off.

**lecturer** *n* declaimer, expounder, haranguer, lector, orator, pedagogue, preacher, prelector, sermoniser, speaker, speechifier, speech-maker, talker, teacher, tutor.

**ledge** *n* berm, mantle, projection, ridge, shelf, shelve, sill, step.

**leech** *n* bloodsucker, freeloader, hanger-on, parasite, sponger, sycophant, usurer.

**leer** *v* eye, fleer, gloat, goggle, grin, ogle, smirk, squint, stare, wink.

*n* grin, ogle, smirk, squint, stare, wink.

**leery** *adj* careful, cautious, chary, distrustful, doubting, dubious, guarded, sceptical, shy, suspicious, uncertain, unsure, wary.

**lees** *n* deposit, draff, dregs, grounds, precipitate, refuse, residue, sediment, settlings.

**leeway** *n* elbow-room, latitude, play, room, scope, space.

**left** *adj* communist, left-hand, leftist, left-wing, liberal, port, progressive, radical, red, sinistral, socialist.
*antonym* right.

**left-handed** *adj* ambiguous, awkward, dubious, equivocal, gauche, sinistral, southpaw, unlucky.
*antonym* right-handed.

**left-overs** *n* dregs, fag-end, leavings, oddments, odds and ends, orts, refuse, remainder, remains, remnants, residue, scraps, surplus, sweepings.

**leg** *n* brace, gam, lap, limb, member, part, pin, portion, prop, section, segment, shank, stage, stretch, stump, support, upright.

**legacy** *n* bequest, birthright, devise, endowment, estate, gift, heirloom, hereditament, heritage, heritance, inheritance, patrimony.

**legal** *adj* above-board, allowable, allowed, authorised, constitutional, forensic, judicial, juridical, lawful, legalised, legitimate, licit, permissible, proper, rightful, sanctioned, valid, warrantable.
*antonym* illegal.

**legalise** *v* allow, approve, authorise, decriminalise, legitimate, legitimise, license, permit, sanction, validate, warrant.

**legality** *n* admissibleness, constitutionality, lawfulness, legitimacy, permissibility, rightfulness, validity.
*antonym* illegality.

**legate** *n* ambassador, delegate, depute, deputy, emissary, envoy, exarch, messenger, nuncio.

**legatee** *n* beneficiary, co-heir(ess), devisee, heir, inheritor, inheritrix, recipient.

**legation** *n* commission, consulate, delegation, deputation, embassy, ministry, mission, representation.

**legend** *n* caption, celebrity, cipher, code, device, fable, fiction, folk-tale, household name, inscription, key, luminary, marvel, motto, myth, narrative, phenomenon, prodigy, saga, spectacle, story, tale, tradition, wonder.

**legendary** *adj* apocryphal, celebrated, fabled, fabulous, famed, famous, fanciful, fictional, fictitious, illustrious, immortal, mythical, renowned, romantic, storied, story-book, traditional, unhistoric(al), well-known.

**legerdemain** *n* artfulness, artifice, chicanery, contrivance, craftiness, cunning, deception, feint, hocus-pocus, manipulation, manoeuvring, prestidigitation, sleight of hand, subterfuge, thaumaturgics, trickery.

**legible** *adj* clear, decipherable, discernible, distinct, intelligible, neat, readable.
*antonym* illegible.

**legion** *n* army, battalion, brigade, cohort, company, division, drove, force, horde, host, mass, multitude, myriad, number, regiment, swarm, throng, troop.
*adj* countless, illimitable, innumerable, multitudinous, myriad, numberless, numerous.

**legislate** *v* authorise, codify, constitute, constitutionalise, enact, establish, ordain, prescribe.

**legislation** *n* act, authorisation, bill, charter, codification, constitutionalisation, enactment, law, law-making, measure, prescription, regulation, ruling, statute.

**legislative** *adj* congressional, judicial, juridical, jurisdictional, jurisdictive, law-giving, law-making, ordaining, parliamentary, senatorial.

**legislator** *n* law-giver, law-maker, nomothete, parliamentarian.

**legislature** *n* assembly, chamber, congress, diet, governing body, house, parliament, senate.

**legitimate** *adj* acknowledged, admissible, authentic, authorised, correct, genuine, just, justifiable, kosher, lawful, legal, legit, licit, logical, proper, real, reasonable, rightful, sanctioned, sensible, statutory, true, true-born, valid, warranted, well-founded.
*antonym* illegitimate.
*v* authorise, charter, entitle, legalise, legitimise, license, permit, sanction.

**legitimise** *v* authorise, charter, entitle, legalise, legitimate, license, permit, sanction.

**leisure** *n* breather, ease, freedom, holiday, let-up, liberty, opportunity, pause, quiet, recreation, relaxation, respite, rest, retirement, spare time, time off, vacation.
*antonyms* toil, work.

**leisurely** *adj* carefree, comfortable, deliberate, easy, gentle, indolent, laid-back, lazy, lingering, loose, relaxed, restful, slow, tranquil, unhasty, unhurried.
*antonyms* hectic, hurried, rushed.

**lend** *v* add, advance, afford, bestow, confer, contribute, furnish, give, grant, impart, lease, loan, present, provide, supply.
*antonym* borrow.

**lend a hand** aid, assist, do one's bit, give a helping hand, help, help out, pitch in.

**lend an ear** give ear, hearken, heed, listen, pay attention, take notice.

**length** *n* distance, duration, elongation, extensiveness, extent, lengthiness, longitude, measure, operoseness, operosity, period, piece, portion, prolixity, protractedness, reach, section, segment, space, span, stretch, tediousness, term.

**lengthen** *v* continue, draw out, eke, eke out, elongate, expand, extend, increase, pad out, prolong, prolongate, protract, spin out, stretch.
*antonym* shorten.

**lengthwise** *adv* endlong, endways, endwise, horizontally, lengthways, longitudinally, vertically.

**lengthy** *adj* diffuse, drawn-out, extended, interminable, lengthened, long, long-drawn-out, long-winded, loquacious, marathon, overlong, prolix, prolonged, protracted, rambling, tedious, verbose, voluble.

*antonym* short.

**leniency** *n* clemency, compassion, forbearance, gentleness, indulgence, lenience, lenity, mercy, mildness, moderation, permissiveness, soft-heartedness, softness, tenderness, tolerance.

*antonym* severity.

**lenient** *adj* clement, compassionate, easy-going, forbearing, forgiving, gentle, indulgent, kind, merciful, mild, soft, soft-hearted, sparing, tender, tolerant.

*antonym* severe.

**lenitive** *adj* alleviating, alleviative, assuaging, calmative, calming, easing, mitigating, mitigative, mollifying, palliative, relieving, soothing.

*antonym* irritant.

**lens** *n* eye, eyeglass, eye-piece, glass, loupe, magnifying-glass, monocle, ocular.

**leper** *n* lazar, outcast, pariah, undesirable, untouchable.

**lesbian** *n* butch, dike, gay, homophile, homosexual, les, lez(z), lezzy, sapphist, tribade.

*adj* butch, dikey, gay, homosexual, lesbic, sapphic, tribadic.

**lesion** *n* abrasion, bruise, contusion, cut, gash, hurt, impairment, injury, scrape, scratch, sore, trauma, wound.

**lessen** *v* abate, abridge, bate, contract, curtail, deaden, decrease, de-escalate, degrade, die down, diminish, dwindle, ease, erode, fail, flag, impair, lighten, lower, minimise, moderate, narrow, reduce, shrink, slack, slow down, weaken.

*antonym* increase.

**lessening** *n* abatement, bating, contraction, curtailment, deadening, decline, decrease, de-escalation, diminution, dwindling, ebbing, erosion, failure, flagging, let-up, minimisation, moderation, petering out, reduction, shrinkage, slackening, waning, weakening.

*antonym* increase.

**lesser** *adj* inferior, lower, minor, secondary, slighter, smaller, subordinate.

*antonym* greater.

**lesson** *n* admonition, assignment, censure, chiding, class, coaching, deterrent, drill, example, exemplar, exercise, homework, instruction, lection, lecture, message, model, moral, pericope, period, practice, precept, punishment, reading, rebuke, recitation, reprimand, reproof, schooling, scolding, task, teaching, tutorial, tutoring, warning.

**let**[1] *v* agree to, allow, authorise, cause, charter, consent to, empower, enable, entitle, give leave, give permission, give the go-ahead, give the green light, grant, hire, lease, make, OK, permit, rent, sanction, tolerate.

*antonym* forbid.

**let down** abandon, betray, desert, disappoint, disenchant, disillusion, dissatisfy, fail, fall short.

*antonym* satisfy.

**let go** free, liberate, manumit, release, set free, unhand.

*antonyms* catch, imprison.

**let in** accept, admit, include, incorporate, receive, take in, welcome.

*antonym* bar.

**let off** absolve, acquit, detonate, discharge, dispense, emit, excuse, exempt, exonerate, explode, exude, fire, forgive, give off, ignore, leak, pardon, release, spare.

*antonym* punish.

**let on** act, admit, counterfeit, disclose, dissemble, dissimulate, divulge, feign, give away, leak, let out, make believe, make known, make out, pretend, profess, reveal, say, simulate.

*antonym* keep mum.

**let out** betray, discharge, disclose, emit, free, give, give vent to, leak, let fall, let go, let slip, liberate, make known, produce, release, reveal, utter.

*antonym* keep in.

**let up** abate, cease, decrease, diminish, ease, ease up, end, halt, moderate, slacken, stop, subside.

*antonym* continue.

**let slip** blab, blurt out, come out with, disclose, divulge, give away, leak, let out, let the cat out of the bag, reveal.

*antonym* keep mum.

**let**[2] *n* check, constraint, hindrance, impediment, interference, obstacle, obstruction, prohibition, restraint, restriction.

*antonym* assistance.

**let-down** *n* anticlimax, betrayal, blow, desertion, disappointment, disillusionment, frustration, lemon, set-back, wash-out.

*antonym* satisfaction.

**lethal** *adj* baleful, dangerous, deadly, deathful, deathly, destructive, devastating, fatal, lethiferous, mortal, mortiferous, murderous, noxious, pernicious, poisonous, virulent.

*antonym* harmless.

**lethargic** *adj* apathetic, comatose, debilitated, drowsy, dull, enervated, heavy, hebetant, hebetated, hebetudinous, inactive, indifferent, inert, languid, lazy, listless, sleepy, slothful, slow, sluggish, somnolent, stupefied, torpid.

*antonym* lively.

**lethargy** *n* apathy, drowsiness, dullness, hebetation, hebetude, hebetudinosity, inaction, indifference, inertia, languor, lassitude, listlessness, sleepiness, sloth, slowness, sluggishness, stupor, torpidity, torpor.

*antonym* liveliness.

**letter**[1] *n* acknowledgement, answer, billet, chit, communication, da(w)k, dispatch, encyclical, epistle, epistolet, line, message, missive, note, reply.

**letter**[2] *n* character, grapheme, lexigram, logogram, logograph, sign, symbol.

**lettered** *adj* accomplished, cultivated, cultured, educated, erudite, highbrow, informed, knowledgeable, learned, literary, literate, scholarly, studied, versed, well-educated, well-read.

*antonym* ignorant.

**letters** *n* academia, belles-lettres, books, culture, erudition, humanities, learning, literature, scholarship, writing.

**let-up** *n* abatement, break, breather, cessation, interval, lessening, lull, pause, recess, remission, respite, slackening.

*antonym* continuation.

**level¹** *adj* abreast, aligned, balanced, calm, champaign, commensurate, comparable, consistent, equable, equal, equivalent, even, even-tempered, flat, flush, horizontal, neck and neck, on a par, plain, proportionate, smooth, stable, steady, uniform.

*antonyms* behind, uneven, unstable.

*v* aim, beam, bulldoze, couch, demolish, destroy, devastate, direct, equalise, even out, flatten, flush, focus, knock down, lay low, plane, point, pull down, raze, smooth, tear down, train, wreck.

*n* altitude, bed, class, degree, echelon, elevation, floor, grade, height, horizontal, layer, plain, plane, position, rank, stage, standard, standing, status, storey, stratum, zone.

**level²** *v* admit, avow, come clean, confess, divulge, open up, tell.

*antonym* prevaricate.

**level-headed** *adj* balanced, calm, collected, commonsensical, composed, cool, dependable, even-tempered, reasonable, sane, self-possessed, sensible, steady, together, unflappable.

**lever** *n* bar, crowbar, handle, jemmy, joy-stick.

*v* dislodge, force, heave, jemmy, move, prise, pry, purchase, raise, shift.

**leverage** *n* advantage, ascendancy, authority, clout, force, influence, pull, purchase, rank, strength, weight.

**leviathan** *n* behemoth, colossus, giant, hulk, mammoth, monster, sea-monster, Titan, whale.

**levity** *n* buoyancy, facetiousness, fickleness, flightiness, flippancy, frivolity, giddiness, irreverence, light-heartedness, silliness, skittishness, triviality, whifflery.

*antonyms* seriousness, sobriety.

**levy** *v* assemble, call, call up, charge, collect, conscript, demand, exact, gather, impose, mobilise, muster, press, raise, summon, tax.

*n* assessment, collection, contribution, duty, exaction, excise, fee, gathering, imposition, impost, subscription, tariff, tax, toll.

**lewd** *adj* bawdy, blue, Cyprian, dirty, harlot, impure, indecent, lascivious, libidinous, licentious, loose, lubric, lubrical, lubricious, lubricous, lustful, obscene, pornographic, profligate, salacious, smutty, unchaste, vile, vulgar, wanton, wicked.

*antonyms* chaste, polite.

**lewdness** *n* bawdiness, carnality, crudity, debauchery, depravity, impurity, indecency, lasciviousness, lechery, licentiousness, lubricity, lustfulness, obscenity, pornography, priapism, profligacy, randiness, salaciousness, smut, smuttiness, unchastity, vulgarity, wantonness.

*antonyms* chasteness, politeness.

**lexicographer** *n* dictionary-writer, glossarist, lexiconist, vocabulist.

**lexicon** *n* dictionary, encyclopaedia, glossary, phrase-book, vocabulary, word-book, word-list.

**liability** *n* accountability, albatross, answerability, arrears, burden, culpability, debit, debt, disadvantage, drag, drawback, duty, encumbrance, handicap, hindrance, impediment, inconvenience, indebtedness, likeliness, millstone, minus, nuisance, obligation, onus, responsibility.

*antonyms* asset(s), unaccountability.

**liable** *adj* accountable, amenable, answerable, apt, bound, chargeable, disposed, exposed, inclined, likely, obligated, open, predisposed, prone, responsible, subject, susceptible, tending, vulnerable.

*antonyms* unaccountable, unlikely.

**liaison** *n* affair, amour, communication, conjunction, connection, contact, entanglement, interchange, intermediary, intrigue, link, love affair, romance, union.

**liar** *n* Ananias, bouncer, deceiver, fabricator, falsifier, fibber, perjurer, prevaricator, storyteller.

**libel** *n* aspersion, calumny, defamation, denigration, obloquy, slander, slur, smear, vilification, vituperation.

*antonym* praise.

*v* blacken, calumniate, defame, derogate, malign, revile, slander, slur, smear, traduce, vilify, vilipend, vituperate.

*antonym* praise.

**libellous** *adj* aspersive, aspersory, calumniatory, calumnious, defamatory, defaming, derogatory, false, injurious, malicious, maligning, scurrilous, slanderous, traducing, untrue, vilifying, vituperative.

*antonyms* laudative, praising.

**liberal** *adj* abundant, advanced, altruistic, ample, beneficent, bounteous, bountiful, broad, broad-minded, catholic, charitable, copious, enlightened, flexible, free, free-handed, general, generous, handsome, high-minded, humanistic, humanitarian, indulgent, inexact, kind, large-hearted, latitudinarian, lavish, lenient, libertarian, loose, magnanimous, munificent, open-handed, open-hearted, permissive, plentiful, profuse, progressive, radical, reformist, rich, tolerant, unbiased, unbigoted, unprejudiced, unstinting, verligte, Whig, Whiggish.

*antonyms* conservative, illiberal, mean, narrow-minded.

**liberalism** *n* free-thinking, humanitarianism, latitudinarianism, libertarianism, progressivism, radicalism, Whiggery, Whiggism.

*antonyms* conservatism, narrow-mindedness.

**liberality** *n* altruism, beneficence, benevolence, bounty, breadth, broad-mindedness, candour, catholicity, charity, free-handedness, generosity, impartiality, kindness, large-heartedness, largess(e), latitude, liberalism, libertarianism, magnanimity, munificence, open-handedness, open-mindedness, permissiveness, philanthropy, progressivism, tolerance, toleration.

*antonyms* illiberality, meanness.

**liberate** *v* affranchise, deliver, discharge, disenthral, emancipate, free, let go, let loose, let out, manumit, ransom, redeem, release, rescue, set free, uncage, unchain, unfetter, unpen, unshackle.

*antonyms* enslave, imprison, restrict.

**liberating** *adj* eleutherian, emancipatory, freeing, redeeming.

*antonym* restricting.

**liberation** *n* deliverance, emancipation, enfranchisement, freedom, freeing, liberating, liberty, manumission, ransoming, redemption, release, uncaging, unchaining, unfettering, unpenning, unshackling.

*antonyms* enslavement, imprisonment, restriction.

**liberator** *n* deliverer, emancipator, freer, manumitter, ransomer, redeemer, rescuer, saviour.

*antonyms* enslaver, jailer.

**libertarian** *n* anarchist, free-thinker, libertine.

*adj* anarchistic.

**liberties** *n* audacity, disrespect, familiarity, forwardness, impertinence, impropriety, impudence, insolence, misuse, overfamiliarity, presumption, presumptuousness.

*antonyms* politeness, respect.

**libertine** *n* debauchee, gay deceiver, lecher, loose fish, loose-liver, lovelace, profligate, rake, reprobate, roué, seducer, sensualist, voluptuary, womaniser.

**liberty** *n* authorisation, autonomy, carte-blanche, dispensation, emancipation, exemption, franchise, free rein, freedom, immunity, independence, latitude, leave, liberation, licence, permission, prerogative, privilege, release, right, sanction, self-determination, sovereignty.

*antonyms* imprisonment, restriction, slavery.

**libidinous** *adj* carnal, concupiscent, cupidinous, debauched, impure, incontinent, lascivious, lecherous, lewd, lickerish, loose, lustful, prurient, randy, ruttish, salacious, sensual, unchaste, wanton, wicked.

*antonyms* modest, temperate.

**library** *n* Athenaeum, bibliotheca, genizah, reading-room, reference-room, stack, study.

**libretto** *n* book, lines, lyrics, script, text, words.

**licence**[1] *n* authorisation, authority, carte blanche, certificate, charter, dispensation, entitlement, exemption, freedom, immunity, imprimatur, independence, indult, latitude, leave, liberty, permission, permit, privilege, right, self-determination, warrant.

*antonyms* banning, dependence, restriction.

**licence**[2] *n* abandon, amorality, anarchy, debauchery, disorder, dissipation, dissoluteness, excess, immoderation, impropriety, indulgence, intemperance, irresponsibility, lawlessness, laxity, profligacy, unruliness.

*antonyms* decorum, temperance.

**license** *v* accredit, allow, authorise, certificate, certify, commission, empower, entitle, permit, sanction, warrant.

*antonym* ban.

**licentious** *adj* abandoned, cupidinous, debauched, disorderly, dissolute, immoral, impure, lascivious, lax, lewd, libertine, libidinous, lickerish, lubric, lubrical, lubricious, lubricous, lustful, profligate, promiscuous, sensual, uncontrollable, uncontrolled, uncurbed, unruly, wanton.

**licentiousness** *n* abandon, cupidinousness, debauchery, dissipation, dissoluteness, lechery, lewdness, libertinism, libidinousness, lubriciousness, lubricity, lust, lustfulness, priapism, profligacy, promiscuity, prurience, salaciousness, salacity, wantonness.

*antonyms* modesty, temperance.

**lick**[1] *v* brush, dart, flick, lap, play over, smear, taste, tongue, touch, wash.

*n* bit, brush, dab, hint, little, sample, smidgeon, speck, spot, stroke, taste, touch.

**lick one's lips** anticipate, drool over, enjoy, relish, savour.

**lick**[2] *v* beat, best, defeat, excel, flog, outdo, outstrip, overcome, rout, skelp, slap, smack, spank, strike, surpass, thrash, top, trounce, vanquish, wallop.

**lick**[3] *n* clip, gallop, pace, rate, speed.

**licking** *n* beating, defeat, drubbing, flogging, hiding, skelping, smacking, spanking, tanning, thrashing, trouncing, whipping.

**lie**[1] *v* dissimulate, equivocate, fabricate, falsify, fib, forswear oneself, invent, misrepresent, perjure, prevaricate.

*n* bam, bounce, caulker, cram, crammer, cretism, deceit, fabrication, falsehood, falsification, falsity, fib, fiction, flam, invention, inveracity, mendacity, plumper, prevarication, stretcher, tar(r)adiddle, untruth, whacker, white lie, whopper.

*antonym* truth.

**lie**[2] *v* be, belong, couch, dwell, exist, extend, inhere, laze, loll, lounge, recline, remain, repose, rest, slump, sprawl, stretch out.

**lie low** go to earth, hide, hide away, hide out, hole up, keep a low profile, lie doggo, lurk, skulk, take cover.

**lie in wait for** ambuscade, ambush, forelay, skulk, waylay.

**life** *n* activity, animation, autobiography, behaviour, being, biography, breath, brio, career, conduct, confessions, continuance, course, creatures, duration, élan vital, energy, entity, essence, existence, fauna, flora and fauna, get-up-and-go, go, growth, heart, high spirits, history, life story, life-blood, life-style, lifetime, liveliness, memoirs, oomph, organisms, sentience, soul, span, sparkle, spirit, story, the world, this mortal coil, time, verve, viability, vigour, vita, vital flame, vital spark, vitality, vivacity, way of life, wildlife, zest.

**lifeless** *adj* abiotic, apathetic, bare, barren, cold, colourless, comatose, dead, deceased, defunct, desert, dull, empty, extinct, flat, heavy, hollow, inanimate, inert, insensate, insensible, insipid, lacklustre, lethargic, listless, nerveless, out cold, out for the count, passive, pointless, slow, sluggish, spent, spiritless, static, sterile, stiff, torpid, unconscious, uninhabited, unproductive, waste, wooden.

*antonyms* alive, lively.

**lifelike** *adj* authentic, exact, expressive, faithful, graphic, natural, photographic, pictorial, picturesque, real, realistic, true, true-to-life, undistorted, vivid.

*antonyms* inexact, unnatural.

**lifelong** *adj* abiding, constant, deep-rooted, deep-seated, enduring, entrenched, inveterate, lasting, lifetime, long-lasting, long-standing, perennial, permanent, persistent.

*antonyms* impermanent, temporary.

**lifetime** *n* career, course, day(s), existence, floruit, life, life span, period, span, time.

**lift¹** *v* advance, ameliorate, annul, appropriate, arrest, ascend, boost, buoy up, cancel, climb, collar, copy, countermand, crib, dignify, disappear, disperse, dissipate, draw up, elevate, end, enhance, exalt, half-inch, heft, hoist, improve, mount, nab, nick, pick up, pilfer, pinch, pirate, plagiarise, pocket, promote, purloin, raise, rear, relax, remove, rescind, revoke, rise, steal, stop, take, terminate, thieve, up, upgrade, uplift, upraise, vanish.

*antonyms* drop, fall, impose, lower.

*n* boost, encouragement, fillip, pick-me-up, reassurance, shot in the arm, spur, uplift.

*antonym* discouragement.

**lift²** *n* drive, hitch, ride, run, transport.

**lift³** *n* elevator, escalator, hoist, paternoster.

**ligature** *n* band, bandage, binding, bond, connection, cord, ligament, link, rope, strap, string, thong, tie, tourniquet.

**light¹** *n* beacon, blaze, brightness, brilliance, bulb, candle, cockcrow, dawn, day, daybreak, daylight, daytime, effulgence, flame, flare, flash, glare, gleam, glim, glint, glow, illumination, incandescence, lambency, lamp, lampad, lantern, lighter, lighthouse, luminescence, luminosity, lustre, match, morn, morning, phosphorescence, radiance, ray, refulgence, scintillation, shine, sparkle, star, sunrise, sunshine, taper, torch, window, Yang.

*antonym* darkness.

*v* animate, beacon, brighten, cheer, fire, floodlight, ignite, illuminate, illumine, inflame, irradiate, kindle, light up, lighten, put on, set alight, set fire to, switch on, turn on.

*antonyms* darken, extinguish.

*adj* bleached, blond, bright, brilliant, faded, faint, fair, glowing, illuminated, lightful, lightsome, lucent, luminous, lustrous, pale, pastel, shining, sunny, well-lit.

*antonym* dark.

**light²** *n* angle, approach, aspect, attitude, awareness, clue, comprehension, context, elucidation, enlightenment, example, exemplar, explanation, hint, illustration, information, insight, interpretation, knowledge, model, paragon, point of view, slant, understanding, viewpoint.

**light³** *adj* agile, airy, amusing, animated, blithe, buoyant, carefree, cheerful, cheery, crumbly, delicate, delirious, digestible, diverting, dizzy, easy, effortless, entertaining, facile, faint, fickle, flimsy, friable, frivolous, frugal, funny, gay, gentle, giddy, graceful, humorous, idle, imponderous, inconsequential, inconsiderable, indistinct, insignificant, insubstantial, light-footed, light-headed, light-hearted, lightweight, lithe, lively, loose, manageable, merry, mild, minute, moderate, modest, nimble, pleasing, porous, portable, reeling, restricted, sandy, scanty, simple, slight, small, soft, spongy, sprightly, sunny, superficial, thin, tiny, trifling, trivial, unchaste, undemanding, underweight, unexacting, unheeding, unsteady, unsubstantial, untaxing, volatile, wanton, weak, witty, worthless.

*antonyms* clumsy, harsh, heavy, important, sad, severe, sober, solid, stiff.

**light on** chance on, come across, discover, encounter, find, happen upon, hit on, spot, stumble on.

**lighten¹** *v* beacon, brighten, illume, illuminate, illumine, light up, shine.

*antonym* darken.

**lighten²** *v* alleviate, ameliorate, assuage, brighten, buoy up, cheer, disburden, disencumber, ease, elate, encourage, facilitate, gladden, hearten, inspire, inspirit, lessen, lift, mitigate, perk up, reduce, relieve, revive, unload, uplift.

*antonyms* burden, depress, oppress.

**light-fingered** *adj* crafty, crooked, dishonest, furtive, pilfering, shifty, sly, thieving, thievish.

*antonym* honest.

**light-footed** *adj* active, agile, buoyant, feat, graceful, lightsome, lithe, nimble, sprightly, spry, swift, tripping, winged.

*antonyms* clumsy, slow.

**light-giving** *adj* luciferous, luminant, luminiferous, luminous.

**light-headed** *adj* bird-brained, delirious, dizzy, faint, feather-brained, fickle, flighty, flippant, foolish, frivolous, giddy, hazy, inane, shallow, silly, superficial, thoughtless, trifling, unsteady, vacuous, vertiginous, woozy.

*antonym* sober.

**light-hearted** *adj* blithe, blithesome, bright, carefree, cheerful, effervescent, elated, frolicsome, gay, glad, gleeful, happy-go-lucky, insouciant, jocund, jolly, jovial, joyful, joyous, light-spirited, merry, perky, playful, sunny, untroubled, upbeat.

*antonym* sad.

**lighthouse** *n* fanal, pharos.

**lightly** *adv* airily, breezily, carelessly, delicately, easily, effortlessly, facilely, faintly, flippantly, frivolously, gaily, gently, gingerly, heedlessly, indifferently, moderately, readily, simply, slightingly, slightly, softly, sparingly, sparsely, thinly, thoughtlessly, timidly, wantonly.

*antonyms* heavily, soberly.

**lightness** *n* agility, airiness, animation, blitheness, buoyancy, cheerfulness, cheeriness, crumbliness, delicacy, delicateness, facileness, faintness, fickleness, flimsiness, frivolity, gaiety, grace, idleness, inconsequentiality, indistinctness, insignificance, legerity, levity, light-heartedness, litheness, liveliness, mildness, minuteness, moderation, nimbleness, porosity, porousness, sandiness, scantiness, slightness, triviality, wantonness.

*antonyms* clumsiness, harshness, heaviness, importance, sadness, severity, sobriety, solidness, stiffness.

**lightning** *n* thunderbolt, thunder-dart, wildfire.

**lightweight** *adj* inconsequential, insignificant, negligible, nugatory, paltry, petty, slight, trifling, trivial, unimportant, worthless.

*antonyms* important, major.

**like**[1] *adj* akin, alike, allied, analogous, approximating, cognate, corresponding, equivalent, homologous, identical, parallel, related, relating, resembling, same, similar.

*antonym* unlike.

*n* counterpart, equal, fellow, match, opposite number, parallel, peer, twin.

*prep* in the same manner as, on the lines of, similar to.

**like**[2] *v* admire, adore, appreciate, approve, care to, cherish, choose, choose to, delight in, desire, dig, enjoy, esteem, fancy, feel inclined, go a bundle on, go for, hold dear, love, prefer, prize, relish, revel in, select, take a shine to, take kindly to, take to, want, wish.

*antonym* dislike.

*n* cup of tea, favourite, liking, love, partiality, penchant, predilection, preference.

*antonym* dislike.

**likeable** *adj* agreeable, amiable, appealing, attractive, charming, congenial, engaging, friendly, genial, loveable, nice, pleasant, pleasing, sympathetic, winning, winsome.

*antonym* disagreeable.

**likelihood** *n* chance, liability, likeliness, possibility, probability, prospect, reasonableness, verisimilitude.

*antonym* unlikeliness.

**likely** *adj* acceptable, agreeable, anticipated, appropriate, apt, befitting, believable, bright, credible, disposed, expected, fair, favourite, feasible, fit, foreseeable, hopeful, inclined, liable, odds-on, on the cards, plausible, pleasing, possible, predictable, probable, promising, prone, proper, qualified, reasonable, suitable, tending, up-and-coming, verisimilar.

*antonyms* unlikely, unsuitable.

*adv* doubtlessly, in all probability, like as not, like enough, no doubt, odds on, presumably, probably, very like.

**like-minded** *adj* agreeing, compatible, harmonious, in accord, in agreement, in harmony, in rapport, of one mind, of the same mind, unanimous.

*antonym* disagreeing.

**liken** *v* associate, compare, equate, juxtapose, link, match, parallel, relate, set beside.

**likeness** *n* affinity, appearance, copy, correspondence, counterpart, delineation, depiction, effigies, effigy, facsimile, form, guise, image, model, photograph, picture, portrait, replica, representation, reproduction, resemblance, semblance, similarity, similitude, simulacrum, study.

*antonym* unlikeness.

**likewise** *adv* also, besides, by the same token, eke, further, furthermore, in addition, moreover, similarly, too.

*antonym* contrariwise.

**liking** *n* affection, affinity, appreciation, attraction, bent, bias, desire, favour, fondness, inclination, love, partiality, penchant, predilection, preference, proneness, propensity, satisfaction, soft spot, stomach, taste, tendency, weakness.

*antonym* dislike.

**lilt** *n* air, beat, cadence, measure, rhythm, song, sway, swing.

**lily-white** *adj* chaste, incorrupt, innocent, irreproachable, milk-white, pure, spotless, uncorrupt, uncorrupted, unsullied, untainted, untarnished, virgin, virtuous.

*antonym* corrupt.

**limb** *n* appendage, arm, bough, branch, extension, extremity, fork, leg, member, offshoot, part, projection, ramus, spur, wing.

**limber** *adj* agile, elastic, flexible, flexile, graceful, lissom, lithe, loose-jointed, loose-limbed, plastic, pliable, pliant, supple.

*antonym* stiff.

**limber up** exercise, loosen up, prepare, warm up, work out.

*antonym* stiffen up.

**limelight** *n* attention, big time, celebrity, fame, prominence, public notice, publicity, recognition, renown, stardom, the public eye, the spotlight.

**limit** *n* bitter end, border, bound, boundary, bourne(e), brim, brink, ceiling, check, compass, confines, curb, cut-off point, deadline, edge, end, extent, frontier, limitation, maximum, mete, obstruction, outrance, perimeter, periphery, precinct, restraint, restriction, rim, saturation point, termination, terminus, terminus a quo, terminus ad quem, threshold, ultimate, utmost, verge.

*v* bound, check, circumscribe, condition, confine, constrain, curb, delimit, delimitate, demarcate, fix, hem in, hinder, ration, restrain, restrict, specify.

*antonyms* extend, free.

**limitation** *n* block, check, condition, constraint, control, curb, definitude, delimitation, demarcation, disadvantage, drawback, impediment, obstruction, qualification, reservation, restraint, restriction, snag.

*antonyms* asset, extension, furtherance.

**limited** *adj* borné, bounded, checked, circumscribed, confined, constrained, controlled, cramped, curbed, defined, determinate, diminished, finite, fixed, hampered, hemmed in, inadequate, insufficient, minimal, narrow, reduced, restricted, short, unsatisfactory.

*antonym* limitless.

**limitless** *adj* boundless, countless, endless, illimitable, illimited, immeasurable, immense, immensurable, incalculable, inexhaustible, infinite, measureless, never-ending, numberless, unbounded, undefined, unending, unlimited, untold, vast.

*antonym* limited.

**limp¹** *v* dot, falter, halt, hamble, hirple, hitch, hobble, hop, shamble, shuffle.

*n* claudication, hitch, hobble, lameness.

**limp²** *adj* debilitated, drooping, enervated, exhausted, flabby, flaccid, flexible, flexile, floppy, hypotonic, lax, lethargic, limber, loose, pliable, pooped, relaxed, slack, soft, spent, tired, toneless, weak, worn out.

*antonym* strong.

**limpid** *adj* bright, clear, comprehensible, crystal-clear, crystalline, glassy, hyaline, intelligible, lucid, pellucid, pure, still, translucent, transparent, unruffled, untroubled.

*antonyms* muddy, ripply, turbid, unintelligible.

**line¹** *n* band, bar, border, borderline, boundary, cable, chain, channel, column, configuration, contour, cord, crease, crocodile, crow's foot, dash, demarcation, disposition, edge, features, figure, filament, file, firing line, formation, front, front line, frontier, furrow, groove, limit, mark, outline, position, procession, profile, queue, rank, rope, row, rule, score, scratch, sequence, series, silhouette, stipe, strand, streak, string, stroke, tail, thread, trail, trenches, underline, wire, wrinkle.

*v* border, bound, crease, cut, draw, edge, fringe, furrow, hatch, inscribe, mark, rank, rim, rule, score, skirt, verge.

**line up** align, arrange, array, assemble, dispose, engage, fall in, form ranks, hire, lay on, marshal, obtain, order, organise, prepare, procure, produce, queue up, range, regiment, secure, straighten.

**line²** *n* activity, approach, area, avenue, axis, belief, business, calling, course, course of action, department, direction, employment, field, forte, ideology, interest, job, line of country, method, occupation, path, policy, position, practice, procedure, profession, province, pursuit, route, scheme, specialisation, specialism, speciality, specialty, system, track, trade, trajectory, vocation.

**line³** *n* ancestry, breed, family, lineage, pedigree, race, stirps, stock, strain, succession.

**line⁴** *n* card, clue, hint, indication, information, lead, letter, memo, memorandum, message, note, postcard, report, word.

**line⁵** *v* ceil, cover, encase, face, fill, reinforce, strengthen, stuff.

**lineage** *n* ancestors, ancestry, birth, breed, descendants, descent, extraction, family, forebears, forefathers, genealogy, heredity, house, line, offspring, pedigree, progeny, race, stirp(s), stock, succession.

**lineaments** *n* appearance, aspect, configuration, countenance, face, features, lines, outline(s), physiognomy, traits, visage.

**lined** *adj* feint, furrowed, lineate(d), lineolate, ruled, wizened, worn, wrinkled.

*antonyms* smooth, unlined.

**linen** *n* bed-linen, napery, sheets, table-linen, white goods.

**lines¹** *n* appearance, configuration, contour, convention, cut, example, model, outline, pattern, plan, principle, procedure, shape, style.

**lines²** *n* book, libretto, part, script, text, words.

**lines³** *n* cross-hatching, hatching, shading.

**line-up** *n* arrangement, array, bill, cast, queue, row, selection, team.

**linger** *v* abide, continue, dally, dawdle, delay, dilly-dally, endure, hang around, hang on, hold out, idle, lag, last out, loiter, persist, procrastinate, remain, stay, stop, survive, tarry, wait.

*antonyms* leave, rush.

**lingerie** *n* frillies, inexpressibles, linen, smalls, underclothes, underclothing, undergarments, underlinen, underset, unmentionables.

**lingering** *adj* dragging, long-drawn-out, persistent, prolonged, protracted, remaining, slow.

*antonym* quick.

**lingo** *n* argot, cant, dialect, idiom, jargon, language, parlance, patois, patter, speech, talk, terminology, tongue, vernacular, vocabulary.

**linguist** *n* linguistic scientist, linguistician, verbalist, vocabularian.

**liniment** *n* balm, balsam, cream, embrocation, emollient, lotion, ointment, salve, unguent, wash.

**lining** *n* backing, encasement, inlay, interfacing, interlining, padding, stiffening.

**link** *n* association, attachment, bond, communication, component, connection, constituent, division, element, joint, knot, liaison, member, part, piece, relationship, tie, tie-up, union.

*v* associate, attach, bind, bracket, catenate, concatenate, connect, couple, fasten, identify, join, relate, tie, unite, yoke.

*antonyms* separate, unfasten.

**link up** ally, amalgamate, connect, dock, hook up, join, join forces, merge, team up, unify.

*antonym* separate.

**link-up** *n* alliance, amalgamation, association, connection, merger, tie-in, union.

*antonym* separation.

**lion-hearted** *adj* bold, brave, courageous, daring, dauntless, dreadless, gallant, heroic, intrepid, resolute, stalwart, stout-hearted, valiant, valorous.

*antonym* cowardly.

**lionise** v acclaim, adulate, aggrandise, celebrate, eulogise, exalt, fête, glorify, hero-worship, honour, idolise, magnify, praise, sing the praises of.

*antonym* vilify.

**lion-like** adj leonine, lion-hearted, lionly.

**lip**[1] n border, brim, brink, edge, margin, rim, verge.

**lip**[2] n backchat, cheek, effrontery, impertinence, impudence, insolence, rudeness, sauce.

*antonym* politeness.

**liquefaction** n deliquescence, dissolution, dissolving, fusion, liquefying, melting, thawing.

*antonym* solidification.

**liquefy** v deliquesce, dissolve, fluidise, flux, fuse, liquesce, liquidise, melt, run, smelt, thaw.

*antonym* solidify.

**liquid** n drink, fluid, juice, liquor, lotion, potation, sap, solution.

*adj* aqueous, clear, convertible, dulcet, flowing, fluid, limpid, liquefied, mellifluent, mellifluous, melted, molten, negotiable, running, runny, serous, shining, smooth, soft, sweet, thawed, translucent, transparent, watery, wet.

*antonyms* harsh, solid.

**liquidate** v abolish, annihilate, annul, assassinate, bump off, cancel, cash, clear, destroy, discharge, dispatch, dissolve, do away with, do in, eliminate, exterminate, finish off, honour, kill, massacre, murder, pay, pay off, realise, remove, rub out, sell off, sell up, settle, silence, square, terminate, wipe out.

**liquor**[1] n aguardiente, alcohol, booze, drink, fire-water, grog, hard stuff, hooch, intoxicant, juice, jungle juice, potation, rotgut, spirits, strong drink, tape.

**liquor**[2] n broth, essence, extract, gravy, infusion, juice, liquid, stock.

**lissom(e)** adj agile, flexible, graceful, light, limber, lithe, lithesome, loose-jointed, loose-limbed, nimble, pliable, pliant, supple, willowy.

*antonym* stiff.

**list**[1] n catalogue, directory, enumeration, file, index, inventory, invoice, leet, listing, litany, matricula, record, register, roll, schedule, series, syllabus, table, tabulation, tally.

*v* alphabeticise, bill, book, catalogue, enrol, enter, enumerate, file, index, itemise, note, record, register, schedule, set down, tabulate, write down.

**list**[2] v cant, careen, heel, heel over, incline, lean, slope, tilt, tip.

*n* cant, leaning, slant, slope, tilt.

**listen** v attend, get a load of, give ear, give heed to, hang on (someone's) words, hang on (someone's) lips, hark, hear, hearken, heed, keep one's ears open, lend an ear, mind, obey, observe, pay attention, pin back one's ears, prick up one's ears, take notice.

**listless** adj apathetic, bored, depressed, enervated, ennuyed, heavy, impassive, inattentive, indifferent, indolent, inert, languid, languishing, lethargic, lifeless, limp, lymphatic, mopish, sluggish, spiritless, supine, torpid, uninterested, vacant.

*antonym* lively.

**listlessness** n accidie, acedia, apathy, enervation, ennui, inattention, indifference, indolence, languidness, languor, lethargy, lifelessness, sloth, sluggishness, spiritlessness, supineness, torpidity, torpor.

*antonym* liveliness.

**litany** n account, catalogue, enumeration, invocation, list, narration, narrative, petition, prayer, recital, recitation, refrain, repetition, supplication, tale.

**literacy** n ability, articulacy, articulateness, cultivation, culture, education, erudition, intelligence, knowledge, learning, proficiency, scholarship.

*antonym* illiteracy.

**literal** adj accurate, actual, boring, close, colourless, down-to-earth, dull, exact, factual, faithful, genuine, matter-of-fact, plain, prosaic, prosy, real, simple, strict, true, unexaggerated, unimaginative, uninspired, unvarnished, verbatim, word-for-word.

*antonym* loose.

**literally** adv actually, closely, exactly, faithfully, literatim, plainly, precisely, really, simply, strictly, to the letter, truly, verbatim, word for word.

*antonym* loosely.

**literary** adj bookish, cultivated, cultured, erudite, formal, learned, lettered, literate, refined, scholarly, well-read.

*antonym* illiterate.

**literature** n belles-lettres, blurb, brochure(s), bumf, circular(s), hand-out(s), information, leaflet(s), letters, lore, pamphlet(s), paper(s), writings.

**lithe** adj double-jointed, flexible, flexile, limber, lissom(e), lithesome, loose-jointed, loose-limbed, pliable, pliant, supple.

*antonym* stiff.

**litigant** n claimant, complainant, contender, contestant, disputant, litigator, party, plaintiff.

**litigation** n action, case, contention, lawsuit, process, prosecution, suit.

**litigious** adj argumentative, belligerent, contentious, disputable, disputatious, quarrelsome.

*antonym* easy-going.

**litter**[1] n clutter, confusion, debris, detritus, disarray, disorder, fragments, jumble, mess, muck, refuse, rubbish, scatter, scoria, shreds, untidiness, wastage.

*v* bestrew, clutter, derange, disarrange, disorder, mess up, scatter, strew.

*antonym* tidy.

**litter**[2] n brood, family, offspring, progeny, quiverful, young.

**litter**[3] n couch, palanquin, stretcher.

**little** *adj* babyish, base, brief, cheap, diminutive, dwarf, elfin, fleeting, hasty, immature, inconsiderable, infant, infinitesimal, insignificant, insufficient, junior, Lilliputian, meagre, mean, microscopic, miniature, minor, minute, negligible, paltry, passing, petite, petty, piccaninny, pint-size(d), pygmy, scant, short, short-lived, skimpy, slender, small, sparse, tiny, transient, trifling, trivial, undeveloped, unimportant, wee, young.

*antonyms* important, large, long.

*adv* barely, hardly, infrequently, rarely, scarcely, seldom.

*antonyms* frequently, greatly.

*n* bit, dab, dash, drib, fragment, hint, modicum, particle, pinch, snippet, speck, spot, taste, touch, trace, trifle.

*antonym* lot.

**little by little** bit by bit, by degrees, gradually, imperceptibly, in penny numbers, piecemeal, progressively, slowly, step by step.

*antonyms* all at one go, quickly.

**liturgical** *adj* ceremonial, eucharistic, formal, hieratic, ritual, sacerdotal, sacramental, solemn.

*antonym* secular.

**liturgy** *n* celebration, ceremony, form, formula, office, rite, ritual, sacrament, service, usage, worship.

**live**[1] *v* abide, breathe, continue, draw breath, dwell, earn a living, endure, exist, fare, feed, get along, hang out, inhabit, last, lead, lodge, make ends meet, pass, persist, prevail, remain, reside, settle, stay, subsist, survive.

*antonyms* cease, die.

**live it up** celebrate, go on the spree, have a ball, make merry, make whoopee, paint the town red, revel.

**live**[2] *adj* active, alert, alight, alive, animate, blazing, breathing, brisk, burning, connected, controversial, current, dynamic, earnest, energetic, existent, glowing, hot, ignited, lively, living, pertinent, pressing, prevalent, relevant, sentient, smouldering, topical, unsettled, vigorous, vital, vivid, wide-awake.

*antonyms* apathetic, dead, out.

**liveable** *adj* acceptable, adequate, bearable, comfortable, endurable, habitable, inhabitable, possible, satisfactory, sufferable, supportable, tolerable, worthwhile.

*antonyms* unbearable, uninhabitable.

**liveable with** bearable, companionable, compatible, congenial, gemütlich, harmonious, passable, sociable, tolerable.

*antonyms* impossible, unbearable.

**livelihood** *n* employment, income, job, living, maintenance, means, occupation, subsistence, support, sustenance, work.

**liveliness** *n* activity, animation, boisterousness, brio, briskness, dynamism, energy, entrain, gaiety, nowness, quickness, smartness, spirit, sprightliness, vitality, vivacity.

*antonyms* apathy, inactivity.

**livelong** complete, enduring, entire, full, long, protracted, whole.

*antonym* partial.

**lively** *adj* active, agile, alert, animated, astir, blithe, blithesome, breezy, bright, brisk, buckish, bustling, busy, buxom, buzzing, canty, cheerful, chipper, chirpy, colourful, crowded, energetic, eventful, exciting, forceful, frisky, frolicsome, galliard, gay, invigorating, keen, lifesome, lightsome, merry, mouvementé, moving, nimble, perky, quick, racy, refreshing, skittish, sparkling, spirited, sprightly, spry, stimulating, stirring, swinging, tit(t)upy, vigorous, vivacious, vivid, zippy.

*antonyms* apathetic, inactive, moribund.

**liven up** animate, brighten, buck up, energise, enliven, hot up, invigorate, pep up, perk up, put life into, rouse, stir, stir up, vitalise, vivify.

*antonyms* deaden, dishearten.

**liverish** *adj* crabbed, crabby, crotchety, crusty, disagreeable, grumpy, ill-humoured, irascible, irritable, peevish, snappy, splenetic, testy, tetchy.

*antonyms* calm, easy-going.

**livery** *n* apparel, attire, clothes, clothing, costume, dress, garb, habit, raiment, regalia, suit, uniform, vestments.

**live-wire** ball of fire, cricket, dynamo, go-getter, grig, hustler, life and soul of the party, self-starter.

*antonym* wet blanket.

**livid**[1] *adj* angry, beside oneself, boiling, enraged, exasperated, fuming, furibund, furious, incensed, indignant, infuriated, irate, ireful, mad, outraged, waxy.

*antonym* calm.

**livid**[2] *adj* angry, ashen, black-and-blue, blanched, bloodless, bruised, contused, discoloured, doughy, greyish, leaden, pale, pallid, pasty, purple, wan, waxen, waxy.

*antonyms* healthy, rosy.

**living** *adj* active, alive, animated, breathing, existing, live, lively, strong, vigorous, vital.

*antonyms* dead, sluggish.

*n* being, benefice, existence, income, job, life, livelihood, maintenance, occupation, profession, property, subsistence, support, sustenance, way of life, work.

**load** *n* affliction, albatross, bale, burden, cargo, consignment, encumbrance, freight, goods, lading, millstone, onus, oppression, pressure, shipment, trouble, weight, worry.

*v* adulterate, burden, charge, cram, doctor, drug, encumber, fill, fortify, freight, hamper, heap, lade, oppress, overburden, pack, pile, prime, saddle with, stack, stuff, trouble, weigh down, weight, worry.

**loaded** *adj* affluent, artful, biased, burdened, charged, distorted, drugged, drunk, fixed, flush, freighted, full, high, inebriated, insidious, intoxicated, laden, manipulative, moneyed, prejudicial, primed, rich, rolling, tight, tipsy, tricky, under the influence, wealthy, weighted, well-heeled, well-off, well-to-do.

*antonyms* poor, sober, straightforward, unloaded.

**loads** *n* a million, dozens, heaps, hordes, hundreds, lots, millions, scores, thousands, tons.

**loaf**[1] *n* block, cake, cube, lump, mass, slab.

**loaf²** *v* idle, laze, lie around, loiter, loll, lounge around, mooch, moon, stand about, take it easy.
*antonym* toil.

**loaf³** *n* brains, chump, common sense, gumption, head, noddle, nous, sense, smeddum.

**loafer** *n* beachcomber, bludger, bum, bummer, burn, corner-boy, do-nothing, drone, idler, layabout, lazybones, lounge-lizard, lounger, ne'er-do-well, shirker, skiver, sluggard, time-waster, wastrel.
*antonym* worker.

**loan** *n* accommodation, advance, allowance, calque, credit, lend-lease, loan translation, loan-word, mortgage, touch.

*v* accommodate, advance, allow, credit, lend, let out, oblige.
*antonym* borrow.

**lo(a)th** *adj* against, averse, backward, counter, disinclined, grudging, hesitant, indisposed, opposed, reluctant, resisting, unwilling.
*antonym* willing.

**loathe** *v* abhor, abominate, despise, detest, dislike, execrate, hate, keck.
*antonym* like.

**loathing** *n* abhorrence, abomination, antipathy, aversion, detestation, disgust, dislike, execration, hatred, horror, nausea, odium, repugnance, repulsion, revulsion.
*antonym* liking.

**loathsome** *adj* abhorrent, abominable, detestable, disgusting, execrable, hateful, horrible, loathful, nasty, nauseating, obnoxious, odious, offensive, repellent, repugnant, repulsive, revolting, vile.
*antonym* likeable.

**lob** *v* chuck, fling, heave, launch, lift, loft, pitch, shy, throw, toss.

**lobby¹** *v* call for, campaign for, demand, influence, persuade, press for, pressure, promote, pull strings, push for, solicit, urge.

*n* ginger group, pressure group.

**lobby²** *n* anteroom, corridor, entrance hall, foyer, hall, hallway, passage, passageway, porch, vestibule, waiting-room.

**local** *adj* community, confined, district, limited, narrow, neighbourhood, parish, parochial, provincial, pump, regional, restricted, small-town, vernacular, vicinal.
*antonym* far-away.

*n* denizen, inhabitant, native, resident, yokel.
*antonym* incomer.

**locale** *n* area, locality, location, locus, place, position, scene, setting, site, spot, venue, zone.

**localise** *v* ascribe, assign, circumscribe, concentrate, confine, contain, delimit, delimitate, limit, narrow down, pin-point, restrain, restrict, specify, zero in on.

**locality** *n* area, district, locale, location, neck of the woods, neighbourhood, place, position, region, scene, setting, site, spot, vicinity, zone.

**locate** *v* detect, discover, establish, find, fix, identify, lay one's hands on, pin-point, place, put, run to earth, seat, set, settle, situate, track down, unearth.

**location** *n* bearings, locale, locus, place, point, position, site, situation, spot, ubiety, venue, whereabouts.

**lock¹** *n* bolt, clasp, fastening, padlock, sneck.

*v* bolt, clasp, clench, close, clutch, disengage, embrace, encircle, enclose, engage, entangle, entwine, fasten, grapple, grasp, hug, join, latch, link, mesh, press, seal, secure, shut, sneck, unite, unlock.

**lock out** ban, bar, debar, exclude, keep out, ostracise, refuse admittance to, shut out.

**lock together** interdigitate, interlock.

**lock up** cage, close up, confine, detain, enlock, imprison, incarcerate, jail, pen, secure, shut, shut in, shut up.
*antonym* free.

**lock²** *n* curl, plait, ringlet, strand, tress, tuft.

**lock-up** *n* brig, can, cell, clink, cooler, gaol, garage, hoos(e)gow, jail, jug, pen, penitentiary, prison, quod, tolbooth.

**locomotion** *n* action, ambulation, headway, motion, movement, moving, progress, progression, travel, travelling.

**locution** *n* accent, articulation, cliché, collocation, diction, expression, idiom, inflection, intonation, phrase, phrasing, style, term, turn of phrase, wording.

**lodge** *n* abode, assemblage, association, branch, cabin, chalet, chapter, club, cot, cot-house, cottage, den, gang-hut, gatehouse, group, haunt, house, hunting-lodge, hut, lair, meeting-place, retreat, shelter, society.

*v* accommodate, billet, board, deposit, dig, entertain, file, get stuck, harbour, imbed, implant, lay, place, put, put on record, put up, quarter, register, room, set, shelter, sojourn, stay, stick, stop, submit.

**lodger** *n* boarder, guest, inmate, paying guest, renter, resident, roomer, tenant.

**lodgings** *n* abode, accommodation, apartments, billet, boarding, digs, dwelling, gite, habitation, pad, quarters, residence, rooms, shelter.

**lofty** *adj* arrogant, condescending, dignified, disdainful, distinguished, elevated, esteemed, exalted, grand, haughty, high, high and mighty, illustrious, imperial, imposing, lordly, majestic, noble, patronising, proud, raised, renowned, sky-high, snooty, soaring, stately, sublime, supercilious, superior, tall, toffee-nosed, towering.
*antonyms* humble, low(ly), modest.

**log¹** *n* billet, block, bole, chunk, loggat, stump, timber, trunk.

**log²** *n* account, chart, daybook, diary, journal, listing, logbook, record, tally.

*v* book, chart, note, record, register, report, tally, write down, write in, write up.

**logic** *n* argumentation, deduction, dialectic(s), ratiocination, rationale, rationality, reason, reasoning, sense.

**logical** *adj* clear, cogent, coherent, consistent, deducible, elenctic, judicious, necessary, obvious, pertinent, plausible, rational, reasonable, relevant, sensible, sound, valid, well-founded, well-grounded, well-organised, wise.

*antonyms* illogical, irrational.

**ogistics** *n* co-ordination, engineering, management, masterminding, orchestration, organisation, planning, plans, strategy.

**oins** *n* genitalia, manliness, potency, power, reins, strength, virility.

**oiter** *v* dally, dawdle, delay, dilly-dally, hang about, idle, lag, lallygag, linger, loaf, loll, lollygag, mooch, mouch, saunter, skulk, stroll.

**oll** *v* dangle, depend, droop, drop, flap, flop, hang, lean, loaf, lounge, recline, relax, sag, slouch, slump, sprawl.

**one** *adj* deserted, isolated, lonesome, one, only, separate, separated, single, sole, solitary, unaccompanied, unattached, unattended.

*antonym* accompanied.

**oneliness** *n* aloneness, desolation, forlornness, friendlessness, isolation, lonesomeness, seclusion, solitariness, solitude.

**onely** *adj* abandoned, alone, apart, companionless, destitute, estranged, forlorn, forsaken, friendless, isolated, lonely-heart, lonesome, outcast, out-of-the-way, remote, secluded, sequestered, solitary, unfrequented, uninhabited, untrodden.

**oner** *n* hermit, individualist, lone wolf, maverick, outsider, pariah, recluse, solitary, solitudinarian.

**onesome** *adj* cheerless, companionless, deserted, desolate, dreary, forlorn, friendless, gloomy, isolated, lone, lonely, solitary.

**ong** *adj* dragging, elongated, expanded, expansive, extended, extensive, far-reaching, interminable, late, lengthy, lingering, long-drawn-out, marathon, prolonged, protracted, slow, spread out, stretched, sustained, tardy.

*antonyms* abbreviated, brief, fleeting, short.

**long for** covet, crave, desire, dream of, hanker for, hunger after, itch for, lust after, pine, thirst for, want, wish, yearn for, yen for.

**ong-drawn-out** *adj* interminable, lengthy, long-drawn, long-winded, marathon, overextended, overlong, prolix, prolonged, protracted, spun out, tedious.

*antonyms* brief, curtailed.

**onging** *n* ambition, aspiration, coveting, craving, desire, hankering, hungering, itch, thirst, urge, wish, yearning, yen.

*adj* anxious, appetence, appetency, ardent, avid, craving, desiderium, desirous, eager, hungry, languishing, pining, wishful, wistful, yearning.

**ong-lasting** *adj* abiding, continuing, enduring, entrenched, established, evergreen, imperishable, lifelong, long-lived, long-standing, perdurable, permanent, prolonged, protracted, unchanging, unfading.

*antonyms* ephemeral, short-lived, transient.

**ong-lived** *adj* durable, enduring, lasting, longevous, long-lasting, long-standing, macrobian, macrobiotic.

*antonyms* brief, ephemeral, short-lived.

**long-standing** *adj* abiding, enduring, established, fixed, hallowed, long-established, long-lasting, long-lived, time-honoured, traditional.

**long-suffering** *adj* easy-going, forbearant, forbearing, forgiving, patient, placid, resigned, stoical, tolerant, uncomplaining.

**long-winded** *adj* circumlocutory, diffuse, discursive, garrulous, lengthy, long-drawn-out, overlong, prolix, prolonged, rambling, repetitious, tedious, verbose, voluble, wordy.

*antonyms* brief, compact, curt, terse.

**long-windedness** *n* diffuseness, discursiveness, garrulity, lengthiness, longueur, macrology, prolixity, repetitiousness, tediousness, verbosity, volubility, wordiness.

*antonyms* brevity, curtness.

**look** *v* appear, behold, consider, contemplate, display, evidence, examine, exhibit, eye, gape, gawk, gawp, gaze, get a load of, glance, goggle, inspect, observe, ogle, peep, regard, rubberneck, scan, scrutinise, see, seem, show, stare, study, survey, take a butcher's, take a gander, take a shufti, view, watch.

*n* air, appearance, aspect, bearing, butcher's, cast, complexion, countenance, decko, demeanour, effect, examination, expression, eyeful, eye-glance, face, fashion, gander, gaze, glance, glimpse, guise, inspection, look-see, manner, mien, observation, once-over, peek, review, semblance, shufti, sight, squint, survey, view.

**look after** attend to, care for, chaperon, guard, keep an eye on, mind, nurse, protect, supervise, take care of, take charge of, tend, watch.

*antonym* neglect.

**look down on** contemn, despise, disdain, hold in contempt, look down one's nose at, misprise, pooh-pooh, scorn, sneer at, spurn, turn one's nose up at.

*antonyms* approve, esteem.

**look for** forage for, hunt, hunt for, hunt out, quest, search for, seek.

**look forward to** anticipate, await, count on, envisage, envision, expect, hope for, long for, look for, wait for.

**look into** check out, delve into, enquire about, examine, explore, fathom, follow up, go into, inspect, investigate, look over, plumb, probe, research, scrutinise, study.

**look like** resemble, take after.

**look out** be careful, be on the qui vive, beware, keep an eye out, keep one's eyes peeled, keep one's eyes skinned, pay attention, watch out.

**look out on** face, front, front on, give on (to), overlook.

**look over** cast an eye over, check, examine, flick through, give a once-over, inspect, look through, monitor, peruse, scan, view.

**look to/for** anticipate, await, count on, expect, hope for, reckon on, rely on.

**look up**[1] call on, drop by, drop in on, find, hunt for, look in on, pay a visit to, research, search for, seek out, stop by, track down, visit.

**look up**[2] ameliorate, come on, get better, improve, meliorate, perk up, pick up, progress, shape up.

**look up to** admire, esteem, have a high opinion of, honour, respect, revere.

**look-alike** n clone, dead ringer, doppel-gänger, double, living image, replica, ringer, spit, spit and image, spitting image, twin.

**look-out** n affair, beacon, business, citadel, concern, funeral, guard, post, problem, readiness, sentinal, sentry, tower, vedette, vigil, watch, watchman, watch-tower, weather-eye, worry.

**loom** v appear, bulk, dominate, emerge, hang over, hover, impend, materialise, menace, mount, overhang, overshadow, overtop, rise, soar, take shape, threaten, tower.

**loop** n arc, bend, circle, coil, convolution, curl, curve, eyelet, hoop, kink, loophole, noose, ring, spiral, turn, twirl, twist, whorl.

v bend, braid, circle, coil, connect, curl, curve round, encircle, fold, gird, join, knot, roll, spiral, turn, twist.

**loophole** n aperture, avoidance, escape, evasion, excuse, get-out, let-out, opening, plea, pretence, pretext, slot, subterfuge.

**loose**¹ adj baggy, crank, diffuse, disconnected, disordered, easy, floating, free, hanging, ill-defined, imprecise, inaccurate, indefinite, indistinct, inexact, insecure, loosened, movable, rambling, random, relaxed, released, shaky, slack, slackened, sloppy, solute, unattached, unbound, unconfined, unfastened, unfettered, unrestricted, unsecured, untied, vague, wobbly.

antonyms close, compact, precise, strict, taut, tense, tight.

v absolve, detach, disconnect, disengage, ease, free, let go, liberate, loosen, release, set free, slacken, unbind, unbrace, unclasp, uncouple, undo, unfasten, unhand, unleash, unlock, unloose, unmew, unmoor, unpen, untie.

antonyms bind, fasten, fix, secure.

**loose**² adj abandoned, careless, debauched, disreputable, dissipated, dissolute, fast, heedless, immoral, imprudent, lax, lewd, libertine, licentious, negligent, profligate, promiscuous, rash, thoughtless, unchaste, unmindful, wanton.

antonyms strict, stringent, tight.

**loosen** v deliver, detach, free, let go, let out, liberate, release, separate, set free, slacken, unbind, undo, unfasten, unloose, unloosen, unstick, untie.

antonym tighten.

**loosen up** ease up, go easy, lessen, let up, mitigate, moderate, relax, soften, unbend, weaken.

**loot** n boodle, booty, cache, goods, haul, plunder, prize, riches, spoils, swag.

v burglarise, despoil, maraud, pillage, plunder, raid, ransack, ravage, rifle, rob, sack.

**lop** v abscind, chop, clip, crop, curtail, cut, detach, detruncate, dock, hack, prune, sever, shorten, trim, truncate.

**lope** v bound, canter, gallop, lollop, run, spring, stride.

**lop-sided** adj askew, asymmetrical, awry, cockeyed, crooked, disproportionate, ill-balanced,

off balance, one-sided, out of true, squint, tiltin, unbalanced, unequal, uneven, warped.

antonyms balanced, straight, symmetrical.

**loquacious** adj babbling, blathering, chatterin, chatty, conversative, gabby, garrulous, gass, gossipy, multiloquent, multiloquous, talkative, voluble, wordy.

antonyms pauciloquent, succinct, taciturn, terse.

**loquacity** n chattiness, effusivenes, garrulity, gassiness, multiloquence, multiloquy, talkativeness, volubility.

antonyms succinctness, taciturnity, terseness.

**lord** n baron, commander, count, daimio, duke, earl, governor, Herr, king, leader, liege, liege-lor, master, monarch, noble, nobleman, overlord, peer, potentate, prince, ruler, seigneur, seignior, sovereign, superior, suzerain, viscount.

**lord it over** act big, boss around, domineer, oppress, order around, pull rank, put on airs, repress, swagger, tyrannise.

**lordly** adj aristocratic, arrogant, authoritarian, condescending, despotic, dictatorial, dignified, disdainful, domineering, exalted, gracious, grand, haughty, high and mighty, high-handed, hoity-toity, imperial, imperious, lofty, majestic, masterful, noble, overbearing, patronising, princely, proud, regal, stately, stuck-up, supercilious, swanky, toffee-nosed, tyrannical.

antonyms humble, low(ly), mean.

**lore** n beliefs, doctrine, erudition, experience, know-how, knowledge, learning, letters, mythus, saws, sayings, scholarship, schooling, teaching, traditions, wisdom.

**lorry** n camion, double-bottom, drag, drawbar outfit, float, juggernaut, pick-up, truck.

**lose** v capitulate, come a cropper, come to grief, consume, default, deplete, displace, dissipate, dodge, drain, drop, duck, elude, escape, evade, exhaust, expend, fail, fall short, forfeit, forget, get the worst of, give (someone) the slip, lap, lavish, leave behind, lose out on, misfile, mislay, misplace, miss, misspend, outdistance, outrun, outstrip, overtake, pass, pass up, shake off, slip away, squander, stray from, suffer defeat, take a licking, throw off, use up, wander from, waste, yield.

**loser** n also-ran, bum, bum steer, bummer, dud, failure, flop, lemon, no-hoper, runner-up, sucker, underdog, wash-out.

antonym winner.

**loss** n bereavement, cost, damage, debit, debt, defeat, deficiency, deficit, depletion, deprivation, destruction, detriment, disadvantage, disappearance, failure, forfeiture, harm, hurt, impairment, injury, losing, losings, misfortune, privation, ruin, shrinkage, squandering, waste, write-off.

antonyms benefit, gain.

**losses** n casualties, dead, death toll, disprofit, fatalities, missing, wounded.

**lost** adj abandoned, abolished, absent, absorbed, abstracted, adrift, annihilated, astray, baffled,

bewildered, confused, consumed, corrupt, damned, demolished, depraved, destroyed, devastated, disappeared, disoriented, dissipated, dissolute, distracted, dreamy, engrossed, entranced, eradicated, exterminated, fallen, forfeited, frittered away, irreclaimable, licentious, misapplied, misdirected, mislaid, misplaced, missed, missing, misspent, misused, mystified, obliterated, off-course, off-track, perished, perplexed, preoccupied, profligate, puzzled, rapt, ruined, spellbound, squandered, strayed, unrecallable, unrecapturable, unrecoverable, untraceable, vanished, wanton, wasted, wayward, wiped out, wrecked.
*antonym* found.

**lot** *n* accident, allowance, assortment, batch, chance, collection, consignment, crowd, cut, destiny, doom, fate, fortune, group, hazard, jingbang, parcel, part, percentage, piece, plight, portion, quantity, quota, ration, set, share, weird.

**loth** *see* **loath**.

**lotion** *n* balm, cream, embrocation, fomentation, liniment, salve, solution.

**lots** *n* a great deal, abundance, oodles, scade, tons.

**lottery** *n* chance, draw, gamble, hazard, raffle, risk, sweepstake, tombola, toss-up, uncertainty, venture.

**loud** *adj* blaring, blatant, boisterous, booming, brash, brassy, brazen, clamorous, coarse, crass, crude, deafening, ear-piercing, ear-splitting, flamboyant, flashy, garish, gaudy, glaring, high-sounding, loud-mouthed, lurid, noisy, offensive, ostentatious, piercing, raucous, resounding, rowdy, showy, sonorous, stentorian, streperous, strepitant, strident, strong, tasteless, tawdry, thundering, tumultuous, turbulent, vehement, vocal, vociferous, vulgar.
*antonyms* low, quiet, soft.

**loudly** *adv* clamorously, deafeningly, fortissimo, lustily, noisily, resoundingly, shrilly, streperously, strepitantly, stridently, strongly, uproariously, vehemently, vigorously, vocally, vociferously.
*antonyms* quietly, softly.

**loudmouth** *n* big mouth, blusterer, boaster, Bobadil, brag, braggadocio, braggart, Drawcansir, gasbag, swaggerer, windbag.

**loud-voiced** *adj* full-throated, leather-lunged, penetrating, piercing, roaring, sonorous, stentorian.
*antonyms* quiet, soft.

**lounge** *v* dawdle, idle, kill time, laze, lie about, lie back, loaf, loiter, loll, potter, recline, relax, slump, sprawl, take it easy, waste time.
*n* day-room, drawing-room, parlour, sitting-room.

**lour, lower** *v* be brewing, blacken, cloud over, darken, frown, give a dirty look, glare, glower, impend, look daggers, loom, menace, scowl, threaten.

**louring, lowering** *adj* black, brooding, browning, clouded, cloudy, dark, darkening, forbidding, foreboding, gloomy, glowering, grey, grim, heavy, impending, menacing, minatory, ominous, overcast, scowling, sullen, surly, threatening.

**lousy** *adj* awful, bad, base, contemptible, crap, despicable, dirty, hateful, inferior, lice-infested, lice-ridden, low, mean, miserable, no good, pedicular, pediculous, poor, rotten, second-rate, shoddy, slovenly, terrible, trashy, vicious, vile.
*antonyms* excellent, superb.

**lout** *n* bear, booby, boor, bull-calf, bumpkin, calf, chuckle-head, churl, clod, dolt, gawk, hallion, hick, hob, hobbledehoy, jake, lager lout, lob, lubber, lummox, oaf, swad, yahoo, yob, yobbo.

**loutish** *adj* bearish, boorish, bungling, churlish, clodhopping, coarse, doltish, gawky, gross, ill-bred, ill-mannered, lubberly, lumpen, lumpish, oafish, rough, stolid, swinish, uncouth, unmannerly, yobbish.

**lovable** *adj* adorable, amiable, attractive, captivating, charming, cuddly, delightful, enchanting, endearing, engaging, fetching, likable, lovely, pleasing, sweet, taking, winning, winsome.
*antonym* hateful.

**love** *v* adore, adulate, appreciate, cherish, delight in, desire, dote on, enjoy, fancy, hold dear, idolise, like, prize, relish, savour, take pleasure in, think the world of, treasure, want, worship.
*antonyms* detest, hate, loathe.
*n* adoration, adulation, affection, agape, aloha, amity, amorosity, amorousness, ardour, attachment, delight, devotion, enjoyment, fondness, friendship, inclination, infatuation, liking, partiality, passion, rapture, regard, relish, soft spot, taste, tenderness, warmth, weakness.
*antonyms* detestation, hate, loathing.

**love-affair** *n* affair, amour, grande passion, intrigue, liaison, love, mania, passion, relationship, romance.

**loveless** *adj* cold, cold-hearted, disliked, forsaken, friendless, frigid, hard, heartless, icy, insensitive, lovelorn, passionless, unappreciated, uncherished, unfeeling, unfriendly, unloved, unloving, unresponsive, unvalued.
*antonym* passionate.

**lovely** *adj* admirable, adorable, agreeable, amiable, attractive, beautiful, captivating, charming, comely, delightful, enchanting, engaging, enjoyable, exquisite, graceful, gratifying, handsome, idyllic, nice, pleasant, pleasing, pretty, sweet, taking, winning.
*antonyms* hideous, ugly, unlovely.

**love-making** *n* amation, carnal knowledge, coition, coitus, congress, copulation, courtship, dalliance, foreplay, gallantry, intercourse, intimacy, mating, sexual intercourse, sexual relations, sexual union, venery.

**lover** *n* admirer, amoretto, amorist, amoroso, beau, beloved, bidie-in, bon ami, boyfriend, Casanova, fancy man, fancy woman, fiancé(e), flame, gigolo, girlfriend, inamorata, inamorato, mistress, paramour, philanderer, suitor, swain, sweetheart.

**lovesick** *adj* desiring, infatuated, languishing, longing, lovelorn, mashed, pining, yearning.

**loving** *adj* affectionate, amative, amatorial, amatorian, amatorious, amorous, ardent, cordial, dear, demonstrative, devoted, doting, fond, friendly, kind, passionate, solicitous, tender, warm, warm-hearted.

**low¹** *adj* abject, base, base-born, blue, brassed off, browned off, cheap, coarse, common, contemptible, crude, dastardly, debilitated, deep, deficient, degraded, dejected, depleted, depraved, depressed, despicable, despondent, disgraceful, disheartened, dishonourable, disreputable, down, down in the dumps, downcast, dying, economical, exhausted, fed up, feeble, forlorn, frail, gloomy, glum, gross, humble, hushed, ignoble, ill, ill-bred, inadequate, inexpensive, inferior, insignificant, little, low-born, low-grade, lowly, low-lying, meagre, mean, mediocre, meek, menial, miserable, moderate, modest, morose, muffled, muted, nasty, obscene, obscure, paltry, plain, plebeian, poor, prostrate, puny, quiet, reasonable, reduced, rough, rude, sad, scant, scurvy, second-rate, servile, shallow, shoddy, short, simple, sinking, small, soft, sordid, sparse, squat, stricken, stunted, subdued, substandard, sunken, trifling, unbecoming, undignified, unhappy, unpretentious, unrefined, unworthy, vile, vulgar, weak, whispered, worthless.

*antonyms* elevated, high, lofty, noble.

**low point** all-time low, low-watermark, nadir, perigee.

**low²** *v* bellow, moo.

**low-born** *adj* mean-born, plebeian, unexalted.

**lowbrow** *adj* crude, ignorant, rude, uncultivated, uncultured, uneducated, unlearned, unlettered, unrefined, unscholarly.

*antonym* highbrow.

**low-down** *n* dope, gen, info, information, inside story, intelligence, news.

**lower¹** *adj* inferior, insignificant, junior, lesser, low-level, lowly, minor, secondary, second-class, smaller, subordinate, subservient, under, unimportant.

*v* abase, abate, belittle, condescend, couch, curtail, cut, debase, decrease, degrade, deign, demean, demolish, depress, devalue, diminish, discredit, disgrace, downgrade, drop, fall, humble, humiliate, lessen, let down, minimise, moderate, prune, raze, reduce, sink, slash, soften, stoop, submerge, take down, tone down.

*antonyms* elevate, increase, raise, rise.

**lower²** *see* **lour**.

**lowering** *see* **louring**.

**low-grade** *adj* bad, cheap-jack, inferior, poor, second-class, second-rate, substandard, third-rate.

*antonyms* good, quality.

**low-key** *adj* downbeat, low-pitched, muffled, muted, quiet, restrained, slight, soft, subdued, understated.

**lowly** *adj* average, common, docile, dutiful, homespun, humble, ignoble, inferior, low-born, mean, mean-born, meek, mild, modest, obscure, ordinary, plain, plebeian, poor, proletarian, simple, submissive, subordinate, unassuming, unexalted, unpretentious.

*antonyms* lofty, noble.

**low-minded** *adj* coarse, crude, depraved, dirty, disgusting, filthy, foul, gross, immoral, indecent, obscene, rude, scurril(e), smutty, uncouth, vulgar.

*antonym* high-minded.

**low-spirited** *adj* apathetic, blue, brassed off, browned off, dejected, depressed, despondent, down, down in the dumps, down-hearted, fed up, gloomy, glum, heavy-hearted, low, miserable, moody, pissed off, sad, unhappy.

*antonyms* cheerful, high-spirited.

**loyal** *adj* attached, constant, dependable, devoted, dutiful, faithful, honest, leal, patriotic, sincere, staunch, steadfast, true, true-blue, true-hearted, trustworthy, trusty, unswerving, unwavering.

*antonyms* disloyal, traitorous.

**loyalty** *n* allegiance, constancy, dependability, devotion, faithfulness, fealty, fidelity, honesty, lealty, patriotism, reliability, sincerity, staunchness, steadfastness, true-heartedness, trueness, trustiness, trustworthiness.

*antonyms* disloyalty, treachery.

**lozenge** *n* cough-drop, jujube, pastille, tablet, troche, trochiscus, trochisk.

**lubberly** *adj* awkward, blundering, bungling, churlish, clodhopping, clownish, clumsy, coarse, crude, dense, doltish, gawky, heavy-handed, loutish, lumbering, lumpen, lumpish, oafish, obtuse, uncouth, ungainly.

**lubricate** *v* grease, lard, oil, smear, wax.

**lucid** *adj* beaming, bright, brilliant, clear, clear-cut, clear-headed, compos mentis, comprehensible, crystalline, diaphanous, distinct, effulgent, evident, explicit, glassy, gleaming, intelligible, limpid, luminous, obvious, pellucid, perspicuous, plain, pure, radiant, rational, reasonable, resplendent, sane, sensible, shining, sober, sound, translucent, transparent.

*antonyms* dark, murky, unclear.

**luck** *n* accident, blessing, break, chance, destiny, fate, fluke, fortuity, fortune, godsend, good fortune, hap, happenstance, hazard, jam, joss, prosperity, serendipity, stroke, success, windfall.

*antonym* misfortune.

**luckily** *adv* feliciter, fortuitously, fortunately, haply, happily, opportunely, propitiously, providentially.

*antonym* unfortunately.

**luckless** *adj* calamitous, catastrophic, cursed, disastrous, doomed, fey, hapless, hopeless, ill-fated, ill-starred, jinxed, star-crossed, unfortunate, unhappy, unlucky, unpropitious, unsuccessful.

*antonym* lucky.

**lucky** *adj* advantageous, adventitious, auspicious, blessed, canny, charmed, favoured, fluk(e)y, fortuitous, fortunate, jammy, opportune, propitious, prosperous, providential, serendipitous, successful, timely.

*antonyms* luckless, unlucky.

**lucky dip** bran tub, grab-bag.

**lucrative** *adj* advantageous, fecund, fertile, fruitful, gainful, paying, productive, profitable, remunerative, well-paid.

*antonym* unprofitable.

**lucre** n gain(s), mammon, money, moolah, pelf, profit, riches, spoils, velvet, wealth.

**ludicrous** adj absurd, amusing, burlesque, comic, comical, crazy, drôle, droll, farcical, funny, incongruous, laughable, nonsensical, odd, outlandish, preposterous, ridiculous, risible, silly, zany.

**lug** v carry, drag, haul, heave, hump, humph, pull, tote, tow, yank.

**luggage** n baggage, bags, cases, gear, impedimenta, paraphernalia, suitcases, things, traps, trunks.

**lugubrious** adj dismal, doleful, dreary, funereal, gloomy, glum, melancholy, morose, mournful, sad, sepulchral, serious, sombre, sorrowful, Wertherian, woebegone, woeful.

*antonyms* cheerful, jovial, merry.

**lukewarm** adj apathetic, cold, cool, half-hearted, indifferent, laodicean, Laodicean, lew, phlegmatic, tepid, unconcerned, unenthusiastic, uninterested, unresponsive, warm.

**lull** v abate, allay, calm, cease, compose, decrease, diminish, dwindle, ease off, hush, let up, lullaby, moderate, pacify, quell, quiet, quieten down, sedate, slacken, soothe, still, subdue, subside, tranquillise, wane.

*antonym* agitate.

n calm, calmness, hush, let-up, pause, peace, quiet, respite, silence, stillness, tranquillity.

*antonym* agitation.

**lullaby** n berceuse, cradle-song, Wiegenlied.

**lumber**[1] n bits and pieces, clutter, jumble, junk, odds and ends, refuse, rubbish, trash, trumpery.

v burden, charge, encumber, hamper, impose, land, load, saddle.

**lumber**[2] v clump, galumph, plod, shamble, shuffle, stump, trudge, trundle, waddle.

**lumbering** adj awkward, blundering, bovine, bumbling, clumsy, elephantine, heavy, heavy-footed, hulking, lubberly, lumpish, massive, overgrown, ponderous, ungainly, unwieldy.

*antonyms* agile, nimble.

**luminary** n celeb, celebrity, dignitary, leader, leading light, lion, notable, personage, star, superstar, VIP, worthy.

**luminescent** adj bright, dayglow, effulgent, fluorescent, glowing, luciferous, luminous, phosphorescent, radiant, shining.

**luminous** adj bright, brilliant, dayglow, glowing, illuminated, lighted, lit, lucent, luminescent, luminiferous, lustrous, radiant, resplendent, shining, vivid.

**lump**[1] n ball, bulge, bump, bunch, cake, chuck, chump, chunk, clod, cluster, cyst, dab, daud, dod, gob, gobbet, group, growth, hunch, hunk, (k)nub, (k)nubble, lob, mass, nugget, piece, protrusion, protuberance, spot, swelling, tuber, tumescence, tumour, wedge, wen, wodge.

v coalesce, collect, combine, consolidate, group, mass, unite.

**lump**[2] v bear (with), brook, endure, put up with, stand, stomach, suffer, swallow, take, thole, tolerate.

**lumpish** adj awkward, boorish, bovine, bungling, clumsy, doltish, dull-witted, elephantine, gawky, heavy, lethargic, lumbering, oafish, obtuse, stolid, stupid, ungainly.

**lumpy** adj bumpy, bunched, cloggy, clotted, curdled, grainy, granular, knobbly, nodose, nodous, nodular, nodulose, nodulous.

*antonyms* even, smooth.

**lunacy** n aberration, absurdity, craziness, dementia, derangement, folly, foolhardiness, foolishness, idiocy, imbecility, insanity, madness, mania, moon-madness, moonraking, psychosis, senselessness, stupidity, tomfoolery.

*antonym* sanity.

**lunatic** n bug, loony, madman, maniac, nut, nutcase, nutter, psychopath.

adj barmy, bonkers, crazy, daft, demented, deranged, insane, irrational, mad, maniacal, moon-stricken, moon-struck, nuts, psychotic, unhinged.

*antonyms* sane, sensible.

**lunch** n dejeune, déjeuner, luncheon, nooning, nuncheon, tiffin.

**lunge** v bound, charge, cut, dash, dive, fall upon, grab (at), hit (at), jab, leap, pitch into, plunge, poke, pounce, set upon, stab, strike (at), thrust.

n charge, cut, jab, pass, pounce, spring, stab, swing, swipe, thrust, venue.

**lurch** v heave, lean, list, pitch, reel, rock, roll, stagger, stumble, sway, tilt, totter, wallow, weave, welter.

**lure** v allure, attract, beckon, decoy, draw, ensnare, entice, inveigle, invite, lead on, seduce, tempt, trepan.

n allurement, attraction, bait, carrot, come-on, decoy, enticement, inducement, magnet, siren, song, temptation, train.

**lurid** adj ashen, bloody, disgusting, exaggerated, fiery, flaming, ghastly, glaring, glowering, gory, graphic, grim, grisly, gruesome, intense, livid, loud, macabre, melodramatic, pale, pallid, revolting, sallow, sanguine, savage, sensational, shocking, startling, unrestrained, violent, vivid, wan.

**lurk** v crouch, hide, hide out, lie in wait, lie low, prowl, skulk, slink, sneak, snook, snoop.

**luscious** adj appetising, delectable, delicious, honeyed, juicy, luxuriant, luxurious, mouth-watering, palatable, rich, savoury, scrumptious, succulent, sweet, tasty, toothsome, yummy.

*antonym* austere.

**lush** adj abundant, dense, elaborate, extravagant, flourishing, grand, green, juicy, lavish, luxuriant, luxurious, opulent, ornate, overgrown, palatial, plush, prolific, rank, ripe, ritzy, succulent, sumptuous, superabundant, teeming, tender, verdant.

**lust** n appetence, appetency, appetite, avidity, carnality, concupiscence, covetousness, craving, cupidity, desire, greed, Kama, Kamadeva, lasciviousness, lech, lechery, lewdness, libido, licentiousness, longing, passion, prurience, randiness, salaciousness, sensuality, thirst, wantonness.

**lust after** crave, desire, have hot-pants for, have the hots for, hunger for, need, slaver over, thirst for, want, yearn for, yen for.

**lustful** *adj* carnal, concupiscent, craving, goatish, hankering, horny, lascivious, lecherous, lewd, libidinous, licentious, passionate, prurient, randy, raunchy, ruttish, sensual, unchaste, venerous, wanton.

**lustily** *adv* forcefully, hard, loudly, powerfully, robustly, stoutly, strongly, vigorously, with all one's might, with might and main.

*antonym* weakly.

**lustiness** *n* energy, haleness, hardihood, hardiness, health, healthiness, power, robustness, stoutness, strength, sturdiness, toughness, vigour, virility.

**lustre** *n* brightness, brilliance, burnish, dazzle, distinction, effulgence, fame, gleam, glint, glitter, glory, gloss, glow, gorm, honour, illustriousness, lambency, luminousness, prestige, radiance, renown, resplendence, sheen, shimmer, shine, sparkle, water.

**lustrous** *adj* bright, burnished, dazzling, gleaming, glistening, glittering, glossy, glowing, lambent, luminous, radiant, shimmering, shining, shiny, sparkling.

*antonyms* dull, lacklustre, matt.

**lusty** *adj* blooming, brawny, energetic, gutsy, hale, healthy, hearty, in fine fettle, muscular, powerful, red-blooded, robust, rugged, stalwart, stout, strapping, strong, sturdy, vigorous, virile.

*antonyms* effete, weak.

**luxuriance** *n* abundance, copiousness, denseness, excess, exuberance, fecundity, fertility, lavishness, lushness, profusion, rankness, richness, sumptuousness.

**luxuriant** *adj* abundant, ample, baroque, copious, dense, elaborate, excessive, extravagant, exuberant, fancy, fecund, fertile, festooned,

flamboyant, florid, flowery, lavish, lush, opulent, ornate, overflowing, plenteous, plentiful, prodigal, productive, profuse, prolific, rank, rich, riotous, rococo, sumptuous, superabundant, teeming, thriving.

*antonyms* barren, infertile.

**luxuriate** *v* abound, bask, bloom, burgeon, delight, enjoy, flourish, grow, have a ball, indulge, live high off the hog, live the life of Riley, prosper, relish, revel, thrive, wallow, wanton.

**luxurious** *adj* comfortable, costly, deluxe, epicurean, expensive, hedonistic, lavish, magnificent, opulent, pampered, plush, plushy, rich, ritzy, self-indulgent, sensual, splendid, sumptuous, sybaritic, voluptuous, well-appointed.

*antonyms* ascetic, austere, economical, frugal, scant(y), spartan.

**luxury** *n* affluence, bliss, comfort, delight, dolce vita, enjoyment, extra, extravagance, flesh-pots, flesh-pottery, frill, gratification, hedonism, indulgence, milk and honey, non-essential, opulence, pleasure, richness, satisfaction, splendour, sumptuousness, treat, voluptuousness, well-being.

*antonym* essential.

**lying** *adj* accumbent, deceitful, decumbent, dishonest, dissembling, double-dealing, duplicitous, false, guileful, mendacious, perfidious, treacherous, two-faced, untruthful.

*antonyms* honest, truthful.

*n* deceit, dishonesty, dissimulation, double-dealing, duplicity, fabrication, falsity, fibbing, guile, mendacity, perjury, prevarication, pseudology, untruthfulness.

*antonyms* honesty, truthfulness.

**lyrical** *adj* carried away, ecstatic, effusive, emotional, enthusiastic, expressive, impassioned, inspired, musical, passionate, poetic, rapturous, rhapsodic.

**lyrics** *n* book, libretto, text, words.

# M

**macabre** *adj* cadaverous, deathlike, deathly, dreadful, eerie, frightening, frightful, ghastly, ghostly, ghoulish, grim, grisly, gruesome, hideous, horrible, horrid, morbid, sick, weird.

**macerate** *v* blend, liquefy, mash, pulp, soak, soften, steep.

**Machiavellian** *adj* amoral, artful, astute, calculating, crafty, cunning, cynical, deceitful, designing, double-dealing, foxy, guileful, intriguing, opportunist, perfidious, scheming, shrewd, sly, underhand, unscrupulous, wily.

**machinate** *v* conspire, contrive, design, devise, engineer, finagle, hatch, intrigue, invent, manoeuvre, plan, plot, scheme, work.

**machination** *n* artifice, cabal, conspiracy, design, device, dodge, finagling, intrigue, manoeuvre, plot, ploy, ruse, scheme, shenanigans, stratagem, trick.

**machine** *n* agency, agent, apparatus, appliance, automaton, contraption, contrivance, device, engine, gadget, gizmo, instrument, machinery, mechanism, organisation, party, puppet, robot, set-up, structure, system, tool, zombi(e).

**machine-gun** *n* Bren (gun), gatling-gun, mitrailleur, mitrailleuse, pompom, tommy-gun.

**machinery** *n* agency, apparatus, channels, enginery, equipment, gear, instruments, kit, machine, mechanism, organisation, procedure, structure, system, tackle, tools, works.

**mad** *adj* abandoned, aberrant, absurd, agitated, angry, ardent, avid, bananas, barmy, bats, batty, berserk, boisterous, bonkers, crackers, crazed, crazy, cuckoo, daft, delirious, demented, deranged, devoted, distracted, dotty, ebullient, enamoured, energetic, enraged, enthusiastic, exasperated, excited, fanatical, fond, foolhardy, foolish, frantic, frenetic, frenzied, fuming, furious, gay, gyte, have bats in the belfry, hooked, impassioned, imprudent, in a paddy, incensed, infatuated, infuriated, insane, irate, irrational, irritated, keen, livid, loony, loopy, ludicrous, lunatic, madcap, mental, moon-stricken, moon-struck, non compos mentis, nonsensical, nuts, nutty, off one's chump, off one's head, off one's nut, off one's rocker, off one's trolley, out of one's mind, possessed, preposterous, psychotic, rabid, raging, raving, resentful, riotous, round the bend, round the twist, screwball, screwy, senseless, unbalanced, uncontrolled, unhinged, unreasonable, unrestrained, unsafe, unsound, unstable, up the pole, waxy, wild, wrathful, zealous.

*antonyms* lucid, rational, sane.

**madcap** *adj* bird-brained, crazy, flighty, foolhardy, hare-brained, heedless, hot-headed, ill-advised, imprudent, impulsive, lively, rash, reckless, silly, thoughtless, wild.

**madden** *v* annoy, craze, dement, dementate, derange, enrage, exasperate, incense, inflame, infuriate, irritate, provoke, unhinge, upset, vex.

*antonyms* calm, pacify, please.

**made-up** *adj* fabricated, fairy-tale, false, fictional, imaginary, invented, make-believe, mythical, specious, trumped-up, unreal, untrue.

**madhouse** *n* asylum, Babel, bedlam, chaos, disarray, disorder, funny farm, loony bin, nut-house, pandemonium, snake-pit, turmoil, uproar.

**madly** *adv* absurdly, crazily, deliriously, dementedly, desperately, devotedly, distractedly, energetically, exceedingly, excessively, excitedly, extremely, fanatically, foolishly, frantically, frenziedly, furiously, hastily, hurriedly, hysterically, insanely, intensely, irrationally, like mad, ludicrously, nonsensically, passionately, quickly, rabidly, rapidly, recklessly, senselessly, speedily, to distraction, unreasonably, violently, wildly.

**madman** *n* bedlamite, détraqué, furioso, loony, lunatic, madling, maniac, mattoid, mental case, nut, nutcase, nutter, psycho, psychopath, psychotic, schizo, screwball.

**madness** *n* abandon, aberration, absurdity, agitation, anger, ardour, craze, craziness, daftness, delusion, dementia, demoniacism, demonomania, derangement, distraction, enthusiasm, exasperation, excitement, fanaticism, folie, folly, fondness, foolhardiness, foolishness, frenzy, furore, fury, infatuation, insanity, intoxication, ire, keenness, lunacy, lycanthropy, mania, monomania, moon-madness, moonraking, nonsense, passion, preposterousness, psychopathy, psychosis, rage, raving, riot, unrestraint, uproar, wildness, wrath, zeal.

*antonym* sanity.

**maelstrom** *n* bedlam, chaos, Charybdis, confusion, disorder, mess, pandemonium, tumult, turmoil, uproar, vortex, whirlpool.

**maestro** *n* expert, genius, master, prodigy, virtuoso, wizard.

**magazine**[1] *n* fanzine, journal, monthly, pamphlet, paper, periodical, quarterly, weekly.

**magazine²** *n* ammunition dump, arsenal, depot, ordnance, powder-room, store, storehouse.

**magic** *n* allurement, black art, charm, conjuring, conjury, diablerie, enchantment, fascination, glamour, goety, gramary(e), hocus-pocus, hoodoo, illusion, jiggery-pokery, jugglery, legerdemain, magnetism, medicine, necromancy, occultism, prestidigitation, sleight of hand, sorcery, sortilege, spell, thaumaturgics, thaumaturgism, thaumaturgy, theurgy, trickery, voodoo, witchcraft, wizardry, wonder-work.

*adj* bewitching, charismatic, charming, enchanting, entrancing, fascinating, goetic, hermetic, magical, magnetic, marvellous, miraculous, mirific, mirifical, sorcerous, spellbinding, spellful.

**magician** *n* archimage, conjurer, conjuror, enchanter, enchantress, genius, illusionist, maestro, mage, Magian, magus, marvel, miracle-worker, necromancer, prestidigitator, prestigiator, sorcerer, spellbinder, thaumaturge, theurgist, virtuoso, warlock, witch, witch-doctor, wizard, wonder-monger, wonder-worker.

**magisterial** *adj* arrogant, assertive, authoritarian, authoritative, bossy, commanding, despotic, dictatorial, domineering, high-handed, imperious, lordly, masterful, overbearing, peremptory.

**magistrate** *n* aedile, bailiff, bail(l)ie, beak, JP, judge, jurat, justice, justice of the peace, mittimus, queer cuffin, stipendiary, tribune.

**magnanimity** *n* beneficence, big-heartedness, bountifulness, charitableness, charity, generosity, high-mindedness, largess(e), liberality, munificence, nobility, open-handedness, selflessness, unselfishness.

*antonym* meanness.

**magnanimous** *adj* altruistic, beneficent, big, big-hearted, bountiful, charitable, free, generous, great-hearted, handsome, high-minded, kind, kindly, large-hearted, large-minded, liberal, munificent, noble, open-handed, philanthropic, selfless, ungrudging, unselfish, unstinting.

*antonyms* mean, paltry, petty.

**magnate** *n* aristocrat, baron, bashaw, big cheese, big noise, big shot, big wheel, bigwig, captain of industry, chief, fat cat, grandee, leader, magnifico, merchant, mogul, nabob, noble, notable, personage, plutocrat, prince, tycoon, VIP.

**magnet** *n* appeal, attraction, bait, draw, enticement, lodestone, lure, solenoid.

*antonym* repellent.

**magnetic** *adj* absorbing, alluring, attractive, captivating, charismatic, charming, enchanting, engrossing, entrancing, fascinating, gripping, hypnotic, irresistible, mesmerising, seductive.

*antonyms* repellent, repugnant, repulsive.

**magnetism** *n* allure, appeal, attraction, attractiveness, charisma, charm, draw, drawing power, enchantment, fascination, grip, hypnotism, lure, magic, mesmerism, power, pull, seductiveness, spell.

**magnification** *n* aggrandisement, amplification, augmentation, blow-up, boost, build-up, deepening, dilation, enhancement, enlargement, exaggeration, expansion, extolment, heightening, increase, inflation, intensification, lionisation.

*antonyms* diminution, reduction.

**magnificence** *n* brilliance, glory, gorgeousness, grandeur, grandiosity, impressiveness, luxuriousness, luxury, majesty, nobility, opulence, pomp, resplendence, splendour, stateliness, sublimity, sumptuousness.

*antonyms* modesty, plainness, simplicity.

**magnificent** *adj* august, brilliant, elegant, elevated, exalted, excellent, fine, glorious, gorgeous, grand, grandiose, imposing, impressive, lavish, luxurious, majestic, noble, opulent, outstanding, plush, posh, princely, regal, resplendent, rich, ritzy, splendid, stately, sublime, sumptuous, superb, superior, transcendent.

*antonyms* humble, modest, plain, simple.

**magnify** *v* aggrandise, aggravate, amplify, augment, blow up, boost, build up, deepen, dilate, dramatise, enhance, enlarge, exaggerate, expand, greaten, heighten, increase, inflate, intensify, lionise, overdo, overemphasise, overestimate, overplay, overrate, overstate, praise.

*antonyms* belittle, play down.

**magniloquence** *n* bombast, euphuism, fustian, grandiloquence, loftiness, orotundity, pomposity, pretentiousness, rhetoric, turgidity.

*antonyms* simplicity, straightforwardness.

**magniloquent** *adj* bombastic, declamatory, elevated, euphuistic, exalted, fustian, grandiloquent, high-flown, high-sounding, lofty, orotund, overblown, pompous, pretentious, rhetorical, sonorous, stilted, turgid.

*antonyms* simple, straightforward.

**magnitude** *n* amount, amplitude, bigness, brightness, bulk, capacity, consequence, dimensions, eminence, enormousness, expanse, extent, grandeur, greatness, hugeness, immensity, importance, intensity, largeness, mark, mass, measure, moment, note, proportions, quantity, significance, size, space, strength, vastness, volume, weight.

*antonym* smallness.

**magnum opus** Almagest, chef d'oeuvre, masterpiece, master-work, pièce de résistance.

**maid** *n* abigail, bonne, damsel, dresser, femme de chambre, fille de chambre, gentlewoman, girl, handmaiden, housemaid, lady's maid, lass, lassie, maiden, maid-of-all-work, maid-servant, miss, nymph, servant, serving-maid, soubrette, tirewoman, tiring-woman, virgin, waitress, wench.

**maiden** *n* damozel, damsel, demoiselle, girl, lass, lassie, maid, may, miss, nymph, virgin, wench.

*adj* chaste, female, first, fresh, inaugural, initial, initiatory, intact, introductory, new, pure, unbroached, uncaptured, undefiled, unmarried, unpolluted, untapped, untried, unused, unwed, virgin, virginal.

*antonyms* defiled, deflowered, unchaste.

**maidenly** *adj* becoming, chaste, decent, decorous, demure, gentle, girlish, modest, proper, pure, reserved, seemly, undefiled, vestal, virginal, virtuous.

*antonym* immodest.

**mail** *n* correspondence, da(w)k, delivery, letters, packages, parcels, post.

*v* air-mail, dispatch, forward, post, send.

**maim** *v* cripple, disable, hack, haggle, hamstring, hurt, impair, incapacitate, injure, lame, mangle, mar, mutilate, savage, wound.

*antonyms* heal, repair.

**main**[1] *adj* absolute, brute, capital, cardinal, central, chief, critical, crucial, direct, downright, entire, essential, extensive, first, foremost, general, great, head, leading, mere, necessary, outstanding, paramount, particular, predominant, pre-eminent, premier, primary, prime, principal, pure, sheer, special, staple, supreme, undisguised, utmost, utter, vital.

*antonyms* minor, unimportant.

*n* effort, foison, force, might, potency, power, puissance, strength, vigour.

*antonym* weakness.

**main**[2] *n* cable, channel, conduit, duct, line, pipe.

**mainly** *adv* above all, as a rule, chiefly, especially, for the most part, generally, in general, in the main, largely, mostly, on the whole, overall, predominantly, primarily, principally, substantially, usually.

**mainspring** *n* cause, driving force, fountainhead, generator, impulse, incentive, inspiration, motivation, motive, origin, prime mover, source, wellspring.

**mainstay** *n* anchor, backbone, bulwark, buttress, linchpin, pillar, prop, support.

**mainstream** *adj* accepted, average, conventional, established, general, normal, orthodox, received, regular, standard.

*antonyms* heterodox, peripheral.

**maintain** *v* advocate, affirm, allege, argue, assert, asseverate, aver, avouch, avow, back, care for, carry on, champion, claim, conserve, contend, continue, declare, defend, fight for, finance, hold, insist, justify, keep, keep up, look after, make good, nurture, observe, perpetuate, plead for, practise, preserve, profess, prolong, provide, retain, stand by, state, supply, support, sustain, take care of, uphold, vindicate.

*antonyms* deny, neglect, oppose.

**maintenance** *n* aliment, alimony, allowance, care, conservation, continuance, continuation, defence, food, keep, keeping, livelihood, living, nurture, perpetuation, preservation, prolongation, protection, provision, repairs, retainment, subsistence, supply, support, sustainment, sustenance, sustention, upkeep.

*antonym* neglect.

**majestic** *adj* august, awesome, dignified, distinguished, elevated, exalted, grand, grandiose, imperial, imperious, imposing, impressive, kingly, lofty, magisterial, magnificent, monumental, noble, pompous, princely, queenly, regal, royal, splendid, stately, sublime, superb.

*antonyms* unimportant, unimpressive.

**majesty** *n* augustness, awesomeness, dignity, exaltedness, glory, grandeur, impressiveness, kingliness, loftiness, magnificence, majesticness, nobility, pomp, queenliness, regalness, resplendence, royalty, splendour, state, stateliness, sublimity.

*antonyms* unimportance, unimpressiveness.

**major** *adj* better, bigger, chief, critical, crucial, elder, grave, great, greater, higher, important, key, keynote, larger, leading, main, most, notable, older, outstanding, pre-eminent, radical, senior, serious, significant, superior, supreme, uppermost, vital, weighty.

*antonym* minor.

**majority** *n* adulthood, bulk, manhood, mass, maturity, plurality, preponderance, seniority, superiority, the many, womanhood, years of discretion.

*antonyms* childhood, minority.

**make** *v* accomplish, acquire, act, add up to, amount to, appoint, arrive at, assemble, assign, attain, beget, bring about, build, calculate, carry out, catch, cause, clear, coerce, compel, compose, conclude, constitute, constrain, construct, contract, contribute, convert, create, designate, do, dragoon, draw up, drive, earn, effect, elect, embody, enact, engage in, engender, establish, estimate, execute, fabricate, fashion, fix, flow, force, forge, form, frame, gain, gar, gauge, generate, get, give rise to, impel, induce, install, invest, judge, lead to, manufacture, meet, mould, net, nominate, oblige, obtain, occasion, ordain, originate, pass, perform, practise, press, pressurise, prevail upon, proceed, produce, prosecute, put together, reach, reckon, render, require, secure, shape, smith(y), suppose, synthesise, take in, tend, think, turn, win.

*antonyms* dismantle, lose, persuade.

*n* brand, build, character, composition, constitution, construction, cut, designation, disposition, form, formation, humour, kind, make-up, manner, manufacture, mark, model, nature, shape, sort, stamp, structure, style, temper, temperament, texture, type, variety.

**make believe** act, dream, enact, fantasise, feign, imagine, play, play-act, pretend.

**make do** cope, get along, get by, improvise, make out, manage, muddle through, scrape by, survive.

**make eyes at** flirt, give (someone) the come-on, leer at, make sheep's eyes at, ogle.

**make for** aim for, conduce to, contribute to, facilitate, favour, forward, further, head for, promote.

**make fun of** deride, lampoon, laugh at, make sport of, mock, parody, poke fun at, queer, quiz, rag, rib, ridicule, roast, rot, satirise, scoff at, send up, sneer at, take off, taunt.

*antonym* praise.

**make inroads into** consume, eat away, eat into, eat up, encroach upon, get on with, make progress with, progress with.

*antonym* add to.

**make it** arrive, come through, get on, prosper, pull through, reach, succeed, survive.

*antonym* fail.

**make love** canoodle, copulate, cuddle, embrace, enjoy, fuck, gender, go to bed, neck, pet, romance, screw, smooch.

**make merry** carouse, celebrate, feast, frolic, junket, make whoopee, paint the town red, revel, whoop it up.

**make no difference** be six and half a dozen, count for nothing, cut no ice.

**make off** abscond, beat a hasty retreat, bolt, clear off, cut and run, decamp, depart, flee, fly, have it on one's toes, leave, make away, run away, run for it, run off, take to one's heels.

**make off with** abduct, appropriate, carry off, filch, kidnap, knock off, nab, nick, pilfer, pinch, purloin, run away, run off with, steal, swipe, walk off with.
*antonym* bring.

**make one's mark** get on, make good, make it, make the big-time, prosper, succeed.
*antonym* fail.

**make out** assert, claim, complete, comprehend, decipher, demonstrate, describe, descry, detect, discern, discover, distinguish, draw up, espy, fare, fathom, fill in, fill out, follow, get on, grasp, imply, infer, inscribe, let on, make as if, manage, perceive, pretend, prosper, prove, realise, recognise, represent, see, show, succeed, survive, thrive, understand, work out, write, write out.
*antonym* fail.

**make sense of** apprehend, comprehend, fathom, figure out, grasp, make head or tail of, make much of, make out, understand.

**make tracks** beat it, dash, dash off, depart, disappear, go, hit the road, hurry, leave, make off, scram, set out, split, take off.

**make up¹** arrange, coin, collect, complement, complete, compose, comprise, concoct, constitute, construct, cook up, create, devise, dream up, fabricate, feign, fill, form, formulate, frame, hatch, invent, meet, originate, parcel, put together, repair, supplement, supply, trump up, write.

**make up²** bury the hatchet, call it quits, come to terms, forgive and forget, make peace, mend one's fences, settle, settle differences, shake hands.

**make up for** atone for, balance, compensate, expiate, make amends for, offset, recompense, redeem, redress, requite.

**make up one's mind** choose, decide, determine, resolve, settle.
*antonym* waver.

**make up to** butter up, chat up, court, curry favour with, fawn on, flirt with, make overtures to, toady to, woo.

**make-believe** *n* charade, dream, fantasy, imagination, play-acting, pretence, role-play, unreality.
*antonym* reality.
*adj* dream, fantasised, fantasy, feigned, imaginary, imagined, made-up, mock, pretend, pretended, sham, simulated, unreal.
*antonym* real.

**maker** *n* architect, author, builder, constructor, contriver, creator, director, fabricator, framer, manufacturer, producer.
*antonym* dismantler.

**makeshift** *adj* band-aid, cutcha, expedient, haywire, improvised, kacha, make-do, provisional, rough and ready, stop-gap, substitute, temporary.
*antonyms* finished, permanent.
*n* band-aid, expedient, fig-leaf, shift, stop-gap, substitute.

**make-up¹** *n* cosmetics, fard, fucus, greasepaint, maquillage, paint, powder, war paint, white-face.

**make-up²** *n* arrangement, assembly, build, cast, character, complexion, composition, configuration, constitution, construction, disposition, figure, form, format, formation, make, nature, organisation, stamp, structure, style, temper, temperament.

**making** *n* assembly, building, composition, construction, creation, fabrication, forging, manufacture, modelling, moulding, production.
*antonym* dismantling.

**makings** *n* beginnings, capability, capacity, earnings, income, ingredients, materials, possibilities, potential, potentiality, proceeds, profits, promise, qualities, returns, revenue, takings.

**maladjusted** *adj* alienated, confused, disturbed, estranged, hung-up, muddled, neurotic, unstable.
*antonym* well-adjusted.

**maladministration** *n* blundering, bungling, corruption, dishonesty, incompetence, inefficiency, malfeasance, malpractice, malversation, misconduct, misfeasance, misgovernment, mismanagement, misrule, stupidity.

**maladroit** *adj* awkward, bungling, cack-handed, clumsy, gauche, graceless, ham-fisted, ill-timed, inconsiderate, inelegant, inept, inexpert, insensitive, tactless, thoughtless, undiplomatic, unhandy, unskilful, untoward.
*antonyms* adroit, tactful.

**malady** *n* affliction, ailment, breakdown, complaint, disease, disorder, illness, indisposition, infirmity, malaise, sickness.
*antonym* health.

**malaise** *n* angst, anguish, anxiety, depression, discomfort, disquiet, distemper, doldrums, enervation, future shock, illness, indisposition, lassitude, melancholy, sickness, unease, uneasiness, weakness.
*antonyms* happiness, well-being.

**malapropos** *adj* ill-timed, inapposite, inappropriate, inapt, inopportune, misapplied, tactless, uncalled-for, unseemly, unsuitable, untimely.
*antonyms* appropriate, tactful.
*adv* inappositely, inappropriately, inaptly, inopportunely, tactlessly, unseasonably, unsuitably.
*antonyms* appropriately, tactfully.

**malapropism** *n* Dogberryism, misapplication, misuse.

**malcontent** *adj* belly-aching, disaffected, discontented, disgruntled, dissatisfied, dissentious, factious, ill-disposed, morose, rebellious, resentful, restive, unhappy, unsatisfied.

*antonym* contented.

*n* agitator, belly-acher, complainer, grouch, grouser, grumbler, mischief-maker, moaner, rebel, troublemaker.

**male** *adj* bull, cock, dog, manlike, manly, masculine, virile.

*antonym* female.

*n* Boy, bull, cock, daddy, dog, father, man.

*antonym* female.

**malediction** *n* anathema, anathematisation, curse, damnation, damning, denunciation, execration, imprecation, malison.

*antonyms* blessing, praise.

**malefactor** *n* convict, criminal, crook, culprit, delinquent, evil-doer, felon, law-breaker, miscreant, misfeasor, offender, outlaw, transgressor, villain, wrong-doer.

**maleficent** *adj* baleful, deleterious, destructive, detrimental, evil, harmful, hurtful, injurious, malefactory, malefic, maleficial, malign, malignant, noxious, pernicious.

*antonyms* beneficent, harmless.

**malevolence** *n* bitterness, hate, hatred, hostility, ill-will, malice, maliciousness, malignance, malignancy, malignity, rancour, spite, spitefulness, vengefulness, venom, viciousness, vindictiveness.

*antonym* benevolence.

**malevolent** *adj* baleful, bitter, despiteful, evil-minded, hostile, ill-natured, malicious, malign, malignant, pernicious, rancorous, spiteful, vengeful, venomous, vicious, vindictive.

*antonym* benevolent.

**malformation** *n* crookedness, deformity, distortion, irregularity, misshape, misshapenness, warp, warpedness, warping.

**malformed** *adj* abnormal, bent, contorted, crooked, deformed, distorted, imperfect, irregular, misshapen, twisted, warped.

*antonym* perfect.

**malfunction** *n* breakdown, defect, failure, fault, flaw, glitch, impairment.

*v* break down, fail, go wrong, misbehave.

**malice** *n* animosity, animus, bad blood, bitterness, despite, enmity, hate, hatred, ill-will, malevolence, maliciousness, malignity, rancour, spite, spitefulness, spleen, vengefulness, venom, viciousness, vindictiveness.

*antonym* kindness.

**malicious** *adj* baleful, bitchy, bitter, catty, despiteful, evil-minded, hateful, ill-natured, injurious, malevolent, malignant, mischievous, pernicious, rancorous, resentful, sham, spiteful, vengeful, venomous, vicious.

*antonyms* kind, thoughtful.

**malign** *adj* bad, baleful, baneful, deleterious, destructive, evil, harmful, hostile, hurtful, injurious, malevolent, malignant, noxious, pernicious, venomous, vicious, wicked.

*antonym* benign.

*v* abuse, badmouth, blacken the name of, calumniate, defame, denigrate, derogate, disparage, harm, injure, libel, revile, run down, slander, smear, traduce, vilify, vilipend.

*antonym* praise.

**malignant** *adj* baleful, bitter, cancerous, cankered, dangerous, deadly, destructive, devilish, evil, fatal, harmful, hostile, hurtful, inimical, injurious, irremediable, malevolent, malicious, malign, pernicious, spiteful, uncontrollable, venomous, vicious, viperish, viperous, virulent.

*antonyms* harmless, kind.

**malignity** *n* animosity, animus, bad blood, balefulness, bitterness, deadliness, destructiveness, gall, harmfulness, hate, hatred, hostility, hurtfulness, ill-will, malevolence, malice, maliciousness, perniciousness, rancour, spite, vengefulness, venom, viciousness, vindictiveness, virulence, wickedness.

*antonyms* harmlessness, kindness.

**malinger** *v* dodge, loaf, shirk, skive, slack, swing the lead.

*antonym* toil.

**malingerer** *n* dodger, lead-swinger, loafer, shirker, skiver, slacker.

*antonym* toiler.

**malleable** *adj* adaptable, biddable, compliant, ductile, governable, impressionable, manageable, plastic, pliable, pliant, soft, tractable, tractile, workable.

*antonyms* intractable, unworkable.

**malnutrition** *n* anorexia (nervosa), hunger, inanition, starvation, undernourishment.

*antonym* nourishment.

**malodorous** *adj* evil-smelling, f(o)etid, foul-smelling, mephitic, miasmal, miasmatic, miasmatous, miasmic, miasmous, nauseating, niffy, noisome, offensive, putrid, rank, reeking, smelly, stinking.

*antonym* sweet-smelling.

**malpractice** *n* abuse, dereliction, malversation, misbehaviour, misconduct, misdeed, mismanagement, negligence, offence, transgression.

**maltreat** *v* abuse, bully, damage, harm, hurt, ill-treat, injure, mistreat, misuse, mousle.

*antonym* care for.

**maltreatment** *n* abuse, bullying, harm, ill-treatment, ill-usage, ill-use, injury, mistreatment, misuse.

*antonym* care.

**mammoth** *adj* Brobdingnag, Brobdingnagian, colossal, enormous, formidable, gargantuan, giant, gigantic, herculean, huge, immense, leviathan, massive, mighty, monumental, mountainous, prodigious, rounceval, stupendous, titanic, vast.

*antonym* small.

**man¹** *n* adult, attendant, beau, bloke, body, boyfriend, cat, chap, chiel, employee, fellow, follower, gentleman, guy, hand, hireling, hombre, human, human being, husband, individual, lover, male, manservant, partner, person, retainer, servant, soldier, spouse, subject, subordinate, valet, vassal, worker, workman.

*v* crew, fill, garrison, occupy, operate, people, staff, take charge of.

**man in the street** homme moyen sensuel, John Doe, Tom Dick or Harry.

**man of fashion** bean, buck, dandy, homme du monde, swell toff.

**man of straw** Jack-straw, nobody, straw man.

**man²** *n* Homo sapiens, human race, humanity, humankind, humans, mankind, mortals, people.

**manacle** *v* bind, chain, check, clap in irons, confine, constrain, curb, fetter, gyve, hamper, hamstring, handcuff, inhibit, put in chains, restrain, shackle, trammel.

*antonym* unshackle.

**manacles** *n* bonds, bracelets, chains, fetters, gyves, handcuffs, irons, shackles.

**manage** *v* accomplish, administer, arrange, bring about, bring off, carry on, command, concert, conduct, contrive, control, cope, cope with, deal with, direct, dominate, effect, engineer, fare, get along, get by, get on, govern, guide, handle, influence, make do, make out, manipulate, muddle through, operate, oversee, pilot, ply, preside over, rule, run, shift, solicit, stage-manage, steer, succeed, superintend, supervise, survive, train, use, wield.

*antonym* fail.

**manageable** *adj* amenable, biddable, compliant, controllable, convenient, docile, easy, governable, handy, submissive, tamable, tractable, wieldable, wieldy.

*antonym* unmanageable.

**management** *n* administration, board, bosses, care, charge, command, conduct, control, direction, directorate, directors, employers, executive, executives, governance, government, governors, guidance, handling, managers, manipulation, operation, oversight, rule, running, stewardry, superintendence, supervision, supervisors.

**manager** *n* administrator, boss, comptroller, conductor, controller, director, executive, factor, gaffer, governor, head, impresario, organiser, overseer, proprietor, steward, superintendent, supervisor.

**mandate** *n* authorisation, authority, bidding, charge, command, commission, decree, dedimus, directive, edict, fiat, firman, injunction, instruction, irade, order, precept, rescript, right, sanction, ukase, warrant.

**mandatory** *adj* binding, compulsory, imperative, necessary, obligatory, required, requisite.

*antonym* optional.

**manful** *adj* bold, brave, courageous, daring, determined, gallant, hardy, heroic, indomitable, intrepid, lion-hearted, manly, noble, noble-minded, powerful, resolute, stalwart, stout, stout-hearted, strong, unflinching, valiant, vigorous.

*antonyms* half-hearted, timid.

**manfully** *adv* boldly, bravely, courageously, desperately, determinedly, gallantly, hard, heroically, intrepidly, nobly, pluckily, powerfully, resolutely, stalwartly, steadfastly, stoutly, strongly, unflinchingly, valiantly, vigorously.

*antonyms* half-heartedly, timidly.

**mangle** *v* butcher, crush, cut, deform, destroy, disfigure, distort, hack, haggle, lacerate, maim, mar, maul, mutilate, rend, ruin, spoil, tear, twist, wreck.

**mangy** *adj* dirty, grotty, mean, moth-eaten, ratty, scabby, scruffy, seedy, shabby, shoddy, squalid, tatty.

*antonyms* clean, neat, spruce.

**manhandle** *v* carry, haul, heave, hump, knock about, lift, maltreat, manoeuvre, maul, mishandle, mistreat, misuse, paw, pull, push, rough up, shove, tug.

**manhood** *n* adulthood, bravery, courage, determination, firmness, fortitude, hardihood, machismo, manfulness, manliness, masculinity, maturity, mettle, resolution, spirit, strength, valour, virility.

*antonym* timidness.

**mania** *n* aberration, cacoethes, compulsion, craving, craze, craziness, delirium, dementia, derangement, desire, disorder, enthusiasm, fad, fetish, fixation, frenzy, infatuation, insanity, itch, lunacy, madness, obsession, partiality, passion, preoccupation, rage, thing.

**maniac** *n* détraqué(e), enthusiast, fan, fanatic, fiend, freak, fruit-cake, loony, lunatic, madman, madwoman, nutcase, nutter, psycho, psychopath.

**manic** *adj* berserk, crazed, crazy, demented, deranged, frenzied, insane, lunatic, mad, maniacal, psychotic, raving, screwy, unbalanced, unhinged, wild.

*antonym* sane.

**manifest** *adj* apparent, clear, conspicuous, distinct, evident, glaring, noticeable, obvious, open, palpable, patent, plain, unconcealed, undeniable, unmistakable, visible.

*antonym* unclear.

*v* demonstrate, display, establish, evidence, evince, exhibit, expose, illustrate, prove, reveal, set forth, show.

*antonym* hide.

**manifestation** *n* appearance, demonstration, disclosure, display, exhibition, exposure, expression, indication, instance, mark, mass-meeting, materialisation, procession, reflex, revelation, show, sign, sit-in, symptom, token.

**manifesto** *n* declaration, platform, policies, policy, pronunciamento.

**manifold** *adj* abundant, assorted, copious, diverse, diversified, kaleidoscopic, many, multifarious, multifold, multiple, multiplex, multiplied, multitudinous, numerous, varied, various.

*antonym* simple.

**manipulate** *v* conduct, control, cook, direct, employ, engineer, gerrymander, guide, handle, influence, juggle with, manoeuvre, negotiate, operate, ply, shuffle, steer, use, wield, work.

**mankind** *n* Everyman, fellow-men, Homo sapiens, human race, humanity, humankind, man, mandom, mortality, people.

**manliness** *n* boldness, bravery, courage, fearlessness, firmness, hardihood, heroism, independence, intrepidity, machismo, manfulness, manhood, masculinity, mettle, resolution, stalwartness, stout-heartedness, valour, vigour, virility.

*antonyms* timidity, unmanliness.

**manly** *adj* bold, brave, courageous, daring, dauntless, fearless, gallant, hardy, heroic, macho, male, manful, masculine, muscular, noble, powerful, resolute, robust, stalwart, stout-hearted, strapping, strong, sturdy, valiant, valorous, vigorous, virile.

*antonyms* timid, unmanly.

**man-made** *adj* artificial, ersatz, imitation, manufactured, simulated, synthetic.

*antonym* natural.

**manner** *n* address, air, appearance, approach, aspect, bearing, behaviour, brand, breed, category, character, comportment, conduct, custom, demeanour, deportment, description, fashion, form, genre, habit, kind, line, look, means, method, mien, mode, nature, practice, presence, procedure, process, routine, sort, style, tack, tenor, tone, type, usage, variety, way, wise, wont.

**mannered** *adj* affected, artificial, euphuistic, posed, precious, pretentious, pseudo, put-on, stilted.

*antonym* natural.

**mannerism** *n* characteristic, feature, foible, habit, idiosyncrasy, peculiarity, quirk, stiltedness, trait, trick.

**mannerly** *adj* civil, civilised, courteous, decorous, deferential, formal, genteel, gentlemanly, gracious, ladylike, polished, polite, refined, respectful, well-behaved, well-bred, well-mannered.

*antonym* unmannerly.

**manners** *n* bearing, behaviour, breeding, carriage, ceremony, comportment, conduct, courtesy, decorum, demeanour, deportment, etiquette, formalities, mores, polish, politeness, politesse, proprieties, protocol, p's and q's, refinement, social graces.

*antonyms* impoliteness, indecorousness.

**mannish** *adj* butch, hoydenish, masculine, tomboyish, unfeminine, unladylike, unwomanly, viraginian, viraginous, viragoish, virilescent.

*antonym* womanish.

**mannishness** *n* butchness, hoydenism, masculinity, unfemininity, unladylikeness, unwomanliness, virilescence, virilism.

*antonym* womanishness.

**manoeuvre** *n* action, artifice, device, dodge, exercise, gambit, intrigue, machination, move, movement, operation, plan, plot, ploy, ruse, scheme, stratagem, subterfuge, tactic, trick.

*v* contrive, deploy, devise, direct, drive, engineer, exercise, guide, handle, intrigue, jockey, machinate, manage, manipulate, move, navigate, negotiate, pilot, plan, plot, pull strings, scheme, steer, wangle.

**man-of-all-work** *n* factotum, famulus, handyman, hobjobber, odd-jobman, orra man, servant.

**manor** *n* barony, big house, château, hall, Hof, schloss, seat, vill.

**manse** *n* glebe-house, vicarage.

**manservant** *n* butler, gentleman's gentleman, retainer, valet, valet-de-chambre.

**mansion** *n* abode, big house, castle, château, dwelling, habitation, hall, home, house, manor, manor-house, residence, schloss, seat, villa.

**mantle** *n* blanket, canopy, cape, cloak, cloud, cover, covering, curtain, envelope, hood, mantlet, pall, pelerine, pelisse, screen, shawl, shroud, veil, wrap.

**manual**[1] *n* bible, book of words, companion, enchi(e)ridion, guide, guide-book, handbook, instructions, primer, vade-mecum.

**manual**[2] *adj* hand, hand-operated, human, physical.

**manufacture** *v* assemble, build, churn out, compose, concoct, construct, cook up, create, devise, fabricate, forge, form, hatch, invent, make, make up, mass-produce, mould, process, produce, shape, think up, trump up, turn out.

*n* assembly, construction, creation, fabrication, facture, formation, making, mass-production, production.

**manufacturer** *n* builder, constructor, creator, fabricant, fabricator, factory-owner, industrialist, maker, mill-owner, producer.

**manure** *n* compost, droppings, dung, fertiliser, guano, muck, ordure.

**manuscript** *n* autograph, deed, document, handwriting, holograph, palimpsest, parchment, scroll, text, vellum.

**many** *adj* abundant, copious, countless, divers, frequent, innumerable, manifold, multifarious, multifold, multitudinous, myriad, n, numerous, profuse, sundry, umpteen, umpty, varied, various.

*antonym* few.

**map** *n* atlas, chart, graph, mappemond, plan, plot, street plan.

**mar** *v* blemish, blight, blot, damage, deface, detract from, disfigure, foul up, harm, hurt, impair, injure, maim, mangle, mutilate, pollute, ruin, scar, spoil, stain, sully, taint, tarnish, temper, vitiate, wreck.

*antonym* enhance.

**maraud** *v* depredate, despoil, forage, foray, harry, loot, pillage, plunder, raid, ransack, ravage, reive, sack, spoliate.

**marauder** *n* bandit, brigand, buccaneer, cateran, corsair, depredator, freebooter, moss-trooper, outlaw, pillager, pirate, plunderer, raider, ravager, reiver, robber, spoliater.

**march** *v* countermarch, file, flounce, goose-step, pace, parade, slog, stalk, stride, strut, stump, tramp, tread, walk.

*n* advance, career, demo, demonstration, development, evolution, footslog, gait, hike, pace, parade, passage, procession, progress, progression, step, stride, tramp, trek, walk.

**margin** *n* allowance, border, bound, boundary, brim, brink, compass, confine, edge, extra, latitude, leeway, limit, marge, perimeter, periphery, play, rand, rim, room, scope, side, skirt, space, surplus, verge.

*antonyms* centre, core.

**marginal** *adj* bordering, borderline, doubtful, infinitesimal, insignificant, low, minimal, minor, negligible, peripheral, slight, small.

*antonyms* central, core.

**marijuana** *n* bhang, cannabis, charas (churrus), dope, ganja, grass, greens, hash, hashish, hemp, kif, mary jane, pot, tea, weed.

**marina** *n* dock, harbour, mooring, port, yacht station.

**marine** *adj* maritime, nautical, naval, ocean-going, oceanic, pelagic, salt-water, sea, seafaring, sea-going, thalassian, thalassic.

*n* galoot, leather-neck, sailor.

**mariner** *n* bluejacket, deckhand, hand, Jack Tar, matelot, matlo(w), navigator, sailor, salt, sea-dog, seafarer, seaman, tar.

**marital** *adj* conjugal, connubial, hymeneal, hymenean, married, matrimonial, nuptial, sponsal, spousal, wedded.

**maritime** *adj* coastal, littoral, marine, nautical, naval, oceanic, pelagic, sea, seafaring, seaside, thalassian, thalassic.

**mark** *n* aim, badge, blaze, blemish, blot, blotch, brand, bruise, character, characteristic, consequence, criterion, dent, device, dignity, distinction, earmark, emblem, eminence, end, evidence, fame, feature, fingermark, footmark, footprint, goal, hallmark, importance, impression, incision, index, indication, influence, label, level, line, lineament, marque, measure, nick, norm, notability, note, noteworthiness, notice, object, objective, pock, prestige, print, proof, purpose, quality, regard, scar, scratch, seal, sign, smudge, splotch, spot, stain, stamp, standard, standing, streak, symbol, symptom, target, token, trace, track, trail, vestige, yardstick.

*v* appraise, assess, attend, betoken, blemish, blot, blotch, brand, bruise, characterise, colour-code, correct, denote, dent, distinguish, evaluate, evince, exemplify, grade, hearken, heed, identify, illustrate, impress, imprint, label, list, listen, mind, nick, note, notice, observe, print, regard, remark, scar, scratch, show, smudge, splotch, stain, stamp, streak, take to heart, traumatise, watch.

**marked** *adj* apparent, clear, considerable, conspicuous, decided, distinct, doomed, emphatic, evident, glaring, indicated, manifest, notable, noted, noticeable, obvious, outstanding, patent, prominent, pronounced, remarkable, salient, signal, striking, strong, suspected, watched.

*antonyms* slight, unnoticeable.

**market** *n* bazaar, demand, fair, market-place, mart, need, outlet, shop, souk.

*v* hawk, peddle, retail, sell, vend.

*antonym* buy.

**marketable** *adj* in demand, merchantable, salable, sellable, sought after, vendible, wanted.

*antonym* unsalable.

**marksman** *n* bersagliere, crack shot, dead shot, sharpshooter, shootist, sniper.

**maroon** *v* abandon, cast away, desert, isolate, leave, put ashore, strand.

*antonym* rescue.

**marriage** *n* alliance, amalgamation, association, confederation, coupling, espousal, link, match, matrimony, matronage, matronhood, merger, nuptials, spousage, spousals, union, wedding, wedlock.

*antonym* divorce.

**married** *adj* conjugal, connubial, hitched, husbandly, joined, marital, matrimonial, nuptial, spliced, spousal, united, wed, wedded, wifely, wived, yoked.

*antonyms* divorced, single.

**marrow** *n* core, cream, essence, gist, heart, kernel, nub, pith, quick, quintessence, soul, spirit, stuff, substance.

**marry** *v* ally, bond, espouse, get hitched, get spliced, join, jump the broomstick, knit, link, match, merge, splice, tie, tie the knot, unify, unite, wed, wive, yoke.

*antonyms* divorce, separate.

**marsh** *n* bayou, bog, carr, fen, maremma, marshland, morass, moss, muskeg, quagmire, slough, slump, soak, swale, swamp, wetland.

**marshal** *v* align, arrange, array, assemble, collect, conduct, convoy, deploy, dispose, draw up, escort, gather, group, guide, lead, line up, muster, order, organise, rank, shepherd, take, usher.

**marshy** *adj* boggy, fennish, fenny, miry, paludal, paludine, paludinous, quaggy, slumpy, spongy, swampy, waterlogged, wet.

*antonym* solid.

**martial** *adj* bellicose, belligerent, brave, combative, heroic, militant, military, soldierly, warlike.

*antonym* pacific.

**martinet** *n* disciplinarian, formalist, slave-driver, stickler, tyrant.

**martyrdom** *n* agony, anguish, death, excruciation, ordeal, persecution, suffering, torment, torture, witness.

**marvel** *n* genius, miracle, non(e)such, phenomenon, portent, prodigy, sensation, spectacle, whiz, wonder.

*v* gape, gaze, goggle, wonder.

**marvellous** *adj* amazing, astonishing, astounding, beyond belief, breathtaking, épatant, excellent, extraordinary, fabulous, fantastic, glorious, great, hell of a, implausible, improbable, incredible, magnificent, miraculous, mirific(al), phenom, phenomenal, prodigious, remarkable, sensational, singular, smashing, spectacular, splendid, stupendous, super, superb, surprising, terrific, unbelievable, unlikely, wonderful, wondrous.

*antonyms* ordinary, plausible, run-of-the-mill.

**masculine** *adj* bold, brave, butch, gallant, hardy, macho, male, manlike, manly, mannish, muscular, powerful, red-blooded, resolute, robust, stout-hearted, strapping, strong, tomboyish, vigorous, virile.

*antonym* feminine.

**masculinity** *n* butchness, hoydenism, maleness, manhood, manliness, mannishness, potency, sexuality, tomboyishness, unladylikeness, unwomanliness, virileness, virilescence, virilism, virility, Yang.

*antonym* femininity.

**mash** *v* beat, champ, comminute, crush, grind, pound, pulverise, pummel, smash, triturate.

**mask** *n* blind, camouflage, cloak, concealment, cover, cover-up, disguise, domino, façade, false face, front, guise, pretence, screen, semblance, show, veil, veneer, visard-mask, visor, vizard.

*v* camouflage, cloak, conceal, cover, disguise, hide, obscure, screen, shield, veil.

*antonym* uncover.

**masked** *adj* camouflaged, cloaked, concealed, covered, disguised, screened, shielded, shrouded, visored, vizarded.

*antonyms* uncovered, unshielded.

**masquerade** *n* cloak, costume, costume ball, counterfeit, cover, cover-up, deception, disguise, dissimulation, domino, fancy dress party, front, guise, imposture, mask, masked ball, masque, mummery, pose, pretence, put-on, revel, screen, subterfuge.

*v* disguise, dissemble, dissimulate, impersonate, mask, pass oneself off, play, pose, pretend, profess.

**mass**[1] *n* accumulation, aggregate, aggregation, assemblage, band, batch, block, body, bulk, bunch, chunk, collection, combination, concretion, congeries, conglomeration, crowd, dimension, entirety, extensity, group, heap, horde, host, hunk, lion's share, load, lot, lump, magnitude, majority, mob, number, piece, pile, preponderance, quantity, size, stack, sum, sum total, throng, totality, troop, welter, whole.

*adj* across-the-board, blanket, comprehensive, extensive, general, indiscriminate, large-scale, pandemic, popular, sweeping, wholesale, widespread.

*antonym* limited.

*v* assemble, cluster, collect, congregate, crowd, for(e)gather, gather, muster, rally.

*antonym* separate.

**mass**[2] *n* communion, eucharist, holy communion, housel, Lord's Supper, Lord's Table, nagmaal.

**massacre** *n* annihilation, blood bath, butchery, carnage, decimation, extermination, holocaust, killing, murder, slaughter.

*v* annihilate, butcher, decimate, exterminate, kill, mow down, murder, slaughter, slay, wipe out.

**massage** *n* effleurage, kneading, malaxage, malaxation, manipulation, petrissage, rubbing, rub-down, shiatsu.

*v* knead, manipulate, rub, rub down.

**mass-book** *n* breviary, missal, prayer-book, service-book.

**massive** *adj* big, bulky, colossal, cyclopean, enormous, extensive, gargantuan, gigantic, great, heavy, hefty, huge, hulking, immense, imposing, impressive, jumbo, mammoth, monster, monstrous, monumental, ponderous, rounceval, solid, substantial, titanic, vast, weighty, whacking, whopping.

*antonyms* slight, small.

**master** *n* ace, adept, baas, boss, bwana, captain, chief, commander, controller, dab hand, deacon, director, doyen, employer, expert, genius, governor, guide, guru, head, Herr, instructor, lord, maestro, manager, overlord, overseer, owner, past master, pedagogue, preceptor, principal, pro, ruler, schoolmaster, skipper, superintendent, swami, teacher, tutor, virtuoso, wizard.

*antonyms* amateur, learner, pupil, servant, slave.

*adj* ace, adept, chief, controlling, crack, expert, foremost, grand, great, leading, main, masterly, predominant, prime, principal, proficient, skilful, skilled.

*antonyms* copy, subordinate, unskilled.

*v* acquire, bridle, check, command, conquer, control, curb, defeat, direct, dominate, get the hang of, govern, grasp, learn, manage, overcome, quash, quell, regulate, rule, subdue, subjugate, suppress, tame, triumph over, vanquish.

**master race** Herrenvolk.

**masterful** *adj* adept, adroit, arrogant, authoritative, autocratic, bossy, clever, consummate, crack, deft, despotic, dexterous, dictatorial, domineering, excellent, expert, exquisite, fine, finished, first-rate, high-handed, imperious, magisterial, masterly, overbearing, overweening, peremptory, powerful, professional, self-willed, skilful, skilled, superior, superlative, supreme, tyrannical.

*antonyms* clumsy, humble, unskilful.

**masterly** *adj* adept, adroit, clever, consummate, crack, dexterous, excellent, expert, exquisite, fine, finished, first-rate, magistral, masterful, skilful, skilled, superb, superior, superlative, supreme.

*antonyms* clumsy, poor, unskilled.

**mastermind** *v* conceive, design, devise, direct, dream up, forge, frame, hatch, manage, organise, originate, plan.

*n* architect, authority, brain(s), creator, director, engineer, genius, intellect, manager, organiser, originator, planner, prime mover, virtuoso.

**masterpiece** *n* chef d'oeuvre, classic, jewel, magnum opus, master-work, museum-piece, pièce de résistance, tour de force.

**mastery** *n* ability, acquirement, advantage, ascendancy, attainment, authority, cleverness, command, comprehension, conquest, control, conversancy, deftness, dexterity, domination, dominion, expertise, familiarity, finesse, grasp, know-how, knowledge, pre-eminence, proficiency, prowess, rule, skill, superiority, supremacy, sway, triumph, understanding, upper hand, victory, virtuosity, whip-hand.

*antonyms* clumsiness, unfamiliarity.

**masticate** *v* champ, chew, crunch, eat, knead, manducate, munch, ruminate.

**masturbate** *v* frig, jerk off, play with oneself, toss (it) off, wank.

**masturbation** *n* auto-eroticism, frig, frigging, frottage, onanism, self-abuse, self-stimulation, tribadism, tribady, wanking.

**mat** *n* carpet, doormat, drugget, felt, rug, under-felt, underlay.

**match**[1] *n* bout, competition, contest, game, main, test, trial, venue.

*v* compete, contend, oppose, pit against, rival, vie.

**match**[2] *n* affiliation, alliance, combination, companion, complement, copy, counterpart, couple, dead ringer, double, duet, duplicate, equal, equivalent, fellow, like, look-alike, marriage, mate, pair, pairing, parallel, partnership, peer, replica, ringer, rival, spit, spitting image, tally, twin, union.

*v* accompany, accord, adapt, agree, ally, blend, combine, compare, co-ordinate, correspond, couple, emulate, equal, fit, gee, go together, go with, harmonise, join, link, marry, mate, measure up to, pair, relate, rival, suit, tally, team, tone with, unite, yoke.

*antonyms* clash, separate.

**match**[3] *n* Congreve-match, fuse, fusee, light, lucifer, lucifer-match, safety match, spill, taper, vesta, vesuvian.

**matching** *adj* analogous, comparable, co-ordinating, corresponding, double, duplicate, equal, equivalent, homochromous, identical, like, parallel, pared, same, similar, toning, twin.

*antonyms* clashing, different.

**matchless** *adj* consummate, excellent, exquisite, incomparable, inimitable, nonpareil, peerless, perfect, superlative, supreme, unequalled, unique, unmatched, unparalleled, unrivalled, unsurpassed.

*antonyms* commonplace, poor.

**mate** *n* assistant, associate, better half, buddy, china, chum, colleague, companion, compeer, comrade, confidant(e), co-worker, crony, double, fellow, fellow-worker, fere, friend, gossip, helper, helpmate, helpmeet, husband, match, pal, partner, repository, side-kick, spouse, subordinate, twin, wife.

*v* breed, copulate, couple, join, marry, match, pair, wed, yoke.

**material** *n* body, cloth, constituents, data, element, evidence, fabric, facts, information, literature, matter, notes, stuff, substance, textile, work.

*adj* applicable, apposite, apropos, bodily, central, concrete, consequential, corporeal, essential, fleshly, germane, grave, gross, hylic, important, indispensable, key, meaningful, momentous, non-spiritual, palpable, pertinent, physical, relevant, serious, significant, substantial, tangible, vital, weighty, worldly.

*antonyms* ethereal, immaterial.

**materialise** *v* appear, arise, happen, occur, take shape, turn up.

*antonym* disappear.

**materialism** *n* hylicism, hylism, mammon, mammonism, money-grubbing.

**materialist** *n* hylicist, hylist, mammonite, money-grubber, mug-hunter, pot-hunter.

**materialistic** *adj* banausic, Kensington, mammonist, mammonistic, mercenary, money-grubbing.

*antonym* spiritual.

**materially** *adv* basically, considerably, essentially, fundamentally, gravely, greatly, much, palpably, physically, seriously, significantly, substantially, tangibly.

*antonym* insignificantly.

**maternal** *adj* loving, matronal, motherly, protective.

*antonym* paternal.

**mating** *n* breeding, coition, copulating, copulation, coupling, fusing, jointing, matching, pangamy, service, sexual intercourse, tupping, twinning, uniting.

**matrimonial** *adj* conjugal, connubial, marital, marriage, married, nuptial, sponsal, spousal, wedded, wedding.

**matrimony** *n* espousals, marriage, nuptials, sponsalia, spousage, spousal, wedlock.

**matron** *n* dame, dowager, matriarch.

**matted** *adj* knotted, tangled, tangly, tousled, uncombed.

*antonyms* tidy, untangled.

**matter**[1] *n* affair, amount, argument, body, business, complication, concern, consequence, context, difficulty, distress, episode, event, hyle, import, importance, incident, issue, material, moment, note, occurrence, problem, proceeding, purport, quantity, question, sense, significance, situation, stuff, subject, substance, sum, text, thesis, thing, topic, transaction, trouble, upset, weight, worry.

*antonym* insignificance.

*v* count, make a difference, mean something, signify.

**matter**[2] *n* discharge, purulence, pus, secretion, suppuration.

*v* discharge, secrete.

**matter-of-fact** *adj* deadpan, direct, down-to-earth, dry, dull, emotionless, flat, lifeless, literal, mundane, plain, prosaic, sober, unembellished, unimaginative, unsentimental, unvarnished.

*antonym* emotional.

**mattress** *n* futon, pallet, palliasse.

**mature** *adj* adult, complete, due, fit, full-blown, full-grown, fully fledged, grown, grown-up, matured, mellow, nubile, perfect, perfected, prepared, ready, ripe, ripened, seasoned, well-thought-out.

*antonym* immature.

*v* accrue, age, bloom, come of age, develop, fall due, grow up, maturate, mellow, perfect, ripen, season.

**maturity** *n* adulthood, completion, experience, fullness, majority, manhood, maturation, matureness, nubility, perfection, readiness, ripeness, wisdom, womanhood.

*antonym* immaturity.

**maudlin** *adj* drunk, emotional, fuddled, half-drunk, icky, lachrymose, mawkish, mushy, sentimental, sickly, slushy, soppy, tearful, tipsy, weepy.

*antonym* matter-of-fact.

**maul** *v* abuse, batter, beat, beat up, claw, ill-treat, knock about, lacerate, maltreat, mangle, manhandle, molest, paw, pummel, rough up, thrash.

**maunder** *v* babble, blather, blether, chatter, drivel, gabble, grumble, mutter, prattle, rabbit, ramble, witter.

**maw** *n* abyss, chasm, craw, crop, gulf, gullet, jaws, mouth, stomach, throat.

**mawkish** *adj* disgusting, emotional, feeble, flat, foul, gushy, icky, insipid, jejune, loathsome, maudlin, mushy, nauseous, offensive, schmaltzy, sentimental, sickly, slushy, soppy, squeamish, stale, vapid.

*antonyms* matter-of-fact, pleasant.

**maxim** *n* adage, aphorism, apophthegm, axiom, byword, epigram, gnome, mot, motto, precept, proverb, rule, saw, saying, sentence.

**maximum** *adj* biggest, greatest, highest, largest, maximal, most, paramount, supreme, topmost, utmost.

*antonym* minimum.

*n* apogee, ceiling, crest, extremity, height, most, ne plus ultra, peak, pinnacle, summit, top (point), upper limit, utmost, zenith.

*antonym* mimimum.

**maybe** *adv* haply, happen, mayhap, peradventure, perchance, perhaps, possibly.

*antonym* definitely.

**maze** *n* confusion, convolutions, imbroglio, intricacy, labyrinth, meander, mesh, mizmaze, puzzle, snarl, tangle, web.

**meadow** *n* field, haugh, holm, inch, lea, ley, mead, pasture.

**meagre** *adj* barren, bony, deficient, emaciated, exiguous, gaunt, hungry, inadequate, infertile, insubstantial, lank, lean, little, negligible, paltry, penurious, poor, puny, scanty, scraggy, scrawny, scrimpy, short, skimpy, skinny, slender, slight, small, spare, sparse, starved, thin, underfed, unfruitful, unproductive, weak.

*antonyms* fertile, substantial.

**meal**[1] *n* banquet, barbecue, beanfeast, beano, blow-out, breakfast, brunch, chota-hazri, collation, déjeuner, déjeuner à la fourchette, dinner, feast, lunch, luncheon, nosh, nosh-up, petit déjeuner, picnic, repast, scoff, snack, spread, supper, tea, tiffin(g), tuck-in.

**meal**[2] *n* farina, flour, grits, oatmeal, powder.

**mealy-mouthed** *adj* equivocal, euphemistic, flattering, glib, hestitant, indirect, mincing, overdelicate, over-squeamish, plausible, prim, reticent, smooth-tongued.

**mean**[1] *adj* abject, bad-tempered, base, base-born, beggarly, callous, cheese-paring, churlish, close, close-fisted, close-handed, common, contemptible, degraded, despicable, disagreeable, disgraceful, dishonourable, down-at-heel, excellent, fast-handed, good, great, hard-hearted, hostile, humble, ignoble, illiberal, inconsiderable, inferior, insignificant, low, low-born, lowly, malicious, malignant, mean-spirited, menial, mercenary, mingy, miserable, miserly, modest, narrow-minded, nasty, near, niggardly, obscure, one-horse, ordinary, paltry, parsimonious, penny-pinching, penurious, petty, plebeian, poor, proletarian, pusillanimous, rude, run-down, scrub, scurvy, seedy, selfish, servile, shabby, shameful, skilful, slink, small-minded, snippy, sordid, sour, squalid, stingy, tawdry, tight, tight-fisted, undistinguished, unfriendly, ungenerous, ungiving, unhandsome, unpleasant, vicious, vile, vulgar, wretched.

*antonyms* generous, kind, noble, superior.

**mean**[2] *v* adumbrate, aim, aspire, augur, betoken, cause, connote, contemplate, convey, denote, design, desire, destine, drive at, engender, entail, express, fate, fit, foreshadow, foretell, get at, give rise to, herald, hint, imply, indicate, insinuate, intend, involve, lead to, make, match, necessitate, omen, plan, portend, predestine, preordain, presage, produce, promise, propose, purport, purpose, represent, result in, say, set out, signify, spell, stand for, suggest, suit, symbolise, want, wish.

**mean**[3] *adj* average, half-way, intermediate, medial, median, medium, middle, middling, moderate, normal, standard.

*antonym* extreme.

*n* aurea mediocritas, average, balance, compromise, golden mean, happy medium, median, middle, middle course, middle way, mid-point, norm, via media.

*antonym* extreme.

**meander** *v* amble, curve, ramble, snake, stravaig, stray, stroll, turn, twist, wander, wind, zigzag.

**meandering** *adj* circuitous, convoluted, indirect, meandrous, roundabout, serpentine, sinuous, snaking, tortuous, twisting, wandering, winding.

*antonym* straight.

**meaning** n aim, connotation, construction, denotation, design, drift, end, explanation, force, gist, goal, idea, implication, import, intention, interpretation, matter, message, object, plan, point, purport, purpose, sense, significance, signification, substance, thrust, trend, upshot, validity, value, worth.

**meaningful** adj eloquent, expressive, important, material, meaningful, pointed, pregnant, purposeful, relevant, serious, significant, speaking, suggestive, useful, valid, warning, worthwhile.

**meaningless** adj absurd, aimless, empty, expressionless, futile, hollow, inane, inconsequential, insignificant, insubstantial, nonsense, nonsensical, nugatory, pointless, purposeless, senseless, trifling, trivial, unmeaning, useless, vain, valueless, worthless.
*antonym* meaningful.

**meanness** n abjectness, baseness, beggarliness, churlishness, close-fistedness, close-handedness, contemptibleness, degradation, despicableness, disagreeableness, disgracefulness, dishonourableness, humbleness, illiberality, insignificance, lowliness, malice, maliciousness, malignity, mean-spiritedness, minginess, miserliness, narrow-mindedness, nastiness, niggardliness, obscurity, paltriness, parsimony, penuriousness, pettiness, poorness, pusillanimity, rudeness, scurviness, seediness, selfishness, servility, shabbiness, shamefulness, sordidness, sourness, squalor, stinginess, tawdriness, tight-fistedness, unfriendliness, unpleasantness, viciousness, vileness, wretchedness.
*antonyms* generosity, kindness, nobility, superiority.

**means** n ability, affluence, agency, avenue, capacity, capital, channel, course, estate, expedient, fortune, funds, income, instrument, machinery, measure, medium, method, mode, money, process, property, resources, riches, substance, way, wealth, wherewithal.

**meantime, meanwhile** advs at the same time, concurrently, en attendant, for now, for the moment, in the interim, in the interval, in the meantime, in the meanwhile, simultaneously.

**measly** adj beggarly, contemptible, meagre, mean, mingy, miserable, miserly, niggardly, paltry, pathetic, petty, piddling, pitiful, poor, puny, scanty, skimpy, stingy, trivial, ungenerous.

**measurable** adj appreciable, assessable, computable, determinable, fathomable, gaugeable, material, mensurable, perceptible, quantifiable, quantitative, significant.
*antonym* measureless.

**measure** n act, action, allotment, allowance, amount, amplitude, beat, bill, bounds, cadence, capacity, control, course, criterion, deed, degree, démarche, enactment, example, expedient, extent, foot, gauge, jigger, law, limit, limitation, magnitude, manoeuvre, means, method, metre, model, moderation, norm, portion, procedure, proceeding, proportion, quantity, quota, range, ration, reach, resolution, restraint, rhythm, rule, scale, scope, share, size, standard, statute, step, system, test, touchstone, verse, yardstick.

v admeasure, appraise, assess, calculate, calibrate, choose, compute, determine, estimate, evaluate, fathom, gauge, judge, mark out, measure off, measure out, plumb, quantify, rate, size, sound, step, survey, value, weigh.

**measure off** circumscribe, delimit, demarcate, determine, fix, lay down, lay off, limit, mark out, measure (out), pace out.

**measure out** allot, apportion, assign, deal out, dispense, distribute, divide, dole out, hand out, issue, measure (off), mete out, parcel out, pour out, proportion, share out.

**measure up** do, fill the bill, make the grade, pass muster, shape up, suffice.

**measure up to** compare with, equal, match, meet, rival, touch.

**measured** adj calculated, considered, constant, deliberate, dignified, even, exact, gauged, grave, leisurely, metronomic, modulated, planned, precise, predetermined, premeditated, quantified, reasoned, regular, regulated, sedate, slow, sober, solemn, standard, stately, steady, studied, unhurried, uniform, verified, well-thought-out.

**measureless** adj bottomless, boundless, endless, immeasurable, immense, incalculable, inestimable, infinite, innumerable, limitless, unbounded, vast.
*antonym* measurable.

**measurement** n amount, amplitude, appraisal, appreciation, area, assessment, calculation, calibration, capacity, computation, depth, dimension, estimation, evaluation, extent, gauging, height, judgement, length, magnitude, mensuration, metage, size, survey, valuation, volume, weight, width.

**meat**[1] n aliment, charqui, cheer, chow, comestibles, eats, fare, flesh, food, grub, jerk, nourishment, nutriment, provender, provisions, rations, subsistence, sustenance, viands, victuals.

**meat**[2] n core, crux, essence, fundamentals, gist, heart, kernel, marrow, nub, nucleus, pith, point, substance.

**meaty** adj beefy, brawny, burly, fleshy, hearty, heavy, husky, interesting, matterful, meaningful, muscular, nourishing, pithy, profound, rich, significant, solid, strapping, sturdy, substantial.

**mechanic** n artificer, engineer, fitter, machinist, mechanician, operative, operator, opificer, repairman, technician.

**mechanical** adj automated, automatic, cold, cursory, dead, dull, emotionless, habitual, impersonal, instinctive, involuntary, lack-lustre, lifeless, machine-driven, machine-like, matter-of-fact, perfunctory, routine, spiritless, unanimated, unconscious, unfeeling, unthinking.

**mechanism** n action, agency, apparatus, appliance, components, contrivance, device, execution, functioning, gadgetry, gears, innards, instrument, machine, machinery, means, medium, method, motor, operation, performance, procedure, process, structure, system, technique, tool, workings, works.

**medal** *n* award, decoration, gong, honour, medalet, medallion, prize, reward, trophy.

**meddle** *v* interfere, interlope, interpose, intervene, intrude, mell, pry, put one's oar in, tamper.

**meddlesome** *adj* interfering, intruding, intrusive, meddling, mischievous, officious, prying, ultracrepidarian.

**medi(a)eval** *adj* antediluvian, antiquated, antique, archaic, old-fashioned, old-world, outmoded, primitive, unenlightened.

**mediate** *v* arbitrate, conciliate, incubate, intercede, interpose, intervene, moderate, negotiate, reconcile, referee, resolve, settle, step in, umpire.

**mediation** *n* arbitration, conciliation, good offices, intercession, interposition, intervention, negotiation, parley, reconciliation.

**mediator** *n* advocate, arbiter, arbitrator, go-between, honest broker, interceder, intermediary, interventor, judge, middleman, moderator, negotiator, ombudsman, ombudswoman, peacemaker, referee, umpire.

**medical** *adj* Hippocratic, iatric(al), medicinal.

**medical practitioner** allopath, consultant, doc, doctor, feldsher, GP, healer, homeopath, intern, medico, MO, physician, sawbones, surgeon.

**medicinal** *adj* adjuvant, analeptic, curative, healing, homeopathic, medical, medicamental, medicamentary, remedial, restorative, roborant, sanatory, therapeutic.

**medicine**[1] *n* cure, diapente, diatessaron, drug, electuary, elixir, febrifuge, Galenical, materia medica, medicament, medication, nostrum, panacea, physic, remedy, specific, tincture, vermifuge.

**medicine**[2] *n* acupuncture, allopathy, homeopathy, leech-craft, surgery, therapeutics.

**medicine-man** *n* angek(k)ok, mystery-man, shaman, witch-doctor.

**mediocre** *adj* amateurish, average, commonplace, indifferent, inferior, insignificant, mean, medium, middling, ordinary, passable, pedestrian, run-of-the-mill, second-rate, so-so, undistinguished, unexceptional, uninspired.

*antonyms* excellent, exceptional, extraordinary.

**mediocrity** *n* amateurishness, cipher, indifference, inferiority, insignificance, lightweight, nobody, nonentity, ordinariness, poorness, second-rater, unimportance.

**meditate** *v* be in a brown study, cerebrate, cogitate, consider, contemplate, deliberate, devise, excogitate, intend, mull over, muse, plan, ponder, purpose, reflect, ruminate, scheme, speculate, study, think, think over.

**meditation** *n* brown study, cerebration, cogitation, concentration, contemplation, excogitation, musing, pondering, reflection, reverie, ruminating, rumination, speculation, study, thought.

**meditative** *adj* cogitative, contemplative, deliberative, museful, pensive, reflective, ruminant, ruminative, studious, thoughtful.

**medium**[1] *adj* average, fair, intermediate, mean, medial, median, mediocre, middle, middling, midway, standard.

*n* aurea mediocritas, average, centre, compromise, golden mean, happy medium, mean, middle, middle ground, midpoint, via media, way.

**medium**[2] *n* agency, avenue, base, channel, excipient, form, instrument, instrumentality, means, mode, organ, vehicle, way.

**medium**[3] *n* clairvoyant, psychic, spiritist, spiritualist.

**medium**[4] *n* ambience, atmosphere, circumstances, conditions, element, environment, habitat, influences, milieu, setting, surroundings.

**medley** *n* assortment, collection, confusion, conglomeration, farrago, galimatias, gallimaufry, hodge-podge, hotchpotch, jumble, macaroni, macédoine, mélange, mingle-mangle, miscellany, mishmash, mixture, olio, olla-podrida, omnium-gatherum, pastiche, patchwork, pot-pourri, quodlibet, salmagundi.

**meek** *adj* acquiescent, compliant, deferential, docile, forbearing, gentle, humble, long-suffering, mild, modest, patient, peaceful, resigned, slavish, soft, spineless, spiritless, subdued, submissive, tame, timid, unambitious, unassuming, unpretentious, unresisting, weak, yielding.

*antonyms* arrogant, rebellious.

**meekness** *n* acquiescence, compliance, deference, docility, forbearance, gentleness, humbleness, humility, long-suffering, lowliness, mildness, modesty, patience, peacefulness, resignation, self-abasement, self-disparagement, self-effacement, softness, spinelessness, spiritlessness, submission, submissiveness, tameness, timidity, weakness.

*antonym* arrogance.

**meet** *v* abut, adjoin, answer, assemble, bear, bump into, chance on, collect, come across, come together, comply, confront, congregate, connect, contact, convene, converge, cross, discharge, encounter, endure, equal, experience, face, find, forgather, fulfil, gather, go through, gratify, handle, happen on, intersect, join, link up, match, measure up to, muster, perform, rally, rencontre, rencounter, run across, run into, satisfy, suffer, touch, undergo, unite.

**meeting** *n* abutment, assembly, assignation, audience, company, conclave, concourse, conference, confluence, confrontation, congregation, conjunction, consult, conventicle, convention, convergence, convocation, crossing, encounter, engagement, forum, gathering, gemot, get-together, gorsedd, indaba, intersection, introduction, junction, meet, moot, rally, rencontre, rencounter, rendezvous, reunion, session, synod, tryst, union, watersmeet.

**meeting-point** *n* confluence, convergence, convergency, crossroads, interface, intersection, junction, watersmeet.

**megalomania** *n* conceitedness, delusions of grandeur, folie de grandeur, overestimation, self-importance.

**melancholy** *adj* blue, dejected, depressed, despondent, disconsolate, dismal, dispirited, doleful, down, down in the dumps, down in the mouth, downcast, down-hearted, gloomy, glum, heavy-hearted, hipped, joyless, low, low-spirited, lugubrious, melancholic, miserable, moody, mournful, pensieroso, pensive, sad, sombre, sorrowful, splenific, unhappy, woebegone, woeful.

*antonyms* cheerful, gay, happy, joyful.

*n* blues, dejection, depression, despondency, dole, dolour, gloom, gloominess, glumness, low spirits, pensiveness, sadness, sorrow, unhappiness, woe.

*antonym* exhilaration.

**mélange** *n* assortment, confusion, farrago, galimatias, gallimaufry, hash, hodge-podge, hotch-potch, jumble, medley, mingle-mangle, miscellany, mishmash, mix, mixed bag, mixture, olio, omnium-gatherum, pastiche, potpourri, salmagundi.

**mêlée** *n* affray, battle royal, brawl, broil, dogfight, donnybrook, fight, fracas, fray, free-for-all, ruckus, ruction, rumpus, scrimmage, scrum, scuffle, set-to, stramash, tussle.

**mellifluous** *adj* canorous, dulcet, euphonious, honeyed, mellow, silvery, smooth, soft, soothing, sweet, sweet-sounding, tuneful.

*antonyms* discordant, grating, harsh.

**mellow** *adj* cheerful, cordial, delicate, dulcet, elevated, expansive, full, full-flavoured, genial, happy, jolly, jovial, juicy, mature, mellifluous, melodious, merry, perfect, placid, relaxed, rich, ripe, rounded, serene, smooth, soft, sweet, tipsy, tranquil, well-matured.

*antonyms* immature, unripe.

*v* improve, mature, perfect, ripen, season, soften, sweeten, temper.

**melodious** *adj* arioso, canorous, concordant, dulcet, euphonious, harmonious, melodic, musical, silvery, sonorous, sweet-sounding, tuneful.

*antonyms* discordant, grating, harsh.

**melodramatic** *adj* blood-and-thunder, exaggerated, hammy, histrionic, overdone, overdramatic, overemotional, overwrought, sensational, stagy, theatrical.

**melody** *n* air, aria, arietta, arriette, euphony, harmony, melisma, melodiousness, music, musicality, refrain, song, strain, theme, tune, tunefulness.

**melt** *v* deliquesce, diffuse, disarm, dissolve, flux, fuse, liquate, liquefy, mollify, relax, soften, thaw, touch, uncongeal, unfreeze.

*antonyms* freeze, harden, solidify.

**melt away** dematerialise, disappear, disperse, dissolve, evanesce, evaporate, fade, vanish.

**member** *n* appendage, arm, associate, component, constituent, element, extremity, fellow, initiate, leg, limb, organ, part, portion, representative.

**membership** *n* adherence, allegiance, associates, body, enrolment, fellows, fellowship, members, participation.

**membrane** *n* diaphragm, fell, film, hymen, integument, partition, septum, skin, tissue, veil, velum.

**memento** *n* keepsake, memorial, record, relic, remembrance, reminder, souvenir, token, trophy.

**memoir** *n* account, biography, essay, journal, life, monograph, narrative, record, register, report.

**memoirs** *n* annals, autobiography, chronicles, confessions, diary, experiences, journals, life, life story, memories, personalia, recollections, records, reminiscences, transactions.

**memorable** *adj* catchy, celebrated, distinguished, extraordinary, famous, historic, illustrious, important, impressive, marvellous, momentous, notable, noteworthy, outstanding, remarkable, signal, significant, striking, unforgettable.

*antonym* forgettable.

**memorial** *n* cairn, cromlech, dolmen, martyry, mausoleum, memento, menhir, monument, plaque, record, remembrance, souvenir, stone.

*adj* celebratory, commemorative, monumental.

**memorise** *v* con, learn, learn by heart, learn by rote, learn off, mug up, swot up.

*antonym* forget.

**memory** *n* bank, celebrity, commemoration, database, fame, glory, honour, memorial, name, recall, recollection, remembrance, reminiscence, renown, reputation, repute, retention, store.

*antonym* forgetfulness.

**menace** *v* alarm, browbeat, bully, comminate, cow, frighten, impend, intimidate, loom, lour (lower), terrorise, threaten.

*n* annoyance, commination, danger, hazard, intimidation, jeopardy, nuisance, peril, pest, plague, scare, terror, threat, troublemaker, warning.

**menacing** *adj* alarming, Damoclean, dangerous, frightening, impending, intimidating, intimidatory, looming, louring (lowering), minacious, minatory, ominous, portentous, threatening.

**mend** *v* ameliorate, amend, better, bushel, cobble, convalesce, correct, cure, darn, emend, fix, heal, improve, patch, recover, rectify, recuperate, refit, reform, remedy, renew, renovate, repair, restore, retouch, revise, solder.

*antonyms* break, destroy, deteriorate.

*n* clout, darn, patch, repair, stitch.

**mendacious** *adj* deceitful, deceptive, dishonest, duplicitous, fallacious, false, fraudulent, insincere, inveracious, lying, perfidious, perjured, untrue, untruthful, unveracious.

*antonyms* honest, truthful.

**mendacity** *n* deceit, deceitfulness, dishonesty, distortion, duplicity, falsehood, falsification, fraudulence, insincerity, inveracity, lie, lying, mendaciousness, misrepresentation, perfidy, perjury, untruth, untruthfulness, unveracity.

*antonyms* honesty, truthfulness.

**mendicant** *adj* begging, cadging, petitionary, scrounging, supplicant.

*n* almsman, beachcomber, beggar, bum, cadger, hobo, moocher, panhandler, pauper, scrounger, tramp, vagabond, vagrant.

**menial** *adj* abject, attending, base, boring, degrading, demeaning, dull, fawning, grovelling, helping, humble, humdrum, ignoble, ignominious, low, lowly, mean, obsequious, routine, servile, slavish, sorry, subservient, sycophantic, unskilled, vile.

*n* attendant, creature, dog's-body, domestic, drudge, eta, flunky, labourer, lackey, peon, serf, servant, skivvy, slave, underling.

**menstruation** *n* catamenia, courses, flow, menorrhoea, menses, monthlies, period, the curse, the usual.

**mensuration** *n* assessment, calculation, calibration, computation, estimation, evaluation, measurement, measuring, metage, survey, surveying, valuation.

**mental**[1] *adj* abstract, cerebral, cognitive, conceptual, ideational, ideative, intellectual, noetic, rational, theoretical.

*antonym* physical.

**mental**[2] *adj* crazy, deranged, disturbed, insane, loony, loopy, lunatic, mad, psychiatric, psychotic, unbalanced, unstable.

*antonyms* balanced, sane.

**mentality** *n* attitude, brains, capacity, character, comprehension, disposition, endowment, faculty, frame of mind, intellect, IQ, make-up, mind, outlook, personality, psychology, rationality, understanding, wit.

**mentally** *adv* emotionally, intellectually, inwardly, psychologically, rationally, subjectively, temperamentally.

**mention** *v* acknowledge, adduce, advise, allude to, apprise, bring up, broach, cite, communicate, declare, disclose, divulge, hint at, impart, intimate, make known, name, point out, recount, refer to, report, reveal, speak of, state, tell, touch on.

*n* acknowledgement, allusion, announcement, citation, indication, notification, observation, recognition, reference, remark, tribute.

**mentioned** *adj* above-mentioned, aforesaid, cited, fore-cited, forementioned, forenamed, fore-quoted, foresaid, quoted, reported, stated.

**mentor** *n* adviser, coach, counsellor, guide, guru, instructor, pedagogue, swami, teacher, tutor.

**menu** *n* bill of fare, card, carte du jour, list, tariff.

**mercantile** *adj* commercial, marketable, merchantable, sal(e)able, trade, trading.

**mercenary** *adj* acquisitive, avaricious, bought, covetous, grasping, greedy, hack, hired, mammonish, mammonistic, materialistic, meretricious, money-grubbing, paid, sordid, venal.

*n* condottiere, free companion, free-lance, hireling, landsknecht, lansquenet, merc, soldier of fortune.

**merchandise** *n* cargo, commodities, freight, goods, produce, products, shipment, staples, stock, stock in trade, truck, vendibles, wares.

*v* carry, deal in, distribute, market, peddle, retail, sell, supply, trade, traffic in, vend.

**merchant** *n* broker, dealer, jobber, négociant, retailer, salesman, seller, shopkeeper, trader, tradesman, trafficker, vendor, wholesaler.

**merciful** *adj* beneficent, benignant, clement, compassionate, condolent, forbearing, forgiving, generous, gracious, humane, humanitarian, kind, lenient, liberal, mild, pitying, soft, sparing, sympathetic, tender-hearted.

*antonyms* cruel, merciless.

**merciless** *adj* barbarous, callous, cruel, hard, hard-hearted, harsh, heartless, implacable, inexorable, inhuman, inhumane, pitiless, relentless, remorseless, ruthless, severe, unappeasable, unforgiving, unmerciful, unpitying, unsparing.

*antonym* merciful.

**mercurial** *adj* active, capricious, changeable, erratic, fickle, flighty, gay, impetuous, impulsive, inconstant, irrepressible, light-hearted, lively, mobile, spirited, sprightly, temperamental, unpredictable, unstable, variable, volatile.

*antonym* saturnine.

**mercy** *n* benevolence, blessing, boon, charity, clemency, compassion, favour, forbearance, forgiveness, godsend, grace, humanitarianism, kindness, leniency, pity, quarter, relief.

*antonyms* cruelty, revenge.

**mere** *adj* absolute, bare, common, complete, entire, paltry, petty, plain, pure, pure and simple, sheer, simple, stark, unadulterated, unmitigated, unmixed, utter, very.

**merge** *v* amalgamate, blend, coalesce, combine, commingle, confederate, consolidate, converge, fuse, incorporate, intermix, join, liquesce, meet, meld, melt into, mingle, mix, unite.

**merger** *n* amalgamation, coalescence, coalition, combination, confederation, consolidation, fusion, incorporation, union.

**merit** *n* advantage, asset, claim, credit, desert, due, excellence, good, goodness, integrity, justification, quality, right, strong point, talent, value, virtue, worth, worthiness.

*antonyms* demerit, fault.

*v* deserve, earn, incur, justify, rate, warrant.

**merited** *adj* appropriate, condign, deserved, due, earned, entitled, fitting, just, justified, rightful, warranted, worthy.

*antonyms* inappropriate, unjustified.

**meritorious** *adj* admirable, commendable, creditable, deserving, estimable, excellent, exemplary, good, honourable, laudable, praiseworthy, right, righteous, virtuous, worthful, worthy.

*antonym* unworthy.

**merriment** *n* amusement, conviviality, elation, exhilaration, festivity, frolic, fun, gaiety, glee, hilarity, jocosity, jocularity, jocundity, jollity, joviality, laughter, levity, liveliness, merry-making, mirth, revelry, sport, waggery.

*antonyms* gloom, gravity, sadness, seriousness.

**merry** *adj* amusing, blithe, blithesome, boon, carefree, cheerful, chirpy, comic, comical, convivial, crank, elevated, facetious, festive, frolicsome, fun-loving, funny, gay, glad, gleeful, happy, heartsome, hilarious, humorous, jocular, jocund, jolly, joyful, joyous, light-hearted, mellow, mirthful, rollicking, rorty, saturnalian, sportful, sportive, squiffy, tiddly, tipsy, vivacious.

*antonyms* gloomy, glum, grave, melancholy, serious, sober, sombre.

**merry-go-round** *n* carousel, joy-wheel, roundabout, whirligig.

**merrymaking** *n* carousal, carouse, carousing, celebration, conviviality, festivity, fun, gaiety, gil(l)ravage, jollification, mafficking, mallemaroking, merriment, mollie, party, rejoicings, revel, revelry.

**mesh** *n* entanglement, lattice, net, netting, network, plexus, reticulation, snare, tangle, toils, tracery, trap, web.

*v* catch, combine, come together, connect, co-ordinate, dovetail, engage, enmesh, entangle, fit, harmonise, inmesh, interlock, knit.

**mesmerise** *v* benumb, captivate, enthral, entrance, fascinate, grip, hypnotise, magnetise, spellbind, stupefy.

**mess** *n* bollocks, botch, chaos, clutter, cock-up, confusion, difficulty, dilemma, dirtiness, disarray, disorder, disorganisation, fix, guddle, hash, imbroglio, jam, jumble, litter, mishmash, mix-up, muddle, muss(e), perplexity, pickle, plight, predicament, shambles, shemozzle, soss, stew, turmoil, untidiness, yuck.

*antonyms* order, tidiness.

*v* befoul, besmirch, clutter, dirty, disarrange, disarray, dishevel, foul, litter, muss(e), pollute, tousle.

*antonyms* order, tidy.

**mess about** amuse oneself, arse about, dabble, fiddle, footle, interfere, meddle, mess around, mess on, muck about, play, play about, play around, potter, tamper, tinker, toy, trifle.

**mess up** botch, bungle, disrupt, jumble, make a hash of, muck up, muddle, spoil, tangle.

**mess with** fiddle with, interfere, meddle with, play with, tamper with, tangle with, tinker with.

**message** *n* bulletin, cable, commission, communication, communiqué, dépêche, dispatch, errand, fax, idea, import, intimation, job, letter, meaning, memorandum, mission, missive, moral, note, notice, point, purport, send, task, Telemessage®, telex, theme, tidings, word.

**messenger** *n* agent, ambassador, bearer, carrier, courier, delivery boy, emissary, envoy, errand-boy, go-between, harbinger, herald, in-between, internuncio, mercury, nuncio, runner, send, vaunt-courier.

**messy** *adj* chaotic, cluttered, confused, dirty, dishevelled, disordered, disorganised, grubby, grungy, littered, muddled, shambolic, sloppy, slovenly, unkempt, untidy, yucky.

*antonyms* neat, ordered, tidy.

**metamorphose** *v* alter, change, convert, modify, mutate, remake, remodel, reshape, transfigure, transform, translate, transmogrify, transmute, transubstantiate.

**metamorphosis** *n* alteration, change, change-over, conversion, modification, mutation, rebirth, transfiguration, transformation, translation, transmogrification, transmutation, transubstantiation.

**metaphor** *n* allegory, analogy, apologue, emblem, figure of speech, image, symbol, trope.

**metaphorical** *adj* allegorical, emblematic, emblematical, figurative, Pickwickian, symbolic, tropical.

**metaphysical** *adj* abstract, abstruse, basic, deep, esoteric, essential, eternal, fundamental, general, high-flown, ideal, immaterial, impalpable, incorporeal, insubstantial, intangible, intellectual, oversubtle, philosophical, profound, recondite, speculative, spiritual, subjective, supernatural, theoretical, transcendental, universal, unreal, unsubstantial.

**mete out** administer, allot, apportion, assign, deal out, dispense, distribute, divide out, dole out, hand out, measure out, parcel out, portion, ration out, share out.

**meteor** *n* aerolite, aerolith, bolide, comet, fire-ball, meteorite, meteoroid, shooting-star.

**meteoric** *adj* brief, brilliant, dazzling, fast, instantaneous, momentary, overnight, rapid, spectacular, speedy, sudden, swift.

**meteorologist** *n* climatologist, met-man, weatherman, weather-prophet.

**method** *n* approach, arrangement, course, design, fashion, form, manner, mode, modus operandi, order, orderliness, organisation, pattern, plan, planning, practice, procedure, process, programme, purpose, regularity, routine, rule, scheme, structure, style, system, technique, way.

**methodical** *adj* business-like, deliberate, disciplined, efficient, meticulous, neat, ordered, orderly, organised, painstaking, planned, precise, punctilious, regular, scrupulous, structured, systematic, tidy.

*antonyms* confused, desultory, irregular.

**meticulous** *adj* accurate, detailed, exact, fastidious, fussy, microscopic, nice, painstaking, particular, perfectionist, precise, punctilious, scrupulous, strict, thorough.

*antonyms* careless, slapdash.

**métier** *n* calling, craft, field, forte, line, occupation, profession, pursuit, speciality, specialty, sphere, trade, vocation.

**metropolis** *n* capital, city, megalopolis.

**mettle** *n* ardour, boldness, bottle, bravery, calibre, character, courage, daring, disposition, fire, fortitude, gallantry, gameness, ginger, grit, guts, hardihood, heart, indomitability, kidney, life, make-up, nature, nerve, pith, pluck, quality, resolution, resolve, spirit, spunk, stamp, temper, temperament, valour, vigour.

**mew** *v* caterwaul, meow, mewl, miaow, miaul, pule, whine.

**mewl** *v* blubber, cry, girn, grizzle, pule, snivel, whimper, whine, whinge.

**miasma** *n* effluvium, fetor, mephitis, odour, pollution, reek, smell, stench, stink.

**miasmal** *adj* fetid, foul, insalubrious, malodorous, mephitic, miasm(at)ic, miasm(at)ous, noisome, noxious, polluted, putrid, reeking, smelly, stinking, unwholesome.

**microbe** *n* bacillus, bacterium, bug, germ, micro-organism, pathogen, virus.

**microscopic** *adj* imperceptible, indiscernible, infinitesimal, invisible, minuscule, minute, negligible, tiny.

*antonyms* huge, vast.

**midday** *n* lunchtime, noon, noonday, noontide, twelve.

**middle** *adj* central, halfway, inner, inside, intermediate, intervening, mean, medial, median, mediate, medium, mid, middle-bracket.

*n* aurea mediocritas, centre, focus, golden mean, halfway mark, halfway point, happy medium, heart, inside, mean, middle way, midpoint, midriff, midsection, midst, thick, via media, waist.

*antonyms* beginning, border, edge, end, extreme.

**middle-class** *adj* bourgeois, conventional, preppy, suburban.

**middleman** *n* broker, distributor, entrepreneur, fixer, go-between, intermediary, negotiator, retailer.

**middling** *adj* adequate, average, fair, indifferent, mean, median, mediocre, medium, moderate, modest, OK, ordinary, passable, run-of-the-mill, so-so, tolerable, unexceptional, unremarkable.

**midget** *n* dwarf, gnome, homuncule, homunculus, manikin, minikin, minnow, pygmy, shrimp, Tom Thumb.

*antonym* giant.

*adj* dwarf, Lilliputian, little, miniature, pocket, pocket-sized, pygmy, small, teeny, tiny.

*antonym* giant.

**midst** *n* bosom, centre, core, depths, epicentre, heart, hub, interior, middle, mid-point, thick.

**midway** *adv* betwixt and between, halfway, in the middle, partially.

**mien** *n* air, appearance, aspect, aura, bearing, carriage, complexion, countenance, demeanour, deportment, look, manner, presence, semblance.

**miffed** *adj* aggrieved, annoyed, chagrined, disgruntled, displeased, hurt, in a huff, irked, irritated, narked, nettled, offended, piqued, put out, resentful, upset, vexed.

*antonyms* chuffed, delighted, pleased.

**might** *n* ability, capability, capacity, clout, efficacy, efficiency, energy, force, heftiness, muscularity, potency, power, powerfulness, prowess, puissance, strength, sway, valour, vigour.

**mightily** *adv* decidedly, energetically, exceedingly, extremely, forcefully, greatly, highly, hugely, intensely, lustily, manfully, much, powerfully, strenuously, strongly, very, very much, vigorously.

**mighty** *adj* bulky, colossal, doughty, enormous, forceful, gigantic, grand, great, hardy, hefty, huge, immense, indomitable, large, lusty, manful, massive, monumental, muscular, potent, powerful, prodigious, puissant, robust, stalwart, stout, strapping, strenuous, strong, stupendous, sturdy, titanic, towering, tremendous, vast, vigorous.

*antonyms* frail, weak.

**migrant** *n* drifter, emigrant, globe-trotter, gypsy, immigrant, itinerant, land-louper, nomad, rover, tinker, transient, traveller, vagrant, wanderer.

*adj* drifting, globe-trotting, gypsy, immigrant, itinerant, migratory, nomadic, roving, shifting, transient, travelling, vagrant, wandering.

**migrate** *v* drift, emigrate, journey, move, roam, rove, shift, transhume, travel, trek, voyage, wander.

**migration** *n* diaspora, emigration, journey, movement, roving, shift, transhumance, travel, trek, Völkerwanderung, voyage, wandering.

**migratory** *adj* gipsy, itinerant, migrant, nomadic, peripatetic, roving, shifting, transient, transitory, travelling, vagrant, wandering.

**mild** *adj* amiable, balmy, bland, calm, clement, compassionate, docile, easy, easy-going, equable, forbearing, forgiving, gentle, indulgent, kind, lenient, meek, mellow, merciful, moderate, pacific, passive, peaceable, placid, pleasant, serene, smooth, soft, temperate, tender, tranquil, warm.

*antonyms* fierce, harsh, stormy, strong, violent.

**mildewy** *adj* fetid, fusty, mucedinous, mucid, musty, rotten.

**mildness** *n* blandness, calmness, clemency, docility, forbearance, gentleness, indulgence, kindness, leniency, lenity, meekness, mellowness, moderation, passivity, placidity, smoothness, softness, temperateness, tenderness, tractability, tranquillity, warmth.

*antonyms* ferocity, harshness, strength, violence.

**mil(e)ometer** *n* hodometer, perambulator, tachograph, waywiser.

**milieu** *n* arena, background, element, environment, locale, location, medium, scene, setting, sphere, surroundings.

**militant** *adj* active, aggressive, assertive, belligerent, combating, combative, contending, embattled, fighting, hawkish, pugnacious, vigorous, warring.

**military** *n* activist, aggressor, belligerent, combatant, fighter, partisan, struggler, warrior.

**military** *adj* armed, martial, service, soldier-like, soldierly, warlike.

*n* armed forces, army, forces, services, soldiers, soldiery.

**militate against** contend, count against, counter, counteract, oppose, resist, tell against, weigh against.

**militate for** advance, aid, back, further, help, promote, speak for.

**militia** *n* fencibles, minutemen, National Guard, reserve, reservists, Territorial Army, train-band, yeomanry.

**milk** *v* bleed, drain, draw off, emulge, exploit, express, extract, impose on, press, pump, siphon, squeeze, tap, use, wring.

**milk-and-water** *adj* bland, feeble, innocuous, insipid, jejune, tasteless, vapid, weak, wishy-washy.

**milksop** *n* chinless wonder, coward, milquetoast, Miss Nancy, molly, mollycoddle, namby-pamby, pansy, sissy, weakling.

**milky** *adj* alabaster, albescent, chalky, clouded, cloudy, milk-white, opaque, white, whitish.

**mill¹** *n* ball-mill, crusher, grinder, quern.

*v* comminute, crush, granulate, grate, grind, pound, powder, press, pulverise, roll.

**mill²** *n* factory, foundry, plant, shop, works.

**mill³** *v* crowd, scurry, seethe, swarm, throng, wander.

**millstone** *n* affliction, burden, drag, encumbrance, grindstone, load, quernstone, weight.

**mime** *n* dumb show, gesture, mimicry, mummery, pantomime.

*v* act out, gesture, impersonate, mimic, represent, signal, simulate.

**mimic** *v* ape, caricature, echo, imitate, impersonate, look like, mirror, parody, parrot, personate, resemble, simulate, take off.

*n* caricaturist, copy, copy-cat, imitator, impersonator, impressionist, parodist, parrot.

*adj* echoic, fake, imitation, imitative, make-believe, mimetic, mock, pseudo, sham, simulated.

**mimicry** *n* apery, burlesque, caricature, copying, imitating, imitation, impersonation, impression, mimesis, mimicking, mockery, parody, parrotry, take-off.

**mince¹** *v* chop, crumble, cut, dice, grind, hash.

*n* hachis, hash.

**mince²** *v* diminish, euphemise, extenuate, hold back, moderate, palliate, play down, soften, spare, suppress, tone down, weaken.

**mince³** *v* attitudinise, ponce, pose, posture, simper.

**mincing** *adj* affected, coxcombic(al), dainty, effeminate, foppish, lah-di-dah, minikin, nice, niminy-piminy, poncy, precious, pretentious, ripperty-tipperty, sissy.

**mind¹** *n* attention, attitude, belief, bent, brains, concentration, desire, disposition, fancy, feeling, genius, grey matter, head, imagination, inclination, inner, intellect, intellectual, intelligence, intention, judgement, leaning, marbles, memory, mentality, notion, opinion, outlook, point of view, psyche, purpose, rationality, reason, recollection, remembrance, sanity, sense, senses, sensorium, sensory, sentiment, spirit, tendency, thinker, thinking, thoughts, understanding, urge, view, will, wish, wits.

**mind's eye** contemplation, head, imagination, memory, mind, recollection, remembrance.

**mind²** *v* care, demur, disapprove, dislike, object, resent, take offence.

**mind³** *v* adhere to, attend, attend to, be careful, be on one's guard, comply with, ensure, follow, guard, have charge of, heed, keep an eye on, listen to, look after, make certain, mark, note, notice, obey, observe, pay attention, pay heed to, regard, respect, take care, take care of, take heed, tend, watch.

**mind out** be careful, be on one's guard, beware, keep one's eyes open, look out, pay attention, take care, watch, watch out.

**mindful** *adj* alert, alive (to), attentive, aware, careful, chary, cognisant, compliant, conscious, heedful, obedient, regardful, remindful, respectful, sensible, thoughtful, wary, watchful.

*antonyms* heedless, inattentive, mindless.

**mindless** *adj* asinine, automatic, brainless, brutish, careless, foolish, forgetful, gratuitous, heedless, idiotic, illogical, imbecilic, inattentive, irrational, mechanical, moronic, neglectful, negligent, oblivious, obtuse, stupid, thoughtless, unintelligent, unmindful, unreasoning, unthinking, witless.

*antonyms* intelligent, mindful, thoughtful.

**mine¹** *n* abundance, coalfield, colliery, deposit, excavation, fund, hoard, lode, pit, reserve, sap, shaft, source, stock, store, supply, treasury, trench, tunnel, vein, wealth, wheal.

*v* delve, dig for, dig up, excavate, extract, hew, quarry, remove, sap, subvert, tunnel, undermine, unearth, weaken.

**mine²** *n* bomb, depth charge, egg, explosive, land-mine.

**miner** *n* coal-miner, collier, pitman.

**mingle** *v* alloy, associate, blend, circulate, coalesce, combine, commingle, compound, hobnob, intermingle, intermix, interweave, join, marry, mell, merge, mix, rub shoulders, socialise, unite.

**miniature** *adj* baby, diminutive, dwarf, Lilliputian, little, midget, mini, minuscule, minute, pint-size(d), pocket, pocket-sized, pygmy, reduced, scaled-down, small, tiny, toy, wee.

*antonym* giant.

**minimal** *adj* least, littlest, minimum, minuscule, minute, nominal, slightest, smallest, token.

**minimise** *v* abbreviate, attenuate, belittle, curtail, decrease, decry, dedramatise, de-emphasise, deprecate, depreciate, diminish, discount, disparage, make light of, make little of, play down, prune, reduce, shrink, underestimate, underrate.

*antonym* maximise.

**minimum** *n* bottom, least, lowest point, nadir, slightest.

*antonym* maximum.

*adj* least, littlest, lowest, minimal, slightest, smallest, tiniest, weeniest, weest.

*antonym* maximum.

**minion** *n* arse-licker, backscratcher, bootlicker, creature, darling, dependant, favourite, flatterer, flunky, follower, hanger-on, heeler, henchman, hireling, lackey, lickspittle, myrmidon, parasite, pet, sycophant, toady, underling, yes-man.

**minister** *n* administrator, agent, aide, ambassador, assistant, churchman, clergyman, cleric, delegate, diplomat, divine, ecclesiastic, envoy, executive, office-holder, official, parson, pastor, plenipotentiary, preacher, priest, servant, subordinate, underling, vicar, vizier.

*v* accommodate, administer, attend, cater to, nurse, pander to, serve, take care of, tend.

**ministration** *n* aid, assistance, care, favour, help, patronage, relief, service, succour, supervision, support.

**ministry**[1] *n* administration, bureau, cabinet, council, department, office.

**ministry**[2] *n* holy orders, the church, the priesthood.

**minor** *adj* inconsequential, inconsiderable, inferior, insignificant, junior, lesser, light, negligible, paltry, petty, piddling, secondary, second-class, slight, small, smaller, subordinate, trifling, trivial, unclassified, unimportant, younger.

*antonym* major.

**minstrel** *n* bard, joculator, jongleur, musician, rhymer, rimer, singer, troubadour.

**mint** *v* cast, coin, construct, devise, fabricate, fashion, forge, invent, make, make up, manufacture, monetise, produce, punch, stamp, strike.

*adj* brand-new, excellent, first-class, fresh, immaculate, perfect, unblemished, undamaged, untarnished.

*n* bomb, bundle, fortune, heap, million, packet, pile, stack.

**minuscule** *adj* diminutive, fine, infinitesimal, itsy-bitsy, Lilliputian, little, microscopic, miniature, minute, teensy-weensy, teeny, tiny.

*antonyms* gigantic, huge.

**minute**[1] *n* flash, instant, jiff, jiffy, mo, moment, sec, second, shake, tick, trice.

**minute**[2] *adj* close, critical, detailed, diminutive, exact, exhaustive, fine, inconsiderable, infinitesimal, itsy-bitsy, Lilliputian, little, meticulous, microscopic, miniature, minim, minuscule, negligible, painstaking, paltry, petty, picayune, piddling, precise, punctilious, puny, slender, slight, small, tiny, trifling, trivial, unimportant.

*antonyms* gigantic, huge, immense.

**minutely** *adv* closely, critically, exactly, exhaustively, in detail, meticulously, painstakingly, precisely, scrupulously, systematically, with a fine-tooth comb.

**minutes** *n* details, memorandum, notes, proceedings, record(s), tapes, transactions, transcript.

**minutiae** *n* details, niceties, particulars, subtleties, trifles, trivialities.

**minx** *n* baggage, coquette, flirt, harpy, harridan, hoyden, hussy, jade, tomboy, wanton.

**miracle** *n* deus ex machina, marvel, miraculum, phenomenon, prodigy, thaumaturgy, wonder, wonder-work.

**miraculous** *adj* amazing, astonishing, astounding, extraordinary, incredible, inexplicable, magical, marvellous, otherworldly, phenomenal, preternatural, prodigious, stupendous, superhuman, supernatural, thaumaturgic, unaccountable, unbelievable, wonderful, wondrous.

*antonyms* natural, normal.

**mirage** *n* fata Morgana, hallucination, illusion, optical illusion, phantasm.

**mire** *n* bog, difficulties, dirt, fen, glaur, marsh, morass, muck, mud, ooze, quag, quagmire, slime, swamp, trouble.

**mirror** *n* copy, double, glass, hand-glass, image, keeking-glass, likeness, looking-glass, pocket-glass, reflection, reflector, replica, representation, speculum, spit and image, spitting image, twin.

*v* copy, depict, echo, emulate, follow, imitate, mimic, reflect, represent, show.

**mirth** *n* amusement, cheerfulness, festivity, frolic, fun, gaiety, gladness, glee, hilarity, jocosity, jocularity, jocundity, jollity, joviality, joyousness, laughter, levity, merriment, merrymaking, pleasure, rejoicing, revelry, sport.

*antonyms* gloom, glumness, melancholy.

**mirthful** *adj* amused, amusing, blithe, cheerful, cheery, festive, frolicsome, funny, gay, glad, gladsome, happy, hilarious, jocose, jocund, jolly, jovial, laughable, laughing, light-hearted, merry, playful, sportive, uproarious, vivacious.

*antonyms* gloomy, glum, melancholy, mirthless.

**miry** *adj* boggy, dirty, fenny, glaury, marshy, mucky, muddy, oozy, slimy, swampy.

**misadventure** *n* accident, calamity, cataclysm, catastrophe, debacle, disaster, failure, ill fortune, ill luck, mischance, misfortune, mishap, reverse, setback, tragedy.

**misanthropic** *adj* antisocial, cynical, egoistic, inhumane, malevolent, surly, unfriendly, unsociable, unsympathetic.

*antonym* philanthropic.

**misanthropy** *n* antisociality, cynicism, egoism, inhumanity, malevolence, unsociableness.

*antonym* philanthropy.

**misapply** *v* abuse, exploit, misappropriate, misemploy, misuse, pervert.

**misapprehend** *v* get the wrong idea, miscomprehend, misconceive, misconstrue, misinterpret, misknow, misread, mistake, misunderstand.

*antonym* apprehend.

**misapprehension** *n* delusion, error, fallacy, misacceptation, misconception, misconstruction, misinterpretation, misreading, mistake, misunderstanding.

*antonym* apprehension.

**misappropriate** *v* abuse, defalcate, embezzle, misapply, misspend, misuse, peculate, pervert, pocket, steal, swindle.

**misappropriation** *n* defalcation, embezzlement, misapplication, misuse, peculation, pocketing, stealing, theft.

**misbegotten** *adj* abortive, dishonest, disreputable, hare-brained, ill-advised, ill-conceived, ill-gotten, illicit, monstrous, poorly thought-out, purloined, shady, stolen, unlawful.

**misbehave** *v* act up, carry on, get up to mischief, kick over the traces, mess about, muck about, offend, transgress, trespass.

*antonym* behave.

**misbehaviour** *n* disobedience, impropriety, incivility, indiscipline, insubordination, mayhem, misconduct, misdeeds, misdemeanour, monkey business, naughtiness, rudeness, shenanigans.

**misbelief** *n* delusion, error, fallacy, heresy, heterodoxy, miscreance, unorthodoxy.

**miscalculate** *v* blunder, boob, err, get wrong, misjudge, overestimate, overrate, overvalue, slip up, underestimate, underrate, undervalue.

**miscarriage** *n* abortion, botch, breakdown, casualty, disappointment, error, failure, misadventure, mischance, misfire, mishap, mismanagement, perversion, thwarting, undoing.

*antonym* success.

**miscarry** *v* abort, bite the dust, come to grief, come to nothing, fail, fall through, flounder, gang agley, misfire, warp.

*antonym* succeed.

**miscellaneous** *adj* assorted, confused, diverse, diversified, farraginous, heterogeneous, indiscriminate, jumbled, manifold, many, mingled, mixed, motley, multifarious, multiform, omnifarious, promiscuous, sundry, varied, various.

**miscellany** *n* anthology, assortment, collection, diversity, farrago, gallimaufry, hash, hotch-potch, jumble, medley, mélange, mixed bag, mixture, olla-podrida, omnium-gatherum, pot-pourri, salmagundi, variety.

**mischance** *n* accident, bad break, blow, calamity, contretemps, disaster, ill-chance, ill-fortune, ill-luck, infelicity, misadventure, misfortune, mishap, tragedy.

**mischief¹** *n* bane, damage, detriment, devilment, deviltry, diablerie, disruption, evil, harm, hurt, impishness, injury, misbehaviour, misfortune, monkey business, naughtiness, pranks, roguery, roguishness, shenanigans, trouble, waggery, waywardness.

**mischief²** *n* devil, imp, monkey, nuisance, pest, rapscallion, rascal, rascallion, rogue, scallywag, scamp, tyke, villain.

*antonym* angel.

**mischievous** *adj* arch, bad, damaging, deleterious, destructive, detrimental, elfish, elvan, elvish, evil, exasperating, frolicsome, harmful, hurtful, impish, injurious, malicious, malignant, naughty, pernicious, playful, puckish, rascally, roguish, sinful, spiteful, sportive, teasing, tricksy, troublesome, vexatious, vicious, wayward, wicked.

*antonyms* good, well-behaved.

**misconceive** *v* misapprehend, misconstrue, misinterpret, misjudge, misread, mistake, misunderstand.

**misconception** *n* delusion, error, fallacy, misapprehension, misconstruction, misreading, misunderstanding, the wrong end of the stick.

**misconduct** *n* delinquency, dereliction, hanky-panky, immorality, impropriety, malfeasance, malpractice, malversation, misbehaviour, misdemeanour, misfeasance, mismanagement, naughtiness, rudeness, transgression, wrong-doing.

**misconstruction** *n* delusion, misapprehension, misinterpretation, misreading, mistake, misunderstanding.

**misconstrue** *v* misapprehend, misconceive, misinterpret, misjudge, misread, misreckon, mistake, mistranslate, misunderstand, take the wrong way.

**miscreant** *n* blackguard, caitiff, criminal, dastard, evil-doer, knave, malefactor, mischief-maker, profligate, rascal, reprobate, rogue, scallywag, scamp, scapegrace, scoundrel, sinner, trouble-maker, vagabond, varlet, villain, wretch, wrong-doer.

*antonym* worthy.

**misdeed** *n* crime, delict, delinquency, error, fault, felony, malefice, misconduct, misdemeanour, offence, peccadillo, sin, transgression, trespass, villainy, wrong.

**misdemeanour** *n* delict, fault, indiscretion, infringement, lapse, malfeasance, misbehaviour, misconduct, misdeed, offence, peccadillo, transgression, trespass.

**miser** *n* cheapskate, curmudgeon, hunks, mammonist, meanie, money-grubber, muck-worm, niggard, penny-pincher, pinchfist, pinchgut, pinchpenny, save-all, screw, Scrooge, skinflint, snudge, tightwad.

*antonym* spendthrift.

**miserable** *adj* abject, agelastic, anguished, bad, broken-hearted, caitiff, cheerless, contemptible, crestfallen, crushed, dejected, deplorable, depressed, depressive, desolate, despicable, despondent, destitute, detestable, disconsolate, disgraceful, dismal, distressed, doleful, dolorous, down, downcast, dreary, forlorn, gloomy, glum, grief-stricken, hapless, heartbroken, ignominious, impoverished, indigent, joyless, lachrymose, lamentable, low, luckless, lugubrious, meagre, mean, melancholic, melancholy, miz, mournful, needy, niggardly, paltry, pathetic, penniless, piteous, pitiable, pitiful, poor, sad, scanty, scurvy, shabby, shameful, sordid, sorrowful, sorrowing, sorry, squalid, star-crossed, stricken, tearful, unhappy, vile, woebegone, worthless, wretched.

*antonyms* cheerful, comfortable, generous, honourable, noble.

**miserliness** *n* avarice, cheese-paring, churlishness, close-fistedness, covetousness, frugality, meanness, minginess, misery, nearness, niggardliness, parsimony, penny-pinching, penuriousness, stinginess, thrift, thriftiness, tight-fistedness.

*antonyms* generosity, lavishness, prodigality.

**miserly** *adj* avaricious, beggarly, cheese-paring, close, close-fisted, close-handed, covetous, curmudgeonly, gare, grasping, grudging, illiberal, mean, mercenary, mingy, money-grubbing, near, niggardly, parsimonious, penny-pinching, penurious, sordid, sparing, stingy, thrifty, tight-fisted, ungenerous.

*antonyms* generous, lavish, prodigal, spendthrift.

**misery**[1] *n* abjectness, adversity, affliction, agony, anguish, bale, bane, bitter pill, blow, burden, calamity, catastrophe, cross, curse, depression, desolation, despair, destitution, disaster, discomfort, distress, dole, dolour, extremity, gloom, grief, hardship, heartache, heartbreak, humiliation, indigence, living death, load, melancholia, melancholy, misfortune, miz, mortification, need, oppression, ordeal, penury, poverty, privation, prostration, sadness, sordidness, sorrow, squalor, suffering, torment, torture, trial, tribulation, trouble, unhappiness, want, woe, wretchedness.

**misery**[2] *n* agelast, grouch, Jeremiah, Job's comforter, killjoy, moaner, moper, pessimist, prophet of doom, ray of sunshine, sourpuss, spoil-sport, Weary Willie, wet blanket, whiner, whinger.

*antonym* sport.

**misfire** *v* abort, bomb, come a cropper, come to grief, fail, fall flat, fall short, fall through, fizzle out, flop, founder, go phut, go wrong, miscarry.

*antonym* succeed.

**misfit** *n* drop-out, eccentric, fish out of water, horse marine, individualist, lone wolf, loner, maverick, nonconformist, odd man out, oddball, rogue, square peg in a round hole, weirdo.

*antonym* conformist.

**misfortune** *n* accident, adversity, affliction, bad luck, blow, buffet, calamity, catastrophe, disaster, failure, grief, hardship, harm, ill-luck, infelicity, infortune, loss, misadventure, mischance, misery, mishap, reverse, setback, sorrow, tragedy, trial, tribulation, trouble, woe.

*antonyms* luck, success.

**misgiving** *n* anxiety, apprehension, backward glance, compunction, distrust, doubt, dubiety,

fear, hesitation, misdoubt, niggle, presentiment, qualm, reservation, scruple, second thoughts, suspicion, uncertainty, unease, worry.

*antonym* confidence.

**misguided** *adj* deluded, erroneous, foolish, ill-advised, ill-considered, ill-judged, imprudent, incautious, injudicious, misconceived, misled, misplaced, mistaken, rash, unreasonable, unsuitable, unwarranted, unwise.

*antonym* sensible.

**mishandle** *v* balls up, bollocks, botch, bungle, fumble, make a balls of, make a hash of, make a mess of, make a pig's ear of, mess up, misguggle, misjudge, mismanage, mousle, muff, screw up.

*antonyms* cope, manage.

**mishap** *n* accident, adversity, balls-up, calamity, contretemps, disaster, hiccup, ill-fortune, ill-luck, misadventure, mischance, misfortune, misventure, setback.

**mishmash** *n* conglomeration, farrago, gallimaufry, hash, hotchpotch, jumble, medley, mess, muddle, olio, olla-podrida, pastiche, pot-pourri, salad, salmagundi.

**misinform** *v* bluff, deceive, give a bum steer, hoodwink, lead up the garden path, misdirect, misguide, mislead, mistell, mizzle, snow, take for a ride.

**misinformation** *n* baloney, bluff, bum steer, disinformation, dope, eyewash, guff, hype, lies, misdirection, misleading, nonsense.

**misinterpret** *v* distort, garble, get the wrong end of the stick, misappreciate, misapprehend, misconceive, misconstruct, misconstrue, misjudge, misread, misrepresent, mistake, misunderstand, pervert, warp, wrest.

**misjudge** *v* miscalculate, miscount, misestimate, misinterpret, misprise, mistake, overestimate, overrate, underestimate, underrate, undervalue.

**mislay** *v* lose, lose sight of, misplace, miss.

**mislead** *v* beguile, bluff, deceive, delude, fool, give a bum steer, hoodwink, lead up the garden path, misadvise, misdirect, misguide, misinform, mizzle, pull the wool over someone's eyes, snow, take for a ride, take in.

**misleading** *adj* ambiguous, biased, casuistical, confusing, deceitful, deceptive, delusive, delusory, disingenuous, distorted, equivocatory, evasive, fallacious, false, falsidical, loaded, mendacious, sophistical, specious, spurious, tricky, unreliable.

*antonyms* authentic, authoritative, informative, plain, unequivocal.

**mismanage** *v* balls up, bollocks, botch, bungle, fluff, foul up, louse up, make a hash of, make a mess of, maladminister, mangle, mar, mess up, misconduct, misdirect, misgovern, mishandle, misjudge, misrule, misspend, muff, screw up, squander, waste.

**mismatched** *adj* antipathetic, clashing, discordant, disparate, ill-assorted, incompatible, incongruous, irregular, misallied, mismated, unmatching, unreconcilable, unsuited.

*antonyms* compatible, matching.

**misogynist** *n* anti-feminist, male chauvinist, male supremacist, misogamist, sexist, woman-hater.

*antonym* feminist.

**misplace** *v* lose, misapply, misassign, misfile, mislay, miss.

**misprint** *n* corrigendum, erratum, error, literal, mistake, transposition, typo.

**misprise** *v* belittle, depreciate, disparage, hold cheap, look down on, mistake, misunderstand, slight, underestimate, underrate, undervalue.

*antonyms* appreciate, understand.

**misquote** *v* distort, falsify, garble, misremember, misreport, misrepresent, misstate, muddle, pervert, twist.

**misrepresent** *v* belie, bend, disguise, distort, exaggerate, falsify, garble, load, minimise, miscolour, misconstrue, misinterpret, misquote, misstate, pervert, slant, twist.

**misrule** *n* anarchy, chaos, confusion, disorder, disorganisation, indiscipline, lawlessness, maladministration, misgovernment, mismanagement, riot, tumult, turbulence, turmoil, unreason.

**miss¹** *v* avoid, bypass, circumvent, err, escape, evade, fail, forego, jump, lack, leave out, let go, let slip, lose, miscarry, mistake, obviate, omit, overlook, pass over, pass up, sidestep, skip, slip, trip.

*n* blunder, error, failure, fault, fiasco, flop, lack, lacuna, loss, mistake, need, omission, oversight, want.

**miss out** bypass, dispense with, disregard, ignore, jump, leave out, omit, pass over, skip.

**miss²** *v* grieve for, lack, lament, long for, mourn, need, pine for, regret, sorrow for, want, wish, yearn for.

**miss³** *n* backfisch, child, damsel, demoiselle, flapper, Fraülein, girl, girly, Jungfrau, junior miss, kid, lass, lassie, mademoiselle, maid, maiden, missy, Ms, nymphet, schoolgirl, spinster, teenager, young thing.

**missal** *n* breviary, euchologion, formulary, mass-book, office-book, prayer-book, service-book, Triodion.

**misshapen** *adj* contorted, crippled, crooked, deformed, distorted, grotesque, ill-made, ill-proportioned, malformed, monstrous, thrawn, twisted, ugly, ungainly, unshapely, unsightly, warped, wry.

*antonyms* regular, shapely.

**missile** *n* arrow, ball, bomb, dart, flying bomb, grenade, projectile, rocket, shaft, shell, shot, torpedo, V-bomb, weapon.

**missing** *adj* absent, astray, disappeared, gone, lacking, lost, minus, misgone, mislaid, misplaced, strayed, unaccounted-for, wanting.

*antonyms* found, present.

**mission** *n* aim, assignment, business, calling, campaign, charge, commission, crusade, delegation, deputation, duty, embassy, errand, goal, job, legation, mandate, ministry, object, office, operation, purpose, pursuit, quest, raison d'être, remit, task, task force, trust, undertaking, vocation, work.

**missionary** *n* ambassador, apostle, campaigner, champion, crusader, emissary, envoy, evangelist, exponent, gospeller, preacher, promoter, propagandist, proselytiser, teacher.

**missish** *adj* affected, arch, bossy, coy, demanding, flighty, giggly, girlish, hoity-toity, impossible, indulged, obstinate, self-willed, sentimental, silly, spoilt, squeamish, wilful.

**missive** *n* bulletin, communication, communiqué, dispatch, epistle, letter, line, memo, memorandum, message, note, report.

**misspent** *adj* dissipated, frittered away, idle, idled away, misapplied, misused, prodigal, profitless, squandered, thrown away, unprofitable, wasted.

*antonym* profitable.

**misstate** *v* distort, falsify, garble, misquote, misrelate, misremember, misreport, misrepresent, mistell, pervert, twist.

**mist** *n* brume, cloud, condensation, dew, dimness, drizzle, exhalation, film, fog, haar, haze, mizzle, roke, smir, smog, spray, steam, vapour, veil, water-smoke.

*v* becloud, bedim, befog, blur, cloud, dim, film, fog, glaze, obscure, steam up, veil.

*antonym* clear.

**mistake** *n* aberration, bêtise, bevue, bish, bloomer, blunder, boner, boob, boo-boo, clanger, clinker, corrigendum, erratum, error, fallacy, false move, fault, faux pas, floater, folly, gaffe, gaucherie, goof, howler, inaccuracy, indiscretion, inexactitude, lapse, lapsus, lapsus calami, lapsus linguae, lapsus memoriae, literal, malapropism, misapprehension, miscalculation, misconception, misjudgement, misprint, misprision, mispronunciation, misreading, misspelling, misunderstanding, mumpsimus, oversight, scape, slip, slip-up, solecism, stumer, tactlessness, trespass.

*v* blunder, confound, confuse, err, get the wrong end of the stick, goof, misapprehend, miscalculate, misconceive, misconstrue, misinterpret, misjudge, misobserve, misprise, misrate, misread, misreckon, misunderstand, slip up.

**mistaken** *adj* deceived, deluded, erroneous, fallacious, false, faulty, ill-judged, inaccurate, inappropriate, inauthentic, incorrect, inexact, misguided, misinformed, misinstructed, mislead, misprised, off base, off beam, unfair, unfounded, unjust, unsound, untrue, wide of the mark, wrong.

*antonyms* correct, justified.

**mistakenly** *adv* by mistake, erroneously, fallaciously, falsely, inaccurately, inappropriately, incorrectly, misguidedly, unfairly, unjustly, wrongly.

*antonyms* appropriately, correctly, fairly, justly.

**mistimed** *adj* ill-timed, inconvenient, infelicitous, inopportune, malapropos, tactless, unfortunate, unseasonable, unsynchronised, untimely.

*antonym* opportune.

**mistreat** *v* abuse, batter, brutalise, bully, harm, hurt, ill-treat, ill-use, injure, knock about, maltreat, manhandle, maul, mishandle, misuse, molest, rough up.

*antonym* pamper.

**mistreatment** *n* abuse, battering, brutalisation, bullying, cruelty, harm, ill-treatment, ill-usage, ill-use, injury, maltreatment, manhandling, mauling, mishandling, misuse, molestation, unkindness.

*antonyms* cosseting, pampering.

**mistress** *n* amante, canary-bird, châtelaine, concubine, courtesan, demi-mondaine, doxy, fancy woman, girlfriend, hetaira, inamorata, kept woman, lady, lady-love, lover, odalisque, owner, paramour, popsy, proprietress, teacher, woman.

**mistrust** *n* apprehension, caution, chariness, distrust, doubt, dubiety, fear, hesitancy, misdoubt, misgiving, reservations, scepticism, suspicion, uncertainty, wariness.

*antonym* trust.

*v* be wary of, beware, disbelieve, distrust, doubt, fear, fight shy of, look askance at, misdoubt, mislippen, question, suspect.

*antonym* trust.

**mistrustful** *adj* apprehensive, cautious, chary, cynical, distrustful, doubtful, dubious, fearful, hesitant, leery, sceptical, shy, suspicious, uncertain, wary.

*antonym* trustful.

**misty** *adj* blear, bleared, bleary, blurred, blurry, cloudy, dark, dim, faint, foggy, fuzzy, gauzy, hazy, indistinct, mistful, murky, muzzy, nebulous, obscure, opaque, roky, smoky, translucent, unclear, vague, veiled.

*antonyms* bright, clear.

**misunderstand** *v* get the wrong end of the stick, get wrong, misapprehend, miscomprehend, misconceive, misconstrue, misesteem, mishear, misinterpret, misjudge, misknow, misprise, misread, miss the point, mistake, take up wrong(ly).

*antonyms* grasp, understand.

**misunderstanding** *n* argument, breach, clash, conflict, difference, difficulty, disagreement, discord, disharmony, dispute, dissension, error, malentendu, misacceptation, misapprehension, misconception, misconstruction, misinterpretation, misjudgement, misknowledge, misprision, misreading, mistake, mix-up, quarrel, rift, rupture, squabble, variance.

*antonyms* agreement, reconciliation.

**misunderstood** *adj* ill-judged, misappreciated, misconstrued, misheard, misinterpreted, misjudged, misprised, misread, misrepresented, mistaken, unappreciated, unrecognised.

**misuse** *n* abusage, abuse, barbarism, catachresis, corruption, desecration, dissipation, distortion, exploitation, harm, ill-treatment, ill-usage, injury, malappropriation, malapropism, maltreatment, manhandling, misapplication, misappropriation, misemployment, mistreatment, misusage, perversion, profanation, prostitution, solecism, squandering, wastage, waste.

*v* abuse, brutalise, corrupt, desecrate, dissipate, distort, exploit, harm, ill-treat, ill-use, injure, malappropriate, maltreat, manhandle, maul, misapply, misappropriate, misemploy, mistreat, molest, overload, overtax, pervert, profane, prostitute, squander, strain, waste, wrong.

**mite** *n* atom, grain, iota, jot, modicum, morsel, ounce, scrap, smidgen, spark, trace, whit.

**mitigate** *v* abate, allay, alleviate, appease, assuage, attemper, blunt, calm, check, decrease, diminish, dull, ease, extenuate, lenify, lessen, lighten, moderate, modify, mollify, pacify, palliate, placate, quiet, reduce, remit, slake, soften, soothe, still, subdue, temper, tone down, weaken.

*antonyms* aggravate, exacerbate, increase.

**mitigating** *adj* exculpatory, extenuating, extenuative, justificatory, justifying, lenitive, mitigative, mitigatory, modifying, palliating, palliative, qualifying, vindicating.

**mitigation** *n* abatement, allaying, alleviation, appeasement, assuagement, decrease, diminution, easement, extenuation, lessening, moderation, mollification, palliation, qualification, reduction, relief, remission, tempering.

*antonyms* aggravation, exacerbation, increase.

**mix** *v* allay, alloy, amalgamate, associate, blend, coalesce, combine, commingle, commix, compound, consort, contemper, cross, dash, fold in, fraternise, fuse, hobnob, homogenise, immingle, incorporate, intermingle, intermix, interweave, join, jumble, mell, merge, mingle, shuffle, socialise, synthesise, unite.

*antonym* separate.

*n* alloy, amalgam, assortment, blend, combination, composite, compound, conglomerate, fusion, medley, mishmash, mixture, pastiche, synthesis.

**mix in** admix, blend, immingle, immix, incorporate, infiltrate, infuse, inject, interject, interlard, intermingle, interpolate, intersperse, introduce, merge.

*antonyms* extract, isolate.

**mix up** bewilder, blend, combine, complicate, confound, confuse, disturb, embroil, entangle, fluster, garble, implicate, involve, jumble, mix, muddle, perplex, puzzle, scramble, snarl up, upset.

**mixed** *adj* alloyed, amalgamated, ambivalent, assorted, blended, combined, composite, compound, cosmopolitan, crossbred, diverse, diversified, ecumenical, equivocal, fused, heterogeneous, hybrid, incorporated, indecisive, integrated, interbred, interdenominational, international, joint, linsey-woolsey, mingled, miscegenate, miscellaneous, mongrel, mongrelly, motley, polyglot, promiscuous, uncertain, united, unsegregated, varied.

**mixed up** bewildered, chaotic, complicated, confused, désorienté, disordered, disoriented, distracted, distraught, disturbed, maladjusted, mingle-mangle, muddled, perplexed, puzzled, upset.

**mixer¹** *n* busybody, disrupter, interferer, makebate, meddler, mischief-maker, stirrer, subversive, trouble-maker.

*antonym* peacemaker.

**mixer²** *n* everybody's friend, extrovert, joiner, life and soul of the party, socialiser.

*antonyms* introvert, loner, recluse.

**mixing** *n* amalgamation, association, blending, coalescence, combination, fraternisation, fusion, hybridisation, interbreeding, intercourse, interflow, intermingling, minglement, miscegenation, socialising, synthesis, union.

*antonym* separation.

**mixture** *n* admixture, alloy, amalgam, amalgamation, association, assortment, blend, brew, coalescence, combination, combine, composite, compost, compound, concoction, conglomeration, cross, fusion, galimatias, gallimaufry, half-breed, hotchpotch, hybrid, jumble, macédoine, medley, mélange, miscegen, miscegenation, miscellany, mix, mixed bag, mongrel, olio, olla-podrida, omnium-gatherum, pastiche, pot-pourri, salad, salmagundi, synthesis, union, variety.

**mix-up** *n* balls-up, chaos, complication, confusion, disorder, fankle, foul-up, jumble, mess, mistake, misunderstanding, muddle, nonsense, snafu, snarl-up, tangle.

**moan** *n* beef, belly-ache, bitch, complaint, gripe, groan, grouch, grouse, grumble, howl, keen, lament, lamentation, sigh, snivel, sob, sough, ululation, wail, whimper, whine, whinge.

*v* beef, belly-ache, bemoan, bewail, bitch, carp, complain, deplore, grieve, gripe, groan, grouch, grouse, grumble, howl, keen, lament, mourn, sigh, snivel, sob, sough, ululate, wail, weep, whimper, whine, whinge, wuther.

*antonym* rejoice.

**mob** *n* assemblage, bevy, body, canaille, class, collection, common herd, commonalty, company, crew, crowd, drove, faex populi, flock, galère, gang, gathering, great unwashed, group, herd, hoi polloi, horde, host, jingbang, lot, many-headed beast, many-headed monster, mass, masses, mobile, multitude, pack, plebs, populace, press, rabble, rent-a-crowd, rent-a-mob, riff-raff, rout, scum, set, swarm, throng, tribe, troop, vulgus.

*v* besiege, charge, cram, crowd, crowd round, descend on, fill, jam, jostle, overrun, pack, pester, set upon, surround, swarm round.

*antonym* shun.

**mobile** *adj* active, agile, ambulatory, animated, changeable, changing, energetic, ever-changing, expressive, flexible, fluid, itinerant, lively, locomobile, locomotive, mercurial, migrant, motile, movable, moving, nimble, peripatetic, portable, roaming, roving, supple, travelling, vagile, vivacious, wandering.

*antonym* immobile.

**mobilise** *v* activate, animate, assemble, call up, enlist, galvanise, levy, marshal, muster, organise, prepare, rally, ready, shift, stir, summon.

**mobility** *n* agility, animation, expressiveness, flexibility, locomobility, locomotion, locomotivity, motility, motion, motivity, movability, movableness, portability, suppleness, vagility, vivacity.

*antonyms* immobility, inflexibility, rigidity.

**mob-rule** *n* lynch-law, mobocracy, ochlocracy, Reign of Terror.

**mock** *v* ape, baffle, befool, burlesque, caricature, chaff, cheat, counterfeit, debunk, deceive, defeat, defy, delude, deride, disappoint, disparage, dupe, elude, explode, fleer, flout, foil, fool, frustrate, guy, imitate, insult, jeer, lampoon, laugh at, laugh in (someone's) face, laugh to scorn, make fun of, make sport of, mimic, parody, parrot, poke fun at, queer, quiz, ridicule, satirise, scoff, scorn, send up, sneer, take the mickey, taunt, tease, thwart, travesty, twit.

*antonyms* flatter, praise.

*adj* artificial, bogus, counterfeit, dummy, ersatz, fake, faked, false, feigned, forged, fraudulent, imitation, phoney, pinchbeck, pretended, pseudo, sham, simulated, spurious, synthetic.

**mocker** *n* derider, detractor, fleerer, flouter, iconoclast, jeerer, lampooner, lampoonist, pasquinader, reviler, ridiculer, satirist, scoffer, scorner, sneerer, tease, tormentor, vilifier.

*antonyms* flatterer, supporter.

**mockery** *n* apology, burlesque, caricature, contempt, contumely, deception, derision, disappointment, disdain, disrespect, farce, fleer, gibes, iconoclasm, imitation, insults, invective, irrision, jeering, joke, lampoon, lampoonery, let-down, mickey-taking, mimesis, mimicry, misrepresentation, parody, pasquinade, pretence, quiz, ridicule, sarcasm, satire, scoffing, scorn, send-up, sham, spoof, take-off, travesty, wisecracks.

**mocking** *adj* contemptuous, contumelious, cynical, derisive, derisory, disdainful, disrespectful, iconoclastic, impudent, insulting, irreverent, irrisory, sarcastic, sardonic, satiric, satirical, scoffing, scornful, snide, taunting.

*antonym* laudatory.

**mode** *n* approach, condition, convention, course, craze, custom, dernier cri, fad, fashion, form, latest thing, look, manner, method, plan, practice, procedure, process, quality, rage, rule, state, style, system, technique, trend, vein, vogue, way.

**model** *n* archetype, configuration, copy, criterion, design, draft, dummy, embodiment, epitome, example, exemplar, facsimile, form, gauge, ideal, image, imitation, kind, loadstar, manikin, mannequin, maquette, mark, miniature, mock-up, mode, mould, original, paradigm, paragon, pattern, personification, plan, poser, praxis, prototype, replica, representation, sitter, sketch, standard, style, subject, template, touchstone, type, variety, version, yardstick.

*adj* archetypal, complete, consummate, dummy, exemplary, facsimile, ideal, illustrative, imitation, miniature, par excellence, paradigmatic, perfect, prototypal, prototypical, representative, standard, typical.

*v* base, carve, cast, create, design, display, fashion, form, make, mould, pattern, plan, sculpt, shape, show off, sport, wear, work.

**moderate** *adj* abstemious, average, calm, centrist, continent, controlled, cool, deliberate, disciplined, equable, fair, fairish, frugal, gentle, indifferent, judicious, limited, mediocre, medium, middle-of-the-road, middling, mild, modest, non-extreme, ordinary, passable, peaceable, quiet, rational, reasonable, restrained, sensible, sober, soft-shell(ed), so-so, steady, temperate, unexceptional, well-regulated.

*v* abate, allay, alleviate, appease, assuage, attemper, blunt, calm, chasten, check, control, curb, cushion, decrease, diminish, dwindle, ease, lenify, lessen, mitigate, modify, modulate, pacify, palliate, play down, quiet, regulate, repress, restrain, slake, soften, soft-pedal, subdue, subside, tame, temper, tone down.

**moderately** *adv* fairly, frugally, gently, in moderation, modestly, passably, pretty, quite, rather, reasonably, slightly, soberly, somewhat, sparingly, to a certain degree, to a certain extent, to some extent, tolerably, unpretentiously, within limits, within measure, within reason.

*antonym* immoderately.

**moderation** *n* abatement, abstemiousness, alleviation, aurea mediocritas, calmness, caution, centrism, chastity, composure, continence, control, coolness, decrease, diminution, discipline, discretion, easing, equanimity, extenuation, fairness, golden mean, judiciousness, justice, justness, let-up, mildness, mitigation, moderateness, modification, modulation, palliation, reasonableness, reduction, restraint, self-control, sobriety, temperance, via media.

*antonyms* increase, intemperance.

**modern** *adj* advanced, avant-garde, contemporary, current, emancipated, fashionable, fresh, go-ahead, goey, innovative, inventive, jazzy, late, latest, mod, modernistic, modish, neoteric, new, newfangled, novel, present, present-day, progressive, recent, stylish, trendy, twentieth-century, up-to-date, up-to-the-minute, with-it.

*antonyms* antiquated, old.

**modernise** *v* do up, improve, modify, neoterise, progress, redesign, reform, refresh, refurbish, regenerate, rejuvenate, remake, remodel, renew, renovate, revamp, streamline, tart up, transform, update.

*antonym* regress.

**modernity** *n* contemporaneity, currency, fashionableness, freshness, goeyness, innovation, innovativeness, newness, novelty, nowness, originality, recentness.

*antonyms* antiquatedness, antiquity.

**modest** *adj* bashful, blushing, chaste, chastened, coy, demure, diffident, discreet, fair, humble, limited, maidenly, meek, middling, moderate,

ordinary, proper, quiet, reserved, reticent, retiring, seemly, self-conscious, self-effacing, shamefaced, shy, simple, small, timid, unassuming, unexceptional, unpresuming, unpresumptuous, unpretending, unpretentious, verecund.

*antonyms* conceited, immodest, pretentious, vain.

**modesty** *n* aidos, bashfulness, coyness, decency, demureness, diffidence, discreetness, humbleness, humility, meekness, propriety, quietness, reserve, reticence, seemliness, self-effacement, shamefacedness, shamefastness, shyness, simplicity, timidity, unobtrusiveness, unpretentiousness.

*antonyms* conceit, immodesty, vanity.

**modicum** *n* atom, bit, crumb, dash, drop, fragment, grain, hint, inch, iota, little, mite, ounce, particle, pinch, scrap, shred, speck, suggestion, tinge, touch, trace.

**modification** *n* adjustment, alteration, change, limitation, moderation, modulation, mutation, qualification, refinement, reformation, restriction, revision, tempering, variation.

**modify** *v* abate, adapt, adjust, allay, alter, attemper, change, convert, improve, lessen, limit, lower, moderate, modulate, qualify, recast, redesign, redo, reduce, refashion, reform, remodel, reorganise, reshape, restrain, restrict, revise, rework, soften, temper, tone down, transform, vary.

**modish** *adj* à la mode, all the rage, avant-garde, chic, contemporary, current, fashionable, goey, hip, in, jazzy, latest, mod, modern, modernistic, now, smart, stylish, trendy, up-to-the-minute, vogue, voguish, with-it.

*antonyms* dowdy, old-fashioned.

**modulate** *v* adjust, alter, attune, balance, harmonise, inflect, lower, moderate, regulate, soften, tone, tune, vary.

*antonyms* increase, raise.

**modulation** *n* accent, adjustment, alteration, inflection, inflexion, intonation, moderation, regulation, shade, shift, tone, tuning, variation.

**modus operandi** manner, method, operation, plan, practice, praxis, procedure, process, rule, rule of thumb, system, technique, way.

**mogul** *n* baron, bashaw, big cheese, big gun, big noise, big pot, big shot, big wheel, bigwig, grandee, magnate, magnifico, Mr Big, nabob, notable, panjandrum, personage, potentate, supremo, top dog, tycoon, VIP.

*antonym* nobody.

**moist** *adj* clammy, damp, dampish, dampy, dank, dewy, dripping, drizzly, humid, marshy, muggy, rainy, soggy, swampy, tearful, vaporous, watery, wet, wettish.

*antonyms* arid, dry.

**moisten** *v* bedew, damp, dampen, embrocate, humect, humectate, humidify, humify, imbue, irrigate, lick, madefy, moistify, moisturise, slake, soak, water, wet.

*antonym* dry.

**moistening** n dampening, damping, humectation, humidification, humification, irrigation, moisturisation, soaking, watering, wetting.

*antonym* drying.

*adj* dampening, damping, humectant, humective, moisturising.

*antonym* drying.

**moisture** n damp, dampness, dankness, dew, humidity, humour, liquid, mugginess, perspiration, sweat, tears, vapour, water, wateriness, wet, wetness.

*antonym* dryness.

**mole**[1] n barrier, breakwater, dike, dyke, embankment, groyne, jetty, jutty, pier.

**mole**[2] n moudiewart, mouldwarp.

**mole**[3] n agent, double agent, infiltrator, secret agent, spy.

**molest** v abuse, accost, afflict, annoy, assail, attack, badger, beset, bother, bug, disturb, faze, harass, harm, harry, hassle, hector, hound, hurt, ill-treat, injure, irritate, maltreat, manhandle, mistreat, persecute, pester, plague, tease, torment, trouble, upset, vex, worry.

**mollify** v abate, allay, appease, assuage, blunt, calm, compose, conciliate, cushion, ease, lessen, lull, mellow, mitigate, moderate, modify, pacify, placate, propitiate, quell, quiet, relax, relieve, soften, soothe, sweeten, temper.

*antonyms* aggravate, anger.

**mollycoddle** v baby, coddle, cosset, indulge, mother, overprotect, pamper, pander to, pet, ruin, spoil, spoon-feed.

*antonyms* ill-treat, neglect.

**moment**[1] n breathing-while, flash, hour, instant, jiff, jiffy, juncture, less than no time, minute, mo, point, second, shake, split second, stage, tick, time, trice, twink, twinkling.

**moment**[2] n concern, consequence, gravity, import, importance, note interest, seriousness, significance, substance, value, weight, weightiness, worth.

*antonym* insignificance.

**momentarily** adv briefly, fleetingly, for a moment, for a second, for an instant, temporarily.

**momentary** adj brief, elusive, ephemeral, evanescent, fleeting, flying, fugitive, hasty, momentaneous, passing, quick, short, short-lived, temporary, transient, transitory.

*antonyms* lasting, permanent.

**momentous** adj apocalyptic, consequential, critical, crucial, decisive, earth-shaking, epoch-making, eventful, fateful, grave, historic, important, major, pivotal, serious, significant, tremendous, vital, weighty.

*antonym* insignificant.

**momentum** n drive, energy, force, impact, impetus, impulse, incentive, power, propulsion, push, speed, stimulus, strength, thrust, urge, velocity.

**monarch** n despot, dynast, emperor, empress, king, potentate, prince, princess, queen, ruler, sovereign, tyrant.

**monarchy** n absolutism, autocracy, despotism, empire, kingdom, kinghood, kingship, majesty, monocracy, princedom, princehood, principality, principate, realm, royalism, rule, sovereignty, tyranny.

**monastery** n abbey, ashram, béguinage, Charterhouse, Chartreuse, cloister, coenobium, convent, fratery, fratry, friary, gompa, house, lamasery, nunnery, priory, vihara, wat.

**monastic** adj anchoritic, ascetic, austere, celibate, cloistered, cloistral, coenobitic, contemplative, conventual, eremital, eremitic, hermitical, monachal, monasterial, monastical, monkish, recluse, reclusive, secluded, sequestered, withdrawn.

*antonyms* gregarious, materialistic, worldly.

**monasticism** n anchoritsm, asceticism, austerity, coenobitism, eremitism, monachism, monkery, monkhood, recluseness, reclusion, seclusion.

**monetary** adj budgetary, bursal, capital, cash, economic, financial, fiscal, money, pecuniary.

**money** n akkas, akkers, baksheesh, banco, banknotes, bankroll, boodle, brass, bread, capital, cash, chips, coin, currency, dibbs, dibs, dough, dumps, fat, filthy lucre, fonds, funds, gelt, gold, gravy, greens, hard cash, hard money, legal tender, lolly, loot, mazuma, mint-sauce, money of account, moolah, oof, pelf, readies, ready money, rhino, riches, scrip, shekels, siller, silver, specie, spondulix (spondulicks), stumpy, sugar, the needful, the ready, the wherewithal, tin, wealth.

**money-box** n cash-box, chest, coffer, penny-pig, pig, piggy-bank, safe.

**moneyed, monied** adj affluent, comfortable, flush, loaded, opulent, prosperous, rich, rolling, stinking, warm, wealthy, well-heeled, well-off, well-to-do.

*antonym* impoverished.

**money-grubber** n mammonist, mammonite, muck-worm, quaestuary.

**money-grubbing** adj acquisitive, grasping, mammonish, mammonistic, mercenary, miserly, quaestuary.

**mongrel** n bigener, cross, crossbreed, half-breed, hybrid, lurcher, mule, mutt, yellow-dog.

*adj* bastard, crossbred, half-breed, hybrid, ill-defined, mixed, mongrelly, nondescript.

*antonyms* pedigree, pure-bred.

**monitor** n adviser, detector, guide, invigilator, overseer, prefect, recorder, scanner, screen, supervisor, watchdog.

*v* check, detect, follow, keep an eye on, keep track of, keep under surveillance, note, observe, oversee, plot, record, scan, supervise, survey, trace, track, watch.

**monk** n beghard, béguin, brother, cloisterer, coenobite, contemplative, conventual, frate, frater, friar, gyrovague, hermit, mendicant, monastic, religieux, religionary, religioner, religious.

**monkey**[1] n ape, primate, simian.

**monkey**[2] *n* ass, butt, devil, dupe, fool, imp, jackanapes, laughing-stock, mug, rapscallion, rascal, rogue, scallywag, scamp.

*v* fiddle, fidget, fool, interfere, meddle, mess, play, potter, tamper, tinker, trifle.

**monkey business** carry-on, chicanery, clowning, dishonesty, foolery, hanky-panky, jiggery-pokery, jugglery, legerdemain, mischief, monkey tricks, pranks, shenanigans, skulduggery, sleight-of-hand, tomfoolery, trickery.

*antonyms* honesty, probity.

**monochrome** *adj* black-and-white, monochroic, monochromatic, monotone, monotonous, sepia, unicolor, unicolorate, unicolorous, unicolour, unicoloured.

*antonym* kaleidoscopic.

**monocle** *n* eyeglass, glass, quiz, quizzing-glass.

**monogamous** *adj* monandrous, monogamic, monogynous.

*antonyms* bigamous, polygamous.

**monogamy** *n* monandry, monogyny.

*antonyms* bigamy, polygamy.

**monolingual** *adj* monoglot, unilingual.

*antonym* polyglot.

**monolith** *n* megalith, menhir, sarsen, shaft, standing stone.

**monolithic** *adj* colossal, faceless, giant, gigantic, huge, immobile, immovable, inflexible, intractable, massive, monumental, rigid, solid, undifferentiated, unvaried, vast.

**monologue** *n* harangue, homily, lecture, oration, sermon, soliloquy, speech, spiel.

*antonyms* conversation, dialogue, discussion.

**monomania** *n* bee in one's bonnet, fanaticism, fetish, fixation, hobby-horse, idée fixe, mania, neurosis, obsession, ruling passion, thing.

**monopolise** *v* appropriate, control, corner, dominate, engross, hog, occupy, preoccupy, take over, take up, tie up.

*antonym* share.

**monopoly** *n* ascendancy, control, corner, domination, exclusive right, monopsony, sole right.

**monotheism** *n* henotheism, unitarianism.

*antonym* polytheism.

**monotonous** *adj* boring, colourless, droning, dull, flat, humdrum, monochrome, plodding, prosaic, repetitious, repetitive, routine, samey, soul-destroying, tedious, tiresome, toneless, unchanging, uneventful, uniform, uninflected, unvaried, unvarying, wearisome.

*antonyms* colourful, lively, varied.

**monotony** *n* boredom, colourlessness, dullness, flatness, humdrumness, monotonousness, prosaicness, repetitiousness, repetitiveness, routine, routineness, sameness, tediousness, tedium, tiresomeness, uneventfulness, uniformity, wearisomeness.

*antonyms* colour, liveliness.

**monster** *n* abortion, barbarian, basilisk, beast, behemoth, bogeyman, brute, centaur, chimera, cockatrice, colossus, Cyclops, demon, devil, fiend, freak, giant, Gorgon, harpy, hellhound, hippocampus, hippogriff, Hydra, jabberwock, kraken, lamia, leviathan, lindworm, mammoth, manticore, Medusa, Minotaur, miscreation, monstrosity, mutant, ogre, ogress, prodigy, rye-wolf, savage, Sphinx, teratism, titan, villain, windigo, wivern.

*adj* Brobdingnagian, colossal, cyclopean, enormous, gargantuan, giant, gigantic, huge, immense, jumbo, mammoth, massive, monstrous, prodigious, rounceval, stupendous, titanic, tremendous, vast.

*antonym* minute.

**monstrosity** *n* abnormality, abortion, atrocity, dreadfulness, enormity, evil, eyesore, freak, frightfulness, heinousness, hellishness, hideousness, horror, loathsomeness, miscreation, monster, mutant, obscenity, ogre, prodigy, teras, teratism.

**monstrous** *adj* abhorrent, abnormal, atrocious, colossal, criminal, cruel, cyclopean, deformed, devilish, diabolical, disgraceful, dreadful, egregious, elephantine, enormous, evil, fiendish, foul, freakish, frightful, gargantuan, giant, gigantic, great, grotesque, gruesome, heinous, hellish, hideous, horrendous, horrible, horrific, horrifying, huge, hulking, immense, infamous, inhuman, intolerable, loathsome, malformed, mammoth, massive, miscreated, misshapen, monster, obscene, odious, outrageous, prodigious, rounceval, satanic, scandalous, shocking, stupendous, teratoid, terrible, titanic, towering, tremendous, unnatural, vast, vicious, villainous, wicked.

**monthly** *adj* mensal, menstrual, mensual.

**monument** *n* ancient monument, antiquity, barrow, cairn, cenotaph, commemoration, cross, dolmen, evidence, gravestone, headstone, marker, martyry, mausoleum, memento, memorial, obelisk, pillar, prehistoric monument, record, relic, remembrance, reminder, shaft, shrine, statue, testament, token, tombstone, tumulus, witness.

**monumental** *adj* abiding, awe-inspiring, awesome, catastrophic, classic, colossal, commemorative, conspicuous, cyclopean, durable, egregious, enduring, enormous, epoch-making, funerary, gigantic, great, historic, horrible, huge, immense, immortal, important, imposing, impressive, indefensible, lasting, magnificent, majestic, massive, memorable, memorial, monolithic, notable, outstanding, overwhelming, prodigious, significant, staggering, statuary, stupendous, terrible, tremendous, vast, whopping.

*antonyms* insignificant, unimportant.

**mood** *n* blues, caprice, depression, disposition, doldrums, dumps, fit, frame of mind, grumps, humour, melancholy, pique, spirit, state of mind, sulk, temper, tenor, the sulks, vein, whim.

**moody** *adj* angry, atrabilious, broody, cantankerous, capricious, cast-down, changeable, choleric, crabbed, crabby, cranky, cross, crotchety, crusty, dejected, depressive, dismal, doleful, dour, downcast, erratic, faddish, fickle, fitful, flighty, gloomy, glum, huffish, huffy, ill-humoured, impulsive, inconstant, introspective, introvert, irascible, irritable, lugubrious, melancholy, mercurial, miserable, mopy, morose, peevish, pensive, petulant, piqued, sad, saturnine, short-tempered, splenetic, sulky, sullen, temperamental, testy, touchy, unpredictable, unsociable, unstable, unsteady, volatile, waspish.

*antonyms* cheerful, equable.

**moon**[1] *v* brood, daydream, dream, fantasise, idle, languish, loaf, mooch, mope, pine, potter.

**moon**[2] *n* crescent, Cynthia, demilune, Diana, full moon, half-moon, lune, lunule, meniscus, Paddy's lantern, Phoebe, Selene.

**moon-like** *adj* crescent, crescentic, lunar, lunate, lunular, meniscoid, moon-shaped, moony, selenic.

**moonshine**[1] *n* baloney, blather, blether, bosh, bullshit, bunk, bunkum, claptrap, crap, eyewash, gas, guff, havers, hogwash, hot air, nonsense, piffle, rot, rubbish, stuff, tarradiddle, tommyrot, tosh, tripe, twaddle.

*antonym* sense.

**moonshine**[2] *n* bootleg, hoo(t)ch, pot(h)een.

**moor**[1] *v* anchor, berth, bind, dock, drop anchor, fasten, fix, hitch, lash, secure, tie up.

*antonym* loose.

**moor**[2] *n* brae, downs, fell, heath, moorland, muir, upland, wold.

**moot** *v* advance, argue, bring up, broach, debate, discuss, introduce, pose, propose, propound, put forward, submit, suggest, ventilate.

*adj* academic, arguable, contestable, controversial, crucial, debatable, disputable, disputed, doubtful, insoluble, knotty, open, open to debate, problematic, questionable, undecided, undetermined, unresolvable, unresolved, unsettled, vexed.

**moot point** controversial issue, crux, difficulty, knot, poser, problem, question mark, stumbling-block, vexata quaestio, vexed question.

**mop** *n* head of hair, mane, mass, mat, shock, sponge, squeegee, swab, tangle, thatch.

*v* absorb, clean, soak, sponge, swab, wash, wipe.

**mop up** absorb, account for, clean up, eliminate, finish off, neutralise, round up, secure, soak up, sponge, swab, take care of, tidy up, wash, wipe.

**mope** *v* agonise, boody, brood, despair, despond, droop, fret, grieve, idle, languish, mooch, moon, pine, sulk.

*n* depressive, grouch, grump, introvert, killjoy, melancholiac, melancholic, misery, moaner, moper, mopus, pessimist, Weary Willie.

**moral** *adj* blameless, chaste, clean-living, decent, equitable, ethical, good, high-minded, honest, honourable, incorruptible, innocent, just, meritorious, moralistic, noble, principled, proper, pure, responsible, right, righteous, square, straight, temperate, upright, upstanding, virtuous.

*antonym* immoral.

*n* adage, aphorism, apophthegm, dictum, epigram, gnome, import, lesson, maxim, meaning, message, motto, point, precept, proverb, saw, saying, significance, teaching.

**morale** *n* confidence, esprit de corps, heart, mettle, mood, resolve, self-esteem, spirit, spirits, state of mind, temper.

**moralise** *v* discourse, edify, ethicise, lecture, pontificate, pontify, preach, sermonise.

**morality** *n* chastity, conduct, decency, deontology, equity, ethicality, ethicalness, ethics, ethos, goodness, habits, honesty, ideals, integrity, justice, manners, morals, mores, philosophy, principle, principles, probity, propriety, rationale, rectitude, righteousness, standards, tightness, uprightness, virtue.

*antonym* immorality.

**morals** *n* behaviour, conduct, deontics, deontology, equity, ethics, ethos, habits, ideals, integrity, manners, morality, mores, principles, probity, propriety, rectitude, scruples, standards.

**morass** *n* bog, can of worms, chaos, clutter, confusion, fen, flow, jam, jumble, marsh, marshland, mess, mire, mix-up, moss, muddle, quag, quagmire, quicksand, slough, swamp, tangle.

**moratorium** *n* ban, delay, embargo, freeze, halt, postponement, respite, standstill, stay, stoppage, suspension.

*antonyms* go-ahead, green light.

**morbid** *adj* ailing, brooding, corrupt, deadly, diseased, dreadful, ghastly, ghoulish, gloomy, grim, grisly, gruesome, hideous, horrid, hypochondriacal, infected, lugubrious, macabre, malignant, melancholy, neurotic, pathological, peccant, pessimistic, putrid, sick, sickly, sombre, unhealthy, unsalubrious, unsound, unwholesome, vicious, Wertherian.

**mordant** *adj* acerbic, acid, acidic, acidulous, acrimonious, astringent, biting, bitter, caustic, corrosive, cutting, edged, harsh, incisive, mordacious, pungent, sarcastic, scathing, sharp, stinging, trenchant, venomous, vicious, waspish, wounding.

*antonyms* gentle, sparing.

**more** *adj* added, additional, alternative, extra, fresh, further, increased, new, other, renewed, repeated, spare, supplementary.

*adv* again, better, further, longer.

**moreover** *adv* additionally, also, as well, besides, further, furthermore, in addition, into the bargain, likewise, may I add, more, more to the point, to boot, too, what is more, withal.

**morgue** *n* deadhouse, mortuary.

**moribund** *adj* at a standstill, caducous, collapsing, comatose, crumbling, dead and alive, declining, doomed, dwindling, dying, ebbing, fading, failing, in extremis, obsolescent, on one's last legs, on the way out, senile, stagnant, stagnating, waning, wasting away, weak, with one foot in the grave.

*antonyms* alive, flourishing, lively, nascent.

**morning** *n* ack emma, am, break of day, cock-crow, dawn, daybreak, daylight, dayspring, first thing, foreday, forenoon, morn, sunrise, sun-up.

*adj* antemeridian, auroral, aurorean, dawn, forenoon, matinal, matutinal, matutive.

**moron** *n* ass, blockhead, bonehead, clot, cretin, daftie, dimwit, dolt, dope, dumbbell, dummy, dunce, dunderhead, fool, halfwit, idiot, imbecile, klutz, mental defective, mooncalf, muttonhead, natural, nong, numbskull, schmo, schmuck, simpleton, thickhead, vegetable, zombie.

**moronic** *adj* asinine, brainless, cretinous, daft, defective, dimwitted, doltish, dopey, foolish, gormless, halfwitted, idiotic, imbecilic, lacking, mindless, retarded, simple, simple-minded, stupid, subnormal, thick, unintelligent.

**morose** *adj* blue, cheerless, churlish, crabbed, crabby, cross, crusty, depressed, dour, down, gloomy, glum, grim, grouchy, gruff, grum, huffy, humourless, ill-humoured, ill-natured, ill-tempered, low, melancholy, misanthropic, moody, mournful, perverse, pessimistic, saturnine, sour, stern, sulky, sullen, surly, taciturn, testy, unsociable.

*antonyms* cheerful, communicative.

**morsel** *n* atom, bit, bite, bonne-bouche, crumb, fraction, fragment, grain, modicum, morceau, mouthful, nibble, part, piece, scrap, segment, slice, smidgen, snack, soupçon, taste, titbit.

**mortal** *adj* agonising, awful, bodily, corporeal, deadly, deathful, dire, earthly, enormous, ephemeral, extreme, fatal, fleshly, grave, great, human, impermanent, implacable, intense, irreconcilable, lethal, lethiferous, mortiferous, passing, perishable, relentless, remorseless, severe, sublunary, sworn, temporal, terrible, transient, unrelenting, worldly.

*antonym* immortal.

*n* being, body, creature, earthling, human, human being, individual, man, person, sublunar, sublunary, woman.

*antonyms* god, immortal.

**mortality** *n* bloodshed, caducity, carnage, corruptibility, death, destruction, ephemerality, fatality, humanity, humans, impermanence, killing, mankind, mortals, perishability, temporality, transience, transitoriness.

*antonym* immortality.

**mortgage** *v* dip, pawn, pledge, put in hock.

*n* bond, debenture, lien, loan, pledge, security, wadset.

**mortification** *n* abasement, annoyance, ascesis, asceticism, chagrin, chastening, confounding, conquering, control, corruption, defeat, denial, discipline, discomfiture, dissatisfaction, embarrassment, festering, gangrene, humiliation, ignominy, loss of face, necrosis, overthrow, punishment, putrescence, shame, subjugation, vexation.

**mortified** *adj* abashed, affronted, annoyed, ashamed, chagrined, chastened, confounded, crushed, dead, decayed, deflated, discomfited, displeased, embarrassed, gangrenous, humbled, humiliated, necrotic, put out, put to shame, putrefied, putrid, rotted, rotten, shamed, vexed.

*antonyms* elated, jubilant.

**mortify** *v* abase, abash, affront, annoy, chagrin, chasten, confound, conquer, control, corrupt, crush, deflate, deny, die, disappoint, discipline, discomfit, embarrass, fester, gangrene, humble, humiliate, macerate, necrose, put to shame, putrefy, shame, subdue, vex.

**mortifying** *adj* chastening, crushing, discomfiting, embarrassing, humbling, humiliating, ignominious, overwhelming, punishing, salutary, shaming, thwarting.

**mortuary** *n* deadhouse, funeral parlour, morgue.

**mostly** *adv* as a rule, characteristically, chiefly, commonly, customarily, feckly, for the most part, generally, largely, mainly, normally, on the whole, particularly, predominantly, primarily, principally, typically, usually.

**mote** *n* atom, grain, iota, jot, mite, particle, speck, spot, trace.

**moth-eaten** *adj* ancient, antiquated, archaic, dated, decayed, decrepit, dilapidated, mangy, moribund, mothed, mouldy, musty, obsolete, old-fashioned, outdated, outworn, ragged, seedy, shabby, stale, tattered, threadbare, worn-out.

*antonyms* fresh, new.

**mother** *n* dam, generatrix, genetrix, ma, mam, mama, mamma, mammy, mater, materfamilias, mom, momma, mommy, mum, mummy, old lady, old woman.

*v* baby, bear, care for, cherish, cosset, foster, fuss over, indulge, nurse, nurture, overprotect, pamper, produce, protect, raise, rear, spoil, tend.

*antonym* neglect.

**motherly** *adj* affectionate, caring, comforting, fond, gentle, indulgent, kind, kindly, loving, maternal, protective, solicitous, tender, warm.

*antonyms* indifferent, neglectful, uncaring.

**motif** *n* concept, decoration, design, device, figure, form, idea, leitmotiv, logo, notion, ornament, pattern, shape, strain, subject, theme.

**motion** *n* action, change, dynamics, flow, flux, gesticulation, gesture, inclination, kinesics, kinetics, locomotion, mechanics, mobility, motility, move, movement, nod, passage, passing, progress, proposal, proposition, recommendation, sign, signal, submission, suggestion, transit, travel, wave.

*v* beckon, direct, gesticulate, gesture, nod, sign, signal, usher, wave.

**motionless** *adj* at a standstill, at rest, calm, fixed, frozen, halted, immobile, inanimate, inert, lifeless, moveless, paralysed, resting, rigid, stagnant, standing, static, stationary, still, stock-still, transfixed, unmoved, unmoving.

*antonym* active.

**motivate** *v* actuate, arouse, bring, cause, draw, drive, encourage, impel, incite, induce, inspire, inspirit, instigate, kindle, lead, move, persuade, prompt, propel, provoke, push, spur, stimulate, stir, trigger, urge.

*antonyms* deter, prevent.

**motivation** *n* ambition, desire, drive, hunger, impulse, incentive, incitement, inducement, inspiration, instigation, interest, momentum, motive, persuasion, provocation, push, reason, spur, stimulus, urge, wish.

*antonyms* discouragement, prevention.

**motive** *n* cause, consideration, design, desire, encouragement, ground(s), impulse, incentive, incitement, inducement, influence, inspiration, intention, mainspring, motivation, object, occasion, purpose, rationale, reason, spur, stimulus, thinking, urge.

*antonyms* deterrent, discouragement, disincentive.

*adj* activating, actuating, agential, driving, impelling, initiating, motivating, moving, operative, prompting, propellent.

*antonyms* deterrent, inhibitory, preventive.

**motley** *adj* assorted, chequered, disparate, dissimilar, diverse, diversified, haphazard, heterogeneous, ill-assorted, kaleidoscopic, mingled, miscellaneous, mixed, multicoloured, particoloured, patchwork, polychromatic, polychrome, polychromous, promiscuous, rainbow, unlike, varied, variegated.

*antonyms* homogeneous, monochrome, uniform.

**mottled** *adj* blotchy, brindled, chequered, dappled, flecked, freaked, freckled, jaspé, marbled, piebald, pied, poikilitic, skewbald, speckled, spotted, stippled, streaked, tabby, variegated, veined, watered.

*antonyms* monochrome, plain, uniform.

**motto** *n* adage, apophthegm, byword, catchword, cry, dictum, epigraph, formula, gnome, golden rule, ichthys, maxim, precept, proverb, rule, saw, saying, sentence, slogan, watchword.

**mould**[1] *n* arrangement, brand, build, calibre, cast, character, configuration, construction, cut, design, die, fashion, form, format, frame, framework, ilk, kidney, kind, line, make, matrix, model, moulage, nature, pattern, quality, shape, sort, stamp, structure, style, template, type.

*v* affect, carve, cast, construct, control, create, design, direct, fashion, fit, forge, form, hew, influence, make, model, sculpt, sculpture, shape, stamp, work.

**mould**[2] *n* black, black spot, blight, fungus, mildew, mouldiness, must, mustiness, rust.

**mould**[3] *n* clods, dirt, dust, earth, ground, humus, loam, soil.

**moulder** *v* corrupt, crumble, decay, decompose, disintegrate, humify, perish, rot, turn to dust, waste.

**mouldy** *adj* bad, blighted, corrupt, decaying, fusty, mildewed, mucedinous, mucid, muggish, muggy, musty, putrid, rotten, rotting, spoiled, stale, vinewed.

*antonyms* fresh, wholesome.

**mound** *n* agger, bank, barrow, bing, bulwark, drift, dune, earthwork, elevation, embankment, heap, hill, hillock, hummock, knoll, mote, motte, pile, rampart, rick, ridge, rise, stack, tuffet, tumulus, tussock, yardang.

**mount** *v* accumulate, arise, ascend, bestride, build, clamber up, climb, climb on, climb up on, copulate, cover, deliver, display, emplace, enchase, escalade, escalate, exhibit, fit, frame, get astride, get on, get up, get up on, go up, grow, horse, increase, install, intensify, jump on, launch, lift, multiply, pile up, place, position, prepare, produce, put in place, put on, ready, ride, rise, rocket, scale, set, set in motion, set off, set up, soar, stage, straddle, swell, tower, tread.

*n* backing, base, fixture, foil, frame, horse, monture, mounting, pedestal, podium, setting, stand, steed, support.

**mountain** *n* abundance, alp, backlog, ben, berg, elevation, eminence, fell, heap, height, mass, massif, mound, mount, Munro, peak, pile, reserve, stack, ton.

**mountainous** *adj* alpine, daunting, enormous, formidable, gigantic, great, gross, high, highland, hilly, huge, hulking, immense, mammoth, mighty, monumental, ponderous, prodigious, rocky, rugged, soaring, steep, towering, unwieldy, upland.

*antonyms* easy, flat, small.

**mountebank** *n* charlatan, cheat, con man, confidence, fake, fraud, huckster, impostor, phoney, pretender, pseud, quack, quacksalver, rogue, spieler, swindler, trickster.

**mourn** *v* bemoan, bewail, beweep, deplore, grieve, keen, lament, miss, regret, rue, sorrow, wail, weep.

*antonyms* bless, rejoice.

**mourner** *n* bereaved, griever, keener, mute, sorrower.

**mournful** *adj* afflicting, broken-hearted, calamitous, cast-down, cheerless, chopfallen, dearnful, dejected, deplorable, depressed, desolate, disconsolate, dismal, distressing, doleful, dolorous, downcast, funereal, gloomy, grief-stricken, grieving, grievous, heartbroken, heavy, heavy-hearted, joyless, lachrymose, lamentable, long-faced, long-visaged, lugubrious, melancholy, miserable, painful, piteous, plaintive, plangent, rueful, sad, sombre, sorrowful, stricken, tragic, unhappy, woeful, woesome.

*antonyms* cheerful, joyful.

**mourning** *n* bereavement, black, desolation, grief, grieving, keening, lamentation, sackcloth and ashes, sadness, sorrow, wailing, weeds, weeping, widow's weeds, woe.

*antonym* rejoicing.

**mouse-like** *adj* cowering, diffident, diminutive, mous(e)y, murine, shy, timid, timorous.

**mous(e)y** *adj* brownish, characterless, colourless, diffident, drab, dull, indeterminate, ineffectual, mouse-like, plain, quiet, self-effacing, shy, timid, timorous, unassertive, unforthcoming, uninteresting, withdrawn.

*antonyms* assertive, bright, extrovert, irrepressible.

**moustache** *n* excrement, face fungus, handlebar moustache, mustachio, mustachios, toothbrush moustache, walrus, whiskers.

**mouth**[1] *n* aperture, cake-hole, cavity, chops, crevice, débouché, debouchment, debouchure, disemboguement, door, embouchure, entrance, estuary, gateway, gob, inlet, jaws, kisser, lips, mandibles, maw, moue, opening, orifice, outlet, portal, potato-trap, pout, proboscis, rattle-trap, scowl, threshold, trap, vent.

*v* articulate, declaim, elegise, enunciate, form, pronounce, shape, spout, utter, whisper.

**mouth**[2] *n* backchat, boasting, braggadocio, bragging, cheek, effrontery, gas, hot air, impudence, insolence, lip, rudeness, sauce.

**mouthful** *n* bit, bite, bonne bouche, drop, forkful, gob, gobbet, gulp, morsel, sample, sip, slug, spoonful, sup, swallow, taste, titbit.

**mouthpiece** *n* agent, delegate, fugleman, journal, organ, propagandist, representative, spokesman, spokeswoman.

**movable** *adj* adjustable, alterable, changeable, detachable, flexible, mobile, portable, portative, transferable, transportable.

*antonyms* fixed, immovable.

**movables** *n* belongings, chattels, effects, furniture, gear, goods, impedimenta, plenishings, possessions, property, stuff, things, traps.

**move** *v* activate, actuate, adjust, advance, advise, advocate, affect, agitate, budge, carry, cause, change, cover the ground, decamp, depart, disturb, drift, drive, ease, edge, excite, flit, get, give rise to, go, go away, gravitate, impel, impress, incite, induce, influence, inspire, instigate, jiggle, lead, leave, locomote, make strides, march, migrate, motivate, move house, operate, persuade, proceed, progress, prompt, propel, propose, pull, push, put forward, quit, recommend, relocate, remove, rouse, run, set going, shift, shove, start, stimulate, stir, submit, suggest, switch, take, touch, transfer, transport, transpose, turn, urge, walk.

*n* act, action, deed, démarche, dodge, draught, flit, flitting, go, manoeuvre, measure, migration, motion, movement, ploy, relocation, removal, ruse, shift, step, stratagem, stroke, tack, tactic, transfer, turn.

**movement** *n* act, action, activity, advance, agitation, beat, cadence, campaign, change, crusade, current, development, displacement, division, drift, drive, evolution, exercise, faction, flow, front, gesture, ground swell, group, grouping, innards, machinery, manoeuvre, measure, mechanism, metre, motion, move, moving, operation, organisation, pace, part, party, passage, progress, progression, rhythm, section, shift, steps, stir, stirring, swing, tempo, tendency, transfer, trend, workings, works.

**movie** *n* feature, film, flick, motion picture, picture, silent, talkie, video.

**movies** *n* cinema, film, films, flicks, pictures, silver screen.

**moving** *adj* affecting, ambulant, ambulatory, arousing, dynamic, emotional, emotive, exciting, impelling, impressive, inspirational, inspiring, locomobile, mobile, motile, motivating, movable, pathetic, persuasive, poignant, portable, propelling, running, stimulating, stimulative, stirring, touching, unfixed.

*antonyms* fixed, stationary, unemotional.

**mow** *v* clip, crop, cut, scythe, shear, trim.

**mow down** butcher, cut down, cut to pieces, decimate, massacre, shoot down, slaughter.

**much** *adv* considerably, copiously, decidedly, exceedingly, frequently, greatly, often.

*adj* a lot of, abundant, ample, considerable, copious, great, plenteous, plenty of, siz(e)able, substantial.

*n* heaps, lashings, loads, lots, oodles, plenty, scads.

*antonym* little.

**muck** *n* dirt, droppings, dung, faeces, filth, gunge, gunk, manure, mire, mud, ooze, ordure, scum, sewage, slime, sludge.

**muck up** botch, bungle, make a mess of, make a muck of, mar, mess up, muff, ruin, screw up, spoil, waste.

**mucky** *adj* begrimed, bespattered, dirty, filthy, grimy, messy, miry, mud-caked, muddy, oozy, soiled, sticky.

*antonym* clean.

**mucous** *adj* gelatinous, glutinous, gummy, mucilaginous, slimy, snotty, viscid, viscous.

**mud** *n* adobe, clabber, clay, dirt, fango, glaur, mire, ooze, silt, slab, sleech, slob, sludge, slush.

**muddle** *v* befuddle, bewilder, confound, confuse, daze, disarrange, disorder, disorganise, disorient(ate), fuddle, fuzzle, jumble, make a mess of, mess, mix up, mull, perplex, scramble, spoil, stupefy, tangle.

*n* bollocks, chaos, clutter, cock-up, confusion, daze, disarray, disorder, disorganisation, fankle, guddle, jumble, mess, mix-up, mull, perplexity, pie, plight, predicament, puddle, snarl-up, tangle.

**muddle through** cope, get along, get by, make it, manage, muddle along, scrape by.

**muddled** *adj* at sea, befuddled, bewildered, chaotic, confused, dazed, disarrayed, disordered, disorganised, disorient(at)ed, higgledy-piggledy, incoherent, jumbled, loose, messy, mixed-up, muddle-headed, perplexed, puzzle-headed, scrambled, stupefied, tangled, unclear, vague, woolly.

**muddy** *adj* bespattered, blurred, boggy, clarty, cloudy, confused, dingy, dirty, dredgy, drumly, dull, foul, fuzzy, glaury, grimy, grouty, hazy, impure, indistinct, marshy, miry, mucky, mud-caked, muddled, opaque, quaggy, slabby, sleechy, sloppy, soiled, swampy, turbid, unclear, vague, woolly.

*antonyms* clean, clear.

*v* bedash, bedaub, begrime, bespatter, cloud, dirty, smear, smirch, soil.

*antonym* clean.

**muff** v botch, bungle, fluff, mess up, mishit, mismanage, miss, spoil.

**muffle** v cloak, conceal, cover, damp down, dampen, deaden, disguise, dull, envelop, gag, hood, hush, mask, mute, muzzle, quieten, shroud, silence, soften, stifle, suppress, swaddle, swathe, wrap up.

antonym amplify.

**mug**[1] n beaker, cup, flagon, jug, pot, stoup, tankard, toby jug.

**mug**[2] n chump, fool, gull, innocent, mark, muggins, sap, saphead, simpleton, soft touch, sucker.

**mug**[3] n clock, countenance, dial, face, features, mush, phiz(og), puss, visage.

**mug up** bone up, con, cram, get up, study, swot.

**mug**[4] v attack, bash, batter, beat up, garrotte, jump (on), mill, rob, roll, set upon, steal from, waylay.

**muggy** adj clammy, close, damp, humid, moist, oppressive, sticky, stuffy, sudorific, sultry, sweltering.

antonym dry.

**mulish** adj bull-headed, cross-grained, defiant, difficult, headstrong, inflexible, intractable, intransigent, obstinate, perverse, pig-headed, recalcitrant, refractory, rigid, self-willed, stiff-necked, stubborn, unreasonable, wilful, wrong-headed.

**mull** v chew, con, consider, contemplate, deliberate, examine, meditate, muse on, ponder, reflect on, review, ruminate, study, think about, think over, weigh up.

**multifarious** adj different, diverse, diversified, legion, manifold, many, miscellaneous, multiform, multiple, multiplex, multitudinous, numerous, sundry, varied, variegated.

**multiple** adj collective, manifold, many, multifarious, multiplex, multitudinous, numerous, several, sundry, various.

**multiplicity** n abundance, array, diversity, heaps, host, loads, lot, lots, manifoldness, mass, multeity, myriad, number, numerousness, oodles, piles, profusion, scores, stacks, tons, variety.

**multiply** v accumulate, augment, boost, breed, build up, expand, extend, increase, intensify, proliferate, propagate, reproduce, spread.

antonyms decrease, lessen.

**multitude** n army, assemblage, assembly, collection, commonalty, concourse, congregation, crowd, herd, hive, hoi polloi, horde, host, legion, lot, lots, mass, mob, myriad, people, populace, proletariat, public, rabble, sea, swarm, throng.

antonyms handful, scattering.

**multitudinous** adj abounding, abundant, considerable, copious, countless, great, infinite, innumerable, legion, manifold, many, myriad, numerous, profuse, swarming, teeming, umpteen.

**mum** adj close-lipped, close-mouthed, dumb, mute, quiet, reticent, secretive, silent, tight-lipped, uncommunicative, unforthcoming.

**mumbo-jumbo** n abracadabra, cant, chant, charm, claptrap, conjuration, double talk, gibberish, gobbledegook, hocus-pocus, humbug, incantation, jargon, magic, mummery, nonsense, rigmarole, rite, ritual, spell, superstition.

**munch** v champ, chew, chomp, crunch, eat, masticate, scrunch.

**mundane** adj banal, commonplace, day-to-day, earthly, everyday, fleshly, human, humdrum, material, mortal, ordinary, prosaic, routine, secular, subastral, sublunar(y), temporal, terrestrial, workaday, worldly.

antonyms cosmic, extraordinary, supernatural.

**municipal** adj borough, burgh(al), city, civic, community, public, town, urban.

**municipality** n borough, burgh, city, département, department, district, precinct, town, township.

**munificence** n beneficence, benevolence, bounteousness, bounty, generosity, generousness, hospitality, largess(e), liberality, magnanimousness, open-handedness, philanthropy.

antonym meanness.

**munificent** adj beneficent, benevolent, big-hearted, bounteous, bountiful, free-handed, generous, hospitable, lavish, liberal, magnanimous, open-handed, philanthropical, princely, rich, unstinting.

antonym mean.

**murder** n agony, assassination, bloodshed, butchery, carnage, danger, deicide, difficulty, filicide, fractricide, hell, homicide, infanticide, killing, manslaughter, massacre, misery, ordeal, parricide, patricide, slaying, trial, trouble.

v abuse, assassinate, bump off, burke, butcher, destroy, dispatch, do in, drub, eliminate, hammer, hit, kill, mangle, mar, massacre, misuse, rub out, ruin, slaughter, slay, spoil, thrash, waste.

**murderer** n assassin, butcher, cut-throat, filicide, hit-man, homicide, killer, matricide, parricide, patricide, slaughterer, slayer.

**murderous** adj ardous, barbarous, bloodthirsty, bloody, brutal, cruel, cut-throat, dangerous, deadly, death-dealing, destructive, devastating, difficult, exhausting, fatal, fell, ferocious, harrowing, hellish, internecine, killing, lethal, sanguinary, sapping, savage, slaughterous, strenuous, unpleasant, withering.

**murky** adj cloudy, dark, dim, dismal, dreary, dull, dusky, enigmatic, foggy, gloomy, grey, misty, mysterious, obscure, overcast, veiled.

antonyms bright, clear.

**murmur** n babble, brool, burble, buzz, buzzing, complaint, croon, drone, grumble, humming, moan, mumble, muttering, purl, purling, purr, rumble, susurrus, undertone, whisper, whispering.

v babble, burble, burr, buzz, drone, gurgle, hum, mumble, mutter, purl, purr, rumble.

**murmuring** adj buzzing, droning, mumbling, murmurous, muttering, purring, rumbling, whispering.

*n* buzz(ing), drone, mumble, mumbling, murmuration, muttering, purr(ing), rumble, rumbling, susurrus, whisper(ing).

**muscle** *n* brawn, clout, depressor, force, forcefulness, levator, might, potency, power, sinew, stamina, strength, sturdiness, tendon, thew, weight.

**muscle in** butt in, elbow one's way in, force one's way in, impose oneself, jostle, push in, shove, strongarm.

**muscular** *adj* athletic, beefy, brawny, hefty, husky, lusty, powerful, powerfully-built, robust, sinewy, stalwart, strapping, strong, sturdy, vigorous, well-knit, wiry.

*antonyms* delicate, feeble, flabby, puny, weak.

**muse** *v* brood, chew, cogitate, consider, contemplate, deliberate, dream, meditate, mull over, ponder, reflect, review, ruminate, speculate, think, think over, weigh.

**mush** *n* corn, dough, hogwash, mash, mawkishness, pap, paste, pulp, schmaltz, sentimentality, slush, swill.

**mushroom** *v* boom, burgeon, expand, flourish, grow, increase, luxuriate, proliferate, shoot up, spread, spring up, sprout.

*n* champignon, chanterelle, fungus, morel, pixy-stool, puffball, toadstool.

**mushy** *adj* doughy, maudlin, mawkish, pappy, pulpous, pulpy, saccharine, schmaltzy, sentimental, sloppy, slushy, soft, squashy, squelchy, squidgy, sugary, syrupy, weepy, wet.

**musical** *adj* canorous, dulcet, euphonious, Euterpean, harmonious, lilting, lyrical, melodic, melodious, sweet-sounding, tuneful.

*antonym* unmusical.

**musician** *n* accompanist, bard, composer, conductor, instrumentalist, minstrel, performer, player, singer, vocalist.

**musing** *n* absent-mindedness, abstraction, brown study, cerebration, cogitation, contemplation, daydreaming, dreaming, introspection, meditation, ponderment, reflection, reverie, rumination, thinking, wool-gathering.

**must** *n* basic, duty, essential, fundamental, imperative, necessity, obligation, prerequisite, provision, requirement, requisite, sine qua non, stipulation.

**muster** *v* assemble, call together, call up, collect, come together, congregate, convene, convoke, enrol, gather, group, marshal, mass, meet, mobilise, rally, round up, summon, throng.

*n* assemblage, assembly, collection, concourse, congregation, convention, convocation, gathering, mass, meeting, mobilisation, rally, round-up, throng.

**musty** *adj* airless, ancient, antediluvian, antiquated, banal, clichéd, dank, decayed, dull, foughty, frowsty, fusty, hackneyed, hoary, mildewed, mildewy, moth-eaten, mouldy, mucedinous, mucid, obsolete, old, old-fashioned, smelly, stale, stuffy, threadbare, trite, vinewed, worn-out.

**mutability** *n* alterability, changeableness, interchangeability, permutability, variability, variation.

**mutable** *adj* adaptable, alterable, changeable, changing, fickle, flexible, inconsistent, inconstant, interchangeable, irresolute, permutable, uncertain, undependable, unreliable, unsettled, unstable, unsteady, vacillating, variable, volatile, wavering.

*antonyms* constant, invariable, permanent.

**mutation** *n* alteration, anomaly, change, deviant, deviation, evolution, metamorphosis, modification, mutant, transfiguration, transformation, variation, vicissitude.

**mute** *adj* aphonic, dumb, mum, noiseless, silent, speechless, unexpressed, unpronounced, unspeaking, unspoken, voiceless, wordless.

*antonyms* articulate, vocal, voluble.

*v* dampen, deaden, lower, moderate, muffle, silence, soften, soft-pedal, subdue, tone down.

**muted** *adj* dampened, dull, faint, low-key, muffled, quiet, soft, stifled, suppressed.

**mutilate** *v* adulterate, amputate, bowdlerise, butcher, censor, cut, cut to pieces, cut up, damage, detruncate, disable, disfigure, dismember, distort, expurgate, hack, hamble, injure, lacerate, lame, maim, mangle, mar, spoil.

**mutilation** *n* amputation, bowdlerisation, damage, detruncation, disfigurement, dismembering, maiming.

**mutinous** *adj* bolshie, bolshy, contumacious, disobedient, insubordinate, insurgent, rebellious, recusant, refractory, revolutionary, riotous, seditious, subversive, turbulent, ungovernable, unmanageable, unruly.

*antonyms* compliant, dutiful, obedient.

**mutiny** *n* defiance, disobedience, insubordination, insurrection, putsch, rebellion, resistance, revolt, revolution, riot, rising, strike, uprising.

*v* disobey, protest, rebel, resist, revolt, rise up, strike.

**mutt** *n* cur, dog, dolt, drongo, dunderhead, fool, idiot, ignoramus, imbecile, mongrel, moron, nong, sap, saphead, thickhead.

**mutter** *v* chunter, complain, grouch, grouse, grumble, mumble, murmur, mussitate, rumble.

**mutual** *adj* common, communal, complementary, exchanged, interchangeable, interchanged, joint, reciprocal, reciprocated, requited, returned, shared.

**muzzle** *n* bit, curb, gag, guard, jaws, mouth, nose, snaffle, snout.

*v* censor, choke, curb, gag, mute, restrain, silence, stifle, suppress.

**muzzy** *adj* addled, befuddled, bewildered, blurred, confused, dazed, hazy, muddled, mused, tipsy.

*antonym* clear.

**myopic** *adj* half-blind, near-sighted, short-sighted.

*antonym* far-sighted.

**myriad** *adj* boundless, countless, immeasurable, incalculable, innumerable, limitless, multitudinous, untold.

*n* army, flood, horde, host, millions, mountain, multitude, scores, sea, swarm, thousands, throng.

**mysterious** *adj* abstruse, arcane, baffling, concealed, covert, cryptic, curious, dark, enigmatic, furtive, hidden, impenetrable, incomprehensible, inexplicable, inscrutable, insoluble, mystical, mystifying, obscure, perplexing, puzzling, recondite, secret, secretive, strange, uncanny, unfathomable, unsearchable, veiled, weird.

*antonyms* comprehensible, frank, straightforward.

**mystery** *n* arcanum, conundrum, enigma, problem, puzzle, question, riddle, secrecy, secret.

**mystical** *adj* abstruse, arcane, cab(b)alistic(al), cryptic, enigmatical, esoteric, hidden, inscrutable, metaphysical, mysterious, mystic, occult, otherworldly, paranormal, preternatural, supernatural, transcendental.

**mystify** *v* baffle, bamboozle, beat, bewilder, confound, confuse, escape, metagrabolise, metagrobolise, perplex, puzzle, stump.

**mystique** *n* appeal, awe, charisma, charm, fascination, glamour, magic, spell.

**myth** *n* allegory, delusion, fable, fairy tale, fancy, fantasy, fiction, figment, illusion, legend, old wives' tale, parable, saga, story, superstition, tradition, untruism.

**mythical** *adj* fabled, fabricated, fabulous, fairy-tale, fanciful, fantasy, fictitious, imaginary, invented, legendary, made-up, make-believe, mythological, non-existent, pretended, unhistoric(al), unreal.

*antonyms* actual, historical, real, true.

**mythological** *adj* fabulous, folkloric, legendary, mythic, mythical, traditional.

**mythology** *n* folklore, folk-tales, legend, lore, myths, mythus, tales, tradition(s).

# N

**nab** *v* apprehend, arrest, capture, catch, collar, grab, nail, nick, seize, snatch.

**nabob** *n* bigwig, billionaire, celebrity, Croesus, financier, luminary, magnate, millionaire, multimillionaire, panjandrum, personage, tycoon, VIP.

**nadir** *n* all-time low, bottom, depths, low point, lowest point, low-watermark, minimum, rock bottom, zero.

*antonyms* acme, apex, peak, zenith.

**nag¹** *v* annoy, badger, berate, chivvy, goad, harass, harry, henpeck, irritate, kvetch, pain, pester, plague, scold, torment, upbraid, vex.

*n* harpy, harridan, kvetch(er), scold, shrew, tartar, termagant, virago.

**nag²** *n* hack, horse, jade, keffel, plug, rip, Rosinante.

**nagging** *adj* continuous, critical, distressing, irritating, painful, persistent, scolding, shrewish, tormenting, upsetting, worrying.

**nail** *v* apprehend, attach, beat, capture, catch, clinch, collar, fasten, fix, hammer, join, nab, nick, pin, secure, seize, tack.

*n* brad, hobnail, peg, pin, rivet, screw, skewer, spike, staple, tack, tacket.

**naïve** *adj* artless, callow, candid, childlike, confiding, credulous, dewy-eyed, facile, frank, green, guileless, gullible, ingenuous, innocent, jejune, natural, open, simple, simplistic, small-town, trusting, unaffected, uncritical, unpretentious, unsophisticated, unsuspecting, unsuspicious, unworldly, verdant, wide-eyed.

*antonyms* experienced, sophisticated.

**naïvety** *n* artlessness, callowness, candour, credulity, experience, frankness, guilelessness, gullibility, inexperience, ingenuousness, innocence, naturalness, openness, simplicity, sophistication.

**naked** *adj* adamic, bare, blatant, defenceless, denuded, disrobed, divested, evident, exposed, helpless, in puris naturalibus, in the altogether, in the buff, insecure, manifest, mother-naked, nude, open, overt, patent, plain, simple, skyclad, stark, starkers, stark-naked, stripped, unadorned, unarmed, unclothed, unconcealed, uncovered, undisguised, undraped, undressed, unexaggerated, unguarded, unmistakable, unprotected, unqualified, unvarnished, vulnerable.

*antonyms* clothed, concealed, covered.

**nakedness** *n* baldness, bareness, nudity, openness, plainness, simplicity, starkness, the altogether, the buff, undress.

**namby-pamby** *adj* anaemic, colourless, feeble, insipid, mawkish, pretty-pretty, prim, prissy, sentimental, spineless, vapid, weak, weedy, wet, white-shoe, wishy-washy.

**name** *n* acronym, agname, agnomen, appellation, character, cognomen, compellation, compellative, credit, denomination, designation, distinction, eminence, epithet, esteem, fame, handle, honour, moni(c)ker, nickname, note, praise, renown, reputation, repute, sobriquet, stage name, term, title, to-name.

*v* appoint, baptise, bename, betitle, call, choose, christen, cite, classify, cognominate, commission, denominate, designate, dub, entitle, identify, label, mention, nominate, select, specify, style, term, title.

**named** *adj* appointed, baptised, called, chosen, christened, cited, classified, commissioned, denominated, designated, dit, dubbed, entitled, identified, known as, labelled, mentioned, nominated, onymous, picked, selected, singled out, specified, styled, termed.

*antonym* nameless.

**nameless** *adj* abominable, anonymous, dreadful, fearsome, horrendous, horrible, incognito, indescribable, ineffable, inexpressible, innominate, obscure, terrible, undesignated, undistinguished, unheard-of, unknown, unmentionable, unnamed, unspeakable, unsung, untitled, unutterable.

*antonym* named.

**namely** *adv* ie, specifically, that is, that is to say, to wit, videlicet, viz.

**nap¹** *v* catnap, doze, drop off, drowse, kip, nod, nod off, rest, sleep, snooze, zizz.

*n* catnap, forty winks, kip, rest, shuteye, siesta, sleep, zizz.

**nap²** *n* down, downiness, fibre, fuzz, grain, pile, shag, weave.

**nappy** *n* diaper, doily, hipping, napkin, serviette, towel.

**narcissistic** *adj* conceited, egocentric, egomaniacal, ego(t)istic, self-centred, self-loving, vain.

**narcotic** *n* anaesthetic, analgesic, anodyne, drug, hop, kef, opiate, pain-killer, sedative, tranquilliser.

*adj* analgesic, calming, dulling, hypnotic, Lethean, numbing, pain-killing, sedative, somniferous, somnific, soporific, stupefacient, stupefactive, stupefying.

**nark** *v* annoy, bother, bug, exasperate, gall, get, irk, irritate, miff, nettle, peeve, pip, pique, provoke, rile.

**narrate** *v* chronicle, describe, detail, recite, recount, rehearse, relate, repeat, report, set forth, state, tell, unfold.

**narration** *n* description, enarration, explanation, reading, recital, recountal, rehearsal, relation, story-telling, telling, voice-over.

**narrative** *n* account, chronicle, detail, history, parable, report, statement, story, tale.

**narrator** *n* annalist, author, bard, chronicler, commentator, raconteur, reciter, relater, relator, reporter, story-teller, writer.

**narrow** *adj* attenuated, avaricious, biased, bigoted, circumscribed, close, confined, constricted, contracted, cramped, dogmatic, exclusive, fine, illiberal, incapacious, intolerant, limited, meagre, mean, mercenary, narrow-minded, near, niggardly, partial, pinched, prejudiced, reactionary, restricted, scanty, select, short-head, simplistic, slender, slim, small-minded, spare, straitened, tapering, thin, tight, ungenerous.

*antonyms* broad, liberal, tolerant, wide.

*v* circumscribe, constrict, constringe, diminish, limit, reduce, simplify, straiten, tighten.

*antonyms* broaden, increase, loosen, widen.

**narrowing** *n* attenuation, compression, constipation, constriction, contraction, curtailment, emaciation, reduction, stenosis, tapering, thinning.

*antonyms* broadening, widening.

**narrowly** *adv* barely, by a hair's breadth, by a whisker, carefully, closely, just, only just, painstakingly, precisely, scarcely, scrutinisingly, strictly.

**narrow-minded** *adj* biased, bigoted, blinkered, borné, conservative, hidebound, illiberal, insular, intolerant, mean, opinionated, parochial, petty, prejudiced, provincial, reactionary, short-sighted, small-minded, strait-laced.

*antonym* broad-minded.

**narrowness** *n* attentuation, closeness, constriction, crowdedness, exclusiveness, insularity, limitation, meagreness, narrow-mindedness, nearness, parochialism, restrictedness, slenderness, thinness, tightness.

*antonyms* breadth, width.

**nascent** *adj* advancing, budding, developing, embryonic, evolving, growing, incipient, naissant, rising, young.

*antonym* dying.

**nastiness** *n* defilement, dirtiness, disagreeableness, filth, filthiness, foulness, impurity, indecency, licentiousness, malice, meanness, obscenity, offensiveness, pollution, porn, pornography, ribaldry, smuttiness, spitefulness, squalor, uncleanliness, unpleasantness, unsavouriness, waspishness.

**nasty** *adj* abusive, annoying, bad, bad-tempered, base, beastly, critical, dangerous, despicable, dirty, disagreeable, disgusting, distasteful, filthy, foul, gross, horrible, impure, indecent, lascivious, lewd, licentious, loathsome, low-down, malicious, malodorous, mean, mephitic, nauseating, noisome, objectionable, obnoxious, obscene, odious, offensive, painful, polluted, pornographic, repellent, repugnant, ribald, serious, severe, sickening, smutty, spiteful, unappetising, unpleasant, unsavoury, vicious, vile, waspish.

*antonyms* agreeable, clean, decent, pleasant.

**nation** *n* citizenry, commonwealth, community, country, people, population, race, realm, society, state, tribe.

**national** *adj* civil, countrywide, domestic, general, governmental, internal, nationwide, public, social, state, widespread.

*n* citizen, indigene, inhabitant, native, resident, subject.

**nationalism** *n* allegiance, chauvinism, ethnocentricity, fealty, jingoism, loyalty, nationality, patriotism, xenophobia, xenophoby.

**nationalistic** *adj* chauvinistic, ethnocentrist, jingoistic, loyal, patriotic, xenophobic.

**nationality** *n* birth, clan, ethnic group, nation, race, tribe.

**native** *adj* aboriginal, autochthonous, built-in, congenital, domestic, endemic, genuine, hereditary, home, home-born, home-bred, home-grown, home-made, inborn, inbred, indigene, indigenous, ingrained, inherent, inherited, innate, instinctive, intrinsic, inveterate, local, mother, natal, natural, original, real, vernacular.

*n* aborigine, autochthon, citizen, countryman, dweller, indigene, inhabitant, national, resident.

*antonyms* foreigner, outsider, stranger.

**nativity** *n* birth, childbirth, delivery, parturition.

**natter** *v* blather, blether, chatter, confab, confabulate, gab, gabble, gossip, jabber, jaw, prate, prattle, talk.

*n* blather, blether, chat, chinwag, chitchat, confab, confabulation, conversation, gab, gabble, gabfest, gossip, jabber, jaw, palaver, prattle, talk.

**natty** *adj* chic, dapper, elegant, fashionable, neat, ritzy, smart, snazzy, spruce, stylish, swanky, trim.

**natural** *adj* artless, candid, characteristic, common, congenital, constitutional, essential, everyday, frank, genuine, inborn, indigenous, ingenuous, inherent, innate, instinctive, intuitive, legitimate, logical, natal, native, normal, open, ordinary, organic, plain, pure, real, regular, simple, spontaneous, typical, unaffected, unbleached, unforced, unlaboured, unlearned, unmixed, unpolished, unpretentious, unrefined, unsophisticated, unstudied, untaught, usual, whole.

*antonyms* abnormal, affected, alien, artificial, pretended, unnatural.

**naturalise** *v* acclimate, acclimatise, acculturate, accustom, adapt, adopt, domesticate, endenizen, enfranchise, familiarise, habituate.

**naturalistic** *adj* graphic, lifelike, natural, photographic, realistic, real-life, representational, true-to-life.

**naturally** *adj* absolutely, artlessly, as a matter of course, candidly, certainly, customarily, frankly, genuinely, informally, normally, of course, plainly, simply, spontaneously, typically, unaffectedly, unpretentiously.

**naturalness** *n* artlessness, candidness, frankness, genuineness, informality, ingenuousness, openness, plainness, pureness, purity, realism, simpleness, simplicity, spontaneity, spontaneousness, unaffectedness, unpretentiousness, wholeness.

**nature**[1] *n* attributes, category, character, complexion, constitution, cosmos, creation, description, disposition, earth, environment, essence, features, humour, inbeing, inscape, kind, make-up, mood, outlook, quality, sort, species, style, temper, temperament, traits, type, universe, variety, world.

**nature**[2] *n* country, countryside, landscape, natural history, scenery.

**naught** *n* nil, nothing, nothingness, nought, zero, zilch.

**naughty** *adj* annoying, bad, bawdy, blue, disobedient, exasperating, fractious, impish, improper, lewd, misbehaved, mischievous, obscene, off-colour, perverse, playful, refractory, remiss, reprehensible, ribald, risqué, roguish, sinful, smutty, teasing, vulgar, wayward, wicked, worthless.

*antonyms* good, polite, well-behaved.

**nausea** *n* abhorrence, aversion, biliousness, disgust, loathing, motion sickness, qualm(s), queasiness, repugnance, retching, revulsion, sickness, squeamishness, vomiting.

**nauseate** *v* disgust, horrify, offend, repel, repulse, revolt, sicken, turn one's stomach.

**nauseating** *adj* abhorrent, detestable, disgusting, distasteful, fulsome, loathsome, nauseous, offensive, repugnant, repulsive, revolting, sickening.

**nautical** *adj* boating, marine, maritime, naval, oceanic, sailing, seafaring, sea-going, yachting.

**naval** *adj* marine, maritime, nautical, sea.

**navel** *n* belly-button, centre, hub, middle, omphalos, tummy-button, umbilicus.

**navigate** *v* con, cross, cruise, direct, drive, guide, handle, helm, journey, manoeuvre, pilot, plan, plot, sail, skipper, steer, voyage.

**navigation** *n* aviation, cruising, helmsmanship, pilotage, sailing, seamanship, steering, voyaging.

**navigator** *n* helmsman, mariner, pilot, seaman.

**navvy** *n* digger, ganger, labourer, worker, workman.

**navy** *n* argosy, armada, fleet, flota, flotilla, navarchy, ships, warships.

**near** *adj* accessible, adjacent, adjoining, akin, allied, alongside, approaching, at close quarters, attached, beside, bordering, close, connected, contiguous, dear, familiar, forthcoming, handy, imminent, impending, in the offing, intimate, looming, near-at-hand, nearby, neighbouring, next, nigh, on the cards, proximal, related, touching.

*antonyms* distant, far, remote.

**near thing** close shave, narrow escape, nasty moment, near miss.

**nearby** *adj* accessible, adjacent, adjoining, convenient, handy, near, neighbouring.

*antonym* faraway.

*adv* at close quarters, close at hand, near, not far away, within reach.

**nearly** *adv* about, all but, almost, approaching, approximately, as good as, closely, just about, not quite, practically, pretty much, pretty well, roughly, virtually, well-nigh.

**nearness** *n* accessibility, availability, chumminess, closeness, contiguity, dearness, familiarity, handiness, immediacy, imminence, intimacy, juxtaposition, propinquity, proximity, vicinity.

**neat** *adj* accurate, adept, adroit, agile, apt, clean-cut, clever, dainty, deft, dexterous, dinky, efficient, effortless, elegant, expert, fastidious, genty, graceful, handy, methodical, nice, nimble, orderly, practised, precise, pure, shipshape, skilful, smart, spick-and-span, spruce, straight, stylish, systematic, tiddley, tidy, trig, trim, uncluttered, undiluted, unmixed, well-judged.

*antonyms* disordered, disorderly, messy, untidy.

**neaten** *v* arrange, clean up, groom, put to rights, smarten, straighten, tidy, trim.

**neatly** *adv* accurately, adeptly, adroitly, agilely, aptly, cleverly, daintily, deftly, dexterously, efficiently, effortlessly, elegantly, expertly, fastidiously, featly, gracefully, handily, methodically, nicely, nimbly, precisely, skilfully, smartly, sprucely, stylishly, systematically, tidily.

*antonyms* inelegantly, inexpertly, unskilfully, untidily.

**neatness** *n* accuracy, adeptness, adroitness, agility, aptness, cleverness, daintiness, deftness, dexterity, disorderliness, efficiency, elegance, expertness, fastidiousness, grace, gracefulness, handiness, inelegance, methodicalness, niceness, nicety, nimbleness, orderliness, preciseness, precision, skilfulness, skill, smartness, spruceness, straightness, style, stylishness, tidiness, trimness, untidyness.

**nebulous** *adj* ambiguous, amorphous, cloudy, confused, dim, fuzzy, hazy, imprecise, indefinite, indeterminate, indistinct, misty, murky, obscure, shadowy, shapeless, uncertain, unclear, unformed, unspecific, vague.

*antonym* clear.

**necessarily** *adv* accordingly, automatically, axiomatically, by definition, certainly, compulsorily, consequently, incontrovertibly, ineluctably, inescapably, inevitably, inexorably, naturally, nolens volens, of course, of necessity, perforce, therefore, thus, willy-nilly.

**necessary** adj certain, compulsory, de rigueur, essential, fated, imperative, indispensable, ineluctable, inescapable, inevitable, inexorable, mandatory, must, needed, needful, obligatory, required, requisite, unavoidable, vital.

antonyms inessential, unimportant, unnecessary.

**necessitate** v call for, coerce, compel, constrain, demand, entail, force, impel, involve, oblige, require.

**necessities** n essentials, exigencies, fundamentals, indispensables, needs, requirements.

**necessity** n ananke, compulsion, demand, desideratum, destiny, destitution, essential, exigency, extremity, fate, fundamental, indigence, indispensability, inevitability, inexorableness, necessary, need, needfulness, obligation, penury, poverty, prerequisite, privation, requirement, requisite, sine qua non, want.

**neck** n halse, nape, scrag, scruff.

**necklace** n carcanet, chain, choker, gorget, lavallière, locket, negligée, pendant, rivière, torc, torque.

**necromancy** n black art, black magic, conjuration, demonology, divination, enchantment, hoodoo, magic, sorcery, thaumaturgy, voodoo, witchcraft, witchery, wizardry.

**need** v call for, crave, demand, lack, miss, necessitate, require, want.

n besoin, demand, deprivation, desideratum, destitution, distress, egence, egency, emergency, essential, exigency, extremity, impecuniousness, inadequacy, indigence, insufficiency, lack, longing, necessity, neediness, obligation, paucity, penury, poverty, privation, requirement, requisite, shortage, urgency, want, wish.

antonym sufficiency.

**needed** adj called for, compulsory, desired, essential, lacking, necessary, obligatory, required, requisite, wanted.

antonyms unnecessary, unneeded.

**needful** adj essential, indispensable, necessary, needed, needy, required, requisite, stipulated, vital.

antonyms excess, needless, superfluous.

**needle** v aggravate, annoy, bait, goad, harass, irk, irritate, nag, nettle, pester, prick, prod, provoke, rile, ruffle, spur, sting, taunt, torment.

**needless** adj causeless, dispensable, excessive, expendable, gratuitous, groundless, inessential, non-essential, pointless, purposeless, redundant, superfluous, uncalled-for, unessential, unnecessary, unwanted, useless.

antonyms necessary, needful.

**needy** adj deprived, destitute, disadvantaged, impecunious, impoverished, indigent, penniless, penurious, poor, poverty-stricken, underprivileged.

antonyms affluent, wealthy, well-off.

**ne'er-do-well** n black sheep, good-for-nothing, idler, layabout, loafer, scapegallows, vaurien, waster, wastrel.

**nefarious** adj abominable, atrocious, base, criminal, depraved, detestable, dreadful, evil, execrable, foul, heinous, horrible, infamous, infernal, iniquitous, monstrous, odious, opprobrious, satanic, shameful, sinful, unholy, vicious, vile, villainous, wicked.

antonym exemplary.

**negate** v abrogate, annul, cancel, contradict, countermand, deny, disallow, disprove, gainsay, invalidate, neutralise, nullify, oppose, quash, refute, repeal, rescind, retract, reverse, revoke, void, wipe out.

antonym affirm.

**negation** n antithesis, cancellation, contradiction, contrary, converse, counterpart, denial, disavowal, disclaimer, inverse, neutralisation, nullification, opposite, rejection, renunciation, repeal, reverse, veto.

antonym affirmation.

**negative** adj annulling, antagonistic, apathetic, below zero, colourless, contradictory, contrary, counteractive, cynical, denying, dissenting, gloomy, invalidating, jaundiced, neutralising, nullifying, opposing, pessimistic, refusing, rejecting, unco-operative, unenthusiastic, uninterested, unwilling, weak.

antonyms optimistic, positive.

n contradiction, denial, opposite, refusal.

**neglect** v contemn, disdain, disprovide, disregard, forget, ignore, leave alone, let slide, omit, overlook, pass by, pigeon-hole, rebuff, scorn, shirk, skimp, slight, spurn.

antonyms cherish, nurture, treasure.

n carelessness, default, dereliction, disdain, disregard, disrespect, failure, forgetfulness, heedlessness, inattention, indifference, laches, laxity, laxness, neglectfulness, negligence, oversight, slackness, slight, slovenliness, unconcern.

**neglected** adj abandoned, derelict, disregarded, overgrown, unappreciated, uncared-for, uncultivated, underestimated, undervalued, unhusbanded, unmaintained, untended, untilled, unweeded.

antonyms cherished, treasured.

**neglectful** adj careless, disregardful, forgetful, heedless, inattentive, indifferent, lax, negligent, oblivious, remiss, thoughtless, uncaring, unmindful.

antonyms attentive, careful.

**negligence** n carelessness, default, dereliction, disregard, failure, forgetfulness, heedlessness, inadvertence, inattention, inattentiveness, indifference, laxity, laxness, neglect, neglectfulness, omission, oversight, remissness, shortcoming, slackness, slight, stupidity, thoughtlessness.

antonyms attentiveness, care, regard.

**neutral**

**negligent** *adj* careless, cursory, disregardful, forgetful, inattentive, indifferent, lax, neglectful, nonchalant, offhand, regardless, remiss, slack, thoughtless, uncareful, uncaring, unmindful, unthinking.

*antonyms* attentive, careful, heedful, scrupulous.

**negligible** *adj* imperceptible, inconsequential, insignificant, minor, minute, neglectable, nugatory, petty, small, trifling, trivial, unimportant.

*antonym* significant.

**negotiate** *v* adjudicate, arbitrate, arrange, bargain, broke, clear, conciliate, confer, consult, contract, cross, deal, debate, discuss, get past, handle, manage, mediate, parley, pass, settle, surmount, transact, traverse, treat, work out.

**negotiation** *n* arbitration, bargaining, debate, diplomacy, discussion, mediation, transaction, wheeler-dealing.

**negotiator** *n* adjudicator, ambassador, arbitrator, broker, delegate, diplomat, go-between, intermediary, mediator, moderator.

**neigh** *v* bray, hinny, whinny.

**neighbourhood** *n* community, confines, district, environs, locale, locality, precincts, proximity, purlieus, quarter, region, surroundings, vicinage, vicinity.

**neighbouring** *adj* abutting, adjacent, adjoining, bordering, connecting, contiguous, near, nearby, nearest, next, surrounding, vicinal.

*antonyms* distant, faraway, remote.

**neighbourly** *adj* amiable, chummy, civil, companionable, considerate, friendly, genial, helpful, hospitable, kind, obliging, sociable, social, solicitous, well-disposed.

**nemesis** *n* destiny, destruction, fate, punishment, retribution, vengeance.

**nerve** *n* audacity, boldness, bottle, brass, bravery, brazenness, cheek, chutzpah, coolness, courage, daring, determination, effrontery, endurance, energy, fearlessness, firmness, force, fortitude, gall, gameness, grit, guts, hardihood, impertinence, impudence, insolence, intrepidity, mettle, might, pluck, resolution, sauce, spirit, spunk, steadfastness, temerity, vigour, will.

*antonyms* cowardice, weakness.

*v* bolster, brace, embolden, encourage, fortify, hearten, invigorate, steel, strengthen.

*antonym* unnerve.

**nerveless** *adj* afraid, cowardly, debilitated, enervated, feeble, flabby, inert, nervous, slack, spineless, timid, unnerved, weak.

*antonyms* bold, grave, strong.

**nerve-racking** *adj* annoying, difficult, disquieting, distressing, frightening, harassing, harrowing, maddening, stressful, tense, trying, worrisome, worrying.

**nerves** *n* anxiety, fretfulness, (h)abdabs, heebie-jeebies, nervousness, strain, stress, tension, worry.

**nervous** *adj* agitated, anxious, apprehensive, edgy, excitable, fearful, fidgety, flustered, hesitant, highly-strung, high-strung, hysterical, jittery, jumpy, nervy, neurotic, on edge, shaky, tense, timid, timorous, twitchy, uneasy, uptight, weak, windy, worried.

*antonyms* bold, calm, confident, cool, relaxed.

**nervousness** *n* agitation, anxiety, disquiet, excitability, fluster, (h)abdabs, heebie-jeebies, perturbation, tension, timidity, touchiness, tremulousness, vapours, willies, worry.

*antonyms* calmness, coolness.

**nervy** *adj* agitated, anxious, excitable, fidgety, jittery, jumpy, nervous, on edge, restless, tense, unquiet.

*antonyms* calm, relaxed.

**nest** *n* breeding-ground, burrow, den, drey, earth, form, formicary, haunt, hideaway, hotbed, nid(e), nidus, refuge, resort, retreat.

**nest-egg** *n* bottom drawer, cache, deposit, fund(s), reserve(s), savings, store.

**nestle** *v* cuddle, curl up, ensconce, huddle, nuzzle, snuggle.

**nestling** *adj* baby, chick, fledgling, suckling, weanling.

**net¹** *n* drag, drag-net, drift, drift-net, drop-net, lattice, mesh, netting, network, open-work, reticulum, tracery, web.

*v* apprehend, bag, benet, capture, catch, enmesh, ensnare, entangle, nab, trap.

**net²** *adj* after tax, clear, final, lowest, nett.

*v* accumulate, bring in, clear, earn, gain, make, obtain, realise, reap, receive, secure.

**nether** *adj* basal, below, beneath, bottom, inferior, infernal, lower, Plutonian, Stygian, under, underground.

**nettle** *v* annoy, chafe, discountenance, exasperate, fret, goad, harass, incense, irritate, needle, pique, provoke, ruffle, sting, tease, vex.

**nettled** *adj* aggrieved, angry, annoyed, chafed, cross, exasperated, galled, goaded, harassed, huffy, incensed, irritable, irritated, miffed, needled, peeved, peevish, piqued, provoked, riled, ruffled, stung, vexed.

**network** *n* arrangement, channels, circuitry, complex, convolution, grid, grill, interconnections, labyrinth, maze, mesh, meshwork, net, nexus, organisation, plexus, rete, reticulation, structure, system, tracks, web.

**neurosis** *n* abnormality, affliction, derangement, deviation, disturbance, instability, maladjustment, obsession, phobia.

**neurotic** *adj* abnormal, anxious, compulsive, deviant, disordered, distraught, disturbed, maladjusted, manic, morbid, nervous, obsessive, overwrought, unhealthy, unstable, wearisome.

*antonyms* normal, stable.

**neuter** *v* caponise, castrate, doctor, dress, emasculate, fix, geld, spay.

**neutral** *adj* colourless, disinterested, dispassionate, dull, even-handed, expressionless, impartial, indeterminate, indifferent, indistinct, indistinguishable, intermediate, non-aligned, non-committal, nondescript, non-partisan, unbia(s)sed, uncommitted, undecided, undefined, uninvolved, unprejudiced.

*antonyms* biased, prejudiced.

**neutralise** *v* cancel, counteract, counterbalance, counterpoise, frustrate, invalidate, negate, nullify, offset, undo.

**neutrality** *n* detachment, disinterest, disinterestedness, impartiality, impartialness, non-alignment, non-intervention, non-involvement, unbiasedness.

**never** *adv* at no time, Greek calends, not at all, not on your life, not on your Nellie, on no account, under no circumstances, when pigs fly.

*antonym* always.

**never-ending** *adj* boundless, ceaseless, constant, continual, continuous, eternal, everlasting, incessant, interminable, non-stop, permanent, perpetual, persistent, relentless, Sisyphean, unbroken, unceasing, unchanging, uninterrupted, unremitting.

*antonyms* fleeting, transitory.

**nevertheless** *adv* anyhow, anyway, but, even so, however, nonetheless, notwithstanding, regardless, still, yet.

**new** *adj* added, advanced, altered, changed, contemporary, current, different, extra, fresh, improved, latest, modern, modernised, modernistic, modish, more, newborn, newfangled, novel, original, recent, redesigned, renewed, restored, supplementary, topical, trendy, ultra-modern, unfamiliar, unknown, unused, unusual, up-to-date, up-to-the-minute, virgin.

*antonyms* hackneyed, old, outdated, out-of-date, usual.

**newcomer** *n* alien, arrival, arriviste, beginner, colonist, foreigner, immigrant, incomer, Johnny-come-lately, novice, outsider, parvenu, settler, stranger.

**newfangled** *adj* contemporary, fashionable, futuristic, gimmicky, modern, modernistic, new, novel, recent, trendy.

*antonym* old-fashioned.

**newly** *adv* afresh, anew, freshly, just, lately, latterly, recently.

**newness** *n* freshness, innovation, novelty, oddity, originality, recency, strangeness, unfamiliarity, uniqueness, unusualness.

*antonyms* oldness, ordinariness.

**news** *n* account, advice, bulletin, communiqué, disclosure, dispatch, exposé, gen, gossip, hearsay, information, intelligence, latest, leak, release, report, revelation, rumour, scandal, statement, story, tidings, update, word.

**newspaper** *n* blat(t), daily, gazette, journal, organ, paper, periodical, publication, rag, sheet, tabloid.

**newsworthy** *adj* arresting, important, interesting, notable, noteworthy, remarkable, reportable, significant, stimulating, unusual.

**next** *adj* adjacent, adjoining, closest, consequent, ensuing, following, later, nearest, neighbouring, sequent, sequential, subsequent, succeeding.

*antonyms* preceding, previous.

*adv* afterwards, later, subsequently, then, thereafter.

**nibble** *n* bit, bite, crumb, morsel, peck, piece, snack, soupçon, taste, titbit.

*v* bite, eat, gnaw, knap, knapple, munch, nip, nosh, peck, pickle.

**nice** *adj* accurate, agreeable, amiable, attractive, careful, charming, commendable, courteous, critical, cultured, dainty, delicate, delightful, discriminating, exact, exacting, fastidious, fine, finical, friendly, genteel, good, kind, lik(e)able, meticulous, neat, particular, pleasant, pleasurable, polite, precise, prepossessing, punctilious, purist, refined, respectable, rigorous, scrupulous, strict, subtle, tidy, trim, virtuous, well-bred, well-mannered.

*antonyms* careless, disagreeable, haphazard, nasty, unpleasant.

**nicely** *adv* acceptably, accurately, agreeable, amiably, attractively, carefully, charmingly, commendably, courteously, critically, daintily, delicately, delightfully, discriminatingly, elegantly, exactingly, exactly, fastidiously, finely, genteelly, kindly, lik(e)ably, meticulously, neatly, pleasantly, pleasingly, pleasurably, politely, precisely, prepossessingly, respectably, rigorously, scrupulously, strictly, subtly, tidily, trimly, virtuously, well.

*antonyms* carelessly, disagreeably, haphazardly, nastily, unpleasantly.

**niceness** *n* accuracy, agreeableness, amiability, attractiveness, care, carefulness, charm, courtesy, daintiness, delicacy, delightfulness, discrimination, exactitude, exactness, fastidiousness, fineness, friendliness, gentility, goodness, kindness, lik(e)ableness, meticulousness, neatness, pleasantness, pleasurableness, politeness, preciseness, precision, punctilio, punctiliousness, purism, refinement, respectability, rigorousness, rigour, scrupulosity, scrupulousness, strictness, subtleness, subtlety, tidiness, trimness, virtue.

*antonyms* carelessness, disagreeableness, haphazardness, nastiness, unpleasantness.

**nicety** *n* accuracy, daintiness, delicacy, discrimination, distinction, exactness, fastidiousness, finesse, finicality, meticulousness, minuteness, nuance, precision, punctilio, quiddit(y), refinement, subtlety.

**niche¹** *n* alcove, corner, cubby, cubby-hole, hollow, nook, opening, recess.

**niche²** *n* calling, métier, pigeon-hole, place, position, slot, vocation.

**nick¹** *n* chip, cut, damage, dent, indent, indentation, mark, notch, scar, score, scratch, snick.

*v* chip, cut, damage, dent, indent, mark, notch, scar, score, scratch, snick.

**nick²** *v* finger, knap, knock off, lag, pilfer, pinch, snitch, steal.

**nickname** *n* cognomen, diminutive, epithet, familiarity, label, moni(c)ker, pet name, sobriquet.

**nifty** *adj* adroit, agile, apt, chic, clever, deft, enjoyable, excellent, neat, nippy, pleasing, quick, sharp, smart, spruce, stylish.

**niggardliness** *n* avarice, avariciousness, beggarliness, cheese-paring, closeness, covetousness, frugality, grudgingness, inadequacy, insufficiency, meagreness, meanness, mercenariness, miserableness, miserliness, nearness, paltriness, parsimony, penuriousness, scantiness, skimpiness, smallness, sordidness, sparingness, stinginess, thrift, tight-fistedness, ungenerousness, wretchedness.

*antonyms* bountifulness, generosity.

**niggardly** *adj* avaricious, beggarly, cheese-paring, close, covetous, frugal, grudging, hard-fisted, inadequate, insufficient, meagre, mean, mercenary, miserable, miserly, near, paltry, parsimonious, penurious, scanty, skimpy, small, sordid, sparing, stinging, stingy, tight-fisted, ungenerous, ungiving, wretched.

*antonyms* bountiful, generous.

**night** *n* dark, darkmans, darkness, dead of night, hours of darkness, night-time.

*antonyms* day, daytime.

**nightclub** *n* cabaret, club, disco, discotheque, nightspot, niterie, nitery, watering-hole.

**nightfall** *n* crepuscule, dusk, eve, evening, eventide, gloaming, moonrise, sundown, sunset, twilight, vespers.

*antonyms* dawn, sunrise.

**nightmare** *n* bad dream, ephialtes, hallucination, horror, incubus, ordeal, succubus, torment, trial, tribulation.

**nightmarish** *adj* agonising, alarming, creepy, disturbing, dreadful, fell, frightening, harrowing, horrible, horrific, scaring, terrifying, unreal.

**nihilism** *n* abnegation, agnosticism, anarchy, atheism, cynicism, denial, disbelief, disorder, emptiness, lawlessness, negation, negativism, non-existence, nothingness, nullity, oblivion, pessimism, rejection, renunciation, repudiation, scepticism, terrorism.

**nihilist** *n* agitator, agnostic, anarchist, antinomian, atheist, cynic, disbeliever, extremist, negationist, negativist, pessimist, revolutionary, sceptic, terrorist.

**nil** *n* duck, goose-egg, love, naught, nihil, none, nothing, zero.

**nimble** *adj* active, agile, alert, brisk, deft, dexterous, light-foot(ed), lissom(e), lively, nippy, proficient, prompt, quick, quick-witted, ready, smart, sprightly, spry, swift, volant.

*antonyms* awkward, clumsy.

**nimbleness** *n* adroitness, agility, alacrity, alertness, deftness, dexterity, finesse, grace, legerity, lightness, niftiness, nippiness, skill, smartness, sprightliness, spryness.

**nimbly** *adv* actively, acutely, agilely, alertly, briskly, deftly, dexterously, easily, fast, featly, fleetly, proficiently, promptly, quickly, quick-wittedly, readily, sharply, smartly, snappily, speedily, spryly, swiftly.

*antonyms* awkwardly, clumsily.

**nincompoop** *n* blockhead, dimwit, dolt, dunce, fool, idiot, ignoramus, ninny, nitwit, noodle, numskull, sap, saphead, simpleton.

**nip**[1] *v* bite, catch, check, clip, compress, grip, nibble, pinch, snag, snap, sneap, snip, squeeze, tweak, twitch.

**nip**[2] *n* dram, draught, drop, finger, mouthful, peg, portion, shot, sip, slug, snifter, soupçon, sup, swallow, taste.

**nipple** *n* breast, dug, mamilla, pap, teat, tit, titty, udder.

**nippy**[1] *adj* astringent, biting, chilly, nipping, pungent, sharp, stinging.

**nippy**[2] *adj* active, agile, fast, nimble, quick, speedy, sprightly, spry.

*antonym* slow.

**nirvana** *n* bliss, ecstasy, exaltation, joy, paradise, peace, serenity, tranquillity.

**nit-picking** *adj* captious, carping, cavilling, finicky, fussy, hair-splitting, hypercritical, pedantic, pettifogging, quibbling.

**nitwit** *n* dimwit, drongo, dummy, fool, half-wit, nincompoop, ninny, numskull, simpleton.

**no doubt** admittedly, assuredly, certainly, doubtless, doubtlessly, presumably, probably, surely, unquestionably.

**nob** *n* aristocrat, big shot, bigwig, fat cat, nabob, personage, toff, VIP.

**nobble** *v* bribe, disable, filch, get at, grab, hamper, handicap, incapacitate, influence, injure, intimidate, knock off, nick, outwit, pilfer, pinch, purloin, snitch, steal, swipe, take, weaken.

**nobility** *n* aristocracy, dignity, élite, eminence, excellence, generosity, gentry, grandeur, greatness, high society, honour, illustriousness, incorruptibility, integrity, loftiness, lords, magnanimity, magnificence, majesty, nobleness, nobles, patricians, peerage, stateliness, sublimity, superiority, uprightness, virtue, worthiness.

*antonyms* baseness, proletariat.

**noble** *n* aristocrat, baron, gentilhomme, grand seigneur, lord, nobleman, patrician, peer.

*antonyms* pleb, prole.

*adj* aristocratic, august, blue-blooded, dignified, distinguished, elevated, eminent, excellent, generous, gentle, grand, great, high-born, honourable, honoured, imposing, impressive, lofty, lordly, magnanimous, magnificent, majestic, patrician, splendid, stately, titled, upright, virtuous, worthy.

*antonyms* base, ignoble, low-born.

**nobody** *n* also-ran, cipher, lightweight, man of straw, menial, minnow, nonentity, no-one, nothing, Walter Mitty.

*antonym* somebody.

**nod** v acknowledge, agree, assent, beckon, bob, bow, concur, dip, doze, droop, drowse, duck, gesture, indicate, nap, salute, sign, signal, sleep, slip up, slump.

n acknowledgement, beck, cue, gesture, greeting, indication, salute, sign, signal.

**node** n bud, bump, burl, caruncle, growth, knob, knot, lump, nodule, process, protuberance, swelling.

**noise** n babble, ballyhoo, blare, brattle, chirm, clamour, clash, clatter, coil, commotion, cry, din, fracas, hubbub, outcry, pandemonium, racket, row, sound, talk, tumult, uproar.

*antonyms* quiet, silence.

v advertise, announce, bruit, circulate, gossip, publicise, repeat, report, rumour.

**noiseless** adj hushed, inaudible, mous(e)y, mute, muted, quiet, silent, soundless, still.

*antonyms* loud, noisy.

**noisome** adj bad, baneful, deleterious, disgusting, fetid, foul, fulsome, harmful, hurtful, injurious, malodorous, mephitic, mischievous, noxious, offensive, pernicious, pestiferous, pestilential, poisonous, putrid, reeking, smelly, stinking, unhealthy, unwholesome.

*antonyms* balmy, pleasant, wholesome.

**noisy** adj boisterous, cacophonous, chattering, clamorous, clangorous, deafening, ear-piercing, ear-splitting, horrisonant, loud, obstreperous, piercing, plangent, rackety, riotous, strepitant, strident, tumultuous, turbulent, uproarious, vocal, vociferous.

*antonyms* peaceful, quiet, silent.

**nom de plume** alias, allonym, assumed name, nom de guerre, pen name, pseudonym.

**nomad** n drifter, itinerant, migrant, rambler, roamer, rover, traveller, vagabond, vagrant, wanderer.

**nomadic** adj drifting, gypsy, itinerant, migrant, migratory, peregrinating, peripatetic, roaming, roving, travelling, unsettled, vagrant, wandering.

**nomenclature** n classification, codification, locution, naming, phraseology, taxonomy, terminology, vocabulary.

**nominal** adj fainéant, figurehead, formal, inconsiderable, insignificant, minimal, ostensible, pretended, professed, puppet, purported, self-styled, small, so-called, soi-disant, supposed, symbolic, theoretical, titular, token, trifling, trivial.

*antonyms* actual, genuine, real, true.

**nominate** v appoint, assign, choose, commission, designate, elect, elevate, empower, mention, name, present, propose, put up, recommend, select, submit, suggest, term.

**nomination** n appointment, choice, designation, election, proposal, recommendation, selection, submission, suggestion.

**nominee** n appointee, assignee, candidate, contestant, entrant, protégé, runner.

**non compos mentis** crazy, deranged, insane, mentally ill, of unsound mind, unbalanced, unhinged.

*antonyms* sane, stable.

**non-aligned** adj impartial, independent, neutral, uncommitted, undecided.

**nonchalance** n aplomb, calm, composure, cool, equanimity, imperturbability, indifference, insouciance, pococurant(e)ism, sang-froid, self-possession, unconcern.

*antonyms* anxiousness, worriedness.

**nonchalant** adj airy, apathetic, blasé, calm, careless, casual, collected, cool, detached, dispassionate, impassive, indifferent, insouciant, offhand, pococurante, unconcerned, unemotional, unperturbed.

*antonyms* anxious, careful, concerned, worried.

**non-committal** adj ambiguous, careful, cautious, circumspect, cunctatious, cunctative, cunctatory, discreet, equivocal, evasive, guarded, indefinite, neutral, politic, reserved, tactful, temporising, tentative, unrevealing, vague, wary.

**nonconformist** n deviant, dissenter, dissentient, eccentric, heretic, iconoclast, individualist, maverick, oddball, protester, radical, rebel, seceder, secessionist.

*antonym* conformist.

**nonconformity** n deviation, dissent, eccentricity, heresy, heterodoxy, secession, unconventionality.

*antonym* conformity.

**nondescript** adj commonplace, dull, featureless, indeterminate, mousy, ordinary, plain, unclassified, undistinctive, undistinguished, unexceptional, uninspiring, uninteresting, unmemorable, unremarkable, vague.

**none** pron nil, nobody, no-one, not any, not one, zero, zilch.

**nonentity** n cipher, dandiprat, drip, drongo, earthworm, gnatling, lightweight, mediocrity, nobody.

**non-essential** adj dispensable, excessive, expendable, extraneous, extrinsic(al), inessential, peripheral, superfluous, supplementary, unimportant, unnecessary.

*antonym* essential.

**none-the-less** adv even so, howbeit, however, natheless, nevertheless, notwithstanding, yet.

**non-existence** n illusiveness, insubtantiality, unbeing, unreality.

*antonym* existence.

**non-existent** adj chimerical, fancied, fictional, hallucinatory, hypothetical, illusory, imaginary, imagined, immaterial, incorporeal, insubstantial, legendary, missing, mythical, null, unreal.

*antonyms* actual, existing, real.

**non-flammable** adj fire-proof, fire-resistant, flame-resistant, incombustible, uninflammable.

*antonyms* flammable, inflammable.

**non-partisan** adj detached, dispassionate, even-handed, impartial, independent, neutral, objective, unbiased, unprejudiced.

*antonym* partisan.

**nonplus** v astonish, astound, baffle, bewilder, confound, confuse, discomfit, disconcert, discountenance, dismay, dumbfound, embarrass, flabbergast, flummox, mystify, perplex, puzzle, stump, stun, take aback.

**nonsense** *n* absurdity, balderdash, balls, baloney, bilge, blah, blather, blethers, bollocks, bombast, bosh, bull, bullshit, bunk, bunkum, claptrap, cobblers, codswallop, crap, double-Dutch, drivel, fadaise, faddle, fandangle, fatuity, fiddle-de-dee, fiddle-faddle, fiddlesticks, flapdoodle, folly, foolishness, fudge, gaff, galimatias, gammon, gas and gaiters, gibberish, gobbledygook, havers, hogwash, hooey, inanity, jabberwock(y), jest, ludicrousness, moonshine, no-meaning, piffle, pulp, ridiculousness, rot, rubbish, senselessness, silliness, squish, squit, stuff, stultiloquence, stupidity, tar(r)adiddle, tommy-rot, tosh, trash, twaddle, twattle, unreason, waffle.

*antonym* sense.

**nonsensical** *adj* absurd, crazy, daft, fatuous, foolish, inane, incomprehensible, irrational, ludicrous, meaningless, ridiculous, senseless, silly.

*antonyms* logical, sensible.

**non-stop** *adj* ceaseless, constant, continuous, direct, endless, incessant, interminable, never-ending, on-going, relentless, round-the-clock, steady, unbroken, unceasing, unending, unfaltering, uninterrupted, unrelenting, unremitting.

*antonyms* intermittent, occasional.

*adv* ceaselessly, constantly, continuously, directly, endlessly, incessantly, interminably, relentlessly, round-the-clock, steadily, unbrokenly, unceasingly, unendingly, unfalteringly, uninterruptedly, unrelentingly, unremittingly.

*antonyms* imtermittently, occasionally.

**non-violent** *adj* dov(e)ish, irenic, pacifist, passive, peaceable, peaceful.

*antonym* violent.

**nook** *n* alcove, cavity, corner, cranny, crevice, cubby-hole, hide-out, ingle-nook, nest, niche, opening, recess, retreat, shelter.

**norm** *n* average, bench-mark, canon, criterion, mean, measure, model, pattern, reference, rule, standard, type, yardstick.

**normal** *adj* accustomed, acknowledged, average, common, common-or-garden, conventional, habitual, mainstream, natural, ordinary, par for the course, popular, rational, reasonable, regular, routine, run-of-the-mill, sane, standard, straight, typical, usual, well-adjusted.

*antonyms* abnormal, irregular, odd, peculiar.

**normality** *n* accustomedness, adjustment, balance, commonness, conventionality, naturalness, ordinariness, popularity, rationality, reason, regularity, routine, routineness, sanity, typicality, usualness.

*antonyms* abnormality, irregularity, oddity, peculiarity.

**normally** *adv* as a rule, characteristically, commonly, habitually, ordinarily, regularly, straight, typically, usually.

*antonym* abnormally.

**northern** *adj* Arctic, boreal, hyperborean, north, northerly, polar, septentrional.

*antonym* southern.

**nose** *n* beak, bill, boko, conk, hooter, neb, proboscis, schnozzle, snitch, snout.

*v* detect, inquire, interface, intrude, meddle, nudge, nuzzle, pry, push, scent, search, shove, smell, sniff, snoop.

**nose-dive** *n* dive, drop, header, plummet, plunge, purler.

*v* dive, drop, plummet, plunge, submerge.

**nosegay** *n* bouquet, boutonnièe, corsage, posy, spray.

**nos(e)y** *adj* curious, eavesdropping, inquisitive, interfering, intermeddling, intrusive, meddlesome, officious, prying, snooping.

**nostalgia** *n* Heimweh, homesickness, longing, mal du pays, pining, regret, regretfulness, remembrance, reminiscence, wistfulness, yearning.

**nostalgic** *adj* emotional, homesick, longing, maudlin, regretful, romantic, sentimental, wistful.

**nosy** *see* **nosey.**

**not bad** all right, average, fair, fair to middling, moderate, OK, passable, reasonable, respectable, satisfactory, so-so, tolerable.

**notability** *n* celebrity, dignitary, distinction, eminence, esteem, fame, luminary, magnate, notable, personage, renown, somebody, VIP, worthy.

*antonym* nonentity.

**notable** *adj* celebrated, conspicuous, distinguished, eminent, evident, extraordinary, famous, impressive, manifest, marked, memorable, noteworthy, noticeable, notorious, outstanding, overt, pre-eminent, pronounced, rare, remarkable, renowned, signal, striking, uncommon, unusual, well-known.

*antonyms* commonplace, ordinary, usual.

*n* celebrity, dignitary, luminary, notability, personage, somebody, VIP, worthy.

*antonyms* nobody, nonentity.

**notably** *adv* conspicuously, distinctly, eminently, especially, impressively, markedly, noticeably, outstandingly, particularly, remarkably, signally, strikingly, uncommonly.

**notation** *n* alphabet, characters, code, noting, record, script, shorthand, signs, symbols, system.

**notch** *n* cleft, cut, degree, grade, incision, indentation, insection, kerf, level, mark, nick, score, sinus, snip, step.

*v* cut, gimp, indent, mark, nick, raffle, scallop, score, scratch.

**notch up** achieve, gain, make, record, register, score.

**notched** *adj* crenellate(d), emarginate, eroded, erose, jagged, jaggy, pinked, serrate(d), serrulate(d).

**note** *n* annotation, apostil(le), billet, celebrity, character, comment, communication, consequence, distinction, eminence, epistle, epistolet, fame, gloss, heed, indication, jotting, letter, line, mark, memo, memorandum, message, minute, notice, observation, prestige, record, regard, remark, reminder, renown, reputation, signal, symbol, token.

*v* denote, designate, detect, enter, indicate, mark, mention, notice, observe, perceive, record, register, remark, see, witness.

**noted** *adj* acclaimed, celebrated, conspicuous, distinguished, eminent, famous, great, illustrious, notable, notorious, prominent, recognised, renowned, respected, well-known.

**notes** *n* draft, impressions, jottings, outline, record, report, sketch, synopsis.

**noteworthy** *adj* exceptional, extraordinary, important, notable, on the map, outstanding, remarkable, significant, unusual, visitable.

*antonyms* commonplace, ordinary, unexceptional, usual.

**nothing** *n* bagatelle, cipher, damn all, emptiness, nada, naught, nix, nobody, nonentity, non-existence, nothingness, nought, nullity, sweet Fanny Adams, (sweet) fuck all, trifle, void, zero.

*antonyms* everything, something.

**nothingness** *n* nada, nihilism, nihility, non-existence, nullity, oblivion, vacuum.

**notice** *v* descry, detect, discern, distinguish, espy, heed, mark, mind, note, observe, perceive, remark, see, spot.

*antonyms* ignore, overlook.

*n* advertisement, advice, affiche, announcement, attention, bill, civility, cognisance, comment, communication, consideration, criticism, heed, instruction, intelligence, intimation, news, note, notification, observation, order, poster, regard, respect, review, sign, warning.

**noticeable** *adj* appreciable, clear, conspicuous, distinct, dramatic, evident, manifest, measurable, observable, obvious, perceptible, plain, significant, striking, unmistakable.

*antonyms* hidden, insignificant, obscure.

**notification** *n* advice, alert, announcement, declaration, disclosure, information, intelligence, message, notice, publication, revelation, statement, telling, warning.

**notify** *v* acquaint, advise, alert, announce, apprise, declare, disclose, inform, publish, reveal, tell, warn.

**notion** *n* apprehension, belief, caprice, conceit, concept, conception, concetto, construct, desire, fancy, idea, image, impression, impulse, inclination, inkling, judgement, knowledge, opinion, sentiment, understanding, view, whim, wish.

**notional** *adj* abstract, classificatory, conceptual, fanciful, hypothetical, ideational, imaginary, speculative, thematic, theoretical, unfounded, unreal, visionary.

*antonym* real.

**notoriety** *n* disfame, dishonour, disrepute, esclandre, infamy, obloquy, opprobrium, scandal.

**notorious** *adj* arrant, blatant, dishonourable, disreputable, egregious, flagrant, glaring, infamous, obvious, open, opprobrious, overt, patent, scandalous, undisputed.

**notoriously** *adv* arrantly, blatantly, dishonourably, disreputably, egregiously, flagrantly, glaringly, infamously, notably, obviously, openly, opprobriously, overtly, particularly, patently, scandalously, spectacularly, undisputedly.

**notwithstanding** *adv* although, despite, howbeit, however, natheless, nevertheless, nonetheless, though, withal, yet.

**nought** *n* naught, nil, nix, nothing, nothingness, zero, zilch.

**nourish** *v* attend, cherish, comfort, cultivate, encourage, feed, foster, furnish, harbour, maintain, nurse, nurture, promote, supply, support, sustain, tend.

**nourishing** *adj* alimentative, beneficial, good, healthful, health-giving, nutritious, nutritive, substantial, wholesome.

**nourishment** *n* aliment, diet, food, goodness, nutriment, nutrition, pabulum, provender, sustenance, viands, victuals.

**novel** *adj* different, fresh, imaginative, innovative, new, original, rare, singular, strange, surprising, uncommon, unconventional, unfamiliar, unusual.

*antonyms* familiar, ordinary.

*n* fiction, narrative, romance, saga, story, tale, yarn.

**novelty** *n* bagatelle, bauble, curiosity, freshness, gadget, gewgaw, gimcrack, gimmick, innovation, knick-knack, memento, neoterism, newness, oddity, originality, peculiarity, souvenir, strangeness, surprise, trifle, trinket, unfamiliarity, uniqueness.

**novice** *n* amateur, apprentice, beginner, catechumen, convert, cub, griffin, Johnny-raw, learner, neophyte, newcomer, novitiate, probationer, proselyte, pupil, tiro.

*antonyms* doyen, expert, professional.

**now** *adv* at once, at present, directly, ek dum, immediately, instanter, instantly, next, nowadays, presently, promptly, straightaway, these days.

**now and then** at times, desultorily, from time to time, infrequently, intermittently, now and again, occasionally, on and off, on occasion, once in a while, periodically, sometimes, spasmodically, sporadically.

**nowadays** *adv* any more, as things are, at the moment, now, these days, today.

**noxious** *adj* baneful, corrupting, deadly, deleterious, destructive, detrimental, foul, harmful, hurtful, injurious, insalubrious, mephitic(al), morbiferous, morbific, noisome, pernicious, pestilential, poisonous, unhealthy, unwholesome.

*antonyms* innocuous, wholesome.

**nuance** *n* degree, distinction, gradation, hint, nicety, overtone, refinement, shade, soupçon, subtlety, suggestion, suspicion, tinge, touch, trace.

**nub** *n* centre, core, crux, essence, gist, heart, kernel, nitty-gritty, nucleus, pith, point.

**nubile** *adj* marriageable, ripe, sexy, voluptuous.

**nucleus** *n* basis, centre, core, crux, focus, heart, heartlet, kernel, nub, pivot.

**nude** *adj* au naturel, bare, disrobed, exposed, in one's birthday suit, in puris naturalibus, in the altogether, in the buff, naked, starkers, stark-naked, stripped, unattired, unclad, unclothed, uncovered, undraped, undressed, without a stitch.

*antonyms* clothed, covered, dressed.

**nudge** *v, n* bump, dig, jog, poke, prod, prompt, push, shove, touch.

**nudity** *n* bareness, deshabille, dishabille, nakedness, nudism, undress.

**nugatory** *adj* bootless, futile, inadequate, inconsequential, ineffectual, inoperative, insignificant, invalid, null and void, trifling, trivial, unavailing, useless, vain, valueless, worthless.
*antonyms* important, significant.

**nugget** *n* chunk, clump, hunk, lump, mass, piece, wodge.

**nuisance** *n* annoyance, bore, bother, desagrement, drag, drawback, inconvenience, infliction, irritation, offence, pain, pest, plague, problem, trouble, vexation.

**null** *adj* characterless, immaterial, incorporeal, ineffectual, inoperative, invalid, non-existent, powerless, useless, vain, valueless, void, worthless.
*antonym* valid.

**nullify** *v* abate, abolish, abrogate, annul, cancel, counteract, countervail, invalidate, negate, neutralise, quash, repeal, rescind, revoke, undermine, veto, vitiate, void.
*antonym* validate.

**nullity** *n* characterlessness, immateriality, incorporeality, ineffectualness, invalidity, non-existence, powerlessness, uselessness, voidness, worthlessness.
*antonym* validity.

**numb** *adj* benumbed, dead, deadened, frozen, immobilised, insensate, insensible, insensitive, paralysed, stunned, stupefied, torpid, unfeeling.
*antonym* sensitive.
*v* anaesthetise, benumb, deaden, dull, freeze, immobilise, obtund, paralyse, stun, stupefy.
*antonym* sensitise.

**number¹** *n* aggregate, amount, character, collection, company, count, crowd, digit, figure, folio, horde, index, integer, many, multitude, numeral, quantity, several, sum, throng, total, unit.
*v* account, add, apportion, calculate, compute, count, enumerate, include, inventory, reckon, tell, total.

**number²** *n* copy, edition, impression, imprint, issue, printing, volume.

**numberless** *adj* countless, endless, infinite, innumerable, multitudinous, myriad, uncounted, unnumbered, unsummed, untold.

**numbness** *n* anaesthetisation, deadness, dullness, insensateness, insensibility, insensitivity, paralysis, stupefaction, torpor, unfeelingness.
*antonym* sensitivity.

**numeral** *n* character, cipher, digit, figure, folio, integer, number.

**numerous** *adj* abundant, copious, divers, many, multitudinous, myriad, plentiful, profuse, several, sundry.
*antonyms* few, scanty.

**numerousness** *n* abundance, copiousness, manifoldness, multiety, multiplicity, multitudinousness, plentifulness, plurality, profusion.
*antonyms* scantiness, scarcity.

**numskull** *n* blockhead, bonehead, buffoon, clot, dimwit, dolt, dope, drongo, dullard, dummy, dunce, dunderhead, fathead, fool, sap, saphead, simpleton, thickhead, twit.

**nun** *n* abbess, anchoress, ancress, bride of Christ, canoness, mother superior, prioress, sister, vestal, vowess.

**nunnery** *n* abbey, cloister, convent, priory.

**nuptial** *adj* bridal, conjugal, connubial, epithalamial, epithalamic, hymeneal, marital, matrimonial, wedded, wedding.

**nuptials** *n* bridal, espousal, marriage, matrimony, spousals, wedding.

**nurse** *v* breast-feed, care for, cherish, cultivate, encourage, feed, foster, harbour, keep, nourish, nurture, preserve, promote, succour, suckle, support, sustain, tend, treat, wet-nurse.
*n* amah, district-nurse, home-nurse, mammy, nanny, nursemaid, sister of mercy, wet nurse.

**nurture** *n* care, cultivation, development, diet, discipline, education, food, instruction, nourishment, rearing, training, upbringing.
*v* bring up, care for, cultivate, develop, discipline, educate, feed, instruct, nourish, nurse, rear, school, support, sustain, tend, train.

**nut¹** *n* kernel, pip, seed, stone.

**nut²** *n* brain, crackpot, crank, eccentric, head, head-banger, loony, lunatic, madman, maniac, mind, nutcase, nutter, psychopath, reason, senses.

**nutriment** *n* aliment, diet, food, foodstuff, nourishment, nutrition, pabulum, provender, subsistence, support, sustenance.

**nutrition** *n* eutrophy, food, nourishment, nutriment, sustenance.

**nutritious** *adj* alimental, alimentative, beneficial, good, healthful, health-giving, invigorating, nourishing, nutritive, strengthening, substantial, wholesome.
*antonyms* bad, unwholesome.

**nuts** *adj* bananas, batty, crazy, demented, deranged, eccentric, insane, irrational, loony, loopy, mad, nutty, psychopathic, unbalanced, unhinged.
*antonym* sane.

**nuts and bolts** basics, bits and pieces, components, details, essentials, fundamentals, nitty-gritty, practicalities.

**nuzzle** *v* burrow, cuddle, fondle, nestle, nudge, pet, snuggle.

**nymph** *n* damsel, dryad, girl, hamadryad, houri, lass, maid, maiden, naiad, oread, sprite, sylph, undine.

# O

**oaf** *n* baboon, blockhead, bonehead, booby, brute, clod, dolt, dullard, dummy, dunce, fool, galoot, gawk, goon, gorilla, half-wit, hick, hobbledehoy, hulk, idiot, imbecile, lout, lummox, moron, nincompoop, oik, sap, schlemiel, schlep, simpleton, yob.

**oafish** *adj* blockish, Boeotian, boneheaded, boorish, bovine, brutish, crass, dense, dim, dimwitted, doltish, dull, dumb, heavy, loutish, lubberly, lumbering, moronic, obtuse, schleppy, stupid, thick.

**oasis** *n* enclave, haven, island, refuge, resting-place, retreat, sanctuary, sanctum, watering-hole.

**oath** *n* affirmation, assurance, avowal, blasphemy, bond, curse, cuss, expletive, imprecation, malediction, pledge, plight, profanity, promise, swear-word, vow, word, word of honour.

**obdurate** *adj* adamant, callous, dogged, firm, fixed, flinty, hard, hard-hearted, harsh, immovable, implacable, inexorable, inflexible, intransigent, iron, mulish, obstinate, perverse, pig-headed, relentless, stiff-necked, stony, stubborn, unbending, unfeeling, unrelenting, unshakable, unyielding.

*antonyms* submissive, tender.

**obedience** *n* accordance, acquiescence, agreement, allegiance, amenableness, compliance, conformability, deference, docility, dutifulness, duty, observance, passivity, respect, reverence, submission, submissiveness, subservience, tractability.

*antonym* disobedience.

**obedient** *adj* acquiescent, amenable, biddable, compliant, deferential, docile, duteous, dutiful, law-abiding, observant, passive, regardful, respectful, sequacious, submissive, subservient, tractable, unquestioning, unresisting, well-trained, yielding.

*antonyms* disobedient, rebellious, refractory, unruly, wilful.

**obeisance** *n* bow, congé, curts(e)y, deference, genuflection, homage, kowtow, respect, reverence, salaam, salutation, salute.

**obese** *adj* bulky, corpulent, Falstaffian, fat, fleshy, gross, heavy, outsize, overweight, paunchy, plump, podgy, ponderous, portly, pursy, roly-poly, rotund, stout, tubby.

*antonyms* skinny, slender, thin.

**obesity** *n* bulk, chubbiness, corpulence, embonpoint, fatness, fleshiness, grossness, middle-age(d) spread, overweight, portliness, stoutness, tubbiness.

*antonyms* skinniness, slenderness, thinness.

**obey** *v* abide by, act upon, adhere to, be ruled by, bow to, carry out, comply, conform, defer (to), discharge, embrace, execute, follow, fulfil, give in, give way, heed, implement, keep, knuckle under, mind, observe, perform, respond, serve, submit, surrender, take orders from, toe the line, yield.

*antonym* disobey.

**object**[1] *n* aim, article, body, butt, design, end, entity, fact, focus, goal, idea, intent, intention, item, motive, objective, phenomenon, point, purpose, raison d'être, reality, reason, recipient, target, thing, victim, visible.

**object**[2] *v* argue, complain, demur, dissent, expostulate, oppose, protest, rebut, refuse, repudiate, take exception.

*antonyms* accede, acquiesce, agree, assent.

**objection** *n* cavil, censure, challenge, complaint, counter-argument, demur, doubt, exception, niggle, opposition, protest, remonstrance, scruple.

*antonyms* agreement, assent.

**objectionable** *adj* abhorrent, antisocial, deplorable, despicable, detestable, disagreeable, dislik(e)able, displeasing, distasteful, exceptionable, indecorous, insufferable, intolerable, loathsome, noxious, obnoxious, offensive, regrettable, repugnant, unacceptable, undesirable, unpleasant, unseemly.

*antonyms* acceptable, pleasant, welcome.

**objective** *adj* calm, detached, disinterested, dispassionate, equitable, even-handed, fair, impartial, impersonal, judicial, just, open-minded, sensible, sober, unbiased, uncoloured, unemotional, unimpassioned, uninvolved, unprejudiced.

*antonyms* biased, subjective.

*n* aim, ambition, aspiration, design, destination, end, goal, intention, mark, object, prize, purpose, target.

**objectivity** *n* detachment, disinterest, disinterestedness, dispassion, equitableness, even-handedness, impartiality, impersonality, open mind, open-mindedness.

*antonyms* bias, subjectivity.

**obligation** *n* accountability, accountableness, agreement, bond, burden, charge, commitment, compulsion, contract, debt, duty, engagement, indebtedness, liability, must, obstriction, onus, promise, requirement, responsibility, stipulation, trust, understanding.

*antonyms* choice, discretion.

**obligatory** *adj* binding, bounden, coercive, compulsory, de rigueur, enforced, essential, imperative, mandatory, necessary, required, requisite, statutory, unavoidable.

*antonym* optional.

**oblige** *v* accommodate, assist, benefit, bind, coerce, compel, constrain, do a favour, favour, force, gratify, help, impel, indulge, make, necessitate, obligate, please, require, serve.

**obliged** *adj* appreciative, beholden, bound, compelled, constrained, forced, grateful, gratified, in debt (to), indebted, obligated, required, thankful, under an obligation, under compulsion.

**obliging** *adj* accommodating, agreeable, aidful, amiable, civil, complaisant, considerate, co-operative, courteous, eager, friendly, good-natured, helpful, kind, polite, willing.

*antonyms* inconsiderate, unhelpful, unkind.

**oblique** *adj* angled, aslant, at an angle, back-handed, circuitous, circumlocutory, evasive, inclined, indirect, roundabout, sidelong, skew, slanted, slanting, sloped, sloping, tilted, transverse.

**obliquely** *adv* askance, askant, aslant, aslope, at an angle, circuitously, diagonally, evasively, in a roundabout way, indirectly, not in so many words, slantwise.

**obliterate** *v* annihilate, blot out, cancel, delete, destroy, efface, eradicate, erase, expunge, extirpate, rub out, vaporise, wipe out.

**obliteration** *n* annihilation, blotting out, deletion, effacement, elimination, eradication, erasure, expunction, extirpation, rasure.

**oblivion** *n* abeyance, blackness, coma, darkness, disregard, eclipse, extinction, forgetfulness, insensibility, Lethe, limbo, neglect, nothingness, obliviousness, obscurity, stupor, unawareness, unconsciousness, void.

*antonyms* awareness, consciousness.

**oblivious** *adj* blind, careless, comatose, deaf, disregardful, forgetful, heedless, ignorant, inattentive, insensible, neglectful, negligent, nescient, regardless, unaware, unconcerned, unconscious, unmindful, unobservant.

*antonyms* aware, conscious.

**obloquy** *n* abuse, animadversion, aspersion, attack, bad press, blame, calumny, censure, contumely, criticism, defamation, detraction, discredit, disfavour, disgrace, dishonour, humiliation, ignominy, infamy, invective, odium, opprobrium, reproach, shame, slander, stigma, vilification.

**obnoxious** *adj* abhorrent, abominable, detestable, disagreeable, disgusting, dislik(e)able, foul, fulsome, hateful, horrid, insufferable, loathsome, nasty, nauseating, nauseous, noisome, objectionable, odious, offensive, repellent, reprehensible, repugnant, repulsive, revolting, sickening, unpleasant.

*antonyms* agreeable, lik(e)able, pleasant.

**obscene** *adj* atrocious, barrack-room, bawdy, blue, coarse, dirty, disgusting, evil, Fescennine, filthy, foul, gross, heinous, immodest, immoral, improper, impure, indecent, lewd, licentious, loathsome, loose, offensive, outrageous, pornographic, prurient, Rabelaisian, ribald, salacious, scabrous, scurrilous, shameless, shocking, sickening, smutty, suggestive, unchaste, unwholesome, vile, wicked.

*antonyms* clean, decent, decorous.

**obscenity** *n* abomination, affront, atrocity, bawdiness, blight, blueness, coarseness, dirtiness, evil, expletive, facetiae, filthiness, foulness, four-letter word, grossness, immodesty, impropriety, impurity, indecency, indelicacy, lewdness, licentiousness, offence, outrage, pornography, profanity, prurience, salacity, scurrility, smut, smuttiness, suggestiveness, swear-word, vileness, vulgarism.

**obscure** *adj* abstruse, ambiguous, arcane, blurred, caliginous, clear as mud, clouded, cloudy, concealed, confusing, cryptic, deep, Delphic, dim, doubtful, dusky, enigmatic, esoteric, faint, gloomy, hazy, hermetic, hidden, humble, incomprehensible, inconspicuous, indefinite, indistinct, inglorious, intricate, involved, little-known, lowly, minor, misty, murky, mysterious, nameless, obfuscated, occult, opaque, oracular, out-of-the-way, recondite, remote, riddling, shadowy, shady, sombre, tenebr(i)ous, tenebrose, twilight, unclear, undistinguished, unheard-of, unhonoured, unimportant, unknown, unlit, unnoted, unobvious, unrenowned, unseen, unsung, vague, veiled.

*antonyms* clear, definite, explicit, famous, lucid.

*v* bedim, befog, block out, blur, cloak, cloud, conceal, cover, darken, dim, disguise, dull, eclipse, hide, mask, muddy, obfuscate, overshadow, screen, shade, shadow, shroud, veil.

*antonyms* clarify, illuminate.

**obscurity** *n* abstruseness, ambiguity, complexity, darkness, dimness, dusk, duskiness, fogginess, gloom, haze, haziness, impenetrability, incomprehensibility, inconspicuousness, indistinctness, ingloriousness, insignificance, intricacy, lowliness, mirk, mirkiness, murk, murkiness, mysticism, namelessness, reconditeness, shadowiness, shadows, unimportance, vagueness.

*antonyms* clarity, fame, lucidity.

**obsequious** *adj* abject, cringing, deferential, dough-faced, fawning, flattering, grovelling, ingratiating, knee-crooking, menial, oily, servile, slavish, slimy, smarmy, submissive, subservient, sycophantic, toadying, unctuous.

*antonym* assertive.

**observable** *adj* apparent, appreciable, clear, detectable, discernible, evident, measurable, noticeable, obvious, open, patent, perceivable, perceptible, recognisable, significant, visible.

**observance** *n* adherence, attention, celebration, ceremonial, ceremony, compliance, custom, discharge, fashion, form, formality, fulfilment, heeding, honouring, notice, obedience, observation, orthodoxy, performance, practice, rite, ritual, service, tradition.

**observant** *adj* alert, attentive, eagle-eyed, eagle-sighted, falcon-eyed, heedful, mindful, perceptive, percipient, quick, sharp-eyed, vigilant, watchful, wide-awake.

*antonyms* inattentive, unobservant.

**observation** *n* annotation, attention, cognition, comment, consideration, discernment, examination, experience, finding, information, inspection, knowledge, monitoring, note, notice, obiter dictum, opinion, perception, pronouncement, reading, reflection, remark, review, scrutiny, study, surveillance, thought, utterance, watching.

**observe** *v* abide by, adhere to, animadvert, celebrate, commemorate, comment, comply, conform to, contemplate, declare, detect, discern, discover, espy, follow, fulfil, heed, honour, keep, keep an eye on, keep tabs on, mention, mind, monitor, note, notice, obey, opine, perceive, perform, regard, remark, remember, respect, say, scrutinise, see, solemnise, spot, state, study, surveille, survey, view, watch, witness.

*antonyms* break, miss, overlook, violate.

**observer** *n* beholder, bystander, commentator, discerner, eyewitness, looker-on, noter, onlooker, spectator, spotter, viewer, watcher, witness.

**obsess** *v* bedevil, consume, dominate, engross, grip, haunt, hold, monopolise, nag, plague, possess, preoccupy, prey on, rule, torment.

**obsessed** *adj* bedevilled, beset, dominated, gripped, hag-ridden, haunted, hounded, hung up on, immersed in, in the grip of, infatuated, plagued, preoccupied.

*antonyms* detached, indifferent, unconcerned.

**obsession** *n* bee in one's bonnet, complex, enthusiasm, fetish, fixation, hang-up, idée fixe, infatuation, mania, monomania, phobia, preoccupation, ruling passion, thing, zelotypia.

**obsessive** *adj* besetting, compulsive, consuming, fixed, gripping, haunting, maddening, nagging, tormenting, unforgettable.

**obsolescent** *adj* ag(e)ing, declining, disappearing, dying out, fading, moribund, on the decline, on the wane, on the way out, past its prime, waning.

**obsolete** *adj* anachronistic, ancient, antediluvian, antiquated, antique, archaic, bygone, dated, dead, démodé, discarded, disused, extinct, fogram, horse-and-buggy, musty, old, old hat, old-fashioned, out, out of date, outmoded, outworn, passé, superannuated.

*antonyms* contemporary, current, modern, new, up-to-date.

**obstacle** *n* bar, barrier, boyg, catch, check, chicane, difficulty, drawback, hindrance, hitch, hurdle, impediment, interference, interruption, obstruction, pons asinorum, remora, snag, stop, stumbling-block, stumbling-stone.

*antonyms* advantage, help.

**obstinacy** *n* doggedness, firmness, frowardness, inflexibility, intransigence, mulishness, obduracy, perseverance, persistence, pertinacity, perversity, pig-headedness, resoluteness, stubbornness, tenacity, wilfulness, wrong-headedness.

*antonyms* co-operativeness, flexibility, submissiveness.

**obstinate** *adj* bullet-headed, bull-headed, bullish, camelish, contumacious, determined, dogged, firm, headstrong, immovable, inflexible, intractable, intransigent, mulish, obdurate, opinionated, persistent, pertinacious, perverse, pervicacious, pig-headed, recalcitrant, refractory, restive, rusty, self-willed, steadfast, stomachful, strong-minded, stubborn, sturdy, tenacious, unadvisable, unyielding, uppity, wilful, wrong-headed.

*antonyms* co-operative, flexible, pliant, submissive.

**obstreperous** *adj* boisterous, clamorous, disorderly, intractable, loud, noisy, out of hand, rackety, rambunctious, rampaging, raucous, refractory, restive, riotous, rip-roaring, roistering, roisterous, rough, rowdy, stroppy, tempestuous, tumultous, turbulent, uncontrolled, undisciplined, unmanageable, unruly, uproarious, vociferous, wild.

*antonyms* calm, disciplined, quiet.

**obstruct** *v* arrest, bar, barricade, block, check, choke, clog, crab, cumber, curb, cut off, frustrate, hamper, hamstring, hide, hinder, hold up, impede, inhibit, interfere with, interrupt, mask, obscure, occlude, prevent, restrict, retard, shield, shut off, slow down, stall, stonewall, stop, stuff, thwart, trammel.

*antonym* help.

**obstruction** *n* bar, barricade, barrier, blockage, check, difficulty, filibuster, hindrance, impediment, snag, stop, stoppage, trammel, traverse.

*antonym* help.

**obstructive** *adj* awkward, blocking, delaying, difficult, hindering, inhibiting, restrictive, stalling, unaccommodating, unco-operative, unhelpful.

*antonym* helpful.

**obtain**[1] *v* achieve, acquire, attain, come by, compass, earn, gain, get, impetrate, procure, secure.

**obtain**[2] *v* be in force, be prevalent, be the case, exist, hold, prevail, reign, rule, stand.

**obtainable** *adj* accessible, achievable, at hand, attainable, available, on call, on tap, procurable, ready, realisable, to be had.

*antonym* unobtainable.

**obtrusive** *adj* blatant, forward, importunate, interfering, intrusive, manifest, meddling, nosy, noticeable, obvious, officious, prominent, protruding, protuberant, prying, pushy.

*antonym* unobtrusive.

**obtuse** *adj* blunt, boneheaded, crass, dense, dopey, dull, dull-witted, dumb, imperceptive, impercipient, inattentive, insensitive, retarded, rounded, slow, stolid, stupid, thick, thick-skinned, uncomprehending, unintelligent.

*antonyms* bright, sharp.

**obviate** *v* anticipate, avert, counter, counteract, divert, forestall, preclude, prevent, remove.

**obvious** *adj* apparent, clear, conspicuous, discernible, distinct, evident, glaring, indisputable, manifest, noticeable, open, open-and-shut, overt, palpable, patent, perceptible, plain, prominent, pronounced, recognisable, self-evident, self-explanatory, straightforward, transparent, unconcealed, undeniable, undisguised, unmistakable, unsubtle, visible.

*antonyms* obscure, unclear.

**obviously** *adv* certainly, clearly, distinctly, evidently, manifestly, of course, palpably, patently, plainly, undeniably, unmistakably, unquestionably, visibly, without doubt.

**occasion** *n* affair, call, case, cause, celebration, chance, convenience, event, excuse, experience, ground(s), incident, inducement, influence, instance, justification, moment, motive, occurrence, opening, opportunity, prompting, provocation, reason, time.

*v* bring about, bring on, cause, create, effect, elicit, engender, evoke, generate, give rise to, induce, influence, inspire, lead to, make, originate, persuade, produce, prompt, provoke.

**occasional** *adj* casual, desultory, fitful, incidental, infrequent, intermittent, irregular, odd, periodic, rare, scattered, sporadic, uncommon.

*antonym* frequent.

**occasionally** *adv* at intervals, at times, every so often, from time to time, infrequently, irregularly, now and again, now and then, off and on, on and off, on occasion, once in a while, periodically, sometimes, sporadically.

*antonym* frequently.

**occult** *adj* abstruse, arcane, cabbalistic, concealed, esoteric, faint, hidden, impenetrable, invisible, magical, mysterious, mystic, mystical, mystifying, obscure, preternatural, recondite, secret, supernatural, unknown, unrevealed, veiled.

*v* conceal, cover (up), enshroud, hide, mask, obscure, screen, shroud, veil.

*antonym* reveal.

**occultism** *n* black magic, diabolism, magic, mysticism, sorcery, spiritualism, supernaturalism, the black arts, witchcraft.

**occupancy** *n* domiciliation, habitation, holding, inhabitancy, occupation, ownership, possession, residence, tenancy, tenure, term, use.

**occupant** *n* addressee, denizen, holder, householder, incumbent, indweller, inhabitant, inmate, lessee, occupier, resident, squatter, tenant, user.

**occupation¹** *n* absorption, activity, business, calling, craft, employment, job, line, post, profession, pursuit, trade, vocation, walk of life, work.

**occupation²** *n* billet, conquest, control, habitation, holding, invasion, occupancy, possession, residence, seizure, subjugation, takeover, tenancy, tenure, use.

**occupied** *adj* absorbed, busy, employed, engaged, engrossed, full, hard at it, in use, inhabited, lived-in, peopled, settled, taken, tenanted, tied up, unavailable, working.

*antonym* unoccupied.

**occupy** *v* absorb, amuse, beguile, busy, capture, conquer, cover, divert, dwell in, employ, engage, engross, ensconce oneself in, entertain, establish oneself in, fill, garrison, hold, immerse, inhabit, interest, invade, involve, keep, keep busy, live in, monopolise, overrun, own, permeate, pervade, possess, preoccupy, reside in, seize, stay in, take over, take possession of, take up, tenant, tie up, use, utilise.

**occur** *v* appear, arise, be found, be met with, be present, befall, betide, chance, come about, come off, come to pass, crop up, develop, eventuate, exist, happen, intervene, manifest itself, materialise, obtain, result, show itself, take place, transpire, turn up.

**occur to** come to mind, come to one, cross one's mind, dawn on, enter one's head, present itself, spring to mind, strike one, suggest itself.

**occurrence** *n* action, adventure, affair, appearance, case, circumstance, development, episode, event, existence, happening, incident, instance, manifestation, materialisation, proceeding, transaction.

**ocean** *n* briny, main, profound, sea, the deep, the drink.

**odd¹** *adj* abnormal, atypical, bizarre, curious, deviant, different, eccentric, exceptional, extraordinary, fantastic, freak, freakish, freaky, funky, funny, irregular, kinky, outlandish, peculiar, quaint, queer, rare, remarkable, singular, strange, uncanny, uncommon, unconventional, unexplained, unusual, weird, whimsical.

*antonym* normal.

**odd²** *adj* auxiliary, casual, fragmentary, ill-matched, incidental, irregular, left-over, lone, miscellaneous, occasional, periodic, random, remaining, seasonal, single, solitary, spare, sundry, surplus, uneven, unmatched, unpaired, varied, various.

**oddity** *n* abnormality, anomaly, bizarreness, card, character, crank, curiosity, eccentricity, extraordinariness, freak, freakishness, idiosyncrasy, incongruity, irregularity, kink, maverick, misfit, oddball, oddness, outlandishness, peculiarity, phenomenon, queerness, quirk, quizziness, rara avis, rarity, screwball, singularity, strangeness, unconventionality, unnaturalness, weirdie, weirdo.

**oddment** *n* bit, end, fragment, leftover, offcut, patch, remnant, scrap, shred, sliver, snippet.

**odds** *n* advantage, allowance, ascendancy, balance, chances, difference, discrepancy, disparity, dissimilarity, distinction, edge, lead, likelihood, probability, superiority.

**odds and ends** bits, bits and pieces, debris, flotsam and jetsam, junk, leavings, litter, oddments, odds and sods, remnants, rubbish, scraps, tatt.

**odious** *adj* abhorrent, abominable, annoying, detestable, disgusting, execrable, foul, hateful, heinous, horrible, horrid, insufferable, loathsome, obnoxious, offensive, repellent, repugnant, repulsive, revolting, unpleasant, vile.

*antonym* pleasant.

**odium** *n* abhorrence, animosity, antipathy, censure, condemnation, contempt, detestation, disapprobation, disapproval, discredit, disfavour, disgrace, dishonour, dislike, disrepute, execration, hatred, infamy, obloquy, opprobrium, reprobation, shame.

**odorous** *adj* aromatic, balmy, fragrant, odoriferous, perfumed, pungent, redolent, scented, sweet-smelling.

*antonym* odourless.

**odour** *n* air, aroma, atmosphere, aura, bouquet, breath, emanation, essence, exhalation, flavour, fragrance, perfume, quality, redolence, scent, smell, spirit, stench, stink.

**odyssey** *n* journey, travels, wandering.

**of course** certainly, definitely, doubtlessly, indubitably, naturally, no doubt, obviously, undoubtedly.

**off** *adj* abnormal, absent, bad, below par, cancelled, decomposed, disappointing, disheartening, displeasing, finished, gone, high, inoperative, mouldy, poor, postponed, quiet, rancid, rotten, slack, sour, substandard, turned, unavailable, unsatisfactory, wrong.

*adv* apart, aside, at a distance, away, elsewhere, out.

**off and on** fitfully, from time to time, intermittently, now and again, now and then, occasionally, on and off, once in a while, periodically, sometimes, sporadically.

**off guard** napping, unprepared, unready, unwary, with one's defences down, with one's pants down.

**off the cuff** ad lib, extempore, impromptu, improvised, offhand, spontaneous, spontaneously, unofficially, unprepared, unrehearsed, unscripted.

**off the hook** acquitted, cleared, exonerated, in the clear, scot free, vindicated.

**off the record** confidential, confidentially, private, privately, sub rosa, unofficial, unofficially.

*antonym* officially.

**off-colour** *adj* faded, ill, indecent, indisposed, off form, out of sorts, pasty-faced, peaky, peelie-wally, poorly, queasy, sick, under the weather, unwell.

**off-duty** *adj* at leisure, at liberty, free, not at work, off, off work, on holiday.

**offence** *n* affront, anger, annoyance, crime, delict, delinquency, displeasure, fault, hard feelings, harm, huff, hurt, indignation, indignity, infraction, infringement, injury, injustice, insult, ire, lapse, misdeed, misdemeanour, needle, outrage, peccadillo, pique, put-down, resentment, sin, slight, snub, transgression, trespass, umbrage, violation, wrath, wrong, wrong-doing.

**offend** *v* affront, annoy, disgruntle, disgust, displease, fret, gall, hip, hurt, insult, irritate, miff, nauseate, outrage, pain, pique, provoke, repel, repulse, rile, sicken, slight, snub, transgress, turn off, upset, vex, violate, wound, wrong.

*antonym* please.

**offended** *adj* affronted, disgruntled, disgusted, displeased, huffy, in a huff, miffed, outraged, pained, piqued, put out, resentful, smarting, stung, upset, wounded.

*antonym* pleased.

**offender** *n* criminal, culprit, delinquent, guilty party, law-breaker, malefactor, miscreant, misfeasor, sinner, transgressor, wrong-doer.

**offensive** *adj* abominable, abusive, aggressive, annoying, attacking, detestable, disagreeable, discourteous, disgusting, displeasing, disrespectful, embarrassing, grisly, impertinent, insolent, insulting, intolerable, invading, irritating, loathsome, nasty, nauseating, noisome, objectionable, obnoxious, odious, rank, repellent, repugnant, revolting, rude, sickening, uncivil, unmannerly, unpalatable, unpleasant, unsavoury, vile.

*antonyms* defensive, pleasing.

*n* attack, drive, onslaught, push, raid, sortie, thrust.

**offer** *v* advance, afford, bid, extend, furnish, give, hold out, make available, move, present, proffer, propose, propound, provide, put forth, put forward, show, submit, suggest, tender, volunteer.

*n* approach, attempt, bid, endeavour, essay, overture, presentation, proposal, proposition, submission, suggestion, tender.

**offering** *n* contribution, donation, gift, oblation, present, sacrifice, subscription, xenium.

**offhand** *adj* abrupt, aloof, brusque, careless, casual, cavalier, curt, glib, informal, offhanded, perfunctory, take-it-or-leave-it, unappreciative, uncaring, unceremonious, unconcerned, uninterested.

*antonyms* calculated, planned.

*adv* at once, extempore, immediately, off the cuff, off the top of one's head, straightaway.

**office** *n* appointment, bath, business, capacity, charge, commission, duty, employment, function, obligation, occupation, place, post, responsibility, role, room, service, situation, station, trust, work.

**officer** *n* administrator, agent, appointee, bureaucrat, dignitary, executive, functionary, office-holder, official, public servant, representative.

**offices** *n* advocacy, aegis, aid, auspices, backing, back-up, favour, help, intercession, intermediation, intervention, mediation, patronage, recommendation, referral, support, word.

**official** *adj* accredited, approved, authentic, authenticated, authorised, authoritative, bona fide, certified, ex cathedra, formal, legitimate, licensed, proper, sanctioned.

*antonym* unofficial.

*n* agent, bureaucrat, executive, fonctionnaire, functionary, gauleiter, hakim, intendant, jack-in-office, mandarin, office-bearer, officer, representative.

**officiate** *v* adjudicate, chair, conduct, emcee, manage, oversee, preside, referee, serve, superintend, umpire.

**officious** *adj* bustling, dictatorial, forward, impertinent, inquisitive, interfering, intermeddling, intrusive, meddlesome, meddling, mischievous, obtrusive, opinionated, over-zealous, pragmatical, pushy, self-important.

**offish** *adj* aloof, cool, haughty, standoffish, stuck-up, unsociable.

*antonyms* friendly, sociable.

**off-key** *adj* discordant, dissonant, inappropriate, indecent, inharmonious, jarring, out of keeping, out of tune, unsuitable.

**offload** *v* deposit, disburden, discharge, drop, dump, get rid of, jettison, shift, transfer, unburden, unload, unship.

**off-putting** *adj* daunting, demoralising, discomfiting, disconcerting, discouraging, disheartening, dismaying, dispiriting, disturbing, formidable, frustrating, intimidating, unnerving, unsettling, upsetting.

**offset** *v* balance out, cancel out, compare, compensate for, counteract, counterbalance, counterpoise, countervail, juxtapose, make up for, neutralise.

*n* balance, compensation, counterbalance, counterweight, equipoise, equivalent, redress.

**offshoot** *n* adjunct, appendage, arm, branch, by-product, development, embranchment, limb, outgrowth, spin-off, sprout, spur.

**offspring** *n* brood, child, children, creation, descendant, descendants, family, fry, heir, heirs, issue, kids, litter, progeny, quiverful, result, scion, seed, spawn, successor, successors, young.

*antonym* parent(s).

**often** *adv* again and again, frequently, generally, habitually, many a time, much, oft, over and over, regularly, repeatedly, time after time, time and again.

*antonym* seldom.

**ogle** *v* eye, eye up, leer, look, make eyes at, stare.

**ogre** *n* bogey, bogeyman, bogle, boyg, bugaboo, bugbear, demon, devil, giant, humgruffi(a)n, monster, spectre.

**oik** *n* bloke, bounder, cad, chap, ignoramus, twerp.

**oil** *v* anoint, embrocate, grease, lubricate.

*n* balm, cream, grease, liniment, lotion, lubricant, ointment, oleum, salve, unguent.

**oily** *adj* fatty, flattering, fulsome, glib, greasy, hypocritical, obsequious, oiled, oleaginous, plausible, sebaceous, servile, slippery, smarmy, smeary, smooth, swimming, unctuous.

**ointment** *n* balm, balsam, cerate, cream, demulcent, embrocation, emollient, liniment, lotion, salve, unction, unguent.

**okay** *adj* acceptable, accurate, adequate, all right, approved, convenient, correct, fair, fine, good, in order, not bad, OK, passable, permitted, reasonable, right as rain, satisfactory, tolerable.

*n* agreement, approbation, approval, assent, authorisation, consent, endorsement, go-ahead, green light, OK, permission, sanction, say-so, seal of approval, support.

*v* accredit, agree to, approve, authorise, consent to, endorse, give the go-ahead to, give the green light to, OK, pass, rubber-stamp, sanction, validate.

*interj* agreed, all right, fine, OK, right, very good, very well, yes.

**old** *adj* aboriginal, aged, age-old, ancient, antediluvian, antiquated, antique, archaic, bygone, cast-off, crumbling, dated, decayed, decrepit, done, earlier, early, elderly, erstwhile, ex-, experienced, familiar, former, grey, grey-haired, grizzled, hackneyed, hardened, hoary, immemorial, long-established, long-standing, mature, obsolete, of old, of yore, Ogygian, olden, old-fashioned, one-time, original, out of date, outdated, outmoded, over the hill, passé, patriarchal, practised, preadamic(al), prehistoric, previous, prim(a)eval, primitive, primordial, pristine, quondam, remote, senescent, senile, skilled, stale, superannuated, time-honoured, time-worn, traditional, unfashionable, unoriginal, venerable, versed, veteran, vintage, worn-out.

*antonym* young.

**old age** advancing years, age, agedness, Anno Domini, dotage, e(i)ld, second childhood, senescence, senility, twilight of one's life.

*antonym* youth.

**old man** boss, elder, elder statesman, employer, father, gaffer, geezer, grandfather, grey, greybeard, hoarhead, husband, OAP, old codger, old stager, oldster, old-timer, patriarch, senior citizen, white-beard, wrinkly.

**old woman** bag, complainer, crone, fag(g)ot, fuss-pot, gammer, grandam, grannam, granny, grouch, grumbler, hag, mother, old dear, wet, wife, wimp, wrinkly.

**old-fashioned** *adj* ancient, antiquated, archaic, arriéré, behind the times, corny, dated, dead, démodé, fog(e)yish, fusty, horse-and-buggy, musty, neanderthal, obsolescent, obsolete, old hat, old-fog(e)yish, old-time, out of date, outdated, outmoded, passé, past, quill-pen, retro, rinky-dink, square, superannuated, unfashionable.

*antonyms* contemporary, modern, up-to-date.

**old-world** *adj* archaic, ceremonious, chivalrous, conservative, courtly, formal, gallant, old-fashioned, picturesque, quaint, traditional.

**Olympian** *adj* elevated, exalted, glorious, godlike, Jovian, lofty, majestic, rarefied, splendid, sublime.

**omen** *n* augury, auspice, boding, foreboding, foretoken, freit, indication, portent, premonition, presage, prognostic, prognostication, sign, straw in the wind, warning, writing on the wall.

**ominous** *adj* baleful, bodeful, dark, fateful, inauspicious, menacing, minatory, portentous, premonitory, presageful, sinister, threatening, unpromising, unpropitious.

*antonym* auspicious.

**omission** *n* avoidance, bowdlerisation, default, ellipsis, exclusion, failure, forgetfulness, gap, lack, neglect, oversight.

*antonyms* addition, inclusion.

**omit** *v* disregard, drop, edit out, eliminate, exclude, fail, forget, give something a miss, leave out, leave undone, let slide, miss out, neglect, overlook, pass over, pretermit, skip.

*antonyms* add, include.

**omnibus** *adj* all-embracing, compendious, comprehensive, encyclop(a)edic, inclusive, wide-ranging.

*antonym* selective.

**omnipotence** *n* divine right, invincibility, mastery, plenipotence, sovereignty, supremacy.

*antonym* impotence.

**omnipotent** *adj* all-powerful, almighty, plenipotent, supreme.

*antonym* impotent.

**omnipresent** *adj* pervasive, ubiquitary, ubiquitous, universal.

**omniscient** *adj* all-knowing, all-seeing, pansophic.

**on and off** discontinuously, fitfully, from time to time, intermittently, now and again, now and then, off and on, on occasion, periodically, sometimes, spasmodically, sporadically.

**on duty** at work, busy, engaged, working.

*antonym* off.

**on edge** apprehensive, eager, edgy, excited, fidgety, ill at ease, impatient, irascible, irritable, keyed up, nervous, on tenterhooks, tense, touchy, uptight.

*antonym* relaxed.

**on fire** ablaze, aflame, alight, ardent, blazing, burning, eager, enthusiastic, excited, fiery, fired, flaming, ignited, in flames, inspired, kindled, passionate.

**on guard** alert, cautious, chary, circumspect, excubant, on the alert, on the lookout, on the qui vive, prepared, ready, vigilant, wary, watchful, wide awake.

**on one's last legs** at death's door, dying, exhausted, fading fast, failing, moribund, with one foot in the grave, worn out.

**on one's own** alone, by oneself, independently, isolated, off one's own bat, on one's tod, singly, unaccompanied, unaided, unassisted.

**on purpose** deliberately, designedly, intentionally, knowingly, premeditatedly, purposely, wilfully, wittingly.

*antonym* accidentally.

**on the ball** alert, attentive, aware, in touch, informed, on one's toes, quick, wide awake.

**on the dot** exactly, on time, precisely, promptly, punctually, spot on, to the minute.

**on the fence** between two stools, dithering, irresolute, shilly-shallying, uncertain, uncommitted, undecided, unsure, vacillating.

**on the increase** accelerating, escalating, expanding, growing, increasing, multiplying, proliferating, rising, spreading.

*antonym* on the wane.

**on the level** above board, candid, fair, frank, genuine, honest, open, sincere, square, straight, straightforward, up front.

**on the mend** convalescent, convalescing, healing, improving, recovering, recuperating, reviving.

**on the move** active, advancing, astir, moving, on the go, progressing, stirring, succeeding.

**on the rampage** amok, berserk, frenzied, in a frenzy, rampageous(ly), rampant(ly), riotous(ly), violent(ly), wild(ly).

**on the scrap-heap** discarded, ditched, dumped, forgotten, jettisoned, redundant, rejected, written off.

**on the sly** clandestinely, covertly, furtively, on the q.t., privately, secretly, surreptitiously, underhandedly.

*antonym* openly.

**on the spur of the moment** capriciously, impetuously, impromptu, impulsively, on impulse, on the spot, thoughtlessly, unpremeditatedly, unthinkingly.

**on the wane** declining, degenerating, deteriorating, dropping, dwindling, ebbing, fading, lessening, moribund, obsolescent, on its last legs, on the decline, on the way out, subsiding, tapering off, weakening, withering.

*antonym* on the increase.

**on the whole** all in all, all things considered, as a rule, by and large, for the most part, generally, generally speaking, in general, in the main, mostly, predominantly.

**on thin ice** at risk, in jeopardy, insecure, open to attack, precarious, unsafe, vulnerable.

**on top of the world** ecstatic, elated, exhilarated, exultant, happy, on cloud nine, over the moon, overjoyed, thrilled.

**once** *adv* at one time, formerly, heretofore, in the old days, in the past, in times gone by, in times past, long ago, once upon a time, previously.

**once (and) for all** conclusively, decisively, definitively, finally, for good, for the last time, permanently, positively.

**once in a blue moon** hardly ever, infrequently, rarely, seldom.

**oncoming** *adj* advancing, approaching, forthcoming, gathering, imminent, impending, looming, onrushing, upcoming.

**one** *adj* alike, compatible, complete, entire, equal, harmonious, identical, like-minded, united, whole.

**oneness** *n* completeness, consistency, distinctness, identicalness, identity, individuality, sameness, singleness, unicity, unity, wholeness.

**onerous** *adj* backbreaking, burdensome, crushing, demanding, difficult, exacting, exhausting, exigent, formidable, grave, hard, heavy, herculean, laborious, oppressive, responsible, taxing, troublesome, weighty.

*antonyms* easy, light.

**one-sided** *adj* asymmetrical, biased, coloured, discriminatory, inequitable, lopsided, partial, partisan, prejudiced, unequal, unfair, unilateral, unjust.

*antonym* impartial.

**one-time** *adj* erstwhile, ex-, former, late, previous, quondam, sometime, umquhile, whilom.

**ongoing** *adj* advancing, continuing, continuous, current, developing, evolving, extant, growing, in progress, lasting, progressing, successful, unfinished, unfolding.

**onlooker** *n* bystander, eye-witness, looker-on, observer, rubber-neck, spectator, viewer, watcher, witness.

**only** *adv* at most, barely, exclusively, just, merely, purely, simply, solely.

*adj* exclusive, individual, lone, single, sole, solitary, unique.

**onrush** *n* career, cascade, charge, flood, flow, onset, onslaught, push, rush, stampede, stream, surge.

**onset** *n* assault, attack, beginning, charge, commencement, inception, kick-off, onrush, onslaught, outbreak, outset, start.

*antonyms* end, finish.

**onslaught** *n* assault, attack, barrage, blitz, bombardment, charge, offensive, onrush, onset.

**onus** *n* burden, duty, encumbrance, liability, load, obligation, responsibility, task.

**onward(s)** *adv* ahead, beyond, forth, forward, frontward(s), in front, on.

*antonym* backward(s).

**oodles** *n* abundance, bags, heaps, lashings, loads, lots, masses, oodlins, tons.

*antonym* scarcity.

**oomph** *n* animation, bounce, energy, enthusiasm, exuberance, get-up-and-go, pep, pizzazz, sex-appeal, sparkle, vigour, vitality, vivacity, zing.

**ooze** *v* bleed, discharge, drain, dribble, drip, drop, emit, escape, exude, filter, leach, leak, osmose, overflow with, percolate, seep, strain, sweat, transude, weep.

*n* alluvium, deposit, mire, muck, mud, sediment, silt, slime, sludge.

**oozy** *adj* dewy, dripping, miry, moist, mucky, muddy, slimy, sloppy, sludgy, sweaty, uliginous, weeping.

**opacity** *n* cloudiness, density, dullness, filminess, impermeability, milkiness, murkiness, obfuscation, obscurity, opaqueness, unclearness.

*antonym* transparency.

**opaque** *adj* abstruse, baffling, clouded, cloudy, cryptic, difficult, dim, dull, enigmatic, filmy, fuliginous, hazy, impenetrable, incomprehensible, inexplicable, lustreless, muddied, muddy, murky, obfuscated, obscure, turbid, unclear, unfathomable, unintelligible.

*antonym* transparent.

**open** *adj* above-board, accessible, agape, airy, ajar, apparent, arguable, artless, available, avowed, bare, barefaced, blatant, bounteous, bountiful, candid, champaign, clear, conspicuous, debatable, disinterested, downright, evident, expanded, exposed, extended, extensive, fair, filigree, flagrant, frank, free, fretted, gaping, general, generous, guileless, holey, honest, honeycombed, impartial, ingenuous, innocent, lacy, liberal, lidless, loose, manifest, moot, munificent, natural, navigable, noticeable, objective, obvious, overt, passable, plain, porous, public, receptive, revealed, rolling, sincere, spacious, spongy, spread out, sweeping, transparent, unbarred, unbiased, unclosed, uncluttered, uncommitted, unconcealed, unconditional, uncovered, uncrowded, undecided, undefended, undisguised, unenclosed, unengaged, unfastened, unfenced, unfolded, unfortified, unfurled, unlidded, unlocked, unobstructed, unoccupied, unprejudiced, unprotected, unqualified, unreserved, unresolved, unrestricted, unroofed, unsealed, unsettled, unsheltered, unwalled, upfront, vacant, visible, wide, wide-open, yawning.

*antonyms* closed, shut.

*v* begin, clear, come apart, commence, crack, disclose, divulge, exhibit, explain, expose, inaugurate, initiate, launch, lay bare, ope, pour out, rupture, separate, set in motion, show, split, spread (out), start, throw wide, unbar, unbare, unblock, unclose, uncork, uncover, undo, unfasten, unfold, unfurl, unlatch, unlid, unlock, unroll, unseal, unshutter.

*antonyms* close, shut.

**open to** accessible, disposed, exposed, liable, susceptible, vulnerable.

**open-air** *adj* alfresco, hypaethral, outdoor, plein-air.

*antonym* indoor.

**open-and-shut** *adj* obvious, simple, straightforward.

**open-handed** *adj* bountiful, eleemosynary, free, generous, large-hearted, lavish, liberal, munificent, unstinting.

*antonym* tight-fisted.

**opening** *n* adit, aperture, beginning, birth, breach, break, chance, chasm, chink, cleft, commencement, crack, dawn, fissure, fistula, foramen, gap, hole, inauguration, inception, initiation, interstice, kick-off, launch, launching, occasion, onset, opportunity, orifice, ostiole, outset, perforation, place, rent, rupture, slot, space, split, start, vacancy, vent, vista.

*antonyms* closing, closure.

*adj* beginning, commencing, early, first, inaugural, inauguratory, inceptive, initial, initiatory, introductory, maiden, primary.

*antonym* closing.

**openly** *adv* blatantly, brazenly, candidly, face to face, flagrantly, forthrightly, frankly, glaringly, in full view, in public, overtly, plainly, publicly, shamelessly, unabashedly, unashamedly, unhesitatingly, unreservedly, wantonly.

*antonyms* secretly, slyly.

**open-minded** *adj* broad, broad-minded, catholic, dispassionate, enlightened, free, impartial, latitudinarian, liberal, objective, reasonable, receptive, tolerant, unbiased, unprejudiced.

*antonyms* bigoted, intolerant, prejudiced.

**open-mouthed** *adj* amazed, astounded, clamorous, dumbfounded, edacious, expectant, flabbergasted, greedy, spellbound, thunderstruck, voracious.

**operate** *v* act, function, go, handle, manage, manoeuvre, perform, run, serve, use, utilise, work.

**operation** *n* action, activity, affair, agency, assault, business, campaign, course, deal, effect, effort, employment, enterprise, exercise, force, influence, instrumentality, manipulation, manoeuvre, motion, movement, performance, procedure, proceeding, process, surgery, transaction, undertaking, use, utilisation, working.

**operational** *adj* functional, going, in service, in working order, on duty, operative, prepared, ready, usable, viable, workable, working.

*antonym* out of order.

**operative** *adj* active, crucial, current, effective, efficient, engaged, functional, functioning, important, in action, in force, in operation, indicative, influential, key, operational, relevant, serviceable, significant, standing, workable.

*antonym* inoperative.

*n* artisan, employee, hand, labourer, machinist, mechanic, operator, worker.

**operator** *n* administrator, conductor, contractor, dealer, director, driver, handler, machinator, machinist, manager, manipulator, mechanic, mover, operant, operative, practitioner, punter, shyster, speculator, technician, trader, wheeler-dealer, worker.

**opiate** *n* anodyne, bromide, depressant, downer, drug, narcotic, nepenthe, pacifier, sedative, soporific, stupefacient, tranquilliser.

**opine** *v* believe, conceive, conclude, conjecture, declare, guess, judge, presume, say, suggest, suppose, surmise, suspect, think, venture, volunteer.

**opinion** *n* assessment, belief, conception, conjecture, conventional wisdom, doxy, estimation, feeling, idea, idée reçue, impression, judgement, mind, notion, perception, persuasion, point of view, sentiment, stance, tenet, theory, view, voice, vox pop, vox populi.

**opinionated** *adj* adamant, biased, bigoted, bull-headed, cocksure, dictatorial, doctrinaire, dogmatic, high-dried, inflexible, obdurate, obstinate, overbearing, partisan, pig-headed, prejudiced, self-assertive, single-minded, stubborn, uncompromising, wilful.

*antonym* open-minded.

**opponent** *n* adversary, antagonist, challenger, competitor, contestant, disputant, dissentient, dissident, enemy, foe, objector, opposer, opposition, rival.

*antonyms* ally, proponent.

**opportune** *adj* advantageous, appropriate, apt, auspicious, convenient, favourable, felicitous, fit, fitting, fortunate, good, happy, lucky, pertinent, proper, propitious, seasonable, suitable, timely, well-timed.

*antonym* inopportune.

**opportunism** *n* adventurism, expediency, exploitation, Machiavellianism, making hay while the sun shines, pragmatism, realism, Realpolitik, taking advantage, trimming, unscrupulousness.

**opportunity** *n* break, chance, convenience, hour, moment, occasion, opening, scope, shot, time, turn.

**oppose** *v* bar, beard, breast, check, combat, compare, confront, contradict, contrary, contrast, contravene, controvert, counter, counterattack, counterbalance, defy, face, fight, fly in the face of, gainsay, hinder, obstruct, pit against, play off, prevent, recalcitrate, resist, stand up to, take a stand against, take issue with, thwart, withstand.

*antonyms* favour, support.

**opposed** *adj* against, agin, antagonistic, anti, antipathetic, antithetical, clashing, conflicting, contrary, contrasted, dissentient, hostile, in opposition, incompatible, inimical, opposing, opposite.

*antonym* in favour.

**opposing** *adj* antagonistic, antipathetic, clashing, combatant, conflicting, contentious, contrary, disputatious, enemy, hostile, incompatible, irreconcilable, opposed, opposite, oppugnant, rival, warring.

**opposite** *adj* adverse, antagonistic, antipodal, antipodean, antithetical, conflicting, contradictory, contrary, contrasted, corresponding, different, differing, diverse, facing, fronting, hostile, inconsistent, inimical, irreconcilable, opposed, reverse, unlike.

*antonym* same.

*n* antipode(s), antipole, antithesis, contradiction, contrary, converse, inverse, reverse.

*antonym* same.

**opposition** *n* antagonism, antagonist, clash, colluctation, competition, contraposition, contrariety, counteraction, counter-stand, counter-time, counter-view, disapproval, foe, hostility, obstruction, obstructiveness, opponent, other side, polarity, prevention, resistance, rival, syzygy, unfriendliness.

*antonyms* co-operation, support.

**oppress** *v* abuse, afflict, burden, crush, depress, dispirit, harass, harry, lie hard on, lie heavy on, maltreat, overpower, overwhelm, persecute, sadden, subdue, subjugate, suppress, torment, trample, tyrannise, vex, weigh heavy.

**oppressed** *adj* abused, browbeaten, burdened, disadvantaged, downtrodden, enslaved, harassed, henpecked, maltreated, misused, persecuted, prostrate, slave, subject, subjugated, troubled, tyrannised, underprivileged.

*antonym* free.

**oppression** *n* abuse, brutality, calamity, cruelty, hardship, harshness, injury, injustice, jackboot, liberticide, maltreatment, misery, persecution, severity, subjection, suffering, tyranny.

**oppressive** *adj* airless, brutal, burdensome, close, cruel, despotic, grinding, harsh, heavy, inhuman, intolerable, muggy, onerous, overbearing, overpowering, overwhelming, repressive, severe, stifling, stuffy, suffocating, sultry, torrid, tyrannical, unendurable, unjust.

*antonym* gentle.

**oppressor** *n* autocrat, bully, coercionist, despot, dictator, harrier, intimidator, liberticide, persecutor, scourge, slave-driver, taskmaster, tormentor, tyrant.

**opprobrious** *adj* abusive, calumniatory, calumnious, contemptuous, contumelious, damaging, defamatory, derogatory, dyslogistic, insolent, insulting, invective, offensive, scandalous, scurrilous, vitriolic, vituperative.

**opprobrium** *n* calumny, censure, contumely, debasement, degradation, discredit, disfavour, disgrace, dishonour, disrepute, ignominy, infamy, obloquy, odium, reproach, scurrility, shame, slur, stigma.

**opt** *v* choose, decide (on), elect, go for, plump for, prefer, select, single out.

**optimistic** *adj* assured, bright, bullish, buoyant, cheerful, confident, encouraged, expectant, heartened, hopeful, idealistic, Panglossian, Panglossic, pollyann(a)ish, positive, sanguine, upbeat, Utopian.

*antonym* pessimistic.

**optimum** *adj* A1, best, choicest, highest, ideal, optimal, peak, perfect, superlative, top.

*antonym* worst.

*n* best, peak, zenith.

**option** *n* alternative, choice, election, possibility, preference, selection.

**optional** *adj* discretionary, elective, extra, open, possible, unforced, voluntary.

*antonym* compulsory.

**opulence** *n* abundance, affluence, copiousness, cornucopia, easy street, fortune, fullness, lavishness, luxuriance, luxury, plenty, pleroma, profusion, prosperity, riches, richness, sumptuousness, superabundance, wealth.

*antonyms* penury, poverty.

**opulent** *adj* abundant, affluent, copious, lavish, luxuriant, luxurious, moneyed, plentiful, profuse, prolific, prosperous, rich, sumptuous, superabundant, wealthy, well-heeled, well-off, well-to-do.

*antonyms* penurious, poor.

**opus** *n* brainchild, composition, creation, lucubration, oeuvre, piece, production, work.

**oracle** *n* adviser, answer, augur, augury, authority, divination, guru, high priest, mastermind, mentor, prediction, prognostication, prophecy, prophet, pundit, python, revelation, sage, seer, sibyl, soothsayer, vision, wizard.

**oracular** *adj* ambiguous, arcane, auspicious, authoritative, cryptic, Delphic, dictatorial, dogmatic, equivocal, grave, haruspical, mantic, mysterious, obscure, ominous, portentous, positive, predictive, prescient, prognostic, prophetic, pythonic, sage, sibylline, significant, two-edged, vatic, vaticinal, venerable, wise.

**oral** *adj* acroamatic(al), spoken, unwritten, verbal, vocal.

*antonym* written.

**orate** *v* declaim, discourse, harangue, hold forth, pontificate, sermonise, speak, speechify, talk.

**oration** *n* address, declamation, discourse, éloge, harangue, homily, lecture, sermon, speech, spiel.

**orator** *n* declaimer, demagogue, lecturer, phrasemaker, phraseman, phrasemonger, phraser, public speaker, rhetorician, speaker, spellbinder, spieler.

**oratorical** *adj* bombastic, Ciceronian, declamatory, Demosthenic, elocutionary, eloquent, grandiloquent, high-flown, magniloquent, rhetorical, silver-tongued, smooth-tongued, sonorous.

**oratory** *n* declamation, diction, elocution, eloquence, grandiloquence, public speaking, rhetoric, speech, speechifying, speech-making.

**orb** *n* ball, circle, globe, globule, mound, ring, round, sphere, spherule.

**orbit** *n* ambit, circle, circumgyration, circumvolution, compass, course, cycle, domain, ellipse, influence, path, range, reach, revolution, rotation, scope, sphere, sphere of influence, sweep, track, trajectory.

*v* circle, circumnavigate, circumvolve, encircle, revolve.

**orchestrate** *v* arrange, compose, concert, co-ordinate, fix, integrate, organise, prepare, present, score, stage-manage.

**ordain** *v* anoint, appoint, call, consecrate, decree, destine, dictate, elect, enact, enjoin, fate, fix, foredoom, foreordain, frock, instruct, intend, invest, lay down, legislate, nominate, order, predestine, predetermine, prescribe, pronounce, require, rule, set, will.

**ordeal** *n* affliction, agony, anguish, nightmare, pain, persecution, suffering, test, torture, trial, tribulation(s), trouble(s).

**order¹** *n* application, arrangement, array, behest, booking, calm, categorisation, chit, classification, codification, command, commission, control, cosmos, decree, dictate, diktat, direction, directive, discipline, disposal, disposition, eutaxy, grouping, harmony, injunction, instruction, law, law and order, layout, line, line-up, mandate, method, neatness, ordering, orderliness, ordinance, organisation, pattern, peace, placement, plan, precept, progression, propriety, quiet, regularity, regulation, request, requisition, reservation, rule, sequence, series, stipulation, structure, succession, symmetry, system, tidiness, tranquillity.

*antonym* disorder.

*v* adjure, adjust, align, arrange, authorise, bid, book, catalogue, charge, class, classify, command, conduct, control, decree, direct, dispose, enact, engage, enjoin, group, instruct, lay out, manage, marshal, neaten, ordain, organise, prescribe, put to rights, regulate, request, require, reserve, sort out, systematise, tabulate, tidy.

*antonym* disorder.

**order²** *n* association, breed, brotherhood, cast, caste, class, community, company, degree, family, fraternity, genre, genus, grade, guild, hierarchy, ilk, kind, league, lodge, organisation, pecking order, phylum, position, rank, sect, sisterhood, society, sodality, sort, species, status, subclass, tribe, type, union.

**orderly** *adj* businesslike, controlled, cosmic, decorous, disciplined, in order, law-abiding, methodical, neat, non-violent, peaceable, quiet, regular, restrained, ruly, scientific, shipshape,

**ordinance**

systematic, systematised, tidy, trim, well-behaved, well-organised, well-regulated.

*antonym* disorderly.

**ordinance** *n* canon, ceremony, command, decree, dictum, directive, edict, enactment, fiat, injunction, institution, law, observance, order, practice, precept, prescript, regulation, rite, ritual, rule, ruling, sacrament, statute, usage.

**ordinarily** *adv* as a rule, commonly, conventionally, customarily, familiarly, generally, habitually, in general, normally, usually.

**ordinary** *adj* accustomed, average, common, common-or-garden, commonplace, conventional, customary, established, everyday, fair, familiar, habitual, homespun, household, humble, humdrum, inconsequential, indifferent, inferior, mean, mediocre, modest, normal, pedestrian, plain, prevailing, prosaic, quotidian, regular, routine, run-of-the-mill, settled, simple, standard, stock, typical, undistinguished, unexceptional, unmemorable, unpretentious, unremarkable, usual, wonted, workaday.

*antonyms* extraordinary, special, unusual.

**ordnance** *n* arms, artillery, big guns, cannon, guns, matériel, missil(e)ry, munitions, weapons.

**ordure** *n* dirt, dung, excrement, filth.

**organ** *n* agency, channel, device, element, forum, harmonium, hurdy-gurdy, implement, instrument, journal, kist of whistles, means, medium, member, mouthpiece, newspaper, paper, part, periodical, process, publication, structure, tool, unit, vehicle, viscus, voice.

**organic** *adj* anatomical, animate, biological, biotic, constitutional, formal, fundamental, inherent, innate, integral, integrated, live, living, methodical, natural, ordered, organised, structural, structured, systematic, systematised.

**organisation** *n* arrangement, assembling, assembly, association, body, business, chemistry, combine, company, composition, concern, confederation, configuration, conformation, consortium, constitution, construction, co-ordination, corporation, design, disposal, federation, firm, format, formation, formulation, framework, group, grouping, institution, league, make-up, management, method, methodology, organism, outfit, pattern, plan, planning, regulation, running, standardisation, structure, structuring, syndicate, system, unity, whole.

*antonym* disorganisation.

**organise** *v* arrange, catalogue, classify, codify, constitute, construct, co-ordinate, dispose, establish, form, frame, group, marshal, pigeonhole, regiment, run, see to, set up, shape, structure, systematise, tabulate.

*antonym* disorganise.

**organised** *adj* arranged, neat, orderly, planned.

*antonym* disorganised.

**organism** *n* animal, being, body, cell, creature, entity, living thing, structure.

**orgy** *n* bacchanal, bacchanalia, binge, bout, carousal, debauch, excess, indulgence, love-in, overindulgence, revel, revelry, saturnalia, splurge, spree, surfeit.

**orient** *v* acclimatise, accommodate, adapt, adjust, align, familiarise, get one's bearings, habituate, orientate.

**orientation** *n* acclimatisation, adaptation, adjustment, assimilation, attunement, bearings, collimation, co-ordination, direction, familiarisation, introduction, location, position, sense of direction, settling in.

**orifice** *n* aperture, cleft, hole, inlet, mouth, opening, perforation, pore, rent, slit, vent.

**origin** *n* ancestry, base, basis, beginning, beginnings, birth, cause, commencement, creation, dawning, derivation, descent, emergence, etymology, etymon, extraction, family, fons et origo, font, foundation, fountain, fountain-head, genesis, heritage, inauguration, inception, incunabula, launch, lineage, occasion, origination, outset, parentage, paternity, pedigree, provenance, root, roots, source, spring, start, stirps, stock, well-spring.

*antonyms* end, termination.

**original** *adj* aboriginal, archetypal, authentic, autochthonous, commencing, creative, earliest, early, embryonic, fertile, first, first-hand, fresh, genuine, imaginative, infant, ingenious, initial, innovative, innovatory, introductory, inventive, master, new, novel, opening, primal, primary, primigenial, primitical, primitive, primordial, pristine, prototypical, resourceful, rudimentary, seminal, starting, unborrowed, unconventional, unhackneyed, unprecedented, unusual.

*antonym* unoriginal.

*n* archetype, case, character, cure, eccentric, master, model, nonconformist, oddity, paradigm, pattern, prototype, queer fish, standard, type, weirdo.

**originality** *n* boldness, cleverness, creative spirit, creativeness, creativity, daring, eccentricity, freshness, imagination, imaginativeness, individuality, ingenuity, innovation, innovativeness, inventiveness, newness, novelty, resourcefulness, singularity, unconventionality, unorthodoxy.

**originally** *adv* at first, at the outset, at the start, by birth, by derivation, first, in origin, in the beginning, initially.

**originate** *v* arise, be born, begin, come, commence, conceive, create, derive, develop, discover, emanate, emerge, establish, evolve, flow, form, formulate, generate, give birth to, inaugurate, initiate, institute, introduce, invent, issue, launch, pioneer, proceed, produce, result, rise, set up, spring, start, stem.

*antonyms* end, terminate.

**originator** *n* architect, author, creator, designer, father, founder, generator, innovator, inventor, mother, pioneer, prime mover, the brains.

**ornament** *n* accessory, adornment, bauble, decoration, doodah, embellishment, fallal, fandangle, figgery, flower, frill, furbelow, garnish, gaud, honour, jewel, leading light, pride, treasure, trimming, trinket.

*v* adorn, beautify, bedizen, bespangle, brighten, caparison, deck, decorate, dress up, embellish, festoon, garnish, gild, grace, prettify, prink, trim.

**ornamental** *adj* attractive, beautifying, decorative, embellishing, flashy, for show, grandiose, showy.

**ornamentation** *n* adornment, decoration, elaboration, embellishment, embroidery, fallalery, frills, garniture, ornateness.

**ornate** *adj* arabesque, aureate, baroque, beautiful, bedecked, busy, convoluted, decorated, elaborate, elegant, fancy, florid, flowery, fussy, ornamented, rococo, sumptuous.

*antonyms* austere, plain.

**oro(ro)tund** *adj* dignified, imposing, magniloquent, pompous, pretentious.

**orthodox** *adj* accepted, approved, conformist, conventional, correct, customary, doctrinal, established, kosher, official, received, sound, traditional, true, usual, well-established.

*antonym* unorthodox.

**orthodoxy** *n* authenticity, authoritativeness, authority, conformism, conformity, conventionality, devotion, devoutness, faithfulness, inflexibility, properness, received wisdom, soundness, traditionalism, trueness.

**oscillate** *v* fluctuate, librate, seesaw, sway, swing, vacillate, vary, vibrate, waver, wigwag, yo-yo.

**oscillation** *n* fluctuation, instability, seesawing, shilly-shallying, swing, swinging, vacillation, variation, wavering.

**ossified** *adj* bony, fixed, fossilised, frozen, hardened, indurate(d), inflexible, petrified, rigid, rigidified, solid, stiff.

**ostensible** *adj* alleged, apparent, avowed, exhibited, manifest, outward, plausible, presumed, pretended, professed, purported, put-on, seeming, so-called, specious, superficial, supposed.

**ostensibly** *adv* apparently, professedly, purportedly, reputedly, seemingly, supposedly.

**ostentation** *n* affectation, boasting, display, exhibitionism, flamboyance, flashiness, flaunting, flourish, foppery, pageantry, parade, pomp, pretension, pretentiousness, show, showiness, showing off, swank, tinsel, trappings, vaunting, window-dressing.

*antonym* unpretentiousness.

**ostentatious** *adj* aggressive, boastful, conspicuous, extravagant, fastuous, flamboyant, flash, flashy, garish, gaudy, loud, obtrusive, pretentious, self-advertising, showy, splashy, swanking, swanky, vain, vulgar.

*antonyms* quiet, restrained.

**ostracise** *v* avoid, banish, bar, black, blackball, blacklist, boycott, cast out, cold-shoulder, cut, debar, disfellowship, exclude, excommunicate, exile, expatriate, expel, reject, segregate, send to Coventry, shun, snub.

*antonyms* accept, receive, reinstate, welcome.

**ostracism** *n* avoidance, banishment, boycott, cold-shouldering, disfellowship, exclusion, excommunication, exile, expulsion, isolation, proscription, rejection.

*antonyms* acceptance, reinstatement, welcome.

**other** *adj* added, additional, alternative, auxiliary, contrasting, different, differing, dissimilar, distinct, diverse, extra, fresh, further, more, new, remaining, separate, spare, supplementary, unrelated.

**otherworldly** *adj* absent-minded, bemused, dreamy, ethereal, fey, preoccupied, rapt.

*antonyms* mundane, solid, substantial, worldly.

**ounce** *n* atom, crumb, drop, grain, iota, jot, modicum, morsel, particle, scrap, shred, speck, spot, trace, whit.

**oust** *v* depose, disinherit, dislodge, displace, dispossess, drive out, eject, evict, expel, overthrow, replace, supplant, throw out, topple, turn out, unseat, upstage.

*antonyms* ensconce, install, reinstate, settle.

**out¹** *adj* abroad, absent, away, disclosed, elsewhere, evident, exposed, gone, manifest, not at home, outside, public, revealed.

**out of bounds** banned, barred, disallowed, forbidden, off-limits, prohibited, taboo.

**out of date** antiquated, archaic, behind the times, dated, fogram, horse-and-buggy, moribund, obsolete, old, old hat, old-fashioned, outmoded, passé.

*antonyms* fashionable, modern, new.

**out of doors** alfresco, en plein air, out, outdoors, outside.

*antonym* indoors.

**out of focus** blurred, blurry, fuzzy, hazy, ill-defined, indistinct, muzzy.

*antonyms* clear, sharp.

**out of order** broken, broken down, burst, conked out, gone phut, haywire, in disrepair, inoperative, kaput, non-functional, on the blink, out of commission.

*antonym* serviceable.

**out of place** disarranged, in disorder, inappropriate, malapropos, tactless, topsy-turvy, unbecoming, unfitting, unseemly, unsuitable.

*antonyms* appropriate, apropos.

**out of sorts** below par, depressed, down in the dumps, down in the mouth, fed up, gloomy, ill, moody, mops and brooms, off-colour, peelie-wally, poorly, sick, under the weather.

*antonyms* cheerful, well.

**out of the blue** all of a sudden, suddenly, unexpectedly.

**out of the wood(s)** home and dry, in the clear, on dry land, out of danger, out of difficulty, safe, safe and sound, secure.

*antonyms* insecure, vulnerable.

**out of this world** excellent, fabulous, fantastic, great, incredible, indescribable, marvellous, phenomenal, remarkable, superb, unbelievable, wonderful.

*antonyms* mundane, ordinary.

**out of work** idle, jobless, laid off, on the dole, redundant, unemployed, workless.

*antonyms* busy, employed, occupied.

**out²** *adj* antiquated, banned, blacked, dated, dead, démodé, disallowed, ended, excluded, exhausted, expired, extinguished, finished, forbidden, impossible, not on, old hat, old-fashioned, out of date, passé, square, taboo, unacceptable, unfashionable, used up.

*antonyms* acceptable, fashionable, in.

**out-and-out** *adj* absolute, arrant, complete, consummate, downright, dyed-in-the-wool, inveterate, outright, perfect, thoroughgoing, total, uncompromising, unmitigated, unqualified, utter, whole-hog.

**outbreak** *n* burst, ebullition, epidemic, eruption, excrescence, explosion, flare-up, flash, outburst, pompholyx, rash, spasm, upsurge.

**outburst** *n* access, attack, boutade, discharge, eruption, explosion, fit, fit of temper, flare-up, gale, gush, outbreak, outpouring, paroxysm, seizure, spasm, storm, surge, volley.

**outcast** *n* abject, castaway, derelict, exile, leper, outsider, pariah, persona non grata, refugee, reject, reprobate, unperson, untouchable, vagabond, wretch.

*antonyms* favourite, idol.

**outclass** *v* beat, eclipse, excel over, leave standing, outdistance, outdo, outrank, outrival, outshine, outstrip, overshadow, put in the shade, surpass, top, transcend.

**outcome** *n* after-effect, aftermath, conclusion, consequence, effect, end, end result, harvest, issue, pay-off, result, sequel, upshot.

**outcry** *n* clamour, commotion, complaint, cry, exclamation, flap, howl, hue and cry, hullaballoo, noise, outburst, protest, row, scream, screech, uproar, vociferation, yell.

**outdated** *adj* antediluvian, antiquated, antique, archaic, behind the times, dated, démodé, fogram, obsolescent, obsolete, old-fashioned, out of date, out of style, outmoded, passé, square, unfashionable, unmodish.

*antonyms* fashionable, modern, modish.

**outdistance** *v* leave behind, leave standing, outpace, outrun, outstrip, overhaul, overtake, pass, pull ahead of, shake off, surpass.

**outdo** *v* beat, best, eclipse, excel over, get the better of, outclass, outdistance, outfox, out-Herod, outmanoeuvre, outshine, outsmart, outstrip, outwit, overcome, surpass, top, transcend.

**outdoor** *adj* alfresco, extraforaneous, open-air, out-of-door(s), outside.

*antonym* indoor.

**outer** *adj* distal, distant, exterior, external, further, outlying, outside, outward, peripheral, remote, superficial, surface.

*antonyms* central, inner, mesial, proximal.

**outface** *v* beard, brave, brazen out, confront, defy, outstare, stare down.

*antonyms* capitulate, succumb.

**outfit¹** *n* accoutrements, clothes, costume, ensemble, equipage, equipment, garb, gear, get-up, kit, paraphernalia, rig, rig-out, set-out, suit, togs, trappings, turn-out.

*v* accoutre, apparel, appoint, attire, equip, fit out, fit up, furnish, kit out, provision, stock, supply, turn out.

**outfit²** *n* business, clan, clique, company, corps, coterie, crew, firm, galère, gang, group, organisation, set, set-out, set-up, squad, team, unit.

**outfitter** *n* clothier, costumer, costumier, couturier, couturière, dressmaker, haberdasher, modiste, sartor, tailor.

**outflow** *n* debouchment, discharge, disemboguement, drainage, ebb, effluence, effluent, effluvium, efflux, effluxion, effusion, emanation, emergence, gush, jet, outfall, outpouring, rush, spout.

**outflowing** *adj* debouching, discharging, effluent, emanant, gushing, leaking, rushing, spurting.

**outgoing** *adj* affable, approachable, chatty, communicative, cordial, demonstrative, departing, easy, ex-, expansive, extrovert, former, friendly, genial, gregarious, informal, last, open, past, retiring, sociable, sympathetic, unreserved, warm, withdrawing.

*antonyms* incoming, introvert, new, unsociable.

**outgoings** *n* costs, disbursal, disbursement, expenditure, expenses, outlay, overheads, spending.

*antonym* income.

**outgrowth** *n* consequence, effect, emanation, excrescence, offshoot, product, protuberance, shoot, sprout, swelling.

**outing** *n* excursion, expedition, jaunt, picnic, pleasure trip, ramble, spin, trip, wayzgoose.

**outlandish** *adj* alien, barbarous, bizarre, eccentric, exotic, extraordinary, fantastic, foreign, grotesque, odd, outré, preposterous, queer, strange, unheard-of, weird.

*antonyms* familiar, ordinary.

**outlandishness** *n* bizarreness, eccentricity, exoticness, grotesqueness, oddness, peregrinity, queerness, strangeness, weirdness.

*antonyms* commonplaceness, familiarity.

**outlast** *v* come through, outlive, outstay, ride, survive, weather.

**outlaw** *n* bandit, brigand, bushranger, cateran, dacoit, desperado, freebooter, fugitive, highwayman, klepht, marauder, outcast, outsider, pariah, proscript, robber.

*v* ban, banish, bar, condemn, debar, decitizenise, disallow, embargo, exclude, excommunicate, forbid, illegalise, illegitimate, interdict, prohibit, proscribe, waive.

*antonyms* allow, legalise.

**outlawed** *adj* banished, banned, condemned, disallowed, embargoed, excommunicated, hors la loi, proscribed.

**outlay** *n* cost, disbursal, disbursement, expenditure, expenses, investment, outgoings, payment, price.

*antonym* income.

**outlet** *n* avenue, channel, débouché, debouchment, duct, egress, emissary, exit, femerall, market, opening, orifice, outfall, release, safety valve, vent, way out.

*antonyms* entry, inlet.

**outline** *n* bare facts, configuration, contorno, contour, croquis, delineation, draft, drawing, figure, form, frame, framework, lay-out, lineament(s), plan, profile, recapitulation, résumé, rough, run-down, scenario, schema, shape, silhouette, skeleton, sketch, summary, synopsis, thumbnail sketch, tracing.

*v* adumbrate, delineate, draft, plan, recapitulate, rough out, sketch, summarise, trace.

**outlive** *v* come through, live through, outlast, survive, weather.

*antonym* predecease.

**outlook** *n* angle, aspect, attitude, expectations, forecast, frame of mind, future, look-out, panorama, perspective, point of view, prognosis, prospect, scene, slant, standpoint, vantage-point, view, viewpoint, views, vista.

**outlying** *adj* distant, far-away, far-flung, far-off, forane, further, outer, outlandish, peripheral, provincial, remote.

*antonyms* central, inner.

**outmanoeuvre** *v* beat, circumvent, get the better of, outdo, outflank, outfox, outgeneral, outsmart, outthink, outwit, put the dead wood on.

**outmoded** *adj* anachronistic, antediluvian, antiquated, antique, archaic, behind the times, bygone, dated, démodé, fogram, fossilised, horse-and-buggy, obsolescent, obsolete, olden, old-fashioned, old-fogeyish, out of date, outworn, passé, square, superannuated, superseded, unfashionable, unmodish, unusable.

*antonyms* fashionable, fresh, modern, modish, new.

**out-of-the-way** *adj* abnormal, abstruse, curious, distant, exceptional, extraordinary, far-away, far-flung, far-off, inaccessible, isolated, little-known, lonely, obscure, odd, outlandish, outlying, peculiar, remote, secluded, strange, uncommon, unfamiliar, unfrequented, unget-at-able, unusual.

**outpace** *v* beat, outdistance, outdo, outrun, outstrip, overhaul, overtake, pass, surpass.

**outpouring** *n* cascade, debouchment, débouchure, deluge, disemboguement, effluence, efflux, effusion, emanation, flow, flux, logorrhoea, outflow, spate, spurt, stream, torrent, word salad.

**output** *n* achievement, manufacture, outturn, print-out, product, production, productivity, read-out, yield.

*antonyms* input, outlay.

**outrage** *n* hurt, abuse, affront, anger, atrocity, barbarism, crime, desecration, disgrace, enormity, evil, fury, grand guignol, horror, indignation, indignity, inhumanity, injury, insult, offence, profanation, rape, ravishing, resentment, scandal, shock, violation, violence, wrath.

*v* abuse, affront, astound, defile, desecrate, disgust, épater le bourgeois, incense, infuriate, injure, insult, madden, make someone's blood boil, maltreat, offend, rape, ravage, ravish, repel, scandalise, shock, violate.

**outrageous** *adj* abominable, atrocious, barbaric, beastly, disgraceful, egregious, excessive, exorbitant, extortionate, extravagant, flagrant, godless, heinous, horrible, immoderate, infamous, inhuman, iniquitous, inordinate, monstrous, nefarious, offensive, preposterous, scandalous, shocking, steep, turbulent, unconscionable, ungodly, unholy, unreasonable, unspeakable, villainous, violent, wicked.

*antonyms* acceptable, irreproachable.

**outrider** *n* advance guard, attendant, bodyguard, escort, guard, harbinger, herald, precursor, scout, squire, vanguard.

**outright** *adj* absolute, arrant, categorical, complete, consummate, definite, direct, downright, flat, out-and-out, perfect, point-blank, pure, straightforward, thorough, thoroughgoing, total, uncompromising, unconditional, undeniable, unequivocal, unmitigated, unqualified, utter, wholesale.

*antonyms* ambiguous, indefinite, provisional.

*adv* absolutely, at once, cleanly, completely, directly, explicitly, immediately, instantaneously, instantly, on the spot, openly, positively, straight away, straightaway, straightforwardly, there and then, thoroughly, unhesitatingly, without restraint.

**outrun** *v* beat, exceed, excel, leave behind, lose, outdistance, outdo, outpace, outstrip, overhaul, overtake, pass, shake off, surpass.

**outset** *n* beginning, commencement, early days, forthgoing, inauguration, inception, kick-off, opening, start.

*antonyms* conclusion, end, finish.

**outshine** *v* beat, best, dwarf, eclipse, excel, outclass, outdo, outrank, outstrip, overshadow, put in the shade, surpass, top, transcend, upstage.

**outside**[1] *adj* exterior, external, extraforaneous, extramural, extraneous, extreme, outdoor, outer, outermost, outward, superficial, surface.

*antonym* inside.

*n* cover, exterior, façade, face, front, skin, superficies, surface, topside.

*antonym* inside.

*prep* furth, outwith, without.

**outside**[2] *adj* distant, faint, infinitesimal, marginal, minute, negligible, remote, slight, slim, small, unlikely.

*antonyms* likely, real, substantial.

**outsider** *n* alien, foreigner, immigrant, incomer, interloper, intruder, layman, misfit, newcomer, non-member, non-resident, observer, odd man out, outcast, outlander, outlier, settler, stranger.

*antonyms* inhabitant, insider, local, member, native, resident, specialist.

**outskirts** *n* borders, boundary, edge, environs, faubourgs, fringes, margin, periphery, purlieus, suburbia, suburbs, vicinity.

*antonyms* centre, city-centre.

**outsmart** *v* beat, best, deceive, dupe, get the better of, outfox, outmanoeuvre, outperform, out-think, outwit, trick.

**outspoken** *adj* abrupt, blunt, candid, direct, explicit, forthright, frank, free, open, plain-spoken, pointed, Rabelaisian, rude, sharp, trenchant, unceremonious, unequivocal, unreserved.

*antonyms* diplomatic, tactful.

**outspread** *adj* expanded, extended, fanned out, flared, open, opened, outstretched, spread out, stretched, unfolded, unfurled, wide, wide-open.

**outstanding**[1] *adj* ace, arresting, celebrated, conspicuous, distinguished, egregious, eminent, excellent, exceptional, extraordinary, eye-catching, great, important, impressive, marked, memorable, notable, noteworthy, pre-eminent, prominent, prosilient, remarkable, salient, signal, singular, special, striking, superior, superlative, surpassing.

*antonyms* ordinary, unexceptional.

**outstanding**[2] *adj* due, left, ongoing, open, over, owing, payable, pending, remaining, uncollected, undone, unpaid, unresolved, unsettled.

**outstrip** *v* beat, best, better, eclipse, exceed, excel, gain on, leave behind, leave standing, outclass, outdistance, outdo, outpace, outperform, outrun, outshine, overhaul, overtake, pass, surpass, top, transcend.

**outward** *adj* alleged, apparent, avowed, evident, exterior, external, noticeable, observable, obvious, ostensible, outer, outside, professed, public, superficial, supposed, surface, visible.

*antonyms* inner, private.

**outwardly** *adv* apparently, at first sight, evidently, externally, in appearance, officially, on the surface, ostensibly, seemingly, superficially, supposedly, to all appearances, to the eye.

*antonyms* internally, inwardly, privately.

**outweigh** *v* cancel out, compensate for, eclipse, make up for, outbalance, overcome, override, overrule, predominate, preponderate, prevail over, take precedence over, tip the scales in favour of, transcend.

**outwit** *v* beat, best, better, cheat, circumvent, deceive, defraud, dupe, get the better of, gull, make a monkey of, outfox, outmanoeuvre, outsmart, outthink, swindle, trick.

**outworn** *adj* abandoned, antiquated, clichéd, defunct, discredited, disused, exhausted, fogeyish, fogram, hackneyed, horse-and-buggy, moth-eaten, obsolete, out of date, outdated, outmoded, overused, rejected, stale, superannuated, threadbare, tired, trite, worn-out.

*antonyms* fresh, new.

**oval** *adj* egg-shaped, ellipsoidal, elliptical, lens-shaped, lenticular, lentiform, lentoid, obovate, obovoid, ovate, oviform, ovoid, ovoidal, vulviform.

**ovation** *n* acclaim, acclamation, applause, bravos, cheering, cheers, clapping, éclat, laudation, plaudits, praises, tribute.

*antonyms* abuse, boos, catcalls, mockery.

**over**[1] *adj* accomplished, bygone, closed, completed, concluded, done with, ended, finished, forgotten, gone, in the past, past, settled, up.

**over**[2] *prep* above, exceeding, in charge of, in command of, in excess of, more than, on, on top of, superior to, upon.

*adv* above, aloft, beyond, extra, in addition, in excess, left, on high, overhead, remaining, superfluous, surplus, unclaimed, unused, unwanted.

**over and above** added to, along with, as well as, besides, in addition to, let alone, not to mention, on top of, plus, together with.

**over and over (again)** ad infinitum, ad nauseam, again and again, continually, endlessly, frequently, often, repeatedly, seventy times seven, time and (time) again.

**over the top** a bit much, excessive, histrionic, immoderate, inordinate, overdone, too much, uncalled-for.

**overabundance** *n* embarras de choix, embarras de richesse, excess, glut, oversupply, plethora, profusion, superabundance, superfluity, surfeit, surplus, too much of a good thing.

*antonyms* dearth, lack.

**overact** *v* emote, exaggerate, ham, ham up, overdo, overplay.

*antonyms* underact, underplay.

**overall** *adj* all-embracing, all-inclusive, all-over, blanket, broad, complete, comprehensive, general, global, inclusive, total, umbrella.

*antonyms* narrow, short-term.

*adv* by and large, generally speaking, in general, in the long term, on the whole.

**overalls** *n* boiler-suit, coverall, dungarees, work-wear.

**overawe** *v* abash, alarm, awe, browbeat, cow, daunt, disconcert, dismay, frighten, intimidate, petrify, scare, terrify, unnerve.

*antonym* reassure.

**overbalance** *v* capsize, fall over, keel over, lose (one's) balance, lose one's footing, overset, overturn, slip, tip over, topple over, trip, tumble, turn turtle, upset.

**overbearing** *adj* arrogant, autocratic, bossy, cavalier, despotic, dictatorial, dogmatic, domineering, haughty, high and mighty, high-handed, imperious, lordly, magisterial, officious, oppressive, overweening, peremptory, pompous, supercilious, superior, tyrannical.

*antonyms* modest, unassertive, unassuming.

**overcast** *adj* black, clouded, clouded over, cloudy, dark, darkened, dismal, dreary, dull, grey, hazy, leaden, lowering, murky, sombre, sunless, threatening.

*antonyms* bright, clear, sunny.

**overcharge** *v* cheat, diddle, do, extort, fleece, mulct, rip off, rook, short-change, sting, surcharge.

*antonym* undercharge.

**overcome** *v* beat, best, better, conquer, crush, defeat, expugn, lick, master, overpower, overthrow, overwhelm, prevail, rise above, subdue, subjugate, surmount, survive, triumph over, vanquish, weather, worst.

*adj* affected, beaten, bowled over, broken, defeated, exhausted, overpowered, overwhelmed, speechless, swept off one's feet.

**over-confident** *adj* arrogant, brash, cocksure, cocky, foolhardy, hubristic, incautious, over-optimistic, overweening, presumptuous, rash, sanguine, temerarious, uppish.

*antonyms* cautious, diffident.

**overcritical** *adj* captious, carping, cavilling, fault-finding, hair-splitting, hard to please, hypercritical, nit-picking, over-nice, overparticular, pedantic, pernickety, purist, ultracrepidarian, Zoilean.

*antonyms* easygoing, tolerant, uncritical.

**overcrowded** *adj* chock-a-block, chock-full, choked, congested, crammed full, hotching, jam-packed, overloaded, overpopulated, packed, packed out, seething, swarming.

*antonyms* deserted, empty.

**overdo** *v* do to death, exaggerate, gild the lily, go to extremes, go too far, labour, lay it on thick, overact, overexert, overindulge, overplay, overreach, overstate, overtax, overuse, overwork.

*antonyms* neglect, underuse.

**overdone** *adj* burnt, burnt to a cinder, charred, dried up, effusive, exaggerated, excessive, fulsome, histrionic, immoderate, inordinate, over the top, overcooked, overelaborate, overplayed, overstated, percoct, preposterous, spoiled, supererogatory, undue, unnecessary.

*antonyms* raw, underdone, underplayed, understated.

**overdue** *adj* behind schedule, behindhand, belated, delayed, late, owing, slow, tardy, unpunctual.

*antonym* early.

**overeat** *v* binge, eat like a horse, gluttonise, gorge, gormandise, guzzle, make a pig of oneself, overindulge, pack away, stuff, stuff oneself.

*antonyms* abstain, starve.

**overeating** *n* bingeing, bulimia, gluttony, gormandise, gormandism, gourmandise, gourmandism, guzzling, hyperphagia, overindulgence.

*antonyms* abstemiousness, abstention.

**overemphasise** *v* belabour, exaggerate, labour, overdramatise, overstress.

*antonyms* belittle, minimise, underplay, understate.

**overexert oneself** break a leg, burn the candle at both ends, drive oneself too hard, fatigue, knock oneself out, overdo it, overstrain oneself, overtax oneself, overtire oneself, overwork, push oneself too hard, strain oneself, wear oneself out, work oneself to death.

*antonyms* idle, laze.

**overflow** *v* brim over, bubble over, cover, deluge, discharge, drown, flood, inundate, pour over, shower, soak, spill, spray, submerge, surge, swamp, well over.

*n* flood, inundation, overabundance, overspill, spill, superfluity, surplus.

**overflowing** *adj* abounding, bountiful, brimful, copious, inundant, plenteous, plentiful, profuse, rife, superabundant, swarming, teeming, thronged.

*antonyms* lacking, scarce.

**overgrowth** *n* escalation, hypertrophy, overabundance, overdevelopment, superabundance.

*antonyms* decline, failure, shrinkage, wasting.

**overhang** *v* beetle, bulge, extend, impend, jut, loom, menace, project, protrude, stick out, threaten.

**overhanging** *adj* beetling, jutting, pensile, projecting, protruding.

**overhaul**[1] *v* check, do up, examine, fix, inspect, mend, recondition, re-examine, repair, restore, service, survey.

*n* check, check-up, examination, going-over, inspection, reconditioning, repair, restoration, service.

**overhaul**[2] *v* gain on, outpace, outstrip, overtake, pass, pull ahead of.

**overhead** *adv* above, aloft, on high, up above, upward.

*antonyms* below, underfoot.

*adj* aerial, elevated, overhanging, roof, upper.

*antonyms* floor, ground, underground.

**overheads** *n* burden, expenses, oncost, operating costs, outgoings, running costs.

*antonyms* income, profit.

**overheated** *adj* agitated, excited, fiery, flaming, impassioned, inflamed, overexcited, overwrought, passionate, roused.

*antonyms* calm, cool, dispassionate, impassive.

**overheating** *n* heatstroke, hyperpyrexia, hyperthermia, sunstroke.

*antonyms* chill, hypothermia.

**overindulge** *v* binge, booze, debauch, gluttonise, gorge, gormandise, guzzle.

*antonym* abstain.

**overindulgence** *n* binge, debauch, excess, immoderation, intemperance, overeating, surfeit.

*antonyms* abstemiousness, abstention.

**overjoyed** *adj* delighted, delirious, ecstatic, elated, enraptured, euphoric, in raptures, joyful, jubilant, on cloud nine, over the moon, rapturous, thrilled, tickled pink, transported.

*antonyms* disappointed, sad.

**overlap** *v* coincide, cover, flap over, imbricate, overlay, overlie, shingle.

**overlapping** *adj* coinciding, covering, imbricated, layered, limbous, overlying, shingled.

**overload** *v* burden, encumber, oppress, overburden, overcharge, overtax, saddle, strain, surcharge, tax, weigh down.

**overlook**[1] *v* condone, disregard, excuse, forget, forgive, ignore, let pass, let ride, miss, neglect, omit, pardon, pass, pass over, skip, slight, turn a blind eye to, wink at.

*antonyms* animadvert, note, notice, penalise, record, remember.

**overlook**[2] *v* command a view of, face, front on to, give upon, look on to.

**overlooked** *adj* unconsidered, unheeded, unhonoured, unnoted, unprized, unregarded, unremarked, unvalued.

*antonyms* appreciated, prized, sought-after, valued.

**overly** *adv* exceedingly, excessively, immoderately, inordinately, over, too, unduly, unreasonably.

*antonyms* inadequately, insufficiently.

**over-nice** *adj* finical, nit-picking, overfastidious, over-meticulous, overparticular, overprecise, overscrupulous, oversensitive, oversubtle, pernickety, rose-water.

*antonyms* casual, uncritical.

**overpower** *v* beat, best, conquer, crush, defeat, floor, immobilise, master, overcome, overthrow, overwhelm, quell, subdue, subjugate, vanquish.

**overpowering** *adj* compelling, convincing, extreme, forceful, insuppressible, invincible, irrefutable, irrepressible, irresistible, nauseating, oppressive, overwhelming, powerful, sickening, strong, suffocating, telling, unbearable, uncontrollable.

**overrate** *v* blow up, magnify, make too much of, overestimate, overpraise, overprize, oversell, overvalue.

*antonym* underrate.

**override** *v* abrogate, annul, cancel, countermand, disregard, ignore, nullify, outweigh, overrule, quash, rescind, reverse, ride roughshod over, set aside, supersede, trample, upset, vanquish.

**overriding** *adj* cardinal, compelling, determining, dominant, essential, final, first, major, number one, overruling, paramount, pivotal, predominant, prevailing, primary, prime, prior, ruling, supreme, ultimate.

*antonyms* insignificant, unimportant.

**overrule** *v* abrogate, annul, cancel, countermand, disallow, invalidate, outvote, override, overturn, recall, repeal, rescind, reverse, revoke, set aside, veto, vote down.

*antonyms* allow, approve.

**overrun**[1] *v* choke, infest, inundate, invade, occupy, overflow, overgrow, overspread, overwhelm, permeate, ravage, run riot, spread over, surge over, swamp, swarm over.

*antonyms* desert, evacuate.

**overrun**[2] *v* exceed, overdo, overshoot, overstep.

**overseas** *adj* exotic, foreign, outland, outlandish, ultramarine.

*antonyms* domestic, home.

*adv* abroad, in/to foreign climes, in/to foreign parts.

*n* foreign climes, foreign parts, outland, outremer.

*antonym* home.

**overseer** *n* boss, chief, foreman, forewoman, gaffer, headman, manager, master, super, superintendent, superior, supervisor, surveyor, workmaster, workmistress.

**overshadow** *v* adumbrate, becloud, bedim, blight, cloud, darken, dim, dominate, dwarf, eclipse, excel, mar, obfuscate, obscure, outshine, outweigh, protect, put in the shade, rise above, ruin, shelter, spoil, surpass, tower above, veil.

**oversight**[1] *n* administration, care, charge, control, custody, direction, guidance, handling, inspection, keeping, management, responsibility, superintendence, supervision, surveillance.

**oversight**[2] *n* blunder, boob, carelessness, delinquency, error, fault, inattention, lapse, laxity, mistake, neglect, omission, slip, slip-up.

**overt** *adj* apparent, avowed, evident, manifest, observable, obvious, open, patent, plain, professed, public, unconcealed, undisguised, visible.

*antonyms* covert, secret.

**overtake** *v* befall, catch up with, come upon, draw level with, engulf, happen, hit, outdistance, outdo, outstrip, overhaul, pass, pull ahead of, strike.

**overthrow** *v* abolish, beat, bring down, conquer, crush, defeat, demolish, depose, destroy, dethrone, displace, knock down, level, master, oust, overcome, overpower, overturn, overwhelm, raze, ruin, subdue, subjugate, subvert, topple, unseat, upset, vanquish.

*antonyms* install, reinstate.

*n* bouleversement, confounding, defeat, deposition, destruction, dethronement, discomfiture, disestablishment, displacement, dispossession, downfall, end, fall, humiliation, labefactation, labefaction, ousting, prostration, rout, ruin, subjugation, subversion, suppression, undoing, unseating.

**overtone** *n* association, connotation, feeling, flavour, hint, implication, innuendo, intimation, nuance, sense, slant, something, suggestion, undercurrent.

**overture** *n* advance, approach, introduction, invitation, motion, move, offer, opening, (opening) gambit, opening move, prelude, proposal, proposition, signal, suggestion, tender.

**overturn** *v* abolish, abrogate, annul, capsize, countermand, depose, destroy, invalidate, keel over, knock down, knock over, overbalance, overset, overthrow, quash, repeal, rescind, reverse, set aside, spill, tip over, topple, tumble, unseat, upend, upset, upturn.

**overused** *adj* bromidic, clichéd, commonplace, hackneyed, platitudinous, played out, stale, stereotyped, threadbare, tired, trite, unoriginal, worn.

*antonyms* fresh, original.

**overweening** *adj* arrogant, cavalier, cocksure, cocky, conceited, egotistical, excessive, extravagant, haughty, high-handed, hubristic, immoderate, inflated, insolent, lordly, opinionated, overblown, pompous, presumptuous, proud, self-confident, supercilious, swollen, uppish, vain, vainglorious.

*antonyms* diffident, unassuming.

**overweight** *adj* ample, bulky, buxom, chubby, chunky, corpulent, fat, flabby, fleshy, gross, heavy, hefty, huge, massive, obese, outsize, plump, podgy, portly, pot-bellied, stout, tubby, well-padded, well-upholstered.

*antonyms* emaciated, skinny, thin, underweight.

**overwhelm** *v* bowl over, bury, confuse, crush, cut to pieces, defeat, deluge, destroy, devastate, engulf, floor, inundate, knock for six, massacre, overcome, overpower, overrun, prostrate, rout, snow under, stagger, submerge, swamp.

**overwhelming** *adj* breathtaking, crushing, devastating, foudroyant, insuppressible, invincible, irrepressible, irresistible, overpowering, shattering, stunning, towering, uncontrollable, vast.

*antonyms* insignificant, negligible, resistible.

**overwork** *v* burden, burn the midnight oil, exhaust, exploit, fatigue, oppress, overburden, overload, overstrain, overtax, overuse, prostrate, strain, sweat, tax, wear out, weary, work one's fingers to the bone.

**overwrought** *adj* agitated, beside oneself, distracted, emotional, excited, frantic, keyed up, on edge, overcharged, overexcited, overheated, overworked, stirred, strung up, tense, uptight, worked up, wound up.

*antonyms* calm, cool, impassive.

**owing** *adj* due, in arrears, outstanding, overdue, owed, payable, unpaid, unsettled.

**owing to** as a result of, because of, imputable to, on account of, thanks to.

**own**[1] *adj* idiosyncratic, individual, inimitable, particular, personal, private.

**own**[2] *v* acknowledge, admit, agree, allow, avow, concede, confess, disclose, enjoy, grant, have, hold, keep, possess, recognise, retain.

**own up** admit, come clean, confess, make a clean breast of it, spill the beans, tell the truth.

**owner** *n* franklin, freeholder, holder, laird, landlady, landlord, lord, master, mistress, possessor, proprietor, proprietress, proprietrix.

**ownership** *n* dominion, freehold, possession, proprietary rights, proprietorship, right of possession, title.

**ox** *n* bison, buffalo, bullock, clod, dolt, gaur, g(a)yal, lout, oaf, steer.

# P

**pace** *n* celerity, clip, gait, lick, measure, momentum, motion, movement, progress, quickness, rapidity, rate, speed, step, stride, tempo, time, tread, velocity, walk.

*v* count, determine, march, mark out, measure, pad, patrol, pound, step, stride, tramp, tread, walk.

**pacific** *adj* appeasing, calm, complaisant, conciliatory, diplomatic, dovelike, dovish, eirenic, equable, friendly, gentle, halcyon, irenic, mild, nonbelligerent, nonviolent, pacificatory, pacifist, peaceable, peaceful, peace-loving, peacemaking, placatory, placid, propitiatory, quiet, serene, smooth, still, tranquil, unruffled.

*antonyms* aggressive, belligerent, contentious, pugnacious.

**pacifism** *n* non-violence, pacificism, passive resistance, satyagraha.

**pacifist** *n* conchie, conscientious objector, dove, pacificist, passive resister, peace-lover, peacemonger, peacenik, satyagrahi.

*antonyms* hawk, warmonger.

**pacify** *v* allay, ameliorate, appease, assuage, calm, chasten, compose, conciliate, crush, humour, lull, moderate, mollify, placate, propitiate, put down, quell, quiet, repress, silence, smooth down, soften, soothe, still, subdue, tame, tranquillise.

*antonyms* aggravate, anger.

**pack** *n* assemblage, back-pack, bale, band, boodle, bunch, bundle, burden, collection, company, crew, crowd, deck, drove, fardel, flock, galère, gang, group, haversack, herd, kit, kitbag, knapsack, load, lot, Matilda, mob, outfit, package, packet, parcel, rucksack, set, troop, truss.

*v* batch, bundle, burden, charge, compact, compress, cram, crowd, empocket, fill, jam, load, mob, package, packet, press, ram, steeve, store, stow, stuff, tamp, throng, thrust, wedge.

**package** *n* agreement, amalgamation, arrangement, bale, box, carton, combination, consignment, container, deal, entity, kit, pack, packet, parcel, proposal, proposition, unit, whole.

*v* batch, box, pack, pack up, packet, parcel, parcel up, wrap, wrap up.

**packed** *adj* brimful, brim-full, chock-a-block, chock-full, congested, cram-full, crammed, crowded, filled, full, hotching, jammed, jam-packed, overflowing, overloaded, seething, swarming.

*antonyms* deserted, empty.

**packet¹** *n* bag, carton, case, container, pack, package, packing, parcel, poke, wrapper, wrapping.

**packet²** *n* a bob or two, bomb, bundle, fortune, king's ransom, lot, lots, mint, pile, pot, pots, pretty penny, small fortune, tidy sum.

**pack-horse** *n* beast of burden, led horse, pack-animal, sumpter, sumpter-horse.

**pact** *n* agreement, alliance, arrangement, bargain, bond, cartel, compact, concord, concordat, contract, convention, covenant, deal, entente, league, protocol, treaty, understanding.

*antonyms* breach, disagreement, quarrel.

**pad¹** *n* block, buffer, cushion, jotter, notepad, pillow, protection, pulvillus, pulvinar, stiffening, stuffing, tablet, wad, writing-pad.

*v* cushion, fill, line, pack, protect, shape, stuff, wrap.

**pad out** amplify, augment, bombast, eke, elaborate, expand, fill out, flesh out, inflate, lengthen, protract, spin out, stretch.

**pad²** *n* foot, footprint, paw, print, sole.

**pad³** *n* apartment, flat, hang-out, home, penthouse, place, quarters, room, rooms.

**pad⁴** *v* lope, move, run, step, tiptoe, tramp, tread, trudge, walk.

**padding** *n* bombast, circumlocution, filling, hot air, packing, perissology, prolixity, stuffing, verbiage, verbosity, wadding, waffle, wordiness.

**paddle¹** *n* oar, scull, sweep.

*v* oar, ply, propel, pull, row, scull, steer.

**paddle²** *v* dabble, plash, slop, splash, stir, trail, wade.

**paddy** *n* bate, fit of temper, fury, paddywhack, passion, pet, rage, taking, tantrum, temper, tiff, wax.

**paean** *n* anthem, dithyramb, doxology, encomium, eulogy, hymn, ovation, panegyric, psalm.

*antonyms* denunciation, satire.

**pagan** *n* atheist, Gentile, heathen, idolater, infidel, nullifidian, polytheist, unbeliever.

*antonym* believer.

*adj* atheistic, Gentile, godless, heathen, heathenish, idolatrous, infidel, irreligious, nullifidian, polytheistic.

**page¹** *n* chapter, episode, epoch, era, event, folio, incident, leaf, period, phase, point, recto, sheet, side, stage, time, verso.

**page²** *n* attendant, bell-boy, bellhop, boy, buttons, cupbearer, footboy, footman, page-boy, servant, squire.

*v* announce, bid, call, call out, preconise, seek, send for, summon.

**pageant** *n* display, extravaganza, masque, parade, play, procession, representation, ritual, scene, show, spectacle, tableau, tableau vivant.

**pageantry** *n* ceremony, display, drama, extravagance, glamour, glitter, grandeur, magnificence, melodrama, ostentation, parade, pomp, show, showiness, spectacle, splash, splendour, state, theatricality.

**pail** *n* bail, bucket, churn, piggin, tub.

**pain** *n* ache, affliction, aggravation, agony, anguish, annoyance, bitterness, bore, bother, burden, cramp, discomfort, distress, dole, dolour, drag, grief, gyp, headache, heartache, heartbreak, hurt, irritation, lancination, misery, nuisance, pang, pest, smart, soreness, spasm, suffering, tenderness, throb, throe, torment, torture, tribulation, trouble, twinge, vexation, woe, wretchedness.

*v* afflict, aggrieve, agonise, annoy, chagrin, cut to the quick, disappont, disquiet, distress, exasperate, gall, grieve, harass, hurt, irritate, nettle, rile, sadden, torment, torture, vex, worry, wound, wring.

*antonyms* gratify, please.

**pained** *adj* aggrieved, chagrined, cut to the quick, cut up, disappointed, distressed, galled, grieved, hurt, injured, miffed, nettled, offended, reproachful, saddened, stung, upset, wounded.

*antonyms* gratified, pleased.

**painful** *adj* aching, achy, afflictive, agonising, arduous, difficult, disagreeable, distasteful, distressing, doloriferous, dolorific, excruciating, grievous, hard, harrowing, laborious, lancinating, saddening, severe, smarting, sore, tedious, tender, troublesome, trying, unpleasant, vexatious.

*antonyms* easy, painless.

**painfully** *adv* alarmingly, clearly, deplorably, distressingly, dreadfully, excessively, markedly, pitiably, pitifully, sadly, unfortunately, woefully, wretchedly.

**painkiller** *n* alleviative, anaesthetic, analgesic, anodyne, drug, lenitive, palliative, paregoric, remedy, sedative.

*antonym* irritant.

**painless** *adj* downhill, easy, effortless, fast, pain-free, plain sailing, quick, simple, trouble-free, undemanding.

*antonyms* difficult, painful.

**pains** *n* assiduity, assiduousness, birth-pangs, bother, care, contractions, diligence, effort, industry, labour, sedulity, sedulousness, throes, trouble.

**painstaking** *adj* assiduous, careful, conscientious, dedicated, devoted, diligent, earnest, exacting, hardworking, industrious, meticulous, perfectionist, persevering,

punctilious, scrupulous, sedulous, strenuous, thorough, thoroughgoing.

*antonyms* careless, negligent.

**paint** *n* colour, colouring, cosmetics, distemper, dye, emulsion, enamel, glaze, greasepaint, lacquer, lake, make-up, maquillage, oils, pigment, primer, stain, tint, undercoat, warpaint, wash, water-colour, whitewash.

*v* apply, coat, colour, cover, daub, decorate, delineate, depict, describe, distemper, evoke, glaze, lacquer, limn, picture, portray, recount, render, represent.

**painter** *n* artist, colourist, dauber, delineator, depicter, limner, miniaturist, muralist, oil-painter, water-colourist.

**painting** *n* aquarelle, camaieu, daubery, depiction, fresco, illustration, kakemono, landscape, miniature, mural, oil, oil-painting, picture, portrait, portraiture, portrayal, representation, scene, seascape, still life, tablature, water-colour.

**pair** *n* brace, combination, couple, doublet, doubleton, duad, duo, dyad, match, span, twins, two of a kind, twosome, yoke.

*v* bracket, couple, join, link, marry, match, match up, mate, pair off, put together, splice, team, twin, wed, yoke.

*antonyms* dissever, sever.

**paired** *adj* associated, bracketed, coupled, didymous, double, in twos, joined, linked, matched, mated, twinned, yoked.

*antonym* single.

**pal** *n* amigo, buddy, china, chum, companion, comrade, confidant(e), crony, friend, gossip, intimate, mate, partner, side-kick, soul mate.

*antonym* enemy.

**palace** *n* alcázar, basilica, château, dome, palazzo, schloss.

*antonym* hovel.

**palatable** *adj* acceptable, agreeable, appetising, attractive, enjoyable, fair, pleasant, sapid, satisfactory, savoury, tasty, toothsome.

*antonyms* unacceptable, unpleasant.

**palate** *n* appetite, appreciation, enjoyment, gout, gusto, heart, liking, relish, stomach, taste, zest.

**palatial** *adj* de luxe, grand, grandiose, illustrious, imposing, luxurious, magnificent, majestic, opulent, plush, posh, regal, spacious, splendid, stately, sumptuous, swanky.

*antonyms* cramped, poky.

**palaver** *n* activity, babble, blather, blether, business, bustle, carry-on, chatter, colloquy, confab, conference, confusion, discussion, fuss, fuss about nothing, get-together, hubbub, natter, parley, performance, pow-wow, prattle, procedure, rigmarole, session, song and dance, to-do, tongue-wagging, yak.

*v* blab, blather, blether, chatter, confab, confer, discuss, gabble, jabber, jaw, natter, parley, powwow, prattle, tattle, yak.

**pale** *adj* anaemic, ashen, ashy, bleached, bloodless, chalky, colourless, dim, etiolated, faded, faint, feeble, inadequate, light, lily-livered, pallid, pasty, poor, sallow, thin, wan, washed-out, waxy, weak, whey-faced, white, white-livered, whitish.

*antonym* ruddy.

*v* blanch, decrease, dim, diminish, dull, etiolate, fade, lessen, whiten.

*antonyms* blush, colour.

**palisade** *n* barricade, bulwark, defence, enclosure, fence, fortification, paling, palisado, stockade.

**pall¹** *n* check, cloud, cold water, damp, damper, dismay, gloom, mantle, melancholy, shadow, shroud, sindon, veil.

**pall²** *v* bore, cloy, glut, jade, lose savour, satiate, sicken, surfeit, tire, weary.

**palliate** *v* abate, allay, alleviate, assuage, cloak, conceal, cover, diminish, ease, excuse, extenuate, lenify, lessen, lighten, minimise, mitigate, moderate, mollify, relieve, soften, soothe, temper.

**palliative** *adj* alleviative, anodyne, assuasive, calmative, calming, demulcent, lenitive, mitigative, mitigatory, mollifying, paregoric, sedative, soothing.

*antonym* irritant.

*n* analgesic, anodyne, calmative, demulcent, lenitive, painkiller, paregoric, sedative, tranquilliser.

**pallid** *adj* anaemic, ashen, ashy, bloodless, cadaverous, colourless, doughy, etiolated, insipid, lifeless, livid, pale, pasty, pasty-faced, peelie-wally, sallow, spiritless, sterile, tame, tired, uninspired, vapid, wan, waxen, waxy, whey-faced, whitish.

*antonyms* high-complexioned, ruddy, vigorous.

**pallor** *n* bloodlessness, chalkiness, etiolation, paleness, pallidness, sallowness, wanness, whiteness.

*antonym* ruddiness.

**pally** *adj* affectionate, chummy, close, familiar, friendly, intimate, palsy, palsy-walsy, thick.

*antonym* unfriendly.

**palm** *n* hand, mitt, paw, vola.

*v* appropriate, conceal, grab, half-inch, nick, sneak, snitch.

**palm off** fob off, foist, foist off, impose, offload, pass off, thrust, unload.

**palmistry** *n* chirognomy, chiromancy, fortune-telling, palm reading.

**palmy** *adj* carefree, flourishing, fortunate, glorious, golden, halcyon, happy, joyous, luxurious, prosperous, salad, thriving, triumphant.

**palpable** *adj* apparent, blatant, clear, concrete, conspicuous, evident, manifest, material, obvious, open, overt, patent, plain, real, solid, substantial, tangible, touchable, unmistakable, visible.

*antonyms* elusive, impalpable, imperceptible, intangible.

**palpitate** *v* beat, flutter, pitapat, pit-pat, pitter-patter, pittypat, pound, pulsate, pulse, quiver, shiver, throb, thump, tremble, vibrate.

**palsied** *adj* agued, arthritic, atonic, crippled, debilitated, disabled, helpless, paralysed, paralytic, rheumatic, sclerotic, shaking, shaky, shivering, spastic, trembling, tremulous.

**paltry** *adj* base, beggarly, contemptible, derisory, despicable, inconsiderable, insignificant, jitney, low, meagre, mean, minor, miserable, negligible, pettifogging, petty, picayunish, piddling, piffling, pimping, pitiful, poor, puny, rubbishy, slight, small, sorry, tinpot, trifling, trivial, two-bit, twopenny-halfpenny, unimportant, worthless, wretched.

*antonyms* significant, substantial.

**pamper** *v* baby, cocker, coddle, cosset, fondle, gratify, humour, indulge, mollycoddle, mother, overindulge, pet, spoil.

*antonyms* ill-treat, neglect.

**pampered** *adj* coddled, cosseted, high-fed, indulged, mollycoddled, overfed, petted, spoilt.

*antonyms* abused, neglected.

**pamphlet** *n* booklet, broadside, brochure, chapbook, folder, leaflet, tract, tractate, treatise.

**pan¹** *n* casserole, container, fryer, marmite, pancheon, pot, saucepan, skillet, spider, stewpot, vessel, wok.

*v* censure, criticise, flay, hammer, knock, pick to pieces, pull to pieces, roast, rubbish, slam, slate.

*antonym* praise.

**pan out** be exhausted, come to an end, culminate, eventuate, happen, result, turn out, work out, yield.

**pan²** *v* circle, follow, move, scan, sweep, swing, track, traverse, turn.

**panacea** *n* catholicon, cure-all, diacatholicon, elixir, nostrum, panpharmacon, theriac, treacle.

**panache** *n* brio, dash, élan, enthusiasm, flair, flamboyance, flourish, grand manner, ostentation, pizzazz, spirit, style, swagger, theatricality, verve, vigour, zest.

**pandemonium** *n* babel, bedlam, chaos, clamour, commotion, confusion, din, disorder, Donnybrook, frenzy, hubbub, hue and cry, hullaballoo, racket, ruckus, ruction, rumpus, to-do, tumult, turbulence, turmoil, uproar.

*antonyms* calm, order, peace.

**pander** *v* cater to, furnish, gratify, indulge, pamper, please, provide, purvey, satisfy.

*n* bawd, go-between, mack, pimp, ponce, procurer, procuress, white-slaver, whoremaster, whoremonger.

**panegyric** *n* accolade, citation, commendation, encomium, eulogium, eulogy, homage, paean, praise, tribute.

*antonym* censure.

*adj* commendatory, complimentary, encomiastic, eulogistic, favourable, flattering, glowing, laudatory, panegyrical, praiseful, praising.

*antonyms* censorious, damning.

**panel** *n* compartment, rectangle, strip, table.

**panelling** *n* dado, panel-work, wainscot, wainscot(t)ing.

**pang** *n* ache, agony, anguish, crick, discomfort, distress, gripe, pain, prick, spasm, stab, sting, stitch, throe, twinge, twitch, wrench.

**panic** *n* agitation, alarm, consternation, dismay, fear, fright, hassle, horror, hysteria, scare, terror, tizzy, to-do.

*antonyms* assurance, confidence.

*v* alarm, get one's knickers in a twist, go to pieces, lose one's cool, lose one's nerve, overreact, put the wind up, scare, startle, terrify, unnerve.

*antonyms* reassure, relax.

**panic-stricken** *adj* affrighted, aghast, agitated, alarmed, appalled, fearful, frenzied, frightened, horrified, horror-stricken, hysterical, in a cold sweat, panicky, perturbed, petrified, scared, scared stiff, startled, stunned, stupefied, terrified, terror-stricken, unnerved.

*antonyms* confident, laid-back, relaxed.

**panoply** *n* armour, array, attire, dress, equipment, garb, gear, get-up, insignia, raiment, regalia, show, trappings, turn-out.

**panorama** *n* bird's-eye view, overview, perspective, prospect, scene, scenery, spectacle, survey, view, vision, vista.

**panoramic** *adj* bird's-eye, comprehensive, extensive, far-reaching, gazy, general, inclusive, overall, panned, scenic, sweeping, universal, wide, widespread.

*antonym* limited.

**pansy** *n* fag, faggot, homo, homosexual, Jessie, milksop, Miss Nancy, molly, mollycoddle, namby-pamby, poof, poofter, queen, queer.

**pant** *v* ache, blow, breathe, covet, crave, desire, flaff, gasp, hanker, heave, huff, hunger, long, palpitate, pine, puff, sigh, thirst, throb, want, wheeze, yearn, yen.

*n* gasp, huff, puff, throb, wheeze.

**panting** *adj* anxious, breathless, eager, gasping, impatient, out of breath, puffed, puffed out, puffing, short-winded, winded.

**pantomime** *n* charade, dumb-show, galantry show, panto.

**pants** *n* briefs, drawers, knickers, panties, shorts, slacks, trews, trousers, trunks, underpants, undershorts, Y-fronts.

**paper** *n* analysis, archive, article, assignment, authorisation, certificate, composition, credential, critique, daily, deed, diary, dissertation, document, dossier, essay, examination, file, gazette, instrument, journal, letter, monograph, news, newspaper, notepaper, organ, rag, record, report, script, stationery, study, thesis, treatise.

**papery** *adj* delicate, flimsy, fragile, frail, insubstantial, light, lightweight, paper-thin, thin, translucent.

**papism** *n* papery, papistry, Roman Catholicism.

**papist** *n* Catholic, Fenian, papisher, Roman Catholic.

*adj* Catholic, Fenian, papish, popish, Roman Catholic.

**par** *n* accordance, average, balance, correspondence, equal footing, equality, equilibrium, equivalence, level, mean, median, norm, parity, similarity, standard, usual.

**parable** *n* allegory, apologue, exemplum, fable, homily, lesson, story.

**parade** *n* array, cavalcade, ceremony, column, corso, display, exhibition, flaunting, march, motorcade, ostentation, pageant, panache, pizzazz, pomp, procession, promenade, review, show, spectacle, train, vaunting.

*v* air, brandish, defile, display, exhibit, flaunt, make a show of, march, peacock, process, show, show off, strut, swagger, vaunt.

**paradigm** *n* archetype, example, exemplar, framework, ideal, model, original, pattern, prototype.

**paradise** *n* bliss, City of God, delight, Eden, Elysian fields, Elysium, felicity, garden of delights, Garden of Eden, heaven, heavenly kingdom, Land o' the Leal, Olympus, Promised Land, seventh heaven, utopia, Valhalla, Zion.

*antonyms* Hades, hell.

**paradox** *n* absurdity, ambiguity, anomaly, contradiction, enigma, equivocation, incongruity, inconsistency, mystery, oddity, puzzle, riddle.

**paradoxical** *adj* absurd, ambiguous, baffling, conflicting, confounding, contradictory, enigmatic, equivocal, Gilbertian, illogical, impossible, improbable, incongruous, inconsistent, puzzling, self-contradictory.

**paragon** *n* apotheosis, archetype, crème de la crème, criterion, cynosure, epitome, exemplar, ideal, jewel, masterpiece, model, non(e)such, nonpareil, paradigm, pattern, prototype, quintessence, standard, the bee's knees.

**paragraph** *n* clause, item, notice, part, passage, portion, section, subdivision, subsection.

**parallel** *adj* akin, aligned, alongside, analogous, co-extensive, collateral, connate, correspondent, corresponding, equidistant, homologous, like, matching, resembling, similar, uniform.

*antonyms* divergent, separate.

*n* analogue, analogy, comparison, corollary, correlation, correspondence, counterpart, duplicate, equal, equivalent, homologue, likeness, match, parallelism, resemblance, similarity, twin.

*v* agree, compare, conform, correlate, correspond, duplicate, emulate, equal, match.

*antonyms* diverge, separate.

**paralyse** *v* anaesthetise, arrest, benumb, clamp down on, cripple, debilitate, disable, freeze, halt, immobilise, incapacitate, lame, numb, obtund, petrify, stun, stupefy, torpefy, transfix.

**paralysis** *n* arrest, break-down, halt, hemiplegia, immobility, monoplegia, palsy, paraplegia, paresis, quadriplegia, shut-down, stagnation, standstill, stoppage, torpor.

**paralytic**[1] *adj* crippled, disabled, hemiplegic, immobile, immobilised, incapacitated, lame, monoplegic, numb, palsied, paralysed, quadriplegic.

**paralytic²** *adj* canned, drunk, inebriated, intoxicated, legless, pie-eyed, pissed, plastered, sloshed, smashed, stewed, stoned, stotious, three sheets in the wind.

*antonym* (stone-cold) sober.

**parameter** *n* boundary, constant, criterion, framework, guideline, indication, limit, limitation, restriction, specification, variable.

**paramount** *adj* capital, cardinal, chief, dominant, eminent, first, foremost, highest, main, outstanding, predominant, pre-eminent, premier, primary, prime, principal, superior, supreme, topmost, top-rank.

*antonyms* inferior, last, lowest.

**paramour** *n* beau, concubine, courtesan, doxy, fancy man, fancy woman, hetaira, inamorata, kept woman, lover, mistress, woman.

**paranoia** *n* delusions, megalomania, monomania, obsession, psychosis.

**parapet** *n* barbican, bartisan, bastion, battlement, bulwark, fortification, rampart.

**paraphernalia** *n* accessories, accoutrements, apparatus, appurtenances, baggage, belongings, bits and pieces, clobber, clutter, effects, equipage, equipment, gear, impedimenta, material, odds and ends, stuff, tackle, things, trappings, traps.

**paraphrase** *n* farse, gloss, interpretation, recapitulation, rehash, rendering, rendition, rephrasing, restatement, rewording, translation, version.

*v* farse, gloss, interpret, recapitulate, rehash, render, rephrase, restate, reword, translate.

**parasite** *n* bloodsucker, cadger, endophyte, endozoon, entozoon, epiphyte, epizoan, epizoon, free-loader, hanger-on, leech, lick-trencher, scrounger, sponge, sponger, sucker.

**parasitic** *adj* biogenous, bloodsucking, cadging, epizoan, epizoic, free-loading, leechlike, parasitical, scrounging, sponging.

**parcel** *n* band, batch, bunch, bundle, carton, collection, company, crew, crowd, da(w)k, gang, group, lot, pack, package, packet, plot, portion, property, quantity, set, tract.

*v* bundle, collect, pack, package, tie up, wrap.

**parcel out** allocate, allot, apportion, carve up, deal out, dispense, disperse, distribute, divide, dole out, mete out, portion out, separate, share out.

**parch** *v* blister, burn, dehydrate, desiccate, dry up, exsiccate, roast, scorch, sear, shrivel, wither.

**parched** *adj* arid, dehydrated, dried up, drouthy, dry, scorched, shrivelled, thirsty, waterless, withered.

**parchment** *n* certificate, charter, diploma, document, palimpsest, scroll, vellum.

**pardon** *v* absolve, acquit, amnesty, condone, emancipate, exculpate, excuse, exonerate,

forgive, free, let off, liberate, overlook, release, remit, reprieve, respite, vindicate.

*n* absolution, acquittal, allowance, amnesty, compassion, condonation, discharge, excuse, exoneration, forgiveness, grace, humanity, indulgence, mercy, release, remission, reprieval, reprieve.

**pardonable** *adj* allowable, condonable, dispensable, excusable, forgivable, justifiable, minor, permissible, remissible, understandable, venial, warrantable.

*antonym* inexcusable.

**pare** *v* clip, crop, cut, cut back, decrease, diminish, dock, flaught, float, lop, peel, prune, reduce, retrench, shave, shear, skin, skive, trim.

**parent** *n* architect, author, begetter, cause, creator, father, forerunner, generant, genetrix, genitor, guardian, mother, origin, originator, procreator, progenitor, progenitress, progenitrix, prototype, root, sire, source.

**parentage** *n* affiliation, ancestry, birth, derivation, descent, extraction, family, filiation, line, lineage, origin, paternity, pedigree, race, source, stirps, stock.

**parenthetic** *adj* adventitious, bracketed, elucidative, explanatory, extraneous, extrinsic, in parenthesis, incidental, inserted, interposed, intervening, parenthetical, qualifying.

*antonyms* basic, original.

**pariah** *n* black sheep, castaway, exile, Ishmael, leper, outcast, outlaw, undesirable, unperson, untouchable.

**paring** *n* clipping, cutting, flake, flaught, fragment, peel, peeling, rind, shaving, shred, skin, slice, sliver, snippet.

**parish** *n* brethren, church, churchgoers, community, congregation, district, flock, fold, parishioners, vicariate.

**parity** *n* affinity, agreement, analogy, conformity, congruence, congruity, consistency, consonance, correspondence, equality, equivalence, likeness, par, parallelism, resemblance, sameness, semblance, similarity, similitude, uniformity, unity.

**park¹** *n* estate, garden, grounds, paddock, parkland, pleasance, pleasure garden, reserve, woodland.

**park²** *v* deposit, dump, leave, position, station.

**parlance** *n* argot, cant, diction, idiom, jargon, language, lingo, phraseology, speech, talk, tongue.

**parley** *n* colloquy, confab, conference, council, deliberation, dialogue, discussion, get-together, meeting, negotiation, palaver, powwow, talk(s), tête-à-tête.

*v* confabulate, confer, consult, deliberate, discuss, get together, negotiate, palaver, powwow, speak, talk.

**parliament** *n* assembly, conclave, congress, convocation, council, Dail, diet, house, legislature, senate, talking-shop, Tynwald.

**parliamentary** *adj* congressional, deliberative, governmental, law-making, legislative, legislatorial, senatorial.

**parlour** *n* drawing-room, living-room, lounge, sitting-room.

**parochial** *adj* blinkered, confined, incestuous, insular, inward-looking, limited, narrow, narrow-minded, parish-pump, petty, provincial, restricted, small-minded.

**parochialism** *n* insularity, narrow-mindedness, pettiness, provincialism.

**parody** *n* burlesque, caricature, imitation, lampoon, mimicry, pasquinade, satire, send-up, skit, spoof, take-off.

*v* burlesque, caricature, lampoon, mimic, pasquinade, satirise, send up, spoof, take off, travesty.

**paroxysm** *n* attack, convulsion, eruption, explosion, fit, flare-up, outbreak, outburst, seizure, spasm, tantrum.

**parrot** *n* ape, copy-cat, imitator, mimic, phraser, repeater.

*v* ape, copy, echo, imitate, mimic, rehearse, reiterate, repeat.

**parrot-fashion** *adv* automatically, by rote, mechanically, mindlessly, unthinkingly.

**parry** *v* avert, avoid, block, circumvent, deflect, divert, dodge, duck, evade, fence, fend off, field, forestall, obviate, rebuff, repel, repulse, shun, sidestep, stave off, ward off.

**parsimonious** *adj* cheese-paring, close, close-fisted, close-handed, frugal, grasping, mean, mingy, miserable, miserly, money-grubbing, niggardly, penny-pinching, penny-wise, penurious, saving, scrimpy, sparing, stingy, stinting, tight-fisted.

*antonyms* generous, liberal, open-handed.

**parsimony** *n* frugality, meanness, minginess, niggardliness, penny-pinching, stinginess, tight-fistedness.

*antonyms* generosity, liberality.

**parson** *n* churchman, clergyman, cleric, divine, ecclesiastic, incumbent, Jack-priest, man of God, mar-text, minister, padre, pastor, preacher, priest, rector, reverend, vicar.

**part** *n* airt, area, behalf, bit, branch, business, capacity, cause, character, charge, clause, complement, component, concern, constituent, department, district, division, duty, element, faction, factor, fraction, fragment, function, heft, ingredient, interest, involvement, limb, lines, lot, member, module, neck of the woods, neighbourhood, office, organ, particle, partwork, party, piece, place, portion, quarter, region, responsibility, role, scrap, section, sector, segment, share, side, slice, task, territory, tip of the iceberg, unit, vicinity, work.

*v* break, break up, cleave, come apart, depart, detach, disband, disconnect, disjoin, dismantle, disperse, disunite, divide, go, go away, leave, part company, quit, rend, scatter, separate, sever, split, split up, sunder, take leave, tear, withdraw.

**part with** abandon, cede, discard, forgo, give up, jettison, let go of, relinquish, renounce, sacrifice, surrender, yield.

**partake** *v* be involved, engage, enter, participate, share, take part.

**partake of** consume, drink, eat, evince, evoke, have, manifest, receive, share, show, suggest, take.

**partial**[1] *adj* fragmentary, imperfect, incomplete, inexhaustive, limited, part, uncompleted, unfinished.

*antonyms* complete, exhaustive, total.

**partial**[2] *adj* affected, biased, coloured, discriminatory, ex parte, influenced, interested, one-sided, partisan, predisposed, prejudiced, tendentious, unfair, unjust.

*antonyms* disinterested, fair, unbiased.

**partial to** crazy about, daft about, fond of, keen on, mad about, taken with.

**partiality** *n* affinity, bias, discrimination, favouritism, fondness, inclination, liking, love, partisanship, penchant, predilection, predisposition, preference, prejudice, proclivity, propensity, soft spot, taste, weakness.

*antonyms* dislike, justice.

**partially** *adv* fractionally, in part, incompletely, partly, somewhat.

**participant** *n* associate, contributor, co-operator, helper, member, partaker, participator, party, shareholder, worker.

**participate** *v* be involved, co-operate, engage, enter, join, muck in, partake, perform, share, take part.

**participation** *n* a piece of the action, assistance, contribution, co-operation, involvement, mucking in, partaking, partnership, sharing.

**particle** *n* atom, atom(y), bit, corn, crumb, drop, electron, grain, iota, jot, kaon, mite, molecule, morsel, mote, neutrino, neutron, piece, pion, proton, scrap, shred, sliver, smidgen, speck, tittle, whit.

**parti-coloured** *adj* motley, piebald, polychromatic, polychromic, variegated, versicoloured.

*antonyms* monochromatic, plain.

**particular**[1] *adj* blow-by-blow, circumstantial, detailed, distinct, especial, exact, exceptional, express, itemised, marked, minute, notable, noteworthy, painstaking, peculiar, precise, remarkable, selective, several, singular, special, specific, thorough, uncommon, unique, unusual, very.

*antonym* general.

*n* circumstance, detail, fact, feature, item, point, specific, specification.

**particular**[2] *adj* choosy, critical, dainty, demanding, discriminating, exacting, fastidious, finical, finicky, fussy, meticulous, nice, overnice, perjink, pernickety, picky.

*antonym* casual.

**particularise** *v* detail, enumerate, individualise, individuate, itemise, specify, stipulate.

**particularity** *n* accuracy, carefulness, characteristic, choosiness, circumstance, detail, distinctiveness, fact, fastidiousness, feature, fussiness, idiosyncrasy, individuality, instance, item, mannerism, meticulousness, peculiarity, point, precision, property, quirk, singularity, thoroughness, trait, uniqueness.

**particularly** *adv* decidedly, distinctly, especially, exceptionally, explicitly, expressly, extraordinarily, in particular, markedly, notably, noticeably, outstandingly, peculiarly, remarkably, singularly, specifically, surprisingly, uncommonly, unusually.

**parting** *n* adieu, breaking, departure, detachment, disjunction, disunion, divergence, division, farewell, going, goodbye, leave-taking, partition, rift, rupture, separation, severance, split, valediction.

*antonyms* convergence, meeting.

*adj* closing, concluding, deathbed, departing, dying, farewell, final, last, stirrup, valedictory.

*antonyms* arriving, first.

**partisan** *n* adherent, backer, champion, devotee, disciple, factionary, factionist, follower, guerrilla, irregular, party-man, stalwart, supporter, upholder, votary.

*adj* biased, discriminatory, factional, guerrilla, interested, irregular, one-sided, partial, predisposed, prejudiced, resistance, sectarian, tendentious, underground.

**partisanship** *n* bias, factionalism, fanaticism, partiality, partyism, sectarianism.

**partition**[1] *n* allocation, allotment, apportionment, distribution, dividing, division, part, portion, rationing out, section, segregation, separation, severance, share, splitting.

*v* allocate, allot, apportion, assign, divide, parcel out, portion, section, segment, separate, share, split up, subdivide.

**partition**[2] *n* barrier, diaphragm, dissepiment, divider, hallan, membrane, room-divider, screen, septum, traverse, wall.

*v* bar, divide, fence off, screen, separate, wall off.

**partly** *adv* halfway, in part, incompletely, moderately, partially, relatively, slightly, somewhat, to a certain degree, to a certain extent, up to a point.

*antonyms* completely, in toto, totally.

**partner** *n* accomplice, ally, associate, bedfellow, butty, collaborator, colleague, companion, comrade, confederate, consort, co-partner, gigolo, helper, helpmate, helpmeet, husband, mate, participant, side-kick, spouse, team-mate, wife.

**partnership** *n* affiliation, alliance, association, brotherhood, combination, combine, companionship, company, conglomerate, connection, co-operation, co-operative, co-partnership, corporation, fellowship, firm, fraternity, house, interest, participation, sharing, society, syndicate, union.

**parts** *n* ability, accomplishments, attributes, calibre, capabilities, endowments, expertise, faculties, genius, gifts, intellect, intelligence, skill, talents.

**party**[1] *n* assembly, at-home, bash, beanfeast, beano, ceilidh, celebration, do, drag, drum, entertainment, -fest, festivity, function, gathering, get-together, hooley, hoot(e)nanny, housewarming, hurricane, jollification, knees-up, rave-up, reception, rout, shindig, social, soirée, thrash.

**party**[2] *n* alliance, association, band, body, bunch, cabal, caucus, clique, coalition, combination, company, confederacy, contingent, contractor, coterie, crew, defendant, detachment, faction, gang, gathering, group, grouping, individual, junto, league, litigant, participant, person, plaintiff, set, side, squad, team, unit.

**parvenu** *n* arriviste, climber, new rich, nouveau riche, pretender, upstart, vulgarian.

*adj* nouveau riche, upstart, vulgarian.

**pass**[1] *v* accept, adopt, answer, approve, authorise, beat, befall, beguile, blow over, cease, come up, come up to scratch, convey, declare, decree, defecate, delate, deliver, depart, develop, devote, die, die away, disappear, discharge, disregard, dissolve, do, dwindle, ebb, elapse, eliminate, employ, empty, enact, end, establish, evacuate, evaporate, exceed, excel, exchange, excrete, expel, experience, expire, express, fade, fall out, fill, flow, get through, give, go, go beyond, go by, go past, graduate, hand, happen, ignore, impersonate, lapse, leave, legislate, melt away, miss, move, neglect, occupy, occur, omit, ordain, outdistance, outdo, outstrip, overlook, overtake, pass muster, proceed, pronounce, qualify, ratify, roll, run, sanction, send, serve as, skip, spend, succeed, suffer, suffice, suit, surmount, surpass, take place, terminate, throw, transcend, transfer, transmit, undergo, utter, validate, vanish, void, waft, wane, while away.

**pass**[2] *n* advances, approach, authorisation, chit, condition, feint, identification, jab, juncture, laissez-passer, licence, lunge, overture, passport, permission, permit, pinch, play, plight, predicament, proposition, push, safe-conduct, situation, stage, state, state of affairs, straits, suggestion, swing, thrust, ticket, warrant.

**pass away** croak, decease, die, expire, give up the ghost, kick the bucket, pass on, pass over, peg out, snuff it.

**pass by** disregard, forget, ignore, leave, miss, neglect, omit, overlook, pass over, pretermit.

**pass muster** be adequate, be up to scratch, fill the bill, make the grade, measure up, qualify.

**pass off** come to an end, counterfeit, die away, disappear, dismiss, disregard, emit, evaporate, fade out, fake, feign, give off, go off, happen, ignore, occur, palm off, pass by, send forth, take place, turn out, utter, vanish, vaporise, wink at.

**pass out**[1] black out, die, drop, faint, flake out, keel over, lose consciousness, swoon.

**pass out**[2] deal out, dispense, distribute, dole out, give out, hand out, share out.

**pass over** ignore, neglect, omit, overlook, pretermit.

**pass**[3] *n* canyon, col, defile, gap, gha(u)t, gorge, halse, nek, ravine.

**passable** *adj* acceptable, adequate, admissible, all right, allowable, average, clear, fair, mediocre, middling, moderate, navigable, OK, open, ordinary, presentable, so-so, tolerable, traversable, unblocked, unexceptional, unobstructed.

**passably** *adv* after a fashion, fairly, moderately, rather, reasonably, relatively, somewhat, tolerably.

**passage** *n* acceptance, access, adit, advance, allowance, authorisation, avenue, change, channel, citation, clause, close, communication, conduit, conversion, corridor, course, crossing, deambulatory, doorway, drift, dromos, duct, enactment, entrance, entrance hall, establishment, excerpt, exit, extract, fistula, flow, freedom, gallery, gut, hall, hallway, journey, lane, legalisation, legislation, lobby, motion, movement, opening, orifice, paragraph, part, passageway, passing, path, permission, piece, portion, progress, progression, quotation, ratification, reading, right, road, route, safe-conduct, section, sentence, spiracle, text, thorough, thoroughfare, tour, transit, transition, trek, trip, vent, verse, vestibule, visa, vista, voyage, warrant, way.

**passageway** *n* aisle, alley, corridor, entrance, exit, hall, hallway, lane, lobby, passage, pend, vennel, wynd.

**passé** *adj* antiquated, dated, démodé, obsolete, old hat, old-fashioned, out, outdated, outmoded, out-of-date, outworn, past one's best, unfashionable.

*antonyms* fashionable, in.

**passenger** *n* commuter, fare, hitch-hiker, pillionist, pillion-rider, rider, traveller.

**passer-by** *n* bystander, looker-on, onlooker, spectator, witness.

**passing** *adj* brief, casual, cursory, ephemeral, evanescent, fleeting, fly-by-night, fugitive, glancing, hasty, impermanent, momentary, quick, shallow, shirt, short, short-lived, slight, superficial, temporary, transient, transitory.

*antonyms* long-lasting, permanent.

*n* death, decease, demise, end, expiration, finish, loss, quietus, termination.

**passion** *n* adoration, affection, anger, animation, ardour, attachment, avidity, bug, chafe, concupiscence, craving, craze, dander, desire, eagerness, emotion, enthusiasm, excitement, fancy, fascination, feeling, fervency, fervour, fire, fit, flare-up, fondness, frenzy, fury, heat, idol, indignation, infatuation, intensity, ire, itch, joy, keenness, love, lust, mania, monomania, obsession, outburst, paroxysm, rage, rapture, resentment, spirit, storm, transport, vehemence, verve, vivacity, warmth, wax, wrath, zeal, zest.

*antonyms* calm, coolness, self-possession.

**passionate** *adj* amorous, animated, ardent, aroused, choleric, desirous, eager, emotional, enthusiastic, erotic, excitable, excited, fervent, fervid, fierce, fiery, frenzied, heartfelt, heated, hot, hot-headed, hot-tempered, impassioned, impetuous, impulsive, incensed, inflamed, inspirited, intense, irascible, irate, irritable, loving, lustful, peppery, quick-tempered, sensual, sexy, stormy, strong, sultry, tempestuous, torrid, vehement, violent, wanton, warm, wild, zealous.

*antonyms* frigid, laid-back, phlegmatic.

**passionless** *adj* apathetic, callous, calm, cold, cold-blooded, cold-hearted, detached, dispassionate, emotionless, frigid, frosty, icy, impartial, impassive, inappetent, indifferent, insensible, neutral, restrained, uncaring, unemotional, unfeeling, uninvolved, unloving, unresponsive, withdrawn.

*antonyms* caring, sensitive, sympathetic.

**passive** *adj* acquiescent, compliant, docile, enduring, impassive, inactive, indifferent, indolent, inert, lifeless, long-suffering, non-participating, non-violent, patient, quiescent, receptive, resigned, submissive, supine, unaffected, unassertive, uninvolved, unresisting.

*antonyms* active, involved, lively.

**passive resistance** non-violence, satyagraha, vis inertiae.

**passport** *n* authorisation, laissez-passer, pass, permit, visa.

**password** *n* countersign, open sesame, parole, shibboleth, signal, watchword.

**past** *adj* accomplished, ancient, bygone, completed, defunct, done, early, elapsed, ended, erstwhile, extinct, finished, foregone, forgotten, former, gone, gone by, late, long-ago, no more, olden, over, over and done with, preceding, previous, prior, quondam, recent, spent, vanished.

*n* antiquity, auld lang syne, background, days of yore, dossier, experience, former times, good old days, history, life, old times, olden days, track record, yesteryear.

**past one's best** not what one was, over the hill, passé.

**paste** *n* adhesive, cement, dope, dough, glue, gum, mastic, mucilage, pastry, putty.

*v* beat, cement, fasten, fix, glue, gum, hammer, stick, thrash, thump, whitewash.

**pastel** *adj* delicate, faint, gentle, light, muted, pale, soft, soft-hued, subdued.

*n* chalk, crayon, drawing, pastille, sketch, vignette, wood.

**pastiche** *n* blend, composition, farrago, gallimaufry, hotchpotch, medley, mélange, miscellany, mixture, motley, olla-podrida, patchwork, pot-pourri.

**pastille** *n* confection, cough drop, cough sweet, jujube, lozenge, pastel, sweet, tablet, troche.

**pastime** *n* activity, amusement, avocation, distraction, diversion, divertisement, entertainment, game, hobby, play, recreation, relaxation, sport, Zeitvertreib.

*antonyms* business, employment, occupation, vocation, work.

**pastmaster** *n* ace, adept, artist, dab hand, expert, old hand, proficient, virtuoso, wizard.

*antonym* incompetent.

**pastor** *n* canon, churchman, clergyman, cleric, divine, ecclesiastic, minister, parson, prebendary, priest, rector, vicar.

**pastoral** *adj* agrarian, Arcadian, bucolic, clerical, countrified, country, ecclesiastical, georgic, idyllic, ministerial, priestly, rural, rustic, simple.

*antonyms* oppidan, urban.

**pasture** *n* alp, eddish, grass, grassland, grazing, herbage, lay, lea, ley, machair, mead, meadow, pasturage, pasture-land, raik, shieling.

**pasty** *adj* anaemic, doughy, gluey, glutinous, mucilaginous, pale, pallid, pasty-faced, peelie-wally, sallow, sickly, starchy, sticky, unhealthy, viscous, wan, waxy, whey-faced.
*antonyms* healthy, rubicund.

**pat** *v* caress, clap, dab, fondle, pet, rub, slap, stroke, tap, touch.
*n* cake, caress, clap, dab, lump, piece, portion, slap, stroke, tap, touch.
*adv* exactly, faultlessly, flawlessly, fluently, glibly, just right, off pat, opportunely, perfectly, plumb, precisely, relevantly, seasonably.
*antonyms* imprecisely, wrongly.
*adj* apposite, appropriate, apropos, apt, automatic, easy, facile, felicitous, fitting, glib, happy, neat, pertinent, ready, relevant, right, simplistic, slick, smooth, spot-on, suitable, to the point, well-chosen.
*antonyms* irrelevant, unsuitable.

**patch** *n* area, bit, clout, ground, land, lot, parcel, piece, plot, scrap, shred, spot, stretch, tract.
*v* botch, cover, fix, mend, reinforce, repair, sew up, stitch, vamp.

**patchwork** *n* confusion, farrago, gallimaufry, hash, hotchpotch, jumble, medley, mishmash, mixture, pastiche.

**patchy** *adj* bitty, erratic, fitful, incongruous, inconsistent, inharmonious, irregular, maculate, random, sketchy, spotty, uneven, variable, varying.
*antonyms* consistent, even, regular, uniform.

**patent** *adj* apparent, blatant, clear, clear-cut, conspicuous, downright, evident, explicit, flagrant, glaring, indisputable, manifest, obvious, open, ostensible, overt, palpable, transparent, unconcealed, unequivocal, unmistakable.
*antonyms* hidden, opaque.
*n* certificate, copyright, invention, licence, privilege, registered trademark.

**paternal** *adj* benevolent, concerned, fatherlike, fatherly, indulgent, patrilineal, patrimonial, patroclinic, patroclinous, protective, solicitous, vigilant.

**paternity** *n* authorship, descent, extraction, family, fatherhood, fathership, lineage, origination, parentage.

**path** *n* avenue, course, direction, footpath, footway, gate, pad, passage, pathway, procedure, ridgeway, road, route, towpath, track, trail, walk, walkway, way.

**pathetic** *adj* affecting, contemptible, crummy, deplorable, dismal-looking, distressing, feeble, heartbreaking, heart-rending, inadequate, lamentable, meagre, melting, miserable, moving, paltry, petty, piteous, pitiable, pitiful, plaintive, poignant, poor, puny, rubbishy, sad, sorry, tender, touching, trashy, uninteresting, useless, woebegone, woeful, worthless.
*antonyms* admirable, cheerful.

**pathos** *n* inadequacy, misery, pitiableness, pitifulness, plaintiveness, poignancy, sadness.

**patience** *n* calmness, composure, constancy, cool, diligence, endurance, equanimity, forbearance, fortitude, long-suffering, perseverance, persistence, resignation, restraint, self-control, serenity, stoicism, submission, sufferance, tolerable, toleration.
*antonyms* impatience, intolerance.

**patient**[1] *adj* accommodating, calm, composed, enduring, even-tempered, forbearing, forgiving, indulgent, lenient, long-suffering, mild, persevering, persistent, philosophical, quiet, resigned, restrained, self-controlled, self-possessed, serene, stoical, submissive, tolerant, uncomplaining, understanding, untiring.
*antonyms* impatient, intolerant.

**patient**[2] *n* case, client, invalid, sufferer.

**patois** *n* argot, cant, dialect, jargon, lingo, lingua franca, patter, slang, vernacular.

**patriarch** *n* elder, father, founder, grand old man, grandfather, greybeard, paterfamilias, sire.

**patrician** *n* aristocrat, gentleman, grandee, noble, nobleman, peer.
*antonyms* commoner, pleb.
*adj* aristocratic, blue-blooded, gentle, high-born, high-class, lordly, noble, thoroughbred, well-born.
*antonyms* common, humble.

**patrimony** *n* bequest, birthright, estate, heritage, inheritance, legacy, portion, revenue, share.

**patriot** *n* chauvinist, flag-waver, jingo, jingoist, loyalist, nationalist.

**patriotic** *adj* chauvinistic, flag-waving, jingoish, jingoistic, loyal, nationalistic.

**patriotism** *n* chauvinism, flag-waving, jingoism, loyalty, nationalism.

**patrol** *n* defence, garrison, guard, guarding, policing, protecting, roundvigilance, sentinel, surveillance, watch, watching, watchman.
*v* cruise, go the rounds, guard, inspect, perambulate, police, range, tour.

**patron** *n* advocate, backer, benefactor, buyer, champion, client, customer, defender, fautor, frequenter, friend, guardian, habitué, helper, Maecenas, partisan, philanthropist, protector, regular, shopper, sponsor, subscriber, supporter, sympathiser.

**patronage** *n* aegis, aid, assistance, backing, benefaction, business, championship, clientèle, commerce, custom, encouragement, help, participation, promotion, sponsorship, subscription, support, sustenance, trade, trading, traffic.

**patronise** *v* assist, back, befriend, encourage, foster, frequent, fund, habituate, help, humour, maintain, promote, shop at, sponsor, support, talk down to.

**patronising** *adj* condescending, contemptuous, disdaining, gracious, haughty, high-handed, imperious, lofty, overbearing, snobbish, stooping, supercilious, superior, toffee-nosed.
*antonym* humble.

**patter**[1] *v* beat, pat, pelt, pitapat, pit-pat, pitter-patter, pittypat, rat-a-rat, scurry, scuttle, skip, spatter, tap, tiptoe, trip.

*n* pattering, pitapat, pit-pat, pitter-patter, pittypat, tapping.

**patter**[2] *n* argot, cant, chatter, gabble, glib talk, jabber, jargon, line, lingo, monologue, patois, pitch, prattle, slang, spiel, vernacular, yak.

**pattern** *n* archetype, arrangement, criterion, cynosure, decoration, delineation, design, device, diagram, examplar, example, figuration, figure, Gestalt, guide, instructions, kind, method, model, motif, norm, order, orderliness, original, ornament, ornamentation, paradigm, paragon, plan, prototype, sample, sequence, shape, sort, specimen, standard, stencil, style, system, template, type, variety.

*v* copy, decorate, design, emulate, follow, form, imitate, match, model, mould, order, shape, stencil, style, trim.

**patterned** *adj* decorated, figured, moiré, ornamented, printed, stamped, watered.

**paucity** *n* dearth, deficiency, exiguousness, fewness, insufficiency, lack, meagreness, paltriness, poverty, rarity, scantiness, scarcity, shortage, slenderness, slightness, smallness, sparseness, sparsity, want.

*antonym* abundance.

**paunch** *n* abdomen, beer-belly, beer-gut, belly, bread-basket, corporation, pot, pot-belly.

**paunchy** *adj* adipose, corpulent, fat, podgy, portly, pot-bellied, pudgy, rotund, tubby.

**pauper** *n* bankrupt, beggar, church-mouse, down-and-out, have-not, indigent, insolvent, mendicant.

**pause** *v* break, cease, cut, delay, desist, discontinue, halt, hesitate, interrupt, rest, take a break, take a breather, take five, wait, waver.

*n* abatement, break, breather, caesura, cessation, delay, discontinuance, dwell, gap, halt, hesitation, interlude, intermission, interruption, interval, let-up, lull, respite, rest, slackening, stay, stoppage, suspension, wait.

**pave** *v* asphalt, concrete, cover, flag, floor, macadamise, revet, slab, surface, tar, tile.

**pavement** *n* bed, causeway, floor, footway, pavé, sidewalk.

**paw** *v* grab, manhandle, maul, mishandle, molest.

*n* foot, forepaw, hand, pad, pud, puddy.

**pawn**[1] *n* cat's-paw, creature, dupe, instrument, plaything, puppet, stooge, tool, toy.

**pawn**[2] *v* deposit, dip, gage, hazard, hock, impawn, impignorate, lay in lavender, mortgage, pledge, pop, stake, wager.

*n* hostage, security.

**pawnbroker** *n* gombeen-man, lender, money-lender, uncle, usurer.

**pawnshop** *n* leaving-shop, mont-de-piété, monte de pietà, pop-shop.

**pay** *v* ante, benefit, bestow, bring in, clear, compensate, cough up, disburse, discharge, extend, foot, get even with, give, grant, honour, indemnify, liquidate, meet, offer, pay out, present, produce, proffer, profit, punish, reciprocate, recompense, reimburse, remit, remunerate, render, repay, requite, return, reward, serve, settle, square, square up, yield.

*n* allowance, compensation, consideration, earnings, emoluments, fee, hire, honorarium, income, payment, recompense, reimbursement, remuneration, reward, salary, stipend, takings, wages.

**pay back** avenge, chasten, get even with, get one's own back, punish, reciprocate, recompense, refund, reimburse, repay, retaliate, return, settle up, settle with, square.

**pay for** answer for, atone, compensate, face the music, get one's deserts, make amends, suffer.

**pay off** clear, discharge, dismiss, fire, lay off, liquidate, sack, satisfy, settle, square, succeed, work.

**pay out** cough up, disburse, dish out, expend, fork out, hand over, lay out, render, shell out, spend.

**payable** *adj* due, in arrears, mature, obligatory, outstanding, owed, owing, receivable, unpaid.

**payment** *n* advance, alimony, ante, consideration, defrayal, deposit, discharge, fee, hire, instalment, outlay, paying, portion, premium, remittance, remuneration, reward, settlement, sub, wage.

**pay-off** *n* climax, clincher, conclusion, consequence, crunch, culmination, day of reckoning, dénouement, judgement, moment of truth, outcome, punch-line, reimbursement, result, retribution, reward, settlement, upshot.

**peace** *n* accord, agreement, amity, armistice, calm, calmness, cease-fire, composure, conciliation, concord, contentment, frith, harmony, hush, pacification, pax, peacefulness, placidity, quiet, quietude, relaxation, repose, rest, serenity, silence, stillness, tranquillity, treaty, truce.

*antonyms* disagreement, disturbance, war.

**peace studies** irenology.

**peaceable** *adj* amiable, amicable, compatible, conciliatory, douce, dovish, easy-going, friendly, gentle, inoffensive, mild, non-belligerent, pacific, peaceful, peace-loving, placid, unwarlike.

*antonyms* belligerent, offensive.

**peaceful** *adj* amicable, at peace, becalmed, calm, conciliatory, friendly, gentle, halcyon, harmonious, irenic (eirenic), non-violent, pacific, peaceable, peace-loving, placatory, placid, quiet, restful, serene, still, tranquil, unagitated, undisturbed, unruffled, untroubled, unwarlike.

*antonyms* disturbed, noisy, troubled.

**peacemaker** *n* appeaser, arbitrator, conciliator, interceder, intercessor, mediator, mediatress, mediatrix, pacifier, peacemonger.

**peacemaking** *adj* appeasing, conciliatory, irenic(al), mediating, mediative, mediatorial, mediatory, pacific.

**peace-pipe** *n* calumet, pipe of peace.

**peak** *n* acme, aiguille, apex, apogee, brow, climax, crest, crown, culmination, cuspid, high noon, high point, maximum, ne plus ultra, pinnacle, point, summit, tip, top, visor, zenith.

*antonyms* nadir, trough.

*v* climax, come to a head, culminate, spire, tower.

**peaky** *adj* drooping, emaciated, ill, off-colour, pale, peelie-wally, pinched, poorly, shilpit, sick, sickly, under the weather, unwell, wan, washed-out, wilting.

*antonyms* healthy, in the pink.

**peal** *n* blast, carillon, chime, clamour, clang, clangour, clap, clash, crash, resounding, reverberation, ring, ringing, roar, rumble, sound, tintinnabulation.

*v* chime, clash, crack, crash, resonate, resound, reverberate, ring, roar, roll, rumble, sound, tintinnabulate, toll, vibrate.

**peanut** *n* goober, ground-nut, monkey-nut.

**peanuts** *n* chickenfeed, pennies, pittance.

**peasant** *n* boor, bumpkin, churl, countryman, fellah, hind, jungli, kulak, lout, moujik, mujik, muzhik, oaf, oik, provincial, rustic, swain, yokel.

*antonym* sophisticate.

**pebble** *n* agate, chip, gallet, stone.

**peccadillo** *n* boob, delinquency, error, fault, indiscretion, infraction, lapse, misdeed, misdemeanour, slip, slip-up.

**peck** *n* criticism, food, jab, kiss, strike.

*v* eat, jab, kiss, nibble.

**peculiar**[1] *adj* abnormal, bizarre, curious, eccentric, exceptional, extraordinary, far-out, freakish, funky, funny, odd, offbeat, outlandish, out-of-the-way, quaint, queer, singular, strange, uncommon, unconventional, unusual, way-out, weird.

*antonyms* normal, ordinary.

**peculiar**[2] *adj* appropriate, characteristic, discriminative, distinct, distinctive, distinguishing, endemic, idiosyncratic, individual, local, particular, personal, private, quintessential, restricted, special, specific, unique.

*antonyms* general, uncharacteristic.

**peculiarity** *n* abnormality, attribute, bizarreness, characteristic, distinctiveness, eccentricity, exception, feature, foible, freakishness, idiosyncrasy, kink, mannerism, mark, oddity, particularity, property, quality, queerness, quirk, singularity, speciality, trait, whimsicality.

**pecuniary** *adj* commercial, financial, fiscal, monetary, nummary, nummulary.

**pedagogue** *n* dogmatist, dominie, don, educationalist, educationist, educator, instructor, master, mistress, pedant, preceptor, schoolmaster, schoolmistress, teacher.

**pedagogy** *n* instruction, pedagogics, teaching, training, tuition, tutelage.

**pedant** *n* casuist, doctrinaire, dogmatist, Dryasdust, gerund-grinder, grammaticaster, grammatist, hair-splitter, literalist, mandarin, nit-picker, pedagogue, pettifogger, precisian, quibbler, scholastic, vocabularian.

**pedantic** *adj* abstruse, academic, bookish, cavilling, didactic, donnish, erudite, finical, formal, fussy, hair-splitting, learned, nit-picking, particular, pedagogic, perfectionist, pompous, precise, punctilious, scholastic, schoolmasterly, sententious, stilted.

*antonyms* casual, imprecise, informal.

**pedantry** *n* bookishness, cavilling, finicality, hair-splitting, pedagogism, pedagoguery, pedagoguishness, pedantism, pomposity, punctiliousness, quibbling, stuffiness.

**peddle** *v* dilly-dally, flog, hawk, huckster, idle, loiter, market, piddle, push, retail, sell, tout, trade, trifle, vend.

**pedestal** *n* base, dado, foot, foundation, mounting, pier, platform, plinth, podium, socle, stand, support, understructure.

**pedestrian** *n* footslogger, foot-traveller, voetganger, walker.

*adj* banal, boring, commonplace, dull, flat, humdrum, indifferent, mediocre, mundane, ordinary, plodding, prosaic, run-of-the-mill, stodgy, tolerable, unimaginative, uninspired, uninteresting.

*antonyms* bright, brilliant, exciting, imaginative.

**pedigree** *n* ancestry, blood, breed, derivation, descent, dynasty, extraction, family, family tree, genealogy, heritage, line, lineage, parentage, race, stemma, stirps, stock, succession.

**pedigreed** *adj* aristocratic, full-blooded, pedigree, pure-bred, thoroughbred.

**pedlar** *n* boxwallah, chapman, cheap-jack, colporteur, gutter-man, gutter-merchant, hawker, huckster, seller, street-trader, vendor, walker, yagger.

**peek** *v* glance, keek, look, peep, peer, spy.

*n* blink, dekko, gander, glance, glimpse, keek, look, look-see, peep, shufti.

**peel** *v* decorticate, denude, desquamate, flake (off), pare, scale, skin, strip (off), undress.

*n* epicarp, exocarp, integument, peeling, rind, skin, zest.

**peep** *v* blink, emerge, glimpse, issue, keek, peek, peer.

*n* blink, dekko, gander, glim, glimpse, keek, look, look-see, peek, shufti.

**peephole** *n* aperture, chink, cleft, crack, crevice, fissure, hole, interstice, keyhole, opening, pinhole, slit, spy-hole.

**peer**[1] *v* appear, blink, emerge, examine, gaze, inspect, peep, scan, scrutinise, snoop, spy, squint.

**peer**[2] *n* aristocrat, baron, count, duke, earl, lord, marquess, marquis, noble, nobleman, thane, viscount.

**peer**[3] *n* compeer, counterpart, equal, equipollent, equivalent, fellow, like, match.

**peerage** *n* aristocracy, lords and ladies, nobility, patriciate, top drawer, upper crust.

**peeress** *n* baroness, countess, dame, duchess, lady, marchioness, noblewoman, viscountess.

**peerless** *adj* beyond compare, excellent, incomparable, matchless, nonpareil, outstanding, paramount, second to none, superlative, supreme, unbeatable, unequalled, unexcelled, unique, unmatched, unparalleled, unrivalled, unsurpassed.

**peeved** *adj* annoyed, exasperated, galled, irked, irritated, miffed, narked, nettled, pipped, piqued, put out, riled, sore, upset, vexed.

**peevish** *adj* acrimonious, cantankerous, captious, childish, churlish, crabbed, cross, crotchety, crusty, dorty, fractious, frampold, franzy, fretful, grumpy, hipped, ill-natured, ill-tempered, irritable, miffy, perverse, pettish, petulant, querulous, ratty, short-tempered, snappy, splenetic, sulky, sullen, surly, testy, touchy, waspish.

*antonym* good-tempered.

**peevishness** *n* acrimony, captiousness, ill-temper, irritability, perversity, pet, petulance, pique, protervity, querulousness, testiness.

**peg** *v* attach, control, fasten, fix, freeze, insert, join, limit, mark, pierce, score, secure, set, stabilise.

*n* dowel, hook, knob, marker, pin, post, stake, thole(-pin), toggle.

**peg away** apply oneself, beaver away, hang in, keep at it, persevere, persist, plod along, plug away, stick at it, work away.

**pejorative** *adj* bad, belittling, condemnatory, damning, debasing, deprecatory, depreciatory, derogatory, detractive, detractory, disparaging, negative, slighting, uncomplimentary, unflattering, unpleasant.

*antonyms* complimentary, laudatory.

**pell-mell** *adv* feverishly, full tilt, hastily, heedlessly, helter-skelter, hurriedly, hurry-scurry, impetuously, posthaste, precipitously, rashly, recklessly.

*adj* chaotic, confused, disordered, disorganised, haphazard, indiscriminate, scrambled, tumultuous.

**pelt¹** *v* assail, batter, beat, belabour, belt, bombard, bucket, career, cast, charge, dash, hit, hurl, hurry, pepper, pour, pummel, rain cats and dogs, rush, shoot, shower, sling, speed, strafe, strike, tear, teem, thrash, throw, wallop, whiz.

**pelt²** *n* coat, fell, fleece, fur, hide, skin.

**pen¹** *v* author, compose, draft, jot down, scribble, write.

**pen name** alias, allonym, nom de plume, pseudonym.

**pen²** *n* cage, coop, crib, cru(i)ve, enclosure, fold, hutch, stall, sty.

*v* cage, confine, coop, corral, crib, enclose, fence, hedge, hem in, hurdle, mew (up), shut up.

**penal servitude** bird, lag, porridge, stretch, time.

**penalise** *v* amerce, correct, disadvantage, discipline, handicap, mulct, punish.

*antonym* reward.

**penalty** *n* amende, amercement, disadvantage, fine, forfeit, forfeiture, handicap, mulct, price, punishment, retribution.

*antonym* reward.

**penance** *n* atonement, mortification, penalty, placation, propitiation, punishment, reparation, sackcloth and ashes.

**penchant** *n* affinity, bent, bias, disposition, fondness, inclination, leaning, liking, partiality, predilection, predisposition, preference, proclivity, proneness, propensity, soft spot, taste, tendency, turn.

*antonym* dislike.

**pendant** *n* drop, lavaliere, locket, medallion, necklace.

**pendent** *adj* dangling, drooping, hanging, nutant, pendulous, pensile, suspended, swinging.

**pending** *adj* awaiting, forthcoming, hanging, imminent, impending, in the balance, in the offing, on the back burner, undecided, undetermined, unfinished, unsettled.

*antonyms* finished, settled.

**pendulous** *adj* dangling, drooping, droopy, hanging, pendent, sagging, suspended, swaying, swinging.

**penetrable** *adj* accessible, clear, comprehensible, explicable, fathomable, intelligible, open, passable, permeable, pervious, porous, understandable.

*antonym* impenetrable.

**penetrate** *v* affect, bore, come across, come home, comprehend, decipher, diffuse, discern, enter, fathom, get through to, get to the bottom of, grasp, impress, infiltrate, perforate, permeate, pervade, pierce, prick, probe, seep, sink, stab, strike, suffuse, touch, understand, unravel.

**penetrating** *adj* acute, astute, biting, carrying, critical, discerning, discriminating, harsh, incisive, intelligent, intrusive, keen, observant, penetrative, perceptive, percipient, perspicacious, pervasive, piercing, profound, pungent, quick, sagacious, searching, sharp, sharp-witted, shrewd, shrill, stinging, strong.

*antonyms* gentle, obtuse, soft.

**penetration** *n* acumen, acuteness, astuteness, discernment, entrance, entry, incision, inroad, insight, interpenetration, invasion, keenness, perception, perforation, perspicacity, piercing, puncturing, sharpness, shrewdness, wit.

**peninsula** *n* cape, chersonese, doab, mull, point, tongue.

**penis** *n* cock, dick, John Thomas, knob, membrum virile, pecker, phallus, pizzle, prick, rod, shaft, tool, winkle.

**penitence** *n* compunction, contrition, regret, regretfulness, remorse, repentance, rue, self-reproach, shame, sorrow.

**penitent** *adj* abject, apologetic, atoning, conscience-stricken, contrite, humble, in sackcloth and ashes, regretful, remorseful, repentant, rueful, sorrowful, sorry.

*antonym* unrepentant.

**penniless** *adj* bankrupt, broke, bust(ed), cleaned out, destitute, flat broke, impecunious, impoverished, indigent, moneyless, necessitous, needy, obolary, on one's uppers, on the rocks, penurious, poor, poverty-stricken, ruined, skint, stoney-broke, strapped.

*antonyms* rich, wealthy.

**pennon** *n* banderol(e), banner, burgee, ensign, gonfalon, jack, oriflamme, pencel, pencil, pennant, pensel, streamer.

**penny-pincher** *n* meany, miser, niggard, pinchfist, pinchgut, pinchpenny, screw, Scrooge, skinflint.

**penny-pinching** *adj* cheeseparing, close, frugal, mean, mingy, miserly, near, niggardly, parsimonious, scrimping, stingy, tight-fisted, ungenerous.

*antonyms* generous, open-handed.

**pension** *n* allowance, annuity, benefit, maintenance, stipend, superannuation.

**pensive** *adj* absent-minded, absorbed, cogitative, contemplative, dreamy, grave, meditative, melancholy, musing, preoccupied, reflective, ruminative, serious, sober, solemn, thoughtful, wistful.

**pent-up** *adj* bottled-up, bridled, checked, constrained, curbed, inhibited, repressed, restrained, smothered, stifled, suppressed.

**penurious** *adj* beggarly, bust(ed), cheeseparing, close, close-fisted, deficient, destitute, flat broke, frugal, grudging, impecunious, impoverished, inadequate, indigent, meagre, mean, miserable, miserly, near, needy, niggardly, obolary, paltry, parsimonious, penniless, poor, poverty-stricken, scanty, skimping, stingy, tight-fisted, ungenerous.

*antonyms* generous, wealthy.

**penury** *n* beggary, dearth, deficiency, destitution, indigence, lack, mendicancy, mendicity, need, paucity, pauperism, poverty, privation, scantiness, scarcity, shortage, sparseness, straitened circumstances, straits, want.

*antonym* prosperity.

**people** *n* citizens, clan, commonalty, community, crowd, demos, family, folk, general public, gens, grass roots, hoi polloi, human beings, humanity, humans, inhabitants, mankind, many-headed beast, many-headed monster, masses, mob, mortals, multitude, nation, persons, plebs, populace, population, public, punters, rabble, race, rank and file, the herd, the million, tribe.

*v* colonise, inhabit, occupy, populate, settle, tenant.

**pep** *n* animation, energy, exuberance, get-up-and-go, gusto, high spirits, life, liveliness, pizzazz, spirit, verve, vigour, vim, vitality, vivacity, zip.

**pep up** animate, energise, enliven, excite, exhilarate, inspire, invigorate, jazz up, quicken, stimulate, vitalise, vivify.

**peppery** *adj* astringent, biting, caustic, choleric, fiery, grumpy, hot, hot-tempered, incisive, irascible, irritable, nippy, piquant, pungent, quick-tempered, sarcastic, sharp, snappish, spicy, stinging, testy, touchy, trenchant, waspish.

**perceive** *v* appreciate, apprehend, be aware of, behold, catch, comprehend, conclude, deduce, descry, discern, discover, distinguish, espy, feel, gather, get, grasp, intuit, know, learn, make out, note, observe, realise, recognise, remark, see, sense, spot, understand.

**perceptible** *adj* apparent, appreciable, clear, conspicuous, detectable, discernible, distinct, distinguishable, evident, noticeable, observable, obvious, palpable, perceivable, recognisable, salient, tangible, visible.

*antonym* imperceptible.

**perception** *n* Anschauung, apprehension, awareness, conception, consciousness, discernment, feeling, grasp, idea, impression, insight, intellection, notion, observation, recognition, sensation, sense, taste, understanding, uptake.

**perceptive** *adj* able to see through a millstone, acute, alert, astute, aware, discerning, insightful, observant, penetrating, percipient, perspicacious, quick, responsive, sagacious, sapient, sensitive, sharp.

*antonym* unobservant.

**perch** *v* alight, balance, drop, land, light, rest, roost, settle, sit on.

**percipience** *n* acuity, acuteness, alertness, astuteness, awareness, discernment, insight, intuition, judgement, penetration, perception, perspicacity, sagacity, sensitivity, understanding.

**percipient** *adj* alert, alive, astute, aware, discerning, discriminating, intelligent, judicious, knowing, penetrating, perceptive, perspicacious, quick-witted, sharp, wide-awake.

*antonyms* obtuse, unaware.

**percolate** *v* drain, drip, exude, filter, filtrate, leach, leak, ooze, osmose, penetrate, permeate, pervade, seep, strain, transfuse.

**perdition** *n* condemnation, damnation, destruction, doom, downfall, hell, hellfire, ruin, ruination.

**peregrination** *n* excursion, expedition, exploration, globe-trotting, journey, odyssey, roaming, roving, tour, travel, travelling, trek, trekking, trip, voyage, wandering, wayfaring.

**peremptory** *adj* abrupt, absolute, arbitrary, assertive, authoritative, autocratic, binding, bossy, categorical, commanding, compelling, curt, decisive, dictatorial, dogmatic, domineering, final, high-handed, imperative, imperious, incontrovertible, intolerant, irrefutable, obligatory, overbearing, summary, undeniable.

**perennial** *adj* abiding, ceaseless, chronic, constant, continual, continuing, deathless, enduring, eternal, evergreen, everlasting, immortal, imperishable, incessant, inveterate, lasting, lifelong, never-ending, never-failing, permanent, perpetual, persistent, recurrent, sempiternal, unceasing, unchanging, undying, unfailing, uninterrupted.

**perfect** *adj* absolute, accomplished, accurate, adept, blameless, close, complete, completed, consummate, copybook, correct, entire, exact, excellent, experienced, expert, faithful, faultless, finished, flawless, full, ideal, immaculate, impeccable, irreproachable, masterly, model, polished, practised, precise, pure, right, sheer, skilful, skilled, splendid, spotless, spot-on, strict, sublime, superb, superlative, supreme, true, unadulterated, unalloyed, unblemished, unerring, unimpeachable, unmarred, unmitigated, untarnished, utter, whole.

*antonyms* flawed, imperfect.

*v* accomplish, achieve, carry out, complete, consummate, effect, elaborate, finish, fulfil, perfectionate, perform, realise, refine.

**perfection** *n* accomplishment, achievement, acme, completeness, completion, consummation, crown, evolution, exactness, excellence, exquisiteness, flawlessness, fulfilment, ideal, integrity, maturity, nonpareil, paragon, perfectness, pinnacle, precision, purity, realisation, sublimity, superiority, wholeness.

*antonyms* flaw, imperfection.

**perfectionist** *n* formalist, idealist, precisian, precisionist, purist, stickler.

**perfectly** *adv* absolutely, admirably, altogether, completely, consummately, entirely, exquisitely, faultlessly, flawlessly, fully, ideally, impeccably, incomparably, irreproachably, quite, superbly, superlatively, supremely, thoroughly, to perfection, totally, unimpeachably, utterly, wholly, wonderfully.

*antonyms* imperfectly, partially.

**perfidious** *adj* corrupt, deceitful, dishonest, disloyal, double-dealing, double-faced, duplicitous, faithless, false, Machiavellian, Punic, recreant, traitorous, treacherous, treasonous, two-faced, unfaithful, untrustworthy.

*antonyms* faithful, honest, loyal.

**perfidy** *n* betrayal, deceit, disloyalty, double-dealing, duplicity, faithlessness, falsity, infidelity, perfidiousness, Punic faith, traitorousness, treachery, treason.

*antonyms* faithfulness, honesty, loyalty.

**perforate** *v* bore, drill, hole, honeycomb, penetrate, pierce, prick, punch, puncture, stab.

**perforated** *adj* bored, drilled, ethmoid, fenestrate(d), fenestrial, foraminous, holed, pierced, porous, punched, punctured.

**perforation** *n* bore, cut, dotted line, fenestration, hole, prick, puncture, slit, space.

**perforce** *adv* inevitably, necessarily, of necessity, unavoidably, willy-nilly.

**perform** *v* accomplish, achieve, act, appear as, bring about, bring off, carry out, complete, depict, discharge, do, effect, enact, execute, fulfil, function, functionate, manage, observe, play, present, produce, pull off, put on, render, represent, satisfy, stage, transact, work.

**performance** *n* accomplishment, account, achievement, act, acting, action, appearance, behaviour, bother, business, carrying out, carry-on, completion, conduct, consummation, discharge, efficiency, execution, exhibition,

exploit, feat, fulfilment, functioning, fuss, gig, implementation, interpretation, melodrama, operation, play, portrayal, practice, presentation, production, rendition, representation, rigmarole, running, show, to-do, work, working.

**performer** *n* actor, actress, artiste, moke, mummer, play-actor, player, Thespian, trouper.

**perfume** *n* aroma, attar, balm, balminess, bouquet, cologne, essence, fragrance, incense, odour, redolence, scent, smell, sweetness, toilet water.

**perfunctory** *adj* automatic, brief, careless, cursory, heedless, hurried, inattentive, indifferent, mechanical, negligent, offhand, routine, sketchy, slipshod, slovenly, stereotyped, superficial, wooden.

*antonym* cordial.

**perhaps** *adv* conceivably, feasibly, happen, maybe, mayhap, peradventure, perchance, possibly, you never know.

**peril** *n* danger, exposure, hazard, imperilment, insecurity, jeopardy, menace, pitfall, risk, threat, uncertainty, vulnerability.

*antonyms* safety, security.

**perilous** *adj* chancy, dangerous, desperate, dicey, difficult, dire, exposed, hairy, hazardous, menacing, parlous, precarious, risky, threatening, unsafe, unsure, vulnerable.

*antonyms* safe, secure.

**perimeter** *n* ambit, border, borderline, boundary, bounds, circumference, confines, edge, fringe, frontier, limit, margin, periphery.

*antonyms* centre, heart, middle.

**period**[1] *n* aeon, age, course, cycle, date, days, end, epoch, era, generation, interval, season, space, span, spell, stage, stint, stop, stretch, term, time, turn, while, years.

**period**[2] *n* menses, menstrual flow, menstruation, monthlies, the curse.

**periodic** *adj* cyclic, cyclical, desultory, etesian, infrequent, intermittent, occasional, periodical, recurrent, regular, repeated, seasonal, spasmodic, sporadic.

**periodical** *n* gazette, journal, magazine, monthly, organ, paper, publication, quarterly, review, serial, weekly.

**peripatetic** *adj* ambulant, ambulatory, itinerant, journeying, migrant, mobile, nomadic, roaming, roving, travelling, vagabond, vagrant, wandering.

*antonym* fixed.

**peripheral** *adj* borderline, exterior, external, incidental, inessential, irrelevant, marginal, minor, outer, outermost, outlying, outside, perimetric, secondary, superficial, surface, tangential, unimportant, unnecessary.

*antonyms* central, crucial.

**periphery** *n* ambit, border, boundary, brim, brink, circuit, circumference, edge, fringe, hem, margin, outskirts, perimeter, rim, skirt, verge.

*antonyms* centre, nub.

**perish** *v* collapse, croak, crumble, decay, decline, decompose, decrease, die, disappear, disintegrate, end, expire, fall, moulder, pass away, rot, vanish, waste, wither.

**perishable** *adj* biodegradable, corruptible, decomposable, destructible, fast-decaying, fast-deteriorating, short-lived, unstable.

**perjury** *n* false oath, false statement, false swearing, false witness, falsification, forswearing, mendacity.

**perk** *n* benefit, bonus, bunce, dividend, extra, freebie, fringe benefit, perquisite, plus.

**perk up** brighten, buck up, cheer up, improve, liven up, look up, pep up, rally, recover, recuperate, revive, take heart, upturn.

**perky** *adj* animated, bouncy, bright, bubbly, buoyant, cheerful, cheery, effervescent, gay, jaunty, lively, peppy, spirited, sprightly, sunny, vivacious.

*antonyms* cheerless, dull, gloomy.

**permanence** *n* constancy, continuance, continuity, deathlessness, dependability, durability, duration, endurance, finality, fixedness, fixity, immortality, imperishability, indestructibility, lastingness, longevity, perdurability, permanency, perpetuity, stability, survival.

*antonym* impermanence.

**permanent** *adj* abiding, constant, durable, enduring, everlasting, fixed, immutable, imperishable, indestructible, ineffaceable, ineradicable, inerasable, invariable, lasting, long-lasting, perennial, perpetual, persistent, stable, standing, steadfast, unchanging, unfading.

*antonyms* ephemeral, fleeting, temporary.

**permanently** *adv* always, ceaselessly, constantly, continually, endlessly, eternally, ever more, everlastingly, for keeps, forever, once and for all, umremittingly, unendingly.

*antonym* temporarily.

**permeable** *adj* absorbent, absorptive, passable, penetrable, pervious, porous, spongeous, spongy.

*antonyms* impermeable, watertight.

**permeate** *v* charge, fill, filter through, imbue, impenetrate, impregnate, infiltrate, interfuse, interpenetrate, pass through, penetrate, percolate, pervade, saturate, seep through, soak through.

**permissible** *adj* acceptable, admissible, all right, allowable, allowed, authorised, kosher, lawful, leal, legit, legitimate, licit, OK, permitted, proper, sanctioned.

*antonym* prohibited.

**permission** *n* allowance, approval, assent, authorisation, consent, dispensation, freedom, go-ahead, green light, imprimatur, indult, leave, liberty, licence, permit, sanction, sufferance.

*antonym* prohibition.

**permissive** *adj* acquiescent, complaisant, easygoing, forbearing, free, indulgent, latitudinarian, lax, lenient, liberal, open-minded, overindulgent, tolerant.

*antonym* strict.

**permit** *v* admit, agree, allow, authorise, consent, empower, enable, endorse, endure, give leave, grant, let, warrant.

*antonym* prohibit.

*n* authorisation, carnet, liberty, licence, pass, passport, permission, sanction, visa, warrant.

*antonym* prohibition.

**permutation** *n* alteration, change, commutation, shift, transformation, transmutation, transposition, transubstantiation.

**pernicious** *adj* bad, baleful, baneful, damaging, dangerous, deadly, deleterious, destructive, detrimental, evil, fatal, harmful, hurtful, injurious, maleficent, malevolent, malicious, malign, malignant, noisome, noxious, offensive, pestilent, poisonous, ruinous, toxic, unhealthy, unwholesome, venomous, wicked.

*antonym* innocuous.

**pernickety** *adj* careful, carping, detailed, exacting, fastidious, fiddly, fikish, fiky, fine, finical, finicky, fussy, hair-splitting, nice, nit-picking, over-precise, painstaking, particular, punctilious, tricky.

**peroration** *n* closing remarks, conclusion, recapitulation, recapping, reiteration, summary, summing-up.

**perpendicular** *adj* plumb, precipitous, sheer, straight, upright, vertical.

*antonym* horizontal.

**perpetrate** *v* carry out, commit, do, effect, enact, execute, inflict, perform, practise, wreak.

**perpetual** *adj* abiding, ceaseless, constant, continual, continuous, deathless, endless, enduring, eternal, everlasting, immortal, incessant, infinite, interminable, lasting, never-ending, never-failing, perennial, permanent, persistent, recurrent, repeated, sempiternal, unceasing, unchanging, undying, unending, unfailing, unflagging, uninterrupted, unremitting, unvarying.

*antonyms* ephemeral, intermittent, transient.

**perpetuate** *v* commemorate, continue, eternalise, immortalise, keep alive, keep up, maintain, preserve, protract, sustain.

**perplex** *v* baffle, befuddle, beset, bewilder, complicate, confound, confuse, dumbfound, embrangle, encumber, entangle, gravel, hobble, involve, jumble, mix up, muddle, mystify, nonplus, pother, pudder, puzzle, stump, tangle, thicken, throw.

**perplexed** *adj* at a loss, baffled, bamboozled, bewildered, confounded, disconcerted, fuddled, muddled, mystified, puzzled, worried.

**perplexing** *adj* amazing, baffling, bewildering, complex, complicated, confusing, difficult, distractive, enigmatic, hard, inexplicable, intricate, involved, knotty, labyrinthine, mysterious, mystifying, paradoxical, puzzling, strange, taxing, thorny, unaccountable, vexatious, weird.

*antonyms* easy, simple.

**perplexity** *n* bafflement, bewilderment, complexity, confusion, difficulty, dilemma, enigma, incomprehension, intricacy, involvement, labyrinth, mystery, mystification, nonplus, obfuscation, obscuration, obscurity, paradox, puzzle, puzzlement, snarl, stupefaction.

**perquisite** *n* ap(p)anage, baksheesh, benefit, bonus, dividend, extra, fringe benefit, gratuity, perk, plus, tip.

**persecute** *v* afflict, annoy, badger, bait, bother, castigate, crucify, distress, dragoon, harass, haze, hound, hunt, ill-treat, injure, maltreat, martyr, molest, oppress, pester, pursue, tease, torment, torture, tyrannise, vex, victimise, worry.

*antonyms* accommodate, humour, indulge, pamper.

**persecution** *n* abuse, baiting, bashing, castigation, discrimination, maltreatment, molestation, oppression, punishment, subjugation, suppression, torture, tyranny.

**perseverance** *n* abidance, assiduity, constancy, dedication, determination, diligence, doggedness, endurance, indefatigability, persistence, pertinacity, purposefulness, resolution, sedulity, stamina, steadfastness, tenacity.

**persevere** *v* adhere, carry on, continue, endure, go on, hang on, hold fast, hold on, keep going, persist, plug away, pursue, remain, soldier on, stand firm, stick at.

*antonyms* desist, discontinue, give up, stop.

**persist** *v* abide, carry on, continue, endure, insist, keep at it, last, linger, perdure, persevere, remain, stand fast, stand firm.

*antonyms* desist, stop.

**persistence** *n* assiduity, assiduousness, constancy, determination, diligence, doggedness, endurance, grit, indefatigableness, perseverance, pertinacity, pluck, resolution, sedulity, stamina, steadfastness, tenacity, tirelessness.

**persistent** *adj* assiduous, constant, continual, continuous, determined, dogged, endless, enduring, fixed, hydra-headed, immovable, incessant, indefatigable, indomitable, interminable, never-ending, obdurate, obstinate, perpetual, persevering, pertinacious, relentless, repeated, resolute, steadfast, steady, stubborn, tenacious, tireless, unflagging, unrelenting, unremitting, zealous.

**person** *n* being, bod, body, cat, chal, character, codger, cookie, customer, human, human being, individual, individuum, living soul, party, soul, specimen, type, wight.

**persona** *n* character, façade, face, front, image, mask, part, personality, public face, role.

**personable** *adj* affable, agreeable, amiable, attractive, charming, good-looking, handsome, lik(e)able, nice, outgoing, pleasant, pleasing, presentable, warm, winning.

*antonyms* disagreeable, unattractive.

**personage** *n* big shot, celebrity, dignitary, headliner, luminary, name, notable, personality, public figure, somebody, VIP, worthy.

**personal** *adj* bodily, corporal, corporeal, derogatory, disparaging, exclusive, exterior, idiosyncratic, individual, inimitable, insulting, intimate, material, nasty, offensive, own, particular, peculiar, pejorative, physical, private, privy, slighting, special, tête-à-tête.

*antonyms* general, public, universal.

**personality** *n* attraction, attractiveness, celebrity, character, charisma, charm, disposition, dynamism, humour, identity, individuality, lik(e)ableness, magnetism, make-up, nature, notable, personage, pleasantness, psyche, selfhood, selfness, star, temper, temperament, traits.

**personally** *adv* alone, idiosyncratically, independently, individually, privately, solely, specially, subjectively.

**personification** *n* delineation, embodiment, image, incarnation, likeness, manifestation, portrayal, recreation, representation, semblance.

**personify** *v* embody, epitomise, exemplify, express, hypostatise, image, incarnate, mirror, personise, represent, symbolise, typify.

**personnel** *n* crew, employees, helpers, human resources, liveware, manpower, members, people, staff, workers, workforce.

**perspective** *n* angle, aspect, attitude, context, objectivity, outlook, overview, panorama, proportion, prospect, relation, scene, slant, view, vista.

**perspicacious** *adj* acute, alert, astute, aware, clear-eyed, clear-sighted, clever, discerning, far-sighted, keen, observant, penetrating, perceptive, percipient, sagacious, sharp, sharp-witted, shrewd.

*antonyms* obtuse, unobservant.

**perspicacity** *n* acuity, acumen, acuteness, brains, cleverness, discernment, discrimination, insight, keenness, penetration, perceptiveness, percipience, perspicaciousness, perspicuity, sagaciousness, sagacity, sharpness, shrewdness, wit.

q**perspicuity** *n* clarity, clearness, comprehensibility, comprehensibleness, distinctness, explicitness, intelligibility, limpidity, limpidness, lucidity, penetrability, plainness, precision, straightforwardness, transparency.

**perspicuous** *adj* apparent, clear, comprehensible, crystal-clear, distinct, explicit, intelligible, limpid, lucid, manifest, obvious, plain, self-evident, straightforward, transparent, unambiguous, understandable.

**perspiration** *n* dew, diaphoresis, exudation, hidrosis, moisture, sudor, sweat, wetness.

**perspire** *v* drip, exude, glow, secrete, sudate, sweat, swelter.

**persuadable** *adj* acquiescent, agreeable, amenable, compliant, flexible, impressionable, malleable, persuasible, pliable, receptive, susceptive.

*antonyms* firm, inflexible, stubborn.

**persuade** *v* actuate, advise, allure, bring round, cajole, coax, convert, convince, counsel, entice, fast-talk, impel, incite, induce, influence, inveigle, lead on, lean on, prevail upon, prompt, satisfy, sway, sweet-talk, talk into, urge, win over.

*antonyms* discourage, dissuade.

**persuasion** *n* belief, blandishment, cajolery, camp, certitude, cogency, come-on, conversion, conviction, credo, creed, cult, denomination, enticement, exhortation, faction, faith, force, inducement, influence, inveiglement, opinion, party, persuasiveness, potency, power, pull, school (of thought), sect, side, suasion, sweet talk, tenet, views, wheedling.

**persuasive** *adj* cogent, compelling, convincing, credible, effective, eloquent, forceful, honeyed, impelling, impressive, inducing, influential, logical, moving, persuasory, plausible, potent, sound, telling, touching, valid, weighty, whilly, whillywha(w), winning.

**pert** *adj* bold, brash, brisk, cheeky, daring, dicacious, flip, flippant, forward, fresh, gay, impertinent, impudent, insolent, jaunty, lively, nimble, perky, presumptuous, saucy, smart, spirited, sprightly, tossy.

*antonyms* coy, shy.

**pertain** *v* appertain, apply, be appropriate, be part of, be relevant, bear on, befit, belong, come under, concern, refer, regard, relate.

**pertinacious** *adj* determined, dogged, headstrong, inflexible, intractable, mulish, obdurate, obstinate, persevering, persistent, perverse, purposeful, relentless, resolute, self-willed, strong-willed, stubborn, tenacious, uncompromising, unyielding, wilful.

**pertinent** *adj* ad rem, admissible, analogous, applicable, apposite, appropriate, apropos, apt, befitting, fit, fitting, germane, material, pat, proper, relevant, suitable, to the point, to the purpose.

*antonyms* inappropriate, irrelevant, unsuitable.

**pertness** *n* audacity, boldness, brashness, brass, brazenness, bumptiousness, cheek, cheekiness, chutzpah, cockiness, didacity, effrontery, forwardness, freshness, impertinence, impudence, insolence, presumption, rudeness, sauciness.

**perturb** *v* aerate, agitate, alarm, bother, confuse, disarrange, discompose, disconcert, discountenance, disorder, disquiet, disturb, faze, feeze, fluster, muddle, ruffle, trouble, unsettle, upset, vex, worry.

*antonyms* compose, reassure.

**perturbed** *adj* agitated, alarmed, anxious, discomposed, disconcerted, disturbed, dithery, fearful, flappable, flurried, flustered, nervous, restless, shaken, troubled, uncomfortable, uneasy, unsettled, upset, worried.

*antonym* unperturbed.

**perusal** *n* browse, check, examination, inspection, look, read, run-through, scrutiny, study.

**peruse** *v* browse, check, examine, inspect, look through, pore over, read, scan, scrutinise, study, vet.

**pervade** *v* affect, charge, diffuse, extend, fill, imbue, infuse, osmose, overspread, penetrate, percolate, permeate, saturate, suffuse.

**pervasive** *adj* common, diffuse, extensive, general, immanent, inescapable, omnipresent, permeating, pervading, prevalent, rife, ubiquitous, universal, widespread.

**perverse** *adj* abnormal, balky, camstairy, cantankerous, churlish, contradictory, contrary, contumacious, crabbed, cross, cross-grained, cussed, delinquent, depraved, deviant, disobedient, dogged, fractious, froward, headstrong, ill-natured, ill-tempered, improper, incorrect, intractable, intransigent, miscreant, mulish, obdurate, obstinate, peevish, petulant, pig-headed, rebellious, recalcitrant, refractory, spiteful, stroppy, stubborn, surly, thrawn, thwart, troublesome, unhealthy, unmanageable, unreasonable, unyielding, uppity, wayward, wilful, wrong-headed, wry.

*antonyms* normal, reasonable.

**perversion** *n* aberration, abnormality, anomaly, corruption, debauchery, depravity, deviance, deviancy, deviation, distortion, falsification, immorality, kink, kinkiness, misapplication, misinterpretation, misrepresentation, misuse, paraphilia, twisting, unnaturalness, vice, vitiation, wickedness.

**perversity** *n* contradictoriness, contrariness, contumacy, cussedness, frowardness, gee, intransigence, obduracy, protervity, refractoriness, waywardness, wrong-headedness.

**pervert** *v* abuse, bend, corrupt, debase, debauch, degrade, deprave, distort, divert, falsify, garble, lead astray, misapply, misconstrue, misinterpret, misrepresent, misuse, subvert, twist, vitiate, warp, wrest.

*n* debauchee, degenerate, deviant, paraphiliac, vert, weirdo.

**perverted** *adj* aberrant, abnormal, corrupt, debased, debauched, depraved, deviant, distorted, evil, freakish, immoral, impaired, kinky, misguided, queer, sick, twisted, unhealthy, unnatural, vicious, vitiated, warped, wicked.

**pessimism** *n* cynicism, dejection, depression, despair, despondency, distrust, doomwatch, gloom, gloominess, glumness, hopelessness, melancholy, Weltschmerz.

*antonym* optimism.

**pessimist** *n* Cassandra, cynic, defeatist, dismal Jimmy, doom-merchant, doomster, doomwatcher, gloom and doom merchant, killjoy, melancholic, wet blanket, worrier.

*antonym* optimist.

**pessimistic** *adj* bleak, cynical, dark, defeatist, dejected, depressed, despairing, despondent, dismal, distrustful, downhearted, fatalistic, gloomy, glum, hopeless, melancholy, misanthropic, morose, resigned, sad, worried.

*antonym* optimistic.

**pest** *n* annoyance, bane, blight, bore, bother, bug, canker, curse, irritation, nuisance, pain (in the neck), scourge, thorn in one's flesh, trial, vexation.

**pester** *v* annoy, badger, bedevil, bother, bug, chivvy, disturb, dog, drive round the bend, drive up the wall, fret, get at, harass, harry, hassle, hector, hound, irk, nag, pick on, plague, ride, torment, worry.

**pestilent** *adj* annoying, bothersome, catching, communicable, contagious, contaminated, corrupting, deleterious, destructive, detrimental, diseased, disease-ridden, evil, galling, harmful, infected, infectious, injurious, irksome, irritating, morbiferous, morbific, pernicious, plague-ridden, plagu(e)y, ruinous, tainted, tiresome, vexing, vicious.

**pestilential** *adj* annoying, catching, contagious, contaminated, dangerous, deadly, deleterious, destructive, detrimental, disease-ridden, evil, foul, harmful, hazardous, infectious, injurious, malignant, morbiferous, morbific, noxious, pernicious, pesky, pestiferous, poisonous, ruinous, troublesome, venomous.

**pet** *n* darling, dautie, dilling, doll, duck, ewe-lamb, favourite, idol, jewel, treasure, whitehead.

*adj* cherished, dearest, favoured, favourite, particular, preferred, special.

*v* baby, canoodle, caress, coddle, cosset, cuddle, daut, dote on, fondle, indulge, kiss, mollycoddle, neck, pamper, pat, smooch, snog, spoil, stroke.

**peter out** cease, dissolve, dwindle, ebb, evaporate, fade, fail, stop, taper off, wane.

**petite** *adj* bijou, dainty, delicate, dinky, elfin, little, slight, small.

*antonyms* big, large.

**petition** *n* address, appeal, application, boon, entreaty, imploration, invocation, plea, prayer, request, rogation, round robin, solicitation, suit, supplication.

*v* appeal, ask, beg, beseech, bid, call upon, crave, entreat, implore, memorialise, plead, pray, press, solicit, sue, supplicate, urge.

**pet-name** *n* diminutive, endearment, hypocorisma, nickname.

**petrified** *adj* aghast, appalled, benumbed, dazed, dumbfounded, fossilised, frozen, horrified, horror-stricken, numb, ossified, scared stiff, shocked, speechless, stunned, stupefied, terrified, terror-stricken.

**petrify** *v* amaze, appal, astonish, astound, benumb, calcify, confound, dumbfound, fossilise, gorgonise, harden, horrify, immobilise, numb, paralyse, set, solidify, stun, stupefy, terrify, transfix, turn to stone.

**petticoat** *n* crinoline, farthingale, half-slip, jupon, kirtle, slip, underskirt.

**pettifogging** *adj* captious, casuistic, cavilling, circumlocutary, equivocating, hair-splitting, mean, niggling, nit-picking, over-refined, paltry, petty, quibbling, sophistical, sophisticated, subtle.

**pettish** *adj* cross, fractious, fretful, grumpy, huffy, ill-humoured, irritable, peevish, petulant, querulous, snappish, splenetic, sulky, tetchy, thin-skinned, touchy, waspish.

**petty** *adj* cheap, contemptible, grudging, inconsiderable, inessential, inferior, insignificant, junior, lesser, little, lower, mean, measly, minor, negligible, one-horse, paltry, picayune, picayunish, piddling, pimping, poking, poky, secondary, shabby, slight, small, small-minded, small-town, spiteful, stingy, subordinate, trifling, trivial, ungenerous, unimportant.

*antonyms* generous, important, large-hearted, significant, vital.

**petulance** *n* bad temper, crabbedness, crabbiness, ill-humour, ill-temper, irritability, peevishness, pettishness, pique, procacity, querulousness, spleen, sulkiness, sullenness, waspishness.

**petulant** *adj* bad-tempered, captious, cavilling, crabbed, cross, crusty, fretful, ill-humoured, impatient, irascible, irritable, moody, peevish, perverse, pettish, procacious, querulous, snappish, sour, sulky, sullen, ungracious, waspish.

**phantom** *n* apparition, chimera, eidolon, figment (of the imagination), ghost, hallucination, illusion, manes, phantasm(a), revenant, shade, simulacrum, spectre, spirit, spook, vision, wraith.

**pharisaical** *adj* canting, formal, goody-goody, holier-than-thou, hypocritical, insincere, moralising, pharisaic, pietistic, preachy, sanctimonious, self-righteous, Tartuf(f)ian, Tartuf(f)ish.

**pharisee** *n* canter, dissembler, dissimulator, fraud, Holy Willie, humbug, hypocrite, phoney, pietist, Tartuf(f)e, whited sepulchre.

**phase** *n* aspect, chapter, condition, development, juncture, period, point, position, season, spell, stage, state, step, time.

**phase out** close, deactivate, dispose of, ease off, eliminate, get rid of, remove, replace, run down, taper off, terminate, wind down, withdraw.

**phenomenal** *adj* amazing, exceptional, extraordinary, fantastic, marvellous, miraculous, outstanding, prodigious, remarkable, sensational, singular, stupendous, uncommon, unique, unparalleled, unusual, wondrous.

**phenomenon** *n* appearance, circumstance, curiosity, episode, event, fact, happening, incident, marvel, miracle, occurrence, prodigy, rarity, sensation, sight, spectacle, wonder.

**philanderer** *n* Casanova, dallier, Don Juan, flirt, gallant, gay deceiver, ladies' man, lady-killer, libertine, Lothario, playboy, stud, trifler, venerean, wencher, wolf, womaniser.

**philanthropic** *adj* alms-giving, altruistic, beneficent, benevolent, benignant, bounteous, bountiful, charitable, eleemosynary, gracious, humane, humanitarian, kind, kind-hearted, kindly, munificent, public-spirited.

*antonym* misanthropic.

**philanthropist** *n* alms-giver, altruist, angel, benefactor, contributor, donor, giver, good fairy, humanitarian, patron.

*antonyms* misanthrope, misanthropist.

**philanthropy** *n* agape, alms-giving, altruism, beneficence, benevolence, benignity, bounty, brotherly love, charitableness, charity, generosity, humanitarianism, kind-heartedness, liberality, munificence, open-handedness, patronage, public-spiritedness, unselfishness.

**Philistine** *n* Babbit, barbarian, Boeotian, boor, bourgeois, Goth, ignoramus, lout, lowbrow, vulgarian, yahoo.

*antonym* aesthete.

*adj* Boeotian, boorish, bourgeois, crass, ignorant, lowbrow, tasteless, uncultivated, uncultured, uneducated, unlettered, unread, unrefined.

**philosopher** *n* deipnosophist, dialectician, epistemologist, logician, metaphysician, sage, theorist, thinker, vocabularian.

**philosophical** *adj* abstract, analytical, calm, collected, composed, cool, dispassionate, equanimous, erudite, impassive, imperturbable, learned, logical, metaphysical, patient, philosophic, rational, resigned, sagacious, serene, stoical, theoretical, thoughtful, tranquil, unruffled, wise.

**philosophy** *n* aesthetics, attitude, beliefs, convictions, doctrine, epistemology, ideology, knowledge, logic, metaphysics, principle, rationale, rationalism, reason, reasoning, tenets, thinking, thought, values, viewpoint, Weltanschauung, wisdom, world-view.

**phlegmatic** *adj* apathetic, bovine, cold, dull, frigid, heavy, impassive, imperturbable, indifferent, lethargic, listless, lymphatic, matter-of-fact, nonchalant, placid, sluggish, stoical, stolid, unconcerned, undemonstrative, unemotional.

*antonyms* demonstrative, passionate.

**phobia** *n* anxiety, aversion, detestation, dislike, distaste, dread, fear, hang-up, hatred, horror, loathing, neurosis, obsession, phobism, repulsion, revulsion, terror, thing.

*antonyms* liking, love.

**phoney** *adj* affected, assumed, bogus, counterfeit, fake, false, forged, imitation, pseudo, put-on, quack, quacksalving, sham, spurious, trick.

*antonyms* real, true.

*n* counterfeit, fake, faker, forgery, fraud, humbug, imposter, mountebank, pretender, pseud, quack, sham.

**phosphorescent** *adj* bright, glowing, luminescent, luminous, noctilucent, noctilucous, radiant, refulgent.

**photograph** *n* ambrotype, angiogram, daguerreotype, ferrotype, image, likeness, photo, picture, print, shot, slide, snap, snapshot, transparency.

*v* film, record, shoot, snap, take, video.

**photographic** *adj* accurate, cinematic, detailed, exact, faithful, filmic, graphic, lifelike, minute, natural, naturalistic, pictorial, precise, realistic, representational, retentive, visual, vivid.

**phrase** *n* construction, expression, idiom, locution, mention, motto, remark, saying, tag, utterance.

*v* couch, express, formulate, frame, present, pronounce, put, say, style, term, utter, voice, word.

**phraseology** *n* argot, cant, diction, expression, idiom, language, parlance, patois, phrase, phrasing, speech, style, syntax, wording.

**physical** *adj* actual, bodily, carnal, concrete, corporal, corporeal, earthly, fleshly, incarnate, material, mortal, natural, palpable, real, sensible, solid, somatic, substantial, tangible, visible.

*antonyms* mental, spiritual.

**physician** *n* doc, doctor, doctor of medicine, general practitioner, GP, hakim, healer, houseman, intern, leech, MD, medic, medical practitioner, medico, registrar, specialist.

**physiognomy** *n* clock, countenance, dial, face, features, look, mug, phiz, phizog, visage, visnomy.

**physique** *n* body, build, chassis, constitution, figure, form, frame, make-up, shape, structure.

**pick** *v* break into, break open, choose, collect, crack, cull, cut, decide on, elect, embrace, espouse, fix upon, foment, gather, harvest, incite, instigate, opt for, pluck, prise, provoke, pull, screen, select, settle on, sift out, single out, start.

*antonym* reject.

*n* best, brightest and best, choice, choicest, choosing, cream, crème de la crème, decision, elect, élite, flower, option, preference, pride, prize, selection, tops.

**pick at** nibble, peck, play with, toy with.

**pick off** detach, drill, hit, kill, plug, remove, shoot, strike.

**pick on** badger, bait, blame, bully, carp at, cavil at, criticise, find fault with, get at, nag, needle, quibble with, tease, torment.

**pick out** choose, cull, differentiate, discriminate, distinguish, hand-pick, notice, perceive, recognise, select, separate, single out, tell apart.

**pick up** acquire, apprehend, arrest, bust, buy, call for, collar, collect, come across, fetch, find, gain, gain ground, garner, gather, grasp, happen on, hoist, improve, learn, lift, master, mend, nab, nick, obtain, perk up, pinch, pull in, purchase, raise, rally, recover, recuperate, run in, score, snap up, uplift.

**picket** *n* demonstrator, dissenter, guard, lookout, outpost, pale, paling, palisade, patrol, peg, picketer, post, protester, scout, sentinel, sentry, spotter, stake, stanchion, upright, vedette, watchman.

*v* blockade, boycott, corral, demonstrate, enclose, fence, hedge in, palisade, pen in, protest.

**pickings** *n* booty, bunce, earnings, gravy, loot, plunder, proceeds, profits, returns, rewards, spoils, take, yield.

**pickle** *n* bind, crisis, difficulty, dilemma, exigency, fix, hot water, jam, pinch, predicament, quandary, scrape, spot, straits, tight spot.

*v* conserve, cure, marinade, preserve, steep.

**pick-me-up** *n* boost, cordial, fillip, refreshment, restorative, roborant, shot in the arm, stimulant, tonic.

**pick-pocket** *n* dip, diver, file, pick-purse, snatcher, wire.

**picnic¹** *n* excursion, fête champêtre, outdoor meal, outing, wayzgoose.

**picnic²** *n* child's play, cinch, doddle, piece of cake, pushover, sinecure, snap, walkover.

**pictorial** *adj* diagrammatic, expressive, graphic, illustrated, picturesque, representational, scenic, schematic, striking, vivid.

**picture** *n* account, archetype, carbon copy, copy, dead ringer, delineation, depiction, description, double, drawing, duplicate, effigy, embodiment, engraving, epitome, essence, film, flick, graphic, illustration, image, impression, kakemono, likeness, living image, lookalike, motion picture, movie, painting, personification, photograph, portrait, portrayal, print, re-creation, replica, report, representation, ringer, scene, similitude, sketch, spit, spitting image, tablature, table, twin, vraisemblance.

*v* conceive of, delineate, depict, describe, draw, envisage, envision, illustrate, image, imagine, paint, photograph, portray, render, represent, see, show, sketch, visualise.

**picturesque** *adj* attractive, beautiful, charming, colourful, descriptive, graphic, pretty, quaint, scenic, striking, vivid.

**piebald** *adj* brindled, dappled, flecked, mottled, pied, pinto, skewbald, speckled, spotted.

**piece** *n* allotment, article, bit, case, chunk, component, composition, constituent, creation, division, element, example, fraction, fragment, instance, item, length, mammock, morsel, mouthful, objet d'art, occurrence, offcut, part, piecemeal, portion, production, quantity, sample, scrap, section, segment, share, shred, slice, snippet, specimen, stroke, study, work, work of art.

**piece together** assemble, attach, compose, fit, fix, join, mend, patch, repair, restore, unite.

**pièce de résistance** *n* chef-d'oeuvre, jewel, magnum opus, masterpiece, masterwork, prize, showpiece.

**piecemeal** *adv* at intervals, bit by bit, by degrees, fitfully, in dribs and drabs, in penny numbers, intermittently, little by little, parcel-wise, partially, slowly.

*antonyms* completely, entirely, wholly.

*adj* discrete, fragmentary, intermittent, interrupted, partial, patchy, scattered, unsystematic.

*antonyms* complete, entire, whole, wholesale.

**pied** *adj* brindle(d), dappled, flecked, irregular, motley, mottled, multicoloured, particoloured, piebald, skewbald, spotted, streaked, varicoloured, variegated.

**pier** *n* buttress, column, jetty, jutty, landing-place, pile, piling, pillar, post, promenade, quay, support, upright, wharf.

**pierce** *v* affect, barb, bore, comprehend, discern, discover, drift, drill, enter, excite, fathom, grasp, gride, hurt, impale, lancinate, move, pain, penetrate, perforate, pink, prick, probe, prog, puncture, realise, rouse, run through, see, spike, stab, stick into, sting, stir, strike, thrill, thrust, touch, transfix, transpierce, understand, wound.

**pierced** *adj* impaled, perforated, pertusate, pertuse(d), punctured, stung.

**piercing** *adj* acute, agonising, alert, algid, arctic, aware, biting, bitter, cold, ear-piercing, ear-splitting, excruciating, exquisite, fierce, freezing, frore, frosty, gelid, high-pitched, intense, keen, loud, nipping, nippy, numbing, painful, penetrating, perceptive, perspicacious, powerful, probing, quick-witted, racking, raw, searching, severe, sharp, shattering, shooting, shrewd, shrill, Siberian, stabbing, wintry.

**piety** *n* devotion, devoutness, dutifulness, duty, faith, godliness, grace, holiness, piousness, religion, religiosity, reverence, saintliness, sanctity, veneration.

*antonym* impiety.

**piffle** *n* balderdash, balls, bullshit, bunk, bunkum, codswallop, drivel, guff, hooey, nonsense, poppycock, rot, rubbish, tarradiddle, tommy-rot, tosh, trash, tripe, twaddle.

**pig** *n* animal, beast, boar, boor, brute, glutton, gormandiser, go(u)rmand, greedy guts, grunter, guzzler, hog, piggy, piglet, porker, shoat, slob, sloven, sow, swine.

**pigeonhole** *n* box, category, class, classification, compartment, cubbyhole, cubicle, locker, niche, place, section, slot.

*v* alphabetise, catalogue, characterise, classify, codify, compartmentalise, defer, file, label, postpone, put off, shelve, slot, sort, typecast.

**pig-headed** *adj* bull-headed, contrary, cross-grained, dense, froward, inflexible, intractable, intransigent, mulish, obstinate, perverse, self-willed, stiff-necked, stubborn, stupid, unyielding, wilful, wrong-headed.

*antonyms* flexible, tractable.

**pigment** *n* colour, colo(u)rant, colouring, colouring matter, dye, dyestuff, hue, paint, stain, tempera, tincture, tint.

**pile¹** *n* accumulation, assemblage, assortment, bing, bomb, building, cock, collection, edifice, erection, fortune, heap, hoard, mass, mint, money, mound, mountain, mow, packet, pot, stack, stockpile, structure, wealth.

*v* accumulate, amass, assemble, build up, charge, climb, collect, crowd, crush, flock, flood, gather, heap, hoard, jam, load up, mass, pack, rush, stack, store, stream.

**pile²** *n* bar, beam, column, foundation, pier, piling, pill, post, rib, stanchion, support, upright.

**pile³** *n* down, fur, fuzz, fuzziness, hair, nap, plush, shag.

**piles¹** *n* a great deal, a lot, loads, millions, oceans, oodles, quantities, stacks.

**piles²** *n* haemorrhoids.

**pilfer** *v* appropriate, embezzle, filch, finger, help oneself to, knock off, lift, mooch, nick, peculate, pickle, pinch, purloin, rifle, rob, steal, thieve.

**pilgrim** n crusader, hadji, palmer, peregrine, traveller, wanderer, wayfarer.

**pilgrimage** n crusade, excursion, expedition, hadj, journey, mission, odyssey, peregrination, tour, trip.

**pill** n ball, bolus, capsule, contraceptive, globule, pellet, pilule, tablet.

**pillage** v depredate, despoil, freeboot, loot, maraud, plunder, raid, ransack, ravage, raze, reive, rifle, rob, sack, spoil, spoliate, strip, vandalise.

n booty, depredation, devastation, harrying, loot, marauding, plunder, rapine, robbery, sack, seizure, spoils, spoliation.

**pillar** n balluster, bastion, cippus, column, leader, leading light, mainstay, mast, pier, pilaster, piling, post, prop, rock, shaft, stanchion, support, supporter, tower of strength, upholder, upright, worthy.

**pillory** v brand, cast a slur on, denounce, hold up to shame, lash, mock, pour scorn on, ridicule, show up, stigmatise.

**pilot** n airman, aviator, captain, conductor, coxswain, director, flier, guide, helmsman, hobbler, hoveller, leader, lodesman, navigator, steersman.

v boss, conduct, control, direct, drive, fly, guide, handle, lead, manage, navigate, operate, run, shepherd, steer.

adj experimental, model, test, trial.

**pimp** n bawd, fancy man, fleshmonger, go-between, mack, pander, panderer, procurer, white-slaver, whoremaster, whoremonger.

**pimple** n black-head, boil, papula, papule, plook, pustule, quat, spot, swelling, whelk, zit.

**pin** v affix, attach, fasten, fix, hold down, hold fast, immobilise, join, nail, pinion, press, restrain, secure, tack.

n bolt, breastpin, brooch, clip, fastener, nail, peg, rivet, screw, spike, spindle, stick pin, tack, tie-pin.

**pin down** bind, compel, confine, constrain, designate, determine, fix, force, hold, hold down, home in on, identify, immobilise, locate, make, nail, nail down, name, pinpoint, press, pressurise, specify, tie down, zero in on.

**pincers** n forceps, forfex, tweezers.

**pinch** v afflict, apprehend, arrest, bust, chafe, check, collar, compress, confine, cramp, crush, distress, do, economise, filch, grasp, hurt, knap, knock off, lay, lift, nab, nick, nip, oppress, pain, pick up, pilfer, press, prig, pull in, purloin, rob, run in, scrimp, skimp, snaffle, snatch, sneap, snitch, spare, squeeze, steal, stint, swipe, tweak.

n bit, crisis, dash, difficulty, emergency, exigency, hardship, jam, jot, mite, necessity, nip, oppression, pass, pickle, plight, predicament, pressure, soupçon, speck, squeeze, strait, stress, taste, tweak.

**pinched** adj careworn, drawn, gaunt, haggard, narrowed, peaky, starved, straightened, thin, worn.

**pine** v ache, covet, crave, decay, decline, desire, droop, dwindle, dwine, fade, flag, hanker, hunger, languish, long, peak, sicken, sigh, sink, thirst, waste, weaken, wilt, wish, wither, yearn, yen.

**pinion** v bind, chain, confine, fasten, fetter, hobble, immobilise, manacle, pin down, shackle, tie, truss.

**pink**[1] n acme, best, extreme, flower, height, peak, perfection, summit, tiptop, top.

adj flushed, reddish, rose, roseate, rosy, salmon.

**pink**[2] v crenellate, incise, notch, perforate, prick, punch, scallop, score, serrate.

**pinnacle** n acme, apex, apogee, cap, cone, crest, crown, eminence, height, needle, obelisk, peak, pyramid, spire, steeple, summit, top, turret, vertex, zenith.

**pin-point** v define, distinguish, home in on, identify, locate, place, spot, zero in on.

**pint-size** adj diminutive, dwarf, little, midget, miniature, pocket, pocket-sized, small, tiny, wee.

*antonyms* giant, huge.

**pioneer** n coloniser, colonist, developer, explorer, founder, founding father, frontiersman, innovator, leader, settler, trail-blazer, voortrekker, way-maker.

v blaze a trail, create, develop, discover, establish, found, initiate, instigate, institute, invent, launch, lead, open up, originate, prepare, start.

**pious** adj dedicated, devoted, devout, God-fearing, godly, good, goody-goody, holier-than-thou, holy, hypocritical, moral, pietistic, religiose, religious, reverent, righteous, saintly, sanctimonious, self-righteous, spiritual, unctuous, virtuous.

*antonym* impious.

**pipe** n briar, clay, conduit, conveyor, duct, fife, fistula, flue, hookah, horn, hose, kalian, line, main, meerschaum, overflow, passage, pipeline, tooter, tube, whistle.

v carry, channel, cheep, chirp, conduct, convey, funnel, peep, play, sing, siphon, sound, supply, tootle, transmit, trill, tweet, twitter, warble, whistle.

**pipe-dream** n castle in Spain, castle in the air, chimera, daydream, delusion, dream, fantasy, mirage, notion, reverie, romance, vagary.

**pipeline** n channel, conduit, conveyor, duct, line, passage, pipe, tube.

**pipsqueak** n creep, hobbledehoy, nobody, nonentity, nothing, oik, squirt, twerp, upstart, whippersnapper.

*antonym* somebody.

**piquancy** n bite, colour, edge, excitement, flavour, ginger, interest, juice, kick, pep, pepperiness, pizzazz, punch, pungency, raciness, relish, sharpness, spice, spiciness, spirit, tang, vigour, vitality, zest, zip.

**piquant** adj biting, interesting, lively, peppery, poignant, provocative, pungent, racy, salty, savoury, scintillating, sharp, sparkling, spicy, spirited, stimulating, stinging, tangy, tart, zesty.

*antonyms* banal, jejune.

**pique** *n* annoyance, displeasure, grudge, huff, irritation, miff, offence, pet, resentment, umbrage, vexation.

*v* affront, annoy, arouse, displease, excite, gall, galvanise, get, goad, incense, irk, irritate, kindle, miff, mortify, nettle, offend, peeve, provoke, put out, rile, rouse, spur, stimulate, sting, stir, vex, whet, wound.

**piracy** *n* bootlegging, buccaneering, freebooting, hijacking, infringement, plagiarism, rapine, robbery, stealing, theft.

**pirate** *n* buccaneer, corsair, filibuster, freebooter, infringer, marauder, marque, picaroon, plagiariser, plagiarist, raider, rover, sallee-man, sea-rat, sea-robber, sea-rover, sea-wolf, water-rat.

*v* appropriate, borrow, copy, crib, lift, nick, pinch, plagiarise, poach, reproduce, steal.

**pirouette** *n* gyration, pivot, spin, turn, twirl, whirl.

*v* gyrate, pivot, spin, turn, twirl, whirl.

**pistol** *n* dag, derringer, gat, gun, hand-gun, iron, Luger, piece, revolver, rod, sidearm, six-shooter.

**pit** *n* abyss, alveole, alveolus, cavity, chasm, coal-mine, crater, dent, depression, dimple, excavation, gulf, hole, hollow, indentation, mine, oubliette, pock-mark, pothole, trench, variole.

**pit against** match, oppose, set against.

**pitch** *v* bung, cast, chuck, dive, drop, erect, fall headlong, fix, fling, flounder, heave, hurl, launch, lob, locate, lurch, peck, place, plant, plunge, raise, roll, set up, settle, sling, stagger, station, throw, topple, toss, tumble, wallow, welter.

*n* angle, cant, degree, dip, gradient, ground, harmonic, height, incline, level, line, modulation, park, patter, playing-field, point, sales talk, slope, sound, spiel, sports field, steepness, summit, tilt, timbre, tone.

**pitch-dark** *adj* black, dark, inky, jet-black, pitch-black, pitchy, Stygian, unilluminated, unlit.

**pitcher** *n* bottle, can, container, crock, ewer, jack, jar, jug, urn, vessel.

**piteous** *adj* affecting, deplorable, distressing, doleful, doloriferous, dolorific, grievous, heartbreaking, heart-rending, lamentable, miserable, mournful, moving, pathetic, pitiable, pitiful, plaintive, poignant, sad, sorrowful, touching, woeful, wretched.

**pitfall** *n* catch, danger, difficulty, downfall, drawback, hazard, peril, pit, snag, snare, stumbling-block, trap.

**pith** *n* consequence, core, crux, depth, essence, force, gist, gravamen, heart, import, importance, kernel, marrow, matter, meat, moment, nub, point, power, quintessence, salient point, significance, strength, substance, value, weight.

**pithy** *adj* aphoristic, apo(ph)thegmatic(al), brief, cogent, compact, concise, epigrammatic, expressive, forceful, laconic, matterful, meaningful, pointed, short, succinct, telling, terse, trenchant.

*antonyms* prolix, verbose, wordy.

**pitiable** *adj* contemptible, distressed, distressful, distressing, doleful, grievous, lamentable, miserable, mournful, pathetic, piteous, poor, sad, sorry, woeful, woesome, wretched.

**pitiful** *adj* abject, base, beggarly, contemptible, deplorable, despicable, distressing, grievous, heartbreaking, heart-rending, hopeless, inadequate, insignificant, lamentable, low, mean, miserable, paltry, pathetic, piteous, pitiable, ruthful, sad, scurvy, shabby, sorry, vile, woeful, worthless, wretched.

**pitiless** *adj* brutal, callous, cold-blooded, cold-hearted, cruel, flinty, hard-hearted, harsh, heartless, implacable, inexorable, inhuman, merciless, obdurate, relentless, ruthless, uncaring, unfeeling, unmerciful, unpitying, unsympathetic.

*antonyms* compassionate, gentle, kind, merciful.

**pittance** *n* chicken-feed, crumb, drop (in the ocean), mite, modicum, peanuts, trifle.

**pitted** *adj* blemished, dented, dinted, gouged, holey, indented, lacunose, marked, nicked, notched, pock-marked, pocky, potholed, punctuate, punctuated, riddled, rough, rutty, scarred, scratched.

**pity** *n* charity, clemency, commiseration, compassion, condolence, crime, crying shame, fellow-feeling, forbearance, kindness, mercy, misfortune, regret, ruth, shame, sin, sympathy, tenderness, understanding.

*antonyms* cruelty, disdain, scorn.

*v* absolve, bleed for, commiserate with, condole with, feel for, forgive, grieve for, pardon, reprieve, sympathise with, weep for.

**pivot** *n* axis, axle, centre, focal point, fulcrum, heart, hinge, hub, kingpin, linchpin, spindle, swivel.

*v* depend, hang, hinge, lie, rely, revolve, rotate, spin, swing, swivel, turn, twirl.

**pivotal** *adj* axial, central, climactic, critical, crucial, decisive, determining, focal, vital.

**pixie** *n* brownie, elf, fairy, goblin, leprechaun, pisky, sprite.

**placard** *n* advertisement, affiche, bill, poster, public notice, sandwich-board, sticker.

**placate** *v* appease, assuage, calm, conciliate, humour, lull, mollify, pacify, propitiate, quiet, satisfy, soothe, win over.

*antonyms* anger, enrage, incense, infuriate.

**placatory** *adj* appeasing, conciliatory, pacificatory, peace-making, propitiative, propitiatory.

**place** *n* abode, accommodation, affair, apartment, appointment, area, berth, billet, charge, city, concern, district, domicile, duty, dwelling, employment, flat, function, grade, home, house, job, locale, locality, location, locus, manor, mansion, neighbourhood, pad, point, position, post, prerogative, property, quarter, rank, region, residence, responsibility, right, role, room, seat, site, situation, space, spot, station, status, stead, town, venue, vicinity, village, whereabouts.

*v* allocate, appoint, arrange, assign, associate, bung, charge, class, classify, commission, deposit, dispose, dump, entrust, establish, fix, give, grade, group, identify, install, know, lay, locate, order, plant, position, put, put one's finger on, rank, recognise, remember, rest, set, settle, situate, sort, stand, station, stick.

**placement** *n* appointment, arrangement, assignment, classification, deployment, disposition, distribution, emplacement, employment, engagement, installation, locating, location, ordering, positioning, ranking, stationing.

**placid** *adj* calm, collected, composed, cool, equable, even, even-tempered, gentle, halcyon, imperturbable, level-headed, mild, peaceful, quiet, reposeful, restful, self-possessed, serene, still, tranquil, undisturbed, unexcitable, unmoved, unruffled, untroubled.

*antonyms* agitated, jumpy.

**plagiarise** *v* appropriate, borrow, counterfeit, crib, infringe, lift, pirate, reproduce, steal, thieve.

**plagiarism** *n* appropriation, borrowing, copying, counterfeiting, cribbing, infringement, lifting, piracy, reproduction, theft.

**plagiarist** *n* Autolycus, copier, imitator, pirate, robber, thief.

**plague** *n* affliction, aggravation, annoyance, bane, blight, bother, calamity, cancer, contagion, curse, death, disease, epidemic, evil, infection, irritant, nuisance, pain, pandemic, pest, pestilence, problem, scourge, thorn in the flesh, torment, trial, vexation, visitation.

*v* afflict, annoy, badger, bedevil, bother, distress, disturb, fret, harass, harry, hassle, haunt, hound, molest, pain, persecute, pester, tease, torment, torture, trouble, vex.

**plain** *adj* apparent, artless, austere, bare, basic, blunt, candid, clear, clinical, common, commonplace, comprehensible, direct, discreet, distinct, downright, even, everyday, evident, flat, forthright, frank, frugal, guileless, home-bred, homely, homespun, honest, ill-favoured, ingenuous, legible, level, lowly, lucid, manifest, modest, muted, obvious, open, ordinary, outspoken, patent, penny-plain, plane, pure, restrained, self-coloured, severe, simple, sincere, smooth, Spartan, stark, straightforward, transparent, ugly, unadorned, unaffected, unambiguous, unattractive, unbeautiful, understandable, undistinguished, unelaborate, unembellished, unfigured, unhandsome, unlovely, unmistakable, unobstructed, unornamented, unpatterned, unprepossessing, unpretentious, untrimmed, unvarnished, visible, whole-coloured, workaday.

*antonyms* abstruse, attractive, elaborate, exaggerated, ostentatious, rich, striking, unclear.

*n* flat, grassland, llano, lowland, maidan, plateau, prairie, steppe, tableland, vega, veld(t).

**plain-spoken** *adj* blunt, candid, direct, downright, explicit, forthright, frank, honest, open, outright, outspoken, straightforward, truthful, unequivocal.

**plaintive** *adj* disconsolate, dismal, doleful, dolorous, grief-stricken, grievous, heart-rending, melancholy, mournful, pathetic, piteous, pitiful, rueful, sad, sorrowful, wistful, woebegone, woeful.

**plan** *n* blueprint, chart, contrivance, delineation, design, device, diagram, drawing, idea, illustration, layout, map, method, plot, procedure, programme, project, proposal, proposition, representation, scenario, schedule, scheme, sketch, strategy, suggestion, system.

*v* aim, arrange, complot, concoct, conspire, contemplate, contrive, design, devise, draft, envisage, foreplan, foresee, formulate, frame, intend, invent, mean, organise, outline, plot, prepare, propose, purpose, represent, scheme.

**plane¹** *n* class, condition, degree, echelon, footing, level, position, rank, rung, stage, stratum.

*adj* even, flat, flush, horizontal, level, plain, planar, regular, smooth, uniform.

**plane²** *n* aeroplane, aircraft, airliner, bomber, fighter, glider, jet, jumbo, jumbo jet, sea-plane, swing-wing, VTOL.

*v* fly, glide, sail, skate, skim, volplane, wing.

**plangent** *adj* clangorous, deep, loud, mournful, plaintive, resonant, resounding, reverberating, ringing, sonorous, vibrant.

**plant¹** *n* bush, flower, herb, shrub, vegetable, weed, wort.

*v* bury, establish, fix, found, imbed, implant, inlay, insert, inset, institute, lodge, put in the ground, root, scatter, seed, set, set out, settle, sow, transplant.

**plant²** *n* apparatus, equipment, factory, foundry, gear, machinery, mill, shop, works, workshop, yard.

**plaque** *n* badge, brooch, cartouche, medal, medallion, panel, plaquette, plate, shield, slab, tablet.

**plaster** *n* bandage, cataplasm, dressing, gypsum, mortar, plaster of Paris, sticking-plaster, stucco.

*v* bedaub, besmear, coat, cover, daub, overlay, parge, parget, smear, spread, teer.

**plastic** *adj* compliant, docile, ductile, fictile, flexible, impressionable, malleable, manageable, mouldable, pliable, pliant, receptive, responsive, soft, supple, tractable.

*antonyms* inflexible, rigid.

**plasticity** *n* flexibility, malleability, pliability, pliableness, pliancy, softness, suppleness, tractability.

*antonyms* inflexibility, rigidity.

**plate** *n* asher, charger, course, dish, helping, illustration, lame, lamella, lath, layer, lithograph, palette, panel, platter, portion, print, scale, serving, sheet, slab, trencher.

*v* anodise, coat, cover, electroplate, face, galvanise, gild, laminate, nickel, overlay, platinise, silver, tin, veneer, zinc, zinc(k)ify.

**plateau** *n* grade, highland, level, mesa, plane, stability, stage, table, tableland, upland.

**platform** *n* dais, estrade, gantry, manifesto, objective(s), party line, podium, policy, principle, programme, rostrum, stage, stand, tenet(s).

**platitude** *n* banality, bromide, chestnut, cliché, commonplace, inanity, stereotype, truism.

**platitudinous** adj banal, clichéd, commonplace, corny, dull, flat, hack, hackneyed, overworked, set, stale, stereotyped, stock, tired, trite, truistic, vapid, well-worn.

**platonic** adj ideal, idealistic, incorporeal, intellectual, non-physical, spiritual, transcendent.

**platoon** n battery, company, group, outfit, patrol, squad, squadron, team.

**platter** n asher, charger, dish, meat-plate, plate, salver, tray, trencher.

**plaudits** n acclaim, acclamation, accolade, applause, approbation, approval, clapping, commendation, congratulations, hand, hurrahs, kudos, ovation, praise, standing ovation.

**plausible** adj believable, colourable, conceivable, convincing, credible, facile, fair-spoken, glib, likely, persuasive, possible, probable, reasonable, smooth, smooth-talking, smooth-tongued, specious, tenable, voluble.

*antonyms* implausible, improbable, unlikely.

**play** v act, bet, caper, challenge, chance, compete, contend, execute, fiddle, fidget, flirt, fool around, frisk, frolic, gamble, gambol, hazard, impersonate, interfere, lilt, participate, perform, personate, portray, punt, represent, revel, risk, rival, romp, speculate, sport, string along, take, take on, take part, take the part of, trifle, vie with, wager.

*antonym* work.

n action, activity, amusement, caper, comedy, diversion, doodle, drama, elbowroom, employment, entertainment, exercise, farce, foolery, frolic, fun, function, gambling, gambol, game, gaming, give, humour, jest, joking, lark, latitude, leeway, margin, masque, motion, movement, operation, pastime, performance, piece, prank, range, recreation, romp, room, scope, show, space, sport, sweep, swing, teasing, tragedy, transaction, working.

**play around** dally, flirt, fool, mess around, philander, trifle, womanise.

**play ball** collaborate, co-operate, go along, play along, reciprocate, respond, show willing.

**play by ear** ad-lib, extemporise, improvisate, improvise.

**play down** gloss over, make light of, make little of, minimise, soft-pedal, underplay, underrate, undervalue.

**play for time** delay, drag one's feet, filibuster, hang fire, hesitate, procrastinate, stall, temporise.

**play havoc with** confuse, demolish, destroy, devastate, disorganise, disrupt, mess up, ruin, wreck.

**play on** abuse, capitalise on, exploit, milk, misuse, profit by, take advantage of, trade on, turn to account, utilise.

**play the fool** act the (giddy) goat, clown around, fool around, horse around, mess about, mess on, monkey around, skylark.

**play the game** acquiesce, conform, keep in step, play by the rules, play fair, toe the line, yield.

**play up** accentuate, begin, bother, emphasise, exaggerate, fool, highlight, hurt, magnify, make

a fool of, malfunction, overemphasise, pain, spotlight, start, stress, strike up, trouble.

**play up to** blandish, bootlick, butter up, fawn, flatter, ingratiate oneself, soft-soap, suck up to, toady.

**playboy** n debauchee, ladies' man, lady-killer, libertine, man about town, philanderer, rake, roué, socialite, womaniser.

**player** n actor, actress, artist(e), bandsman, competitor, contestant, cricketer, entertainer, footballer, instrumentalist, musician, participant, performer, sportsman, sportswoman, Thespian, trouper.

**playful** adj arch, cheerful, coltish, coquettish, coy, espiègle, flirtatious, frisky, frolicsome, gamesome, gay, good-natured, humorous, impish, jesting, jokey, joking, joyous, kittenish, kitteny, larkish, larky, lively, ludic, merry, mischievous, puckish, reasing, roguish, rollicking, spirited, sportive, sprightly, tongue-in-cheek, toyish, toysome, vivacious, waggish.

*antonyms* serious, stern.

**playmate** n buddy, chum, companion, comrade, friend, marrow, neighbour, pal, playfellow.

**plaything** n amusement, bauble, game, gewgaw, gimcrack, pastime, puppet, toy, trifle, trinket.

**playwright** n dramatist, dramaturge, dramaturgist, screen-writer, scriptwriter.

**plea** n action, allegation, apology, appeal, begging, cause, claim, defence, entreaty, excuse, explanation, extenuation, imploration, intercession, invocation, justification, overture, petition, placit(um), prayer, pretext, request, suit, supplication, vindication.

**plead** v adduce, allege, appeal, argue, ask, assert, beg, beseech, crave, entreat, implore, importune, maintain, moot, petition, put forward, request, solicit, supplicate.

**pleasant** adj acceptable, affable, agreeable, amene, amiable, amusing, charming, cheerful, cheery, congenial, cool, delectable, delightful, delightsome, engaging, enjoyable, fine, friendly, genial, good-humoured, gratifying, likeable, listenable, lovely, nice, pleasing, pleasurable, refreshing, satisfying, sunshiny, toothsome, welcome, winsome.

*antonyms* distasteful, nasty, repugnant, unpleasant.

**pleasantry** n badinage, banter, bon mot, jest, joke, persiflage, quip, sally, witticism.

**please** v amuse, captivate, charm, cheer, choose, content, delight, desire, enchant, entertain, gladden, go for, gratify, humour, indulge, like, opt, prefer, rejoice, satisfy, see fit, suit, think fit, tickle, tickle pink, want, will, wish.

*antonyms* anger, annoy, displease.

**pleased** adj chuffed, contented, delighted, elated, euphoric, glad, gratified, gruntled, happy, in high spirits, over the moon, satisfied, thrilled, tickled, tickled pink.

*antonyms* annoyed, displeased.

**pleasing** adj acceptable, agreeable, amiable, amusing, attractive, charming, congenial, delightful, engaging, enjoyable, entertaining, good, gratifying, likable, nice, pleasurable, polite, satisfying, welcome, winning.

*antonym* unpleasant.

**pleasurable** *adj* agreeable, amusing, congenial, delightful, diverting, enjoyable, entertaining, fun, good, gratifying, groovy, lovely, nice, pleasant, welcome.

*antonyms* bad, disagreeable.

**pleasure** *n* amusement, bliss, choice, comfort, command, complacency, contentment, delectation, delight, desire, diversion, ease, enjoyment, gladness, gratification, happiness, inclination, joy, mind, option, preference, purpose, recreation, satisfaction, solace, will, wish.

*antonyms* displeasure, pain, sorrow, trouble.

**pleat** *v* crease, crimp, flute, fold, gather, goffer, plait, pucker, shirr, tuck.

**plebeian** *adj* base, coarse, common, ignoble, low, low-born, lower-class, mean, non-U, peasant, proletarian, uncultivated, unrefined, vulgar, working-class.

*antonyms* aristocratic, noble, patrician.

*n* common man, commoner, man in the street, peasant, pleb, prole, proletarian, roturier, worker.

*antonyms* aristocrat, noble, patrician.

**plebiscite** *n* ballot, poll, referendum, straw poll, vote.

**pledge** *n* assurance, bail, bond, collateral, covenant, deposit, earnest, gage, guarantee, health, oath, pawn, promise, security, surety, toast, undertaking, vow, wadset(t), warrant, word, word of honour.

*v* bind, contract, drink to, engage, ensure, gage, guarantee, mortgage, plight, promise, secure, swear, toast, undertake, vouch, vow.

**plenary** *adj* absolute, complete, entire, full, general, integral, open, sweeping, thorough, unconditional, unlimited, unqualified, unrestricted, whole.

**plenipotentiary** *n* ambassador, dignitary, emissary, envoy, legate, minister, nuncio, plenipo.

**plenitude** *n* abundance, amplitude, bounty, completeness, copiousness, cornucopia, entireness, excess, fullness, plenteousness, plentifulness, plenty, plethora, profusion, repletion, wealth.

*antonym* scarcity.

**plenteous** *adj* abounding, abundant, ample, bounteous, bountiful, bumper, copious, fertile, fruitful, generous, inexhaustible, infinite, lavish, liberal, luxuriant, overflowing, plentiful, productive, profuse, prolific.

*antonym* scarce.

**plentiful** *adj* abounding, abundant, ample, bounteous, bountiful, bumper, complete, copious, fertile, fruitful, generous, inexhaustible, infinite, lavish, liberal, luxuriant, overflowing, plenteous, productive, profuse, prolific.

*antonyms* rare, scanty, scarce.

**plenty** *n* abundance, affluence, copiousness, enough, fertility, fruitfulness, fund, heap(s), lots, luxury, mass, masses, milk and honey, mine, mountain(s), oodles, opulence, pile(s), plenitude, plenteousness, plentifulness, plethora, profusion, prosperity, quantities, quantity, stack(s), store, sufficiency, volume, wealth.

*antonyms* lack, need, scarcity, want.

**plethora** *n* excess, glut, overabundance, overful(l)ness, profusion, superabundance, superfluity, surfeit, surplus.

**pliability** *n* adaptability, amenability, bendability, compliance, docility, ductility, elasticity, flexibility, impressionableness, malleability, mobility, plasticity, pliancy, suggestibility, susceptibility, tractableness.

*antonyms* inflexibilty, rigidity.

**pliable** *adj* accommodating, adaptable, bendable, bendy, compliant, docile, ductile, flexible, impressionable, influenceable, limber, lithe, malleable, manageable, persuadable, plastic, pliant, receptive, responsive, suggestible, supple, susceptible, tractable, yielding.

*antonyms* inflexible, rigid.

**pliant** *adj* adaptable, bendable, bendy, biddable, compliant, ductile, easily led, flexible, impressionable, influenceable, lithe, manageable, persuadable, plastic, pliable, supple, susceptible, tractable, whippy, yielding.

*antonyms* inflexible, intractable.

**plight**[1] *n* case, circumstances, condition, difficulty, dilemma, extremity, galère, hole, jam, perplexity, pickle, predicament, quandary, scrape, situation, spot, state, straits, trouble.

**plight**[2] *n* affiance, contract, covenant, engage, guarantee, pledge, promise, propose, swear, vouch, vow.

**plod** *v* clump, drag, drudge, grind, grub, labour, lumber, moil, peg, persevere, plough through, plug, slog, soldier on, stomp, sweat, toil, tramp, tread, trudge.

**plodder** *n* drudge, dullard, mug, sap, slogger, toiler.

*antonym* high-flier.

**plot**[1] *n* action, cabal, conspiracy, covin, design, intrigue, machination(s), narrative, outline, plan, scenario, scheme, story, story line, stratagem, subject, theme, thread.

*v* brew, cabal, calculate, chart, collude, compass, compute, conceive, concoct, conspire, contrive, cook up, design, devise, draft, draw, frame, hatch, imagine, intrigue, lay, locate, machinate, manoeuvre, map, mark, outline, plan, project, scheme.

**plot**[2] *n* allotment, area, erf, green, ground, lot, parcel, patch, tract.

**plotter** *n* caballer, conspirator, intriguer, Machiavellian, machinator, schemer, strategist.

**plough** *v* break, cultivate, dig, furrow, ridge, spade, till.

**ploy** *n* artifice, contrivance, device, dodge, gambit, game, manoeuvre, move, ruse, scheme, stratagem, subterfuge, tactic, trick, wile.

**pluck**[1] *n* backbone, boldness, bottle, bravery, courage, determination, fortitude, gameness, grit, guts, hardihood, heart, intrepidity, mettle, nerve, resolution, spirit, spunk, tenacity.

**pluck**[2] *v* catch, clutch, collect, depilate, deplume, displume, draw, evulse, gather, harvest, jerk, pick, plunk, pull, pull off, pull out, snatch, strum, thrum, tug, twang, tweak, unplume, yank.

**plucky** *adj* bold, brave, courageous, daring, doughty, game, gamy, gritty, gutsy, hardy, heroic, intrepid, mettlesome, spirited, spunky, tenacious, unflinching, valiant.
*antonyms* feeble, weak.

**plug** *n* advert, advertisement, bung, cake, chew, cork, dook, dossil, dottle, good word, hype, mention, pigtail, publicity, puff, push, quid, spigot, spile, stopper, stopple, studdle, tamp(i)on, twist, wad.
*v* advertise, block, build up, bung, choke, close, cork, cover, drudge, fill, grind, hype, labour, mention, pack, peg away, plod, promote, publicise, puff, push, seal, slog, stop, stop up, stopper, stopple, stuff, tamp, toil.

**plum** *n* bonus, cushy number, find, pick, prize, sinecure, treasure.
*adj* best, choice, cushy, first-class, prize.

**plumb** *n* lead, plumb bob, plummet, sinker, weight.
*adv* bang, dead, exactly, perpendicularly, precisely, slap, spot-on, square, up and down, vertically.
*v* delve, explore, fathom, gauge, investigate, mark, measure, penetrate, probe, search, sound, unravel.

**plume** *n* aigrette, crest, feather, pappus, pinion, quill, tuft.
**plume oneself on** boast about, congratulate oneself, exult in, pat oneself on the back, pique oneself, preen oneself, pride oneself.

**plummet** *v* crash, descend, dive, drop, fall, hurtle, nose-dive, plunge, stoop, swoop, tumble.
*antonym* soar.

**plump**[1] *adj* beefy, burly, buxom, chopping, chubby, corpulent, dumpy, embonpoint, endomorphic, fat, fleshy, full, matronly, obese, podgy, portly, roly-poly, rotund, round, stout, tubby, well-upholstered.
*antonyms* skinny, thin.

**plump**[2] *v* collapse, descend, drop, dump, fall, flop, sink, slump.
*adv* abruptly, directly, straight.
**plump for** back, choose, favour, opt for, select, side with, support.

**plumpness** *n* chubbiness, corpulence, embonpoint, fatness, fleshiness, obesity, podginess, portliness, pudginess, rotundity, stoutness, tubbiness.
*antonyms* skinniness, thinness.

**plunder** *v* depredate, despoil, devastate, loot, pillage, raid, ransack, ravage, reive, rifle, rob, sack, spoil, spoliate, steal, strip.
*n* booty, despoilment, ill-gotten gains, loot, pickings, pillage, prey, prize, rapine, spoils, swag.

**plunge** *v* career, cast, charge, dash, demerge, demerse, descend, dip, dive, dive-bomb, dook, douse, drop, fall, go down, hurtle, immerse, jump, lurch, nose-dive, pitch, plummet, rush, sink, submerge, swoop, tear, throw, tumble.
*n* collapse, descent, dive, dook, drop, fall, immersion, jump, submersion, swoop, tumble.

**plurality** *n* bulk, diversity, galaxy, majority, mass, most, multiplicity, multitudinousness, numerousness, preponderance, profusion, variety.

**plus** *n* advantage, asset, benefit, bonus, credit, extra, gain, good point, perk, surplus.
*antonym* minus.

**plush** *adj* affluent, costly, de luxe, lavish, luxurious, luxury, opulent, palatial, rich, ritzy, sumptuous.

**plutocrat** *n* billionaire, capitalist, Croesus, Dives, fat cat, magnate, millionaire, moneybags, multimillionaire, rich man, tycoon.

**ply**[1] *v* assail, beseige, beset, bombard, carry on, employ, exercise, feed, follow, furnish, handle, harass, importune, manipulate, practise, press, provide, pursue, supply, swing, urge, utilise, wield, work at.

**ply**[2] *n* bend, fold, layer, leaf, sheet, strand, thickness.

**poach** *v* appropriate, encroach, infringe, intrude, pilfer, plunder, rob, steal, trespass.

**pocket** *n* bag, compartment, envelope, hollow, pouch, receptacle, reticule, sack.
*adj* abridged, compact, concise, dwarf, little, mini, miniature, pint-size(d), portable, potted, small.
*v* appropriate, filch, help oneself to, impocket, lift, nick, pilfer, pinch, purloin, snaffle, steal, take.

**pockmark** *n* blemish, pit, pock, pockpit, scar.

**pod** *n* case, hull, husk, legume, shell, shuck.

**podgy** *adj* chubby, chunky, corpulent, dumpy, fat, fleshy, paunchy, plump, roly-poly, rotund, squat, stout, stubby, stumpy, tubby.
*antonym* skinny.

**podium** *n* dais, platform, rostrum, stage, stand.

**poem** *n* acrostic, ballad(e), dit(t), ditty, eclogue, elegy, epicede, epicedium, epinicion, epithalamion, epithalamium, epopee, fabliau, genethliac(on), idyll, jingle, lay, limerick, lipogram, lyric, madrigal, monody, ode, palinode, rhyme, song, sonnet, verse, verselet, verset, versicle.

**poet** *n* bard, griot, iambist, iambographer, idyllist, lyricist, makar, maker, Meistersinger, metrician, metricist, minnesinger, minstrel, monodist, odist, Parnassian, poetaster, poeticule, rhymer, rhymester, rhymist, rimer, skald, verse-man, verse-monger, verser, verse-smith, versificator, versifier, verslibrist.

**poetic** *adj* artistic, elegiac, flowing, graceful, lyric, lyrical, metrical, moving, rhythmical.
*antonym* prosaic.

**poetry** *n* free verse, gay science, iambics, lyrics, macaronics, muse, Parnassus, pennill, poems, poesy, rhyme, rhyming, vers libre, verse, versing.

**poignancy** *n* bitterness, emotion, emotionalism, evocativeness, feeling, intensity, keenness, painfulness, pathos, piquancy, piteousness, plaintiveness, pungency, sadness, sentiment, sharpness, tenderness.

**poignant** *adj* acrid, acute, affecting, agonising, biting, bitter, caustic, distressing, heartbreaking, heart-rending, intense, keen, moving, painful, pathetic, penetrating, piercing, piquant, pointed, pungent, sad, sarcastic, severe, sharp, stinging, tender, touching, upsetting.

**point**[1] *n* aim, aspect, attribute, burden, characteristic, circumstance, condition, core, crux, degree, design, detail, dot, drift, end, essence, extent, facet, feature, full stop, gist, goal, import, instance, instant, intent, intention, item, juncture, location, mark, marrow, matter, meaning, moment, motive, nicety, nub, object, objective, particular, peculiarity, period, pith, place, position, property, proposition, purpose, quality, question, reason, respect, score, side, site, speck, spot, stage, station, stop, subject, tally, text, theme, thrust, time, trait, unit, use, usefulness, utility.

*v* aim, denote, designate, direct, draw attention to, hint, indicate, level, show, signal, signify, suggest, train.

**point of view** angle, approach, attitude, belief, judgement, opinion, orientation, outlook, perspective, position, slant, stance, standpoint, view, viewpoint.

**point out** allude to, bring up, call attention to, identify, indicate, mention, remind, reveal, show, specify.

**point up** accentuate, emphasise, headline, spotlight, stress, underline, underscore.

**point**[2] *n* apex, bill, cacumen, cape, end, fastigium, foreland, head, headland, neb, ness, nib, promontory, prong, spike, spur, summit, tang, tine, tip, top.

**point-blank** *adj* abrupt, blunt, categorical, direct, downright, explicit, express, forthright, plain, plain-spoken, straightforward, unreserved.

*adv* bluntly, brusquely, candidly, directly, explicitly, forthrightly, frankly, openly, plainly, straight, straightforwardly, unequivocally.

**pointed** *adj* accurate, acicular, aciform, aculeate(d), acuminate, acute, barbed, biting, cuspidate, cutting, edged, fastigiate(d), incisive, keen, lanceolate(d), lancet, lanciform, mucronate, penetrating, pertinent, sharp, telling, trenchant.

**pointer** *n* advice, caution, fingerpost, guide, hand, hint, indication, indicator, information, needle, recommendation, suggestion, tip, warning.

**pointless** *adj* absurd, aimless, bootless, fruitless, futile, inane, ineffectual, irrelevant, meaningless, nonsensical, profitless, senseless, silly, stupid, unavailing, unbeneficial, unproductive, unprofitable, useless, vague, vain, worthless.

*antonyms* meaningful, profitable.

**poise** *n* aplomb, assurance, calmness, collectedness, composure, cool, coolness, dignity, elegance, equanimity, equilibrium, grace, presence, presence of mind, sangfroid, savoir-faire, self-possession, serenity.

*v* balance, float, hang, hold, hover, librate, position, support, suspend.

**poised** *adj* calm, collected, composed, cool, dignified, expectant, graceful, nonchalant, prepared, ready, self-confident, self-possessed, serene, suave, unruffled, urbane, waiting.

**poison** *n* aconite, aconitum, bane, blight, cancer, canker, contagion, contamination, corruption, malignancy, miasma, toxin, venom, virus.

*v* adulterate, contaminate, corrupt, defile, deprave, empoison, envenom, infect, kill, murder, pervert, pollute, subvert, taint, undermine, vitiate, warp.

**poisonous** *adj* aconitic, baleful, baneful, corruptive, deadly, evil, fatal, lethal, malicious, mephitic, mortal, muscarinic, noxious, pernicious, pestiferous, pestilential, toxic, venomous, vicious, virose, virous, virulent.

**poke** *v* butt, butt in, dig, elbow, hit, interfere, intrude, jab, meddle, nose, nudge, peek, prod, prog, pry, punch, push, shove, snoop, stab, stick, tamper, thrust.

*n* butt, dig, dunt, jab, nudge, prod, punch, shove, thrust.

**poke fun at** chaff, guy, jeer, make fun of, mock, parody, prog, rag, rib, ridicule, send up, spoof, take the mickey, tease.

**poky** *adj* confined, cramped, crowded, incommodious, narrow, small, tight, tiny.

*antonym* spacious.

**polarity** *n* ambivalence, contradiction, contrariety, dichotomy, duality, oppositeness, opposition, paradox.

**pole**[1] *n* bar, lug, mast, post, rod, shaft, spar, staff, stake, standard, stang, stick.

**pole**[2] *n* antipode, extremity, limit, terminus, (ultima) Thule.

**poles apart** at opposite extremes, incompatible, irreconcilable, like chalk and cheese, like night and day, worlds apart.

**polemic** *n* argument, controversy, debate, dispute.

*adj* argumentative, contentious, controversial, disputatious, eristic(al), polemical.

**polemicist** *n* arguer, contender, controversialist, debater, disputant, disputer, logomachist, polemist.

**polemics** *n* argument, argumentation, contention, controversy, debate, disputation, dispute, logomachy.

**police** *n* boys in blue, constabulary, fuzz, gendarmerie, law, myrmidons of the law, (the) Old Bill.

*v* check, control, defend, guard, keep a check on, keep guard on, keep in order, keep the peace, monitor, observe, oversee, patrol, protect, regulate, stand guard over, supervise, watch.

**policeman** *n* beetle-crusher, bluebottle, bobby, bogey, bull, catchpole, constable, cop, copper, crusher, flatfoot, flic, fuzz, garda, gendarme, gumshoe, hammer(-beak), headborough, mountie, officer, peeler, pig, rozzer, sepoy, slop.

**policy** *n* action, approach, code, course, custom, discretion, good sense, guideline, line, plan, position, practice, procedure, programme, protocol, prudence, rule, sagacity, scheme, shrewdness, stance, stratagem, theory, wisdom.

**polish** *v* brighten, brush up, buff, burnish, clean, correct, cultivate, emend, emery, enhance, file, finish, furbish, improve, lustre, perfect, planish, refine, rub, rub up, shine, shine up, slick, slicken, smooth, touch up, wax.

*antonyms* dull, tarnish.

*n* breeding, brightness, brilliance, class, cultivation, elegance, eutrapelia, expertise, finesse, finish, glaze, gloss, grace, lustre, perfectionism, politesse, proficiency, refinement, savoir-faire, sheen, smoothness, sophistication, sparkle, style, suavity, urbanity, varnish, veneer, wax.

*antonyms* clumsiness, dullness, gaucherie.

**polish off** bolt, bump off, consume, devour, dispose of, down, eat, eliminate, finish, gobble, kill, liquidate, murder, put away, rub out, shift, stuff, wolf.

**polished** *adj* accomplished, adept, bright, burnished, civilised, courtly, cultivated, educated, elegant, expert, faultless, fine, finished, flawless, furbished, genteel, glassy, gleaming, glossy, graceful, gracious, impeccable, lustrous, masterly, outstanding, perfected, polite, professional, refined, sheeny, shining, skilful, slippery, smooth, sophisticated, suave, superlative, urbane, well-bred.

*antonyms* clumsy, dull, gauche, inexpert, tarnished.

**polite** *adj* affable, attentive, civil, civilised, complaisant, considerate, cordial, courteous, courtly, cultured, deferential, diplomatic, discreet, elegant, genteel, gentlemanly, gracious, Grandisonian, ladylike, mannerly, obliging, polished, refined, respectful, tactful, thoughtful, urbane, well-behaved, well-bred, well-mannered.

*antonyms* impolite, uncultivated.

**politeness** *n* attention, civility, complaisance, considerateness, cordiality, courtesy, courtliness, cultivation, culture, deference, diplomacy, discretion, elegance, gentilesse, gentility, gentlemanliness, grace, graciousness, mannerliness, manners, polish, refinement, respect, respectfulness, tact, thoughtfulness.

*antonym* impoliteness.

**politic** *adj* advantageous, advisable, artful, astute, canny, crafty, cunning, designing, diplomatic, discreet, expedient, ingenious, intriguing, judicious, Machiavellian, opportune, prudent, sagacious, sage, scheming, sensible, shrewd, sly, subtle, tactful, unscrupulous, wise.

*antonym* impolitic.

**politician** *n* agitator, legislator, Machiavellian, machinator, manipulator, Member of Parliament, MP, opportunist, politicaster, politico, statesman, statist, stirrer, tactician, wheeler-dealer.

**politics** *n* affairs of state, civics, diplomacy, government, ideology, Machiavellianism, Machiavellism, machination, Machtpolitik, manipulation, political science, polity, power-politics, Realpolitik, statecraft, statesmanship, Weltpolitik, wheeler-dealing.

**poll**[1] *n* ballot, canvass, census, count, figures, kite-flying, plebiscite, returns, sampling, straw-poll, survey, tally, vote, voting.

**poll**[2] *v* clip, dishorn, dod, pollard, shear, trim.

**pollute** *v* adulterate, befoul, besmirch, canker, contaminate, corrupt, debase, debauch, defile, deprave, desecrate, dirty, dishonour, foul, infect, mar, poison, profane, soil, spoil, stain, sully, taint, violate, vitiate.

**pollution** *n* adulteration, befouling, contamination, corruption, defilement, desecration, dirtying, foulness, impurity, infection, profanation, soilure, stain, taint, uncleanness, violation, vitiation.

*antonyms* purification, purity.

**polychromatic** *adj* kaleidoscopic, many-coloured, many-hued, motley, mottled, multicoloured, parti-coloured, poikilitic, polychrome, rainbow, varicoloured, variegated.

*antonyms* monochromatic, monochrome.

**polyglot** *adj* cosmopolitan, international, multilingual, multiracial, polyglottal, polyglottic.

*antonym* monoglot.

*n* linguist, multilinguist.

**polymath** *n* all-rounder, know-all, mine of information, oracle, pansophist, polyhistor, Renaissance man, walking encyclopaedia.

*antonym* ignoramus.

**pomp** *n* ceremonial, ceremoniousness, ceremony, display, éclat, flourish, formality, grandeur, grandiosity, magnificence, ostentation, pageant, pageantry, parade, pomposity, ritual, show, solemnity, splendour, state, vainglory.

*antonyms* austerity, simplicity.

**pomposity** *n* affectation, airs, arrogance, bombast, euphuism, fustian, grandiloquence, grandiosity, loftiness, magniloquence, oro(ro)tundity, pompousness, pontificating, portentousness, preachiness, presumption, pretension, pretentiousness, ranting, rhetoric, self-importance, stuffiness, turgidity, vainglory, vanity.

*antonyms* economy, simplicity.

**pompous** *adj* affected, aldermanlike, aldermanly, arrogant, bloated, bombastic, budge, chesty, euphuistic, flatulent, fustian, grandiloquent, grandiose, high-flown, imperious, inflated, magisterial, magniloquent, oro(ro)tund, ostentatious, overbearing, overblown, pontifical, portentous, pretentious, prosy, ranting, self-important, stilted, stuffy, supercilious, turgid, vainglorious, windy.

*antonyms* economical, modest, simple, unaffected, unassuming.

**ponder** *v* analyse, brood, cerebrate, cogitate, contemplate, consider, deliberate, examine, excogitate, give thought to, incubate, meditate, mull over, muse, ponderate, puzzle over, ratiocinate, reason, reflect, ruminate over, study, think, volve, weigh.

**ponderous** *adj* awkward, bulky, clumsy, cumbersome, cumbrous, dreary, dull, elephantine, graceless, heavy, heavy-footed, heavy-handed, hefty, huge, humourless, laborious, laboured, lifeless, long-winded, lumbering, massive, pedantic, pedestrian, plodding, portentous, prolix, slow-moving, stilted, stodgy, stolid, tedious, unwieldy, verbose, weighty.

*antonyms* delicate, light, simple.

**ponderousness** *n* gravitas, heaviness, humourlessness, laboriousness, seriousness, stodginess, stolidity, tedium, unwieldiness, weightiness.

*antonyms* delicacy, lightness, subtlety.

**poniard** *n* bodkin, dagger, dirk, misericord, skene, stiletto, stylet.

**pontifical** *adj* apostolic, bloated, condescending, didactic, dogmatic, ecclesiastical, homiletical, imperious, magisterial, overbearing, papal, pompous, portentous, preachy, prelatic, pretentious, self-important, sermonising.

*antonyms* reticent, unassuming.

**pontificate** *v* declaim, dogmatise, expertise, expound, harangue, hold forth, lay down the law, lecture, moralise, perorate, pontify, preach, pronounce, sermonise, sound off.

**pooh-pooh** *v* belittle, brush aside, deride, disdain, dismiss, disparage, disregard, make little of, minimise, play down, reject, ridicule, scoff, scorn, slight, sneer, sniff at, spurn, turn up one's nose at.

*antonyms* consider, exaggerate, magnify, regard.

**pool**[1] *n* dub, lake, lasher, leisure pool, linn, mere, pond, puddle, splash, stank, swimming bath, swimming pool, tarn, water-hole, watering-hole.

**pool**[2] *n* accumulation, bank, cartel, collective, combine, consortium, funds, group, jackpot, kitty, pot, purse, reserve, ring, stakes, syndicate, team, trust.

*v* amalgamate, chip in, combine, contribute, dob in, merge, muck in, put together, share.

**poor**[1] *adj* badly off, bankrupt, beggared, beggarly, broke, deficient, destitute, distressed, embarrassed, exiguous, hard up, impecunious, impoverished, in reduced circumstances, inadequate, indigent, insufficient, lacking, meagre, miserable, moneyless, necessitous, needy, niggardly, obolary, on one's beam-ends, on one's uppers, on the rocks, pauperised, penniless, penurious, pinched, pitiable, poverty-stricken, reduced, scanty, skimpy, skint, slight, sparse, stony-broke, straitened, without means, without the wherewithal.

*antonyms* affluent, opulent, rich, wealthy.

**poor**[2] *adj* bad, bare, barren, below par, depleted, exhausted, faulty, feeble, fruitless, grotty, humble, imperfect, impoverished, inferior, infertile, insignificant, jejune, low-grade, lowly, mean, mediocre, modest, paltry, pathetic, pitiful, plain, ropy, rotten, rubbishy, second-rate, shabby, shoddy, sorry, spiritless, sterile, substandard, third-rate, trivial, unfruitful, unimpressive, unproductive, unsatisfactory, valueless, weak, worthless.

*antonym* superior.

**poor**[3] *adj* accursed, cursed, forlorn, hapless, ill-fated, luckless, miserable, pathetic, pitiable, star-crossed, unfortunate, unhappy, unlucky, wretched.

*antonym* lucky.

**poorly** *adv* badly, crudely, faultily, feebly, inadequately, incompetently, inexpertly, inferiorly, insufficiently, meanly, rottenly, shabbily, shoddily, unjustly, unsatisfactorily, unsuccessfully.

*antonym* well.

*adj* ailing, below par, dicky, frail, groggy, ill, indisposed, off colour, out of sorts, rotten, seedy, shaky, sick, sickly, under the weather, unhealthy, unwell.

*antonyms* healthy, robust, well.

**pop** *v* appear, bang, bulge, burst, call, come, crack, drop, drop in, explode, go, go bang, go off, go phut, insert, jump, nip, protrude, push, put, report, shove, slide, slip, snap, spring, step, stick, thrust, tuck, visit.

*n* bang, burst, crack, explosion, noise, report, snap.

**pope** *n* Bishop of Rome, His Holiness, Holy Father, papa, pontiff, sovereign pontiff, Vicar of Christ.

**popinjay** *n* beau, buck, coxcomb, dandy, dude, exquisite, fop, fopling, jackanapes, macaroni, pansy, peacock, princox, spark, swell, toff.

*antonyms* he-man, macho.

**poppycock** *n* babble, balderdash, balls, baloney, bullshit, bunk, bunkum, drivel, eyewash, gibberish, gobbledegook, guff, hooey, nonsense, rot, rubbish, tommyrot, tosh, trash, twaddle.

*antonym* sense.

**populace** *n* canaille, common herd, commonalty, crowd, general public, hoi polloi, inhabitants, masses, mob, multitude, people, plebs, proletariat, public, punters, rabble, rank and file, throng, vulgus.

*antonyms* aristocracy, élite, nobility.

**popular** *adj* accepted, approved, celebrated, common, conventional, current, democratic, demotic, famous, fashionable, favoured, favourite, fêted, general, hip, household, idolised, in, in demand, in favour, liked, lionised, modish, overpopular, overused, prevailing, prevalent, public, sought-after, standard, stock, trite, ubiquitous, universal, vernacular, voguey, voguish, vulgar, well-liked, widespread.

*antonyms* exclusive, unpopular, unusual.

**popularise** *v* debase, democratise, disseminate, familiarise, give currency to, propagate, simplify, spread, universalise, vulgarise.

*antonym* discredit.

**popularity** *n* acceptance, acclaim, adoration, adulation, approbation, approval, celebrity, currency, esteem, fame, favour, glory, idolisation, kudos, lionisation, mass appeal, recognition, regard, renown, reputation, repute, vogue, worship.

*antonym* unpopularity.

**popularly** *adv* commonly, conventionally, customarily, generally, in the vernacular, ordinarily, regularly, traditionally, universally, usually, vernacularly, vulgarly, widely.

**populate** *v* colonise, establish oneself in, habit, inhabit, live in, occupy, overrun, people, put down roots in, settle, tenant.

**population** *n* citizenry, citizens, community, denizens, folk, inhabitants, natives, occupants, people, populace, residents, society.

**populous** *n* crawling, crowded, frequented, overpeopled, overpopulated, packed, populated, swarming, teeming, thickly populated, thronged.

*antonyms* deserted, unfrequented.

**pore** *v* brood, con, contemplate, devour, dwell on, examine, go over, peruse, ponder, read, scan, scrutinise, study.

**pornographic** *adj* bawdy, blue, coarse, dirty, filthy, girlie, gross, indecent, lewd, nudie, obscene, off-colour, offensive, porn, porno, prurient, risqué, salacious, smutty.

*antonyms* innocent, inoffensive.

**pornography** *n* bawdiness, dirt, erotica, facetiae, filth, grossness, indecency, obscenity, porn, porno, sexploitation, smut.

**porous** *adj* absorbent, absorptive, cellular, foraminous, foveate, honeycombed, penetrable, permeable, pervious, pitted, sponge-like, spongy.

*antonyms* impermeable, impervious.

**port** *n* anchorage, harbour, harbourage, haven, hithe, roads, roadstead, seaport.

**portable** *adj* carriageable, compact, convenient, handy, light, lightweight, manageable, movable, portatile, portative, transportable.

*antonyms* fixed, immovable.

**portend** *v* adumbrate, announce, augur, bespeak, betoken, bode, forebode, forecast, foreshadow, foretell, foretoken, forewarn, harbinger, herald, indicate, omen, point to, predict, presage, prognosticate, promise, signify, threaten, warn of.

**portent** *n* augury, foreboding, forecast, forerunner, foreshadowing, forewarning, harbinger, indication, omen, precursor, prefiguration, premonition, presage, presentiment, prodrome, prognostic, prognostication, sign, signification, threat, warning.

**portentous** *adj* alarming, amazing, astounding, awe-inspiring, bloated, charged, consequential, crucial, earth-shaking, epoch-making, extraordinary, fateful, heavy, important, menacing, minatory, miraculous, momentous, ominous, phenomenal, pompous, ponderous, pontifical, pregnant, prodigious, remarkable, significant, sinister, solemn, threatening.

*antonyms* insignificant, unimportant, unimpressive.

**porter**[1] *n* baggage attendant, baggage man, bearer, caddie, carrier.

**porter**[2] *n* caretaker, commissionaire, concierge, door-keeper, doorman, doors-man, dvornik, gatekeeper, huissier, janitor, porteress, portress.

**portion** *n* allocation, allotment, allowance, assignment, bit, cup, destiny, division, fate, fortune, fraction, fragment, helping, kismet, lot, luck, measure, meed, moiety, morsel, parcel, part, piece, quantity, quota, rake-off, ration, scrap, section, segment, serving, share, slice, something, tranche, whack.

*v* allocate, allot, apportion, assign, carve up, deal, distribute, divide, divvy up, dole, parcel, partion, partition, share out, slice up.

**portliness** *n* ampleness, beefiness, chubbiness, corpulence, dumpiness, embonpoint, fleshiness, fullness, heaviness, obesity, paunchiness, plumpness, rotundity, roundness, stoutness, tubbiness.

**portly** *adj* ample, beefy, bulky, chubby, corpulent, dumpy, embonpoint, fat, fleshy, full, gaucie, heavy, large, obese, overweight, paunchy, plump, rotund, round, stout, tubby.

*antonyms* slight, slim.

**portrait** *n* account, caricature, characterisation, depiction, description, icon, image, likeness, miniature, mug shot, painting, photograph, picture, portraiture, portrayal, profile, representation, sketch, thumbnail, vignette.

**portray** *v* act, capture, characterise, delineate, depict, describe, draw, emblazon, encapsulate, evoke, figure, illustrate, impersonate, limn, paint, personate, personify, picture, play, present, render, represent, sketch, suggest.

**portrayal** *n* characterisation, delineation, depiction, description, evocation, hypotyposis, impersonation, interpretation, performance, picture, presentation, rendering, representation, sketch.

**pose** *v* advance, affect, arrange, assert, attitudinise, claim, feign, impersonate, masquerade, model, pass oneself off, place, posit, position, posture, present, pretend, profess to be, propound, put, put forward, put on an act, set, sham, sit, state, strike an attitude, submit.

*n* act, affectation, air, attitude, bearing, con, façade, front, mark, masquerade, mien, position, posture, pretence, role, sham, stance, take-in.

**poser**[1] *n* brain-teaser, chinese puzzle, conundrum, enigma, mystery, problem, puzzle, question, riddle, vexed question.

**poser**[2] *n* attitudiniser, poseur, poseuse, posturer, posturist.

**poseur** *n* attitudiniser, charlatan, con, exhibitionist, impostor, masquerader, mountebank, phoney, poser, poseuse, posturer, posturist, pseud, quack.

**posh** *adj* classy, de-luxe, elegant, exclusive, fashionable, grand, high-class, lavish, luxurious, luxury, opulent, plummy, ritzy, select, smart, stylish, sumptuous, swanky, swell, swish, up-market, upper-class.

*antonyms* cheap, inferior.

**posit** *v* advance, assert, assume, pose, postulate, predicate, presume, propound, put forward, state, submit.

**position** n angle, area, arrangement, attitude, bearings, belief, berth, billet, capacity, character, circumstances, condition, deployment, disposition, duty, employment, function, grade, importance, job, level, locale, locality, location, niche, occupation, office, opinion, outlook, pass, perspective, pinch, place, placement, placing, plight, point, point of view, pose, positioning, post, posture, predicament, prestige, rank, reference, reputation, role, set, setting, site, situation, slant, slot, spot, stance, stand, standing, standpoint, state, station, stature, status, ubiety, view, viewpoint, whereabouts.

v arrange, array, deploy, dispose, fix, lay out, locate, place, pose, put, range, set, settle, stand, stick.

**positive** adj absolute, actual, affirmative, arrant, assertive, assured, authoritative, beneficial, categorical, certain, clear, clear-cut, cocksure, complete, conclusive, concrete, confident, constructive, consummate, convinced, decided, decisive, definite, direct, dogmatic, downright, effective, efficacious, emphatic, explicit, express, firm, forceful, forward-looking, helpful, hopeful, incontestable, incontrovertible, indisputable, irrefragable, irrefutable, open-and-shut, opinionated, optimistic, out-and-out, peremptory, perfect, practical, productive, progressive, promising, rank, real, realistic, resolute, secure, self-evident, sheer, stubborn, sure, thorough, thoroughgoing, uncompromising, undeniable, unequivocal, unmistakable, unmitigated, unquestioning, useful, utter.

antonyms indecisive, indefinite, negative, uncertain.

**positively** adv absolutely, assuredly, authoritatively, categorically, certainly, conclusively, constructively, decisively, definitely, dogmatically, emphatically, expressly, finally, firmly, incontestably, incontrovertibly, indisputably, surely, uncompromisingly, undeniably, unequivocally, unmistakably, unquestionably.

**possess** v acquire, be endowed with, control, dominate, enjoy, have, hold, obtain, occupy, own, possess oneself of, seize, take, take over, take possession of.

**possessed** adj bedevilled, berserk, besotted, bewitched, consumed, crazed, cursed, demented, dominated, enchanted, entêté, frenzied, hag-ridden, haunted, infatuated, maddened, mesmerised, obsessed, raving.

**possession** n colony, control, custody, dependency, dominion, enjoyment, fruition, hold, mandate, occupancy, occupation, ownership, proprietorship, protectorate, province, tenure, territory, title.

**possessions** n assets, belongings, chattels, effects, estate, goods, goods and chattels, junk, meum et tuum, movables, paraphernalia, property, riches, stuff, things, traps, wealth, worldly wealth.

**possessive** adj acquisitive, clinging, covetous, dominating, domineering, grasping, jealous, overprotective, proprietorial, selfish.

antonyms generous, sharing, unassertive.

**possibilities** n advantages, capabilities, expectations, potential, potentiality, promise, prospects, talent.

antonyms disadvantages, liabilities.

**possibility** n achievability, chance, conceivability, feasibility, hazard, hope, liability, likelihood, odds, plausibility, potentiality, practicability, probability, prospect, realisability, risk, workableness.

antonym impossibility.

**possible** adj accomplishable, achievable, alternative, attainable, available, conceivable, credible, doable, feasible, hopeful, hypothetical, imaginable, likely, on, potential, practicable, probable, promising, realisable, tenable, viable, workable.

antonym impossible.

**possibly** adv at all, by any chance, by any means, Deo volente, DV, God willing, haply, happen, hopefully, in any way, maybe, mayhap, peradventure, perchance, perhaps, very like(ly).

**post**[1] n baluster, banister, column, leg, newel, pale, palisade, picket, pier, pillar, pin, pole, shaft, stake, stanchion, standard, stock, strut, support, upright.

v advertise, affix, announce, denounce, display, make known, placard, preconise, proclaim, promulgate, publicise, publish, report, stick up.

**post**[2] n appointment, assignment, beat, berth, billet, employment, incumbency, job, office, place, position, situation, station, vacancy.

v appoint, assign, establish, locate, move, place, position, put, second, send, shift, situate, station, transfer.

**post**[3] n collection, delivery, dispatch, mail, postal service, uplifting.

v acquaint, advise, apprise, brief, dispatch, fill in on, inform, keep posted, mail, notify, report to, send, transmit.

**poster** n advertisement, affiche, announcement, bill, handbill, notice, placard, sign, sticker.

**posterior** adj after, back, behind, dorsal, ensuing, following, hind, hinder, later, latter, posticous, rear, rearward, subsequent, succeeding.

antonyms anterior, front, previous.

n backside, behind, bottom, bum, buttocks, haunches, hinder end, hindquarters, rear, rump, seat, tail.

**posterity** n children, descendants, epigons, family, future, heirs, issue, offspring, progeny, scions, seed, successors.

antonyms ancestors, antiquity, forebears, past.

**posthaste** adv at once, directly, double-quick, ek dum, full tilt, hastily, immediately, promptly, pronto, quickly, speedily, straightaway, swiftly, with all speed.

antonyms eventually, gradually, slowly.

**postman** n letter-carrier, mail-carrier, post, postie.

**postmortem** n analysis, autopsy, dissection, examination, necropsy, review.

**postpone** v adjourn, defer, delay, freeze, hold over, pigeonhole, prorogue, put back, put off, put on ice, shelve, suspend, table, waive.

antonyms advance, forward.

**postponed** *adj* adjourned, deferred, frozen, in abeyance, on ice, pigeonholed, shelved, suspended.

*antonym* advanced.

**postponement** *n* adjournment, deferment, deferral, delay, freeze, moratorium, prorogation, put-off, respite, stay, suspension.

**postscript** *n* addendum, addition, afterthought, afterword, appendix, codicil, epilogue, PS, supplement.

*antonyms* introduction, prologue.

**postulate** *v* advance, assume, hypothesise, lay down, posit, predicate, presuppose, propose, stipulate, suppose, take for granted, theorise.

**posture** *n* attitude, bearing, carriage, decubitus, disposition, mien, port, pose, position, set, stance.

*v* affect, attitudinise, ponce, pose, put on airs, show off, strike attitudes, strut.

**posy** *n* bouquet, boutonniere, buttonhole, corsage, inscription, motto, nosegay, spray, verse, verselet.

**pot** *n* basin, beaker, bowl, coffee-pot, crock, crucible, cruse, cupel, flask, gallipot, jar, marmite, pan, pig, pipkin, planter, receptacle, samovar, teapot, test, urn, vase, vessel.

**potato** *n* murphy, pratie, praty, spud, tater, tattie.

**pot-bellied** *adj* bloated, corpulent, distended, fat, gor-bellied, obese, overweight, paunchy, portly, tubby.

**pot-belly** *n* beer belly, belly, corporation, gor-belly, gut, paunch, pot, spare tyre.

**potency** *n* authority, capacity, cogency, control, effectiveness, efficaciousness, efficacy, energy, force, headiness, influence, kick, might, muscle, persuasiveness, potential, power, puissance, punch, strength, sway, vigour.

*antonyms* impotence, weakness.

**potent** *adj* authoritative, cogent, commanding, compelling, convincing, dominant, dynamic, effective, efficacious, eloquent, forceful, formidable, heady, impressive, influential, intoxicating, mighty, moving, persuasive, powerful, puissant, pungent, strong, telling, vigorous, weighty.

*antonyms* impotent, weak.

**potentate** *n* chief, chieftain, despot, dictator, dynast, emperor, empress, head of state, king, leader, mogul, monarch, overlord, prince, queen, ruler, sovereign, tyrant.

**potential** *adj* budding, concealed, conceivable, dormant, embryonic, future, hidden, imaginable, in embryo, in posse, inherent, latent, likely, possible, probable, promising, prospective, undeveloped, unrealised.

*n* ability, aptitude, capability, capacity, flair, possibility, potentiality, power, talent, the makings, what it takes, wherewithal.

**potentiality** *n* ability, aptitude, capability, capacity, likelihood, possibilities, potential, promise, prospect, virtuality.

**potion** *n* beverage, brew, concoction, cup, dose, draught, drink, electuary, elixir, medicine, mixture, philtre, potation, tonic, treacle.

**pot-pourri** *n* collection, combination, gallimaufry, hotchpotch, jumble, medley, mélange, miscellany, mixture, motley, olio, olla-podrida, pastiche, patchwork, salad, salmagundi.

**potter** *v* dabble, da(c)ker, dodder, fettle, fiddle, fidget, footle, fribble, frig, fritter, mess about, mooch, moon, tinker.

**pottery** *n* ceramics, china, China-ware, crockery, delf, earthenware, pig, porcelain, stoneware, terra cotta, ware.

*adj* ceramic, china, clay, earthenware, fictile, figuline, porcelain, stoneware, wally.

**potty** *adj* bananas, barmy, bonkers, crackers, crazy, daft, demented, dippy, dotty, eccentric, foolish, footling, insignificant, nuts, nutty, petty, piddling, silly, soft, touched, trifling, trivial.

**pouch** *n* bag, container, marsupium, pocket, poke, purse, reticule, sac, sack, sporran, wallet.

**pounce** *v* ambush, attack, dash at, dive on, drop, fall upon, grab, jump, leap at, lunge at, snatch, spring, strike, swoop.

*n* assault, attack, bound, dive, grab, jump, leap, lunge, spring, swoop.

**pound**[1] *v* bang, bash, baste, batter, beat, belabour, bray, bruise, clobber, clomp, clump, comminute, crush, drum, hammer, levigate, march, palpitate, pelt, powder, pulsate, pulse, pulverise, pummel, smash, stomp, strike, strum, thrash, throb, thrum, thud, thump, thunder, tramp, triturate.

**pound**[2] *n* compound, corral, enclosure, fank, fold, pen, yard.

**pour** *v* bucket, cascade, course, crowd, decant, effuse, emit, exude, flow, gush, rain, rain cats and dogs, run, rush, sheet, spew, spill, spout, stream, swarm, teem, throng, tumble.

**pour out** debouch, decant, discharge, disembogue, disgorge, embogue, emit, issue, lave, spew forth.

**pout** *v* glower, grimace, lower, mope, pull a face, scowl, sulk.

*antonyms* grin, smile.

*n* glower, grimace, long face, moue, scowl.

*antonyms* grin, smile.

**poverty** *n* aridity, bareness, barrenness, beggary, dearth, deficiency, depletion, destitution, distress, exhaustion, hardship, ill-being, impoverishment, inadequacy, indigence, infertility, insolvency, insufficiency, jejuneness, lack, meagreness, necessitousness, necessity, need, paucity, pauperism, pennilessness, penury, poorness, poortith, privation, proletarianism, scarcity, shortage, sterility, thinness, unfruitfulness, want.

*antonyms* affluence, fertility, fruitfulness, riches, richness.

**poverty-stricken** *adj* bankrupt, beggared, broke, destitute, distressed, impecunious, impoverished, indigent, necessitous, needy, obolary, on one's beam-ends, on one's uppers, penniless, penurious, poor, skint, stony, stony-broke, strapped.

*antonyms* affluent, rich.

**powder** *n* bran, dust, pounce, pulvil, pulville, pulvil(l)io, talc, triturate.

*v* bray, comminute, cover, crush, dredge, dust, granulate, grind, levigate, pestle, pound, pulverise, scatter, sprinkle, strew, triturate.

**powdery** *adj* chalky, crumbling, crumbly, dry, dusty, fine, friable, grainy, granular, levigate, loose, powder, pulverised, pulverous, pulverulent, sandy.

**power** *n* ability, ascendancy, autarchy, authorisation, authority, brawn, capability, capacity, clout, clutches, command, competence, competency, control, dominance, domination, dominion, efficience, energy, faculty, force, forcefulness, heavy metal, hegemony, imperium, influence, intensity, juice, kami, licence, mana, mastery, might, muscle, omnipotence, plenipotence, potency, potential, prerogative, privilege, right, rule, sovereignty, strength, supremacy, sway, teeth, vigour, virtue, vis, voltage, vroom, warrant, weight.

**powerful** *adj* ascendant, authoritative, cogent, commanding, compelling, controlling, convincing, dominant, effective, effectual, energetic, forceful, forcible, impressive, influential, leading, masterful, mighty, muscular, omnipotent, persuasive, plutocratic, potent, pre-eminent, prepotent, prevailing, puissant, robust, souped-up, sovereign, stalwart, strapping, strong, sturdy, supreme, telling, vigorous, weighty, winning.

*antonyms* impotent, ineffective, weak.

**powerfully** *adv* cogently, convincingly, forcefully, forcibly, hard, impressively, mightily, persuasively, potently, strongly, tellingly, vigorously, with might and main.

**powerless** *adj* adynamic, debilitated, defenceless, dependent, disabled, effete, feeble, frail, helpless, impotent, incapable, incapacitated, ineffective, ineffectual, inefficacious, inerm, infirm, nerveless, paralysed, prostrate, subject, tied, unarmed, vulnerable, weak, weak-headed.

*antonyms* commanding, potent, powerful.

**practicability** *n* feasibility, handiness, operability, possibility, practicality, use, usefulness, utility, value, viability, workability, workableness.

*antonym* impracticability.

**practicable** *adj* accomplishable, achievable, attainable, compassable, doable, effectible, feasible, negotiable, passable, performable, possible, viable, workable.

*antonym* impracticable.

**practical** *adj* accomplished, active, applicative, applied, businesslike, commonsense, commonsensical, down-to-earth, efficient, empirical, everyday, expedient, experienced, experimental, factual, feasible, functional, hands-on, hard-headed, hard-nosed, material, matter-of-fact, mundane, nuts-and-bolts, ordinary, practicable, practive, pragmatic, proficient, qualified, realistic, seasoned, sensible,

serviceable, skilled, sound, trained, unsentimental, useful, utilitarian, workable, workaday, working.

*antonym* impractical.

**practicality** *n* basics, common sense, experience, feasibility, nitty-gritty, nuts and bolts, practicability, practicalities, practicalness, practice, pragmatism, realism, sense, serviceability, soundness, usefulness, utility, workability.

**practically**[1] *adv* actually, all but, almost, essentially, fundamentally, in effect, in practice, in principle, just about, nearly, not quite, pretty nearly, pretty well, very nearly, virtually, well-nigh.

**practically**[2] *adv* clearly, from a commonsense angle, matter-of-factly, rationally, realistically, reasonably, sensibly, unsentimentally.

**practice** *n* action, application, business, career, clientèle, convention, custom, discipline, drill, dry run, dummy run, effect, exercise, experience, habit, ism, method, mode, modus operandi, operation, patronage, performance, policy, practic, practicalities, practicum, praxis, preparation, procedure, profession, rehearsal, repetition, routine, rule, run-through, study, system, tradition, training, usage, use, vocation, way, wont, work, work-out.

**practise** *v* apply, carry out, discipline, do, drill, enact, engage in, execute, exercise, follow, implement, live up to, observe, perfect, perform, ply, prepare, pursue, put into practice, rehearse, repeat, run through, study, train, undertake, warm up.

**practised** *adj* able, accomplished, consummate, experienced, expert, finished, highly-developed, knowing, knowledgeable, perfected, proficient, qualified, refined, seasoned, skilled, trained, versed, veteran, well-trained.

*antonyms* inexpert, unpractised.

**pragmatic** *adj* businesslike, efficient, factual, hard-headed, opportunistic, practical, realistic, sensible, unidealistic, unsentimental, utilitarian.

*antonyms* idealistic, romantic, unrealistic.

**pragmatism** *n* ad hocery, hard-headedness, humanism, opportunism, practicalism, practicality, realism, unidealism, utilitarianism.

*antonyms* idealism, romanticism.

**pragmatist** *n* humanist, opportunist, practicalist, realist, utilitarian.

*antonyms* idealist, romantic.

**praise** *n* acclaim, acclamation, accolade, acknowledgement, adoration, adulation, applause, approbation, approval, bouquet, cheering, commend, commendation, compliment, compliments, congratulation, devotion, encomium, eulogium, eulogy, extolment, flattery, glory, homage, honour, kudos, laud, laudation, ovation, panegyric, plaudit, puff, rave, recognition, salvoes, testimonial, thanks, thanksgiving, tribute, worship.

*antonyms* criticism, revilement.

*v* acclaim, acknowledge, admire, adore, applaud, approve, belaud, bless, celebrate, cheer, compliment, congratulate, cry up, eulogise, exalt, extol, flatter, give thanks to, glorify, hail, honour, laud, magnify, panegyrise, pay tribute to, promote, puff, rave over, recognise, tout, wax lyrical, worship.

*antonyms* criticise, revile.

**praiseworthy** *adj* admirable, commendable, creditable, deserving, estimable, excellent, exemplary, fine, honourable, laudable, meritorious, reputable, sterling, worthy.

*antonyms* discreditable, dishonourable, ignoble.

**praising** adj, adulatory, approbatory, approving, commendatory, complimentary, congratulatory, encomiastic, eulogistic, favourable, flattering, laudative, laudatory, panegyric, plauditory, promotional, recommendatory, worshipful.

*antonyms* condemnatory, critical.

**prance** *v* bound, caper, capriole, caracole, cavort, curvet, dance, frisk, frolic, gambol, jump, leap, parade, prank, prankle, romp, show off, skip, spring, stalk, strut, swagger, swank, vault.

**prank** *n* antic, caper, dido, escapade, fredaine, frolic, galliardise, guy, jape, joke, lark, piece of mischief, practical joke, rig, spree, stunt, trick, vagary.

**prate** *v* babble, blather, bleat, blether, boast, brag, burble, chatter, drivel, gab, gas, haver, jabber, jaw, maunder, palaver, prattle, ramble, witter, yak.

**prattle** *v* babble, blather, blether, chat, chatter, clack, clash, drivel, gabble, gossip, jabber, patter, rattle, twitter, witter.

*n* bavardage, bletheration, blethers, chat, chatter, clack, clash, claver, drivel, foolishness, gab, gabnash, gibberish, gossip, gup, haverings, havers, hot air, jaw, maundering, nashgab, nonsense, prating, talk, tattle.

**prattler** *n* babbler, blabbermouth, blatherskite, blether, bletherskate, chatterbox, chatterer, gabbler, gabnash, gossip, loudmouth, magpie, nashgab, pie, prater, prattlebox, rattle-brain, talker, tatler, tattler, windbag.

*antonym* clam.

**pray** *v* adjure, ask, beg, beseech, call on, crave, entreat, implore, importune, invoke, obsecrate, petition, plead, press, request, solicit, sue, supplicate, urge.

**prayer** *n* appeal, collect, communion, devotion, entreaty, invocation, kyrie, kyrie eleison, litany, orison, paternoster, petition, plea, request, solicitation, suffrage, suit, supplication.

**prayer-book** *n* breviary, euchologion, euchologue, euchology, ma(c)hzor, missal, ordinal, siddur.

**preach** *v* address, admonish, advocate, ethicise, evangelise, exhort, harangue, lecture, moralise, orate, pontificate, pontify, preachify, prose, sermonise, urge.

**preacher** *n* canter, clergyman, devil-dodger, evangelist, homilist, mar-text, minister, missionary, moraliser, parson, pontificater, predicant, pulpite(e)r, ranter, revivalist, sermoniser.

**preachiness** *n* cant, didacticism, dogmatism, moralising, pharisaism, pietism, pomposity, portentousness, preachment, pulpitry, religiosity, sanctimoniousness, sanctimony, self-righteousness, sermonising.

**preaching** *n* doctrine, dogma, evangel, evangelism, exhortation, gospel, homiletics, homilies, instruction, kerygma, message, pontificating, precepts, sermonising, sermons, teaching.

**preachy** *adj* canting, didactic, dogmatic, edifying, exhortatory, holier-than-thou, homiletic, hortatory, moralising, pharisaic, pietistic, pontifical, pontificating, preceptive, religiose, sanctimonious, self-righteous, sermonising.

**preamble** *n* exordium, foreword, introduction, lead-in, overture, preface, preliminaries, prelude, preparation, proem, prolegomenon, prologue.

*antonyms* epilogue, postscript.

**precarious** *adj* chancy, dangerous, delicate, dicey, dodgy, doubtful, dubious, hairy, hazardous, iffy, insecure, parlous, periculous, perilous, problematic, risky, shaky, slippery, ticklish, tricky, uncertain, unpredictable, unreliable, unsafe, unsettled, unstable, unsteady, unsure, vulnerable.

*antonyms* certain, safe, secure.

**precaution** *n* anticipation, backstop, buffer, care, caution, circumspection, foresight, forethought, insurance, preparation, prophylaxis, protection, providence, provision, prudence, safeguard, safety measure, security, surety, wariness.

**precautionary** *adj* anticipatory, cautious, foresighted, foresightful, judicious, preliminary, preparatory, preventive, prophylactic, protective, provident, provisional, prudent, safety, self-protective.

**precede** *v* antecede, antedate, anticipate, come first, forerun, front, go before, head, herald, introduce, lead, preface, prefix, prelude, premise, prevene, take precedence.

*antonym* follow.

**precedence** *n* antecedence, first place, lead, pre-eminence, preference, pride of place, primacy, priority, rank, seniority, superiority, supremacy.

**precedent** *n* antecedent, authority, citation, criterion, example, exemplar, guideline, instance, judgement, model, paradigm, past instance, pattern, prototype, ruling, standard, yardstick.

**preceding** *adj* above, aforementioned, aforesaid, antecedent, anterior, earlier, foregoing, former, past, precedent, precursive, previous, prior, supra.

*antonyms* following, later.

**precept** *n* axiom, behest, bidding, byword, canon, charge, command, commandment, convention, decree, dictum, direction, directive, guideline, injunction, institute, instruction, law, mandate, maxim, motto, order, ordinance, principle, regulation, rubric, rule, saying, sentence, statute.

**precinct** *n* area, banlieue, bound, boundary, confine, district, division, enclosure, limit, peribolos, quarter, section, sector, zone.

**precincts** n area, borders, bounds, confines, district, environs, limits, locality, milieu, neighbourhood, purlieus, region, surrounds, vicinity.

**preciosity** n affectation, alembication, artificiality, chichi, floweriness, Marivaudage, over-refinement, tweeness.

**precious** adj adored, affected, artificial, arty-farty, beloved, cherished, chichi, choice, costly, darling, dear, dearest, expensive, exquisite, fastidious, favourite, fine, flowery, greenery-yallery, idolised, inestimable, invaluable, irreplaceable, loved, namby-pamby, overnice, over-refined, priceless, prized, rare, recherché, treasured, twee, valuable, valued.

**precipice** n bluff, brink, cliff, cliff face, crag, drop, escarp, escarpment, height, krantz, scarp, steep.

**precipitate** v accelerate, advance, bring on, cast, cause, chuck, discharge, drive, expedite, fling, further, hasten, hurl, hurry, induce, launch, occasion, pitch, press, project, quicken, speed, throw, trigger.
adj abrupt, breakneck, brief, frantic, Gadarene, hasty, headlong, heedless, hot-headed, hurried, impatient, impetuous, impulsive, incautious, indiscreet, madcap, pell-mell, plunging, precipitous, quick, quixotic, rapid, rash, reckless, rushing, sudden, swift, unannounced, unexpected, violent.
antonym cautious.

**precipitous** adj abrupt, dizzy, giddy, high, perpendicular, sheer, steep, vertiginous.
antonyms gradual, sloping.

**précis** n abbreviation, abridgement, abstract, aperçu, compendium, condensation, conspectus, contraction, digest, encapsulation, epitome, outline, résumé, run-down, sketch, summary, synopsis, table.
v abbreviate, abridge, abstract, compress, condense, contract, digest, encapsulate, epitomise, outline, shorten, sum up, summarise, synopsise.
antonyms amplify, expand.

**precise** adj absolute, accurate, actual, authentic, blow-by-blow, buckram, careful, ceremonious, clear-cut, correct, definite, delimitative, determinate, distinct, exact, explicit, express, expressis verbis, factual, faithful, fastidious, finical, finicky, fixed, formal, identical, literal, meticulous, minute, nice, particular, prim, punctilious, puritanical, rigid, scrupulous, specific, strict, succinct, unequivocal, verbatim, word-for-word.
antonym imprecise.

**precisely** adv absolutely, accurately, bang, blow by blow, correctly, dead, distinctly, exactly, expressis verbis, just, just so, literally, minutely, plumb, slap, smack, square, squarely, strictly, verbatim, word for word.

**precision** n accuracy, care, correctness, definiteness, detail, exactitude, exactness, explicitness, expressness, faithfulness, fastidiousness, fidelity, meticulousness, minuteness, neatness, niceness, nicety,

particularity, preciseness, punctilio, punctiliousness, rigour, scrupulosity, specificity.
antonym imprecision.

**preclude** v avoid, check, debar, eliminate, exclude, forestall, hinder, inhibit, obviate, prevent, prohibit, restrain, rule out, stop.
antonyms incur, involve.

**precocious** adj advanced, ahead, bright, clever, developed, fast, forward, gifted, mature, precocial, premature, quick, smart.
antonym backward.

**preconceive** v anticipate, assume, conceive, conceptualise, envisage, ideate, imagine, picture, presume, presuppose, project, visualise.

**preconception** n anticipation, assumption, bias, conjecture, notion, predisposition, prejudice, prenotion, prepossession, presumption, presupposition.

**precondition** n essential, must, necessity, need, prerequisite, proviso, requirement, requisite, sine qua non, stipulation.

**precursor** n antecedent, forebear, forerunner, harbinger, herald, indication, messenger, originator, pathfinder, pioneer, predecessor, prodrome, prodromus, sign, trail-blazer, usher, vanguard, warning, way-maker.
antonyms after-effect, aftermath.

**precursory** adj antecedent, anterior, introductory, preambulatory, preceding, precursive, prefatory, preliminary, preludial, prelusive, premonitory, preparatory, prevenient, previous, prior, prodromal, warning.
antonyms following, resulting, subsequent.

**predatory** adj acquisitive, avaricious, carnivorous, covetous, despoiling, greedy, hunting, lupine, marauding, pillaging, plundering, predacious, predative, preying, rapacious, raptatorial, raptorial, ravaging, ravening, thieving, voracious, vulturine, vulturous, wolfish.

**predecessor** n ancestor, antecedent, antecessor, forebear, forefather, forerunner, precursor, progenitor.
antonyms descendant, successor.

**predestination** n ananke, destiny, doom, election, fate, foreordainment, foreordination, karma, lot, necessity, portion, predestiny, predetermination, preordainment, preordination, weird.

**predestine** v destine, doom, fate, foredoom, foreordain, intend, mean, predestinate, predetermine, pre-elect, preordain.

**predetermined** adj agreed, cut and dried, decided beforehand, deliberate, fixed, foregone, foreordained, prearranged, preordained, preplanned, set, set up, settled.

**predicament** n can of worms, corner, crisis, dilemma, embarrassment, emergency, fix, galère, hole, hot water, impasse, jam, kettle of fish, mess, pickle, pinch, plight, quandary, scrape, situation, spot, state, trouble.

**predicate** v affirm, assert, aver, avouch, avow, base, build, contend, declare, establish, found, ground, maintain, posit, postulate, premise, proclaim, rest, state.

**predict** v augur, auspicate, divine, forebode, forecast, foresay, foresee, foreshow, forespeak, foretell, portend, presage, prognosticate, project, prophesy, second-guess, soothsay, vaticinate.

**predictable** adj anticipated, calculable, certain, dependable, determinate, expected, finite, foregone, foreseeable, foreseen, imaginable, likely, presumable, probable, reliable, sure.

antonym unpredictable.

**prediction** n augury, auspication, divination, forecast, fortune-telling, prognosis, prognostication, prophecy, second sight, soothsaying, vaticination.

**predictive** adj augural, diagnostic, divinatory, foretelling, prognostic, prophetic.

**predilection** n affection, affinity, bent, bias, enthusiasm, fancy, fondness, inclination, leaning, liking, love, partiality, penchant, predisposition, preference, proclivity, proneness, propensity, soft spot, taste, tendency, weakness.

antonyms antipathy, disinclination.

**predispose** v affect, bias, dispose, head, incline, induce, influence, lead, lean, make, make liable, prejudice, prepare, prime, prompt, sway.

**predisposed** adj agreeable, amenable, biased, disposed, favourable, inclined, liable, minded, not unwilling, nothing loth, prejudiced, prepared, prone, ready, subject, susceptible, well-disposed, willing.

**predisposition** n bent, bias, disposition, inclination, leaning, liability, likelihood, mind, penchant, potentiality, predilection, preference, prejudice, proclivity, proneness, propensity, susceptibility, tendency, vulnerability, willingness.

**predominance** n ascendancy, control, dominance, dominion, edge, hegemony, hold, influence, leadership, mastery, numbers, paramountcy, power, prepollence, prepollency, preponderance, prepotence, prepotency, prevalence, superiority, supremacy, sway, upper hand, weight.

antonyms ineffectiveness, weakness.

**predominant** adj ascendant, capital, chief, controlling, dominant, forceful, important, influential, leading, main, paramount, potent, powerful, prepollent, preponderant, prepotent, prevailing, prevalent, primary, prime, principal, prominent, ruling, sovereign, strong, superior, supreme.

antonyms ineffective, lesser, minor, weak.

**predominate** v dominate, obtain, outnumber, outweigh, override, overrule, overshadow, preponderate, prevail, reign, rule, tell, transcend.

**pre-eminence** n distinction, excellence, fame, incomparability, matchlessness, paramountcy, peerlessness, predominance, prestige, prominence, renown, repute, superiority, supremacy, transcendence.

**pre-eminent** adj chief, consummate, distinguished, excellent, exceptional, facile

princeps, foremost, incomparable, inimitable, leading, matchless, nonpareil, outstanding, paramount, passing, peerless, predominant, prominent, renowned, superior, superlative, supreme, surpassing, transcendent, unequalled, unmatched, unrivalled, unsurpassed.

antonyms undistinguished, unknown.

**pre-eminently** adv conspicuously, eminently, emphatically, especially, exceptionally, exclusively, incomparably, inimitably, matchlessly, notably, par excellence, particularly, peerlessly, signally, singularly, strikingly, superlatively, supremely, surpassingly.

**pre-empt** v acquire, anticipate, appropriate, arrogate, assume, bag, forestall, secure, seize, usurp.

**preen** v adorn, array, beautify, clean, deck, do up, doll up, dress up, fig out, groom, plume, prank, prettify, primp, prink, slick, spruce up, tart up, titivate, trick out, trim.

**preen (oneself)** bask, congratulate, exult, gloat, pique, plume, pride.

**preface** n exordium, foreword, intro, introduction, preamble, preliminaries, prelims, prelude, proem, prolegomena, prolegomenon, prologue, prooemion, prooemium.

antonyms afterthought, epilogue, postscript.

v begin, introduce, launch, lead up to, open, precede, prefix, prelude, premise, start.

antonyms append, complete, finish.

**prefatory** adj antecedent, exordial, explanatory, introductory, opening, preambulatory, precursory, prefatorial, preliminary, preludial, prelusive, prelusory, preparatory, proemial, prolegomenal.

antonyms closing, final.

**prefect** n administrator, monitor, praefect, praeposter, prepositor, supervisor.

**prefer**[1] v adopt, advocate, back, be partial to, choose, desire, elect, endorse, fancy, favour, go for, incline towards, like better, opt for, pick, plump for, recommend, select, single out, support, want, wish, would rather, would sooner.

antonym reject.

**prefer**[2] v bring, file, lodge, place, present, press.

**prefer**[3] v advance, aggrandise, dignify, elevate, exalt, promote, raise, upgrade.

antonym demote.

**preferable** adj advantageous, advisable, best, better, choice, chosen, desirable, eligible, expedient, favoured, nicer, preferred, stronger, superior, worthier.

antonyms ineligible, inferior, undesirable.

**preferably** adv first, for choice, for preference, rather, sooner.

**preference**[1] n choice, desire, election, fancy, favourite, first choice, inclination, liking, option, partiality, pick, predilection, selection, wish.

**preference**[2] n advantage, favour, favouritism, precedence, preferential treatment, priority, special consideration, special treatment.

**preferential** *adj* advantageous, better, biased, favourable, favoured, partial, partisan, prior, privileged, special, superior.

*antonym* equal.

**preferment** *n* advancement, aggrandisement, betterment, dignity, elevation, exaltation, furtherance, improvement, promotion, rise, step up, upgrading.

*antonym* demotion.

**preferred** *adj* approved, authorised, choice, chosen, desired, favoured, predilect, recommended, sanctioned, selected.

*antonyms* rejected, undesirable.

**pregnancy** *n* child-bearing, conception, family way, fertilisation, gestation, gravidity, impregnation.

**pregnant**[1] *adj* big, big-bellied, enceinte, expectant, expecting, gravid, impregnated, in an interesting condition, in the club, in the family way, in the pudding club, parturient, preggers, teeming, with child.

**pregnant**[2] *adj* charged, eloquent, expressive, full, heavy, loaded, meaning, meaningful, ominous, pithy, pointed, significant, suggestive, telling, weighty.

*antonym* jejune.

**prehistoric** *adj* ancient, antediluvian, antiquated, archaic, earliest, early, fogram, hoary, obsolete, Ogygian, old, outmoded, out-of-date, primeval, primitive, primordial.

*antonym* modern.

**prejudge** *v* anticipate, assume, forejudge, judge prematurely, predetermine, prejudicate, presume, presuppose.

**prejudice**[1] *n* bias, bigotry, chauvinism, discrimination, injustice, intolerance, narrow-mindedness, partiality, partisanship, preconception, prejudgement, racism, sexism, unfairness, viewiness, warp.

*antonyms* fairness, tolerance.

*v* bias, colour, condition, distort, incline, indoctrinate, influence, jaundice, load, poison, predispose, prepossess, slant, sway, warp, weight.

**prejudice**[2] *n* damage, detriment, disadvantage, harm, hurt, impairment, injury, loss, mischief, ruin, vitiation, wreck.

*antonyms* advantage, benefit.

*v* damage, harm, hinder, hurt, impair, injure, mar, ruin, spoil, undermine, vitiate, wreck.

*antonyms* advance, benefit, help.

**prejudiced** *adj* biased, bigoted, chauvinist, conditioned, discriminatory, distorted, ex parte, illiberal, influenced, intolerant, jaundiced, loaded, narrow-minded, one-sided, opinionated, partial, partisan, prepossessed, racist, sexist, subjective, unenlightened, unfair, verkrampte, viewy, warped, weighted.

*antonyms* fair, tolerant.

**prejudicial** *adj* counter-productive, damaging, deleterious, detrimental, disadvantageous, harmful, hostile, hurtful, inimical, injurious, mischievous, noxious, pernicious, ruinous, undermining, unfavourable.

*antonyms* advantageous, beneficial.

**preliminaries** *n* basics, beginning, first round, formalities, foundations, groundwork, initiation, introduction, opening, preamble, preface, prelims, prelude, preparation, proem, prolegomena, rudiments, start.

**preliminary** *adj* earliest, early, embryonic, exordial, experimental, exploratory, first, inaugural, initial, initiative, initiatory, introductory, opening, pilot, precursory, prefatory, prelusive, preparatory, primary, prior, qualifying, test, trial.

*antonyms* closing, final.

**prelude** *n* beginning, commencement, curtain-raiser, exordium, foreword, introduction, intro, opener, overture, praeludium, preamble, precursor, preface, preliminary, preludio, prelusion, preparation, prodrome, proem, prolegomenon, prologue, prooemion, prooemium, start, taster, verset, Vorspiel.

*antonyms* aftermath, epilogue, postscript.

**premature** *adj* abortive, early, embryonic, forward, green, half-formed, hasty, ill-considered, ill-timed, immature, imperfect, impulsive, incomplete, inopportune, overhasty, precipitate, precocious, preterm, previous, rash, raw, undeveloped, unfledged, unripe, unseasonable, untimely.

*antonyms* late, tardy.

**premeditated** *adj* aforethought, calculated, cold-blooded, conscious, considered, contrived, deliberate, intended, intentional, planned, plotted, prearranged, predetermined, prepense, preplanned, studied, wilful.

*antonyms* spontaneous, unpremeditated.

**premeditation** *n* deliberateness, deliberation, design, determination, forethought, intention, malice aforethought, planning, plotting, prearrangement, predetermination, purpose, scheming.

*antonyms* impulse, spontaneity.

**premier** *n* chancellor, chief minister, first minister, head of government, prime minister, secretary of state.

*adj* arch, cardinal, chief, earliest, first, foremost, head, highest, initial, leading, main, original, paramount, pre-eminent, primary, prime, principal, supreme, top.

**premiere** *n* début, first night, opening, opening night.

**premise** *v* assert, assume, hypothesise, lay down, posit, postulate, predicate, presuppose, state, stipulate, take as true.

*n* argument, assertion, assumption, ground, hypothesis, postulate, postulation, predication, premiss, presupposition, proposition, statement, stipulation, supposition, thesis.

**premises** *n* building, establishment, estate, grounds, office, place, property, site.

**premonition** *n* anxiety, apprehension, fear, feeling, foreboding, forewarning, hunch, idea, intuition, misgiving, niggle, omen, portent, presage, presentiment, sign, suspicion, unease, uneasiness, warning, worry.

**preoccupation** *n* absence of mind, absent-mindedness, absorption, abstraction, brown study, concern, daydreaming, distraction, engrossment, enthusiasm, fixation, hang-up, hobby-horse, idée fixe, immersion, inattention, inattentiveness, musing, oblivion, obliviousness, obsession, pensiveness, raptness, reverie, wool-gathering.

**preoccupied** *adj* absent-minded, absorbed, abstracted, daydreaming, distracted, distrait, engrossed, entêté, faraway, fixated, heedless, immersed, intent, oblivious, obsessed, pensive, rapt, taken up, unaware, visited, wrapped up.

**preordain** *v* destine, doom, fate, foreordain, prearrange, predestine, predetermine.

**preparation**[1] *n* alertness, anticipation, arrangement, assignment, basics, development, expectation, foresight, foundation, groundwork, homework, imposition, lesson, measure, plan, precaution, preliminaries, prep, preparedness, provision, readiness, revision, rudiments, safeguard, schoolwork, study, task.

**preparation**[2] *n* application, composition, compound, concoction, lotion, medicine, mixture, potion, tincture.

**preparatory** *adj* basic, elementary, exordial, fundamental, initial, introductory, opening, prefatory, preliminary, preparative, primary, proemial, rudimentary.

**preparatory to** before, in advance of, in anticipation of, in expectation of, previous to, prior to.

**prepare** *v* accoutre, adapt, adjust, anticipate, arrange, assemble, boun, brace, brief, busk, coach, compose, concoct, confect, construct, contrive, develop, devise, dispose, do one's homework, draft, draw up, dress, equip, fashion, fettle, fit, fit out, fix up, forearm, form, format, fortify, furnish, get up, gird, groom, instruct, limber up, make, make ready, outfit, plan, practise, predispose, prime, produce, provide, psych up, ready, rehearse, rig out, steel, strengthen, supply, train, trim, warm up.

**prepare oneself** brace oneself, fortify oneself, get psyched up, gird oneself, limber up, psych oneself up, ready oneself, steel oneself.

**prepared** *adj* able, arranged, briefed, disposed, expectant, fit, forearmed, inclined, minded, planned, predisposed, primed, psyched up, ready, set, waiting, well-rehearsed, willing, word-perfect.

*antonyms* unprepared, unready.

**preparedness** *n* alertness, anticipation, expectancy, fitness, order, preparation, readiness.

*antonym* unreadiness.

**preponderance** *n* ascendancy, bulk, dominance, domination, dominion, extensiveness, force, lion's share, majority, mass, power, predominance, prevalence, superiority, supremacy, sway, weight.

**preponderant** *adj* ascendant, controlling, dominant, extensive, foremost, greater, important, larger, overriding, overruling, paramount, predominant, prevailing, prevalent, significant, superior.

**preponderate** *v* dominate, outnumber, override, overrule, predominate, prevail, rule, tell, turn the balance, turn the scale, weigh with.

**prepossessing** *adj* alluring, amiable, appealing, attractive, beautiful, bewitching, captivating, charming, delightful, disarming, enchanting, engaging, fair, fascinating, fetching, good-looking, handsome, inviting, likable, lovable, magnetic, pleasing, striking, taking, winning, winsome.

*antonyms* unattractive, unprepossessing.

**prepossession** *n* absorption, bias, engrossment, inclination, leaning, liking, partiality, predilection, predisposition, prejudice, preoccupation.

**preposterous** *adj* absurd, asinine, bizarre, crazy, derisory, excessive, exorbitant, extravagant, extreme, fatuous, foolish, imbecile, impossible, inane, incredible, insane, intolerable, irrational, laughable, ludicrous, monstrous, nonsensical, outrageous, ridiculous, risible, senseless, shocking, unbelievable, unconscionable, unreasonable, unthinkable.

*antonyms* reasonable, .h prerequisite.

*adj* basic, essential, fundamental, imperative, indispensable, mandatory, necessary, needed, needful, obligatory, required, requisite, vital.

*antonym* unnecessary.

*n* condition, essential, imperative, must, necessity, precondition, provision, proviso, qualification, requirement, requisite, sine qua non.

*antonym* extra.

**prerogative** *n* advantage, authority, birthright, carte blanche, choice, claim, droit, due, exemption, immunity, liberty, licence, perquisite, privilege, right, sanction, title.

**presage** *v* adumbrate, augur, betoken, bode, divine, feel, forebode, forecast, forefeel, foreknow, forepoint, foresee, foreshadow, foretell, forethink, foretoken, forewarn, intuit, omen, point to, portend, predict, previse, prognosticate, prophesy, sense, signify, soothsay, vaticinate, warn.

*n* apprehension, augury, auspice, bad vibes, bodement, boding, feeling, foreboding, forecast, forewarning, harbinger, intimation, intuition, misgiving, omen, portent, prediction, premonition, presentiment, prodrome, prodromus, prognostic, prognostication, prophecy, sign, warning.

**prescience** *n* clairvoyance, far-sightedness, foreknowledge, foresight, precognition, prevision, prophecy, propheticness, second sight.

**prescient** *adj* clairvoyant, discerning, divinatory, divining, far-seeing, far-sighted, foreknowing, foresighted, mantic, perceptive, previsional, prophetic, psychic.

*antonym* imperceptive.

**prescribe** *v* appoint, assign, command, decree, define, dictate, direct, enjoin, fix, impose, lay down, limit, ordain, order, require, rule, set, set bounds to, specify, stipulate.

**prescribed** *adj* assigned, decreed, formulary, laid down, ordained, set, specified, stipulated.

**prescription** *n* direction, drug, formula, instruction, medicine, mixture, preparation, recipe, remedy, treatment.

**prescriptive** *adj* authoritarian, customary, dictatorial, didactic, dogmatic, legislating, preceptive, prescribing, rigid.

**presence** *n* air, apparition, appearance, aspect, attendance, aura, bearing, carriage, closeness, companionship, company, comportment, demeanour, ease, existence, ghost, habitation, inhabitance, manifestation, mien, nearness, neighbourhood, occupancy, personality, poise, propinquity, proximity, residence, revenant, self-assurance, shade, spectre, spirit, statuesqueness, vicinity.

*antonym* absence.

**presence of mind** alertness, aplomb, calmness, composure, cool, coolness, gumption, imperturbability, level-headedness, nous, quickness, sang-froid, self-assurance, self-command, self-possession, wits.

*antonyms* agitation, confusion.

**present**[1] *adj* at hand, attending, available, contemporary, current, existent, extant, here, immediate, instant, near, ready, there, to hand.

*antonyms* absent, out-of-date, past.

**present**[2] *v* acquaint with, adduce, advance, award, bestow, confer, declare, demonstrate, display, donate, entrust, exhibit, expound, extend, furnish, give, grant, hand over, hold out, introduce, mount, offer, porrect, pose, produce, proffer, put on, raise, recount, relate, show, stage, state, submit, suggest, tender.

*antonym* take.

*n* benefaction, boon, bounty, cadeau, compliment, donation, endowment, favour, gift, grant, gratuity, largess, nuzzer, offering, pressie, prezzie, refresher.

**presentable** *adj* acceptable, becoming, clean, decent, neat, passable, proper, respectable, satisfactory, suitable, tidy, tolerable.

*antonyms* unpresentable, untidy.

**presentation** *n* appearance, arrangement, award, bestowal, conferral, delivery, demonstration, display, donation, exhibition, exposition, giving, introduction, investiture, offering, pageant, performance, production, rendition, representation, show, staging, submission.

**present-day** *adj* contemporary, current, existing, fashionable, hodiernal, living, modern, present, up-to-date.

*antonyms* future, past.

**presenter** *n* anchorman, compère, frontman, host, master of ceremonies, MC.

**presentiment** *n* anticipation, apprehension, bad vibes, expectation, fear, feeling, forebodement, foreboding, forecast, forethought, hunch, intuition, misgiving, premonition, presage.

**presently** *adv* anon, before long, by and by, directly, immediately, in a minute, shortly, soon.

**preservation** *n* conservation, defence, keeping, maintenance, perpetuation, protection, retention, safeguarding, safekeeping, safety, salvation, security, storage, support, upholding, upkeep.

*antonyms* destruction, ruination.

**preserve** *v* care for, confect, conserve, continue, defend, embalm, entreasure, guard, keep, maintain, perpetuate, protect, retain, safeguard, save, secure, shelter, shield, store, sustain, uphold.

*antonyms* destroy, ruin.

*n* area, confection, confiture, conserve, domain, field, game park, game reserve, jam, jelly, konfyt, marmalade, pigeon, realm, reservation, reserve, safari park, sanctuary, specialism, speciality, specialty, sphere, thing.

**preside** *v* administer, chair, conduct, control, direct, govern, head, lead, manage, officiate, run, supervise.

**press**[1] *v* adpress, afflict, appress, assail, beg, beset, besiege, calendar, clasp, cluster, compel, compress, condense, constrain, crowd, crush, demand, depress, disquiet, dun, embrace, encircle, enfold, enforce, enjoin, entreat, exhort, finish, flatten, flock, force, force down, gather, harass, hasten, herd, hug, hurry, implore, importune, insist on, iron, jam, mangle, mash, mill, petition, plague, plead, pressurise, push, reduce, rush, seethe, smooth, squeeze, steam, stuff, sue, supplicate, surge, swarm, throng, torment, trouble, urge, vex, worry.

*antonyms* expand, hang back, lighten, relieve.

*n* bunch, bustle, crowd, crush, demand, flock, hassle, herd, horde, host, hurry, mob, multitude, pack, pressure, push, strain, stress, swarm, throng, urgency.

**press**[2] *n* columnists, correspondents, Fleet Street, fourth estate, hacks, journalism, journalists, news media, newsmen, newspapers, paparazzi, papers, photographers, pressmen, reporters, writers.

**pressed** *adj* browbeaten, bullied, coerced, constrained, forced, harassed, hurried, pressured, pressurised, pushed, rushed, short.

*antonyms* unhurried, well-off.

**pressing** *adj* burning, constraining, crowding, crucial, essential, exigent, high-priority, imperative, important, importunate, serious, thronging, urgent, vital.

*antonyms* trivial, unimportant.

**pressure** *n* adversity, affliction, burden, coercion, compressing, compression, compulsion, constraint, crushing, demands, difficulty, distress, exigency, force, hassle, heat, heaviness, hurry, influence, load, obligation, power, powerplay, press, pression, squeezing, strain, stress, sway, urgency, weight.

*v* browbeat, bulldoze, bully, coerce, compel, constrain, dragoon, drive, force, impel, induce, lean on, oblige, persuade, press, pressurise, squeeze.

**pressurise** *v* browbeat, bulldoze, bully, coerce, compel, constrain, dragoon, drive, force, impel, induce, lean on, oblige, persuade, press, pressure, squeeze.

**prestige** *n* authority, cachet, celebrity, clout, credit, distinction, eminence, esteem, fame, honour, importance, influence, kudos, pull, regard, renown, reputation, standing, stature, status, weight.

*antonyms* humbleness, unimportance.

**prestigious** *adj* blue-chip, celebrated, eminent, esteemed, exalted, great, illustrious, important, imposing, impressive, influential, prominent, renowned, reputable, respected, up-market.

*antonyms* humble, modest.

**presumably** *adv* apparently, as like as not, doubtless, doubtlessly, in all likelihood, in all probability, most likely, no doubt, probably, seemingly.

**presume** *v* assume, bank on, believe, conjecture, count on, dare, depend on, go so far, have the audacity, hypothesise, hypothetise, infer, make bold, make so bold, posit, postulate, presuppose, rely on, suppose, surmise, take for granted, take it, take the liberty, think, trust, undertake, venture.

**presumption**[1] *n* assurance, audacity, boldness, brass, brass neck, cheek, effrontery, forwardness, gall, impudence, insolence, neck, nerve, presumptuousness, temerity.

*antonyms* humility, politeness.

**presumption**[2] *n* anticipation, assumption, basis, belief, chance, conjecture, grounds, guess, hypothesis, likelihood, opinion, plausibility, premiss, presupposition, probability, reason, supposition, surmise.

**presumptive** *adj* assumed, believable, believed, conceivable, credible, designate, expected, hypothetical, inferred, likely, plausible, possible, probable, prospective, reasonable, supposed, understood.

*antonyms* known, unlikely.

**presumptuous** *adj* arrogant, audacious, big-headed, bold, conceited, foolhardy, forward, impertinent, impudent, insolent, over-confident, over-familiar, overweening, presuming, pushy, rash, uppish.

*antonym* modest.

**presuppose** *v* accept, assume, consider, imply, posit, postulate, premise, presume, suppose, take for granted.

**presupposition** *n* assumption, belief, hypothesis, preconception, premise, premiss, presumption, supposition, theory.

**pretence** *n* acting, affectation, aim, allegation, appearance, artifice, blague, bounce, charade, claim, cloak, colour, cover, deceit, deception, display, excuse, fabrication, façade, faking, falsehood, feigning, garb, guise, humbug, invention, make-believe, mask, masquerade, posing, posturing, pretentiousness, pretext, profession, pseudery, purpose, ruse, semblance, sham, show, simulation, subterfuge, trickery, veil, veneer, wile.

*antonyms* honesty, openness, reason.

**pretend** *v* act, affect, alge, allege, aspire, assume, claim, counterfeit, dissemble, dissimulate, fake, falsify, feign, go through the motions, imagine, impersonate, make believe, pass oneself off, profess, purport, put on, sham, simulate, suppose.

**pretended** *adj* alleged, avowed, bogus, counterfeit, fake, false, feigned, fictitious, imaginary, ostensible, phoney, pretend, professed, pseudo, purported, sham, so-called, specious, spurious, supposed, supposititious.

*antonym* real.

**pretender** *n* aspirant, claimant, claimer, pretendant.

**pretension** *n* affection, airs, aspiration, assertion, assumption, claim, conceit, demand, hypocrisy, ostentation, pomposity, pretence, pretentiousness, pretext, profession, self-importance, show, showiness, snobbery, snobbishness, vainglory, vanity.

*antonyms* humility, modesty, simplicity, straightforwardness.

**pretentious** *adj* affected, ambitious, assuming, bombastic, chichi, conceited, euphemistic, exaggerated, extravagant, flaunting, grandiloquent, grandiose, highfalutin, high-flown, high-sounding, hollow, inflated, magniloquent, mannered, oro(ro)tund, ostentatious, overambitious, overassuming, pompous, pseud, pseudish, pseudo, showy, snobbish, specious, uppish, vainglorious.

*antonyms* humble, modest, simple, straightforward.

**pretentiousness** *n* attitudinising, flamboyance, floridness, floweriness, ostentation, posing, posturing, pretension, pseudery, show, theatricality.

*antonyms* humbleness, modesty, simplicity, straightforwardness.

**pretext** *n* appearance, cloak, cover, device, excuse, guise, mask, ploy, pretence, rationale, ruse, semblance, show, simulation, umbrage, veil.

**prettify** *v* adorn, beautify, bedeck, deck, deck out, decorate, do up, doll up, embellish, garnish, gild, ornament, primp, prink up, smarten up, tart up, titivate, trick out, trim.

*antonyms* mar, uglify.

**pretty** *adj* appealing, attractive, beautiful, bijou, bonny, charming, comely, cute, dainty, delicate, elegant, fair, fine, good-looking, graceful, lovely, neat, nice, personable, pleasing, sightly, tasteful, trim.

*antonyms* tasteless, ugly.

*adv* fairly, moderately, passably, quite, rather, reasonably, somewhat, tolerably.

**prevail** *v* abound, obtain, overcome, overrule, predominate, preponderate, reign, rule, succeed, triumph, win.

*antonym* lose.

**prevail upon** bring round, convince, dispose, dissuade, incline, induce, influence, persuade, prompt, sway, talk into, talk out of, talk round, win over.

**prevailing** *adj* common, controlling, current, customary, dominant, established, fashionable, general, in style, in vogue, influential, main, mainstream, operative, ordinary, popular, predominating, preponderating, prepotent, prevalent, principal, ruling, set, usual, widespread.

*antonyms* minor, uncommon.

**prevalence** *n* acceptance, ascendancy, commonness, currency, frequency, hold, mastery, omnipresence, pervasiveness, popularity, predominance, preponderance, primacy, profusion, regularity, rule, sway, ubiquity, universality.

*antonym* uncommonness.

**prevalent** *adj* accepted, ascendant, common, commonplace, compelling, current, customary, dominant, epidemic, established, everyday, extensive, frequent, general, governing, habitual, popular, powerful, predominant, prevailing, rampant, regnant, rife, successful, superior, ubiquitous, universal, usual, victorious, widespread.

*antonyms* subordinate, uncommon.

**prevaricate** *v* cavil, deceive, dodge, equivocate, evade, fib, hedge, lie, palter, quibble, shift, shuffle, temporise, tergiversate.

**prevarication** *n* cavil, cavillation, cavilling, deceit, deception, equivocation, evasion, falsehood, falsification, fibbing, fib(s), half-truth, lie, misrepresentation, pretence, quibbling, tergiversation, untruth.

**prevaricator** *n* Ananias, casuist, caviller, deceiver, dissembler, dodger, equivocator, evader, fibber, hypocrite, liar, pettifogger, quibbler, sophist.

**prevent** *v* anticipate, avert, avoid, balk, bar, block, check, counteract, debar, defend against, foil, forestall, frustrate, hamper, head off, hinder, impede, inhibit, intercept, obstruct, obviate, preclude, restrain, stave off, stop, stymie, thwart, ward off.

*antonyms* cause, foster, help.

**prevention** *n* anticipation, avoidance, bar, check, deterrence, elimination, forestalling, forethought, frustration, hindrance, impediment, interruption, obstacle, obstruction, obviation, precaution, preclusion, prophylaxis, safeguard, stoppage, thwarting.

*antonyms* causing, fostering, help.

**preventive** *adj* counteractive, deterrent, hampering, hindering, impeding, inhibitory, obstructive, precautionary, prevenient, preventative, prophylactic, protective, shielding.

*antonyms* causative, fostering.

*n* block, condom, deterrent, hindrance, impediment, neutraliser, obstacle, obstruction, prevention, prophylactic, protection, protective, remedy, safeguard, shield.

*antonyms* cause, encouragement, incitement.

**previous** *adj* antecedent, anterior, arranged, earlier, erstwhile, ex-, foregoing, former, one-time, past, preceding, precipitate, premature,

prior, quondam, sometime, umwhile, untimely, whilom.

*antonyms* later, timely.

**previously** *adv* before, beforehand, earlier, formerly, heretofore, hitherto, once.

*antonym* later.

**prey** *n* booty, dupe, fall guy, game, kill, mark, mug, plunder, quarry, target, victim.

**prey on** blackmail, bleed, bully, burden, devour, distress, eat, eat away, exploit, feed on, gnaw at, haunt, hunt, intimidate, live off, moth-eat, oppress, seize, take advantage of, terrorise, trouble, victimise, waste, weigh down, weigh heavily, worry.

**price** *n* amount, assessment, bill, bounty, charge, consequences, cost, damage, estimate, expenditure, expense, fee, figure, levy, odds, outlay, payment, penalty, rate, reward, sacrifice, sum, toll, valuation, value, worth.

*v* assess, cost, estimate, evaluate, offer, put, rate, valorise, value.

**priceless**[1] *adj* beyond price, cherished, costly, dear, expensive, incalculable, incomparable, inestimable, invaluable, irreplaceable, precious, prized, rare, rich, treasured, without price.

*antonyms* cheap, run-of-the-mill.

**priceless**[2] *adj* a hoot, a scream, absurd, amusing, comic, droll, funny, hilarious, killing, rib-tickling, ridiculous, riotous, risible, side-splitting.

**price-list** *n* catalogue, menu, price(s)-current.

**pric(e)y** *adj* costly, dear, excessive, exorbitant, expensive, extortionate, high-priced, over the odds, steep.

*antonym* cheap.

**prick** *v* bite, bore, itch, jab, jag, pain, perforate, pierce, pink, point, prickle, prog, punch, puncture, raise, rise, smart, stab, sting, thorn, tingle, touch, trouble.

*n* jag, pang, perforation, pinhole, prickle, prog, puncture, smart, spasm, sting, twinge, wound.

**prickle** *n* acantha, barb, formication, needle, point, smart, spike, spine, spur, thorn, tickle, tingle, tingling.

*v* itch, jab, nick, nip, prick, smart, sting, tingle.

**prickly** *adj* acanaceous, aculeate(d), barbed, brambly, bristly, cantankerous, complicated, crawling, difficult, echinate, edgy, fractious, grumpy, intricate, involved, irritable, itchy, jaggy, knotty, peevish, pettish, petulant, pricking, prickling, scratchy, sharp, short-tempered, smarting, spiny, stinging, tetchy, thorny, ticklish, tingling, touchy, tricky, troublesome, trying, waspish.

*antonyms* easy-going, simple, smooth.

**pricy** *see* **pric(e)y**.

**pride** *n* amour-propre, arrogance, best, big-headedness, boast, choice, conceit, cream, delight, dignity, egotism, élite, flower, gem, glory, gratification, haughtiness, hauteur, high spirits, honour, hubris, jewel, joy, loftiness, magnificence, mettle, morgue, ostentation, pick, pleasure, presumption, pretension, pretensiousness, pride and joy, prize, satisfaction, self-esteem, self-importance, self-love, self-respect, smugness, snobbery, splendour, superciliousness, treasure, vainglory, vanity.

*antonym* humility.

**pride (oneself on)** boast, brag, congratulate oneself, crow, exult, flatter oneself, glory, pat oneself on the back, pique, plume, preen, revel, take pride, vaunt.

*antonyms* belittle, humble.

**priest** *n* abbé, churchman, clergyman, cleric, curate, divine, ecclesiast, ecclesiastic, father, father confessor, flamen, holy man, Jack-priest, lama, Levite, Magus, man of God, man of the cloth, mar-text, masspriest, minister, padre, priestling, vicar.

**priestess** *n* abbess, beguine, canoness, clergywoman, deaconess, mambo, nun, prioress, religious, sister, vestal.

**priestly** *adj* Aaronic(al), canonical, clerical, ecclesiastical, flaminical, hieratic, pastoral, priestlike, sacerdotal.

**prig** *n* goody-goody, holy Joe, Holy Willie, Mrs Grundy, old maid, precisian, prude, puritan.

**priggish** *adj* goody-goody, holier-than-thou, narrow-minded, pedantic, prim, prudish, pudibund, puritanical, self-righteous, self-satisfied, smug, starchy, stiff, stuffy.

*antonyms* broad-minded, informal.

**prim** *adj* demure, fastidious, formal, fussy, governessy, old-maidish, old-maidist, particular, perjink, po-faced, precise, priggish, prissy, proper, prudish, pudibund, puritanical, schoolmarmish, sedate, starchy, stiff, strait-laced.

*antonyms* broad-minded, informal.

**primacy** *n* ascendancy, command, dominance, dominion, leadership, paramoun(t)cy, pre-eminence, seniority, sovereignty, superiority, supremacy.

*antonym* inferiority.

**primal** *adj* central, chief, earliest, first, fundamental, greatest, highest, initial, main, major, original, paramount, primary, prime, primeval, primitive, primordial, principal, pristine.

*antonyms* later, minor.

**primarily** *adv* at first, basically, chiefly, especially, essentially, fundamentally, generally, initially, mainly, mostly, originally, principally.

*antonym* secondarily.

**primary** *adj* aboriginal, basic, beginning, best, capital, cardinal, chief, dominant, earliest, elemental, elementary, essential, first, first-formed, first-made, fundamental, greatest, highest, initial, introductory, leading, main, original, paramount, primal, prime, primeval, primigenial, primitial, primitive, primordial, principal, pristine, radical, rudimentary, simple, top, ultimate, underlying.

*antonym* secondary.

**prime¹** *adj* basic, best, capital, chief, choice, earliest, excellent, first-class, first-rate, fundamental, highest, leading, main, original, predominant, pre-eminent, primary, principal, quality, ruling, select, selected, senior, superior, top, underlying.

*antonyms* minor, secondary, second-rate.

*n* beginning, flowering, height, heyday, maturity, morning, opening, peak, perfection, spring, springtide, springtime, start, zenith.

**prime²** *v* brief, charge, clue up, coach, cram, fill, fill in, gen up, groom, inform, notify, post up, prepare, train.

**primer** *n* Donat, introduction, manual, prodrome, prodromus, text-book.

**primeval** *adj* ancient, earliest, early, first, Ogygian, old, original, prehistoric, primal, primitial, primitive, primordial, pristine.

*antonyms* developed, later, modern.

**primitive** *adj* aboriginal, barbarian, barbaric, childlike, crude, earliest, early, elementary, first, naïve, neanderthal, original, primal, primary, primeval, primordial, pristine, rough, rude, rudimentary, savage, simple, uncivilised, uncultivated, undeveloped, unrefined, unsophisticated, untrained, untutored.

*antonyms* advanced, civilised, developed.

**primordial** *adj* basic, earliest, elemental, first, first-formed, first-made, fundamental, original, prehistoric, primal, primeval, primigenial, primitial, primitive, pristine, radical.

*antonyms* developed, later, modern.

**prince** *n* lord, mogul, monarch, nabob, nawab, potentate, ruler, sovereign.

**princely** *adj* august, bounteous, bountiful, dignified, generous, gracious, grand, imperial, imposing, lavish, liberal, lofty, magnanimous, magnificent, majestic, munificent, noble, open-handed, regal, rich, royal, sovereign, stately, sumptuous.

*antonyms* humble, mean.

**principal¹** *adj* capital, cardinal, chief, controlling, decuman, dominant, essential, first, foremost, highest, key, leading, main, paramount, pre-eminent, primary, prime, strongest, truncal.

*antonyms* least, lesser, minor.

*n* boss, chief, dean, director, first violin, head, head teacher, headmaster, headmistress, lead, leader, master, prima ballerina, prima donna, rector, star, superintendent.

**principal²** *n* assets, capital, capital funds, money.

**principality** *n* princedom, principate.

**principally** *adv* above all, chiefly, especially, mainly, mostly, particularly, predominantly, primarily.

**principle** *n* assumption, attitude, axiom, belief, canon, code, conscience, credo, criterion, dictum, doctrine, dogma, duty, element, ethic, formula, fundamental, golden rule, honour, institute, integrity, law, maxim, moral, morality, morals, opinion, precept, principium, probity, proposition, rectitude, rule, scruples, standard, tenet, truth, uprightness, verity.

*antonyms* corruption, wickedness.

**principled** adj clear, clear-cut, conscientious, correct, decent, ethical, high-minded, honourable, just, logical, moral, rational, reasoned, righteous, right-minded, scrupulous, sensible, thought-out, upright, virtuous.

antonym unprincipled.

**print** v engrave, impress, imprint, issue, mark, produce, publish, put to bed, reproduce, run off, stamp, write.

n book, characters, copy, dab, engraving, face, fingerprint, font, fount, impression, lettering, letters, magazine, mould, newspaper, newsprint, periodical, photo, photograph, picture, publication, reproduction, stamp, type, typeface, typescript.

**prior** adj aforementioned, antecedent, anterior, earlier, foregoing, former, preceding, pre-existent, previous.

antonym later.

**prior to** before, earlier than, preceding, preparatory to, previous to.

antonym after.

**priority** n precedence, pre-eminence, preference, prerogative, privilege, rank, right of way, seniority, superiority, supremacy, the lead.

antonyms inferiority, subordinateness.

**priory** n abbey, béguinage, cloister, convent, monastery, nunnery, religious house.

**prise** see **prize**.

**prison** n bagnio, bastille, borstal(l), bridewell, brig, cage, calaboose, can, cell, chok(e)y, clink, confinement, cooler, coop, dungeon, gaol, glasshouse, gulag, hoos(e)gow, house of correction, imprisonment, jail, jug, lock-up, panopticon, penal institution, penitentiary, pokey, porridge, prison-house, prison-ship, quod, slammer, slink, stalag, stir, tank, tol(l)booth.

**prisoner** n canary-bird, captive, collegian, con, convict, detainee, détenu(e), forçat, hostage, inmate, internee, jail-bird, lag.

**prissy** adj effeminate, fastidious, finicky, fussy, old-maidish, overnice, po-faced, precious, prim, prim and proper, prudish, pudibund, school-marmish, squeamish, starchy, strait-laced.

antonyms broad-minded, informal.

**pristine** adj earliest, first, former, initial, original, primal, primary, primeval, primigenial, primitial, primitive, primordial, uncorrupted, undefiled, unspoiled, unsullied, untouched, virgin.

antonyms developed, later, spoiled.

**privacy** n clandestineness, concealment, confidentiality, isolation, privateness, quietness, quietude, retirement, retreat, seclusion, secrecy, separateness, sequestration, solitude.

antonym publicness.

**private** adj clandestine, closet, concealed, confidential, exclusive, home-felt, hush-hush, in camera, independent, individual, inside, intimate, intraparietal, inward, isolated, off the record, own, particular, personal, privy, reserved, retired, secluded, secret, separate, sequestrated, solitary, special, unofficial, withdrawn.

antonyms open, public.

n enlisted man, private soldier, squaddy, swad, swaddy, tommy, Tommy Atkins.

**private detective** pinkerton, private eye, private investigator, shamus.

**private parts** fanny, genitalia, genitals, privates, pudenda, pussy, quim.

**privateer** n buccaneer, corsair, freebooter, marque, pirate, sea-robber, sea-wolf.

**privation** n affliction, austerity, destitution, distress, hardship, indigence, lack, loss, misery, necessary, need, neediness, penury, poverty, suffering, want.

antonyms affluence, wealth.

**privatise** v denationalise.

antonym nationalise.

**privilege** n advantage, benefit, birthright, claim, concession, droit, due, entitlement, franchise, freedom, immunity, liberty, licence, prerogative, right, sanction, title.

antonym disadvantage.

**privileged** adj advantaged, allowed, authorised, élite, empowered, entitled, exempt(ed), favoured, free, granted, honoured, indulged, licensed, permitted, powerful, ruling, sanctioned, special, vested.

antonyms disadvantaged, under-privileged.

**privy** n bog, cloaca, closet, cludge, earth-closet, head, John, latrine, lavatory, loo, reredorter, toilet, water-closet.

adj confidential, hidden, hush-hush, intimate, off the record, personal, private, secret, top secret.

antonym public.

**privy to** apprised of, aware of, cognisant of, in on, in the know, informed about, wise to.

antonym unaware.

**prize**[1] n accolade, aim, ambition, award, conquest, desire, gain, goal, haul, honour, hope, jackpot, premium, purse, reward, stake(s), trophy, windfall, winnings.

adj award-winning, best, champion, excellent, first-rate, outstanding, top, top-notch, winning.

antonym second-rate.

v appreciate, cherish, esteem, hold dear, revere, reverence, set store by, treasure, value.

antonyms despise, undervalue.

**prize**[2] n booty, capture, loot, pickings, pillage, plunder, spoils, trophy.

**prize**[3], prise¢prize, prise" v force, jemmy, lever, pry, winkle.

**prize-winner** n champ, champion, cup-winner, dux, medallist, prize-man, winner.

**probability** n assumption, chance, chances, expectation, liability, likelihood, likeliness, odds, presumption, prospect.

antonym improbability.

**probable** adj apparent, credible, feasible, likely, odds-on, on the cards, plausible, possible, presumed, reasonable, seeming, verisimilar.

antonym improbable.

**probably** *adv* as likely as not, doubtless, happen, in all likelihood, in all probability, likely, maybe, most likely, perhaps, possibly, presumably.

*antonym* improbably.

**probation** *n* apprenticeship, examination, initiation, noviciate, proof, test, testing, trial, trial period.

**probe** *v* examine, explore, go into, investigate, look into, pierce, poke, prod, query, scrutinise, search, sift, sound, test, verify.

*n* bore, detection, drill, examination, exploration, inquest, inquiry, investigation, research, scrutiny, study, test.

**probity** *n* equity, fairness, fidelity, goodness, honesty, honour, honourableness, integrity, justice, morality, rectitude, righteousness, sincerity, trustworthiness, truthfulness, uprightness, virtue, worth.

*antonym* improbity.

**problem** *n* boyg, brain-teaser, complication, conundrum, difficulty, dilemma, disagreement, dispute, doubt, enigma, no laughing matter, poser, predicament, puzzle, quandary, question, riddle, trouble, vexata quaestio, vexed question.

*adj* delinquent, difficult, intractable, perverse, refractory, uncontrollable, unmanageable, unruly.

*antonyms* manageable, well-behaved.

**problematic** *adj* chancy, debatable, doubtful, dubious, enigmatic, moot, problematical, puzzling, questionable, tricky, uncertain, unestablished, unsettled, unsure.

*antonym* certain.

**procedure** *n* action, conduct, course, custom, form, formula, method, modus operandi, move, operation, performance, plan of action, policy, practice, process, routine, scheme, step, strategy, system, transaction.

**proceed** *v* advance, arise, carry on, come, continue, derive, emanate, ensue, flow, follow, go ahead, issue, move on, originate, press on, progress, result, set in motion, spring, start, stem.

*antonyms* retreat, stop.

**proceedings** *n* account, action, affair, affairs, annals, archives, business, course of action, dealings, deeds, doings, event(s), matters, measures, minutes, moves, procedure, process, records, report, steps, transactions, undertaking.

**proceeds** *n* earnings, emoluments, gain, income, motser, motza, produce, products, profit, receipts, returns, revenue, takings, yield.

*antonyms* losses, outlay.

**process**[1] *n* action, advance, case, course, course of action, development, evolution, formation, growth, manner, means, measure, method, mode, movement, operation, performance, practice, procedure, proceeding, progress, progression, stage, step, suit, system, transaction, trial, unfolding.

*v* alter, convert, deal with, digitise, dispose of, fulfil, handle, prepare, refine, transform, treat.

**process**[2] *n* node, nodosity, nodule, projection, prominence, protuberance, protusion.

**processing** *n* conversion, datamation, handling, preparation, refinement.

**procession** *n* cavalcade, column, concatenation, cortege, course, cycle, file, march, motorcade, parade, run, sequence, series, skimmington, string, succession, train.

**proclaim** *v* advertise, affirm, announce, annunciate, blaze, blazon, circulate, declare, enounce, enunciate, give out, herald, indicate, make known, preconise, profess, promulgate, publish, show, testify, trumpet.

**proclamation** *n* announcement, annunciation, ban, declaration, decree, edict, firman, hatti-sherif, indiction, interlocution, irade, manifesto, notice, notification, proclaim, promulgation, pronouncement, pronunciamento, publication, ukase.

**proclivity** *n* bent, bias, disposition, facility, inclination, leaning, liability, liableness, penchant, predilection, predisposition, proneness, propensity, tendency, weakness.

*antonym* disinclination.

**procrastinate** *v* adjourn, dally, defer, delay, dilly-dally, drag one's feet, gain time, penelopise, play for time, postpone, prolong, protract, put off, retard, stall, temporise.

*antonyms* advance, proceed.

**procrastination** *n* dallying, deferral, delaying, dilly-dallying, foot-dragging, stalling, temporising.

**procreate** *v* beget, breed, conceive, engender, father, generate, mother, produce, propagate, reproduce, sire, spawn.

**procure** *v* acquire, appropriate, bag, buy, come by, earn, effect, find, gain, get, induce, lay hands on, obtain, pander, pick up, pimp, purchase, secure, win.

*antonym* lose.

**procurer** *n* bawd, madam, pander, panderer, pimp, procuress, white-slaver, whoremonger.

**prod** *v* dig, drive, egg on, elbow, goad, impel, incite, jab, motivate, move, nudge, poke, prick, prog, prompt, propel, push, rouse, shove, spur, stimulate, urge.

*n* boost, cue, dig, elbow, jab, nudge, poke, prog, prompt, push, reminder, shove, signal, stimulus.

**prodigal** *adj* bounteous, bountiful, copious, excessive, extravagant, exuberant, immoderate, improvident, intemperate, lavish, luxuriant, profligate, profuse, reckless, spendthrift, squandering, sumptuous, superabundant, teeming, unsparing, unthrift, unthrifty, wanton, wasteful.

*antonyms* modest, parsimonious, thrifty.

*n* big spender, profligate, spendall, spendthrift, squanderer, waster, wastrel.

**prodigality** *n* abandon, abundance, amplitude, bounteousness, bounty, copiousness, dissipation, excess, extravagance, exuberance, immoderation, intemperance, lavishness, luxuriance, plenteousness, plenty, profligacy, profusion, recklessness, richness, squandering, sumptuousness, unthrift, unthriftiness, wantonness, waste, wastefulness.

*antonyms* modesty, parsimony, thrift.

**prodigious** *adj* abnormal, amazing, astounding, colossal, enormous, exceptional, extraordinary, fabulous, fantastic, flabbergasting, giant, gigantic, huge, immeasurable, immense, impressive, inordinate, mammoth, marvellous, massive, miraculous, monstrous, monumental, phenomenal, remarkable, spectacular, staggering, startling, striking, stupendous, tremendous, unusual, vast, wonderful.

*antonyms* commonplace, small, unremarkable.

**prodigy** *n* abnormality, child genius, curiosity, freak, genius, grotesque, marvel, matermind, miracle, monster, monstrosity, mutation, phenomenon, rara avis, rarity, sensation, spectacle, talent, whiz, whiz kid, wizard, wonder, wonder child, wonder-work, wunderkind.

**produce**[1] *v* advance, afford, bear, beget, breed, bring forth, cause, compose, construct, create, deliver, demonstrate, develop, direct, effect, engender, exhibit, fabricate, factify, factuate, furnish, generate, give, give rise to, invent, make, manufacture, mount, occasion, offer, originate, present, provoke, put forward, put on, render, result in, show, stage, supply, throw, yield.

*antonyms* consume, result from.

*n* crop, harvest, product, yield.

**produce**[2] *v* continue, elongate, extend, lengthen, prolong, protract.

**producer** *n* director, farmer, grower, impresario, maker, manager, manufacturer, presenter, régisseur.

**product** *n* artefact, commodity, concoction, consequence, creation, effect, facture, fruit, goods, invention, issue, legacy, merchandise, offshoot, offspring, outcome, output, produce, production, result, returns, spin-off, upshot, work, yield.

*antonym* cause.

**production** *n* assembly, construction, creation, direction, fabrication, facture, formation, fructification, making, management, manufacture, manufacturing, origination, preparation, presentation, producing, staging.

*antonym* consumption.

**productive** *adj* advantageous, beneficial, constructive, creative, dynamic, effective, energetic, fecund, fertile, fructiferous, fructuous, fruitful, gainful, generative, gratifying, inventive, plentiful, producing, profitable, prolific, rewarding, rich, teeming, uberous, useful, valuable, vigorous, voluminous, worthwhile.

*antonyms* fruitless, unproductive.

**productivity** *n* abundance, output, production, productiveness, uberty, work-rate, yield.

*antonym* unproductiveness.

**profane** *adj* abusive, blasphemous, coarse, crude, disrespectful, filthy, forbidden, foul, godless, heathen, idolatrous, impious, impure, irreligious, irreverent, lay, obscene, pagan, sacrilegious, secular, sinful, temporal, terefa(h), unclean, unconsecrated, ungodly, unhallowed, unholy, uninitiated, unsanctified, vulgar, wicked, worldly.

*antonyms* initiated, permitted, religious, sacred.

*v* abuse, contaminate, debase, defile, degrade, desecrate, misemploy, misuse, pervert, pollute, prostitute, violate, vitiate.

*antonym* revere.

**profanity** *n* abuse, blasphemy, curse, cursing, execration, expletive, four-letter word, impiety, imprecation, inquination, irreverence, malediction, obscenity, profaneness, sacrilege, swearing, swear-word.

*antonyms* politeness, reverence.

**profess** *v* acknowledge, admit, affirm, allege, announce, assert, asseverate, aver, avow, certify, claim, confess, confirm, declare, enunciate, fake, feign, maintain, make out, own, pretend, proclaim, propose, propound, purport, sham, state, vouch.

**professed** *adj* acknowledged, avowed, certified, confirmed, declared, ostensible, pretended, proclaimed, purported, self-acknowledged, self-confessed, self-styled, so-called, soi-disant, supposed, would-be.

**profession** *n* acknowledgement, affirmation, assertion, attestation, avowal, business, calling, career, claim, confession, declaration, employment, job, line (of work), manifesto, métier, occupation, office, position, sphere, statement, testimony, vocation, vow, walk of life.

**professional** *adj* adept, competent, crack, efficient, experienced, expert, finished, masterly, polished, practised, proficient, qualified, skilled, slick, trained, virtuose, virtuosic, well-skilled.

*antonyms* amateur, unprofessional.

*n* adept, authority, dab hand, expert, maestro, master, pastmaster, pro, proficient, specialist, virtuoso, wizard.

**proffer** *v* advance, extend, hand, hold out, offer, present, propose, propound, submit, suggest, tender, volunteer.

**proficiency** *n* ability, accomplishment, aptitude, competence, conversancy, dexterity, expertise, expertness, facility, finesse, knack, know-how, mastery, skilfulness, skill, talent, virtuosity.

*antonyms* clumsiness, incompetence.

**proficient** *adj* able, accomplished, adept, apt, capable, clever, competent, conversant, efficient, experienced, expert, gifted, masterly, qualified, skilful, skilled, talented, trained, versed, virtuose, virtuosic.

*antonyms* clumsy, incompetent.

**profile** *n* analysis, biography, biopic, characterisation, chart, contour, diagram, drawing, examination, figure, form, graph, outline, portrait, review, shape, side view, silhouette, sketch, study, survey, table, thumbnail sketch, vignette.

**profit** *n* a fast buck, advancement, advantage, avail, benefit, boot, bottom line, bunce, earnings, emoluments, fruit, gain, gelt, good, graft, gravy, grist, interest, melon, percentage, proceeds, receipts, return, revenue, surplus, takings, use, value, velvet, winnings, yield.

*antonym* loss.

*v* advance, advantage, aid, avail, benefit, better, boot, contribute, gain, help, improve, line one's pockets, promote, serve, stand in good stead.

*antonyms* harm, hinder.

**profit by/from** capitalise on, cash in on, exploit, learn from, put to good use, reap the benefit of, take advantage of, turn to account, turn to advantage, use, utilise.

*antonym* lose by.

**profitable** *adj* advantageable, advantageous, beneficial, commercial, cost-effective, emolumental, emolumentary, fruitful, gainful, lucrative, money-making, paying, plummy, productive, remunerative, rewarding, serviceable, useful, utile, valuable, worthwhile.

*antonym* unprofitable.

**profiteer** *n* exploiter, extortioner, extortionist, racketeer.

*v* exploit, extort, fleece, make a fast buck, make a quick killing, overcharge, racketeer.

**profiteering** *n* exploitation, extortion, Rachmanism, racketeering.

**profitless** *adj* bootless, fruitless, futile, gainless, idle, ineffective, ineffectual, pointless, thankless, unavailing, unproductive, unprofitable, unremunerative, useless, vain, worthless.

*antonym* profitable.

**profligacy** *n* abandon, corruption, debauchery, degeneracy, depravity, dissipation, dissoluteness, excess, extravagance, immorality, improvidence, lavishness, laxity, libertinism, licentiousness, prodigality, promiscuity, recklessness, squandering, unrestraint, unthrift, unthriftiness, wantonness, waste, wastefulness.

*antonyms* morality, parsimony, thrift, uprightness.

**profligate** *adj* abandoned, corrupt, Cyprian, debauched, degenerate, depraved, dissipated, dissolute, extravagant, immoderate, immoral, improvident, iniquitous, libertine, licentious, loose, prodigal, promiscuous, reckless, shameless, spendthrift, squandering, unprincipled, vicious, vitiated, wanton, wasteful, whorish, wicked, wild.

*antonyms* moral, parsimonious, thrifty, upright.

*n* debauchee, degenerate, libertine, prodigal, racketeer, rake, reprobate, roué, spendthrift, squanderer, waster, wastrel.

**profound** *adj* abject, absolute, abstruse, abysmal, acute, awful, bottomless, cavernous, complete, consummate, deep, deep-seated, discerning, erudite, exhaustive, extensive, extreme, far-reaching, fathomless, great, heartfelt, heart-rending, hearty, intense, keen, learned, penetrating, philosophical, pronounced, recondite, sagacious, sage, serious, sincere, skilled, subtle, thoroughgoing, thoughtful, total, utter, weighty, wise, yawning.

*antonyms* mild, shallow, slight.

**profoundly** *adv* abjectly, acutely, awfully, deeply, dreadfully, extremely, greatly, heartily, intensely, keenly, seriously, sincerely, thoroughly.

*antonym* slightly.

**profundity** *n* abstruseness, acuity, acumen, depth, erudition, extremity, insight, intelligence, intensity, learning, penetration, perceptiveness, perspecuity, perspicacity, profoundness, sagacity, seriousness, severity, strength, wisdom.

*antonym* shallowness.

**profuse** *adj* abundant, ample, bountiful, copious, excessive, extravagant, exuberant, fulsome, generous, immoderate, large-handed, lavish, liberal, luxuriant, open-handed, over the top, overflowing, plentiful, prodigal, prolific, teeming, unstinting.

*antonyms* sparing, sparse.

**profusion** *n* abundance, bounty, copiousness, cornucopia, excess, extravagance, exuberance, glut, lavishness, luxuriance, multitude, plenitude, pleroma, plethora, prodigality, quantity, riot, superabundance, superfluity, surplus, wealth.

*antonyms* sparingness, sparsity.

**progenitor** *n* ancestor, antecedent, begetter, father, forebear, forefather, forerunner, founder, instigator, mother, originator, parent, precursor, predecessor, primogenitor, procreator, source.

**progeny** *n* breed, children, descendants, family, issue, lineage, offspring, posterity, quiverful, race, scions, seed, stock, young.

**prognosis** *n* diagnosis, expectation, forecast, outlook, prediction, prognostication, projection, prospect, speculation, surmise.

**prognosticate** *v* augur, betoken, divine, forebore, forecast, foreshadow, foretell, harbinger, herald, indicate, portend, predict, presage, prophesy, soothsay.

**prognostication** *n* expectation, forecast, horoscope, prediction, prognosis, projection, prophecy, speculation, surmise.

**programme** *n* agenda, broadcast, curriculum, design, line-up, list, listing, order of events, order of the day, performance, plan, plan of action, presentation, procedure, production, project, schedule, scheme, show, syllabus, transmission.

*v* arrange, bill, book, brainwash, design, engage, formulate, itemise, lay on, line up, list, map out, plan, prearrange, schedule, work out.

**progress** *n* advance, advancement, amelioration, betterment, breakthrough, circuit, continuation, course, development, gain, growth, headway, improvement, increase, journey, movement, passage, procession, progression, promotion, step forward, way.

*antonyms* decline, deterioration.

*v* advance, ameliorate, better, blossom, come on, continue, develop, forge ahead, gain, gather momentum, grow, improve, increase, make headway, make strides, mature, proceed, prosper, travel.

*antonyms* decline, deteriorate.

**progression** *n* advance, advancement, chain, concatenation, course, cycle, furtherance, gain, headway, order, progress, sequence, series, string, succession.

*antonyms* decline, deterioration.

**progressive** *adj* accelerating, advanced, advancing, avant-garde, continuing, continuous, developing, dynamic, enlightened, enterprising, escalating, forward-looking, go-ahead, growing, increasing, intensifying, liberal, modern, ongoing, radical, reactionary, reformist, regressive, revolutionary, up-and-coming.

**prohibit** v ban, bar, constrain, debar, disallow, forbid, hamper, hinder, impede, interdict, obstruct, outlaw, preclude, prevent, proscribe, restrict, rule out, stop, veto.

*antonym* permit.

**prohibited** *adj* banned, barred, disallowed, embargoed, forbidden, interdicted, off-limits, proscribed, taboo, verboten, vetoed.

*antonym* permitted.

**prohibition** *n* ban, bar, constraint, disallowance, embargo, exclusion, forbiddal, forbiddance, injunction, interdict, interdiction, negation, obstruction, prevention, proscription, restruction, veto.

*antonym* permission.

**prohibitionist** *n* abolitionist, dry, pussyfoot, teetotaller.

**prohibitive** *adj* excessive, exorbitant, extortionate, forbidding, impossible, preposterous, prohibiting, prohibitory, proscriptive, repressive, restraining, restrictive, sky-high, steep, suppressive.

*antonyms* encouraging, reasonable.

**project** *n* activity, assignment, conception, design, enterprise, idea, job, occupation, plan, programme, proposal, purpose, scheme, task, undertaking, venture, work.

v beetle, bulge, calculate, cast, contemplate, contrive, design, devise, discharge, draft, estimate, exsert, extend, extrapolate, extrude, fling, forecast, frame, gauge, hurl, jut, launch, map out, outline, overhang, plan, predetermine, predict, propel, prophesy, propose, protrude, purpose, reckon, scheme, shoot, stand out, stick out, throw, transmit.

**projectile** *n* ball, bullet, grenade, missile, mortar-bomb, rocket, shell, shot.

**projecting** *adj* beetling, exsertile, extrusive, extrusory, overhanging, protrudent, protruding, protrusive.

**projection** *n* blueprint, bulge, calculation, computation, diagram, eaves, estimate, estimation, extrapolation, forecast, jut, jutty, ledge, map, nab, outjet, outjut, outline, overhang, plan, prediction, process, prominence, protrusion, protuberance, reckoning, representation, ridge, shelf, sill.

**proletariat** *n* canaille, common people, commonalty, commoners, great unwashed, herd, hoi polloi, lower classes, masses, mob, plebs, proles, rabble, working class.

**proliferate** *v* breed, burgeon, escalate, expand, exuberate, increase, multiply, mushroom, run riot, snowball.

*antonym* dwindle.

**proliferation** *n* build-up, concentration, duplication, escalation, expansion, extension, increase, intensification, multiplication, mushrooming, snowballing, spread.

*antonym* decrease.

**prolific** *adj* abounding, abundant, bountiful, copious, fecund, fertile, fertilising, fruitful, generative, luxuriant, productive, profuse, rank, reproductive, rich, teeming, voluminous.

*antonyms* infertile, scarce.

**prolix** *adj* diffuse, digressive, discursive, lengthy, long, long-winded, prolonged, prosy, protracted, rambling, tedious, tiresome, verbose, windy, wordy.

*antonym* succinct.

**prolixity** *n* boringness, circuity, diffuseness, discursiveness, long-windedness, macrology, maundering, pleonasm, prosiness, rambling, tediousness, verbiage, verboseness, verbosity, wandering, windiness, wordiness.

*antonym* succinctness.

**prologue** *n* exordium, foreword, introduction, preamble, preface, preliminary, prelude, proem, prolegomena, prooemion, prooemium.

**prolong** *v* continue, delay, drag out, draw out, extend, lengthen, lengthen out, perpetuate, produce, protract, spin out, stretch.

*antonym* shorten.

**promenade**[1] *n* boulevard, esplanade, front, parade, prom, sea-front, terrace, walkway.

**promenade**[2] *n* airing, breather, constitutional, saunter, stroll, turn, walk, walkabout.

v flaunt, mosey, parade, perambulate, sally forth, saunter, stroll, strut, swagger, walk.

**prominence**[1] *n* bulge, bump, cliff, crag, crest, elevation, headland, height, hummock, hump, jutting, lump, mound, pinnacle, process, projection, prominency, promontory, protrusion, protuberance, rise, spur, swelling.

**prominence**[2] *n* celebrity, conspicuousness, distinction, eminence, fame, greatness, importance, markedness, name, notability, outstandingness, precedence, pre-eminence, prestige, rank, reputation, salience, specialness, standing, top billing, visibility, weight.

*antonyms* inconspicuousness, unimportance.

**prominent** *adj* beetling, bulging, celebrated, chief, conspicuous, distinguished, eminent, eye-catching, famous, foremost, high-profile, important, jutting, leading, main, noted, noticeable, obtrusive, obvious, outstanding, popular, pre-eminent, projecting, pronounced, protruding, protrusive, protuberant, remarkale, renowned, respected, salient, standing out, striking, top, unmistakable, weighty, well-known.

*antonyms* inconspicuous, unimportant.

**promiscuity** *n* abandon, amorality, debauchery, depravity, dissipation, immorality, laxity, laxness, lechery, libertinism, licentiousness, looseness, permissiveness, profligacy, promiscuousness, protervity, wantonness, whoredom, whoring, whorishness.

*antonym* chastity.

**promiscuous** *adj* abandoned, accidental, careless, casual, chaotic, confused, debauched, disordered, dissipated, dissolute, diverse, fast, haphazard, heterogeneous, ill-assorted, immoral, indiscriminate, intermingled, intermixed, jumbled, libertine, licentious, loose, mingled, miscellaneous, mixed, motley, of easy virtue, profligate, random, unbridled, unchaste, uncontrolled, undiscriminating, unselective, wanton, whoremasterly, whorish, wild.

*antonyms* chaste, controlled, selective.

**promise** *v* assure, augur, bespeak, betoken, bid fair, contract, denote, engage, guarantee, hint at, indicate, look like, pledge, plight, predict, presage, prophesy, stipulate, suggest, swear, take an oath, undertake, vouch, vow, warrant.

*n* ability, aptitude, assurance, bond, capability, capacity, commitment, compact, covenant, engagement, flair, guarantee, oath, pledge, pollicitation, potential, talent, undertaking, vow, word, word of honour.

**promised land** land of milk and honey, paradise, Shangri-la, Zion.

**promising** *adj* able, auspicious, bright, encouraging, favourable, gifted, good, hopeful, likely, propitious, reassuring, rising, rosy, talented, up-and-coming.

*antonym* unpromising.

**promontory** *n* cape, foreland, head, headland, hoe, mull, nab, naze, ness, peninsula, point, projection, ridge, spur.

**promote** *v* advance, advertise, advocate, aggrandise, aid, assist, back, blazon, boost, champion, contribute to, develop, dignify, elevate, encourage, endorse, espouse, exalt, forward, foster, further, help, honour, hype, kick upstairs, nurture, plug, popularise, prefer, publicise, puff, push, raise, recommend, sell, sponsor, stimulate, support, trumpet, upgrade, urge.

*antonyms* demote, disparage, obstruct.

**promotion** *n* advancement, advertising, advocacy, aggrandisement, backing, ballyhoo, boosting, campaign, cultivation, development, elevation, encouragement, ennoblement, espousal, exaltation, fanfare, furtherance, honour, hype, plugging, preferment, promo, propaganda, publicity, puffery, pushing, rise, support, trumpeting, upgrading.

*antonyms* demotion, disparagement, obstruction.

**prompt**[1] *adj* alert, brisk, eager, early, efficient, expeditious, immediate, instant, instantaneous, on time, punctual, quick, rapid, ready, responsive, smart, speedy, swift, timely, timeous, unhesitating, willing.

*antonym* slow.

*adv* exactly, on the dot, promptly, punctually, sharp, to the minute.

**prompt**[2] *v* advise, assist, call forth, cause, cue, elicit, evoke, give rise to, impel, incite, induce, inspire, instigate, motivate, move, occasion, prod, produce, provoke, remind, result in, spur, stimulate, urge.

*antonym* dissuade.

*n* cue, help, hint, instigation, jog, jolt, prod, reminder, spur, stimulus.

**prompting** *n* admonition, advice, assistance, encouragement, hint, incitement, influence, jogging, persuasion, pressing, pressure, prodding, protreptic, pushing, reminder, reminding, suggestion, urging.

*antonym* dissuasion.

**promptly** *adv* directly, ek dum, forthwith, immediately, instantly, on time, posthaste, pronto, punctually, quickly, speedily, swiftly, unhesitatingly.

**promptness** *n* alacrity, alertness, briskness, dispatch, eagerness, expedition, haste, promptitude, punctuality, quickness, readiness, speed, swiftness, willingness.

*antonym* tardiness.

**promulgate** *v* advertise, announce, broadcast, circulate, communicate, declare, decree, disseminate, issue, notify, preconise, proclaim, promote, publicise, publish, spread.

**promulgation** *n* announcement, communication, declaration, dissemination, issuance, proclamation, promulgating, publication, publicising.

**prone**[1] *adj* apt, bent, disposed, given, inclined, liable, likely, predisposed, propense, subject, susceptible, tending, vulnerable.

*antonym* unlikely.

**prone**[2] *adj* face down, flat, full-length, horizontal, procumbent, prostrate, recumbent, stretched.

*antonym* upright.

**proneness** *n* aptness, bent, bias, disposition, inclination, leaning, liability, penchant, proclivity, propensity, susceptibility, tendency, weakness.

*antonym* dislike.

**prong** *n* fork, grain, point, projection, spike, spur, tine, tip.

**pronounce** *v* accent, affirm, announce, articulate, assert, breathe, declaim, declare, decree, deliver, enunciate, judge, proclaim, say, sound, speak, stress, utter, vocalise, voice.

**pronounceable** *adj* articulable, enunciable, expressible, sayable, speakable, utterable, vocable.

*antonym* unpronounceable.

**pronounced** *adj* broad, clear, conspicuous, decided, definite, distinct, evident, marked, noticeable, obvious, positive, striking, strong, unmistakable.

*antonyms* unnoticeable, vague.

**pronouncement** *n* announcement, assertion, declaration, decree, dictum, edict, ipse dixit, ipsissima verba, judgement, manifesto, notification, proclamation, promulgation, pronunciamento, statement.

**pronunciation** *n* accent, accentuation, articulation, diction, elocution, enunciation, inflection, intonation, modulation, speech, stress.

**proof** *n* assay, attestation, authentication, certification, confirmation, corroboration, demonstration, documentation, evidence, examination, experiment, ordeal, scrutiny, substantiation, test, testimony, trial, verification, voucher.

*adj* impenetrable, impervious, proofed, rainproof, repellent, resistant, strong, tight, treated, waterproof, weatherproof, windproof.

*antonyms* permeable, untreated.

**prop** *v* bolster, buttress, lean, maintain, rest, set, shore, stand, stay, strut, support, sustain, truss, underpin, uphold.

*n* brace, buttress, mainstay, stanchion, stay, strut, studdle, support, truss.

**propaganda** *n* advertising, agitprop, ballyhoo, brainwashing, hype, promotion, publicity, puffery, puffs.

**propagandist** *n* advocate, canvasser, evangelist, indoctrinator, pamphleteer, plugger, promoter, proponent, proselytiser, publicist.

**propagate** *v* beget, breed, broadcast, circulate, diffuse, disseminate, engender, generate, increase, multiply, proclaim, procreate, produce, proliferate, promote, promulgate, provine, publicise, publish, reproduce, spawn, spread, transmit.

**propagation** *n* breeding, circulation, communication, diffusion, dissemination, distribution, generation, increase, issuance, multiplication, procreation, proliferation, promotion, promulgation, reproduction, spawning, spread, spreading, transmission.

**propel** *v* drive, force, impel, launch, push, send, shoot, shove, start, thrust, waft.

*antonyms* slow, stop.

**propensity** *n* aptness, bent, bias, disposition, foible, inclination, leaning, liability, penchant, predisposition, proclivity, proneness, readiness, susceptibility, tendency, weakness.

*antonym* disinclination.

**proper** *adj* accepted, accurate, appropriate, apt, becoming, befitting, characteristic, conventional, correct, decent, decorous, established, exact, fit, fitting, formal, genteel, gentlemanly, gradely, graithly, individual, kosher, ladylike, legitimate, mannerly, meet, orthodox, own, particular, peculiar, perjink, personal, polite, precise, prim, prissy, punctilious, refined, respectable, respective, right, sedate, seemly, special, specific, suitable, suited, well-becoming, well-beseeming.

*antonyms* common, general, improper.

**property**[1] *n* acres, assets, belongings, building(s), capital, chattels, effects, estate, freehold, goods, holding, holdings, house(s), land, means, meum et tuum, possessions, real estate, realty, resources, riches, title, wealth.

**property**[2] *n* ability, affection, attribute, characteristic, feature, hallmark, idiosyncrasy, mark, peculiarity, quality, trait, virtue.

**prophecy** *n* augury, divination, forecast, foretelling, hariolation, prediction, prognosis, prognostication, revelation, second-sight, soothsaying, taghairm, vaticination.

**prophesy** *v* augur, divine, forecast, foresee, foretell, forewarn, hariolate, predict, presage, prognosticate, soothsay, vaticinate.

**prophet** *n* augur, Cassandra, clairvoyant, divinator, diviner, forecaster, foreteller, Nostradamus, oracle, prognosticator, prophesier, seer, sibyl, soothsayer, tipster, vaticinator.

**prophet of doom** Cassandra, doomwatcher, Jeremiah, pessimist.

**prophetic** *adj* augural, divinatory, fatidical, fey, foreshadowing, mantic, oracular, predictive, presaging, prescient, prognostic, sibylline, vatic, vaticidal.

*antonym* unprophetic.

**propinquity** *n* adjacency, affiliation, affinity, blood, closeness, connection, consanguinity, contiguity, kindredness, kindredship, kinship, nearness, neighbourhood, proximity, relation, relationship, tie, vicinity.

*antonym* remoteness.

**propitiate** *v* appease, conciliate, mollify, pacify, placate, reconcile, satisfy, soothe.

*antonyms* anger, provoke.

**propitiation** *n* appeasement, conciliation, mollification, pacification, pacifying, peacemaking, placation, reconciliation.

*antonyms* angering, provocation.

**propitiatory** *adj* appeasing, assuaging, conciliatory, mollifying, pacificatory, pacifying, peacemaking, placative, placatory, propitiative, reconciliatory, soothing.

*antonym* provocative.

**propitious** *adj* advantageous, auspicious, beneficial, benevolent, benign, bright, encouraging, favourable, fortunate, friendly, gracious, happy, kindly, lucky, opportune, promising, prosperous, reassuring, rosy, timely, well-disposed.

*antonym* inauspicious.

**proponent** *n* advocate, apologist, backer, champion, defender, enthusiast, exponent, friend, partisan, patron, proposer, propounder, subscriber, supporter, upholder, vindicator.

*antonym* opponent.

**proportion** *n* agreement, amount, balance, congruity, correspondence, cut, distribution, division, eurhythmy, fraction, harmony, measure, part, percentage, quota, ratio, relationship, segment, share, symmetry.

*antonyms* disproportion, imbalance.

**proportional** *adj* balanced, commensurate, comparable, compatible, consistent, correspondent, corresponding, equitable, even, fair, just, logistical, proportionate.

*antonyms* disproportionate, unjust.

**proportionally** *adv* commensurately, comparably, correspondingly, evenly, pro rata, proportionately.

*antonym* disproportionately.

**proportions** *n* amplitude, breadth, bulk, capacity, dimensions, expanse, extent, magnitude, measurements, range, scope, size, volume.

**proposal** *n* bid, design, draft, manifesto, motion, offer, outline, overture, plan, platform, presentation, proffer, programme, project, proposition, recommendation, scheme, sketch, suggestion, suit, tender, terms.

**propose** *v* advance, aim, bring up, design, enunciate, have in mind, intend, introduce,

**prostrate**

invite, lay before, mean, move, name, nominate, pay suit, plan, pop the question, present, proffer, propound, purpose, put forward, put up, recommend, scheme, submit, suggest, table, tender.

*antonyms* oppose, withdraw.

**proposition** *n* manifesto, motion, plan, programme, project, proposal, recommendation, scheme, suggestion, tender.

*v* accost, solicit.

**propound** *v* advance, advocate, contend, enunciate, lay down, move, postulate, present, propose, put forward, set forth, submit, suggest.

*antonym* oppose.

**proprietor** *n* châtelaine, deed holder, freeholder, landlady, landlord, landowner, owner, patron, patronne, possessor, proprietary, proprietress, proprietrix, title-holder.

**propriety** *n* appropriateness, aptness, becomingness, breeding, correctness, courtesy, decency, decorum, delicacy, etiquette, fitness, gentlemanliness, manners, modesty, politeness, protocol, punctilio, rectitude, refinement, respectability, rightness, seemliness, suitableness.

*antonym* impropriety.

**proprieties** *n* civilities, conventions, decencies, decorum, etiquette, niceties, protocol, p's and q's, social graces.

*antonym* boorishness.

**propulsion** *n* drive, impetus, impulse, impulsion, momentum, power, pressure, push, thrust.

**prosaic** *adj* banal, boring, bromidic, commonplace, dry, dull, everyday, flat, hackneyed, humdrum, matter-of-fact, mundane, ordinary, pedestrian, routine, stale, tame, trite, unimaginative, uninspired, uninspiring, unpoetical, vapid, workaday.

*antonyms* imaginative, interesting.

**proscribe** *v* attant, ban, banish, bar, black, blackball, boycott, censure, condemn, damn, denounce, deport, doom, embargo, exclude, excommunicate, exile, expatriate, expel, forbid, interdict, ostracise, outlaw, prohibit, reject.

*antonyms* admit, allow.

**proscription** *n* attander, ban, banishment, bar, barring, boycott, censure, condemnation, damning, denunciation, deportation, ejection, embargo, eviction, exclusion, excommunication, exile, expatriation, expulsion, interdict, ostracism, outlawry, prohibition, rejection.

*antonyms* admission, allowing.

**prosecute** *v* arraign, bring suit against, bring to trial, carry on, conduct, continue, direct, discharge, engage in, execute, follow through, indict, litigate, manage, perform, persevere, persist, practise, prefer charges, pursue, put on trial, see through, sue, summon, take to court, try, work at.

*antonym* desist.

**proselytise** *v* bring into the fold, bring to God, convert, evangelise, make converts, persuade, propagandise, spread the gospel, win over.

**prospect** *n* calculation, chance, contemplation, expectation, future, hope, landscape, likelihood, odds, opening, outlook, panorama, perspective, plan, possibility, presumption, probability, promise, proposition, scene, sight, spectacle, thought, view, vision, vista.

*antonym* unlikelihood.

*v* explore, fossick, nose, quest, search, seek, survey.

**prospective** *adj* anticipated, approaching, awaited, coming, designate, designated, destined, eventual, expected, forthcoming, future, imminent, intended, likely, possible, potential, soon-to-be, to come, -to-be.

*antonyms* agreed, current.

**prospectus** *n* account, announcement, catalogue, conspectus, list, manifesto, outline, pamphlet, plan, platform, programme, scheme, syllabus, synopsis.

**prosper** *v* advance, bloom, boom, burgeon, fare well, flourish, flower, get on, grow rich, make good, progress, succeed, thrive, turn out well.

*antonym* fail.

**prosperity** *n* affluence, boom, ease, fortune, good fortune, luxury, plenty, prosperousness, riches, success, the good life, weal, wealth, well-being.

*antonym* poverty.

**prosperous** *adj* affluent, blooming, booming, burgeoning, flourishing, fortunate, in the money, lucky, moneyed, opulent, palmy, profitable, rich, successful, thriving, wealthy, well-heeled, well-off, well-to-do.

*antonym* poor.

**prostitute** *n* bawd, brass, broad, call-girl, cocotte, courtesan, dolly-mop, drab, fallen woman, fille de joie, fille des rues, floosie, grande cocotte, harlot, hooker, hustler, loon, loose woman, loose-fish, lorette, moll, Paphian, pro, punk, rent-boy, street-walker, strumpet, tart, trollop, trull, vizard-mask, wench, white slave, whore, woman of the town, working girl.

*v* cheapen, debase, degrade, demean, devalue, misapply, misuse, pervert, profane.

**prostitution** *n* harlotry, meretriciousness, street-walking, the game, the oldest profession, vice, whoredom, whoring.

**prostrate** *adj* abject, brought to one's knees, crushed, defenceless, dejected, depressed, desolate, disarmed, done, drained, exhausted, fagged, fallen, flat, helpless, horizontal, impotent, inconsolable, knackered, kowtowing, overcome, overwhelmed, paralysed, pooped, powerless, procumbent, prone, reduced, shattered, spent, worn out.

*antonyms* elated, erect, hale, happy, strong, triumphant.

*v* crush, depress, disarm, drain, exhaust, fag out, fatigue, knacker, lay low, overcome, overthrow, overturn, overwhelm, paralyse, poop, reduce, ruin, sap, shatter, tire, wear out, weary.

*antonyms* elate, exalt, strengthen.

**prostrate oneself** abase oneself, bend the knee, bow down, cringe, grovel, kneel, kowtow, submit.

*antonym* exalt oneself.

**prostration** *n* abasement, bow, collapse, dejection, depression, desolation, despair, despondency, exhaustion, genuflection, grief, helplessness, kneeling, kowtow, obeisance, paralysis, slough of despond, submission, weakness, weariness.

*antonyms* elation, exaltation, happiness, triumph.

**protagonist** *n* advocate, champion, chief character, exponent, hero, heroine, lead, leader, mainstay, prime mover, principal, proponent, standard-bearer, supporter.

**protean** *adj* amoebic, changeable, ever-changing, inconstant, many-sided, mercurial, multiform, mutable, polymorphic, polymorphous, variable, volatile.

*antonyms* stable, unchanging.

**protect** *v* care for, chaperon, convoy, cover, cover up for, defend, escort, guard, harbour, keep, look after, preserve, safeguard, save, screen, secure, shelter, shield, stand guard over, support, watch over.

*antonyms* attack, threaten.

**protection** *n* aegis, armour, backstop, barrier, buffer, bulwark, care, charge, cover, custody, defence, guard, guardianship, guarding, preservation, protecting, refuge, safeguard, safekeeping, safety, screen, security, shelter, shield, umbrella, wardship.

*antonyms* attack, threat.

**protective** *adj* careful, conservationist, covering, custodial, defensive, fatherly, insulating, jealous, maternal, motherly, paternal, possessive, safeguarding, sheltering, shielding, tutelary, vigilant, warm, watchful.

*antonyms* aggressive, threatening.

**protector** *n* advocate, benefactor, bodyguard, champion, counsel, defender, father-figure, guard, guardian, patron, protectress, protectrix, safeguard.

*antonyms* attacker, threat.

**protégé(e)** *n* blue-eyed boy, charge, dependant, discovery, pupil, student, ward, white-headed boy.

*antonym* guardian.

**protest** *n* complaint, declaration, demur, demurral, dharna, disapproval, dissent, formal complaint, objection, obtestation, outcry, protestation, remonstrance.

*antonym* acceptance.

*v* affirm, argue, assert, asseverate, attest, avow, complain, contend, cry out, declare, demonstrate, demur, disagree, disapprove, expostulate, insist, maintain, object, obtest, oppose, profess, remonstrate, squawk, take exception, testify, vow.

*antonym* accept.

**protestation** *n* affirmation, asseveration, assurance, avowal, complaint, declaration, disagreement, dissent, expostulation, oath, objection, outcry, pledge, profession, protest, remonstrance, remonstration, statement, vow.

**protester** *n* agitator, demonstrator, dissenter, dissident, rebel, remonstrant, remonstrator.

**protocol** *n* conventions, courtesies, customs, decorum, etiquette, formalities, good form, manners, politesse, procedure, propriety, p's and q's.

*antonym* boorishness.

**prototype** *n* archetype, example, exemplar, mock-up, model, original, paradigm, pattern, precedent, standard, type.

**protract** *v* continue, draw out, extend, keep going, lengthen, prolong, spin out, stretch out, sustain.

*antonym* shorten.

**protracted** *adj* dragged out, drawn-out, extended, interminable, lengthy, long, long-drawn-out, overlong, prolix, prolonged, wearisome, wordy.

*antonym* shortened.

**protrude** *v* bulge, come through, exsert, extend, extrude, jut out, obtrude, point, pop, project, protuberate, stand out, start, stick out, strout.

**protruding** *adj* astrut, exsertive, extrusive, extrusory, jutting, prominent, protrudent, protrusive, protuberant, proud.

*antonyms* flat, flush.

**protrusion** *n* bulge, bump, jut, lump, outgrowth, process, projection, protuberance, swelling.

**protuberance** *n* apophysis, bulb, bulge, bump, excrescence, knob, lump, mamelon, mamilla, outgrowth, process, projection, prominence, protrusion, swelling, tuber, tubercle, tumour, umbo, venter, wart, welt.

**protuberant** *adj* astrut, beetling, bulbous, bulging, bunched, exsertive, extrusive, extrusory, gibbous, jutting, popping, prominent, protrudent, protruding, protrusive, proud, swelling, swollen.

*antonym* flat.

**proud** *adj* appreciative, arrogant, august, boastful, conceited, content, contented, dicky, disdainful, distinguished, egotistical, eminent, exalted, glad, glorious, grand, gratified, gratifying, great, haughty, high and mighty, honoured, illustrious, imperious, imposing, lofty, lordly, magnificent, majestic, memorable, misproud, noble, orgulous, overbearing, overweening, pleased, pleasing, presumptuous, prideful, projecting, raised, red-letter, rewarding, satisfied, satisfying, self-important, self-respecting, snobbish, snobby, snooty, splendid, stately, stuck-up, supercilious, toffee-nosed, vain.

*antonym* humble.

**provable** *adj* attestable, confirmable, corroborable, demonstrable, establishable, evincible, testable, verifiable.

*antonym* unprovable.

**prove** *v* analyse, ascertain, assay, attest, authenticate, bear out, check, confirm, corroborate, demonstrate, determine, document, establish, evidence, evince, examine, experience, experiment, justify, show, substantiate, suffer, test, try, turn out, verify.

*antonyms* discredit, disprove, falsify.

**proven** *adj* accepted, attested, authentic, certified, checked, confirmed, corroborated, definite, dependable, established, proved, reliable, tested, tried, trustworthy, undoubted, valid, verified.

*antonym* unproven.

**provenance** *n* birthplace, derivation, origin, provenience, source.

**provender** *n* comestibles, eatables, eats, edibles, fare, feed, fodder, food, foodstuffs, forage, groceries, grub, nosh, provand, proviant, provisions, rations, supplies, sustenance, victuals.

**proverb** *n* adage, aphorism, apophthegm, bromide, byword, dictum, gnome, maxim, precept, saw, saying.

**proverbial** *adj* accepted, acknowledged, apophthegmatic, archetypal, axiomatic, bromidic, conventional, current, customary, famed, famous, legendary, notorious, self-evident, time-honoured, traditional, typical, unquestioned, well-known.

**provide** *v* accommodate, add, afford, anticipate, arrange for, bring, cater, contribute, determine, equip, forearm, furnish, give, impart, lay down, lend, outfit, plan for, prepare for, present, produce, provision, render, require, serve, specify, state, stipulate, stock up, suit, supply, take measures, take precautions, yield.

*antonyms* remove, take.

**provide for** dower, endow, fend, keep, maintain, support, sustain.

*antonyms* ignore, neglect.

**providence** *n* care, caution, destiny, discretion, divine intervention, far-sightedness, fate, foresight, forethought, fortune, God's will, karma, kismet, perspicacity, predestination, predetermination, presence of mind, prudence.

*antonym* improvidence.

**provident** *adj* canny, careful, cautious, discreet, economical, equipped, far-seeing, far-sighted, frugal, imaginative, long-sighted, prudent, sagacious, shrewd, thrifty, vigilant, wary, well-prepared, wise.

*antonym* improvident.

**providential** *adj* convenient, fortuitous, fortunate, happy, heaven-sent, lucky, opportune, timely, welcome.

*antonym* untimely.

**provider** *n* angel, benefactor, breadwinner, donor, earner, funder, giver, mainstay, source, supplier, supporter, wage-earner.

**providing** *conj* as long as, contingent upon, given, on condition, on the assumption, on the understanding, provided, subject to, with the proviso.

**province** *n* area, bailiwick, business, capacity, charge, colony, concern, county, department, dependency, district, division, domain, duty, employment, field, function, line, orbit, part, pigeon, post, region, responsibility, role, section, sphere, territory, tract, zone.

**provincial** *adj* bucolic, country, home-grown, homespun, insular, inward-looking, limited, local, mofussil, narrow, narrow-minded, parish-pump, parochial, rural, rustic, small-minded, small-town, uninformed, unsophisticated.

*antonyms* sophisticated, urban.

**provincialism** *n* insularity, localism, narrow-mindedness, parochialism, provinciality, regionalism, sectionalism.

*antonym* sophistication.

**provision** *n* accoutrement, agreement, arrangement, catering, clause, condition, demand, equipping, fitting out, furnishing, plan, prearrangement, precaution, preparation, prerequisite, providing, proviso, purveyance, purveying, requirement, specification, stipulation, supplying, term, victualling.

*antonyms* neglect, removal.

**provisional** *adj* conditional, contingent, interim, limited, pro tem, provisory, qualified, stop-gap, temporary, tentative, transitional.

*antonyms* definite, fixed, permanent.

**provisionally** *adv* for the time being, interim, meanwhile, pro tem, pro tempore.

**provisions** *n* comestibles, eatables, eats, edibles, fare, food, foodstuff, groceries, grub, piece, prog, provand, provender, proviant, rations, stores, supplies, sustenance, viands, viaticum, victuallage, victuals, vittles.

**proviso** *n* clause, condition, limitation, provision, qualification, requirement, reservation, restriction, rider, small print, stipulation.

**provisory** *adj* conditional, interim, provisional, qualified, temporary, tentative.

*antonyms* definite, fixed, permanent.

**provocation** *n* affront, aggravation, annoyance, casus belli, cause, challenge, dare, grievance, grounds, incitement, indignity, inducement, injury, instigation, insult, justification, motivation, motive, offence, reason, red rag, stimulus, taunt, vexation.

**provocative** *adj* abusive, aggravating, alluring, annoying, arousing, challenging, disturbing, erotic, exciting, galling, goading, incensing, insulting, inviting, offensive, outrageous, provocatory, provoking, seductive, sexy, stimulating, suggestive, tantalising, tempting.

*antonyms* pacificatory, unprovocative.

**provoke** *v* affront, aggravate, anger, annoy, cause, chafe, elicit, enrage, evoke, exasperate, excite, fire, gall, generate, give rise to, incense, incite, induce, inflame, infuriate, inspire, instigate, insult, irk, irritate, kindle, madden, motivate, move, occasion, offend, pique, precipitate, produce, promote, prompt, put out, rile, rouse, stimulate, stir, vex.

*antonyms* pacify, please, result.

**provoking** *adj* aggravating, annoying, exasperating, galling, infuriating, irking, irksome, irritating, maddening, obstructive, offensive, pesky, pestiferous, tiresome, vexatious, vexing.

*antonyms* pacificatory, pleasing.

**prow** *n* bow(s), cut-water, fore, forepart, front, head, nose, prore, stem.

*antonym* stern.

**prowess** *n* ability, accomplishment, adeptness, adroitness, aptitude, attainment, bravery, command, daring, dauntlessness, dexterity, doughtiness, excellence, expertise, expertness, facility, genius, heroism, mastery, skill, talent, valour.

*antonyms* clumsiness, mediocrity.

**prowl** *v* creep, cruise, hunt, lurk, nose, patrol, range, roam, rove, scavenge, search, skulk, slink, sneak, snook, stalk, steal.

**proximity** *n* adjacency, closeness, contiguity, juxtaposition, nearness, neighbourhood, propinquity, proximation, vicinity.

*antonym* remoteness.

**proxy** *n* agent, attorney, delegate, deputy, factor, locum, representative, stand-in, substitute, surrogate.

**prude** *n* Mrs Grundy, old maid, prig, puritan, school-marm, Victorian.

**prudence** *n* canniness, care, caution, circumspection, common sense, discretion, economy, far-sightedness, foresight, forethought, frugality, good sense, heedfulness, husbandry, judgement, judiciousness, planning, policy, precaution, preparedness, providence, sagacity, saving, thrift, vigilance, wariness, wisdom.

*antonym* imprudence.

**prudent** *adj* canny, careful, cautious, circumspect, discerning, discreet, economical, far-sighted, frugal, judicious, politic, provident, sagacious, sage, sensible, shrewd, sparing, thrifty, vigilant, wary, well-advised, wise, wise-hearted.

*antonym* imprudent.

**prudish** *adj* demure, narrow-minded, old-maidish, overmodest, overnice, po-faced, priggish, prim, prissy, proper, pudibund, puritanical, school-marmish, squeamish, starchy, strait-laced, stuffy, ultra-virtuous, Victorian.

*antonyms* easy-going, lax.

**prudishness** *n* Grundyism, old-maidishness, overmodesty, priggishness, primness, prissiness, prudery, pudibundity, puritanism, squeamishness, starchiness, strictness, stuffiness.

*antonym* laxness.

**prune** *v* clip, cut, dehorn, dock, lop, pare, reduce, shape, shorten, snip, trim.

**prurient** *adj* concupiscent, cupidinous, desirous, dirty, erotic, indecent, itching, lascivious, lecherous, lewd, libidinous, lickerish, lustful, obscene, pornographic, salacious, smutty, voyeuristic.

*antonym* decent.

**pry** *v* delve, dig, ferret, interfere, intrude, meddle, nose, peep, peer, poke, poke one's nose in, snoop.

*antonym* mind one's own business.

**prying** *adj* curious, inquisitive, interfering, intrusive, meddlesome, meddling, nosy, peering, peery, snooping, snoopy, spying.

*antonym* uninquisitive.

**psalm** *n* canticle, chant, hymn, paean, paraphrase, song.

**pseud** *n* fraud, humbug, phoney, poser, poseur, trendy.

**pseudo** *adj* artificial, bogus, counterfeit, ersatz, fake, false, imitation, mock, phoney, pretended, pseud, quasi-, sham, spurious, ungenuine.

*antonym* genuine.

**pseudonym** *n* alias, allonym, anonym, assumed name, false name, incognito, monicker, nom de guerre, nom de plume, pen name, stage name.

**psyche** *n* anima, awareness, consciousness, individuality, intellect, intelligence, mind, personality, pneuma, self, soul, spirit, subconscious, understanding.

**psychiatrist** *n* analyst, headshrinker, psychoanalyser, psychoanalyst, psychologist, psychotherapist, shrink, therapist, trick-cyclist.

**psychic** *adj* clairvoyant, cognitive, extra-sensory, intellectual, mental, mystic, mystical, occult, preternatural, psychogenic, psychological, spiritual, spiritualistic, supernatural, telekinetic, telepathic.

**psychological** *adj* affective, cerebral, cognitive, emotional, imaginary, intellectual, irrational, mental, psychosomatic, subconscious, subjective, unconscious, unreal.

**psychology** *n* brains, craft, craftiness, cunning, psychiatry, psychics, slyness, subtlety, wiliness.

**psychopath** *n* lunatic, madman, maniac, psycho, psychotic, sociopath.

**psychotic** *adj* certifiable, demented, deranged, insane, lunatic, mad, mental, psychopathic, unbalanced.

*antonym* sane.

**puberty** *n* adolescence, juvenescence, maturity, nubility, pubescence, teens, youth.

*antonyms* childhood, immaturity.

**public** *adj* accessible, acknowledged, circulating, civic, civil, common, communal, community, exposed, general, high-profile, important, known, national, notorious, obvious, open, overt, patent, plain, popular, prominent, published, recognised, respected, social, state, universal, unrestricted, well-known, widespread.

*antonym* private.

*n* audience, buyers, citizens, clientèle, commonalty, community, country, electorate, everyone, followers, following, masses, multitude, nation, patrons, people, populace, population, punters, society, supporters, voters.

**public house** alehouse, bar, bierkeller, bodega, boozer, brasserie, cantina, dram-shop, hostelry, inn, jerry-shop, local, lush-house, pot-house, pot-shop, pub, roadhouse, tap-house, tavern, tippling-house, vaults.

**publican** *n* barman, inn-keeper, mine host, padrone, taverner.

**publication** *n* advertisement, airing, announcement, appearance, book, booklet, broadcasting, brochure, declaration, disclosure, dissemination, divulgation, handbill, issue, leaflet, magazine, newspaper, notification, pamphlet, periodical, proclamation, promulgation, publishing, publishment, reporting, vent.

**publicise** v advertise, blaze, blazon, broadcast, hype, plug, promote, puff, push, spotlight, spread about, write off.

*antonym* keep secret.

**publicity** n advertising, attention, ballyhoo, boost, build-up, hype, plug, press, promotion, public notice, puff, puffery, réclame, splash.

*antonym* secrecy.

**public-spirited** adj altruistic, charitable, community-minded, conscientious, generous, humanitarian, philanthropic, unselfish.

*antonym* selfish.

**publish** v advertise, announce, bring out, broadcast, circulate, communicate, declare, diffuse, disclose, distribute, divulgate, divulge, evulgate, issue, leak, part, print, proclaim, produce, promulgate, publicise, reveal, spread, vent.

*antonym* keep secret.

**pucker** v compress, contract, crease, crinkle, crumple, furrow, gather, purse, ruck, ruckle, ruffle, screw up, shirr, shrivel, tighten, wrinkle.

n crease, crinkle, crumple, fold, ruck, ruckle, shirr, wrinkle.

**puckered** adj creased, gathered, pursy, rucked, ruckled, wrinkled.

*antonym* smooth.

**puckish** adj frolicsome, impish, mischievous, naughty, pawky, playful, roguish, sly, sportive, teasing, waggish, whimsical.

*antonym* solemn.

**pudding** n afters, dessert, dumpling, pud, sweet.

**puddle** n dub, plash, plashet, pool, slop, sop, soss.

**pudenda** n fanny, genitalia, genitals, private parts, privates, pussy, quim.

**puerile** adj babyish, childish, foolish, immature, inane, infantile, irresponsible, jejune, juvenile, naïve, petty, ridiculous, silly, trifling, trivial, weak.

*antonym* mature.

**puff** n advertisement, blast, breath, commendation, drag, draught, emanation, flurry, gust, mention, plug, pull, smoke, waft, whiff.

v bloat, blow, breathe, dilate, distend, drag, draw, exhale, expand, gasp, gulp, hype, inflate, inhale, pant, plug, praise, promote, publicise, pull, push, smoke, suck, swell, waft, wheeze, whiff, whiffle.

**puffed** adj breathless, done in, exhausted, gasping, out of breath, panting, winded.

*antonym* vigorous.

**puffed up** arrogant, big-headed, full of oneself, high and mighty, prideful, proud, swollen-headed, too big for one's boots.

*antonym* modest.

**puffy** adj bloated, distended, enlarged, inflamed, inflated, oedematous, puffed up, pursy, swollen.

*antonym* flat.

**pugilism** n boxing, fighting, fistiana, prize-fighting, the fancy, the noble art, the noble science, the prize-ring, the ring.

**pugilist** n boxer, bruiser, fighter, prize-fighter, pug, pugil.

**pugnacious** adj aggressive, antagonistic, argumentative, bare-knuckle, bellicose, belligerent, choleric, combative, contentious, disputatious, hostile, hot-tempered, irascible, petulant, quarrelsome.

*antonym* easy-going.

**puke** v disgorge, heave, posset, regurgitate, retch, spew, throw up, vomit.

**pull** v attract, cull, dislocate, drag, draw, draw out, entice, extract, gather, haul, jerk, lure, magnetise, pick, pluck, remove, rend, rip, schlep, sprain, strain, stretch, take out, tear, tow, track, trail, tug, tweak, uproot, weed, whang, wrench, yank.

*antonyms* deter, push, repel.

n advantage, allurement, attraction, clout, drag, drawing power, effort, exertion, force, forcefulness, influence, inhalation, jerk, leverage, lure, magnetism, muscle, power, puff, seduction, tug, twitch, weight, yank.

*antonyms* deterring, push, repelling.

**pull a face** frown, glower, grimace, knit one's brows, lower, pout, scowl, sulk.

**pull a fast one on** cheat, con, deceive, defraud, grift, hoodwink, put one over on, sting, swindle, take for a ride, trick.

**pull apart** attack, carp at, criticise, dismember, divellicate, find fault, flay, knock, lay into, pan, part, pick holes in, pull to pieces, run down, separate, slam, slate, sunder.

*antonym* praise.

**pull down** bulldoze, demolish, destroy, dismantle, knock down, raze, remove.

*antonym* put up.

**pull in** arrest, arrive, attract, bring in, bust, clear, collar, come in, draw, draw in, draw up, earn, gain, gross, make, nab, nail, net, park, pinch, pocket, reach, run in, stop, take home.

*antonyms* lose, pull away, repel.

**pull off** accomplish, achieve, bring off, carry out, manage, succeed, swing.

*antonym* fail.

**pull out** abandon, depart, draw out, evacuate, evulse, leave, quit, retreat, withdraw.

*antonym* join.

**pull someone's leg** chaff, deceive, fool, make fun of, tease, trick.

**pull the wool over someone's eyes** bamboozle, con, deceive, delude, dupe, fool, hoodwink, lead up the garden path, pull a fast one on, put one over on, snow, take in, trick.

**pull through** rally, recover, recuperate, survive, weather.

*antonym* fail.

**pull together** collaborate, co-operate, team up, work together.

*antonym* fight.

**pull up** admonish, brake, carpet, castigate, draw in, draw up, halt, lift, raise, rebuke, reprimand, reprove, stop, take to task, tell off, tick off, uproot.

**pulp** *n* flesh, marrow, mash, mush, pap, paste, pomace, soft part, triturate.

*v* crush, liquidise, mash, pulverise, squash.

**pulpit** *n* dais, lectern, platform, rostrum, soap-box, wood.

**pulpy** *adj* fleshy, mushy, pappy, sloppy, soft, squashy, succulent.

*antonym* hard.

**pulsate** *v* beat, drum, hammer, oscillate, palpitate, pound, pulse, quiver, throb, thud, thump, tick, vibrate.

**pulsating** *adj* oscillating, palpitating, pulsatile, pulsative, pulsatory, pulsing, vibratile, vibrating, vibrative.

**pulsation** *n* ictus, oscillation, palpitation, vibration, vibratiuncle.

**pulse** *n* beat, beating, drumming, oscillation, pulsation, rhythm, stroke, throb, throbbing, thudding, vibration.

*v* beat, drum, pulsate, throb, thud, tick, vibrate.

**pulverise** *v* annihilate, bray, comminute, crush, defeat, demolish, destroy, flatten, granulate, grind, hammer, levigate, mill, pestle, pound, smash, triturate, vanquish, wreck.

**pummel** *v* bang, batter, beat, fib, hammer, knead, knock, nevel, pound, punch, strike, thump.

**pump** *v* catechise, cross-examine, debrief, drive, force, grill, inject, interrogate, pour, probe, push, question, quiz, send, supply.

**pump out** bail out, drain, draw off, empty, force out, siphon.

**pump up** blow up, dilate, distend, inflate, puff up.

**pun** *n* clinch, double entendre, equivoke, jeu de mots, paronomasia, paronomasy, play on words, quip, witticism.

**punch**[1] *v* bash, biff, bop, box, clout, fib, hit, plug, pummel, slam, slug, smash, sock, strike, wallop.

*n* bash, biff, bite, blow, bop, clout, drive, effectiveness, force, forcefulness, hit, impact, jab, knock, knuckle sandwich, lander, muzzler, panache, pizzazz, plug, point, sock, thump, verve, vigour, wallop.

*antonym* feebleness.

**punch**[2] *v* bore, cut, drill, perforate, pierce, pink, prick, puncture, stamp.

**punch-drunk** *adj* befuddled, confused, dazed, dizzy, groggy, punchy, reeling, slap-happy, staggering, stupefied, unsteady, woozy.

**punch-up** *n* argument, brawl, ding-dong, Donnybrook, dust-up, fight, free-for-all, row, ruckus, scrap, set-to, shindy, stand-up fight.

**punchy** *adj* aggressive, dynamic, effective, forceful, incisive, lively, powerful, spirited, vigorous, zappy.

*antonyms* feeble, weak.

**punctilio** *n* ceremony, convention, delicacy, distinction, exactitude, exactness, fine point, finickiness, formality, meticulousness, nicety, particular, particularity, preciseness, precision, punctiliousness, refinement, scrupulousness, strictness.

*antonyms* boorishness, informality.

**punctilious** *adj* careful, ceremonious, conscientious, exact, finicky, formal, formalist, fussy, meticulous, nice, overnice, particular, precise, proper, scrupulous, strict.

*antonyms* boorish, easy-going, informal.

**punctual** *adj* early, exact, in good time, on the dot, on time, precise, prompt, punctilious, strict, timely, up to time.

*antonym* unpunctual.

**punctuality** *n* promptitude, promptness, readiness, regularity, strictness.

*antonym* unpunctuality.

**punctually** *adv* on the dot, on time, precisely, prompt, promptly, sharp.

*antonym* unpunctually.

**punctuate** *v* accentuate, break, emphasise, interject, interrupt, intersperse, pepper, point, sprinkle.

**puncture** *n* break, cut, fissure, flat, flat tyre, hole, leak, nick, opening, perforation, rupture, slit.

*v* bore, cut, deflate, discourage, disillusion, flatten, humble, nick, penetrate, perforate, pierce, prick, rupture, take down a peg or two.

**pundit** *n* authority, buff, deipnosophist, expert, guru, maestro, master, teacher.

**pungent** *adj* acid, acrid, acrimonious, acute, aromatic, barbed, biting, bitter, caustic, cutting, fell, hot, incisive, keen, mordant, painful, penetrating, peppery, piercing, piquant, poignant, pointed, sarcastic, scathing, seasoned, sharp, sour, spicy, stinging, stringent, strong, tangy, tart, telling, trenchant.

*antonyms* feeble, mild, tasteless.

**punish** *v* abuse, amerce, batter, beat, castigate, chasten, chastise, correct, crucify, discipline, flog, give a lesson to, give someone laldie, harm, hurt, injure, keelhaul, knee-cap, lash, maltreat, manhandle, masthead, misuse, oppress, penalise, rough up, scour, scourge, sort, strafe, trounce.

**punishable** *adj* blameworthy, chargeable, convictable, criminal, culpable, indictable, unlawful.

**punishing** *adj* arduous, backbreaking, burdensome, demanding, exhausting, fatiguing, grinding, gruelling, hard, strenuous, taxing, tiring, wearing.

*antonym* easy.

**punishment** *n* abuse, beating, chastening, chastisement, come-uppance, correction, damnation, deserts, discipline, jankers, knee-capping, laldie, maltreatment, manhandling, medicine, pain, pay-off, penalty, penance, punition, retribution, sanction, toco, torture, victimisation.

**punitive** *adj* penal, punitory, retaliative, retaliatory, retributive, revengeful, vindictive.

**punter** *n* backer, better, bloke, buffer, chap, client, cove, customer, fellow, gambler, guy, individual, josser, oik, person, shaver.

**puny** *adj* diminutive, dwarfish, feeble, frail, inconsequential, inferior, insignificant, little, meagre, minor, paltry, petty, piddling, pimping, reckling, runted, runtish, runty, sickly, stunted, tiny, trifling, trivial, underfed, undersized, undeveloped, weak, weakly, worthless.

*antonyms* important, large, strong.

**pupil** *n* beginner, catechumen, disciple, learner, neophyte, novice, protégé, scholar, schoolboy, schoolgirl, student, tiro, tutee.

*antonym* teacher.

**puppet** *n* cat's-paw, creature, doll, dupe, figurehead, gull, instrument, marionette, mouthpiece, pawn, quisling, stooge, tool.

**puppet-show** *n* bunraku, fantoccini, Punch and Judy show, puppet-play, puppetry.

**puppy** *n* braggart, cub, jackanapes, popinjay, pup, shaver, whelp, whippersnapper.

**purchase** *v* achieve, acquire, attain, buy, earn, gain, invest in, obtain, pay for, procure, ransom, realise, secure, win.

*antonym* sell.

*n* acquisition, advantage, asset, buy, edge, emption, foothold, footing, gain, grasp, grip, hold, influence, investment, lever, leverage, possession, property, ransoming, support, toehold.

*antonym* sale.

**purchaser** *n* buyer, chap, chapman, client, consumer, customer, emptor, hirer, shopper, vendee.

**pure** *adj* absolute, abstract, academic, antiseptic, authentic, blameless, chaste, clean, clear, disinfected, flawless, genuine, germ-free, guileless, high-minded, honest, hygienic, immaculate, innocent, intemerate, maidenly, modest, natural, neat, pasteurised, perfect, philosophical, real, refined, sanitary, Saturnian, sheer, simple, sincere, snow-white, speculative, spiritous, spotless, stainless, sterile, sterilised, straight, taintless, theoretical, thorough, true, unadulterate, unadulterated, unalloyed, unblemished, uncontaminated, uncorrupted, undefiled, unmingled, unmitigated, unmixed, unpolluted, unqualified, unsoiled, unspoilt, unspotted, unstained, unsullied, untainted, untarnished, upright, utter, virgin, virginal, virginly, virtuous, wholesome.

*antonyms* adulterated, applied, defiled, immoral, impure, polluted, tainted.

**pure-bred** *adj* blooded, full-blooded, pedigree, pedigreed, pure-blood, pure-blooded, thoroughbred.

*antonyms* cross-bred, hybrid, mixed, mongrel.

**purely** *adv* absolutely, completely, entirely, exclusively, just, merely, only, plainly, sheerly, simply, solely, thoroughly, totally, utterly, wholly.

**purgation** *n* abstersion, catharsis, cleansing, clearing, depuration, evacuation, exculpation, exoneration, justification, purge, purging, purification, riddance, ridding, vindication.

**purgative** *n* abstersive, aperient, cathartic, clyster, depurative, diacatholicon, eccoprotic, emetic, enema, evacuant, laxative, purge.

*adj* abstersive, aperient, cathartic, cathartical, cleansing, depurative, eccoprotic, evacuant, laxative, purging.

**purge** *v* absolve, absterge, catharise, clean out, cleanse, clear, dismiss, eject, eradicate, exonerate, expel, expiate, exterminate, extract, forgive, get rid of, kill, liquidate, oust, pardon, purify, remove, rid, root out, scour, wash, wipe out.

*n* aperient, catharsis, cathartic, clyster, depurative, ejection, elimination, emetic, enema, eradication, expulsion, extermination, laxative, liquidation, purgative, removal, witch hunt.

**purification** *n* absolution, beneficiation, catharsis, clarification, cleaning, cleansing, decontamination, deodorisation, depuration, desalination, disinfection, epuration, filtration, fumigation, furbishing, lustration, lustre, lustrum, mundification, purgation, redemption, refinement, sanctification, sanitisation.

*antonyms* contamination, defilement, pollution.

**purify** *v* absolve, beneficiate, catharise, chasten, clarify, clean, cleanse, decontaminate, deodorise, depurate, desalinate, disinfect, epurate, filter, fumigate, furbish, lustrate, mundify, redeem, refine, sanctify, sanitise, shrive, sublimise, wash.

*antonyms* contaminate, defile, pollute.

**purifying** *adj* cathartic, cleansing, depurative, lustral, mundificative, purgative, purging, purificatory, refining.

*antonyms* contaminating, defiling, polluting.

**purism** *n* Atticism, austerity, classicism, fastidiousness, formalism, fussiness, orthodoxy, over-precision, pedantry, restraint, strictness.

*antonyms* liberality, open-mindedness, tolerance.

**purist** *n* Atticist, classicist, formalist, grammaticaster, grammatist, mandarin, nit-picker, pedant, precisian, precisianist, precisionist, quibbler, stickler, vocabularian.

*antonym* liberal.

*adj* austere, captious, fastidious, finicky, fussy, hypercritical, nit-picking, over-exact, over-fastidious, over-meticulous, over-particular, over-precise, pedantic, puristic, quibbling, strict, uncompromising.

*antonyms* liberal, open-minded, tolerant.

**puritan** *n* bluenose, disciplinarian, fanatic, kill-joy, moralist, pietist, prude, rigorist, spoil-sport, zealot.

*antonyms* hedonist, libertarian.

*adj* ascetic, austere, disciplinarian, hard-line, hide-bound, intolerant, moralistic, narrow, narrow-minded, prim, prudish, puritanical, self-disciplined, severe, stern, strait-laced, strict, uncompromising.

*antonyms* broad-minded, hedonistic, indulgent, liberal.

**puritanical** *adj* abstemious, abstinent, ascetic, austere, bigoted, disapproving, disciplinarian, fanatical, narrow, narrow-minded, prim, proper, prudish, puritan, rigid, severe, stern, stiff, strait-laced, strict, stuffy, uncompromising, zealous.

*antonyms* broad-minded, hedonistic, indulgent, liberal.

**puritanism** *n* abstemiousness, abstinence, asceticism, austerity, bigotry, fanaticism, narrow-mindedness, narrowness, priggishness, primness, propriety, prudishness, rigidity, rigorousness, self-denial, self-discipline, severity, sternness, stiffness, strictness, uncompromisingness, zealotry.

*antonyms* broad-mindedness, hedonism, indulgence, liberality.

**purity** *n* blamelessness, chasteness, chastity, clarity, classicism, cleanliness, clearness, decency, faultlessness, fineness, genuineness, immaculateness, incorruption, innocence, integrity, morality, piety, pureness, rectitude, refinement, sanctity, simplicity, sincerity, spotlessness, stainlessness, truth, unspottedness, untaintedness, uprightness, virginity, virtue, virtuousness, wholesomeness.

*antonyms* immorality, impurity.

**purlieus** *n* banlieue, borders, bounds, confines, environs, fringes, limits, neighbourhood, outskirts, perimeter, periphery, precincts, suburbs, vicinity.

**purloin** *v* abstract, appropriate, filch, finger, half-inch, lift, nick, nobble, palm, pilfer, pinch, pocket, prig, remove, rob, snaffle, snitch, steal, swipe, take, thieve.

**purport** *v* allege, argue, assert, betoken, claim, convey, declare, denote, express, give out, imply, import, indicate, intend, maintain, mean, portend, pose as, pretend, proclaim, profess, seem, show, signify, suggest.

*n* bearing, direction, drift, gist, idea, implication, import, meaning, point, significance, spirit, substance, tendency, tenor, theme, thrust.

**purpose** *n* advantage, aim, ambition, aspiration, assiduity, avail, benefit, constancy, contemplation, decision, dedication, design, determination, devotion, drive, effect, end, firmness, function, gain, goal, good, hope, idea, ideal, intention, motive, object, objective, outcome, persistence, pertinacity, plan, point, principle, profit, project, rationale, reason, resolution, resolve, result, return, scheme, service, single-mindedness, steadfastness, target, telos, tenacity, use, usefulness, utility, view, vision, will, wish, zeal.

*v* aim, aspire, contemplate, decide, design, desire, determine, ettle, intend, mean, meditate, plan, propose, resolve.

**purposeful** *adj* assiduous, decided, deliberate, determined, firm, fixed, hormic, motivated, persevering, persistent, pertinacious, positive, purposive, resolute, resolved, sedulous, settled, single-minded, steadfast, strong-willed, teleological, tenacious, unfaltering, unswerving.

*antonym* purposeless.

**purposeless** *adj* aimless, empty, goalless, gratuitous, motiveless, needless, nonsensical, objectless, pointless, senseless, thoughtless, unasked-for, uncalled-for, unnecessary, useless, vacuous, vain, wanton.

*antonym* purposeful.

**purposely** *adv* by design, calculatedly, consciously, deliberately, designedly, expressly, intentionally, knowingly, on purpose, premeditatedly, specifically, wilfully, with malice aforethought.

*antonyms* impulsively, spontaneously, unpremeditatedly.

**purse** *n* award, burse, coffers, exchequer, finances, fisc, funds, means, money, money-bag, monkey-bag, pocket-book, porte-monnaie, pouch, prize, resources, reward, sporran, treasury, wallet, wealth.

*v* close, compress, contract, draw together, pucker, tighten, wrinkle.

**pursuance** *n* accomplishment, achievement, completion, discharge, effecting, effectuation, execution, following, fulfilment, performance, prosecution, pursuing.

**pursue** *v* accompany, adhere to, aim at, aim for, aspire to, attend, bedevil, beset, besiege, carry on, chase, check out, conduct, continue, course, court, cultivate, desire, dog, engage in, follow, follow up, go for, gun for, harass, harry, haunt, hold to, hound, hunt, inquire into, investigate, keep on, maintain, perform, persecute, persevere in, persist in, plague, ply, practise, proceed, prosecute, purpose, seek, set one's cap at, shadow, stalk, strive for, tackle, tail, track, trail, try for, wage, woo.

*antonyms* eschew, shun.

**pursuit**[1] *n* chase, chevy, hounding, hue and cry, hunt, hunting, inquiry, investigation, quest, search, seeking, stalking, tracking, trail, trailing.

**pursuit**[2] *n* activity, craft, hobby, interest, line, occupation, parergon, pastime, pleasure, side-line, speciality, vocation.

**purvey** *v* cater, communicate, deal in, disseminate, furnish, pass on, propagate, provide, provision, publicise, publish, put about, retail, sell, spread, stock, supply, trade in, transmit, victual.

**purveyor** *n* communicator, dealer, disseminator, propagater, provider, provisor, retailer, stockist, supplier, trader, transmitter, victualler.

**push** *v* advance, advertise, boost, browbeat, bulldoze, bully, coerce, constrain, depress, dragoon, drive, edge, egg on, elbow, encourage, expedite, force, hurry, hype, incite, influence, inveigle, jockey, jog, joggle, jostle, manhandle, manoeuvre, oblige, peddle, persuade, plug, poke, press, prod, promote, propagandise, propel, publicise, puff, ram, shoulder, shove, speed, spur, squeeze, thrust, urge, wedge, whang.

*n* advance, ambition, assault, attack, bunt, butt, charge, determination, discharge, dismissal, drive, dynamism, effort, energy, enterprise, go, impetus, impulse, initiative, jolt, knock, notice, nudge, offensive, one's books, one's cards, one's marching orders, onset, onslaught, poke, pressure, prod, shove, the axe, the boot, the bum's rush, the chop, the sack, thrust, vigour, vim, vitality, zip.

**push off** depart, go away, leave, make a move, make tracks, move, push along, shift, shove off.

**pushed** *adj* harassed, hard-pressed, hard-up, harried, hurried, in difficulties, pinched, pressed, rushed, short of, strapped, stretched, under pressure.

**pushing** *adj* aggressive, ambitious, assertive, bold, brash, bumptious, determined, driving, dynamic, enterprising, forceful, forward, go-ahead, high-powered, impertinent, intrusive, presumptuous, purposeful, pushful, pushy, resourceful, self-assertive, thrusting.

*antonyms* conservative, diffident, unassertive, unassuming, unenterprising.

**push-over** *n* child's play, cinch, doddle, dupe, easy mark, fall guy, gull, mug, picnic, piece of cake, sinecure, sitting duck, sitting target, soft mark, soft touch, stooge, sucker, walk-over.

*antonyms* challenge, labour.

**pushy** *adj* aggressive, ambitious, arrogant, assertive, assuming, bold, bossy, brash, bumptious, forceful, forward, loud, obtrusive, offensive, officious, over-confident, presumptuous, pushing, self-assertive.

*antonyms* quiet, restrained, unassertive, unassuming.

**pusillanimity** *n* cowardliness, cravenness, faint-heartedness, fearfulness, feebleness, gutlessness, poltroonery, recreancy, spinelessness, timidity, timorousness, weakness, yellow-streak.

**pusillanimous** *adj* caitiff, chicken, chicken-hearted, cowardly, craven, faint-hearted, fearful, feeble, gutless, lily-livered, mean-spirited, poltroon, recreant, scared, spineless, timid, timorous, unassertive, unenterprising, weak, weak-kneed, yellow.

*antonyms* ambitious, courageous, forceful, strong.

**pussyfoot** *v* beat about the bush, creep, equivocate, hedge, mess about, pad, prevaricate, prowl, sidestep, slink, steal, tergiversate, tiptoe.

**pustule** *n* abscess, blister, boil, bulla, carbuncle, eruption, fester, furuncle, gathering, imposthume, papilla, papule, pimple, pock, ulcer, whelk, whitlow.

**put** *v* advance, apply, assign, bring, bring forward, cast, commit, condemn, consign, constrain, couch, deploy, deposit, dispose, drive, employ, enjoin, establish, express, fit, fix, fling, force, formulate, forward, frame, heave, hurl, impel, impose, induce, inflict, land, lay, levy, lob, make, oblige, offer, park, phrase, pitch, place, plonk, pose, position, post, present, propose, push, render, require, rest, send, set, set down, settle, situate, state, station, subject, submit, suggest, tender, throw, thrust, toss, utter, voice, word, write.

**put across** bring home to, communicate, convey, explain, express, get through to, put over, spell out.

**put an end to** abolish, annihilate, annul, cancel, check, destroy, discontinue, jugulate, kibosh,

knock on the head, nullify, put a stop to, put paid to, put the kibosh on, put the lid on, put the mockers on, stem, stop, terminate.

**put aside**[1] cache, deposit, hoard, keep, lay by, put by, reserve, retain, salt away, save, set aside, stash, stockpile, store, stow.

**put aside**[2] abandon, bury, discard, discount, dispense with, disregard, forget, ignore, set aside.

**put away** certify, commit, consume, divorce, eat, imprison, institutionalise, kill, put aside, remove, renounce, replace, repudiate, return, save, shift, store, tidy, wolf.

**put back** delay, postpone, replace, repulse, reschedule, return.

**put down**[1] enter, inscribe, log, note, record, register, report, state, transcribe, write down.

**put down**[2] abash, condemn, crush, defeat, deflate, degrade, destroy, dismiss, disparage, humble, humiliate, kill, mortify, put to sleep, quash, quell, reject, repress, shame, silence, slight, snub, suppress, take down a peg, topple.

**put down**[3] ascribe, assign, attribute, impute.

**put forward** advance, introduce, move, nominate, offer, present, press, proffer, propose, recommend, submit, suggest, table, tender.

**put in** enter, input, insert, key in.

**put off** abash, confuse, daunt, defer, delay, demoralise, deter, discomfit, disconcert, discourage, dishearten, dismay, dispirit, dissuade, distress, divert, nonplus, perturb, postpone, put out, rattle, reschedule, throw, unnerve, unsettle.

*antonym* encourage.

**put on** add, affect, affix, apply, assume, attach, back, bet, deceive, do, don, dress, fake, feign, gain, impose, increase by, lay, make believe, mislead, mount, place, present, pretend, produce, sham, show, simulate, stage, stake, wager.

**put one's finger on** discover, find out, hit the nail on the head, hit upon, identify, indicate, isolate, locate, pin down, pinpoint, place, recall, remember.

**put out** affront, anger, announce, annoy, bother, broadcast, circulate, confound, discomfit, discommode, discompose, disconcert, discountenance, dislocate, dismiss, disturb, douse, embarrass, exasperate, exert, expel, extinguish, give out, harass, hurt, impose on, incommode, inconvenience, irk, irritate, issue, nettle, offend, perturb, produce, provoke, publish, quench, release, smother, trouble, upset, vex.

**put the wind up** agitate, alarm, daunt, discourage, frighten, panic, perturb, scare, sound the alarm, startle, unnerve.

*antonym* reassure.

**put through** accomplish, achieve, bring off, conclude, effect, execute, finalise, manage.

**put to death** execute, exterminate, kill, liquidate, martyr.

**put to shame** disgrace, eclipse, humble, humiliate, outclass, outdo, outstrip, shame, show up, surpass.

**put up** accommodate, advance, assemble, board, build, construct, entertain, erect, fabricate, float, give, house, invest, lodge, nominate, offer, pay, pledge, present, propose, provide, put forward, quarter, raise, recommend, shelter, submit, supply.

**put up to** abet, encourage, goad, incite, instigate, prompt, urge.

*antonyms* discourage, dissuade.

**put up with** abide, allow, bear, brook, endure, lump, stand, stand for, stomach, suffer, swallow, take, take lying down, thole, tolerate.

*antonyms* object to, protest against, reject.

**put upon** exploit, impose on, inconvenience, take a loan of, use.

**put wise** alert, apprise, clue in, fill in, inform, intimate to, make wise to, notify, put in the picture, tell, tip off, warn, wise up.

**putative** *adj* alleged, assumed, conjectural, hypothetical, imputed, presumed, presumptive, reported, reputative, reputed, supposed, suppositional, supposititious.

**put-down** *n* affront, dig, disparagement, gibe, humiliation, insult, rebuff, sarcasm, slap in the face, slight, sneer, snub.

**put-off** *n* constraint, curb, damper, deterrent, discouragement, disincentive, hindrance, obstacle, restraint.

*antonyms* encouragement, incentive.

**putrefy** *v* addle, corrupt, decay, decompose, deteriorate, fester, foost, gangrene, go bad, mortify, mould, necrose, perish, rot, spoil, stink, taint.

**putrescent** *adj* decaying, decomposing, festering, mephitic, perishing, putrefying, rotting, stinking.

**putrid** *adj* addle, addled, bad, contaminated, corrupt, decayed, decomposed, fetid, foosty, foul, gangrenous, mephitic, mouldy, necrosed, noisome, off, putrefied, rancid, rank, reeking, rotten, rotting, sphacelate(d), spoiled, stinking, tainted.

*antonyms* fresh, wholesome.

**put-upon** *adj* abused, beset, exploited, harassed, harried, henpecked, ill-used, imposed on, inconvenienced, overworked, persecuted.

**puzzle¹** *v* baffle, bamboozle, beat, bewilder, confound, confuse, fickle, floor, flummox, gravel, metagrobolise, mystify, nonplus, perplex, pother, pudder, stump, worry.

*n* acrostic, anagram, brain-teaser, confusion, conundrum, crossword, difficulty, dilemma, enigma, jigsaw, knot, koan, logogram, logograph, logogriph, maze, mind-bender, mystery, paradox, poser, problem, quandary, question, rebus, riddle, Sphinx, tickler.

**puzzle²** *v* brood, cogitate, consider, deliberate, figure, meditate, mull over, muse, ponder, rack one's brains, ratiocinate, reason, ruminate, study, think, wonder, worry.

**puzzle out** clear up, crack, decipher, decode, excogitate, figure out, metagrobolise, reason out, resolve, see, solve, sort out, think out, unravel, unriddle, untangle, work out.

**puzzled** *adj* at a loss, at sea, baffled, bamboozled, beaten, bemused, bewildered, confounded, confused, disorientated, doubtful, flummoxed, in a haze, lost, mixed up, mizzled, mystified, nonplussed, perplexed, stuck, stumped, stymied, uncertain.

*antonyms* certain, clear.

**puzzlement** *n* astonishment, bafflement, bamboozlement, bewilderment, confusion, disorientation, doubt, doubtfulness, incertitude, mystification, perplexity, surprise, uncertainty, wonder.

*antonyms* certainty, clarity, lucidity.

**puzzling** *adj* abstruse, ambiguous, baffling, bewildering, bizarre, cabalistic, circuitous, confusing, cryptic, curious, enigmatic, equivocal, impenetrable, inexplicable, intricate, involved, knotty, labyrinthine, mind-bending, mind-boggling, misleading, mysterious, mystical, mystifying, peculiar, perplexing, queer, riddling, Sphinx-like, strange, tangled, tortuous, unaccountable, unclear, unfathomable.

**pygmy** *n* dwarf, fingerling, half-pint, homunculus, hop-o'-my-thumb, Lilliputian, manikin, midget, runt, shrimp, thumbling, Tom Thumb.

*antonym* giant.

*adj* baby, diminutive, dwarf, dwarfish, elfin, half-pint, Lilliputian, midget, miniature, minuscule, minute, pint-sized, pocket, pygmaean, small, stunted, tiny, toy, undersized, wee.

*antonym* gigantic.

**pyromaniac** *n* arsonist, firebug, fire-raiser, incendiary, pétroleur, pétroleuse.

# Q

**quack** *n* charlatan, cowboy, empiric, fake, fraud, humbug, impostor, masquerader, medicaster, mountebank, phoney, pretender, pseud, quacksalver, sham, spieler, swindler, trickster, witch-doctor.

*adj* bogus, counterfeit, fake, false, fraudulent, phoney, pretended, sham, so-called, spurious, supposed, unqualified.

*antonym* genuine.

**quackery** *n* charlatanism, charlatanry, empiricism, fraud, fraudulence, humbug, imposture, mountebankery, mountebankism, phoniness, sham.

**quaff** *v* booze, carouse, down, drain, drink, gulp, guzzle, imbibe, knock back, swallow, swig, swill, tipple, tope, toss off.

*n* bevvy, cup, dram, draught, drink, jorum, slug, snifter, swig.

**quagmire** *n* bog, everglade, fen, marsh, mire, morass, moss, mudflat, quag, quicksand, slough, swamp.

**quail** *v* back away, blanch, blench, cower, droop, faint, falter, flinch, quake, recoil, shake, shrink, shudder, shy away, tremble, wince.

**quaint** *adj* absurd, antiquated, antique, bizarre, charming, curious, droll, eccentric, fanciful, fantastic, freaky, funky, Heath-Robinson, ingenious, odd, old-fashioned, old-time, old-world, peculiar, picturesque, queer, rum, singular, strange, unconventional, unusual, weird, whimsical.

**quake** *v* convulse, heave, jolt, move, pulsate, quail, quiver, rock, shake, shiver, shudder, sway, throb, totter, tremble, vibrate, waver, wobble.

**qualification**[1] *n* ability, accomplishment, adequacy, aptitude, attribute, capability, capacity, certification, competence, eligibility, fitness, skill, suitability, suitableness, training.

**qualification**[2] *n* adaptation, adjustment, allowance, caveat, condition, criterion, exception, exemption, limitation, modification, objection, provision, proviso, reservation, restriction, stipulation.

**qualified**[1] *adj* able, accomplished, adept, adequate, capable, certificated, certified, competent, efficient, eligible, equipped, experienced, expert, fit, habilitated, knowledgeable, licensed, practised, proficient, skilful, talented, trained.

*antonym* unqualified.

**qualified**[2] *adj* bounded, cautious, circumscribed, conditional, confined, contingent, equivocal, guarded, limitative, limited, modificatory, modified, provisional, qualificatory, reserved, restricted.

**qualify**[1] *v* authorise, capacitate, certificate, empower, endow, equip, fit, graduate, habilitate, permit, prepare, sanction, shape, train.

*antonym* unfit.

**qualify**[2] *v* abate, adapt, adjust, alleviate, assuage, categorise, characterise, circumscribe, classify, define, delimit, describe, designate, diminish, distinguish, ease, lessen, limit, mitigate, moderate, modify, modulate, reduce, regulate, restrain, restrict, soften, temper, vary, weaken.

**quality** *n* aspect, attribute, calibre, character, characteristic, class, complexion, condition, constitution, deal, description, distinction, essence, excellence, feature, fineness, grade, kidney, kind, make, mark, merit, nature, peculiarity, position, pre-eminence, property, rank, refinement, sort, standing, status, superiority, talent, timbre, tone, trait, value, water, worth.

**qualm** *n* anxiety, apprehension, compunction, disquiet, doubt, fear, hesitation, misgiving, pang, presentiment, regret, reluctance, remorse, scruple, twinge, uncertainty, unease, uneasiness, worry.

**quandary** *n* bewilderment, confusion, corner, difficulty, dilemma, doubt, embarrassment, entanglement, fix, hole, imbroglio, impasse, jam, kettle of fish, mess, perplexity, plight, predicament, problem, puzzle, uncertainty.

**quantity** *n* aggregate, allotment, amount, breadth, bulk, capacity, content, dosage, expanse, extent, greatness, length, lot, magnitude, mass, measure, number, part, portion, proportion, quantum, quota, share, size, spread, strength, sum, total, volume, weight.

**quarantine** *n* detention, isolation, lazaret, lazaretto, segregation.

**quarrel** *n* affray, altercation, argument, barney, beef, bicker, brattle, brawl, breach, breeze, broil, clash, commotion, conflict, contention, controversy, coolness, debate, difference, disagreement, discord, disputation, dispute, dissension, dissidence, disturbance, dust-up, estrangement, feud, fight, fracas, fratch, fray, misunderstanding, row, rupture, schism, scrap, shouting match, slanging match, spat, split, squabble, strife, tiff, tumult, vendetta, wrangle.

*antonyms* agreement, harmony.

QR

*v* altercate, argue, be at loggerheads, be at variance, bicker, brawl, carp, cavil, clash, contend, differ, disagree, dispute, dissent, fall out, fight, find fault, object, pick holes, question, row, spar, spat, squabble, take exception, tiff, vitilitigate, wrangle.

*antonym* agree.

**quarrelling** *n* altercation, argumentation, argy-bargying, bickering, contention, discord, disharmony, disputation, dissension, feuding, rowing, strife, variance, vitilitigation, wrangling.

*antonyms* concord, harmony.

*adj* at loggerheads, at odds, at variance, bickering, contending, discordant, dissentient, feuding, fighting, rowing, scrapping, squabbling, waring, wrangling.

*antonyms* amicable, friendly.

**quarrelsome** *adj* altercative, antagonistic, argumentative, bellicose, belligerent, cantankerous, captious, choleric, combative, contentious, contrary, cross, disputatious, fractious, ill-tempered, irascible, irritable, peevish, perverse, petulant, pugnacious, querulous, stroppy, testy, truculent, turbulent, wranglesome.

*antonyms* peaceable, placid.

**quarry** *n* game, goal, kill, object, objective, prey, prize, target, victim.

**quarter**[1] *n* area, direction, district, division, locality, location, neighbourhood, part, place, point, position, province, quartier, region, section, sector, side, spot, station, territory, vicinity, zone.

**quarter**[2] *n* clemency, compassion, favour, forgiveness, grace, indulgence, leniency, mercy, pardon, pity.

**quarter**[3] *n* fardel, forpit, fourth, quartern, term.

*v* decussate, divide in four, quadrisect.

**quarter**[4] *v* accommodate, bed, billet, board, house, install, lodge, place, post, put up, shelter, station.

**quarters** *n* abode, accommodation, apartment, barracks, billet, cantonment, caserne, chambers, digs, domicile, dwelling, habitation, lodging, lodgings, post, quarterage, residence, rooms, station.

**quash** *v* annul, cancel, crush, declare null and void, defeat, disannul, disenact, invalidate, nullify, overrule, overthrow, quell, repress, rescind, reverse, revoke, set aside, squash, subdue, suppress, void.

*antonyms* confirm, justify, reinstate, vindicate.

**quaver** *v* break, crack, flicker, flutter, oscillate, pulsate, quake, quiver, shake, shudder, tremble, trill, twitter, vibrate, warble.

*n* break, quaveriness, quiver, shake, sob, throb, tremble, trembling, tremolo, tremor, trill, vibration, vibrato, warble.

**quay** *n* dock, harbour, jetty, levee, pier, wharf.

**queasy** *adj* bilious, dizzy, faint, giddy, green, groggy, ill, indisposed, nauseated, off-colour, qualmish, qualmy, queer, sick, sickened, squeamish, unwell.

**queen** *n* beauty, belle, consort, diva, doyenne, empress, goddess, grande dame, idol, maharani, mistress, monarch, nonpareil, prima donna, princess, rani, ruler, sovereign, star, sultana, tsarina, Venus.

**queenly** *adj* dignified, gracious, grand, imperial, imperious, majestic, noble, regal, royal, sovereign, stately.

*antonym* undignified.

**queer** *adj* aberrant, abnormal, absurd, anomalous, atypical, bizarre, cranky, crazy, curious, daft, demented, deranged, deviant, disquieting, dizzy, doubtful, droll, dubious, eccentric, eerie, eldritch, erratic, exceptional, extraordinary, faint, fanciful, fantastic, fey, fishy, freakish, funny, giddy, grotesque, homosexual, idiosyncratic, ill, irrational, irregular, light-headed, mad, mysterious, odd, offbeat, outlandish, outré, peculiar, preternatural, puzzling, quaint, queasy, questionable, reeling, remarkable, rum, screwy, shady, shifty, singular, strange, suspect, suspicious, touched, unaccountable, unbalanced, uncanny, uncommon, unconventional, uneasy, unhinged, unnatural, unorthodox, unusual, unwell, unwonted, weird.

*antonyms* common, ordinary, straightforward, unexceptional, usual.

*v* botch, cheat, endanger, foil, frustrate, harm, impair, imperil, injure, jeopardise, mar, ruin, spoil, stymie, thwart, upset, wreck.

**queerness** *n* aberrance, abnormality, absurdity, anomalousness, atypicalness, bizarreness, crankiness, craziness, curiousness, deviance, drollness, dubiety, dubiousness, eccentricity, eeriness, fishiness, grotesqueness, idiosyncrasy, individuality, irrationality, irregularity, light-headedness, madness, mysteriousness, mystery, oddity, oddness, outlandishness, peculiarity, puzzle, quaintness, shadiness, shiftiness, singularity, strangeness, suspiciousness, uncanniness, uncommonness, unconventionality, unnaturalness, unorthodoxy, unusualness, unwontedness.

**quell** *v* allay, alleviate, appease, assuage, blunt, calm, compose, conquer, crush, deaden, defeat, dull, extinguish, hush, mitigate, moderate, mollify, overcome, overpower, pacify, put down, quash, quench, quiet, reduce, silence, soothe, squash, stifle, subdue, subjugate, suppress, vanquish.

**quench** *v* allay, appease, check, cool, crush, damp down, destroy, douse, end, extinguish, overcome, put out, quash, quell, sate, satisfy, silence, slake, smother, snuff out, stifle, suppress.

**querulous** *adj* cantankerous, captious, carping, cavilling, censorious, complaining, crabbed, critical, cross, cross-grained, crusty, discontented, dissatisfied, exacting, fault-finding, fretful, fussy, grouchy, grumbling, hypercritical, intolerant, irascible, irritable, peevish, perverse, petulant, plaintive, quarrelsome, querimonious, sour, testy, thrawn, waspish, whingeing, whining.

*antonyms* contented, equable, placid, uncomplaining.

**querulousness** *n* cantankerousness, captiousness, censoriousness, crabbedness, criticalness, crossness, crustiness, discontent, discontentedness, dissatisfaction, fault-finding, fretfulness, fussiness, grouchiness, intolerance, irrascibility, irritability, peevishness, perversity, petulance, querimony, sourness, testiness, waspishness.

*antonyms* contentedness, equableness, placidity.

**query** *v* ask, be sceptical of, call in question, challenge, disbelieve, dispute, distrust, doubt, enquire, misdoubt, mistrust, quarrel with, question, suspect.

*antonym* accept.

*n* demand, doubt, hesitation, inquiry, misdoubt, misgiving, objection, problem, quaere, question, quibble, reservation, scepticism, suspicion, uncertainty.

**quest** *n* adventure, crusade, enterprise, expedition, exploration, hunt, inquiry, investigation, journey, mission, pilgrimage, pursuit, search, undertaking, venture, voyage.

**question** *v* ask, be sceptical of, catechise, challenge, controvert, cross-examine, debrief, disbelieve, dispute, distrust, doubt, enquire, examine, grill, impugn, interpellate, interrogate, interview, investigate, misdoubt, mistrust, oppose, probe, pump, quarrel with, query, quiz, suspect.

*n* argument, confusion, contention, controversy, debate, difficulty, dispute, doubt, dubiety, erotema, erotesis, examination, inquiry, interpellation, interrogation, investigation, issue, misdoubt, misgiving, motion, point, problem, proposal, proposition, quaere, query, quibble, scepsis, subject, theme, topic, uncertainty.

**questionable** *adj* arguable, borderline, controversial, debatable, disputable, doubtful, dubious, dubitable, equivocal, fishy, iffy, impugnable, moot, problematical, queer, shady, suspect, suspicious, uncertain, undetermined, unproven, unreliable, unsettled, vexed.

*antonyms* certain, indisputable, straightforward.

**questioner** *n* agnostic, catechiser, catechist, disbeliever, doubter, examiner, inquirer, inquisitor, interlocutor, interrogator, interviewer, investigator, sceptic.

**questionnaire** *n* answer-sheet, catechism, form, questionary, quiz, test.

**queue** *n* file, line, line-up, order, procession, sequence, series, string, succession, tail, tail-back, train.

**quibble** *v* carp, cavil, chop logic, equivocate, pettifog, prevaricate, shift, split hairs.

*n* carriwitchet, casuistry, cavil, complaint, criticism, equivocation, equivoke, evasion, niggle, objection, pettifoggery, prevarication, query, quiddit, quiddity, quillet, quip, quirk, sophism, subterfuge.

**quibbler** *n* casuist, caviller, chop-logic, criticaster, equivocator, hair-splitter, logic-chopper, niggler, nit-picker, pettifogger, sophist.

**quibbling** *adj* ambiguous, captious, carping, casuistic, cavilling, critical, equivocating, evasive, hair-splitting, logic-chopping, niggling, nit-picking, overnice, pettifogging, quidditative, sophistical.

**quick** *adj* able, active, acute, adept, adroit, agile, alert, animated, apt, astute, awake, brief, bright, brisk, clever, cursory, deft, dexterous, discerning, energetic, expeditious, express, fast, fleet, flying, hasty, headlong, hurried, immediate, instant, instantaneous, intelligent, keen, lively, nifty, nimble, nippy, penetrating, perceptive, perfunctory, precipitate, prompt, quick-witted, rapid, ready, receptive, responsive, sharp, shrewd, skilful, smart, snappy, speedy, spirited, sprightly, spry, sudden, summary, swift, unhesitating, vivacious, wide-awake, winged.

*antonyms* dull, slow.

**quicken** *v* accelerate, activate, advance, animate, arouse, dispatch, energise, enliven, excite, expedite, galvanise, hasten, hurry, impel, incite, inspire, invigorate, kindle, precipitate, reactivate, refresh, reinvigorate, resuscitate, revitalise, revive, revivify, rouse, sharpen, speed, stimulate, strengthen, vitalise, vivify.

*antonyms* dull, retard.

**quickly** *adv* abruptly, at a rate of knots, at the double, before you can say Jack Robinson, briskly, by leaps and bounds, cursorily, ek dum, expeditiously, express, fast, hastily, hell for leather, hotfoot, hurriedly, immediately, instantaneously, instantly, lickety-split, like a bat out of hell, perfunctorily, posthaste, promptly, pronto, quick, rapidly, readily, soon, speedily, swiftly, unhesitatingly.

*antonyms* slowly, tardily, thoroughly.

**quickness** *n* acuteness, agility, alertness, aptness, astuteness, briskness, deftness, dexterity, expedition, hastiness, immediacy, instantaneousness, intelligence, keenness, liveliness, nimbleness, penetration, precipitation, promptitude, promptness, quick-wittedness, rapidity, readiness, receptiveness, sharpness, shrewdness, speed, speediness, suddenness, summariness, swiftness, turn of speed.

*antonyms* dullness, slowness, tardiness.

**quick-tempered** *adj* choleric, excitable, explosive, fiery, hot-tempered, impatient, impulsive, irascible, irritable, petulant, quarrelsome, shrewish, snappy, splenetic, temperamental, testy, touchy, volcanic, waspish.

*antonyms* cool, dispassionate.

**quick-witted** *adj* acute, alert, astute, bright, clever, crafty, ingenious, intelligent, keen, nimble-witted, penetrating, perceptive, ready-witted, resourceful, sharp, shrewd, smart, wide-awake, witty.

*antonyms* dull, slow, stupid.

**quiescent** *adj* asleep, calm, dormant, in abeyance, inactive, inert, latent, motionless, passive, peaceful, placid, quiet, reposeful, resting, serene, silent, sleeping, smooth, still, tranquil, undisturbed, untroubled.

*antonym* active.

**quiet** *adj* calm, composed, conservative, contemplative, contented, docile, dumb, even-tempered, gentle, hushed, inaudible, isolated, lonely, low, low-pitched, meek, mild, modest, motionless, noiseless, pacific, passive, peaceable, peaceful, placid, plain, private, removed, reserved, restful, restrained, retired, retiring, secluded, secret, sedate, self-contained, sequestered, serene, shtoom, shy, silent, simple, smooth, sober, soft, soundless, still, stilly, subdued, taciturn, thoughtful, tranquil, uncommunicative, unconversable, undisturbed, uneventful, unexcitable, unexciting, unforthcoming, unfrequented, uninterrupted, unobtrusive, untroubled.

*antonyms* busy, noisy, obtrusive.

*n* calm, calmness, ease, hush, lull, peace, quiescence, quietness, quietude, repose, rest, serenity, silence, stillness, tranquillity.

*antonyms* bustle, disturbance, noise.

**quieten** *v* abate, allay, alleviate, appease, assuage, blunt, calm, compose, deaden, diminish, dull, hush, lull, mitigate, mollify, muffle, mute, pacify, palliate, quell, quiet, reduce, silence, smooth, sober, soothe, stifle, still, stop, subdue, tranquillise.

*antonyms* aggravate, discompose, disturb, exacerbate.

**quietly** *adv* calmly, composedly, confidentially, contentedly, demurely, diffidently, dispassionately, docilely, gently, humbly, inaudibly, meekly, mildly, modestly, mutely, noiselessly, obediently, patiently, peacefully, placidly, privately, secretly, serenely, silently, softly, soundlessly, surreptitiously, tranquilly, undemonstratively, unobtrusively, unostentatiously, unpretentiously.

*antonyms* noisily, obtrusively.

**quietness** *n* calm, calmness, composure, dullness, hush, inactivity, inertia, lull, peace, placidity, quiescence, quiet, quietude, repose, serenity, silence, still, stillness, tranquillity, uneventfulness.

*antonyms* activity, bustle, commotion, disturbance, noise, racket.

**quietus** *n* acquittance, coup de grâce, death, death-blow, death-stroke, decease, demise, discharge, dispatch, end, extinction, finishing stroke, quittance, silencing.

**quilt** *n* bed quilt, bedcover, bedspread, comforter, counterpane, coverlet, Downie®, duvet, eiderdown, Federbett.

**quintessence** *n* core, distillation, embodiment, essence, exemplar, extract, gist, heart, kernel, marrow, pattern, pith, quiddity, soul, spirit, sum and substance.

**quintessential** *adj* archetypical, complete, consummate, definitive, entire, essential, ideal, perfect, prototypical, ultimate.

**quip** *n* bon mot, carriwitchet, crack, epigram, gag, gibe, jest, jeu d'esprit, joke, mot, one-liner, pleasantry, quirk, retort, riposte, sally, wisecrack, witticism.

*v* gag, gibe, jest, joke, quirk, retort, riposte, wisecrack.

**quirk** *n* aberration, caprice, characteristic, curiosity, eccentricity, fancy, fetish, foible, freak, habit, idiosyncrasy, kink, mannerism, oddity, oddness, peculiarity, singularity, trait, turn, twist, vagary, warp, whim.

**quisling** *n* betrayer, collaborationist, collaborator, fifth columnist, Judas, puppet, renegade, traitor, turncoat.

**quit** *v* abandon, abdicate, apostatise, cease, conclude, decamp, depart, desert, disappear, discontinue, drop, end, exit, forsake, give up, go, halt, leave, relinquish, renege, renounce, repudiate, resign, retire, stop, surrender, suspend, vamoose, vanish, withdraw.

**quit of** clear of, discharged from, done with, finished with, free of, released from, rid of.

**quite** *adv* absolutely, comparatively, completely, entirely, exactly, fairly, fully, moderately, perfectly, precisely, rather, relatively, somewhat, totally, utterly, wholly.

**quits** *adj* equal, even, level, square.

**quitter** *n* apostate, defector, delinquent, deserter, rat, recreant, renegade, shirker, skiver.

**quiver** *v* agitate, bicker, convulse, flichter, flicker, flutter, oscillate, palpitate, pulsate, quake, quaver, shake, shiver, shudder, tremble, vibrate, wobble.

*n* convulsion, flicker, flutter, oscillation, palpitation, pulsation, shake, shiver, shudder, spasm, throb, tic, tremble, tremor, vibration, wobble.

**quixotic** *adj* chivalrous, extravagant, fanciful, fantastical, idealistic, impetuous, impracticable, impulsive, romantic, starry-eyed, unrealistic, unworldly, Utopian, visionary.

*antonyms* hard-headed, practical, realistic.

**quiz** *n* catechism, examination, investigation, questioning, questionnaire, test.

*v* ask, catechise, cross-examine, cross-question, debrief, examine, grill, interrogate, investigate, pump, question.

**quizzical** *adj* amused, arch, bantering, curious, humorous, inquiring, mocking, questioning, sardonic, satirical, sceptical, teasing, waggish, whimsical.

**quizzicality** *n* archness, humorousness, humour, mockery, satiricalness, scepticism, teasing, waggishness, whimsicality.

**quota** *n* allocation, allowance, assignment, cut, part, percentage, portion, proportion, quotum, ration, share, slice, whack.

**quotation**[1] *n* citation, crib, cutting, excerpt, extract, gobbet, locus classicus, passage, piece, quote, reference, remnant.

**quotation**[2] *n* charge, cost, estimate, figure, price, quote, rate, tender.

**quote** *v* adduce, attest, cite, detail, echo, Hansardise, instance, name, parrot, recall, recite, recollect, refer to, repeat, reproduce, retell.

**quoted** *adj* above-mentioned, cited, fore-cited, forementioned, instanced, referred to, reported, reproduced, stated.

**quotidian** *adj* common, commonplace, customary, daily, day-to-day, diurnal, everyday, habitual, normal, ordinary, recurrent, regular, repeated, routine, workaday.

# R

**rabbit** *n* bunny, bunny rabbit, cony, cottontail, daman, dassie, hyrax.

**rabble** *n* canaille, clamjamphrie, colluvies, commonalty, commoners, crowd, doggery, dregs, faex populi, galère, herd, hoi polloi, horde, masses, mob, peasantry, plebs, populace, proles, proletariat, raffle, raggle-taggle, rag-tag (and bobtail), rascality, riffraff, scum, swarm, tagrag, throng, trash.

*antonyms* aristocracy, elite, nobility.

**rabble-rouser** *n* agitator, demagogue, firebrand, fomenter, incendiary, mischief-maker, mob-orator, ringleader, troublemaker, tub-thumper.

**Rabelaisian** *adj* barrack-room, bawdy, blue, broad, coarse, earthy, extravagant, exuberant, gross, indecent, lewd, lusty, racy, ribald, risqué, robust, salacious, satirical, scabrous, uninhibited, unrestrained, vulgar.

**rabid** *adj* berserk, bigoted, crazed, extreme, fanatical, fervent, frantic, frenzied, furious, hydrophobic, hysterical, infuriated, intemperate, intolerant, irrational, mad, maniacal, narrow-minded, obsessive, overzealous, raging, unreasoning, violent, wild, zealous.

**rabies** *n* hydrophobia, rabidity, rabidness.

**race¹** *n* chase, competition, contention, contest, corso, dash, derby, foot-race, kermesse, marathon, pursuit, quest, rat race, regatta, rivalry, scramble, sprint, steeplechase.

*v* career, compete, contest, dart, dash, fly, gallop, hare, hasten, hurry, run, rush, speed, sprint, tear, zoom.

**race²** *n* ancestry, blood, breed, clan, descent, family, folk, house, issue, kin, kindred, line, lineage, nation, offspring, people, progeny, seed, stirps, stock, strain, tribe, type.

**race-course** *n* circuit, circus, course, dromos, flaptrack, hippodrome, race-track, route, speedway, track, turf.

**racial** *adj* ancestral, avital, ethnic, ethnological, folk, genealogical, genetic, inherited, national, tribal.

**raciness** *n* animation, bawdiness, boisterousness, breeziness, buoyancy, doubtfulness, dubiousness, dynamism, ebullience, energy, exhilaration, freshness, gaminess, indecency, indelicacy, jauntiness, lewdness, naughtiness, piquancy, pungency, relish, ribaldry, richness, salaciousness, sharpness, smuttiness, spiciness,

suggestiveness, tanginess, tastiness, zest, zestfulness.

**rack¹** *n* frame, framework, gantry, gondola, hack, shelf, stand, structure.

**rack²** *n* affliction, agony, anguish, distress, misery, pain, pangs, persecution, suffering, torment, torture.

*v* afflict, agonise, convulse, crucify, distress, excruciate, harass, harrow, lacerate, oppress, pain, shake, strain, stress, stretch, tear, torment, torture, wrench, wrest, wring.

**racket¹** *n* babel, ballyhoo, clamour, clangour, commotion, din, disturbance, fuss, hubbub, hullabaloo, hurly-burly, kerfuffle, noise, outcry, pandemonium, row, shouting, tumult, uproar.

**racket²** *n* business, con, deception, dodge, fiddle, fraud, game, scheme, swindle, trick.

**racy** *adj* animated, bawdy, blue, boisterous, breezy, broad, buoyant, distinctive, doubtful, dubious, dynamic, ebullient, energetic, entertaining, enthusiastic, exciting, exhilarating, gamy, heady, immodest, indecent, indelicate, jaunty, lewd, lively, naughty, piquant, pungent, Rabelaisian, ribald, rich, risqué, salacious, sharp, smutty, sparkling, spicy, spirited, stimulating, strong, suggestive, tangy, tasty, vigorous, zestful.

*antonyms* dull, ponderous.

**radiance** *n* brightness, brilliance, delight, effulgence, gaiety, glare, gleam, glitter, glow, happiness, incandescence, joy, lambency, light, luminosity, lustre, pleasure, rapture, refulgence, resplendence, shine, splendour, warmth.

**radiant** *adj* aglow, alight, beaming, beamish, beamy, beatific, blissful, bright, brilliant, delighted, ecstatic, effulgent, gleaming, glittering, glorious, glowing, happy, illuminated, incandescent, joyful, joyous, lambent, luminous, lustrous, profulgent, rapturous, refulgent, resplendent, shining, sparkling, splendid, sunny.

*antonym* dull.

**radiate** *v* branch, diffuse, disseminate, divaricate, diverge, emanate, emit, eradiate, gleam, glitter, issue, pour, scatter, shed, shine, spread, spread out.

**radiation** *n* emanation, emission, insolation, rays.

**radical** *adj* basic, complete, comprehensive, constitutional, deep-seated, entire, essential, excessive, extreme, extremist, fanatical, far-reaching, fundamental, inherent, innate, intrinsic, native, natural, organic, primary, profound, revolutionary, rooted, severe, sweeping, thorough, thoroughgoing, total, violent.

*antonym* superficial.

*n* extremist, fanatic, jacobin, left-winger, militant, reformer, reformist, revolutionary.

**raffish** *adj* bohemian, careless, casual, cheap, coarse, dashing, devil-may-care, disreputable, dissipated, dissolute, flamboyant, flashy, garish, gaudy, gross, improper, jaunty, loud, meretricious, rakish, showy, sporty, tasteless, tawdry, trashy, uncouth, vulgar.

*antonyms* decorous, proper, sedate, staid.

**raffle** *n* draw, lottery, sweep, sweepstake, tombola.

**rag** *v* badger, bait, bullyrag, chaff, chiack, haze, jeer, mock, rib, ridicule, taunt, tease, torment, twit.

**ragamuffin** *n* dandiprat, gamin, guttersnipe, mudlark, scarecrow, street arab, tatterdemalion, urchin, waif.

**ragbag** *n* assemblage, confusion, hotchpotch, jumble, medley, miscellany, mixture, olio, olla podrida, omnium-gatherum, pastiche, pot-pourri, salad.

**rage** *n* agitation, anger, bate, chafe, conniption, craze, dernier cri, enthusiasm, fad, fashion, frenzy, fury, ire, madness, mania, obsession, paddy, passion, style, tantrum, vehemence, violence, vogue, wrath.

*v* chafe, explode, fret, fulminate, fume, inveigh, ramp, rampage, rant, rave, seethe, storm, surge, thunder.

**ragged** *adj* broken, deckled, desultory, disorganised, down-at-heel, duddie, erratic, fragmented, frayed, irregular, jagged, moth-eaten, notched, patchy, raguly, rent, ripped, rough, rugged, scraggy, serrated, shabby, shaggy, tattered, tattery, tatty, threadbare, torn, uneven, unfinished, unkempt, worn-out.

**raging** *adj* enraged, fizzing, frenzied, fulminating, fuming, furibund, furious, incensed, infuriated, irate, ireful, mad, rabid, rampageous, raving, seething, wrathful.

**rags** *n* clouts, duddery, duds, raggedness, remnants, shreds, tats, tatters.

**raid** *n* attack, break-in, bust, descent, foray, incursion, inroad, invasion, irruption, onset, onslaught, razzia, sally, seizure, sortie, strike, swoop.

*v* attack, bust, descend on, do, forage, foray, invade, loot, maraud, pillage, plunder, ransack, reive, rifle, rush, sack.

**raider** *n* attacker, brigand, cateran, depredator, despoiler, forager, freebooter, invader, looter, marauder, pirate, plunderer, ransacker, reiver, robber, rustler, sacker, thief.

**rail** *v* abuse, arraign, attack, castigate, censure, criticise, decry, denounce, fulminate, inveigh, jeer, mock, revile, ridicule, scoff, upbraid, vituperate, vociferate.

**railing** *n* balustrade, barrier, fence, paling, parapet, rail, rails.

**raillery** *n* badinage, banter, chaff, chiacking, diatribe, dicacity, invective, irony, jeering, jesting, joke, joking, kidding, mockery, persiflage, pleasantry, ragging, repartee, ribbing, ridicule, satire, sport, teasing.

**railway** *n* line, metro, permanent way, railroad, rails, subway, track, tramway, tube, underground.

**rain** *n* cloudburst, deluge, downpour, drizzle, fall, flood, hail, mizzle, precipitation, raindrops, rainfall, rains, serein, shower, spate, squall, stream, torrent, volley.

*v* bestow, bucket, deluge, deposit, drizzle, drop, expend, fall, heap, lavish, mizzle, pour, shower, spit, sprinkle, teem.

**rainbow** *n* arc, iris, prism, spectrum.

*adj* iridescent, irisated, irised, kaleidoscopic, nacreous, opalescent, prismatic, rainbow-like, shot, spectral, variegated.

*antonym* monochrome.

**rainy** *adj* damp, dripping, drizzly, hyetal, mizzly, pluviose, pluvious, showery, wet.

*antonym* dry.

**raise** *v* abandon, activate, advance, aggrade, aggrandise, aggravate, amplify, arouse, assemble, augment, awaken, boost, breed, broach, build, cause, collect, construct, create, cultivate, develop, discontinue, elate, elevate, emboss, embourgeoise, end, engender, enhance, enlarge, erect, escalate, evoke, exaggerate, exalt, excite, foment, form, foster, gather, gentrify, get, grow, heave, heighten, hoist, incite, increase, inflate, instigate, intensify, introduce, kindle, levy, lift, loft, magnify, mass, mobilise, moot, motivate, muster, nurture, obtain, occasion, originate, pose, prefer, produce, promote, propagate, provoke, rally, rear, recruit, reinforce, relinquish, remove, sky, start, strengthen, sublime, suggest, terminate, up, upgrade, uplift.

*antonyms* debase, decrease, degrade, dismiss, lower, reduce, suppress.

**raised** *adj* applied, appliqué, cameo, embossed, relief, rilievo.

*antonyms* engraved, incised, intaglio.

**raising** *n* abandonment, advancement, aggradation, ascension, assumption, breeding, construction, development, elation, elevation, enhancement, erection, exaltation, fostering, increase, intensification, levitation, lifting, mobilisation, nurture, preferment, promotion, rearing, recruitment, rise, rising, upgrading, upping.

**rake¹** *v* accumulate, amass, bombard, collect, comb, drag, enfilade, examine, gather, graze, harrow, haul in, hoe, hunt, make, pepper, ransack, remove, scan, scour, scrape, scratch, scrutinise, search, strafe, sweep.

**rake²** *n* blood, debauchee, degenerate, dissolute, hedonist, lecher, libertine, loose-liver, playboy, pleasure-seeker, prodigal, profligate, rakehell, roué, sensualist, spendthrift, swinger, voluptuary.

*antonyms* ascetic, puritan.

**rakish** *adj* abandoned, breezy, dapper, dashing, debauched, debonair, degenerate, depraved, devil-may-care, dissipated, dissolute, flamboyant, flashy, immoral, jaunty, lecherous, libertine, licentious, loose, natty, prodigal, profligate, raffish, sharp, sinful, smart, snazzy, sporty, stylish, wanton.

**rally**[1] *v* assemble, bunch, cheer, cluster, collect, congregate, convene, embolden, encourage, gather, hearten, improve, marshal, mass, mobilise, muster, organise, pick up, rally round, reassemble, recover, recuperate, reform, regroup, reorganise, revive, round up, summon, unite.

*n* assembly, comeback, concourse, conference, congregation, convention, convocation, gathering, improvement, jamboree, meeting, recovery, recuperation, regrouping, renewal, reorganisation, resurgence, reunion, revival, stand.

**rally**[2] *v* chaff, mock, rag, rib, ridicule, send up, taunt, tease, twit.

**ram** *v* beat, butt, cram, crash, crowd, dash, drive, drum, force, hammer, hit, impact, jam, pack, pound, pun, slam, smash, strike, stuff, tamp, thrust.

**ramble** *v* amble, babble, chatter, digress, divagate, dodder, drift, expatiate, maunder, meander, perambulate, peregrinate, range, roam, rove, saunter, snake, straggle, stravaig, stray, stroll, traipse, walk, wander, wind, zigzag.

*n* divagation, excursion, hike, perambulation, peregrination, roaming, roving, saunter, stroll, tour, traipse, trip, walk.

**rambler** *n* drifter, globe-trotter, hiker, peregrinator, roamer, rover, stroller, walker, wanderer, wayfarer.

**rambling** *adj* circuitous, desultory, diffuse, digressive, disconnected, discursive, disjointed, excursive, incoherent, irregular, long-drawn-out, long-winded, periphrastic, prolix, sprawling, spreading, straggling, trailing, wordy.

*antonym* direct.

**ramification** *n* branch, complication, consequence, development, dichotomy, divarication, division, excrescence, extension, fork, offshoot, outgrowth, ramulus, ramus, result, sequel, subdivision, upshot.

**ramp** *n* grade, gradient, incline, rise, slope.

**rampage** *v* rage, rant, rave, run amuck, run riot, run wild, rush, storm, tear.

*n* destruction, frenzy, furore, fury, rage, storm, tempest, tumult, uproar, violence.

**rampant** *adj* aggressive, dominant, epidemic, erect, excessive, exuberant, fierce, flagrant, luxuriant, outrageous, prevalent, prodigal, profuse, raging, rampaging, rank, rearing, rife, riotous, standing, unbridled, unchecked, uncontrollable, uncontrolled, ungovernable, unrestrained, upright, vehement, violent, wanton, widespread, wild.

**rampart** *n* barricade, bastion, breastwork, bulwark, defence, earthwork, embankment, fence, fort, fortification, guard, parapet, security, stronghold, vallum, wall.

**ramshackle** *adj* broken-down, crumbling, decrepit, derelict, dilapidated, flimsy, haywire, jerry-built, rickety, shaky, tottering, tumbledown, unsafe, unsteady.

*antonyms* solid, stable.

**ranch** *n* estancia, estate, farm, hacienda, plantation, station.

**rancid** *adj* bad, fetid, foul, frowsty, fusty, musty, off, putrid, rank, reasty, rotten, sour, stale, strong-smelling, tainted.

*antonym* sweet.

**rancorous** *adj* acrimonious, bitter, hostile, implacable, malevolent, malignant, resentful, spiteful, splenetic, vengeful, venomous, vindictive, virulent.

**rancour** *n* acrimony, animosity, animus, antipathy, bitterness, enmity, grudge, hate, hatred, hostility, ill-feeling, ill-will, malevolence, malice, malignity, resentfulness, resentment, spite, spleen, venom, vindictiveness.

**random** *adj* accidental, adventitious, aimless, arbitrary, casual, chance, desultory, fortuitous, haphazard, incidental, indiscriminate, purposeless, scattershot, spot, stray, unfocused, unplanned, unpremeditated.

*antonyms* deliberate, systematic.

**randy** *adj* amorous, aroused, concupiscent, goatish, horny, hot, lascivious, lecherous, lustful, raunchy, satyric, sexy, turned-on.

**range** *n* amplitude, area, assortment, band, bounds, chain, class, collection, compass, confines, diapason, distance, domain, extent, field, file, gamme, gamut, kind, latitude, limits, line, lot, orbit, order, palette, parameters, province, purview, radius, raik, rank, reach, row, scale, scope, selection, sequence, series, sort, span, spectrum, sphere, string, sweep, tessitura, tier, variety.

*v* aim, align, arrange, array, bracket, catalogue, categorise, class, classify, cruise, direct, dispose, explore, extend, file, fluctuate, go, grade, group, level, order, pigeonhole, point, raik, ramble, rank, reach, roam, rove, run, straggle, stravaig, stray, stretch, stroll, sweep, train, traverse, wander.

**rangy** *adj* gangling, lanky, leggy, long-legged, rawboned, skinny, weedy.

*antonyms* compact, dumpy.

**rank**[1] *n* caste, class, classification, column, condition, degree, dignity, division, echelon, estate, état, file, formation, grade, group, level, line, nobility, order, position, quality, range, row, series, sort, standing, station, status, stratum, tier, type.

*v* align, arrange, array, class, classify, dispose, grade, locate, marshal, order, organise, place, position, range, sort.

**rank**[2] *adj* absolute, abundant, abusive, arrant, atrocious, bad, blatant, coarse, complete, crass, dense, disagreeable, disgusting, downright, egregious, excessive, extravagant, exuberant, fetid, filthy, flagrant, flourishing, foul, fusty, gamy, glaring, gross, indecent, lush, luxuriant, mephitic, musty, nasty, noisome, noxious, obscene, off, offensive, out-and-out, outrageous, productive, profuse, pungent, putrid, rampant, rancid, repulsive, revolting, scurrilous, sheer, shocking, stale, stinking, strong-smelling, thorough, thoroughgoing, total, undisguised, unmitigated, utter, vigorous, vulgar.

*antonyms* sparse, sweet.

**rankle** *v* anger, annoy, chafe, embitter, fester, gall, irk, irritate, nettle, peeve, rile.

**ransack** *v* comb, depredate, despoil, explore, gut, loot, maraud, pillage, plunder, raid, rake, ravage, rifle, rummage, sack, scour, search, strip.

**ransom** *n* deliverance, liberation, money, payment, pay-off, price, redemption, release, rescue.

*v* buy out, deliver, extricate, liberate, redeem, release, rescue.

**rant** *v* bellow, bluster, cry, declaim, mouth it, rave, roar, shout, slang-whang, spout, tub-thump, vociferate, yell.

*n* bluster, bombast, declamation, diatribe, fanfaronade, harangue, philippic, rhetoric, storm, tirade, tub-thumping, vociferation.

**rap** *v* bark, castigate, censure, chat, confabulate, converse, crack, criticise, discourse, flirt, hit, knock, pan, reprimand, scold, strike, talk, tap.

*n* blame, blow, castigation, censure, chat, chiding, clout, colloquy, confabulation, conversation, crack, dialogue, discourse, discussion, knock, punishment, rebuke, reprimand, responsibility, sentence, talk, tap.

**rapacious** *adj* avaricious, esurient, extortionate, grasping, greedy, insatiable, marauding, plundering, predatory, preying, ravening, ravenous, usurious, voracious, vulturine, vulturish, vulturous, wolfish, wolvish.

**rapacity** *n* avarice, avidity, cupidity, esurience, esuriency, graspingness, greed, greediness, insatiableness, predatoriness, rapaciousness, ravenousness, shark's manners, usury, voraciousness, voracity, wolfishness.

**rape** *n* abuse, defilement, deflowering, depredation, desecration, despoilment, despoliation, maltreatment, outrage, perversion, pillage, plundering, rapine, ravaging, ravishment, sack, spoliation, violation.

*v* assault, despoil, loot, pillage, plunder, ransack, ravish, sack, spoliate, stuprate, violate.

**rapid** *adj* brisk, expeditious, express, fast, fleet, flying, hasty, headlong, hurried, precipitate, prompt, quick, speedy, swift, tantivy.

*antonyms* leisurely, slow, sluggish.

**rapidity** *n* alacrity, briskness, celerity, dispatch, expedition, expeditiousness, fleetness, haste, hurry, precipitateness, promptitude, promptness, quickness, rush, speed, speediness, swiftness, velocity.

*antonym* slowness.

**rapidly** *adv* briskly, expeditiously, fast, hastily, hurriedly, lickety-split, precipitately, promptly, quickly, speedily, swiftly.

*antonym* slowly.

**rapids** *n* dalles, white water, wild water.

**rapine** *n* depredation, despoilment, despoliation, looting, marauding, pillage, plunder, ransacking, rape, ravaging, robbery, sack, sacking, seizure, spoliation, theft.

**rapport** *n* affinity, bond, compatibility, empathy, harmony, link, relationship, sympathy, understanding.

**rapprochement** *n* agreement, détente, harmonisation, reconcilement, reconciliation, reunion, softening.

**rapscallion** *n* blackguard, cad, cur, disgrace, good-for-nothing, knave, ne'er-do-well, rascal, reprobate, rogue, scallywag, scamp, scoundrel, wastrel, wretch.

**rapt** *adj* absorbed, beatific, bewitched, captivated, charmed, delighted, ecstatic, enchanted, engrossed, enraptured, enthralled, entranced, fascinated, gripped, held, intent, preoccupied, rapturous, ravished, spellbound, transported.

**rapture** *n* beatitude, bliss, delectation, delight, ecstasy, enthusiasm, entrancement, euphoria, exaltation, felicity, happiness, joy, ravishment, rhapsody, spell, transport.

**rapturous** *adj* blissful, delighted, ecstatic, enthusiastic, entranced, euphoric, exalted, happy, joyful, joyous, overjoyed, ravished, rhapsodic, transported.

**rare** *adj* admirable, choice, curious, excellent, exceptional, exquisite, extreme, few, fine, great, incomparable, infrequent, invaluable, peerless, precious, priceless, recherché, rich, scarce, singular, sparse, sporadic, strange, superb, superlative, uncommon, unusual.

*antonyms* abundant, common, usual.

**rarefied** *adj* clannish, cliquish, elevated, esoteric, exalted, exclusive, high, lofty, noble, occult, private, refined, select, spiritual, sublime.

**rarely** *adv* atypically, exceptionally, extraordinarily, finely, hardly, infrequently, little, notably, remarkably, seldom, singularly, uncommonly, unusually.

*antonyms* frequently, often.

**raring** *adj* agog, athirst, avid, desperate, eager, enthusiastic, impatient, itching, keen, longing, ready, willing, yearning.

**rarity** *n* choiceness, curio, curiosity, excellence, exquisiteness, find, fineness, gem, incomparability, incomparableness, infrequency, object of virtu, one-off, pearl, peerlessness, preciousness, pricelessness, quality, richness, scarcity, shortage, singularity, sparseness, strangeness, treasure, uncommonness, unusualness, value, worth.

*antonyms* commonness, commonplace.

**rascal** *n* blackguard, caitiff, cullion, devil, disgrace, good-for-nothing, hellion, hempy, imp, knave, loon, lorel, losel, miscreant, ne'er-do-well, rake, ra(p)scallion, reprobate, rogue, scallywag, scamp, scoundrel, skeesicks, spalpeen, toe-rag, toe-ragger, varmint, villain, wastrel, wretch.

**rascally** *adj* bad, base, crooked, dishonest, disreputable, evil, furciferous, good-for-nothing, knavish, low, mean, reprobate, scoundrelly, unscrupulous, vicious, villainous, wicked.

**rash**[1] *adj* adventurous, audacious, brash, careless, foolhardy, harebrained, harum-scarum, hasty, headlong, headstrong, heedless, helter-skelter, hot-headed, ill-advised, ill-considered, impetuous, imprudent, impulsive, incautious, indiscreet, injudicious, insipient, madcap, precipitant, precipitate, premature, reckless, slap-dash, temerarious, temerous, thoughtless, unguarded, unthinking, unwary, venturesome.

*antonyms* calculating, careful, considered, wary.

**rash**[2] *n* epidemic, eruption, exanthem(a), flood, hives, nettlerash, outbreak, plague, pompholyx, series, spate, succession, urticaria, wave.

**rashness** *n* adventurousness, audacity, brashness, carelessness, foolhardiness, hastiness, heedlessness, incaution, incautiousness, indiscretion, precipitance, precipitation, precipitency, recklessness, temerity, thoughtlessness.

*antonyms* carefulness, cautiousness.

**rasp** *n* croak, grating, grinding, harshness, hoarseness, scrape, scratch.

*v* abrade, croak, excoriate, file, grate, grind, irk, irritate, jar, rub, sand, scour, scrape.

**rasping** *adj* creaking, croaking, croaky, grating, gravelly, gruff, harsh, hoarse, husky, jarring, raspy, raucous, rough, scratchy, stridulant.

**rat** *n* cad, ratfink, renegade, swine, turncoat.

**rate**[1] *n* basis, charge, class, classification, cost, degree, dues, duty, fee, figure, gait, grade, hire, measure, pace, percentage, position, price, proportion, quality, rank, rating, ratio, reckoning, relation, scale, speed, standard, status, tariff, tax, tempo, time, toll, value, velocity, worth.

*v* adjudge, admire, appraise, assess, class, classify, consider, count, deserve, esteem, estimate, evaluate, figure, grade, judge, measure, measure up, merit, perform, rank, reckon, regard, respect, value, weigh.

**rate**[2] *v* admonish, berate, blame, castigate, censure, chide, criticise, lecture, rebuke, reprimand, reprove, roast, scold, tongue-lash, upbraid.

**rather** *adv* a bit, fairly, instead, kinda, kind of, moderately, noticeably, preferably, pretty, quite, relatively, significantly, slightly, somewhat, sooner, sort of, very.

**ratify** *v* affirm, approve, authenticate, authorise, bind, certify, confirm, corroborate, endorse, establish, homologate, legalise, recognise, sanction, sign, uphold, validate.

*antonyms* reject, repudiate.

**rating**[1] *n* class, classification, degree, designation, estimate, evaluation, grade, grading, order, placing, position, rank, rate, sort, sorting, standing, status.

**rating**[2] *n* castigation, chiding, dressing-down, lecture, rebuke, reprimand, reproof, roasting, row, scolding, telling-off, ticking-off, tongue-lashing, upbraiding, wigging.

**ratio** *n* arrangement, balance, correlation, correspondence, equation, fraction, percentage, proportion, quotient, rate, relation, relationship.

**ration** *n* allocation, allotment, allowance, amount, dole, helping, measure, part, portion, provision, quota, share.

*v* allocate, allot, apportion, budget, conserve, control, deal, dispense, distribute, dole, issue, limit, mete, restrict, save, supply.

**rational** *adj* balanced, cerebral, cognitive, compos mentis, dianoetic, enlightened, intelligent, judicious, logical, lucid, normal, ratiocinative, realistic, reasonable, reasoning, sagacious, sane, sensible, sound, thinking, well-founded, well-grounded, wise.

*antonyms* crazy, illogical, irrational.

**rationale** *n* excuse, exposition, grounds, logic, motivation, philosophy, pretext, principle, raison d'être, reasons, theory.

**rationalise** *v* elucidate, excuse, extenuate, justify, reason out, reorganise, resolve, streamline, trim, vindicate.

**rations** *n* commons, étape, food, prog, provender, provisions, stores, supplies.

**rattle** *v* bang, bounce, bump, clank, clatter, clitter, crepitate, discomfit, discompose, disconcert, discountenance, disturb, faze, frighten, jangle, jiggle, jolt, jounce, perturb, scare, shake, upset, vibrate.

**rattle off** anote, enumerate, itemise, list, recite, reel off, rehearse, repeat, run through.

**rattle on** blether, cackle, chatter, gab, gabble, gibber, jabber, prate, prattle, rabbit on, witter, ya(c)k.

**ratty** *adj* angry, annoyed, crabbed, cross, impatient, irritable, peeved, short, short-tempered, snappy, testy, touchy.

*antonyms* calm, patient.

**raucous** *adj* grating, harsh, hoarse, husky, loud, noisy, rasping, rough, rusty, strident.

**ravage** *v* demolish, depredate, desolate, despoil, destroy, devastate, gut, lay waste, loot, pillage, plunder, ransack, raze, ruin, sack, shatter, spoil, wreck.

*n* damage, defilement, demolition, depredation, desecration, desolation, destruction, devastation, havoc, pillage, plunder, rapine, ruin, ruination, spoliation, waste, wreckage.

**ravaged** *adj* battle-torn, desolate, destroyed, devastated, ransacked, shattered, spoilt, war-torn, war-wasted, war-worn, wrecked.

*antonym* unspoilt.

**rave** *v* babble, declaim, fulminate, fume, harangue, rage, ramble, rant, roar, splutter, storm, thunder.

*adj* ecstatic, enthusiastic, excellent, fantastic, favourable, laudatory, wonderful.

**ravenous** *adj* avaricious, covetous, devouring, esurient, famished, ferocious, gluttonous, grasping, greedy, insatiable, insatiate, predatory, rapacious, ravening, starved, starving, voracious, wolfish, wolvish.

**rave-up** *n* bash, blow-out, carousal, celebration, debauch, do, orgy, party, shindig, thrash, wing-ding.

**ravine** *n* arroyo, canyon, chine, clough, defile, flume, gap, gorge, grike, gulch, gully, khor, khud, kloof, linn, lin(n), pass.

**raving** *adj* berserk, bonkers, crazed, crazy, delirious, frantic, frenzied, furious, hysterical, insane, irrational, mad, manic, rabid, raging, wild.

**ravish** *v* abuse, captivate, charm, deflorate, deflower, delight, enchant, enrapture, entrance, fascinate, outrage, overjoy, rape, spellbind, transport, violate.

**ravishing** *adj* alluring, beautiful, bewitching, charming, dazzling, delightful, enchanting, entrancing, gorgeous, lovely, radiant, seductive, stunning.

**raw** *adj* abraded, bare, basic, biting, bitter, bleak, bloody, blunt, brutal, callow, candid, chafed, chill, chilly, coarse, cold, crude, damp, frank, freezing, fresh, grazed, green, harsh, ignorant, immature, inexperienced, naked, natural, new, open, organic, piercing, plain, realistic, rough, scraped, scratched, sensitive, skinned, sore, tender, unadorned, uncooked, undisciplined, undisguised, undressed, unfinished, unpleasant, unpractised, unprepared, unprocessed, unrefined, unripe, unseasoned, unskilled, untrained, untreated, untried, unvarnished, verdant, wet.

*antonyms* cooked, experienced, refined.

**ray** *n* bar, beam, flash, flicker, gleam, glimmer, glint, hint, indication, scintilla, shaft, spark, stream, trace.

**raze** *v* bulldoze, delete, demolish, destroy, dismantle, efface, erase, expunge, extinguish, extirpate, flatten, level, obliterate, remove, ruin.

**re** *prep* about, anent, apropos, concerning, regarding, respecting, touching, with reference to, with regard to.

**reach** *v* amount to, arrive at, attain, contact, drop, fall, get to, grasp, hand, land at, make, move, pass, rise, sink, stretch, strike, touch.

*n* ambit, capacity, command, compass, distance, extension, extent, grasp, influence, jurisdiction, latitude, mastery, power, purview, range, scope, spread, stretch, sweep.

**react** *v* acknowledge, act, answer, behave, emote, function, operate, proceed, reply, respond, work.

**reaction** *n* acknowledgement, answer, antiperistasis, backwash, compensation, conservatism, counteraction, counterbalance, counterbuff, counterpoise, counter-revolution, feedback, obscurantism, recoil, reply, response, swing-back.

**reactionary** *adj* blimpish, conservative, counter-revolutionary, obscurantist, obstructive, reactionist, rightist.

*antonyms* progressive, radical, revolutionary.

*n* Colonel Blimp, conservative, counter-revolutionary, die-hard, obscurantist, obstructionist, reactionist, rightist, right-winger.

*antonyms* progressive, radical, revolutionary.

**read** *v* announce, comprehend, con, construe, decipher, declaim, deliver, discover, display, indicate, interpret, peruse, pore over, recite, record, refer to, register, scan, see, show, speak, study, understand, utter.

**readable** *adj* clear, compelling, comprehensible, compulsive, decipherable, enjoyable, entertaining, enthralling, gripping, intelligible, interesting, legible, plain, pleasant, understandable, unputdownable.

*antonyms* illegible, unreadable.

**readily** *adv* cheerfully, eagerly, easily, effortlessly, fain, freely, gladly, lief, promptly, quickly, smoothly, speedily, unhesitatingly, voluntarily, willingly.

**readiness** *n* adroitness, alacrity, aptitude, aptness, dexterity, eagerness, ease, facility, fitness, gameness, handiness, inclination, keenness, maturity, preparation, preparedness, promptitude, promptness, quickness, rapidity, ripeness, skill, willingness.

**reading** *n* book-learning, conception, construction, edification, education, emendation, erudition, examination, grasp, homily, impression, inspection, interpretation, knowledge, learning, lecture, lesson, performance, pericope, perusal, recital, rendering, rendition, review, scholarship, scrutiny, sermon, study, treatment, understanding, version.

**ready** *adj* à la main, about, accessible, acute, ad manum, adroit, agreeable, alert, apt, arranged, astute, available, bright, clever, close, completed, convenient, deft, dexterous, disposed, eager, expert, facile, fit, game, glad, handy, happy, inclined, intelligent, keen, liable, likely, minded, near, on call, on tap, organised, overflowing, perceptive, predisposed, prepared, present, primed, prompt, prone, quick, quick-witted, rapid, resourceful, ripe, set, sharp, skilful, smart, willing.

*antonyms* unprepared, unready.

*v* alert, arrange, equip, order, organise, prepare, prime, set.

**real** *adj* absolute, actual, authentic, bona fide, certain, dinkum, dinky-di(e), essential, existent, factual, genuine, heartfelt, honest, intrinsic, legitimate, positive, right, rightful, simon-pure, sincere, substantial, substantive, sure-enough, tangible, thingy, true, unaffected, unfeigned, valid, veritable.

*antonyms* imaginary, unreal.

**realisation** *n* accomplishment, achievement, actualisation, appreciation, apprehension, awareness, cognisance, completion, comprehension, conception, concretisation, consciousness, consummation, effectuation, fulfilment, grasp, imagination, perception, recognition, understanding.

**realise** *v* accomplish, achieve, acquire, actualise, appreciate, apprehend, catch on, clear, complete, comprehend, conceive, concretise, consummate, do, earn, effect, effectuate, fulfil, gain, get, grasp, imagine, implement, make, net, obtain, perform, produce, recognise, reify, take in, twig, understand.

**realism** *n* actuality, practicality, pragmatism, rationality, saneness, sanity, sensibleness.

**realistic** *adj* authentic, businesslike, clear-eyed, clear-sighted, common-sense, detached, down-to-earth, faithful, genuine, graphic, hard-headed, level-headed, lifelike, matter-of-fact, natural, naturalistic, objective, practical, pragmatic, rational, real, real-life, representational, sensible, sober, true, truthful, unromantic, unsentimental.

*antonyms* fanciful, impractical, irrational, unrealistic.

**reality** *n* actuality, authenticity, certainty, corporeality, fact, factuality, genuineness, materiality, nitty-gritty, palpability, realism, tangibility, truth, validity, verisimilitude, verity.

**really** *adv* absolutely, actually, assuredly, categorically, certainly, essentially, genuinely, indeed, intrinsically, positively, surely, truly, undoubtedly, verily.

**realm** *n* area, bailiwick, branch, country, department, domain, dominion, empire, field, jurisdiction, kingdom, land, monarchy, orbit, principality, province, region, sphere, state, territory, world, zone.

**reap** *v* acquire, collect, crop, cut, derive, gain, garner, gather, get, harvest, mow, obtain, realise, secure, win.

**rear**[1] *n* back, backside, bottom, buttocks, croup, end, hindquarters, posterior, rearguard, rump, stern, tail.

*antonym* front.

*adj* aft, after, back, following, hind, hindmost, last.

*antonym* front.

**rear**[2] *v* breed, build, construct, cultivate, educate, elevate, erect, fabricate, foster, grow, hoist, lift, loom, nurse, nurture, parent, raise, rise, soar, tower, train.

**rearrange** *v* adjust, alter, rejig, rejigger, reorder, reposition, shift, vary.

**reason** *n* aim, apologia, apology, apprehension, argument, basis, bounds, brains, case, cause, common sense, comprehension, consideration, defence, design, end, excuse, explanation, exposition, goal, ground, grounds, gumption, impetus, incentive, inducement, intellect, intention, judgement, justification, limits, logic, mentality, mind, moderation, motive, nous, object, occasion, propriety, purpose, ratiocination, rationale, rationality, reasonableness, reasoning, sanity, sense, sensibleness, soundness, target, understanding, vindication, warrant, wisdom.

*v* conclude, deduce, infer, intellectualise, ratiocinate, resolve, solve, syllogise, think, work out.

**reason with** argue, debate, dispute, dissuade, expostulate, make representations, move, persuade, protest, remonstrate, talk, urge.

**reasonable** *adj* acceptable, advisable, arguable, average, believable, credible, equitable, fair, fit, honest, inexpensive, intelligent, judicious, just, justifiable, logical, moderate, modest, OK, passable, plausible, possible, practical, proper, rational, reasoned, right, sane, satisfactory, sensible, sober, sound, tenable, tolerable, viable, well-advised, well-thought-out, wise.

*antonyms* crazy, extravagant, irrational, outrageous, unreasonable.

**reasoned** *adj* clear, judicious, logical, methodical, rational, sensible, sound, systematic, well-thought-out.

*antonyms* illogical, unsystematic.

**reasoning** *n* analysis, argument, case, cogitation, deduction, explication, exposition, hypothesis, interpretation, logic, proof, ratiocination, reason, supposition, thinking, thought.

**reassure** *v* bolster, brace, comfort, encourage, hearten, inspirit, nerve, rally.

**rebate** *n* allowance, bonus, deduction, discount, reduction, refund, repayment.

**rebel** *v* defy, disobey, dissent, flinch, kick over the traces, mutiny, recoil, resist, revolt, rise up, run riot, shrink.

*n* apostate, dissenter, heretic, insurgent, insurrectionary, Jacobin, malcontent, mutineer, nonconformist, revolutionary, revolutionist, schismatic, secessionist.

*adj* insubordinate, insurgent, insurrectionary, malcontent(ed), mutinous, rebellious, revolutionary.

**rebellion** *n* apostasy, defiance, disobedience, dissent, heresy, inqilab, insubordination, insurgence, insurgency, insurrection, intifada, Jacquerie, mutiny, nonconformity, resistance, revolt, revolution, rising, schism, sedition, uprising.

**rebellious** *adj* contumacious, defiant, difficult, disaffected, disloyal, disobedient, disorderly, incorrigible, insubordinate, insurgent, insurrectionary, intractable, malcontent(ed), mutinous, obstinate, rebel, recalcitrant, refractory, resistant, revolutionary, seditious, turbulent, ungovernable, unmanageable, unruly.

*antonyms* obedient, submissive.

**rebirth** *n* reactivation, reanimation, regeneration, reincarnation, rejuvenation, renaissance, renascence, renewal, restoration, resurgence, resurrection, revitalisation, revival.

**rebound** *v* backfire, boomerang, bounce, misfire, recoil, redound, resile, resound, return, ricochet.

*n* back-wash, bounce, reflection, repercussion, return, reverberation, ricochet.

**rebuff** *v* cold-shoulder, cut, decline, deny, discourage, put someone's nose out of joint, refuse, reject, repulse, resist, slight, snub, spurn, turn down.

*n* brush-off, check, cold shoulder, defeat, denial, discouragement, flea in one's ear, noser, opposition, refusal, rejection, repulse, rubber, set-down, slight, snub.

**rebuild** *v* haussmannise, reassemble, reconstruct, re-edify, refashion, remake, remodel, renovate, restore.

*antonyms* demolish, destroy.

**rebuke** *v* admonish, berate, blame, carpet, castigate, censure, chide, countercheck, jobe, keelhaul, lecture, lesson, rate, reprehend, reprimand, reproach, reprove, scold, slap down, tell off, tick off, trim, trounce, upbraid.

*antonyms* compliment, praise.

*n* admonition, blame, castigation, censure, countercheck, dressing-down, lecture, reprimand, reproach, reproof, reproval, row, slap, telling-off, ticking-off, tongue-lashing, wigging.

*antonyms* compliment, praise.

**rebut** *v* confute, defeat, discredit, disprove, explode, give the lie to, invalidate, negate, overturn, quash, refute.

**rebuttal** *n* confutation, defeat, disproof, invalidation, negation, overthrow, refutation.

**recalcitrant** *adj* contrary, contumacious, defiant, disobedient, insubordinate, intractable, obstinate, refractory, renitent, stubborn, uncontrollable, unco-operative, ungovernable, unmanageable, unruly, unsubmissive, unwilling, wayward, wilful.

*antonym* amenable.

**recall** *v* abjure, annul, cancel, cast one's mind back, countermand, evoke, mind, nullify, place, recognise, recollect, remember, repeal, rescind, retract, revoke, withdraw.

*n* abrogation, annulment, cancellation, memory, nullification, recision, recollection, remembrance, repeal, rescission, retraction, revocation, withdrawal.

**recant** *v* abjure, abrogate, apostatise, deny, disavow, disclaim, disown, forswear, recall, renounce, repudiate, rescind, retract, revoke, unsay, withdraw.

**recantation** *n* abjuration, apostasy, denial, disavowal, disclaimer, disownment, renunciation, repudiation, retractation, retraction, revocation, revoke, withdrawal.

**recapitulate** *v* give a resumé, recap, recount, reiterate, repeat, restate, review, sum up, summarise.

**recede** *v* abate, decline, decrease, diminish, dwindle, ebb, fade, lessen, regress, retire, retreat, retrogress, return, shrink, sink, slacken, subside, wane, withdraw.

*antonyms* advance, proceed.

**receipt** *n* acceptance, acknowledgement, counterfoil, delivery, receiving, reception, recipience, slip, stub, ticket, voucher.

**receipts** *n* gains, gate, income, proceeds, profits, return, take, takings.

**receive** *v* accept, accommodate, acquire, admit, apprehend, bear, collect, derive, encounter, entertain, experience, gather, get, greet, hear, meet, obtain, perceive, pick up, react to, respond to, suffer, sustain, take, undergo, welcome.

*antonyms* donate, give.

**receiver** *n* beneficiary, donee, Fagin, fence, handset, radio, recipient, tuner, wireless.

*antonym* donor.

**recent** *adj* contemporary, current, fresh, late, latter, latter-day, modern, neoteric(al), new, novel, present-day, up-to-date, young.

*antonyms* dated, old, out-of-date.

**recently** *adv* currently, freshly, lately, latterly, newly.

**receptacle** *n* container, holder, pantechnicon, repository, reservatory, vessel.

**reception** *n* acceptance, acknowledgement, admission, do, durbar, entertainment, function, greeting, levee, party, reaction, receipt, receiving, recipience, recognition, response, shindig, soirée, treatment, welcome.

**receptive** *adj* accessible, alert, amenable, approachable, bright, favourable, friendly, hospitable, interested, open, open-minded, perceptive, responsive, sensitive, suggestible, susceptible, sympathetic, welcoming.

**recess** *n* alcove, apse, apsidiole, bay, break, cavity, cessation, closure, corner, depression, embrasure, holiday, hollow, indentation, intermission, interval, loculus, niche, nook, oriel, respite, rest, vacation.

**recesses** *n* bowels, depths, heart, innards, interior, penetralia, reaches, retreats.

**recession** *n* decline, depression, downturn, slump, stagflation.

*antonyms* boom, upturn.

**recherché** *adj* abstruse, arcane, choice, esoteric, exotic, far-fetched, rare, refined, select.

*antonym* commonplace.

**recipe** *n* directions, formula, ingredients, instructions, method, prescription, procedure, process, programme, receipt, system, technique.

**recipient** *n* assignee, beneficiary, donee, grantee, legatee, receiver, suscipient.

*antonyms* donor, giver.

**reciprocal** *adj* alternate, complementary, correlative, corresponding, equivalent, give-and-take, interchangeable, interdependent, mutual, reciprocative, reciprocatory, shared.

**reciprocate** *v* alternate, barter, correspond, equal, exchange, interchange, match, reply, requite, respond, return, swap, trade.

**recital** *n* account, convert, description, detailing, enumeration, interpretation, narration, narrative, performance, reading, recapitulation, recitation, rehearsal, relation, rendering, rendition, repetition, statement, story, tale, telling.

**recitation** *n* lecture, narration, party piece, passage, performance, piece, reading, recital, rendering, rendition, telling.

**recite** *v* articulate, declaim, deliver, describe, detail, enumerate, itemise, narrate, orate, perform, recapitulate, recount, rehearse, relate, repeat, speak, tell.

**reckless** *adj* careless, daredevil, devil-may-care, foolhardy, harebrained, hasty, headlong, heedless, ill-advised, imprudent, inattentive, incautious, indiscreet, irresponsible, madcap, mindless, negligent, precipitate, rantipole, rash, regardless, tearaway, thoughtless, wild.

*antonyms* calculating, careful, cautious.

**recklessness** *n* carelessness, foolhardiness, gallowsness, heedlessness, imprudence, inattention, incaution, irresponsibleness, irresposibility, madness, mindlessness, motorway madness, negligence, rashness, thoughtlessness.

*antonym* carefulness.

**reckon** *v* account, add up, adjudge, appraise, assess, assume, believe, calculate, compute, conjecture, consider, count, deem, enumerate, esteem, estimate, evaluate, expect, fancy, gauge, guess, hold, imagine, judge, number, opine, rate, regard, suppose, surmise, tally, think, total.

**reckon on** bank, calculate, count, depend, figure on, hope for, rely, trust in.

**reckon with** anticipate, bargain for, consider, cope with, deal with, expect, face, foresee, handle, plan for, take into account, treat.

**reckoning** *n* account, adding, addition, bill, calculation, charge, computation, count, counting, doom, due, enumeration, estimate, judgement, retribution, score, settlement, summation, working.

**reclaim** *v* impolder, recapture, recover, redeem, reform, regain, regenerate, reinstate, rescue, restore, retrieve, salvage.

**recline** *v* couch, lean, lie, loll, lounge, repose, rest, sprawl, stretch out.

**recluse** *n* anchoress, anchoret, anchorite, ancress, ascetic, eremite, hermit, monk, solitaire, solitarian, solitary, stylite.

**reclusive** *adj* anchoretic(al), anchoritic(al), ascetic, cloistered, eremitic, hermitical, isolated, monastic, recluse, retiring, secluded, sequestered, solitary, withdrawn.

**recognise** *v* accept, acknowledge, admit, allow, appreciate, approve, avow, concede, confess, grant, greet, honour, identify, know, notice, own, perceive, place, realise, recall, recollect, remember, respect, salute, see, spot, understand, wot.

**recognition** *n* acceptance, acknowledgement, admission, allowance, appreciation, approval, avowal, awareness, cognisance, confession, detection, discovery, enlightenment, gratitude, greeting, honour, identification, notice, perception, realisation, recall, recollection, remembrance, respect, salute, understanding.

**recoil** *v* backfire, boomerang, falter, flinch, kick, misfire, quail, react, rebound, redound, resile, shrink.

*n* backlash, kick, reaction, rebound, redound(ing), repercussion.

**recollect** *v* call up, cast one's mind back, mind, place, recall, remember, reminisce.

**recollection** *n* image, impression, memory, recall, remembrance, reminiscence, souvenir.

**recommend** *v* advance, advise, advocate, approve, commend, counsel, endorse, enjoin, exhort, plug, praise, propose, puff, suggest, urge, vouch for.

*antonyms* disapprove, veto.

**recommendation** *n* advice, advocacy, approbation, approval, blessing, commendation, counsel, endorsement, plug, praise, proposal, puff, reference, sanction, suggestion, testimonial, urging.

*antonyms* disapproval, veto.

**recompense** *v* compensate, guerdon, indemnify, pay, redress, reimburse, remunerate, repay, requite, reward, satisfy.

*n* amends, compensation, damages, emolument, guerdon, indemnification, indemnity, pay, payment, remuneration, reparation, repayment, requital, restitution, return, reward, satisfaction, wages.

**reconcile** *v* accept, accommodate, accord, adjust, appease, compose, conciliate, harmonise, pacify, placate, propitiate, rectify, resign, resolve, reunite, settle, square, submit, yield.

*antonym* estrange.

**reconciliation** *n* accommodation, adjustment, agreement, appeasement, bridge-building, compromise, conciliation, détente, harmony, pacification, propitiation, rapprochement, reconcilement, rectification, reunion, settlement, understanding.

*antonyms* estrangement, separation.

**recondite** *adj* abstruse, arcane, cabbalistic, complicated, concealed, dark, deep, difficult, esoteric, hidden, intricate, involved, mysterious, mystical, obscure, occult, profound, secret.

*antonyms* simple, straightforward.

**recondition** *v* fix, overhaul, refurbish, remodel, renew, renovate, repair, restore, revamp, sort.

**reconnaissance** *n* examination, exploration, inspection, investigation, observation, patrol, probe, recce, reconnoitring, scan, scouting, scrutiny, survey.

**reconnoitre** *v* case, examine, explore, inspect, investigate, observe, patrol, probe, recce, scan, scout, scrutinise, spy out, survey.

**reconsider** *v* modify, reassess, re-examine, rethink, review, revise, think better of, think over, think twice.

**reconstruct** *v* reassemble, rebuild, recreate, re-establish, refashion, reform, reformulate, regenerate, remake, remodel, renovate, reorganise, restore.

**record** *n* account, album, annals, archives, background, career, chronicle, curriculum vitae, diary, disc, document, documentation, dossier, entry, EP, evidence, file, form, forty-five, gramophone record, history, journal, log, LP, memoir, memorandum, memorial, minute, noctuary, performance, platter, recording, register, release, remembrance, report, single, talky, testimony, trace, tracing, track record, witness.

*v* annalise, chalk up, chronicle, contain, cut, diarise, document, enregister, enrol, enter, indicate, inscribe, log, minute, note, preserve, read, register, report, say, score, show, tape, tape-record, transcribe, video, video-tape, wax.

**recorder** *n* annalist, archivist, chronicler, chronographer, chronologer, clerk, diarist, historian, registrar, score-keeper, scorer, scribe, stenographer.

**recording** *n* cut, disc, gramophone record, performance, record, recordation, release, tape, video.

**recount** *v* communicate, delineate, depict, describe, detail, enumerate, narrate, portray, recite, rehearse, relate, repeat, report, tell.

**recoup** v compensate, indemnify, make good, recover, redeem, refund, regain, reimburse, remunerate, repay, requite, retrieve, satisfy.

**recourse** n access, alternative, appeal, choice, expedient, option, refuge, remedy, resort.

**recover** v convalesce, heal, improve, mend, pick up, pull through, rally, recapture, reclaim, recoup, recuperate, redeem, regain, repair, replevy, repossess, restore, retake, retrieve, revive.

*antonyms* forfeit, lose, worsen.

**recovery** n amelioration, betterment, convalescence, healing, improvement, mending, rally, recapture, reclamation, recoupment, recuperation, redemption, rehabilitation, repair, repossession, restoration, retrieval, revival, upturn.

*antonyms* forfeit, loss, worsening.

**recreation** n amusement, distraction, diversion, enjoyment, entertainment, exercise, fun, games, hobby, leisure activity, pastime, play, pleasure, refreshment, relaxation, relief, sport.

**recrimination** n accusation, bickering, counter-attack, counterblast, countercharge, name-calling, quarrel, retaliation, retort, squabbling.

**recruit** v augment, draft, engage, enlist, enrol, gather, headhunt, impress, levy, mobilise, muster, obtain, procure, proselytise, raise, refresh, reinforce, renew, replenish, restore, strengthen, supply, trawl.

n apprentice, beginner, conscript, convert, draftee, greenhorn, helper, initiate, learner, neophyte, nig-nog, novice, proselyte, rookie, trainee, tyro, yob.

**rectify** v adjust, amend, correct, distil, emend, fix, improve, mend, purify, redress, refine, reform, remedy, repair, right, separate, square, straighten.

**rectitude** n accuracy, correctness, decency, equity, exactness, goodness, honesty, honour, incorruptibility, integrity, irreproachability, justice, morality, precision, principle, probity, righteousness, rightness, scrupulousness, sinlessness, soundness, unimpeachability, uprightness, verity, virtue.

**recumbent** adj flat, horizontal, leaning, lounging, lying, prone, prostrate, reclining, resting, sprawling, supine.

*antonyms* erect, upright.

**recuperate** v convalesce, get better, improve, mend, pick up, rally, recoup, recover, regain, revive.

*antonym* worsen.

**recur** v persist, reappear, repeat, return.

**recurrent** adj continued, cyclical, frequent, habitual, haunting, periodic, recurring, regular, repeated, repetitive.

**recycle** v reclaim, reconstitute, reprocess, reuse, salvage, save.

**red** adj bay, bloodshot, bloodstained, bloody, blooming, blushing, cardinal, carmine, carroty, cherry, chestnut, coral, crimson, damask, embarrassed, ensanguined, flame-coloured, flaming, florid, flushed, foxy, glowing, gory, gules, healthy, horseflesh, incarnadine, inflamed, Judas-coloured, lateritious, maroon, pink, reddish, rose, roseate, rosy, rubicund, rubied, rubineous, rubious, ruby, ruby-red, ruddy, sandy, sanguine, scarlet, shamefaced, suffused, titian, vermeil, vermilion, wine.

**red-blooded** adj hearty, lively, lusty, manly, robust, strong, vigorous, virile, vital.

**redden** v blush, colour, crimson, flush, rubefy, suffuse.

**reddish** adj bloodshot, ginger, pink, rosy, rubicund, ruddy, rufescent, rufous, russet, sandy.

**redeem** v absolve, acquit, atone for, cash (in), change, compensate for, defray, deliver, discharge, emancipate, exchange, extricate, free, fulfil, keep, liberate, make good, make up for, meet, offset, outweigh, perform, ransom, reclaim, recoup, recover, recuperate, redress, regain, rehabilitate, reinstate, repossess, repurchase, rescue, retrieve, salvage, satisfy, save, trade in.

**redemption** n amends, atonement, compensation, deliverance, discharge, emancipation, exchange, expiation, fulfilment, liberation, performance, ransom, reclamation, recovery, rehabilitation, reinstatement, release, reparation, repossession, repurchase, rescue, retrieval, salvation, trade-in.

**redolent** adj aromatic, evocative, fragrant, odorous, perfumed, remindful, reminiscent, scented, suggestive, sweet-smelling.

**redoubtable** adj courageous, doughty, dreadful, fearful, fearsome, formidable, heroic, mighty, powerful, resolute, strong, terrible, valiant.

**redound** v accrue, conduce, contribute, effect, ensue, rebound, recoil, reflect, resile, result, tend.

**redress** v adjust, amend, balance, correct, ease, expiate, mend, recompense, rectify, reform, regulate, relieve, remedy, repair, square.

n aid, amends, assistance, atonement, compensation, correction, cure, ease, expiation, help, indemnification, justice, payment, quittance, recompense, rectification, relief, remedy, reparation, requital, restitution, satisfaction.

*antonyms* boost, fatten, increase.

**reduce** v abate, abridge, bankrupt, break, cheapen, conquer, contract, curtail, cut, debase, decimate, decrease, degrade, demote, deoxidate, deoxidise, depress, diet, dilute, diminish, discount, downgrade, drive, force, humble, humiliate, impair, impoverish, lessen, lower, master, moderate, overpower, pauperise, rebate, ruin, scant, shorten, slake, slash, slenderise, slim, subdue, trim, truncate, vanquish, weaken.

*antonyms* boost, fatten, increase, upgrade.

**reduction** n abbreviation, abridgement, abstraction, alleviation, attenuation, compression, condensation, constriction, contraction, curtailment, cut, cutback, decline, decrease, deduction, degradation, demotion, deoxidation, deoxidisation, deposal, depreciation, devaluation, diminution, discount, drop, easing, ellipsis, limitation, loss, miniature, mitigation, moderation, modification, muffling, muting, narrowing, rebate, rebatement, refund, restriction, shortening, shrinkage, slackening, softening, subtraction, summarisation, summary, syncope.

*antonyms* enlargement, improvement, increase.

**redundancy** *n* battology, excess, pleonasm, prolixity, repetition, superfluity, surplus, tautology, uselessness, verbosity, wordiness.

**redundant** *adj* de trop, diffuse, excessive, extra, inessential, inordinate, padded, periphrastic, pleonastical, prolix, repetitious, supererogatory, superfluous, supernumerary, surplus, tautological, unemployed, unnecessary, unneeded, unwanted, verbose, wordy.

*antonyms* concise, essential, necessary.

**reef** *n* cay, key, ridge, sand-bank, sand-bar.

**reek** *v* exhale, fume, hum, pong, smell, smoke, stink.

*n* effluvium, exhalation, fetor, fume(s), malodour, mephitis, odour, pong, smell, smoke, stench, stink, vapour.

**reel** *v* gyrate, lurch, pitch, revolve, rock, roll, spin, stagger, stumble, sway, swim, swirl, totter, twirl, waver, wheel, whirl, wobble.

**refer** *v* accredit, adduce, advert, allude, apply, ascribe, assign, attribute, belong, cite, commit, concern, consign, consult, credit, deliver, direct, go, guide, hint, impute, invoke, look up, mention, pertain, point, recommend, relate, send, speak of, submit, touch on, transfer, turn to.

**referee** *n* adjudicator, arbiter, arbitrator, arbitratrix, arbitress, judge, ref, umpire.

*v* adjudicate, arbitrate, judge, ref, umpire.

**reference** *n* allusion, applicability, bearing, certification, character, citation, concern, connection, consideration, credentials, endorsement, illustration, instance, mention, note, quotation, recommendation, regard, relation, remark, respect, testimonial.

**refine** *v* chasten, civilise, clarify, cultivate, distil, elevate, exalt, filter, hone, improve, perfect, polish, process, purify, rarefy, spiritualise, sublimise, subtilise, temper.

**refined** *adj* Attic, Augustan, civil, civilised, clarified, clean, courtly, cultivated, cultured, delicate, discerning, discriminating, distilled, elegant, exact, fastidious, filtered, fine, genteel, gentlemanly, gracious, ladylike, nice, polished, polite, precise, processed, punctilious, pure, purified, sensitive, sophisticated, sublime, subtle, urbane, well-bred, well-mannered.

*antonyms* brutish, coarse, earthy, rude, vulgar.

**refinement** *n* breeding, chastity, civilisation, civility, clarification, cleansing, courtesy, courtliness, cultivation, culture, delicacy, discrimination, distillation, elegance, fastidiousness, filtering, fineness, finesse, finish, gentility, grace, graciousness, manners, nicety, nuance, polish, politeness, politesse, precision, processing, purification, rarefaction, rectification, sophistication, style, subtlety, taste, urbanity.

*antonyms* coarseness, earthiness, vulgarity.

**reflect** *v* bespeak, cogitate, communicate, consider, contemplate, deliberate, demonstrate, display, echo, evince, exhibit, express, imitate, indicate, manifest, meditate, mirror, mull (over), muse, ponder, reproduce, return, reveal, ruminate, show, think, wonder.

**reflection** *n* aspersion, censure, cerebration, cogitation, consideration, contemplation, counterpart, criticism, deliberation, derogation, echo, idea, image, impression, imputation, meditation, musing, observation, opinion, pondering, reflex, reproach, rumination, slur, study, thinking, thought, view.

**reflective** *adj* absorbed, cogitating, contemplative, deliberative, dreamy, meditative, pensive, pondering, reasoning, ruminative, thoughtful.

**reform** *v* ameliorate, amend, better, correct, emend, improve, mend, purge, rebuild, reclaim, reconstitute, reconstruct, rectify, regenerate, rehabilitate, remodel, renovate, reorganise, repair, restore, revamp, revolutionise.

*n* amelioration, amendment, betterment, correction, improvement, purge, rectification, rehabilitation, renovation, shake-out.

**reformer** *n* do-gooder, revolutionary, whistle-blower.

**refractory** *adj* balky, cantankerous, contentious, contumacious, difficult, disobedient, disputatious, headstrong, intractable, mulish, obstinate, perverse, recalcitrant, resistant, restive, stubborn, uncontrollable, unco-operative, unmanageable, unruly, wilful.

*antonyms* co-operative, malleable, obedient.

**refrain¹** *v* abstain, avoid, cease, desist, eschew, forbear, leave off, quit, renounce, stop, swear off.

**refrain²** *n* burden, chorus, epistrophe, falderal, melody, song, tune, undersong, wheel.

**refresh** *v* brace, cheer, cool, energise, enliven, freshen, inspirit, jog, prod, prompt, reanimate, reinvigorate, rejuvenate, renew, renovate, repair, replenish, restore, revitalise, revive, revivify, stimulate.

*antonyms* exhaust, tire.

**refreshing** *adj* bracing, cooling, different, energising, fresh, inspiriting, invigorating, new, novel, original, refrigerant, restorative, revivifying, stimulating, thirst-quenching.

*antonyms* exhausting, tiring.

**refreshment** *n* enlivenment, freshening, reanimation, reinvigoration, renewal, renovation, repair, restoration, revitalisation, revival, stimulation.

**refreshments** *n* aliment, drinks, food, provisions, snacks, sustenance, titbits.

**refrigerate** *v* chill, congeal, cool, freeze.

*antonyms* heat, warm.

**refuge** *n* asylum, bolthole, funk-hole, harbour, haven, hide-away, hideout, holt, protection, resort, retreat, sanctuary, security, shelter.

**refugee** *n* absconder, deserter, displaced person, émigré, escapee, exile, fugitive, runaway.

**refulgent** *adj* beaming, bright, brilliant, gleaming, glistening, glittering, irradiant, lambent, lustrous, radiant, resplendent, shining.

**refund** *v* rebate, reimburse, repay, restore, return.

*n* rebate, reimbursement, repayment, return.

**refurbish** *v* mend, overhaul, recondition, re-equip, refit, remodel, renovate, repair, restore, revamp.

**refusal** *n* choice, consideration, defiance, denial, incompliance, nay-say, negation, no, opportunity, option, rebuff, rejection, repudiation.
*antonym* acceptance.

**refuse**[1] *v* decline, deny, nay-say, reject, repel, repudiate, spurn, withhold.
*antonyms* accept, allow.

**refuse**[2] *n* chaff, dregs, dross, excrementa, garbage, hogwash, husks, junk, lag(s), landfill, leavings, lees, left-overs, litter, mullock, offscourings, rejectamenta, riddlings, rubbish, scum, sediment, slops, sordes, sullage, sweepings, tailings, trash, waste, wastrel.

**refutation** *n* confutation, disproof, elenchus, negation, overthrow, rebuttal.

**refute** *v* confute, counter, discredit, disprove, give the lie to, negate, overthrow, rebut, silence.

**regain** *v* reattain, recapture, reclaim, recoup, recover, redeem, re-establish, repossess, retake, retrieve, return to.

**regal** *adj* kingly, magnificent, majestic, monarch(i)al, monarchic(al), noble, princely, proud, queenly, royal, sovereign, stately.

**regale** *v* amuse, captivate, delight, divert, entertain, fascinate, feast, gratify, ply, refresh, serve.

**regard** *v* account, adjudge, attend, behold, believe, concern, consider, deem, esteem, estimate, eye, heed, hold, imagine, interest, judge, mark, mind, note, notice, observe, pertain to, rate, relate to, remark, respect, scrutinise, see, suppose, think, treat, value, view, watch.
*antonyms* despise, disregard.

*n* account, advertence, advertency, affection, aspect, attachment, attention, bearing, care, concern, connection, consideration, deference, detail, esteem, feature, gaze, glance, heed, honour, item, look, love, matter, mind, note, notice, particular, point, reference, relation, relevance, reputation, repute, respect, scrutiny, stare, store, sympathy, thought.
*antonyms* contempt, disapproval, disregard.

**regardful** *adj* attentive, aware, cany, careful, circumspect, considerate, dutiful, heedful, mindful, observant, respectful, thoughtful, watchful.
*antonyms* heedless, inattentive, regardless, unobservant.

**regarding** *prep* about, apropos, as regards, as to, concerning, in re, in respect of, in the matter of, on the subject of, re, respecting, touching, with reference to, with regard to.

**regardless** *adj* disregarding, heedless, inattentive, inconsiderate, indifferent, neglectful, negligent, nonchalant, rash, reckless, remiss, uncaring, unconcerned, unmindful.
*antonyms* attentive, heedful, regardful.

*adv* anyhow, anyway, come what may, despite everything, in any case, nevertheless, no matter what, nonetheless, willy-nilly.

**regards** *n* compliments, devoirs, greetings, respects, salutations.

**regenerate** *v* change, inspirit, invigorate, reawaken, reconstitute, reconstruct, re-establish, refresh, reinvigorate, rejuvenate, renew, renovate, reproduce, restore, revive, revivify, uplift.

**regeneration** *n* homomorphosis, reconstitution, reconstruction, re-establishment, reinvigoration, rejuvenation, renewal, renovation, reproduction, restoration.

**regime** *n* administration, command, control, establishment, government, leadership, management, reign, rule, system.

**regiment** *n* band, battery, body, brigade, cohort, company, crew, gang, group, platoon, squadron.

**regimented** *adj* controlled, co-ordinated, disciplined, methodical, ordered, organised, regulated, severe, standardised, stern, strict, systematic.
*antonyms* disorganised, free, lax, loose.

**region** *n* area, clime, country, district, division, domain, expanse, field, land, locality, neighbourhood, part, place, province, quarter, range, realm, scope, section, sector, sphere, terrain, terrene, territory, tract, vicinity, world, zone.

**regional** *adj* district, local, localised, parochial, provincial, sectional, zonal.

**register** *n* almanac, annals, archives, catalogue, chronicle, diary, file, ledger, list, log, matricula, memorandum, notitia, record, roll, roster, schedule.

*v* bespeak, betray, catalogue, chronicle, display, enlist, enrol, enter, exhibit, express, indicate, inscribe, list, log, manifest, mark, note, read, record, reflect, reveal, say, score, show, sign on.

**registrar** *n* administrator, annalist, archivist, cataloguer, chronicler, clerk, greffier, protocolist, recorder, secretary.

**regress** *v* backslide, degenerate, deteriorate, ebb, lapse, recede, relapse, retreat, retrocede, retrogress, return, revert, wane.
*antonym* progress.

**regret** *v* bemoan, bewail, deplore, grieve, lament, miss, mourn, repent, rue, sorrow.

*n* bitterness, compunction, contrition, disappointment, grief, lamentation, penitence, remorse, repentance, ruefulness, self-reproach, shame, sorrow.

**regretful** *adj* apologetic, ashamed, conscience-stricken, contrite, disappointed, mournful, penitent, remorseful, repentant, rueful, sad, sorrowful, sorry.
*antonyms* impenitent, unashamed.

**regrettable** *adj* deplorable, disappointing, distressing, ill-advised, lamentable, pitiable, sad, shameful, sorry, unfortunate, unhappy, unlucky, woeful, wrong.
*antonyms* fortunate, happy.

**regular** *adj* approved, balanced, bona fide, classic, common, commonplace, consistent, constant, consuetudinary, conventional, correct, customary, daily, dependable, efficient, established, even, everyday, fixed, flat, formal, habitual, level, methodical, normal, official, ordered, orderly, ordinary, orthodox, periodic, prevailing, proper, rhythmic, routine, sanctioned, set, smooth, standard, standardised, stated, steady, straight, symmetrical, systematic, time-honoured, traditional, typical, uniform, unvarying, usual.

*antonyms* irregular, sporadic, unconventional.

**regulate** *v* adjust, administer, arrange, balance, conduct, control, direct, fit, govern, guide, handle, manage, moderate, modulate, monitor, order, organise, oversee, regiment, rule, run, settle, square, superintend, supervise, systematise, tune.

**regulation** *n* adjustment, administration, arrangement, commandment, control, decree, dictate, direction, edict, governance, government, law, management, modulation, order, ordinance, precept, prodecure, regimentation, requirement, rule, statute, supervision, tuning.

*adj* accepted, customary, mandatory, normal, official, prescribed, required, standard, stock, usual.

**regurgitate** *v* disgorge, puke, regorge, spew, throw up, vomit.

**rehabilitate** *v* adjust, clear, convert, mend, normalise, rebuild, recondition, reconstitute, reconstruct, redeem, redintegrate, re-establish, reform, reinstate, reintegrate, reinvigorate, renew, renovate, restore, save.

**rehash** *n* rearrangement, rejig, rejigging, reshuffle, restatement, reworking, rewrite.

*v* alter, change, rearrange, refashion, rejig, rejigger, reshuffle, restate, rework, rewrite.

**rehearsal** *n* account, catalogue, description, drill, dry-run, enumeration, list, narration, practice, preparation, reading, recital, recounting, relation, run-through, telling.

**rehearse** *v* act, delineate, depict, describe, detail, drill, enumerate, list, narrate, practise, prepare, ready, recite, recount, relate, repeat, review, run through, spell out, study, tell, train, trot out.

**reign** *n* ascendancy, command, control, dominion, empire, hegemony, influence, monarchy, power, rule, sovereignty, supremacy, sway.

*v* administer, authority, command, govern, influence, kingship, obtain, predominate, prevail, rule.

**reimburse** *v* compensate, indemnify, recompense, refund, remunerate, repay, requite, restore, return, square up.

**rein** *n* brake, bridle, check, check-rein, control, curb, harness, hold, overcheck, restraint, restriction.

*v* arrest, bridle, check, control, curb, halt, hold, hold back, limit, restrain, restrict, stop.

**reincarnation** *n* metempsychosis, palingenesis, rebirth, transmigration.

**reinforce** *v* augment, bolster, buttress, emphasise, fortify, harden, increase, prop, recruit, steel, stiffen, strengthen, stress, supplement, support, toughen, underline.

*antonyms* undermine, weaken.

**reinforcement** *n* addition, amplification, augmentation, brace, buttress, emphasis, enlargement, fortification, hardening, increase, prop, shore, stay, strengthening, supplement, support.

**reinforcements** *n* auxiliaries, back-up, reserves, support.

**reinstate** *v* reappoint, recall, re-establish, rehabilitate, reinstall, replace, restore, return.

**reiterate** *v* ding, iterate, recapitulate, repeat, resay, restate, retell.

**reject** *v* athetise, condemn, decline, deny, despise, disallow, discard, eliminate, exclude, explode, jettison, jilt, pip, rebuff, refuse, renounce, repel, reprobate, repudiate, repulse, scrap, spike, spurn, veto.

*antonyms* accept, select.

*n* cast-off, discard, failure, second.

**rejection** *n* athetesis, brush-off, dear John letter, denial, dismissal, elimination, exclusion, rebuff, refusal, renunciation, repudiation, veto.

*antonyms* acceptance, selection.

**rejoice** *v* celebrate, delight, exult, glory, joy, jubilate, maffick, revel, triumph.

**rejoicing** *n* celebration, cheer, delight, elation, exultation, festivity, gaiety, gladness, happiness, joy, jubilation, mafficking, mallemaroking, merrymaking, revelry, triumph.

**rejoin** *v* answer, quip, repartee, reply, respond, retort, riposte.

**rejoinder** *n* answer, come-back, counter, countercharge, counter-claim, quip, repartee, reply, response, retort, riposte.

**rejuvenate** *v* reanimate, recharge, refresh, regenerate, reinvigorate, rekindle, renew, restore, revitalise, revivify.

**relapse** *v* backslide, degenerate, deteriorate, fade, fail, lapse, regress, retrogress, revert, sicken, sink, weaken, worsen.

*n* backsliding, deterioration, hypostrophe, lapse, recidivism, recurrence, regression, retrogression, reversion, setback, weakening, worsening.

**relate** *v* ally, appertain, apply, associate, chronicle, concern, connect, co-ordinate, correlate, couple, describe, detail, empathise, feel for, identify with, impart, join, link, narrate, pertain, present, recite, recount, refer, rehearse, report, sympathise, tell, understand.

**related** *adj* accompanying, affiliated, affine(d), agnate, akin, allied, associated, cognate, concomitant, connected, consanguine, consanguineous, correlated, interconnected, joint, kin, kindred, linked.

*antonyms* different, unconnected, unrelated.

**relation** *n* account, affiliation, affine, affinity, agnate, agnation, application, bearing, bond, comparison, connection, consanguinity, correlation, description, german, interdependence, kin, kindred, kinship, kinsman, kinswoman, link, narration, narrative, pertinence, propinquity, recital, recountal, reference, regard, relationship, relative, report, sib, similarity, story, tale, tie-in.

**relations** *n* affairs, associations, clan, communications, connections, contact, dealings, doings, family, interaction, intercourse, kin, kindred, kinsmen, liaison, meetings, rapport, relationship, relatives, terms, tribe, truck.

**relationship** *n* affaire, association, bond, communications, conjunction, connection, contract, correlation, dealings, exchange, intercourse, kinship, liaison, link, parallel, proportion, rapport, ratio, similarity, tie-up.

**relative** *adj* allied, applicable, apposite, appropriate, appurtenant, apropos, associated, comparative, connected, contingent, correlative, corresponding, dependent, germane, interrelated, pertinent, proportionate, reciprocal, related, relevant, respective.

*n* cognate, connection, german, kinsman, kinswoman, relation, sib.

**relatively** *adv* comparatively, fairly, quite, rather, somewhat.

**relax** *v* abate, diminish, disinhibit, ease, ebb, lessen, loosen, lower, mitigate, moderate, reduce, relieve, remit, rest, slacken, soften, tranquillise, unbend, unclench, unwind, weaken.

*antonyms* intensify, tighten.

**relaxation** *n* abatement, amusement, délassement, détente, diminution, disinhibition, distraction, easing, emollition, enjoyment, entertainment, fun, leisure, lessening, let-up, moderation, pleasure, recreation, reduction, refreshment, rest, slackening, weakening.

*antonyms* intensification, tension.

**relaxed** *adj* calm, carefree, casual, collected, composed, cool, downbeat, easy-going, even-tempered, happy-go-lucky, informal, insouciant, laid-back, mellow, mild, nonchalant, placid, serene, together, tranquil, unhurried.

*antonyms* edgy, nervous, stiff, tense, uptight.

**relay** *n* broadcast, communication, dispatch, message, programme, relief, shift, transmission, turn.

*v* broadcast, carry, communicate, rebroadcast, send, spread, supply, transmit.

**release** *v* absolve, acquit, break, circulate, declassify, decontrol, deliver, discage, discharge, disengage, disenthral, disimprison, disinhibit, disoblige, dispense, disprison, disseminate, distribute, drop, emancipate, exempt, excuse, exonerate, extricate, free, furlough, issue, launch, liberate, loose, manumit, present, publish, unbind, uncage, unchain, undo, unfasten, unfetter, unhand, unleash, unloose, unmew, unpen, unshackle, untie, unveil.

*antonyms* check, detain.

*n* absolution, acquittal, acquittance, announcement, deliverance, delivery, discharge, disimprisonment, disinhibition, dispensation, emancipation, exemption, exoneration, freedom,

issue, let-off, liberation, liberty, manumission, offering, proclamation, publication, quittance, relief.

*antonym* detention.

**relegate** *v* assign, banish, consign, delegate, demote, deport, dispatch, downgrade, eject, entrust, exile, expatriate, expel, refer, transfer.

*antonym* promote.

**relent** *v* acquiesce, capitulate, drop, ease, fall, forbear, give in, melt, relax, slacken, slow, soften, unbend, weaken, yield.

**relentless** *adj* cruel, fierce, grim, hard, harsh, implacable, incessant, inexorable, inflexible, merciless, non-stop, persistent, pitiless, punishing, remorseless, ruthless, stern, sustained, unabated, unbroken, uncompromising, undeviating, unfaltering, unflagging, unforgiving, unrelenting, unrelieved, unremitting, unstoppable, unyielding.

*antonyms* submissive, yielding.

**relevant** *adj* ad rem, admissible, applicable, apposite, appropriate, appurtenant, apt, congruous, fitting, germane, material, pertinent, proper, related, relative, significant, suitable, suited.

*antonym* irrelevant.

**reliable** *adj* banker, certain, constant, copper-bottomed, dependable, faithful, honest, predictable, regular, responsible, safe, solid, sound, stable, staunch, sure, true, trustworthy, trusty, unfailing, upright, white.

*antonyms* doubtful, suspect, unreliable, untrustworthy.

**reliance** *n* assurance, belief, confidence, credence, credit, dependence, faith, trust.

**relic** *n* fragment, keepsake, memento, potsherd, remembrance, remnant, scrap, souvenir, survival, token, trace, vestige.

**relief** *n* abatement, aid, alleviation, assistance, assuagement, balm, break, breather, comfort, cure, deliverance, diversion, ease, easement, help, let-up, load off one's mind, mitigation, palliation, refreshment, relaxation, release, remedy, remission, respite, rest, solace, succour, support, sustenance.

**relieve** *v* abate, aid, alleviate, appease, assist, assuage, break, brighten, calm, comfort, console, cure, deliver, diminish, discharge, disembarrass, disencumber, dull, ease, exempt, free, help, interrupt, lighten, mitigate, mollify, palliate, relax, release, salve, slacken, soften, solace, soothe, spell, stand in for, substitute for, succour, support, sustain, take over from, take the place of, unburden, vary.

*antonyms* aggravate, intensify.

**religious** *adj* church-going, conscientious, devotional, devout, divine, doctrinal, exact, faithful, fastidious, God-fearing, godly, holy, meticulous, pious, punctilious, pure, reverent, righteous, rigid, rigorous, sacred, scriptural, scrupulous, sectarian, spiritual, strict, theological, unerring, unswerving.

*antonyms* irreligious, lax, ungodly.

**relinquish** *n* abandon, abdicate, cede, desert, discard, drop, forgo, forsake, hand over, leave, quit, release, renounce, repudiate, resign, surrender, vacate, waive, yield.

*antonyms* keep, retain.

**relish** *v* appreciate, degust, enjoy, fancy, lap up, like, prefer, revel in, savour, taste.

*n* appetiser, appetite, appreciation, condiment, enjoyment, fancy, flavour, fondness, gout, gusto, liking, love, partiality, penchant, piquancy, predilection, sauce, savour, seasoning, smack, spice, stomach, tang, taste, trace, zest.

**reluctance** *n* aversion, backwardness, disinclination, dislike, distaste, hesitancy, indisposition, loathing, recalcitrance, repugnance, unwillingness.

*antonyms* eagerness, willingness.

**reluctant** *adj* averse, backward, disinclined, grudging, hesitant, indisposed, loath, loathful, loth, recalcitrant, renitent, slow, squeamish, unenthusiastic, unwilling.

*antonyms* eager, willing.

**rely** *v* bank, bet, count, depend, lean, reckon, swear by, trust.

**remain** *v* abide, bide, cling, continue, delay, dwell, endure, last, linger, persist, prevail, rest, sojourn, stand, stay, survive, tarry, wait.

*antonyms* depart, go, leave.

**remainder** *n* balance, dregs, excess, leavings, remanent, remanet, remnant, residuum, rest, surplus, trace, vestige(s).

**remaining** *adj* abiding, extant, lasting, left, lingering, outstanding, persisting, residual, surviving, unfinished, unspent, unused.

**remains** *n* ashes, balance, body, cadaver, carcass, corpse, crumbs, debris, detritus, dregs, fragments, leavings, left-overs, oddments, pieces, relics, reliquiae, remainder, remnants, residue, rest, scraps, traces, vestiges.

**remark** *v* animadvert, comment, declare, espy, heed, mark, mention, note, notice, observe, perceive, reflect, regard, say, see, state.

*n* acknowledgement, assertion, attention, comment, consideration, declaration, heed, mention, notice, observation, opinion, recognition, reflection, regard, say, statement, thought, utterance, word.

**remarkable** *adj* amazing, conspicuous, distinguished, exceptional, extraordinary, famous, impressive, miraculous, notable, noteworthy, odd, outstanding, phenomenal, pre-eminent, prominent, rare, signal, singular, strange, striking, surprising, unco, uncommon, unusual, wonderful.

*antonyms* average, commonplace, ordinary.

**remedy** *n* antidote, corrective, counteractive, countermeasure, cure, magistery, medicament, medicine, nostrum, panacea, physic, prescript, redress, relief, restorative, simillimum, solution, specific, therapy, treatment.

*v* alleviate, ameliorate, assuage, control, correct, counteract, cure, ease, fix, heal, help, mitigate, palliate, put right, rectify, redress, reform, relieve, repair, restore, solve, soothe, treat.

**remember** *v* commemorate, place, recall, recognise, recollect, reminisce, retain, summon up, think back.

*antonym* forget.

**remembrance** *n* anamnesis, commemoration, keepsake, memento, memorial, memory, mind, monument, recall, recognition, recollection, recordation, regard, relic, remembrancer, reminder, reminiscence, retrospect, souvenir, testimonial, thought, token.

**remind** *v* bring to mind, call to mind, call up, cue, hint, jog one's memory, prompt, put in mind, refresh one's memory.

**reminder** *n* aide-mémoire, cue, hint, memo, memorandum, nudge, prompt(ing), suggestion.

**reminisce** *v* hark back, look back, recall, recollect, remember, retrospect, review, think back.

**reminiscence** *n* anecdote, memoir, memory, personalia, recall, recollection, reflection, remembrance, retrospection, review.

**reminiscent** *adj* evocative, nostalgic, redolent, remindful, similar, suggestive.

**remiss** *adj* careless, culpable, delinquent, derelict, dilatory, fainéant, forgetful, heedless, inattentive, indifferent, lackadaisical, lax, neglectful, negligent, regardless, slack, slipshod, sloppy, slothful, slow, tardy, thoughtless, unmindful.

*antonyms* careful, scrupulous.

**remission** *n* abatement, abeyance, absolution, acquittal, alleviation, amelioration, amnesty, decrease, diminution, discharge, ebb, excuse, exemption, exoneration, forgiveness, indulgence, lessening, let-up, lull, moderation, pardon, reduction, relaxation, release, relinquishment, reprieve, respite, slackening, suspension.

**remit** *v* abate, alleviate, cancel, decrease, defer, delay, desist, desist from, diminish, dispatch, dwindle, forbear, forward, halt, mail, mitigate, moderate, post, postpone, put back, reduce, relax, repeal, rescind, send, send back, shelve, sink, slacken, soften, stop, suspend, transfer, transmit, wane, weaken.

*n* authorisation, brief, guidelines, instructions, orders, responsibility, scope, terms of reference.

**remittance** *n* allowance, consideration, dispatch, fee, payment, sending.

**remnant** *n* balance, bit, end, fent, fragment, hangover, left-overs, piece, remainder, remains, remane(n)t, residue, residuum, rest, rump, scrap, shred, survival, trace, vestige.

**remonstrance** *n* complaint, exception, expostulation, grievance, objection, petition, protest, protestation, reprimand, reproof.

**remonstrate** *v* argue, challenge, complain, dispute, dissent, expostulate, gripe, object, protest.

**remorse** *n* anguish, bad conscience, compassion, compunction, contrition, grief, guilt, penitence, pity, regret, repentance, ruefulness, ruth, self-reproach, shame, sorrow.

**remorseful** *adj* apologetic, ashamed, chastened, compunctious, conscience-stricken, contrite, guilt-ridden, guilty, penitent, regretful, repentant, rueful, sad, sorrowful, sorry.

*antonyms* impenitent, remorseless.

**remorseless** *adj* callous, cruel, hard, hard-hearted, harsh, impiacable, inexorable, inhumane, merciless, pitiless, relentless, ruthless, savage, stern, undeviating, unforgiving, unmerciful, unrelenting, unremitting, unstoppable.

*antonyms* remorseful, sorry.

**remote** *adj* abstracted, alien, aloof, backwoods, cold, detached, distant, doubtful, dubious, extraneous, extrinsic, faint, far, faraway, far-off, foreign, god-forsaken, immaterial, implausible, inaccessible, inconsiderable, indifferent, introspective, introverted, irrelevant, isolated, lonely, meagre, negligible, outlying, out-of-the-way, outside, poor, removed, reserved, secluded, slender, slight, slim, small, standoffish, unconnected, uninterested, uninvolved, unlikely, unrelated, withdrawn.

*antonyms* adjacent, close, nearby, significant.

**removal** *n* ablation, abstraction, demigration, departure, dislodgement, dismissal, displacement, dispossession, ejection, elimination, eradication, erasure, expulsion, expunction, extraction, flitting, metastasis, move, purge, purging, relocation, riddance, stripping, subtraction, transfer, uprooting, withdrawal.

**remove** *v* ablate, abolish, abstract, amove, amputate, assassinate, delete, depart, depose, detach, dethrone, discharge, dislodge, dismiss, displace, doff, efface, eject, eliminate, erase, execute, expunge, extract, flit, flit (move house), guy, kill, liquidate, move, murder, oust, purge, quit, relegate, relocate, shave, shear, shed, shift, sideline, strike, subduct, transfer, transmigrate, transport, unseat, vacate, withdraw.

**remunerate** *v* compensate, fee, guerdon, indemnify, pay, recompense, redress, reimburse, repay, requite, reward.

**remuneration** *n* compensation, earnings, emolument, fee, guerdon, income, indemnity, pay, payment, profit, recompense, reimbursement, remittance, reparation, repayment, retainer, return, reward, salary, stipend, wages.

**remunerative** *adj* fruitful, gainful, lucrative, moneymaking, paying, profitable, rewarding, rich, worthwhile.

**renaissance** *n* awakening, new birth, new dawn, reappearance, reawakening, rebirth, recrudescence, re-emergence, regeneration, rejuvenation, renascence, renewal, restoration, resurgence, resurrection, revival.

**renascent** *adj* born-again, reanimated, reawakened, reborn, redivivus, re-emergent, renewed, resurgent, resurrected, revived.

**rend** *v* afflict, anguish, break, burst, cleave, crack, dissever, distress, disturb, disunite, divide, fracture, hurt, lacerate, pain, pierce, pull, rip, rive, rupture, separate, sever, shatter, smash, splinter, split, stab, sunder, tear, torment, wound, wrench, wring.

**render** *v* act, cede, clarify, construe, contribute, deliver, depict, display, do, evince, exchange, exhibit, explain, furnish, give, give back, give up, hand over, interpret, leave, make, make up, manifest, melt, pay, perform, play, portray, present, provide, put, relinquish, repay, represent, reproduce, restate, restore, return, show, show forth, submit, supply, surrender, swap, tender, trade, transcribe, translate, yield.

**rendezvous** *n* appointment, assignation, date, engagement, haunt, meeting, meeting-place, resort, tryst, trysting-place, venue.

*v* assemble, collect, convene, converge, gather, meet, muster, rally.

**rendition** *n* arrangement, construction, delivery, depiction, execution, explanation, interpretation, metaphrase, metaphrasis, performance, portrayal, presentation, reading, rendering, transcription, translation, version.

**renegade** *n* apostate, backslider, betrayer, defector, deserter, dissident, mutineer, outlaw, rebel, recreant, renegado, renegate, runaway, tergiversator, traitor, turncoat.

*antonyms* adherent, disciple, follower.

*adj* apostate, backsliding, disloyal, dissident, mutinous, outlaw, perfidious, rebel, rebellious, recreant, runaway, traitorous, unfaithful.

**renegue** *v* apostatise, cross the floor, default, renege, renig, repudiate, welsh.

**renew** *v* continue, extend, mend, modernise, overhaul, prolong, reaffirm, recommence, recreate, re-establish, refashion, refit, refresh, refurbish, regenerate, rejuvenate, remodel, renovate, reopen, repair, repeat, replace, replenish, restate, restock, restore, resume, revitalise, transform.

**renewal** *n* instauration, kiss of life, recommencement, reconditioning, reconstitution, reconstruction, recreation, recruit, recruital, refurbishment, reinvigoration, reiteration, rejuvenation, renovation, repair, replenishment, resumption, resurrection, resuscitation, revitalisation, revivification.

**renounce** *v* abandon, abdicate, abjure, abnegate, decline, deny, discard, disclaim, disown, disprofess, eschew, forgo, forsake, forswear, put away, quit, recant, reject, relinquish, repudiate, resign, spurn.

**renovate** *v* do up, furbish, improve, modernise, overhaul, recondition, reconstitute, recreate, refit, reform, refurbish, rehabilitate, remodel, renew, repair, restore, revamp.

**renovation** *n* face-lift, improvement, modernisation, reconditioning, refit, refurbishment, renewal, repair, restoration.

**renown** *n* acclaim, celebrity, distinction, eminence, fame, glory, honour, illustriousness, kudos, lustre, mark, note, reputation, repute, stardom.

*antonyms* anonymity, obscurity.

**renowned** *adj* acclaimed, celebrated, distinguished, eminent, esteemed, famed, famous, illustrious, notable, noted, pre-eminent, supereminent, well-known.

*antonyms* anonymous, obscure, unknown.

**rent**[1] *n* fee, gale, hire, lease, payment, rental, tariff.

*v* charter, farm out, hire, lease, let, sublet, take.

**rent**[2] *n* breach, break, chink, cleavage, crack, dissension, disunion, division, flaw, gash, hole, opening, perforation, rift, rip, rupture, schism, slash, slit, split, tear.

**renunciation** *n* abandonment, abdication, abjuration, abnegation, abstention, denial, disavowal, disclaimer, eschewal, forgoing, forswearing, recantation, rejection, relinquishment, repudiation, resignation, spurning, surrender, waiver.

**repair**[1] *v* debug, fix, heal, mend, patch up, recover, rectify, redress, renew, renovate, restore, retrieve, square.

*n* adjustment, condition, darn, fettle, form, improvement, mend, nick, overhaul, patch, restoration, shape, state.

**repair**[2] *v* go, wend one's way, move, remove, resort, retire, turn, withdraw.

**reparable** *adj* corrigible, curable, recoverable, rectifiable, remediable, restorable, retrievable, salvageable, savable.

*antonym* irreparable.

**reparation** *n* amends, atonement, compensation, damages, indemnity, propitiation, recompense, redress, renewal, repair, requital, restitution, satisfaction, solatium.

**repartee** *n* badinage, banter, jesting, persiflage, pleasantry, raillery, riposte, sally, waggery, wit, witticism, wittiness, wordplay.

**repast** *n* collation, feed, food, meal, nourishment, refection, snack, spread, victuals.

**repay** *v* avenge, compensate, get even with, make restitution, reciprocate, recompense, refund, reimburse, remunerate, requite, restore, retaliate, return, revenge, reward, settle the score, square.

**repayment** *n* amends, avengement, compensation, rebate, reciprocation, recompense, redress, refund, reimbursement, remuneration, reparation, requital, restitution, retaliation, retribution, revenge, reward, ultion, vengeance.

**repeal** *v* abolish, abrogate, annul, cancel, countermand, invalidate, nullify, quash, recall, rescind, reverse, revoke, set aside, void, withdraw.

*antonyms* enact, establish.

*n* abolition, abrogation, annulment, cancellation, invalidation, nullification, quashing, rescinding, rescindment, rescission, reversal, revocation, withdrawal.

*antonyms* enactment, establishment.

**repeat** *v* duplicate, echo, iterate, quote, rebroadcast, recapitulate, recite, re-do, rehearse, reiterate, relate, renew, replay, reproduce, rerun, reshow, restate, retell.

*n* duplicate, echo, rebroadcast, recapitulation, reiteration, repetition, replay, reproduction, rerun, reshowing.

**repeatedly** *adv* again and again, frequently, often, oftentimes, ofttimes, over and over, recurrently, time after time, time and (time) again.

**repel** *v* check, confront, decline, disadvantage, disgust, fight, hold off, nauseate, offend, oppose, parry, rebuff, refuse, reject, repulse, resist, revolt, sicken, ward off.

*antonym* attract.

**repellent** *adj* abhorrent, abominable, discouraging, disgusting, distasteful, hateful, horrid, loathsome, nauseating, noxious, obnoxious, odious, offensive, off-putting, rebarbative, repugnant, repulsive, revolting, sickening.

*antonym* attractive.

**repent** *n* atone, bewail, deplore, lament, regret, relent, rue, sorrow.

**repentance** *n* compunction, contrition, grief, guilt, metanoia, penitence, regret, remorse, self-reproach, sorriness, sorrow.

**repentant** *adj* apologetic, ashamed, chastened, compunctious, contrite, penitent, regretful, remorseful, rueful, sorry.

*antonym* unrepentant.

**repercussion** *n* aftermath, backlash, backwash, consequence, echo, rebound, recoil, result, reverberation, side effect.

**repertory** *n* collection, list, range, repertoire, repository, reserve, reservoir, stock, store, supply.

**repetition** *n* anaphora, dittography, duplication, echo, echolalia, epanalepsis, epanaphora, iteration, reappearance, recapitulation, recital, recurrence, redundancy, rehearsal, reiteration, relation, renewal, repeat, repetitiousness, replication, restatement, return, tautology.

**repetitious** *adj* battological, long-winded, pleonastic(al), prolix, redundant, tautological, tedious, verbose, windy, wordy.

**repetitive** *adj* boring, dull, interminable, mechanical, monotonous, recurrent, samey, tedious, unchanging, unvaried.

**rephrase** *v* paraphrase, recast, reword, rewrite.

**repine** *v* beef, brood, complain, fret, grieve, grouse, grumble, lament, languish, moan, mope, murmur, sulk.

**replace** *v* deputise, follow, make good, oust, re-establish, reinstate, restore, substitute, succeed, supersede, supplant, supply.

**replacement** *n* double, fill-in, proxy, replacer, stand-in, substitute, succedaneum, successor, surrogate, understudy.

**replenish** *v* fill, furnish, provide, recharge, recruit, refill, reload, renew, replace, restock, restore, stock, supply, top up.

**replete** *adj* abounding, brimful, brimming, charged, chock-a-block, chock-full, crammed, filled, full, full up, glutted, gorged, jammed, jam-packed, sated, satiated, stuffed, teeming, well-provided, well-stocked.

**repletion** *n* completeness, fullness, glut, overfullness, plethora, satiation, satiety, superabundance, superfluity.

**replica** *n* clone, copy, duplicate, facsimile, imitation, model, reproduction.

**replicate** *v* ape, clone, copy, duplicate, follow, mimic, recreate, reduplicate, repeat, reproduce.

**reply** *v* acknowledge, answer, counter, echo, react, reciprocate, rejoin, repartee, respond, retaliate, retort, return, riposte.

*n* acknowledgement, answer, comeback, counter, echo, reaction, reciprocation, rejoinder, repartee, response, retaliation, retort, return, riposte.

**report** *n* account, announcement, article, bang, blast, boom, bruit, character, communication, communiqué, crack, crash, declaration, description, detail, detonation, discharge, dispatch, esteem, explosion, fame, gossip, hearsay, information, message, narrative, news, noise, note, paper, piece, procès-verbal, recital, record, regard, relation, reputation, repute, reverberation, rumour, sound, statement, story, summary, tale, talk, tidings, version, word, write-up.

*v* air, announce, appear, arrive, broadcast, bruit, circulate, come, communicate, cover, declare, describe, detail, document, mention, narrate, note, notify, proclaim, publish, recite, record, recount, relate, relay, state, tell.

**reporter** *n* announcer, correspondent, hack, Jenkins, journalist, leg-man, leg-woman, newscaster, newshound, newspaperman, newspaperwoman, pressman, stringer, writer.

**repose**[1] *n* aplomb, calm, calmness, composure, dignity, ease, equanimity, inactivity, peace, poise, quiet, quietness, quietude, relaxation, respite, rest, restfulness, self-possession, serenity, sleep, slumber, stillness, tranquillity.

*antonyms* activity, strain, stress.

*v* laze, recline, relax, rest, sleep, slumber.

**repose**[2] *v* confide, deposit, entrust, invest, lodge, place, put, set, store.

**repository** *n* archive, depository, depot, emporium, magazine, promptuary, receptacle, repertory, store, storehouse, treasury, vault, warehouse.

**reprehensible** *adj* bad, blamable, blameworthy, censurable, condemnable, culpable, delinquent, discreditable, disgraceful, errant, erring, ignoble, objectionable, opprobrious, remiss, shameful, unworthy.

*antonyms* creditable, good, praiseworthy.

**represent** *v* act, appear as, be, betoken, delineate, denote, depict, depicture, describe, designate, embody, enact, epitomise, equal, evoke, exemplify, exhibit, express, illustrate, mean, outline, perform, personify, picture, portray, produce, render, reproduce, show, sketch, stage, symbolise, typify.

**representation** *n* account, argument, bust, committee, delegates, delegation, delineation, depiction, description, embassy, exhibition, explanation, exposition, expostulation, icon, idol, illustration, image, likeness, model, narration, narrative, performance, petition, picture, play, portrait, portrayal, production, relation, remonstrance, resemblance, show, sight, sketch, spectacle, statue.

**representative** *n* agent, archetype, commissioner, councillor, delegate, depute, deputy, embodiment, epitome, exemplar, member, MP, personification, proxy, rep, representant, salesman, spokesman, spokesperson, spokeswoman, traveller, type.

*adj* archetypal, characteristic, chosen, delegated, elected, elective, emblematic, evocative, exemplary, illustrative, normal, symbolic, typical, usual.

*antonyms* atypical, unrepresentative.

**repress** *v* bottle up, chasten, check, control, crush, curb, hamper, hinder, impede, inhibit, master, muffle, overcome, overpower, quash, quell, reprime, restrain, silence, smother, stifle, subdue, subjugate, suppress, swallow.

**repression** *n* authoritarianism, censorship, coercion, constraint, control, denial, despotism, domination, gagging, inhibition, restraint, subjugation, suffocation, suppression, tyranny.

**repressive** *adj* absolute, authoritarian, autocratic, coercive, despotic, dictatorial, harsh, iron-handed, oppressive, severe, tough, tyrannical.

**reprieve** *v* abate, allay, alleviate, mitigate, palliate, pardon, redeem, relieve, rescue, respite.

*n* abatement, abeyance, alleviation, amnesty, deferment, let-up, mitigation, palliation, pardon, postponement, redemption, relief, remission, rescue, respite, suspension.

**reprimand** *n* admonition, blame, bollocking, castigation, censure, dressing-down, jawbation, jobation, lecture, rebuke, reprehension, reproach, reproof, row, schooling, talking-to, telling-off, ticking-off, tongue-lashing, wigging.

*v* admonish, bawl out, blame, bollock, bounce, castigate, censure, check, chide, jobe, keelhaul, lecture, lesson, rebuke, reprehend, reproach, reprove, scold, slate, tongue-lash, upbraid.

**reprisal** *n* counter-stroke, recaption, requital, retaliation, retribution, revenge, ultion, vengeance.

**reproach** *v* abuse, blame, censure, chide, condemn, criticise, defame, discredit, disparage, dispraise, rebuke, reprehend, reprimand, reprove, scold, upbraid.

*n* abuse, blame, blemish, censure, condemnation, contempt, disapproval, discredit, disgrace, dishonour, disrepute, ignominy, indignity, nayword, obloquy, odium, opprobrium, reproof, scorn, shame, slight, slut, stain, stigma, upbraiding.

**reproachful** *adj* abusive, admonitory, aggrieved, castigatory, censorious, condemnatory, contemptuous, critical, disappointed, disapproving, fault-finding, opprobrious, reproving, scolding, upbraiding.

*antonym* complimentary.

**reprobate** *adj* abandoned, bad, base, condemnatory, corrupt, damned, degenerate, depraved, dissolute, hardened, immoral, incorrigible, profligate, reprobative, reprobatory, shameless, sinful, unprincipled, vile, wicked.

*antonym* upright.

*n* blackguard, degenerate, evildoer, knave, miscreant, ne'er-do-well, outcast, pariah, profligate, rake, rakehell, rascal, rogue, roué, scamp, scoundrel, sinner, villain, wastrel, wretch, wrongdoer.

**reproduce** v ape, breed, copy, duplicate, echo, emulate, facsimile, generate, imitate, match, mirror, multiply, parallel, parrot, print, procreate, proliferate, propagate, recreate, regurgitate, repeat, replicate, represent, simulate, spawn, transcribe.

**reproduction** n amphimixis, breeding, copy, duplicate, ectype, facsimile, fructuation, gamogenesis, generation, imitation, increase, multiplication, picture, print, procreation, proliferation, propagation, replica.

*antonym* original.

**reproductive** adj generative, genital, procreative, progenitive, propagative, sex, sexual.

**reproof** n admonition, blame, castigation, censure, chiding, condemnation, criticism, dressing-down, rebuke, reprehension, reprimand, reproach, reproval, reproving, scolding, ticking-off, tongue-lashing, upbraiding.

*antonym* praise.

**reprove** v abuse, admonish, berate, blame, censure, check, chide, condemn, rap, rate, rebuke, reprehend, reprimand, scold, upbraid.

*antonym* praise.

**repudiate** v abandon, abjure, cast off, deny, desert, disaffirm, disavow, discard, disclaim, disown, disprofess, divorce, forsake, reject, renounce, rescind, retract, reverse, revoke.

*antonyms* admit, own.

**repudiation** n abjuration, denial, disaffirmance, disaffirmation, disavowal, disclaimer, disowning, recantation, rejection, renouncement, renunciation, retraction.

*antonym* acceptance.

**repugnance** n abhorrence, abhorring, antipathy, aversion, disgust, dislike, disrelish, distaste, hatred, inconsistency, loathing, reluctance, repugnancy, repulsion, revulsion.

*antonyms* liking, pleasure.

**repugnant** adj abhorrent, abominable, adverse, antagonistic, antipathetic, averse, contradictory, disgusting, distasteful, foul, hateful, horrid, hostile, incompatible, inconsistent, inimical, loathsome, nauseating, objectionable, obnoxious, odious, offensive, opposed, repellent, revolting, sickening, unacceptable, vile.

*antonyms* acceptable, consistent, pleasant.

**repulse** v beat off, check, defeat, disdain, disregard, drive back, rebuff, refuse, reject, repel, snub, spurn.

n check, defeat, disappointment, failure, rebuff, refusal, rejection, repudiation, reverse, snub, spurning.

*antonyms* acceptance, success.

**repulsion** n abhorrence, aversion, detestation, disgust, disrelish, distaste, hatred, loathing, repellence, repellency, repugnance, revulsion.

*antonym* liking.

**repulsive** adj abhorrent, abominable, cold, disagreeable, disgusting, distasteful, forbidding, foul, hateful, hideous, horrid, ill-faced, loathsome, nauseating, objectionable, obnoxious, odious, offensive, repellent, reserved, revolting, sickening, ugly, unpleasant, vile.

*antonyms* friendly, pleasant.

**reputable** adj creditable, dependable, estimable, excellent, good, honourable, honoured, irreproachable, legitimate, principled, reliable, respectable, trustworthy, unimpeachable, upright, worthy.

*antonyms* disreputable, infamous.

**reputation** n bad name, character, credit, distinction, esteem, estimation, fame, good name, honour, infamy, name, opinion, renown, repute, standing, stature.

**repute** n celebrity, distinction, esteem, estimation, fame, good name, name, renown, reputation, standing, stature.

*antonym* infamy.

**reputed** adj accounted, alleged, believed, considered, deemed, estimated, held, ostensible, putative, reckoned, regarded, reputative, rumoured, said, seeming, supposed, thought.

*antonym* actual.

**reputedly** adv allegedly, apparently, ostensibly, reputatively, seemingly, supposedly.

*antonym* actually.

**request** v ask, ask for, beg, beseech, demand, desire, entreat, impetrate, importune, petition, pray, requisition, seek, solicit, supplicate.

n appeal, application, asking, begging, call, demand, desire, entreaty, impetration, petition, prayer, representation, requisition, solicitation, suit, supplication.

**require** v ask, beg, beseech, bid, command, compel, constrain, crave, demand, desire, direct, enjoin, exact, force, instruct, involve, lack, make, miss, necessitate, need, oblige, order, request, take, want, wish.

**required** adj compulsory, demanded, essential, mandatory, necessary, needed, obligatory, prescribed, recommended, requisite, set, stipulated, unavoidable, vital.

*antonyms* inessential, optional.

**requirement** n demand, desideratum, essential, lack, must, necessity, need, precondition, prerequisite, provision, proviso, qualification, requisite, sine qua non, specification, stipulation, term, want.

*antonym* inessential.

**requisite** adj essential, imperative, indispensable, mandatory, necessary, needed, needful, obligatory, prerequisite, required, vital.

*antonyms* inessential, optional.

n condition, desiderative, desideratum, essential, must, necessity, need, precondition, prerequisite, requirement, sine qua non.

*antonym* inessential.

**requisition** v appropriate, commandeer, confiscate, demand, occupy, put in for, request, seize, take.

*n* application, appropriation, call, commandeering, demand, occupation, order, request, seizure, summons, takeover, use.

**requital** *n* amends, compensation, indemnification, indemnity, payment, pay-off, quittance, recompense, redress, reparation, repayment, restitution, satisfaction.

**requite** *v* avenge, compensate, pay, reciprocate, recompense, redress, reimburse, remunerate, repay, respond, retaliate, return, reward, satisfy.

**rescind** *v* abrogate, annul, cancel, countermand, invalidate, negate, nullify, overturn, quash, recall, repeal, retract, reverse, revoke, void.

*antonym* enforce.

**rescission** *n* abrogation, annulment, cancellation, invalidation, negation, nullification, recall, repeal, rescindment, retraction, reversal, revocation, voidance.

*antonym* enforcement.

**rescue** *v* deliver, extricate, free, liberate, ransom, recover, redeem, release, salvage, save.

*antonym* capture.

*n* deliverance, delivery, extrication, liberation, recovery, redemption, release, relief, salvage, salvation, saving.

*antonym* capture.

**research** *n* analysis, delving, examination, experimentation, exploration, fact-finding, groundwork, inquiry, investigation, probe, quest, scrutiny, search, study.

*v* analyse, examine, experiment, explore, ferret, investigate, probe, scrutinise, search, study.

**researcher** *n* analyst, boffin, field worker, inquirer, inspector, investigator, student.

**resemblance** *n* affinity, analogy, assonance, closeness, comparability, comparison, conformity, correspondence, counterpart, facsimile, image, kinship, likeness, parallel, parity, sameness, semblance, similarity, similitude.

*antonym* dissimilarity.

**resemble** *v* approach, duplicate, echo, favour, mirror, parallel, take after.

*antonym* differ from.

**resent** *v* begrudge, chafe at, dislike, grudge, grumble at, object to, take amiss, take exception to, take offence at, take the huff, take umbrage at.

*antonyms* accept, like.

**resentful** *adj* aggrieved, angry, bitter, embittered, exasperated, grudging, huffish, huffy, hurt, incensed, indignant, irate, ireful, jealous, miffed, offended, peeved, piqued, put out, resentive, revengeful, stomachful, unforgiving, wounded.

*antonym* contented.

**resentment** *n* anger, animosity, bitterness, disaffection, discontentment, displeasure, fury, grudge, huff, hurt, ill-feeling, ill-will, indignation, ire, irritation, malice, pique, rage, rancour, umbrage, vexation, vindictiveness, wrath.

*antonym* contentment.

**reservation**¹ *n* arrière pensée, condition, demur, doubt, hesitancy, hesitation, inhibition, proviso,

qualification, restraint, scepticism, scruple, second thought, stipulation.

**reservation**² enclave, homeland, park, preserve, reserve, sanctuary, territory, tract.

**reserve**¹ *v* bespeak, book, conserve, defer, delay, engage, hoard, hold, husband, keep, postpone, prearrange, preserve, retain, save, secure, set apart, spare, stockpile, store, withhold.

*antonym* use up.

*n* backlog, cache, capital, fund, hoard, park, preserve, reservation, reservoir, sanctuary, savings, stock, stockpile, store, substitute, supply, tract.

**reserve**² aloofness, constraint, coolness, formality, limitation, modesty, reluctance, reservation, restraint, restriction, reticence, secretiveness, shyness, silence, taciturnity.

*antonyms* friendliness, informality.

*adj* additional, alternate, auxiliary, extra, secondary, spare, substitute.

**reserved**¹ *adj* booked, bound, designated, destined, earmarked, engaged, fated, held, intended, kept, meant, predestined, restricted, retained, set aside, spoken for, taken.

*antonym* unreserved.

**reserved**² aloof, cautious, close-mouthed, cold, cool, demure, formal, modest, prim, restrained, reticent, retiring, secretive, shy, silent, stand-offish, taciturn, unapproachable, unclub(b)able, uncommunicative, uncompanionable, unconversable, undemonstrative, unforthcoming, unresponsive, unsociable.

*antonyms* friendly, informal.

**reservoir** *n* accumulation, basin, container, fund, holder, lake, pond, pool, receptacle, repository, reservatory, reserves, source, stock, stockpile, store, supply, tank.

**reshuffle** *n* change, interchange, realignment, rearrangement, redistribution, regrouping, reorganisation, restructuring, revision, shake-up, upheaval.

*v* change, interchange, realign, rearrange, redistribute, regroup, reorganise, restructure, revise, shake up, shift, shuffle.

**reside** *v* abide, consist, dwell, exist, inhabit, inhere, lie, live, lodge, remain, settle, sit, sojourn, stay.

**residence** *n* abode, country-house, country-seat, domicile, dwelling, habitation, hall, home, house, household, lodging, manor, mansion, occupancy, occupation, pad, palace, place, quarters, seat, sojourn, stay, tenancy, villa.

**resident** *n* citizen, commorant, denizen, habitant, indweller, inhabitant, local, lodger, occupant, tenant.

*antonym* non-resident.

*adj* dwelling, en poste, gremial, inhabiting, living, local, neighbourhood, permanent, settled.

*antonym* non-resident.

**residential** *adj* commuter, exurban, suburban.

**residential area** commuter belt, dormitory town, exurbia, suburbia, suburbs.

**residual** adj left-over, net(t), reliquary, remaining, residuary, residuous, unconsumed, unused, vestigial.

*antonym* core.

**residue** n balance, difference, dregs, excess, extra, left-overs, overflow, overplus, remainder, remains, remnant, residuum, rest, surplus.

*antonym* core.

**resign** v abandon, abdicate, cede, forgo, forsake, leave, quit, relinquish, renounce, sacrifice, stand down, surrender, vacate, waive, yield.

*antonyms* join, maintain.

**resign oneself** accede, accept, acquiesce, bow, comply, reconcile, submit, yield.

*antonym* resist.

**resignation** n abandonment, abdication, acceptance, acquiescence, compliance, defeatism, demission, departure, endurance, forbearing, fortitude, leaving, non-resistance, notice, passivity, patience, relinquishment, renunciation, retirement, submission, sufferance, surrender.

*antonym* resistance.

**resigned** adj acquiescent, compliant, defeatist, long-suffering, patient, stoical, subdued, submissive, unprotesting, unresisting.

*antonym* resisting.

**resilience** n adaptability, bounce, buoyancy, elasticity, flexibility, give, hardiness, plasticity, pliability, recoil, spring, springiness, strength, suppleness, toughness, unshockability.

*antonyms* inflexibility, rigidity.

**resilient** adj adaptable, bouncy, buoyant, elastic, flexible, hardy, irrepressible, plastic, pliable, springy, strong, supple, tough, unshockable.

*antonyms* downcast, rigid.

**resist** v avoid, battle, check, combat, confront, counteract, countervail, curb, defy, dispute, fight back, forbear, forgo, hinder, oppose, recalcitrate, refuse, repel, thwart, weather, withstand.

*antonyms* accept, submit.

**resistance** n antiperistasis, battle, combat, contention, counteraction, counter-stand, counter-time, defiance, fight, fighting, hindrance, impedance, impediment, intransigence, Maquis, obstruction, opposition, partisans, refusal, resistant, resistors, struggle, underground.

*antonyms* acceptance, submission.

**resistant** adj antagonistic, combative, defiant, dissident, hard, hostile, impervious, insusceptible, intractible, intransigent, opposed, recalcitrant, renitent, resistive, stiff, strong, tough, unsusceptible, unwilling, unyielding.

*antonyms* compliant, yielding.

**resolute** adj bold, constant, determined, dogged, firm, fixed, indissuadable, indivertible, inflexible, obstinate, persevering, purposeful, relentless, set, staunch, steadfast, stout, strong-minded, strong-willed, stubborn, sturdy, tenacious, unbending, undaunted, unflinching, unshakable, unshaken, unwavering.

*antonym* irresolute.

**resolution** n aim, answer, boldness, constancy, courage, decision, declaration, dedication, dénouement, determination, devotion, doggedness, earnestness, end, energy, finding, firmness, fortitude, intent, intention, judgement, motion, obstinacy, outcome, perseverance, pertinacity, purpose, relentlessness, resoluteness, resolve, settlement, sincerity, solution, solving, staunchness, steadfastness, stubbornness, tenacity, unravelling, verdict, will power, zeal.

*antonym* indecision.

**resolve** v agree, alter, analyse, anatomise, answer, banish, break up, change, clear, conclude, convert, crack, decide, design, determine, disentangle, disintegrate, dispel, dissect, dissipate, dissolve, elucidate, explain, fathom, fix, intend, liquefy, melt, metamorphose, purpose, reduce, relax, remove, separate, settle, solve, transform, transmute, undertake, unravel.

*antonyms* blend, waver.

n boldness, conclusion, conviction, courage, decision, design, determination, earnestness, firmness, intention, objective, project, purpose, resoluteness, resolution, sense of purpose, steadfastness, undertaking, will power.

*antonym* indecision.

**resonant** adj booming, canorous, echoing, full, plummy, resounding, reverberant, reverberating, rich, ringing, sonorous, vibrant.

*antonym* faint.

**resort** v frequent, go, haunt, hie, repair, visit.

*antonym* avoid.

n alternative, chance, course, expedient, haunt, health resort, hope, howf(f), possibility, recourse, reference, refuge, retreat, spa, spot, watering-place.

**resort to** employ, exercise, go so far as to, lower oneself to, stoop to, use, utilise.

**resound** v boom, echo, re-echo, resonate, reverberate, ring, sound, thunder.

**resounding** adj booming, conclusive, crushing, decisive, echoing, full, plangent, powerful, reboant, resonant, reverberating, rich, ringing, sonorous, sounding, thorough, vibrant, vocal.

*antonyms* faint, slight.

**resource** n ability, appliance, cache, capability, cleverness, contrivance, course, device, expedient, hoard, ingenuity, initiative, inventiveness, means, quick-wittedness, reserve, resort, resourcefulness, shift, source, stockpile, supply, talent.

*antonym* unimaginativeness.

**resourceful** adj able, bright, capable, clever, creative, fertile, imaginative, ingenious, innovative, inventive, originative, quick-witted, sharp, slick, talented.

**resourceless** adj feckless, feeble, fushionless, helpless, hopeless, inadequate, shiftless, useless.

*antonym* unimaginative.

**resources** n assets, capital, fisc, funds, holdings, materials, means, money, pelf, property, purse, reserves, riches, supplies, wealth, wherewithal.

**respect** n admiration, appreciation, approbation, aspect, bearing, characteristic, connection, consideration, deference, detail, esteem, estimation, facet, feature, homage, honour, matter, particular, point, recognition, reference, regard, relation, reverence, sense, veneration, way.

*antonym* disrespect.

v admire, appreciate, attend, esteem, follow, heed, honour, notice, obey, observe, pay homage to, recognise, regard, revere, reverence, value, venerate.

*antonym* scorn.

**respectable** *adj* admirable, ample, appreciable, clean-living, considerable, decent, decorous, dignified, estimable, fair, good, goodly, honest, honourable, large, passable, presentable, proper, reasonable, reputable, respected, seemly, sizable, substantial, tidy, tolerable, upright, venerable, well-to-do, worthy.

*antonyms* disreputable, miserly, unseemly.

**respectful** *adj* civil, courteous, courtly, deferential, dutiful, filial, gracious, humble, mannerly, obedient, polite, regardful, reverent, reverential, self-effacing, solicitous, submissive, subservient, well-mannered.

*antonym* disrespectful.

**respecting** *prep* about, concerning, considering, in respect of, regarding, with regard to, with respect to.

**respective** *adj* corresponding, individual, own, particular, personal, relevant, separate, several, special, specific, various.

**respects** n compliments, devoirs, duty, greetings, regards, salutations.

**respite** n adjournment, break, breather, cessation, delay, gap, halt, hiatus, intermission, interruption, interval, let-up, lull, moratorium, pause, postponement, recess, relaxation, relief, remission, reprieve, rest, stay, suspension.

**resplendent** *adj* beaming, bright, brilliant, dazzling, effulgent, fulgent, gleaming, glittering, glorious, irradiant, luminous, lustrous, radiant, refulgent, shining, splendid, splendiferous.

*antonym* dull.

**respond** v acknowledge, answer, answer back, come back, counter, react, reciprocate, rejoin, reply, retort, return.

**response** n acknowledgement, answer, comeback, counterblast, feedback, reaction, rejoinder, reply, respond, retort, return, riposte.

*antonym* query.

**responsibility** n accountability, amenability, answerability, authority, blame, burden, care, charge, conscientiousness, culpability, dependability, duty, fault, guilt, importance, level-headedness, liability, maturity, obligation, onus, power, rationality, reliability, sense, sensibleness, soberness, stability, trust, trustworthiness.

*antonym* irresponsibility.

**responsible** *adj* accountable, adult, amenable, answerable, authoritative, bound, chargeable, conscientious, culpable, decision-making, dependable, duty-bound, ethical, executive, guilty, high, important, level-headed, liable, mature, public-spirited, rational, reliable, right, sensible, sober, sound, stable, steady, subject, trustworthy.

*antonym* irresponsible.

**responsive** *adj* alive, awake, aware, forthcoming, impressionable, open, perceptive, reactive, receptive, respondent, responsorial, sensitive, sharp, susceptible, sympathetic.

*antonym* unresponsive.

**rest**[1] n base, break, breather, breathing-space, breathing-time, breathing-while, calm, cessation, cradle, doze, halt, haven, holder, holiday, idleness, inactivity, interlude, intermission, interval, leisure, lie-down, lie-in, lodging, lull, motionlessness, nap, pause, prop, refreshment, refuge, relaxation, relief, repose, retreat, shelf, shelter, shut-eye, siesta, sleep, slumber, snooze, somnolence, spell, stand, standstill, stillness, stop, support, tranquillity, trestle, vacation.

*antonyms* action, activity, restlessness.

v alight, base, cease, continue, depend, desist, discontinue, doze, found, halt, hang, hinge, idle, keep, land, lay, laze, lean, lie, lie back, lie down, lie in, perch, prop, recline, relax, rely, remain, repose, reside, settle, sit, sleep, slumber, snooze, spell, stand, stay, stop, turn.

*antonyms* change, continue, work.

**rest**[2] n balance, core, excess, left-overs, majority, others, remainder, remains, remnants, residue, residuum, rump, surplus.

**restaurant** n automat, bistro, brasserie, buffet, café, cafeteria, diner, dining-car, dining-room, eatery, eating-house, grill-room, grub-shop, porter-house, snack bar, steak-house.

**restful** *adj* calm, calming, comfortable, easeful, languid, pacific, peaceful, placid, quiet, relaxed, relaxing, serene, sleepy, soothing, tranquil, tranquillising, undisturbed, unhurried.

*antonyms* disturbed, disturbing.

**restitution** n amends, compensation, damages, indemnification, indemnity, recompense, redress, refund, reimbursement, remuneration, reparation, repayment, requital, restoration, restoring, return, satisfaction.

**restive** *adj* agitated, edgy, fidgety, fractious, fretful, impatient, jittery, jumpy, nervous, obstinate, recalcitrant, refractory, restless, uneasy, unquiet, unruly.

*antonyms* calm, relaxed.

**restless** *adj* active, agitated, anxious, bustling, changeable, disturbed, edgy, fidgety, fitful, footloose, fretful, hurried, inconstant, irresolute, jumpy, moving, nervous, nomadic, restive, roving, shifting, sleepless, transient, troubled, turbulent, uneasy, unquiet, unresting, unruly, unsettled, unstable, unsteady, wandering, worried.

*antonyms* calm, relaxed.

**restlessness** n activity, agitation, anxiety, bustle, disquiet, disturbance, edginess, fitfulness, fretfulness, heebie-jeebies, hurry, hurry-scurry, inconstancy, inquietude, insomnia, instability, jitters, jumpiness, movement, nervousness, restiveness, transience, turbulence, turmoil, uneasiness, unrest, unsettledness, wanderlust, worriedness.

*antonyms* calmness, relaxation.

**restoration** *n* instauration, kiss of life, reconstruction, recovery, recruit, recruital, re-establishment, refreshment, refurbishing, rehabilitation, reinstallation, reinstatement, rejuvenation, renewal, renovation, repair, replacement, restitution, return, revitalisation, revival.

*antonyms* damage, removal, weakening.

**restore** *v* fix, mend, reanimate, rebuild, recondition, reconstitute, reconstruct, recover, recruit, redintegrate, re-enforce, re-establish, refresh, refurbish, rehabilitate, reimpose, reinstate, reintroduce, rejuvenate, renew, renovate, repair, replace, retouch, return, revitalise, revive, revivify, strengthen.

*antonyms* damage, remove, weaken.

**restrain** *v* arrest, bind, bit, bridle, chain, check, cohibit, confine, constrain, control, curb, curtail, debar, detain, fetter, govern, hamper, hamshackle, handicap, harness, hinder, hold, imprison, inhibit, jail, keep, limit, manacle, muzzle, pinion, prevent, repress, restrict, stay, subdue, suppress, tie.

*antonyms* encourage, liberate.

**restrained** *adj* calm, controlled, discreet, low-key, mild, moderate, muted, quiet, reasonable, reticent, self-controlled, soft, steady, subdued, tasteful, temperate, undemonstrative, understated, unemphatic, unobtrusive.

*antonym* unrestrained.

**restraint** *n* arrest, ban, bondage, bonds, bridle, captivity, chains, check, coercion, cohibition, command, compulsion, confinement, confines, constraint, control, cramp, curb, curtailment, dam, detention, embargo, fetters, grip, hindrance, hold, imprisonment, inhibition, interdict, lid, limit, limitation, manacles, moderation, pinions, prevention, rein, restriction, self-control, self-discipline, self-possession, self-restraint, stint, straitjacket, suppression, taboo, tie.

*antonym* freedom.

**restrict** *v* astrict, bound, circumscribe, condition, confine, constrain, contain, cramp, demarcate, hamper, handicap, impede, inhibit, limit, regulate, restrain, restringe, scant, thirl, tie.

*antonyms* broaden, encourage, free.

**restriction** *n* check, condition, confinement, constraint, containment, control, curb, demarcation, handicap, inhibition, limitation, regulation, restraint, rule, squeeze, stint, stipulation.

*antonyms* broadening, encouragement, freedom.

**result** *n* conclusion, consequence, decision, development, effect, end, end-product, event, fruit, issue, outcome, produce, reaction, sequel, termination, upshot.

*antonyms* beginning, cause.

*v* appear, arise, culminate, derive, develop, emanate, emerge, end, ensue, eventuate, finish, flow, follow, happen, issue, proceed, spring, stem, terminate.

*antonyms* begin, cause.

**resume** *v* continue, pick up, proceed, recommence, reinstitute, reopen, restart, take up.

*antonym* cease.

**résumé** *n* abstract, digest, epitome, overview, précis, recapitulation, review, run-down, summary, synopsis.

**resumption** *n* continuation, epanalepsis, re-establishment, renewal, reopening, restart, resurgence.

*antonym* cessation.

**resurgence** *n* rebirth, recrudescence, re-emergence, renaissance, renascence, resumption, resurrection, return, revival, revivification, risorgimento.

*antonym* decrease.

**resurrect** *v* come to life, disinter, reintroduce, renew, restore, revive.

*antonyms* bury, kill off, quash.

**resurrection** *n* comeback, reactivation, reappearance, rebirth, renaissance, renascence, renewal, restoration, resurgence, resuscitation, return, revival, revivification.

*antonyms* burying, killing off, quashing.

**resuscitate** *v* quicken, reanimate, reinvigorate, renew, rescue, restore, resurrect, revitalise, revive, revivify, save.

**resuscitated** *adj* redintegrate(d), redivivus, restored, resurrected, revived.

**retain** *v* absorb, commission, contain, detail, employ, engage, grasp, grip, hire, hold, hold back, keep, keep in mind, keep up, maintain, memorise, pay, preserve, recall, recollect, remember, reserve, restrain, save.

*antonyms* release, spend.

**retainer**[1] *n* attendant, dependant, domestic, flunky, footman, galloglass, lackey, menial, servant, supporter, valet, vassal.

**retainer**[2] *n* advance, deposit, fee, retaining fee.

**retaliate** *v* fight back, get back at, get even with, get one's own back, give as good as one gets, hit back, reciprocate, repay in kind, return like for like, revenge oneself, strike back, take revenge.

*antonyms* accept, submit.

**retaliation** *n* a taste of one's own medicine, counterblow, counterstroke, reciprocation, repayment, reprisal, requital, retort, retortion, retribution, revenge, tit for tat, vengeance.

*antonyms* acceptance, submission.

**retard** *v* arrest, brake, check, clog, decelerate, defer, delay, detain, encumber, handicap, hinder, impede, keep back, obstruct, slow, stall.

*antonym* advance.

**retardation** *n* deficiency, delay, dullness, hindering, hindrance, impeding, incapability, incapacity, lag, mental handicap, obstruction, retardment, slowing, slowness.

*antonym* advancement.

**retch** *v* disgorge, gag, heave, puke, reach, regurgitate, spew, throw up, vomit.

**retching** *n* gagging, nausea, puking, reaching, vomiting, vomiturition.

**reticence** *n* muteness, quietness, reserve, restraint, secretiveness, silence, taciturnity, uncommunicativeness, unforthcomingness.

*antonyms* communicativeness, forwardness, frankness.

**reticent** *adj* boutonné, close-lipped, close-mouthed, mum, mute, quiet, reserved, restrained, secretive, silent, taciturn, tight-lipped, uncommunicative, unforthcoming, unspeaking.

*antonyms* communicative, forward, frank.

**retinue** *n* aides, attendants, cortège, entourage, escort, followers, following, personnel, servants, staff, suite, train.

**retiral** *n* abdication, decumbiture, departure, exit, flight, resignation, retirement, retreat, withdrawal.

*antonym* advance.

**retire** *v* decamp, depart, draw back, ebb, exit, leave, recede, remove, retreat, withdraw.

*antonyms* enter, join.

**retired** *adj* emeritus, ex-, former, past.

**retirement** *n* loneliness, obscurity, privacy, retiral, retreat, seclusion, solitude, withdrawal.

*antonyms* company, limelight.

**retiring** *adj* bashful, coy, demure, diffident, humble, meek, modest, mousy, quiet, reclusive, reserved, reticent, self-effacing, shamefaced, shrinking, shy, timid, timorous, unassertive, unassuming.

*antonyms* assertive, forward.

**retort** *v* answer, counter, rejoin, repartee, reply, respond, retaliate, return, riposte.

*n* answer, backword, come-back, quip, rejoinder, repartee, reply, response, riposte, sally.

**retract** *v* abjure, cancel, deny, disavow, disclaim, disown, recall, recant, renounce, repeal, repudiate, rescind, reverse, revoke, unsay, unspeak, withdraw.

*antonym* maintain.

**retreat** *v* depart, ebb, leave, quit, recede, recoil, retire, shrink, turn tail, withdraw.

*antonym* advance.

*n* asylum, den, departure, ebb, evacuation, flight, funk-hole, growlery, haunt, haven, hibernacle, hibernaculum, hideaway, privacy, refuge, resort, retirement, sanctuary, seclusion, shelter, withdrawal.

*antonyms* advance, company, limelight.

**retrench** *v* curtail, cut, decrease, diminish, economise, husband, lessen, limit, pare, prune, reduce, save, slim down, trim.

*antonym* increase.

**retrenchment** *n* contraction, cost-cutting, curtailment, cut, cutback, economy, pruning, reduction, run-down, shrinkage.

*antonym* increase.

**retribution** *n* compensation, justice, Nemesis, payment, punishment, reckoning, recompense, redress, repayment, reprisal, requital, retaliation, revenge, reward, satisfaction, talion, vengeance.

**retrieve** *v* fetch, make good, recall, recapture, recoup, recover, redeem, regain, repair, repossess, rescue, restore, return, salvage, save.

*antonym* lose.

**retrograde** *adj* backward, declining, degenerative, denigrating, deteriorating, downward, inverse, negative, regressive, relapsing, retreating, retrogressive, reverse, reverting, waning, worsening.

*antonym* progressive.

**retrogress** *v* backslide, decline, degenerate, deteriorate, drop, ebb, fall, recede, regress, relapse, retire, retreat, retrograde, return, revert, sink, wane, withdraw, worsen.

*antonym* progress.

**retrogression** *n* decline, deterioration, drop, ebb, fall, recidivism, regress, relapse, retrogradation, return, worsening.

*antonyms* increase, progress.

**retrospect** *n* afterthought, contemplation, hindsight, recollection, re-examination, reference, regard, remembrance, reminiscence, review, survey.

*antonym* prospect.

**retrospective** *adj* backward-looking, retroactive, retro-operative.

**return** *v* announce, answer, choose, communicate, convey, deliver, earn, elect, make, net, pick, reappear, rebound, reciprocate, recoil, recompense, recur, redound, re-establish, refund, reimburse, reinstate, rejoin, remit, render, repair, repay, replace, reply, report, requite, respond, restore, retort, retreat, revert, send, submit, transmit, volley, yield.

*antonyms* leave, take.

*n* account, advantage, answer, benefit, comeback, compensation, form, gain, home-coming, income, interest, list, proceeds, profit, quip, reappearance, rebound, reciprocation, recoil, recompense, recrudescence, recurrence, redound, re-establishment, reimbursement, reinstatement, rejoinder, reparation, repayment, replacement, reply, report, requital, response, restoration, retaliation, retort, retreat, revenue, reversion, reward, riposte, sally, statement, summary, takings, yield.

*antonyms* disappearance, expense, loss, payment.

**re-use** *v* reconstitute, recycle.

**revamp** *v* do up, overhaul, rebuild, recast, recondition, reconstruct, refit, refurbish, rehabilitate, renovate, repair, restore, revise.

**reveal** *v* announce, bare, betray, broadcast, communicate, disbosom, disclose, dismask, display, divulge, exhibit, expose, impart, leak, lift the lid off, manifest, open, proclaim, publish, show, spill a bibful, tell, unbare, unbosom, uncover, unearth, unfold, unmask, unshadow, unveil.

*antonym* hide.

**revel** *v* carouse, celebrate, live it up, make merry, paint the town red, push the boat out, raise the roof, roist, roister, whoop it up.

*n* bacchanal, carousal, carouse, celebration, comus, debauch, festivity, gala, jollification, merry-make, merrymaking, party, saturnalia, spree.

**revel in** bask, crow, delight, gloat, glory, indulge, joy, lap up, luxuriate, rejoice, relish, savour, take pleasure, thrive on, wallow.

*antonym* dislike.

**revelation** *n* announcement, apocalypse, betrayal, broadcasting, communication, disclosure, discovery, display, exhibition, exposé, exposition, exposure, giveaway, leak, manifestation, news, proclamation, publication, telling, uncovering, unearthing, unveiling.

**reveller** *n* bacchanal, bacchant, carouser, celebrator, merrymaker, party-goer, pleasure-seeker, roister, roisterer, royster, roysterer, wassailer.

**revelry** *n* carousal, carouse, celebration, debauch, debauchery, festivity, fun, jollification, jollity, merrymaking, party, revel-rout, riot, roistering, saturnalia, spree, wassail, wassailing, wassailry.

*antonym* sobriety.

**revenge** *n* a dose/taste of one's own medicine, ravanche, reprisal, requital, retaliation, retribution, revengement, satisfaction, ultion, vengeance, vindictiveness.

*v* avenge, even the score, get one's own back, get satisfaction, repay, requite, retaliate, vindicate.

**revengeful** *adj* bitter, implacable, malevolent, malicious, malignant, merciless, pitiless, resentful, spiteful, unforgiving, unmerciful, vengeful, vindictive, wreakful.

*antonym* forgiving.

**revenue** *n* gain, income, interest, proceeds, profits, receipts, returns, rewards, take, takings, yield.

*antonym* expenditure.

**reverberate** *v* echo, rebound, recoil, re-echo, reflect, resound, ring, vibrate.

**reverberation** *n* echo, rebound, recoil, re-echoing, reflection, resonance, resounding, ringing, vibration, wave.

**reverberations** *n* consequences, effects, repercussions, results, ripples, shock wave.

**revere** *v* adore, defer to, exalt, honour, pay homage to, respect, reverence, venerate, worship.

*antonyms* despise, scorn.

**reverence** *n* admiration, adoration, awe, deference, devotion, dulia, esteem, genuflection, homage, honour, hyperdulia, latria, puja, respect, veneration, worship.

*antonym* scorn.

*v* acknowledge, admire, adore, honour, respect, revere, venerate, worship.

*antonyms* despise, scorn.

**reverent** *adj* adoring, awed, decorous, deferential, devout, dutiful, humble, loving, meek, pious, respectful, reverential, solemn, submissive.

*antonym* irreverent.

**reverie** *n* absent-mindedness, abstraction, brown study, daydream, daydreaming, dreamery, inattention, musing, preoccupation, trance, woolgathering.

**reversal** *n* abrogation, annulment, cancellation, countermanding, defeat, delay, difficulty, disaster, enantiodromia, misfortune, mishap, nullification, problem, repeal, rescinding, rescission, reverse, revocation, set-back, turnabout, turnaround, turnround, upset, U-turn, volte-face.

*antonyms* advancement, progress.

**reverse** *v* alter, annul, back, backtrack, cancel, change, countermand, hark back, invalidate, invert, negate, overrule, overset, overthrow, overturn, quash, repeal, rescind, retract, retreat, revert, revoke, transpose, undo, up-end, upset.

*antonym* enforce.

*n* adversity, affliction, antithesis, back, blow, check, contradiction, contrary, converse, defeat, disappointment, failure, hardship, inverse, misadventure, misfortune, mishap, opposite, rear, repulse, reversal, setback, trial, underside, verso, vicissitude, woman.

*adj* backward, contrary, converse, inverse, inverted, opposite, verso.

**revert** *v* backslide, lapse, recur, regress, relapse, resume, retrogress, return, reverse.

*antonym* progress.

**review** *v* assess, criticise, discuss, evaluate, examine, inspect, judge, reassess, recall, recapitulate, recollect, reconsider, re-evaluate, re-examine, rehearse, remember, rethink, revise, scrutinise, study, weigh.

*n* analysis, assessment, commentary, criticism, critique, evaluation, examination, journal, judgement, magazine, notice, periodical, reassessment, recapitulation, recension, reconsideration, re-evaluation, re-examination, report, rethink, retrospect, revision, scrutiny, study, survey.

**reviewer** *n* arbiter, commentator, connoisseur, critic, essayist, judge, observer.

**revile** *v* abuse, blackguard, calumniate, defame, denigrate, libel, malign, miscall, reproach, scorn, slander, smear, traduce, vilify, vilipend, vituperate.

*antonym* praise.

**revise** *v* alter, amend, change, correct, edit, emend, memorise, modify, recast, recense, reconsider, reconstruct, redo, re-examine, reread, revamp, review, rewrite, study, swot up, update.

**revision** *n* alteration, amendment, change, correction, editing, emendation, homework, memorising, modification, recast, recasting, recension, reconstruction, re-examination, rereading, review, rewriting, rifacimento, studying, swotting, updating.

**revitalise** *v* reactivate, reanimate, refresh, rejuvenate, renew, restore, resurrect, revive, revivify.

*antonyms* dampen, suppress.

**revival** *n* awakening, quickening, reactivation, reanimation, reawakening, rebirth, recrudescence, renaissance, renascence, renewal, restoration, resurgence, resurrection, resuscitation, revitalisation, revivification, risorgimento.

*antonym* suppression.

**revive** *v* animate, awaken, cheer, comfort, invigorate, quicken, rally, reactivate, reanimate, recover, refresh, rekindle, renew, renovate, restore, resuscitate, revitalise, revivify, rouse.

*antonyms* suppress, weary.

**revivify** *v* inspirit, invigorate, reactivate, reanimate, refresh, renew, restore, resuscitate, revive.

*antonyms* dampen, depress.

**reviving** *adj* bracing, enheartening, exhilarating, invigorating, reanimating, refreshening, regenerating, reinvigorating, revivescent, revivifying, reviviscent, stimulating, tonic.

*antonyms* disheartening, exhausting.

**revocation** *n* abolition, annulment, cancellation, countermanding, nullification, quashing, repeal, repealing, repudiation, rescinding, rescission, retractation, retraction, reversal, revoking, withdrawal.

*antonym* enforcement.

**revoke** *v* abolish, abrogate, annul, cancel, countermand, disclaim, dissolve, invalidate, negate, nullify, quash, recall, recant, renounce, repeal, repudiate, rescind, retract, reverse, withdraw.

*antonym* enforce.

**revolt**[1] *n* breakaway, defection, inqilab, insurgency, insurrection, Jacquerie, mutiny, putsch, rebellion, revolution, rising, secession, sedition, uprising.

*v* defect, mutiny, rebel, resist, riot, rise.

*antonym* submit.

**revolt**[2] *v* disgust, nauseate, offend, outrage, repel, repulse, scandalise, shock, sicken.

*antonym* please.

**revolting** *adj* abhorrent, abominable, appalling, disgusting, distasteful, fetid, foul, horrible, horrid, loathsome, nasty, nauseating, nauseous, noisome, obnoxious, obscene, offensive, repellent, repugnant, repulsive, shocking, sickening, sickly.

*antonym* pleasant.

**revolution** *n* cataclysm, change, circle, circuit, coup, coup d'état, cycle, gyration, innovation, inqilab, insurgency, Jacquerie, lap, metamorphosis, metanoia, mutiny, orbit, putsch, rebellion, reformation, revolt, rising, rotation, round, shift, spin, transformation, turn, upheaval, uprising, volution, wheel, whirl.

**revolutionary** *n* anarchist, insurgent, insurrectionary, insurrectionist, Jacobin, mutineer, rebel, revolutionist, Trot, Trotskyite.

*adj* anarchistic, avant-garde, different, drastic, experimental, extremist, fundamental, innovative, insurgent, insurrectionary, mutinous, new, novel, progressive, radical, rebel, seditious, subversive, thoroughgoing.

*antonyms* commonplace, establishment.

**revolve** *v* circle, circumgyrate, circumvolve, gyrate, orbit, rotate, spin, turn, wheel, whirl.

**revolver** *n* air-gun, firearm, gun, hand-gun, heater, peace-maker, piece, pistol, rod, shooter, six-shooter.

**revolving** *adj* gyral, gyrating, gyratory, rotating, spinning, turning, whirling.

*antonym* stationary.

**revulsion** *n* abhorrence, abomination, aversion, detestation, disgust, dislike, distaste, hatred, loathing, recoil, repugnance, repulsion.

*antonym* pleasure.

**reward** *n* benefit, bonus, bounty, come-up(p)ance, compensation, desert, gain, guerdon, honour, meed, merit, payment, pay-off, premium, prize, profit, punishment, recompense, remuneration, repayment, requital, retribution, return, wages.

*antonym* punishment.

*v* compensate, guerdon, honour, pay, recompense, remunerate, repay, requite.

*antonym* punish.

**rewarding** *adj* advantageous, beneficial, edifying, enriching, fruitful, fulfilling, gainful, gratifying, pleasing, productive, profitable, remunerative, rewardful, satisfying, valuable, worthwhile.

*antonym* unrewarding.

**rewording** *n* metaphrase, metaphrasis, paraphrase, rephrasing, revision.

**rewrite** *v* correct, edit, emend, recast, redraft, revise, reword, rework.

**rhetoric** *n* bombast, declamation, eloquence, fustian, grandiloquence, hyperbole, magniloquence, oratory, pomposity, rant, verbosity, wordiness.

**rhetorical** *adj* artificial, bombastic, declamatory, false, flamboyant, flashy, florid, flowery, grandiloquent, high-flown, high-sounding, hyperbolic, inflated, insincere, linguistic, magniloquent, oratorical, over-decorated, pompous, pretentious, rhetoric, showy, silver-tongued, stylistic, verbal, verbose, windy.

*antonym* simple.

**rhyme** *n* chime, ditty, doggerel, jingle, limerick, ode, poem, poesie, poetry, song, verse.

**rhythm** *n* accent, beat, cadence, cadency, eurhythmy, flow, lilt, measure, metre, movement, pattern, periodicity, pulse, rhythmicity, swing, tempo, time.

**rhythmic** *adj* cadenced, flowing, harmonious, lilting, melodious, metric, metrical, musical, periodic, pulsating, rhythmical, throbbing.

*antonym* unrhythmical.

**rib** *n* band, bar, bone, costa, moulding, purlin(e), ribbing, ridge, shaft, support, vein, wale.

**ribald** *adj* base, bawdy, blue, broad, coarse, derisive, earthy, filthy, foul-mouthed, gross, indecent, irrisory, jeering, licentious, low, mean, mocking, naughty, obscene, off-colour, Rabelaisian, racy, risqué, rude, scurrilous, smutty, vulgar.

*antonym* polite.

**ribaldry** *n* baseness, bawdiness, billingsgate, coarseness, derision, earthiness, filth, grossness, indecency, irrision, jeering, licentiousness, lowness, mockery, naughtiness, obscenity, raciness, rudeness, scurrility, smut, smuttiness, vulgarity.

**ribbon** *n* band, cord, fillet, hair-band, head-band, jag, sash, shred, strip, taenia, tatter.

**rich** *adj* abounding, abundant, affluent, ample, bright, copious, costly, creamy, deep, delicious, dulcet, elaborate, elegant, expensive, exquisite, exuberant, fatty, fecund, fertile, fine, flavoursome, flush, fruitful, full, full-bodied, full-flavoured, full-toned, gay, gorgeous, heavy, highly-flavoured, humorous, in the money, intense, juicy, laughable, lavish, loaded, ludicrous, luscious, lush, luxurious, mellifluous, mellow, moneyed, opulent, palatial, pecunious, plenteous, plentiful, plutocratic, precious, priceless, productive, prolific, propertied, property, prosperous, resonant, ridiculous, risible, rolling, savoury, side-splitting, spicy, splendid, strong, succulent, sumptuous, superb, sweet, tasty, uberous, valuable, vibrant, vivid, warm, wealthy, well-heeled, well-off, well-provided, well-stocked, well-supplied, well-to-do.

*antonyms* harsh, miserly, plain, poor, simple, tasteless, thin, unfertile.

**riches** *n* a long purse, abundance, affluence, assets, fortune, gold, mint, money, opulence, pelf, plenty, property, resources, richness, substance, treasure, uberty, wealth.

*antonym* poverty.

**richly** *adv* amply, appropriately, condignly, elaborately, elegantly, expensively, exquisitely, fully, gorgeously, lavishly, luxuriously, opulently, palatially, properly, splendidly, suitably, sumptuously, thoroughly, well.

*antonyms* poorly, scantily.

**rickety** *adj* broken, broken-down, decrepit, derelict, dilapidated, feeble, flimsy, frail, imperfect, infirm, insecure, jerry-built, precarious, ramshackle, shaky, shoogly, tottering, tottery, unsound, unstable, unsteady, weak, wobbly.

*antonyms* stable, strong.

**rid** *v* clear, deliver, disabuse, disburden, disembarrass, disencumber, expel, free, purge, relieve, unburden.

*antonym* burden.

**riddance** *n* clearance, deliverance, disposal, ejection, elimination, expulsion, extermination, freedom, purgation, release, relief, removal.

*antonym* burdening.

**riddle¹** *n* brain-teaser, charade, conundrum, enigma, logogram, logograph, logogriph, mystery, poser, problem, puzzle, rebus.

**riddle²** *v* boult, corrupt, damage, fill, filter, impair, infest, invade, mar, pepper, perforate, permeate, pervade, pierce, puncture, screen, sieve, sift, spoil, strain, winnow.

*n* boulter, sieve, strainer.

**ride** *v* control, dominate, enslave, float, grip, handle, haunt, hurl, journey, manage, move, oppress, progress, sit, survive, travel, weather.

*n* drive, hurl, jaunt, journey, lift, outing, spin, trip, whirl.

**ridge** *n* arête, band, costa, crinkle, drum, drumlin, escarpment, eskar, hill, hog's back, hummock, lump, reef, ripple, saddle, wale, weal, welt, yardang, zastruga.

**ridicule** *n* banter, chaff, derision, gibe, irony, irrision, jeering, jeers, laughter, mockery, raillery, sarcasm, satire, scorn, sneers, taunting.

*antonym* praise.

*v* banter, burlesque, caricature, cartoon, chaff, crucify, deride, humiliate, jeer, josh, lampoon, mock, parody, pillory, pooh-pooh, queer, quiz, rib, satirise, scoff, send up, sneer at, take the mickey out of, taunt.

*antonym* praise.

**ridiculous** *adj* absurd, comical, contemptible, damfool, derisory, farcical, foolish, funny, hilarious, incredible, laughable, laughworthy, ludicrous, nonsensical, outrageous, preposterous, risible, silly, stupid, unbelievable.

*antonym* sensible.

**riding-school** *n* manège, school of equitation.

**rife** *adj* abounding, abundant, common, commonplace, current, epidemic, frequent, general, plentiful, prevailing, prevalent, raging, rampant, teeming, ubiquitous, universal, widespread.

*antonym* scarce.

**riff-raff** *n* canaille, hoi polloi, mob, rabble, raffle, raggle-taggle, rag-tag, rag-tag and bobtail, rascality, rent-a-mob, scum, undesirables.

**rifle¹** *v* burgle, despoil, gut, loot, maraud, pillage, plunder, ransack, rob, rummage, sack, strip.

**rifle²** *n* air-gun, bundook, carbine, firearm, firelock, flintlock, fusil, gun, musket, shotgun.

**rift** *n* alienation, beach, breach, break, chink, cleavage, cleft, crack, cranny, crevice, difference, disaffection, disagreement, dissure, division, estrangement, fault, flaw, fracture, gap, opening, quarrel, schism, separation, space, split.

*antonym* unity.

**rig¹** *v* accoutre, equip, fit up, furnish, kit out, outfit, provision, supply.

*n* accoutrements, apparatus, ensemble, equipage, equipment, fitments, fittings, fixtures, gear, machinery, outfit, tackle.

**rig out** accoutre, array, attire, caparison, clothe, costume, dress, dress up, equip, fit, fit out, fit up, furnish, kit out, outfit.

**rig up** arrange, assemble, build, construct, erect, fit up, fix up, improvise, knock up.

*antonym* dismantle.

**rig²** *v* arrange, cook, doctor, engineer, fake, falsify, fiddle, fix, gerrymander, juggle, manipulate, tamper with, trump up.

**right** *adj* absolute, accurate, admissible, advantageous, appropriate, authentic, balanced, becoming, characteristic, comme il faut, complete, compos mentis, conservative, correct, deserved, desirable, dexter, dextral, direct, done, due, equitable, ethical, exact, factual, fair, favourable, fine, fit, fitting, genuine, good, healthy, honest, honourable, ideal, just, lawful, lucid, moral, normal, opportune, out-and-out, perpendicular, precise, proper, propitious, rational, reactionary, real, reasonable, righteous, rightful, rightist, rightward, right-wing, sane, satisfactory, seemly, sound, spot-on, straight, suitable, thorough, thoroughgoing, Tory, true, unerring, unimpaired, upright, utter, valid, veracious, veritable, virtuous, well.

*antonyms* left, left-wing, mad, unfit, wrong.

*adv* absolutely, accurately, advantageously, altogether, appropriate, aptly, aright, bang, befittingly, beneficially, completely, correctly, directly, entirely, ethically, exactly, factually, fairly, favourably, fittingly, fortunately, genuinely, honestly, honourably, immediately, instantly, justly, morally, perfectly, precisely, promptly, properly, quickly, quite, righteously, rightward(s), satisfactorily, slap-bang, squarely, straight, straightaway, suitably, thoroughly, totally, truly, utterly, virtuously, well, wholly.

*antonyms* incorrectly, left, unfairly, wrongly.

*n* authority, business, claim, droit, due, equity, freedom, good, goodness, honour, integrity, interest, justice, lawfulness, legality, liberty, licence, morality, permission, power, prerogative, privilege, propriety, reason, rectitude, righteousness, rightfulness, rightness, title, truth, uprightness, virtue.

*antonyms* depravity, wrong.

*v* avenge, correct, fix, rectify, redress, repair, righten, settle, stand up, straighten, vindicate.

**right away** at once, chop-chop, directly, forthwith, immediately, instantly, now, promptly, right off, straight off, straightaway, straightway, this instant, tout de suite, without delay, without hesitation.

*antonym* eventually.

**righteous** *adj* blameless, equitable, ethical, fair, God-fearing, good, guiltless, honest, honourable, incorrupt, just, law-abiding, moral, pure, rectitudinous, saintly, sinless, upright, virtuous.

*antonym* unrighteous.

*n* Holy Willies, just, Pharisees, saints, unco guid, well-doers.

*antonym* unrighteous.

**righteousness** *n* blamelessness, dharma, equity, ethicalness, faithfulness, goodness, honesty, honour, integrity, justice, morality, probity, purity, rectitude, uprightness, virtue.

*antonym* unrighteousness.

**rightful** *adj* authorised, bona fide, correct, de jure, due, just, lawful, legal, legitimate, licit, prescribed, proper, real, suitable, true, valid.

*antonyms* incorrect, unlawful.

**rightfully** *adv* correctly, de jure, justifiably, justly, lawfully, legally, legitimately, properly, rightly.

*antonyms* incorrectly, unjustifiably.

**right-handed** *adj* dext(e)rous.

*antonym* left-handed.

**right-handedness** *n* dexterity, dextrality.

*antonym* left-handedness.

**rigid** *adj* adamant, austere, cast-iron, exact, fixed, harsh, inflexible, intransigent, invariable, rigorous, set, severe, starch(y), stern, stiff, stony, strict, stringent, tense, unalterable, unbending, uncompromising, undeviating, unrelenting, unyielding.

*antonym* flexible.

**rigmarole** *n* balderdash, bother, carry-on, gibberish, hassle, jargon, nonsense, palaver, performance, red tape, riddle-me-ree, to-do, trash, twaddle.

**rigorous** *adj* accurate, austere, challenging, conscientious, demanding, exact, exacting, extreme, firm, hard, harsh, inclement, inflexible, inhospitable, meticulous, nice, painstaking, precise, punctilious, Rhadamanthine, rigid, scrupulous, severe, spartan, stern, strict, stringent, thorough, tough, unsparing.

*antonyms* lenient, mild.

**rigour** *n* accuracy, asperity, austerity, conscientiousness, exactitude, exactness, firmness, hardness, hardship, harshness, inflexibility, meticulousness, ordeal, preciseness, precision, privation, punctiliousness, rigidity, rigorism, rigourousness, sternness, strictness, stringency, suffering, thoroughness, trial.

*antonyms* leniency, mildness.

**rig-out** *n* apparel, clobber, clothing, costume, dress, ensemble, garb, gear, get-up, habit, livery, outfit, raiment, rig, togs, uniform.

**rile** *v* anger, annoy, bug, exasperate, gall, get, irk, irritate, miff, nark, nettle, peeve, pique, provoke, put out, upset, vex.

*antonym* soothe.

**rim** *n* border, brim, brink, circumference, edge, lip, margin, skirt, verge.

*antonym* centre.

**rind** *n* crust, epicarp, husk, integument, peel, skin, zest.

**ring**[1] *n* annulation, annulet, annulus, arena, association, band, cabal, cartel, cell, circle, circuit, circus, clique, collar, collet, combine, coterie, crew, enclosure, gang, group, gyre, halo, hoop, knot, loop, mob, organisation, rink, round, rundle, syndicate.

*v* circumscribe, encircle, enclose, encompass, gash, gird, girdle, mark, score, surround.

**ring**[2] *v* bell, buzz, call, chime, clang, clink, peal, phone, resonate, resound, reverberate, sound, tang, telephone, ting, tinkle, tintinnabulate, toll.

*n* buzz, call, chime, clang, clink, knell, peal, phone-call, tang, ting, tinkle, tintinnabulation.

**ringleader** *n* bell-wether, brains, chief, fugleman, leader, spokesman.

**rinse** *v* bathe, clean, cleanse, dip, sluice, splash, swill, synd, wash, wet.

*n* bath, dip, dye, splash, tint, wash, wetting.

**riot** *n* anarchy, bagarre, boisterousness, carousal, commotion, confusion, debauchery, disorder, display, disturbance, Donnybrook, émeute, excess, extravaganza, festivity, flourish, fray, frolic, high, insurrection, jinks, jollification, road

lawlessness, merry-make, merrymaking, quarrel, revelry, riotousness, riotry, romp, rookery, rout, row, ruction, ruffle, shindig, shindy, show, splash, strife, tumult, turbulence, turmoil, uproar.

*antonyms* calm, order.

*v* carouse, frolic, rampage, rebel, revel, revolt, rise up, roister, romp, run riot, run wild.

**riotous** *adj* anarchic, boisterous, disorderly, insubordinate, insurrectionary, lawless, loud, luxurious, mutinous, noisy, orgiastic, rambunctious, rampageous, rebellious, refractory, roisterous, rollicking, rowdy, saturnalian, side-splitting, tumultuous, ungovernable, unrestrained, unruly, uproarious, violent, wanton, wild.

*antonyms* orderly, restrained.

**rip** *v* burst, claw, cut, gash, hack, lacerate, rend, rupture, score, separate, slash, slit, split, tear.

*n* cleavage, cut, gash, hole, laceration, rent, rupture, slash, slit, split, tear.

**rip off** cheat, con, defraud, diddle, do, dupe, exploit, filch, fleece, lift, mulct, overcharge, pilfer, pinch, rob, rogue, steal, sting, swindle, swipe, thieve, trick.

**ripe** *adj* accomplished, auspicious, complete, developed, favourable, finished, grown, ideal, mature, mellow, opportune, perfect, prepared, promising, propitious, ready, right, ripened, seasoned, suitable, timely.

*antonyms* inopportune, untimely.

**ripen** *v* age, burgeon, develop, mature, mellow, prepare, season.

**rip-off** *n* cheat, con, con trick, daylight robbery, diddle, exploitation, fraud, robbery, sting, swindle, theft.

**riposte** *n* answer, come-back, quip, rejoinder, repartee, reply, response, retort, return, sally.

*v* answer, quip, reciprocate, rejoin, reply, respond, retort, return.

**ripple** *n* babble, burble, disturbance, eddy, gurgle, lapping, pirl, purl, ripplet, undulation, wave, wimple.

**rise** *v* advance, appear, arise, ascend, buoy, climb, crop up, emanate, emerge, enlarge, eventuate, flow, get up, grow, happen, improve, increase, intensify, issue, kite, levitate, lift, mount, mutiny, occur, originate, progress, prosper, rebel, resist, revolt, slope, slope up, soar, spring, spring up, stand up, surface, swell, tower, volume, wax.

*antonyms* descend, fall.

*n* acclivity, advance, advancement, aggrandisement, ascent, climb, elevation, hillock, improvement, incline, increase, increment, origin, progress, promotion, raise, rising, upsurge, upswing, upturn, upward turn.

*antonyms* descent, fall.

**risible** *adj* absurd, amusing, comic, comical, droll, farcical, funny, hilarious, humorous, laughable, ludicrous, rib-tickling, ridiculous, side-splitting.

*antonyms* serious, unfunny.

**rising** *n* émeute, insurrection, revolt, revolution, riot, uprising.

*adj* advancing, approaching, ascending, assurgent, emerging, growing, increasing, intensifying, mounting, soaring, swelling.

*antonym* decreasing.

**risk** *n* adventure, chance, danger, gamble, hazard, jeopardy, peril, possibility, speculation, uncertainty, venture.

*antonyms* certainty, safety.

*v* adventure, chance, dare, endanger, gamble, hazard, imperil, jeopardise, speculate, venture.

**risky** *adj* chancy, dangerous, dicey, dodgy, fraught, hazardous, iffy, perilous, precarious, riskful, touch-and-go, tricky, uncertain, unsafe.

*antonym* safe.

**risqué** *adj* bawdy, blue, coarse, crude, daring, earthy, immodest, improper, indecent, indecorous, indelicate, naughty, near the knuckle, off colour, Rabelaisian, racy, ribald, suggestive.

*antonym* decent.

**rite** *n* act, ceremonial, ceremony, custom, form, formality, liturgy, mystery, observance, office, ordinance, practice, procedure, ritual, sacrament, service, solemnity, usage, worship.

**ritual** *n* ceremonial, ceremony, communion, convention, custom, form, formality, habit, liturgy, mystery, observance, ordinance, practice, prescription, procedure, rite, routine, sacrament, service, solemnity, tradition, usage, wont.

*adj* ceremonial, ceremonious, conventional, customary, formal, formulary, habitual, prescribed, procedural, routine, stereotyped.

*antonyms* informal, unusual.

**rival** *n* adversary, antagonist, challenger, collateral, compeer, competitor, contender, contestant, corrival, emulator, equal, equivalent, fellow, match, opponent, peer, rivaless.

*antonyms* associate, colleague, co-worker.

*adj* competing, competitive, conflicting, corrival, emulating, emulous, opposed, opposing.

*antonyms* associate, co-operating.

*v* compete, contend, emulate, equal, match, oppose, rivalise, vie with.

*antonym* co-operate.

**rivalry** *n* antagonism, competition, competitiveness, conflict, contention, contest, duel, emulation, opposition, rivality, rivalship, struggle, vying.

*antonym* co-operation.

**river** *n* beck, burn, creek, ea, flood, flow, gush, riverway, rush, spate, stream, surge, tributary, waterway.

*adj* fluvial, riverain, riverine.

**river-bank** *n* rivage.

**river-mouth** *n* broads, delta, estuary, firth, frith, ostium.

**riveting** *adj* absorbing, arresting, captivating, engrossing, enthralling, fascinating, gripping, hypnotic, magnetic, spellbinding.

*antonym* boring.

**road** *n* Autobahn, autopista, autoroute, autostrada, avenue, boulevard, camino real, carriageway, clearway, course, crescent, direction, drift, drive, driveway, freeway, highway, lane, motorway, path, pathway, roadway, route, street, thoroughfare, track, way.

**roam** *v* drift, meander, peregrinate, prowl, ramble, range, rove, squander, stravaig, stray, stroll, travel, walk, wander.

*antonym* stay.

**roar** *v* bawl, bay, bell, bellow, blare, clamour, crash, cry, guffaw, hoot, howl, rumble, shout, thunder, vociferate, wuther, yell.

*antonym* whisper.

*n* bellow, belly-laugh, blare, clamour, crash, cry, guffaw, hoot, howl, outcry, rumble, shout, thunder, yell.

*antonym* whisper.

**rob** *v* bereave, blag, bunko, cheat, con, defraud, deprive, despoil, dispossess, do, flake, flimp, gyp, heist, hold up, loot, mill, pillage, plunder, raid, ramp, ransack, reive, rifle, rip off, roll, sack, sting, strip, swindle, thieve.

*antonyms* give, provide.

**robber** *n* bandit, brigand, burglar, cateran, cheat, con man, dacoit, fraud, highwayman, hijacker, klepht, ladrone, land-pirate, latron, looter, motorbandit, pirate, plunderer, raider, reiver, stealer, swindler, thief, vulture.

**robbery** *n* blag, burglary, dacoitage, dacoity, depredation, embezzlement, filching, fraud, heist, high toby, hold-up, larceny, low toby, pillage, plunder, purse-snatching, purse-taking, raid, rapine, rip-off, spoliation, stealing, stick-up, swindle, theft, thievery.

**robe** *n* bathrobe, costume, dressing-gown, gown, habit, housecoat, peignoir, vestment, wrap, wrapper.

*v* apparel, attire, clothe, drape, dress, garb, vest.

**robot** *n* android, automaton, Dalek, golem, machine, zombie.

**robust** *adj* able-bodied, athletic, boisterous, brawny, coarse, down-to-earth, earthy, fit, hale, hard-headed, hardy, healthy, hearty, husky, indecorous, lusty, muscular, over-hearty, powerful, practical, pragmatic, raw, realistic, robustious, roisterous, rollicking, rough, rude, rugged, sensible, sinewy, sound, staunch, sthenic, stout, straightforward, strapping, strong, sturdy, thick-set, tough, unsubtle, vigorous, well.

*antonyms* mealy-mouthed, unhealthy, unrealistic, weak.

**rock**[1] *n* anchor, boulder, bulwark, cornerstone, danger, foundation, hazard, logan, log(g)anstone, mainstay, obstacle, pebble, problem, protection, stone, support.

**rock**[2] *v* astonish, astound, daze, dumbfound, jar, lurch, pitch, reel, roll, shake, shock, stagger, stun, surprise, sway, swing, tilt, tip, toss, wobble.

**rocky**[1] *adj* craggy, flinty, hard, pebbly, rocklike, rough, rugged, stony.

*antonyms* smooth, soft.

**rocky**[2] *adj* dizzy, doubtful, drunk, ill, inebriated, intoxicated, rickety, shaky,

sick, sickly, staggering, tipsy, tottering, uncertain, undependable, unpleasant, unreliable, unsatisfactory, unstable, unsteady, unwell, weak, wobbly, wonky.

*antonyms* dependable, steady, well.

**rod** *n* bar, baton, birch, cane, dowel, ferula, ferule, mace, pole, sceptre, shaft, spoke, staff, stick, strut, switch, verge, wand.

**rogue** *n* blackguard, charlatan, cheat, con man, crook, deceiver, devil, fraud, Greek, knave, miscreant, mountebank, nasty piece/bit of work, ne'er-do-well, picaroon, rapscallion, rascal, reprobate, saltimbanco, scamp, scapegallows, scoundrel, sharper, swindler, vagrant, villain, wag.

*antonym* saint.

**roguish** *adj* arch, bantering, cheeky, confounded, coquettish, criminal, crooked, deceitful, deceiving, dishonest, espiègle, fraudulent, frolicsome, hempy, impish, knavish, mischievous, playful, puckish, raffish, rascally, roguing, shady, sportive, swindling, unprincipled, unscrupulous, villainous, waggish.

*antonyms* honest, serious.

**roguishly** *adv* archly, cheekily, coquettishly, en badinant, impishly, mischievously, playfully.

*antonym* seriously.

**roguishness** *n* archness, badinage, bantering, cheekiness, coquettishness, deceitfulness, dishonesty, espièglerie, fraud, impishness, mischief, mischievousness, playfulness, roguery, tricks, unscrupulousness, villainy, waggishness.

*antonym* seriousness.

**roister** *v* bluster, boast, brag, carouse, celebrate, frolic, make merry, paint the town red, revel, roist, rollick, romp, strut, swagger, whoop it up.

**roisterer** *n* blusterer, boaster, braggart, carouser, ranter, reveller, roister, swaggerer.

**roisterous** *adj* boisterous, clamorous, disorderly, exuberant, loud, noisy, obstreperous, roisting, rowdy, uproarious, wild.

*antonyms* orderly, restrained.

**role** *n* capacity, character, duty, function, impersonation, job, job of work, part, portrayal, position, post, representation, task.

**roll** *v* billow, bind, boom, coil, curl, drum, echo, elapse, enfold, entwine, envelop, even, flatten, flow, furl, grumble, gyrate, level, lumber, lurch, pass, peel, pivot, press, reel, resound, reverberate, revolve, roar, rock, rotate, rumble, run, smooth, spin, spread, stagger, swagger, swathe, sway, swing, swivel, thunder, toss, trill, trindle, trundle, tumble, turn, twirl, twist, undulate, volume, waddle, wallow, wander, welter, wheel, whirl, wind, wrap.

*n* annals, ball, bobbin, boom, catalogue, census, chronicle, cycle, cylinder, directory, drumming, growl, grumble, gyration, index, inventory, list, notitia, record, reel, register, resonance, reverberation, revolution, roar, roller, roster, rotation, rumble, run, schedule, scroll, spin, spool, table, thunder, turn, twirl, undulation, volume, wheel, whirl.

**roll up** arrive, assemble, cluster, congregate, convene, forgather, gather.

*antonyms* leave, scatter.

**rollicking** *adj* boisterous, carefree, cavorting, devil-may-care, exuberant, frisky, frolicsome, hearty, jaunty, jovial, joyous, lively, merry, playful, rip-roaring, roisterous, roisting, romping, spirited, sportive, sprightly, swashbuckling.

*antonyms* restrained, serious.

**rolling** *adj* heaving, rippling, surging, undulant, undulating, waving.

*antonym* flat.

**roly-poly** *adj* buxom, chubby, fat, overweight, plump, podgy, pudgy, roll-about, rotund, roundabout, rounded, tubby.

*antonym* slim.

**romance** *n* absurdity, adventure, affair(e), amour, attachment, charm, colour, exaggeration, excitement, fabrication, fairy tale, falsehood, fantasy, fascination, fiction, gest(e), glamour, idyll, intrigue, invention, legend, liaison, lie, love affair, love story, melodrama, mystery, novel, passion, relationship, sentiment, story, tale, tear-jerker.

*v* exaggerate, fantasise, lie, overstate.

**romantic** *adj* amorous, charming, chimerical, colourful, dreamy, exaggerated, exciting, exotic, extravagant, fabulous, fairy-tale, fanciful, fantastic, fascinating, fictitious, fond, glamorous, high-flown, idealistic, idyllic, imaginary, imaginative, impractical, improbable, legendary, lovey-dovey, loving, made-up, mushy, mysterious, passionate, picturesque, quixotic, romantical, sentimental, sloppy, soppy, starry-eyed, tender, unrealistic, utopian, visionary, whimsical, wild.

*antonyms* humdrum, practical, real, sober, unromantic.

*n* Don Quixote, dreamer, idealist, romancer, sentimentalist, utopian, visionary.

*antonym* realist.

**Romeo** *n* Casanova, Don Juan, gigolo, ladies' man, lady-killer, Lothario, lover.

**romp** *v* caper, cavort, frisk, frolic, gambol, revel, rig, roister, rollick, skip, sport.

*n* caper, frolic, lark, rig, spree.

**rook** *v* bilk, cheat, clip, con, defraud, diddle, do, fleece, mulct, overcharge, rip off, soak, sting, swindle.

**room** *n* allowance, apartment, area, capacity, chamber, chance, compartment, compass, elbow-room, expanse, extent, house-room, latitude, leeway, margin, occasion, office, opportunity, play, range, salon, saloon, scope, space, territory, volume.

**roomy** *adj* ample, broad, capacious, commodious, extensive, generous, large, sizable, spacious, voluminous, wide.

*antonym* cramped.

**root¹** *n* base, basis, beginnings, bottom, cause, core, crux, derivation, essence, foundation, fountainhead, fundamental, germ, heart, mainspring, more, nub, nucleus, occasion, origin, radicle, radix, rhizome, root-cause, rootlet, seat, seed, source, starting point, stem, tuber.

*v* anchor, embed, entrench, establish, fasten, fix, ground, implant, moor, set, sink, stick.

**root and branch** completely, entirely, finally, radically, thoroughly, totally, utterly, wholly.

*antonyms* not at all, slightly.

**root²** *v* burrow, delve, dig, ferret, forage, grout, hunt, nose, poke, pry, rootle, rummage.

**root out** abolish, clear away, destroy, dig out, discover, efface, eliminate, eradicate, erase, exterminate, extirpate, produce, remove, root up, turn out, uncover, unearth, uproot.

*antonyms* cover, establish.

**rooted** *adj* confirmed, deep, deeply, deep-seated, entrenched, established, felt, firm, fixed, ingrained, radical, rigid, root-fast.

*antonyms* superficial, temporary.

**roots** *n* background, beginning(s), birthplace, cradle, family, heritage, home, origins.

**rope** *n* cable, cord, fake, hawser, lariat, lasso, line, marline, strand, warp, widdy.

*v* bind, catch, fasten, hitch, lash, lasso, moor, pinion, tether, tie.

**rope in** embroil, engage, enlist, inveigle, involve, lure, persuade.

*antonym* keep out.

**ropy** *adj* below par, deficient, inadequate, indifferent, inferior, off colour, poorly, rough, sketchy, stringy, substandard, unwell.

*antonyms* good, well.

**roster** *n* bead-roll, list, listing, register, roll, rota, schedule, table.

**rostrum** *n* dais, hustings, platform, podium, stage.

**rosy** *adj* auspicious, blooming, blushing, bright, cheerful, encouraging, favourable, fresh, glowing, healthy-looking, hopeful, optimistic, pink, promising, reassuring, red, reddish, rose, roseate, rose-coloured, rose-hued, roselike, rose-pink, rose-red, rose-scented, rosy-fingered, rubicund, ruddy, sunny.

*antonyms* depressed, depressing, sad.

**rot** *v* corrode, corrupt, crumble, decay, decline, decompose, degenerate, deteriorate, disintegrate, fester, go bad, languish, moulder, perish, putrefy, ret, spoil, taint.

*n* balderdash, blight, bosh, bunk, bunkum, canker, claptrap, codswallop, collapse, corrosion, corruption, decay, decomposition, deterioration, disintegration, drivel, flapdoodle, guff, hogwash, moonshine, mould, nonsense, poppycock, putrefaction, putrescence, rubbish, tommyrot, tosh, twaddle.

**rotary** *adj* gyrating, gyratory, revolving, rotating, rotational, rotatory, spinning, turning, whirling.

*antonym* fixed.

**rotate** *v* alternate, gyrate, interchange, pirouette, pivot, reel, revolve, spell, spin, switch, swivel, turn, twiddle, wheel.

**rotation** *n* alternation, cycle, gyration, interchanging, orbit, pirouette, reel, revolution, sequence, spin, spinning, succession, switching, turn, turning, volution, wheel.

**rotten** *adj* addle(d), bad, base, below par, bent, contemptible, corroded, corrupt, crooked, crumbling, crummy, decayed, decaying, deceitful, decomposed, decomposing, degenerate, deplorable, despicable, dirty, disagreeable, disappointing, dishonest, dishonourable, disintegrating, disloyal, faithless, festering, fetid, filthy, foul, grotty, ill-considered, ill-thought-out, immoral, inadequate, inferior, lousy, low-grade, manky, mean, mercenary, mouldering, mouldy, nasty, off colour, perfidious, perished, poor, poorly, punk, putid, putrescent, putrid, rank, regrettable, ropy, rough, scurrilous, sick, sorry, sour, stinking, substandard, tainted, treacherous, unacceptable, unfortunate, unlucky, unpleasant, unsatisfactory, unsound, untrustworthy, unwell, venal, vicious, vile, wicked.

*antonyms* good, honest, practical, sensible, well.

**rotter** *n* bastard, blackguard, blighter, bounder, cad, cur, dastard, fink, louse, rat, scoundrel, stinker, swine.

*antonym* saint.

**rotund** *adj* bulbous, chubby, corpulent, fat, fleshy, full, globular, grandiloquent, heavy, magniloquent, obese, orbed, orbicular, orby, oro(ro)tund, plump, podgy, portly, resonant, rich, roly-poly, rotundate, round, rounded, sonorous, spheral, spheric, spherical, spherular, sphery, stout, tubby.

*antonyms* flat, gaunt, slim.

**roué** *n* debauchee, lecher, libertine, profligate, rake, rakehell, sensualist, wanton.

**rough** *adj* agitated, amorphous, approximate, arduous, austere, basic, bearish, bluff, blunt, boisterous, bristly, broken, brusque, bumpy, bushy, cacophonous, choppy, churlish, coarse, craggy, crude, cruel, cursory, curt, discordant, discourteous, dishevelled, disordered, drastic, estimated, extreme, foggy, formless, fuzzy, general, grating, gruff, hairy, hard, harsh, hasty, hazy, husky, ill, ill-bred, ill-mannered, imperfect, impolite, imprecise, inclement, incomplete, inconsiderate, indelicate, inexact, inharmonious, irregular, jagged, jarring, loutish, nasty, off colour, poorly, quick, rasping, raspy, raucous, raw, rocky, ropy, rotten, rough-and-ready, rowdy, rude, rudimentary, rugged, rusty, scabrous, severe, shaggy, shapeless, sharp, sick, sketchy, spartan, squally, stony, stormy, tangled, tempestuous, tough, tousled, tousy, turbulent, unceremonious, uncivil, uncomfortable, uncouth, uncultured, uncut, undressed, uneven, unfeeling, unfinished, ungracious, unjust, unmannerly, unmusical, unpleasant, unpolished, unprocessed, unrefined, unshaven, unshorn, untutored, unwell, unwrought, upset, vague, violent, wild.

*antonyms* accurate, calm, harmonious, mild, polite, smooth, well.

*n* bruiser, bully, corner-boy, draft, hooligan, keelie, mock-up, model, outline, roughneck, rowdy, ruffian, sketch, thug, tough, yob, yobbo.

**rough up** bash, batter, beat up, do, knock about, maltreat, manhandle, mistreat, mug, thrash.

**rough-and-ready** *adj* adequate, approximate, crude, impoverished, makeshift, provisional, sketchy, stop-gap, unpolished, unrefined.

*antonyms* exact, refined.

**rough-and-tumble** *n* affray, bagarre, barney, brawl, Donnybrook, dust-up, fight, fracas, mêlée, punch-up, rookery, rout, ruction, ruffle, rumpus, scrap, scuffle, shindy, struggle.

**roughen** *v* abrade, asperate, coarsen, granulate, graze, harshen, rough, scuff.

*antonym* smooth.

**roughneck** *n* apache, bruiser, bully boy, corner-boy, hooligan, keelie, lout, Mohock, myrmidon, rough, rowdy, ruffian, thug, toe-rag, toe-ragger, tough.

**round** *adj* ample, annular, ball-shaped, blunt, bowed, bulbous, candid, circular, complete, curved, curvilinear, cylindrical, direct, discoid, disc-shaped, entire, fleshy, frank, full, full-fleshed, globular, mellifluous, orbed, orbicular, orby, orotund, outspoken, plain, plump, resonant, rich, ring-shaped, roly-poly, rotund, rotundate, rounded, solid, sonorous, spheral, spheric, spherical, spherular, sphery, straightforward, unbroken, undivided, unmodified, whole.

*antonyms* evasive, niggardly, partial, thin.

*n* ambit, ball, band, beat, bout, bullet, cartridge, circle, circuit, compass, course, cycle, disc, discharge, division, globe, lap, level, orb, period, ring, routine, schedule, sequence, series, session, shell, shot, sphere, spheroid, spherule, stage, succession, tour, turn.

*v* bypass, circle, circumnavigate, encircle, flank, sail round, skirt, turn.

**round off** cap, close, complete, conclude, crown, end, finish, finish off, settle.

*antonym* begin.

**round on** abuse, assail, attack, bite (someone's) head off, retaliate, snap at, turn on.

**round the bend** barmy, batty, bonkers, crazy, cuckoo, daft, dotty, eccentric, insane, mad, nuts, nutty, off one's rocker, screwy.

*antonym* sane.

**round up** assemble, collect, drive, gather, gather in, group, herd, marshal, muster, rally.

*antonym* disperse.

**roundabout** *adj* ambagious, circuitous, circumlocutory, devious, discursive, evasive, indirect, meandering, oblique, periphrastic, tortuous, twisting, winding.

*antonyms* direct, straight, straightforward.

**roundly** *adv* bluntly, completely, fiercely, forcefully, frankly, intensely, openly, outspokenly, rigorously, severely, sharply, thoroughly, vehemently, violently.

*antonym* mildly.

**round-up** *n* assembly, collation, collection, gathering, herding, marshalling, muster, overview, précis, rally, summary, survey.

*antonym* dispersal.

**rouse** *v* agitate, anger, animate, arouse, awaken, bestir, call, disturb, enkindle, excite, exhilarating, firk, flush, galvanise, incite, inflame, instigate, move, provoke, rise, start, startle, stimulate, stir, suscitate, unbed, wake, whip up.

*antonym* calm.

**rousing** *adj* brisk, electrifying, excitant, excitative, excitatory, exciting, exhilarating, hypnopompic, inflammatory, inspiring, lively, moving, spirited, stimulating, stirring, vigorous.

*antonym* calming.

**rout** *n* beating, brawl, clamour, crowd, debacle, defeat, disturbance, Donnybrook, drubbing, flight, fracas, fuss, herd, hiding, licking, mob, overthrow, pack, rabble, riot, rookery, ruffle, ruin, shambles, stampede, thrashing.

*antonyms* calm, win.

*v* beat, best, chase, conquer, crush, defeat, destroy, discomfit, dispel, drub, fleme, fley, hammer, lick, overthrow, scatter, thrash, worst.

**route** *n* avenue, beat, circuit, course, direction, flightpath, itinerary, journey, passage, path, road, round, run, way.

*v* convey, direct, dispatch, forward, send.

**routine** *n* act, bit, custom, formula, grind, groove, heigh, jog-trot, line, method, order, pattern, performance, piece, practice, procedure, programme, spiel, usage, way, wont.

*adj* banal, boring, clichéd, conventional, customary, day-by-day, dull, everyday, familiar, habitual, hackneyed, humdrum, mundane, normal, ordinary, predictable, run-of-the-mill, standard, tedious, tiresome, typical, unimaginative, uninspired, unoriginal, usual, wonted, workaday.

*antonyms* exciting, unusual.

**rove** *v* cruise, drift, gallivant, meander, ramble, range, roam, stravaig, stray, stroll, traipse, waltz Matilda, wander.

*antonym* stay.

**rover** *n* drifter, gadabout, gypsy, itinerant, nomad, rambler, ranger, stravaiger, transient, traveller, vagrant, wanderer.

*antonym* stay-at-home.

**row**[1] *n* bank, colonnade, column, file, line, queue, range, rank, sequence, series, string, tier.

**row**[2] *n* altercation, brawl, castigation, commotion, controversy, dispute, disturbance, Donnybrook, dressing-down, falling-out, fracas, fray, fuss, lecture, noise, quarrel, racket, rammy, reprimand, reproof, rhubarb, rollicking, rookery, rout, ruckus, ruction, ruffle, rumpus, scrap, shemozzle, shindig, shindy, slanging match, squabble, talking-to, telling-off, ticking-off, tiff, tongue-lashing, trouble, tumult, uproar.

*antonym* calm.

*v* argue, argufy, brawl, dispute, fight, scrap, squabble, wrangle.

**rowdy** *adj* boisterous, disorderly, loud, loutish, noisy, obstreperous, roisterous, roisting, rorty, rough, rumbustious, stroppy, unruly, uproarious, wild.

*antonyms* quiet, restrained.

*n* brawler, corner-boy, hoodlum, hooligan, keelie, lout, rough, ruffian, tearaway, tough, yahoo, yob, yobbo.

**royal** *adj* august, basilical, grand, imperial, impressive, kinglike, kingly, magnificent, majestic, monarchical, princely, queenlike, queenly, regal, sovereign, splendid, stately, superb, superior.

**rub** *v* abrade, apply, caress, chafe, clean, embrocate, fray, grate, knead, malax, malaxate, massage, polish, put, scour, scrape, shine, smear, smooth, spread, stroke, wipe.

*n* caress, catch, difficulty, drawback, hindrance, hitch, impediment, kneading, malaxage, malaxation, massage, obstacle, polish, problem, shine, snag, stroke, trouble, wipe.

**rub out** assassinate, cancel, delete, efface, erase, expunge, kill, murder, obliterate, remove.

**rub up the wrong way** anger, annoy, bug, get, get one's goat, get to, get under one's skin, irk, irritate, needle, niggle, peeve, vex.

*antonym* calm.

**rubbish** *n* balderdash, balls, baloney, bosh, bunkum, clamjamphrie, claptrap, cobblers, codswallop, crap, dead-wood, debris, draff, dreck, drivel, dross, flotsam and jetsam, garbage, gibberish, gobbledegook, guff, havers, hogwash, junk, kibosh, kitsch, landfill, leavings, litter, lumber, moonshine, mullock, nonsense, offal, offscourings, offscum, piffle, poppycock, raffle, refuse, riddlings, rot, scoria, scrap, stuff, sullage, sweepings, tommyrot, tosh, trash, trashery, truck, trumpery, twaddle, vomit, waste.

*antonym* sense.

**rubbish-dump** *n* kitchen-midden, landfill, laystall, tip.

**rubbishy** *adj* brummagem, cheap, draffish, draffy, gimcrack, grotty, paltry, petty, shoddy, tatty, tawdry, third-rate, throw-away, trashy, twopenny-halfpenny, valueless, worthless.

*antonym* classy.

**ruction** *n* altercation, brawl, commotion, dispute, disturbance, Donnybrook, fracas, fuss, quarrel, racket, rookery, rout, row, ruffle, rumpus, scrap, storm, to-do, trouble, uproar.

*antonym* calm.

**ruddy** *adj* blooming, blushing, crimson, flammulated, florid, flushed, fresh, glowing, healthy, pink, red, reddish, roseate, rose-hued, rose-pink, rosy, rosy-cheeked, rubicund, rubineous, rubious, ruby, sanguine, scarlet, sunburnt.

*antonyms* pale, unhealthy.

**rude** *adj* abrupt, abusive, artless, barbarous, blunt, boorish, brusque, brutish, cheeky, churlish, coarse, crude, curt, discourteous, disrespectful, graceless, gross, harsh, ignorant, illiterate, ill-mannered, impertinent, impolite, impudent, inartistic, inconsiderate, inelegant, insolent, insulting, loutish, low, makeshift, oafish, obscene, offhand, peremptory, primitive, raw, rough, savage, scurrilous, sharp, short, simple, startling, sudden, uncivil, uncivilised, uncouth, uncultured, uneducated, ungracious, unmannerly, unpleasant, unpolished, unrefined, untutored, violent, vulgar.

*antonyms* graceful, polished, polite, smooth.

**rudeness** *n* abruptness, abuse, abusiveness, bad manners, barbarism, bluntness, boorishness, brusqueness, cheek, churlishness, curtness, discourtesy, disrespect, grossièreté, ill-manners, impertinence, impoliteness, impudence, incivility, insolence, oafishness, sharpness, uncouthness, vulgarity.

*antonym* politeness.

**rudimentary** *adj* abecedarian, basic, early, elementary, embryonic, fundamental, germinal, immature, inchoate, initial, introductory, primary, primitive, primordial, undeveloped, vestigial.

*antonyms* advanced, developed.

**rudiments** *n* ABC, basics, beginnings, elements, essentials, foundation, fundamentals, germin, principia, principles, prolegomena.

**rue** *v* bemoan, bewail, beweep, deplore, grieve, lament, mourn, regret, repent.

*antonym* rejoice.

**rueful** *adj* conscience-stricken, contrite, dismal, doleful, grievous, long-visaged, lugubrious, melancholy, mournful, penitent, pitiable, pitiful, plaintive, regretful, remorseful, repentant, sad, self-reproachful, sorrowful, sorry, woebegone, woeful.

*antonym* glad.

**ruffian** *n* apache, bruiser, brute, bully, bully-boy, corner-boy, cut-throat, hoodlum, hooligan, keelie, lout, miscreant, Mohock, myrmidon, plug-ugly, rascal, rogue, rough, roughneck, rowdy, scoundrel, thug, toe-rag, toe-ragger, tough, villain, yob, yobbo.

**ruffle** *v* agitate, annoy, confuse, derange, disarrange, discompose, disconcert, dishevel, disorder, disquiet, disturb, fluster, harass, irritate, mess up, muss up, muss(e), nettle, peeve, perturb, rattle, rumple, stir, torment, tousle, trouble, unsettle, upset, vex, worry, wrinkle.

*antonym* smooth.

**rugged** *adj* arduous, austere, barbarous, beefy, blunt, brawny, broken, bumpy, burly, churlish, crabbed, craggy, crude, demanding, difficult, dour, exacting, graceless, gruff, hale, hard, hard-featured, hardy, harsh, husky, irregular, jagged, laborious, muscular, ragged, rigorous, robust, rocky, rough, rude, severe, sour, stark, stern, strenuous, strong, sturdy, surly, taxing, tough, trying, uncompromising, uncouth, uncultured, uneven, unpolished, unrefined, vigorous, weather-beaten, weathered, worn.

*antonyms* easy, refined, smooth.

**ruin** *n* bankruptcy, bouleversement, breakdown, collapse, crash, damage, decay, defeat, destitution, destruction, devastation, disintegration, disrepair, dissolution, downfall, failure, fall, havoc, heap, insolvency, nemesis, overthrow, ruination, subversion, undoing, Waterloo, wreck, wreckage.

*antonyms* development, reconstruction.

*v* banjax, bankrupt, botch, break, crush, damage, defeat, demolish, destroy, devastate, disfigure, impoverish, injure, jigger, mangle, mar, mess up, overthrow, overturn, overwhelm, pauperise, raze, scupper, scuttle, shatter, smash, spoil, unmake, unshape, wreck.

*antonyms* develop, restore.

**ruinous** *adj* baleful, baneful, broken-down, calamitous, cataclysmic, catastrophic, crippling,

deadly, decrepit, deleterious, derelict, destructive, devastating, dilapidated, dire, disastrous, extravagant, fatal, immoderate, injurious, murderous, noxious, pernicious, ramshackle, ruined, shattering, wasteful, withering.

*antonym* beneficial.

**ruins** *n* chaos, debris, devastation, havoc, shambles.

**rule** *n* administration, ascendancy, authority, axiom, canon, command, condition, control, convention, course, criterion, custom, decree, direction, domination, dominion, empire, form, formula, governance, government, guide, guideline, habit, influence, institute, jurisdiction, law, leadership, mastery, maxim, method, order, ordinance, policy, power, practice, precept, prescript, principle, procedure, raj, regime, regulation, reign, routine, ruling, standard, supremacy, sway, tenet, way, wont.

*v* adjudge, adjudicate, administer, command, control, decide, decree, determine, direct, dominate, establish, find, govern, guide, judge, lead, manage, obtain, predominate, preponderate, prevail, pronounce, regulate, reign, resolve, settle.

**rule out** ban, debar, disallow, dismiss, eliminate, exclude, forbid, obviate, preclude, prevent, prohibit, proscribe, reject.

**ruler** *n* commander, controller, emperor, empress, gerent, governor, gubernator, head of state, imperator, king, leader, lord, monarch, potentate, prince, princess, queen, sovereign, suzerain.

*antonym* subject.

**ruling** *n* adjudication, decision, decree, finding, firman, hatti-sherif, indiction, interlocution, irade, judgement, pronouncement, resolution, ukase, verdict.

*adj* boss, chief, commanding, controlling, dominant, governing, leading, main, predominant, pre-eminent, preponderant, prevailing, prevalent, principal, regnant, reigning, supreme, upper.

**rum** *adj* abnormal, bizarre, curious, freakish, funny, funny-peculiar, odd, peculiar, queer, singular, strange, suspect, suspicious, unusual, weird.

**rumbustious** *adj* boisterous, clamorous, disorderly, exuberant, loud, noisy, obstreperous, refractory, robust, roisterous, roisting, rorty, rough, rowdy, unmanageable, unruly, uproarious, wayward, wild, wilful.

*antonyms* quiet, restrained, sensible.

**ruminate** *v* brood, chew over, chew the cud, cogitate, consider, contemplate, deliberate, meditate, mull over, muse, ponder, reflect, revolve, think.

**rummage** *v* delve, examine, explore, hunt, poke around, ransack, root, rootle, rout, search.

**rumour** *n* breeze, bruit, bush telegraph, buzz, canard, fame, furphy, gossip, grapevine, hearsay, kite, news, on-dit, report, story, talk, tidings, underbreath, whisper, word.

*v* bruit, circulate, gossip, publish, put about, report, say, tell, whisper.

**rump** *n* backside, bottom, bum, buttocks, croup, dock, haunch, hindquarters, nache, posterior, rear, seat.

**rumple** *v* crease, crinkle, crumple, crush, derange, dishevel, disorder, muss up, muss(e), pucker, ruffle, scrunch, tousle, wrinkle.

*antonym* smooth.

**rumpus** *n* bagarre, barney, brouhaha, commotion, confusion, disruption, disturbance, Donnybrook, fracas, furore, fuss, kerfuffle, noise, rhubarb, rookery, rout, row, ruction, shemozzle, shindig, shindy, tumult, uproar.

*antonym* calm.

**run** *v* abscond, administer, bear, beat it, bleed, bolt, boss, career, carry, cascade, challenge, circulate, clear out, climb, compete, conduct, contend, continue, control, convey, co-ordinate, course, creep, dart, dash, decamp, depart, direct, discharge, display, dissolve, drive to, escape, extend, feature, flee, flow, function, fuse, gallop, glide, go, gush, hare, hasten, head, hie, hotfoot, hurry, issue, jog, ladder, last, lead, leak, lie, liquefy, lope, manage, manoeuvre, mastermind, melt, mix, move, operate, oversee, own, pass, perform, ply, pour, print, proceed, propel, publish, race, range, reach, regulate, roll, rush, scamper, scarper, scramble, scud, scurry, skedaddle, skim, slide, speed, spill, spout, spread, sprint, stand, stream, stretch, superintend, supervise, tear, tick, trail, transport, unravel, work.

*antonyms* stay, stop.

*n* application, category, chain, class, coop, course, current, cycle, dash, demand, direction, drift, drive, enclosure, excursion, flow, gallop, jaunt, jog, journey, joy, kind, ladder, lift, motion, movement, order, outing, passage, path, pen, period, pressure, progress, race, ride, rip, round, rush, season, sequence, series, snag, sort, spell, spin, sprint, spurt, streak, stream, stretch, string, tear, tendency, tenor, tide, trend, trip, type, variety, way.

**run after** chase, follow, pursue, stalk, tail.

*antonym* flee.

**run away** abscond, beat it, bolt, clear out, decamp, elope, escape, flee, scarper, scoot, scram, skedaddle, take it on the lam.

*antonym* stay.

**run down** belittle, capture, criticise, curtail, cut, debilitate, decrease, decry, defame, denigrate, disparage, drop, exhaust, hit, knock, knock over, reduce, revile, run over, strike, tire, trim, vilify, weaken.

*antonyms* increase, miss, praise.

**run for it** bolt, do a bunk, escape, flee, fly, have it on one's toes, make off, retreat, scarper, scram, skedaddle.

*antonym* stay.

**run in** apprehend, arrest, bust, collar, feel (someone's) collar, jail, lift, nab, nick, pick up, pinch.

**run into** bash, encounter, hit, meet, ram, strike.

*antonym* miss.

**run off** abscond, bleed, bolt, decamp, drain, duplicate, elope, escape, have it on one's toes, make off, print, produce, scarper, siphon, skedaddle, tap.

*antonym* stay.

**run out** cease, close, dry up, end, expire, fail, finish, terminate.

**run over** hit, knock down, overflow, rehearse, reiterate, review, run down, spill, strike, survey.

**run riot** cut loose, go on the rampage, kick over the traces, rampage, sow one's wild oats, spread.

**run through** blow, check, dissipate, examine, exhaust, fritter away, pierce, practise, read, rehearse, review, spit, squander, stab, stick, survey, transfix, waste.

**run together** amalgamate, blend, coalesce, combine, commingle, fuse, intermingle, intermix, join, merge, mingle, mix, unite.

*antonym* separate.

**runaway** *n* absconder, deserter, escapee, escaper, fleer, fugitive, refugee, truant.

*adj* escaped, fleeing, fugitive, loose, uncontrolled, wild.

**rundown** *n* briefing, cut, decrease, drop, lessening, outline, précis, recap, reduction, résumé, review, run-through, sketch, summary, synopsis.

**run-down** *adj* broken-down, debilitated, decrepit, dilapidated, dingy, drained, enervated, exhausted, fatigued, grotty, peaky, ramshackle, scabby, seedy, shabby, tumble-down, unhealthy, weak, weary, worn-out.

*antonym* well-kept.

**run-in** *n* altercation, argument, brush, confrontation, contretemps, difference of opinion, dispute, dust-up, encounter, fight, quarrel, set-to, skirmish, tussle, wrangle.

**runner**[1] *n* athlete, competitor, courier, harrier, jogger, messenger, miler, participant, sprinter.

**runner**[2] *n* flagellum, offshoot, sarmentum, shoot, sprig, sprout, stem, stolon, tendril.

**running** *adj* consecutive, constant, continuous, current, flowing, incessant, moving, perpetual, streaming, successive, together, unbroken, unceasing, uninterrupted.

*antonyms* broken, ceased, occasional.

*n* administration, charge, competition, conduct, contention, contest, control, co-ordination, direction, functioning, going, leadership, maintenance, management, operation, organisation, pace, performance, regulation, superintendency, supervision, working.

**runny** *adj* dilute, diluted, flowing, fluid, liquefied, liquid, melted, molten, watery.

*antonym* solid.

**run-of-the-mill** *adj* average, common, commonplace, everyday, fair, mediocre, middling, modest, ordinary, passable, routine, tolerable, undistinguished, unexceptional, unexciting, unimaginative, unimpressive, unremarkable.

*antonym* exceptional.

**rupture** *n* altercation, breach, break, breaking, burst, bust-up, cleavage, cleft, contention, crack, disagreement, disruption, dissolution, estrangement, falling-out, feud, fissure, fracture, hernia, hostility, quarrel, rent, rift, schism, split, splitting, tear.

*v* break, burst, cleave, crack, disrupt, dissever, divide, fracture, puncture, rend, separate, sever, split, sunder, tear.

**rural** *adj* agrarian, agrestic, agricultural, Arcadian, bucolic, countrified, country, forane, mofussil, pastoral, pr(a)edical, rustic, sylvan, yokelish.

*antonym* urban.

**ruse** *n* artifice, blind, deception, device, dodge, hoax, imposture, manoeuvre, ploy, sham, stall, stratagem, subterfuge, trick, wile.

**rush** *v* accelerate, attack, bolt, capture, career, charge, dart, dash, dispatch, expedite, fly, hasten, hightail it, hotfoot, hurry, hustle, overcome, press, push, quicken, race, run, scour, scramble, scurry, shoot, speed, speed up, sprint, stampede, storm, tear, wallop, w(h)oosh.

*n* assault, charge, dash, dispatch, expedition, flow, haste, hurry, onslaught, push, race, scramble, speed, stampede, storm, streak, surge, swiftness, tantivy, tear, urgency.

*adj* brisk, careless, cursory, emergency, expeditious, fast, hasty, hurried, prompt, quick, rapid, superficial, swift, urgent.

**rush about** rampage.

**rust** *n* blight, corrosion, fungus, mildew, mould, must, oxidation, patina, rot, stain, verdigris.

*v* atrophy, corrode, corrupt, decay, decline, degenerate, deteriorate, oxidise, rot, stagnate, tarnish.

**rust-coloured** *adj* auburn, chestnut, copper, coppery, ginger, gingery, red, reddish, reddish-brown, russet, rusty, sandy, tawny, titian.

**rustic** *adj* agrarian, agrestic, Arcadian, artless, awkward, boorish, bucolic, churlish, cloddish, clodhopping, clownish, clumsy, coarse, countrified, country, crude, georgic, graceless, hick, hodden, homely, homespun, loutish, lumpish, maladroit, oafish, pastoral, plain, provincial, rough, rude, rural, silvatic, silvestrian, simple, sylvan, unaffected, uncouth, uncultured, unmannerly, unpolished, unrefined, unsophisticated, yokelish.

*antonyms* cultivated, polished, sophisticated, urban, urbane.

*n* boor, bumpkin, carl, chaw-bacon, chuff, churl, clod, clodhopper, clown, Corydon, country cousin, countryman, countrywoman, hayseed, hick, hillbilly, hind, hob, Hobinoll, Hodge, kern, oaf, peasant, provincial, swain, yokel.

*antonyms* dandy, man-about-town, sophisticate.

**rustle** *v* crackle, crepitate, susurrate, swish, whisper, whoosh.

*n* crackle, crepitation, crepitus, crinkling, rustling, susurration, susurrus, swish, whisper, whispering, whoosh.

**rusty** *adj* aeruginous, ancient, antiquated, antique, corroded, creaking, creaky, croaking, croaky, dated, deficient, discoloured, dull, encrusted, fogram, hoarse, impaired, old-fashioned, outmoded, oxidised, passé, patinated, raucous, rough, rust-covered, rusted, sluggish, stagnated, stale, stiff, tarnished, time-worn, unpractised, weak.

**rut** *n* channel, ditch, furrow, gouge, groove, gutter, habit, indentation, pattern, pothole, routine, score, sulcus, system, track, trough, vallecula, wheelmark.

*v* channel, cut, furrow, gouge, groove, hole, indent, mark, score.

**ruthless** *adj* adamant, adamantine, barbarous, brutal, callous, cruel, cut-throat, dog-eat-dog, ferocious, fierce, hard, hard-hearted, harsh, heartless, implacable, inexorable, inhuman, merciless, pitiless, relentless, remorseless, savage, severe, stern, stony, unfeeling, unmerciful, unpitying, unrelenting.

*antonyms* compassionate, merciful.

# S

**sable** *adj* black, coal-black, dark, dusky, ebon, ebony, inky, jet, jetty, midnight, pitch-black, pitch-dark, pitchy, reven, sombre.

**sabotage** *v* cripple, damage, destroy, disable, disrupt, incapacitate, mar, nullify, ratten, scupper, subvert, thwart, undermine, vandalise, vitiate, wreck.

*n* damage, destruction, disablement, disruption, impairment, marring, rattening, subversion, treachery, treason, undermining, vandalism, vitiation, wrecking.

**sac** *n* bag, bladder, bursa, capsule, cyst, follicle, pocket, pod, pouch, saccule, theca, vesica, vesicle, vesicula.

**saccharine** *adj* cloying, honeyed, maudlin, mawkish, nauseating, oversweet, schmaltzy, sentimental, sickly, sickly-sweet, sloppy, soppy, sugary, syrupy, treacly.

*antonyms* bitter, tart.

**sack**[1] *v* axe, discharge, dismiss, fire, lay off, make redundant.

*n* discharge, dismissal, notice, one's books, one's cards, one's marching orders, the axe, the boot, the bum's rush, the chop, the elbow, the push.

**sack**[2] *v* demolish, depredate, desecrate, despoil, destroy, devastate, lay waste, level, loot, maraud, pillage, plunder, raid, rape, ravage, raze, rifle, rob, ruin, spoil, strip, waste.

*n* depredation, desecration, despoliation, destruction, devastation, levelling, looting, marauding, pillage, plunder, plundering, rape, rapine, ravage, razing, ruin, waste.

**sacred** *adj* blessed, consecrated, dedicated, devotional, divine, ecclesiastical, godly, hallowed, heavenly, holy, inviolable, inviolate, invulnerable, priestly, protected, religious, revered, sacrosanct, saintly, sanctified, secure, solemn, venerable, venerated.

*antonyms* mundane, profane, temporal.

**sacredness** *n* divinity, godliness, holiness, inviolability, invulnerability, sacrosanctity, saintliness, sanctity, solemnity.

*antonyms* profaneness, worldliness.

**sacrifice** *v* abandon, forego, forfeit, immolate, let go, lose, offer, relinquish, renounce, slaughter, surrender.

*n* corban, destruction, hecatomb, holocaust, host, immolation, loss, mactation, oblation, offering, renunciation, surrender, victim, votive offering.

**sacrificial** *adj* atoning, expiatory, oblatory, piacular, propitiatory, reparative, votive.

**sacrilege** *n* blasphemy, defilement, desecration, disrespect, heresy, impiety, impiousness, irreverence, mockery, outrage, profanation, profaneness, profanity, violation.

*antonyms* piety, respect, reverence.

**sacrilegious** *adj* blasphemous, desecrating, disrespectful, godless, heretical, impious, irreligious, irreverent, profanatory, profane, ungodly, unholy.

*antonyms* pious, respectful, reverent.

**sacrosanct** *adj* hallowed, impregnable, inviolable, inviolate, sacred, sanctified, untouchable.

**sad** *adj* bad, blue, calamitous, cheerless, chopfallen, crestfallen, crushed, dark, dejected, deplorable, depressed, depressing, desolated, despondent, disastrous, disconsolate, dismal, dispirited, distressed, distressing, doleful, dolesome, doloriferous, dolorific, doughy, dour, dowie, downcast, down-hearted, drear, dreary, gloomy, glum, grave, grief-stricken, grieved, grieving, grievous, heart-rending, heavy, heavy-hearted, jaw-fallen, joyless, lachrymose, lamentable, long-faced, low, low-spirited, lugubrious, melancholy, miserable, mournful, moving, painful, pathetic, pensive, piteous, pitiable, pitiful, poignant, regrettable, serious, shabby, sober, sober-minded, sombre, sorrowful, sorry, sportless, stiff, tearful, touching, tragic, triste, uncheerful, unfortunate, unhappy, unsatisfactory, upsetting, wan, wistful, woebegone, woeful, wretched.

*antonyms* cheerful, fortunate, happy, lucky.

**sadden** *v* aggrieve, dash, deject, depress, desolate, discourage, dishearten, dispirit, distress, grieve, hurt, oppress, upset.

*antonyms* cheer, delight, gratify, please.

**saddle** *v* burden, charge, encumber, impose, land, load, lumber, task, tax.

*n* demipique, pack-saddle, pigskin, pillion, seat.

**sadism** *n* barbarity, bestiality, brutality, callousness, cruelty, heartlessness, inhumanity, malevolence, ruthlessness, sado-masochism, savagery, spite, unnaturalness, viciousness.

**sadistic** *adj* barbarous, bestial, brutal, cruel, heartless, inhuman, malevolent, perverted, ruthless, savage, spiteful, unnatural, vicious.

S

**sadness** n bleakness, cheerlessness, darkness, dejection, depression, desolation, despondency, disconsolateness, dismalness, distress, dole, dolefulness, dolour, gloominess, glumness, gravity, grief, joylessness, low spirits, lugubriousness, melancholy, misery, misfortune, mournfulness, pain, pathos, poignancy, regret, sombreness, sorrow, sorrowfulness, tearfulness, tragedy, unhappiness, wanness, wistfulness, woe, wretchedness.

*antonyms* cheerfulness, delight, happiness.

**safe** adj alive and well, all right, cautious, certain, circumspect, conservative, dependable, discreet, foolproof, guarded, hale, harmless, immune, impregnable, innocuous, intact, invulnerable, non-poisonous, non-toxic, OK, out of harm's way, protected, proven, prudent, pure, realistic, reliable, scatheless, secure, sound, sure, tame, tested, tried, trustworthy, unadventurous, uncontaminated, undamaged, unfailing, unharmed, unhurt, uninjured, unscathed, wholesome.

*antonyms* exposed, harmful, unsafe, vulnerable.

n cash-box, chest, coffer, deposit box, peter, repository, strongbox, vault.

**safe-conduct** n authorisation, convoy, laissez-passer, licence, pass, passport, permit, safeguard, warrant.

**safeguard** v assure, defend, guard, insure, preserve, protect, screen, secure, shelter, shield.

*antonyms* endanger, jeopardise.

n armour, assurance, bulwark, convoy, cover, defence, escort, guarantee, guard, insurance, long-stop, Palladium, precaution, preventive, protection, security, shield, surety.

**safekeeping** n aegis, care, charge, custody, guard, guardianship, keeping, lock and key, protection, supervision, surveillance, trust, tutelage, vigilance, ward, wardship, watch.

**safety** n assurance, cover, deliverance, dependability, harmlessness, immunity, impregnability, invulnerability, protection, refuge, reliability, safeguard, salvation, sanctuary, security, shelter, sureness, via trita, via tuta.

*antonyms* danger, jeopardy.

adj fail-safe, precautionary, preventative, protective.

**sag** v bag, decline, dip, drag, droop, drop, dwindle, fail, fall, flag, give, give way, hang, settle, sink, slide, slip, slump, wane, weaken, wilt.

*antonyms* bulge, rise.

n decline, depression, dip, downturn, drop, dwindling, fall, low, low point, reduction, slide, slip, slump.

*antonyms* peak, rise.

**saga** n adventure, chronicle, epic, epopee, epopeia, epos, history, narrative, romance, roman-fleuve, soap opera, story, tale, yarn.

**sagacious** adj able, acute, apt, astute, canny, cute, discerning, downy, far-sighted, fly, insightful, intelligent, judicious, knowing, long-headed, long-sighted, penetrating, perceptive, percipient, perspicacious, quick, sage, sapient, sharp, shrewd, smart, wary, wide-awake, wily, wise.

*antonyms* foolish, obtuse, short-sighted.

**sagacity** n acumen, acuteness, astuteness, canniness, discernment, foresight, insight, judgement, judiciousness, knowingness, penetration, percipience, perspicacity, prudence, sapience, sense, sharpness, shrewdness, understanding, wariness, wiliness, wisdom.

*antonyms* folly, foolishness, obtuseness.

**sage** adj astute, canny, discerning, intelligent, judicious, knowing, knowledgeable, learned, perspicacious, politic, prudent, sagacious, sapient, sensible, wise.

*antonym* foolish.

n acharya, authority, elder, expert, guru, hakam, maharishi, mahatma, master, Nestor, oracle, philosopher, pundit, rishi, savant, Solomon, Solon, teacher, wise man.

*antonym* ignoramus.

**sail** v captain, cruise, drift, embark, float, fly, glide, navigate, pilot, plane, put to sea, scud, shoot, skim, skipper, soar, steer, sweep, take ship, voyage, waft, weigh anchor, wing.

**sail into** assault, attack, belabour, lambaste, lay into, let fly, set about, tear into, turn on.

**sailor** n AB, able seaman, able-bodied seaman, galiongee, gob, hearty, Jack Tar, lascar, leatherneck, limey, marine, mariner, matelot, matlow, navigator, rating, salt, sea dog, sea-dog, seafarer, seaman, tar, tarpaulin, tarry-breeks, water-rat.

**saintliness** n asceticism, blessedness, chastity, devoutness, faith, godliness, goodness, holiness, morality, piety, purity, righteousness, sanctity, self-denial, selflessness, self-sacrifice, spirituality, spotlessness, unselfishness, uprightness, virtue.

*antonyms* godlessness, unholiness, wickedness.

**saintly** adj angelic, beatific, blameless, blessed, blest, celestial, devout, god-fearing, godly, holy, immaculate, innocent, pious, pure, religious, righteous, sainted, saintlike, seraphic, sinless, spotless, stainless, upright, virtuous, worthy.

*antonyms* godless, unholy, unrighteous, wicked.

**sake** n account, advantage, aim, behalf, benefit, cause, consideration, end, gain, good, interest, motive, object, objective, principle, profit, purpose, reason, regard, respect, score, welfare, wellbeing.

**salacious** adj bawdy, blue, carnal, coarse, concupiscent, erotic, horny, improper, indecent, lascivious, lecherous, lewd, libidinous, lickerish, lubricious, lustful, obscene, pornographic, prurient, randy, raunchy, ribald, ruttish, scurrilous, smutty, steamy, wanton.

*antonyms* clean, decent, proper.

**salaried** adj emolumental, emolumentary, paid, remunerated, stipendiary, waged.

*antonyms* honorary, unpaid, voluntary.

**salary** n earnings, emolument, honorarium, income, pay, remuneration, screw, stipend, wage, wages.

**sale** *n* auction, deal, disposal, marketing, sell, selling, trade, traffic, transaction, vending, vendition, vendue.

**saleable** *adj* desirable, marketable, merchantable, sought-after, vendible.

*antonyms* unmarketable, unsaleable.

**salesperson** *n* bagman, clerk, counter-jumper, counter-skipper, sales assistant, salesclerk, salesgirl, saleslady, salesman, saleswoman, shop assistant, shop-boy, shopgirl, shop-keeper, vendeuse.

**salient** *adj* arresting, chief, conspicuous, important, jutting, main, marked, noticeable, obvious, outstanding, principal, projecting, prominent, pronounced, protruding, remarkable, signal, significant, striking.

**sallow** *adj* anaemic, bilious, colourless, pale, pallid, pasty, sickly, unhealthy, wan, yellowish.

*antonyms* rosy, sanguine.

**sally**[1] *v* breeze, charge, erupt, foray, issue, mosey, promenade, rush, saunter, sortie, stroll, surge, venture.

*antonym* retreat.

*n* assault, dash, drive, escapade, excursion, foray, frolic, incursion, jaunt, offensive, raid, rush, sortie, surge, thrust, trip, venture.

*antonyms* retire, retreat.

**sally**[2] *n* bon mot, crack, jest, jeu d'esprit, joke, quip, retort, riposte, wisecrack, witticism.

**salt** *n* acuteness, Attic salt, Attic wit, bite, dryness, flavour, liveliness, merum sal, pawkiness, piquancy, punch, pungency, relish, sarcasm, savour, seasoning, sharpness, smack, taste, trenchancy, vigour, wit, zest, zip.

*adj* brackish, briny, saline, salted, saltish, salty.

*antonym* fresh.

**salt away** accumulate, amass, bank, cache, collect, hide, hoard, save, stash, stockpile, store up.

*antonyms* spend, squander.

**salty** *adj* brackish, briny, colourful, dry, humorous, keen, lively, pawky, piquant, pungent, racy, saline, salsuginous, salt, salted, saltish, spicy, tangy, tart, witty, wry, zestful.

**salubrious** *adj* beneficial, bracing, healthful, health-giving, healthy, hygienic, invigorating, refreshing, restorative, salutary, sanitary, wholesome.

*antonyms* insalubrious, unwholesome.

**salutary** *adj* advantageous, beneficial, good, healthful, healthy, helpful, much-needed, practical, profitable, salubrious, seasonable, timely, useful, valuable, wholesome.

**salutation** *n* address, greeting, homage, obeisance, respects, reverence, salaam, salute, welcome.

**salute** *v* accost, acknowledge, address, bow, greet, hail, honour, kiss, knuckle, nod, recognise, salaam, wave, welcome.

*n* acknowledgement, address, bow, gesture, greeting, hail, handclap, handshake, hello, kiss, nod, obeisance, recognition, reverence, salaam, salutation, salve, salvo, tribute, wave.

**salvage** *v* conserve, glean, preserve, reclaim, recover, recuperate, redeem, repair, rescue, restore, retrieve, salve, save.

*antonyms* abandon, lose, waste.

**salvation** *n* deliverance, escape, liberation, lifeline, preservation, reclamation, redemption, rescue, restoration, retrieval, safety, saving, soteriology.

*antonyms* damnation, loss.

**salve** *n* application, balm, cream, dressing, embrocation, emollient, liniment, lotion, lubricant, medication, ointment, preparation, unguent.

**same** *adj* aforementioned, aforesaid, alike, analogous, changeless, comparable, consistent, corresponding, duplicate, equal, equivalent, homologous, identical, indistinguishable, interchangeable, invariable, matching, mutual, reciprocal, selfsame, similar, substitutable, synonymous, twin, unaltered, unchanged, undiminished, unfailing, uniform, unvarying, very.

*antonyms* changeable, different, incompatible, inconsistent, variable.

*n* ditto, the above-mentioned, the above-named, the aforementioned, the aforesaid.

**sameness** *n* changelessness, consistency, deja vu, duplication, identicalness, identity, indistinguishability, invariability, likeness, monotony, oneness, predictability, repetition, resemblance, similarity, standardisation, tedium, uniformity.

*antonyms* difference, variety.

**sample** *n* cross section, demonstration, ensample, example, exemplification, foretaste, free sample, freebie, illustration, indication, instance, model, pattern, representative, sign, specimen, swatch.

*v* experience, inspect, investigate, pree, sip, taste, test, try.

*adj* demonstration, illustrative, pilot, representative, specimen, test, trial.

**sanctify** *v* anoint, bless, cleanse, consecrate, dedicate, divinify, divinise, exalt, hallow, make holy, purify, sanction.

*antonyms* defile, degrade, desecrate.

**sanctimonious** *adj* canting, false, goody-goody, holier-than-thou, holy, hypocritical, moralising, pharisaical, pi, pietistic, pious, preaching, priggish, righteous, self-righteous, self-satisfied, smug, superior, Tartuffian, Tartuffish, unctuous.

*antonym* humble.

**sanctimoniousness** *n* cant, canting, complacency, holiness, humbug, hypocrisy, moralising, pharisaism, pietism, preachiness, priggishness, righteousness, self-righteousness, self-satisfaction, smugness, Tartuffism, unctuousness.

*antonym* humility.

**sanction** *n* accreditation, agreement, allowance, approbation, approval, authorisation, authority, backing, cachet, confirmation, countenance, endorsement, go-ahead, green light, imprimatur, licence, OK, permission, ratification, seal, support.

*antonyms* disapproval, veto.

*v* accredit, allow, approve, authorise, back, confirm, countenance, countersign, endorse, fiat, license, permit, ratify, support, underwrite, warrant.

*antonyms* disallow, disapprove, veto.

**sanctions** *n* ban, boycott, embargo, interdict, penalty, prohibition, proscription, restrictions.

**sanctity** *n* devotion, godliness, goodness, grace, holiness, inviolability, piety, purity, religiousness, righteousness, sacredness, sacrosanctity, saintliness, saintship, sanctitude, solemnity, spirituality, venerableness.

*antonyms* godlessness, impurity, secularity, unholiness, worldliness.

**sanctuary** *n* adytum, altar, ark, asylum, chancel, church, delubrum, frith, grith, harbourage, haven, holy of holies, naos, presbytery, protection, refuge, retreat, sacrarium, sanctum, sanctum sanctorum, seclusion, shelter, shrine, tabernacle, temple.

**sanctum** *n* cubby-hole, den, growlery, hideaway, holy of holies, refuge, retreat, sanctuary, sanctum sanctorum, shrine, snug, snuggery, study.

**sand** *n* arena, beach, gravel, grit, sands, shore, strand.

**sand-bank** *n* bar, cay, dune, hurst, key, reef, sand-bar, sand-hill, yardang.

**sandy** *adj* arenaceous, auburn, coppery, ginger, gingerous, gingery, gritty, psammitic, red, reddish, reddish-yellow, rusty, tawny, titian, xanthous, yellow, yellowish, yellowy.

**sane** *adj* all there, balanced, compos mentis, dependable, judicious, level-headed, lucid, moderate, normal, rational, reasonable, reliable, right-minded, sensible, sober, sound, stable.

**sang-froid** *n* aplomb, assurance, calmness, composure, cool, cool-headedness, coolness, dispassion, equanimity, imperturbability, indifference, nerve, nonchalance, phlegm, poise, self-control, self-possession, unflappability.

*antonyms* discomposure, excitability, hysteria, panic.

**sanguinary** *adj* bloodied, bloodthirsty, bloody, brutal, cruel, fell, gory, grim, merciless, murderous, pitiless, ruthless, savage.

**sanguine**[1] *adj* animated, ardent, assured, buoyant, cheerful, confident, expectant, hopeful, lively, optimistic, over-confident, over-optimistic, Panglossian, roseate, spirited, unabashed, unappalled, unbowed.

*antonyms* cynical, depressive, gloomy, melancholy, pessimistic, realistic.

**sanguine**[2] *adj* florid, flushed, fresh, fresh-complexioned, pink, red, rosy, rubicund, ruddy.

*antonyms* pale, sallow.

**sanitary** *adj* aseptic, clean, disinfected, germ-free, healthy, hygienic, pure, salubrious, uncontaminated, unpolluted, wholesome.

*antonyms* insanitary, unwholesome.

**sanity** *n* balance of mind, common sense, dependability, judiciousness, level-headedness, lucidity, normality, rationality, reason, reasonableness, reliability, saneness, sense, soundness, stability.

*antonyms* foolishness, insanity.

**sap** *v* bleed, deplete, devitalise, diminish, drain, enervate, exhaust, impair, reduce, rob, undermine, weaken.

*antonyms* build up, increase, strengthen.

**sarcasm** *n* acidity, bitterness, contempt, cynicism, derision, diatribe, invective, irony, mockery, mordancy, satire, scorn, sneering, venom, vitriol.

**sarcastic** *adj* acerbic, acid, acrimonious, biting, caustic, contemptuous, cutting, cynical, derisive, disparaging, incisive, ironical, mocking, mordant, sardonic, sarky, satirical, scathing, sharp, sharp-tongued, sneering, taunting, withering.

**sardonic** *adj* biting, bitter, cynical, derisive, dry, heartless, ironical, jeering, malevolent, malicious, malignant, mocking, mordant, quizzical, sarcastic, satirical, scornful, sneering, wry.

**sash** *n* baldric, belt, cincture, cummerbund, girdle, surcingle, vitta, waistband, zone.

**Satan** *n* Abaddon, Apollyon, Beelzebub, Belial, Clootie, Cloots, Hornie, Lucifer, Mephistopheles, Old Nick, Prince of Darkness, The Adversary, The Devil, The Enemy, The Evil One, The Tempter.

**satanic** *adj* accursed, black, demoniac, demoniacal, demonic, devilish, diabolic, diabolical, evil, fell, fiendish, hellish, infernal, inhuman, iniquitous, malevolent, malignant, Mephistophelian, satanical, wicked.

*antonyms* benevolent, benign, divine, godlike, godly, heavenly, holy.

**sate** *v* cloy, fill, glut, gorge, gratify, overfill, satiate, satisfy, saturate, sicken, slake, surfeit, weary.

*antonyms* deprive, dissatisfy, starve.

**satellite** *n* adherent, aide, attendant, dependant, disciple, follower, hanger-on, lackey, minion, moon, moonlet, parasite, puppet, retainer, sidekick, sputnik, subordinate, sycophant, tributary, vassal, votary.

**satiate** *v* cloy, engorge, glut, gorge, jade, nauseate, overfeed, overfill, sate, satisfy, slake, stuff, surfeit.

*antonyms* deprive, dissatisfy, underfeed.

**satiety** *n* fullness, gratification, over-fullness, overindulgence, repleteness, repletion, satiation, satisfaction, saturation, surfeit.

**satire** *n* burlesque, caricature, diatribe, invective, irony, lampoon, parody, Pasquil, Pasquin, pasquinade, raillery, ridicule, sarcasm, send-up, skit, spoof, squib, takeoff, travesty, wit.

**satirical** *adj* biting, bitter, burlesque, caustic, cutting, cynical, derisive, Hudibrastic, iambic, incisive, ironical, irreverent, mocking, mordant, pungent, sarcastic, sardonic, satiric, taunting.

**satirise** *v* abuse, burlesque, caricature, censure, criticise, deride, lampoon, make fun of, make sport of, mock, parody, Pasquil, Pasquin, pasquinade, pillory, ridicule, send up, squib, take off, travesty.

*antonyms* acclaim, celebrate, honour.

**satirist** *n* caricaturist, cartoonist, lampooner, lampoonist, mocker, parodist, pasquilant, pasquiler, pasquinader, ridiculer.

**satisfaction** *n* achievement, amends, appeasing, assuaging, atonement, comfort, compensation, complacency, content, contentedness, contentment, conviction, damages, ease, enjoyment, fulfilment, fullness, gratification, guerdon, happiness, indemnification, justice, payment, pleasure, pride, quittance, recompense, redress, reimbursement, remuneration, reparation, repleteness, repletion, requital, resolution, restitution, reward, satiety, self-satisfaction, sense of achievement, settlement, vindication, well-being.

*antonyms* discontent, displeasure, dissatisfaction, frustration.

**satisfactory** *adj* acceptable, adequate, all right, average, competent, fair, fit, OK, passable, proper, sufficient, suitable, tickety-boo, up to the mark.

*antonyms* inadequate, unacceptable, unsatisfactory.

**satisfied** *adj* appeased, complacent, content, contented, convinced, full, happy, mollified, pacified, persuaded, pleased, positive, reassured, replete, sated, satiated, self-satisfied, smug, sure.

*antonyms* dissatisfied, hungry, unconvinced.

**satisfy** *v* answer, appease, assuage, assure, atone, compensate, content, convince, delight, discharge, do, fill, fulfil, glut, gratify, guerdon, indemnify, indulge, meet, mollify, pacify, pay, persuade, placate, please, qualify, quench, quiet, reassure, recompense, reimburse, remunerate, replete, requite, reward, sate, satiate, serve, settle, slake, square up, suffice, surfeit.

*antonyms* disappoint, dissatisfy, fail, frustrate, thwart.

**satisfying** *adj* cheering, convincing, cool, filling, fulfilling, gratifying, persuasive, pleasing, pleasurable, satisfactory.

*antonyms* dissatisfying, frustrating, thwarting, unsatisfactory.

**saturate** *v* douse, drench, drouk, imbue, impregnate, infuse, permeate, ret, soak, souse, steep, suffuse, waterlog.

**saturated** *adj* drenched, dripping, droukit, imbued, impregnated, permeated, soaked, soaking, sodden, soggy, sopping, soused, steeped, suffused, waterlogged, wringing.

**saturnine** *adj* austere, dismal, dour, dull, gloomy, glum, grave, heavy, melancholy, mirthless, moody, morose, phlegmatic, severe, sombre, stern, taciturn, uncommunicative, withdrawn.

*antonyms* cheerful, jovial.

**satyr** *n* faun, goat, lecher, Pan, philanderer, womaniser, wood-house, woodwose.

**sauce** *n* archness, assurance, audacity, backchat, brass, brazenness, cheek, cheekiness, disrespect, disrespectfulness, flippancy, freshness, impertinence, impudence, insolence, irreverence, lip, malapertness, nerve, pertness, presumption, presumptuousness, rudeness, sass, sauciness.

*antonyms* politeness, respectfulness.

**saucy** *adj* arch, audacious, cheeky, dashing, disdainful, disrespectful, flip, flippant, forward, fresh, gay, impertinent, impudent, insolent, irreverent, jaunty, lippy, malapert, natty, perky, pert, presumptuous, provocative, rakish, rude, sassy, sporty.

*antonyms* polite, respectful.

**saunter** *v* amble, dacker, dally, dander, daunder, dawdle, linger, loiter, meander, mooch, mosey, perambulate, promenade, ramble, roam, rove, sally forth, stravaig, stroll, wander.

*n* airing, amble, breather, constitutional, outing, perambulation, promenade, ramble, sally, stroll, turn, walk.

**savage** *adj* barbarous, beastly, bestial, blistering, bloodthirsty, bloody, brutal, brutish, catamountain, cruel, devilish, diabolical, dog-eat-dog, fell, feral, ferocious, fierce, harsh, immane, inhuman, merciless, murderous, pitiless, primitive, ravening, rough, rude, rugged, ruthless, sadistic, sanguinary, uncivilised, uncultivated, undomesticated, uneducated, unenlightened, unsparing, untamed, untaught, vicious, wild.

*antonyms* benign, civilised, humane.

*n* aboriginal, aborigine, ape, autochthon, barbarian, bear, beast, boor, brute, fiend, heathen, illiterate, indigene, lout, monster, native, oaf, philistine, primitive, roughneck, yahoo, yobbo.

*v* attack, claw, hammer, lacerate, mangle, maul, pan, scarify, tear.

**savagery** *n* barbarity, bestiality, bloodthirstiness, brutality, brutishness, cruelty, ferity, ferocity, fierceness, inhumanity, mercilessness, murderousness, pitilessness, primitiveness, roughness, ruthlessness, sadism, viciousness, wildness.

*antonyms* civilisation, civility, humanity.

**savant** *n* authority, guru, intellectual, man of letters, master, mastermind, philosopher, pundit, rishi, sage, savante, scholar.

*antonyms* amateur, duffer, ignoramus.

**save** *v* cache, collect, conserve, cut back, deliver, economise, free, gather, guard, hinder, hoard, hold, husband, keep, lay up, liberate, obviate, preserve, prevent, protect, put aside, put by, reclaim, recover, redeem, rescue, reserve, retain, retrench, safeguard, salt away, salvage, screen, shield, spare, squirrel, stash, store.

*antonyms* discard, spend, squander, waste.

**saving** *adj* careful, compensatory, economical, extenuating, frugal, mitigating, qualifying, redeeming, soterial, sparing, thrifty.

*n* bargain, conservation, cut, discount, economy, preservation, reclamation, redemption, reduction, rescue, retrenchment, salvage, salvation.

*antonyms* expense, loss, waste.

**savings** *n* capital, fund, nest egg, reserve fund, reserves, resources, store.

**saviour** *n* champion, defender, emancipator, guardian, knight-errant, liberator, messiah, preserver, protector, rescuer, salvation.

*antonyms* destroyer, enemy.

**savoir-faire** *n* ability, accomplishment, address, assurance, capability, confidence, diplomacy, discretion, expertise, finesse, know-how, poise, tact, urbanity.

*antonyms* awkwardness, clumsiness, incompetence, inexperience.

**savour** *n* excitement, fascination, flavour, interest, piquancy, relish, salt, sapor, smack, smell, spice, tang, taste, zest.

*v* appreciate, dwell on, enjoy, gloat over, like, luxuriate in, partake, rehearse, relish, revel in.

*antonyms* shrink from, wince at.

**savoury** *adj* agreeable, appetising, aromatic, dainty, decent, delectable, delicious, edifying, full-flavoured, gamy, good, gusty, honest, luscious, mouthwatering, palatable, piquant, reputable, respectable, rich, salubrious, scrumptious, spicy, tangy, tasty, toothsome, wholesome.

*antonyms* insipid, tasteless, unappetising.

*n* appetiser, bonne bouche, canape, hors d'oeuvre.

**saw** *n* adage, aphorism, apophthegm, axiom, byword, commonplace, dictum, epigram, gnome, maxim, mot, proverb, saying.

**say** *v* add, affirm, allege, announce, answer, assert, assume, bruit, claim, comment, communicate, conjecture, convey, declare, deliver, disclose, divulge, do, enunciate, estimate, express, guess, imagine, imply, intimate, judge, maintain, mention, opine, orate, perform, presume, pronounce, read, recite, reckon, rehearse, rejoin, remark, render, repeat, reply, report, respond, retort, reveal, rumour, signify, speak, state, suggest, surmise, tell, utter, voice.

*n* authority, chance, clout, crack, go, influence, power, sway, turn, voice, vote, weight, word.

**saying** *n* adage, aphorism, apophthegm, axiom, byword, dictum, gnome, maxim, mot, motto, precept, proverb, remnant, saw, slogan.

**sayings** *n* analects, bon mots, dicta, gems, logia, mots, obiter dicta, quotations, quotes, remarks, remnants, tags, words of wisdom.

**say-so** *n* affirmation, agreement, approval, assertion, asseveration, assurance, authorisation, authority, backing, consent, dictum, guarantee, OK, permission, ratification, sanction, word.

**scald** *v* blister, burn, sear.

**scale**[1] *n* calibration, compass, continuum, degree, degrees, extent, gamut, gradation, grading, graduation, hierarchy, ladder, measure, order, progression, proportion, range, ranking, ratio, reach, register, scope, sequence, series, spectrum, spread, steps.

*v* adjust, level, move, proportion, prorate, regulate, shift.

**scale**[2] *n* crust, encrustation, film, flake, furfur, lamella, lamina, layer, plate, scutellum, shield, squama, squamella, squamula, squamule.

*v* clean, desquamate, exfoliate, flake, peel, scrape.

**scale**[3] *v* ascend, clamber, climb, escalade, mount, scramble, shin up, surmount, swarm.

**scaliness** *n* dandruff, flakiness, furfur, scabrousness, scurfiness, squamosity.

**scaly** *adj* branny, desquamative, desquamatory, flaky, furfuraceous, furfurous, lepidote, leprose, leprous, scabby, scabrous, scurfy, squamose, squamous, squamulose.

**scamp** *n* blighter, caitiff, devil, fripon, imp, knave, lorel, losel, mischief-maker, monkey, prankster, rascal, rogue, ruffian, scallywag, scapegrace, toe-rag, tyke, whippersnapper, wretch.

**scamper** *v* chevy, dart, dash, fly, frisk, frolic, gambol, hasten, hurry, pelt, romp, run, rush, scoot, scurry, scuttle, skedaddle, sprint.

**scan** *v* check, con, examine, glance through, investigate, pan, pan over, scrutinise, search, skim, survey, sweep.

*n* check, examination, investigation, probe, review, screening, scrutiny, search, survey.

**scandal** *n* abuse, aspersion, backbiting, calumniation, calumny, crime, defamation, detraction, dirt, discredit, disgrace, dishonour, embarrassment, enormity, evil, furore, gossip, gossiping, ignominy, infamy, muck-raking, obloquy, odium, offence, opprobrium, outcry, outrage, reproach, rumours, shame, sin, slander, stigma, talk, tattle, traducement, uproar, Watergate, wrongdoing.

**scandalise** *v* affront, appal, astound, disgust, dismay, horrify, nauseate, offend, outrage, repel, revolt, shock, sicken.

**scandalmonger** *n* busybody, calumniator, defamer, gossip, gossip-monger, muck-raker, quidnunc, scandal-bearer, tabby, tabby-cat, tale-bearer, tattle, tattler, traducer.

**scandalous** *adj* abominable, atrocious, calumnious, defamatory, disgraceful, disreputable, evil, exorbitant, extortionate, gamy, gossiping, immoderate, improper, infamous, libellous, monstrous, odious, opprobrious, outrageous, scurrilous, shameful, shocking, slanderous, unseemly, unspeakable, untrue.

**scant** *adj* bare, deficient, hardly any, inadequate, insufficient, limited, little, little or no, minimal, sparse.

*antonyms* adequate, ample, sufficient.

**scanty** *adj* bare, beggarly, deficient, exiguous, inadequate, insubstantial, insufficient, light, meagre, narrow, parsimonious, poor, restricted, scant, scrimp, scrimpy, short, shy, skimped, skimpy, slender, sparing, sparse, thin.

*antonyms* ample, plentiful, substantial.

**scapegoat** *n* fall guy, patsy, victim, whipping-boy.

**scapegrace** *n* blighter, good-for-nothing, imp, ne'er-do-well, rapscallion, rascal, reprobate, rogue, scallywag, scamp, toe-rag.

**scar** *n* blemish, cicatrix, injury, lesion, mark, proud flesh, scar tissue, scarring, stigma, trauma, ulosis, wound.

*v* brand, cicatrise, damage, disfigure, mark, stigmatise, traumatise.

**scarce** *adj* deficient, few, infrequent, insufficient, lacking, rare, scanty, sparse, thin on the ground, uncommon, unusual, wanting.

*antonyms* common, copious, plentiful.

**scarcely** *adv* barely, hardly, just and no more, not readily, not willingly, only just, scarce.

**scarcity** *n* dearth, deficiency, infrequency, insufficiency, lack, niggardliness, paucity, poverty, rareness, rarity, scantiness, shortage, sparseness, uncommonness, want.

*antonyms* abundance, enough, glut, plenty, sufficiency.

**scare** *v* affright, alarm, appal, daunt, dismay, frighten, gally, intimidate, panic, shock, startle, terrify, terrorise, unnerve.

*antonym* reassure.

*n* agitation, alarm, alarm and despondency, alert, consternation, dismay, fright, hysteria, panic, shock, start, terror.

*antonym* reassurance.

**scarecrow** *n* craw-bogle, craw-deil, crowboggart, crow-keeper, fright, gally-bagger, gally-crow, mess, sight, tatterdemalion.

**scared** *adj* affrighted, affrightened, agitated, anxious, appalled, dismayed, fearful, frightened, nervous, panicky, panic-stricken, petrified, shaken, startled, terrified, worried.

*antonyms* confident, reassured.

**scaremonger** *n* alarmist, Cassandra, doom and gloom merchant, doomsman, doomwatcher, jitterbug, pessimist, prophet of doom.

**scarf** *n* babushka, boa, cravat, fichu, headscarf, headsquare, kerchief, muffler, neckerchief, necktie, shawl, stole, tawdry-lace.

**scarper** *v* abscond, absquatulate, beat it, bolt, bunk off, clear off, decamp, depart, disappear, do a bunk, escape, flee, flit, go, hightail it, run away, run for it, scram, skedaddle, vamoose, vanish.

**scary** *adj* alarming, anxious, bloodcurdling, chilling, creepy, disturbing, eldritch, frightening, hair-raising, hairy, horrendous, horrible, horrifying, intimidating, shocking, spine-chilling, spooky, terrifying, unnerving, upsetting, worrying.

**scathing** *adj* acid, biting, bitter, brutal, caustic, critical, cutting, excoriating, harsh, lacerating, mordant, sarcastic, savage, scornful, searing, trenchant, unsparing, virulent, vitriolic, withering, wounding.

*antonym* complimentary.

**scatter** *v* bestrew, break up, broadcast, diffuse, disband, disintegrate, disject, dispel, disperse, disseminate, dissipate, disunite, divide, fling, flurr, litter, propagate, separate, shower, sow, spatter, splutter, spread, sprinkle, squander, strew.

*antonyms* collect, concentrate.

**scatter-brained** *adj* bird-brained, careless, dizzy, empty-headed, feather-brained, flighty, forgetful, frivolous, giddy, inattentive, irresponsible, madcap, scatty, silly, slap-happy, thoughtless, undependable, unreliable.

*antonyms* careful, efficient, sensible, sober.

**scattering** *n* break-up, diaspora, diffusion, disgregation, disjection, dispersal, dispersion, dissemination, dissipation, dissolution, few, fistful, handful, propagation, scatter, separation, smatter, smattering, sprinkling.

*antonyms* abundance, mass.

*adj* disintegrative, dispersive, disseminative, dissipative, divisive.

*antonym* unifying.

**scavenger** *n* Autolycus, cleaner, dustman, forager, garbage collector, raker, rummager, scavager, scrounger, street orderly, street-cleaner, sweeper.

**scenario** *n* outline, plan, plot, projection, resume, rundown, scheme, sequence, situation, skeleton, sketch, story line, summary, synopsis.

**scene** *n* act, area, arena, backdrop, background, business, carry-on, chapter, circumstances, commotion, confrontation, display, disturbance, division, drama, environment, episode, exhibition, focus, fuss, incident, landscape, locale, locality, location, melodrama, milieu, mise en scène, outburst, pageant, panorama, part, performance, picture, place, position, prospect, representation, row, set, setting, show, sight, site, situation, spectacle, spot, stage, tableau, tantrum, to-do, upset, view, vista, whereabouts, world.

**scenery** *n* backdrop, background, decor, flats, landscape, mise en scène, outlook, panorama, set, setting, sight, surroundings, terrain, tormentors, view, vista.

**scenic** *adj* awe-inspiring, beautiful, breathtaking, grand, impressive, magnificent, panoramic, picturesque, pretty, spectacular, striking, stupendous.

*antonyms* dreary, dull, unspectacular.

**scent** *n* aroma, bouquet, fragrance, fumet, odour, perfume, redolence, smell, spoor, trace, track, trail, waft, whiff.

*antonym* stink.

*v* detect, discern, nose, nose out, perceive, recognise, sense, smell, sniff, sniff out.

**scented** *adj* aromatic, fragrant, odoriferous, perfumed, redolent, sweet-smelling.

*antonyms* malodorous, noisome, stinking.

**sceptic** *n* agnostic, atheist, cynic, disbeliever, doubter, doubting Thomas, nullifidian, Pyrrhonist, questioner, questionist, rationalist, scoffer, unbeliever.

*antonym* believer.

**sceptical** *adj* cynical, disbelieving, distrustful, doubtful, doubting, dubious, hesitating, incredulous, mistrustful, pessimistic, questioning, quizzical, scoffing, suspicious, unbelieving, unconvinced, unpersuaded, untrustful.

*antonyms* convinced, naïve, trusting.

**scepticism** *n* agnosticism, atheism, cynicism, disbelief, distrust, doubt, incredulity, pessimism, Pyrrhonism, rationalism, suspicion, unbelief, Voltairianism, Voltairism.

*antonyms* belief, faith, naïvety.

**schedule** *n* agenda, calendar, catalogue, diary, form, inventory, itinerary, list, plan, programme, scheme, scroll, table, timetable.

*v* appoint, arrange, book, list, organise, plan, programme, slot, table, time.

**schematic** *adj* diagrammatic, diagrammatical, graphic, illustrative, representational, simplified, simplistic, symbolic.

**scheme** *n* arrangement, blueprint, chart, codification, configuration, conformation, conspiracy, contrivance, dart, design, device, diagram, disposition, dodge, draft, game, idea, intrigue, lay-out, machinations, manoeuvre, method, outline, pattern, plan, plot, ploy, procedure, programme, project, proposal, proposition, racket, ruse, schedule, schema, shape, shift, stratagem, strategy, subterfuge, suggestion, system, tactics, theory.

*v* collude, conspire, contrive, design, devise, frame, imagine, intrigue, machinate, manipulate, manoeuvre, mastermind, plan, plot, project, pull strings, pull wires, work out.

**schemer** *n* conniver, deceiver, eminence grise, fox, intriguer, Machiavelli, Machiavellian, machinator, mastermind, plotter, politician, wangler, wheeler-dealer, wire-puller.

**scheming** *adj* artful, calculating, conniving, crafty, cunning, deceitful, designing, devious, duplicitous, foxy, insidious, Machiavellian, slippery, sly, tricky, underhand, unscrupulous, wily.

*antonyms* artless, honest, open, transparent.

**schism** *n* breach, break, cleavage, discord, disunion, division, estrangement, faction, quarrel, rift, rupture, sect, separation, severance, splinter group, splintering, split, sunderance.

**scholar** *n* academe, academic, authority, bookman, bookworm, egghead, intellectual, man of letters, maulvi, pupil, savant, scholastic, schoolboy, schoolchild, schoolgirl, schoolman, student.

*antonyms* dullard, dunce, ignoramus, illiterate, philistine.

**scholarly** *adj* academic, analytical, bookish, clerk-like, clerkly, conscientious, critical, erudite, intellectual, knowledgeable, learned, lettered, scholastic, scientific, studious, well-read, wissenschaftlich.

*antonyms* illiterate, unscholarly.

**scholarship**[1] *n* attainments, book-learning, education, erudition, insight, knowledge, learnedness, learning, lore, scholarliness, wisdom, Wissenschaft.

**scholarship**[2] *n* award, bursary, endowment, exhibition, fellowship, grant.

**scholastic** *adj* academic, analytical, bookish, learned, lettered, literary, pedagogic, pedantic, precise, scholarly, subtle.

**school** *n* academy, adherents, alma mater, circle, class, clique, college, creed, denomination, department, devotees, disciples, discipline, doctrine, dogma, externat, faction, faculty, faith, followers, following, group, gymnasium, institute, institution, lycee, outlook, pedagoguery, persuasion, pupils, sect, seminary, set, students, teaching, view, votaries.

*v* coach, discipline, drill, educate, habituate, harden, indoctrinate, instruct, inure, prepare, prime, train, tutor, verse.

**schooling** *n* book-learning, booklore, coaching, drill, education, grounding, guidance, inculcation, indoctrination, instruction, preparation, schoolcraft, teaching, training, tuition.

**schoolteacher** *n* dominie, educator, instructor, master, mistress, pedagogue, school-dame, school-ma'am, schoolmarm, schoolmaster, schoolmistress, teacher, usher.

**science** *n* art, discipline, knowledge, ology, proficiency, skill, specialisation, technique, technology, Wissenschaft.

**scientific** *adj* accurate, analytical, controlled, exact, mathematical, methodical, precise, scholarly, systematic, thorough, wissenschaftlich.

**scintillate** *v* blaze, coruscate, flash, gleam, glint, glisten, glitter, shine, spark, sparkle, twinkle, wink.

**scintillating** *adj* animated, blazing, blinding, bright, brilliant, coruscant, coruscating, dazzling, ebullient, exciting, flashing, glittering, lively, shining, sparkling, stimulating, vivacious, winking, witty.

*antonym* dull.

**scion** *n* branch, child, descendant, graft, heir, imp, offshoot, offspring, shoot, slip, sprig, sprout, successor, twig.

**scoff**[1] *v* belittle, deride, despise, fleer, flout, geck, gibe, jeer, knock, mock, poke fun, pooh-pooh, rail, revile, rib, ridicule, scorn, sneer, taunt, twit.

*antonyms* compliment, flatter, praise.

**scoff**[2] *v* bolt, consume, cram, devour, fill one's face, gobble, gulp, guzzle, pig, put away, shift, wolf.

*antonym* abstain.

*n* chow, comestibles, commons, eatables, eats, edibles, fare, feed, fodder, food, grub, meal, nosh, nosh-up, provisions, rations, scran, tuck, victuals.

**scoffing** *adj* cynical, fiendish, Mephistophelian, sarcastic.

**scold** *v* admonish, bawl out, berate, blame, castigate, censure, chide, find fault with, flyte, jaw, jawbone, lecture, nag, rate, rebuke, remonstrate, reprimand, reproach, reprove, rollick, take to task, tell off, tick off, upbraid, vituperate, wig.

*antonyms* commend, praise.

*n* battle-axe, beldam, fishwife, Fury, harridan, nag, shrew, termagant, virago, vixen, Xanthippe.

**scolding** *n* a piece of one's mind, castigation, dirdum, dressing-down, earful, flyting, jaw, jawbation, jawing, jobation, lecture, rebuke, reprimand, reproof, rollicking, row, siserary, talking-to, telling-off, throughgoing, ticking-off, tongue-lashing, upbraiding, wigging.

*antonym* commendation.

**scoop**[1] *n* backhoe, bail, bailer, bucket, dipper, lade, ladle, spoon.

*v* bail, dig, dip, empty, excavate, gather, gouge, hollow, ladle, lift, pick up, remove, scrape, shovel, sweep.

**scoop**[2] *n* coup, exclusive, expose, inside story, latest, low-down, revelation, sensation.

**scoot** *v* beat it, bolt, bowl, career, dart, dash, hurry, run, scamper, scarper, scud, scurry, scuttle, shoot, skedaddle, sprint, tootle, vamoose, zip.

**scope** *n* ambit, application, area, breadth, capacity, compass, competence, confines, coverage, elbow-room, extent, freedom, latitude, liberty, opportunity, orbit, outlook, purview, range, reach, remit, room, space, span, sphere, terms of reference, tessitura.

**scorch** *v* blacken, blister, burn, char, parch, roast, scald, sear, shrivel, singe, sizzle, torrefy, wither.

**scorched** *adj* arid, baked, blackened, blistered, burnt, charred, cracked, parched, sear, seared, shrivelled, torrid, withered.

**scorching** *adj* baking, blistering, boiling, broiling, burning, fiery, flaming, parching, red-hot, roasting, scalding, searing, sizzling, sweltering, torrid, tropical, withering.

**score** *n* a bone to pick, account, amount, basis, bill, cause, charge, debt, due, gash, grade, gravamen, grievance, ground, grounds, grudge, injury, injustice, line, mark, notch, obligation, outcome, points, reason, reckoning, record, result, scratch, sum total, tab, tally, total, wrong.

*v* achieve, adapt, amass, arrange, attain, be one up, benefit, chalk up, count, cut, deface, earn, engrave, furrow, gain, gouge, grave, graze, groove, hatch, have the advantage, have the edge, impress, incise, indent, knock up, make, make a hit, mark, nick, notch, notch up, orchestrate, profit, realise, record, register, scrape, scratch, set, slash, tally, total, win.

**score out** cancel, cross out, delete, efface, erase, expunge, obliterate, remove, strike out.

*antonyms* reinstate, restore.

**scores** *n* crowds, droves, hosts, hundreds, legions, lots, masses, millions, multitudes, myriads, shoals, swarms.

**scorn** *n* contempt, contemptuousness, contumely, derision, despite, disdain, disgust, dismissiveness, disparagement, geck, mockery, sarcasm, scornfulness, slight, sneer.

*antonyms* admiration, respect.

*v* contemn, deride, despise, disdain, dismiss, flout, hold in contempt, laugh at, laugh in the face of, look down on, misprise, pooh-pooh, refuse, reject, scoff at, slight, sneer at, spurn.

*antonyms* admire, respect.

**scornful** *adj* arrogant, contemptuous, contumelious, defiant, derisive, disdainful, dismissive, disparaging, haughty, insulting, jeering, mocking, sarcastic, sardonic, scathing, scoffing, slighting, sneering, supercilious, withering.

*antonyms* admiring, complimentary, respectful.

**scornfully** *adv* arrogantly, contemptuously, derisively, disdainfully, dismissively, disparagingly, haughtily, scathingly, slightingly, sneeringly, superciliously, witheringly.

*antonyms* admiringly, respectfully.

**scot-free** *adj* clear, ininjured, safe, scatheless, undamaged, unharmed, unhurt, unpunished, unrebuked, unreprimanded, unreproached, unscathed, without a scratch.

**scoundrel** *n* blackguard, blighter, bounder, caitiff, cheat, cur, dastard, good-for-nothing, heel, hound, knave, louse, miscreant, ne'er-do-well, picaroon, rascal, rat, reprobate, rogue, rotter, ruffian, scab, scallywag, scamp, scapegrace, stinker, swine, vagabond, villain.

**scour**[1] *v* abrade, buff, burnish, clean, cleanse, flush, furbish, polish, purge, rub, scrape, scrub, wash, whiten.

**scour**[2] *v* beat, comb, drag, forage, go over, hunt, rake, ransack, search, turn upside-down.

**scourge** *n* affliction, bane, cat, cat-o'-nine-tails, curse, evil, flagellum, infliction, knout, lash, menace, misfortune, penalty, pest, pestilence, plague, punishment, strap, switch, terror, thong, torment, visitation, whip.

*antonyms* benefit, blessing, boon, godsend.

*v* afflict, beat, belt, cane, castigate, chastise, curse, devastate, discipline, excoriate, flagellate, flail, flog, harass, horsewhip, lambast, lash, lather, leather, plague, punish, tan, terrorise, thrash, torment, trounce, verberate, visit, wallop, whale, whip.

**scout** *v* case, check out, do a recce, explore, hunt, investigate, look, observe, pickeer, probe, reconnoitre, search, seek, snoop, spy, spy out, survey, track, watch.

*n* emissary, escort, lookout, outrider, pickeerer, precursor, reconnoitrer, spy, vanguard.

**scowl** *v* frown, glare, glower, grimace, lower.

*n* frown, glare, glower, grimace, moue.

*antonyms* beam, grin, smile.

**scrabble** *v* clamber, claw, dig, grope, grub, paw, root, scramble, scrape, scratch.

**scraggy** *adj* angular, bony, emaciated, gangling, gaunt, lank, lanky, lean, meagre, rawboned, scranny, scrawny, skinny, spare, undernourished, wasted.

*antonyms* plump, rounded, sleek.

**scram** *v* beat it, bolt, clear off, clear out, depart, disappear, do a bunk, flee, get lost, go away, leave, quit, scarper, scoot, shove off, skedaddle, take to one's heels, vamoose.

**scramble** *v* clamber, climb, contend, crawl, hasten, jostle, jumble, push, run, rush, scale, scrabble, shuffle, sprawl, strive, struggle, swarm, vie.

*n* climb, commotion, competition, confusion, contention, free-for-all, hustle, mêlée, muddle, race, rat race, rivalry, rush, strife, struggle, trek, trial, tussle.

**scrap¹** *n* atom, bit, bite, crumb, fraction, fragment, grain, iota, junk, mite, modicum, morsel, mouthful, part, particle, piece, portion, remnant, shard, shred, sliver, snap, snatch, snippet, trace, vestige, waste, whit.

*v* abandon, axe, break up, cancel, chuck, demolish, discard, ditch, drop, jettison, junk, shed, throw out, write off.

*antonyms* reinstate, restore, resume.

**scrap²** *n* argument, bagarre, barney, battle, brawl, disagreement, dispute, dust-up, fight, quarrel, row, ruckus, ruction, rumpus, scuffle, set-to, shindy, squabble, tiff, wrangle.

*antonyms* agreement, peace.

*v* argue, argufy, bicker, clash, fall out, fight, spat, squabble, wrangle.

*antonym* agree.

**scrape** *v* abrade, bark, claw, clean, erase, file, grate, graze, grind, pinch, rasp, remove, rub, save, scour, scrabble, scratch, screech, scrimp, scuff, skimp, skin, squeak, stint.

*n* abrasion, difficulty, dilemma, distress, fix, graze, mess, pickle, plight, predicament, pretty kettle of fish, rub, scratch, scuff, shave, spot, trouble.

**scrappy** *adj* bitty, disjointed, fragmentary, incomplete, perfunctory, piecemeal, sketchy, slapdash, slipshod, superficial.

*antonyms* complete, finished.

**scraps** *n* bits, leavings, leftovers, remains, scrapings.

**scratch** *v* annul, cancel, claw, curry, cut, damage, delete, eliminate, erase, etch, grate, graze, incise, lacerate, mark, race, retire, rub, scarify, score, scrab, scrabble, scrape, withdraw.

*n* blemish, claw mark, gash, graze, laceration, mark, race, scrape, streak.

*adj* haphazard, impromptu, improvised, rough, rough-and-ready, unrehearsed.

*antonym* polished.

**scrawl** *n* cacography, scrabble, scratch, scribble, squiggle, writing.

**scrawny** *adj* angular, bony, emaciated, gaunt, lanky, lean, rawboned, scraggy, skeletal, skinny, thin, underfed, under-nourished.

*antonym* plump.

**scream¹** *v* bawl, clash, cry, holler, jar, roar, screak, screech, shriek, shrill, squeal, wail, yell, yelp, yowl.

*n* howl, outcry, roar, screak, screech, shriek, squeal, wail, yell, yelp, yowl.

*antonym* whisper.

**scream²** *n* card, caution, character, comedian, comic, cure, hoot, joker, laugh, riot, sensation, wit.

*antonym* bore.

**screech** *v* cry, screak, scream, shriek, squawk, squeal, ululate, yelp.

*antonym* whisper.

**screen** *v* cloak, conceal, cover, cull, defend, evaluate, examine, filter, gauge, grade, guard, hide, mask, process, protect, riddle, safeguard, scan, shade, shelter, shield, shroud, sieve, sift, sort, veil, vet.

*antonyms* broadcast, present, show, uncover.

*n* abat-jour, awning, canopy, cloak, concealment, cover, divider, guard, hallan, hedge, hoarding, mantle, mesh, net, partition, shade, shelter, shield, shroud.

**screw** *v* adjust, bleed, cheat, coerce, compress, constrain, contort, contract, crumple, distort, extort, extract, fasten, force, oppress, pressurise, pucker, squeeze, tighten, turn, twist, wind, wrest, wring, wrinkle.

**screw up** botch, bungle, close, contort, contract, crumple, disrupt, distort, knot, louse up, make a hash of, mess up, mishandle, mismanage, pucker, queer, spoil, tighten, wrinkle.

*antonyms* manage, unscrew.

**screwy** *adj* batty, cracked, crackers, crazy, daft, dotty, eccentric, mad, nutty, odd, queer, round the bend, round the twist, weird.

*antonym* sane.

**scribble** *v* dash off, doodle, jot, pen, scratch, scrawl, write.

**scribbler** *n* hack, ink-slinger, paper-stainer, pen-driver, penny-a-liner, pen-pusher, pot-boiler, quill-driver, quillman, writer.

**scribe** *n* amanuensis, clerk, copyist, hierographer, notary, penman, scrivener, secretary, tabellion, writer.

**scrimmage** *n* affray, bovver, brawl, disturbance, dust-up, fight, fray, free-for-all, mêlée, riot, row, scrap, scuffle, set-to, shindy, skirmish, squabble, stramash, struggle.

*antonym* calmness.

**scrimp** *v* curtail, economise, limit, pinch, reduce, restrict, save, scrape, shorten, skimp, stint.

*antonym* spend.

**script** *n* book, calligraphy, cheirography, copy, hand, handwriting, letters, libretto, lines, longhand, manuscript, penmanship, text, words, writing.

**scripture** *n* Analects, Bhagavad Gita, Granth, Holy Bible, Holy Scripture, Holy Writ, Koran, New Testament, Old Testament, Pentateuch, shaster, shastra, sutra(s), the Bible, the Good Book, the Gospels, the Scriptures, the Word, the Word of God, Tripitaka, Upanishad(s), Veda(s), Zend-Avesta.

**scroll** *n* inventory, list, parchment, roll, volume, volute.

**Scrooge** *n* cheapskate, meanie, miser, money-grubber, niggard, penny-pincher, skinflint, tightwad.

*antonym* spendthrift.

**scrounge** v beg, bludge, bum, cadge, freeload, purloin, sponge, wheedle.

**scrounger** n bludger, bum, cadger, freeloader, parasite, scunge, sponger.

**scrub** v abandon, abolish, cancel, clean, cleanse, delete, discontinue, ditch, drop, forget, give up, rub, scour.

**scruff** n draggle-tail, ragamuffin, ragbag, scarecrow, sloven, slut, tatterdemalion, tramp.

**scruffy** adj disreputable, dog-eared, draggletailed, frowzy, grotty, ill-groomed, mangy, messy, ragged, run-down, scrubby, seedy, shabby, slatternly, slovenly, sluttish, squalid, tattered, ungroomed, unkempt, untidy.

*antonyms* tidy, well-dressed.

**scrumptious** adj appetising, delectable, delicious, delightful, exquisite, luscious, magnificent, moreish, mouth-watering, succulent, yummy.

*antonym* unappetising.

**scrunch** v champ, chew, crumple, crunch, crush, grate, grind, mash, squash.

**scruple** v balk at, demur at, falter, hesitate, object to, recoil from, shrink from, stick at, vacillate, waver.

n caution, compunction, difficulty, doubt, hesitation, misgiving, pang, perplexity, qualm, reluctance, squeamishness, uneasiness.

**scrupulous** adj careful, conscientious, conscionable, exact, fastidious, honourable, meticulous, minute, moral, nice, painstaking, precise, principled, punctilious, rigorous, squeaky-clean, strict, upright.

*antonym* careless.

**scrutinise** v analyse, dissect, examine, explore, give a once-over, inspect, investigate, peruse, probe, scan, search, sift, study.

**scrutiny** n analysis, docimasy, examination, exploration, inquiry, inspection, investigation, once-over, perusal, search, sifting, study.

**scud** v blow, dart, fly, hasten, race, sail, shoot, skim, speed.

**scuff** v abrade, brush, drag, graze, rub, scratch, shuffle, skin.

**scuffle** v clash, contend, fight, grapple, hocus, jostle, struggle, tussle.

n affray, bagarre, barney, brawl, commotion, disturbance, dog-fight, fight, fray, ruck, ruckus, ruction, rumpus, scrap, set-to, tussle.

**sculpt** v carve, chisel, cut, fashion, form, hew, model, mould, represent, sculp, sculpture, shape.

**scum** n algae, canaille, crust, dregs, dross, film, froth, impurities, offscourings, offscum, pellicle, rabble, rag-tag and bobtail, riff-raff, rubbish, scruff, spume, sullage, trash, vomit.

**scupper** v defeat, demolish, destroy, disable, overthrow, overwhelm, put a spanner in the works, ruin, torpedo, wreck.

*antonyms* advance, promote.

**scurf** n dandruff, flakiness, furfur, scabrousness, scaliness.

**scurfy** adj furfuraceous, furfurous, lepidote, leprose, leprous, scaberulous, scabrid, scabrous, scaly.

**scurrility** n abuse, abusiveness, billingsgate, coarseness, grossness, indecency, invective, nastiness, obloquy, obscenity, offensiveness, rudeness, scurrilousness, vituperation, vulgarity.

*antonym* politeness.

**scurrilous** adj abusive, coarse, defamatory, Fescennial, foul, foul-mouthed, gross, indecent, insulting, low, nasty, obscene, offensive, Rabelaisian, ribald, rude, salacious, scabrous, scandalous, slanderous, vituperative, vulgar.

*antonym* polite.

**scurry** v dart, dash, fly, hurry, race, scamper, scoot, scud, scuttle, skedaddle, skelter, skim, sprint, trot, whisk.

*antonym* stroll.

n flurry, hustle and bustle, scampering, whirl.

*antonym* calm.

**scurvy** adj abject, bad, base, caddish, contemptible, despicable, dirty, dishonourable, ignoble, low, low-down, mean, pitiful, rotten, scabby, shabby, sorry, vile, worthless.

*antonyms* good, honourable.

**scuttle** v bustle, hare, hasten, hurry, run, rush, scamper, scoot, scramble, scud, scurry, scutter, trot.

*antonym* stroll.

**sea** n abundance, briny, deep, ditch, drink, expanse, main, mass, multitude, ocean, oggin, plethora, profound, profusion, waves.

adj aquatic, marine, maritime, naval, ocean, ocean-going, oceanic, pelagic, salt, saltwater, sea-going.

*antonyms* air, land.

**seafaring** adj marine, maritime, nautical, naval, oceanic, sailing.

*antonym* land.

**seal** v assure, attest, authenticate, bung, clinch, close, conclude, confirm, consummate, cork, enclose, establish, fasten, finalise, plug, ratify, secure, settle, shake hands on, shut, stamp, stop, stopper, validate, waterproof.

*antonym* unseal.

n assurance, attestation, authentication, bulla, confirmation, imprimatur, insignia, notification, ratification, sigil, signet, stamp.

**seal off** block up, close off, cut off, fence off, isolate, quarantine, segregate, shut off.

*antonym* open up.

**sealed** adj closed, corked, hermetic, plugged, shut.

*antonym* unsealed.

**seam** n closure, crack, furrow, joint, layer, line, lode, ridge, scar, stratum, suture, vein, wrinkle.

**seaman** n AB, deck-hand, hand, Jack tar, lascar, matelot, matlo(w), sailor, seacunny, sea-dog, seafarer, steersman, tar.

**seamy** *adj* corrupt, dark, degraded, disagreeable, disreputable, low, nasty, rough, sleazy, sordid, squalid, unpleasant, unwholesome.

*antonyms* pleasant, respectable.

**sear** *v* blight, brand, brown, burn, cauterise, desiccate, dry up, harden, scorch, seal, shrivel, sizzle, wilt, wither.

**search** *v* check, comb, examine, explore, ferret, forage, frisk, inquire, inspect, investigate, jerque, look, probe, pry, quest, ransack, rifle, rummage, scour, scrutinise, sift, test.

*n* examination, exploration, going-over, hunt, inquiry, inspection, investigation, perquisition, perscrutation, pursuit, quest, researches, rummage, scrutiny, zetetic.

**searching** *adj* close, intent, keen, minute, penetrating, piercing, probing, quizzical, severe, sharp, thorough, zetetic.

*antonyms* superficial, vague.

**seasickness** *n* mal de mer, nausea, queasiness.

**season** *n* division, interval, period, span, spell, term, time.

*v* acclimatise, accustom, anneal, colour, condiment, condition, discipline, enliven, flavour, habituate, harden, imbue, inure, lace, leaven, mature, mitigate, moderate, prepare, qualify, salt, spice, temper, toughen, train.

**seasonable** *adj* appropriate, convenient, fit, opportune, providential, suitable, timely, timeous, welcome, well-timed.

*antonym* unseasonable.

**seasoned** *adj* acclimatised, battle-scarred, experienced, hardened, long-serving, mature, old, practised, time-served, veteran, weathered, well-versed.

*antonym* novice.

**seasoning** *n* condiment, dressing, flavouring, pepper, relish, salt, sauce, spice.

**seat** *n* abode, axis, base, bed, bench, bottom, capital, cause, centre, chair, constituency, cradle, footing, foundation, ground, groundwork, headquarters, heart, house, hub, incumbency, location, mansion, membership, pew, place, residence, seat-stick, sedes, settle, shooting-stick, site, situation, source, stall, station, stool, throne.

*v* accommodate, assign, contain, deposit, fit, fix, hold, install, locate, place, set, settle, sit, slot, take.

**seating** *n* accommodation, chairs, gradin(e), places, room, seats.

**seaweed** *n* arame, gulf-weed, kelp, laver, laverbread, sargasso, sea-moss, sea-tang, sea-tangle, sea-ware, sea-wrack, varec(h), wrack.

**secede** *v* apostatise, disaffiliate, leave, quit, resign, retire, separate, split off, withdraw.

*antonyms* join, unite with.

**secession** *n* apostasy, break, defection, disaffiliation, schism, schismatics, seceders, seceding, split, withdrawal.

*antonyms* amalgamation, unification.

**secluded** *adj* claustral, cloistered, cloistral, cut off, isolated, lonely, out-of-the-way, private, reclusive, remote, retired, sequestered, sheltered, solitary, umbratile, umbratilous, unfrequented.

*antonyms* busy, public.

**seclusion** *n* concealment, hiding, isolation, privacy, purdah, recluseness, remoteness, retirement, retreat, shelter, solitude.

**second**[1] *adj* additional, alternate, alternative, double, duplicate, extra, following, further, inferior, lesser, lower, next, other, repeated, reproduction, secondary, subordinate, subsequent, succeeding, supplementary, supporting, twin.

*n* assistant, backer, helper, supporter.

*v* advance, agree with, aid, approve, assist, back, encourage, endorse, forward, further, help, promote, support.

**second coming** parousia.

**second**[2] *n* instant, jiff, jiffy, minute, mo, moment, sec, tick, trice, twinkling.

**secondary** *adj* alternate, auxiliary, back-up, consequential, contingent, derivative, derived, extra, indirect, inferior, lesser, lower, minor, relief, reserve, resultant, resulting, second, second-hand, second-rate, spare, subordinate, subsidiary, supporting, unimportant.

*antonym* primary.

**second-class** *adj* declasse(e), indifferent, inferior, mediocre, second-best, second-rate, undistinguished, uninspired, uninspiring.

**second-hand** *adj* borrowed, derivative, hand-me-down, old, plagiarised, used, vicarious, worn.

*antonym* new.

**second-rate** *adj* cheap, cheap and nasty, grotty, inferior, low-grade, mediocre, poor, rubbishy, shoddy, substandard, tacky, tawdry, undistinguished, uninspired, uninspiring.

*antonym* first-rate.

**secrecy** *n* clandestineness, concealment, confidence, confidentiality, covertness, furtiveness, hugger-mugger, mystery, privacy, retirement, seclusion, secretiveness, silence, solitude, stealth, stealthiness, surreptitiousness.

*antonym* openness.

**secret** *adj* abstruse, arcane, back-door, backstairs, cabbalistic(al), camouflaged, clandestine, classified, cloak-and-dagger, close, closet, concealed, conspiratorial, covered, covert, cryptic, deep, discreet, disguised, esoteric, furtive, hidden, hole-and-corner, hush-hush, inly, mysterious, occult, out-of-the-way, private, privy, recondite, reticent, retired, secluded, secretive, sensitive, shrouded, sly, stealthy, tête-à-tête, undercover, underground, underhand, under-the-counter, undisclosed, unfrequented, unknown, unpublished, unrevealed, unseen.

*antonyms* open, public.

*n* arcanum, code, confidence, enigma, formula, key, mystery, recipe.

**secretary** *n* assistant, clerk, famulus, girl Friday, PA, person Friday, personal assistant, stenographer, typist.

**secrete¹** v appropriate, bury, cache, conceal, cover, disguise, harbour, hide, screen, secure, shroud, stash away, stow, veil.

*antonym* reveal.

**secrete²** v emanate, emit, extravasate, extrude, exude, osmose, secern, separate.

**secretion** n discharge, emission, excretion, extravasation, exudation, osmosis, secernment.

**secretive** adj cagey, close, close-lipped, close-mouthed, cryptic, deep, enigmatic, quiet, reserved, reticent, tight-lipped, uncommunicative, unforthcoming, withdrawn.

*antonyms* communicative, open.

**secretly** adv clandestinely, confidentially, covertly, furtively, in camera, in confidence, in private, in secret, on the q.t., on the quiet, on the sly, privately, privily, quietly, stealthily, surreptitiously, unobserved.

*antonym* openly.

**sect** n camp, denomination, division, faction, group, party, school, splinter group, subdivision, wing.

**sectarian** adj bigoted, clannish, cliquish, doctrinaire, dogmatic, exclusive, factional, fanatic, fanatical, insular, limited, narrow, narrow-minded, parochial, partisan, rigid, ultra.

*antonyms* broad-minded, cosmopolitan, non-sectarian.

n adherent, bigot, disciple, dogmatist, extremist, fanatic, fractionalist, partisan, zealot.

**section** n area, article, component, cross section, department, district, division, fraction, fractionlet, fragment, instalment, part, passage, piece, portion, region, sample, sector, segment, slice, subdivision, wing, zone.

*antonym* whole.

**sectional** adj class, divided, exclusive, factional, local, localised, partial, racial, regional, sectarian, separate, separatist.

*antonyms* general, universal.

**sector** n area, category, district, division, part, quarter, region, section, stratum, subdivision, zone.

*antonym* whole.

**secular** adj civil, laic, laical, lay, non-religious, profane, state, temporal, worldly.

*antonym* religious.

**secularise** v deconsecrate.

**secure** adj absolute, assured, certain, conclusive, confident, definite, dependable, easy, fast, fastened, firm, fixed, fortified, immovable, immune, impregnable, on velvet, over-confident, protected, reassured, reliable, safe, sheltered, shielded, solid, stable, steadfast, steady, sure, tight, unassailable, undamaged, unharmed, well-founded.

*antonyms* insecure, uncertain.

v acquire, assure, attach, batten down, bolt, chain, ensure, fasten, fix, gain, get, get hold of, guarantee, insure, land, lash, lock, lock up, moor, nail, obtain, padlock, procure, rivet, seize.

*antonyms* lose, unfasten.

**security** n assurance, asylum, care, certainty, collateral, confidence, conviction, cover, custody, defence, gage, guarantee, guards, hostage, immunity, insurance, pawn, pledge, positiveness, precautions, preservation, protection, refuge, reliance, retreat, safeguards, safe-keeping, safety, sanctuary, sureness, surety, surveillance, warranty.

*antonym* insecurity.

**sedate** adj calm, collected, composed, cool, decorous, deliberate, demure, dignified, douce, earnest, grave, imperturbable, middle-aged, placed, proper, quiet, seemly, serene, serious, slow-moving, sober, solemn, staid, tranquil, unflappable, unruffled.

*antonyms* flippant, hasty, undignified.

**sedative** adj allaying, anodyne, calmative, calming, depressant, lenitive, relaxing, soothing, soporific, tranquillising.

*antonym* rousing.

n anodyne, calmative, downer, narcotic, opiate, quietive, sleeping-pill, tranquilliser.

**sedentary** adj desk, desk-bound, inactive, motionless, seated, sedent, sitting, stationary, still, torpid, unmoving.

*antonym* active.

**sediment** n deposit, draff, dregs, faeces, fecula, grounds, lees, precipitate, residium, settlings, warp.

**sedition** n agitation, disloyalty, rabble-rousing, ruckus, rumpus, subversion, treason, tumult.

*antonyms* calm, loyalty.

**seditious** adj disloyal, dissident, insubordinate, mutinous, rebellious, refractory, revolutionary, subversive, traitorous.

*antonyms* calm, loyal.

**seduce** v allure, attract, beguile, betray, bewitch, corrupt, debauch, deceive, decoy, deflower, deprave, dishonour, ensnare, entice, inveigle, lure, mislead, ruin, tempt.

**seducer** n cad, Casanova, charmer, deceiver, Don Juan, flirt, gay deceiver, goat, libertine, Lothario, philanderer, wolf, womaniser.

**seduction** n allure, allurement, come-on, corruption, defloration, enticement, lure, ruin, seducement, snare, temptation.

**seductive** adj alluring, attractive, beguiling, bewitching, captivating, come-hither, come-on, enticing, flirtatious, honeyed, inviting, irresistible, page-three, provocative, ravishing, seducing, sexy, siren, specious, tempting.

*antonym* unattractive.

**seductress** n Circe, femme fatale, Lorelei, siren, temptress, vamp.

**sedulous** adj assiduous, busy, conscientious, constant, determined, diligent, industrious, laborious, painstaking, persevering, persistent, resolved, tireless, unflagging, unremitting, untiring.

*antonym* half-hearted.

**see** *v* accompany, anticipate, appreciate, ascertain, attend, behold, comprehend, consider, consult, court, date, decide, deem, deliberate, descry, determine, discern, discover, distinguish, divine, encounter, ensure, envisage, escort, espy, experience, fathom, feel, follow, foresee, foretell, get, glimpse, grasp, guarantee, heed, identify, imagine, interview, investigate, judge, know, lead, learn, look, make out, mark, meet, mind, note, notice, observe, perceive, picture, realise, receive, recognise, reflect, regard, show, sight, spot, take, understand, usher, view, visit, visualise, walk, witness.

**see eye to eye** accord, agree, coincide, concur, get along, get on, harmonise, jibe, speak the same language, subscribe.

*antonym* disagree.

**see red** blow one's top, blow up, boil, go mad, go off one's head, lose one's rag, lose one's temper.

**see to** arrange, attend to, deal with, do, fix, look after, manage, organise, repair, sort out, take care of, take charge of.

**seed** *n* beginning, children, descendants, egg, embryo, germ, grain, heirs, inkling, issue, kernel, nucleus, offspring, ovule, ovum, pip, progeny, quiverful, race, scions, semen, source, spawn, sperm, spore, start, successors, suspicion.

*antonym* ancestors.

**seedy** *adj* ailing, crummy, decaying, dilapidated, faded, grotty, grubby, ill, mangy, manky, off-colour, old, peelie-wally, poorly, run-down, scruffy, shabby, sickly, sleazy, slovenly, squalid, tatty, unkempt, unwell, worn.

*antonyms* posh, well.

**seek** *v* aim, ask, aspire to, attempt, beg, busk, desire, endeavour, entreat, essay, follow, hunt, inquire, invite, petition, pursue, request, solicit, strive, try, want.

**seeker** *n* chela, disciple, inquirer, novice, searcher, student, zetetic.

**seem** *v* appear, look, look like, pretend, sound like.

**seeming** *adj* apparent, appearing, illusory, ostensible, outward, pseudo, quasi-, specious, surface.

*antonym* real.

**seemingly** *adv* allegedly, apparently, as far as one can see, on the face of it, on the surface, ostensibly, outwardly, superficially.

*antonym* really.

**seemly** *adj* appropriate, attractive, becoming, befitting, comely, comme il faut, decent, decorous, fit, fitting, handsome, maidenly, meet, nice, proper, suitable, suited.

*antonym* unseemly.

**seep** *v* exude, leak, ooze, osmose, percolate, permeate, soak, trickle, weep, well.

**seepage** *n* exudation, leak, leakage, oozing, osmosis, percolation.

**seer** *n* augur, prophet, sibyl, soothsayer, spaeman, spaewife.

**seesaw** *v* alternate, fluctuate, oscillate, pitch, swing, teeter.

*n* pendulum, wild mare.

**seethe** *v* boil, bubble, churn, ferment, fizz, foam, foam at the mouth, froth, fume, hotch, marinate, rage, rise, saturate, simmer, smoulder, soak, souse, steep, storm, surge, swarm, swell, teem.

**see-through** *adj* diaphanous, filmy, flimsy, gauzy, gossamer(y), sheer, translucent, transparent.

*antonym* opaque.

**segment** *n* articulation, bit, compartment, division, part, piece, portion, section, slice, wedge.

*antonym* whole.

*v* anatomise, cut up, divide, halve, separate, slice, split.

**segregate** *v* cut off, discriminate against, dissociate, isolate, quarantine, separate, set apart.

*antonym* unite.

**segregation** *n* apartheid, discrimination, isolation, quarantine, separation.

*antonym* unification.

**seize** *v* abduct, annex, apprehend, appropriate, arrest, capture, catch, claw, clutch, cly, collar, commander, confiscate, crimp, distrain, distress, fasten, fix, for(e)hent, get, grab, grasp, grip, hijack, impound, nab, prehend, smug, snatch, take.

*antonym* let go.

**seizure** *n* abduction, annexation, apprehension, arrest, attachment, attack, capture, commandeering, confiscation, convulsion, distraint, distress, fit, grabbing, paroxysm, spasm, taking.

*antonym* liberation.

**seldom** *adv* infrequently, occasionally, rarely, scarcely.

*antonym* often.

**select** *v* choose, cull, pick, prefer, single out.

*adj* choice, elite, excellent, exclusive, first-class, first-rate, hand-picked, limited, picked, posh, preferable, prime, privileged, rare, selected, special, superior, top, top-notch.

*antonyms* general, second-rate.

**selection** *n* anthology, assortment, choice, choosing, collection, line-up, medley, miscellany, option, palette, pick, potpourri, preference, range, variety.

**selective** *adj* careful, discerning, discriminating, discriminatory, eclectic, elitist, particular.

*antonym* unselective.

**self** *n* ego, egoity, I, identity, person, personality, soul.

**self-assertive** *adj* aggressive, authoritarian, bossy, commanding, dictatorial, domineering, forceful, heavy-handed, high-handed, overbearing, overweening, peremptory, pushing, pushy.

*antonym* compliant.

**self-assurance** *n* assurance, cockiness, cocksureness, confidence, overconfidence, positiveness, self-confidence, self-possession.

*antonyms* humility, unsureness.

**self-assured** *adj* assured, cocksure, cocky, confident, overconfident, self-collected, self-possessed, sure of oneself.

*antonyms* humble, unsure.

**self-centred** *adj* egotistic(al), narcissistic, self-absorbed, self-interested, selfish, self-seeking, self-serving.

*antonym* altruistic.

**self-confidence** *n* aplomb, assurance, confidence, nerve, poise, self-assurance, self-possession, self-reliance.

*antonyms* humility, unsureness.

**self-confident** *adj* assured, confident, fearless, poised, secure, self-assured, self-collected, self-possessed, self-reliant.

*antonyms* humble, unsure.

**self-conscious** *adj* affected, awkward, bashful, coy, diffident, embarrassed, ill at ease, insecure, nervous, retiring, self-effacing, shamefaced, sheepish, shrinking, uncomfortable.

*antonyms* natural, unaffected.

**self-control** *n* calmness, composure, cool, coolness, discipline, encraty, restraint, self-command, self-discipline, self-government, self-mastery, self-restraint, temperance, will-power.

**self-denial** *n* abstemiousness, asceticism, moderation, renunciation, self-abandonment, self-abnegation, selflessness, self-renunciation, self-sacrifice, temperance, unselfishness.

*antonym* self-indulgence.

**self-esteem** *n* amour-propre, dignity, pride, self-assurance, self-confidence, self-pride, self-regard, self-respect.

*antonym* humility.

**self-evident** *adj* axiomatic, clear, incontrovertible, inescapable, manifest, obvious, undeniable, unquestionable.

**self-glorification** *n* egotheism, egotism, self-admiration, self-advertisement, self-aggrandisement, self-exaltation.

*antonym* humility.

**self-government** *n* autarchy, autonomy, democracy, home rule, independence, self-sovereignty.

*antonym* subjection.

**self-importance** *n* arrogance, big-headedness, bumptiousness, cockiness, conceit, conceitedness, pomposity, pompousness, pushiness, self-consequence, self-opinion, vanity.

*antonym* humility.

**self-important** *adj* arrogant, big-headed, bumptious, cocky, conceited, consequential, overbearing, pompous, pushy, self-consequent, strutting, swaggering, swollen-headed, vain.

*antonym* humble.

**self-indulgence** *n* dissipation, dissoluteness, excess, extravagance, high living, incontinence, intemperance, profligacy, self-gratification, sensualism.

*antonym* self-denial.

**self-indulgent** *adj* dissipated, dissolute, extravagant, intemperate, profligate, sensualistic.

*antonym* abstemious.

**self-interest** *n* self, selfishness, self-love, self-regard, self-serving.

*anto*⁓⁓ ⁓elflessness.

**selfish** *adj* egoistic, egoistical, egotistic, egotistical, greedy, mean, mercenary, narrow, self-centred, self-interested, self-seeking, self-serving.

*antonym* unselfish.

**selfishness** *n* egoism, egotism, greed, meanness, self-centredness, self-interest, self-love, self-regard, self-seeking, self-serving.

*antonym* selflessness.

**selfless** *adj* altruistic, generous, magnanimous, self-denying, self-forgetful, self-sacrificing, ungrudging, unselfish.

*antonym* selfish.

**self-possessed** *adj* calm, collected, composed, confident, cool, poised, self-assured, self-collected, together, unruffled.

*antonym* worried.

**self-possession** *n* aplomb, calmness, composure, confidence, cool, coolness, poise, sang-froid, self-command, self-confidence, unflappability.

*antonym* worry.

**self-propelling** *adj* automobile, locomobile, self-moving.

**self-reliance** *n* autarky, independence, self-sufficiency, self-support, self-sustainment, self-sustenance, self-sustentation.

*antonym* dependence.

**self-reliant** *adj* autarkic(al), independent, self-sufficient, self-supporting, self-sustaining.

*antonym* dependent.

**self-respect** *n* amour-propre, dignity, pride, self-assurance, self-confidence, self-esteem, self-pride, self-regard.

*antonym* self-doubt.

**self-restraint** *n* abstemiousness, encraty, forbearance, moderation, patience, self-command, self-control, self-denial, self-discipline, self-government, temperance, will-power.

*antonym* licence.

**self-righteous** *adj* complacent, goody-goody, holier-than-thou, hypocritical, pharisaical, pi, pietistic(al), pious, priggish, sanctimonious, self-satisfied, smug, superior, Tartuffian, Tartuffish.

*antonym* understanding.

**self-righteousness** *n* goodiness, goody-goodiness, pharisaicalness, pharisaism, piousness, priggishness, sanctimoniousness.

*antonyms* humility, understanding.

**self-sacrifice** *n* altruism, generosity, self-abandonment, self-abnegation, self-denial, selflessness, self-renunciation.

*antonym* selfishness.

**self-satisfaction** *n* complacency, contentment, pride, self-appreciation, self-approbation, self-approval, smugness.

*antonym* humility.

**self-satisfied** *adj* complacent, puffed up, self-approving, self-congratulatory, self-righteous, smug.

*antonym* humble.

**self-seeking** *adj* acquisitive, calculating, careerist, fortune-hunting, gold-digging, mercenary, on the make, opportunistic, self-endeared, self-interested, selfish, self-loving, self-serving.

*antonym* altruistic.

**self-styled** *adj* professed, pseudo, self-appointed, so-called, soi-disant, would-be.

**self-supporting** *adj* autarkic(al), self-financing, self-reliant, self-sufficient, self-sustaining.

*antonym* dependent.

**self-willed** *adj* bloody-minded, cussed, headstrong, intractable, obstinate, opinionated, pig-headed, refractory, self-opinionated, self-opinionative, stiff-necked, stubborn, ungovernable, wilful.

*antonym* complaisant.

**sell** *v* barter, cheat, convince, deal in, exchange, handle, hawk, impose on, market, merchandise, peddle, persuade, promote, retail, sell out, stock, surrender, trade, trade in, traffic in, trick, vend.

*antonym* buy.

**sell out** betray, double-cross, fail, fink on, rat on, sell down the river, stab in the back.

*antonym* back.

**seller** *n* agent, dealer, merchant, rep, representative, retailer, salesgirl, saleslady, salesman, saleswoman, shopkeeper, storekeeper, tradesman, traveller, vendor.

*antonym* buyer.

**selling** *n* dealing, marketing, merchandising, merchanting, promotion, salesmanship, trading, traffic, transactions, vendition.

*antonym* buying.

**semblance** *n* air, apparition, appearance, aspect, bearing, façade, figure, form, front, guise, image, likeness, mask, mien, pretence, resemblance, show, similarity, veneer.

**semen** *n* jism, seed, spawn, sperm, spunk.

**semicircle** *n* half-round, hemicycle.

**seminal** *adj* creative, formative, imaginative, important, influential, innovative, major, original, productive, seminary.

*antonym* derivative.

**seminary** *n* academy, college, institute, institution, school, training-college.

**send** *v* broadcast, cast, charm, communicate, consign, convey, delight, deliver, direct, discharge, dispatch, electrify, emit, enrapture, enthrall, excite, exude, fire, fling, forward, grant, hurl, intoxicate, move, please, propel, radiate, ravish, remit, shoot, stir, thrill, titillate, transmit.

**send for** call for, call out, command, order, request, summon.

*antonym* dismiss.

**send up** burlesque, imitate, lampoon, mickey-take, mimic, mock, parody, satirise, spook, take off, take the mickey out of.

**send-off** *n* departure, farewell, going-away, leave-taking, start, valediction.

*antonym* arrival.

**send-up** *n* imitation, mickey-take, mockery, parody, satire, skit, spoof, take-off.

**senile** *adj* anile, decrepit, doddering, doited, doting, failing, imbecile, senescent.

**senility** *n* anility, caducity, decrepitude, dotage, eld, infirmity, paracme, second childhood, senescence, senile dementia.

**senior** *adj* aîne(e), doyen(ne), elder, first, higher, high-ranking, major, older, superior.

*antonym* junior.

**seniority** *n* eldership, precedence, priority, rank, standing, superiority.

*antonym* juniority.

**sensation** *n* agitation, awareness, commotion, consciousness, emotion, Empfindung, excitement, feeling, furore, hit, impression, perception, scandal, sense, stir, surprise, thrill, tingle, vibes, vibrations, wow.

**sensational** *adj* amazing, astounding, blood-and-thunder, breathtaking, dramatic, electrifying, excellent, exceptional, exciting, fabulous, gamy, hair-raising, horrifying, impressive, lurid, marvellous, melodramatic, mind-blowing, revealing, scandalous, sensationalistic, shocking, smashing, spectacular, staggering, startling, superb, thrilling.

*antonym* run-of-the-mill.

**sense** *n* advantage, appreciation, atmosphere, aura, awareness, brains, clear-headedness, cleverness, consciousness, definition, denotation, direction, discernment, discrimination, drift, faculty, feel, feeling, gist, good, gumption, implication, import, impression, intelligence, interpretation, intuition, judgement, logic, marbles, meaning, message, mother wit, nous, nuance, opinion, perception, point, premonition, presentiment, purport, purpose, quickness, reason, reasonableness, sagacity, sanity, savvy, sensation, sensibility, sentiment, sharpness, significance, signification, smeddum, substance, tact, understanding, use, value, wisdom, wit(s), worth.

*antonym* foolishness.

*v* appreciate, comprehend, detect, divine, feel, grasp, notice, observe, perceive, realise, suspect, understand.

**senseless** *adj* absurd, anaesthetised, asinine, crazy, daft, deadened, dotty, fatuous, foolish, halfwitted, idiotic, illogical, imbecilic, inane, incongruous, inconsistent, insensate, insensible, irrational, ludicrous, mad, meaningless, mindless, moronic, nonsensical, numb, numbed, out, out for the count, pointless, ridiculous, silly, simple, stunned, stupid, unconscious, unfeeling, unintelligent, unreasonable, unwise.

*antonym* sensible.

**sensibilities** *n* emotions, feelings, sensitivities, sentiments, susceptibilities.

**sensibility** *n* appreciation, awareness, delicacy, discernment, insight, intuition, perceptiveness, responsiveness, sensitiveness, sensitivity, susceptibility, taste.

*antonym* insensibility.

**sensible** *adj* appreciable, canny, considerable, delicate, discernable, discreet, discriminating, down-to-earth, far-sighted, intelligent, judicious, level-headed, matter-of-fact, noticeable, palpable, perceptible, practical, prudent, rational, realistic, reasonable, right-thinking, sagacious, sage, sane, senseful, shrewd, significant, sober, solid, sound, tangible, visible, well-advised, well-thought-out, wise.

*antonyms* imperceptible, senseless.

**sensible of** acquainted with, alive to, aware of, cognisant of, conscious of, convinced of, mindful of, observant of, sensitive to, understanding.

*antonym* unaware of.

**sensitive** *adj* acute, controversial, delicate, fine, hyper(a)esthesic, hyper(a)esthetic, hyperconscious, impressionable, irritable, keen, nociceptive, perceptive, precise, reactive, responsive, secret, sensitised, sentient, susceptible, temperamental, tender, thin-skinned, touchy, umbrageous.

*antonym* insensitive.

**sensitivity** *n* delicacy, hyper(a)esthesia, hyperconsciousness, reactiveness, reactivity, receptiveness, responsiveness, sensitiveness, susceptibility.

*antonym* insensitivity.

**sensual** *adj* animal, bodily, carnal, epicurean, erotic, fleshly, lascivious, lecherous, lewd, libidinous, licentious, lustful, luxurious, pandemian, physical, randy, raunchy, self-indulgent, sexual, sexy, voluptuous, worldly.

*antonyms* ascetic, Puritan.

**sensualist** *n* bon vivant, bon viveur, debauchee, epicure, Epicurean, gourmand, gourmet, hedonist, libertine, profligate, roue, sybarite, voluptuary.

*antonyms* ascetic, Puritan.

**sensuality** *n* animal magnetism, animalism, carnality, debauchery, eroticism, gourmandise,

lasciviousness, lecherousness, lewdness, libertinism, libidinousness, licentiousness, lustfulness, profligacy, prurience, salaciousness, sexiness, voluptuousness.

*antonyms* asceticism, Puritanism.

**sensuous** *adj* epicurean, gratifying, hedonistic, lush, luxurious, pleasurable, rich, sensory, sumptuous, sybaritic, voluptuous.

*antonyms* ascetic, plain, simple.

**sentence** *n* aphorism, apophthegm, condemnation, decision, decree, doom, gnome, judgement, maxim, opinion, order, pronouncement, ruling, saying, verdict.

*v* condemn, doom, judge, pass judgement on, penalise, pronounce judgement on.

**sententious** *adj* aphoristic, axiomatic, brief, canting, compact, concise, epigrammatic, gnomic, laconic, moralising, moralistic, pithy, pointed, pompous, ponderous, preachy, sanctimonious, short, succinct, terse.

*antonyms* humble, prolix.

**sentient** *adj* aware, conscious, live, living, reactive, responsive, sensitive.

*antonym* insentient.

**sentiment** *n* attitude, belief, emotion, emotionalism, feeling, idea, judgement, mawkishness, maxim, opinion, persuasion, romanticism, saying, sensibility, sentimentalism, sentimentality, slush, soft-heartedness, tenderness, thought, view.

*antonyms* hard-heartedness, straightforwardness.

**sentimental** *adj* corny, dewy-eyed, drippy, emotional, gushing, gushy, gutbucket, impressionable, lovey-dovey, maudlin, mawkish, mushy, nostalgic, pathetic, romantic, rose-water, schmaltzy, simpering, sloppy, slushy, soft-hearted, tearful, tear-jerking, tender, too-too, touching, treacly, weepy, wertherian.

*antonym* unsentimental.

**sentimentality** *n* bathos, corniness, emotionalism, gush, mawkishness, mush, nostalgia, pulp, romanticism, schmaltz, sentimentalism, sloppiness, slush, tenderness.

**sentry** *n* guard, look-out, picket, sentinel, vedette, watch, watchman.

**separable** *adj* detachable, discerptible, distinguishable, divisible, partible, scissile, severable.

*antonym* inseparable.

**separate** *v* abstract, bifurcate, decouple, deglutinate, demerge, departmentalise, detach, disaffiliate, disally, discerp, disconnect, disentangle, disjoin, dislink, dispart, dissever, distance, disunite, divaricate, diverge, divide, divorce, eloi(g)n, estrange, exfoliate, isolate, part, part company, prescind, remove, secede, secern, seclude, segregate, sever, shear, split, split up, sunder, uncouple, winnow, withdraw.

*antonyms* join, unite.

*adj* alone, apart, autonomous, detached, disconnected, discrete, disjointed, disjunct, disparate, distinct, divided, divorced, independent, individual, isolated, particular, several, single, solitary, sundry, unattached, unconnected.

*antonyms* attached, together.

**separated** *adj* apart, disassociated, disconnected, disunited, divided, isolated, parted, segregated, separate, split up, sundered.

*antonyms* attached, together.

**separately** *adv* alone, apart, discretely, discriminately, divisim, independently, individually, personally, severally, singly.

*antonym* together.

**separating** *adj* discretive, disjunctive, divellent, dividing, divisive, divulsive, intervening, isolating, partitioning, segregating.

*antonym* unifying.

**separation** *n* break, break-up, demerger, detachment, diaeresis, dialysis, diaspora, diastasis, discerption, disconnection, disengagement, disgregation, disjunction, disjuncture, disseverance, disseveration, disseverment, dissociation, disunion, division, divorce, estrangement, farewell, gap, leave-taking, parting, rift, segregation, severance, solution, split, split-up.

*antonyms* togetherness, unification.

**septic** *adj* festering, infected, poisoned, purulent, putrefactive, putrefying, putrid, pyogenic, pyoid, suppurating.

**sepulchral** *adj* cheerless, deep, dismal, funereal, gloomy, grave, hollow, lugubrious, melancholy, morbid, mournful, reverberating, sad, sepultural, sepulchrous, sombre, sonorous, woeful.

*antonym* cheerful.

**sepulchre** *n* grave, mausoleum, tomb, vault.

**sequel** *n* conclusion, consequence, continuation, development, end, follow-up, issue, outcome, pay-off, prequel, result, upshot.

**sequence** *n* arrangement, chain, consequence, course, cycle, order, procession, progression, series, set, succession, track, train.

**sequestered** *adj* backveld, cloistered, isolated, lonely, outback, out-of-the-way, private, quiet, remote, retired, secluded, unfrequented.

*antonyms* busy, frequented, public.

**seraphic** *adj* angelic, beatific, blissful, celestial, divine, heavenly, holy, innocent, pure, saintly, seraphical, sublime.

*antonym* demonic.

**serene** *adj* calm, composed, cool, halcyon, imperturbable, peaceful, placid, tranquil, unclouded, undisturbed, unflappable, unruffled, untroubled.

*antonym* troubled.

**serenity** *n* calm, calmness, composure, cool, peace, peacefulness, placidity, quietness, quietude, stillness, tranquillity, unflappability.

*antonyms* anxiety, disruption.

**serf** *n* bondmaid, bondservant, bond-slave, bon(d)sman, bond(s)-woman, helot, servant, slave, thrall, villein.

*antonym* master.

**series** *n* arrangement, catena, chain, concatenation, consecution, course, cycle, enfilade, line, order, progression, run, scale, sequence, set, string, succession, train.

**serious** *adj* acute, alarming, critical, crucial, dangerous, deep, deliberate, determined, difficult, earnest, far-reaching, fateful, genuine, grave, grim, heavy, honest, humourless, important, long-faced, momentous, pensive, pressing, resolute, resolved, sedate, severe, significant, sincere, sober, solemn, staid, stern, thoughtful, unsmiling, urgent, weighty, worrying.

*antonyms* facetious, light, slight, smiling, trivial.

**seriously** *adv* acutely, badly, critically, dangerously, distressingly, earnestly, gravely, grievously, joking apart, severely, sincerely, solemnly, sorely, thoughtfully.

*antonyms* casually, slightly.

**seriousness** *n* danger, earnestness, gravitas, gravity, humourless, importance, moment, sedateness, significance, sobriety, solemnity, staidness, sternness, urgency, weight.

*antonyms* casualness, slightness, triviality.

**sermon** *n* address, dressing-down, exhortation, harangue, homily, lecture, preachment, talking-to.

**sermonise** *v* preach, preachify.

**sermonising** *n* pi-jaw, preachifying, preachment, pulpitry.

**serpentine** *adj* coiling, crooked, meandering, serpentiform, sinuous, snakelike, snaking, snaky, tortuous, twisting, winding.

*antonym* straight.

**serrated** *adj* notched, sawlike, saw-toothed, serrate, serratulate, serriform, serrulate(d), toothed.

*antonym* smooth.

**serried** *adj* close, close-set, compact, crowded, dense, massed.

*antonym* scattered.

**servant** *n* aia, amah, ancillary, attendant, ayah, bearer, boy, daily, day, day-woman, domestic, drudge, esne, flunkey, footman, galopin, garçon, gentleman's gentleman, gossoon, gyp, haiduk, handmaid, handmaiden, help, helper, hind, hireling, Jeeves, khidmutgar, kitchen-maid, knave, lackey, lady's maid, livery-servant, maid, maid of all work, maître d'hôtel, major-domo, man, manservant, menial, ministrant, retainer, scout, seneschal, servitor, skivvy, slave, slavey, steward, valet, vassal, woman.

*antonyms* master, mistress.

**serve** *v* act, aid, answer, arrange, assist, attend, avail, complete, content, dance attendance, deal, deliver, discharge, distribute, do, fulfil, further, handle, help, minister to, oblige, observe, officiate, pass, perform, present, provide, satisfy, succour, suffice, suit, supply, undergo, wait on, work for.

**service** *n* advantage, assistance, avail, availability, benefit, business, ceremony, check, disposal, duty, employ, employment, expediting, function, help, labour, maintenance, ministrations, observance, office, overhaul, performance, rite, servicing, set, supply, use, usefulness, utility, work, worship.

*v* check, maintain, overhaul, recondition, repair, tune.

**serviceable** *adj* advantageous, beneficial, convenient, dependable, durable, efficient, functional, hard-wearing, helpful, operative, plain, practical, profitable, simple, strong, tough, unadorned, usable, useful, utilitarian.

*antonym* unserviceable.

**servile** *adj* abject, base, bootlicking, controlled, craven, cringing, fawning, grovelling, humble, low, mean, menial, obsequious, slavish, subject, submissive, subservient, sycophantic, toadying, toadyish, unctuous.

*antonyms* aggressive, bold.

**servility** *n* abjection, abjectness, arse-licking, baseness, bootlicking, fawning, grovelling, meanness, obsequiousness, self-abasement, slavishness, submissiveness, subservience, sycophancy, toad-eating, toadyism, unctuousness.

*antonyms* aggressiveness, boldness.

**servitude** *n* bondage, bonds, chains, enslavement, obedience, serfdom, slavery, subjugation, thraldom, thrall, vassalage, villeinage.

*antonym* freedom.

**session** *n* assembly, conference, discussion, get-together, go, hearing, meeting, period, semester, sitting, term, year.

**set**[1] *v* adjust, aim, allocate, allot, apply, appoint, arrange, assign, cake, conclude, condense, congeal, co-ordinate, crystallise, decline, decree, deposit, designate, determine, dip, direct, disappear, embed, establish, fasten, fix, fix up, gelatinise, harden, impose, install, jell, lay, locate, lodge, mount, name, ordain, park, place, plant, plonk, plump, position, prepare, prescribe, propound, put, rectify, regulate, resolve, rest, schedule, seat, settle, sink, situate, solidify, specify, spread, stake, station, stick, stiffen, subside, synchronise, thicken, turn, vanish.

*n* attitude, bearing, carriage, fit, hang, inclination, mise-en-scène, position, posture, scene, scenery, setting, turn.

*adj* agreed, appointed, arranged, artificial, conventional, customary, decided, definite, deliberate, entrenched, established, firm, fixed, formal, hackneyed, immovable, inflexible, intentional, prearranged, predetermined, prescribed, regular, rehearsed, rigid, routine, scheduled, settled, standard, stereotyped, stock, strict, stubborn, traditional, unspontaneous, usual.

*antonyms* free, movable, spontaneous, undecided.

**set about** assail, assault, attack, bash, beat up, begin, belabour, lambaste, mug, start, tackle, wade into.

**set against** alienate, balance, compare, contrast, disunite, divide, estrange, juxtapose, mix, oppose, weigh.

**set apart** choose, elect, peculiarise, put aside, separate.

**set aside** abrogate, annul, cancel, discard, dismiss, keep, keep back, lay aside, nullify, overrule, overturn, put aside, quash, reject, repudiate, reserve, reverse, save, select, separate.

**set back** delay, hamper, hinder, hold up, impede, interrupt, retard, slow.

**set eyes on** behold, clap eyes on, come across, come upon, encounter, lay eyes on, meet, meet with, notice, observe, see.

**set free** decontrol, deliver, disembarrass, disentangle, disimprison, disprison, emancipate, extricate, free, liberate, loose, manumit, ransom, release, rescue, rid, save, unpen.

*antonyms* confine, enslave.

**set off** depart, detonate, display, embark, enhance, explode, ignite, leave, light, make tracks, present, sally forth, show off, touch off, trigger off.

**set on** assail, assault, attack, beat up, fall upon, fly at, go for, incite, instigate, lay into, mug, pitch into, sail into, set about, set upon, turn on, urge.

**set out** arrange, array, begin, describe, detail, display, dispose, elaborate, elucidate, embark, exhibit, explain, lay out, make a move, make tracks, present, sally forth, set off, start, start out.

**set up** arrange, assemble, back, begin, boost, build, cheer, compose, construct, create, elate, elevate, erect, establish, finance, form, found, gratify, inaugurate, initiate, install, institute, introduce, organise, prearrange, prepare, promote, raise, revivify, start, strengthen, subsidise.

**set**[2] *n* apparatus, assemblage, assortment, band, batch, circle, class, clique, collection, company, compendium, coterie, covey, crew, crowd, faction, gang, group, kit, outfit, sect, sequence, series.

**setback** *n* blow, check, defeat, delay, disappointment, hiccup, hitch, hold-up, knock-back, misfortune, problem, rebuff, relapse, reverse, snag, throw-back, upset.

*antonyms* advance, advantage, boost, help.

**setting** *n* adjustment, age, backcloth, backdrop, background, context, environment, frame, locale, location, milieu, mise en scène, mounting, period, perspective, position, scene, scenery, set, site, surround, surroundings.

**setting-up** *n* creation, establishment, foundation, founding, inauguration, inception, institution, introduction, start.

*antonyms* abolition, termination.

**settle** *v* adjust, agree, alight, appoint, arrange, bed, calm, choose, clear, colonise, compact, complete, compose, conclude, confirm, decide, decree, descend, determine, discharge, dispose, dower, drop, dwell, endow, establish, fall, fix, found, hush, inhabit, land, light, liquidate, live, lower, lull, occupy, ordain, order, pacify, pay, people, pioneer, plant, plump, populate, quell, quiet, quieten, quit, reassure, reconcile, relax, relieve, reside, resolve, sedate, sink, soothe, square, square up, subside, tranquillise.

**settlement**[1] *n* accommodation, adjustment, agreement, allowance, arrangement, Ausgleich, clearance, clearing, completion, conclusion, confirmation, decision, defrayal, diktat, discharge, disposition, establishment, income, liquidation, payment, resolution, satisfaction, termination.

**settlement**[2] *n* colonisation, colony, community, encampment, hamlet, immigration, kibbutz, nahal, occupation, outpost, peopling, plantation, population.

**settlement**[3] *n* compacting, drop, fall, sinkage, subsidence.

**settler** *n* coloniser, colonist, frontiersman, immigrant, incomer, kibbutznik, newcomer, pioneer, planter, squatter.

*antonym* native.

**set-to** *n* altercation, argument, argy-bargy, barney, brush, conflict, contest, disagreement, dust-up, exchange, fight, fracas, quarrel, row, scrap, spat, squabble, wrangle.

**set-up** *n* arrangement, business, circumstances, conditions, menage, organisation, regime, structure, system.

**sever** *v* alienate, bisect, cleave, cut, detach, disconnect, disjoin, dissever, dissociate, dissolve, dissunder, disunite, divide, estrange, part, rend, separate, split, sunder, terminate.

*antonyms* join, unite.

**several** *adj* assorted, different, discrete, disparate, distinct, divers, diverse, individual, many, particular, respective, separate, single, some, some few, specific, sundry, various.

**severally** *adv* discretely, individually, particularly, respectively, separately, seriatim, specifically.

*antonyms* simultaneously, together.

**severe** *adj* acute, arduous, ascetic, astringent, austere, biting, bitter, Catonian, caustic, chaste, classic, classical, cold, critical, cruel, cutting, dangerous, demanding, difficult, disapproving, distressing, dour, Draconian, Draconic, Dracontic, eager, exacting, extreme, fierce, flinty, forbidding, functional, grave, grim, grinding, hard, harsh, inclement, inexorable, intense, iron-handed, oppressive, pitiless, plain, punishing, relentless, restrained, Rhadamanthine, rigid, rigorous, satirical, scathing, serious, shrewd, simple, sober, Spartan, stern, strait-laced, strict, stringent, taxing, tight-lipped, tough, trying, unadorned, unbending, unembellished, ungentle, unrelenting, unsmiling, unsparing, unsympathetic, violent.

*antonyms* compassionate, kind, lenient, mild, sympathetic.

**severely** *adv* acutely, austerely, badly, bitterly, coldly, critically, dangerously, disapprovingly, dourly, extremely, gravely, grimly, hard, harshly, rigorously, sharply, sorely, sternly, strictly, unsympathetically.

**severity** *n* acuteness, asceticism, austerity, coldness, gravity, hardness, harshness,

plainness, rigour, seriousness, severeness, sharpness, sternness, stringency, strictness, toughness, ungentleness.

*antonyms* compassion, kindness, leniency, mildness.

**sex** *n* coition, coitus, congress, copulation, desire, fornication, gender, intercourse, intimacy, libido, lovemaking, nookie, poontang, reproduction, screw, sexual intercourse, sexual relations, sexuality, union, venery.

**sex appeal** allure, desirability, glamour, it, magnetism, nubility, oomph, seductiveness, sensuality, sex attraction, sexiness, voluptuousness.

**sexless** *adj* asexual, neuter, parthenogenetic, undersexed, unfeminine, unmasculine, unsexed, unsexual.

**sexpot** *n* enchantress, houri, Lolita, nymphet, seductress, sex goddess, sex-bomb, siren.

**sexton** *n* caretaker, fossor, grave-digger, grave-maker, sacristan, verger.

**sexual** *adj* carnal, coital, erotic, gamic, genital, intimate, procreative, reproductive, sensual, sex, sex-related, venereal.

*antonym* asexual.

**sexual intercourse** bonk, carnal knowledge, coition, coitus, commerce, congress, consummation, copulation, coupling, fuck, fucking, greens, mating, nookie, penetration, poontang, pussy, screw, screwing, sex, shag, shagging, tail, union.

**sexuality** *n* carnality, desire, eroticism, lust, sensuality, sexiness, sexual instincts, sexual urge, virility, voluptuousness.

**sexy** *adj* arousing, beddable, come-hither, cuddly, curvaceous, epigamic, erotic, flirtatious, inviting, kissable, naughty, nubile, pornographic, provocative, provoking, seductive, sensual, sensuous, slinky, suggestive, titillating, virile, voluptuous.

*antonym* sexless.

**shabby** *adj* cheap, contemptible, dastardly, despicable, dilapidated, dingy, dirty, dishonourable, disreputable, dog-eared, down-at-heel, faded, frayed, ignoble, low, low-down, low-life, low-lived, mangy, mean, moth-eaten, neglected, paltry, poking, poky, poor, ragged, raunchy, rotten, run-down, scruffy, seedy, shameful, shoddy, tacky, tattered, tatty, threadbare, ungentlemanly, unworthy, worn, worn-out.

*antonyms* honourable, smart.

**shack** *n* bothy, but and ben, cabin, dump, hole, hovel, hut, hutch, lean-to, shanty, shed, shiel, shieling.

**shackle** *n* bond, bracelets, chain, darbies, fetter, gyve, hamper, handcuff, hobble, iron, leg-iron, manacle, rope, shackles, tether, trammel.

*v* bind, chain, constrain, embarrass, encumber, fetter, gyve, hamper, hamstring, handcuff, handicap, hobble, hogtie, impede, inhibit, limit, manacle, obstruct, pinion, restrain, restrict, secure, tether, thwart, tie, trammel.

**shade** *n* amount, apparition, blind, canopy, colour, coolness, cover, covering, curtain, darkness, dash, degree, difference, dimness, dusk, eidolon, ghost, gloaming, gloom, gloominess, gradation, hint, hue, manes, murk, nuance, obscurity, phantasm, phantom, screen, semblance, semi-darkness, shadiness, shadow, shadows, shelter, shield, shroud, spectre, spirit, stain, suggestion, suspicion, tinge, tint, tone, trace, twilight, umbra, umbrage, variation, variety, veil, wraith.

*v* cloud, conceal, cover, darken, dim, hide, inumbrate, mute, obscure, overshadow, protect, screen, shadow, shield, shroud, veil.

**shadow** *n* affliction, blight, caliginosity, cloud, companion, cover, darkness, detective, dimness, dusk, ghost, gloaming, gloom, hint, image, inseparable, obscurity, pal, phantom, protection, remnant, representation, sadness, shade, shelter, sidekick, sleuth, spectre, spirit, suggestion, suspicion, tenebrity, tenebrosity, trace, umbrage, vestige.

*v* darken, dog, follow, obscure, overhang, overshadow, screen, shade, shield, stalk, tail, tail-up, trail, watch.

**shadowy** *adj* caliginous, crepuscular, dark, dim, dreamlike, dusky, faint, ghostly, gloomy, half-remembered, hazy, illusory, imaginary, impalpable, indistinct, intangible, murky, nebulous, obscure, shaded, shady, spectral, tenebrious, tenebrose, tenebrous, umbratile, umbratilous, undefined, unreal, unsubstantial, vague, wraithlike.

**shady**[1] *adj* bosky, bowery, caliginous, cool, dark, dim, leafy, shaded, shadowy, tenebrous, umbrageous, umbratile, umbratilous, umbriferous, umbrose, umbrous.

*antonyms* bright, sunlit, sunny.

**shady**[2] *adj* crooked, discreditable, dishonest, disreputable, dubious, fishy, louche, questionable, shifty, slippery, suspect, suspicious, underhand, unethical, unscrupulous, untrustworthy.

*antonyms* honest, trustworthy.

**shaft** *n* arbor, arrow, barb, beam, cut, dart, gibe, gleam, haft, handle, missile, pole, ray, rod, shank, stem, stick, sting, streak, thrust, upright, well, winze.

**shaggy** *adj* crinose, hairy, hirsute, long-haired, nappy, rough, tousled, tousy, unkempt, unshorn.

*antonyms* bald, shorn.

**shake** *n* agitation, convulsion, disturbance, instant, jar, jerk, jiffy, jolt, jounce, moment, no time, pulsation, quaking, second, shiver, shock, shudder, tick, trembling, tremor, trice, twitch, vellication, vibration.

*v* agitate, brandish, bump, churn, concuss, convulse, didder, discompose, distress, disturb, flourish, fluctuate, frighten, heave, impair, intimidate, jar, joggle, jolt, jounce, move, oscillate, quake, quiver, rattle, rock, rouse, shimmy, shiver, shock, shog, shoggle, shudder, split, stir, succuss, sway, totter, tremble, twitch, undermine, unnerve, unsettle, upset, vellicate, vibrate, wag, waggle, wave, waver, weaken, wobble.

**shake a leg** get a move on, get cracking, hurry, look lively, step on it, stir one's stumps.

**shake off** dislodge, elude, get rid of, give the slip, leave behind, lose, outdistance, outpace, outstrip.

**shake-up** *n* disturbance, rearrangement, reorganisation, reshuffle, upheaval.

**shaky** *adj* dubious, faltering, inexpert, insecure, precarious, questionable, quivery, rickety, rocky, shoogly, suspect, tottering, tottery, uncertain, undependable, unreliable, unsound, unstable, unsteady, unsupported, untrustworthy, weak, wobbly.

*antonyms* firm, strong.

**shallow** *adj* empty, flimsy, foolish, frivolous, idle, ignorant, meaningless, puerile, simple, skin-deep, slight, superficial, surface, trivial, unanalytical, unintelligent, unscholarly.

*antonyms* analytical, deep.

**sham** *n* charlatan, counterfeit, feint, forgery, fraud, gold-brick, hoax, humbug, imitation, impostor, imposture, mountebank, phoney, pretence, pretender, pseud, stumer.

*adj* artificial, bogus, Brummagem, counterfeit, ersatz, faked, false, feigned, imitation, mock, pasteboard, phoney, pinchbeck, pretended, pseud, pseudo, put-on, simulated, snide, spurious, synthetic.

*antonym* genuine.

*v* affect, counterfeit, fake, feign, malinger, pretend, put on, simulate.

**shaman** *n* angekkok, magician, medicine-man, pawaw, powwow, sorcerer, witch-doctor.

**shambles** *n* anarchy, bedlam, chaos, confusion, disarray, disorder, disorganisation, havoc, madhouse, mess, muddle, pigsty, wreck.

**shambling** *adj* awkward, clumsy, disjointed, loose, lumbering, lurching, shuffling, unco-ordinated, ungainly, unsteady.

*antonyms* agile, neat, nimble, spry.

**shame** *n* aidos, bashfulness, blot, chagrin, compunction, contempt, degradation, derision, discredit, disgrace, dishonour, disrepute, embarrassment, humiliation, ignominy, infamy, mortification, obloquy, odium, opprobrium, reproach, scandal, shamefacedness, stain, stigma.

*antonyms* distinction, honour, pride.

*v* abash, blot, confound, debase, defile, degrade, discomfit, disconcert, discredit, disgrace, dishonour, embarrass, humble, humiliate, mortify, put to shame, reproach, ridicule, show up, smear, stain, sully, taint.

*interj* fi donc, fie, fie upon you, for shame, fy, shame on you.

**shamefaced** *adj* abashed, apologetic, ashamed, bashful, blushing, chagrined, conscience-stricken, contrite, diffident, discomfited, embarrassed, hesitant, humiliated, modest, mortified, pudibund, red-faced, remorseful, shamefast, sheepish, shrinking, shy, timid, uncomfortable.

*antonyms* proud, unashamed.

**shameful** *adj* abominable, atrocious, base, contemptible, dastardly, degrading, discreditable, disgraceful, dishonourable, embarrassing, humiliating, ignominious, indecent, infamous, low, mean, mortifying, outrageous, reprehensible, scandalous, shaming, unbecoming, unworthy, vile, wicked.

*antonyms* creditable, honourable.

**shameless** *adj* abandoned, abashless, audacious, barefaced, blatant, brash, brazen, corrupt, defiant, depraved, dissolute, flagrant, hardened, immodest, improper, impudent, incorrigible, indecent, insolent, ithyphallic, profligate, reprobate, unabashed, unashamed, unblushing, unprincipled, unscrupulous, wanton.

*antonyms* ashamed, contrite, shamefaced.

**shanty** *n* bothy, cabin, hovel, hut, hutch, lean-to, shack, shed.

**shape** *n* apparition, appearance, aspect, build, condition, configuration, conformation, contours, cut, dimensions, fettle, figure, form, format, frame, Gestalt, guise, health, kilter, likeness, lines, make, model, mould, outline, pattern, physique, profile, semblance, silhouette, state, template, trim.

*v* accommodate, adapt, brute, construct, create, define, develop, devise, embody, fashion, forge, form, frame, girdle, guide, make, model, modify, mould, plan, prepare, produce, redact, regulate, remodel.

**shapeless** *adj* amorphous, asymmetrical, battered, characterless, dumpy, embryonic, formless, inchoate, indeterminate, indigest, irregular, misshapen, nebulous, undeveloped, unformed, unshapely, unstructured.

*antonym* shapely.

**shapely** *adj* comely, curvaceous, elegant, featous, gainly, graceful, neat, pretty, trim, voluptuous, well-formed, well-proportioned, well-set-up, well-turned.

*antonym* shapeless.

**share** *v* allot, apportion, assign, chip in, distribute, divide, divvy, divvy up, go Dutch, go fifty-fifty, go halves, muck in, partake, participate, split, whack.

*n* a piece of the action, allotment, allowance, contribution, cut, dividend, division, divvy, due, finger, lot, part, portion, proportion, quota, ration, snap, snip, stint, whack.

**share out** allot, apportion, assign, distribute, divide up, give out, parcel out, prorate.

*antonym* monopolise.

**shark** *n* chiseller, crook, extortioner, fleecer, parasite, politician, sharper, slicker, sponger, swindler, wheeler-dealer.

**sharp** *adj* abrupt, acerbic, acicular, acid, acidulous, acrid, acrimonious, acute, alert, apt, artful, astute, barbed, biting, bitter, bright, burning, canny, caustic, chic, chiselled, classy, clear, clear-cut, clever, crafty, crisp, cunning, cutting, discerning, dishonest, distinct, dressy, eager, edged, excruciating, extreme, fashionable, fierce, fit, fly, harsh, honed, hot, hurtful, incisive, intense, jagged, keen, knife-edged, knifelike, knowing, long-headed, marked, natty, nimble-witted, noticing, observant, painful, penetrating, peracute, perceptive, piercing, piquant, pointed, pungent, quick, quick-witted, rapid, razor-sharp, ready, sarcastic, sardonic, saw-edged, scathing, serrated, severe, sharpened, shooting, shrewd, sly, smart, snappy, snazzy, sour, spiky, stabbing, stinging, stylish, subtle, sudden, tart, trenchant, trendy, unblurred, undulled, unscrupulous, vinegary, violent, vitriolic, waspish, wily.

*antonyms* blunt, dull, mild, obtuse, slow, stupid.

*adv* abruptly, exactly, on the dot, out of the blue, precisely, promptly, punctually, suddenly, unexpectedly.

**sharpen** *v* acuminate, de-blur, edge, file, grind, hone, strop, taper, whet.

*antonym* blunt.

**sharpness** *n* acuity, acuteness, astuteness, discernment, eagerness, fierceness, incisiveness, intensity, keenness, observation, penetration, perceptiveness, pungency, quickness, severity, shrewdness, whet.

*antonyms* dullness, sloth.

**sharp-sighted** *adj* eagle-eyed, gimlet-eyed, hawk-eyed, keen-sighted, lyncean, lynx-eyed, noticing, observant, perceptive.

*antonyms* short-sighted, unobservant.

**shatter** *v* blast, blight, break, burst, crack, crush, demolish, destroy, devastate, disable, disshiver, dumbfound, exhaust, explode, impair, implode, overturn, overwhelm, pulverise, ruin, shiver, smash, smithereen, split, stun, torpedo, undermine, upset, wreck.

**shattered** *adj* all in, crushed, dead beat, devastated, dog-tired, done in, exhausted, jiggered, knackered, overwhelmed, undermined, weary, worn out, zonked.

**shattering** *adj* crushing, damaging, devastating, foudroyant, overwhelming, paralysing, severe, stunning.

**shave** *v* barber, brush, crop, fleece, graze, pare, plane, plunder, scrape, shear, tonsure, touch, trim.

**sheaf** *n* armful, bunch, bundle, dorlach, gait, garbe, truss.

**sheath** *n* armour, carapace, case, casing, coat, coating, condom, covering, envelope, French letter, protective layer, rubber, safe, shell, sleeve, vagina, vaginula.

**shed**[1] *v* afford, cast, cast off, diffuse, discard, drop, emit, exuviate, give, moult, pour, radiate, scatter, shower, slough, spill, throw.

**shed light on** clarify, clear up, effuse, elucidate, exfoliate, explain, illuminate, simplify.

**shed**[2] *n* barn, hut, lean-to, lock-up, outhouse, shack.

**shedding** *n* casting, diffusion, discarding, ecdysis, effusion, emission, exfoliation, exuviation, moulting, radiation, scattering, sloughing.

**sheen** *n* brightness, brilliance, burnish, gleam, gloss, lustre, patina, polish, shimmer, shine, shininess.

*antonyms* dullness, tarnish.

**sheep** *n* bell-wether, eanling, ewe, jumbuck, lamb, ram, tup, wether, yow.

**sheepish** *adj* abashed, ashamed, chagrined, chastened, embarrassed, foolish, mortified, self-conscious, shamefaced, silly, uncomfortable.

*antonym* unabashed.

**sheer**[1] *adj* abrupt, absolute, arrant, complete, downright, mere, out-and-out, perpendicular, precipitous, pure, rank, steep, thorough, thoroughgoing, total, unadulterated, unalloyed, unmingled, unmitigated, unqualified, utter, vertical.

**sheer**[2] diaphanous, fine, flimsy, gauzy, gossamer, pellucid, see-through, thin, translucent, transparent.

*antonyms* heavy, thick.

**sheet** *n* blanket, broadsheet, broadside, circular, coat, covering, expanse, film, flyer, folio, handbill, handout, lamina, layer, leaf, leaflet, membrane, nappe, news-sheet, overlay, pane, panel, piece, plate, shroud, skin, slab, stratum, surface, veneer.

**shelf** *n* bank, bar, bench, bracket, ledge, mantel, mantelpiece, platform, projection, reef, sandbank, sand-bar, shoal, step, terrace.

**shell** *n* carapace, case, casing, chassis, covering, crust, dop, frame, framework, hull, husk, nacelle, pod, rind, shuck, skeleton, structure.

*v* attack, barrage, batter, blitz, bomb, bombard, cannonade, hull, husk, shuck, strafe, strike.

**shell out** ante, contribute, cough up, disburse, donate, expend, fork out, give, lay out, pay out, subscribe.

**shelter** *v* accommodate, cover, defend, ensconce, guard, harbour, hide, protect, put up, safeguard, screen, shade, shadow, shield, shroud, skug.

*antonym* expose.

*n* accommodation, aegis, asylum, bield, bunker, cover, covert, coverture, defence, dugout, funk-hole, guard, gunyah, harbourage, haven, lean-to, lee, lodging, protection, refuge, retreat, roof, safety, sanctuary, sconce, screen, screening, security, shade, shadow, shiel, umbrage, umbrella.

*antonym* exposure.

**sheltered** *adj* cloistered, conventual, cosy, hermitic, isolated, lee, protected, quiet, reclusive, retired, screened, secluded, shaded, shielded, snug, unworldly, warm, withdrawn.

*antonym* exposed.

**shelve** *v* defer, dismiss, freeze, halt, mothball, pigeonhole, postpone, put aside, put in abeyance, put off, put on ice, suspend, table.

*antonyms* expedite, implement.

**shepherd** *n* guardian, herd, herdboy, herd-groom, herdsman, protector, shepherd boy, shepherdess, shepherdling.

*v* conduct, convoy, escort, guide, herd, lead, marshal, steer, usher.

**shield** *n* aegis, ancile, buckler, bulwark, cover, defence, escutcheon, guard, pelta, protection, rampart, safeguard, screen, scutum, shelter, targe, ward.

*v* cover, defend, guard, protect, safeguard, screen, shade, shadow, shelter.

*antonym* expose.

**shift** *v* adjust, alter, budge, change, dislodge, displace, fluctuate, manoeuvre, move, quit, rearrange, relocate, remove, reposition, rid, scoff, swallow, swerve, switch, transfer, transpose, vary, veer, wolf.

*n* alteration, artifice, change, contrivance, craft, device, displacement, dodge, equivocation, evasion, expedient, fluctuation, manoeuvre, modification, move, permutation, rearrangement, removal, resource, ruse, shifting, sleight, stratagem, subterfuge, switch, transfer, trick, veering, wile.

**shiftless** *adj* aimless, directionless, feckless, goalless, good-for-nothing, idle, incompetent, indolent, ineffectual, inefficient, inept, irresponsible, lackadaisical, lazy, resourceless, slothful, unambitious, unenterprising.

*antonyms* ambitious, aspiring, eager, enterprising.

**shifty** *adj* contriving, crafty, deceitful, devious, dishonest, disingenuous, dubious, duplicitous, evasive, fly-by-night, furtive, scheming, shady, slippery, tricky, underhand, unprincipled, untrustworthy, wily.

*antonyms* honest, open.

**shilly-shally** *v* dilly-dally, dither, falter, fluctuate, haver, hem and haw, hesitate, mess about, prevaricate, seesaw, shuffle, swither, teeter, vacillate, waver.

**shimmer** *v* coruscate, gleam, glisten, glitter, phosphoresce, scintillate, twinkle.

*n* coruscation, gleam, glimmer, glitter, glow, incandescence, iridescence, lustre, phosphorescence.

**shimmering** *adj* aventurine, gleaming, glistening, glittering, glowing, incandescent, iridescent, luminous, lustrous, shining, shiny.

*antonyms* dull, matt.

**shin** *v* ascend, clamber, climb, mount, scale, scramble, shoot, soar, swarm.

**shine** *v* beam, brush, buff, burnish, coruscate, effulge, excel, flash, glare, gleam, glimmer, glisten, glitter, glow, lustre, polish, radiate, resplend, scintillate, shimmer, sparkle, stand out, star, twinkle.

*n* brightness, burnish, effulgence, glare, glaze, gleam, gloss, glow, lambency, light, luminosity, lustre, patina, polish, radiance, sheen, shimmer, sparkle.

**shininess** *n* brightness, burnish, effulgence, gleam, glitter, glossiness, lustre, polish, sheen, shine.

*antonym* dullness.

**shining** *adj* beaming, bright, brilliant, celebrated, conspicuous, distinguished, effulgent, eminent, fulgent, gleaming, glistening, glittering, glorious, glowing, illustrious, lamping, leading, lucent, luminous, nitid, outstanding, profulgent, radiant, resplendent, rutilant, shimmering, sparkling, splendid, twinkling.

**shiny** *adj* agleam, aglow, bright, burnished, gleaming, glistening, glossy, lustrous, nitid, polished, satiny, sheeny, shimmery, sleek.

*antonyms* dark, dull.

**ship** *n* argosy, bark, barque, boat, ferry, galleon, galley, liner, prore, prow, steamer, tanker, trawler, vessel, yacht.

**shipshape** *adj* businesslike, neat, orderly, seamanlike, spick-and-span, spruce, tidy, trig, trim, well-organised, well-planned, well-regulated.

*antonyms* disorderly, untidy.

**shirk** *v* avoid, bludge, dodge, duck, duck out of, evade, funk, shun, sidestep, skive, skrimshank, slack, swing the lead.

**shirker** *n* absentee, bludger, clock-watcher, dodger, embusque, idler, layabout, loafer, malingerer, quitter, shirk, skiver, skrimshanker, slacker.

**shiver** *v* palpitate, quake, quiver, shake, shudder, tremble, vibrate.

*n* flutter, frisson, grue, quiver, shudder, start, thrill, tremble, trembling, tremor, twitch, vibration.

**shivery** *adj* chilled, chilly, cold, fluttery, nervous, quaking, quivery, shaking, shuddery, trembly.

**shoal** *n* assemblage, flock, horde, mass, mob, multitude, swarm, throng.

**shock** *v* agitate, appal, astound, confound, disgust, dismay, disquiet, horrify, jar, jolt, nauseate, numb, offend, outrage, paralyse, revolt, scandalise, shake, sicken, stagger, startle, stun, stupefy, traumatise, unnerve, unsettle.

*antonyms* delight, gratify, please, reassure.

*n* blow, bombshell, breakdown, clash, collapse, collision, concussion, consternation, dismay, distress, disturbance, encounter, fright, impact, jarring, jolt, perturbation, prostration, stupefaction, stupor, succussion, thunderbolt, trauma, turn, upset.

*antonyms* delight, pleasure.

**shocking** *adj* abhorrent, abominable, appalling, astounding, atrocious, deplorable, detestable, disgraceful, disgusting, disquieting, distressing, dreadful, execrable, foul, frightful, ghastly, hideous, horrible, horrific, horrifying, insufferable, intolerable, loathsome, monstrous, nauseating, nefandous, odious, offensive, outrageous, repugnant, repulsive, revolting, scandalous, sickening, stupefying, unbearable, unspeakable.

*antonyms* acceptable, delightful, pleasant, satisfactory.

**shoddy** *adj* cheap, cheap-jack, flimsy, gimcrack, inferior, junky, poor, rubbishy, second-rate, slipshod, tacky, tatty, tawdry, trashy, trumpery.

*antonyms* fine, well-made.

**shoemaker** *n* bootmaker, cobbler, cordiner, cordwainer, snab, snob, souter.

**shoemaking** *n* bootmaking, cobblery, cobbling, gentle craft.

**shoot**[1] *v* bag, blast, bolt, charge, dart, dash, discharge, dump, emit, enfilade, film, fire, flash, flung, gun down, hit, hurl, hurtle, kill, launch, open fire, photograph, pick off, plug, precipitate, project, propel, race, rake, rush, scoot, speed, spring, sprint, streak, take, tear, whisk, whiz, zap.

**shoot**[2] *n* branch, bud, germen, offshoot, scion, slip, sprig, sprout, tendron, twig.

*v* bolt, bud, burgeon, detonate, germinate, grow, shoot up, sprout, stretch, tower.

**shop** *n* boutique, chain, dolly-shop, emporium, hypermarket, hypermart, market, mart, megastore, store, superette, supermarket, workshop.

**shopping precinct** arcade, complex, mall, market, plaza.

**shore**[1] *n* beach, coast, foreshore, lakeside, littoral, margin, offing, promenade, rivage, sands, seaboard, sea-front, seashore, strand, waterfront, water's edge, waterside.

**shore**[2] *v* brace, buttress, hold, prop, reinforce, shore up, stay, strengthen, support, underpin.

**shorn** *adj* bald, beardless, crew-cut, cropped, deprived, nott, polled, shaved, shaven, stripped.

**short** *adj* abbreviated, abridged, abrupt, blunt, brief, brittle, brusque, compendious, compressed, concise, crisp, crumbly, crusty, curt, curtailed, deficient, diminutive, direct, discourteous, dumpy, ephemeral, evanescent, fleeting, friable, gruff, impolite, inadequate, insufficient, lacking, laconic, limited, little, low, meagre, momentary, murly, offhand, passing, petite, pithy, poor, precised, sawn-off, scant, scanty, scarce, sententious, sharp, shortened, short-handed, short-lived, short-term, slender, slim, small, snappish, snappy, sparse, squat, straight, succinct, summarised, summary, tart, terse, tight, tiny, transitory, uncivil, understaffed, unplentiful, wanting, wee.

*antonyms* adequate, ample, expansive, large, lasting, long, long-lived, polite, tall.

**short of** apart from, deficient in, except, lacking, less than, low on, missing, other than, pushed for, short on, wanting.

**shortage** *n* absence, dearth, deficiency, deficit, failure, inadequacy, insufficiency, lack, leanness, meagreness, paucity, poverty, scantiness, scarcity, shortfall, sparseness, want, wantage.

*antonyms* abundance, sufficiency.

**shortcoming** *n* defect, drawback, faible, failing, fault, flaw, foible, frailty, imperfection, inadequacy, weakness.

**shorten** *v* abbreviate, abridge, crop, curtail, cut, decrease, diminish, dock, foreshorten, lessen, lop, precis, prune, reduce, take up, telescope, trim, truncate.

*antonyms* amplify, enlarge, lengthen.

**shortened** *adj* abbreviated, abbreviatory, abridged, abstracted, compendious, condensed, summarised.

*antonym* amplified.

**shorthand** *n* brachygraphy, phonography, stenography, tachygraphy.

*antonym* longhand.

**short-lived** *adj* brief, caducous, ephemeral, evanescent, fleeting, fugacious, impermanent, momentary, passing, short, temporary, transient, transitory.

*antonyms* abiding, enduring, lasting, long-lived.

**shortly** *adv* abruptly, anon, briefly, concisely, curtly, directly, laconically, presently, sharply, soon, succinctly, tartly, tersely.

**short-sighted** *adj* careless, hasty, ill-advised, ill-considered, impolitic, impractical, improvident, imprudent, injudicious, myopic, near-sighted, unimaginative, unthinking.

*antonyms* far-sighted, hypermetropic, long-sighted.

**short-tempered** *adj* choleric, crusty, fiery, hot-tempered, impatient, irascible, irritable, peppery, quick-tempered, ratty, testy, touchy.

*antonyms* calm, patient, placid.

**short-winded** *adj* breathless, gasping, panting, peching, puffing, pursy.

**shot**[1] *n* attempt, ball, bash, blast, bullet, cannon-ball, chance, conjecture, contribution, crack, discharge, dram, effort, endeavour, essay, go, guess, injection, lead, lob, marksman, opportunity, pellet, projectile, range, reach, shooter, shy, slug, spell, stab, stroke, surmise, throw, try, turn.

**shot in the arm** boost, encouragement, fillip, fresh talent, impetus, lift, stimulus, uplift.

**shot in the dark** blind guess, conjecture, guess, guesswork, speculation.

**shot**[2] *adj* iridescent, moire, mottled, variegated, watered.

**shoulder** *v* accept, assume, barge, bear, carry, elbow, jostle, press, push, shove, sustain, take on, thrust.

**shout** *n* bay, bellow, belt, call, cheer, cry, roar, scream, shriek, yell.

*v* bawl, bay, bellow, call, cheer, cry, holler, roar, scream, shriek, yell.

**shove** *v* barge, crowd, drive, elbow, force, impel, jostle, press, propel, push, shoulder, thrust.

**shove off** beat it, clear off, clear out, depart, do a bunk, get lost, leave, push off, put out, scarper, scram, skedaddle, vamoose.

**shovel** *n* backhoe, bail, bucket, scoop, spade.

*v* convey, dredge, heap, ladle, load, move, scoop, shift, spade, spoon, toss.

**show** *v* accompany, accord, assert, attend, attest, bestow, betray, clarify, conduct, confer, demonstrate, disclose, display, divulge, elucidate, escort, evidence, evince, exemplify, exhibit, explain, grant, guide, illustrate, indicate, instruct, lead, manifest, offer, present, prove, register, reveal, teach, usher, witness.

*n* affectation, air, appearance, array, dash, demonstration, display, eclat, elan, entertainment, exhibition, exhibitionism, expo, exposition, extravaganza, façade, fair, feerie, flamboyance, gig, illusion, indication, likeness, manifestation, ostentation, pageant, pageantry, panache, parade, performance, pizzazz, plausibility, pose, presentation, pretence, pretext, production, profession, razzle-dazzle, representation, semblance, sight, sign, spectacle, swagger, view.

**show off** advertise, boast, brag, brandish, demonstrate, display, enhance, exhibit, flaunt, grandstand, parade, peacock, set off, strut, swagger, swank.

**show up** appear, arrive, come, disgrace, embarrass, expose, highlight, humiliate, lay bare, let down, mortify, pinpoint, reveal, shame, show, stand out, turn up, unmask.

**show-down** *n* clash, climax, confrontation, crisis, culmination, denouement, expose, face-off.

**shower**[1] *n* barrage, deluge, douche, down-come, drift, fusillade, hail, plethora, precipitation, rain, spout, stream, torrent, volley.

*v* deluge, douche, douse, heap, inundate, lavish, load, overwhelm, pour, rain, sparge, spray, sprinkle.

**shower**[2] *n* crew, galère, gang, mob, rabble.

**showiness** *n* flamboyance, flashiness, glitter, glitz, ostentation, pizzazz, razzle-dazzle, razzmatazz, swank.

*antonym* restraint.

**showing** *n* account, appearance, display, evidence, exhibition, impression, past performance, performance, presentation, record, representation, show, staging, statement, track record.

*adj* demonstrative, descriptive, elucidative, endeictic, explanatory, explicatory, illustrative, indicative, representative, revelatory, significant, symbolic.

**showing-off** *n* boasting, braggadocio, bragging, egotism, exhibitionism, hokum, peacockery, self-advertisement, swagger, swank, vainglory.

*antonym* modesty.

**showman** *n* entertainer, impresario, performer, publicist, ring-master, self-advertiser, show-off.

**show-off** *n* boaster, braggadocio, braggart, egotist, exhibitionist, peacock, self-advertiser, swaggerer, swanker, vaunter.

**showy** *adj* epideictic, euphuistic, exotic, flamboyant, flash, flashy, florid, flossy, garish, gaudy, glitzy, loud, ostentatious, pompous, pretentious, sparkish, specious, splashy, swanking, swanky, tawdry, tinselly.

*antonyms* quiet, restrained.

**shred** *n* atom, bit, fragment, grain, iota, jot, mammock, mite, piece, rag, ribbon, scrap, sliver, snippet, tatter, trace, whit, wisp.

**shrew** *n* bitch, dragon, Fury, harridan, henpecker, nag, scold, spitfire, termagant, virago, vixen, Xanthippe.

**shrewd** *adj* acute, arch, argute, artful, astucious, astute, calculated, calculating, callid, canny, clever, crafty, cunning, discerning, discriminating, downy, far-seeing, far-sighted, fly, gnostic, intelligent, judicious, keen, knowing, long-headed, observant, perceptive, perspicacious, sagacious, sharp, sly, smart, well-advised, wily.

*antonyms* naïve, obtuse, unwise.

**shrewdly** *adv* artfully, astutely, cannily, cleverly, craftily, far-sightedly, judiciously, knowingly, perceptively, perspicaciously, sagaciously, wisely.

**shrewdness** *n* acumen, acuteness, astucity, astuteness, callidity, canniness, discernment, grasp, intelligence, judgement, penetration, perceptiveness, perspicacity, sagacity, sharpness, smartness, wisdom.

*antonyms* foolishness, naïvety, obtuseness.

**shrewish** *adj* bad-tempered, captious, complaining, discontented, fault-finding, henpecking, ill-humoured, ill-natured, ill-tempered, nagging, peevish, petulant, quarrelsome, querulous, scolding, sharp-tongued, vixenish.

*antonyms* affectionate, peaceable, placid, supportive.

**shriek** *v* bellow, caterwaul, cry, holler, howl, scream, screech, shout, squeal, wail, yell.

*n* bellow, caterwaul, cry, howl, scream, screech, shout, squeal, wail.

**shrill** *adj* acute, argute, carrying, ear-piercing, ear-splitting, high, high-pitched, penetrating, piercing, piping, screaming, screeching, screechy, sharp, strident, treble.

*antonyms* gentle, low, soft.

**shrine** *n* chapel, dagoba, darga, delubrum, dome, fane, martyry, sanctuary, stupa, tabernacle, temple, tope, vimana.

**shrink** *v* back away, balk, contract, cower, cringe, decrease, deflate, diminish, dwindle, flinch, lessen, narrow, quail, recoil, retire, shorten, shrivel, shun, shy away, wince, withdraw, wither, wrinkle.

*antonyms* embrace, expand, stretch, warm to.

**shrivel** *v* burn, dehydrate, desiccate, dwindle, frizzle, gizzen, parch, pucker, scorch, sear, shrink, wilt, wither, wizen, wrinkle.

**shrivelled** *adj* desiccated, dried up, dry, emaciated, gizzen, puckered, sere, shrunken, withered, wizened, wrinkled, writhled.

**shroud** *v* blanket, cloak, conceal, cover, enshroud, envelop, enwrap, hide, screen, sheet, swathe, veil, wrap.

*antonyms* expose, uncover.

*n* cerecloth, cerement, cloud, covering, grave-clothes, mantle, pall, screen, sindon, veil, winding-sheet.

**shrouded** *adj* blanketed, cloaked, clouded, concealed, covered, enshrouded, enveloped, hidden, swathed, veiled, wrapped.

*antonyms* exposed, uncovered.

**shrunken** *adj* cadaverous, contracted, emaciated, gaunt, reduced, shrivelled, shrunk.

*antonyms* full, generous, rounded, sleek.

**shudder** *v* convulse, heave, quake, quiver, shake, shiver, tremble.

*n* convulsion, frisson, grue, horror, quiver, spasm, trembling, tremor.

**shuffle**[1] *v* drag, hobble, limp, scrape, scuff, scuffle, shamble.

**shuffle**[2] chop and change, confuse, disarrange, disorder, intermix, jumble, mix, rearrange, reorganise, shift, shift around, switch around.

**shun** *v* avoid, cold-shoulder, elude, eschew, evade, ignore, ostracise, shy away from, spurn, steer clear of.

*antonyms* accept, embrace.

**shut** *v* bar, bolt, cage, close, fasten, latch, lock, seal, secure, slam, spar.

*antonym* open.

**shut down** cease, close, discontinue, halt, inactivate, shut up, stop, suspend, switch off, terminate.

**shut in** box in, circumscribe, confine, enclose, hedge round, hem in, imprison, incarcerate.

**shut off** cut off, isolate, remove, seclude, segregate, separate, sequester.

**shut out** banish, bar, conceal, cover, debar, exclude, hide, lock out, mask, muffle, ostracise, screen, veil.

**shut up** cage, clam up, confine, coop up, gag, gaol, hold one's tongue, hush up, immure, imprison, incarcerate, intern, jail, muzzle, pipe down, silence.

**shutter** *n* abat-jour, jalousie, louvre, screen.

**shuttle** *v* alternate, commute, go to and fro, seesaw, shunt, shuttlecock, travel.

**shy** *adj* backward, bashful, cautious, chary, coy, diffident, distrustful, farouche, hesitant, inhibited, modest, mousy, nervous, reserved, reticent, retiring, self-conscious, self-effacing, shrinking, suspicious, timid, unassertive, wary.

*antonyms* bold, confident.

*v* back away, balk, buck, flinch, quail, rear, recoil, shrink, start, swerve, wince.

**shyness** *n* bashfulness, constraint, coyness, diffidence, hesitancy, inhibition, modesty, mousiness, nervousness, reticence, self-consciousness, timidity, timidness, timorousness.

*antonyms* boldness, confidence.

**sibling** *n* brother, german, sib, sister, twin.

**sibyl** *n* oracle, prophetess, Pythia, pythoness, seer, seeress, sorceress, wise woman.

**sick** *adj* ailing, black, blasé, bored, diseased, disgusted, displeased, dog-sick, fed up, feeble, ghoulish, glutted, ill, indisposed, jaded, laid up, morbid, mortified, nauseated, pining, poorly, puking, qualmish, queasy, sated, satiated, sickly, tired, under the weather, unwell, vomiting, weak, weary.

*antonyms* healthy, well.

**sicken** *v* disgust, nauseate, put off, repel, revolt, scunner, turn off.

*antonyms* attract, delight.

**sickening** *adj* disgusting, distasteful, foul, loathsome, mephitic, offensive, putrid, repulsive, revolting, vile.

*antonyms* attractive, delightful, pleasing.

**sickly** *adj* ailing, bilious, bloodless, cloying, delicate, faint, feeble, frail, icky, indisposed, infirm, lacklustre, languid, mawkish, nauseating, pallid, peaked, peaky, peelie-wally, pimping, pining, puly, revolting, saccharine, sweet, syrupy, treacly, unhealthy, wan, weak, weakly.

*antonyms* robust, sturdy.

**sickness** *n* affliction, ailment, bug, complaint, derangement, disease, disorder, dwam, ill-health, illness, indisposition, infirmity, insanity, malady, nausea, pestilence, qualmishness, queasiness, vomiting.

*antonym* health.

**side** *n* airs, angle, arrogance, aspect, bank, border, boundary, brim, brink, camp, cause, department, direction, division, edge, elevation, face, facet, faction, flank, flitch, fringe, gang, hand, insolence, light, limit, margin, opinion, ostentation, page, part, party, perimeter, periphery, position, pretentiousness, quarter, region, rim, sect, sector, slant, stand, standpoint, surface, team, twist, verge, view, viewpoint.

*adj* flanking, incidental, indirect, irrelevant, lateral, lesser, marginal, minor, oblique, roundabout, secondary, subordinate, subsidiary.

**side with** agree with, befriend, favour, second, support, team up with, vote for.

**sidelong** *adj* covert, indirect, oblique, sideward, sideways.

*antonyms* direct, overt.

**sidestep** *v* avoid, bypass, circumvent, dodge, duck, elude, evade, find a way round, shirk, skip, skirt.

*antonym* tackle.

**sidetrack** *v* deflect, distract, divert, head off.

**sideways** *adv* askance, crabwise, edgeways, edgewise, laterally, obliquely, sidelong, sidewards.

*adj* oblique, side, sidelong, sideward, slanted.

**sidle** *v* creep, edge, inch, ingratiate, insinuate, slink, sneak, steal, wriggle.

**siesta** *n* catnap, doze, forty winks, nap, relaxation, repose, rest, sleep, snooze.

**sieve** *v* boult, remove, riddle, separate, sift, strain.

*n* boulter, colander, riddle, screen, sifter, strainer.

**sift** *v* analyse, boult, discuss, examine, fathom, filter, investigate, pan, part, probe, review, riddle, screen, scrutinise, separate, sieve, sort, sprinkle, temse, winnow.

*n* analysis, colation, examination, filtering, filtration, review, screening, separation, sort, sorting, straining.

**sigh** *n* moan, sough, suspiration, wuther.

*v* breathe, complain, grieve, lament, moan, sorrow, sough, suspire, wuther.

**sigh for** grieve, lament, languish, long, mourn, pine, weep, yearn.

**sight** *n* appearance, apprehension, decko, display, estimation, exhibition, eye, eyes, eye-shot, eyeshot, eyesight, eyesore, field of vision, fright, gander, glance, glimpse, judgement, ken, look, mess, monstrosity, observation, opinion, pageant, perception, range, scene, seeing, show, spectacle, view, viewing, visibility, vision, vista.

*v* behold, discern, distinguish, glimpse, observe, perceive, see, spot.

**sights** *n* amenities, beauties, curiosities, features, marvels, Sehenswürdigkeiten, splendours, videnda, wonders.

**sightseer** *n* excursionist, holidaymaker, rubber-neck, tourist, tripper, visitor.

**sign** *n* augury, auspice, badge, beck, betrayal, board, character, cipher, clue, device, emblem, ensign, evidence, figure, foreboding, forewarning, gesture, giveaway, grammalogue, hierogram, hint, indication, indicium, insignia, intimation, lexigram, logo, logogram, logograph, manifestation, mark, marker, miracle, note, notice, omen, placard, pointer, portent, presage, proof, reminder, representation, rune, signal, signature, signification, signpost, spoor, suggestion, symbol, symptom, token, trace, trademark, vestige, warning.

*v* autograph, beckon, endorse, gesticulate, gesture, indicate, initial, inscribe, motion, signal, subscribe, wave.

**sign over** consign, convey, deliver, entrust, make over, surrender, transfer, turn over.

**sign up** appoint, contract, employ, engage, enlist, enrol, hire, join, join up, recruit, register, sign on, take on, volunteer.

**signal** *n* alarm, alert, beacon, beck, cue, flare, flash, gesture, go-ahead, griffin, impulse, indication, indicator, light, mark, OK, password, rocket, sign, tip-off, token, transmitter, waft, warning, watchword.

*adj* conspicuous, distinguished, eminent, exceptional, extraordinary, famous, glorious, impressive, memorable, momentous, notable, noteworthy, outstanding, remarkable, significant, striking.

*v* beckon, communicate, gesticulate, gesture, indicate, motion, nod, sign, telegraph, waft, wave.

**signature** *n* autograph, endorsement, initials, inscription, mark, sign.

**significance** *n* consequence, consideration, force, implication, implications, import, importance, impressiveness, interest, matter, meaning, message, moment, point, purport, relevance, sense, signification, solemnity, weight.

*antonym* unimportance.

**significant** *adj* critical, denoting, eloquent, expressing, expressive, important, indicative, knowing, material, meaning, meaningful, momentous, noteworthy, ominous, pregnant, senseful, serious, solemn, suggestive, symbolic, symptomatic, vital, weighty.

*antonyms* meaningless, unimportant.

**significantly** *adj* appreciably, considerably, critically, crucially, eloquently, knowingly, materially, meaningfully, meaningly, noticeably, perceptibly, suggestively, vitally.

**signify** v announce, augur, betoken, carry weight, communicate, connote, convey, count, denote, evidence, exhibit, express, imply, indicate, intimate, matter, mean, omen, portend, presage, proclaim, represent, show, stand for, suggest, symbolise, transmit.

**signpost** n clue, fingerpost, guidepost, hand-post, pointer, sign, way-post.

**silence** n calm, dumbness, hush, lull, muteness, noiselessness, obmutescence, peace, quiescence, quiet, quietness, reserve, reticence, secretiveness, speechlessness, stillness, taciturnity, uncommunicativeness.
v deaden, dumbfound, extinguish, gag, muffle, muzzle, quell, quiet, quieten, stifle, still, strike dumb, subdue, suppress.

**silent** adj aphonic, aphonous, dumb, hushed, idle, implicit, inaudible, inoperative, mum, mute, muted, noiseless, quiet, reticent, shtoom, soundless, speechless, still, stilly, tacit, taciturn, tongue-tied, uncommunicative, understood, unexpressed, unforthcoming, unpronounced, unsounded, unspeaking, unspoken, voiceless, wordless.
*antonyms* loud, noisy, talkative.

**silently** adv dumbly, ex tacito, inaudibly, mutely, noiselessly, quietly, soundlessly, speechlessly, tacitly, unheard, wordlessly.

**silhouette** n configuration, delineation, form, outline, profile, shadow-figure, shadowgraph, shape.

**silky** adj fine, satiny, silken, sleek, smooth, soft, velvety.

**silly** adj absurd, addled, asinine, benumbed, bird-brained, brainless, childish, cuckoo, daft, dazed, dopey, drippy, fatuous, feather-brained, flighty, foolhardy, foolish, frivolous, gaga, giddy, groggy, hen-witted, idiotic, illogical, immature, imprudent, inane, inappropriate, inept, irrational, irresponsible, meaningless, mindless, muzzy, pointless, preposterous, puerile, ridiculous, scatter-brained, senseless, spoony, stunned, stupefied, stupid, unwise, witless.
*antonyms* collected, mature, sane, sensible, wise.
n clot, dope, duffer, goose, half-wit, ignoramus, ninny, silly-billy, simpleton, twit, wally.

**silt** n alluvium, deposit, mud, ooze, residue, sediment, sludge.

**silt up** block, choke, clog, congest, dam.

**silvan** adj arboreous, bosky, forestal, forested, forestine, leafy, tree-covered, wooded, woodland.
*antonym* treeless.

**similar** adj alike, analogous, close, comparable, compatible, congruous, corresponding, homogeneous, homogenous, homologous, related, resembling, self-like, uniform.
*antonym* different.

**similarity** n affinity, agreement, analogy, closeness, coincidence, comparability, compatibility, concordance, congruence, correspondence, equivalence, homogeneity, likeness, relation, resemblance, sameness, similitude, uniformity.
*antonym* difference.

**similarly** adv by analogy, by the same token, correspondingly, likewise, uniformly.

**simmer** v boil, burn, fizz, fume, rage, seethe, smart, smoulder.

**simmer down** calm down, collect oneself, contain oneself, control oneself, cool down, cool off, recollect oneself, settle down, take it easy.

**simpering** adj affected, arch, coy, giggling, missish, schoolgirlish, self-conscious, silly.

**simple** adj artless, bald, basic, brainless, childlike, classic, classical, clean, clear, credulous, dense, direct, dumb, easy, elementary, feeble, feeble-minded, foolish, frank, green, guileless, half-witted, homely, honest, humble, idiot-proof, inelaborate, ingenuous, innocent, inornate, intelligible, lowly, lucid, manageable, modest, moronic, naïf, naive, naïve, naked, natural, obtuse, one-fold, plain, pure, rustic, Saturnian, shallow, silly, sincere, single, slow, Spartan, stark, straightforward, stupid, thick, unadorned, unaffected, unalloyed, unblended, uncluttered, uncombined, uncomplicated, undeniable, understandable, undisguised, undivided, unelaborate, unembellished, unfussy, uninvolved, unlearned, unmixed, unornate, unpretentious, unschooled, unskilled, unsophisticated, unsuspecting, unvarnished, user-friendly.
*antonyms* artful, clever, complicated, difficult, fancy, intricate.

**simple-minded** adj addle-brained, artless, backward, brainless, cretinous, dim-witted, dopey, feeble-minded, foolish, goofy, idiot, idiotic, imbecile, moronic, natural, retarded, simple, stupid, unsophisticated.
*antonyms* bright, clever.

**simpleton** n Abderite, blockhead, booby, daftie, dizzard, dolt, dope, dullard, dunce, dupe, flat, flathead, fool, gaby, gander, gomeril, goon, goop, goose, goose-cap, goosy, Gothamist, Gothamite, green goose, greenhorn, gump, gunsel, idiot, imbecile, jackass, Johnny, juggins, maffling, moron, nincompoop, ninny, ninny-hammer, numskull, soft-head, spoon, stupid, twerp.
*antonym* brain.

**simplicity** n artlessness, baldness, candour, clarity, classicism, clearness, directness, ease, easiness, elementariness, guilelessness, innocence, intelligibility, modesty, naïvete, naïvety, naturalness, obviousness, openness, plainness, purity, restraint, simpleness, sincerity, straightforwardness, uncomplicatedness.
*antonyms* difficulty, guile, intricacy, sophistication.

**simplify** v abridge, decipher, disentangle, facilitate, prune, reduce, streamline.
*antonyms* complicate, elaborate.

**simplistic** adj naïve, oversimplified, schematic, shallow, simple, superficial, sweeping, unanalytical.
*antonyms* analytical, detailed.

**simply** adv absolutely, altogether, artlessly, baldly, clearly, completely, directly, easily, intelligibly, just, merely, modestly, naturally, obviously, only, plainly, purely, quite, really, simpliciter, sincerely, solely, straightforwardly, totally, unaffectedly, undeniably, unpretentiously, unquestionably, unreservedly, utterly, wholly.

**simulate** *v* act, affect, assume, counterfeit, duplicate, echo, fabricate, fake, feign, imitate, mimic, parrot, pretend, put on, reflect, reproduce, sham.

**simulated** *adj* artificial, assumed, bogus, fake, feigned, imitation, inauthentic, insincere, make-believe, man-made, mock, phoney, pinchbeck, pretended, pseudo, put-on, sham, spurious, substitute, synthetic, ungenuine.

*antonyms* genuine, real.

**simultaneous** *adj* accompanying, coincident, coinciding, concomitant, concurrent, contemporaneous, parallel, synchronic, synchronous.

*antonyms* asynchronous, separate.

**sin** *n* crime, damnation, debt, error, evil, fault, guilt, hamartia, impiety, iniquity, lapse, misdeed, offence, sinfulness, transgression, trespass, ungodliness, unrighteousness, wickedness, wrong, wrongdoing.

*v* err, fall, fall from grace, go astray, lapse, misbehave, offend, stray, transgress, trespass.

**sincere** *adj* artless, bona fide, candid, deep-felt, earnest, frank, genuine, guileless, heartfelt, heart-whole, honest, natural, open, plain-hearted, plain-spoken, pure, real, serious, simple, simple-hearted, single-hearted, soulful, straightforward, true, true-hearted, truthful, unadulterated, unaffected, unfeigned, unmixed, wholehearted.

*antonym* insincere.

**sincerely** *adv* earnestly, genuinely, honestly, in earnest, really, seriously, simply, truly, truthfully, unaffectedly, wholeheartedly.

**sincerity** *n* artlessness, bona fides, candour, earnestness, frankness, genuineness, good faith, guilelessness, honesty, plain-heartedness, probity, seriousness, straightforwardness, truth, truthfulness, wholeheartedness.

*antonym* insincerity.

**sinecure** *n* cinch, cushy job, doddle, gravy train, money for jam, picnic, plum job, soft option.

**sinewy** *adj* athletic, brawny, lusty, muscular, powerful, robust, stringy, strong, sturdy, tendinous, vigorous, wiry.

**sinful** *adj* bad, corrupt, criminal, depraved, erring, fallen, guilty, immoral, impious, iniquitous, irreligious, peccable, peccant, ungodly, unholy, unrighteous, unvirtuous, wicked, wrongful.

*antonyms* righteous, sinless.

**sinfulness** *n* corruption, depravity, guilt, immorality, impiety, iniquity, peccability, peccancy, sin, transgression, ungodliness, unrighteousness, wickedness.

*antonym* righteousness.

**sing** *v* betray, bizz, blow the whistle, cantillate, carol, caterwaul, chant, chirp, croon, finger, fink, grass, hum, inform, intone, lilt, melodise, peach, pipe, purr, quaver, rat, render, serenade, spill the beans, squeal, talk, trill, vocalise, warble, whine, whistle, yodel.

**sing out** bawl, bellow, call, cooee, cry, halloo, holler, shout, yell.

**singe** *v* blacken, burn, cauterise, char, scorch, sear.

**singer** *n* balladeer, balladist, bard, cantabank, cantatrice, cantor, caroller, chanteuse, choirboy, choirgirl, choirman, chorister, crooner, diva, griot, jongleur, Meistersinger, minstrel, precentor, prima donna, psalmodist, songster, troubadour, vocalist.

**single** *adj* celibate, distinct, exclusive, free, individual, lone, man-to-man, one, one-fold, one-to-one, only, particular, separate, simple, sincere, single-minded, singular, sole, solitary, unattached, unblended, unbroken, uncombined, uncompounded, undivided, unique, unmarried, unmixed, unshared, unwed, wholehearted.

**single out** choose, cull, distinguish, hand-pick, highlight, isolate, pick, pinpoint, select, separate, set apart.

**single-handed** *adj, adv* alone, independently, solo, unaccompanied, unaided, unassisted.

**single-minded** *adj* dedicated, determined, dogged, fixed, hell-bent, monomaniacal, resolute, steadfast, stubborn, tireless, undeviating, unswerving, unwavering.

**singular** *adj* atypical, conspicuous, curious, eccentric, eminent, exceptional, extraordinary, individual, noteworthy, odd, out-of-the-way, outstanding, peculiar, pre-eminent, private, prodigious, proper, puzzling, queer, rare, remarkable, separate, single, sole, strange, uncommon, unique, unparalleled, unusual.

*antonyms* normal, usual.

**singularity** *n* abnormality, curiousness, eccentricity, extraordinariness, idiosyncrasy, irregularity, oddity, oddness, oneness, particularity, peculiarity, queerness, quirk, strangeness, twist, unicity, uniqueness.

*antonym* normality.

**singularly** *adv* bizarrely, conspicuously, especially, exceptionally, extraordinarily, notably, outstandingly, particularly, prodigiously, remarkably, signally, surprisingly, uncommonly, unusually.

**sinister** *adj* dire, disquieting, evil, inauspicious, injurious, left, louche, malevolent, malign, malignant, menacing, ominous, threatening, underhand, unlucky.

*antonyms* harmless, innocent.

**sink** *v* abandon, abate, abolish, bore, collapse, conceal, decay, decline, decrease, defeat, degenerate, degrade, delapse, descend, destroy, dig, diminish, dip, disappear, drill, drive, droop, drop, drown, dwindle, ebb, engulf, excavate, fade, fail, fall, finish, flag, founder, invest, lapse, lay, lessen, lower, merge, overwhelm, pay, penetrate, plummet, plunge, relapse, retrogress, ruin, sag, scupper, slip, slope, slump, stoop, submerge, subside, succumb, suppress, weaken, worsen.

*antonyms* float, rise, uplift.

**sinless** *adj* faultless, guiltless, immaculate, impeccable, innocent, pure, unblemished, uncorrupted, undefiled, unspotted, unsullied, virtuous.

*antonym* sinful.

**sinner** *n* backslider, evil-doer, malefactor, miscreant, offender, reprobate, transgressor, trespasser, wrong-doer.

**sinuous** *adj* coiling, crooked, curved, curvy, lithe, mazy, meandering, serpentine, slinky, supple, tortuous, undulating, winding.

*antonym* straight.

**sip** *v* delibate, sample, sup, taste.

*n* drop, mouthful, spoonful, swallow, taste, thimbleful.

**siren** *n* charmer, Circe, femme fatale, houri, Lorelei, seductress, temptress, vamp, witch.

**sissy** *n* baby, coward, milksop, mollycoddle, mummy's boy, namby-pamby, pansy, softy, weakling, wet.

*adj* cowardly, effeminate, feeble, namby-pamby, pansy, sissified, soft, unmanly, weak, wet.

**sit** *v* accommodate, assemble, befit, brood, contain, convene, deliberate, hold, meet, officiate, perch, pose, preside, reside, rest, seat, settle.

**site** *n* ground, location, lot, place, plot, position, setting, spot, station.

*v* dispose, install, locate, place, position, set, situate, station.

**sitting** *n* assembly, consultation, get-together, hearing, meeting, period, seat, session, spell.

**situation** *n* ball-game, berth, case, circumstances, condition, employment, galère, job, kettle of fish, lie of the land, locale, locality, location, office, place, plight, position, post, predicament, rank, scenario, seat, setting, set-up, site, sphere, spot, state, state of affairs, station, status.

**sizable** *adj* biggish, considerable, decent, decent-sized, goodly, large, largish, respectable, significant, substantial, tidy.

*antonym* small.

**size** *n* amount, amplitude, bigness, bulk, dimensions, extent, greatness, height, hugeness, immensity, largeness, magnitude, mass, measurement(s), proportions, range, vastness, volume.

**size up** appraise, assess, evaluate, gauge, measure.

**sizzle** *v* crackle, frizzle, fry, hiss, scorch, sear, spit, sputter.

**skedaddle** *v* abscond, beat it, bolt, decamp, disappear, do a bunk, flee, hop it, run away, scarper, scoot, scram, split, vamoose.

**skeletal** *adj* cadaverous, drawn, emaciated, fleshless, gaunt, haggard, hollow-cheeked, shrunken, skin-and-bone, wasted.

**skeleton** *n* bare bones, draft, endoskeleton, frame, framework, outline, sketch, structure.

**sketch** *v* block out, delineate, depict, draft, draw, outline, paint, pencil, plot, portray, represent, rough out.

*n* croquis, delineation, design, draft, drawing, ebauche, esquisse, outline, plan, scenario, skeleton, vignette.

**sketchily** *adv* cursorily, hastily, imperfectly, inadequately, incompletely, patchily, perfunctorily, roughly, vaguely.

*antonym* fully.

**sketchy** *adj* bitty, crude, cursory, imperfect, inadequate, incomplete, insufficient, outline, perfunctory, rough, scrappy, skimpy, slight, superficial, unfinished, vague.

*antonym* full.

**skilful** *adj* able, accomplished, adept, adroit, apt, canny, clever, competent, dexterous, experienced, expert, handy, masterly, nimble-fingered, practised, professional, proficient, quick, ready, skilled, tactical, trained.

*antonyms* awkward, clumsy, inept.

**skill** *n* ability, accomplishment, adroitness, aptitude, art, cleverness, competence, dexterity, experience, expertise, expertness, facility, finesse, handiness, ingenuity, intelligence, knack, proficiency, quickness, readiness, savoir-faire, savvy, skilfulness, talent, technique, touch.

**skilled** *adj* able, accomplished, crack, experienced, expert, masterly, practised, professional, proficient, schooled, skilful, trained.

*antonym* unskilled.

**skim** *v* brush, coast, cream, dart, despumate, float, fly, glide, plane, sail, scan, separate, skip, soar.

**skimp** *v* conserve, cut corners, economise, pinch, scamp, scant, scrimp, stint, withhold.

**skimpy** *adj* beggarly, exiguous, inadequate, insufficient, meagre, measly, miserly, niggardly, scanty, short, sketchy, sparse, thin, tight.

*antonym* generous.

**skin** *n* casing, coating, crust, deacon, epidermis, fell, film, hide, husk, integument, membrane, mouton, outside, peel, pellicle, pelt, rind, tegument.

*v* abrade, bark, excoriate, flay, fleece, graze, peel, scrape, strip.

**skin-deep** *adj* artificial, empty, external, meaningless, outward, shallow, superficial, surface.

**skinflint** *n* cheese-parer, meanie, miser, niggard, penny-pincher, Scrooge, tightwad.

**skinny** *adj* attenuate(d), emaciated, lean, scragged, scraggy, skeletal, skin-and-bone, thin, twiggy, underfed, undernourished, weedy.

*antonym* fat.

**skip** *v* bob, bounce, caper, cavort, cut, dance, eschew, flisk, flit, frisk, gambol, hop, miss, omit, overleap, play truant, prance, trip.

**skirmish** *n* affair, affray, battle, brush, clash, combat, conflict, contest, dust-up, encounter, engagement, fracas, incident, scrap, scrimmage, set-to, spat, tussle, velitation.

*v* clash, collide, pickeer, scrap, tussle.

**skirt** *v* avoid, border, bypass, circle, circumambulate, circumnavigate, circumvent, detour, edge, evade, flank, steer clear of.

**skit** *n* burlesque, caricature, parody, satire, sketch, spoof, take-off, travesty, turn.

**skittish** *adj* coltish, excitable, fickle, fidgety, frivolous, highly-strung, jumpy, kittenish, kitteny, lively, nervous, playful, restive.

**skittles** *n* kettle-pins, kittle-pins, ninepins, pins, tenpins.

**skive** *v* dodge, dodge the column, idle, malinger, shirk, skrimshank, skulk, slack, swing the lead.

**skiver** *n* dodger, do-nothing, idler, loafer, malingerer, scrimshanker, shirker, slacker.

**skulduggery** *n* chicanery, double-dealing, duplicity, fraudulence, jiggery-pokery, machinations, shenanigan(s), swindling, trickery, underhandedness, unscrupulousness.

**skulk** *v* creep, lie in wait, loiter, lurk, pad, prowl, pussyfoot, slink, sneak.

**sky** *n* air, ambient, atmosphere, azure, blue, empyrean, firmament, heavens, vault of heaven, welkin.

**slab** *n* briquette, chunk, hunk, lump, piece, planch, portion, slice, wedge, wodge.

**slack** *adj* baggy, crank, dull, easy, easy-going, flaccid, flexible, idle, inactive, inattentive, lax, lazy, limp, loose, neglectful, negligent, permissive, quiet, relaxed, remiss, slow, slow-moving, sluggish, tardy.

*antonyms* busy, diligent, quick, rigid, stiff, taut.

*n* excess, give, inactivity, leeway, looseness, play, relaxation, room.

*v* dodge, idle, malinger, neglect, relax, shirk, skive, slacken.

**slacken off** abate, decrease, diminish, fail, flag, lessen, loosen, moderate, reduce, relax, release, slow, slow down, tire.

*antonyms* increase, quicken, tighten.

**slacker** *n* clock-watcher, dawdler, dodger, do-nothing, embusque, faineant, good-for-nothing, idler, layabout, loafer, malingerer, passenger, shirk(er), skiver, skrimshanker.

**slag** *v* abuse, berate, criticise, deride, insult, lambaste, malign, mock, slam, slang, slate.

**slake** *v* abate, allay, assuage, deaden, extinguish, gratify, mitigate, moderate, moisten, quench, reduce, sate, satiate, satisfy, slacken, subside.

**slam** *v* attack, bang, castigate, clap, crash, criticise, damn, dash, excoriate, fling, hurl, lambaste, pan, pillory, slate, smash, swap, swop, throw, thump, vilify.

**slander** *n* aspersion, backbiting, calumniation, calumny, defamation, detraction, libel, misrepresentation, muck-raking, obloquy, scandal, smear, traducement, traduction.

*v* asperse, backbite, calumniate, decry, defame, detract, disparage, libel, malign, muck-rake, scandalise, slur, smear, traduce, vilify, vilipend.

*antonyms* glorify, praise.

**slanderous** *adj* abusive, aspersive, aspersory, calumnious, damaging, defamatory, libellous, malicious.

**slang** *v* abuse, berate, castigate, excoriate, insult, lambaste, malign, revile, scold, slag, vilify, vituperate.

*antonym* praise.

**slanging match** altercation, argument, argy-bargy, barney, dispute, quarrel, row, set-to, shouting match, spat.

**slant** *v* angle, bend, bevel, bias, cant, colour, distort, incline, lean, list, shelve, skew, slope, tilt, twist, warp, weight.

*n* angle, attitude, bias, camber, declination, diagonal, emphasis, gradient, incline, leaning, obliquity, pitch, prejudice, rake, ramp, slope, tilt, viewpoint.

**slanting** *adj* angled, askew, aslant, asymmetrical, bent, canted, cater-cornered, diagonal, inclined, oblique, sideways, skew-whiff, slanted, slantwise, sloping, tilted, tilting.

*antonym* level.

**slap** *n* bang, blow, clap, clout, cuff, paddy-whack, skelp, smack, spank, wallop, whack.

*v* bang, clap, clout, cuff, daub, hit, plaster, plonk, skelp, spank, spread, strike, whack.

*adv* bang, dead, directly, exactly, plumb, precisely, right, slap-bang, smack.

**slap down** berate, keelhaul, rebuke, reprimand, restrain, squash, upbraid.

**slap in the face** affront, blow, humiliation, indignity, insult, put-down, rebuff, rebuke, rejection, repulse, snub.

**slap-dash** *adj* careless, clumsy, disorderly, haphazard, hasty, hurried, last-minute, messy, negligent, offhand, perfunctory, rash, slipshod, sloppy, slovenly, thoughtless, thrown-together, untidy.

*antonyms* careful, orderly.

**slap-happy** *adj* boisterous, casual, dazed, giddy, haphazard, happy-go-lucky, hit-or-miss, irresponsible, nonchalant, punch-drunk, reckless, reeling, slap-dash, woozy.

**slapstick** *n* buffoonery, comedy, farce, horseplay, knockabout, tomfoolery.

**slap-up** *adj* elaborate, excellent, first-class, first-rate, lavish, luxurious, magnificent, princely, splendid, sumptuous, superb, superlative.

**slash** *v* criticise, cut, drop, gash, hack, lacerate, lash, lower, reduce, rend, rip, score, slit.

*n* cut, gash, incision, laceration, lash, rent, rip, slit.

**slashing** *adj* aggressive, biting, brutal, ferocious, harsh, savage, searing, unsparing, vicious.

**slate** *v* abuse, berate, blame, castigate, censure, criticise, lambaste, pan, rebuke, reprimand, roast, scold, slag, slam, slang.

*antonym* praise.

**slatternly** *adj* bedraggled, dirty, dowdy, draggle-tailed, frowzy, frumpish, frumpy, slipshod, sloppy, slovenly, sluttish, unclean, unkempt, untidy.

**slaughter** *n* battue, blood-bath, bloodshed, butchery, carnage, extermination, holocaust, killing, liquidation, massacre, murder, schechita(h), shochet, slaying.

*v* butcher, crush, defeat, destroy, exterminate, halal, hammer, kill, liquidate, massacre, murder, overwhelm, rout, scupper, slay, thrash, trounce, vanquish.

**slave** *n* abject, bondservant, bond-slave, bond(s)man, bond(s)woman, captive, drudge, esne, helot, Mameluke, scullion, serf, servant, skivvy, slavey, thrall, vassal, villein.

*v* drudge, grind, labour, skivvy, slog, struggle, sweat, toil.

**slaver** *v* dribble, drivel, drool, salivate, slabber, slobber.

**slavery** *n* bondage, captivity, duress(e), enslavement, impressment, serfdom, servitude, subjugation, thraldom, thrall, vassalage, yoke.

*antonym* freedom.

**slavish** *adj* abject, base, conventional, cringing, despicable, fawning, grovelling, imitative, laborious, literal, low, mean, menial, obsequious, servile, strict, submissive, sycophantic, unimaginative, uninspired, unoriginal.

*antonyms* independent, original.

**slay** *v* amuse, annihilate, assassinate, butcher, destroy, dispatch, eliminate, execute, exterminate, impress, kill, massacre, murder, rub out, slaughter, wow.

**slaying** *n* annihilation, assassination, butchery, destruction, dispatch, elimination, extermination, killing, mactation, massacre, murder, shambles, slaughter.

**sleazy** *adj* crummy, disreputable, low, run-down, seedy, sordid, squalid, tacky.

**sleek** *adj* glossy, insinuating, lustrous, plausible, shiny, smooth, smug, well-fed, well-groomed.

**sleep** *v* catnap, doss (down), doze, drop off, drowse, hibernate, nod off, repose, rest, slumber, snooze, snore, zizz.

*n* coma, dormancy, doss, doze, forty winks, hibernation, nap, repose, rest, shut-eye, siesta, slumber(s), snooze, sopor, zizz.

**sleepiness** *n* doziness, drowsiness, heaviness, lethargy, oscitancy, somnolence, torpor.

*antonyms* alertness, wakefulness.

**sleeping** *adj* asleep, becalmed, daydreaming, dormant, dormient, hibernating, idle, inactive, inattentive, off guard, passive, slumbering, unaware.

*antonyms* alert, awake.

**sleepless** *adj* alert, disturbed, insomniac, insomnious, restless, unsleeping, vigilant, wakeful, watchful, wide-awake.

**sleeplessness** *n* insomnia, insomnolence, wakefulness.

**sleep-walker** *n* noctambulist, somnambulist.

**sleep-walking** *n* noctambulation, noctambulism, somnambulation, somnambulism.

**sleepy** *adj* drowsy, dull, heavy, hypnotic, inactive, lethargic, quiet, slow, sluggish, slumb(e)rous, slumbersome, slumbery, somnolent, soporific, soporose, soporous, torpid.

*antonyms* alert, awake, restless, wakeful.

**sleight of hand** adroitness, artifice, dexterity, legerdemain, magic, manipulation, prestidigitation, skill, trickery.

**slender** *adj* acicular, faint, feeble, flimsy, fragile, gracile, inadequate, inconsiderable, insufficient, lean, little, meagre, narrow, poor, remote, scanty, slight, slim, small, spare, svelte, sylph-like, tenuous, thin, thready, wasp-waisted, weak, willowish, willowy.

*antonyms* considerable, fat, thick.

**sleuth** *n* bloodhound, detective, dick, gumshoe, private eye, private investigator, shadow, tail, tracker.

**slice** *n* cut, frustum, helping, piece, portion, rasher, section, segment, share, sheave, shive, slab, sliver, tranche, wafer, wedge, whack, whang.

*v* carve, chop, cut, divide, segment, sever, sliver, whittle.

**slick** *adj* adroit, deft, dexterous, glib, meretricious, plausible, polished, professional, sharp, skilful, sleek, smooth, sophistical, specious, trim.

*antonyms* amateurish, clumsy, coarse.

**slide** *v* coast, glide, glissade, lapse, skate, skim, slidder, slip, slither, toboggan, veer.

**slight** *adj* delicate, feeble, flimsy, fragile, gracile, inconsiderable, insignificant, insubstantial, meagre, minor, modest, negligible, paltry, scanty, slender, slim, small, spare, superficial, trifling, trivial, unimportant, weak.

*antonyms* considerable, large, major, significant.

*v* affront, cold-shoulder, cut, despise, disdain, disparage, disrespect, ignore, insult, neglect, scorn, snub.

*antonyms* compliment, flatter.

*n* affront, contempt, discourtesy, disdain, disregard, disrespect, inattention, indifference, insult, neglect, rebuff, rudeness, slur, snub.

**slighting** *adj* abusive, belittling, defamatory, derogatory, disdainful, disparaging, disrespectful, insulting, offensive, scornful, slanderous, supercilious, uncomplimentary.

*antonym* complimentary.

**slim** *adj* ectomorphic, faint, gracile, lean, narrow, poor, remote, slender, slight, svelte, sylph-like, thin, trim.

*antonyms* chubby, fat, strong.

*v* bant, diet, lose weight, reduce, slenderise.

**slime** *n* bitumen, cludge, filth, gleet, glit, goo, gunk, mess, muck, mucus, mud, ooze.

**slimy** *adj* clammy, creeping, disgusting, glutinous, grovelling, miry, mucous, muddy, obsequious, oily, oozy, servile, smarmy, soapy, sycophantic, toadying, uliginous, unctuous, viscous.

**sling** v cast, catapult, chuck, dangle, fling, hang, heave, hurl, lob, pitch, shy, suspend, swing, throw, toss.

n band, bandage, catapult, loop, parbuckle, selvagee, strap, support.

**slink** v creep, prowl, pussyfoot, scunge, sidle, skulk, slip, sneak, steal.

**slinky** adj clinging, close-fitting, feline, figure-hugging, lean, sinuous, skin-tight, sleek.

**slip**[1] v blunder, boob, conceal, creep, disappear, discharge, dislocate, elude, err, escape, fall, get away, glide, hide, lapse, loose, miscalculate, misjudge, mistake, skate, skid, slidder, slide, slink, slither, sneak, steal, trip.

n bloomer, blunder, boob, error, failure, fault, imprudence, indiscretion, lapsus, lapsus calami, lapsus linguae, lapsus memoriae, mistake, omission, oversight, slip-up.

**slip**[2] n certificate, coupon, cutting, offshoot, pass, piece, runner, scion, shoot, sliver, sprig, sprout, strip.

**slipper** n flip-flop, loafer, moccasin, mule, pabouche, pantable, pantof(f)le, panton, pantoufle, pump, sandal.

**slippery** adj crafty, cunning, devious, dishonest, duplicitous, evasive, false, foxy, glassy, greasy, icy, lubric(al), lubric(i)ous, perilous, shifty, skiddy, sliddery, slippy, smooth, sneaky, treacherous, tricky, two-faced, unpredictable, unreliable, unsafe, unstable, unsteady, untrustworthy.

**slippy** adj elusive, evasive, greasy, icy, lubric(i)ous, smooth, uncertain, unstable.

**slipshod** adj careless, casual, loose, negligent, slap-dash, sloppy, slovenly, unsystematic, untidy.

*antonyms* careful, fastidious, neat, tidy.

**slit** v cut, gash, knife, lance, pierce, rip, slash, slice, split.

n cut, fent, fissure, gash, incision, opening, rent, split, tear, vent.

adj cut, pertusate, pertuse(d), rent, split, torn.

**slither** v glide, skitter, slidder, slide, slink, slip, snake, undulate.

**sliver** n chip, flake, fragment, paring, shaving, shiver, shred, slip, splinter.

**slob** n boor, brute, churl, lout, oaf, philistine, sloven, yahoo, yob.

**slobber** v dribble, drivel, drool, salivate, slabber, slaver, splutter, water at the mouth.

**slog** v bash, belt, hit, labour, persevere, plod, plough through, slave, slosh, slug, smite, sock, strike, thump, toil, tramp, trek, trudge, wallop, work.

n effort, exertion, grind, hike, labour, struggle, tramp, trek, trudge.

**slogan** n battle-cry, catch-phrase, catchword, chant, jingle, motto, rallying-cry, war cry, watchword.

**slop** v overflow, slobber, slosh, spatter, spill, splash, splatter, wash away.

**slope** v batter, delve, fall, incline, lean, pitch, rise, slant, tilt, verge, weather.

n bajada, brae, cant, declination, declivity, descent, downgrade, escarp, glacis, gradient, inclination, incline, ramp, rise, scarp, slant, tilt, versant.

**sloping** adj acclivitous, acclivous, bevelled, canting, declivitous, declivous, inclined, inclining, leaning, oblique, slanting.

*antonym* level.

**sloppy** adj amateurish, banal, careless, clumsy, gushing, hit-or-miss, inattentive, mawkish, messy, mushy, schmaltzy, sentimental, slipshod, slovenly, sludgy, slushy, soppy, splashy, trite, unkempt, untidy, watery, weak, wet.

*antonyms* careful, exact, precise.

**slosh** v bash, biff, flounder, hit, plash, pour, punch, shower, slap, slog, slop, slug, sock, splash, spray, strike, swash, swipe, thump, thwack, wade, wallop.

**slot** n aperture, channel, gap, groove, hole, niche, opening, place, position, slit, space, time, vacancy.

v adjust, assign, fit, insert, pigeonhole, place, position.

**sloth** n accidie, acedia, faineance, idleness, inactivity, indolence, inertia, laziness, listlessness, slackness, slothfulness, sluggishness, torpor.

*antonyms* diligence, industriousness, sedulity.

**slothful** adj do-nothing, faineant, idle, inactive, indolent, inert, lazy, listless, skiving, slack, sluggish, torpid, workshy.

*antonyms* diligent, industrious, sedulous.

**slouch** v droop, hunch, loll, shamble, shuffle, slump, stoop.

**slouching** adj careless, disorderly, heedless, loose, negligent, shambling, shuffling, slack, slap-dash, slatternly, slipshod, sloppy, unkempt, untidy.

**slow** adj adagio, backward, behind, behindhand, boring, bovine, conservative, creeping, dawdling, dead, dead-and-alive, delayed, deliberate, dense, dilatory, dim, dull, dull-witted, dumb, easy, gradual, inactive, lackadaisical, laggard, lagging, late, lazy, leaden, leisurely, lingering, loitering, long-drawn-out, measured, obtuse, one-horse, pedetentous, plodding, ponderous, prolonged, protracted, quiet, retarded, slack, sleepy, slow-moving, slow-witted, sluggardly, sluggish, stagnant, stupid, tame, tardy, tedious, thick, time-consuming, uneventful, unhasty, unhurried, uninteresting, unproductive, unprogressive, unpunctual, unresponsive, wearisome.

*antonyms* active, fast, quick, rapid, swift.

v brake, check, curb, decelerate, delay, detain, draw rein, handicap, hold up, lag, relax, restrict, retard.

**slow to** averse, disinclined, hesitant, indisposed, loath, reluctant, unwilling.

**slowly** *adv* adagio, gradually, inchmeal, larghetto, largo, lazily, leisurely, lento, ploddingly, ponderously, sluggishly, steadily, unhurriedly.

*antonym* quickly.

**sludge** *n* dregs, gunge, gunk, mire, muck, mud, ooze, residue, sediment, silt, slag, slime, slop, slush, swill.

**sluggish** *adj* dull, heavy, inactive, indolent, inert, lethargic, lifeless, listless, lurdan, lymphatic, phlegmatic, slothful, slow, slow-moving, torpid, unresponsive.

*antonyms* brisk, dynamic, eager, quick, vigorous.

**sluggishness** *n* apathy, drowsiness, dullness, faineance, heaviness, indolence, inertia, languor, lassitude, lethargy, listlessness, slothfulness, slowness, somnolence, stagnation, torpor.

*antonyms* dynamism, eagerness, quickness.

**sluice** *v* cleanse, drain, drench, flush, irrigate, slosh, swill, wash.

**slumber** *v* doze, drowse, nap, repose, rest, sleep, snooze.

**slummy** *adj* decayed, dirty, overcrowded, ramshackle, run-down, seedy, sleazy, sordid, squalid, wretched.

**slump** *v* bend, collapse, crash, decline, deteriorate, droop, drop, fall, hunch, loll, plummet, plunge, sag, sink, slip, slouch, worsen.

*n* collapse, crash, decline, depreciation, depression, downturn, drop, failure, fall, falling-off, low, recession, reverse, stagnation, trough, worsening.

*antonym* boom.

**slur** *n* affront, aspersion, blot, brand, calumny, discredit, disgrace, innuendo, insinuation, insult, reproach, slander, slight, smear, stain, stigma.

**slut** *n* dolly-map, drab, d(r)aggle-tail, dratchell, jade, slattern, sloven, trollop.

**sly** *adj* arch, artful, astute, canny, clever, conniving, covert, crafty, cunning, devious, foxy, furtive, guileful, impish, insidious, knowing, mischievous, peery, roguish, scheming, secret, secretive, shifty, sleeky, stealthy, subtle, surreptitious, underhand, vulpine, wily.

*antonyms* frank, honest, open, straightforward.

**smack** *v* box, clap, cuff, hit, pandy, pat, skelp, slap, sock, spank, strike, tap, thwack, whack.

*n* blow, box, crack, cuff, hit, pandy, pat, skelp, slap, sock, spank, strike, tap, thwack, whack.

*adv* directly, exactly, plumb, point-blank, precisely, right, slap, slap-bang, squarely, straight.

**smack one's lips** anticipate, delight in, drool over, enjoy, relish, savour.

**small** *adj* bantam, base, dilute, diminutive, dwarf(ish), grudging, humble, illiberal, immature, inadequate, incapacious, inconsiderable, insignificant, insufficient, itsy-bitsy, lesser, limited, little, meagre, mean, mignon(ne), mini, miniature, minor, minuscule, minute, modest, narrow, negligible, paltry, petite, petty, pigmean, pint-

size(d), pocket, pocket-sized, puny, pygmaean, pygmean, scanty, selfish, slight, small-scale, tichy, tiddl(e)y, tiny, trifling, trivial, undersized, unimportant, unpretentious, wee, young.

*antonyms* big, huge, large.

**small-minded** *adj* bigoted, envious, grudging, hidebound, insular, intolerant, mean, narrow-minded, parochial, petty, rigid, ungenerous.

*antonyms* broad-minded, liberal, tolerant.

**small-time** *adj* inconsequential, insignificant, minor, no-account, petty, piddling, unimportant.

*antonyms* important, major.

**smarminess** *n* obsequiousness, oiliness, servility, suavity, sycophancy, toadying, unctuosity, unctuousness.

**smarmy** *adj* bootlicking, crawling, fawning, fulsome, greasy, ingratiating, obsequious, oily, servile, smooth, soapy, suave, sycophantic, toadying, unctuous.

**smart¹** *adj* acute, adept, agile, apt, astute, bright, brisk, canny, chic, clever, cracking, dandy, effective, elegant, fashionable, fine, impertinent, ingenious, intelligent, jaunty, keen, lively, modish, natty, neat, nimble, nimble-witted, nobby, pert, pointed, quick, quick-witted, rattling, ready, ready-witted, saucy, sharp, shrewd, smart-alecky, snappy, spanking, spirited, spruce, stylish, swagger, swish, tippy, trim, vigorous, vivacious, well-appointed, witty.

*antonyms* dowdy, dumb, slow, stupid, unfashionable, untidy.

**smart Alec(k)** Besserwisser, clever clogs, clever dick, know-all, smart-arse, smartyboots, smartypants, wise guy, wiseacre.

**smart²** *v* burn, hurt, nip, pain, sting, throb, tingle, twinge.

*adj* hard, keen, nipping, nippy, painful, piercing, resounding, sharp, stinging.

*n* nip, pain, pang, smarting, soreness, sting, twinge.

**smarten** *v* beautify, clean, groom, neaten, polish, primp, prink, spruce up, tidy.

**smash** *v* break, collide, crash, crush, defeat, demolish, destroy, disintegrate, lay waste, overthrow, prang, pulverise, ruin, shatter, shiver, squabash, wreck.

*n* accident, collapse, collision, crash, defeat, destruction, disaster, downfall, failure, pile-up, prang, ruin, shattering, smash-up.

**smashing** *adj* braw, excellent, exhilarating, fab, fabulous, fantastic, first-class, first-rate, great, magnificent, marvellous, sensational, stupendous, super, superb, superlative, terrific, tremendous, wonderful.

**smattering** *n* basics, bit, dash, elements, modicum, rudiments, smatter, soupçon, sprinkling.

**smear** *v* asperse, bedaub, bedim, besmirch, blacken, blur, calumniate, coat, cover, dab, daub, dirty, drag (someone's) name through the mud, gaum, malign, patch, plaster, rub on, slubber, smarm, smudge, soil, spread over, stain, sully, tarnish, traduce, vilify.

*n* blot, blotch, calumny, daub, defamation, gaum, libel, mudslinging, slander, smudge, splodge, streak, vilification, whispering campaign.

**smell** *n* aroma, bouquet, fetor, fragrance, fumet(te), funk, malodour, mephitis, nose, odour, perfume, pong, redolence, scent, sniff, stench, stink, whiff.

*v* be malodorous, hum, inhale, nose, pong, reek, scent, sniff, snuff, stink, stink to high heaven, whiff.

**smelly** *adj* bad, evil-smelling, fetid, foul, foul-smelling, frowsty, funky, graveolent, high, malodorous, mephitic, noisome, off, pongy, putrid, reeking, stinking, strong, strong-smelling, whiffy.

**smirk** *n* grin, leer, simper, sneer, snigger.

**smitten** *adj* afflicted, beguiled, beset, bewitched, bowled over, burdened, captivated, charmed, enamoured, infatuated, plagued, struck, troubled.

**smoke** *n* exhaust, film, fog, fume, funk, gas, mist, reek, roke, smog, vapour.

*v* cure, dry, fume, fumigate, reek, roke, smoulder, vent.

**smoky** *adj* begrimed, black, caliginous, grey, grimy, hazy, murky, reechy, reeky, roky, sooty, thick.

**smooth** *adj* agreeable, bland, calm, classy, easy, effortless, elegant, equable, even, facile, fair-spoken, flat, flowing, fluent, flush, frictionless, glassy, glib, glossy, hairless, horizontal, ingratiating, level, levigate, mellow, mild, mirror-like, peaceful, persuasive, plain, plane, pleasant, polished, regular, rhythmic, serene, shiny, silken, silky, sleek, slick, slippery, smarmy, smug, soft, soothing, steady, suave, tranquil, unbroken, unctuous, undisturbed, uneventful, uniform, uninterrupted, unpuckered, unruffled, unrumpled, untroubled, unwrinkled, urbane, velvety, well-ordered.

*antonyms* coarse, harsh, irregular, rough, unsteady.

*v* allay, alleviate, appease, assuage, calm, dub, ease, emery, extenuate, facilitate, flatten, iron, level, levigate, mitigate, mollify, palliate, plane, polish, press, slicken, soften, unknit, unwrinkle.

*antonym* roughen.

**smoothly** *adv* calmly, easily, effortlessly, equably, evenly, fluently, ingratiatingly, legato, mildly, peacefully, pleasantly, serenely, slickly, soothingly, steadily, suavely, tranquilly.

**smoothness** *n* calmness, ease, efficiency, effortlessness, evenness, facility, felicity, finish, flow, fluency, glassiness, glibness, levelness, lubricity, oiliness, placidity, polish, regularity, rhythm, serenity, silkiness, sleekness, slickness, smarminess, softness, stillness, suavity, unbrokenness, urbanity, velvetiness.

*antonyms* coarseness, harshness, roughness.

**smooth-talking** *adj* bland, facile, glib, logodaedalic, persuasive, plausible, slick, smooth, suave.

**smother** *v* choke, cocoon, conceal, cover, envelop, extinguish, heap, hide, inundate, muffle, overlie, overwhelm, repress, shower, shroud, snuff, stifle, strangle, suffocate, suppress, surround.

**smoulder** *v* boil, burn, fester, fume, rage, seethe, simmer, smoke.

**smudge** *v* blacken, blur, daub, dirty, mark, smear, smirch, soil, spot, stain.

*n* blemish, blot, blur, smear, smut, smutch, spot, stain.

**smug** *adj* cocksure, complacent, conceited, holier-than-thou, priggish, self-opinionated, self-righteous, self-satisfied, superior, unctuous.

*antonym* modest.

**smuggler** *n* bootlegger, contrabandist, courier, moonshiner, mule, rum-runner, runner, wrecker.

**smutty** *adj* bawdy, blue, coarse, crude, dirty, filthy, gross, improper, indecent, indelicate, lewd, obscene, off colour, pornographic, prurient, racy, raunchy, ribald, risqué, salacious, suggestive, vulgar.

*antonyms* clean, decent.

**snack** *n* bite, break, elevens, elevenses, nacket, nibble, nocket, quick-lunch, refreshment(s), rere-supper, running-banquet, titbit, zakuska.

**snag** *n* bug, catch, complication, difficulty, disadvantage, drawback, hitch, inconvenience, obstacle, problem, snub, stick, stumbling block.

*v* catch, hole, ladder, rip, tear.

**snap** *v* bark, bite, break, catch, chop, click, crack, crackle, crepitate, flash, grip, growl, knap, nip, pop, retort, seize, separate, snarl, snatch.

*n* bite, break, crack, crackle, energy, fillip, flick, get-up-and-go, go, grabe, liveliness, nip, pizazz, pop, vigour, zip.

*adj* abrupt, immediate, instant, offhand, on-the-spot, sudden, unexpected, unpremeditated.

**snap up** grab, grasp, nab, pick up, pluck, pounce on, seize, snatch.

**snappy** *adj* brusque, chic, crabbed, cross, dapper, edgy, fashionable, hasty, ill-natured, irritable, modish, natty, quick-tempered, smart, snappish, stylish, tart, testy, touchy, trendy, up-to-the-minute, waspish.

**snare** *v* catch, ensnare, entrap, illaqueate, net, seize, springe, trap, trepan, wire.

*n* catch, cobweb, gin, lime, lime-twig, net, noose, pitfall, springe, springle, toils, trap, wire.

**snarl**[1] *v* complain, gnarl, gnar(r), growl, grumble, knar.

**snarl**[2] *v* complicate, confuse, embroil, enmesh, entangle, entwine, jam, knot, muddle, ravel, tangle.

**snarl-up** *n* confusion, entanglement, jumble, mess, mix-up, muddle, tangle, traffic jam.

**snatch** *v* clutch, gain, grab, grasp, grip, kidnap, nab, pluck, pull, ramp, rap, rescue, seize, spirit, take, win, wrench, wrest.

*n* bit, fraction, fragment, part, piece, section, segment, smattering, snippet, spell.

**snazzy** *adj* attractive, dashing, fashionable, flamboyant, flashy, jazzy, raffish, ritzy, showy, smart, snappy, sophisticated, sporty, stylish, swinging, with-it.

*antonyms* drab, unfashionable.

**sneak** *v* cower, cringe, grass on, inform on, lurk, pad, peach, sidle, skulk, slink, slip, smuggle, spirit, steal, tell tales.

*n* informer, snake in the grass, sneaker, telltale.

*adj* clandestine, covert, furtive, quick, secret, stealthy, surprise, surreptitious.

**sneaking** *adj* contemptible, dim, furtive, half-formed, hidden, intuitive, mean, nagging, niggling, persistent, private, secret, sly, sneaky, suppressed, surreptitious, two-faced, uncomfortable, underhand, unexpressed, unvoiced, worrying.

**sneaky** *adj* base, contemptible, cowardly, deceitful, devious, dishonest, disingenuous, double-dealing, furtive, guileful, low, low-down, malicious, mean, nasty, shady, shifty, slippery, sly, snide, unethical, unreliable, unscrupulous, untrustworthy.

*antonyms* honest, open.

**sneer** *v* deride, disdain, fleer, gibe, jeer, laugh, look down on, mock, ridicule, scoff, scorn, sniff at, snigger.

*n* derision, disdain, fleer, gibe, jeer, mockery, ridicule, scorn, smirk, snidery, snigger.

**sneezing** *adj* errhine, sternutatory.

**snide** *adj* base, cynical, derogatory, dishonest, disparaging, hurtful, ill-natured, insinuating, malicious, mean, nasty, sarcastic, scornful, sneering, spiteful, unkind.

**sniff** *v* breathe, inhale, nose, smell, snuff, snuffle, vent.

**sniffy** *adj* condescending, contemptuous, disdainful, haughty, scoffing, sneering, supercilious, superior.

**snigger** *v, n* giggle, laugh, sneer, snicker, snort, titter.

**snip** *v* clip, crop, cut, nick, notch, prune, shave, slit, trim.

*n* bargain, bit, clipping, fragment, giveaway, piece, scrap, shred, slit, snippet.

**snippet** *n* fragment, part, particle, piece, portion, scrap, section, segment, shred, snatch.

**snivelling** *adj* blubbering, crying, girning, grizzling, mewling, moaning, sniffling, snuffling, weeping, whimpering, whingeing, whining.

**snobbery** *n* airs, arrogance, condescension, loftiness, lorliness, pretension, pride, side, snobbishness, snootiness, uppishness.

**snobbish** *adj* arrogant, condescending, dicky, high and mighty, high-hat, hoity-toity, lofty, lordly, patronising, pretentious, snooty, stuck-up, superior, toffee-nosed, uppish, uppity, upstage.

**snoop** *v* interfere, prodnose, pry, sneak, spy.

**snooper** *n* busybody, meddler, nosy parker, Paul Pry, prodnose, pry, snoop, spy.

**snooze** *v* catnap, doze, drowse, kip, nap, nod off, sleep.

*n* catnap, doze, forty winks, kip, nap, shut-eye, siesta, sleep.

**snout** *n* muzzle, neb, proboscis, schnozzle, snitch, trunk.

**snub** *v* check, cold-shoulder, cut, humble, humiliate, mortify, rebuff, rebuke, shame, slight, sneap, squash, squelch, wither.

*n* affront, brush-off, check, humiliation, insult, put-down, rebuff, rebuke, slap in the face, sneap.

**snug** *adj* close, close-fitting, comfortable, comfy, compact, cosy, homely, intimate, neat, sheltered, trim, warm.

**snuggle** *v* cuddle, embrace, hug, nestle, nuzzle.

**so far** hitherto, thus far, till now, to date.

**soak** *v* bathe, damp, drench, imbue, immerse, infuse, interfuse, marinate, moisten, penetrate, permeate, saturate, sog, souse, steep, wet.

**soaking** *adj* drenched, dripping, drookit, saturated, soaked, sodden, sopping, streaming, waterlogged, wringing.

*antonym* dry.

**soar** *v* ascend, climb, escalate, fly, mount, plane, rise, rocket, tower, wing.

*antonym* plummet.

**sob** *v* bawl, blubber, boohoo, cry, greet, howl, mewl, moan, shed tears, snivel, weep.

**sober** *adj* abstemious, abstinent, calm, clear-headed, cold, composed, cool, dark, dispassionate, douce, drab, grave, level-headed, lucid, moderate, peaceful, plain, practical, quiet, rational, realistic, reasonable, restrained, sedate, serene, serious, severe, solemn, sombre, sound, staid, steady, subdued, temperate, unexcited, unruffled.

*antonyms* drunk, excited, frivolous, gay, intemperate, irrational.

**sobriety** *n* abstemiousness, abstinence, calmness, composure, continence, coolness, gravity, level-headedness, moderation, reasonableness, restraint, sedateness, self-restraint, seriousness, soberness, solemnity, staidness, steadiness, temperance.

*antonyms* drunkenness, excitement, frivolity.

**so-called** *adj* alleged, nominal, ostensible, pretended, professed, self-styled, soi-disant, supposed.

**sociability** *n* affability, chumminess, companionability, congeniality, conviviality, cordiality, friendliness, gregariousness, neighbourliness.

**sociable** *adj* accessible, affable, approachable, chummy, companionable, conversable, convivial, cordial, familiar, friendly, genial, gregarious, neighbourly, outgoing, social, viscerotonic, warm.

*antonyms* unfriendly, unsociable, withdrawn.

**social** *adj* collective, common, communal, community, companionable, friendly, general, gregarious, group, neighbourly, organised, public, sociable, societal.

*n* ceilidh, do, gathering, get-together, hoolly, hoot(e)nanny, party.

**socialise** *v* entertain, fraternise, get together, go out, hang out, mix, party.

**socialism** *n* communism, leftism, Leninism, Marxism, Stalinism, Trotskyism, welfarism.

**socialist** *adj* commie, communist, leftie, leftist, left-wing, pink, red, Trot, Trotskyist, Trotskyite.

*n* commie, communist, leftie, leftist, left-winger, parlour pink, pink(o), red, Trot, Trotskyist, Trotskyite, welfarist.

**society** *n* association, beau monde, brotherhood, camaraderie, circle, civilisation, club, companionship, company, corporation, culture, elite, fellowship, fraternity, fratry, friendship, gentry, Gesellschaft, group, guild, haut monde, humanity, institute, league, mankind, organisation, people, population, sisterhood, the nobs, the public, the smart set, the swells, the toffs, the top drawer, the world, union, upper classes, upper crust, Verein.

**sodden** *adj* boggy, drenched, drookit, marshy, miry, saturated, soaked, soggy, sopping, waterlogged, wet.

*antonym* dry.

**soft** *adj* balmy, bendable, bland, caressing, comfortable, compassionate, cottony, creamy, crumby, cushioned, cushiony, cushy, daft, delicate, diffuse, diffused, dim, dimmed, doughy, downy, ductile, dulcet, easy, easy-going, effeminate, elastic, faint, feathery, feeble-minded, flabby, flaccid, fleecy, flexible, flowing, fluid, foolish, furry, gelatinous, gentle, impressible, indulgent, kind, lash, lax, lenient, liberal, light, limp, low, malleable, mellifluous, mellow, melodious, mild, mouldable, murmured, muted, namby-pamby, non-alcoholic, overindulgent, pale, pampered, pastel, permissive, pitying, plastic, pleasant, pleasing, pliable, pulpy, quaggy, quiet, restful, sensitive, sentimental, shaded, silky, silly, simple, smooth, soothing, soppy, spineless, spongy, squashy, subdued, supple, swampy, sweet, sympathetic, temperate, tender, tender-hearted, undemanding, understated, unprotected, velvety, weak, whispered, yielding.

*antonyms* hard, harsh, heavy, loud, rigid, rough, severe, strict.

**soft spot** fondness, liking, partiality, penchant, weakness.

**soften** *v* abate, allay, alleviate, anneal, appease, assuage, calm, cushion, digest, diminish, ease, emolliate, intenerate, lessen, lighten, lower, macerate, malax, malaxate, melt, mitigate, moderate, modify, mollify, muffle, palliate, quell, relax, soothe, still, subdue, temper.

**soften up** conciliate, disarm, melt, persuade, soft-soap, weaken, win over.

**soft-hearted** *adj* benevolent, charitable, clement, compassionate, generous, indulgent, kind, merciful, sentimental, sympathetic, tender, tender-hearted, warm-hearted.

*antonym* hard-hearted.

**soft-pedal** *v* de-emphasise, go easy, moderate, play down, subdue, tone down.

*antonyms* emphasise, play up.

**soggy** *adj* boggy, dripping, heavy, moist, mushy, pulpy, saturated, soaked, sodden, sopping, soppy, spiritless, spongy, waterlogged.

**soil**[1] *n* clay, country, dirt, dust, earth, glebe, ground, humus, land, loam, region, terra firma.

**soil**[2] *v* bedaggle, bedraggle, befoul, begrime, besmirch, besmut, defile, dirty, foul, maculate, muddy, pollute, smear, spatter, spot, stain, sully, tarnish.

**soiled** *adj* dirty, grimy, maculate, manky, polluted, spotted, stained, sullied, tarnished.

*antonyms* clean, immaculate.

**sojourn** *n* peregrination, rest, stay, stop, stopover, visit.

*v* abide, dwell, lodge, reside, rest, stay, stop, tabernacle, tarry.

**solace** *n* alleviation, assuagement, comfort, consolation, relief, succour, support.

*v* allay, alleviate, comfort, console, mitigate, soften, soothe, succour, support.

**soldier** *n* buff-coat, buff-jerkin, fighter, gallo(w)glass, galoot, ghazi, GI, guardee, guardsman, hoplite, Ironside, jackman, jäger, janissary, jawan, kern(e), lancer, landsknecht, lansquenet, leather-neck, Mameluke, man-at-arms, marine, poilu, redcoat, rifleman, sepoy, serviceman, soldado, squaddy, swad(dy), sweat, Tommy, trooper, warrior.

**sole** *adj* alone, exclusive, individual, one, only, single, singular, solitary, unique.

*antonyms* multiple, shared.

**solecism** *n* absurdity, anacoluthon, blunder, boo-boo, cacology, faux pas, gaffe, gaucherie, impropriety, incongruity, indecorum, lapse, mistake.

**solely** *adv* alone, completely, entirely, exclusively, merely, only, single-handedly, singly, uniquely.

**solemn** *adj* august, awed, awe-inspiring, ceremonial, ceremonious, devotional, dignified, earnest, formal, glum, grand, grave, hallowed, holy, imposing, impressive, majestic, momentous, pompous, portentous, religious, reverential, ritual, sacred, sanctified, sedate, serious, sober, sombre, staid, stately, thoughtful, venerable.

*antonyms* frivolous, gay, light-hearted.

**solemnise** *v* celebrate, commemorate, dignify, honour, keep, observe.

**solemnities** *n* celebration, ceremonial, ceremony, formalities, observance, proceedings, rite, ritual.

**solemnity** *n* dignity, earnestness, grandeur, gravity, impressiveness, momentousness, portentousness, sacredness, sanctity, seriousness, stateliness.

*antonym* frivolity.

**solicit** *v* ask, beg, beseech, canvass, crave, entreat, implore, importune, petition, pray, seek, sue, supplicate, tout.

**solicitor** *n* advocate, attorney, barrister, DA, law-agent, lawmonger, lawyer, notary (public), QC, silk.

**solicitous** *adj* anxious, apprehensive, ardent, attentive, careful, caring, concerned, eager, earnest, fearful, troubled, uneasy, worried, zealous.

**solicitude** *n* anxiety, attentiveness, care, concern, considerateness, consideration, disquiet, regard, uneasiness, worry.

**solid** *adj* agreed, compact, complete, concrete, constant, continuous, cubic(al), decent, dense, dependable, estimable, firm, genuine, good, hard, law-abiding, level-headed, massed, pure, real, reliable, sensible, serious, sober, sound, square, stable, stocky, strong, sturdy, substantial, trusty, unalloyed, unanimous, unbroken, undivided, uninterrupted, united, unmixed, unshakeable, unvaried, upright, upstanding, wealthy, weighty, worthy.

*antonyms* broken, insubstantial, liquid.

**solidarity** *n* accord, camaraderie, cohesion, concord(ance), consensus, consentaneity, esprit de corps, harmony, like-mindedness, soundness, stability, team spirit, unanimity, unification, unity.

*antonyms* discord, division, schism.

**solidify** *v* cake, clot, coagulate, cohere, congeal, harden, jell, jellify, set.

*antonyms* dissolve, liquefy, soften.

**solitary** *adj* alone, cloistered, companionless, de(a)rnful, desolate, friendless, hermitical, hidden, isolated, lone, lonely, lonesome, out-of-the-way, reclusive, remote, retired, secluded, separate, sequestered, single, sole, unfrequented, unsociable, unsocial, untrodden, unvisited.

*antonyms* accompanied, gregarious.

**solitude** *n* aloneness, desert, emptiness, isolation, loneliness, privacy, reclusiveness, retirement, seclusion, waste, wasteland, wilderness.

*antonym* companionship.

**solution** *n* answer, blend, clarification, compound, decipherment, denouement, disconnection, dissolution, elucidation, emulsion, explanation, explication, key, liquefaction, melting, mix, mixture, resolution, result, solvent, solving, suspension, unfolding, unravelling.

**solve** *v* answer, clarify, crack, decipher, disentangle, dissolve, elucidate, explain, expound, interpret, resolve, settle, unbind, unfold, unravel, work out.

**sombre** *adj* dark, dim, dismal, doleful, drab, dull, dusky, funereal, gloomy, grave, joyless, lugubrious, melancholy, mournful, obscure, sad, sepulchral, shadowy, shady, sober, sombrous, subfusc.

*antonyms* bright, cheerful, happy.

**somebody** *n* big noise, big shot, big wheel, bigwig, celebrity, dignitary, heavyweight, household name, luminary, magnate, mogul, nabob, name, notable, panjandrum, personage, quidam, star, superstar, VIP.

*antonym* nobody.

**someday** *adv* eventually, one day, sometime, ultimately.

*antonym* never.

**somehow** *adv* by fair means or foul, by hook or by crook, come hell or high water, come what may, one way or another.

**sometimes** *adv* at times, from time to time, now and again, now and then, occasionally, off and on, once in a while, otherwhiles.

*antonyms* always, never.

**somnolent** *adj* comatose, dozy, drowsy, half-awake, heavy-eyed, oscitant, sleepy, soporific, torpid.

**son** *n* boy, descendant, disciple, inhabitant, lad(die), native, offspring.

**song** *n* air, anthem, ballad, barcarol(l)e, canticle, cantilena, canto, canzone, canzonet, carol, chanson, chansonette, chant, chorus, ditty, elegy, epicede, epicedium, epinicion, epithalamion, epithalamium, fit, folk-song, hymn, lay, lied, lilt, lullaby, lyric, madrigal, melody, number, ode, paean, poem, psalm, shanty, strain, tune, volkslied, war-song, wassail.

**song and dance** ado, commotion, flap, furore, fuss, hoo-ha, kerfuffle, performance, pother, shindig, shindy, squall, stir, tizzy, to-do, tumult, variety, vaudeville.

**songster** *n* balladeer, chanteuse, chorister, crooner, minstrel, singer, troubadour, vocalist, warbler.

**sonorous** *adj* full, full-mouthed, full-throated, full-voiced, grandiloquent, high-flown, high-sounding, loud, oro(ro)tund, plangent, resonant, resounding, rich, ringing, rounded, sounding.

**soon** *adv* anon, betimes, in a minute, in a short time, in the near future, presently, shortly.

**soothe** *v* allay, alleviate, appease, assuage, calm, coax, comfort, compose, ease, hush, lull, mitigate, mollify, pacify, quiet, relieve, salve, settle, soften, still, tranquillise.

*antonyms* annoy, irritate, vex.

**soothing** *adj* anetic, assuasive, balmy, balsamic, calming, demulcent, easeful, emollient, lenitive, palliative, relaxing, restful.

*antonyms* annoying, irritating, vexing.

**soothsayer** *n* augur, Chaldee, diviner, foreteller, haruspex, prophet, seer, sibyl.

**sophisticated** *adj* advanced, blase, citified, complex, complicated, cosmopolitan, couth, cultivated, cultured, delicate, elaborate, highly-developed, intricate, jet-set, mondain, multifaceted, refined, seasoned, subtle, urbane, worldly, worldly-wise, world-weary.

*antonyms* artless, naïve, simple, unsophisticated.

**sophistication** *n* culture, elegance, experience, finesse, poise, savoir-faire, savoir-vivre, urbanity, worldliness.

*antonyms* naïvety, simplicity.

**sophistry** *n* casuistry, elenchus, fallacy, paralogism, quibble, sophism.

**soporific** *adj* dormitive, hypnagogic, hypnic, hypnogenetic, hypnogenic, hypnogenous, hypnotic, poppied, sedative, sleep-inducing, sleepy, somniferous, somnolent, tranquillising.

*antonyms* invigorating, stimulating.

*n* anaesthetic, hypnic, hypnotic, narcotic, opiate, sedative, tranquilliser.

*antonym* stimulant.

**soppy** *adj* cloying, corny, daft, drippy, gushy, lovey-dovey, mawkish, mushy, pathetic, schmaltzy, sentimental, silly, slushy, soft, weepy.

**sorcerer** *n* angek(k)ok, enchanter, mage, Magian, magician, magus, necromancer, reim-kennar, sorceress, voodoo, warlock, witch, wizard.

**sorcery** *n* black art, black magic, charm, diablerie, divination, enchantment, hoodoo, incantation, magic, necromancy, pishogue, spell, voodoo, warlockry, witchcraft, witchery, witching, wizardry.

**sordid** *adj* avaricious, base, corrupt, covetous, debauched, degenerate, degraded, despicable, dingy, dirty, disreputable, filthy, foul, grasping, low, mean, mercenary, miserly, niggardly, rapacious, seamy, seedy, selfish, self-seeking, shabby, shameful, sleazy, slovenly, slummy, squalid, tawdry, unclean, ungenerous, venal, vicious, vile, wretched.

**sore** *adj* acute, afflicted, aggrieved, angry, annoyed, annoying, burning, chafed, critical, desperate, dire, distressing, extreme, grieved, grievous, harrowing, hurt, inflamed, irked, irritable, irritated, pained, painful, peeved, pressing, raw, reddened, resentful, sensitive, severe, sharp, smarting, stung, tender, touchy, troublesome, upset, urgent, vexed.

*n* abscess, boil, canker, carbuncle, chafe, gathering, inflammation, swelling, ulcer, wound.

**sorrow** *n* affliction, anguish, blow, distress, dole, grief, hardship, heartache, heartbreak, lamentation, misery, misfortune, mourning, regret, ruth, sadness, trial, tribulation, trouble, unhappiness, woe, worry.

*antonyms* happiness, joy.

*v* agonise, bemoan, bewail, beweep, grieve, lament, moan, mourn, pine, weep.

*antonym* rejoice.

**sorrowful** *adj* affecting, afflicted, dejected, depressed, disconsolate, distressing, doleful, grievous, heartbroken, heart-rending, heavy-hearted, lamentable, lugubrious, melancholy, miserable, mournful, painful, piteous, rueful, ruthful, sad, sorry, tearful, unhappy, wae, woebegone, woeful, wretched.

*antonyms* happy, joyful.

**sorry** *adj* abject, apologetic, base, commiserative, compassionate, conscience-stricken, contrite, deplorable, disconsolate, dismal, distressed, distressing, grieved, guilt-ridden, mean, melancholy, miserable, mournful, moved, paltry, pathetic, penitent, piteous, pitiable, pitiful, pitying, poor, regretful, remorseful, repentant, ruthful, sad, self-reproachful, shabby, shamefaced, sorrowful, sympathetic, unhappy, unworthy, vile, wretched.

*antonym* glad.

**sort** *n* alphasort, brand, breed, category, character, class, denomination, description, family, genre, genus, group, ilk, kidney, kind, make, nature, order, quality, race, species, stamp, style, type, variety.

*v* alphasort, arrange, assort, catalogue, categorise, choose, class, classify, distribute, divide, file, grade, group, neaten, order, rank, screen, select, separate, systematise, tidy.

**sort out** clarify, clear up, divide, organise, resolve, segregate, select, separate, sift, tidy up.

**so-so** *adj* adequate, average, fair, fair to middling, indifferent, middling, moderate, neutral, not bad, OK, ordinary, passable, respectable, run-of-the-mill, tolerable, undistinguished, unexceptional.

**soul** *n* alma, animation, ardour, being, body, courage, creature, element, embodiment, energy, essence, feeling, fervour, force, incarnation, individual, inner man, inspiration, inspirer, intellect, leader, life, man, mind, mortal, nobility, person, personification, pneuma, psyche, quintessence, reason, spirit, type, vital force, vitality, vivacity, woman.

**soulful** *adj* eloquent, emotional, expressive, heartfelt, meaningful, mournful, moving, profound, sensitive.

**soulless** *adj* callous, cold, cruel, dead, ignoble, inhuman, lifeless, mean, mean-spirited, mechanical, soul-destroying, spiritless, unfeeling, uninteresting, unkind, unsympathetic.

**sound¹** *n* description, din, earshot, hearing, idea, implication, impression, look, noise, range, report, resonance, reverberation, tenor, tone, utterance, voice.

*v* announce, appear, articulate, chime, declare, echo, enunciate, express, knell, look, peal, pronounce, resonate, resound, reverberate, ring, seem, signal, toll, utter, voice.

**sound²** *adj* complete, copper-bottomed, correct, deep, entire, established, fair, fere, firm, fit, hale, healthy, hearty, intact, just, level-headed, logical, orthodox, peaceful, perfect, proper, proven, prudent, rational, reasonable, recognised, reliable, reputable, responsible, right, right-thinking, robust, safe, secure, sensible, solid, solvent, stable, sturdy, substantial, thorough, tried-and-true, true, trustworthy, unbroken, undamaged, undisturbed, unhurt, unimpaired, uninjured, untroubled, valid, vigorous, wakeless, well-founded, well-grounded, whole, wise.

*antonyms* shaky, unfit, unreliable, unsound.

**sound³** *v* examine, fathom, inspect, investigate, measure, plumb, probe, test.

**sound out** ask, canvass, examine, probe, pump, question.

**sound⁴** *n* channel, estuary, firth, fjord, inlet, passage, strait, voe.

**soup** *n* bisque, broth, chowder, consomme, julienne, potage.

**sour** *adj* acerb(ic), acetic, acid, acidulated, acrid, acrimonious, bad, bitter, churlish, crabbed, curdled, cynical, disagreeable, discontented, embittered, fermented, grouchy, grudging, ill-natured, ill-tempered, inharmonious, jaundiced, off, peevish, pungent, rancid, rank, sharp, tart, turned, ungenerous, unpleasant, unsavoury, unsuccessful, unsweet, unwholesome, vinegarish, vinegary, waspish.

*antonyms* good-natured, sweet.

*v* alienate, curdle, disenchant, embitter, envenom, exacerbate, exasperate, spoil.

**source** *n* author, authority, begetter, beginning, cause, commencement, derivation, fons et origo, fountain-head, informant, klondike, milch-cow, mine, origin, originator, primordium, quarry, rise, spring, water-head, well-head, ylem.

**sourpuss** *n* crosspatch, grouse, grumbler, grump, killjoy, kvetch, misery, shrew, whiner, whinger.

**souse** *v* douse, drench, dunk, immerse, marinate, pickle, plunge, soak, steep.

**souvenir** *n* fairing, gift, keepsake, memento, memory, relic, remembrance(r), reminder, token.

**sovereign** *n* autarch, chief, dynast, emperor, empress, kaiser, king, monarch, potentate, prince, queen, ruler, shah, tsar.

*adj* absolute, august, chief, dominant, effectual, efficacious, efficient, excellent, imperial, kingly, majestic, monarch(ic)al, paramount, predominant, principal, queenly, regal, royal, ruling, supreme, unlimited.

**sovereignty** *n* ascendancy, domination, imperium, kingship, primacy, raj, regality, supremacy, suzerainty, sway.

**sow** *v* broadcast, disseminate, drill, implant, inseminate, lodge, plant, scatter, seed, spread, strew.

**space** *n* accommodation, amplitude, berth, blank, capacity, chasm, diastema, distance, duration, elbow-room, expanse, extension, extent, gap, house-room, interval, lacuna, leeway, margin, omission, period, place, play, room, scope, seat, spaciousness, span, time, volume.

**spacious** *adj* ample, big, broad, capacious, comfortable, commodious, expansive, extensive, huge, large, roomy, sizable, uncrowded, vast, wide.

*antonyms* confined, cramped, narrow, small.

**spadework** *n* donkey-work, drudgery, foundation, groundwork, labour, preparation.

**span** *n* amount, compass, distance, duration, extent, length, period, reach, scope, spell, spread, stretch, term.

*v* arch, bridge, cover, cross, encompass, extend, link, overarch, traverse, vault.

**spank** *v* belt, cane, cuff, leather, slap, slipper, smack, tan, wallop, whack.

**spanking** *adj* brand-new, brisk, energetic, fast, fine, gleaming, invigorating, lively, quick, smart, snappy, speedy, swift, vigorous.

*antonym* slow.

**spar** *v* argue, bicker, contend, contest, dispute, fall out, scrap, skirmish, spat, squabble, tiff, wrangle, wrestle.

**spare** *adj* additional, economical, emergency, extra, free, frugal, gash, gaunt, lank, lean, leftover, meagre, modest, odd, over, remaining, scanty, slender, slight, slim, sparing, superfluous, supernumerary, surplus, unoccupied, unused, unwanted, wiry.

*antonyms* corpulent, necessary, profuse.

*v* afford, allow, bestow, give quarter, grant, leave, let off, pardon, part with, refrain from, release, relinquish.

**sparing** *adj* careful, chary, cost-conscious, economical, frugal, lenten, prudent, saving, thrifty.

*antonyms* lavish, liberal, unsparing.

**spark** *n* atom, flake, flare, flash, flaught, flicker, gleam, glint, hint, jot, scintilla, scintillation, scrap, spit, trace, vestige.

*v* animate, cause, excite, inspire, kindle, occasion, precipitate, provoke, set off, start, stimulate, stir, trigger.

**sparkle** *v* beam, bubble, coruscate, dance, effervesce, emicate, fizz, fizzle, flash, gleam, glint, glisten, glister, glitter, glow, scintillate, shimmer, shine, spark, twinkle, wink.

*n* animation, brilliance, coruscation, dash, dazzle, effervescence, elan, emication, flash, flicker, gaiety, gleam, glint, glitter, life, panache, pizzazz, radiance, scintillation, spark, spirit, twinkle, vim, vitality, vivacity, wit, zip.

**sparkling** *adj* animated, bubbly, carbonated, coruscating, effervescent, emicant, fizzy, flashing, frizzante, gleaming, glistening, glittering, scintillating, twinkling, witty.

*antonyms* dull, flat.

**sparse** *adj* infrequent, meagre, scanty, scarce, scattered, sporadic.

*antonyms* dense, lush, thick.

**spartan** *adj* abstemious, abstinent, ascetic, austere, bleak, disciplined, extreme, frugal, hardy, joyless, plain, rigorous, self-denying, severe, stern, strict, stringent, temperate, unflinching.

**spasm** *n* access, burst, contraction, convulsion, eruption, fit, frenzy, jerk, outburst, paroxysm, seizure, throe, twitch.

**spasmodic** *adj* convulsive, erratic, fitful, intermittent, irregular, jerky, occasional, paroxysmal, sporadic.

*antonyms* continuous, uninterrupted.

**spate** *n* deluge, epidemic, flood, flow, outpouring, rush, torrent.

**spatter** *v* bedaub, bespatter, bespot, besprinkle, bestrew, daub, dirty, scatter, soil, speckle, splash, splodge, spray, sprinkle.

**speak** *v* address, advert to, allude to, argue, articulate, breathe, comment on, communicate, converse, deal with, declaim, declare, discourse, discuss, enunciate, express, harangue, lecture, mention, plead, pronounce, refer to, say, speechify, spiel, state, talk, tell, utter, voice.

**speak to** accost, address, admonish, apostrophise, bring to book, dress down, lecture, rebuke, reprimand, scold, tell off, tick off, upbraid, warn.

**speaker** *n* lecturer, mouthpiece, orator, prolocutor, speechifier, speech-maker, spieler, spokesman, spokesperson, spokeswoman.

**spearhead** *v* front, head, initiate, launch, lead, pioneer.

**special** *adj* appropriate, certain, characteristic, chief, choice, detailed, distinctive, distinguished, especial, exceptional, exclusive, extraordinary, festive, gala, important, individual, intimate, main, major, memorable, momentous, particular, peculiar, precise, primary, red-letter, select, significant, specialised, specific, uncommon, unique, unusual.

*antonyms* common, normal, ordinary, usual.

**specialist** *n* adept, authority, connoisseur, consultant, expert, master, professional, proficient.

**speciality** *n* bag, forte, metier, pièce de resistance, scene, special, specialty, strength.

**species** *n* breed, category, class, collection, denomination, description, genus, group, kind, sort, type, variety.

**specific** *adj* characteristic, clear-cut, definite, delimitative, distinguishing, especial, exact, explicit, express, limited, particular, peculiar, precise, special, unambiguous, unequivocal.

*antonyms* general, vague.

**specification** *n* condition, description, detail, enumeration, item, itemisation, listing, particular, qualification, requirement, stipulation.

**specify** *v* cite, define, delineate, describe, designate, detail, enumerate, indicate, individualise, itemise, list, mention, name, particularise, spell out, stipulate.

**specimen** *n* copy, embodiment, ensample, example, exemplar, exemplification, exhibit, illustration, individual, instance, model, paradigm, pattern, person, proof, representative, sample, type.

**specious** *adj* casuistic, deceptive, fallacious, false, misleading, pageant, plausible, sophistic, sophistical, unsound, untrue.

*antonym* valid.

**speck** *n* atom, bit, blemish, blot, defect, dot, fault, flaw, fleck, grain, iota, jot, macula, mark, mite, modicum, mote, particle, shred, speckle, spot, stain, tittle, trace, whit.

**speckled** *adj* brinded, brindle(d), dappled, dotted, flecked, fleckered, freckled, lentiginous, mottled, spotted, spotty, sprinkled, stippled.

**spectacle** *n* curiosity, display, event, exhibition, extravaganza, marvel, pageant, parade, performance, phenomenon, scene, show, sight, wonder.

**spectacles** *n* cheaters, eyeglasses, glasses, goggles, lorgnette, lorgnon, opera-glasses, pince-nez, specs.

**spectacular** *adj* amazing, breathtaking, daring, dazzling, dramatic, eye-catching, fabulous, fantastic, grand, impressive, magnificent, marked, remarkable, sensational, splendid, staggering, striking, stunning.

*antonyms* ordinary, unspectacular.

*n* display, extravaganza, pageant, show, spectacle.

**spectator** *n* beholder, bystander, eye-witness, looker-on, observer, onlooker, passer-by, viewer, watcher, witness.

*antonyms* contestant, participant, player.

**spectral** *adj* disembodied, eerie, ghostly, incorporeal, insubstantial, phantasmal, phantom, shadowy, spooky, supernatural, uncanny, unearthly, weird.

**spectre** *n* apparition, ghost, larva, lemur, phantom(a), presence, revenant, shade, shadow, spirit, vision, wraith.

**speculate** *v* cogitate, conjecture, consider, contemplate, deliberate, gamble, guess, hazard, hypothesise, meditate, muse, reflect, risk, scheme, suppose, surmise, theorise, venture, wonder.

**speculation** *n* conjecture, consideration, contemplation, deliberation, flight of fancy, gamble, gambling, guess, guesswork, hazard, hypothesis, ideology, land-jobbing, opinion, risk, supposition, surmise, theory.

**speculative** *adj* abstract, academic, chancy, conjectural, dicey, hazardous, hypothetical, iffish, iffy, notional, projected, risky, suppositional, tentative, theoretical, uncertain, unpredictable.

**speech** *n* address, articulation, colloquy, communication, conversation, dialect, dialogue, diction, discourse, discussion, disquisition, enunciation, harangue, homily, idiom, intercourse, jargon, language, lecture, lingo, oration, parlance, parole, peroration, say, spiel, talk, tongue, utterance, voice, winged words.

**speechless** *adj* aghast, amazed, astounded, dazed, dumb, dumbfounded, dumbstruck, inarticulate, mum, mute, obmutescent, shocked, silent, thunderstruck, tongue-tied, wordless.

**speed** *n* acceleration, celerity, dispatch, expedition, fleetness, haste, hurry, lick, momentum, pace, precipitation, quickness, rapidity, rush, swiftness, tempo, velocity.

*v* advance, aid, assist, belt, bomb, boost, bowl along, career, dispatch, expedite, facilitate, flash, fleet, further, gallop, hasten, help, highball, hurry, impel, lick, press on, promote, put one's foot down, quicken, race, rush, sprint, step on it, step on the gas, step on the juice, tear, urge, vroom, zap, zoom.

*antonyms* delay, hamper, restrain, slow.

**speedily** *adv* fast, hastily, hurriedly, posthaste, promptly, quickly, rapidly, swiftly, ventre à terre.

*antonym* slowly.

**speedy** *adj* clipping, expeditious, express, fast, fleet, hasty, headlong, hurried, immediate, nimble, precipitate, prompt, quick, rapid, summary, swift, winged, zappy.

*antonyms* dilatory, slow, tardy.

**spell**[1] *n* bout, course, innings, interval, patch, period, season, stint, stretch, term, time, turn.

**spell**[2] *n* abracadabra, allure, bewitchment, charm, conjuration, enchantment, exorcism, fascination, glamour, hex, incantation, jettatura, love-charm, magic, open sesame, paternoster, philtre, rune, sorcery, trance, weird, witchery.

**spell**[3] *v* augur, herald, imply, indicate, mean, portend, presage, promise, signal, signify, suggest.

**spell out** clarify, elucidate, emphasise, explain, specify.

**spellbound** *adj* bemused, bewitched, captivated, charmed, enchanted, enthralled, entranced, fascinated, gripped, hooked, mesmerised, possessed, rapt, transfixed, transported.

**spend** *v* apply, bestow, blow, blue, concentrate, consume, cough up, deplete, devote, disburse, dispense, dissipate, drain, employ, empty, exhaust, expend, fill, fork out, fritter, invest, lavish, lay out, occupy, pass, pay out, shed, shell out, splash out, squander, use, use up, waste.

*antonyms* hoard, save.

**spendthrift** *n* big spender, prodigal, profligate, spendall, spender, squanderer, unthrift, waster, wastrel.

*antonyms* hoarder, miser, saver.

*adj* extravagant, improvident, prodigal, profligate, thriftless, wasteful.

**spent** *adj* all in, burnt out, bushed, consumed, dead beat, debilitated, dog-tired, done in, drained, exhausted, expended, fagged (out), finished, gone, jiggered, knackered, played out, prostrate, shattered, tired out, used up, weakened, wearied, weary, whacked, worn out, zonked.

**spew** *v* belch, disgorge, posset, puke, regurgitate, retch, spit out, throw up, vomit.

**sphere** *n* ball, capacity, circle, compass, department, domain, employment, field, function, globe, globule, milieu, orb, province, range, rank, realm, scope, spheroid, spherule, station, stratum, territory.

**spherical** *adj* globate, globed, globe-shaped, globoid, globose, globular, orbicular, rotund, round.

**spice** *n* colour, excitement, flavouring, gusto, kick, life, pep, piquancy, relish, savour, seasoning, tang, zap, zest, zip.

**spick and span** clean, immaculate, neat, polished, scrubbed, shipshape, spotless, spruce, tidy, trim, well-kept.

*antonyms* dirty, untidy.

**spicy** *adj* aromatic, flavoursome, fragrant, hot, improper, indecorous, indelicate, off-colour, piquant, pointed, pungent, racy, ribald, risque, savoury, scandalous, seasoned, sensational, showy, suggestive, tangy, titillating, unseemly.

*antonym* bland.

**spiel** *v* harangue, hold forth, lecture, orate, recite, sermonise, speechify, spout.

*n* harangue, oration, patter, pitch, recital, sales patter, sermon, speech.

**spike** *n* barb, nail, point, prong, spine, spire, tine.

*v* block, foil, frustrate, impale, reject, spear, spit, stick, thwart.

**spill** *v* discharge, disgorge, overflow, overturn, scatter, shed, slop, slosh, upset.

*n* accident, cropper, fall, overturn, tumble, upset.

**spill the beans** blab, blow the gaff, give the game away, grass, inform, let the cat out of the bag, rat, split, squeal, tattle.

**spin** *v* birl, concoct, develop, gyrate, gyre, hurtle, invent, narrate, pirouette, purl, recount, reel, relate, revolve, rotate, spirt, swim, swirl, tell, turn, twirl, twist, unfold, wheel, whirl.

*n* agitation, commotion, drive, flap, gyration, hurl, panic, pirouette, revolution, ride, roll, run, state, tizzy, turn, twist, whirl.

**spin out** amplify, delay, extend, lengthen, maintain, pad out, prolong, prolongate, protract, sustain.

**spindle** *n* arbor, axis, axle, fusee, pivot.

**spindly** *adj* attenuate(d), gangling, gangly, lanky, leggy, skeletal, skinny, spidery, spindle-shanked, thin, twiggy, weedy.

*antonyms* stocky, thickset.

**spine** *n* backbone, barb, needle, quill, rachis, ray, spicule, spiculum, spike, spur, vertebrae, vertebral column.

**spine-chilling** *adj* bloodcurdling, eerie, frightening, hair-raising, horrifying, scary, spine-tingling, spooky, terrifying.

**spineless** *adj* cowardly, faint-hearted, feeble, gutless, inadequate, ineffective, irresolute, lily-livered, soft, spiritless, squeamish, submissive, vacillating, weak, weak-kneed, weak-willed, wet, wishy-washy, yellow.

*antonyms* brave, strong.

**spiny** *adj* acanthaceous, acanthous, briery, prickly, spicular, spiculate, spiniferous, spinigerous, spinose, spinous, thistly, thorny.

**spiral** *adj* circular, cochlear, cochleate, coiled, corkscrew, gyral, gyroidal, helical, scrolled, spiraliform, voluted, volutoid, whorled, winding.

*n* coil, convolution, corkscrew, curlicue, gyre, helix, screw, volute, volution, whorl.

**spire** *n* cone, flèche, peak, pinnacle, point, shoot, spike, sprout, stalk, steeple, summit, tip, top.

**spirit** *n* air, animation, apparition, ardour, Ariel, atmosphere, attitude, backbone, bravura, breath, brio, character, complexion, courage, daemon, dauntlessness, deva, disposition, div, djinni, earnestness, energy, enterprise, enthusiasm, entrain, Erdgeist, esprit follet, essence, familiar, faun, feeling, feelings, fire, foison, force, gameness, geist, genie, genius, genius loci, ghost, ghoul, gist, grit, guts, humour, intent, intention, jinnee, jinni, ka, kobold, life, liveliness, manito(u), marid, meaning, mettle, mood, morale, motivation, outlook, phantom, pneuma, psyche, purport, purpose, python, quality, resolution, resolve, revenant, sense, shade, shadow, soul, sparkle, spectre, spook, sprite, spunk, stout-heartedness, substance, sylph, temper, temperament, tenor, tone, verve, vigour, vision, vivacity, warmth, water-horse, water-nymph, water-rixie, water-sprite, Weltgeist, wili, will, will power, Zeitgeist, zest.

*v* abduct, abstract, capture, carry, convey, kidnap, purloin, remove, seize, snaffle, steal, whisk.

**spirited** *adj* active, animated, ardent, bold, courageous, energetic, game, gamy, high-spirited, lively, mettlesome, plucky, sparkling, sprightly, spunky, stomachful, vigorous, vivacious.

*antonyms* lazy, spiritless, timid.

**spiritless** *adj* anaemic, apathetic, dejected, depressed, despondent, dispirited, droopy, dull, lacklustre, languid, lifeless, listless, low, melancholic, melancholy, mopy, torpid, unenthusiastic, unmoved, wishy-washy.

*antonym* spirited.

**spirits** *n* alcohol, fire-water, hooch, liquor, moonshine, strong drink, strong liquor, the hard stuff.

**spiritual** *adj* aery, devotional, divine, ecclesiastical, ethereal, ghostly, holy, immaterial, incorporeal, otherwordly, pneumatic, pure, religious, sacred, unfleshly, unworldly.

*antonyms* material, physical.

**spit** *v* discharge, drizzle, eject, expectorate, hawk, hiss, spew, splutter, sputter.

*n* dribble, drool, expectoration, phlegm, saliva, slaver, spittle, sputum.

**spite** *n* animosity, bitchiness, despite, gall, grudge, hate, hatred, ill-nature, malevolence, malice, malignity, pique, rancour, spitefulness, spleen, venom, viciousness.

*antonyms* affection, goodwill.

*v* annoy, discomfit, gall, harm, hurt, injure, irk, irritate, needle, nettle, offend, peeve, pique, provoke, put out, vex.

**spiteful** *adj* barbed, bitchy, catty, cruel, ill-disposed, ill-natured, malevolent, malicious, malignant, nasty, rancorous, snide, splenetic, vengeful, venomous, vindictive, waspish.

*antonyms* affectionate, charitable.

**spitting image** clone, dead ringer, dead spit, double, likeness, lookalike, picture, replica, ringer, spit, twin.

**splash** *v* bathe, batter, bespatter, blazon, break, broadcast, buffet, dabble, dash, flaunt, flouse, floush, headline, paddle, plash, plaster, plop, plunge, publicise, shower, slop, slosh, smack, spatter, splodge, spray, spread, sprinkle, squirt, strew, strike, surge, tout, trumpet, wade, wallow, wash, wet.

*n* burst, dash, display, effect, excitement, impact, ostentation, patch, publicity, sensation, spattering, splatter, splodge, splurge, stir, touch.

**splash out** invest in, lash out, push the boat out, spend, splurge.

**spleen** *n* acrimony, anger, animosity, animus, bad temper, bile, biliousness, bitterness, gall, hatred, hostility, ill-humour, ill-will, malevolence, malice, malignity, peevishness, petulance, pique, rancour, resentment, spite, spitefulness, venom, vindictiveness, wrath.

**splendid** *adj* admirable, beaming, bright, brilliant, costly, dazzling, excellent, exceptional, fantastic, fine, first-class, glittering, glorious, glowing, gorgeous, grand, great, heroic, illustrious, imposing, impressive, lavish, lustrous, luxurious, magnificent, marvellous, ornate, outstanding, phenom, pontific(al), radiant, rare, refulgent, remarkable, renowned, resplendent, rich, splendiferous, splend(o)rous, sterling, sublime, sumptuous, superb, supreme, tiptop, top-hole, top-notch, topping, wonderful.

*antonyms* drab, ordinary, run-of-the-mill.

**splendour** *n* brightness, brilliance, ceremony, dazzle, display, effulgence, fulgo(u)r, glory, gorgeousness, grandeur, lustre, magnificence, majesty, pomp, radiance, refulgence, renown, resplendence, richness, show, solemnity, spectacle, stateliness, sumptuousness.

**splenetic** *adj* acid, atrabilious, bilious, bitchy, choleric, churlish, crabbed, crabby, cross, envenomed, fretful, irascible, irritable, morose, peevish, petulant, rancorous, sour, spiteful, sullen, testy, touchy.

**splice** *v* bind, braid, entwine, graft, interlace, interlink, intertwine, intertwist, interweave, join, knit, marry, mesh, plait, tie, unite, wed, yoke.

**splinter** *n* chip, flake, flinder, fragment, needle, paring, shaving, sliver, spall, spalt, spicule, stob.

*v* disintegrate, fracture, fragment, shatter, shiver, smash, spalt, split.

**split** *v* allocate, allot, apportion, betray, bifurcate, branch, break, burst, cleave, crack, delaminate, disband, distribute, disunite, divaricate, diverge, divide, divulge, fork, gape, grass, halve, inform on, open, parcel out, part, partition, peach, rend, rip, separate, share out, skive, slash, slice up, slit, sliver, snap, spell, splinter, squeal.

*n* breach, break, break-up, cleft, crack, damage, dichotomy, difference, discord, disruption, dissension, disunion, divergence, division, estrangement, fissure, gap, partition, race, rent, rift, rip, rupture, schism, scissure, separation, slash, slit, tear.

*adj* ambivalent, bisected, broken, cleft, cloven, cracked, divided, dual, fractured, ruptured, twofold.

**split hairs** cavil, find fault, nit-pick, over-refine, pettifog, quibble.

**split up** break up, disband, dissolve, divorce, part, part company, separate.

**spoil** *v* addle, baby, blemish, bugger, butcher, cocker, coddle, cosset, curdle, damage, debase, decay, decompose, deface, despoil, destroy, deteriorate, disfigure, go bad, go off, harm, impair, indulge, injure, jigger, louse up, mar, mildew, mollycoddle, pamper, plunder, putrefy, queer, rot, ruin, screw, spoon-feed, turn, upset, wreck.

**spoils** *n* acquisitions, boodle, booty, gain, haul, loot, pickings, pillage, plunder, prey, prizes, rapine, spoliation, swag, winnings.

**spoil-sport** *n* damper, dog in the manger, killjoy, mar-sport, meddler, misery, party-pooper, wet blanket, wowser.

**spoken** *adj* declared, expressed, oral, phonetic, said, stated, told, unwritten, uttered, verbal, viva voce, voiced.

*antonyms* unspoken, written.

**sponge** *v* cadge, freeload, mooch, scrounge, shool.

**sponger** *n* bloodsucker, cadge, cadger, freeloader, hanger-on, leech, moocher, parasite, scrounger, smell-feast.

**spongy** *adj* absorbent, bibulous, cushioned, cushiony, elastic, fozy, light, porous, springy.

**sponsor** *n* angel, backer, godparent, guarantor, patron, promoter, surety, underwriter.

*v* back, finance, fund, guarantee, patronise, promote, subsidise, underwrite.

**spontaneous** *adj* extempore, free, impromptu, impulsive, instinctive, natural, ultroneous, unbidden, uncompelled, unconstrained, unforced, unhesitating, unlaboured, unpremeditated, unprompted, unstudied, untaught, voluntary, willing.

*antonyms* forced, planned, studied.

**spontaneously** *adv* ex mero motu, ex proprio motu, extempore, freely, impromptu, impulsively, instinctively, of one's own accord, off the cuff, on impulse, unprompted, voluntarily, willingly.

**spoof** *n* bluff, burlesque, caricature, con, deception, fake, game, hoax, joke, lampoon, leg-pull, mockery, parody, prank, satire, send-up, take-off, travesty, trick.

**spooky** *adj* chilling, creepy, eerie, eldritch, frightening, ghostly, hair-raising, mysterious, scary, spine-chilling, supernatural, uncanny, unearthly, weird.

**spoonerism** *n* marrowsky, transposition.

**spoon-feed** *v* baby, cosset, featherbed, indulge, mollycoddle, pamper, spoil.

**sporadic** *adj* erratic, infrequent, intermittent, irregular, isolated, occasional, random, scattered, spasmodic, uneven.

*antonyms* frequent, regular.

**sport** *n* activity, amusement, badinage, banter, brick, buffoon, butt, dalliance, derision, diversion, entertainment, exercise, fair game, frolic, fun, game, jest, joking, kidding, laughing-stock, merriment, mirth, mockery, pastime, play, plaything, raillery, recreation, ridicule, sportsman, teasing.

*v* caper, dally, display, disport, exhibit, flirt, frolic, gambol, philander, play, romp, show off, toy, trifle, wear.

**sporting** *adj* considerate, fair, gentlemanly, sportsmanlike.

*antonyms* unfair, ungentlemanly, unsporting.

**sportive** *adj* coltish, frisky, frolicsome, gamesome, gay, jaunty, joyous, kittenish, lively, merry, playful, prankish, rollicking, skittish, sprightly.

**sporty** *adj* athletic, casual, energetic, flamboyant, flashy, gay, hearty, informal, jaunty, jazzy, loud, natty, outdoor, raffish, rakish, showy, snazzy, stylish, trendy.

**spot** *n* bit, blemish, blot, blotch, daub, difficulty, discoloration, flaw, little, locality, location, macula, maculation, macule, mark, mess, morsel, pimple, place, plight, plook, point, position, predicament, pustule, quandary, scene, site, situation, smudge, speck, splash, stain, stigma, taint, trouble.

*v* besmirch, blot, descry, detect, dirty, discern, dot, espy, fleck, identify, maculate, mark, mottle, observe, recognise, see, sight, soil, spatter, speckle, splodge, splotch, stain, sully, taint, tarnish.

**spotless** *adj* blameless, chaste, faultless, flawless, gleaming, immaculate, innocent, irreproachable, pure, shining, snowy, spick and span, unblemished, unimpeachable, unstained, unsullied, untarnished, virgin, virginal, white.

*antonyms* dirty, impure, spotted.

**spotlight** *v* accentuate, emphasise, feature, focus on, highlight, illuminate, point up, throw into relief.

*n* attention, emphasis, fame, interest, limelight, notoriety, public eye.

**spotted** *adj* brinded, brindle(d), dappled, dotted, flecked, fleckered, guttate(d), macled, macular, maculate, maculose, mottled, parded, pied, polka-dot, specked, speckled.

*antonym* spotless.

**spotty** *adj* blotchy, pimpled, pimply, plooky, speckled, spotted.

**spouse** *n* better half, companion, consort, fere, helpmate, husband, mate, partner, wife.

**spout** *v* declaim, discharge, emit, erupt, expatiate, gush, jet, orate, pontificate, rabbit on, ramble (on), rant, sermonise, shoot, speechify, spiel, spray, spurt, squirt, stream, surge.

*n* chute, fistula, fountain, gargoyle, geyser, jet, nozzle, outlet, rose, spray.

**sprawl** *v* flop, loll, lounge, ramble, recline, repose, slouch, slump, spread, straggle, trail.

**spray**[1] *v* atomise, diffuse, douse, drench, scatter, shower, sprinkle, wet.

*n* aerosol, atomiser, drizzle, droplets, foam, froth, mist, moisture, spindrift, spoondrift, sprinkler.

**spray**[2] *n* bough, branch, corsage, garland, shoot, sprig, wreath.

**spread** *v* advertise, arrange, array, blazon, bloat, broadcast, broaden, bruit, cast, circulate, couch, cover, diffuse, dilate, dispread, disseminate, distribute, divulgate, divulge, effuse, escalate, expand, extend, fan out, furnish, lay, metastasise, multiply, mushroom, open, overlay, prepare, proclaim, proliferate, promulgate, propagate, publicise, publish, radiate, scatter, set, shed, sprawl, stretch, strew, swell, transmit, unfold, unfurl, unroll, widen.

*antonyms* close, compress, contain, fold.

*n* advance, advancement, array, banquet, blow-out, compass, cover, development, diffusion, dispersion, dissemination, divulgation, divulgence, escalation, expanse, expansion, extent, feast, increase, period, proliferation, ranch, reach, repast, span, spreading, stretch, suffusion, sweep, term, transmission.

**spree** *n* bacchanalia, bender, binge, blind, bum, carouse, debauch, fling, jag, jamboree, junketing, orgy, randan, razzle-dazzle, revel, splurge, tear.

**sprightly** *adj* active, agile, airy, alert, animated, blithe, brisk, cheerful, energetic, frolicsome, gamesome, gay, hearty, jaunty, joyous, lively, nimble, perky, playful, spirited, sportive, spry, vivacious.

*antonym* inactive.

**spring**[1] *v* appear, arise, bounce, bound, burgeon, come, dance, derive, descend, develop, emanate, emerge, grow, hop, issue, jump, leap, mushroom, originate, proceed, rebound, recoil, shoot up, sprout, start, stem, vault.

*n* bounce, bounciness, bound, buck, buoyancy, elasticity, flexibility, gambado, give, hop, jump, leap, rebound, recoil, resilience, saltation, springiness, vault.

**spring**[2] *n* beginning, cause, eye, fountain-head, origin, root, source, well, well-spring.

**springy** *adj* bouncy, buoyant, elastic, flexible, resilient, rubbery, spongy, stretchy.

*antonyms* rigid, stiff.

**sprinkle** *v* asperge, diversify, dot, dredge, dust, pepper, powder, scatter, seed, shower, sparge, spatter, spray, strew.

**sprinkling** *n* admixture, dash, dusting, few, handful, scatter, scattering, smattering, sprinkle, touch, trace.

**sprint** *v* belt, dart, dash, gallop, hare, hotfoot, race, run, scamper, shoot, tear, whiz.

**sprite** *n* apparition, brownie, dryad, elf, fairy, goblin, imp, kelpie, leprechaun, naiad, nymph, pixie, pouke, puck, spirit, sylph.

**sprout** *v* bud, develop, germinate, grow, pullulate, push, shoot, spring, vegetate.

**spruce** *adj* dainty, dapper, elegant, natty, neat, sleek, slick, smart, smirk, trig, trim, well-groomed, well-turned-out.

*antonyms* dishevelled, untidy.

**spruce up** groom, neaten, preen, primp, smarten up, tidy, titivate.

**spry** *adj* active, agile, alert, brisk, energetic, nimble, nippy, peppy, quick, ready, sprightly, supple.

*antonyms* doddering, inactive, lethargic.

**spunk** *n* backbone, bottle, chutzpah, courage, gameness, grit, guts, heart, mettle, nerve, pluck, resolution, spirit, toughness.

*antonym* funk.

**spur** *v* animate, drive, goad, impel, incite, poke, press, prick, prod, prompt, propel, stimulate, urge.

*antonym* curb.

*n* fillip, goad, impetus, impulse, incentive, incitement, inducement, motive, prick, rowel, stimulus.

*antonym* curb.

**spurious** *adj* adulterate, adulterine, apocryphal, artificial, bastard, bogus, contrived, counterfeit, deceitful, dog, fake, false, feigned, forged, illegitimate, imitation, mock, phoney, pretended, pseudish, pseudo, sham, simulated, specious, supposititious, unauthentic.

*antonyms* authentic, genuine, real.

**spurn** *v* cold-shoulder, contemn, cut, despise, disdain, disregard, rebuff, reject, repulse, scorn, slight, snub, turn down.

*antonym* embrace.

**spurt** *v* burst, effuse, erupt, gush, jet, shoot, spew, squirt, surge.

*n* access, burst, effusion, fit, rush, spate, surge.

**spy** *n* beagle, double agent, fifth columnist, foreign agent, mole, scout, secret agent, secret service man, snooper, spook, undercover agent.

*v* descry, discover, espy, glimpse, notice, observe, spot.

**squabble** *v* argue, bicker, brawl, clash, dispute, fall out, fight, quarrel, row, scrap, spat, tiff, wrangle.

*n* argument, barney, clash, disagreement, dispute, fight, rhubarb, row, scrap, set-to, spat, tiff.

**squad** *n* band, brigade, company, crew, force, gang, group, outfit, team, troop.

**squalid** *adj* broken-down, decayed, dingy, dirty, disgusting, fetid, filthy, foul, low, nasty, neglected, poverty-stricken, repulsive, run-down, seedy, sleazy, slovenly, slummy, sordid, uncared-for, unclean, unkempt.

*antonyms* clean, pleasant.

**squall** *n* blow, drow, gale, gust, hurricane, storm, tempest, williwaw, wind-storm.

**squally** *adj* blowy, blustery, gusty, rough, stormy, tempestuous, turbulent, wild, windy.

**squalor** *n* decay, dinginess, filth, foulness, meanness, neglect, sleaziness, squalidness, wretchedness.

**squander** *v* blow, blue, consume, dissipate, expend, fritter away, lavish, misspend, misuse, scatter, spend, splurge, throw away, waste.

**square** *v* accommodate, accord, adapt, adjust, agree, align, appease, balance, bribe, conform, correspond, corrupt, discharge, fit, fix, harmonise, level, liquidate, match, quit, reconcile, regulate, rig, satisfy, settle, suborn, suit, tailor, tally, true.

*adj* above-board, bourgeois, broad, complete, conservative, conventional, decent, equitable, ethical, even, exact, fair, fitting, full, genuine, honest, just, old-fashioned, on the level, opposed, orthodox, quadrate, right-angled, satisfying, solid, straight, straightforward, strait-laced, stuffy, suitable, thick-set, traditional, true, unequivocal, unhip, upright.

*n* antediluvian, conformer, conformist, conservative, conventionalist, die-hard, fuddy-duddy, (old) fogy, stick-in-the-mud, traditionalist.

**squash** v annihilate, compress, crowd, crush, distort, flatten, humiliate, mash, pound, press, pulp, quash, quell, silence, smash, snub, squelch, stamp, suppress, trample.

*antonyms* elongate, stretch.

**squashy** adj mushy, pappy, pulpy, soft, spongy, squelchy, squishy, yielding.

*antonym* firm.

**squat** adj chunky, dumpy, fubby, short, squabby, stocky, stubby, stumpy, thickset.

*antonyms* lanky, slender.

v absquatulate, bend, camp out, crouch, hunch, hunker, ruck, settle, stoop.

**squawk** v cackle, complain, crow, cry, grouse, hoot, protest, screech, shriek, squeal, yelp.

**squeak** v chirk, peep, pipe, shrill, squeal, whine, yelp.

**squeal** n scream, screech, shriek, ululation, wail, yell, yelp, yowl.

v betray, blab, complain, grass, inform on, moan, peach, protest, rat on, scream, screech, shout, shriek, shrill, snitch, squawk, ululate, wail, yelp.

**squeamish** adj coy, delicate, fastidious, finicky, nauseous, particular, prissy, prudish, punctilious, qualmish, queasy, queer, reluctant, scrupulous, sick, sickish, strait-laced.

**squeeze** v bleed, chirt, clasp, clutch, compress, cram, crowd, crush, cuddle, embrace, enfold, extort, force, grip, hug, jam, jostle, lean on, milk, nip, oppress, pack, pinch, press, pressurise, ram, scrounge, squash, strain, stuff, thrust, wedge, wrest, wring.

n clasp, congestion, crowd, crush, embrace, grasp, handclasp, hold, hug, jam, press, pressure, restriction, squash.

**squint** adj askew, aslant, awry, cockeyed, crooked, indirect, oblique, off-centre, skew-whiff, strabismic.

*antonym* straight.

**squire** v accompany, attend, conduct, escort.

**squirm** v agonise, fidget, flounder, move, shift, squiggle, twist, wiggle, wriggle, writhe.

**squirt** v chirt, discharge, ejaculate, eject, emit, expel, jet, shoot, spout, spurt.

n chirt, jet, spray, spurt.

**stab** v bayonet, cut, dirk, gore, injure, jab, knife, pierce, pink, puncture, spear, stick, thrust, transfix, wound.

n ache, attempt, endeavour, essay, gash, incision, jab, pang, pink, prick, puncture, rent, thrust, try, twinge, venture, wound.

**stab in the back** betray, deceive, double-cross, inform on, let down, sell out, slander.

**stabbing** adj acute, lancinating, piercing, shooting, stinging.

**stability** n constancy, durability, firmness, fixity, permanence, solidity, soundness, steadfastness, steadiness, strength, sturdiness.

*antonyms* insecurity, instability, unsteadiness, weakness.

**stable** adj abiding, constant, deep-rooted, durable, enduring, established, fast, firm, fixed, immutable, invariable, lasting, permanent, reliable, secure, self-balanced, sound, static, steadfast, steady, strong, sturdy, sure, unalterable, unchangeable, unwavering, well-founded.

*antonyms* shaky, unstable, weak, wobbly.

**stack** n accumulation, clamp, cock, heap, hoard, load, mass, mound, mountain, pile, ruck, stockpile.

v accumulate, amass, assemble, gather, load, pile, save, stockpile, store.

**staff** n caduceus, cane, crew, employees, lecturers, lituus, officers, organisation, personnel, pole, prop, rod, stave, teachers, team, wand, workers, workforce.

**stage** n division, floor, juncture, lap, leg, length, level, period, phase, point, shelf, step, storey, subdivision, tier.

v arrange, do, engineer, give, mount, orchestrate, organise, perform, present, produce, put on, stage-manage.

**stagger** v alternate, amaze, astonish, astound, confound, daddle, daidle, dumbfound, falter, flabbergast, hesitate, lurch, nonplus, overlap, overwhelm, reel, shake, shock, step, stun, stupefy, surprise, sway, teeter, titubate, totter, vacillate, waver, wobble, zigzag.

**stagnant** adj becalmed, brackish, lethargic, motionless, sluggish, stale, standing, still, torpid.

**stagnate** v decay, decline, degenerate, deteriorate, fester, idle, languish, rot, rust, vegetate.

**staid** adj calm, composed, decorous, demure, grave, quiet, sedate, self-restrained, serious, sober, sober-blooded, solemn, steady, Victorian.

*antonyms* debonair, frivolous, jaunty, sportive.

**stain** v bedye, besmirch, blacken, blemish, blot, colour, contaminate, corrupt, defile, deprave, dirty, discolour, disgrace, distain, dye, imbue, mark, smutch, soil, spot, sully, taint, tarnish, tinge.

n blemish, blot, discoloration, disgrace, dishonour, dye, infamy, reproach, shame, slur, smirch, smutch, soil, splodge, spot, stigma, tint.

**stake¹** n loggat, pale, paling, picket, pile, pole, post, spike, standard, stang, stave, stick.

v brace, fasten, pierce, prop, secure, support, tether, tie, tie up.

**stake out** define, delimit, demarcate, keep an eye on, mark out, outline, reserve, stake off, survey, watch.

**stake²** n ante, bet, chance, claim, concern, hazard, interest, investment, involvement, peril, pledge, prize, risk, share, venture, wager.

v ante, bet, chance, gage, gamble, hazard, imperil, jeopardise, pledge, risk, venture, wager.

**stale** adj antiquated, banal, cliche'd, cliche-ridden, common, commonplace, decayed, drab, dry, effete, faded, fetid, flat, fozy, fusty, hackneyed, hard, insipid, musty, old, old hat, overused, platitudinous, repetitious, sour, stagnant, stereotyped, tainted, tasteless, threadbare, trite, unoriginal, vapid, worn-out.

*antonym* fresh.

**stalemate** *n* deadlock, draw, halt, impasse, standstill, stop, tie, zugzwang.

*antonym* progress.

**stalk¹** *v* approach, follow, haunt, hunt, march, pace, pursue, shadow, stride, strut, tail, track.

**stalk²** *n* bole, branch, kex, shoot, spire, stem, sterigma, trunk.

**stall¹** *v* delay, equivocate, hedge, obstruct, penelopise, play for time, prevaricate, stonewall, temporise.

*antonym* advance.

**stall²** *n* bay, bench, booth, compartment, cowshed, pew, seat, stable, table.

**stalwart** *adj* athletic, beefy, brawny, daring, dependable, determined, hefty, husky, indomitable, intrepid, lusty, manly, muscular, redoubtable, resolute, robust, rugged, sinewy, staunch, stout, strapping, strong, sturdy, valiant, vigorous.

*antonyms* timid, weak.

**stamina** *n* energy, fibre, force, grit, indefatigability, lustiness, power, resilience, resistence, staying power, strength, vigour.

*antonym* weakness.

**stammer** *v* falter, gibber, hesitate, splutter, stumble, stutter.

**stamp** *v* beat, brand, bray, categorise, characterise, crush, engrave, exhibit, fix, identify, impress, imprint, inscribe, label, mark, mint, mould, pound, print, pronounce, reveal, strike, trample.

*n* attestation, authorisation, brand, breed, cast, character, cut, description, earmark, evidence, fashion, form, hallmark, impression, imprint, incuse, kind, mark, mould, sign, signature, sort, stomp, type.

**stamp out** crush, destroy, eliminate, end, eradicate, extinguish, extirpate, kill, quell, quench, scotch, suppress.

*antonym* encourage.

**stampede** *n* charge, dash, debacle, flight, rout, rush, scattering, sprint.

*v* charge, dash, flee, fly, gallop, hightail it, hot-foot it, run, rush, scurry, shoot, sprint, tear.

*antonyms* walk, wander.

**stance** *n* angle, attitude, bearing, carriage, deportment, point of view, position, posture, stand, standpoint, station, viewpoint.

**stanch** *v* arrest, block, check, dam, halt, plug, stay, stem, stop.

*antonyms* increase, promote.

**stand** *v* abide, allow, bear, belong, brook, continue, cost, countenance, demur, endure,

erect, exist, experience, halt, handle, hold, mount, obtain, pause, place, position, prevail, put, rank, remain, rest, rise, scruple, set, stay, stomach, stop, suffer, support, sustain, take, thole, tolerate, undergo, wear, weather, withstand.

*antonym* advance.

*n* attitude, base, booth, bracket, cradle, dais, determination, erection, frame, grandstand, halt, holder, loss, opinion, place, platform, position, rack, rank, resistance, rest, stage, staging, stall, stance, standpoint, standstill, stay, stop, stop-over, stoppage, support, table, tub, vat, witness-box.

*antonym* progress.

**stand by** adhere to, back, befriend, champion, defend, hold to, reiterate, repeat, speak for, stick up for, support, uphold.

*antonym* let down.

**stand down** abdicate, cede, give away, give up, quit, resign, step down, withdraw.

*antonyms* ascend, join.

**stand for** bear, betoken, brook, champion, countenance, denote, embody, endure, epitomise, exemplify, indicate, mean, personify, represent, signify, suffer, symbolise, tolerate, typify, wear.

**stand in for** cover for, deputise for, hold the fort for, replace, substitute for, understudy.

**stand out** bulk large, catch the eye, jut out, project, stare one in the face, stick out, stick out a mile, stick out like a sore thumb.

**stand up** cohere, hold up, hold water, stand, wash.

**stand up for** champion, defend, fight for, side with, speak for, speak up for, stick up for, support, uphold.

*antonym* attack.

**stand up to** brave, confront, defy, endure, face, front, oppose, resist, withstand.

*antonym* give in to.

**standard¹** *n* average, bench-mark, canon, criterion, example, exemplar, gauge, grade, guide, guideline, level, measure, model, norm, norma, pattern, principle, requirement, rule, sample, specification, touchstone, type, yardstick.

*adj* accepted, approved, authoritative, average, basic, classic, customary, definitive, established, mainstream, normal, official, orthodox, popular, prevailing, recognised, regular, set, staple, stock, typical, usual.

*antonyms* abnormal, irregular, unusual.

**standard²** *n* banner, colours, ensign, flag, gonfalon, gonfanon, labarum, pennant, pennon, rallying-point, streamer, vexillum.

**standard-bearer** *n* cornet, ensign, gonfalonier, standard, vexillary.

**standardise** *v* assimilate, equalise, institutionalise, mass-produce, normalise, regiment, stereotype.

*antonym* differentiate.

**standards** *n* ethics, ideals, morals, principles.

**standing** *n* condition, continuance, credit, duration, eminence, estimation, existence, experience, footing, position, prestige, rank, reputation, repute, seniority, station, status.

*adj* erect, fixed, lasting, on one's feet, permanent, perpendicular, perpetual, rampant, regular, repeated, up-ended, upright, vertical.

*antonyms* horizontal, lying.

**standing-stone** *n* megalith, menhir, monolith.

**stand-offish** *adj* aloof, cold, distant, haughty, remote, reserved, unapproachable, uncommunicative, unsociable, untalkative.

*antonym* friendly.

**standpoint** *n* angle, point of view, position, post, stance, station, vantage-point, viewpoint, Weltanschauung.

**standstill** *n* arrest, cessation, dead-finish, deadlock, halt, hold-up, impasse, lapse, log-jam, lull, moratorium, pause, reprieve, respite, rest, stalemate, stay, stop, stoppage, termination.

*antonym* progress.

**staple** *adj* basic, chief, essential, fundamental, key, leading, main, major, predominant, primary, principle.

*antonym* minor.

**star**[1] *n* asterisk, asteroid, comet, etoile, meteor, meteorite, nova, planet, pulsar, quasar, red dwarf, red giant, satellite, shooting-star, starlet, sun, supernova, white dwarf.

**star**[2] *n* celebrity, draw, idol, lead, leading, leading lady, leading man, luminary, main attraction, name, starlet, vedette.

*adj* brilliant, celebrated, illustrious, leading, major, paramount, pre-eminent, principal, prominent, talented, well-known.

*antonym* minor.

**starchy** *adj* ceremonious, conventional, formal, prim, punctilious, stiff, strait-laced, stuffy.

*antonym* informal.

**stare** *v* gape, gawk, gawp, gaze, glare, goggle, look, watch.

*n* fish-eye, gaze, glare, glower, leer, look, ogle, scowl.

**stark** *adj* absolute, arrant, austere, bald, bare, barren, bleak, blunt, cold, consummate, depressing, desolate, downright, drear, dreary, entire, flagrant, forsaken, grim, harsh, out-and-out, palpable, patent, plain, pure, severe, sheer, simple, solitary, stern, stiff, strong, unadorned, unalloyed, unmitigated, unyielding, utter.

*antonyms* mild, slight.

*adv* absolutely, altogether, clean, completely, entirely, quite, stoutly, totally, utterly, wholly.

*antonyms* mildly, slightly.

**stark-naked** *adj* in one's birthday suit, in the altogether, in the buff, in the nude, in the raw, naked, nude, stark, starkers, stripped, unclad, undressed.

*antonym* clothed.

**start** *v* activate, appear, arise, begin, blench, break away, commence, create, dart, depart, engender, establish, father, flinch, found, inaugurate, initiate, instigate, institute, introduce, issue, jerk, jump, kick off, launch, leave, open, originate, pioneer, recoil, sally forth, set off, set out, set up, shoot, shy, spring forward, twitch.

*antonyms* finish, stop.

*n* advantage, backing, beginning, birth, break, chance, commencement, convulsion, dawn, edge, fit, foundation, inauguration, inception, initiation, introduction, jar, jump, kick-off, lead, onset, opening, opportunity, outburst, outset, spasm, sponsorship, spurt, twitch.

*antonyms* finish, stop.

**startle** *v* affray, agitate, alarm, amaze, astonish, astound, electrify, flush, frighten, scare, shock, spook, start, surprise.

*antonym* calm.

**startling** *adj* alarming, astonishing, astounding, dramatic, electric, electrifying, extraordinary, shocking, staggering, sudden, surprising, unexpected, unforeseen.

*antonyms* boring, calming, ordinary.

**starvation** *n* famishment, hunger, inanition, malnutrition, underfeeding, undernourishment.

*antonym* plenty.

**starve** *v* clem, deny, deprive, die, diet, fast, hunger, perish, refuse.

*antonym* provide.

**starving** *adj* famished, hungering, hungry, ravenous, sharp-set, starved, underfed, undernourished.

*antonym* fed.

**stash** *v* cache, closet, conceal, hide, hoard, lay up, salt away, save up, secrete, stockpile, stow.

*antonyms* bring out, uncover.

**state**[1] *v* affirm, articulate, assert, asseverate, aver, declare, enumerate, explain, expound, express, formalise, formulate, formulise, present, propound, put, report, say, specify, voice.

*n* attitude, bother, case, category, ceremony, circumstances, condition, dignity, display, flap, glory, grandeur, humour, majesty, mode, mood, panic, pass, phase, plight, pomp, position, pother, predicament, shape, situation, spirits, splendour, stage, station, style, tizzy.

*antonym* calmness.

**state of affairs** case, circumstances, condition, crisis, galère, juncture, kettle of fish, lie of the land, plight, position, predicament, situation.

**state**[2] *n* body politic, commonwealth, country, federation, government, kingdom, land, leviathan, nation, republic, territory.

*adj* ceremonial, ceremonious, formal, governmental, magnificent, national, official, pompous, public, solemn.

**stately** *adj* august, ceremonious, deliberate, dignified, elegant, grand, imperial, imposing, impressive, Junoesque, kingly, lofty, majestic, measured, noble, pompous, princely, queenly, regal, royal, solemn.

*antonyms* informal, unimpressive.

**statement** *n* account, announcement, bulletin, communication, communique, constatation, declaration, explanation, factoid, ipse dixit, ipsissima verba, proclamation, recital, relation, report, testimony, utterance, verbal.

**statesman** *n* diplomat, Elder Statesman, GOM, homme d'etat, politician.

**static** *adj* changeless, constant, fixed, immobile, inert, motionless, resting, stable, stagnant, stationary, still, unmoving, unvarying.

*antonyms* active, dynamic, moving.

**station** *n* appointment, base, business, calling, depot, employment, grade, habitat, head-quarters, location, occupation, office, place, position, post, rank, seat, situation, sphere, stance, standing, standing-place, status, stopping-place.

*v* appoint, assign, establish, fix, garrison, install, locate, post, send, set.

**stationary** *adj* fixed, inert, moored, motionless, parked, resting, settled, standing, static, stock-still, unmoving.

*antonym* moving.

**statue** *n* acrolith, bronze, bust, carving, caryatid, effigy, figure, figurine, head, idol, statuette, xoanon.

**statuesque** *adj* dignified, imposing, majestic, regal, stately, statuary.

*antonym* small.

**stature** *n* consequence, eminence, importance, prestige, prominence, rank, size, standing, weight.

*antonym* unimportance.

**status** *n* character, condition, consequence, degree, distinction, eminence, grade, importance, position, prestige, rank, standing, state, weight.

*antonym* unimportance.

**statute** *n* act, decree, edict, enactment, firman, hatti-sherif, indiction, interlocution, irade, law, ordinance, regulation, rescript, rule, ukase.

**staunch¹** *adj* constant, dependable, faithful, firm, hearty, loyal, reliable, resolute, sound, steadfast, stout, strong, sure, true, true-blue, trustworthy, trusty, watertight, yeomanly, zealous.

*antonyms* unreliable, wavering, weak.

**staunch²** *same as* **stanch**.

**stave off** avert, delay, evade, fend off, foil, hold off, keep at bay, keep back, parry, ward off.

*antonyms* cause, encourage.

**stay¹** *v* abide, adjourn, allay, arrest, check, continue, curb, defer, delay, detain, discontinue, dwell, endure, halt, hinder, hold, hold out, hover, impede, last, linger, live, lodge, loiter, obstruct, pause, prevent, prorogue, remain, reside, restrain, settle, sojourn, stand, stop, suspend, tarry, visit, wait.

*antonyms* advance, leave.

*n* continuance, deferment, delay, halt, holiday, pause, postponement, remission, reprieve,

sojourn, stop, stopover, stopping, suspension, visit.

**stay²** *n* brace, buttress, prop, reinforcement, shoring, stanchion, support.

*v* buttress, prop, prop up, shore up, support, sustain.

**steadfast** *adj* constant, dedicated, dependable, established, faithful, fast, firm, fixed, intent, loyal, perseverant, persevering, reliable, resolute, single-minded, stable, staunch, steady, unfaltering, unflinching, unswerving, unwavering.

*antonyms* unreliable, wavering, weak.

**steady** *adj* balanced, calm, ceaseless, confirmed, consistent, constant, continuous, dependable, equable, even, faithful, firm, fixed, habitual, immovable, imperturbable, incessant, industrious, level-headed, non-stop, persistent, regular, reliable, rhythmic, safe, sedate, sensible, serene, serious-minded, settled, sober, stable, staid, steadfast, substantial, unbroken, unchangeable, unfaltering, unfluctuating, unhasting, unhasty, unhurried, uniform, uninterrupted, unremitting, unswerving, unvarying, unwavering.

*antonyms* unsteady, wavering.

*v* balance, brace, firm, fix, secure, stabilise, support.

**steal** *v* appropriate, bone, cly, convey, creep, embezzle, filch, flit, half-inch, heist, knap, knock off, lag, lift, mill, misappropriate, nab, nick, peculate, pilfer, pinch, pirate, plagiarise, poach, purloin, relieve someone of, rip off, shoplift, slink, slip, smouch, smug, snaffle, snatch, sneak, snitch, swipe, take, thieve, tiptoe.

*antonym* return.

**stealing** *n* embezzlement, larceny, misappropriation, peculation, pilferage, pilfering, plagiarism, rip-off, robbery, shoplifting, theft, thievery, thieving.

**stealth** *n* covertness, furtiveness, secrecy, slyness, sneakiness, stealthiness, surreptitiousness, unobtrusiveness.

*antonym* openness.

**stealthy** *adj* cat-like, clandestine, covert, furtive, quiet, secret, secretive, skulking, sly, sneaking, sneaky, surreptitious, underhand.

*antonym* open.

**steam** *n* condensation, dampness, fumes, haze, mist, moisture, roke, vapour.

**steamboat** *n* packet, packet-boat, packet-ship, paddle-boat, paddle-steamer, puffer, steamer, steam-packet, steamship, steam-tug, steam-vessel, steam-yacht, vaporetto.

**steamy** *adj* close, damp, gaseous, hazy, humid, misty, muggy, roky, steaming, stewy, sticky, sultry, sweaty, sweltering, vaporiform, vaporous, vapourish, vapoury.

**steed** *n* charger, hack, horse, jade, mount, nag, Rosinante.

**steel** *v* brace, fortify, harden, nerve, toughen.

*antonym* weaken.

**steep¹** *adj* abrupt, bluff, excessive, exorbitant, extortionate, extreme, headlong, high, overpriced, precipitious, sheer, stiff, uncalled-for, unreasonable.

*antonyms* gentle, moderate.

**steep²** *v* brine, damp, drench, fill, imbrue, imbue, immerse, infuse, macerate, marinate, moisten, permeate, pervade, pickle, saturate, seethe, soak, souse, submerge, suffuse.

**steer** *v* con, conduct, control, direct, govern, guide, pilot.

**steer clear of** avoid, bypass, circumvent, dodge, escape, eschew, evade, shun, skirt.

*antonym* seek.

**stem¹** *n* axis, branch, family, house, line, lineage, peduncle, race, shoot, stalk, stock, trunk.

**stem from** arise from, come from, derive from, develop from, emanate from, flow from, issue from, originate in, spring from.

*antonym* give rise to.

**stem²** *v* check, contain, curb, dam, oppose, resist, restrain, stanch, stay, stop, tamp.

*antonyms* encourage, increase.

**stench** *n* mephitis, odour, pong, reek, stink, whiff.

**step** *n* act, action, advance, advancement, deed, degree, demarche, doorstep, expedient, footfall, footprint, footstep, gait, halfpace, impression, level, manoeuvre, means, measure, move, pace, phase, point, print, procedure, proceeding, process, progression, rank, remove, round, rung, stage, stair, stride, trace, track, tread, walk.

*v* move, pace, stalk, stamp, tread, walk.

**step by step** gradatim, gradually, slowly.

**step down** abdicate, bow out, leave, quit, resign, retire, stand down, withdraw.

*antonyms* ascend, join.

**step up** accelerate, augment, boost, build up, escalate, increase, intensify, raise, speed up, up.

*antonym* decrease.

**stereotype** *n* convention, formula, mould, pattern.

*v* categorise, conventionalise, dub, mass-produce, pigeonhole, standardise, typecast.

*antonym* differentiate.

**stereotyped** *adj* banal, cliche'd, cliche-ridden, conventional, corny, hackneyed, mass-produced, overused, platitudinous, stale, standard, standardised, stock, threadbare, tired, trite, unoriginal.

*antonyms* different, unconventional.

**sterile** *adj* abortive, acarpous, antiseptic, aseptic, bare, barren, disinfected, dry, empty, fruitless, germ-free, infecund, pointless, sterilised, unfruitful, unimaginative, unproductive, unprofitable, unprolific.

*antonyms* fruitful, septic.

**sterilise** *v* clean, cleanse, disinfect, fumigate, purify.

*antonyms* contaminate, infect.

**sterility** *n* asepsis, atocia, barrenness, cleanness, fruitlessness, futility, impotence, ineffectiveness,

inefficacy, pointlessness, purity, unfecundity, unfruitfulness, uselessness.

*antonyms* fertility, fruitfulness.

**sterling** *adj* authentic, excellent, first-class, genuine, great, pure, real, sound, standard, substantial, superlative, true, worthy.

*antonyms* false, poor.

**stern** *adj* austere, authoritarian, bitter, cruel, flinty, forbidding, frowning, grim, hard, harsh, inflexible, relentless, rigid, rigorous, serious, severe, stark, steely, strict, unrelenting, unsmiling, unsparing, unyielding.

*antonym* mild.

**stew** *v* agonise, boil, braise, fret, fricassee, fuss, jug, perspire, seethe, simmer, sweat, swelter, worry.

*n* agitation, bother, bouillabaisse, chowder, daube, fluster, fret, fuss, goulash, hash, lobscouse, pot-au-feu, pother, ragout, tizzy, worry.

**steward** *n* chamberlain, dewan, factor, grieve, homme d'affaires, maître d'hôtel, major-domo, manciple, marshal.

**stick¹** *v* abid, adhere, affix, attach, bind, bond, bulge, catch, cement, cleave, cling, clog, deposit, dig, drop, endure, extend, fasten, fix, fuse, glue, gore, hold, insert, install, jab, jam, join, jut, lay, linger, lodge, obtrude, paste, penetrate, persist, pierce, pin, place, plant, plonk, poke, position, prod, project, protrude, puncture, put, put up with, remain, set, show, snag, spear, stab, stand, stay, stomach, stop, store, stuff, take, thole, thrust, tolerate, transfix, weld.

*antonym* unstick.

**stick at¹** continue, hang on in, keep at, persevere in, persist, plug away at.

*antonym* give up.

**stick at²** balk, demur, doubt, draw the line at, hesitate, pause, recoil, scruple, shrink from, stop at.

**stick to** adhere to, cleave to, honour, keep to, persevere in, stand by.

*antonyms* give up, quit.

**stick up for** champion, defend, speak for, speak up for, stand up for, support, take the part or side of, uphold.

*antonym* attack.

**stick²** *n* baton, bavin, birch, bludgeon, branch, cane, lathi, lug, pole, quarterstaff, rod, sceptre, staff, stake, stave, switch, twig, waddy, wand, whip, withy.

**stick³** *n* abuse, blame, criticism, flak, hostility, punishment, reproof.

*antonym* praise.

**stickiness** *n* adhesiveness, gaum, glueyness, glutinousness, goo, gooeyness, gumminess, syrupiness, tack, tackiness, viscidity.

**stick-in-the-mud** *adj* antediluvian, antiquated, conservative, fogram, fogyish, fossilised, outmoded, unadventurous, Victorian.

*antonyms* adventurous, modern.

*n* conservative, fog(e)y, fogram, fogramite, fossil.

**stickler** *n* fanatic, fusspot, maniac, martinet, nut, pedant, perfectionist, precisianist, purist.

**sticky** *adj* adhesive, awkward, claggy, clammy, clinging, clingy, cloggy, close, dauby, delicate, difficult, discomforting, embarrassing, gluey, glutinous, gooey, gummy, hairy, humid, muggy, nasty, oppressive, painful, smeary, sultry, sweltering, syrupy, tacky, tenacious, thorny, tricky, unpleasant, viscid, viscous.

*antonyms* cool, dry, easy.

**stiff** *adj* arduous, arthritic, artificial, austere, awkward, brisk, brittle, buckram, budge, ceremonious, chilly, clumsy, cold, constrained, creaky, crude, cruel, difficult, drastic, exacting, excessive, extreme, fatiguing, firm, forced, formal, formidable, fresh, graceless, great, hard, hardened, harsh, heavy, inelastic, inelegant, inexorable, inflexible, jerky, laborious, laboured, mannered, oppressive, pertinaceous, pitiless, pokerish, pompous, powerful, priggish, prim, punctilious, resistant, rheumaticky, rigid, rigorous, severe, sharp, solid, solidified, stand-offish, starch(y), stark, stilted, strict, stringent, strong, stubborn, taut, tense, tight, toilsome, tough, trying, unbending, uneasy, ungainly, ungraceful, unnatural, unrelaxed, unsupple, unyielding, uphill, vigorous, wooden.

*antonyms* flexible, graceful, informal, mild.

**stiffen** *v* ankylose, brace, coagulate, congeal, crystallise, harden, jell, reinforce, rigidify, rigidise, set, solidify, starch, tauten, tense, thicken.

**stiff-necked** *adj* arrogant, contumacious, haughty, obstinate, opinionated, proud, stubborn, uncompromising.

*antonyms* flexible, humble.

**stifle** *v* asphyxiate, check, choke, curb, dampen, extinguish, hush, muffle, prevent, repress, restrain, silence, smother, stop, strangle, suffocate, suppress.

*antonym* encourage.

**stigma** *n* blemish, blot, brand, disgrace, dishonour, imputation, mark, reproach, shame, slur, smirch, spot, stain.

*antonym* credit.

**stigmatise** *v* brand, condemn, denounce, discredit, fame, label, mark, pillory, vilify, vilipend.

*antonym* praise.

**still** *adj* calm, hushed, inert, lifeless, motionless, noiseless, pacific, peaceful, placid, quiet, restful, serene, silent, smooth, stagnant, stationary, stilly, tranquil, undisturbed, unruffled, unstirring.

*antonyms* agitated, busy, disturbed, noisy.

*v* allay, alleviate, appease, calm, hold back, hush, lull, pacify, quiet, quieten, restrain, settle, silence, smooth, soothe, subdue, tranquillise.

*antonyms* agitate, stir up.

*n* hush, peace, peacefulness, quiet, quietness, silence, stillness, tranquillity.

*antonyms* agitation, disturbance, noise.

*adv* but, even so, even then, however, nevertheless, nonetheless, notwithstanding, yet.

**stilted** *adj* artificial, bombastic, constrained, forced, grandiloquent, high-flown, high-sounding, inflated, laboured, mannered, pedantic, pompous, pretentious, stiff, unnatural, wooden.

*antonyms* flowing, fluent.

**stimulant** *n* analeptic, bracer, excitant, hype, incitant, oestrus, pep pill, pick-me-up, restorative, reviver, tonic, upper, whetstone.

*antonym* depressant.

**stimulate** *v* animate, arouse, dynamise, encourage, fan, fire, foment, get psyched up, goad, hop up, hype up, impel, incite, inflame, instigate, jog, prompt, provoke, psych oneself up, quicken, rouse, spur, titillate, urge, whet.

*antonym* discourage.

**stimulating** *adj* excitant, excitative, excitatory, exciting, exhilarating, galvanic, inspiring, intriguing, provocative, provoking, rousing, stirring, thought-provoking.

*antonyms* boring, depressing, uninspiring.

**stimulus** *n* carrot, encouragement, fillip, ginger, goad, incentive, incitement, inducement, prick, provocation, spur.

*antonym* discouragement.

**sting** *v* anger, burn, cheat, con, defraud, do, fleece, gall, hurt, incense, inflame, infuriate, nettle, overcharge, pain, pique, provoke, rile, rip off, smart, swindle, tingle, urticate, wound.

*antonym* soothe.

*n* agony, anguish, bite, bitterness, distress, goad, incentive, incitement, nip, prick, pungency, smarting, spur, stimulus, tingle, torment, torture, woe.

**stinging** *adj* aculeate(d), burning, nippy, smarting, tingling, urent, urticant.

*antonyms* mild, soothing.

**stingy** *adj* avaricious, cheeseparing, close-fisted, covetous, illiberal, inadequate, insufficient, meagre, mean, measly, mingy, miserly, near, niggardly, parsimonious, penny-pinching, penurious, save-all, scanty, scrimping, small, tightfisted, ungenerous, ungiving.

*antonym* generous.

**stink** *v* niff, pong, reek, whiff.

*n* brouhaha, commotion, disturbance, fetor, foulness, fuss, hubbub, malodour, mephitis, niff, odour, pong, row, rumpus, scandal, stench, stir, to-do, uproar, upset, whiff.

**stinker** *n* affliction, beast, bounder, cad, creep, cur, dastard, difficulty, fink, heel, horror, impediment, plight, poser, predicament, problem, rat, rotter, scab, scoundrel, shocker, sod, swine.

**stinking** *adj* boozed, canned, contemptible, disgusting, drunk, fetid, foul-smelling, graveolent, grotty, ill-smelling, intoxicated, low, low-down, malodorous, mean, mephitic, noisome, pissed, plastered, pongy, reeking, rotten, smashed, smelly, sozzled, stenchy, stewed, stoned, unpleasant, vile, whiffy, wretched.

*antonyms* good, pleasant, sober.

**stint** *n* assignment, bit, period, quota, share, shift, spell, stretch, term, time, tour, trick, turn.

*v* begrudge, economise, pinch, save, scrimp, skimp on, withhold.

**stipulate** *v* agree, contract, covenant, engage, guarantee, insist upon, lay down, pledge, postulate, promise, provide, require, settle, specify.

*antonym* imply.

**stipulation** *n* agreement, clause, condition, contract, engagement, precondition, prerequisite, provision, proviso, qualification, requirement, restriction, settlement, sine qua non, small print, specification, term.

*antonym* implication.

**stir** *v* affect, agitate, beat, bestir, budge, disturb, electrify, emove, excite, fire, flutter, hasten, inspire, look lively, mix, move, quiver, rustle, shake, shake a leg, thrill, touch, tremble.

*antonyms* bore, calm, stay.

*n* activity, ado, agitation, bustle, commotion, disorder, disturbance, excitement, ferment, flurry, fuss, hustle and bustle, movement, to-do, toing and froing, tumult, uproar.

*antonym* calm.

**stir up** animate, arouse, awaken, excite, incite, inflame, instigate, jog, kindle, mix, prompt, provoke, quicken, raise, spur, stimulate, urge.

*antonyms* calm, discourage.

**stirring** *adj* animating, dramatic, emotive, exciting, exhilarating, heady, impassioned, inspiring, intoxicating, lively, martial, moving, rousing, spirited, stimulating, thrilling.

*antonyms* calming, uninspiring.

**stock** *n* ancestry, array, assets, assortment, background, beasts, block, breed, cache, capital, cattle, choice, commodities, descent, equipment, estimation, extraction, family, flocks, forebears, fund, funds, goods, handle, herds, hoard, horses, house, inventory, investment, kindred, line, lineage, livestock, log, merchandise, parentage, pedigree, post, property, race, range, repertoire, repute, reserve, reservoir, selection, sheep, source, stem, stockpile, store, strain, stump, supply, trunk, type, variety, wares.

*adj* banal, basic, bromidic, cliche'd, commonplace, conventional, customary, formal, hackneyed, ordinary, overused, regular, routine, run-of-the-mill, set, standard, staple, stereotyped, traditional, trite, usual, worn-out.

*antonym* original.

*v* deal in, handle, keep, sell, supply, trade in.

**stock up** accumulate, amass, equip, fill, furnish, gather, hoard, lay in, pile up, provision, replenish, save, store (up), supply.

**stocky** *adj* blocky, chunky, dumpy, mesomorphic, short, solid, stubby, stumpy, sturdy, thickset.

*antonyms* skinny, tall.

**stodgy** *adj* boring, dull, filling, formal, fuddy-duddy, heavy, laboured, leaden, solemn, spiritless, staid, starchy, stuffy, substantial, tedious, turgid, unenterprising, unexciting, unimaginative, uninspired.

*antonyms* exciting, informal, light.

**stoical** *adj* calm, cool, dispassionate, impassive, imperturbable, indifferent, long-suffering, patient, philosophic(al), phlegmatic, resigned, stoic, stolid.

*antonyms* anxious, depressed, furious, irascible.

**stoicism** *n* acceptance, ataraxia, ataraxy, calmness, dispassion, fatalism, forbearance, fortitude, impassivity, imperturbability, indifference, long-suffering, patience, resignation, stolidity.

*antonyms* anxiety, depression, fury.

**stolid** *adj* apathetic, beefy, blockish, bovine, doltish, dull, heavy, impassive, lumpish, obtuse, po, po-faced, slow, stoic(al), stupid, unemotional, wooden.

*antonyms* interested, lively.

**stomach** *n* abdomen, appetite, belly, bread-basket, craw, desire, gizzard, gut, inclination, inner man, inside(s), king's-hood, little Mary, maw, mind, paunch, pot, potbelly, relish, spare tyre, taste, tummy.

*v* abide, bear, endure, submit to, suffer, swallow, take, thole, tolerate.

**stone** *n* boulder, cobble, concretion, endocarp, flagstone, gem, gemstone, gravestone, headstone, jewel, kernel, lapis, pebble, pip, pit, rock, seed, set(t), slab, tombstone.

**stone circle** henge, peristalith.

**stony** *adj* adamant, blank, callous, chilly, expressionless, frigid, hard, heartless, hostile, icy, indifferent, inexorable, lapideous, lapilliform, lithoid(al), merciless, obdurate, pitiless, steely, stonelike, unfeeling, unforgiving, unresponsive.

*antonyms* forgiving, friendly, soft-hearted.

**stooge** *n* butt, cat's paw, dupe, fall guy, foil, henchman, lackey, patsy, pawn, puppet.

**stoop** *v* bend, bow, couch, crouch, descend, duck, hunch, incline, kneel, lean, squat.

*n* droop, inclination, round-shoulderedness, sag, slouch, slump.

**stoop to** condescend, deign, descend, go so far as, go so low as, lower oneself, resort, sink, vouchsafe.

**stop** *v* arrest, bar, block, break, cease, check, close, conclude, desist, discontinue, embar, end, finish, forestall, frustrate, halt, hinder, impede, intercept, intermit, interrupt, knock off, leave off, lodge, obstruct, pack (it) in, pack in, pack up, pause, plug, poop out, prevent, quit, refrain, repress, rest, restrain, scotch, seal, silence, sojourn, stall, staunch, stay, stem, stymie, suspend, tarry, terminate.

*antonyms* advance, continue, start.

*n* bar, block, break, bung, cessation, check, conclusion, control, depot, destination, discontinuation, end, finish, halt, hindrance, impediment, plug, rest, sojourn, stage, standstill, station, stay, stop-over, stoppage, termination, terminus, ventage, visit.

*antonyms* continuation, start.

*interj* avast, cease, cut it out, desist, easy, give over, halt, hang on, hold it, hold on, hold your horses, lay off, leave it out, refrain, stop it, wait, wait a minute, whoa.

**stop-gap** *n* expedient, improvisation, makeshift, resort, shift, substitute.

*adj* emergency, expediential, impromptu, improvised, makeshift, provisional, rough-and-ready, temporary.

*antonyms* finished, permanent.

**stoppage** *n* abeyance, arrest, blockage, check, close, closure, curtailment, cut-off, deduction, desistance, discontinuance, halt, hartal, hindrance, interruption, lay-off, obstruction, occlusion, shut-down, sit-in, standstill, stasis, stopping, strike, walk-out.

*antonyms* continuation, start.

**stopper** *n* bung, cork, plug, stopple.

**store** *v* accumulate, cupboard, deposit, garner, hive, hoard, husband, keep, lay aside, lay by, lay in lavender, lay up, put aside, reserve, salt away, save, stash, stock, stockpile, treasure.

*antonym* use.

*n* abundance, accumulation, bank, cache, cupboard, database, depository, emporium, esteem, fund, hoard, keeping, lot, market, mart, memory, mine, outlet, panary, plenty, plethora, provision, quantity, repository, reserve, reservoir, shop, stock, stockpile, storehouse, storeroom, supermarket, supply, value, warehouse, wealth.

*antonym* scarcity.

**storehouse** *n* armoury, arsenal, barn, cellar, depository, depot, elevator, entrepot, etape, fund, garderobe, garner, granary, hold, larder, pantry, repertory, repository, silo, treasury, vault, warehouse.

**storey** *n* deck, etage, flight, floor, level, stage, stratum, tier.

**storm** *n* agitation, anger, assault, attack, blast, blitz, blitzkrieg, blizzard, clamour, commotion, cyclone, disturbance, dust-devil, furore, gale, gust, haboob, hubbub, hurricane, offensive, onset, onslaught, outbreak, outburst, outcry, paroxysm, passion, roar, row, rumpus, rush, sandstorm, squall, stir, strife, tempest, tornado, tumult, turmoil, violence, whirlwind.

*antonym* calm.

*v* assail, assault, beset, bluster, charge, complain, expugn, flounce, fly, fume, rage, rampage, rant, rave, rush, scold, stalk, stamp, stomp, thunder.

**stormy** *adj* blustering, blustery, boisterous, choppy, dirty, foul, gustful, gusty, inclement, oragious, raging, rough, squally, tempestuous, turbulent, wild, windy.

*antonym* calm.

**story** *n* account, ancedote, article, chronicle, episode, fable, fairy-tale, falsehood, feature, fib, fiction, historiette, history, legend, lie, Märchen, - myth, narration, narrative, news, novel, plot, recital, record, relation, report, romance, scoop, spiel, tale, untruth, version, yarn.

**storyteller** *n* anecdotist, author, bard, chronicler, clype, fabulist, fibber, liar, narrator, novelist, raconteur, raconteuse, romancer, tell-tale.

**stout** *adj* able-bodied, athletic, beefy, big, bold, brave, brawny, bulky, burly, chopping, corpulent, courageous, dauntless, doughty, embonpoint, enduring, fat, fearless, fleshy, gallant, hardy, heavy, hulking, husky, intrepid, lion-hearted, lusty, manly, muscular, obese, overweight, plucky, plump, portly, resolute, robust, rotund, stalwart, strapping, strong, sturdy, substantial, thick, tough, tubby, valiant, valorous, vigorous.

*antonyms* slim, timid, weak.

**stove** *n* calefactor, chauffer, cockle, cooker, furnace, grill, heater, kiln, oven, range.

**stow** *v* bundle, cram, deposit, dump, jam, load, pack, secrete, sling, stash, store, stuff, tuck.

*antonym* unload.

**straggle** *v* amble, dilly-dally, drift, lag, loiter, ramble, range, roam, rove, scatter, spread, stray, string out, trail, wander.

**straggly** *adj* aimless, disorganised, drifting, irregular, loose, rambling, random, spreading, straggling, straying, strung out, untidy.

*antonyms* grouped, organised, tidy.

**straight** *adj* accurate, aligned, arranged, authentic, balanced, blunt, bourgeois, candid, consecutive, conservative, continuous, conventional, decent, direct, downright, equitable, erect, even, fair, forthright, frank, honest, honourable, horizontal, just, law-abiding, level, near, neat, non-stop, normal, orderly, organised, orthodox, outright, perpendicular, plain, plumb, point-blank, pure, reliable, respectable, right, running, settled, shipshape, short, smooth, solid, square, straightforward, successive, sustained, through, tidy, traditional, true, trustworthy, unadulterated, undeviating, undiluted, uninterrupted, unmixed, unqualified, unrelieved, unswerving, upright, vertical.

*antonyms* circuitous, dilute, dishonest, evasive, indirect, roundabout.

*adv* candidly, directly, frankly, honestly, outspokenly, point-blank, upright.

**straightaway** *adv* at once, directly, immediately, instanter, instantly, now, right away, straightway, there and then, this minute, tout de suite.

*antonym* eventually.

**straighten** *v* arrange, neaten, order, untwist.

*antonyms* bend, twist.

**straighten out** clear up, correct, disentangle, rectify, regularise, resolve, settle, sort out, unfankle, unsnarl, work out.

*antonym* muddle.

**straightforward** *adj* candid, clear-cut, direct, easy, elementary, forthright, genuine, guileless, honest, open, open-and-shut, penny-plain, routine, simple, sincere, truthful, uncomplicated, undemanding.

*antonyms* complicated, devious, evasive.

**strain**[1] *v* compress, distend, drive, embrace, endeavour, exert, express, extend, fatigue, filter, injure, labour, overtax, overwork, percolate, pull, purify, restrain, retch, riddle, screen, seep, separate, sieve, sift, sprain, squeeze, stretch, strive, struggle, tauten, tax, tear, tighten, tire, tug, twist, weaken, wrench, wrest, wrick.

*n* anxiety, burden, effort, exertion, force, height, injury, key, pitch, pressure, pull, sprain, stress, struggle, tautness, tension, wrench.

**strain²** *n* ancestry, blood, descent, extraction, family, humour, lineage, manner, pedigree, race, spirit, stem, stock, streak, style, suggestion, suspicion, temper, tendency, tone, trace, trait, vein, way.

**strained** *adj* artificial, awkward, constrained, difficult, embarrassed, epitonic, false, forced, laboured, self-conscious, stiff, tense, uncomfortable, uneasy, unnatural, unrelaxed.

*antonym* natural.

**strains** *n* air, lay, measure, melody, song, theme, tune.

**strait** *n* channel, gat, gut, kyle, narrows, sound.

**straitened** *adj* difficult, distressed, embarrassed, impoverished, limited, poor, reduced, restricted.

*antonyms* easy, well-off.

**strait-laced** *adj* moralistic, narrow, narrow-minded, old-maidish, prim, proper, prudish, puritanical, strict, stuffy, upright, Victorian.

*antonyms* broad-minded, easy-going.

**straits** *n* crisis, difficulty, dilemma, distress, embarrassment, emergency, extremity, hardship, hole, mess, perplexity, plight, poverty, predicament.

**strand** *n* fibre, fibril, fibrilla, filament, length, lock, rope, string, thread, tress, twist.

**stranded** *adj* abandoned, aground, ashore, beached, grounded, helpless, high and dry, homeless, in the lurch, marooned, penniless, shipwrecked, wrecked.

**strange** *adj* abnormal, alien, astonishing, awkward, bewildered, bizarre, curious, disorientated, disoriented, eccentric, eerie, exceptional, exotic, extraordinary, fantastic(al), ferly, foreign, frain, fremd, fremit, funny, irregular, lost, marvellous, mystifying, new, novel, odd, out-of-the-way, peculiar, perplexing, queer, rare, remarkable, remote, singular, sinister, unaccountable, unacquainted, uncanny, unco, uncomfortable, uncommon, unexplained, unexplored, unfamiliar, unheard of, unknown, untried, unversed, weird, wonderful.

*antonyms* comfortable, common, familiar, ordinary.

**strangeness** *n* abnormalism, abnormality, abnormity, bizarreness, bizarrerie, eccentricity, eeriness, exoticness, extraordinariness, fantasticality, fantasticalness, irregularity, oddity, oddness, peculiarity, queerness, singularity, uncanniness.

*antonym* ordinariness.

**stranger** *n* alien, foreigner, fraim, fremd, fremit, guest, incomer, newcomer, non-member, outlander, unknown, visitor.

*antonyms* local, native.

**strangle** *n* asphyxiate, choke, constrict, gag, garrotte, inhibit, jugulate, repress, smother, stifle, strangulate, suffocate, suppress, throttle.

**strap** *n* belt, leash, selvagee, thong, tie, vitta.

*v* beat, belt, bind, buckle, fasten, flog, lash, scourge, secure, tie, truss, whip.

**strapping** *adj* beefy, big, brawny, burly, hefty, hulking, hunky, husky, powerful, robust, stalwart, strong, sturdy, well-built.

*antonym* puny.

**stratagem** *n* artifice, device, dodge, feint, fetch, intrigue, manoeuvre, plan, plot, ploy, ruse, ruse de guerre, scheme, subterfuge, trick, wile.

**strategic** *adj* calculated, cardinal, critical, crucial, decisive, deliberate, diplomatic, important, key, planned, politic, strategetical, vital.

*antonym* unimportant.

**strategy** *n* approach, design, manoeuvring, plan, planning, policy, procedure, programme, scheme, way.

**stratum** *n* bed, bracket, caste, category, class, grade, group, layer, level, lode, rank, region, seam, station, stratification, table, tier, vein.

**stray** *v* deviate, digress, diverge, drift, err, get lost, meander, ramble, range, roam, rove, straggle, wander (off).

*adj* abandoned, accidental, chance, erratic, forwandered, freak, homeless, lost, odd, random, roaming, scattered, vagrant.

**streak** *n* band, dash, element, freak, layer, line, slash, smear, strain, strip, stripe, stroke, touch, trace, vein.

*v* band, dart, daub, flash, fleck, fly, gallop, hurtle, slash, smear, speed, sprint, striate, stripe, sweep, tear, whistle, whizz, zoom.

**streaked** *adj* banded, barred, brinded, brindle(d), flecked, fleckered, lined, streaky, striate, veiny.

**stream** *n* beck, brook, burn, course, creek, current, drift, flow, freshet, ghyll, gill, gush, outpouring, rill, rillet, river, rivulet, run, runnel, rush, surge, tide, torrent, tributary.

*v* cascade, course, emit, flood, flow, glide, gush, issue, pour, run, shed, spill, spout, surge, well out.

**streamer** *n* banner, ensign, flag, gonfalon, gonfanon, pennant, pennon, plume, ribbon, standard.

**streamlined** *adj* efficient, graceful, modernised, organised, rationalised, sleek, slick, smooth, smooth-running, superior, time-saving, up-to-the-minute, well-run.

*antonyms* clumsy, inefficient, old-fashioned.

**street** *n* avenue, boulevard, carriageway, corso, crescent, drive, gate, highway, lane, prospect, road, roadway, row, terrace, thoroughfare.

**strength** *n* advantage, anchor, asset, backbone, brawn, brawniness, cogency, concentration, courage, effectiveness, efficacy, energy, firmness, foison, force, fortitude, fushion, health, intensity, lustiness, mainstay, might, muscle, potency, power, resolution, robustness, security, sinew, spirit, stamina, stoutness, sturdiness, thew, toughness, vehemence, vigour, virtue.

*antonyms* timidness, weakness.

**strengthen** *v* afforce, bolster, brace, buttress, confirm, consolidate, corroborate, edify, encourage, enhance, establish, fortify, harden, hearten, heighten, increase, intensify, invigorate, justify, nerve, nourish, reinforce, rejuvenate, restore, steel, stiffen, substantiate, support, toughen.

*antonym* weaken.

**strenuous** *adj* active, arduous, bold, demanding, determined, eager, earnest, energetic, exhausting, hard, Herculean, laborious, persistent, resolute, spirited, strong, taxing, tireless, toilful, toilsome, tough, uphill, urgent, vigorous, warm, zealous.

*antonyms* easy, effortless.

**stress** *n* accent, accentuation, anxiety, beat, burden, emphasis, emphaticalness, force, hassle, importance, oppression, pressure, significance, strain, tautness, tension, trauma, urgency, weight, worry.

*antonym* relaxation.

*v* accentuate, belabour, emphasise, repeat, strain, tauten, underline, underscore.

*antonym* relax.

**stretch** *n* area, bit, distance, exaggeration, expanse, extensibility, extension, extent, period, reach, run, space, spell, spread, stint, strain, sweep, term, time, tract.

*v* cover, distend, elongate, expand, extend, inflate, lengthen, pull, rack, reach, spread, strain, swell, tauten, tighten, unfold, unroll.

*antonyms* relax, squeeze.

**stretch one's legs** exercise, go for a walk, move about, promenade, stroll, take a breather, take a walk, take the air.

**stretch out** hold out, lie down, porrect, put out, reach, relax, stretch forth.

*antonym* draw back.

**strew** *v* bespread, besprinkle, bestrew, disperse, litter, scatter, spread, sprinkle, toss.

*antonym* gather.

**stricken** *adj* affected, afflicted, expunged, hit, injured, smitten, struck, wounded.

*antonym* unaffected.

**strict** *adj* absolute, accurate, austere, authoritarian, close, complete, exact, faithful, firm, harsh, meticulous, no-nonsense, particular, perfect, precise, religious, restricted, rigid, rigorous, scrupulous, severe, stern, stringent, thoroughgoing, total, true, unsparing, utter, Victorian.

*antonyms* easy-going, flexible, mild.

**strictness** *n* accuracy, austerity, authoritarianism, exactness, firmness, harshness, martinetism, meticulousness, rigidity, rigidness, rigorousness, rigour, scrupulousness, severity, sternness, stringency, stringentness.

*antonyms* flexibility, mildness.

**stricture** *n* animadversion, blame, censure, criticism, flak, rebuke, reproof.

*antonym* praise.

**strident** *adj* cacophonous, clamorous, clashing, discordant, grating, harsh, jangling, jarring, loud, rasping, raucous, screeching, shrill, stridulant, stridulous, unmusical, vociferous.

*antonyms* quiet, sweet.

**strife** *n* animosity, battle, bickering, brigue, colluctation, combat, conflict, contention, contest, contestation, controversy, discord, dissension, friction, quarrel, rivalry, row, squabbling, struggle, warfare, wrangling.

*antonym* peace.

**strike** *n* attack, buffet, hartal, hit, mutiny, raid, refusal, stoppage, thump, walk-out, wallop, work-to-rule.

*v* achieve, affect, afflict, arrange, assail, assault, assume, attack, attain, bang, beat, bop, box, buff, buffet, cancel, chastise, clap, clash, clobber, clout, clump, cob, coin, collide with, cuff, dart, dash, delete, devastate, discover, dismantle, douse, down tools, drive, dunt, effect, encounter, find, force, hammer, hit, impel, impress, interpose, invade, knock, mutiny, penetrate, pierce, pound, print, punish, ratify, reach, register, remove, revolt, seem, shoot, slap, slat, smack, smite, sock, stamp, stumble across, stumble upon, surrender, swap, swipe, swop, thrust, thump, touch, trap, turn up, uncover, unearth, walk out, wallop, whack, wham, work to rule, zap.

**strike down** afflict, assassinate, destroy, kill, murder, ruin, slay, smite.

**strike out** cancel, cross out, delete, efface, erase, excise, expunge, remove, score off, score out, strike off, strike through.

*antonym* add.

**striking** *adj* arresting, astonishing, conspicuous, dazzling, distingue(e), extraordinary, forcible, foudroyant, frappant, impressive, memorable, noticeable, outstanding, salient, stunning, wonderful.

*antonym* unimpressive.

**string** *n* bunch, chain, cord, fibre, file, line, number, procession, queue, row, sequence, series, strand, succession, train, twine.

*v* festoon, hang, link, loop, sling, stretch, suspend, thread, tie up.

**string along¹** accompany, agree, assent, collaborate, co-operate, go along.

*antonym* dissent.

**string along²** bluff, deceive, dupe, fool, hoax, humbug, play (someone) false, play fast and loose with, put one over on, take (someone) for a ride.

**string out** disperse, extend, fan out, lengthen, protract, space out, spread out, straggle, stretch out, wander.

*antonyms* gather, shorten.

**stringent** *adj* binding, demanding, exacting, flexible, inflexible, mild, rigid, rigorous, severe, strict, tight, tough.

**strings** *n* catches, conditions, limitations, obligations, prerequisites, provisos, qualifications, requirements, restrictions, stipulations.

**stringy** *adj* chewy, fibrous, gristly, ropy, sinewy, tough, wiry.

*antonym* tender.

**strip**[1] *v* bare, clear, defoliate, denude, deprive, despoil, devest, disadorn, disembellish, disgarnish, disinvest, disleaf, disleave, dismantle, displenish, disrobe, divest, doff, empty, excoriate, excorticate, expose, gut, husk, lay bare, loot, peel, pillage, plunder, ransack, rob, sack, skin, spoil, unclothe, uncover, undress, widow.

*antonyms* cover, provide.

**strip**[2] *n* band, belt, bit, fillet, lath, list, piece, ribbon, sash, screed, shred, slat, slip, spline, strake, strap, swathe, tape, thong, tongue, vitta.

**stripe** *n* band, bar, belt, chevron, flash, fleck, striation, vitta.

**striped** *adj* banded, barred, streaky, striated, stripy, vittate.

**stripling** *n* adolescent, boy, fledgling, hobbledehoy, lad, shaver, teenager, youngling, youngster, young'un, youth.

**strive** *v* attempt, compete, contend, endeavour, fight, labour, push oneself, strain, struggle, toil, try, work.

**stroke** *n* accomplishnment, achievement, apoplexy, attack, blow, clap, collapse, effleurage, feat, fit, flourish, hit, knock, move, movement, pat, rap, seizure, shock, swap, swop, thump.

*v* caress, clap, fondle, pat, pet, rub.

**stroll** *v* amble, da(c)ker, dander, dawdle, mosey, promenade, ramble, saunter, stooge, toddle, wander.

*n* airing, bummel, constitutional, dawdle, excursion, promenade, ramble, saunter, toddle, turn, walk.

**stroller** *n* dawdler, flâneur, rambler, saunterer, walker, wanderer.

**strong** *adj* acute, aggressive, athletic, beefy, biting, bold, brave, brawny, bright, brilliant, burly, capable, clear, clear-cut, cogent, compelling, competent, concentrated, convincing, courageous, dazzling, dedicated, deep, deep-rooted, determined, distinct, drastic, durable, eager, effective, efficient, emphasised, excelling, extreme, fast-moving, fervent, fervid, fierce, firm, forceful, forcible, formidable, glaring, great, grievous, gross, hale, hard, hard-nosed, hard-wearing, hardy, heady, healthy, hearty, heavy-duty, Herculean, highly-flavoured, highly-seasoned, hot, intemperate, intense, intoxicating, keen, loud, lusty, marked, muscular, nappy, numerous, offensive, overpowering, persuasive, petrous, piquant, pithy, plucky, pollent, potent, powerful, pungent, pure, rank, redoubtable, reinforced, resilient, resolute, resourceful, robust, self-assertive, severe, sharp, sinewy, sound, spicy, stalwart, stark, staunch, steadfast, sthenic, stout, stouthearted, strapping, stressed, sturdy, substantial, telling, tenacious, thewy, tough, trenchant, undiluted, unmistakable, unseemly, unyielding, urgent, vehement, violent, virile, vivid, weighty, well-armed, well-built, well-established, well-founded, well-knit, well-protected, well-set, well-versed, zealous.

*antonyms* mild, weak.

**strong point** advantage, aptitude, asset, bag, bent, forte, gift, long suit, metier, speciality, specialty, strength, strong suit, talent, thing.

**strongarm** *adj* aggressive, bullying, coercive, forceful, intimidatory, oppressive, physical, terror, threatening, thuggish, violent.

*antonym* gentle.

**stronghold** *n* bastion, bulwark, castle, centre, citadel, fastness, fort, fortress, hedgehog, keep, redoubt, refuge.

**strong-minded** *adj* determined, firm, independent, iron-willed, resolute, steadfast, strong-willed, tenacious, unbending, uncompromising, unwavering.

*antonym* weak-willed.

**stroppy** *adj* awkward, bad-tempered, bloody-minded, cantankerous, difficult, obstreperous, perverse, quarrelsome, refractory, rowdy, unco-operative, unhelpful.

*antonyms* co-operative, sweet-tempered.

**structural** *adj* configurational, constructional, design, formational, organisational, tectonic.

**structure** *n* arrangement, building, compages, configuration, conformation, construction, contexture, design, edifice, erection, fabric, form, formation, make-up, organisation, pile, set-up.

*v* arrange, assemble, build, construct, design, form, organise, shape.

**struggle** *v* agonise, battle, compete, contend, fight, grapple, labour, scuffle, strain, strive, toil, work, wrestle.

*antonyms* give in, rest.

*n* agon, agony, battle, brush, clash, combat, conflict, contest, effort, encounter, exertion, grind, hostilities, labour, luctation, pains, scramble, skirmish, strife, toil, tussle, work.

*antonyms* ease, submission.

**strut** *v* brank, cock, parade, peacock, prance, stalk, swagger.

**stub** *n* butt, counterfoil, dog-end, doup, end, fag-end, remnant, snub, stump, tail, tail-end.

**stubborn** *adj* bull-headed, contumacious, cross-grained, difficult, dogged, dour, fixed, headstrong, inflexible, intractable, intransigent, mulish, obdurate, obstinate, opinionated, persistent, pertinacious, pig-headed, recalcitrant, refractory, rigid, self-willed, stiff, stiff-necked, tenacious, unbending, unmanageable, unshakable, unyielding, wilful.

*antonym* compliant.

**stubby** *adj* bristling, bristly, chunky, dumpy, knobbly, knubbly, knubby, nubbly, nubby, prickly, rough, short, squat, stocky, stubbly, stumpy, thickset.

*antonyms* long, tall, thin.

**stuck** *adj* baffled, beaten, cemented, fast, fastened, firm, fixed, glued, joined, nonplussed, stumped, stymied.

*antonym* loose.

**stuck on** crazy about, dotty about, enthusiastic about, infatuated with, keen on, mad on, nuts on, obsessed with, wild about.

*antonym* indifferent to.

**stuck-up** *adj* arrogant, big-headed, conceited, condescending, exclusive, haughty, high and mighty, hoity-toity, overweening, patronising, prideful, proud, snobbish, snooty, swollen-headed, toffee-nosed, uppish, uppity.

*antonym* humble.

**studded** *adj* bejewelled, bespangled, dotted, flecked, ornamented, scattered, set, spangled, speckled, spotted, sprinkled.

**student** *n* apprentice, bajan, bejant, bookman, chela, co-ed, collegianer, contemplator, disciple, fresher, freshman, learner, observer, pupil, scholar, seminarist, soph, sophomore, undergraduate, undergraduette.

**studied** *adj* calculated, conscious, deliberate, forced, intentional, over-elaborate, planned, premeditated, purposeful, unnatural, voulu, wilful.

*antonyms* natural, unplanned.

**studio** *n* atelier, school, workroom, workshop.

**studious** *adj* academic, assiduous, attentive, bookish, careful, diligent, eager, earnest, hard-working, heedful, intellectual, intent, meditative, reflective, scholarly, sedulous, serious, solicitous, thoughtful.

*antonym* lazy.

**study** *v* analyse, cogitate, con, consider, contemplate, cram, deliberate, dig, examine, investigate, learn, lucubrate, meditate, mug up, peruse, ponder, pore over, read, read up, research, scan, scrutinise, survey, swot.

*n* analysis, application, attention, cogitation, consideration, contemplation, cramming, critique, examination, inclination, inquiry, inspection, interest, investigation, learning, lessons, lucubration, memoir, monograph, prolusion, reading, report, research, reverie, review, scrutiny, survey, swotting, thesis, thought, zeal.

**stuff** *v* binge, bombast, compress, cram, crowd, fill, force, gobble, gorge, gormandise, guzzle, jam, load, overindulge, pack, pad, push, ram, sate, satiate, shove, squeeze, steeve, stodge, stow, trig, wedge.

*antonyms* nibble, unload.

*n* belongings, clobber, cloth, effects, equipment, essence, fabric, furniture, gear, goods, impedimenta, junk, kit, luggage, material, materials, materiel, matter, objects, paraphernalia, pith, possessions, provisions, quintessence, staple, substance, tackle, textile, things, trappings.

**stuffing** *n* bombast, farce, farcing, filler, force-meat, kapok, packing, quilting, wadding.

**stuffy** *adj* airless, close, conventional, deadly, dreary, dull, fetid, fogram, fogyish, frowsty, frowzy, fuggy, fusty, heavy, humourless, muggy, musty, old-fashioned, oppressive, poking, poky, pompous, priggish, prim, staid, stale, stifling, stilted, stodgy, strait-laced, suffocating, sultry, uninteresting, unventilated, Victorian.

*antonyms* airy, informal, interesting, modern.

**stultify** *v* benumb, blunt, dull, hebetate, invalidate, negate, nullify, numb, smother, stifle, stupefy, suppress, thwart.

*antonyms* prove, sharpen.

**stultifying** *adj* dulling, hebetant, hebetating, numbing, stupefying.

*antonym* electrifying.

**stumble** *v* blunder, fall, falter, flounder, fluff, hesitate, lurch, reel, slip, stagger, stammer, stutter, titubate, trip.

**stumble on** blunder upon, chance upon, come across, discover, encounter, find, happen upon, light upon.

**stumbling-block** *n* bar, barrier, crux, difficulty, hindrance, hurdle, impediment, obstacle, obstruction, pons asinorum, snag.

*antonym* boost.

**stump** *v* baffle, bamboozle, bewilder, clomp, clump, confound, confuse, defeat, dumbfound, flummox, foil, lumber, mystify, nonplus, outwit, perplex, plod, puzzle, stamp, stomp, stop, stymie, trudge.

*antonym* assist.

**stump up** contribute, cough up, donate, fork out, hand over, pay, pay out, pay up, shell out.

*antonym* receive.

**stumped** *adj* baffled, bamboozled, floored, flummoxed, nonplussed, perplexed, stuck, stymied.

**stumpy** *adj* chunky, dumpy, dwarf, dwarfish, heavy, short, squat, stocky, stubby, thick, thickset.

*antonyms* long, tall, thin.

**stun** *v* amaze, astonish, astound, bedeafen, bewilder, confound, confuse, daze, deafen, dumbfound, flabbergast, overcome, overpower, shock, stagger, stupefy.

**stung** *adj* angered, bitten, exasperated, goaded, hurt, incensed, irked, needled, nettled, peeved, piqued, resentful, roused, wounded.

*antonym* soothed.

**stunned** *adj* astounded, dazed, devastated, dumbfounded, flabbergasted, floored, numb, shocked, staggered, stupefied.

*antonym* indifferent.

**stunner** *n* beauty, charmer, dazzler, dish, dolly, eye-catcher, eyeful, femme fatale, good-looker, heart-throb, honey, knock-out, looker, lovely, peach, sensation, siren, smasher, stotter, wow.

*antonym* dog.

**stunning** *adj* beautiful, brilliant, dazing, dazzling, devastating, gorgeous, great, heavenly, impressive, lovely, marvellous, ravishing, remarkable, sensational, smashing, spectacular, stotting, striking, wonderful.

*antonyms* poor, ugly.

**stunt**[1] *n* act, campaign, deed, enterprise, exploit, feat, feature, gest(e), performance, tour de force, trick, turn.

**stunt**[2] *v* arrest, check, dwarf, hamper, hinder, impede, restrict, slow, stop.

*antonym* promote.

**stunted** *adj* diminutive, dwarfed, dwarfish, little, runtish, runty, small, tiny, undersized.

*antonyms* large, sturdy.

**stupefaction** *n* amaze, amazement, astonishment, awe, bafflement, bewilderment, wonder, wonderment.

**stupefy** *v* amaze, astound, baffle, benumb, bewilder, confound, daze, drowse, dumbfound, hocus, numb, shock, stagger, stun.

**stupendous** *adj* amazing, astounding, breathtaking, colossal, enormous, fabulous, fantastic, gigantic, huge, marvellous, mind-blowing, mind-boggling, overwhelming, phenomenal, prodigious, staggering, stunning, superb, tremendous, vast, wonderful.

*antonym* unimpressive.

**stupid** *adj* anserine, asinine, beef-brained, beef-witted, blockish, Boeotian, boobyish, boring, bovine, brainless, chuckle-headed, clueless, crackbrained, cretinous, cuckoo, damfool, dazed, deficient, dense, dilly, dim, doltish, donnart, donnered, dopey, dovie, dozy, drippy, dull, dumb, fat-witted, foolish, fozy, futile, gaumless, glaikit, gormless, groggy, gullible, half-baked, half-witted, hammer-headed, idiotic, ill-advised, imbecilic, inane, indiscreet, insensate, insensible, insulse, irrelevant, irresponsible, laughable, looby, ludicrous, lumpen, lurdan, meaningless, mindless, moronic, naïve, nonsensical, obtuse, opaque, pointless, puerile, punch-drunk, rash, semiconscious, senseless, short-sighted, simple, simple-minded, slow, slow-witted, sluggish, stolid, stunned, stupefied, thick, thick-headed, thick-witted, trivial, unintelligent, unthinking, vacuous, vapid, witless, wooden-headed.

*antonyms* alert, clever.

**stupidity** *n* absurdity, asininity, betise, brainlessness, crassitude, crassness, denseness, dimness, dopiness, doziness, dullness, dumbness, duncery, fatuity, fatuousness, feeble-mindedness, folly, foolhardiness, foolishness, futility, goosery, idiocy, imbecility, impracticality, inaneness, inanity, indiscretion, ineptitude, insipience, irresponsibility, ludicrousness, lunacy, madness, naïvete, naivety, obtuseness, oscitancy, pointlessness, puerility, rashness, senselessness, silliness, simplicity, slowness, thick-headedness, thickness, vapidity.

*antonyms* alertness, cleverness.

**stupor** *n* coma, daze, inertia, insensibility, kef, lethargy, numbness, stupefaction, torpor, trance, unconsciousness, wonder.

*antonym* alertness.

**sturdy** *adj* athletic, brawny, determined, durable, firm, flourishing, hardy, hearty, husky, lusty, muscular, obstinate, powerful, resolute, robust, secure, solid, stalwart, staunch, steadfast, stout, strong, substantial, vigorous, well-built, well-made.

*antonyms* decrepit, puny.

**stutter** *v* falter, hesitate, mumble, splutter, stammer, stumble.

**style** *n* affluence, appearance, approach, bon ton, category, chic, comfort, cosmopolitanism, custom, cut, dash, design, diction, dressiness, dress-sense, ease, elan, elegance, expression, fashion, fashionableness, flair, flamboyance, form, genre, grace, grandeur, hand, haut ton, kind, luxury, manner, method, mode, panache, pattern, phraseology, phrasing, pizzazz, polish, rage, refinement, savoir-faire, smartness, sophistication, sort, spirit, strain, stylishness, taste, technique, tenor, tone, treatment, trend, type, urbanity, variety, vein, vogue, way, wording.

*antonym* inelegance.

*v* adapt, address, arrange, call, christen, create, cut, denominate, design, designate, dress, dub, entitle, fashion, label, name, shape, tailor, term, title.

**stylish** *adj* a la mode, chic, chichi, classy, dapper, dressy, fashionable, groovy, in vogue, modish, natty, polished, smart, snappy, snazzy, trendy, urbane, voguish.

*antonym* unstylish.

**stylus** *n* gnomon, graphium, graver, hand, index, needle, pen, pointer, probe, style.

**stymie** *v* baffle, balk, bamboozle, confound, defeat, flummox, foil, frustrate, hinder, mystify, nonplus, puzzle, snooker, stump, thwart.

*antonym* assist.

**suave** *adj* affable, agreeable, bland, charming, civilised, courteous, diplomatic, gracious, obliging, pleasing, polite, smooth, smooth-tongued, soft-spoken, sophisticated, unctuous, urbane, worldly.

*antonym* unsophisticated.

**suavity** *n* blandness, charm, sophistication, unctuosity, unctuousness, urbanity.

*antonym* coarseness.

**subaquatic** *adj* demersal, subaqua, subaqueous, submarine, submersed, undersea, underwater.

**subconscious** *adj* hidden, inner, innermost, intuitive, latent, repressed, subliminal, suppressed, unconscious.

*antonym* conscious.

*n* id, super-ego, unconscious, underself.

**subdue** *v* allay, break, check, conquer, control, crush, damp, dampen, daunt, defeat, discipline, humble, master, mellow, moderate, overcome, overpower, overrun, quell, quieten, reduce, repress, soften, soft-pedal, subact, subject, suppress, tame, trample, vanquish.

*antonym* arouse.

**subdued** *adj* abated, chastened, crestfallen, dejected, dim, downcast, grave, hushed, low-key, muted, quiet, repentant, repressed, restrained, sad, serious, shaded, sober, soft, solemn, sombre, subfusc, subtle, unobtrusive.

*antonyms* aroused, lively.

**subject** *n* affair, business, case, chapter, citizen, client, dependant, ground, issue, liegeman, matter, mind, national, object, participant, patient, point, question, subordinate, substance, theme, topic, vassal, victim.

*antonym* master.

*adj* answerable, captive, cognisable, conditional, contingent, dependent, disposed, enslaved, exposed, heteronomous, inferior, liable, obedient, open, prone, satellite, subjugated, submissive, subordinate, subservient, susceptible, vulnerable.

*antonyms* free, insusceptible, superior.

*v* expose, lay open, subdue, submit, subordinate, treat.

**subjection** *n* bondage, captivity, chains, crushing, defeat, domination, enslavement, mastery, oppression, quelling, servitude, shackles, slavery, subduing, subjugation, thraldom, thrall, vassalage.

**subjective** biased, emotional, idiosyncratic, individual, instinctive, introspective, intuitive, personal, prejudiced.

*antonym* objective.

**subjugate** *v* conquer, crush, defeat, enslave, enthrall, master, overcome, overpower, overthrow, quell, reduce, subdue, suppress, tame, thrall, vanquish.

*antonym* free.

**sublimate** *v* channel, divert, elevate, exalt, heighten, purify, redirect, refine, sublime, transfer, transmute, turn.

*antonym* let out.

**sublime** *adj* Dantean, Dantesque, elevated, eminent, empyreal, empyrean, exalted, glorious, grand, great, high, imposing, lofty, magnificent, majestic, noble, transcendent.

*antonym* lowly.

**submerge** *v* deluge, demerge, dip, drown, duck, dunk, engulf, flood, immerse, implunge, inundate, overflow, overwhelm, plunge, sink, submerse, swamp.

*antonym* surface.

**submerged** *adj* concealed, demersal, demersed, drowned, hidden, immersed, inundated, obscured, subaquatic, subaqueous, submarine, submersed, sunk, sunken, swamped, undersea, underwater, unseen.

**submission** *n* acquiescence, argument, assent, capitulation, compliance, contention, deference, docility, entry, meekness, obedience, passivity, presentation, proposal, resignation, resignedness, submissiveness, submitting, suggestion, surrender, tendering, tractability, yielding.

*antonym* intractability.

**submissive** *adj* abject, accommodating, acquiescent, amenable, biddable, bootlicking, complaisant, compliant, deferential, docile, dutiful, humble, ingratiating, malleable, meek, obedient, obeisant, obsequious, passive, patient, pliant, resigned, subdued, subservient, supine, tractable, uncomplaining, unresisting, yielding.

*antonym* intractable.

**submit** *v* accede, acquiesce, advance, agree, argue, assert, bend, bow, capitulate, claim, commit, comply, contend, defer, endure, knuckle under, move, present, proffer, propose, propound, put, refer, state, stoop, succumb, suggest, surrender, table, tender, tolerate, volunteer, yield.

*antonym* struggle.

**subnormal** *adj* cretinous, ESN, feeble-minded, imbecilic, inferior, low, moronic, retarded, slow, unteachable.

*antonym* gifted.

**subordinate** *adj* ancillary, auxiliary, dependent, inferior, junior, lesser, lower, menial, minor, secondary, servient, subject, subservient, subsidiary, supplementary.

*antonym* superior.

*n* adjunct, aide, assistant, attendant, dependant, inferior, junior, second, second banana, stooge, sub, subaltern, underdog, underling, underman, under-workman, weakling.

*antonym* superior.

**subordination** *n* inferiority, servitude, subjection, submission, subservience.

*antonym* superiority.

**subscribe** *v* acquiesce, advocate, agree, approve, consent, contribute, cough up, countenance, donate, endorse, fork out, give, offer, pledge, promise, shell out, support.

**subscription** *n* abonnement, contribution, donation, dues, fee, gift, offering, payment.

**subsequent** *adj* after, consequent, consequential, ensuing, following, later, postliminary, postliminous, resulting, succeeding.

*antonym* previous.

**subsequently** *adv* after, afterwards, consequently, later.

*antonym* previously.

**subservient** *adj* abject, accessory, ancillary, auxiliary, bootlicking, conducive, cringing, deferential, dough-faced, helpful, inferior, instrumental, obsequious, serviceable, servile, slavish, subject, submissive, subordinate, subsidiary, sycophantic, truckling, useful.

*antonyms* domineering, rebellious, unhelpful.

**subside** *v* abate, collapse, decline, decrease, descend, diminish, drop, dwindle, ease, ebb, fall, lessen, lower, moderate, quieten, recede, settle, sink, slacken, slake, wane.

*antonym* increase.

**subsidence** *n* abatement, decline, decrease, de-escalation, descent, detumescence, diminution, ebb, lessening, settlement, settling, sinking, slackening.

*antonym* increase.

**subsidiary** *adj* adjective, aiding, ancillary, assistant, auxiliary, branch, contributory, co-operative, helpful, lesser, minor, secondary, serviceable, subordinate, subservient, succursal, supplemental, supplementary, useful.

*antonym* chief.

*n* affiliate, branch, division, offshoot, part, section.

**subsidise** *v* aid, back, finance, fund, promote, sponsor, support, underwrite.

**subsidy** *n* aid, allowance, assistance, backing, contribution, finance, grant, help, sponsorship, subvention, support.

**subsist** v continue, endure, exist, hold out, inhere, last, live, remain, survive.

**subsistence** n aliment, existence, food, keep, livelihood, living, maintenance, nourishment, prog, provision, rations, support, survival, sustenance, upkeep, victuals.

**substance** n actuality, affluence, assets, body, burden, concreteness, consistence, element, entity, essence, estate, fabric, force, foundation, gist, gravamen, ground, hypostasis, import, material, matter, meaning, means, nitty-gritty, pith, property, reality, resources, significance, solidity, stuff, subject, subject-matter, texture, theme, wealth.

**substandard** adj damaged, imperfect, inadequate, inferior, poor, second-rate, shoddy, tawdry, unacceptable.

antonym first-rate.

**substantial** adj actual, ample, big, bulky, considerable, corporeal, durable, enduring, essential, existent, firm, full-bodied, generous, goodly, hefty, important, large, massive, material, positive, real, significant, sizable, solid, sound, stout, strong, sturdy, tidy, true, valid, weighty, well-built, worthwhile.

antonyms insignificant, small.

**substantially** adv essentially, largely, materially, significantly, to all intents and purposes.

antonym slightly.

**substantiate** v affirm, authenticate, confirm, corroborate, embody, establish, prove, support, validate, verify.

antonym disprove.

**substitute** v change, commute, exchange, interchange, replace, subrogate, swap, switch.

n agent, alternate, depute, deputy, equivalent, ersatz, locum, locum tenens, makeshift, proxy, relief, replacement, replacer, reserve, stand-by, stop-gap, sub, succedaneum, supply, surrogate, temp, vicar.

adj acting, additional, alternative, ersatz, proxy, replacement, reserve, second, surrogate, temporary, vicarious.

**substitute for** act for, cover for, deputise, double for, fill in for, relieve, stand in for, sub.

**substitution** n change, exchange, interchange, replacement, swap, swapping, switch, switching.

**subterfuge** n artifice, deception, deviousness, dodge, duplicity, evasion, excuse, expedient, machination, manoeuvre, ploy, pretence, pretext, quibble, ruse, scheme, shift, stall, stratagem, trick.

antonyms honesty, openness.

**subtle** adj artful, astute, crafty, cunning, deep, delicate, designing, devious, discriminating, elusive, faint, fine-drawn, fine-spun, impalpable, implied, indirect, ingenious, insinuated, intriguing, keen, Machiavellian, nice, obstruse, over-refined, penetrating, profound, rarefied, refined, scheming, shrewd, slight, sly, sophisticated, tenuous, understated, wily.

antonyms open, unsubtle.

**subtlety** n acumen, acuteness, artfulness, astuteness, cleverness, craftiness, cunning, delicacy, deviousness, discernment, discrimination, finesse, guile, intricacy, nicety, openness, penetration, refinement, sagacity, skill, slyness, sophistication, unsubtlety, wiliness.

**subtract** v debit, deduct, detract, diminish, remove, withdraw.

antonyms add, add to.

**suburbs** n banlieue, commuter belt, dormitory, environs, exurbia, faubourg, neighbourhood, outskirts, precincts, purlieus, stockbroker belt, suburbia, villadom.

antonyms centre, heart.

**subversive** adj destructive, disruptive, incendiary, inflammatory, insurrectionary, overthrowing, perversive, riotous, seditious, treasonous, underground, undermining.

antonym loyal.

n deviationist, dissident, fifth columnist, freedom fighter, insurrectionary, quisling, saboteur, seditionary, seditionist, terrorist, traitor.

**subvert** v confound, contaminate, corrupt, debase, demolish, demoralise, deprave, destroy, disrupt, invalidate, overturn, pervert, poison, raze, ruin, sabotage, undermine, upset, vitiate, wreck.

antonyms boost, uphold.

**subway** n metro, tube, underground.

**succeed** v arrive, ensue, fadge, flourish, follow, make good, make it, prosper, result, supervene, thrive, triumph, work.

antonyms fail, precede.

**succeed to** accede, come into, enter upon, inherit, replace, supersede, take over.

antonyms abdicate, precede.

**succeeding** adj coming, ensuing, following, later, next, subsequent, successive, to come.

antonym previous.

**success** n ascendancy, bestseller, celebrity, eminence, fame, fortune, happiness, hit, luck, prosperity, sensation, somebody, star, triumph, VIP, well-doing, winner.

antonym failure.

**successful** adj acknowledged, bestselling, booming, efficacious, favourable, flourishing, fortunate, fruitful, lucky, lucrative, moneymaking, paying, profitable, prosperous, rewarding, satisfactory, satisfying, soaraway, thriven, thriving, top, unbeaten, victorious, wealthy, well-doing.

antonym unsuccessful.

**successfully** adv beautifully, famously, fine, great, swimmingly, victoriously, well.

antonym unsuccessfully.

**succession** n accession, assumption, chain, concatenation, continuation, course, cycle, descendants, descent, elevation, flow, inheritance, line, lineage, order, procession, progression, race, run, sequence, series, train.

**successive** adj consecutive, following, in succession, sequent, succeeding.

**succinct** *adj* brief, compact, compendious, concise, condensed, gnomic, laconic, pithy, short, summary, terse.

*antonym* wordy.

**succour** *v* aid, assist, befriend, comfort, encourage, foster, help, help out, nurse, relieve, support.

*antonym* undermine.

*n* aid, assistance, comfort, help, helping hand, ministrations, relief, support.

**succulent** *adj* fleshy, juicy, luscious, lush, mellow, moist, mouthwatering, rich, sappy.

*antonym* dry.

**succumb** *v* capitulate, collapse, deteriorate, die, fall, give in, knuckle under, submit, surrender, yield.

*antonym* overcome.

**suck** *v* absorb, drain, draw in, extract, imbibe.

**sucker** *n* butt, cat's-paw, dupe, fool, mark, mug, patsy, pushover, sap, stooge, victim.

**sucking-up** *n* arse-licking, bootlicking, currying favour, fawning, flattering, ingratiating, toadying, truckling.

**sudden** *adj* abrupt, hasty, hurried, impulsive, prompt, quick, rapid, rash, snap, startling, subitaneous, swift, unexpected, unforeseen, unusual.

*antonym* slow.

**suddenness** *n* abruptness, haste, hastiness, hurriedness, impulsiveness.

*antonym* slowness.

**sue** *v* apply, beg, beseech, charge, entreat, indict, petition, plead, prosecute, solicit, summon, supplicate.

**suffer** *v* ache, agonise, allow, bear, brook, deteriorate, endure, experience, feel, grieve, hurt, let, permit, sorrow, support, sustain, tolerate, undergo.

**suffering** *n* ache, affliction, agony, anguish, discomfort, distress, hardship, martyrdom, misery, ordeal, pain, pangs, torment, torture.

**suffice** *v* answer, content, do, measure up, satisfy, serve.

**sufficiency** *n* adequacy, adequateness, competence, conceit, enough, enow, plenty, quantum suffice, satiety, sufficience.

*antonym* insufficiency.

**sufficient** *adj* adequate, competent, effective, enough, satisfactory, sufficing, well-off, well-to-do.

*antonyms* insufficient, poor.

**suffocate** *v* asphyxiate, choke, smother, stifle, strangle, throttle.

**suffuse** *v* bathe, colour, cover, flood, imbue, infuse, mantle, permeate, pervade, redden, steep, transfuse.

**suggest** *v* advise, advocate, connote, evoke, hint, imply, indicate, inkle, innuendo, insinuate, intimate, move, propose, recommend.

*antonyms* demonstrate, order.

**suggestion** *n* breath, hint, incitement, indication, innuendo, insinuation, intimation, motion, plan, proposal, proposition, recommendation, suspicion, temptation, trace, whisper.

*antonyms* demonstration, order.

**suggestive** *adj* bawdy, blue, evocative, expressive, immodest, improper, indecent, indelicate, indicative, insinuating, meaning, off-colour, page-three, provocative, prurient, racy, redolent, reminiscent, ribald, risque, rude, smutty, spicy, titillating, unseemly.

*antonyms* clean, unevocative.

**suicide** *n* felo de se, hara-kiri, kamikaze, self-destruction, self-immolation, self-murder, self-slaughter, suttee.

**suit** *v* accommodate, adapt, adjust, agree, answer, become, befit, correspond, do, fashion, fit, gee, gratify, harmonise, match, modify, please, proportion, satisfy, tailor, tally.

*antonyms* clash, displease.

*n* action, addresses, appeal, attentions, case, cause, clothing, costume, courtship, dress, ensemble, entreaty, get-up, habit, invocation, kind, lawsuit, outfit, petition, prayer, proceeding, prosecution, request, rig-out, series, trial, type.

**suitability** *n* appositeness, appropriateness, aptness, fitness, fittingness, opportuneness, rightness, timeliness.

*antonym* unsuitability.

**suitable** *adj* acceptable, accordant, adequate, applicable, apposite, appropriate, apt, becoming, befitting, competent, conformable, congenial, congruent, consonant, convenient, correspondent, due, fit, fitting, opportune, pertinent, proper, relevant, right, satisfactory, seemly, square, suited, well-becoming, well-beseeming.

*antonym* unsuitable.

**suitably** *adv* acceptably, accordingly, appropriately, fitly, fittingly, properly, quite.

*antonym* unsuitably.

**suite** *n* apartment, attendants, collection, entourage, escort, followers, furniture, household, retainers, retinue, rooms, sequence, series, servants, set, train.

**suitor** *n* admirer, beau, follower, pretendant, swain, wooer, young man.

**sulk** *v* boody, brood, grouch, grump, mope, pet, pout.

**sulky** *adj* aloof, churlish, cross, disgruntled, grouty, ill-humoured, moody, morose, perverse, pettish, petulant, put out, resentful, sullen.

*antonym* cheerful.

**sullen** *adj* baleful, brooding, cheerless, cross, dark, dismal, dull, farouche, gloomy, glowering, glum, heavy, lumpish, malignant, moody, morose, obstinate, perverse, silent, sombre, sour, stubborn, sulky, surly, unsociable.

*antonym* cheerful.

**sullenness** *n* brooding, glowering, glumness, heaviness, moodiness, moroseness, sourness, sulkiness, surliness.

*antonym* cheerfulness.

**sully** v befoul, besmirch, blemish, contaminate, darken, defile, dirty, disgrace, dishonour, distain, mar, pollute, spoil, spot, stain, taint, tarnish.

*antonyms* cleanse, honour.

**sultry** *adj* close, come-hither, erotic, hot, humid, indecent, lurid, muggy, oppressive, passionate, provocative, seductive, sensual, sexy, sticky, stifling, stuffy, sweltering, torrid, voluptuous.

*antonyms* cold, cool.

**sum** *n* aggregate, amount, completion, culmination, entirety, height, quantity, reckoning, result, score, substance, sum total, summary, tally, total, totality, whole.

**sum up** close, conclude, perorate, precis, recapitulate, review, summarise.

**summarily** *adv* abruptly, arbitrarily, expeditiously, forthwith, hastily, immediately, peremptorily, promptly, speedily, swiftly.

**summarise** v abbreviate, abridge, condense, encapsulate, epitomise, outline, precis, review, shorten, sum up.

*antonym* expand (on).

**summary** *n* abridgement, abstract, compendium, digest, epitome, essence, extract, outline, precis, recapitulation, resume, review, rundown, summation, summing-up, synopsis.

*adj* arbitrary, brief, compact, compendious, concise, condensed, cursory, expeditious, hasty, laconic, perfunctory, pithy, short, succinct.

*antonym* lengthy.

**summer-house** *n* belvedere, gazebo, pavilion.

**summit** *n* acme, apex, apogee, crown, culmination, head, height, high noon, peak, pinnacle, point, top, vertex, zenith.

*antonyms* bottom, nadir.

**summon** v accite, arouse, assemble, beckon, bid, call, cite, convene, convoke, gather, hist, invite, invoke, mobilise, muster, preconise, rally, rouse.

*antonym* dismiss.

**sumptuous** *adj* costly, dear, expensive, extravagant, gorgeous, grand, lavish, luxurious, magnificent, opulent, plush, posh, princely, rich, ritzy, splendid, superb.

*antonym* mean.

**sun** *n* daystar, star, sun-disc, sunlight, sunshine.

v bake, bask, brown, insolate, sunbathe, tan.

**sunbathe** v bake, bask, brown, insolate, take the sun, tan.

**sunburnt** *adj* blistered, bronzed, brown, burnt, peeling, red, ruddy, scarlet, tanned, weather-beaten.

*antonym* pale.

**sunder** v chop, cleave, cut, dissever, dissunder, divide, part, separate, sever, split.

*antonym* join.

**sundry** *adj* a few, assorted, different, divers, miscellaneous, separate, several, some, varied, various.

**sunk** *adj* done for, doomed, finished, lost, ruined, up the creek, up the spout.

**sunken** *adj* buried, concave, depressed, drawn, emaciated, gaunt, haggard, hollow, hollowed, immersed, lower, recessed, submerged.

**sunless** *adj* bleak, cheerless, cloudy, dark, depressing, dismal, dreary, gloomy, grey, hazy, overcast, sombre.

*antonym* sunny.

**sunny** *adj* beaming, blithe, bright, brilliant, buoyant, cheerful, cheery, clear, cloudless, fine, genial, happy, joyful, light-hearted, luminous, optimistic, pleasant, radiant, smiling, summery, sun-bright, sunlit, sunshiny.

*antonym* gloomy.

**sunrise** *n* aurora, cock-crow, crack of dawn, dawn, daybreak, daylight, dayspring, sun-up.

**sunset** *n* crepuscule, dusk, evening, eventide, gloaming, nightfall, sundown, twilight.

**super** *adj* excellent, glorious, incomparable, magnificent, marvellous, matchless, outstanding, peerless, sensational, smashing, superb, terrific, top-notch, wizard, wonderful.

*antonym* poor.

**superannuated** *adj* aged, antiquated, decrepit, fogram, moribund, obsolete, old, past it, pensioned off, put out to grass, retired, senile, superannuate.

*antonym* young.

**superb** *adj* admirable, breathtaking, choice, clipping, excellent, exquisite, fine, first-rate, gorgeous, grand, magnificent, marvellous, splendid, superior, unrivalled.

*antonym* poor.

**supercilious** *adj* arrogant, condescending, contemptuous, disdainful, haughty, highty-tighty, hoity-toity, imperious, insolent, lofty, lordly, overbearing, patronising, proud, scornful, snooty, snotty, snouty, stuck-up, toffee-nosed, uppish, uppity, upstage, vainglorious.

*antonym* humble.

**superficial** *adj* apparent, casual, cosmetic, cursory, desultory, empty, empty-headed, evident, exterior, external, frivolous, hasty, hurried, lightweight, nodding, ostensible, outward, passing, perfunctory, peripheral, seeming, shallow, silly, sketchy, skin-deep, slapdash, slight, surface, trivial, unanalytical, unreflective.

*antonym* detailed.

**superficially** *adv* apparently, externally, ostensibly, seemingly.

*antonym* in depth.

**superfluity** *n* excess, exuberance, glut, perissology, pleonasm, plethora, postiche, redundancy, superabundance, surfeit, surplus.

*antonym* lack.

**superfluous** *adj* de trop, excess, excessive, extra, needless, otiose, pleonastic(al), postiche, redundant, remaining, residuary, spare, superabundant, supererogatory, supernumerary, surplus, uncalled-for, unnecessary, unneeded, unneedful, unwanted.

*antonym* necessary.

**superhuman** *adj* divine, great, herculean, heroic, immense, paranormal, phenomenal, preternatural, prodigious, stupendous, supernatural, valiant.

*antonyms* average, ordinary.

**superintend** *v* administer, control, direct, guide, inspect, manage, overlook, oversee, run, steer, supervise.

**superintendence** *n* administration, care, charge, control, direction, government, guidance, inspection, management, supervision, surveillance.

**superintendent** *n* administrator, chief, conductor, controller, curator, director, gaffer, governor, inspector, manager, overseer, supervisor.

**superior** *adj* admirable, airy, better, choice, condescending, de luxe, disdainful, distinguished, excellent, exceptional, exclusive, fine, first-class, first-rate, good, grander, greater, haughty, high-class, higher, highty-tighty, hoity-toity, lofty, lordly, par excellence, patronising, predominant, preferred, pretentious, prevailing, respectable, snobbish, snooty, snotty, snouty, stuck-up, supercilious, superordinate, surpassing, top-flight, top-notch, transcendent, unrivalled, upper, uppish, uppity, upstage, worthy.

*antonyms* humble, inferior.

*n* boss, chief, director, foreman, gaffer, higher-up, manager, principal, senior, supervisor.

*antonyms* inferior, junior.

**superiority** *n* advantage, ascendancy, edge, excellence, lead, predominance, pre-eminence, preponderance, prevalence, supremacy, vis major.

*antonym* inferiority.

**superlative** *adj* consummate, crack, excellent, greatest, highest, magnificent, matchless, nonpareil, outstanding, peerless, supreme, surpassing, transcendent, unbeatable, unbeaten, unparalleled, unrivalled, unsurpassed.

*antonym* poor.

**superman** *n* colossus, giant, Übermensch.

**supernatural** *adj* abnormal, dark, ghostly, hidden, hyperphysical, metaphysical, miraculous, mysterious, mystic, occult, paranormal, phantom, preternatural, psychic, spectral, spiritual, superlunary, supersensible, supersensory, uncanny, unearthly, unnatural.

*antonym* natural.

**supernumerary** *adj* excess, excessive, extra, extraordinary, redundant, spare, superfluous, surplus.

*antonym* necessary.

**supersede** *v* annul, displace, oust, overrule, remove, replace, succeed, supplant, supplement, suspend, usurp.

**superstition** *n* Aberglaube, delusion, fable, fallacy, illusion, myth, old wives' tale, voodooism.

**superstitious** *adj* delusive, fallacious, false, fetishistic, groundless, illusory, voodooistic.

**supervise** *v* administer, conduct, control, direct, general, handle, inspect, keep tabs on, manage, oversee, preside over, run, superintend.

**supervision** *n* administration, auspices, care, charge, control, direction, guidance, instruction, leading-strings, management, oversight, stewardship, superintendence, surveillance.

**supervisor** *n* administrator, boss, chief, foreman, gaffer, inspector, manager, overseer, steward, superintendent.

**supervisory** *adj* administrative, directorial, executive, managerial, overseeing, superintendent.

**supine** *adj* apathetic, bored, careless, flat, heedless, horizontal, idle, inactive, incurious, indifferent, indolent, inert, languid, lazy, lethargic, listless, negligent, passive, prostrate, recumbent, resigned, slothful, sluggish, spineless, spiritless, torpid, uninterested, unresisting.

*antonyms* alert, upright.

**supplant** *v* displace, dispossess, oust, overthrow, remove, replace, supersede, topple, undermine, unseat.

**supple** *adj* bending, double-jointed, elastic, flexible, limber, lithe, loose-limbed, plastic, pliable, pliant, whippy, willowish, willowy.

*antonym* rigid.

**supplement** *n* addendum, addition, appendix, codicil, complement, extra, insert, postscript, pull-out, rider, sequel, supplemental, supplementary, suppletion.

*v* add, add to, augment, complement, eke, eke out, extend, fill up, reinforce, supply, top up.

*antonym* deplete.

**supplementary** *adj* accompanying, additional, ancillary, auxiliary, complementary, extra, secondary, supplemental, suppletive, suppletory.

*antonym* core.

**suppliant** *adj* begging, beseeching, craving, entreating, imploring, importunate, supplicating.

*n* applicant, petitioner, pleader, postulant, suitor, supplicant.

**supplication** *n* appeal, entreaty, invocation, orison, petition, plea, pleading, prayer, request, rogation, solicitation, suit, supplicat.

**supplicatory** *adj* begging, beseeching, imploring, imprecatory, petitioning, precative, precatory, supplicating.

**supplier** *n* dealer, hawker, Italian warehouseman, pedlar, provider, purveyor, retailer, seller, shop-keeper, sutler, vendor, vivandier, vivandière, wholesaler.

**supplies** *n* equipment, food, foodstuffs, materials, materiel, necessities, provender, provisions, rations, stores, victuals, vittles.

**supply** *v* afford, contribute, endow, equip, fill, furnish, give, grant, minister, outfit, produce, provide, purvey, replenish, satisfy, stock, store, victual, yield.

*antonym* take.

*n* cache, fund, hoard, materials, necessities, provender, provisions, quantity, rations, reserve, reservoir, service, source, stake, stock, stockpile, store, stores.

*antonym* lack.

**support** *v* adminiculate, advocate, aid, appui, appuy, assist, authenticate, back, bear, bolster, brace, brook, buttress, carry, champion, cherish, confirm, corroborate, countenance, crutch, defend, document, endorse, endure, finance, foster, fund, help, hold, keep, maintain, nourish, promote, prop, rally round, reinforce, second, stand (for), stay, stomach, strengthen, strut, submit, subsidise, substantiate, succour, suffer, sustain, take (someone's) part, thole, tolerate, underpin, underwrite, uphold, verify.

*antonyms* contradict, oppose.

*n* abutment, adminicle, aid, aidance, approval, appui, assistance, back, backbone, backer, backing, backstays, backstop, blessing, brace, championship, comfort, comforter, crutch, encouragement, foundation, friendship, fulcrum, furtherance, help, jockstrap, keep, lining, livelihood, loper, loyalty, mainstay, maintenance, patronage, pillar, post, prop, protection, relief, second, sheet-anchor, shore, stanchion, stay, stiffener, subsistence, succour, supporter, supportment, supporture, sustenanace, sustenance, underpinning, upkeep.

*antonym* opposition.

**supporter** *n* adherent, advocate, ally, apologist, bottle-holder, champion, co-worker, defender, fan, follower, friend, heeler, helper, patron, seconder, sponsor, upholder, well-wisher.

*antonym* opponent.

**supportive** *adj* attentive, caring, encouraging, helpful, reassuring, sympathetic, understanding.

*antonym* discouraging.

**suppose** *v* assume, believe, calculate, conceive, conclude, conjecture, consider, expect, fancy, guess, hypothesise, hypothetise, imagine, infer, judge, opine, posit, postulate, presume, presuppose, pretend, surmise, think.

*antonym* know.

**supposed** *adj* accepted, alleged, assumed, conjectured, hypothetical, imagined, presumed, presupposed, professed, putative, reported, reputed, rumoured.

*antonym* known.

**supposed to** expected to, intended to, meant to, obliged to, required to.

**supposedly** *adv* allegedly, assumedly, avowedly, hypothetically, ostensibly, presumably, professedly, purportedly, theoretically.

*antonym* really.

**supposition** *n* assumption, conjecture, doubt, guess, guesstimate, guesswork, hypothesis, idea, notion, opinion, postulate, presumption, speculation, surmise, theory.

*antonym* knowledge.

**suppress** *v* censor, check, conceal, conquer, contain, crush, extinguish, muffle, muzzle, overpower, overthrow, quash, quell, repress, restrain, silence, smother, snuff out, squelch, stamp out, stifle, stop, strangle, subdue, submerge, vote down, withhold.

*antonyms* encourage, incite.

**suppression** *n* censorship, check, clampdown, crackdown, crushing, dissolution, elimination, extinction, inhibition, prohibition, quashing, quelling, smothering, termination.

*antonyms* encouragement, incitement.

**suppurate** *v* discharge, fester, gather, matter, maturate, ooze, weep.

**suppuration** *n* diapyesis, festering, mattering, pus, pussiness.

**supremacy** *n* ascendancy, dominance, domination, dominion, hegemony, lordship, mastery, paramountcy, predominance, pre-eminence, primacy, sovereignty, sway.

**supreme** *adj* cardinal, chief, consummate, crowning, culminating, extreme, final, first, foremost, greatest, head, highest, incomparable, leading, matchless, nonpareil, paramount, peerless, predominant, pre-eminent, prevailing, prime, principal, second-to-none, sovereign, superlative, surpassing, top, transcendent, ultimate, unbeatable, unbeaten, unsurpassed, utmost, world-beating.

*antonyms* lowly, poor, slight.

**sure** *adj* accurate, assured, banker, bound, certain, clear, confident, convinced, decided, definite, dependable, effective, fast, firm, fixed, foolproof, guaranteed, honest, indisputable, ineluctable, inescapable, inevitable, infallible, irrevocable, persuaded, positive, precise, reliable, safe, satisfied, secure, solid, stable, steadfast, steady, sure-fire, trustworthy, trusty, undeniable, undoubted, unerring, unfailing, unmistakable, unswerving, unwavering.

*antonyms* doubtful, unsure.

**surely** *adv* assuredly, certainly, confidently, definitely, doubtlessly, firmly, indubitably, inevitably, inexorably, safely, undoubtedly, unquestionably.

**surety** *n* bail, bond, bondsman, certainty, deposit, guarantee, guarantor, hostage, indemnity, insurance, mortgagor, pledge, safety, security, sponsor, warrant, warranty.

**surface** *n* covering, day, exterior, façade, face, facet, grass, outside, plane, side, skin, superficies, top, veneer, working-surface, worktop.

*antonym* interior.

*adj* apparent, exterior, external, outer, outside, outward, superficial.

*antonym* interior.

*v* appear, come to light, emerge, materialise, rise, transpire.

*antonyms* disappear, sink.

**surfeit** *n* bellyful, excess, glut, overindulgence, plethora, satiety, superabundance, superfluity.

*antonym* lack.

*v* cram, fill, glut, gorge, overcloy, overfeed, overfill, satiate, stuff.

**surge** *v* billow, eddy, gush, heave, rise, roll, rush, seethe, swell, swirl, tower, undulate.

*n* access, billow, breaker, efflux, flood, flow, gurgitation, gush, intensification, outpouring, roller, rush, swell, uprush, upsurge, wave.

**surly** *adj* bearish, brusque, chuffy, churlish, crabbed, cross, crusty, curmudgeonly, grouchy, gruff, grum, gurly, ill-natured, morose, perverse, sulky, sullen, testy, uncivil, ungracious.

*antonym* pleasant.

**surmise** *v* assume, conclude, conjecture, consider, deduce, fancy, guess, imagine, infer, opine, presume, speculate, suppose, suspect.

*antonym* know.

*n* assumption, conclusion, conjecture, deduction, guess, hypothesis, idea, inference, notion, opinion, possibility, presumption, speculation, supposition, suspicion, thought.

*antonym* certainty.

**surmount** *v* conquer, exceed, get over, master, overcome, surpass, triumph over, vanquish.

**surpass** *v* beat, best, ding, eclipse, exceed, excel, outdo, outshine, outstrip, override, overshadow, surmount, top, tower above, transcend.

**surpassing** *adj* exceptional, extraordinary, incomparable, inimitable, matchless, outstanding, phenomenal, rare, supreme, transcendent, unrivalled, unsurpassed.

*antonym* poor.

**surplus** *n* balance, excess, overplus, remainder, residue, superabundance, superfluity, surfeit, surplusage.

*antonym* lack.

*adj* excess, extra, odd, redundant, remaining, spare, superfluous, unused.

*antonym* essential.

**surprise** *v* amaze, astonish, astound, bewilder, confuse, disconcert, dismay, flabbergast, nonplus, stagger, startle, stun.

*n* amazement, astonishment, bewilderment, bombshell, dismay, eye-opener, incredulity, jolt, revelation, shock, start, stupefaction, wonder.

*antonym* composure.

**surprised** *adj* amazed, astonished, confounded, disconcerted, incredulous, nonplussed, open-mouthed, shocked, speechless, staggered, startled, thunderstruck.

*antonyms* composed, unsurprised.

**surprising** *adj* amazing, astonishing, astounding, extraordinary, incredible, marvellous, remarkable, staggering, startling, stunning, unexpected, unlooked-for, unusual, unwonted, wonderful.

*antonyms* expected, unsurprising.

**surrender** *v* abandon, capitulate, cede, concede, forego, give in, give up, quit, relinquish, remise, renounce, resign, submit, succumb, waive, yield.

*antonym* fight on.

*n* appeasement, capitulation, decheance, delivery, Munich, relinquishment, remise, rendition, renunciation, resignation, submission, white flag, yielding.

**surreptitious** *adj* behind-door, clandestine, covert, fraudulent, furtive, secret, sly, sneaking, stealthy, unauthorised, underhand, veiled.

*antonym* open.

**surrogate** *n* deputy, proxy, replacement, representative, stand-in, substitute.

**surround** *v* begird, besiege, compass, embosom, encase, encincture, encircle, enclose, encompass, envelop, environ, girdle, invest, ring.

**surrounding** *adj* adjacent, adjoining, ambient, bordering, circumambient, circumjacent, encircling, enclosing, environing, environmental, nearby, neighbouring.

**surroundings** *n* ambience, background, entourage, environment, environs, locale, location, milieu, neighbourhood, setting, vicinity.

**surveillance** *n* care, charge, check, control, direction, guardianship, inspection, monitoring, observation, regulation, scrutiny, stewardship, superintendence, supervision, vigilance, watch.

**survey** *v* appraise, assess, consider, contemplate, estimate, examine, inspect, measure, observe, peruse, plan, plot, prospect, reconnoitre, research, review, scan, scrutinise, study, supervise, surview, triangulate, view.

*n* appraisal, assessment, conspectus, examination, geodesy, inquiry, inspection, measurement, overview, perusal, review, sample, scrutiny, study, triangulation.

**surveying** *n* geodesy, geodetics, measurement, triangulation.

**surveyor** *n* assessor, examiner, geodesist, inspector.

**survive** *v* endure, exist, last, last out, live, live out, live through, outlast, outlive, ride, stay, subsist, weather, withstand.

*antonym* succumb.

**susceptibility** *n* defencelessness, liability, openness, predisposition, proclivity, proneness, propensity, responsiveness, sensitivity, suggestibility, tendency, vulnerability, weakness.

*antonyms* impregnability, resistance.

**susceptible** *adj* defenceless, disposed, given, impressible, impressionable, inclined, liable, open, predisposed, pregnable, prone, receptive, responsive, sensitive, subject, suggestible, tender, vulnerable.

*antonyms* impregnable, resistant.

**suspect** *v* believe, call in question, conclude, conjecture, consider, distrust, doubt, fancy, feel, guess, infer, mistrust, opine, speculate, suppose, surmise.

*adj* debatable, dodgy, doubtful, dubious, fishy, questionable, suspicious, unauthoritative, unreliable.

*antonyms* acceptable, innocent, straightforward.

**suspend** v adjourn, append, arrest, attach, cease, dangle, debar, defer, delay, disbar, discontinue, dismiss, expel, freeze, hang, hold off, interrupt, postpone, shelve, sideline, stay, swing, unfrock, withhold.

*antonyms* continue, expedite, reinstate, restore.

**suspended** adj abeyant, dangling, hanging, pendent, pending, pensile, put on ice, shelved.

**suspense** n anticipation, anxiety, apprehension, doubt, excitement, expectancy, expectation, incertitude, indecision, insecurity, irresolution, tension, uncertainty, wavering.

*antonyms* certainty, knowledge.

**suspension** n abeyance, abeyancy, adjournment, break, cessation, deferment, deferral, delay, diapause, disbarment, discontinuation, dormancy, intermission, interruption, moratorium, postponement, remission, respite, standstill, stay.

*antonyms* continuation, reinstatement, restoration.

**suspicion** n apprehension, chariness, conjecture, distrust, doubt, glimmer, guess, hint, hunch, idea, impression, intuition, jealousy, misgiving, mistrust, notion, presentiment, qualm, scepticism, shade, shadow, soupçon, strain, streak, suggestion, supposition, surmise, suspiciousness, tinge, touch, trace, wariness.

*antonym* trust.

**suspicious** adj apprehensive, chary, distrustful, dodgy, doubtful, dubious, fishy, incredulous, irregular, jealous, louche, mistrustful, peculiar, queer, questionable, sceptical, shady, suspect, suspecting, unbelieving, uneasy, wary.

*antonyms* innocent, trustful, unexceptionable.

**sustain** v aid, approve, assist, bear, carry, comfort, confirm, continue, endorse, endure, experience, feel, foster, help, hold, keep going, maintain, nourish, nurture, prolong, protract, provide for, ratify, relieve, sanction, stay, suffer, support, survive, sustenate, undergo, uphold, validate, verify, withstand.

**sustained** adj constant, continuous, long-drawn-out, non-stop, perpetual, prolonged, protracted, steady, unremitting.

*antonyms* broken, intermittent, interrupted, occasional, spasmodic.

**sustenance** n aliment, board, comestibles, commons, eatables, edibles, etape, fare, food, freshments, livelihood, maintenance, nourishment, nutriment, pabulum, provender, provisions, rations, refection, subsistence, support, viands, victuals.

**svelte** adj elegant, graceful, lissom, lithe, polished, shapely, slender, slinky, smooth, sophisticated, streamlined, sylphlike, urbane, willowy.

*antonyms* bulky, ungainly.

**swagger** v bluster, boast, brag, brank, bully, cock, crow, gasconade, hector, parade, prance, roist, roister, strut, swank.

n arrogance, bluster, boastfulness, boasting, braggadocio, display, fanfaronade, gasconade, gasconism, ostentation, rodomontade, show, showing off, swank, vainglory.

*antonyms* diffidence, modesty, restraint.

**swaggerer** n attitudiniser, blusterer, boaster, braggadocio, braggart, fanfaron, gascon, gasconader, loudmouth, peacock, poser, poseur, poseuse, posturer, rodomontader, roister, roisterer, scaramouch, show-off, strutter, swank, swashbuckler, whiffler.

**swallow** v absorb, accept, assimilate, believe, buy, consume, devour, down, drink, eat, englut, engulf, gulp, imbibe, ingest, ingurgitate, knock back, quaff, stifle, suppress, swig, swill, wash down.

**swallow up** absorb, consume, deplete, dissipate, drain, eat up, engulf, envelop, exhaust, gobble up, guzzle, ingurgitate, overrun, overwhelm, use up, waste.

**swamp** n bog, dismal, everglades, fen, marsh, mire, morass, moss, quagmire, quicksands, slough, vlei.

v beset, besiege, capsise, deluge, drench, engulf, flood, inundate, overload, overwhelm, saturate, sink, submerge, waterlog.

**swampy** adj boggy, fenny, marish, marshy, miry, mushy, paludal, quaggy, soggy, squelchy, uliginous, waterlogged, wet.

*antonyms* arid, dehydrated, dry.

**swank** v attitudinise, boast, parade, posture, preen oneself, show off, strut, swagger.

n boastfulness, conceit, conceitedness, display, ostentation, pretentiousness, self-advertisement, show, showing-off, swagger, vainglory.

*antonyms* modesty, restraint.

**swanky** adj de luxe, epideictic, exclusive, expensive, fancy, fashionable, flash, flashy, glamorous, grand, lavish, luxurious, ostentatious, plush, plushy, posh, pretentious, rich, ritzy, showy, smart, stylish, sumptuous, swish.

*antonyms* discreet, unobtrusive.

**swap, swop** v bandy, barter, exchange, interchange, substitute, switch, trade, traffic, transpose.

**swarm** n army, bevy, concourse, crowd, drove, flock, herd, horde, host, mass, mob, multitude, myriad, shoal, throng.

v congregate, crowd, flock, flood, mass, stream, throng.

**swarm with** abound, bristle, crawl, hotch, teem.

**swarthy** adj black, brown, dark, dark-complexioned, dark-skinned, dusky, swart, swarth, tawny.

*antonyms* fair, pale.

**swashbuckling** adj adventurous, bold, daredevil, dashing, exciting, flamboyant, gallant, lusty, mettlesome, rip-roaring, robust, roisterous, spirited, swaggering.

*antonyms* tame, unadventurous, unexciting.

**swastika** n fylfot, gammadion, gammation, Hakenkreuz.

**swathe** v bandage, bind, cloak, drape, enshroud, envelop, enwrap, fold, furl, lap, sheathe, shroud, swaddle, wind, wrap.

*antonyms* unwind, unwrap.

**sway** v affect, bend, control, direct, divert, dominate, fluctuate, govern, guide, incline, induce, influence, lean, lurch, oscillate, overrule, persuade, rock, roll, swerve, swing, titter, veer, wave.

n ascendency, authority, cloud, command, control, dominion, government, hegemony, influence, jurisdiction, leadership, power, predominance, preponderance, rule, sovereignty, sweep, swerve, swing.

**swear**[1] v affirm, assert, asseverate, attest, avow, declare, depose, insist, promise, testify, vow, warrant.

**swear**[2] v blaspheme, blind, curse, cuss, eff, imprecate, maledict, take the Lord's name in vain, turn the air blue.

**swearing** n bad language, billingsgate, blasphemy, coprolalia, cursing, cussing, effing and blinding, expletives, foul language, imprecations, maledictions, profanity.

**swear-word** n blasphemy, curse, expletive, four-letter word, imprecation, oath, obscenity, profanity.

**sweat** n agitation, anxiety, chore, dew, diaphoresis, distress, drudgery, effort, exudation, fag, flap, hidrosis, labour, panic, perspiration, strain, sudation, sudor, worry.

v agonise, chafe, exude, fret, glow, perspirate, perspire, swelter, worry.

**sweaty** adj clammy, damp, glowing, moist, perspiring, sticky, sudorous, sweating.

*antonyms* cool, dry.

**sweep** v brush, career, clean, clear, dust, flounce, fly, glance, glide, hurtle, pass, remove, sail, scud, skim, tear, whisk, zoom.

n arc, bend, clearance, compass, curve, expanse, extent, gesture, impetus, move, movement, onrush, range, scope, span, stretch, stroke, swing, vista.

**sweeping** adj across-the-board, all-embracing, all-inclusive, blanket, broad, comprehensive, exaggerated, extensive, far-reaching, global, indiscriminate, overdrawn, oversimplified, overstated, radical, simplistic, thoroughgoing, unanalytical, unqualified, wholesale, wide, wide-ranging.

**sweepstake** n draw, lottery, sweep, sweepstakes.

**sweet**[1] adj affectionate, agreeable, amabile, amiable, appealing, aromatic, attractive, balmy, beautiful, beloved, benign, charming, cherished, clean, cloying, darling, dear, dearest, delightful, dulcet, engaging, euphonic, euphonious, fair, fragrant, fresh, gentle, gracious, harmonious, honeyed, icky, kin, lovable, luscious, mellow, melodious, melting, mild, musical, new, perfumed, pet, precious, pure, redolent, saccharine, sickly, silver-toned, silvery, soft, suave, sugary, sweetened, sweet-smelling,

sweet-sounding, sweet-tempered, syrupy, taking, tender, toothsome, treasured, tuneful, unselfish, wholesome, winning, winsome.

*antonyms* acid, bitter, cacophonous, discordant, malodorous, salty, sour, unpleasant.

n afters, dessert, pudding, second course, sweet course.

**sweet**[2] n bonbon, candy, comfit, confect, confection, confectionery, sweetie, sweetmeat.

**sweeten** v alleviate, appease, cushion, dulcify, edulcorate, honey, mellow, mollify, pacify, soften, soothe, sugar, sugar-coat, take the sting out of, temper.

*antonyms* aggravate, embitter, jaundice.

**sweetheart** n admirer, beau, beloved, betrothed, boyfriend, darling, dear, dona, Dulcinea, flame, follower, girlfriend, inamorata, inamorato, lady-love, leman, love, lover, Romeo, steady, suitor, swain, sweetie, truelove, valentine.

**sweetness** n amiability, balminess, charm, dulcitude, euphony, fragrance, freshness, harmony, kindness, love, loveliness, lusciousness, mellowness, suavity, succulence, sugariness, sweet temper, syrup, tenderness, winsomeness.

*antonyms* acidity, bitterness, cacophony, nastiness, saltness, sourness.

**sweet-smelling** adj ambrosial, aromatic, balmy, fragrant, odoriferous, odorous, perfumed, redolent, sweet-scented.

*antonyms* fetid, malodorous.

**swell**[1] v aggravate, augment, balloon, belly, billow, blab, bloat, boll, bulb, bulge, dilate, distend, enhance, enlarge, expand, extend, fatten, grow, heave, heighten, hove, increase, intensify, intumesce, louden, mount, protrude, reach a crescendo, rise, strout, surge, tumefy, volume.

*antonyms* contract, dwindle, shrink.

n billow, bore, bulge, distension, eagre, enlargement, loudening, rise, surge, swelling, undulation, wave.

**swell**[2] n adept, beau, bigwig, blade, cockscomb, dandy, dude, fop, nob, popinjay, toff.

*antonyms* down-and-out, scarecrow, tramp.

adj de luxe, dude, exclusive, fashionable, flashy, grand, posh, ritzy, smart, stylish, swanky.

*antonyms* seedy, shabby.

**swelling** n blister, boll, botch, bruise, bulb, bulge, bump, dilation, distension, emphysema, enlargement, gall, gathering, gout, inflammation, intumescence, lump, oedema, protuberance, puffiness, tuber, tubercle, tumescence, tumour, venter.

**sweltering** adj airless, baking, broiling, burning, hot, humid, oppressive, perspiring, scorching, steamy, stifling, suffocating, sultry, sweating, torrid, tropical.

*antonyms* airy, breezy, chilly, cold, cool, fresh.

**swerve** v bend, carve, deflect, deviate, diverge, incline, sheer, shift, skew, stray, sway, swing, turn, veer, wander, warp, wind.

**swift** *adj* abrupt, agile, expeditious, express, fast, fleet, fleet-footed, flying, hurried, light-heeled, light-legged, limber, nimble, nimble-footed, nippy, precipitate, prompt, quick, rapid, ready, short, spanking, speedy, sudden, winged.

*antonyms* slow, sluggish, tardy.

**swiftly** *adj* at full tilt, double-quick, expeditiously, express, fast, hotfoot, hurriedly, instantly, posthaste, promptly, quickly, rapidly, speedily.

*antonyms* slowly, tardily.

**swiftness** *n* alacrity, celerity, dispatch, expedition, fleetness, immediacy, immediateness, instantaneity, promptness, quickness, rapidity, readiness, speed, speediness, suddenness, velocity.

*antonyms* delay, slowness, tardiness.

**swill** *v* consume, drain, drink, gulp, guzzle, imbibe, knock back, quaff, swallow, swig, toss off.

*n* hogwash, mash, mush, offal, pigswill, refuse, scourings, slops, waste.

**swill out** cleanse, drench, flush, rinse, sluice, wash down, wash out.

**swimming-pool** *n* Jacuzzi®, leisure pool, lido, swimming-bath, swimming-pond.

**swimsuit** *n* bathers, bathing-costume, bathing-dress, bathing-suit, bikini, cossie, maillot, swimming costume, swimwear, trunks.

**swindle** *v* bamboozle, bilk, bunko, cheat, chicane, chouse, con, deceive, defraud, diddle, do, dupe, finagle, financier, fleece, grift, gyp, hand someone a lemon, hornswoggle, overcharge, ramp, rip off, rook, sell smoke, sell someone a pup, skelder, trick.

*n* chicanery, con, deceit, deception, double-dealing, fakery, fiddle, fraud, gold-brick, grift, gyp, imposition, knavery, racket, rip-off, roguery, scam, sharp practice, shenanigans, skin-game, swizz, swizzle, trickery.

**swindler** *n* charlatan, cheat, chicaner, con man, escroc, fraud, fraudster, grifter, impostor, jackman, knave, mountebank, rascal, rogue, rook, shark, sharper, slicker, spieler, trickster.

**swine** *n* beast, boar, boor, brute, cad, heel, pig, reptile, rotter, scoundrel.

**swing** *v* arrange, brandish, control, dangle, fix, fluctuate, hang, hurl, influence, librate, oscillate, pendulate, rock, suspend, sway, swerve, vary, veer, vibrate, wave, whirl.

*n* fluctuation, impetus, libration, motion, oscillation, rhythm, scope, stroke, sway, swaying, sweep, sweeping, vibration, waving.

**swing round** curve, gyrate, pivot, revolve, rotate, spin, swivel, turn, twirl, wheel.

**swingeing** *adj* Draconian, drastic, excessive, exorbitant, extortionate, harsh, heavy, huge, oppressive, punishing, severe, stringent, thumping.

*antonym* mild.

**swinging** *adj* contemporary, dynamic, fashionable, fast, groovy, hip, jet-setting, lively, modern, stylish, toney, trendy, up-to-date, up-to-the-minute, with it.

*antonyms* old-fashioned, square.

**swipe** *v* appropriate, clip, filch, half-inch, hit, lift, pilfer, pinch, purloin, slap, slosh, snaffle, snitch, sock, steal, strike, thwack, wallop, whack.

*n* blow, clip, clout, cuff, gobble, gowff, slap, smack, thwack, wallop, whack.

**swirl** *v* agitate, boil, churn, eddy, purl, scud, spin, surge, swish, twirl, twist, wheel, whirl.

**swish¹** *v* birch, brandish, flog, flourish, lash, rustle, swing, swirl, swoosh, thrash, twirl, wave, whip, whirl, whisk, whistle, whiz(z), whoosh.

**swish²** *adj* de luxe, dude, elegant, exclusive, fashionable, flash, grand, plush, posh, ritzy, smart, sumptuous, swanky, swell.

*antonyms* seedy, shabby.

**switch¹** *v* change, change course, change direction, chop and change, deflect, deviate, divert, exchange, interchange, put, rearrange, replace, shift, shunt, substitute, swap, trade, turn, veer.

*n* about-turn, alteration, change, change of direction, exchange, interchange, shift, substitution, swap.

**switch off** inactivate, put off, turn off.

**switch²** *v* birch, flog, jerk, lash, swish, twitch, wave, whip, whisk.

*n* birch, cane, jerk, rod, whip, whisk.

**swivel** *v* gyrate, pirouette, pivot, revolve, rotate, spin, swing round, turn, twirl, wheel.

**swollen** *adj* bloated, bolled, bulbous, distended, dropsical, emphysematous, enlarged, inflamed, intumescent, oedematose, oedematous, puffed up, puffy, tumescent, tumid, turgid, ventricose, ventricous.

*antonyms* contracted, emaciated, shrunken.

**swoop** *v* descend, dive, drop, fall, lunge, pounce, rush, stoop, sweep.

*n* attack, descent, drop, lunge, onslaught, plunge, pounce, rush, stoop, sweep.

**swop** *see* **swap**.

**sword** *n* bilbo, blade, broadsword, claymore, cutlass, foil, gladius, machete, rapier, sabre, schiavone, scimitar.

**sworn** *adj* attested, confirmed, devoted, eternal, implacable, inveterate, relentless.

**swot** *v* bone up, burn the midnight oil, con, cram, dig, learn, lucubrate, memorise, mug up, pore over, revise, study, work.

*n* bluestocking, bookworm, crammer, dig, worker.

*antonym* idler.

**sybarite** *n* bon vivant, epicure, epicurean, hedonist, one of the idle rich, parasite, playboy, pleasurer, pleasure-seeker, sensualist, voluptuary.

*antonyms* ascetic, toiler.

**sybaritic** *adj* easy, epicurean, hedonistic, Lucullan, luxurious, parasitic, pleasure-loving, pleasure-seeking, self-indulgent, sensual, voluptuous.

*antonym* ascetic.

**sycophancy** *n* adulation, arse-licking, backscratching, bootlicking, cringing, fawning, flattery, grovelling, kowtowing, obsequiousness, servility, slavishness, toadyism, truckling.

**sycophant**     *n*     arse-licker,     backscratcher, bootlicker, cringer, fawner, flatterer, flunky, groveller, hanger-on, lickspittle, parasite, slave, sponger, toad-eater, toady, truckler, yes-man.

**sycophantic** *adj* arse-licking, backscratching, bootlicking, cringing, fawning, flattering, grovelling, ingratiating, obsequious, parasitical, servile, slavish, slimy, smarmy, timeserving, toad-eating, toadying, truckling, unctuous.

**syllabus** *n* course, curriculum, plan, programme, schedule, table.

**syllogism** *n* argument, deduction, epicheirema, proposition.

**sylph-like** *adj* elegant, graceful, lithe, slender, slight, slim, streamlined, svelte, willowy.

*antonyms* bulky, plump.

**symbiotic** *adj* commensal, co-operative, emphytic, endophytic, epizoan, epizoic, epizootic, interactive, interdependent, synergetic.

**symbol** *n* badge, character, emblem, figure, grammalogue, ideogram, ideograph, image, logo, logogram, logograph, mandala, mark, representation, rune, sign, token, type.

**symbolic** *adj* allegorical, allusive, aniconic, emblematic, figurative, metaphorical, representative, ritual, significant, symbolical, token, typical.

**symbolise** *v* allude to, betoken, connote, denote, emblem, emblematise, emblemise, exemplify, mean, personate, personify, represent, signify, typify.

**symmetrical** *adj* balanced, corresponding, isometric, parallel, proportional, regular, well-balanced, well-proportioned, well-rounded.

*antonyms* asymmetrical, irregular.

**symmetry** *n* agreement, balance, correspondence, evenness, form, harmony, isometry, order, parallelism, proportion, regularity.

*antonyms* asymmetry, irregularity.

**sympathetic** *adj* affectionate, agreeable, appreciative, caring, comforting, commiserating, companionable, compassionate, compatible, concerned, congenial, consoling, empathetic, empathic, exorable, feeling, friendly, interested, kind, kindly, like-minded, pitying, responsive, supportive, tender, understanding, warm, warm-hearted, well-intentioned.

*antonyms* antipathetic, callous, indifferent, unsympathetic.

**sympathetically** *adv* appreciatively, comfortingly, compassionately, consolingly, feelingly, kindly, pityingly, responsively, sensitively, supportively, understandingly, warm-heartedly, warmly.

**sympathise** *v* agree, commiserate, condole, empathise, feel for, identify with, pity, rap, respond to, side with, understand.

*antonyms* disapprove, dismiss, disregard, ignore, oppose.

**sympathiser** *n* adherent, admirer, backer, condoler, fan, fellow-traveller, friend in need, partisan, supporter, well-wisher.

*antonyms* enemy, opponent.

**sympathy** *n* affinity, agreement, comfort, commiseration, compassion, condolement, condolence, condolences, congeniality, correspondence, empathy, fellow-feeling, harmony, pity, rapport, responsiveness, tenderness, thoughtfulness, understanding, warmth.

*antonyms* callousness, disharmony, incompatibility, indifference.

**symptom** *n* concomitant, diagnostic, evidence, expression, feature, indication, manifestation, mark, note, sign, syndrome, token, warning.

**symptomatic** *adj* associated, characteristic, indicative, suggestive, typical.

**syndicate** *n* alliance, bloc, cartel, combination, combine, group, ring.

**synonymous** *adj* co-extensive, comparable, corresponding, equal, equivalent, exchangeable, identical, identified, interchangeable, parallel, similar, substitutable, tantamount, the same.

*antonyms* antonymous, dissimilar, opposite.

**synopsis** *n* abridgement, abstract, aperçu, compendium, condensation, conspectus, digest, epitome, outline, precis, recapitulation, resume, review, run-down, sketch, summary, summation.

**synthesis** *n* alloy, amalgam, amalgamation, blend, coalescence, combination, composite, compound, fusion, integration, pastiche, unification, union, welding.

**synthesise** *v* amalgamate, blend, coalesce, combine, compound, fuse, integrate, manufacture, merge, unify, unite, weld.

*antonyms* analyse, resolve, separate.

**synthetic** *adj* artificial, bogus, ersatz, fake, imitation, man-made, manufactured, mock, pseud, pseudo, put-on, sham, simulated.

*antonyms* genuine, real.

**syphilis** *n* clap, French pox, gonorrhoea, pip, pox, venereal disease.

**system** *n* arrangement, classification, co-ordination, logic, method, methodicalness, methodology, mode, modus operandi, orderliness, organisation, plan, practice, procedure, process, regularity, routine, rule, scheme, set-up, structure, systematisation, tabulation, taxis, taxonomy, technique, theory, usage.

**systematic** *adj* businesslike, efficient, habitual, intentional, logical, methodical, ordered, orderly, organised, planned, precise, standardised, systematical, systematised, well-ordered, well-planned.

*antonyms* disorderly, inefficient, unsystematic.

**systematise** *v* arrange, classify, dispose, make uniform, methodise, order, organise, rationalise, regiment, regulate, schematise, standardise, tabulate.

# T

**tab** *n* docket, flag, flap, label, marker, sticker, tag, ticket.

**tabby** *adj* banded, brindled, mottled, streaked, striped, stripy, variegated, wavy.

**table** *n* agenda, altar, bench, board, catalogue, chart, counter, diagram, diet, digest, fare, flat, flatland, food, graph, index, inventory, list, mahogany, paradigm, plain, plan, plateau, record, register, roll, schedule, slab, spread, stall, stand, syllabus, synopsis, tableland, victuals.

*v* postpone, propose, put forward, submit, suggest.

**tableau** *n* diorama, picture, portrayal, representation, scene, spectacle, tableau vivant, vignette.

**taboo** *adj* accursed, anathema, banned, forbidden, inviolable, outlawed, prohibited, proscribed, sacrosanct, unacceptable, unmentionable, unthinkable, verboten.

*antonym* acceptable.

*n* anathema, ban, curse, disapproval, interdict, interdiction, prohibition, proscription, restriction.

**tabulate** *v* arrange, catalogue, categorise, chart, classify, codify, index, list, order, range, sort, systematise, table, tabularise.

**tacit** *adj* implicit, implied, inferred, silent, ulterior, undeclared, understood, unexpressed, unprofessed, unspoken, unstated, unuttered, unvoiced, voiceless, wordless.

*antonyms* explicit, express, spoken, stated.

**taciturn** *adj* aloof, antisocial, cold, distant, dumb, mute, pauciloquent, quiet, reserved, reticent, saturnine, silent, tight-lipped, uncommunicative, unconversable, unforthcoming, withdrawn.

*antonyms* communicative, forthcoming, sociable, talkative.

**tack** *n* approach, attack, bearing, course, direction, drawing-pin, heading, line, loop, method, nail, path, pin, plan, procedure, route, staple, stitch, tactic, thumb-tack, tin-tack, way.

*v* add, affix, annex, append, attach, baste, fasten, fix, join, nail, pin, staple, stitch, tag.

**tackle¹** *n* accoutrements, apparatus, equipment, gear, harness, implements, outfit, paraphernalia, rig, rigging, tackling, tools, trappings.

*v* harness.

**tackle²** *n* attack, block, challenge, interception, intervention, stop.

*v* attempt, begin, block, challenge, clutch, confront, deal with, embark upon, encounter, engage in, essay, face up to, grab, grapple with, grasp, halt, intercept, seize, set about, stop, take on, throw, try, undertake, wade into.

*antonyms* avoid, side-step.

**tacky** *adj* adhesive, cheap, gimcrack, gluey, gummy, messy, nasty, scruffy, seedy, shabby, shoddy, sleazy, sticky, tasteless, tatty, tawdry, vulgar, wet.

**tact** *n* address, adroitness, consideration, delicacy, diplomacy, discernment, discretion, finesse, grace, judgement, perception, prudence, savoir-faire, sensitivity, skill, thoughtfulness, understanding.

*antonyms* clumsiness, indiscretion, tactlessness.

**tactful** *adj* careful, considerate, delicate, diplomatic, discerning, discreet, graceful, judicious, perceptive, polished, polite, politic, prudent, sensitive, skilful, subtle, thoughtful, understanding.

*antonym* tactless.

**tactic** *n* approach, course, device, line, manoeuvre, means, method, move, ploy, policy, ruse, scheme, shift, stratagem, subterfuge, tack, trick, way.

**tactical** *adj* adroit, artful, calculated, clever, cunning, diplomatic, judicious, politic, prudent, shrewd, skilful, smart, strategic.

*antonym* impolitic.

**tactician** *n* brain, campaigner, co-ordinator, director, mastermind, orchestrator, planner, politician, strategist.

**tactics** *n* approach, campaign, game plan, line of attack, manoeuvres, moves, plan, plan of campaign, plans, ploys, policy, procedure, shifts, stratagems, strategy.

**tactless** *adj* blundering, boorish, careless, clumsy, discourteous, gauche, hurtful, ill-timed, impolite, impolitic, imprudent, inappropriate, inconsiderate, indelicate, indiscreet, inept, insensitive, maladroit, rough, rude, thoughtless, uncivil, undiplomatic, unfeeling, unkind, unsubtle.

*antonym* tactful.

**tactlessness** *n* bad timing, boorishness, clumsiness, discourtesy, gaucherie, impoliteness, indelicacy, indiscretion, ineptitude, insensitivity, maladdress, maladroitness, rudeness, thoughtlessness.

*antonym* tact.

**tag**[1] *n* aglet, aiglet, aiguillette, appellation, dag, designation, docket, epithet, flap, identification, label, mark, marker, name, note, slip, sticker, tab, tally, ticket.

*v* add, adjoin, affix, annex, append, call, christen, designate, dub, earmark, fasten, identify, label, mark, name, nickname, style, tack, term, ticket.

**tag along** accompany, attend, dog, follow, hang round, shadow, tail, trail.

**tag**[2] *n* dictum, fadaise, gnome, gobbet, maxim, moral, motto, proverb, quotation, quote, remnant, saw, saying.

**tail** *n* appendage, backside, behind, bottom, bum, buttocks, conclusion, croup, detective, empennage, end, extremity, file, follower, fud, line, posterior, queue, rear, rear end, retinue, rump, scut, suite, tailback, tailpiece, tailplane, train.

*v* dog, follow, keep with, shadow, spy on, stalk, track, trail.

**tail off** decrease, die, die out, drop, dwindle, fade, fail, fall away, peter out, tail away, taper off, wane.

*antonyms* grow, increase.

**tailless** *adj* acaudal, acaudate, anurous, ecaudate, excaudate, Manx.

**tailor** *n* clothier, costumer, costumier, couturier, couturière, darzi, dressmaker, modiste, outfitter, seamstress, whipcat, whip-stitch.

*v* accommodate, adapt, adjust, alter, convert, cut, fashion, fit, modify, mould, shape, style, suit, trim.

**tailor-made** *adj* bespoke, custom-built, custom-made, fitted, ideal, made-to-measure, perfect, right, suitable, suited.

*antonyms* ill-adapted, unsuitable.

**taint** *v* adulterate, besmirch, blacken, blemish, blight, blot, brand, contaminate, corrupt, damage, defile, deprave, dirty, disgrace, dishonour, envenom, foul, infect, muddy, poison, pollute, ruin, shame, smear, smirch, soil, spoil, stain, stigmatise, sully, tarnish, vitiate.

*n* blemish, blot, contagion, contamination, corruption, defect, disgrace, dishonour, fault, flaw, infamy, infection, obloquy, odium, opprobium, pollution, shame, smear, smirch, spot, stain, stigma.

**take** *v* abduct, abide, abstract, accept, accommodate, accompany, acquire, adopt, appropriate, arrest, ascertain, assume, attract, bear, believe, betake, bewitch, blight, book, brave, bring, brook, buy, call for, captivate, capture, carry, cart, catch, charm, clutch, conduct, consider, consume, contain, convey, convoy, deduct, deem, delight, demand, derive, detract, do, drink, eat, effect, eliminate, enchant, endure, engage, ensnare, entrap, escort, execute, fascinate, ferry, fetch, filch, gather, glean, grasp, grip, guide, haul, have, have room for, hire, hold, imbibe, ingest, inhale, lead, lease, make, measure, misappropriate, necessitate, need, nick, observe, obtain, operate, perceive, perform, photograph, pick, pinch, please, pocket, portray, presume, purchase, purloin, receive, regard, remove, rent, require, reserve, secure, seize, select, stand, steal, stomach, strike, subtract, succeed, suffer, swallow, swipe, thole, tolerate, tote, transport, undergo, understand, undertake, usher, weather, win, withstand, work.

*n* catch, gate, haul, income, proceeds, profits, receipts, return, revenue, takings, yield.

**take aback** astonish, astound, bewilder, disconcert, dismay, flabbergast, floor, nonplus, stagger, startle, stun, surprise, upset.

**take apart** analyse, disassemble, dismantle, resolve, take down, take to pieces.

**take back** deny, disavow, disclaim, eat one's words, recant, reclaim, regain, renounce, repossess, repudiate, retract, unsay, withdraw.

**take down** deflate, demolish, disassemble, dismantle, humble, humiliate, level, lower, minute, mortify, note, put down, raze, record, reduce, set down, strike, transcribe, unstep, write.

**take effect** be effective, become operative, begin, come into force, work.

**take heart** brighten up, buck up, cheer up, perk up, rally, revive.

*antonym* despond.

**take in** absorb, accommodate, admit, annex, appreciate, assimilate, bamboozle, bilk, bluff, cheat, comprehend, comprise, con, contain, cover, cozen, deceive, digest, do, dupe, embrace, enclose, encompass, fool, furl, grasp, gull, hoodwink, imagine, include, incorporate, kid, mislead, realise, receive, shelter, subdue, swindle, tighten, trick, understand.

**take issue** call in question, challenge, disagree, dispute, object, oppose, quarrel, question, take exception.

**take it ill** be miffed, be offended, miff, object, protest, take the huff.

**take off** beat it, bloom, burgeon, caricature, decamp, depart, disappear, discard, divest, doff, drop, expand, flourish, go, imitate, lampoon, leave, mimic, mock, parody, remove, satirise, scarper, send up, soar, spoof, strip, take wing, travesty, vamoose.

**take offence** be miffed, miff, sulk, take it ill, take the huff.

**take on** accept, acquire, assume, complain, contend with, employ, engage, enlist, enrol, face, fight, grieve, hire, lament, oppose, retain, tackle, undertake, vie with.

**take part** associate oneself, be instrumental, be involved, join, partake, participate, play a part, share, take a hand.

**take pity on** feel compassion for, forgive, give quarter, have mercy on, melt, pardon, pity, relent, reprieve, show mercy, spare.

**take place** befall, betide, come about, come off, come to pass, fall, happen, occur.

**take stock** appraise, assess, estimate, size up, survey, weigh up.

**take the plunge** commit oneself, cross the Rubicon, decide, pop the question.

**take to task** blame, censure, criticise, lecture, rebuke, reprimand, reproach, reprove, scold, tell off, tick off, upbraid.

*antonyms* commend, praise.

**take up** absorb, accept, adopt, affect, arrest, assume, begin, borrow, carry on, consume,

T-V

continue, cover, engage in, engross, fasten, fill, interrupt, lift, monopolise, occupy, proceed, raise, recommence, restart, resume, secure, start, use up.

**take-off** *n* burlesque, caricature, imitation, lampoon, mickey-take, mimicry, parody, spoof, travesty.

**takeover** *n* amalgamation, coalition, combination, coup, incorporation, merger.

**taking** *adj* alluring, appealing, attractive, beguiling, captivating, catching, charming, compelling, delightful, enchanting, engaging, fascinating, fetching, intriguing, pleasing, prepossessing, winning, winsome.

*antonyms* repellent, repulsive, unattractive.

*n* agitation, alarm, coil, commotion, consternation, flap, fuss, panic, passion, pother, state, sweat, tiz-woz, tizzy, turmoil, wax.

**takings** *n* earnings, emoluments, gain, gate, haul, income, pickings, proceeds, profits, receipts, returns, revenue, take, yield.

**tale** *n* account, anecdote, fable, fabrication, falsehood, fib, fiction, legend, lie, Märchen, Munchausen, myth, narration, narrative, old wives' tale, relation, report, rigmarole, romance, rumour, saga, spiel, story, superstition, tall story, tradition, untruth, yarn.

**talent** *n* ability, aptitude, bent, capacity, endowment, faculty, feel, flair, forte, genius, gift, knack, long suit, nous, parts, power, strength.

*antonyms* inability, ineptitude, weakness.

**talented** *adj* able, accomplished, adept, adroit, apt, artistic, brilliant, capable, clever, deft, gifted, ingenious, inspired, well-endowed.

*antonyms* clumsy, inept, maladroit.

**talisman** *n* abraxas, amulet, charm, fetish, juju, mascot, periapt, phylactery, telesm.

**talk** *v* articulate, blab, blether, chat, chatter, chinwag, commune, communicate, confabulate, confer, converse, crack, gab, gossip, grass, inform, jaw, natter, negotiate, palaver, parley, prate, prattle, rap, say, sing, speak, squeak, squeal, utter, verbalise, witter.

*n* address, argot, bavardage, blather, blether, causerie, chat, chatter, chinwag, chitchat, clash, claver, colloquy, conclave, confab, confabulation, conference, consultation, conversation, crack, dialect, dialogue, discourse, discussion, disquisition, dissertation, gab, gossip, gup, harangue, hearsay, jargon, jaw, jawing, language, lecture, lingo, meeting, natter, negotiation, oration, palabra, palaver, parley, patois, rap, rumour, seminar, sermon, slang, speech, spiel, symposium, tittle-tattle, utterance, words.

**talk big** bluster, boast, brag, crow, exaggerate, swank, vaunt.

**talk into** bring round, coax, convince, encourage, overrule, persuade, sway, win over.

*antonym* dissuade.

**talk out of** caution, deter, discourage, dissuade, expostulate, head off, protest, put off, remonstrate, urge against.

**talkative** *adj* chatty, communicative, conversational, conversative, effusive, expansive, forthcoming, gabby, garrulous, gossipy, long-tongued, long-winded, loquacious, prating, prolix, unreserved, verbose, vocal, voluble, wordy.

*antonyms* pauciloquent, reserved, taciturn.

**talker** *n* chatterbox, communicator, conversationalist, lecturer, orator, speaker, speech-maker.

**talking-to** *n* criticism, dressing-down, earful, jaw, jawbation, lecture, rebuke, reprimand, reproach, reproof, row, scolding, slating, telling-off, ticking-off, wigging.

*antonyms* commendation, congratulation, praise.

**tall** *adj* absurd, big, dubious, elevated, embellished, exaggerated, far-fetched, giant, grandiloquent, great, high, implausible, improbable, incredible, lanky, leggy, lofty, overblown, preposterous, remarkable, soaring, steep, topless, towering, unbelievable, unlikely.

*antonyms* low, reasonable, short, small.

**tallness** *n* altitude, height, loftiness, procerity, stature.

**tally** *v* accord, agree, coincide, compute, concur, conform, correspond, figure, fit, harmonise, jibe, mark, match, parallel, reckon, record, register, square, suit, tie in, total.

*antonyms* differ, disagree.

*n* account, count, counterfoil, counterpart, credit, duplicate, label, mark, match, mate, notch, reckoning, record, score, stub, tab, tag, tick, total.

**tame** *adj* amenable, anaemic, biddable, bland, bloodless, boring, broken, compliant, cultivated, disciplined, docile, domesticated, dull, feeble, flat, gentle, humdrum, insipid, lifeless, manageable, meek, obedient, prosaic, spiritless, subdued, submissive, tedious, tractable, unadventurous, unenterprising, unexciting, uninspired, uninspiring, uninteresting, unresisting, vapid, wearisome.

*antonyms* exciting, rebellious, unmanageable, wild.

*v* break in, bridle, calm, conquer, curb, discipline, domesticate, enslave, gentle, house-train, humble, master, mellow, mitigate, mute, pacify, quell, repress, soften, subdue, subjugate, suppress, temper, train.

**tamper** *v* alter, bribe, cook, corrupt, damage, fiddle, fix, influence, interfere, intrude, juggle, manipulate, meddle, mess, rig, tinker.

**tang** *n* aroma, bite, flavour, hint, kick, overtone, piquancy, pungency, reek, savour, scent, smack, smell, suggestion, taste, tinge, touch, trace, whiff.

**tangible** *adj* actual, concrete, corporeal, definite, discernible, evident, manifest, material, objective, observable, palpable, perceptible, physical, positive, real, sensible, solid, substantial, tactile, touchable.

*antonym* intangible.

**tangle** *n* burble, coil, complication, confusion, convolution, embroglio, embroilment, entanglement, fankle, fix, imbroglio, jam, jumble, jungle, knot, labyrinth, mass, mat, maze, mesh, mess, mix-up, muddle, raffle, snarl, snarl-up, twist, web.

v catch, coil, confuse, convolve, embroil, enmesh, ensnare, entangle, entrap, hamper, implicate, interlace, interlock, intertwine, intertwist, interweave, involve, jam, knot, mat, mesh, muddle, snarl, trap, twist.

*antonym* disentangle.

**tangled** *adj* complex, complicated, confused, convoluted, dishevelled, entangled, intricate, involved, jumbled, knotted, knotty, matted, messy, mixed-up, scrambled, snarled, tortuous, tousled, twisted.

*antonyms* clear, free.

**tangy** *adj* biting, bitter, fresh, gamy, piquant, pungent, savoury, sharp, spicy, strong, tart.

*antonym* insipid.

**tank¹** *n* aquarium, basin, cistern, container, reservoir, vat.

**tank²** *n* armoured car, armoured vehicle, panzer.

**tantalise** *v* baffle, bait, balk, disappoint, entice, frustrate, lead on, play upon, provoke, taunt, tease, thwart, titillate, torment, torture.

*antonym* satisfy.

**tantamount** *adj* as good as, commensurate, equal, equivalent, synonymous, the same as, virtually.

**tantrum** *n* bate, fit, flare-up, fury, hysterics, outburst, paddy, paroxysm, rage, scene, storm, temper, wax.

**tap¹** *v* beat, chap, drum, knock, pat, rap, strike, tat, touch.

*n* beat, chap, knock, pat, rap, rat-tat, touch.

**tap²** *n* bug, bung, faucet, plug, receiver, spigot, spile, spout, stop-cock, stopper, valve.

*v* bleed, broach, bug, drain, exploit, milk, mine, open, pierce, quarry, siphon, unplug, use, utilise, wiretap.

**tape** *n* band, binding, magnetic tape, riband, ribbon, strip, tape-measure.

*v* assess, bind, measure, record, seal, secure, stick, tape-record, video, wrap.

**taper²** *v* attenuate, decrease, die away, die out, dwindle, fade, lessen, narrow, peter out, reduce, slim, subside, tail off, thin, wane, weaken.

*antonyms* increase, swell, widen.

**taper²** *n* bougie, candle, spill, wax-light, wick.

**tardily** *adv* at the eleventh hour, at the last minute, belatedly, late, late in the day, slowly, sluggishly, unpunctually.

*antonyms* promptly, punctually.

**tardiness** *n* belatedness, dawdling, delay, dilatoriness, lateness, procrastination, slowness, sluggishness, unpunctuality.

*antonyms* promptness, punctuality.

**tardy** *adj* backward, behindhand, belated, dawdling, delayed, dilatory, eleventh-hour, lag, last-minute, late, loitering, overdue, procrastinating, retarded, slack, slow, sluggish, unpunctual.

*antonyms* prompt, punctual.

**target** *n* aim, ambition, bull's-eye, butt, destination, end, goal, intention, jack, mark, object, objective, prey, prick, purpose, quarry, scapegoat, victim.

**tariff** *n* assessment, bill of fare, charges, customs, duty, excise, impost, levy, menu, price list, rate, schedule, tax, toll.

**tarnish** *v* befoul, blacken, blemish, blot, darken, dim, discolour, dislustre, dull, mar, rust, soil, spoil, spot, stain, sully, taint.

*antonyms* brighten, enhance, polish up.

*n* blackening, blemish, blot, discoloration, film, patina, rust, spot, stain, taint.

*antonyms* brightness, polish.

**tarry** *v* abide, bide, dally, dawdle, delay, dwell, lag, linger, loiter, pause, remain, rest, sojourn, stay, stop, wait.

**tart¹** *n* pastry, pie, quiche, tartlet.

**tart²** *adj* acerb, acerbic, acid, acidulous, acrimonious, astringent, barbed, biting, bitter, caustic, cutting, incisive, piquant, pungent, sardonic, scathing, sharp, short, sour, tangy, trenchant, vinegary.

**tart³** *n* broad, call girl, drab, fallen woman, fille de joie, fille publique, floosie, harlot, hooker, prostitute, slut, street-walker, strumpet, trollop, whore.

**task** *n* assignment, aufgabe, burden, business, charge, chore, darg, duty, employment, enterprise, exercise, imposition, job, job of work, labour, mission, occupation, pensum, toil, undertaking, work.

*v* burden, charge, commit, encumber, entrust, exhaust, load, lumber, oppress, overload, push, saddle, strain, tax, test, weary.

**taste** *n* appetite, appreciation, bent, bit, bite, choice, correctness, cultivation, culture, dash, decorum, delicacy, desire, discernment, discretion, discrimination, drop, elegance, experience, fancy, finesse, flavour, fondness, gout, grace, gustation, inclination, judgement, leaning, liking, morsel, mouthful, nibble, nicety, nip, palate, partiality, penchant, perception, polish, politeness, predilection, preference, propriety, refinement, relish, restraint, sample, sapor, savour, sensitivity, sip, smack, smatch, soupçon, spoonful, style, swallow, tact, tactfulness, tang, tastefulness, titbit, touch.

*v* assay, degust, degustate, differentiate, discern, distinguish, encounter, experience, feel, know, meet, nibble, perceive, relish, sample, savour, sip, smack, test, try, undergo.

**tasteful** *adj* aesthetic, artistic, beautiful, charming, comme il faut, correct, cultivated, cultured, delicate, discreet, discriminating, elegant, exquisite, fastidious, graceful, handsome, harmonious, judicious, polished, refined, restrained, smart, stylish, well-judged.

*antonym* tasteless.

**tasteless** *adj* barbaric, bland, boring, cheap, coarse, crass, crude, dilute, dull, flashy, flat, flavourless, garish, gaudy, graceless, gross, improper, inartistic, indecorous, indelicate, indiscreet, inelegant, inharmonious, insipid, low, mild, naff, rude, stale, tacky, tactless, tame, tatty, tawdry, thin, uncouth, undiscriminating, uninspired, uninteresting, unseemly, untasteful, vapid, vulgar, watered-down, watery, weak, wearish.

*antonym* tasteful.

**tasting** *n* assay, assessment, gustation, sampling, testing, trial.

**tasty** *adj* appetising, delectable, delicious, flavorous, flavourful, flavoursome, gusty, luscious, mouthwatering, palatable, piquant, sapid, saporous, savoury, scrumptious, succulent, toothsome, yummy.

*antonyms* disgusting, insipid, tasteless.

**tattered** *adj* duddie, frayed, in shreds, lacerated, ragged, raggy, rent, ripped, tatty, threadbare, torn.

*antonyms* neat, trim.

**tatters** *n* duddery, duds, flitters, rags, ribbons, shreds.

**tattle** *v* babble, blab, blather, blether, chat, chatter, clash, claver, gab, gash, gossip, jabber, natter, prate, prattle, talk, tittle-tattle, yak, yap.

*n* babble, blather, blether, chat, chatter, chitchat, clash, claver, gossip, hearsay, jabber, prattle, rumour, talk, tittle-tattle, yak, yap.

**tattler** *n* busybody, gossip, newsmonger, quidnunc, rumour-monger, scandalmonger, talebearer, tale-teller, tell-tale.

**taunt** *v* bait, chiack, deride, fleer, flout, flyte, gibe, insult, jeer, mock, provoke, reproach, revile, rib, ridicule, sneer, tease, torment, twit.

*n* barb, catcall, censure, cut, derision, dig, fling, gibe, insult, jeer, poke, provocation, reproach, ridicule, sarcasm, sneer, teasing.

**taut** *adj* contracted, rigid, strained, stressed, stretched, tense, tensed, tight, tightened, unrelaxed.

*antonyms* loose, relaxed, slack.

**tautological** *adj* iterative, otiose, pleonastic, redundant, repetitious, repetitive, superfluous, truistic.

*antonyms* economical, succinct.

**tautology** *n* duplication, iteration, otioseness, perissology, pleonasm, redundancy, repetition, repetitiousness, repetitiveness, superfluity.

*antonyms* economy, succinctness.

**tavern** *n* alehouse, bar, boozer, bush, dive, doggery, fonda, hostelry, inn, joint, local, pub, public house, roadhouse, tap-house.

**tawdry** *adj* brummagem, cheap, cheap-jack, flashy, garish, gaudy, gimcrack, gingerbread, glittering, meretricious, pinchbeck, plastic, raffish, showy, tacky, tasteless, tatty, tinsel, tinselly, vulgar.

*antonyms* excellent, fine, superior.

**tawny** *adj* fawn, fulvid, fulvous, golden, sandy, tan, xanthous, yellow.

**tax** *n* agistment, assessment, burden, charge, contribution, customs, demand, drain, duty,

excise, geld, imposition, impost, levy, load, octroi, pressure, rate, scat, scot, strain, tariff, tithe, toll, tribute, weight.

*v* accuse, arraign, assess, blame, burden, censure, charge, demand, drain, enervate, exact, exhaust, extract, geld, impeach, impose, impugn, incriminate, load, overburden, overtax, push, rate, reproach, sap, strain, stretch, task, tithe, try, weaken, weary.

**taxi** *n* cab, fiacre, hackney-coach, hansom-cab, taxicab.

**taxing** *adj* burdensome, demanding, draining, enervating, exacting, exhausting, heavy, onerous, punishing, stressful, tiring, tough, trying, wearing, wearisome.

*antonyms* easy, gentle, mild.

**teach** *v* accustom, advise, coach, counsel, demonstrate, direct, discipline, drill, edify, educate, enlighten, ground, guide, impart, implant, inculcate, inform, instil, instruct, school, show, train, tutor, verse.

**teacher** *n* abecedarian, coach, dominie, don, educator, guide, guru, instructor, khodja, kindergartener, kindergärtner, lecturer, luminary, maharishi, master, mentor, mistress, pedagogue, professor, pundit, school-marm, schoolmaster, schoolmistress, school-teacher, trainer, tutor, usher.

**teaching** *n* didactics, doctrine, dogma, education, gospel, grounding, indoctrination, instruction, pedagoguism, pedagogy, precept, principle, schooling, tenet, training, tuition.

**team** *n* band, body, bunch, company, crew, écurie, équipe, gang, group, line-up, pair, set, shift, side, span, squad, stable, troupe, yoke.

*v* combine, couple, join, link, match, yoke.

**team up** band together, combine, co-operate, join, unite.

**teamwork** *n* collaboration, co-operation, co-ordination, esprit de corps, fellowship, joint effort, team spirit.

*antonyms* disharmony, disunity.

**tear** *v* belt, bolt, career, charge, claw, dart, dash, dilacerate, divide, drag, fly, gallop, gash, grab, hurry, lacerate, mangle, mutilate, pluck, pull, race, rend, rip, rive, run, rupture, rush, scratch, seize, sever, shoot, shred, snag, snatch, speed, split, sprint, sunder, wrench, wrest, yank, zoom.

*n* hole, laceration, rent, rip, run, rupture, scratch, snag, split.

**tearaway** *n* daredevil, delinquent, good-for-nothing, hoodlum, hooligan, hothead, madcap, rascal, rough, roughneck, rowdy, ruffian, tityre-tu, tough.

**tearful** *adj* blubbering, crying, distressing, dolorous, emotional, lachrymose, lamentable, maudlin, mournful, pathetic, pitiable, pitiful, poignant, sad, sobbing, sorrowful, upsetting, weeping, weepy, whimpering, woeful.

**tears** *n* blubbering, crying, distress, lamentation, mourning, pain, regret, sadness, sobbing, sorrow, wailing, water-drops, waterworks, weeping, whimpering, woe.

**tease** v aggravate, annoy, badger, bait, banter, bedevil, chaff, chiack, chip, gibe, goad, grig, guy, irritate, josh, mock, needle, pester, plague, provoke, rag, rib, ridicule, take a rise out of, tantalise, taunt, torment, twit, vex, worry.

**technique** n address, adroitness, approach, art, artistry, course, craft, craftsmanship, delivery, executancy, execution, expertise, facility, fashion, knack, know-how, manner, means, method, mode, modus operandi, performance, procedure, proficiency, skill, style, system, touch, way.

**tedious** adj annoying, banal, boring, deadly, drab, draggy, dreary, dreich, dull, fatiguing, humdrum, irksome, laborious, lifeless, long-drawn-out, longsome, long-spun, monotonous, prosaic, prosy, soporific, tiring, unexciting, uninteresting, vapid, wearisome.

*antonyms* exciting, interesting.

**tedium** n banality, boredom, drabness, dreariness, dullness, ennui, lifelessness, monotony, prosiness, routine, sameness, tediousness, vapidity.

**teem** v abound, bear, brim, bristle, burst, increase, multiply, overflow, overspill, produce, proliferate, pullulate, swarm.

*antonyms* lack, want.

**teeming** adj abundant, alive, brimful, brimming, bristling, bursting, chock-a-block, chock-full, crawling, fruitful, full, numerous, overflowing, packed, pregnant, proliferating, pullulating, replete, swarming, thick.

*antonyms* lacking, rare, sparse.

**teenage** adj adolescent, immature, juvenile, pubescent, teen, young, youthful.

**teenager** n adolescent, bobbysoxer, boy, girl, juvenile, minor, youth.

**teeny** adj diminutive, microscopic, miniature, minuscule, minute, teensy-weensy, teeny-weeny, tichy, tiny, tottie, wee.

**teeter** v balance, lurch, pitch, pivot, rock, seesaw, stagger, sway, titubate, totter, tremble, waver, wobble.

**teetotaller** n abstainer, nephalist, non-drinker, Rechabite, water-drinker.

**telegram** n cable, telegraph, telemessage, telex, wire.

**telegraph** n cable, radiotelegraph, telegram, teleprinter, telex, wire.

v cable, send, signal, telex, transmit, wire.

**telepathy** n clairvoyance, ESP, mind-reading, sixth sense, thought transference.

**telephone** n blower, dog and bone, handset, line, phone.

v buzz, call, call up, contact, dial, get in touch, get on the blower, give someone a tinkle, phone, ring (up).

**telescope** v abbreviate, abridge, compress, concertina, condense, contract, crush, curtail, cut, reduce, shorten, shrink, squash, trim, truncate.

**television** n boob tube, goggle-box, idiot box, receiver, set, small screen, telly, the box, the tube, TV, TV set.

**tell** v acquaint, announce, apprise, authorise, bid, calculate, chronicle, command, communicate, comprehend, compute, confess, count, depict, describe, differentiate, direct, discern, disclose, discover, discriminate, distinguish, divulge, enjoin, enumerate, express, foresee, identify, impart, inform, instruct, mention, militate, narrate, notify, number, order, portray, predict, proclaim, reckon, recount, register, rehearse, relate, report, require, reveal, say, see, speak, state, summon, tally, understand, utter, weigh.

**tell off** bawl out, berate, censure, chide, dress down, lecture, objurgate, rebuke, reprimand, reproach, reprove, scold, take to task, tear off a strip, tick off, upbraid.

**telling-off** n bawling-out, castigation, dressing-down, jawbation, jawing, jobation, lecture, rebuke, reprimand, reproach, reproof, row, scolding, tongue-lashing.

**temerity** n assurance, audacity, boldness, brass neck, chutzpah, daring, effrontery, forwardness, gall, heedlessness, impudence, impulsiveness, intrepidity, nerve, pluck, rashness, recklessness.

*antonym* caution.

**temper** n anger, annoyance, attitude, bait, calm, calmness, character, composure, constitution, cool, coolness, disposition, equanimity, fury, heat, humour, ill-humour, irascibility, irritability, irritation, mind, moderation, mood, nature, paddy, passion, peevishness, pet, petulance, rage, resentment, sang-froid, self-control, surliness, taking, tantrum, temperament, tenor, tranquillity, vein, wax, wrath.

v abate, admix, allay, anneal, assuage, calm, harden, indurate, lessen, mitigate, moderate, modify, mollify, palliate, restrain, soften, soothe, strengthen, toughen.

**temperament** n anger, bent, character, complexion, constitution, crasis, disposition, excitability, explosiveness, hot-headedness, humour, impatience, make-up, mettle, moodiness, moods, nature, outlook, personality, petulance, quality, soul, spirit, stamp, temper, tendencies, tendency, volatility.

**temperamental** adj capricious, congenital, constitutional, emotional, erratic, excitable, explosive, fiery, highly-strung, hot-headed, hypersensitive, impatient, inborn, inconsistent, ingrained, inherent, innate, irritable, mercurial, moody, natural, neurotic, over-emotional, passionate, petulant, sensitive, touchy, undependable, unpredictable, unreliable, volatile, volcanic.

*antonyms* calm, serene, steady.

**temperance** n abstemiousness, abstinence, continence, discretion, forbearance, moderation, prohibition, restraint, self-abnegation, self-control, self-denial, self-discipline, self-restraint, sobriety, teetotalism.

*antonyms* excess, intemperance.

**temperate** adj abstemious, abstinent, agreeable, balanced, balmy, calm, clement, composed, continent, controlled, cool, dispassionate, equable, even-tempered, fair, gentle, mild, moderate, pleasant, reasonable, restrained, sensible, sober, soft, stable.

*antonyms* excessive, extreme, intemperate.

**tempest** *n* bourasque, commotion, cyclone, disturbance, ferment, furore, gale, hurricane, squall, storm, tornado, tumult, typhoon, upheaval, uproar.

**tempestuous** *adj* agitated, blustery, boisterous, breezy, emotional, excited, feverish, furious, gusty, heated, hysterical, impassioned, intense, passionate, raging, squally, stormy, troubled, tumultuous, turbulent, uncontrolled, violent, wild, windy.

*antonyms* calm, quiet.

**temple** *n* church, delubrum, fane, gompa, haffet, joss-house, mandir(a), masjid, monopteron, monopteros, mosque, pagoda, sanctuary, shrine, tabernacle, vihara, wat.

**tempo** *n* beat, cadence, measure, metre, pace, pulse, rate, rhythm, speed, time, velocity.

**temporal** *adj* carnal, civil, earthly, evanescent, fleeting, fleshly, fugacious, fugitive, impermanent, lay, material, momentary, mortal, mundane, passing, profane, secular, short-lived, sublunary, temporary, terrestrial, transient, transitory, unspiritual, worldly.

*antonym* spiritual.

**temporarily** *adv* briefly, fleetingly, for the nonce, for the time being, in the interim, momentarily, pro tem, transiently, transitorily.

*antonym* permanently.

**temporary** *adj* brief, ephemeral, evanescent, fleeting, fugacious, fugitive, impermanent, interim, makeshift, momentary, passing, pro tem, pro tempore, provisional, short-lived, stop-gap, transient, transitory.

*antonyms* everlasting, permanent.

**temporise** *v* delay, equivocate, hang back, hum and haw, pause, play for time, procrastinate, stall, tergiversate.

**tempt** *v* allure, attract, bait, coax, dare, decoy, draw, enamour, entice, incite, inveigle, invite, lure, provoke, risk, seduce, tantalise, test, try, woo.

*antonyms* discourage, dissuade.

**temptation** *n* allurement, appeal, attraction, attractiveness, bait, blandishments, coaxing, come-on, decoy, draw, enticement, fascination, forbidden fruit, inducement, invitation, lure, persuasion, pull, seduction, snare.

**tempting** *adj* alluring, appetising, attractive, enticing, inviting, lickerish, liquorish, mouthwatering, seductive, tantalising, temptatious.

*antonyms* unattractive, uninviting.

**temptress** *n* Circe, coquette, Delilah, enchantress, femme fatale, flirt, seductress, siren, sorceress, vamp.

**tenable** *adj* arguable, believable, credible, defendable, defensible, justifiable, maintainable, plausible, rational, reasonable, sound, supportable, viable.

*antonyms* indefensible, unjustifiable, untenable.

**tenacious** *adj* adamant, adhesive, backboned, clinging, coherent, cohesive, determined, dogged, fast, firm, forceful, gluey, glutinous, inflexible, intransigent, mucilaginous, obdurate, obstinate, persistent, pertinacious, resolute, retentive, single-minded, solid, staunch, steadfast, sticky, strong, strong-willed, stubborn, sure, tight, tough, unshakeable, unswerving, unwavering, unyielding, viscous.

*antonyms* loose, slack, weak.

**tenacity** *n* adhesiveness, application, clinginess, coherence, cohesiveness, determination, diligence, doggedness, fastness, firmness, force, forcefulness, indomitability, inflexibility, intransigence, obduracy, obstinacy, perseverance, persistence, pertinacity, power, resoluteness, resolution, resolve, retention, retentiveness, single-mindedness, solidity, solidness, staunchness, steadfastness, stickiness, strength, stubbornness, toughness, viscosity.

*antonyms* looseness, slackness, weakness.

**tenancy** *n* holding, incumbency, lease, leasehold, occupancy, occupation, possession, renting, residence, tenure.

**tenant** *n* gavelman, inhabitant, landholder, leaseholder, lessee, occupant, occupier, renter, resident.

**tend**[1] *v* affect, aim, bear, bend, conduce, contribute, go, gravitate, head, incline, influence, lead, lean, move, point, trend, verge.

**tend**[2] *v* attend, comfort, control, cultivate, feed, guard, handle, keep, maintain, manage, minister to, nurse, nurture, protect, serve, succour.

*antonym* neglect.

**tendency** *n* bearing, bent, bias, conatus, course, direction, disposition, drift, drive, heading, inclination, leaning, liability, movement, partiality, penchant, predilection, predisposition, proclivity, proneness, propensity, purport, readiness, susceptibility, tenor, thrust, trend, turning.

**tender**[1] *adj* aching, acute, affectionate, affettuoso, amoroso, amorous, benevolent, breakable, bruised, callow, caring, chary, compassionate, complicated, considerate, dangerous, delicate, difficult, emotional, evocative, feeble, fond, fragile, frail, gentle, green, humane, immature, impressionable, inexperienced, inflamed, irritated, kind, loving, merciful, moving, new, painful, pathetic, pitiful, poignant, raw, risky, romantic, scrupulous, sensitive, sentimental, smarting, soft, soft-hearted, sore, sympathetic, tender-hearted, ticklish, touching, touchy, tricky, vulnerable, warm, warm-hearted, weak, young, youthful.

*antonyms* callous, chewy, hard, harsh, rough, severe, tough.

**tender**[2] *v* advance, extend, give, offer, present, proffer, propose, submit, suggest, volunteer.

*n* bid, currency, estimate, medium, money, offer, payment, proffer, proposal, proposition, specie, submission, suggestion.

**tender-hearted** *adj* affectionate, benevolent, benign, caring, compassionate, considerate, feeling, fond, gentle, humane, kind, kind-hearted, kindly, loving, merciful, mild, pitying, responsive, sensitive, sentimental, soft-hearted, sympathetic, warm, warm-hearted.

*antonyms* callous, cruel, hard-hearted, unfeeling.

**tenderness** *n* ache, aching, affection, amorousness, attachment, benevolence, bruising, callowness, care, compassion, consideration, delicateness, devotion, discomfort, feebleness, fondness, fragility, frailness, gentleness, greenness, humaneness, humanity, immaturity, impressionableness, inexperience, inflammation, irritation, kindness, liking, love, loving-kindness, mercy, newness, pain, painfulness, pity, rawness, sensitiveness, sensitivity, sentimentality, soft-heartedness, softness, soreness, sweetness, sympathy, tender-heartedness, vulnerability, warm-heartedness, warmth, weakness, youth, youthfulness.

*antonyms* cruelty, hardness, harshness.

**tenet** *n* article of faith, belief, canon, conviction, credo, creed, doctrine, dogma, maxim, opinion, precept, presumption, principle, rule, teaching, thesis, view.

**tenor** *n* aim, burden, course, direction, drift, essence, evolution, gist, intent, meaning, path, point, purport, purpose, sense, spirit, substance, tendency, theme, trend, way.

**tense** *adj* anxious, apprehensive, edgy, electric, exciting, fidgety, jittery, jumpy, moving, nerve-racking, nervous, overwrought, restless, rigid, strained, stressful, stretched, strung up, taut, tight, uneasy, uptight, worrying.

*antonyms* calm, lax, loose, relaxed.

*v* brace, contract, strain, stretch, tauten, tighten.

*antonyms* loosen, relax.

**tension** *n* anxiety, apprehension, edginess, hostility, nervousness, pressure, restlessness, rigidity, stiffness, strain, straining, stress, stretching, suspense, tautness, tightness, tone, unease, worry.

*antonyms* calm(ness), laxness, looseness, relaxation.

**tent** *n* big top, canvas, marquee, marquise, tabernacle, tepee, wigwam, y(o)urt.

**tentative** *adj* cautious, conjectural, diffident, doubtful, experimental, faltering, hesitant, indefinite, peirastic, provisional, speculative, timid, uncertain, unconfirmed, undecided, unformulated, unsettled, unsure.

*antonyms* conclusive, decisive, definite, final.

**tenuous** *adj* attenuated, delicate, doubtful, dubious, fine, flimsy, gossamer, insignificant, insubstantial, nebulous, questionable, rarefied, shaky, sketchy, slender, slight, slim, thin, weak.

*antonyms* significant, strong, substantial.

**tenure** *n* habitation, holding, incumbency, occupancy, occupation, possession, proprietorship, residence, tenancy, term, time.

**tepid** *adj* apathetic, cool, half-hearted, indifferent, lew, lukewarm, unenthusiastic, warmish.

*antonyms* animated, cold, hot, passionate.

**tergiversation** *n* apostasy, defection, desertion, equivocation, fencing, hedging, prevarication, shilly-shallying, vacillation, wavering.

**term**[1] *n* appellation, denomination, designation, epithet, epitheton, expression, locution, name, phrase, title, word.

*v* call, denominate, designate, dub, entitle, label, name, style, tag, title.

**term**[2] *n* bound, boundary, close, conclusion, confine, course, culmination, duration, end, finish, fruition, half, interval, limit, period, season, session, space, span, spell, terminus, time, while.

**terminal** *adj* bounding, concluding, deadly, desinent, desinential, extreme, fatal, final, incurable, killing, last, lethal, limiting, mortal, ultimate, utmost.

*antonym* initial.

*n* boundary, depot, end, extremity, limit, termination, terminus.

**terminate** *v* abort, cease, close, complete, conclude, cut off, discontinue, drop, end, expire, finish, issue, lapse, result, stop, wind up.

*antonyms* begin, initiate, start.

**termination** *n* abortion, cessation, close, completion, conclusion, consequence, dénouement, discontinuation, effect, end, ending, expiry, finale, finis, finish, issue, result, wind-up.

*antonyms* beginning, initiation, start.

**terminology** *n* argot, cant, jargon, language, lingo, nomenclature, patois, phraseology, terms, vocabulary, words.

**terminus** *n* boundary, close, depot, destination, end, extremity, furthermost point, garage, goal, limit, station, target, termination.

**terms** *n* agreement, charges, compromise, conditions, fees, footing, language, particulars, payment, phraseology, position, premises, price, provisions, provisos, qualifications, rates, relations, relationship, specifications, standing, status, stipulations, terminology, understanding.

**terrain** *n* country, countryside, ground, land, landscape, territory, topography.

**terrestrial** *adj* earthly, global, mundane, subastral, sublunary, tellurian, terrene, worldly.

*antonyms* cosmic, empyreal, heavenly.

**terrible** *adj* abhorrent, appalling, awful, bad, beastly, dangerous, desperate, dire, disgusting, distressing, dread, dreaded, dreadful, extreme, fearful, foul, frightful, god-awful, gruesome, harrowing, hateful, hideous, horrendous, horrible, horrid, horrific, horrifying, loathsome, monstrous, obnoxious, odious, offensive, outrageous, poor, repulsive, revolting, rotten, serious, severe, shocking, unpleasant, vile.

*antonyms* great, pleasant, superb, wonderful.

**terribly** *adv* awfully, decidedly, desperately, exceedingly, extremely, frightfully, gravely, greatly, much, seriously, shockingly, thoroughly, very.

**terrific** *adj* ace, amazing, awesome, awful, breathtaking, brilliant, dreadful, enormous, excellent, excessive, extreme, fabulous, fantastic, fearful, fierce, fine, gigantic, great, harsh, horrific, huge, intense, magnificent, marvellous, monstrous, outstanding, prodigious, sensational, severe, smashing, stupendous, super, superb, terrible, tremendous, wonderful.

**terrified** *adj* alarmed, appalled, awed, dismayed, frightened, horrified, horror-struck, intimidated, panic-stricken, petrified, scared.

**terrify** *v* affright, alarm, appal, awe, dismay, frighten, horrify, intimidate, petrify, scare, shock, terrorise.

**territorial** *adj* area, district, domainal, geographical, localised, regional, sectional, topographic, zonal.

**territory** *n* area, bailiwick, country, dependency, district, domain, jurisdiction, land, park, preserve, province, region, sector, state, terrain, tract, zone.

**terror** *n* affright, alarm, anxiety, awe, blue funk, bogeyman, bugbear, consternation, devil, dismay, dread, fear, fiend, fright, horror, intimidation, monster, panic, rascal, rogue, scourge, shock, tearaway.

**terrorise** *v* alarm, appal, awe, browbeat, bully, coerce, dismay, frighten, horrify, intimidate, menace, oppress, petrify, scare, shock, strongarm, terrify, threaten.

**terse** *adj* abrupt, aphoristic, brief, brusque, clipped, compact, concise, condensed, crisp, curt, economical, elliptical, epigrammatic, gnomic, incisive, laconic, neat, pithy, sententious, short, snappy, succinct.

*antonyms* long-winded, prolix, repetitious.

**test** *v* analyse, assay, assess, check, examine, experiment, investigate, prove, screen, try, verify.

*n* analysis, assessment, attempt, catechism, check, evaluation, examination, hurdle, investigation, moment of truth, ordeal, pons asinorum, probation, proof, shibboleth, trial, try-out.

**testament** *n* attestation, demonstration, devise, earnest, evidence, exemplification, proof, testimony, tribute, will, witness.

**testicles** *n* balls, bollocks, gonads, goolies, knackers, nuts, pills, stones.

**testify** *v* affirm, assert, asseverate, attest, avow, certify, corroborate, declare, depone, depose, evince, show, state, swear, vouch, witness.

**testimonial** *n* certificate, character, commendation, credential, endorsement, gift, memorial, plug, recommendation, reference, tribute.

**testimony** *n* affidavit, affirmation, asseveration, attestation, avowal, confirmation, corroboration, declaration, demonstration, deposition, evidence, indication, information, manifestation, profession, proof, statement, submission, support, verification, witness.

**testy** *adj* bad-tempered, cantankerous, captious, carnaptious, crabbed, cross, crusty, fretful, grumpy, impatient, inflammable, irascible, irritable, peevish, peppery, petulant, quarrelsome, quick-tempered, short-tempered, snappish, snappy, splenetic, sullen, tetchy, touchy, waspish.

*antonyms* even-tempered, good-humoured.

**tether** *n* bond, chain, cord, fastening, fetter, halter, lead, leash, line, restraint, rope, shackle.

*v* bind, chain, fasten, fetter, lash, leash, manacle, picket, restrain, rope, secure, shackle, tie.

**text** *n* argument, body, contents, lection, libretto, matter, motif, paragraph, passage, reader, reading, script, sentence, source, subject, textbook, theme, topic, verse, wordage, wording, words.

**texture** *n* character, composition, consistency, constitution, fabric, feel, grain, quality, structure, surface, tissue, weave, weftage, woof.

**thankful** *adj* appreciative, beholden, contented, grateful, indebted, obliged, pleased, relieved.

*antonyms* thankless, unappreciative, ungrateful.

**thankless** *adj* fruitless, unappreciated, ungrateful, unprofitable, unrecognised, unrequited, unrewarding, useless.

*antonym* rewarding.

**thanks** *n* acknowledgement, appreciation, credit, grace, gratefulness, gratitude, recognition, thank-offering, thanksgiving.

*interj* cheers, danke (schön), gracias, gramercy, grand merci, grazie, merci, merci beaucoup, merci bien, ta.

**thanks to** as a result of, because of, by reason of, due to, in consequence of, on account of, owing to, through.

**thaw** *v* defreeze, defrost, dissolve, liquefy, melt, soften, unbend, uncongeal, unfreeze, unthaw, warm.

*antonym* freeze.

**the end** beyond endurance, enough, insufferable, intolerable, the final blow, the last straw, the limit, the worst, too much, unbearable, unendurable.

**the limit** enough, it, the end, the final blow, the last straw, the worst.

**the masses** hoi polloi, the admass, the common people, the commonalty, the crowd, the majority, the many, the multitude, the people, the plebs, the proles, the proletariat, the rank and file.

**theatre** *n* amphitheatre, auditorium, hall, lyceum, odeon, opera house, penny gaff, playhouse.

**theatrical** *adj* affected, artificial, ceremonious, dramatic, dramaturgic, exaggerated, extravagant, hammy, histrionic, mannered, melodramatic, ostentatious, overdone, pompous, scenic, showy, stagy, stilted, theatric, Thespian, unreal.

**theft** *n* abstraction, blag, embezzlement, fraud, heist, kleptomania, larceny, pilfering, plunderage, purloining, rip-off, robbery, stealing, thievery, thieving.

**thematic** *adj* conceptual, notional, taxonomic, classificatory.

**theme** *n* argument, burden, composition, dissertation, essay, exercise, idea, keynote, leitmotiv, lemma, matter, motif, mythos, paper, subject, subject-matter, text, thesis, topic, topos.

**theological** *adj* divine, doctrinal, ecclesiastical, hierological, religious.

**theorem** *n* deduction, dictum, formula, hypothesis, postulate, principle, proposition, rule, statement, thesis.

**theoretical** *adj* abstract, academic, conjectural, doctrinaire, doctrinal, hypothetical, ideal, impractical, on paper, pure, speculative.

*antonyms* applied, concrete, practical.

**theorise** *v* conjecture, formulate, guess, hypothesise, postulate, project, propound, speculate, suppose.

**theory** *n* abstraction, assumption, conjecture, guess, hypothesis, ism, philosophy, plan, postulation, presumption, proposal, scheme, speculation, supposition, surmise, system, thesis.

*antonyms* certainty, practice.

**therapeutic** *adj* ameliorative, analeptic, beneficial, corrective, curative, good, healing, recuperative, remedial, restorative, salubrious, salutary, sanative, tonic.

*antonym* harmful.

**therapy** *n* cure, healing, prophylaxis, tonic, treatment.

**therefore** *adv* accordingly, as a result, consequently, ergo, for that reason, hence, so, then, thence, thus.

**thesaurus** *n* dictionary, encyclopedia, lexicon, repository, storehouse, synonymicon, synonymy, treasury, vocabulary, wordbook.

**thesis** *n* argument, assumption, composition, contention, disquisition, dissertation, essay, hypothesis, idea, monograph, opinion, paper, postulate, premiss, proposal, proposition, statement, subject, supposition, surmise, theme, theory, topic, tract, tractate, treatise, view.

**thick** *adj* abundant, brainless, brimming, bristling, broad, bulky, bursting, chock-a-block, chock-full, chummy, close, clotted, coagulated, compact, concentrated, condensed, confidential, covered, crass, crawling, crowded, decided, deep, dense, devoted, dim-witted, distinct, distorted, dopey, dull, excessive, familiar, fat, foggy, frequent, friendly, full, gross, guttural, heavy, hoarse, husky, impenetrable, inarticulate, indistinct, insensitive, inseparable, intimate, marked, matey, moronic, muffled, numerous, obtuse, opaque, packed, pally, pronounced, replete, rich, slow, slow-witted, solid, soupy, squabbish, strong, stupid, substantial, swarming, teeming, thick-headed, throaty, turbid, wide.

*antonyms* brainy, clever, slender, slight, slim, thin, watery.

*n* centre, focus, heart, hub, middle, midst.

**thicken** *v* cake, clot, coagulate, condense, congeal, deepen, gel, incrassate, inspissate, jell, set.

*antonym* thin.

**thicket** *n* bosket, brake, clump, coppice, copse, covert, dead-finish, greave, grove, macchie, maquis, spinney, wood, woodland.

**thickhead** *n* blockhead, bonehead, chump, clot, dimwit, dolt, dope, dullard, dummy, dunce, dunderhead, fathead, fool, idiot, imbecile, moron, nitwit, numskull, pinhead, thick, twit.

**thick-headed** *adj* asinine, blockheaded, brainless, dense, dim-witted, doltish, dopey, dull-witted, idiotic, imbecilic, moronic, obtuse, slow, slow-witted, stupid, thick.

*antonyms* brainy, clever, intelligent, sharp.

**thickness** *n* body, breadth, bulk, bulkiness, density, diameter, layer, ply, sheet, spissitude, stratum, viscosity, width.

*antonym* thinness.

**thickset** *adj* beefy, brawny, bulky, burly, dense, heavy, muscular, nuggety, powerful, solid, squabbish, squabby, squat, stocky, strong, stubby, sturdy, thick, well-built.

*antonym* lanky.

**thick-skinned** *adj* callous, case-hardened, hard-boiled, hardened, impervious, insensitive, inured, obdurate, pachydermatous, stolid, tough, unfeeling.

*antonym* thin-skinned.

**thief** *n* abactor, Autolycus, bandit, burglar, cheat, cracksman, crook, cut-purse, embezzler, filcher, hoister, house-breaker, kleptomaniac, ladrone, land-rat, larcener, larcenist, latron, mugger, pickpocket, pilferer, plunderer, prigger, purloiner, robber, shop-lifter, snatch-purse, St Nicholas's clerk, stealer, swindler.

**thieve** *v* abstract, cheat, embezzle, filch, half-inch, heist, knock off, lift, misappropriate, nick, peculate, pilfer, pinch, plunder, poach, purloin, rip off, rob, steal, swindle, swipe.

**thieving** *n* banditry, burglary, crookedness, embezzlement, larceny, mugging, peculation, pilferage, pilfering, piracy, plundering, robbery, shop-lifting, stealing, theft, thievery.

**thievish** *adj* crooked, dishonest, fraudulent, furacious, larcenous, light-fingered, piratical, predatory, rapacious, sticky-fingered, thieving.

**thin** *adj* attenuate, attenuated, bony, deficient, delicate, diaphanous, dilute, diluted, emaciated, feeble, filmy, fine, fine-drawn, flimsy, gaunt, gossamer, inadequate, insubstantial, insufficient, lanky, lean, light, meagre, narrow, poor, rarefied, runny, scant, scanty, scarce, scattered, scragged, scraggy, scrawny, see-through, shallow, sheer, skeletal, skimpy, skinny, slender, slight, slim, spare, sparse, spindly, superficial, tenuous, translucent, transparent, unconvincing, undernourished, underweight, unsubstantial, washy, watery, weak, wishy-washy, wispy.

*antonyms* broad, dense, fat, solid, strong, thick.

*v* attenuate, decrassify, dilute, diminish, emaciate, extenuate, prune, rarefy, reduce, refine, trim, water down, weaken, weed out.

**thing** *n* act, action, affair, apparatus, article, aspect, attitude, being, body, circumstance, concept, contrivance, creature, deed, detail, device, dislike, entity, event, eventuality, facet, fact, factor, feat, feature, fetish, fixation, gadget, hang-up, happening, idée fixe, implement, incident, instrument, item, liking, machine, mania, matter, means, mechanism, monomania, object, obsession, occurrence, part, particular, phenomenon, phobia, point, portion, possession, preoccupation, problem, proceeding, quirk, something, statement, substance, thought, tool.

**things** *n* baggage, belongings, bits and pieces, clobber, clothes, effects, equipment, gear, goods, impedimenta, junk, luggage, odds and ends, paraphernalia, possessions, stuff, traps, utensils.

**think** *v* anticipate, be under the impression, believe, brood, calculate, cerebrate, cogitate, conceive, conclude, consider, contemplate, deem, deliberate, design, determine, envisage, esteem, estimate, expect, foresee, hold, ideate, imagine, intellectualise, judge, meditate, mull over, muse, ponder, presume, purpose, ratiocinate, reason, recall, reckon, recollect, reflect, regard, remember, revolve, ruminate, suppose, surmise.

*n* assessment, cogitation, consideration, contemplation, deliberation, meditation, reflection.

**think much of** admire, esteem, prize, rate, respect, set store by, think highly of, value.

*antonym* abominate.

**think over** chew over, consider, contemplate, meditate, mull over, ponder, reflect upon, ruminate, weigh up.

**think up** conceive, concoct, contrive, create, design, devise, dream up, imagine, improvise, invent, visualise.

**thinkable** *adj* cogitable, conceivable, feasible, imaginable, likely, possible, reasonable, supposable.

*antonym* unthinkable.

**thinker** *n* brain, ideologist, imaginist, intellect, mastermind, philosopher, sage, theorist.

**thinking** *n* assessment, cogitation, conclusions, conjecture, idea, judgement, opinion, outlook, philosophy, position, ratiocination, reasoning, theory, thoughts, view.

*adj* analytical, cerebral, contemplative, cultured, dianoetic, intelligent, meditative, philosophical, ratiocinative, rational, reasoning, reflective, sophisticated, thoughtful.

**thin-skinned** *adj* hypersensitive, irascible, irritable, sensitive, snappish, soft, susceptible, tender, testy, touchy, vulnerable.

*antonym* thick-skinned.

**third-rate** *adj* bad, cheap and nasty, cheap-jack, duff, indifferent, inferior, low-grade, mediocre, poor, ropy, shoddy.

**thirst** *n* appetite, craving, desire, drought, drouth, drouthiness, dryness, eagerness, hankering, hunger, hydromania, keenness, longing, lust, passion, thirstiness, yearning.

**thirsty** *adj* adry, appetitive, arid, athirst, avid, burning, craving, dehydrated, desirous, drouthy, dry, dying, eager, greedy, hankering, hungry, hydropic, itching, longing, lusting, parched, thirsting, yearning.

**thorn** *n* acantha, affliction, annoyance, bane, barb, bother, curse, doorn, irritant, irritation, nuisance, pest, plague, prickle, scourge, spike, spine, torment, torture, trouble.

**thorny** *adj* acanthous, awkward, barbed, bristly, difficult, fraught, harassing, hard, irksome, pointed, prickly, problematic, sharp, spiky, spinous, spiny, sticky, ticklish, tough, troublesome, trying, unpleasant, upsetting, vexatious, vexed, worrying.

**thorough** *adj* absolute, all-embracing, all-inclusive, arrant, assiduous, careful, complete, comprehensive, conscientious, deep-seated, downright, efficient, entire, exhaustive, full, in-depth, intensive, meticulous, out-and-out, painstaking, perfect, pure, root-and-branch, scrupulous, sheer, sweeping, thoroughgoing, total, unmitigated, unqualified, utter.

*antonyms* careless, haphazard, partial.

**thoroughfare** *n* access, avenue, boulevard, concourse, highway, motorway, passage, passageway, road, roadway, street, turnpike, way.

**thoroughly** *adv* à fond, absolutely, assiduously, carefully, completely, comprehensively, conscientiously, downright, efficiently, entirely, every inch, exhaustively, fully, inside out, intensively, meticulously, painstakingly, perfectly, point-device (-devise), quite, root and branch, scrupulously, sweepingly, totally, utterly, with a fine-tooth comb.

*antonyms* carelessly, haphazardly, partially.

**though** *conj* albeit, allowing, although, even if, granted, howbeit, notwithstanding, while.

*adv* all the same, even so, for all that, however, in spite of that, nevertheless, nonetheless, notwithstanding, still, yet.

**thought** *n* aim, anticipation, anxiety, aspiration, assessment, attention, attentiveness, belief, brainwork, care, cerebration, cogitation, compassion, concept, conception, concern, conclusion, conjecture, considerateness, consideration, contemplation, conviction, dash, deliberation, design, dream, estimation, excogitation, expectation, heed, hope, idea, intention, introspection, jot, judgement, kindness, little, meditation, mentation, muse, musing, notion, object, opinion, plan, prospect, purpose, reflection, regard, resolution, rumination, scrutiny, solicitude, study, sympathy, thinking, thoughtfulness, touch, trifle, view, whisker.

**thoughtful** *adj* absorbed, abstracted, astute, attentive, canny, careful, caring, cautious, circumspect, considerate, contemplative, deliberate, deliberative, discreet, heedful, helpful, introspective, kind, kindly, meditative, mindful, musing, pensieroso, pensive, prudent, rapt, reflective, ruminative, serious, solicitous, studious, thinking, unselfish, wary, wistful.

*antonym* thoughtless.

**thoughtless** *adj* absent-minded, careless, étourdi(e), foolish, heedless, ill-considered, impolite, imprudent, inadvertent, inattentive, inconsiderate, indiscreet, injudicious, insensitive, mindless, neglectful, negligent, rash, reckless, regardless, remiss, rude, selfish, silly, stupid, tactless, uncaring, undiplomatic, unkind, unmindful, unobservant, unreflecting, unthinking.

*antonym* thoughtful.

**thraldom** *n* bondage, enslavement, serfdom, servitude, slavery, subjection, subjugation, vassalage, ville(i)nage.

*antonym* freedom.

**thrash** v  beat, belt, bethump, bethwack, birch, cane, chastise, clobber, crush, defeat, drub, flagellate, flail, flog, hammer, heave, horse-whip, jerk, lam, lambaste, larrup, lather, lay into, leather, maul, overwhelm, paste, plunge, punish, quilt, rout, scourge, slaughter, spank, squirm, swish, tan, thresh, toss, towel, trim, trounce, wallop, whale, whap, whip, writhe.

**thrash out**  debate, discuss, negotiate, resolve, settle, solve.

**thrashing** n  beating, belting, caning, chastisement, defeat, dressing, drubbing, flogging, hammering, hiding, laldie, lamming, lashing, leathering, mauling, pasting, punishment, quilting, rout, strap-oil, tanning, trouncing, whaling, whipping, whopping.

**thread** n  cotton, course, direction, drift, fibre, filament, film, fimbria, line, motif, plot, story-line, strain, strand, string, tenor, theme, yarn.

v  ease, inch, meander, pass, string, weave, wind.

**threadbare** adj  clichéd, cliché-ridden, commonplace, conventional, corny, down-at-heel, frayed, hackneyed, moth-eaten, old, overused, overworn, ragged, scruffy, shabby, stale, stereotyped, stock, tattered, tatty, tired, trite, used, well-worn, worn, worn-out.

antonyms  fresh, luxurious, new, plush.

**thread-like** adj  fibriform, fibrillar(y), fibrillate(d), filaceous, filamentary, filamentous, filiform, filose, fine, slender, stringy, thin, thready.

**threat** n  commination, danger, foreboding, foreshadowing, frighteners, hazard, menace, omen, peril, portent, presage, risk, sabre-rattling, warning.

**threaten** v  browbeat, bully, comminate, cow, endanger, forebode, foreshadow, impend, imperil, intimidate, jeopardise, menace, portend, presage, pressurise, terrorise, warn.

**threatening** adj  baleful, bullying, cautionary, comminatory, Damoclean, grim, inauspicious, intimidatory, menacing, minacious, minatory, ominous, sinister, terrorising, warning.

**threesome** n  trey, triad, trilogy, trine, trinity, trio, triple, triplet, triplex, triptych, triumvirate, triune, troika.

**threshold** n  beginning, brink, dawn, door, door-sill, door-stead, doorstep, doorway, entrance, inception, minimum, opening, outset, sill, start, starting-point, verge.

**thrift** n  carefulness, conservation, economy, frugality, husbandry, parsimony, prudence, saving, thriftiness.

antonyms  profligacy, waste.

**thriftless** adj  dissipative, extravagant, improvident, imprudent, lavish, prodigal, profligate, spendthrift, unthrifty, wasteful.

antonym  thrifty.

**thrifty** adj  careful, conserving, economical, frugal, parsimonious, provident, prudent, saving, sparing.

antonyms  prodigal, profligate, thriftless, wasteful.

**thrill** n  adventure, buzz, charge, flutter, fluttering, frisson, glow, kick, pleasure, quiver, sensation, shudder, stimulation, throb, tingle, titillation, tremble, tremor, vibration.

v  arouse, electrify, excite, flush, flutter, glow, move, quake, quiver, send, shake, shudder, stimulate, stir, throb, tingle, titillate, tremble, vibrate, wow.

**thrilling** adj  electrifying, exciting, exhilarating, gripping, hair-raising, heart-stirring, quaking, rip-roaring, riveting, rousing, sensational, shaking, shivering, shuddering, soul-stirring, stimulating, stirring, trembling, vibrating.

**thrive** v  advance, bloom, blossom, boom, burgeon, develop, flourish, gain, grow, increase, profit, prosper, succeed, wax.

antonyms  die, fail, languish, stagnate.

**thriving** adj  affluent, blooming, blossoming, booming, burgeoning, comfortable, developing, flourishing, growing, healthy, prosperous, successful, wealthy, well.

antonyms  ailing, dying, failing, languishing, stagnating.

**throat** n  craw, fauces, gorge, gullet, halse, oesophagus, the Red Lane, thropple, throttle, weasand, windpipe.

**throaty** adj  deep, gruff, guttural, hoarse, husky, low, rasping, raucous, thick.

**throb** v  beat, palpitate, pound, pulsate, pulse, thump, vibrate.

n  beat, palpitation, pounding, pulsating, pulsation, pulse, thump, thumping, vibration, vibrato.

**throe** n  convulsion, fit, pain, pang, paroxysm, seizure, spasm, stab.

**throes** n  agony, anguish, death-agony, distress, pain, suffering, torture, travail.

**throng** n  assemblage, bevy, concourse, congregation, crowd, crush, flock, herd, horde, host, jam, mass, mob, multitude, pack, press, swarm.

v  bunch, congregate, converge, cram, crowd, fill, flock, herd, jam, mill around, pack, press, swarm.

**throttle** v  asphyxiate, choke, control, gag, garrotte, inhibit, silence, smother, stifle, strangle, strangulate, suppress.

**through** prep  as a result of, because of, between, by, by means of, by reason of, by virtue of, by way of, during, in, in and out of, in consequence of, in the middle of, past, thanks to, throughout, using, via.

adj  completed, direct, done, ended, express, finished, non-stop, terminated.

**through and through**  altogether, completely, entirely, from top to bottom, fully, thoroughly, to the core, totally, unreservedly, utterly, wholly.

**throughout** adv  everywhere, extensively, ubiquitously, widely.

**throw** v  astonish, baffle, bemuse, bring down, cast, chuck, confound, confuse, defeat, discomfit, disconcert, dislodge, dumbfound, elance, execute, fell, fling, floor, heave, hurl, jaculate, launch, lob, overturn, perform, perplex, pitch, produce, project, propel, put, send, shy, sling, slug, toss, unhorse, unsaddle, unseat, upset, whang.

*n* attempt, cast, chance, essay, fling, gamble, hazard, heave, lob, pitch, projection, put, shy, sling, spill, toss, try, venture, wager.

**throw away** blow, blue, cast off, discard, dispense with, dispose of, ditch, dump, fritter away, jettison, lose, reject, scrap, squander, waste.

*antonyms* keep, preserve, rescue, salvage.

**throw dust in the eyes of** con, confuse, cozen, deceive, delude, dupe, fool, have on, hoodwink, mislead, take in.

**throw off** abandon, cast off, confuse, discard, disconcert, disturb, doff, drop, shake off, throw, unsaddle, unseat, unsettle, upset.

**throw out** confuse, diffuse, discard, disconcert, dismiss, disseminate, disturb, ditch, dump, egurgitate, eject, emit, evict, expel, give off, jettison, radiate, reject, scrap, throw, turf out, turn down, unhouse, unsettle, upset, utter.

**throw over** abandon, chuck, desert, discard, drop, finish with, forsake, jilt, leave, quit, reject.

**throw up** abandon, chuck, disgorge, egurgitate, give up, heave, jack in, leave, produce, puke, quit, regurgitate, relinquish, renounce, resign, retch, reveal, spew, vomit.

**throwaway** *adj* careless, casual, cheap, disposable, offhand, passing, undramatic, unemphatic.

**thrust** *v* bear, butt, drive, force, impel, intrude, jab, jam, lunge, pierce, plunge, poke, press, prod, propel, push, ram, shove, stab, stick, urge, wedge.

*n* drive, flanconade, impetus, lunge, momentum, poke, prod, prog, push, shove, stab, stoccado.

**thud** *n* clonk, clump, clunk, crash, knock, smack, thump, thwack, wallop, wham.

*v* bash, clonk, clump, clunk, crash, knock, smack, thump, thunder, thwack, wallop, wham.

**thug** *n* animal, assassin, bandit, bangster, bruiser, bully-boy, cut-throat, gangster, goon, gorilla, heavy, highbinder, hood, hoodlum, hooligan, killer, mugger, murderer, phansigar, robber, ruffian, tough.

**thumb one's nose at** cock a snook at, deride, flout, guy, jeer at, laugh at, mock, ridicule, scoff.

**thumb through** browse through, flick through, flip through, glance at, leaf through, peruse, riffle through, scan, skim.

**thumbnail** *adj* brief, compact, concise, miniature, pithy, quick, short, small, succinct.

**thumbs down** disapproval, negation, no, rebuff, refusal, rejection, turn-down.

*antonym* thumbs up.

**thumbs up** acceptance, affirmation, approval, encouragement, go-ahead, green light, OK, sanction, yes.

*antonym* thumbs down.

**thump** *n* bang, blow, box, clout, clunk, crash, cuff, knock, rap, smack, thud, thwack, wallop, whack.

*v* bang, batter, beat, belabour, box, clout, crash, cuff, daud, ding, dunt, dush, hit, knock, lambaste, pound, rap, smack, strike, thrash, throb, thud, thwack, wallop, whack.

**thumping** *adj* big, colossal, enormous, excessive, exorbitant, gargantuan, gigantic, great, huge, immense, impressive, mammoth, massive, monumental, terrific, thundering, titanic, towering, tremendous, whooping.

*antonyms* insignificant, petty, piddling, trivial.

**thunder** *n* boom, booming, clap, cracking, crash, crashing, detonation, explosion, pealing, roll, rumble, rumbling.

*v* bark, bellow, blast, boom, clap, crack, crash, curse, declaim, denounce, detonate, explode, fulminate, inveigh, peal, rail, resound, reverberate, roar, rumble, shout, threaten, yell.

**thundering** *adj* enormous, excessive, great, monumental, remarkable, tremendous, unmitigated.

**thunderous** *adj* booming, deafening, ear-splitting, loud, noisy, resounding, reverberating, roaring, stentorian, tumultuous.

**thunderstruck** *adj* agape, aghast, amazed, astonished, astounded, dazed, dumbfounded, flabbergasted, floored, flummoxed, nonplussed, open-mouthed, paralysed, petrified, shocked, staggered, stunned.

**thus** *adv* accordingly, as follows, consequently, ergo, hence, in this way, like so, like this, so, then, therefore, thuswise.

**thwack** *v* bash, beat, buffet, clout, cuff, flog, hit, slap, smack, thump, wallop, whack.

*n* bash, blow, buffet, cloud, cuff, slap, smack, thump, wallop, whack.

**thwart** *v* baffle, balk, check, defeat, foil, frustrate, hinder, impede, obstruct, oppose, outwit, prevent, spite, stonker, stop, stymie, transverse, traverse.

*antonyms* abet, aid, assist.

**tic** *n* jerk, spasm, tic douloureux, twitch.

**tick** *n* clack, click, clicking, dash, flash, instant, jiffy, mark, minute, moment, sec, second, shake, stroke, tap, tapping, tick-tick, tick-tock, trice, twinkling.

*v* beat, choose, clack, click, indicate, mark (off), select, tally, tap.

**tick off** bawl out, berate, censure, chide, haul over the coals, keelhaul, lecture, rebuke, reprimand, reproach, reprove, scold, take to task, tear off a strip, tell off, upbraid.

*antonym* praise.

**ticket** *n* card, certificate, coupon, docket, label, marker, pass, slip, sticker, tab, tag, tessera, token, voucher.

**tickle** *v* amuse, cheer, delight, divert, enchant, entertain, excite, gratify, please, thrill, titillate.

**ticklish** *adj* awkward, critical, delicate, difficult, dodgy, hazardous, nice, precarious, risky, sensitive, thorny, touchy, tricky, uncertain, unstable, unsteady.

*antonyms* easy, straightforward.

**tide** *n* course, current, direction, drift, ebb, flow, flux, movement, stream, tendency, tenor, trend.

**tidings** *n* advice, bulletin, communication, dope, gen, greetings, information, intelligence, message, news, report, word.

**tidy** *adj* ample, businesslike, clean, cleanly, considerable, fair, generous, good, goodly, handsome, healthy, large, largish, methodical, neat, ordered, orderly, respectable, shipshape, siz(e)able, spick, spick-and-span, spruce, substantial, systematic, trim, uncluttered, well-groomed, well-kept.

*antonyms* disorganised, untidy.

*v* arrange, clean, fettle, groom, neaten, order, spruce up, straighten.

**tie** *v* attach, bind, confine, connect, draw, equal, fasten, hamper, hinder, hold, interlace, join, knot, lash, ligature, limit, link, match, moor, oblige, restrain, restrict, rope, secure, strap, tether, truss, unite.

*n* affiliation, allegiance, band, bond, commitment, connection, contest, copula, cord, dead heat, deadlock, draw, duty, encumbrance, fastening, fetter, fixture, game, hindrance, joint, kinship, knot, liaison, ligature, limitation, link, match, obligation, relationship, restraint, restriction, rope, stalemate, string.

**tie up** attach, bind, conclude, end, engage, engross, finish off, lash, ligate, moor, occupy, pinion, restrain, rope, secure, settle, terminate, tether, truss, wind up, wrap up.

**tie-in** *n* affiliation, association, connection, co-ordination, hook-up, liaison, link, relation, relationship, tie-up.

**tier** *n* band, belt, echelon, floor, gradin(e), layer, level, line, rank, row, stage, storey, stratification, stratum, zone.

**tiff** *n* barney, difference, disagreement, dispute, falling-out, huff, ill-humour, pet, quarrel, row, scrap, set-to, spat, squabble, sulk, tantrum, temper, words.

**tight**[1] *adj* close, close-fitting, compact, competent, constricted, cramped, dangerous, difficult, even, evenly-balanced, fast, firm, fixed, grasping, harsh, hazardous, hermetic, impervious, inflexible, mean, miserly, narrow, near, niggardly, parsimonious, penurious, perilous, precarious, precise, problematic, proof, rigid, rigorous, sealed, secure, severe, snug, sound, sparing, stern, sticky, stiff, stingy, stretched, strict, stringent, taut, tense, ticklish, tight-fisted, tough, tricky, trig, troublesome, uncompromising, unyielding, watertight, well-matched, worrisome.

*antonyms* lax, loose, slack.

**tight**[2] *adj* blotto, drunk, half cut, half-seas-over, in one's cups, inebriated, intoxicated, pickled, pie-eyed, pissed, plastered, smashed, sozzled, stewed, stoned, three sheets in the wind, tiddly, tipsy, under the influence.

*antonym* sober.

**tighten** *v* close, constrict, constringe, cramp, crush, fasten, fix, narrow, rigidify, screw, secure, squeeze, stiffen, stretch, tauten, tense.

*antonyms* loosen, relax.

**tight-fisted** *adj* cheese-paring, close, close-fisted, grasping, mean, mingy, miserly, niggardly, parsimonious, penny-pinching, penurious, sparing, stingy, tight.

*antonym* generous.

**tight-lipped** *adj* close-lipped, close-mouthed, mum, mute, quiet, reserved, reticent, secretive, silent, taciturn, uncommunicative, unforthcoming.

*antonyms* garrulous, talkative.

**till** *v* cultivate, dig, dress, plough, work.

**tilt** *v* attack, cant, clash, contend, duel, encounter, fight, heel, incline, joust, lean, list, overthrow, pitch, slant, slope, spar, tip.

*n* angle, cant, clash, combat, duel, encounter, fight, inclination, incline, joust, list, lists, pitch, set-to, slant, slope, thrust, tournament, tourney.

**timber** *n* beams, boarding, boards, forest, logs, planking, planks, trees, wood.

**timbre** *n* colour, klang, resonance, ring, tonality, tone, voice quality.

**time** *n* age, beat, chronology, date, day, duration, epoch, era, generation, heyday, hour, instance, interval, juncture, life, lifespan, lifetime, measure, metre, occasion, peak, period, point, rhythm, season, space, span, spell, stage, stretch, tempo, term, tide, while.

*v* clock, control, count, judge, measure, meter, regulate, schedule, set.

**time and again** frequently, many times, often, on many occasions, over and over again, recurrently, repeatedly, time after time.

**time-honoured** *adj* accustomed, age-old, ancient, conventional, customary, established, fixed, historic, long-established, old, traditional, usual, venerable.

**timeless** *adj* abiding, ageless, amaranthine, ceaseless, changeless, deathless, endless, enduring, eternal, everlasting, immortal, immutable, imperishable, indestructible, lasting, permanent, perpetual, persistent, undying.

**timely** *adj* appropriate, convenient, judicious, opportune, prompt, propitious, punctual, seasonable, suitable, tempestive, well-timed.

*antonyms* ill-timed, inappropriate, unfavourable.

**timetable** *n* agenda, calendar, curriculum, diary, list, listing, programme, roster, rota, schedule.

**time-worn** *adj* aged, ancient, broken-down, bromidic, cliché'd, dated, decrepit, dog-eared, hackneyed, hoary, lined, old hat, out of date, outworn, passé, ragged, ruined, run-down, shabby, stale, stock, threadbare, tired, trite, weathered, well-worn, worn, wrinkled.

*antonyms* fresh, new.

**timid** *adj* afraid, apprehensive, bashful, cowardly, coy, diffident, faint-hearted, fearful, hen-hearted, irresolute, modest, mousy, nervous, pavid, pusillanimous, retiring, shrinking, shy, spineless, timorous.

*antonyms* audacious, bold, brave.

**timorous** *adj* afraid, apprehensive, aspen, bashful, cowardly, coy, diffident, faint-hearted, fearful, inadventurous, irresolute, modest, mousy, nervous, pusillanimous, retiring, shrinking, shy, tentative, timid, trembling.

*antonyms* assertive, assured, bold.

**tincture** *n* aroma, colour, dash, flavour, hint, hue, seasoning, shade, smack, stain, suggestion, tinct, tinge, tint, touch, trace.

*v* colour, dye, flavour, imbue, infuse, permeate, scent, season, stain, suffuse, tinge, tint.

**tinge** *n* bit, cast, colour, dash, drop, dye, flavour, pinch, shade, smack, smatch, smattering, sprinkling, stain, suggestion, tinct, tincture, tint, touch, trace, wash.

*v* colour, dye, encolour, imbue, shade, stain, suffuse, tint.

**tingle** *v* dindle, itch, prickle, ring, sting, thrill, throb, tickle, vibrate.

*n* frisson, gooseflesh, goose-pimples, itch, itching, pins and needles, prickling, quiver, shiver, stinging, thrill, tickle, tickling.

**tinker** *v* dabble, fiddle, meddle, monkey, play, potter, putter, toy, trifle.

*n* botcher, bungler, diddicoy, fixer, itinerant, mender.

**tinsel** *adj* brummagem, cheap, clinquant, flashy, gaudy, gimcrack, meretricious, ostentatious, pinchbeck, plastic, sham, showy, specious, superficial, tawdry, trashy.

*n* artificiality, clinquant, display, flamboyance, frippery, garishness, gaudiness, glitter, insignificance, meaninglessness, ostentation, pinchbeck, pretension, sham, show, spangle, triviality, worthlessness.

**tint** *n* cast, colour, dye, hint, hue, rinse, shade, stain, streak, suggestion, tinct, tincture, tinge, tone, touch, trace, wash.

*v* affect, colour, dye, influence, rinse, stain, streak, taint, tincture, tinge.

**tiny** *adj* diminutive, dwarfish, infinitesimal, insignificant, itsy-bitsy, Lilliputian, little, microscopic, mini, miniature, minute, negligible, petite, pint-size(d), pocket, puny, pygmy, slight, small, teensy, teentsy, teeny, teeny-weeny, tiddl(e)y, tottie, totty, trifling, wee, weeny.

*antonyms* big, immense.

**tip¹** *n* acme, apex, cap, crown, end, extremity, ferrule, head, nib, peak, pinnacle, point, summit, top.

*v* cap, crown, finish, pinnacle, poll, pollard, prune, surmount, top.

**tip²** *v* cant, capsize, ditch, dump, empty, heel, incline, lean, list, overturn, pour out, slant, spill, tilt, topple over, unload, up-end, upset.

*n* bing, coup, dump, midden, refuse-heap, rubbish-heap, slag-heap.

**tip³** *n* baksheesh, clue, forecast, gen, gift, gratuity, hint, information, inside information, lagniappe, perquisite, pointer, pourboire, refresher, suggestion, tip-off, warning, word, word of advice, wrinkle.

*v* advise, caution, forewarn, inform, remunerate, reward, suggest, tell, warn.

**tipple** *v* bib, drink, imbibe, indulge, quaff, swig, tope.

*n* alcohol, booze, drink, liquor, poison, wet.

**tippler** *n* bibber, boozer, dipso(maniac), drinker, drunk, drunkard, inebriate, lush, soak, sot, sponge, toper, wine-bag.

**tipsy** *adj* a peg too low, a pip out, cockeyed, corny, drunk, elevated, fuddled, happy, mellow, merry, moony, moppy, mops and brooms, nappy, pixil(l)ated, rocky, screwed, screwy, slewed, sprung, squiff(y), tiddled, tiddley, tiddly, tight, totty, wet, woozy.

*antonym* sober.

**tirade** *n* abuse, denunciation, diatribe, fulmination, harangue, invective, lecture, outburst, philippic, rant.

**tire** *v* annoy, betoil, bore, cook, drain, droop, enervate, exasperate, exhaust, fag, fail, fatigue, flag, harass, irk, irritate, jade, knacker, sink, weary.

*antonyms* energise, enliven, exhilarate, invigorate, refresh.

**tired** *adj* all in, awearied, aweary, beat, bone-weary, bushed, clapped-out, clichéd, conventional, corny, dead-beat, disjaskit, dog-tired, drained, drooping, drowsy, enervated, épuisé(e), exhausted, fagged, familiar, fatigued, flagging, forfairn, forfough(t)en, forjeskit, hackneyed, jaded, knackered, old, outworn, shagged, shattered, sleepy, spent, stale, stock, threadbare, trite, weary, well-worn, whacked, worn out.

*antonyms* active, energetic, fresh, lively, rested.

**tireless** *adj* determined, diligent, energetic, indefatigable, industrious, resolute, sedulous, unflagging, untiring, unwearied, vigorous.

*antonyms* tired, unenthusiastic, weak.

**tiresome** *adj* annoying, boring, bothersome, dull, exasperating, fatiguing, flat, irksome, irritating, laborious, monotonous, pesky, tedious, troublesome, trying, uninteresting, vexatious, wearing, wearisome.

*antonyms* easy, interesting, stimulating.

**tiring** *adj* arduous, demanding, draining, enervating, enervative, exacting, exhausting, fagging, fatiguing, laborious, strenuous, tough, wearing, wearying.

**tiro** *n* apprentice, beginner, catechumen, freshman, greenhorn, initiate, learner, neophyte, novice, novitiate, pupil, starter, student, tenderfoot, trainee.

*antonyms* old hand, veteran.

**tissue** *n* accumulation, agglomeration, collection, combination, concatenation, conglomeration, fabric, fabrication, gauze, mass, mesh, network, pack, paper, series, structure, stuff, texture, tissue-paper, web.

**tit for tat** a Roland for an Oliver, counterblow, counterbuff, countercharge, lex talionis, measure for measure, quid pro quo, requital, retaliation, revenge, talion.

**titan** *n* Atlas, colossus, giant, Hercules, leviathan, superman.

**titanic** *adj* Brobdingnagian, colossal, cyclopean, enormous, giant, gigantic, herculean, huge, immense, jumbo, mammoth, massive, mighty, monstrous, monumental, mountainous, prodigious, stupendous, towering, vast.

*antonyms* insignificant, small.

**titbit** *n* appetiser, bonne bouche, dainty, delicacy, goody, morsel, scrap, snack, tidbit, treat.

**tithe** *n* assessment, duty, impost, levy, rent, tariff, tax, tenth, toll, tribute.

*v* assess, charge, give, hand over, levy, pay, rate, take in, tax.

**titillate** *v* arouse, captivate, excite, interest, intrigue, provoke, stimulate, tantalise, tease, thrill, tickle, turn on.

**titillating** *adj* arousing, captivating, exciting, interesting, intriguing, lewd, lurid, provocative, sensational, stimulating, suggestive, teasing, thrilling.

**titivate** *v* doll up, make up, prank, preen, primp, prink, refurbish, smarten up, tart up, touch up.

**title** *n* appellation, caption, championship, claim, crown, denomination, designation, entitlement, epithet, handle, heading, inscription, label, laurels, legend, letter-head, moniker, name, nickname, nom de plume, ownership, prerogative, privilege, pseudonym, right, sobriquet, style, term.

*v* call, christen, designate, dub, entitle, label, name, style, term.

**titter** *v* chortle, chuckle, giggle, laugh, mock, snigger, tee-hee.

**tittle-tattle** *n* babble, blather, blether, cackle, chatter, chitchat, clishmaclaver, gossip, hearsay, jaw, natter, prattle, rumour, twaddle, ya(c)k, yackety-yak.

*v* babble, blather, blether, cackle, chat, chatter, chitchat, gossip, jaw, natter, prattle, tell tales, witter, ya(c)k, yackety-yak.

**titular** *adj* formal, honorary, nominal, puppet, putative, so-called, token.

**to a fault** excessively, immoderately, in the extreme, needlessly, out of all proportion, over the top, overly, overmuch, preposterously, ridiculously, to extremes, unduly.

**to a man** bar none, every one, nem con, one and all, unanimously, without exception.

**to a turn** correctly, exactly, perfectly, precisely, to perfection.

**to all intents and purposes** as good as, practically, pretty much, pretty well, virtually.

**to be reckoned with** consequential, considerable, formidable, important, influential, powerful, significant, strong, weighty.

**to the full** completely, entirely, fully, thoroughly, to the utmost, utterly.

**to the hilt** absolutely, completely, entirely, fully, totally, wholly.

**to the letter** accurately, exactly, literally, literatim, precisely, spot on, strictly, word for word.

**to the point** applicable, apposite, appropriate, apropos, apt, brief, fitting, germane, pertinent, pithy, pointed, relevant, short, suitable, terse.

*antonym* irrelevant.

**toady** *n* arse-licker, bootlicker, clawback, crawler, creep, fawner, flatterer, flunky, groveller, hanger-on, jackal, Jenkins, lackey, lick-platter, lickspittle, lick-spittle, minion, nark, parasite, pick-thank, running dog, spaniel, sucker, sycophant, toad-eater, truckler, tuft-hunter, yes-man.

*v* bootlick, bow and scrape, butter up, crawl, creep, cringe, curry favour, fawn, flatter, grovel, kiss the feet, kowtow, suck up, truckle.

**toast¹** *v* broil, brown, grill, heat, roast, warm.

**toast²** *n* compliment, darling, drink, favourite, grace cup, health, hero, heroine, pledge, salutation, salute, tribute, wassail.

**to-do** *n* agitation, bother, brouhaha, bustle, commotion, disturbance, excitement, flap, flurry, furore, fuss, hoo-ha, performance, pother, quarrel, ruction, rumpus, stew, stir, stramash, tumult, turmoil, unrest, uproar.

**together** *adv* all at once, arranged, as one, as one man, at the same time, cheek by jowl, closely, collectively, concurrently, consecutively, contemporaneously, continuously, en masse, fixed, hand in glove, hand in hand, in a body, in a row, in concert, in co-operation, in fere, in mass, in succession, in unison, jointly, mutually, on end, ordered, organised, pari passu, settled, shoulder to shoulder, side by side, simultaneously, sorted out, straight, successively.

*antonym* separately.

*adj* calm, commonsensical, composed, cool, down-to-earth, level-headed, sensible, stable, well-adjusted, well-balanced, well-organised.

**toil** *n* application, donkey-work, drudgery, effort, elbow grease, exertion, graft, industry, labor improbus, labour, pains, slog, sweat, travail, yakka.

*v* drudge, graft, grind, grub, labour, persevere, plug away, slave, slog, strive, struggle, sweat, tew, work.

**toiler** *n* donkey, drudge, grafter, labourer, menial, navvy, slave, slogger, struggler, workaholic, worker, workhorse, workman.

*antonyms* idler, loafer, shirker.

**toilet** *n* ablutions, bathing, bathroom, bog, can, closet, comfort station, convenience, dressing, gents', grooming, john, karsey, kazi, ladies', latrine, lavatory, loo, outhouse, powder-room, privy, reredorter, rest-room, smallest room, thunder-box, toilette, urinal, washroom, water closet, WC.

**toilsome** *adj* arduous, backbreaking, burdensome, difficult, fatiguing, hard, herculean, laborious, painful, severe, strenuous, taxing, tedious, tiresome, tough, uphill, wearisome.

**token** *n* badge, clue, demonstration, earnest, evidence, expression, index, indication, keepsake, manifestation, mark, memento, memorial, note, pledge, proof, remembrance, reminder, representation, sign, souvenir, symbol, tessera, testimony, voucher, warning.

*adj* emblematic, hollow, inconsiderable, minimal, nominal, perfunctory, superficial, symbolic.

**tolerable** *adj* acceptable, adequate, all right, allowable, average, bearable, endurable, fair, fair to middling, indifferent, liv(e)able, mediocre, middling, not bad, OK, ordinary, passable, run-of-the-mill, so-so, sufferable, supportable, unexceptional.

*antonym* intolerable.

**tolerance** *n* allowance, broad-mindedness, charity, endurance, fluctuation, forbearance, fortitude, hardiness, hardness, indulgence, lenity, magnanimity, open-mindedness, patience, permissiveness, play, resilience, resistance, rope, stamina, sufferance, swing, sympathy, toughness, variation.

*antonyms* bigotry, intolerance, narrow-mindedness, prejudice.

**tolerant** *adj* biddable, broad-minded, catholic, charitable, complaisant, compliant, easy-going, fair, forbearing, indulgent, kind-hearted, latitudinarian, lax, lenient, liberal, long-suffering, magnanimous, open-minded, patient, permissive, soft, sympathetic, understanding, unprejudiced.

*antonyms* biased, bigoted, intolerant, prejudiced, unsympathetic.

**tolerate** *v* abear, abide, accept, admit, allow, bear, brook, condone, connive at, countenance, endure, indulge, permit, pocket, put up with, receive, sanction, stand, stomach, suffer, swallow, take, thole, turn a blind eye to, undergo, wear, wink at.

**toleration** *n* acceptance, allowance, condonation, connivance, endurance, indulgence, permissiveness, sanction, sufferance, tholing, wearing.

**toll¹** *v* announce, call, chime, clang, knell, peal, ring, send, signal, sound, strike, summon, warn.

**toll²** *n* assessment, charge, cost, customs, damage, demand, duty, fee, impost, inroad, levy, loss, payment, penalty, rate, tariff, tax, tithe, tribute.

**tomb** *n* burial-place, catacomb, cenotaph, crypt, dolmen, grave, mastaba, mausoleum, sepulchre, sepulture, speos, vault.

**tomboy** *n* gamine, gilp(e)y, hempy, hoyden, minx, randie, randy, romp.

**tombstone** *n* gravestone, headstone, marker, memorial, monument, stone.

**tome** *n* book, opus, volume, work.

**tomfoolery** *n* balderdash, baloney, bilge, bosh, buffoonery, bunk, bunkum, childishness, claptrap, clowning, foolishness, hogwash, hooey, horseplay, idiocy, inanity, larking about, larks, messing about, messing on, nonsense, poppycock, rot, rubbish, shenanigans, silliness, skylarking, stupidity, tommyrot, tosh, trash, twaddle.

**tone** *n* accent, air, approach, aspect, attitude, cast, character, colour, drift, effect, emphasis, feel, force, frame, grain, harmony, hue, inflection, intonation, klang, manner, modulation, mood, note, pitch, quality, shade, spirit, strength, stress, style, temper, tenor, timbre, tinge, tint, tonality, vein, volume.

*v* blend, harmonise, intone, match, sound, suit.

**tone down** alleviate, assuage, dampen, dim, mitigate, moderate, modulate, palliate, play down, reduce, restrain, soften, soft-pedal, subdue, temper.

**tone up** brighten, freshen, invigorate, limber up, shape up, sharpen up, touch up, trim, tune up.

**tongue** *n* argot, articulation, clack, clapper, dialect, discourse, idiom, language, languet(te), lath, lingo, parlance, patois, red rag, speech, talk, utterance, vernacular, voice.

**tongue-tied** *adj* dumb, dumbstruck, inarticulate, mute, silent, speechless, voiceless.

*antonyms* garrulous, talkative, voluble.

**tonic** *n* analeptic, boost, bracer, cordial, fillip, inspiration, livener, pick-me-up, refresher, restorative, roborant, shot in the arm, stimulant.

**too¹** *adv* also, as well, besides, further, in addition, into the bargain, likewise, moreover, to boot, what's more.

**too²** *adv* excessively, exorbitantly, extremely, immoderately, inordinately, over, overly, ridiculously, to excess, to extremes, unduly, unreasonably, very.

**tool** *n* agency, agent, apparatus, appliance, cat's-paw, contraption, contrivance, creature, device, dupe, flunkey, front, gadget, hireling, implement, instrument, intermediary, jackal, lackey, machine, means, medium, minion, pawn, puppet, stooge, toady, utensil, vehicle, weapon, widget.

*v* chase, cut, decorate, fashion, machine, ornament, shape, work.

**tooth** *n* cog, denticle, denticulation, dentil, fang, incisor, jag, masticator, molar, prong, tush, tusk.

**toothless** *adj* edentate, edentulous, fangless, gummy, powerless.

**toothsome** *adj* agreeable, ambrosial, appetising, dainty, delectable, delicious, flavoursome, luscious, mouthwatering, nice, palatable, sapid, savoury, scrumptious, sweet, tasty, tempting, yummy.

*antonyms* disagreeable, unpleasant.

**top** *n* acme, apex, apogee, cacumen, cap, cop, cork, cover, crest, crown, culmen, culmination, head, height, high point, lead, lid, meridian, peak, pinnacle, stopper, summit, upside, vertex, zenith.

*antonyms* base, bottom, nadir.

*adj* best, chief, crack, crowning, culminating, dominant, elite, finest, first, foremost, greatest, head, highest, lead, leading, pre-eminent, prime, principal, ruling, sovereign, superior, topmost, upmost, upper, uppermost.

*v* ascend, beat, best, better, cap, climb, command, cover, crest, crown, decorate, eclipse, exceed, excel, finish, finish off, garnish, head, lead, outdo, outshine, outstrip, roof, rule, scale, surmount, surpass, tip, transcend.

**topic** *n* issue, lemma, matter, motif, point, question, subject, subject-matter, talking-point, text, theme, thesis.

**topical** *adj* contemporary, current, familiar, newsworthy, popular, relevant, up-to-date, up-to-the-minute.

**topmost** *adj* apical, dominant, foremost, highest, leading, loftiest, maximum, paramount, principal, supreme, top, upper, uppermost.

*antonyms* bottom, bottommost, lowest.

**topple** *v* capsize, collapse, oust, overbalance, overthrow, overturn, totter, tumble, unseat, upset.

**topsy-turvy** *adj* arsy-versy, backside-foremost, chaotic, confused, disarranged, disorderly, disorganised, inside-out, jumbled, messy, mixed-up, untidy, upside-down.

*antonyms* ordered, tidy.

**torch** *n* brand, cresset, firebrand, flambeau, flashlight, lampad, link.

**torment** *v* afflict, agitate, agonise, annoy, bedevil, bother, chivvy, crucify, devil, distort, distress, excruciate, harass, harrow, harry, hound, irritate, nag, pain, persecute, pester, plague, provoke, rack, tease, torture, trouble, vex, worry, wrack.

*n* affliction, agony, angst, anguish, annoyance, bane, bother, distress, harassment, hassle, hell, irritation, misery, nag, nagging, nuisance, pain, persecution, pest, plague, provocation, scourge, suffering, torture, trouble, vexation, worry.

**torn** *adj* cut, dithering, divided, havering, irresolute, lacerated, ragged, rent, ripped, slit, split, swithering, uncertain, undecided, unsure, vacillating, wavering.

**tornado** *n* cyclone, gale, hurricane, monsoon, squall, storm, tempest, twister, typhoon, whirlwind.

**torpid** *adj* apathetic, benumbed, dormant, drowsy, dull, fainéant, hebetudinous, inactive, indolent, inert, lackadaisical, languid, languorous, lazy, lethargic, listless, lymphatic, motionless, numb, passive, slothful, slow, slow-moving, sluggish, somnolent, stagnant, supine.

*antonyms* active, lively, vigorous.

**torpor** *n* accidie, acedia, apathy, dormancy, drowsiness, dullness, hebetude, inactivity, inanition, indolence, inertia, inertness, languor, laziness, lethargy, listlessness, numbness, passivity, sloth, sluggishness, somnolence, stagnancy, stupidity, stupor, torpidity.

*antonyms* activity, animation, vigour.

**torrent** *n* barrage, cascade, deluge, downpour, effusion, flood, flow, gush, outburst, rush, spate, stream, tide, volley.

**torrid** *adj* ardent, arid, blistering, boiling, broiling, burning, dried, dry, emotional, erotic, fervent, fiery, hot, intense, parched, parching, passionate, scorched, scorching, sexy, sizzling, steamy, stifling, sultry, sweltering, tropical.

*antonym* arctic.

**tortuous** *adj* ambagious, ambiguous, bent, Byzantine, circuitous, complicated, convoluted, crooked, cunning, curved, deceptive, devious, indirect, involved, mazy, meandering, misleading, roundabout, serpentine, sinuous, tricky, twisted, twisting, winding, zigzag.

*antonyms* straight, straightforward.

**torture** *v* afflict, agonise, crucify, distress, excruciate, harrow, lacerate, martyr, martyrise, pain, persecute, rack, torment, wrack.

*n* affliction, agony, anguish, distress, gyp, hell, laceration, martyrdom, misery, pain, pang(s), persecution, rack, suffering, torment.

**toss** *v* agitate, cant, cast, chuck, disturb, fling, flip, heave, hurl, jiggle, joggle, jolt, labour, launch, lob, lurch, pitch, project, propel, rock, roll, shake, shy, sling, thrash, throw, tumble, wallow, welter, wriggle, writhe.

*n* cast, chuck, fling, lob, pitch, shy, sling, throw.

**tot** *n* baby, bairn, child, dram, finger, infant, measure, mite, nip, shot, slug, snifter, toddler, toothful, wean.

**tot up** add (up), calculate, compute, count (up), reckon, sum, tally, total.

**total** *n* aggregate, all, amount, ensemble, entirety, lot, mass, sum, totality, whole.

*adj* absolute, all-out, complete, comprehensive, consummate, downright, entire, full, gross, integral, out-and-out, outright, perfect, root-and-branch, sheer, sweeping, thorough, thoroughgoing, unconditional, undisputed, undivided, unmitigated, unqualified, utter, whole, whole-hog.

*antonyms* limited, partial, restricted.

*v* add (up), amount to, come to, count (up), reach, reckon, sum (up), tot up.

**totalitarian** *adj* authoritarian, despotic, dictatorial, monocratic, monolithic, omnipotent, one-party, oppressive, tyrannous, undemocratic.

*antonym* democratic.

**totality** *n* aggregate, all, completeness, cosmos, entireness, entirety, everything, fullness, pleroma, sum, total, universe, whole, wholeness.

**totally** *adv* absolutely, completely, comprehensively, consummately, entirely, fully, perfectly, quite, thoroughly, unconditionally, undisputedly, undividedly, unmitigatedly, utterly, wholeheartedly, wholly.

*antonym* partially.

**totter** *v* daddle, daidle, falter, lurch, quiver, reel, rock, shake, stagger, stumble, sway, teeter, titter, tremble, waver.

**touch** *n* ability, acquaintance, adroitness, approach, art, artistry, awareness, bit, blow, brush, caress, characteristic, command, communication, contact, correspondence, dash, deftness, detail, direction, drop, effect, facility, familiarity, feel, feeling, flair, fondling, hand, handiwork, handling, hit, hit, influence, intimation, jot, knack, manner, mastery, method, palpation, pat, pinch, push, skill, smack, smattering, soupçon, speck, spot, stroke, style, suggestion, suspicion, tactility, tap, taste, technique, tig, tincture, tinge, trace, trademark, understanding, virtuosity, way, whiff.

*v* abut, adjoin, affect, attain, border, brush, caress, cheat, compare with, concern, consume, contact, converge, disturb, drink, eat, equal, feel, finger, fondle, graze, handle, hit, hold a candle to, impress, influence, inspire, interest, mark, match, meet, melt, move, palp, palpate, parallel, pat, pertain to, push, reach, regard, rival, soften, stir, strike, stroke, tap, tat, tinge, upset, use, utilise.

**touch off** actuate, arouse, begin, cause, fire, foment, ignite, inflame, initiate, light, provoke, set off, spark off, trigger (off).

**touch on** allude to, broach, cover, deal with, mention, refer to, remark on, speak of.

**touch up** arouse, brush up, enhance, finish off, fondle, improve, patch up, perfect, polish up, renovate, retouch, revamp, round off, stimulate, titivate.

**touch-and-go** *adj* close, critical, dangerous, dodgy, hairy, hazardous, near, nerve-racking, offhand, parlous, perilous, precarious, risky, sticky, tricky.

**touched** *adj* affected, barmy, batty, bonkers, crazy, cuckoo, daft, disturbed, dotty, eccentric, impressed, mad, melted, moved, nuts, nutty, softened, stirred, swayed, upset.

**touchiness** *n* bad temper, captiousness, crabbedness, grouchiness, grumpiness, irascibility, irritability, peevishness, pettishness, petulance, surliness, testiness, tetchiness.

**touching** *adj* affecting, emotional, emotive, haptic, heartbreaking, libant, melting, moving, pathetic, piteous, pitiable, pitiful, poignant, sad, stirring, tender.

**touchstone** *n* bench-mark, criterion, gauge, measure, norm, proof, standard, yardstick.

**touchy** *adj* bad-tempered, captious, crabbed, cross, feisty, grouchy, grumpy, huffy, irascible, irritable, miffy, peevish, pettish, petulant, querulous, quick-tempered, sensitive, snippety, snuffy, sore, splenetic, surly, testy, tetchy, thin-skinned.

*antonyms* calm, imperturbable, serene, unflappable.

**tough** *adj* adamant, arduous, bad, baffling, brawny, butch, callous, cohesive, difficult, durable, exacting, exhausting, firm, fit, hard, hard-bitten, hard-boiled, hardened, hard-nosed, hardy, herculean, inflexible, intractable, irksome, knotty, laborious, lamentable, leathery, merciless, obdurate, obstinate, perplexing, pugnacious, puzzling, refractory, regrettable, resilient, resistant, resolute, rigid, rough, ruffianly, rugged, ruthless, seasoned, severe, solid, stalwart, stern, stiff, stout, strapping, strenuous, strict, strong, stubborn, sturdy, tenacious, thorny, troublesome, unbending, unforgiving, unfortunate, unlucky, unyielding, uphill, vicious, vigorous, violent.

*antonyms* brittle, delicate, fragile, liberal, soft, tender, vulnerable, weak.

*n* bravo, bruiser, brute, bully, bully-boy, bully-rook, droog, gorilla, hooligan, rough, roughneck, rowdy, ruffian, thug, yob, yobbo.

**toughness** *n* arduousness, callousness, difficulty, durability, firmness, fitness, grit, hardiness, hardness, inflexibility, intractability, laboriousness, obduracy, obstinacy, pugnacity, resilience, resistance, rigidity, roughness, ruggedness, ruthlessness, severity, solidity, sternness, stiffness, strength, strenuousness, strictness, sturdiness, tenacity, viciousness.

*antonyms* fragility, liberality, softness, vulnerability, weakness.

**tour** *n* circuit, course, drive, excursion, expedition, jaunt, journey, outing, peregrination, progress, ride, round, trip.

*v* drive, explore, journey, ride, sightsee, travel, visit.

**tourist** *n* emmet, excursionist, globe-trotter, grockle, holidaymaker, journeyer, rubber-neck, sightseer, sojourner, traveller, tripper, voyager.

**tournament** *n* championship, competition, contest, event, joust, lists, match, meeting, series, tourney.

**tourniquet** *n* garrot.

**tousled** *adj* disarranged, dishevelled, disordered, messed up, ruffled, rumpled, tangled, tumbled.

**tow** *v* drag, draw, haul, lug, pull, tote, trail, transport, trawl, tug, yank.

**towards** *prep* a little short of, about, almost, approaching, close to, coming up to, concerning, for, getting on for, in the direction of, in the vicinity of, just before, nearing, nearly, on the way to, regarding, to, -wards, with regard to, with respect to.

**tower** *n* barbican, bastille, bastion, belfry, castle, citadel, column, donjon, fort, fortification, fortress, keep, minar, minaret, mirador, obelisk, pillar, refuge, skyscraper, steeple, stronghold, turret.

*v* ascend, dominate, exceed, loom, mount, overlook, overtop, rear, rise, soar, surpass, top, transcend, uprise.

**towering** *adj* burning, colossal, elevated, excessive, extraordinary, extreme, fiery, gigantic, great, high, immoderate, imposing, impressive, inordinate, intemperate, intense, lofty, magnificent, mighty, monumental, outstanding, overpowering, paramount, passionate, prodigious, soaring, sublime, superior, supreme, surpassing, tall, transcendent, vehement, violent.

*antonyms* minor, small, trivial.

**town** *n* borough, bourg, burg, burgh, city, metropolis, municipality, settlement, township.

*antonym* country.

**town-dweller** *n* burgher, citizen, oppidan, townsman, towny, urbanite.

*antonyms* country-dweller, rustic.

**toxic** *adj* baneful, deadly, harmful, lethal, morbific, noxious, pernicious, pestilential, poisonous, septic, unhealthy.

*antonym* harmless.

**toy** *n* bauble, doll, game, gewgaw, kickshaw(s), knick-knack, plaything, trifle, trinket.

*v* dally, fiddle, flirt, play, potter, putter, sport, tinker, trifle, wanton.

**trace** *n* bit, dash, drop, evidence, footmark, footprint, footstep, hint, indication, iota, jot, mark, path, record, relic, remains, remnant, scintilla, shadow, sign, smack, soupçon, spoor, spot, suggestion, survival, suspicion, tincture, tinge, token, touch, track, trail, trifle, vestige, whiff.

*v* ascertain, chart, copy, delineate, depict, detect, determine, discover, draw, find, follow, map, mark, outline, pursue, record, seek, shadow, show, sketch, stalk, track, trail, traverse, unearth, write.

**track** *n* course, drift, footmark, footprint, footstep, line, mark, orbit, path, pathway, piste, rail, rails, ridgeway, road, scent, sequence, slot, spoor, tack, trace, trail, train, trajectory, wake, wavelength, way.

*v* chase, dog, follow, hunt, pursue, shadow, spoor, stalk, tail, trace, trail, travel, traverse.

**track down** apprehend, capture, catch, dig up, discover, expose, ferret out, find, hunt down, locate, run to earth, sniff out, trace, unearth.

**tract**[1] *n* area, district, estate, expanse, extent, lot, plot, quarter, region, section, stretch, territory, zone.

**tract**[2] *n* booklet, brochure, discourse, disquisition, dissertation, essay, homily, leaflet, monograph, pamphlet, sermon, tractate, treatise.

**tractable** *adj* amenable, biddable, complaisant, compliant, controllable, docile, ductile, fictile, governable, malleable, manageable, obedient, persuadable, plastic, pliable, pliant, submissive, tame, tractile, willing, workable, yielding.

*antonyms* headstrong, intractable, obstinate, refractory, stubborn, unruly, wilful.

**traction** *n* adhesion, drag, draught, drawing, friction, grip, haulage, propulsion, pull, pulling, purchase, resistance.

**trade** *n* avocation, barter, business, calling, clientele, commerce, commodities, craft, custom, customers, deal, dealing, employment, exchange, interchange, job, line, market, métier, occupation, patrons, profession, public, pursuit, shopkeeping, skill, swap, traffic, transactions, truck.

*v* bargain, barter, commerce, deal, do business, exchange, peddle, swap, switch, traffic, transact, truck.

**trademark** *n* badge, brand, crest, emblem, hallmark, identification, idiograph, insignia, label, logo, logotype, name, sign, symbol.

**trader** *n* barrow-boy, barterer, broker, buyer, dealer, marketer, merchandiser, merchant, seller, sutler.

**tradesman** *n* artisan, craftsman, dealer, journeyman, mechanic, merchant, retailer, seller, shopkeeper, shopman, vendor, workman.

**tradition** *n* convention, custom, customs, folklore, habit, institution, lore, praxis, ritual, usage, usance, way, wony.

**traditional** *adj* accustomed, ancestral, conventional, customary, established, fixed, folk, historic, long-established, new, old, oral, time-honoured, tralaticious, transmitted, unconventional, unwritten, usual.

**traduce** *v* abuse, asperse, blacken, calumniate, decry, defame, denigrate, deprecate, depreciate, detract, disparage, knock, malign, misrepresent, revile, run down, slag, slander, smear, vilify.

**traducer** *n* abuser, asperser, calumniator, defamer, denigrator, deprecator, detractor, disparager, knocker, mud-slinger, slanderer, smearer, vilifier.

**traffic** *n* barter, business, commerce, communication, dealing, dealings, doings, exchange, freight, intercourse, movement, passengers, peddling, relations, toing and froing, trade, transport, transportation, truck, vehicles.

*v* bargain, barter, deal, do business, exchange, intrigue, market, merchandise, peddle, trade, truck.

**trafficker** *n* broker, dealer, merchant, monger, peddler, trader.

**tragedy** *n* adversity, affliction, blow, calamity, catastrophe, disaster, misfortune, unhappiness.

*antonyms* prosperity, success, triumph.

**tragic** *adj* anguished, appalling, awful, calamitous, catastrophic, deadly, dire, disastrous, doleful, dreadful, fatal, grievous, heartbreaking, heart-rending, ill-fated, ill-starred, lamentable, miserable, mournful, pathetic, pitiable, ruinous, sad, shocking, sorrowful, thespian, unfortunate, unhappy, woeful, wretched.

*antonyms* comic, successful, triumphant.

**trail** *v* chase, dangle, dawdle, drag, draw, droop, extend, follow, hang, haul, hunt, lag, linger, loiter, pull, pursue, shadow, stalk, straggle, stream, sweep, tail, tow, trace, track, traipse.

*n* abature, appendage, drag, footpath, footprints, footsteps, mark, marks, path, road, route, scent, spoor, stream, tail, trace, track, train, wake, way.

**trail away** decrease, die away, diminish, disappear, dwindle, fade (away), fall away, lessen, peter out, shrink, sink, subside, tail off, taper off, trail off, weaken.

**train** *v* aim, coach, direct, discipline, drill, educate, excercise, focus, guide, improve, instruct, lesson, level, point, prepare, rear, rehearse, school, teach, tutor.

*n* appendage, attendants, caravan, chain, choo-choo, column, concatenation, convoy, cortege, course, court, entourage, file, followers, following, household, lure, order, process, procession, progression, retinue, sequence, series, set, staff, string, succession, suite, tail, trail.

**trainer** *n* coach, drill-master, handler, instructor, teacher, tutor, walker.

**training** *n* coaching, discipline, dressage, education, exercise, grounding, guidance, instruction, manège, practice, preparation, schooling, teaching, tuition, tutelage, upbringing, working-out.

**traipse** *v* plod, slouch, trail, tramp, trudge.

*n* plod, slog, tramp, trek, trudge.

**trait** *n* attribute, characteristic, feature, idiosyncrasy, lineament, mannerism, peculiarity, quality, quirk, thew.

**traitor** *n* apostate, back-stabber, betrayer, deceiver, defector, deserter, double-crosser, fifth columnist, informer, Judas, miscreant, nithing, proditor, quisling, rebel, renegade, turncoat.

**traitorous** *adj* apostate, dishonourable, disloyal, double-crossing, double-dealing, faithless, false, perfidious, proditorious, renegade, seditious, treacherous, treasonable, unfaithful, untrue.

*antonyms* faithful, loyal, patriotic.

**trajectory** *n* course, flight, line, path, route, track, trail.

**trammel** *n* bar, block, bond, chain, check, clog, curb, fetter, hamper, handicap, hindrance, impediment, obstacle, rein, shackle, stumbling-block.

*v* bar, block, capture, catch, check, clog, curb, enmesh, ensnare, entrammel, entrap, fetter, hamper, handicap, hinder, impede, inhibit, net, pinion, restrain, restrict, shackle, snag, tie.

**tramp** *v* crush, footslog, hike, march, plod, ramble, range, roam, rove, slog, stamp, stomp, stump, toil, traipse, trample, tread, trek, trudge, walk, yomp.

*n* clochard, derelict, dosser, down-and-out, drifter, drummer, footfall, footstep, hike, hobo, march, piker, plod, ramble, slog, stamp, toe-rag(ger), tread, trek, vagabond, vagrant, weary willie.

**trample** *v* crush, flatten, hurt, infringe, insult, squash, stamp, tread, violate.

**trance** *n* abstraction, catalepsy, daze, dream, ecstasy, muse, rapture, reverie, spell, stupefaction, stupor, unconsciousness.

**tranquil** *adj* at peace, calm, composed, cool, disimpassioned, dispassionate, pacific, peaceful, placid, quiet, reposeful, restful, sedate, serene, still, undisturbed, unexcited, unperturbed, unruffled, untroubled.

*antonyms* agitated, disturbed, noisy, troubled.

**tranquillise** *v* calm, compose, lull, narcotise, opiate, pacify, quell, quiet, relax, sedate, soothe.

*antonyms* agitate, disturb, upset.

**tranquilliser** *n* barbiturate, bromide, downer, narcotic, opiate, opium, sedative.

**tranquillity** *n* ataraxia, ataraxy, calm, calmness, composure, coolness, equanimity, hush, imperturbability, peace, peacefulness, placidity, quiet, quietness, quietude, repose, rest, restfulness, sedateness, serenity, silence, stillness.

*antonyms* agitation, disturbance, noise.

**transact** *v* accomplish, carry on, carry out, conclude, conduct, discharge, dispatch, do, enact, execute, handle, manage, negotiate, perform, prosecute, settle.

**transaction** *n* action, affair, arrangement, bargain, business, coup, deal, deed, enterprise, event, execution, matter, negotiation, occurrence, proceeding, undertaking.

**transactions** *n* affairs, annals, concerns, doings, goings-on, minutes, proceedings, record.

**transcend** *v* eclipse, exceed, excel, outdo, outrival, outshine, outstrip, overleap, overstep, overtop, surmount, surpass.

**transcendence** *n* ascendancy, excellence, greatness, incomparability, matchlessness, paramoun(t)cy, predominance, pre-eminence, sublimity, superiority, supremacy, transcendency.

**transcendent** *adj* consummate, exceeding, extraordinary, foremost, incomparable, matchless, peerless, pre-eminent, sublime, superior, transcendental, unequalled, unique, unparalleled, unrivalled, unsurpassed.

**transcribe** *v* copy, engross, exemplify, interpret, note, record, render, reproduce, rewrite, take down, tape, tape-record, transfer, translate, transliterate.

**transcript** *n* carbon, copy, duplicate, manuscript, note, notes, record, recording, reproduction, tenor, transcription, translation, transliteration, version.

**transfer** *v* carry, cede, change, consign, convey, decal, decant, demise, displace, grant, hand over, move, relocate, remove, second, shift, translate, transmit, transplant, transport, transpose.

*n* change, changeover, crossover, decantation, displacement, handover, move, relocation, removal, shift, switch, switch-over, transference, translation, transmission, transposition, virement.

**transfigure** *v* alter, apotheosise, change, convert, exalt, glorify, idealise, metamorphose, transform, translate, transmute.

**transfix** *v* engross, fascinate, fix, hold, hypnotise, impale, mesmerise, paralyse, petrify, pierce, puncture, skewer, spear, spellbind, spike, spit, stick, stun, transpierce.

*antonym* bore.

**transform** *v* alter, change, convert, metamorphose, reconstruct, remodel, renew, revolutionise, transfigure, translate, transmogrify, transmute, transverse.

*antonym* preserve.

**transformation** *n* alteration, change, conversion, metamorphosis, metanoia, metastasis, renewal, revolution, sea-change, transfiguration, translation, transmogrification, transmutation.

*antonym* preservation.

**transfuse** *v* imbue, instil, permeate, pervade, suffuse, transfer.

**transgress** *v* breach, break, contravene, defy, disobey, encroach, err, exceed, infringe, lapse, misbehave, offend, overstep, sin, trespass, violate.

*antonym* obey.

**transgression** *n* breach, contravention, crime, debt, encroachment, error, fault, infraction, infringement, iniquity, lapse, misbehaviour, misdeed, misdemeanour, offence, peccadillo, peccancy, sin, trespass, violation, wrong, wrongdoing.

**transgressor** *n* criminal, culprit, debtor, delinquent, evil-doer, felon, lawbreaker, malefactor, miscreant, offender, sinner, trespasser, villain, wrong-doer.

**transience** *n* brevity, briefness, caducity, deciduousness, ephemerality, evanescence, fleetingness, fugacity, fugitiveness, impermanence, shortness, transitoriness.

*antonym* permanence.

**transient** *adj* brief, caducous, deciduous, ephemeral, evanescent, fleeting, flying, fugacious, fugitive, impermanent, momentary, passing, short, short-lived, short-term, temporary, transitory.

*antonym* permanent.

**transit** *n* alteration, carriage, cartage, carting, change, changeover, conversion, conveyance, crossing, haulage, motion, movement, passage, portage, shift, shipment, transfer, transition, transport, transportation, travel, traverse.

**transition** *n* alteration, change, changeover, conversion, development, evolution, flux, metabasis, metamorphosis, metastasis, passage, passing, progress, progression, shift, transformation, transit, transmutation, upheaval.

*antonyms* beginning, end.

**transitional** *adj* changing, developmental, fluid, intermediate, metabatic, passing, provisional, temporary, transition, transitionary, unsettled.

*antonyms* final, initial.

**transitory** *adj* brief, deciduous, ephemeral, evanescent, fleeting, flying, fugacious, fugitive, impermanent, momentary, passing, short, short-lived, short-term, temporary, transient, vanishing.

*antonym* lasting.

**translate** *v* alter, carry, change, construe, convert, convey, decipher, decode, do, do up, elucidate, enrapture, explain, improve, interpret, metamorphose, move, paraphrase, remove, render, renovate, send, simplify, spell out, transcribe, transfer, transfigure, transform, transliterate, transmogrify, transmute, transplant, transport, transpose, turn.

**translation** *n* alteration, change, conversion, conveyance, crib, decoding, elucidation, explanation, gloss, interpretation, metamorphosis, metaphrase, metaphrasis, move, paraphrase, removal, rendering, rendition, rephrasing, rewording, simplification, transcription, transference, transfiguration, transformation, transliteration, transmutation, transposition, version.

**translator** *n* dragoman, exegete, exegetist, glossarist, glossator, glosser, interpreter, linguist, metaphrast, paraphraser, paraphrast.

**translucent** *adj* clear, diaphanous, limpid, lucent, pellucid, translucid, transparent.

*antonym* opaque.

**transmigration** *n* metempsychosis, Pythagoreanism, rebirth, reincarnation, transformation.

**transmission** *n* broadcast, broadcasting, carriage, communication, conveyance, diffusion, dispatch, dissemination, passage, programme, relaying, remission, sending, shipment, show, showing, signal, spread, trajection, transfer, transference, transit, transport, transportation.

*antonym* reception.

**transmit** *v* bear, broadcast, carry, communicate, convey, diffuse, dispatch, disseminate, forward, impart, network, radio, relay, remit, send, spread, traject, transfer, transport.

*antonym* receive.

**transmute** *v* alter, change, convert, metamorphose, remake, transfigure, transform, translate, transmogrify, transverse.

*antonym* retain.

**transparency**[1] *n* apparentness, candidness, clarity, clearness, diaphanousness, directness, distinctness, explicitness, filminess, forthrightness, frankness, gauziness, limpidity, limpidness, obviousness, openness, patentness, pellucidity, pellucidness, perspicuousness, plainness, sheerness, straightforwardness, translucence, translucency, translucidity, transparence, unambiguousness, visibility, water.

*antonyms* ambiguity, opacity, unclearness.

**transparency**[2] *n* photograph, picture, plate, slide.

**transparent** *adj* apparent, candid, clear, crystalline, diaphanous, dioptric, direct, distinct, easy, evident, explicit, filmy, forthright, frank, gauzy, hyaline, hyaloid, ingenuous, limpid, lucent, lucid, manifest, obvious, open, patent, pellucid, perspicuous, plain, plain-spoken, recognisable, see-through, sheer, straight, straightforward, translucent, transpicuous, unambiguous, understandable, undisguised, unequivocal, visible.

*antonyms* ambiguous, opaque, unclear.

**transpire** *v* appear, arise, befall, betide, chance, come out, come to light, emerge, happen, leak out, occur, take place, turn up.

**transplant** *v* displace, pot on, relocate, remove, repot, resettle, shift, transfer, uproot.

*antonym* leave.

**transport** *v* banish, bear, bring, captivate, carry, carry away, convey, delight, deport, ecstasise, electrify, enchant, enrapture, entrance, exile, fetch, haul, move, ravish, remove, run, ship, spellbind, take, transfer, waft.

*antonyms* bore, leave.

*n* bliss, carriage, cartage, carting, conveyance, delight, ecstasy, enchantment, euphoria, happiness, haulage, heaven, rapture, ravishment, removal, shipment, shipping, transference, transportation, vehicle, waterage.

*antonym* boredom.

**transportation** *n* carriage, cartage, carting, conveyance, haulage, postage, transfer, transport, transportal.

**transpose** *v* alter, change, exchange, interchange, metathesise, move, rearrange, relocate, reorder, shift, substitute, swap, switch, transfer.

*antonym* leave.

**transverse** *adj* cross, crossways, crosswise, diagonal, oblique, transversal.

**transvestism** *n* cross-dressing, drag, eonism, travesty.

**trap** *n* ambush, artifice, bunker, danger, deception, device, gin, hazard, net, noose, pitfall, ruse, snare, spring, springe, springle, stratagem, subterfuge, toils, trap-door, trepan, trick, trickery, wile.

*v* ambush, beguile, benet, catch, corner, deceive, dupe, enmesh, ensnare, entrap, illaqueate, inveigle, lime, snare, take, tangle, trepan, trick.

**trapped** *adj* ambushed, beguiled, caught, cornered, deceived, duped, ensnared, illaqueated, inveigled, netted, snared, stuck, surrounded, trepanned, tricked.

*antonym* free.

**trapper** *n* backwoodsman, frontiersman, hunter, huntsman, voyageur.

**trappings** *n* accompaniments, accoutrements, adornments, clothes, decorations, dress, equipment, finery, fittings, fixtures, fripperies, furnishings, gear, housings, livery, ornaments, panoply, paraphernalia, raiment, things, trimmings.

**trash** *n* balderdash, draff, dreck, dregs, drivel, dross, garbage, hogwash, inanity, junk, kitsch, litter, nonsense, offscourings, offscum, refuse, riddlings, rot, rubbish, scoria, sullage, sweepings, trashery, tripe, trumpery, twaddle, waste.

*antonym* sense.

**trashy** *adj* brummagem, catchpenny, cheap, cheap-jack, flimsy, grotty, inferior, kitschy, meretricious, pinchbeck, rubbishy, shabby, shoddy, tawdry, third-rate, tinsel, worthless.

*antonym* first-rate.

**trauma** *n* agony, anguish, damage, disturbance, hurt, injury, jolt, lesion, ordeal, pain, scar, shock, strain, suffering, torture, upheaval, upset, wound.

*antonyms* healing, relaxation.

**traumatic** *adj* agonising, damaging, distressing, disturbing, frightening, hurtful, injurious, painful, scarring, shocking, unpleasant, upsetting, wounding.

*antonyms* healing, relaxed, relaxing.

**travail** *n* birth-pangs, childbirth, distress, drudgery, effort, exertion, grind, hardship, labour, labour pains, pain, slavery, slog, strain, stress, suffering, sweat, tears, throes, toil, tribulation.

*antonym* rest.

**travel** *v* carry, commute, cross, excursionise, go, hump the bluey, journey, locomote, move, peregrinate, proceed, progress, ramble, roam, rove, tour, traverse, trek, voyage, walk, wander, wayfare, wend.

*antonym* stay.

**traveller** *n* agent, drummer, excursionist, explorer, globetrotter, gypsy, hiker, holiday-maker, itinerant, journeyer, migrant, nomad, passenger, peregrinator, rep, representative, salesman, saleswoman, tinker, tourist, tripper, vagrant, viator, voyager, wanderer, wayfarer.

**travelling** *adj* itinerant, migrant, migratory, mobile, movable, moving, multivagrant, nomadic, on the move, peripatetic, roaming, roving, touring, vagrant, viatorial, wandering, wayfaring.

*antonyms* fixed, stay-at-home.

**travels** *n* excursion, expedition, globetrotting, journey, passage, peregrination, ramble, tour, travel, trip, voyage, walk, wanderings, wayfare.

**travel-worn** *adj* footsore, jet-lagged, saddle-sore, travel-weary, waygone, wayworn, weary.

*antonym* fresh.

**traverse** *v* balk, bridge, check, consider, contradict, contravene, counter, counteract, cover, cross, deny, dispute, examine, eye, frustrate, hinder, impede, inspect, investigate, move, negotiate, obstruct, oppose, peregrinate, ply, range, review, roam, scan, scrutinise, span, study, swing, thwart, turn, wander.

*antonyms* aid, confirm.

**travesty** *n* apology, botch, burlesque, caricature, distortion, lampoon, mockery, parody, perversion, send-up, sham, take-off.

*v* burlesque, caricature, deride, distort, lampoon, mock, parody, pervert, pillory, ridicule, send up, sham, spoof, take off.

**treacherous** *adj* dangerous, deceitful, deceptive, disloyal, double-crossing, double-dealing, double-hearted, double-tongued, duplicitous, faithless, false, hazardous, icy, perfidious, perilous, precarious, proditorious, proditory, Punic, recreant, risky, slippery, slippy, traitorous, treasonable, tricky, unfaithful, unreliable, unsafe, unstable, untrue, untrustworthy.

*antonyms* dependable, loyal.

**treacherously** *adv* deceitfully, disloyally, faithlessly, falsely, perfidiously.

*antonym* loyally.

**treachery** *n* betrayal, disloyalty, double-cross, double-dealing, duplicity, faithlessness, falseness, infidelity, Judas-kiss, laesa majestas, Medism, perfidiousness, perfidy, Punic faith, Punica fides, trahison, treason.

*antonyms* dependability, loyalty.

**tread** *v* crush, hike, march, oppress, pace, pad, plod, press, quell, repress, squash, stamp, step, stride, subdue, subjugate, suppress, tramp, trample, trudge, walk, walk on.

*n* footfall, footstep, gait, pace, step, stride, walk.

**tread on someone's toes** affront, annoy, bruise, discommode, disgruntle, hurt, inconvenience, infringe, injure, irk, offend, upset, vex.

*antonym* soothe.

**treason** *n* disaffection, disloyalty, duplicity, laesa majestas, lese-majesty, mutiny, perfidy, sedition, subversion, trahison, traitorousness, treachery.

*antonym* loyalty.

**treasonable** *adj* disloyal, false, insurrectionary, mutinous, perfidious, seditious, subversive, traitorous, treacherous.

*antonym* loyal.

**treasure** *n* cash, darling, ewe-lamb, flower, fortune, funds, gem, gold, jewel, jewels, money, nonpareil, paragon, pearl, precious, pride and joy, prize, riches, valuables, wealth.

*v* adore, cherish, esteem, idolise, love, preserve, prize, revere, value, venerate, worship.

*antonym* disparage.

**treasurer** *n* bursar, cashier, purser, quaestor.

**treasury** *n* assets, bank, cache, capital, chrestomathy, coffers, corpus, exchequer, finances, fisc, funds, hoard, money, Parnassus, repository, resources, revenues, store, storehouse, thesaurus, vault.

**treat** *n* banquet, celebration, delight, enjoyment, entertainment, excursion, feast, fun, gift, gratification, joy, outing, party, pleasure, refreshment, satisfaction, surprise, thrill, wayzgoose.

*antonym* drag.

*v* attend to, bargain, care for, confer, consider, contain, deal with, discourse upon, discuss, doctor, entertain, feast, give, handle, manage, medicament, medicate, medicine, negotiate, nurse, parley, provide, regale, regard, stand, use.

**treatise** *n* disquisition, dissertation, essay, exposition, monograph, pamphlet, pandect, paper, prolegomena, prolusion, study, thesis, tract, tractate, work, writing.

**treatment** *n* care, conduct, cure, deal, dealing, discussion, handling, healing, management, manipulation, medication, medicine, prescript, reception, regimen, remedy, surgery, therapeutics, therapy, usage, use.

**treble** *adj* high, high-pitched, piping, sharp, shrill, threefold, triple.

*antonym* deep.

**treaty** *n* agreement, alliance, bargain, bond, compact, concordat, contract, convention, covenant, entente, negotiation, pact.

**tree** *n* arbor, bush, conifer, cross, evergreen, frutex, gallows, pollard, sampling, seedling, shrub.

**trek** *n* expedition, footslog, hike, journey, march, migration, odyssey, safari, slog, tramp, walk.

*v* footslog, hike, journey, march, migrate, plod, range, roam, rove, slog, traipse, tramp, trudge, yomp.

**tremble** *v* heave, oscillate, quake, quiver, rock, shake, shiver, shudder, teeter, totter, vibrate, wobble.

*n* heart-quake, oscillation, quake, quiver, shake, shiver, shudder, tremblement, tremor, vibration.

*antonym* steadiness.

**trembling** *n* heart-quake, oscillation, quaking, quavering, quivering, rocking, shakes, shaking, shivering, shuddering, tremblement, trepidation, vibration.

*antonym* steadiness.

**tremendous** *adj* ace, amazing, appalling, awe-inspiring, awesome, awful, colossal, deafening, dreadful, enormous, excellent, exceptional, extraordinary, fabulous, fantastic, fearful, formidable, frightful, gargantuan, gigantic, great, hell of a, herculean, huge, immense, incredible, mammoth, marvellous, monstrous, prodigious, sensational, spectacular, stupendous, super, terrible, terrific, titanic, towering, vast, whopping, wonderful.

*antonyms* boring, dreadful, run-of-the-mill, tiny.

**tremor** *n* agitation, earthquake, quake, quaking, quaver, quavering, quiver, quivering, shake, shaking, shiver, shock, thrill, tremble, trembling, trepidation, trillo, vibration, wobble.

*antonym* steadiness.

**tremulous** *adj* afraid, agitated, agog, anxious, aspen, dithery, excited, fearful, frightened, jittery, jumpy, nervous, quavering, quivering, quivery, scared, shaking, shivering, timid, trembling, trembly, tremulant, trepid, trepidant, vibrating, wavering.

*antonyms* calm, firm.

**trench** *n* channel, cut, ditch, drain, earthwork, entrenchment, excavation, fosse, furrow, grip, gullet, gutter, pit, rill, sap, trough, waterway.

**trenchant** *adj* acerbic, acid, acidulous, acute, astringent, biting, caustic, clear, clear-cut, cogent, crisp, cutting, distinct, driving, effective, effectual, emphatic, energetic, explicit, forceful, forthright, hurtful, incisive, keen, mordant, penetrating, piquant, pointed, potent, powerful, pungent, sarcastic, scratching, severe, sharp, strong, tart, unequivocal, vigorous.

*antonym* woolly.

**trend** *n* bias, course, crazed, current, dernier cri, direction, drift, fad, fashion, flow, inclination, leaning, look, mode, rage, style, tendency, thing, vogue.

**trendy** *adj* fashionable, funky, groovy, hip, in, latest, modish, stylish, up to the minute, voguish, with it.

*antonym* unfashionable.

**trepidation** *n* agitation, alarm, anxiety, apprehension, butterflies, cold sweat, consternation, dismay, disquiet, disturbance, dread, emotion, excitement, fear, fright, jitters, misgivings, nervousness, palpitation, perturbation, qualms, quivering, shaking, trembling, tremor, unease, uneasiness, worry.

*antonym* calm.

**trespass** *v* encroach, err, infringe, injure, intrude, invade, obtrude, offend, poach, sin, transgress, violate, wrong.

*antonyms* keep to, obey.

*n* breach, contravention, crime, debt, delinquency, encroachment, error, evil-doing, fault, infraction, infringement, iniquity, injury, intrusion, invasion, misbehaviour, misconduct, misdeed, misdemeanour, offence, poaching, sin, transgression, wrong-doing.

**trespasser** *n* criminal, debtor, delinquent, evil-doer, infringer, interloper, intruder, invader, malefactor, offender, poacher, sinner, transgressor, wrong-doer.

**tress** *n* braid, bunch, curl, lock, pigtail, plait, queue, ringlet, tail.

**trial** *n* adversity, affliction, assay, attempt, audition, bane, bother, burden, check, contest, crack, distress, effort, endeavour, examination, experience, experiment, go, grief, hardship, hassle, hearing, irritation, litigation, load, misery, nuisance, ordeal, pain, pest, plague, probation, proof, shot, sorrow, stab, suffering, taster, temptation, test, testing, tribulation, tribunal, trouble, try, trying, unhappiness, venture, vexation, whack, woe, worry, wretchedness.

*antonyms* happiness, rest.

*adj* dry, dummy, experimental, exploratory, pilot, probationary, provisional, testing.

**triangular** *adj* cuneiform, three-cornered, three-sided, trigonal, trigonic, trigonous, trilateral.

**tribal** adj class, ethnic, family, gentilitial, gentilitian, gentilitious, group, narrow, native, parochial, primitive, savage, sectarian, sectional, uncivilised, uncultured.

**tribe** n blood, branch, caste, clan, class, division, dynasty, family, gens, group, house, ilk, nation, people, phratry, race, seed, sept, stock.

**tribulation** n adversity, affliction, blow, burden, care, curse, distress, grief, heartache, misery, misfortune, ordeal, pain, reverse, sorrow, suffering, travail, trial, trouble, unhappiness, vexation, woe, worry, wretchedness.

*antonyms* happiness, rest.

**tribunal** n bar, bench, court, examination, hearing, inquisition, trial.

**tribute** n accolade, acknowledgement, annates, applause, charge, commendation, compliment, contribution, cornage, credit, customs, duty, encomium, esteem, eulogy, excise, first-fruits, gavel, gift, gratitude, homage, honour, horngeld, impost, laudation, offering, panegyric, payment, praise, ransom, recognition, respect, subsidy, tax, testimonial, testimony, toll.

*antonym* blame.

**trice** n flash, instant, jiff, jiffy, minute, moment, sec, second, shake, tick, twinkling, whiff.

**trick** n antic, art, artifice, cantrip, caper, characteristic, chicane, command, con, craft, deceit, deception, device, dodge, dog-trick, expedient, expertise, feat, feint, foible, fraud, frolic, gag, gambol, gift, gimmick, habit, hang, hoax, idiosyncrasy, imposition, imposture, jape, joke, josh, knack, know-how, legerdemain, leg-pull, mannerism, manoeuvre, peculiarity, ploy, practical joke, practice, prank, put-on, quirk, quiz, rig, ruse, secret, shot, skill, sleight, spell, stall, stratagem, stunt, subterfuge, swindle, technique, toy, trait, trap, trinket, turn, wile.

adj artificial, bogus, counterfeit, ersatz, fake, false, feigned, forged, imitation, mock, pretend, sham.

*antonym* genuine.

v bamboozle, beguile, cheat, con, cozen, deceive, defraud, delude, diddle, dupe, fool, gull, hoax, hocus-pocus, hoodwink, hornswoggle, illude, lead on, mislead, outwit, pull a fast one on, pull someone's leg, sell, swindle, trap.

**trick out** adorn, array, attire, bedeck, bedizen, decorate, do up, doll up, dress up, ornament, prank, prink, spruce up, tart up, trick up.

**trickery** n cheating, chicanery, con, conveyance, deceit, deception, dishonesty, dodgery, double-dealing, dupery, flim-flam, fraud, funny business, guile, hanky-panky, hoax, hocus-pocus, imposture, jiggery-pokery, jugglery, monkey business, pretence, shennanigans, skulduggery, sleight, sleight-of-hand, swindling, trickstering.

*antonym* honesty.

**trickle** v dribble, drip, drop, exude, filter, gutter, leak, ooze, percolate, run, seep.

*antonyms* gush, stream.

n drib, dribble, driblet, dribs and drabs, drip, seepage.

*antonyms* gush, stream.

**trickster** n cheat, con man, cozener, deceiver, diddler, fraud, hoaxer, impostor, joker, pretender, quiz, quizzer, swindler, tregetour, tricker.

**tricky** adj artful, complicated, crafty, cunning, deceitful, deceptive, delicate, devious, difficult, foxy, Gordian, knotty, legerdemain, problematic, risky, scheming, slippery, sly, sticky, subtle, thorny, ticklish, touch-and-go, trickish, tricksome, tricksy, wily.

*antonyms* easy, honest.

**trifle** n bagatelle, bauble, bit, concetto, dash, drop, falderal, finicality, foolishness, gewgaw, jot, knick-knack, little, nonsense, nothing, pinch, plaything, spot, touch, toy, trace, trinket, triviality, whigmaleerie, whim-wham.

v coquet, dabble, dally, dawdle, faddle, fiddle-faddle, flirt, fool, fribble, fritter, frivol, idle, meddle, niggle, palter, play, play with, sport, toy, wanton, waste.

**trifler** n dallier, dilettante, fribbler, futilitarian, good-for-nothing, idler, layabout, loafer, ne'er-do-well, piddler, waster.

**trifles** n inessentials, minor considerations, minutiae, nugae, trivia, trivialities.

*antonym* essentials.

**trifling** adj empty, footling, foozling, fribbling, fribblish, frivolous, idle, inconsiderable, insignificant, minuscule, negligible, nugatory, paltry, petty, piddling, piffling, puny, shallow, silly, slight, small, tiny, trivial, unimportant, valueless, worthless.

*antonym* important.

n desipience, fiddling, fooling, footling, frivolity, piddling, piffling, whiffery.

**trigger** v activate, actuate, cause, elicit, generate, initiate, produce, prompt, provoke, set off, spark off, start.

n catch, goad, lever, release, spur, stimulus, switch.

**trill** v cheep, chirp, chirrup, sing, tweet, twitter, warble, whistle.

**trim** adj clean-limbed, compact, dapper, natty, neat, orderly, shipshape, slender, slim, smart, smirk, soigné, spick-and-span, spruce, streamlined, svelte, trig, well-dressed, well-groomed, willowy.

*antonym* scruffy.

v adjust, adorn, arrange, array, balance, barb, barber, beautify, bedeck, clip, crop, curtail, cut, decorate, distribute, dock, dress, dub, embellish, embroider, garnish, lop, order, ornament, pare, prepare, prune, settle, shave, shear, tidy, trick.

n adornment, array, attire, border, clipping, condition, crop, cut, decoration, disposition, dress, edging, embellishment, equipment, fettle, fitness, fittings, form, frill, fringe, garnish, gear, health, humour, nick, order, ornament, ornamentation, piping, pruning, repair, shape, shave, shearing, situation, state, temper, trappings, trimming.

**trimmer** n time-server, vicar of Bray, weathercock.

**trimming** n adornment, border, braid, decoration, edging, embellishment, falbala, fimbriation, frill, fringe, frou-frou, furbelow, garnish, ornamentation, passament, passementerie, piping, trim.

**trimmings** n accessories, accompaniments, additions, appurtenances, clippings, cuttings, ends, extras, frills, garnish, ornaments, paraphernalia, parings, remnants, shavings, trappings.

**trinity** n threefoldness, threesome, triad, trilogy, trio, tripersonality, triple, triplet, triumvirate, triune, triunity, troika.

**trinket** n bagatelle, bauble, bibelot, bijou, doodad, fairing, gewgaw, gimcrack, kickshaws, knick-knack, nothing, ornament, toy, trifle, trinkum-trankum, whigmaleerie, whim-wham.

**trio** n terzetto, threesome, triad, trilogy, trine, trinity, triple, triplet, triptych, triumvirate, triune.

**trip** n blunder, boob, errand, error, excursion, expedition, fall, faux pas, foray, indiscretion, jaunt, journey, lapse, misstep, outing, ramble, run, skip, slip, step, stumble, tour, travel, voyage.

v activate, blunder, boob, caper, confuse, dance, disconcert, engage, err, fall, flip, flit, frisk, gambol, go, hop, lapse, miscalculate, misstep, pull, ramble, release, set off, skip, slip, slip up, spring, stumble, switch on, throw, tilt up, tip up, tour, trap, travel, tumble, unsettle, voyage.

**tripe** n balderdash, balls, blah, bosh, bullshit, bunkum, claptrap, drivel, garbage, guff, hogwash, inanity, nonsense, poppycock, rot, rubbish, tosh, trash, trumpery, twaddle.

*antonym* sense.

**triple** adj ternal, three-branched, threefold, three-ply, three-way, treble, trigeminal, trinal, trinary, tripartite, triplex, triplicate, triploid.

n threefoldness, threesome, triad, trilogy, trine, trinity, trio, triplet, triplicity, triumvirate, triune, triunity.

v treble, triplicate.

**triplet** n tercet, terzetta, threesome, triad, trilling, trilogy, trin, trine, trinity, trio, triple, triplicity, tripling, triumvirate, triune, troika.

**tripper** n emmet, excursionist, grockle, holiday-maker, sightseer, tourist, voyager.

**trite** adj banal, bromidic, cliché'd, common, commonplace, corny, dull, hack, hackneyed, Mickey Mouse, ordinary, overworn, pedestrian, rinky-dink, routine, run-of-the-mill, stale, stereotyped, stock, threadbare, tired, uninspired, unoriginal, well-trodden, well-worn, worn, worn out.

*antonym* original.

**triumph** n accomplishment, achievement, ascendancy, attainment, conquest, coup, elation, exultation, feat, happiness, hit, joy, jubilation, masterstroke, mastery, pride, rejoicing, sensation, smash, smash-hit, success, tour de force, victory, walk-away, walk-over, win.

*antonym* disaster.

v best, celebrate, crow, defeat, dominate, exult, gloat, glory, have the last laugh, humble, humiliate, jubilate, overcome, overwhelm, prevail, prosper, rejoice, revel, subdue, succeed, swagger, vanquish, win.

*antonym* fail.

**triumphant** adj boastful, celebratory, cock-a-hoop, conquering, dominant, elated, epinikian, exultant, gloating, glorious, joyful, jubilant, proud, rejoicing, successful, swaggering, triumphal, undefeated, victorious, winning.

*antonyms* defeated, humble.

**trivia** n details, irrelevancies, minutiae, nugae, pap, trifles, trivialities.

*antonym* essentials.

**trivial** adj commonplace, dinky, everyday, frivolous, incidental, inconsequential, inconsiderable, insignificant, little, meaningless, Mickey Mouse, minor, negligible, nugatory, paltry, pettifogging, petty, piddling, piffling, puny, slight, small, snippety, trifling, trite, unimportant, valueless, worthless.

*antonym* significant.

**trivialise** v belittle, depreciate, devalue, minimise, play down, scoff at, underestimate, underplay, undervalue.

*antonym* exalt.

**triviality** n detail, frivolity, futility, inconsequence, inconsequentiality, insignificance, littleness, meaninglessness, minor matter, negligibility, nothing, nugatoriness, paltriness, pettiness, slightness, smallness, technicality, trifle, triteness, unimportance, valuelessness, worthlessness.

*antonyms* essential, importance.

**troop** n assemblage, band, body, bunch, company, contingent, crew, crowd, division, drove, flock, gang, gathering, group, herd, horde, multitude, pack, squad, squadron, swarm, team, throng, trip, unit.

v crowd, flock, go, march, pack, parade, stream, swarm, throng, traipse, turn.

**troops** n army, men, military, servicemen, soldiers, soldiery.

**trophy** n award, booty, cup, laurels, memento, memorial, prize, souvenir, spoils.

**tropical** adj equatorial, hot, humid, lush, luxuriant, steamy, stifling, sultry, sweltering, torrid.

*antonyms* arctic, cold, cool, temperate.

**trot** v bustle, canter, jog, lope, pace, run, scamper, scurry, scuttle.

n canter, jog, jog-trot, lope, run.

**trot out** adduce, bring forward, bring up, drag up, exhibit, recite, rehearse, reiterate, relate, repeat.

**troubadour** n balladeer, cantabank, jongleur, minnesinger, minstrel, poet, singer, trouvère, trouveur.

**trouble** n affliction, agitation, ailment, annoyance, anxiety, attention, bother, care, commotion, complaint, concern, danger, defect, difficulty, dilemma, disability, discontent, discord, disease, disorder, disquiet, dissatisfaction, distress, disturbance, effort, exertion, failure, grief, heartache, illness, inconvenience, irritation, labour, malfunction, mess, misfortune, nuisance, pain, pains, pest, pickle, predicament, problem, row, scrape, shtook, solicitude, sorrow, spot, strife, struggle, suffering, thought, torment, travail, trial, tribulation, tumult, uneasiness, unrest, upheaval, upset, vexation, woe, work, worry.

*antonyms* calm, peace.

*v* afflict, agitate, annoy, bother, burden, discomfort, discommode, discompose, disconcert, disquiet, distress, disturb, fash, fret, grieve, harass, incommode, inconvenience, molest, muddy, pain, perplex, perturb, pester, plague, sadden, torment, upset, vex, worry.

*antonyms* help, reassure.

**troublemaker** *n* agent provocateur, agitator, bell-wether, bolshevik, bovver boy, firebrand, heller, incendiary, instigator, meddler, mischief-maker, rabble-rouser, ringleader, stirrer, tub-thumper.

*antonym* peace-maker.

**troublesome** *adj* annoying, arduous, bothersome, burdensome, demanding, difficult, disorderly, fashious, harassing, hard, importunate, inconvenient, insubordinate, irksome, irritating, laborious, oppressive, pestilential, plaguesome, plaguey, poxy, rebellious, recalcitrant, refractory, rowdy, spiny, taxing, thorny, tiresome, tricky, trying, turbulent, unco-operative, undisciplined, unruly, upsetting, vexatious, violent, wearisome, worrisome, worrying.

*antonyms* easy, helpful, polite.

**trough** *n* back, channel, conduit, crib, depression, ditch, duct, flume, furrow, gully, gutter, hollow, manger, trench, tub.

**trounce** *v* beat, best, censure, clobber, crush, drub, hammer, lick, overwhelm, paste, punish, rebuke, rout, slaughter, thrash, whale, whitewash.

**troupe** *n* band, cast, company, group, set, troop.

**trouper** *n* actor, artiste, entertainer, old hand, performer, player, Roscius, theatrical, thespian, veteran.

**trousers** *n* bags, bloomers, breeches, breeks, culottes, denims, ducks, dungarees, flannels, indescribables, inexpressibles, jeans, knickerbockers, lederhosen, Levis"trade", pantaloons, pants, pedal-pushers, plus-fours, shorts, slacks, trews, trunk-breeches, trunk-hose, unmentionables, unutterables.

**truancy** *n* absence, dodging, malingering, shirking, skiving.

*antonyms* attendance, effort.

**truant** *n* absentee, deserter, dodger, hookey, malingerer, runaway, shirker, skiver, wag.

*adj* absent, malingering, missing, runaway, skiving.

*v* desert, dodge, malinger, play truant, shirk, skive, skive off.

**truce** *n* armistice, break, cease-fire, cessation, intermission, interval, let-up, lull, moratorium, peace, respite, rest, stay, suspension, treaty, Truce of God.

*antonym* hostilities.

**truck**[1] *n* business, commerce, communication, connection, contact, dealings, exchange, intercourse, relations, trade, traffic.

**truck**[2] *n* barrow, bogie, camion, cart, drag, float, hand-cart, lorry, trailer, trolley, van, wag(g)on, water-cart, water-wagon, wheelbarrow.

**truculent** *adj* aggressive, antagonistic, bad-tempered, bellicose, belligerent, combative, contentious, cross, defiant, fierce, hostile, ill-tempered, obstreperous, pugnacious, quarrelsome, savage, scrappy, sullen, violent.

*antonyms* co-operative, good-natured.

**trudge** *v* clump, footslog, hike, labour, lumber, march, mush, plod, slog, stump, traipse, tramp, trek, walk.

*n* footslog, haul, hike, march, mush, slog, traipse, tramp, trek, walk.

**true** *adj* absolute, accurate, actual, apod(e)ictic, authentic, bona fide, confirmed, conformable, constant, correct, corrected, dedicated, devoted, dutiful, exact, factual, faithful, fast, firm, genuine, honest, honourable, legitimate, loyal, natural, perfect, precise, proper, pure, real, right, rightful, sincere, sooth, spot-on, square, staunch, steady, true-blue, true-born, true-hearted, trustworthy, trusty, truthful, typical, unerring, unswerving, upright, valid, veracious, veridical, veritable.

*antonyms* faithless, false, inaccurate.

*adv* accurately, correctly, exactly, faithfully, honestly, perfectly, precisely, properly, rightly, truly, truthfully, unerringly, veraciously, veritably.

*antonyms* falsely, inaccurately.

**true-blue** *adj* card-carrying, committed, confirmed, constant, dedicated, devoted, dyed-in-the-wool, faithful, loyal, orthodox, staunch, true, trusty, uncompromising, unwavering.

*antonyms* superficial, wavering.

**truism** *n* axiom, bromide, cliché, commonplace, platitude, saw, truth, verity.

**truly** *adv* accurately, authentically, constantly, correctly, devotedly, dutifully, en verité, exactly, exceptionally, extremely, factually, faithfully, fegs, firmly, genuinely, greatly, honestly, honourably, in good sooth, in reality, in truth, indeed, indubitably, legitimately, loyally, precisely, properly, really, rightly, sincerely, soothly, staunchly, steadfastly, steadily, truthfully, undeniably, veraciously, verily, veritably, very.

*antonyms* faithlessly, falsely, incorrectly, slightly.

**trump up** *v* concoct, contrive, cook up, create, devise, fabricate, fake, invent, make up.

**trumped-up** *adj* concocted, contrived, cooked-up, fabricated, fake, faked, false, falsified, invented, made-up, phoney, spurious, untrue.

*antonym* genuine.

**trumpery** *adj* brummagem, cheap, flashy, grotty, meretricious, nasty, pinchbeck, rubbishy, shabby, shoddy, tawdry, trashy, trifling, useless, valueless, worthless.

*antonym* first-rate.

**trumpet** *n* bellow, blare, blast, bray, bugle, call, clarion, cry, honk, horn, roar.

*v* advertise, announce, bellow, blare, blast, bray, broadcast, call, extol, honk, preconise, proclaim, publish, roar, shout, tout.

**truncate** v abbreviate, clip, crop, curtail, cut, cut short, lop, maim, pare, prune, shorten, trim.
*antonym* lengthen.

**truncheon** n baton, club, cosh, cudgel, knobkerrie, life-preserver, night-stick, shillela(g)h, staff.

**trunk**[1] n bin, box, case, chest, coffer, crate, Gladstone bag, kist, locker, portmanteau, suitcase.

**trunk**[2] n body, bole, frame, shaft, stalk, stem, stock, torso, tube.

**trunk**[3] n nose, proboscis, snout.

**truss** v bind, bundle, fasten, hogtie, pack, pinion, secure, strap, tether, tie.
*antonym* untie.
n bale, bandage, beam, binding, brace, bundle, buttress, joist, prop, shore, stanchion, stay, strut, support.

**trust** n affiance, assurance, belief, care, certainty, certitude, charge, confidence, conviction, credence, credit, custody, duty, expectation, faith, fidelity, guard, guardianship, hope, obligation, protection, reliance, responsibility, safekeeping, trusteeship, uberrima fides.
*antonym* mistrust.
v assign, assume, bank on, believe, command, commit, confide, consign, count on, credit, delegate, depend on, entrust, expect, give, hope, imagine, presume, rely on, suppose, surmise, swear by.
*antonym* mistrust.

**trustee** n administrator, agent, custodian, depositary, executor, executrix, fiduciary, guardian, keeper.

**trusting** adj confiding, credulous, gullible, innocent, naïve, optimistic, simple, trustful, unguarded, unquestioning, unsuspecting, unsuspicious, unwary.
*antonyms* cautious, distrustful.

**trustworthy** adj authentic, dependable, ethical, four-square, honest, honourable, level-headed, mature, principled, reliable, responsible, righteous, sensible, steadfast, true, trusty, truthful, upright.
*antonym* unreliable.

**trusty** adj dependable, faithful, firm, honest, loyal, reliable, responsible, solid, staunch, steady, straightforward, strong, supportive, true, trustworthy, upright.
*antonym* unreliable.

**truth** n accuracy, actuality, axiom, candour, certainty, constancy, dedication, devotion, dutifulness, exactness, fact, facts, factuality, factualness, faith, faithfulness, fidelity, frankness, genuineness, historicity, honesty, integrity, law, legitimacy, loyalty, maxim, naturalism, precision, realism, reality, sooth, truism, truthfulness, uprightness, validity, veracity, verdicality, verity.
*antonym* falsehood.

**truthful** adj accurate, candid, correct, exact, faithful, forthright, frank, honest, literal, naturalistic, plain-spoken, precise, realistic, reliable, sincere, sooth, soothfast, soothful, straight, straightforward, true, trustworthy, veracious, veridicous, verist, veristic, veritable.
*antonym* untruthful.

**truthfulness** n candour, frankness, honesty, openness, righteousness, sincerity, straightness, uprightness, veracity, verism.
*antonym* untruthfulness.

**try** v adjudge, adjudicate, afflict, aim, annoy, appraise, attempt, catechise, endeavour, essay, evaluate, examine, experiment, hear, inconvenience, inspect, investigate, irk, irritate, pain, plague, prove, sample, seek, strain, stress, strive, struggle, taste, tax, test, tire, trouble, undertake, upset, venture, vex, wear out, weary.
n appraisal, attempt, bash, crack, effort, endeavour, essay, evaluation, experiment, fling, go, inspection, sample, shot, stab, taste, taster, test, trial, whack.

**try out** appraise, check out, evaluate, inspect, sample, taste, test, try on.

**trying** adj aggravating, annoying, arduous, bothersome, difficult, distressing, exasperating, fatiguing, hard, irksome, irritating, searching, severe, stressful, taxing, testing, tiresome, tough, troublesome, upsetting, vexing, wearisome.
*antonym* calming.

**tub** n back, barrel, basin, bath, bathtub, bucket, butt, cask, hogshead, keeve, keg, kid, kit, pail, puncheon, stand, tun, vat.

**tubby** adj buxom, chubby, corpulent, fat, obese, overweight, paunchy, plump, podgy, portly, pudgy, roly-poly, stout, well-upholstered.
*antonym* slim.

**tube** n channel, conduit, cylinder, duct, hose, inlet, main, outlet, pipe, shaft, spout, trunk, vas.

**tuberculosis** n consumption, phthisis, TB.

**tubular** adj pipelike, pipy, tubate, tubelike, tubiform, tubulate, tubulous, vasiform.

**tuck**[1] v cram, crease, fold, gather, insert, push, stuff.
n crease, fold, gather, pinch, pleat, pucker.

**tuck**[2] n comestibles, eats, food, grub, nosh, prog, scoff, victuals, vittles.

**tuck in** devour, dine, eat, eat up, fall to, feast, gobble, gorge, scoff, sup.

**tuft** n beard, bunch, clump, cluster, collection, crest, dag, daglock, dollop, floccule, flocculus, floccus, flock, knot, shock, tassle, topknot, truss, tussock.

**tug** v drag, draw, haul, heave, jerk, jigger, lug, pluck, pull, tow, wrench, yank.
n drag, haul, heave, jerk, pluck, pull, tow, traction, wrench, yank.

**tuition** n education, instruction, lessons, pedagogics, pedagogy, schooling, teaching, training, tutelage, tutoring.

**tumble** v disorder, drop, fall, flop, jumble, overthrow, pitch, plummet, roll, rumple, stumble, topple, toss, trip up.

*n* collapse, drop, fall, flop, plunge, roll, spill, stumble, toss, trip.

**tumbledown** *adj* broken-down, crumbling, crumbly, decrepit, dilapidated, disintegrating, ramshackle, rickety, ruined, ruinous, shaky, tottering.

*antonym* well-kept.

**tumbler**[1] *n* acrobat, contortionist, gymnast, voltigeur.

**tumbler**[2] *n* beaker, cup, drinking-glass, glass, goblet, mug, schooner.

**tumid** *adj* affected, bloated, bombastic, bulbous, bulging, distended, enlarged, euphuistic, flowery, fulsome, fustian, grandiloquent, grandiose, high-flown, inflated, magniloquent, oro(ro)tund, overblown, pompous, pretentious, protuberant, puffed up, puffy, sesquipedalian, stilted, swollen, tumescent, turgid.

*antonyms* flat, simple.

**tumour** *n* cancer, carcinoma, growth, lump, lymphoma, melanoma, myeloma, neoplasm, sarcoma, swelling, tubercle, tubercule, tuberculoma, tuberculum.

**tumult** *n* ado, affray, agitation, altercation, bedlam, brattle, brawl, brouhaha, bustle, clamour, coil, commotion, deray, din, disorder, disturbance, Donnybrook, émeute, excitement, fracas, hubbub, hullabaloo, outbreak, pandemonium, quarrel, racket, riot, rookery, rout, row, ruction, ruffle, stir, stramash, strife, turmoil, unrest, upheaval, uproar.

*antonym* calm.

**tumultuous** *adj* agitated, boisterous, clamorous, confused, disorderly, disturbed, excited, fierce, hectic, irregular, lawless, noisy, obstreperous, passionate, raging, restless, riotous, rowdy, rumbustious, stormy, tempestuous, troubled, turbulent, unrestrained, unruly, uproarious, violent, vociferous, wild.

*antonym* calm.

**tune** *n* agreement, air, attitude, concert, concord, consonance, demeanour, disposition, euphony, frame of mind, harmony, melisma, melody, mood, motif, pitch, song, strain, sympathy, temper, theme, unison.

*v* adapt, adjust, attune, harmonise, pitch, regulate, set, synchronise, temper.

**tuneful** *adj* canorous, catchy, euphonious, harmonious, mellifluous, mellow, melodic, melodious, musical, pleasant, sonorous.

*antonym* tuneless.

**tuneless** *adj* atonal, cacophonous, clashing, discordant, dissonant, harsh, horrisonant, unmelodic, unmelodious, unmusical.

*antonym* tuneful.

**tunnel** *n* burrow, channel, chimney, drift, flue, gallery, hole, passage, passageway, sap, shaft, subway, underpass.

*v* burrow, dig, excavate, mine, penetrate, sap, undermine.

**turbid** *adj* clouded, cloudy, confused, dense, dim, disordered, feculent, foggy, foul, fuzzy, hazy, impure, incoherent, muddled, muddy, murky, opaque, roily, thick, unclear, unsettled.

*antonym* clear.

**turbulence** *n* agitation, boiling, chaos, commotion, confusion, disorder, disruption, instability, pandemonium, roughness, storm, tumult, turmoil, unrest, upheaval.

*antonym* calm.

**turbulent** *adj* agitated, anarchic, blustery, boiling, boisterous, choppy, confused, disordered, disorderly, foaming, furious, insubordinate, lawless, mutinous, obstreperous, raging, rebellious, refractory, riotous, rough, rowdy, seditious, stormy, tempestuous, tumultuous, unbridled, undisciplined, ungovernable, unruly, unsettled, unstable, uproarious, violent, wild.

*antonym* calm.

**turf** *n* clod, divot, glebe, grass, green, sod, sward.

**turf out** banish, bounce, chuck out, discharge, dismiss, dispossess, eject, elbow, evict, expel, fire, fling out, give the elbow to, kick out, oust, sack, throw out, turn out.

**turgid** *adj* affected, bloated, bombastic, bulging, congested, dilated, distended, extravagant, flowery, fulsome, fustian, grandiloquent, grandiose, high-flown, inflated, magniloquent, oro(ro)tund, ostentatious, overblown, pompous, pretentious, protuberant, puffy, sesquipedalian, stilted, swollen, tumescent, tumid, windy.

*antonyms* flat, simple.

**turmoil** *n* agitation, bedlam, brouhaha, bustle, chaos, combustion, commotion, confusion, disorder, disquiet, disturbance, Donnybrook, dust, émeute, ferment, flurry, hubbub, hubbuboo, noise, pandemonium, pother, pudder, rookery, rout, row, ruffle, stir, stour, stramash, strife, tracasserie, trouble, tumult, turbulence, uproar, violence, welter.

*antonym* calm.

**turn** *v* adapt, alter, apostatise, appeal, apply, approach, become, caracol, change, circle, construct, convert, corner, curdle, defect, deliver, depend, desert, divert, double, execute, fashion, fit, form, frame, go, gyrate, hang, hinge, infatuate, influence, issue, look, make, metamorphose, mould, move, mutate, nauseate, negotiate, pass, perform, persuade, pivot, prejudice, remodel, renege, resort, retract, return, reverse, revolve, roll, rotate, shape, shift, sicken, sour, spin, spoil, swerve, switch, swivel, taint, transfigure, transform, translate, transmute, twirl, twist, upset, veer, wheel, whirl, write.

*n* act, action, airing, aptitude, bend, bent, bias, bout, caracol, cast, chance, change, circle, circuit, constitutional, crack, crankle, crisis, culmination, curve, cycle, deed, departure, deviation, direction, distortion, drift, drive, excursion, exigency, fashion, favour, fling, form, format, fright, gesture, go, guise, gyration, heading, innings, jaunt, make-up, manner, mode, mould, occasion, opportunity, outing, performance, performer, period, pivot, promenade, reversal, revolution, ride, rotation, round, saunter, scare, service, shape, shift, shock, shot, spell, spin, start, stint, stroll, style, succession, surprise, swing, tendency, time, trend, trick, try, turning, twist, uey, U-turn, vicissitude, walk, warp, way, whack, whirl.

**turn away** avert, deflect, depart, deviate, discharge, dismiss.

*antonym* accept.

**turn back** beat off, do a uey, drive back, drive off, force back, go back, rebuff, repel, repulse, resist, retrace one's steps, return, revert.

*antonyms* go on, stay.

**turn down** decline, diminish, fold, invert, lessen, lower, muffle, mute, quieten, rebuff, refuse, reject, repudiate, soften, spurn.

*antonyms* accept, turn up.

**turn in** deliver, enter, give back, give up, go to bed, hand in, hand over, hit the sack, register, retire, return, submit, surrender, tender.

*antonyms* get up, give out, keep.

**turn inside out** evaginate, evert, extravert, introvert.

**turn of events** affair, galère, happening, incident, occurrence, outcome, phenomenon, result.

**turn of phrase** diction, expression, idiom, locution, metaphor, phraseology, saying, style.

**turn off** alienate, bore, branch off, cut out, depart from, deviate, discourage, disenchant, disgust, dismiss, displease, divert, irritate, kill, leave, nauseate, offend, put off, put out, quit, repel, shut, shut down, sicken, stop, switch off, turn out, unplug.

*antonym* turn on.

**turn on** activate, arouse, assail, assault, attack, attract, balance, depend, energise, excite, expose, fall on, hang, hinge, ignite, inform, initiate, introduce, pivot, please, rest, round on, rouse, show, start, start up, stimulate, switch on, thrill, titillate, trip, turn against, work up.

*antonym* turn off.

**turn out** accoutre, apparel, appear, assemble, attend, attire, banish, become, cashier, clean out, clear, clothe, come, come about, crop up, deport, develop, discharge, dishome, dishouse, dismiss, displant, dispossess, dress, drive out, drum out, emerge, empty, end up, eventuate, evict, evolve, expel, fabricate, finish, fire, fit, gather, go, happen, kick out, make, manufacture, muster, oust, outfit, process, produce, result, sack, show up, switch off, throw out, transpire, turf out, turn off, turn up, unplug, unseat.

*antonyms* stay away, turn on.

**turn over** activate, assign, break up, capsize, commend, commit, consider, contemplate, crank, deliberate, deliver, dig, examine, give over, give up, hand over, keel over, mull over, overturn, pass on, plough, ponder, reflect on, render, reverse, revolve, rob, ruminate, start up, surrender, switch on, think about, think over, transfer, upend, upset, yield.

*antonym* stand firm.

**turn over a new leaf** amend, begin anew, change, change one's ways, improve, mend one's ways, pull one's socks up, reform.

*antonym* persist.

**turn tail** escape, flee, hightail it, make off, retreat, run away, run for it, run off, scarper, skedaddle, take off, take to one's heels, vamoose.

*antonym* stand firm.

**turn up** amplify, appear, arrive, attend, boost, come, crop up, dig up, disclose, discover, disgust, enhanse, expose, find, increase, intensify, invert, pop up, raise, reveal, show, show up, transpire, unearth.

*antonyms* stay away, turn down.

**turncoat** *n* apostate, backslider, blackleg, defector, deserter, fink, rat, recreant, renegade, renegate, scab, seceder, tergiversator, traitor.

**turning** *n* bend, crossroads, curve, flexure, fork, junction, turn, turn-off.

**turning-point** *n* change, climacteric, crisis, crossroads, crux, cusp, moment of truth, watershed.

**turn-out** *n* array, assemblage, assembly, attendance, attire, audience, company, congregation, costume, crowd, dress, equipage, equipment, gate, gear, get-up, number, outfit, output, outturn, product, production, productivity, rig-out, team, throng, turnover, volume, yield.

**turnover** *n* business, change, flow, income, movement, output, outturn, production, productivity, profits, replacement, volume, yield.

**turpitude** *n* badness, baseness, corruption, corruptness, criminality, degeneracy, depravity, evil, flagitiousness, foulness, immorality, iniquity, nefariousness, rascality, sinfulness, viciousness, vileness, villainy, wickedness.

*antonym* honour.

**tussle** *v* battle, brawl, compete, contend, fight, grapple, scramble, scrap, scuffle, struggle, vie, wrestle.

*n* battle, bout, brawl, competition, conflict, contention, contest, dust-up, fight, fracas, fray, mêlée, punch-up, race, scramble, scrap, scrimmage, scrum, scuffle, set-to, struggle.

**tutelage** *n* aegis, care, charge, custody, education, eye, guardianship, guidance, instruction, patronage, preparation, protection, schooling, teaching, tuition, vigilance, wardship.

**tutor** *n* coach, director of studies, educator, governor, guardian, guide, guru, instructor, lecturer, master, mentor, preceptor, répétiteur, supervisor, teacher.

*v* coach, control, direct, discipline, drill, edify, educate, guide, instruct, lecture, school, supervise, teach, train.

**tutorial** *n* class, lesson, seminar, teach-in.

*adj* coaching, didactic, educative, educatory, guiding, instructional, teaching.

**twaddle** *n* balderdash, balls, blather, blether, bunk, bunkum, chatter, claptrap, drivel, fadaise, gabble, garbage, gobbledegook, gossip, guff, havers, hogwash, hot air, inanity, nonsense, piffle, poppycock, rigmarole, rot, rubbish, stuff, tattle, tosh, trash, trumpery, waffle.

*antonym* sense.

**tweak** *v, n* jerk, nip, pull, punch, snatch, squeeze, tug, twist, twitch.

**twee** *adj* affected, bijou, cute, cutesy, dainty, kitschy, precious, pretty, quaint, sentimental, sweet.

**tweezers** *n* forceps, pincers, tongs, vulsella.

**twiddle** *v* adjust, fiddle, finger, jiggle, juggle, swivel, turn, twirl, twist, wiggle.

**twig**[1] *n* branch, offshoot, ramulus, shoot, spray, spring, stick, wattle, whip, withe, withy.

**twig**[2] *v* catch on, comprehend, cotton on, fathom, get, grasp, rumble, savvy, see, tumble to, understand.

**twilight** *n* crepuscle, crepuscule, decline, demi-jour, dimness, dusk, ebb, evening, eventide, gloaming, half-light, sundown, sunset.

*adj* crepuscular, darkening, declining, dim, dying, ebbing, evening, final, last, shadowy.

**twin** *n* clone, corollary, counterpart, doppelgänger, double, duplicate, fellow, gemel, likeness, lookalike, match, mate, ringer.

*adj* balancing, corresponding, didymous, double, dual, duplicate, geminate, geminous, identical, matched, matching, paired, parallel, symmetrical, twofold.

*v* combine, couple, join, link, match, pair, yoke.

**twine** *n* cord, string, twist, yarn.

*v* bend, braid, coil, curl, encircle, entwine, interlace, interweave, knit, loop, meander, plait, snake, spiral, splice, surround, tie, twist, weave, wind, wrap, wreathe, wriggle, zigzag.

**twinge** *n* bite, gripe, pain, pang, pinch, prick, qualm, spasm, stab, stitch, throb, throe, tweak, twist, twitch.

**twinkle** *v* blink, coruscate, flash, flicker, gleam, glint, glisten, glitter, scintillate, shimmer, shine, sparkle, vibrate, wink.

*n* amusement, blink, coruscation, flash, flicker, gleam, glimmer, glistening, glitter, glittering, light, quiver, scintillation, shimmer, shine, spark, sparkle, wink.

**twinkling** *adj* blinking, bright, coruscating, flashing, flickering, gleaming, glimmering, glistening, glittering, nitid, polished, scintillating, shimmering, shining, sparkling, winking.

*n* flash, instant, jiff, jiffy, mo, moment, no time, sec, second, shake, tick, trice, twinkle, two shakes.

**twirl** *v* birl, coil, gyrate, gyre, pirouette, pivot, revolve, rotate, spin, swivel, turn, twiddle, twist, wheel, whirl, wind.

*n* coil, convulution, gyration, gyre, helix, pirouette, revolution, rotation, spin, spiral, turn, twiddle, twist, wheel, whirl, whorl.

**twirling** *adj* gyral, gyratory, pirouetting, pivotal, pivoting, revolving, rotating, rotatory, spinning, swivelling, whirling.

**twist** *v* alter, change, coil, contort, corkscrew, crankle, crinkle, crisp, curl, distort, encircle, entangle, entwine, garble, intertwine, misquote, misrepresent, pervert, pivot, revolve, rick, screw, spin, sprain, squirm, strain, swivel, turn, tweak, twine, warp, weave, wigwag, wind, wrap, wreathe, wrench, wrest, wrick, wriggle, wring, writhe.

*n* aberration, arc, bend, bent, braid, break, change, characteristic, coil, confusion, contortion, convolution, crankle, curl, curlicue, curve, defect, deformation, development, distortion, eccentricity, entanglement, fault, flaw, foible, hank, idiosyncrasy, imperfection, intortion, jerk, kink, knot, meander, mess, mix-up, nuance, oddity, peculiarity, plug, proclivity, pull, quid, quirk, revelation, roll, screw, slant, snarl, spin, sprain, squiggle, surprise, swivel, tangle, tortion, trait, turn, twine, undulation, variation, warp, wind, wrench, wrest, zigzag.

**twist someone's arm** bulldoze, bully, coerce, dragoon, force, intimidate, lean on, persuade, pressurise.

**twisted** *adj* bent, biased, bitter, coiled, contorted, convoluted, curled, deformed, deviant, devious, distorted, garbled, intertwined, intorted, jaundiced, misshapen, perverse, perverted, quirky, thrawn, torqued, tortile, tortuous, unnatural, warped, wound, woven, wry.

*antonyms* straight, straightforward.

**twister** *n* blackguard, cheat, con man, crook, deceiver, fraud, phoney, rogue, rotter, scoundrel, swindler, trickster.

**twit**[1] *v* banter, berate, blame, censure, chiack, deride, jeer, mock, rib, scorn, taunt, tease, upbraid.

**twit**[2] *n* ass, blockhead, buffoon, chump, clot, clown, dope, fool, halfwit, idiot, muggins, nerd, nincompoop, ninny, nitwit, noodle, nurd, silly ass, simpleton, twerp.

**twitch** *v* blink, flutter, jerk, jump, pinch, pluck, pull, snatch, tug, tweak, vellicate, yank.

*n* blink, convulsion, flutter, jerk, jump, pluck, pull, spasmytic, subsultus, tremor, tweak, twinge, vellication.

**twitter** *v* chatter, cheep, chirp, chirrup, giggle, prattle, simper, sing, snigger, titter, trill, tweet, warble, whistle.

*n* agitation, anxiety, call, chatter, cheeping, chirping, chirruping, cry, dither, excitement, flurry, fluster, flutter, nervousness, song, tizz, tizzy, trill, tweeting, warble.

**two-faced** *adj* deceitful, deceiving, devious, dissembling, double-dealing, double-tongued, duplicitous, false, hypocritical, insincere, Janus-faced, lying, mendacious, perfidious, treacherous, untrustworthy.

*antonyms* candid, frank, honest.

**tycoon** *n* baron, big cheese, big noise, big shot, capitalist, captain of industry, Croesus, Dives, entrepreneur, fat cat, financier, gold-bug, industrialist, magnate, mogul, nabob, plutocrat, potentate, supremo.

**type**[1] *n* archetype, breed, category, class, classification, description, designation, emblem, embodiment, epitome, essence, example, exemplar, form, genre, group, ilk, insignia, kidney, kind, mark, model, order, original, paradigm, pattern, personification, prototype, quintessence, sort, species, specimen, stamp, standard, strain, subdivision, variety.

**type**[2] *n* case, characters, face, font, fount, lettering, print, printing.

**typhoon** *n* baguio, cordonazo, cyclone, hurricane, squall, storm, tempest, tornado, twister, whirlwind, willy-willy.

**typical** *adj* archetypal, average, characteristic, classic, conventional, distinctive, essential, illustrative, indicative, model, normal, orthodox, quintessential, representative, standard, stock, symptomatic, usual, vintage.

*antonyms* atypical, untypical.

**typify** *v* characterise, embody, encapsulate, epitomise, exemplify, illustrate, incarnate, personify, represent, symbolise.

**tyrannical** *adj* absolute, arbitrary, authoritarian, autocratic, coercive, despotic, dictatorial, domineering, high-handed, imperious, inexorable, iron-handed, magisterial, Neronian, oppressive, overbearing, overpowering, overweening, peremptory, ruthless, severe, tyrannous, unjust, unreasonable.

*antonyms* liberal, tolerant.

**tyrannise** *v* browbeat, bully, coerce, crush, dictate, domineer, enslave, intimidate, lord it, oppress, subjugate, terrorise.

**tyranny** *n* absolutism, authoritarianism, autocracy, coercion, despotism, dictatorship, harshness, high-handedness, imperiousness, injustice, liberticide, monocracy, oppression, peremptoriness, relentlessness, ruthlessness.

*antonyms* democracy, liberality.

**tyrant** *n* absolutist, authoritarian, autocrat, bully, despot, dictator, Hitler, liberticide, martinet, monarch, oppressor, satrap, slave-driver, sovereign, taskmaster.

**tyro** *see* **tiro.**

# U

**ubiquitous** *adj* all-over, common, commonly-encountered, ever-present, everywhere, frequent, global, omnipresent, pervasive, universal.

*antonym* rare.

**ubiquity** *n* commonness, frequency, omnipresence, pervasiveness, popularity, prevalence, universality.

*antonym* rarity.

**ugliness** *n* danger, deformity, disgrace, enormity, evil, frightfulness, heinousness, hideosity, hideousness, homeliness, horridness, horror, menace, monstrosity, monstrousness, nastiness, offensiveness, plainness, repulsiveness, unattractiveness, unloveliness, unpleasantness, unsightliness, vileness.

*antonyms* beauty, charm, goodness, pleasantness.

**ugly** *adj* angry, bad-tempered, dangerous, dark, disagreeable, disgusting, distasteful, evil, evil-favoured, forbidding, frightful, hagged, haggish, hard-favoured, hard-featured, hideous, homely, horrid, ill-faced, ill-favoured, ill-looking, malevolent, menacing, misshapen, monstrous, nasty, objectionable, offensive, ominous, plain, repugnant, repulsive, revolting, shocking, sinister, spiteful, sullen, surly, terrible, threatening, truculent, unattractive, unlovely, unpleasant, unprepossessing, unsightly, vile.

*antonyms* beautiful, charming, good, pretty.

**ulcer** *n* abscess, canker, fester, imposthume, noma, sore, ulceration.

**ulterior** *adj* concealed, covert, hidden, personal, private, secondary, secret, selfish, undisclosed, unexpressed.

*antonyms* declared, overt.

**ultimate** *adj* basic, conclusive, consummate, decisive, elemental, end, eventual, extreme, final, fundamental, furthest, greatest, highest, last, maximum, paramount, perfect, primary, radical, remotest, superlative, supreme, terminal, topmost, utmost.

*n* consummation, culmination, daddy of them all, dinger, epitome, extreme, granddaddy, greatest, height, peak, perfection, summit.

**ultimately** *adv* after all, at last, basically, eventually, finally, fundamentally, in origin, in the end, originally, primarily, sooner or later.

**ultra** *adj* avant-garde, excessive, extravagant, extreme, fanatical, immoderate, rabid, radical, revolutionary, way-out.

**ultra-** *adv* especially, exceptionally, excessively, extra, extraordinarily, extremely, remarkably, unusually.

**ululate** *v* cry, holler, hoot, howl, keen, lament, moan, mourn, scream, screech, sob, wail, weep.

**umbrage** *n* anger, chagrin, disgruntlement, displeasure, grudge, high dudgeon, huff, indignation, offence, pique, resentment, sulks.

**umbrella** *n* aegis, agency, brolly, bumbershoot, chatta, cover, en tout cas, gamp, mush, mushroom, parasol, patronage, protection, sunshade, umbel.

**umpire** *n* adjudicator, arbiter, arbitrator, daysman, judge, linesman, mediator, moderator, ref, referee.

*v* adjudicate, arbitrate, call, control, judge, moderate, ref, referee.

**umpteen** *adj* a good many, a thousand, considerable, countless, innumerable, millions, n, numerous, plenty, uncounted.

*antonym* few.

**unabashed** *adj* blatant, bold, brazen, composed, confident, unawed, unblushing, unconcerned, undaunted, undismayed, unembarrassed.

*antonyms* abashed, sheepish.

**unable** *adj* impotent, inadequate, incapable, incompetent, ineffectual, powerless, unequipped, unfit, unfitted, unqualified.

*antonym* able.

**unabridged** *adj* complete, entire, full, full-length, uncondensed, uncut, unexpurgated, unshortened, whole.

*antonym* abridged.

**unacceptable** *adj* before the pale, disagreeable, displeasing, distasteful, improper, inadmissible, insupportable, objectionable, offensive, ugly, undesirable, unpleasant, unsatisfactory, unwelcome.

*antonym* acceptable.

**unaccommodating** *adj* disobliging, inflexible, intransigent, obstinate, perverse, rigid, stubborn, unbending, uncomplaisant, uncompromising, unco-operative, unyielding.

*antonyms* flexible, obliging.

**unaccompanied** *adj* a cappella, alone, lone, solo, unattended, unescorted.

*antonym* accompanied.

**unaccountable** *adj* astonishing, baffling, extraordinary, impenetrable, incomprehensible, inexplicable, inscrutable, mysterious, odd, peculiar, puzzling, singular, strange, uncommon, unexplainable, unfathomable, unheard-of, unintelligible, unusual, unwonted.

*antonyms* accountable, explicable.

**unaccustomed** *adj* different, green, inexperienced, new, remarkable, special, strange, surprising, unacquainted, uncommon, unexpected, unfamiliar, unpractised, unprecedented, unused, unusual, unwonted.

*antonyms* accustomed, customary.

**unacquainted** *adj* ignorant, strange, unaccustomed, unfamiliar.

**unadorned** *adj* austere, outright, plain, restrained, severe, simple, stark, straightforward, undecorated, unembellished, unornamented, unvarnished.

*antonyms* decorated, embellished, ornate.

**unaffected¹** *adj* aloof, impervious, naïf, natural, proof, spontaneous, unaltered, unchanged, unimpressed, unmoved, unresponsive, untouched.

*antonyms* affected, unnatural.

**unaffected²** *adj* artless, blasé, genuine, honest, indifferent, ingenuous, naive, plain, simple, sincere, straightforward, unassuming, unconcerned, unpretentious, unsophisticated, unspoilt, unstudied.

*antonyms* affected, impressed, moved.

**unafraid** *adj* confident, daring, dauntless, fearless, imperturbable, intrepid, unshakeable.

*antonym* afraid.

**unalterable** *adj* final, fixed, immutable, inflexible, invariable, permanent, rigid, steadfast, unchangeable, unchanging, unyielding.

*antonyms* alterable, flexible.

**unanimity** *n* accord, agreement, chorus, concert, concord, concurrence, consensus, consent, correspondence, harmony, like-mindedness, unison, unity.

*antonyms* disagreement, disunity.

**unanimous** *adj* agreed, common, concerted, concordant, harmonious, in accord, in agreement, joint, united.

*antonyms* disunited, split.

**unanimously** *adv* at one man, by common consent, conjointly, in concert, nem con, unopposed, without exception, without opposition.

**unanswerable** *adj* absolute, conclusive, final, incontestable, incontrovertible, indisputable, irrefragable, irrefutable, unarguable, undeniable.

*antonyms* answerable, refutable.

**unappetising** *adj* disagreeable, distasteful, insipid, off-putting, tasteless, unappealing, unattractive, unexciting, uninteresting, uninviting, unpalatable, unpleasant, unsavoury.

*antonym* appetising.

**unapproachable** *adj* aloof, distant, forbidding, formidable, frigid, godforsaken, inaccessible, remote, reserved, stand-offish, unbending,

unfriendly, un-get-at-able, unreachable, unsociable, withdrawn.

*antonym* approachable.

**unapt** *adj* inapplicable, inapposite, inappropriate, inapt, malapropos, unfit, unfitted, unseasonable, unsuitable, unsuited, untimely.

*antonym* apt.

**unarmed** *adj* assailable, defenceless, exposed, helpless, inerm, open, pregnable, unarmoured, unprotected, vulnerable, weak, weaponless.

*antonym* armed.

**unashamed** *adj* impenitent, open, shameless, unabashed, unconcealed, undisguised, unrepentant.

**unasked** *adj* gratuitous, spontaneous, unbidden, undemanded, undesired, uninvited, unprompted, unrequested, unsolicited, unsought, unwanted, voluntary.

*antonyms* invited, solicited.

**unassailable** *adj* absolute, conclusive, impregnable, incontestable, incontrovertible, indisputable, invincible, inviolable, invulnerable, irrefutable, positive, proven, sacrosanct, secure, sound, undeniable, well-armed, well-fortified.

*antonym* assailable.

**unassertive** *adj* backward, bashful, diffident, meek, mousy, quiet, retiring, self-effacing, shy, timid, timorous, unassuming.

*antonym* assertive.

**unassuming** *adj* diffident, humble, meek, modest, natural, quiet, restrained, retiring, self-effacing, simple, unassertive, unobtrusive, unostentatious, unpresuming, unpretentious.

*antonyms* assuming, presumptuous, pretentious.

**unattached** *adj* autonomous, available, fancy-free, footloose, free, independent, non-aligned, single, unaffilated, uncommitted, unengaged, unmarried, unspoken for.

*antonyms* attached, committed, engaged.

**unattended** *adj* abandoned, alone, disregarded, ignored, unaccompanied, unescorted, unguarded, unsupervised, unwatched.

*antonyms* attended, escorted.

**unattractive** *adj* disagreeable, disgusting, distasteful, homely, ill-favoured, objectionable, offensive, off-putting, plain, repellent, ugly, unappealing, unappetising, uncomely, undesirable, unexciting, uninviting, unlovely, unpalatable, unpleasant, unprepossessing, unsavoury, unsightly, unwelcome.

*antonym* attractive.

**unauthorised** *adj* illegal, illicit, irregular, unlawful, unofficial, unsanctioned, unwarranted.

*antonym* authorised.

**unavailing** *adj* abortive, barren, bootless, fruitless, futile, idle, ineffective, ineffectual, inefficacious, pointless, unproductive, unprofitable, unsuccessful, useless, vain.

*antonyms* productive, successful.

**unavoidable** *adj* certain, compulsory, fated, ineluctable, inescapable, inevitable, inexorable, mandatory, necessary, obligatory.

*antonym* avoidable.

**unaware** *adj* blind, deaf, forgetful, heedless, ignorant, incognisant, oblivious, unconscious, unenlightened, uninformed, unknowing, unmindful, unsuspecting, unsuspicious.

*antonym* aware.

**unawares** *adv* aback, abruptly, accidentally, by surprise, imperceptibly, inadvertently, insidiously, mistakenly, off guard, on the hop, suddenly, unconsciously, unexpectedly, unintentionally, unknowingly, unprepared, unthinkingly, unwittingly.

**unbalanced** *adj* asymmetrical, biased, crazy, demented, deranged, disturbed, dysharmonic, eccentric, erratic, inequitable, insane, irrational, irregular, lopsided, lunatic, mad, off-balance, off-centre, one-sided, partial, partisan, prejudiced, shaky, touched, unequal, uneven, unfair, unhinged, unjust, unsound, unstable, unsteady, wobbly.

*antonym* balanced.

**unbearable** *adj* insufferable, insupportable, intolerable, outrageous, unacceptable, unendurable, unspeakable.

*antonyms* acceptable, bearable.

**unbeatable** *adj* indomitable, invincible, matchless, nonpareil, supreme, unconquerable, unstoppable, unsurpassable.

*antonyms* inferior, weak.

**unbeaten** *adj* supreme, triumphant, unbowed, unconquered, undefeated, unsubdued, unsurpassed, unvanquished, victorious, winning.

*antonyms* defeated, vanquished.

**unbecoming** *adj* discreditable, dishonourable, ill-suited, improper, inappropriate, incongruous, indecorous, indelicate, offensive, tasteless, unattractive, unbefitting, unfit, unflattering, unmaidenly, unmeet, unseemly, unsightly, unsuitable, unsuited.

*antonyms* becoming, seemly.

**unbelief** *n* agnosticism, atheism, disbelief, distrust, doubt, incredulity, scepticism.

*antonyms* belief, faith.

**unbelievable** *adj* astonishing, far-fetched, implausible, impossible, improbable, inconceivable, incredible, outlandish, preposterous, questionable, staggering, unconvincing, unimaginable, unlikely, unthinkable.

*antonyms* believable, credible.

**unbeliever** *n* agnostic, atheist, disbeliever, doubter, doubting Thomas, infidel, nullifidian, sceptic.

*antonyms* believer, supporter.

**unbelieving** *adj* disbelieving, distrustful, doubtful, doubting, dubious, incredulous, nullifidian, sceptical, suspicious, unconvinced, unpersuaded.

*antonyms* credulous, trustful.

**unbend** *v* loosen up, relax, straighten, thaw, unbutton, uncoil, uncurl, unfreeze.

*antonyms* stiffen, withdraw.

**unbending** *adj* aloof, distant, firm, forbidding, formal, formidable, hard-line, inflexible, intransigent, reserved, resolute, Rhadamanthine, rigid, severe, stiff, strict, stubborn, tough, uncompromising, unyielding.

*antonyms* approachable, friendly, relaxed.

**unbiased** *adj* disinterested, dispassionate, equitable, even-handed, fair, fair-minded, impartial, independent, just, neutral, objective, open-minded, uncoloured, uninfluenced, unprejudiced.

*antonym* biased.

**unbidden** *adj* free, spontaneous, unasked, unforced, uninvited, unprompted, unsolicited, unwanted, unwelcome, voluntary, willing.

*antonyms* invited, solicited.

**unbind** *v* free, liberate, loose, loosen, release, unchain, undo, unfasten, unfetter, unloose, unloosen, unshackle, untie, unyoke.

*antonyms* bind, restrain.

**unblemished** *adj* clear, flawless, immaculate, irreproachable, perfect, pure, spotless, unflawed, unimpeachable, unspotted, unstained, unsullied, untarnished.

*antonyms* blemished, flawed, imperfect.

**unblinking** *adj* assured, calm, composed, cool, emotionless, fearless, impassive, imperturbable, steady, unafraid, unemotional, unfaltering, unflinching, unshrinking, unwavering.

*antonyms* cowed, faithful, fearful.

**unblushing** *adj* amoral, blatant, bold, brazen, conscience-proof, immodest, shameless, unabashed, unashamed, unembarrassed.

*antonyms* abashed, ashamed.

**unborn** *adj* awaited, coming, embryonic, expected, foetal, future, hereafter, in utero, later, subsequent, succeeding.

**unbosom** *v* admit, bare, confess, confide, disburden, disclose, divulge, lay bare, let out, pour out, reveal, tell, unburden, uncover.

*antonyms* conceal, suppress.

**unbounded** *adj* absolute, boundless, endless, immeasurable, infinite, lavish, limitless, prodigal, unbridled, unchecked, unconstrained, uncontrolled, unlimited, unrestrained, vast.

*antonym* limited.

**unbreakable** *adj* armoured, durable, indestructible, infrangible, lasting, permanent, proof, resistant, rugged, shatter-proof, solid, strong, tough, toughened.

*antonyms* breakable, fragile.

**unbridled** *adj* excessive, immoderate, intemperate, licentious, profligate, rampant, riotous, unchecked, unconstrained, uncontrolled, uncurbed, ungovernable, ungoverned, unrestrained, unruly, violent, wanton.

**unbroken** *adj* ceaseless, complete, constant, continuous, endless, entire, incessant, intact, integral, perpetual, progressive, serried, solid, successive, total, unbowed, unceasing, undivided, unimpaired, uninterrupted, unremitting, unsubdued, untamed, whole.

*antonyms* cowed, fitful, intermittent.

**unburden** *v* confess, confide, disburden, discharge, disclose, discumber, disencumber, empty, lay bare, lighten, offload, pour out, relieve, reveal, tell all, unbosom, unload.

*antonyms* conceal, hide, suppress.

**uncalled-for** *adj* gratuitous, inappropriate, needless, undeserved, unheeded, unjust, unjustified, unmerited, unnecessary, unprovoked, unwanted, unwarranted, unwelcome.

*antonym* timely.

**uncanny** *adj* astonishing, astounding, bizarre, creepy, eerie, eldritch, exceptional, extraordinary, fantastic, incredible, inspired, miraculous, mysterious, preternatural, prodigious, queer, remarkable, scary, singular, spooky, strange, supernatural, unaccountable, unco, unearthly, unerring, unheard-of, unnatural, unusual, weird.

**uncaring** *adj* callous, inconsiderate, indifferent, negligent, unconcerned, unfeeling, uninterested, unmoved, unresponsive, unsympathetic.

*antonyms* concerned, solicitous.

**unceasing** *adj* ceaseless, constant, continual, continuing, continuous, endless, incessant, never-ending, non-stop, perpetual, persistent, relentless, unbroken, unending, unfailing, uninterrupted, unrelenting, unremitting.

*antonyms* intermittent, spasmodic.

**uncertain** *adj* ambiguous, ambivalent, chancy, changeable, conjectural, dicky, dithery, doubtful, dubious, erratic, fitful, hazardous, hazy, hesitant, iffy, in the lap of the gods, incalculable, inconstant, indefinite, indeterminate, indistinct, insecure, irregular, irresolute, on the knees of the gods, precarious, problematic, questionable, risky, shaky, slippy, speculative, unclear, unconfirmed, undecided, undetermined, unfixed, unforeseeable, unpredictable, unreliable, unresolved, unsettled, unsure, vacillating, vague, variable, wavering.

*antonym* certain.

**uncertainty** *n* ambiguity, bewilderment, confusion, diffidence, dilemma, doubt, dubiety, hesitancy, hesitation, incalculability, inconclusiveness, indecision, insecurity, irresolution, misgiving, peradventure, perplexity, puzzlement, qualm, quandary, risk, scepticism, unpredictability, vagueness.

*antonym* certainty.

**unchallengeable** *adj* absolute, conclusive, final, impregnable, inappellable, incontestable, incontrovertible, indisputable, irrefragable, irrefutable.

*antonyms* contestable, inconclusive.

**unchangeable** *adj* changeless, eternal, final, immutable, intransmutable, irreversible, permanent, unchanging.

*antonym* changeable.

**unchanging** *adj* abiding, changeless, constant, continuing, enduring, eternal, fixed, immutable, imperishable, lasting, permanent, perpetual, phaseless, steadfast, steady, unchanged, unfading, unvarying.

*antonyms* changeable, changing.

**uncharitable** *adj* callous, captious, cruel, hard-hearted, hypercritical, inhumane, insensitive, mean, merciless, pitiless, stingy, unchristian, unfeeling, unforgiving, unfriendly, ungenerous, unkind, unsympathetic.

*antonym* charitable.

**uncharted** *adj* foreign, mysterious, new, novel, strange, undiscovered, unexplored, unfamiliar, unknown, unplumbed, virgin.

*antonyms* familiar, well-known.

**unchaste** *adj* defiled, depraved, dishonest, dissolute, fallen, immodest, immoral, impure, lewd, licentious, loose, promiscuous, wanton.

*antonym* chaste.

**uncivil** *adj* abrupt, bad-mannered, bearish, boorish, brusque, churlish, curt, discourteous, disrespectful, gruff, ill-bred, ill-mannered, impolite, rude, surly, uncouth, ungracious, unmannerly.

*antonym* civil.

**uncivilised** *adj* antisocial, barbarian, barbaric, barbarous, boorish, brutish, churlish, coarse, gross, heathenish, ill-bred, illiterate, philistine, primitive, savage, tramontane, uncouth, uncultivated, uncultured, uneducated, unpolished, unsophisticated, untamed, vulgar, wild.

*antonym* civilised.

**unclassifiable** *adj* doubtful, elusive, etypic(al), ill-defined, indefinable, indefinite, indescribable, indeterminate, indistinct, uncertain, unconformable, undefinable, unidentifiable, vague.

*antonyms* conformable, definable, identifiable.

**unclean** *adj* contaminated, corrupt, defiled, dirty, evil, filthy, foul, impure, insalubrious, nasty, polluted, soiled, spotted, stained, sullied, tainted, unhygienic, unwholesome.

*antonym* clean.

**unclear** *adj* ambiguous, as clear as mud, dim, doubtful, dubious, equivocal, hazy, indefinite, indiscernible, indistinguishable, multivocal, obscure, uncertain, vague.

*antonym* clear.

**unclothed** *adj* bare, disrobed, en cuerpo, in one's birthday suit, in the altogether, in the buff, naked, nude, stark naked, starkers, stripped, unclad, undressed.

*antonyms* clothed, dressed.

**uncomfortable** *adj* awkward, bleak, confused, conscience-stricken, cramped, disagreeable, discomfited, discomfortable, discomposed, disquieted, distressed, disturbed, embarrassed, hard, ill-fitting, incommodious, irritating, painful, poky, self-conscious, sheepish, troubled, troublesome, uneasy.

*antonyms* comfortable, easy.

**uncommitted** *adj* available, fancy-free, floating, free, neutral, non-aligned, non-partisan, unattached, undecided, uninvolved.

*antonym* committed.

**uncommon** *adj* abnormal, atypical, bizarre, curious, distinctive, exceptional, extraordinary, incomparable, infrequent, inimitable, notable, noteworthy, novel, odd, outstanding, peculiar, queer, rare, recherché, remarkable, scarce, singular, special, strange, superior, unfamiliar, unparalleled, unprecedented, unusual, unwonted.

*antonym* common.

**uncommonly** *adv* abnormally, exceptionally, extremely, infrequently, occasionally, outstandingly, particularly, peculiarly, rarely, remarkably, seldom, singularly, strangely, unusually, very.

*antonyms* commonly, frequently.

**uncommunicative** *adj* brief, close, curt, guarded, laconic, reserved, reticent, retiring, secretive, short, shy, silent, taciturn, tight-lipped, unforthcoming, unresponsive, unsociable, withdrawn.

*antonym* communicative.

**uncompromising** *adj* decided, die-hard, firm, hard-core, hard-line, hardshell, inexorable, inflexible, intransigent, obdurate, obstinate, rigid, steadfast, strict, stubborn, tough, unaccommodating, unbending, unyielding.

*antonyms* flexible, open-minded.

**unconcealable** *adj* clear, insistent, insuppressible, irrepressible, manifest, obvious, plain, uncontrollable, undistinguishable.

**unconcealed** *adj* admitted, apparent, blatant, conspicuous, evident, frank, ill-concealed, manifest, naked, noticeable, obvious, open, overt, patent, self-confessed, unashamed, undistinguished, visible.

*antonyms* hidden, secret.

**unconcern** *n* aloofness, apathy, callousness, detachment, indifference, insouciance, jauntiness, negligence, nonchalance, pococurantism, remoteness, uninterestedness.

*antonym* concern.

**unconcerned** *adj* aloof, apathetic, blithe, callous, carefree, careless, complacent, composed, cool, detached, dispassionate, distant, easy, incurious, indifferent, insouciant, joco, nonchalant, oblivious, pococurante, relaxed, serene, uncaring, uninterested, uninvolved, unmoved, unperturbed, unruffled, unsympathetic, untroubled, unworried.

*antonym* concerned.

**unconditional** *adj* absolute, categorical, complete, downright, entire, full, implicit, out-and-out, outright, plenary, positive, thoroughgoing, total, unequivocal, unlimited, unqualified, unreserved, unrestricted, utter, whole-hearted.

*antonym* conditional.

**unconformity** *n* disconformity, discontinuity, irregularity, unconformability.

*antonym* conformability.

**uncongenial** *adj* antagonistic, antipathetic, disagreeable, discordant, displeasing, distasteful, incompatible, unappealing, unattractive, uninviting, unpleasant, unsavoury, unsuited, unsympathetic.

*antonym* congenial.

**unconnected** *adj* detached, disconnected, disjointed, divided, illogical, incoherent, independent, irrational, irrelevant, off-line, separate, unattached, unrelated.

*antonyms* connected, relevant.

**unconquerable** *adj* enduring, indomitable, ingrained, insuperable, insurmountable, inveterate, invincible, irrepressible, irresistible, overpowering, unbeatable, undefeatable, unyielding.

*antonyms* weak, yielding.

**unconscionable** *adj* amoral, criminal, excessive, exorbitant, extravagant, extreme, immoderate, inordinate, outrageous, preposterous, unethical, unjustifiable, unpardonable, unprincipled, unreasonable, unscrupulous, unwarrantable.

**unconscious** *adj* accidental, automatic, blind to, comatose, concussed, deaf to, heedless, ignorant, inadvertent, innate, insensible, instinctive, involuntary, knocked out, latent, oblivious, out, out cold, out for the count, reflex, repressed, senseless, stunned, subconscious, subliminal, suppressed, unaware, unintended, unintentional, unknowing, unmindful, unsuspecting, unwitting.

*antonym* conscious.

**unconstraint** *n* abandon, freedom, laissez-aller, laissez-faire, liberality, openness, relaxation, unreserve, unrestraint.

**uncontrollable** *adj* frantic, furious, intractable, irrepressible, irresistible, irrestrainable, mad, masterless, recalcitrant, refractory, strong, ungovernable, unmanageable, unruly, violent, wild.

*antonyms* controllable, manageable.

**uncontrolled** *adj* boisterous, furious, masterless, rampant, riotous, unbridled, unchecked, uncurbed, undisciplined, ungoverned, unhindered, unrestrained, unruly, untrammelled, violent, wild.

*antonyms* contained, controlled.

**unconventional** *adj* abnormal, alternative, atypical, bizarre, bohemian, different, eccentric, freakish, idiosyncratic, individual, individualistic, informal, irregular, nonconforming, odd, offbeat, original, spacy, unconformable, unorthodox, unusual, way-out, wayward.

*antonym* conventional.

**unconvincing** *adj* doubtful, dubious, feeble, fishy, flimsy, implausible, improbable, inconclusive, lame, questionable, specious, suspect, tall, thin, unlikely, unpersuasive, weak.

*antonyms* convincing, plausible.

**unco-ordinated** *adj* awkward, bumbling, clodhopping, clumsy, desultory, diffuse, disjointed, disorganised, graceless, inept, lumbering, maladroit, unconcerted, ungainly, ungraceful.

*antonyms* concerted, graceful, systematic.

**uncouth** *adj* awkward, barbarian, barbaric, boorish, clownish, clumsy, coarse, crude, gauche, gawky, graceless, gross, ill-mannered, loutish, lubberly, oafish, rough, rude, rustic, uncivilised, uncultivated, ungainly, unrefined, unseemly, vulgar.

*antonyms* polished, polite, refined, urbane.

**uncover** *v* bare, detect, disclose, discover, dismask, disrobe, divulge, exhume, expose, leak, lift the lid off, open, reveal, show, strip, unearth, unmask, unveil, unwrap.

*antonyms* conceal, cover, suppress.

**uncritical** *adj* accepting, credulous, indiscriminate, naïve, non-judgemental, superficial, trusting, undiscerning, undiscriminating, unexacting, unfussy, unscholarly, unselective, unthinking.

*antonyms* critical, discriminating, sceptical.

**unctuous** *adj* fawning, glib, greasy, gushing, ingratiating, insincere, obsequious, oily, pietistic, plausible, religiose, sanctimonious, slick, smarmy, smooth, suave, sycophantic.

**uncultivated** *adj* fallow, incult, natural, rough, uncultured, wild.

*antonym* cultivated.

**uncultured** *adj* awkward, boorish, coarse, crude, hick, raw, rustic, uncivilised, uncouth, uncultivated, unrefined, unsophisticated.

*antonym* cultured.

**undaunted** *adj* bold, brave, courageous, dauntless, fearless, gallant, indomitable, intrepid, resolute, steadfast, unbowed, undashed, undeterred, undiscouraged, undismayed, unfaltering, unflinching, unperturbed, unshrinking.

*antonyms* cowed, timorous.

**undecided** *adj* ambivalent, debatable, dithering, doubtful, dubious, hesitant, in two minds, indefinite, irresolute, moot, open, pending, swithering, tentative, torn, uncertain, uncommitted, unconcluded, undetermined, unfixed, unsettled, unsure, vague, vexed, wavering.

*antonyms* certain, decided, definite.

**undecorated** *adj* austere, classical, functional, inornate, plain, severe, simple, stark, unadorned, unembellished, unornamented.

*antonyms* decorated, ornate.

**undefended** *adj* defenceless, exposed, expugnable, inerm, naked, open, pregnable, unarmed, unfortified, unguarded, unprotected, vulnerable.

*antonyms* armed, defended, fortified.

**undefiled** *adj* chaste, clean, clear, flawless, immaculate, intact, intemerate, inviolate, pure, sinless, spotless, unblemished, unsoiled, unspotted, unstained, unsullied, virginal.

**undefined** *adj* formless, hazy, ill-defined, imprecise, indefinite, indeterminate, indistinct, inexact, nebulous, shadowy, tenuous, unclear, unexplained, unspecified, vague, woolly.

*antonyms* definite, precise.

**undemonstrative** *adj* aloof, cold, contained, cool, distant, formal, impassive, phlegmatic, reserved, restrained, reticent, stiff, stolid, unbending, uncommunicative, unemotional, unresponsive, withdrawn.

*antonym* demonstrative.

**undeniable** *adj* certain, clear, evident, incontestable, incontrovertible, indisputable, indubitable, irrefragable, irrefutable, manifest, obvious, patent, proven, sound, sure, unassailable, undoubted, unmistakable, unquestionable.

**undependable** *adj* capricious, changeable, erratic, fair-weather, fickle, inconsistent, inconstant, irresponsible, mercurial, treacherous, uncertain, unpredictable, unreliable, unstable, untrustworthy, variable.

*antonyms* dependable, reliable.

**under** *prep* belonging to, below, beneath, governed by, included in, inferior to, junior to, lead by, less than, lower than, secondary to, subject to, subordinate to, subservient to, underneath.

*adv* below, beneath, down, downward, less, lower.

**under an obligation** beholden, bound, duty-bound, grateful, honour-bound, in debt to, in honour bound, indebted, obligated, obliged, thankful.

**under the weather** ailing, below par, groggy, hung over, ill, indisposed, mops and brooms, nauseous, off-colour, out of sorts, peelie-wally, poorly, queer, seedy, sick, squeamish, the worse for wear.

**under way** afoot, begun, going, in motion, in operation, in progress, launched, moving, on the go, on the move, started.

**underclothes** *n* frillies, lingerie, smalls, underclothing, undergarments, underlinen, underwear, undies, unmentionables.

**undercover** *adj* clandestine, concealed, confidential, covert, furtive, hidden, hush-hush, intelligence, private, secret, spy, stealthy, surreptitious, underground.

*antonyms* open, unconcealed.

**undercurrent** *n* atmosphere, aura, cross-current, drift, eddy, feeling, flavour, hint, movement, murmur, overtone, rip, riptide, sense, suggestion, tendency, tenor, tide, tinge, trend, underflow, undertone, undertow, vibes, vibrations.

**undercut** *v* excavate, gouge out, hollow out, mine, sacrifice, scoop out, underbid, undercharge, undermine, underprice, undersell.

**underestimate** *v* belittle, dismiss, fail to appreciate, minimise, miscalculate, misprise, sell short, underrate, undervalue.

*antonyms* exaggerate, overestimate.

**undergo** *v* bear, brook, endure, experience, run the gauntlet, stand, submit to, suffer, sustain, weather, withstand.

**underground** *adj* alternative, avant-garde, buried, clandestine, concealed, covered, covert, experimental, hidden, hypogeal, hypogean, hypogene, hypogeous, radical, revolutionary, secret, subterranean, subversive, surreptitious, undercover.

*n* métro, subway, tube.

**undergrowth** *n* bracken, brambles, briars, brush, brushwood, firth, frith, ground cover, scrub, underbrush.

**underhand** *adj* clandestine, crafty, crooked, deceitful, deceptive, devious, dishonest, dishonourable, fraudulent, furtive, immoral, improper, shady, shifty, sly, sneaky, stealthy, surreptitious, treacherous, underhanded, unethical, unscrupulous.

*antonym* above board.

**underline** v accentuate, emphasise, highlight, italicise, labour, mark, point up, press, reiterate, stress, underscore, urge.

*antonyms* play down, soft-pedal.

**underling** n flunkey, hireling, inferior, lackey, menial, minion, nobody, nonentity, retainer, servant, slave, subordinate, understrapper, weakling.

*antonyms* boss, leader, master.

**underlying** adj basal, basic, concealed, elementary, essential, fundamental, hidden, intrinsic, latent, lurking, primary, prime, root, subjacent, substral, substructural, veiled.

**undermine** v debilitate, disable, erode, excavate, impair, mar, mine, sabotage, sap, subvert, threaten, tunnel, undercut, vitiate, weaken, wear away.

*antonyms* fortify, strengthen.

**underprivileged** adj deprived, destitute, disadvantaged, impecunious, impoverished, needy, poor, poverty-stricken.

*antonyms* affluent, fortunate, privileged.

**underrate** v belittle, depreciate, discount, dismiss, disparage, misprise, underestimate, undervalue.

*antonyms* exaggerate, overrate.

**undersell** v cut, depreciate, disparage, mark down, play down, reduce, slash, undercharge, undercut, understate.

**undersized** adj achondroplastic, atrophied, dwarfed, dwarfish, miniature, minute, puny, pygmy, runtish, runty, small, stunted, tiny, underdeveloped, underweight.

*antonyms* big, oversized, overweight.

**understand** v accept, appreciate, apprehend, assume, believe, commiserate, comprehend, conceive, conclude, cotton on, discern, fathom, follow, gather, get, get the message, get the picture, grasp, hear, know, learn, penetrate, perceive, presume, realise, recognise, savvy, see, see daylight, suppose, sympathise, think, tolerate, tumble, twig.

*antonym* misunderstand.

**understanding** n accord, agreement, appreciation, awareness, belief, comprehension, conclusion, discernment, estimation, grasp, idea, impression, insight, intellect, intellection, intelligence, interpretation, judgement, knowledge, notion, opinion, pact, penetration, perception, reading, sense, view, viewpoint, wisdom.

adj accepting, compassionate, considerate, discerning, forbearing, forgiving, kind, kindly, loving, patient, perceptive, responsive, sensitive, sympathetic, tender, tolerant.

*antonyms* impatient, insensitive, intolerant, unsympathetic.

**understate** v belittle, dismiss, make light of, make little of, minimise, play down, soft-pedal, underplay, undersell.

**understatement** n dismissal, litotes, meiosis, minimisation, restraint, underplaying.

**understood** adj accepted, assumed, axiomatic, implicit, implied, inferred, presumed, tacit, unspoken, unstated, unwritten.

**understudy** n alternate, deputy, double, fill-in, replacement, reserve, stand-in, substitute.

**undertake** v accept, agree, assume, attempt, bargain, begin, commence, contract, covenant, embark on, endeavour, engage, guarantee, pledge, promise, shoulder, stipulate, tackle, try.

**undertaker** n funeral director, funeral furnisher, mortician.

**undertaking** n adventure, affair, assurance, attempt, business, commitment, effort, emprise, endeavour, enterprise, game, operation, pledge, project, promise, task, venture, vow, word.

**undertone** n atmosphere, current, feeling, flavour, hint, murmur, suggestion, tinge, touch, trace, undercurrent, undervoice, whisper.

**undervalue** v depreciate, discount, dismiss, disparage, disprize, minimise, misjudge, misprice, misprise, underestimate, underrate.

*antonyms* exaggerate, overrate.

**underwater** adj subaquatic, subaqueous, submarine, submerged, sunken, undersea.

**underwear** n frillies, lingerie, smalls, underclothes, underclothing, undergarments, underlinen, undies, unmentionables.

**underweight** adj emaciated, half-starved, puny, skinny, thin, undernourished, undersized.

*antonym* overweight.

**underworld** n Avernus, criminal fraternity, gangland, gangsterland, Hades, hell, nether world, the Inferno.

**underwrite** v approve, authorise, back, consent, countenance, countersign, endorse, finance, fund, guarantee, initial, insure, okay, sanction, sign, sponsor, subscribe, subsidise, validate.

**undesirable** adj disagreeable, disliked, disreputable, distasteful, dreaded, objectionable, obnoxious, offensive, repugnant, unacceptable, unattractive, unpleasant, unpopular, unsavoury, unsuitable, unwanted, unwelcome, unwished-for.

*antonym* desirable.

**undeveloped** adj dwarfed, embryonic, immature, inchoate, latent, potential, primordial, stunted, unformed.

*antonyms* developed, mature.

**undignified** adj foolish, improper, inappropriate, indecorous, inelegant, infra dig, petty, unbecoming, ungentlemanly, unladylike, unrefined, unseemly, unsuitable.

*antonym* dignified.

**undisciplined** adj disobedient, disorganised, obstreperous, uncontrolled, unpredictable, unreliable, unrestrained, unruly, unschooled, unsteady, unsystematic, untrained, wayward, wild, wilful.

*antonym* disciplined.

**undisguised** *adj* apparent, blatant, confessed, evident, explicit, frank, genuine, ill-concealed, manifest, naked, obvious, open, out-and-out, outright, overt, patent, stark, thoroughgoing, transparent, unadorned, unashamed, unconcealed, unmistakable, utter, whole-hearted.

*antonyms* concealed, hidden, secret.

**undisguisedly** *adj* blatantly, frankly, obviously, openly, outright, overtly, patently, transparently, unreservedly.

*antonym* secretly.

**undisputed** *adj* accepted, acknowledged, certain, conclusive, incontestable, incontrovertible, indisputable, irrefragable, irrefutable, recognised, sure, unchallenged, uncontested, undeniable, undoubted, unequivocal, unmistakable, unquestioned.

*antonyms* dubious, uncertain.

**undistinguished** *adj* banal, commonplace, everyday, indifferent, inferior, mediocre, ordinary, pedestrian, prosaic, run-of-the-mill, so-so, unexceptional, unexciting, unimpressive, unremarkable.

*antonyms* distinguished, exceptional.

**undisturbed** *adj* calm, collected, composed, equable, even, motionless, placid, quiet, serene, tranquil, unaffected, unconcerned, uninterrupted, unperturbed, unruffled, untouched, untroubled.

*antonyms* disturbed, interrupted.

**undivided** *adj* combined, complete, concentrated, concerted, entire, exclusive, full, individuate, solid, thorough, tight-knit, unanimous, unbroken, united, whole, whole-hearted.

**undo** *v* annul, cancel, defeat, destroy, disengage, dislink, invalidate, loose, loosen, mar, neutralise, nullify, offset, open, overturn, quash, reverse, ruin, separate, shatter, spoil, subvert, unbutton, undermine, unfasten, unlink, unlock, unloose, unloosen, untie, unwind, unwrap, upset, vitiate, wreck.

*antonym* fasten.

**undoing** *n* besetting sin, blight, collapse, curse, defeat, destruction, disgrace, downfall, hamartia, humiliation, misfortune, overthrow, overturn, reversal, ruin, ruination, shame, tragic fault, trouble, weakness.

**undomesticated** *adj* ferae naturae, feral, natural, savage, uncivilised, unhouseproud, unhousewifely, unmaternal, unmotherly, unpractical, untamed, wild.

*antonyms* domesticated, home-loving, tame.

**undone**[1] *adj* betrayed, destroyed, lost, ruined.

**undone**[2] *adj* forgotten, incomplete, left, neglected, omitted, outstanding, unaccomplished, uncompleted, unfinished, unfulfilled, unperformed.

*antonyms* accomplished, complete, done.

**undone**[3] *adj* loose, open, unbraced, unbuttoned, unfastened, unlaced, unlocked, untied.

*antonyms* fastened, secured.

**undoubted** *adj* acknowledged, certain, definite, evident, incontrovertible, indisputable, indubitable, obvious, patent, sure, unchallenged, undisputed, unquestionable, unquestioned.

**undoubtedly** *adv* assuredly, certainly, definitely, doubtless, indubitably, of course, surely, undeniably, unmistakably, unquestionably.

**undreamed-of** *adj* astonishing, inconceivable, incredible, miraculous, undreamt, unexpected, unforeseen, unheard-of, unhoped-for, unimagined, unsuspected.

**undress** *v* disrobe, divest, peel off, remove, shed, strip, take off.

*n* déshabillé, disarray, dishabille, nakedness, nudity.

**undressed** *adj* disrobed, en cuerpo, naked, nude, stark naked, starkers, stripped, unclad, unclothed.

**undue** *adj* disproportionate, excessive, extravagant, extreme, immoderate, improper, inordinate, intemperate, needless, overmuch, supererogatory, uncalled-for, undeserved, unnecessary, unreasonable, unseemly, unwarranted.

*antonym* reasonable.

**undulate** *v* billow, heave, ripple, rise and fall, roll, surge, swell, wave.

**undulating** *adj* billowing, flexuose, flexuous, rippling, rolling, sinuous, undate, undulant, wavy.

*antonym* flat.

**unduly** *adv* disproportionately, excessively, extravagantly, immoderately, inordinately, over, overly, overmuch, too, unjustifiably, unnecessarily, unreasonably.

*antonym* reasonably.

**undutiful** *adj* careless, defaulting, delinquent, disloyal, neglectful, negligent, remiss, slack, unfilial.

*antonym* dutiful.

**undutifulness** *n* default, defection, delinquency, dereliction, desertion, disloyalty, incivism, neglect, negligence, remissness.

*antonyms* dutifulness, loyalty.

**undying** *adj* abiding, constant, continuing, deathless, eternal, everlasting, immortal, imperishable, indestructible, inextinguishable, infinite, lasting, perennial, permanent, perpetual, sempiternal, undiminished, unending, unfading.

*antonyms* impermanent, inconstant.

**unearth** *v* detect, dig up, discover, disinter, dredge up, excavate, exhume, expose, ferret out, find, reveal, uncover.

**unearthly** *adj* abnormal, eerie, eldritch, ethereal, extraordinary, ghostly, haunted, heavenly, nightmarish, other-worldly, phantom, preternatural, spectral, spine-chilling, strange, sublime, supernatural, uncanny, ungodly, unreasonable, weird.

**uneasiness** *n* agitation, alarm, anxiety, apprehension, apprehensiveness, dis-ease, disquiet, doubt, dysphoria, inquietude, misgiving, nervousness, perturbation, qualms, suspicion, unease, worry.

*antonyms* calm, composure.

**uneasy** *adj* agitated, anxious, apprehensive, awkward, constrained, discomposed, disquieting, disturbed, disturbing, edgy, impatient, insecure, jittery, nervous, niggling, on edge, perturbed, precarious, restive, restless, shaky, strained, tense, troubled, troubling, uncomfortable, unquiet, unsettled, unstable, upset, upsetting, worried, worrying.

*antonyms* calm, composed.

**uneconomic** *adj* loss-making, non-profit-making, uncommercial, unprofitable.

*antonyms* economic, profitable.

**uneducated** *adj* benighted, ignorant, illiterate, low-brow, philistine, uncultivated, uncultured, uninstructed, unlessoned, unlettered, unread, unschooled, untaught.

*antonym* educated.

**unembellished** *adj* austere, bald, bare, functional, modest, plain, severe, simple, stark, unadorned, undecorated, unelaborated, unornamented, unvarnished.

*antonyms* embellished, ornate.

**unemotional** *adj* apathetic, cold, cool, dispassionate, impassive, indifferent, laid-back, low-key, objective, passionless, phlegmatic, reserved, undemonstrative, unexcitable, unfeeling, unimpassioned, unresponsive.

*antonyms* emotional, excitable.

**unemphatic** *adj* down-beat, played-down, soft-pedalled, underplayed, understated, unobtrusive, unostentatious.

**unemployed** *adj* idle, jobless, on the dole, out of work, redundant, resting, unoccupied, workless.

*antonym* employed.

**unending** *adj* ceaseless, constant, continual, endless, eternal, everlasting, incessant, interminable, never-ending, perpetual, unceasing, undying, unrelenting, unremitting.

*antonyms* intermittent, transient.

**unendurable** *adj* insufferable, insupportable, intolerable, overwhelming, shattering, unbearable.

*antonyms* bearable, endurable.

**unenthusiastic** *adj* apathetic, blasé, bored, cool, half-hearted, indifferent, laodicean, lukewarm, neutral, nonchalant, unimpressed, uninterested, unmoved, unresponsive.

*antonym* enthusiastic.

**unenviable** *adj* disagreeable, painful, thankless, uncomfortable, uncongenial, undesirable, unpalatable, unpleasant, unsavoury.

*antonyms* desirable, enviable.

**unequal** *adj* asymmetrical, different, differing, disparate, disproportionate, dissimilar, ill-equipped, ill-matched, inadequate, incapable, incompetent, insufficient, irregular, unbalanced, uneven, unlike, unmatched, variable, varying.

*antonym* equal.

**unequalled** *adj* exceptional, incomparable, inimitable, matchless, nonpareil, paramount, peerless, pre-eminent, supreme, surpassing, transcendent, unmatched, unparalleled, unrivalled, unsurpassed.

**unequivocal** *adj* absolute, certain, clear, clear-cut, crystal-clear, decisive, definite, direct, distinct, evident, explicit, express, incontrovertible, indubitable, manifest, plain, positive, straight, unambiguous, uncontestable, unmistakable.

*antonyms* ambiguous, vague.

**unerring** *adj* accurate, certain, dead, exact, faultless, impeccable, infallible, perfect, sure, uncanny, unfailing.

*antonym* fallible.

**unerringly** *adv* accurately, bang, dead, infallibly, unfailingly.

**unethical** *adj* dirty, discreditable, dishonest, dishonourable, disreputable, illegal, illicit, immoral, improper, shady, underhand, unfair, unprincipled, unprofessional, unscrupulous, wrong.

*antonym* ethical.

**uneven** *adj* accidented, asymmetrical, broken, bumpy, changeable, desultory, disparate, erratic, fitful, fluctuating, ill-matched, inconsistent, intermittent, irregular, jerky, lopsided, notchy, odd, one-sided, patchy, rough, spasmodic, unbalanced, unequal, unfair, unsteady, variable.

*antonym* even.

**uneventful** *adj* boring, commonplace, dull, humdrum, monotonous, ordinary, quiet, routine, tame, tedious, unexceptional, unexciting, uninteresting, unmemorable, unremarkable, unvaried.

*antonyms* eventful, memorable.

**unexampled** *adj* incomparable, never before seen, novel, unequalled, unheard-of, unique, unmatched, unparalleled, unprecedented.

**unexceptional** *adj* average, commonplace, conventional, indifferent, insignificant, mediocre, normal, ordinary, pedestrian, run-of-the-mill, typical, undistinguished, unimpressive, unmemorable, unremarkable, usual.

*antonyms* exceptional, impressive.

**unexcitable** *adj* calm, composed, contained, cool, dispassionate, easy-going, impassive, imperturbable, laid-back, passionless, phlegmatic, relaxed, self-possessed, serene, unimpassioned.

*antonym* excitable.

**unexpected** *adj* abrupt, accidental, amazing, astonishing, chance, fortuitous, startling, sudden, surprising, unaccustomed, unanticipated, unforeseen, unlooked-for, unpredictable, unusual, unwonted.

*antonyms* expected, normal, predictable.

**unexpectedly** *adv* abruptly, by chance, ex improviso, fortuitously, out of the blue, suddenly, surprisingly, unpredictably, without warning.

**unexpressive** *adj* blank, dead-pan, emotionless, expressionless, immobile, impassive, inexpressive, inscrutable, vacant.

*antonyms* expressive, mobile.

**unfading** *adj* abiding, durable, enduring, fadeless, fast, immarcescible, imperishable, lasting, undying, unfailing.

*antonyms* changeable, transient.

**unfailing** *adj* certain, constant, dependable, faithful, infallible, loyal, reliable, staunch, steadfast, steady, sure, true, undying, unfading.

*antonyms* fickle, impermanent, transient.

**unfair** *adj* arbitrary, biased, bigoted, crooked, discriminatory, dishonest, dishonourable, inequitable, one-sided, partial, partisan, prejudiced, uncalled-for, undeserved, unethical, unjust, unmerited, unprincipled, unscrupulous, unsporting, unwarranted, wrongful.

*antonym* fair.

**unfairness** *n* bias, bigotry, discrimination, inequity, injustice, maldistribution, one-sidedness, partiality, partisanship, prejudice.

*antonyms* equity, fairness.

**unfaithful** *adj* adulterous, deceitful, dishonest, disloyal, faithless, false, false-hearted, fickle, godless, inconstant, perfidious, recreant, traitorous, treacherous, treasonable, two-timing, unbelieving, unchaste, unreliable, untrue, untrustworthy.

*antonyms* faithful, loyal.

**unfaltering** *adj* constant, firm, fixed, indefatigable, pertinacious, resolute, steadfast, steady, tireless, unfailing, unflagging, unflinching, unswerving, untiring, unwavering.

*antonyms* faltering, uncertain, wavering.

**unfamiliar** *adj* alien, curious, different, foreign, new, novel, out-of-the-way, strange, unaccustomed, unacquainted, uncharted, uncommon, unconversant, unexplored, unknown, unpractised, unskilled, unusual, unversed.

*antonyms* customary, familiar.

**unfashionable** *adj* antiquated, dated, démodé, demoded, dismoded, fogram, obsolete, old hat, old-fashioned, out, out of date, outmoded, passé, square, unpopular.

*antonym* fashionable.

**unfasten** *v* detach, disconnect, loosen, open, separate, uncouple, undo, unlace, unlock, unloose, unloosen, untie.

*antonym* fasten.

**unfathomable** *adj* abstruse, baffling, bottomless, deep, esoteric, fathomless, hidden, immeasurable, impenetrable, incomprehensible, indecipherable, inexplicable, mysterious, profound, unknowable, unplumbed, unsounded.

*antonyms* comprehensible, explicable, penetrable.

**unfavourable** *adj* adverse, bad, contrary, critical, disadvantageous, discouraging, hostile, ill-suited, inauspicious, infelicitous, inimical, inopportune, low, negative, ominous, poor, threatening, uncomplimentary, unfortunate, unfriendly, unlucky, unpromising, unpropitious, unseasonable, unsuited, untimely, untoward.

*antonym* favourable.

**unfeeling** *adj* apathetic, callous, cold, cruel, hard, hardened, hard-hearted, harsh, heartless, inhuman, insensitive, pitiless, soulless, stony, uncaring, unsympathetic.

*antonym* concerned.

**unfeigned** *adj* frank, genuine, heartfelt, natural, pure, real, sincere, spontaneous, unaffected, unforced, whole-hearted.

*antonyms* feigned, insincere, pretended.

**unfettered** *adj* free, unbridled, unchecked, unconfined, unconstrained, unhampered, unhindered, uninhibited, unrestrained, unshackled, untrammelled.

*antonyms* constrained, fettered.

**unfinished** *adj* bare, crude, deficient, half-done, imperfect, incomplete, incondite, lacking, natural, raw, rough, rude, sketchy, unaccomplished, uncompleted, undone, unfulfilled, unpolished, unrefined, wanting.

*antonyms* finished, polished, refined.

**unfit** *adj* debilitated, decrepit, feeble, flabby, flaccid, hypotonic, ill-adapted, ill-equipped, inadequate, inappropriate, incapable, incompetent, ineffective, ineligible, unequal, unhealthy, unprepared, unqualified, unsuitable, unsuited, untrained, useless.

*antonyms* competent, fit, suitable.

**unflagging** *adj* constant, fixed, indefatigable, never-failing, persevering, persistent, single-minded, staunch, steady, tireless, unceasing, undeviating, unfailing, unfaltering, unremitting, unswerving, untiring.

*antonyms* faltering, inconstant.

**unflappable** *adj* calm, collected, composed, cool, equable, impassive, imperturbable, level-headed, phlegmatic, self-possessed, unexcitable, unruffled, unworried.

*antonyms* excitable, nervous, temperamental.

**unflattering** *adj* blunt, candid, critical, honest, outspoken, unbecoming, uncomplimentary, unfavourable, unprepossessing.

*antonyms* complimentary, flattering.

**unflinching** *adj* bold, constant, determined, firm, fixed, resolute, stalwart, staunch, steadfast, steady, sure, unblinking, unfaltering, unshaken, unshrinking, unswerving, unwavering.

*antonyms* cowed, scared.

**unfold** *v* clarify, describe, develop, disclose, disentangle, divulge, elaborate, evolve, expand, explain, flatten, grow, illustrate, mature, open, present, reveal, show, spread, straighten, stretch out, uncoil, uncover, undo, unfurl, unravel, unroll, unwrap.

*antonyms* fold, suppress, withhold, wrap.

**unforeseen** *adj* abrupt, accidental, fortuitous, startling, sudden, surprise, surprising, unanticipated, unavoidable, unexpected, unheralded, unlooked-for, unpredicted.

*antonyms* expected, predictable.

**unforgettable** *adj* exceptional, extraordinary, historic, impressive, memorable, momentous, notable, noteworthy.

*antonyms* unexceptional, unmemorable.

**unforgivable** *adj* deplorable, disgraceful, indefensible, inexcusable, reprehensible, shameful, unconscionable, unjustifiable, unpardonable, unwarrantable.

*antonyms* forgivable, venial.

**unforgiven** *adj* unabsolved, unredeemed, unregenerate, unrepentant, unshrived, unshriven.

*antonyms* absolved, forgiven.

**unfortunate** *adj* adverse, calamitous, cursed, deplorable, disadventurous, disastrous, doomed, hapless, hopeless, ill-advised, ill-fated, ill-starred, ill-timed, inappropriate, infelicitous, inopportune, lamentable, luckless, poor, regrettable, ruinous, star-crossed, tactless, unbecoming, unfavourable, unhappy, unlucky, unprosperous, unsuccessful, unsuitable, untimely, untoward, wretched.

*antonym* fortunate.

**unfortunately** *adv* miserabile dictu, regrettably, sad to relate, sad to say, sadly, unhappily, unluckily, worse luck.

*antonym* fortunately.

**unfounded** *adj* baseless, fabricated, false, gratuitous, groundless, idle, spurious, trumped-up, unjustified, unmerited, unproven, unsubstantiated, unsupported.

*antonym* justified.

**unfrequented** *adj* deserted, desolate, god-forsaken, isolated, lone, lonely, remote, secluded, sequestered, solitary, uninhabited, unvisited.

*antonyms* busy, crowded, populous.

**unfriendly** *adj* alien, aloof, antagonistic, chilly, cold, critical, disagreeable, distant, hostile, ill-disposed, inauspicious, inhospitable, inimical, quarrelsome, sour, stand-offish, surly, unapproachable, unbending, uncongenial, unfavourable, unneighbourly, unsociable, unwelcoming.

*antonyms* agreeable, amiable, friendly.

**unfrock** *v* degrade, demote, depose, disfrock, disgown, dismiss, suspend.

*antonyms* reinstate, restore.

**unfruitful** *adj* arid, barren, exhausted, fruitless, impoverished, infecund, infertile, infructuous, sterile, unproductive, unprofitable, unprolific, unrewarding.

*antonym* fruitful.

**ungainly** *adj* awkward, clumsy, gangling, gauche, gawky, inelegant, loutish, lubberly, lumbering, slouching, unco-ordinated, uncouth, unwieldy.

*antonyms* elegant, graceful.

**ungirded** *adj* discinct, unbelted, ungirt, unprepared, unready.

**ungodly** *adj* blasphemous, corrupt, depraved, dreadful, godless, horrendous, immoral, impious, intolerable, irreligious, outrageous, profane, sinful, unearthly, unreasonable, unseasonable, unseemly, unsocial, vile, wicked.

**ungovernable** *adj* disorderly, masterless, rebellious, refractory, uncontrollable, ungoverned, unmanageable, unrestrainable, unruly, wild.

**ungracious** *adj* bad-mannered, boorish, churlish, discourteous, disrespectful, graceless, ill-bred, impolite, offhand, rude, uncivil, unmannerly.

*antonyms* gracious, polite.

**ungrateful** *adj* heedless, ill-mannered, ingrate, selfish, thankless, unappreciative, ungracious, unmindful.

*antonym* grateful.

**unguarded**[1] *adj* careless, foolhardy, foolish, heedless, ill-considered, impolitic, imprudent, incautious, indiscreet, rash, thoughtless, uncircumspect, undiplomatic, unheeding, unthinking, unwary.

*antonyms* cautious, guarded.

**unguarded**[2] *adj* defenceless, exposed, pregnable, undefended, unpatrolled, unprotected, vulnerable.

*antonyms* guarded, protected.

**unhandy** *adj* awkward, bungling, cack-handed, clumsy, cumbersome, fumbling, heavy-handed, ill-contrived, incompetent, inconvenient, inept, inexpert, maladroit, unco-ordinated, unskilful, unwieldy.

*antonyms* adroit, deft, handy.

**unhappy** *adj* awkward, blue, clumsy, contentless, crestfallen, cursed, dejected, depressed, despondent, disconsolate, dismal, dispirited, down, downcast, gauche, gloomy, hapless, ill-advised, ill-chosen, ill-fated, ill-omened, ill-timed, inappropriate, inapt, inept, infelicitous, injudicious, long-faced, luckless, lugubrious, malapropos, melancholy, miserable, mournful, sad, sorrowful, sorry, tactless, uneasy, unfortunate, unlucky, unsuitable, wretched.

*antonyms* fortunate, happy.

**unharmed** *adj* intact, safe, scot-free, sound, undamaged, unhurt, unimpaired, uninjured, unscarred, unscathed, untouched, whole.

*antonyms* damaged, harmed, impaired.

**unhealthy** *adj* ailing, bad, baneful, corrupt, corrupting, degrading, deleterious, delicate, demoralising, detrimental, epinosic, feeble, frail, harmful, infirm, insalubrious, insalutary, insanitary, invalid, morbid, noisome, noxious, polluted, poorly, sick, sickly, undesirable, unhygienic, unsound, unwell, unwholesome, weak.

*antonyms* healthy, hygienic, robust, salubrious.

**unheard-of** *adj* disgraceful, extreme, inconceivable, new, novel, obscure, offensive, out of the question, outrageous, preposterous, shocking, singular, unacceptable, unbelievable, undiscovered, undreamed-of, unexampled, unfamiliar, unimaginable, unique, unknown, unprecedented, unregarded, unremarked, unsung, unthinkable, unthought-of, unusual.

*antonyms* famous, normal, usual.

**unheeded** *adj* disobeyed, disregarded, forgotten, ignored, neglected, overlooked, unnoticed, unobserved, unremarked.

*antonyms* heeded, noted, observed.

**unheralded** *adj* surprise, unadvertised, unannounced, unexpected, unforeseen, unnoticed, unproclaimed, unpublicised, unrecognised, unsung.

*antonyms* advertised, publicised, trumpeted.

**unhesitating** *adj* automatic, immediate, implicit, instant, instantaneous, prompt, ready, resolute, spontaneous, steadfast, unfaltering, unquestioning, unreserved, unswerving, unwavering, whole-hearted.

*antonyms* hesitant, tentative, uncertain.

**unhinge** *v* confuse, craze, derange, disorder, distract, drive mad, madden, unbalance, unnerve, unsettle, upset.

**unholy** *adj* appalling, base, corrupt, depraved, dishonest, evil, heinous, immoral, iniquitous, irreligious, outrageous, profane, shocking, sinful, taboo, unconscionable, unearthly, ungodly, unnatural, unreasonable, vile, wicked.

*antonyms* godly, holy, pious, reasonable.

**unhoped-for** *adj* incredible, surprising, unanticipated, unbelievable, undreamed-of, unexpected, unforeseen, unimaginable, unlooked-for.

**unhurried** *adj* calm, deliberate, easy, easy-going, laid-back, leisurely, relaxed, sedate, slow.

*antonyms* hasty, hurried.

**unicorn** *n* monoceros.

**unidentified** *adj* anonymous, incognito, mysterious, nameless, unclaimed, unclassified, unfamiliar, unknown, unmarked, unnamed, unrecognised, unspecified.

*antonyms* identified, known, named.

**unification** *n* alliance, amalgamation, coalescence, coalition, combination, confederation, enosis, federation, fusion, incorporation, merger, union, uniting.

*antonyms* separation, split.

**uniform** *n* costume, dress, garb, gear, habit, insignia, livery, outfit, regalia, regimentals, rig, robes, suit.

*adj* alike, consistent, constant, equable, equal, even, homochromous, homogeneous, homomorphic, homomorphous, identical, like, monochrome, montonous, of a piece, regular, same, selfsame, similar, smooth, unbroken, unchanging, undeviating, unvarying.

*antonyms* changing, colourful, varied.

**uniformity** *n* constancy, drabness, dullness, evenness, flatness, homogeneity, homomorphism, invariability, monotony, regularity, sameness, similarity, similitude, tedium.

*antonyms* difference, dissimilarity, variation.

**unify** *v* amalgamate, bind, combine, confederate, consolidate, federate, fuse, join, marry, merge, unite, weld.

*antonyms* separate, split.

**unifying** *adj* combinatory, consolidative, esemplastic, henotic, reconciling, unific, uniting.

*antonym* divisive.

**unimaginable** *adj* fantastic, impossible, inconceivable, incredible, indescribable, ineffable, mind-boggling, unbelievable, undreamed-of, unheard-of, unhoped-for, unknowable, unthinkable.

**unimaginative** *adj* banal, barren, blinkered, commonplace, derivative, dry, dull, hackneyed,

lifeless, matter-of-fact, myopic, ordinary, pedestrian, predictable, prosaic, routine, short-sighted, tame, uncreative, uninspired, unoriginal.

*antonyms* imaginative, original.

**unimpeachable** *adj* blameless, faultless, immaculate, impeccable, irreproachable, perfect, spotless, unassailable, unblemished, unchallengeable, unexceptionable, unquestionable.

*antonyms* blameworthy, faulty.

**unimpeded** *adj* all-round, clear, free, open, unblocked, unchecked, unconstrained, unhampered, unhindered, uninhibited, unrestrained, untrammelled.

*antonyms* hampered, impeded.

**unimportant** *adj* immaterial, inconsequential, insignificant, irrelevant, low-ranking, Mickey Mouse, minor, minuscule, negligible, nugatory, off the map, paltry, paravail, petty, slight, small-time, trifling, trivial, worthless.

*antonym* important.

**unimpressive** *adj* average, commonplace, dull, indifferent, mediocre, undistinguished, unexceptional, uninteresting, unremarkable, unspectacular.

*antonyms* impressive, memorable, notable.

**uninhibited** *adj* abandoned, candid, emancipated, frank, free, informal, instinctive, liberated, natural, open, relaxed, spontaneous, unbridled, unchecked, unconstrained, uncontrolled, uncurbed, unrepressed, unreserved, unrestrained, unrestricted, unselfconscious.

*antonyms* constrained, inhibited, repressed.

**uninspired** *adj* boring, commonplace, dull, humdrum, indifferent, ordinary, pedestrian, prosaic, stale, stock, trite, undistinguished, unexciting, unimaginative, uninspiring, uninteresting, unoriginal.

*antonyms* inspired, original.

**unintelligent** *adj* brainless, dense, dull, dumb, empty-headed, fatuous, foolish, gormless, half-witted, obtuse, silly, slow, stupid, thick, unreasoning, unthinking.

*antonym* intelligent.

**unintelligible** *adj* double Dutch, garbled, illegible, inapprehensible, inarticulate, incoherent, incomprehensible, indecipherable, indistinct, jumbled, meaningless, muddled, unfathomable.

*antonym* intelligible.

**unintentional** *adj* accidental, fortuitous, inadvertent, involuntary, unconscious, undeliberate, unintended, unpremeditated, unthinking, unwitting.

*antonyms* deliberate, intentional.

**uninterested** *adj* apathetic, blasé, bored, distant, impassive, incurious, indifferent, listless, pococurante, unconcerned, unenthusiastic, uninvolved, unresponsive.

*antonyms* concerned, enthusiastic, interested, responsive.

**uninteresting** *adj* boring, commonplace, corny, drab, dreary, dry, dull, flat, humdrum, monotonous, tame, tedious, tiresome, uneventful, unexciting, unimpressive, uninspiring, wearisome.

*antonyms* exciting, interesting.

**uninterrupted** *adj* constant, continual, continuous, non-stop, peaceful, prolonged, quiet, steady, sustained, unbroken, undisturbed, unending.

*antonyms* broken, intermittent.

**uninvited** *adj* unasked, unbidden, unsolicited, unsought, unwanted, unwelcome.

*antonyms* invited, solicited.

**uninviting** *adj* disagreeable, distasteful, offensive, off-putting, repellent, repulsive, unappealing, unappetising, unattractive, undesirable, unpleasant, unsavoury, unwelcoming.

*antonyms* inviting, welcome.

**uninvolved** *adj* disengaged, fancy-free, footloose, free, heart-free, heart-whole, independent, unattached, uncommitted, unengaged, unhampered, unhindered, untrammelled.

*antonyms* attached, committed.

**union** *n* accord, agreement, alliance, amalgam, amalgamation, Anschluss, association, blend, Bund, coalition, coition, coitus, combination, compact, concord, concrescence, concurrence, confederacy, confederation, conjugation, conjunction, copulation, couplement, coupling, enosis, federation, fusion, harmony, intercourse, junction, juncture, league, marriage, matrimony, mixture, symphysis, synthesis, unanimity, unison, uniting, unity, wedlock.

*antonyms* alienation, disunity, estrangement, separation.

**unique** *adj* incomparable, inimitable, lone, matchless, nonpareil, one-off, only, peerless, single, singular, sole, solitary, sui generis, unequalled, unexampled, unmatched, unparalleled, unprecedented, unrivalled.

*antonym* commonplace.

**unison** *n* accord, accordance, aggreement, concert, concord, co-operation, harmony, homophony, monophony, unanimity, unity.

*antonyms* disharmony, polyphony.

**unit** *n* ace, assembly, component, constituent, detachment, element, entity, Gestalt, group, item, measure, measurement, member, module, monad, monas, one, part, piece, portion, quantity, section, segment, system, whole.

**unite** *v* accrete, ally, amalgamate, associate, band, blend, coadunate, coalesce, combine, confederate, conglutinate, conjoin, conjugate, consolidate, cooperate, couple, fay, fuse, incorporate, join, join forces, league, link, marry, merge, pool, splice, unify, wed.

*antonyms* separate, sever.

**united** *adj* affiliated, agreed, allied, collective, combined, concerted, concordant, conjoined, conjoint, conjunctive, corporate, in accord, in agreement, leagued, like-minded, one, pooled, unanimous, unified.

*antonyms* differing, disunited, separated, unco-ordinated.

**unity** *n* accord, agreement, community, concord, concurrence, consensus, entity, harmony, integrity, oneness, peace, singleness, solidarity, unanimity, unification, union, wholeness.

*antonyms* disagreement, disunity.

**universal** *adj* across-the-board, all-embracing, all-inclusive, all-round, catholic, common, ecumenic, ecumenical, entire, general, global, omnipresent, total, ubiquitous, unlimited, whole, widespread, worldwide.

**universality** *n* all-inclusiveness, commonness, completeness, comprehensiveness, entirety, generalisation, generality, predominance, prevalence, totality, ubiquity.

**universally** *adv* always, everywhere, invariably, ubiquitously, uniformly.

**universe** *n* cosmos, creation, firmament, heavens, macrocosm, nature, world.

**university** *n* academia, academy, Athenaeum, college, institute, multiversity, varsity.

**unjust** *adj* biased, gratuitous, groundless, inequitable, one-sided, partial, partisan, prejudiced, undeserved, unethical, unfair, unjustified, unmerited, wrong, wrongful.

*antonym* just.

**unjustifiable** *adj* excessive, immoderate, indefensible, inexcusable, outrageous, steep, unacceptable, unforgivable, unjust, unpardonable, unreasonable, unwarrantable, wrong.

*antonym* justifiable.

**unkempt** *adj* bedraggled, blowsy, disarranged, dishevelled, disordered, frowsy, mal soigné, messy, mop-headed, ratty, rumpled, scruffy, shabby, shaggy, slatternly, sloppy, slovenly, sluttish, tousled, uncombed, ungroomed, untidy.

*antonyms* neat, tidy.

**unkind** *adj* callous, cruel, disobliging, hard-hearted, harsh, inconsiderate, inhuman, inhumane, insensitive, malevolent, malicious, mean, nasty, spiteful, thoughtless, unamiable, uncaring, uncharitable, unchristian, unfeeling, unfriendly, unsympathetic.

*antonyms* considerate, kind.

**unkindness** *n* callousness, cruelty, disobligingness, hard-heartedness, harshness, ill-turn, inhumanity, insensitivity, maliciousness, meanness, spite, uncharitableness, unfriendliness.

*antonyms* friendship, kindness.

**unknowable** *adj* in the lap of the gods, incalculable, incognisable, infinite, on the knees of the gods, unascertainable, unfathomable, unforeseeable, unimaginable, unpredictable, untold.

**unknown** *adj* alien, anonymous, concealed, dark, foreign, hidden, humble, incognito, mysterious, nameless, new, obscure, secret, strange, uncharted, undisclosed, undiscovered, undistinguished, unexplored, unfamiliar, unheard-of, unidentified, unnamed, unrecognised, unsung, untold.

*antonyms* familiar, known.

**unladylike** *adj* boyish, coarse, hoydenish, ill-bred, impolite, indelicate, inelegant, rough, rude, tomboyish, uncivil, unfeminine, ungracious, unmannerly, unrefined, unseemly.

*antonyms* ladylike, seemly.

**unlawful** *adj* actionable, banned, criminal, forbidden, illegal, illegitimate, illicit, outlawed, prohibited, unauthorised, unconstitutional, unlicensed, unsanctioned.

*antonym* lawful.

**unleash** *v* free, loose, release, unloose, untether, untie.

*antonym* restrain.

**unlettered** *adj* ignorant, illiterate, uneducated, unlearned, unlessoned, unschooled, untaught, untutored.

*antonym* educated.

**unlike** *adj* contrasted, different, difform, disparate, dissimilar, distinct, divergent, diverse, ill-matched, incompatible, opposed, opposite, unequal, unrelated.

*antonyms* related, similar.

**unlikely** *adj* doubtful, dubious, faint, implausible, improbable, incredible, questionable, remote, slight, suspect, suspicious, tall, unbelievable, unconvincing, unexpected, unimaginable.

*antonyms* likely, plausible.

**unlikeness** *n* contrast, difference, disparity, dissemblance, dissimilarity, divergence, diversity, incompatibility.

*antonym* similarity.

**unlimited** *adj* absolute, all-encompassing, boundless, complete, countless, endless, extensive, full, great, illimitable, immeasurable, immense, incalculable, infinite, limitless, total, unbounded, uncircumscribed, unconditional, unconstrained, unfettered, unhampered, unqualified, unrestricted, vast.

*antonyms* circumscribed, limited.

**unload** *v* disburden, discharge, discumber, disencumber, disload, dump, empty, offload, relieve, unburden, unpack.

**unlock** *v* bare, disengage, free, open, release, unbar, unbolt, undo, unfasten, unlatch.

*antonyms* fasten, lock.

**unlooked-for** *adj* chance, fortuitous, fortunate, lucky, surprise, surprising, unanticipated, undreamed-of, unexpected, unforeseen, unhoped-for, unpredicted, unthought-of.

*antonyms* expected, predictable.

**unloved** *adj* detested, disliked, forsaken, hated, loveless, neglected, rejected, spurned, uncared-for, uncherished, unpopular, unwanted.

*antonyms* beloved, loved.

**unlucky** *adj* cursed, disastrous, doomed, hapless, ill-fated, ill-omened, ill-starred, inauspicious, infaust, jinxed, left-handed, luckless, mischanceful, miserable, ominous, unfavourable, unfortunate, unhappy, unsuccessful, untimely, wretched.

*antonym* lucky.

**unman** *v* daunt, demoralise, discourage, disman, dispirit, effeminate, effeminise, emasculate, emolliate, enervate, enfeeble, evirate, intimidate, unnerve, weaken.

*antonyms* brace, nerve, steel.

**unmanageable** *adj* awkward, bulky, cumbersome, difficult, disorderly, fractious, inconvenient, intractable, obstreperous, recalcitrant, refractory, stroppy, uncontrollable, unco-operative, unhandy, unruly, unwieldy, wild.

*antonyms* docile, manageable.

**unmanly** *adj* chicken-hearted, cowardly, craven, dishonourable, effeminate, epicene, feeble, ignoble, namby-pamby, sissy, soft, weak, weak-kneed, weedy, wet, womanish, yellow.

*antonym* manly.

**unmannerly** *adj* badly-behaved, bad-mannered, boorish, discourteous, disrespectful, graceless, ill-bred, ill-mannered, impolite, low-bred, rude, uncivil, uncouth, ungracious.

*antonym* polite.

**unmarried** *adj* available, bachelor, celibate, fancy-free, footloose, maiden, single, unattached, unwed, unwedded, virgin.

*antonym* married.

**unmask** *v* bare, detect, disclose, discover, dismask, expose, reveal, show, uncloak, uncover, unveil.

**unmatched** *adj* beyond compare, consummate, incomparable, matchless, nonpareil, paramount, peerless, supreme, unequalled, unexampled, unparalleled, unrivalled, unsurpassed.

**unmentionable** *adj* abominable, disgraceful, disreputable, immodest, indecent, innominable, nefandous, scandalous, shameful, shocking, taboo, unnameable, unspeakable, unutterable.

**unmerciful** *adj* brutal, callous, cruel, hard, heartless, implacable, merciless, pitiless, relentless, remorseless, ruthless, sadistic, uncaring, unfeeling, unrelenting, unsparing.

*antonym* merciful.

**unmethodical** *adj* confused, desultory, disorderly, haphazard, illogical, immethodical, irregular, muddled, random, unco-ordinated, unorganised, unsystematic.

*antonym* methodical.

**unmindful** *adj* blind, careless, deaf, forgetful, heedless, inattentive, indifferent, lax, neglectful, negligent, oblivious, regardless, remiss, slack, unaware, unconscious, unheeding.

*antonyms* aware, heedful, mindful.

**unmistakable** *adj* certain, clear, conspicuous, crystal-clear, decided, distinct, evident, explicit, glaring, indisputable, manifest, obvious, palpable, patent, plain, positive, pronounced, sure, unambiguous, undeniable, undisputed, unequivocal, unquestionable.

*antonyms* ambiguous, unclear.

**unmitigated** *adj* absolute, arrant, complete, consummate, downright, grim, harsh, intense, oppressive, out-and-out, outright, perfect, persistent, pure, rank, relentless, sheer, thorough, thoroughgoing, unabated, unalleviated, unbroken, undiminished, unmodified, unqualified, unredeemed, unrelenting, unrelieved, unremitting, utter.

**unmoved** *adj* adamant, cold, determined, dispassionate, dry-eyed, fast, firm, impassive, indifferent, inflexible, obdurate, phlegmatic, resolute, resolved, steadfast, steady, unaffected, unchanged, undeviating, unfeeling, unimpressed, unresponsive, unshaken, untouched, unwavering.

*antonyms* affected, moved, shaken.

**unnatural** *adj* aberrant, abnormal, absonant, affected, anomalous, artificial, assumed, bizarre, brutal, callous, cataphysical, cold-blooded, contrived, cruel, disnatured, evil, extraordinary, factitious, false, feigned, fiendish, forced, freakish, heartless, inhuman, insincere, irregular, laboured, mannered, monstrous, odd, outlandish, perverse, perverted, phoney, queer, ruthless, sadistic, savage, self-conscious, stagy, stiff, stilted, strained, strange, studied, supernatural, theatrical, unaccountable, uncanny, unfeeling, unspontaneous, unusual, wicked.

*antonyms* acceptable, natural, normal.

**unnecessary** *adj* dispensable, expendable, inessential, needless, non-essential, otiose, pleonastic, redundant, supererogatory, superfluous, supernumerary, tautological, uncalled-for, unjustified, unneeded, useless.

*antonyms* indispensable, necessary.

**unnerve** *adj* confound, daunt, demoralise, disconcert, discourage, dishearten, dismay, dispirit, fluster, frighten, intimidate, rattle, scare, shake, unhinge, unman, upset, worry.

*antonyms* brace, nerve, steel.

**unnoticed** *adj* disregarded, ignored, neglected, overlooked, passed over, unconsidered, undiscovered, unheeded, unobserved, unperceived, unrecognised, unrecorded, unremarked, unseen.

*antonyms* noted, remarked.

**unobtrusive** *adj* humble, inconspicuous, low-key, meek, modest, quiet, restrained, retiring, self-effacing, subdued, unassertive, unassuming, unemphatic, unnoticeable, unostentatious, unpretentious.

*antonyms* obtrusive, ostentatious.

**unobtrusively** *adv* inconspicuously, modestly, on the q.t., on the quiet, quietly, surreptitiously, unostentatiously.

*antonyms* obtrusively, ostentatiously.

**unoccupied** *adj* désoevré, disengaged, empty, free, idle, inactive, jobless, unemployed, uninhabited, untenanted, vacant, workless.

*antonyms* busy, occupied.

**unofficial** *adj* backyard, confidential, illegal, informal, personal, private, ulterior, unauthorised, unconfirmed, undeclared, wildcat.

*antonym* official.

**unoriginal** *adj* cliché-ridden, copied, cribbed, derivative, derived, second-hand, stale, trite, unimaginative, uninspired.

*antonyms* imaginative, original.

**unorthodox** *adj* abnormal, alternative, fringe, heterodox, irregular, nonconformist, unconventional, unusual, unwonted.

*antonyms* conventional, orthodox.

**unpaid** *adj* due, free, honorary, outstanding, overdue, owing, payable, unremunerative, unsalaried, unsettled, voluntary.

*antonym* paid.

**unpalatable** *adj* bitter, disagreeable, displeasing, distasteful, inedible, insipid, offensive, repugnant, unappetising, unattractive, uneatable, unenviable, unpleasant, unrelished, unsavoury.

*antonyms* palatable, pleasant.

**unparalleled** *adj* consummate, exceptional, incomparable, matchless, peerless, rare, singular, superlative, supreme, surpassing, unequalled, unexampled, unique, unmatched, unprecedented, unrivalled, unsurpassed.

**unpardonable** *adj* deplorable, disgraceful, indefensible, inexcusable, irremissible, outrageous, scandalous, shameful, shocking, unconscionable, unforgivable.

*antonyms* forgivable, understandable.

**unperturbed** *adj* calm, collected, composed, cool, impassive, placid, poised, self-possessed, serene, tranquil, undisturbed, unexcited, unflinching, unflustered, unruffled, untroubled, unworried.

*antonyms* anxious, perturbed.

**unpleasant** *adj* abhorrent, bad, disagreeable, displeasing, distasteful, god-awful, ill-natured, irksome, nasty, objectionable, obnoxious, poxy, repulsive, rocky, sticky, traumatic, troublesome, unattractive, unpalatable.

*antonym* pleasant.

**unpleasantness** *n* annoyance, bother, embarrassment, esclandre, furore, fuss, ill-feeling, nastiness, scandal, trouble, upset.

**unpolished** *adj* coarse, crude, home-bred, rough, rough and ready, rude, sketchy, uncivilised, uncouth, uncultivated, uncultured, unfashioned, unfinished, unrefined, unsophisticated, unworked, vulgar.

*antonyms* finished, polished, refined.

**unpopular** *adj* avoided, detested, disliked, hated, neglected, rejected, shunned, undesirable, unfashionable, unloved, unsought-after, unwanted, unwelcome.

*antonyms* fashionable, popular.

**unprecedented** *adj* abnormal, exceptional, extraordinary, freakish, new, novel, original, remarkable, revolutionary, singular, unexampled, unheard-of, unknown, unparalleled, unrivalled, unusual.

**unpredictable** *adj* chance, changeable, doubtful, erratic, fickle, fluky, iffy, in the lap of the gods, inconstant, on the knees of the gods, random, scatty, unforeseeable, unreliable, unstable, variable.

*antonym* predictable.

**unprejudiced** *adj* balanced, detached, dispassionate, enlightened, even-handed, fair,

fair-minded, impartial, just, non-partisan, objective, open-minded, unbiased, uncoloured.

*antonyms* narrow-minded, prejudiced.

**unpremeditated** *adj* extempore, fortuitous, impromptu, impulsive, offhand, off-the-cuff, spontaneous, spur-of-the-moment, unintentional, unplanned, unprepared, unrehearsed.

*antonym* premeditated.

**unprepared** *adj* ad-lib, extemporaneous, half-baked, ill-considered, improvised, incomplete, napping, off-the-cuff, spontaneous, surprised, unawares, unfinished, ungirded, unplanned, unready, unrehearsed, unsuspecting.

*antonyms* prepared, ready.

**unpretentious** *adj* homely, honest, humble, modest, natural, penny-plain, plain, simple, straightforward, unaffected, unassuming, unimposing, unobtrusive, unostentatious, unpretending, unsophisticated, unspoiled.

*antonym* pretentious.

**unprincipled** *adj* amoral, corrupt, crooked, deceitful, devious, discreditable, dishonest, dishonourable, immoral, underhand, unethical, unprofessional, unscrupulous.

*antonym* ethical.

**unproductive** *adj* arid, barren, bootless, dry, fruitless, futile, idle, ineffective, inefficacious, infertile, otiose, sterile, unavailing, unfruitful, unprofitable, unprolific, unremunerative, unrewarding, useless, vain, valueless, worthless.

*antonyms* fertile, productive.

**unprofessional** *adj* amateur, amateurish, improper, inadmissible, incompetent, inefficient, inexperienced, inexpert, lax, negligent, unacceptable, unbecoming, unethical, unfitting, unprincipled, unseemly, unskilled, untrained, unworthy.

*antonyms* professional, skilful.

**unpromising** *adj* adverse, depressing, discouraging, dispiriting, doubtful, gloomy, inauspicious, ominous, unfavourable, unpropitious.

*antonym* promising.

**unprotected** *adj* defenceless, exposed, helpless, inerm, liable, naked, open, pregnable, unarmed, unattended, undefended, unfortified, unguarded, unsheltered, unshielded, unvaccinated, vulnerable.

*antonyms* immune, protected, safe.

**unprovable** *adj* indemonstrable, indeterminable, unascertainable, undemonstrable, unverifiable.

*antonym* verifiable.

**unqualified** *adj* absolute, categorical, complete, consummate, downright, ill-equipped, incapable, incompetent, ineligible, out-and-out, outright, thorough, thoroughgoing, total, uncertificated, unconditional, unfit, unmitigated, unmixed, unprepared, unreserved, unrestricted, untrained, utter, whole-hearted.

*antonyms* conditional, tentative.

**unquestionable** *adj* absolute, certain, clear, conclusive, definite, faultless, flawless, incontestable, incontrovertible, indisputable, indubitable, irrefutable, manifest, obvious, patent, self-evident, sure, unchallenged, undeniable, unequivocal, unmistakable.

*antonyms* dubious, questionable.

**unquestioning** *adj* implicit, questionless, unconditional, unhesitating, unqualified, whole-hearted.

*antonym* doubtful.

**unravel** *v* disentangle, explain, extricate, figure out, free, interpret, penetrate, puzzle out, ravel out, resolve, separate, solve, sort out, undo, unknot, untangle, unwind, work out.

*antonyms* complicate, tangle.

**unreal** *adj* academic, artificial, chimerical, fabulous, fairy-tale, fake, false, fanciful, fantastic, fictitious, hypothetical, illusory, imaginary, immaterial, impalpable, insincere, insubstantial, intangible, made-up, make-believe, mock, moonshiny, mythical, nebulous, ostensible, phantasmagorical, pretended, seeming, sham, storybook, synthetic, vaporous, visionary.

*antonyms* genuine, real.

**unrealistic** *adj* half-baked, idealistic, impracticable, impractical, improbable, quixotic, romantic, starry-eyed, theoretical, unworkable.

*antonyms* pragmatic, realistic.

**unreasonable** *adj* absurd, arbitrary, biased, blinkered, capricious, cussed, erratic, excessive, exorbitant, extortionate, extravagant, far-fetched, foolish, froward, headstrong, illogical, immoderate, inconsistent, irrational, mad, nonsensical, opinionated, perverse, preposterous, quirky, senseless, silly, steep, stupid, thrawn, uncalled-for, undue, unfair, unjust, unjustifiable, unjustified, unwarranted.

*antonyms* moderate, rational, reasonable.

**unrecognisable** *adj* altered, changed, disguised, incognisable, incognito, unidentifiable, unknowable.

**unrefined** *adj* boorish, coarse, crude, imperfect, inelegant, raw, rude, uncultivated, uncultured, unfinished, unperfected, unpolished, unpurified, unsophisticated, untreated, vulgar.

*antonyms* finished, refined.

**unregenerate** *adj* abandoned, hardened, impenitent, incorrigible, intractable, obdurate, obstinate, persistent, recalcitrant, refractory, shameless, sinful, stubborn, unconverted, unreformed, unrepentant, wicked.

*antonyms* reformed, repentant.

**unrelated** *adj* different, disparate, dissimilar, distinct, extraneous, inapplicable, inappropriate, irrelevant, unassociated, unconnected, unlike.

*antonyms* related, similar.

**unrelenting** *adj* ceaseless, constant, continual, continuous, cruel, endless, implacable, incessant, inexorable, insistent, intransigent, merciless, perpetual, pitiless, relentless, remorseless, ruthless, steady, stern, tough, unabated, unalleviated, unbroken, unceasing, uncompromising, unmerciful, unremitting, unsparing.

*antonyms* intermittent, spasmodic.

**unreliable** *adj* deceptive, delusive, disreputable, erroneous, fair-weather, fallible, false, implausible, inaccurate, inauthentic, irresponsible, mistaken, specious, uncertain, unconvincing, undependable, unsound, unstable, untrustworthy.

*antonym* reliable.

**unremitting** *adj* assiduous, ceaseless, conscientious, constant, continual, continuous, diligent, incessant, indefatigable, perpetual, relentless, remorseless, sedulous, tireless, unabated, unbroken, unceasing, unrelenting.

*antonym* spasmodic.

**unrepentant** *adj* callous, hardened, impenitent, incorrigible, obdurate, shameless, unabashed, unashamed, unregenerate, unremorseful, unrepenting.

*antonyms* penitent, repentant.

**unreserved** *adj* absolute, candid, complete, demonstrative, direct, entire, extrovert, forthright, frank, free, full, open, open-hearted, outgoing, outspoken, total, unconditional, unhesitating, uninhibited, unlimited, unqualified, unrestrained, whole-hearted.

*antonyms* inhibited, tentative.

**unreservedly** *adv* completely, entirely, outright, plump, unhesitatingly, utterly, whole-heartedly.

**unresisting** *adj* docile, like a lamb to the slaughter, meek, obedient, passive, submissive.

*antonyms* protesting, resisting.

**unresolved** *adj* doubtful, indefinite, moot, pending, problematical, unanswered, undecided, undetermined, unsettled, unsolved, up in the air, vague, vexed.

*antonyms* definite, determined.

**unresponsive** *adj* aloof, apathetic, cool, echoless, indifferent, unaffected, uninterested, unmoved, unsympathetic.

*antonyms* responsive, sympathetic.

**unrest** *n* agitation, anxiety, apprehension, disaffection, discontent, discord, disquiet, dissatisfaction, dissension, distress, perturbation, protest, rebellion, restlessness, sedition, strife, tumult, turmoil, unease, uneasiness, worry.

*antonyms* calm, peace.

**unrestrained** *adj* abandoned, boisterous, free, immoderate, inordinate, intemperate, irrepressible, natural, rampant, unbounded, unbridled, unchecked, unconstrained, uncontrolled, unhindered, uninhibited, unrepressed, unreserved, uproarious.

*antonym* inhibited.

**unrestricted** *adj* absolute, all-round, clear, free, free-for-all, free-wheeling, open, public, unbounded, uncircumscribed, unconditional, unhindered, unimpeded, unlimited, unobstructed, unopposed, unregulated.

*antonyms* limited, restricted.

**unripe** *adj* green, immature, undeveloped, unready, unripened.

*antonyms* mature, ripe.

**unrivalled** *adj* incomparable, inimitable, matchless, nonpareil, peerless, superlative, supreme, surpassing, unequalled, unexcelled, unmatched, unparalleled, unsurpassed, without equal.

**unruffled** *adj* calm, collected, composed, cool, even, imperturbable, level, peaceful, placid, serene, smooth, tranquil, unbroken, undisturbed, unflustered, unmoved, unperturbed, untroubled.

*antonyms* anxious, troubled.

**unruly** *adj* camstairy, disobedient, disorderly, fractious, headstrong, insubordinate, intractable, lawless, mutinous, obstreperous, rebellious, refractory, riotous, rowdy, ruleless, turbulent, uncontrollable, ungovernable, unmanageable, wayward, wild, wilful.

*antonym* manageable.

**unsafe** *adj* dangerous, exposed, hazardous, insecure, parlous, perilous, precarious, risky, threatening, treacherous, uncertain, unreliable, unsound, unstable, vulnerable.

*antonyms* safe, secure.

**unsaid** *adj* undeclared, unexpressed, unmentioned, unpronounced, unspoken, unstated, unuttered, unvoiced.

*antonym* spoken.

**unsaleable** *adj* invendible, unmarketable, unsellable.

*antonyms* marketable, saleable.

**unsatisfactory** *adj* deficient, disappointing, displeasing, dissatisfying, frustrating, inadequate, inferior, insufficient, leaving a lot to be desired, mediocre, poor, rocky, thwarting, unacceptable, unsatisfying, unsuitable, unworthy, weak.

*antonym* satisfactory.

**unsavoury** *adj* disagreeable, distasteful, nasty, nauseating, objectionable, obnoxious, offensive, repellent, repugnant, repulsive, revolting, sickening, sordid, squalid, unappetising, unattractive, undesirable, unpalatable, unpleasant.

*antonyms* palatable, pleasant.

**unscathed** *adj* intact, safe, scot-free, sound, unharmed, unhurt, uninjured, unmarked, unscarred, unscratched, untouched, whole.

*antonyms* harmed, injured.

**unscrupulous** *adj* corrupt, crooked, cynical, discreditable, dishonest, dishonourable, immoral, improper, ruthless, shameless, unethical, unprincipled.

*antonym* scrupulous.

**unseasonable** *adj* ill-timed, inappropriate, inopportune, intempestive, malapropos, mistimed, unsuitable, untimely.

*antonyms* seasonable, timely.

**unseasoned** *adj* green, unmatured, unprepared, unprimed, untempered, untreated.

**unseat** *v* depose, dethrone, discharge, dishorse, dismiss, dismount, displace, disseat, oust, overthrow, remove, throw, topple, unhorse, unsaddle.

**unseemly** *adj* discreditable, disreputable, improper, inappropriate, indecorous, indelicate, shocking, unbecoming, unbefitting, undignified, undue, ungentlemanly, unladylike, unrefined, unsuitable.

*antonyms* decorous, seemly.

**unseen** *adj* concealed, hidden, invisible, lurking, obscure, overlooked, undetected, unnoticed, unobserved, unobtrusive, unperceived, veiled.

*antonyms* observed, visible.

**unselfish** *adj* altruistic, charitable, dedicated, devoted, disinterested, generous, humanitarian, kind, liberal, magnanimous, noble, philanthropic, self-denying, selfless, self-sacrificing, single-eyed, ungrudging, unstinting.

*antonym* selfish.

**unsentimental** *adj* cynical, hard as nails, hard-headed, level-headed, practical, pragmatic, realistic, shrewd, tough.

*antonyms* sentimental, soft.

**unsettle** *v* agitate, bother, confuse, destabilise, discompose, disconcert, disorder, disturb, fluster, flutter, perturb, rattle, ruffle, shake, throw, trouble, unbalance, upset.

*antonyms* compose, settle.

**unsettled** *adj* agitated, anxious, changeable, changing, confused, debatable, disorderly, disoriented, disturbed, doubtful, due, edgy, flustered, iffy, inconstant, insecure, moot, open, outstanding, overdue, owing, payable, pending, perturbed, problematical, restive, restless, shaken, shaky, tense, troubled, uncertain, undecided, undetermined, uneasy, unnerved, unpredictable, unresolved, unstable, unsteady, upset, variable.

*antonyms* certain, composed, settled.

**unshakable** *adj* absolute, adamant, constant, determined, firm, fixed, immovable, resolute, stable, staunch, steadfast, sure, unassailable, unswerving, unwavering, well-founded.

*antonym* insecure.

**unsheathe** *v* dissheathe, draw, evaginate, expose, reveal, uncover.

*antonyms* retract, sheathe.

**unshod** *adj* barefooted, discalced, shoeless.

*antonym* shod.

**unsightly** *adj* disagreeable, displeasing, hideous, horrid, off-putting, repellent, repugnant, repulsive, revolting, ugly, unattractive, unpleasant, unprepossessing.

*antonym* pleasing.

**unskilful** *adj* amateurish, awkward, bungling, clumsy, fumbling, gauche, incompetent, inept, inexperienced, inexpert, maladroit, unapt, uneducated, unhandy, unpractised, unprofessional, unqualified, unskilled, untalented, untaught, untrained.

*antonyms* skilful, skilled.

**unsociable** *adj* aloof, chilly, cold, distant, farouche, hostile, inconversable, inhospitable, introverted, reclusive, reserved, retiring, stand-offish, taciturn, uncommunicative, uncongenial, unforthcoming, unfriendly, unneighbourly, unsocial, withdrawn.

*antonyms* friendly, sociable.

**unsolicited** *adj* gratuitous, spontaneous, unasked, uncalled-for, unforced, uninvited, unrequested, unsought, unwanted, unwelcome, voluntary.

*antonyms* invited, solicited.

**unsophisticated** *adj* artless, childlike, funky, guileless, hick, homespun, inexperienced, ingenuous, innocent, naïve, natural, plain, simple, small-town, straightforward, unaffected, uncomplicated, uninvolved, unpretentious, unrefined, unspecialised, unspoilt, untutored, unworldly.

*antonyms* complex, pretentious, sophisticated.

**unsound** *adj* ailing, defective, delicate, deranged, dicky, diseased, erroneous, fallacious, fallible, false, faulty, flawed, frail, ill, ill-founded, illogical, insecure, invalid, shaky, specious, unbalanced, unhealthy, unhinged, unreliable, unsafe, unstable, unsteady, unwell, weak, wobbly.

*antonyms* safe, sound.

**unsparing** *adj* abundant, bountiful, generous, hard, harsh, implacable, inexorable, lavish, liberal, merciless, munificent, open-handed, plenteous, prodigal, profuse, relentless, rigorous, ruthless, scathing, severe, stern, stringent, uncompromising, unforgiving, ungrudging, unmerciful, unstinting.

*antonyms* forgiving, mean, sparing.

**unspeakable** *adj* abhorrent, abominable, appalling, dreadful, evil, execrable, frightful, heinous, horrible, inconceivable, indescribable, ineffable, inexpressible, loathsome, monstrous, nefandous, odious, overwhelming, repellent, shocking, unbelievable, unimaginable, unutterable, wonderful.

**unspectacular** *adj* boring, dull, methodical, ordinary, plodding, systematic, unexciting, unimpressive, unremarkable.

**unspoilt** *adj* artless, innocent, intact, natural, perfect, preserved, scatheless, unaffected, unaltered, unassuming, unblemished, unchanged, undamaged, unharmed, unimpaired, unscathed, unsophisticated, unspoiled, unstudied, untouched, wholesome.

*antonyms* affected, spoilt.

**unspoken** *adj* assumed, implicit, implied, inferred, mute, silent, speechless, tacit, undeclared, understood, unexpressed, unsaid, unstated, unuttered, voiceless, wordless.

*antonym* explicit.

**unstable** *adj* astable, capricious, changeable, erratic, fitful, fluctuating, inconsistent, inconstant, insecure, irrational, labile, precarious, rickety, risky, shaky, shoogly, slippy, ticklish, tottering, unpredictable, unsettled, unsteady, untrustworthy, vacillating, variable, volatile, wobbly.

*antonyms* stable, steady.

**unsteady** *adj* changeable, dicky, erratic, flickering, flighty, fluctuating, frail, inconstant, infirm, insecure, irregular, precarious, reeling, rickety, shaky, shoogly, skittish, tittupy, tottering, totty, treacherous, tremulous, unreliable, unsafe, unstable, unsteeled, vacillating, variable, volatile, wavering, wobbly.

*antonyms* firm, steady.

**unstinting** *adj* abounding, abundant, ample, bountiful, full, generous, large, lavish, liberal, munificent, plentiful, prodigal, profuse, ungrudging, unsparing.

*antonyms* grudging, mean.

**unsubstantial** *adj* airy, chimerical, dreamlike, erroneous, fanciful, flimsy, fragile, frail, ill-founded, illusory, imaginary, immaterial, impalpable, inadequate, insubstantial, light, slight, superficial, tenuous, thin, unsound, unsupported, vaporous, visionary, weak.

*antonyms* real, valid.

**unsubstantiated** *adj* debatable, dubious, questionable, unattested, unconfirmed, uncorroborated, unestablished, unproved, unproven, unsupported, unverified.

*antonyms* proved, proven.

**unsuccessful** *adj* abortive, bootless, failed, foiled, fruitless, frustrated, futile, ill-fated, inadequate, ineffective, ineffectual, losing, luckless, manqué, otiose, sterile, thwarted, unavailing, unfortunate, unlucky, unproductive, unsatisfactory, useless, vain.

*antonyms* effective, successful.

**unsuitable** *adj* improper, inapposite, inappropriate, inapt, incompatible, incongruous, inconsistent, indecorous, ineligible, infelicitous, malapropos, unacceptable, unbecoming, unbefitting, unfitting, unlikely, unseasonable, unseemly, unsuited.

*antonyms* seemly, suitable.

**unsullied** *adj* clean, immaculate, intact, perfect, pristine, pure, spotless, stainless, unblackened, unblemished, uncorrupted, undefiled, unsoiled, unspoiled, unspotted, unstained, untarnished, untouched.

*antonyms* dirty, stained.

**unsung** *adj* anonymous, disregarded, forgotten, neglected, obscure, overlooked, unacknowledged, uncelebrated, unhailed, unhonoured, unknown, unnamed, unrecognised, unrenowned.

*antonyms* famous, renowned.

**unsure** *adj* agnostic, distrustful, doubtful, dubious, hesitant, insecure, irresolute, mistrustful, sceptical, suspicious, tentative, uncertain, unconvinced, undecided, unpersuaded.

*antonyms* resolute, sure.

**unsurpassed** *adj* consummate, exceptional, incomparable, matchless, nonpareil, paramount, peerless, sublime, superlative, supreme, surpassing, transcendent, unequalled, unexcelled, unparalleled, unrivalled.

**unsuspecting** *adj* childlike, confiding, credulous, green, gullible, inexperienced, ingenuous, innocent, naïve, trustful, trusting, unconscious, uncritical, unsuspicious, unwary, unwitting.

*antonyms* conscious, knowing.

**unswerving** *adj* constant, dedicated, devoted, direct, firm, fixed, immovable, resolute, single-minded, staunch, steadfast, steady, sure, true, undeviating, unfaltering, unflagging, untiring, unwavering.

*antonyms* irresolute, tentative.

**unsympathetic** *adj* antagonistic, antipathetic, apathetic, callous, cold, compassionless, cruel, hard, hard as nails, hard-hearted, harsh, heartless, indifferent, inhuman, insensitive, soulless, stony, uncharitable, uncompassionate, unconcerned, unfeeling, unkind, unmoved, unpitying, unresponsive.

*antonyms* compassionate, sympathetic.

**unsystematic** *adj* chaotic, confused, desultory, disorderly, disorganised, haphazard, illogical, indiscriminate, irregular, jumbled, muddled, random, shambolic, slapdash, sloppy, unco-ordinated, unmethodical, unorganised, unplanned, untidy.

*antonyms* logical, systematic.

**untamed** *adj* barbarous, ferae naturae, feral, fierce, haggard, savage, unbroken, undomesticated, unmellowed, untameable, wild.

*antonyms* domesticated, tame.

**untangle** *v* disentangle, explain, extricate, ravel out, resolve, solve, undo, unravel, unsnarl.

*antonyms* complicate, tangle.

**untarnished** *adj* bright, burnished, clean, glowing, immaculate, impeccable, intact, polished, pristine, pure, shining, spotless, stainless, unblemished, unimpeachable, unsoiled, unspoilt, unspotted, unstained, unsullied.

*antonyms* blemished, tarnished.

**untenable** *adj* fallacious, flawed, illogical, indefensible, insupportable, rocky, shaky, unmaintainable, unreasonable, unsound, unsustainable.

*antonyms* sound, tenable.

**unthinkable** *adj* absurd, illogical, implausible, impossible, improbable, incogitable, inconceivable, incredible, insupportable, outrageous, preposterous, shocking, unbelievable, unheard-of, unimaginable, unlikely, unreasonable.

**unthinking** *adj* automatic, careless, heedless, impulsive, inadvertent, incautious, inconsiderate, indiscreet, insensitive, instinctive, mechanical, negligent, oblivious, rash, rude, selfish, senseless, tactless, thoughtless, unconscious, undiplomatic, unguarded, vacant, witless.

*antonyms* conscious, deliberate, witting.

**untidy** *adj* bedraggled, chaotic, cluttered, dishevelled, disorderly, higgledy-piggledy, jumbled, littered, messy, muddled, ratty, raunchy, rumpled, scruffy, shambolic, slatternly, slipshod, sloppy, slovenly, sluttish, topsy-turvy, unkempt, unsystematic.

*antonyms* systematic, tidy.

**untie** *v* free, loosen, release, unbind, undo, unfasten, unknot, unlace, unloose, unloosen, untether.

*antonyms* fasten, tie.

**untimely** *adj* awkward, early, ill-timed, inappropriate, inauspicious, inconvenient, inopportune, intempestive, malapropos, mistimed, premature, unfortunate, unseasonable, unsuitable.

*antonyms* opportune, timely.

**untiring** *adj* constant, dedicated, determined, devoted, dogged, incessant, indefatigable, patient, persevering, persistent, staunch, steady, tenacious, tireless, unfailing, unfaltering, unflagging, unremitting, unwearied.

*antonym* inconstant.

**untold** *adj* boundless, countless, hidden, incalculable, indescribable, inexhaustible, inexpressible, infinite, innumerable, measureless, myriad, numberless, private, secret, uncountable, uncounted, undisclosed, undreamed-of, unimaginable, unknown, unnumbered, unpublished, unreckoned, unrecounted, unrelated, unrevealed, unthinkable, unutterable.

**untouched** *adj* indifferent, intact, safe, scatheless, unaffected, unaltered, unconcerned, undamaged, unharmed, unhurt, unimpaired, unimpressed, uninjured, unmoved, unscathed, unstirred.

*antonyms* affected, impaired, moved.

**untoward** *adj* adverse, annoying, awkward, contrary, disastrous, ill-timed, improper, inappropriate, inauspicious, inconvenient, indecorous, inimical, inopportune, irritating, ominous, troublesome, unbecoming, unexpected, unfavourable, unfitting, unfortunate, unlucky, unpropitious, unseemly, unsuitable, untimely, vexatious, worrying.

*antonyms* auspicious, suitable.

**untrained** *adj* amateur, green, inexperienced, inexpert, raw, uneducated, unpractised, unprofessional, unqualified, unschooled, unskilled, untaught, untutored.

*antonyms* expert, trained.

**untried** *adj* experimental, exploratory, innovative, innovatory, new, novel, unestablished, unproved, untested.

*antonyms* proven, tested.

**untroubled** *adj* calm, composed, cool, impassive, peaceful, placid, serene, steady, tranquil, unconcerned, undisturbed, unexcited, unflappable, unflustered, unperturbed, unruffled, unstirred, unworried.

*antonyms* anxious, troubled.

**untrue** *adj* deceitful, deceptive, deviant, dishonest, disloyal, distorted, erroneous, faithless, fallacious, false, forsworn, fraudulent, inaccurate, inauthentic, inconstant, incorrect, lying, mendacious, misleading, mistaken, perfidious, sham, specious, spurious, traitorous, treacherous, two-faced, unfaithful, untrustworthy, untruthful, wrong.

*antonyms* honest, true.

**untrustworthy** *adj* capricious, deceitful, devious, dishonest, disloyal, dubious, duplicitous, fair-weather, faithless, false, fickle, fly-by-night, shady, slippery, treacherous, tricky, two-faced, undependable, unfaithful, unreliable, unsafe, untrue, untrusty.

*antonyms* reliable, trustworthy.

**untruth** *n* deceit, deceitfulness, duplicity, fabrication, falsehood, falsification, falsism, falsity, fib, fiction, inexactitude, invention, inveracity, lie, lying, mendacity, perjury, prevarication, story, tale, trick, truthlessness, untruthfulness, whopper.

*antonym* truth.

**untruthful** *adj* crooked, deceitful, deceptive, dishonest, dissembling, false, hypocritical, lying, mendacious, untrustworthy, unveracious.

*antonym* truthful.

**untwine** *v* disentwine, uncoil, unravel, untwist, unwind.

*antonyms* twine, wind.

**untwist** *v* detort, ravel out, uncoil, unravel, untwine, unwind.

*antonym* twist.

**untutored** *adj* artless, ignorant, illiterate, inexperienced, inexpert, simple, uneducated, unlearned, unlessoned, unpractised, unrefined, unschooled, unsophisticated, untrained, unversed.

*antonyms* educated, trained.

**unused** *adj* available, extra, fresh, idle, intact, left, left-over, new, pristine, remaining, unaccustomed, unconsumed, unemployed, unexploited, unfamiliar, untouched, unutilised.

**unusual** *adj* abnormal, anomalous, atypical, bizarre, curious, different, eccentric, exceptional, extraordinary, odd, phenomenal, queer, rare, remarkable, singular, strange, surprising, uncommon, unconventional, unexpected, unfamiliar, unwonted.

*antonyms* normal, usual.

**unutterable** *adj* egregious, extreme, indescribable, ineffable, nefandous, overwhelming, unimaginable, unspeakable.

**unvarnished** *adj* bare, candid, frank, honest, naked, plain, pure, sheer, simple, sincere, stark, straightforward, unadorned, undisguised, unembellished.

*antonyms* disguised, embellished.

**unveil** *v* bare, disclose, discover, disenshroud, divulge, expose, reveal, uncover, unfold, unshroud.

*antonyms* cover, hide.

**unwanted** *adj* de trop, extra, otiose, outcast, rejected, superfluous, surplus, unasked, undesired, uninvited, unnecessary, unneeded, unrequired, unsolicited, unwelcome, useless.

*antonyms* necessary, needed, wanted.

**unwarranted** *adj* baseless, gratuitous, groundless, indefensible, inexcusable, uncalled-for, unjust, unjustified, unprovoked, unreasonable, vain, wrong.

*antonyms* justifiable, warranted.

**unwary** *adj* careless, credulous, hasty, heedless, imprudent, incautious, indiscreet, rash, reckless, thoughtless, unchary, uncircumspect, unguarded, unthinking, unwatchful.

*antonyms* cautious, wary.

**unwavering** *adj* consistent, dedicated, determined, resolute, single-minded, staunch, steadfast, steady, sturdy, tenacious, undeviating, unfaltering, unflagging, unquestioning, unshakable, unshaken, unswerving, untiring.

*antonyms* fickle, wavering.

**unwelcome** *adj* disagreeable, displeasing, distasteful, excluded, rejected, thankless,

**unacceptable,** undesirable, uninvited, unpalatable, unpleasant, unpopular, unwanted, upsetting, worrying.

*antonyms* desirable, welcome.

**unwell** *adj* ailing, ill, indisposed, mops and brooms, nohow, nohowish, off-colour, poorly, sick, sickly, unhealthy.

*antonyms* healthy, well.

**unwholesome** *adj* anaemic, bad, corrupting, degrading, deleterious, demoralising, depraving, epinosic, evil, harmful, immoral, innutritious, insalubrious, insalutary, insanitary, junk, noxious, pale, pallid, pasty, perverting, poisonous, sickly, tainted, unhealthy, unhygienic, wan, wicked.

*antonyms* salubrious, wholesome.

**unwieldy** *adj* awkward, bulky, burdensome, clumsy, cumbersome, cumbrous, gangling, hefty, hulking, inconvenient, massive, ponderous, ungainly, unhandy, unmanageable, weighty.

*antonyms* dainty, neat, petite.

**unwilling** *adj* averse, disinclined, grudging, indisposed, laggard, loath, loathful, opposed, reluctant, resistant, slow, unenthusiastic.

*antonyms* enthusiastic, willing.

**unwillingness** *n* backwardness, disinclination, hesitancy, indisposition, lack of enthusiasm, loathfulness, nolition, reluctance, slowness.

*antonyms* enthusiasm, willingness.

**unwind** *v* calm down, detort, disentangle, quieten down, relax, slacken, uncoil, undo, unravel, unreel, unroll, unswathe, untwine, untwist, unwrap, wind down.

*antonyms* twist, wind.

**unwise** *adj* foolhardy, foolish, ill-advised, ill-considered, ill-judged, impolitic, improvident, imprudent, inadvisable, indiscreet, inexpedient, injudicious, irresponsible, rash, reckless, senseless, short-sighted, silly, stupid, thoughtless, unintelligent.

*antonyms* prudent, wise.

**unwitting** *adj* accidental, chance, ignorant, inadvertent, innocent, involuntary, unaware, unconscious, unintended, unintentional, unknowing, unmeant, unplanned, unsuspecting, unthinking.

*antonyms* conscious, deliberate, knowing, witting.

**unwonted** *adj* atypical, exceptional, extraordinary, infrequent, peculiar, rare, singular, strange, unaccustomed, uncommon, uncustomary, unexpected, unfamiliar, unheard-of, unusual.

*antonyms* usual, wonted.

**unworldly** *adj* abstract, celestial, ethereal, extramundane, extra-physical, extra-terrestrial, green, idealistic, impractical, inexperienced, innocent, metaphysical, naïve, otherworldly, religious, spiritual, transcendental, unearthly, unsophisticated, visionary.

*antonyms* materialistic, practical, worldly.

**unworried** *adj* collected, composed, downbeat, unabashed, undismayed, unperturbed, unruffled, untroubled.

*antonym* anxious.

**unworthy** *adj* base, contemptible, degrading, desertless, discreditable, disgraceful, dishonourable, disreputable, ignoble, improper, inappropriate, ineligible, inferior, shameful, unbecoming, unbefitting, undeserving, unfitting, unprofessional, unseemly, unsuitable, unsuited.

*antonyms* commendable, worthy.

**unwritten** *adj* accepted, conventional, customary, implicit, oral, recognised, tacit, traditional, understood, unformulated, unrecorded, verbal, vocal, word-of-mouth.

*antonyms* recorded, written.

**unyielding** *adj* adamant, determined, firm, hardline, immovable, implacable, inexorable, inflexible, intractable, intransigent, obdurate, obstinate, relentless, resolute, rigid, solid, staunch, steadfast, stubborn, tough, unbending, uncompromising, unrelenting, unwavering.

*antonyms* flexible, yielding.

**up to one's eyes** busy, engaged, inundated, overwhelmed, preoccupied, tied up.

*antonyms* free, idle.

**up to scratch** acceptable, adequate, capable, comme il faut, competent, OK, satisfactory, sufficient.

*antonym* unsatisfactory.

**up-and-coming** ambitious, assertive, eager, enterprising, go-getting, promising, pushing.

**upbeat** *adj* bright, bullish, buoyant, cheerful, cheery, encouraging, favourable, forward-looking, heartening, hopeful, optimistic, positive, promising, rosy.

*antonyms* down-beat, gloomy.

**upbraid** *v* admonish, berate, blame, carpet, castigate, censure, chide, condemn, criticise, dress down, jaw, lecture, rate, rebuke, reprimand, reproach, reprove, scold, take to task, tell off, tick off.

*antonyms* commend, praise.

**upbringing** *n* breeding, bringing-up, care, cultivation, education, instruction, nurture, parenting, raising, rearing, tending, training.

**update** *v* amend, correct, modernise, renew, renovate, revamp, revise.

**upgrade** *v* advance, ameliorate, better, elevate, embourgeoise, enhance, gentilise, gentrify, improve, promote, raise.

*antonyms* degrade, downgrade.

**upgrading** *n* advancement, amelioration, betterment, elevation, embourgeoisement, enhancement, gentrification, improvement, promotion.

**upheaval** *n* cataclysm, chaos, confusion, disorder, disruption, disturbance, earthquake, eruption, overthrow, revolution, shake-up, turmoil, upset.

**uphill** *adj* acclivious, acclivitous, arduous, ascending, climbing, difficult, exhausting, gruelling, hard, laborious, mounting, punishing, rising, strenuous, taxing, tough, upward, wearisome.

*antonyms* downhill, easy.

**uphold** v advocate, aid, back, champion, countenance, defend, encourage, endorse, fortify, hold to, justify, maintain, promote, stand by, stengthen, support, sustain, vindicate.

**upkeep** n care, conservation, expenditure, expenses, keep, maintenance, oncosts, operating costs, outgoing, outlay, overheads, preservation, repair, running, running costs, subsistence, support, sustenance.

*antonym* neglect.

**uplift** v advance, ameliorate, better, boost, civilise, cultivate, edify, elate, elevate, enlighten, exalt, heave, hoist, improve, inspire, lift, raise, refine, upgrade.

n advancement, betterment, boost, cultivation, edification, enhancement, enlightenment, enrichment, improvement, lift, refinement.

**upper** adj elevated, eminent, exalted, greater, high, higher, important, loftier, senior, superior, top, topmost, uppermost.

*antonyms* inferior, junior, lower.

**upper hand** advantage, ascendancy, control, dominance, domination, dominion, edge, mastery, superiority, supremacy, sway.

**upper-class** adj aristocratic, blue-blooded, educated, élite, exclusive, gentle, high-born, high-class, noble, patrician, swanky, top-drawer, tweedy, well-born, well-bred.

*antonyms* humble, working-class.

**uppermost** adj chief, dominant, first, foremost, greatest, highest, leading, loftiest, main, paramount, predominant, pre-eminent, primary, principal, prominent, supreme, top, topmost, upmost.

*antonyms* bottommost, lowest.

**uppish** adj affected, arrogant, assuming, big-headed, bumptious, cocky, conceited, hoity-toity, impertinent, overweening, presumptuous, self-important, snobbish, stuck-up, supercilious, swanky, toffee-nosed, uppity.

*antonyms* diffident, unassertive.

**upright** adj arrect, bluff, conscientious, erect, ethical, faithful, four-square, good, high-minded, honest, honourable, incorruptible, just, noble, perpendicular, principled, righteous, straight, straightforward, true, trustworthy, unimpeachable, upstanding, vertical, virtuous.

*antonyms* dishonest, flat, horizontal, prone, supine.

**uprising** n inqilab, insurgence, insurgency, insurrection, mutiny, putsch, rebellion, revolt, revolution, rising, sedition, upheaval.

**uproar** n brawl, brouhaha, clamour, commotion, confusion, din, disorder, furore, hubbub, hullabaloo, hurly-burly, katzenjammer, noise, outcry, pandemonium, racket, rammy, randan, riot, ruckus, ruction, rumpus, stramash, tumult, turbulence, turmoil.

**uproarious** adj boisterous, clamorous, confused, convulsive, deafening, disorderly, gleeful, hilarious, hysterical, killing, loud, noisy, rib-tickling, riotous, rip-roaring, roistering, rollicking, rowdy, rowdy-dowdy, side-splitting, tempestuous, tumultuous, turbulent, unrestrained, wild.

*antonym* sedate.

**uproot** v deracinate, destroy, disorient, displace, disroot, eliminate, eradicate, exile, exterminate, extirpate, grub up, remove, rip up, root out, weed out, wipe out.

**upset** v agitate, bother, capsize, change, conquer, defeat, destabilise, discombobulate, discompose, disconcert, dismay, disorder, disorganise, disquiet, distress, disturb, fluster, grieve, hip, overcome, overset, overthrow, overturn, perturb, ruffle, shake, spill, spoil, tip, topple, trouble, unnerve, unsteady.

n agitation, bother, bug, complaint, defeat, disorder, disruption, disturbance, illness, indisposition, malady, purl, reverse, shake-up, shock, sickness, surprise, trouble, upheaval, worry.

adj agitated, bothered, capsized, chaotic, choked, confused, disconcerted, dismayed, disordered, disquieted, distressed, disturbed, frantic, gippy, grieved, hurt, ill, messed up, muddled, overturned, overwrought, pained, poorly, qualmish, queasy, ruffled, shattered, sick, spilled, toppled, topsy-turvy, troubled, tumbled, worried.

**upshot** n conclusion, consequence, culmination, end, event, finale, finish, issue, outcome, pay-off, result.

**upside down** at sixes and sevens, chaotic, confused, disordered, higgledy-piggledy, inverted, jumbled, muddled, overturned, topsy-turvy, upset, upturned, wrong side up.

*antonym* shipshape.

**upstanding** adj erect, ethical, firm, four-square, good, hardy, healthy, hearty, honest, honourable, incorruptible, lusty, moral, principled, robust, stalwart, strong, sturdy, true, trustworthy, upright, vigorous.

*antonyms* puny, untrustworthy.

**upstart** n arriviste, mushroom, nobody, nouveau riche, parvenu, social climber.

**uptight** adj anxious, edgy, hung-up, irritated, nervy, prickly, tense, uneasy.

*antonyms* calm, cool, relaxed.

**up-to-date** adj à la mode, all the rage, contemporary, current, fashionable, in, latest, modern, modish, newest, now, popular, smart, stylish, swinging, trendy, up-to-the-minute, vogue, voguish, with it.

*antonym* old-fashioned.

**upturn** n advancement, amelioration, boost, improvement, increase, recovery, revival, rise, upsurge, upswing.

*antonyms* downturn, drop, setback.

**urban** adj built-up, burghal, city, civic, inner-city, metropolitan, municipal, oppidan, town, urbanised.

*antonyms* country, rural, rustic.

**urbane** adj bland, civil, civilised, cosmopolitan, courteous, cultivated, cultured, debonair, easy, elegant, mannerly, polished, refined, smooth, sophisticated, suave, well-bred, well-mannered.

*antonyms* gauche, uncouth.

**urbanity** n blandness, charm, civility, courtesy, cultivation, culture, ease, elegance, eutrapelia, grace, mannerliness, polish, refinement, smoothness, sophistication, suavity, worldliness.

*antonyms* awkwardness, gaucheness.

**urchin** *n* brat, gamin, gutter-snipe, kid, mudlark, ragamuffin, street Arab, tatterdemalion, waif.

**urge** *v* advise, advocate, beg, beseech, champion, compel, constrain, counsel, drive, emphasise, encourage, entreat, exhort, force, goad, hasten, hist, impel, implore, incite, induce, instigate, nag, plead, press, propel, push, recommend, solicit, spur, stimulate, support, underline, underscore.

*antonyms* deter, dissuade.

*n* compulsion, desire, drive, eagerness, fancy, impulse, inclination, itch, libido, longing, wish, yearning, yen.

*antonym* disinclination.

**urgency** *n* exigence, exigency, extremity, gravity, hurry, imperativeness, importance, importunity, instancy, necessity, need, pressure, seriousness, stress.

**urgent** *adj* clamorous, cogent, compelling, critical, crucial, eager, earnest, emergent, exigent, immediate, imperative, important, importunate, insistent, instant, intense, persistent, persuasive, pressing, top-priority.

**urinal** *n* gents, pissoir.

**urinate** *v* ease oneself, leak, make water, micturate, pass water, pee, piddle, piss, relieve oneself, spend a penny, stale, tinkle, wee, wee-wee.

**urination** *n* emiction, Jimmy, micturition, run-off.

**urine** *n* pee, piddle, piss, stale, water.

**usable** *adj* available, current, exploitable, functional, operating, operational, practical, serviceable, utilisable, valid, working.

*antonyms* unusable, useless.

**usage** *n* application, control, convention, custom, employment, etiquette, form, habit, handling, management, method, mode, operation, practice, procedure, protocol, régime, regulation, routine, rule, running, tradition, treatment, use, wont.

**use** *v* apply, bring, consume, employ, enjoy, exercise, exhaust, expend, exploit, handle, manipulate, misuse, operate, ply, practise, spend, treat, usufruct, utilise, waste, wield, work.

*n* advantage, application, avail, benefit, call, cause, custom, employment, end, enjoyment, exercise, good, habit, handling, help, meaning, mileage, necessity, need, object, occasion, operation, point, practice, profit, purpose, reason, service, treatment, usage, usefulness, usufruct, utility, value, way, wont, worth.

**use up** absorb, consume, deplete, devour, drain, eat into, exhaust, finish, fritter, sap, squander, swallow, waste.

**used** *adj* accustomed, cast-off, dog-eared, familiar, hand-me-down, nearly new, reach-me-down, second-hand, shop-soiled, soiled, worn.

*antonyms* fresh, new, unused.

**useful** *adj* advantageous, all-purpose, beneficial, convenient, effective, fruitful, general-purpose, handy, helpful, practical, productive, profitable, salutary, serviceable, valuable, worthwhile.

*antonym* useless.

**useless** *adj* bootless, clapped-out, disadvantageous, effectless, feckless, fruitless, futile, hopeless, idle, impractical, incompetent, ineffective, ineffectual, inefficient, inept, naff, of no use, pointless, profitless, shiftless, spastic, stupid, unavailing, unproductive, unworkable, vain, valueless, weak, worthless.

*antonym* useful.

**uselessness** *n* futility, hopelessness, idleness, impracticality, incompetence, ineffectiveness, ineffectuality, ineptitude, inutility.

*antonyms* effectiveness, usefulness.

**usher** *n* attendant, doorkeeper, escort, guide, huissier, usherette.

*v* conduct, direct, escort, guide, lead, pilot, shepherd, steer.

**usher in** announce, herald, inaugurate, initiate, introduce, launch, precede, ring in.

**usual** *adj* accepted, accustomed, common, constant, conventional, customary, everyday, expected, familiar, fixed, general, habitual, nomic, normal, ordinary, recognised, regular, routine, standard, stock, typical, unexceptional, wonted.

*antonyms* unheard-of, unusual.

**usually** *adv* as a rule, by and large, chiefly, commonly, customarily, generally, generally speaking, habitually, in the main, mainly, mostly, normally, on the whole, ordinarily, regularly, routinely, traditionally, typically.

*antonym* exceptionally.

**usurer** *n* extortionist, gombeen-man, loan-shark, money-lender, note-shaver, Shylock.

**usurp** *v* annex, appropriate, arrogate, assume, commandeer, seize, steal, take, take over, wrest.

**usury** *n* extortion, gombeen, interest, loan-sharking, money-lending, usance.

**utensil** *n* apparatus, contrivance, device, gadget, gismo, implement, instrument, tool.

**utilise** *v* adapt, appropriate, employ, exploit, make use of, put to use, resort to, take advantage of, turn to account, use.

**utilitarian** *adj* convenient, down-to-earth, effective, efficient, functional, lowly, practical, pragmatic, sensible, serviceable, unpretentious, useful.

*antonyms* decorative, impractical.

**utilitarianism** *n* eudaemonism.

**utility** *n* advantage, advantageousness, avail, benefit, convenience, efficacy, expedience, fitness, point, practicality, profit, satisfactoriness, service, serviceableness, use, usefulness, value.

*antonym* inutility.

**utmost** *adj* extreme, farthest, final, first, greatest, highest, last, maximum, outermost, paramount, remotest, supreme, ultimate, uttermost.

*n* best, hardest, maximum, most, uttermost.

**Utopia** *n* bliss, Eden, Elysium, Erewhon, Garden of Eden, heaven, heaven on earth, paradise, seventh heaven, Shangri-la.

**Utopian** *adj* airy, chimerical, dream, Elysian, fanciful, fantastic, ideal, idealistic, illusory, imaginary, impractical, perfect, romantic, unworkable, visionary, wishful.

**utter**[1] *adj* absolute, arrant, complete, consummate, dead, downright, entire, out-and-out, perfect, sheer, stark, thorough, thoroughgoing, total, unalleviated, unmitigated, unqualified.

**utter**[2] *v* articulate, declare, deliver, divulge, enounce, enunciate, express, proclaim, promulgate, pronounce, publish, reveal, say, sound, speak, state, tell, tongue, verbalise, vocalise, voice.

**utterance** *n* announcement, articulation, comment, declaration, delivery, ejaculation, expression, gift of tongues, glossolalia, illocution, opinion, pronouncement, remark, speaking with tongues, speech, statement, verbalisation, vocalisation, vociferation.

**utterly** *adv* absolutely, completely, dead, diametrically, entirely, extremely, fully, perfectly, thoroughly, totally, wholly.

**U-turn** *n* about-turn, backtrack, enantiodromia, reversal, tergiversation, uey, volte-face.

# V

**vacancy** *n* accommodation, emptiness, gap, job, opening, opportunity, place, position, post, room, situation, space, vacuity, vacuousness, vacuum, void.

**vacant** *adj* absent, absent-minded, abstracted, available, blank, disengaged, dreaming, dreamy, empty, expressionless, free, idle, inane, inattentive, incurious, thoughtless, to let, unemployed, unengaged, unfilled, unoccupied, untenanted, unthinking, vacuous, void.

*antonyms* engaged, occupied.

**vacate** *v* abandon, depart, evacuate, leave, quit, withdraw.

**vacillate** *v* fluctuate, haver, hesitate, oscillate, shilly-shally, shuffle, sway, swither, temporise, tergiversate, waver.

**vacillating** *adj* hesitant, irresolute, oscillating, shilly-shallying, shuffling, swithering, temporising, uncertain, unresolved, wavering.

*antonyms* resolute, unhesitating.

**vacillation** *n* fluctuation, hesitancy, hesitation, inconstancy, indecision, indecisiveness, irresolution, shilly-shallying, temporisation, tergiversation, unsteadiness, wavering.

**vacuity** *n* apathy, blankness, emptiness, inanity, incognisance, incomprehension, incuriosity, nothingness, space, vacuousness, vacuum, void.

**vacuous** *adj* apathetic, blank, empty, idle, inane, incurious, stupid, uncomprehending, unfilled, unintelligent, vacant, void.

**vacuum** *n* chasm, emptiness, gap, nothingness, space, vacuity, void.

**vagabond** *n* beggar, bum, down-and-out, hobo, itinerant, land-louper, migrant, nomad, outcast, palliard, rascal, rover, runabout, runagate, tramp, vagrant, wanderer, wayfarer.

**vagary** *n* caprice, crotchet, fancy, fegary, humour, megrim, notion, prank, quirk, whim, whimsy.

**vagrant** *n* beggar, bum, gangrel, hobo, itinerant, land-louper, rolling stone, stroller, tramp, wanderer.

*adj* footloose, homeless, itinerant, nomadic, roaming, rootless, roving, shiftless, travelling, vagabond, wandering.

**vague** *adj* amorphous, blurred, dim, doubtful, evasive, fuzzy, generalised, hazy, ill-defined, imprecise, indefinite, indeterminate, indistinct, inexact, lax, loose, misty, nebulous, obscure, shadowy, uncertain, unclear, undefined, undetermined, unknown, unspecific, unspecified, woolly.

*antonyms* certain, clear, definite.

**vaguely** *adv* absent-mindedly, dimly, faintly, imprecisely, inexactly, obscurely, slightly, vacantly.

**vagueness** *n* ambiguity, amorphousness, dimness, faintness, fuzziness, haziness, imprecision, inexactitude, looseness, obscurity, uncertainty, woolliness.

*antonyms* clarity, precision.

**vain** *adj* abortive, affected, arrogant, baseless, bigheaded, conceited, egotistical, empty, fruitless, futile, groundless, hollow, idle, inflated, mindless, narcissistic, nugatory, ostentatious, overweening, peacockish, pointless, pretentious, proud, purposeless, self-important, self-satisfied, senseless, stuck-up, swaggering, swanky, swollen-headed, time-wasting, trifling, trivial, unavailing, unimportant, unproductive, unprofitable, unsubstantial, useless, vainglorious, vaporous, worthless.

*antonyms* modest, self-effacing.

**valediction** *n* adieu, farewell, godspeed, goodbye, leave-taking, send-off, vale.

*antonyms* greeting, welcome.

**valet** *n* body servant, gentleman's gentleman, man, man-servant, valet de chambre.

**valetudinarian** *adj* delicate, feeble, frail, hypochondriac, infirm, invalid, neurotic, sickly, weakly.

*antonym* stoical.

**valiant** *adj* bold, brave, courageous, dauntless, doughty, fearless, gallant, heroic, indomitable, intrepid, plucky, redoubtable, stalwart, staunch, stout, stout-hearted, valorous, worthy.

*antonym* cowardly.

**valid** *adj* approved, authentic, binding, bona fide, cogent, conclusive, convincing, efficacious, efficient, genuine, good, just, lawful, legal, legitimate, logical, official, potent, powerful, proper, rational, reliable, sound, substantial, telling, weighty, well-founded, well-grounded.

*antonym* invalid.

**validate** *v* attest, authenticate, authorise, certify, confirm, corroborate, endorse, legalise, ratify, substantiate, underwrite.

**validity** *n* authority, cogency, force, foundation, grounds, justifiability, lawfulness, legality, legitimacy, logic, point, power, soundness, strength, substance, weight.

*antonym* invalidity.

**valley** *n* clough, coomb, cwm, dale, dean, dell, den, depression, dingle, glen, graben, griff, gulch, hollow, hope, slade, strath, vale.

**valorous** *adj* bold, brave, courageous, dauntless, doughty, fearless, gallant, hardy, heroic, intrepid, lion-hearted, mettlesome, plucky, redoubtable, stalwart, valiant.

*antonyms* cowardly, weak.

**valour** *n* boldness, bravery, courage, derring-do, doughtiness, fearlessness, fortitude, gallantry, hardiness, heroism, intrepidity, lion-heartedness, mettle, spirit.

*antonyms* cowardice, weakness.

**valuable** *adj* advantageous, beneficial, blue-chip, cherished, costly, dear, esteemed, estimable, expensive, fruitful, handy, helpful, high-priced, important, invaluable, precious, prizable, prized, productive, profitable, serviceable, treasured, useful, valued, worthwhile, worthy.

*antonyms* useless, valueless.

**valuation** *n* appraisement, assessment, computation, estimate, evaluation, survey.

**value** *n* account, advantage, avail, benefit, cost, desirability, equivalent, good, help, importance, merit, price, profit, rate, significance, use, usefulness, utility, worth.

*v* account, appraise, appreciate, apprize, assess, cherish, compute, esteem, estimate, evaluate, hold dear, price, prize, rate, regard, respect, survey, treasure.

*antonyms* disregard, neglect, undervalue.

**valued** *adj* beloved, cherished, dear, esteemed, highly regarded, loved, prized, respected, treasured.

**values** *n* ethics, morals, principles, standards.

**vamoose** *v* absquatulate, clear off, decamp, disappear, do a bunk, make oneself scarce, quit, scarper, scram, skedaddle, vanish.

**vanish** *v* dematerialise, depart, die out, disappear, disperse, dissolve, evanesce, evaporate, exit, fade, fizzle out, melt, peter out.

*antonyms* appear, materialise.

**vanity** *n* affectation, airs, arrogance, bigheadedness, conceit, conceitedness, egotism, emptiness, frivolity, fruitlessness, fume, futility, hollowness, idleness, inanity, narcissism, ostentation, peacockery, pointlessness, pretension, pride, self-admiration, self-conceit, self-love, self-satisfaction, swollen-headedness, triviality, unreality, unsubstantiality, uselessness, vainglory, worthlessness.

*antonyms* modesty, worth.

**vanquish** *v* beat, confound, conquer, crush, defeat, humble, master, overcome, overpower, overwhelm, quell, reduce, repress, rout, subdue, subjugate, triumph over.

**vapid** *adj* banal, bland, bloodless, boring, colourless, dead, dull, flat, flavourless, insipid, jejune, lifeless, limp, stale, tame, tasteless,

tedious, tiresome, trite, uninspiring, uninteresting, watery, weak, wishy-washy.

*antonyms* interesting, vigorous.

**vaporous** *adj* brumous, chimerical, fanciful, flimsy, foggy, fumous, fumy, gaseous, insubstantial, misty, steamy, vain.

*antonym* substantial.

**vapour** *n* breath, brume, damp, dampness, exhalation, fog, fumes, halitus, haze, miasm, miasma, mist, reek, roke, smoke, steam.

**variable** *adj* capricious, chameleonic, changeable, fickle, fitful, flexible, fluctuating, inconstant, mercurial, moonish, mutable, protean, shifting, temperamental, unpredictable, unstable, unsteady, vacillating, varying, versiform, wavering.

*antonym* invariable.

*n* factor, parameter.

**variance** *n* difference, disagreement, discord, discrepancy, disharmony, dissension, dissent, divergence, division, inconsistency, quarrelling, strife, variation.

*antonyms* agreement, harmony.

**variant** *adj* alternative, derived, deviant, different, divergent, exceptional, modified.

*antonyms* normal, standard, usual.

*n* alternative, development, deviant, modification, rogue, sport, variation.

**variation** *n* alteration, change, departure, deviation, difference, discrepancy, diversification, diversity, elaboration, inflection, innovation, modification, modulation, novelty, variety.

*antonyms* monotony, similitude, uniformity.

**varied** *adj* accidented, assorted, different, diverse, heterogeneous, manifold, miscellaneous, mixed, motley, multifarious, sundry, various.

*antonyms* similar, uniform.

**variegated** *adj* diversified, freaked, jaspé, many-coloured, motley, mottled, multicoloured, parti-coloured, pied, poikilitic, polychrome, streaked, varicoloured, veined, versicoloured.

*antonyms* monochrome, plain.

**variety** *n* array, assortment, brand, breed, category, change, class, collection, difference, discrepancy, diversification, diversity, intermixture, kind, make, manifoldness, many-sidedness, medley, miscellany, mixture, multifariousness, multiplicity, olio, olla-podrida, order, pot-pourri, range, sort, species, strain, type, variation.

*antonyms* monotony, similitude, uniformity.

**various** *adj* assorted, different, differing, disparate, distinct, divers, diverse, diversified, heterogeneous, many, many-sided, miscellaneous, multifarous, omnifarous, several, sundry, varied, variegated, varying.

**varnish** *n* coating, glaze, gloss, japan, lac, lacquer, polish, resin, shellac.

**vary** *v* alter, alternate, change, depart, differ, disagree, diverge, diversify, fluctuate, inflect, intermix, modify, modulate, permutate, reorder, transform.

**vase** n amphora, container, ewer, hydria, jar, jug, pitcher, urn, vessel.

**vassal** n bondman, bondservant, bondsman, galloglass, liege, liegeman, retainer, serf, slave, subject, thrall, villein.

**vassalage** n bondage, dependence, serfdom, servitude, slavery, subjection, subjugation, thraldom, villeinage.

**vast** adj astronomical, boundless, capacious, colossal, cyclopean, enormous, extensive, far-flung, fathomless, gigantic, great, huge, illimitable, immeasurable, immense, limitless, mammoth, massive, measureless, monstrous, monumental, never-ending, prodigious, stupendous, sweeping, tremendous, unboudned, unlimited, vasty, voluminous, wide.

**vat** n container, keeve, kier, tank, tub.

**vault**[1] v bound, clear, hurdle, jump, leap, leap-frog, spring.

**vault**[2] n arch, camera, cavern, cellar, concave, crypt, depository, mausoleum, repository, roof, span, strongroom, tomb, undercroft, wine-cellar.

**vaunt** v blazon, boast, brag, crow, exult in, flaunt, parade, show off, trumpet.

*antonyms* belittle, minimise.

**veer** v change, sheer, shift, swerve, tack, turn, wheel.

**vegetables** n greens, greenstuff, legumes.

**vegetarian** adj grass-eating, herbivorous, Pythagorean, vegan.

**vegetate** v degenerate, deteriorate, go to seed, idle, languish, moulder, rust, rusticate, stagnate.

**vehemence** n animation, ardour, eagerness, earnestness, emphasis, energy, enthusiasm, fervency, fervour, fire, force, forcefulness, heat, impetuosity, intensity, keenness, passion, urgency, verve, vigour, violence, warmth, zeal.

*antonym* indifference.

**vehement** adj animated, ardent, eager, earnest, emphatic, enthusiastic, fervent, fervid, fierce, forceful, forcible, heated, impassioned, impetuous, intense, passionate, powerful, strong, urgent, violent, zealous.

*antonyms* apathetic, indifferent.

**vehicle** n apparatus, channel, conveyance, means, mechanism, medium, organ.

**veil** v cloak, conceal, cover, dim, disguise, dissemble, dissimulate, hide, mantle, mask, obscure, screen, shade, shadow, shield.

*antonyms* expose, uncover.

n blind, cloak, cover, curtain, disguise, film, humeral, integument, mask, screen, shade, shroud, velum.

**vein** n blood vessel, course, current, dash, frame of mind, hint, humour, lode, mode, mood, note, seam, strain, stratum, streak, stripe, style, temper, tenor, thread, tone, trait.

**veined** adj freaked, jaspé, marbled, mottled, streaked, variegated.

**velocity** n celerity, fleetness, impetus, pace, quickness, rapidity, rate, speed, swiftness.

**venal** adj bent, bribable, buyable, corrupt, corruptible, grafting, mercenary, purchasable, simoniacal.

*antonym* incorruptible.

**vendetta** n bad blood, bitterness, blood-feud, enmity, feud, quarrel, rivalry.

**veneer** n appearance, coating, façade, front, gloss, guise, layer, mask, pretence, semblance, show, surface.

**venerable** adj aged, august, dignified, esteemed, grave, honoured, respected, revered, reverenced, reverend, sage, sedate, venerated, wise, worshipful.

**venerate** v adore, esteem, hallow, honour, respect, revere, reverence, worship.

*antonyms* anathematise, disregard, execrate.

**veneration** n adoration, awe, deference, devotion, dulia, esteem, hyperdulia, latria, respect, reverence, worship.

**vengeance** n avengement, lex talionis, reprisal, requital, retaliation, retribution, revanche, revenge, talion, tit for tat.

*antonym* forgiveness.

**vengeful** adj avenging, implacable, punitive, rancorous, relentless, retaliatory, retributive, revanchist, revengeful, spiteful, unforgiving, vindictive.

*antonym* forgiving.

**venial** adj excusable, forgivable, insignificant, minor, negligible, pardonable, slight, trifling, trivial.

*antonyms* mortal, unforgivable, unpardonable.

**venom** n acrimony, bane, bitterness, gall, grudge, hate, hatred, ill-will, malevolence, malice, maliciousness, malignity, poison, rancour, spite, spitefulness, spleen, toxin, venin, vindictiveness, virulence, virus, vitrio.

**venomous** adj baleful, baneful, envenomed, hostile, malicious, malign, malignant, mephitic, noxious, poison, poisonous, rancorous, savage, spiteful, toxic, vicious, vindictive, virulent, vitriolic.

**vent** n aperture, blowhole, duct, hole, opening, orifice, outlet, passage, spiracle, split.

v air, discharge, emit, express, let fly, release, unloose, utter, voice.

**ventilate** v air, broadcast, debate, discuss, examine, expound, express.

*antonym* suppress.

**venture** v advance, adventure, chance, dare, endanger, hazard, imperil, jeopardise, make bold, presume, put forward, risk, speculate, stake, suggest, take the liberty, volunteer, wager.

n adventure, chance, endeavour, enterprise, fling, gamble, hazard, operation, project, risk, speculation, undertaking.

**venturesome** adj adventurous, audacious, bold, courageous, daredevil, daring, dauntless, doughty, enterprising, fearless, intrepid, plucky, spirited.

*antonyms* pusillanimous, unenterprising.

**veracious** adj accurate, credible, dependable, exact, factual, faithful, frank, genuine, honest, reliable, straightforward, true, trustworthy, truthful, veridical.

*antonym* untruthful.

**veracity** *n* accuracy, candour, credibility, exactitude, frankness, honesty, integrity, precision, probity, rectitude, trustworthiness, truth, truthfulness, verity.

*antonym* untruthfulness.

**verbal** *adj* lexical, oral, spoken, unwritten, verbatim, word-of-mouth.

**verbatim** *adv* exactly, literally, precisely, to the letter, (verbatim et) literatim, word for word.

**verbiage** *n* circumlocution, periphrasis, perissology, pleonasm, prolixity, repetition, verbosity.

*antonyms* economy, succinctness.

**verbose** *adj* ambagious, circumlocutory, diffuse, garrulous, long-winded, loquacious, multiloquent, periphrastic, phrasy, pleonastic, prolix, windy, wordy.

*antonyms* economical, laconic, succinct.

**verbosity** *n* garrulity, logorrhoea, long-windedness, loquaciousness, loquacity, multiloquy, prolixity, verbiage, verboseness, windiness, wordiness.

*antonyms* economy, succinctness.

**verdant** *adj* fresh, graminaceous, gramineous, grassy, green, leafy, lush, virid, viridescent.

**verdict** *n* adjudication, assessment, conclusion, decision, finding, judgement, opinion, sentence.

**verdure** *n* foliage, grass, greenery, greenness, greenth, herbage, leafage, meadows, pasture, verdancy, vert, viridescence, viridity.

**verge** *n* border, boundary, brim, brink, edge, edging, extreme, limit, lip, margin, roadside, threshold.

**verge on** approach, border on, come close to, near.

**verification** *n* attestation, authentication, checking, confirmation, corroboration, proof, substantiation, validation.

**verify** *v* attest, authenticate, check, confirm, corroborate, prove, substantiate, support, testify, validate.

*antonyms* discredit, invalidate.

**verisimilitude** *n* authenticity, colour, credibility, likeliness, plausibility, realism, resemblance, ring of truth, semblance.

*antonym* implausibility.

**verity** *n* actuality, authenticity, factuality, soundness, truth, truthfulness, validity, veracity.

*antonym* untruth.

**vernacular** *adj* colloquial, common, endemic, indigenous, informal, local, mother, native, popular, vulgar.

*n* argot, cant, dialect, idiom, jargon, language, lingo, parlance, patois, speech, tongue.

**versatile** *adj* adaptable, adjustable, all-round, flexible, functional, general-purpose, handy, many-sided, multifaceted, multipurpose, protean, Renaissance, resourceful, variable.

*antonym* inflexible.

**verse** *n* canto, doggerel, elegaics, fit, iambics, jingle, poesy, poetastery, poetry, rhyme, stanza, stave, strophe, verse-making, verse-mongering, versicle, versification.

**versed** *adj* accomplished, acquainted, au fait, competent, conversant, experienced, familiar, knowledgeable, learned, practised, proficient, qualified, seasoned, skilled.

**versifier** *n* poet, poetaster, poetess, poeticule, rhymer, rhymester, rhymist, verse-maker, verse-monger, verser, verse-smith, versificator.

**version** *n* account, adaptation, design, form, interpretation, kind, model, paraphrase, portrayal, reading, rendering, rendition, style, translation, type, variant.

**vertex** *n* acme, apex, apogee, crown, culmination, extremity, height, peak, pinnacle, summit, top, zenith.

*antonym* nadir.

**vertical** *adj* erect, on end, perpendicular, upright, upstanding.

*antonym* horizontal.

**vertigo** *n* dizziness, giddiness, light-headedness, megrim.

**verve** *n* animation, brio, dash, élan, energy, enthusiasm, force, gusto, life, liveliness, pizzazz, punch, relish, sparkle, spirit, vigour, vim, vitality, vivacity, zeal, zip.

*antonym* apathy.

**very** *adv* absolutely, acutely, awfully, decidedly, deeply, dogged, dooms, eminently, exceeding(ly), excessively, extremely, fell, gey, greatly, highly, jolly, noticeably, particularly, passing, rattling, really, remarkably, superlatively, surpassingly, terribly, truly, uncommonly, unusually, wonderfully.

*antonyms* hardly, scarcely, slightly.

*adj* actual, appropriate, bare, exact, express, identical, mere, perfect, plain, precise, pure, real, same, selfsame, sheer, simple, unqualified, utter.

**vessel** *n* barque, boat, canister, container, craft, holder, jar, pot, receptacle, ship, utensil.

**vestibule** *n* anteroom, entrance, entrance-hall, entrance-way, foyer, hall, lobby, porch, portico.

**vestige** *n* evidence, glimmer, hint, indication, print, relic, remainder, remains, remnant, residue, scrap, sign, suspicion, token, trace, track, whiff.

**vestigial** *adj* functionless, imperfect, incomplete, reduced, rudimentary, surviving, undeveloped.

**vet¹** *v* appraise, audit, check, examine, inspect, investigate, review, scan, scrutinise, survey.

**vet²** *n* dog-leech, farrier, hippiatrist, horse-doctor, horse-leech, veterinarian, veterinary, veterinary surgeon.

**veteran** *n* master, old hand, old soldier, old stager, old-timer, pastmaster, pro, trouper, war-horse.

*antonyms* novice, recruit.

*adj* adept, battle-scarred, experienced, expert, long-serving, masterly, old, practised, professional, proficient, seasoned.

*antonyms* inexperienced, raw.

**veto** v ban, blackball, disallow, forbid, interdict, kill, negative, prohibit, reject, rule out, turn down.

*antonyms* approve, sanction.

n ban, embargo, interdict, prohibition, rejection, thumbs down.

*antonyms* approval, assent.

**vex** v afflict, aggravate, agitate, annoy, bother, bug, chagrin, deave, displease, distress, disturb, exasperate, fret, gall, get (to), harass, hump, irritate, molest, needle, nettle, offend, peeve, perplex, pester, pique, plague, provoke, rile, spite, tease, torment, trouble, upset, worry.

*antonym* soothe.

**vexation** n aggravation, anger, annoyance, bore, bother, chagrin, difficulty, displeasure, dissatisfaction, exasperation, frustration, fury, headache, irritant, misfortune, nuisance, pique, problem, trouble, upset, worry.

**vexatious** adj afflicting, aggravating, annoying, bothersome, burdensome, disagreeable, disappointing, distressing, doggone, exasperating, fashious, harassing, infuriating, irksome, irritating, nagging, pesky, pestful, pestiferous, pestilent, plaguesome, plagu(e)y, provoking, teasing, tormenting, troublesome, trying, unpleasant, upsetting, worrisome, worrying.

*antonyms* pleasant, soothing.

**vexed** adj afflicted, aggravated, agitated, annoyed, bedevilled, bored, bothered, chagrined, confused, contested, controversial, deaved, displeased, disputed, distressed, disturbed, exasperated, harassed, irritated, miffed, moot, nettled, peeved, perplexed, provoked, put out, riled, ruffled, tormented, troubled, upset, worried.

**viable** adj achievable, applicable, feasible, operable, possible, practicable, usable, workable.

*antonyms* impossible, unworkable.

**vibes** n ambience, atmosphere, aura, emanation, emotions, feel, feelings, reaction, response, vibrations.

**vibrant** adj alive, animated, bright, colourful, dynamic, electric, electrifying, jazzy, oscillating, palpitating, peppy, pulsating, quivering, responsive, sensitive, sparkling, spirited, trembling, vivacious, vivid.

**vibrate** v dinnle, dirl, fluctuate, judder, oscillate, pendulate, pulsate, pulse, quiver, resonate, reverberate, shake, shimmy, shiver, shudder, sway, swing, throb, tremble, undulate.

**vibration** n diadrom, fremitus, frisson, judder, juddering, oscillation, pulsation, pulse, quiver, resonance, reverberation, shaking, shudder, throb, throbbing, trembling, tremor.

**vicarious** adj acting, commissioned, delegated, deputed, empathetic, indirect, second-hand, substituted, surrogate.

**vice** n bad habit, besetting sin, blemish, corruption, defect, degeneracy, depravity, evil, evil-doing, failing, fault, hamartia, immorality, imperfection, iniquity, profligacy, shortcoming, sin, venality, weakness, wickedness.

*antonym* virtue.

**vicinity** n area, circumjacency, district, environs, locality, neighbourhood, precincts, propinquity, proximity, purlieus, vicinage.

**vicious** adj abhorrent, atrocious, backbiting, bad, barbarous, bitchy, brutal, catty, corrupt, cruel, dangerous, debased, defamatory, depraved, diabolical, fiendish, foul, heinous, immoral, infamous, malicious, mean, monstrous, nasty, perverted, profligate, rancorous, savage, sinful, slanderous, spiteful, unprincipled, venomous, vile, vindictive, violent, virulent, vitriolic, wicked, worthless, wrong.

*antonyms* gentle, good, virtuous.

**viciousness** n badness, bitchiness, brutality, corruption, cruelty, depravity, ferocity, immorality, malice, profligacy, rancour, savagery, sinfulness, spite, spitefulness, venom, virulence, wickedness.

*antonyms* gentleness, goodness, virtue.

**vicissitude** n alteration, alternation, change, deviation, divergence, fluctuation, mutation, revolution, shift, turn, twist, variation.

**victim** n casualty, dupe, fall guy, fatality, gull, innocent, mark, martyr, patsy, sacrifice, scapegoat, sitting target, sucker, sufferer.

**victimise** v bully, cheat, deceive, defraud, discriminate against, dupe, exploit, fool, gull, hoodwink, oppress, persecute, pick on, prey on, swindle, use.

**victor** n champ, champion, conqueror, first, prize-winner, subjugator, top dog, vanquisher, victor ludorum, victrix, winner.

*antonyms* loser, vanquished.

**victorious** adj champion, conquering, first, prize-winning, successful, top, triumphant, unbeaten, winning.

*antonyms* losing, unsuccessful.

**victory** n conquest, laurels, mastery, palm, prize, subjugation, success, superiority, triumph, vanquishment, win.

*antonyms* defeat, loss.

**victuals** n aliment, bread, comestibles, eatables, eats, edibles, food, grub, meat, nosh, provisions, rations, stores, supplies, sustenance, viands, vittles.

**vie** v compete, contend, contest, corrival, fight, rival, strive, struggle.

**view** n aspect, attitude, belief, contemplation, conviction, display, estimation, examination, feeling, glimpse, impression, inspection, judgement, landscape, look, notion, opinion, outlook, panorama, perception, perspective, picture, prospect, scan, scene, scrutiny, sentiment, sight, spectacle, survey, viewing, vision, vista.

v behold, consider, contemplate, deem, examine, explore, eye, inspect, judge, observe, perceive, read, regard, scan, speculate, survey, watch, witness.

**viewer** n looker-in, observer, onlooker, spectator, watcher.

**viewpoint** n angle, Anschauung, attitude, feeling, opinion, perspective, position, slant, stance, standpoint.

**vigil** *n* lookout, pernoctation, sleeplessness, stake-out, wake, wakefulness, watch.

**vigilance** *n* alertness, attentiveness, carefulness, caution, circumspection, guardedness, observation, wakefulness, watchfulness.

**vigilant** *adj* alert, Argus-eyed, attentive, careful, cautious, circumspect, guarded, on one's guard, on one's toes, on the alert, on the lookout, on the qui vive, sleepless, unsleeping, wakeful, watchful, wide-awake.

*antonyms* careless, forgetful, lax, negligent.

**vigorous** *adj* active, brisk, dynamic, effective, efficient, energetic, enterprising, flourishing, forceful, forcible, full-blooded, hale, hardy, healthy, hearty, intense, lively, lusty, mettlesome, powerful, red-blooded, robust, sound, spanking, spirited, stout, strenuous, strong, virile, vital, zippy.

*antonyms* feeble, lethargic, weak.

**vigorously** *adv* briskly, eagerly, energetically, forcefully, hard, heartily, lustily, powerfully, strenuously, strongly.

*antonyms* feebly, weakly.

**vigour** *n* activity, animation, dash, dynamism, energy, force, forcefulness, gusto, health, liveliness, might, oomph, pep, potency, power, punch, robustness, snap, soundness, spirit, stamina, strength, verve, vim, virility, vitality, zip.

*antonyms* impotence, sluggishness, weakness.

**vile** *adj* abandoned, abject, appalling, bad, base, coarse, contemptible, corrupt, debased, degenerate, degrading, depraved, despicable, disgraceful, disgusting, earthly, evil, foul, horrid, humiliating, ignoble, impure, loathsome, low, mean, miserable, nasty, nauseating, nefarious, noxious, offensive, perverted, repellent, repugnant, repulsive, revolting, scabbed, scabby, scandalous, scurvy, shocking, sickening, sinful, ugly, vicious, vulgar, wicked, worthless, wretched.

**vileness** *n* baseness, coarseness, corruption, degeneracy, depravity, dreadfulness, enormity, evil, foulness, meanness, noxiousness, offensiveness, outrage, profanity, ugliness, wickedness.

**vilification** *n* abuse, aspersion, calumniation, calumny, contumely, criticism, defamation, denigration, disparagement, invective, mud-slinging, revilement, scurrility, vituperation.

**vilify** *v* abuse, asperse, bad-mouth, berate, calumniate, criticise, debase, decry, defame, denigrate, denounce, disparage, malign, revile, slander, smear, stigmatise, traduce, vilipend, vituperate.

*antonyms* adore, compliment, eulogise, glorify.

**village** *n* clachan, community, dorp, hamlet, kampong, kraal, pueblo, settlement, township.

**villain** *n* anti-hero, baddy, blackguard, bravo, caitiff, criminal, devil, evil-doer, heavy, knave, libertine, malefactor, miscreant, profligate, rapscallion, rascal, reprobate, rogue, scoundrel, wretch.

*antonyms* angel, goody, hero, heroine.

**villainous** *adj* atrocious, bad, base, blackguardly, criminal, cruel, debased, degenerate, depraved, detestable, diabolical, disgraceful, evil, fiendish, hateful, heinous, ignoble, infamous, inhuman, malevolent, mean, nefarious, opprobrious, outrageous, ruffianly, scoundrelly, sinful, terrible, thievish, vicious, vile, wicked.

*antonyms* angelic, good, heroic.

**villainy** *n* atrocity, badness, baseness, crime, criminality, delinquency, depravity, devilry, iniquity, knavery, rascality, roguery, sin, turpitude, vice, viciousness, wickedness.

**vindicate** *v* absolve, acquit, advocate, assert, clear, defend, establish, exculpate, excuse, exonerate, justify, maintain, rehabilitate, support, uphold, verify.

*antonyms* accuse, convict.

**vindication** *n* apology, assertion, defence, exculpation, excuse, exoneration, extenuation, justification, maintenance, plea, rehabilitation, substantiation, support, verification.

*antonyms* accusation, conviction.

**vindictive** *adj* implacable, malevolent, malicious, malignant, merciless, punitive, rancorous, relentless, resentful, retributive, revengeful, spiteful, unforgiving, unrelenting, vengeful, venomous.

*antonyms* charitable, forgiving, merciful.

**vintage** *n* collection, crop, epoch, era, generation, harvest, origin, period, year.

*adj* best, choice, classic, fine, mature, old, prime, quintessential, rare, ripe, select, superior, venerable, veteran.

**violate** *v* abuse, assault, befoul, break, contravene, debauch, defile, desecrate, dishonour, disobey, disregard, flout, infract, infringe, invade, outrage, pollute, profane, rape, ravish, transgress.

*antonyms* obey, observe, uphold.

**violation** *n* abuse, breach, contravention, defilement, desecration, disruption, encroachment, infraction, infringement, offence, profanation, rapine, sacrilege, spoliation, transgression, trespass.

*antonyms* obedience, observance.

**violence** *n* abandon, acuteness, bestiality, bloodshed, bloodthirstiness, boisterousness, brutality, conflict, cruelty, destructiveness, ferocity, fervour, fierceness, fighting, force, frenzy, fury, harshness, hostilities, intensity, murderousness, passion, power, roughness, savagery, severity, sharpness, storminess, terrorism, thuggery, tumult, turbulence, vehemence, wildness.

*antonyms* passivity, peacefulness.

**violent** *adj* acute, agonising, berserk, biting, bloodthirsty, blustery, boisterous, brutal, cruel, destructive, devastating, excruciating, extreme, fiery, forceful, forcible, furious, harsh, headstrong, homicidal, hot-headed, impetuous, intemperate, intense, maddened, maniacal, murderous, outrageous, painful, passionate, peracute, powerful, raging, riotous, rough, ruinous, savage, severe, sharp, strong, tempestuous, tumultuous, turbulent, uncontrollable, ungovernable, unrestrained, vehement, vicious, wild.

*antonyms* calm, gentle, moderate, passive, peaceful.

**VIP** *n* big cheese, big name, big noise, big shot, bigwig, celebrity, dignitary, headliner, heavyweight, lion, luminary, notable, personage, somebody, star.

*antonyms* nobody, nonentity.

**virago** *n* battle-axe, dragon, fury, gorgon, harridan, hell-cat, randy, scold, shrew, tartar, termagant, vixen, Xanthippe.

**virgin** *n* bachelor, celibate, damsel, girl, maid, maiden, spinster, vestal, virgo intacta.
*adj* chaste, fresh, immaculate, intact, maidenly, modest, new, pristine, pure, snowy, spotless, stainless, uncorrupted, undefiled, unsullied, untouched, unused, vestal, virginal.

**virginal** *adj* celibate, chaste, fresh, immaculate, maidenly, pristine, pure, snowy, spotless, stainless, uncorrupted, undefiled, undisturbed, untouched, vestal, virgin, white.

**virginity** *n* chasteness, chastity, maidenhead, maidenhood, purity, virtue.

**virile** *adj* forceful, husky, lusty, macho, male, man-like, manly, masculine, potent, red-blooded, robust, rugged, strong, vigorous.

*antonyms* effeminate, impotent, weak.

**virility** *n* huskiness, machismo, manhood, manliness, masculinity, potency, ruggedness, vigour.

*antonyms* effeminacy, impotence, weakness.

**virtual** *adj* effective, essential, implicit, implied, indirect, potential, practical, tacit.

*antonym* actual.

**virtually** *adv* almost, as good as, effectively, effectually, in effect, in essence, nearly, practically, to all intents and purposes.

**virtue** *n* advantage, asset, attribute, chastity, credit, excellence, goodness, high-mindedness, honour, incorruptibility, innocence, integrity, justice, merit, morality, plus, probity, purity, quality, rectitude, redeeming feature, righteousness, strength, uprightness, virginity, worth, worthiness.

*antonym* vice.

**virtuosity** *n* bravura, brilliance, éclat, expertise, finesse, finish, flair, mastery, panache, polish, skill, wizardry.

**virtuoso** *n* ace, artist, crackerjack, dabster, genius, maestro, magician, master, prodigy, whiz, wizard.
*adj* bravura, brilliant, crackerjack, dazzling, expert, masterly, wizard.

**virtuous** *adj* blameless, celibate, chaste, clean-living, continent, ethical, excellent, exemplary, good, high-principled, honest, honourable, incorruptible, innocent, irreproachable, moral, praiseworthy, pure, righteous, spotless, squeaky-clean, unimpeachable, upright, virginal, worthy.

*antonyms* bad, dishonest, immoral, vicious, wicked.

**virulence** *n* acrimony, antagonism, bitterness, deadliness, harmfulness, hatred, hostility, hurtfulness, infectiousness, malevolence, malice, malignancy, poison, rancour, resentment, spite, spleen, toxicity, venom, viciousness, vindictiveness, virulency, vitriol.

**virulent** *adj* acrimonious, baneful, bitter, deadly, envenomed, hostile, infective, injurious, lethal, malevolent, malicious, malignant, noxious, pernicious, poisonous, rancorous, resentful, septic, spiteful, splenetic, toxic, venomous, vicious, vindictive, vitriolic.

**viscera** *n* bowels, chitterlings, entrails, gralloch, harigal(d)s, ha(r)slet, innards, insides, intestines, vitals.

**viscous** *adj* adhesive, clammy, gelatinous, gluey, glutinous, gooey, gummy, mucilaginous, mucous, sticky, syrupy, tacky, tenacious, thick, treacly, viscid.

*antonyms* runny, thin, watery.

**visible** *adj* apparent, aspectable, clear, conspicuous, detectable, discernible, discoverable, distinguishable, evident, manifest, noticeable, observable, obvious, open, palpable, patent, perceivable, perceptible, plain, unconcealed, undisguised, unmistakable.

*antonym* invisible.

**vision** *n* aisling, apparition, chimera, concept, conception, construct, daydream, delusion, discernment, dream, eyes, eyesight, fantasy, far-sightedness, foresight, ghost, hallucination, idea, ideal, illusion, image, imagination, insight, intuition, mirage, penetration, perception, phantasm, phantasma, phantom, picture, prescience, revelation, seeing, sight, spectacle, spectre, view, wraith.

**visionary** *adj* chimerical, delusory, dreaming, dreamy, fanciful, fantastic, ideal, idealised, idealistic, illusory, imaginary, impractical, moonshiny, prophetic, quixotic, romantic, speculative, starry-eyed, unreal, unrealistic, unworkable, utopian.
*n* daydreamer, Don Quixote, dreamer, enthusiast, fantasist, idealist, mystic, prophet, rainbow-chaser, romantic, seer, theorist, utopian, zealot.

*antonym* pragmatist.

**visit** *v* afflict, assail, attack, befall, call in, call on, drop in on, haunt, inspect, look in, look up, pop in, punish, see, smite, stay at, stay with, stop by, take in, trouble.
*n* call, excursion, sojourn, stay, stop.

**visitation** *n* appearance, bane, blight, calamity, cataclysm, catastrophe, disaster, examination, infliction, inspection, manifestation, nemesis, ordeal, punishment, retribution, scourge, trial, visit.

**visitor** *n* caller, company, emmet, grockle, guest, holidaymaker, tourist, visitant.

**vista** *n* enfilade, panorama, perspective, prospect, view.

**visual** *adj* discernible, observable, ocular, optic, optical, perceptible, specular, visible.

**visualise** *v* conceive, envisage, ideate, imagine, picture.

**vital** *adj* alive, animate, animated, animating, basic, cardinal, critical, crucial, decisive, dynamic, energetic, essential, forceful, fundamental, generative, imperative, important, indispensable, invigorating, key, life-giving, life-or-death, live, lively, living, necessary, quickening, requisite, significant, spirited, urgent, vibrant, vigorous, vivacious, zestful.

*antonyms* inessential, peripheral, unimportant.

**vitality** *n* animation, energy, exuberance, foison, go, life, liveliness, lustiness, oomph, pep, robustness, sparkle, stamina, strength, vigour, vim, vivaciousness, vivacity.

**vitiate** *v* blemish, blight, contaminate, corrupt, debase, defile, deprave, deteriorate, devalue, harm, impair, injure, invalidate, mar, nullify, pervert, pollute, ruin, spoil, sully, taint, undermine.

*antonym* purify.

**vitriolic** *adj* acerbic, acid, bitchy, biting, bitter, caustic, destructive, envenomed, malicious, sardonic, scathing, venomous, vicious, virulent, withering.

**vituperate** *v* abuse, berate, blame, castigate, censure, denounce, rate, reproach, revile, slag, slam, slang, slate, upbraid, vilify.

*antonyms* applaud, eulogise, extol, praise.

**vituperation** *n* abuse, blame, castigation, censure, contumely, diatribe, fault-finding, flak, invective, objurgation, obloquy, phillipic, rebuke, reprimand, reproach, revilement, scurrility, stick, vilification.

*antonyms* acclaim, eulogy, praise.

**vituperative** *adj* abusive, belittling, calumniatory, censorious, defamatory, denunciatory, derogatory, fulminatory, harsh, insulting, malign, objurgatory, opprobrious, sardonic, scornful, scurrilous, withering.

*antonym* laudatory.

**vivacious** *adj* animated, bubbling, bubbly, cheerful, chipper, ebullient, effervescent, frisky, frolicsome, gay, high-spirited, jolly, light-hearted, lively, merry, scintillating, sparkling, spirited, sportive, sprightly, vital.

*antonym* languid.

**vivacity** *n* animation, brio, bubbliness, ebullience, effervescence, energy, friskiness, gaiety, high spirits, jollity, life, liveliness, pep, quickness, sparkle, spirit, sprightliness.

*antonym* languor.

**vivid** *adj* active, animated, bright, brilliant, clear, colourful, distinct, dramatic, dynamic, eidetic, energetic, expressive, flamboyant, glowing, graphic, highly-coloured, intense, lifelike, lively, memorable, powerful, quick, realistic, rich, sharp, spirited, stirring, striking, strong, telling, vibrant, vigorous.

*antonyms* dull, lifeless.

**vividness** *n* brightness, brilliancy, clarity, distinctness, glow, immediacy, intensity, life, liveliness, lucidity, radiance, realism, refulgence, resplendence, sharpness, sprightliness, strength.

*antonyms* dullness, lifelessness.

**vixen** *n* beldam, bitch, fury, harpy, harridan, hell-cat, scold, shrew, spitfire, termagant, virago, Xanthippe.

**vocabulary** *n* dictionary, glossary, idiom, idioticon, language, lexicon, lexis, nomenclature, thesaurus, word-book, words.

**vocal** *adj* articulate, clamorous, eloquent, expressive, forthright, frank, free-spoken, noisy, oral, outspoken, plain-spoken, said, shrill, spoken, strident, uttered, vociferous, voiced.

*antonyms* inarticulate, quiet.

**vocation** *n* bag, business, calling, career, employment, job, métier, mission, niche, office, post, profession, pursuit, role, trade, work.

**vociferous** *adj* clamant, clamorous, loud, loud-mouthed, noisy, obstreperous, ranting, shouting, shrill, stentorian, strident, thundering, uproarious, vehement, vocal.

*antonyms* quiet, silent.

**vogue** *n* acceptance, craze, currency, custom, day, dernier cri, fashion, fashionableness, favour, haut ton, last word, mode, popularity, prevalence, style, the latest, the rage, the thing, trend, usage, use.

*adj* current, fashionable, in, modish, now, popular, prevalent, stylish, trendy, up-to-the-minute, voguish, with it.

**voice** *n* agency, articulation, decision, expression, inflection, instrument, intonation, language, medium, mouthpiece, organ, part, say, sound, speech, spokesman, spokesperson, spokeswoman, tone, utterance, vehicle, view, vote, will, wish, words.

*v* air, articulate, assert, bruit, convey, declare, disclose, divulge, enunciate, express, say, speak of, utter, ventilate.

**void** *adj* bare, blank, cancelled, clear, dead, drained, emptied, empty, free, inane, ineffective, ineffectual, inoperative, invalid, nugatory, null, tenantless, unenforceable, unfilled, unoccupied, useless, vacant, vain, worthless.

*antonyms* full, valid.

*n* blank, blankness, cavity, chasm, emptiness, gap, hiatus, hollow, lack, opening, space, vacuity, vacuum, want.

*v* abnegate, annul, cancel, defecate, discharge, drain, eject, elimate, emit, empty, evacuate, invalidate, nullify, rescind.

*antonyms* fill, validate.

**volatile** *adj* airy, changeable, erratic, explosive, fickle, flighty, gay, giddy, hot-headed, hot-tempered, inconstant, lively, mercurial, sprightly, temperamental, unsettled, unstable, unsteady, variable, volcanic.

*antonyms* constant, steady.

**volition** *n* choice, choosing, determination, discretion, election, option, preference, purpose, resolution, taste, velleity, will.

**volley** *n* barrage, blast, bombardment, burst, cannonade, discharge, enfilade, explosion, fusillade, hail, salvo, shower.

**voluble** *adj* articulate, fluent, forthcoming, garrulous, glib, loquacious, talkative.

*antonym* pauciloquent.

**volume** *n* aggregate, amount, amplitude, bigness, body, book, bulk, capacity, compass, dimensions, fascic(u)le, heft, mass, part, publication, quantity, tome, total, treatise.

**voluminous** *adj* abounding, ample, big, billowing, bulky, capacious, cavernous, commodious, copious, full, large, massive, prolific, roomy, vast.

*antonyms* scanty, slight.

**voluntarily** *adv* by choice, consciously, deliberately, freely, intentionally, of one's own accord, of one's own free will, on one's own initiative, purposely, spontaneously, willingly.

*antonyms* involuntarily, unwillingly.

**voluntary** *adj* conscious, deliberate, discretional, free, gratuitous, honorary, intended, intentional, optional, purposeful, purposive, spontaneous, unconstrained, unforced, unpaid, volunteer, wilful, willing.

*antonyms* compulsory, forced, involuntary, unwilling.

**volunteer** *v* advance, communicate, extend, offer, present, proffer, propose, put forward, step forward, suggest, tender.

**voluptuary** *n* bon vivant, debauchee, epicurean, hedonist, libertine, playboy, pleasure-seeker, profligate, sensualist, sybarite.

*antonym* ascetic.

**voluptuous** *adj* ample, buxom, curvaceous, effeminate, enticing, epicurean, erotic, goluptious, hedonistic, licentious, luscious, luxurious, pleasure-loving, provocative, seductive, self-indulgent, sensual, shapely, sybaritic.

*antonym* ascetic.

**voluptuousness** *n* buxomness, carnality, curvaceousness, licentiousness, lusciousness, opulence, seductiveness, sensuality, shapeliness.

*antonym* asceticism.

**vomit** *v* barf, boak, boke, bring up, cat, chunder, disgorge, egurgitate, eject, emit, heave, posset, puke, regurgitate, retch, sick up, spew out, spew up, throw up.

**vomiting** *n* chundering, egurgitation, ejection, emesis, emission, puking, regurgitation, retching, sickness, spewing.

**voracious** *adj* acquisitive, avid, devouring, edacious, gluttonous, greedy, hungry, insatiable, omnivorous, pantophagous, prodigious, rapacious, ravening, ravenous, uncontrolled, unquenchable.

**voracity** *n* acquisitiveness, avidity, eagerness, edacity, greed, hunger, pantophagy, rapacity, ravenousness.

**vortex** *n* eddy, maelstrom, whirl, whirlpool, whirlwind.

**votary** *n* addict, adherent, aficionado, believer, devotee, disciple, follower, monk.

**vote** *n* ballot, election, franchise, plebiscite, poll, referendum, show of hands, suffrage.

*v* ballot, choose, declare, elect, judge, opt, plump for, pronounce, propose, recommend, return, suggest.

**voucher** *n* certificate, check, coupon, ticket, token, warrant.

**vouch for** affirm, assert, asseverate, attest to, avouch, back, certify, confirm, endorse, guarantee, support, swear to, uphold.

**vouchsafe** *v* accord, bestow, cede, confer, deign, grant, impart, yield.

**vow** *v* affirm, avouch, bename, consecrate, dedicate, devote, maintain, pledge, profess, promise, swear.

*n* avouchment, oath, pledge, promise, troth.

**voyage** *n* crossing, cruise, expedition, journey, passage, peregrination, travels, trip.

**vulgar** *adj* banausic, blue, boorish, cheap and nasty, coarse, common, crude, dirty, flashy, gaudy, general, gross, ill-bred, impolite, improper, indecent, indecorous, indelicate, low, low-life, low-lived, low-minded, low-thoughted, naff, nasty, native, naughty, ordinary, pandemian, plebby, plebeian, ribald, risqué, rude, suggestive, tacky, tasteless, tawdry, uncouth, unmannerly, unrefined, vernacular.

*antonyms* correct, decent, elegant, noble, polite, refined.

**vulgarian** *n* arriviste, barbarian, boor, nouveau riche, parvenu, philistine, upstart.

**vulgarity** *n* coarseness, crudeness, crudity, dirtiness, gaudiness, grossness, indecency, indecorum, indelicacy, ribaldry, rudeness, suggestiveness, tastelessness, tawdriness.

*antonyms* decency, politeness.

# W

**wacky** *adj* crazy, daft, eccentric, erratic, goofy, irrational, loony, loopy, nutty, odd, screwy, silly, unpredictable, wild, zany.

*antonym* sensible.

**wad** *n* ball, block, bundle, chunk, hump, hunk, mass, pledget, plug, roll.

**wadding** *n* cotton-wool, filler, lining, packing, padding, stuffing.

**waddle** *v* rock, shuffle, sway, toddle, totter, wiggle, wobble.

**waffle** *v* blather, fudge, jabber, prate, prattle, prevaricate, rabbit on, spout, witter on.

*n* blather, gobbledegook, guff, jabber, nonsense, padding, prating, prattle, prolixity, verbiage, verbosity, wordiness.

**waft** *v* bear, carry, convey, drift, float, ride, transmit, transport, whiffle, winnow.

*n* breath, breeze, current, draught, puff, scent, whiff.

**wag¹** *v* bob, bobble, flutter, jiggle, nod, oscillate, pendulate, quiver, rock, shake, stir, vibrate, waggle, wave, wiggle.

*n* bob, bobble, flutter, jiggle, nod, oscillation, quiver, shake, toss, vibration, waggle, wave, wiggle.

**wag²** *n* banterer, card, clown, comedian, comic, droll, fool, humorist, jester, joker, wit.

**wage** *n* allowance, compensation, earnings, emolument, fee, guerdon, hire, pay, payment, penny-fee, recompense, remuneration, reward, salary, screw, stipend, wage-packet, wages.

*v* carry on, conduct, engage in, practise, prosecute, pursue, undertake.

**wager** *n* bet, flutter, gage, gamble, hazard, pledge, punt, speculation, stake, venture.

*v* bet, chance, gamble, hazard, lay, lay odds, pledge, punt, risk, speculate, stake, venture.

**waggish** *adj* amusing, arch, bantering, comical, droll, espiègle, facetious, frolicsome, funny, humorous, impish, jesting, jocose, jocular, merry, mischievous, playful, puckish, risible, roguish, sportive, witty.

*antonyms* grave, serious, staid.

**waggle** *v* bobble, flutter, jiggle, oscillate, shake, wag, wave, wiggle, wobble.

*n* bobble, flutter, jiggle, oscillation, shake, wag, wave, wiggle, wobble.

**wagon** *n* buggy, carriage, cart, dray, float, train, truck, tumbrel, van.

**waif** *n* foundling, orphan, stray, wastrel.

**wail** *v* bemoan, bewail, complain, cry, deplore, grieve, howl, keen, lament, mewl, moan, ululate, weep, yammer, yowl.

*n* caterwaul, complaint, cry, grief, howl, keen, lament, lamentation, moan, ululation, weeping, yowl.

**wait** *v* abide, dally, delay, hang fire, hesitate, hold back, hover, linger, loiter, mark time, pause, remain, rest, stay, tarry.

*antonyms* depart, go, leave.

*n* delay, halt, hesitation, hiatus, hold-up, interval, pause, rest, stay.

**waive** *v* abandon, defer, disclaim, forgo, postpone, relinquish, remit, renounce, resign, surrender.

*antonyms* claim, maintain.

**waiver** *n* abandonment, abdication, deferral, disclaimer, postponement, relinquishment, remission, renunciation, resignation, surrender.

**wake¹** *v* activate, animate, arise, arouse, awake, awaken, bestir, enliven, excite, fire, galvanise, get up, kindle, provoke, quicken, rise, rouse, stimulate, stir, unbed.

*antonyms* relax, sleep.

*n* death-watch, funeral, pernoctation, vigil, watch.

**wake²** *n* aftermath, backwash, path, rear, track, trail, train, wash, waves.

**wakeful** *adj* alert, alive, attentive, heedful, insomniac, observant, restless, sleepless, unblinking, unsleeping, vigilant, wary, watchful.

*antonyms* inattentive, sleepy, unwary.

**waken** *v* activate, animate, arouse, awake, awaken, enliven, fire, galvanise, get up, ignite, kindle, quicken, rouse, stimulate, stir, whet.

**walk** *v* accompany, advance, amble, convoy, escort, go by Shanks's pony, hike, hoof it, march, move, pace, pedestrianise, perambulate, plod, promenade, saunter, step, stride, stroll, take, traipse, tramp, tread, trek, trog, trudge.

*n* aisle, alley, ambulatory, avenue, carriage, constitutional, esplanade, footpath, frescade, gait, hike, lane, mall, march, pace, path, pathway, pavement, pawn, perambulation, promenade, ramble, saunter, sidewalk, step, stride, stroll, trail, traipse, tramp, trek, trudge, turn.

**walk of life** activity, area, arena, calling, career, course, field, line, métier, profession, pursuit, sphere, trade, vocation.

**walker** n ambulator, backpacker, footslogger, hiker, pedestrian, rambler, wayfarer.

**walk-out** n industrial action, protest, rebellion, revolt, stoppage, strike.

**walk-over** n child's play, cinch, doddle, picnic, piece of cake, pushover, snap, walk-away.

**walkway** n ambulatory, esplanade, footpath, lane, path, pathway, pavement, promenade, sidewalk.

**wall** n bailey, barricade, barrier, block, breastwork, bulk-head, bulwark, dike, divider, dyke, embankment, enclosure, fence, fortification, hedge, impediment, membrane, obstacle, obstruction, palisade, panel, parapet, partition, rampart, screen, septum, stockade.

**wallet** n bill-fold, case, holder, note-case, pochette, pocket-book, pouch, purse.

**wallop** v batter, beat, belt, best, buffet, clobber, crush, defeat, drub, hammer, hit, lambaste, lick, paste, pound, pummel, punch, rout, slug, smack, strike, swat, swipe, thrash, thump, thwack, trounce, vanquish, whack, worst.

n bash, belt, blow, haymaker, hit, kick, punch, slug, smack, swat, swipe, thump, thwack, whack.

**wallow** v bask, delight, enjoy, flounder, glory, indulge, lie, lurch, luxuriate, relish, revel, roll, splash, stagger, stumble, tumble, wade, welter.

**wan** adj anaemic, ashen, bleak, bloodless, cadaverous, colourless, dim, discoloured, faint, feeble, ghastly, livid, lurid, mournful, pale, pallid, pasty, sickly, waxen, weak, weary, whey-faced, white.

**wand** n baton, mace, rod, sceptre, sprig, staff, stick, twig, verge, withe, withy.

**wander** v aberrate, babble, cruise, depart, deviate, digress, divagate, diverge, drift, err, hump the bluey, lapse, meander, mill around, peregrinate, ramble, range, rave, roam, rove, saunter, squander, straggle, stravaig, stray, stroll, swerve, traipse, veer, wilder.

n cruise, excursion, meander, peregrination, ramble, saunter, stroll, traipse.

**wanderer** n drifter, gypsy, itinerant, nomad, rambler, ranger, rolling stone, rover, strag, straggler, stray, stroller, traveller, vagabond, vagrant, voyager.

**wandering** n aberration, deviation, digression, divagation, divergence, drift(ing), evagation, journey(ing), meander(ing), odyssey, peregrination, travels, walkabout.

adj aberrant, circumforaneous, drifting, homeless, itinerant, migratory, nomadic, peregrinatory, peripatetic, rambling, rootless, roving, strolling, travelling, vagabond, vagrant, voyaging, wayfaring.

**wane** v abate, atrophy, contract, decline, decrease, dim, diminish, droop, drop, dwindle, ebb, fade, fail, lessen, shrink, sink, subside, taper off, weaken, wither.

*antonyms* increase, wax.

n abatement, atrophy, contraction, decay, decline, decrease, diminution, drop, dwindling, ebb, fading, failure, fall, lessening, sinking, subsidence, tapering off, weakening.

*antonym* increase.

**wangle** v arrange, contrive, engineer, fiddle, finagle, fix, flam, manage, manipulate, manoeuvre, pull off, scheme, work, work the oracle.

**want** v call for, covet, crave, demand, desiderate, desire, fancy, hanker after, hunger for, lack, long for, miss, need, pine for, require, thirst for, wish, yearn for, yen.

n absence, appetite, besoin, craving, dearth, default, deficiency, demand, desideratum, desire, destitution, famine, fancy, hankering, hunger, indigence, insufficiency, lack, longing, necessity, need, neediness, paucity, pauperism, penury, poverty, privation, requirement, scantiness, scarcity, shortage, thirst, wish, yearning, yen.

*antonyms* abundance, plenty, riches.

**wanting** adj absent, defective, deficient, disappointing, faulty, imperfect, inadequate, incomplete, inferior, insufficient, lacking, less, missing, patchy, poor, short, shy, sketchy, substandard, unsatisfactory, unsound.

*antonyms* adequate, sufficient.

**wanton** adj abandoned, arbitrary, careless, coltish, cruel, dissipated, dissolute, evil, extravagant, fast, gratuitous, groundless, heedless, immoderate, immoral, intemperate, lavish, lecherous, lewd, libertine, libidinous, licentious, loose, lubricious, lustful, malevolent, malicious, motiveless, needless, outrageous, promiscuous, rakish, rash, reckless, senseless, shameless, spiteful, uncalled-for, unchaste, unjustifiable, unjustified, unprovoked, unrestrained, vicious, wicked, wild, wilful.

n Casanova, debauchee, Don Juan, gammerstang, giglet, giglot, gillet, gillflirt, harlot, jillet, jillflirt, lecher, libertine, mort, profligate, prostitute, rake, roué, slut, strumpet, tart, trollop, voluptuary, whore.

**war** n battle, bloodshed, combat, conflict, contention, contest, enmity, fighting, hostilities, hostility, jihad, strife, struggle, ultima ratio regum, warfare.

*antonym* peace.

v battle, clash, combat, contend, contest, fight, skirmish, strive, struggle, take up arms, wage war.

**war cry** battle cry, rallying-cry, slogan, war-song, war-whoop, watchword.

**warble** v chirp, chirrup, quaver, sing, trill, twitter, yodel.

n call, chirp, chirrup, cry, quaver, song, trill, twitter.

**ward** n apartment, area, care, charge, cubicle, custody, dependant, district, division, guardianship, keeping, minor, precinct, protection, protégé, pupil, quarter, room, safe-keeping, vigil, watch, zone.

**ward off** avert, avoid, beat off, block, deflect, disperse, evade, fend off, forestall, parry, repel, repulse, stave off, thwart, turn aside, turn away.

**warden** *n* administrator, captain, caretaker, castellan, châtelaine, concierge, curator, custodian, guardian, janitor, keeper, ranger, steward, superintendent, warder, watchman.

**warder** *n* custodian, gaoler, guard, jailer, keeper, prison officer, screw, turnkey, wardress.

**wardrobe** *n* apparel, attire, closet, clothes, cupboard, garderobe, outfit.

**warehouse** *n* depository, depot, entrepot, freightshed, godown, hong, repository, stockroom, store, storehouse.

**wares** *n* commodities, goods, lines, manufactures, merchandise, produce, products, stock, stuff, vendibles.

**warfare** *n* arms, battle, blows, combat, conflict, contention, contest, discord, fighting, hostilities, passage of arms, strife, struggle, war.

*antonyms* harmony, peace.

**warily** *adv* apprehensively, cagily, carefully, cautiously, charily, circumspectly, distrustfully, gingerly, guardedly, hesitantly, leerily, suspiciously, uneasily, vigilantly, watchfully.

*antonyms* heedlessly, recklessly, thoughtlessly, unwarily.

**wariness** *n* alertness, apprehension, attention, caginess, care, carefulness, caution, circumspection, discretion, distrust, foresight, heedfulness, hesitancy, mindfulness, prudence, suspicion, unease, vigilance, watchfulness.

*antonyms* heedlessness, recklessness, thoughtlessness.

**warlike** *adj* aggressive, antagonistic, bellicose, belligerent, bloodthirsty, combative, hawkish, hostile, inimical, jingoistic, martial, militaristic, military, pugnacious, sabre-rattling, truculent, unfriendly.

*antonym* peaceable.

**warlock** *n* conjurer, demon, enchanter, magician, magus, necromancer, sorcerer, witch, wizard.

**warm** *adj* affable, affectionate, amiable, amorous, animated, ardent, balmy, calid, cheerful, cordial, dangerous, disagreeable, earnest, effusive, emotional, enthusiastic, excited, fervent, friendly, genial, glowing, happy, hazardous, hearty, heated, hospitable, impassioned, incalescent, intense, irascible, irritable, keen, kindly, lively, loving, lukewarm, passionate, perilous, pleasant, quick, sensitive, short, spirited, stormy, sunny, tender, tepid, thermal, touchy, tricky, uncomfortable, unpleasant, vehement, vigorous, violent, zealous.

*antonyms* cool, indifferent, unfriendly.

*v* animate, awaken, excite, heat, heat up, interest, melt, mull, put some life into, reheat, rouse, stimulate, stir, thaw, turn on.

*antonym* cool.

**warm-blooded** *adj* ardent, earnest, emotional, enthusiastic, excitable, fervent, homothermic, homothermous, hot-blooded, idiothermous, impetuous, lively, passionate, rash, red-blooded, spirited, vivacious.

**warm-hearted** *adj* affectionate, ardent, compassionate, cordial, generous, genial, kind-hearted, kindly, loving, sympathetic, tender, tender-hearted.

*antonyms* cold, unsympathetic.

**warmth** *n* affability, affection, amorousness, animation, ardour, calidity, cheerfulness, cordiality, eagerness, earnestness, effusiveness, empressement, enthusiasm, excitement, fervency, fervour, fire, happiness, heartiness, heat, hospitableness, hotness, intensity, kindliness, love, passion, spirit, tenderness, transport, vehemence, vigour, violence, warmness, zeal, zest.

*antonyms* coldness, coolness, unfriendliness.

**warn** *v* admonish, advise, alert, apprise, caution, counsel, forewarn, inform, notify, put on one's guard, tip off.

**warning** *n* admonishment, admonition, advance notice, advice, alarm, alert, augury, caution, caveat, forenotice, foretoken, forewarning, griffin, hint, larum, larum-bell, lesson, monition, notice, notification, omen, premonition, presage, prodrome, sign, signal, siren, threat, tip, tip-off, token, vigia, word, word to the wise.

*adj* admonitory, aposematic, cautionary, in terrorem, monitive, monitory, ominous, premonitory, prodromal, prodromic, threatening.

**warp** *v* bend, contort, deform, deviate, distort, kink, misshape, pervert, twist.

*antonym* straighten.

*n* bend, bent, bias, contortion, deformation, deviation, distortion, irregularity, kink, perversion, quirk, turn, twist.

**warrant** *n* authorisation, authority, commission, guarantee, licence, permission, permit, pledge, sanction, security, voucher, warranty.

*v* affirm, answer for, approve, assure, attest, authorise, avouch, be bound, call for, certify, commission, declare, demand, empower, entitle, excuse, guarantee, justify, license, necessitate, permit, pledge, require, sanction, secure, underwrite, uphold, vouch for.

**warrantable** *adj* accountable, allowable, defensible, excusable, justifiable, lawful, legal, necessary, permissible, proper, reasonable, right.

*antonyms* indefensible, unjustifiable, unwarrantable.

**warranty** *n* assurance, authorisation, bond, certificate, contract, covenant, guarantee, justification, pledge.

**warring** *adj* at daggers drawn, at war, belligerent, combatant, conflicting, contending, embattled, fighting, hostile, opposed, opposing.

**warrior** *n* champion, combatant, fighter, fighting man, gallo(w)glass, ghazi, man-at-arms, soldier, wardog, war-horse.

**wart** *n* excrescence, growth, lump, protuberance, verruca.

**wary** *adj* alert, apprehensive, attentive, cagey, careful, cautious, chary, circumspect, distrustful, guarded, hawk-eyed, heedful, leery, on one's guard, on the lookout, on the qui vive, prudent, suspicious, vigilant, watchful, wide-awake.

*antonyms* careless, foolhardy, heedless, reckless, unwary.

**wash**[1] *v* bath, bathe, clean, cleanse, launder, moisten, rinse, scrub, shampoo, shower, sluice, swill, wet.

*n* a lick and a promise, ablution, bath, bathe, cleaning, cleansing, coat, coating, ebb and flow, film, flow, laundering, layer, overlay, rinse, roll, screen, scrub, shampoo, shower, souse, stain, suffusion, surge, sweep, swell, washing, wave.

**wash one's hands** abandon, abdicate responsibility, give up on, have nothing to do with, leave to one's own devices.

**wash**[2] *v* bear examination, bear scrutiny, carry weight, hold up, hold water, pass muster, stand up, stick.

**washed-out** *adj* all in, blanched, bleached, colourless, dead on one's feet, dog-tired, drained, drawn, etiolated, exhausted, faded, fatigued, flat, haggard, knackered, lacklustre, mat, pale, pallid, peelie-wally, spent, tired-out, wan, weary, worn-out.

**wash-out** *n* disappointment, disaster, dud, failure, fiasco, flop, incompetent, lead balloon, lemon, loser, mess.

*antonyms* success, triumph, winner.

**waspish** *adj* bad-tempered, bitchy, cantankerous, captious, crabbed, crabby, cross, crotchety, fretful, grouchy, grumpy, ill-tempered, irascible, irritable, peevish, peppery, pettish, petulant, prickly, snappish, splenetic, testy, touchy, waxy.

**waste** *v* atrophy, blow, consume, corrode, crumble, debilitate, decay, decline, deplete, despoil, destroy, devastate, disable, dissipate, drain, dwindle, eat away, ebb, emaciate, enfeeble, exhaust, fade, fritter away, gnaw, lavish, lay waste, misspend, misuse, perish, pillage, prodigalise, rape, ravage, raze, rig, ruin, sack, sink, spend, spoil, squander, tabefy, throw away, undermine, wane, wanton, wear out, wither.

*n* debris, desert, desolation, destruction, devastation, dissipation, dregs, dross, effluent, expenditure, extravagance, garbage, havoc, leavings, leftovers, litter, loss, misapplication, misuse, mullock, offal, offscouring(s), prodigality, ravage, recrement, refuse, rubbish, ruin, scrap, slops, solitude, spoilage, squandering, sweepings, trash, void, wastefulness, wasteland, wild, wilderness.

*adj* bare, barren, desolate, devastated, dismal, dreary, empty, extra, left-over, superfluous, supernumerary, uncultivated, uninhabited, unproductive, unprofitable, unused, unwanted, useless, wild, worthless.

**wasted** *adj* abandoned, atrophied, cadaverous, debauched, depleted, dissipated, dissolute, emaciated, exhausted, finished, gaunt, profligate, shrivelled, shrunken, spent, tabescent, tabid, wanton, war-worn, washed-out, withered.

*antonyms* healthy, robust.

**wasteful** *adj* dissipative, extravagant, improvident, lavish, prodigal, profligate, ruinous, spendthrift, thriftless, uneconomical, unthrifty.

*antonyms* economical, frugal, thrifty.

**wasteland** *n* barrenness, desert, solitude, void, waste, wilderness, wild(s).

**waster** *n* drone, good-for-nothing, idler, layabout, loafer, lounger, malingerer, ne'er-do-well, profligate, shirker, skiver, spendthrift, wastrel.

*antonym* worker.

**wasting** *n* atrophy, degeneration, dystrophy, emaciation, marasmus, tubefaction, tubes, tubescence.

*adj* destroying, devastating, dystrophic, emaciating, enfeebling, marasmic, tubescent, tubetic, tubid.

*antonym* strengthening.

**watch**[1] *v* attend, contemplate, eye, gaze at, guard, keep, keep an eye open, look, look after, look at, look on, look out, mark, mind, note, observe, ogle, pay attention, peer at, protect, regard, see, spectate, stare at, superintend, take care of, take heed, tend, view, wait.

*n* alertness, attention, eye, heed, inspection, lookout, notice, observation, pernoctation, supervision, surveillance, vigil, vigilance, wake, watchfulness.

**watch out** have a care, keep a weather eye open, keep one's eyes open, keep one's eyes peeled, keep one's eyes skinned, mind oneself.

**watch over** defend, guard, keep an eye on, look after, mind, preserve, protect, shelter, shield, stand guard over, tend.

**watch**[2] *n* chronometer, clock, ticker, tick-tick, tick-tock, timepiece, wristwatch.

**watch-dog** *n* custodian, guard dog, guardian, house-dog, inspector, monitor, ombudsman, protector, scrutineer, vigilante.

**watcher** *n* Argus, looker-on, lookout, member of the audience, observer, onlooker, peeping Tom, spectator, spy, viewer, voyeur, witness.

**watchful** *adj* alert, attentive, cautious, circumspect, guarded, heedful, observant, on one's guard, on the lookout, on the qui vive, on the watch, suspicious, unmistaking, vigilant, wary, wide awake.

*antonym* inattentive.

**watchfulness** *n* alertness, attention, attentiveness, caution, cautiousness, circumspection, heedfulness, suspicion, suspiciousness, vigilance, wariness.

*antonym* inattention.

**watchman** *n* caretaker, custodian, guard, security guard, security man, sentry, wakeman.

**watchword** *n* battle-cry, buzz-word, byword, catch phrase, catchword, countersign, magic word, maxim, motto, password, rallying-cry, shibboleth, signal, slogan.

**water** *n* Adam's ale, Adam's wine, aqua, lake, ocean, rain, river, saliva, sea, stream, sweat, tears, urine.

*v* adulterate, damp, dampen, dilute, douse, drench, drink, flood, hose, irrigate, moisten, soak, souse, spray, sprinkle, thin, water down, weaken.

*antonyms* dry out, purify, strengthen.

**water down** adulterate, dilute, mitigate, mix, qualify, soften, thin, tone down, water, weaken.

*antonyms* purify, strengthen.

**water-closet** *n* bog, cludge, convenience, gents', head, john, ladies', lav, lavatory, loo, powder-room, privy, public convenience, toilet, urinal, wash-room, WC.

**watercourse** *n* arroyo, channel, ditch, khor, river, stream, wadi, water-channel.

**water-diviner** *n* dowser, water-finder.

**waterfall** *n* cascade, cataract, chute, fall, force, lash, lin(n), torrent.

**water-power** *n* white coal.

**waterproof** *adj* coated, damp-proof, impermeable, impervious, proofed, rubberised, water-repellent, water-resistant.

*antonym* leaky.

**watertight** *adj* airtight, firm, flawless, foolproof, hermetic, impregnable, incontrovertible, sound, unassailable, waterproof.

*antonyms* leaky, unsound.

**watery** *adj* adulterated, aqueous, damp, dilute, diluted, flavourless, fluid, humid, hydatoid, insipid, liquid, marshy, moist, poor, rheumy, runny, soggy, squelchy, tasteless, tear-filled, tearful, thin, washy, watered-down, waterish, weak, weepy, wet, wishy-washy.

*antonyms* solid, strong.

**wave**[1] *v* beckon, brandish, direct, flap, flourish, flutter, gesticulate, gesture, indicate, oscillate, quiver, ripple, shake, sign, signal, stir, sway, swing, undulate, waft, wag, waver, weave, wield.

**wave**[2] *n* billow, breaker, comber, current, drift, flood, ground swell, movement, outbreak, rash, ripple, roller, rush, stream, surge, sweep, swell, tendency, tidal wave, trend, tsunami, undulation, unevenness, upsurge, water-wave, wavelet, white horse.

**waver** *v* blow hot and cold, dither, falter, flicker, fluctuate, haver, hesitate, hum and haw, quiver, reel, rock, seesaw, shake, shilly-shally, sway, swither, totter, tremble, undulate, vacillate, vary, waffle, wave, weave, wobble.

*antonyms* decide, stand.

**waverer** *n* ditherer, doubter, haverer, invertebrate, shilly-shallier, wobbler.

**wavering** *adj* dithering, dithery, doubtful, doubting, havering, hesitant, in two minds, shilly-shallying.

*antonym* determined.

**wavy** *adj* curly, curvy, flamboyanat, ridged, ridgy, rippled, ripply, sinuate(d), sinuous, undate, undulate, undulated, winding, wrinkled, zigzag.

*antonyms* flat, smooth.

**wax** *v* become, develop, dilate, enlarge, expand, fill out, grow, increase, magnify, mount, rise, swell.

*antonym* wane.

**waxen** *adj* anaemic, ashen, bloodless, colourless, ghastly, livid, pale, pallid, wan, white, whitish.

*antonym* ruddy.

**waxy** *adj* ceraceous, cereous, impressible, impressionable, pallid, pasty, soft, waxen.

**way** *n* access, advance, aim, ambition, approach, aspect, avenue, channel, characteristic, choice, circumstance, condition, conduct, course, custom, demand, desire, detail, direction, distance, elbow-room, fashion, feature, fettle, gate, goal, habit, headway, highway, idiosyncrasy, journey, lane, length, manner, march, means, method, mode, movement, nature, opening, particular, passage, path, pathway, personality, plan, pleasure, point, practice, procedure, process, progress, respect, road, room, route, scheme, sense, shape, situation, space, state, status, street, stretch, style, system, technique, thoroughfare, track, trail, trait, usage, will, wish, wont.

**way of life** life-style, modus vivendi.

**wayfarer** *n* bird of passage, dusty-foot, globetrotter, gypsy, itinerant, journeyer, nomad, piepowder, rover, traveller, trekker, viator, voyager, walker, wanderer.

*antonyms* resident, stay-at-home.

**wayfaring** *adj* drifting, itinerant, journeying, multivagant, nomadic, peripatetic, rambling, roving, travelling, viatorial, voyaging, walking, wandering.

*antonyms* resident, stay-at-home.

**waylay** *v* accost, ambush, attack, buttonhole, catch, hold up, intercept, lie in wait for, seize, set upon, surprise.

**way-out** *adj* advanced, amazing, avant-garde, bizarre, crazy, eccentric, excellent, experimental, fantastic, far-out, freaky, great, marvellous, off-beat, outlandish, progressive, satisfying, tremendous, unconventional, unorthodox, unusual, weird, wild, wonderful.

*antonym* ordinary.

**ways and means** capability, capacity, capital, cash, funds, methods, procedure, resources, resources, tools, way, wherewithal.

**wayward** *adj* capricious, changeable, contrary, contumacious, cross-grained, disobedient, erratic, fickle, flighty, froward, headstrong, inconstant, incorrigible, insubordinate, intractable, mulish, obdurate, obstinate, perverse, rebellious, refractory, self-willed, stubborn, undependable, ungovernable, unmanageable, unpredictable, unruly, uppity, wilful.

*antonyms* complaisant, good-natured.

**weak** *adj* anaemic, asthenic, atonic, cowardly, debile, debilitated, decrepit, defenceless, deficient, delicate, diluted, disturbant, dull, effete, enervated, exhausted, exposed, faint, faulty, feeble, fibreless, flimsy, fragile, frail, helpless, hollow, imperceptible, impotent, inadequate, inconclusive, indecisive, ineffective, ineffectual, infirm, insipid, invalid, irresolute, lacking, lame, languid, low, milk-and-water, muffled, namby-pamby, pathetic, poor, powerless, puny, quiet, runny, shaky, shallow, sickly, slight, small, soft, spent, spineless, substandard, tasteless, tender, thin, timorous, toothless, unconvincing, under-strength, unguarded, unprotected, unresisting, unsafe, unsatisfactory, unsound, unsteady, unstressed, untenable, vulnerable, wanting, wasted, watery, weak-hearted, weak-kneed, weakly, weak-minded, weak-spirited, wishy-washy.

*antonym* strong.

**weaken** *v* abate, adulterate, craze, cut, debase, debilitate, depress, dilute, diminish, disinvigorate, droop, dwindle, ease up, effeminate, effeminise, emasculate, enervate, enfeeble, eunuchise, fade, fail, flag, give way, impair, invalidate, lessen, lower, mitigate, moderate, reduce, sap, soften up, temper, thin, tire, undermine, wane, water down.

*antonym* strengthen.

**weakening** *n* abatement, dilution, diminishment, dwindling, easing, fading, failing, flagging, labefactation, labefaction, lessening, lowering, moderation, reduction, waning.

*antonym* strengthening.

**weakling** *n* coward, doormat, drip, milksop, milquetoast, mouse, sissy, softling, underdog, underling, wally, weed, wet, wimp, windlestraw, wraith.

*antonyms* hero, stalwart.

**weakness** *n* Achilles' heel, asthenia, atonicity, atony, blemish, debility, decrepitude, defect, deficiency, enervation, enfeeblement, faible, failing, faintness, fault, feebleness, flaw, foible, fondness, fragility, frailty, imperfection, impotence, inclination, infirmity, irresolution, lack, liking, passion, penchant, powerlessness, predilection, proclivity, proneness, shortcoming, soft spot, soft underbelly, underbelly, vulnerability, weakpoint, weediness.

*antonyms* dislike, strength.

**weak-willed** *adj* complaisant, compliant, faint-hearted, irresolute, persuadable, persuasible, pliable, pusillanimous, spineless, submissive, weak-hearted, weak-kneed, weak-minded.

*antonym* strong-willed.

**weal** *n* cicatrice, cicatrix, contusion, mark, ridge, scar, streak, stripe, wale, welt, wheal, wound.

**wealth** *n* abundance, affluence, assets, bounty, capital, cash, copiousness, cornucopia, estate, fortune, fullness, funds, golden calf, goods, klondike, lucre, mammon, means, money, opulence, pelf, plenitude, plenty, possessions, profusion, property, prosperity, resources, riches, richness, store, substance.

*antonym* poverty.

**wealthy** *adj* affluent, comfortable, easy, filthy rich, flush, living in clover, loaded, moneyed, opulent, prosperous, rich, rolling in it, well-heeled, well-off, well-to-do.

*antonym* poor.

**wear** *v* abrade, accept, allow, annoy, bear, bear up, believe, brook, carry, consume, corrode, countenance, deteriorate, display, don, drain, dress in, endure, enervate, erode, exasperate, exhibit, fall for, fatigue, fly, fray, grind, harass, have on, hold up, irk, last, permit, pester, put on, put up with, rub, show, sport, stand for, stand up, stomach, swallow, take, tax, tolerate, undermine, use, vex, waste, weaken, weary.

*n* abrasion, apparel, attire, attrition, clothes, corrosion, costume, damage, depreciation, deterioration, dress, durability, employment, erosion, friction, garb, garments, gear, habit, mileage, outfit, service, things, use, usefulness, utility, wear and tear.

**wear down** abrade, chip away at, consume, corrode, diminish, erode, grind down, lessen, macerate, overcome, reduce, rub away, undermine.

**wear off** abate, abrade, decrease, diminish, disappear, dwindle, ebb, efface, fade, lessen, peter out, rub away, subside, wane, weaken.

*antonym* increase.

**wear out** consume, deteriorate, enervate, erode, exhaust, fag out, fatigue, fray, impair, knacker, prostrate, rub through, sap, tire (out), tucker (out), use up, wear through, weary.

*antonyms* refresh, replenish.

**weariness** *n* drowsiness, enervation, ennui, exhaustion, fatigue, languor, lassitude, lethargy, listlessness, prostration, sleepiness, tiredness.

*antonym* freshness.

**wearing** *adj* abradant, abrasive, exasperating, exhausting, fatiguing, irksome, oppressive, taxing, tiresome, tiring, trying, wearisome.

*antonym* refreshing.

**wearisome** *adj* annoying, boring, bothersome, burdensome, dreary, dull, ennuying, exasperating, exhausting, fatiguing, humdrum, irksome, monotonous, oppressive, pestilential, prolix, prosaic, protracted, tedious, troublesome, trying, vexatious, weariful, wearing.

*antonym* refreshing.

**weary** *adj* all in, arduous, aweared, aweary, beat, bored, browned-off, dead beat, dead on one's feet, discontented, dog-tired, drained, drooping, drowsy, enervated, enervative, ennuied, ennuyé, exhausted, fagged, fatigued, fed up, flagging, impatient, indifferent, irksome, jaded, knackered, laborious, sick, sick and tired, sleepy, spent, taxing, tired, tiresome, tiring, wayworn, wearied, wearing, wearisome, whacked, worn out.

*antonyms* excited, fresh, lively.

*v* annoy, betoil, bore, bug, burden, debilitate, drain, droop, enervate, ennui, exasperate, fade, fag, fail, fatigue, irk, irritate, jade, plague, sap, sicken, tax, tire, tire out, wear out.

**wearying** *adj* ennuying, exhausting, fatiguing, taxing, tiring, trying, wearing, wearisome.

*antonym* refreshing.

**weather** *n* climate, conditions, rainfall, temperature.

*v* brave, come through, endure, expose, harden, live through, overcome, pull through, resist, ride out, rise above, season, stand, stick out, suffer, surmount, survive, toughen, weather out, withstand.

*antonym* succumb.

**weave** *v* blend, braid, build, construct, contrive, create, criss-cross, entwine, fabricate, fuse, incorporate, intercross, interdigitate, interlace, intermingle, intertwine, introduce, knit, make, mat, merge, plait, put together, spin, twist, unite, wind, zigzag.

**weaver** *n* brabener, wabster, webster.

**web** *n* interlacing, lattice, mesh, mesh-work, net, netting, network, palama, screen, snare, tangle, tela, texture, toils, trap, weave, webbing, weft.

**wed** *v* ally, blend, coalesce, combine, commingle, dedicate, espouse, fuse, get hitched, interweave, join, jump the broomstick, link, marry, merge, splice, tie the knot, unify, unite, wive, yoke.

*antonym* divorce.

**wedding** *n* bridal, espousals, marriage, matrimony, nuptials.

*antonym* divorce.

*adj* bridal, epithalamial, epithalamic, hymeneal, hymenean, marriage, matrimonial, nuptial.

**wedge** *n* block, chock, chunk, cleat, lump, wodge.

*v* block, cram, crowd, force, jam, lodge, pack, push, ram, squeeze, stuff, thrust.

*antonyms* dislodge, space out, take out.

**wedlock** *n* holy matrimony, marriage, matrimony, union.

**wee** *adj* diminutive, insignificant, itsy-bitsy, Lilliputian, little, microscopic, midget, miniature, minuscule, minute, negligible, small, teeny, teeny-weeny, tiny, weeny.

*antonym* large.

**weed** *v* hoe.

**weed out** eliminate, eradicate, extirpate, get rid of, purge, remove, root out.

*antonyms* add, fix, infiltrate.

**weedy** *adj* feeble, frail, ineffectual, insipid, lanky, namby-pamby, puny, skinny, thin, undersized, ungainly, weak, weak-kneed, wet, white-shoe, wimpish.

*antonym* strong.

**week** *n* hebdomad, sennight.

**weekly** *adv* by the week, every week, hebdomadally, once a week.

*adj* hebdomadal, hebdomadary.

**weep** *v* bemoan, bewail, blub, blubber, boo-hoo, bubble, complain, cry, drip, exude, greet, keen, lament, leak, moan, mourn, ooze, pipe, pipe one's eye, pour forth, pour out, rain, snivel, sob, tune one's pipes, ululate, whimper, whinge.

*antonym* rejoice.

*n* blub, bubble, cry, greet, lament, moan, snivel, sob.

**weepie** *n* melodrama, sob-stuff, tear-jerker.

**weepy** *adj* blubbering, crying, labile, lachrymose, sobbing, tearful, teary, weeping.

*antonym* dry-eyed.

**weigh** *v* bear down, burden, carry weight, consider, contemplate, count, deliberate, evaluate, examine, give thought to, impress, matter, meditate on, mull over, oppress, ponder, ponderate, prey, reflect on, study, tell, think over.

*antonyms* cut no ice, hearten.

**weigh down** afflict, bear down, burden, depress, get down, load, oppress, overburden, overload, press down, trouble, weigh upon, worry.

*antonyms* hearten, lighten, refresh.

**weigh up** assess, chew over, cogitate, consider, contemplate, deliberate, discuss, examine, mull over, perpend, ponder, ruminate on, think over.

**weight** *n* authority, avoirdupois, ballast, burden, clout, consequence, consideration, efficacy, emphasis, force, gravity, heaviness, heft, impact, import, importance, impressiveness, influence, load, mass, millstone, moment, onus, oppression, persuasiveness, ponderance, ponderancy, poundage, power, preponderance, pressure, significance, strain, substance, tonnage, value.

*antonym* lightness.

*v* ballast, bias, burden, charge, encumber, freight, handicap, hold down, impede, keep down, load, oppress, overburden, slant, unbalance, weigh down.

*antonym* lighten.

**weightless** *adj* airy, imponderous, insubstantial, light, unsubstantial.

*antonym* heavy.

**weighty** *adj* backbreaking, burdensome, consequential, considerable, critical, crucial, crushing, cumbersome, demanding, dense, difficult, exacting, forcible, grave, heavy, hefty, important, leading, massive, momentous, onerous, oppressive, ponderous, portentous, respected, revered, serious, significant, solemn, substantial, taxing, worrisome, worrying.

*antonyms* trivial, unimportant.

**weir** *n* dam, fence, garth, lash, wear.

**weird** *adj* bizarre, creepy, eerie, eldritch, freakish, ghostly, grotesque, mysterious, odd, outlandish, preternatural, queer, spooky, strange, superlunar, supernatural, uncanny, unco, unearthly, unnatural, witching.

*antonym* normal.

**weirdo** *n* crackpot, crank, cure, eccentric, freak, fruitcake, loony, nut, nutcase, nutter, oddball, queer fish, weirdie.

**welcome** *adj* able, acceptable, accepted, agreeable, allowed, appreciated, delightful, desirable, entitled, free, gratifying, permitted, pleasant, pleasing, refreshing.

*antonym* unwelcome.

*n* acceptance, greeting, hospitality, reception, red carpet, salaam, salutation.

*v* accept, approve of, embrace, greet, hail, meet, receive, roll out the red carpet for.

*antonyms* reject, snub.

**weld** *v* bind, bond, cement, connect, fuse, join, link, seal, solder, unite.

*antonym* separate.

*n* bond, joint, seal, seam.

**welfare** *n* advantage, benefit, good, happiness, heal, health, interest, profit, prosperity, success, weal, well-being.

*antonym* harm.

**well**[1] *n* bore, cavity, fount, fountain, hole, lift-shaft, mine, pit, pool, repository, shaft, source, spring, waterhole, well-spring.

*v* brim over, flood, flow, gush, jet, ooze, pour, rise, run, seep, spout, spring, spurt, stream, surge, swell, trickle.

**well**[2] *adv* ably, abundantly, accurately, adeptly, adequately, admirably, agreeably, amply, approvingly, attentively, capitally, carefully, clearly, closely, comfortably, completely, conscientiously, considerably, correctly, deeply, easily, effectively, efficiently, expertly, fairly, famously, favourably, fittingly, flourishingly, fully, glowingly, graciously, greatly, happily, heartily, highly, intimately, justly, kindly, nicely, personally, pleasantly, possibly, proficiently, profoundly, properly, prosperously, readily, rightly, satisfactorily, skilfully, smoothly, splendidly, substantially, successfully, sufficiently, suitably, thoroughly, warmly.

*antonym* badly.

*adj* A1, able-bodied, advisable, agreeable, bright, fine, fit, fitting, flourishing, fortunate, good, great, hale, happy, healthy, hearty, in fine fettle, in good health, lucky, on the top of the world, pleasing, profitable, proper, prudent, right, robust, satisfactory, sound, strong, thriving, up to par, useful.

*antonyms* bad, ill.

**well done!** brava, bravo, euge.

**well-balanced** *adj* graceful, harmonious, judicious, level-headed, nutritious, proportional, rational, reasonable, sane, sensible, sober, sound, symmetrical, together, well-adjusted, well-proportioned.

*antonym* unbalanced.

**well-being** *n* comfort, contentment, good, happiness, prosperity, weal, welfare.

*antonyms* discomfort, harm.

**well-bred** *adj* aristocratic, blue-blooded, civil, courteous, courtly, cultivated, cultured, gallant, genteel, gentle, gentlemanly, highborn, ladylike, mannerly, noble, patrician, polished, polite, refined, titled, upper-crust, urbane, well-born, well-brought-up, well-mannered.

*antonym* ill-bred.

**well-deserved** *adj* appropriate, condign, deserved, due, just, justified, meet, merited, rightful.

*antonym* undeserved.

**well-disposed** *adj* agreeable, amicable, favourable, friendly, sympathetic, well-aimed, well-arranged, well-minded, well-placed.

*antonym* ill-disposed.

**well-dressed** *adj* dapper, natty, neat, smart, spruce, tidy, trim, well-groomed.

*antonym* scruffy.

**well-equipped** *adj* well-appointed, well-found.

**well-known** *adj* celebrated, famed, familiar, famous, illustrious, notable, noted, popular, renowned.

*antonym* unknown.

**well-off** *adj* affluent, comfortable, flourishing, flush, fortunate, in the money, loaded, lucky, moneyed, prosperous, rich, successful, thriving, warm, wealthy, well-heeled, well-to-do.

*antonym* poor.

**well-thought-of** *adj* admired, esteemed, highly regarded, honoured, reputable, respected, revered, venerated, weighty.

*antonym* despised.

**well-to-do** *adj* affluent, comfortable, flush, loaded, moneyed, prosperous, rich, warm, wealthy, well-heeled, well-off.

*antonym* poor.

**well-wisher** *n* fan, supporter, sympathiser, well-willer.

**well-worn** *adj* bromidic, commonplace, hackneyed, overused, stale, stereotyped, threadbare, timeworn, tired, trite.

*antonym* original.

**welsh** *v* cheat, defraud, diddle, do, swindle, welch.

**welt** *n* cicatrice, cicatrix, contusion, mark, ridge, scar, streak, stripe, wale, weal, wheal.

**welter** *v* billow, flounder, heave, lie, pitch, roll, splash, stumble, toss, tumble, wade, wallow, writhe.

*n* confusion, hotchpotch, jumble, mess, mish-mash, mixter-maxter, muddle, tangle, web.

**wend one's way** go, hike, meander, move, plod, proceed, progress, travel, trudge, walk, wander.

*antonym* stay.

**werewolf** *n* lycanthrope, lycanthropist, werwolf.

**western** *adj* Hesperian, occidental.

*antonym* eastern.

*n* horse opera, spaghetti western.

**wet** *adj* boggy, clammy, damp, dank, drenched, dripping, drizzling, effete, feeble, foolish, humid, ineffectual, irresolute, misty, moist, moistened, namby-pamby, pouring, raining, rainy, saturated, showery, silly, sloppy, soaked, soaking, sodden, soft, soggy, sopping, soppy, soused, spineless, spongy, teeming, timorous, waterlogged, watery, weak, weedy, white-shoe, wimpish, wimpy.

*antonyms* dry, resolute, strong.

*n* clamminess, condensation, damp, dampness, drip, drizzle, humidity, liquid, milksop, milquetoast, moisture, rain, rains, sap, water, weakling, weed, wetness, wimp.

*antonym* dryness.

*v* bedabble, bedew, bedrench, damp, dampen, dip, douse, drench, humidify, imbue, irrigate, moisten, saturate, sluice, soak, splash, spray, sprinkle, steep, water.

*antonym* dry.

**wet behind the ears** callow, green, immature, inexperienced, innocent, naïve, new, raw, untrained.

*antonym* experienced.

**wetness** *n* clamminess, condensation, damp, dampness, dankness, humidity, liquid, moisture, soddenness, sogginess, water, wet.

*antonym* dryness.

**wet-nurse** *n* amah.

**whack** *v* bang, bash, beat, belabour, belt, biff, box, buffet, clobber, clout, cuff, hit, lambaste, rap, slap, slug, smack, sock, strike, thrash, thump, thwack, wallop, whale, whang.

*n* allotment, attempt, bang, bash, belt, biff, bit, blow, box, buffet, clout, crack, cuff, cut, go, hit, part, portion, quota, rap, share, shot, slap, slug, smack, sock, stab, stroke, thump, thwack, try, turn, wallop, wham, whang.

**wham** *n* bang, bash, blow, clout, concussion, hit, impact, slam, smack, splat, thump, thwack, wallop, whack, whang.

**wharf** *n* dock, dockyard, jetty, landing-stage, marina, pier, quay, quayside.

**what's-its-name** *n* dingus, doodad, jigamaree, jiggumbob, thingumajig, thingumbob, thingummy, what-d'ye-call-it, whatsit, what-you-may-call-it.

**wheedle** *v* cajole, charm, coax, court, draw, entice, flatter, importune, inveigle, persuade, whilly, whillywha(w).

*antonym* force.

**wheel** *n* birl, circle, gyration, pivot, revolution, roll, rotation, spin, turn, twirl, whirl.

*v* birl, circle, gyrate, orbit, pirouette, revolve, roll, rotate, spin, swing, swivel, turn, twirl, whirl.

**wheelbarrow** *n* ball-barrow, barrow, hand-cart, monotroch.

**wheeze**[1] *v* cough, gasp, hiss, rasp, whiss, whistle, whiz(z).

*n* cough, gasp, hiss, rasp, whistle, whiz(z).

**wheeze**[2] *n* anecdote, catch-phrase, chestnut, crack, expedient, gag, idea, joke, one-liner, plan, ploy, practical joke, prank, ruse, scheme, story, stunt, trick, wrinkle.

**whereabouts** *n* location, place, position, site, situation, vicinity.

**wherewithal** *n* capital, cash, funds, means, money, necessary, readies, resources, supplies.

**whet** *v* acuminate, arouse, awaken, file, grind, hone, incite, increase, kindle, pique, provoke, quicken, rouse, sharpen, stimulate, stir, strop, titillate.

*antonyms* blunt, dampen.

**whiff** *n* aroma, blast, breath, draught, gale, gust, hint, niff, odour, pong, puff, reek, scent, smell, sniff, stench, stink.

**whim** *n* caprice, chimera, conceit, concetto, crank, craze, crotchet, fad, fancy, fizgig, flam, freak, humour, impulse, maggot, notion, quirk, sport, urge, vagary, whims(e)y.

**whimper** *v* blub, blubber, cry, girn, grizzle, mewl, moan, pule, snivel, sob, weep, whine, whinge.

*n* girn, moan, snivel, sob, whine.

**whimsical** *adj* capricious, chimeric(al), crotchety, curious, dotty, droll, eccentric, fanciful, fantastic(al), freakish, funny, Gilbertian, maggoty, mischievous, odd, peculiar, playful, quaint, queer, singular, unusual, waggish, weird, whimmy.

*antonym* sensible.

**whine** *n* beef, belly-ache, complaint, cry, girn, gripe, grouch, grouse, grumble, moan, sob, wail, whimper.

*v* beef, belly-ache, carp, complain, cry, girn, gripe, grizzle, grouch, grouse, grumble, kvetch, moan, sob, wail, whimper, whinge.

**whinge** *v* beef, belly-ache, carp, complain, gripe, grouse, grumble, kvetch, moan.

*n* beef, belly-ache, complaint, gripe, grouse, grumble, moan.

**whip** *v* agitate, beat, best, birch, cane, castigate, clobber, compel, conquer, dart, dash, defeat, dive, drive, drub, flagellate, flash, flit, flog, flounce, fly, foment, goad, hammer, hound, incite, instigate, jambok, jerk, knout, k(o)urbash, lash, leather, lick, outdo, overcome, overpower, overwhelm, paddle, prick, prod, produce, provoke, pull, punish, push, quirt, remove, rout, rush, scourge, shoot, sjambok, snatch, spank, spur, stir, strap, switch, tan, tear, thrash, trounce, urge, whale, whisk, whop, worst.

*n* birch, bullwhip, cane, cat, cat-o'-nine-tails, crop, flagellum, horsewhip, jambok, knout, k(o)urbash, lash, paddle, quirt, rawhide, riding-crop, scourge, sjambok, switch, thong.

**whip up** agitate, arouse, excite, foment, incite, inflame, instigate, kindle, provoke, psych up, stir up, work up.

*antonyms* dampen, deter.

**whippersnapper** *n* hobbledehoy, nipper, shaver, whiffet.

**whipping** *n* beating, belting, birching, caning, castigation, flagellation, flogging, hiding, lashing, leathering, paddling, punishment, quilting, spanking, tanning, thrashing.

**whirl** *v* birl, circle, gyrate, gyre, pirouette, pivot, reel, revolve, roll, rotate, spin, swirl, swivel, turn, twirl, twist, wheel.

*n* agitation, birl, bustle, circle, commotion, confusion, daze, dither, flurry, giddiness, gyration, gyre, hubbub, hubbuboo, hurly-burly, merry-go-round, pirouette, reel, revolution, roll, rotation, round, series, spin, stir, succession, swirl, tumult, turn, twirl, twist, uproar, vortex, wheel, whorl.

*antonym* calm.

**whirling** *adj* birling, gyral, gyrating, gyratory, pirouetting, pivoting, reeling, revolving, rotating, spinning, turning, twirling, vertiginous, vortical, vorticular, vorticuse, vortiginous, wheeling.

*antonym* stationary.

**whirlpool** *n* maelstrom, vortex, weel.

**whirlwind** *n* cyclone, dust-devil, tornado, vortex, waterspout.

*adj* hasty, headlong, impetuous, impulsive, lightning, precipitate, quick, rapid, rash, short, speedy, split-second, swift.

*antonyms* deliberate, slow.

**whisk** *v* beat, brush, dart, dash, flick, fly, grab, hasten, hurry, race, rush, scoot, shoot, speed, sweep, swipe, tear, twitch, whip, wipe.

*n* beater, brush, swizzle-stick.

**whisker** *n* bristle, hair, hair's breadth, vibrissa.

**whisk(e)y** *n* barley-bree, bourbon, John Barleycorn, malt, mountain dew, peat-reek, rye, Scotch, usquebaugh.

**whisper** *v* breathe, buzz, divulge, gossip, hint, hiss, insinuate, intimate, murmur, rustle, sigh, sough, susurrate, tittle.

*antonym* shout.

*n* breath, buzz, gossip, hint, hiss, innuendo, insinuation, murmur, report, rumour, rustle, shadow, sigh, sighing, soughing, soupçon, suggestion, suspicion, susurration, susurrus, swish, tinge, trace, underbreath, undertone, whiff, word.

*antonym* roar.

**whistle** *n* call, cheep, chirp, hooter, siren, song, warble.

*v* call, cheep, chirp, pipe, siffle, sing, warble, wheeze, whiss.

**whit** *n* atom, bit, crumb, damn, dash, drop, fragment, grain, hoot, iota, jot, little, mite, modicum, particle, piece, pinch, scrap, shred, speck, tittle, trace.

*antonym* lot.

**white** *adj* ashen, auspicious, bloodless, bright, canescent, Caucasian, clean, colourless, dealbate, favourable, ghastly, grey, grizzled, hoar, hoary, honest, immaculate, innocent, pale, pallid, pasty, pure, purified, reliable, silver, snowy, spotless, stainless, unblemished, unsullied, wan, waxen, whey-faced.

*antonyms* black, dark, dishonest, ruddy, unclean, unreliable.

*n* albumen, gub, gubbah, honkie, whitey.

**white-collar** *adj* clerical, executive, non-manual, office, professional, salaried.

*antonyms* blue-collar, manual.

**whiten** *v* blanch, bleach, blench, decolour, etiolate, fade, pale, whitewash.

*antonyms* blacken, colour, darken.

**whitewash**[1] *n* camouflage, concealment, cover-up, deception, extenuation.

*antonym* exposure.

*v* camouflage, conceal, cover up, euphemise, extenuate, gloss over, make light of, suppress.

*antonym* expose.

**whitewash**[2] *v* beat, best, clobber, crush, drub, hammer, lick, paste, thrash, trounce, whale.

**whitlow** *n* paronychia.

**whittle** *v* carve, consume, cut, destroy, diminish, eat away, erode, hew, pare, reduce, scrape, shape, shave, trim, undermine, wear away.

**whole** *adj* better, complete, cured, entire, faultless, fit, flawless, full, good, hale, healed, healthy, in one piece, intact, integral, integrate, inviolate, mint, perfect, recovered, robust, sound, strong, total, unabbreviated, unabridged, unbroken, uncut, undamaged, undivided, unedited, unexpurgated, unharmed, unhurt, unimpaired, uninjured, unmutilated, unscathed, untouched, well.

*antonyms* damaged, ill, partial.

*n* aggregate, all, ensemble, entirety, entity, everything, fullness, Gestalt, lot, piece, total, totality, unit, unity.

*antonym* part.

**whole-hearted** *adj* committed, complete, dedicated, determined, devoted, earnest, emphatic, enthusiastic, genuine, heartfelt, hearty, passionate, real, sincere, true, unfeigned, unqualified, unreserved, unstinting, warm, whole-souled, zealous.

*antonym* half-hearted.

**wholesale** *adj* broad, comprehensive, extensive, far-reaching, indiscriminate, mass, massive, sweeping, total, wide-ranging.

*antonym* partial.

*adv* comprehensively, en bloc, extensively, indiscriminately, massively, totally.

*antonym* partially.

**wholesome** *adj* advantageous, beneficial, clean, decent, edifying, exemplary, good, healthful, health-giving, healthy, helpful, honourable, hygienic, improving, innocent, invigorating, moral, nice, nourishing, nutritious, propitious, pure, respectable, righteous, salubrious, salutary, sanitary, squeaky-clean, uplifting, virtuous, worthy.

*antonym* unwholesome.

**wholly** *adv* absolutely, all, altogether, completely, comprehensively, entirely, exclusively, fully, in toto, only, perfectly, solely, thoroughly, through and through, totally, utterly.

*antonym* partly.

**whoop** *v, n* cheer, cry, holler, hoop, hoot, hurrah, roar, scream, shout, shriek, yell.

**whooping-cough** *n* pertussis.

**whopper** *n* colossus, cracker, fable, fabrication, fairy story, falsehood, giant, lie, monster, plumper, tall story, untruth.

**whopping** *adj* big, enormous, extraordinary, giant, gigantic, great, huge, large, mammoth, massive, mighty, monstrous, monumental, prodigious, staggering, tremendous, whacking.

*antonym* tiny.

**whore** *n* brass, broad, call girl, courtesan, demimondaine, demirep, drab, fallen woman, fille de joie, harlot, hooker, hustler, loon, loose fish, lorette, Paphian, prostitute, scarlet woman, strange woman, street-walker, strumpet, succubus, tart, tramp, trollop, waistcoateer, wench, woman of the town, working girl.

**whorehouse** *n* bagnio, bawdy-house, bordello, brothel, cat-house, house of ill repute, knocking-shop, stew.

**whorl** *n* coil, convolution, corkscrew, helix, spiral, turn, twist, vortex.

**wicked** *adj* abandoned, abominable, acute, agonising, amoral, arch, atrocious, awful, bad, black-hearted, bothersome, corrupt, debased, depraved, destructive, devilish, difficult, dissolute, distressing, dreadful, egregious, evil, facinorous, fearful, fiendish, fierce, flagitious, foul, galling, guilty, harmful, heinous, immoral, impious, impish, incorrigible, inexpiable, iniquitous, injurious, intense, irreligious, mighty, mischievous, nasty, naughty, nefarious, nefast, offensive, painful, piacular, rascal-like, rascally, roguish, scandalous, severe, shameful, sinful, spiteful, terrible, troublesome, trying, ungodly, unpleasant, unprincipled, unrighteous, vicious, vile, villainous, worthless.

*antonyms* good, harmless, modest, upright.

**wickedness** *n* abomination, amorality, atrocity, corruption, corruptness, depravity, devilishness, dissoluteness, enormity, evil, facinorousness, fiendishness, foulness, heinousness, immorality, impiety, iniquity, pravity, reprobacy, shamefulness, sin, sinfulness, unrighteousness, vileness, villainy.

*antonym* uprightness.

**wickerwork** *n* basket-work, wattle, wattle-work.

**wide** *adj* ample, away, baggy, broad, capacious, catholic, commodious, comprehensive, diffuse, dilated, distant, distended, encyclopaedic, expanded, expansive, extensive, far-reaching, full, general, immense, inclusive, large, latitudinous, loose, off, off-course, off-target, outspread, outstretched, remote, roomy, spacious, sweeping, vast.

*antonyms* limited, narrow.

*adv* aside, astray, off course, off target, off the mark, out.

*antonym* on target.

**wide-awake** *adj* alert, astute, aware, conscious, fully awake, heedful, keen, observant, on one's toes, on the alert, on the ball, on the qui vive, quick-witted, roused, sharp, vigilant, wakened, wary, watchful.

*antonym* asleep.

**widely** *adv* extensively, generally, ubiquitously, universally.

**widen** *v* broaden, dilate, distend, enlarge, expand, extend, open out, splay, spread, stretch.

*antonym* narrow.

**wide-open** *adj* defenceless, expansive, exposed, gaping, indeterminate, open, outspread, outstretched, splayed, spread, susceptible, uncertain, unfortified, unpredictable, unprotected, unsettled, vulnerable, wide.

*antonyms* closed, narrow.

**widespread** *adj* broad, common, epidemic, extensive, far-flung, far-reaching, general, pervasive, popular, prevailing, prevalent, rife, sweeping, universal, unlimited, wholesale.

*antonyms* limited, uncommon.

**widowed** *adj* bereaved, viduous.

**widowhood** *n* viduage, viduity.

**width** *n* amplitude, beam, breadth, compass, diameter, extent, girth, measure, range, reach, scope, span, thickness, wideness.

**wield** *v* apply, brandish, command, control, employ, exercise, exert, flourish, handle, have, hold, maintain, manage, manipulate, ply, possess, swing, use, utilise, wave, weave.

**wife** *n* better half, bride, consort, dutch, helpmate, helpmeet, little woman, mate, missis, missus, old lady, old woman, partner, rib, spouse, woman.

*antonym* husband.

**wifely** *adj* uxorial.

**wig** *n* caxon, dalmahoy, gizz, Gregorian, hair-piece, jas(e)y, jazy, jiz, merkin, peruke, postiche, tie-wig, toupee.

**wiggle** *v, n* jerk, jiggle, shake, shimmy, squirm, twist, twitch, wag, waggle, wriggle, writhe.

**wild** *adj* agrest(i)al, barbaric, barbarous, berserk, blustery, boisterous, brutish, chaotic, chimeric(al), choppy, crazed, crazy, daft, delirious, demented, desert, deserted, desolate, dishevelled, disordered, disorderly, eager, empty, enthusiastic, excited, extravagant, fantastic, ferae naturae, feral, feralised, ferine, ferocious, fierce, flighty, foolhardy, foolish, frantic, free, frenzied, furious, giddy, god-forsaken, howling, hysterical, ill-considered, impetuous, impracticable, imprudent, inaccurate, indigenous, intense, irrational, lawless, mad, madcap, maniacal, native, natural, noisy, nuts, outrageous, potty, preposterous, primitive, rabid, raging, rash, raving, reckless, riotous, rough, rowdy, rude, savage, self-willed, tempestuous, tousled, trackless, turbulent, unbridled, unbroken, uncheated, uncivilised, uncontrollable, uncontrolled, uncultivated, undisciplined, undomesticated, unfettered, ungovernable, uninhabited, unjustified, unkempt, unmanageable, unpopulated, unpruned, unrestrained, unruly, unsubstantiated, untamed, untidy, uproarious, violent, virgin, wayward, woolly.

*antonyms* civilised, peaceful, sane, sensible, tame, unenthusiastic.

**wilderness** *n* clutter, confusion, congeries, desert, jumble, jungle, mass, maze, muddle, tangle, waste, wasteland, welter, wild, wild-land.

**wildlife** *n* animals, fauna.

**wilds** *n* back-veld, desert, outback, the back of beyond, the boondocks, the middle of nowhere, the sticks, wasteland, wilderness.

**wile** *n* artfulness, artifice, cheating, chicanery, contrivance, craft, craftiness, cunning, deceit, device, dodge, expedient, fraud, guile, hanky-panky, imposition, lure, manoeuvre, ploy, ruse, slyness, stratagem, subterfuge, trick, trickery.

*antonym* guilelessness.

**wilful** *adj* adamant, bloody-minded, bull-headed, conscious, deliberate, determined, dogged, froward, headstrong, inflexible, intended, intentional, intractable, intransigent, mulish, obdurate, obstinate, persistent, perverse, pig-headed, purposeful, refractory, self-willed, stubborn, thrawn, uncompromising, unyielding, volitional, voluntary.

*antonyms* complaisant, good-natured.

**will** *n* aim, attitude, choice, command, decision, declaration, decree, desire, determination, discretion, disposition, fancy, feeling, inclination, intention, mind, option, pleasure, preference, prerogative, purpose, resolution, resolve, testament, velleity, volition, will power, wish, wishes.

*v* bequeath, bid, cause, choose, command, confer, decree, desire, determine, devise, direct, dispose of, elect, give, leave, opt, ordain, order, pass on, resolve, transfer, want, wish.

**willing** *adj* agreeable, amenable, biddable, compliant, consenting, content, desirous, disposed, eager, enthusiastic, favourable, game, happy, inclined, nothing lo(a)th, pleased, prepared, ready, so-minded, volitient, willing-hearted.

*antonym* unwilling.

**willingly** *adv* by choice, cheerfully, eagerly, freely, gladly, happily, nothing lo(a)th, readily, unhesitatingly, voluntarily.

*antonym* unwillingly.

**willingness** n agreeableness, agreement, complaisance, compliance, consent, desire, disposition, enthusiasm, favour, inclination, volition, will, wish.

*antonym* unwillingness.

**will-o'-the-wisp** n fatuous fire, fen-fire, friar's lantern, ignis fatuus, wisp.

**willowy** adj graceful, gracile, limber, lissom, lithe, lithesome, slender, slim, supple, svelte, sylph-like.

*antonym* buxom.

**will-power** n determination, drive, grit, resolution, resolve, self-command, self-control, self-discipline, self-mastery, single-mindedness.

**willy-nilly** adv compulsorily, necessarily, nolens volens, of necessity, perforce.

**wilt** v atrophy, diminish, droop, dwindle, ebb, fade, fail, flag, flop, languish, melt away, sag, shrivel, sink, wane, weaken, wither.

*antonym* perk up.

**wily** adj arch, artful, astute, cagey, crafty, crooked, cunning, deceitful, deceptive, designing, fly, foxy, guileful, intriguing, long-headed, Machiavellian, scheming, sharp, shifty, shrewd, sly, streetwise, tricky, underhand, versute, wileful.

*antonym* guileless.

**wimp** n clot, clown, drip, fool, jerk, marshmallow, milksop, milquetoast, nebbich, neb(b)ish, nyaff, sap, softy, wally, wet.

**win** v accomplish, achieve, acquire, attain, bag, capture, catch, collect, come away with, conquer, earn, gain, get, net, obtain, overcome, pick up, prevail, procure, receive, secure, succeed, sweep the board, triumph.

*antonym* lose.

n conquest, mastery, success, triumph, victory.

*antonym* defeat.

**win over** allure, attract, carry, charm, convert, convince, disarm, dissuade, induce, influence, persuade, prevail upon, sway, talk round.

**wince** v blench, cower, cringe, draw back, flinch, funk, jerk, quail, recoil, shrink, start.

n cringe, flinch, jerk, start.

**wind¹** n air, air-current, babble, blast, blather, bluster, boasting, breath, breeze, clue, current, cyclone, draught, flatulence, flatus, gab, gale, gas, gregale, gust, harmattan, hint, hot air, humbug, hurricane, idle talk, inkling, intimation, khamsin, levanter, libeccio, mistral, monsoon, notice, puff, report, respiration, rumour, scirocco, sirocco, suggestion, talk, tidings, tornado, warning, whisper, williwaw, windiness, zephyr.

**wind²** v bend, coil, curl, curve, deviate, encircle, furl, loop, meander, ramble, reel, roll, serpent, serpentine, serpentinise, snake, spiral, turn, twine, twist, wreath, zigzag.

n bend, curve, meander, turn, twist, zigzag.

**wind down** decline, diminish, dwindle, lessen, quieten down, reduce, relax, slacken off, slow, slow down, subside, unwind.

*antonyms* increase, tense.

**wind up** close, close down, coil, conclude, crank up, end, end one's days, end up, excite, finalise, find oneself, finish, finish up, hoist, liquidate, raise, settle, terminate, tighten, work up, wrap up.

*antonym* begin.

**wind-bag** n big-mouth, blether, boaster, bore, braggart, gas-bag, gossip, rodomontader.

**winded** adj breathless, out of breath, out of puff, panting, pooped, puffed, puffed out.

*antonym* fresh.

**windfall** n bonanza, find, godsend, jackpot, manna, pennies from heaven, stroke of luck, treasure-trove.

**windiness** n borborygmus, breeziness, flatulence, flatulency, gassiness, gustiness, storminess, ventosity.

*antonym* calm.

**winding** adj anfractuous, bending, circuitous, convoluted, crooked, curving, flexuose, flexuous, indirect, meandering, meandrous, roundabout, serpentine, sinuate(d), sinuous, spiral, tortuous, turning, twisting.

*antonym* straight.

**window** n dormer, dormer-window, fenestella, fenestra, fenestral, glass, light, loop-light, lucarne, opening, oriel, oriel-window, pane, rosace, rose-window, skylight, ventana.

**windpipe** n pharynx, throat, trachea, weasand.

**wind-sock** n drogue, wind-cone, wind-sleeve.

**windy** adj afraid, blowy, blustering, blustery, boastful, boisterous, bombastic, breezy, changeable, chicken, conceited, cowardly, diffuse, empty, fearful, flatulent, flatuous, frightened, garrulous, gusty, long-winded, loquacious, meandering, nervous, pompous, prolix, rambling, scared, squally, stormy, tempestuous, thrasonic, timid, turgid, ventose, verbose, wild, windswept, wordy.

*antonyms* calm, fearless, modest.

**wine** n champagne, claret, plonk, port, rosé, vin, vin ordinaire, vinho verde, vino, vintage.

**wine-glass** n flute, glass, goblet, schooner.

**wine-grower** n vigneron, viniculturist, viticulturist.

**wine-growing** n viniculture, viticulture.

**wing** n adjunct, annexe, arm, branch, circle, clique, coterie, extension, faction, flank, group, grouping, mudguard, pinion, protection, section, segment, set, side.

v clip, fleet, flit, fly, glide, hasten, hit, hurry, move, nick, pass, race, soar, speed, travel, wound, zoom.

**wink** v bat, blink, flash, flicker, flutter, gleam, glimmer, glint, nictate, nictitate, pink, sparkle, twinkle.

n blink, flash, flutter, gleam, glimmering, glint, hint, instant, jiffy, moment, nictation, nictitation, second, sparkle, split second, twinkle, twinkling.

**winner** n champ, champion, conqueror, corker, cracker, daisy, dinger, first, humdinger, master, vanquisher, victor, world-beater, wow.

*antonym* loser.

**winning** *adj* alluring, amiable, attractive, bewitching, captivating, charming, conquering, delectable, delightful, disarming, enchanting, endearing, engaging, fascinating, fetching, lovely, on top, pleasing, prepossessing, successful, sweet, taking, triumphant, unbeaten, undefeated, victorious, winsome.

*antonyms* losing, unappealing.

**winnings** *n* booty, gains, motser, motza, prize(s), proceeds, profits, spoils, takings, velvet.

*antonym* losses.

**winnow** *v* comb, cull, diffuse, divide, fan, part, screen, select, separate, sift, waft.

**winsome** *adj* agreeable, alluring, amiable, attractive, bewitching, captivating, charming, cheerful, comely, delectable, disarming, enchanting, endearing, engaging, fair, fascinating, fetching, graceful, pleasant, pleasing, prepossessing, pretty, sweet, taking, winning.

*antonym* unattractive.

**wintry** *adj* algid, bleak, brumous, cheerless, chilly, cold, desolate, dismal, freezing, frore, frosty, frozen, gelid, harsh, hibernal, hiemal, icy, rimy, Siberian, snowy, winterly.

*antonym* summery.

**wipe** *v* absterge, brush, clean, clear, deterge, dicht, dry, dust, erase, mop, remove, rub, sponge, swab, take away, take off.

*n* brush, dicht, lick, rub, swab.

**wipe out** abolish, annihilate, blot out, destroy, efface, eradicate, erase, expunge, exterminate, extirpate, massacre, obliterate, put paid to, raze.

*antonym* establish.

**wire-pulling** *n* clout, conspiring, influence, intrigue, Machiavellianism, manipulation, plotting, pull, scheming.

**wiry** *adj* bristly, lean, sinewy, stiff, strong, tough, withy.

*antonym* puny.

**wisdom** *n* anthroposophy, astuteness, circumspection, comprehension, discernment, enlightenment, erudition, foresight, gnosis, intelligence, judgement, judiciousness, knowledge, learning, penetration, prudence, reason, sagacity, sapience, sence, sophia, understanding.

*antonym* folly.

**wise** *adj* aware, clever, discerning, enlightened, erudite, informed, intelligent, judicious, knowing, long-headed, long-sighted, perceptive, politic, prudent, rational, reasonable, sagacious, sage, sapient, sensible, shrewd, sound, understanding, well-advised, well-informed.

*antonym* foolish.

**wiseacre** *n* clever dick, smart Alec(k), smartypants, wise guy, wiseling.

**wisecrack** *n* barb, funny, gag, jest, jibe, joke, one-liner, quip, witticism.

**wish** *v* ask, aspire, bid, command, covet, crave, desiderate, desire, direct, greet, hanker, hope, hunger, instruct, long, need, order, require, thirst, want, whim, yearn, yen.

*antonyms* dislike, fear.

*n* aspiration, bidding, command, desire, hankering, hope, hunger, inclination, intention, liking, order, request, thirst, urge, velleity, voice, want, whim, will, yearning, yen.

*antonyms* dislike, fear.

**wishbone** *n* furcula, merry-thought.

**wishy-washy** *adj* bland, feeble, flat, ineffective, ineffectual, insipid, jejune, namby-pamby, tasteless, thin, vapid, watered-down, watery, weak, wersh.

*antonym* strong.

**wisp** *n* jag, lock, piece, shred, snippet, strand, thread, twist.

**wispy** *adj* attenuate, attenuated, delicate, diaphanous, ethereal, faint, fine, flimsy, flyaway, fragile, frail, gossamer, insubstantial, light, thin, unsubstantial.

*antonym* substantial.

**wistful** *adj* contemplative, disconsolate, dreaming, dreamy, forlorn, longing, meditative, melancholy, mournful, musing, pensive, reflective, sad, soulful, thoughtful, wishful, yearning.

**wit** *n* acumen, badinage, banter, brains, card, cleverness, comedian, common sense, comprehension, conceit, discernment, drollery, epigrammatist, eutrapelia, facetiousness, farceur, fun, homme d'esprit, humorist, humour, ingenuity, insight, intellect, intelligence, jocularity, joker, judgement, levity, merum sal, mind, nous, perception, pleasantry, punster, quipster, raillery, reason, repartee, sense, smeddum, understanding, wag, wisdom, wit-cracker, wordplay.

*antonyms* seriousness, stupidity.

**witch** *n* enchantress, galdregon, gyre-carline, hag, hex, lamia, magician, necromancer, occultist, pythoness, reim-kennar, sorceress, sortileger, weird, wise woman, witch-wife.

**witchcraft** *n* black magic, conjuration, divination, enchantment, glamour, goety, incantation, invultuation, magic, myalism, necromancy, occultism, pishogue, sorcery, sortilege, sortilegy, spell, the black art, the occult, voodoo, witchery, witching, wizardry.

**witch-doctor** *n* angek(k)ok, magician, medicine-man, shaman.

**witch-hunt** *n* hounding, hue and cry, McCarthyism.

**with it** fashionable, groovy, hep, hip, in, modern, modish, progressive, trendy, up-to-date, up-to-the-minute, vogue.

*antonym* out-of-date.

**withdraw** *v* abjure, absent oneself, back out, depart, disavow, disclaim, disengage, disenrol, disinvest, draw back, draw out, drop out, extract, fall back, go, go away, hive off, leave, pull back, pull out, recall, recant, remove, repair, rescind, retire, retract, retreat, revoke, secede, subduct, subtract, take away, take back, take off, unsay, waive.

*antonyms* advance, deposit, persist.

**withdrawal** *n* abjuration, departure, disavowal, disclaimer, disengagement, disinvestment, Dunkirk, exit, exodus, extraction, recall, recantation, removal, repudiation, rescission, retirement, retraction, retreat, revocation, secession, waiver, withdrawment.

*antonyms* advance, deposit, persistence.

**withdrawn** *adj* aloof, detached, distant, hidden, introvert, isolated, out-of-the-way, private, quiet, remote, reserved, retiring, secluded, shrinking, shy, silent, solitary, taciturn, uncommunicative, unforthcoming, unsociable.

*antonym* outgoing.

**wither** *v* abash, blast, blight, decay, decline, desiccate, disintegrate, droop, dry, fade, humiliate, languish, miff, mortify, perish, put down, shame, shrink, shrivel, snub, wane, waste, welt, wilt.

*antonyms* boost, thrive.

**wither away** decrease, die, die off, disappear, dwindle, fade away, miff, shrink, shrivel, wilt.

**withering** *adj* deadly, death-dealing, destructive, devastating, humiliating, killing, mortifying, murderous, scathing, scornful, searing, slaughterous, snubbing, wounding.

*antonym* supportive.

**withhold** *v* check, conceal, deduct, detain, hide, keen, keep back, refuse, repress, reserve, resist, restrain, retain, sit on, suppress, suspend.

*antonyms* accord, give.

**without delay** at once, immediately, pronto, quick-stick(s), right away, straight away, straightway, there and then, tout de suite.

**without doubt** certainly, doubtless, no doubt, questionless, unquestionably.

**without fail** conscientiously, constantly, dependably, faithfully, like clockwork, predictably, punctually, regularly, reliably, religiously, unfailingly, without exception.

*antonyms* unpredictably, unreliably.

**withstand** *v* bear, brave, combat, confront, cope with, defy, endure, face, grapple with, hold off, hold one's ground, hold out, last out, oppose, put up with, resist, stand, stand fast, stand one's ground, stand up to, survive, take, take on, thwart, tolerate, weather.

*antonyms* collapse, yield.

**witless** *adj* crazy, cretinous, daft, dull, empty-headed, foolish, gormless, half-witted, idiotic, imbecilic, inane, moronic, obtuse, senseless, silly, stupid.

*antonym* intelligent.

**witness** *n* attestant, beholder, bystander, corroborator, deponent, eye-witness, looker-on, observer, onlooker, spectator, testifier, viewer, vouchee, voucher, watcher, witnesser.

*v* attend, attest, bear out, bear witness, confirm, corroborate, countersign, depone, depose, endorse, look on, mark, note, notice, observe, perceive, see, sign, testify, view, watch.

**wits** *n* acumen, astuteness, brains, cleverness, comprehension, faculties, gumption, ingenuity, intelligence, judgement, marbles, mother-wit, nous, reason, sense, understanding.

*antonym* stupidity.

**witticism** *n* bon mot, epigram, jeu d'esprit, mot, one-liner, pleasantry, pun, quip, repartee, riposte, sally.

**witty** *adj* amusing, brilliant, clever, comic, droll, epigrammatic, facetious, fanciful, funny, humorous, ingenious, jocular, lively, original, piquant, salty, sparkling, waggish, whimsical.

*antonyms* dull, unamusing.

**wizard**[1] *n* conjurer, enchanter, mage, magician, magus, necromancer, occultist, reim-kennar, shaman, sorcerer, sortileger, thaumaturge, warlock, witch.

**wizard**[2] *n* ace, adept, dabster, deacon, expert, genius, hotshot, maestro, master, prodigy, star, virtuoso, whiz.

*antonym* duffer.

*adj* ace, brilliant, enjoyable, fab, fantastic, good, great, marvellous, sensational, smashing, super, superb, terrif, terrific, tiptop, top-hole, topping, tremendous, wonderful.

*antonym* rotten.

**wizardry** *n* black magic, conjuration, divination, enchantment, glamour, goety, incantation, invultuation, magic, myalism, necromancy, occultism, pishogue, sorcery, sortilege, sortilegy, the black art, the occult, voodoo, warlockry, witchcraft, witchery, witching.

**wizened** *adj* dried up, gnarled, lined, sere, shrivelled, shrunken, thin, weazen, weazened, withered, wizen, worn, wrinkled.

*antonyms* plump, smooth.

**wobble** *v* dither, dodder, fluctuate, haver, heave, hesitate, oscillate, quake, rock, seesaw, shake, shilly-shally, shoggle, sway, swither, teeter, totter, tremble, vacillate, vibrate, waver.

*n* oscillation, quaking, rock, shake, tremble, tremor, unsteadiness, vibration.

**wobbly** *adj* doddering, doddery, rickety, shaky, shoogly, teetering, tottering, unbalanced, uneven, unsafe, unstable, unsteady, wonky.

*antonym* stable.

**woe** *n* adversity, affliction, agony, anguish, burden, curse, dejection, depression, disaster, distress, dole, dolour, dule, gloom, grief, hardship, heartache, heartbreak, melancholy, misery, misfortune, pain, sadness, sorrow, suffering, tears, trial, tribulation, trouble, unhappiness, wretchedness.

*antonym* joy.

**woebegone** *adj* blue, crestfallen, dejected, disconsolate, dispirited, doleful, down in the mouth, downcast, downhearted, forlorn, gloomy, grief-stricken, hangdog, long-faced, lugubrious, miserable, mournful, sad, sorrowful, tearful, tear-stained, troubled, wretched.

*antonym* joyful.

**woeful** *adj* agonising, appalling, awful, bad, calamitous, catastrophic, cruel, deplorable, disappointing, disastrous, disconsolate, disgraceful, distressing, doleful, dreadful, feeble, gloomy, grieving, grievous, heartbreaking, heart-rending, hopeless, inadequate, lamentable, lousy, mean, miserable, mournful, paltry, pathetic, piteous, pitiable, pitiful, plaintive, poor, rotten, sad, shocking, sorrowful, sorry, terrible, tragic, unhappy, woesome, wretched.

*antonym* joyful.

**wolf** *n* Casanova, dallier, Don Juan, ladies' man, lady-killer, lecher, Lothario, philanderer, Romeo, seducer, womaniser.

**wolf down** bolt, cram, devour, gobble, gorge, gormandise, gulp, pack away, put away, scoff, shift, stuff.

*antonym* nibble.

**wolf-man** *n* lycanthrope, lycanthropist, werewolf.

**woman** *n* bimbo, bint, bird, bride, broad, chambermaid, char, charwoman, chick, dame, daughter, domestic, fair, female, feme, femme, Frau, gimmer, girl, girlfriend, handmaiden, housekeeper, kept woman, lady, lady-in-waiting, ladylove, lass, lassie, maid, maiden, maidservant, mate, miss, mistress, mort, old lady, partner, piece, placket, she, sheila, spouse, sweetheart, vrouw, wife, woman-body.

*antonym* man.

**womanhood** *n* muliebrity, woman, womankind, womenfolk(s), womenkind.

**womaniser** *n* Casanova, dallier, Don Juan, ladies' man, lady-killer, lecher, Lothario, philanderer, Romeo, seducer, wolf.

**womanising** *n* dalliance, lechery, philandering, venery, wenching, whoring.

**womanly** *adj* female, feminine, ladylike, matronly, motherly, weak, womanish.

*antonym* manly.

**womb** *n* matrix, uterus.

**women** *n* distaff side, muliebrity, muslin, womanhood, womankind, womenfolk(s), womenkind.

**wonder** *n* admiration, amaze, amazement, astonishment, awe, bewilderment, curiosity, fascination, marvel, miracle, nonpareil, phenomenon, portent, prodigy, rarity, sight, spectacle, stupefaction, surprise, wonderment, wunderkind.

*antonyms* disinterest, ordinariness.

*v* ask oneself, boggle, conjecture, doubt, gape, gaup, gawk, inquire, marvel, meditate, ponder, puzzle, query, question, speculate, stare, think.

**wonderful** *adj* ace, admirable, amazing, astonishing, astounding, awe-inspiring, awesome, brilliant, épatant, excellent, extraordinary, fab, fabulous, fantastic, great, incredible, magnificent, marvellous, miraculous, mirific(al), odd, oustanding, peculiar, phenomenal, remarkable, sensational, smashing, staggering, startling, strange, stupendous, super, superb, surprising, terrif, terrific, tiptop, top-hole, topping, tremendous, unheard-of, wizard, wondrous.

*antonyms* ordinary, rotten.

**wonders** *n* curiosities, magic, marvels, mirabilia, miracles, phenomena, prodigies, sights.

**wonky** *adj* amiss, askew, awry, groggy, infirm, shaky, skew-whiff, squint, unsound, unsteady, weak, wobbly, wrong.

*antonyms* stable, straight.

**wont** *adj* accustomed, given, habituated, used.

*n* custom, habit, practice, routine, rule, use, way.

**wonted** *adj* accustomed, common, conventional, customary, daily, familiar, frequent, habitual, normal, regular, routine, usual.

*antonym* unwonted.

**woo** *v* chase, court, cultivate, importune, look for, pay court to, pursue, seek, seek the hand of.

**wood**[1] *n* hyle, lumber, planks, timber.

**wood**[2] *n* bosk, coppice, copse, forest, grove, hanger, holt, hurst, plantation, thicket, trees, underwood, woodland, woods.

**wooded** *adj* bosky, forested, nemorous, silvan, timbered, tree-covered, woody.

*antonym* open.

**wooden** *adj* awkward, blank, clumsy, colourless, deadpan, dense, dim, dim-witted, dull, dull-witted, emotionless, empty, expressionless, gauche, gawky, glassy, graceless, inelegant, inflexible, lifeless, ligneous, maladroit, muffled, oaken, obstinate, obtuse, rigid, slow, spiritless, stiff, stupid, thick, timber, treen, unbending, unemotional, ungainly, unresponsive, unyielding, vacant, woody, xyloid.

*antonyms* bright, lively.

**woodland** *n* boscage, forest, frith (firth), wood(s).

**woody** *adj* bosky, forested, ligneous, sylvan, tree-covered, wooded, wooden, xyloid.

*antonym* open.

**wool** *n* down, fleece, floccus, fluff, hair, yarn.

**woolly** *adj* blurred, clouded, confused, fleecy, floccose, flocculent, foggy, frizzy, fuzzy, hairy, hazy, ill-defined, indefinite, indistinct, lanate, laniferous, lanigerous, lanose, muddled, nappy, nebulous, shaggy, ulotrichous, unclear, vague, woolled, woollen, woolly-haired.

*n* cardigan, guernsey, jersey, jumper, pullover, sweater.

**woozy** *adj* befuddled, bemused, blurred, confused, dazed, dizzy, fuddled, nauseated, pickled, pixil(l)ated, rocky, tipsy, unsteady, vague, wobbly, woolly.

*antonyms* alert, sober.

**word** *n* account, advice, affirmation, assertion, assurance, bidding, bulletin, chat, colloquy, command, commandment, comment, communication, communiqué, confab, confabulation, consultation, conversation, countersign, declaration, decree, dicky-bird, discussion, dispatch, edict, expression, firman, go-ahead, green light, guarantee, hatti-sherif, hint, information, intelligence, interlocution, intimation, lexigram, locution, mandate, message, news, notice, oath, order, palabra, parole, password, pledge, promise, remark, report, rescript, rumour, sign, signal, slogan, talk, term, tête-à-tête, tidings, ukase, undertaking, utterance, vocable, vow, war-cry, watch-word, will.

*v* couch, explain, express, phrase, put, say, write.

**wordiness** *n* bafflegab, logorrhoea, perissology, verbal diarrhoea, verbiage, wordage.

**wording** *n* choice of words, diction, language, phraseology, phrasing, style, terminology, verbiage, wordage, words.

**word-lover** *n* logodaedalus, philologist, philologue, verbalist, verbarian, vocabularian, wordsmith.

**word-perfect** *adj* accurate, exact, faithful, letter-perfect, spot-on.

*antonym* inaccurate.

**word-play** *n* paronomasia, punning, puns, repartee, wit, witticisms.

**words** *n* altercation, argument, barney, bickering, contention, disagreement, dispute, libretto, lyrics, quarrel, row, run-in, set-to, squabble, text.

**wordy** *adj* diffuse, discursive, garrulous, longiloquent, long-winded, loquacious, phrasy, pleonastic, prolix, rambling, verbose, windy.

*antonyms* concise, laconic.

**work** *n* achievement, art, assignment, book, business, calling, chore, commission, composition, craft, creation, darg, deed, doings, drudgery, duty, effort, elbow grease, employ, employment, exertion, graft, grind, handiwork, industry, job, labour, line, livelihood, métier, occupation, oeuvre, office, opus, ouvrage, performance, piece, play, poem, production, profession, pursuit, service, skill, slog, stint, sweat, task, toil, trade, travail, undertaking, workload, workmanship.

*antonyms* hobby, play, rest.

*v* accomplish, achieve, act, arrange, beaver, bring about, bring off, cause, contrive, control, convulse, create, cultivate, dig, direct, drive, drudge, effect, encompass, execute, exploit, farm, fashion, fiddle, fix, force, form, function, go, graft, handle, implement, knead, labour, make, manage, manipulate, manoeuvre, mould, move, operate, peg away, perform, ply, process, progress, pull off, run, shape, slave, slog, sweat, swing, till, toil, twitch, use, wield, writhe.

*antonyms* fail, play, rest.

**work on** butter up, cajole, coax, dissuade, influence, inveigle, persuade, soft-soap, sweet-talk, talk round, wheedle.

**work out** accomplish, achieve, add up to, amount to, arrange, attain, calculate, clear up, come out, come to, construct, contrive, develop, devise, drill, effect, elaborate, evolve, excogitate, exercise, exhaust, expiate, figure out, flourish, form, formulate, go, happen, pan out, plan, practise, prosper, put together, puzzle out, reach, resolve, result, solve, succeed, train, turn out, warm up, win, worry out.

**work up** agitate, animate, arouse, elaborate, enkindle, excite, expand, foment, generate, incite, increase, inflame, instigate, move, rouse, spur, stir up, wind up.

**workable** *adj* doable, effectible, feasible, possible, practicable, practical, realistic, viable.

*antonym* unworkable.

**workaday** *adj* common, commonplace, dull, everyday, familiar, humdrum, labouring, mundane, ordinary, practical, prosaic, routine, run-of-the-mill, toiling, work-day, working.

*antonym* exciting.

**worker** *n* artisan, craftsman, employee, hand, labourer, proletarian, staffer, tradesman, work-girl, workhorse, working man, working woman, workman, work-woman.

*antonym* idler.

**workforce** *n* employees, hands, labour, labour force, personnel, shop-floor, staff, workers, workfolk(s), work-people.

**working** *n* action, functioning, manner, method, operation, routine, running.

*adj* active, employed, functioning, going, labouring, operational, operative, running.

*antonyms* idle, inoperative, retired, unemployed.

**workings** *n* diggings, excavations, mine, pit, quarry, shaft.

**workman** *n* artificer, artisan, craftsman, employee, hand, journeyman, labourer, mechanic, navvy, operative, tradesman, worker.

**workmanlike** *adj* adept, careful, efficient, expert, masterly, painstaking, professional, proficient, satisfactory, skilful, skilled, thorough, workmanly.

*antonym* amateurish.

**workmanship** *n* art, artistry, craft, craftsmanship, execution, expertise, facture, finish, handicraft, handiwork, manufacture, skill, technique, work.

**work-mate** *n* associate, colleague, co-worker, fellow-worker, work-fellow, yoke-fellow, yoke-mate.

**works**[1] *n* factory, foundry, mill, plant, shop, workshop.

**works**[2] *n* actions, acts, books, canon, deeds, doings, oeuvre, output, plays, poetry, productions, writings.

**works**[3] *n* action, gearing, guts, innards, insides, machinery, mechanism, movement, parts, workings.

**workshop** *n* atelier, class, discussion group, factory, mill, plant, school, seminar, shop, studio, symposium, workroom, works.

**world** *n* age, area, class, creation, days, division, domain, earth, environment, epoch, era, existence, field, globe, human race, humanity, humankind, kingdom, life, man, mankind, men, nature, people, period, planet, province, public, realm, society, sphere, star, system, terrene, times, universe, Welt.

**worldly** *adj* ambitious, avaricious, blasé, carnal, cosmopolitan, covetous, earthly, experienced, fleshly, grasping, greedy, knowing, lay, materialistic, mondain, mundane, physical, politic, profane, secular, selfish, sophisticated, sublunary, temporal, terrene, terrestrial, unspiritual, urbane, worldly-minded, worldly-wise.

*antonym* unworldly.

**worldwide** *adj* catholic, general, global, international, mondial, pandemic, ubiquitous, universal.

*antonym* local.

**worn** *adj* attrite, bromidic, careworn, cliché'd, drawn, exhausted, fatigued, frayed, hackneyed, haggard, jaded, lined, pinched, played-out, ragged, shabby, shiny, spent, tattered, tatty, threadbare, tired, trite, wearied, weary, wizened, woe-wearied, woe-worn, worn-out.

*antonyms* fresh, new.

**worn out** all in, clapped out, clapped-out, dead on one's feet, decrepit, dog-tired, done, done in, épuisé(e), exhausted, fatigued, finished, fit to drop, forswunk, frayed, jiggered, knackered, moth-eaten, on its last legs, played-out, prostrate, ragged, shabby, spent, tattered, tatty, threadbare, tired, tired out, used, useless, warby, weary, worn, zonked.

*antonym* fresh.

**worried** *adj* afraid, agonised, anxious, apprehensive, bothered, concerned, distracted, distraught, distressed, disturbed, fearful, frabbit, fretful, frightened, ill at ease, nervous, on edge, overwrought, perturbed, strained, tense, tormented, troubled, uneasy, unquiet, upset.

*antonyms* calm, unconcerned, unworried.

**worrisome** *adj* agonising, anxious, apprehensive, bothersome, disquieting, distressing, disturbing, fretful, frightening, insecure, irksome, jittery, nail-biting, nervous, perturbing, troublesome, uneasy, upsetting, vexing, worrying.

*antonyms* calm, reassuring, unworried.

**worry** *v* agonise, annoy, attack, badger, bite, bother, brood, deave, disquiet, distress, disturb, faze, feeze, frab, fret, get one's knickers in a twist, gnaw at, go for, harass, harry, hassle, hector, importune, irritate, kill, lacerate, nag, perturb, pester, plague, savage, tantalise, tear, tease, torment, trouble, unsettle, upset, vex.

*antonyms* comfort, reassure.

*n* agitation, annoyance, anxiety, apprehension, care, concern, disturbance, fear, irritation, misery, misgiving, perplexity, pest, plague, problem, stew, tew, tizz, tizzy, torment, trial, trouble, unease, vexation, woe, worriment.

*antonyms* comfort, reassurance.

**worrying** *adj* anxious, disquieting, distressing, disturbing, harassing, nail-biting, perturbing, troublesome, trying, uneasy, unsettling, upsetting, worrisome.

*antonym* reassuring.

**worsen** *v* aggravate, damage, decay, decline, degenerate, deteriorate, disimprove, exacerbate, go downhill, pejorate, retrogress, sink, take a turn for the worse.

*antonym* improve.

**worsening** *n* decay, decline, degeneration, deterioration, exacerbation, pejoration, retrogression.

*antonym* improvement.

**worship** *v* adore, adulate, deify, exalt, glorify, honour, idolatrise, idolise, kanticoy, laud, love, misworship, praise, pray to, respect, revere, reverence, venerate.

*antonym* despise.

*n* adoration, adulation, allotheism, deification, devotion(s), dulia, exaltation, glorification, glory, homage, honour, hyperdulia, image-worship, knee-drill, latria, latry, laudation, love, misdevotion, misworship, monolatry, praise,

prayer(s), puja, regard, respect, reverence, will-worship.

*antonym* vilification.

**worst** *v* beat, best, conquer, crush, defeat, drub, master, overcome, overpower, overthrow, subdue, subjugate, vanquish, whitewash.

**worth** *n* aid, assistance, avail, benefit, cost, credit, desert(s), excellence, goodness, help, importance, merit, price, quality, rate, significance, use, usefulness, utility, value, virtue, worthiness.

*antonym* worthlessness.

**worthless** *adj* abandoned, abject, base, beggarly, Brummagem, contemptible, depraved, despicable, draffish, draffy, futile, good-for-nothing, grotty, ignoble, ineffectual, insignificant, littleworth, meaningless, miserable, naff, no use, no-account, no-good, nugatory, paltry, pointless, poor, rubbishy, scabbed, scabby, screwy, stramineous, trashy, trifling, trivial, unavailing, unimportant, unusable, useless, valueless, vaurien, vile, wretched.

*antonym* valuable.

**worthwhile** *adj* beneficial, constructive, furthersome, gainful, good, helpful, justifiable, productive, profitable, useful, utile, valuable, worthy.

*antonym* useless.

**worthy** *adj* admirable, appropriate, commendable, creditable, decent, dependable, deserving, estimable, excellent, fit, good, honest, honourable, laudable, meritorious, praiseworthy, reliable, reputable, respectable, righteous, suitable, upright, valuable, virtuous, worthwhile.

*antonyms* disreputable, unworthy.

*n* big cheese, big noise, big pot, big shot, big-wig, dignitary, luminary, name, notable, personage.

**wound** *n* anguish, cut, damage, distress, gash, grief, harm, heartbreak, hurt, injury, insult, laceration, lesion, offence, pain, pang, scar, shock, slash, slight, torment, torture, trauma.

*v* annoy, bless, cut, cut to the quick, damage, distress, gash, grieve, harm, hit, hurt, injure, irritate, lacerate, mortify, offend, pain, pierce, pip, shock, slash, sting, traumatise, wing, wring someone's withers.

**wraith** *n* apparition, ghost, larva, lemur, phantom, revenant, shade, spectre, spirit, spook.

**wrangle** *n* altercation, argument, argy-bargy, barney, bickering, brawl, clash, contest, controversy, dispute, quarrel, row, set-to, slanging match, squabble, tiff, tussle.

*antonym* agreement.

*v* altercate, argue, argufy, bicker, brawl, contend, digladiate, disagree, dispute, ergotise, fall out, fight, quarrel, row, scrap, squabble.

*antonym* agree.

**wrap** *v* absorb, bind, bundle up, cloak, cocoon, cover, encase, enclose, enfold, envelop, fold, hap, immerse, muffle, pack, package, roll up, sheathe, shroud, surround, swathe, wind.

*antonym* unwrap.

*n* cape, cloak, mantle, pelisse, robe, shawl, stole.

**wrap up**[1] bring to a close, complete, conclude, end, finish off, pack up, package, parcel, round off, terminate, wind up.

*antonym* begin.

**wrap up**[2] be quiet, hold one's tongue, hold one's wheesht, put a sock in it, shoosh, shut it, shut one's cakehole, shut one's face, shut one's mouth, shut one's trap, shut up, wheesht.

**wrapper** *n* cover, dust-jacket, envelope, jacket, packaging, paper, sheath, sleeve, wrapping.

**wrapping** *n* blister card, blister pack, bubble pack, carton, case, cellophane®, envelope, Jiffybag®, packaging, paper, silver-paper, swathe, tinfoil, wrappage.

**wrath** *n* anger, bitterness, choler, displeasure, exasperation, fury, indignation, ire, irritation, passion, rage, resentment, spleen, temper.

*antonyms* calm, pleasure.

**wrathful** *adj* angry, bitter, displeased, enraged, furibund, furious, gusty, in a paddy, incensed, indignant, infuriated, irate, ireful, on the warpath, raging, waxy, wrathy, wroth.

*antonyms* calm, pleased.

**wreak** *v* bestow, bring about, carry out, cause, create, effect, execute, exercise, express, inflict, perpetrate, unleash, vent, visit, work.

**wreath** *n* anadem, band, chaplet, coronet, crown, festoon, garland, lei, loop, ring.

**wreathe** *v* adorn, coil, crown, encircle, enfold, entwine, envelop, enwrap, festoon, intertwine, interweave, surround, swathe, twine, twist, wind, wrap, writhe.

**wreck** *v* break, crab, demolish, destroy, devastate, mar, play havoc with, ravage, ruin, shatter, smash, spoil, torpedo, write off.

*antonyms* repair, save.

*n* derelict, desolation, destruction, devastation, disruption, hulk, mess, overthrow, ruin, ruination, shipwreck, undoing, write-off.

**wreckage** *n* debris, flotsam, fragments, pieces, remains, rubble, ruin, waveson, wrack.

**wrench** *v* distort, force, jerk, pull, rax, rick, rip, sprain, strain, tear, tug, wrest, wring, yank.

*n* ache, blow, jerk, monkey-wrench, pain, pang, pliers, pull, sadness, shock, sorrow, spanner, sprain, tear, tug, twist, upheaval, uprooting.

**wrest** *v* extract, force, pervert, pull, seize, strain, take, twist, win, wrench, wring.

**wrestle** *v* battle, combat, contend, contest, fight, grapple, scuffle, strive, struggle, tussle, vie.

**wretch** *n* blackguard, cad, caitiff, cullion, cur, good-for-nothing, insect, miscreant, no-good, outcast, pilgarlick, profligate, rapscallion, rascal, rascallion, rat, rogue, rotter, ruffian, scoundrel, swine, vagabond, villain, wight, worm.

**wretched** *adj* abject, base, broken-hearted, caitiff, calamitous, cheerless, comfortless, contemptible, crestfallen, dejected, deplorable, depressed, despicable, disconsolate, distressed, doggone, doleful, downcast, forlorn, gloomy, grotty, hapless, hopeless, inferior, low, low-down, mean, melancholy, miserable, paltry, pathetic, pesky, pitiable, pitiful, poor, ratty, scurvy, shabby, shameful, sorry, unfortunate, unhappy, vile, woebegone, woeful, worthless.

*antonyms* excellent, happy.

**wriggle** *v* crawl, dodge, edge, extricate, jerk, jiggle, manoeuvre, scriggle, sidle, slink, snake, sneak, squiggle, squirm, talk one's way out, turn, twist, wag, waggle, wiggle, worm, writhe, zigzag.

*n* jerk, jiggle, squirm, turn, twist, twitch, wag, waggle, wiggle.

**wring** *v* coerce, distress, exact, extort, extract, force, hurt, lacerate, mangle, pain, pierce, rack, rend, screw, squeeze, stab, tear, torture, twist, wound, wrench, wrest.

**wrinkle** *n* corrugation, crease, crinkle, crow's-foot, crumple, fold, furrow, gather, line, pucker, rumple, wimple.

*v* corrugate, crease, crinkle, crumple, fold, furrow, gather, line, pucker, rivel, ruck, rumple, runkle, shrivel.

**wrinkled** *adj* creased, crinkled, crinkly, crumpled, furrowed, puckered, ridged, rivelled, rugate, rugose, rugous, rumpled, wrinkly.

*antonym* smooth.

**writ** *n* court order, decree, subpoena, summons.

**write** *v* compose, copy, correspond, create, draft, draw up, indite, inscribe, jot down, pen, record, screeve, scribble, scribe, set down, take down, tell, transcribe.

**write off** cancel, crash, cross out, destroy, disregard, scrub, smash up, wreck.

**writer** *n* amanuensis, author, authoress, clerk, columnist, copyist, crime writer, detectivist, dialogist, diarist, diatribist, dramatist, dramaturg, dramaturgist, elegiast, elegist, encomiast, epigrammatist, epistler, epistolarian, epistoler, epistolist, epitapher, epitaphist, epitomist, essayist, farceur, fictionist, hack, librettist, littérateur, man of letters, memoirist, novelist, panegyrist, paper-stainer, pen, penman, penny-a-liner, penpusher, penwoman, periodicalist, playwright, prosaist, proseman, proser, prose-writer, quill-driver, scribbler, scribe, secretary, wordsmith, writeress.

**writhe** *v* coil, contort, jerk, squirm, struggle, thrash, thresh, toss, twist, wiggle, wreathe, wriggle.

**writing** *n* autography, belles-lettres, book, calligraphy, chirography, composition, document, exaration, hand, handwriting, letter, letters, literature, opus, penmanship, print, publication, scrawl, scribble, script, work.

**written** *adj* documental, documentary, drawn up, recorded, set down, transcribed.

*antonyms* unwritten, verbal.

**wrong** *adj* abusive, amiss, askew, awry, bad, blameworthy, criminal, crooked, defective, dishonest, dishonourable, erroneous, evil, fallacious, false, faulty, felonious, funny, illegal, illicit, immoral, improper, in error, in the wrong, inaccurate, inappropriate, inapt, incongruous, incorrect, indecorous, infelicitous, iniquitous, inner, inside, inverse, malapropos, misinformed, mistaken, off base, off beam, off target, opposite, out, out of commission, out of order, reprehensible, reverse, sinful, unacceptable, unbecoming, unconventional, under, undesirable, unethical, unfair, unfitting, unhappy, unjust, unlawful, unseemly, unsound, unsuitable, untrue, wicked, wide of the mark, wrongful, wrongous.

*antonym* right.

*adv* amiss, askew, astray, awry, badly, erroneously, faultily, improperly, inaccurately, incorrectly, mistakenly, wrongly.

*antonym* right.

*n* abuse, crime, error, grievance, immorality, inequity, infraction, infringement, iniquity, injury, injustice, misdeed, offence, sin, sinfulness, transgression, trespass, unfairness, wickedness, wrong-doing.

*antonym* right.

*v* abuse, cheat, discredit, dishonour, harm, hurt, ill-treat, ill-use, impose on, injure, malign, maltreat, misrepresent, mistreat, oppress, traduce.

**wrong-doer** *n* criminal, culprit, delinquent, evildoer, felon, law-breaker, malefactor, miscreant, offender, sinner, transgressor, trespasser.

**wrong-doing** *n* crime, delinquency, error, evil, fault, felony, immorality, iniquity, maleficence, mischief, misdeed, offence, sin, sinfulness, transgression, wickedness.

**wrongful** *adj* blameworthy, criminal, dishonest, dishonourable, evil, felonious, illegal, illegitimate, illicit, immoral, improper, reprehensible, unethical, unfair, unjust, unlawful, wicked, wrong, wrongous.

*antonym* rightful.

**wrongly** *adv* badly, by mistake, erroneously, in error, inaccurately, incorrectly, mistakenly.

*antonym* rightly.

**wrought** *adj* beaten, decorative, fashioned, hammered, made, manufactured, ornamental, ornamented, ornate, shaped.

**wry** *adj* askew, aslant, awry, contorted, crooked, deformed, distorted, droll, dry, ironic, mocking, pawky, perverse, sarcastic, sardonic, thrawn, twisted, uneven, warped.

*antonym* straight.

# XYZ

**xenophobia** *n* ethnocentrism, racialism, racism, xenophoby.

*antonym* xenomania.

**xenophobic** *adj* ethnocentrist, parochial, racialist, racist.

**ya(c)k** *v* blather, chatter, gab, gossip, jabber, jaw, prattle, run on, tattle, twattle, witter on, yap, yatter.

*n* blah, blather, chat, chinwag, confab, gossip, hot air, jaw, prattle, twattle, ya(c)kety-ya(c)k, yatter.

**yank** *v, n* haul, heave, jerk, pull, snatch, tug, wrench.

**yap** *v* babble, blather, chatter, go on, gossip, jabber, jaw, prattle, talk, tattle, twattle, ya(c)k, yammer, yatter, yelp, yip.

**yard** *n* court, court-yard, garden, garth, Hof, hypaethron, quad, quadrangle.

**yardstick** *n* benchmark, comparison, criterion, gauge, measure, standard, touchstone.

**yarn¹** *n* abb, fibre, fingering, gimp, lisle, thread.

**yarn²** *n* anecdote, cock-and-bull story, fable, fabrication, story, tale, tall story.

**yawn** *v* gape, ga(u)nt, open, split.

**yawning** *adj* cavernous, gaping, hiant, huge, vast, wide, wide-open.

*antonym* narrow.

**yearly** *adj* annual, per annum, per year.

*adv* annually, every year, once a year.

**yearn for** ache for, covet, crave, desire, hanker for, hunger for, itch for, languish for, long for, lust for, pant for, pine for, want, wish for, yen for.

*antonym* dislike.

**yell** *v* bawl, bellow, holler, hollo, howl, roar, scream, screech, shout, shriek, squawl, squeal, whoop, yelp, yowl.

*antonym* whisper.

*n* bellow, cry, holler, hollo, howl, roar, scream, screech, shriek, squawl, whoop, yelp.

*antonym* whisper.

**yellow** *adj* flavescent, flaxen, fulvid, fulvous, gold, golden, lemon, primrose, saffron, vitellary, vitelline, xanthic, xanthochroic, xanthomelanous, xanthous.

**yelp** *v* bark, bay, cry, yap, yell, yip, yowl.

*n* bark, cry, yap, yell, yip, yowl.

**yen** *n* craving, desire, hankering, hunger, itch, longing, lust, passion, thing, yearning.

*antonym* dislike.

**yes** *interj* absolutely, affirmative, agreed, aye, quite, right, uh-huh, yea, yeah, yep.

*antonym* no.

**yes-man** *n* arse-licker, bootlicker, crawler, creature, lackey, minion, sycophant, toad-eater, toady.

**yesterday's** *adj* bygone, hesternal, passé, past, stale.

*antonym* tomorrow's.

**yield¹** *v* abandon, abdicate, accede, acquiesce, admit defeat, agree, allow, bow, capitulate, cave in, cede, comply, concede, consent, cry quits, give, give in, give way, go along with, grant, knuckle under, part with, permit, relinquish, resign, resign oneself, submit, succumb, surrender, throw in the towel.

*antonym* withstand.

**yield²** *v* afford, bear, bring forth, bring in, earn, fructify, fructuate, fruit, furnish, generate, give, net, pay, produce, provide, return, supply.

*n* crop, earnings, harvest, income, output, proceeds, produce, product, profit, return, revenue, takings.

**yielding** *adj* accommodating, acquiescent, amenable, biddable, complaisant, compliant, docile, easy, elastic, flexible, obedient, obliging, pliable, pliant, quaggy, resilient, soft, spongy, springy, submissive, supple, tractable, unresisting.

*antonyms* obstinate, solid.

**yobbo** *n* apache, corner-boy, hoodlum, hooligan, keelie, lager lout, loafer, lout, rough, rowdy, ruffian, thug, tough, yahoo, yob.

**yoke** *n* bond, bondage, burden, chain, coupling, enslavement, helotry, ligament, link, oppression, serfdom, service, servility, servitude, slavery, subjugation, thraldom, tie, vassalage.

*v* bracket, connect, couple, enslave, harness, hitch, inspan, join, link, tie, unite.

*antonym* unhitch.

**yokel** *n* boor, bucolic, bumpkin, clodhopper, cornball, country cousin, hick, hillbilly, jake, joskin, peasant, rustic.

*antonyms* sophisticate, towny.

**young** *adj* adolescent, baby, callow, cub, early, fledgling, green, growing, immature, infant, junior, juvenile, little, new, recent, unblown, unfledged, youthful.

*antonym* old.

*n* babies, brood, chicks, cubs, family, fledglings, issue, litter, little ones, offspring, progeny, quiverful.

*antonym* parents.

**youngster** *n* boy, girl, juvenile, kid, lad, laddie, lass, lassie, nipper, shaver, teenybopper, urchin, young pup, youth.

*antonym* oldie.

**youth** *n* adolescence, adolescent, boy, boyhood, colt, ephebe, ephebus, girlhood, halflin(g), hobbledehoy, immaturity, juvenescence, juvenile, kid, lad, salad days, shaveling, springal(d), stripling, swain, teenager, the young, young man, young people, young shaver, younger generation, youngster, younker.

*antonyms* old age, oldie.

**youthful** *adj* active, boyish, childish, ephebic, fresh, girlish, immature, inexperienced, juvenescent, juvenile, lively, pubescent, puerile, sprightly, spry, vigorous, vivacious, well-preserved, young.

*antonyms* aged, languorous.

**youthfulness** *n* freshness, juvenileness, juvenility, liveliness, sprightliness, spryness, vigour, vivaciousness, vivacity.

*antonyms* agedness, languor.

**yowl** *v* bay, caterwaul, cry, howl, screech, squall, ululate, wail, yell, yelp.

*n* cry, howl, screech, wail, yell, yelp.

**yucky** *adj* beastly, dirty, disgusting, filthy, foul, grotty, horrible, messy, mucky, revolting, saccharine, sentimental, sickly, unpleasant.

*antonym* nice.

**zany** *adj* amusing, clownish, comical, crazy, daft, droll, eccentric, funny, goofy, kooky, loony, madcap, nutty, screwy, wacky.

*antonym* serious.

*n* buffoon, card, clown, comedian, cure, droll, fool, jester, joker, kook, laugh, merry-andrew, nut, nutcase, nutter, screwball, wag.

**zeal** *n* ardour, dedication, devotion, eagerness, earnestness, enthusiasm, fanaticism, fervency, fervour, fire, gusto, keenness, militancy, passion, spirit, verve, warmth, zelotypia, zest.

*antonym* apathy.

**zealot** *n* bigot, devotee, enthusiast, extremist, fanatic, fiend, freak, maniac, militant.

**zealous** *adj* ardent, burning, devoted, eager, earnest, enthusiastic, fanatical, fervent, fervid, fired, gung-ho, impassioned, keen, militant, passionate, rabid, spirited.

*antonym* apathetic.

**zenith** *n* acme, apex, apogee, climax, culmination, height, high point, meridian, peak, pinnacle, summit, top, vertex.

*antonym* nadir.

**zero** *n* bottom, cipher, duck, goose-egg, love, nadir, naught, nil, nothing, nought.

**zero in on** aim for, concentrate on, converge on, direct at, fix on, focus on, head for, home in on, level at, pinpoint, train on.

**zest** *n* appetite, charm, delectation, élan, enjoyment, flavour, gusto, interest, joie de vivre, keenness, kick, peel, piquancy, pungency, relish, rind, savour, smack, spice, tang, taste, zeal, zing.

*antonym* apathy.

**zigzag** *v* meander, snake, wind, yaw.

*adj* meandering, serpentine, sinuous, zigzagging, zigzaggy.

*antonym* straight.

**zing** *n* animation, brio, dash, élan, energy, go, joie de vivre, life, liveliness, oomph, pizazz, sparkle, spirit, vigour, vitality, zest, zip.

*antonym* listlessness.

**zip** *n* brio, drive, élan, energy, enthusiasm, get-up-and-go, go, gusto, life, liveliness, oomph, pep, pizzazz, punch, sparkle, spirit, verve, vigour, vim, vitality, zest, zing.

*antonym* listlessness.

*v* dash, flash, fly, gallop, hurry, race, rush, scoot, shoot, speed, tear, whiz, whoosh, zoom.

**zone** *n* area, belt, district, region, section, sector, sphere, stratum, territory, tract, zona, zonule, zonulet.

**zoo** *n* animal park, aquarium, aviary, menagerie, safari park, zoological gardens.

**zoom** *v* buzz, dash, dive, flash, fly, gallop, hare, hurtle, pelt, race, rush, scoot, shoot, speed, streak, tear, whirl, whiz, whoosh, zip.

# Appendices

## Appendix I: classified word lists

air and space vehicles   707
alphabets, writing systems   707
anatomical   707
architecture and building   708
art   709
canonical hours   710
cattle breeds   710
cheeses   710
chemical elements   710
cloths, fabrics   711
coins, currencies   712
collective nouns   713
collectors, enthusiasts   713
colours   713
confections, dishes, foods   714
dances   715
dog breeds   716
drinks, alcoholic   716
French Revolutionary calendar   717
furniture, furnishings   717
garments, vestments   717

heraldry   720
herbs, spices   721
jewels, gems   721
Jewish calendar   721
languages   721
legal   722
minerals   724
musical instruments   725
parliaments   726
prosody   726
ranks in armed forces   727
rhetoric   727
titles of rulers   727
tools   728
units of measurement   729
vehicles   729
vessels, ships   730
weapons, armour   731
wine-bottle sizes   732
zodiac signs   732

## Appendix II: words listed by suffix

-ast   733
-aster   733
-cide   733
-cracy   733
-crat   733
-cratic   733
-cultural   733
-culture   733
-cyte   733
-dom   734
-ferous   734
-gamy   734
-genesis   734
-genic   735
-gon   735
-gram   735
-graph   735
-graphical   736
-graphy   736
-hedron   737

-hood   737
-iac   737
-iatric   737
-iatry   737
-ician   737
-ics   738
-iform   739
-ism   739
-itis   745
-latrous   746
-latry   746
-logical   746
-logous   746
-logue   746
-logy   747
-lysis   748
-lytic   748
-mancy   748
-mania   748
-mantic   749

-mathic   749
-mathy   749
-meter   749
-metry   750
-monger   750
-morphic   750
-morphous   750
-onym   750
-onymic   750
-osis   750
-path   751
-pathic   751
-pathy   751
-phage   751
-phagous   751
-phagy   751
-phile   752
-philia   752
-philist   752
-phily   752

-phobe   752
-phobia   752
-phobic   752
-phone   752
-phonic   752
-phony   753
-phorous   753
-phyte   753
-saurus   753
-scope   753
-scopic   753
-scopy   753
-ship   754
-sophy   755
-stat   755
-therapy   755
-tomy   755
-urgy   755
-vorous   755

# Classified word-lists

## air and space vehicles

aerobus
aerodrome
aerodyne
aerohydroplane
aeroplane
aerostat
air-ambulance
air-bus
airship
all-wing aeroplane
amphibian
autogiro
balloon
biplane
blimp
bomber
cable-car
camel
canard
chopper
comsat
convertiplane
crate
delta-wing
dirigible
dive bomber
fan-jet
fighter
fire-balloon
flying boat
flying saucer
flying wing
glider
gondola
gyrocopter
gyroplane
helibus
helicopter
hoverbus
hovercar
hovercraft
hovertrain
hydro-aeroplane
hydrofoil
hydroplane
intercepter
jet
jetliner
jetplane
lem
microlight
module
monoplane
multiplane
plane
rocket
rocket-plane
runabout
sailplane
satellite
seaplane
space platform
space probe
space shuttle
spacecraft
spaceship
spitfire
sputnik
step-rocket
stol
strato-cruiser
stratotanker
swingtail cargo aircraft
swing-wing
tanker
taube
téléférique
tow-plane
tractor
triplane
troop-carrier
tube
tug
turbojet
turbo-jet
twoseater
UFO
warplane
zeppelin

## alphabets, writing systems

Chalcidian alphabet
cuneiform
Cyrillic
devanagari
estrang(h)elo
finger-alphabet
futhark
Glagol
Glossic
Greek
Gurmukhi
hieroglyphs
hiragana
ideograph
kana
katakana
Kufic
linear A
linear B
logograph
nagari
naskhi
og(h)am
pictograph
Roman
runic
syllabary

## anatomical

abductor
acromion
adductor
alvine
ancon
astragalus
atlas
aural
auricular
axilla
biceps
blade-bone
bone
brachial
bregma
buccal
calcaneum
calcaneus
capitate
cardiac
carpal
carpus
cartilage
cephalic
cerebral
cholecyst
clavicle
coccyx
c(o)eliac
collar-bone
concha
coracoid
crural
cuboid
cuneiform
deltoid
dental
derm
derma
dermal
dermic
diaphragm
diencephalon
digital
diploe
diverticulum
dorsal
dorsolumbar
dorsum
duodenal
duodenum
dura mater
earlap
elbow
enarthrosis
encephalic
encephalon
endocardiac
endocardial
endocardium
endocrinal
endocrine
epencephalic
epencephalon
epidermal
epidermic
epidermis
epididymis
epigastric
epigastrium
epiglottic
epiglottis
epithelium
eponychium
erythrocyte
ethmoid
extensor
Fallopian tubes
false rib
femur
fenestra ovalis
fenestra rotunda
fibula
flexor
floating rib
fontanel(le)
fonticulus
foramen magnum
forearm
forebrain
forefinger
foreskin
fourchette
fr(a)enum
frontal
funiculus
funny bone
gastric
gastrocnemius
gena
genal
genial
genitalia
genu
gingival
glabella
glabellar
gladiolus
glossa
glossal
glottal
glottic
glottis
glut(a)eus
gnathal
gnathic
gonion
gracilis
gremial
gristle

## anatomical (contd.)

groin
gula
gular
gullet
guttural
h(a)emal
haematic
hallux
ham
hamate
hamstring
helix
hepatic
hind-brain
hindhead
hip-bone
hip-girdle
hock
huckle-bone
humeral
humerus
hyoid
hypogastrium
hypothalamus
iliac
ilium
incus
inguinal
innominate
innominate bone
intercostal
ischium
jugular
labial
lachrymal
lacrimal
leucocyte
ligament
lumbar
lumbrical
lunate
luz
malar
malleolus
malleus
mamillar(y)
mammary
mandible
mandibular
manubrium
marriage-bone
mastoid
maxilla
maxillary
membral
mental
merrythought
metacarpal
metatarsal
mons veneris
mount of Venus
muscle
nasal
nates
navicular
neural
obturators
occipital
occiput
occlusal

occlusion
occlusor
ocular
odontic
(o)esophagus
omentum
omohyoid
omoplate
optical
orbicularis
orbit(a)
origin
os innominatum
oscheal
oscular
ossicle
otic
otolith
palatal
palatine
palpebral
parasphenoid
parietal
paroccipital
parotid
patella
patellar
pecten
pectoral
pedal
pelvic girdle
pelvis
periotic
perone
phalanges
pisiform
plantar
popliteal
poplitic
prefrontal
premaxilla
premaxillary
pronator
prootic
prosencephalon
psoas
pubis
pudenda
pulmonary
quadriceps
radius
renal
rhomboid
rib
rictal
sacrocostal
sacrum
sartorius
scaphoid
scapula
sesamoid
shoulder-blade
shoulder-bone
skull
soleus
spade-bone
sphenoid
spine
splinter-bone
stapes
sternum

stirrup-bone
supinator
sural
talus
tarsal
temporal
tendon
thigh-bone
tibia
trapezium
trapezius
trapezoid
triceps
triquetral
turbinal
tympanic
ulna
umbilicus
unguis
urachus
uterus
uvula
vagus
vas deferens
velum
vermis
vertebra
vertebrae
vertex
vesica
voice-box
vomer
vulva
windpipe
wisdom tooth
womb
wrist
xiphisternum
xiphoid
zygapophysis
zygoma
zygomatic

## architecture and building

abacus
abutment
acrolith
acroter
acroterial
acroterion
acroterium
alcove
annulet
anta
antefix
araeostyle
architrave
ashlar
ashler
astragal
baguette
bandelet
banderol(e)
barge-board
barge-couple
barge-stones
battlement
bellcote
bema

bratticing
canephor
canton
cartouche
caryatid
Catherine-wheel
cavetto
centering
cinque-foil
concha
corbeil
corbel
corner-stone
corona
cradling
crenel
crocket
crossette
cruck
cul-de-four
dado
decorated
demi-bastion
demi-lune
dentil
diaconicon
diaper
diastyle
diglyph
dimension work
dinette
dipteros
distyle
ditriglyph
dodecastyle
dog-leg(ged)
dogtooth
dome
domed
domical
donjon
Doric
dormer
double-glazing
doucine
drawbridge
drawing-room
dreamhole
dressing
drip
dripstone
dromic
dromos
drum
dry-stone
duplex
Early English
eaves
echinus
egg-and-anchor
egg-and-dart
egg-and-tongue
egg-box
el
elevation
Elizabethan
embattlement
embrasure
emplection
encarpus
engage

**architecture and building** *(contd.)*
engaged
engrail
enneastyle
entresol
epaule
epaulement
epistyle
eustyle
exedra
extrados
eye-catcher
façade
fan tracery
fan vaulting
fanlight
fascia
fastigium
feathering
fenestella
fenestra
fenestral
fenestration
festoon
fillet
finial
flamboyant
flèche
Flemish bond
fletton
fleuron
foliation
fornicate
fortalice
French sash/window
frieze
fronton
furring
fusarol(e)
fust
gable
gablet
galilee
gambrel roof
gargoyle
gatehouse
giacis
glyph
gopura(m)
gorgerin
Gothic
gradin(e)
griff(e)
groin
groundplan
groundsel
guilloche
gutta
hagioscope
half-timbered
hammer-beam
hammer-brace
hance
hanging buttress
harling
haunch
haute époque
headstone
heart
helix

herringbone
hexastyle
hip
hip-knob
holderbat
hood-mould(ing)
hypostyle
imbrex
imbricate
imbrication
imperial
impost
impostume
intercolumniation
intrados
jamb
javelin
jerkinhead
knosp
lierne
linen-fold
linen-scroll
lintel
mansard(-roof)
mascaron
merlon
metope
modillion
monostyle
mullion
muntin(g)
mutule
Norman
oeil-de-boeuf
ogee
opisthodomos
oriel
out-wall
ovolo
ox-eye
pagoda
pantile
parget
patera
paternoster
patten
pediment
Persian
pilaster
pineapple
pinnacle
plafond
platband
plateresque
plinth
poppy-head
predella
propylaeum
propylon
prostyle
pylon
quatrefeuille
quatrefoil
queen-post
quirk
rear-arch
reglet
regula
rere-arch
retrochoir
reredos

revet
rocaille
rococo
Romanesque
rood-loft
rood-screen
rood-steeple
rood-tower
roof
roof-tree
rosace
rose
rosette
rotunda
roughcast
sacristy
skew-back
socle
soffit
solidum
spandrel
strap-work
stria
string-course
subbasal
surbase
swag
systyle
tabernacle-work
table
telamon
terrazzo
tierceron
tondino
toroid
torsel
torus
trabeation
tracery
triforium
trumeau
tympanum
vault
vaultage
vaulted
vaulting
Venetian mosaic
vermiculate(d)
vice
vitrail
vitrailled
Vitruvian
volute
voussoir
wainscot
wall-plate
water-joint
water-table
weathering
xystus

**art**

abstract
abstraction
action painting
anaglyph
anastasis
anastatic
anthemion
aquarelle

bas relief
Bauhaus
camaieu
cire perdue
dadaism
decal
decoupage
Der Blaue Reiter
diaglyph
Die Brücke
diptych
dry-point
duotone
écorché
enamel
encaustic
engraving
etch
etchant
faience
fashion-plate
Fauve
Fauvism
fête champêtre
figurine
filigree
flambé
flannelgraph
Flemish
flesh-tint
Florentine
free-hand
fresco
fret
frit
futurism
futurist
gadroon
genre
gesso
glyptics
glyptography
Gobelin
gouache
graphic
graphics
graphium
graticulation
gravure
grecque
grisaille
gumption
hachure
hatch
hatching
haut relief
herm(a)
historiated
hound's-tooth
intaglio
linocut
literalism
litho
lithochromatic(s)
lithochromy
lithograph
lithoprint
lost wax
mandorla
meander
monotint

**art** *(contd.)*
monotype
morbidezza
Parian
paysage
phylactery
pietra-dura
piqué
pochoir
pompier
putto
quattrocento
relievo
repoussage
repoussé
reserved
retroussage
rilievo
sculp(t)
scumble
sea-piece
seascape
secco
serigraph
statuary
stipple
stylus
surrealism
symbolism
tachism(e)
tempera
tenebrism
tessellated
tessera
tondo
trecento
triptych
ukiyo-e
velatura
Venetian mosaic
Venetian red
verditer
verism
vermiculate(d)
versal
vitrail
vitraillist
vitrifacture
vitrine
vitro-di-trina
volute
vorticism
woodblock
wood-carving
woodcut
wood-engraving
xoanon
zoomorphic

**canonical hours**
compline
lauds
matins
none
orthros
prime
sext
terce
undern
vespers

**cattle breeds**
Africander
Alderney
Angus
Ankole
Ayrshire
Blonde d'Aquitaine
Brahman
Brown Swiss
cattabu
cattalo
Charol(l)ais
Chianina
Chillingham
Devon
dexter
Durham
Friesian
Galloway
Guernsey
Hereford
Highland
Holstein
Jersey
Latvian
Limousin
Luing
Red Poll
Romagnola
Santa Gertrudis
short-horn
Simmenthal(er)
Teeswater
Ukrainian
Welsh Black

**cheeses**
Amsterdam
Bel Paese
Blarney
Bleu d'Auvergne
Blue Vinny
Boursin
Brie
brynza
Caboc
Caerphilly
Camembert
Carré
Cheddar
Cheshire
Chevrotin
Colwick
Coulommiers
crowdie
Danish blue
Derby
Dolcelatte
Dorset Blue
double Gloucester
Dunlop
Edam
Emmental
Emment(h)al(er)
Esrom
ewe-cheese
Feta
Fynbo
Gammelost

G(j)etost
Gloucester
Gorgonzola
Gouda
Grana
Grevé
Gruyère
Handkäse
Havarti
Herrgårdsost
Herve
Huntsman
Hushållsost
Islay
Jarlsberg
Killarney
Kryddost
Lancashire
Leicester
Limburg(er)
Lymeswold®
mouse-trap
mozzarella
Munster
Mysost
Neufchâtel
Parmesan
Petit Suisse
pipo creme
Pont-l'Éveque
Port(-du-)Salut
Prästost
Provolone
Pultost
Raclette
Red Windsor
Reggiano
ricotta
Romadur
Roquefort
sage Derby
Saint-Paulin
Samsø
sapsago
Stilton
stracchino
Tilsit(er)
Vacherin
Wensleydale
Wexford

**chemical elements**
actinium
aluminium
americium
antimony
argon
arsenic
astatine
barium
berkelium
beryllium
bismuth
boron
bromine
cadmium
caesium
calcium
californium
carbon

cerium
chlorine
chromium
cobalt
copper
curium
dysprosium
einsteinium
erbium
europium
fermium
fluorine
francium
gadolinium
gallium
germanium
gold
hafnium
hahnium
helium
holmium
hydrogen
indium
iodine
iridium
iron
krypton
lanthanum
lawrencium
lead
lithium
lutetium
magnesium
manganese
mendelevium
mercury
molybdenum
neodymium
neon
neptunium
nickel
niobium
nitrogen
nobelium
osmium
oxygen
palladium
phosphorus
platinum
plutonium
polonium
potassium
praseodymium
promethium
protoactinium
radium
radon
rhenium
rhodium
rubidium
ruthenium
rutherfordium
samarium
scandium
selenium
silicon
silver
sodium
strontium
sulphur
tantalum

**chemical elements**
*(contd.)*
technetium
tellurium
terbium
thallium
thorium
thulium
tin
titanium
tungsten
uranium
vanadium
xenon
ytterbium
yttrium
zinc
zirconium

**cloths, fabrics**

abaca
abb
alamode
alepine
alpaca
American cloth
angora
armozine
armure
arrasene
astrakhan
atlas
baft
bagging
Balbriggan
baldachin
balzarine
barathea
barege
barracan
batiste
batting
bayadère
bearskin
beaver
beige
bengaline
Binca®
blanket
blanketing
blonde(e)-lace
bobbinet
bobbin-lace
bombasine
bone-lace
botany
bouclé
bo(u)lting cloth
box-cloth
broadcloth
brocade
brocatel(le)
broché
Brussels lace
buckram
buckskin
budge
buff
bunting
Burberry

burlap
burnet
burrel
butter-cloth
butter-muslin
byssus
caddis
calamanco
calico
cambric
cameline
camlet
candlewick
canvas
carmelite
carpeting
casement-cloth
cashmere
cassimere
catgut
(cavalry) twill
challis
chamois
chantilly (lace)
charmeuse
cheesecloth
Dacron®
damask
damassin
delainè
denim
devil's dust
dhoti
d(h)urrie
diamanté
diaper
dimity
doe-skin
doily
domett
dornick
dowlas
drab
drabbet
Dralon®
drap-de-Berry
dreadnought
drill
droguet
drugget
duchesse lace
duck
duffel
dungaree
dupion
durant
Dutch carpet
duvetyn
ecru
éolienne
façonné
faille
far(r)andine
fearnought
felt
ferret
filet
flannel
flannelette
foulard
foulé

frieze
frocking
fustian
gaberdine
galatea
galloon
gambroon
gauze
genappe
georgette
gingham
Gobelin(s)
gold-cloth
gold-lace
grass cloth
grenadine
grogram
grosgrain
guipure
gunny
gurrah
habit-cloth
haircloth
harn
Hessian
hodden
holland
homespun
Honiton
hopsack
horsehair
huckaback
humhum
jaconet
Jaeger®
jamdani
jean
jeanette
jersey
kalamkari
karakul
kente cloth
kersey
kerseymere
khaddar
khaki
kid
kidskin
kilt
kincob
kip-skin
lamé
lampas
lawn
leather
leather-cloth
leatherette
leghorn
leno
levant
Lincoln-green
linen
linsey
linsey-woolsey
llama
lockram
loden
longcloth
lovat
Lurex®
lustre

lustring
lutestring
Lycra®
mac(k)intosh
madras
mantling
marcella
marocain
maroquin
marquisette
mazarine
Mechlin
medley
melton
merino
Mexican
mignonette
mohair
moire
moleskin
monk's cloth
moreen
morocco
mourning-stuff
mousseline
mousseline-de-laine
mousseline-de-soie
Moygashel®
mull
mulmul(l)
mungo
musk-rat
muslin
muslinet
musquash
nacarat
nainsook
nankeen
ninon
nitro-silk
nun's-veiling
nylon
oilcloth
organdie
organza
organzine
orleans
osnaburg
orris
ottoman
overcoating
paduasoy
paisley
panne
paper-cloth
paper-muslin
par(r)amatta
peau-de-soie
penistone
percale
percaline
perse
petersham
piña-cloth
pin-stripe
piqué
plaid
plush
point-lace
polycotton
poplin

## cloths, fabrics *(contd.)*

poplinette
prunella
purple
quilting
rabanna
ratine (ratteen)
raven('s)-duck
rep (repp)
roan
russel
russel-cord
russet
sackcloth
sacking
sagathy
sail-cloth
samite
sarsenet
satara
sateen
satin
satinette
satin-sheeting
saxony
say
scarlet
schappe
scrim
seersucker
sendal
serge
shagreen
shalloon
shammy(-leather)
shantung
sharkskin
sheepskin
Shetland wool
shoddy
Sicilian
sicilienne
silesia
silk
slipper satin
soneri
split
sponge-cloth
spun silk
stammel
strouding
suede
suedette
suiting
surah
surat
swansdown
swan-skin
tabaret
tabbinet
tabby
taffeta
tamin(e)
tamise
tammy
tarlatan
tarpaulin
tartan
tat
Tattersall (check)
T-cloth

tentage
tent-cloth
terry
Terylene®
thibet
thickset
thrown-silk
thunder-and-lightning
ticken
tick(ing)
tiffany
toile
toilinet(te)
torchon lace
towelling
tram
tricot
troll(e)y
tulle
tusser(-silk)
tweed
union
Valenciennes
veiling
Velcro®
velour(s)
veloutine
velveret
velvet
velveteen
velveting
vicuña
voile
wadmal
waistcoating
watchet
waterwork
waxcloth
webbing
whipcord
wigan
wild silk
wincey
winceyette
wire gauze
woolsey
worcester
worsted
zanella
zephyr

## coins, currencies

agora
antoninianus
as
asper
aureus
baht
balboa
bawbee
bekah
belga
bezant
bit
bod(d)le
bolivar
boliviano
bonnet-piece
broad(piece)
buck

cardecu(e)
Carolus
cash
cent
centavo
centime
chiao
colon
conto
cordoba
couter
crown
crusado
cruzeiro
dam
daric
deaner
décime
denarius
denier
Deutschmark
didrachm(a)
dime
dinar
dirham
doit
dollar
double
doubloon
drachma
ducat
dupondius
duro
eagle
écu
eighteen-penny piece
ekuele
escudo
farthing
fen
fifty-pence piece
fifty-penny piece
five-pence piece
five-penny piece
florin
forint
franc
geordie
gerah
gourde
groat
groschen
guinea
gulden
haler
half-crown
half-dollar
halfpenny
half-sovereign
heller
jacobus
jane
jiao
jitney
joe
joey
jo(h)annes
kina
knife-money
koban(g)
kopeck

koruna
kreutzer
krona
krone
Krugerrand
kwacha
kyat
lek
lempira
leone
lepton
leu
lev
lilangeni
lion
lira
litre
livre
louis
louis-d'or
mag
maik
make
manch
mancus
maravedi
mark
markka
mawpus
merk
metical
mil
millième
millime
milreis
mina
mite
mna
mohur
moidore
mopus
naira
napoleon
(naya) paisa
(new) cedi
ngwee
nickel
nicker
obang
obol
obolus
öre
øre
Paduan
pagoda
pänga
paolo
para
pataca
patrick
paul
peseta
pesewa
peso
pfennig
piastre
picayune
pice
piece of eight
pine-tree money
pistareen

**coins, currencies**
**(contd.)**
pistole
pistolet
plack
portague
portcullis
pound
pula
punt
qintar
quetzal
quid
rag
rand
real
red
red cent
reichsmark
reis
renminbi
rial
rider
riel
ringgit
rix-dollar
riyal
rose-noble
r(o)uble
royal
ruddock
ruddy
rupee
rupiah
ryal
saw-buck
sceat(t)
schilling
scudo
semis
semuncia
sen
sequin
sesterce
sestertium
sextans
shekel
shilling
silverling
sixpence
skilling
smacker
sol
soldo
solidus
sou
sovereign
spade-guinea
spur-royal
stater
sterling
stiver
sucre
sword-dollar
sycee
tael
taka
talent
tanner
tenner
tenpence

ten-pence piece
ten-penny piece
tester(n)
testo(o)n
testril(l)
tetradrachm
thaler
thick'un
thin'un
three-farthings
three-halfpence
threepence
threepenny bit/piece
tical
tick(e)y
tizzy
toman
turner
twenty-pence piece
twenty-penny piece
two bits
twopence
two-pence piece
two-penny piece
unicorn
ure
vellon
wakiki
wampum
won
xerafin
yen
yuan
zack
zaire
zecchino
zimbi
zloty
zuz
zwanziger

**collective nouns**

building of rooks
cast of hawks
cete of badgers
charm of goldfinches
chattering of choughs
clamour of rooks
clowder of cats
company of widgeon
covert of coots
covey of partridges
down of hares
drift of swine
drove of cattle
dule of doves
exaltation of larks
fall of woodcock
fesnyng of ferrets
gaggle of geese
gam of whales
gang of elks
grist of bees
husk of hares
kindle of kittens
leap of leopards
leash of bucks
murder of crows
murmuration of starlings
muster of peacocks

mute of hounds
nide of pheasants
pace of asses
pod of seals
pride of lions
school of porpoises
siege of herons
skein of geese
skulk of foxes
sloth of bears
sounder of boars
spring of teals
stand of plovers
stud of mares
team of ducks
tok of capercailzies
troop of kangaroos
unkindness of ravens
walk of snipe
watch of nightingales

**collectors, enthusiasts**

abolitionist
ailurophile
antiquary
antivaccinationist
antivivisectionist
arachnologist
arctophile
audiophil(e)
balletomane
bibliolatrist
bibliomane
bibliopegist
bibliophagist
bibliophile
bibliophilist
bicameralist
campanologist
canophilist
cartophile
cartophilist
cheirographist
coleopterist
conservationist
cynophilist
Dantophilist
deltiologist
discophile
dog-fancier
ecclesiologist
egger
entomologist
environmentalist
ephemerist
epicure
ex-librist
feminist
Francophile
Gallophile
gastronome
gemmologist
Germanophil(e)
gourmet
herpetologist
hippophile
homoeopathist
iconophilist
incunabulist
Kremlinologist

lepidopterist
medallist
miscegenationist
monarchist
myrmecologist
negrophile
negrophilist
notaphilist
numismatist
oenophile
oenophilist
ophiophilist
orchidomaniac
ornithologist
orthoepist
orthographist
ostreiculturist
pangrammatist
Panhellenist
panislamist
Pan-Slavist
paragrammatist
paroemographer
perfectionist
philanthrope
philatelist
philhellene
phillumenist
philogynist
philologist
philologue
prohibitionist
pteridophilist
reincarnationist
Russophile
Russophilist
scripophile
scripophilist
sericulturist
Sinophile
Slavophile
spelaeologist
steganographist
stegophilist
supernaturalist
tege(s)tologist
timbrologist
timbromaniac
timbrophilist
tulipomane
tulipomaniac
Turcophile
ufologist
ultramontanist
vexillologist
virtuoso
vulcanologist
xenophile
zoophile
zoophilist

**colours**

anthochlore
anthocyan(in)
anthoxanthin
aquamarine
argent
aurora
avocado
badious

**colours** *(contd.)*
Berlin blue
beryl
biscuit
black
blae
blood-red
blue
bottle-green
brick-red
buff
caesious
canary
caramel
carmine
carnation
celadon
celeste
cerise
cerulean
cervine
champagne
charcoal
cobalt-blue
coral
cyan
dove
drab
dun
Dutch pink
dwale
eau de Nil
ebony
emerald
fawn
feldgrau
ferrugin(e)ous
filemot
flame
flavescent
flaxen
flesh-colour
fulvous
fuscous
ginger
glaucous
gold
golden
green
greige (grège)
grey (gray)
gridelin
griseous
grizzle(d)
gules
guly
hoar
horse-flesh
hyacinth
hyacinthine
ianthine
icterine
icteritious
incarnadine
indigo
isabel
isabella
isabelline
jacinth
khaki
lake

lateritious
lemon
lilac
lovat
lurid
luteolous
luteous
lutescent
magenta
mahogany
maize
mandarin(e)
maroon
mauve
mazarine
miniate
minium
modena
morel
mouse-colour(ed)
mous(e)y
mulberry
murrey
nacarat
Naples-yellow
nattier blue
Nile green
nut-brown
ochroleucous
off-white
orange
oxblood
Oxford blue
palatinate
pansy
peach
peach-bloom
peacock
peacock-blue
perse
philomot
piceous
pink
plum
plumbeous
pompadour
ponceau
pongee
porphyry
porraceous
puce
purple
purpure
pyrrhous
red
reseda
roan
rose
rose-coloured
rose-pink
rose-red
rosy
rubicund
rubied
rubiginous
rubineous
rubious
ruby
ruby-red
ruddy
rufescent

rufous
russet
rust-coloured
rusty
sable
saffron
sage
salmon
sand
sapphire
saxe blue
scarlet
sepia
siena
silver
sky
slate
smalt
straw
tan
taupe
tawny
tenné
Titian
tomato
tusser
Tyrian
ultramarine
vermeil
vermilion
vinous
violet
virescent
vitellary
vitreous
watchet
white
wine
xanthic
xanthous
yellow

**confections,
dishes, foods**

andouillette
angels-on-horseback
battalia pie
bir(i)yani
blanquette
Bombay duck
borsch(t)
bouillabaisse
bubble-and-squeak
bummalo
burgoo
calzone
cannelloni
carbon(n)ade
carpet-bag (steak)
cassoulet
cecils
charlotte russe
chilli con carné
chocolate vermicelli
chop-suey
chorizo
chowder
chow-mein
cockaleekie
colcannon

consommé
Danish pastry
dariole
devil
devil's food cake
devils-on-horseback
Devonshire cream
diet-bread
dika-bread
dimsum
dough-boy
doughnut
dragée
drammock
drisheen
duff
dumpling
dunderfunk
Eccles cake
éclair
Edinburgh rock
egg custard
enchilada
eryngo
escalope
escargot
espangole
faggot
fancy-bread
farle
fedelini
felafel
fettuc(c)ine
feuilleté
fishball
fishcake
fishfinger
flan
flapjack
floater
flummery
foie gras
fondant
fondue
forcemeat
fortune cookie
fraise
frankfurter
French bread
French dressing
French fry
French stick
French toast
fricandeau
fricassee
friedcake
fritter
fritto misto
friture
froise
fruit cocktail
fruit salad
fruitcake
frumenty
fu yung
fudge
fumado
galantine
game chips
garam masala
garbanzo

**confections, dishes,**
**foods** *(contd.)*
Garibaldi biscuit
gateau
gazpacho
gefilte fish
Genoa cake
ghee
ginger nut
gingerbread
gingersnap
gnocchi
gofer
goulash
graham bread
graham crackers
grits
gruel
guacamole
gumdrop
gundy
haberdine
haggis
halva(h)
hamburger
hard sauce
hardbake
hardtack
hoe-cake
hominy
hoosh
hot dog
hot-cross-bun
hotpot
howtowdie
humbug
hummus
hundreds-and-thousands
hyson
jemmy
kedgeree
knish
lardy-cake
latke
laverbread
linguini
matelote
millefeuille(s)
minestrone
mous(s)aka
na(a)n
navarin
nuoc mam
olla-podrida
opsonium
paella
pakora
panada
panettone
pastrami
pavlova
pem(m)ican
pep(p)eroni
pesto
pettitoes
pilaff
pilau
pinole
piri-piri
pirozhki
pizza

ploughman's lunch
plum-duff
plum-porridge
plum-pudding
poi
polenta
polony
popover
pop(p)adum
porterhouse(-steak)
pot-au-feu
prairie-oyster
profiterole
prosciutto
pumpernickel
queen of puddings
queen's pudding
quenelle
quiche
raclette
ragout
ramekin
ratatouille
ravioli
remoulade
rijst(t)afel
rillettes
risotto
rissole
roly-poly pudding
Sachertorte
salmagundi
salmi(s)
saltimbocca
sambal
samosa
sashimi
sauce hollandaise
sauerkraut
scampi
schnitzel
sch(t)chi
Scotch woodcock
shashlik
shepherd's pie
smørbrød
smörgåsbord
soufflé
spaghetti (alla) bolognese
spotted dick
spring roll
stovies
stroganoff
succotash
sukiyaki
summer pudding
sundae
sup(p)awn
sushi
syllabub
Tabasco®
tabbouleh
tablet
taco
tagliarini
tamal(e)
tandoori
tapioca
taramasalata
tempura
timbale

toad-in-the-hole
torte
tortellini
tortilla
trifle
tsamba
turtle-soup
tutti-frutti
tzimmes
velouté sauce
vermicelli
vichyssoise
vienna loaf
vienna steak
vindaloo
vol-au-vent
wafer
waffle
warden pie
wastel-bread
water-biscuit
water-gruel
welsh rabbit (rarebit)
white sauce
white-pot
white-pudding
Wiener schnitzel
Wimpy®
wine-biscuit
wonder
Worcestershire sauce
wurst
yoghurt
Yorkshire pudding
zabaglione
Zwieback

**dances**

allemande
beguine
belly-dance
bergamask
black bottom
bolero
bossa nova
bourree
branle
breakdown
bunny-hug
cachucha
cakewalk
canary
cancan
carioca
carmagnole
carol
cha-cha
chaconne
Charleston
cinque-pace
Circassian circle
clogdance
conga
coranto
corroboree
cotill(i)on
country-dance
courant
cracovienne
csárdás (czardas)

dos-à-dos (dosi-do)
dump
écossaise
egg-dance
fading
fado
fandango
farruca
figure-dance
flamenco
fling
flip-flap(-flop)
forlana
fox-trot
galliard
gallopade
galop
gavotte
gigue
gopak
habanera
haka
halling
haymaker
hey (hay)
hey-de-guy
Highland fling
hoedown
hoolachan
hula-hula
jig
jitterbug
jive
John Canoe
joncanoe
jota
juba
kathek
kazatzke
kolo
lancers
loure
malagueña
mambo
matachin
maxixe
mazurka
minuet
Moresco
morris-dance
musette
onestep
Paduan
paso doble
passacaglia
passepied
passy-measure
Paul Jones
pavan(e)
pericon
petronella
planxty
polacca
polka
polo
polonaise
poule
poussette
quadrille
quickstep
redowa

**dances** *(contd.)*
reel
r(h)umba
rigadoon
ring-dance
romaika
ronggeng
roundel
roundelay
roundle
rumba
salsa
saltarello
samba
sand-dance
saraband
sardana
schottische
sequidilla
shimmy(-shake)
siciliano
spring
square-dance
stomp
strathspey
sword-dance
tamborin
tango
tap-dance
tarantella
the twist
toe-dance
tripudium
turkey-trot
two-step
Tyrolienne
valeta
valse
varsovienne
volta
waltz
war dance
zapateado
ziganka

**dog breeds**
affenpinscher
badger-dog
basenji
basset(-hound)
Bedlington (terrier)
Blenheim spaniel
boar-hound
Border terrier
borzoi
Boston terrier
Briard
Brussels griffon
bull mastiff
bulldog
bull-terrier
cairn terrier
Cavalier King Charles
 spaniel
chihuahua
chow
clumber spaniel
coach-dog
cocker spaniel
collie

corgi
dachshund
Dalmatian
Dandie Dinmont
Dane
deerhound
dhole
dingo
Doberman(n) pinscher
elkhound
Eskimo dog
foxhound
fox-terrier
German police dog
German Shepherd dog
Great Dane
greyhound
griffon
harlequin
(Irish) water-spaniel
Jack Russell
keeshond
King Charles spaniel
Labrador
laika
lhasa apso
lurcher
lyam-hound
malemute
Maltese
mastiff
peke
Pekin(g)ese
pinscher
pointer
Pomeranian
poodle
pug
pug-dog
retriever
Rottweiler
saluki
Samoyed(e)
sausage-dog
schipperke
schnauzer
Scotch-terrier
Sealyham
setter
sheltie
Shetland sheepdog
shih tzu
shough
Skye (terrier)
spaniel
Spartan
spitz
St Bernard
staghound
Sussex spaniel
talbot
teckel
terrier
vizsla
volpino
warragal
water-dog
Weimaraner
whippet
wire-hair(ed terrier)
wolf-dog

wolf-hound
Yorkshire terrier
zorro

**drinks, alcoholic**
absinth(e)
aguardiente
akvavit
amontillado
anisette
apple-jack
aqua-mirabilis
aquavit
aqua-vitae
arak
Armagnac
arrack
audit ale
ava
bacharach
badminton
barley-bree
Beaujolais
Beaune
Benedictine
bingo
bishop
black velvet
bloody Mary
blue ruin
bourbon
brandy-pawnee
bride-ale
Bristol-milk
bucellas
bumbo
burgundy
Calvados
Campari
canary
catawba
Chablis
chain-lightning
Chambertin
Champagne
Chardonnay
Chartreuse
cherry brandy
cherry-bounce
Chianti
chicha
cider
claret
claret-cup
cobbler
cobbler's punch
Cognac
Cointreau®
cold-without
Constantia
cool-tankard
cooper
cordial
corn-brandy
daiquiri
demerara
dog's-nose
dop
Drambuie®
eau de vie

eau des creoles
egg-flap
eggnog
enzian
espumoso
fine
fino
flip
four-ale
geneva
genevrette
geropiga
gimlet
gin
gin and it
gin-fizz
ginger wine
ginsling
glogg
glühwein
gooseberry wine
grappa
Graves
grog
haoma
heavy wet
herb-beer
hermitage
hippocras
hock
hollands
hoo(t)ch
it
Johannisberger
John Barleycorn
John Collins
kaoliang
kava
kefir
kir
kirsch
kirschwasser
k(o)umiss
kümmel
kvass
London particular
madeira
malmsley
manzanilla
maraschino
marc brandy
Marcobrunner
margarita
Marsala
Martini®
Médoc
metheglin
mirabelle
mobbie
Moselle
mountain
mountain dew
muscat
muscatel
negus
Nipa
noyau
oenomel
Old Tom
oloroso
olykoek

**drinks, alcoholic**
*(contd.)*
Orvieto
ouzo
pastis
peach-brandy
Pernod®
perry
persico(t)
Peter-see-me
pils(e)ner
Pinot
plottie
pombe
port
pot(h)een
pousse-café
pulque
punch
purl
quetsch
ratafia
resinata
retsina
Rhine-wine
Riesling
Rioja
rosé
Rudesheimer
Rüdesheimer
rum
rumbo
rumfustian
rum-punch
rum-shrub
rye
rye-whisky
sack
sack-posset
sake
samshoo
sangaree
sangria
Sauterne(s)
Sauvignon
schiedam
schnapps
Scotch
shandy
sherry
sherry-cobbler
shrub
sidecar
Sillery
skokiaan
sling
slivovitz
sloe-gin
small beer
small-ale
sour
spruce-beer
St Julien
Steinberger
stengah
stinger
stingo
swipes
swizzle
tafia
Tarragona

tent
tequil(l)a
tipper
toddy
Tokay
Tom Collins
Tom-and-Jerry
twankay
twopenny
usquebaugh
vermouth
vin blanc
vin ordinaire
vin rosé
vinho verde
vodka
wassail
water-brose
whisk(e)y
whisky toddy
white wine
white-ale
Xeres
zythum

**French Revolutionary calendar**

Brumaire
Floréal
Frimaire
Fructidor
Germinal
Messidor
Nivôse
Pluviôse
Prairial
Thermidor
Vendémiaire
Ventôse

**furniture, furnishings**

andiron
banquette
basket-chair
basketwork
bergama
bergamot
bolster
bonheur-du-jour
box-bed
bracket clock
brise-soleil
buffet
buhl
bureau
cabriolet
camp-bed
canterbury
chair-bed
chaise-longue
chesterfield
cheval-glass
chiffonier
coaster
coffee-table
commode
continental quilt
credence (table/shelf)
credenza

davenport
day-bed
desk
deuddarn
dinner-table
dinner-wagon
divan
dos-à-dos
drape
drawer
drawing-table
draw-leaf table
dresser
dressing-table
dumb-waiter
easy-chair
elbow-chair
electrolier
encoignure
escritoire
étagere
faldstool
fauteuil
fender
fender-stool
festoon-blind
fire-dog
fireguard
firescreen
four-poster
gasalier
girandole
girnel
guéridon
hallstand
hassock
hearth-rug
highboy
high-chair
hip-bath
humpty
jardinière
lectern
looking-glass
lounge
lounger
love-seat
lowboy
lug-chair
mirror
mobile
ottoman
overmantel
pelmet
pembroke (table)
picture rail
piecrust table
pier-glass
pier-table
plaque
plenishings
pouf(fe)
prie-dieu
pulpit
pulvinar
radiator
rocking chair  ·
sag-bag
scatter rug/cushion
sconce
secretaire

settee
settle
settle-bed
sideboard
side-table
sofa
sofa-bed
sofa-table
squab
standard lamp
studio couch
swivel-chair
table
tallboy
tapestry
tatami
teapoy
tea-service
tea-set
tea-table
tea-tray
tea-trolley
tent-bed
tête-à-tête
toilet-table
toilet(te)
torchère
tridarn
tringle
umbrella-stand
Vanitory®
vanity unit
vargueño
veilleuse
vis-à-vis
vitrine
wall-unit
wardrobe
washhand-stand
wash-stand
water bed
Welsh dresser
whatnot
writing-desk
writing-table

**garments, vestments**

aba
abaya
abba
abolla
achkan
acton
Afghan
alb
alpargata
amice
anorak
antigropelo(e)s
ascot
babouche
babushka
balaclava
Balbriggan
balibuntal
balmoral
bandan(n)a
bania(n)
barret
basher

**garments, vestments (contd.)**

bashlyk
basinet
basque
basquine
bathing-costume
bauchle
beanie
bearskin
beaver
bed-jacket
bedsocks
beetle-crushers
belcher
benjamin
benny
Bermuda shorts
Bermudas
bertha
bikini
billycock
biretta
blanket
blouson
blucher
boa
boater
bobbysock
bodice
body stocking
body-warmer
bolero
bomber jacket
bongrace
bonnet
bonnet-rouge
boob-tube
bootee
bottine
box-coat
bow-tie
bra
brassière
breeches
breeks
breton
broad-brim
brogue(s)
buckskins
buff
buffalo-robe
buff-coat
buff-jerkin
bumfreezer
Burberry
burdash
burk(h)a
burnous(e)
busby
bush jacket
bush shirt
buskin
bustle
bustle
bycoket
caftan
cagoul(e)
calamanco
calash
calceamentum

calotte
calyptra
camiknickers
camise
camisole
capa
cape
capel(l)ine
capote
capuche
capuchin
carcanet
car-coat
cardigan
cardinal
carmagnole
cashmere
casque
cassock
casuals
catsuit
caul
cere-cloth
cerement
chadar
chaparajos
chapeau
chapeau-bras
chaperone
chapka
chaplet
chaps
chasuble
cimar
collar of esses
corset
corslet
cummerbund
cymar
dalmahoy
Dalmatic
dashiki
décolletage
derby
diadem
diaper
dick(e)y
dinner-gown
dinner-jacket
dirndl
dishabille
dittos
divided skirt
djellaba(h)
djibbah
dog-collar
Dolly Varden
dolman
donkey jacket
doublet
drainpipes
drapesuit
drawers
dreadnought
dress uniform
dress-coat
dress-improver
dressing-gown
dressing-jacket
dressing-sack
dress-shirt

dress-suit
dress-tie
duffel coat
dungarees
earmuffs
encolpion
epaulet(te)
ephod
epitrachelion
espadrille
Eton collar
Eton jacket
Etons
evening dress
evening-dress
exomis
faldetta
falling band
fannel(l)
fanon
farthingale
fascinator
fatigues
fedora
ferronnière
fez
fibula
fichu
filibeg
fillet
finnesko
flat-cap
flip-flop
fob
fontange
fore-and-after
fraise
French knickers
frock
frock-coat
frog
frontlet
fustanella
gaberdine
gaiter
galligaskins
galoshes
gamash
gambeson
garibaldi
gauchos
gay deceivers
gee-string (G-string)
geneva bands
geta
gibus
gi(e)
gilet
girandole
gizz
grego
gremial
g-suit
guernsey
gumboot
gum(shoe)
habergeon
hacqueton
haik
hair-net
hair-piece

half-boot
hat
hatband
hatpin
hattock
hauberk
havelock
headcloth
head-hugger
headsquare
hejab
hennin
himation
hip-huggers
hipsters
hogger
Homburg
hood
hotpants
housecoat
hug-me-tight
humeral veil
hummel
hunting cap
ihram
indescribables
jabot
jacket
Jap-silk
jeans
jersey
jiz
jubbah (djibbah)
jumper
jump-suit
jupon
kabaya
kaffiyeh
kaftan
kagoul
kalpak
kalyptra
kamees
kamik
kanzu
kell
kerchief
k(h)anga
k(h)urta
Kilmarnock
Kilmarnock cowl
kimono
kirtle
kiss-me
kiss-me-quick
knickerbockers
knickers
lammy
lava-lava
lederhosen
leggings
leghorn
leg-warmers
leotard
Levis®
liberty bodice
lingerie
loden
lounger
lounge-suit
lungi

**garments, vestments**
*(contd.)*
mac(k)
mackinaw
mac(k)intosh
madras
manta
manteau
mantilla
mantle
mantlet
manto
matinee
matinee jacket/coat
maud
mazarine
mazarine hood
middy (blouse)
mink
mitre
mitt
mitten
mob
mob-cap
mode
modius
mohair
moleskins
monkey-jacket
monteith
montero
montero-cap
morning-dress
morning-gown
mortar-board
Mother Hubbard
mourning-cloak
mousquetaire
moz(z)etta
muff
muffin-cap
muffler
mutch
muu-muu
netherstock
newmarket
nightingale
Nithsdale
Norfolk jacket
nubia
obi
omophorion
orarion
orarium
overcoat
overgarment
Oxonian
paduasoy
paenula
pagri
paletot
pall
palla
pallium
paludament
pantable
pantalets
pantaloons
panties
pantihose
pantof(f)le

panton
pantoufle
pants
pants suit
pareu
pea-coat
pea-jacket
pearlies
pectoral
pedal-pushers
pelerine
pelisse
pencil skirt
penitentials
peplos
peplum
petasos
petersham
petticoat
petticoat
petticoat-breeches
ph(a)elonion
Phrygian cap
picture-hat
pierrot
pilch
pileus
pill-box
pinafore
pinafore-dress
pinafore-skirt
pinner
piupiu
pixie-hood
plaid
plimsoll
plus-fours
plushes
pneumonia-blouse
poke-bonnet
polonaise
polo-neck
poncho
pontificals
pos(h)teen
powdering-gown
pressure-helmet
pressure-suit
pressure-waistcoat
princess(e)
pumps
puttee
rabato
raglan
raincoat
rami(e)
Ramil(l)ie(s)
ra-ra skirt
rat-catcher
rational
rationals
rebater
rebato
redingote
reefer
reefing-jacket
riding-breeches
riding-cloak
riding-clothes
riding-coat
riding-glove

riding-habit
riding-hood
riding-robe
riding-skirt
riding-suit
robe
robe-de-chambre
rochet
roll-neck sweater
roll-on
rompers
romper-suit
roquelaure
ruff
rug-gown
sabot
sack
sack-coat
safari jacket
safari suit
sagum
sailor-hat
sakkos
salopette
samfoo
sanbenito
sandal
sarafan
sari
sarong
sash
sayon
scapular
scarf
scarpetto
schema
scotch bonnet
screen
sea-boots
sealskin
semmit
separates
shalwar
shako
shaps
shauchle
shawl
shawl-waistcoat
shell suit
shift
shirt
shirt dress
shirtwaist
shirtwaister
shoe
shooting-jacket
short-clothes
short-coats
shortgown
shorts
shovel-hat
silk-hat
silly-how
singlet
siren suit
skeleton suit
skin-tights
skirt
skullcap
slacks
slicker

sling-back
slip
slip-over
slipper(s)
slipslop
sloppy Joe
slop(s)
slouch(-hat)
small-clothes
smalls
smicket
smock
smock-frock
smoking cap
smoking jacket
sneaker(s)
snood
snow-boots
snow-shoe(s)
sock
sola(r) topi/helmet
solitaire
solleret
sombrero
sontag
soubise
soutane
sou'-wester
space-suit
spat
spattee
spatterdash
spencer
sphendone
sponge-bags
sporran
sports jacket
sports shirt
start-up
stays
steenkirk
steeple-crown
steeple-hat
stephane
step-in
Stetson
sticharion
stock
stockinet(te)
stockingette
stocking(s)
stola
stole
stomacher
stovepipe (hat)
strait-jacket
strait-waistcoat
straw (hat)
string vest
string-tie
strip
stuff-gown
subfusc
subucula
succinctorium
sun-bonnet
sundown
sun-dress
sunhat
sunsuit
superhumeral

**garments, vestments**
*(contd.)*
surcingle
surcoat
surplice
surtout
suspender-belt
suspenders
swaddling-band/cloth/
  clothes
swagger-coat
swallow-tail
sweat band
sweat suit
sweater
sweat-shirt
swimming costume
swimsuit
swimwear
sword-belt
tabard
taglioni
tail-coat
tails
taj
talar
talaria
tall hat
tallith
talma
tam
Tam O'Shanter
tammy
tanga
tank top
tarboosh
tarpaulin
tasse
tawdry-lace
tea-gown
Teddy suit
tee-shirt
ten-gallon hat
terai
thrum-cap
tiar(a)
tie
tights
tile(-hat)
tippet
toga
tonnag
top-boots
topcoat
topee
topi
topper
tops
toque
toreador pants
tournure
tower
toy
tozie
track shoe
track suit
trenchard
trench-coat
trencher-cap
trews
tricorn(e)

trilby
trollopee
trot-cozy
trouser suit
trousers
trouse(s)
trunk-breeches
trunk-hose
trunks
truss(es)
trusty
T-shirt
tube-skirt
tunic
tunicle
tuque
turban
turtle-neck
tuxedo
twin-set
ugly
ulster
ulsterette
undercoat
underpants
undershorts
undervest
upper-stock
Vandyke (collar)
vareuse
veil
veld(-)schoen
vest
victorine
visite
vitta
volet
waistcloth
waistcoat
wam(p)us
war bonnet
warm
watch cap
watch chain
Watteau bodice
weeper
wellie
wellington
wet-suit
whisk
white tie
wide-awake
wig
wimple
windcheater
windjammer
wing collar
winkle-pickers
woggle
wrap
wraparound
wrapover
wrapper
wrap-rascal
wristlet
wylie-coat
yarmulka
yashmak
Y-fronts
zamarra
zoot suit

zoster
zucchetto

**heraldry**

abatement
addorsed
affrontee
Albany Herald
allusive
annulet
armorist
assurgent
augmentation
baton-sinister
bendlet
bend-sinister
bendwise
bendy
bezant
bicorporate
billet
bordure
botoné
brisure
caboched
cabré
cadency
canting
canton
catherine-wheel
champ
chequy
chevron
chevrony
chief
coupé
debased
debruised
declinant
delf
device
dexter
difference
dimidiate
dismembered
displayed
dormant
double
doubling
dragonné
dwale
eightfoil
embattled
emblaze
emblazon
emblazoner
emblazonment
emblazonry
enarched
enarmed
engouled
engrail
engrailed
engrailment
enveloped
escrol(l)
escutcheon
extendant
fess(e)
fesse-point

fetterlock
field
fimbriate
fitché(e)
flanch
flanched
flotant
fracted
fret
fructed
fur
fusil
gale
gamb
garb(e)
gemel
gerbe
golp(e)
gorged
grieced
g(u)ardant
gules
gyron
gyronny
hatchment
haurient
herisson
honour-point
impale
impalement
increscent
inescutcheon
interfretted
invected
jessant
langued
lioncel
lis
lozenge
lozengy
manche
mantling
martlet
mascle
mascled
masculy
moline
morné
morned
mounted
mullet
naiant
naissant
nombril
nowed
nowy
opinicus
or
orle
palewise
pall
passant
patonce
patté(e)
pean
percussant
pheon
pile
point
pommelé
pommelled

**heraldry** *(contd.)*
pommetty
portate
portcullis
posé
potencé
potent
primrose
quarter
quartering
quarterly
queue
ragged staff
raguled
raguly
rampant
raping
rebate
regardant
respect
respectant
roundel
rustre
saltire
sans nombre
satyral
scarp
segreant
sej(e)ant
semé(e)
square-pierced
statant
tenné
trangle
tressure
trippant
umbrated
undee
undifferenced
unguled
urinant
vair
vairé
verdoy
vert
voided
vol
volant
vorant
vuln
vulned
waved
weel
wivern
woodwose
(wood-house)

**herbs, spices**

amaracus
basil thyme
caraway seeds
cardamom
cassia
cayenne
chervil
chilli
chive
cinnamon
cloves
coriander

cum(m)in
dill
dittany
endive
eyebright
fennel
fenugreek
finoc(c)hio
galega
garlic
gentian
ginger
groundsel
hellebore
henbane
horehound
horseradish
Hyoscyamus
hyssop
isatis
juniper
lemon thyme
liquorice
lovage
lungwort
mace
marjoram
mint
motherwort
mustard
myrrh
nutmeg
oregano
orpine
paprika
parsley
peppermint
purslane
rampion
rape
rosemary
rue
saffron
sage
savory
stacte
tarragon
thyme
turmeric
vanilla
verbena
watercress
wintergreen
wormwood
woundwort
yerba

**jewels, gems**

agate
amber
amethyst
aquamarine
asteria
balas ruby
baroque
beryl
bloodstone
brilliant
cairngorm
cameo

carbuncle
chalcedony
chrysolite
coral
cornelian
crystal
diamond
draconites
dumortierite
emerald
fire-opal
garnet
girasol(e)
grossular(ite)
heliodor
hyacinth
hyalite
hydrophane
intaglio
jacinth
jade
jango(o)n
jasper
jet
lapis lazuli
ligure
marcasite
marquise
Mocha stone
moonstone
morganite
mother-of-pearl
nacre
olivet
olivine
onyx
opal
oriental amethyst
paragon
pearl
peridot(e)
pyreneite
pyrope
Rhinestone
rhodolite
rose
rose-cut
rose-diamond
ruby
sapphire
sard
sardine
sardonyx
smaragd
topaz
tourmaline
turquoise
water-sapphire
wood-opal
yu
yu-stone
zircon

**Jewish calendar**

Ab
Abib
Adar
Adar Sheni
Elul
Hes(h)van

ly(y)ar
Kislev
Nisan
S(h)ebat
Sivan
Tammuz
Tebet(h)
Tis(h)ri
Veadar

**languages**

Aeolic
Afghan
Afrikaans
Akkadian
Albanian
Alemannic
Algonki(a)n
Altaic
Ameslan
Amharic
Anatolian
Anglo-Saxon
Arabic
Aramaic
Armenian
Armoric
Aryan
Assyrian
Attic
Austric
Austroasiatic
Austronesian
Avestan
Bahasa Indonesia
Balinese
Baltoslav(on)ic
Baluch(i)
Bantu
Basque
Basuto
Bengali
Berber
Bohemian
bohunk
Breton
Brezonek
British
Brythonic
Bulgarian
Bulgaric
Burmese
B(y)elorussian
Cajun
Carib
Catalan
Celtic
Chaldaic
Cherokee
Chinese
Choctaw
Circassian
Cornish
creole
Croat(ian)
Cushitic
Czech
Danish
Dardic
Doric

**languages** *(contd.)*
Dravidian
Dutch
Early English
Efik
English
Erse
Eskimo
Esperanto
Est(h)onian
Ethiopic
Etruscan
Euskarian
Fanti
Farsi
Finnish
Finno-Ugric (-Ugrian)
Flemish
Franglais
French
Frisian
Gadhelic (Goidelic)
Gaelic
Gaulish
Geëz (Giz)
Gentoo
Georgian
German
Germanic
Greek
Guaraní
Gujarat(h)i
Gullah
Hausa
Hawaiian
Hebrew
Hellenic
Herero
High German
Hindi
Hindustani
Hittite
Hottentot
Hungarian
Icelandic
Idiom Neutral
Ido
I(g)bo
Indian
Indic
Indo-European
Indo-Germanic
In(n)uit
Interlingua
Ionic
Iranian
Iraqi
Irish
Iroquoian
Italian
Italic
Japanese
Kalmuck
Kanarese
Kannada
Karen
Kennick
Khmer
Koine
Kolarian

Kuo-yü
Kurdish
Ladin
Ladino
Lallans
Landsmaal
Langue d'oc
Langue d'oil
Langue d'oui
Laplandish
Lapp
Lappish
Latin
Latvian
Lettic
Lettish
lingua franca
lingua geral
Lithuanian
Low German
Magyar
Malagasy
Malay
Malayala(a)m
Maltese
Manchu
Mandaean
Mandarin
Mandingo
Manx
Maori
Marathi
Median
Melanesian
Mexican
Micmac
Middle English
Moeso-gothic
Mohawk
Mohican
Mon
Mongolian
Moto
Munda
Nahuatl
Navaho
Neo
Newspeak
Norwegian
Novial
Nynorsk
Old English
Old Norse
Oriya
Oscan
Ostyak
Pali
Papiamento
Pawnee
Pehlevi
Pekin(g)ese
Pennsylvania Dutch
Persian
Persic
Phoenician
Pictish
pig Latin
Pilipino
Platt-Deutsch
Polabian

Polish
Portuguese
Prakrit
Provençal
Provinçal
Prussian
Punic
Punjabi
Pushtu
Quechua
Rabbinic
Rhaetic
Rhaeto-Romance
Rhaeto-Romanic
Rock English
rogues' Latin
Romaic
Romance
Romanes
Romanic
Roman(n)y
Romans(c)h
Rumanian
Russian
Russniak
Ruthenian
Sakai
Samnite
Samoyed(e)
Sanskrit
Saxon
Scots
Scythian
Semitic
Serb(ian)
Serbo-Croat(ian)
Shan
Shona
Siamese
Sinhalese
Siouan
Slavonic
Slovak
Slovenian
Somali
Sorbian
Sorbish
Spanish
Sudanic
Sumerian
Suomi
Swahili
Swedish
Swiss
Syriac
Taal
Tagálog
Taino
Tamil
Tataric
Telugu
Teutonic
Thai
Tibetan
Tocharian
Tswana
Tuareg
Tungus(ian)
Tupí
Turki

Turkish
Twi
Ugrian
Ugro-finnic
Ukrainian
Umbrian
Uralic
Urdu
Uzbeg
Vaudois
Vietnamese
Volapük
Volga-Baltic
Volscian
Welsh
Wendic
Wendish
West-Saxon
Wolof
Xhosa
Yakut
Yiddish
Yoruba
Zulu

**legal**

abate
abatement
absolvitor
abstract of title
acceptilation
accession
accessory
accessory after the fact
accessory before the fact
Acts of Adjournal
(ad) avizandum
adeem
adhere
adjudication
adminicle
administrator
afforce
alienee
alienor
allenarly
allodial
amicus curiae
amove
appointer
apprize
apprizer
assumpsit
attorn
back-bond
bairn's-part
capias
certiorari
chaud-mellé
cognosce
cognovit
compear
compulsitor
copyhold
cross-examine
decree absolute
decree nisi
decreet
decretals

**legal** *(contd.)*
decretist
dedimus
deed
deed of accession
defalcate
defeasance
defeasanced
defeasible
defendant
defender
deforce
deforcement
deforciant
delapidation
delate
delation
delator
delict
demurrer
deodand
detainer
detinue
devastavit
devest
diet
dimissory
disapply
disbar
disbench
discovert
discoverture
disentail
disgavel
disinherison
dispone
disponee
disposition
disseise
disseisin
disseisor
distinguish
distrain
distrainee
distrainer
distrainment
distrainor
distraint
distress
distringas
dittay
dole
donatary
droit
droit du Seigneur
duplicand
duply
dying declaration
easement
ejectment
embracer
embracery
emendals
emphyteusis
en ventre sa mère
enfeoff
enfeoffment
enjoin
enlevé
enlevement

entry
eric
escheat
escrow (escroll)
escuage
esnecy
esrepe
essoin
estate
estop
estoppel
estover
estray
estreat
estrepement
examination
excamb
excambion
excambium
executry
exemplify
expromission
extend
extent
extinguishment
extract
extradition
facile
facility
factorise
faldage
felo de se
felony
feme
feme covert
feme sole
feoff
feoffee
feoffer (feoffor)
feoffment
feu
feuar
fief
filacer
fire-bote
fiscal
folio
force and fear
force majeure
foreclose
foreclosure
forinsec
forisfamiliate
forjudge
frankalmoign
free-bench
frontager
fugitation
fungibles
garnishee
garnisheement
garnisher
gavelkind
gavelman
granter (grantor)
grassum
hamesucken
hedge-bote
hide
homologation

horning
house-bote
hypothec
hypothecary
hypothecate
hypothecation
improbation
indenture
indict
indictment
induciae
infangthief
infeft
inquirendo
institorial
insucken
interlocutor
interplead
interpleader
interpose
irrepleviable
irreplevisable
ish
John Doe and
  Richard Roe
joinder
jointure
jus primae noctis
laches
law-agent
law-burrows
legitim
lenocinium
letters of administration
lien
life-rent
malfeasance
mens rea
mesne
messuage
misdemeanant
misfeasance
misfeasor
misprision
mittimus
mora
mortmain
multiplepoinding
nolle prosequi
nolo contendere
non-access
nonage
non-compearance
non-entry
nonsuit
non-user
notour
novalia
noverint
novodamus
noxal
obligant
obligation
obligor
obreption
onus probandi
ouster
outfangthief
overt act
owelty

oyer
pactum nudum
Pandect
panel
pernancy
personalty
pickery
plaint
plaintiff
porteous roll
portioner
practic
prima facie
privy
prorogate
pupil
quadruply
realty
recaption
recusation
reddendo
relator
relaxation
remise
replevin
replevy
repone
reprobator
res gestae
retour
retroact
retroactive
reverser
right of drip
rout
scutage
stillicide
supersedeas
supplicavit
surrebut
surrebuttal
surrebutter
surrejoin
surrejoinder
terminer
tolt
tort
tortfeasor
tortious
udal
udaller
ultimus haeres
unlaw
uses
usucapient
usucapion (usucaption)
usucapt
usucaptible
usufruct
usufructuary
ultimogeniture
vacatur
venire (facias)
venter
venue
vert
vest
vested
visne
voidable

**legal** *(contd.)*
voir dire
volunteer
wage
waive
waste
watch
watching brief
water-privilege
wit

**minerals**
adularia
aegirine
aegirite
alabandine
almandine
alum-shale
alum-slate
alum-stone
alunite
amazonite
amazon-stone
amianthus
amosite
amphibole
analcime
anatase
andesine
aplite
argil
arkose
asbestos
asparagus-stone
asphalt(um)
aventurine
baetyl
balas
Barbados earth
barilla
baryta
barytes
basalt
Bath stone
bath-brick
bezoar
bitter-earth
bitter-spar
bitumen
blackjack
blacklead
blaes
blende
bloodstone
blue ground
blue John
blue vitriol
bluestone
Bologna phosphorus
borane
borax
borazon
boride
bornite
boulder-clay
breccia
Bristol-brick
Bristol-diamond
brown spar
brownstone

buhrstone
cacholong
caen-stone
cairngorm
calamine
calc-sinter
calcspar
calc-tuff
caliche
calp
Carborundum®
cat's-eye
cat-silver
cauk
celestine
cement-stone
ceruse
chalcedony
chalcedonyx
chalk
chert
Chile saltpetre
china clay
china stone
chrome-alum
chrome-spinel
chrysoberyl
chrysocolla
chrysoprase
chrysotile
cinnabar
cinnamon-stone
cipollino
corundum
cryolite
cymophane
dacite
dendrite
Derbyshire spar
diabase
diallage
dialogite
diaspore
diatomite
dice-coal
diopside
dioptase
diorite
dogger
dogtooth-spar
dolerite
dolomite
dopplerite
dropstone
dunite
dyscrasite
dysodyle
eagle-stone
earthflax
earthwax
eclogite
electric calamine
elvan
emery
encrinite
enhydrite
enhydros
epidiorite
epidosite
epidote
epistilbite

epsomite
erinite
erionite
erubescite
erythrite
euclase
eucrite
eudialyte
eutaxite
euxenite
fahlerz
fahlore
fakes
fayalite
fel(d)spar
felsite
felstone
flint
fluorite
fluorspar
franklinite
French chalk
fuchsite
fulgurite
fuller's earth
gabbro
gadolinite
gahnite
galena
galenite
gangue
gan(n)ister
garnet-rock
gibbsite
glance
glauberite
glauconite
glimmer
gmelinite
gneiss
goldstone
goslarite
gossan
göthite
granite
granitite
granodiorite
granophyre
granulite
graphic granite
graphite
green earth
greenockite
greensand
greenstone
greisen
greywacke
gummite
gypsum
haematite
hälleflinta
halloysite
harmotome
hatchettite
haüyne
heavy spar
hedyphane
hemimorphite
hepatite
hercynite
(h)essonite

heulandite
hiddenite
honey-stone
hornblende
hornfels
hornstone
horseflesh ore
humite
hyacinth
hyalophane
hypersthene
ice-spar
ice-stone
idocrase
ironstone
jacinth
keratophyre
kermes
kermesite
kieselguhr
knotenschiefer
kunkur
kupferschiefer
lamprophyre
lapis lazuli
lepidomelane
limestone
lithomarge
narlstone
meerschaum
mellite
mica
microlite
microlith
mispickel
morion
moss-agate
mundic
nail-head-spar
needle-tin
nepheline
nickel-bloom
nickel-ochre
Norway saltpetre
nosean
noselite
obsidian
omphacite
onyx
onyx-marble
ophiolite
orthoclase
orthophyre
ottrelite
ozokerite
peacock-ore
pencil-ore
pencil-stone
peperino
periclase
pericline
petuntse
piedmontite
pipeclay
pipestone
plagioclose
pleonaste
porphyry
potstone
prase
protogine

**minerals** *(contd.)*
pyrites
quartz
realgar
rock-oil
rubicelle
ruby-spinel
rutile
saltpetre
sandstone
sanidine
sapphire
sapphire-quartz
sapphirine
sard
sardonyx
satin-spar
satin-stone
scaglia
scawtite
schalstein
schiller-spar
schist
schorl
serpentine
serpentine(-rock)
shale
shell-limestone
shell-marl
silica
silver-glance
sinter
slate
soapstone
spar
speiss-cobalt
spelter
sphene
spiegeleisen
spinel
spinel-ruby
spodumene
stinkstone
strontian(ite)
sunstone
surturbrand
swinestone
sylvine
tabular spar
tachylyte
talc
talc-schist
terne
terpene
terpineol
terra alba
terracotta
terra-japonica
terramara
terra-rossa
terra-sigillata
terts
thulia
tiger(s)-eye
till
tin-stone
toad-stone
tombac
touchstone
tourmaline
trass

travertin(e)
tripoli
troutstone
tufa
tuff
Turkey hone
Turkey stone
turquoise
tutty
uinta(h)ite
umber
Uralian emerald
uralite
uraninite
uranite
uvarovite
vanadinite
variolite
variscite
veinstone
veinstuff
Venice talc
verd-antique
vesuvianite
vitrain
vivianite
vulpinite
wacke
wad(d)
wallsend
wavellite
Wernerite
whet-slate
whewellite
whinstone
white pyrites
willemite
witherite
wolfram
wollastonite
wood-coal
wulfenite
wurtzite
zaratite
zarnich
zeolite
zeuxite
zinkenite
zircon
zoisite
zorgite

**musical instruments**

aeolian harp
aerophone
alpenhorn
alphorn
althorn
alto
Amati
American organ
apollonicon
archlute
arpeggione
atabal
autoharp
balalaika
bandore
bandura
banjulele

baryton(e)
bass clarinet
bass drum
bass fiddle
bass horn
bass tuba
bass viol
basset horn
bazooka
bombard
bombardon
bongo (drum)
bouzouki
buccina
bugle
buglet
bull fiddle
calliope
castanets
celeste
cello
cembalo
chair-organ
chalumeau
chamber organ
chikara
Chinese pavilion
chitarrone
chordophone
cinema-organ
cithara
cither(n)
citole
cittern
clarichord
clarinet
clarino
clarion
clarsach
clave
clavichord
cornet
cornettino
crwth
cymbal
cymbalo
decachord
dichord
didgeridoo
digitorium
double bass
drum
dulcimer
Dulcitone®
dumb-piano
echo
electric guitar
electric organ
euphonium
fagotto
fife
fipple-flute
flageolet
flügel
flügelhorn
flute
flûte-à-bec
flutina
French horn
gamelan
German flute

gimbard
gittern
glass harmonica
glockenspiel
grand piano
gu
guiro
guitar
gusla
Hammerklavier
hand-horn
hand-organ
harmonica
harmonicon
harmoniphone
harmonium
harp
harpsichord
hautboy
heckelphone
heptachord
horn
hornpipe
humstrum
hunting-horn
hurdy-gurdy
idiophone
jingling Johnny
kantele
kazoo
kent-bugle
keyboard(s)
keybugle
klavier
koto
krummhorn
Kuh-horn
langsp(i)el
lituus
lur(e)
lyra-viol
lyre
mandola
mandolin(e)
mandora
manzello
maraca
marimba
marimbaphone
marine trumpet
melodeon
metallophone
mirliton
monochord
Moog synthesizer
mouth-harp
mouth-organ
mridangam
musette
musical glasses
naker
nose-flute
nun's-fiddle
oboe
oboe d'amore
oboe di caccia
ocarina
octachord
octave-flute
ophicleide
organ-harmonium

**musical instruments**
*(contd.)*
orpharion
orpheorion
pandora
panharmonicon
Pan-pipes
Pan's pipes
pantaleon
pianette
pianino
piano
piano-accordion
pianoforte
Pianola®
piano-organ
piffero
pipe
pipeless organ
pipe-organ
player piano
polyphon(e)
poogye
posaune
psaltery
pyrophone
quena
quint(e)
racket(t)
rebec(k)
regal
rote
sackbut
salpinx
sambuca
sancho
sang
santir
sarangi
sarod
sarrusophone
sausage-bassoon
saxhorn
saxophone
seraphine
serinette
serpent
s(h)amisen
shawm
side-drum
sitar
small-pipes
sourdeline
sousaphone
spinet(te)
squeeze-box
squiffer
steel drum
sticcado
stock-and-horn
strad
Stradivari(us)
string bass
sultana
symphonion
symphony
synthesiser
syrinx
tabla
tabor
tabo(u)rin

tabret
tambour
tamboura
tambourine
tam-tam
testudo
tetrachord
theatre organ
theorbo
timbal
timbrel
timpano
tin whistle
traps
triangle
trichord
tromba marina
trombone
trump
trumpet
trumpet marine
tuba
tubular bells
tympan
uillean pipes
ukulele
vibraharp
vibraphone
vielle
vihuela
vina
viol
viola
viola da braccio
(viola da) gamba
viola da gamba
viola da spalla
viola d'amore
violin
violoncello
violone
virginal(s)
vocalion
waldflute
waldhorn
Welsh harp
xylophone
xylorimba
zambomba
zampogna
zanze
zel
zeze
zinke
zither
zufolo

**parliaments**

Althing (Iceland)
Cortes (Spain
Portugal)
Dáil (Ireland)
d(o)uma (Russia)
ecclesia (Athens)
eduskunta (Finland)
Folketing (Denmark)
House of Commons (UK)
House of Keys (Isle of Man)
House of Lords (UK)

Knesset (Israel)
Lagt(h)ing (Norway)
Lagting (Norway)
Landst(h)ing (Denmark)
Landtag (Germany)
Løgting (Faroes)
Lok Sabha (India)
Majlis (Iran)
Odelst(h)ing (Norway)
Oireachtas (Ireland)
Parliament (UK)
Pnyx (Athens)
Porte (Turkey)
Rajya Sabha (India)
Reichsrat(h) (Austria)
Reichstag (Germany)
Rigsdag (Denmark)
Riksdag (Sweden)
Seanad (Ireland)
Senate (Rome
USA
etc.)
Skupshtina (Yugoslavia)
Sobranje (Bulgaria)
Stort(h)ing (Norway)
Tynwald (Isle of Man)
witenagemot (England)

**prosody**

Alcaic
alexandrine
amphibrach
amphibrachic
amphimacer
Anacreontic
anacrusis
anacrustic
anapaest
anapaestic
antibacchius
antispast
antispastic
antistrophe
Archilochian
arsis
Asclepiad
asynartete
atonic
bacchius
catalectic
choliamb
choree
choriamb
cinquain
cretic
dactyl
decastich
decasyllabic
decasyllable
dipody
dispondaic
dispondee
distich
disyllable
ditrochean
ditrochee
dizain
dochmiac
dochmius
dodecasyllabic

dodecasyllable
dolichurus
duan
ectasis
ecthlipsis
elide
elision
enjamb(e)ment
envoy
epic
epirrhema
epistrophe
epitrite
epode
epopee
epopoeia
epos
epyllion
extrametrical
eye-rhyme
false quantity
feminine caesura
feminine ending
feminine rhyme
fifteener
free verse
galliambic
g(h)azal
glyconic
gradus
haiku
head-rhyme
hendecasyllabic
hendecasyllable
hephthemimer
heptameter
heptapody
heptasyllabic
heterostrophic
heterostrophy
hexameter
hexametric(al)
hexapody
hexastich
Hudibrastic
huitain
hypercatalectic
hypercatalexis
hypermetrical
iamb
iambus
ictus
Ionic
irrational
kyrielle
laisse
Leonine
limerick
limma
linked verse
logaoedic
long-measure
macaronic(s)
masculine ending
masculine rhyme
meliboean
miurus
monometer
monorhyme
monostich
monostrophic

**prosody** *(contd.)*
mora
outride
oxytone
pantoum
pentameter
pentastich
penthemimer
Pherecratean
Pherecratic
Pindaric
poulters' measure
proceleusmatic
pyrrhic
Pythian
quatorzain
quatrain
reported verses
rhopalic
rhyme-royal
rich rhyme
riding-rhyme
rime riche
rime suffisante
rondeau
rondel
rove-over
rubaiyat
run-on
Sapphics
scazon
semeion
senarius
septenarius
sestina
spondee
strophe
synaphe(i)a
tetrameter
tetrapody
tetrasemic
tetrastich
thesis
tirade
tribrach
trimeter
tripody
triseme
trochee
villanelle
virelay

**ranks in armed forces**

able seaman
acting sub-lieutenant
admiral
admiral of the fleet
air chief marshal
air commandant
air commodore
air vice marshal
aircraftman
air-marshal
brigadier
captain
chief officer
chief petty officer
chief technician
colonel
commandant

commander
commodore
corporal
field marshal
first officer
fleet chief petty officer
flight lieutenant
flight officer
flight sergeant
flying
officer
general
group captain
group officer
junior seaman
junior technician
lance-corporal
lance-jack
lance-sergeant
leading aircraftman
leading seaman
lieutenant
lieutenant-colonel
lieutenant-commander
lieutenant-general
major
major-general
marshal
marshal of the Royal
    Air Force
master-at-arms
midshipman
ordinary seaman
petty officer
pilot officer
post-captain
private
purser
quartermaster
quartermaster-general
quartermaster-sergeant
quartermistress
rear-admiral
risaldar
ritt-master
second lieutenant
second officer
senior aircraftman
sergeant
sergeant-major
squadron leader
squadron officer
staff sergeant
sub-lieutenant
superintendent
third officer
vice admiral
warrant officer
wing commander
wing officer

**rhetoric**

abscission
alliteration
amoebaean
anacoluthia
anacoluthon
anadiplosis
anaphora
anaphoric

anastrophe
antimetabole
antimetathesis
antiphrasis
antiphrastic(al)
antithesis
antithetic(al)
antonomasia
aporia
asteism
asyndeton
auxesis
catachresis
chiasmus
climax
diallage
diegesis
dissimile
double entendre
dramatic irony
dysphemism
ecbole
echoic
ecphonesis
ellipsis
enallage
enantiosis
enumeration
epanadiplosis
epanalepsis
epanaphora
epanodos
epanorthosis
epexegesis
epiphonema
epizeuxis
erotema
erotetic
figure
flower
head-rhyme
hendiadys
holophrase
hypallage
hyperbaton
hyperbole
hypobole
hypostrophe
hypotyposis
hysteron-proteron
increment
irony
litotes
meiosis
metalepsis
metaphor
metonym
metonymy
mixed metaphor
onomatopoeia
oxymoron
parabole
paral(e)ipsis
parenthesis
prolepsis
simile
syllepsis
symploce
synchoresis
synchysis
synecdoche

synoeciosis
trope
vicious circle
zeugma

**titles of rulers**

abuna
adelantado
ag(h)a
alderman
amir
amman
amtman
ard-ri(gh)
atabeg
atabek
ataman
atheling
ayatollah
Ban
beglerbeg
begum
bey
boyar
burgrave
caboceer
cacique
caliph
caudillo
Cid
Dan
Dauphin
Dauphine
Dauphiness
dey
diadochus
doge
duce
duke
ealdorman
elector
emir
emperor
empress
ethnarch
exarch
gospodar
Graf
Gräfin
grave
Great Mogul
harmost
heptarch
hospodar
huzoor
imperator
Inca
infanta
infante
jarl
kaid
kaiser
kalif
khan
khedive
king
kinglet
kingling
landgrave
landgravine

**titles of rulers** *(contd.)*
maharaja(h)
maharani
mandarin
marchesa
marchese
marchioness
margrave
margravine
marquess
marquis
marquise
mikado
Mirza
Monseigneur
monsieur
Monsignor
Monsignore
mormaor
mpret
nabob
naik
nawab
nizam
nomarch
omrah
padishah
palatine
palsgrave
pasha
pendragon
pentarch
pharaoh
prince
prince-bishop
prince-imperial
princess
raja(h)
rajpramukh
rana
rani
Rhinegrave
Rhinegravine
sachem
sagamore
satrap
shah
sheik(h)
sherif
shogun
sirdar
sovereign
stad(t)holder
starosta
suba(h)dar
sultan
suzerain
taoiseach
theocrat
toiseach
toparch
tsar
tuchun
voivode
waldgrave

**tools**

about-sledge
aiguille
auger

auger-bit
awl
boaster
bodkin
bolster
bradawl
broach
bucksaw
burin
burr
buzz-saw
card
caschrom
caulking-iron
celt
centre-bit
chaser
chisel
chopper
clamp
cleaver
cold-chisel
cradle-scythe
crosscut-saw
crown-saw
diamond-drill
dibble
dividers
dolly
drawing-knife
draw-knife
drill
drove
els(h)in
extirpator
fillister
float
forceps
forfex
fork
fraise
frame-saw
fretsaw
gad
gang-saw
gavelock
gimlet
gouge
grapnel
grapple
graver
gurlet
hacksaw
hammer
handsaw
hawk
hay fork
hay knife
helve-hammer
hod
hoe
holing-axe
jackhammer
jack-plane
jointer
laster
level
levelling-rod
levelling-staff
loy
mace

madge
maker
mall
mallet
mattock
maul
monkey
moon-knife
mortar
muller
oliver
oustiti
pachymeter
pad-saw
palstave
panel saw
panga
paper-cutter
paper-knife
pattle
pecker
peel
pestle
pick
pickaxe
pincers
pinch
pinking-shears
piolet
pitchfork
plane
planer
plessor
plexor
pliers
plough
plow
plugger
plumb
plumb-line
plumb-rule
plummet
pocket-knife
pointel
pricker
priest
priming-iron
priming-wire
probang
probe
probing-scissors
prod
prog
pruning-bill
pruning-hook
pruning-knife
pruning-shears
prunt
punch
puncheon
punty
quadrant
quannet
rabble
rake
raspatory
reed-knife
repositor
retractor
ricker
rickstick

riddle
riffle
ripper
ripping-saw
ripple
rip-saw
risp
router
rule
ruler
sash-tool
saw
sax
scalpel
scauper
scissors
scoop
scooper
scorper
scraper
screwdriver
screwjack
screw-wrench
scribe(r)
scutch(er)
scythe
seam-set
serving-mallet
shave
shears
shovel
sickle
slane
slate-axe
slater
slicker
smoother
snap
snarling-iron
snarling-rod
snips
soldering-bolt
soldering-iron
spade
spanner
spider
spokeshave
spud
squeegee
stadda
stake
stapler
stapling-machine
steel
stithy
stone-hammer
stretching-iron
strickle
strigil
stubble-rake
style
stylet
swage
swingle(-hand)
switch
tedder
tenon-saw
threshel
thresher
thrust-hoe
tint-tool

**tools** *(contd.)*
tongs
trepan
trowel
T-square
turfing-iron
turf-spade
turning-saw
tweezers
twist drill
upright
van
vice
vulsella
waster
whip-saw
widener
wimble
wood-shears
wortle
xyster
Y-level

**units of measurement**

acre
ampere
angstrom
anker
ardeb
are
arpent
arroba
arshin
as
bar
barleycorn
barn
barrel
bath
baud
becquerel
bel
bigha
bit
Board of Trade Unit/BTU
board-foot
boll
bolt
braccio
bushel
butt
cab
cable
calorie
candela
candle
candy
carat
catty
cell
cental
centner
chain
chalder
chaldron
ch(o)enix
chopin
chronon
clove
co(o)mb

cor
cord
coss
coulomb
cran
crith
cubit
cumec
curie
cusec
cyathus
daraf
Debye (unit)
degree
demy
dessiatine
digit
dirham
dra(ch)m
dyne
ell
em
en
epha(h)
erg
farad
faraday
fathom
fermium
firkin
firlot
foot
fother
fou
furlong
gal
gallon
gerah
gilbert
gill
grain
gram(me)
hectare
henry
hertz
hin
hogshead
homer
hoppus foot
hundredweigh
inch
joule
kaneh
kantar
kelvin
k(h)at
kilderkin
kin
knot
league
leaguer
li
liang
liard
ligne
link
lippy
lire
lisp(o)und
litre
log

lux
maneh
maund
metre
mho
micrometre
micron
mile
mil(l)
mina
minim
minute
mna
modius
mole
morgen
muid
mutchkin
nail
neper
nepit
newton
nit (information)
nit (luminance)
noggin
obol
oersted
ohm
oke
omer
ounce
oxgang
parasang
pascal
peck
perch
picul
pin
pint
pipe
poise
pole
pood
pound
poundal
quart
quarter
quartern
quintal
quire
radian
ream
rem
rod
rood
rote
rotolo
run(d)let
rutherford
sabin
s(a)eculum
sazhen
scruple
second
seer
semuncia
shekel
shippound
siemens
sievert
sone

span
square
stadium
steradian
stere
stilb
stoke(s)
stone
tael
talent
tare
tesla
therm
tical
tierce
tod
toise
tola
ton
tonne
tonneau
tor
truss
tun
vara
verst
virgate
volt
watt
weber
wey
yard
yardland
yojan

**vehicles**

aerotrain
air-car
amtrack
araba
arba
aroba
barouche
Bath chair
berlin(e)
bicycle
biga
bobsled
bobsleigh
bogie
boneshaker
brake
britzka
brougham
brute
bubble-car
buckboard
buckcart
buck-wagon
buggy
bus
cab
caboose
cabriolet
caisson
calash
camper
car
caravan
caravanette

**vehicles** *(contd.)*
caroche
car(r)iole
carry-all
catafalque
chair
chaise
chaise-cart
chapel cart
charabanc
chariot
clarence
coach
coaler
convertible
conveyance
cycle
dandy-cart
dandy-horse
dennet
désobligeante
dhooly
diesel
diligence
dilly
Dodgem(s)®
dog-cart
dogcart
dolly
doolie
dormitory-car
drag
dray
dros(h)ky
duck
ekka
fiacre
fly
fork-lift truck
four-in-hand
gharri
gig
glass-coach
go-kart
Green Goddess
gyrocar
gyrodyne
hack
hackery
hackney-carriage/coach
hatchback
herdic
honey-cart
honey-wag(g)on
HUMV
hurley-hacket
ice-yacht
inside-car
jeep
jingle
jinricksha(w)
jitney
juggernaut
kago
kajawah
kart
kibitka
landau
landaulet(te)
limousine
litter

lorry
mail-cart
minibus
monorail
motor caravan
motor-bicycle
motor-bike
motor-bus
motor-car
motor-coach
motor-cycle
motor-lorry
motor-scooter
norimon
omnibus
outside-car
palanquin (palankeen)
palki
pantechnicon
pedal cycle
pedicab
people mover
phaeton
pick-up
pill-box
pincers
post-chaise
prairie schooner
pulka
quad
quadriga
rail-bus
rail-car
rail-motor
ricksha(w)
roadster
rockaway
runabout
safety bicycle
saloon-car
saloon-carriage
samlor
scooter
sedan
sedan-chair
shandry(dan)
shooting-brake
sidecar
single-decker
skateboard
ski-bob
sled
sledge
sleeper
sleeping-car
sleeping-carriage
sleeping-coach
sleigh
slip-carriage
slip-coach
slipe
snowmobile
snow-plough
sociable
solo
speedster
spider
spring-carriage
spring-cart
squad car
stage-coach

stage-wagon
stanhope
station-wagon
steam-car
steam-carriage
steamer
steam-roller
stillage
stone boat
straddle carrier
street-car
sulky
surrey
tally-ho
tandem
tank
tank-car
tank-engine
tanker
tank-wagon
tarantas(s)
tartana
tax(ed)-cart
taxi
taxicab
T-cart
telega
telpher
tender
thoroughbrace
through-train
tilbury
tim-whisk(e)y
tin Lizzie
tip
tip-cart
tipper
toboggan
tonga
tourer
touring-car
tractor
trailer
train
tram
tramway-car
transporter
transport-rider
trap
tricar
tricycle
trike
triplet
trishaw
troika
trolley
trolley-bus
trolley-car
troop-carrier
tru:k
tube
tumble-car(t)
tumbrel
turbocar
two-decker
twoseater
two-wheeler
velocipede
vettura
victoria
village cart

vis-à-vis
volante
wag(g)on
wagonette
wagon-lit
wain
water-cart
water-wagon
weasel
wheelbarrow
wheel-chair
whisk(e)y
Whitechapel cart

**vessels, ships**
argosy
barca
barque
barquentine
bateau
bawley
Berthon-boat
bilander
billyboy
bireme
birlinn
boat
bomb-ketch
bomb-vessel
brig
brigantine
Bucentaur
budgerow
bum-boat
buss
butty
cabin cruiser
caique
canal-boat
canoe
caravel
Carley float
carrack
casco
cat
catamaran
catboat
clipper
coaler
coaster
cob(b)le
cockboat
cockleshell
cog
collier
commodore
coracle
corocore
corvette
cot
crare
crayer
currach
cutter
dandy
deep-sinker
deepwaterman
destroyer
d(h)ow
dinghy

**vessels, ships** *(contd.)*
diving-bell
dogger
drake
dreadnought
dredger
drog(h)er
dromond
dugout
East-Indiaman
E-boat
faltboat
felucca
flatboat
floating battery
flyboat
flying bridge
fore-and-after
frigate
frigatoon
funny
gabbart
galleass
galleon
galley
gal(l)iot
gallivat
gay-you
geordie
gondola
grab
hatch boat
herringer
hooker
hovercraft
hoy
hydrofoil
hydroplane
hydrovane
ice-boat
Indiaman
iron-clad
jigger
jollyboat
junk
kayak
ketch
koff
laker
landing-craft
lapstreak
launch
liberty-ship
lighter
line-of-battle-ship
liner
long-boat
longship
lorcha
lugger
lymphad
mackinaw
masoolah
merchantman
mistico
monitor
monkey-boat
monohull
monoxylon
montaria
motor-boat

motor-launch
motor-ship
motoscafo
mud-boat
mudscow
multihull
nacelle
nuggar
outrigger
packet
packet-boat
packet-ship
pair-oar
patamar
pedalo
penteconter
periagua
peter-boat
pink
pinkie
pinky
pinnace
piragua
pirogue
pleasure-boat
pocket battleship
polacca
polacre
pontoon
powerboat
praam
pra(h)u
pram
privateer
puffer
pulwar
punt
puteli
quadrireme
quinquereme
randan
razee
river-boat
river-craft
row-barge
row-boat
rowing-boat
saic
sail-boat
sailing-boat
sailing-ship
salmon-coble
sampan
schooner
schuit
scooter
scow
scull
sculler
sea-boat
seaplane-carrier
settee
shallop
ship
ship-of-the-line
shore-boat
show-boat
skiff
sloop
sloop-of-war
smack

smuggler
snow
speed-boat
speedster
square rigger
steamboat
steamer
steam-launch
steam-packet
steamship
steam-tug
steam-vessel
steam-yacht
stern-wheeler
stew-can
sub
submarine
super-Dreadnought
supertanker
surface-craft
surf-board
surf-boat
surf-canoe
surfing-board
swamp boat
tanker
tartane(e)
tender
tern
three-decker
three-master
tilt-boat
torpedo-boat
torpedo-boat destroyer
track-boat
tracker
trader
train ferry
tramp
transport-ship
trawler
trek-schuit
triaconter
trimaran
trireme
troop-carrier
trooper
troop-ship
tub
tug
tug-boat
turbine-steamer
turret-ship
two-decker
two-master
U-boat
umiak
vaporetto
vedette(-boat)
vessel
wager-boat
warship
water-bus
well-boat
well-smack
whaleboat
whaler
wherry
whiff
windjammer
xebec

yacht
yawl
zabra
zulu

## weapons, armour

A-bomb
ack-ack
aerodart
ailette
air rifle
amusette
an(e)lace
arbalest
arblast
Archibald
Archie
arcubalist
armet
arquebus(e)
baldric(k)
ballista
ballistic missile
bandolier
basilisk
baton gun
bazooka
beaver
bill
Biscayan
blackjack
blowgun
blowpipe
bludgeon
blunderbuss
boarding-pike
bodkin
Bofors gun
bolas
bomb
bombard
boomerang
bowie knife
brassard
breastplate
breech-loader
Bren (gun)
bricole
brigandine
broadsword
brown Bess
brown bill
buckler
buckshot
bulldog
bullet
bundook
Bungalore torpedo
burganet
byrnie
caltrop
cannon
carbine
carronade
casque
cataphract
catapult
chain-armour
chain-mail
chamfrain

**weapons, armour**
*(contd.)*
Chassepot
chausses
cheval-de-frise
chokebore
claymore
cluster-bomb
coal-box
co(e)horn
Colt
Congreve
corium
dag
dagger
dah
Damascus blade
Damascus sword
demi-cannon
demi-culverin
demi-lance
depth-bomb
depth-charge
dirk
dragoon
elephant gun
épée
escopette
Exocet®
express rifle
falchion
falconet
field gun
fire-arm
fire-arrow
firebomb
firelock
firepot
fission bomb
flail
flame-thrower
flick-knife
flintlock
foil
fougade
fougasse
four-pounder
fusee
fusil
Garand rifle
gatling-gun
gavelock
genouillère
gisarme
gladius
gorget
grapeshot
greave
Greek fire
grenade
gun
habergeon
hackbut
hacqueton
hailshot
halberd
half-pike
hand-grenade
hand-gun
han(d)jar
handstaff

harquebus
hauberk
H-bomb
heaume
helm
helmet
hielaman
howitzer
jack
jamb(e)
jazerant
jesserant
Jethart staff
kalashnikov
katana
kirpan
kris
lamboys
lame
lance
Lochaber-axe
Long Tom
machete
machine-gun
mangonel
martel
Martini (-Henry)
matchlock
Mauser
Maxim(-gun)
mesail
Mills bomb
Mills grenade
mine
mine-thrower
mini-rocket launcher
minnie
mitrailleur
mitrailleuse
morgenstern
morglay
morning-star
mor(r)ion
mortar
musket
musketoon
nulla-nulla
oerlikon
panga
partisan
Patriot
pauldron
pavis(e)
peasecod-cuirass
pederero
pelican
pelta
perrier
petrary
petronel
pickelhaube
pike
pilum
pistol
pistolet
placket
plastron
plate-armour
pocket-pistol
poitrel
pole-ax(e)

poleyn
pompom
poniard
potgun
quarter-staff
queen's-arm
rapier
rerebrace
rest
revolver
rifle
rifle-grenade
sabaton
sabre
saker
sallet
saloon-pistol
saloon-rifle
sap
sarbacane
schiavone
schläger
scimitar
scorpion
Scud
scutum
serpentine
sharp
shell
shield
shillela(g)h
shortsword
shotgun
shrapnel
siege-artillery
siege-gun
siege-piece
singlestick
six-gun
six-shooter
skean(dhu)
sling
slung-shot
small-arm
small-sword
smoke-ball
smoke-bomb
snickersnee
spadroon
sparth(e)
spear
spear gun
splint-armour
spontoon
spring-gun
squid
steel
sten gun
Sterling
stern-chaser
stiletto
stone axe
stone-bow
stylet
submachine-gun
sumpit(an)
switch-blade (knife)
swivel-gun
sword
sword bayonet
sword-cane

sword-stick
tace
targe
target
taslet
tasse
tasset
testudo
three-pounder
threshel
throw-stick
time-bomb
toc emma
toggle-iron
tomahawk
Tomahawk
tomboc
tommy-gun
tormentum
torpedo
tortoise
trecento
trench-mortar
trident
truncheon
tuille
tuillette
tulwar
turret-gun
twibill
vambrace
vamplate
V-bomb
visor
vou(l)ge
war-wolf
waster
water-cannon
water-pistol
Welsh hook
white-arm
Winchester (rifle)
wind-gun
wo(o)mera(ng)
yatag(h)an
zumbooruk

**wine-bottle sizes**

baby
balthasar
jeroboam
magnum
Methuselah
nebuchadnezzar
nip
rehoboam
salmanazar

**zodiac signs**

Aquarius
Aries
Cancer
Capricorn
Gemini
Leo
Libra
Pisces
Sagittarius
Scorpio
Taurus
Virgo

# Words listed by suffix

**-ast**

chiliast
diaskeuast
dicast
dikast
dynast
ecclesiast
ecdysiast
elegiast
encomiast
enthusiast
fantast
gymnasiast
gymnast
Hesychast
hypochondriast
iconoclast
idoloclast
metaphrast
orgiast
paederast
pancratiast
paraphrast
peltast
phantasiast
pleonast
scholiast
utopiast

**-aster**

criticaster
grammaticaster
medicaster
philosophaster
poetaster
politicaster
theologaster

**-cide**

aborticide
acaricide
algicide
aphicide
aphidicide
bacillicide
bactericide
biocide
deicide
ecocide
ethnocide
feticide
filicide
foeticide
fratricide
fungicide
genocide
germicide
giganticide
herbicide

homicide
infanticide
insecticide
larvicide
liberticide
matricide
menticide
molluscicide
ovicide
parasiticide
parasuicide
parricide
patricide
pesticide
prolicide
regicide
rodenticide
sororicide
spermicide
suicide
taeniacide
trypanocide
tyrannicide
uxoricide
vaticide
verbicide
vermicide
viricide
viticide
vulpicide
weedicide

**-cracy**

aristocracy
autocracy
bureaucracy
chrysocracy
cottonocracy
democracy
demonocracy
despotocracy
dollarocracy
doulocracy
dulocracy
ergatocracy
Eurocracy
gerontocracy
gynaecocracy
hagiocracy
hierocracy
isocracy
kakistocracy
meritocracy
millocracy
mobocracy
monocracy
nomocracy
ochlocracy
pantisocracy
pedantocracy

physiocracy
plantocracy
plutocracy
plutodemocracy
pornocracy
ptochocracy
slavocracy
snobocracy
squattocracy
stratocracy
technocracy
thalassocracy
thalattocracy
theocracy
timocracy.

**-crat**

aristocrat
autocrat
bureaucrat
cosmocrat
democrat
hierocrat
meritocrat
millocrat
mobocrat
monocrat
ochlocrat
pantisocrat
pedantocrat
physiocrat
plutocrat
slavocrat
stratocrat
technocrat
theocrat.

**-cratic**

aristocratic
autocratic
bureaucratic
cosmocratic
democratic
Eurocratic
gerontocratic
gynaecocratic
hierocratic
isocratic
meritocratic
mobocratic
monocratic
ochlocratic
pancratic
pantisocratic
pedantocratic
physiocratic
plutocratic
stratocratic
technocratic

theocratic
timocratic
undemocratic

**-cultural**

accultural
agricultural
arboricultural
crinicultural
cultural
floricultural
horticultural
piscicultural
subcultural
vinicultural
vocicultural

**-culture**

agriculture
apiculture
aquaculture
aquiculture
arboriculture
aviculture
culture
electroculture
floriculture
horticulture
mariculture
monoculture
ostreiculture
pisciculture
pomiculture
self-culture
sericiculture
sericulture
silviculture
stirpiculture
subculture
sylviculture
viniculture
viticulture
water-culture
zooculture

**-cyte**

athrocyte
cyte
erythrocyte
fibrocyte
gonocyte
granulocyte
haemocyte
leucocyte
lymphocyte
macrocyte
microcyte
oocyte

**-cyte** *(contd.)*
phagocyte
poikilocyte
spermatocyte
thrombocyte
thymocyte

**-dom**

Anglo-Saxondom
apedom
archdukedom
attorneydom
babeldom
babudom
bachelordom
beadledom
beggardom
birthdom
bishopdom
boredom
Bumbledom
chiefdom
Christendom
clerkdom
cockneydom
crippledom
cuckoldom
czardom
demirepdom
devildom
Dogberrydom
dolldom
dufferdom
dukedom
duncedom
earldom
enthraldom
fairydom
fandom
filmdom
flunkeydom
fogydom
freedom
fresherdom
Greekdom
gypsydom
halidom
heathendom
heirdom
hobbledehoydom
hobodom
junkerdom
kaiserdom
kingdom
kitchendom
leechdom
liegedom
mandom
martyrdom
masterdom
newspaperdom
niggerdom
noodledom
noveldom
officialdom
overfreedom
penny-wisdom
popedom
princedom
puppydom

puzzledom
Quakerdom
queendom
queerdom
rascaldom
rebeldom
sachemdom
saintdom
savagedom
Saxondom
scoundreldom
serfdom
sheikdom
sheikhdom
sheriffdom
Slavdom
spinsterdom
squiredom
stardom
subkingdom
swelldom
thanedom
thraldom
thralldom
topsyturvydom
tsardom
underkingdom
unwisdom
villadom
whoredom
wisdom
Yankeedom

**-ferous**

aluminiferous
amentiferous
antenniferous
argentiferous
auriferous
bacciferous
balsamiferous
bulbiferous
calciferous
carboniferous
celliferous
celluliferous
cheliferous
cobaltiferous
conchiferous
coniferous
coralliferous
corniferous
cruciferous
culmiferous
cupriferous
cupuliferous
diamantiferous
diamondiferous
doloriferous
dorsiferous
ferriferous
flagelliferous
flammiferous
floriferous
foraminiferous
fossiliferous
frondiferous
fructiferous
frugiferous
furciferous

garnetiferous
gemmiferous
glandiferous
glanduliferous
globuliferous
glumiferous
granuliferous
guaniferous
gummiferous
guttiferous
lactiferous
laniferous
laticiferous
lethiferous
luciferous
luminiferous
mammaliferous
mammiferous
manganiferous
manniferous
margaritiferous
melliferous
metalliferous
morbiferous
mortiferous
moschiferous
muciferous
nectariferous
nickeliferous
nubiferous
nuciferous
odoriferous
oleiferous
omniferous
ossiferous
oviferous
ovuliferous
ozoniferous
papilliferous
papuliferous
Permo-Carboniferous
pestiferous
petaliferous
petroliferous
piliferous
platiniferous
plumbiferous
polliniferous
pomiferous
poriferous
proliferous
pyritiferous
quartziferous
reptiliferous
resiniferous
rotiferous
sacchariferous
saliferous
salutiferous
sanguiferous
sebiferous
seminiferous
septiferous
siliciferous
soboliferous
somniferous
soporiferous
spiniferous
spinuliferous
splendiferous
staminiferous

stanniferous
stelliferous
stigmatiferous
stoloniferous
strombuliferous
styliferous
sudoriferous
tentaculiferous
thuriferous
titaniferous
tuberiferous
umbelliferous
umbriferous
unfossiliferous
uriniferous
vitiferous
vociferous
yttriferous
zinciferous
zinkiferous

**-gamy**

allogamy
apogamy
autogamy
bigamy
chalazogamy
chasmogamy
cleistogamy
clistogamy
cryptogamy
deuterogamy
dichogamy
digamy
endogamy
exogamy
geitonogamy
hercogamy
herkogamy
heterogamy
homogamy
hypergamy
isogamy
misogamy
monogamy
oogamy
pangamy
pantagamy
plasmogamy
plastogamy
polygamy
porogamy
siphonogamy
syngamy
trigamy
xenogamy
zoogamy

**-genesis**

abiogenesis
agamogenesis
anthropogenesis
autogenesis
biogenesis
blastogenesis
carcinogenesis
chondrogenesis
cytogenesis
diagenesis

**-genesis** *(contd.)*
diplogenesis
dynamogenesis
ectogenesis
electrogenesis
embryogenesis
epeirogenesis
epigenesis
gametogenesis
gamogenesis
haematogenesis
heterogenesis
histogenesis
homogenesis
hylogenesis
hypnogenesis
merogenesis
metagenesis
monogenesis
morphogenesis
mythogenesis
neogenesis
noogenesis
ontogenesis
oogenesis
organogenesis
orogenesis
orthogenesis
osteogenesis
paedogenesis
palingenesis
pangenesis
paragenesis
parthenogenesis
pathogenesis
perigenesis
petrogenesis
phylogenesis
phytogenesis
polygenesis
psychogenesis
pyogenesis
schizogenesis
spermatogenesis
sporogenesis
syngenesis
thermogenesis
xenogenesis

**-genic**

aesthesiogenic
allergenic
androgenic
anthropogenic
antigenic
biogenic
blastogenic
carcinogenic
cariogenic
cryogenic
dysgenic
ectogenic
electrogenic
endogenic
epeirogenic
erogenic
erotogenic
eugenic
genic
glycogenic

hallucinogenic
histogenic
hypnogenic
hysterogenic
iatrogenic
lactogenic
lysigenic
mammogenic
mutagenic
myogenic
neurogenic
odontogenic
oestrogenic
oncogenic
ontogenic
orogenic
orthogenic
osteogenic
pathogenic
photogenic
phytogenic
polygenic
psychogenic
pyogenic
pyrogenic
pythogenic
radiogenic
rhizogenic
saprogenic
schizogenic
somatogenic
spermatogenic
telegenic
teratogenic
thermogenic
tumorgenic
tumorigenic
visiogenic
zoogenic
zymogenic

**-gon**

chiliagon
decagon
dodecagon
endecagon
enneagon
hendecagon
heptagon
hexagon
isogon
nonagon
octagon
pentagon
perigon
polygon
tetragon
trigon

**-gram**

aerogram
anagram
anemogram
angiogram
audiogram
ballistocardiogram
barogram
cablegram
calligram

cardiogram
cartogram
centigram
centimetre-gram
chromatogram
chromogram
chronogram
cryptogram
dactylogram
decagram
decigram
dendrogram
diagram
echogram
electrocardiogram
electroencephalogram
encephalogram
engram
epigram
ergogram
ferrogram
harmonogram
hectogram
hexagram
hierogram
histogram
hologram
ideogram
indicator-diagram
isogram
kilogram
lexigram
lipogram
logogram
lymphogram
marconigram
marigram
meteorogram
microgram
monogram
myogram
nanogram
nephogram
neurogram
nomogram
organogram
oscillogram
pangram
paragram
parallelogram
pentagram
phonogram
photogram
phraseogram
pictogram
program
psychogram
pyelogram
radiogram
radiotelegram
röntgenogram
scintigram
seismogram
sialogram
skiagram
sociogram
spectrogram
spectroheliogram
sphenogram
sphygmogram
steganogram

stereogram
tachogram
telegram
tephigram
tetragram
thermogram
tomogram
trigram

**-graph**

Addressograph®
aerograph
airgraph
allograph
anemograph
apograph
audiograph
autograph
autoradiograph
ballistocardiograph
bar-graph
barograph
biograph
cardiograph
cathodograph
cerograph
chirograph
choreograph
chromatograph
chromolithograph
chromoxylograph
chronograph
cinematograph
coronagraph
coronograph
cryptograph
cyclograph
cymagraph
cymograph
diagraph
Dictograph®
digraph
dynamograph
eidograph
electrocardiograph
electroencephalograph
electrograph
electromyograph
ellipsograph
encephalograph
epigraph
ergograph
evaporograph
flannelgraph
glyphograph
harmonograph
hectograph
helicograph
heliograph
hierograph
hodograph
holograph
homograph
hydrograph
hyetograph
hyetometrograph
hygrograph
ideograph
idiograph
jellygraph

**-graph** *(contd.)*
keraunograph
kinematograph
kinetograph
kymograph
lithograph
logograph
magnetograph
marconigraph
marigraph
meteorograph
micrograph
microphotograph
microseismograph
mimeograph
monograph
myograph
nephograph
nomograph
odograph
odontograph
oleograph
opisthograph
orthograph
oscillograph
pantograph
paragraph
pentagraph
phonautograph
phonograph
photograph
photolithograph
photomicrograph
phototelegraph
photozincograph
phraseograph
pictograph
planigraph
plethysmograph
polygraph
pseudograph
psychograph
pyrophotograph
radioautograph
radiograph
radiometeorograph
radiotelegraph
rotograph
seismograph
selenograph
serigraph
shadowgraph
skiagraph
spectrograph
spectroheliograph
sphygmograph
spirograph
steganograph
stenograph
stereograph
Stevengraph
stylograph
syngraph
tachograph
tachygraph
Telautograph®
telegraph
telephotograph
thermograph
thermometrograph
tomograph

torsiograph
trigraph
vectograph
vibrograph
xylograph
zincograph

**-graphical**

autobiographical
bathygraphical
bathyorographical
bibliographical
biobibliographical
biogeographical
biographical
cacographical
calligraphical
cartographical
cerographical
chorographical
cinematographical
climatographical
cosmographical
geographical
glossographical
graphical
hagiographical
hierographical
historiographical
hydrographical
hyetographical
hygrographical
ichnographical
ideographical
lexicographical
lexigraphical
lithographical
logographical
monographical
myographical
oceanographical
oreographical
orographical
orthographical
palaeographical
palaeontographical
pantographical
paragraphical
pasigraphical
petrographical
photographical
physiographical
prosopographical
pseudepigraphical
psychobiographical
psychographical
pterylographical
seismographical
selenographical
spectrographical
stenographical
stereographical
stratigraphical
tachygraphical
topographical
typographical
xylographical
zincographical
zoogeographical
zoographical

**-graphy**

aerography
ampelography
angiography
anthropogeography
anthropography
areography
autobiography
autography
autoradiography
autotypography
ballistocardiography
bibliography
biogeography
biography
brachygraphy
cacography
calligraphy
cardiography
cartography
cathodography
ceramography
cerography
chalcography
chartography
cheirography
chirography
cholangiography
choregraphy
choreography
chorography
chromatography
chromolithography
chromotypography
chromoxylography
chronography
cinematography
cinemicrography
climatography
cometography
cosmography
cryptography
crystallography
dactyliography
dactylography
demography
dermatography
dermography
discography
dittography
doxography
echocardiography
ectypography
electrocardiography
electroencephalography
electrography
electromyography
electrophotography
encephalography
enigmatography
epigraphy
epistolography
ethnography
ferrography
filmography
geography
glossography
glyphography
glyptography
hagiography

haplography
heliography
heresiography
hierography
historiography
holography
horography
hydrography
hyetography
hymnography
hypsography
ichnography
ichthyography
iconography
ideography
lexicography
lexigraphy
lipography
lithography
logography
lymphography
mammography
metallography
microcosmography
micrography
microphotography
mimography
monography
morphography
myography
mythography
nomography
nosography
oceanography
odontography
oleography
opisthography
orchesography
oreography
organography
orography
orthography
osteography
palaeogeography
palaeography
palaeontography
pantography
paroemiography
pasigraphy
pathography
petrography
phonography
photography
photolithography
photomicrography
phototelegraphy
photoxylography
photozincography
physiography
phytogeography
phytography
pictography
polarography
polygraphy
pornography
prosopography
pseudepigraphy
pseudography
psychobiography
psychography
pterylography

**-graphy** *(contd.)*
pyelography
pyrography
pyrophotography
radiography
radiotelegraphy
reprography
rhyparography
röntgenography
scenography
scintigraphy
seismography
selenography
serigraphy
sialography
snobography
spectrography
sphygmography
steganography
stenography
stereography
stratigraphy
stylography
symbolography
tachygraphy
technography
telautography
telegraphy
telephotography
thalassography
thanatography
thaumatography
thermography
tomography
topography
typography
ultrasonography
uranography
urography
ventriculography
xerography
xeroradiography
xylography
xylopyrography
xylotypography
zincography
zoogeography
zoography

**-hedron**

chiliahedron
decahedron
dihedron
dodecahedron
enneahedron
hemihedron
hexahedron
holohedron
icosahedron
icositetrahedron
leucitohedron
octahedron
octohedron
pentahedron
polyhedron
pyritohedron
rhombohedron
scalenohedron
tetrahedron
tetrakishexahedron

trapezohedron
triakisoctahedron
trihedron
trisoctahedron

**-hood**

adulthood
angelhood
apehood
apprenticehood
babyhood
bachelorhood
beadlehood
beasthood
bountihood
boyhood
brotherhood
cathood
childhood
Christhood
companionhood
cousinhood
cubhood
deaconhood
dollhood
drearihood
elfhood
fairyhood
falsehood
fatherhood
flapperhood
flesh-hood
gawkihood
gentlehood
gentlemanhood
gianthood
girlhood
godhood
hardihood
high-priesthood
hobbledehoyhood
hoghood
hoydenhood
idlehood
invalidhood
jealoushood
kinghood
kinglihood
knighthood
ladyhood
likelihood
livelihood
lustihood
maidenhood
maidhood
manhood
masterhood
matronhood
misshood
monkhood
motherhood
nationhood
needy-hood
neighbourhood
novicehood
nunhood
old-maidhood
orphanhood
pagehood
parenthood

popehood
priesthood
princehood
prophethood
puppyhood
queenhood
sainthood
selfhood
serfhood
sisterhood
spinsterhood
squirehood
statehood
swinehood
tabbyhood
thanehood
thinghood
traitorhood
unlikelihood
virginhood
waiterhood
widowerhood
widowhood
wifehood
wivehood
womanhood
youthhood

**-iac**

ammoniac
amnesiac
anaphrodisiac
anglomaniac
Anglophobiac
antaphrodisiac
anthomaniac
aphasiac
aphrodisiac
archgenethliac
bacchiac
bibliomaniac
cardiac
celiac
Cluniac
coeliac
coprolaliac
demoniac
dextrocardiac
Dionysiac
dipsomaniac
dochmiac
dysthymiac
egomaniac
elegiac
endocardiac
erotomaniac
etheromaniac
Genesiac
genethliac
haemophiliac
hebephreniac
heliac
hypochondriac
iliac
insomniac
intracardiac
Isiac
kleptomaniac
maniac
megalomaniac

melancholiac
melomaniac
monomaniac
morphinomaniac
mythomaniac
necrophiliac
neurastheniac
nymphomaniac
opsomaniac
orchidomaniac
paedophiliac
Pandemoniac
paradisiac
paranoiac
paraphiliac
paroemiac
pericardiac
phrenesiac
pyromaniac
sacroiliac
scopophiliac
scoriac
simoniac
symposiac
Syriac
theomaniac
theriac
timbromaniac
toxiphobiac
zodiac
zygocardiac

**-iatric**

chemiatric
chemopsychiatric
geriatric
hippiatric
kinesiatric
paediatric
psychiatric
psychogeriatric

**-iatry**

chemopsychiatry
geriatry
hippiatry
neuropsychiatry
orthopsychiatry
paediatry
podiatry
psychiatry

**-ician**

academician
acoustician
aeroelastician
aesthetician
arithmetician
audiometrician
beautician
biometrician
clinician
cosmetician
diagnostician
dialectician
dietician
econometrician
ekistician

**-ician** *(contd.)*

electrician
geometrician
geopolitician
geriatrician
informatician
linguistician
logician
logistician
magician
magnetician
mathematician
mechanician
metaphysician
metrician
mortician
musician
obstetrician
optician
paediatrician
patrician
Paulician
phonetician
physician
politician
practician
psychogeriatrician
psychometrician
rhetorician
rubrician
statistician
systematician
tactician
technician
theoretician

**-ics**

acoustics
acrobatics
aerobatics
aerobics
aerodynamics
aeronautics
aerostatics
aesthetics
agogics
agonistics
ambisonics
apologetics
aquabatics
aquanautics
astrodynamics
astronautics
astrophysics
athletics
atmospherics
autonomics
avionics
axiomatics
ballistics
bioastronautics
biodynamics
bioethics
biomathematics
biomechanics
biometrics
bionics
bionomics
biophysics
biorhythmics

biosystematics
cacogenics
calisthenics
callisthenics
catacoustics
catallactics
cataphonics
catechetics
catoptrics
ceroplastics
chemotherapeutics
chrematistics
chromatics
civics
cliometrics
conics
cosmonautics
cosmopolitics
cryogenics
cryonics
cryophysics
cybernetics
cytogenetics
deontics
dermatoglyphics
diacoustics
diagnostics
dialectics
dianetics
didactics
dietetics
dioptrics
dogmatics
dramatics
dynamics
dysgenics
eclectics
econometrics
economics
ecumenics
ekistics
electrodynamics
electrokinetics
electromechanics
electronics
electrostatics
electrotechnics
electrotherapeutics
electrothermics
energetics
entoptics
environics
epigenetics
epistemics
epizootics
ergonomics
ethics
ethnolinguistics
eudaemonics
eudemonics
eugenics
eurhythmics
euthenics
exegetics
floristics
fluidics
forensics
genetics
geodetics
geodynamics
geophysics

geopolitics
geoponics
geostatics
geotectonics
geriatrics
gerontotherapeutics
glyptics
gnomonics
gnotobiotics
graphemics
graphics
gyrostatics
halieutics
haptics
harmonics
hedonics
hermeneutics
hermetics
hippiatrics
histrionics
homiletics
hydraulics
hydrodynamics
hydrokinetics
hydromagnetics
hydromechanics
hydroponics
hydrostatics
hydrotherapeutics
hygienics
hypersonics
hysterics
informatics
irenics
isagogics
isometrics
kinematics
kinesics
kinetics
linguistics
lithochromatics
liturgics
logistics
loxodromics
macrobiotics
macroeconomics
magnetics
magneto-hydrodynamics
magneto-optics
maieutics
mathematics
mechanics
melodics
metalinguistics
metamathematics
metaphysics
metapsychics
meteoritics
microeconomics
microelectronics
microphysics
mnemotechnics
mole-electronics
monostrophics
morphemics
morphophonemics
nautics
nucleonics
numismatics
obstetrics
olympics

onomastics
optics
optoelectronics
orchestics
orthodontics
orthodromics
orthogenics
orthopaedics
orthopedics
orthoptics
orthotics
paedeutics
paediatrics
paedodontics
paideutics
pantopragmatics
paralinguistics
party-politics
pataphysics
patristics
pedagogics
peptics
periodontics
pharmaceutics
pharmacodynamics
pharmacokinetics
phelloplastics
phonemics
phonetics
phonics
phonocamptics
phonotactics
photics
photochromics
photoelectronics
phototherapeutics
photovoltaics
psionics physics
physiotherapeutics
plastics
pneumatics
pneumodynamics
polemics
politico-economics
politics
power-politics
problematics
prosthetics
prosthodontics
psionics
psychics
psychodynamics
psychogeriatrics
psycholinguistics
psychometrics
psychonomics
psychophysics
psychosomatics
psychotherapeutics
pyrotechnics
quadraphonics
quadrophonics
radionics
radiophonics
radiotherapeutics
rhythmics
robotics
semantics
semeiotics
semiotics
Semitics

**-ics** *(contd.)*
sferics
significs
sociolinguistics
sonics
sophistics
spherics
sphragistics
statics
stereoptics
strategics
stylistics
subatomics
subtropics
syllabics
symbolics
synectics
systematics
tactics
technics
tectonics
telearchics
thaumaturgics
theatrics
therapeutics
thermionics
thermodynamics
thermotics
toponymics
toreutics
transonics
transsonics
ultrasonics
vitrics
zoiatrics
zootechnics
zymotechnics

**-iform**

aciform
acinaciform
aciniform
aeriform
alphabetiform
amoebiform
anguiform
anguilliform
antenniform
asbestiform
auriform
aviform
bacciform
bacilliform
biform
bursiform
cactiform
calcariform
calceiform
calyciform
cambiform
campaniform
campodeiform
cancriform
capriform
cauliform
cerebriform
cirriform
claviform
clypeiform
cobriform

cochleariform
coliform
colubriform
conchiform
coniform
coralliform
cordiform
corniform
corolliform
cotyliform
crateriform
cribriform
cristiform
cruciform
cteniform
cubiform
cucumiform
culiciform
cultriform
cumuliform
cuneiform
curviform
cyathiform
cylindriform
cymbiform
cystiform
deiform
dendriform
dentiform
digitiform
dolabriform
elytriform
ensiform
equisetiform
eruciform
falciform
fibriform
filiform
flabelliform
flagelliform
floriform
fringilliform
fungiform
fusiform
gangliform
gasiform
glandiform
granitiform
granuliform
hydatidiform
incisiform
infundibuliform
insectiform
janiform
jelliform
lamelliform
lanciform
lapilliform
larviform
lentiform
limaciform
linguiform
lumbriciform
lyriform
malleiform
mamilliform
mammiform
maniform
medusiform
mitriform
monadiform

moniliform
morbilliform
multiform
mummiform
muriform
mytiliform
napiform
natiform
naupliiform
nubiform
omniform
oviform
paliform
panduriform
papilliform
patelliform
pelviform
penicilliform
penniform
perciform
phialiform
piliform
pisciform
pisiform
placentiform
planuliform
plexiform
poculiform
proteiform
pulvilliform
pyriform
quadriform
radiciform
raduliform
raniform
reniform
restiform
retiform
sacciform
sagittiform
salpiform
scalariform
scalpelliform
scalpriform
scoleciform
scolopendriform
scutiform
scyphiform
securiform
septiform
serpentiform
spiniform
spongiform
squamiform
stalactiform
stalactitiform
stelliform
stratiform
strigiform
strobiliform
strombuliform
styliform
tauriform
tectiform
telescopiform
thalliform
triform
tuberiform
tubiform
tympaniform
umbraculiform

unciform
unguiform
uniform
vaporiform
variform
vasculiform
vasiform
vermiform
verruciform
versiform
villiform
viperiform
vitriform
vulviform
ypsiliform
zeolitiform

**-ism**

abnormalism
abolitionism
aboriginalism
absenteeism
absolutism
academicalism
academicism
accidentalism
achromatism
acosmism
acrobatism
acrotism
actinism
activism
Adamitism
adiaphorism
adoptianism
Adoptionism
adventurism
aeroembolism
aerotropism
aestheticism
Africanism
ageism
agnosticism
agrarianism
Albigensianism
albinism
albinoism
alcoholism
algorism
alienism
allelomorphism
allotropism
alpinism
altruism
amateurism
Americanism
ametabolism
amoralism
amorism
amorphism
anabaptism
anabolism
anachronism
anagrammatism
anarchism
anastigmatism
androdioecism
andromonoecism
aneurism
Anglicanism

**-ism** *(contd.)*
anglicism
Anglo-Catholicism
aniconism
animalism
animatism
animism
annihilationism
antagonism
anthropomorphism
anthropomorphitism
anthropopathism
anthropophuism
anthropopsychism
antichristianism
anticivism
anticlericalism
antidisestablish-
  mentarianism
anti-federalism
anti-Gallicanism
anti-Jacobinism
antinomianism
antiochianism
antiquarianism
anti-Semitism
antisepticism
antisocialism
antitheism
antitrinitarianism
antivaccinationism
antivivisectionism
anythingarianism
apheliotropism
aphorism
apism
aplanatism
apochromatism
apogeotropism
apoliticism
Apollinarianism
apostolicism
apriorism
Arabism
Aramaism
Arcadianism
archaicism
archaism
Arianism
aristocratism
Aristotelianism
Aristotelism
Arminianism
asceticism
asepticism
Asiaticism
aspheterism
asteism
asterism
astigmatism
asynchronism
asystolism
atavism
atheism
athleticism
Atlanticism
atomism
atonalism
atropism
Atticism
attorneyism

Augustinianism
Australianism
authorism
authoritarianism
autism
autochthonism
autoeroticism
autoerotism
automatism
automobilism
automorphism
autotheism
avant-gardism
Averrhoism
Averroism
Baalism
Baathism
Ba'athism
Babbitism
Babeeism
babelism
Babiism
Babism
babuism
bacchanalianism
bachelorism
Baconianism
Bahaism
bantingism
baptism
barbarism
bashawism
bastardism
bathmism
bedlamism
behaviourism
Benthamism
Bergsonism
Berkeleianism
bestialism
betacism
biblicism
bibliophilism
bilateralism
bilingualism
bimetallism
bipedalism
blackguardism
blepharism
bogeyism
bogyism
Bohemianism
bolshevism
Bonapartism
bonism
boobyism
Boswellism
botulism
Bourbonism
bowdlerism
bradyseism
braggartism
Brahmanism
Brahminism
Braidism
Briticism
Britishism
Brownism
bruxism
Buchmanism
Buddhism

bullyism
Burschenism
Byronism
Byzantinism
cabalism
cabbalism
Caesarism
caesaropapism
caffeinism
caffeism
Calvinism
cambism
Camorrism
cannibalism
capitalism
Carbonarism
careerism
Carlism
Carlylism
carnalism
Cartesianism
casualism
catabolism
catastrophism
catechism
catechumenism
Catharism
catheterism
catholicism
causationism
cauterism
cavalierism
Celticism
centenarianism
centralism
centripetalism
centrism
cerebralism
ceremonialism
chaldaism
characterism
charism
charlatanism
chartism
Chasidism
Chassidism
Chaucerism
chauvinism
chemism
chemotropism
chloralism
Christianism
chromaticism
churchism
Ciceronianism
cicisbeism
cinchonism
civism
cladism
classicism
clericalism
cliquism
clubbism
coalitionism
Cobdenism
cocainism
cockneyism
coenobitism
collectivism
collegialism
colloquialism

colonialism
commensalism
commercialism
communalism
communism
compatriotism
comstockism
Comtism
conacreism
conceptualism
concettism
concretism
confessionalism
confrontationism
Confucianism
Congregationalism
conservatism
consortism
constitutionalism
constructionism
constructivism
consubstantialism
consumerism
contact-metamorphism
continentalism
contortionism
contrabandism
conventionalism
conversationism
convictism
copyism
corporatism
corporealism
corybantism
cosmeticism
cosmism
cosmopolitanism
cosmopolitism
cosmotheism
cottierism
Couéism
courtierism
creatianism
creationism
cretinism
cretism
criticism
cronyism
crotalism
cubism
cultism
curialism
cyclicism
cynicism
czarism
Dadaism
Daltonism
dandyism
Darwinism
deaf-mutism
decimalism
defeatism
deism
demagogism
demagoguism
demoniacism
demonianism
demonism
denominationalism
departmentalism
descriptivism

**-ism** *(contd.)*
despotism
deteriorism
determinism
deviationism
devilism
diabolism
diachronism
diageotropism
diaheliotropism
dialecticism
diamagnetism
diaphototropism
diastrophism
diatropism
dichroism
dichromatism
dichromism
diclinism
dicrotism
didacticism
diffusionism
dilettanteism
dilettantism
dimerism
dimorphism
dioecism
diorism
diothelism
diphysitism
dirigism
dissenterism
dissolutionism
disyllabism
ditheism
ditheletism
dithelism
dithelitism
divisionism
Docetism
doctrinairism
doctrinarianism
Dogberryism
dogmatism
do-goodism
dolichocephalism
donatism
donnism
do-nothingism
Doricism
Dorism
dowdyism
draconism
dragonism
dramaticism
drudgism
druidism
dualism
dudism
dufferism
dunderheadism
dynamism
dyotheletism
dyothelism
dysphemism
ebionism
ebionitism
echoism
eclecticism
ecumenicalism
ecumenicism

ecumenism
Edwardianism
egalitarianism
egoism
egotheism
egotism
electromagnetism
electromerism
elementalism
elitism
Elizabethanism
embolism
emotionalism
empiricism
enantiomorphism
Encratism
encyclopaedism
endemism
Englishism
entrism
environmentalism
eonism
epicism
Epicureanism
epicurism
epiphenomenalism
epiphytism
epipolism
episcopalianism
episcopalism
equalitarianism
equestrianism
Erastianism
eremitism
erethism
ergotism
eroticism
erotism
erythrism
escapism
esotericism
esoterism
Essenism
essentialism
etacism
etherism
ethicism
ethnicism
ethnocentrism
eudaemonism
eugenism
euhemerism
eumerism
eunuchism
eunuchoidism
euphemism
euphuism
Eurocommunism
Europeanism
evangelicalism
evangelicism
evangelism
evolutionism
exclusionism
exclusivism
exhibitionism
existentialism
ex-librism
exorcism
exotericism
exoticism

expansionism
experientialism
experimentalism
expressionism
extensionalism
externalism
extremism
Fabianism
factionalism
faddism
fairyism
fakirism
falangism
familism
fanaticism
fantasticism
faradism
fascism
fatalism
Fauvism
favism
favouritism
Febronianism
federalism
femininism
feminism
Fenianism
fetichism
fetishism
feudalism
feuilletonism
fideism
fifth-monarchism
filibusterism
finalism
fissiparism
flagellantism
flunkeyism
fogyism
formalism
fortuitism
Fourierism
fractionalism
Froebelism
functionalism
fundamentalism
fusionism
futurism
gaelicism
Galenism
Gallicanism
gallicism
galvanism
gamotropism
ganderism
gangsterism
Gargantuism
gargarism
gargoylism
Gasconism
Gaullism
generationism
Genevanism
genteelism
gentilism
geocentricism
geomagnetism
geophagism
geotropism
Germanism
giantism

gigantism
Girondism
Gnosticism
Gongorism
gormandism
Gothicism
gourmandism
gradualism
Graecism
grammaticism
Grangerism
Grecism
gregarianism
griffinism
Grobianism
Grundyism
gynandrism
gynandromorphism
gynodioecism
gynomonoecism
gypsyism
gyromagnetism
haptotropism
Hasidism
Hassidism
heathenism
Hebraicism
Hebrewism
hectorism
hedonism
Hegelianism
hegemonism
heliotropism
Hellenism
helotism
hemihedrism
hemimorphism
henotheism
hermaphroditism
heroism
hetaerism
hetairism
heterochronism
heteroecism
heteromorphism
heterostylism
heterothallism
heurism
Hibernianism
Hibernicism
hidalgoism
hierarchism
highbrowism
High-Churchism
Hildebrandism
Hinduism
Hippocratism
hispanicism
historicism
historism
histrionicism
histrionism
Hitlerism
Hobbesianism
Hobbianism
Hobbism
hobbledehoyism
hobbyism
hobgoblinism
hoboism
holism

**-ism** *(contd.)*
holohedrism
holometabolism
holophytism
homeomorphism
homoeomorphism
homoeroticism
homoerotism
homomorphism
homothallism
hooliganism
hoydenism
humanism
humanitarianism
Humism
humoralism
hybridism
hydrargyrism
hydrotropism
hylicism
hylism
hylomorphism
hylopathism
hylotheism
hylozoism
hyperadrenalism
hyperbolism
hypercriticism
hyperthyroidism
hyphenism
hypnotism
hypochondriacism
hypocorism
hypognathism
hypothyroidism
Ibsenism
iconomaticism
iconophilism
idealism
idiotism
idolism
illuminism
illusionism
imagism
immanentism
immaterialism
immediatism
immersionism
immobilism
immoralism
imperialism
impossibilism
impressionism
incendiarism
incivism
incorporealism
indeterminism
indifferentism
individualism
industrialism
infallibilism
infantilism
inflationism
Infralapsarianism
inquilinism
inspirationism
institutionalism
instrumentalism
insularism
insurrectionism
intellectualism

interactionism
internationalism
interventionism
intimism
intransigentism
intuitionalism
intuitionism
intuitivism
invalidism
iodism
Ionism
iotacism
irenicism
Irishism
irrationalism
irredentism
Irvingism
Islamism
ism
Ismailism
isochronism
isodimorphism
isolationism
isomerism
isomorphism
isotropism
itacism
Italianism
italicism
Jacobinism
Jacobitism
Jainism
Jansenism
Jesuitism
jingoism
jockeyism
Johnsonianism
Johnsonism
journalism
Judaism
junkerism
kaiserism
Kantianism
Kantism
karaism
katabolism
Kelticism
Keynesianism
klephtism
know-nothingism
Krishnaism
labdacism
labialism
labourism
laconicism
laconism
ladyism
Lamaism
Lamarckianism
Lamarckism
lambdacism
landlordism
Laodiceanism
larrikinism
lathyrism
Latinism
latitudinarianism
laxism
leftism
legalism
leggism

Leibnitzianism
Leibnizianism
Leninism
lesbianism
liberalism
liberationism
libertarianism
libertinism
lichenism
lionism
lipogrammatism
Listerism
literalism
literaryism
localism
Lollardism
Londonism
Low-Churchism
Luddism
luminarism
Lutheranism
Lutherism
lyricism
lyrism
Lysenkoism
macarism
Machiavellianism
Machiavellism
Magianism
Magism
magnetism
Magyarism
Mahdiism
Mahdism
maidism
malapropism
Malthusianism
mammonism
Manichaeanism
Manichaeism
Manicheanism
Manicheism
mannerism
Maoism
Marcionitism
Marinism
martialism
martinetism
Marxianism
Marxism
masochism
materialism
mathematicism
matriarchalism
maudlinism
Mazdaism
Mazdeism
McCarthyism
mechanism
mediaevalism
medievalism
Medism
melanism
meliorism
memoirism
Mendelism
mentalism
mephitism
mercantilism
mercenarism
mercurialism

merism
merycism
mescalism
mesmerism
mesocephalism
mesomerism
Messianism
metabolism
metachronism
metamerism
metamorphism
metasomatism
metempiricism
meteorism
methodism
metopism
Micawberism
Michurinism
micro-organism
microseism
militarism
millenarianism
millenarism
millennianism
millenniarism
Miltonism
minimalism
minimism
misoneism
Mithraicism
Mithraism
mithridatism
modalism
moderatism
modernism
Mohammedanism
Mohammedism
Molinism
monachism
monadism
monarchianism
monarchism
monasticism
monergism
monetarism
mongolism
mongrelism
monism
monkeyism
monochromatism
monoecism
monogenism
monolingualism
monometallism
monophysitism
monorchism
monosyllabism
monotheism
monotheletism
monothelism
monothelitism
Monroeism
Montanism
moralism
Moravianism
Morisonianism
Mormonism
morphinism
mosaicism
Mosaism
Moslemism

**-ism** *(contd.)*
mountebankism
multiracialism
Munichism
municipalism
Muslimism
mutism
mutualism
myalism
mysticism
mythicism
mythism
namby-pambyism
nanism
Napoleonism
narcissism
narcotism
nationalism
nativism
naturalism
naturism
navalism
Nazaritism
Naziism
Nazism
necessarianism
necessitarianism
necrophilism
negativism
negroism
negrophilism
neoclassicism
neocolonialism
Neo-Darwinism
Neofascism
Neohellenism
Neo-Impressionism
Neo-Kantianism
Neo-Lamarckism
neologism
Neo-Malthusianism
neo-Nazism
neonomianism
neopaganism
neoplasticism
Neo-Plasticism
Neoplatonism
Neopythagoreanism
neoterism
neovitalism
nephalism
Nestorianism
neuroticism
neutralism
newspaperism
nicotinism
Nietzscheanism
niggerism
nihilism
noctambulism
Noetianism
nomadism
nominalism
nomism
northernism
notaphilism
nothingarianism
nothingism
Novatianism
novelism
nudism

nyctitropism
obeahism
obeism
obiism
objectivism
obscurantism
obsoletism
Occamism
occasionalism
Occidentalism
occultism
Ockhamism
odism
odylism
oecumenicalism
oecumenicism
oecumenism
officialism
old-maidism
onanism
oneirocriticism
onirocriticism
Ophism
Ophitism
opportunism
optimism
Orangeism
Orangism
organicism
organism
Orientalism
Origenism
Orleanism
orphanism
Orphism
orthognathism
orthotropism
ostracism
ostrichism
Owenism
pacificism
pacifism
Paddyism
paedobaptism
paedomorphism
paganism
palaeomagnetism
palladianism
paludism
panaesthetism
Pan-Africanism
Pan-Americanism
Pan-Arabism
panchromatism
pancosmism
panderism
panegoism
Pan-Germanism
Panhellenism
panislamism
panlogism
panpsychism
pansexualism
Pan-Slavism
pansophism
panspermatism
panspermism
Pantagruelism
pantheism
papalism
papism

parabaptism
parachronism
paragnathism
paraheliotropism
parallelism
paralogism
paramagnetism
paramorphism
parapsychism
parasitism
Parkinsonism
parliamentarism
Parnassianism
Parnellism
parochialism
Parseeism
Parsiism
Parsism
partialism
particularism
partyism
passivism
pasteurism
pastoralism
paternalism
patrialism
patriarchalism
patriarchism
patriotism
Patripassianism
patristicism
Paulinism
pauperism
pedagogism
pedagoguism
pedanticism
pedantism
pedestrianism
Pelagianism
pelmanism
pelorism
pennalism
penny-a-linerism
pentadactylism
pentamerism
pentaprism
peonism
perfectibilism
perfectionism
peripateticism
perpetualism
Persism
personalism
perspectivism
pessimism
petalism
Petrarchianism
Petrarchism
Petrinism
phaeism
phagocytism
phalansterianism
phalansterism
phallicism
phallism
pharisaism
phariseeism
phenakism
phenomenalism
phenomenism
philhellenism

philistinism
philosophism
phobism
phoneticism
phonetism
phosphorism
photism
photochromism
photoperiodism
phototropism
physicalism
physicism
physitheism
pianism
pietism
piezomagnetism
Pindarism
Pittism
plagiarism
plagiotropism
Platonicism
Platonism
plebeianism
pleiotropism
pleochroism
pleomorphism
plumbism
pluralism
Plutonism
Plymouthism
pococuranteism
pococurantism
poeticism
pointillism
polonism
polychroism
polycrotism
polydactylism
polygenism
polymastism
polymerism
polymorphism
polynomialism
polysyllabicism
polysyllabism
polysyllogism
polysyntheticism
polysynthetism
polytheism
Pooterism
populism
porism
Porphyrogenitism
positivism
possibilism
Post-Impressionism
post-millennialism
Poujadism
Powellism
practicalism
pragmatism
precisianism
predestinarianism
predeterminism
preferentialism
preformationism
prelatism
premillenarianism
premillennialism
Pre-Raphaelism
Pre-Raphaelitism

**-ism** *(contd.)*
Presbyterianism
presentationism
preternaturalism
prettyism
priapism
priggism
primitivism
primordialism
probabiliorism
probabilism
prochronism
professionalism
prognathism
progressionism
progressism
progressivism
prohibitionism
proletarianism
propagandism
prophetism
prosaicism
prosaism
proselytism
prostatism
prosyllogism
protectionism
Protestantism
proverbialism
provincialism
prudentialism
Prussianism
psellism
psephism
pseudo-archaism
pseudoclassicism
pseudomorphism
psilanthropism
psychism
psychologism
psychopannychism
psychoticism
ptyalism
puerilism
pugilism
puppyism
purism
puritanism
Puseyism
pyrrhonism
Pythagoreanism
Pythagorism
Quakerism
quattrocentism
quietism
quixotism
rabbinism
Rabelaisianism
racemism
Rachmanism
racialism
racism
radicalism
Ramism
ranterism
rascalism
rationalism
reactionarism
realism
rebaptism
Rebeccaism

Rechabitism
recidivism
red-tapism
reductionism
reformism
regalism
regionalism
reincarnationism
relationism
relativism
religionism
Rembrandtism
representationalism
representationism
republicanism
restitutionism
restorationism
resurrectionism
reunionism
revanchism
revisionism
revivalism
revolutionism
rheotropism
rheumatism
rhopalism
rhotacism
Ribbonism
rigorism
ritualism
Romanism
romanticism
Rosicrucianism
Rosminianism
Rotarianism
routinism
rowdyism
royalism
ruffianism
ruralism
Russianism
Russophilism
Sabaism
Sabbatarianism
sabbatism
Sabellianism
Sabianism
sacerdotalism
sacramentalism
sacramentarianism
Sadduceeism
Sadducism
sadism
sado-masochism
saintism
Saint-Simonianism
Saint-Simonism
Saivism
Saktism
salvationism
Samaritanism
sanitarianism
sansculottism
sapphism
saprophytism
Saracenism
satanism
saturnism
Saxonism
scepticism
schematism

scholasticism
scientism
sciolism
Scotism
Scotticism
scoundrelism
scribism
scripturalism
scripturism
secessionism
sectarianism
sectionalism
secularism
self-criticism
self-hypnotism
selfism
semi-Arianism
semi-barbarism
Semi-Pelagianism
Semitism
sensationalism
sensationism
sensism
sensualism
sensuism
sentimentalism
separatism
serialism
servilism
servo-mechanism
sesquipedalianism
sexism
sexualism
Shaivism
shakerism
Shaktism
shamanism
shamateurism
Shiism
Shintoism
Shivaism
shunamitism
sigmatism
Sikhism
simplism
sinapism
sinecurism
singularism
Sinicism
Sinophilism
Sivaism
Slavism
snobbism
socialism
Socinianism
sociologism
Sofism
solarism
solecism
sol-faism
solidarism
solidism
solifidianism
solipsism
somatism
somnambulism
somniloquism
sophism
southernism
sovietism
specialism

speciesism
Spencerianism
Spinozism
spiritism
spiritualism
spoonerism
spread-eagleism
Stahlianism
Stahlism
Stakhanovism
Stalinism
stand-pattism
statism
stercoranism
stereoisomerism
stereotropism
stibialism
stigmatism
stoicism
strabism
structuralism
strychninism
strychnism
Stundism
subjectivism
sublapsarianism
subordinationism
substantialism
suburbanism
suffragism
Sufiism
Sufism
suggestionism
supernationalism
supernaturalism
superrealism
Supralapsarianism
supremacism
suprematism
surrealism
sutteeism
Swadeshism
swarajism
Swedenborgianism
swingism
sybaritism
sybotism
syllabism
syllogism
symbolism
symphilism
synaposematism
synchronism
syncretism
syndactylism
syndicalism
synecdochism
synergism
synoecism
syntheticism
Syriacism
Syrianism
systematism
tachism
tactism
Tammanyism
tantalism
Tantrism
Taoism
tarantism
Tartuffism

**-ism** *(contd.)*
Tartufism
tautochronism
tautologism
tautomerism
teetotalism
teleologism
tenebrism
teratism
terminism
territorialism
terrorism
tetramerism
tetratheism
Teutonicism
Teutonism
textualism
thanatism
Thatcherism
thaumaturgism
theanthropism
theatricalism
theatricism
theism
theomorphism
Theopaschitism
theophilanthropism
theosophism
therianthropism
theriomorphism
thermotropism
thigmotropism
Thomism
thrombo-embolism
thuggism
tigerism
Timonism
Titanism
Titoism
toadyism
tokenism
Toryism
totalitarianism
totemism
tourism
tractarianism
trade-unionism
traditionalism
Traducianism
traitorism
transcendentalism
transformism
transmigrationism
transsexualism
transvestism
transvestitism
traumatism
trialism
tribadism
tribalism
trichroism
trichromatism
tricrotism
triliteralism
trimorphism
Trinitarianism
trinomialism
tripersonalism
tritheism
triticism
trituberculism

trivialism
troglodytism
troilism
trophotropism
tropism
Trotskyism
truism
tsarism
tuism
Turcophilism
tutiorism
tutorism
tychism
ultra-Conservatism
ultraism
ultramontanism
undenominationalism
unicameralism
unidealism
uniformitarianism
unilateralism
unionism
unitarianism
universalism
unrealism
unsectarianism
unsocialism
untruism
uranism
utilitarianism
utopianism
utopism
Utraquism
vagabondism
Valentinianism
valetudinarianism
vampirism
vandalism
Vansittartism
Vaticanism
Vedism
veganism
vegetarianism
ventriloquism
verbalism
verism
vernacularism
Victorianism
vigilantism
vikingism
virilism
virtualism
vitalism
viviparism
vocalism
vocationalism
volcanism
Voltaireanism
Voltairianism
Voltairism
voltaism
voltinism
voluntarism
voluntaryism
voodooism
vorticism
voyeurism
vulcanism
vulgarism
vulpinism
vulturism

Wagnerianism
Wagnerism
Wahabiism
Wahabism
welfarism
werewolfism
Wertherism
werwolfism
Wesleyanism
westernism
Whiggism
whiteboyism
wholism
witticism
Wodenism
Wolfianism
xanthochroism
Yankeeism
yogism
zanyism
Zarathustrianism
Zarathustrism
zealotism
Zionism
Zoilism
zoism
Zolaism
zombiism
zoomagnetism
zoomorphism
zoophilism
zootheism
Zoroastrianism
Zwinglianism
zygodactylism
zygomorphism

**-itis**

adenitis
antiaditis
aortitis
appendicitis
arteritis
arthritis
balanitis
blepharitis
bronchitis
bursitis
carditis
cellulitis
cephalitis
ceratitis
cerebritis
cholecystitis
colitis
conchitis
conjunctivitis
crystallitis
cystitis
dermatitis
diaphragmatitis
diphtheritis
diverticulitis
duodenitis
encephalitis
endocarditis
endometritis
enteritis
fibrositis
gastritis

gastroenteritis
gingivitis
glossitis
hamarthritis
hepatitis
hysteritis
ileitis
iritis
keratitis
labyrinthitis
laminitis
laryngitis
lymphangitis
mastitis
mastoiditis
meningitis
metritis
myelitis
myocarditis
myositis
myringitis
nephritis
neuritis
onychitis
oophoritis
ophthalmitis
orchitis
osteitis
osteo-arthritis
osteomyelitis
otitis
ovaritis
panarthritis
pancreatitis
panophthalmitis
papillitis
parotiditis
parotitis
pericarditis
perigastritis
perihepatitis
perinephritis
perineuritis
periostitis
peritonitis
perityphlitis
pharyngitis
phlebitis
phrenitis
pleuritis
pneumonitis
poliomyelitis
polyneuritis
proctitis
prostatitis
pyelitis
pyelonephritis
rachitis
rectitis
retinitis
rhachitis
rhinitis
rhinopharyngitis
salpingitis
scleritis
sclerotitis
sinuitis
sinusitis
splenitis
spondylitis
staphylitis

**-itis** *(contd.)*
stomatitis
strumitis
synovitis
syringitis
tendonitis
tenosynovitis
thrombo-phlebitis
thyroiditis
tonsilitis
tonsillitis
tracheitis
trachitis
tympanitis
typhlitis
ulitis
ureteritis
urethritis
uteritis
uveitis
uvulitis
vaginitis
valvulitis
vulvitis

**-latrous**

bibliolatrous
heliolatrous
ichthyolatrous
idolatrous
litholatrous
Mariolatrous
Maryolatrous
monolatrous
ophiolatrous
zoolatrous

**-latry**

angelolatry
anthropolatry
astrolatry
autolatry
bardolatry
bibliolatry
Christolatry
cosmolatry
demonolatry
dendrolatry
ecclesiolatry
epeolatry
geolatry
hagiolatry
heliolatry
hierolatry
ichthyolatry
iconolatry
idolatry
litholatry
lordolatry
Mariolatry
Maryolatry
monolatry
necrolatry
ophiolatry
physiolatry
plutolatry
pyrolatry
symbololatry
thaumatolatry

theriolatry
zoolatry

**-logical**

aerobiological
aerological
aetiological
agrobiological
agrological
agrostological
algological
alogical
amphibological
analogical
anthropological
arachnological
archaeological
astrological
atheological
audiological
autecological
axiological
bacteriological
batological
battological
biological
bryological
campanological
carcinological
cartological
chorological
Christological
chronological
climatological
codicological
conchological
cosmological
craniological
cryobiological
cryptological
cytological
demonological
dendrological
deontological
dermatological
dysteleological
ecclesiological
ecological
Egyptological
electrophysiological
embryological
entomological
epidemiological
epistemological
eschatological
ethnological
ethological
etymological
futurological
gastrological
gemmological
gemological
genealogical
genethlialogical
geochronological
geological
geomorphological
gerontological
glaciological
glossological

gnotobiological
graphological
gynaecological
hagiological
helminthological
hepaticological
herpetological
histological
histopathological
homological
horological
hydrobiological
hydrological
ichthyological
ideological
illogical
immunological
laryngological
limnological
lithological
logical
malacological
mammalogical
martyrological
metapsychological
meteorological
micrological
mineralogical
monological
morphological
musicological
mycological
myological
myrmecological
mythological
necrological
neological
nephological
nephrological
neurological
nomological
nosological
nostological
oceanological
odontological
oenological
ontological
ophiological
ophthalmological
oreological
ornithological
orological
osteological
paedological
palaeontological
palaeozoological
palynological
parapsychological
pathological
pedological
penological
pestological
petrological
phaenological
phenological
phenomenological
philological
phonological
phraseological
phrenological
phycological

physiological
phytological
phytopathological
pneumatological
poenological
pomological
posological
potamological
protozoological
psephological
psychobiological
psychological
radiological
reflexological
rheumatological
rhinological
scatological
sedimentological
seismological
selenological
serological
Sinological
sociobiological
sociological
somatological
soteriological
Sovietological
spectrological
spelaeological
stoechiological
stoicheiological
stoichiological
synecological
tautological
technological
teleological
teratological
terminological
theological
topological
toxicological
traumatological
trichological
tropological
typological
unlogical
untheological
urological
virological
volcanological
vulcanological
zoological
zoophytological
zymological

**-logous**

analogous
antilogous
dendrologous
heterologous
homologous
isologous
tautologous

**-logue**

aeglogue
analogue
apologue
catalogue

**-logue** *(contd.)*
collogue
decalogue
dialogue
duologue
eclogue
epilogue
grammalogue
homologue
idealogue
ideologue
isologue
monologue
philologue
prologue
Sinologue
theologue
travelogue
trialogue

**-logy**

acarology
aerobiology
aerolithology
aerology
aetiology
agriology
agrobiology
agrology
agrostology
algology
amphibology
anaesthesiology
analogy
andrology
anemology
angelology
anthology
anthropobiology
anthropology
antilogy
apology
arachnology
archaeology
archeology
archology
aristology
Assyriology
astacology
astrogeology
astrology
atheology
atmology
audiology
autecology
autology
axiology
bacteriology
balneology
batology
battology
bibliology
bioecology
biology
biotechnology
brachylogy
bryology
bumpology
cacology
caliology

campanology
carcinology
cardiology
carphology
cartology
cetology
characterology
cheirology
chirology
choreology
chorology
Christology
chronobiology
chronology
cine-biology
climatology
codicology
cometology
conchology
coprology
cosmetology
cosmology
craniology
criminology
cryobiology
cryptology
cytology
dactyliology
dactylology
deltiology
demology
demonology
dendrochronology
dendrology
deontology
dermatology
diabology
diabolology
dialectology
diplomatology
dittology
docimology
dogmatology
dosiology
dosology
doxology
dyslogy
dysteleology
ecclesiology
eccrinology
ecology
edaphology
Egyptology
electrobiology
electrology
electrophysiology
electrotechnology
elogy
embryology
emmenology
endemiology
endocrinology
entomology
enzymology
epidemiology
epistemology
escapology
eschatology
ethnology
ethnomusicology
ethology

Etruscology
etymology
euchology
eulogy
exobiology
festilogy
festology
folk-etymology
futurology
gastroenterology
gastrology
gemmology
gemology
genealogy
genethlialogy
geochronology
geology
geomorphology
gerontology
gigantology
glaciology
glossology
glottology
gnomonology
gnoseology
gnosiology
gnotobiology
graphology
gynaecology
haematology
hagiology
hamartiology
haplology
heliology
helminthology
heortology
hepaticology
hepatology
heresiology
herpetology
heterology
hierology
hippology
histiology
histology
histopathology
historiology
homology
hoplology
horology
hydrobiology
hydrogeology
hydrology
hydrometeorology
hyetology
hygrology
hymnology
hypnology
ichnology
ichthyology
iconology
ideology
immunology
insectology
irenology
kidology
kinesiology
koniology
Kremlinology
laryngology
lepidopterology

lexicology
lichenology
limacology
limnology
lithology
liturgiology
macrology
malacology
malariology
mammalogy
Mariology
martyrology
Maryology
Mayology
menology
metapsychology
meteorology
methodology
microbiology
microclimatology
micrology
micro-meteorology
microtechnology
mineralogy
misology
monadology
monology
morphology
muscology
museology
musicology
mycetology
mycology
myology
myrmecology
mythology
necrology
nematology
neology
nephology
nephrology
neurobiology
neurohypnology
neurology
neuropathology
neurophysiology
neuroradiology
neurypnology
nomology
noology
nosology
nostology
numerology
numismatology
oceanology
odonatology
odontology
oenology
olfactology
oncology
oneirology
onirology
ontology
oology
ophiology
ophthalmology
optology
orchidology
oreology
ornithology
orology

**-logy** *(contd.)*
orthopterology
oryctology
osteology
otolaryngology
otology
otorhinolaryngology
ourology
paedology
palaeanthropology
palaeethnology
palaeichthyology
palaeoclimatology
palaeolimnology
palaeontology
palaeopedology
palaeophytology
palaeozoology
palillogy
palynology
pantheology
papyrology
paradoxology
paralogy
parapsychology
parasitology
paroemiology
pathology
patrology
pedology
pelology
penology
pentalogy
periodontology
perissology
pestology
petrology
phaenology
pharmacology
pharyngology
phenology
phenomenology
philology
phonology
photobiology
photogeology
phraseology
phrenology
phycology
physiology
phytology
phytopathology
planetology
plutology
pneumatology
podology
poenology
pomology
ponerology
posology
potamology
primatology
proctology
protistology
protozoology
psephology
pseudology
psychobiology
psychology
psychopathology
psychophysiology

pteridology
pyramidology
pyretology
pyroballogy
radiobiology
radiology
reflexology
rheology
rheumatology
rhinology
röntgenology
sarcology
satanology
scatology
Scientology
sedimentology
seismology
selenology
selenomorphology
semasiology
semeiology
semiology
serology
sexology
sindonology
Sinology
sitiology
sitology
skatology
sociobiology
sociology
somatology
soteriology
spectrology
spelaeology
sphagnology
sphygmology
spongology
stichology
stoechiology
stoicheiology
stoichiology
stomatology
storiology
symbology
symbolology
symptomatology
synchronology
synecology
synoecology
syphilology
systematology
tautology
technology
teleology
teratology
terminology
terotechnology
tetralogy
thanatology
theology
thermology
therology
thremmatology
timbrology
tocology
tokology
topology
toxicology
traumatology
tribology

trichology
trilogy
trophology
tropology
typhlology
typology
ufology
uranology
urbanology
urinology
urology
venereology
vexillology
victimology
vinology
virology
volcanology
vulcanology
xylology
zoopathology
zoophytology
zoopsychology
zymology

**-lysis**

analysis
atmolysis
autocatalysis
autolysis
bacteriolysis
catalysis
cryptanalysis
cytolysis
dialysis
electroanalysis
electrolysis
haematolysis
haemodialysis
haemolysis
histolysis
hydrolysis
hypno-analysis
leucocytolysis
microanalysis
narco-analysis
neurolysis
paralysis
photolysis
plasmolysis
pneumatolysis
proteolysis
psephoanalysis
psychoanalysis
pyrolysis
radiolysis
thermolysis
uranalysis
urinalysis
zincolysis
zymolysis

**-lytic**

analytic
anxiolytic
autocatalytic
autolytic
bacteriolytic
catalytic
dialytic

electrolytic
haemolytic
histolytic
hydrolytic
paralytic
photolytic
plasmolytic
pneumatolytic
proteolytic
psychoanalytic
pyrolytic
sympatholytic
tachylytic
thermolytic
unanalytic

**-mancy**

aeromancy
axinomancy
belomancy
bibliomancy
botanomancy
capnomancy
cartomancy
ceromancy
cheiromancy
chiromancy
cleromancy
coscinomancy
crithomancy
crystallomancy
dactyliomancy
gastromancy
geomancy
gyromancy
hieromancy
hydromancy
lampadomancy
lithomancy
myomancy
necromancy
nigromancy
oenomancy
omphalomancy
oneiromancy
oniromancy
onychomancy
ornithomancy
pyromancy
rhabdomancy
scapulimancy
spodomancy
tephromancy
theomancy
zoomancy

**-mania**

acronymania
anglomania
anthomania
arithmomania
balletomania
bibliomania
Celtomania
demonomania
dipsomania
egomania
eleutheromania
erotomania

**-mania** *(contd.)*
etheromania
flagellomania
francomania
gallomania
graphomania
hydromania
hypomania
hysteromania
kleptomania
megalomania
melomania
methomania
metromania
monomania
morphinomania
mythomania
nostomania
nymphomania
oenomania
opsomania
orchidomania
petalomania
phyllomania
potichomania
pteridomania
pyromania
squandermania
technomania
theatromania
theomania
timbromania
toxicomania
trichotillomania
tulipomania
typomania
xenomania

**-mantic**
cheiromantic
chiromantic
geomantic
hydromantic
myomantic
necromantic
ornithomantic
pyromantic
scapulimantic
spodomantic
theomantic
zoomantic

**-mathic**
chrestomathic
philomathic
polymathic

**-mathy**
chrestomathy
opsimathy
philomathy
polymathy

**-meter**
absorptiometer
accelerometer
acidimeter

actinometer
aerometer
alcoholometer
alkalimeter
altimeter
ammeter
anemometer
araeometer
areometer
arithmometer
atmometer
audiometer
auxanometer
auxometer
barometer
bathometer
bathymeter
bolometer
bomb-calorimeter
calorimeter
cathetometer
centimeter
chlorimeter
chlorometer
chronometer
clinometer
colorimeter
Comptometer®
coulombmeter
coulometer
craniometer
cryometer
cyanometer
cyclometer
decelerometer
declinometer
dendrometer
densimeter
densitometer
diagometer
diameter
diaphanometer
diffractometer
dimeter
dose-meter
dosimeter
drosometer
dynamometer
effusiometer
electrodynamometer
electrometer
endosmometer
ergometer
eriometer
evaporimeter
extensimeter
extensometer
fathometer
flowmeter
fluorimeter
fluorometer
focimeter
galactometer
galvanometer
gas-meter
gasometer
geometer
geothermometer
goniometer
gradiometer
gravimeter

harmonometer
heliometer
heptameter
hexameter
hodometer
hydrometer
hyetometer
hygrometer
hypsometer
iconometer
inclinometer
interferometer
isoperimeter
katathermometer
konimeter
kryometer
lactometer
luxmeter
lysimeter
machmeter
magnetometer
manometer
mekometer
meter
micrometer
microseismometer
mileometer
milometer
monometer
nephelometer
Nilometer
nitrometer
octameter
odometer
oenometer
ohmmeter
ombrometer
oncometer
ophthalmometer
opisometer
opsiometer
optometer
osmometer
oximeter
pachymeter
parameter
passimeter
pedometer
pelvimeter
pentameter
perimeter
permeameter
phonmeter
phonometer
photometer
piezometer
planimeter
planometer
plessimeter
pleximeter
pluviometer
pneumatometer
polarimeter
potentiometer
potometer
psychometer
psychrometer
pulsimeter
pulsometer
pycnometer
pyknometer

pyrheliometer
pyrometer
quantometer
radiogoniometer
radiometer
radiotelemeter
refractometer
rheometer
rhythmometer
saccharimeter
saccharometer
salimeter
salinometer
scintillometer
sclerometer
seismometer
semi-diameter
semiperimeter
sensitometer
slot-meter
solarimeter
spectrophotometer
speedometer
spherometer
sphygmomanometer
sphygmometer
spirometer
stactometer
stalagmometer
stereometer
strabismometer
strabometer
swingometer
sympiesometer
tacheometer
tachometer
tachymeter
taseometer
tasimeter
taximeter
telemeter
tellurometer
tetrameter
thermometer
Tintometer®
tonometer
torque-meter
tribometer
trigonometer
trimeter
trocheameter
trochometer
tromometer
udometer
urinometer
vaporimeter
variometer
viameter
vibrometer
viscometer
viscosimeter
voltameter
voltmeter
volumenometer
volumeter
volumometer
water-barometer
water-meter
water-thermometer
wattmeter
wavemeter

**-meter** *(contd.)*
weatherometer
xylometer
zymometer
zymosimeter

**-metry**
acidimetry
aerometry
alcoholometry
alkalimetry
anemometry
anthropometry
araeometry
asymmetry
barometry
bathymetry
biometry
bolometry
calorimetry
chlorimetry
chlorometry
chronometry
clinometry
colorimetry
coulometry
craniometry
densimetry
densitometry
dissymmetry
dosimetry
dynamometry
electrometry
galvanometry
gasometry
geometry
goniometry
gravimetry
hodometry
horometry
hydrometry
hygrometry
hypsometry
iconometry
interferometry
isometry
isoperimetry
micrometry
microseismometry
nephelometry
noometry
odometry
ophthalmometry
optometry
pelvimetry
perimetry
photometry
planimetry
plessimetry
pleximetry
polarimetry
pseudosymmetry
psychometry
psychrometry
pyrometry
saccharimetry
seismometry
sociometry
spectrometry
spectrophotometry

spirometry
stalagmometry
stereometry
stichometry
stoechiometry
stoicheiometry
stoichiometry
symmetry
tacheometry
tachometry
tachymetry
telemetry
tensiometry
thermometry
trigonometry
unsymmetry
uranometry
viscometry
viscosimetry
zoometry

**-monger**

balladmonger
barber-monger
borough-monger
carpetmonger
cheese-monger
costardmonger
costermonger
fellmonger
fishmonger
flesh-monger
gossip-monger
ironmonger
lawmonger
love-monger
maxim-monger
meal-monger
miracle-monger
mystery-monger
newsmonger
panic-monger
peace-monger
pearmonger
peltmonger
phrasemonger
place-monger
prayer-monger
relic-monger
scandalmonger
scaremonger
sensation-monger
species-monger
starmonger
state-monger
system-monger
verse-monger
warmonger
whoremonger
wit-monger
wonder-monger

**-morphic**

actinomorphic
allelomorphic
allotriomorphic
anamorphic
anthropomorphic
automorphic

biomorphic
dimorphic
ectomorphic
enantiomorphic
endomorphic
ergatomorphic
gynandromorphic
hemimorphic
heteromorphic
homeomorphic
homoeomorphic
homomorphic
hylomorphic
idiomorphic
isodimorphic
isomorphic
lagomorphic
mesomorphic
metamorphic
monomorphic
morphic
ophiomorphic
ornithomorphic
paedomorphic
paramorphic
perimorphic
pleomorphic
polymorphic
protomorphic
pseudomorphic
tetramorphic
theomorphic
theriomorphic
trimorphic
xenomorphic
xeromorphic
zoomorphic
zygomorphic

**-morphous**
amorphous
anamorphous
anthropomorphous
dimorphous
enantiomorphous
gynandromorphous
heteromorphous
homeomorphous
homoeomorphous
homomorphous
isodimorphous
isomorphous
lagomorphous
mesomorphous
monomorphous
ophiomorphous
perimorphous
pleomorphous
polymorphous
pseudomorphous
rhizomorphous
tauromorphous
theriomorphous
trimorphous
xeromorphous
zygomorphous

**-onym**
acronym
anonym

antonym
autonym
cryptonym
eponym
exonym
heteronym
homonym
metonym
paronym
polyonym
pseudonym
synonym
tautonym
toponym
trionym

**-onymic**

acronymic
Hieronymic
homonymic
matronymic
metonymic
metronymic
patronymic
polyonymic
synonymic
toponymic

**-osis**

abiosis
acidosis
actinobacillosis
actinomycosis
aerobiosis
aeroneurosis
alkalosis
amaurosis
amitosis
anabiosis
anadiplosis
anaerobiosis
anamorphosis
anaplerosis
anastomosis
anchylosis
ankylosis
anthracosis
anthropomorphosis
antibiosis
apodosis
aponeurosis
apotheosis
arteriosclerosis
arthrosis
asbestosis
aspergillosis
ateleiosis
atherosclerosis
athetosis
autohypnosis
avitaminosis
bacteriosis
bagassosis
bilharziosis
biocoenosis
bromhidrosis
bromidrosis
brucellosis
byssinosis

**-osis** *(contd.)*
carcinomatosis
carcinosis
chlorosis
cirrhosis
coccidiosis
cyanosis
cyclosis
dermatosis
diarthrosis
diorthosis
diverticulosis
dulosis
ecchymosis
enantiosis
enarthrosis
endometriosis
endosmosis
enosis
enteroptosis
epanadiplosis
epanorthosis
exosmosis
exostosis
fibrosis
fluorosis
furunculosis
gliomatosis
gnotobiosis
gomphosis
gummosis
haematosis
halitosis
hallucinosis
heliosis
heterosis
hidrosis
homeosis
homoeosis
homomorphosis
homozygosis
hydronephrosis
hyperhidrosis
hyperidrosis
hyperinosis
hypersarcosis
hypervitaminosis
hypinosis
hypnosis
hypotyposis
ichthyosis
kenosis
keratosis
ketosis
kurtosis
kyllosis
kyphosis
leishmaniosis
leptospirosis
leucocytosis
limosis
listeriosis
lipomatosis
lordosis
madarosis
marmarosis
meiosis
melanosis
metachrosis
metamorphosis
metempsychosis

miosis
mitosis
molybdosis
mononucleosis
monosis
morphosis
mucoviscidosis
mycosis
mycotoxicosis
myosis
myxomatosis
narcohypnosis
narcosis
necrobiosis
necrosis
nephroptosis
nephrosis
neurosis
onychocryptosis
ornithosis
osmidrosis
osmosis
osteoarthrosis
osteoporosis
otosclerosis
paedomorphosis
parabiosis
paraphimosis
parapsychosis
parasitosis
pediculosis
phagocytosis
phimosis
pholidosis
phytosis
pneumoconiosis
pneumokoniosis
pneumonokoniosis
pneumonoultramicroscopic-
  silicovolcanoconiosis
pollenosis
polyposis
porosis
proptosis
psilosis
psittacosis
psychoneurosis
psychosis
pterylosis
ptilosis
ptosis
pyrosis
resinosis
salmonellosis
sarcoidosis
sarcomatosis
sclerosis
scoliosis
self-hypnosis
siderosis
silicosis
sorosis
spirillosis
spirochaetosis
spondylosis
steatosis
stegnosis
stenosis
strongylosis
sycosis
symbiosis

symptosis
synarthrosis
synchondrosis
syndesmosis
synoeciosis
synostosis
syntenosis
syssarcosis
thanatosis
theriomorphosis
thrombosis
thylosis
thyrotoxicosis
torulosis
toxoplasmosis
trichinosis
trichophytosis
trichosis
trophobiosis
trophoneurosis
tuberculosis
tylosis
ulosis
urosis
virosis
visceroptosis
xerosis
zoonosis
zygosis
zymosis

**-path**

allopath
homeopath
homoeopath
kinesipath
naturopath
neuropath
osteopath
psychopath
sociopath
telepath

**-pathic**

allopathic
anthropopathic
antipathic
empathic
homoeopathic
hydropathic
idiopathic
kinesipathic
naturopathic
neuropathic
osteopathic
protopathic
psychopathic
sociopathic
telepathic

**-pathy**

allopathy
anthropopathy
antipathy
apathy
cardiomyopathy
dyspathy
empathy

enantiopathy
homeopathy
homoeopathy
hydropathy
idiopathy
kinesipathy
myocardiopathy
naturopathy
neuropathy
nostopathy
osteopathy
psychopathy
sociopathy
sympathy
telepathy
theopathy
zoopathy

**-phage**

bacteriophage
macrophage
ostreophage
xylophage

**-phagous**

anthropophagous
autophagous
carpophagous
coprophagous
creophagous
endophagous
entomophagous
exophagous
geophagous
hippophagous
hylophagous
ichthyophagous
lithophagous
mallophagous
meliphagous
monophagous
myrmecophagous
necrophagous
omophagous
ophiophagous
ostreophagous
pantophagous
phyllophagous
phytophagous
polyphagous
rhizophagous
saprophagous
sarcophagous
scatophagous
theophagous
toxicophagous
toxiphagous
xylophagous
zoophagous

**-phagy**

anthropophagy
autophagy
coprophagy
dysphagy
endophagy
entomophagy
exophagy

## -phagy (contd.)

geophagy
hippophagy
ichthyophagy
monophagy
mycophagy
omophagy
ostreophagy
pantophagy
polyphagy
sarcophagy
scatophagy
theophagy
xerophagy

## -phile

ailurophile
arctophile
audiophile
bibliophile
cartophile
discophile
francophile
gallophile
Germanophile
gerontophile
halophile
hippophile
homophile
iodophile
logophile
Lusophile
lyophile
myrmecophile
necrophile
negrophile
oenophile
ombrophile
paedophile
psammophile
Russophile
scripophile
Sinophile
Slavophile
spermophile
thermophile
Turcophile
xenophile
zoophile

## -philia

ailurophilia
anglophilia
canophilia
coprophilia
ephebophilia
Germanophilia
gerontophilia
haemophilia
necrophilia
neophilia
paedophilia
paraphilia
scopophilia
scoptophilia
zoophilia

## -philist

bibliophilist
canophilist
cartophilist
Dantophilist
iconophilist
negrophilist
notaphilist
oenophilist
ophiophilist
pteridophilist
Russophilist
scripophilist
stegophilist
timbrophilist
zoophilist

## -phily

acarophily
anemophily
bibliophily
cartophily
entomophily
halophily
hydrophily
myrmecophily
necrophily
notaphily
oenophily
ornithophily
photophily
scripophily
Sinophily
symphily
timbrophily
toxophily
xerophily

## -phobe

ailurophobe
anglophobe
francophobe
gallophobe
Germanophobe
gerontophobe
hippophobe
hygrophobe
lyophobe
negrophobe
ombrophobe
photophobe
Russophobe
Slavophobe
Turcophobe
xenophobe

## -phobia

acrophobia
aerophobia
agoraphobia
aichmophobia
ailurophobia
algophobia
anemophobia
anglophobia
anthropophobia
arachnophobia
arithmophobia
astraphobia
astrapophobia
bathophobia
bibliophobia
canophobia
claustrophobia
clinophobia
cynophobia
dromophobia
dysmorphophobia
ecophobia
ergophobia
euphobia
francophobia
gallophobia
gerontophobia
graphophobia
gynophobia
hierophobia
homophobia
hydrophobia
hypsophobia
kenophobia
monophobia
mysophobia
necrophobia,
negrophobia
neophobia
nosophobia
nyctophobia
ochlophobia
ophthalmophobia
panophobia
pantophobia
pathophobia
phagophobia
phengophobia
phonophobia
photophobia
Russophobia
satanophobia
scopophobia
sitiophobia
sitophobia
symmetrophobia
syphilophobia
taphephobia
taphophobia
technophobia
thanatophobia
theophobia
toxicophobia
toxiphobia
triskaidecaphobia
triskaidekaphobia
xenophobia
zelophobia
zoophobia

## -phobic

aerophobic
agoraphobic
anglophobic
claustrophobic
heliophobic
hydrophobic
lyophobic
monophobic

phobic
photophobic

## -phone

aerophone
allophone
anglophone
Ansaphone®
audiphone
chordophone
detectophone
diaphone
dictaphone
diphone
earphone
Entryphone®
francophone
geophone
gramophone
harmoniphone
headphone
heckelphone
homophone
hydrophone
idiophone
interphone
kaleidophone
megaphone
metallophone
microphone
monotelephone
optophone
phone
photophone
Picturephone®
polyphone
pyrophone
radiogramophone
radiophone
radiotelephone
sarrusophone
saxophone
sousaphone
speakerphone
sphygmophone
stentorphone
telephone
theatrophone
triphone
vibraphone
videophone
videotelephone
viewphone
xylophone

## -phonic

acrophonic
allophonic
anglophonic
antiphonic
aphonic
cacophonic
cataphonic
chordophonic
dodecaphonic
dysphonic
euphonic
gramophonic
homophonic

## -phonic (contd.)

microphonic
monophonic
paraphonic
photophonic
quadraphonic
quadrophonic
radiophonic
stentorophonic
stereophonic
symphonic
telephonic
xylophonic

## -phony

acrophony
antiphony
aphony
autophony
cacophony
colophony
dodecaphony
euphony
gramophony
homophony
laryngophony
monophony
photophony
polyphony
quadraphony
quadrophony
radiophony
radiotelephony
stereophony
symphony
tautophony
telephony

## -phorous

discophorous
Eriophorous
galactophorous
hypophosphorous
mastigophorous
necrophorous
odontophorous
phosphorous
pyrophorous
rhynchophorous
sporophorous

## -phyte

aerophyte
bryophyte
cormophyte
dermatophyte
ectophyte
endophyte
entophyte
epiphyte
gametophyte
geophyte
halophyte
heliophyte
heliosciophyte
holophyte
hydrophyte
hygrophyte

hylophyte
lithophyte
mesophyte
microphyte
neophyte
oophyte
osteophyte
phanerophyte
phreatophyte
protophyte
psammophyte
pteridophyte
saprophyte
schizophyte
spermaphyte
spermatophyte
spermophyte
sporophyte
thallophyte
tropophyte
xerophyte
zoophyte
zygophyte

## -saurus

Allosaurus
Ankylosaurus
Apatosaurus
Atlantosaurus
brachiosaurus
brontosaurus
Ceteosaurus
Dolichosaurus
Ichthyosaurus
megalosaurus
Plesiosaurus
Stegosaurus
Teleosaurus
Titanosaurus
tyrannosaurus

## -scope

aethrioscope
auriscope
baroscope
bathyscope
benthoscope
bioscope
bronchoscope
chromoscope
chronoscope
colposcope
cryoscope
cystoscope
dichrooscope
dichroscope
dipleidoscope
ebullioscope
electroscope
endoscope
engiscope
engyscope
epidiascope
episcope
fluoroscope
galvanoscope
gastroscope
gyroscope
hagioscope

helioscope
hodoscope
horoscope
hydroscope
hygroscope
iconoscope
iriscope
kaleidoscope
kinetoscope
koniscope
lactoscope
laparoscope
laryngoscope
lychnoscope
megascope
microscope
mutoscope
myringoscope
myrioscope
nephoscope
opeidoscope
ophthalmoscope
oscilloscope
otoscope
pantoscope
periscope
pharyngoscope
phenakistoscope
phonendoscope
polariscope
poroscope
praxinoscope
proctoscope
pseudoscope
pyroscope
radarscope
radioscope
rhinoscope
scintilloscope
scope
seismoscope
sigmoidoscope
somascope
spectrohelioscope
spectroscope
sphygmoscope
spinthariscope
statoscope
stereofluoroscope
stereoscope
stethoscope
stroboscope
tachistoscope
teinoscope
telescope
thermoscope
triniscope
ultramicroscope
vectorscope
Vertoscope®
vitascope

## -scopic

autoscopic
bronchoscopic
cryoscopic
deuteroscopic
dichrooscopic
dichroscopic
ebullioscopic

electroscopic
endoscopic
gyroscopic
hagioscopic
helioscopic
horoscopic
hygroscopic
kaleidoscopic
laryngoscopic
macroscopic
megascopic
metoposcopic
microscopic
necroscopic
ophthalmoscopic
orthoscopic
pantoscopic
periscopic
poroscopic
rhinoscopic
seismoscopic
spectroscopic
stethoscopic
stroboscopic
submicroscopic
tachistoscopic
telescopic
thermoscopic
ultramicroscopic
zooscopic

## -scopy

autoscopy
bronchoscopy
colposcopy
cranioscopy
cryoscopy
cystoscopy
dactyloscopy
deuteroscopy
ebullioscopy
endoscopy
episcopy
fluoroscopy
foetoscopy
hepatoscopy
hieroscopy
horoscopy
laparoscopy
laryngoscopy
metoposcopy
microscopy
necroscopy
omoplatoscopy
oneiroscopy
oniroscopy
ophthalmoscopy
ornithoscopy
ouroscopy
peritoneoscopy
pharyngoscopy
poroscopy
proctoscopy
radioscopy
retinoscopy
rhinoscopy
röntgenoscopy
skiascopy
spectroscopy
stereoscopy

**-scopy** *(contd.)*
stethoscopy
telescopy
tracheoscopy
ultramicroscopy
urinoscopy
uroscopy
zooscopy

**-ship**

abbotship
accountantship
acquaintanceship
administratorship
admiralship
advisership
aedileship
airmanship
aldermanship
amateurship
ambassadorship
apostleship
apprenticeship
archonship
assessorship
associateship
attorneyship
auditorship
augurship
authorship
bachelorship
bailieship
baillieship
bardship
barristership
bashawship
batsmanship
beadleship
bedellship
bedelship
benchership
bondmanship
brinkmanship
bursarship
bushmanship
butlership
cadetship
Caesarship
candidateship
captainship
cardinalship
catechumenship
censorship
chairmanship
chamberlainship
championship
chancellorship
chaplainship
chelaship
chiefship
chieftainship
citizenship
clanship
clerkship
clientship
clownship
coadjutorship
colleagueship
collectorship
colonelship

commandantship
commandership
commissaryship
commissionership
committeeship
companionship
compotationship
comradeship
conductorship
confessorship
connoisseurship
conservatorship
constableship
consulship
controllership
copartnership
co-rivalship
corporalship
counsellorship
countship
courtship
cousinship
cowardship
craftmanship
craftsmanship
creatorship
creatureship
curateship
curatorship
custodianship
deaconship
dealership
deanship
demyship
denizenship
devilship
dictatorship
directorship
discipleship
disfellowship
doctorship
dogeship
dogship
dollarship
donship
draftsmanship
dukeship
editorship
eldership
electorship
emperorship
endship
ensignship
entrepreneurship
envoyship
executorship
factorship
fathership
fellowship
foxship
freshmanship
friendship
gamesmanship
generalship
gentlemanship
giantship
gladiatorship
goddess-ship
godship
good-fellowship
governor-generalship

governorship
grandeeship
guardianship
guideship
hardship
headship
hectorship
heirship
heraldship
heroship
hership
hetmanship
horsemanship
hostess-ship
housewifeship
huntsmanship
inspectorship
interpretership
interrelationship
janitorship
jockeyship
judgeship
justiceship
kaisership
keepership
kindredship
kingship
kinship
knaveship
ladyship
lairdship
land-ownership
laureateship
leadership
lectorship
lectureship
legateship
legislatorship
librarianship
lieutenant-
  commandership
lieutenant-generalship
lieutenant-governorship
lieutenantship
lifemanship
logship
lordship
ludship
mageship
major-generalship
majorship
managership
marshalship
mastership
matronship
mayorship
mediatorship
membership
Messiahship
milk-kinship
minorship
mistress-ship
moderatorship
monitorship
multi-ownership
musicianship
noviceship
nunship
oarsmanship
one-upmanship
overlordship

ownership
partisanship
partnership
pastorship
patroonship
peatship
pendragonship
penmanship
physicianship
poetship
popeship
possessorship
postmastership
praetorship
preachership
precentorship
prefectship
prelateship
premiership
prenticeship
presbytership
presidentship
pretendership
priestship
primateship
primogenitureship
principalship
priorship
probationership
proconsulship
proctorship
procuratorship
professorship
progenitorship
prolocutorship
prophetship
proprietorship
prosectorship
protectorship
provostship
pursership
quaestorship
queenship
rajahship
rajaship
rangership
readership
recordership
rectorship
regentship
registrarship
relationship
residentiaryship
residentship
retainership
rivalship
rogueship
rulership
sachemship
saintship
salesmanship
scholarship
school-friendship
schoolmastership
scrivenership
seamanship
secretaryship
seigniorship
sempstress-ship
senatorship
seneschalship

**-ship** *(contd.)*
serfship
sergeantship
serjeantship
servantship
servitorship
sextonship
sheriffship
showmanship
sibship
sizarship
soldiership
solicitorship
sonship
speakership
spectatorship
spinstership
sponsorship
sportsmanship
squireship
statesmanship
stewardship
studentship
subahship
subdeaconship
subeditorship
subinspectorship
subjectship
successorship
suffraganship
sultanship
superintendentship
superiorship
supervisorship
suretyship
surgeonship
surrogateship
surveyorship
survivorship
swordsmanship
teachership
tellership
tenantship
thaneship
thwartship
tide-waitership
township
traineeship
traitorship
treasurership
treeship
tribuneship
truantship
trusteeship
tutorship
twinship
umpireship
uncleship
under-clerkship
undergraduateship
under-secretaryship
unfriendship
ushership
vaivodeship
vergership
vicarship
vice-chairmanship
vice-chancellorship
vice-consulship
viceroyship

virtuosoship
viscountship
viziership
vizirship
voivodeship
waivodeship
wardenship
wardship
watermanship
Whigship
workmanship
worship
wranglership
writership
yachtsmanship

**-sophy**

anthroposophy
gastrosophy
gymnosophy
pansophy
philosophy
sciosophy
theosophy

**-stat**

aerostat
antistat
appestat
bacteriostat
barostat
chemostat
coccidiostat
coelostat
cryostat
gyrostat
haemostat
heliostat
humidistat
hydrostat
hygrostat
klinostat
pyrostat
rheostat
siderostat
thermostat

**-therapy**

actinotherapy
aromatherapy
balneotherapy
chemotherapy
cryotherapy
curietherapy
electrotherapy
heliotherapy
hydrotherapy
hypnotherapy
immunotherapy
kinesitherapy
musicotherapy
narcotherapy
opotherapy
organotherapy
pelotherapy
phototherapy
physiotherapy
psychotherapy

pyretotherapy
radiotherapy
röntgenotherapy
serotherapy
serum-therapy
zootherapy

**-tomy**

adenectomy
adenoidectomy
anatomy
anthropotomy
appendectomy
appendicectomy
arteriotomy
autotomy
cephalotomy
cholecystectomy
cholecystotomy
colotomy
cordotomy
craniectomy
craniotomy
cystotomy
dichotomy
duodenectomy
embryotomy
encephalotomy
enterectomy
enterostomy
enterotomy
gastrectomy
gastrotomy
gingivectomy
glossectomy
hepatectomy
herniotomy
hysterectomy
hysterotomy
iridectomy
iridotomy
keratotomy
laparotomy
laryngectomy
laryngotomy
leucotomy
lipectomy
lithotomy
lobectomy
lobotomy
lumpectomy
mastectomy
meniscectomy
microtomy
myringotomy
necrotomy
nephrectomy
nephrotomy
neurectomy
neuroanatomy
neurotomy
oophorectomy
orchidectomy
orchiectomy
osteotomy
ovariotomy
patellectomy
pharyngotomy
ph\*botomy

phytotomy
pleurotomy
pneumonectomy
pogonotomy
prostatectomy
rhytidectomy
salpingectomy
sclerotomy
splenectomy
stapedectomy
stereotomy
strabotomy
sympathectomy
symphyseotomy
symphysiotomy
syringotomy
tenotomy
tetrachotomy
thymectomy
tonsilectomy
tonsillectomy
tonsillotomy
tonsilotomy
topectomy
tracheotomy
trichotomy
tubectomy
ultramicrotomy
uterectomy
uterotomy
varicotomy
vasectomy
zootomy

**-urgy**

chemurgy
dramaturgy
electrometallurgy
hierurgy
hydrometallurgy
liturgy
metallurgy
micrurgy
theurgy
zymurgy

**-vorous**

apivorous
baccivorous
carnivorous
fructivorous
frugivorous
graminivorous
granivorous
herbivorous
insectivorous
lignivorous
mellivorous
myristicivorous
nucivorous
omnivorous
ossivorous
piscivorous
radicivorous
ranivorous
sanguinivorous
sanguivorous
vermivorous